WILSON'S

OLD TESTAMENT
WORD STUDIES

WILSON'S
OLD TESTAMENT WORD STUDIES

*A valuable aid that will help you
understand the precise meaning
of Hebrew words used in the Bible*

WILLIAM WILSON

HENDRICKSON
PUBLISHERS

WILSON'S OLD TESTAMENT WORD STUDIES
William Wilson

Hendrickson Publishers
P.O. Box 3473
Peabody, Massachusetts 01961–3473

Printed in the United States of America

ISBN 0-917006-27-5

PREFACE

THE work now presented to the Public has been the result of almost incredible labour bestowed on it during many years. It was commenced for the purpose of illustrating the precise meaning of Hebrew words; to be a kind of manual of consultation when longer time could not be spared for further investigation. The force of an English word could not be depended on for giving a correct and precise meaning to it in any explanation of Scripture. It was felt, also, that many Hebrew words are rendered by the same English word, which being in a certain degree synonymous, yet require a distinction of meaning according to their use in the original. And sometimes a fair and suitable meaning may be assigned to an expression viewed only in the English translation, as Cruden has done in his Concordance, which is not borne out by the original, or may even be found contrary to it: so that deductions drawn from that meaning must be altogether unwarranted or absolutely erroneous. Taylor's illustrations of the meaning of the original are frequently very striking, and the explication of certain phrases very happy. The Author had collected these under the corresponding English words, when it occurred to him that the undertaking might be made useful to others, and improved by consulting other works, especially philological, such as the late editions of Gesenius's Lexicon, and modern critical commentaries on the Sacred Books.

His next object was to give the construction of the original, and so to arrange the work that the reader might be able at once to find it. For this purpose "The Englishman's Hebrew Concordance" was referred to, and found indispensable for carrying out this object. The Author begs to acknowledge the great use of this invaluable work. He is bound also to express his obligation to Mr. Bagster, of Paternoster-row, for many suggestions in the arrangement of the references. Few can be aware of the immense labour required to carry out this part of the plan, and to insure anything like accuracy. The Author will not attempt to detail the means used to obtain this accuracy, the labour of which has been very greatly enhanced by the disappointment he has from time to time experienced in the use of such works as he hoped to find auxiliary to

his undertaking. Suffice it to say, that he believes the present work is the nearest approach to a complete Concordance of every word in the original that has yet been made: and as a Concordance, it may be found of great use to the Bible student, while at the same time it serves the important object of furnishing the means of comparing synonymous words, and of eliciting their precise and distinctive meaning.

The knowledge of the Hebrew language is not absolutely necessary to the profitable use of this work; and it is believed that many devout and accurate students of the Bible, entirely unacquainted with it, will derive great advantage from frequent reference to these pages. The Author earnestly recommends it to the adoption of all ministers of God's Word, and that they would make it the depository of such critical remarks as may occur to them in the course of their reading. For this purpose an interleaved copy would further serve this purpose, and induce the habit of accurate attention to the Sacred Scriptures, by the care taken to note down every verbal criticism of importance.

It is related of Coleridge, that he devoted a certain portion of time periodically to the verbal examination of the Bible, in which he directed his attention especially to the proper and primary meaning of the original; and that he received great profit and interest from the employment.

The use of this work will shew in a very convincing manner the disadvantage in our Version of a more uniform rendering not having been adopted by the translators. Different renderings of the same word have in many cases been resorted to, as it would seem, rather for the sake of variety than for the purpose of conveying any precise meaning in distinction. The Author has no intention of invalidating a Version so long consecrated by the reverend study of many generations since it was first given to the Church with a providential blessing, nor would he propose to substitute any other Version for one so long used; but an edition in which a more uniform translation of certain words, and a more literal version of certain expressions and phrases, might be appended to the text, would be a boon to most readers.

The present undertaking has been pursued under the growing conviction of the plenary inspiration of the language of the Sacred Scriptures. What Professor Gaussen has said in his invaluable work on this subject, in respect to the result of his labour in answering objections, the Author can fully adopt as the result of his own attention, "in compelling us by a more attentive examination to test the diamonds of Holy Scripture, they have sent forth unexpected lustre, which has led us

PREFACE

to fresh discoveries of more brilliant reflections of its divinity ." The use of this "Help" is earnestly recommended to those who, with the light of so important a truth as the verbal inspiration of the Sacred Oracles, desire to compare our Version with the text, and to correct from time to time their apprehension of the truths which have emanated from the Divine Mind, by reference to their model and type presented in the revealed Word. There may be some who speak with contempt of the letter of the Old Testament; but those who have examined it most closely will not fail to discover rays of light, which will, in " the glory of the day of Jesus," burst forth with a refulgence which will disclose to us yet hidden treasures in the Scriptures. It is hoped and believed that there is an increasing attention to the only standard of Christian faith and practice; but the Author feels constrained to say that much, very much, is yet needed for the elucidation of the primitive language of man. If this humble effort to prepare the way for more knowledge of the Sacred Tongue may be instrumental to revive so important a pursuit, he will render unfeigned thanks to God that health and strength have been vouchsafed for the completion of an object in which he has experienced an unusual interest and delight. And he has no greater desire, next to the fulfilling of the ministry of the Word, than to be spared for any further service he may be enabled to render to the Scriptures in unfolding their literal meaning, or aiding the search of others.

At a time when the authority and character of the Sacred Record is sadly assailed on various grounds; when devout attention is denounced as Bibliolatry, and other standards of opinion referred to, it is a paramount duty in all that cleave to the Word of God, to " search the Scriptures" more intelligently. And it is believed that a more reverent attention to the Old Testament would be the means of reviving a more spiritual apprehension of many great and overwhelming truths, in the present day too much lost sight of.

May He, without whose blessing even the written Word avails nothing to saving knowledge, bestow His favour on this undertaking, and direct its use and advantage to His own glory, and the edification of His Church!

" A SHORT statement of the nature and construction of Hebrew for the guidance of such as need it," was promised in the Prospectus of this work. It is proposed to fulfil this intention only so far as the use of this undertaking may seem to require, for the direction of those who are not acquainted with the peculiarities of that language. It is necessary to premise that pronouns and particles are not included in the following work, and need not to be noticed on the present occasion. Nor is it intended to produce the paradigms of the several forms of the verbs. The reader who desires to pursue the grammatical knowledge of the sacred language of the Old Testament, is referred to the valuable publication of Gesenius's Hebrew Grammar, by Bagster and Sons, Paternoster-row, London; from which the following notices are chiefly taken, with the kind consent of those publishers. It cannot be doubted that this volume is the very best introduction to the study of this important language that has yet appeared; and Bible students are greatly indebted to the literary labours which have issued from the same establishment for the promotion of Biblical learning.

INTRODUCTION
TO HEBREW
FOR ENGLISH READERS

₊ The reader is requested to refer to the body of the work for the original of those tenses referred to in the course of this statement; which being given only for the information of the English reader, does not include the Hebrew that may be in most cases found in Gesenius's Grammar.

THE Hebrew alphabet consists of twenty-two letters. The language itself is read from right to left.

Form.

ל	כ	י	ט	ח	ז	ו	ה	ד	ג	ב	א
l	k, or kh	y	t	ch	z	v	h	d	g	b	a

ת	ש	ר	ק	צ	פ	ע	ס	נ	מ
t, or th	sh, or s	r	q	ts	p, or ph	o	s	n	m

Final.

ץ	ף	ן	ם	ך
ts	p, or ph	n	m	k, or kh

As it is not designed in this grammatical sketch to enter on the nature of the vowel-points, the letters of the English alphabet may represent in a general way to the English reader the power of the several characters.

There are certain Hebrew words which are denominated Roots, consisting usually of three letters,—called Roots because from the primary meaning of such words are deduced many others, as well nouns, adjectives, adverbs, &c., as the several forms of Hebrew verbs. The third person singular of the preterite is commonly the root here referred to, which is varied by the vowel-points to form nouns, &c., *e. g.* אָדַם *he was red,* אָדֹם *red,* אָדָם *man.*

The verb is, in Hebrew, the most elaborated part of speech, and in the understanding of any sentence, requires our chief attention. The ground-form or root of the third person preterite admits of various modifications to give a definite change in signification; so that its primary meaning shall become intensive, frequentative, causative, passive, reflexive, reciprocal. This is the general account of what are usually called conjugations in Hebrew, now to be explained.

They may be illustrated thus:—

Kal	. .	קָטַל	to kill.
Niphal	.	נִקְטַל	to be killed.
Piel	. .	קִטֵּל	to murder.
Pual	. .	קֻטַּל	to be murdered.
Hiphil	.	הִקְטִיל	to cause to kill.
Hophal	.	הֻקְטַל	to be caused to kill.
Hithpael	.	הִתְקַטֵּל	to kill oneself.

By reference to the Index at the end of this volume, it will be seen that there are few verbs which admit of their being used in every one of these forms: and very frequently it is difficult to ascertain the signification of the ground-form, Kal not occurring in the sacred writings.

KAL being the simplest form of the verb, we are to look to it for the primary signification, usually in an active sense, but not always so rendered. The simple primary idea in every verb is matter of curious investigation with the learned in philology; but, as may be seen by the Index, that primary meaning has gone through many modifications. Sometimes the first meaning is better traced in the other conjugations; to which argument Gesenius has had recourse not seldom in his Lexicon.

The tenses in Hebrew are not to be estimated according to their use in modern languages, in which we find *time* distinctly involved. In Hebrew they are intended to refer more particularly to action, and may be either definite or indefinite in their use. Thus it will be found that the preterite is sometimes rendered by a *future* tense in English, or even by a *present*, the time being relative to some specification already made in the text, upon which the idea of time to be maintained in the mind of the reader depends.

THE USE OF THE PRETERITE

The Preterite stands,—

1. In itself and properly, for *absolutely* and *fully* past time, *e.g.* Gen. iv. 10, *What hast thou done?* Being preceded by a word or particle which in itself fixes the time, it may be considered as an *imperfect* tense. Gen. i. 1, *In the beginning God created the heaven and the earth: in the beginning*, notes the time, and *created*, simply states a past action; Josh. x. 33, *Then Horam king of Gezer came up to help Lachish:* the particle *then* gives the note of time, and to the verb *came*, an *imperfect* or even *present* tense, implying that Horam came at the very time that Joshua was attacking Lachish.

2. For the *pluperfect*, 1 Sam. ix. 15, *Now the Lord had told Samuel in his ear a day before Saul came;* Gen. ii. 2, *His work which he had done.*

3. For our *present*, where this denotes (A) a condition or attribute already long continued and still existing, as Job ix. 2, *I know;* Gen. iv. 9, *I know not;* Job xxxiv. 5, *I am righteous:* or (B) a permanent or habitual action (often in statements of general experience), *e.g.* Job vii. 13, *when I say;* Ps. i. 1, *walketh—standeth—sitteth.*

4. Even for the *future*, in *protestations* and *assurances*, in which the mind of the speaker views the action as already accomplished, being as good as done. In English the present is sometimes used, in this case, for the future. So in stipulations or promises in the way of a compact, Gen. xxiii. 11, *The field give I thee*, ver. 13, *I will give thee money for the field;* particularly in promises made by God, Gen. xv. 18, *Unto thy seed have I given, i.e.* I will give, *this land.*

5. For those *relative tenses*, in which the past is the principal idea, viz. (A) for the *imperfect subjunctive* (which is however expressed by the future also), *e.g.* Isa. i. 9, *We should have been as Sodom, &c.;* Job iii. 13. (B) For the *pluperfect subjunctive*, Isa. i. 9, *Except the Lord of hosts had left;* Num. xiv. 2, *Would God we had died*, lit. *if we had but died* (with the future it would have been, *if we might but die*); Job x. 19, *as though I had not been.* (C) For the *future* perfect, *e.g.* Isa. iv. 4, *When the Lord shall have washed away;* Gen. xiv. 14, *If I be bereaved* (for *if I shall be*), *then I am bereaved.*

*   *   *   *   *   *

In all the foregoing cases we have viewed the preterite in its independent use, when not connected with preceding verbs. But its use is no less diversified when it is joined to preceding verbs by the conjunction ו (*vau conversive of the preterite*). It then takes the tense and mood of the verb going before. Hence it stands,—

(A) Most frequently for the *future*, when that tense goes before it, *e.g.* Gen. xxiv. 40, *The Lord will send his angel with thee, and prosper thy way;* Judg. vi. 16, *I will be with thee, and thou shalt smite*, &c.

(B) For the *present subjunctive*, when the preceding future form has this sense, *e.g.* Gen. iii. 22, *Lest he put forth his hand, and take, and eat;* xxxii. 12, *I will surely do thee good, and make, &c.;* Gen. xix. 19, *Lest some evil take me, and I die;* Prov. xxx. 10, *Lest he curse thee, and thou be found guilty.*

(C) For the *imperative*, when a verb in that form goes before, Gen. xxvii. 43, 44, *Flee thou, &c., and tarry with him*, &c.

(D) For the *past* or the *present* time, according as the preceding *pret.* or *fut.* may require.

THE USE OF THE FUTURE

The Hebrew future forms, in general, the exact contrary of the preterite, and expresses, accordingly, what is unfinished, what is coming to pass and future, but also what is continued and in progress at any point of time, even of the past. Hence the future stands,—

1. For strictly *future* time; Gen. ix. 11, *Neither shall there any more be a flood;* also in narrative for the future with relation to some past point of time, as 2 Kings iii. 27, *His eldest son that should have reigned.*

2. For *present* time; 1 Kings iii. 7, *I know not;* Isa. i. 13, *I cannot away with;* Gen. xxxvii. 15, *What seekest thou?* It is employed especially in the expression of permanent states, which exist now and always will exist; hence also in the expression of general truths, *e.g.* Gen. xliii. 32, *The Egyptians might not eat bread with the Hebrews;* Job iv. 17, *Shall mortal man be more just than God?* ii. 4; Prov. xv. 20, *A wise son maketh a glad father;* and very often so in Job and Proverbs.

3. For a series of relations which in Latin are expressed by the subjunctive, especially by the present subjunctive. In this way is expressed what is future, or what is expected to occur, according to a subjective view, or according to some objective condition. It stands,—

(A) For the subjunctive after particles, signifying *that, that not,* *e.g.* Gen. xi. 7, *that they may not understand;* xxxviii. 16, *What wilt thou give, that thou mayest come in unto me?* Deut. iv. 1, *that ye may live;* Gen. iii. 22, *lest he put forth his hand.*

(B) For the optative, Job iii. 3, *let the day perish.*

(C) For the imperative, the place of which it always supplies in negative commands (prohibitions); dehortatory, Gen. xlvi. 3, *fear not;* Job iii. 4, 6, 7, prohibitory: Exod. xx. 15, *Thou shalt not steal.* It is also used for the imperative when the third person is required, and for the imperatives of the passive voice, so far as these are not in use, *e.g.* Gen. i. 3, *Let there be light;* Exod. xxxv. 2, *shall be put to death, i. e.* let him be put to death.

(D) For the so-called potential, where we use *may, can, might, could, &c., e.g.* Gen. ii. 16, *thou mayest freely eat;* Prov. xx. 9, *Who can say?* Gen. xliii. 7, *Could we certainly know?*

4. Even for time past: it is thus used chiefly in these cases,—

(A) After the particles, *then, not yet, before;* Josh. x. 12, *Then spake Joshua;* Gen. ii. 5, *before it was;* xxxvii. 18, *before he came near;* Jer. i. 5 (compare the use of *pret.* and *fut.* in the same sentence); 1 Sam. iii. 7 (see margin).

(B) Often also of customary or continued action, and in extended representation, like the imperfect of the Latin and French languages. Repeated or customary action, as it involves the conception of something yet to be, is properly expressed by the future; Job i. 5, *Thus did Job continually;* xxii. 6, 7, 8; xxix. 12, 13: Judg. xiv. 10: 1 Sam. i. 7: 1 Kings v. 25: Ps. xlii. 4.

(C) Of single acts that are done and passed, where the preterite might be expected. Such is the case, at least in poetry, on the same principle as we employ the present tense, in lively representations of the past; Job iii. 3, *wherein I was born;* ver. 11, *Why died I not from the womb?* iv. 12, 15, 16; x. 10, 11.

5. For the imperfect subjunctive, especially in conditional sen-

tences, Ps. xxiii. 4, *Though I walk . . . . I will fear no evil;* Job v. 8, *I would seek unto God* (were I in thy place); ix. 21, *Would I not know my soul* (if I spoke otherwise); x. 18, *O that I had given up the ghost, and no eye had seen me;* iii. 16; vi. 14.

USE OF THE FUTURE WITH VAU CONVERSIVE

1. The future with *vau conversive* (the conjunction ן, *and*, prefixed to verbs), stands only in connexion with something preceding. Most commonly a narrative begins with a *preterite*, and proceeds in the *future* with *vau conversive*, which is the most usual way of relating past events, *e.g.* Gen. iv. 1, *And Adam knew Eve his wife, and she conceived and bare Cain;* vi. 9, 10, &c.; x. 9, 10, 15, 19; xi. 12–15, 27, 28; xiv. 5, &c.; xv. 1, 2; xvi. 1, 2; xxi. 1, &c.; xxiv. 1, 2; xxv. 19, 20, &c.; xxxvi. 2–4; xxxvii. 2. The preceding *preterite* is at times only implied in the sense, *e.g.* Gen. xi. 10; x. 1.

2. If there be, however, any connexion with an earlier event, the *fut.* with *vau conv.* may even begin a narrative, or a section of one. In this case we find a very frequent use of ויהי; *And it came to pass, and there was,* &c., Gen. xi. 1; xiv. 1; xvii. 1; xxii. 1; xxvi. 1; xxvii. 1: xii. 1, *Now the Lord had said.*

The use of the future is found also especially (A) after an antecedent clause, *e.g.* after BECAUSE; 1 Sam. xv. 23, *Because thou hast rejected the word of the Lord, he hath also rejected thee;* Gen. xxxiii. 10, (B) after an absolute noun, *e.g.* 1 Kings xii. 17; ix. 21; Dan. viii. 22.

The *vau conv.* may be rendered *that* in sentences like the following :—Ps. cxliv. 3, *What is man that thou takest knowledge of him !*

3. As to the relations of time indicated by this future denoting sequence or progress, we may remark that it, in accordance always with the preceding tense, may refer,—

(A) To the present time, namely, in continued descriptions of it, when preceded by a *preterite* (in the sense of a *present*), Gen. xxxii. 5 : Isa. ii. 7, 8 : Job vii. 9; xiv. 2 : or a *future* (as a *present*), Job xiv. 10 : 1 Sam. ii. 29 : or a *participle,* Nah. i. 4 : 2 Sam. xix. 1 : Amos ix. 6.

(B) Less frequently to futurity, when preceded by a *preterite* (as a *future*), Isa. v. 15, 16; xxii. 7, 8 : Joel ii. 23 : Micah ii. 13 : or by a proper *future,* Isa. ix. 10 : Joel ii. 18, 19 : or by an *imperative,* Ps. l. 6 (also when joined to a clause without a verb, *e.g.* Gen. xlix. 15 ; or to an absolute noun, *e.g.* Isa. ix. 12 ; or when it turns to the *future, e.g.* Isa. ii. 9; ix. 13).

OF THE IMPERATIVE

1. The imperative expresses not only command in the strict sense, but also exhortation (Hos. x. 12); entreaty (2 Kings v. 22 : Isa. v. 3) ; wish (Gen. xxiii. 13) ; permission (2 Sam. xviii. 23 : Isa. xlv. 11). It is employed especially in strong assurances, and hence in prophetic declarations, as Isa. vi. 10. These may be either (A) *promises,* Ps. cxxviii. 5 : Isa. xxxvii. 30; lxv. 18 : Ps. xxii. 26 : Gen. xx. 7 : or (B) *threatenings,* Isa. xxiii. 1, 2, 4; x. 30; xiii. 6.

2. We may, from the above, explain the peculiar use of the two imperatives joined by *and.* (A) Where they are employed in a good sense, the first containing an admonition or exhortation, and the second a promise made on the condition implied in the first (like *divide et impera*), *e.g.* Gen. xlii. 18, *This do and live;* Prov. xx. 13, *Open thine eyes and thou shalt be satisfied;* Ps. xxxvii. 27 : Prov. vii. 2; ix. 6: Job xxii. 21: Isa. xxxvi. 16; xlv. 22: Hos. x. 12 : Amos v. 4, 6. (B) Where a threat is expressed, and the first *imp.* tauntingly permits an act, while the second denounces the consequences, Isa. viii. 9; xxix. 9. In the second member, the *fut.* also may be used, Isa. vi. 9; viii. 10: 1 Sam. xvii. 44.

USE OF THE INFINITIVE ABSOLUTE

The infinitive absolute is employed when there is occasion to express the action of the verb by itself, neither connected with something following nor dependent on a preceding noun or particle. The most important cases of its use are,—

1. When it is governed by a *transitive verb,* and consequently stands as an accusative, Isa. xlii. 24, *they would not walk,* &c. Sometimes rendered as a noun, Isa. xxii. 13, *slaying, killing,* &c., *prop.* to slay, &c.

2. When it is in the accusative, and used *adverbially,* hence,—

3. When it is used for emphasis, in connexion with a *finite verb.* (A) It then stands most commonly *before* the finite verb, to which it gives, in general, *strength* or *intensity.* 1 Sam. xx. 6, *He earnestly asked;* Gen. xliii. 3 : Amos ix. 8. Its effect is often merely to give a certain prominence to the thought contained in the finite verb, which in other languages is done chiefly by the expression of the voice or by particles, as in assurances, questions (such especially as express excitement in view · of something strange and improbable), contrasts, Gen. xliii. 7; xxxvii. 8; xxxi. 30: Judg. xv. 13 : 2 Sam. xxiv. 24 : 1 Sam. ix. 6: Hab. ii. 3.

(B) When the *inf.* stands after the finite verb, this connexion generally indicates *continued* or *lasting* action; Isa. vi. 9 : Jer. xxiii. 17 : Gen. xix. 9. Two infinitives absolute may be thus used ; 1 Sam. vi. 12, *went along, lowing as they went;* 1 Kings xx. 37. Instead of the second *inf.* is sometimes used a finite verb (Josh. vi. 13), or a participle (2 Sam. xvi. 5).

4. When it stands in place of the *finite verb.* We must here distinguish the following cases, viz.—

(A) When it is preceded by a finite verb. This is frequent, especially among the later writers, in the expression of several successive acts or states, where only the first of the verbs employed takes the required form in respect to *tense* and *person,* the others being simply put in the infinitive with the same tense and person implied; Dan. ix. 5, *by departing,* or (we have) *departed;* Jer. xiv. 5, *calved in the field and forsook it.* With the *fut.,* Jer. xxxii. 44, *Men shall buy (fut.) fields, and subscribe evidences, and seal them, and take witnesses* (three infinitives) ; Num. xv. 35.

(B) It may stand at the beginning of the sentence, without a preceding finite verb. The infinitive (being the pure abstract idea of the verb) may serve as a short and emphatic expression for any tense and person which the connexion requires, *e.g.* it stands (*a*) for the *pret.* in lively narration and description, Isa. xxi. 5; Hos. iv. 2 ; also (*β*) for the *fut.* in its proper sense, 2 Kings iv. 43 ; (*γ*) most frequently for the emphatic *imp.,* Deut. v. 12; Exod. xx. 8. For the cohortative, Isa. xxii. 13, *Let us eat and drink :* 1 Kings xxii. 30, *lit.* to disguise myself and go (will I do).

INFINITIVE CONSTRUCT

The *inf. const.* as a verbal substantive is subject to the same relations of case with the noun.

The infinitive may be construed with the case of its verb, and hence in transitive verbs it takes the accusative of the object.

The same construction takes place with a verbal noun analogous to the infinitive, as Isa. xi. 9, *the knowledge of Jehovah* (prop. *the knowing Jehovah*).

USE OF THE PARTICIPLE

The only existing form of the participle is used to express all the tenses.

NIPHAL

Significations of Niphal.—It has similarity to the Greek *middle voice*, and hence (A) it is primarily *reflexive* of Kal, e.g. נִשְׁמַר, *to look to one's self, to beware;* נִסְתַּר, *to hide oneself;* often in verbs which express passion or feeling, as נִחַם, *to trouble one's self, to grieve;* נֶאֱנַח, *to bemoan one's self.* (B) Next it frequently expresses *reciprocal action,* as נִשְׁפַּט, *to contend with one another at law;* יָעַץ, *to counsel;* Niph., *to consult together.* (C) It has also, like Hithpael, the signification of the active with the addition of *self* for one's self, e.g. נִשְׁאַל, *to ask for one's self* (1 Sam. xx. 6, 28). (D) It is often also *passive* of Kal, e.g. יָלַד, *to bear;* Niph., *to be born;* likewise of Piel and Hiphil, when Kal is intransitive or not in use, e.g. כָּבֵד, *to be in honour;* Niph., *to be honoured;* כָּתַד, in Piel, *to conceal;* Hiph., *to make disappear, to destroy;* Niph., passive of both: and in this case its meaning may again coincide with Kal (חָלָה Kal, and Niph., *to be sick*).

PIEL AND PUAL

Significations of Piel.—(A) It denotes *intensity* and *repetition,* e.g. צָחַק, *to laugh;* Piel, *to sport, to jest* (to laugh repeatedly); שָׁאַל, *to ask;* Piel, *to beg:* hence it denotes that the action is *performed upon many,* as קָבַר, *to bury* (one), Gen. xxiii. 4; Piel, *to bury* (many), 1 Kings xi. 15. This signification of Piel is found with various shades of difference, פָּתַח, *to open;* Piel, *to loose:* סָפַר, *to count;* Piel, *to relate.* With the eager pursuit of an object is connected the influence which the subject of it exerts upon others. Hence (B) it has a *causative* signification (like Hiphil), e.g. לָמַד, *to learn;* Piel, *to teach.* It often takes the modifications expressed by *to permit, to declare,* or *to regard, to help,* as חָיָה, *to let live;* צָדַק, *to declare innocent;* יָלַד, *to assist in child-bearing.*

(C) *Denominatives* are frequently found in this conjugation, which in general mean *to make a thing* (sc. that which the noun expresses), or *to be in any way occupied with it,* as from קֵן, *nest;* קִנֵּן, *to make a nest:* from עָפָר, *dust;* עִפֵּר, *to throw dust, to dust.* It also expresses the *taking away* or *injuring* that thing or part of which the noun is the name (as in English, *to behead, to skin, to bone*), e.g. שֵׁרֵשׁ (from שֹׁרֶשׁ, *a root*), *to root out, extirpate;* זִנֵּב (from זָנָב *tail*), properly, *to injure the tail,* hence *to rout the rearguard of an army;* דִּשֵּׁן, *to remove the ashes.* So also in verbs whose origin cannot be traced to a noun, e.g. סָקַל, *to stone,* and also, *to remove the stones,* sc. from a field.

The significations of the passive will present themselves spontaneously, e.g. גָּנַב, *to steal;* Piel, *to steal;* Pual, *to be stolen.*

HIPHIL AND HOPHAL

Significations of Hiphil.—It is properly *causative of Kal,* and in this sense is more frequently employed than Piel, e.g. יָצָא, *to go forth;* Hiph., *to bring out of, to lead forth;* קָדַשׁ, *to be holy;* Hiph., *to sanctify.* When Kal is transitive, Hiph. takes two accusatives. Frequently Piel and Hiph. are both in use in the same signification, as אָבַד, *to perish;* Piel and Hiph., *to destroy;* but generally only one of them is found; or they have some difference of signification, as in כָּבֵד, *to be heavy;* Piel, *to honour;* Hiph., *to make heavy.* Intransitive verbs merely become transitive, e.g. נָטָה, *to bow* (intrans.); Hiph., *to bow* (trans.). The signification of *Hophal,* as of Niphal, may sometimes coincide with that of Kal, e.g. יָכֹל, *potuit;* fut., Hoph., *potens fiet, i.e. poterit.*

HITHPAEL

Significations of Hithpael.—(A) Most frequently it is *reflexive,* but chiefly of Piel, as הִתְקַדֵּשׁ, *to sanctify one's self;* הִתְנַקֵּם, *to avenge one's self;* הִתְאַזֵּר, *to gird one's self.* Then farther it means, *to make one's self that* which is expressed by the first conjugation: hence, *to conduct one's self* as such, *to shew one's self, to imagine one's self* to be such; properly, *to make one's self* so and so, *to act* so and so, e.g. הִתְגַּדֵּל, *to make one's self great, to act proudly;* הִתְחַכֵּם, *to shew one's self cunning, crafty,* also Eccles. vii. 16, *to think one's self wise;* הִתְעַשֵּׁר, *to make, i.e. to feign one's self rich.* Its signification sometimes coincides with that of Kal, and both forms are in use with the same meaning, e.g. אָבַל Kal, *to mourn,* is found only in poetry; Hithp. in the same sense, is more common in prose, and even takes an accusative. (B) It expresses *reciprocal action,* as הִתְרָאָה, *to look upon one another,* Gen. xlii. 1. More frequently (C) it expresses what one does indirectly *to* or *for himself.* It has then an active signification, and governs an accusative. Only seldom (D) it is *passive,* Judges xx. 15, 17; xxi. 9.

UNUSUAL CONJUGATIONS

Of the unusual conjugations some are connected, in form, with Piel, as—

1. *Poel.*—Its *signification,* like that of Piel, is often causative of Kal. Sometimes both are in use in the same signification, as רוֹצֵץ, and רָצַץ, *to oppress;* sometimes each has its peculiar modification of meaning, as סָבַב, *to turn about, to change;* סוֹבֵב, *to go about, to surround.*

2. *Pilel, Pulal, Hithpalel;* used especially of permanent states or conditions, e.g. of colours; as שַׁאֲנַן, *to be at rest;* רַעֲנַן, *to be green, pass.;* אֻמְלָל, *to be withered.* Of these verbs there is no example in Kal.

3. *Pealal;* as קְטַלְטַל, with repetition of the last two stem-letters, used especially of slight motions repeated in quick succession, e.g. סְחַרְחַר, *to go about with quick motion,* hence (of the heart), *to palpitate;* Ps. xxxviii. 10, from סָחַר, *to go about;* pass. חֳמַרְמָר, *to ferment with violence, to make a rumbling sound,* Lam. i. 20. Nouns of this form are *diminutives.* Nearly related to this is—

4. *Pilpel.*—This also is used of *motion rapidly repeated,* which all languages are prone to express by repetition of the same sound, as צִפְצֵף, *to chirp;* צִלְצֵל, *to tinkle;* גִּרְגֵּר, *to gurgle;* עִפְעֵף, *to flutter* (from עוּף, *to fly*).

With Hiphil are connected,—

5. *Tiphel;* as תִּקְטֵל, with ת prefixed, as תִּרְגַּל, *to teach one to walk, to lead* (denom. from רֶגֶל, *a foot*); תַּחֲרֶה, *fut.* יִתְחֲרֶה, *to emulate,* Jer. xii. 5; xxii. 15 (from חָרָה, *to be ardent, eager*).

6. *Shaphel;* שַׁקְטֵל, frequent in Syriac, as שַׁלְהֵב, *to flame,* from לָהַב. In Heb. it is found only in the noun שַׁלְהֶבֶת, *flame.*

OF GRAMMATICAL STRUCTURE

The formation of the parts of speech from the roots, and their inflexion, are effected in two ways: (1) by changes in the stem itself, particularly in its vowels; (2) by the addition of the formative syllables.

OF THE PERSONAL OR SEPARATE PRONOUN

1. The personal pronoun (as well as the pronouns generally) is among the oldest and simplest elements of the language.

2. The pronouns in their separate and chief forms, or as expressing the nominative, are the following:—

	Singular.			*Plural.*	
1. comm.	אָנֹכִי אֲנִי	*I*	1. comm.	אֲנַחְנוּ	*we*
2. { m.	אַתָּה	} *thou*	2. { m.	אַתֶּם	} *ye*
f.	אַתְּ		f.	אַתֵּן	
3. { m.	הוּא	*he*	3. { m.	הֵם	} *they*
f.	הִיא	*she*	f.	הֵן	

SUFFIX PRONOUN

1. The full and separate forms of the pronoun express only the nominative; the accusative and genitive, on the contrary, are expressed by shortened forms of fragments which are joined to the end of verbs, nouns, and particles (*suffix pronouns,* usually *suffixes*), *e.g.* הוּ *him,* and וֹ *his* (from הוּא *he*); thus קְטַלְתִּיהוּ *I have killed him,* סוּסוֹ *his horse.*

2. Concerning the *cases* which these suffixes denote, let it be remarked,—

(A) When joined to verbs, they denote the accusative, קְטַלְתִּיהוּ *I have killed him.*

(B) When joined to substantives, they denote the genitive, and then serve as *possessive pronouns,* as אָבִי *my father.*

(C) When joined to particles, they denote either the genitive or the accusative, according as the particle has the meaning of a noun or verb, *e.g.* אִתִּי (prop. *my vicinity*) *with me;* on the contrary, הִנְנִי *behold me.*

(D) The dative and ablative of the pronoun are expressed by combining the prepositions that are signs of these cases, (לְ, sign of the dative, בְּ *in,* מִן *from*); with the suffixes, as לוֹ *to him;* בּוֹ *in him;* מִכֶּם *from you.*

OF THE NOUN

A regular *inflexion* of the noun by *cases* does not exist in Hebrew, although perhaps some ancient traces of case-endings remain. The relation of case in a noun is either learned simply from its position in the clause, or indicated by prepositions. In the *form* of the noun there is no change.

OF FORMS WHICH MARK THE GENDER OF NOUNS

1. The Hebrew, like all the Shemitish languages, has but two genders, the *masculine* and *feminine.* Inanimate objects, properly of the neuter gender, and abstract ideas, for which other languages have a *neuter form,* are regarded in Hebrew as either masculine or feminine, particularly the latter.

2. The *masculine,* as being the most common and important form of the noun, has no peculiar mark of distinction. The ending for the *feminine* was originally ת—, as in the 3 *sing. pret.* of verbs. But when the noun stands without a genitive following (*i.e.* when it is not in the *construct state*), the ת— usually appears in the weakened form ה—, or is shortened to ת— unaccented.

DERIVATION OF NOUNS

Nouns are either *primitive,* as אָב, *father,* אֵם, *mother,* or *derivative.* The latter are derived either from the verb, as צַדִּיק *just,* צֶדֶק, צְדָקָה, *righteousness,* from צָדַק, *to be just;* רָם *high,* רָמָה, *high place,* מָרוֹם *height,* from רוּם, *to be high,* or from another noun (*denominatives*), as רֶגֶל, *foot;* מַרְגְּלוֹת, *place at the feet.* The verbals are by far the most numerous class.

PRIMITIVE NOUNS

1. The number of primitives is very small, the nouns which are in most languages primitive being here usually derived from verbal ideas, *e.g.* most of the names of natural objects, as שָׂעִיר, *he-goat* (prop. *shaggy,* from שָׂעַר); חֲסִידָה, *stork* (prop. *pious*); שְׂעֹרָה, *barley* (prop. *bearded,* also from שָׂעַר); זָהָב, *gold* (from צָהַב, זָהַב, *to be yellow*). Decidedly primitive are the cardinal numbers, and there are many names of the members of the body, in men and beasts, for which no stem-verb can be found, as קֶרֶן, *horn,* שַׁד, *female breast.*

2. The *form* of the primitives is that of the simplest verbals, as קֶטֶל, קְטָל, and it makes no difference, in the grammatical treatment, to which class the nouns belong.

OF VERBAL NOUNS IN GENERAL

1. In Hebrew, as in Greek and Latin, the *verbal nouns* are connected in form and signification with certain forms of the verb, namely, the participles and infinitives, which even without any change are often employed as nouns, *e.g.* דַּעַת (*to know*), *knowledge;* אֹיֵב (*hating*), *enemy.*

2. As to *signification,* it follows from the nature of the case, that nouns which have the form of infinitives regularly denote the *action* or *state,* with other closely related ideas (such as *the place* of the action), and are, therefore, mostly *abstract;* that participial nouns, on the contrary, denote, for the most part, the *subject* of the action, or of the state, and hence are *concrete.* It often happens, however, that a certain signification is found in single examples, which is not characteristic of the form.

OF THE PLURAL

1. The *plural* termination for the *masculine gender* is ◌ִים, *e. g.* סוּס, *horse*, pl. סוּסִים, *horses*. Nouns in ◌ֶה lose this termination when they take the plural ending, *e.g.* חֹזֶה, *seer*, pl. חֹזִים.

2. The plural termination for the *feminine gender* is וֹת. This takes the place of the feminine termination ◌ָת, ◌ֶת, ◌ָה, ◌ֶה, when the noun in the singular ends with one of these; otherwise it is merely appended to the form of the singular.

3. Words which are of two genders have often, in the plural, both the masculine and feminine terminations, *e.g.* נֶפֶשׁ, *soul*, pl. נְפָשׁוֹת, and נְפָשִׁים.

4. A considerable number of masculines form their plural in וֹת, while many feminines have a plural in ◌ִים. In both cases, however, the gender of the singular is usually retained in the plural.

5. It is chiefly only in adjectives and participles that we find the plural endings regularly and constantly distinguished according to the gender, *e.g.* טוֹבִים *boni*; טוֹבוֹת *bonæ*; קְטֻלִים *masc.*, קְטֻלוֹת *fem.* So also in substantives of the same stem, when the difference depends on sex, בָּנִים *sons*; בָּנוֹת *daughters*; מְלָכִים *kings*; מְלָכוֹת *queens.*

OF THE DUAL

1. As a modification of the plural we have the *dual*, which, however, is used only in substantives (not in adjectives, verbs, and pronouns). It is indicated in both genders by the ending ◌ַיִם, appended to the singular, as יָדַיִם, *both hands*; יוֹמַיִם, *two days.*

2. The use of the *dual* is in Hebrew confined chiefly to such objects as are by nature or art in *pairs*, as יָדַיִם, *both hands.*

THE GENITIVE AND THE CONSTRUCT STATE

The Hebrew has no more the living use of *case-endings*, but indicates *the relations of case*, either by no outward means, as that of the nominative and generally also of the accusative, or by prepositions; but the *genitive* relation is indicated by a close connexion between two nouns. The noun, which serves as genitive to limit the other, remains unchanged, and is only uttered in more close connexion with the preceding *nomen regens*. Thus in Hebrew, the noun which stands *before a genitive* suffers the change (when there is any) by which this relation is indicated, and in grammatical language it is said to be in the *construct state*, while a noun which is not thus followed by a genitive is said to be in the *absolute state.*

SYNTAX OF THE NOUN

RELATION OF THE SUBSTANTIVE TO THE ADJECTIVE,—OF THE ABSTRACT TO THE CONCRETE.

In the Hebrew language there is a want of adjectives in proportion to substantives, and some classes of adjectives (*e.g.* those of *material*) are almost wholly wanting. This deficiency is supplied by substantives, and especially in the following ways :—

1. The substantive employed to express some quality in another is placed after it in the genitive. So constantly in designating the material, *e.g.* כְּלִי כֶסֶף, *vessels of silver, silver vessels.*

2. In Hebrew many of our adjectives denoting a property, attribute, or habit, are expressed by circumlocution, viz., by an abstract noun or name of a thing, which designates the attribute, preceded by some general name of a person as the subject of the attribute. The subject is expressed by several words.

OF THE PLURAL, AND OF COLLECTIVE NOUNS

1. Besides the proper plural endings, the language employs some other means for the expression of plurality, viz. (A) certain words whose appropriate signification is *collective*, designating an indefinite number of a class of objects, and having their corresponding *nomina unitatis*, or nouns which designate an individual of the class, as שׁוֹר, *an ox* (*an individual of the ox kind*); בָּקָר, *oxen, e.g.* חֲמִשָּׁה בָקָר, *five oxen*, Exod. xxi. 37 ; צֹאן, *small cattle*, viz. *sheep or goats*; שֶׂה, *an individual of the same, a sheep or a goat* (comp. in Eng. *twenty people*). (B) The feminine ending. (C) Nouns which have the proper signification of the singular, but which are often used as collectives, *e.g.* אָדָם, *man, the human race*, Gen. i. 26 ; אִישׁ, *collect. for men ;* דָּבָר, *words ;* אֹיֵב, *the enemy*, for *enemies.* These words take the article when all the individuals of the class are included.

2. When a substantive is followed by a genitive, and this compound idea is to be expressed in the plural, it is done (A) most naturally by the plural form in the *governing noun*, as גִּבֹּרֵי חַיִל, *strong heroes ;* so also in compounds, as בֶּן־יְמִינִי, *Benjaminite*, pl. בְּנֵי יְמִינִי, 1 Sam. xxii. 7. (B) *In both*, as גִּבֹּרֵי חֲיָלִים, 1 Chron. vii. 5 ; and hence בְּנֵי אֵלִים, Ps. xxix. 1, sons of Gods for sons of God. (C) Even only *in the noun governed*, as בֵּית אָב, *family ;* בֵּית אָבוֹת, *families.* On this remark, which has hitherto been overlooked by grammarians, compare Judg. vii. 25, (*the head of Oreb and Zeeb*, for *the heads*), 2 Kings xvii. 29 : Dan. xi. 15. Here the two words by which the compound idea is expressed are treated as a *nomen compositum.*

3. To the modes of expressing plurality belongs also the *repetition* of a noun, with or without a conjunction. By this is indicated the *whole, all, every*, as יוֹם יוֹם, *day by day, every day ;* אִישׁ אִישׁ, *every man ;* hence *distributively*, as עֵדֶר עֵדֶר לְבַדּוֹ, *each flock by itself*, Gen. xxxii. 16 ; also, *a great multitude*, even with the plural form, Gen. xiv. 10, בְּאֵרֹת בֶּאֱרֹת חֵמָר, *asphalt-pits in abundance*, nothing but asphalt-pits, 2 Kings iii. 16 : Joel iii. 14 ; finally, *diversity, more than one kind*, as כֹּל signifies *all* and *every* kind, *e.g.* אֶבֶן וָאָבֶן, *two kinds of weights*, Deut. xxv. 13 ; לֵב וָלֵב, *a double heart*, Ps. xii. 2 : 1 Chron. xii. 33.

CONNEXION OF THE SUBSTANTIVE WITH THE ADJECTIVE

1. The adjective which serves to qualify the substantive stands *after* it, and agrees with it in *gender* and *number*, as אִישׁ גָּדוֹל, אִשָּׁה יָפָה.

2. An adjective, when its meaning is more fully determined by a substantive, is followed by it in the genitive case, as יְפֵה־תֹאַר, *beautiful in form*, Gen. xxxix. 6 ; נְקִי כַפַּיִם, *pure in hands*, Ps. xxiv. 4 ; אֻמְלַל נֶפֶשׁ, *sorrowful in spirit*, Isa. xix. 10. But *verbal adjectives* govern also the cases of their verbs, as Deut. xxxiv. 9,

מָלֵא רוּחַ חָכְמָה, *full of the spirit of wisdom* (where רוּחַ is accusative).

OF APPOSITION

By this is meant the placing together of two substantives, so that one of them (commonly the second) serves to limit or qualify the other, as אִשָּׁה אַלְמָנָה, *a woman* (who is) *a widow*, 1 Kings vii. 14; נַעֲרָה בְתוּלָה, *a damsel* (who is) *a virgin*, Deut. xxii. 28; אֲמָרִים אֱמֶת, *words* (which are) *truth*, Prov. xxii. 21.

OF THE GENITIVE

1. Apart from the obsolete ending of the genitive, the Hebrew regularly expresses the genitive relation by the *construct state*. When several successive genitives depend on each other, the repetition of the *construct state* is often avoided by adopting a periphrastic construction; yet this is not always done, *e.g.* יְמֵי שְׁנֵי חַיֵּי אֲבֹתַי, *the days of the years of the life of my fathers*, Gen. xlvii. 9; שְׁאָר מִסְפַּר־קֶשֶׁת גִּבּוֹרֵי בְנֵי־קֵדָר, *the residue of the number of the bows of the mighty ones of the children of Kedar*, Isa. xxi. 17.

2. The noun in the genitive expresses not only the subject, but at times also the object, *e.g.* Ezek. xii. 19, חֲמַס הַיֹּשְׁבִים, *the wrong which the inhabitants did*; on the contrary, Obad. 10, חֲמַס אָחִיךָ, *the wrong against thy brother*; Prov. xx. 2, אֵימַת מֶלֶךְ, *the fear of a king*; זַעֲקַת סְדֹם, *the cry concerning Sodom*, Gen. xviii. 20. Other applications of the genitive are, דֶּרֶךְ עֵץ, *way to the tree*, Gen. iii. 24; קְצִינֵי סְדֹם, *judges like those in Sodom*, Isa. i. 10; זִבְחֵי אֱלֹהִים, *sacrifices pleasing to God*, Ps. li. 19.

3. Not unfrequently the genitive construction also stands in the place of apposition, as נְהַר פְּרָת, *river of Euphrates*.

USE OF THE ACCUSATIVE

The accusative is employed (A) to express the object of the transitive verbs, and also (B) in certain adverbial designations, where it is no longer governed immediately by the verb. We shall here treat only of the latter.

Accordingly, the accusative is employed,—

1. In designations of *place*. (A) In answer to the question *Whither?* After verbs of motion, as נֵצֵא הַשָּׂדֶה, *let us go out into the field*, 1 Sam. xx. 11; 2 Chron. xx. 36; Ps. cxxxiv. 2. (B) In answer to the question *Where?* After verbs of rest, as בֵּית אָבִיךְ, *in the house of thy father*, Gen. xxxviii. 11; פֶּתַח הָאֹהֶל, *in the door of the tent*, xviii. 1. It is then employed also with reference to *space* and *measure*, in answer to the question, *How far?* Gen. vii. 20, *the water rose fifteen cubits*.

2. In designations of *time*. (A) In answer to the question *When?* as הַיּוֹם, *the day*, i.e. *on the day, then*, or, *on this day, to-day*; עֶרֶב, *at evening*; הַלַּיְלָה, *by night*; צָהֳרַיִם, *at noon*, Ps. xci. 6. (B) In answer to the question *How long?* שֵׁשֶׁת יָמִים, *six days* (*long*), Exod. xx. 9.

3. In other adverbial designations, Gen. xli. 40, רַק הַכִּסֵּא אֶגְדַּל, *only in respect to the throne will I be greater*; 2 Sam. xxi. 20, *four-and-twenty* מִסְפָּר *in number*. With a following genitive, יִרְאַת שָׁמִיר, *for fear of thorns*, Isa. vii. 25; Job i. 5, *he brought burnt-offerings* מִסְפָּר כֻּלָּם *according to the number of them all*. Here belong also cases like מִשְׁנֶה כֶסֶף, *the double in money*, Gen. xlii. 15; אֵיפָה שְׂעֹרִים, *an ephah of barley*, Ruth ii. 17.

MODES OF EXPRESSING THE COMPARATIVE AND SUPERLATIVE

1. When the *comparative* is to be expressed, the particle מִן (מִ·) is prefixed to the word with which the comparison is made, *e.g.* 1 Sam. ix. 2, נָּבֹהַּ מִכָּל־הָעָם, *taller than any of the people*; Judg. xiv. 18, מָתוֹק מִדְּבַשׁ, *sweeter than honey*; so also after a verb denoting an attribute, as וַיִּגְבַּהּ מִכָּל־הָעָם, *and he was taller than any of the people*, 1 Sam. x. 23.

2. The several modes of expressing the *superlative* are in principle the same: thus in all of them the *positive form*, by means of the article, or a suffix, or a following genitive, is made to designate an *individual* as preeminently the possessor of the quality expressed (comp. *le plus grand*), *e.g.* 1 Sam. xvii. 14, *And David was* הַקָּטָן *the small* (one), i.e. *the smallest*, and *the three great* (ones), i.e. *greater*, &c.; Gen. xlii. 13; Jonah iii. 5, מִגְּדוֹלָם וְעַד קְטַנָּם, *from the greatest among them* (lit. *their great one*) *even unto the least among them* (lit. *their little one*).

TO THE READER

THIS work is commended to your intelligent use for gaining a correct understanding of the text of the Sacred Scriptures. The present work was undertaken for the purpose of attaining a more definite idea of the import of certain words in the text of our version than could be obtained without reference to the original, and then of discriminating the use of the same English word when used in the rendering of different Hebrew words. A reference to this work by those who are not grammatically acquainted with the original, will be found to serve this purpose. For the direction of such it must be noticed, that where the Hebrew is rendered by a phrase, *to keep silence, to hold fast, to take hold,* &c., the reader will find the reference only under one of these words; and a little consideration will sometimes be necessary as to what word should be consulted. It is believed, however, that every verb and noun in Hebrew will be found referred to. Very considerable labour has been applied to the making the references correct and the whole complete; but it must be understood that many phrases will not be found which are the rendering of particles, adverbs, and prepositions. It was found impracticable to include the renderings of the verb-substantive הָיָה, *to be,* except in some few cases. A Concordance of all such phrases might yet be considered a desideratum by those who appreciate the present work.

In the Indexes to the references where the same English word occurs more than once, the order has been pointed out, *e. g. know,* 2 Sam. iii. 25, 25, 25, 2 a b b, *knowest* is *pret.,* and *to know* occurs twice as *inf.;* but in Gen. iii. 5, 2 e, *doth know,* and *knowing,* are both *part. Poel.* It is of importance to mark the part of speech in the original, since verbs and nouns in Hebrew are not always rendered by verbs and nouns in English. An occasional reference to the Index of the varied renderings of the same original Hebrew, and a comparison of the explanation of that word in the body of this work, may frequently be of use.

Thankful will the Author be if those who use the present work may find it instrumental to an increase in the knowledge of the Divine Will, as made known to us in the writings of "Holy men of God, who spake as they were moved by the Holy Ghost;" "not in the words which man's wisdom teacheth, but which the Holy Ghost teacheth."

THE BIBLE STUDENT'S GUIDE TO OLD TESTAMENT WORD STUDIES

A, AN

אֶחָד *adj.* one. ^a חַד Ch. *adj.* one.

Exod. xvi. 33, xxxiii. 5, xxxvi. 21.	2 Sam. ii. 18, β 25, vi. 19, 19, 19, xviii. 11.	Jer. li. 60, lii. 25.
Lev. viii. 26.	1 Kings vii. 32, xiii. 11, xix. 4, 5, xx. 13, xxii. 9.	Ezek. viii. 7, 8, xxxiii. 2, xl. 42, 42, 43, xliii. 13, xlviii. 1, 2, 3, 4, 5, 6, 7, 23,γ 24, 25, 26, 27.
Num. vii. 43, xiii. 2.		
Josh. iii. 12, 13, 16, iv. 2, 4, 5, vii. 21, 21, xxii. 14.	2 Kings vi. 2, xii. 9, xxv. 19.	Dan. ii. 31. a
Judg. iv. 16, a xv. 4.	2 Chron. ix. 8.	vi. 17. a
1 Sam. i. 5, vi. 7, vii. 9, 12, ix. 15, xvi. 20, xxiv. 14, xxvi. 20.	Ezra iv. 8. a	viii. 3.
	vi. 2. a	Jonah iii. 4.
	Job xlii. 11, 11.	Zech. v. 7.

α *lit.* unto one.   β *lit.* as one of the roes.   γ *lit.* one.

ABASE

עָנָה to labour, to suffer ; to be afflicted, to humble oneself. KAL *fut.* Is. xxxi. 4, *i.e.* does not submit himself.

שָׁפֵל to be low ; to depress, cast down. HIPHIL *inf.* Ezek. xxi. 26. *imp.* Job xl. 11. שְׁפַל Ch. Aphel, to bring down. *inf.* Dan. iv. 37.

ABATE

גָּרַע to take from or away. NIPHAL *pret.* Lev. xxvii. 18.

חָסֵר to diminish ; to fail, to be lessened. KAL *fut.* Gen. viii. 3.

נוּס to flee. KAL *pret.* Deut. xxxiv. 7, *marg.* fled. See Gen. xxvii. 1.

קָלַל to be light ; to be lessened. KAL *pret.* Gen. viii. 8, 11.

רָפָה to cast down ; to let fall ; with מִן to cease from, of anger. KAL *pret.* Judg. viii. 3.

ABHOR

1 בָּאַשׁ to stink, as a dead body, Exod. vii. 18, 21, viii. 14 ; as the manna that has bred worms, Exod. xvi. 20 ; as ointment corrupted by flies, Eccles. x. 1 ; as fish when dead, Is. l. 2. Ps. xxxviii. 5 ; my wounds, *i. e.* my sins stink and are corrupt, as a wound that has become very offensive, like an envenomed ulcer discharging a fetid odour ; and which the suffering sinner himself can no longer bear. Hence the force of this word when translated 'abhor.' NIPHAL ^a*pret.* HIPHIL ^b*pret.* ^c*inf.*

2 בָּחַל to loathe and abhor ; with בְּ. KAL *pret.*

3 גָּעַל to loathe, to reject with aversion, or cast away : that kind of aversion is implied, which is often ascribed to the soul or mind, as when the wicked abhor the statutes and judgments of God ; and God abhors the disobedient and unbelieving. It is used in other cases of that aversion which is chiefly to be referred to feeling or instinct : see *Loathe.* KAL ^a*pret.* ^b*fut.*

4 דְּרָאוֹן *m.* The primary meaning seems to be that of thrusting back. The noun is used twice of those who are thrust out of the kingdom of heaven and everlasting life as objects of abhorrence or detestation.

5 זָהַם to loathe, to nauseate, as that which is fetid and filthy. Only in PIEL *pret.*

6 זָעַם to be indignant. KAL ^a*fut.* ^b*part.* Paül.

7 מָאַס to refuse, to reject as useless or troublesome, or with aversion ; to despise, *opp.* בָּחַר to choose, *comp.* Is. xli. 9, Job xxxiv. 33 : see *Despise ;* sometimes rendered ἀποδοκιμάζειν. KAL *fut.*

8 נָאַץ to treat with scorn and contumely : this word is stronger than the preceding, as implying provocation on the part of the object, and is used of God's abhorrence of perverse sinners in each instance of this rendering, except 1 Sam. ii. 17. It sometimes means wantonly to provoke to anger ; lxx. παροξύνειν, παροργίζειν. So it is used of God's being provoked to anger by the contemptuous rejection of his counsel, his abhorring with anger. KAL ^a*fut.* PIEL ^b*pret.*

9 נָאַר to reject with abhorrence and detestation. PIEL *pret.* This word seems to have something in common with אָרַר to execrate, and is always used in connection with נָנֵה to cast off.

10 קוּץ to be weary of, to be greatly disgusted at, to loathe, with בְּ ; to be grieved and distressed as by something painful and oppressive : so Is. vii. 16 and 1 Kings xi. 25 may be understood, *moleste ferre ;* lxx. ἐβαρυθύμησεν, to be distressed on account of. מִפְּנֵי Is. vii. 16 may be rendered, "the land by whose two kings thou art distressed." KAL ^a*fut.* ^b*part.*

11 שָׁקַץ to be abominable, filthy, impure, chiefly through idolatry, or the eating of things unclean ; to detest, abhor, nauseate. PIEL *pret.*

12 תָּאַב to desire earnestly, eagerly, as a hungry man desires food; in PIEL it is once used in a contrary sense; that which we strongly desire, and do not obtain, we may loathe; or it may be for the following root by the change of one letter. PIEL *part.*

13 תָּעַב to be averse to, as to that which is offensive to all the senses; to detest, hate with indignation, as the Israelites, things accursed; as David, false doctrine, Ps. cxix. 163; as the wicked, an upright speaker, Amos v. 10; and judgment, Mic. iii. 9; as God abhors the man of blood and deceit, Ps. v. 6; *comp.* Job xv. 16; Ps. cvi. 40. PIEL ^a*pret.* ^b*inf.* ^c*fut.* ^d*part.*

Exod. v. 21.	1 b	Job xxx. 10.	13 a	Prov. xxii. 14.	6 b
Lev. xx. 23.	10 a	xxxiii. 20.	5	xxiv. 24.	6 a
xxvi. 11, 15.	3 b	xlii. 6.	7	Is. vii. 16.	10 b
xxvi. 30, 43, 44.	3 a	Ps. v. 6.	13 c	xlix. 7.	13 d
Deut. vii. 26. a	13 b c	x. 3.	8 b	lxvi. 24.	4
xxiii. 7, 7.	13 c	xxii. 24.	11	Jer. xiv. 21.	8 a
xxxii. 19. β	8 a	xxxvi. 4.	7	Lam. ii. 7.	9
1 Sam. ii. 17. γ	8 b	lxxviii. 59.	7	Ezek. xvi. 25.	13 c
xxvii. 12. δ	1 c b	lxxxi. 38.	7	Amos v. 10.	13 c
2 Sam. xvi. 21.	1 a	cvi. 40.	13 c	vi. 8.	12
1 Kings xi. 25.	10 a	cvii. 18.	13 c	Mic. iii. 9.	13 d
Job ix. 31. ε	13 a	cxix. 163.	13 c	Zech. xi. 8.	2
xix. 19.	13 a				

a lit. and abhorring thou shalt abhor it.   β *or,* despised.   γ lxx. ἠθέτουν.
δ *lit.* in making himself to stink he hath made himself stink.   ε *or,* make me to be abhorred.

ABI

אָב *m.* father: Judg. vi. 11, 24; viii. 32: *lit.* father of.

ABIB

אָבִיב *m.* the name of a month, so called because corn was then forming the ear, a few weeks before harvest; falling somewhere about March or April; afterwards called Nisan, the first month of the Hebrew year: Exod. xiii. 4; xxiii. 15; xxxiv. 18, 18: Deut. xvi. 1, 1: Ezek. iii. 15, Tel-abib, *i.e.* a corn-hill.

ABIDE

1 בּוֹא to come in, to enter. KAL *fut.*

2 גּוּר to sojourn as a stranger, a guest; in Ps. xv. 1, some understand it of a temporary abode in the church below, as distinguished from a fixed dwelling, of the next clause, in the church for ever. KAL *fut.*

3 דָּבַק to cleave; with עַ to abide fast, to remain with. KAL *fut.*

4 חוּל to stay, rest, or abide, implying action which has attained its object, which does not however cease, but now dwells on the purpose to which it is directed: let the following passages be consulted as to the import of this meaning, where evil is said to fall and stay to fulfil its commission on some object of vengeance: Jer. xxiii. 19; xxx. 23: Lam. iv. 6: 2 Sam. iii. 29. KAL *pret.*

5 חָנָה to abide, rest, after travelling or marching, or as opposed to removing; to abide in tents. KAL ^a*imp.* ^b*fut.*

6 יָשַׁב to sit, to remain in a place, mostly with בְּ. See *Sit.* KAL ^a*pret.* ^b*inf.* ('thy abode,' *lit.* thy sitting, is to be understood with the phrases that follow of all the actions of a man's life: *comp.* Ps. cxxxix. 2.) ^c*imp.* ^d*fut.* ^e*part.* Poel. HIPHIL ^f*fut.*

7 כּוּל to contain; to sustain or endure heavy judgments, implying suffering: see *Contain, Presence.* PILP. ^a*part.* HIPHIL ^b*fut.*

8 לָוָה to be joined, to adhere to, to accompany. KAL ^b*fut.*

9 לִין to lodge, to stay all night; to continue in a settled state. KAL ^a*fut.* HITHPALP. ^b*fut.*

10 סָפַח to adjoin oneself: HITHPAEL *inf.;* with בְּ. I Sam. xxvi. 19, *marg.* cleaving; have driven me from abiding, from associating myself and being associated with the inheritance of the Lord, *i. e.* from abiding in it: *comp.* Deut. xxxii. 9.

11 עָמַד to stand; *opp.* to pass away, Eccles. i. 4; to abide, to be situate, with עַל, in a place; to abide behind. KAL ^a*fut.* ^b*part.* Poel.

12 מִקְוֶה *m.* hope, expectation: I Chron. xxix. 15; no abiding, no expectation of a fixed or continued state.

13 קוּם to rise; to stand up, to keep one's ground. KAL *fut.*

14 שׁוּב to return. KAL *inf.* Paronomasia.

15 שָׁכַן to dwell, to remain, to continue where one is; to rest after motion; to rest or remain in a state of inactivity; applied to the presence of God among his people, and hence, Shechinah: see *Tabernacle.* KAL ^a*pret.* ^b*fut.* ^c*part.* Poel.

16 הָיָה to be. KAL *fut.*

Gen. xix. 2.	9 a	Judg. xi. 17.	6 d	2 Chron. xxxii. 10.	6 e
xxii. 5.	6 c	xvi. 9, 12.	6 e	Ezra viii. 15. β	5 b
xxiv. 55.	6 d	xix. 4.	6 d	viii. 32.	6 d
xxix. 14.	6 d	xx. 47.	6 d	Job xxxix. 13.	6 a
xxix. 19.	6 c	xxi. 2.	6 d	xxxviii. 40.	6 a
xliv. 33.	6 d	Ruth ii. 8.	3	xxxix. 9.	9 a
xlix. 24.	6 d	1 Sam. i. 22.	6 a	xxxix. 28.	9 b
Exod. xvi. 29.	6 c	i. 23.	6 d	Ps. xv. 1.	2
xxiv. 16.	15 b	v. 7.	6 d	xlix. 12.	9 a
xl. 35.	15 a	vii. 2.	6 b	lv. 19.	6 e
Lev. viii. 35.	6 d	xiii. 16.	6 a	lxi. 4.	2
xix. 13.	9 a	xix. 2.	6 a	lxi. 7.	6 d
Num. ix. 17, 18.	15 b	xxii. 5.	6 d	xci. 1.	9 b
ix. 20, 22.	5 b	xxii. 6.	6 e	cxix. 90.	11 a
ix. 21.	16	xxii. 23.	6 d	cxxv. 1.	6 d
xi. 35.	16	xxiii. 14, 18, 25.	6 d	Prov. vii. 11.	15 b
xx. 1.	6 d	xxv. 13.	6 a	xv. 31.	9 a
xxii. 5.	6 e	xxvi. 7.	6 e	xix. 23.	9 a
xxii. 8.	6 d	xxvi. 19.	10	Eccles. i. 4.	11 b
xxiv. 2.	15 c	xxx. 10.	11 a	viii. 15.	8
xxv. 1.	6 d	xxx. 21.	6 f	Is. xxxvii. 28.	6 b
xxxi. 19.	5 a	2 Sam. i. 1.	6 d	Jer. x. 10.	7 b
xxxii. 23, 23. a	1	xi. 11.	6 e	xxi. 9.	6 e
xxxv. 25.	6 a	xi. 12.	6 d	xxxviii. 28.	6 e
Deut. i. 46, 46.	6 d a	xv. 8.	6 b	xlii. 10. γ	14, 6 d
iii. 19, 29.	6 d	xv. 19.	6 c	xlix. 18, 33.	6 d
ix. 9.	6 d	xvi. 3.	6 e	l. 40.	6 d
Josh. ii. 22.	6 d	xvi. 18.	6 d	Hos. iii. 3, 4.	4
v. 8.	6 d	1 Kings viii. 13.	6 b	xi. 6.	4
viii. 9.	6 d	xvii. 19.	6 e	Joel ii. 11.	7 b
xviii. 5, 5.	11 a	2 Kings xix. 27.	6 b	Mic. v. 4.	6 a
Judg. v. 16.	6 a	1 Chron. xxix. 15.	12	Nah. i. 6.	13
v. 17, 17.	15 a b	2 Chron. xxv. 19.	6 c	Mal. iii. 2.	7 a

a lit. shall go into the fire.   β *or,* pitched.   γ *lit.* returning ye will abide.

ABJECTS

נָכֶה *adj.* one that smites, a smiter with the tongue, calumniator: Ps. xxxv. 15. lxx. *Vulg. Syr. flagella. Symm.* πλῆκται. *Hieron.* percutientes. *Targ.* impii qui percutiunt me verbis suis. *Comp.* Jer. xviii. 18; Job v. 21. Our version takes it in a passive sense, smitten, *i. e.* lowest of men, despised, contemptible: *comp. Vile,* in Job xxx. 8.

ABLE, ABILITY

1 דַּי *m.* sufficiency; the full ability of a person; with a genitive of the person or thing to or for which there is a sufficiency.

2 חַיִל *m.* strength, power ; strength of body or mind.

3 יָד *com.* hand.

4 יָכֹל to be able ; constr. with acc. more freq. with a gerund ; to be able to do anything, with a simple inf.; also with a finite verb ; to be able to effect, to accomplish, to prevail. KAL [a]*pret.* [b]*inf.* [c]*fut.* יָכֹל Ch. P'AL, to be able. [d]*pret.* [e]*part.*

5 כְּהַל Ch. to be able. P'AL *part. active.*

6 כֹּחַ *m.* strength of body and vigour.

7 מָצָא to find. KAL [a]*pret.* [b]*fut.*

8 נָשַׂג to move oneself to ; to reach, to attain to. HIPHIL [a]*pret.* [b]*fut.*

9 עָצַר to shut up ; to hold back, to detain ; with כֹּחַ expressed or understood, to retain strength ; with לְ to have strength for anything, to be able. KAL [a]*pret.* [b]*fut.*

10 יֵשׁ to be : 2 Chron. xxv. 9 ; *lit.* it is to Jehovah to give.

ABLE, followed by an infinitive in English, has frequently no corresponding Hebrew, and will be found under the latter word ; as, able to endure. See *Endure,* &c.

Gen. xv. 5.	4 c	Deut. xiv. 24.	4 c	Ps. xxi. 11.	4 c
Exod. x. 5.	4 c	xvi. 17. κ	3	xxxvi. 12.	4 a
xviii. 18.	4 c	Judg. viii. 3.	4 a	xl. 12.	4 a
xviii. 21, 25.	2	1 Sam. vi. 20.	4 c	Eccles. viii. 17.	4 c
xviii. 23.	4	xvii. 9, 33.	4 c	Is. xxxvi. 8, 14.	4 c
xl. 35.	4 a	1 Kings iii. 9.	4 c	xlvii. 11, 12.	4 c
Lev. v. 7. α	3, 1	ix. 21.	4 a	Jer. xi. 11.	4 c
v. 11. β	3, 8	2 Kings xviii. 23, 29.	4 c	xlix. 10.	4 c
xii. 8. γ	3, 7 b 1	1 Chron. xiii. λ	2	Lam. i. 14.	4 c
xiv. 22. δ	3, 8 b	xxvi. 8.	2	Ezek. vii. 19.	4 c
xiv. 31. δ	3, 8 b	xxix. 14. μ	9 b, 6	xxxiii. 12.	4 c
xxv. 26. ε	3, 8 a, 7 a, 1	2 Chron. ii. 6. ν	9 b, 6	xlvi. 5, o 11.	3
xxv. 28. ζ	3, 7 a, 1	vii. 7.	4 a	Dan. i. 4.	6
xxv. 49. η	3, 8 a	xx. 37.	9 a	ii. 26.	5
xxvii. 8. θ	3, 8 b	xxxii. 14, 15.	4 c	iii. 17.	4 b, a
Num. xi. 14.	4 c	Ezra ii. 69.	6	iv. 18, 18.	4 e, 5
xiii. 30, 31.	4 c	x. 13. ξ	6	iv. 37.	4 e
xiv. 16.	4 b	Neh. iv. 10.	4 c	vi. 20.	4 d
xxii. 11, ι 37.	4 c	v. 8.	1	Amos vii. 10.	4 c
Deut. i. 9.	4 c	Ps. lxxviii. 38.	4 e	Zeph. i. 18.	4 c
ix. 28.	4 b				

α *lit.* his hand cannot reach to the sufficiency of ; see also *Bring.* β *lit.* his hand reach not. γ *lit.* her hand find not sufficiency of. δ *lit.* his hand can reach. ε *lit.* his hand hath attained and found sufficiency. ζ *lit.* If his hand hath not found a sufficiency. η *lit.* his hand hath attained. θ *lit.* as the hand of him, &c. can attain. ι *lit.* I shall prevail in fighting against him. κ *lit.* according to the gift of his hand. λ *lit.* mighty men of valour. μ *lit.* retain, or, obtain strength. ν *lit.* hath retained, or obtained strength. ξ *lit.* not power. o *lit.* the gift of his hand.

ABOLISH

חָלַף to pass, to pass away. KAL *fut.* Is. ii. 18 : *lit.* the idols shall utterly pass away.

חָתַת to be broken, so as to be quite disabled ; applied to the righteousness or saving power and goodness of God, which shall never be broken, disabled, or rendered in any respect incapable of making his faithful servants happy. NIPHAL *fut.* Is. li. 6.

מָחָה to blot or wipe out. NIPHAL *pret.* Ezek. vi. 6.

ABOMINABLE, ABOMINATION

1 בָּאַשׁ to stink, to be loathsome and odious, to be had in abomination. See *Abhor.* NIPHAL *pret.*

2 זָעַם to be indignant ; to account abominable, the object of the warmest resentment. KAL *part.* Paül.

3 פִּגּוּל *m.* impurity, uncleanness, abomination ; spoken of food.

4 שָׁקַץ to detest ; to be abominable, unclean, chiefly used of idolatry, and of things that one may not touch, eat, or worship ; PIEL, to make abominable, to have in abomination. PIEL [a]*fut.* [b]שֶׁקֶץ *m.* abomination, an abominable thing ; [c]שִׁקּוּץ *m.* of garments, of meats offered to idols, abominable filthy idols.

5 תָּעַב See *Abhor.* NIPHAL [a]*pret.* [b]*part.* HIPHIL, to do abominably, chiefly in things connected with idolatry. [c]*pret.* [d]*fut.* [e]תּוֹעֵבָה *f.* an abomination ; abominable deed or practice.

Gen. xliii. 32.	5 e	2 Chron. xv. 8.	4 c	Jer. viii. 12.	5 e
xlvi. 34.	5 e	xxviii. 3.	5 e	xiii. 27.	4 c
Exod. viii. 26, 26.	5 e	xxxiii. 2.	5 e	xvi. 18.	4 c
Lev. vii. 18.	3	xxxiv. 33.	5 e	xxxii. 34.	5 e
vii. 21.	4 b	xxxvi. 8, 14.	5 e	xxxii. 35.	4 c
xi. 10, 12, 20, 23, 41,		Ezra ix. 1, 11, 14.	5 b	xliv. 4, 22.	5 e
42.	4 b	Job xv. 16.	5 b	Ezek. iv. 14.	3
xi. 11, 11.	4 b a	Ps. xiv. 1.	5 c	v. 9, 11.	5 e
xi. 13, 13.	4 a b	liii. 1.	5 c	vii. 9, 11.	5 e
xi. 43.	4 a	lxxxviii. 8.	5 e	vii. 3, 4, 8, 9, 20.	5 e
xviii. 22, 26, 27, 29,		Prov. iii. 32.	5 e	viii. 6, 6, 9, 13, 15, 17.	5 e
30.	5 e	vi. 16.	5 e	viii. 10.	4 b
xix. 7.	3	viii. 7.	5 e	ix. 4.	5 e
xx. 13.	5 e	xi. 1, 20.	5 e	xi. 18, 21.	5 e
xx. 25.	4 a	xii. 22.	5 e	xii. 16.	5 e
Deut. vii. 25, 26.	5 e	xiii. 19.	5 e	xiv. 6.	5 e
xii. 31.	5 e	xv. 8, 9, 26.	5 e	xvi. 2, 22, 36, 43,	
xiii. 14.	5 e	xvi. 5, 12.	5 e	47, 50, 51, 51, }	5 e
xiv. 3.	5 e	xvii. 15.	5 e	58.	
xvii. 1, 4.	5 e	xx. 10, 23.	5 e	xvi. 52.	5 c
xviii. 9, 12, 12.	5 e	xxi. 27.	5 e	xviii. 12, 13, 24.	5 e
xx. 18.	5 e	xxiv. 9.	5 e	xx. 4.	5 e
xxii. 5.	5 e	xxvi. 25.	5 e	xx. 7, 8, 30.	4 c
xxiii. 18.	5 e	xxviii. 9.	5 e	xxii. 2, 11.	5 e
xxiv. 4.	5 e	xxix. 27, 27.	5 e	xxiii. 36.	5 e
xxv. 16.	5 e	Is. i. 13.	5 e	xxxiii. 26, 29.	5 e
xxvii. 15.	5 e	xix. 19.	5 b	xxxvi. 31.	5 e
xxix. 17.	5 e	xli. 24.	5 e	xliii. 8.	5 e
xxxii. 16.	5 e	xlix. 19.	5 e	xliv. 6, 7, 13.	5 e
1 Sam. xiii. 4.	1	lxv. 4.	5 e	Dan. ix. 27.	4 c
1 Kings xi. 5, 7, 7.	4 c	lxvi. 3.	4 c	xi. 31.	4 c
xiv. 24.	5 e	lxvi. 17.	4 b	xii. 11.	4 c
xxi. 26.	5 d	Jer. ii. 7.	5 e	Hos. ix. 10.	4 c
2 Kings xvi. 3.	5 e	iv. 1.	4 c	Mic. vi. 10.	2
xxi. 2, 11.	5 e	vi. 15.	5 e	Nah. iii. 6.	4 c
xxiii. 13, 13, 13.	4 c c, 5 e	vii. 10.	5 e	Zech. ix. 7.	4 c
xxiii. 24.	4 c	vii. 30.	4 c	Mal. ii. 11.	5 e
1 Chron. xxi. 6.	5 a				

ABOUND, ABUNDANCE, ABUNDANT

1 הָמוֹן a multitude ; plenty or abundance of anything, especially of riches.

2 זִיז *m.* The primary meaning of the root זוז, nowhere used, is doubtful. Ges. refers it to the idea of quick motion. Lee renders the noun, *essentia,* from which he deduces the idea of abundance, riches. Füerst gives to the root the meaning of prolific existence, fecundity ; and also that of radiating motion, whence the noun comes to mean beasts that roam about, devastate the vineyards, Ps. lxxx. 13, and wander in the open field, Ps. l. 11. Critics are divided as to the meaning in Is. lxvi. 11, whether it is brightness or abundance. The whole context implies an abundance of consolations, which may be supposed to flow in upon Israel in rapid motion. Ges. renders it 'full breasts.'

3 יָרַד to come down. KAL *part.* Poel.

4 יֶתֶר *m.* residue, abundance. [a]יִתְרָה *f.* Is. xv. 7, *i. e.* what is left after the necessaries of life have been supplied ; what, according to the next clause, they lay up.

5 כָּבֵד to be heavy ; to be abundant ; to abound with. NIPHAL *part.* Prov. viii. 24, of fountains abounding with water, or, according to Geier, in reference to their excellence, as living, flowing, and pure.

6 כָּבַר to be great, much. HIPHIL, to multiply; part.

7 מִסְפָּר m. number; in abundance: lit. without number.

8 עָצְמָה f. strength. Is. xlvii. 9: or, in the midst of the vigour of.

9 עָתֶרֶת f. riches, abundance.

10 רַב adj. many, much, numerous. a רֹב m. multitude.

11 רָבָה to multiply, to bring in abundance. HIPHIL a pret. b inf. c fut.

12 שֶׂבַע m. plenty, abundance of food.

13 שַׁלְוָה f. quietness, peace; abundance of idleness.

14 שֶׂפַע m. abundance. a שִׁפְעָה f. id. multitude.

ABUNDANTLY is frequently the translation of the infinitive of verbs. See *Breed, Bring forth,* &c.

Exod. xxxiv. 6.	10	2 Chron. xiv. 15.	10 a	Prov. viii. 24.	5
Num. xx. 11.	10	xv. 9.	10 a	xxviii. 20.	10
Deut. xxviii. 47.	10 a	xvii. 5.	10 a	xxix. 22.	10
xxxiii. 19.	14	xviii. 1, 2.	10 a	Eccles. v. 10.	1
1 Sam. i. 16.	10 a	xx. 25.	10 a	v. 12.	12
2 Sam. xii. 30. α	11 b	xxiv. 11.	10 a	Is. vii. 22.	10 a
1 Kings i. 19, 25.	10 a	xxix. 35.	10 a	xv. 3. δ	3
x. 10, 27.	10 a	xxxi. 5, 5.	11 a, 10 a	xv. 7.	4 a
xviii. 41. β	1	xxxii. 5, 29.	10 a	xlvii. 9. ε	8
1 Chron. xii. 40.	10 a	Neh. ix. 25.	10 a	lv. 7. ζ	11 c
xxii. 3, 3, 5, 8, 14,		Esth. i. 7.	10	lvi. 12. η	4
15.	10 a	Job xxii. 11.	14 a	lx. 5. θ	1
xxii. 4. γ	7	xxxvi. 28.	10	lxvi. 11. ι	4
xxix. 2, 21.	10 a	xxxvi. 31.	6	Jer. xxxiii. 6.	9
2 Chron. i. 15.	10 a	xxxviii. 34.	14 a	li. 13.	10
ii. 9.	10 a	Ps. xxxvii. 11.	10 a	Ezek. xvi. 49. κ	13
iv. 18.	10 a	lii. 7.	10 a	xxvi. 10.	14 a
ix. 1, 9, 27.	10 a	lxxii. 7.	10 a	Zech. xiv. 14.	10 a
xi. 23.	10 a				

α *lit.* very great abundance. β *lit.* or, a sound of noise of rain. γ *lit.* without number. δ *lit.* flowing in weeping; *marg.* descending into weeping; or, coming down with weeping. ε *lit.* with strength. ζ *lit.* multiply to pardon. η *lit.* a very great residue. θ *lit.* or, the noise of the sea shall be turned to thee. ι *lit.* or brightness. κ *lit.* in the security of ease.

ABOUT

סָבַב to turn oneself; to go about in a place; to surround, encompass; to be about on every side; to make about, to cast about. KAL a pret. b fut. HIPHIL c fut. d סָבִיב m. round about.

ABOUT enters into the rendering of many verbs; as, bring about, &c.

Num. ii. 2.	d	Neh. v. 17.	d	Jer. xlviii. 17, 39.	d
xvi. 24.	d	vi. 16.	d	xlix. 5.	d
Deut. xvii. 14.	d	Job xxix. 5.	d	Ezek. i. 4.	d
2 Sam. xxiv. 6.	d	Ps. lxxxix. 7.	d	v. 2.	d
1 Kings v. 3.	a	Cant. iii. 7.	d	xii. 14.	d
vii. 23.	d	Jer. xvii. 26.	d	xxxii. 22.	d
xviii. 32.	d	xxxii. 44.	d	xxxvi. 7.	d
2 Chron. xiv. 7.	c	xxxiii. 13.	d	xliii. 17, 17.	d
Ezra i. 6.	d	xli. 14.	b	Dan. ix. 16.	d

ABOVE

מָרוֹם m. height; something remote or far off: 2 Sam. xxii. 17: Ps. x. 5; xviii. 16; cxliv. 7: Lam. i. 13.

ABROAD

חוּץ m. any space that lieth without, in contradistinction to that which lieth within, or which lies beyond any supposed bounds or precincts: Gen. xv. 5; xix. 17: Exod. xii. 46; xxi. 19: Lev. xiv. 8; xviii. 9: Deut. xxiii. 10, 12, 13; xxiv. 11, 11: Judges xii. 9, 9: 1 Sam. ix. 26: 2 Kings ix. 3: 2 Chron. xxix. 16: Ps. xli. 6: Prov. v. 16: Jer. vi. 11: Lam. i. 20: Ezek. xxxiv. 21.

פָּרַץ to break forth. KAL fut. 1 Chr. xiii. 2. "Let us send abroad;" *marg.* let us break forth and send.

See also the verb with which it is connected, as *Cast,* &c.

ABSENT

סָתַר to hide. NIPHAL fut. Gen. xxxi. 49; lit. hidden from, i. e. shall not see one another.

ABUSE

עָלַל to do, perform. Hithpael with ב to perform a mighty deed on, or to abuse any one, to treat any one ill, to do violence, to use with indignity, insolence, and scorn. HITHPAEL pret. 1 Sam. xxxi. 4; marg. mock. 1 Chron. x. 4; marg. id. fut. Judg. xix. 25.

ACCEPT, ACCEPTABLE, ACCEPTANCE

1 בָּחַר to choose, select, prefer. NIPHAL part.

2 דָּשֵׁן to be or become fat; to make fat, to regard as fat; or, from דֶּשֶׁן m. ashes, to turn to ashes. PIEL fut.

3 חֵפֶץ m. delight: acceptable words; lit. words of delight.

4 יָטַב to be well; to be pleasing, agreeable, right, acceptable. KAL fut.

5 לָקַח to take, accept, &c. KAL pret.

6 נָפַל to fall; to let fall a supplication, to present it in a humble manner; as we say, to lay it at one's feet. KAL fut.

7 נָשָׂא to lift up; with פָּנִים to accept the person of any one, to be gracious to him; either in a good sense favourably, or in a bad sense partially. The expression arises from an Eastern custom of prostrating themselves in making a request, which being granted, the prince orders the suppliant to rise, i. e. to lift up his face. KAL a pret. b inf. c fut. d שְׂאֵת m. a raising, exaltation, dignity; precedence, pre-eminence, of the birthright. Gen. iv. 7; comp. xlix. 3.

8 פָּנִים m. pl. face.

9 רוּחַ to smell, to smell with pleasure, to smell a sweet savour. HIPHIL fut.

10 רָצָה to be well pleased with, to take delight in a person or thing; particularly to accept graciously one with a present, or with offerings and prayers, spoken of the Deity. To bear with a patient, acquiescing, submissive mind; in opposition to reluctance, impatience, distrust, or despair; Lev. xxvi. 41, 43. KAL a pret. b imp. c fut. d part. Poel. e part. Paül. NIPHAL f pret. g fut. h רָצוֹן m. delight, acceptance, approbation; good will, favour, grace.

11 שְׁפַר Ch. to be beautiful, acceptable, with עַל. P'AL fut.

Gen. iv. 7.	7 d	1 Sam. xxvi. 19.	9	Is. xlix. 8. β	10 h
xix. 21.	7 a, 8	2 Sam. xxiv. 23.	10 c	lvi. 7. γ	10 h
xxxii. 20.	7 c, 8	Esth. x. 3.	10 e	lviii. 5. δ	10 h
xxviii. 38.	5	Job xiii. 8, 10.	7 c	lx. 7.	10 h
Exod. xxii. 11.	10 h	xxxii. 21.	7 c	lxi. 2.	10 h
Lev. i. 4.	10 f	xxxiv. 19.	7 a	Jer. vi. 20.	10 h
vii. 18.	10 g	xxxiv. 8, 9.	7 c, 8	xiv. 10.	10 a
x. 19.	4	Ps. xix. 14.	10 h	xiv. 12.	10 d
xix. 7.	10 g	xx. 3.	2	xxxvii. 20.	6
xxii. 20, 21.	10 h	lxix. 13. β	7 c	Ezek. xx. 40, 41.	10 c
xxii. 23, 25, 27.	10 g	lxxxii. 2.	7 c	xliii. 27.	10 a
xxiii. 11. a	10 h	cxix. 108.	10 b	Dan. iv. 27.	11
xxvi. 41, 43.	10 c	Prov. xi. 32.	10 h	Hos. viii. 13.	10 a
Deut. xxxiii. 11.	10 c	xviii. 5.	7 b	Amos v. 22.	10 c
xxxiii. 24.	10 e	xxi. 3.	1	Mal. i. 8.	7 c
1 Sam. xviii. 5.	4	Eccles. ix. 7.	10 a	i. 10, 13.	10 c
xxv. 35.	7 c	xii. 10.	3		

α *lit.* for your acceptance. β *lit.* a time of acceptance. γ *lit.* unto favour. δ *lit.* a day of acceptance.

ACCOMPLISH

1 כָּלָה to be completed, finished. PIEL, to accomplish. KAL [a] pret. [b] inf. PIEL [c] pret. [d] inf.

2 מָלֵא to be or become full; to fill, to make full. Job xv. 32: "it shall be accomplished," i. e. vanity, or, the recompense; or, impers. there shall be a filling up, before his time, i. e. when his days are not accomplished. KAL [a] pret. [b] inf. [c] fut. NIPHAL [d] fut. PIEL [e] inf.

3 עָשָׂה to make, do, act; to execute or accomplish anything. KAL [a] pret. [b] fut.

4 פָּלָא to separate; to consecrate, to pay a vow. PIEL inf.

5 קוּם to rise; to raise up, to fulfil. HIPHIL [a] inf. [b] fut.

6 רָצָה to be well pleased, to take delight in. KAL fut. Job xiv. 6: till he shall accomplish as an hireling his day; till he be delighted as a labourer in having finished his day.

7 תָּמַם to be finished, complete; to be consumed. KAL pret.

8 הָיָה to be. NIPHAL, to be accomplished, pret.

Lev. xxii. 21.	4	Isa. lv. 11.	3 a	Ezek. v. 13, 13.	1 a d
1 Kings v. 9.	3 b	Jer. xxv. 12.	2 b	vi. 12.	1 c
2 Chron. xxxvi. 22.	1 b	xxv. 34.	2 a	vii. 8.	1 c
Esth. ii. 12.	2 c	xxix. 10.	2 b	xiii. 15.	1 c
Job xiv. 6.	6	xliv. 25. β	5 a b	xx. 8, 21.	1 d
xv. 32. a	2 d	Lam. iv. 11.	1 c	Dan. ix. 2.	2 e
Ps. lxiv. 6.	7	iv 22.	7	xi. 36.	1 a
Prov. xiii. 9.	8	Ezek. iv. 6.	1 c	xii. 7.	1 d
Isa. xl. 2.	2 a				

a lit. or, cut off, as if from מָלַל   β lit. accomplishing ye will accomplish.

ACCORD

פֶּה m. mouth : Josh. ix. 2, "with one accord."

To grow of its own accord : see Grow.

ACCOUNT

1 חָשַׁב to think; to account, esteem; to make account of. NIPHAL [a] fut. [b] part. PIEL [c] fut. [d] חֶשְׁבּוֹן m. reason.

2 טַעַם Ch. m. commandment, decree; intelligence, reason.

3 סָפַר to count, number. PUAL [a] fut. [b] מִסְפָּר m. number.

4 עָנָה to answer; to give account. KAL fut.

5 פְּקֻדָּה f. muster, enumeration.

Deut. ii. 11, 20.	1 a	2 Chron. xxvi. 11.	5	Eccles. vii. 27.	1 d
1 Kings x. 21.	1 b	Job xxxiii. 13.	4	Isa. ii. 22.	1 b
1 Chron. xxvii. 24.	3 b	Ps. xxii. 30.	3 a	Dan. vi. 2.	2
2 Chron. ix. 20.	1 b	cxliv. 3.	1 c		

ACCURSED

1 חָרַם see Destroy. HIPHIL, to make devoted or accursed. [a] fut. [b] חֵרֶם m. devoted to destruction.

2 קָלַל to be light; PIEL, to vilify, to curse, to blaspheme. PUAL [a] fut. Isa. lxv. 20, i. e. shall be evil spoken of, as dying young, because of sin. [b] קְלָלָה f. a cursing.

Deut. xxi. 23.	2 b	Josh. ii. 9, 11, 12,	1 b	1 Chron. ii. 7.	1 b
Josh. vi. 17.	1 b	12, 13, 13, 15.	1 b	Isa. lxv. 20.	2 a
vi. 18, 18, 18.	1 b a b	xxii. 20.	1 b		

ACCUSE, ACCUSATION

אֲכַל Ch. to eat. P'AL pret. Dan. iii. 8; vi. 24.

לָשַׁן to tongue, i. e. to use the tongue freely; to slander a person. HIPHIL fut. Prov. xxx. 10.

קְרַץ Ch. m. a piece torn or gnawed off : found only in connection with אֲכַל above : meaning to slander, inform

against; as in Lat., mordere, dente carpere, dente rodere. Dan. iii. 8; vi. 24. lit. to eat the pieces of.

שִׂטְנָה f. accusation, of an adversary : Ezra iv. 6.

ACCUSTOMED

לִמּוּד adj. used to anything, practised, expert : Jer. xiii. 23.

ACHMETHA

אַחְמְתָא Ch. Ecbatana, the metropolis of ancient Media, and the summer residence of the kings of Persia; situated in the same place where afterwards was, and still is, Hamedan, the Parthian metropolis. Jarchi and Aben Ezra suppose it to be a chest or coffer in which writings are kept. Ezra vi. 2.

ACKNOWLEDGE

1 אָשֵׁם to be guilty; to acknowledge an offence. KAL fut.

2 יָדַע to know. KAL [a] pret. [b] imp. [c] fut. HIPHIL [d] fut.

3 נָכַר see Know; in Hiphil, to know, own as an acquaintance or friend, to treat as an acquaintance; to distinguish by marks. HIPHIL [a] pret. [b] fut.

Gen. xxxviii. 26.	3 b	Prov. iii. 6.	2 b	Jer. xiv. 20.	2 a
Deut. xxi. 17.	3 b	Isa. xxxiii. 13.	2 b	xxiv. 5.	3 b
xxxiii. 9.	3 a	lxi. 9.	3 b	Dan. xi. 39.	3 b
Ps. xxxii. 5.	2 d	lxiii. 16.	3 b	ל 39	3 a
li. 3.	2 c	Jer. iii. 13.	2 b	Hos. v. 15.	1

ACQUAINT, ACQUAINTANCE

1 יָדַע to know. KAL [a] part. [b] part. Paül. PUAL [c] part.

2 מְכָר m. acquaintance, friend.

3 נָהַג to urge; to lead, guide, conduct; implying something of force. KAL part. Poel : Eccles. ii. 3, "yet acquainting mine heart," urging on my heart at the same time in wisdom, so as not to endanger my integrity.

4 סָכַן to be useful, profitable, or to dwell with; to attend upon a person in a large sense; to become familiar with, to be reconciled. HIPHIL [a] pret. [b] imp.

2 Kings xii. 5, 7.	2	Ps. xxxi. 11.	1 c	Eccles. ii. 3.	3
Job xix. 13.	1 a	lv. 13.	1 c	Isa. liii. 3.	1 b
xxii. 21.	4 b	lxxxviii. 8, 18.	1 c		
xlii. 11.	1 a	cxxxix. 3.	4 a		

ACQUIT

נָקָה to be clean; to clear, hold guiltless, innocent. PIEL inf., Nah. i. 3, lit. acquitting will not acquit. fut. Job x. 14; Nah. i. 3.

ACRE

מַעֲנָה m. a furrow : 1 Sam. xiv. 14, marg. or, half a furrow of an acre, or of a yoke of land.

צֶמֶד m. a yoke of oxen; as much as a yoke of oxen would plough in a day, Isa. v. 10.

ACT, ACTION

1 דָּבָר m. word, matter, affair, &c.

2 עֲבוֹדָה f. labour, service.

3 עֲלִילָה f. action, deed, work, facinus; usually in a bad sense.

4 מַעֲשֶׂה m. a deed, action, concern, business.

5 פֹּעַל *m.* an action, deed (of God) ; an action in a moral sense.

See also *Mighty, Righteous, Terrible, &c.*

Deut. xi. 3, 7.	4	2 Kings xiv. 15, 18, 28.	1	2 Chron. xvi. 11.	1
1 Sam. ii. 3.	3	xv. 6, 11, 15, 21, 26,		xx. 34.	1
2 Sam. xxiii. 20.	5	31, 36.	1	xxv. 26.	1
1 Kings x. 6.	1	xvi. 19.	1	xxvi. 22.	1
xi. 41, 41.	1	xx. 20.	1	xxvii. 7.	1
xiv. 19, 29.	1	xxi. 17, 25.	1	xxviii. 26.	1
xv. 7, 23, 31.	1	xxiii. 19.	4	xxxii. 32.	1
xvi. 5, 14, 20, 27.	1	xxiii. 28.	1	xxxiii. 18.	1
xxii. 39, 45.	1	xxiv. 5.	1	xxxv. 26.	1
2 Kings i. 18.	1	1 Chron. xi. 22.	5	xxxvi. 8.	1
viii. 23.	1	xxix. 29.	1	Esth. x. 2.	4
x. 34.	1	2 Chron. ix. 5, 29.	1	Ps. ciii. 7.	3
xii. 19.	1	xii. 15.	1	Isa. xxviii. 21, 21.	2
xiii. 8, 12.	1	xiii. 22.	1	lix. 6.	5

ACTIVITY

חַיִל *m.* strength, courage ; integrity : Gen. xlvii. 6.

ADAM

אָדָם *m.* man ; so named, as most commonly supposed, from being of a ruddy colour ; others more suitably derive the word from אֲדָמָה earth, as made of the earth. Some have referred this appellation to דָּמָה to be like, formed in the likeness of God. It is especially the denominative of the first man, who was the figure of the second Adam, the image of the invisible God. Col. i. 15.

ADAMANT

שָׁמִיר *m.* sharp point ; see *Diamond.* Ezek. iii. 9 ; Zech. vii. 12.

ADAR

אֲדָר *m.* the month of blossoms ; the sixth month of the civil year, and the twelfth month of the ecclesiastical year ; from the new moon of March to that of April ; or, according to the Rabbins, from the new moon of February to that of March : Esth. iii. 7, 13 ; viii. 12 ; ix. 1, 15, 17 ; xix. 21. אֲדָר Ch. *id.,* Ezra vi. 15.

ADD

1 יָסַף to add, with *accus.* of the thing added, and עַל of that to which it is added ; to add to, to increase ; the phrase of adding to do, signifies not only to do the same thing again, but to do it with a greater intention of spirit ; thus, to add to sin is to sin more grievously, to be more vile and sinful in sinning : Judg. vii. 12 ; x. 6. 1 Sam. iii. 21 : "The Lord added to appear," *i. e.* he appeared more fully and clearly, in a more glorious discovery of himself. KAL [a] *pret.* [b] *part.* Poel. NIPHAL [c] *pret.* HIPHIL [d] *pret.* [e] *inf.* [f] *fut.* [g] יְסַף Ch. *id.* HOPHAL *pret.*

2 נָתַן to give. KAL [a] *imp.* [b] *fut.*

3 סָפָה to add, to add one thing to another with אֶל. KAL [a] *inf.* [b] *imp.*

Gen. xxx. 24.	1 f	Deut. xix. 9.	1 a	Prov. iii. 2.	1 f		
Lev. v. 16.	1 f	xxix. 19.	3 a	x. 22.	1 f		
vi. 5.	1 f	1 Sam. xii. 19.	1 a	xvi. 23.	1 f		
xxvii. 13, 15, 19,		2 Sam. xxiv. 3.	1 a	xxx. 6.	1 f		
27.	1 a	1 Kings xii. 11, 14.	1 d	Isa. xxix. 1.	3 b		
xxvii. 31.	1 f	2 Kings xx. 6.	1 d	xxx. 1.	3 a		
Num. v. 7.	1 f	1 Chron. xxii. 14.	1 f	xxxviii. 5.	1 b		
xxxv. 6.	2 b	2 Chron. x. 14.	1 f	Jer. xxxvi. 32.	1 c		
Deut. iv. 2.	1 f	xxviii. 13.	1 e	xlv. 3.	1 a		
v. 22.	1 a	Job xxxiv. 37.	1 f	Dan. iv. 36.	1 g		
xii. 32.	1 f	Ps. lxix. 27.	2 a				

ADDER

עַכְשׁוּב *m.* asp, adder ; derived perhaps from עָכַשׁ to bend back, and עָקַב to lie in wait, *i. e.* an animal coiling itself and lying in wait. When intending to bite, it is said to swell its skin, till it suddenly rises up, and strikes backward, as if it fell over. Cycloped. of Bib. Literature : *Adder.* Ps. cxl. 3.

פֶּתֶן *m.* an asp, a serpent whose poison is incurable, as it quickly penetrates to the vitals. A great number of authors, historians as well as poets, agree that serpents may be charmed with certain musical sounds, and so made tame and harmless ; but some were so fierce that no art could have any effect upon them. Bochart asserts that they lay one ear on the ground and stop the other with the tail, or repel the incantation by violent hissing. Ps. lviii. 4 ; xci. 13.

צִפְעוֹנִי *m.* the basilisk, the most poisonous of all serpents, said to breathe poison. Prov. xxiii. 32.

שְׁפִיפֹן *m.* a serpent of the viper kind, of a sandy colour, which lurks in sand, and the tracks of wheels in the road ; and which infects with its deadly bite, not only the unwary traveller, but also horses and others ; according to Jerome, the horned serpent, or cerastes. Gen. xlix. 17.

ADDITION

לֹיוֹת *f. pl.* see *Join; prob.* wreaths, festoons, or some additional ornaments : 1 Kings vii. 29, 30, 36.

ADJURE

אָלָה to swear. HIPHIL *fut.* 1 Sam. xiv. 24.

שָׁבַע to swear. HIPHIL *fut.* Josh. vi. 26. *part.* 1 Kings xxii. 16 : 2 Chron. xviii. 15.

ADMONISH

זָהַר to shine ; hence, to instruct, to admonish : see *Warn.* NIPHAL *inf.* Eccles. iv. 13. *imp.* Eccles. xii. 12.

עוּד to say again and again ; to testify, to admonish. HIPHIL *seq.* בְּ to testify against. *pret.* Jer. xlii. 19.

ADONI

אֲדֹנִי the Lord ; used in the composition of names : Judg. i. 5, 6, 7.

ADORN

עָדָה to pass ; to cause to pass over upon ; to dress in a splendid manner. KAL *fut.* Isa. lxi. 10 : Jer. xxxi. 4.

ADULTERY, ADULTERER

1 אִשָּׁה *f.* woman, wife.

2 נָאַף to commit adultery ; this word is confined to adultery in the exclusive sense of the term, or to fornication by a married person : Lev. xx. 10 : Ezek. xvi. 32 : Hos. iv. 14 : Prov. vi. 32 ; applied to spiritual adultery or idolatry ; *seq. acc.* to commit adultery *with* a woman. KAL [a] *inf.* [b] *fut.* [c] *part.* Poel. PIEL [d] *pret.* [e] *fut.* [f] *part.* [g] נַאֲפוּפִים *m. pl.* adulteries. [h] נַאֲפִים *m. pl. id.*

Exod. xx. 14.	2 b	Jer. iii. 8.	2 d	Ezek. xxiii. 37, 37.	2 d
Lev. xx. 10, 10, 10,		iii. 9.	2 b	xxiii. 43.	2 h
10.	2 b b c c	v. 7.	2 b	xxiii. 45, 45.	2 c
Deut. v. 18.	2 b	vii. 9.	2 a	Hos. ii. 2.	2 g
Job xxiv. 15.	2 c	x. 2.	2 f	iii. 1.	2 a
Ps. l. 18.	2 f	xiii. 27.	2 h	iv. 2.	2 f
Prov. vi. 26.	1	xxiii. 10.	2 f	iv. 13, 14.	2 e
vi. 32.	2 c	xxiii. 14.	2 a	vii. 4.	2 f
xxx. 20.	2 f	xxix. 23.	2 e	Mal. iii. 5.	2 f
Isa. lvii. 3.	2 f	Ezek. xvi. 32.	2 f		

ADVANCE

גָּדַל to be great; to make great. PIEL *pret.* Esth. x. 2.

נָשָׂא to lift up. PIEL *pret.* Esth. v. 11. *fut.* Esth. iii. 1.

עָשָׂה to make. KAL *pret.* 1 Sam. xii. 6.

ADVANTAGE

סָכַן to benefit; to be profitable; *seq.* לְ. KAL *fut.* Job xxxv. 3.

ADVENTURE

נָסָה to try; to attempt, to assay. PIEL *pret.* Deut. xxviii. 56.

שָׁלַךְ to cast; *seq.* מִנֶּגֶד to cast away, to expose to great danger. HIPHIL *fut.* Judg. ix. 17.

ADVERSARY

1 אִישׁ *m.* man.

2 בַּעַל *m.* owner, master; implying dominion.

3 צוּר to press, straiten; to persecute. KAL *pret.*

4 צָרַר to bind; to be hostile to, to persecute. KAL a *part.* Poel. b צַר and צָר *m.* an adversary, enemy, persecutor. c צָרָה *f.* a female adversary.

5 רִיב to strive, contend. HIPHIL a *part.* b רִיב *m.* strife.

6 שָׂטַן to be hostile, to oppose, persecute. KAL a *fut.* b *part.* Poel. c שָׂטָן *m.* an adversary, opponent, in war, before a court, and generally one who obstructs another's way; with the article הַשָּׂטָן the adversary by way of eminence, Satan, an evil angel, who excites men to evil (1 Chron. xxi. 1; *comp.* 2 Sam. xxiv. 1), and accuses and calumniates them before God (Zech. iii. 1, 2, &c.; *comp.* Rev. xii. 10). It implies hatred, great hostility, and endeavours to injure; persevering persecution.

7 מִשְׁפָּט *m.* judgment.

Exod. xxiii. 22, 22.	3, 4 a	Job xxxi. 35. a	1, 5 b	Isa. lix. 18.	4 b
Num. xxii. 22.	6 c	Ps. xxxviii. 20.	6 a	lxiii. 18.	4 b
Deut. xxxii. 27, 43.	4 b	lxix. 19.	4 a	lxiv. 2.	4 b
Josh. v. 13.	4 b	lxxi. 13.	6 b	Jer. xxx. 16.	4 b
1 Sam. i. 6.	4 c	lxxiv. 10.	4 b	xlvi. 10.	4 b
ii. 10.	5 a	lxxxi. 14.	4 b	l. 7.	4 b
xxix. 4.	6 c	lxxxix. 42.	4 b	Lam. i. 5, 7, 10, 17.	4 b
2 Sam. xix. 22.	6 c	cix. 4.	6 b	ii. 4, 17.	4 b
1 Kings v. 4.	6 c	cix. 20, 29.	6 b	iv. 12.	4 b
xi. 14, 23, 25.	6 c	Isa. i. 24.	4 b	Amos iii. 11.	4 b
Ezra iv. 1.	4 b	ix. 11.	4 b	Mic. v. 9.	4 b
Neh. iv. 11.	4 b	xi. 13.	4 a	Nah. i. 2.	4 b
Esth. vii. 6.	1, 4 b	l. 8.	2, 7		

a lit. the man of my strife.

ADVERSITY

1 צֶלַע *m.* a halting, falling. Ps. xxxv. 15.

2 צָרָה *f.* distress, trouble. צַר *m.* adversary, enemy.

3 רַע *adj.* evil.

1 Sam. x. 19.	3	Ps. xxxi. 7.	2	Prov. xxiv. 10.	2
2 Sam. iv. 9.	2	xciv. 13.	3	Eccles. vii. 14.	3
2 Chron. xv. 6.	2	Prov. xvii. 17.	2	Isa. xxx. 20.	2 a
Ps. x. 6.	2				

ADVERTISE

אֹזֶן *m.* the ear. Ruth iv. 4.

גָּלָה to open, uncover. KAL *fut.* Ruth iv. 4.

יָעַץ to counsel. KAL *fut.* Num. xxiv. 14.

ADVICE, ADVISE, ADVISEMENT

1 דָּבָר *m.* matter, business, advice, &c.

2 תַּחְבֻּלוֹת *f. pl.* a leading, guidance, direction; the art of leading, &c.; hence, a wise plan or counsel; "good advice."

3 טַעַם *m.* taste; judgment, discernment, &c.; judicious, discreet counsel.

4 יָדַע to know. KAL *imp.*

5 יָעַץ to deliberate, to give counsel, to take advice. NIPHAL a *fut.* b *part.* "well-advised." c עֵצָה *f.* counsel.

6 עוּץ *i. q.* יָעַץ to take advice. KAL *imp.*

7 רָאָה to see, look. KAL *imp.* "advise thyself."

Judg. xix. 30.	6	1 Kings xii. 6.	5 b	2 Chron. x. 14.	5 c
xx. 7.	1	1 Chron. xix. 19.	5 c	xxv. 17.	5 a
1 Sam. xxv. 33.	3	xxi. 12.	5	Prov. xiii. 10.	5 b
2 Sam. xix. 43.	1	2 Chron. x. 9.	5 b	xx. 18.	2
xxiv. 13.	4				

AFAR OFF

רָחַק to be far off, far away. HIPHIL a *inf.* b רָחוֹק *adj.* far off. c מֶרְחָק *m.* what is far off, a place far off.

Gen. xxii. 4.	b	Neh. xii. 43.	b	Isa. xxiii. 7.	b
xxxvii. 18.	b	Job ii. 12.	b	lix. 14.	b
Exod. ii. 4.	b	xxxvi. 3, 25.	b	lxvi. 19.	b
xx. 18, 21.	b	xxxix. 25, 29.	b	Jer. xxiii. 23.	b
xxiv. 1.	b	Ps. x. 1.	b	xxx. 10.	b
xxxiii. 7.	a	xxxviii. 11.	b	xxxi. 10.	c
Num. ix. 10.	b	lxv. 5.	b	xlvi. 27.	b
1 Sam. xxvi. 13.	b	cxxxviii. 6.	b	li. 50.	b
2 Kings ii. 7.	b	cxxxix. 2.	b	Mic. iv. 3.	b
Ezra iii. 13.	b	Prov. xxxi. 14.	c		

AFFAIRS

דָּבָר *m.* word, matter, business, &c. 1 Chron. xxvi. 32: Ps. cxii. 5.

עֲבִידָה Ch. *f.* work, business, administration of affairs. Dan. ii. 49; iii. 12.

AFFECT

עָלַל to do, perform; in Poel *seq.* לְ to do evil, to vex. POEL *pret.* Lam. iii. 51, *lit.* mine eye causes pain to my soul.

רָצָה to take delight in, to set affection on. KAL *inf.* 1 Chron. xxix. 3.

AFFINITY

חָתַן to make marriages, to join in affinity. HITHPAEL *inf.* Ezra ix. 14. *fut.* 1 Kings iii. 1: 2 Chron. xviii. 1.

AFFLICT

1 אָוֶן *m.* see *Iniquity, Vanity.*

2 בֵּן *m.* son.

3 דַּךְ *adj.* crushed; hence oppressed.

4 יָגָה to be afflicted with grief and anguish, which galls and tears the heart, and causes the most painful sorrow. NIPHAL a *part.* HIPHIL b *pret.* c *part.*

5 כָּבַד to be heavy; to afflict grievously. HIPHIL *pret.*, Is.

ix. 1, or to make honoured, as the word may be translated, and as the connection seems to require.

6 לָחַץ to press or squeeze very hard; to oppress a people by laying them under heavy contributions, or such constraints and restraints as make life miserable. KAL *pret.* ᵇ לַחַץ *m.* oppression; calamities, distresses.

7 מָס *adj.* see *Melt;* of one who pines away, and is consumed by calamity.

8 מוּעָקָה *f.* heavy burden: see *Press.*

9 עַיִן *com.* the eye, put for state or condition.

10 עָנָה to labour; to suffer, to be afflicted, depressed, oppressed. Piel, to oppress, to afflict, to humble. Sept. ταπεινόω, κακόω. KAL *pret.* ᵇ*fut.* NIPHAL ᶜ*pret.* ᵈ*part.* PIEL ᵉ*pret.* ᶠ*inf.* ᵍ*fut.* ʰ*part.* PUAL ⁱ*pret.* ʲ*inf.* ᵏ*fut.* ˡ*part.* HIPHIL ᵐ*fut.* HITHPAEL ⁿ*pret.* ᵒ*inf.* ᵖ*fut.* עֱנוּת *f.* affliction. ʳ עָנִי *adj.* poor, helpless, humble, lowly. ˢ עֲנִי *m.* affliction; oppression, suffering, misery.

11 צָרַר to bind up; to be hostile to, persecute. KAL *pret.* ᵇ*part.* Poel. HIPHIL ᶜ*inf.* ᵈ צַר *m.* an adversary; affliction, distress. ᵉ צָרָה *f.* distress, trouble.

12 קָלַל to be light; to make light, despise, to bring into contempt; to afflict lightly. HIPHIL *pret.*

13 רָעַע to break, to break in pieces; to do ill, to afflict. HIPHIL *pret.* ᵇ*inf.* ᶜ*fut.* ᵈ רַע *adj.* See *Evil.*

14 שֶׁבֶר *m.* breach; destruction. Jer. xxx. 15; comp. v. 12.

Gen. xv. 13.	10 e	Job v. 6.	1	Prov. xxxi. 5.	2, 10 s
xvi. 11.	10 s	vi. 14.	7	Isa. ix. 1, 1.	12, 5
xxix. 32.	10 s	x. 15.	10 s	xxx. 20.	6 b
xxxi. 42.	10 s	xxx. 11.	10 g	xlviii. 10.	10 s
xxxi. 50.	10 g	xxx. 16, 27.	10 s	xlix. 13.	10 r
xli. 52.	10 s	xxxiv. 28.	10 s	li. 21.	10 r
Exod. i. 11.	10 f	xxxvi. 8, 15, 21.	10 s	li. 23.	4 c
i. 12.	10 g	xxxvii. 23.	10 g	liii. 4.	10 l
iii. 7, 17.	10 s	Ps. xviii. 27.	10 r	liii. 7.	10 d
iv. 31.	10 s	xxii. 24, 24.	10 q r	liv. 11.	10 r
xxii. 22.	10 g	xxv. 16.	10 s	lviii. 3.	10 e
xxii. 23. α	10 f g	xxv. 18.	10 s	lviii. 5.	10 f
Lev. xvi. 29.	10 e	xxxiv. 19.	13 d	lviii. 10.	10 d
xvi. 31.	10 e	xliv. 2.	13 c	lx. 14.	10 h
xxiii. 27, 32.	10 s	xliv. 24.	10 s	lxiii. 9, 9. ε	11 e d
xxiii. 29.	10 k	lv. 19. γ	10 b	lxiv. 12.	10 g
Num. xi. 11.	13 a	lxvi. 11.	8	Jer. iv. 15.	1
xxiv. 24, 24.	10 e	lxxxii. 3.	10 r	xv. 11.	11 e
xxix. 7.	10 e	lxxxviii. 7.	10 e	xvi. 19.	11 e
xxx. 13.	10 f	lxxxviii. 9.	10 s	xxx. 15.	14
Deut. xvi. 3.	10 s	lxxxviii. 15.	10 r	xxxi. 28.	13 b
xxvi. 6.	10 s	lxxxix. 22.	10 g	xlviii. 16.	13 d
xxvi. 7.	10 s	xc. 15.	10 e	Lam. i. 3, 7, 9.	10 s
Judg. xvi. 5, 6, 19.	10 f	xciv. 5.	10 g	i. 4.	4 a
Ruth i. 21.	13 a	cii. title.	10 r	i. 5, 12.	4 b
1 Sam. i. 11.	10 s	cvi. 44.	11 d	iii. 1, 19.	10 s
2 Sam. vii. 10. β	10 f	cvii. 10, 41.	10 s	iii. 33.	10 e
xvi. 12.		cvii. 17.	10 p	Hos. v. 15.	11 d
12 כ	10 s	cvii. 39.	13 d	Amos v. 12.	11 b
xxii. 18.	10 g	cxvi. 10.	10 a	vi. 6.	14
1 Kings ii. 26, 26.	10 n	cxix. 50, 92, 153.	10 s	vi. 14.	6 a
viii. 35.	10 m	cxix. 67.	10 b	Obad. 13.	13 d
xi. 39.	10 g	cxix. 71.	10 i	Jonah ii. 2.	11 e
xxii. 27, 27.	6 b	cxix. 75.	10 e	Mic. iv. 6.	13 a
2 Kings xiv. 26.	10 s	cxix. 107.	10 c	Nah. i. 9.	11 e
xvii. 20.	10 g	cxxix. 1, 2.	11 a	i. 12, 12.	10 e g
2 Chron. vi. 26.	10 m	cxxxi. 1.	10 j	Hab. iii. 7.	1
xviii. 26, 26.	6 b	cxl. 12.	10 r	Zeph. iii. 12.	10 r
xx. 9.	11 e	cxliii. 12.	11 b	iii. 19.	10 h
xxxiii. 12.	11 c	Prov. xv. 15.	10 r	Zech. i. 15.	13 d
Ezra viii. 21.	10 o	xxii. 22.	10 s	viii. 10.	11 d
Neh. i. 3.	13 d	xxvi. 28. δ	3	x. 11.	11 e
xi. 9.	10 s				

α *lit.* afflicting thou afflictest.   β *lit.* add to afflict.   γ or, answer.
δ *i.e.* its victims.   ε *lit.* affliction was to him.

AFFORD

פּוּק to draw, to bring out for use and service, as from a storehouse. HIPHIL *part.* Ps. cxliv. 13.

AFRAID, AFFRIGHT

1 אָחַז to take hold, to take, to seize; *metaph.* ascribed to terror, fear; but also *vice versa* one is said, as in English, to take fright, *i. q.* to be affrighted. KAL. *pret.*

2 בָּהַל to tremble, to shake; to be in trepidation, to be amazed, confounded, struck with terror, consternation; to make afraid. NIPHAL ᵃ*pret.* PIEL ᵇ*fut.*

3 בָּעַת to fear, with great consternation of mind, as at the sight of an angel, or for the wrath of a king; to make afraid. NIPHAL ᵃ*pret.* PIEL ᵇ*pret.* ᶜ*fut.*

4 גּוּר to sojourn as a stranger; to fear as a stranger, or as one who turns aside; to fear, to be sore afraid; with מִן and מִפְּנֵי implying mostly reverence. KAL ᵃ*imp.* ᵇ*fut.*

5 דָּאַב to melt, to become liquid; to fear, implying solicitude as to some approaching event; with *acc.* and מִן. KAL ᵃ*pret.* ᵇ*part.* Poel.

6 דְּחַל Ch. to creep along timidly, to fear, to be afraid; the same as זָחַל; to make afraid. PAEL *fut.*

7 זָחַל to creep, or skulk like a snake, to approach with hesitating step. KAL *pret.*

8 חָגַר to gird. This root and חָרַג seem to have similar primary meanings, viz. to straiten or shut in, so to be brought into great and pressing difficulties, and constrained through fear to do this or that. KAL *fut.* 2 Sam. xxii. 46. See the corresponding passage under חָרַג.

9 חוּל to fear and tremble. KAL and HIPHIL *fut.* Ps. lxxvii. 16. The waters are represented as fearing the majesty of God, and trembling, so as to rise contrary to their nature, and stand as a wall on either side.

10 חָרַג to tremble, to be in trepidation; to be constrained to do a thing through fear and dread. KAL *fut.* See חָגַר.

11 חָרַד to tremble. The word includes not only anxiety and solicitude, coupled with fear of some evil, but also such a violent commotion of the mind as agitates the body also; as in the fear of the brethren of Joseph, Gen. xlii. 28, lxx. ἐταράχθησαν; of the Israelites when God descended on the mount, Exod. xix. 16, lxx. ἐπτοήθη; fear of an enemy approaching, 1 Sam. xiii. 7, lxx. ἐξέστη; spoken of Boaz, Ruth iii. 8; Abimelech, 1 Sam. xxi. 1; Saul, xxviii. 5; Elihu terrified by the thunder, Job xxxvii. 1; Adonijah, 1 Kings i. 49; to make afraid. KAL ᵃ*pret.* ᵇ*fut.* HIPHIL ᶜ*pret.* ᵈ*inf.* ᵉ*part.* ᶠ חָרֵד *adj.*

12 חָתַת to be broken; to be broken with fear, to be terrified, in consternation; often joined with יָרֵא and translated to be dismayed; sometimes with בּוּשׁ, and then it implies perturbation of mind, or expectation disappointed, Isa. xx. 5. KAL ᵃ*pret.* NIPHAL ᵇ*pret.* ᶜ*fut.* HIPHIL ᵈ*fut.*

13 יָגֹר see *Fear.* This root seems to imply fear in anticipation. KAL ᵃ*pret.* ᵇ*part.*

14 יָרֵא see *Fear;* to be timorous, apprehensive, sore afraid; with לְ to fear for, Josh. ix. 24, Prov. xxxi. 21; with מִן to be afraid of, Lev. xix. 14, 32; so with מִפְּנֵי, 1 Kings i. 50, 2 Kings xxv. 26, Jer. xli. 18; and מִלְּפָנֵי, Eccles. viii. 12, 13. KAL ᵃ*pret.* ᵇ*inf.* ᶜ*fut.* PIEL ᵈ*pret.* ᵉ*inf.* ᶠ*part.* ᵍ יָרֵא *adj.* ʰ יִרְאָה *f.* fear.

15 יָרֵהּ to tremble; to be astonished, amazed. KAL *fut.*; see also רָהָה.

16 עָרַץ see *Fear*; to terrify, to make afraid; to fear, to be afraid; with מִפְּנֵי of the person feared; also with an accusative. The primary signification seems to have been to quake. KAL ^a*fut.* HIPHIL ^b*fut.*

17 פָּחַד see *To fear*; to be afraid; with מִן and מִפְּנֵי of the person feared; also with אֶל of the thing for which one fears, Isa. xix. 17. KAL ^a*pret.* ^b*fut.*

18 רָגַז to be moved, or thrown into commotion; to be moved with any violent emotion, as fear; to tremble, to quake. KAL *fut.*

19 רָהָה to be afraid; the proper root seems to be יָרֵהּ; see above. KAL *pret.*

20 רָעַשׁ to tremble, to quake; to be moved, to shake. Ges., to cause to leap. HIPHIL *fut.*

21 שָׂעַר to shudder, shiver, from fear, alarm, to be horribly afraid; *seq.* עַל of the cause; construed also with an acc. like Gr. φρίσσω τινά, to fear, reverence, Deut. xxxii. 17. KAL ^a*pret.* ^b*imp.* ^c*fut.* ^dשַׂעַר *m.* shuddering, horror.

Gen. iii. 10.	14 c	1 Kings i. 49.	11 b	Isa. x. 29.	11 a	
xviii. 15. α	14 a	2 Kings i. 15.	14 c	xii. 2.	17 b	
xx. 8.	14 c	x. 4.	14 c	xiii. 8.	2 a	
xxviii. 17.	14 c	xix. 6.	14 c	xvii. 2.	11 a	
xxxi. 31.	14 a	xxv. 26.	14 a	xix. 16.	11 a	
xxxii. 7.	14 c	1 Chron. x. 4.	14 a	xix. 17.	17 b	
xlii. 28.	11 b	xiii. 12.	14 c	xx. 5.	12 a	
xlii. 35.	14 c	xxi. 30.	3 a	xxi. 4.	3 b	
xliii. 18.	14 c	2 Chron. xx. 15.	14 c	xxxi. 4.	12 c	
Exod. iii. 6.	14 a	xxxii. 7.	14 c	xxxi. 9.	12 a	
xiv. 10.	14 c	xxxii. 18.	14 e	xxxiii. 14.	17 a	
xv. 14.	18	Neh. ii. 2.	14 c	xxxvii. 6.	14 c	
xxxiv. 30.	14 c	iv. 14.	14 c	xl. 9.	14 c	
Lev. xxvi. 6.	11 e	vi. 9.	14 f	xli. 5.	11 b	
Num. xii. 8.	14 a	vi. 13.	14 c	xliv. 8.	15, 19	
xxii. 3.	4 b	Esth. vii. 6.	3 a	li. 7.	12 c	
Deut. i. 17.	4 b	Job iii. 25.	13 a	li. 12.	14 c	
i. 29.	14 c	v. 21, 22.	14 a	lvii. 11.	5 a	
ii. 4.	14 c	vi. 21.	14 c	Jer. i. 8.	14 c	
v. 5.	14 a	ix. 28.	13 a	ii. 12.	21 b	
vii. 18.	14 c	xi. 19.	11 e	x. 5.	14 c	
vii. 19.	14 g	xiii. 11, 21.	3 c	xxvi. 21.	14 c	
vii. 21.	16 a	xv. 24.	3 c	xxx. 10.	11 e	
ix. 19.	13 a	xviii. 11.	3 b	xxxvi. 16, 24.	17 a	
xviii. 22.	4 b	xviii. 20.	1, 21 d	xxxviii. 19.	5 b	
xx. 1.	14 c	xix. 29.	4 a	xxxix. 17.	13 b	
xxviii. 10.	14 a	xxi. 6.	2 a	xli. 18.	14 a	
xxviii. 60.	13 a	xxiii. 15.	17 b	lii. 11, 11, 11.	14 c g c	
xxxi. 6.	16 a	xxxii. 6.	7	xlii. 16.	5 b	
Josh. i. 9.	16 a	xxxiii. 7.	3 c	xlvi. 27.	11 e	
ix. 24.	14 c	xxxix. 20.	20	li. 32.	2 a	
xi. 3.	14 c	xxxix. 22.	12 c	Ezek. ii. 6, 6.	14 c	
Judg. vii. 3.	11 f	xli. 25.	14 c	xxvii. 35.	21 a	
Ruth iii. 8.	11 b	Ps. iii. 6.	14 c	xxx. 9.	11 d	
1 Sam. iv. 7.	14 c	xviii. 4.	3 c	xxxii. 10.	21 c	
vii. 7.	14 c	xviii. 45. γ	10	xxxiv. 28.	11 e	
xvii. 11, 24.	14 c	xxvii. 1.	17 b	xxxvi. 29.	11 e	
xviii. 12.	14 c	xlix. 16.	14 c	Dan. iv. 5.	6	
xviii. 15.	4 b	lvi. 11, 11.	14 c	viii. 17.	3 a	
xviii. 29. β	14 b	lxv. 8.	14 c	Joel ii. 22.	14 c	
xxi. 1.	11 b	lxxvii. 16.	14 c	Amos iii. 6.	11 b	
xxi. 12.	14 c	lxxxiii. 15.	2 b	Jonah i. 5.	14 c	
xxiii. 3.	14 g	xci. 5.	14 c	i. 10. δ	14 h c	
xxviii. 5, 13, 20.	14 a	cxii. 7, 8.	14 c	Mic. iv. 4.	14 c	
xxxi. 4.	14 a	cxix. 120.	14 a	vii. 17.	17 b	
2 Sam. i. 14.	14 a	Prov. iii. 24.	17 b	Nah. ii. 11.	11 e	
vi. 9.	14 c	iii. 25.	14 c	Hab. ii. 17.	12 d	
xiv. 15.	14 d	xxxi. 21.	14 c	iii. 2.	14 a	
xvii. 2.	11 c	Eccles. xii. 5.	14 c	Zeph. iii. 13.	11 e	
xxii. 5.	3 c	Isa. viii. 12.	16 b	Mal. ii. 5.	12 b	
xxii. 46.	14 c	x. 24.	14 c			

^a *vulg.* timore perterrita, *comp.* 1 Pet. iii. 6.   β *lit.* added to fear. γ *i.e.* forced through fear to come out.   δ *lit.* with a great fear afraid.

AFORE, AFORETIME

1 פָּנִים *m. pl.* face; with לְ prefix aforetime; afore.

---

2 קֶדֶם *m.* what is before. ^a קַדְמָה *f.* beginning, origin; *constr.*, used as a preposition. ^b קַדְמָה Ch. *f.* former time.

3 רֹאשֹׁן *adj.* first in time and order; with בְּ aforetime.

Neh. xiii. 5.	1	Isa. xviii. 5.	1	Ezek. xxxiii. 22.	1
Job xvii. 6.	1	Jer. xxx. 20.	2	Dan. vi. 10. α	2 b
Ps. cxxix. 6.	2 a				

^a *lit.* from before this.

AFTER

1 אַחֲרוֹן *adj.* hinder, following, last; after, later, following. ^a אָחוֹר *m.* the hinder part.

2 יָצָא to go out. KAL *inf.*

3 עֵת *com.* time; with לְ at the return of; with מְ after, at the end.

4 קֵץ *m.* an end, either of space or time. ^a קָצֶה *m. id.* with מְ.

5 רֶגֶל *f.* foot.

Gen. xvi. 3.	4	1 Kings xvii. 13.	5	Prov. xxix. 11. γ	1 a
xxxiii. 2.	1	1 Chron. xx. 1.	3	Eccles. i. 11.	1
Num. xiii. 25.	4	2 Chron. xviii. 2.	4	iv. 16.	1
Josh. iii. 2.	4 a	xxi. 19. β	2	Isa. ix. 1.	1
1 Sam. xxv. 42. α	5	Neh. xiii. 6.	4	Jer. xiii. 1.	4
2 Sam. xv. 7.	4	Esth. ii. 12.	4	xlii. 7.	4
xv. 16, 17, 18. α	5	Job xviii. 20.	4	Dan. xi. 13.	4
1 Kings xvii. 7.	4				

^a *lit.* at his or her foot.   β *lit.* at the period of the going out of the end. γ or keepeth it backwards.

AFTERNOON

יוֹם *m.* day: Judg. xix. 8.

נָטָה to decline. KAL *inf.* Judg. xix. 8.

AGAIN

1 יָלַךְ to go. KAL *inf.*

2 יָסַף to add, with another verb in the *inf.* rendered again. KAL ^a*pret.* HIPHIL ^b*pret.* ^c*fut.*

3 שׁוּב to return. Followed by another verb in the *inf.*, or with ו copulative, it is often translated again, and implies either a repetition of an action, the doing it a second time; or it denotes an action contrary to one already referred to, as in Jer. xviii. 4: Zech. viii. 15: Mal. iii. 18. The copulative ו is sometimes omitted, as 1 Sam. iii. 5. KAL ^a*pret.* ^b*inf.* ^c*imp.* ^d*fut.* HIPHIL ^e*fut.*

4 שֵׁנִי *adj. ord.* second.

5 תִּנְיָנוּת Ch. *adv.* a second time.

(See also the verb with which *Again* is connected, as *Bring*, &c.)

Gen. iv. 2.	2 c	Judg. xi. 14.	2 c	2 Kings i. 11. β	3 d
viii. 10, 21, 21.	2 c	xiii. 1.	2 c	i. 13. β	3 d
viii. 12. α	2 a	xix. 7.	3 d	xiii. 25. β	3 d
xviii. 29.	2 c	xx. 22, 23, 28.	2 c	xix. 9. β	3 d
xxv. 1.	2 c	1 Sam. iii. 5. γ	3 c	xix. 36.	2 a
xxvi. 18. β	3 d	iii. 6, 6.	2 c, 3 c	xxi. 3. β	3 d
xxx. 31. γ	3 d	iii. 8, 21.	2 c	1 Chron. xiv. 13.	2 c
xxxviii. 5. β	2 c	ix. 8.	2 c	2 Chron. xix. 4. δ	3 d
xxxviii. 26.	2 c	xvii. 30. ε	3 e	xxxiii. 3. δ	3 d
Exod. x. 29.	2 c	xx. 17.	2 c	Ezra ix. 14. δ	3 d
xiv. 13.	2 c	xix. 8, 21.	2 c	Neh. ix. 28. δ	3 d
Lev. xiii. 6, 7.	4	xxiii. 4.	2 c	Esth. viii. 3.	2 c
Num. iv. 4. β	3 d	xxvii. 4.	2 c	Job x. 16. γ	3 d
xxii. 15, 25.	2 a	xxvii. 4 כ	2 a	Ps. lxxi. 20, 20. γ	3 d
xxxii. 15.	2 a	2 Sam. ii. 22.	2 c	lxxxv. 6.	3 d
Deut. xviii. 16.	2 c	iii. 34.	2 c	Prov. xix. 19.	2 c
xxiv. 4. δ	3 b	v. 22.	2 c	Eccles. i. 7.	1
xxx. 9. δ	3 d	xvi. 19.	4	Isa. vii. 10.	2 c
Josh. v. 2. δ	3 c	xviii. 22.	2 c	viii. 5.	2 c
Judg. iii. 12.	2 c	1 Kings xiii. 33. β	3 d	xi. 11.	2 c
iv. 1.	2 c	xix. 6. β	3 d	xxiv. 20.	2 c
ix. 37. β	2 c	xix. 20.	2 c	xxxvii. 31.	2 a
x. 6.	2 c				

Jer. xviii. 4. β	3 a	Dan. x. 18.	2 c	Hag. ii. 20.	4
xxxvi. 28. ζ	3 c	Amos vii. 8, 13.	2 c	Zech. iv. 12.	4
Ezek. iv. 6.	4	viii. 2.	2 c	viii. 15. γ	3 a
ii. 7.	5	Jonah ii. 4.	2 c	Mal. ii. 13.	4
Dan. ix. 25. β	3 d				

a *lit.* added.   β *Heb.* with וֹ   γ *Heb.* without וֹ   δ *Heb.* with *inf.*
ϵ *lit.* returned word.   ζ *lit.* return, take thee.

AGAINST

קָרָא to meet. KAL *inf.* used as a preposition. Gen. xv. 10: Exod. vii. 15, "against he come," *lit.* to meet him; xiv. 27. Numb. xx. 18, 20; xxi. 23, 33; xxii. 34: Deut. i. 44; ii. 32; iii. 1; xxix. 7: Josh. viii. 5, 14, 22; xi. 20: Judg. vii. 24; xiv. 5, *marg.* in meeting him; xv. 14; xx. 25, 31: 1 Sam. iv. 1, 2; ix. 14; xvii. 2, 21, 55; xxiii. 28; xxv. 20: 2 Sam. x. 9, 10, 17; xviii. 6: 1 Kings xx. 27: 2 Kings ix. 21; xxiii. 29: 1 Chron. xix. 10, 11, 17: 2 Chron. xxxv. 20: Ps. xxxv. 3.

נֹכַח *m.* obsolete root, used as a prep. and adverb. "Over against," Exod. xxvi. 35; xl. 24: Josh. xviii. 17: Judg. xix. 10; xx. 43: 1 Kings xx. 29: Ezek. xlvii. 20. "Against," 1 Kings xxii. 35: 2 Chron. xviii. 34.

עֻמָּה *f.* pr. union, used as prep. "Over against," Exod. xxv. 27, &c. "Against," 1 Chron. xxv. 8, &c.

(See also the verb with which it is connected, as *Come against*, &c.)

AGATE

כַּדְכֹּד *m.* name of a precious stone, most probably of a red colour, and sparkling; see *Sparks.* Isa. liv. 12: Ezek. xxvii. 16, *marg.* chrysoprase.

שְׁבוֹ *m.* name of a precious stone; lxx. ἀχάτης. Vulg. achates. Exod. xxviii. 19; xxxix. 12.

AGE

1   אֱנוֹשׁ *m.* man; "in the flower of their age;" Heb. men.

2   בֵּן *m.* son; "from the age of fifty years;" Heb. from the son of, &c.

3   דּוּר to dwell; properly, in a tent. דּוֹר *m.* an age, or generation of men; a dwelling. In Isa. xxxviii. 12, Vitringa thinks that it means the body as the abode of animal life, that in which the soul sojourns for a time, like one living in a tent rather than in a fixed abode. Cocceius (Anecdota) explains it by οἰκητήριον habitaculum, sive ἐνδιαίτημα τοῦ αἰῶνος τούτου, mansio hujus seculi, comp. 2 Cor. v. 1.

4   זָקֵן to be old. KAL a*pret.* b זָקֵן *adj.* aged. זֹקֶן *m.* age.

5   חַי *adj.* living, life.

6   חֶלֶד *m.* short, transitory; the world, the age of man as transitory and of short duration, Job xi. 17. Thy transient age, or thine age though transient, shall be brighter than the noonday.

7   יוֹם *m.* day; days used for age. Heb. gone into days.

8   יָשִׁישׁ *m.* a very old person.

9   כֶּלַח *m.* that old age, which purely in a natural way, without the violence of distemper, is at length weakened and spent into a ripeness for the grave, as corn for its maturity is fit to be brought into the barn; Job v. 26, "in a full age;" Job xxx. 2, "in whom old age was perished," *i. e.* as to its maturity and wisdom, or as to its existence, since they die of a premature old age.

10   שֵׂיב *m.* gray hairs; old age.

11   שָׁנָה *f.* year.

Gen. xviii. 11.	7	1 Kings xiv. 4. a	10	Job xxix. 8.	8
xxiv. 1.	7	1 Chron. xxiii. 3, 24.	2	xxx. 2.	9
xlvii. 28.	7, 11, 5	Job v. 26.	9	xxxii. 9.	4 b
xlviii. 10.	4 c	viii. 8.	3	Ps. xxxix. 5.	6
Num. viii. 25.	2	xi. 17.	6	Isa. xxxviii. 12.	3
Josh. xxiii. 1, 2.	7	xii. 20.	4 b	Jer. vi. 11.	4 b
1 Sam. ii. 33.	1	xv. 10.	8	Zech. viii. 4.	7
2 Sam. xix. 32.	4 a				

a lit. for his hoariness.

AGO

יוֹם *m.* day; 1 Sam. ix. 20, three days ago, *lit.* to-day three days, xxx. 13.

קַדְמָה Ch. *f.* what is before: Ezra v. 11.

AGREEMENT

חֹזֶה a seer, a vision. Isa. xxviii. 15.   חָזוּת *f.* a vision. Isa. xxviii. 18. In these passages agreement, or compact, or truce, is certainly implied, and the word might take this meaning from the idea of a vision of God being a vision of peace; or from enemies seeing each other during a truce.

יָעַד to appoint; to come together by appointment. NIPHAL *pret.* Amos iii. 3.

מֵישָׁרִים *m. pl.* things that are right. Dan. xi. 16. *marg.* rights.

עָשָׂה to make. KAL *pret.* Isa. xxviii. 15. *lit.* made agreement.

AID

חָזַק to be strong. PIEL *pret.* Judg. ix. 24.

AIJELETH-SHAHAR

אַיֶּלֶת *f.* hind: Ps. xxii. 1, an emblem of the suffering Messiah. שַׁחַר *m.* morning. See the meaning of this title fully discussed in Sontag and Irhoven de Titulis Psalmorum; also Hengstenberg on the Psalms.

AIL

מַה־לָּךְ "what aileth, ailed, thee?" Heb. what to thee. Gen. xxi. 17: Judg. xviii. 23: 2 Sam. xiv. 5: 2 Kings vi. 28: Ps. cxiv. 5: Isa. xxii. 1. "What aileth the people?" Heb. what to the people? 1 Sam. xi. 5.

AIR

רוּחַ *com.* wind, air; spirit; breath: Job xli. 16.

שָׁמַיִם *m.* dual; heaven or heavens; the air in which birds fly. Gen. i. 26, &c.

ALAMOTH

עֲלָמוֹת *f. pl.* a kind of tune or harmony in music; perhaps the female voice or treble: 1 Chron. xv. 20: Ps. xlvi. title. Others, the virgins, *i. e. fig.* the people of God, Cant. i. 3.

ALARM

רוּעַ to make a loud noise; to blow an alarm: see *Sound.* HIPHIL a*pret.* b*inf.* c*imp.* d*fut.* ϵ תְּרוּעָה *f.* a cry of jubilee; a shout for battle.

Numb. x. 5, 6, 6.	e	2 Chron. xiii. 12.	b	Joel ii. 1.	ϵ
x. 7.	d	Jer. iv. 19.	c	Zeph. i. 16.	ϵ
x. 9.	a	xlix. 2.	c		

ALGUM TREES

אַלְגּוּמִּים *m. pl.* a costly wood, which Solomon obtained from Ophir, and employed for the ornaments of the temple and palace, and for making musical instruments : 2 Chron. ii. 8 ; ix. 10, 11. See *Almug-tree.*

ALIEN

1   גֵּר *m.* see *Stranger.*

2   נֵכָר *m.* see *Stranger.*   ª נָכְרִי *adj.* strange.

Exod. xviii. 3.	1 | Job xix. 15.	2 a | Isa. lxi. 5.	2
Deut. xiv. 21.	2 a | Ps. lxix. 8.	2 a | Lam. v. 2.	2 a

ALIENATE

1   יָקַע to be rent or torn away ; to be separated from through disgust and aversion ; *seq.* מִן and מֵעַל. KAL *fut.*

2   נָקַע *id.* ; to move oneself away ; to be alienated. KAL *pret.*

3   עָבַר to pass over. KAL ª *fut.* כתיב. HIPHIL ᵇ *fut.*

Ezek. xxiii. 17.	1 | Ezek. xlviii. 14.	3 a	
xxiii. 18, 18.	1, 2 | xlviii. 14.	3 b	
xxiii. 22, 28.	2		

ALIKE   (See also LIKE)

1   אֶחָד *adj.* one ; alike, *lit.* as one.

2   יַחַד *m.* see *Together:* alike, one as well as another.

Deut. xii. 22.	2 | 1 Sam. xxx. 24.	2 | Ps. xxxiii. 15.	2
xv. 22.	2 | Job xxi. 26.	2 | Eccles. xi. 6.	1

ALIVE   (See LIFE)

ALL

כֹּל *part.* all : Gen. iii. 17, &c.

כָּלִיל *adj.* complete ; the whole : Exod. xxviii. 31 ; xxxix. 22.

מִסְפָּר *m.* number : Eccles. ii. 3 ; v. 18 ; vi. 12.

רֹב *m.* multitude : Job iv. 14, *lit.* the multitude of.

ALL THAT IS THEREIN

מְלֹא *m.* fulness ; "all therein ;" Heb., the fulness thereof. Isa. xxxiv. 1 ; xlii. 10 : Jer. viii. 16 ; xlvii. 2 : Ezek. xii. 19 ; xxx. 12 : Amos vi. 8 : Mic. i. 2.

ALL TO BE

תָּמַם to be finished. KAL *pret.* 1 Sam. xvi. 11, "are here all?" *inf.* 1 Kings xiv. 10, "to be all gone."

ALLIED

קָרוֹב *adj.* near, nigh ; of space, of kindred, of time ; *seq.* לְ, Neh. xiii. 4.

ALLON-BACHUTH

אַלּוֹן *m.* an oak. }   Gen. xxxv. 8, *lit.* The oak of weeping ; where

בָּכוּת *f.* weeping. }   relatives came to weep at stated times, for which the shade of the oak was favourable.

ALLOWANCE

אֲרֻחָה *f.* see *Victuals.* 2 Kings xxv. 30, 30.

ALLURE

פָּתָה to open ; to be open. Piel, to persuade, to allure by tender persuasion, to entice. PIEL *part.* Hos. ii. 14.

ALMIGHTY

שַׁדַּי Learned men greatly differ in the explanation of this word. See Hottingeri. Dissertatt. Theol. Philol. Fasc. p. 275, Ikenii Dissertatt. p. 9, sqq. Deyling, Observ. Sacr. p. 1, 43, sqq. The meaning most generally adopted is that of our translation ; yet many ancient and modern critics have derived it from דַּי sufficiency and שׁ the prefix, who is, denoting his infinite sufficiency for himself and all other beings ; so Glassii Onomatologia, of the Messiah ; others from שַׁד a breast, implying the All-bountiful Being. The lxx. certainly translate it by ἱκανός occasionally. Gen. xvii. 1, &c. ; Isa. xiii. 6. Paronomasia כְּשֹׁד מִשַּׁדַּי.

ALMOND

שָׁקֵד *m.* almond-tree ; almond ; so called from its bringing forth blossoms early in January, as if it were in haste, or took the first opportunity to blossom, before any other tree ; to which there is an allusion in Jer. i. 12 ; see *Hasten.* A rod of almond seems to be an emblem of vigilance. The idea of not being anticipated may be implied, and so the blossom of the almond is a fit emblem of the hastening and sudden appearing of God's judgments, and of the unperceived advances of old age : Gen. xliii. 11 : Numb. xvii. 8 : Eccles. xii. 5 : Jer. i. 11. שָׁקַד to have the form of almond flowers. PUAL *part.* Exod. xxv. 33, 33, 34 ; xxxvii. 19, 19, 20.

ALMOST

מְעַט *m.* few, little : Exod. xvii. 4, *lit.* yet a little and they will stone me : Ps. lxxiii. 2 ; xciv. 17, *marg.* or, quickly, cxix. 87 : Prov. v. 14.

ALMUG-TREE

אַלְמֻגִּים *m. pl.* see *Algum.* 1 Kings x. 11, 12, 12.

ALOES

אֲהָלִים *m.* and אֲהָלוֹת *f. pl.* Lign-aloes, or Agollachum. An Indian aromatic tree. Cels. Hierobot. Pt. I. p. 1, 135. It is like an olive-tree ; sometimes larger : Raii Hist. Plant. Tom. II. p. 1808. In all places it implies perfume, and figuratively (Numb. xxiv. 6) it applies to the fame of the Israelites diffused far and wide. Numb. xxiv. 6 : Ps. xlv. 8 : Prov. vii. 17 : Cant. iv. 14.

ALONE   (See LET)

1   אֶחָד *adj.* one : Isa. li. 2. I called him alone, *i. e.* as one ; before he had children ; *comp.* Mal. ii. 15.

2   בָּדַד to be, live, or act alone, separate from others. KAL ª *part.* Poel. ᵇ בָּדָד *m.* alone. To sit or dwell alone imports, I. a solitary, desolate, sad, afflicted condition, Jer. xv. 17 : Lam. iii. 28. II. sometimes a state of safety and security, separate from and unmolested by others, Deut. xxxiii. 28 : Jer. xlix. 31. III. it is used to signify the separate condition of the Israelites, as God had singled them out, and distinguished them from other nations, Numb. xxiii. 9. בַּד *m.* separation. לְבַדִּי alone, Numb. xi. 14, &c.

Lev. xiii. 46.	2 b	Josh. xxii. 20. a	1	Jer. xv. 17.	2 b
Numb. xxiii. 9.	2 b	Ps. cii. 7.	2 a	xlix. 31.	2 b
Deut. xxxii. 12.	2 b	Isa. xiv. 31.	2 a	Lam. iii. 28.	2 b
xxxiii. 28.	2 b	li. 2.	1	Hos. viii. 9.	2 a

a *lit.* and he, one man, perisheth not.

ALONG

1 דֶּרֶךְ *com.* way; "along that way," "along by."
2 הָלַךְ to go. KAL *inf.* went along, *lit.* going.
3 מָלֵא *m.* fulness: 1 Sam. xxviii. 20.
4 קוֹמָה *f.* height, stature.

| Judg. ix. 25, 37. | 1 | 1 Sam. xxviii. 20. | 3, 4 | Jer. xli. 6. | 2 |
| 1 Sam. vi. 12. | 2 | 2 Sam. iii. 16. | 2 | | |

ALOUD

1 גָּדוֹל *adj.* great.
2 גָּרוֹן *m.* the throat; "with the throat," *i. e.* with open mouth, the voice coming from the throat and breast.
3 חַיִל Ch. *m.* might; aloud, *marg.* with might.
4 נָתַן to give. KAL *fut.*
5 קוֹל *m.* voice.
6 רום to be lifted up. HIPHIL *inf.*
7 רֵעַ *m.* shouting; outcry, noise.

Gen. xlv. 2.	4, 5	Isa. lviii. 1.	2	Dan. v. 7.	3
1 Kings xviii. 27, 28.	1, 5	Dan. iii. 4.	3	Mic. iv. 9.	7
Ezra iii. 12. a	5, 6	iv. 14.	3		

a *lit.* in the shouting for joy unto lifting up the voice. See *Shout.*

ALREADY

כְּבָר *adv.* of time, long ago, formerly. Eccles. i. 10; ii. 12; iii. 15; iv. 2; v. 10.

ALTAR

1 אֲרִיאֵל *m.* Ezek. xliii. 15, *marg.* lion of God, 16; so called, perhaps, because it devoured the sacrifices.—*Bochart.*
2 הַרְאֵל *m.* Ezek. xliii. 15, prop. the mount of God, put for the altar of burnt offering.
3 מַדְבַּח Ch. *m.* an altar, from דְּבַח to sacrifice.
4 מִזְבֵּחַ *m.* altar; used of the altar of burnt offering, and of the altar of incense: Gen. viii. 20, &c.
5 לְבֵנָה *f.* brick, altar of brick; *marg.* bricks.
6 מְקַטְּרוֹת *f. pl.* altars for incense.

מִזְבֵּחַ No. 4, occurs very frequently, and is not included.

| 2 Chron. xxx. 14, 14. | 4, 6 | Isa. lxv. 3. | 5 | Ezek. xliii. 16. | 1 |
| Ezra vii. 17. | 3 | Ezek. xliii. 15, 15. | 2, 1 | | |

AL-TASCHITH

שָׁחַת to be corrupt. HIPHIL, to destroy: *fut.* Ps. lvii. and lviii. and lix. and lxxv. title, *marg.* or, destroy not. See Irhovii Conjectanea in Psalm. Titulos, p. 118, who regards it as a title to prayers similar to Deut. ix. 26–29.

ALTER

1 חָלַף to pass; to change, to alter. HIPHIL *fut.*
2 עָבַר to pass away. KAL *fut.*
3 עֲדָה Ch. to pass over or away, to pass by. P'AL *fut.*
4 שָׁנָה to do a second time, to change, to alter. PIEL a *fut.* שְׁנָא Ch. to change. APHEL b *inf.* c *fut.*

| Lev. xxvii. 10. | 1 | Ezra vi. 12. | 4 b | Ps. lxxxix. 34. | 4 a |
| Ezra vi. 11. | 4 c | Esth. i. 19. | 2 | Dan. vi. 8, 12. | 3 |

ALTOGETHER

אֶחָד *adj.* one. Jer. x. 8, *marg.* in one, or, at once.
הֶבֶל *com.* vanity. Job xxvii. 12, *lit.* in vanity.
יַחַד together, alike. Ps. xix. 9; liii. 3; lxii. 9: *marg.* alike, Isa. x. 8: Jer. v. 5.
כָּלָה *f.* see *End.* Gen. xviii. 21: Exod. xi. 1: 2 Chron. xii. 12.

ALTOGETHER is frequently the translation of infinitives used intensively. See the verb to which it is attached.

ALWAY

1 יוֹם *m.* day; alway, Heb. all days.
2 נֶצַח *m.* for ever.
3 עוֹלָם *m.* perpetual.
4 עֵת *com.* time, season; alway, Heb. in all time.
5 תָּמִיד *m.* constant, continuance.

Gen. vi. 3.	3	Deut. xxviii. 33.	1	Ps. xvi. 8.	5
Exod. xxv. 30.	5	2 Sam. ix. 10.	5	ciii. 9.	2
xxvii. 20.	5	1 Kings xi. 36.	1	cxix. 112.	3
xxviii. 38.	5	2 Kings viii. 19.	1	Prov. v. 19.	5
Num. ix. 16.	5	1 Chron. xvi. 15.	3	viii. 30.	4
Deut. v. 29.	1	2 Chron. xviii. 7.	1	xxviii. 14.	5
vi. 24.	1	Job vii. 16.	3	Eccles. ix. 8.	4
xi. 1.	1	xxvii. 10.	4	Isa. lvii. 16.	2
xi. 12.	5	Ps. ix. 18.	2	Ezek. xx. 17.	3
xiv. 23.	1	x. 5.	1	Ezek. xxxviii. 8.	5

AMAZE

1 בָּהַל to be terrified; to flee in great trepidation. NIPHAL a *pret.* Exod. xv. 15. b *fut.* Judg. xx. 41.
2 חָתַת to be broken; to be dismayed. KAL *pret.* Job xxxii. 15.
3 שָׁמֵם to be laid waste, made desolate; to be amazed, astonished. HIPHIL *pret.* Ezek. xxxii. 10.
4 תָּמַה to wonder. KAL *fut.* Isa. xiii. 8.

AMBASSADOR

1 לִיץ see *Interpret.* HIPHIL *part.* interpreter: (an ambassador, who negotiates friendship between two parties; see 2 Kings xx. 12.)
2 מַלְאָךְ *m.* angel, messenger.
3 צִיר *m.* a messenger, or ambassador. צִיר to go as ambassador. HITHPAEL a *fut.*

Josh. ix. 4.	3 a	Isa. xviii. 2.	3	Jer. xlix. 14.	3
2 Chron. xxxii. 31.	1	xxx. 4.	2	Ezek. xvii. 15.	2
xxxv. 21.	2	xxxiii. 7.	2	Obad. 1.	3
Prov. xiii. 17.	3				

AMBER

חַשְׁמַל *m.* Sept. ἤλεκτρον. Vulg. *electrum;* meaning prob. thereby a bright metal compounded of gold and silver, much esteemed in ancient times; supposed to be compounded of נָחֻשׁ and מַל, a syllable which seems to imply smoothness and polish as combined, in such words as מָלַם and מַלְץ. There is apparently an allusion to it in Rev. i. 15, χαλκολίβανον. The rendering of amber is, on the authority of Jerome, expressive of the colour, but not sufficiently setting forth the brilliancy implied. See Plin. xxxiii. 4, 23, &c.: Ges. Lexicon: Ezek. i. 4, 27; viii. 2.

AMBUSH

אָרַב to lie in wait, concealed in some secret place, watching an opportunity to make a sudden unexpected attack, in

order to rob or kill.   KAL ^a*part.* Poel.   PIEL ^b*part.*
^c מַאֲרָב *m.* ambushment ; "to lie in ambush."

Josh. viii. 2, 7, 12, 14, 19,	Josh. viii. 9.	c	2 Chron. xx. 22. b
21. a	2 Chron. xiii. 13, 13.	c	Jer. li. 12. a

AMEN

אָמַן to be true. אָמֵן amen, let it be granted, let it be done,
and unalterably confirmed : Num. v. 22, &c. Used of
the Messiah, "God of truth," Isa. lxv. 16. comp. Rev.
iii. 14.

AMEND

חָזַק to be strong ; to make strong, repair. PIEL *inf.*
יָטַב to be well, in any respect. HIPHIL ^a*inf.* ^b*imp.* ^c*fut.*

2 Chron. xxxiv. 10. 1	Jer. vii. 5. a	2 a c	Jer. xxxv. 15. 2 b
Jer. vii. 3. 2 b	xxvi. 13.	2 b	

a lit. in mending, amend.

AMENDS

שָׁלַם to be completed. PIEL, to complete ; to restore, make
good : *fut.* Lev. v. 16.

AMERCE

עָנַשׁ to amerce, or impose a fine on any one ; construed with
two accusatives. KAL *pret.* Deut. xxii. 19.

AMETHYST

אַחְלָמָה *f.* name of a precious stone, which the Lxx. and Vulg. have
translated ἀμέθυστος, amethystus. In its form it is a
verbal from the Hiphil of חָלַם to dream ; hence the
story of the Rabbins that this gem has the property of
causing dreams : Exod. xxviii. 19 ; xxxix. 12.

AMIABLE

יָדִיד *adj. const.* beloved : Ps. lxxxiv. 1.

AMISS

עָוָה to be crooked, to be perverted ; to do perversely. HIPHIL
pret. 2 Chron. vi. 37.
שָׁלָה Ch. *f.* error : Dan. iii. 29, כְּתִיב. שָׁלוּ Ch. *f.*, Dan. iii. 29.

AMMI

עַם *com.* people : Hos. i. 9, and ii. 1, *lit.* my people.

AMMINADIB

עַם *com.* people }
נָדִיב *adj.* willing } Cant. vi. 12, *lit.* my willing people.

AMONG

בְּדִי Job xxxix. *lit.* in the sufficiency of.
בְּתוֹךְ used as a prep., in the midst of ; in, within ; among : Gen.
iii. 8, &c.
גֵּו back ; middle : Job xxx. 5, from the midst (of men) they
are driven.
קֶרֶב in the interior, midst of anything. בְּקֶרֶב among, as a
preposition, Gen. xxiv. 3, &c.

ANCESTOR

רִאשׁוֹן *adj.* first, in time, order, or dignity : Lev. xxvi. 45.

ANCIENT

1 זָקֵן *adj.* old, in wisdom, as well as age ; elders, &c. Füerst
defines this word as implying hoary with age.
2 יָשִׁישׁ *m.* a very aged person.
3 עוֹלָם perpetual : also of time past, days of old, former times.
4 עַתִּיק *adj.* old ; advanced in age. עַתִּיק Ch. *id.*
5 קֶדֶם *m.* east, what is before ; spoken also of time, former.
קַדְמֹנִי *adj. id.* ^b קְדוּמִים *m. pl.* antiquity.

Deut. xxxiii. 15.	5	Isa. iii. 2, 5, 14.	1	Isa. li. 9.	5
Judg. v. 21.	5 b	ix. 15.	1	Jer. v. 15.	3
1 Sam. xxiv. 13.	5 a	xix. 11.	5	xviii. 15.	3
2 Kings xix. 25.	5	xxiii. 7.	5	xix. 1, 1.	1
1 Chron. iv. 22.	4	xxiv. 23.	1	Ezek. vii. 26.	1
Ezra iii. 12.	1	xxxvii. 26.	5	viii. 11, 12.	1
Job xii. 12.	2	xliv. 7.	5	ix. 6.	1
Ps. lxxvii. 5.	3	xlv. 21.	5	xxvii. 9.	1
cxix. 100.	1	xlvi. 10.	5	xxxvi. 2.	3
Prov. xxii. 28.	3	xlvii. 6.	1	Dan. vii. 9, 13, 22.	4 a

ANCLE

אֶפֶס *m.* end or remote part : Ezek. xlvii. 3. *Heb.* waters of the
ancles.

ANGEL

אַבִּיר *adj.* mighty : Ps. lxxviii. 25, *marg.* the bread of the
mighty. Pfeiffer, in Dub. Vex., supposes manna might
be called the bread of the mighty, from its peculiar
nutritive power, as well as from its delicious flavour.
Cocceius thinks that אַבִּירִים may be the name of God,
the Mighty One of Israel, who gave them this food.
אֱלֹהִים *m. pl.* a name of God, given also to angels. Ps. viii. 5.
מַלְאָךְ *m.* a messenger of God, an angel, prophet ; a name of
office, not of nature, given generally to the ministering
servants of God, to prophets, and holy men acting
under the divine direction, or in the service of religion. Gen. xvi. 7, &c. : The "angel of Jehovah" is
evidently appropriated to an uncreated being, and the
designation of the Messiah ; called the angel of Jehovah, Exod. iii. 2 : Judg. vi. 11 : angel of God, Gen.
xxxi. 11 : Exod. xiv. 19 : angel of his presence, Isa. lxiii.
9 : angel, or messenger of the covenant, Mal. iii. 1.
מַלְאַךְ Ch. *m. id.* Dan. iii. 28 ; vi. 22.
שִׁנְאָן *m.* repetition : Ps. lxviii. 17, *lit.* thousands of repetitions,
i. e. thousands upon thousands.

ANGER

1 אָנַף to blow hard in the nostrils, to be angry : it is used only
of God's displeasure against sin, and implies his aversion
to it, and readiness to punish it. אַף differs from קִנְאָה
a stronger affection ; from כַּעַס and from חֵמָה ; see Prov.
xxvii. 3, 4.—Cocc. KAL ^a*pret.* ^b*fut.* HITHPAEL ^c*pret.*
^d*fut.* ^e אַף *m.* nostrils, anger : Gen. xxvii. 45, &c.
2 בְּנַס Ch. to be angry, indignant. P'AL *pret.*
3 זָעַם see *Indignation ;* is used in general of the anger of God

against his people in punishing them. KAL [a] *part.* Poel. NIPHAL [b] *part.* [c] זַעַם *m.* foam; wrath, anger.

4 חֵמָה *f.* indignation, wrath, fury, with heat: this word differs from אַף in being the expression of anger more fierce, lasting, and cruel.

5 חָרָה to be warm, to fume; to be greatly angry with resentment, indignation; sometimes it implies any sorrowful perturbation of mind, as in Jonah's case, iv. 1, &c. KAL [a] *pret.* [b] *fut.*

6 חָרַר to be burnt to a red-hot coal; applied to the heat of the mind. NIPHAL *pret.*

7 כָּעַם to be under any turbulent, uneasy commotion of mind. KAL [a] *inf.* [b] *fut.* [c] כַּעַם *m.* vexation.

8 מַר *adj.* bitter.

9 נֶפֶשׁ *com.* soul, life.

10 עֶבְרָה *f.* that which exceeds (applied to anger, wrath.)

11 עַיִן *com.* eye.

12 עָשֵׁן to smoke: metaphor of the anger of God. KAL *pret.*

13 פָּנִים *m. pl.* face; sometimes of an angry countenance.

14 קָצַף to breathe short; to foam, to be wroth. KAL [a] *fut.* HIPHIL [b] *fut.*

15 קָצֵר *adj.* short.

16 רוּחַ wind, breath, spirit.

Provoke to anger. See *Provoke.*

אַף anger, No. 1 e, not included.

Gen. xviii. 30, 32.	5 b	Neh. v. 6.	5 b	Prov. xxii. 8.	10
xlv. 5.	5 b, 11	Esth. i. 12.	4	xxii. 24.	1 e
Lev. x. 16.	14 a	Ps. ii. 12.	1 b	xxv. 23.	3 b
Deut. i. 37.	1 c	vii. 11.	3 a	xxix. 22.	1 e
iv. 21.	1 c	xxi. 9.	13	Eccles. v. 6.	14 a
ix. 8.	1 c	xxxviii. 3.	3 c	vii. 9, 9.	7 a c
ix. 20.	1 c	lxxvi. 7. α	1 e	Cant. i. 6.	6
Judg. viii. 3.	16	lxxix. 5.	1 b	Isa. xii. 1, 1.	1 a e
xviii. 25.	8, 9	lxxx. 4.	12	Jer. iii. 12.	13
2 Sam. xix. 42.	5 a	lxxxv. 4.	7 c	Lam. iv. 16.	13
1 Kings viii. 46.	1 a	lxxxv. 5.	1 b	Ezek. xvi. 42.	7 b
xi. 9.	1 d	cvi. 32.	14 b	Dan. ii. 12.	2
2 Kings xvii. 18.	1 d	Prov. xiv. 17. β	15, 1 e	Jonah iv. 1.	5 b
2 Chron. vi. 36.	1 a	xxi. 19. γ	7 c	iv. 4, 9, 9.	5 a
Ezra ix. 14.	1 b				

α *lit.* in the time of thy anger.　β *lit.* short of nostrils.　γ *lit.* woman of anger.

ANGLE

חַכָּה *f.* hook; Isa. xix. 8: Hab. i. 15.

ANGUISH

1 חוּל to travail, to tremble for pain (see *Pain*); to be in great pain, pangs, anguish, &c. KAL *pret.*

2 צוּקָה *f.* straitness, distress, trouble. [a] מָצוֹק *m.* straitness, distress. [b] מְצוּקָה *f.* distress.

3 צַר *m.* an adversary; affliction, distress, trouble. [a] צָרָה *f.* distress.

4 קֹצֶר *m.* shortness. Gr., feeble-mindedness; *comp.* 1 Thess. v. 14. The word seems to imply extreme dejection, with impatience.

5 שָׁבָץ *m.* according to the Targums, perplexity, terror; *pr.* confusion of mind; *marg.* coat of mail, or, embroidered coat. See *Embroider.*

Gen. xlii. 21.	3 a	Job xv. 24.	2 b	Jer. iv. 31.	3 a
Exod. vi. 9.	4	Ps. cxix. 143.	2 a	vi. 24.	3 a
Deut. ii. 25.	1	Prov. i. 27.	2	xlix. 24.	3 a
2 Sam. i. 9.	3	Isa. viii. 22.	2	l. 43.	3 a
Job vii. 11.	3	xxx. 6.	2		

ANOINT

1 בָּלַל to pour over; intrans. to overflow with. See also *Mingle.* The being anointed with "fresh oil," in Ps. xcii. 10, seems also to imply a penetrating power. KAL *pret.*

2 בֵּן *m.* son; anointed ones, *lit.* sons of oil.

3 דִּשֵּׁן to make fat. PIEL *pret.*, *i. e.* poured largely the oil.

4 מָשַׁח to spread over, to anoint. It is applied chiefly to the anointing of kings, priests, prophets, and sacred things. KAL [a] *pret.* [b] *inf.* [c] *imp.* [d] *fut.* [e] *part.* Poel. [f] *part.* Paül. NIPHAL [g] *pret.* [h] *inf.* [i] מָשִׁיחַ *adj. m.* anointed, Messiah: title (frequent in the Targums) of the expected Deliverer and Saviour. [k] מָשְׁחָה *f.* anointing. [l] מִשְׁחָה *f.* anointing. [m] מִמְשַׁח *m.* anointed: Ezek. xxviii. 14, anointed cherub. Ges., cherub of expansion. Vulg., *cherub extentus, i. e.* with expanded wings, in allusion to the cherubim over the mercy-seat; *comp.* Exod. xxv. 20.

5 סוּךְ to anoint the body after washing. KAL [a] *pret.* [b] *inf.* [c] *fut.* HIPHIL [d] *fut.*

6 יִצְהָר *m.* oil; especially new, of the same year's growth, so named from its bright and clear colour; *prob.* such as was always used in the Golden Candlestick.

7 שֶׁמֶן *com.* fat, fatness; oil: Isa. x. 27. It is difficult to get at any certainty in the interpretation of these words, in which expositors widely differ. The Heb. is literally, from the face of the oil. Chald., before the Messiah, the Anointed. Vitringa understands it of the Holy Spirit.

Gen. xxxi. 13.	4 a	Num. xviii. 8.	4 l	2 Kings ix. 3, 6, 12.	4 a
Exod. xxv. 6.	4 k	xxxv. 25.	4 a	xi. 12.	4 d
xxviii. 41.	4 a	Deut. xxviii. 40.	5 c	xxiii. 30.	4 d
xxix. 2.	4 f	Judg. ix. 8.	4 b	1 Chron. xi. 3.	4 a
xxix. 7, 7.	4 k a	ix. 15.	4 e	xiv. 8.	4 g
xxix. 21.	4 k	Ruth iii. 3.	4 a	xvi. 22.	4 i
xxix. 29.	4 l	1 Sam. ii. 10, 35.	4 a	xxix. 22.	4 d
xxix. 36.	4 a	ix. 16.	4 a	2 Chron. vi. 42.	4 i
xxx. 25, 31.	4 k	x. 1.	4 a	xxii. 7. β	4 d
xxx. 26.	4 a	xii. 3, 5.	4 a	xxiii. 11.	4 d
xxx. 30.	4 d	xv. 1.	4 b	xxviii. 15.	5 c
xxxi. 11.	4 k	xv. 17.	4 a	Ps. ii. 2.	4 i
xxxv. 8, 15, 28.	4 k	xvi. 3, 13.	4 a	xviii. 50.	4 i
xxxvii. 29.	4 k	xvi. 6. α	4 a	xx. 6.	4 i
xxxix. 38.	4 k	xvi. 12.	4 a	xxiii. 5.	3
xl. 9, 9.	4 k a	xvi. 13.	4 d	xxviii. 8.	4 i
xl. 10, 11, 13.	4 a	xix. 6, 6, 10.	4 i	xlv. 7.	4 a
xl. 15, 15, 15.	4 a a l	xxvi. 9, 11, 16, 23.	4 i	lxxxiv. 9.	4 i
Lev. i. 4.	4 f	2 Sam. i. 14, 16, 21.	4 a	lxxxix. 20.	4 a
iv. 3, 5, 16.	4 i	ii. 4.	4 d	lxxxix. 38, 51.	4 a
vi. 20.	4 h	ii. 7.	4 a	xcii. 10.	1
vi. 22.	4 i	iii. 39.	4 f	cv. 15.	4 i
vii. 12.	4 f	v. 3.	4 a	cxxxii. 10, 17.	4 i
vii. 35, 35.	4 k	v. 17.	4 a	Isa. x. 27.	7
vii. 36.	4 k	xii. 7.	4 a	xxi. 5.	4 i
viii. 2, 30.	4 k	xii. 20.	5 d	xlv. 1.	4 i
viii. 10, 10.	4 k d	xiv. 2.	5 c	lxi. 1.	4 a
viii. 11.	4 d	xix. 10.	4 a	Lam. iv. 20.	4 i
viii. 12, 12.	4 k d	xix. 21.	4 a	Ezek. xvi. 9.	5 c
x. 7.	4 k	xxii. 51.	4 i	xxviii. 14.	4 m
xvi. 32.	4 i	xxiii. 1.	4 i	Dan. ix. 24.	4 b
xxi. 10, 12.	4 k	1 Kings i. 34.	4 a	x. 3. γ	5 b a
Num. iii. 3.	4 f	i. 39, 45.	4 d	Amos vi. 6.	4 d
iv. 16.	4 k	v. 1.	4 a	Mic. vi. 15.	5 c
vi. 15.	4 f	xix. 15.	4 a	Hab. iii. 13.	4 i
vii. 1, 1.	4 a	xix. 16, 16.	4 a	Zech. iv. 14.	2, 6
vii. 10, 84, 88.	4 h				

α *lit.* before the Lord is his anointed.　β *lit.* anointed him.　γ *lit.* anointing I did not anoint myself.

ANOTHER

1 אָדָם *m.* man. Eccles. viii. 9, *lit.* over man.

2 אָח *m.* brother; one—another, preceded by אִישׁ.

3   אֶחָד   *adj.* one: repeated, one—another.

4   אָחוֹת   *f.* sister; after אִשָּׁה one—another.

5   אַחֵר   *adj.* another, other, &c., frequent.   אַחֲרִי ᵃ Ch. *adj.* ᵇ אָחֳרָן Ch. *adj.*

6   אִישׁ   *m.* man: repeated, one—another.

7   אֱנוֹשׁ   *m.* man: Job xiii. 9. "mocketh another," *lit.* as the mocking at a man.

8   דּוֹר   *m.* generation.

9   זוּר   to be strange. KAL *part.* See *Strange.*

10   חֹדֶשׁ   moon.

11   כְּלִי   *m.* vessels.

12   כָּנָף   *com.* wing.

13   נָגַד   to tell. HIPHIL *part.* See *Messenger.*

14   עָמִית   *m.* neighbour.

15   רֵעַ   *m.* neighbour; a friend, companion, acquaintance. רְעוּת ᵃ *f. id.*

16   שֵׁנִי   *adj. ord.* second.

אַחֵר another, No. 5, not included.

Gen. xi. 3, 7.	15	Judg. xvi. 11.	3	Jer. xiii. 14.	2
xv. 10.	15	Ruth iii. 14.	15	xviii. 14. η	9
xxvi. 31.	2	1 Sam. ii. 25.	6	xxv. 26.	2
xxxi. 49.	15	x. 3, 3.	3	xlvi. 16.	15
xxxvii. 19.	2	x. 11. β	15	li. 31.	13
xlii. 21, 28.	2	xiii. 18, 18.	3	Ezek. i. 9.	4
xliii. 33.	15	xx. 41, 41.	15	i. 11.	16
Exod. x. 23.	2	1 Kings vi. 27. γ	12	iii. 13.	4
xvi. 15.	2	xviii. 6.	3	iv. 17.	2
xviii. 16.	15	2 Kings iii. 23.	15	x. 9, 9.	3
xxi. 18, 35.	15	vii. 3, 9.	15	xvii. 7.	3
xxv. 20.	2	vii. 6.	15	xix. 5.	3
xxvi. 3, 3, 5, 17.	4	1 Chron. xxvi. 12. δ	2	xxii. 11.	6
xxvi. 19, 21, 25.	2	2 Chron. xx. 23.	15	xxiv. 23.	3
xxxvi. 10, 10, 12, 13, 22, 24, 26.	3	Neh. iii. 19, 21, 24, 27, 30.	16	xxxiii. 30.	3
				xxxvii. 16, 17.	3
xxxvii. 8, 19.	3	iv. 19.	2	xl. 26, 49.	3
xxxvii. 9.	2	Esth. i. 7. ε	11	xli. 11.	3
Lev. vii. 10.	2	i. 19.	15 a	xlvii. 14.	2
xix. 11.	14	ix. 19, 22.	15	Dan. ii. 39, 39.	5 a
xxv. 14, 46.	2	Job xix. 27.	9	v. 17.	5 b
xxv. 17.	14	xli. 16.	2	vii. 5, 6, 8.	5 a
xxvi. 37.	2	xli. 17.	2	vii. 24.	5 b
Num. viii. 8.	16	Ps. cxlv. 4. ζ	8	viii. 13.	3
xiv. 4.	2	Prov. xxvii. 1.	9	Hos. iv. 4.	6
Deut. xxi. 15.	3	Eccles. iv. 10.	16	Joel ii. 8.	2
xxv. 11.	2	viii. 9.	1	Amos iv. 7.	2
Judg. vi. 29.	15	Isa. iii. 5.	6	Zech. viii. 21.	3
ix. 37. a	3	xiii. 8.	15	xi. 9.	15 a
x. 18.	15	lxvi. 23.	10	Mal. iii. 16.	15
xvi. 7.	3				

ᵃ *lit.* one head.   β *lit.* a man to his neighbour.   γ *lit.* wing to wing. δ *lit.* opposite their brethren.   ε *lit.* and vessels different from vessels. ζ *lit.* generation to generation shall, &c.   η *lit.* "that come from another place."

ANSWER

1   אָמַר   to say. KAL ᵃ *pret.* ᵇ *fut.* ᶜ אֹמֶר *m.* word.

2   דָּבַר   to say, to speak. PIEL ᵃ *fut.* ᵇ דָּבָר *m.* word.

3   יָדַע   to know. HIPHIL *imp.*

4   מִלָּה   *m.* words, speech.

5   עָנָה   The various significations derived from this root make it very difficult to catch the primary idea conveyed by it. Most lexicographers suppose the general idea to be, that act which has respect to others. Koerber, in the Lexicon attached to Noldius, says it is derived from an Arabic word, meaning to express the likeness of anything, to assimilate, or to signify. The general idea involved in the word may therefore be the act or operation which corresponds to, assimilates with, or expresses

and signifies the act of another; or to cause that act in another. Thus, to answer in speaking, singing, &c., by hearing a request, to be suitable, to comply or submit willingly or unwillingly, to labour, to be afflicted. Hence these several significations: (1) to act suitably, to relieve, &c., as the sense of the place requireth; Gen. xxxv. 3, Ps. lxv. 5, Eccles. v. 10, Isa. xli. 17: (2) to act suitably to exhortations, &c.; Isa. lxv. 12, Jer. xxxv. 17: (3) to speak suitably to the occasion, &c.; Deut. xxi. 7, xxvi. 5, xxvii. 15, Job iii. 2, Cant. ii. 10: (4) to speak alternately, Isa. xiii. 22; to sing responsively: (5) to speak suitably to a question, &c., to answer: (6) to answer in litigious or judicial cases, to plead, &c.; to give an account, to vindicate; to confute; to answer as a witness; to testify against. KAL ᵃ *pret.* ᵇ *inf.* ᶜ *imp.* ᵈ *fut.* ᵉ *part.* Poel. NIPHAL ᶠ *pret.* ᵍ *fut.* ʰ *part.* עָנָה to afflict, humble. HIPHIL ⁱ *part.* Eccles. v. 20, God answereth, or, humbleth him in the joy of his heart; others, if God hears him through the joy of his heart, *i. e.* imparts to him through the joy of his heart. עֲנָה Ch. P'AL ᵏ *pret.* ˡ *part.* מַעֲנֶה *m.* answer, always, good, or proper: Prov. xv. 23.

6   פִּתְגָּם   Ch. *m.* a word, an order, a letter, a matter.

7   שׁוּב   to return. Hiphil, to bring again. HIPHIL ᵃ *inf.* ᵇ *imp.* ᶜ *fut.* ᵈ *part.* ᵉ תְּשׁוּבָה *f.* return.

8   תּוּב   Ch. to return, to return answer, with an accusative of the person. APHIL ᵃ *pret.* ᵇ *inf.* ᶜ *fut.*

9   עֻמָּה   *f.* conjunction, communion; *prep.* over against; equally with, even as; answerable to, Exod. xxxviii. 18.

Gen. xviii. 27.	5 d	Ruth ii. 6, 11.	5 d	2 Sam. xviii. 3, 29, 32.	1 b
xxiii. 5, 10, 14.	5 d	iii. 11.	1 b	xix. 21, 42, 43.	5 d
xxiv. 50.	5 d	1 Sam. i. 15, 17.	5 d	xxi. 26. 38.	1 b
xxvii. 37, 39.	5 d	iii. 4, 6, 10, 16.	1 a	xx. 17, 17.	1 b
xxx. 33.	5 a	iii. 4, 6, 10, 16.	1 b	xx. 20.	5 d
xxxi. 31, 36, 43.	5 d	iv. 17.	5 d	xxi. 1, 5, 3.	1 b
xxxiv. 13.	5 a	iv. 20.	5 a	xxii. 42.	5 a
xxxv. 3.	5 e	v. 8.	5 a	xxiv. 13.	2 b
xl. 18.	5 d	vi. 4.	1 b	1 Kings i. 28, 36, 43.	5 d
xli. 16, 16.	5 d	ix. 8.	5 b	ii. 22.	1 b
xlii. 22.	5 d	ix. 12, 19, 21.	5 d	ii. 30.	5 d
xliii. 28.	1 b	x. 12.	5 d	iii. 27.	5 d
xlv. 3.	5 b	xi. 2.	1 b	ix. 9.	1 a
Exod. iv. 1.	5 d	xii. 5.	1 b	ix. 22.	1 b
xv. 21.	5 d	xiii. 12, 28.	5 d	xii. 6. α	7 a, 2 b
xix. 8, 19.	5 d	xiv. 12, 28.	5 d	xii. 7.	5 a
xxiv. 3.	5 d	xiv. 37.	5 a	xix. 9. α	7 c, 2 b
xxxviii. 18.	9	xiv. 39.	5 e	xii. 13.	5 d
Num. xi. 28.	5 d	xiv. 44.	1 b	xii. 16. α	7 c, 2 b
xxii. 18.	5 d	xvi. 18.	5 d	xiii. 6.	5 d
xxiii. 12, 26.	5 d	xvii. 27, 58.	5 b	xviii. 18, 18.	1 b
xxxii. 31.	5 d	xvii. 30.	7 c, 2 b	xviii. 21.	5 a
Deut. i. 14, 41.	5 d	xvii. 7.	1 b	xviii. 24, 24.	5 d
xx. 11.	5 a	xix. 17.	1 b	xviii. 26.	5 e
xxi. 7.	5 a	xx. 10, 28, 32.	5 d	xviii. 29.	5 e
xxv. 9.	5 a	xxi. 4, 5.	5 d	xx. 4, 11.	5 d
xxvii. 15.	5 a	xxi. 9, 14.	5 d	xxii. 14.	1 b
Josh. i. 16.	1 b	xxii. 12.	1 b	xxi. 6, 20.	1 b
iv. 7.	1 a	xxiii. 4.	5 d	xxii. 15.	1 b
vii. 20.	5 d	xxv. 10.	5 d	2 Kings i. 8.	1 b
ix. 24.	5 d	xxvi. 6, 14, 14, 22.	5 d	i. 10, 11, 12.	5 d
xv. 19.	1 b	xxviii. 6.	5 a	ii. 5.	1 b
xvii. 15.	1 b	xxviii. 15, 15.	1 b, 5 a	iii. 8.	1 b
xxii. 21.	1 b	xxix. 9.	5 d	iii. 11.	5 d
xxiv. 16.	5 d	xxx. 8.	1 b	iv. 13, 14, 26.	1 b
Judg. v. 29, 29.	5 d, 1 c	2 Sam. i. 4, 7, 8, 13.	1 b	iv. 29.	5 d
vii. 14.	5 d	ii. 20.	1 b	vi. 2, 3, 16, 22, 28.	1 b
viii. 8, 8.	5 d a	iii. 11.	7 a	viii. 12, 13, 14.	5 d
viii. 18, 25.	1 b	iv. 9.	5 d	ix. 19, 22.	1 b
xi. 13.	1 b	ix. 6.	1 a	x. 13, 15.	1 b
xv. 6, 10.	1 b	xiii. 12.	5 d	xviii. 36, 36.	5 a d
xviii. 14.	5 d	xiii. 32.	5 d	xx. 10, 15.	1 b
xix. 28.	5 e	xv. 5, 32.	5 d	1 Chron. iv. 17.	5 d
xx. 4.	1 b	xvii. 8, 19.	5 d	xxi. 3.	1 b
Ruth ii. 4.	1 b	xv. 21.	5 d	xxi. 26.	5 d

Reference	Code	Reference	Code	Reference	Code
1 Chron. xxi. 28.	5 a	Job xxxi. 14.	7 c	Isa. xxxvi. 21, 21.	5 a d
2 Chron. ii. 11.	1 b	xxxi. 35.	5 d	xxxix. 4.	1 b
vii. 22.	1 a	xxxii. 1.	5 b	xli. 28.	7 c
x. 6, 9.	2 b	xxxii. 3, 5.	5 d	xlvi. 7.	5 d
x. 10.	1 b	xxxii. 6, 17, 20.	5 d	l. 2.	5 e
x. 13.	5 d	xxxii. 12.	5 e	lviii. 9.	5 d
x. 14.	2 a	xxxii. 14.	7 c	lxv. 12.	5 a
x. 16.	7 c	xxxii. 15, 16.	5 a	lxv. 24.	5 d
xviii. 3.	1 b	xxxiii. 5.	7 a	lxvi. 4.	5 e
xxv. 9.	1 b	xxxiii. 12.	5 d	Jer. v. 19.	1 a
xxix. 31.	5 d	xxxiii. 32.	7 b	vii. 13.	5 a
xxxi. 10.	1 b	xxxiv. 1.	5 d	vii. 27.	5 d
xxxiv. 15.	5 d	xxxiv. 36.	7 c, 4	xxii. 9.	1 a
xxxiv. 23.	1 b	xxxv. 4.	5 d	xxiii. 35, 37.	5 a
Ezra iv. 17.	6	xxxviii. 1.	5 d	xxxiii. 3.	5 a
v. 5.	8 c	xxxviii. 3.	3	xxxv. 17.	5 a
v. 11.	6	xl. 1, 2, 3, 5, 6.	5 d	xxxvi. 18.	1 b
x. 2, 12.	5 d	xl. 4.	7 c	xlii. 4.	5 d
Neh. ii. 20. β	7 c, 2 b	xlii. 1.	5 d	xliv. 15.	5 d
vi. 4.	7 c	Ps. xviii. 41.	5 a	xliv. 20.	5 e, 2 b
viii. 6.	5 d	xxvii. 7.	5 c	Ezek. xiv. 4.	5 f
Esth. i. 16.	1 b	lxv. 5.	5 d	xiv. 7.	5 h
iv. 13.	7 a	lxxxi. 7.	5 d	xxi. 7.	1 a
v. 4.	1 b	lxxxvi. 7.	5 d	xxiv. 20.	1 b
v. 7.	5 d	xci. 15.	5 d	xxxvii. 3.	1 b
vi. 7.	1 b	xcix. 6.	5 d	xxxviii. 18.	9
vii. 3.	5 d	xcix. 8.	5 a	Dan. ii. 5, 8, 15, 20,	
vii. 5.	1 b	cii. 2.	5 c	26, 27, 47.	5 l
Job i. 7, 9.	5 d	cviii. 6.	5 c	ii. 7, 10.	5 k
ii. 2, 4.	5 d	cxviii. 5.	5 a	ii. 14.	8 a
iv. 1.	5 d	cxix. 42.	5 d	iii. 16, 16.	5 k, 8 b
v. 1.	5 e	cxxxviii. 3.	5 d	iii. 24, 25.	5 l
vi. 1.	5 d	cxliii. 1.	5 c	iv. 19.	5 l
viii. 1.	5 d	Prov. i. 28.	5 d	v. 17.	5 l
ix. 1, 3, 14, 15, 16,		xv. 1, 23.	5 m	vi. 12.	5 l
32.	5 d	xv. 28.	5 b	vi. 13.	5 k
xi. 1.	5 d	xvi. 1.	5 m	Joel ii. 19.	5 d
xi. 2.	5 g	xviii. 13.	7 d	Amos vii. 14.	5 d
xii. 1, 4.	5 d	xviii. 23.	5 d	Mic. iii. 7.	5 m
xiii. 22, 22.	5 d, 7 b	xxii. 21.	7 a	vi. 5.	5 a
xiv. 15.	5 d	xxiv. 26.	7 d, 2 b	Hab. ii. 1.	7 c
xv. 1.	5 d	xxvi. 4.	5 d	ii. 2, 11.	5 d
xvi. 1, 3.	5 d	xxvi. 5.	5 c	Hag. ii. 12, 13, 14.	5 d
xviii. 1.	5 d	xxvii. 11. γ	7 c, 2 b	Zech. i. 10, 11, 12, 13.	5 d
xix. 1, 16.	5 d	xxix. 19.	5 m	i. 19.	1 b
xx. 1, 3.	5 d	Eccles. v. 20.	5 i	iii. 4.	5 d
xx. 2.	7 c	x. 19.	5 d	iv. 4, 5, 6, 11, 12.	5 d
xxi. 1.	5 d	Cant. v. 6.	5 a	iv. 13.	1 b
xxi. 34.	7 e	Isa. vi. 11.	1 b	v. 2.	1 b
xxii. 1.	5 d	xiv. 32.	5 d	vi. 4, 5.	5 d
xxiii. 1, 5.	5 d	xxi. 9.	5 d	xiii. 6.	1 a
xxv. 1.	5 d	xxx. 19.	5 a		
xxvi. 1.	5 d				

a lit. return word to.   *β lit.* returned a word.   *γ lit.* return a word.

ANT

נְמָלָה *f.* a small insect, very sagacious, provident, and industrious, which is said to cut or nibble the sprouts of grains of corn before stowing them up: Prov. vi. 6; xxx. 25.

ANTIQUITY

קַדְמָה *f.* former state: Isa. xxiii. 7.

ANVIL

פַּעַם *com.* an anvil, from פָּעַם to strike: Isa. xli. 7.

ANY

1   אֶחָד *adj.* one, any one, some one.

2   מְאוּמָה *f.* whatever, something, anything.

3   אִישׁ *m.* man, any one, every one.

4   דָּבָר *m.* word, matter, "anything."

5   הֵם *m.* found only in the *pl.,* Ezek. vii. 11, "any of theirs," *marg.* or, their tumultuous persons, from הָמָה to make a tumultuous noise: Ges. riches, wealth; [there shall remain] nothing of them, neither of their multitude, nor of their wealth. The Paronomasia of the words,

מֶהֱמֶה, מַהֲמוֹנָם, מֵהֶם, seems to have given occasion for the new or unusual form of this word. See APP.

6   יָסַף to add; translated throughout "any more." See *More.*

7   נֶפֶשׁ *com.* soul; person; 'any person,' being, individual.

8   עוֹלָם *m.* ever; 'any more,' *lit.* for ever.

Nos. 1, 3, 4, and 6, occurring so frequently, are not included.

Reference	Code	Reference	Code	Reference	Code
Gen. xxii. 12.	2	Num. xxxi. 19.	7	2 Sam. xiii. 2.	2
xxx. 31.	2	xxxv. 11, 15, 30, 30.	7	2 Chron. xx. 20.	2
xxxix. 9, 23.	2	Deut. xxiv. 7.	7	Eccles. ix. 5.	2
Lev. ii. 1.	7	xxiv. 10.	2	Ezek. vii. 11.	5
xxiv. 17.	7	1 Sam. xx. 26, 39.	7	xxvii. 36.	8
Num. xix. 11.	2	xxi. 2.	2	xxviii. 19.	8
xxii. 38.	2	xxv. 15.	2	Jonah iii. 7.	2

APART

נִדָּה *f.* separation; Lev. xv. 19, "put apart:" *lit.* in her separation; xviii. 19, *lit.* in the separation of; Ezek. xxii. 10, "set apart for pollution," *lit.* unclean by separation.

APE

קוֹף *m.* the marmoset, or Ethiopian monkey: Shaw's Supp. p. 95: 1 Kings x. 22: 2 Chron. ix. 21.

APIECE

אֶחָד *adj.* one: 1 Kings vii. 15, *lit.* eighteen cubits was the height of one pillar.

כַּף a spoon: Num. vii. 86, apiece, *lit.* (each) spoon.

עַמּוּד *m.* pillar: 1 Kings vii. 15, *lit.* as above.

APOTHECARY

רָקַח to spice, season; to compound drugs. KAL *part.* Poel: Exod. xxx. 25, *marg.* or, perfumer, 35; xxxvii. 29: Eccles. x. 1. רֹקַח *m.* apothecary, perfumer, Neh. iii. 8. מִרְקַחַת *f.* ointment; "prepared by the apothecaries' art," 2 Chron. xvi. 14.

APPAREL   (See also CHANGE)

1   בֶּגֶד *m.* see Garment.

2   בְּרוֹמִים *m. pl.* "rich apparel," Ezek. xxvii. 24. Ges., variegated stuffs, damask cloths, in which threads of various colours are woven together in figures.

3   לָבַשׁ to put on clothes, or armour; to be clothed. KAL a *fut.* PUAL b *part.* c לְבוּשׁ *m.* a garment, clothing. d מַלְבּוּשׁ *m.* a garment.

4   שִׂמְלָה *f.* a garment, for men and women; see *Clothes.*

Reference	Code	Reference	Code	Reference	Code
Judg. xvii. 10.	1	1 Kings x. 5.	3 d	Isa. iv. 1.	4
1 Sam. xxvii. 9.	1	2 Chron. ix. 4, 4.	3 d	lxiii. 1, 2.	3 c
2 Sam. i. 24.	3 c	Ezra iii. 10.	3 b	Ezek. xxvii. 24.	2
xii. 20.	4	Esth. vi. 8, 9, 10, 11.	3 c	Zeph. i. 8.	3 d
xiii. 18.	3 a	viii. 15.	3 c	Zech. xiv. 14.	1
xiv. 2.	1				

APPEAR, APPARENTLY

1   גָּלָה to open, uncover, reveal, discover, disclose. KAL a *pret.* NIPHAL b *pret.* c *inf.*

2   גָּלַשׁ to pasture, to crop the grass, according to Buxtorf; to to have a shining beautiful appearance, according to Coccieus. Bochart Hieron. part i. lib. xi. c. li. p. 626, supposes the proper meaning to be, to ascend; supported by the lxx., the versions of Jerome, and

the Syriac. Gesenius and Fürst, from the Arabic, derive the meaning of lying down, *quæ discumbunt in monte Gilead.* KAL *pret.*

3 מַחְשֹׂף *m.* a peeling, decortication. See *Bare.*

4 יָצָא to come out. KAL *inf.*

5 עַיִן *com.* eye; appearance, form; "outward appearance."

6 פָּנָה to turn toward; of the approach of day. KAL *inf.*

7 פָּתַח to open. PIEL *pret.*

8 רָאָה to see, look; Niph., to be seen, to show oneself, appear. NIPHAL a *pret.* b *inf.* c *fut.* d *part.* e מַרְאֶה *m.* a looking, seeing; appearance, form; vision as granted to the prophets, and preeminently to Moses, the vision of God.

9 שָׁקַף to lie out over, to project; to look forth. NIPHAL *pret.*

Gen. i. 9.	8 c	Num. xvi. 19, 42.	8 c	Cant. vi. 5.	2
xii. 7, 7.	8 c d	xx. 6.	8 c	vii. 12.	7
xvii. 1.	8 c	Deut. xvi. 16, 16.	8 c	Isa. i. 12.	8 b
xviii. 1.	8 c	xxxi. 11.	8 b	lxvi. 5.	8 d
xxvi. 2, 24.	8 c	xxxi. 15.	8 c	Jer. vi. 1. ι	9
xxx. 37. α	3	Judg. vi. 12.	8 c	xiii. 26.	8 a
xxxv. 1.	8 d	xiii. 3.	8 c	xxxi. 3.	8 c
xxxv. 7.	1 b	xiii. 10.	8 c	Ezek. i. 5, 13, 13, 14,	
xxxv. 9.	8 c	xiii. 21. δ	8 b	16, 16, 26, 26, 27,	
xlviii. 3. β	8 a	1 Sam. i. 22.	8 a	27, 27, 27, 28, 28,	
Exod. iii. 2.	8 c	ii. 27. ε	1 c b	28.	8 e
iii. 16.	8 a	iii. 21. ζ		viii. 2, 2, 2.	8 e
iv. 1, 5.	8 a	xvi. 7.	8 b	x. 1, 1.	8 a
vi. 3.	8 c	2 Sam. xxii. 16.	5	x. 8.	8 c
xiv. 27.	6	1 Kings iii. 5.	8 a	x. 9, 10, 22.	8 e
xvi. 10.	8 c	ix. 2.	8 c a	xix. 11.	8 c
xxiii. 15, 17.	8 c	xi. 9.	8 a	xxi. 24.	8 b
xxxiv. 20, 23.	8 c	2 Chron. i. 7.	8 a	xl. 3, 3.	8 e
xxxiv. 24.	8 b	iii. 1.	8 c	xli. 21, 21.	8 e
Lev. ix. 4.		vii. 12.		xli. 11.	8 e
ix. 6, 23.	8 c	Neh. iv. 21. η	4	xliii. 3.	8 e
xiii. 14. γ	8 b	Ps. xlii. 2.	8 c	Dan. i. 15.	8 a
xiii. 43.	8 e	lxxxiv. 7.	8 c	viii. 1, 1.	8 a
xiii. 57.	8 e	xc. 16.	8 c	viii. 15.	8 e
xvi. 2.	8 c	cii. 16.	8 e	x. 6, 18.	8 e
Num. ix. 15, 16.	8 e	Prov. xxvii. 25. θ	1 a	Joel ii. 4, 4.	8 e
xii. 8.	8 e	Cant. ii. 12.	8 a	Mal. iii. 2.	8 b
xiv. 10.	8 a	iv. 1.	2		

a *lit.* by a making bare of the white.   β *lit.* was seen.   γ *lit.* and in the day of appearing.   δ *lit.* added not to appear.   ε *lit.* appearing did I appear.   ζ *lit.* added to appear.   η *lit.* the coming forth of the stars.   θ Ges. is gone away.   ι *i.e.* impendeth, approacheth.

APPEASE

כָּפַר to cover; see *Atonement.* PIEL *fut.* Gen. xxxii. 20, *lit.* appease his face, *or* propitiate his countenance.

שָׁכַךְ to settle, to subside, spoken of water, anger. KAL *inf.* Esth. ii. 1.

שָׁקַט to rest, to have repose. Hiph., to still, appease, *e.g.* strife. HIPHIL *fut.* Prov. xv. 18.

APPERTAIN

יָאָה to become any one, to be due as that which is fit and proper. *Impers. seq.* לְ, it is becoming, suitable for any one. KAL *pret.*, Jer. x. 7. *Sept. ed. Compl.* σοὶ γὰρ πρέπει.

APPETITE

חַי *adj.* living, life: Job xxxviii. 39.

נֶפֶשׁ *com.* animal life, soul, Prov. xxiii. 2; Eccles. vi. 7.

שָׁקַק to be desirous, eager; to long. KAL *part.* Poel, Isa. xxix. 8.

APPLE

אִישׁוֹן blackness, obscurity; the pupil of the eye. Schultens supposes it has reference to the little image of a man that is seen in the black of the eye: Schultens on Prov. Gesenius says the derivation from the figure seen in the eye is common to many other languages. Deut. xxxii. 10: Ps. xvii. 8: Prov. vii. 2.

בָּבָה *f.* the black or pupil of the eye: Zech. ii. 8. Ges. and Fürst, the gate of the eye, from נָבַב to be hollow, hence, *m.* a hole, gate, or door.

בַּת *f.* daughter: Ps. xvii. 8, *lit.* as the apple the daughter of the eye; Lam. ii. 18, *lit.* the daughter of thine eye.

APPLE-TREE

תַּפּוּחַ *m.* an apple-tree; apples, some of which are known to be very pleasant to sight, smell, and taste. But Celsius (Hierobot. Part I. p. 255) contends that the apples celebrated in Scripture were Mala Cydonia, or quinces; which, from various ancient authors, he shews were golden in colour, delicious in taste, of a fragrant and refreshing smell, far beyond our quinces, and particularly that they are the apples of gold in Prov. xxv. 11. See also Ray's Hist. of Plants, tom. II. ch. iii. p. 1453. Others think the citron is intended, a large and beautiful tree, always green, perfuming the air, and extending a deep and refreshing shade, and loaded with gold-coloured apples. Prov. xxv. 11: Cant. ii. 3, 5; vii. 8; viii. 5: Joel i. 12.

APPLY

בּוֹא to come. HIPHIL, to cause to come; *imp.*, Prov. xxiii. 12. *fut.*, Ps. xc. 12.

לֵב *m.* heart: Eccles. vii. 25; *lit.* I and my heart compassed.

נָטָה to turn aside. HIPHIL *fut.*, Prov. ii. 2.

נָתַן to give. KAL *pret.*, Eccles. viii. 16; *inf.*, Eccles. viii. 9.

סָבַב to turn about, to compass about. KAL *pret.*, Eccles. vii. 25.

שִׁית to set or put; with לְ to lay to heart. KAL *fut.*, Prov. xxii. 17.

APPOINT

1 אָמַר to speak, command, design. KAL a *pret.* b *fut.* c אֹמֶר *m.* word, command. d מַאֲמַר Ch. *m.* appointment.

2 בָּחַר to choose; to select, to prefer. KAL *fut.*

3 בֵּן *m.* child, son: Ps. lxxix. 11.

4 דָּבַר to tell, to bid, to command. PIEL *pret.*

5 זָמַן to determine, fix, appoint. PUAL *part.*

6 חָגַר to gird. KAL *part.* Paül.

7 חָקַק to prescribe, decree. KAL a *inf.* b חֹק *m.* a portion. c חֻקָּה *f.* that which is established or defined.

8 חֵרֶם *m.* appointed to utter destruction. See *Devote.*

9 יָדַע to know; to make to know, to appoint. POAL *pret.*

10 יָכַח to be right; to shew to be right, to decide, to adjudge to any one. HIPHIL *pret.*

11 יָסַד to lay a foundation; to ordain, decree. PIEL *pret.*

12 יָעַד to define, appoint; to come together at an appointed place. KAL *a* *pret.* NIPHAL *b* *fut.* Hiphil, to appoint a time in a forensic sense. *c* *fut.* *d* מוֹעֵד *m.* appointed time; assembly; a place in which an assembly is held; an appointed sign. *e* מוֹעֵד *m.* assembly, a troop of soldiers. *f* מוּעָדָה *f.* appointed place of meeting.

13 כֶּסֶא Cocceius and Schultens understand Prov. vii. 20 of the new moon, a time appointed for extraordinary solemnities of religion. The most probable derivation is from כָּסַס to number, to reckon; and so it refers to specially appointed feasts, as of the Passover, of the Feast of Tabernacles. *a* כֶּסֶה *m.* *id.*

14 מָנָה to assign, allot. PIEL *a* *pret.* *b* *fut.* PUAL *c* *part.*

15 נָצַב to place. NIPHAL *part.*

16 נָקַב to pierce; to mark or note an account; to declare or specify. KAL *imp.*

17 נָתַן to give. KAL *a* *pret.* *b* *imp.* *c* *fut.* *d* *part.* Paül.

18 סָמַן to designate, to mark off. NIPHAL *part.* Isa. xxviii. 25. Ges., and (he plants) barley in the appointed place. According to the *Sept. Aqu. Theod. Vulg.* Isa. xxviii. 25 is understood of millet, though without confirmation from the kindred dialects.

19 עָמַד to stand. Hiphil, to set before, to appoint. *a* *pret.* *b* *inf.* *c* *fut.*

20 עָשָׂה to make. KAL *pret.*

21 פֶּה *m.* mouth.

22 פָּקַד to look after; to give the oversight, to place a person over anything, with עַל and אֶת; to give commission, to command, with עַל of the person; Hiphil, to appoint, with עַל over anything, and with לְ to appoint to have the charge. KAL *a* *pret.* *b* *imp.* *c* *fut.* NIPHAL *d* *fut.* HIPHIL *e* *pret.* *f* *imp.* *g* *fut.* *h* מִפְקָד *m.* command, appointed place.

23 צָבָא *m.* host, warfare, hard service: Job vii. 1, xiv. 14, my appointed service, or warfare; Dan. x. 1, "the time appointed was long," or the warfare was long, probably that series of wars described in the next chapter.

24 צָוָה to command, with an accusative of the person, and עַל of the thing, to appoint over; to appoint, ordain. PIEL *a* *pret.* *b* *inf.*

25 קָדַשׁ see *Sanctify.* HIPHIL *fut.*

26 קוּם Ch. to rise up. Aphel, to set up, *fut.*

27 קָרָה to meet. Hiphil, to cause to meet, to make opportune; to make a suitable selection. HIPHIL *pret.*

28 שׂוּם to set, place, put, in any manner; to ordain, establish; to appoint; with עַל of the thing, to place or appoint over anything. KAL *a* *pret.* *b* *inf.* *c* *imp.* *d* *fut.*

29 שִׁית to lay, put, set, place; to constitute, appoint, with עַל over a thing. KAL *a* *pret.* *b* *fut.*

30 שָׁלַח to send; to send on a commission, a charge. KAL *fut.*

Judg. xviii. 11, 16, 17.	6	2 Chron. xxiii. 18.	28 d	Prov. vii. 20.	13
xx. 38.	12 d	xxxi. 2.	19 c	viii. 29.	7 a
1 Sam. viii. 11.	28 a	xxxiii. 8.	19 a	xxxi. 8.	3
viii. 12.	28 b	Ezra iii. 8.	19 c	Isa. i. 14.	12 d
xiii. 11.	12 d	vi. 9.	1 d	xiv. 31.	12 e
xix. 20.	15	viii. 20.	17 a	xxvi. 1.	29 b
xx. 35.	12 d	x. 14.	5	xxviii. 25. γ	18
xxi. 2.	9	Neh. v. 14. β	24 a	xliv. 7.	28 b
xxv. 30.	24 a	vi. 7.	19 a	lxi. 3.	28 b
2 Sam. vi. 21.	24 b	vii. 1.	22 d	Jer. v. 24.	7 c
vii. 10.	28 a	vii. 3.	19 b	viii. 7.	12 d
xiii. 32.	21	ix. 17.	17 c	xv. 3.	22 a
xv. 15.	2	x. 34.	5	xxxiii. 25.	28 a
xvii. 14.	24 a	xii. 31.	19 c	xlvi. 17.	12 d
xx. 5.	12 a	xii. 44.	22 d	xlvii. 7.	12 a
xxiv. 15.	12 d	xiii. 30.	19 c	xlix. 19, 19.	22 c, 12 c
1 Kings i. 35.	24 a	xiii. 31.	5	l. 44, 44.	22 c, 12 c
v. 6.	1 b	Esth. i. 8.	11	li. 27.	22 b
v. 9.	30	ii. 3.	22 g	Ezek. iv. 6. δ	17 a
v. 18.	1 a	ii. 15.	1 b	xxi. 19.	28 c
xii. 12.	4	iv. 5.	19 a	xxi. 20.	28 d
xx. 42.	8	Job ii. 11.	12 b	xxi. 22, 22.	28 b
2 Kings vii. 17.	22 e	vii. 1.	23	xxxvi. 5.	17 a
viii. 6.	17 c	vii. 3.	14 a	xliii. 21.	22 h
x. 24.	28 a	xiv. 5.		xlv. 6.	17 c
xi. 18.	28 d	xiv. 13.	29 b	Dan. i. 5.	14 b
xviii. 14.	28 d	xiv. 14.	23	i. 10.	14 a
1 Chron. vi. 48.	17 d	xx. 29.	1 c	v. 21.	26
ix. 29.	14 c	xxiii. 14.	7 b	viii. 19.	12 d
xv. 16.	19 b	xxx. 23.	12 d	x. 1.	23
xv. 17.	19 c	Ps. lxxvii. 5.	28 a	xi. 27, 29, 35.	12 d
vi. 4.	17 c	lxxix. 11.	3	Hos. i. 11.	28 a
2 Chron. viii. 14.	19 c	lxxxi. 3.	13 a	Mic. vi. 9.	12 a
xx. 21.	19 c	cii. 20.	3	Hab. ii. 3.	12 d
		civ. 19.	20		

a *lit.* of appointment. β *lit.* he appointed me. γ *i.e.* selected or designated as seed barley.   δ *lit.* given it.

APPROACH

1 נָגַשׁ to come near, or close. KAL *a* *inf.* NIPHAL *b* *pret.* HIPHIL *c* *fut.*

2 קָרַב to draw near; to be at hand. KAL *a* *pret.* *b* *fut.* PIEL *c* *fut.* *d* קָרֵב *adj.* drawing near. *e* קָרְבָה *f.* approach. *f* קָרוֹב *adj.* near.

Lev. xviii. 6, 14, 19.	2 b	Deut. xxxi. 14.	2 a	Isa. lviii. 2.	2 e
xx. 16.	2 b	Josh. viii. 5.	2 b	Jer. xxx. 21, 21.	1 b a
xxi. 17, 18.	2 b	2 Sam. xi. 20.	1 b	Ezek. xlii. 13.	2 f
Num. iv. 19.	1 a	2 Kings xvi. 12.	2 b	xlii. 14.	2 f
Deut. xx. 2.	1 b	Job xl. 19.	1 c	xliii. 19.	2 f
xx. 3.	2 d	Ps. lxv. 4.	2 c		

APPROVE

רָאָה to see, look on. KAL *pret.* Lam. iii. 36.

רָצָה to be well pleased with, or to take delight in. KAL *fut.* Ps. xlix. 13.

APRON

חֲגוֹרָה *f.* that which girds about: Gen iii. 7.

APT

עָשָׂה to make, do, act; to wage (war). KAL *part.* Poel. 2 Kings xxiv. 16, *lit.* doers of.

ARABAH

עֲרָבָה *f.* a plain: Josh. xv. 6; xviii. 18, 18.

ARABIA

עֶרֶב *m.* evening: 1 Kings x. 15, perhaps, *lit.* of the mingled people; see *Mix.*

ARCH

אֵילָם *m.* a porch, a gallery; an arch which is bound to or connected with the main building: Ezek. xl. 21, 22, 22, 24, 25, 26, 29, 29, 31, 33, 33, 34, 36. אֵלַמּוֹת *f. id. pl.* Ezek. xl. 16, 30.

Gen iv. 25.		29 a	Exod. xxiii. 15.	12 d	Num. ix. 2, 3, 7, 13.	12 d
xviii. 19.	12 d	xxx. 16.	17 a	xxxv. 6.	17 c
xxiv. 14, 44.	10	Lev. xxvi. 16.	22 e	xxxv. 11.	27
xxx. 28.	16	Num. i. 50.	22 f	Josh. viii. 14.	12 d
xli. 34.	22 g	iii. 10.	22 c	xx. 2.	17 b
Exod. ix. 5.	28 d	iv. 19.	28 a	xx. 7.	25
xxi. 13.	28 a	iv. 27, 27.	21, 22 a	xx. 9. α	12 f

ARCHER

1 אֱנוֹשׁ *m.* man.

2 בַּעַל *m.* owner, master.

3 דָּרַךְ to tread; to bend the bow by setting the foot or knee upon it. KAL *part.* Poel.

4 חָצַץ to shoot with an arrow. PIEL ᵃ*part.* ᵇ חֵץ *m.* arrow.

5 יָרָה to throw darts, shoot arrows or stones out of an engine in a regular manner, aiming directly at a mark. KAL ᵃ*part.* Poel. HIPHIL ᵇ*part.*

6 רַב *m.* in all the ancient versions of Job xvi. 13 is rendered arrows; by others, archers.

7 רָבָה to multiply; also to shoot. KAL *part.* Poel. Gen. xxi. 20, *lit.* a shooter with a bow.—Taylor. Another rendering, however, is given by Ges.: he grew up an archer; see קֶשֶׁת ᵃ. Fürst, *adolescens sagittarius, uti bene Vulg. factusque est juvenis sagittarius sive jaculans sagittarius.* lxx. τοξότης.

8 קֶשֶׁת *com.* bow. ᵃ קַשָּׁת *m.* a bowman.

Gen. xxi. 20.	7, 8 a	1 Chron. viii. 40. β	3, 8	Isa. xxi. 17.	8
xlix. 23. α	2, 4 b	x. 3.	5 b, 8	xxii. 3.	8
Judg. v. 11.	4 a	xi. 18.	5 a	Jer. l. 29.	6
1 Sam. xxxi. 3.	5 b, 1, 8	2 Chron. xxxv. 23.	5 a	li. 3.	3
xxxi. 3.	5 b	Job xvi. 13.	6		

α *lit.* masters of arrows.   β *lit.* benders of the bow.

ARCTURUS

עָשׁ *m.* and עַיִשׁ *f.* the constellation which we call the Great Bear, Ursa Major, the Wain, from the Greeks and Romans; its sons are the three stars in the tail of the bear: Job ix. 9; xxxviii. 32.

ARGUE

יָכַח to shew, to prove in order to convince or refute by reasons, arguments, or actions. HIPHIL *inf.* Job vi. 25. תּוֹכַחַת *f.* a proving, arguments: Job xxiii. 4.

ARIEL

אֲרִיאֵל and אַרְאֵל *m.* lion of God; altar of God. So the altar of burnt offering is called, Ezek. xliii. 15, 17; and Jerusalem, because the altar was there. Fürst derives it from אָרָא to be strong, &c., ἀρήϊον εἶναι, and supposes it to be the name of Jerusalem, as the abode of mighty men. Isa. xxix. 1, 1, 2, 2, 7. Ges. supposes אֲרִי means hearth; but 'lion of God' is probably the true meaning, and that it is put for Jerusalem, as Nineveh is described under this figure, Nah. ii. 11, 12.

ARIGHT

יָטַב to be well, to use well; to 'use aright.' HIPHIL *fut.* Prov. xv. 2.

מֵישָׁרִים *m. pl.* uprightness: Prov. xxiii. 31.

כּוּן to set things right, or in good order. HIPHIL *pret.* Ps. lxxviii. 8. כֵּן *adj.* aright: Jer. viii. 6.

ARISE

1 זָרַח to arise, to spring forth; applied chiefly to the light, to the sun, to the glory or favour of God. KAL ᵃ*pret.* ᵇ*inf.* ᶜ*fut.* ᵈ*part.* Poel.

2 נָשָׂא to lift up, to lift up oneself. KAL *inf.*

3 עוּר to awake, to rouse oneself. KAL *imp.*

4 עָלָה to ascend, to go up. KAL ᵃ*pret.* ᵇ*inf.* ᶜ*fut.* ᵈ*part.* Poel.

5 עָמַד to stand. KAL *fut.*; or, continued.

6 קוּם see *Rise:* to apply to action; hence, arise, a word of excitation to action. Figuratively, to arise, to begin to exist, to come to pass, connoting power and prevalency, Hos. x. 14; to stand firm and upright, Prov. xxxi. 28; her children arise up, stand, *i. e.* flourish in wisdom, virtue, wealth, or reputation; and so call her, *i. e.* give others occasion to call her blessed: to stand or rise up in succession, Gen. xli. 30. KAL ᵃ*pret.* ᵇ*inf.* ᶜ*imp.* ᵈ*fut.* HIPHIL ᵉ*pret.* קוּם Ch. P'AL ᶠ*imp.* ᵍ*fut.*

7 קִיץ to awake from sleep, death. HIPHIL *imp.*

8 שָׁכַם to rise up early. HIPHIL *fut.*

Gen. xiii. 17.	6 c	2 Sam. ii. 14, 14, 15.	6 d	Ps. vii. 6.	6 c
xix. 15, 15.	4 a, 6 c	iii. 21.	6 d	ix. 19.	6 c
xix. 33.	6 b	vi. 2.	6 d	x. 12.	6 c
xix. 35, 35.	6 d b	xi. 2.	6 d	xii. 5.	6 c
xxiv. 10, 61.	6 c	xi. 20.	4 c	xvii. 13.	6 d
xxvii. 19, 43.	6 c	xii. 17, 20.	6 d	xliv. 23.	6 c
xxvii. 31.	6 c	xiii. 15.	6 c	xliv. 26.	7
xxviii. 11.	6 c	xiii. 29, 31.	6 d	lxviii. 1.	6 d
xxxi. 13.	6 c	xiv. 23, 31.	6 d	lxxiv. 22.	6 c
xxxv. 1.	6 c	xv. 9.	6 d	lxxvi. 9.	6 b
xxxv. 3.	6 a	xv. 14.	6 c	lxxviii. 6.	6 b
xxxvii. 7.	6 a	xvii. 1, 22, 23.	6 c	lxxxii. 8.	6 c
xxxviii. 19.	6 c	xvii. 21.	6 c	lxxxviii. 10.	6 d
xli. 30.	6 a	xix. 7.	6 a	lxxxix. 9.	2
xliii. 8.	6 d	xix. 8.	6 a	cii. 13.	6 d
xliii. 13.	6 d	xxii. 39.	6 a	civ. 22.	1 c
Exod. i. 8.	6 d	xxiii. 10.	6 a	cix. 28.	6 a
Deut. ix. 12.	6 c	1 Kings i. 50.	6 a	cxii. 4.	1 a
x. 11.	6 c	ii. 40.	6 d	cxxxii. 8.	6 c
xiii. 1.	6 d	iii. 12, 20.	6 d	Prov. vi. 9.	6 a
xvii. 8.	6 a	viii. 54.	6 a	xxxi. 28.	6 a
xxxiv. 10.	6 a	xi. 18, 40.	6 d	Eccles. i. 5, 5.	1 a d
Josh. i. 2.	6 c	xiv. 2, 12.	6 c	Cant. ii. 13.	6 c
viii. 1.	6 c	xiv. 4, 17.	6 d	Isa. ii. 19, 21.	6 b
viii. 3.	6 a	xvii. 9.	6 c	xxi. 5.	6 c
viii. 19.	6 a	xvii. 10.	6 a	xxiii. 12.	6 c
xviii. 8.	6 d	xviii. 44.	4 d	xxvi. 19.	6 d
xxiv. 9.	6 d	xix. 3, 8, 21.	6 d	xxxi. 2.	6 a
Judg. ii. 10.	6 d	xix. 5, 7.	6 c	xxxvii. 36.	8
iii. 20.	6 d	xxi. 7, 15, 18.	6 d	lxiii. 7.	6 a
iv. 9.	6 d	2 Kings i. 3.	6 c	lii. 2.	6 a
v. 7, 7.	6 a	iii. 24.	6 d	lx. 1.	6 c
v. 12.	8	iv. 30.	6 d	lx. 2.	1 c
vi. 28.	6 d	vii. 7, 12.	6 d	Jer. i. 17.	6 a
vii. 9, 15.	6 d	viii. 1.	6 c	ii. 27.	6 d
viii. 21.	6 d	ix. 2.	6 d	ii. 28.	6 d
x. 3.	6 d	ix. 6.	6 e	vi. 4, 5.	6 d
xiii. 11.	6 d	x. 12.	6 d	viii. 4.	6 d
xvi. 3.	6 d	xi. 1.	6 d	xiii. 4, 6.	6 c
xviii. 9.	6 c	xii. 20.	6 d	xviii. 2.	6 c
xix. 5, 8.	6 d	xix. 35.	4 d	xxxi. 6.	6 d
xx. 8, 18.	6 d	xxiii. 25.	6 a	xli. 2.	6 d
xx. 40.	6 d	xxv. 26.	6 d	xlvi. 16.	6 d
Ruth i. 6.	4 b	1 Chron. x. 12.	6 d	xlix. 28, 31.	6 c
1 Sam. iii. 6, 8.	6 d	xx. 4.	5	Lam. ii. 19.	6 c
v. 3, 4.	8	xxii. 16, 19.	6 c	Ezek. iii. 22.	6 c
ix. 3.	6 c	2 Chron. vi. 41.	6 c	iii. 23.	6 d
ix. 26, 26.	8, 6 d	vii. 10.	6 d	Dan. ii. 39.	6 g
xiii. 15.	6 d	xxix. 12.	6 d	vi. 19.	6 g
xvi. 12.	6 c	xxx. 14, 27.	6 a	vii. 5.	6 f
xvii. 35, 52.	6 d	xxxvi. 16.	4 b	vii. 17, 24.	6 g
xvii. 48.	6 a	Ezra iii. 5.	6 a	Hos. x. 14.	6 a
xviii. 27.	6 a	x. 4.	6 c	Amos vii. 2, 5.	6 d
xx. 25, 34, 42.	6 d	Neh. ii. 12, 20.	6 d	Obad. 1.	6 c
xx. 41.	6 d	Esth. iv. 14.	6 a	Jonah i. 2, 6.	6 c
xxi. 10.	6 d	vii. 7.	6 d	iii. 2.	6 c
xxiii. 4.	6 d	Job i. 20.	6 d	iii. 3, 6.	6 d
xxiii. 13, 16, 24.	6 d	vii. 4.	6 d	iv. 8.	1 b
xxiv. 4, 8.	6 d	xix. 18.	6 d	Mic. ii. 10.	6 c
xxv. 1, 41, 42.	6 d	xxv. 3.	6 d	iv. 13.	6 c
xxvi. 2, 5.	6 d	xxix. 8.	6 a	vi. 1.	6 c
xxvii. 8.	6 d	Ps. iii. 7.	6 c	vii. 8.	6 a
xxviii. 23.	6 d			Nah. iii. 17.	1 a
xxxi. 12.	6 d			Hab. ii. 19.	3
				Mal. iv. 2.	1 a

ARK

אָרוֹן and אָרֹן *c.* an ark, chest, box, coffer, coffin; in which anything is laid up and preserved: this is the word applied to the ark of the covenant, in which were laid up the tables of the law, over which was the divine manifestation; called the ark of the testimony, because it contained the written law, Exod. xxxi. 18; xxxiv. 29; the ark of the strength of God, because it was the symbol of the power of God, going forth against the enemies of Israel; and the ark of holiness, dedicated to a holy God, and containing his holy law, Exod. xxv. 10, &c.

תֵּבָה *f.* strictly a box, chest; hence a vessel, boat, ship, *e. g.* that of Noah, that wherein Moses was exposed when an infant: lxx. κιβῶτος. Vulg. *arca.* Gen. vi. 14, 14, 15, 16, 16, 18, 19; vii. 1, 7, 9, 13, 15, 17, 18, 23; viii. 1, 4, 6, 9, 9, 10, 13, 16, 19; ix. 10, 18: Exod. ii. 3, 5.

ARM

דְּרָע Ch. *f.* an arm: Dan. ii. 32.

זְרוֹעַ *com.* an arm; the shoulder of any animal. Figuratively, power, strength; any kind of help or support, as riches, friends, &c., Job xxii. 8, 9. The power and operation of God; Isa. li. 9; lii. 10; where some think the doctrine of the Gospel is referred to, others Christ himself, who is the arm of the Lord to vindicate his truth and glory in the salvation of men. Isa. xliv. 12, the strength of his arms; *lit.* the arm of his strength; Gen. xlix. 24, &c.; אֶזְרוֹעַ *f.* Jer. xxxi. 22; xxxii. 21.

חֹצֶן *m.* the grasp of both the arms; Isa. xlix. 22. See *Bosom, Lap.*

כָּתֵף *f.* the shoulder; Job xxxi. 22, or, let my shoulder fall from its blade.

ARM-HOLES

אַצִּיל joining; the joining of the hand or of the arm, the wrist; Jer. xxxviii. 12: Ezek. xiii. 18.

יָד *com.* hand; arm-holes; *lit.* holes of my hands: Jer. xxxviii. 12: Ezek. xiii. 18.

ARMED

1   חָלַץ to draw out, to draw off: it is used of armed men, as it has been supposed, because they are drawn out or draughted for war; but as the word means to strip, so it may come to have been used of men prepared for war, corresponding with the Latin word *expediti;* translated in Josh. iv. 13, εὔζωνος, elsewhere by lxx. ἐνωπλισμένος, ὁπλίτης, πολεμιστής, μάχιμος. KAL [a] *part.* Paül. NIPHAL [b] *imp.* [c] *fut.*

2   חֲמֻשִׁים *adj. pl.* by fives; armed, in battle array: others, divided into companies of fifty: see Patrick's Com. on Exod. xiii. 18. He saith that the Hebrew word *chomaseh* signifies those parts that are under the five small ribs about which men were wont to be girt, when they went to fight or travel; and so it signifies to be armed, accoutred. Fürst regards the word as a verb denom. in *part. pass. plur.*, and so Ges.

3   לָבַשׁ to put on clothes or armour. KAL [a] *part.* Paül. HIPHIL [b] *fut.*

4   מָגֵן *m.* a shield; "armed man," *lit.* a man of shield, *i. e.* not to be resisted.

5   נָשַׁק to join or close together; hence applied to those who meet in battle. Ancient versions, however, render this word of the use of the bow: see Ges. Thes. Heb. in v. The noun, therefore, may rather be understood of *tela* than *arma.* KAL [a] *part.* Poel. [b] נֶשֶׁק and נֵשֶׁק *m.* armour, armoury.

6   רוּק to draw out. HIPHIL *fut.*

Gen. xiv. 14.	6	Josh. iv. 12.	2	2 Chron. xvii. 17.	5 a
Num. xxxi. 3. a	1 b	vi. 7, 9, 13.	1 a	xxviii. 14.	1 a
xxxi. 5.	1 a	Judg. vii. 11.	2	Job xxxix. 21.	5 b
xxxii. 17, 20.	1 c	1 Sam. xvii. 5.	3 a	Ps. lxxviii. 9.	5 a
xxxii. 21, 27, 29, 30,		xvii. 38, 38.	3 b	Prov. vi. 11.	4
32.	1 a	1 Chron. xii. 2.	5 a	Isa. xv. 4.	1 a
Deut. iii. 18.	1 a	xii. 23, 24.	1 a		
Josh. i. 14.	2				

a lit. arm men.

ARMY

1   גְּדוּד *m.* see *Troop;* a band of warriors, or robbers.

2   חַיִל *m.* strength, &c., valour in war; forces, an army. [a] חַיִל Ch. *m. id.* [b] חֵיל *m. id.*

3   חָלָץ see *Armed.* KAL part. Paül.

4   מַחֲנֶה *com.* the encamping of an army, either in a field or in the siege of a town; hence, a host or any company of men.

5   מַצָּבָה *f.* a post or garrison.

6   מַעֲרָכָה *m.* an army set in battle array. [a] מַעֲרוֹת *f. pl. id.*

7   צָבָא *m.* an army, a host, a body of men marshalled, set in array, properly disposed, where every one is appointed to his proper station and duty, and obliged to attend upon it.

Gen. xxvi. 26.	7	1 Kings xx. 19, 25, 25.	2	Isa. xxxiv. 2.	7
Exod. vi. 26.	7	2 Kings xxv. 5, 5, 10,		xxxvi. 2.	2 b
vii. 4.	7	23, 26.	2	xliii. 17.	2
xii. 17, 51.	7	1 Chron. xi. 26.	2	Jer. xxxii. 2.	2
xiv. 9.	2	xx. 1.	7	xxxiv. 1, 7, 21.	2
Num. i. 3.	7	xxvii. 34.	7	xxxv. 11, 11.	2
ii. 3, 9, 10, 16, 18,		2 Chron. xiii. 3.	2	xxxvii. 5, 7, 10, 11, 11.	2
24, 25.	7	xiv. 8.	2	xxxviii. 3.	2
x. 14, 18, 22, 28.	7	xvi. 4.	2	xxxix. 1, 5.	2
xxxiii. 1.	7	xx. 21.	3	xlvi. 2, 22.	2
Deut. xi. 4.	7	xxiv. 24.	2	lii. 4, 8, 8, 14.	2
xx. 9.	7	xxv. 9.	1	Ezek. xvii. 17.	2
Judg. iv. 7.	7	xxv. 10, 13.	1	xxvii. 10, 11.	2
viii. 6.	7	xxvi. 13.	2, 7	xxix. 18, 18, 19.	2
ix. 29.	7	Neh. ii. 9.	2	xxxii. 31.	2
1 Sam. iv. 2, 12, 16, 16.	6	iv. 2.	1	xxxvii. 10.	2
xvii. 1.	4	Job xxv. 3.	1	xxxviii. 4, 15.	2
xvii. 8, 10, 21, 21, 22,		xxix. 25.	7	Dan. iii. 20.	2 a
23, 26, 36, 45, 48.	6	Ps. xciv. 9.	7	iv. 35.	2 a
xvii. 23. ל	6 a	lx. 10.	7	xi. 7, 13, 25, 25, 26.	2
xxiii. 3.	6	lxviii. 12.	7	Joel ii. 11, 25.	2
xxviii. 1.	4	Cant. vi. 13.	3	Zech. ix. 8.	5
xxix. 1.	4				

ARMOUR, ARMOURY

1   אוֹצָר *m.* see *Treasure.*

2   זֵנוֹת *f. pl.* defensive armour, encompassing and surrounding the body. The passage in 1 Kings xxii. 38 may be rendered, 'and the harlots washed,' *i. e.* in the same pool; which is mentioned to the disgrace of Ahab: so the Rabbins and many commentators understand the passage.—*Keil.*

3   חֲגוֹרָה *f.* a girdle.

4   חֲלִיצָה   *f.* spoil stripped from an enemy, booty ; see *Armed*.

5   כְּלִי   *m.* a general name for all kinds of tools, armour, weapons, &c.

6   מַד   *m.* an upper garment. See *Raiment*.

7   נֵשֶׁק   *f.* see *Armed*.

8   תַּלְפִּיוֹת   *f. pl.* an armoury, a place where weapons were hung up, as on the turrets and walls of eastern cities : Cant. iv. 4, comp. Ezek. xxvii. 10, 11. Probably compounded of תַּל (from תָּלָה to hang up,) and פִּיוֹת edges, *sc.* of swords, comp. Prov. v. 4. Gesenius derives it from תָּלַח to destroy ; *i. e.* destructive weapons.

Judg. ix. 54.	5	2 Sam. xviii. 15.	5	1 Chron. x. 4, 4, 5, 9, 10.	5
1 Sam. xiv. 1, 6, 7, 12,	5	xxiii. 37.	5	xi. 39.	5
13, 13, 14, 17.	5	1 Kings x. 25.	7	Neh. iii. 19.	7
xvi. 21.	5	xxii. 38.	2	Cant. iv. 4.	8
xvii. 38, 39.	6	2 Kings iii. 21.	3	Isa. xxii. 8.	7
xvii. 54.	5	x. 2.	7	xxxix. 2.	5
xxxi. 4, 4, 5, 6, 9, 10.	5	xx. 13.	5	Jer. l. 25.	1
2 Sam. ii. 21.	4				

ARRAY

1   אָסַר   to bind ; to draw men up in battle array, to bind them together in order, in rank and file. KAL *fut.*

2   לָבַשׁ   to put on clothes and armour. KAL *a fut.* PUAL *b part.* HIPHIL *c pret.* *d fut.*

3   עָטָה   to cover, to wrap oneself up with a cloak or upper garment. KAL *a pret.* Jer. xliii. 12, of Nebuchadnezzar, who shall get possession of Egypt as easily as a person puts on a garment ; or the import may be, the Egyptians may procure assistance and supplies and wealth, but he shall clothe himself with all their preparation.

4   עָרַךְ   to set things in a regular disposition, as they suit or match one another, or to place them in equal corresponding ranks ; as soldiers are drawn up in battle array, with אֵת and לִקְרַאת against any one : intrans., to put oneself in battle array, with עַל, ל, לִקְרַאת, against any one. KAL *a pret.* *b inf.* *c imp.* *d fut.* ? *part.* Paül.

5   שִׁית   to set, put, place. KAL *a pret.* *b inf.*

Gen. xli. 42.	2 d	2 Chron. v. 12.	2 b	Job xl. 10.	2 a
Judg. xx. 20, 30, 33.	4 d	xiii. 3.	1	Isa. xxii. 7. β	5 a b
xx. 22, a 22.	4 b a	xiii. 3.	4 a	Jer. vi. 23.	4 e
1 Sam. iv. 2.	4 d	xiv. 10.	4 d	xliii. 12.	3
xvii. 2.	4 d	xxviii. 15.	2 d	l. 9.	4 a
xvii. 8.	4 d	Esth. vi. 9.	2 c	l. 14.	4 c
xvii. 21.	4 b	vi. 11.	2 d	l. 42.	4 e
2 Sam. x. 8, 9, 10, 17.	4 d	Job vi. 4.	4 d	Joel ii. 5.	4 e
1 Chron. xix. 9, 10, 11,					
17, 17.	4 d				

a lit. added to set in array.   *β lit.* setting, shall set themselves.

ARROGANCY

גָּאוֹן   *m.* elevation, exaltation ; excellence ; swelling pride ; as of waves, and of self-exaltation, arrogance, pride, and haughtiness : Prov. viii. 13 : Isa. xiii. 11 : Jer. xlviii. 29.

עָתָק   *adj.* that which is grown old, hard, and durable ; it seems to denote an obstinate, unrelenting disposition, showing itself in insolence, pride, and violence : 1 Sam. ii. 3.

ARROW

1   בֵּן   *m.* a son ; arrows, *lit.* sons of the bow or the quiver.

2   חֵץ   *m.* an arrow, or dart. Arrows were usually made of light wood, with a head of brass or iron, which was commonly barbed : sometimes they were armed with two, or three, or four hooks. The heads of arrows were also occasionally dipped in poison (to which distinct allusion is made in Job vi. 4) of the deadliest kind : the fatal effect, it is said, usually takes place at sunset, to which there may be reference in 2 Chron. xviii. 34. Figuratively, arrows are put for calamities, pains, or sorrows inflicted by God, Deut. xxxii. 23, Job vi. 4 ; the tortures of famine, Ezek. v. 16. Thunders, lightning, hail, are God's arrows, Ps. lxxvii. 17, cxliv. 6. The Gospel is an arrow in the hand of Christ to subdue his enemies, Ps. xlv. 5, *comp.* Rev. vi. 2. Arrows were used in drawing lots to assign to persons their particular shares or stations, to decide purposes of war, Ezek. xxi. 21. Arrows were shot into an enemy's country as a signal of war, 2 Kings xiii. 17. Children of a family are called arrows of their parents, from the protection they afford, Ps. cxxvii. 4. In some places, says Paxton, the birth of a son is announced by an arrow being hung up before the house. Whatever greatly injures is compared to an arrow ; as a false witness, Prov. xxv. 18 ; a false tongue, Ps. cxx. 4, Jer. ix. 8 ; bitter words, Ps. lxiv. 3. *a* חֲצִי *m. id.* *b* חָצָץ *m. id.*

3   קֶשֶׁת   *com.* bow.

4   רֶשֶׁף   *m.* spark ; a flame, strong heat ; lightning : Ps. lxxvi. 3, the lightnings of the bow, *i. e.* arrows : some the sparks of the bow, because arrows fly from the bow like sparks.

Num. xxiv. 8.	2	Ps. xi. 2.	2	Prov. xxvi. 18.	2
Deut. xxxii. 23, 42.	2	xviii. 14.	2	Isa. v. 28.	2
1 Sam. xx. 20, 21, 21,		xxxviii. 2.	2	vii. 24.	2
22, 36, 38.	2	xlv. 5.	2	xxxvii. 33.	2
xx. 36, 37, 37.	2 a	lviii. 4.	2	Jer. ix. 8.	2
xx. 38. ל	2	lviii. 7.	2	l. 9, 14.	2
2 Sam. xxii. 15.	2	lxiv. 3, 7.	2	li. 11.	2
2 Kings ix. 24.	2 a	lxxvi. 3.	2	Lam. iii. 12.	2
xiii. 15, 15, 17, 17, 18.	2	lxxvii. 17.	2 b	iii. 13.	1
xix. 32.	2	xci. 5.	2	Ezek. v. 16.	2
1 Chron. xii. 2.	2	cxx. 4.	2	xxi. 21.	2
2 Chron. xxvi. 15.	2	cxxvii. 4.	2	xxxix. 3, 9.	2
Job vi. 4.	2	cxliv. 6.	2	Hab. iii. 11.	2
xli. 28.	1, 3	Prov. xxv. 18.	2	Zech. ix. 14.	2
Ps. vii. 13.	2				

ART

מַעֲשֶׂה   *m.* work, labour ; business, occupation : Exod. xxx. 25, 35 : 2 Chron. xvi. 14.

ARTIFICER

חָרָשׁ   *m.* graver ; workman in brass, &c., 1 Chron. xxix. 5 ; 2 Chron. xxxiv. 11. חָרָשׁ *m.* cutting, graving ; graver : Gen. iv. 22. חֲרָשׁ *m.* artificial work ; used of magic arts, Isa. iii. 3. Gesenius understands this passage of magic arts ; but Sept., Vulg., &c., of a skilful artist.

ARTILLERY

כְּלִי   *m.* a general name for tools, armour, &c.: 1 Sam. xx. 40.

ASCEND

1   נָסַק   occurs only in one passage, but is allowed to mean, to climb. KAL *fut.*

2   עָלָה   to go or come up, to mount. KAL *a pret.* *b fut.* *c part.* Poel. HIPHIL *d fut.* *e part.* *f* מַעֲלָה *m.* ascent. *g* עֹלָה *f.* ascent. *h* עֲלִיָּה *f.* way up to the temple.

Gen. xxviii. 12.	2 c	Judg. xiii. 20.	2 b	Ps. cxxxv. 7.	2 e		
Exod. xix. 18.	2 b	xx. 40.	2 a		2 l		
Num. xiii. 22.	2 b	1 Sam. xxviii. 13.	2 c	Prov. xxx. 4.	2 a		
xxxiv. 4.	2 f	2 Sam. xv. 30.	2 f	Isa. xiv. 13, 14.	2 b		
Josh. vi. 5.	2 a	1 Kings x. 5.	2 g	Jer. x. 13.	2 d		
viii. 20, 21.	2 a	2 Chron. ix. 4.	2 h	li. 16.	2 d		
x. 7.	2 b	Ps. xxiv. 3.	2 b	Ezek. xxxviii. 9.	2 a		
xv. 3.	2 a	lxviii. 18.	2 a				

ASCRIBE

יָהַב   to supply or give. See *Give*. KAL *imp.* Deut. xxxii. 3.

נָתַן   to give. KAL *pret.* 1 Sam. xviii. 8, 8.   *imp.* Ps. lxviii. 34. *fut.* Job xxxvi. 3.

ASHDOTH

אַשְׁדוֹת   *m.* springs; Ashdoth-Pisgah, *marg.* springs of Pisgah, or the hill: Deut. iii. 17: Josh. xii. 3; xiii. 20.

ASH

אֹרֶן   *m.* a timber-tree, but of what species is uncertain; Gesenius, a pine, so called because when agitated it emits a tremulous sound. Sept. πίτυς. Vulg. *pinus.* Isa. xliv. 14.

ASHAMED

1   בּוּשׁ   to be ashamed, to feel shame; denoting, more than the following, that shame which is internal; and therefore sometimes that which may or ought to prevent an action: Ezra viii. 22: Job xix. 3:—but most commonly that which follows upon disappointment of opinion, hope, or expectation. Its primary idea seems to lie in paleness caused by fear; it is therefore used of confusion and consciousness of disgrace and ignominy, or in respect of anything which causes a degree of disgrace, as of a son causing shame: Prov. x. 5, &c., *comp.* Isa. xxix. 22. Applied to enemies and wicked men who are put to flight after vain attempts, and to persons oppressed with sudden calamity. Joined with כָּלַם of outward shame or ignominy, it adds great force to Jer. viii. 12, *i. e.* they were not brought to repentance by inward shame or outward disgrace. The phrase עַד בּוֹשׁ applies to that importunity which exceeds the bounds of reason and modesty, Judg. iii. 25, 2 Kings ii. 17, or which cannot for shame be refused. KAL [a] *pret.* [b] *inf.* [c] *imp.* [d] *fut.* [e] *part.* POEL. HIPHIL [f] *fut.* [g] *part.* HITHPOLEL [h] *fut.* [i] בֹּשֶׁת *f.*

2   חָפֵר   to hang down the head, and hide the face, to blush with shame and confusion: it is frequently joined with the previous word to express the greatest confusion and shame internally and externally. KAL [a] *pret.* [b] *fut.* HIPHIL [c] *pret.*

3   יָבֵשׁ   to be made dry; to become pale; to be ashamed from disappointment of hope. HIPHIL [a] *pret.* [b] *imp.*

4   כָּלַם   probably to wound; always referred to threats, reproaches, injury; to reproach, to shame, to harm; to be in a state of dishonour, disgrace, ignominy. This word expresses a higher degree of shame than בּוֹשׁ, with which it is often joined to express a twofold shame, internal and external: Isa. xlv. 16. It is used of shame from public divine punishment, Ezek. xvi. 52, Jer. xiv. 3; from public and notorious ignominy, Num. xii. 14, 2 Sam. xix. 3, x. 5. It answers frequently very nearly to the Latin

word, *calumniare*, Ps. iv. 2.   NIPHAL [a] *pret.*   [b] *inf.* [c] *fut.*   [d] *part.* HIPHIL [e] *part.*

Gen. ii. 25.	1 h	Ps. cxix. 6, 46, 78, 80.	1 d	Jer. viii. 9.	3 a	
Num. xii. 14.	4 c	cxix. 116.	1 f	viii. 12, 12.γ	3 a, 1 b d	
Judg. iii. 25.	1 b	cxxvii. 5.	1 d	xii. 13.	1 a	
2 Sam. x. 5.	4 d	Prov. xii. 4.	1 d	xiv. 3, 4.	1 a	
xix. 3.	4 d	Isa. i. 29.	1 d	xv. 9.	1 d	
2 Kings ii. 17.	1 b	xx. 5.	1 a	xvii. 13.	1 d	
viii. 11.	1 b	xxiii. 4.	1 c	xx. 11.	1 a	
1 Chron. xix. 5.	4 d	xxiv. 23.	1 a	xxii. 22.	1 d	
2 Chron. xxx. 15.	4 a	xxvi. 11.	1 d	xxxi. 19.	1 d	
Ezra viii. 22.	1 a	xxix. 22.	1 d	xlviii. 13, 13.	1 a	
ix. 6.	1 a	xxx. 5.	3 a	l. 12.	2 a	
Job vi. 20.	2 b	xxxiii. 9.	2 c	Ezek. xvi. 27.	4 d	
xi. 3.	4 e	xli. 11.	1 d	xvi. 61.	4 a	
xix. 3.	1 d	xlii. 17.α	1 d i	xxxii. 30.	1 e	
Ps. vi. 10, 10.	1 d	xliv. 9, 11, 11.	1 d	xxxvi. 32.	1 c	
xxv. 2, 3, 3, 20.	1 d	xlv. 16.	1 a	xliii. 10.	4 c	
xxxi. 1, 17, 17.	1 d	xlv. 17, 24.	1 d	xliii. 11.	4 a	
xxxiv. 5.	2 b	xlix. 23.	1 d	Hos. iv. 19.	1 d	
xxxv. 26.	1 d	l. 7.	1 d	x. 6.	1 d	
xxxvii. 19.	1 d	liv. 4.	1 d	Joel ii. 26, 27.	1 d	
xl. 14.	1 d	lxv. 13.	1 d	Mic. iii. 7.	1 a	
lxix. 6.	1 d	lxvi. 5.	1 d	Zeph. iii. 11.	1 a	
lxx. 2.	1 d	Jer. ii. 26.β 26.	1 i, 3 a	Zech. ix. 5.	3 a	
lxxiv. 22.	1 d	ii. 36, 36.	1 d, a	xiii. 4.	1 d	
lxxxvi. 17.	1 d	iii. 3.	4 b			
cix. 28.	1 d	vi. 15, 15.γ	3 a, 1 b d			

α *lit.* be ashamed a shame.   β *lit.* as the shame of a thief.   γ *lit.* in being ashamed they were not ashamed.

ASHES

1   אֵפֶר   *m.* the ashes to which any substance burned in the fire is reduced; by paranomasia עָפָר וָאֵפֶר, dust and ashes: Job xxx. 19; xlii. 6.   פְּאֵר תַּחַת אֵפֶר, Isa. lxi. 3. [a] אֲפֵר *m.* according to our version, ashes; but according to Jewish interpreters and modern critics, a covering of the head, or bandage with which the prophet covered his wound and disguised himself.

2   דֶּשֶׁן   *m.* fatness; ashes of the fat and other parts of the sacrifice burned on the altar; also the ashes of corpses burned: Jer. xxxi. 40. Hence the verb דָּשֵׁן to take away ashes. PIEL [a] *pret.* [b] *inf.*

3   עָפָר   *m.* any dust, ashes, or powder; the dust of the earth.

4   פִּיחַ   *m.* ashes that may be blown away.

Gen. xviii. 27.	1	1 Kings xx. 38, 41.	1 a	Isa. lviii. 5.	1
Exod. ix. 8, 10.	4	2 Kings xxiii. 4.	1	lxi. 3.	1
xxvii. 3.	2 b	Esth. iv. 1, 3.	1	Jer. vi. 26.	1
Lev. i. 16.	2	Job ii. 8.	1	xxxi. 40.	2
iv. 12, 12.	2	xiii. 12.	1	Lam. iii. 16.	1
vi. 10, 11.	2	xxx. 19.	1	Ezek. xxvii. 30.	1
Num. iv. 13.	2 a	xlii. 6.	1	xxviii. 18.	1
xix. 9, 10.	1	Ps. cii. 9.	1	Dan. ix. 3.	1
xix. 17.	3	cxlvii. 16.	1	Jonah iii. 6.	1
2 Sam. xiii. 19.	2	Isa. xliv. 20.	1	Mal. iv. 3.	1
1 Kings xiii. 3, 5.	1				

ASK   (See also MUCH)

1   בְּעָה   Ch. to request, desire earnestly. P'AL *pret.*

2   בָּקַשׁ   to seek; to desire and search after. PIEL [a] *inf.* [b] *fut.*

3   דָּרַשׁ   to seek or search after anything; to inquire: to ask advice, help, or direction. KAL *inf. seq.* מִמְּ.

4   שָׁאַל   to ask, demand, require, seek, with an accusative of the thing; the person of whom anything is asked is preceded by מִן, or put in an accusative (like αἰτεῖν τινά τι); hence with two accusatives, Ps. cxxxvii. 3, Deut. xiv. 26: to ask, beg, request, with an accusative of the thing, and מִן, מֵעִם, מֵאֵת, of the person; to inquire of, to interrogate, with an accusative of the person, and with לְ: the thing for which one inquires is

preceded by לְ, by עַל, or put in an accusative: particularly to inquire of or consult, as an oracle, to ask counsel, and then construed with בְּ; with לְ for a person; to inquire after the health of any one, particularly as a salutation, with לְ; to ask as a loan, to ask alms. Niph., to ask for oneself (like the Greek, αἰτοῦμαι, mihi peto, different from αἰτέω). KAL ª *pret.* ᵇ *inf.* ᶜ *imp.* ᵈ *fut.* ᵉ *part.* Poel. NIPHAL ᶠ *pret.* ᵍ *inf.* PIEL ʰ *fut.* שְׁאַל Ch. P'AL ⁱ *pret.*

Gen. xxiv. 47.	4 d	1 Sam. viii. 10.	4 e	Ps. xxi. 4.	4 a
xxvi. 7.	4 d	xii. 17, 19.	4 b	lxxviii. 18.	4 b
xxxii. 17.	4 a	xiv. 37.	4 d	cv. 40.	4 a
xxxii. 29, 29.	4 d	xix. 22.	4 d	Isa. vii. 11, 11.	4 c b
xxxvii. 15.	4 d	xx. 6, 28.	4 g f	vii. 12.	4 d
xxxviii. 21.	4 d	xxv. 8.	4 c	xxx. 2.	4 a
xl. 7.	4 d	xxviii. 16.	4 d	xli. 28.	4 d
xliii. 7.	4 a b	2 Sam. xiv. 18.	4 e	xlv. 11.	4 c
xliii. 27.	4 d	xx. 18.	4 b h	lviii. 2.	4 d
xliv. 19.	4 a	1 Kings ii. 16.	4 e	lxv. 1.	4 a
Exod. xiii. 14.	4 d	ii. 20.	4 d	Jer. vi. 16.	4 c
xviii. 7.	4 d	ii. 22, 22.	4 e c	xv. 5.	4 a
Num. xxvii. 21.	4 a	iii. 5.	4 c	xviii. 13.	4 c
Deut. iv. 32.	4 c	iii. 10, 11, 11, 11, 11,		xxiii. 33.	4 c
vi. 20.	4 d	11, 13.	4 a	xxx. 6.	4 c
xiii. 14.	4 a	x. 13.	4 a	xxxvi. 17.	4 a
xxxii. 7.	4 c	xiv. 5.	3	xxxvii. 17.	4 a
Josh. iv. 6, 21.	4 a	2 Kings ii. 9.	4 c	xxxviii. 14.	4 d
ix. 14.	4 a	ii. 10.	4 b	xxxviii. 27.	4 e
xv. 18.	4 b	viii. 6.	4 b	l. 5.	4 d
xix. 50.	4 a	1 Chron. x. 13.	4 b	Lam. iv. 4.	4 a
Judg. i. 1.	4 d	2 Chron. i. 7.	4 c	Dan. ii. 10.	4 i
i. 14.	4 b	i. 11, 11, 11.	4 a a d	vi. 7, 12.	1
v. 25.	4 a	ix. 12.	4 a	vii. 16.	1
vi. 29.	2 b	xx. 4.	2 a	Hos. iv. 12.	4 d
xiii. 6.	4 a	Ezra v. 9, 10.	4 i	Mic. vii. 3.	4 e
xiii. 18.	4 a	Neh. i. 2.	4 d	Hag. ii. 11.	4 c
xviii. 5.	4 c	Job xii. 7.	4 a	Zech. x. 1.	4 c
xx. 18, 23.	4 d	xxi. 29.	4 a		
1 Sam. i. 17, 20, 27.	4 a	Ps. ii. 8.	4 c		

ASP

פֶּתֶן see *Adder.* Deut. xxxii. 33: Job xx. 14, 16: Isa. xi. 8.

ASS

1 אָתוֹן *f.* an ass, so called from its slow gait; or more probably from its strength and patience.

2 חֲמוֹר *m.* an ass, so called from its reddish colour, being that of the wild ass, and often of the domestic ass. Bryant remarks (Observations, p. 61), that a great part of the wealth of the inhabitants of the East often consisted of she-asses, the males being few, and not held in equal estimation.

3 עַיִר *m.* a young ass, an ass colt; the wild ass colt: it is applied also to the animal when grown, so as to be used for riding and bearing burdens. ª עֲיָרִים *m.*

4 עָרוֹד *m.* the wild ass; the mere Aramean name for פֶּרֶא. ª עֲרָד Ch. *m. id.*

5 פֶּרֶא *com.* the wild ass, now chiefly found in Tartary, under the name of Kulan.

No. 2 not included.

Gen. xii. 16, 16.	2, 1	1 Sam. ix. 3, 3, 5, 20.	1	Ps. civ. 11.	5
xxxii. 15.	1	x. 2, 2, 14, 16.	1	Isa. xxx. 6. 'כ	3 a
xlv. 23, 23.	2, 1	2 Kings iv. 22, 24.	1	xxx. 6.	3
xlix. 11.	1	1 Chron. xxvii. 30.	1	xxx. 24.	3
Num. xxii. 21, 22, 23,		Job i. 3, 14.	1	xxxii. 14.	5
23, 23, 25, 27, 27,		vi. 5.	1	Jer. ii. 24.	5
28, 29, 30, 30, 32,		xi. 12.	5	xiv. 6.	5
33.	1	xxiv. 5.	1	Dan. v. 21.	4 a
Judg. v. 10.	1	xxxix. 5, 5.	5, 4	Hos. viii. 9.	5
x. 4.	3	Job xlii. 12.	1	Zech. ix. 9, 9.	2, 1
xii. 14.	3				

ASSAULT

צוּר to press upon, to urge, to assail. KAL *part.* Poel. Esth. viii. 11, *lit.* assailants, *i. e.* persecutors.

ASSAY

יָאַל to will; to undertake, to venture, to begin. HIPHIL *fut.* 1 Sam. xvii. 39.

נָסָה in Piel, to try, prove; to make trial, to attempt. PIEL *pret.* Deut. iv. 34: Job iv. 2.

ASSEMBLE

1 אָסַף to gather; to gather together. KAL ª *pret.* ᵇ *inf.* ᶜ *imp.* ᵈ *fut.* NIPHAL ᵉ *pret.* ᶠ *imp.* ᵍ *fut.* ʰ אֲסֻפּוֹת *f. pl.* assemblies, especially of learned and wise men discussing divine things.—*Gesenius.*

2 גּוּר to gather themselves together; of those who assemble to supplicate idols for the fertility of their fields. HITHPOLEL *fut.*

3 זָעַק see *Cry;* to gather, *i. e.* to call men together by proclamation, for help in time of danger, or in order to resist or fall upon an enemy. NIPHAL ª *fut.* HIPHIL ᵇ *inf.* ᶜ *imp.*

4 יָעַד to appoint; Niph., to assemble together by appointment or agreement. NIPHAL ª *pret.* ᵇ *part.* ᶜ מוֹעֵד *m.* congregation, assembly; place of assembly; solemn assembly. ᵈ עֵדָה *f.* an appointed meeting.

5 מוֹשָׁב *m.* a sitting down, an assembly of persons.

6 סוֹד *m. consessus,* divan, circle of persons sitting together; a secret assembly.

7 עוּשׁ to assemble. KAL *imp.* LXX. συναθροίζεσθε, perhaps to hasten together.

8 עָצַר to restrain; to close; to be gathered together. ª עֲצָרָה *f.* a solemn assembly, or day of restraint, when people, restrained from the common business of life, assembled together for the duties of religion. Some think there is reference to the concluding assembly of great festivals. See *Solemn.* ᵇ עֲצֶרֶת *f. id.*

9 צָבָא to attend on duty, in a regular, ordered manner, as soldiers on service; to assemble by troops. KAL ª *pret.* ᵇ *part.* Poel.

10 קָבַץ to gather together persons or things. KAL ª *inf.* ᵇ *imp.* NIPHAL ᶜ *pret.* ᵈ *imp.*

11 קָהַל to assemble together in a great body, either upon a civil or religious account. NIPHAL ª *pret.* ᵇ *fut.* ᶜ *part.* HIPHIL ᵈ *pret.* ᵉ *fut.* ᶠ קָהָל *m.* an assembly, congregation, particularly of the Israelitish people. ᵍ קְהִלָּה *f. id.*

12 מִקְרָא *m.* see *Convocation.*

13 רְגַשׁ Ch. to run together in a tumult. APHEL *pret.*

Gen. xlix. 6.	11 f	Num. xx. 8.	4 d	2 Sam. xx. 4.	3 c
Exod. xii. 6.	11 f	xxix. 35.	8 b	xx. 5.	3 b
xvi. 3.	11 f	Deut. v. 22.	11 f	1 Kings viii. 1.	11 e
xxxviii. 8, 8.	9 b a	ix. 10.	11 f	viii. 2.	11 b
Lev. iv. 13.	11 f	x. 4.	11 f	viii. 5.	4 b
viii. 4.	4 d	xviii. 16.	11 f	xii. 21.	11 e
xxiii. 36.	8 b	Josh. xviii. 1.	11 b	2 Kings x. 20.	8 a
Num. i. 18.	11 d	Judg. x. 17.	1 g	1 Chron. xv. 4.	1 d
viii. 9.	4 d	xxi. 8.	11 f	xxviii. 1.	11 e
x. 2.	4 d	1 Sam. ii. 22.	8 b	2 Chron. v. 2.	11 e
x. 3, 3.	4 d a	xiv. 20.	4 d	v. 3.	11 b
xvi. 3.	4 d	xvii. 47.	11 f	v. 6.	4 b
xx. 6.	11 f			vii. 9.	8 b
				xx. 26.	11 a

2 Chron. xxx. 13.	1 g	Isa. xi. 12.	1 a	Ezek. xxiii. 24.	11 f	Lev. xxvi. 32.	4 a	Jer. iv. 9.	4 d	Ezek. iv. 16.	4 k
xxx. 23.	11 f	xliii. 9.	1 g	xxxviii. 7.	11 c	Deut. xxviii. 28.	6 b	viii. 21.	1	iv. 17.	4 d
Ezra ix. 4.	1 g	xlv. 20.	10 d	xxxix. 17.	10 d	xxviii. 37.	4 l	xiv. 9.	1	v. 15.	4m
x. 1.	10 c	xlviii. 14.	10 d	xliv. 24.	4	1 Kings ix. 8.	4 c	xviii. 16.	4 c	xii. 19.	4 k
Neh. v. 7.	11 g	Jer. iv. 5.	1 f	Dan. vi. 6, 11, 15.	13	2 Chron. vii. 21.	4 c	xix. 8.	4 c	xxiii. 33.	4 l
viii. 18.	8 b	vi. 11.	6	xi. 10.	1 a	xxix. 8.	4 l	xxv. 9, 11, 18.	4 l	xxvi. 16.	4 a
ix. 1.	1 e	viii. 14.	1 f	Hos. vii. 14.	2	Ezra ix. 3, 4.	4 e	xxix. 18.	4 l	xxvii. 35.	4 a
Esth. ix. 18.	11 a	ix. 2.	8 b	Joel i. 14.	8 a	Job xvii. 8.	4 c	xlii. 18.	4 l	xxviii. 19.	4 a
Ps. xxii. 16.	4 d	xii. 9.	1 c	ii. 15.	8 a	xviii. 20.	4 d	xliv. 12, 22.	4 l	Dan. iii. 24.	5
xlviii. 4.	4 a	xv. 17.	6	ii. 16.	10 b	xxi. 5.	4 a	xlix. 17.	4 c	iv. 19.	4 i
lxxvi. 14.	4 d	xxi. 4.	1 a	iii. 11.	7	xxvi. 11.	6 a	l. 13.	4 c	v. 9.	3
lxxxix. 7.	6	xxvi. 17.	11 f	Amos iii. 9.	1 f	Ps. lx. 3.	2	li. 37, 41.	4 l	vi. 27.	4 d
cvii. 32.	5	l. 9.	11 f	v. 21.	8 b	Isa. lii. 14.	4 a	Ezek. iii. 15.	4 f	Zech. xii. 4.	6 b
cxi. 1.	6	Lam. i. 15.	4 c	Mic. ii. 12.	1 b d	Jer. ii. 12.	4 b				
Prov. v. 14.	4 d	ii. 6.	4 c	iv. 6.	1 d						
Eccles. xii. 11.	1 h	Ezek. xi. 17.	1 a	Zeph. iii. 8.	10 a						
Isa. i. 13.	12	xiii. 9.	6	iii. 18.	4 c						
iv. 5.	12										

ASSENT

פֶּה *m.* mouth : 2 Chron. xviii. 12, *lit.* with one mouth.

ASSIGN

נָתַן to give. Kal *pret.* Josh. xx. 8. *fut.* 2 Sam. xi. 16.

ASSOCIATE

רָעַע the primary meaning of this verb is supposed to be, to tumultuate, to rage ; and the rendering which best suits the connection in which it is used, is tumultuously to confederate. Kal *imp.* Isa. viii. 9.

ASSUAGE

חָשַׂךְ to hold back, to restrain. Kal *fut.* Job xvi. 5. Niphal *fut.* Job xvi. 6.

שָׁכַךְ to settle down, subside. Kal *fut.* Gen. viii. 1.

ASSURE, ASSURANCE

אָמַן to be firm, secure ; true, faithful. Hiphil *fut.* Deut. xxviii. 66. אֱמֶת *f.* truth, faithfulness : Jer. xiv. 13, *lit.* of truth ; Jer. xxxii. 41.

בֶּטַח *m.* confidence, security. Isa. xxxii. 17.

קוּם to rise, to be sure. See *Sure.* Kal *pret.*

'Assuredly' is sometimes used as the translation of the inf. intensitive.

ASTONISHED, ASTONIED

1   דָּהַם found only in Niphal, *part.* Jer. xiv. 9, as one taken by surprise, perplexed, and astonished by a sudden calamity.

2   תַּרְעֵלָה *f.* trembling, horror ; or giddiness, intoxication.

3   שְׁבַשׁ Ch. to perplex, disturb, trouble. Ithpael *part.*

4   שָׁמֵם the primary idea in this word is thought to be that of silence, to be dumb ; and so to be astonished, amazed, affrighted ; see also *Desolate.* Kal ᵃ*pret.* ᵇ*imp.* ᶜ*fut.* Niphal ᵈ*pret.* Polel ᵉ*part.* Hiphil ᶠ*part.* Hophal ᵍ*imp.* Hithpolel ʰ*fut.* שָׁמֵם Ch. Ithpolel ⁱ*fut.* ᵏ שִׁמָּמוֹן *m.* astonishment. ˡ שַׁמָּה *f. id.* astonishment, object of astonishment ; often joined with שְׁרֵקָה hissing, derision. ᵐ מְשַׁמָּה *f. id.*

5   תְּוַהּ Ch. to be astonished, terrified, to tremble from fear. P'al *pret.*

6   תָּמַהּ to wonder, to be struck with fear and amazement, to be in consternation. Kal ᵃ*fut.* ᵇ תִּמָּהוֹן *m.* fear, terror.

ASTROLOGER

1   אַשָּׁף *m.* enchanter, magician. ᵃ אַשָּׁף Ch. *id.*

2   הָבַר to cut out, to divide ; to divide the heavens for astrological observations. Kal *part.* Poel.

3   שָׁמַיִם *m. pl.* the heavens ; astrologers, *lit.* viewers of the heavens.

Isa. xlvii. 13.	2, 3	Dan. ii. 2.	1	Dan. iv. 7.	1 a
Dan. i. 20.	1	ii. 10, 27.	1 a	v. 7, 11, 15.	1 a

ASUNDER

(See the verb with which it is connected.)

ASUPPIM

אֲסֻפִּים *m. pl.* stores, with or without בַּיִת, storehouse ; an apartment of the outer temple towards the south : 1 Chron. xxvi. 15, *marg.* gatherings, 17.

AT ALL, AT ONCE

יַחַד *m.* see *Together.* Hos. xi. 7 : Ps. lxxiv. 6 : Isa. xlii. 14.

'At all' also frequently occurs as the translation of the inf. intensitive.

ATONEMENT

כָּפַר to cover, to cover sin, or to secure the sinner from guilt and punishment ; to atone for an offence, *seq. acc.*, בְּעַד, עַל, and מִן ; for an offender, *seq.* עַל of *pers.* בְּעַד and בְּ. This word conveys the idea both of pacification of wrath, and of the covering of transgression, but does not seem to express of itself the idea of full and adequate satisfaction for sin. Piel ᵃ*pret.* ᵇ*inf.* ᶜ*imp.* ᵈ*fut.* Pual ᵉ*pret.* ᶠ כְּפֻרִים *m. pl.* redemptions.

Exod. xxix. 33.	e	Lev. xii. 7, 8.	a	Num. vi. 11.	a
xxix. 36, 36.	f b	xiv. 18, 19, 20, 31, 53.	a	viii. 12, 19.	b
xxix. 37.	f	xv. 21, 29.	b	viii. 21.	d
xxx. 10, 10, 10.	a f d	xv. 15, 30.	a	xv. 25.	a
xxx. 15.	d	xvi. 6, 11, 16, 18, 24, 32.	a	xv. 28, 28.	a b
xxx. 16, 16.	f b	xvi. 10, 27, 34.	b	xvi. 46.	c
xxxii. 30.	d	xvi. 17, 17.	b a	xvi. 47.	d
Lev. i. 4.	b	xvi. 30.	d	xxv. 13.	b
iv. 20, 26, 31, 35.	a	xvii. 33, 33, 33.	a d d	xxviii. 22, 30.	b
v. 6, 10, 13, 18.	a	xvii. 11, 11.	b d	xxix. 5.	b
v. 16.	d	xix. 22.	a	xxix. 11.	f
vi. 7.	a	xxiii. 27.	b	xxxi. 50.	b
vii. 7.	d	xxiii. 28, 28.	f b	1 Chron. vi. 49.	b
viii. 34.	b	xxv. 9.	f	2 Chron. xxix. 24.	b
ix. 7, 7.	c	Num. v. 8, 8.	f d	Neh. x. 33.	b
x. 17.	b				

ATTAIN

בּוֹא to come, with עַד or אֶל to reach, to be equal to any one. Kal *pret.* 2 Sam. xxiii. 19, 23 : 1 Chron. xi. 21, 25.

יָכֹל see *Able;* to prevail, to attain, to accomplish, *seq.* לְ, and *acc.* Kal *fut.* Ps. cxxxix. 6 : Hos. viii. 5.

נָשַׂג to reach, to extend to. HIPHIL *pret.* Gen. xlvii. 9 ; *inf.* Ezek. xlvi. 7.

קָנָה to get, gain, acquire. KAL *fut.* Prov. i. 3.

ATTEND, ATTENT, ATTENTIVE, ATTENDANCE

1 בִּין to understand, to consider. HITHPOLEL *fut.*

2 מַעֲמָד *m.* attendance.

3 קָשַׁב to give attention, to be attentive. Hiphil, joined with אֹזֶן, to incline one's ear attentively. HIPHIL [a] *pret.* [b] *imp.* [c] קַשָּׁב *adj.* attent, attentive. [d] קֶשֶׁב *adj. id.*

4 שָׁמַע to hear. KAL *inf.* attentively ; *lit.* in hearing.

To appoint to attend; see *Appoint.*

1 Kings x. 5.		2	Job xxxvii. 2.		4	Ps. cxxx. 2.		3 c
2 Chron. vi. 40.	3 c	Ps. xvii. 1.		3 b	cxlii. 6.		3 b
vii. 15.	3 c	lv. 2.		3 b	Prov. iv. 1, 20.	3 b
ix. 4.		2	lxi. 1.		3 b	v. 1.		3 b
Neh. i. 6, 11.	3 d	lxvi. 19.		3 a	vii. 24.		3 b
Job xxxii. 12.	1	lxxxvi. 6.		3 b		

ATTIRE

צָנַף to wrap round. KAL *fut.* Lev. xvi. 4.

קִשֻּׁרִים *m. pl.* a girdle worn by women, Jer. ii. 32.

שִׁית *m.* something put on, dress, Prov. vii. 10.

See also *Dye.*

AUDIENCE

אֹזֶן *m.* the ear ; 'in the audience ;' *lit.* in the ears: Gen. xxiii. 10, 13, 16 : Exod. xxiv. 7 : 1 Sam. xxv. 24 : 1 Chron. xxviii. 8 : Neh. xiii. 1.

AUGMENT

סָפָה to add, to add to, *seq.* עַל. KAL *inf.* Num. xxxii. 14.

AUNT

דּוֹדָה *f.* father's sister ; also, an uncle's wife : Lev. xviii. 14.

AUTHORITY

רָבָה to multiply, increase, to be in authority. KAL *inf.* Prov. xxix. 2.

תֹּקֶף *m.* might, power, authority : Esth. ix. 29.

AVAIL

שָׁוָה to be even, to be equal, to be sufficient as an equivalent. KAL *part.* Poel., Esth. v. 13.

AVEN

אָוֶן *m.* nothingness, vanity, specially of idols, and of everything pertaining to idolatry. Hence, in Hos. x. 5, 8, the city בֵּית־אֵל house of God, as being given to idolatry, is scornfully called בֵּית־אָוֶן house of vanity, *i. e.* of idols; Ezek. xxx. 17, *marg.* or, Heliopolis ; Hos. iv. 15, or, house of iniquity, v. 8 ; x. 5, 8 : Amos i. 5. The site of Beth-el is now called Bet-een, very probably a contraction of Beth-aven.

AVENGE

1 גָּאַל see *Redeem* ; *seq.* דָּם to redeem blood, to avenge bloodshed. KAL *part.* Poel.

2 יָשַׁע to save. HIPHIL *inf., lit.* from saving thyself.

3 נָקַם to revenge, to take vengeance ; with *acc.* of person or thing avenged ; the person of or from whom vengeance is taken is put with מֵאֵת, מִן, לְ, and *acc.* Niph., to avenge oneself, to be avenged, *seq.* בְּ of person on whom vengeance is taken ; *seq.* מִן in the same sense ; sometimes *seq. dupl.* מִן of person from whom and of the thing for which vengeance is taken. The word seems always to imply great rage and fury, as of one seeking revenge. KAL [a] *pret.* [b] *imp.* [c] *fut.* [d] *part.* Poel. NIPHAL [e] *pret.* [f] *inf.* [g] *fut.* PIEL [h] *pret.* HOPHAL [i] *fut.* HITHPAEL [k] *fut.* [l] *part.* [m] נָקָם *m.* vengeance. [n] נְקָמָה *f. id.* These two nouns often joined with the verb for emphasis, as below.

4 נָתַן to give. KAL [a] *inf.* [b] *fut.* [c] *part.* Poel.

5 פָּקַד to visit, to punish. KAL *pret.*

6 פָּרַע to set free, to make loose, to deliver from oppression, &c. ; to avenge. KAL [a] *inf.* [b] פְּרָעוֹת *m.* Judg. v. 2, *lit.* for avenging the avenges of.

7 שָׁפַט to judge ; *seq.* מִיַּד to set free, to deliver from the hand of. KAL *pret.*

Gen iv. 24.	3 i	Judg. v. 2.	6 a b	2 Kings ix. 7.		3 h
Lev. xix. 18.	3 c	xv. 7.	3 e	Esth. viii. 13.	3 f
xxvi. 25.	3 d	xvi. 28.γ	3 gm	Ps. viii. 2.		3 l
Num. xxxi. 2. α	3 b n	1 Sam. xiv. 24.	3 e	xviii. 47.	4 c, 3 n
xxxi. 3. β	4 a, 3 n	xviii. 25.	3 f	xliv. 16.		3 l
xxxv. 12.	1	xxv. 26, 31, 33.	2	Isa. i. 24.		3 g
Deut. xix. 6, 12.	1	2 Sam. viii. δ	3 a	Jer. v. 9, 29.	3 k
xxxii. 43.	3 c	xiv. 9.	4 b, 3 n	ix. 9.		3 k
Josh. x. 13.	3 c	xviii. 19, 31.	7	xlvi. 10.		3 f
xx. 3, 5, 9.	1	xxii. 48.	4	Hos. i. 4.		5

α *lit.* avenge the vengeance of. β *lit.* give the vengeance of. γ *lit.* may be avenged the vengeance. δ *lit.* hath given avengements to.

AVERSE

שׁוּב to turn ; *seq.* מִ to turn from, as averse to it. KAL *part.* Paül, Mic. ii. 8.

AVOID

סָבַב to turn about, to turn aside. NIPHAL *fut.* 1 Sam. xviii. 11.

פָּרַע to set free ; to refuse, reject. KAL *imp.* Prov. iv. 15.

AVOUCH

אָמַר to say, &c. ; HIPHIL, to make to say, to declare solemnly, to promise : *pret.* Deut. xxvi. 17, 18.

AWAKE

1 יָקַץ to awake, to awake or rouse up to action. KAL *fut.*

2 עוּר to awake out of sleep or inactivity ; to excite to action or attention ; to keep the heart awake or ready for action. KAL [a] *imp.* POLEL [b] *fut.* HIPHIL [c] *fut.* HITHPOLEL [d] *imp.*

3 עִיר *m.* this word is supposed to mean anger, wrath, and in Ps. lxxiii. 20, may be rendered 'with wrath ;' but according to Gesenius, בָּעִיר stands for בְּהָעִיר, HIPHIL *inf.*, from עוּר. Hengstenberg however rejects this, and renders it 'in the city ;' as also Cocceius, 'in the city,' *i. e.* 'in the church their image wilt thou despise.'

4 קִיץ to awake out of sleep; applied to the awakening out of the sleep of death. HIPHIL [a]pret. [b]inf. [c]imp. [d]fut. [e]part.

Gen. ix. 24.	1	Ps. xxxv. 23.	4 c	Cant. iv. 16.	2 a
xxviii. 16.	1	xliv. 23.	2 a	viii. 4.	2 b
xli. 4, 7, 21.	1	lvii. 8, 8, 8.	2 a a c	Isa. xxvi. 19.	4 c
Judg. v. 12,12,12,12.	2 a	lix. 4.	2 a	xxix. 8, 8.	4 a
xvi. 14, 20.	1	lix. 5.	4 c	li. 9, 9, 9.	2 a
1 Sam. xxvi. 12.	4 e	lxxiii. 20, 20.	4 b, 3	li. 17, 17.	2 d
1 Kings iii. 15.	1	lxxviii. 65.	1	Jer. li. 1, 1.	2 a
xviii. 27.	1	cviii. 2, 2.	2 a, 2 c	Jer. xxxi. 26.	4 a
2 Kings iv. 31.	4 a	cxxxix. 18.	4 a	Dan. xii. 2.	4 d
Job viii. 6.	2 c	Prov. vi. 22.	4 a	Joel i. 5.	4 c
xiv. 12.	4 d	xxiii. 35.	4 d	Hab. ii. 7.	1
Ps. iii. 5.	4 a	Cant. ii. 7.	2 b	ii. 19.	4 c
vii. 6.	2 a	iii. 5.	2 b	Zech. xiii. 7.	2 a
xvii. 15.	4 b				

AWARE

יָדַע to know. KAL pret. Cant. vi. 12 : Jer. l. 24.

AWAY

דֶּרֶךְ com. a way: 1 Sam. xxiv. 19, lit. in a good way.

יָכֹל to be able, to endure. KAL fut. Isa. i. 13, "I cannot away with."

יָלַךְ to walk, to go, to depart. KAL imp. Exod. xix. 24.

עָבַר to pass over. HIPHIL imp. 2 Chron. xxxv. 23, "Have me away."

AWE

גּוּר see Afraid, Fear. KAL fut. Ps. xxxiii. 8, "stand in awe."

פָּחַד to fear. KAL pret. Ps. cxix. 161, "standeth in awe."

רָגַז to be disturbed, to be moved (with anger). KAL imp. Ps. iv. 4, "Stand in awe;" Lxx. ὀργίζεσθε, Eph. iv. 26.

AWL

מַרְצֵעַ m. awl to bore with: Exod. xxi. 6 : Deut. xv. 17.

AXE, AX-HEAD

בַּרְזֶל iron, ax-head: 2 Kings vi. 5, lit. iron.

מַגְזֵרָה f. an axe: 2 Sam. xii. 31.

גַּרְזֶן m. an axe: Deut. xix. 5 ; xx. 19 : 1 Kings vi. 7 : Isa. x. 15.

מְגֵרָה f. a saw or axe: 1 Chron. xx. 3.

חֶרֶב f. sword, knife, mattock, &c.: Ezek. xxvi. 9.

כַּשִּׁיל m. an axe, a maul, or great hammer: Ps. lxxiv. 6.

מַעֲצָד m. an axe or hatchet: Jer. x. 3.

קַרְדֹּם m. an axe: Judg. ix. 48 : 1 Sam. xiii. 20, 21 : Ps. lxxiv. 5 : Jer. xlvi. 22.

AXLETREE

יָד com. hand; things resembling hands: 1 Kings vii. 32, 33.

BAALI

בַּעַל m. master, owner, lord: Hos. ii. 16, lit. my lord.

BABBLE

בַּעַל m. master: Eccles. x. 11, lit. master of the tongue.

לָשׁוֹן com. tongue: Eccles. x. 11.

שִׂיחַ m. meditation; complaint; melancholy reflections: Prov. xxiii. 29. It is doubtful whether in this passage the word should be taken of that meditation which after intoxication reviews past folly; or of that idle and pitiful babbling to which the drunkard is liable. Cocceius takes the former meaning, Vatablus the latter. See Geier.

BABE

נַעַר m. a young man; an infant, a child: Exod. ii. 6.

עוֹלֵל m. a sucking child: Ps. viii. 2 ; xvii. 14. תַּעֲלוּלִים m. pl. Isa. iii. 4, lit. children.

BACA

בָּכָא m. mulberry-tree: Ps. lxxxiv. 6, marg. mulberry-trees.

BACK, BACKSIDE, BACKWARD

1 אַחַר frequently used as a preposition, behind, after; in Exod. iii. 1, used of the interior of the desert; Vulg. ad interiora deserti, i.e. a great way into the desert; the further part from Egypt or Palestine. [a] אָחוֹר m. back, back parts, backward; as applied to the divine vision, in Exod. xxxiii. 23, it is understood of God's manifest and visible works; or it may imply the imperfect vision of God, which alone can be vouchsafed to us. [b] אֲחֹרַנִּית adv. backward.

2 גַּב m. any part which rises above the rest; a bunch on the back; the back of animals. [a] גַּב m. Ch. id.

3 גֵּו m. the body, back; 'to cast behind the back' is to forget or disregard, to forgive sin. [a] גֵּו m. id.

4 הָלְאָה adv. implies distance both of time and space.

5 עֹרֶף m. neck; marg. the hinder part of the neck.

6 שְׁכֶם m. see Shoulder.

Gen. ix. 23, 23.	1 b	Ps. ix. 3.	1 a	Isa. l. 5.	1 a
xix. 9.	1	xxi. 12.	6	l. 6.	3 a
xlix. 17.	1 a	xxxv. 4.	1 a	lix. 14.	1 a
Exod. iii. 1.	1	xl. 14.	1 a	Jer. ii. 27.	5
xxiii. 27.	5	xliv. 10, 18.	1 a	vii. 24.	1 a
xxvi. 12.	1	lvi. 9.	1 a	xv. 6.	1 a
xxxiii. 23.	1 a	lxx. 2.	1 a	xviii. 17.	5
Josh. vii. 8.	5	cxiv. 3, 5.	1 a	xxxii. 33.	1 a
vii. 12.	5	cxxiii. 3.	2	xxxviii. 22.	1 a
1 Sam. iv. 18.	1 b	cxxix. 5.	1 a	xlvi. 5.	1 a
x. 9.	6	Prov. x. 13.	3 a	xlviii. 39.	5
2 Sam. i. 22.	1 a	xix. 29.	3 a	Lam. i. 8, 13.	1 a
1 Kings xiv. 9.	3	xxvi. 3.	3 a	ii. 3.	1 a
xviii. 37.	1 b	Isa. i. 4.	1 a	Ezek. viii. 16.	1 a
2 Kings ii. 24.	1	xxxviii. 8.	1 b	x. 12.	2
xx. 10, 11.	1 b	xxxviii. 17.	3 a	xxiii. 35.	3
2 Chron. xxix. 6.	5	xlii. 17.	3 a	Dan. vii. 8.	2 a
Neh. ix. 26.	3	xliv. 25.	1 a	Zeph. i. 6.	1
Job xxiii. 8.	1 a				

BACKBITE

סֵתֶר m. a hiding, something hidden, or to be secretly communicated; secret calumny: Prov. xxv. 23, see marg. (comp. Judg. iii. 19: Deut. xiii. 6: Ps. ci. 5).

רָגַל to run about as a talebearer, to calumniate. KAL pret. Ps. xv. 3.

BACKBONE

עָצֶה m. the chine, spine, backbone: Lev. iii. 9.

BACKSLIDE

1 סוּג to go off from, to draw back. KAL part. Paůl, of one who departs from God in heart.

2 סָרַר to act like a refractory untractable heifer, that turneth backwards or sideways, and cannot be made to go forward and draw regularly in the plough or wagon. KAL *part.* Poel.

3 מְשׁוּבָה *f.* a turning away; apostasy. ª שׁוֹבֵב *adj.* rebellious, backsliding. ᵇ שׁוֹבָב *adj. id.*

Prov. xiv. 14.	1	Jer. v. 6.	3	Jer. xlix. 4.	3 b
Jer. ii. 19.	3	viii. 5.	3	Hos. iv. 16.	2
iii. 6, 8, 11, 12.	3	xiv. 7.	3	xi. 7.	3
iii. 14.	3 a	xxxi. 22.	3 b	xiv. 4.	3
iii. 22, 22.	3 a, 3				

BAD

1 בְּאִשׁ Ch. *adj.* bad, having respect to disposition.

2 רַע *adj.* bad, evil, worthless. ª רֹעַ *m.* badness, bad quality.

Gen. xxiv. 50.	2	Num. xiii. 19.	2	1 Kings iii. 9.	2
xxxi. 24, 29.	2	xx. 23.	2	Ezra iv. 12.	1
xli. 19.	2 a	2 Sam. xiii. 22.	2	Jer. xxiv. 2.	2 a
Lev. xxvii. 10, 10, 12,		xiv. 17.	2		
14, 33.	2				

BADGER

תַּחַשׁ *m.* the various and very different interpretations of this word render the true meaning very uncertain; but this at least is generally admitted, that the badger is not the animal intended by the Hebrew. A writer in the Cyclopedia of Biblical Literature gives it as his opinion, that the term designates some animal of the antelope family, whose skin is of a slaty or purple-gray colour, used for boots: Ezek. xvi. 10. Ancient interpreters and Bochart suppose the term to imply only the colour of the outer covering of the ark, &c. Gesenius's Thesaurus does not agree to this. Exod. xxv. 5; xxvi. 14; xxxv. 7, 23; xxxvi. 19; xxxix. 34: Num. iv. 6, 8, 10, 11, 12, 14, 25: Ezek. xvi. 10.

BAG

חֲרִיטִים *m. pl.* casket, pocket, purse; Gesenius *loculi.* 2 Kings v. 3.

כִּיס *m.* a bag for money or weights. See *Cup.* Deut. xxv. 13: Prov. xvi. 11: Isa. xlvi. 6: Mic. vi. 11.

כְּלִי *m.* a general name for vessels, &c.: 1 Sam. xvii. 40, 49.

צוּר to bind, to bind up in bags. KAL *fut.* 2 Kings xii. 10.

צְרוֹר *m.* a bundle, purse. Job xiv. 17: Prov. vii. 20: Hag. i. 6.

BAKE

1 אָפָה to bake in the oven, or on the hearth. KAL ª *pret.* ᵇ *imp.* ᶜ *fut.* ᵈ *part.* Poel. NIPHAL ᵉ *fut.* ᶠ מַאֲפֶה *m.* a baking. ᵍ תְּפִינִים *m. pl.* baken (pieces).

2 בָּשַׁל to be cooked; Piel, to cook, to bake. PIEL ª *pret.* ᵇ *fut.*

3 עוּג to bake cakes of bread on a gridiron, and sometimes upon coals. KAL *fut.* Ezek. iv. 12, dung dried was the fuel to be put under the gridiron.

4 רָבַךְ to bake. Gesenius and others, to mingle, to dip (as bread in oil). Fürst, *bene parare jusculo confrictum intritumque panem.* HOPHAL *part.*

5 רָצַף *m.* see *Coal;* "baken on the coals."

Gen. xix. 3.	1 a	Lev. vi. 21, 21.	4, 1 g	2 Sam. xiii. 8.	2 b
xl. 1, 2, 5, 16, 17. a	1 d	vii. 9.	1 e	1 Kings xix. 6.	5
xl. 20, 22.	1 d	xxiii. 17.	1 e	Isa. xliv. 15, 19.	1 a
xli. 10.	1 d	xxiv. 5.	1 a	Jer. xxxvii. 21.	1 d
Exod. xii. 39.	1 c	xxvi. 26.	1 a	Ezek. iv. 12.	3
xvi. 23, 23.	1 b c	Num. xi. 8.	2 a	xlvi. 20.	1 c
Lev. ii. 4.	1 f	1 Sam. viii. 13.	1 d	Hos. vii. 4, 6.	1 d
vi. 17.	1 e	xxviii. 24.	1 c		

ª See *Meat.*

BALANCE

1 מֹאזְנַיִם *dual,* balances, a balance. ª מֹאזְנִין Ch. *id.*

2 מִפְלָשׂ *m.* a poising, balancing (of the clouds).

3 קָנֶה *m.* a reed; rod or beam of a balance, including also the κανών of the balance, derived from קָנָה to set upright.

Lev. xix. 36.	1	Prov. xvi. 11.	1	Ezek. xlv. 10.	1
Job vi. 2.	1	xx. 23.	1	Dan. v. 27.	1 a
xxxi. 6.	1	Isa. xl. 12, 15.	1	Hos. xii. 7.	1
xxxvii. 16.	2	xlvi. 6.	3	Amos viii. 5.	1
Ps. lxii. 9.	1	Jer. xxxii. 10.	1	Mic. vi. 11.	1
Prov. xi. 1.	1	Ezek. v. 1.	1		

BALD

1 גִּבֵּחַ *adj.* one whose forehead is bald; *opp.* קֵרֵחַ bald behind. ª גַּבַּחַת *f.* bald forehead.

2 קָרַח to make smooth, to shave, make baldness. KAL ª *imp.* ᵇ *fut.* NIPHAL ᶜ *fut.* HIPHIL ᵈ *pret.* 'made bald baldness.' HOPHAL ᵉ *part.* ᶠ קֵרֵחַ *m.* one that has baldness on the hinder part of his head. ᵍ קָרְחָה *f.* baldness. ʰ קָרַחַת *f.* baldness, bald spot.

Lev. xiii. 40.	2 f	2 Kings ii. 23, 23.	2 f	Jer. xlviii. 37.	2 g
xiii. 41.	1	Isa. iii. 24.	2 g	Ezek. vii. 18.	2 g
xiii. 42, 42, 42.	2 h, 1 a	xv. 2.	2 g	xxvii. 31.	2 d g
42.	2 h, 1 a	xxii. 12.	2 g	xxix. 18.	2 e
xiii. 43, 43.	2 g, 1 a	Jer. xvi. 6.	2 c	Amos viii. 10.	2 g
xxi. 5.	2 b g	xlvii. 5.	2 g	Mic. i. 16, 16.	2 a g
Deut. xiv. 1.	2 g				

BALL

דּוּר *m.* anything round, a ball: Isa. xxii. 18.

BALM

צְרִי *m.* the gum of the balsam-bush, a production of Gilead of great medicinal virtue: Gen. xxxvii. 25; xliii. 11: Jer. viii. 22; xlvi. 11; li. 8: Ezek. xxvii. 17, *marg.* or, rosin.

BAMAH, BAMOTH

בָּמָה *f.* high place: Josh. xiii. 17: Ezek. xx. 29.

BAND

1 אָסַר to bind, to put in bands. KAL ª *fut.* ᵇ אֵסוּר *m.* a band, bond. ᶜ אֱסוּר Ch. *m. id.* ᵈ מוֹסֵר *m.* bonds, fetters.

2 חָבַל to bind, as with a cord. KAL *part.* Poel.

3 חַרְצֻבּוֹת *f. pl.* bands tightly drawn; pains, pangs, torments.

4 מוֹטָה *f.* pole, staff, bar, for bearing; yoke, bars bound to the collar.

5 מוֹשְׁכוֹת *f. pl.* the drawing-bands of Orion, figuratively represented as binding up the earth and vegetation by the rigours of winter. Others think there is an allusion to the belt of Orion; but the former is the more general interpretation, as making a striking contrast between the two constellations, and effects produced by them: Job xxxviii. 31, *i. e.* Canst thou bind up the spring, or loosen the rigour of winter?

6 עֲבֹת *com.* wreathen cords, &c.

7 שָׂפָה *f.* a lip, a border, a band.

Exod. xxxix. 23.	7	Ps. ii. 3.	1 d	Jer. ii. 20.	1 d
Lev. xxvi. 13.	4	lxxiii. 4.	3	Ezek. iii. 25.	6
Judg. xv. 14.	1 b	cvii. 14.	1 d	iv. 8.	6
2 Kings xxiii. 33.	1 a	Eccles. vii. 26.	1 b	xxxiv. 27.	4
Job xxxviii. 31.	5	Isa. xxviii. 22.	1 d	Dan. iv. 15, 23.	1 c
xxxix. 5.	1 d	lii. 2.	1 d	Hos. xi. 4.	6
xxxix. 10.	6	lviii. 6.	3	Zech. xi. 7, 14.	2

BAND (i. e. COMPANY)

1 אֲגַף *m.* the wing of an army; and in the plural the several corps of which an army consists.

2 גְּדוּד *m.* see *Troop*.

3 חֶבֶל *m.* see *Company*.

4 חַיִל *m.* strength, valour in war, forces, an army; 'band of men, of soldiers.'

5 חָצַץ to divide, to go forth by bands, *i. e.* in divisions. KAL *part.* Poel.

6 מַחֲנֶה *com.* a host or company of men encamping.

7 רֹאשׁ *m.* head; captain, company, multitude, host, particularly of warriors.

Gen. xxxii. 7, 10.	6	1 Chron. vii. 4.	2	Ps. cxix. 61.	3
1 Sam. x. 26.	4	xii. 18, 21.	2	Prov. xxx. 27.	5
2 Sam. iv. 2.	2	xii. 23.	7	Ezek. xii. 14.	1
1 Kings xi. 24.	2	2 Chron. xxii. 1.	2	xvii. 21.	1
2 Kings vi. 23.	2	xxvi. 11.	2	xxxviii. 6, 6, 9, 22.	1
xiii. 20, 21.	2	Ezra viii. 22.	4	xxxix. 4.	1
xxiv. 2, 2, 2, 2.	2	Job i. 17.	7		

BANISH

נָדַח to cast out. NIPHAL *part.*, 2 Sam. xiv. 13, 14.

מַדּוּחִים *m. pl.* "causes of banishment," Lam. ii. 14.

שָׁרֹשִׁי (ק) or שְׁרֹשׁוּ (כ) Ch. *f.* a rooting out, or, *metaph.* a banishment: Ezra vii. 26, comp. x. 8.

BANK

1 גָּדָה *f.* banks of a river, so called as cut away and torn by the stream. ᵃ גִּדְיָה (כ) *id.* implying a great overflow.

2 סֹלְלָה *f.* a bank cast up, a military mound or bank thrown up in besieging a city.

3 שָׂפָה *f.* lip, border, bank.

Gen. xli. 17.	3	Josh. xiii. 9, 16.	3	Isa. viii. 7.	1
Deut. iv. 48.	3	2 Sam. xx. 15.	2	xxxvii. 33.	2
Josh. iii. 15.	1	2 Kings ii. 13.	3	Ezek. xlvii. 7, 12.	3
iv. 18.	1	xix. 32.	2	Dan. xii. 5, 5.	3
xii. 2.	3	1 Chron. xii. 15.	1, 1 a		

BANNER

דָּגַל to set up banners, which are conspicuous and may be seen afar off; some think the idea of exultation and triumph is implied. KAL *fut.*, Ps. xx. 5. NIPHAL *part.*, Cant. vi. 4, 10, *i. e.* furnished with banners. דֶּגֶל *m.* see *Standard*, Cant. ii. 4.

נֵס *m.* see *Standard*: Ps. lx. 4, Isa. xiii. 2, or ensign, of the Messiah.

BANQUET

1 יַיִן *m.* wine: "banqueting-house," *lit.* house of wine.

2 בָּרָה to prepare, to make ready, to provide. KAL *fut.*, Job xli. 6. Perhaps splendid and costly entertainments are intended, for which a man's own stores do not suffice, so that he must purchase more.

3 מַרְזֵחַ *m.* a banquet; particularly an entertainment made for friends who come to comfort such as have lost a near relation. See *Mourning*, and *Cup of Consolation*.

4 שָׁתָה to drink, to banquet. KAL ᵃ *inf.* ᵇ מִשְׁתֶּה *m.* a feast, drinking. ᶜ מִשְׁתֶּה Ch. *m. id.*

Esth. v. 4, 5, 6, 8, 12,		Esth. vii. 1.	4 a	Cant. ii. 4.	1
14.	4 b	vii. 2, 7, 8.	4 b	Dan. v. 10.	4 c
vi. 14.	4 b	Job xli. 6.	2	Amos vi. 7.	3

BAR

אָחַז to lay hold of, to hold fast; to close or shut a gate. KAL *imp.*, Neh. vii. 3.

בַּדִּים *m. pl.* staves, bars; bars of the pit are gates of the unseen world: Job xvii. 16.

בְּרִיחַ *m.* a cross-bar to strengthen a tent, or secure the gates of a city. The tabernacle Moses built had such bars running all round to keep it steady and firm. Metaphorically, the strength or defences of a city or nation: Exod. xxvi. 26, &c.

מוֹט *m.* staff, or pole for bearing; it seems also to mean a frame for the same purpose: Num. iv. 10, 12.

מְטִיל *m.* a staff, a pole (of iron): Job xl. 18.

BARBED

שֻׂכָּה *f.* a sharp instrument, a dart; *pr.* a thorn, a goad; "barbed irons:" Job xli. 7.

BARBER

גַּלָּב *m.* one that shaves or scrapes off the beard: Ezek. v. 1.

BARE

חָמַס to do violence; to tear away with violence; to treat with violence. NIPHAL *pret.*, Jer. xiii. 22, where the idea of making bare is taken from the context; and the rendering might have been, 'shall be violently made bare.'

חָשַׂף to lay bare by removing that which covers. See *Discover*, *Uncover*. To make bare the arm is to exert and show power. Upper garments having anciently no sleeves, the arms were wrapped up and covered under them; and therefore when the right arm was used, it must be disengaged and made bare. Applied to a nation stripped of all its treasures and defences. KAL *pret.* Isa. lii. 10: Jer. xlix. 10: Joel i. 7. *inf.* Joel i. 7. *lit.* 'in making bare he hath made it bare.' *imp.* Isa. xlvii. 2.

יָחֵף *adj.* unshod: 2 Sam. xv. 30: Isa. xx. 2, 3, 4.

עֶרְוָה *f.* naked: Ezek. xvi. 7, 22, 39; xxiii. 29.

עָרַר to be naked; to make bare. KAL *imp.* Isa. xxxii. 11.

פָּרַע to set free, to uncover. KAL *part.* Paül. Lev. xiii. 45.

קָרַחַת *f.* bald head behind: Lev. xiii. 55, *lit.* 'bald in the head thereof.'

BARK

נָבַח to bark. KAL *inf.*, Isa. lvi. 10. Whatever be the proper meaning of this word occurring only here, is it not used on this occasion because of its similarity to נָבָא to prophesy? It is common in the Arabic and Rabbinical Hebrew, says Henderson.

BARK (of a Tree)

קְצָפָה *f.* a fragment, a broken thing, especially of foliage, boughs: Joel i. 7.

BARLEY

שְׂעֹרָה *f.* barley; so called from its long hairy beard in the ear: Exod. ix. 31, &c.

BARN, BARNFLOOR

אֲסָמִים *m. pl.* places where corn or any fruits are stored up; or storehouses, sometimes underground: Prov. iii. 10.

מְגוּרָה *f.* a barn into which corn, &c. is gathered : Hag. ii. 19. מַמְּגֻרוֹת *f. pl.* places or buildings where there are granaries, or cells for keeping grain : Joel i. 17.

גֹּרֶן *m.* threshing-floor : 2 Kings vi. 27 : Job xxxix. 12, 'barn,' rather 'to thy threshing-floor.'

BARREL

כַּד *f.* a great earthen vessel, or jar, to hold water or meal ; not a barrel of wood. See *Pitcher.* 1 Kings xvii. 12, 14, 16 ; xviii. 33.

BARREN

1 מְלֵחָה *f.* salt land.

2 עֹצֶר *m.* a shutting up.

3 עָקָר *adj.* rooted out ; unfruitful, sterile.

4 צִיָּה *f.* drought.

5 שָׁכֵל to lose children, to become childless ; of land, to be barren. PIEL ᵃ *part.* ᵇ שַׁכּוּל bereaved of children.

Gen. xi. 30.	3	1 Sam. ii. 5.	3	Prov. xxx. 16.		2
xxv. 21.	3	2 Kings ii. 19, 21.	5 a	Cant. iv. 2.		5 b
xxix. 31.	3	Job xxiv. 21.	3	vi. 6.		5 b
Exod. xxiii. 26.	3	xxxix. 6.	1	Isa. liv. 1.		3
Deut. vii. 14.	3, 3	Ps. cvii. 34.	1	Joel ii. 20.		4
Judg. xiii. 2, 3.	3	cxiii. 9.	3			

BASE

מְכוֹנָה and מְכֹנָה *f.* a place, a base ; a stand for the lavers in the court of Solomon's temple. 1 Kings vii. 27, &c. ; 38, *lit.* upon one base of ten bases.

כֵּן *m.* a stand, base, pedestal : 1 Kings vii. 29, 31.

BASE (*i.e.* VILE)

קָלָה to be light, mean, vile ; despised, ignoble, low. NIPHAL *part.* Isa. iii. 5.

שֵׁם *m.* name ; 'base,' of no name : Job xxx. 8.

שָׁפָל *adj.* low, mean, contemptible : 2 Sam. vi. 22 : Ezek. xvii. 14 ; xxix. 14, 15 : Mal. ii. 9. שְׁפַל Ch. *id.* Dan. iv. 17.

BASKET

דּוּד *m.* a basket for carrying fruit ; also a pot or kettle ; a caldron : 2 Kings x. 7 : Jer. xxiv. 2, 2. דּוּדַי *m. id.* Jer. xxiv. 1.

טֶנֶא a basket, from being woven : Deut. xxvi. 2, 4 ; xxviii. 5, 17.

כְּלוּב *m.* a cage ; a basket, probably from its similarity in form : Amos viii. 1, 2.

סַל *m.* a wicker basket, bread-basket : Gen. xl. 16, &c. סַלְסִלּוֹת *f. pl. id.* Jer. vi. 9.

BASON

1 אַגָּן *m.* a cup, bowl, or bason.

2 כְּפוֹר *m.* a large cup or bowl, probably with a cover or lid, used in the temple service, I suppose, to hold wine for the priests and sacrificers, when they did eat and drink before the Lord. (Deut. xiv. 26 ; xv. 19, 20.)—*Taylor.*

3 מִזְרָק *m.* large basons or bowls, which received the blood of the sacrifices, and out of which it was sprinkled upon the altar, &c. ; any bason or bowl like or as large as those.

4 סַף *m.* dish, bowl.

Exod. xii. 22, 22.	4	43, 49, 55, 61, 67, 73,		1 Chron. xxviii. 17.β		2
xxiv. 6.	1	79, 84, 85.	3	2 Chron. iv. 8, 11, 22.		3
xxvii. 3.	3	2 Sam. xvii. 28.	4	Ezra i. 10, 10.		2
xxviii. 3.	3	1 Kings vii. 40, 45, 50.	3	viii. 27.		2
Num. iv. 14.	3	2 Kings xii. 13.	3	Neh. vii. 70.		3
vii. 13, 19, 25, 31, 37,		1 Chron. xxviii.17,17.α	2	Jer. lii. 19.		4

ᵅ *lit.* for bason and bason. ᵝ *lit.* and for the basons of silver for bason and bason.

BASTARD

מַמְזֵר *m. pr.* mixed ; one born of a mixed or unlawful marriage, or of fornication ; a stranger, foreigner ; perhaps born of marriage with a stranger, and therefore considered spurious : Deut. xxiii. 2 : Zech. ix. 6.

BAT

עֲטַלֵּף *m.* the bat.—*Bochart.* Greatly abounding in the East, and inhabiting forsaken houses or caves, which become in consequence very offensive and useless : it is still a proverbial saying, 'given to the bats.'—*Roberts.* Lev. xi. 19 : Deut. xiv. 18 : Isa. ii. 20. See Paxton's Illustrations of Scripture Natural History, p. 402.

BATH

בַּת *com.* a measure of fluids, containing near eight gallons, wine measure ; its contents are the same with the ephah, viz. seven gallons, two quarts, and half a pint. —*Taylor.* See also Gesenius, 1 Kings vii. 26, 38, &c. בַּת Ch. *id.* Ezra vii. 22, 22.

BATHE

רָוָה to be thoroughly wet, moistened ; to be satiated, or drunk. PIEL *pret.* Isa. xxxiv. 5 ; *comp.* Jer. xlvi. 10, and Deut. xxxii. 42.

רָחַץ to wash, cleanse ; to bathe. KAL *pret.* Lev. xv. 5, 6, 7, 8, 10, 11, 13, 18, 21, 22, 27 ; xvi. 26, 28 ; xvii. 15 : Num. xix. 7, 8, 19. *fut.* Lev. xvii. 16.

BATH-RABBIM

בַּת *f.* daughter. רַבִּים *adj.* many ; Cant. vii. 4, *lit.* daughter of many ; or, of mighty ones.

BATTER

שָׁחַת to corrupt, destroy, mar. HIPHIL *part.* 2 Sam. xx. 15, *marg.* marred to throw down.

BATTLE

כִּידוֹר *m.* tumult, especially warlike tumult, war. Job xv. 24.

מַחֲנֶה *com.* a camp. 1 Sam. xxviii. 1, *lit.* into the camp.

מִלְחָמָה *f.* war : Gen. xiv. 8, &c. : 1 Chron. xxvi. 27, *lit.* out of the battles and spoils.

נֶשֶׁק *m.* arms, weapons, and armour. See *Armed.* Ps. cxl. 7.

סְאוֹן *m.* Gesenius and others take this word to mean the higher prepared shoe of the soldier, fitted for passing over rough and miry places ; or the greaves which covered the feet and legs : Isa. ix. 5. Fürst, every weapon is sharp, *i. e.* pierces with warlike tumult. See *War.*

פָּנִים *m. pl.* face. 1 Chron. xix. 10, *lit.* the face of the battle.

צָבָא *m.* an host, an army: Num. xxxi. 14, *lit.* host of war; xxxi. 27, 28: Josh. xxii. 32: 1 Chron. xii. 33, 36.

קְרָב *m.* a coming near in a hostile manner: 2 Sam. xvii. 11: Job xxxviii. 23: Ps. lv. 18; lxxviii. 9: Zech. xiv. 3.

BATTLE-AX

מַפֵּץ *m.* a hammer, or battle-ax: Jer. li. 20, strictly *part.* HIPHIL, from נָפַץ to dash in pieces.

BATTLEMENTS

נְטִישׁוֹת *f. pl.* see *Branch:* battlements extending or spreading themselves. Jer. v. 10.

מַעֲקֶה *m.* a battlement or balustrade round the flat roof of an oriental house: Deut. xxii. 8.

BAY

אֲמֻצִּים see *Strong;* or, *pr.* sharp, active; hence of colours that which is lively or bright: the context seems to require that the word be understood of colour. Zech. vi. 3, *marg.* strong; 7, *lit. id.*

BAY (OF THE SEA)

לָשׁוֹן *com.* the tongue; tongue of the sea: Josh. xv. 2, *marg.* tongue, 5; xviii. 19, *marg.* tongue.

BAY-TREE

אֶזְרָח *m.* that which springs up without being transplanted: Ps. xxxvii. 35, *marg.* or, a green tree that groweth in his own soil, *i.e.* native and luxuriant.

BDELLIUM

בְּדֹלַח *m.* a white transparent oily gum which flows from a tree about the bigness of an olive. Cels. Hierobot.: Gen. ii. 12: Num. xi. 7. Gesenius, a pearl, white, like grains of manna. See Bush on Gen. ii. 12.

TO BE

1 הָוָה the less common form of the verb substantive. KAL [a] *imp.* [b] *fut.* [c] *part.* Poel. הָוָה Ch. P'AL [d] *pret.* [e] *fut.*

2 הָיָה to come to pass, to happen; to be; to begin to be, *i.e.* to become, especially with לְ to be made or done; to be, *i.e.* the substantive verb, occurring so frequently as to preclude the being introduced in this work.

3 יֵשָׁה *est sunt.* Schultens upon Prov. xix. 18, saith that "the Hebrew word יֵשׁ is not a verb, but a noun substantive, signifying solidity:" and Koerber before him, in his small Lexicon of the Hebrew particles, printed at the end of Noldius's Concordance in the Jena edition, affirms that it is a noun derived from the same root as אִישׁ a man, and signifies force, power, firmness, and existence; and as an adjective, firm, strong, existing; and adds the following examples: Gen. xviii. 24, "Peradventure there be fifty;" Heb., perhaps there is the existence of fifty righteous persons: xxiv. 42, "If now thou do prosper;" Heb., if firmness, or firm purpose, is to thee prospering my way: ver. 49, "If you will deal kindly;" Heb., if firmness is to your dealing

kindly: Gen. xxxi. 29, "It is in the power;" Heb., force is to the power of my hand: Ruth iii. 12, "There is a kinsman;" Heb., there is the power of a kinsman. I believe this criticism is right. We render it in one place ' substance,' Prov. viii. 21: and in 2 Chron. xxv. 9, "The Lord is able;" Heb., power is to the Lord. But in the form of a noun it cannot well be translated in many places. It stands under a strong emphasis, and may be translated, in reality, certainly, truly, sincerely, wholly, entirely. It may import the reality, entireness, solidity, completeness, of existence, and is to be understood and translated according to the nature of the subject to which it is applied; and it may be applied to any subject.—*Taylor's Concordance.*

Gen. xviii. 24.	3	Ezra iv. 20.	1 d	Prov. xxiii. 18.	3
xxiii. 8.	3	v. 5, 11.	1 d	xxiv. 14.	3
xxiv. 23.	3	v. 8.	1 e	Eccles. i. 10.	3
xxvii. 29.	1 a	vi. 6.	1 d	ii. 21.	3
xxviii. 16.	3	vi. 8, 9.	1 e	iv. 8.	3
xxxi. 29.	3	vii. 23, 26.	1 e	v. 13.	3
xlii. 1, 2.	3	x. 2.	3	vi. 1, 11.	3
xliv. 26.	3	Neh. v. 2, 3, 4, 5.	3	vii. 15, 15.	3
Exod. xvii. 7.	3	vi. 6.	1 c	viii. 6, 14, 14, 14.	3
Num. ix. 20, 21.	3	Esth. iii. 8.	3	ix. 4.	3
xiii. 20.	3	Job v. 1.	3	x. 5.	3
xxii. 29.	3	vi. 6, 30.	3	xi. 3.	1 b
Deut. xxix. 18, 18.	3	ix. 33.	3	Isa. xvi. 4.	1 a
Judg. iv. 20.	3	xi. 18.	3	xliv. 8.	3
vi. 13.	3	xiv. 7.	3	Jer. v. 1.	3
xviii. 14.	3	xvi. 4.	3	xiv. 22.	3
xix. 19, 19.	3	xxv. 3.	3	xxiii. 26.	3
Ruth iii. 12.	3	xxviii. 1.	3	xxvii. 18.	3
1 Sam. ix. 11, 12.	3	xxxiii. 23.	3	xxxi. 6, 16, 17.	3
xiv. 39.	3	xxxvii. 6.	1 a	xxxvii. 17, 17.	3
xvii. 46.	3	Ps. vii. 3.	3	Lam. i. 12.	3
xx. 8.	3	xiv. 2.	3	iii. 29.	3
xxi. 3, 4, 8.	3	liii. 2.	3	Dan. ii. 20, 28, 40.	1 e
xxiii. 23.	3	lviii. 11.	3	ii. 41, 41, 42.	1 e
2 Sam. ix. 1.	3	lxxiii. 11.	3	iii. 18.	1 e
xiv. 32.	3	cxxxv. 17.	3	iv. 4.	1 d
1 Kings xviii. 10.	3	Prov. xi. 24.	3	iv. 25, 27.	1 e
2 Kings ii. 16.	3	xii. 18.	3	v. 17, 29.	1 e
iii. 12.	3	xiii. 7, 23.	3	vi. 1.	1 e
v. 8.	3	xiv. 12.	3	vi. 3.	1 d
ix. 15.	3	xvi. 25.	3	vii. 19.	1 e
x. 15, 15, 15, 23.	3	xviii. 24.	3	vii. 23.	1 e
2 Chron. xv. 7. *a*	3	xix. 18.	3	Jonah iv. 11.	3
xxv. 9.	3	xx. 15.	3	Mic. ii. 1.	3
Ezra iv. 12, 13.	1 e				

a lit. there is reward.

BEACON

תֹּרֶן *m.* the mast of a ship; a long pole erected upon a hill as a signal: Isa. xxx. 17, *marg.* ' or, a tree bereft of branches, or, boughs; or, a mast.' Gesenius and others, a signal-pole.

BEAM

אֶרֶג *m.* a weaver's beam, to which the warp is fastened; in Judg. xvi. 14, it is very difficult to obtain the correct meaning of this word, unless it be considered as used of the whole weaving apparatus, being of a very simple construction, and secured, for the sake of firmness, by a pin fastened in the ground. Samson took away the whole with the web in which his hair had been woven. Judg. xvi. 14.

גֵּב *m.* a pit; the vaulting of a building, or beams cut and hewn for the roof of a house, &c.: 1 Kings vi. 9.

כְּפִיס *m.* a cross-beam, for joining together: Hab. ii. 11.

כְּרֻתוֹת *f. pl.* hewed beams: 1 Kings vi. 36; vii. 2, 12.

מָנוֹר *m.* a yoke; *trop.* a weaver's beam: 1 Sam. xvii. 7: 2 Sam. xxi. 19: 1 Chron. xi. 23; xx. 5.

עָב *m.* a thick beam; supposed to be a term of architecture for the threshold or step; Gesenius, collectively, the ascent into a portico: 1 Kings vii. 6.

צֶלָע *f.* a rib. See *Board.* 1 Kings vii. 3.

קָרָה to meet. Piel, to frame or lay beams together for a house or gate; *Lat.* contignare, *lit.* to make the beams meet together. PIEL *pret.* Neh. iii. 3, 6. *inf.* Neh. ii. 8. *part.* Ps. civ. 3. קוֹרָה *f.* a beam, or roof where timbers meet and cross each other: 2 Kings vi. 2, 5: 2 Chron. iii. 7: Cant. i. 17.

BEAN

פֹּל *m.* bean: 2 Sam. xvii. 28: Ezek. iv. 9.

BEAR (See WITNESS, &c.)

1 אִישׁ a man; "bear tidings," *lit.* be a man of tidings.

2 זֶרַע to sow; to produce seed. KAL *part.* Poel.

3 יָלַךְ to go. HIPHIL, to lead, convey: *part.*

4 יָצָא to go out. HIPHIL, to bear out: *inf.*

5 כּוּל see *Contain.* HIPHIL *inf.*

6 נָטַל to bear, to have a burden laid upon one, and to bear it as a slave doth, who is confined to it by a shoulder-yoke. See *Yoke, Staff.* Lam. iii. 28, "It is good for a man to bear the yoke in his youth. He sitteth alone, and keepeth silence, because he hath borne it upon him." Heb., because it is yoked, or in that manner laid upon him; the providence of God confineth it to him. See *Offer, Take up.* KAL ᵃ*pret.* PIEL ᵇ*fut.* ᶜ נָטִיל *adj.* laden.

7 נָשָׂא to lift or raise up; Lxx. αἴρω, ἐξαίρω, ἐπαίρω, ὑψόω; to lift up so as to bear upon oneself, to contract guilt: Lev. xxii. 9; Num. xviii. 32: to bear away, to take away sin, as the priest by bearing it, Lev. x. 17; and God in pardoning it, when he takes it away, Gen. iv. 13. In the N. T. we have αἴρω τὴν ἁμαρτίαν for *expio,* John i. 29. The Lxx. use ἐξαίρω ἁμάρτημα, Exod. xxviii. 38; ἀφαιρέω τὴν ἁ. Lev. x. 17, Num. xiv. 18; ἀνίημι, Isa. i. 14; ἀφίημι, Gen. iv. 13. To take up, to take hold of, Josh. vi. 4, 6; to take up, to carry as a load; to suffer, to endure with patience; to suffer oneself to bear. KAL ᵃ*pret.* ᵇ*inf.* ᶜ*imp.* ᵈ*fut.* ᵉ*part.* Poel. NIPHAL ᶠ*pret.* ᵍ*fut.* HIPHIL ʰ*pret.* Lev. xxii. 16, 'suffer to bear.'

8 סָבַל to bear or carry a burden as a porter; to 'bear iniquity' is to suffer on account of it, comp. Lam. v. 7; Isa. liii. 4, 11, 'he shall bear their iniquities,' as a heavy burden on his shoulders, with great pain and suffering, and so atone for them. KAL ᵃ*pret.* ᵇ*inf.* ᶜ*fut.* ᵈ סַבָּל *m.* bearer of burdens.

9 סָמַךְ to lean upon; to be supported. NIPHAL *fut.*

10 עָמַס to lift up, to carry as a load. KAL *part.* Paül.

11 עָנָה to answer, to bear (witness). KAL ᵃ*fut.* ᵇ*part.* Poel.

12 עָשָׂה to do; to make; to bear (fruit). KAL ᵃ*pret.* ᵇ*fut.*

13 פָּרָה to be fruitful, to bear (fruit). KAL *part.* Poel.

14 צָמַח to spring up; to make to grow. HIPHIL *fut.*

15 תָּכַן to rectify; to fix, establish. PIEL *pret.*

Gen. i. 29.	2	Deut. xxix. 23.	14	Prov. xxx. 21.	7 b
iv. 13.a	7 b	xxxi. 9, 25.	7 e	Isa. i. 14.	7 a
vii. 17.	7 d	xxxii. 11.	7 d	xxii. 6.	7 a
xiii. 6.	7 a	Josh. iii. 3, 8, 13, 14,	7 e	xxxvii. 31.	12 a
xxxvi. 7.	7 b	15, 15, 17.	7 e	xlvi. 3.	10
xxxvii. 25.	7 e	iv. 9, 10, 16, 18.	7 d	xlvi. 4, 7.	7 b
xlix. 15.	8 b	vi. 4, 6.	7 d	lii. 11.	7 d
Exod. xviii. 22.	7 a	vi. 8, 13.	7 e	liii. 4, 12.	7 a
xix. 4.	7 d	viii. 33.	7 e	liii. 11.	8 c
xx. 16.	11 a	Judg. iii. 18.	7 e	lxiii. 9.	6 b
xxv. 14, 27.	7 b	ix. 54.	7 e	lxvi. 12.	7 g
xxv. 28.	7 d	1 Sam. xiv. 1, 6, 7, 12,	7 e	Jer. x. 5.δ	7 b g
xxvii. 7.β	7 b	12, 13, 13, 14, 17.	7 d	x. 19.	7 d
xxviii. 12, 29, 30, 38.	7 a	xvi. 21.	7 d	xvii. 21.	7 b
xxviii. 43.	7 b	xvii. 7, 41.	7 e	xvii. 27.	7 b
xxx. 4.	7 b	2 Sam. vi. 13.	7 e	xxxi. 19.	7 b
xxxvii. 5, 14, 15, 27.	7 b	v. 24.	7 e	xliv. 22.	7 b
xxxviii. 7.	7 b	xviii. 15.	7 e	Lam. iii. 27.	7 b
Lev. v. 1, 17.	7 a	xviii. 20.	1	iii. 28.	6 a
x. 17.	7 b	xxiii. 37.	7 e	v. 7.	8 a
xi. 25, 28, 40.	7 e	1 Kings ii. 26.	7 a	Ezek. iv. 4.	7 d
xv. 10.	7 e	v. 15.	7 e	iv. 5, 6.	7 d
xvi. 22.	7 a	x. 2.	7 d	xii. 6, 12.	7 d
xvii. 16.	7 a	xiv. 28.	7 d	xii. 7.	7 d
xix. 8.	7 d	2 Kings v. 23.	7 d	xiv. 10.	7 d
xx. 17, 19, 20.	7 d	xviii. 14.	7 d	xvi. 52, 52.	7 d
xxii. 9.	7 a	xix. 30.	12 a	xvi. 54.	7 d
xxii. 16.	7 h	1 Chron. v. 18.	7 e	xvi. 58.	7 d
xxiv. 15.	7 a	x. 4, 4, 5.	7 e	xvii. 8.	7 d
Num. i. 50.	7 d	xi. 39.	7 e	xvii. 23.	12 a
iv. 15.	7 b	xii. 24.	7 e	xviii. 19.	7 d
iv. 25.	7 a	xv. 15.	7 d	xviii. 20, 20.	7 d
v. 31.	7 a	v. 26, 27.	7 d	xxiii. 35.	7 d
vii. 9.	7 d	2 Chron. ii. 2, 18.	8 d	xxiii. 49.	7 c
ix. 13.	7 d	ix. 1.	7 d	xxxii. 24, 25, 30.	7 d
x. 17, 21.	7 e	xiv. 8, 8.	7 e	xxxiv. 29.	7 d
xi. 12.	7 d	xxxiv. 13.	8 d	xxxvi. 6.	7 d
xi. 14.	7 d	Neh. iv. 10.	8 d	xxxvi. 7, 15.	7 a
xi. 17, 17.	7 a d	iv. 17.	7 d	xxxix. 26.	7 a
xiii. 23.	7 b	Job xxxiv. 31.	7 a	xliv. 10, 12, 13.	7 a
xiv. 33.	7 a	Ps. lv. 12.	7 d	xlvi. 20.	4
xiv. 34.	7 a	lxix. 7.	7 a	Hos. ix. 16.	12 b
xviii. 1, 1, 23, 32.	7 d	lxxv. 3.	15	Joel ii. 22.	7 a
xviii. 22.	7 b	lxxxix. 50.γ	7 a	Amos v. 26.	7 a
xxx. 15.	7 a	xci. 12.	7 d	vii. 10.	5
Deut. i. 9.	7 b	xcvi. 6.	7 e	Mic. vi. 16.	7 d
i. 12.	7 d	Prov. ix. 12.	7 d	vii. 9.	7 d
i. 31, 31.	7 a d	xviii. 14.	7 b	Zeph. i. 11.	6 c
v. 20.	11 a	xxv. 18.	11 b	Hag. ii. 12.	7 d
x. 8.	7 b			Zech. v. 10.	3
xxix. 18.	13			vi. 13.	7 d

a lit. from to pardon, *i.e.* too great to be forgiven.   *β lit.* in bearing it.   *γ lit.* my bearing.   *δ lit.* bearing they must be borne.

BEAR (A CHILD)

1 הָרָה to conceive in the womb, to be with child, to bring forth. KAL *fut.*

2 חוּל to travail in childbirth, to bring forth; see *Form.* POLEL *fut.*

3 יָלַד to beget as a father, to bear or bring forth as a mother; applied also to spiritual birth: Ps. xxii. 31; lxxxvii. 4, 5, 6: from God the Father, Isa. lxvi. 9: by the church the mother, Isa. liv. 1; lxvi. 7, 8. KAL ᵃ*pret.* ᵇ*inf.* ᶜ*fut.* ᵈ*part.* Poel. ᵉ*part.* Paül. NIPHAL ᶠ*pret.* ᵍ*inf.* ʰ*fut.* ⁱ*part.* PUAL ᵏ*pret.* HOPHAL ˡ*inf.* ᵐ יוֹלֵד *adj.* born. ⁿ יָלִיד *m. constr.* born. ᵒ מוֹלֶדֶת *f.* birth, 'born at.'

Gen. iv. 1, 17, 20, 25.	3 c	Gen. xvii. 12, 13, 23, 27.	3 n	Gen. xxiv. 15.	3 k
iv. 2.a	3 b	xvii. 17, 17.	3 h c	xxiv. 24, 47.	3 a
iv. 18.	3 h	xvii. 19.	3 d	xxiv. 36.	3 c
iv. 22.	3 a	xvii. 21.	3 c	xxv. 2.	3 c
iv. 26.	3 k	xviii. 13.	3 c	xxv. 12.	3 a
vi. 1.	3 k	xix. 37.	3 c	xxv. 19.	3 b
vi. 4.	3 a	xix. 38.	3 a	xxv. 26.	3 a
x. 1.	3 h	xx. 17.	3 h	xxix. 32, 33.	3 a
xii. 25.	3 k	xxi. 2.	3 c	xxix. 34, 34.	3 c a
xiv. 14.	3 n	xxi. 3, 3.	3 i a	xxix. 35, 35.β	3 c b
xvi. 1.	3 a	xxi. 5.	3 g	xxx. 1, 5, 7, 10, 12, 17, 19, 23.	3 a
xvi. 2, 16.	3 b	xxi. 7, 9.	3 c	xxx. 9.β	3 b
xvi. 11.	3 d	xxii. 20, 23.	3 a	xxxi. 8, 8, 43.	3 a
xvi. 15, 15.	3 e a	xxii. 24.	3 c		

Gen. xxxiv. 1.	3	a	1 Sam. i. 20.	3	c	Job iii. 3.	3	h
xxxv. 26.	3	k	ii. 5	3	a	v. 7.	3	k
xxxvi. 4, 4.	3 c	a	ii. 21.	3	a	xi. 12.	3	h
xxxvi. 5, 5.	3 a	k	iv. 20.	3	a	xiv. 1.	3	e
xxxvi. 12, 14.	3	c	2 Sam. iii. 2.	3	h	xv. 7.	3	h
xxxviii. 3, 4.	3	c	iii. 2ר.	3	k	xv. 14.	3	e
xxxviii. 5, 5.	3 c	b	iii. 5.	3	k	xxiv. 21.	3	c
xli. 50, 50.	3 k	a	v. 13.	3	h	xxv. 4.	3	e
xliv. 27.	3	a	v. 14.	3	a	xxxviii. 21.	3	h
xlvi. 15.	3	c	xi. 27.	3	c	Ps. xxii. 31.	3	i
xlvi. 18, 25.	3	c	xii. 14.	3	m	lxxviii. 6.	3	h
xlvi. 20, 20.	3 h	a	xii. 15.	3	a	lxxxvii. 4, 5, γ 6.	3	k
xlvi. 22, 27.	3 k	a	xii. 24.	3	c	Prov. xvii. 17.	3	h
xlviii. 5.	3	i	xiv. 27.	3	h	xvii. 25.	3	d
Exod. i. 22.	3 m		xxi. 8.	3	a	xxiii. 25.	3	d
ii. 2, 22.	3	c	xxi. 20, 22.	3	k	Eccles. iii. 2.δ	3	b
vi. 20, 23, 25.	3 c	l	1 Kings i. 6.	3	a	iv. 14.	3	f
xxi. 4.	3	a	iii. 21.	3	a	Cant. vi. 9.	3	d
Lev. xii. 2.	3	a	xi. 20.	3	c	Isa. vii. 14.	3	a
xii. 5.	3	c	xiii. 2.	3	i	viii. 3.	3	d
xii. 7.	3 d		2 Kings iv. 17.	3	c	ix. 6.	3	k
xviii. 9, 9.	3	o	1 Chron. i. 19.	3	k	li. 2.		2
xxii. 11.	3	n	i. 32.	3	a	liv. 1.	3	h
Num. xxvi. 59, 59.	3 a	c	ii. 3, 9.	3	f	lxvi. 8.	3	n
xxvi. 60.	3	h	ii. 4, 17, 46, 48.	3	a	Jer. ii. 14.	3	d
Deut. xxi. 15.	3	a	ii. 19, 21, 24, 29, 35, 49.	3	c	xv. 9.	3	d
xxv. 6.	3	c	iv. 6.	3	c	xv. 10.	3	a
xxviii. 57.	3	c	iv. 9, 18.	3	a	xvi. 3, 3.	3 m	d
Josh. v. 5.	3 m		iv. 17.		1	xx. 14, 14.	3 k	a
Judg. viii. 31.	3	a	vii. 14, 14, 18.	3	a	xx. 15.	3	k
xi. 2.	3	c	vii. 16, 23.	3	c	xxii. 26, 26.	3 a	k
xiii. 2, 3, 3.	3	a	vii. 21.	3	i	xxix. 6.	3	i
xiii. 5, 7.	3	d	xx. 8.	3	f	l. 12.	3	d
xiii. 8.	3 k		xxvi. 6.	3	f	Ezek. xvi. 4, 5.	3	l
xiii. 24.	3	c	2 Chron. xi. 19, 20.	3	c	xvi. 20.	3	a
xviii. 29.	3 k		Ezra x. 3.	3	i	xxiii. 4.	3	a
Ruth i. 12.	3	a	Job i. 2.	3	h	xxiii. 37.	3	a
iv. 12, 15.	3	a				Hos. i. 3, 6, 8.	3	a
iv. 13.	3	c				ii. 3.	3	g
iv. 17.	3	k						

a lit. added to bear.   *β lit.* from bearing.   *γ lit.* a man and a man was born, &c.   *δ lit.* to bear.

BEAR (AN ANIMAL)

דָּבַב the original idea of this verb seems to be, to do anything slowly and deliberately; hence the name of a bear from its slow and insidious movements. דֹּב and דּוֹב *m.* a bear: *metaph.,* a cruel and vindictive man, 2 Sam. xvii. 8, Prov. xxviii. 15; the Medo-Persian kingdom, Dan. vii. 5, &c. דֹּב *Ch. m.* Dan. vii. 5.

BEARD

זָקָן *com.* the beard, on which Orientals set a high value; to shave or pluck the beard is the highest indignity. Lev. xiii. 29, 30; xiv. 9; xix. 27; xxi. 5: 1 Sam. xvii. 35; xxi. 13: 2 Sam. x. 4, 5; xx. 9: 1 Chron. xix. 5: Ezra ix. 3: Ps. cxxxiii. 2, 2: Isa. vii. 20; xv. 2: Jer. xli. 5; xlviii. 37: Ezek. v. 1.

שָׂפָם *m.* the beard; perhaps the whole chin, or that on which the beard grows; hence sometimes rendered the upper lip: 2 Sam. xix. 24.

BEAST

1 בְּהֵמָה *f.* when opposed to man, as in Ps. xxxvi. 6, it signifies any brute creature: when opposed to creeping things, as Lev. xi. 2-7, 29, 30, it signifies fourfooted land animals from the size of the hare and upwards; for the mouse, weasel, ferret, are reckoned among the creeping things, Lev. xi. 29, 30: when opposed to wild beasts of the earth, as Gen. i. 25, it signifies cattle or tame animals.—*Bochart.* Gen. vi. 7, &c.

2 בְּעִיר *m.* see *Brutish.*

3 חַי *adj.* any living thing. חֵיוָא *Ch. f. id.*

4 מֶבַח *m.* slaughter.

5 נְבֵלָה *f.* see *Carcase;* "beast that dieth of itself."

6 נֶפֶשׁ *com.* animal life.

7 מְרִיא *m.* fat beasts, fed beasts.

No. 1 not included.

Gen. i. 24, 25, 30.	3	1 Sam. xvii. 46.	3	Ezek. v. 17.	3
ii. 19, 20.	3	2 Sam. xxi. 10.	3	xiv. 15, 15.	3
iii. 1, 14.	3	2 Kings xiv. 9.	3	xiv. 21, 21.	3, 1
vii. 14, 21.	3	2 Chron. xxv. 18.	3	xxix. 5.	3
viii. 19.	3	Job v. 22, 23.	3	xxxi. 6, 13.	3
ix. 2, 5, 10, 10.	3	xxxvii. 8.	3	xxxii. 4.	3
xxxvi. 20, 23.	3	xxxix. 15.	3	xxxiii. 27.	3
xlv. 17.	2	xl. 20.	3	xxxiv. 5, 8, 25, 28.	3
Exod. xxii. 5.	2	Ps. l. 10.	2	xxxviii. 20.	3
xxiii. 11, 29.	3	lxxix. 2.	3	xxxix. 4, 17.	3
Lev. v. 2.	3	civ. 11, 20, 25.	3	Dan. ii. 38.	3 a
vii. 24.	3	cxlviii. 10.	5	iv. 12, 14, 15, 16, 21, 23, 25, 32.	3 a
xi. 2, 2.	3, 1	Prov. ix. 2.	4	v. 21.	3
xi. 27, 47, 47.	3	Isa. i. 11.	7	vii. 3, 5, 6, 7, 7, 11, 12, 17, 19, 23.	3 a
xvii. 13.	3	xxxv. 9.	3	viii. 4.	3
xxiv. 18.a	6, 1	xl. 16.	3	Hosea ii. 12, 18.	3
xxiv. 18, 18.	3	xliii. 20.	3	iv. 3.	3
xxv. 7.	3	xlvi. 1.	3	xiii. 8.	3
xxvi. 6, 22.	3	lvi. 9, 9.	3	Amos v. 22.	7
Num. xx. 8, 11.	3	Jer. xii. 9.	3	Zeph. ii. 14, 15.	3
xxxv. 3.	3	xxvii. 6.	3		
Deut. vii. 22.	3	xxviii. 14.	3		

a lit. smiteth the life of a beast.

BEAT

1 גֶּרֶשׁ *m.* something put forth, produce; "corn beaten out of full ears," or green ears; roasted corn, bruised, is a favourite dish in the East.

2 דּוּךְ to pound in a mortar. KAL *pret.*

3 דָּכָא to break into small pieces. PIEL *fut.*

4 דָּפַק to force forward, to push against; to thrust, to beat, to knock. HITHPAEL *part.*

5 דָּקַק to beat small and thin. KAL *a fut.* HIPHIL *b pret.*

6 הָלַם to smite or strike as with a hammer; *intrans.* to break up, to be beaten. KAL *a pret. b inf.*

7 הָרַס to pull or tear down, overthrow or demolish. KAL *fut.*

8 חָבַט to beat olives from the tree; to beat or lash corn out of the ear with a stick, by which means the best and ripest grains and olives are taken; or it may imply the beating out a smaller quantity, in distinction from threshing the whole, as in Isa. xxvii. 12, the taking a portion only; *i. e.* when he shall restore the children of Israel, the Lord will beat, shake, or sever the righteous from the wicked, and gather them, &c. KAL *a fut.* NIPHAL *b fut.*

9 חָתַת to be broken, so as to be quite disabled. NIPHAL *fut.*

10 כָּתַת to beat, to crush; applied to bruising in a mortar: Exod. xxvii. 20; as of olives, and the oil left to run freely and leisurely, and therefore more pure and free from dregs than that which was pressed; to beating iron on an anvil; to crushing or beating down foes, or a nation. KAL *a pret. b imp.* PIEL *c pret.* HOPHAL *d fut.* כָּתִית *f.* beaten, of oil from the olive.

11 נָגַע to touch, to touch with a heavy hostile hand; to be beaten in battle. NIPHAL *fut.*

12 נָגַף to strike, smite. NIPHAL *fut.*

13 נָכָה to beat, to smite, to scourge; to strike home, to strike deep, so as to wound or kill; applied to the stroke of the sun on the head of Jonah, iv. 8. HIPHIL *a pret.*

[b] *inf.* [c] *fut.* HOPHAL [d] *fut.* [e] *part.* [f] מַכָּה *f.* a beating; used of wheat threshed.

14 נָפַץ to break, to dash in pieces. PUAL *part.*

15 נָתַץ to break down so as totally to demolish. KAL [a] *pret.* [b] *fut.*

16 רָקַע to stamp, to beat out. PIEL *fut.*

17 מִקְשָׁה *f.* that which is hard and solid; beaten, beaten work, beaten out of one piece. It appears, from comparing 1 Kings vi. 23 with ver. 28, that the cherubim of the Temple were made of olive wood covered with solid gold.

18 שָׁחַט to kill, to slay: its use, in 1 Kings x. 16, 17, and 2 Chron. ix. 15, 15, 16, in respect to gold, is variously interpreted. Our translators seem to have taken the word for שָׁחַט to expand, to spread out, the letters being transposed. Others suppose that mixed gold is meant. KAL *part.* Poel.

19 שָׁחַק to beat in pieces, to pound fine. KAL [a] *pret.* [b] *fut.*

Exod. v. 14.	13 d	Josh. viii. 15.		Ps. lxxxix. 23.	10 a
v. 16.	13 e	Judg. viii. 17.	15 a	Prov. xxiii. 13, 14.	13 c
xxv. 18, 31, 36.	17	ix. 45.	15 b	xxiii. 35.	6 a
xxvii. 20.	10 e	xix. 22.	4	Isa. ii. 4.	10 c
xxix. 40.	10 e	Ruth ii. 17.	8 a	iii. 15.	3
xxx. 36.	19 a	1 Sam. xiv. 16.	6 b	xxvii. 9.	14
xxxvii. 7, 17, 22.	17	2 Sam. ii. 17.	12	xxvii. 12.	8 a
xxxix. 3.	16	xxii. 43.	19 b	xxviii. 27.	8 b
Lev. ii. 14, 16.	1	1 Kings vi. 17.	18	xxx. 31.	9
xxiv. 2.	10 e	2 Kings iii. 25.	7	xli. 15.	5 a
Num. viii. 4, 4.	17	xiii. 25.	13 a	Jer. xlvi. 5.	10 d
xi. 8.	2	xxiii. 12.	15 b	Joel iii. 10.	10 b
xxviii. 5.	10 e	2 Chron. ii. 10.	13 f	Jonah iv. 8.	13 c
Deut. xxiv. 20.		ix. 15, 15, 16.	18	Micah i. 7.	10 c
xxv. 2, 2.	13 b a	xxxiv. 7.	10 c	iv. 3.	10 c
xxv. 3.	13 b	Ps. xviii. 42.	19 b	iv. 13.	5 b

BEAUTY

1 הָדָר *m.* glory, honour, majesty, splendour, beauty. [a] הֲדָרָה *f. id.* ornament; "beauty of holiness," *marg.* glorious sanctuary.

2 הוֹד *m.* any good quality or endowment, for which a person is admired, &c.; splendour, beauty.

3 חָמַד to desire strongly. KAL *part.* Paul.

4 טוֹב *adj.* good.

5 יָפָה to be fair, beautiful, comely in person, by nature or art; beautiful in action, in wisdom, in season, and in suitableness: it implies beauty internal as well as external. KAL [a] *pret.* [b] *fut.* [c] יָפֶה *adj.* fair, beautiful. [d] יְפִי *m.* and [e] יֳפִי *m.* splendour, brightness; beauty, gracefulness.

6 נָאָה see *Become.* PILEL *pret.*

7 נָעֵם to be pleasant, delightful; with מִן to pass in beauty. KAL [a] *pret.* [b] נֹעַם *m.* pleasantness, grace, favour: the beauty of the Lord denotes whatever in the Lord is sweet, pleasant, and salutary to the sinner, and therefore his virtues of goodness and grace together with all their signs and effects.— *Venema in Hengstenberg.*

8 פָּאַר to adorn, beautify, the sanctuary, the church of God, the poor by great benefits (*comp.* the Latin phrase *ornare beneficiis*), see also *Glorify.* PIEL [a] *inf.* [b] *fut.* [c] פְּאֵר *m.* ornament of the head; a paronomasia with ashes: Isa. lxi. 3 (see APPENDIX, Paronomasia). [d] תִּפְאָרָה *f.* in Isa. xxviii. 5, Jer. xlviii. 17; elsewhere תִּפְאֶרֶת *f.* absol. and constr.: ornament, splendour, beauty; glory and beauty together imply great splendour.

9 צְבִי *m.* honour, majesty; see *Glory.* Isa. lxi. 3.

10 צוּר *m.* a rock, strength of the rich and powerful, all that belongs to such in outward form or condition; by some rendered 'form' in Ps. xlix. 14. (כתיב) צִיר *id.*

11 מַרְאֶה *m.* appearance.

12 תֹּאַר *m.* form, visage; beautiful, *lit.* fair of form or visage.

Gen. xxix. 17. a	5 c, 12	Ps. l. 2.	5 e	Isa. lx. 13.	8 a
Exod. xxviii. 2, 40.	8 d	xc. 17.	7 b	lxi. 3.	8 c
Deut. xxi. 11. a	5 c, 12	xcvi. 6.	8 d	lxiv. 11.	8 d
1 Sam. xvi. 12.	5 c	xcvi. 9.	1 a	Jer. xiii. 20.	8 d
xxv. 3.	5 c	cx. 3.	1	xlviii. 17.	8 d
2 Sam. i. 19.	9	cxlix. 4.	8 b	Lam. i. 6.	1
xi. 2.	4	Prov. vi. 25.	5 e	ii. 1.	8 d
1 Chron. xvi. 29.	1 a	xx. 29.	1	ii. 15.	8 c
2 Chron. iii. 6.	8 d	xxxi. 30.	5 e	Ezek. vii. 20.	5 e 9
xx. 21.	1 a	Eccles. iii. 11.	5 c	xvi. 12.	8 d
Ezra vii. 27.	8 a	Cant. vi. 4.	5 c	xvi. 13.	5 b
Esth. i. 11.	5 e	Isa. iii. 24.	5 e	xvi. 14, 15, 25.	5 e
ii. 7.	4, 11	iv. 2.	9	xxiii. 42.	8 d
Job xl. 10.	1	xiii. 19.	8 d	xxvii. 3, 4, 11.	5 d
Ps. xxvii. 4.	7 b	xxviii. 1, 4, 5.	8 d	xxvii. 7.	5 e
xxix. 2.	1 a	xxxiii. 17.	5 c	xxviii. 12, 17.	5 e
xxxix. 11.	3	xliv. 13.	5 e	xxxii. 19.	7 a
xlv. 11.	5 e	lii. 1.	8 d	Hos. xiv. 6.	2
xlvii. 2.	5 e	lii. 7.	6	Zech. ix. 17.	5 e
xlix. 14.	10	liii. 2.	10	xi. 7, 10.	7 b

a. lit. fair of form.

BECAUSE

אוֹדוֹת *f. pl.* causes; with עַל because of: Gen. xxi. 11, 25: Num. xii. 1; xiii. 24: Judg. vi. 7.

דֶּרֶךְ *com.* way, Ps. cvii. 17, *lit.* from the way, *i. e.* habit, custom, of their iniquity.

BECOME

הָיָה to be; frequently rendered 'become' in construction with לְ, to, (hence in the Greek Testament γίνεσθαι εἰς, Matt. xxi. 42, and elsewhere) not included.

הָפַךְ to turn. NIPHAL *fut.* Job xxx. 21, Heb. turned to be cruel.

נָאָה The primary meaning may be, to sit, to dwell at ease, with pleasure and tranquillity; hence, to become one, to sit well upon one, as we say of a garment, &c.: *comp.* Plin. Panegyr. 10, *quam bene humeris tuis sederet imperium.* PILEL *pret.* Ps. xciii. 5. נָאוֶה *adj.* becoming, seemly: Prov. xvii. 7.

עָרַב to be surety, to become (surety). KAL *part.* Poel. Prov. xvii. 18.

עָשָׂה to do. NIPHAL *fut.* Esth. ii. 11.

BED

1 יָצַע to spread clothes or anything to lie down and rest upon, to make a bed. HIPHIL *fut.* יָצוּעַ *m.* couch, chamber. מַצָּע *m.* a couch, a bed.

2 מִטָּה *f.* a bed which consists of clothes stretched out or spread, and upon which the human body is stretched out, in sleep or sickness, at table or for rest.

3 מִשְׁכָּב *m.* a lying down, a bed: Gen. xlix. 4, &c. מִשְׁכַּב Ch. *m. id.*

4 עֲרוּגָה *f.* a ridge or raised bed, upon which vines &c. are planted.

5 עֶרֶשׂ *m.* a bed, a couch, prop. covered with a hanging curtain; a bedstead.

No 3. not included.

Gen. xlvii. 31.	2	1 Chron. v. 1.	1 a	Prov. xxvi. 14.	2
xlviii. 2.	2	2 Chron. xxii. 11.	2	Cant. i. 16.	5
xlix. 33.	2	xxiv. 25.	2	iii. 7.	2
Exod. viii. 3, 3.	3, 2	Esth. i. 6.	2	v. 13.	4
Deut. iii. 11.	5	vii. 8.	2	vi. 2.	4
1 Sam. xix. 13, 15, 16.	2	Job vii. 13.	2	Isa. xxviii. 20.	1 b
xxvii. 23.	2	xvii. 13.	2	Ezek. xxiii. 41.	2
2 Sam. iv. 7, 7.	2, 3	Ps. vi. 6.	2	Dan. ii. 28, 29.	3 a
1 Kings xvii. 19.	2	xli. 3, 3.	5, 3	iv. 5, 10, 13.	3 a
xxi. 4.	2	lxiii. 6.	1 a	vii. 1.	3 a
2 Kings i. 4, 6, 16.	2	cxxxii. 3. a	5, 1 a	Amos iii. 12.	2
iv. 10, 21, 32.	2	cxxxix. 8.	1	vi. 4.	2
xi. 2.	2	Prov. vii. 16.	2		

a lit. the couch of my bed.

BEE

דְּבוֹרָה *f.* a bee, a gregarious insect living under a kind of government of its own; from דָּבַר to order, lead, and govern.—*Bochart.* They not only make honey in hives, but naturally and originally in hollow trees and other convenient lodgments in the rocks: Deut. i. 44: Judg. xiv. 8: Ps. cxviii. 12: Isa. vii. 18.

BEER-LAHAI-ROI

בְּאֵר *m.* a well. חַי *adj.* living. רֹאִי *m.* seeing: Gen. xvi. 14, *lit.* the well of the living one that seeth me. Chald. 'the well of the angel of life who appeared there.'

BEETLE

חַרְגֹּל *m.* a species of the locust, according to Gesenius, so called from its leaping. It does not appear that beetles were ever an article of food, which the locust was: Lev. xi. 22.

BEEVES

בָּקָר *com.* horned cattle, at full age when fit for the plough: Lev. xxii. 19, 21: Num. xxxi. 28, 30, 33, 38, 44.

BEFALL

1 אָנָה to cause to come, to meet: to happen unfortunately. See *Happen.* PUAL *fut.*

2 בּוֹא to come, *seq.* עַל to befall. KAL *pret.*

3 מָצָא to find. KAL a *pret.* b *fut.* c *part.* Poel.

4 קָרָא to meet, befall; spoken of an event, &c. KAL a *pret.* b *fut.*

5 קָרָה to meet, befall. KAL a *pret.* b *fut.* c *part.* Poel. d מִקְרָה *m.* an event.

Gen. xlii. 4.	4 b	Num. xx. 14.	3 a	1 Sam. xx. 26.	5 d
xlii. 29.	5 c	Deut. xxxi. 17.	3 a	2 Sam. xix. 7.	2
xlii. 38.	4 a	xxxi. 21.	3 b	Esth. vi. 13.	5 a
xliv. 29.	5 a	xxxi. 29.	4 a	Ps. xci. 10.	1
xlix. 1.	4 b	Josh. ii. 23.	3 c	Eccles. iii. 19, 19, 19.	5 d
Lev. x. 19.	4 b	Judg. vi. 13.	3 a	Dan. x. 14.	5 b

BEG

בָּקַשׁ to seek. PIEL *part.* Ps. xxxvii. 25.

שָׁאַל to ask. KAL *pret.* Prov. xx. 4. *fut.* Prov. xx. 4. כ׳. PIEL *pret.* Ps. cix. 10.

BEGGAR

אֶבְיוֹן *adj.* a poor needy person: 1 Sam. ii. 8.

BEGET

1 יָלַד to beget as a father, or to bear and bring forth as a mother.

KAL a *pret.* b *part.* Poel. NIPHAL c *fut.* HIPHIL d *pret.* e *inf.* f *imp.* g *fut.* h *part.* i מוֹלֶדֶת *f.* nativity, kindred; offspring.

2 יָצָא to go forth. KAL *part.* Poel, Judg. viii. 30. Heb., going out of his thigh.

Gen. iv. 18, 18, 18.	1 a	Gen. xlviii. 6.	1 d	1 Chron. viii. 1, 7, 8, 11, 32, 33, 33, 33, 34, 36, 36, 36, 37.	1 d
v. 3, 6, 9, 12, 15, 18, 21, 25, 28, 32.	1 g	Lev. xviii. 11.	1 i	viii. 38.	1 a
v. 4, 4.	1 e g	xxv. 45.	1 d	ix. 38, 39, 39, 39, 40, 42, 42, 42, 43.	1 d
v. 7, 7.	1 e g	Num. xi. 12.	1 a	xiv. 3.	1 g
v. 10, 10.	1 e g	xxvi. 29, 58.	1 d	2 Chron. xi. 21.	1 g
v. 13, 13.	1 e g	Deut. iv. 25.	1 g	xiii. 21.	1 g
v. 16, 16.	1 e g	xxiii. 8.	1 c	xxiv. 3.	1 g
v. 19, 19.	1 e g	xxviii. 41.	1 g	Neh. xii. 10, 10, 10, 11, 11.	1 d
v. 22, 22.	1 e g	xxxii. 18.	1 a	Job xxxviii. 28.	1 d
v. 26, 26.	1 e g	Judg. viii. 30.	2	Prov. xvii. 21.	1 a
v. 30.	1 e	xi. 1.	1 g	xxiii. 22.	1 a
vi. 10.	1 g	Ruth iv. 18, 19, 19, 20, 20, 21, 21, 22, 22.	1 d	xxiii. 24.	1 b
x. 8, 13, 15, 24, 24, 26.	1 a	2 Kings xx. 18.	1 a	Eccles. v. 14.	1 d
xi. 10, 12, 14, 16, 18, 20, 22, 24.	1 g	1 Chron. i. 10, 11, 13, 18, 18, 20.	1 a	vi. 3.	1 g
xi. 11, 11.	1 e g	i. 34.	1 g	Isa. xxxix. 7.	1 g
xi. 13, 13.	1 e g	ii. 10, 10, 11, 11, 12, 12, 13, 18, 20, 20, 22, 36, 36, 37, 37, 38, 38, 39, 39, 40, 40, 41, 41, 44, 44, 46.	1 d	xlv. 10.	1 a
xi. 15, 15.	1 e g			xlix. 21.	1 a
xi. 17, 17.	1 e g	iv. 2, 2, 8, 11, 12, 14,	1 d	Jer. xvi. 3.	1 h
xi. 19, 19.	1 e g	vi. 4, 4, 5, 5, 6, 6, 7, 7, 8, 8, 9, 9, 10, 12, 12, 13, 13, 14, 14.	1 d	xxix. 6.	1 a
xi. 21, 21.	1 e g			Ezek. xviii. 10, 14.	1 b
xi. 23, 23.	1 e g	vii. 11, 11.	1 g d	xlvii. 22.	1 b
xi. 25, 25.	1 e g	vii. 32.	1 d	Dan. xi. 6.	1 b
xi. 27, 27.	1 d			Hos. v. 7.	1 b
xvii. 20.	1 g			Zech. xiii. 3, 3.	1 b
xxii. 23.	1 a				
xxv. 3.	1 a				
xxv. 19.	1 d				

BEGIN

1 חָלַל to penetrate; figuratively, to make an opening or entrance into an affair; to begin, Num. xvi. 46, 47, "the plague is begun," hath penetrated into, made an entrance among the people; to enter upon an action, *seq.* infinitive with or without לְ; rarely followed by a finite verb. Neut., to have a beginning, to be begun. HIPHIL a *pret.* b *inf.* c *imp.* d *fut.* e *part.* HOPHAL f *pret.* g תְּחִלָּה *f.* beginning: Prov. ix. 10, "the beginning of wisdom," the first act of wisdom.

2 יָאַל to will, to undertake. See *Content.* HIPHIL *pret.* Deut. i. 5, Moses began, settled his resolution to declare, or, undertook the arduous duty of, &c.

3 יְסֹד *m.* foundation; figuratively, the foundation is put for the beginning of an undertaking.

4 רֹאשׁ *m.* head. a רֵאשָׁה *f.* beginning. b רִאשׁוֹן *adj.* first. c רֵאשִׁית *f.* beginning; a former state; first in time or dignity: Ps. cxi. 10, "the beginning of wisdom," the chief part of wisdom, that which perfects the whole habit.

5 שְׁרָא Ch. to loose, to begin. POEL *pret.*

Beginning. See *World.*

Gen. i. 1.	4 c	Num. xxv. 1.	1 d	Judg. xvi. 19, 22.	1 d
iv. 26.	1 f	xxviii. 11.	4	xx. 31.	1 d
vi. 1.	1 d	Deut. i. 5.	2	xx. 39, 40.	1 a
ix. 20.	1 a	ii. 24.	1 c	Ruth i. 22.	1 g
x. 8.	1 a	ii. 25.	1 d	iii. 10.	4 b
x. 10.	4 c	ii. 31, 31.	1 a c	1 Sam. iii. 2.	1 a
xi. 6.	1 b	iii. 24.	1 a	iii. 12.	1 a
xiii. 3.	1 a	iii. 12.	4 c	xxii. 15.	1 a
xli. 21.	1 g	xvi. 9, 9.	1 d b	2 Sam. xxi. 9, 10.	1 g
xli. 54.	1 a	xxi. 17.	4 c	2 Kings x. 32.	1 g
xliv. 12.	1 a	xxxii. 42.	1 d	xv. 37.	1 g
Exod. xii. 2.	4 c	Josh. iii. 7.	1 a	vii. 25.	1 g
Num. x. 10.	4	Judg. vii. 19.	4 c	1 Chron. i. 10.	4 b
xvi. 46, 47.	1 a	x. 18.	1 d	vii. 9.	4 b
		xiii. 5, 25.	1 d	xxvii. 24.	1 a

2 Chron. iii. 1, 2.	1 d	Job xlii. 12.	4 c	Isa. xlviii. 16.	4		
xx. 22.	1 a	Ps. cxi. 10.	4 c	Jer. xvii. 12.	4 b		
xxix. 17.	1 d	cxix. 160.	4	xxv. 29.	1 e		
xxix. 27, 27.	1 a	Prov. i. 7.	4 c	xxvi. 1.	4 c		
xxxi. 7, 21.	1 a	viii. 22.	4	xxvii. 1.	4 c		
xxxi. 10.	1 b	viii. 23.	4	xxviii. 1.	4 c		
xxxiv. 3, 3.	1 a	ix. 10.	1 g	xlix. 34.	4 c		
Ezra iii. 6, 8.	1 a	xvii. 14.	4 c	Lam. ii. 19.	4		
iv. 6.	1 g	Eccles. iii. 11.	4 b	Ezek. ix. 6, 6.	1 d		
v. 2.	5	vii. 8.	4	xxxvi. 11.	4 a		
vii. 9.	3	x. 13.	1 g	xl. 1.	4		
Neh. iv. 7.	1 a	Isa. i. 26.	1 g	Dan. ix. 21, 23.	1 g		
xi. 17.	1 g	xl. 21.	4	Hos. i. 2.	1 g		
Esth. vi. 13.	1 a	xli. 4, 26.	4	Amos vii. 1.	4		
ix. 23.	1 a	xlvi. 10.	4 c	Jonah iii. 4.	1 d		
Job viii. 7.	4 c			Micah i. 13.	4 c		

with accuracy, as from a high situation. KAL *a* *imp.* *b* *fut.* POLEL *c* *pret.*

7 שִׁיר to sing, to praise. POLEL *pret.* Job xxxvi. 24, or from the former root; either sense will suit the context. *Vulg. cecinerunt.* So Coverdale, Schultens, Herder, Noyes.

'Behold,' as the rendering of particles, not included.

Gen. xii. 14.	5 d	Job xli. 34.	5 d	Jer. iv. 23, 24, 25, 26.	5 a		
xiii. 10.	5 d	Ps. x. 14.	2 c	xiii. 20.	5 c		
xix. 28.	5 d	xi. 4, 7.	1 c	xx. 4.	5 e		
xxxi. 2.	5 d	xvii. 2, 15.	1 c	xxix. 32.	5 d		
xlviii. 8.	5 d	xxvii. 4.	1 a	xxxi. 26.	5 d		
Num. xii. 8.	2 c	xxxiii. 13.	5 a	xxxii. 4.	5 d		
xxi. 9.	2 a	xxxvii. 37.	5 c	xxxiv. 3.	5 d		
xxiii. 9.	2 a	xlvi. 8.	1 b	xl. 4.	5 c		
xxiii. 21.	2 a	lix. 4.	5 c	xlii. 2.	5 c		
xxiv. 17.	6 b	lxvi. 7.	4 a	Lam. i. 9, 18, 20.	5 c		
Deut. i. 8, 21.	5 c	lxxx. 14.	5 c	i. 12.	2 b		
ii. 24, 31.	5 c	lxxxiv. 9.	5 c	ii. 20.	5 c		
iii. 27.	5 c	xci. 8.	2 c	iii. 50.	5 d		
iv. 5.	5 c	cii. 19.	2 a	iii. 63.	2 b		
xi. 26.	5 c	cxiii. 6.	5 b	v. 1.	5 c		
xxxii. 49.	5 c	cxix. 18.	2 c	Ezek. i. 15.	5 c		
Josh. viii. 4.	5 c	cxix. 37.	5 b	viii. 2.	5 d		
xxii. 28.	5 c	cxix. 158.	5 a	viii. 9.	5 d		
xxiii. 4.	5 c	cxlii. 4.	5 c	xxviii. 17.	5 b		
Judg. xvi. 27.	5 e	Prov. vii. 7.	5 d	xxviii. 18.	5 c		
1 Sam. xxvi. 5.	5 d	xv. 3.	4 b	xxxvii. 8.	5 a		
2 Sam. xxiv. 22.	5 c	xxiii. 33.	5 c	xl. 4.	5 c		
1 Chron. xxi. 15.	5 a	Eccles. ii. 12.	5 b	xliv. 5.	5 c		
Job xix. 27.	5 a	v. 11.	5 f	Dan. vii. 4, 6, 9, 11,			
xx. 9.	6 b	vii. 27.	5 c	11, 21.	1 d		
xxii. 12.	5 c	viii. 17.	5 a	ix. 18.	1 c		
xxiii. 9.	1 c	xi. 7.	5 c	Amos iii. 9.	5 c		
xxiv. 18.	3	Cant. iii. 11.	5 c	Micah vii. 9, 10.	5 d		
xxxi. 26.	5 d	Isa. xxvi. 10.	5 d	Hab. i. 8.	2 c		
xxxiv. 29.	6 b	xxxiii. 17.	5 d	i. 5.	5 b		
xxxv. 5.	6 a	xxxviii. 11.	2 c	i. 13.	5 b		
xxxvi. 24.	7, or 6 c	xl. 26.	5 c	iii. 6.	5 a		
xxxvi. 25.	2 c	xli. 23, 28.	5 d	Zech. iii. 4.	5 c		
xxxix. 29.	5 c	xlix. 18.	5 c	vi. 8.	5 c		
xl. 11.	5 c	lxiii. 15.	5 c				

BEGUILE

נָכַל to act deceitfully; Piel, to practise deceit against any one, with לְ. PIEL *pret.* Num. xxv. 18.

נָשָׁא the meaning of Kal may have been, to err, forget; hence, Hiphil, to lead astray, to deceive, impose upon, lead into a pernicious error. See *Deceive.* HIPHIL *pret.* Gen. iii. 13.

רָמָה to throw; Piel, to deceive, to cause to fall, to trip up. PIEL *pret.* Gen. xxix. 25: Josh. ix. 22.

BEHAVE, BEHAVIOUR

הָלַךְ to walk. HITHPAEL, to walk to and fro, applied to conduct: *pret.* Ps. xxxv. 14.

טַעַם *m.* taste; judgment, reason; to conceal reason, *i. e.* to feign madness: 1 Sam. xxi. 13: Ps. xxxiv. title.

שָׁוָה to be even; Piel, to make plain and even, joined with נֶפֶשׁ to quiet one's spirit, to compose the mind, by humility, patience, &c., Ps. cxxxi. 2, in contrast with the pretensions of the proud, ver. 1. PIEL *pret.*

BEHEAD

סוּר to turn away; to take off, remove. HIPHIL *fut.* 2 Sam. iv. 7.

עָרַף to break the neck; to take off the head. KAL *part.* Paül. Deut. xxi. 6.

רֹאשׁ *m.* head: 2 Sam. iv. 7.

BEHEMOTH

בְּהֵמָה see *Beast;* in the *pl.* or with an Egyptian termination, בְּהֵמוֹת the great beast, huge quadruped, the hippopotamus: Job xl. 15, *marg.* 'or, the elephant, as some think.'

BEHOLD

1 חָזָה to see; mostly mentally or prophetically. KAL *a* *inf.* *b* *imp.* *c* *fut.* חֲזָא Ch. P'AL *d* *part. active.*

2 נָבַט to look earnestly. HIPHIL *a* *pret.* *b* *imp.* *c* *fut.*

3 פָּנָה to turn, to look. KAL *fut.*

4 צָפָה to look about, to watch, to observe narrowly. KAL *a* *fut.* *b* *part.* Poel.

5 רָאָה to see, look; the act of the senses. KAL *a* *pret.* *b* *inf.* *c* *imp.* *d* *fut.* *e* *part.* Poel. *f* רְאוּת *f.* sight-seeing. רְאִית *id.* כְּתִיב.

6 שׁוּר to view, to look with attention and earnestness, to survey

BEKAH

בֶּקַע *m.* a half; a half shekel: Exod. xxxviii. 26.

BELCH

נָבַע to gush out; to pour forth. HIPHIL *fut.* Ps. lix. 7.

BELIAL

בְּלִיַּעַל *m.* used of wicked, ungodly men; implies in the formation of the word worthlessness, and according to Gesenius, perniciousness. Lxx. mostly render it by παράνομος, λοιμὸς, once ἀσεβής, Judg. xx. 13: *abstr:* ἀνόμημα, ἀνομία, ἀποστασία, Aqu. ἀποστασία, ἀποστάτης: Deut. xiii. 13, or, naughty men: Judg. xix. 22; xx. 13: 1 Sam. i. 16; ii. 12; x. 27; xxv. 17, 25; xxx. 22: 2 Sam. xvi. 7; xx. 1; xxiii. 6: 1 Kings xxi. 10, 13, 13: 2 Chron. xiii. 7.

BELIE (See LIE)

BELIEVE

אָמַן to be firm, fixed, stable, sure; to be true, faithful: in Hiphil, *seq.* בְּ of person, to have confidence in, answering to the dative in Greek, Rom. iv. 3, James ii. 23: *seq.* לְ has respect to words or motive for confidence, answering to εἰς in Greek, John xiv. 1. HIPHIL *a* *pret.* *b* *imp.* *c* *fut.* *d* *part.* אָמַן Ch. APHEL *e* *pret.*

Gen. xv. 6.	a	Exod. xiv. 31.	c	Deut. i. 32.			d
xlv. 26.	a	xix. 9.	c	ix. 23.			a
Exod. iv. 1, 5, 9, 31.	a	Num. xiv. 11.	c	1 Sam. xxvii. 12.			a
iv. 8, 8.	c, a	xx. 12.	a	1 Kings x. 7.			a

2 Kings xvii. 14.	a	Ps. lxxviii. 22, 32.	a	Isa. xliii. 10.	c
2 Chron. ix. 6.	a	cvi. 12.	a	liii. 1.	a
xx. 20, 20.	b	cvi. 24.	c	Jer. xii. 6.	c
xxxii. 15.	c	cxvi. 10.	a	xl. 14.	a
Job ix. 16.	c	cxix. 66.	a	Lam. iv. 12.	a
xv. 22.	c	Prov. xiv. 15.	c	Dan. vi. 23.	a
xxix. 24.	c	xxvi. 26.	c	Jonah iii. 5.	c
xxxix. 12, 24.	c	Isa. vii. 9. a	c	Hab. i. 5.	c
Ps. xxvii. 13.	d	xxviii. 16.	d		

a marg. ' or, Do ye not believe? it is because ye are not stable.'

BELL

פַּעֲמוֹן m. a bell, from פָּעַם to strike; of the bells on Aaron's robes : Exod. xxviii. 33, 34, 34 ; xxxix. 25, 25, 26, 26.

מְצִלּוֹת f. pl. bells, from their tinkling: Zech. xiv. 20, marg. ' or, bridles ;' according to the Rabbins, the Lxx., and the Vulg. Henderson says they were small metallic plates suspended from the necks or heads of horses or camels for the sake of ornament, and making a tinkling noise by striking against each other like cymbals. It is certain however that bells have always in the East been a part of the trappings of horses. See Paxton's Manners and Customs, ii. p. 237.

BELLOW

צָהַל to neigh as a horse ; metaph. to rejoice, as men. KAL fut. Jer. l. 11.

BELLOWS

מַפֻּחַ m. bellows, from נָפַח to blow : Jer. vi. 29.

BELLY

בֶּטֶן f. the belly, the womb ; prominent or swelling, the middle or inward part of anything ; the inward part of our constitution, the mind, the thoughts and affections of the mind : Num. v. 21, &c.

גָּחוֹן m. the belly of creeping things, which drags along the ground : Gen. iii. 14 : Lev. xi. 42.

כָּרֵשׂ m. the belly or maw of a dragon : Jer. li. 34.

מֵעִים m. pl. the bowels : Cant. v. 14 : Jonah i. 17 ; ii. 1. מְעִין Ch. m. pl. id. Dan ii. 32.

קֵבָה f. the part between the ribs and the loins : Num. xxv. 8.

BELONG

מָנָה f. part, portion : Esth. ii. 9.

BELOVED, WELL-BELOVED

1 אָהַב to love. KAL part. Paül.

2 דּוֹד m. any person that is esteemed or loved. See Love.

3 יָדִיד adj. const. probably implies a more vehement affection of love. ◦ יְדִדוּת f. delight, that which is loved ; 'dearly beloved.'

4 מַחְמָד m. that which is greatly desirable. ◦ חֲמוּדוֹת f. pl. precious things ; 'greatly beloved.'

Deut. xxi. 15, 15, 16.	1	Cant. ii. 3, 8, 9, 10, 16, 17.	2	Isa. v. 1, 1, 1.	3, 2, 3
xxxiii. 12.	3	iv. 16.	2	Jer. xi. 15.	3
Neh. xiii. 26.	1	v. 1, 2, 4, 5, 6, 6, 8, 9,		xii. 7.	3 a
Ps. lx. 5.	3	vi. 9, 9, 10, 16,	2	Dan. ix. 23.	4 a
cviii. 6.	3	vi. 1, 1, 2, 3, 3.	2	x. 11, 19.	4 a
cxxvii. 2.	3	vii. 9, 10, 11, 13.	2	Hos. iii. 1.	1
Cant. i. 13, 14, 16.	2	viii. 5, 14.	2	ix. 16.	4

BEMOAN

נוּד to be shaken, to be agitated ; the shaking or motion of the head, or other parts of the body, expressive of sorrow, the same word used of condolence ; to condole, to bemoan, with a dat. to pity ; also, to comfort, seq. לְ of pers. KAL a imp. b fut. HITHPOLEL c part.

Job xlii. 11.		Jer. xxii. 10.	b	Jer. xlviii. 17.	a
Jer. xv. 5.	b	xxxi. 18.	c	Nah. iii. 7.	b
xvi. 5.	b				

BENCH

קֶרֶשׁ m. a board, a plank : Ezek. xxvii. 6. See Company.

BEND

1 דָּרַךְ to tread ; to tread or bend the bow, when it is large and strong, by setting the foot or knee upon it : the word is also used with arrows following, either by an ellipsis supplied in our translation, or, as Gesenius observes, the origin of the expression being overlooked : "They bend (the bow to shoot) arrows," Ps. lviii. 7 ; lxiv. 3. Gussetius would rather take דָּרַךְ to mean elliptically to shoot as with a bow ; and connect ' arrows' with the following words ; as in Ps. lviii. 7, "Their arrows (are) bitter words ;" Zech. ix. 13, "When I have bent Judah for me," used Judah as a well-directed bow, i.e. to scatter my enemies. KAL a pret. b fut. c part. Poel. d part. Paül. HIPHIL e fut.

2 כָּפַן to extend, or twist around ; Lxx. περιπλέκειν. Gesenius and others, from oriental sources, suppose that the idea of thirst or eager desire is implied in the word, with a pregnant meaning in Ezek. xvii. 7, i. e. did thirst, and so bend her roots towards him, seeking nourishment. KAL pret.

3 שָׁחַח to stoop, to be bowed down, to bend oneself. KAL inf.

4 תָּלָא to hang, to hang in inclination or suspense, to be inclined to, with לְ. KAL part. Paül.

Ps. vii. 12.	1 a	Isa. xxi. 15.	1 d	Lam. ii. 4.	1 a
xi. 2.	1 b	lx. 14.	3	iii. 12.	1 a
xxxvii. 14.	1 a	Jer. ix. 3.	1 e	Ezek. xvii. 7.	2
lviii. 7.	1 b	xlvi. 9.	1 c	Hos. xi. 7.	4
lxiv. 3.	1 a	l. 14, 29.	1 c	Zech. ix. 13.	1 a
Isa. v. 28.	1 d	li. 3, a 3.	1 b		

a וְלֹא (ק׳ ב׳) i.e. found in the text, but accounted superfluous by the Masorites.

BENEFIT

גְּמוּל m. see Reward. 2 Chron. xxxii. 25 : Ps. ciii. 2. תַּגְמוּל m. id. Ps. cxvi. 12.

יָטַב to be good ; to do good. HIPHIL inf. Jer. xviii. 10.

BENJAMIN

בֵּן m. son. יָמִין m. right hand. Gen. xxxv. 18.

BENONI

בֵּן m. son. אָוֶן m. evil, trouble, sorrow : Gen. xxxv. 18.

BERACHAH

בְּרָכָה f. blessing : 2 Chron. xx. 26, 26.

BEREAVE

1 חָסֵר to be diminished, to want, to cause to want. PIEL part.

2 כָּשַׁל see *Fall*. PIEL *fut.*

3 שָׁכֹל to lose children, to become childless. KAL ᵃ *pret.* PIEL ᵇ *pret.* ᶜ *inf.* ᵈ *fut.* ᵉ *part.* ᶠ שַׁכּוּל *adj.* bereaved of young.

Gen. xlii. 36.	3 b	Lam. i. 20.	3 b	Ezek. xxxvi. 14. כ	2
xliii. 14, 14.	3 a	Ezek. v. 17.	3 b	xxxvi. 14.	3 d
Eccles. iv. 8.	1	xxxvi. 12.	3 c	Hos. ix. 12.	3 b
Jer. xv. 7.	3 b	xxxvi. 13.	3 e	xiii. 8.	3 f
xviii. 21.	3 f				

BERRIES

גַּרְגַּר *m.* berries of the olive : Isa. xvii. 6.

BERYL

תַּרְשִׁישׁ *m.* a precious stone, perhaps from Tartessus ; LXX. and Josephus make it the chrysolite, which is the topaz of the moderns : adopted by Braun, de Vestitu Sacerdot. ii. 7. Exod. xxviii. 20 ; xxxix. 13 : Cant. v. 14 : Ezek. i. 16 ; x. 9 ; xxviii. 13 : Dan. x. 6.

BESEECH

1 בָּקַשׁ to seek. PIEL *fut.*

2 חָלָה to be smooth ; in Piel, taking after it פָּנִים the face, it signifies to smoothe the countenance, *i. e.* to appease wrath and procure favour by humble submission, supplication, or deprecation. PIEL ᵃ *pret.* ᵇ *imp.* ᶜ *fut.* The word means also to be sick, affected with grief ; and the use of the phrase above may have its origin in the idea of affecting the countenance by entreaties, so as to produce sympathy there and in the heart ; as we say a pitiful man is *misericors.*

3 חָנַן to show favour ; to pray or supplicate favour. HITHPAEL ᵃ *inf.* ᵇ *fut.*

Gen. xlii. 21.	3 a	1 Kings xiii. 6.	2 c	Ezra viii. 23.	1
Exod. xxxii. 11.	2 c	2 Kings i. 13.	3 b	Esth. viii. 3.	3 b
Deut. iii. 23.	3 b	xiii. 4.	2 c	Jer. xxvi. 19.	2 c
2 Sam. xii. 16.	1	2 Chron. xxxiii. 12.	2 a	Mal. i. 9.	2 b

I BESEECH

אָנָּא an interjection of entreaty : 2 Kings xx. 3 : Neh. i. 5, 11 : Ps. cxvi. 4 ; cxviii. 25, 25 : Isa. xxxviii. 3 : Jonah i. 14.

נָא see *Pray*, Exod. iii. 18 ; xxxiii. 18 : Num. xii. 11 : Neh. i. 8 : Amos vii. 5 : Jonah iv. 3 : Job x. 9 ; xlii. 4 : Ps. cxix. 108 : Dan. i. 12 ; ix. 16.

BESET

כָּתַר to surround, beset round. PIEL *pret.* Ps. xxii. 12.

סָבַב to compass about. KAL *pret.* Hos. vii. 2. *fut.* Judg. xx. 5. NIPHAL *pret.* Judg. xix. 22.

צוּר to bind up ; to besiege. KAL *pret.* Ps. cxxxix. 5.

BESIEGE

1 בּוֹא to come ; to be besieged ; Heb. to come into siege. KAL *fut.*

2 נָצַר to keep ; to watch closely ; to be besieged or shut up close within the walls of a city. KAL *part.* Paül. Isa. i. 8, "as a besieged city," closely watched ; or, according to some, with difficulty preserved, so Ezek. vi. 12 ; "he that remaineth," from the pestilence, "and is besieged," or preserved from the sword, &c.

3 סָבַב to compass about. KAL *pret.*

4 צוּר to press, straiten ; to besiege ; with *acc. sc.* עַל. KAL ᵃ *pret.* ᵇ *inf.* ᶜ *imp.* ᵈ *fut.* ᵉ *part.* Poel. ᶠ מָצוֹר *m.* siege ; fortification, fortress.

5 צָרַר to bind up close, to shut up, to besiege. HIPHIL ᵃ *pret.* ᵇ *fut.*

Deut. xx. 12.	4 a	2 Kings xvi. 5.	4 d	Isa. xxi. 2.	4 c
xx. 19.	4 d	xvii. 5.	4 d	xxxvii. 25.	4 f
xxviii. 52, 52.	5 a	xviii. 9.	4 d	Jer. xxi. 4, 9.	4 e
1 Sam. xxiii. 8.	4 b	xix. 24.	4 f	xxxii. 2.	4 e
2 Sam. xi. 1.	4 d	xxiv. 10.	1, 4 f	xxxvii. 5.	4 e
xx. 15.	4 d	xxiv. 11.	4 e	xxxix. 1.	4 d
1 Kings viii. 37.	5 b	xxv. 2.	1, 4 f	lii. 5.	1, 4 f
xvi. 17.	4 d	1 Chron. xx. 1.	4 d	Ezek. iv. 3.α	4 f
xx. 1.	4 d	2 Chron. vi. 28.	5 b	vi. 12.	2
2 Kings vi. 24.	4 d	Eccles. ix. 14.	3	Dan. i. 1.	4 d
vi. 25.	4 e	Isa. i. 8.	2		

α *lit.* in a siege.

BESOM

מַטְאֲטֵא *m.* see *Sweep*. Isa. xiv. 23.

BEST

1 זִמְרָה *f.* choice select things, most praised and esteemed ; 'best fruits.'

2 חֵלֶב *m.* fat.

3 טוֹב *adj.* good.

4 יָטַב to be good, to seem good, to seem best. KAL ᵃ *fut.* ᵇ מֵיטַב *m.* the good or best part of anything.

5 נָצַב to place, to settle. NIPHAL *part.* Ps. xxxix. 5, "in his best state."

6 פָּז to purify. HOPHAL *part.* best gold, *lit.* purified ; *comp.* 2 Chron. ix. 17, pure.

Gen. xliii. 11.	1	Deut. xxiii. 16.α	3	Esth. ii. 9.	3
xlvii. 6, 11.	4 b	1 Sam. viii. 14.	3	Ps. xxxix. 5.γ	5
Exod. xxii. 5, 5.	4 b	xv. 9, 15.	4 b	Cant. vii. 9.	3
Num. xviii. 12, 12, 29,	2	2 Sam. xviii. 4.β	4	Ezek. xxxi. 16.	3
30, 32.		1 Kings x. 18.	6	Mic. vii. 4.	3
xxxvi. 6.	3	2 Kings x. 3.	3		

a marg. is good for him. *β lit.* is good in your eyes. *γ marg.* settled.

BESTEAD (See HARD)

BESTIR

חָרַץ to be sharp ; applied to activity, &c. ; see *Move, Decide*. KAL *fut.* 2 Sam. v. 24 : it may here be understood either of a command to cut short all delay and deliberation, so as at once to attack the enemy ; or, that David should rouse himself to courage and exertion.

BESTOW

1 גָּמַל see *Reward*. KAL *pret.*

2 יָנַח to lay up, and leave it to be or lie where it is placed. HIPHIL *fut.*

3 נָחָה to lead, guide, direct ; to lead forth in order to place troops. HIPHIL *fut.*

4 נָתַן to give. KAL ᵃ *pret.* ᵇ *inf.* ᶜ *fut.* נְתַן Ch. P'AL ᵈ *inf.* ᵉ *fut.*

5 עָשָׂה to do ; to make, to prepare or appoint to a new purpose, as when the holy things of the house of God were made the holy things of Baalim ; *comp.* Hos. ii. 8. KAL *pret.*

6 פָּקַד to commit to the care of another, to lay up. KAL *fut.*

Exod. xxxii. 29.	4 b	2 Kings xii. 15.	4 b	2 Chron. xxiv. 7.	5
Deut. xiv. 26.	4 a	1 Chron. xxix. 25.	4 c	Ezra vii. 20, 20.	4 d e
1 Kings x. 26.	3	2 Chron. ix. 25.	2	Isa. lxiii. 7, 7.	1
2 Kings v. 24.	6				

BETH

בַּיִת *m.* house ; used frequently in the composition of proper names, to signify house or place.

BETHER

בֶּתֶר *m.* a section, division ; of a country divided by mountains and valleys, rugged and abrupt : Cant. ii. 17, *marg.* 'or, of division ;' LXX. ἐπὶ ὄρη κοιλωμάτων, *i.e.* mountains divided by valleys.

BETHINK

לֵב *m.* the heart : 1 Kings viii. 47 ; לָבָב *m.* 2 Chron. vi. 37.

שׁוּב to turn. HIPHIL *pret.* 1 Kings viii. 47 : 2 Chron. vi. 37.

BETIMES

שָׁחַר to seek early, betimes, &c. PIEL *pret. seq. dat.* of person, Prov. xiii. 24, "chasteneth him betimes," *lit.* seeketh for him chastening betimes.

BETRAY

רָמָה to throw ; Piel, to cause to fall, to deceive, beguile. PIEL *inf.* 1 Chron. xii. 17, *i.e.* to deceive in order to betray.

BETROTH

1 אָרַשׂ to espouse, solemnly to promise marriage. PIEL ᵃ *pret.* ᵇ *fut.* PUAL ᶜ *pret.* ᵈ *part.*

2 חָרַף to pluck or strip off fruit ; to reproach ; to deflower virginity. NIPHAL *part.* Lev. xix. 20, *marg.* reproached by or for man ; or, abused by any. Gesenius, *pr.* to be abandoned, *i.e.* to be delivered over to a husband, *i.e.* betrothed. Is not the meaning to be understood of a bondmaid made a concubine by her master and not married to him, or redeemed, and therefore not free ? Exod. xxi. 7–11.

3 יָעַד to appoint, set ; to agree to marry, to betroth. KAL ᵃ *pret.* ᵇ *fut.*

Exod. xxi. 8.	3 a	Lev. xix. 20.	2	Deut. xxii. 28.	1 c
xxi. 9.	3 b	Deut. xx. 7.	1 a	xxviii. 30.	1 b
xxii. 16.	1 c	xxii. 23, 25, 27.	1 d	Hos. ii. 19, 19, 20.	1 a

BETTER

1 טוֹב to be good. KAL ᵃ *pret.* HIPHIL, to do good, to confer benefits, ᵇ *pret.* טוֹב ᶜ *adj.* good. Gen. xxix. 19, &c.

2 יָטַב to be good, &c. KAL ᵃ *fut.* HIPHIL ᵇ *fut.*

3 יִתְרוֹן *f.* profit, excellency. יוֹתֵר ᵃ *m.* gain, emolument.

No. 1 c not included.

1 Kings i. 47.	2 b	Eccles. x. 11.β	3	Ezek. xxxvi. 11.	1 b
Eccles. vi. 11.α	3 a	Cant. iv. 10.	1 a	Nah. iii. 8.	2 b
vii. 3.	1 c, 2 a				

α *lit.* what gain to a man?   β *lit.* no excellency to a babbler.

BEULAH

בָּעַל to marry. KAL *part.* Paül, Isa. lxii. 4, *marg.* 'married,' *i.e.* enjoying all the privileges of a married state.

BEWAIL

בָּכָה to weep. KAL *pret.* Deut. xxi. 13. *fut.* Lev. x. 6 : Judg. xi. 37, 38 : Isa. xvi. 9.

יָפַח to break or issue forth with strength and vehemence, as the breath or voice in lamenting. HITHPAEL *fut.* Jer. iv. 31.

BEWARE

עָרַם to be crafty, prudent. HIPHIL *fut.* Prov. xix. 25, *marg.* 'will be cunning.'

שָׁמַר to keep, to watch, to guard. KAL *imp.* 2 Sam. xviii. 12. NIPHAL *imp.* Gen. xxiv. 6 : Exod. xxiii. 21 : Deut. vi. 12 ; viii. 11 ; xv. 9 : Judg. xiii. 4 : 2 Kings vi. 9. *fut.* Judg. xiii. 13.

BEWRAY

גָּלָה to open, reveal, discover. PIEL *fut.* Isa. xvi. 3.

נָגַד to show. HIPHIL *fut.* Prov. xxix. 24.

קָרָא to cry out. KAL *fut.* Prov. xxvii. 16. This expression is used of ointment bewraying its odour, from its being intended to represent the unrestrained clamour of a contentious wife.

BEYOND

עָבַר to pass over. HIPHIL *inf.* 1 Sam. xx. 36.

BID

1 אָמַר to say, to command. KAL ᵃ *pret.* ᵇ *inf.* ᶜ *imp.* ᵈ *fut.*

2 דָּבַר to say, speak ; to command, prescribe. KAL ᵃ *part.* Poel. PIEL ᵇ *pret.*

3 צָוָה to charge, to command. PIEL *pret.*

4 קָדַשׁ to be holy. HIPHIL, to sanctify, to sanctify others for a solemnity, festival, or sacrifice, *i.e.* to order them to sanctify themselves, or to bid and invite them. Henderson explains this use of the word, of the selection of troops for war, and the religious rites engaged in when they set out upon a military expedition. HIPHIL *pret.*

5 קָרָא to call. KAL *part.* Paül.

6 מִשְׁמַעַת *f.* hearing, obedience : 1 Sam. xxii. 14, at thy bidding, *i.e.* at the hearing of thy commands : according to others, at thy private audience.

Gen. xxvii. 19.	2 b	1 Sam. ix. 13, 22.	5	2 Kings iv. 24.	1 a
xliii. 17.	1 a	ix. 27.	1 c	v. 13.	2 b
Exod. xvi. 24.	3	xxii. 14.	6	x. 5.	1 d
Num. xiv. 10.	1 d	2 Sam. i. 18.	1 a	2 Chron. x. 12.	2 b
xv. 38.	1 a	ii. 16.	1 d	Esth. iv. 15.	1 d
Josh. vi. 10.	1 b	xiv. 19.	1 d	Jonah iii. 2.	2 a
xi. 9.	1 a	xvi. 11.	3	Zeph. i. 7.	4
Ruth iii. 6.	3		1 a		

BIER

מִטָּה *f.* (see *Bed ;*) a bier upon which a corpse was carried to be interred : 2 Sam. iii. 31.

BILL

סֵפֶר *m.* a writing, bill, book, &c. : Deut. xxiv. 1, 3 : Isa. l. 1 : Jer. iii. 8.

BILLOW

גַּל *m.* heap, wave : Ps. xlii. 7.

מִשְׁבָּר *m.* breakers, waves, billows : Jonah ii. 3.

BLAMELESS

נָקָה to be clear; innocent. NIPHAL *pret.* Judg. xv. 3. נָקִי *adj.* pure; innocent; clear, quit, free from blame: Gen. xliv. 10: Josh. ii. 17.

BLASPHEME

1 בָּרַךְ to bless; sometimes the word means to blaspheme, to curse; not from its natural force, but because pious persons of old accounted blasphemy so abominable, that they abhorred to express it by its proper name; and therefore, by an *euphemismus* or decent manner of speaking, instead of 'curse God,' said 'bless God.' See also *Curse*. In 1 Kings xxi. 10, 13, the accusers are said to have accused Naboth of some blasphemous imprecation against God, which they would describe by saying he blessed God, in a way that was understood by his judges. *Euphemismus* is a figure of speech which only applies to language where the subject and other circumstances make the meaning of the speaker sufficiently evident. PIEL *pret.*

2 גָּדַף to reproach, to revile; to treat contumeliously by words or deeds; always used of blaspheming God: joined with חָרַף it denotes the highest degree of reproach and blasphemy that can be offered to God: 2 Kings xix. 22. PIEL a *pret.* b *part.*

3 חָרַף to reproach, rail on, blaspheme. PIEL *pret.*

4 נָאַץ to treat with scorn and contumely, to irritate, to provoke to anger. See *Abhor, Provoke.* PIEL a *pret.* b *inf.* c *fut.* HITHPOLEL d *part.* e נְאָצָה *f.* contumely, reproach. f נֶאָצוֹת *f. pl.* provocations, reviling.

5 נָקַב to pierce; to note or mark with dishonour or infamy, to stigmatize, to blaspheme, to curse: the use of this word to mark more especially the blasphemy to be punished by stoning (Lev. xxiv. 23), is thought by Gussetius to imply that the fearful name of Jehovah was opprobriously profaned, and that a greater guilt was incurred than that referred to in ver. 15, where קָלַל is used.

Lev. xxiv. 11.	5 b	2 Kings xix. 6, 22.	2 a	Isa. xxxvii. 6, 23.	2 a
xxiv. 16, 16.	5 c a	Ps. xliv. 16.	2 b	lii. 5.	4 d
2 Sam. xii. 14.	4 b a	lxxiv. 10.	4 a	lxv. 7.	3
1 Kings xxi. 10, 13.	1	lxxiv. 18.	4 a	Ezek. xx. 27.	2 a
2 Kings xix. 3.	4 e	Isa. xxxvii. 3.	4 e	xxxv. 12.	4 f

BLAST

נְשָׁמָה *f.* breath, a blast: 2 Sam. xxii. 16: Job iv. 9: Ps. xviii. 15.

רוּחַ *com.* breath, wind; Exod. xv. 8: 2 Kings xix. 7: Isa. xxv. 4; xxxvii. 7.

BLASTED

1 שְׁדֵמָה *f.* a field: Isa. xxxvii. 27, (as corn) blasted: this place may be thus rendered, 'and as a field before there is standing corn in it:' see *Grow up*. Cocceius and Alexander. Otherwise it may be put for שְׁדֵפָה in the parallel passage, 2 Kings xix. 26.

2 שָׁדַף to burn, blacken, blast, blight. KAL a *part.* Paül. b שְׁדֵפָה *f.* blasting, blight, *e. g.* of grain by the east wind. c שִׁדָּפוֹן *m. id.*

Gen. xli. 6, 23, 27.	2 a	2 Kings xix. 26.	2 b	Amos iv. 9.	2 c
Deut. xxviii. 22.	2 c	2 Chron. vi. 28.	2 c	Hag. ii. 17.	2 c
1 Kings viii. 37.	2 c	Isa. xxxvii. 27.	1		

BLEATING

קוֹל *m.* voice: 1 Sam. xv. 14.

שְׁרִיקוֹת *f. pl.* bleatings; hissing: Judg. v. 16; here it may mean the piping of the herdsmen with their flocks. Lxx. σύρισμος.

BLEMISH

1 תְּבַלֻּל *m.* found only in Lev. xxi. 20, having a white spot (λεύκωμα) in his eye. Vulg. *albuginem habens in oculo.* Comp. Tobit ii. 9; iii. 17; vi. 8, where the Hebrew interpreter has rendered the Greek λεύκωμα by this word.— *Gesenius.*

2 מוּם *m.* any defect or blemish in the body. a מאום *m. id.*

3 תָּמִים *adj.* perfect, "without blemish."

Exod. xii. 5.	3	Lev. xxi. 29.	1	Deut. xv. 21, 21.	2
xxix. 1.	3	xxii. 19.	3	xvii. 1.	2
Lev. i. 3, 10.	3	xxii. 20, 21, 25.	2	2 Sam. xiv. 25.	2
iii. 1, 6.	3	xxiii. 12, 18.	3	Ezek. xliii. 22, 23, 23,	
iv. 3, 23, 28, 32.	3	xxiv. 19, 20.	3	25.	3
v. 15, 18.	3	Num. vi. 14, 14, 14.	3	xlv. 18, 23.	3
vi. 6.	3	xix. 2.	2	xlvi. 4, 4, 6, 6, 13.	3
ix. 2, 3.	3	xxviii. 19, 31.	3	Dan. i. 4.	2
xiv. 10, 10.	3	xxix. 2, 8, 13, 20, 23,		i. 4. ב.	2 a
xxi. 17, 18, 21, 21, 23.	2	29, 32, 36.	3		

BLESS

1 אָשַׁר to walk straight on: the word that signifies to go, signifies also to be happy or blessed, because our way or motion showeth what our end or rest shall be; our happiness in the end lieth virtually in our way.—*Taylor.* Piel, to call blessed. Pual, to be blessed. PIEL a *pret.* b *fut.* PUAL c *pret.* d אַשְׁרֵי *m. pl. const.* blessednesses: this word is always applied to man; בָּרַךְ to bless, to God and man. Blessedness is attributed to man under the several names by which man is expressed in Hebrew: אֱנוֹשׁ Job v. 17: אִישׁ Ps. i. 1: אָדָם Ps. xxxii. 1: and גֶּבֶר Ps. xciv. 12.

2 בָּרַךְ to kneel; to kneel for prayer, praise, &c., hence to praise, to thank, to salute, to wish well to. The most extensive use and meaning is found in Piel; in Hithpael, it is used of the wicked blessing himself in the persuasion that he shall have peace and favour, Deut. xxix. 19; and of the Gentiles blessing themselves, or rejoicing in and receiving all the blessings of the promised redemption, Gen. xxii. 18; xxvi. 4. A blessing is a bountiful gift, as the word εὐλογία is used in 2 Cor. ix. 5. The blessed of (Heb. to) the Lord (Ps. cxv. 15) are blessed with all solid and permanent felicity of every kind; as the people of God are blessed above all other people, Deut. vii. 14; Christ is the blessed seed of Abraham, and the fountain of all blessing, Ps. cxviii. 26. The word is used in various ways of one blessing another in different relations; of the consecration of a sacrifice, 1 Sam. ix. 13. Opposed to קָלַל Prov. xxx. 11; to אָרַר Gen. xii. 3. As a salutation, it is used by one arriving or departing; to one arriving or departing. KAL a *inf.* b *part.* Paül. NIPHAL c *pret.* PIEL d *pret.* e *inf.* f *imp.* g *fut.* h *part.*

PUAL [1] *fut.* [k] *part.* **HITHPAEL** [1] *pret.* [m] *fut.* [n] *part.* בָּרַךְ
Ch. P'AL [o] *part. passive.* **PAEL** [p] *pret.* [q] *part.* [r] בְּרָכָה *f.*
blessing ; a gift or present.

Gen. i. 22, 28.	2 g	Deut. xxviii. 3, 3, 4,		Ps. xxi. 3, 6.	2 r
ii. 3.	2 g	5, 6, 6.	2 b	xxiv. 5.	2 r
v. 2.	2 g	xxviii. 8, 8.	2 r d	xxvi. 12.	2 g
ix. 1.	2 g	xxviii. 12.	2 e	xxviii. 6.	2 b
ix. 26.	2 b	xxix. 19.	2 l	xxviii. 9.	2 r
xii. 2, 2.	2 g r	xxx. 1, 19.	2 r	xxix. 11.	2 b
xii. 3, 3, 3.	2 g h c	xxx. 16.	2 d	xxxi. 21.	2 b
xiv. 19, 19.	2 g b	xxxiii. 1, 1.	2 r d	xxxii. 1, 2.	1 d
xiv. 20.	2 b	xxxiii. 11.	2 f	xxxiii. 12.	1 d
xvii. 16, 16, 20.	2 d	xxxiii. 13.	2 k	xxxiv. 1.	2 g
xviii. 18.	2 c	xxxiii. 20, 24.	2 b	xxxiv. 8.	1 d
xxii. 17, 17.	2 e g	xxxiii. 23.	2 r	xxxvi. 22.	2 k
xxii. 18.	2 l	Josh. viii. 33.	2 e	xxxvii. 26. γ	2 r
xxiv. 1, 35.	2 d	viii. 34.	2 r	xl. 4.	1 d
xxiv. 27, 31.	2 b	xiv. 13.	2 g	xli. 1.	1 d
xxv. 11.	2 g	xv. 19.	2 r	xli. 2.	1 c
xxvi. 3, 12.	2 g	xvii. 14.	2 d	xli. 13.	2 b
xxvi. 4. α	2 l	xxii. 6, 7, 33.	2 g	xlv. 2.	2 g
xxvi. 24.	2 d	xxiv. 10.	2 a g	xlix. 18.	2 g
xxvi. 29.	2 b	Judg. i. 15.	2 r	lxii. 4.	2 g
xxvii. 4, 7, 10, 19, 23,		v. 9.	2 f	lxiii. 4.	2 g
25, 31.	2 g	v. 24, 24.	2 i	lxv. 4.	1 d
xxvii. 12, 35, 36, 36.	2 r	xiii. 24.	2 g	lxv. 10.	2 g
xxvii. 27, 27.	2 g d	xvii. 2.	2 b	lxvi. 8.	2 f
xxvii. 29, 29.	2 b h	Ruth ii. 4.	2 g	lxvi. 20.	2 b
xxvii. 30.	2 e	ii. 19, 20.	2 b	lxvii. 1, 6, 7.	2 g
xxvii. 33, 33.	2 g b	iii. 10.	2 b	lxviii. 19, 35.	2 f
xxvii. 34.	2 f	iv. 14.	2 b	lxviii. 26.	2 f
xxvii. 38, 38.	2 r f	1 Sam. ii. 20.	2 d	lxxii. 17, 17.	2 m, 1 b
xxvii. 41, 41.	2 r d	ix. 13.	2 g	lxxii. 18, 19.	2 b
xxviii. 1, 3.	2 g	xv. 13.	2 b	lxxxiv. 4, 5, 12.	1 d
xxviii. 4.	2 r	xxiii. 21.	2 b	lxxxix. 15.	2 b
xxviii. 6, 6.	2 d e	xxv. 27.	2 r	lxxxix. 52.	2 b
xxviii. 14.	2 c	xxv. 32, 33, 33, 39.	2 g	xciv. 12.	1 d
xxx. 13.	1 a	2 Sam. ii. 5.	2 b	xcvi. 2.	2 f
xxx. 27, 30.	2 g	vi. 11, 18.	2 g	c. 4.	2 f
xxxi. 55.	2 g	vi. 12.	2 d	ciii. 1, 2, 20, 21, 22,	
xxxii. 26.	2 d	vi. 20.	2 e	22.	2 f
xxxii. 29.	2 g	vii. 29, 29, 29.	2 f r i	civ. 1, 35.	2 f
xxxiii. 11.	2 r	viii. 10.	2 e	cvi. 3.	1 d
xxxv. 9.	2 g	xiii. 25.	2 g	cvi. 48.	2 b
xxxix. 5, 5.	2 g r	xviii. 28.	2 b	cvii. 38.	2 g
xlvii. 7, 10.	2 d	xix. 39.	2 g	cix. 17.	2 r
xlviii. 3, 9, 15, 16,		xxi. 3.	2 f	cix. 28.	2 d
20, 20.	2 g	xxii. 47.	2 b	cxii. 1.	1 d
xlix. 25, 25, 25,		1 Kings i. 47.	2 e	cxii. 2.	2 i
25.	2 g r r r	i. 48.	2 b	cxiii. 2.	2 k
xlix. 26, 26.	2 r	ii. 45.	2 b	cxv. 12, 12, 12, 13,	
xlix. 28, 28, 28.	2 g r d	v. 7.	2 b	18.	2 g
Exod. xii. 32.	2 d	viii. 14, 55, 66.	2 g	cxv. 15.	2 b
xviii. 10.	2 b	viii. 15, 56.	2 b	cxviii. 26, 26.	2 b d
xx. 11, 24.	2 d	x. 9.	2 b	cxix. 1, 2.	1 d
xxiii. 25.	2 d	2 Kings v. 15.	2 f	cxix. 12.	2 b
xxxii. 29.	2 r	1 Chron. iv. 10.	2 e g	cxxiv. 6.	2 b
xxxix. 43.	2 g	xiii. 14.	2 g	cxxviii. 1.	1 d
Lev. ix. 22, 23.	2 g	xvi. 2.	2 g	cxxviii. 4.	2 i
xxv. 21.	2 r	xvi. 36.	2 b	cxxviii. 5.	2 g
Num. vi. 23, 24, 27.	2 g	xvi. 43.	2 e	cxxix. 8, 8.	2 r d
xxii. 6, 6.	2 g k	xvii. 27, 27, 27.	2 e d k	cxxxii. 15.	2 e g
xxii. 12.	2 b	xxiii. 13.	2 e	cxxxiii. 3.	2 r
xxiii. 11.	2 d e	xxvi. 5.	2 d	cxxxiv. 1, 2.	2 f
xxiii. 20, 20.	2 e r	xxix. 10, 10.	2 g b	cxxxiv. 3.	2 g
xxiii. 25.	2 e g	xxix. 20, 20.	2 f g	cxxxv. 19, 19, 20, 20.	2 f
xxiv. 1.	2 e	2 Chron. ii. 12.	2 b	cxxxv. 21.	2 b
xxiv. 9, 9.	2 b h	vi. 3.	2 g	cxliv. 1.	2 g
xxiv. 10.	2 e d	vi. 4.	2 b	cxlv. 1, 2, 10, 21.	2 g
Deut. i. 11.	2 g	ix. 8.	2 b	cxlvii. 13.	2 d
ii. 7.	2 d	xx. 26.	2 d	Prov. iii. 33.	2 g
vii. 13, 13.	2 d	xxx. 27.	2 g	v. 18.	2 b
vii. 14.	2 b	xxxi. 8.	2 g	viii. 32, 34.	1 d
viii. 10.	2 d	xxxi. 10.	2 d	x. 6, 7, γ 22.	2 r
x. 8.	2 e	Ezra vii. 27.	2 b	xi. 11, 26.	2 r
xi. 26, 27, 29.	2 r	Neh. viii. 6.	2 g	xx. 7.	1 d
xii. 7.	2 d	ix. 5, 5, β 5.	2 f g r	xx. 21.	2 i
xii. 15.	2 r	xi. 2.	2 g	xxii. 9.	2 i
xiv. 24, 29.	2 d	xiii. 2.	2 r	xxiv. 25.	2 r
xv. 4.	2 e g	Job i. 10.	2 d	xxvii. 14.	2 h
xv. 10.	2 g	i. 21.	2 k	xxviii. 20.	2 b
xv. 6, 14, 18.	2 d	xxix. 11.	1 b	xxxi. 11.	2 g
xvi. 10, 15.	2 g	xxix. 13.	2 b	xxxi. 28.	1 b
xvi. 17.	2 r	xxxi. 20.	1 d	Eccles. x. 17.	1 d
xxi. 5.	2 e	xlii. 12.	2 d	Cant. vi. 9.	1 b
xxiii. 5.	2 r	Ps. i. 1.	1 d	Isa. xix. 24.	2 r
xxiii. 20.	3 g	ii. 12.	1 d	xix. 25, δ 25.	2 b d
xxiii. 20.	2 d	iii. 8.	1 d	xix. 18.	1 d
xxiv. 19.	2 g	v. 12.	1 d	xxxii. 20.	1 d
xxvi. 15.	2 f	x. 3.	2 g	xliv. 3.	2 r
xxvii. 12.	2 e	xvi. 7.	2 g	li. 2.	2 g
xxviii. 2.	2 r	xviii. 46.	2 b	lvi. 2.	1 d
				lxi. 9.	2 d

Isa. lxv. 8.	2 r	Ezek. iii. 12.	2 b	Joel ii. 14.	2 r
lxv. 16, 16.	2 n m	xxxiv. 26, 26.	2 r	Hag. ii. 19.	2 g
lxv. 23.	2 b	xliv. 30.	2 r	Zech. viii. 13.	2 r
lxvi. 3.	2 h	Dan. ii. 19.	2 p	xi. 5.	2 b
Jer. iv. 2.	2 l	ii. 20.	2 q	Mal. ii. 2.	2 r
xvii. 7.	2 b	iii. 28.	2 p	iii. 10.	2 r
xx. 14.	2 b	iv. 34.	2 p	iii. 12.	1 a
xxxi. 23.	2 g	xii. 12.	1 d		

α *lit.* shall bless themselves.   β *lit.* they shall bless.   γ *lit.* for a
blessing.   δ *lit.* shall bless him.

BLIND, BLINDNESS

1   סַנְוֵרִים   *m. pl.* blindness, or confusion of sight ; Lxx. ἀορασία, so
that everything appears wrong, inflicted by the sud-
den and immediate stroke of God : *pr.* dazzled blindnesses. *Ch.* fatuity of vision. *Syr.* with illusions.

2   עָוַר   to make blind ; to draw, as it were, a skin or film over
the sight ; to be in the condition of one who hath his
sight so obscured ; or, to dig out the eyes. PIEL
[a] *fut.* [b] עִוֵּר *adj.* blind ; *metaph.* used of men who walk
in the darkness of ignorance or of misery. [c] עִוָּרוֹן *m.*
[d] עַוֶּרֶת *f.* blindness.

3   עָלַם   to hide. HIPHIL *fut.*

Gen. xix. 11.α	1	Deut. xxviii. 29.	2 b	Isa. xliii. 8.	2 b
Exod. iv. 11.	2 b	1 Sam. xii. 3.	3	lvi. 10.	2 b
xxiii. 8.	2 a	2 Sam. v. 6, 8, 8.	3	lix. 10.	2 b
Lev. xix. 14.	2 b	2 Kings vi. 18, 18.α	1	Jer. xxxi. 8.	2 b
xxi. 18.	2 b	Job xxix. 15.	2 b	Lam. iv. 14.	2 b
xxii. 22.	2 d	Ps. cxlvi. 8.	2 b	Zeph. i. 17.	2 b
Deut. xv. 21.	2 b	Isa. xxix. 18.	2 b	Zech. xii. 4.	2 c
xvi. 19.	2 a	xxxv. 5.	2 b	Mal. i. 8.	2 b
xxvii. 18.	2 b	xlii. 7, 16, 18, 19, 19,			
xxviii. 28.	2 c	19.	2 b		

α *lit.* with blindnesses.

BLOOD, BLOODTHIRSTY, BLOODGUILTY

1   אֱנוֹשׁ   *m.* a man.

2   דָּם   blood ; the guilt of murder ; any atrocious crime, especially
in the plural ; ' bloody,' *Heb.* of bloods.

3   דָּמָה   to be like, or, to be silent, quiet ; from which may be
deduced Ezek. xix. 10, *marg.* ' or, in thy quietness, or, in
thy likeness.'

4   נֵצַח   *m.* (see *Strength,*) Isa. lxiii. 3, "and their blood shall be
sprinkled," &c. ; ver. 6, "and I will bring down their
strength to the earth." In both places the same word
is used : blood seems to be intended, and here means
the purest heart's blood, in which the strength or life
of the body consists. Henderson says it properly signifies the juice or liquor which is spirted from the grape.

No. 2 not included, except where the plural is rendered as a singular.

Gen. iv. 10, 11.	2	2 Chron. xxiv. 25.	2	Ezek. vii. 23.	2
Exod. iv. 25, 26.	2	Ps. v. 6.	2	ix. 9.	2
xxii. 2, 3.	2	ix. 12.	2	xvi. 6, 6, 6, 9, 36.	2
Lev. xii. 4, 5, 7.	2	xxvi. 9.	2	xviii. 13.	2
xx. 9, 11, 12, 13, 16,		li. 14.	2	xix. 10.	2, 3
18, 27.	2	lv. 23.	2	xxii. 2.	2
Deut. xix. 10.	2	lix. 2.	2	xxiv. 6, 9.	2
xxii. 8.	2	cvi. 38.	2	Hos. i. 4.	2
1 Sam. xxv. 26, 33.	2	cxxxix. 19.	2	iv. 2, 2.	2
2 Sam. iii. 28.	2	Prov. xxix. 10.	1, 2	xii. 14.	2
xvi. 7, 8, 8.	2	Isa. i. 15.	2	Mic. iii. 10.	2
1 Kings ii. 5, 5, 31, 33.	2	iv. 4.	2	vii. 2.	2
2 Kings ix. 7, 7, 26, 26.	2	ix. 5.	2	Nah. iii. 1.	2
1 Chron. xxii. 8.	2	xxvi. 21.	2	Hab. ii. 8, 12, 17.	2
xxviii. 3.	2	xxxiii. 15.	2	Zech. ix. 7.	2
		lxiii. 3.	4		

BLOOM, BLOSSOM

1   נֵץ   *m.* blossoms, buddings.

2   פָּרַח   to grow, to bud, to flourish in all the stages and forms of

vegetation, according to the nature of each tree and plant. KAL ^a *inf.* ^b *fut.* ^c פֶּרַח *m.* a bud, flower, blossom, the product of vegetation.

3 צִיץ to put forth flowers, to blossom. KAL ^a *pret.* HIPHIL ^b *fut.* ^c צִיץ *m.* a flower.

Gen. xl. 10.	1	Isa. v. 24.	2 c	Isa. xxxv. 2.	2 a b
Num. xvii. 5.	2 b	xxvii. 6.	3 b	Ezek. vii. 10.	3 a
xvii. 8, 8.	3 b c	xxxv. 1.	2 b	Hab. iii. 17.	2 b

BLOT, BLOT OUT

1 מוּם *m.* any defect or blemish in the body. ^a מְאוּם *m. id.*

2 מָחָה to wipe off, to wash out as ink might be ; see *Ink ; comp.* Num. v. 23, to blot out or erase, to blot out or pardon. This word seems to imply both the blotting out of sin as a debt, and the wiping away or cleansing of the pollution of sin. The prophet Isaiah (xliv. 22) uses two words to express sin in this view, פֶּשַׁע and חֵטָא ; the former applies more especially to open sins, and particularly to idolatry ; the latter to sins of the heart. So the ideas of wiping out and blotting out are there further illustrated by sin being compared to a cloud, either a thick or lighter cloud. See Vitringa in loc. KAL ^a *pret.* ^b *inf.* ^c *imp.* ^d *fut.* ^e *part.* Poel. NIPHAL ^f *fut.* HIPHIL ^g *fut.*

Exod. xxxii. 32.	2 c	2 Kings xiv. 27.	2 b	Prov. ix. 7.	1
xxxii. 33.	2 d	Neh. iv. 5.	2 f	Isa. xliii. 25.	2 e
Num. v. 23.	2 a	Job xxi. 7.	1 a	xliv. 22.	2 a
Deut. ix. 14.	2 d	Ps. li. 1, 9.	2 c	Jer. xviii. 23.	2 g
xxv. 19.	2 d	lxix. 28.	2 f		
xxix. 20.	2 a	cix. 13, 14.	2 f		

BLOW

תִּגְרָה *f.* strife, contention, conflict : Ps. xxxix. 10.

מַכָּה *f.* a smiting, stroke, plague : Jer. xiv. 17.

BLOW (V)

1 חָצַר to sound a trumpet. HIPHIL *part.*

2 חָצֹצֵר the same. PIEL *part.*

3 נָסַע to remove, to go forth ; peculiarly applied to a wind issuing forth, sent forth, discharged, or driving forward with violence, from God. HIPHIL *fut.*

4 נָפַח to breathe, to blow ; to blast, to blow upon ; to blow up, to blow away. KAL ^a *pret.* ^b *inf.* ^c *part.* Poel. PUAL ^d *pret.*

5 נָשַׁב to breathe, to blow (of the wind) ; to blast or dissipate by blowing ; *seq.* בּ upon. KAL ^a *pret.* HIPHIL ^b *fut.*

6 נָשַׁף to blow with violence. KAL *pret.*

7 פּוּחַ to blow upon, to breathe out with a degree of vehemence or force ; *seq.* בּ to kindle up a fire. HIPHIL ^a *imp.* ^b *fut.*

8 רוּעַ to cry aloud, to blow (with a trumpet), to blow an alarm. HIPHIL ^a *pret.* ^b תְּרוּעָה *f.* blowing of trumpets.

9 תָּקַע to blow in a trumpet, with בּ or without ; in Num. x. 6, 7, תָּקַע שׁוֹפָר to blow the trumpet once (as a signal for calling the people together), is distinguished from הָרִיעַ and תָּקַע תְּרוּעָה to sound an alarm (as a signal for moving). KAL ^a *pret.* ^b *inf.* ^c *imp.* ^d *fut.* ^e *part.* NIPHAL ^f *fut.*

Exod. xv. 10.	6	1 Sam. xiii. 3.	9 a	Isa. xl. 7.	5 a
Lev. xxiii. 24.	8 b	2 Sam. ii. 28.	9 d	xl. 24.	6
Num. x. 3, 5, 10.	9 a	xviii. 16.	9 d	liv. 16.	4 c
x. 4, 7, 8.	9 d	xx. 1, 22.	9 d	Jer. iv. 5.	9 c
x. 6, 6.	9 a d	1 Kings i. 34.	9 a	vi. 1.	9 c
x. 9.	8 a	i. 39.	9 d	li. 27.	9 c
xxix. 1.	8 b	2 Kings ix. 13.	9 d	Ezek. vii. 14.	9 a
xxxi. 6.	8 b	xi. 14.	9 e	xxi. 31.	7 b
Josh. vi. 4, 20.	9 d	1 Chron. xv. 24.a	1	xxii. 20.	4 b
vi. 8, 16.	9 a	xv. 24.b	2	xxii. 21.	4 a
vi. 9, 9.	9 e b	Job xx. 26.	4 d	xxxiii. 3, 6.	9 a
vi. 13, 13.	9 a b	Ps. lxxviii. 26.	3	Hos. v. 8.	9 c
Judg. iii. 27.	9 d	lxxxi. 3.	9 c	Joel ii. 1, 15.	9 c
i. 34.	9 d	cxlvii. 18.	5 b	Amos iii. 6.	9 f
vii. 18, 18.	9 a	Cant. iv. 16.	7 a	Hag. i. 9.	4 a
vii. 19, 22.	9 d	Isa. xviii. 3.	9 b	Zech. ix. 14.	9 d
vii. 20, 20.	9 d b	xxvii. 13.	9 f		

a lit. were trumpeting.

BLUE

חַבּוּרָה *f.* wound, bruise, causing blueness : Prov. xx. 30, or stripes (and) wounds.

שֵׁשׁ *m.* white marble ; also fine white linen : Esth. i. 6, *marg.* ' marble.'

תְּכֵלֶת *f.* a shell-fish ; bluish purple, azure, sky-colour ; according to Maimonides, "this colour is like the firmament ;" also cloth or thread so coloured ; LXX. generally ὑάκινθος, ὑακίνθινος ; so Jerome, Vulg. This colour distinguished the dress of princes, &c., imported from remote countries, and is supposed to have been procured from the juice of a purple shell-fish in the Mediterranean sea, conchylium of the ancients, helix ianthina, Linn. ; or from indigo. This word is almost constantly joined with אַרְגָּמָן reddish purple : Exod. xxv. 4, &c.

BLUNT

קָהָה to be set on edge, as teeth ; to be blunted, as iron. PIEL *pret.* Eccles. x. 10.

BLUSH

כָּלַם see *Ashamed.* NIPHAL *pret.* Ezra ix. 6. *inf.* Jer. viii. 12, *lit.* they knew not to blush. HIPHIL *inf.* Jer. vi. 15.

BOAR

חֲזִיר *m.* swine, Ps. lxxx. 13, which devours and destroys an immense quantity of grapes, when it finds its way into a vineyard.

BOARD

לוּחַ *m.* a smooth even board, or plank of wood : Exod. xxvii. 8 ; xxxviii. 7 : Cant. viii. 9 : Ezek. xxvii. 5.

צֵלָע *f.* a rib ; hence beams or planks in a ceiling, which are as the ribs of a house : 1 Kings vi. 15, 16.

קֶרֶשׁ a board or plank : frequent in the book of Exodus, as used of the boards of the tabernacle, made to be compact or fastened together, which is probably the primary meaning of the root ; and in Num. iii. 36 ; iv. 31 : Exod. xxvi. 15, &c.

שְׂדֵרָה *f.* row, rank, of soldiers, of stories or chambers : 1 Kings vi. 9, *marg.* ' ceilings ;' "and covered the house with beams and boards of cedar ;" Heb. and covered the house, the vaultings (see *Beams*), and the piazzas or cloisters, with cedar.

BOAST

1 אָמַר to speak, say, &c. ; to speak emphatically, to relate as

great ; hence, in Hithpael, to talk big, to boast, to speak of oneself as great in any respect. HITHPAEL *fut.*

2 גָּדַל to be great. HIPHIL, to magnify : *fut.*

3 הָלַל to shine ; to make oneself shine, to boast of oneself. PIEL [a] *pret.* HITHPAEL [b] *fut.* [c] *part.*

4 יָמַר to change ; to be changed or substituted in the place of another. HITHPAEL *fut.* Isa. lxi. 6, *lit.* in their glory shall ye substitute yourselves : see Alexander in loc. The interpretation sanctioned by ancient versions and our own, supposes the form הִתְיַמֵּר to be used for הִתְאַמֵּר.

5 כָּבֵד to be heavy ; to honour, to honour oneself. HIPHIL *inf.*

6 פָּאַר to adorn, to beautify. HITHPAEL, to boast oneself, to glory, with עַל. *fut.*

1 Kings xx. 11.	3 b	Ps. xlix. 6.	3 b	Prov. xxv. 14.	3 c
2 Chron. xxv. 19.	5	lii. 1.	3 b	xxvii. 1.	3 b
Ps. x. 3.	3 a	xciv. 4.	1	Isa. x. 15.	6
xxxiv. 2.	3 b	xcvii. 7.	3 c	lxi. 6.	4
xliv. 8.	3 a	Prov. xx. 14.	3 b	Ezek. xxxv. 13.	2

BOCHIM

בָּכָה to weep. KAL *part.* Poel, Judg. ii. 1, 5, *marg.* 'weepers.'

BODY　(See also DIE, DEAD)

1 בֶּטֶן *f.* belly, the womb.

2 בָּשָׂר *m.* flesh ; the human body.

3 גַּב any part of a thing which rises above the rest ; *metaph.* eminence in point of argument or evidence. Job xiii. 12, 12, your repeating of wise sayings is dust, your best arguments are but heaps of clay ; your eminences for eminences of clay ; or the word implying that which is strong and solid, it is here asserted that the solidity of their arguments is that of clay. Gesenius, bulwarks, intrenchment.

4 גֵּו *m.* the back. [a] גֵּוָה *f.* the body. [b] גְּוִיָּה *f.* a body, a carcase.

5 גּוּפָה *f.* a dead body, corpse, so called from its hollowness. [a] גַּף *m.* body ; rendered in our version, " by himself," *marg.* 'with his body,' Exod. xxi. 3, 3, 4.

6 גֶּשֶׁם Ch. *m.* the body.

7 יָרֵךְ *f.* the thigh.

8 נְבֵלָה *f.* a carcase, bereft of life and fallen to the ground.

9 נִדְנֶה Ch. *m.* a sheath : *trop.* of the body, the sheath of the spirit.

10 נֶפֶשׁ *com.* the soul, life, &c.　Sometimes of the mere body.

11 עֶצֶם *f.* a bone ; the body in its strength, Lam. iv. 7 ; the body of heaven, the perfection, the highest degree of it, the sky in its clearness, Exod. xxiv. 10.

12 שְׁאָר *m.* see *Flesh* : *pr.* remains.

Gen. xlvii. 18.	4 b	Neh. ix. 37.	4 b	Jer. xxxvi. 30.	8
Exod. xxi. 3, 3, 4.	5 a	Job xiii. 12, 12.	3	Lam. iv. 7.	11
xxiv. 10.	11	xix. 17.	1	Ezek. i. 11, 23.	4 b
Lev. xxi. 11.α	10	xx. 25.	4 a	x. 12.	2
Num. vi. 6.β	10	Ps. lxxix. 2.	8	Dan. iii. 27, 28.	6
ix. 6, 7, 10.	10	cx. 6.	4 b	iv. 33.	6
xix. 13.γ	10	cxxxii. 11.	1	v. 21.	6
Deut. xxi. 23.	8	Prov. v. 11.	12	vii. 11.	6
xxviii. 4, 11, 18, 53.	1	xxvi. 19.	8	vii. 15.	9
xxx. 9.	1	li. 23.	4	x. 6.	4 b
Judg. viii. 30.	7	Jer. xxvi. 23.	8	Micah vi. 7.	1
1 Sam. xxxi. 10, 12, 12.	4 b	xxxiv. 20.	8	Hag. ii. 13.	10
1 Chron. x. 12, 12.	5				

[a] *lit.* souls of the dead.　　[β] *lit.* dead soul.　　[γ] *lit.* the dead, the soul of.

BOIL

שְׁחִין *m.* a burning sore, an ulcer ; the botch of Egypt is thought to be the elephantiasis, which is endemic in Egypt. It affects particularly the feet, which immediately swell up, lose their flexibility, and become stiff like the feet of elephants. It is used of the sores of the leprosy, or of the elephantiasis, Job ii. 7.—Exod. ix. 9, 10, 11, 11 : Lev. xiii. 18, 19, 20, 23 : 2 Kings xx. 7 : Job ii. 7 ; Isa. xxxviii. 21.

BOIL

1 בָּעָה to swell as a bulging wall, or a boiling pot. KAL *fut.*

2 בָּשַׁל to be cooked, ripened ; to cook. PIEL [a] *pret.* [b] *imp.* [c] *fut.* [d] *part.* [e] מְבַשְּׁלוֹת *f. pl.* boiling-places.

3 רָתַח to boil, to be hot ; of the bowels, put for commotion of mind. PIEL [a] *imp.* PUAL [b] *pret.* HIPHIL [c] *fut.* [d] רֶתַח *m.* boiling 'well,' *lit.* its boilings.

Lev. viii. 31.	2 b	Job xli. 31.	3 c	Ezek. xlvi. 20.	2 c
1 Kings xix. 21.	2 a	Isa. lxiv. 2.	1	xlvi. 23.	2 e
2 Kings vi. 29.	2 c	Ezek. xxiv. 5.	3 a d	xlvi. 24, 24.	2 d c
Job xxx. 27.	3 b				

BOLD

בָּטַח to trust ; to be assured or confident. KAL *fut.* Prov. xxviii. 1. בֶּטַח *m.* confidence : Gen. xxxiv. 25.

עֹז *m.* strength ; applied to a bold, daring, fierce temper and aspect : Eccles. viii. 1.

BOLLED

גִּבְעוֹל *m.* Exod. ix. 31, the flax was bolled, in the calyx or flower. —*Gesenius :* in the pod.—*Bush.*

BOLSTER

מְרַאֲשׁוֹת *f. pl.* pillow for the head : 1 Sam. xix. 13, 16 ; xxvi. 7, 11, 16. רַאֲשׁוֹת *m. id.* 1 Sam. xxvi. 12.

BOLT

נָעַל to make a door fast, or a place secure, with bolts and bars. KAL *pret.* 2 Sam. xiii. 18. *imp.* 2 Sam. xiii. 17.

BOND

1 אִסָּר *m.* a binding, prohibition, interdict ; a vow of abstinence. [a] אֱסָר *m.* מָסֹרֶת [b] *f.* band, bond. [c] מוֹסֵר *m.*

2 מוּסָר *m.* correction, chastisement : Job xii. 18, *i. e.* discipline, authority.

Num. xxx. 2, 3, 10,		Job xii. 18.	2	Jer. xxx. 8.	1 c
11, 12.	1	Ps. cxvi. 16.	1 c	Ezek. xx. 37.	1 b
xxx. 4, 4.	1, 1 a	Jer. v. 5.	1 c	Nah. i. 13.	1 c
xxx. 5, 7, 14.	1 a	xxvii. 2.	1 c		

BONDAGE, BONDMAN, ETC.

1 אָמָה *f.* a maidservant, a bondmaid, a bondservant.

2 כָּבַשׁ to subdue ; to bring into bondage. KAL [a] *part.* Poel. NIPHAL [b] *part.*

3 עָבַד to serve, with בּ to serve oneself upon. Hiphil, to keep in bondage. KAL [a] *fut.* [b] *part.* Poel. HIPHIL [c] *part.* [d] עֶבֶד *m.* servant, bondman, &c. [e] עֲבֹדוּת *f.* bondage. [f] עֲבוֹדָה *f.* bondage, service.

4 שִׁפְחָה *f.* a maidservant, or slave ; " a bondmaid, bondwomen."

Gen. xxi. 10, 10, 12, 13.	1	Lev. xxv. 46.	3 a	Judg. vi. 8.	3 d
xliii. 18.	3 d	xxvi. 13.	3 d	1 Kings ix. 21. a	3 b
xliv. 9, 33.	3 d	Deut. v. 6.	3 d	ix. 22.	3 d
Exod. i. 14.	3 f	vi. 12, 21.	3 d	2 Kings iv. 1.	3 d
ii. 23, 28.	3 f	vii. 8.	3 d	2 Chron. xxviii. 10,	
vi. 5.	3 c	viii. 14.	3 d	10.	3 d, 4
vi. 6, 9.	3 f	xiii. 5, 10.	3 d	Ezra ix. 8.	3 e
xiii. 3, 14.	3 d	xv. 15.	3 d	ix. 9, 9.	3 d e
xx. 2.	3 d	xvi. 12.	3 d	Neh. v. 5, 5.	2 a b
Lev. xix. 20.	4	xxiv. 18, 22.	3 d	v. 18.	3 f
xxv. 39.	3 f	xxvi. 6.	3 f	ix. 17.	3 e
xxv. 42.	3 d	xxviii. 68, 68.	3 d, 4	Esth. vii. 4, 4.	3 d, 4
xxv. 44, 44, 44.	3 d	Josh. ix. 23.	3 d	Isa. xiv. 3.	3 f
44.	3 d, 1, 3 d, 1	xxiv. 17.	3 d	Jer. xxxiv. 13.	3 d

a lit. servile tribute.

BONE

1 גֶּרֶם m. a bone ; anything hard and strong. a גֵּרֵם to break or gnaw bones. KAL pret. b גְּרַם Ch. m.

2 עֶצֶם f. a bone which is the strongest and most durable part of the body ; see *Strength*: Ezek. xxxvii. 11, our bones, our national prosperity, are dried. This is the general name for bones : Gen. ii. 23, &c. : hence also the verb עָצַם to break or gnaw bones. PIEL a pret.

3 קָנֶה m. a reed ; the channel bone. Gesenius, the upper bone of the arm, *os humeri*.

No. 2 not included.

Job xxxi. 22.	3	Prov. xxv. 15.	1	Dan. vi. 24.	1 b
xl. 18, 18.	2, 1	Jer. l. 17.	2 a	Zeph. iii. 3.	1 a
Prov. xvii. 22.	1				

BONNET

מִגְבָּעוֹת f. pl. a bonnet or turban : Exod. xxviii. 40 ; xxix. 9 ; xxxix. 28 : Lev. viii. 13.

פְּאֵר m. beauty, ornament ; a headdress, turban, worn by the priests, by the bridegroom, by women ; Isa. iii. 20 : Ezek. xliv. 18.

BOOK

דָּבָר m. a word, &c., a book, Heb. words, marg. a history ; it may be equivalent to our word journal.

סֵפֶר m. a book, letter, &c. ; narration, historical records : Gen. v. 1, &c. a סְפַר m. Ch. id. b סִפְרָה f. id.

No. 2 not included.

1 Chron. xxix. 29, 29, 29.	1	2 Chron. xxxiv. 34, 34.	1, 2	Ezra vi. 18.	2 a
2 Chron. ix. 29.	1	xxxiii. 18.	1	Ps. lvi. 8.	2 b
xii. 15.	1	Ezra iv. 15, 15.	2 a	Dan. vii. 10.	2 b

BOOTH

סֻכָּה f. tabernacle, pavilion, booth, &c. : Gen. xxxiii. 17 : Lev. xxiii. 42, 42, 43 : Neh. viii. 14, 15, 16, 17, 17 : Job xxvii. 18 : Jonah iv. 5.

BOOTY

בַּז m. prey, spoil, plundered by an enemy : Jer. xlix. 32.

מַלְקוֹחַ m. prey, especially of cattle and animals : Num. xxxi. 32.

מְשִׁסָּה f. plunder, spoil : Hab. ii. 7 : Zeph. i. 13.

BORDER

1 גָּבַל to set a bound, to be the border. KAL a fut. b גְּבוּל m. a boundary ; the limits, coasts, or confines of a place or country ; a place or country lying within its limits or borders : frequent, especially in Joshua. c גְּבוּלָה f. border, margin.

2 גְּלִילָה f. circuit, region ; a sinuous portion of land by a river.

3 יָד com. the hand ; sides or coasts of a country.

4 תוֹצָאוֹת f. pl. goings forth.

5 יַרְכָה f. a side, hinder part, as of a country.

6 כָּנָף a wing of a fowl; figuratively applied to the border of a garment.

7 מִסְגֶּרֶת f. a border or work drawn about the circumference, which enclosed the table of shewbread and the lavers in Solomon's temple.

8 נָפָה f. any district elevated and conspicuous.

9 קֵץ m. an end, extremity ; 'utmost border.' a קָצֶה m.

10 שָׂפָה f. a lip ; a border, of a vessel, of a garment, of a river, of the sea, of a country.

11 תּוֹר m. row, order ; row or string of pearls, or of gold and silver beads, as an ornament for the head.

No. 1 b not included.

Gen. xxiii. 17. a	1 b	Josh. iv. 19.	9 a	2 Kings xvi. 17.	7
xlix. 13.	1 b	xi. 13.	8	xix. 23.	9
Exod. xvi. 35.	9 a	xiii. 2.	2	1 Chron. v. 16.	4
xix. 12.	9 a	xviii. 20.	1 a	vii. 29.	3
xxv. 25, 25, 27.	7	xxii. 10, 11.	2	Ps. lxxiv. 17.	1 c
xxviii. 26.	10	Judg. vii. 22.	10	Cant. i. 11.	11
xxxvii. 12, 12, 14.	9	2 Sam. viii. 3.	9	Isa. xxxvii. 24.	9
xxxix. 19.	10	1 Kings vii. 28, 29,		Jer. l. 26.	9
Num. xv. 38, 38.	6	31, 32, 35, 36.	9	Zech. ix. 2.	1 a

a lit. border thereof.

BORE

נָקַב to bore a hole, to perforate. KAL fut. 2 Kings xii. 9 : Job xli. 2.

רָצַע to pierce through, to transfix. KAL pret. Exod. xxi. 6.

BORN (See BEAR, HOMEBORN)

בֶּטֶן f. belly, womb : Ps. lviii. 3, "as soon as they be born," marg. 'from the belly.'

בֵּן m. son : Gen. xv. 3, lit. the son of. Eccles. ii. 7, servants born, lit. sons of my house.

אֶזְרָח m. a native, one born in a place, not a foreigner, indigena, homeborn, born in the country, &c. : Exod. xii. 19, 48, 49 : Lev. xix. 34 ; xxiii. 42 ; xxiv. 16 : Num. ix. 14 ; xv. 13, 29, 30 : Josh. viii. 33 : Ezek. xlvii. 22.

BORROW

1 לָוָה to adhere to any one ; hence to borrow of any one, to be bound (*nexum esse*) as a creditor. KAL a pret. b fut. c part.

2 מָעַט to be few or little. HIPHIL fut. See Few.

3 עָבַט probably, to change, exchange ; to borrow by giving a pledge, *mutuum accipere*. KAL fut.

4 שָׁאַל to ask ; demand, petition, request. KAL a pret. b imp. c fut. d part. Paül.

Exod. iii. 22.	4 a	Deut. xv. 6.	3	Neh. v. 4.	1 a
xi. 2.	4 c	xxviii. 12.	1 b	Ps. xxxvii. 21.	1 c
xii. 35.	4 c	2 Kings iv. 3, 3.	4 b, 2	Prov. xxii. 7.	1 c
xxii. 14.	4 c	vi. 5.	4 d	Isa. xxiv. 2.	1 c

BOSOM

חֹב m. the bosom, in which we hide or cherish. See *Love*. Job xxxi. 33.

חֵיק *m.* the bosom, of a garment, of a person; or inward part of anything; the embracing of the arms to the breast is implied: it is put for the inward recesses of the mind, Eccles. vii. 9; for what is dear and tenderly cared for, Deut. xiii. 6, 2 Sam. xii. 3, Num. xi. 12; to render reproach, iniquity into the bosom, is to strike home and fill the heart with shame and sorrow, Ps. lxxix. 12, Isa. lxv. 6; to bear in the bosom is to conceal, Ps. lxxxix. 50; a gift or reward in the bosom, what is given secretly, Prov. xvii. 23, xxi. 14: this means the bosom of the garment, the open part of the tunic, or long outer robe above the girdle, into which gifts were dropped: so in Latin, *sinum laxare, et sinum expedire,* is said of those who look for rewards.—Sen. Epist. 119, Sen. Thyest. 430. —Gen. xvi. 5, &c.   חֹק *m.* Ps. lxxiv. 11, ‍כ׳.

חֹצֶן *m.* the grasp of both the arms folded and meeting before the breast, as in carrying a sheaf of corn: Ps. cxxix. 7. Gesenius, the arm, forearm, as the symbol of strength.

צַלַּחַת *f.* a dish, a bowl; hence used of the cavity of the bosom. Some understand the word in Prov. xix. 24, xxvi. 15, of the dish into which it was customary to dip the hand in eating, which a man is too slothful to raise again to his mouth.

BOSSES

גַּב *m.* anything that rises above; the middle of a shield opposed to an enemy: Job xv. 26.

BOTCH

שְׁחִין *m.* see *Boil.* Deut. xxviii. 27, 35.

BOTH

יַחְדָּו together, *lit.* they together; together at the same time: Ps. iv. 8, I lie down and sleep at once, *i. e.* under an assurance of divine protection.

שְׁנַיִם *adj. num. dual,* two: Gen. ii. 25, &c.

BOTTLE

1 אוֹב *m.* a bottle or bag to hold liquor, made of skins.

2 בַּקְבֻּק *m.* a jug or earthen vessel with a narrow mouth; from the sound which such a bottle makes when emptied.

3 חֵמֶת *m.* a bag of goat-skin, fitted to hold water and other liquors.

4 חֵמָה heat; *constr.* חֲמַת. Hos. vii. 5, *marg.* 'or, with heat through wine.'

5 נֵבֶל *m.* see *Carcase.* From the similarity of the word, Taylor supposes that it means the whole skin of a goat or bullock, made to hold wine, to be kept at home, in distinction from the lesser vessels fitted to carry abroad, and being closed, was hung on hooks or beams, and filled with wine would resemble the carcase of an animal. Thus also we may judge of the propriety of Job's comparing the clouds suspended on high to these leathern bottles, with means of drawing off the wine as wanted. The word is also used of vessels made by the potter; see *Pitcher.*

6 נֹאד *m.* a bottle, probably of skin, in which milk was shaken to make butter: it was used also for wine.

Gen. xxi. 14, 15, 19.		3	1 Sam. xxv. 18.	5	Jer. xiii. 12, 12.	5
Josh. ix. 4, 13.	6	2 Sam. xvi. 1.	5	xix. 1, 10.	2
Judg. iv. 19.	6	Job xxxii. 19.	1	xlviii. 12.	5
1 Sam. i. 24.	5	xxxviii. 37.	5	Hos. vii. 5.	4
x. 3.	5	Ps. lvi. 8.	6	Hab. ii. 15.	3
xvi. 20.	6	cxix. 83.	6		

BOTTOM

אַרְעִית Ch. *f.* the earth, or floor; the lowest part: Dan. vi. 24.

חֵיק *m.* (see *Bosom:*) the middle or inward part of anything; the hearth of an altar: Ezek. xliii. 13, 14, 17.

יְסוֹד *m.* foundation: Exod. xxix. 12, &c.

מְצוֹלָה *f.* a deep hollow place: Exod. xv. 5.   מְצֻלָה *f.* the bottom of a hollow place: Zech. i. 8.

קֶצֶב *m.* size, to which a thing is cut; also, prob. end, extremity: Jonah ii. 6, *marg.* 'cuttings off,' *i. e.* the foundations of the mountains. Vulg. *extrema montium.*

קַרְקַע *m.* the ground, floor, bottom of the sea: Amos ix. 3.

רְפִידָה *f.* that which is spread under: Cant. iii. 10, probably the frame of a couch.

שֹׁרֶשׁ *m.* a root; the lowest part of anything, bottom of the sea: Job xxxvi. 30.

BOUGH

1 אָמִיר *m.* the highest branch of a tree.

2 בֵּן *m.* a son; metaphorically, the branch is a son with respect to the tree: Gen. xlix. 22, 22, or, son of a fruitful (vine), or, a son of fructifying. See *Fruitful.*

3 חֹרֶשׁ *m.* wood, or a bough, fit to be cut for the carpenter's use.

4 סַנְסִנִּים *m. pl.* the shoot of the palm-tree, on which the fruit hangs like bunches of grapes. See *Palm.*

5 סְעַפָּה *f.* a branch, as branching out or divided from the tree.

6 סַרְעַפָּה *f.* a tender shoot, or bough.

7 עֲבֹת *com.* wreathen; boughs of a tree intertwined in each other; "thick bough."

8 עָנָף *m.* a bough, a branch full of leaves. [a] עֲנַף Ch. *m.*

9 פֹּארָה *f.* a branch or bough with leaves, *lit.* the ornament of the trees; like the Lat. *coma arborum.* [a] פֻּארָה foliage (*pr.* glory) of a tree. Hence the verb פָּאַר to search the branches, to glean; to go over the boughs. PIEL [b] *fut.*

10 פְּרִי *m.* fruit.

11 קָצִיר *m.* harvest; boughs from which a harvest is gathered.

12 שׂוֹבֶךְ *m.* thick boughs, a thicket.

13 שׂוֹךְ *m.* a bough, such as is used for hedges. [a] שׂוֹכָה *f. id.*

Gen. xlix. 22, 22.	2	Ps. lxxx. 10.	8	Ezek. xvii. 23.	8
Lev. xxiii. 40, 40.	10, 8	lxxx. 11.	11	xxxi. 3, 10, 14.	7
Deut. xxiv. 20.	9 b	Cant. vii. 8.	4	xxxi. 5.	6
Judg. ix. 48.	13 a	Isa. x. 33.	9 a	xxxi. 6, 8.	5
ix. 49.	13	xvii. 6.	1	xxxi. 12.	9
2 Sam. xviii. 9.	12	xvii. 6.	3	Dan. iv. 12.	8 a
Job xiv. 9.	11	xxvii. 11.	11		

BOUND

1 גְּבוּל *m.* see *Border.* [a] גְּבוּלָה *f. id.* גָּבַל HIPHIL, to set bounds: [b] *pret.* [c] *imp.*

2 חֹק *m.* prescribed bounds or limits as to space or time.

3 תְּאֵוָה *f.* some derive this word from תָּוָה to mark, to set out the limits of a country ; and so it is translated, Gen. xlix. 26, "utmost bound ;" but it may rather be understood of the desirable productions of the ancient hills : see *Desire* אָוָה. Thus Moses seems to explain this part of Joseph's blessing, Deut. xxxiii. 15. See Dr. Patrick.

Gen. xlix. 26.		3	Deut. xxxii. 8.		1 a	Ps. civ. 9.		1
Exod. xix. 12.		1 b	Job xiv. 5.		2	Isa. x. 13.		1 a
xix. 23.		1 c	xxvi. 10.		2	Jer. v. 22.		1
xxiii. 31.		1	xxxviii. 20.		1	Hos. v. 11.		1

BOUNTY, BOUNTIFUL

גָּמַל to reward, to deal bountifully. KAL *pret.* Ps. xiii. 6 ; cxvi. 7. *imp.* Ps. cxix. 17. *fut.* Ps. cxlii. 7.

טוֹב *adj.* good : Prov. xxii. 9.

יָד *com.* the hand : 1 Kings x. 13, *marg.* gave her 'according to the hand of king Solomon,' as became royal bounty.

שׁוֹעַ *m.* rich, opulent ; noble, liberal : Isa. xxxii. 5.

BOW

קֶשֶׁת *m.* a bow, from which arrows are discharged ; it is put for the effects of divine anger against the wicked, Lam. ii. 4, iii. 12 ; divine power, Hab. iii. 9 : applied to men, it denotes their power, and strength, and attempts to injure, Ps. xi. 2, xxxvii. 14, 15 : a bow of brass is the emblem of great power and strength, Job xx. 24 ; a deceitful bow represents a man or assistance which disappoints, like a weak or broken bow, Ps. lxxviii. 57, Hos. vii. 16 ; it is sometimes put for military armour, or for warlike strength, Ps. xliv. 6, Job xxix. 20 ; it is used for the bow in the clouds, Gen. ix. 13, &c.

BOWMAN

רָמָה to cast or throw. KAL *part.* Poel, Jer. iv. 29, *lit.* that cast with the bow. There may be something sudden and unexpected implied in the word, as it is used of that which deceives.

BOW (V)

1 אַבְרֵךְ Gen. xli. 43, "Bow the knee," *marg.* 'or, Tender father, as if compounded of אָב *m.* father, and רַךְ tender. Father of the King seems to have been a title of the chief counsellor of the state : *comp.* Gen. xlv. 8. Our translation takes the word for, HIPHIL *fut.* אַבְרִיךְ I will cause to bow the knee ; or, for הַבְרֵךְ HIPHIL *inf.* of בָּרַךְ.

2 כָּפַף to bow, to bend as the top of a bulrush, or the branches of a palm-tree ; to bow the body in worship ; *seq.* לְ to submit oneself to any one ; figuratively, to be bowed down with affliction and sorrow. KAL ᵃ*pret.* ᵇ*inf.* ᶜ*part.* Paül. NIPHAL ᵈ*fut.*

3 כָּרַע to bow the knee, to kneel ; to sink down the body by bowing the knee ; to bow in adoration ; to sink or drop down as a man that is mortally wounded ; to bow down in subjection and submission to a conqueror. KAL ᵃ*pret.* ᵇ*fut.* ᶜ*part.* Poel.

4 נָטָה to stretch out, applied to the stretching or exerting the whole body : Judg. xvi. 30, Samson bowed, stretched himself with all his might ; to the stretching or extend-

ing the several parts of the body, as the eye, Ps. xvii. 11, "they have set their eyes bowing down," or, to stretch or extend them to the earth, to the land, to every part of the country, to discover and destroy me ; or rather, to turn them away, *i. e.* our steps in the earth, to make us stumble, *comp.* Ps. lxxiii. 2 ; figuratively, the ear is bowed down to hear instruction, Prov. xxii. 17; the shoulder is bowed, extended, to bear (Gen. xlix. 15), as porters do when they receive a burden ; to the stretching out of a wall when it boweth or declineth out of the perpendicular, Ps. lxii. 3 ; so, bowing the heavens is making them stretch out or decline from their proper position, 2 Sam. xxii. 10 ; to the stretching out or extending the heart towards an object in regard, favour, mercy, compassion, 2 Sam. xix. 14. KAL ᵃ*inf.* ᵇ*fut.* ᶜ*part.* Paül. HIPHIL ᵈ*imp.* ᵉ*fut.*

5 עָוָה to turn away, to be distorted, to writhe : it is applied to distortions of the body by racking pains. NIPHAL *pret.*

6 עָוַת to be crooked, applied to the body. HITHPAEL *pret.*

7 קָדַד to bow or stoop low with the head in order to do honour to a person : it is usually followed by הִשְׁתַּחֲוָה KAL *fut.*

8 שׁוּחַ to sink down ; to be bowed down. KAL *pret.*

9 שָׁחָה to bow down ; to sink down ; HITHPAEL (with a doubling of the third radical), to bow down, to prostrate oneself, as a testimony of respect and reverence, προσκυνεῖν ; often with the addition of אַפַּיִם אַרְצָה with the face to the earth. The person before whom one prostrates himself is preceded by לְ, more rarely by לִפְנֵי. This token of respect was shown sometimes to equals, sometimes to superiors, kings, and princes, and especially to the Deity ; hence to worship, to adore. KAL ᵃ*imp.* HITHPAEL ᵇ*pret.* ᶜ*inf.* ᵈ*fut.*

10 שָׁחַח to stoop, bow down, couch ; to be brought low, bowed down (with sorrow) ; to sink : Hab. iii. 6. KAL ᵃ*pret.* NIPHAL ᵇ*fut.*

Gen. xviii. 2.	9 d	Ruth ii. 10.	9 d	Ps. xvii. 11.	4 a
xix. 1.	9 d	1 Sam. iv. 19.	3 b	xviii. 9.	4 b
xxiii. 7, 12.	9 d	xx. 41.	9 d	xxii. 29.	3 b
xxiv. 26, 48.	7	xxiv. 8.	9 d	xxxi. 2.	4 d
xxvii. 29, 29.	9 d	xxv. 23, 41.	9 d	xxxv. 14.	10 a
xxxiii. 3, 6, 7, 7.	9 d	xxviii. 14.	9 d	xxxvii. 6.	10 a
xxxvii. 10.	9 c	2 Sam. ix. 8.	9 d	xliv. 25.	8
xli. 43.	1	xiv. 22, 33.	9 d	lvii. 6.a	2 a
xlii. 6.	9 d	xviii. 21.	9 d	lxii. 3.	4 c
xliii. 26.	9 d	xix. 14.	4 e	lxxii. 9.	3 b
xlvii. 31.	7	xxii. 10.	4 b	lxxxvi. 1.	4 d
xlviii. 12.	9 d	xxiv. 20.	9 d	xcv. 6.	3 b
xlix. 8.	9 d	1 Kings i. 16, 31.	7	cxliv. 5.	4 d
xlix. 8.	4 b	i. 23, 47, 53.	9 d	cxlv. 14.	2 c
xlix. 15.	7	ii. 19.	9 d	cxlvi. 8.	2 c
Exod. iv. 31.	7	ii. 18.	3 a	Prov. v. 1.	4 d
xi. 8.	9 b	xix. 18.	7	xiv. 19.	10 a
xii. 27.	7	2 Kings ii. 15.	9 d	xxii. 17.	4 d
xx. 5.	9 d	iv. 37.	9 d	Eccles. xii. 3.	6
xxiii. 24.	9 d	v. 18, 18.	9 b c	Isa. ii. 9.	10 b
xxxiv. 8.	9 d	xvii. 35.	9 d	ii. 11, 17.	10 a
Lev. xxvi. 1.	9 c	xix. 16.	4 d	x. 4.	3 a
Num. xxii. 31.	7	1 Chron. xxi. 21.	9 d	xxi. 3.	5
xxv. 2.	9 d	xxix. 20.	7	xlv. 23.	3 b
Deut. v. 9.	9 d	2 Chron. vii. 3.	3 b	xlvi. 1, 2.	3 a
Josh. xxiii. 7.	9 d	xx. 18.	7	xlix. 23.	9 d
xxiii. 16.	9 b	xxv. 14.	9 d	li. 23.	9 a
Judg. ii. 12, 17.	9 c	xxix. 29.	3 a	lviii. 5.	2 b
ii. 19.	9 c	xxxv. 30.	7	lx. 14.	9 b
v. 27, 27, 27.	3 a	Neh. viii. 6.	7	lxv. 12.	3 b
vii. 5.	3 b	Esth. iii. 2, 2.	3 b	Micah vi. 6.	2 d
vii. 6.	3 a	iii. 5.	3 c	Hab. iii. 6.	10 a
xvi. 30.	4 b	Job xxxi. 10.	3 b		
		xxxix. 3.	3 b		

a or, he (the enemy) bows down.

BOWELS

מֵעִים the bowels; figuratively, the innermost recesses of the mind; the affections, tenderness, pity, compassion: Gen. xv. 4, &c.

קֶרֶב *m.* the middle or inward part; the inner part of the body: Ps. cix. 18, *marg.* or, 'within him.'

רַחֲמִים *m. pl.* the chief intestines; tender love or affection, chiefly towards relatives; favour, grace; mercy, compassion: Gen. xliii. 30: 1 Kings iii. 26.

BOWL

1   גְּבִיעַ *m.* a cup, goblet, bowl, of a large size. See *Pot.*

2   גֻּלָּה *f.* anything round; a bowl of chapiters; of the candle-stick. ᵃ גֹּל *m.* a bowl, oil-vessel of a lamp.

3   מִזְרָק *m.* large bason or bowl which received the blood of the sacrifices, and out of which it was sprinkled upon the altar, &c. Any bason or bowl of a like or large size.

4   מְנַקִּיּוֹת *f. pl.* sacrificial dishes, bowls for libation. Ainsworth shows, from Hebrew doctors, that they were reeds of gold laid between the shewbread cakes, to admit the air and keep them clear of mustiness.

5   סַף *m.* a bason; also, a threshold, which is sometimes worn hollow in the middle, and may have given the name to some particular kind of cup.

6   סֵפֶל *m.* a dish, probably shallow in form.

Exod. xxv. 29.	4	Judg. vi. 38.	6	Jer. iii. 18, 19.		3
xxv. 31, 33, 34.	1	1 Kings vii. 41, 41, 42.	2	Amos vi. 6.		3
xxxvii. 16.	4	vii. 50.	5	Zech. iv. 2.		2 a
xxxvii. 17, 19, 19, 20.	1	2 Kings xii. 13.	5	iv. 3.		2
Num. iv. 7.	4	xxv. 15.	3	ix. 15.		3
vii. 13, 19, 25, 31, 37,		1 Chron. xxviii. 17.	3	xiv. 20.		3
43, 49, 55, 61, 67,		Eccles. xii. 6.	2			
73, 79, 84, 85.	3					

BOX

פַּךְ *m.* a vial, flask, bottle: 2 Kings ix. 1, 3.

BOX-TREE

תְּאַשּׁוּר *m.* name of a tree which the ancient versions render variously, cedar, fir, poplar, &c.; most probably a species of cedar of Lebanon, called in the East, *sherbin*: Isa. xli. 19; lx. 13.

BOY

יֶלֶד *m.* a child, a young man: Joel iii. 3: Zech. viii. 5.

נַעַר *m.* a young person: Gen. xxv. 27.

BOZRAH

בָּצְרָה *f.* a fold, a sheepfold; or a fortress, stronghold; one of the chief cities of the Edomites: Mic. ii. 12.

BRACELET

חָח see *Chain.* Probably a hook or pin for securing the garment round the neck: Exod. xxxv. 22.

פָּתִיל *m.* a thread, string, cord: used of the cord by which the orientalist suspends his seal-ring; see *Signet.* Gen. xxxviii. 18, 25.

צָמִיד *m.* a bracelet, where two parts are joined or fastened together: Gen. xxiv. 22, 30, 47: Num. xxxi. 50: Ezek. xvi. 11; xxiii. 42.

אֶצְעָדָה *f.* clasp, bracelet; for the arm: 2 Sam. i. 10.

שֵׁרוֹת *f.* chains, bracelets: Isa. iii. 19.

BRAMBLE

אָטָד *m.* a brier or bramble: Judg. ix. 14, 15, 15.

חוֹחַ *m.* see *Thorns, Thickets*: Isa. xxxiv. 13.

BRANCH

1   אָמִיר *m.* the highest branch of a tree.

2   בַּדִּים *m. pl.* staves, bars; large strong branches.

3   בֵּן *m.* a son; metaphorically, the branch is a son with respect to the tree.

4   בַּת *f.* daughter.

5   דָּלִיּוֹת *f. pl.* branches that hang down. See *Draw.*

6   זְמוֹרָה *f.* a branch pruned or cut off; vine-branch. ᵃ זָמִיר *m.* Gesenius, song of triumph; which is clearly the sense in Isa. xxv. 5.

7   יוֹנֶקֶת *f.* a tender branch, deriving its nutriment from the tree.

8   כַּף *f.* the branch of a palm-tree, which hangs down or bends over, resembling a hand partly closed. ᵃ כִּפָּה *f.* a palm branch, and any similar branch. "Branch and rush" seems to be a proverbial expression for the highest and lowest. It is to be remarked that כַּף means both the palm of the hand and a branch of the palm-tree, as *palma* in Latin.

9   נְטִישׁוֹת *f. pl.* that which is spread abroad and extended: it is applied to branches of the vine spreading wide and extended.

10   נֵצֶר *m.* a slip, scion, or young sucker of a tree, selected and reserved for planting, and which when planted required to be attended and guarded with care; *metaph.* a descendant of a family: Isa. xi. 1, of the Messiah. Nazareth or Nazarene is supposed to be derived from this root.

11   סָעִיף *m.* a branch as dividing itself from the tree.

12   עֲבֹת *com.* wreathen; bushy boughs of trees interwoven with each other.

13   עָלֶה *m.* a leaf, a branch, from its sprouting forth.

14   עָנָף *m.* a bough, a branch full of leaves. ᵃ עֲנַף Ch. *m. id.* ᵇ עָנֵף *adj.* 'full of branches.'

15   עֳפָאִים *m. pl.* boughs, foliage.

16   פֹּארָה *f. pl.* branches, as the ornament of a tree; as in Latin *coma arborum.*

17   צֶמַח *m.* that which springeth up, a shoot, a branch. The Messiah is a Branch of Jehovah, either as to his eternal generation, or as the restorer of his chosen people.

18   קָנֶה *m.* a reed, stalk, branch: in this rendering only applied to the branches of the candlestick in the tabernacle: Exod. xxv. 31, &c.; xxx. 23; xxxvii. 17, &c.

19   קָצִיר *m.* harvest, a branch from which a harvest is gathered. The most flourishing circumstances, or the height of temporal prosperity, is implied.

20 שִׁבֹּלֶת *f.* ears of corn, or branches, from mounting up or spreading out.

21 שְׁלֻחוֹת *f. pl.* shoots, branches, tendrils.

22 שָׂרִיגִים *m. pl.* vine-branches, from their interweaving with each other.

23 צַמֶּרֶת *f.* highest branch. See *High.*

No. 18 not included.

Gen. xl. 10, 12.	22	Isa. xi. 1.	10	Ezek. xvii. 8.	14
xlix. 22.	4	xiv. 19.	10	xix. 10.	14 b
Lev. xxiii. 40.	8	xvi. 8.	21	xix. 11, 11.	12, 5
Num. xiii. 23.	6	xvii. 6.	11	xiv. 14.	2
Neh. viii. 15, 15, 15,		xvii. 9.	1	xxxi. 3.	14
15, 15.	13	xviii. 5.	9	xxxi. 5, 6, 8, 13.	16
Job viii. 16.	7	xix. 15.	8 a	xxxi. 7, 9, 12.	5
xiv. 7.	7	xxv. 5.	6 a	xxxvi. 8.	14
xv. 30.	7	xxvii. 10.	11	Dan. iv. 14, 14, 21.	14 a
xv. 32.	8 a	lx. 21.	10	xi. 7.	10
xviii. 16.	19	Jer. xi. 16.	5	Hos. xi. 6.	2
xxix. 19.	19	xxiii. 5.	17	xiv. 8.	7
Ps. lxxx. 11.	7	xxxiii. 15.	17	Joel i. 7.	22
lxxv. 15.	3	Ezek. viii. 17.	6	Nah. ii. 2.	6
civ. 12.	15	xv. 2.	6	Zech. iii. 8.	17
Prov. xi. 28.	13	xvii. 3, 22.	23	iv. 12.	20
Isa. iv. 2.	17	xvii. 6, 6.	5, 2	vi. 12.	17
ix. 14.	8 a	xvii. 7, 23.	5	Mal. iv. 1.	14

BRAND

אוּד *m.* a firebrand; a brand partly consumed but snatched from the fire: Zech. iii. 2.

לַפִּיד *m.* a burning lamp or torch: Judg. xv. 5.

BRANDISH

עוּף to fly; to whirl about. POLEL *inf.* Ezek. xxxii. 10.

BRASS

נְחָשׁ Ch. *m.* Dan. ii. 32, 35, 39, 45; iv. 15, 23; v. 4, 23; vii. 19. נְחֹשֶׁת *com.* brass, brasen; copper seems frequently intended, when translated brass, and may therefore be the proper meaning of the word, as brass is a factitious preparation: figuratively, that which is common and vile, in opposition to that which is more pure and precious, as silver and gold, which represent truth and excellency: Isa. i. 22. This word occurs frequently. נָחוּשׁ *adj.* Job vi. 12, *marg.* 'brasen.' נְחוּשָׁה *f. id.* Lev. xxvi. 19: Job xxviii. 2; xl. 18; xli. 27: Isa. xlv. 2; xlviii. 4: Mic. iv. 13.

BRAVERY

תִּפְאָרָה *f.* ornament, splendour, beauty: Isa. iii. 18, perhaps used ironically.

BRAWLING

מִדְיָנִים *m. pl.* contentions, Prov. xxi. 9; xxv. 24. מָדוֹן *m. id.* 'p.

BRAY

כָּתַשׁ to bray in a mortar. KAL *fut.* Prov. xxvii. 22.

נָהַק to bray as an ass, to make a foul noise. KAL *fut.* Job vi. 5; xxx. 7.

BREACH

1 בֶּדֶק *m.* a crack, chink, or breach in a building that needs to be repaired.

2 בָּקַע (see *Break*); to make a breach. PUAL [a] *part.* HIPHIL [b] *fut.* [c] בָּקִיעַ *m.* a breach.

3 תְּנוּאָה *f.* a forsaking, withdrawing; "breach of promise."

4 פֶּרֶץ to break forth. KAL [a] *pret.* [b] *part.* Paül. [c] פֶּרֶץ *m.* a gap, breach; a breaking out of water; a breaking in upon, a sudden and destructive attack; an overthrow. [d] מִפְרָץ *m.* haven, harbour.

5 רְסִיסִים *m. pl.* droppings.

6 שֶׁבֶר *m.* a breaking; a wound, injury, breach; ruin, destruction, of a state, or persons.

Gen. xxxviii. 29.	4 c	2 Kings xxii. 5.	1	Isa. xxii. 9.	2 c
Lev. xxiv. 20, 20.	6	1 Chron. xiii. 11.	4 a c	xxx. 13.	4 c
Num. xiv. 34.	3	xv. 13.	4 a	xxx. 26.	6
Judg. v. 17.	4 d	Neh. iv. 7.	4 b	lviii. 12.	4 c
xxi. 15.	4 c	vi. 1.	4 c	Jer. xiv. 17.	6
2 Sam. v. 20.	4 c	Job xvi. 14, 14.	4 c	Lam. ii. 13.	2 a
vi. 8.	4 a c	Ps. lx. 2.	6	Ezek. xxvi. 10.	2 a
1 Kings xi. 27.	4 c	cvi. 23.	4 c	Amos iv. 3.	4 c
2 Kings xii. 5, 5, 6, 7,		Prov. xv. 4.	6	vi. 11.	5
7, 8, 12.	1	Isa. vii. 6.	2 b	ix. 11.	4 c

BREAD (See also UNLEAVENED)

לֶחֶם *m. pr.* bread; also any kind of victuals, meat, provision, whether bread, flesh, or fruit, Jer. xi. 19; but bread is principally intended, as the eastern people are in general great eaters of bread; it being computed, saith Dr. Shaw in his Travels, that three persons in four live upon it, or upon such compositions as are made of barley and wheat flour: bread is put for corn, of which bread is made, Isa. xxviii. 28. Figuratively, provision for the mind, good instructions and principles by which it is nourished, refreshed, and made happy: Prov. ix. 5: Isa. lv. 2. Bread of men, Ezek. xxiv. 17, 22, that which is sent to near friends, &c. in a time of mourning, called in the Targum the bread of mourning. Bread of God, *i. e.* sacrifices, Lev. xxi. 6, 8, 17, 21, 22. This, the only word translated bread, occurs frequently; Lev. xxi. 17, *marg.* 'food,' &c.

BREADTH

מִדְרָךְ *m.* a place which is trodden: Deut. ii. 5.

כַּף *f.* palm of the hand, sole of the foot: Deut. ii. 5.

פְּתָי Ch. *m.* width, breadth: Ezra vi. 3: Dan. iii. 1.

רֹחַב *m.* largeness, breadth; frequent. רַחַב *m.* a broad place: Job xxxviii. 18. מֶרְחָב *m.* a large place: Hab. i. 6.

BREAK

1 אָבַד to perish. KAL *part.* Poel.

2 אוֹר to be or become light, of the break of day. NIPHAL *fut.*

3 בָּקַע to cleave asunder, to rend, divide; to lay open anything enclosed that it may break forth, as light, waters, &c.; to break in or penetrate, *seq.* בְּ; to break through, *seq.* אֶל. KAL [a] *fut.* NIPHAL [b] *pret.* [c] *fut.* HIPHIL [d] *inf.* HOPHAL [e] *pret.*

4 נִיחַ or נֻוחַ to break or burst forth. KAL *inf.*

5 גָּרַם to break bones: also to gnaw or pick them; hence to lick: Ezek. xxiii. 34, "Thou shalt drink it (the cup) and suck it out, and break (or, lick) the sherds thereof." PIEL *fut.*

6   גָּרַם   to bruise, to wear, to weaken, to unfit for action and for use. KAL [a]*pret.* HIPHIL [b]*fut.*

7   דּוּק   Ch. to bruise. P'AL *pret.*

8   דּוּשׁ   to bruise, to crush by treading. KAL *fut.*

9   דָּכָא   to bray, bruise, and break into small pieces: the word implies the solidity of that which is so broken, and with that its entire comminution, the being crushed: as applied to the mind it imports debility of tone, the breaking down of stubbornness, the spirit bruised and broken as with a hammer, made contrite. PIEL [a]*pret.* [b]*fut.* PUAL [c]*fut.* [d]*part.*

10   דְּקַק   Ch. to bruise and beat very small. P'AL [a]*pret.* APHEL [b]*pret.* [c]*fut.* [d]*part.*

11   דָּכָה   nearly of the same signification as דָּכָא. NIPHAL [a]*pret.* PIEL [b]*pret.*

12   הָיָה   to be. NIPHAL *pret.*

13   הָלַם   to smite or strike as with a hammer, to beat the ground with the hoof, to smite. KAL [a]*pret.* [b]*fut.*

14   הָמַם   to vex, to destroy, to discomfit. KAL *pret.* Isa. xxviii. 28. Ges., or drive the wheels of his (threshing) car.

15   הָרַס   to pull or tear down; to tear out; to overthrow, demolish; to break through: applied to the rushing and pressure of a crowd, who trample down every fence or barrier: Exod. xix. 21. KAL [a]*pret.* [b]*imp.* [c]*fut.* [d]*part.* Poel. [e]*part.* Paül. NIPHAL [f]*pret.*

16   חָלַל   to penetrate, to wound, to slay (see *Slay*); hence to dissolve, to make void (see *Profane*). Agreeably to this sense, Bp. Pearson on the Creed (after Grotius) says: " One ancient custom of cancelling bonds was by striking a nail through the writing;" to which the apostle may allude: Col. ii. 14. PIEL [a]*pret.* [b]*fut.* HIPHIL [c]*fut.*

17   חָתַת   to be broken, so as to be quite disabled; applied to a bow that is broken and deprived of its elasticity and spring to throw the arrow, 1 Sam. ii. 4, 2 Sam. xxii. 35 (see נָחַת); applied to a nation, people, or person, that is quite broken, and disabled from doing either good or evil, Isa. vii. 8, 1 Sam. ii. 10; or that is rendered weak, dispirited, and incapable in any or in every respect of resisting an enemy or defending themselves, Jer. xlviii. 20.—*Taylor.* KAL [a]*pret.* [b]*imp.* NIPHAL [c]*fut.* PIEL [d]*pret.* HIPHIL [e]*pret.* [f] חַת *adj.* broken.

18   יָצָא   to go out; to break out. KAL *fut.*

19   כָּאָה   to be made sad, to be dispirited; to be dejected and broken, or wounded in spirit. NIPHAL *part.*

20   כָּתַת   to beat, to crush, to knock in pieces. KAL [a]*inf.* PIEL [b]*pret.*

21   מַחְתֶּרֶת   *f.* a breaking in.

22   מָרוֹחַ   *adj. m. const.* broken, *i. e.* bruised.

23   נָאַף   to commit adultery; to break (wedlock). KAL *part.* Poel.

24   נוֹא   the true meaning of this word seems to be, to disallow, reject, refuse; it usually applies to persons: so the construction of HIPHIL *pret.* Ps. cxli. 5, may be, Let not my head reject it, according to Schmidt and others.

25   נָחַת   to come down; to cause to come down, as the bow when it is about to be used. PIEL *pret.*

26   נִיר   to till, to cultivate; applied in a moral sense. KAL *imp.*

27   נָכָא   *adj.* that which is smitten or wounded.

28   מַסָּח   *m.* a removing, a keeping off, a people, a crowd; which is admitted by critics to be the force of the word in 2 Kings xi. 6, *lit.* by keeping off; *comp.* ver. 8.

29   נָפַץ   to dash, to break and shatter, so as to scatter abroad and disperse all the parts and pieces. KAL [a]*inf.* [b]*part.* Paül. PIEL [c]*pret.* [d]*fut.*

30   נָתַע   to strike out: the same with נָתַץ by a change of the last letter. NIPHAL *pret.*

31   נָתַץ   to tear down, to destroy, *e. g.* buildings, walls, &c.; to break or strike out. KAL [a]*pret.* [b]*inf.* [c]*fut.* NIPHAL [d]*pret.* PIEL [e]*pret.* [f]*fut.* HOPHAL [g]*fut.*

32   נָתַק   to draw or pull asunder; to separate what is joined together: applied to the breaking of a string, cord, or ligature; figuratively, to the pulling or snapping asunder a chain, or purposes or designs formed in the mind: Job xvii. 11. KAL [a]*part.* Paül. NIPHAL [b]*pret.* [c]*fut.* PIEL [d]*fut.*

33   עָבַט   to change. PIEL *fut.*

34   עָלָה   to rise, ascend. KAL [a]*pret.* [b]*inf.* NIPHAL [c]*inf.* of the breaking up of an army, with מֵעַל.

35   עָרַף   to break the neck; to throw down an altar by taking away the top. KAL [a]*pret.* [b]*fut.*

36   עָרַר   to make bare, to destroy, by making bare to the foundation. PILPEL [a]*inf.* [b]*fut.*

37   עָרַץ   to terrify, to make afraid; to break terribly, to break with power. KAL *fut.*

38   פּוּחַ   to blow, to breathe. KAL *fut.* " until the day break," becomes cool in the evening.

39   פּוּץ   to smite or dash in pieces. POLEL *fut.*

40   פּוּר   to break; Hiphil, to break; figuratively, to violate. HIPHIL *pret.*

41   פָּצַח   to break in pieces with a noise; to break out into joy. KAL [a]*pret.* [b]*imp.* [c]*fut.* PIEL [d]*pret.*

42   פָּצַם   only in PIEL, to break, cleave: *pret.*

43   פָּרַח   to break out, as a bud or blossom; used also of sores, or the leprosy. KAL [a]*pret.* [b]*inf.* abroad. [c]*fut.* [d]*part.* Poel.

44   פָּרַץ   to tear or break forth, to break down a wall; to disperse, or spread abroad; to break in, in mining; with בְ to break in, or cause an overthrow among a people; applied to a sudden and destructive bursting forth of judgments; to act with violence; to break away. KAL [a]*pret.* [b]*inf.* [c]*fut.* [d]*part.* Poel. [e]*part.* Paül. PUAL [f]*part.* HITHPAEL [g]*part.* [h] פֶּרֶץ *m.* breach of a wall; dispersion.

45   פָּרַק   to break off with rending; construed with מֵעַל; Piel, to tear off; Hithpael, to break off from oneself. KAL [a]*pret.* PIEL [b]*imp.* HITHPAEL [c]*pret.* [d]*imp.* [e]*fut.* פְּרַק Ch. P'AL [f]*imp.*

46 פָּרַר to break, to violate; to annul a covenant. See נוֹא. PILPEL [a]*fut.* to break asunder. HIPHIL [b]*pret.* [c]*inf.* [d]*imp.* [e]*fut.* HOPHAL [f]*fut.*

47 פָּרַשׂ to spread or stretch out; to break, divide in pieces. KAL *part.* Poel.

48 פָּתַח to open. NIPHAL *fut.*

49 צָלַח to pass on or through, to advance, to fall on. KAL *fut.*

50 קוּר to dig, particularly for water. PILPEL, to destroy, to overturn by digging under: *part.*

51 רָגַע to shake, to tremble; to burst, to divide with a noise. KAL *pret.* Job vii. 5. Very different interpretations are given of this word, and it is not easy to arrive at the primary meaning. Jerome renders it *aruit*, dries up. Goode thinks it includes the idea of stiffness, rigidity.

52 רוּץ to run. KAL *fut.* 2 Kings xxiii. 12, *marg.* 'ran down.'

53 רָעָה to feed, to feed on. KAL *fut.* Jer. ii. 16, *lit.* have fed on thee (as to) the head, implying great devastation.

54 רָעַע to break or dash in pieces; to make good for nothing; to be reduced to a weak and wretched condition, to be ruined. KAL [a]*pret.* [b]*inf.* [c]*fut.* HITHPOLEL [d]*pret.* רְעַע Ch. P'AL [e]*part.* [f] רֹעָה *f.* a breakage.

55 רָצַץ to dash in pieces; to oppress, treat with violence. KAL [a]*fut.* [b]*part.* Paül. NIPHAL [c]*pret.* [d]*fut.* PIEL [e]*pret.* HIPHIL [f]*fut.*

56 שָׂדַד to harrow, to break clods. PIEL *fut.*

57 שְׁבָבִים *m. pl.* small pieces.

58 שָׁבַר to break, a bow, a bone, an earthen vessel, a ship in a storm; a nation is broken when its power is weakened or ruined; the limbs of an animal are broken when disabled; Lev. xxi. 19, Zech. xi. 16; Ezek. xxi. 6, "with the breaking of thy loins," *i.e.* walking as if thy loins were broken or disabled: pride is broken when humbled; broken in heart are the humble and truly penitent, Ps. cxlvii. 3; the heart is also broken when quite dispirited and discouraged, Ps. lxix. 20. In this sense it is applied, speaking after the manner of men, to the great God, Ezek. vi. 9: "I am broken," *Heb.* have been broken, quite tired out, "with their whorish heart," and despairing, as it were, of their amendment, have sent them into captivity.—*Taylor.* In reference to Job xxxviii. 10, Gesenius adds, to measure off, to define; which accords with the marginal rendering, but is of doubtful authority. KAL [a]*pret.* [b]*inf.* [c]*imp.* [d]*fut.* [e]*part.* Poel. [f]*part.* Paül. NIPHAL [g]*pret.* [h]*inf.* [i]*fut.* [k]*part.* PIEL [l]*pret.* [m]*inf.* [n]*fut.* [o]*part.* [p] שֶׁבֶר *m.* Job xli. 25, breakings, *i.e.* terrors. [q] שִׁבָּרוֹן *m.* a breaking. [r] מַשְׁבֵּר *m.* place of breaking forth.

59 שׁוּף to break upon, to batter and bruise. See *Bruise.* KAL *fut.*

60 תְּבַר Ch. P'AL *part.* broken, fragile, frail.

Gen. vii. 11.	3 b
xvii. 14.	46 b
xix. 9.	58 b
xxvii. 40.	45 a
xxxii. 24.	34 b
xxxii. 26.	34 a
Gen. xxxviii. 29.	44 a
Exod. ix. 9, 10.	43 d
ix. 25.	58 l
xii. 46.	58 d
xiii. 13.	35 a
xix. 21.	15 c
Exod. xix. 22.	44 c
xix. 24, 24.	15 c, 44 c
xxii. 2.	21
xxii. 6.	18
xxiii. 24.	58 m n
xxxii. 2.	45 b
Exod. xxxii. 3.	45 e
xxxii. 19.	58 n
xxxii. 24.	45 d
xxxiv. 1.	58 l
xxxiv. 13.	58 n
xxxiv. 20.	35 a
Lev. vi. 28.	58 i
xi. 33.	58 d
xi. 35.	31 g
xiii. 12. α	43 b c
xiii. 20, 25.	43 a
xiv. 43.	43 a
xiv. 45.	31 a
xv. 12.	58 i
xxi. 19, 19.	58 p
xxi. 20.	22
xxii. 22.	58 f
xxii. 24.	32 a
xxvi. 13.	58 d
xxvi. 15, 44.	46 c
xxvi. 19.	58 a
xxvi. 26.	58 b
Num. ix. 12.	58 d
xv. 31.	46 b
xxiv. 8.	5
xxx. 2.	16 c
Deut. vii. 5.	58 n
ix. 17.	58 n
x. 2.	58 l
xii. 3.	58 l
xxxi. 16, 20.	46 b
Judg. ii. 1.	46 e
v. 22.	13 a
vii. 19.	29 a
vii. 20.	58 d
viii. 9.	31 c
ix. 53. β	55 f
xvi. 9, 9.	32 d c
xvi. 12.	32 d
1 Sam. ii. 4.	17 f
ii. 10.	17 c
iv. 18.	58 i
xxv. 10.	44 g
2 Sam. ii. 32. γ	2
v. 20.	44 a
xxii. 35. δ	25
xxiii. 16.	3 a
1 Kings xv. 19.	46 d
xviii. 30.	15 e
xix. 11.	58 o
xxii. 48.	58 g
2 Kings iii. 26.	3 d
x. 27, 27.	31 c
xi. 6.	28
xi. 18, 18.	31 c, 58 l
xiv. 13.	44 c
xviii. 4, 4.	58 l, 20 b
xxiii. 7.	31 c
xxiii. 8, 15.	31 a
xxiii. 12.	55 a, or 52
xxiii. 14.	58 l
xxv. 4.	3 c
xxv. 10.	31 a
xxv. 13.	58 l
1 Chron. xi. 18.	3 a
xiv. 11, 11.	44 a h
2 Chron. xiv. 3.	58 n
xvi. 3.	46 d
xx. 37, 37.	44 a, 58 i
xxi. 17.	3 a
xxiii. 17, 17.	31 c, 58 l
xxiv. 7.	44 a
xxv. 12.	3 b
xxv. 23.	44 c
xxvi. 6.	44 c
xxxi. 1.	58 n
xxxii. 5.	44 e
xxxiii. 3.	31 e
xxxiv. 4, 4.	31 f, 58 l
xxxiv. 7.	31 f
xxxvi. 19.	31 f
Ezra ix. 14. ε	46 c
Neh. i. 3.	44 f
ii. 13.	44 e
iv. 3.	44 a
Job iv. 10.	30
vii. 5.	51
ix. 17.	59
xii. 14.	15 c
xiii. 25.	37
xvi. 12.	46 a
xvi. 14.	44 c
xvii. 11.	32 b
xix. 2.	9 b
xxii. 9.	9 c
xxiv. 20.	58 i
Job xxviii. 4.	44 a
xxix. 17.	58 n
xxx. 14.	44 h
xxxi. 22.	58 i
xxxiv. 24.	54 c
xxxviii. 8.	4
xxxviii. 10.	58 d
xxxviii. 15.	58 i
xxxix. 15.	8
xli. 25.	58 p
Ps. ii. 3.	32 d
ii. 9.	54 c
iii. 7.	58 l
x. 15.	58 c
xviii. 34. δ	25
xxix. 5, 5.	58 e n
xxxi. 12.	1
xxxiv. 18.	58 k
xxxiv. 20.	58 g
xxxvii. 15, 17.	58 i
xxxviii. 8.	11 a
xliv. 19.	11 b
xlvi. 9.	58 n
xlviii. 7.	58 n
li. 8.	11 b
li. 17, 17.	58 k
lv. 20.	16 a
lviii. 6, 6.	15 b, 31 b
lx. 2.	42
lxix. 20.	58 a
lxxii. 4.	9 b
lxxiv. 6.	13 b
lxxiv. 13.	58 l
lxxiv. 14.	55 e
lxxvi. 3.	58 l
lxxx. 12.	44 a
lxxxix. 10.	9 a
lxxxix. 31, 34.	16 b
lxxxix. 40.	44 a
xciv. 5.	9 b
cv. 16.	58 a
cv. 33.	58 n
cvi. 29.	44 c
cvii. 14.	32 d
cvii. 16.	58 l
cix. 16.	19
cxix. 20.	6 a
cxxiv. 7.	58 g
cxli. 5.	24
cxliv. 14.	44 h
cxlvii. 3.	58 f
Prov. iii. 20.	3 b
vi. 15.	58 c
xv. 13.	27
xvii. 22.	27
xxiv. 31.	15 f
xxv. 15.	58 d
xxv. 19.	54 f
xxv. 28.	44 e
Eccles. iii. 3.	44 b
iv. 12.	32 c
x. 8.	44 d
xii. 6, 6, 6.	55 a, 58 i, 55 c
Cant. ii. 17.	38
iv. 6.	38
Isa. v. 5.	44 b
v. 27.	32 b
vii. 8.	17 c
viii. 9, 9, 9.	17 b
viii. 15.	58 g
ix. 4.	17 e
xiv. 5.	58 a
xiv. 7.	41 a
xiv. 25.	58 b
xiv. 29.	58 g
xvi. 8.	13 a
xix. 10.	9 d
xxi. 9.	58 l
xxii. 5.	50
xxii. 10.	31 c
xxiv. 5.	46 b
xxiv. 10.	58 g
xxiv. 19.	54 b d
xxvii. 11.	58 i
xxviii. 13.	58 g
xxviii. 24.	56
xxviii. 28.	14
xxx. 13.	58 p
xxx. 14, 14, 14.	58 a p, 20 a
xxxiii. 8.	46 b
xxxiii. 20.	32 c
xxxv. 6.	3 b
xxxvi. 6.	55 b
xxxviii. 13.	58 n
Isa. xlii. 3.	58 d
xliv. 23.	14 b
xlv. 2.	58 n
xlix. 13.	41 b
lii. 9.	41 b
liv. 1.	41 b
liv. 3.	44 c
lv. 12.	41 c
lviii. 6.	32 d
lviii. 8.	3 c
lix. 5.	3 c
lxi. 1.	58 k
Jer. i. 14.	48
ii. 13.	58 k
ii. 16.	53
ii. 20.	58 a
iv. 3.	26
iv. 26.	31 d
v. 5.	58 a
x. 20.	32 b
xi. 10.	46 b
xi. 16.	54 a
xiv. 17.	58 g
xiv. 21.	46 e
xv. 12.	54 c
xix. 10.	58 a
xix. 11, 11.	58 d
xxii. 28.	29 b
xxiii. 9.	58 g
xxiii. 29.	39
xxviii. 2, 13.	58 a
xxviii. 4, 10, 11.	58 d
xxviii. 12.	58 b
xxx. 8.	58 d
xxxi. 28.	31 b
xxxi. 32.	46 b
xxxiii. 20.	46 e
xxxiii. 21.	46 f
xxxvii. 11.	34 c
xxxix. 2.	3 e
xxxix. 8.	31 a
xliii. 13.	58 l
xlv. 4.	15 d
xlviii. 12.	29 d
xlviii. 17, 25.	58 g
xlviii. 20, 39.	17 a
xlviii. 38.	58 a
xlix. 35.	58 e
l. 2, 2.	17 a
l. 23.	58 i
li. 20, 21, 21, 22, 22, 22, 23, 23, 23.	29 c
li. 30.	58 g
li. 56.	17 d
li. 58.	36 a b
lii. 7.	3 c
lii. 14.	31 a
lii. 17.	58 l
Lam. ii. 9.	58 l
iii. 4.	58 l
iii. 16.	6 b
iv. 4.	47
Ezek. iv. 16.	58 e
v. 16.	58 a
vi. 4, 6, 9.	58 g
xiii. 14.	15 a
xiv. 13.	58 a
xvi. 38.	23
xvi. 39.	31 e
xvi. 59.	46 c
xvii. 15, 16.	46 b
xvii. 18.	46 c
xvii. 19.	40
xix. 12.	45 c
xxi. 6.	58 q
xxiii. 34.	5
xxvi. 2.	58 g
xxvi. 4, 12.	15 a
xxvi. 9.	31 c
xxvii. 26.	58 a
xxvii. 34.	58 k
xxix. 7, 7.	55 d, 58 i
xxx. 4.	15 f
xxx. 18.	58 b
xxx. 21, 24.	58 a
xxx. 22, 22.	58 a k
xxxi. 12.	58 i
xxxii. 28.	58 i
xxxiv. 4, 16.	58 k
xxxiv. 27.	58 b
xliv. 7.	46 e
Dan. ii. 1. ζ	12
ii. 34.	10 b
ii. 35.	7, or 10 a
ii. 40, 40, 40.	10 d, 54 e, 10 c

Dan. ii. 42.	60	Dan. xi. 4, 22.	58 i	Joel ii. 7. η	33	Jer. li. 17.		5	Ezek. xxxvii. 5, 6, 8, 10. 5	Dan. x. 17. 4
ii. 44.	10 c	Hos. i. 5.	58 a	Amos i. 5.	58 a	Lam. iii. 56.		5 a	xxxvii. 9, 9. 5, 2 a	Hab. ii. 19. 5
ii. 45.	10 b	ii. 18.	58 d	v. 6.	49	iv. 20.		5	Dan. v. 23. 4 a	
iv. 27.	45 f	iv. 2.	44 a	Jonah i. 4.	58 h					
vi. 24.	10 b	v. 11.	55 b	Micah ii. 13, 13.	44 d a					
vii. 7, 19.	10 d	viii. 6.	57	iii. 3.	41 d					
vii. 23.	10 c	x. 2.	35 b	Nah. i. 13.	58 d					
viii. 7.	58 n	x. 11.	56	Zech. ix. 10, 14.	46 c					
viii. 8.	58 g	x. 12.	26	xi. 11.	46 f					
viii. 22.	58 k	xiii. 13.	58 r	xi. 16.	58 k					
viii. 25.	58 i	Joel i. 17.	15 f							

a comp. Prov. vi. 19. *Heb.*, and Acts ix. 1.

a lit. breaking out break out. *β lit.* and she brake. *γ lit.* and it became light to them. *δ* or is bent, *i.e.* by the strength of mine arm; rather than from חָתַת. *ε lit.* should we turn to break. *ζ lit.* had been upon him, *i.e.* was now departed. *η i.e.* they shall not change their course, but go straight forward.

BREAST

1 דַּד *m.* the breasts of a woman.

2 חֲדִין Ch. *m. pl.* of the same meaning with the following.

3 חָזֶה *m.* the breast from the throat to the belly; the most conspicuous part of an animal.

4 לֵבָב *m.* the heart.

5 עֲטִין *m.* there is a variety of renderings to this word. Gesenius renders it, sides; Lxx., ἔγκατα; Vulg., *viscera*; Syr., *latera ejus;* Aben-Ezra, places where camels kneel down to drink.

6 שַׁד *m.* breasts of women, or animals. ⁴ שֹׁד *m.* a mother's breast.

Gen. xlix. 25.	6	Job xxiv. 9.	6 a	Lam. iv. 3.	6	
Exod. xxix. 26, 27.	3	Ps. xxii. 9.	6	Ezek. xvi. 7.	6	
Lev. vii. 30, 30, 31, 34.	6	Prov. v. 19.	1	xxiii. 3, 34.	6	
viii. 29.	3	Cant. i. 13.	6	xxiii. 8.	1	
ix. 20, 21.	3	iv. 5.	6	Dan. ii. 32.	2	
x. 14, 15.	3	vii. 3, 7, 8.	6	Hos. ii. 2.	6	
Num. vi. 20.	3	viii. 1, 8, 10.	6	ix. 14.	6	
xviii. 18.	3	Isa. xxviii. 9.	6	Joel ii. 16.	6	
Job iii. 12.	3	lx. 16.	6 a	Nah. ii. 7.	4	
xxi. 24.	5	lxvi. 11.	6 a			

BREASTPLATE

חֹשֶׁן *m.* part of the high priest's vestments, a span square when doubled; inserted in the ephod, just over the breast; having twelve precious stones set in gold, engraven with the names of the twelve tribes. This he wore when he went to consult the oracle: in this were placed the Urim and Thummim: only in Exod. and Lev. viii. 8, 8.

שִׁרְיֹן *m.* a coat of mail, habergeon: Isa. lix. 17.

BREATH

1 יָפֵחַ *adj.* breathing with difficulty or force.

2 נָפַח to breathe with force. KAL ⁴ *imp.* ᵇ *fut.*

3 נֶפֶשׁ *com.* animal life, nearly connected with the breath.

4 נְשָׁמָה *f.* the breath by which animal life is supported, but used only of man; soul or spirit of man; the breath of God denotes his grace or wrath. ⁴ נִשְׁמָא Ch. *f.*

5 רוּחַ *com.* the wind, air, breath. ⁴ רְוָחָה *f.* respite.

Gen. ii. 7, 7.	2 b, 4	Job xii. 10.	5	Ps. civ. 29.	5
vi. 17.	5	xv. 30.	5	cxxxv. 17.	5
vii. 15.	5	xvii. 1.	5	cxlvi. 4.	5
vii. 22.	4, 5	xix. 17.	5	cl. 6.	4
Deut. xx. 16.	4	xxvii. 3.	4	Eccles. iii. 19.	5
Josh. x. 40.	4	xxxiii. 4.	4	Isa. ii. 22.	4
xi. 11, 14.	4	xxxiv. 14.	4	xi. 4.	5
2 Sam. xxii. 16.	5	xxxvii. 10.	4	xxx. 28.	5
1 Kings xv. 29.	4	xli. 21.	4	xxx. 33.	5
xvii. 17.	4	Ps. xviii. 15.	5	xxxiii. 11.	5
Job ix. 9.	5	xxvii. 12.a	1	xlii. 5.	4
ix. 18.	5	xxxiii. 6.	5	Jer. x. 14.	5

BREECHES

מִכְנָסַיִם *m. dual,* a part of the garments of the priests, a covering: Exod. xxviii. 42; xxxix. 28: Lev. vi. 10; xvi. 4: Ezek. xliv. 18.

BREED (N)

בֵּן *m.* son: Deut. xxxii. 14.

BREED (V)

מִמְשַׁק *m.* Zeph. ii. 9, prob. the possession of nettles: *comp.* Isa. xiv. 23.

רוּם to lift up oneself; to rise up, as in growth; to breed. KAL *fut.* Exod. xvi. 20.

שָׁרַץ to bring forth abundantly. KAL *pret.* Gen. viii. 17.

BRIDE

כֹּפֶר *m.* ransom, satisfaction: 1 Sam. xii. 3: Amos v. 12.

שֹׁחַד *m.* gift, present: 1 Sam. viii. 3: Job xv. 34: Ps. xxvi. 10: Isa. xxxiii. 15.

BRICK

לְבֵנָה *f.* brick, from the white clay of which they were made: Vitruv. ii. 3: Gen. xi. 3, 3: Exod. i. 14; v. 7, 8, 16, 18, 19: Isa. ix. 10; lxv. 3, "altars of brick," *marg.* 'bricks;' hence לָבַן, with or without the noun, to make brick. KAL *inf.* Exod. v. 7, 14. *fut.* Gen. xi. 3. מַלְבֵּן *m.* brick-kiln: 2 Sam. xii. 31: Jer. xliii. 9: Nah. iii. 14.

BRIDE

כַּלָּה *f.* a bride, supposed to imply beauty of dress and appearance: Isa. xlix. 18; lxi. 10; lxii. 5: Jer. ii. 32; vii. 34; xvi. 9; xxv. 10; xxxiii. 11: Joel ii. 16.

BRIDEGROOM

חָתָן *m.* son-in-law, husband, bridegroom: Ps. xix. 5: Isa. lxi. 10; lxii. 5: Jer. vii. 34; xvi. 9; xxv. 10; xxxiii. 11: Joel ii, 16.

BRIDLE

מַחְסוֹם *m.* "a bridle, or muzzle for the mouth:" Ps. xxxix. 1.

מֶתֶג *m.* a bit or bridle: 2 Kings xix. 28: Prov. xxvi. 3: Isa. xxxvii. 29.

רֶסֶן *m.* a rein, bridle, which goes over a horse's nose: Job xxx. 11: Ps. xxxii. 9: Isa. xxx. 28. Also the mouth, with the double row of teeth within which the bridle goes: Job xli. 13.

BRIER

בַּרְקָנִים *m. pl.* briers; but, according to others, a threshing instrument, armed with sharp points underneath, to be drawn over the grain: Judg. viii. 7, 16.

חֵדֶק *m.* a species of thorn, or thornbush: Micah vii. 4.

סַלּוֹן *m.* a thorn, brier; Lxx. σκόλοψ: Ezek. xxviii. 24.

סָרָבִים *m. pl.* refractory, rebellious : the rendering of briers does not seem to be warranted : Ezek. ii. 6.

סִרְפָּד *m.* name of a plant which cannot be determined with certainty : Lxx. Theod. Aqu. κόνυζα. Vulg. *urtica.* The context requires us to understand the word of some mean and useless plant. Isa. lv. 13.

שָׁמִיר *m.* briers or thorns, used for fences to preserve the grain, &c. Isa. v. 6; vii. 23, 24, 25; ix. 18; x. 17; xxvii. 4; xxxii. 13.

BRIGANDINE

סִרְיוֹן *m.* a kind of armour, a coat of mail : Jer. xlvi. 4; li. 3.

BRIGHT, BRIGHTNESS

1 אוֹר light. ᵃ מָאוֹר *m.* light; *lit.* lights of the light.

2 בָּהִיר *adj.* bright, shining.

3 בָּרָק glittering, lightning.

4 בָּרַר to purge, to make clean, pure. HIPHIL *imp.*

5 זֹהַר *m.* splendour. Michaelis understands this, not of the brightness of the heavens, but of the bright morning star, or the planet Venus.

6 זִיו Ch. *m.* brightness, clearness.

7 חָזִיז *m.* an arrow : hence lightning; " bright clouds."

8 יִפְעָה brightness, beauty, of a city.

9 יָקָר *adj.* costly, precious, excellent, majestic.

10 לַהַב *m.* flame.

11 מָרַט to polish, to make smooth and bright. PUAL *part.*

12 מָרַק to clean metal from rust by scouring. KAL *part.* Paül.

13 נֹגַהּ *f.* brightness, shining, particularly of the fire, of the sun, of the moon, of a sword or spear, of the Shechinah or presence of Jehovah. ᵃ נְגֹהוֹת *f. pl.* brightnesses.

14 עֶשֶׁת *m.* forged, laboured, wrought. ᵃ עָשׁוּת *adj.* fabricated, wrought; bright.

15 קָלַל to be light. Pilpel, to move, shake; to polish. PILPEL *pret.* Ezek. xxi. 21, has been variously translated in reference to different modes of divination : Ges., he shakes or waves with arrows.

2 Sam. xxii. 13.	13	Isa. lx. 3, 19.	13	Ezek. xviii. 7, 17.	8	
1 Kings vii. 45.	11	lxii. 1.	13	xxxii. 8.	1 a, 1	
2 Chron. iv. 16.	12	Jer. li. 11.	4	Dan. ii. 31.	6	
Job xxxi. 26.	9	Ezek. i. 4, 13, 27, 28.	13	iv. 36.	6	
xxxvii. 11.	1	viii. 2.	13	xii. 3.	6	
xxxvii. 21.	2	x. 4.	13	Amos v. 20.	13	
Ps. xviii. 12.	13	xxi. 15.α	3	Nah. iii. 3.	10	
Cant. v. 14.	14	xxi. 21.	15	Hab. iii. 4.	13	
Isa. lix. 9.	13 a	xxvii. 19.	14 a	Zech. x. 1.	7	

a lit. unto glittering.

BRIM

קָצֶה *m.* end, edge, border : Josh. iii. 15.

שָׂפָה *f.* lip : 1 Kings vii. 23, 24, 26, 26 : 2 Chron. iv. 2, 2, 5, 5.

BRIMSTONE

גָּפְרִית *f.* (see *Gopher*); sulphur, bitumen, or pitch : figuratively, God's severe punishment of the wicked : Gen. xix. 24 :

Deut. xxix. 23 : Job xviii. 15 : Ps. xi. 6 : Isa. xxx. 33; xxxiv. 9 : Ezek. xxxviii. 22.

BRING

1 אָמַן to bring up. See *Nurse.* KAL ᵃ *part.* Poel. ᵇ *part.* Paül. ᶜ אָמְנָה *f.* a bringing up. ᵈ אָמוֹן *m. nutricius, alumnus;* one brought up : spoken of the hypostatic Wisdom of God, the second person of the Trinity, by which name some understand the Architect of the world; *comp.* Cant. vii. 1.

2 אָסַף to gather; used also of bringing into any sort of communion. KAL ᵃ *pret.* ᵇ *fut.* NIPHAL ᶜ *inf.* ᵈ *fut.*

3 אָתָה to come; poetic for בּוֹא. HIPHIL ᵃ *pret.* אָתָה Ch. APHEL ᵇ *pret.* ᶜ *inf.* HOPHAL ᵈ *pret.*

4 בּוֹא to go or come in, to enter; to cause to come in, to bring in, into, forth; to pass up. KAL ᵃ *pret.* ᵇ *fut.* ᶜ *part.* Poel. HIPHIL ᵈ *pret.* ᵉ *inf.* ᶠ *imp.* ᵍ *fut.* ʰ *part.* HOPHAL ⁱ *pret.* ᵏ *fut.* ˡ *part.*

5 בָּכַר to bring forth new or excellent fruit; to bring forth a first child. PIEL ᵃ *fut.* HIPHIL ᵇ *part.*

6 בָּעַר to consume; to remove entirely out of the way. PIEL *pret.*

7 גָּדַל to be or become great; to grow, to grow up, to be brought up. KAL ᵃ *pret.* PIEL ᵇ *pret.* ᶜ *fut.* ᵈ *part.*

8 גּוּז to pass away; to cause to pass away, to bring over. KAL *fut.*

9 גּוּחַ to break forth; to labour to bring forth. KAL *imp.*

10 גָּלָה to carry away into captivity. HIPHIL ᵃ *pret.* גְּלָה Ch. APHEL ᵇ *pret.*

11 דָּשָׁא to spring up as new grass. HIPHIL *fut.*

12 הוּךְ Ch. to go up; to bring again. P'AL *fut.*

13 חָיָה to be, to be brought to pass. NIPHAL *pret.*

14 חָבַל to travail, to bring forth. PIEL *pret.*

15 חוּל (see *Form*); to bring forth : it is applied to the eternal generation of the Son of God, Prov. viii. 24, 25; to the production of rain, Prov. xxv. 23; also to the formation of some curious work. HIPHIL ᵃ *fut.* PULAL ᵇ *pret.* HOPHAL ᶜ *fut.*

16 יָבַל to flow as water : applied to continuous motion of any kind, of the presents flowing in or solemnly brought to the Messiah, Ps. lxviii. 29. HIPHIL ᵃ *fut.* HOPHAL ᵇ *fut.* ᶜ יְבַל Ch. APHEL *pret.*

17 יָהַב to give, put, place; used (except once, see *Burden*) as an imperative, give, give here. KAL *imp.*

18 יָלַד to bring forth children, to beget; to bring up : Gen. l. 23, " brought up upon Joseph's knees," *i. e.* laid on his knees to be owned and blessed. KAL ᵃ *pret.* ᵇ *inf.* ᶜ *fut.* NIPHAL ᵈ *fut.* PUAL ᵉ *pret.* HIPHIL ᶠ *pret.* ᵍ *inf.* ʰ *fut.* ⁱ *part.*

19 יָלַךְ to go; to make to go, to lead, to bring. HIPHIL ᵃ *pret.* ᵇ *fut.*

20 יָסַף to add, to bring more. KAL ᵃ *pret.* HIPHIL ᵇ *part.*

21 יָצָא to go out, go forth; to lead forth, to bring out, forth, up. KAL [a] *part.* Poel. HIPHIL [b] *pret.* [c] *inf.* [d] *imp.* [e] *fut.* [f] *part.* HOPHAL [g] *pret.* [h] *part.* [i] מוֹצָא *m.* the going forth: used of the bringing of horses from Egypt for Solomon; *comp.* 2 Chron. ix. 28.

22 יָרַד to go down, to be brought down; to bring down. HIPHIL [a] *pret.* [b] *imp.* [c] *fut.* [d] *part.* HOPHAL [e] *pret.* [f] *fut.*

23 יָשַׁב to dwell; to make to dwell. HIPHIL *pret.* Zech. x. 6, "I will bring them again to place them." Aben-Ezra and Kimchi think that the word is compounded of שׁוּב and יָשַׁב; and so our translators seem to have taken it: the expression implies at least secure habitation.

24 כָּלָה to finish, to bring to pass. PIEL *pret.*

25 כָּנַע to be bowed down; to bow down, to humble, to bring down, under. NIPHAL [a] *fut.* HIPHIL [b] *fut.*

26 כָּרַע to bow, to be brought down. KAL *pret.*

27 לָקַח to take, to take away; frequently with the import of to take and bring, to take and give, &c. KAL [a] *pret.* [b] *imp.* [c] *fut.* NIPHAL [d] *fut.*

28 מָצָא to find. KAL *fut.*

29 נָגַע to touch, to reach to. HIPHIL [a] *pret.* [b] *fut.*

30 נָגַשׁ to touch, to near; to bring near, forth, hither. HIPHIL [a] *pret.* [b] *imp.* [c] *fut.* [d] *part.*

31 נָדַח to thrust; to bring upon; *seq.* עַל. HIPHIL *pret.*

32 נָהַג to lead, guide, conduct, to bring away. KAL [a] *fut.* [b] *part.* Paül. PIEL [c] *pret.* [d] *fut.*

33 נוּב to sprout, to bring forth; to bring forth words. KAL *fut.*

34 נָחָה to lead, to lead out or away. HIPHIL *fut.*

35 נָסַע to pull up (the tent-pins); to depart, to remove. HIPHIL [a] *fut.* [b] מַסָּע *m.* a removing.

36 נָשָׂא to lift up, to take away. KAL [a] *pret.* [b] *imp.* [c] *fut.* [d] *part.* Poel. HIPHIL [e] *pret.*

37 נָתַן to give. KAL [a] *pret.* [b] *inf.* [c] *imp.* [d] *fut.* [e] *part.* Poel.

38 סָבַב to go about, to bring about, again. HIPHIL [a] *pret.* [b] *inf.* [c] *fut.*

39 סוּר to turn aside out of the way. HIPHIL *pret.*

40 עָבַד to serve, to work, to perform. KAL *inf.*

41 עָבַר to pass over; to bring over, through. HIPHIL [a] *pret.* [b] *inf.* [c] *fut.*

42 עָלָה to ascend, to go up; to bring up. KAL [a] *inf.* [b] *fut.* NIPHAL [c] *inf.* HIPHIL [d] *pret.* [e] *inf.* [f] *imp.* [g] *fut.* [h] *part.* HOPHAL [i] *pret.*

43 עֲלַל Ch. to go in; to bring in. APHEL [a] *pret.* [b] *inf.* [c] *imp.* HOPHAL [d] *pret.*

44 עָנַן to bring (a cloud). PIEL *inf.*

45 עָשָׂה to do; taking its meaning from the word to which it refers: Ps. xxxvii. 5, "he shall bring to pass," *i. e.* the object of thy way. KAL [a] *pret.* [b] *inf.* [c] *fut.* [d] *part.* Poel.

46 פָּלַח to cleave; to let break forth, to bring forth. PIEL *fut.*

47 פָּרָה to bear fruit, to bring forth. KAL [a] *pret.* [b] *fut.*

48 צָמַח to spring or grow up; to bring forth. KAL [a] *part.* Poel. HIPHIL [b] *fut.*

49 צָעַר to go up; to cause to advance. HIPHIL *fut.*

50 קָבַץ to gather; to bring together. PIEL *part.*

51 קָרַב to draw or come near; to bring near, bring, bring forth. NIPHAL [a] *pret.* PIEL [b] *pret.* HIPHIL [c] *pret.* [d] *inf.* [e] *imp.* [f] *fut.* קְרֵב Ch. APHEL [g] *pret.*

52 קָרָה to meet. HIPHIL *pret.*

53 רָבָה to be many, to increase, to grow up; to bring up; to bring in abundance. PIEL [a] *pret.* HIPHIL [b] *pret.*

54 רוּם to be lifted up; Polel, to bring up, nourish, educate; or to exalt in spiritual and temporal blessings. POLEL *pret.*

55 רוּץ to run; to bring hastily. HIPHIL *fut.*

56 רָכַב to ride; to cause to ride, to bring, to bring on horseback. HIPHIL [a] *pret.* [b] *fut.*

57 שָׁבַר to break, to cause to break forth, bring to the birth. HIPHIL *fut.*

58 שׁוּב to return; to bring again, bring back, bring home again. KAL [a] *pret.* [b] *inf.* [c] *fut.* [d] *part.* Poel. POLEL [e] *pret.* [f] *inf.* PULAL [g] *part.* HIPHIL [h] *pret.* [i] *inf.* [k] *imp.* [l] *fut.* [m] *part.* HOPHAL [n] *fut.* [o] *part.*

59 שָׁוָה to be even; to make even, to set, "to bring forth" (fruit), to prepare fruit for himself. PIEL *fut.*

60 שׂוּם to set, place, put. KAL [a] *pret.* [b] *fut.*

61 שָׁחַח to bow down; to be brought low, brought down. NIPHAL [a] *fut.* HIPHIL [b] *pret.*

62 שִׁית to set, to lay, to put. KAL [a] *fut.*

63 שָׁלַח to send; to bring on the way; *comp.* 3 John 6: Rom. xv. 24: 1 Cor. xvi. 11: Acts xx. 38. PIEL [a] *pret.* [b] *inf.*

64 שָׁפֵל to be made low; to bring down. KAL [a] *pret.* HIPHIL [b] *pret.* [c] *fut.*

65 שָׁפַת to set, put, or place. See *Set, Burden, Pot, Hook.* If the view given under *Burden* be the just one, in Ps. xxii. 15 the idea is that of being brought to the dust of death in a degraded condition, as of one who usually lies among the pots.—*Schultens.* KAL *fut.*

66 שָׁרַץ this word seems to have nearly the same meaning as *scateo* in Latin, and signifies to swarm in respect to production, to bring forth abundantly. KAL [a] *pret.* [b] *imp.* [c] *fut.*

In many cases the verb *Bring* will be found under the noun connected with it, as *Desolation, Distress, Evil, Fruit,* &c.

Gen. i. 11.	11	Gen. xv. 5.	21 e	Gen. xxvii. 14, 31, 33.	4 g
i. 12, 24.	21 e	xv. 7.	21 b	xxvii. 20.	52
i. 20.	66 c	xviii. 16.	63 b	xxvii. 25, 25, 25.	30 b c
i. 21.	66 a	xviii. 19.	4 e		4 g
ii. 19, 22.	4 g	xix. 5, 12.	21 d	xxviii. 15.	58 h
iii. 16.	18 c	xix. 8, 16.	21 e	xxix. 13, 23.	4 g
iii. 18.	48 b	xix. 17.	21 c	xxx. 14.	4 g
iv. 3.	4 g	xx. 9.	4 d	xxx. 39.	18 o
iv. 4.	4 g	xxiv. 5.	58 i l	xxxi. 39.	4 d
vi. 17.	4 h	xxiv. 6, 8.	58 l	xxxiii. 11.	4 i
vi. 19.	4 g	xxiv. 53.	21 e	xxxvii. 2, a 28, 32.	4 g
viii. 17.	21 d	xxiv. 67.	4 g	xxxvii. 14.	58 k
ix. 7.	66 b	xxvi. 10.	4 d	xxxviii. 24.	21 d
ix. 14.	44	xxvii. 4, 7.	4 f	xxxviii. 25.	21 h
xiv. 16, 16.	58 l h	xxvii. 5.	4 e	xxxix. 1, 1.	22 e, a
xiv. 18.	21 b	xxvii. 10, 12.	4 d	xxxix. 14, 17.	4 d

Gen. xl. 14. 21 b
xli. 14. 55
xli. 32. 45 b
xli. 47. 45 c
xlii. 20. 4 g
xlii. 34. 4 f
xlii. 37, 37. 4 g, 58 l
xlii. 38. 22 a
xliii. 2, 9. 4 d
xliii. 7. 22 b
xliii. 12. 58 o
xliii. 16. 4 f
xliii. 17, 24, 26. 4 g
xliii 18, 18. 4 i l
xliii. 21. 58 l
xliii. 22. 22 a
xliii. 23. 21 e
xliv. 8. 58 h
xliv. 21. 22 b
xl. v. 29, 31. 22 a
xliv. 32. 4 g
xlv. 13. 22 a
xlv. 19. 36 a
xlvi. 4. 42 a
xlvi. 7, 32. 4 d
xlv i. 7, 14, 17. 4 g
xlviii. 9. 27 b
xlviii. 10, 13. 30 c
xlviii. 12. 21 e
xlviii. 21. 58 h
l. 20. 45 b
l. 23. 18 e
l. 24 42 d
Exod. ii. 10. 4 g
iii. 8. 42 e
iii. 10. 21 d
iii. 11. 21 e
iii. 12. 21 c
iii. 17. 42 g
vi. 6. 21 b
vi. 7. 21 f
vi. 8. 4 d
vi. 13, 27. 21 c
vi. 26. 21 d
vii. 4, 5. 21 b
viii. 3. 66 a
viii. 7. 42 g
viii. 18. 60 a
viii. 18. 21 c
ix. 19. 2 d
x. 4. 4 h
x. 8. 58 n
x. 13, 13. 32 c, 36 a
xi. 1. 4 g
xii. 17, 39, 51. 21 b
xii. 42. 21 c
xiii. 3, 9, 14, 16. 21 b
xiii. 5, 11. 4 g
xv. 17. 4 g
xv. 19. 58 l
xv. 22. 35 a
xv. 26. 60 a
xvi. 3, 6. 21 b
x· i. 5. 4 g
xvi. 32. 21 c
xvii. 3. 42 d
xviii. 1. 21 b
xviii 19. 4 d
xviii 22, 26. 4 g
xix. 4. 4 h
xix. 17. 21 e
xx. 2. 21 b
xxi. 6, 6. 30 a
xxii. 8. 51 a
xxii. 13. 4 g
xxiii. 4. 58 i l
xxiii. 19. 4 e
x· iii. 20. 4 e
xxiii. 23. 4 d
xxv. 2. 27 c
xxvi. 33. 4 d
xxvii. 20. 27 c
xxix. 3, 10. 51 c
xxix. 4, 8. 51 f
xxix. 46. 21 b
xxxii. 1, 4, 7, 8, 23. 42 d
xxxii. 2. 4 f
xxxii. 3. 4 g
xxxii. 6. 30 c
xxxii. 11, 12. 21 b
xxxii. 21. 4 d
xxxiii. 1. 42 d
xxxiii. 12. 42 f
xxxiv. 26. 4 g
xxxv. 5, 25. 4 g

Exod. xxxv. 21, 22, 23, 24, 24, 27. 4 d
xxxv. 29, 29. 4 d e
xxxvi. 3, 3. 4 d
xxxvi. 5,β 6. 4 e
xxxix. 33. 4 g
xl. 4, 4. 4 d
xl. 12. 51 c
xl. 14. 51 f
xl. 21. 4 g
Lev. i. 2, 2, 10. 51 f
i. 5, 13, 14, 15. 51 c
ii. 2. 4 g
ii. 4, 11. 51 f
ii. 8, 8. 4 d, 30 a
iv. 3. 51 c
iv. 4, 5, 14, 16, 23, 28. 4 d
iv. 32, 32. 4 g
v. 6, 8, 11, 12, 15, 18. 4 d
v. 7, 7. 29 b, 4 d
vi. 6, 21. 4 g
vi. 30. 4 k
vii. 29, 30, 30. 4 g
viii. 6, 13, 18, 22, 24. 51 f
viii. 14. 30 c
ix. 5. 27 c
ix. 9, 15, 16, 17. 51 f
x. 15. 4 g
x. 18. 4 i
xi. 45. 42 h
xii. 6. 4 g
xii. 8, 8. 27 a, 28
xiii. 2, 9. 4 i
xiv. 2. 4 i
xiv. 23. 4 d
xiv. 29. 4 g
xvi. 9, 11, 20. 51 c
xvi. 12, 15. 4 d
xvi. 27. 4 i
xvii 4. 4 d
xvii. 5, 5. 4 g d
xvii. 9. 4 g
xviii. 3. 4 h
xix. 21. 21 b
xix. 36. 21 b
xx. 22. 4 h
xxii. 27. 18 d
xxiii. 33. 21 f
xxiii. 10. 4 d
xxiii. 14, 15. 4 e
xxiii. 17. 4 g
xxiii. 43. 21 c
xxiv. 2. 27 c
xxiv. 11. 4 g
xxiv. 14. 21 d
xxiv. 23. 21 e
xxv. 21. 45 a
xxv. ? 8, 42, 55. 21 b
xxvi. 10. 21 e
xxvi. 13, 45. 21 b
xxvi. 21.γ 20 a
xxvi. 25, 41. 4 d
xxvii. 9. 51 f
Num. iii. 6. 51 e
v. 9. 51 f
v. 15, 15. 4 d
v. 16. 51 c
vi. 10, 13.δ 4 g
vi. 12. 4 d
vi. 16. 51 c
vii. 3, 3. 4 g, 51 f
viii. 9, 10. 51 c
ix. 13. 51 c
xi. 16. 27 a
xi. 31. 8
xii. 15. 2 c
xiii. 20. 27 a
xiii. 26. 58 l
xiii. 32. 21 e
xiv. 3. 4 h
xiv. 8, 24, 31. 4 d
xiv. 13. 42 d
xiv. 16. 4 e
xiv. 36. 21 c
xiv. 37. 21 f
xv. 4, 9, 27. 51 c
xv. 10, 33. 51 f
xv. 18. 4 h
xv. 25. 4 d
xv. 36. 21 b
xv. 41. 21 b
xvi. 9. 51 d
xvi. 10. 51 f
xvi. 13. 42 d
xvi. 14. 4 d

Num. xvi. 17. 51 c
xvii. 8, 9. 21 e
xvii. 10. 58 k
xviii. 2. 51 e
xviii. 13. 4 g
xviii. 15. 51 f
xix. 2. 27 c
xix. 3. 21 b
xx. 4. 4 d
xx. 5. 4 e
xx. 8. 21 b
xx. 12. 4 g
xx. 16. 21 c
xx. 25. 42 f
xxi. 5. 42 d
xxii. 8. 58 h
xxii. 41. 42 g
xxiii. 14, 27, 28. 27 c
xxiii. 22. 21 f
xxiv. 8. 21 f
xxv. 6. 51 f
xxvii. 5. 51 f
xxvii. 17. 4 g
xxviii. 26. 51 d
xxxi. 12, 54. 4 g
xxxi. 50. 51 f
xxxii. 5. 41 c
xxxii. 17. 4 d
Deut. i. 17. 51 f
i. 22. 58 l
i. 25, 25. 58 l, 22 c
i. 27. 21 b
iv. 20, 37. 21 e
iv. 38. 4 e
v. 6. 21 b
v. 15. 21 e
vi. 10. 4 g
vi. 12. 21 b
vi. 21. 21 e
vi. 23, 23. 21 b, 4 e
vii. 1, 26. 4 g
vii. 8, 19. 21 b
viii. 7. 4 h
viii. 14, 15. 21 f
ix. 3. 25 b
ix. 4. 4 d
ix. 12, 26, 29. 21 b
ix. 28, 28, 28. 21 b, 4 e, 21 b
xi. 29. 4 g
xii. 6. 4 g
xii. 11. 4 g
xiii. 5, 10. 21 f
xiv. 22.ε 21 a
xiv. 28. 21 e
xvi. 1. 21 b
xvii. 5. 21 b
xx. 1. 42 h
xxi. 4. 22 a
xxi. 12. 4 d
xxi. 19. 21 b
xxii. 1.ζ 58 i l
xxii. 2. 2 a
xxii. 8. 60 b
xxii. 14, 15, 19, 21, 24. 21 b
xxiii. 18. 4 g
xxiv. 11. 21 e
xxvi. 2, 9. 4 g
xxvi. 8. 21 e
xxvii. 10. 4 d
xxvii. 13. 6
xxviii. 36. 19 b
xxviii. 60, 68. 58 h
xxviii. 49. 36 c
xxviii. 61. 42 g
xxix. 25. 21 c
xxix. 27. 4 e
xxx. 5. 4 d
xxx. 12, 13. 27 c
xxxi. 20, 21, 23. 4 g
xxxiii. 7. 21 d
Josh. ii. 3. 21 d
ii. 6. 42 d
ii. 18. 2 b
vi. 22. 21 d
vi. 23, 23. 21 e b
vii. 7. 41 a b
vii. 14. 51 a
vii. 16, 17, 17, 18. 51 f
vii. 23. 4 g
vii. 24. 42 g
viii. 23. 51 f
x: 22. 21 b

Josh. x. 23. 21 e
x. 24. 21 c
xiv. 7. 58 l
xviii. 6.η 4 d
xxii. 32. 58 l
xxiii. 15. 4 g
xxiv. 5. 21 b
xxiv. 6. 21 e
xxiv. 7, 8. 4 g
xxiv. 17. 42 h
xxiv. 32. 42 d
Judg. i. 7. 4 g
ii. 1. 4 g
ii. 12. 21 f
iii. 17. 51 f
v. 25. 51 c
vi. 8. 8. 42 d, 21 e
vi. 13. 42 d
vi. 18. 21 b
vi. 19. 21 e
vi. 30. 21 d
vii. 4. 22 b
vii. 5. 22 c
vii. 25. 4 d
xi. 9. 58 m
xiv. 11. 27 c
xv. 13. 42 g
xvi. 8, 18. 42 g
xvi. 21. 22 c
xvi. 31.θ 42 b
xviii. 3. 4 d
xix. 3, 3. 58 i, 4 g
xix. 21. 4 g
xxii. 22. 21 d
xix. 24, 25. 21 e
xx. 12. 4 g
Ruth i. 21. 58 h
ii. 18. 21 e
iii. 15. 17
1 Sam. i. 22. 4 d
i. 24, 25. 4 g
ii. 6, 6. 22 d, 42 g
ii. 14. 42 g
ii. 19. 42 d
iv. 4. 36 c
v. 1, 2. 4 g
v. 10. 38 a
vi. 7, 21. 58 h
vii. 1. 4 g
viii. 8. 42 e
ix. 7, 7. 4 g, 4 e
ix. 22. 4 g
ix. 23. 37 c
x. 18. 42 d
x. 27. 4 d
xi. 12. 37 c
xii. 6. 42 d
xii. 8. 21 e
xiii. 9. 30 b
xiv. 18. 30 b
xiv. 34, 34. 30 b c
xv. 15. 4 d
xv. 20. 4 g
xv. 32. 30 b
xvi. 12. 4 g
xvi. 17. 4 d
xvii. 54, 57. 4 g
xviii. 27. 4 g
xix. 7. 4 g
xix. 15. 42 f
xix. 8, 8. 4 d, g
xxi. 8. 27 a
xxi. 14. 4 g
xxi. 15. 4 d
xxii. 4. 34
xxiii. 5. 32 a
xxiii. 9. 30 b
xxv. 27, 35. 4 d
xxvii. 11. 4 e
xxviii. 11, 11. 42 g f
xxviii. 15. 42 e
xxviii. 25. 30 c
xxx. 7, 7. 30 b c
xxx. 11. 27 c
2 Sam. i. 10. 4 g
ii. 3. 4 g
ii. 8. 41 c
iii. 11. 38 b
iii. 13. 4 e
iii. 22. 4 d
iii. 26. 58 l
iv. 8. 4 g
v. 2. 4 h

2 Sam. vi. 2. 42 e
vi. 3, 4. 36 c
vi. 12. 42 g
vi. 15. 42 h
vi. 17. 4 g
vii. 6. 42 e
vii. 18. 4 d
viii. 2, 6. 36 d
vii. 7. 4 g
ix. 10. 4 d
x. 16. 21 e
xii. 23. 58 i
xii. 30, 31. 21 b
xiii. 10, 10. 4 f g
xiii. 11. 30 c
xiii. 18. 21 e
xiv. 10. 4 d
xiv. 21. 58 k
xiv. 23. 4 g
xv. 8. 58 c
xv. 14. 31
xv. 25. 58 h
xvii. 3. 58 l
xvii. 13. 36 e
xvii. 14. 4 e
xvii. 28. 30 a
xix. 10, 11, 12, 43. 58 i
xix. 41. 41 c
xxi. 8. 18 a
xxi. 13. 42 g
xxii. 20. 21 e
xxii. 48. 22 d
xxii. 49. 21 f
xxiii. 16. 4 g
1 Kings i. 3. 22 a
i. 33. 22 a
i. 38. 19 b
i. 53. 22 c
ii. 9. 22 a
ii. 30. 58 l
ii. 40. 4 g
iii. 1. 4 g
iii. 24, 24. 27 b, 4 g
iv. 21. 30 d
iv. 28. 4 g
v. 9. 22 c
v. 17. 35 a
vi. 7. 35 b
vii. 51. 4 g
viii. 1. 4 g
viii. 4, 4. 42 g
viii. 6. 4 g
viii. 16, 51. 21 b
viii. 21, 53. 21 c
viii. 32. 37 b
viii. 34. 58 h
ix. 9, 9. 21 b, 4 d
ix. 28. 4 g
x. 11, 11. 36 a, 4 d
x. 22. 36 d
x. 25. 4 h
x. 28. 21 i
xii. 28. 42 d
xiii. 18. 58 k
xiii. 20, 23, 26. 4 g
xiii. 29. 58 l
xiv. 10. 4 h
xiv. 28. 58 h
xv. 15. 4 g
xvii. 6. 4 h
xvii. 11. 27 b
xvii. 13. 21 b
xvii. 23. 22 c
xvii. 27. 10 a
xviii. 40. 22 c
xx. 9. 58 l
xx. 39. 4 g
xxi. 21. 4 g
xxi. 29, 29. 4 g
xxii. 37. 4 g
2 Kings ii. 20, 20. 27 b c
iii. 15. 27 b
iv. 5. 30 d
iv. 6. 30 b
iv. 20, 42. 4 g
iv. 41. 27 b
v. 20. 4 d
vi. 13. 58 l
x. 1, 5. 1 a
x. 6. 7 d

2 Kings x. 8. 4 d
x. 22, 22. 21 d e
x. 24. 4 h
x. 26. 21 e
xi. 4. 4 g
xi. 12. 21 e
xi. 19. 22 c
xii. 4, 4. 4 k e
xii. 9, 13. 4 l
xii. 16. 4 k
xiv. 20. 36 c
xvi. 14. 51 f
xvii. 4, 36. 42 d
xvii. 7. 42 h
xvii. 24. 4 g
xvii. 27. 10
xix. 3. 18 b
xix. 25. 4 d
xx. 11. 58 l
xx. 20. 4 g
xxi. 12. 4 h
xxii. 4. 4 l
xxii. 9. 58 l
xxii. 16. 4 h
xxii. 20, 20. 4 h, 58 l
xxiii. 4. 21 c
xxiii. 6. 21 e
xxiii. 8, 30. 4 g
xxiv. 16. 4 g
xxv. 6. 42 g
xxv. 20. 19 b
1 Chron. v. 26. 4 g
ix. 28. 4 g, 21 e
x. 12. 4 h
xi. 2. 4 h
xi. 18. 4 g
xi. 19. 4 d
xii. 40. 4 h
xiii. 3. 38 c
xiii. 5. 4 e
xiii. 6. 4 g
xiii. 12. 4 g
xiii. 13. 39
xiv. 17. 37 a
xv. 3, 14, 25. 42 e
xv. 12. 42 d
xv. 28. 42 h
xvi. 1. 4 g
xvi. 29. 36 b
xvii. 5. 42 d
xvii. 16. 4 d
xviii. 2, 6. 36 d
xviii. 7. 27 a
xviii. 11. 36 a
xx. 2, 3. 21 b
xxi. 2. 4 f
xxi. 12. 58 l
xxii. 4. 4 d
xxiii. 19. 4 e
2 Chron. i. 4. 42 d
i. 16. 21 i
i. 17, 17. 21 e
ii. 16. 4 g
v. 1, 7. 4 g
v. 2. 42 e
v. 5, 5. 42 d g
vi. 5. 21 b
vi. 25. 58 h
vii. 22, 22. 21 b, 4 d
viii. 11. 42 d
viii. 18. 4 g
ix. 10, 10, 12. 4 d
ix. 14, 14, 24. 4 h
ix. 21. 36 d
ix. 28. 21 f
x. 8, 10. 7 a
xi. 1. 58· i
xi. 11. 58 h
xiii. 18. 25 a
xv. 11. 4 d
xv. 18. 4 g
xvi. 2. 21 e
xvii. 5. 37 d
xvii. 11, 11. 4 h
xix. 4. 58 l
xxii. 9. 21 e
xxiii. 11, 14. 21 e
xxiii. 20. 22 c
xxiv. 5, 9. 4 e
xxiv. 10, 11. 4 d
xxiv. 14. 4 d
xxiv. 19. 58 i
xxv. 12, 14, 23. 4 g
xxv. 28. 36 c

2 Chron. xxviii.5, 8, 13, 15.	4 g
xxviii. 27.	4 d
xxix. 4, 21.	4 g
xxix. 16.	21 e
xxix. 23.	30 c
xxix. 31, 31.	4 f g
xxix. 32.	4 d
xxx. 15.	4 g
xxxi. 5, 5.	53 b, 4 d
xxxi. 6.	4 d
xxxi. 10.	4 e
xxxi. 12.	4 g
xxxii. 23.	4 h
xxxiii. 11.	4 g
xxxiii. 13.	58 l
xxxiv. 9.	4 l
xxxiv. 14, 14.	21 c, 4 l
xxxiv. 16.	58 l
xxxiv. 24.	4 h
xxxiv. 28, 28.	4 h, 58 l
xxxv. 24.	19 b
xxxvi. 10.	4 g
xxxvi. 17.	42 g
xxxvi. 18.	4 d
Ezra i. 7, 7.	21 b
i. 8.	21 e
i. 11, 11.	42 d c
iii. 7.	4 e
iv. 2.	42 h
iv. 10.	10 b
v. 14.	16 c
vi. 5, 5.	16 c, 12
viii. 17, 30.	4 e
viii. 17כ.	21 e
viii. 18.	4 g
Neh. i. 9.	4 d
viii. 1.	4 e
viii. 2, 16.	4 g
ix. 7, 15.	21 b
ix. 18.	42 d
ix. 23.	4 g
ix. 29.	58 l
ix. 33.	4 c
x. 31.	4 h
x. 34, 35, 36.	4 e
x. 37, 39.	4 d
x. 38.	42 g
xi. 1.	4 e
xii. 27.	4 e
xii. 31.	42 g
xiii. 9.	58 l
xiii. 12.	4 d
xiii. 15, 15, 16.	4 h
xiii. 18, 18.	4 g, 20 b
xiii. 19.	4 b
Esth. i. 11, 17.ι	4 e
ii. 7.	1 a
ii. 8.	27 d
ii. 20.	1 c
iii. 9.	4 e
vi. 1, 14.	4 e
vi. 8.	4 g
vi. 9.	56 a
vi. 11.	56 b
ix. 11.	4 a
Job vi. 22.	17
x. 9.	58 l
x. 18.	21 h
xii. 6.	4 d
xii. 22.	21 e
xiv. 3.	4 g
xiv. 4.	37 d
xiv. 9.	45 a
xv. 35.	18 b
xviii. 14.	49
xxi. 30, 32.	16 b
xxviii. 11.	21 e
xxx. 23.	58 l
xxxi. 18.	7 a
xxxiii. 30.	58 l
xxxviii. 32.	21 e
xxxix. 1, 2.	18 b
xxxix. 3.	46
xxxix. 12.	58 l
xl. 20.	36 c
xli. 11.	4 d
Ps. i. 3.	37 d
vii. 14.	18 a
xiv. 7.	58 b
xviii. 19.	21 e
xviii. 27.	64 c
xx. 8.	26
xxii. 15.	65
xxv. 17.	21 d

Ps. xxx. 3.	42 d
xxxvii. 5.	45 c
xxxvii. 6.	21 b
xxxvii. 7.	45 d
xl. 2.	42 g
xliii. 3.	4 g
xlv. 14, 14.	16 b, 4 l
xlv. 15.	16 b
liii. 6.	58 b
lv. 23.	22 c
lix. 11.	22 b
lx. 9.	16 a
lxvi. 11.	4 d
lxvi. 12.	21 e
lxviii. 6.	21 f
lxviii. 22, 22.	58 l
lxviii. 29.	16 a
lxxi. 20.	42 g
lxxii. 3.	36 c
lxxvi. 11.	16 a
lxxviii. 16.	21 e
lxxviii. 26.	32 d
lxxviii. 54.	4 g
lxxviii. 71.	4 d
lxxx. 8.	35 a
lxxxi. 2.	37 c
lxxxi. 10.	42 h
lxxxix. 1.	58 a
lxxxix. 40.	60 a
xc. 2.	18 e
xcii. 14.	33
xciv. 23.	58 l
xcvi. 8.	36 b
civ. 14.	21 c
cv. 30.	66 a
cv. 37, 43.	21 e
cv. 40.	4 g
cvii. 12.	25 b
cvii. 14, 28.	21 e
cvii. 30.	34
cviii. 10.	16 a
cxxvi. 6.	36 d
cxxxv. 7.	21 f
cxxxvi. 11.	21 e
cxlii. 7.	21 d
cxliii. 11.	21 e
Prov. viii. 24, 25.	15 b
viii. 30.	1 d
x. 31.	33
xvi. 30.	24
xviii. 16.	34
xix. 24.	58 l
xx. 26.	58 l
xxi. 27.	4 g
xxvi. 15.	58 l
xxvii. 1.	18 c
xxix. 25.	37 d
xxx. 33, 33, 33.	21 e
xxxi. 14.	4 g
Eccles. ii. 6.	48 a
iii. 22.	4 g
xi. 9.	4 g
Cant. i. 4.	4 d
ii. 4.	4 d
iii. 4.	4 d
viii. 2, 11.	4 g
viii. 5, 5.	14
Isa. i. 2.	54
i. 13.κ	4 e
v. 2, 2.	45 b c
v. 4, 4.	45 b c
v. 15.	61 a
vii. 17.	4 g
viii. 7.	42 h
xiv. 2.	4 d
xiv. 11.	22 e
xiv. 15.	22 f
xv. 9.	62
xviii. 7.	16 b
xxi. 14.	3 a
xxiii. 4, 4.	18 a, 54
xxiii. 13.	60 a
xxv. 5.	25 b
xxv. 11.	64 b
xxv. 12, 12.	61 b, 29 a
xxvi. 5, 5.	61 b, 29 a
xxvi. 18.	18 a
xxviii. 21.	40
xxix. 4.	64 a
xxxi. 2.	4 g
xxxiii. 11.	18 c
xxxvii. 3.	18 b
xxxvii. 26.	4 d

Isa. xxxviii. 8.	58 m
xl. 23.	37 e
xl. 26.	21 f
xli. 21.	30 b
xli. 22.	30 c
xlii. 1, 3.	21 e
xlii. 7.	21 c
xlii. 16.	19 a
xliii. 5.	4 g
xliii. 6.	4 f
xliii. 8.	21 d
xliii. 9.	37 d
xliii. 14.	22 a
xliii. 17.	21 f
xliii. 23.	4 d
xlv. 8.	47 b
xlv. 10.	15 a
xlv. 21.	30 b
xlvi. 8.	58 k
xlvi. 11.	4 g
xlvi. 13.	51 b
xlviii. 15.	4 d
xlix. 5.	58 f
xlix. 21.	7 b
xlix. 22.	4 d
li. 18, 18.	18 a, 7 b
lii. 8.	58 b
liii. 7.	16 b
liv. 16.	21 f
lv. 10.	18 f
lvi. 7.	4 d
lviii. 7.	4 g
lx. 4.	18 g
lx. 6.	36 c
lx. 9.	4 e
lx. 11, 11.	4 e, 32 b
lx. 17, 17.	4 g
lxi. 11.	21 e
lxii. 9.	50
lxiii. 6.	22 c
lxiii. 11.	42 h
lxv. 9.	21 b
lxv. 23.	18 c
lxvi. 4.	4 g
lxvi. 7.	18 a
lxvi. 8, 8.	15 c, 18 a
lxvi. 9, 9, 9.	57, 18 h i
lxvi. 20, 20.	4 d g
Jer. ii. 6.	42 h
ii. 7.	4 g
ii. 27.λ	18 a
iii. 14.	4 d
iv. 6.	4 h
iv. 31.	5 b
v. 15.	4 h
vii. 22.	4 h
viii. 1.	21 c
x. 9.	4 k
x. 13.	21 e
xi. 4.	21 c
xi. 7.	42 e
xi. 8, 23.	4 g
xi. 11.	4 h
xi. 19.	16 b
xii. 2.	45 a
xii. 15.	58 h
xv. 8.	4 d
xv. 19.	58 l
xvi. 14.	42 d
xvi. 15, 15.	42 d, 58 h
xvii. 18, 24.	4 e
xvii. 21.	4 d
xvii. 26, 26.	4 h
xviii. 22.	4 g
xix. 3, 15.	4 h
xx. 3.	21 e
xxiii. 3.	58 h
xxiii. 7, 8.	42 d
xxiii. 12.	4 g
xxiii. 40.	37 a
xxiv. 1.	4 g
xxiv. 6.	58 h
xxv. 9, 13.	4 d
xxvi. 15.	37 e
xxvi. 23.	4 g
xxvii. 11.	4 g
xxvii. 12.	58 f
xxvii. 16.	58 o
xxvii. 22.	42 d
xxviii. 3, 4.	58 m
xxviii. 6.	58 i
xxix. 14.	58 h
xxx. 3.	58 a
xxx. 18.	58 d

Jer. xxxi. 8.	4 h
xxxi. 23.	58 b
xxxi. 32.	21 c
xxxii. 21.	21 e
xxxii. 37.	58 h
xxxiii. 42, 42.	4 d h
xxxiii. 6.	42 h
xxxiii. 11.	4 h
xxxiv. 13.	21 c
xxxv. 2.	4 d
xxxv. 4.	4 g
xxxv. 17.	4 d
xxxvi. 31.	4 d
xxxvii. 14.	4 g
xxxviii. 22.	21 h
xxxviii. 23.	21 f
xxxix. 5.	42 g
xxxix. 16.	4 h
xl. 3.	4 g
xli. 5.	4 e
xli. 16.	58 h
xlii. 17.	4 h
xliv. 2.	4 d
xlv. 5.	4 h
xlviii. 44.	4 g
xlviii. 47.	58 a
xlix. 5.	4 h
xlix. 6, 39.	58 l
xlix. 8, 36, 37.	4 d
xlix. 16.	22 c
xlix. 32.	4 g
l. 19.	58 e
l. 25.	21 e
li. 10, 44.	21 b
li. 16.	21 e
li. 40.	22 c
li. 64.	4 h
lii. 26.	19 b
lii. 31.	21 e
Lam. i. 21.	4 d
ii. 2.	29 a
ii. 22.	53 a
iii. 2.	19 b
iv. 5.	1 b
Ezek. v. 17.	4 g
vi. 3.	4 h
vii. 24.	4 d
viii. 3, 7, 14, 16.	4 d
xi. 1, 8, 24.	4 g
xi. 7, 9.	21 b
xii. 4, 7, 7.	21 b
xii. 13.	4 d
xiii. 14.	29 a
xiii. 17.	4 g
xiv. 22, 22, 22.	21 h, 4 d d
xvi. 40.	42 d
xvi. 53.	58 a
xvi. 6.	45 c
xvii. 8.	45 b
xvii. 20.	4 d
xvii. 23.	36 a
xvii. 24.	64 b
xix. 3.	42 g
xix 4, 9, 9.	4 g
xx. 6, 9, 41.	21 c
xx. 10, 28.	4 h

Ezek. xx. 14, 22, 34.	21 b
xx. 15, 42.	4 e
xx. 35, 37.	4 d
xx. 38.	21 e
xxi. 7.	13
xxi. 29.	37 b
xxiii. 22.	4 d
xxiii. 42.	4 l
xxiii. 46.	42 e
xxiv. 6.	21 d
xxvi. 7.	4 h
xxvi. 19.	42 e
xxvi. 20.	22 a
xxvii. 15.	58 h
xxvii. 26.	4 d
xxviii. 7.	4 h
xxviii. 8.	22 c
xxviii. 18, 18.	21 e, 37 d
xxix. 4.	42 d
xxix. 5.	2 d
xxix. 8.	4 h
xxix. 14.	58 a
xxx. 11.	4 l
xxxi. 6.	18 a
xxxi. 18.	22 e
xxxii. 3.	42 d
xxxii. 9.	4 e
xxxiii. 2.	4 g
xxxiv. 4.	58 h
xxxiv. 13, 13.	21 b, 4 d
xxxvi. 11.	47 a
xxxvi. 24.	4 d
xxxvi. 26.	58 l
xxxvii. 6.	42 d
xxxvii. 12, 21.	4 d
xxxvii. 13.	42 e
xxxvii. 23.	4 g
xxxviii. 4.	4 h
xxxviii. 8, 8.	58 g, 21 g
xxxviii. 16.	4 d
xxxviii. 17.	4 d
xxxix. 2.	4 d
xxxix. 25.	58 l
xxxix. 27.	58 f
xl. 1, 3, 17, 28, 32, 35, 48.	4 g
xl. 2.	4 d
xl. 4.	4 i
xl. 24.	19 b
xli. 1.	4 g
xlii. 1, 1.	21 e, 4 g
xlii. 15.	21 b
xliii. 1.	19 b
xliii. 5.	4 g
xliv. 1.	58 l
xlv. 4.	4 g
xlvi. 19.	4 g
xlvi. 21.	21 e
xlvii. 1.	58 l
xlvii. 2.	21 e
xlvii. 3, 4, 4.	41 c
xlvii. 6.	19 b
xlvii. 8.	21 h
xlvii. 12.	5 a
Dan. i. 2.	4 d
i. 3.	4 h

Dan. i. 9.	37 d
i. 18, 18.	4 e g
ii. 24.	43 c
ii. 25.	43 a
iii. 13, 13.	3 c d
iii. 16.	43 b
v. 2.	3 c
v. 3, 23.	3 b
v. 7.	43 b
v. 13, 13.	43 d, 3 b
v. 15.	3 d
vi. 16, 24.	3 b
vi. 17.	3 d
vi. 18.	43 a
vii. 13.	51 g
ix. 12, 24.	4 g
ix. 14.	4 g
ix. 15.	21 b
xi. 6.	4 h
Hos. ii. 14.	19 a
vii. 12.	22 c
ix. 12.	7 c
ix. 13.	21 c
ix. 16.	18 c
x. 1.	59
xii. 13.	42 d
Joel iii. 1.	58 l
iii. 2.	22 a
Amos ii. 10.	42 d
iii. 1.	42 d
iii. 11.	22 a
iv. 1, 4.	4 f
vi. 10.	21 c
viii. 10.	42 d
ix. 2.	22 c
ix. 7.	42 d
ix. 14.	58 a
Obad. 3, 4.	22 c
7.	63 a
Jonah i. 13.μ	58 i
ii. 6.	42 g
Micah i. 15.	4 g
v. 3.	18 a
v. 4.	42 d
vii. 9.	21 e
Nah. i. 7.	42 i
Zeph. ii. 2.	18 b
iii. 5.	37 d
iii. 10.	16 a
iii. 20.	4 g
Hag. i. 6.	4 e
i. 8, 9.	4 d
i. 11.	21 e
ii. 19.	36 a
Zech. iii. 8.	4 h
iv. 7.	21 b
v. 4.	21 b
viii. 8.	4 d
x. 6.	23
x. 10, 10.	4 g, 58 h
x. 11.	22 e
xiii. 9.	4 d
Mal. i. 13, 13.	4 d
iii. 10.	4 f

α *lit.* brought to their father. β *lit.* increase to bring. γ *lit.* and I will add. δ *lit.* (one) shall bring him. ε *lit.* which cometh forth of the field. ζ *lit.* bringing again thou shalt bring them again. η *lit.* and bring them. θ or, went up. ι *lit.* to bring Vashti. κ *lit.* add not to bring. λ כתיב *mary.* or, hath begotten me, קרי hath begotten us. μ *lit.* to make to return.

BRINK

קָצֶה end, border, extremity : Josh. iii. 8.

שָׂפָה lip : Gen. xli. 3 : Exod. ii. 3 ; vii. 15 : Deut. ii. 36 : Ezek. xlvii. 6.

BROAD

1 יָד *com.* hand.

2 רָחָב *adj.* large, wide, spacious, extensive. ᵃ רַחַב *m.* broad place. ᵇ רֹחַב *m.* breadth. ᶜ רְחוֹב *f.* strictly, broad ways.

3 רָקַע to beat out metal into broad plates. PIEL *fut.* ᵃ רְקָעִים *m. pl.* broad (plates).

Exod. xxvii. 1.	2 b	Job xi. 9.	2	Ezek. xl. 6, 6, 7, 29,		
Num. xvi. 38.	3 a	xxxvi. 16.	2 a	30, 33, 42, 47.	2 b	
xvi. 39.	3	Ps. cxix. 96.	2	xli. 1, 1, 12.	2 b	
1 Kings vi. 6, 6, 6.	2 b	Isa. xxxiii. 21. a	2, 1	xlii. 11, β 20.	2 c	
2 Chron. vi. 13.	2 b	Jer. v. 1.	2 c	xliii. 16, 17.	2 b	
Neh. iii. 8.	2	li. 58.	2	xlv. 6.	2 b	
xii. 38.	2	Nah. ii. 4.		xlvi. 22.	2 b	
				Nah. ii. 4.	2 c	

a lit. broad of spaces, or, hands. *β lit.* so the breadth of them.

BROIDERED

רִקְמָה *f.* variegation of colour; party-coloured cloth or garment, broidered work: Ezek. xvi. 10, 13, 18; xxvi. 16; xxvii. 7, 16, 24.

שָׁבַץ Piel, to work with chequer-work on white cloth, so that the cheques or cells resembled the settings of precious stones.—*Gesenius.* תַּשְׁבֵּץ *m.* tesselated stuff: Exod. xxviii. 4. Gesenius, made of chequer-work.

BROOK

אָפִיק *m.* see *Channel:* Ps. xlii. 1.

יְאוֹר *m.* river. See *River.* Isa. xix. 6, 7, 7, 7, 8.

מִיכַל *m.* a small brook: 2 Sam. xvii. 20.

נַחַל *m.* a valley with a brook; a brook, stream. Most of the streams in Palestine are torrents, flowing only in winter (χειμάρροι), and such an one is meant in Job vi. 15, My brethren are deceitful like the torrent, which dries up unexpectedly, and so disappoints the traveller.—*Gesenius.* Gen. xxxii. 23, &c.

BROTH

מָרָק *m.* broth, soup: Judg. vi. 19, 20: Isa. lxv. 4.

פָּרָק the same as above by a change of the first letter; or more probably from פָּרַק to break in pieces: Isa. lxv. 4, כתיב.

BROTHER

אָח *m.* a brother, whether of the same father, or mother, or of both; a relation generally, whether by affinity or blood, as uncle, cousin, nephew; one of the same country, tribe, or neighbourhood; a fellow or familiar; any person or thing like another; a term of affection generally: Gen. iv. 2, &c.; very frequent. אַח Ch. *m.* Ezra vii. 18. אַחֲוָה *f.* brotherhood: Zech. xi. 14.

אֱנוֹשׁ see *Man.* Gen. xiii. 8, *lit.* men brethren.

דּוֹד *m.* father's brother: Num. xxxvi. 11: 2 Kings xxiv. 17.

יָבַם to marry as the nearest relation, or in right of affinity. PIEL *inf.* Deut. xxv. 7. *fut.* Deut. xxv. 5. יָבָם *m.* the brother of a woman's husband, which brother, if her husband died childless, was obliged to marry her: Deut. xxv. 5, 7.

רֵעַ *m.* a companion, acquaintance, friend; one beloved: Deut. xxiv. 10.

BROW

גַּב *m.* that part which rises above the rest; the arch of the eye, eyebrow: Lev. xiv. 9.

מֵצַח *com.* forehead: Isa. xlviii. 4.

BROWN

חוּם *adj.* a dark brown or black colour: Gen. xxx. 32, 33, 35, 40.

BRUISE

1 דָּכָא to bruise, break in small pieces; to smite; applied to the mind, and used of the Messiah, it designates the most severe inward and outward suffering: Isa. liii. 5. PIEL *a inf.* PUAL *b part.*

2 דָּקַק to beat small or thin. KAL *a fut.* HOPHAL *b fut.*

3 חַבּוּרָה *f.* a stripe, weal, or wound.

4 מָעַךְ to press, squeeze, crush. KAL *part.* Paül.

5 עָשָׂה to work, or labour; to press the breasts. KAL *a inf.* PIEL *b pret.*

6 רְעַע Ch. to break in pieces. P'AL *fut.*

7 רָצַץ to break, to crush; differs from שָׁבַר, see Isa. xlii. 3. KAL *part.* Paül.

8 שֶׁבֶר *m.* breaking.

9 שׁוּף to break or smite in pieces; greatly to injure or wound. KAL *fut.*

Gen. iii. 15, 15.		9	Isa. xlii. 3.	7	Ezek. xxiii. 3, 8.	5 b	
Lev. xxii. 24.		4	liii. 5.	1 b	xxiii. 21.	5 a	
2 Kings xviii. 21.		7	liii. 10.	1 a	Dan. ii. 40.	6	
Isa. i. 6.		3	Jer. xxx. 12.	8	Nah. iii. 19.	8	
xxviii. 28, 28.	2 b a						

BRUIT

שֵׁמַע *m.* report, tidings, fame: Nah. iii. 19. שְׁמוּעָה *f.* message, tidings: Jer. x. 22.

BRUTISH

בָּעַר to consume, either by burning or eating: the latter sense seems to be the root of בְּעִיר, whence has recurred the meaning of brutish to the verb, to act like a brute, without regard to reason or propriety. KAL *a fut.* *b part.* Poel. NIPHAL *c pret.* *d part.* *e* בַּעַר *m.* stupid, brutish.

Ps. xlix. 10.		Prov. xxx. 2.	e	Jer. x. 14, 21.	c	
xcii. 6.	e	Isa. xix. 11.	b	li. 17.	c	
xciv. 8.	b	Jer. x. 8.	a	Ezek. xxi. 31.	b	
Prov. xii. 1.						

BUCKET

דְּלִי *m.* a vessel to draw water with: Isa. xl. 15. דְּלִי *m.* Num. xxiv. 7, *id.*

BUCKLER

1 מָגֵן *m.* a shield.

2 סֹחֵרָה *f.* a buckler or target, which protects the body on every side.

3 צִנָּה *f.* a shield of the larger size, which covered the whole person, not only from hostile attacks, but from the heat of the sun.

4 רֹמַח *m.* a spear, javelin.

2 Sam. xxii. 31.	1	Ps. xviii. 2, 30.	1	Jer. xlvi. 3.	1	
1 Chron. v. 18.	1	xxxv. 2.	3	Ezek. xxiii. 24.	3	
xii. 8.	4	xci. 4.	2	xxvi. 8.	3	
2 Chron. xxiii. 9.	1	Prov. ii. 7.	1	xxxviii. 4.	3	
Job xv. 26.	1	Cant. iv. 4.	1	xxxix. 9.	3	

BUD

1 מוֹצָא *m.* going out.

2 נָצַץ to send out rays, to shine; *trop.* to put forth flowers or blossoms. HIPHIL *pret.*

3 פָּרַח to sprout, blossom. KAL ᵃ*pret.* ᵇ*part.* Poel. HIPHIL ᶜ*fut.* ᵈ פֶּרַח *m.* flower, blossoms.

4 צָמַח to sprout or spring up. HIPHIL ᵃ*pret.* ᵇ*fut.* ᶜ צֶמַח *m.* a sprout, shoot.

Gen. xl. 10.	3 b	Cant. vi. 11.	2	Isa. lxi. 11.	4 c
Num. xvii. 8, 8.	3 a d	vii. 12.	2	Ezek. vii. 10.	3 a
Job xiv. 9.	3 c	Isa. xviii. 5.	3 d	xvi. 7.	4 c
xxxviii. 27.	1	xxvii. 6.	3 a	xxxi. 21.	4 b
Ps. cxxxii. 17.	4 b	lv. 10.	4 a	Hos. viii. 7.	4 c

BUILD

1 בָּנָה to build or repair a house or town, with an accusative of the *material,* and of the *place;* with an accusative of the *person,* to build a house for any one, to cause him to prosper; it also applies to having offspring and descendants: see *Child.* To begin to build: 1 Kings vi. 1, *comp.* 2 Chron. iii. 1, 2. To be advanced in honour and wealth; to be enlarged in knowledge; teachers are called builders for the same reason. KAL ᵃ*pret.* ᵇ*inf.* ᶜ*imp.* ᵈ*fut.* ᵉ*part.* Poel. ᶠ*part.* Paül. NIPHAL ᵍ*pret.* ʰ*inf.* ⁱ*fut.* ᵏ*part.* בְּנָה and בְּנָא Ch. P'AL ˡ*pret.* ᵐ*inf.* ⁿ*part.* ᵒ*part. pass.* ITHP'IL ᵠ*fut.* ʳ*part.* ˢ בִּנְיָה *f.* a building. ᵗ בִּנְיָן *m.* ᵘ בִּנְיָן Ch. *m.*

2 מְקָרֶה *m.* the beams of a house, framework.

Gen. iv. 17.α	1 e	2 Sam. xxiv. 21.	1 b	1 Chron. xvii. 25.	1 b
viii. 20.	1 d	xxiv. 25.	1 d	xxi. 22, 26.	1 d
x. 11.	1 d	1 Kings ii. 36.	1 c	xxii. 2, 5, 6, 7.	1 b
xi. 4.	1 d	iii. 1.	1 b	xxii. 8, 10.	1 d
xi. 5.	1 a	iii. 2.	1 g	xxii. 11.	1 a
xi. 8.	1 b	v. 3.	1 b	xxii. 19, 19.	1 c k
xii. 7, 8.	1 d	v. 5, 5.	1 b d	xxviii. 2, 10.	1 b
xiii. 18.	1 d	v. 18, 18, 18.	1 e e b	xxviii. 3, 6.	1 b
xxii. 9.	1 d	vi. 1, 5, 9, 10, 14, 15,		2 Chron. ii. 1, 3.	1 b
xxvi. 25.	1 d	16, 16, 36, 38.	1 d	ii. 4, 5, 9.	1 a
xxxiii. 17.	1 d	vi. 2.	1 a	ii. 6, 6.	1 d
xxxv. 7.	1 d	vi. 7, 7, 7.	1 h g h	ii. 12.	1 a
Exod. i. 11.	1 d	vi. 12.	1 e	iii. 1, 2, 3.	1 b
xvii. 15.	1 d	vii. 1.	1 a	vi. 2, 18, 33, 34, 38.	1 a
xx. 25.	1 d	vii. 2.	1 d	vi. 5, 7, 8.	1 b
xxiv. 4.	1 d	viii. 13.	1 b a	vi. 9, 9, 10.	1 d
xxxii. 5.	1 d	viii. 27, 43, 44, 48.	1 a	viii. 1, 2, 11, 12.	1 a
Num. xiii. 22.	1 g	viii. 16, 17, 18.	1 b	viii. 4, 4.	1 d a
xxi. 27.	1 i	viii. 19, 19, 20.	1 d	viii. 5.	1 d
xxiii. 1, 29.	1 c	ix. 1, 15, 19.	1 b	viii. 6.	1 b
xxiii. 14.	1 d	ix. 3, 10, 24, 24, 25.	1 a	ix. 3.	1 a
xxxii. 16, 34.	1 d	ix. 17.	1 d	xi. 5, 6.	1 a
xxxii. 24.	1 c	x. 4.	1 a	xiv. 6, 7, 7.	1 d
xxxii. 37, 38.	1 a	xi. 7.	1 d	xvi. 1.	1 a
Deut. vi. 10.	1 a	xi. 27, 38, 38.	1 a	xvi. 5.	1 d
viii. 12.	1 d	xii. 25, 25.	1 d	xvi. 6, 6.	1 a d
xiii. 16.	1 i	xiv. 23.	1 a	xvii. 12.	1 d
xx. 5, 20.	1 a	xv. 17.	1 d	xx. 8.	1 d
xxii. 8.	1 d	xv. 21.	1 b	xxvi. 2.	1 a
xxv. 9.	1 d	xv. 22, 22.	1 a d	xxvi. 6, 9, 10.	1 d
xxvii. 5.	1 a	xv. 23.	1 a	xxvii. 3, 3, 4, 4.	1 a
xxvii. 6.	1 a	xvi. 24, 24.	1 d a	xxxii. 5.	1 d
xxviii. 30.	1 d	xvi. 32, 34.	1 a	xxxiii. 3, 5.	1 d
Josh. vi. 26.	1 a	xviii. 32.	1 a	xxxiii. 4, 14, 15, 19.	1 d
viii. 30.	1 d	xxii. 39.	1 a	xxxiv. 11.	1 e
xix. 50.	1 d	2 Kings xii. 11.	1 e	xxxv. 3.	1 a
xxii. 10.	1 a	xii. 22.	1 a	xxxvi. 23.	1 b
xxii. 11.	1 a	xv. 35.	1 a	Ezra i. 2, 5.	1 b
xxii. 16, 19.β	1 b	xvi. 11.	1 d	i. 3.	1 d
xxii. 23, 26, 29.	1 b	xvi. 18.	1 a	iii. 2.	1 d
xxiv. 13.	1 a	xvii. 9.	1 d	iii. 10.	1 e
Judg. i. 26.	1 d	xxi. 3, 5.	1 a	iv. 1.	1 e
vi. 24.	1 a	xxi. 4.	1 a	iv. 2.	1 d
vi. 26.	1 a	xxii. 6.	1 e	iv. 3, 3.	1 b d
vi. 28.	1 f	xxiii. 13.	1 b d	iv. 4.	1 b
xviii. 28.	1 a	xxv. 1.	1 b	iv. 12.	1 o
xxi. 4.	1 d	1 Chron. vi. 10.	1 a	iv. 13, 16, 21.	1 q
Ruth iv. 11.	1 a	vi. 32.	1 d	v. 2, 3, 9, 13, 17.	1 m
1 Sam. ii. 35.	1 a	vi. 48.	1 d	v. 4.	1 u
vii. 17.	1 d	viii. 12.	1 a	v. 8, 16.	1 q
xiv. 35.	1 d b	xiv. 1.	1 b	v. 11, 11, 11.	1 o p l
2 Sam. v. 9, 11.	1 d	xvii. 4, 10, 12.	1 d	v. 15.	1 q
vii. 5, 13, 27.	1 d	xvii. 6.	1 a	vi. 3.	1 q
vii. 7.	1 a				

Ezra vi. 7.	1 n	Eccles. ix. 14.	1 a	Ezek. iv. 2.	1 a		
vi. 8.	1 m	x. 18.	2	xi. 3.	1 b		
vi. 14, 14.	1 o l	Cant. iv. 4.	1 f	xiii. 10.	1 e		
Neh. ii. 5, 17.	1 d	viii. 9.	1 a	xvi. 24.	1 d		
ii. 18, 20.	1 a	Isa. v. 2.	1 d	xvi. 25.	1 a		
iii. 1, 14, 15.	1 d	ix. 10.	1 d	xvi. 31.	1 b		
iii. 2, 2, 3, 13.	1 a	xxv. 2.	1 i	xvii. 17.	1 b		
iv. 1, 3, 5, 17, 18, 18.	1 e	xliv. 26, 28.	1 i	xxi. 22.	1 d		
iv. 6.	1 d	xlv. 13.	1 d	xxvi. 14.	1 i		
iv. 10.	1 b	lviii. 12.	1 a	xxvii. 4.	1 e		
vi. 1.	1 a	lx. 10.	1 a	xxviii. 26.	1 a		
vi. 6.	1 e	lxi. 4.	1 a	xxxvi. 10.	1 i		
vii. 1.	1 g	lxv. 21.	1 a	xxxvi. 33.	1 g		
vii. 4.	1 f	lxv. 22.	1 a	xxxvi. 36.	1 a		
xii. 29.	1 d	lxvi. 1.	1 d	xl. 5.	1 a		
Job iii. 14.	1 e	Jer. i. 10.	1 b	xli. 12, 12, 15.	1 t		
xii. 14.	1 i	xii. 16.	1 a	xli. 13.	1 t		
xx. 19.	1 d	xviii. 9.	1 b	xlii. 1, 5, 10.	1 t		
xxii. 23.	1 i	xix. 5.	1 a	Dan. iv. 30.	1 l		
xxvii. 18.	1 a	xxii. 13.	1 a	ix. 25, 25.	1 b g		
Ps. xxviii. 5.	1 d	xxii. 14.	1 a	Hos. viii. 14.	1 d		
li. 18.	1 d	xxiv. 6.	1 a	Amos v. 11.	1 a		
lxix. 35.	1 d	xxix. 5, 28.	1 c	ix. 6.	1 a		
lxxviii. 69.	1 d	xxx. 18.	1 a	ix. 11, 14.	1 a		
lxxxix. 2.	1 a	xxxi. 4, 4.	1 d g	Micah iii. 10.	1 b		
lxxxix. 4.	1 a	xxxi. 28.	1 b	vii. 11.	1 b		
cii. 16.	1 e	xxxi. 38.	1 a	Hab. ii. 12.	1 a		
cxviii. 22.	1 e	xxxii. 31.	1 a	Zeph. i. 13.	1 a		
cxxii. 3.	1 f	xxxii. 35.	1 a	Hag. i. 2.	1 h		
cxxvii. 1, 1.	1 d e	xxxiii. 7.	1 d	i. 8.	1 c		
cxlvii. 2.	1 d	xxxv. 7.	1 d	Zech. i. 16.	1 b		
Prov. ix. 1.	1 a	xxxv. 9.	1 d	v. 11.	1 b		
xiv. 1.	1 a	xlii. 10.	1 a	vi. 12, 15.	1 a		
xxiv. 3.	1 i	xlv. 4.	1 a	vi. 13.	1 d		
xxiv. 27.	1 a	lii. 4.	1 d	viii. 9.	1 h		
Eccles. ii. 4.	1 a	Lam. iii. 5.	1 a	ix. 3.	1 h		
iii. 3.	1 b			Mal. i. 4, 4.	1 d		

α *lit.* he was building.   β *lit.* in your building for you.

BUL

בּוּל *m.* the name of a month, beginning with the new moon of November; so called from its being a rainy month: 1 Kings vi. 38.

BULL, BULLOCK

1 אַבִּיר (see *Mighty*), strong, powerful; that which is the strongest; *metaph.* enemies of Christ and his church.

2 בֵּן *m.* son.

3 בָּקָר *com.* horned cattle (most commonly) at full age, when fit for the plough.—*Bochart.*

4 עֵגֶל *com.* a steer, a young bull or bullock, from its round plump form.

5 פַּר *m.* a bull, bullock, "young bullock," steer ox.

6 שׁוֹר *m.* an animal of the ox kind, without respect to age or sex. See *Ox.* The word itself is strictly generic.

7 תּוֹא *m.* a wild bull, or rather a species of gazelle or wild goat; Lxx. Vulg. in Deut. Aqu. Symm. Theod. Vulg. in Isa. ὄρυξ. The Targums, *bos sylvestris,* a kindred idea. Comp. *Unicorn.* See Bocharti Hierozoicon. lib. iii. cap. xxviii.

8 תּוֹר Ch. *m.* an ox, *i. q.* Heb. שׁוֹר.

No. 5 not all included.

Exod. xxix. 1.α	5, 2, 3	Num. xv. 24.α	5, 2, 3	Ps. lxvi. 15.	3
Lev. i. 5.β	2, 3	xxviii. 11, 19, 27.α	5, 2, 3	lxviii. 30.	1
iv. 10.	6	xxix. 2, 8, 13, 17.α	5, 2, 3	Isa. xxxiv. 7.	5, 1
iv. 14.α	5, 2, 3	Deut. 15, 19.	6	li. 20.	7
ix. 4, 18, 19.	6	xvii. 1.	6	lxv. 25.	3
xvi. 3.α	5, 2, 3	xxxiii. 17.	6	Jer. xxxi. 18.	4
xxii. 23, 27.	6	Judg. vi. 25, 25.γ	6, 5	xlvi. 21.	4
xxiii. 18.α	5, 2, 3	2 Chron. xiii. 9.α	5, 3	l. 11.	1
Num. vii. 15, 21, 27, 33,		xxix. 22, 32.	3	lii. 20.	3
39, 45, 51, 57, 63,	5, 2, 3	xxxv. 7.	3	Ezek. xliii. 19, 23, 25.α	5, 2, 3
69, 75, 81.α	5, 2, 3	Ezra vi. 9, 17.	8		
viii. 8, 8.α	5, 2, 3	vii. 17.	8	xlv. 18.α	5, 2, 3
viii. 8, 8.β	2, 3	Job xxi. 10.	6	xlv. 23.α	5, 2, 3
xv. 11.	6	Ps. l. 13.	6	Hos. xii. 11.	6

α *lit.* a steer the son of a bull.   β *lit.* the son of a bull.   γ *lit.* steer ox.

BULRUSH

אַגְמוֹן *m.* a rush: Isa. lviii. 5.

גֹּמֶא the Egyptian papyrus. See *Rush.* Exod. ii. 3: Isa. xviii. 2. Pliny takes notice of the "naves papyraceas armentaque Nili." Lucan has, "Conseritur bibula memphitis cymba papyro."

BULWARK

חֵיל *m.* see *Trench.* Isa. xxvi. 1. חֵילָה *f. id.* Ps. xlviii. 13, *lit.* her bulwark.

מָצוֹר *m.* a fortress, entrenchment, a besieging tower: Eccles. ix. 14.

פִּנָּה *f.* a corner, a battlement in a wall, *pinna:* 2 Chron. xxvi. 15.

מָצוֹר *m.* a mound, entrenchment, of the besiegers: Deut. xx. 20.

BUNCH

אֲגֻדָּה *f.* a collection, a bundle: Exod. xii. 22.

דַּבֶּשֶׁת *f.* bunch on a camel's back: Isa. xxx. 6.

BUNDLE

צְרוֹר *m.* that which is bound up fast and close, a bundle: Gen. xlii. 35, 35: 1 Sam. xxv. 29: Cant. i. 13.

BURDEN

1 אֲגֻדָּה *f.* a collection, a bunch: Isa. lviii. 6, "heavy burdens," *marg.* 'bundles of the yoke.'

2 מוֹטָה *f.* see *Yoke.* Isa. lviii. 6, *marg.* as above. The translators would seem to have rendered אֲגֻדּוֹת burdens, and מוֹטָה heavy; at least, so Taylor supposes in his Hebrew Concordance.

3 יָהַב to give, to supply. KAL *pret.* Ps. lv. 22, thy burden, *lit.* which he hath given thee, *i. e.* thy lot; or thy care, anxiety; LXX. μέριμνα; comp. 1 Pet. v. 7. Or יְהָב *m.* lot.

4 מַשָּׂא *m.* a burden or load; figuratively, a judgment which lies heavy on a people. Gesenius however takes the meaning in a more favourable sense of oracle uttered, as in Zech. xii. 1, and Mal. i. 1, it stands in a good sense. Exod. xxiii. 5, &c. ᵃ מַשָּׂאָה *f.* burden; or rising up, ascent of smoke and flame. ᵇ מַשֵּׂאת *f.* burden or oracle, either in the figurative sense as above, or burdens imposed, tribute, &c.

5 סָבַל to bear or to carry a burden as a porter. HITHPAEL to be a burden: ᵃ *fut.* ᵇ סֵבֶל *m.* a charge or burden. ᶜ סֹבֶל *m. id.* ᵈ סְבָלָה *f.* this word seems to imply heavier burdens. ᵉ סַבָּל *m.* a bearer (of burdens), a porter, in 1 Kings v. 29, with נֹשֵׂא by apposition; *lit.* a bearer of burdens bearing.

6 עָמַס to lay on a burden, to load. KAL ᵃ *part.* Poel, Zech. xii. 3. ᵇ מַעֲמָסָה *f.* a burden: Zech. xii. 3, *lit.* of burden. Gesenius quotes Jerome on this passage, to illustrate its meaning; who informs us that it was the custom in Palestine, and in the villages &c. of Judea, to place round heavy stones with which the young men might exercise themselves, some raising them to the knees, others higher, and others to the head or shoulders; and some, with uplifted arms and united hands, to show their strength, would raise them above their heads. Which

may be applied to the passage in question in this way,— Jerusalem shall be a burdensome stone to all who contend with her or attempt to remove her; they shall be cut and torn by it, while they accomplish nothing against her. Comp. Matt. xxi. 44.

7 שָׁפַת to place, to put. מִשְׁפְּתַיִם *dual,* may be intended to mean rails or bars placed on each side, to keep cattle asunder and in order, as in a stable or fold: Gen. xlix. 14, Issachar is a strong ass, couching, lying at his ease (see *Couch*), between two rails, enclosing him on each side, *i. e.* submitting to labours of husbandry, and extraordinary taxes, that they might be exempted from the avocations and perils of war. See Patrick *in loc.* Various other interpretations have been given of this word, as that it means panniers, boundaries, *i. e.* of the country of Issachar; but I adhere to the opinion of Schultens, that it refers to the hearth-irons, or stones, on which the pot was set for boiling, and that the figure there used is that of shepherds or nomad tribes, who prefer that kind of life to the more active and patriotic occupation of defending the country against their enemies; and we are to suppose the meanest and most inactive stretched on the ground where the cooking has been carried on. The charge brought against this tribe is that of disgraceful inactivity in preferring an inglorious occupation.

No. 4 not included.

Gen. xlix. 14.	7	Ps. lv. 22.	3	Isa. xxx. 27.	4 a
Exod. i. 11.	5 d	lxxxi. 6.	5 b	lviii. 6.	1, 2
ii. 11.	5 d	Eccles. xii. 5.	5 a	Lam. ii. 14.	4 b
v. 4, 5.	5 d	Isa. ix. 4.	5 c	Amos v. 11.	4 b
vi. 6, 7.	5 d	x. 27.	5 c	Zeph. iii. 18.	4 b
1 Kings v. 15.	5 e	xiv. 25.	5 c	Zech. xii. 3, 3.	6 b a
Neh. iv. 17.	5 b				

BURIAL (See BURY)

BURN

1 אָכַל to eat, to consume or destroy in any way, especially by fire or sword. KAL *fut.*

2 אֵשׁ *com.* fire.

3 בָּעַר to burn, said of fire, and of the fuel of fire; properly to burn in order to waste, consume, and clear away; it implies therefore raging and increasing flame. A distinction is to be made in the use of this word when applied to fire or to the material; as the bush burned though not consumed, with the appearance of fire, which did not consume the wood. KAL ᵃ *pret.* ᵇ *fut.* ᶜ *part.* Poel. PIEL ᵈ *pret.* ᵉ *inf.* ᶠ *fut.* PUAL ᵍ *part.* HIPHIL ʰ *pret.* ⁱ *fut.*

4 דּוּר *m.* anything round; a heap of wood or bones for the fire.

5 דָּלַק to burn; to pursue with a hot malicious mind: yet in one instance it is used evidently in a good sense, applied to the lips when professing ardent friendship. KAL ᵃ *part.* דְּלַק Ch. ᵇ P'AL *part. active.*

6 זָכַר to remember; to make to be remembered; to offer a memorial sacrifice. HIPHIL *part.*

7 חָרָה to kindle. KAL *fut.*

8 חָרַר to be burned to a coal: figuratively applied to extreme heat of the body in a fever. KAL ᵃ *pret.* NIPHAL ᵇ *pret.*

ᶜ*fut.* ᵈ*part.* ᵉ חַרְחֻר *m.* scorching heat in the air causing great drought.

9   יָצַת to burn with a destructive conflagration, as a forest, city, or cornfield set on fire: hence to be reduced to a ruined desolate condition. KAL ᵃ*fut.* NIPHAL ᵇ*pret.* HIPHIL ᶜ*pret.*

10   יָקַד to burn as common culinary fire, which burns slow and steady, but may spread wide, consume much, and continue long. KAL ᵃ*fut.* ᵇ*part.* Poel. HOPHAL ᶜ*fut.* יְקַד Ch. P'AL ᵈ*part. active.* ᵉ יְקֵדָה Ch. *f.* a burning. ᶠ יְקוֹד *m. id.* ᵍ מוֹקֵד *m. id.* ʰ מוֹקְדָה *f. id.* Gesenius, perhaps, heap of fuel.

11   כָּוָה only in Niphal, to be burnt with fire in any part of the body. NIPHAL ᵃ*fut.* ᵇ כִּי *m.* the mark of a hot iron brand on the forehead or cheek as a token of servility. ᶜ כְּוִיָה *f.* a burning. ᵈ מִכְוָה *f.* a place burnt on the body.

12   לָהַט to burn, or be burnt, with the vehement heat of a strong penetrating flame: applied to God's dreadful judgments burning up the wicked. PIEL ᵃ*pret.* ᵇ*fut.*

13   מָזֶה *adj.* emaciated, dried up, reduced to skin and bone.

14   נָשָׂא to lift up; to burn as a bonfire or conflagration. KAL *fut.*

15   נָשַׂק to kindle a fire, to set on fire. HIPHIL *pret.*

16   סָרַף see below שָׂרַף. PIEL *part.*

17   עָלָה to ascend; a lamp ascends when it is lighted or burneth; so also what is burnt on the altar ascends in flame and smoke. KAL ᵃ*fut.* HIPHIL ᵇ*inf.* ᶜ עֹלָה *f.* a burnt-offering and sacrifice. ᵈ עֲלָה Ch. *f. id.*

18   צוּת to kindle, set on fire. HIPHIL *fut.*

19   צָרַב to burn, to scorch. NIPHAL ᵃ*pret.* ᵇ צָרֶבֶת *f.* a burning.

20   קָדַח to kindle, to cause to burn; to kindle itself. KAL ᵃ*inf.* ᵇ קַדַּחַת *f.* burning ague, fever.

21   קָטַר Piel, to burn incense or fat; to cause the smoke to ascend as vapour of incense. PIEL ᵃ*pret.* ᵇ*inf.* ᶜ*fut.* ᵈ*part.* HIPHIL ᵉ*pret.* ᶠ*inf.* ᵍ*imp.* ʰ*fut.* ⁱ*part.* HOPHAL ᵏ*fut.* ˡ מִקְטָר *m.* a burning.

22   רֶשֶׁף *m.* a flame, a burning heat; a burning pestilence; burning heat, burning coals.

23   שָׂרַף to burn, *e.g.* cities, houses, altars. KAL ᵃ*pret.* ᵇ*inf.* ᶜ*fut.* ᵈ*part.* Poel. ᵉ*part.* Paül. NIPHAL ᶠ*fut.* PUAL ᵍ*pret.* ʰ שְׂרֵפָה *f.* a burning. ⁱ מַשְׂרָפוֹת *f. pl.* burnings.

No. 17 c not included.

Gen. xi. 3.	23 c h	Lev. iii. 5, 11, 16.	21 e	Lev. xiii. 23.	19 b
xv. 17.	2	iv. 10, 19, 31, 35.	21 e	xiii. 24, 24, 25, 28, 28.	11 d
xxxviii. 24.	23 f	iv. 12, 12.	23 a f	xiii. 52, 52.	23 a f
xliv. 18.	7	iv. 21, 21.	23 a	xiii. 55, 57.	23 c
Exod. iii. 2.	3 c	iv. 26.	21 h	xvi. 25.	21 h
iii. 3.	3 b	v. 12.	21 e	xvi. 27.	23 a
xii. 10.	23 c	vi. 9, 9.	10 h c	xvi. 28.	23 d
xxi. 25, 25.	11 c	vi. 12, 12, 12.	10c,3d,21e	xvii. 6.	21 e
xxvii. 20.	17 b	vi. 13.	10 c	xix. 6.	23 f
xxix. 13, 18, 25.	21 e	vi. 15.	21 e	xx. 14.	23 c
xxix. 14.	23 c	vi. 22.	21 k	xxi. 9.	23 f
xxix. 34.	23 a	vi. 30.	23 f	xxiv. 2.	17 b
xxx. 1.	21 l	vii. 5, 31.	21 e	xxvi. 16.	20 b
xxx. 7, 7.	21 e h	vii. 17, 19.	23 f	Num. v. 26.	21 e
xxx. 8.	21 h	viii. 16, 20, 21, 28.	21 h	xi. 1.	3 b
xxx. 20.	21 f	viii. 17.	23 a	xi. 3.	3 a
xxxii. 20.	23 c	viii. 32.	23 c	xvi. 37.	23 h
xl. 27.	21 h	ix. 10.	21 e	xvi. 39.	23 e
Lev. i. 9, 13, 15, 17.	21 e	ix. 11.	21 e	xviii. 17.	21 e
ii. 2, 9, 16.	21 e	ix. 13, 14, 17, 20.	21 h	xix. 5, 5.	23 a c
ii. 11.	21 h	x. 6.	23 h	xix. 6, 17.	23 h
ii. 12.	17 a	x. 16.	23 g	xix. 8.	23 d

Num. xxxi. 10.	23 a	2 Chron. xxi. 19, 19.	23 h	Jer. xi. 13.	21 b
Deut. iv. 11.	3 c	xxv. 14.	21 c	xv. 14.	10 c
v. 23.	3 c	xxvi. 16, 18, 18, 19.	21 f	xvii. 4.	10 c
vii. 5, 25.	23 c	xxviii. 3, 3.	21 e, 3 i	xviii. 15.	21 c
ix. 15.	3 c	xxviii. 4.	21 c	xix. 4.	21 c
ix. 21.	23 c	xxviii. 25.	21 b	xix. 5.	23 b
xii. 3, 31.	23 c	xxix. 7.	21 e	xix. 13.	21 a
xiii. 16.	23 a	xxix. 11.	21 i	xx. 9.	3 c
xxviii. 22.	8 e	xxxii. 12.	21 h	xxi. 10.	23 a
xxix. 23.	23 h	xxxiv. 5.	23 a	xxii. 12.	3 a
xxxii. 22.	10 a	xxxiv. 25.	21 c	xxxii. 29.	23 a
xxxii. 24, 24.	13, 22	xxxvi. 19, 19.	23 c a	xxxiv. 2, 22.	23 a
Josh. vi. 24.	23 a	Ezra vi. 9.	17 d	xxxiv. 5, 5.	23 i c
vii. 15.	23 f	Neh. i. 3.	9 b	xxxvi. 22.	3 g
vii. 25.	23 c	ii. 17.	9 b	xxxvi. 25, 27.	23 b
viii. 28.	23 c	iv. 2.	23 e	xxxvi. 28, 29, 32.	23 a
xi. 6.	23 c	x. 34.	3 e	xxxvii. 8, 10.	23 a
xi. 9, 11, 13, 13.	23 a	Esth. i. 12.	3 a	xxxviii. 17.	23 f
Judg. ix. 52.	23 b	Job i. 16.	3 b	xxxviii. 18.	23 a
xii. 1.	23 c	xxx. 30.	8 a	xxxviii. 23.	23 a
xiv. 15.	23 c	Ps. xxxix. 3.	3 b	xxxix. 8.	23 a
xv. 5.	3 i	xlvi. 9.	23 c	xliii. 12.	23 a
xv. 6.	23 c	lxxiv. 8.	23 a	xliii. 13.	23 a
xv. 14.	3 a	lxxix. 5.	3 b	xliv. 3, 5, 8, 17, 18,	
xviii. 27.	23 a	lxxx. 16.	23 e	25.	21 b
1 Sam. ii. 15.	21 h	lxxxiii. 14.	3 b	xliv. 15, 19.	21 d
ii. 16.	21 h	lxxxix. 46.	3 b	xliv. 21, 23.	21 a
ii. 28.	21 f	xcvii. 3.	12 b	xlviii. 35.	21 i
xxx. 1.	23 c	cii. 3.	8 b	xlix. 2.	9 a
xxx. 3.	23 e	cvi. 18.	12 b	li. 25.	23 h
xxx. 14.	23 a	Prov. vi. 27.	23 f	li. 30.	9 c
xxxi. 12.	23 c	vi. 28.	11 a	li. 32.	23 a
2 Sam. v. 21.	23 a	vi. 29.	11 a	li. 58.	9 a
xxiii. 7.	23 b f	xxvi. 23.	5 a	lii. 13, 13.	23 c a
1 Kings iii. 3.	21 i	Isa. i. 7.	23 e	Lam. ii. 3.	3 b
ix. 16.	23 c	i. 31.	3 a	Ezek. i. 13.	23 c
ix. 25.	21 f	iii. 24.	11 b	v. 2.	3 i
xi. 8.	21 i	iv. 4.	3 e	v. 4.	23 a
xii. 33.	21 f	ix. 5.	23 h	xv. 4.	8 c
xiii. 1.	21 f	ix. 18.	3 a	xv. 5.	8 c
xiii. 2, 2. a	21 i, 23 c	x. 16, 16.	10 f	xvi. 41.	23 a
xv. 13.	23 c	x. 17.	3 a	xx. 47.	19 a
xvi. 18.	23 a	xxiv. 6.	8 a	xxiii. 47.	23 c
xxii. 43.	21 d	xxvii. 4.	18 v	xxiv. 5.	4
2 Kings i. 14.	1	xxx. 27.	3 c	xxiv. 10.	8 c
x. 26.	23 c	xxxiii. 12, 12.	23 i, 9 a	xxiv. 11.	8 a
xii. 3.	21 d	xxxiii. 14.	10 g	xxxix. 9, 9.	15, 3 d
xiv. 4.	21 d	xxxiv. 9.	3 c	xxxix. 10.	23 a
xv. 4, 35.	21 d	xl. 16.	3 e	xliii. 21.	23 a
xvi. 4.	21 c	xlii. 25.	3 b	Dan. iii. 6, 11, 15, 17,	
xvi. 13.	21 h	xliii. 2. β	11 a	20, 21, 23, 26.	10 d
xvi. 15.	21 g	xliv. 15.	3 e	vii. 9.	9 b
xvii. 11.	21 c	xliv. 16, 19.	23 a	vii. 11	10 e
xvii. 31.	23 d	xlvii. 14.	23 a	Hos. ii. 13.	21 h
xviii. 4.	21 d	lxii. 1.	3 b	iv. 13.	21 c
xxii. 17.	21 c	lxiv. 2.	20 a	vii. 6.	3 c
xxiii. 4, 6, 16, 20.	23 c	lxiv. 11. γ	23 h	xi. 2.	21 c
xxiii. 5, 5.	21 c d	lxv. 3.	21 d	Joel i. 19.	12 a
xxiii. 8.	21 a	lxv. 5.	10 b	ii. 3.	12 b
xxiii. 11.	23 a	lxv. 7.	21 a	Amos ii. 1.	23 b
xxv. 9, 9.	23 c a	lxvi. 2.	6	iv. 11.	23 h
1 Chron. xiv. 12.	23 f	Jer. i. 16.	21 c	vi. 10.	16
xxiii. 13.	21 f	ii. 15.	9 b	Mic. i. 7.	23 f
2 Chron. ii. 4, 6.	21 f	iv. 4.	3 a	Nah. i. 5.	14
iv. 20.	3 e	vi. 29.	8 b	ii. 13.	3 h
xiii. 11, 11.	21 i, 3 e	vii. 9.	21 b	Hab. i. 16.	21 c
xv. 16.	23 c	vii. 20.	3 a	iii. 5. δ	22
xvi. 14.	23 c h	ix. 10, 12.	9 b	Mal. iv. 1, 1.	3 c, 12 a

α *lit.* they shall burn.   β *lit.* it shall not burn thee.   γ *lit.* for burning of fire.   δ or, burning diseases, Deut. xxxii. 24.

BURNISHED

קָלָל *adj.* smooth, polished: Ezek. i. 7.

BURST

בָּקַע to cleave asunder with a noise. NIPHAL *fut.* Job xxxii. 19, "ready to burst."

מְכִתָּה *f.* a breaking in pieces: Isa. xxx. 14.

נָתַק to draw or pull asunder; to tear off. PIEL *pret.* Jer. ii. 20; v. 5. *fut.* Jer. xxx. 8: Nah. i. 13.

פָּרַץ to break out violently, as water breaks through a bank or any forced passage, and diffuseth itself all abroad. KAL *fut.* Prov. iii. 10.

BURY

קָבַר to bury; an act of kindness and humanity which none dared to perform for one who had been executed : Ps. lxxix. 3. KAL [a]*pret.* [b]*inf.* [c]*imp.* [d]*fut.* [e]*part.* Poel. [f]*part.* Paül. NIPHAL [g]*fut.* PIEL [h]*inf.* [i]*fut.* [k]*part.* PUAL [l]*pret.* [m]קֶבֶר *m.* buryingplace. [n]קְבוּרָה *f.* burial ; grave, sepulchre.

Gen. xv. 15.	g	1 Sam. xxviii. 3.	d	2 Kings xxi. 26.a	d
xxiii. 4, 4.	m d	xxxi. 13.	d	xxiii. 30.	d
xxiii. 6, 6.	c b	2 Sam. ii. 4.	a	1 Chron. x. 12.	d
xxiii. 8.	b	ii. 5, 32.	d	2 Chron. xxi. 31.a	d
xxiii. 9, 20.	m	iii. 32.	d	xii. 16.	g
xxiii. 11, 15.	c	iv. 12.	d	xiv. 1.	d
xxiii. 13.	d	xvii. 23.	g	xvi. 14.	d
xxiii. 19.	a	xxi. 14.	d	xxi. 1.	g
xxv. 9.	d	1 Kings ii. 10, 34.	g	xxi. 20.	d
xxv. 10	l	ii. 31.	a	xxii. 9.	d
xxxv. 8, 19.	g	xi. 15.	h	xxiv. 16.	d
xxxv. 29.	d	xi. 43.	d	xxiv. 25, 25.	d a
xlvii. 29.	d	xiii. 29.	b	xxv. 28.	d
xlvii. 30, 30.	a n	xiii. 31, 31, 31.	b a f	xxvi. 23, 23.	d n
xlviii. 7.	d	xiv. 13.	a	xxvii. 9.	d
xlix. 29.	c	xiv. 18.	d	xxviii. 27.	d
xlix. 30.	m	xiv. 31.	d	xxxii. 33.	d
xlix. 31, 31, 31.	a	xv. 8.	d	xxxiii. 20.	d
l. 5, 5.	d	xv. 24.	g	xxxv. 24.	g
l. 6.	c	xvi. 6, 28.	d	Job xxvii. 15.	g
l. 7, 14, 14.	b	xxii. 37.	d	Ps. lxxix. 3.	e
l. 13, 13.	d m	xxii. 50.	g	Eccles. vi. 3.	n
Num. xi. 34.	a	2 Kings viii. 24.	g	viii. 10.	f
xx. 1.	g	ix. 10.	e	Isa. xiv. 20.	n
xxxiii. 4.	k	ix. 28.	d	Jer. vii. 32.	a
Deut. x. 6.	g	ix. 34.	c	viii. 2.	g
xxi. 23.	b d	ix. 35.	b	xiv. 16.	k
xxxiv. 6.	d	x. 35.	d	xvi. 4, 6.	g
Josh. xxiv. 30, 33.	d	xii. 21.	d	xix. 11, 11.	d b
xxiv. 32.	a	xiii. 9, 20.	d	xx. 6.	g
Judg. ii. 9.	d	xiii. 13.	g	xxii. 19, 19.	g n
viii. 32.	g	xiii. 21.	e	xxv. 33.	g
x. 2, 5.	g	xiv. 16, 20.	d	Ezek. xxxix. 11, 12, 13.	a
xii. 7, 10, 12, 15.	g	xv. 7.	d	xxxix. 14.	k
xvi. 31, 31.	d m	xv. 38.	g	xxxix. 15, 15.	k a
Ruth i. 17.	g	xvi. 20.	d	Hos. ix. 6.	i
1 Sam. xxv. 1.	d	xxi. 18.	g		

a lit. one buried him.

BUSH, BUSHY

נַהֲלֹלִים *m.* pastures to which flocks are led : Isa. vii. 19. Our translation gives in the *marg.* 'commendable trees,' as if the word were derived from הָלַל to praise ; but this is not admitted by modern critics.

סְנֶה *m.* a thorny bush : Exod. iii. 2, 2, 2, 3, 4 : Deut. xxxiii. 16 : whence prob. the name of Mount Sinai.

שִׂיחַ *m.* plant, shrub, bush : Job xxx. 4, 7.

תַּלְתַּלִּים *m. pl.* hanging down, flowing ; spoken of the hair : Cant. v. 11.

BUSINESS

דָּבָר *m.* a thing, matter, business, &c. : Deut. xxiv. 5 : Josh. ii. 14, 20 : Judg. xviii. 7, 28 : 1 Sam. xxi. 2, 2, 8.

עִנְיָן *m.* see *Travail :* Eccles. v. 3.

מְלָאכָה *f.* any work, business, or affair ; an occupation, employment : Gen. xxxix. 11, &c.

מַעֲשֶׂה *m.* work, labour : 1 Sam. xx. 19.

BUSY

עָשָׂה to do. KAL *part.* Poel : 1 Kings xx. 40.

BUTLER

שָׁקָה HIPHIL, to give to drink : *part.* cupbearer : Gen. xl. 1, 2,

5, 9, 13, 20, 21, 23 ; xli. 9. מַשְׁקֶה *m.* butlership : Gen. xl. 21, "he again gave the chief cupbearer charge over the giving of drink."

BUTTER

חֶמְאָה *f.* thick or curdled milk, or cream : in Prov. xxx. 33, it is thought to mean cheese. Gen. xviii. 8 : Deut. xxxii. 14 : Judg. v. 25 : 2 Sam. xvii. 29 : Job xx. 17 : Prov. xxx. 33 : Isa. vii. 15, 22, 22. מַחֲמָאֹת *f. pl.* Ps. lv. 21, *lit.* smooth are the milkinesses of his mouth : but, observes Gesenius, it would better suit the parallelism to read with Kimchi and others, מְחֶמְאֹת his mouth is smoother than cream or butter.

חֵמָה *f.* the same : Job xxix. 6.

BUTTOCKS

מִפְשָׂעָה *f.* the thigh, the hip, the part on which the step chiefly depends : 1 Chron. xix. 4.

שֵׁת *m.* the posteriors, the seat : 2 Sam. x. 4 : Isa. xx. 4.

BUY

1 כָּרָה to prepare, to provide ; to provide by purchasing. KAL *fut.*

2 לָקַח to take, as a possession ; as ware is taken or bought. KAL *fut.*

3 קָנָה to get, gain, acquire, possess, in any manner. KAL [a]*pret.* [b]*inf.* [c]*imp.* [d]*fut.* [e]*part.* Poel. NIPHAL [f]*pret.* קְנָה Ch. P'AL [g]*fut.* [h]מִקְנָה *f.* bought.

4 שָׁבַר *m. com.* whence שֶׁבֶר to buy or sell, corn, food. KAL [a]*inf.* [b]*imp.* [c]*fut.* [d]*part.* Poel.

Gen. xvii. 12, 13, 23,		Lev. xxv. 14.	3 b	1 Chron. xxi. 24.	3 b d
27.	3 h	xxv. 15, 44, 45.	3 d	2 Chron. xxxiv. 11.	3 b
xxiii. 19.	3 d	xxv. 28, 30, 50.	3 e	Ezra vii. 17.	3 g
xxxix. 1.	3 d	xxv. 51.	3 h	Neh. v. 3.	2
xli. 57.	4 a	xxvii. 22.	3 h	v. 16.	3 a
xlii. 2.	4 b	xxvii. 24.	3 a	x. 31.	2
xlii. 3, 5, 7, 10,	4 a	Deut. ii. 6, 6.	4 c, 1	Prov. xx. 14.	3 e
xliii. 2.	4 b	xxviii. 68.	3 e	xxiii. 23.	3 c
xliii. 4.	4 c	xxxii. 6.	3 a	xxxi. 16.	2
xliii. 20, 22.	4 a	Josh. xxiv. 32.	3 a	Isa. xxiv. 2.	3 e
xliv. 25.	4 b	Ruth iv. 4, 8.	3 c	xliii. 24.	3 a
xlvii. 14.	4 d	iv. 5, 5.	3 b a	lv. 1, 1.	3 a
xlvii. 19.	3 c	iv. 9.	3 a	Jer. xxxii. 7, 7.	3 c b
xlvii. 20.	3 d	2 Sam. xii. 3.	3 a	xxxii. 8, 8, 25.	3 c
xlvii. 22, 23.	3 a	xxiv. 21.	3 b	xxxii. 9, 44.	3 d
xlix. 30.	3 a	xxiv. 24.	3 b d	xxxii. 43.	3 f
l. 13.	3 a	xxiv. 24.	3 d	Ezek. vii. 12.	3 e
Exod. xii. 44.	3 h	1 Kings xvi. 24.	3 d	Hos. iii. 2.	1
xxi. 2.	3 d	2 Kings xii. 12.	3 b	Amos viii. 6.	3 b
Lev. xxii. 11.	3 d	xxii. 6.	3 b		

BYWAYS

עֲקַלְקַל *adj.* crooked. אֹרַח *com.* a way, road or path : Judg. v. 6.

BYWORD

מִלָּה *f.* word, speech ; the subject of talk and conversation : Job xxx. 9.

מָשָׁל *m.* parable, proverb : Ps. xliv. 14. מְשֹׁל *m.* proverb : Ges., a song of derision : Job xvii. 6.

שְׁנִינָה *f.* mockery, scorn, derision ; *lit.* sharp, pungent speech : Deut. xxviii. 37 : 1 Kings ix. 7 : 2 Chron. vii. 20.

CAB

קַב *m.* a measure, the eighteenth part of an ephah, containing something more than three pints : 2 Kings vi. 25.

CABIN

חָנוּת *f.* a vault, cell, so called from its curved or arched form ; a dungeon : Jer. xxxvii. 16.

CAGE

כְּלוּב *m.* a cage or basket ; a trap-cage : Jer. v. 27.

CAKE

1 דְּבֵלָה *f.* dry figs worked into one mass or cake : in which form they grew hard, and would keep for a long time : Cels. Hierobot. part ii. p. 377.

2 חַלָּה *f.* a cake, especially such as was offered in sacrifices, similar to the unleavened cakes still made by the Jews, which are perforated or punctured to prevent fermentation.

3 כַּוָּנִים *m. pl.* cakes prepared in a certain way for an idol.

4 לְבִבוֹת *f. pl.* cakes shaped like a heart; whence לָבַב to make cakes. PIEL [a] *fut.*

5 עֻגָה and עֻגָּה *f.* a cake baked on the hearth ; or upon hot stones, and covered with ashes, such as could be hastily prepared. [a] מָעוֹג *m. id.*

6 צַלּוּל, *in keri* צְלִיל *m.* a round cake (of barley bread).

7 רָקִיק *m.* wafer.

See *Unleavened.*

Gen. xviii. 6.	5	Num. xv. 20.	2	1 Kings xvii. 13.	5
Exod. xii. 39.	5	Judg. vii. 13.	6	xix. 6.	5
xxix. 2, 23.	2	1 Sam. xxv. 18.	1	1 Chron. xii. 40.	5
Lev. ii. 4.	2	xxx. 12.	1	xxiii. 29.	7
vii. 12, 13.	2	2 Sam. vi. 19.	3	Jer. vii. 18.	3
viii. 26, 26.	2	xiii. 6.	4 a, 4	xliv. 19.	3
xxiv. 5, 5.	2	xiii. 8, 8.	4 a, 4	Ezek. iv. 12.	5
Num. vi. 15, 19.	2	xiii. 10.	4	Hos. vii. 8.	8
xi. 8.	5	1 Kings xvii. 12.	5 a		

CALAMITY

1 אֵיד *m.* a heavy calamity, which crusheth and ruineth ; great distress, which surrounds and straitens ; or, as serenity and light are the symbols of joy, so vapour, fog, clouds, and darkness, of distress and perplexity.—*Taylor.*

2 הַוָּה *f.* any troublesome evil, sad event or accident ; a ruinous downfall ; a very great misfortune. See *Wicked.* כ' הַיָּה [a]

3 רַע *adj.* evil, unfortunate, calamitous.

Deut. xxxii. 35.	1	Prov. i. 26.	1	Jer. xviii. 17.	1
2 Sam. xxii. 19.	1	vi. 15.	1	xlvi. 21.	1
Job vi. 2.	2	xvii. 5.	1	xlviii. 16.	1
xxx. 13.	2	xix. 13.	2	xlix. 8, 32.	1
Ps. xviii. 18.	1	xxiv. 22.	1	Ezek. xxxv. 5.	1
lvii. 1.	2	xxvii. 10.	1	Obad. 13, 13, 13.	1
cxli. 5.	3				

CALAMUS

קָנֶה *m.* a reed ; the word is also used to signify *calamus aromaticus*, sometimes alone, sometimes with the addition of בֹּשֶׂם *aromatis* or *aromaticus*, sometimes of הַטּוֹב *optimus.* The *calamus aromaticus* is a reed growing in India and Arabia, scenting the air with a fragrant smell ; and when cut down, dried, and powdered, making an ingredient in the richest perfumes : Exod. xxx. 23 : Cant. iv. 14 : Ezek. xxvii. 19.

CALDRON

אַגְמוֹן *m.* a pool, a caldron : Job xli. 20.

דּוּד *m.* a basket ; a pot or kettle : 2 Chron. xxxv. 13.

סִיר *com.* a pot, kettle, caldron ; a fleshpot : Jer. lii. 18, 19 : Ezek. xi. 3, 7, 11, *lit.* be for a caldron to you.

קַלַּחַת *f.* a pot, kettle : 1 Sam. ii. 14 : Micah iii. 3.

CALF

1 בֵּן *m.* a son, calf, *lit.* son of.

2 בָּקָר *com.* a beeve, male or female.

3 עֵגֶל *com.* a calf, male and female ; sometimes a heifer, in its round and fleshy state. [a] עֶגְלָה *f. id.*

4 פַּר and פָּר *m.* a young bull.

Gen. xviii. 7.		1, 2	1 Kings xii. 28, 32.	3	Isa. xxvii. 10.	3
xviii. 8.	1, 2	2 Kings x. 29.	3	Jer. xxxiv. 18, 19.	3
Exod. xxxii. 4, 8, 19,		xvii. 16.	3	Ezek. i. 7.	3
20, 24, 35.	3	2 Chron. xi. 15.	3	Hos. viii. 5, 6.	3
Lev. ix. 2.	3, 1, 2	xiii. 8.	3	x. 5.	3 a
ix. 3, 8.	3	Neh. ix. 18.	3	xiii. 2.	3
Deut. ix. 16, 21.	3	Ps. xxix. 6.	3	xiv. 2.	4
1 Sam. vi. 7, 10.	1	lxviii. 30.	3	Amos vi. 4.	3
xiv. 32.	1, 2	cvi. 19.	3	Micah vi. 6.	3
xxviii. 24.	3	Isa. xi. 6.	3	Mal. iv. 2.	3

CALKER

בֶּדֶק *m.* that which repairs a breach, from בָּדַק to make a breach : Ezek. xxvii. 9, 27, *marg.* 'stoppers of chinks.'

חָזַק to bind fast, to strengthen, repair ; or stop a chink. HIPHIL *part.* Ezek. xxvii. 9, *marg.* 'strengtheners, or stoppers of chinks ;' 27, *lit.* repairers of thy chinks.

CALL

1 אָמַר to say. KAL [a] *fut.* [b] *part.* Poel. NIPHAL [c] *fut.*

2 בּוֹא to come. HIPHIL *fut.* cause to come.

3 זָעַק to cry out, to call. See *Cry.* KAL [a] *fut.* NIPHAL [b] *fut.* HIPHIL [c] *fut.*

4 סוּר to turn aside. HIPHIL *pret.* call back, remove.

5 צָעַק to cry, particularly for help ; Hiphil, to call together. NIPHAL [a] *fut.* HIPHIL [b] *fut.*

6 קָרָא to cry, call out, shout ; with אַחֲרֵי, עַל, אֶל to, after any one ; to cry for help, to call upon, to invoke ; to call upon God, with אֶל, לְ ; and with עַל of the person against whom help is asked ; with בְּשֵׁם to call on the name Jehovah ; to proclaim, to publish, to praise, celebrate. The most common meaning of this word answers to the Greek word καλεῖν, to call, call for, to summon or invite ; to call together or convoke ; to call to an office ; to call to judgment ; to call or give a name to another ; to read aloud ; Niphal, to be called, &c. We have the following forms of expression : to be called by the name of, to be numbered with, Isa. xliii. 7 ; to be called by the name of, *lit.* the name of to be called upon, is equivalent to the being accounted the people of Jehovah : to be called is sometimes equivalent to the verb, to be, or to be in a settled, authorised manner. KAL [a] *pret.* [b] *inf.* [c] *imp.* [d] *fut.* [e] *part.* Poel. [f] *part.* Paül. NIPHAL [g] *pret.* [h] *fut.* [i] *part.* PUAL [k] *pret.* [l] *part.* קְרָא Ch. to call, ITHP'EL [m] *fut.* [n] מִקְרָא *m.* convocation.

7 שׁוּב to return. HIPHIL *pret.* call, cause to return.

8 שׂוּם to set. KAL *fut., lit.* and he set his name.

9 שָׁמַע to hear; Piel and Hiphil, to call together. PIEL [a] *fut.* HIPHIL [b] *imp.*

See *Blessed, Happy, Record, Remembrance, Witness.*

Gen. i. 5, 5.	6 d	Num. xvi. 12.	6 b	2 Sam. xv. 2.	6 d
i. 8.	6 d	xxi. 3.	6 d	xv. 11.	6 f
i. 10, 10.	6 d a	xxii. 5, 20, 37.	6 b	xvii. 5.	6 d
ii. 19, 19.	6 d	xxiv. 10.	6 a	xviii. 18, 18.	6 d h
ii. 23.	6 h	xxv. 2.	6 d	xviii. 26, 28.	6 d
iii. 9, 20.	6 d	xxxii. 41, 42.	6 d	xxi. 2.	6 d
iv. 17, 25.	6 d	Deut. ii. 11, 20.	6 d	xxii. 4, 7.	6 d
iv. 26, 26.	6 d b	iii. 9, 9, 14.	6 d	1 Kings i. 9, 25.	6 d
v. 2, 3, 29.	6 d	iii. 13.	6 h	i. 10, 26.	6 d
xi. 9.	6 a	iv. 7.	6 b	i. 19, 19.	6 d a
xii. 8, 18.	6 d	v. 1.	6 d	i. 28, 32.	6 c
xiii. 4.	6 d	xv. 2.	6 a	ii. 36, 42.	6 d
xvi. 11, 14.	6 a	xxv. 8.	6 a	vii. 21, 21.	6 d
xvi. 13, 15.	6 d	xxv. 10.	6 g	viii. 43, 43.	6 d g
xvii. 5.	6 h	xxviii. 10.β	6 g	viii. 52.	6 b
xvii. 15.	6 d	xxix. 2.	6 d	ix. 13.	6 d
xvii. 19.	6 a	xxx. 1.	7	xii. 3, 20.	6 d
xix. 5, 37, 38.	6 d	xxxi. 7.	6 d	xvi. 24.	6 d
xix. 22.	6 a	xxxi. 14.	6 c	xvii. 10, 11.	6 d
xx. 8, 9.	6 d	xxxiii. 19.	6 d	xviii. 3, 26.	6 d
xxi. 3, 17, 33.	6 d	Josh. iv. 4.	6 d	xviii. 24, 24.	6 a d
xxi. 12.α	6 h	v. 9.	6 d	xviii. 25.	6 d
xxi. 31.	6 a	vi. 6.	6 d	xx. 7.	6 d
xxii. 11, 14, 15.	6 d	vii. 26.	6 a	xxii. 9.	6 d
xxiv. 57, 58.	6 d	viii. 16.	3 b	xxii. 13.	6 d
xxv. 25, 26.	6 d	ix. 22.	6 d	2 Kings iii. 10, 13.	6 a
xxv. 30.	6 a	x. 24.	6 d	iv. 12, 12.	6 c d
xxvi. 9, 20, 21, 22,		xix. 47.	6 d	iv. 15, 15.	6 c d
25, 33.	6 d	xxii. 1, 34.	6 d	iv. 22.	6 c
xxvi. 18, 18.	6 d a	xxiii. 2.	6 d	iv. 36, 36, 36.	6 d c d
xxvii. 1, 42.	6 d	xxiv. 1, 9.	6 d	v. 11.	6 a
xxviii. 1, 19.	6 d	Judg. i. 17, 26.	6 d	vi. 11.	6 d
xxix. 32, 33.	6 a	ii. 5.	6 d	vii. 10, 11.	6 d
xxix. 34, 35.	6 a	iv. 6.	6 d	viii. 1.	6 a
xxx. 6.	6 a	iv. 10.	3 c	ix. 1.	6 a
xxx. 8, 11, 13, 18, 20,		vi. 24, 32.	6 d	x. 19.	6 c
21, 24.	6 d	viii. 1.	6 b	xii. 7.	6 d
xxxi. 4, 54.	6 d	viii. 31.	8	xiv. 7.	6 d
xxxi. 47, 47.	6 d a	ix. 54.	6 d	xviii. 4, 18.	6 d
xxxi. 48.	6 a	x. 4.	6 d	1 Chron. iv. 9.	6 a
xxxii. 2, 30.	6 d	xii. 1.	6 a	iv. 10.	6 d
xxxii. 28.	1 c	xii. 2.	3 a	vi. 65.	6 d
xxxiii. 17.	6 a	xiii. 24.	6 d	vii. 16, 23.	6 d
xxxiii. 20.	6 d	xiv. 15.	6 a	xi. 7.	6 a
xxxv. 7, 8, 15.	6 d	xv. 17, 18.	6 a	xiii. 6.	6 g
xxxv. 10, 10.	6 h d	xv. 19.	6 a	xiii. 11.	6 d
xxxv. 18, 18.	6 d	xvi. 18, 19, 28.	6 d	xiv. 11.	6 a
xxxviii. 3, 4, 5, 29, 30.	6 d	xvi. 25, 25.	6 c d	xv. 11.	6 d
xxxix. 14.	6 d	xviii. 12.	6 a	xvi. 8.	6 c
xli. 8, 14, 45, 51.	6 d	xviii. 29.	6 d	xxi. 26.	6 a
xli. 52.	6 a	xxi. 13.	6 d	xxiii. 6.	6 d
xlvi. 33.	6 d	Ruth i. 20, 20.	6 d c	2 Chron. iii. 17.	6 d
xlvii. 29.	6 d	i. 21.	6 d	vi. 33, 33.	6 d g
xl iii. 6.	6 h	iv. 17.	6 d	vii. 14.β	6 g
xlix. 1.	6 d	1 Sam. i. 20.	6 d	x. 3.	6 d
l. 11.	6 a	iii. 4, 9, 10, 16.	6 d	xviii. 8.	6 d
Exod. i. 18.	6 d	iii. 5, 5.	6 a	xviii. 12.	6 b
ii. 7.	6 a	iii. 6, 6, 6.	6 b a a	xx. 26.	6 a
ii. 8, 10, 22.	6 d	iii. 8, 8, 8.	6 b a e	xxii. 6.	6 d
ii. 20.	6 c	vi. 2.	6 d	Ezra ii. 61.	6 h
iii. 4.	6 d	vii. 12.	6 d	Neh. v. 12.	6 d
vii. 11.	6 d	ix. 9.	6 h	vii. 63.	6 h
viii. 8, 25.	6 d	ix. 26.	6 d	Esth. ii. 14.	6 g
ix. 27.	6 d	x. 17.	5 b	iii. 12.	6 h
x. 16.	6 d	xii. 17, 18.	6 d	iv. 5.	6 d
x. 24.	6 d	xiii. 4.	5 a	iv. 11, 11.	6 h g
xii. 21, 31.	6 d	xvi. 3.	6 a	v. 10.	2
xv. 23.	6 a	xvi. 5, 8.	6 d	viii. 9.	6 h
xvi. 31.	6 d	xix. 7.	6 d	ix. 26.	6 a
xvii. 7, 15.	6 d	xxii. 11.	6 b	Job i. 4.	6 a
xix. 3, 7, 20.	6 d	xxiii. 8.	9 a	v. 1.	6 c
xxiv. 16.	6 d	xxiii. 28.	6 a	ix. 16.	6 d
xxxi. 2.	6 a	xxviii. 15.	6 d	xii. 4.	6 e
xxxiii. 7.	6 a	xxix. 6.	6 d	xiii. 22.	6 d
xxxiv. 15.	6 a	2 Sam. i. 7, 15.	6 d	xiv. 15.	6 a
xxxiv. 31.	6 d	ii. 16, 26.	6 d	xix. 16.	6 a
xxxv. 30.	6 a	v. 9.	6 d	xxvii. 10.	6 a
xxxvi. 2.	6 d	v. 20.	6 a	xxx. 28.	6 a
Lev. i. 1.	6 d	vi. 2.	6 g	Ps. iv. 1, 3.	6 b
ix. 1.	6 a	vi. 8.	6 d	xiv. 4.	6 a
x. 4.	6 d	ix. 2, 9.	6 d	xvii. 6.	6 a
Num. x. 2.	6 n	xi. 13.	6 d	xviii. 3, 6.	6 a
xi. 3, 34.	6 d	xii. 24, 25.	6 a	xx. 9.	6 b
xii. 5.	6 d	xii. 28.	6 d	xxxi. 17.	6 a
xiii. 16.	6 a	xiii. 17.	6 d	xlii. 7.	6 d
xiii. 24.	6 a	xiv. 33.	6 d	xlix. 11.	6 a

Ps. l. 1, 4.	6 d	Isa. xliii. 1, 22.	6 a
l. 15.	6 c	xliii. 7.	6 i
liii. 4.	6 a	xliv. 5, 7.	6 d
lv. 16.	6 d	xlv. 3.	6 e
lxxix. 6.	6 a	xlv. 4.	6 d
lxxx. 18.	6 d	xlvi. 11.	6 e
lxxxi. 7.	6 a	xlvii. 1, 5.	6 d
lxxxvi. 5.	6 e	xlviii. 1.	6 i
lxxxvi. 7.	6 d	xlviii. 2.	6 g
lxxxviii. 9.	6 a	xlviii. 8.	6 k
xci. 15.	6 d	xlviii. 12.	6 l
xcix. 6, 6.	6 e	xlviii. 13.	6 e
cii. 2.	6 d	xlviii. 15.	6 a
cv. 1.	6 c	xlix. 1.	6 a
cv. 16.	6 d	l. 2.	6 a
cxvi. 2, 4, 13, 17.	6 d	li. 2.	6 a
cxviii. 5.	6 d	liv. 5.	6 a
cxlv. 18, 18.	6 e d	liv. 6.	6 a
cxlvii. 4.	6 d	lv. 5.	6 d
Prov. i. 24.	6 a	lv. 6.	6 c
i. 28.	6 d	lvi. 7.	6 h
vii. 4.	6 d	lviii. 5, 9.	6 d
viii. 4.	6 d	lviii. 12.δ	6 k
ix. 15.	6 b	lix. 4.	6 e
xvi. 21.	6 h	lix. 4.	6 e
xviii. 6.	6 d	lx. 14, 18.	6 a
xxiv. 8. γ	6 d	lxi. 3.	6 k
Cant. v. 6.	6 a	lxii. 2.δ	6 k
Isa. i. 13.	6 b	lxii. 6.	6 k
i. 26.δ	6 h	lxii. 12, 12.	6 a h
iv. 1.β	6 h	lxiii. 19.β	6 g
iv. 3.	1 c	lxiv. 7.	6 e
v. 20.	1 b	lxiv. 12.	6 e
vii. 14.	6 a	lxv. 1.	6 k
viii. 3.	6 c	lxv. 12.	6 a
ix. 6.	6 d	lxv. 15, 24.	6 d
xii. 4.	6 c	lxvi. 4.	6 d
xiii. 3.	6 a	Jer. i. 15.	6 e
xix. 18.	1 c	iii. 17, 19.	6 e
xxi. 11.	6 e	vi. 30.	6 h
xxii. 12.	6 d	vii. 10, 11, 14, 30.	6 g
xxii. 20.	6 a	vii. 13.	6 d
xxxi. 2.	4	vii. 27.	6 a
xxxi. 4.	6 a	vii. 32.	1 c
xxxii. 5.	6 h	ix. 17.	6 c
xxxiv. 12.	6 h	x. 25.	6 d
xxxv. 8.	6 h	xi. 16.	6 a
xl. 26.	6 d	xii. 6. e	6 d
xli. 2, 25.	6 d	xiv. 9.β	6 g
xli. 4.	6 a	xv. 16.β	6 e
xli. 9.	6 a	xix. 6.	6 h
xlii. 6.	6 a		

Jer. xx. 3.	6 a		
xxiii. 6.ζ	6 d		
xxv. 29, 29.	6 g e		
xxix. 12.	6 a		
xxx. 17.	6 a		
xxxii. 34.β	6 g		
xxxiii. 3.	6 c		
xxxiii. 16.η	6 d		
xxxiv. 15.β	6 g		
xxxv. 17.	6 d		
xxxvi. 4.	6 d		
xlii. 8.	6 d		
i. 29.	9 b		
li. 27.	9 b		
Lam. i. 15, 19, 21.	1 a		
ii. 15.	6 a		
ii. 22.	6 d		
iii. 55.	6 a		
iii. 57.	6 d		
Ezek. ix. 3.	6 d		
xx. 29.	6 h		
xxxvi. 29.	6 a		
xxxviii. 21.	6 a		
xxxix. 11.	6 a		
Dan. ii. 2.	6 b		
v. 12.	6 m		
viii. 16.	6 d		
ix. 18,β 19.	6 g		
x. 1.	6 g		
Hos. i. 4, 6, 9.	6 c		
ii. 16, 16.	6 d		
vii. 7.	6 e		
vii. 11.	6 e		
xi. 1, 2.	6 d		
xi. 7.	6 d		
Joel i. 14.	6 c		
ii. 15.	6 c		
ii. 32, 32.	6 d e		
Amos v. 8.	6 e		
v. 16.	6 a		
vii. 4.	6 e		
ix. 6.	6 e		
ix. 12.β	6 g		
Jonah i. 6.	6 d		
Zeph. iii. 9.	6 b		
Hag. i. 11.	6 d		
Zech. iii. 10.	6 d		
viii. 3.	6 d		
xi. 7, 7.	6 a		
xiii. 9.	6 d		
Mal. i. 4.	6 a		

α *lit.* it shall be called to thee.   β *lit.* name called upon.   γ *lit.* they shall call.   δ *lit.* be called to thee.   ε or, cried after thee fully.   ζ *lit.* (one) shall call him.   η *lit.* (one) shall call to her.

CALM

דְּמָמָה *f.* silence, stillness : Ps. cvii. 29.

שָׁתַק to be still and quiet after disturbance or vehement tossings. KAL *fut.* Jonah i. 11, 12.

CALVE

חוּל to travail, to be in pain. POLEL *pret.* Job xxxix. 1. *fut.* Ps. xxix. 9.

יָלַד to bring forth. KAL *pret.* Jer. xiv. 5.

פָּלַט to let escape : to bring forth. PIEL *fut.* Job xxi. 10.

CAMEL

גָּמָל *com.* a large beast of burden singularly adapted to bear labour and fatigue in hot and dry countries : it can travel four or five days together without water ; and half a gallon of beans and barley, or a few balls made of the flour, will nourish it for the whole day.— *Shaw's Travels*, p. 230. The Arabs employed camels anciently in war, in their caravans, and for food. They are not unfrequently called "ships of the desert." Gen. xii. 16, &c.

אֲחַשְׁתְּרָנִים *m. pl.* camel or dromedary : Esth. viii. 10, 14.

CAMP, ENCAMP

חָנָה to abide, settle; applied to the encamping of an army, either in the field or besieging a town. KAL [a] *pret.* [b] *inf.* [c] *imp.* [d] *fut.* [e] *part.* Poel. [f] מַחֲנֶה *com.* a camp for soldiers, hence an army or host, for pastoral tribes, and of the children of Israel in the wilderness : Exod. xiv. 19, &c. [g] תַּחֲנֹת *f. pl.* a place where a camp is pitched.

No. f not included.

Exod. xiii. 20.	d	Josh. iv. 19.	d	1 Kings xvi. 16, 16.	e f	
xiv. 2, 2.	d	v. 10.	d	2 Kings vi. 8.	g	
xiv. 9.	e	x. 5, 31, 34.	d	1 Chron. xi. 15.	d	
xv. 27.	d	Judg. vi. 4.	d	2 Chron. xxxii. 1.	d	
xviii. 5.	e	ix. 50.	d	Job xix. 12.	d	
xix. 2.	e	x. 17, 17.	d	Ps. xxvii. 3.	d	
Num. i. 50.	d	xx. 19.	d	xxxiv. 7.	e	
ii. 17, 17, 17.	f f d	1 Sam. xi. 1.	d	liii. 5.	e	
ii. 27.	e	xiii. 16.	a	Isa. xxix. 3.	a	
iii. 38.	e	2 Sam. xi. 11.	e	Jer. l. 29.	c	
x. 31.	b	xii. 28.	c	Nah. iii. 17.	a	
xxxiii. 10, 11, 12, 13,		1 Kings xvi. 15.	e	Zech. ix. 8.	a	
14, 17, 24, 26, 30,						
32, 34, 35, 46.	d					

CAMPHIRE

כֹּפֶר *m.* a shrub, ten or fifteen feet high, like privet, whose flowers grow in bunches, and have a very sweet and grateful smell; with the powder of the leaves or flowers, mixed with water, women smeared their hands, feet, &c., to give them a golden colour : Cels. Hierobot. part i. p. 225 : Hiller. Hieroph. part i. cap. 54 : Raii Hist. Plant. tom. ii. p. 1604 : Cant. i. 14; iv. 13.

CAN

1   יָדַע   to know. KAL *pret.* rendered can, could.

2   יָכֹל   this word admits of all the senses in which we say a man can or cannot, is or is not able. KAL [a] *pret.* [b] *fut.* יָכֹל Ch. P'AL [c] *pret.* [d] *fut.* [e] *part.*

3   כְּהַל   Ch. to be able. P'AL *part. active.*

4   נָדַד   to flee away. KAL *pret.*

5   נָכַר   see *Discern.* HIPHIL *part.*

Gen. xiii. 6.	2 a	Ruth iv. 6, 6.	2 b	Isa. i. 13.	2 b
xiii. 16.	2 b	1 Sam. iii. 2.	2 b	vii. 1.	2 a
xix. 19, 22.	2 b	iv. 15.	2 b	xxix. 11.	2 b
xxiv. 50.	2 b	xvii. 39.	2 b	xlvi. 2.	2 a
xxix. 8.	2 b	2 Sam. iii. 11.	2 b	lvi. 10.	2 b
xxxi. 35.	2 b	xii. 23.	2 b	lvi. 11, 11.α	1
xxxiv. 14.	2 b	1 Kings v. 3.	2 a	lvii. 20.	2 b
xxxvi. 7.	2 a	viii. 11.	2 a	lix. 14.	2 b
xxxvii. 4.	2 a	xiii. 4.	2 a	Jer. i. 6,β	1
xliv. 1, 22, 26.	2 b	xiv. 4.	2 a	iii. 5.	2 b
xlv. 1, 3.	2 a	2 Kings iii. 26.	2 a	vi. 10.	2 b
xlviii. 10.	2 b	iv. 40.	2 a	vi. 15.γ	1
Exod. iii. 3.	2 a	xvi. 5.	2 a	viii. 12.γ	1
vii. 21, 24.	2 a	1 Chron. xxi. 30.	2 a	xiv. 9.	2 b
viii. 18.	2 a	2 Chron. v. 14.	2 a	xviii. 6.	2 b
ix. 11.	2 a	vii. 2.	2 a	xix. 11.	2 b
xii. 39.	2 a	xxix. 34.	2 a	xx. 9.	2 b
xv. 23.	2 a	xxx. 3.	2 a	xxxvi. 5.	2 b
xix. 23.	2 b	xxxii. 14.	2 a	xxxviii. 5.	2 b
xxxiii. 20.	2 b	Ezra ii. 59.	2 a	xliv. 22.	2 b
Num. ix. 6.	2 a	Neh. vi. 3.	2 b	xlix. 23.	2 b
xxii. 18.	2 b	vii. 61.	2 a	Lam. iv. 14.	2 b
xxiv. 13.	2 b	xiii. 24.	5	Ezek. xlvii. 5.	2 b
Deut. vii. 17.	2 b	Esth. vi. 1.	4	Dan. iii. 10.	2 d
xxviii. 27, 35.	2 b	Job iv. 2.	2 b	ii. 27.	2 e
xxxi. 2.	2 b	xxxiii. 5.	2 b	ii. 47.	2 c
Josh. vii. 12, 13.	2 b	xlii. 2.	2 b	iii. 29.	2 d
xv. 63.	2 a	Ps. lxxvii. 19, 20.	2 b	v. 8, 15.	3
xvii. 12.	2 a	cxxxix. 6.	2 b	v. 16, 16.	2 d
xxiv. 19.	2 b	Prov. xxx. 21.	2 b	vi. 4.	2 e
Judg. ii. 14.	2 a	Eccles. i. 8, 15, 15.	2 b	x. 17.	2 b
xi. 35.	2 b	vii. 13.	2 b	Hos. v. 13.	2 b
xiv. 13.	2 b	viii. 17.	2 b	Jonah i. 13.	2 a
xiv. 14.	2 a	Cant. viii. 7.		Hab. i. 13.	2 b

a lit. know not to understand.   *β lit.* I know not to speak.
γ lit. they know not to blush.

CANAANITE

כְּנַעֲנִי *m.* inhabitant of the country west of Jordan : the Canaanites were celebrated merchants : Zech. xiv. 21.

CANDLE

נֵר *m.* a lamp, candle, light, which was always kept burning in the apartment night and day, the putting out of which was therefore equivalent to desolation or destruction, Jer. xxv. 10, Job xxi. 17 ; as the contrary is the symbol of prosperity, Job xxix. 2, 3, 4 ; xviii. 6, *marg.* ' or, lamp;' xxi. 17, *marg. id.* ; xxix. 3, *marg. id.*, Ps. xviii. 28, *marg. id.* : Prov. xx. 27, *marg. id.* ; xxiv. 20, *marg. id.* ; xxxi. 18 : Jer. xxv. 10 : Zeph. i. 12.

מְנוֹרָה *f.* a candlestick, particularly that in the tabernacle : Exod. xxv. 31, &c. : 1 Chron. xxviii. 15, "every candlestick," *lit.* candlestick and candlestick ; 15, *lit. id.*

נֶבְרַשְׁתָּה Ch. *f.* a candlestick : Dan. v. 5.

CANE

קָנֶה *m.* see *Calamus :* Isa. xliii. 24 : Jer. vi. 20.

CANKERWORM

יֶלֶק *m.* the *scarabæus arboreus,* or hedge-chafer : Philos. Trans. No. 234, p. 741. A species of locust, so called from its gnawing herbage and trees.—*Bochart.* Called also *attilabus,* being a locust before it has cast its fourth covering, and having short wings, with which it can pass from one place to another on the surface : in this state it devours much herbage, and then assumes its more perfect state, and flies away : see Ges. Thes. The English word cankerworm is probably used simply to mean any insect that feeds largely on herbage : Joel i. 4, 4 ; ii. 25 : Nah. iii. 15, 15, 16.

CAPTAIN

1   אַלּוּף   *m.* head of a family or tribe.

2   בַּעַל   *m.* owner, master.

3   טִפְסָר   *m.* name of a military officer among the Assyrians and Medes.

4   כַּר   *m.* ram ; *metaph.* captain or chief leader ; also a battering-ram.

5   כָּרִי   *m. pl.* according to Gesenius, a description of a body-guard under the later kings. See *Cherethites.* Derived from כָּרָה or כַּר *obsol.* and denoting a part of their office to act as executioners.

6   נָגִיד   *m.* a person raised, eminent, and conspicuous in fortitude and magnanimity, that goes before, directs and guards others. See *Ruler.*

7   נָשִׂיא   *m.* one lifted up in power, &c., a prince, ruler, captain.

8   פֶּחָה   *m.* see *Governor.* [a] פֶּחָה Ch. *m.*

9   קָצִין   *m.* a ruler ; a leader in war.

10   רֹאשׁ   *m.* the head ; a head, chief, leader.

11   רַב   *adj.* great ; a chief, head, captain ; or, chief marshal ; chief of the executioners, or, slaughterer. [a] רַב Ch. *adj.*

12   שַׁלִּיט   Ch. *adj.* that hath power.

13 שָׁלִישׁ *m.* a distinguished kind of warriors or combatants; perhaps strictly the riders in the war-chariots, ἀναβάται, παραβάται. Exod. xiv. 7, "He took all the chariots of Egypt," וְשָׁלִשִׁים עַל כֻּלּוֹ, "and warriors in each of them," xv. 4. Lxx. in xiv. 7, τρίστάται; and in xv. 4, ἀναβάται παραβάται. (Τρίστάτης has this meaning, according to Origen, because there were three in each chariot, of whom the first fought, the second protected him with a shield, and the third guided the horses.) In 1 Kings ix. 22, שָׁלִשִׁים and שָׂרֵי־רֶכֶב are joined together: *comp.* 2 Kings ix. 25. In other passages they appear to make a part of the bodyguard of the Israelitish kings: 1 Kings ix. 22: 2 Kings x. 25: 1 Chron. xi. 11; xii. 18. These may indeed be the same, only having a different employment in time of peace. שָׁלִישׁ in the singular is often probably the same as רֹאשׁ הַשָּׁלִשִׁים, and occurs as a high officer attending on the king: 2 Kings ix. 25, 25; xv. 25; vii. 2, 17, 19. The etymology in Hebrew seems to be analogous to that of the Greek word τρίστάτης. a שְׁלוֹשִׁים *pl. adj. num.*

14 שַׂר *m.* a commander, chief, or prince: Josh. v. 14, Captain of the LORD's host, or prince, identified with Jehovah, vi. 2. Gen. xxi. 22, &c. See *Guard.*

No. 14 not included.

Exod. xiv. 7.	13	2 Kings x. 25, 25.	13	Jer. xiii. 21.	1
xv. 4.	13	xi. 4, 19.	5	xxxvii. 13.	2
Num. ii. 3, 5, 7, 10,		xv. 25.	13	xxxix. 9, 10, 11, 13.	11
12, 14, 18, 20, 22,		xviii. 24.	8	xl. 1, 2, 5.	11
25, 27, 29.	7	xx. 5.	6	xli. 10.	11
xiv. 4.	10	xxv. 8, 10, 11, 12, 15,		xlii. 8.	11
Deut. xxix. 10.	10	18, 20.	11	li. 23, 28, 57.	8
Josh. x. 24.	9	1 Chron. iv. 42.	10	li. 27.	8
Judg. xi. 6, a 11.	9	xi. 11.	13	lii. 12, 14, 15, 16, 19,	
1 Sam. ix. 16.	6	xi. 15, β 42.	10	24, 26, 30.	11
x. 1.	6	xii. 14, 20.	10	Ezek. xxi. 22.	4
xiii. 14.	6	xxi. 18, 18.	13, 10	xxiii. 6, 12, 23.	8
2 Sam. v. 2.	6	2 Chron. viii. 9, 9.	13, 14	Dan. ii. 14.	11 a
xxiii. 8.	13	xi. 11.	6	ii. 15.	12
1 Kings ix. 22.	13	xiii. 12.	10	iii. 2, 3, 27.	8 a
xx. 24.	8	Neh. ix. 17.	10	vi. 7.	8 a
2 Kings ix. 25.	13	Isa. xxxvi. 9.	8	Nah. iii. 17.	3

a lit. for captain to us. *β* or, three captains over the thirty.

CAPTIVE, CAPTIVITY

1 בֵּן Ch. *m.* son : Dan. ii. 25, *marg.* 'children of the captivity.'

2 גָּלָה to uncover; to strip a land of its inhabitants, to carry, lead, &c. into captivity; also, to go into captivity, but seldom of going voluntarily. KAL a *pret.* b *inf.* c *fut.* d *part.* Poel. PUAL e *pret.* HIPHIL f *pret.* g *inf.* h *fut.* HOPHAL i *pret.* k *part.* l גָּלוּת *f.* captivity, captives. m גָּלוּת Ch. *f.* n גּוֹלָה *f.*

3 מַלְטָלָה *f.* a throwing or casting away. See *Cast,* and *Carry.*

4 צָעָה see *Exile.* KAL *part.* Poel, "captive exile," or bowed down, *i. e.* with chains.

5 שָׁבָה to take away, to carry away captive. KAL a *pret.* b *inf.* c *imp.* d *fut.* e *part.* Poel. f *part.* Paül. NIPHAL g *pret.* h שְׁבוּת *f.* captivity. i שְׁבִי *m.* (also *adj.*) captivity; captive. k שִׁבְיָה *f.* captivity; *meton.* captives. l שְׁבִית *f.* captivity. m שִׁבְיָה *f.* captivity.

Gen. xiv. 14.	5 g	Num. xxiv. 22.	5 d	Deut. xxviii. 41.	5 i
xxxi. 26.	5 f	xxxi. 9.	5 d	xxx. 3.	5 h
xxxiv. 29.	5 a	xxi. 12, 19.	5 b	xxxii. 42.	5 i
Exod. xii. 29.	5 i	Deut. xxi. 10, 13.	5 i	Judg. v. 12, 12.	5 k
Num. xxi. 29.	5 l	xxi. 11.	5 k	xviii. 30.	2 b

---

1 Sam. xxx. 2.	5 d	Isa. xx. 4.	2 l	Jer. lii. 27.	2 c
xxx. 3, 5.	5 g	xxii. 17.	3	lii. 31.	2 l
1 Kings viii. 46.a	5 e	xlv. 13.	2 l	Lam. i. 3.	2 a
viii. 47, 47.	5 g e	xlvi. 2.	5 i	i. 5, 18.	5 i
viii. 48.	5 a	xlix. 21.	2 d	ii. 14.	5 h
viii. 50.	5 e	xlix. 24, γ 25.	5 i	iv. 22.	2 g
2 Kings v. 2.	5 d	li. 14.	4	Ezek. i. 1.	2 n
vi. 22.	5 a	lii. 2.	5 i	i. 2.	2 l
xv. 29.	2 h	lxi. 1.	5 f	iii. 11, 15.	2 n
xvi. 9.	2 h	Jer. i. 3.	2 b	vi. 9.	5 g
xxiv. 14.	2 d	xiii. 17.	5 g	xi. 24, 25.	2 n
xxiv. 15, 16,β	2 n	xiii. 19, 19.	2 i	xii. 4, 7.	2 n
xxv. 27.	2 l	xv. 2, 2.	5 i	xii. 11.	5 i
1 Chron. v. 22.	2 n	xx. 4.	2 f	xvi. 53, 53, 53, 53,	
2 Chron. vi. 36.	5 e	xx. 6.	5 i	53.	5 l h h h l
vi. 37, 37.	5 g i	xxii. 12.	2 f	xxv. 3.	2 n
vi. 38, 38.	5 i a	xxii. 22.	5 i	xxix. 14.	5 h
xxv. 12.	5 e	xxiv. 1.	2 g	xxx. 17, 18.	5 i
xxviii. 5, 13, 14, 15.	5 k	xxiv. 5.	2 l	xxxiii. 21.	2 l
xxviii. 8.	5 h	xxvii. 20.	2 g	xxxix. 23.	2 a
xxviii. 11, 11.	5 k a	xxviii. 4.	2 l	xxxix. 25.	5 h
xxviii. 17.	5 i	xxviii. 6.	2 n	xxxix. 28.	2 g
xxix. 9.	5 e	xxix. 1, 1.	2 n f	xl. 1.	2 l
xxx. 9.	5 e	xxix. 4, 16, 20, 31.	2 n	Dan. ii. 25.	1, 2 m
Ezra i. 11.	2 n	xxix. 7.	2 f	v. 13.	2 m
ii. 1.	5 i	xxix. 14, 14.	5 h, 2 f	vi. 13.	2 m
iii. 8.	5 i	xxix. 22.	2 l	xi. 8, 33.	5 i
iv. 1.	2 n	xxx. 3, 18.	5 h	Hos. vi. 11.	5 h
vi. 16.	2 m	xxx. 10, 16.	5 i	Joel iii. 1.	5 h
vi. 19, 20, 21.	2 n	xxxi. 23.	5 h	Amos i. 5.	2 a
viii. 35.	5 i	xxxii. 44.	5 h	i. 6. 6.	2 g l
ix. 7.	2 n	xxxiii. 7, 7, 11, 26.	5 h	i. 9.	2 l
x. 7, 16.	2 n	xxxix. 9.	2 f	i. 15.	2 n
Neh. i. 2, 3.	5 i	xl. 1, 1.	2 l k	v. 5.	2 b c
iv. 4.	5 k	xl. 7.	2 i	v. 27.	2 f
vii. 6.	5 i	xli. 10, 10.	5 d	vii. 7, 7.	2 c d
viii. 17.	5 i	xli. 14.	5 a	vii. 11, 17.	2 b c
Esth. ii. 6.	2 n	xliii. 3.	2 g	ix. 4.	5 i
Job xlii. 10.	5 h	xliii. 11, 11.	5 i	ix. 14.	5 h
Ps. xiv. 7.	5 h	xliii. 12.	5 a	Obad. 11.	5 b
liii. 6.	5 h	xlvi. 19.	2 n	20, 20.	2 l
lxviii. 18, 18.	5 a i	xlvi. 27.	5 i	Mic. i. 16.	2 a
lxxviii. 61.	5 i	xlvii. 7, 11.	2 n	Nah. iii. 1.	2 e
lxxxv. 1.	5 l	xlviii. 46, 46.	5 i k	iii. 10.	5 i
cvi. 46.	5 h	xlviii. 47.	5 h	Hab. i. 9.	5 i
cxxvi. 1.	5 m	xlix. 3.	2 n	Zeph. ii. 7.	5 l
cxxvi. 4.	5 l	xlix. 6, 39.	5 h	iii. 20.	5 h
cxxxvii. 3.	5 e	l. 33.	5 e	Zech. vi. 10.	2 n
Isa. v. 13.	2 a	lii. 15, 28, 29, 30.	2 f	xiv. 2.	2 n
xiv. 2, 2.	2 e				

a lit. their captors captivate them. *β lit.* into captivity. *γ lit.* the captivity of the just.

CARBUNCLE

אֶבֶן *f.* stone : Isa. liv. 12 ; *lit.* stones of a sparkling gem.

אֶקְדָּח *m.* name of a precious stone, perhaps a carbuncle ; from קָדָה to kindle. The derivation shows it to be of a fiery sparkling nature : Isa. liv. 12, or, stones of carbuncles.

בָּרֶקֶת *f.* a precious stone, so called from its glittering brightness : see *Glittering.* According to Braun (de Vestitu Sacerdotum Hebræorum, p. 518), the emerald : Exod. xxviii. 17; xxxix. 10. בָּרְקַת *f. id.* Ezek. xxviii. 13.

CARCASE

1 גְּוִיָה *f.* a body, corpse, or carcase.

2 נְבֵלָה *f.* the body of a man or beast bereft of the inward principle of life, and fallen to the ground : Lev. v. 2, &c.

3 מַפֶּלֶת *f.* something fallen, a dead body, a corpse ; like *cadaver* from *cadere; πτῶμα* from *πίπτω.*

4 פֶּגֶר *m.* that which is exhausted of life. See *Faint.*

No 2 not included.

Gen. xv. 11.	4	Judg. xiv. 9.	1	Isa. lxvi. 24.	4
Lev. xxvi. 30, 30.	4	1 Sam. xvii. 46.	4	Ezek. vi. 5.	4
Num. xiv. 29, 32, 33.	4	Isa. xiv. 19.	4	xliii. 7, 9.	4
Judg. xiv. 8, 8.	3, 1	xxxiv. 3.	4	Nah. iii. 3.	4

CARE, CARELESS, CAREFUL

1 בָּטַח to trust. KAL a *part.* Poel, careless. b בֶּטַח *m.* security ; with לְ carelessly, without care.

2 דָּאַג to be anxiously solicitous or fearful. KAL ᵃ *fut.* ᵇ דְּאָנָה *f.* fear, dread, anxious care.

3 דָּבָר *m.* word, matter, affair, &c.

4 דָּרַשׁ to seek or search after ; to look after ; take care of. KAL *part.* Poel.

5 חָרַד to tremble ; to have care or concern for. KAL ᵃ *pret.* ᵇ חֲרָדָה *f.* terror, fear ; care, concern.

6 חֲשַׁח Ch. to think necessary. P'AL *part.*

7 לֵב *m.* the heart.

8 שׂוּם to set. KAL *fut.*

9 שָׁמַע to hear. KAL *inf.* carefully.

Deut. xi. 12.	4	Ps. cxlii. 4.	4	Ezek. xii. 18, 19.	2 b
xv. 5.	9	Isa. xxxii. 9, 10, 11.	1 a	xxx. 9.	1 b
Judg. xviii. 7.	1 b	xlvii. 8.	1 b	xxxix. 6. a	1 b
1 Sam. x. 2.	3	Jer. xvii. 8.	2 a	Dan. iii. 16.	6
2 Sam. xviii. 3, 3.	8, 7	xlix. 31.	1 b	Zeph. ii. 15.	1 b
2 Kings iv. 13, 13.	5 a b	Ezek. iv. 16.	2 b		

a or, confidently.

CARMEL

כַּרְמֶל *m.* a fruitful field ; proper name of a fruitful promontory on the Mediterranean sea, on the southern boundary of the tribe of Asher : 2 Kings xix. 23, *marg.* 'or, and his fruitful field :' 2 Chron. xxvi. 10 : Cant. vii. 5, *marg.* 'or, crimson :' Isa. xxxvii. 24, *marg.* ' or, (and) his fruitful field :' Amos i. 2 ; ix. 3 : Micah vii. 14.

CARNALLY

זֶרַע *m.* seed : Lev. xviii. 20, *lit.* giving thy lying for seed ; xix. 20, *lit.* with the lying of seed : Num. v. 13, *lit. id.*

שְׁכָבָה *f.* lying : Lev. xix. 20, *lit.* the lying of seed : Num. v. 13, *lit. id.*

CARPENTER

חָרָשׁ *m.* an artificer : 2 Sam. v. 11, *lit.* workers of wood : 2 Kings xii. 11, *lit. id.* ; xxii. 6 : 1 Chron. xiv. 1, *lit.* workers of wood : 2 Chron. xxiv. 12 : Ezra iii. 7, *marg.* ' or, workmen :' Isa. xli. 7, xliv. 13, *lit.* workman of wood : Jer. xxiv. 1 ; xxix. 2 : Zech. i. 20.

עֵץ *m.* tree, wood : 2 Sam. v. 11, *lit.* workers of wood : 2 Kings xii. 11, *lit. id.* : 1 Chron. xiv. 1, *lit. id.* : Isa. xliv. 13, *lit. id.*

CARRIAGE

כְּבוּדָּה *adj. f.* that which is heavy or costly : Judg. xviii. 21, luggage or baggage.

כְּלִי *m.* vessels, &c. : 1 Sam. xvii. 22, 22 : Isa. x. 28.

נְשׂוּאָה *m.* carriage for bearing, from נָשָׂא : Isa. xlvi. 1.

CARRY

1 בּוֹא to come in ; to bring, to carry. HIPHIL ᵃ *pret.* ᵇ *inf.* ᶜ *imp.* ᵈ *fut.* HOPHAL ᵉ *fut.*

2 גָּלָה to carry into captivity, to carry away. KAL ᵃ *fut.* HIPHIL ᵇ *pret.* ᶜ *inf.* ᵈ *fut.* HOPHAL ᵉ *pret.* ᶠ גְּלָה Ch. APHEL *pret.* ᵍ גּוֹלָה *f.* captivity.

3 גָּנַב to steal, to withdraw, or convey away privately. KAL *pret.*

4 זָרַם to flow down, to rush down or out suddenly with violence. KAL *pret.*

5 טוּל to cast out, to carry away. PILPEL *part.* Isa. xxii. 17, *marg.* 'who covered thee with an excellent covering ;' rather, who cast thee out with a mighty casting, or the casting of a mighty man.

6 יָבַל to lead along, to bring, to carry, generally as a present, or in a pleasant agreeable manner. HIPHIL ᵃ *fut.* HOPHAL ᵇ *fut.* יְבַל Ch. *id.* APHEL ᶜ *inf.*

7 יָלַךְ to go ; to lead, to carry. HIPHIL ᵃ *pret.* ᵇ *inf.* ᶜ *imp.* ᵈ *fut.*

8 יָצָא to go out ; to bring forth, to carry forth. HIPHIL ᵃ *pret.* ᵇ *inf.* ᶜ *imp.* ᵈ *fut.*

9 יָרַד to go down ; to bring down, to carry down. HIPHIL ᵃ *inf.* ᵇ *imp.*

10 לָקַח to take, to take away. KAL ᵃ *pret.* ᵇ *fut.*

11 מָהַר to hasten. NIPHAL *part.* "carried headlong;" *lit.* become hurried, or thrown into confusion ; illustrated by the following verse.

12 מוֹט see *Move.* KAL *inf.*

13 נָהַג to lead, to guide, to conduct. KAL ᵃ *fut.* PIEL ᵇ *fut.*

14 נָהַל to lead as a flock. PIEL *fut.*

15 נְחַת Ch. to come down. APHEL *imp.*

16 נָטָה to incline, to turn aside. HIPHIL *fut.*

17 נָשָׂא to lift up, to take, to take away. KAL ᵃ *pret.* ᵇ *inf.* ᶜ *imp.* ᵈ *fut.* ᵉ *part.* Poel. ᶠ *part.* Paül. NIPHAL ᵍ *pret.* ʰ *fut.* PIEL ⁱ *fut.* ᵏ נְשָׂא Ch. P'AL *pret.* ˡ מַשָּׂא *m.* a lifting up.

18 סָבַב to compass, to carry about. NIPHAL ᵃ *fut.* HIPHIL ᵇ *pret.* ᶜ *fut.*

19 סָבַל to bear or carry a heavy burden. KAL ᵃ *pret.* ᵇ *fut.*

20 עָבַר to pass on, over, &c. HIPHIL ᵃ *pret.* ᵇ *inf.* ᶜ *fut.*

21 עָלָה to ascend. HIPHIL ᵃ *pret.* ᵇ *fut.*

22 פָּלַט to escape ; to deliver. HIPHIL *fut.* "carry away safe."

23 רָכַב to ride. HIPHIL *fut.*

24 רָמָה to cast, to throw, to shoot with a bow. KAL *part.* Poel.

25 שָׁבָה to take away captive, to carry away. KAL ᵃ *pret.* ᵇ *fut.*

26 שׁוּב to turn, return ; to carry back. HIPHIL ᵃ *imp.* ᵇ *fut.*

See *Captive, Tales, Tidings,* &c.

Gen. xxxi. 18.	13 a	1 Sam. x. 3, 3, 3.	17 e	2 Kings xxiv. 15, 15.	2 d,
xxxi. 26.	13 b	xvii. 18.	1 d		7 a
xxxvii. 25.	9 a	xx. 40.	1 c	xxv. 7.	1 d
xlii. 19.	1 c	xxx. 2.	13 a	xxv. 11.	2 b
xliii. 11.	9 b	xxx. 18.	10 a	xxv. 13.	17 d
xliii. 12.	26 b	2 Sam. vi. 10.	16	xxv. 21.	2 a
xliv. 1.	17 b	xv. 25.	26 a	1 Chron. v. 6.	2 b
xlv. 27.	17 b	xv. 29.	26 b	v. 26.	2 b
xlvi. 5, 5.	17 d b	xix. 18.	20 b	vi. 15.	2 c
xlvii. 30.	17 a	1 Kings viii. 46.	25 a	ix. 1.	2 e
l. 13.	17 d	xvii. 19.	21 b	xiii. 7. a	23
l. 25.	21 a	xviii. 12.	17 d	xiii. 13.	16
Exod. xii. 46.	8 d	xxi. 10.	8 a	xv. 2, 2.	17 b
xiii. 19.	21 a	xxi. 13.	8 d	xxiii. 26.	17 b
xiv. 11.	8 b	xxii. 26.	26 a	2 Chron. ii. 16.	21 b
xxxiii. 15.	21 b	xxii. 34.	8 c	vi. 36.	25 a
Lev. iv. 12, 12.	8 a	2 Kings iv. 19.	17 c	xii. 9.	10 b
vi. 11.	8 a	vii. 8, 8.	17 d	xiv. 13.	17 d
x. 4.	17 c	ix. 2.	1 a	xv. 11.	25 b
x. 5.	17 d	ix. 28. a	23	xvi. 6.	17 d
xiv. 45.	8 a	xvii. 6.	2 b	xviii. 25.	26 a
xvi. 27.	8 d	xvii. 11, 28, 33.	2 b	xviii. 33.	8 a
Num. xi. 12.	17 c	xvii. 23.	2 a	xx. 25.	17 1
Deut. xiv. 24.	17 b	xvii. 27.	7 c	xxi. 17.	25 b
xxviii. 38.	8 d	xvii. 11.	2 d	xxiv. 11.	26 b
Josh. iv. 3.	20 a	xx. 17.	17 g	xxviii. 5, 17.	25 b
iv. 8.	20 c	xxiii. 4.	1 b	xxviii. 15.	14
Judg. xvi. 3.	21 b	xxiii. 30. a	23	xxix. 5.	8 c
1 Sam. v. 8, 8.	18 a c	xxiv. 13.	8 d	xxix. 16.	8 b
v. 9.	18 b	xxiv. 14.	2 b	xxxiii. 11.	7 d

2 Chron. xxxiv. 16.	1 d	Ps. xlix. 17.	10 b	Jer. xxvii. 22.	1 e
xxxvi. 4.	1 d	lxxviii. 9.	24	xxviii. 3.	1 d
xxxvi. 6.	7 b	xc. 5.	4	xxix. 4.	2 b
xxxvi. 7.	1 a	Eccles. v. 15.	7 d	xxxix. 7.	1 b
xxxvi. 20.	2 d	x. 20.	7 d	xxxix. 14.	8 b
Ezra ii. 1, 1.	2 g b	Isa. v. 29.	22	lii. 9.	21 b
v. 12.	2 f	xv. 7.	17 d	lii. 11.	1 d
v. 15.	15	xxii. 17.	5	lii. 17.	17 d
vii. 15.	6 c	xxiii. 7.	6 a	Ezek. xii. 5.	8 a
viii. 35.	2 g	xxx. 6.	17 d	xii. 6.	8 d
ix. 4.	2 g	xxxix. 6.	17 g	xii. 12.	8 b
x. 6, 8.	2 g	xl. 11.	17 d	xvii. 4.	1 d
Neh. vii. 6, 6.	2 g b	xli. 16.	17 d	xxxvii. 1.	8 d
Esth. ii. 6, 6, 6.	2 e e b	xlvi. 3.	17 f	xxxvii. 13.	17 b
Job i. 17.	10 b	xlvi. 4, 4, 7.	19 b	Dan. i. 2.	1 d
v. 13.	11	xlix. 22.	17 h	ii. 35.	17 k
x. 19.	6 b	liii. 4. β	19 a	xi. 8.	1 d
xv. 12.	10 b	lvii. 13.	17 d	Hos. x. 6.	6 b
xxi. 18.	3	lxiii. 9.	17 i	xii. 1.	6 b
xxvii. 21.	17 d	Jer. xvii. 22.	8 d	Joel iii. 5.	1 a
Ps. xlvi. 2.	12	xx. 5.	1 a	Nah. iii. 10.	2 g

α *lit.* and made him to ride. β *lit.* carried them.

CART

עֲגָלָה *f.* a cart, wagon; the threshing-wagon: 1 Sam. vi. 7, 7, 8, 10, 11, 14, 14: 2 Sam. vi. 3, 3: 1 Chron. xiii. 7, 7: Isa. v. 18; xxviii. 27, 28: Amos ii. 13.

CARVE

1 חֲטֻבוֹת *f. pl.* carved, from חָטַב to hew: Prov. vii. 16. Gesenius and Fürst, variegated with the thread of Egypt.

2 חָקָה to engrave. PUAL *part.*

3 חֲרֹשֶׁת *f.* labouring or working in wood or stone.

4 פֶּסֶל *m.* graven image. ª פְּסִילִים *m. pl. id.*

5 פִּתּוּחַ *m.* engraving.

6 קָלַע to cut in, to engrave. KAL *pret.* ª מִקְלַעַת *f.* sculpture.

Exod. xxxi. 5.	3	1 Kings vi. 29, 29.β	6, 5	2 Chron. xxxiii. 22.	4 a
xxxv. 33.	3	vi. 32, 32.	6, 6 a	xxxiv. 3, 4.	4 a
Judg. xviii. 18.	4	vi. 35, 35.	6, 2	Ps. lxxiv. 6.	5
1 Kings vi. 18.α	6 a	2 Chron. xxxiii. 7.	4	Prov. vii. 16.	1

α *lit.* the carving. β *lit.* the engravings of figures.

CASE

דָּבָר *m.* word, matter, affair, &c.: Deut. xix. 4, " case of the slayer," *i. e.* what is to be said of the slayer.

CASEMENT

אֶשְׁנָב *m.* a lattice window for the admission of cool air: Prov. vii. 6.

CASSIA

קִדָּה *f.* the Arabian cassia: Exod. xxx. 24: Ezek. xxvii. 19.

קְצִיעוֹת *f. pl.* the Arabian cassia, a bark resembling cinnamon: Ps. xlv. 8.

CAST

1 בָּרַק to lighten, to cast forth (lightning). KAL *imp.*

2 נָהַר to bow oneself down, first kneeling down, and then placing the head on the ground. KAL *fut.*

3 גָּעַל to reject with abhorrence (see *Abhor*); to cast away vilely. NIPHAL *pret.*

4 גָּרַשׁ to drive, thrust; to cast, to expel. KAL ª *fut.* NIPHAL ᵇ *pret.* PIEL ᶜ *inf.* ᵈ *imp.* ᵉ *fut.* ᶠ מִגְרָשׁ *m.* or according to Gesenius *inf.* after the Aramæan form.

5 הוּחַ to thrust away, to cast quite out. HIPHIL *pret.*

6 דָּחָה to thrust, push, or knock down, sometimes without the hope of rising again; to be an outcast. PUAL *pret.*

7 הָדַף to thrust away, expel, drive out totally. KAL ª *inf.* ᵇ *fut.*

8 הָלְא implies distance both of space and time; to be cast far off. NIPHAL *part.*

9 זָנַח to forsake, cast away, reject, abandon, as God a people, or man that which is good; the word implies the breaking of relative bonds, and the consequent misery or ruin of that which had been the object of care. KAL ª *pret.* ᵇ *fut.* HIPHIL ᶜ *pret.* ᵈ *fut.*

10 זָרָה to scatter. KAL *fut.*

11 חָלַל (see *Profane*), to cast as profane. PIEL *fut.*

12 חֲתַת *m.* terror, dismay, casting down.

13 טוּל Hiphil, to cast, cast down, out, forth; implying no apparent recovery or remedy, utterly to cast down: Jer. xxii. 26, Ps. xxxvii. 24; of the ejection of the Jews out of their own land, of the casting a spear with force, of casting into the sea. HIPHIL ª *pret.* ᵇ *imp.* ᶜ *fut.* HOPHAL ᵈ *pret.* ᵉ *fut.*

14 יָדַד to throw or cast, e. g. lots. KAL *pret.*

15 יָרָה to cast or throw, e. g. stones, darts, &c. PIEL ª *inf.* ᵇ *fut.*

16 יָנַח to set down, to cast down and leave there. HIPHIL *pret.*

17 יָצַק to pour out; to cast metal. KAL ª *pret.* ᵇ *inf.* ᶜ *fut.* ᵈ *part.* Paül. ᵉ יְצֻקָה *f.* a casting. ᶠ מוּצָק *m.* something fused. ᵍ מוּצֶקֶת *f.* a fusion, casting.

18 יָרַד to go down; to be cast down; to bring down. HIPHIL ª *inf.* ᵇ *imp.* ᶜ *fut.*

19 יָרָה to cast or throw with order and aim; to throw darts, to shoot arrows or stones out of an engine; to shoot down, to cast down with sudden violence: it is once used of casting lots; to lay a foundation, to found or erect. KAL ª *pret.* ᵇ *part.* Poel. HIPHIL ᶜ *pret.*

20 יָרַשׁ to take possession; to be dispossessed, driven out of one's possessions; to dispossess, to expel. HIPHIL ª *pret.* ᵇ *fut.*

21 יֶשַׁח *m.* casting down, bowing down: 'depression' is probably the primary meaning of this word, but how it is to be applied in this case is doubtful; whether to disease or the sensation of hunger, or, according to Fürst, to the bowing down of the body by disease consequent on famine: Mic. vi. 14. Gussetius, corruptio tui.

22 בָּרַע to bow down; to cast down, bring low. HIPHIL *imp.*

23 כָּשַׁל to faint, to stumble; to be cast down. NIPHAL ª *fut.* HIPHIL ᵇ *inf.*

24 לוּט to wrap up, to cover. KAL *part.* Poel.

25 מָאַס to reject with contempt and disdain, as hateful, greatly disagreeable, or not worth regard; to abhor. KAL ª *pret.* ᵇ *fut.*

26 מָנַר to thrust down. PIEL *pret.*

27 מוֹט to move, to shake; to cause to fall upon with injury. See *Move.* HIPHIL *fut.*

28 נָגַע to reach, to touch; to make to touch, to bring near. HIPHIL *fut.*

29 נָדָה to remove, to put away from one as a thing filthy and separate. PIEL *part.*

30 נָדַח to drive, force, expel; to cast down with a violent shock. See *Outcast.* NIPHAL ᵃ*part.* HIPHIL ᵇ*pret.* ᶜ*inf.* ᵈ*imp.*

31 נָטַשׁ (see *Forsake*); to cast off, to reject, as God his people, and as man rejects God. KAL *fut.*

32 נָכָה to beat; to strike deep. HIPHIL *fut.*

33 נָפַל to fall; to cause to fall, to throw, to cast as a birth, to cast away, down, to cast lots. KAL ᵃ*fut.* HIPHIL ᵇ*pret.* ᶜ*inf.* ᵈ*imp.* ᵉ*fut.* HITHPAEL ᶠ*part.*

34 נָשָׂא to lift up. KAL *fut.* See *Lift.*

35 נָשַׁל to draw out or off; to cast out, eject. KAL ᵃ*pret.* ᵇ*fut.*

36 נָתַן to give. KAL ᵃ*pret.* ᵇ*inf.* NIPHAL ᶜ*pret.*

37 נָתַץ to tear or break down (walls, buildings, &c.) KAL ᵃ*pret.* PUAL ᵇ*pret.*

38 סָבַב to compass, to cast about. KAL *fut.*

39 סָלַל to be cast up into a heap. KAL ᵃ*imp.* ᵇ*part.* Paül.

40 סָקַל to stone; to cast (stones). PIEL *fut.*

41 עָלָה to go up; to make to go up, to cast up on. HIPHIL ᵃ*pret.* ᵇ*fut.*

42 עָפַר to throw dust at. PIEL *pret.*

43 פּוּץ to break in pieces; to scatter, disperse. HIPHIL ᵃ*pret.* ᵇ*imp.*

44 פָּנָה to turn; to cause to turn and go away, to remove, destroy. PIEL *pret.*

45 פָּרַר to break asunder; to make void. HIPHIL *fut.*

46 צוּר *i. q.* יָצַר to form, make. KAL *fut.*

47 צָרַף to melt, fuse. KAL *part.* Poel.

48 קוּר to dig for water; to let water flow forth. HIPHIL ᵃ*pret.* ᵇ*inf.*

49 מָרוּד *m.* wandering, having no home.

50 רוּק to pour out, to empty. HIPHIL *fut.*

51 רְמָה Ch. to cast, to throw. P'AL ᵃ*pret.* ᵇ*inf.* ᶜ*part. passive.* ITHP'EL ᵈ*fut.*

52 שׂוּם to set, put, place. KAL *pret.*

53 שָׁחַח to bow down. HITHPOLEL *fut.*

54 שָׁחַת to corrupt, or be corrupt. PIEL *pret.*

55 שָׁכַב to lie down; to cause to lie down. HIPHIL *inf.*

56 שָׁכַל to be bereaved; to cast the young. PIEL ᵃ*pret.* ᵇ*fut.* ᶜ*part.*

57 שָׁלַח to send; to throw, cast, or send a thing away, or at a distance from one. PIEL ᵃ*pret.* ᵇ*imp.* ᶜ*fut.* ᵈ*part.* PUAL ᵉ*pret.* ᶠ*part.*

58 שָׁלַךְ perhaps 'to fling,' in the somewhat obsolete use of this English word, best expresses the general meaning of this root; to cast down, away, out; to be cast down, in a neglected, abandoned condition: it often implies contempt and disgust, especially followed by אַחֲרֵי; in one case it is applied to God's pardoning sin, Isa. xxxviii. 17: it is frequently used in the Psalms, of God's desertion, which is deprecated in the fear of divine displeasure; with עַל to commit to another, Ps. lv. 22. HIPHIL ᵃ*pret.*

ᵇ*inf.* ᶜ*imp.* ᵈ*fut.* ᵉ*part.* HOPHAL ᶠ*pret.* ᵍ*fut.* ʰ*part.* ⁱ שַׁלֶּכֶת *f.* casting.

59 שָׁפַךְ to pour out; of things dry, to cast up. KAL ᵃ*pret.* ᵇ*inf.* ᶜ*imp.* ᵈ*fut.*

60 שָׁפֵל to be brought low. HIPHIL ᵃ*pret.* ᵇ*part.*

61 תָּקַע to strike; to fasten by driving a nail (as of a tent); to cast into the sea, and fasten them there so that they cannot return. KAL *fut.*

Gen. xxi. 10.	4 d	2 Kings xiii. 21.	58 d	Ps. lxxiii. 18.	33 b
xxi. 15.	58 d	xiii. 23.	58 a	lxxiv. 1.	9 a
xxxi. 38.	56 a	xvi. 3.	20 a	lxxiv. 7.	57 a
xxxi. 51.	19 a	xvii. 8.	20 a	lxxvii. 7.	9 b
xxxvii. 20, 24.	58 a	xvii. 20.	58 a	lxxvii. 49.	57 c
xxxvii. 22.	58 c	xix. 18.	36 a	lxxviii. 55.	4 e
xxxix. 7.	34	xix. 32.	59 d	lxxx. 8.	4 e
Exod. i. 22.	58 c d	xxi. 2.	20 a	lxxxviii. 14.	9 b
iv. 3, 3.	58 c d	xxiii. 6.	58 d	lxxxix. 38.	9 a
iv. 25.	28	xxiii. 12.	58 a	lxxxix. 44.	26
vii. 9.	58 c	xxiii. 27.	25 a	xciv. 14.	31
vii. 10, 12.	58 d	xxiv. 20.	58 a	cii. 10.	58 d
x. 19.	61	1 Chron. xxiv. 31.	33 e	cviii. 9.	58 d
xv. 4.	19 a	xxv. 8.	33 e	cviii. 11.	9 a
xv. 25.	58 d	xxvi. 13.	33 e	cxl. 10.	33 e
xxii. 31.	58 d	xxvi. 14.	33 b	cxliv. 6.	1
xxiii. 26.	56 c	xxviii. 9.	9 d	cxlvii. 6.	60 b
xxv. 12.	17 a	2 Chron. iv. 3, 3.	17 d	cxlvii. 17.	58 e
xxvi. 37.	17 a	iv. 77.	17 a	Prov. i. 14.	33 e
xxxii. 19, 24.	58 d	vii. 20.	58 d	vii. 26.	33 b
xxxiv. 24.	20 b	xi. 14.	9 c	x. 3.	7 b
xxxvi. 36.	17 a	xiii. 9.	30 b	xvi. 33.	13 e
xxxvii. 3, 13.	17 c	xx. 11.	4 c	xix. 15.	33 e
xxxviii. 5.	17 c	xxiv. 10.	58 d	xxi. 22.	18 c
xxxviii. 27.	17 b	xxv. 8.	23 b	xxii. 10.	4 c
Lev. i. 16.	58 a	xxv. 12.	58 d	xxvi. 18.	19 b
xiv. 40.	58 a	xxviii. 3.	20 a	Eccles. iii. 5, 6.	58 b
xvi. 8.	36 a	xxix. 19.	9 c	xi. 1.	57 b
xviii. 24.	57 d	xxx. 14.	58 d	Isa. ii. 20.	58 d
xx. 23.	57 d	xxxiii. 2.	20 a	v. 24.	25 a
xxvi. 30.	36 a	xxxiii. 15.	58 d	vi. 13.	58 i
xxvi. 44.	25 a	Ezra x. 1.	33 f	xiv. 19.	58 f
Num. xix. 6.	58 a	Neh. i. 9.	30 a	xvi. 2.3	57 f
xxxv. 22.	58 a	vi. 16.	33 a	xix. 8.	58 e
xxxv. 23.	33 e	ix. 26.	58 d	xxv. 7.	24
Deut. vi. 19.	7 a	x. 34.	33 b	xxvii. 19.	33 e
vii. 1.	35 a	xi. 1.	33 b	xxviii. 2.	16
ix. 4.	7 a	xiii. 8.	58 d	xxviii. 25, 25.	43 a, 52
ix. 17, 21.	58 d	Esth. iii. 7.	33 b	xxx. 22.	10
xxviii. 40.	35 b	ix. 24.	33 b	xxxi. 7.	25 b
xxix. 28.	58 d	Job vi. 21.	12	xxxiv. 3.	58 g
Josh. viii. 29.	58 d	viii. 4.	57 c	xxxvii. 17.	33 b
x. 11.	58 a	viii. 20.	25 b	xxxvii. 19.	36 b
x. 27.	58 d	xv. 4.	45	xxxvii. 33.	59 d
xiii. 12.	20 b	xv. 33.	58 d	xxxviii. 17.	58 a
xviii. 6.	19 a	xviii. 7.	58 d	xl. 19.	47
xviii. 8, 10.	58 d	xviii. 8.	57 e	xli. 9.	25 a
Judg. vi. 28.	37 b	xx. 15.	20 b	lvii. 14, 14.	39 a
vi. 30, 31.	37 a	xx. 23. γ	57 c	lvii. 20.	4 a
viii. 25.	58 d	xxi. 10.	56 b	lviii. 7.	49
ix. 53.	58 d	xxii. 29.	60 a	lxii. 10, 10.	39 a
xv. 17.	58 d	xxvii. 22.	58 d	lxvi. 5.	29
1 Sam. xiv. 42.	33 d	xxix. 24.	33 e	Jer. vi. 6.	59 c
xviii. 11.	13 c	xxx. 19.	19 c	vi. 7, 7.	48 b a
xx. 33.	13 c	xxxix. 3.	57 c	vi. 15.	23 a
2 Sam. i. 21.	3	xl. 11.	43 b	vii. 15, 15.	58 a
viii. 2. α	55	xli. 9.	13 e	vii. 29.	58 c
xi. 21.	58 a	Ps. ii. 3.	58 d	viii. 12.	23 a
xvi. 6. β	40	v. 10.	30 d	ix. 19.	58 a
xvi. 13.	42	xvii. 13.	22	xiv. 16.	58 h
xviii. 17.	58 d	xviii. 42.	50	xv. 1.	57 b
xx. 12, 22.	58 d	xxii. 10.	58 f	xvi. 13.	13 a
xx. 15.	58 d	xxii. 18.	33 e	xviii. 15.	39 b
1 Kings vii. 15.	46	xxxvi. 12.	6	xxii. 7.	33 b
vii. 24, 24.	17 d e	xxxvii. 14.	33 c	xxii. 19.	58 b
vii. 37.	17 f	xxxvii. 24.	13 e	xxii. 26.	13 a
vii. 46.	17 a	xlii. 5, 6, 11.	53	xxii. 28, 28.	13 d, 58 f
ix. 7.	57 c	xliii. 2.	9 a	xxvi. 23.	58 d
xii. 24, 25, 28.	58 h	xliii. 5.	53	xxviii. 16.	57 d
xiv. 9.	58 a	xliv. 2.	57 c	xxxi. 37.	25 b
xiv. 24.	20 a	xliv. 9.	9 a	xxxiii. 24, 26.	25 b
xviii. 42.	2	xliv. 23.	9 b	xxxvi. 23.	58 h
xix. 19.	58 d	l. 17.	58 d	xxxvi. 30.	58 h
xxi. 26.	20 a	li. 11.	58 d	xxxviii. 6.	58 a
2 Kings ii. 16, 21.	58 d	lv. 3.	27	xxxviii. 9.	58 a
iii. 25.	58 d	lv. 22.	58 c	xli. 9.	58 a
iv. 41.	58 d	lvi. 7.	18 b	xli. 14.	38
vi. 6.	58 d	lx. 1, 10.	9 a	l. 26.	39 a
vii. 15.	58 a	lx. 8.	58 d	l. 34.	5
ix. 25, 26.	58 c	lxii. 4.	30 c	li. 63.	58 a
x. 25.	58 d	lxxi. 9.	58 d	lii. 3.	58 b

Lam. ii. 1.	58 a	Ezek. xxxii. 4.	13 c	Amos viii. 3.	58 a	2 Sam. ii. 16.	5 c	2 Kings iv. 27.	5 c	Prov. vii. 13.	5 b
ii. 7.	9 a	xxxii. 18.	18 b	viii. 8.	4 b	xviii. 9.	5 a	vii. 12.	13 a	Eccles. ix. 12.	1 c
ii. 10.	41 a	xxxvi. 5.	4 f	Obad. 11.	14	1 Kings i. 50.	5 c	2 Chron. xxii. 9.	9	Jer. v. 26.	9
iii. 31.	9 b	xliii. 24.	58 a	Jonah i. 5, 15.	13 c	i. 51.	1 a	Ps. x. 9, 9.	6 b c	l. 24.	13 b
iii. 53.	15 b	Dan. iii. 6, 11, 15.	51 d	i. 7, 7.	33 e	ii. 28.	5 c	xxxv. 8.	9	Ezek. xix. 3, 6.	8
Ezek. iv. 2.	59 a	iii. 20.	51 b	i. 12.	13 b	xi. 30.	13 a	cix. 11.	11	Hab. i. 15.	4
v. 4.	58 a	iii. 21.	51 c	ii. 3.	58 d	xx. 33.					
vi. 4.	33 b	iii. 24.	51 a	ii. 4.	4 b						
vii. 19.	58 d	vi. 7, 12.	51 d	Micah ii. 5.	58 e						
xv. 4.	36 c	vi. 16, 24.	51 a	ii. 9.	4 e						
xvi. 5.	58 g	vii. 9.	51 c	iv. 7.	8						
xvii. 17.	59 b	viii. 7, 12.	58 d	vi. 14.	21						
xviii. 31.	58 c	viii. 10.	33 e	vii. 19.	58 d						
xix. 12.	58 f	viii. 11.	58 f	Nah. iii. 6.	58 a						
xx. 7.	58 c	xi. 12.	33 b	iii. 10.	14						
xx. 8.	58 a	xi. 15.	59 d	Zeph. iii. 15.	44						
xxi. 22.	59 a	Hos. viii. 3, 5.	9 a	Zech. i. 21.	15 a						
xxiii. 35.	58 d	ix. 17.	25 b	v. 8, 8.	58 d						
xxvi. 8.	59 a	xiv. 5.	32	ix. 4.	20 b						
xxvii. 30.	41 b	Joel i. 7.	58 a	x. 6.	9 a						
xxviii. 16.	11	iii. 3.	14	xi. 13, 13.	58 c d						
xxviii. 17.	58 a	Amos i. 11.	54	Mal. iii. 11.	56 b						
xxxi. 16.	18 a	iv. 3.	58 a								

a *lit.* making them to lie down.   β *lit.* he stoned with stones.
γ *lit.* send forth.   δ *marg.* 'or, a nest forsaken.'

CASTLE

1   אַרְמוֹן   *m.* a high place, a palace.

2   בִּירָנִיּוֹת   *f. pl.* castle, fortress, citadel.   See *Palace.*

3   מִגְדָּל   *m.* see *Tower.*

4   טִירָה   *f.* a tower, palace, goodly castle.

5   מְצָד   *m.* a fortress, stronghold, castle on a mountain; probably used frequently of places strong by nature, as high mountains or rocks.   מְצוּדָה   *f. id.*

Gen. xxv. 16.	4	1 Chron. xi. 5.	5 a	2 Chron. xvii. 12.	2
Num. xxxi. 10.	4	xi. 7.	5	xxvii. 4.	2
1 Chron. vi. 54.	4	xxvii. 25.	3	Prov. xviii. 19.	1

CATCH, TO CATCH HOLD, TO CATCH SELF

1   אָחַז   to seize, lay hold of, take, with בְּ. KAL a *pret.* b *fut.* c *part.* Paül. NIPHAL d *part.*

2   בָּזַז   to take; to spoil, plunder. KAL *pret.*

3   גָּזַל   to take away by force. KAL *pret.*

4   גָּרַר   to draw, to sweep away. KAL *fut.*

5   חָזַק   to take and keep strong fast hold. KAL a *fut.* HIPHIL b *pret.* c *fut.*

6   חָטַף   to seize upon suddenly and unawares. KAL a *pret.* b *inf.* c *fut.*

7   חָלַט   it is difficult to attain the precise meaning of this word, of which so many renderings have been given by the learned; comparing and combining which leaves this idea, to seize on eagerly for confirmation. HIPHIL *fut.* 1 Kings xx. 33. Lxx., ἀνελέξαντο τὸν λόγον ἐκ τοῦ στόματος αὐτοῦ. Vulg., " rapuit verbum ex ore ejus."

8   טָרַף   to tear or rend in pieces prey, as a wild animal. KAL *inf.*

9   לָכַד   to lay fast hold of. KAL *fut.*

10   מָצָא   to find, to come to. KAL *pret.*

11   נָקַשׁ   to lay snares. PIEL to lay snares, with לְ for, &c. *fut.*

12   צַיִד   *m.* a hunting; "hunteth and catcheth," *lit.* hunteth a hunting. See *Hunt.*

13   תָּפַשׂ   to lay hold of with the hand. KAL a *fut.* NIPHAL b *pret.*

Gen. xxii. 13.	1 d	Lev. xvii. 13.	12	Judg. xv. 4.	9
xxxix. 12.	13 a	Num. xxxi. 32.	2	xxi. 21.	6 a
Exod. iv. 4.	5 c	Judg. i. 6.	1 b	xxi. 23.	3
xxii. 6.	10	viii. 14.	9	1 Sam. xvii. 35.	5 b

CATERPILLAR

חָסִיל   *m.* a waster, devourer, *vorax;* hence the name of a species of locust: 1 Kings viii. 37 : 2 Chron. vi. 28 : Ps. lxxviii. 46 : Isa. xxxiii. 4 : Joel i. 4 ; ii. 25.

יֶלֶק   *m.* a species of locust, "cankerworm," which gnaws and destroys herbage and trees: Ps. cv. 34 : Jer. li. 14, 27.

CATTLE

1   בְּהֵמָה   *f.* (see *Beast*), cattle collectively: Gen. i. 24, &c.

2   בְּעִיר   *m.* see *Brute.*

3   בָּקָר   *com.* collectively cattle, oxen, herd; בָּקָר וָצֹאן "great and small cattle."

4   מְלָאכָה   *f.* work, goods, substance, cattle.

5   מְרִיא   *m.* fatlings, fat cattle.

6   צֹאן   *com.* a collective noun denoting small cattle, *i. e.* sheep and goats.

7   מִקְנֶה   *m.* a possession, substance, but used only of cattle, which among nomadic tribes is the principal and almost the only property. This word denotes both oxen and sheep, but does not include horses or asses.

8   שֶׂה   *com.* one of the smaller cattle, a sheep or a goat; the *nomen unitatis* corresponding to צֹאן small cattle.

No 1 not included.

Gen. iv. 20.	7	Exod. ix. 3, 4, 4, 6, 6,		1 Kings i. 9, 19, 25.	5
xiii. 2, 7, 7.	7	7, 19, 20, 21.	7	2 Kings iii. 17.	7
xxix. 7.	7	x. 26.	7	vii. 21.	7
xxx. 29.	7	xii. 38.	7	1 Chron. v. 9, 21.	7
xxx. 32. 32.	8	xvii. 3.	7	2 Chron. xiv. 15.	7
xxx. 39, 40, 41, 41,		xxxiv. 19.	7	xxvi. 10.	7
42, 43.	6	Num. xx. 4.	2	Job xxxvi. 33.	7
xxxi. 8, 8, 10, 10, 12,		xx. 19.	7	Ps. lxxviii. 48.	2
41, 43, 43.	6	xxxii. 1, 1, 4, 4, 16.	7	Eccles. ii. 7.α	3, 6
xxxi. 9, 18, 18.	7	Deut. iii. 19, 19.	7	Isa. viii. 25.β	8
xxxiii. 14.	4	Josh. i. 14.	7	xxx. 23.	7
xxxiii. 17.	7	xiv. 4.	7	xliii. 23.	7
xxxiv. 5, 23.	7	xxii. 8.	7	Jer. ix. 10.	7
xxxvi. 6, 7.	7	Judg. vi. 5.	7	xlix. 32.	7
xlvi. 6, 32, 34.	7	xviii. 21.	7	Ezek. xxxiv. 17, 17.	8
xlvii. 6, 16, 16, 17,		1 Sam. xxiii. 5.	7	xxxiv. 20, 20, 22, 22.	8
17, 17.	7	xxx. 20.	7	xxxviii. 12, 13.	7
				Joel i. 18.	3

α *lit.* oxen, and sheep.   β "lesser cattle."

CAUL

יֹתֶרֶת   *f.* the diaphragm or midriff, which stretches above the liver from the ribs, all across the whole extent of the thorax : Exod. xxix. 13, 22 : Lev. iii. 4, 10, 15 ; iv. 9 ; vii. 4 ; viii. 16, 25 ; ix. 10, 19.

סְגוֹר   *m.* the caul, or that which encloses the heart, the pericardium : Hos. xiii. 8.

שְׁבִיסִים   *m. pl.* caps of network, cauls : Isa. iii. 18.

CAUSE   (See PLEAD, &c.)

1   אוֹדוֹת   *f. pl.* circumstances, reasons, causes.

2   דָּבָר   *m.* word, matter, affair, &c.   a דִּבְרָה *f.* in a forensic sense.

3   דִּין   *m.* plea, judgment.

4　חִנָּם　freely ; causeless, without a cause.

5　נָתַן　to give. KAL [a] *pret.* [b] *fut.* NIPHAL [c] *part.*

6　סִבָּה　*f.* a turn of events. [a] נְסִבָּה *f.* turn, course of things, from God.

7　עָשָׂה　to make. KAL *pret.*

8　רִיב　*m.* strife, contention ; a cause, matter of contention.

9　רֵיקָם　without cause, vainly, void.

10　מִשְׁפָּט　*m.* judgment, cause, right.

11　שֶׁקֶר　*m.* vain, false, a lie ; without a cause.

Exod. xviii. 19, 26.	2	Job xiii. 18.	10	Prov. xxv. 9.		8
xxii. 9.	2	xxiii. 4.	10	xxvi. 2.		4
xxiii. 2, 3, 6.	8	xxix. 16.	8	xxix. 7.		3
Lev. xxiv. 19, 20.	5 b	xxxi. 13.	10	xxxi. 8.		3
Num. xxvii. 5.	10	Ps. vii. 4.	9	Isa. i. 23.		8
Deut. i. 17.	2	ix. 4.	3	xli. 21.		8
xxviii. 7, 25.	5 b	xxv. 3.	7	Jer. iii. 8.		1
Josh. v. 4.	2	xxxv. 7, 7, 19.	4	v. 28, 28.		3
xx. 4.	2	xxxv. 23.	8	xi. 20.		3
1 Sam. xvii. 29.	2	xliii. 1.	8	xv. 4.	5 a	8
xix. 5.	6	lxix. 4.	8	xx. 12.		8
xxiv. 15.	8	lxxiv. 22.	8	xxii. 16.		3
xxv. 31.	4	cix. 3.	8	xxx. 13.		3
xxv. 39.	8	cxix. 78.	11	l. 34.		8
2 Sam. xiii. 16.	1	cxix. 154.	8	li. 36.		8
xv. 4.	10	cxix. 161.	4	Lam. iii. 36, 58.		8
1 Kings viii. 45, 49,		cxl. 12.	3	iii. 52.		8
59, 59.	10	Prov. i. 11.	4	iii. 49.		10
xi. 27.	2	iii. 30.	4	Ezek. xiv. 23.		4
xii. 15.	6	x. 10.	5 b	xvi. 7.	5 a	
2 Chron. vi. 35, 39.	10	xviii. 17.	4	xxvi. 17.	5 a	
x. 15.	6 a	xxii. 21.	8	xxxii. 23, 24, 26, 32.	5 a	
xix. 10.	8	xxiii. 11.	8	xxxii. 25.	5 c	
Job ii. 3.	4	xxiii. 29.	4	xxxvi. 27.		7
v. 8.	2 a	xxiv. 28.	4	Micah vii. 9.		8
ix. 17.	4					

CAUSEWAY

מְסִלָּה　*f.* a way cast up. See *Highway.*　1 Chron. xxvi. 16, 18.

CAVE

חוֹר　*m.* a hole (as of a serpent, &c.) : Job xxx. 6.

מְחִלּוֹת　*f. pl.* holes, caves : Isa. ii. 19.

מְעָרָה　*f.* a hole, cave, cavern : Gen. xix. 30, &c.

CEASE

1　בָּטֵל　to leave, to cease from labour ; to be unfit for use. KAL [a] *pret.* בְּטֵל Ch. P'AL [b] *pret.* [c] *inf.* [d] *part.*

2　גָּמַר　to finish ; to come to an end. KAL *pret.*

3　דָּמָה　to be quiet or still, to rest, cease. KAL *fut.*

4　דָּמַם　to be silent ; to rest, to be quiet, to keep still. KAL [a] *pret.* [b] *fut.*

5　חָדַל　to cease, to leave off, to desist to act ; to cease to be, involving a negation of act or existence, so as to be equivalent to 'not to do this or that :' 1 Sam. xii. 23, in ceasing to pray, *i.e.* in not praying (see *Forbear*) ; as when the hungry are no more hungry : 1 Sam. ii. 5. KAL [a] *pret.* [b] *inf.* [c] *imp.* [d] *fut.*

6　חָרַשׁ　to be silent ; to withdraw from. HIPHIL *fut.*

7　יָסַף　to add. KAL *pret.*

8　כָּלָה　to be finished ; to act, or be capable of acting, no more. KAL *pret.*

9　מוּשׁ　to depart, to remove. HIPHIL *fut.*

10　נוּחַ　to rest. KAL *fut.*

11　נָפַל　to fall. Hiphil, to leave off, **to cease.** HIPHIL *pret.*

12　עָמַד　to stand, stand still, cease. KAL *fut.*

13　פּוּג　to be cold ; to be languid, infirm. KAL *fut.*

14　פָּרַר　to break asunder ; *fig.* to frustrate, disannul. HIPHIL *imp.*

15　רָפָה　to be slack, hang down ; with מִן to desist from. HIPHIL *imp.*

16　שָׁבַת　to cease to do anything, with מִן and an *inf.* wholly to rest from labour, to cease to be. KAL [a] *pret.* [b] *fut.* NIPHAL [c] *pret.* HIPHIL [d] *pret.* [e] *imp.* [f] *fut.* [g] *part.* [h] שָׁבָת *m.* ceasing.

17　שׁוּב　to return. KAL *fut.* shall cease, *lit.* return from.

18　שָׁכַךְ　to settle, subside ; to still. HIPHIL *pret.*

19　שָׁתַק　to be still, to rest. KAL *fut.*

20　תָּמַם　to be finished, completed ; to end, leave off, cease, HIPHIL *inf.*

Gen. viii. 22.	16 b	Job xxxii. 1.	16 b	Isa. xxxiii. 8.	16 a
xviii. 11.	5 a	Ps. xii. 1.	2	Jer. vii. 34.	16 d
Exod. ix. 29, 33.	5 d	xxxv. 15.	4 a	xiv. 17.	3
ix. 34.	5 a	xxxvii. 8.	15	xv. 9.	16 g
Num. viii. 25.	17	xlvi. 9.	16 g	xvii. 8.	9
xi. 25. α	7	xlix. 8. γ	5 a	xxxi. 36.	16 b
xvii. 5.	18	lxxvii. 2.	13	xxxvi. 29.	16 d
Deut. xv. 11.	5 d	lxxxv. 4.	14	xlviii. 35.	16 d
xxxii. 26.	16 f	lxxxix. 44.	16 d	Lam. ii. 18.	4 b
Josh. v. 12.	16 b	Prov. xviii. 18	16 f	iii. 49.	3
xxii. 25.	16 d	xix. 27.	5 c	v. 14, 15.	16 d
Judg. ii. 19.	11	xx. 3.	16 h	Ezek. vi. 6.	16 c
v. 7, 7.	5 d	xxii. 10.	16 b	vii. 24.	16 d
xv. 7.	5 d	xxiii. 4.	5 c	xii. 23.	16 d
xx. 28.	5 d	xxvi. 20.	19	xvi. 41.	16 d
1 Sam. ii. 5.	5 a	Eccles. xii. 3.	1 a	xxiii. 27, 48.	16 d
vii. 8.	6	Isa. i. 16.	5 c	xxvi. 13.	16 d
xii. 23.	5 b	x. 25.	8	xxx. 10, 13.	16 d
xxv. 9.	10	2 Chron. xvi. 5.	16 f	xxx. 18.	16 c
Ezra iv. 21.	1 c	xiv. 4, 4.	16 a	xxxiii. 28.	16 c
iv. 23.	1	xvi. 4.	8	xxxiv. 10, 25.	16 c
iv. 24, 24. β	1 b d	xvi. 10.	16 d	Dan. ix. 27.	16 f
v. 5.	1 b d	vii. 10.	16 c	xi. 18.	16 d
Neh. iv. 11.	16 d	xxi. 2.	16 d	Hos. i. 4.	16 d
vi. 3.	16 b	xxiv. 8, 8.	16 a	ii. 11.	16 d
Job iii. 17.	5 a	xxxiii. 1.	20	vii. 4.	16 b
x. 20.	5 c			Amos vii. 10.	5 c
xiv. 7.	5 c			Jonah i. 15.	12

α *lit.* and added not.　β *lit.* so it was ceasing.　γ "so that he must let that alone for ever."—*Prayer-Book version.*

CEDAR

אֶרֶז　*m.* the cedar-tree, tall, beautiful, wide spreading ; growing on the mountains ; symbolically representing kings, princes, and nobles ; and so called from the firmness of its roots : Lev. xiv. 4, &c. אַרְזָה *f.* cedarwork : Zeph. ii. 14. אֲרֻזִים *adj.* made of cedar : Ezek. xxvii. 24. The wood is odoriferous and exceedingly durable, and therefore was much used in the temple and the king's palaces for ornamental work, and especially for the wainscot and ceiling.

CELEBRATE

הָלַל　to praise. PIEL *fut.* Isa. xxxviii. 18.

חָנַג　to keep (a feast). KAL *fut.* Lev. xxiii. 41.

שָׁבַת　to rest. KAL *fut.* Lev. xxiii. 32, *or,* celebrate the rest of.

CELLAR

אוֹצָר　*m.* treasures, storehouse : 1 Chron. xxvii. 27, 28.

CENSER

מַחְתָּה　*f.* a censer filled with burning coals from the altar : Lev.

x. 1 ; xvi. 12 : Num. iv. 14 ; xvi. 6, 17, 17, 17, 17, 18, 37, 38, 39, 46 : 1 Kings vii. 50 : 2 Chron. iv. 22.

מִקְטֶרֶת *f.* a censer, to burn incense : 2 Chron. xxvi. 19 : Ezek. viii. 11.

CEREMONIES

מִשְׁפָּט *m.* judgment ; law, custom ; prescribed rules : Num. ix. 3.

CERTAIN

1 אֶחָד *adj.* one.
2 אִישׁ a man.
3 אֲמָנָה *f.* see *Portion.*
4 אֱנוֹשׁ *m.* man.
5 גְּבַר Ch. *m.* see *Man.*
6 יָדַע to know ; certainly, for a certainty, *lit.* knowing. KAL *inf.*
7 יַצִּיב Ch. *adj.* fixed ; sure, true.
8 כֵּן to establish. NIPHAL *part.*
9 עֵת see *Time.*
10 פְּלֹמוֹנִי *m.* see *Such.* פְּלֹנִי and אַלְמֹנִי are joined in one word.
11 קֹשְׁט *m.* truth, certainty, purity.

Gen. xxxviii. 1, 2.	2	2 Sam. xviii. 10.	1	Jer. xiii. 12.	6
xliii. 7.	6	1 Kings ii. 37, 42.	6	xxvi. 15.	6
Num. ix. 6.	4	xi. 17.	4	xxvi. 17.	4
xvi. 2.	4	xx. 35.	1	xl. 14.	6
Deut. xiii. 14.	8	2 Kings iv. 1.	1	xli. 5.	4
xvii. 4.	8	viii. 6.	1	xlii. 19, 22.	6
Josh. xxiii. 13.	6	2 Chron. xxviii. 12.	4	Ezek. xiv. 1.	4
Judg. ix. 53.	1	Ezra i. 4.	4	xx. 1.	4
xiii. 2. α	1	Neh. xi. 23.	3	Dan. ii. 8, 45.	7
xix. 1.	2	xiii. 25.	4	iii. 8, 12.	5
xix. 22. β	4	Esth. ii. 5. γ	2	viii. 13.	10
1 Sam. i. 1.	1	iii. 8.	1	x. 5. α	1
xx. 3, 9.	6	Prov. xxii. 21.	11	xi. 13.	9
xxiii. 23.	8				

α *lit.* one man. β *lit.* men of the sons of. γ *lit.* a man a Jew.

CERTIFY

אָמַר to say, to tell. KAL *fut.* Esth. ii. 22.
יְדַע Ch. to know ; to make known. APHEL *pret.* Ezra iv. 14. *inf.* Ezra v. 10. *part.* Ezra iv. 16 ; vii. 24.
נָגַד to tell, to declare. HIPHIL *inf.* 2 Sam. xv. 28.

CHAFED

מַר *adj.* bitter, fierce : 2 Sam. xvii. 8.

CHAFF

חָשַׁשׁ *m.* hay, dried grass : Isa. v. 24 ; xxxiii. 11.
מֹץ *m.* chaff, winnowed from the grain : Job xxi. 18 : Ps. i. 4 ; xxxv. 5 : Isa. xvii. 13 ; xxix. 5 ; xli. 15 : Hos. xiii. 3 : Zeph. ii. 2.
עוּר Ch. *m.* chaff or light straw : Dan. ii. 35.
תֶּבֶן *m.* straw, as broken up by threshing : Jer. xxiii. 28, *lit.* what to the straw the wheat.

CHAIN

1 אֲזִקִּים *m. pl.* manacles or handcuffs : *i.q.* זִקִּים.
2 אֶצְעָדָה *f.* see *Bracelet.*
3 הַמְנִיךָ Ch. a chain for the neck or arm.

4 זִקִּים *m. pl.* fetters, chains.
5 חָח *m.* see *Hook.*
6 חֲרוּזִים *m. pl.* a string of pearls, or such like ornaments.
7 כֹּשָׁרוֹת *f. pl.* chains or bands, as if from קָשַׁר to bind : according to others, prosperity, from כָּשֵׁר to prosper.
8 נְחֹשֶׁת *com.* brass, fetters of brass.
9 נְטִיפוֹת *f.* ear-pendants, so called from the pearls in the form of a drop.
10 עֲנָק *m.* an ornament of the neck, a badge of honour or distinction. עָנַק to surround like a necklace ; as pride is on the neck like a chain of ornament, so the *collum resupinum* was significative of pride. KAL ª *pret.*
11 רָבִיד *m.* collar, chain for the neck.
12 רַתּוֹק *m.* a chain. ª רַתּוּקָה *f.* רְתֻקוֹת ᵇ *f. pl.*
13 שַׁרְשְׁרָה *m.* a little chain ; reduplication of שָׁרָה, (see *Bracelet*); by contraction ª שַׁרְשָׁה *f.*

Gen. xli. 42.		11	Ps. lxviii. 6.		7	Jer. xxxix. 7.	8
Exod. xxviii. 14, 14.		13	lxviii. 6.		10 a	xl. 1, 4.	1
xxviii. 22.		13 a	cxlix. 8.		4	lii. 11.	8
xxxix. 15.		13	Prov. i. 9.		9	Lam. iii. 7.	8
Num. xxxi. 50.		2	Cant. i. 10.		6	Ezek. vii. 23.	12
Judg. viii. 26.		10	iv. 9.		9	xvi. 11.	11
1 Kings vi. 21.		12 a	Isa. iii. 19. α		9	xix. 4, 9.	5
vii. 17.		13	xl. 19.		12 b	Dan. v. 7, 16, 29.	3
2 Chron. iii. 5, 16, 16.		13	xlv. 14.		4	Nah. iii. 10.	4

a See *Stacte.*

CHALK-STONES

גִּיר *m.* lime ; אֶבֶן *m.* stone : Isa. xxvii. 9.

CHALLENGE

אָמַר to say. KAL *fut.* Exod. xxii. 9.

CHAMBER

1 חֶדֶר *m.* the inmost and most retired part of any place ; the retired part of a large chamber called a bedchamber, separated by a curtain ; hence an inner chamber, *marg.* 'a chamber within a chamber.' Dr. Shaw, describing the structure of houses in Barbary, says, "Their chambers are large and spacious ; one of them frequently serving a whole family. At one end of each chamber there is a little gallery, raised four or five feet, with a balustrade in the front of it : here they place their beds."—*Taylor.*
2 חֻפָּה *f.* a bridal canopy or covering, at a marriage ceremony.
3 יָצִיעַ *com.* a chamber, or chamber floor.—*Gesenius.* This name is given in Solomon's temple to the three stories of side chambers, which were built around the temple on three sides, five cubits in height, one above another.
4 לִשְׁכָּה *f.* a chamber in the temple ; these were used as storerooms for tithes, offerings, vessels, &c., as dining-rooms, and probably as lodging-rooms ; also the secretary's office in the king's house : Jer. xxxvi. 12.
5 נִשְׁכָּה *f.* a chamber or cell in the temple.
6 עֲלִיָּה *f.* a chamber or upper room ; independent houses annexed to the greater, consisting of one or two rooms and terrace above them. See *Roof.* Sometimes they were built over the porch or gallery, and had private stairs

down into the porch or street, by which they might pass without giving any disturbance to the family. In these separate private back houses strangers were lodged and entertained : 2 Kings iv. 10. The men retired from the hurry and noise of their families for devotion or diversion.—*Shaw's Travels*, p. 280. One of the rooms of these separate houses among the Jews, much used for devotion and other purposes, was called ὑπερῷον, an upper room, Acts i. 13. See Dan. vi. 10, and *Windows*. עֲלִית [a] Ch. *f. id.*

7   צֵלָע   *f.* a rib ; a side chamber (of the temple) ; also collectively, a whole story of side chambers, or even the three stories : Ezek. xli. 5, &c. בֵּית צְלָעוֹת Ezek. xli. 9, is the space for these side chambers between the two walls of the temple. *Comp.* Josephi Antiq. Jud. iii. 3, 2.

8   תָּא   *m.* a chamber, *thalamus.*

No. 1 not included.

2 Sam. xviii. 33.	6	1 Chron. xxviii. 12.	4	Jer. xxxvi. 10, 12, 20, 21.	4
1 Kings vi. 5, 5.	3, 7	2 Chron. iii. 9.	6	Ezek. xl. 7, 7, 10, 12, 12,	
vi. 6.	6	xii. 11.	8	13, 16, 21, 29, 33,	
vi. 8.	7	xxxi. 11.	4	36.	8
vi. 10.	8	Ezra viii. 29.	4	xl. 17, 17, 38, 44, 45, 46.	4
xiv. 28.	8	x. 6.	4	xli. 5, 6, 6, 7, 8, 9, 9,	
xvii. 23.	6	Neh. iii. 30.	5	11, 26.	7
2 Kings i. 2.	6	x. 37, 38, 39.	4	xli. 10.	4
iv. 10, 11.	6	xii. 44.	5	xlii. 1, 4, 5, 7, 7, 8, 9,	
xxiii. 11.	4	xiii. 4, 5, 8, 9.	4	10, 11, 12, 13, 13,	
xxiii. 12.	6	xiii. 7.	5	13.	4
1 Chron. ix. 26.	4	Ps. xix. 5.	2	xliv. 19.	4
ix. 33.	4	civ. 3, 13.	6	xlv. 5.	4
xxiii. 28.	4	Jer. xxii. 13, 14.	6	xlvi. 19.	4
xxviii. 11.	6	xxxv. 2, 4, 4, 4.	4	Dan. vi. 10.	6 a

CHAMBERLAIN

סָרִים   *m.* an eunuch ; and because eunuchs were employed as chamberlains and in other great offices in the courts of kings, hence it came to be a general name for such officers, though they were not eunuchs : 2 Kings xxiii. 11 : Esth. i. 10, 12, 15 ; ii. 3, 14, 15, 21 ; iv. 4, 5 ; vi. 2, 14 ; vii. 9.

CHAMELEON

כֹּחַ   *m.* a large kind of lizard : Lev. xi. 30.

CHAMOIS

זֶמֶר   *m.* the *camelopardalis* or giraffe : Shaw's Sup. pp. 78, 88. A horned animal, mild like the sheep, spotted like the leopard ; its neck seven feet long ; from head to tail eighteen feet ; its head when lifted up reaches sixteen feet from the ground ; the fore legs are much longer than the hind legs, which makes it difficult to eat grass, and obliges it to jump in running : Raii Syn. Quadrup. p. 90. As it lives chiefly by cropping, and as it were pruning the leaves and under branches of trees, probably it took its name from this circumstance, and might be called the pruner : Deut. xiv. 5.

CHAMPAIGN

עֲרָבָה   *f.* see *Plain.* Deut. xi. 30.

CHAMPION

אִישׁ   *m.* a man ; בְּנַיִם *dual,* the interval between two armies : 1 Sam. xvii. 4, 23, a champion, *lit.* a middle-man ; or, man of the two intermediates.

נִבּוֹר   *adj.* one mighty in valour : 1 Sam. xvii. 51.

CHANCE

פֶּגַע   *m.* an occurrence, incident : Eccles. ix. 11.

קָרָא   to meet, befall ; to happen, to be by chance. NIPHAL *inf.* 2 Sam. i. 6, *lit.* happening I happened. *fut.* Deut. xxii. 6.

קָרָה   *m.* chance, accident : Deut. xxiii. 10.   מִקְרֶה *m.* fortuitous chance : 1 Sam. vi. 9.

CHANCELLOR

בְּעֵל   Ch. *m.* master. טְעֵם Ch. *m.* decree, commandment : Ezra iv. 8, 9, 17, *lit.* master of counsel, or decrees.

CHANGE

1   הָפַךְ   (see *Turn*) to change, to change one thing for another ; to change or turn into a different substance, form, quality, or place ; to change into a ruinous desolate condition. It is used in Kal both transitively and neutrally. KAL [a] *pret.* [b] *fut.* NIPHAL [c] *pret.*

2   חָלַף   to pass ; to pass from one thing, degree, condition, or station, to another ; hence—(1) to change or alter, in Matt. xxiv. 35 : the force of this word in Ps. cii. 26 is well expressed by παρελεύσονται, yet the context implies a change, as of old garments for new ; (2) to renew, Job xiv. 14, "till my change," renewal, the happy change of my condition, "come ;" (3) to take in turns or courses by succession, Job x. 17, "changes and war are against me," *i.e.* a war in which one body of men succeeds another, and makes a fresh attack ; meaning the variety of afflictions which had befallen him. With *inf.* change at all. KAL [a] *pret.* [b] *fut.* PIEL [c] *fut.* HIPHIL [d] *pret.* [e] *imp.* [f] *fut.* [g] חֲלִיפָה *f.* change, change for the better, as in Job xiv. 14, in the sense of restoration, as also in Job xiv. 7.

3   מַחֲלָצוֹת   *f.* change of raiment, changeable suits of apparel, so called because they are gently drawn off and laid aside when not used : Zech. iii. 4, *i.e.* costly and beautiful garments, not worn in common.

4   חָפַשׂ   to search for that which is hid ; to let oneself be sought, to be hid, concealed, disguised ; to disguise oneself. HITHPAEL [a] *fut.* Job xxx. 18, "by the great force of my disease is my garment changed," or disguised so that it cannot be known. This very difficult verse has not yet received any better explication.

5   יָמַר   to change, to exchange. HIPHIL *pret.*

6   מוּר   to change ; to substitute one thing in the place of another ; to change, alter, or turn to the reverse. With *inf.* change at all. NIPHAL [a] *pret.* HIPHIL [b] *pret.* [c] *inf.* [d] *fut.* [e] תְּמוּרָה *f.* exchange.

7   מָרָה   to rebel ; to resist, to oppose : Ezek. v. 6, "hath changed ;" rather, hath rebelled against. Our version is from מוּר to change. HIPHIL *fut.*

8   סָבַב   to compass, to turn about. HIPHIL [a] *fut.* HOPHAL [b] *part.*

9   שׂוּם   to put or set with design, care, &c. KAL *fut.*

10 שָׁנָה to double; to do a thing over again; to do it in a different manner; to alter, to change. KAL ᵃpret. ᵇpart. Poel. PIEL ᶜpret. ᵈinf. ᵉfut. ᶠpart. שָׁנָא, after the Chaldaic form. KAL ᵍfut. PIEL ʰpret. PUAL ⁱfut.

11 שְׁנָא Ch. P'AL ᵃpret. ᵇfut. ᶜpart. PAEL ᵈpret. ᵉfut. ITHPAEL ᶠpret. ᵍfut. APHEL ʰinf. ⁱpart.

Gen. xxxi. 7.	2 d	Job x. 17.	2 g	Lam. iv. 1.	10 g
xxxi. 41.	2 f	xiv. 14.	2 g		7
xxxv. 2.	2 f	xiv. 20.	10 f	Ezek. vi. 6.	
xli. 14.	2 c	xvii. 12.	9	Dan. ii. 9.	11 g
xlv. 22, 22.	2 g	xxx. 18.	4	ii. 21.	11 i
Lev. xiii. 16.	1 c	Ps. xv. 4.	6 d	iii. 19.	11 f
xiii. 55.	1 a	xxxiv. title.	10 d	iii. 27.	11 a
xxvii. 10.	6 d	lv. 19.	2 g	iii. 28.	11 d
xxvii. 10.	6 c d	cii. 26, 26.	2 f b	iv. 16.	11 e
xxvii. 33.	6 d	cvi. 20.	6 d	v. 6.	11 a
xxvii. 33.	6 c d	Prov. xxiv. 21. a	10 b	v. 9.	11 c
xxvii. 33.	6 e	Eccles. viii. 1.	10 i	v. 10.	11 g
Num. xxxii. 38.	8 b	Isa. iii. 22.	3	vi. 8, 15.	11 h
Judg. xiv. 12, 13, 19.	2 g	ix. 10.	2 f	vi. 17.	11 b
1 Sam. xxi. 13.	10 e	xxiv. 5.	2 a	vii. 25.	11 h
2 Sam. xii. 20.	2 c	Jer. ii. 11, 11.	5, 6 b	vii. 28.	11 g
Ruth iv. 7.	6 e	ii. 36.	10 d	Hos. vi. 7.	6 d
2 Kings v. 5, 22, 23.	2 g	xiii. 23.	1 b	Micah ii. 4.	6 d
xxiv. 17.	8 a	xlviii. 11.	6 a	Hab. i. 11.	2 a
xxv. 29.	10 h	lii. 33.	10 c	Zech. iii. 4.	3
				Mal. iii. 6.	10 a

a "given to change."

CHANNEL

אָפִיק a stream, held in by the banks; a channel or cavity of the earth in which it flows: 2 Sam. xxii. 16: Ps. xviii. 15: Isa. viii. 7.

שִׁבֹּלֶת *f.* a stream (see *Flood*): Isa. xxvii. 12.

CHANT

פָּרַם to part, to separate; to open wide the lips as in singing, to sing, to chant. KAL *part.* Poel, Amos vi. 5.

CHAPEL

מִקְדָּשׁ *m.* a sanctuary, holy place: Amos vii. 13.

CHAPITER

כֹּתֶרֶת *f.* a chapiter, or ornament in architecture, encompassing the top of a pillar: 1 Kings vii. 16, 16, 16, 17, 17,17, 18, 18, 19, 20, 20, 31, 41, 41, 42: 2 Kings xxv. 17, 17, 17: 2 Chron. iv. 12, 12, 13: Jer. lii. 22, 22, 22.

צֶפֶת *f.* the capital of a column: 2 Chron. iii. 15.

רֹאשׁ *m.* head: Exod. xxxvi. 38; xxxviii. 17, 19, 28.

CHAPMAN

תּוּר see *Merchant.* KAL *part.* Poel. אֱנוֹשׁ *m.* man: 2 Chron. ix. 14.

CHAPT

חָתַת to be broken. KAL *pret.* Jer. xiv. 4.

CHARGE

1 אָמַר to say, &c. KAL *fut.*

2 יָד *com.* hand.

3 נָתַן to give. KAL ᵃ*pret.* ᵇ*inf.* ᶜ*fut.* with בְּקֶרֶב to lay to people's charge.

4 סֵבֶל *m.* burden; tax.

5 עָבַר to pass. KAL *fut.*

6 עוּד see *Testify.* HIPHIL ᵃ*pret.* ᵇ*imp.*

7 עָשָׂה to do; to have charge of. KAL *part.* Poel.

8 פָּקַד to look on or after a thing, particularly with a concern for it, *prospicere alicui rei;* to give the oversight, to place a person over anything, to command, with עַל of the person. Hiphil, to appoint, with עַל of the thing, and with לְ; to commit to a person, with עַל ,יַד ,בְּיַד, and with אֵת (אֶת) *penes* (like *deponere apud aliquem*). KAL ᵃ*pret.* ᵇ*fut.* HIPHIL ᶜ*pret.* ᵈפְּקֻדָּה *f.* care, oversight; or visitation in a way of punishment: so Ezek. ix. 1, cause visitations to draw near. ᵉפָּקִיד *m.* overseer.

9 צָוָה to command to do; to give a charge. PIEL ᵃ*pret.* ᵇ*inf.* ᶜ*imp.* ᵈ*fut.*

10 קֶרֶב *m.* the middle or inner part; "unto," *lit.* in the midst of my people.

11 שָׁאַל to ask, to lay to charge of, to demand in a way of inquiry. KAL *fut.*

12 שָׁבַע to swear; Hiphil, to charge with an oath. With *inf.* straitly charged. HIPHIL ᵃ*pret.* ᵇ*inf.*

13 שׂוּם to put or set with care, regard. KAL *fut.*

14 מִשְׁמֶרֶת *f.* a watching, keeping or preserving, command, care or management of a business; *marg.* 'ward,' 'ordinance.'

15 מִשְׁפָּט *m.* judgment, law, custom, mode or manner.

Gen. xxvi. 5.	14	Josh. xxii. 3.	14	Ezra i. 2.	8 a
xxvi. 11.	9 d	xxii. 5.	9 a	Neh. viii. 2.	9 d
xxviii. 1, 6.	9 d	Ruth ii. 9.	9 a	x. 32.	3 b
xl. 4.	8 b	1 Sam. xiv. 27.	12 b	xiii. 19.	1
xlix. 29.	9 d	xiv. 28.	12 b a	Esth. ii. 10, 20.	9 a
Exod. i. 22.	9 d	2 Sam. iii. 8.	8 b	iii. 19.	7
vi. 13.	9 d	xi. 19.	9 d	iv. 8.	9 b
xix. 21.	6 b	xiv. 8.	9 d	Job i. 22.	3 a
xix. 23.	6 a	xviii. 5.	9 b	iv. 18.β	13
Lev. viii. 35.	14	xviii. 5.	9 b	xxxiv. 13.	8 a
Num. i. 53.	14	1 Kings ii. 1.	9 d	Ps. xxxv. 11.	11
iii. 7, 7, 8, 25, 28, 31, 32, 36, 38, 38.	14	ii. 3.	14	xci. 11.	9 d
iv. 27, 28, 31, 32.	14	ii. 43.	9 a	Cant. ii. 7.	12 a
v. 19, 21.	12 a	iv. 28.	15	iii. 5.	12 a
viii. 26, 26.	14	xi. 28.	4	v. 8, 9.	12 a
ix. 19, 23.	14	xiii. 9.	9 a	viii. 4.	12 a
xviii. 3, 3, 4, 5, 5, 8.	14	2 Kings vii. 17. a	8 c	Isa. x. 6.	9 d
xxvii. 19.	9 a	xvii. 15.	9 a	Jer. xxxii. 13.	9 d
xxvii. 23.	9 d	xvii. 35.	9 a	xxxv. 8.	9 a
xxxi. 30, 47.	14	1 Chron. ix. 27.	14	xxxix. 11.	9 d
xxxi. 49.	2	xxii. 6, 12.	9 d	xlvii. 7.	9 a
Deut. i. 16.	9 d	xxii. 13.	9 a	lii. 25.	8 e
iii. 28.	9 c	2 Chron. viii. 14.	14	Ezek. ix. 1.	8 d
xi. 1.	14	xiii. 11.	14	xl. 45, 46.	14
xxi. 8.	3 c, 10	xix. 9.	9 d	xliv. 8, 8.	14
xxiv. 5.	5	xxxi. 16, 17.	14	xliv. 11.	8 d
xxvii. 11.	9 d	xxxv. 2.	14	xliv. 14, 15, 16.	14
xxxi. 14, 23.	9 d	xxxvi. 23.	8 a	xlviii. 11.	14
Josh. xviii. 8.	9 d			Zech. iii. 7.	14

a "appointed to have the charge."   β See *Folly*, No. 9.

CHARGEABLE

כָּבֵד to be heavy, to lie or fall heavy on any one, to be chargeable or troublesome to him. KAL *fut.* 2 Sam. xiii. 25. HIPHIL *pret.* Neh. v. 15.

CHARGER

אֲגַרְטָל *m.* a bason or bowl: Ezra i. 9, 9.

קְעָרָה *f.* a dish, charger: Num. vii. 13, 19, 25, 31, 37, 43, 49, 55, 61, 67, 73, 79, 84, 85.

CHARIOT

1 הֹצֶן *m.* some warlike machine, perhaps a chariot armed with scythes.

2 עֲגָלָה f. a wagon or chariot.

3 אַפִּרְיוֹן m. sedan, litter, portable couch. LXX. φορεῖον. Vulg. *ferculum*. In Talmudic this word signifies a nuptial bed.

4 רָכַב to ride, to ride in a chariot. KAL a *fut*. b רֶכֶב m. driver of a chariot. c רֶכֶב *com*. chariot: Gen. l. 9, &c. d רִכְבָּה f. riding, driving. e רְכוּב m. vehicle, chariot. f מֶרְכָּב m. chariot. g מֶרְכָּבָה f. chariot, especially a war-chariot: Gen. xli. 43, &c. Chariots of iron were armed with scythes of about two cubits long, fastened to long axletrees on both wheels. Often רֶכֶב refers mostly to the horses yoked to the chariots, and to the soldiers riding in the chariots, as 2 Sam. viii. 4; x. 18.

No. 4 c g not included.

1 Kings iv. 26.	4 f	2 Chron. xviii. 33.	4 b	Cant. iii. 9.	3
xxii. 34.	4 b	Ps. xlvi. 9.	2	Ezek. xxiii. 24.	1
2 Kings ix. 16.	4 a	civ. 3.	4 e	xxvii. 20.	4 d

CHARM

1 אִטִּים m. pl. sorcerers, jugglers; alluding perhaps to their soft and silent motions, or their low and slow manner of speaking.

2 חָבַר to join together, to bind, to fascinate. KAL part. Poel. a חֶבֶר m. an incantation.

3 לַחַשׁ to speak in a soft gentle manner; applied to the charming of serpents, probably by soft and gentle sounds. PIEL part. a לַחַשׁ m. charm.

Deut. xviii. 11.α	2, 2 a	Isa. xix. 3.β	1
Ps. lviii. 5, 5.	3, 2 2 a	Jer. viii. 17.γ	3 a

α *lit*. one that charms a charming. β Lxx. their idols. γ *lit*. for whom there is no charm.

CHASE

1 בָּרַח to flee away; to drive away. HIPHIL *fut*. Neh. xiii. 28, with מֵעָלַי as one troublesome.

2 דָּחָה to push, thrust, drive. KAL part. Poel.

3 דָּלַק to burn; to pursue or persecute with a hot malicious mind. KAL *inf*.

4 נָדַד to move oneself, to flee away. HIPHIL a *fut*. HOPHAL b *fut*.

5 נָדַח to expel, drive away, banish. HOPHAL part.

6 צוּד to lie in wait, to hunt. With *fut*. chase sore. KAL a *pret*. b *inf*.

7 רָדַף to run or follow after; to pursue, persecute; to chase, to put to flight. KAL a *pret*. b *fut*. PUAL c *pret*. HIPHIL d *pret*.

Lev. xxvi. 7, 8, 36.	7 a	Josh. xxiii. 10.	7 b	Job xx. 8.	4 b
Deut. i. 44.	7 b	Judg. ix. 40.	7 b	Ps. xxxv. 5.α	2
xxxii. 30.	7 b	xx. 48.	7 d	Prov. xix. 26.	1
Josh. vii. 5.	7 b	1 Sam. xvii. 53.	3	Isa. xiii. 14.	5
viii. 24.	7 a	Neh. xiii. 28.	1	xvii. 13.	7 c
x. 10.	7 b	Job xviii. 18.	4 a	Lam. iii. 52.β	6 b a
xi. 8.	7 b				

α *lit*. chasing them. β *lit*. chasing chased me.

CHASTISE, CHASTEN

1 יָכַח see *Reprove, Rebuke*. HIPHIL a *pret*. HOPHAL b *pret*. c תּוֹכַחָה f. punishment, chastening.

2 יָסַר to bind; to discipline, to correct, to chasten, to restrain from doing wrong, to reduce to duty and obedience, to reform by words or actions. With *inf*. chasten sore. KAL a *fut*. b *part*. Poel. NIPHAL c *fut*. PIEL d *pret*. e *inf*. f *imp*. g *fut*. h *part*. HIPHIL i *fut*. k מוּסָר m. correction.

3 עָנָה to afflict. HITHP. *inf*.

Lev. xxvi. 28.	2 d	Job v. 17.	2 k	Prov. xiii. 24.β	2 k
Deut. viii. 5, 5.	2 g h	xxxiii. 19.	1 b	xix. 18.	2 f
xi. 2.	2 k	Ps. vi. 1.	2 g	Isa. xxvi. 16.	2 k
xxi. 18.	2 d	xxxviii. 1.	2 g	liii. 5.	2 k
xxii. 18.	2 d	lxxiii. 14.	1 c	Jer. xxx. 14.	2 k
2 Sam. vii. 14.	1 a	xciv. 10.	2 b	xxxi. 18, 18.	2 d c
1 Kings xii. 11, 11.	2 d g	xciv. 12.	2 g	Dan. x. 12.	3
xii. 14, 14.	2 d g	cxviii. 18.α	2 d e	Hos. vii. 12.	2 i
2 Chron. x. 11, 14.	2 d	Prov. iii. 11.	2 k	x. 10.	2 a

α *lit*. in chastening hath chastened. β *lit*. betimes seeketh correction for him.

CHATTER

צָפַף to chirp, as a bird. PILPEL *fut*. Isa. xxxviii. 14.

CHECK

יָסַר see *Chasten*. מוּסָר m. correction: Job xx. 3.

CHECKER

שְׂבָכָה f. a net; lattice, lattice-work: 1 Kings vii. 17.

CHEEK

לְחִי m. the cheek, from its fresh colour: Deut. xviii. 3: 1 Kings xxii. 24: 2 Chron. xviii. 23: Job xvi. 10, *lit*. my cheeks: Ps. iii. 7, "cheek bone:" Cant. i. 10; v. 13: Isa. l. 6: Lam. i. 2; iii. 30: Micah v. 1.

CHEER, CHEERFUL

1 טוֹב to be well, to be good. HIPHIL a *fut*. b טוֹב *adj*. good. יָטַב to be good. Hiphil, to make cheerful. HIPH. c *fut*.

2 נוּב to grow as plants; to give forth words. PILEL *fut*.

3 שָׂמַח to rejoice; to cheer up. PIEL a *pret*. b *part*.

Deut. xxiv. 5.	3 a	Prov. xv. 13.	1 c	Zech. viii. 19.	1 b
Judg. ix. 13.	3 b	Eccles. xi. 9.	1 a	ix. 17.	2

CHEESE

גְּבִינָה f. cheese, i. e. curdled milk: Job x. 10.

חָלָב m. milk: 1 Sam. xvii. 18.

חָרִיץ m. a cutting: 1 Sam. xvii. 18, perhaps cuttings, slices of curdled milk, or soft cheese.

שְׁפָה f. according to the Targum, Syriac, and the Jewish interpreters, cheese of kine: 2 Sam. xvii. 29.

CHERETHITES

כְּרֵתִי m. a part of the king's bodyguard, and supposed to be executioners; or, by some, hewers of wood, as the Gibeonites: 2 Sam. viii. 18; xv. 18; xx. 7, 23: 1 Kings i. 38, 44: 1 Chron. xviii. 17: Ezek. xxv. 16: Zeph. ii. 5.

CHERISH

סָכַן to profit; to attend upon a person as a nurse, providing and ordering things proper for nourishment and refreshment. KAL part. Poel, 1 Kings i. 2, 4.

CHERUBIM

כְּרוּב m. The primary meaning of this word is undoubtedly involved in obscurity, which has never been cleared

away by the very numerous discussions to which it has given rise ; and the present undertaking cannot afford an opportunity of even noticing the elaborate opinions of learned writers on the nature and import of the Cherubim. Ode, in his learned work, *De Angelis*, has given a long chapter to the consideration of the various opinions of others, and the demonstration of his own, that they were symbolical of angels, and typical of the faithful. Fairbairn, on the Typology of Scripture, refers to Bahr's Symbolik, "whose skilful and elaborate treatment of this symbol surpasses everything he has seen on the subject," and devotes many pages to the discussion. He comes to the conclusion, which seems to me generally most satisfactory, that they represent redeemed and glorified manhood—the highest perfection of creature life. They were intended, in Paradise, to direct the hope of our fallen parents to eternal life, in the revelation of mercy by the Redeemer. In the most holy place of the tabernacle, the same life, identified in union with the Mediator, is typified by the mercyseat, with which the Cherubim were connected, beaten out of the same mass of gold. In the temple they were made of wood covered with plates of gold, which might typify human nature glorified. In the visions of Ezekiel they symbolise glorified saints and angels, who serve God day and night, and shall stand before Him and minister unto Him in a world of glory for ever and ever. In Rev. v. 9, the four living creatures, corresponding in description with the visions of Ezekiel, are clearly identified with the redeemed by the blood of Christ. See Fairbairn's Typology, vol. i. p. 296–323 ; vol. ii. p. 402–404 ; Gen. iii. 24, &c.

CHEST

אָרוֹן *c.* an ark, chest, &c.: 2 Kings xii. 9, 10 ; 2 Chron. xxiv. 8, 10, 11, 11.

גְּנָזִים *m. pl.* treasures ; chests in which precious goods are stored : Ezek. xxvii. 24.

CHESTNUT-TREE

עַרְמוֹן *m.* properly the plane-tree, so called from shedding its bark : Gen. xxx. 37 : Ezek. xxxi. 8.

CHEW

גָּרַר to ruminate, to chew the cud ; *pr.* to bring up again through the gullet. NIPHAL *fut.* Lev. xi. 7.

גֵּרָה *f.* rumination : Deut. xiv. 8, *lit.* and not rumination. Some, as our translators, consider it a verb, "and cheweth not the cud."

כָּרַת to cut off. NIPHAL *fut.* Num. xi. 33, *lit.* cut off.

עָלָה to ascend ; to chew the cud, *lit.* to make the cud ascend. HIPHIL *part.* Lev. xi. 3, 4, 4, 5, 6, 26 : Deut. xiv. 6, 7, 7.

CHIDE

רִיב to contend or strive. KAL *fut.* Gen. xxxi. 36 : Exod. xvii. 2, 2 : Num. xx. 3 : Judg. viii. 1 : Ps. ciii. 9.

רִיב *m.* strife, contention : Exod. xvii. 7.

CHIEF

1 אָב *m.* father ; chief house, *Heb.* house of a father.

2 אַבִּיר *adj.* that which is strongest and most excellent.

3 אֲצִילִים *m. pl.* nobles, chiefs ; select persons of distinction and eminence ; or, those on whom the state leans for support. Fürst : *fundamenta terræ* (see Exod. xxiv. 11). Modern critics give the meaning of sides or extremities of the earth.

4 בַּעַל *m.* owner, husband, father of a family. The argument in Lev. xxi. 4 seems to be that the high priest shall not defile himself even for his own wife when dead, since he is the husband of the people, or father of that family, and must not let this interfere with his sacred duties.

5 גִּבּוֹר *adj.* see *Mighty.*

6 דָּגַל to carry a standard. KAL *part.* Paül. Ges., lifted up as a standard, *i. e.* conspicuous, distinguished, spoken of a noble youth.

7 כֹּהֵן *m.* a priest, or prince ; chief ruler, *marg.* 'or, prince.'

8 נָגִיד *m.* see *Captain.* Chief ruler, or prince.

9 נָצַח Piel, to be placed over, to have the oversight of ; used in reference to music, probably, to preside over the singing, to lead in the singing. Here belongs the expression לַמְנַצֵּחַ in the superscription of fifty-five Psalms, (PIEL *part.*), and in Hab. iii. 19, a precentor, chorister. So Rashi, Aben-Ezra, Kimchi, and most of the moderns. Others make it the Syr. *inf.* Pa. (*comp.* in Chald. Dan. v. 12), to lead in singing. Targ. *ad laudandum.* The former interpretation is favoured by the frequent use of the word, to oversee.—*Gesenius.*

10 נָשִׂיא *m.* a prince, a ruler.

11 מַעֲלֶה *m.* ascent.

12 עַתּוּד *m.* a he-goat ; *metaph.* a leader of the people, a prince.

13 פִּנָּה *f.* a corner, cornerstone ; a principal person, the chief support of a community.

14 רֹאשׁ *m.* head ; a chief, ruler, captain, &c. (frequent). רֹאש [a] Ch. *m.* רֵאשִׁית [b] *f.* beginning, first, &c. רִאשׁוֹן [c] *adj.*

15 רַב Ch. *adj.* great.

16 שַׂר *m.* a captain, commander, chief ; prince, courtier.

No. 14, *Chief,* and No. 9, *Chief Musician,* not included.

Gen. xl. 2, 2, 9, 16, 20, 20, 21, 22, 23.	16	1 Kings viii. 1.	16	Ezra v. 10.	16
xli. 9, 10.	16	ix. 23.	16	viii. 24, 29, 29.	16
Lev. xxi. 4.	4	xiv. 27.	16	ix. 2.	14 c
Num. iii. 24, 30, 32, 32, 35.	10	1 Chron. v. 2.	4	x. 5.	16
iv. 34, 46.	10	ix. 26.	16	Job xl. 19.	14 b
xxv. 14, 15.	1	xv. 5, 6, 7, 8, 9, 10, 16, 22.	14 b	Ps. lxxviii. 51.	14 b
Josh. xxii. 14.	1	xviii. 17.	14 c	cv. 36.	14 b
Judg. xx. 2.	13	xxix. 6.	16	Cant. v. 10.	6
1 Sam. ii. 29.	14 b	xxix. 22.	8	Isa. xiv. 9.	12
xiv. 38.	13	2 Chron. v. 2.	10	xli. 9.	3
xv. 21.	14 b	viii. 9, 10.	16	Jer. xx. 1.	8
xxi. 7.	2	xii. 10.	16	xlix. 35.	14 b
2 Sam. viii. 18.	7	xvii. 14.	16	Dan. ii. 48.	15
xx. 26.	7	xxxii. 33.	11	x. 13.	14 c
1 Kings v. 16.	16	xxxv. 9.	16	xi. 41.	14 b
		xxxvi. 14.	16	Amos vi. 1, 6.	14 b
				Hab. iii. 19.	9

CHILD, CHILDHOOD

1 בָּנָה to build ; Niphal, to obtain, to have children, because by them a house is built. NIPHAL *fut.* בֵּן *m.* a son, a

child ; sometimes used of either sex : Deut. xxv. 5. comp. Matt. xxii. 24. Exod. ix. 4, &c. ^b בֶּן Ch. *m. id.*

2   הָרָה   to conceive, to be with child. KAL ^a *pret.* ^b *fut.* ^c הָרָה *adj. f.* with child, woman with child. ^d הָרִיָה *adj. f. id.*

3   וָלָד   *m.* offspring. ^a וָלָד *m. id.*

4   זֶרַע   *m.* seed ; child.

5   טַף   *m.* see *Little Ones.*

6   יָלַד   to bring forth children. KAL ^a *part.* Paül. ^b יֶלֶד a child. ^c יַלְדוּת *f.* childhood. ^d יָלִיד *m. const.* one born, a son.

7   מָלֵא   *adj.* full, "with child."

8   נַעַר   *m.* a young man, a child. ^a נַעַר *m.* boyhood, youth. נְעוּרִים *m. pl.* youth.

9   עוּל   a sucking child. ^a מְעוֹלֵל *m. id.* ^b עֲוִיל *m.* young children, *marg.* 'or, the wicked :' see *Wicked.* ^c עוֹלֵל, and עֹלָל *m.* infants, babes.

No. 1 a not included.

Gen. xi. 30.	3	2 Sam. xii. 15, 18, 18,		Isa. iii. 4, 5.	8	
xvi. 2.	1	18, 18, 19, 19, 21,		iii. 12.	9 d	
xvi. 11.	2 c	21, 22, 22.	6 b	vii. 16.	8	
xix. 36.	2 b	xii. 16.	8	viii. 4.	8	
xxi. 8, 14, 15, 16.	6 b	1 Kings iii. 7.	8	viii. 18.	6 b	
xxx. 3.	1	iii. 25.	6 b	ix. 6.	6 b	
xxx. 26.	6 b	iii. 26, 26.	1 a, 6 a	x. 19.	8	
xxxiii. 1, 2, 2, 5, 5,		iii. 27.	6 a	xi. 6.	8	
6, 7, 13, 14.	6 b	xi. 17.	8	xiii. 16.	9 c	
xxxvii. 30.	6 b	xiv. 3, 17.	8	xxvi. 17.	8	
xxxviii. 24, 25.	2 c	xiv. 12.	8	xxvi. 18.	2 a	
xlii. 20.	6 b	xvii. 21, 22, 22, 23.	6 b	xxix. 23.	6 b	
xliv. 20.	6 b	2 Kings ii. 23.	8	xlix. 15.	9 a	
Exod. i. 17, 18.	6 b	ii. 24.	6 b	lvii. 4, 5.	6 b	
ii. 3, 6, 6, 7, 8, 9, 9,		iv. 18, 26, 34, 34, 34.	6 b	lxv. 20.	8	
10.	6 b	iv. 29, 30, 31, 31, 32,		Jer. i. 6, 7.	8	
xii. 37, 37.	1 a, 5	35, 35.	8	vi. 11.	9 c	
xxi. 4.	6 b	v. 14.	8	ix. 21.	9 c	
xxi. 22.	2 c	viii. 12, 12, 12.	1 a, 9 c, 2 c	xxxi. 8.	2 c	
Lev. xxii. 13.	4	xv. 16.	2 c	xxxi. 10.	6 b	
Num. xiii. 22, 28.	6 d	1 Chron. xiv. 4.	6 a	xl. 7.	5	
xiv. 3.	5	xx. 4.	6 d	xli. 16.	5	
xvi. 27.	5	Ezra vi. 16, 16.	1 b	xliii. 6.	5	
xxxi. 18.	5	x. 1.	6 b	xliv. 7.	9 c	
Deut. iii. 6.	5	Neh. xii. 43.	6 b	Lam. i. 5.	9 c	
xxxi. 12.	5	Esth. iii. 13.	5	ii. 11, 19, 20.	9 c	
Josh. xv. 14.	6 d	Job xix. 18.	9 b	iv. 4.	9 c	
Judg. xiii. 5, 7, 8, 12, 24.	8	xxi. 11.	6 b	iv. 10.	6 b	
xxi. 10.	5	xxiv. 5.	8	v. 13.	8	
Ruth iv. 16.	6 b	xxix. 5.	8	Ezek. ix. 6.	5	
1 Sam. i. 2, 2.	6 b	xxxiii. 25.	8 a	Dan. i. 4, 10, 13, 15,		
i. 11.	4	Ps. cxlviii. 12.	8	17.	6 b	
i. 22, 24, a 25, 27.	8	Prov. xx. 11.	8	ii. 38.	1 b	
ii. 11, 18, 21, 26.	8	xxii. 6, 15.	8	v. 13.	1 b	
iii. 1, 8.	8	xxiii. 13.	8	xiii. 24.	1 b	
iv. 19.	2 c	xxix. 15.	8	Hos. i. 2.	6 b	
iv. 21.	8	Eccles. iv. 13, 15.	6 b	xi. 1.	8	
xii. 2.	8 b	x. 16.	8	xiii. 16.	2 d	
xvi. 11.	8	xi. 5.	7	Joel ii. 16.	9 c	
xxii. 19.β	9 c	xi. 5.	8	Amos i. 13, 13.	1 a, 2 c	
2 Sam. vi. 23.	3 a, 6 b כ	Isa. ii. 6.	6 c	Micah i. 9.	9 c	
xi. 5.	2 c	Isa. ii. 6.	6 b	Nah. iii. 10.	9 c	

a *lit.* and the child was a child.   β *lit.* from children.

CHILDLESS

עֲרִירִי *adj.* solitary, forsaken, childless : Gen. xv. 2 : Lev. xx. 20, 21 : Jer. xxii. 30.

שָׁכֵל to lose children. KAL *fut.* 1 Sam. xv. 33. PIEL *pret.* 1 Sam. xv. 33.

CHIMNEY

אֲרֻבָּה *f.* an outlet ; a latticed window, a chimney : Hos. xiii. 3, perhaps closed with lattice-work.

CHISLEU

כִּסְלֵו *m.* name of a month beginning with the new moon of December : Neh. i. 1 : Zech. vii. 1.

CHOOSE, CHOICE

1   בָּחַר   to choose, select, prefer ; and that which is mostly implied in choice, to examine, explore. There is a fulness in this word, which includes all these ideas, as must be evident in many passages in which it is used : Job xxxiv. 4, let us choose to us, prefer, and adhere to judgment ; let us be sincerely desirous to understand, and with impartiality and accuracy to discuss the subject in debate : xxix. 25, I chose out their way, showing my approbation or disapprobation : Ps. cxix. 30, I have chosen, preferred, and take pleasure in the way of truth : Isa. lxvi. 3, they have chosen, preferred their own ways before mine : 1 Sam. xx. 30, thou hast chosen, preferred before me, esteemed more than me, the son of Jesse : it is opposed to מָאַס to reject, pass by, despise, Isa. vii. 15, 16 ; xli. 9 : Job xxxiv. 33. Often *c. dat.* לֹ to chose for oneself. The thing chosen is put in the *accus. ;* also more freq. with בְּ ; once with עַל as marking desire, Job xxxvi. 21 ; also מִן implying preference, Ps. lxxxiv. 11. KAL ^a *pret.* ^b *inf.* ^c *imp.* ^d *fut.* ^e *part.* Poel. ^f *part.* Paül. NIPHAL ^g *pret.* ^h *part.* ⁱ בָּחוּר *m.* chosen, choice young man. ^k בָּחִיר *adj.* chosen. ^l מִבְחוֹר *m.* choice. ^m מִבְחָר *m.* choice.

2   בָּרַר   to separate ; to select ; that which is choice and set apart. KAL ^a *part.* Paül. ^b בַּר *adj.* chosen, beloved.

3   בָּרָה   to choose, select ; from the idea of cutting out and separating, corresponding in sense with בָּרַר.

4   בָּרָא   to hew, or cut ; to form, make, produce ; Piel, to mark out. PIEL *imp.* Ezek. xxi. 19, 19. *parall.* שִׂים לְךָ in the same verse.

5   קָבַל   to receive, to take anything offered. PIEL *imp.*

Gen. vi. 2.	1 a	1 Sam. xvii. 8.	3	2 Chron. xiii. 3, 3, 17.	1 f
xiii. 11.	1 d	xvii. 40.	1 d	xxv. 5.	1 f
xxiii. 6.	1 m	xx. 30.	1 e	xxix. 11.	1 a
Exod. xiv. 7.	1 f	xxiv. 2.	1 f	xxxiii. 7.	1 a
xv. 4.	1 m	xxvi. 2.	1 f	Neh. i. 9.	1 a
xvii. 9.	1 c	2 Sam. vi. 1.	1 f	v. 18.	2 a
xviii. 25.	1 d	vi. 21.	1 a	ix. 7.	1 a
Num. xvi. 5, 7.	1 d	x. 9, 9.	1 d f	Job viii. 15.	1 d
xvii. 5.	1 d	xvi. 18.	1 d	ix. 14.	1 d
Deut. iv. 37.	1 d	xvii. 1.	1 d	xv. 5.	1 d
vii. 6.	1 d	xxi. 6.	1 k	xxix. 25.	1 d
vii. 7.	1 d	xxiv. 12.	1 c	xxxiv. 4, 33.	1 d
x. 15.	1 d	1 Kings iii. 8.	1 a	xxxvi. 21.	1 d
xii. 5, 14, 18, 21, 26.	1 d	viii. 16, 16.	1 a d	Ps. xxv. 12.	1 d
xii. 11, 11.	1 d m	viii. 44, 48.	1 a	xxxiii. 12.	1 d
xiv. 2.	1 a	xi. 13, 32, 34, 36.	1 a	xlvii. 4.	1 d
xiv. 23, 24, 25.	1 d	xii. 21.	1 f	lxv. 4.	1 d
xv. 20.	1 d	xiv. 21.	1 a	lxxviii. 31.	1 i
xvi. 2, 6, 7, 11, 15,		xviii. 23.	1 d	lxxviii. 67.	1 a
16.	1 d	xviii. 25.	1 c	lxxviii. 68, 70.	1 d
xvii. 8, 10, 15.	1 d	2 Kings iii. 19.	1 l	lxxxix. 3.	1 k
xviii. 5.	1 a	xix. 23.	1 l	lxxxix. 19.	1 k
xviii. 6.	1 d	xxi. 7.	1 a	cv. 6, 43.	1 k
xxi. 5.	1 d	xxiii. 27.	1 a	cv. 26.	1 k
xxiii. 16.	1 d	1 Chron. vii. 40.	2 a	cvi. 5, 23.	1 k
xxvi. 2.	1 d	ix. 22.	2 a	cxix. 30, 173.	1 k
xxx. 19.	1 d	xv. 2.	1 a	cxxxii. 13.	1 a
xxxi. 11.	1 d	xvi. 13.	1 k	cxxxv. 4.	1 a
Josh. viii. 3.	1 d	xvi. 41.	2 a	Prov. i. 29.	1 d
ix. 27.	1 d	xix. 10, 10.	1 d f	iii. 31.	1 d
xxiv. 15.	1 c	xxi. 10.	1 c	viii. 10, 19.	1 h
xxiv. 22.	1 a	xxi. 11.	5	x. 20.	1 h
Judg. v. 8.	1 d	xxviii. 4, 4.	1 d a	xvi. 16.	1 h
x. 14.	1 d	xxviii. 5.	1 d	xxii. 1.	1 h
xx. 15, 16, 34.	1 f	xxviii. 6, 10.	1 a	Cant. xi. 9.	2 b
1 Sam. ii. 28.	1 b	xxix. 1.	1 d	Isa. i. 29.	1 a
viii. 18.	1 a	2 Chron. vi. 5, 5, 34,		vii. 15, 16.	1 b
ix. 2.	1 i	38.	1 a	xiv. 1.	1 a
x. 24.	1 d	vi. 6, 6.	1 d	xxii. 7.	1 m
xii. 13.	1 a	vii. 12, 16.	1 a	xxxvii. 24.	1 m
xiii. 2.	1 d	xi. 1.	1 f	xl. 20.	1 d
xvi. 8, 9, 10.	1 a	xii. 13.	1 a	xli. 8, 9.	1 a

Isa. xli. 24.	1 d	Isa. lxvi. 3.	1 a	Ezek. xxi. 19, 19.	4		
xliii. 10.	1 a	lxvi. 4, 4.	1 d a	xxiii. 7.	1 m		
xliii. 20.	1 k	Jer. viii. 3.	1 g	xxiv. 4, 5.	1 m		
xliv. 1, 2.	1 a	xxii. 7.	1 m	xxxi. 16.	1 m		
xlviii. 10.	1 a	xxxiii. 24.	1 a	Dan. xi. 15.	1 m		
xlix. 7.	1 d	xlviii. 15.	1 m	Hag. ii. 23.	1 a		
lvi. 4.	1 a	xlix. 19.	1 f	Zech. i. 17.	1 a		
lviii. 5, 6.	1 d	l. 44.	1 f	ii. 12.	1 a		
lxv. 12.	1 a	Ezek. xx. 5.	1 b	iii. 2.	1 e		
lxv. 15.	1 k						

CHOLER

מָרַר to be in bitterness, to be grieved, vexed. HITHPALPEL, to be moved with choler : *fut.* Dan. viii. 7 ; xi. 11.

CHOP

פָּרַשׁ to break, divide. KAL *pret.* Micah iii. 3.

CHRONICLES

דָּבָר *m.* a word; יוֹם *m.* day. Chronicles, דִּבְרֵי הַיָּמִים *lit.* words of the days : 1 Kings xiv. 19, &c.

CHURL

כִּילַי and כֵּלַי *m.* a tenacious, covetous person, from כּוּל, or rather, a deceitful, fraudulent person, from נָכַל to deceive, as described in Isa. xxxii. 5, 7. Lowth, niggard : Noyes, crafty. In v. 7, obs. paronomasia.

קָשֶׁה *adj.* hard, rough, harsh : 1 Sam. xxv. 3.

CHURN

מִיץ *m.* to force, press, squeeze, wring ; translated in the same verse, churning, wringing, forcing : Prov. xxx. 33.

CIEL

חָפָה to overlay. PIEL *pret.* 2 Chron. iii. 5.

סָפַן to cover or line the inside arched roof of a building with boards closely jointed. KAL *part.* Paül. Jer. xxii. 14 : Hag. i. 4. סִפֻּן *m.* cieling : 1 Kings vi. 15.

שָׁחִיף *m.* board, as made thin by hewing, planing, &c. : Ezek. xli. 16.

CINNAMON

קִנָּמוֹן *m.* the bark of a tree resembling the willow, dried, and coming in rolls like a cane or tube ; according to Herodotus, a word of Phenician origin : Exod. xxx. 23 : Prov. vii. 17 : Cant. iv. 14.

CIRCLE, CIRCUIT

חוּג *m.* circle, sphere, the arch or vault of the heavens ; the circle of the earth, *orbis terrarum :* Job xxii. 14 : Isa. xl. 22.

סָבַב to compass about. KAL *pret.* 1 Sam. vii. 16. סָבִיב *m.* circuit : Eccles. i. 6.

תְּקוּפָה *f.* a going round, coming about : Ps. xix. 6.

CIRCUMCISE

1 מוּל to cut off, to circumcise. With *inf.*, must needs be circumcised. KAL ᵃ *pret.* ᵇ *imp.* ᶜ *fut.* ᵈ *part.* Paül. NIPHAL ᵉ *pret.* ᶠ *inf.* ᵍ *imp.* ʰ *fut.* ⁱ *part.* ᵏ מולה *f. pl.* circumcision.

2 נָמַל to cut off, to circumcise. KAL *pret.*

Gen. xvii. 10, 24, 25.	1 f	Gen. xxxiv. 22, 22.	1 f i	Josh. v. 2.	1 b
xvii. 11.	2	xxxiv. 24.	1 h	v. 3.	1 c
xvii. 12, 14.	1 h	Exod. iv. 26.	1 k	v. 4, 7, 7.	1 a
xvii. 13.	1 f h	xii. 44.	1 k	v. 5, 5.	1 d a
xvii. 23.	1 c	xii. 48.	1 f	v. 8.	1 f
xvii. 26, 27.	1 e	Lev. xii. 3.	1 h	Jer. iv. 4.	1 f
xxi. 4.	1 c	Deut. x. 16.	1 a	ix. 25.	1 d
xxxiv. 15, 17.	1 f	xxx. 6.	1 a		

CIRCUMSPECT

שָׁמַר to watch, mark, observe ; take heed. NIPHAL *fut.* Exod. xxiii. 13.

CISTERN

בּוֹר *m.* a pit, a well, &c. ; a cistern hewn in stone : 2 Kings xviii. 31 : Prov. v. 15 : Eccles. xii. 6 : Isa. xxxvi. 16.

בְּאֵר *m.* the same : Jer. ii. 13, 13.

CITY

1 עִיר *f.* this is a word of large signification : in its primary use it may have applied to any place of look-out, especially such as was fortified ; to any place in which shepherds defended themselves and their flocks in the wilderness from wild beasts, robbers, &c. ; also to towns defended, of no large size, as is evident from the enumeration of so many in Josh. xv., no less than 124 in the tribe of Judah ; it is used also of a portion of a city more particularly fortified, as the city of David on Mount Zion : 2 Sam. v. 7, 9 ; vi. 10, 12. This word occurs very frequently. ᵃ עָר *m. id.* ᵇ עִיר *m.* according to Gesenius, heat ; anger, wrath ; anxiety, anguish, terror : Hos. xi. 9 ; Ges., I will not come in wrath. Jer. xv. 8, Lxx. ἐπέρριψα ἐπ' αὐτὴν ἐξαίφνης τρόμον καὶ σπουδήν.

2 קִרְיָה *f.* a city, so called from the concourse of people. ᵃ קִרְיָה and קִרְיָא Ch. *f.* ᵇ קֶרֶת *f.*

3 שַׁעַר *m.* a gate ; the great gate of a royal citadel or palace. Gate seems sometimes put for the people that pass through or assemble there.

No. 1 not included.

Num. xxi. 28.	2	Prov. viii. 3.	2 b	Isa. xxv. 3.	2
Deut. ii. 36, 36.	1, 2	ix. 3.	2 b	xxvi. 5.	2
iii. 4, 4, 4.	1, 2, 1	x. 15.	2	xxix. 1. α	2
Ruth iii. 11.	3	xi. 10.	2	xxxii. 13.	2
1 Kings i. 41, 45.	2	xi. 11.	2 b	xxxiii. 20.	2
viii. 37.	3	xviii. 11, 19.	2	Jer. xv. 8.	1, 1 b
2 Chron. vi. 28.	3	xxix. 8.	2	xlix. 25, 25.	1, 2
Ezra iv. 10, 12, 13, 15,		Isa. i. 21.	2	Lam. ii. 11.	2
15, 15, 16, 19, 21.	2 a	i. 26, 26.	1, 2	Hos. vi. 8.	2
Job xxiv. 12.	1, 1 b	xiv. 21.	1 a	xi. 9.	1 a, or b
xxix. 7.	2 b	xxii. 2, 2.	1, 2	Micah iv. 10.	2
xxxix. 7.	2	xxiv. 10.	2	v. 11, 14.	1 a
Ps. ix. 6.	1 a	xxiv. 2, 2, 2.	1, 2, 1	Hab. ii. 8, 12, 17.	2
xlviii. 2.	2				

α marg. 'or, of the city.'

CLAD

כָּסָה to cover. HITHPAEL *part.* 1 Kings xi. 29.

עָטָה to cover or wrap oneself with a cloke ; figuratively, with zeal. KAL *fut.* Isa. lix. 17.

CLAMOROUS

הָמָה to rage, to roar. See *Noise.* KAL *part.* Poel, Prov. ix. 13.

CLAP

1   מָחָא   to strike, to smite ; applied to the striking of the hands against each other in token of joy. KAL ^a *fut.* PIEL ^b *inf.*

2   נָכָה   to smite, to clap the hands, either in exultation, indignation, or lamentation. HIPHIL *fut.*

3   סָפַק   to smite, to clap the hands in token of exultation, insolence, contempt, scorn, and derision. KAL ^a *pret.* ^b *fut.*

4   שָׁפַק   *id.* KAL *fut.*

5   תָּקַע   to smite ; to clap the hands as a token of rejoicing ; also at the calamities of others, with עַל. KAL ^a *pret.* ^b *imp.*

2 Kings xi. 12.	2	Ps. xlvii. 1.		Lam. ii. 15.	3 a
Job xxvii. 23.	4	xcviii. 8.		Ezek. xxv. 6.	1 b
xxxiv. 37.	3 b	Isa. lv. 12.	1 a	Nah. iii. 19.	5 a

CLAW

פַּרְסָה   *f.* the divided or cloven hoof of animals : Deut. xiv. 6 : Zech. xi. 16.

CLAY

1   חֹמֶר   *m.* clay, mud, slime, mortar ; from its red colour.

2   חֲסַף   Ch. *m.* potter's clay, burnt clay.

3   טִיט   *m.* mire, dirt, clay thick and adhesive. See *Mire.*

4   מֶלֶט   *m.* clay or mortar, from its slipperiness.

5   מַעֲבֶה   *m.* density, compactness ; clay ground.

6   עָב   *com.* thickness.

7   עַבְטִיט   *m.* thick clay (Hab. ii. 6), as if composed of עָב and טִים (see above) : others suppose it to mean pledges, from עָבַט (see *Lend*) ; others, guilt, criminality, from acts of rapine, which will be demanded of him again ; or property wrested from the right owner, to which it must return. The signification given by Lee is, " an accumulation of pledges in the hand of an unfeeling usurer." See also Gussetius.

1 Kings vii. 46.	5	Job xxxviii. 14.	1	Jer. xviii. 4, 6.	1
2 Chron. iv. 17.	6	Ps. xl. 2.	3	xliii. 9.	4
Job iv. 19.	1	Isa. xxix. 16.	3	Dan. ii. 33, 34, 35, 41,	
x. 9.	1	xli. 25.	3	41, 42, 43, 45.	2
xiii. 12.	1	xlv. 9.	1	Nah. iii. 14.	3
xxvii. 16.	1	lxiv. 8.	1	Hab. ii. 6.	7
xxxiii. 6.	1				

CLEAN, CLEANSE, CLEAR

1   אוֹר   *m.* light.

2   בָּרַר   to separate, to separate that which is impure. KAL ^a *part.* Paül. NIPHAL ^b *imp.* HIPHIL ^c *inf.* ^d בַּר *adj.* clear, pure ; empty. ^e בֹּר *m.* purity.

3   זָכָה   to be clean or pure. It occurs only in a moral sense, but of a twofold cleanness : (1) a perfect, entire, and legal purity, such as belongs not to man, Job xv. 14 ; xxv. 4 ; Prov. xx. 9 ; but only to God, Ps. li. 4 : (2) an evangelical purity from grosser sins, and in the pursuit of holiness, in those who are pure in comparison with those who sin of purpose, Ps. lxxiii. 13 ; cxix. 9. KAL ^a *fut.* PIEL ^b *pret.* ^c *fut.* HITHPAEL ^d *imp.*

4   זָכַךְ   to be pure physically and morally : used of oil and frankincense : *metaph.* of faith, of prayer, of the ways of a man, of sincerity towards God and man, of purity, integrity, and sincerity of life, of the rectitude of a

child. KAL ^a *pret.* HIPHIL ^b *pret.* ^c זַךְ *adj.* pure ; figuratively, of the soul.

5   חָטָא   to sin. PIEL, of persons, to expiate, atone for ; of things, to cleanse, to purify : ^a *pret.* ^b *inf.*

6   חָמִיץ   *adj.* salted : Isa. xxx. 24, clean provender, *marg.* 'leavened or savoury ;' which seems to have been done to render it more acceptable to cattle.

7   טָהַר   to be clear, bright, and shining ; to be pure, clean, purged ; to be clean from all pollution or defilement, as opposed to טָמֵא, and implying that purity which religion requires, and is necessary for communion with God. As there is impurity in sin, so there is a purity arising out of reconciliation with God : Job xiv. 4 : Ezek. xxxvi. 25. In Hithpael, to wash with water, to be baptized : Gen. xxxv. 2. Jacob commands his household to put away idols, and to wash themselves in token of being purified from idolatry. Baptism, in the N. T., is called καθαρισμός, in accordance with this Heb. expression. KAL ^a *pret.* ^b *imp.* ^c *fut.* PIEL, to pronounce clean, ^d *pret.* ^e *inf.* ^f *imp.* ^g *fut.* ^h *part.* PUAL ⁱ *part.* HITHPAEL ^k *pret.* ^l *imp.* ^m *part.* ⁿ טָהוֹר *adj.* pure, clear, and as opposed to unclean. ^o טֹהַר *m.* purity. ^p טֹהַר *m.* clearness, purity of the air. ^q טָהֳרָה *f.* cleansing, purification.

8   יָקָר   *adj.* precious, splendid : Zech. xiv. 6. Hengstenberg renders the latter part of this verse, " it will not be light, the precious will become mean," in reference to the great changes in the heavens, &c.

9   כָּפַר   to cover. PIEL, to make atonement ; PUAL, to be cleansed, *fut.*

10   תַּמְרוּק   *m.* scouring, cleansing ; the means of correction.

11   נָקָה   to be clean or free from whatever staineth or fouleth : Amos iv. 6, cleanness of teeth, *i.e.* teeth free from the relics of food adhering to them after eating. Figuratively, to be cleared, freed, or exempted from an obligation or from service : Gen. xxiv. 8, to be clean, blameless, innocent ; to be cleared or exempted from punishment. NIPHAL ^a *pret.* ^b *fut.* PIEL ^c *pret.* ^d *inf.* ^e *imp.* ^f *fut.* ^g נָקִי *adj.* pure, free from blame. ^h נִקָּיוֹן *m.* purity, cleanness.

12   צָדַק   to be righteous, to be justified. NIPHAL ^a *pret.* HITHPAEL, to clear oneself, ^b *fut.*

13   צַח   *adj.* white and shining ; clear bright air, free from clouds and fogs.

14   קוּם   to rise. KAL *fut.*

15   תָּמַם   to be finished. KAL *pret.*

Clean is often used as the rendering of the infinitive intensive.

Gen. vii. 2, 2, 8, 8.	7 n	Lev. xi. 32.	7 a	Lev. xiv. 2, 23, 32.	7 q
viii. 20, 20.	7 n	xi. 36, 37, 47.	7 n	xiv. 4, 4.	7 m n
xxiv. 8.	11 a	xii. 7, 8.	7 n	xiv. 7, 7.	7 m d
xxiv. 41, 41.	11 b g	xiii. 6, 6.	7 d a	xiv. 8, 8.	7 m a
xxxv. 2.	7 k	xiii. 7, 35.	7 q	xiv. 9, 20, 53.	7 m
xlix. 16.	12 b	xiii. 13, 13.	7 d n	xiv. 11, 11.	7 h m
Exod. xxiv. 10.	7 p	xiii. 17, 17.	7 d n	xiv. 14, 17, 18, 19,	
xxix. 36.	5 a	xiii. 23, 28.	7 d	25, 28, 29, 31.	7 m
xxxiv. 7. a	11 d f	xiii. 34, 34.	7 d a	xiv. 48.	7 d
Lev. iv. 12.	7 n	xiii. 37, 37.	7 n	xiv. 49.	5 b
vi. 11.	7 n	xiii. 39, 40, 41.	7 n	xiv. 52.	5 a
vii. 19.	7 n	xiii. 58.	7 n	xiv. 57.	7 n
x. 10, 14.	7 n	xiii. 59.	7 e	xv. 8.	7 n

Lev. xv. 13, 13, 13.	7 c q a	2 Kings v. 14.	7 c	Prov. xiv. 4.	2 d
xv. 28, 28.	7 a c	2 Chron. xxix. 15, 16.	7 e	xvi. 2.	4 c
xvi. 19.	7 d	xxix. 18.	7 d	xx. 9.	3 b
xvi. 30, 30.	7 e c	xxx. 17.	7 n	xx. 30.	10
xvii. 15.	7 a	xxx. 18.	7 k	Eccles. ix. 2.	7 n
xx. 25, 25.	7 n	xxxiv. 5.	7 g	Cant. vi. 10.	3 a
xxii. 4.	7 c	Neh. xiii. 9.	7 g	Isa. i. 16.	3 d
xxii. 7.	7 a	xiii. 22. γ	7 m	xviii. 4.	13
Num. v. 28.	7 n	xiii. 30.	7 d	xxx. 24.	6
vi. 9.	7 q	Job ix. 30.δ	4 b, 2 e	lii. 11.	2 b
viii. 6, 15.	7 d	xi. 4.	2 d	lxvi. 20.	7 n
viii. 7, 7.	7 e k	xi. 17.	14	Jer. iv. 11.	2 c
viii. 21.	7 e	xiv. 4.	7 n	xiii. 27.	7 c
ix. 13.	7 n	xv. 14.	3 a	xxxiii. 8.	7 n
xiv. 18.α	11 d f	xv. 15.	4 a	Ezek. xxii. 24.	7 i
xviii. 11, 13.	7 n	xvii. 19.	7 o	xxii. 36.	7 n
xix. 9, 9, 18.	7 n	xxv. 4.	3 a	xxxvi. 25, 25, 25.	7 n a g
xix. 12, 12.	7 c	xxxiii. 3.	2 a	xxxvi. 33.	7 e
xix. 19, 19.	7 n a	xxxiii. 9.	4 c	xxxvii. 23.	7 d
xxxi. 23, 24.	7 a	xxxvii. 21.	7 n	xxxix. 12, 14.	7 d
xxxv. 33.	9	Ps. xviii. 20, 24.	2 e	xxxix. 16.	7 d
Deut. xii. 15, 22.	7 n	xix. 9.	7 h	xliii. 20, 22, 22.	5 b
xiv. 11, 20.	7 n	xix. 12.	11 e	xliii. 23.	5 b
xv. 22.	7 n	xxiv. 4.	11 g	xliv. 23.	7 q
xxiii. 10.	7 n	li. 2.	7 f	xliv. 26.	5 a
Josh. iii. 17.β	15	li. 4.	3 a	xlv. 18.	5 a
iv. 1, 11.	15	li. 7.	7 c	Dan. viii. 14.	12 a
xxii. 17.	7 k	li. 10.	7 n	Joel iii. 21, 21.	11 c
1 Sam. xx. 26, 26.	7 n	lxxiii. 1.	2 d	Amos iv. 6.	11 h
2 Sam. xxii. 21, 25.	2 e	lxxiii. 13.	3 b	viii. 9.ε	11 h 1
2 Kings v. 10, 13.	7 b	cxix. 19.	2 e	Zech. xiv. 4.	7 a
v. 12.	7 a				

α *lit.* and clearing will not clear. β *lit.* had finished to pass over. γ *lit.* should be cleansing, &c. δ *lit.* cleanse my hands in purity. ε *lit.* day of light.

See the verb to which *Clean* is attached: *Riddance, Dry, Bare, Shine.*

CLEAVE, CLEFT, CLIFT

1 בָּקַע to break, tear, rip up, cleave or split asunder with a noise; to break through or into: applied to the cleaving of wood; to the cleaving of the ground; to the breaking forth of light; to the cleaving or opening of an enclosure, in order to make a passage out of it, particularly to open a passage for waters. KAL a *pret.* b *fut.* c *part.* Poel. NIPHAL d *pret.* e *fut.* PIEL f *fut.* HITHPAEL g *fut.* h בָּקִיעַ *m.* clefts of houses into which water introduces itself, and so destroys them.

2 חֲגָוִים *m. pl.* clefts of the rock, in which doves make their nests, and where people retreat from their enemies.

3 נְקָרָה *f.* a cleft or clift in a rock dug out.

4 סָעִיף *m.* the top of a rock.

5 פֶּלַח to cleave, cut, furrow. PIEL, to divide, cleave, *fut.*

6 פַּרְסָה *f.* hoof; cloven-footed. Heb., cleaving the cleft of the hoof.

7 שָׁסַע to cleave, split, so that the parts are not totally separated. KAL a *part.* Poel. b *part.* Paül. PIEL c *pret.* d שֶׁסַע *m.* cleft.

Gen. xxii. 3.	1 f	Judg. xv. 19.	1 b	Isa. xlviii. 21.	1 b
Exod. xxiii. 22.	3	1 Sam. vi. 14.	1 f	lvii. 5.	4
Lev. i. 17.	7 c	Job xvi. 13.	5	Jer. xlix. 16.	2
xi. 3.	7 a d 6	Ps. lxxiv. 15.	1 a	Amos vi. 11.	1 h
xi. 7.	7 a d 6	lxxviii. 15.	1 f	Obad. 3.	2
xi. 26.	7 a d	cxli. 7.	1 c	Micah i. 4.	1 g
Num. xvi. 31.	1 e	Eccles. x. 9.	1 c	Hab. iii. 9.	1 f
Deut. xiv. 6, 6.	7 a d	Cant. ii. 14.	2	Zech. xiv. 4.	1 d
xiv. 7.	7 b	Isa. ii. 21.	1 b		

CLEAVE

1 דָּבַק and דְּבֵק to stick, as things that are glued together, as clods of earth, Job xxxviii. 38; to be closely joined together, as the scales and flakes of Leviathan, Job xli. 17, 23; to adhere, as the tongue to the roof of the mouth, unable to give utterance to words, Ps. xxii. 15, Lam. iv. 4: the same phrase is used to express deep silence, Job xxix. 10, Ps. cxxxvii. 6, Ezek. iii. 26; as the bones to the skin in the emaciated, Job xix. 20, Ps. cii. 5; as a girdle to the loins of a man, Jer. xiii. 11, by which figure God expresses the near union into which he had brought his people to himself, in love and favour; as a disease cleaves to a man, Deut. xxviii. 60, 2 Kings v. 27: to adhere in affection, duty, fidelity—so men are said to cleave to each other as companions, Ruth ii. 8, 21, 23; to cleave to God, to their king, to the law of God, to a friend, to a wife; men cleave to the sins of others by imitating them, 2 Kings iii. 3; to follow hard after is expressed by the same word, as also to overtake, Gen. xxxi. 23, cf. xix. 19; that which has been stolen is said to cleave to the hands, Deut. xiii. 17, Job xxxi. 7; the belly cleaveth to the earth when one lies prostrate on the ground: seq. בְּ, אֶל, לְ, and אַחֲרֵי. KAL a *pret.* b *inf.* c *fut.* PUAL d *fut.* HIPHIL e *prct.* f *fut.* HOPHAL g *part.* דְּבַק Ch. P'AL h *part. active.* i דָּבֵק *adj.* adhering.

2 חָזַק to lay hold, to hold fast to anything. HIPHIL *part.* seq. עַל.

3 יָצַק to pour out molten and liquid metal, which afterwards becomes hard and sets; seq. בְּ. KAL *part.* Paül. See צוּק.

4 לָוָה see *Join.* NIPHAL *pret.*

5 סָפַח to cleave or adhere, as a scab to the skin. NIPHAL *pret.* seq. עַל.

6 צוּק to be straitened, press close upon; to cleave to. KAL *fut.* seq. בְּ.

7 צָפַד to adhere, stick fast. KAL *pret.* See יָצַק.

Gen. ii. 24.	1 a	2 Sam. xx. 2.	1 a	Ps. xliv. 25.	1 a
xxxiv. 3.	1 c	xxiii. 10.	1 c	ci. 3.	1 c
Deut. iv. 4.	1 i	1 Kings xi. 2.	1 a	cii. 5.	1 a
x. 20.	1 c	2 Kings iii. 3.	1 a	cxix. 25.	1 a
xi. 22.	1 c	v. 27.	1 a	cxxxvii. 6.	1 c
xiii. 4, 17.	1 c	xviii. 6.	1 a	Isa. xix. 1.	5
xxviii. 21.	1 f	Neh. x. 29.	1	Jer. xiii. 11, 11.	1 c e
xxviii. 60.	1 a	Job xix. 20.	2	Lam. iv. 4.	1 a
xxx. 20.	1 b	xxix. 10.	1 a	iv. 8.	7
Josh. xxii. 5.	1 b	xxxi. 7.	1 a	Ezek. iii. 26.	1 f
xxiii. 8.	1 c	xxxviii. 38.	1 d	Dan. ii. 43.	1 h
xxiii. 12.	1 d	Ps. xxii. 15.	1 d	xi. 34.	1 h
Ruth i. 14.	1 a	xli. 8.	3 or 6		4

CLIFF

עָרִיץ *m.* anything which inspires terror, here applied to valleys: Job xxx. 6, *lit.* horror of valleys, *i.e.* horrid valleys.

מַעֲלָה *m.* ascent: 2 Chron. xx. 16.

CLIMB

עָלָה to ascend. KAL *pret.* Jer. iv. 29. *fut.* 1 Sam. xiv. 13: Joel ii. 7, 9: Amos ix. 2.

CLIP

גָּרַע to lessen, to diminish; to take from. KAL *part.* Paül, Jer. xlviii. 37.

CLOD

גּוּשׁ *m.* a clod of earth: Job vii. 5.

מְגְרָפָה *f.* a clod, such as is turned over and moved: Joel i. 17.

רֶגֶב *m.* soft, moist clods of the earth.—*Schultens.* Job xxi. 33; xxxviii. 38.

CLOKE

מְעִיל *m.* see *Robe.* Isa. lix. 17.

CLOSE

1   גָּדַר   to fence up, enclose. KAL *pret.*

2   דָּבַק   to cleave, to stick close; to follow close. KAL [a] *fut.* [b] דָּבֵק *adj.* cleaving, adhering.

3   זוּר   to dress a wound or sore by pressing out the matter or blood, closing and binding it up. KAL *pret.*

4   כָּסָה   to cover, to conceal. PIEL *fut.*

5   סָבַב   to compass. POEL *fut.*

6   סָגַר   to shut up; to be enclosed, shut up, confined in any respect, so that one cannot escape one way or other; see *Shut.* KAL [a] *fut.* [b] מִסְגֶּרֶת *f.* close place, fortified.

7   סָתַם   to stop, to obstruct, to close up. KAL *part.* Paül.

8   סָתַר   to hide, to conceal, to keep close. NIPHAL *pret.*

9   עָצַם   to shut the eyes strongly, so that a person either is not able, or will not be prevailed upon, to open them. PIEL *fut.*

10   עָצַר   to restrain, to stop, to hinder, &c.; to close up, with *inf.* close up fast. KAL [a] *pret.* [b] *inf.* [c] *part.* Paül.

11   צַר   *adj.* strait, narrow, compressed.

12   תַּחְרָה   to mix with or among; others, to walk amongst, as an owner in his domain: Gussetius, to fortify oneself with. PIEL *part.* Jer. xxii. 15; by others derived from חָרָה to be warm; to emulate, to rival. TIPHEL *part.* Jer. xxii. 15.

Gen. ii. 21.	6 a	1 Chron. xii. 1.	10 c	Isa. xxix. 10.	9
xx. 18. a	10 b a	Job xxviii. 21.	8	Jer. xlviii. 15.	12
Num. v. 13.	8	xli. 15.	11	xlii. 16.	2 a
xvi. 33.	4	Ps. xviii. 45.	6 b	Dan. xi. 9.	7
Judg. iii. 22.	6 a	Prov. xviii. 24.	2 b	Amos ix. 11.	1
2 Sam. xxii. 46.	6 b	Isa. i. 6.	3	Jonah ii. 5.	5

a lit. closing up had closed.

CLOSET

חֻפָּה *f.* the covert of a chamber or closet: Joel ii. 16. See *Chamber.*

CLOTH, CLOTHING

1   בֶּגֶד   see *Garment.* Gen. xxxvii. 29, &c.

2   גְּלוֹם   *m.* garments with foldings.

3   מִכְבָּר   *m.* a thick sort of cloth.

4   מַד   *m.* see *Raiment.*

5   סוּת   *m.* a garment; Ges., from סָוָה to veil oneself.

6   שַׂלְמָה   *f.* by transposition for the following.

7   שִׂמְלָה   *f.* a garment for men or women, Deut. xxii. 5; particularly the broad robe of the Orientals, Gen. ix. 23, 1 Sam. xxi. 9, which served him also for his bed-covering, Deut. xxii. 17.

No. 1 not included.

Gen. xxxvii. 34.	7	Deut. xxii. 17.	7	2 Kings viii. 15.	3
xliv. 13.	7	xxix. 5.	7	Neh. ix. 21.	6
xlix. 11.	7	Josh. vii. 6.	5	Job xxxi. 31.	6
Exod. xii. 34.	7	1 Sam. iv. 12.	4	Isa. iii. 6, 7.	7
xix. 10, 14.	7	xxi. 9.	7	Ezek. xxvii. 24.	2

CLOTHE

1   כָּסָה   to cover, conceal. PUAL [a] *part.* [b] מְכַסֶּה *m.* covering, clothing.

2   כִּרְבֵּל   to gird, to clothe: *part. pass.*

3   לָבַשׁ and לָבֵשׁ to put on clothes and armour; to clothe; to be clothed. Figuratively, when anything lies very thick upon the surface of another; as flesh clothed with worms, Job vii. 5; pastures clothed with flocks, Ps. lxv. 13; the heavens clothed with blackness, Isa. l. 3: to be clothed with majesty, honour, excellency, is to be perfect in them severally, Job xl. 10, Ps. xciii. 1, civ. 1: to be clothed with vengeance, is to be in every respect prepared to execute the most dreadful vengeance, Isa. lix. 17: to clothe, or to be clothed, with salvation, implies full possession of all the blessings of divine goodness, 2 Chron. vi. 41, *comp.* Gal. iii. 27: to put on, and to be clothed with righteousness, is to attend and adhere to it strictly, and to be filled with it; the word is used in this twofold sense in Job xxix. 14: to be clothed with shame and dishonour, is to be in the most shameful and dishonourable condition. KAL [a] *pret.* [b] *inf.* [c] *fut.* [d] *part.* Poel. [e] *part.* Paül. PUAL [f] *part.* HIPHIL [g] *pret.* [h] *inf.* [i] *fut.* [k] *part.* לְבַשׁ Ch. P'AL [l] *fut.* APHEL [m] *pret.* [n] לְבוּשׁ *m.* a garment, clothing. [o] תִּלְבֹּשֶׁת *f.* a garment.

Gen. iii. 21.	3 i	Ps. xxxv. 26.	3 c	Jer. x. 9.	3 n
Exod. xl. 14.	3 g	xlv. 13.	3 n	Ezek. vii. 27.	3 c
Lev. viii. 7.	3 a	lxv. 13.	3 a	ix. 2, 3, 11.	3 e
2 Sam. i. 24.	3 k	xciii. 1, 1.	3 a	x. 2, 6, 7.	3 e
1 Chron. xv. 27.	2	civ. 1.	3 a	xvi. 10.	3 i
xxi. 16.	1 a	cix. 18, 29.	3 c	xxiii. 6, 12.	3 i
2 Chron. vi. 41.	3 c	cxxxii. 9.	3 c	xxvi. 16.	3 c
xviii. 9.	3 f	cxxxii. 16, 18.	3 i	xxxiv. 3.	3 c
xxviii. 15.	3 i	Prov. xxxi. 21.	3 i	xxxviii. 4.	3 c
Esth. iv. 2. a	3 n	xxxvii. 26.	3 n	xlv. 17.	3 c
iv. 4.	3 h	xxxi. 21.	3 e	Dan. v. 7, 16.	3 l
Job vii. 5.	3 a	xxxi. 22, 25.	3 n	v. 29.	3 m
viii. 22.	3 c	Isa. xxxi. 21.	3 g	x. 5.	3 e
x. 11.	3 i	xxiii. 18.	1 b	iii. 6, 7.	3 e
xxiv. 7, 10.	3 n	xlix. 18.	3 c	Zeph. i. 8.	3 d
xxix. 14.	3 c	l. 3.	3 i	Hag. i. 6.	3 b
xxxi. 19.	3 n	lix. 17.	3 o	Zech. iii. 3.	3 e
xxxix. 19.	3 i	lxi. 10.	3 n	iii. 4. β	3 h
Ps. xxxv. 13.	3 n	Jer. iv. 30.	3 c	iii. 5.	3 i

a lit. in clothing of.   *β lit.* and to clothe.

CLOUD

1   חָזִין   *m.* (see *Lightning*), bright clouds.

2   כַּף   *f.* the hand: *clouds* seems to have no relation to the other meanings of the word. Schultens renders the place more probably thus, "He covers both his hands with lightning." Cocceius too gives nearly the same sense. LXX. "He covereth the light in his hands." Our translators seem to have given the meaning of clouds to this word, from the idea that clouds at their first rising are like a man's hand (1 Kings xviii. 44); and then the passage denotes the approach of rain.

3   נָשִׂיא   *m.* clouds or vapours lifted up into the sky.

4   עוּב   to be in a dark, cloudy state. HIPHIL [a] *fut.* [b] עָב *com.* darkness, a cloud, a thick cloud.

5   עָנָן   *m.* a cloud; "cloudy," *lit.* of cloud: Gen. ix. 13, &c. [a] עֲנָן Ch. *m. id.* [b] עֲנָנָה *f. collect.* clouds: Job iii. 5, *i. e.* gathered tempest. Theodot. συννεφία. LXX. γνόφος.

6   עֲרָפֶל   *m.* a thick mist, darkness; a dark cloud.

7 שַׁחַק *m.* the clouds, the heavens : in the former sense rain and thunder are ascribed to them.

No. 5 not included.

Judg. v. 4.	4 b	Job xxxvii. 21.	7	Prov. xvi. 15.	4 b
2 Sam. xx. 12.	4 b	xxxviii. 34.	4 b	xxv. 14.	3
xxiii 4.	4 b	xxxviii. 37.	7	Eccles. xi. 3, 4.	4 b
1 Kings xviii. 44, 45.	4 b	Ps. xviii. 11, 12.	4 b	xii. 2.	4 b
Job iii. 5.	5 b	xxxvi. 5.	7	Isa. v. 6.	4 b
xx. 6.	4 b	lvii. 10.	7	xiv. 14.	4 b
xxii. 13.	6	lxviii. 34.	7	xviii. 4.	4 b
xxii. 14.	7	lxxvii. 17.	4 b	xix. 1.	4 b
xxvi. 8, 8.	4 b, 5	lxxviii. 23.	7	xxv. 5.	4 b
xxx. 15.	4 b	civ. 3.	4 b	xliv. 22, 22.	4 b, 5
xxxvi. 28.	7	cviii. 4.	7	lx. 8.	4 b
xxxvi. 29.	4 b	cxlvii. 8.	4 b	Lam. ii. 1.	4 a
xxxvi. 32.	2	Prov. iii. 20.	7	Dan. vii. 13.	5 a
xxxvii. 11, 11.	4 b, 5	viii. 28.	7	Zech. x. 1.	1
xxxvii. 16.	4 b				

CLOUT

טָלָא to be spotted. Pual, to join a patch to a shoe: *part.* Josh. ix. 5.

סְתַבוֹת *f. pl.* "cast clouts;" such as have been torn and rendered useless : Jer. xxxviii. 11, 12.

CLUSTER

אֶשְׁכֹּל and אֶשְׁכּוֹל *m.* strictly the stem or stalk on which berries or flowers grow in clusters, *racemus,* spoken of the vine and other similar plants ; *e. g.* of the plant called by Arabians *alhenna* : Cant. i. 14 ;—a cluster of the *alhenna,* of the palm, or date tree; vii. 8, clusters (of dates) ;— of a vine-stem with flowers and unripe grapes, Gen. xl. 10, *lit.* the unripe grapes ripened into ripe grapes. So the Latin *racemus* stands for unripe grapes. On account of this extended use of the word, in order to restrict its meaning to clusters of the vine, it is followed sometimes by הַגֶּפֶן, or עֲנָבִים : Gen. xl. 10 : Num. xiii. 23, 24 : Deut. xxxii. 32 : Cant. i. 14 : vii. 7, 8 : Isa. lxv. 8 : Micah vii. 1.

COAL

1 גַּחֶלֶת *f.* burning coals ; or as kept in order to preserve fire ; put for the last hope or scion of a race or family.

2 פֶּחָם *m.* coal, charcoal ; also a burning coal.

3 רֶצֶף *m.* a stone which is heated in order to roast meat or bake bread upon ; a cake baken on hot stones. רִצְפָּה *f.* a hot stone : Isa. vi. 6. Vulg. *calculus.* The Rabbins explain this and the preceding word by, a hot or live coal. —*Gesenius.*

4 רֶשֶׁף *m.* flame ; lightning ; fever, burning plague.

5 שָׁחוֹר *m.* blackness.

Lev. xvi. 12.	1	Prov. vi. 28.	1	Isa. xlvii. 14.	1
2 Sam. xiv. 7.	1	xxv. 22.	1	liv. 16.	2
xxii 9, 13.	1	xxvi. 21, 21.	2, 1	Lam. iv. 8.	5
1 Kings xix. 6.	3	Cant. viii. 6, 6.	4	Ezek. i. 13.	1
Job xli. 21.	1	Isa. vi. 6.	3 a	x. 2.	1
Ps. xviii. 8, 12, 13.	1	xliv. 12.	2	xxiv. 11.	1
cxx. 4.	1	xliv. 19.	1	Hab. iii. 5.	4
cxl. 10.	1				

COAST

1 גְּבוּל *m.* see *Border*: Exod. x. 4, &c. גְּבוּלָה *f. id.*

2 גְּלִילָה *f.* the round or compass of a country.

3 חֶבֶל *com.* a plot, lot, or tract of land measured or laid out.

4 חוֹף *m.* coast or shore as washed by the sea.

5 יָד *com.* hand, side, coast, or border.

6 יַרְכָה *f.* side, hinder part ; remote regions.

7 נָפָה *f.* high place ; any district whose situation is remarkably elevated and conspicuous.

8 קָצֶה *f.* end, extremity. קָצֶה *m.* utmost coast.

No. 1 not included.

Num. xiii. 29.	5	Judg. xi. 26.	5	Ezek. xxv. 16.	4
xxiv. 24.	5	xviii. 2.	8	xxxiii. 2.	8 a
xxxiv. 3, 3.	5, 8 a	Jer. xxv. 32.	6	xlviii. 1, 1.	5
Josh. ix. 1.	4	xxxi. 8.	6	Joel iii. 4.	2
xii. 23.	7	l. 41.	6	Zeph. ii. 5, 6, 7.	3
xix. 29, 29, 29.	1, 1, 3				

COAT

כֻּתֹּנֶת and כְּתֹנֶת *f.* a tunic, worn next the skin, Lev. xvi. 4, by men and women, 2 Sam. xiii. 18 : Cant. v. 3 ; chiefly by the priests and Levites, Exod. xxviii. 4 ; xxix. 5 : Neh. vii. 70, 72 ; generally with sleeves, to the knees, but seldom to the ancles, Gen. iii. 21, &c.

מְעִיל *m.* see *Robe.* 1 Sam. ii. 19.

סַרְבְּלִין Ch. *m. pl.* Dan. iii. 21, *marg.* 'or, mantles,' 27. But all the ancient versions apply the word to the wide Persian covering of the thighs and legs, with which original word the name in various languages still agrees.

שִׁרְיוֹן *m.* coat of mail, probably so called from its glittering : 1 Sam. xvii. 5, 5, 38.

COCKATRICE

צֶפַע *m.* a viper, so called from its hissing ; perhaps with Aquil. and Vulg. *basiliscus regulus,* a small serpent of Africa, exceedingly venomous, which was also called *sibilus* : Isa. xiv. 29.

צִפְעוֹנִי *m.* Isa. xi. 8, *marg.* 'or, adder ;' lix. 5, *marg. id.* Jer. viii. 17.

COCKLE

בָּאְשָׁה *f.* Job xxxi. 40, *marg.* 'or, noisome weeds ;' darnel is supposed to be meant, which very much resembles wheat ; *comp.* Matt. xiii. 30.

COGITATION

רַעְיוֹן Ch. *m.* thought : Dan. vii. 28.

COFFER, COFFIN

אַרְגַּז *m.* a box, chest, coffer, fixed to the side of a wagon : 1 Sam. vi. 8, 11, 15.

אָרוֹן *c.* an ark, chest, box, coffer, coffin : Gen. l. 26.

COLD

חֹרֶף *m.* see *Winter.* Prov. xx. 4.

צִנָּה *f.* cold : Prov. xxv. 13.

קַר *adj.* cold, cool : Prov. xxv. 25 : Jer. xviii. 14. קֹר *m.* cold : Gen. viii. 22. קָרָה *f.* cold : Job xxiv. 7 ; xxxvii. 9 : Ps. cxlvii. 17 : Prov. xxv. 20 : Nah. iii. 17 : perhaps day or time of cooling.

COLLAR

נְטִיפוֹת *f. pl.* perhaps pendants for the ears ; *lit.* drops, of precious stone or metal ; but the margin of our translation seems

to refer the word to some sweet aromatic. See *Stacte*. Judg. viii. 26.

פֶּה *m.* mouth; mouth or collar of a garment: Job xxx. 18.

COLLECTION

מַשְׂאֵת *f.* lifting up; gift, present; tribute; a tax or duty laid on as a burden: 2 Chron. xxiv. 6, 9.

COLLEGE

מִשְׁנֶה *m.* second place: 2 Kings xxii. 14, *marg.* ' or, in the second part,' *i.e.* of the city: 2 Chron. xxxiv. 22. Targ. *in domo doctrinæ.* The Rabbins derive this word from שָׁנָה *i.q.* תָּנָא Ch. to teach: hence school or college of the prophets.

COLLOP

פִּימָה *f.* fat, fatness: Job xv. 27.

COLOUR

1 טָלָא to patch; to be patched or spotted with different colours. KAL *part.* Paül.

2 עַיִן *com.* the eye; the aspect, colour, or surface of an object.

3 פּוּךְ see *Paint.* Isa. liv. 11, stones of paint, probably a more costly kind or species of marble, used in ornamenting buildings.

4 פַּסִּים *m. pl.* pieces, so of various colours. כְּתֹנֶת פַּסִּים was a tunic reaching to the palms of the hands and soles of the feet; the long tunic with sleeves worn by young men and maidens of the better class; in the case of Joseph, supposed by Bush, notes *in loc.*, to have been the badge of the birthright which had been forfeited by Reuben and transferred to Joseph; see 1 Chron. v. 1. According to Braunius, De Vestitu Sacerdotum, an ornamented coat; a coat of distinction, of different colours.

5 צֶבַע *m.* a dyeing, dyed garments.

6 רִקְמָה *f.* work in colours, embroidery.

Gen. xxxvii. 3, 23.	4	2 Sam. xiii. 18, 19.	4	Ezek. viii. 2.	2
xxxvii. 32.	4	1 Chron. xxix. 2.	6	x. 9.	2
Lev. xiii. 55.	2	Prov. xxiii. 31.	2	xvi. 16.	1
Num. xi. 7, 7.	2	Isa. liv. 11.	2	xvii. 3.	6
Judg. v. 30, 30, 30.	5	Ezek. i. 4, 7, 16, 22, 27.	2	Dan. x. 6.	2

COLT

בֵּן *m.* a son: Gen. xxxii. 15; xlix. 11.

עַיִר *m.* a foal or colt; an ass colt: Judg. x. 4; xii. 14: Job xi. 12: Zech. ix. 9.

COME, TO COME

1 אָחַז to take hold of. KAL *pret.*

2 אָחוֹר *m.* latter time, future. • אַחֲרוֹן *adj.* following, future.

3 אָתָה and אָתָא to come, to come with speed, to approach. KAL ᵃ*pret.* ᵇ*imp.* ᶜ*fut.* ᵈ*part.* Poel. HIPHIL ᵉ*imp.* אֵתָה and אֵתָא Ch. P'AL ᶠ*pret.* ᵍ*inf.* ʰ*imp.* ⁱ*part.*

4 בּוֹא to go or come in, to enter; frequently opposed to יָצָא; to come, opposed to הָלַךְ; sometimes to go. The sense is very extensive. To come into, is to engage in an affair; 1 Sam. xxv. 26, "from coming to shed blood," *lit.* from

coming into bloods, *i.e.* from engaging in bloody work. Ps. lxxi. 16, I will go, enter upon this work, in the strength of the Lord. The going out and coming in, is the doing or carrying on of business, going about the affairs of life. To come, is sometimes to come home, to come as to a dwellingplace or residence: 1 Sam. xi. 5: Ps. xlv. 15: Prov. ii. 10: Isa. xxiii. 1. To go or come with persons, is to enter into society, friendship, familiarity, or commerce with them. To come into one's use and service: Exod. xxii. 15. To come unto a teacher for instruction: Ezek. xxxiii. 31. To come unto God, is to come to his worship and service, &c. God cometh unto us to bless us and to dwell with us. So mercy, good, come unto us, to continue with us. To come before, or to be brought before a person, denotes acceptance and favour: Job xiii. 16: Ps. xlv. 14. To come into any blessing, is to have a part in it: Ps. lxix. 27. To come in a hostile or distressing manner. To come unto, to come after, are used in making comparisons: 2 Sam. xxiii. 19: Eccles. ii. 12. With *inf.* indeed, surely to pass, doubtless, certainly, come. KAL ᵃ*pret.* ᵇ*inf.* ᶜ*imp.* ᵈ*fut.* ᵉ*part.* Poel. HIPHIL ᶠ*pret.* ᵍ*inf.* ʰ מָבוֹא *com.* entering, entrance. ⁱ מוֹבָא *m. id.* a word irregularly formed, so as to have a resemblance to מוֹצָא occurring in the same passages, by paronomasia.

5 בֵּן *m.* son.

6 גַּד *m.* a troop: Gen. xxx. 11, "a troop cometh," *lit.* in a troop, according to כתיב, but קרי has בָּא גָד a troop has come.

7 גִּיחַ or גּוּחַ to sally forth. KAL ᵃ*fut.* HIPHIL ᵇ*part.*

8 דָּרַךְ to tread upon, to walk, to come. KAL *pret.*

9 הוּךְ Ch. to go. P'AL *fut.*

10 הָלַךְ to walk, to go, &c. KAL ᵃ*pret.* ᵇ*inf.* ᶜ*fut.* ᵈ*part.* Poel.

11 הָפַךְ to turn. NIPHAL *pret.*

12 זָעַק see *Gather.* NIPHAL *pret.*

13 יָדַע to know. KAL *pret.*

14 יָהַב to supply, or contribute joint endeavours where advice or assistance is wanting. See *Give.* Hence in the imperative an interjection of encouragement or excitation, which we translate well enough, go to, come on; but in its strict original propriety it imports, supply, give your assistance, join heart and hand. KAL *imp.*

15 יָלַד to bear, to be born. NIPHAL *fut.*

16 יָלַךְ to go, to walk; to go to, to come, &c. The imperative is often used as an adverb of exhorting, exciting, encouraging, inviting, advising; come, come on. KAL ᵃ*imp.* ᵇ*fut.*

17 יָסַף to add; to do a thing again; to come again. KAL ᵃ*pret.* ᵇ*fut.*

18 יָצָא to go out, to come out, to depart. KAL ᵃ*pret.* ᵇ*inf.* ᶜ*imp.* ᵈ*fut.* ᵉ*part.* Poel. ᶠ יָצִיא *adj.* מוֹצָא *m.* ʰ צֵאָה *f.* excrement. ⁱ צֶאֱצָאִים *m. pl.* offspring.

19 יָרַד to go down, to come down from a higher to a lower place. God comes down, when he reveals or manifests himself in some tokens of his presence or operation. KAL

pret. ᵇ*inf.* ᶜ*imp.* ᵈ*fut.* ᵉ*part.* Poel. With *inf.* indeed come. HIPHIL ᶠ*pret.* ᵍ*fut.*

20 לָבַשׁ to put on, to clothe. KAL *pret.*

21 מָחָר to-morrow; time to come; Heb. day of to-morrow; or, to-morrow.

22 מְטָא Ch. to reach. P'AL *pret.*

23 מָצָא to find, to come upon. KAL ᵃ*pret.* ᵇ*fut.* NIPHAL ᶜ*part.* HIPHIL ᵈ*fut.*

24 נָגַע (see *Touch*) to reach to, to extend to. KAL ᵃ*pret.* ᵇ*fut.* HIPHIL ᶜ*pret.* ᵈ*inf.* ᵉ*fut.* ᶠ*part.*

25 נָגַשׁ to be close together; to advance, to approach near to. KAL ᵃ*inf.* ᵇ*imp.* ᶜ*fut.* NIPHAL ᵈ*pret.* ᵉ*part.* HIPHIL ᶠ*fut.*

26 נָחַת to come down, as a stroke, a violent hand, threats and punishments; and so to make an impression in a hostile manner upon a place or people. KAL ᵃ*fut.* HIPHIL ᵇ*imp.* נְחַת Ch. P'AL ᶜ*part.* ᵈ נָחֵת *adj.* a coming down.

27 נְפַק Ch. to go forth. P'AL ᵃ*pret.* ᵇ*imp.* ᶜ*part.*

28 נָתַן to give. KAL *fut.* It appears to be used impersonally, there cometh or ariseth, or one causeth.

29 סָבַב to encompass, to come round about. KAL ᵃ*pret.* HIPHIL ᵇ*pret.*

30 סְלַק Ch. to mount up. P'AL ᵃ*pret.* ᵇ*part. active.* P'IL ᶜ*pret.*

31 עָבַר to pass over. KAL ᵃ*pret.* ᵇ*inf.* ᶜ*imp.* ᵈ*fut.* ᵉ*part.* Poel.

32 עָלָה to ascend, to go up, to come up: a king marching to attack another is said to go or come up against him: 2 Chron. xxxvi. 6. Growth of vegetables is expressed by ascending or coming up: Jonah iv. 6. Flesh cometh up or groweth upon bones: Ezek. xxxvii. 8. Wrath ariseth or starteth up in the mind: Ps. lxxviii. 21. A thought cometh up into the mind: Jer. vii. 31. When people are talked of in a reproachful way, they are said to come upon the lip or tongue: Ezek. xxxvi. 3. Garments cover, ascend, or come upon a person: Lev. xix. 19. A lot cometh up upon a person or thing: Josh. xix. 10. The smell of putrid bodies ascendeth or cometh up, when it infecteth the air: Joel ii. 20, 20. A shock of corn ascendeth, when it is cut down and afterwards taken from the earth and stacked; so *metaph.* a body ascendeth when it is carried and laid in the high tombs used by the ancients, either as built high or cut out of high rocks. KAL ᵃ*pret.* ᵇ*inf.* ᶜ*imp.* ᵈ*fut.* ᵉ*part.* Poel. HIPHIL ᶠ*pret.* ᵍ*inf.* ʰ*imp.* ⁱ*fut.* ᵏ*part.* ˡ מַעֲלֶה *f.* a going up.

33 עֲלַל Ch. to go in, to enter. P'AL ᵃ*pret.* ᵇ*part.*

34 עָשָׂה to do; to be done, to come to pass. NIPHAL *fut.*

35 עָתִיד *adj.* ready, prepared.

36 פָּגַע to strike upon or against; to fall upon, to light upon; to reach unto. KAL ᵃ*pret.* HIPHIL ᵇ*part.*

37 פָּנָה to turn. KAL *inf.*

38 פָּרַץ to break forth. KAL *inf.*

39 צָלַח to go over or through; to come upon suddenly. KAL ᵃ*pret.* ᵇ*fut.*

40 קָדַם to prevent, to come before. PIEL *fut.*

41 תְּקוּפָה *f.* circuit, as of the sun; hence the coming about, or return of seasons, lapse of time.

42 קָרָא to encounter, to meet. KAL ᵃ*pret.* ᵇ*inf.* ᶜ*part.* Poel. HIPHIL ᵈ*fut.*

43 קָרַב to come near, to approach. KAL ᵃ*pret.* ᵇ*inf.* ᶜ*imp.* ᵈ*fut.* HIPHIL ᵉ*pret.* ᶠ*fut.* ᵍ קָרֵב *adj.* קְרָב Ch. P'AL ʰ*pret.* ⁱ*inf.* ᵏ קָרוֹב *adj.*

44 קָרָה to meet, to befall, to happen. KAL ᵃ*fut.* NIPHAL ᵇ*fut.*

45 רֶגֶל *f.* foot.

46 שֶׁגֶר *m.* that which is cast forth at birth; young, offspring.

47 שׁוּב to return, come again. KAL ᵃ*pret.* ᵇ*inf.* ᶜ*imp.* ᵈ*fut.* ᵉ*part.* Poel.

To come to pass, the rendering of הָיָה, is not included.

Gen. vi. 4, 20.	4 d	Gen. xxxv. 9, 16.	4 b	Exod. viii. 5.	32 h
vi. 13, 18.	4 a	xxxv. 11.	18 d	viii. 20.	18 e
vii. 1.	4 c	xxxvii. 10.	4 b d	viii. 24.	4 d
viii. 11.	4 d	xxxvii. 13, 20, 27.	16 a	ix. 19.	19 a
x. 14.	18 a	xxxvii. 14.	4 d	x. 3.	4 d
x. 19.	4 b	xxxvii. 18.	43 d	x. 12.	32 d
xi. 5.	19 d	xxxvii. 19, 25.	4 a	x. 26.	4 b
xi. 31.	4 d	xxxvii. 23.	4 a	xi. 8.	19 a
xii. 1.	4 d	xxxviii. 16, 16, 18.	4 d	xii. 23.	4 b
xii. 11.	43 e	xxxviii. 28, 29, 30.	18 a	xii. 25.	4 b
xii. 14.	4 b	xxxix. 14, 17.	4 a	xii. 48.	43 d
xiii. 10.	4 b	xxxix. 16.	4 b	xiii. 3.	18 a
xiii. 18.	4 d	xl. 6.	4 d	xiii. 8.	18 e
xiv. 5.	4 a	xli. 2, 3, 5, 18, 19,		xiii. 8.	18 b
xiv. 7, 13.	4 d	22, 27.	32 e	xiii. 12.	46
xv. 4, 14.	18 d	xli. 14, 50.	4 d	xiii. 14.	21
xv. 11.	19 d	xli. 29, 35.	4 b	xiv. 29, 20.	4 d, 43 a
xv. 16.	47 d	xli. 54.	4 b	xiv. 26.	47 d
xvi. 8.	4 a	xli. 57.	4 a	xiv. 28.	4 e
xvii. 6.	18 d	xlii. 5, 5.	4 d e	xv. 23, 27.	4 d
xviii. 5.	31 a	xlii. 6, 29.	4 d	xvi. 1, 22.	4 d
xviii. 21.	4 e	xlii. 7, ⁹, 10, 12, 21.	4 a	xvi. 9.	43 c
xix. 1.	4 d	xlii. 15.	4 b	xvi. 13.	32 d
xix. 5, 8.	4 a, 25 c	xliii. 19.	25 c	xvi. 35, 35.	4 b
xix. 9, 9.	4 a, 25 c	xliii. 20.	19 b a	xvii. 6.	18 a
xix. 22, 31.	4 b	xliii. 21.	4 a	xvii. 8.	4 d
xix. 32.	16 a	xliii. 25.	4 b	xviii. 5, 7, 12, 15.	4 d
xx. 3, 13.	4 d	xliii. 26.	4 d	xviii. 6, 16.	4 e
xx. 4.	43 a	xliv. 14.	4 d	xviii. 8.	23 a
xxii. 5.	47 d	xliv. 18.	25 c	xix. 1.	4 a
xxii. 9.	4 d	xliv. 22.	19 d	xix. 2, 7.	4 d
xxiii. 2.	4 d	xliv. 24.	32 a	xix. 9.	4 e
xxiv. 5.	18 a	xliv. 30.	4 b	xix. 11, 20.	19 d
xxiv. 13, 15, 43, 45.	18 e	xliv. 34.	23 b	xix. 13.	32 d
xxiv. 16.	32 d	xlv. 4, 4.	25 b c	xix. 15.	25 c
xxiv. 30, 32, 41, 42.	4 d	xlv. 9.	19 c	xix. 22.	25 e
xxiv. 31.	4 c	xlv. 16, 19.	4 a	xix. 23.	32 b
xxiv. 62.	4 a	xlv. 18.	4 c	xix. 24, 24.	32 a b
xxiv. 63.	4 e	xlv. 25.	4 d	xx. 20.	4 a
xxv. 25.	18 d	xlvi. 1, 6, 28.	4 d	xx. 24.	4 d
xxv. 26.	18 a	xlvi. 8.	4 e	xxi. 3.	4 d
xxv. 29.	4 d	xlvi. 26, 26.	4 e, 18 e	xxii. 9.	4 d
xxvi. 27.	4 a	xlvi. 27.	4 e	xxii. 15.	4 d
xxvi. 32.	4 d	xlvi. 31.	4 a	xxiii. 15.	18 a
xxvii. 18, 33.	4 d	xlvii. 1, 1.	4 d a	xxiii. 27.	4 d
xxvii. 21, 26.	25 b	xlvii. 4, 5.	4 a	xxiv. 1, 12.	32 c
xxvii. 27.	25 c	xlvii. 15, 18.	4 d	xxiv. 2, 2.	25 d c
xxvii. 30, 35.	4 a	xlviii. 2.	4 e	xxiv. 3.	4 d
xxviii. 21.	47 a	xlviii. 5, 7, 7.	4 b	xxiv. 14, 14.	47 d, 25 c
xxix. 1.	16 b	xlix. 6, 10.	4 d	xxv. 32, 33.	18 e
xxix. 6.	4 e	l. 5.	47 d	xxviii. 35.	18 b
xxix. 9.	4 a	l. 10.	4 d	xxviii. 43, 43.	4 b, 25 a
xxx. 16, 16.	4 a, 6	Exod. i. 1, 1.	4 d	xxix. 30.	4 d
xxx. 30.	45	i. 5.	18 e	xxx. 20.	25
xxx. 33, 33.	21, 4 d	i. 10.	14	xxxii. 1.	19 b
xxx. 38, 38.	4 d b	i. 19.	4 d	xxxii. 24.	43 a
xxxi. 24.	4 d	ii. 5.	19 d	xxxiii. 5.	18 d
xxxi. 44.	16 a	ii. 16, 17.	4 a	xxxiii. 7.	32 d
xxxii. 6, 6.	4 a, 10 d	ii. 23.	32 d	xxxiv. 2.	32 a
xxxii. 8, 11.	4 d	iii. 1.	4 d	xxxiv. 18.	32 d
xxxii. 13.	4 e	iii. 8.	19 d	xxxiv. 29, 29.	19 b
xxxiii. 1.	4 a	iii. 9, 18.	4 a	xxxiv. 30.	25 a
xxxiii. 3.	25 a	iii. 10.	16 a	xxxiv. 32.	25 d
xxxiii. 6, 7.	25 c	iii. 13.	4 e	xxxiv. 34, 34.	18 b a
xxxiii. 7, 7.	25 c d	iv. 14.	18 e	xxxv. 10, 21, 22.	4 d
xxxiii. 14.	4 d	v. 15.	4 d	xxxvi. 2.	43 b
xxxiii. 18, 18.	4 d b	v. 20.	18 b	xxxvii. 4.	4 d
xxxiv. 5.	4 b	v. 23.	4 a	xl. 32.	43 b
xxxiv. 7, 27.	4 a	vii. 15.	42 b	Lev. ix. 22.	19 d
xxxiv. 20, 25.	4 d	viii. 3.	4 a	ix. 23, 24.	18 d
xxxv. 6, 27.	4 d	viii. 4, 6.	32 d	x. 3.	43 k

Lev. xi. 34. 4 d
xii. 4. 4 d
xiii. 16. 4 a
xiv. 8, 34. 4 d
xiv. 35, 44. 4 a
xiv. 39. 47 a
xiv. 43. 47 d
xiv. 48. 4 b d
xv. 14. 4 a
xvi. 2, 3, 26, 28. 4 d
xvi. 17. 18 b
xvi. 23. 4 a
xvi. 24. 18 a
xix. 19. 32 d
xix. 23. 4 d
xxi. 21, 21, 23. 25 c
xxiii. 10. 4 d
xxv. 2. 4 d
xxv. 22. 4 b
xxv. 25. 4 a
Num. i. 1. 18 b
i. 51. 43 g
iii. 10, 38. 43 g
iv. 5. 4 a
iv. 15. 4 d
iv. 47. 4 e
v. 14, 14. 31 a
v. 30. 31 d
vi. 5. 31 d
vi. 6. 4 d
viii. 19. 25 a
ix. 1. 18 b
ix. 6. 43 d
x. 21. 4 b
x. 29. 16 a
xi. 17. 19 a
xi. 20, 20. 18 d a
xi. 23. 44 a
xi. 25. 19 d
xii. 4, 4. 18 c d
xii. 5, 5. 19 d, 18 d
xii. 12. 18 b
xiii 21. 4 b
xiii. 22, 23, 26. 4 d
xiii. 27. 4 a
xiv. 30. 4 d
xiv. 45. 19 d
xv. 2. 4 d
xv. 18. 4 b
xvi. 5, 5. 43 e f
xvi. 12, 14. 32 d
xvi. 27, 35. 18 a
xvi. 40. 43 d
xvi. 43. 4 d
xvii. 13.α 43 g
xviii. 3, 4, 22. 43 d
xviii. 7. 43 g
xix. 2. 32 a
xix. 7. 4 d
xix. 14. 4 e
xx. 1, 22. 4 d
xx. 5. 32 f
xx. 11, 18, 20. 18 d
xx. 28. 19 d
xxi. 1. 4 e
xxi. 7, 23. 4 d
xxi. 13. 18 e
xxi. 27. 4 c
xxii. 5. 18 a
xxii. 6, 17. 16 a
xxii. 7, 9, 39. 4 d
xxii. 11, 11. 18 e, 16 a
xxii. 14. 10 b
xxii. 16, 16. 4 d, 10 b
xxii. 20, 20. 4 d a
xxii. 36. 4 e
xxii. 37. 10 a
xxii. 38. 4 a
xxiii. 3. 44 b
xxiii. 7, 7, 13, 27. 16 a
xxiii. 17. 4 d
xxiv. 14. 16 a
xxiv. 17. 8
xxv. 6. 4 e
xxvii. 1. 43 d
xxvii. 21. 4 d
xxxi. 14. 4 e
xxxi. 24. 4 d
xxxi. 48. 43 d
xxxii. 2. 4 d
xxxii. 11. 32 e
xxxii. 16. 25 c
xxxiii. 9. 4 d
xxxiii. 38. 18 b
xxxiii. 40. 4 b
Num. xxxiv. 2. 4 e
xxxv. 10. 31 e
xxxv. 26, 26. 18 b d
xxxv. 32. 47 d
xxxvi. 1. 43 d
Deut. i. 19, 24. 4 d
i. 20. 4 a
i. 22, 22. 43 d, 4 d
i. 31. 4 b
i. 44. 18 d
ii. 14, 14. 10 a, 31 a
ii. 19, 37. 43 a
ii. 23. 18 e
ii. 32. 18 d
iii. 1. 18 d
iv. 11. 43 d
iv. 30. 23 a
iv. 45, 46. 18 b
v. 23. 43 d
vi. 10. 21
ix. 7. 4 b
ix. 15. 19 d
x. 1. 32 c
x. 5. 19 d
xi. 5. 4 b
xi. 10. 18 a
xii. 5, 9. 4 a
xiii. 2. 4 a
xiv. 29. 4 a
xv. 19. 15
xvi. 3, 3. 18 a b
xvi. 6. 18 b
xvii. 9. 4 a
xvii. 14. 4 d
xviii. 6, 6. 4 d a
xviii. 9. 4 e
xviii. 22. 4 d
xx. 2. 43 b
xx. 10. 43 d
xxi. 2. 18 a
xxi. 5. 25 d
xxii. 14. 43 d
xxiii. 4. 18 b
xxiii. 10, 24, 25. 4 d
xxiii. 11, 11. 37, 4 d
xxiii. 13. 18 h
xxiv. 9. 18 b
xxv. 1, 9. 25 d
xxv. 17. 18 b
xxvi. 1. 4 d
xxvi. 3. 4 d
xxvii. 12. 31 b
xxviii. 2, 15, 45. 4 a
xxviii. 6, 19. 4 b
xxviii. 7. 18 d
xxviii. 24, 43. 19 d
xxviii. 52. 19 b
xxviii. 57. 18 e
xxix. 7, 7. 4 d, 18 d
xxix. 16. 31 a
xxix. 22, 22. 2 a, 4 d
xxx. 1. 4 d
xxxi. 2, 11. 4 b
xxxi. 17. 23 a
xxxii. 17. 4 a
xxxii. 35. 35
xxxii. 44. 4 d
xxxiii. 2, 2. 4 a, 3 a
xxxiii. 16. 4 d
xxxiii. 21. 3 c
Josh. ii. 1, 22, 23. 4 d
ii. 2, 4. 4 a
ii. 3, 3. 4 e a
ii. 8. 32 a
ii. 10. 18 b
ii. 18. 4 e
iii. 1. 4 d
iii. 4. 43 b
iii. 8, 15. 4 b
iii. 9. 25 b
iii. 13, 16, 16. 19 e
iv. 6, 21. 21
iv. 16. 32 d
iv. 17. 32 c
iv. 18. 32 b
iv. 19. 32 a
iv. 22. 31 a
v. 4, 4. 18 e b
v. 5, 5. 18 e b
v. 6. 18 e
v. 14. 4 a
vi. 1. 4 e
vi. 9, 13. 10 d
vi. 11, 19. 4 d
vii. 14, 14, 14. 43 d
Josh. viii. 5. 18 d
viii. 6. 18 a
viii. 11. 4 d
ix. 6, 9. 4 a
ix. 8, 17. 4 d
ix. 12. 18 b
x. 4, 6. 32 c
x. 9. 4 d
x. 24, 24. 43 c d
x. 33. 32 a
xi. 5, 7, 21. 4 d
xiv. 6. 25 c
xiv. 11. 4 b
xv. 18. 4 b
xvi. 7. 36 a
xvii. 4. 43 d
xviii. 4, 9. 4 d
xviii. 8. 47 c
xviii. 11, 11. 32 d, 18 d
xviii. 16. 19 a
xix. 1, 24. 18 d
xix. 10. 32 d
xix. 17, 32, 40. 18 a
xx. 6. 4 a
xxi. 1. 25 c
xxi. 4. 18 d
xxi. 45. 4 a
xxii. 10, 15. 4 d
xxii. 24, 27, 28. 21
xxiii. 7. 4 b
xxiii. 14, 15. 4 a
xxiv. 6, 11. 4 d
Judg. i. 3. 32 c
i. 14. 4 b
i. 24. 18 e
i. 34. 19 b
ii. 1. 32 d
iii. 20, 24. 4 a
iii. 22. 18 d
iii. 27. 4 b
iv. 5. 32 d
iv. 20. 43 d
iv. 22, 22, 22. 18 d, 16 a, 4 d
v. 14. 19 a
v. 19, 23. 4 a
v. 28. 4 b
vi. 3, 3. 32 a
vi. 4. 4 b
vi. 5, 5. 32 d, 4 a
vi. 11. 4 d
vi. 18, 18. 4 b, 47 b
vi. 34. 20
vi. 35. 32 d
vii. 13, 13, 19. 4 d
vii. 17. 4 e
vii. 24. 19 c
viii. 4, 15. 4 d
viii. 9. 47 b
ix. 10, 12, 14. 16 a
ix. 15, 15. 4 c, 18 d
ix. 20, 20. 18 d
ix. 24. 4 b
ix. 25. 31 d
ix. 26, 52, 57. 4 d
ix. 29. 18 c
ix. 31. 4 e
ix. 33, 43. 18 e
ix. 36. 19 e
ix. 37, 37. 19 e, 4 a
xi. 6. 16 a
xi. 7, 12. 4 a
xi. 13. 32 b
xi. 16, 16. 32 b, 4 d
xi. 18, 18. 4 d a
xi. 31. 18 e d
xi. 33. 4 b
xi. 34, 34. 4 d, 18 e
xii. 3. 32 a
xiii. 5. 32 d
xiii. 6, 6. 4 d a
xiii. 8, 9, 11, 12, 17. 4 d
xiii. 10. 4 a
xiii. 14. 18 d
xiv. 2. 32 d
xiv. 5. 4 d
xiv. 6, 19. 39 b
xiv. 9. 16 b
xiv. 14, 14. 18 a
xv. 6. 32 d
xv. 10, 10. 32 a
xv. 12. 19 a
xv. 14, 14. 4 a, 39 b
xv. 19, 19. 18 d, 47 d
xvi. 2. 4 a
Judg. xvi. 5. 32 d
xvi. 17. 32 a
xvi. 18, 18. 32 c a
xvi. 31. 19 d
xvii. 8, 9. 4 d
xviii. 2, 7, 8, 10, 13, 15, 27. 4 d
xviii. 17. 4 a
xviii. 23. 12
xix. 10, 17, 26, 29. 4 d
xix. 11, 13. 16 a
xix. 16, 22, 23. 4 a
xix. 30. 32 b
xx. 4. 4 a
xx. 10. 4 b
xx. 21. 18 d
xx. 24. 43 d
xx. 26, 34. 4 d
xx. 33. 7 b
xx. 41. 24 a
xx. 48, 48. 23 c
xxi. 2, 22. 4 d
xxi. 5, 5. 32 a
xxi. 8, 8. 32 a, 4 a
xxi. 14. 47 d
xxi. 21, 21. 18 d a
Ruth i. 2. 4 d
i. 19, 19. 4 b
i. 22. 4 a
ii. 3, 7. 4 d
ii. 4. 4 e
ii. 6. 47 a
ii. 11. 16 b
ii. 12. 4 a
ii. 14. 25 b
iii. 7, 16. 4 d
iii. 14. 4 a
iv. 1. 31 e
iv. 3. 47 a
iv. 11. 4 e
1 Sam. i. 11. 32 d
i. 19. 4 d
i. 20. 41
ii. 3. 18 d
ii. 13, 15. 4 a
ii. 14, 31. 4 e
ii. 19. 32 b
ii. 27, 34, 36. 4 d
iii. 10. 4 d
iv. 3, 3, 12, 14. 4 d
iv. 5. 4 b
iv. 6, 7. 4 a
iv. 13, 13. 4 d e
iv. 16. 4 e
iv. 19. 11
v. 5. 4 e
v. 10. 4 b
vi. 7. 32 a
vi. 14. 4 e
vi. 21. 19 c
vii. 1. 4 d
vii. 13.β 4 b
viii. 4. 4 b
ix. 5, 5. 4 a, 16 a
ix. 6. 4 b d
ix. 9, 10. 16 a
ix. 12, 16. 4 a
ix. 13, 13, 15. 4 b
ix. 14, 14. 4 e, 18 e
ix. 25. 19 d
x. 3, 22. 4 a
x. 5, 5, 5. 4 d, 4 b, 19 e
x. 6. 39 a
x. 7, 9, 13, 14. 4 d
x. 8, 8. 19 e, 4 b
x. 10, 10. 4 d, 39 b
x. 20, 21. 43 f
xi. 1. 32 d
xi. 3. 18 a
xi. 4, 11. 4 d
xi. 5. 4 a
xi. 6. 39 b
xi. 7, 7. 18 e d
xi. 9, 9. 4 e d
xi. 10. 18 d
xi. 14. 16 a
xii. 8, 12. 4 a
xiii. 5. 32 d
xiii. 8, 11. 4 a
xiii. 10. 4 e
xiii. 12. 19 d
xiii. 17. 18 d
xiv. 1, 6. 16 a
xiv. 9. 24 d
xiv. 10, 12, 12. 32 c
1 Sam. xiv. 11. 18 e
xiv. 20, 26. 4 d
xiv. 25. 4 a
xv. 2, 6. 32 b
xv. 5, 13. 4 d
xv. 7. 4 b
xv. 12. 4 a
xv. 32. 16 b
xv. 35. 17 a
xvi. 2, 5, 5. 4 a
xvi. 4, 4, 4. 4 d, 42 b, 4 b
xvi. 6, 11. 4 b
xvi. 13. 39 b
xvi. 21. 4 d
xvii. 8, 8. 18 d, 19 d
xvii. 20, 22. 4 d
xvii. 23, 25, 25. 32 e
xvii. 28, 28. 19 a
xvii. 34. 4 a
xvii. 41.γ 16 b, 10 d
xvii. 43, 45, 45. 4 e
xvii. 44. 16 a
xvii. 48. 16 b
xvii. 52. 4 b
xviii. 6, 6. 4 b, 18 d
xviii. 10. 39 b
xviii. 13. 4 d
xviii. 16. 4 e
xix. 16, 18, 22. 4 d
xix. 23. 4 b
xx. 1, 37, 38. 4 d
xx. 9. 4 b
xx. 11. 16 a
xx. 19, 27, 29. 4 a
xx. 21. 4 c
xxi. 1, 15. 4 d
xxi. 5. 18 b
xxii. 3. 18 d
xxii. 5, 11. 4 d
xxii. 9. 4 e
xxiii. 3. 16 b
xxiii. 6. 19 a
xxiii. 7. 4 a
xxiii. 10. 4 b
xxiii. 11, 11, 25. 19 d
xxiii. 15. 18 a
xxiii. 19. 32 d
xxiii. 20, 20. 19 c b
xxiii. 23. 47 a
xxiii. 27, 27. 4 a, 16 a
xxiv. 3. 4 d
xxiv. 14. 18 a
xxv. 8, 8.δ 4 a, 23 b
xxv. 9, 12, 34, 36, 40. 4 d
xxv. 19. 4 e
xxv. 20, 20. 19 e
xxv. 26, 33. 4 b
xxvi. 1, 5, 7, 10. 4 d
xxvi. 3, 4, 15. 4 a
xxvi. 20. 18 a
xxvi. 22. 31 d
xxvii. 9. 4 d
xxviii. 4, 8, 21. 4 d
xxviii. 14. 32 e
xxix. 6, 6. 4 b
xxix. 10. 4 b
xxx. 1. 4 b
xxx. 3, 9, 26. 4 d
xxx. 12. 47 d
xxx. 21, 21. 4 d, 25 c
xxx. 23. 4 e
xxxi. 4, 7, 8, 12. 4 d
2 Sam. i. 2, 2. 4 e b
i. 3. 4 d
i. 9. 1
ii. 4, 29. 4 d
ii. 23, 23. 18 d, 4 e
ii. 24. 4 a
iii. 13. 4 b
iii. 20, 35. 4 d
iii. 22. 4 e
iii. 23, 23. 4 a
iii. 24, 24. 4 d e
iii. 25, 25. 4 a h i
iii. 26. 18 a
iv. 4. 4 b
iv. 5, 7. 4 d
iv. 6. 4 a
v. 1, 3, 6, 6, 8, 20. 4 d
v. 13, 25. 4 b
v. 17. 32 d
v. 18, 23. 4 a
v. 22.ε 32 b
vi. 6, 9. 4 d
vi. 16. 4 e
2 Sam. vi. 20. 18 d
viii. 5. 4 d
ix. 6. 4 d
x. 2, 14, 16, 17. 4 d
x. 8. 18 d
x. 11. 10 a
xi. 4, 7, 22. 4 d
xi. 10. 4 e
xi. 23. 18 d
xii. 1, 20, 20. 4 d
xii. 4, 4, 4. 4 d e e
xiii. 5, 5. 4 a d
xiii. 6, 6, 24. 4 d
xiii. 11. 4 c
xiii. 30, 35, 36. 4 a
xiii. 34. 10 d
xiv. 3, 15. 4 a
xiv. 29, 29. 4 b
xiv. 31, 33, 33. 4 d
xiv. 32, 32. 4 c a
xv. 2, 20, 28. 4 b
xv. 4, 6, 13, 37, 37. 4 d
xv. 5. 43 b
xv. 18, 32. 4 a
xvi. 5, 5, 5, 5. 4 a, 18 e e b
xvi. 7, 7. 18 c
xvi. 11. 18 a
xvi. 14. 4 a
xvi. 15, 16. 4 a
xvii. 2, 6, 18, 20. 4 d
xvii. 12, 24. 4 a
xvii. 17, 27. 4 b
xvii. 21. 32 d
xviii. 4. 18 a
xviii. 25.ζ 16 b, 10 b
xviii. 27. 4 d
xviii. 31. 4 e
xix. 5, 8. 4 d
xix. 11, 20, 25, 30. 4 a
xix. 15, 15. 4 d a
xix. 16. 19 d
xix. 18. 31 b
xix. 24, 24. 19 a, 4 a
xix. 31. 19 a
xix. 33. 31 c
xix. 39. 31 a
xix. 41. 4 e
xx. 3, 15. 4 d
xx. 12. 4 e
xx. 16. 43 c
xx. 17. 43 d
xxii. 10. 19 d
xxiii. 13. 4 d
xxiv. 6, 6, 7, 8, 13, 13, 18. 4 d
xxiv. 20. 31 e
xxiv. 21. 4 a
1 Kings i. 12. 16 a
i. 14, 23, 28, 32, 53. 4 d
i. 22, 47. 4 a
i. 35, 35. 32 a, 4 a
i. 40, 45. 32 d
i. 42, 42. 4 c a
ii. 7. 43 a
ii. 8. 19 a
ii. 13, 13. 4 b d
ii. 28. 4 a
ii. 30, 30. 4 d, 18 c
ii. 41. 47 d
iii. 7. 4 b
iii. 15, 16. 4 d
iv. 27. 43 g
iv. 34. 4 d
vi. 1. 18 b
vii. 14. 4 d
viii. 3. 4 d
viii. 9, 10. 18 b
viii. 19. 18 e
viii. 31,η 41, 42. 4 a
ix. 12. 18 d
ix. 24. 32 a
ix. 28. 4 d
x. 1, 2, 2, 22. 4 d
x. 7, 10, 12, 14. 4 a
x. 29. 32 d
xi. 2, 18, 18. 4 d
xii. 1. 4 a
xii. 3, 21. 4 d
xii. 5. 47 c
xii. 12, 12. 4 d, 47 c
xii. 20. 47 a
xiii. 1, 10, 12, 14, 21. 4 a
xiii. 7. 4 c
xiii. 9, 17. 10 a

1 Kings xiii. 11, 25, 29. 4 d
xiii. 15. 16 a
xiii. 22, 22. 47 d, 4 d
xiv. 4, 13. 4 d
xiv. 5, 5. 4 e b
xiv. 6, 6. 4 e c
xiv. 17, 17. 4 d e
xiv. 25. 32 a
xv. 17. 4 e
xv. 19. 16 a
xvii. 10. 4 d
xvii. 18. 4 d
xvii. 21, 22. 47 d
xviii. 12. 4 a
xviii. 21, 36. 25 c
xviii. 30, 30. 25 b c
xix. 3, 4, 9. 4 d
xix. 7. 47 d
xix. 15. 4 a
xx. 5. 25 d
xx. 17, 18, 18, 19. 18 a
xx. 22, 22. 25 c, 32 e
xx. 28. 25 c
xx. 30, 32, 43. 4 d
xx. 33, 33. 18 d, 32 i
xxi. 4, 5, 13. 4 d
xxii. 2. 19 d
xxii. 15. 4 d
xxii. 21. 18 d
xxii. 27. 4 b

2 Kings i. 4, 10, 10, 12, 12, 16. 19 d
i. 6, 6. 32 a, 19 d
i. 7. 32 a
i. 9, 11. 19 c
i. 13. 4 d
i. 14. 19 a
ii. 3, 24. 18 d
ii. 4, 15. 4 d
ii. 5. 25 c
ii. 18. 47 d
ii. 23. 18 a
iii. 20. 4 e
iii. 21. 32 a
iii. 24. 4 d
iv. 1, 4. 4 a
iv. 7, 11, 25, 32, 36, 39. 4 d
iv. 10. 4 b
iv. 22. 4 d
iv. 27, 27. 4 d, 25 c
iv. 38. 47 a
iv. 42. 4 d
v. 6. 4 d
v. 8, 9, 15, 24. 4 d
v. 10, 14. 47 d
v. 11. 18 b d
v. 13. 25 c
v. 22. 4 d
vi. 4, 14. 4 d
vi. 9. 26 d
vi. 18. 19 d
vi. 20. 4 b
vi. 23. θ 4 b
vi. 32, 32. 4 d b
vi. 33. 19 e
vii. 4. 16 a
vii. 5. 4 d
vii. 6. 4 b
vii. 8, 8. 4 d, 47 d
vii. 9, 9. 23 a, 16 a
vii. 10, 10. 4 d
vii. 12. 18 d
vii. 17. 19 b
viii. 1. 4 a
viii. 7, 7. 4 d a
viii. 9, 14. 4 d
ix. 2. 4 a
ix. 5, 19, 30, 34. 4 d
ix. 11, 11. 18 a, 4 a
ix. 16. 19 a
ix. 17. 4 b
ix. 18, 18. 4 a, 47 a
ix. 20, 20. 4 a, 47 a
ix. 36. 47 d
x. 2, 7. 4 b
x. 6. 4 c
x. 8, 17. 16 a
x. 12. 16 b
x. 16. 16 a
x. 21, 21, 21. 4 d a d
x. 25. 18 d
xi. 8, 8. 4 e b
xi. 9, 9. 4 e d

2 Kings xi. 13, 19. 4 d
xi. 16. 4 h
xii. 4, 10. 32 d
xii. 9. 4 b
xiii. 14. 19 d
xiii. 20. 4 e
xiv. 8. 16 a
xiv. 13. 4 d
xv. 14. 4 d
xv. 19, 29. 4 a
xvi. 5. 32 d
xvi. 6. 4 a
xvi. 7. 32 c
xvi. 11. 4 b
xvi. 12. 4 d
xvii. 3. 32 a
xvii. 5. 32 d
xvii. 28. 4 d
xvii. 9, 13, 25. 32 a
17. 4 d, 32 d, 4 d
xviii. 18. 18 d
xviii. 31. 18 c
xviii. 32. 4 b
xviii. 37. 4 d
xix. 3. 4 a
xix. 5, 33, 33. 4 d
xix. 9. 18 a
xix. 23. 32 a
xix. 27. 4 b
xix. 28, 28. 32 a, 4 a
xix. 32, 32. 4 d, 40
xx. 1. 4 a
xx. 14, 14, 14. 4 d d a
xx. 17. 4 e
xxi. 15. 18 a
xxii. 9. 4 d
xxiii. 9. 32 d
xxiii. 17, 18. 4 a
xxiii. 34. 4 d
xxiv. i. 10. 32 a
xxiv. 7. κ 18 b
xxiv. 11. 4 d
xxv. 1, 8, 25. 4 a
xxv. 23, 26. 4 d

1 Chron. i. 12. 18 a
ii. 53. 18 a
ii. 55. 4 e
iv. 41. 4 d
vii. 21. 19 a
vii. 22. 4 d
ix. 22. 4 d
ix. 25. 4 d
x. 4, 7, 8. 4 d
xi. 3, 5. 4 d
xii. 1. 4 e
xii. 16, 22. 4 a
xii. 17, 23, 38. 4 a
xii. 18. 20
xii. 19, 31. 4 d
xiii. 9. 4 d
xiv. 9, 14. 4 a
xiv. 11. 32 d
xv. 29. 4 a
xvi. 29. 4 c
xvi. 33. 4 a
xvii. 16. 4 d
xviii. 5. 4 d
xix. 2, 7, 7, 15, 17. 4 d
xix. 3. 4 a
xix. 9, 9. 18 d, 4 a
xx. 1. 4 d
xxi. 4, 11, 21. 4 d
xxiv. 7. 18 d
xxiv. 19. 4 b
xxv. 9. 18 d
xxvi. 14. 18 d
xxvii. 1. 4 e

2 Chron. i. 10, 13. 4 d
v. 4. 4 d
v. 10, 11. 18 b
vi. 9. 18 e
vi. 22, 32, 32. 4 a c e
vii. 1. 19 a
vii. 3. 19 b
vii. 11. 4 a
viii. 11. 4 a
ix. 1, 1, 21. 4 d
ix. 6, 13. 4 a
x. 1. 4 a
x. 3. 4 d
x. 5. 47 c
x. 12, 12. 4 d, 47 c
xi. 1. 4 d
xi. 14. 16 b

2 Chron. xi. 16. 4 a
xii. 2. 32 a
xii. 3, 5, 11. 4 a
xii. 4. 4 d
xii. 9. 32 d
xii. 9. 4 e
xiii. 13. 29 b, 4 b
xiv. 9, 9. 18 d, 4 d
xv. 5. 4 e
xvi. 1, 1. 32 a, 4 e
xvi. 7. 4 a
xviii. 14. 4 d
xviii. 20. 18 d
xviii. 23. 25 c
xix. 10. 4 d
xx. 1, 4, 24. 4 a
xx. 2, 2. 4 d e
xx. 9, 25, 28. 4 d
xx. 10, 11. 4 b
xx. 12, 22. 4 e
xx. 16. 32 e
xxi. 12. 4 a
xxi. 17. 32 d
xxii. 1. 4 e
xxii. 7, 7. 4 b
xxiii. 2, 6, 12, 15, 20. 4 d
xxiii. 7, 7. 4 e b
xxiii. 8. 4 e
xxiv. 11, 17, 24. 4 a
xxiv. 20. 20
xxiv. 23, 23. 32 a, 4 d
xxv. 7, 10. 4 a
xxv. 14. 4 b
xxv. 17. 16 a
xxviii. 9, 12. 4 a
xxviii. 17. 4 a
xxviii. 20. 4 d
xxix. 15. 4 d
xxix. 17. 4 a
xxix. 31. 25 b
xxx. 1, 5. 4 b
xxx. 9. 47 b
xxx. 11, 27. 4 d
xxx. 25, 25. 4 e
xxxi. 5. 38
xxxi. 8. 4 a
xxxii. 1, 2, 26. 4 a
xxxii. 4. 4 d
xxxii. 21, 21. 4 d, 18 f
xxxiv. 9. 4 d
xxxv. 20. 32 a
xxxv. 22. 4 d
xxxvi. 6. 32 a

Ezra ii. 1. 47 d
ii. 2. 4 a
ii. 68. 4 b
iii. 1. 24 b
iii. 8, 8. 4 b e
iv. 2. 25 c
iv. 12, 12. 30 c, 3 f
v. 3, 16. 3 f
v. 5. 9
vi. 21. 47 e
vii. 8. 4 d
vii. 9. 4 a
viii. 32. 4 d
viii. 35. 4 e
ix. 1. 25 d
ix. 13. 4 e
x. 6. 16 b
x. 8, 14. 4 d

Neh. i. 2. 4 d
ii. 7, 9, 11. 4 d
ii. 10. 4 a
iii. 17. 16 a
iv. 8. 4 b
iv. 11. 4 d
iv. 12. 4 a
v. 17. 4 e
vi. 2, 7. 16 a
vi. 3, 3. 19 b a
vi. 10, 10, 10. 4 a c e
vi. 17. 4 e
vii. 5. 32 e
vii. 6. 47 d
vii. 7. 4 e
vii. 73. 24 b
viii. 17. 47 e
ix. 13. 19 a
ix. 32. 23 a
xiii. 1. 4 d
xiii. 6, 21. 4 a
xiii. 22. 4 e

Esth. i. 12. 4 b
i. 17, 17. 18 d, 4 e

Esth. i. 19. 4 d
ii. 12, 15. 24 d
ii. 13. 4 e
ii. 14. 4 d
iv. 2, 4, 9. 4 d
iv. 3. 24 f
iv. 11, 11. 4 d b
iv. 14. 24 c
v. 4, 5, 8, 10. 4 d
v. 12. 4 f
vi. 4. 4 a
vi. 5, 6. 4 d
vi. 12. 47 d
vi. 14. 24 c
vii. 1. 4 d
viii. 1. 4 a
viii. 6. 23 b
viii. 17. 24 f
ix. 25. 4 b
ix. 26. 24 c

Job i. 6, 6, 7. 4 a
i. 14, 19. 4 a
i. 16, 17, 18. 4 a
i. 21. 18 a
ii. 1, 1, 2. 4 a
ii. 11, 11, 11. 4 e d b
iii. 6, 7, 24, 26. 4 d
iii. 11. 18 a
iii. 25, 25. 3 c, 4 d
iv. 5. 42 a
iv. 14. 42 a
v. 6. 18 d
v. 21. 4 d
v. 26, 26. 4 d, 32 b
vi. 20. 4 a
vii. 9. 32 d
ix. 32. 4 a
xiii. 13. 31 d
xiii. 16. 4 d
xiv. 2. 18 a
xiv. 14. 4 b
xv. 21. 4 d
xvi. 22. 3 c
xvii. 10. 4 c
xviii. 20. 2 a
xix. 12. 4 d
xx. 22. 4 d
xx. 25, 25. 18 d, 10 c
xxi. 17. 4 d
xxii. 21. 4 d
xxiii. 3. 4 d
xxiii. 10. 18 d
xxvi. 4. 18 a
xxvii. 5. 4 d
xxviii. 20. 18 d
xxix. 13. 4 d
xxx. 14. 3 c
xxx. 26, 26. 4 d
xxxiv. 28. 4 g
xxxvi. 32. 36 b
xxxvii. 9. 4 d
xxxvii. 13. 23 d
xxxvii. 22. 4 d
xxxviii. 11. 4 d
xxxviii. 29. 18 a
xli. 13, 16. 4 d
xlii. 11. 4 d

Ps. v. 7. 4 d
vii. 12. 19 d
xvii. 2. 18 d
xviii. 6. 4 d
xviii. 9. 19 d
xix. 5. 18 e
xxii. 31. 4 d
xxiv. 7. 9. 4 d
xxvii. 2. 43 b
xxix. 9. 4 d
xxxii. 6. 24 e
xxxii. 9. 43 b
xxxiv. 11. 16 a
xxxv. 8. 4 d
xxxvi. 11. 4 d
xxxvii. 13. 4 d
xl. 7. 4 a
xli. 6. 4 a
xlii. 7. 4 d
xliv. 17. 4 a
xlvi. 8. 16 a
l. 3. 4 d
li. title, liv. title. 4 b a
lii. title, title. 4 b a
lv. 5. 4 d
lxv. 2. 4 d
lxvi. 5, 16. 16 a
lxviii. 31. 3 c

Ps. lxix. 1, 2. 4 a
lxix. 27. 4 d
lxxi. 18. 4 d
lxxii. 10. 19 d
lxxviii. 4, 6. 2 a
lxxviii. 21, 31. 32 a
lxxviii. 39. 47 d
lxxix. 1. 4 a
lxxix. 11. 4 d
lxxx. 2. 16 a
lxxxiii. 4. 16 a
lxxxvi. 9. 4 d
lxxxviii. 2. 4 d
lxxxviii. 8. 18 d
lxxxviii. 17. 29 a
xci. 7. 25 c
xci. 10. 4 d
xcv. 2. 16 a
xcv. 6. 40
xcvi. 8. 4 c
xcvi. 13, 13. 4 a
xcviii. 9. 4 a
c. 2. 4 c
ci. 2. 4 d
cii. 1. 4 d
cii. 13. 4 a
cii. 18. 2 a
cv. 19. 4 b
cv. 23, 31, 34. 4 d
cix. 17, 18. 4 d
cxviii. 26. 4 e
cxix. 41, 77, 170. 4 d
cxix. 169. 43 d
cxxi. 1. 4 d
cxxi. 8. 4 b
cxxvi. 6. 4 b d
cxxxii. 3. 4 d
cxliv. 5. 19 d

Prov. i. 11. 16 a
i. 26. 4 d
i. 27, 27, 27. 4 b, 3 c, 4 b
iii. 28. 47 c
v. 8. 43 d
vi. 3, 11. 4 a
vi. 15. 4 d
vii. 15. 18 a
vii. 18. 16 a
viii. 3. 4 h
ix. 5. 16 a
x. 24. 4 d
xi. 2. 4 a d
xi. 8, 27. 4 d
xii. 13. 18 d
xiii. 10. 28
xiii. 12. 4 d
xviii. 3, 3. 4 b a
xviii. λ 4 d
xxiv. 25. 4 d
xxv. 4. 18 d
xxv. 7. 32 c
xxvi. 2. 4 d
xxviii. 22. 4 d
xxxi. 25. 2 a

Eccles. i. 4. 4 d
i. 7. 10 d
i. 11, 11. 2 a a
ii. 16. 4 e
iv. 14. 18 a
iv. 16. 2 a
v. 15, 15. 18 a, 4 a
v. 16. 4 a
vi. 4. 4 a
vii. 18. 16 a
viii. 10. 4 a
ix. 14. 4 a
xi. 8. 4 a

Cant. ii. 8. 4 e
ii. 10, 13. 16 a
ii. 12. 24 c
iii. 6. 32 a
iv. 2. 32 a
iv. 8. 4 d
iv. 16, 16. 4 c d
v. 1. 4 a
vii. 11. 16 a
viii. 5. 32 e

Isa. i. 12, 23. 4 d
i. 18. 16 a

Isa. ii. 3, 5. 16 a
v. 6. 32 a
v. 19, 26. 4 d
vii. 17, 19. 4 a
vii. 24, 25. 4 d
viii. 7. 32 a
x. 3. 4 d
x. 28. 4 a
xi. 1. 18 a
xi. 16. 32 b
xiii. 5. 4 e
xiii. 6. 4 d
xiii. 22. 4 a
xiv. 8. 32 d
xiv. 9. 4 b
xiv. 29. 18 d
xiv. 31. 4 a
xvi. 8. 24 a
xvi. 12. 4 a
xix. 1, 23. 4 a
xx. 1. 4 b
xxi. 1, 9. 4 a
xxi. 12. 12. 3 a b
xxiv. 10. 4 b
xxiv. 18. 32 a
xxvi. 20. 16 a
xxvi. 21. 18 e
xxvii. 6, 11. 4 e
xxvii. 13. 4 a
xxviii. 15. 4 d
xxviii. 29. 18 a
xxix. 31. 13
xxx. 4. 24 e
xxx. 8. 2 a
xxx. 13. 4 d
xxx. 27. 4 a
xxx. 29. 4 b
xxxi. 4. 19 d
xxxii. 10. 4 d
xxxii. 13. 32 d
xxxii. 19. 19 b
xxxiv. 1, 1. 43 c, 18 i
xxxiv. 3. 32 d
xxxiv. 5. 19 d
xxxiv. 7. 19 a
xxxiv. 13. 32 a
xxxv. 4, 4. 4 d
xxxv. 10. 4 a
xxxvi. 1, 10. 32 a
xxxvi. 3. 18 d
xxxvi. 16. 18 c
xxxvi. 17. 4 b
xxxvi. 22. 4 d
xxxvii. 3. 4 a
xxxvii. 5. 4 d
xxxvii. 9. 18 a
xxxvii. 24. 32 a
xxxvii. 28. 4 b
xxxvii. 29, 29. 32 a, 4 a
xxxvii. 33, 33. 4 d, 40
xxxvii. 34, 34. 4 a d
xxxviii. 1. 4 d
xxxix. 3, 3, 3. 4 d d a
xxxix. 6. 4 e
xl. 10. 4 e
xli. 1, 1. 25, 43 d
xli. 5. 3 c
xli. 22. 4 e
xli. 23. 3 d
xli. 25, 25. 3 c, 4 d
xlii. 5. 18 i
xlii. 9. 4 a
xlii. 23. 2
xliv. 7, 7. 3 d, 4 d
xlv. 11. 3 d
xlv. 14, 14, 14. 31 d, 16 b, 31 d
xlv. 20. 4 c
xlv. 24. 4 d
xlvii. 1. 19 c
xlvii. 9, 9. 4 d a
xlvii. 11, 11. 4 a d
xlviii. 1. 4 d
xlviii. 3, 5. 4 d
xlviii. 16. 43 c
xlix. 12. 4 d
xlix. 18. 4 a
l. 2. 4 a
l. 8. 25 c
li. 11. 4 a
li. 19. 42 c
lii. 1. 4 d
liv. 14. 43 d

Reference	Code
Isa. lv. 1, 1, 1, 8.	16 a
lv. 10.	19 d
lv. 13, 13.	32 d
lvi. 1.	4 b
lvi. 9, 12.	3 b
lix. 19.	4 d
lix. 20.	4 a
lx. 1.	4 a
lx. 3, 14.	10 a
lx. 4, 4.	4 a d
lx. 5, 6, 13.	4 d
lx. 7.	32 d
lxii. 11.	4 e
lxiii. 1, 4.	4 a
lxiv. 1, 3.	19 a
lxv. 5.	25 c
lxv. 17.	32 d
lxvi. 7, 15, 23.	4 d
lxvi. 18, 18.	4 e a
Jer. i. 5.	18 d
i. 15.	4 a
ii. 3, 31.	4 d
iii. 18.	32 d
iii. 18.	4 d
iii. 22.	3 a
iv. 4.	18 d
iv. 7.	32 a
iv. 12.	4 d
iv. 13.	32 d
iv. 16.	4 e
v. 12.	4 d
vi. 3, 20, 26.	4 d
vi. 22.	4 e
vii. 10.	4 a
vii. 25.	18 a
vii. 31.	32 a
vii. 32.	4 e
viii. 7.	4 b
viii. 16.	4 d
ix. 17, 17.	4 d
ix. 21.	32 a
ix. 25.	4 e
x. 22.	4 e
xii. 9, 9.	16 a, 3 e
xii. 12.	4 a
xiii. 18.	19 a
xiii. 20.	42 a
xiii. 22.	4 d
xiv. 3.	4 a
xvi. 14.	4 e
xvi. 19.	4 d
xvii. 6, 8, 15, 19.	4 d
xvii. 16.	18 g
xvii. 26.	4 a
xviii. 18, 18.	16 a
xix. 5.	32 a
xix. 6.	4 e
xix. 13.	4 d
xx. 6.	4 d
xx. 18.	18 a
xxi. 13.	26 a
xxii. 23.	4 b
xxiii. 5, 7.	4 e
xxiii. 17.	4 d
xxv. 31.	4 a
xxvi. 2.	4 e
xxvi. 10.	32 d
xxvii. 3.	4 e
xxvii. 7.	4 b
xxviii. 9.	4 b
xxx. 3.	4 e
xxxi. 9.	4 d
xxxi. 12.	4 e
xxxi. 16, 17.	47 a
xxxi. 27, 31, 38.	4 e
xxxii. 7.	4 e
xxxii. 8.	4 d
xxxii. 23, 23.	4 d, 42 d
xxxii. 24, 29.	4 a
xxxii. 35.	32 a
xxxiii. 5, 14.	32 b, 4 c
xxxvi. 6, 9.	4 e
xxxvi. 14, 14.	16 a, 4 d
xxxvi. 29.	4 b d
xxxvii. 4.	4 a
xxxvii. 5.	18 a
xxxvii. 7.	18 e
xxxviii. 8.	47 a
xxxviii. 19.	4 d
xxxviii. 25.	4 a
xxxviii. 27.	4 d
xxxix. 1.	4 d
xxxix. 3.	4 a
xl. 4, 4, 4.	4 b c b

Reference	Code
Jer. xl. 8, 10, 12.	4 d
xl. 13.	4 a
xli. 1.	4 a
xli. 5.	4 d
xli. 6.	4 c
xli. 7.	4 b
xlii. 1.	25 c
xliii. 7, 7.	4 d
xliii. 11.	4 a
xliv. 21.	32 d
xlvi. 7.	32 d
xlvi. 9, 9.	32 a, 18 d
xlvi. 13.	4 b
xlvi. 18.	4 a
xlvi. 20, 20, 21, 22.	4 a
xlvii. 4.	4 e
xlvii. 5.	4 a
xlviii. 2.	16 a
xlviii. 6.	4 d
xlviii. 12.	4 e
xlviii. 16.	4 b
xlviii. 18, 18.	19 c, 32 a
xlviii. 21.	4 a
xlviii. 45.	18 a
xlix. 2.	4 e
xlix. 4, 36.	4 d
xlix. 9.	4 a
xlix. 14.	4 c
xlix. 19, 22.	32 d
l. 3.	32 a
l. 4.	4 d
l. 5, 26.	4 c
l. 9.	32 k
l. 27, 31, 41.	4 a
l. 44.	32 d
li. 10.	4 c
li. 13, 47, 52.	4 a
li. 27.	32 h
li. 33, 46, 51, 56.	4 a
li. 42.	32 a
li. 48, 53, 60.	4 a
li. 50.	32 d
li. 61.	4 b
lii. 4, 12.	4 a
Lam. i. 4.	4 a
i. 9.	19 d
i. 14.	32 a
i. 22.	4 d
iv. 18.	4 a
Ezek. i. 4.	4 e
iii. 15.	18 h
iv. 12.	4 a
iv. 14.	18 d
v. 4.	4 a
vii. 2, 12, 25.	4 e
vii. 5, 10.	4 e
vii. 6, 6, 6.	4 a a e
vii. 7, 7.	4 a e
vii. 26.	4 d
ix. 2.	4 e
ix. 6.	25 c
xi. 5.	32 l
xi. 16, 18.	4 a
xii. 16.	34
xii. 25.	4 d
xiv. 1.	4 d
xiv. 4, 4, 7.	4 a
xiv. 22.	18 e
xvi. 7.	4 a
xvi. 16.	4 e
xvi. 33.	4 b
xvii. 3.	4 a
xvii. 12.	4 e
xviii. 6.	43 d
xx. 1.	4 a
xx. 3.	4 e
xx. 32.	32 e
xxi. 7, 7.	4 e
xxi. 19, 19.	4 b, 18 d
xxi. 20, 27.	4 b
xxi. 25, 29.	4 a
xxii. 3.	4 b
xxiii. 4.	4 d
xxiii. 17, 39.	4 d
xxiii. 24.	4 a
xxiii. 40, 40.	4 e a
xxiv. 8.	32 g
xxiv. 14.	4 d
xxiv. 24.	4 b
xxiv. 26.	4 d
xxvi. 3, 3.	32 f g
xxvi. 16.	19 a
xxvii. 29.	19 a
xxx. 6.	19 a

Reference	Code
Ezek. xxx. 9.	4 e
xxxii. 2.	7 a
xxxii. 11.	4 d
xxxiii. 3.	4 e
xxxiii. 4.	4 d
xxxiii. 6, 6.	4 e d
xxxiii. 21.	4 a
xxxiii. 22, 22, 23.	4 b
xxxiii. 30, 30.	4 c, 18 e
xxxiii. 31, 31.	4 d h
xxxiii. 33, 33.	4 b e
xxxiv. 26.	19 f
xxxvi. 8.	4 b
xxxvii. 7.	43 d
xxxvii. 8.	32 a
xxxvii. 9.	4 c
xxxvii. 10.	4 d
xxxvii. 12.	32 f
xxxviii. 8, 9.	4 a
xxxviii. 10.	32 d
xxxviii. 13.	4 e
xxxviii. 15.	4 a
xxxviii. 16.	32 a
xxxviii. 18, 18.	4 b, 32 d
xxxix. 2.	32 f
xxxix. 8.	4 a
xxxix. 17.	4 c
xl. 6.	4 d
xl. 46.	43 g
xliii. 2, 4.	4 a
xliii. 3.	4 b
xliii. 11.	4 i
xliv. 13, 13.	25 c a
xliv. 15, 16.	43 d
xliv. 17.	32 d
xliv. 25.	4 d
xlv. 4.	43 g
xlvi. 9, 9.	4 b
xlvii. 1.	19 e
xlvii. 9, 9, 9.	4 d a d
xlvii. 20.	4 b
Dan. i. 1.	4 a
ii. 2.	4 a
ii. 29.	30 c
iii. 2.	3 g
iii. 8.	43 h
iii. 26, 26, 26, 26.	43 h, 27 b, 3 h, 27 c
iv. 7.	33 b
iv. 13, 23.	26 c
iv. 24, 28.	22
v. 5.	27 a
v. 8.	33 b
v. 10.	33 a
vi. 12.	43 h
vi. 20.	43 i
vi. 24.	22
vii. 3.	30 b
vii. 8, 20.	30 a
vii. 10.	27 c
vii. 13, 13.	3 i, 22
vii. 16.	43 h
vii. 22, 22.	3 f, 22
viii. 3.	32 e
viii. 5.	4 e
viii. 7.	24 f
viii. 8.	32 d
viii. 9.	18 a
viii. 17, 17.	4 d b
ix. 13.	4 a
ix. 22.	18 a
ix. 23, 23.	18 a, 4 a
ix. 26.	4 e
x. 3, 12, 13, 14, 20, 20.	4 a
x. 18.	17 b
xi. 6, 7, 15.	4 d
xi. 9, 21, 29, 30.	45, 4 a
xi. 10.	4 b a
xi. 11.	18 a
xi. 13.	4 b d
xi. 16.	4 e
xi. 23.	32 a
xi. 12.	24 e
Hos. i. 11.	32 a
ii. 15.	32 b
iv. 15.	4 d
vi. 1.	16 a
vi. 3.	4 d
vii. 1.	4 d
ix. 4.	4 d
ix. 7, 7.	4 a
x. 8.	32 d
x. 12.	4 d

Reference	Code
Hos. xiii. 13.	4 d
xiii. 15, 15.	4 d, 32 e
Joel i. 6.	32 a
i. 13.	4 c
i. 15.	4 d
ii. 1.	4 a
ii. 20, 20.	32 a d
ii. 23.	19 g
ii. 31.	4 b
iii. 9, 12.	4 c, 26 b
iii. 11, 11.	4 d
iii. 13.	4 d
iii. 18.	18 d
Amos iv. 2.	4 e
iv. 4.	4 c
iv. 10.	32 i
v. 9.	4 d
vi. 1.	25 f
vi. 3.	25 f
viii. 2.	4 a
viii. 11.	4 e
ix. 13.	4 e
Obad. 5, 5.	4 a
21.	32 a
Jonah i. 2.	32 a
i. 6.	43 a
i. 7.	16 a
i. 8.	4 d

Reference	Code
Jonah ii. 7.	4 d
iii. 6.	24 b
iv. 6.	32 d
iv. 10.	5
Micah i. 3, 3.	18 e, 19 a
i. 9, 9.	4 a, 24 a
i. 11.	18 a
i. 12.	19 a
i. 15.	32 a
ii. 13.	4 d
iii. 11.	4 d
iv. 2, 2.	10 a, 16 a
iv. 8, 8.	3 c, 4 a
v. 2.	18 d
v. 5, 6.	4 d
vi. 6, 6.	40
vii. 4.	4 a
vii. 12.	4 d
vii. 15.	18 b
Nah. i. 11.	18 a
ii. 1.	32 a
Hab. i. 8, 8.	4 b d
ii. 3.	4 b
iii. 3.	4 d
iii. 16.	32 b
Zeph. ii. 2, 2.	4 d
Hag. i. 2.	4 b
i. 14.	4 d

Reference	Code
Hag. ii. 5.	18 b
ii. 7, 16, 16.	4 a
ii. 22.	19 a
Zech. i. 21, 21.	4 e d
ii. 10.	4 e
iv. 1.	47 d
v. 9.	18 e
vi. 1.	18 e
vi. 10, 10.	4 a
vi. 15.	4 d
viii. 10.	4 d
viii. 20.	4 d
viii. 22.	4 a
ix. 9.	4 d
x. 4.	18 d
xi. 2.	19 a
xii. 9.	4 e
xiv. 1, 5, 21.	4 a
xiv. 16.	4 e
xiv. 17, 19.	32 d
xiv. 18, 18.	4 a, 32 d
Mal. iii. 1, 1.	4 d a
iii. 2.	4 b
iii. 5.	43 a
iv. 1, 1.	4 e
iv. 5.	4 b
iv. 6.	4 d

α *lit.* cometh near cometh near.   β *lit.* they added not yet to come. γ *lit.* went going and, &c.   δ *lit.* thy hand shall find.   ε *lit.* added to come up.   ζ *lit.* he went going.   η *or,* he enter into an oath before thine altar.   θ *lit.* added not yet to come.   ι *lit.* the way of the entrance of the horses.   κ *lit.* added not to come.   λ The קרי reads in *pret.*, which the English version follows; the *lit.* of כתיב is, his neighbour shall come in.

COMELY

1   הָדָר   *m.* honour, majesty, splendour, beauty; whatever commands reverence.

2   הוֹד   *m.* glow, beauty, vigour; that which commands praise.

3   חֵן   *m.* grace, fulness, beauty.

4   יָטַב   to be well in any respect. HIPHIL *part.*

5   יָפֶה   see *Fair;* comely, *i.e.* proper, suitable, becoming.

6   נָאָה   see *Become.* PILEL a *pret.* b נָאָה *adj.* becoming, seemly, beautiful. c נָוָה *f.* contraction of the previous *adj.*, or from נָוָה to keep at home.

7   תִּפְאָרֶת   *f.* ornament, beauty.

8   תֹּאַר   *m.* form, figure of the body.

1 Sam. xvi. 18.	8		Cant. i. 5.	6 a		Isa. liii. 2.	1
Job xli. 12. a	3		i. 10.	6 b		Jer. vi. 2.	6 c
Ps. xxxiii. 1.	6 b		ii. 14.	6 b		Ezek. xvi. 14.	1
cxlvii. 1.	6 b		iv. 3.	6 b		xxvii. 10.	1
Prov. xxx. 29.	4		vi. 4.	6 b		Dan. x. 8.	2
Eccles. v. 18.	5		Isa. iv. 2.	7			

α *lit.* not the grace of his structure; or, of his armature. See *Proportion.*

COMFORT

1   בָּלַג   to be bright; to shine forth; to make cheerful, to enliven; to revive, to refresh, to strengthen. HIPHIL a *fut.* b מַבְלִיגִית *f.* a cheering, exhilaration.

2   לֵב   *m.* the heart; comfortably; Heb. to the heart.

3   לֵבָב   *m. id.*

4   מְנוּחָה   *f.* rest, quiet.

5   נָחַם   this word seems to denote some strong impulse of the mind, and so is understood of sympathy, comfort, revenge, &c., and applied to those acts by which it finds ease for itself; hence to console oneself. NIPHAL a *pret.* b *inf.* c *fut.* PIEL d *pret.* e *inf.* f *imp.* g *fut.* h *part.* PUAL i *fut.* k *part.* HITHPAEL l *pret.* m *inf.* n *fut.*

° part. נֶחָמָה f. consolation. ⁹ נִחוּמִים m. pl. conso-lations. ʳ תַּנְחוּמִים m. pl. consolations ; pity, mercy.

6 סָעַד to support ; applied to refreshing the heart with food. KAL imp.

7 רָפַד to strew, to spread ; to stay up, to support, pr. with pillows ; hence to refresh. PIEL imp.

Gen. v. 29.	5 g	Job xvi. 2.	5 h	Isa. lii. 9.	5 d
xviii. 5.	6	xxi. 34.	5 g	liv. 11.	5 k
xxiv. 67.	5 c	xxix. 25.	5 g	lvii. 6.	5 c
xxvii. 42.	5 o	xlii. 11.	5 g	lvii. 18.	5 q
xxxvii. 35, 35.	5 e m	Ps. xxiii. 4.	5 g	lxi. 2.	5 e
xxxviii. 12.	5 c	lxix. 20.	5 h	lxvi. 13, 13, 13.	5 g g i
l. 21.	5 g	lxxi. 21.β	5 g	Jer. viii. 18.γ	1 b
Judg. xix. 5, 8.	6	lxxvii. 2.	5 b	xvi. 7.	5 e
Ruth ii. 13.	5 d	lxxxvi. 17.	5 d	xxxi. 13.	5 a
2 Sam. x. 2.	5 e	xciv. 19.	5 r	xxxi. 15.	5 b
x. 3.	5 h	cxix. 50.	5 p	Lam. i. 2, 9, 16, 17, 21.	5 h
xii. 24.	5 g	cxix. 52.	5 n	ii. 13.	5 g
xiii. 39.	5 a	cxix. 76.	5 e	Ezek. v. 13.	5 l
xiv. 17.	4	cxix. 82.	5 g	xiv. 22.	5 a
xix. 7.	2	Eccles. iv. 1. 1.	5 h	xiv. 23.	5 d
1 Chron. vii. 22.	5 e	Cant. ii. 5.	7	xvi. 54.	5 e
2, 2.	5 e	Isa. xii. 1.	5 g	xxxii. 31.	5 a
xix. 3.	5 h	xxii. 4.	5 e	Hos. ii. 14.	2
2 Chron. xxx. 22.	2	xl. 1, 1.	5 f	Nah. iii. 7.	5 h
xxxii. 6.	3	xl. 2.	2	Zech. i. 13.	5 q
Job ii. 11.	5 e	xlix. 13.	5 d	i. 17.	5 d
vi. 10.a	5 p	li. 3, 3.	5 d	x. 2.	5 g
vii. 13.	5 g	li. 12.	5 h		
ix. 27.	1 a	li. 19.	5 g		
x. 20.	1 a				

α lit. my comfort yet would be me. β lit. and shall go about and comfort γ lit. my consolation.

COMMAND

1 אָמַר to speak, to say ; to command. KAL a pret. b fut. c part. Poel. אֹמֵר Ch. P'AL d pret. e part. f אִמְרָה f. word, speech. g מַאֲמַר m. an edict, a mandate.

2 דָּבַר to speak, &c. PIEL a pret. b דָּבָר m. word, precept.

3 דָּת f. an imperial law, &c., enforced by the highest and most absolute authority.

4 חֹק m. a statute, ordinance.

5 טַעַם Ch. m. will, command. a טְעֵם Ch. m. will, command, royal edict.

6 מִלָּה Ch. a word, a thing.

7 פֶּה mouth ; word, command, precept, order.

8 פִּקּוּדִים m. pl. mandates, precepts, sc. of God. a מִפְקָד m. appoint-ment, mandate.

9 צָוָה to set up, to put, to place ; to constitute, appoint ; to command, to charge ; absol. Ps. xxxiii. 9 ; seq. acc. of person ; more rarely עַל, אֶל, לְ; so with the express words of command after לֵאמֹר. Further, that which one commands to be done is put in the acc. with acc. of person, also with dat. of person, and the inf. with לְ. Where one is commanded not to do anything, i.e. where anything is forbidden, it is put with מִן seq. inf., or with לְבִלְתִּי seq. inf., in the fut. with אֲשֶׁר that, oftener with vav. With an acc. of person, without mention of the thing commanded, to give charge to any one, to send with commands, to command to go : the person to whom one is thus sent is put with אֶל עַל; the person or thing concerning which charge is given is put with עַל, אֶל, and לְ. PIEL a pret. b inf. c imp. d fut. e part. PUAL f pret. g fut. h מִצְוָה f. commandment : Gen. xxvi. 5, &c. i צַו m. precept.

10 שׂוּם Ch. to set. P'AL a pret. b part. pass.

No. 9 h, *Commandment*, not included.

Gen. ii. 16.	9 d	Num. xxviii. 2.	9 c	Ruth ii. 15.	9 d
iii. 11, 17.	9 a	xxix. 40.	9 a	1 Sam. ii. 29.	9 a
vi. 22.	9 a	xxx. 1, 16.	9 a	xii. 14, 15.	7
vii. 5, 9, 16.	9 a	xxxi. 7, 21, 31, 41, 47.	9 a	xiii. 13.	9 a
xii. 20.	9 d	xxxii. 25.	9 e	xiii. 14, 14.	9 d a
xviii. 19.	9 a	xxxii. 28.	9 d	xv. 11, 13.	2 b
xxi. 4.	9 a	xxxiii. 2, 38.	7	xv. 24.	7
xxvii. 8.	9 e	xxxiv. 2.	9 a	xvi. 16.	1 b
xxxii. 4, 17, 19.	9 d	xxxiv. 13, 13.	9 d	xvii. 20.	9 a
xlii. 25.	9 d	xxxiv. 29.	9 d	xviii. 22.	9 d
xliv. 1.	9 d	xxxv. 2.	9 a	xx. 29.	9 a
xlv. 19.	9 f	xxxvi. 2, 2.	9 a f	xxi. 2, 2.	9 a
xlv. 21.	7	xxxvi. 5.	9 a	2 Sam. iv. 12.	9 a
xlvii. 11.	9 a	xxxvi. 6, 10, 13.	9 a	v. 25.	9 a
xlix. 33.	9 b	Deut. i. 3, 19, 41.	9 a	vii. 7, 11.	9 a
l. 2.	9 a	i. 18.	9 d	ix. 11.	9 d
l. 12, 16.	9 a	i. 26, 43.	7	xii. 9.	2 b
Exod. i. 17.	2 a	ii. 4.	9 c	xiii. 28, 28.	9 d a
iv. 28.	9 a	iii. 18.	9 d	xiii. 29.	9 a
v. 6.	9 d	iii. 21.	9 a	xviii. 5.	9 d
vii. 2.	9 a	iv. 2, 2, 40.	9 a	xxi. 14.	9 d
vii. 6, 10, 20.	9 d	iv. 5, 14.	9 a	xxiv. 19.	9 a
viii. 27.	1 b	vi. 1, 17, 20, 25.	9 a	1 Kings ii. 46.	9 a
xii. 28, 50.	9 a	vi. 2, 24.	9 d	v. 6.	9 c
xvi. 16, 32, 34.	9 d	vii. 11.	9 a	v. 17.	9 d
xvii. 1.	7	viii. 1, 11.	9 a	viii. 58.	9 a
xviii. 23.	9 a	ix. 12, 16.	9 a	ix. 4.	2
xix. 7.	9 a	ix. 23.	9 d	xi. 10, 10, 11.	9 a
xxiii. 15.	9 a	x. 4.	9 a	xi. 38.	9 d
xxv. 22.	9 d	x. 5.	9 a	xiii. 21.	9 a
xxvii. 20.	9 e	xi. 8, 13, 22, 27, 28.	9 e	xv. 5.	9 a
xxix. 35.	9 a	xi. 14, 28, 32.	9 e	xvii. 4, 9.	9 a
xxxi. 6, 11.	9 a	xii. 21.	9 a	xviii. 31.	9 a
xxxiv. 4, 18.	9 a	xiii. 5.	9 a	2 Kings xi. 5, 15.	9 d
xxxiv. 11.	2 e	xiii. 18.	9 e	xi. 9.	9 a
xxxiv. 28.	9 e	xv. 5, 11, 15.	9 a	xiv. 6.	9 a
xxxiv. 32.	9 d	xviii. 18.	9 d	xvi. 15.	9 a
xxxiv. 34.	9 d	xviii. 20.	9 a	xvii. 13, 34.	9 d
xxxv. 1, 4, 10, 29.	9 g	xx. 7, 9.	9 a	xvii. 27.	9 d
xxxvi. 1, 5.	9 a	xxiv. 8.	9 e	xxi. 8, 8.	9 a
xxxvi. 6.	9 d	xxiv. 18, 22.	9 e	xxii. 12.	9 a
xxxvii. 21.	7	xxvi. 13, 14.	9 a	xxiii. 4, 21.	9 d
xxxviii. 22.	9 a	xxvi. 16.	9 a	xxiii. 35.	7
xxxix. 1, 5, 7, 21.	9 a	xxvii. 1, 1.	9 d e	xxiv. 3.	7
xxxix. 26, 29, 31, 32, 42, 43.	9 a	xxvii. 4, 10.	9 e	1 Chron. vi. 49.	9 a
xl. 16, 19, 21, 23, 25, 27, 29, 32.	9 a	xxvii. 11, 13, 14, 15.	9 e	vi. 12.	1 b
Lev. vi. 9.	9 c	xxviii. 8.	9 e	xiv. 16.	9 a
vii. 36.	9 a	xxviii. 45.	9 a	xv. 15.	9 a
vii. 38, 38.	9 a b	xxix. 1.	9 a	xvi. 15, 40.	9 a
viii. 4, 5, 9, 13, 17, 21, 29, 31, 34, 36.	9 a	xxx. 2, 8, 11, 16.	9 e	xvi. 6, 10.	9 a
viii. 35.	9 f	xxxi. 5, 29.	9 a	xxi. 17, 18.	1 a
ix. 5, 6, 7, 10, 21.	9 a	xxxi. 10, 25.	9 d	xxi. 27.	1 b
x. 1, 15, 18.	9 a	xxxii. 46.	9 d	xxii. 12.	9 d
x. 13.	9 f	xxxiii. 4.	9 a	xxii. 17.	9 d
xiii. 54.	9 a	Josh. i. 7, 9, 13, 16.	9 a	xxiv. 19.	9 a
xiv. 4, 5, 36, 40.	9 a	i. 10.	9 a	xxviii. 21.	2 b
xvi. 34.	9 a	i. 11.	9 c	2 Chron. vii. 13.	9 d
xvii. 2.	9 a	i. 18, 18.	7, 9 d	vii. 17.	9 a
xxiv. 2.	9 c	iii. 3, 8.	9 a	viii. 14.	9 h
xxiv. 23.	9 a	iv. 8, 10, 16.	9 a	xiv. 4.	1 b
xxv. 21.	9 a	iv. 17.	9 d	xviii. 30.	9 a
xxvii. 34.	9 a	vi. 10.	9 d	xxiii. 8.	9 a
Num. i. 19, 54.	9 a	vii. 11.	9 a	xxiv. 8.α	1 b
ii. 33, 34.	9 a	viii. 4.	9 d	xxv. 4.	9 a
iii. 16.	9 f	viii. 8, 8.	2 b, 9 a	xxix. 21, 27, 30.	9 a
iii. 39.	7	viii. 27, 29, 31, 33, 35.	9 a	xxix. 24.	1 a
iii. 42, 51.	9 a	ix. 24.	9 d	xxxi. 4, 11.	9 a
iv. 37, 41.	7	x. 27.α	9 d	xxxi. 5.	2 b
iv. 49, 49.	7, 9 a	xi. 12, 15, 15, 15, 20.	9 a	xxxii. 12.	8 a
v. 2.	9 c	xiii. 6.	9 a	xxxiii. 8.	1 b
viii. 3, 20, 22.	9 a	xiv. 2, 5.	9 a	xxxiii. 16.	9 a
ix. 5.	9 a	xv. 13.	7	xxxiv. 20.	9 d
ix. 8.	9 d	xvii. 4, 4.	9 a, 7	xxxv. 21.	9 a
ix. 18, 18, 20, 20, 23, 23, 23.	7	xxi. 2, 8.	9 a	Ezra iv. 3.	9 a
x. 13.	7	xxi. 3.	7	iv. 19.	5 a, 10 b
xiii. 3.	9 a	xxii. 2, 2.	9 a	iv. 21, 21.	5 a, 5
xiv. 10.	9 a	xxii. 9.	9 a	v. 3.β	10 a, 5 a
xv. 23, 23, 36.	9 a	Judg. ii. 20.	9 a	v. 9.β	10 a, 5 a
xvi. 47.	2 a	iii. 4.	9 a	vi. 14, 14.	5, 5 a
xvii. 11.	9 a	iv. 6.	9 a	vii. 23.	5 a
xix. 2.	9 a	xiii. 14.	9 a	viii. 17.	9 d
xx. 9, 27.	9 a	xxi. 10, 20.	9 d	ix. 11.	9 d
xxiv. 13.	7			Neh. i. 7, 8.	9 a
xxvi. 4.	9 a			viii. 1, 14.	9 a
xxvii. 11, 22.	9 a			ix. 14.	9 a
xxvii. 14.	7			xiii. 5.	9 a
xxvii. 23.	2 a			xiii. 9, 19, 22.	1 b
				Esth. i. 10, 17.	1 a

Esth. i. 12, 19.	2 b	Ps. cv. 8.	9 a	Jer. xxxvi. 5, 26.	9 d
i. 15.	1 g	cvi. 34.	1 b	xxxvi. 8.	9 d
ii. 8.	2 b	cvii. 25.	1 b	xxxvii. 21.	9 d
ii. 20.	1 g	cxi. 7.	8	xxxviii. 10.	9 a
iii. 2, 12.	9 a	cxi. 9.	9 a	xxxviii. 27.	9 a
iii. 14.	3	cxix. 4, 138.	9 a	l. 21.	9 a
iii. 15.	2 b	cxxxiii. 3.	9 a	li. 59.	9 a
iv. 3.	2 b	cxlvii. 15.	1 f	Lam. i. 10, 17.	9 a
iv. 5, 10.	9 d	cxlviii. 5.	9 a	i. 18.	7
iv. 13.	1 b	Prov. viii. 29.	7	ii. 17.	9 a
iv. 17.	9 a	Eccles. viii. 2.	7	iii. 37.	9 a
vi. 1.	1 b	Isa. v. 6.	9 d	Ezek. ix. 11.	9 a
viii. 9.	9 a	xiii. 3.	9 a	x. 6.	9 b
viii. 13.	3	xxiii. 11.	9 a	xii. 7.	9 f
viii. 14, 17.	2 b	xxxiv. 16.	9 a	xxiv. 18.	9 f
ix. 1.	2 b	xlv. 11.	9 a	xxxvii. 7.	9 f
ix. 14.	1 b	xlv. 12.	9 a	xxxvii. 10.	9 a
ix. 25.	1 a	xlviii. 5.	9 a	Dan. ii. 12, 46.	1 b
Job ix. 7.	1 c	lv. 4.	9 e	iii. 4, 19.	1 e
xxxvi. 32.	1 b	Jer. i. 7, 17.	9 d	iii. 13, 20.	1 d
xxxvii. 12.	9 d	vii. 22, 31.	9 a	iii. 22.	6
xxxviii. 12.	9 d	vii. 23, 23.	9 a d	iv. 26.	1 d
xxxix. 27.	7	xi. 4, 4.	9 a d	v. 2, 29.	1 d
xlii. 9.	2 a	xi. 8.	9	vi. 16, 23, 24.	1 d
Ps. vii. 6.	9 a	xiii. 5, 6.	9 a	ix. 23, 25.	2 b
xxxiii. 9.	9 a	xiv. 14.	9 a	Hos. v. 11.	9 i
xlii. 8.	9 d	xvii. 22.	9 a	Amos ii. 4.	4
xliv. 4.	9 c	xix. 5.	9 a	ii. 12.	9 e
lxviii. 28.	9 a	xxiii. 32.	9 a	vi. 11.	9 e
lxxi. 3.	9 a	xxvi. 2, 8.	9 a	ix. 3, 4.	9 d
lxxviii. 5.	9 a	xxvii. 4.	9 a	ix. 9.	9 e
lxxviii. 23.	9 d	xxix. 23.	9 a	Nah. i. 14.	9 a
ciii. 18.	8	xxxi. 23, 35.	9 a	Zech. i. 6.	9 a
ciii. 20.	2 b	xxxiv. 22.	9 a	Mal. ii. 4.	9 a
		xxxv. 6,10,14,16,18.	9 a		

a lit. and the king said, and they made.   *β lit.* hath set a decree.

COMMEND

הָלַל to praise. PIEL *fut.* Gen. xii. 15. PUAL *fut.* Prov. xii. 8.

שָׁבַח to soothe; to praise; to pronounce happy. PIEL *pret.* Eccles. viii. 15.

COMMISSION

דָּת *f.* an imperial law: Ezra viii. 36.

COMMIT

1   גָּלַל to roll, to devolve one's self, way, &c. upon God. KAL *imp.*

2   הָיָה to be, to exist, to be one. KAL a *fut.* NIPHAL b *pret.*

3   זָנָה to commit fornication, &c.: see *Fornication,* &c. KAL *fut.*

4   חָטָא to sin. KAL *pret.*

5   מָסַר to deliver; to give occasion to; Gesenius, to separate, to separate oneself, to fall away treacherously. KAL *inf.* Num. xxxi. 16. See *Deliver.* Fürst renders this passage, "Tradendo prevaricationem in manus Jehovæ, h.e. ut a Deo vivo desciscerent." Others, to dare a defection from the Lord.

6   מָעַל see *Trespass.*

7   נָתַן to give. KAL a *pret.* b *fut.* NIPHAL c *pret.*

8   עָזַב to leave; to commit to another. KAL *fut.*

9   עָשָׂה to labour in anything. KAL a *pret.* b *inf.* c *fut.* d *part.* Poel. NIPHAL e *pret.*

10   פָּעַל to make, to do, in an emphatic sense. KAL *pret.*

11   פָּקַד to visit; to give in charge, to commit. HIPHIL a *pret.* b *fut.*

12   שׂוּם to set, put, place. KAL *fut.*

Gen. xxxix. 8.	7 a	Lev. xviii. 26.	9 c	Num. xxxi. 16.	5
xxxix. 22.	7 b	xviii. 29, 29.	9 c d	Deut. xvii. 5.	9 a
Lev. iv. 35.	4	xx. 30, 30.	9 b e	xix. 20. α	9 b
v. 7.	4	xx. 13, 23.	9 a	xxi. 22. β	2 a
v. 15.	6 c	Num. v. 6.	9 c	Josh. vii. l.	6 c
v. 17.	9 a	v. 12.	6 a	xxii. 16, 20, 31.	9 a
vi. 2.	6 a	xv. 24.	9 e	Judg. xx. 6.	9 a

1 Kings xiv. 22.	4	Jer. xvi. 10.	4	Ezek. xviii. 12, 21, 22, 24, 26, 27, 28.	9 a
xiv. 27.	11 a	xxix. 23.	9 a	xx. 27.	6 b
1 Chron. x. 13.	6 a	xxxvii. 21.	11 b	xx. 43.	9 a
2 Chron. xii. 10.	11 a	xxxix. 14.	7 b	xxii. 9, 11.	9 a
xxxiv. 16.	7 c	xl. 7.	11 a	xxiii. 7.	7 b
Job v. 8.	12	xli. 10.	11 a	xxiii. 43.	3
Ps. x. 14.	8	xliv. 3, 9, 22.	9 a	xxxiii. 13, 13, 18, 29.	9 d
xxxi. 5.	11 b	xliv. 7.	9 d	xxxiii. 15.	9 b
xxxvii. 5.	1	Ezek. iii. 20.	9 a	xxxiii. 16.	4
Prov. xvi. 3.	1	vi. 9.	9 a	xliii. 8.	9 a
xvi. 12.	9 b	viii. 6.	9 a	xliv. 13.	9 a
Isa. xxii. 21.	7 b	viii. 17, 17.	9 b a	Hos. vi. 9.	9 a
Jer. ii. 13.	9 a	xv. 8.	6 a	vii. 1.	10
v. 30.	2 b	xvi. 43.	9 a	Mal. ii. 11.	9 e
vi. 15.	9 a	xvi. 50.	9 c		
viii. 11.	9 a	xvi. 51.	4		

a lit. shall not add to commit.   *β lit.* if there be in man a sin.

COMMON

אָדָם *m.* man: Ezek. xxiii. 42, "of the common sort," *marg.* 'of the multitude of men.'

אֶרֶץ *com.* the land, earth: Lev. iv. 27, *marg.* 'people of the land.'

בֵּן *m.* son: Jer. xxvi. 23; *marg.* 'sons of the people.'

הָלַל (see *Profane,* and *Gather*), to eat as common. PIEL *pret.* Jer. xxxi. 5, *marg.* 'profane.' חֹל *adj.* profane, unholy, common: 1 Sam. xxi. 4, 5.

מוּת *m.* death: Num. xvi. 29, *marg.* 'as every man dieth.'

רֹב *m.* multitude: Ezek. xxiii. 42. רַב *adj.* many. Eccles. vi. 1.

COMMOTION

רַעַשׁ *m.* a trembling, shaking; tumult, noise, as of battle: Jer. x. 22.

COMMUNE, COMMUNICATION

1   אָמַר to say, speak. KAL *imp.*

2   דָּבַר see *Speak.* In Exod. xxv. 22 there is an evident allusion to the oracle of the mercyseat, called דְּבִיר, or speaking-place. KAL a *part.* Poel. PIEL b *pret.* c *inf.* d *imp.* e *fut.* דָּבָר f *m.* word.

3   סָפַר to number, to tell, to relate, to declare. PIEL *fut.*

4   שִׂיחַ to speak, talk, converse; to talk with oneself, to meditate. KAL a *fut.* b שִׂיחַ *m.* speech, discourse.

Gen. xviii. 33.	2 c	1 Sam. ix. 25.	2 e	2 Chron. ix. 1.	2 e
xxiii. 8.	2 e	xviii. 22.	2 d	Job iv. 2.	2 f
xxxiv. 6.	2 c	xix. 3.	2 e	Ps. iv. 4.	1
xxxiv. 8, 20.	2 e	xxv. 39.	2 e	iv. 5.	3
xlii. 24.	2 e	2 Sam. iii. 17.	2 f	lxxvii. 6.	4 a
xliii. 19.	2 e	1 Kings ix. 2.	2 e	Eccles. i. 16.	2 b
Exod. xxv. 22.	2 b	2 Kings ix. 11.	4 b	Dan. i. 19.	2 e
xxxi. 18.	2 e	xxii. 14.	2 e	Zech. i. 14.	2 a
Judg. ix. 1.	2 e				

COMPACT

חָבַר to join or couple together. PUAL *pret.* Ps. cxxii. 3.

COMPANY, COMPANION

1   אֹרַח to travel. KAL *part.* Poel, a caravan, or company of travellers, especially of merchants.

2   בַּת *f.* a daughter; daughter of a city, or region, or people, "company of the Assyrians:" Ezek. xxvii. 6. The margin, on the authority of Buxtorf probably, gives the rendering 'well trodden:' *Heb.* the daughter of goings, of ivory that has been long under the earth, and thought to have been improved by this; at least much ivory in former times was so found. The whole

marginal rendering stands thus : 'They have made thy hatches of ivory well trodden ;' hatches, or deck, being supposed more appropriate in this view of the meaning of the passage.

3 גְּדוּד *m.* see *Troop.*

4 הֲלִיכָה *f.* goings, progress ; ways ; companies of travellers, caravans.

5 הָמוֹן see *Multitude, Tumult.*

6 זָעַק to cry, to gather. NIPHAL *pret.*

7 חֶבֶל *com.* a cord, &c. ; a company of men bound together in a society, or walking in a train ; so a company of soldiers is called σπεῖρα : Matt. xxvii. 27.

8 חָבֵר *m.* associate, companion. [b] חָבֵר *adj.* companion. [c] חֶבֶר Ch. *m. id.* [d] חֶבֶר *m.* company. [e] חֶבְרָה *f.* company. [f] חֲבֶרֶת *f.* companion.

9 חַי *adj.* a living creature, beast, &c. ; *collect.*, a band of men, troop : Ps. lxviii. 30, "the company of spearmen," *marg.* 'the beasts of the reeds ;' Jer. li. 32 ; some wild animals dwelling among reeds ; crocodile, lion, boar, &c.

10 חַיִל *m.* host.

11 מְחוֹלָה *f.* dance ; a company, showing public exultation or joy, with dancing.

12 מַחֲלֹקֶת *f.* divisions, courses ; companies by course.

13 מַחֲנֶה *com.* an army, a host ; any company of men.

14 תּוֹדָה *f.* thanksgiving ; choir of singers ; rendered *company of them who give " thanks."*

15 כְּנָת *m.* fellow labourers, colleagues. כְּנָת Ch. *m. id.*

16 לַהֲקָה *f.* assembly ; only in 1 Sam. xix. 20, probably *i. q.* קַהֲלָה so the Lxx. Syr. Arab. Chald.

17 סוּסָה *f.* a company of horses.

18 עֵדָה *f.* see *Congregation.* Job xvi. 7, *i. e.* family, or those congregated about his tent.

19 צָבָא *m.* host, army.

20 מִצְעָר *m.* anything small, a small company.

21 קִבֻּץ *m.* a gathering, throng.

22 קָהָל *m.* see *Congregation.* Gen. xxxv. 11, *Gr.* synagogues ; Ch. a congregation of tribes.

23 רֹאשׁ *m.* head ; sum, amount ; a body, band, company, especially of soldiers.

24 רֶגֶשׁ *m. pr.* a noisy crowd ; hence, generally, a crowd, company.

25 רָעָה to associate together. KAL [a] *part.* Poel. [b] רֵעַ *m.* a friend, companion, acquaintance. [c] רֵעָה *f.* companion. [d] מֵרֵעַ *m.* a friend, companion.

26 שִׁפְעָה *f.* abundance, multitude, of men, camels.

Gen. xxxii. 8, 8, 21.	13	Judg. xi. 38.	25 c	1 Chron. ix. 18.	13	
xxxv. 11.	22	xiv. 11, 20.	25 d	xxvii. 33.	25 b	
xxxvii. 25.	1	xv. 2, 6.	25 d	xxxviii. 1.	12	
l. 9.	13	xviii. 23.	6	2 Chron. ix. 1.	10	
Exod. xxxii. 27.	25 b	1 Sam. x. 5, 10.	7	xx. 12.	5	
Num. xiv. 7.	18	xi. 11.	23	xxiv. 24.	20	
xvi. 5, 6, 11, 16, 40.	18	xiii. 17, 17, 18, 18.	23	Ezra iv. 7.	15	
xxii. 4.	18	xix. 20.	16	iv. 9, 17, 23.	15	
xxvi. 9, 10.	18	xxx. 15, 15, 23.	3	v. 3, 6.	15	
xxvii. 3, 3.	18	2 Kings v. 2.	3	vi. 6, 13.	15	
Judg. vii. 16, 20.	23	v. 15.	13	Neh. xii. 31, 38, 40	14	
ix. 34, 37, 43, 44, 44.	23	ix. 17, 17.	26	Job vi. 19.	4	

Job xvi. 7.	18	Prov. xiii. 20.	25 a	Ezek. xvi. 40.	22		
xxx. 29.	25 b	xxviii. 7.	25 a	xvii. 17.	22		
xxxiv. 8.	8 e	xxviii. 24.	8 b	xxiii. 46, 47.	22		
xxxv. 4.	25 b	xxix. 3.	25 a	xxvi. 7.	22		
xli. 6.	8 a	Cant. i. 7.	8 b	xxvii. 6.	2		
Ps. xlv. 14.	25 c	i. 9.	17	xxvii. 27, 34.	22		
lv. 14.	24	vi. 13.	11	xxxii. 3, 22, 23.	22		
lxviii. 11.	19	viii. 13.	8 b	xxxvii. 16, 16.	8 b		
lxviii. 30.	9	Isa. i. 23.	8 b	xxxviii. 4, 7, 13, 15.	22		
cvi. 17, 18.	18	xxi. 13.	1	Dan. ii. 17.	8 c		
cxix. 63.	8 b	viii. 13.	21	Hos. vi. 9.	8 d		
cxxii. 8.	25 b	Jer. xxxi. 8.	22	Mal. ii. 14.	8 f		

COMPARABLE

סְלָא to weigh. PUAL *part.* Lam. iv. 2.

COMPARE

דָּמָה to be like. PIEL *pret.* Cant. i. 9.

מָשַׁל to compare ; to use a proverb. HIPHIL *fut.* Isa. xlvi. 5.

עָרַךְ to lay in order ; *seq.* לְ to place together with anything alongside of it, to compare. KAL *fut.* Ps. lxxxix. 6 : Isa. xl. 18.

שָׁוָה to be equal ; to be like, to resemble ; *seq.* לְ. KAL *fut.* Prov. iii. 15 ; viii. 11.

COMPASS

1 אָזַר to gird ; to be armed. PIEL *part.*

2 אָפַף to compass about, to attack with violence and terror. KAL *pret.*

3 זָרָה to disperse, to fan ; hence to sift or search ; or from זֵר a crown or border around the ark ; to gird round, as God compasseth all things by his omniscience. PIEL *pret.*

4 חוּג to draw a circle, to measure with a compass. KAL [a] *pret.* [b] חוּג *m.* circuit. [c] מְחוּגָה *f.* a compass.

5 כַּרְכֹּב *m.* the margin round the altar above the grating, upon which the priests could walk in attending upon it.

6 כָּתַר to compass about, as a crown compasseth the head. HIPHIL [a] *fut.* [b] *part.*

7 נָקַף to go round, to make a circle ; to surround. HIPHIL [a] *pret.* [b] *fut.* [c] *part.*

8 סָבַב to turn about, to compass about, to besiege ; to go about, to fetch a compass ; to beset, to compass about in a distressing manner ; to attend upon diligently and frequently, Ps. xxvi. 6. To compass about with songs of deliverance, *dupl. acc.* Ps. xxxii. 7, is to afford complete joy, without any mixture of sorrow : in Jer. xxxi. 22, "A woman shall compass a man," is a prophecy of the birth of the Messiah from a virgin. KAL [a] *pret.* [b] *inf.* [c] *imp.* [d] *fut.* [e] *part.* Poel. NIPHAL [f] *pret.* POEL [g] *fut.* HIPHIL [h] *imp.* [i] *fut.* [k] סָבִיב *m.* round about. [l] מֵסַב *m.* circle ; Gesenius, couches set in a circle, a divan ; or the word, in Ps. cxl. 9, may be taken as HIPHIL *part.* of סָבַב.

9 עָטַר to crown ; to encompass. KAL [a] *fut.* [b] *part.* Poel.

10 עָנַק to adorn with a neckchain or collar. KAL *pret.*

Gen. ii. 11, 13.	8 e	Deut. ii. 1.	8 d	Josh. vi. 15, 15.	8 d a
xix. 4.	8 f	ii. 3.	8 b	xv. 3, 10.	8 f
Exod. xxvii. 5.	5	Josh. vi. 3.	8 a	xviii. 14.	8 f
xxxviii. 4.	5	vi. 4, 14.	8 d	xix. 14.	8 f
Num. xxi. 4.	8 b	vi. 7.	8 c	Judg. xi. 18.	8 f
xxiv. 5.	8 f	vi. 11.	8 i	xvi. 2.	8 d

1 Sam. xxiii. 26.	9 b	2 Chron. xxxiii. 14.	8 a	Ps. cix. 3.	8 a	
2 Sam. v. 23.	8 h	Job xvi. 13.	8 d	cxvi. 3.		2
xviii. 15.	8 d	xix. 6.	7 a	cxviii. 10, 11, 11,		
xxii. 5.	2	xxvi. 10.	4 a	12.	8 a	
xxii. 6.	8 a	xl. 12.	8 d	cxxxix. 3.	3	
1 Kings vii. 15, 23.	8 d	Ps. v. 12.	9 a	cxl. 9.	8 l	
vii. 24, 24.	8 e, 7 c	vii. 7.	8 g	cxlii. 7.	6 a	
vii. 35.	8 k	xvii. 9.	7 b	Prov. viii. 27.	4 b	
2 Kings iii. θ.	8 d	xviii. 4.	8 a	Isa. xliv. 13.	4 c	
vi. 14.	7 b	xviii. 5.	2	l. 11.	1	
vi. 15.	8 e	xviii. 15.	8 a	Jer. xxxi. 22.	8 g	
viii. 21.	8 e	xxii. 12, 16.	8 a	xxxi. 39.	8 f	
xi. 8.	7 a	xxvi. 6.	8 g	lii. 21.	8 d	
2 Chron. iv. 2, 2.	8 k d	xxxii. 7, 10.	8 g	Lam. iii. 5.	7 b	
iv. 3, 3.	8 e, 7 c	xl. 12.	2	Hos. xi. 12.	8 a	
xviii. 31. α	8 d	xlix. 5.	8 d	Jonah ii. 3.	8 a	
xxi. 9.	8 e	lxxiii. 6.	10	ii. 5.	8 g	
xxiii. 7.	7 a	lxxxviii. 17.	7 a	Hab. i. 4.	6 b	

a or, compassed against him.

COMPASSION

1   חָמַל   to be mild and gentle ; to treat with tenderness ; to have compassion. See *Spare*. KAL [a] *pret.* [b] *inf.* [c] *fut.*

2   רָחַם   to be tender ; to have mercy, compassion upon any one ; to pity, from an idea of fondness, cherishing : strictly of compassion towards the needy and helpless, as widows, infants ; also of parents towards their infant children ; especially of God pitying his afflicted people. PIEL [a] *pret.* [b] *inf.* [c] *fut.* [d] רַחוּם *adj.* merciful, only used of God ; "full of compassion." [e] רַחֲמִים *m. pl.* very tender affection, pity, grace, favour.

Exod. ii. 6.	1 c	2 Chron. xxxvi. 15, 17.	1 a	Jer. xii. 15.	2 a
Deut. xiii. 17.	2 a	Ps. lxxvii. 38.	2 d	Lam. iii. 22.	2 e
xxx. 3.	2 a	lxxxvi. 15.		iii. 32.	2 a
1 Sam. xxiii. 21.	1 a	cxi. 4.	2 d	Ezek. xvi. 5.	1 b
1 Kings viii. 50, 50.	2 e a	cxii. 4.	2 d	Micah vii. 19.	2 c
2 Kings xiii. 23.	2 c	cxlv. 8.	2 d	Zech. vii. 9.	2 e
2 Chron. xxx. 9.	2 e	Isa. xlix. 15.	2 d		

COMPEL

אָנַס   to press, constrain, compel. KAL *part.* Poel, Esth. i. 8.

נָדַח   to push, thrust, force. HIPHIL *fut.* 2 Chron. xxi. 11.

עָבַד   to serve. KAL *fut.* Lev. xxv. 39, *lit.* thou shalt not make him to serve the service of a bond servant.

פָּרַץ   to break ; to break forth upon, to urge. KAL *fut.* 1 Sam. xxviii. 23.

COMPLAIN

אָנַן   to groan, murmur, complain. HITHPAEL *fut.* Lam. iii. 39, *marg.* 'murmur.' *part.* Num. xi. 1.

בָּכָה   to weep. KAL *fut.* Job xxxi. 38.

צְוָחָה   *f.* outcry, of lamentation. See *Cry.* Ps. cxliv. 14.

רִיב   to contend, to strive ; to plead. KAL *inf.* Judg. xxi. 22.

שִׂיחַ   to speak, discourse ; to meditate, to lament. KAL *fut.* Job vii. 11 : Ps. lxxvii. 3. שִׂיחַ *m.* the inward or outward expression of sorrow, on which the mind enlarges : 1 Sam. i. 16 : Job vii. 13 ; ix. 27 ; x. 1 ; xxi. 4 ; xxiii. 2 : Ps. lv. 2 ; cii. title ; cxlii. 2.

COMPLETE

תָּמִים   *adj.* perfect : Lev. xxiii. 15.

COMPOUND, COMPOSITION

מַתְכֹּנֶת   *f.* measure : Exod. xxx. 32, 37, *i. e.* according to the proportion of the parts of which it is composed.

רָקַח   to season, to spice, *e. g.* oil for making ointments ; to perfume. KAL *fut.* Exod. xxx. 33.

מִרְקַחַת   *f.* compounding of ointment : Exod. xxx. 25, *lit.* an ointment of compounding.

COMPREHEND

יָדַע   to know. KAL *fut.* Job xxxvii. 5.

כּוּל   to hold or keep together. KAL *pret.* Isa. xl. 12.

CONCEAL

חָרַשׁ   to keep silence. HIPHIL *fut.* Job xli. 12.

כָּחַד   to hide ; to conceal from sight and from hearing. PIEL *pret.* Job vi. 10 : Ps. xl. 10. *fut.* Job xxvii. 11 : Jer. l. 2.

כָּסָה   to cover. KAL *part.* Poel, Prov. xii. 23. PIEL *pret.* Gen. xxxvii. 26. *fut.* Deut. xiii. 8. *part.* Prov. xi. 13.

סָתַר   to hide, to cover from the sight. HIPHIL *inf.* Prov. xxv. 2.

CONCEIT

עַיִן   *com.* the eye : Prov. xxvi. 5 (*marg.* 'his own eyes'), 12, 16 ; xxviii. 11.

מַשְׂכִּית   *f.* image, figure ; imagination, idea, thought : Prov. xviii. 11.

CONCEIVE

1   הָרָה   to conceive in the womb ; figuratively, to form designs and counsels in the mind. KAL [a] *pret.* [b] *inf.* [c] *fut.* [d] *part.* Poel. PUAL [e] *pret.* POEL [f] *inf.* [g] הָרֶה *adj.* pregnant, with child. The import of the sign in Isa. vii. 14 lies in the use of this word, and in its being the *part.* of 'bear :' behold a virgin pregnant and bearing. This is the sign ; and the future fulfilment is denoted by "shall give." [h] הֵרוֹן *m.* conception. [i] הֵרָיוֹן *m. id.*

2   זָרַע   to sow seed ; to be sown, to conceive. NIPHAL [a] *pret.* HIPHIL [b] *fut.*

3   חָשַׁב   to devise. KAL *pret.*

4   יָחַם   to be in heat ; *coire.* KAL [a] *fut.* PIEL [b] *pret.* [c] *inf.*

5   יָסַף   to add. HIPHIL *fut.*

Gen. iii. 16.	1 h	Exod. ii. 2.	1 c	Job xv. 35. β	1 b		
iv. 1, 17.	1 c	Lev. xii. 2.	2 b	Ps. vii. 14.	1 a		
xvi. 4, 4.	1 c a	Num. v. 28.	2 a	li. 5.	4 b		
xvi. 5.	1 a	xi. 12.	1 a	Cant. iii. 4.	1 d		
xxi. 2.	1 c	Judg. xiii. 3.	1 a	Isa. vii. 14.	1 g		
xxv. 21.	1 c	xiii. 5, 7.	1 g	viii. 3.	1 c		
xxix. 32, 33, 34, 35.	1 c	Ruth iv. 13.	1 i	xxxiii. 11.	1 c		
xxx. 38, 39.	4 a	ii. 21.	1 c	lix. 4.	1 b		
xxx. 5, 7, 17, 19, 23.	1 c	1 Sam. i. 20.	1 c	lix. 13.	1 f		
xxx. 41, 41.	4 c	2 Sam. xi. 5.	1 c	Jer. xlix. 30.	3		
xxxi. 10.	4 c	2 Kings iv. 17.	1 c	Hos. i. 3, 6, 8.	1 c		
xxxviii. 3, 4, 18.	1 c	1 Chron. vii. 23.	1 c	ii. 5.	1 d		
xxxviii. 5. α	1 c	Job iii. 3.	1 e	ix. 11.	1 i		

a lit. and she added yet and bare.   β *lit.* to conceive ; implying continued action.

CONCLUSION

סוֹף   *m.* end : Eccles. xii. 13.

CONCOURSE

הָמָה   to make a great noise ; applied to a tumultuous concourse of people. KAL *part.* Poel, Prov. i. 21.

CONCUBINE

אִשָּׁה   *f.* a woman, a wife : Judg. xix. 1.

לְחֵנָה   Ch. *f.* a concubine : Dan. v. 2, 3, 23.

פִּילֶגֶשׁ   *com.* a concubine without the authority and dignity of a

wife ; spoken commonly of a female slave, who was also usually a legal concubine : Gen. xxii. 24 ; xxxv. 22 : Judg. xix. 2, &c. Fully אִשָּׁה פִילֶגֶשׁ, Judg. xix. 1 : 2 Sam. xv. 16 ; xx. 3. Opp. to wives of higher rank : 1 Kings xi. 3 : Cant. vi. 8, 9.

CONDEMN

1 יָצָא to go out. KAL *fut.*

2 עָנַשׁ to amerce. KAL ᵃ *fut.* ᵇ *part.* Paül.

3 רָשַׁע to be wicked, guilty ; to pronounce guilty. HIPHIL ᵃ *pret.* ᵇ *inf.* ᶜ *fut.* ᵈ *part.* ᵉ רָשָׁע *adj.* wicked.

4 שָׁפַט to judge. KAL *part.* Poel.

Exod. xxii. 9.	3 c	Job xxxii. 3.	3 c	Ps. cix. 31.	4
Deut. xxv. 1.	3 a	xxxiv. 17.	3 c	Prov. xii. 2.	3 c
1 Kings viii. 32.	3 b	xl. 8.	3 c	xvii. 15.	3 d
2 Chron. xxxvi. 3.	2 a	Ps. xxxvii. 33.	3 c	Isa. l. 9.	3 c
Job ix. 20.	3 c	xciv. 21.	3 c	liv. 17.	3 c
x. 2.	3 c	cix. 7.	1, 3 e	Amos ii. 8.	2 b
xv. 6.	3 c				

CONDUCT

עָבַר to pass, to cause to pass. HIPHIL *pret.* 2 Sam. xix. 40. *inf.* 2 Sam. xix. 15. *fut.* 2 Sam. xix. 40 כ׳.

שָׁלַח to send. PIEL *inf.* 2 Sam. xix. 31.

CONDUIT

תְּעָלָה *f.* trench; watercourse, channel for conducting water : 2 Kings xviii. 17; xx. 20 : Isa. vii. 3 ; xxxvi. 2.

CONEY

שָׁפָן *m.* a quadruped, chewing the cud in the manner of the hare, living in flocks, and distinguished for its cunning : Lev. xi. 5 : Deut. xiv. 7 : Ps. civ. 18 : Prov. xxx. 26.

CONFECTION

רֹקַח *m.* ointment, perfume : Exod. xxx. 35. רַקָּחָה *f.* ointment-maker, perfumer : 1 Sam. viii. 13.

CONFEDERATE

בַּעַל *m.* owner, master : Gen. xiv. 13.

בְּרִית *f.* a covenant : Gen. xiv. 13, *lit.* masters of a covenant, *i. e.* allies or sworn friends : Ps. lxxxiii. 5 : Obad. 7.

כָּרַת to cut off, to make (a covenant). KAL *fut.* Ps. lxxxiii. 5, *lit.* they have made a covenant.

נוּחַ to rest on, *seq.* עַל. KAL *pret.* Isa. vii. 2.

קֶשֶׁר *m.* conspiracy : Isa. viii. 12, 12.

CONFER

דָּבָר *m.* a word : 1 Kings i. 7, *lit.* his words were with.

CONFESS

יָדָה to own, acknowledge, confess ; to praise ; to make confession by holding out or extending the hand. HIPHIL ᵃ *pret.* ᵇ *fut.* ᶜ *part.* HITHPAEL ᵈ *pret.* ᵉ *inf.* ᶠ *fut.* ᵍ *part.* ʰ תּוֹדָה *f.* confession, thanksgiving.

Lev. v. 5.	d	2 Chron. vi. 24, 26.	a	Neh. ix. 3.		
xvi. 21.	d	xxx. 22.	g	Job xl. 14.	b	
xxvi. 40.	d	Ezra x. 1.	e	Ps. xxxii. 5.	b	
Num. v. 7.	a	x. 11.	h	Prov. xxviii. 13.	c	
Josh. vii. 19.	h	Neh. i. 6.	g	Dan. ix. 4.	c	
1 Kings viii. 33, 35.	g	ix. 2.	f	ix. 20.	g	

CONFIDENCE

1 בָּטַח to trust, to confide in ; *abs.* to be confident, *i. e.* to be secure, without fear. KAL ᵃ *inf.* ᵇ *fut.* ᶜ *part.* Poel. ᵈ בֶּטַח *m.* confidence. ᵉ בִּטְחָה *f. id.* ᶠ בִּטָּחוֹן *m. id.* ᵍ מִבְטָח *m. id.*

2 כֶּסֶל *m.* hope, confidence, what a man depends on, as the loins are the strength and firmness of the body. ᵃ כִּסְלָה *f.* confidence, hope.

Judg. ix. 26.	1 b	Ps. cxviii. 8, 9.	1 a	Isa. xxxvi. 4.	1 f		
2 Kings xviii. 19.	1 f	Prov. iii. 26.	2	Jer. ii. 37.	1 g		
Job iv. 6.	2 a	xiv. 16.	1 c	xlviii. 13.	1 g		
xviii. 14.	1 g	xiv. 26.	1 g	Ezek. xxviii. 26.	1 d		
xxxi. 24.	1 g	xxi. 22.	1 g	xxix. 16.	1 g		
Ps. xxvii. 3.	1 c	xxv. 19.	1 g	Micah vii. 5.	1 b		
lxv. 5.	1 g	Isa. xxx. 15.	1 e				

CONFIRM

1 אָמֵץ to be strong. PIEL *imp.*

2 גָּבַר to be strong ; to make firm. HIPHIL *pret.*

3 חָזַק to be strong in a prevailing degree, by soundness and cohesion of every part, so as to be firm and compact : opp. to רָפָה, Isa. xxxv. 3 : Job xxvii. 6 : Prov. iv. 13 : and חָלָה, Isa. xxxix. 1, &c. It is said, Judg. i. 28, "Israel was strong," *i. e.* after they had increased so as to fill the land, being at first scattered and dispersed through it. A kingdom is confirmed by the union of mind and strength, 2 Kings xiv. 5. KAL ᵃ *pret.* HIPHIL ᵇ *inf.* ᶜ *part.*

4 כּוּן to establish. POLEL ᵃ *pret.* ᵇ *fut.* HIPHIL ᶜ *pret.*

5 מָלֵא to fill. PIEL *pret.* 1 Kings i. 14.

6 עָמַד to stand ; to make to stand. HIPHIL *fut.*

7 קוּם to stand upright ; to establish. PIEL ᵃ *pret.* ᵇ *inf.* HIPHIL ᶜ *pret.* ᵈ *fut.* ᵉ *part.*

Num. xxx. 14.	7 c	1 Chron. xiv. 2.	4 c	Isa. xxxv. 3.	1	
Deut. xxvii. 26.	7 d	xvi. 17.	6	xliv. 26.	7 e	
Ruth iv. 7.	7 b	Esth. ix. 29, 31.	7 b	Ezek. xiii. 6.	7 e	
2 Sam. vii. 24.	4 b	ix. 32.	7 a	Dan. xi. 12.	7 d	
1 Kings i. 14.	5	Ps. lxviii. 9. a	4 a	ix. 27.	2	
2 Kings xiv. 5.	3 a	cv. 10.	6	xi. 1.	3 c	
xv. 19.	3 b					

ᵃ *lit.* confirm it.

CONFISCATION

עֲנַשׁ Ch. *m.* fine, mulct : Ezra vii. 26.

CONFOUND, CONFUSION, CONFUSED

1 בּוּשׁ see *Ashamed.* KAL ᵃ *pret.* ᵇ *imp.* ᶜ *fut.* ᵈ בֹּשֶׁת *f.* shame.

2 בָּלַל seems to combine all the meanings included in *affusio, perfusio,* and *confusio,* and so to mix things together that the substance of each remains, and so to confound by such mixture ; to confound language by its pronunciation, or rather by the introduction of strange words, miraculously caused. Thus we may deduce the probability that the original language, the Hebrew, remained unchanged with some : *comp.* Latin, *balbus, balbutio ;* and *Gr.* βάρβαρος for βάλβαλος. KAL ᵃ *pret.* ᵇ *fut.* ᶜ תֶּבֶל *m.* foul pollution.

3 חָפֵר (see *Ashamed*), to bring to confusion. KAL ᵃ *pret.* ᵇ *fut.*

4 חָתַת to be broken to pieces, to be dismayed. HIPHIL, to break to pieces, *fut.*

5 יָבֵשׁ see *Ashamed.* HIPHIL *pret.*

6   כָּלַם see *Ashamed*. NIPHAL [a] *pret.* [b] *imp.* [c] *fut.* HOPHAL [d] *pret.*
    [e] כְּלִמָּה [f]. shame, reproach.

7   קָלוֹן *m.* contempt, shame, dishonour.

8   תֹּהוּ *m.* emptiness, vanity ; wasteness, desolation.

Gen. xi. 7.	2 b	Ps. cxxix. 5.	1 c	Jer. xv. 9.	3 a	
xi. 9.	2 a	Isa. i. 29.	3 b	xvii. 18, 18.	1 c	
Lev. xviii. 23.	2 c	xix. 9.	1 a	xx. 11.	6 e	
xx. 12.	2 c	xxiv. 10.	8	xxii. 22.	6 a	
1 Sam. xx. 30, 30.	1 d	xxiv. 23.	3 a	xxxi. 19.	6 a	
2 Kings xix. 26.	1 c	xxx. 3.	6 e	xlvi. 24.	5	
Ezra ix. 7.	1 d	xxxiv. 11.	8	xlviii. 1, 1, 20.	5	
Job vi. 20.	1 a	xxxvii. 27.	1 a	xlix. 23.	1 a	
x. 15.	7	xli. 11.	6 e	l. 2, 2.	5	
Ps. xxii. 5.	1 a	xli. 29.	8	l. 12.	1 a	
xxxv. 4, 4.	1 c, 3 b	xlv. 16, 16.	6 a e	li. 17.	5	
xxxv. 26.	3 b	xlv. 17.	6 c	li. 47.	1 c	
xl. 14.	3 b	l. 7.	6 a	li. 51.	1 a	
xliv. 15.	6 e	liv. 4.	6 c	Ezek. xvi. 52.	1 b	
lxix. 6.	6 c	lxi. 7.	6 e	xvi. 54.	6 a	
lxx. 2, 2.	3 b, 6 a	Jer. i. 17.	4	xvi. 63.	1 a	
lxxi. 1, 13.	1 c	iii. 25.	6 e	xxxvi. 32.	6 b	
lxxi. 24.	1 a	vii. 19.	1 d	Dan. ix. 7, 8.	1 d	
lxxxiii. 17.	1 c	ix. 19.	1 a	Micah iii. 7.	3 a	
xcvii. 7.	1 c	x. 14.	5	vii. 16.	1 c	
cix. 29.	1 d	xiv. 3.	6 d	Zech. x. 5.	5	

CONGEAL

  קָפָא to draw in oneself, to contract ; to concrete, to coagulate,
as milk ; *poet.* of the sea. KAL *pret.* Exod. xv. 8.

CONGRATULATE

  בֵּרַךְ to bless ; to salute, to greet. PIEL *inf.* 1 Chron. xviii. 10.

CONGREGATION

1   אֵלֶם *m.* from אָלַם to bind in a bundle, a congregation or collection of people, Ps. lviii. 1 : but the word might perhaps be rendered silence, and then the translation may be, "Do ye indeed speak silence of justice ?" Silence of justice is the suppression of that which is just and right in the representations supposed to have been made. In respect to David this was undoubtedly the case in the court of Saul.

2   חַי *adj.* anything living ; *collect.* a family or body of people that live in one community and under one head.

3   עֵדָה *f.* an appointed meeting, assembly ; assembly, congregation, community of the Israelites ; a domestic or private company, family, household, Job xvi. 7, xv. 34 ; any assembly, multitude, often in a bad sense, troop, band, gang, of wicked men : found chiefly in Num. and also in Exod. and Lev. ; Exod. xii. 3, &c. [a] מוֹעֵד *m.* appointment of time ; a coming together, assembly ; also the place of assembly, a synagogue, Ps. lxxiv. 4 : it occurs in the expression 'tent or tabernacle of congregation' frequently, and in Num. xvi. 2 : Ps. lxxiv. 4 ; lxxv. 2 : Isa. xiv. 13.

4   קָהָל *m.* a coming together, an assembling, the act ; an assembly, congregation, convocation, *spec.* of the assembly or congregation of the people of Israel for any cause, mostly for religious purposes ; in a wider sense, of any assembly or multitude of men, of troops, of nations, of the wicked, of the righteous, of angels, of the dead. [a] קְהִלָּה *f.* an assembly. [b] מַקְהֵלוֹת *f. pl.* assemblies, especially of those who praise God. [c] מַקְהֵלִים *m. pl. id.*

No. 3, *Congregation*, and No. 3 a, when occurring in the expression "the tent or tabernacle of the congregation," not included.

Lev. iv. 14, 21.	4	2 Chron. i. 3, 5.	4	Ps. xxvi. 12.	4 c
xvi. 17, 33.	4	vi. 3, 3, 12, 13.	4	xxxv. 18.	4
Num. x. 7.	4	vii. 8.	4	xl. 9, 10.	4
xv. 15.	4	xx. 5, 14.	4	lviii. 1.	1
xvi. 2.	3 a	xxiii. 3.	4	lxviii. 10.	2
xvi. 3, 3.	3, 4	xxiv. 6.	4	lxviii. 26.	4 b
xvi 33, 47.	4	xxviii. 14.	4	lxxiv. 4.	3 a
xix. 20.	4	xxix. 23, 28, 31, 32.	4	lxxiv. 19.	2
xx. 4, 10, 12.	4	xxx. 2, 4, 13, 17, 24,		lxxv. 2. a	3 a
Deut. xxiii. 1, 2, 2, 3,		24, 25, 25.	4	lxxxix. 5.	4
3, 8.	4	xxxi. 18.	4	cvii. 32.	4
xxxi. 30.	4	Ezra ii. 64.	4	cxlix. 1.	4
xxxiii. 4.	4 a	x. 1, 8, 12, 14.	4	Prov. v. 14.	4
Josh. viii. 35.	4	Neh. v. 13.	4	xxi. 16.	4
Judg. xxi. 5.	4	vii. 66.	4	xxvi. 26.	4
1 Kings viii. 14, 14, 22,		viii. 2, 17.	4	Isa. xiv. 13.	3 a
55, 65.	4	xiii. 1.	4	Lam. i. 10.	4
xii. 3.	4	Job xxx. 28.	4	Joel ii. 16.	4
1 Chron. xiii. 2, 4.	4	Ps. xxii. 22, 25.	4	Micah ii. 5.	4
xxviii. 8.	4	xxvi. 5.	4		
xxix. 1, 10, 20, 20.	4				

a marg. 'or, when I shall take a set time.' See Acts i. 7 ; *comp.* Rev. xi. 17.

CONSECRATE

1   חָרַם see *Destroy, Devote*. HIPHIL *pret.*

2   מָלֵא to fill ; to consecrate, *lit.* to fill the hand יָד ; some of the sacrifice being put into the hand, to be waved, and then borne to the altar. KAL [a] *imp.* PIEL [b] *pret.* [c] *inf.* [d] *fut.* [e] מִלֻּאִים *m. pl.* consecration.

3   נָזַר to separate. HIPHIL [a] *pret.* [b] נֵזֶר *m.* see *Crown*.

4   קָדַשׁ to be holy ; to regard or treat as holy, to consecrate. PIEL [a] *pret.* [b] *inf.* PUAL [c] *part.* [d] קֹדֶשׁ *m.* holy.

5   יָד *com.* hand, is used with מָלֵא in passages marked *.

Exod. xxviii. 3.	4 b	Lev. viii. 33, 33.*	2 e d	1 Chron. xxix. 5.*	2 c
xxviii. 41.*	2 b	xvi. 32.*	2 d	2 Chron. xiii. 9.*	2 c
xxix. 9.a	2 b	xxi. 10.*	2 b	xxvi. 18.	4 c
xxix. 22, 26, 27, 31,		Num. iii. 3.*	2 b	xxix. 31.*	2 b
34.	2 c	vi. 7.	3 b	xxix. 33.	4 d
xxix. 29,* 33.*	2 c	vi. 9.	3 b	xxxi. 6.	4 c
xxix. 35.*	2 d	vi. 12.	3 a	Ezra iii. 5.	4 c
xxx. 30.	4 a	Josh. vi. 19.	4 d	Ezek. xliii. 26.*	2 b
xxxii. 29.*	2 a	Judg. xvii. 5,* 12.*	2 d	Micah iv. 13.	1
Lev. vii. 37.	4 d	1 Kings xiii. 33.*	2 d		
viii. 22, 28, 29, 31.	2 e				

a lit. fill the hand of Aaron and the hand of his sons.

CONSENT

1   אָבָה to be willing, to acquiesce. See *Will*. KAL *fut.*

2   אוֹת to consent, acquiesce, submit. NIPHAL *fut.*

3   אִישׁ *m.* a man.

4   לֵב *m.* the heart.

5   רָצָה to delight in ; to approve. KAL *fut.*

6   שְׁכֶם *m.* shoulder.

7   שָׁמַע to hear, obey. KAL *fut.*

Gen. xxxiv. 15, 22, 23.	2	2 Kings xii. 8.	2	Dan. i. 14.	7
Deut. xiii. 8.	1	Ps. l. 18.	5	Hos. vi. 9.	6
1 Sam. xi. 7.	3	lxxxiii. 5.	4	Zeph. iii. 9.	6
1 Kings xx. 8.	1	Prov. i. 10.	1		

CONSIDER

1   אָמַר to say. KAL *fut.*

2   בִּין to distinguish ; to consider, to understand, which depends on the power of discerning. With *inf.*, consider diligently. KAL [a] *inf.* [b] *imp.* KAL and HIPHIL [c] *fut.* HIPHIL [d] *imp.* [e] *part.* HITHPOLEL [f] *pret.* [g] *imp.* [h] *fut.*

3 זָמַם to devise, to purpose: to consider with a fixed deliberate purpose. KAL *pret.*

4 חָשַׁב to think, count, reflect. PIEL *pret.*

5 יָדַע to know, to be sensible of. KAL [a] *pret.* [b] *imp.* [c] *fut.* [d] *part.* Poel.

6 לֵב m. the heart ; to consider, *lit.* to set the heart on.

7 לֵבָב m: id.

8 נָבַט to look with consideration and attention. HIPHIL [a] *imp.* [b] *fut.*

9 נָתַן to give. KAL *pret.*

10 פָּסַג to cut up, or divide ; to take a distinct view or survey (hence Pisgah) ; some, to extol, to raise up. PIEL *imp.*

11 רָאָה to see, with thought and reflection, with attention ; to take good notice ; to look upon with a kind, friendly, compassionate affection ; to respect, to regard. KAL [a] *pret.* [b] *imp.* [c] *fut.*

12 שׁוּב to return. HIPHIL [a] *pret.* [b] *fut.*

13 שׂוּם to put, set, or place ; to consider ; Heb. to set the heart on ; sometimes without לֵב, the heart. KAL [a] *pret.* [b] *imp.* [c] *fut.*

14 שִׁית to set ; with לֵב to consider. KAL *fut.*

15 שָׂכַל to look at, to look at with the mind, to consider, to attend to ; to be or become intelligent, prudent, wise ; it implies maturity of understanding or judgment. HIPHIL [a] *pret.* [b] *part.* [c] שְׂכַל Ch. ITHPAEL *part.*

16 שָׁמַע to hear, to hearken. KAL *pret.*

Exod. xxxiii. 13.	11 b	Ps. xxxiii. 15.	2 e	Isa. xiv. 16.	2 h	
Lev. xiii. 13.	11 a	xxxvii. 10.	2 f	xviii. 4. γ	8 b	
Deut. iv. 39. α	12 a	xli. 1.	15 b	xli. 20.	13 a	
viii. 5.	5 a	xlv. 10.	11 b	xli. 22.	13 a, 6	
xxxii. 7.	2 b	xlviii. 13.	10	xliii. 18.	2 h	
xxxii. 29.	2 b	i. 22.	2	xliv. 19.	12 b	
Judg. xviii. 14.	5 b	lxiv. 9.	15 a	lii. 15.	2 f	
xix. 30. β	13 b	lxxvii. 5.	4	lvii. 1.	2 e	
1 Sam. xii. 24.	11 b	cxix. 95.	2 h	Jer. ii. 10.	2 g	
xxv. 17.	11 b	cxix. 153, 159.	11 b	ix. 17.	2 g	
1 Kings iii. 21.	2 h	Prov. vi. 6.	11 b	xxiii. 20.	2 h	
v. 8.	16	xxi. 12.	15 b	xxx. 24.	2 h	
2 Kings v. 7.	5 b	xxiii. 1.	2 a c	xxxiii. 24.	11 a	
Job i. 8.	13 a, 6	xxiv. 12.	2 c	Lam. i. 11.	8 a	
ii. 3.	13 a, 6	xxiv. 32.	14, 6	ii. 20.	8 a	
xi. 11.	2 h	xxviii. 22.	5 c	v. 1.	8 a	
xxiii. 15.	2 h	xxix. 7.	5 d	Ezek. xii. 3.	11 c	
xxxiv. 27.	15 a	xxxi. 16.	3	xviii. 14, 28.	11 c	
xxxvii. 14.	2 g	Eccles. iv. 1.	11 c	xxiii. 5.	15 c	
Ps. v. 1.	2 b	iv. 4, 15.	11 a	viii. 5.	2 e	
viii. 3.	11 c	v. 1.	5 d	ix. 23.	2 d	
ix. 13.	11 b	vii. 13, 14.	11 b	Hos. vii. 2.	1	
xiii. 3.	8 a	ix. 1.	9	Hag. i. 5.	13 b, 7	
xxv. 19.	11 b	Isa. i. 3.	2 f	i. 7.	13 b, 7	
xxxi. 7.	11 a	v. 12.	11 a	ii. 15, 18, 18.	13 b, 7	

α *lit.* cause to return to. β *lit.* put to yourselves upon it. γ *marg.*
'or, regard my set dwelling-place.' δ *lit.* was considering.

CONSOLATION

תַּנְחוּמוֹת f. pl. compassion, consolations ; see *Comfort, Cup.* Job xv. 11 ; xxi. 2. תַּנְחוּמִים m. pl. Isa. lxvi. 11 ; Jer. xvi. 7.

CONSPIRE

1 נָכַל to deceive. HITHPAEL *fut.*

2 קָשַׁר to bind, to join together ; to conspire ; with the noun, to make a conspiracy. KAL [a] *pret.* [b] *fut.* [c] *part.* Poel. HITHPAEL [d] *pret.* [e] *fut.* [f] *part.* [g] קֶשֶׁר m. conspiracy.

Gen. xxxvii. 18. α	1	2 Kings xii. 20.	2 b g	2 Chron. xxiv. 25.	2 d	
1 Sam. xxii. 8, 13.	2 a	xiv. 19.	2 b g	xxiv. 26.	2 f	
2 Sam. xv. 12.	2 g	xv. 10, 25.	2 b	xxv. 27.	2 b g	
xv. 31.	2 c	xv. 15.	2 a g	xxxiii. 24.	2 b	
1 Kings xv. 27.	2 b	xv. 30.	2 b g	xxxiii. 25.	2 c	
xvi. 9.	2 b	xvii. 4.	2 g	Neh. iv. 8.	2 b	
xvi. 16.	2 a	xxi. 23.	2 b	Jer. xi. 9.	2 g	
2 Kings ix. 14.	2 e	xxi. 24.	2 b	Ezek. xxii. 25.	2 g	
x. 9.	2 a	2 Chron. xxiv. 21.	2 b	Amos vii. 10.	2 a	

α i.e. craftily conspired ; Gr. ἐπονηρεύοντο, they malignantly plotted.

CONSTANT

חָזַק to be strong; implying diligence and perseverance ; *seq.* לְ c. infin. KAL *fut.* 1 Chron. xxviii. 7.

נֶצַח m. perpetuity : Prov. xxi. 28, constantly, *i.e.* shall not be silenced. *Comp.* xii. 19.

CONSTELLATION

כְּסִיל m. see *Orion :* Isa. xiii. 10.

CONSTRAIN

חָזַק to be strong ; to take fast hold. HIPHIL *fut.* 2 Kings iv. 8 ; *marg.* 'laid hold on him.'

צוּק to be straitened ; to press, to urge. HIPHIL *pret.* Job xxxii. 18.

CONSULT

1 יְעַט Ch. to counsel. ITHPAEL *pret.*

2 יָעַץ to consult, to advise ; *i. e.* both to take and give counsel. KAL [a] *pret.* NIPHAL [b] *pret.* [c] *fut.* HITHPAEL [d] *fut.*

3 מָלַךְ to reign : the sense is uniform, except in one place where it is figuratively applied to a man's own heart or spirit. NIPHAL *fut.*

4 שָׁאַל to ask, to inquire ; to ask counsel. KAL [a] *pret.* [b] *part.* Poel.

Deut. xviii. 11.	4 b	Neh. v. 7. α	3	Ezek. xxi. 21.	4 a	
1 Kings xii. 6, 8.	2 c	Ps. lxii. 4.	2 a	Dan. vi. 7.	1	
1 Chron. xiii. 1.	2 c	lxxxiii. 3.	2 d	Micah vi. 5.	2 a	
2 Chron. xx. 21.	2 c	lxxxiii. 5.	2 b	Hab. ii. 10.	2 a	

α *marg.* 'my heart consulted in me,' *i.e.* my resolution prevailed over my fear; I took courage.

CONSUME, CONSUMPTION, CONSUMMATION

1 אָכַל to eat, to consume, &c. KAL [a] *pret.* [b] *fut.* [c] *part.* Poel. NIPHAL [d] *pret.* [e] *fut.* PIEL [f] *fut.* PUAL [g] *part.* [h] *part.* HIPHIL [i] *inf.* [k] אָכְלָה f. meat, fuel, &c.

2 אָסַף to take away, to remove, to gather. KAL [a] *inf.* [b] *part.* Paül.

3 בָּלָה (see *Old*), to be worn out with age and use, to be wasted. KAL [a] *fut.* PIEL [b] *inf.*

4 גָּזַל to take away by force ; to spoil, to rob, to plunder. KAL *fut.*

5 דָּעַךְ to be extinguished. NIPHAL *pret.*

6 הָמַם to harass, to throw into confusion in order to destroy. KAL *inf.*

7 חָסַל to waste and consume, as locusts and caterpillars. KAL *fut.*

8 יָרַשׁ to possess. PIEL *fut.*

9 כָּלָה to be quite done, to be finished, to be brought to an end. KAL [a] *pret.* [b] *inf.* [c] *fut.* PIEL [d] *pret.* [e] *inf.*

imp. ᵍ *fut.* ʰ *part.* ⁱ כָּלָה *f.* completion; destruction. ᵏ כִּלָּיוֹן *m.* that which terminates, destruction.

10   מוּג   to melt, to flow down; to cause to melt away and perish. KAL *fut.*

11   מָסָה   to flow down; to dissolve. HIPHIL *fut.*

12   מָקַק   to melt, to pine away. NIPHAL ᵃ *pret.* ᵇ *fut.* HIPHIL ᶜ *inf.*

13   סוּף   to snatch away; to make an end of, to cause to cease; to destroy. KAL ᵃ *pret.* ᵇ *fut.* HIPHIL ᶜ *fut.* ᵈ סוּף Ch. APHEL *fut.*

14   סָפָה   to scrape, to take clean away, to destroy. KAL ᵃ *pret.* ᵇ *fut.* NIPHAL ᶜ *fut.*

15   עָשָׂה   to make. KAL *pret.*

16   עָשֵׁשׁ   to fall away, to pine away, to become old. KAL *pret.*

17   צָמַת   to cut off. PIEL *pret.*

18   רָפָה   to be relapsed, slackened, to collapse; of grass consumed by the flame. KAL *fut.*

19   שַׁחֶפֶת   *f.* consumption, wasting away of the body.

20   שְׁמַד   Ch. to destroy. APHEL *inf.*

21   תָּמַם   to complete, to finish; to be exhausted, spent. KAL ᵃ *pret.* ᵇ *inf.* ᶜ *fut.* NIPHAL ᵈ *fut.* HIPHIL ᵉ *pret.* ᶠ *inf.*

Gen. xix. 15, 17.	14 c	2 Kings i. 10, 10, 12,		Isa. xxviii. 22.	9 i
xxxi. 40.	1 a	12.	1 b	xxix. 20.	9 a
xli. 30.	9 d	vii. 13.	21 a	lxiv. 7.	10
Exod. iii. 2.	1 h	vii. 17, 19.	9 e	lxvi. 17.	13 b
xv. 7.	1 b	2 Chron. vii. 1.	1 b	Jer. v. 3.	9 d
xxii. 6.	1 d	viii. 8.	9 d	vi. 29.	21 a
xxxii. 10.	9 g	xviii. 10.	9 e	viii. 13.	2 a, 13 c
xxxii. 12.	9 e	Ezra ix. 14.	9 e	ix. 16.	9 e
xxxiii. 3.	9 g	Neh. ii. 3, 13.	1 g	x. 25.	9 g
xxxiii. 5.	9 d	ix. 31.α	15, 9 i	xii. 4.	14 a
Lev. vi. 10.	1 b	Esth. ix. 24.	6	xiv. 12.	9 h
ix. 24.	1 b	Job i. 16.	1 b	xiv. 15.	21 d
xxvi. 16, 16.	19, 9 h	iv. 9.	9 c	xvi. 4.	9 c
Num. xi. 1.	1 b	vi. 11.	5	xx. 18.	9 c
xii. 12.	1 e	vii. 9.	9 a	xxiv. 10.	21 b
xiv. 35.	21 d	xiii. 28.	3 a	xxvii. 8.	21 b
xvi. 21, 45.	9 g	xv. 34.	1 a	xxxvi. 23.	21 b
xvi. 26.	14 c	xix. 27.	9 a	xliv. 12, 12.	21 a
xvi. 35.	1 b	xx. 26.	1 f	xliv. 18, 27.	21 a.
xvii. 13.	21 a	xxii. 20.	1 a	xlix. 27.	9 e
xxi. 28.	1 a	xxiv. 19.	4	xlix. 37.	9 e
xxv. 11.	9 d	xxxi. 12.	1 b	Lam. ii. 22.	9 d
xxxii. 13.	21 b	xxxiii. 21.	9 c	iii. 22.	21 a
Deut. ii. 15.	21 b	Ps. vi. 7.	16	Ezek. iv. 17.	12 a
ii. 16.	21 a	xviii. 37.	9 e	v. 12.	9 c
iv. 24.	1 c	xxxi. 9, 10.	16	xiii. 13.	9 i
v. 25.	1 b	xxxvii. 20, 20.	9 a	xiii. 14.	9 a
vii. 16.	1 a	xxxix. 10.	9 a	xix. 12.	1 a
vii. 16.	9 e	xxxix. 11.	11	xx. 13.	9 e
ix. 3.	1 c	xlix. 14.	3 b	xxi. 28.γ	1 i
xxviii. 21.	9 e	lix. 13, 13.	9 f	xxii. 15.	21 e
xxviii. 22.	19	lxxi. 13.	9 c	xxii. 31.	9 d
xxviii. 38.	7	lxxiii. 19.β	13 a, 21 a	xxiv. 10.	21 f
xxviii. 42.	8	lxxviii. 33.	9 g	xxiv. 11.	21 c
xxxii. 22.	1 b	lxxviii. 63.	1 a	xxxiv. 29.	2 b
Josh. v. 6.	21 b	xc. 7.	9 a	xxxv. 12.	1 k
viii. 24.	21 b	cii. 3.	9 a	xliii. 8.	9 g
x. 20.	21 b	civ. 35.	21 d	xlvii. 12.	21 c
xxiv. 20.	9 d	cxix. 87.	9 d	Dan. ii. 44.	13 d
Judg. vi. 21.	1 b	cxix. 139.	17	vii. 26.	20
1 Sam. ii. 33.	9 e	Prov. v. 11.	9 b	ix. 27.	9 i
xii. 25.	14 c	Isa. i. 28.	9 c	xi. 16.δ	9 i
xv. 18.	9 e	v. 24.	18	Hos. xi. 6.	9 d
2 Sam. xxi. 5.	9 d	vii. 20.	14 b	Zeph. i. 2.	2 a, 13 c
xxii. 38.	9 e	x. 18.	9 g	i. 3, 3.	13 c
xxii. 39.	9 g	x. 22.	9 k	Zech. v. 4.	9 d
1 Kings xviii. 38.	1 b	x. 23.	9 i	xiv. 12, 12, 12.	12 c b b
xxii. 11.	9 e	xvi. 4.	21 a	Mal. iii. 6.	9 a
		xxvii. 10.	9 d		

ᵃ *lit.* didst not make them a consumption.   β *lit.* they are at an end, they are consumed.   γ *lit.* to cause to eat, or consume; *comp.* 2 Sam. ii. 26.   δ *lit.* and destruction in his hand

CONTAIN

1   בַּיִת   *m.* a house, a container of anything.

2   כּוּל   to hold or contain; the primary meaning may have been that which is given to 1 Kings viii. 27, and 2 Chron. vi. 18, by the Lxx. ἀρκεῖν, to be sufficient. PILPEL ᵃ *fut.* HIPHIL ᵇ *inf.* ᶜ *fut.*

3   נָשָׂא   to bear; to contain, to be sufficient for. KAL *inf.*

1 Kings vii. 26, 38.	2 c	2 Chron. ii. 6.	2 a	Ezek. xxiii. 32.β	2 b
viii. 27.	2 a	vi. 18.	2 a	xlv. 11.	3
xviii. 32.a	1				

ᵃ *lit.* as the house of two measures.   β *lit.* it is great to contain.

CONTEMN, CONTEMPT

1   בּוּז   to despise with mockery, and openly: with *inf.*, utterly contemn. See *Despise.* KAL ᵃ *inf.* ᵇ *fut.* ᶜ בּוּז *m.* contempt.

2   בָּזָה   to despise through pride; see *Despise.* NIPHAL ᵃ *part.* ᵇ בִּזָּיוֹן *m.* contempt.

3   דִּרְאוֹן   *m.* a thrusting away; see *Abhor.*

4   מָאַס   to refuse, reject as vile and worthless, with disdain and aversion; see *Abhor, Reject.* KAL ᵃ *part.* Poel. It belongs not to this work to explain the two very obscure verses in Ezek. xxi. 10, 13; the reader must consult the best commentators. See *Fairbairn.*

5   נָאַץ   to treat with scorn and contumely; see *Abhor.* KAL ᵃ *pret.* PIEL ᵇ *pret.*

6   קָלָה   to be light, to be made light of. NIPHAL *pret.*

7   קָלַל   to be light; to be lightly esteemed; to bring into contempt. HIPHIL *inf.*

Esth. i. 18.	2 b	Ps. cvii. 11.	5 a	Isa. xvi. 14.	6
Job xii. 21.	1 c	cvii. 40.	1 c	xxiii. 9.	7
xxxi. 34.	1 c	cxix. 22.	1 c	Ezek. xxi. 10, 13.	4
Ps. x. 13.	5 b	cxxiii. 3, 4.	1 c	Dan. xii. 2.	3
xv. 4.	4 b	Prov. xviii. 3.	1 c	Mal. i. 7, 12.	2 a
xxxi. 18.	1 c	Cant. viii. 7.	1 a b	ii. 9.	2 a

CONTEND, CONTENTION

1   גָּרָה   to throw things into confusion, to stir up strife or war; to contend with, *seq.* בְּ. HITHPAEL ᵃ *imp.* ᵇ *fut.*

2   דִּין   to judge; to plead, to debate; to strive, to wrangle. KAL ᵃ *inf.* ᵇ מָדוֹן *m.* strife, discord: a man of contention may be taken, either actively of one ready to contend, or passively of one who is liable to contentions with and from others; so Jer. xv. 10, it seems, ought to be understood. Schmidt conceives both meanings may be included: "Ego habeor et videor vir rixosus, et cum quo illi vicissim rixentur, ut reprehendam illos, illique vicissim me." ᶜ מִדְיָנִים *m. pl.* strifes, contentions.

3   חָרָה   to burn, to be wroth, to contend eagerly. HIPHIL *fut.*

4   מַצָּה   *f.* strife, contention; see *Strife.* ᵃ מַצּוּת *f. id.*

5   רִיב   to contend, to strive, to quarrel; to plead a cause; see *Strive.* KAL ᵃ *inf.* ᵇ *imp.* ᶜ *fut.* ᵈ יָרִיב *m.* an adversary. ᵉ רִיב *m.* strife, quarrel; cause, suit.

6   שָׁפַט   see *Plead.* NIPHAL, to contend before a judge, *part.*

Deut. ii. 9.	1 b	Job xiii. 8.	5 c	Prov. xviii. 6.	5 e
ii. 24.	1 a	xxxi. 13.	5 e	xviii. 18, 19.	2 c
Neh. xiii. 11, 17, 25.	5 c	xl. 2.a	5 a	xix. 13.	2 c
Job ix. 3.	5 a	Prov. xiii. 10.	4	xxi. 19.β	2 c
x. 2.	5 c	xvii. 14.	5 c	xxii. 10.	2 b

Prov. xxiii. 29.	2 c	Isa. xli. 12.	4 a	Jer. xv. 10.	2 b
xxvi. 21.	2 c	xlix. 25, 25.	5 c d	xviii. 19.	5 d
xxvii. 15.	2 c	l. 8.	5 c	Amos vii. 4.	5 a
xxviii. 4.	1 b	lvii. 16.	5 c	Micah vi. 1.γ	5 b
xxix. 9.	6	Jer. xii. 5.	3	Hab. i. 3.	2 b
Eccles. vi. 10.	2 a				

α *lit.* contending.   β *lit.* a woman of contention.   γ *lit.* or, contend with.

CONTENT

1 אָבָה to acquiesce, to rest content ; see *Will.* KAL *fut.*

2 יָאַל to be willing ; see *Will.* Hiphil, implying a force applied to the will, to undertake, to attempt what is difficult or painful ; see *Begin,* &c.; to yield to entreaties, to allow, not to refuse ; to yield to temptation (see *Will*) ; of God, who yields to prayers or his own pity (see *Please*). HIPHIL [a] *pret.* [b] *imp.* [c] *fut.*

3 יָטַב to be good. KAL *fut.*

4 עַיִן *com.* eye.

5 שָׁמַע to hear. KAL *fut.*

Gen. xxxvii. 27.	5	Judg. xvii. 11.	2 c	2 Kings vi. 3.	2 b
Exod. ii. 21.	2 c	xix. 6.	2 b	Job vi. 28.	2 b
Lev. x. 20.α	3, 4	2 Kings v. 23.	2 b	Prov. vi. 35.	1
Josh. vii. 7.	2 a				

α *lit.* it was good in his eyes.

CONTINUE, CONTINUANCE, CONTINUAL

1 אָחַר to tarry. PIEL *part.*

2 אָמַן to sustain. NIPHAL, to be of long continuance : *part.*

3 בְּכִי *m.* weeping.

4 גּוּר to sojourn. HITHPAEL *part.*

5 גָּרַר to sweep away. HITHPAEL *part.* of a whirlwind sweeping all before it.

6 הָלַךְ to walk, to go. KAL [a] *inf.* [b] *part.* Poel.

7 חָזַק to hold fast, to hold to anything. HIPHIL *pret.*

8 טָרַד to thrust ; to follow one another continually. KAL *part.* Poel.

9 יוֹם *m.* a day, continually ; *Heb.* all the days, all day, every day.

10 יָסַף to add. HIPHIL *fut.*

11 יָשַׁב to sit, to dwell ; to remain. KAL [a] *pret.* [b] *fut.*

12 לָן to lodge, remain. KAL *fut.*

13 מָשַׁךְ to draw out, to protract, prolong. KAL *imp.*

14 נִן to have offspring ; to be propagated, to flourish. NIPHAL *fut.* or HIPHIL *fut.* כתיב, which Gussetius adopts, and renders the sentence "his name shall beget sons." Comp. Isa. liii. 10, 11.

15 נָשָׂא to lift up, to utter aloud, to lift up the voice in. KAL *inf.*

16 סָרָה *f.* a turning away.

17 עוֹלָם *m.* for ever ; perpetual.

18 עָמַד to stand, to stay ; remain, remain alive. KAL [a] *pret.* [b] *fut.*

19 עֵת *com.* time, season ; continually ; *lit.* in all time.

20 קוּם to rise up ; to stand, to stand fast, remain. KAL [a] *fut.* HIPHIL [b] *fut.*

21 רָבָה to multiply. HIPHIL *pret.*

22 שׁוּב to return. KAL *inf.*

23 שָׁכַן to dwell. KAL *fut.*

24 תְּדִירָא Ch. *f.* circuit ; continuity, perpetuity.

25 תָּמִיד *m.* continuance, perpetuity, *i. e.* perpetual time, as moving on continually without interruption : Ezek. xxxix. 14, "continual employment," *marg.* 'continuance ;' continual, continually : Exod. xxviii. 29, &c.

הָיָה to be, is sometimes rendered to continue.

No. 25 not included.

Gen. vi. 5.	9	1 Kings xxii. 1.	11 b	Ps. cxxxix. 16.	9
viii. 3.	6 a, 22	2 Chron. xii. 15.β	9	cxl. 2.ε	9
viii. 5.	6 a	Neh. v. 16.	7	Prov. vi. 14.	19
Exod. xxi. 21.	18 b	Job i. 5.β	9	xix. 13.	8
Lev. xii. 4, 5.	11 b	xiv. 2.	18 b	xxvii. 15.	8
Deut. xxviii. 59, 59.	2	xv. 29.	20 a	Isa. v. 11.	1
Josh. viii. 13.α	6 a	xvii. 2.	12	xiv. 6.	16
Judg. v. 17.	11 a	xxvii. 1.	10, 15	lxiv. 5.	17
Ruth ii. 7.	18 b	xxix. 1.	10, 15	Jer. xxx. 23.	4 or 5
1 Sam. i. 12.	21	Ps. xxxvi. 10.	13	xxxii. 14.	18 b
xiii. 14.	20 a	xlii. 3.γ	9	xxxiii. 18.β	9
xviii. 29.β.	9	xliv. 15.γ	9	xlviii. 5.	3
2 Sam. vi. 11.	11 b	lii. 1.δ	9	Ezek. xxxix. 14.	25
xv. 12.	6 b	lxxii. 17.	14	Dan. vi. 16, 20.	24
xix. 13.β	9	cii. 28.	23	xi. 8.	18 b
1 Kings ii. 4.	20 b	cxix. 91.	18 a		

α *lit.* went on to go.   β *lit.* all the days.   γ *lit.* all the day.   δ *lit.* every day.   ε *lit.* all day.

CONTRARY

הָפַךְ to turn. NIPHAL, turned to the contrary : *inf.* Esth. ix. 1. הָפֵךְ and הֶפֶךְ *m.* Ezek. xvi. 34, 34.

קְרִי *m.* hostile encounter : Lev. xxvi. 21, 23, 24, 27, 28, 40, 41.

CONTRITE

דָּכָא to bruise, to break ; see *Break.* NIPHAL *part.* Isa. lvii. 15. דַּכָּא *adj.* crushed, broken in spirit : Ps. xxxiv. 18 ; Isa. lvii. 15.

דָּכָה nearly the same. NIPHAL *part.* Ps. li. 17.

נְכֵה *adj.* smitten in spirit : Isa. lxvi. 2.

CONTROVERSY

רִיב *m.* strife, contention : Deut. xvii. 8 ; xix. 17 ; xxi. 5 ; xxv. 1 : 2 Sam. xv. 2 : 2 Chron. xix. 8 : Isa. xxxiv. 8 : Jer. xxv. 31 : Ezek. xliv. 24 : Hos. iv. 1 ; xii. 2 : Micah vi. 2, 2.

CONVENIENT

חֹק *m.* see *Portion.* Prov. xxx. 8, *marg.* 'of my allowance,' *i.e.* give me so much as the law of nature, or the law of my necessity or convenience, calls for, to fit me for duty ; with this statute bread let me be fed ; let others have their full tables, this shall serve my turn.—*Caryl in loc.*

יָשָׁר *adj.* right : Jer. xl. 4, 5, *lit.* right in thine eyes.

CONVERSANT

הָלַךְ to walk ; to be conversant. KAL *part.* Poel, Josh. viii. 35. HITHPAEL *pret.* 1 Sam. xxv. 15.

CONVERSATION

דֶּרֶךְ *com.* way : Ps. xxxvii. 14 ; l. 23.

CONVERT

הָפַךְ to turn. NIPHAL *fut.* Isa. lx. 5.

שׁוּב to return. KAL *fut.* Ps. li. 13 : *part.* Poel, Isa. i. 27 ; vi. 10. HIPHIL *part.* restoring, Ps. xix. 7.

CONVEY

עָבַר to pass ; to cause to pass. HIPHIL *fut.* Neh. ii. 7.

שׂוּם to put, set, place. KAL *fut.* 1 Kings v. 9.

CONVINCE

יָכַח to show, to prove in order to convince. HIPHIL *part.* Job xxxii. 12.

CONVOCATION

מִקְרָא *m.* a calling together, convocation ; convocation, assembly, *sc.* for worship and for the performance of sacred rites : Exod. xii. 16, 16 : Lev. xxiii. 2, 3, 4, 7, 8, 21, 24, 27, 35, 36, 37 : Num. xxviii. 18, 25, 26 ; xxix. 1, 7, 12.

COOK

טַבָּח *m.* a slaughterer ; a cook : 1 Sam. ix. 23, 24. מַבָּחוֹת *f.* 1 Sam. viii. 13.

COOL

רוּחַ *com.* wind : Gen. iii. 8, cool breeze.

COPING

טֶפַח *m.* the expanded open palm of the hand ; in architecture, prob. the *corbel*, projecting stone on which timber is laid : 1 Kings vii. 9.

COPPER

נְחֹשֶׁת see *Brass.* Ezra viii. 27, *marg.* 'yellow, *or,* shining brass.'

COPULATION

שְׁכָבָה *f.* lying : Lev. xv. 16, 17, 18.

COPY

עָתַק see (*To Remove*) ; to transfer, to transcribe. HIPHIL *pret.* Prov. xxv. 1.

פַּרְשֶׁגֶן *m.* a transcript, copy, *e.g.* of a letter : Ezra vii. 11. Ch. *m.* פַּרְשֶׁגֶן Ezra iv. 11, 23 ; v. 6. פַּתְשֶׁגֶן *m.* Esth. iii. 14 ; iv. 8 ; viii. 13.

מִשְׁנֶה *m.* second, double ; copy : Deut. xvii. 18 ; Josh. viii. 32.

COR

בֹּר *m.* see *Measure.* Ezek. xlv. 14.

CORAL

רָאמוֹת *f. pl.* high priced or precious things ; according to the Rabbins, red coral : Job xxviii. 18, *marg.* ' *or,* Ramoth :' Ezek. xxvii. 16.

CORD

1   חֶבֶל and חֵבֶל *com.* a cord, a rope.

2   חוּט *m.* a thread, a twine, a line, a cord.

3   יֶתֶר *m.* a cord fastened to the upper part of a tent, and tied upon full stretch to a pin driven into the ground at a convenient distance from the tent, to keep it firm and steady ; see *Pin.* ᵃ מֵיתָר *m.* string, cord.

4   עֲבֹת *com.* wreathen chains or cords, such as captives were bound with.

Exod. xxxv. 18.	3 a	Job xli. 1.	1	Isa. v. 18.	1
xxxix. 40.	3 a	Ps. ii. 3.	4	xxxiii. 20.	1
Num. iii. 26, 37.	3 a	cxviii. 27.	4	liv. 2.	3 a
iv. 26, 32.	3 a	cxxix. 4.	4	Jer. x. 20.	3 a
Josh. ii. 15.	1	cxl. 5.	4	xxxviii. 6, 11, 12, 13.	1
Judg. xv. 13, 14.	4	Prov. v. 22.	1	Ezek. xxvii. 24.	1
Esth. i. 6.	1	Eccles. iv. 12.	1	Hos. xi. 4.	1
Job xxx. 11.	3	xii. 6.	2	Micah ii. 5.	1
xxxvi. 8.	1				

CORIANDER

גַּד *m.* an aromatic seed, round ; to which manna is compared : Exod. xvi. 31 ; Num. xi. 7.

CORMORANT

קָאַת *f.* see *Pelican.* Isa. xxxiv. 11 ; Zeph. ii. 14.

שָׁלָךְ *m.* a sea-fowl, a species of pelican which casts itself from high rocks into the water after fish : Lev. xi. 17 ; Deut. xiv. 17.

CORN

1   בָּלִיל *m.* that which has been mixed.

2   בֶּן *m.* a son : Isa. xxi. 10, *marg.* 'the son of my floor,' *i.e.* threshed grain ; used also as a meat-offering.

3   בַּר and בַּר *m.* wheat, and every kind of grain.

4   גֹּרֶן *m.* a threshingfloor.

5   גֶּרֶשׂ *m.* corn beaten out of the ear, or bruised, previous to being roasted.

6   דָּגָן *m.* corn of any kind, wheat, barley, &c. : Gen. xxvii. 28, 37, &c.

7   עָבוּר *m.* old corn, the produce of the past year, as תְּבוּאָה the produce of the present year, Josh. v. 12, 13 ; or, the produce of the earth, opposed to manna, the bread of heaven.

8   קָמָה *f.* standing corn.

9   רִיפוֹת *f. pl.* pounded corn, or grains, grits, *polenta ;* or boiled wheat, which was afterwards pounded, and then laid out to dry.

10   שֶׁבֶר *m.* grain, corn.

See also *Shock, Stack, Ears,* &c.

No. 6 not included.

Gen. xli. 35, 49.	3	Lev. ii. 14, 16.	10	Job xxxix. 4.	3
xlii. 1, 2, 19, 26.	10	Deut. xvi. 9.	8	Ps. lxv. 13.	3
xliii. 3, 25.	3	xvi. 13.	4	lxxii. 16.	3
xliii. 2.	10	xxiii. 25, 25.	8	Prov. xi. 26.	3
xliv. 2.	10	Josh. v. 11, 12.	7	Isa. xvii. 5.	8
xlv. 23.	3	Judg. xv. 5, 5.	8	xxi. 10.β	2
xlvii. 14.	10	2 Sam. xvii. 19.	8	Amos viii. 5.	10
Exod. xxii. 6.	8	Job xxiv. 6.α	1		

α *marg.* 'mingled corn, *or,* dredge.'   β *marg.* ' son of my floor.'

CORNER

1   זָוִיֹּת *f. pl.* corners, corners of an altar ; cornerstones ; the corner columns of a palace, beautifully sculptured.

2   כָּנָף *com.* a wing ; remoter parts of the earth or a country.

3   כָּתֵף *f.* the shoulder ; side or corner of a building.

4   פָּאָה according to Gesenius, to blow away ; or, scatter as with the wind : our version considers it as a denominative from the following noun, to scatter into corners. HIPHIL ᵃ *fut.* ᵇ פֵּאָה *f.* side, quarter, region ; extreme part, extremity, corner. In Amos iii. 12, supposed to mean the corner where the bed is put aside in the daytime.

5 פָּנָה to turn; to look towards. KAL [a] *part.* Poel. [b] פִּנָּה *f.* a corner, an angle, *pr.* exterior, as of a house, of a street; also interior, as of a roof, of a court, of a city : *metaph.* prince, chief of a people, on whom as a cornerstone the burden of a state rests. [c] פֵּן *m.* a corner.

6 פַּעַם *com.* tread of the foot; foot of man : Gesenius, *pl.* artificial feet, of the corners of the ark.

7 צֵלָע *f.* rib.

8 קָצֶה *m.* end, extremity.

9 קָצַע to scrape off; applied to the corner or bend of a building. HOPHAL [a] *part.* [b] מְקֻצֹעַ *m.* an angle, corner. [c] מְקֻצְעָת *f. pl. id.*

Exod. xxv. 12.	6	Josh. xviii. 14.	4 b	Isa. xi. 12.	2
xxv. 26.	4 b	1 Kings vii. 30.	6	xxviii. 16.	5 b
xxvi. 23.	9 c	vii. 34.	5 b	Jer. ix. 26.	4 b
xxvi. 24.	9 b	2 Kings xi. 11, 11.	3	xxv. 23.	4 b
xxvii. 2.	5 b	xiv. 13.		xxxi. 38, 40.	4 b
xxvii. 4.	8	2 Chron. xxv. 23.	5 a	xlviii. 45.	4 b
xxx. 4.	7	xxvi. 9.	5 b	xlix. 32.	4 b
xxxvi. 25.	4 b	xxviii. 24.	5 b	li. 26.	5 b
xxxvi. 28.	9 c	Neh. iii. 24, 31, 32.	5 b	Ezek. vii. 2.	2
xxxvi. 29.	9 b	ix. 22.	4 b	xli. 22.	9 b
xxxvii. 3.	6	Job i. 19.	5 b	xlii. 20.	5 b
xxxvii. 13.	4 b	xxxviii. 6.	5 b	xlv. 19.	5 b
xxxvii. 27.	7	Ps. cxviii. 22.	5 b	xlvi. 22, 22.	9 b a
xxxviii. 2.	5 b	cxliv. 12.	1	Amos iii. 12.	4 b
Lev. xix. 9, 27, 27.	4 b	Prov. vii. 8.	5 c	Zech. ix. 15.	1
xxi. 5.	4 b	vii. 12.	5 b	x. 4.	5 b
xxiii. 22.	4 b	xxi. 9.	5 b	xiv. 10.	5 c
Num. xxiv. 17.	4 b	xxv. 24.	5 b		
Deut. xxxii. 26.	4 a				

CORNET

מְנַעַנְעִים *m. pl.* a musical instrument or rattle which gave a tinkling sound on being shaken; so Gr. σεῖστρα from σείω. The sistrum was used in Egypt in the worship of Isis; see the description and figures of it in Wilkinson's Mann. and Cust. of the Ancient Egyptians, ii. p. 323, &c.; 2 Sam. vi. 5. Vulg. *sistra.*

קֶרֶן Ch. *f.* a wind instrument, horn, cornet : Dan. iii. 5, 7, 10, 15.

שׁוֹפָר *m.* a trumpet with a clear shrill sound : 1 Chron. xv. 28; 2 Chron. xv. 14 : Ps. xcviii. 6 : Hos. v. 8.

CORPSE

גְּוִיָּה *f.* body; dead body, carcase, of men or animals : Nah. iii. 3, 3.

פֶּגֶר *m.* a corpse, exhausted body, of man, of beast : 2 Kings xix. 35 : Isa. xxxvii. 36.

CORRECT

1 יָכַח to show, to prove; to correct, reprove, convince; to rebuke, to punish. HIPHIL [a] *inf.* [b] *fut.* [c] תּוֹכַחַת *f.* correction.

2 יָסַר to correct, chastise; to instruct, admonish. NIPHAL [a] *fut.* PIEL [b] *pret.* [c] *imp.* [d] *fut.* [e] מוּסָר *m.* correction, admonition, instruction.

3 שֵׁבֶט *com.* rod.

Job v. 17.	1 b	Prov. xv. 10.	2 e	Jer. v. 3.	2 e
xxxvii. 13.	3	xxii. 15.	2 e	vii. 28.	2 e
Ps. xxxix. 11.	2 b	xxiii. 13.	2 e	x. 24.	2 e
xciv. 10.	1 b	xxix. 17.	2 c	xxx. 11.	2 b
Prov. iii. 11.	1 c	xxix. 19.	2 a	xlvi. 28.	2 b
iii. 12.	1 b	Jer. ii. 19.	2 d	Hab. i. 12.	1 a
vii. 22.	2 e	ii. 30.	2 e	Zeph. iii. 2.	2 e

CORRUPT

1 בְּלִי consumption, destruction : wasted away.

2 גָּעַר see *Rebuke.* Applied to God's judgment in rebuking the seed that it shall not produce a harvest. KAL *part.* Poel.

3 חָבַל to deal perversely or corruptly; to spoil; to be destroyed. With *inf.*, to deal very corruptly. KAL [a] *pret.* [b] *inf.* PUAL [c] *pret.*

4 חָנֵף see *Defile*; also *Hypocrite.* HIPHIL *fut.*

5 מוּג to waste away; to cause to waste away, *i. e.* gradually to ruin others by oppression : according to modern lexicographers, to mock and deride. HIPHIL *fut.*

6 מָקַק to waste away, as bodies that are putrid : Gesenius, run with corrupt matter. NIPHAL *pret.*

7 שָׁחַת to destroy, to ruin, to lay in ruins (see *Destroy*); to destroy one's way, *i. e.* to corrupt or pervert it, and hence to act wickedly : *metaph.* to mar, to spoil, to make good for nothing; to corrupt wisdom, to pervert it to the purposes of craft and deceit; Ezek. xxviii. 17. Moral corruption implies the loss of integrity and of virtue. With *inf.*, utterly corrupt. NIPHAL [a] *pret.* [b] *fut.* [c] *part.* PIEL [d] *pret.* HIPHIL [e] *pret.* [f] *inf.* [g] *fut.* [h] *part.* HOPHAL [i] *part.* Ch. P'AL [k] *part. pass.* [l] שַׁחַת *f.* a pit; the sepulchre, a grave; corruption. LXX., διαφθορά. [m] מַשְׁחִית *f.* destruction. [n] מָשְׁחָת *m.* that which is corrupt.

Gen. vi. 11.	7 d	Job xvii. 1. a	3 c	Ezek. xx. 44.	7 c
vi. 12, 12.	7 a e	xvii. 14.	7 l	xxiii. 11.	7 g
Exod. viii. 24.	7 b	Ps. xiv. 1.	7 e	xxviii. 17.	7 d
xxxii. 7.	7 d	xvi. 10.	7 l	Dan. ii. 9.	7 k
Lev. xxii. 25.	7 n	xxxviii. 5.	6	x. 8.	7 m
Deut. iv. 16.	7 g	xlix. 9.	7 l	xi. 17.	7 f
iv. 25.	7 e	liii. 1.	7 e	xi. 32.	4
ix. 12.	7 d	lxxiii. 8.	5	Hos. ix. 9.	7 d
xxxi. 29.	7 f g	Prov. xxv. 26.	7 i	Jonah ii. 6.	7 l
xxxii. 5.	7 e	xxxviii. 17.	7 h	Zeph. iii. 7.	7 l
Judg. ii. 19.	7 e		1	Mal. i. 14.	7 i
2 Kings xxiii. 13.	7 m	Jer. vi. 28.	7 h	ii. 3.	7 2
2 Chron. xxvii. 2.	7 h	Ezek. xvi. 47.	7 g	ii. 8.	7 d
Neh. i. 7.	3 b a				

a t.e. has lost its power, is exhausted.

COST

חִנָּם *adv.* freely; to no purpose; without cause; without cost : 2 Sam. xxiv. 24 : 1 Chron. xxi. 24.

יָקָר *adj.* precious, costly : 1 Kings v. 17; vii. 9, 10, 11.

COTE

אֲוֵרוֹת *f. pl.* for אֻרְווֹת, stalls, cribs : 2 Chron. xxxii. 28, *lit.* and flocks for stalls.

גְּדֵרָה *f.* fold : 1 Sam. xxiv. 3.

COTTAGE

כְּרֹת *f. pl. const.* cottages, accommodations for shepherds : Gesenius, pits, cisterns, wells : Zeph. ii. 6. In כְּרֹת (Zeph. ii. 6) is an allusion to the Cherethites in v. 5.

מְלוּנָה *f.* a lodge; a temporary shed for the watchman of a garden or vineyard while the fruit is ripening : Isa. xxiv. 20.

סֻכָּה *f.* booth, hut : a temporary habitation or shelter : Isa. i. 8.

COUCH

יָצֻעַ *m.* a bed, couch : Gen. xlix. 4.

עֶרֶשׂ *m.* a bed, couch, probably with canopy and curtains; a sofa, divan : Ps. vi. 6 : Amos iii. 12 ; vi. 4.

מִשְׁכָּב *m.* a bed to lie down on ; Job vii. 13.

COUCH (*V*)

כָּרַע to bend, to bow down. KAL *pret.* Num. xxiv. 9.

רָבַץ to lie down, as beasts, quadrupeds. KAL *pret.* Gen. xlix. 9. *part.* Poel, Gen. xlix. 14 : Deut. xxxiii. 13. מִרְבָּץ *m.* couching-place : Ezek. xxv. 5.

שָׁחַח to bow down. KAL *fut.* Job xxxviii. 40.

COULTER

אֵת an agricultural instrument of iron, having an edge, and requiring to be sometimes sharpened ; according to most of the ancient interpreters, a ploughshare or coulter ; according to Symmachus and the Rabbins, a mattock ; Lxx., σκεῦος. 1 Sam. xiii. 20, 21.

COUNSEL, COUNSELLOR, COUNCIL

1 אִישׁ *m.* man.

2 אֱנוֹשׁ *m.* man.

3 דִּבֵּר *m.* word.

4 הַדָּבָר *m.* Ch. counsellor of state, minister, vizier ; *i. e.* one skilled in the law.

5 הַדָּבְרִין Ch. *m. pl.* counsellors.

6 תַּחְבֻּלוֹת *f. pl.* steering ; art of steering or guiding ; wise counsel, prudent measures ; cunning devices.

7 יָסַד to set or lay a foundation. NIPHAL, to be set, as in counsel, to take counsel : ᵃ*pret.* ᵇ*inf.*

8 יְעַט Ch. to counsel. PᵃAL *part.*

9 יָעַץ to deliberate : Ps. xiii. 2, to lay a scheme, to form a design ; to give counsel, to ask counsel ; to take counsel ; with or without עֵצָה. KAL ᵃ*pret.* ᵇ*fut.* ᶜ*part.* Poel, Isa. ix. 6, of the Messiah. NIPHAL ᵈ*pret.* ᵉ*fut.* ᶠ*part.* ᵍ מוֹעֵצוֹת *f. pl.* ʰ עֵצָה *f.* counsel, including both deliberation and the purpose of doing anything ; implying also wisdom, reflection, and skill : Deut. xxxii. 28, &c.

10 מְלַךְ Ch. *m.* advice, counsel.

11 סוֹד *m.* an assembly ; consultation ; confidential talk, a secret ; "secret counsel."

12 עֵטָא Ch. *f.* counsel, wisdom, understanding.

13 רִגְמָה *f.* heap ; throng, band ; *marg.* 'company.'

14 שָׁאַל to ask, to inquire, to ask for ; to interrogate, to ask counsel. KAL ᵃ*imp.* ᵇ*fut.*

No. 9 h not all included.

Exod. xviii. 19.	9 b	1 Chron. xxvii. 32, 33.	9 c	Ps. ii. 2.	7 a
Num. xxxi. 16.	3	2 Chron. x. 6, 6.	9 e f	v. 10.	9 g
Judg. xviii. 5.	14 a	x. 8, 8.	9 h a e	xvi. 7.	9 a
xx. 18.	14 b	xxiii. 3, 4.	9 e	xxxi. 13.	7 b
1 Sam. xiv. 37.	14 b	xxv. 16, a 16.	9 c h	lv. 14.	11
2 Sam. xv. 12.	9 f	xxx. 2, 23.	9 e	lxiv. 2.	11
xvi. 23, 23, 23.	9 h a h	xxxii. 3.	9 e	lxviii. 27.	13
xvii. 7.	9 a	Ezra iv. 5.	9 c	lxxi. 10.	9 d
xvii. 11, 15, 15, 21.	9 a	vii. 14, 15.	9 b	lxxxi. 12.	9 g
1 Kings i. 12.	9 b h	vii. 28.	9 e	lxxxiii. 3.	11
xii. 8.	9 h a	viii. 25.	9 c	cxix. 24.	2, 9 h
xii. 9.	9 f	Neh. vi. 7.	9 e	Prov. i. 5.	6
xii. 13.	9 h a	Job iii. 14.	9 e	xi. 14, 14.	6, 9 c
xii. 28.	9 e	xii. 17.	9 a	xii. 5.	9 c
2 Kings vi. 8.	9 e	xxvi. 3.	9 a	xiii. 20.	9 c
1 Chron. xxvi. 14.	9 c	xxxvii. 12.	6	xv. 22, 22.	11, 9 c

Prov. xxii. 20.	9 g	Isa. xlv. 21.	9 e	Dan. iii. 2, 3.	4
xxiv. 6, 6.	6, 9 c	xlvi. 11.β	9 h	iii. 24, 27.	5
Isa. i. 26.	9 c	Jer. vii. 24.	9 g	iv. 27.	10
iii. 3.	9 c	xxiii. 18, 22.	11	iv. 36.	5
vii. 5.	9 a	xxxviii. 15.	9 b	vi. 7.	5
ix. 6.	9 c	xlix. 20.	9 h a	Hos. iv. 12.	14 b
xix. 11, 11.	9 h c	xlix. 30.	9 a h	xi. 6.	9 g
xxiii. 8.	9 a	l. 45.	9 h a	Micah iv. 9.	9 c
xl. 13.	1, 9 h	Ezek. xi. 2.γ	9 c h	vi. 16.	9 g
xl. 14.	9 d	Dan. ii. 14.	12	Nah. i. 11.	9 c
xli. 28.	9 c				

a lit. for counsellor to the king.   β *lit.* the man of my counsel.
γ *lit.* counsellors of wicked counsel.

COUNT

1 חָשַׁב to think, &c., to account, esteem ; to count or number ; to impute, to reckon to any, *seq.* לְ of person and *acc.* of thing. KAL ᵃ*fut.* NIPHAL ᵇ*pret.* ᶜ*fut.* PIEL ᵈ*pret.*

2 כָּסַס to count, to reckon. KAL *fut.*

3 מָנָה to number. KAL *pret.*

4 נָתַן to give (see *Make*) ; to make like ; so τίθεσθαι for νομίζειν, ἡγεῖσθαι. KAL *fut.*

5 סָפַר to relate, to number. KAL ᵃ*pret.* ᵇ*fut.* ᶜ*part.* Poel. NIPHAL ᵈ*fut.*

6 פָּקַד to number ; to take particular notice or account of. KAL ᵃ*pret.* ᵇ*part.* Paül. PUAL ᶜ*pret.*

Gen. xv. 6.	1 a	1 Kings iii. 8.	5 d	Ps. lxxxviii. 4.	1 b
xxxi. 15.	1 b	1 Chron. xxi. 6.	6 a	cvi. 31.	1 c
Exod. xii. 4.	2	xxiii. 24.	6 b	cxxxix. 18.	5 b
xxxviii. 21.	6 c	Neh. xiii. 13.	1 b	Prov. xvii. 28.	1 c
Lev. xxiii. 15.	5 a	Job xviii. 3.	1 b	xxvii. 14.	1 c
xxv. 27, 52.	1 d	xix. 11, 15.	1 a	Isa. x. 28.	1 b
xxv. 31.	1 c	xxxi. 4.	5 b	xxxii. 15.	1 c
Num. xviii. 30.	1 b	xxxiii. 10.	1 a	xxxiii. 18.	5 c
xxiii. 10.	3	xli. 29.	1 b	xl. 15, 17.	1 b
Josh. xiii. 3.	1 c	Ps. xliv. 22.	1 b	Hos. viii. 12.	1 b
1 Sam. i. 16.	4	lxxxvii. 6.	5 b		

COUNTENANCE

1 אַף *m.* face ; anger.

2 הָדַר to honour, to countenance. KAL *fut.*

3 זִיו Ch. brightness, countenance.

4 עַיִן *com.* the eye.

5 פָּנִים *m. pl.* the face, countenance, the part turned towards any one : 2 Kings viii. 11, "he settled his countenance steadfastly," *i. e.* beheld him with a fixed look. The face, countenance, is also put for the look, mien, air of a person, as expressing the affections or emotions of the mind : Gen. xxxi. 2, 5. Gen. iv. 5, &c.

6 מַרְאֶה *m.* sight, aspect, view ; appearance, form.

7 תֹּאַר *m.* form, figure.

No. 5 not included.

Exod. xxiii. 3.	2	1 Sam. xxv. 3.	7	Cant. v. 15.	6
Judg. xviii. 6, 6.	6	Sam. xxvii. 37.	6	Dan. i. 13, 13, 15.	6
1 Sam. xvi. 7.	6	Ps. x. 4.	1	v. 6, 9, 10.	3
xvi. 12.	4	Cant. ii. 14, 14.	6	vii. 28.	3
xvii. 42.	6				

COUNTERVAIL

שָׁוָה to be made even, level ; to be equal, to countervail, to be equivalent. KAL *part.* Poel, Esth. vii. 4, *i. e.* cannot make it good.

COUNTRY   (See also **FAR**)

1 אֲדָמָה *f.* earth, ground ; land, a country.

2 אִי *m.* see *Isle.*

3 אֶרֶץ *com.* the earth, the ground; a land, a country: Gen. x. 20, &c.

4 גְּלִילָה *f.* border, coast.

5 אֶזְרָח *m.* one who lives in the place where he arose or was born; "one of your own country;" "born in the country."

6 חֶבֶל *com.* a cord; a tract of land measured or laid out.

7 נֶפֶת *f.* (see *Situation*), elevated country.

8 מָקוֹם *com.* place, *pr.* station, from standing.

9 פְּרָזִי one dwelling in the country; joined with villages.

10 שָׂדֶה *m.* field, country, open fields; the field or country of a people is their territory.

No. 3 not included.

Gen. xiv. 7.	10	Deut. iii. 14.	6	1 Sam. xxvii. 5, 7, 11.	10
xxix. 26.	8	Josh. xvii. 11.	7	1 Chron. viii. 8.	10
xxxii. 3.	10	Judg. xx. 6.	10	Jer. xlvii. 2.	2
Lev. xvi. 29.	5	Ruth i. 1, 2, 6, 22.	10	Ezek. xlvii. 8.	4
xvii. 15.	5	ii. 6.	10	xlvii. 22.	5
xxiv. 22.	5	iv. 3.	10	Hos. xii. 12.	10
Num. xv. 13.	10	1 Sam. vi. 1.	10	Jonah iv. 2.	1
xxi. 20.	10	vi. 18.	9		

COUPLE, COUPLING

1 חָבַר to join or couple together things of the same sort. See *Join.* KAL [a] *part.* Poel. PIEL [b] *pret.* [c] *inf.* [d] *fut.* PUAL [e] *pret.* [f] חֹבֶרֶת *f.* junction, place of union. [g] מְחַבְּרוֹת *f. pl.* beams of wood used for joining. [h] מַחְבֶּרֶת *f.* joining.

2 צֶמֶד *m.* a pair, a yoke, of oxen and of asses.

3 שְׁנַיִם *adj. num. dual,* two.

4 תָּאַם to be double, twain. KAL [a] *part.* Poel. [b] תָּאֳמִים *m. pl. constr.* for תְּאֳמִים twins.

Exod. xxvi. 3, 3.	3	Exod. xxxvi. 10, 10.	1 d b	Exod. xxix. 20.	1 h
xxvi. 4, 4.	1 f h	xxxvi. 11, 11, 12.	1 h	Judg. xix. 3.	2
xxvi. 5.	1 b	xxxvi. 13, 16.	1 d	2 Sam. xiii. 6.	3
xxvi. 6, 9, 11.	1 b	xxxvi. 17, 17.	1 h f	xvi. 1.	2
xxvi. 10, 10.	1 f	xxxvi. 18.	1 c	2 Chron. xxxiv. 11.	1 g
xxvi. 24, 24.	4 a b	xxxvi. 29, 29.	4 a b	Isa. xxi. 7, 9.	2
xxviii. 27.	1 h	xxxix. 4, 4.	1 a e		

COURAGE

1 אָמַץ to be strong, resolute, and vigorous; to act with great spirit and undaunted courage: in certain passages it seems to have been rendered, "to be of good courage," because of its being joined with חָזַק, usually translated, to be strong: these two words are combined to denote intrepidity, fearlessness, and a resolute mind. KAL [a] *imp.* [b] אַמִּיץ *adj.* firm, strong.

2 חָזַק to bind fast; to make firm; to be strong, firm, undaunted. See *Strong, Sure.* KAL [a] *pret.* [b] *imp.* HITHPAEL [c] *pret.*

3 לֵב the heart. [a] לְבָב *m. id.*

4 רוּחַ *com.* breath, spirit, mind; spirit, courage.

Num. xiii. 20.	2 c	2 Sam. xiii. 28.	2 b	Ezra x. 4.	2 b
Deut. xxxi. 6, 7, 23.	1 a	1 Chron. xix. 13.	2 b	Ps. xxvii. 14.	2 b
Josh. i. 6, 7, 9, 18.	1 a	xxii. 13.	1 a	xxxi. 24.	2 b
ii. 11.	4	xxviii. 20.	1 a	Isa. xli. 6.	2 b
x. 25.	1 a	2 Chron. xv. 8.	2 c	Dan. xi. 25.	3 a
xxiii. 6.	2 a	xix. 11. a	2 b	Amos ii. 16.	1 b, 3
2 Sam. x. 12.	2 b	xxxii. 7.	1 a		

[a] "deal courageously," *lit.* take courage and do.

COURSE

1 חָלַף to pass, to change, to take by courses in succession. [a] חֲלִיפָה *f.* change.

2 מַחֲלֹקָה Ch. *f.* division, class, course; specially of the twenty-four classes of the Levites and priests. [a] מַחֲלֹקֶת *f.* divisions.

3 יָבָל *m.* a stream; a channel in which a stream flows.

4 מוֹצָא *m.* place of going forth, a fountain of waters.

5 מוֹט to be moved, to be out of course, with danger of ruin. NIPHAL *fut.*

6 מְסִלָּה *f.* highway, path: as used of the stars, it seems to mean their orbits; *lit.* from their highways or elevations.

7 עָנָה to answer; to sing together by courses. KAL *fut.*

8 מְרוּצָה *f.* a running, a course of action. The marginal reading of Jer. xxiii. 10 is probably taken from רָצַץ to break; to oppress.

No. 2 a not included.

Judg. v. 20.	6	Ezra iii. 11.	7	Isa. xliv. 4.	3
1 Kings v. 14.	1 a	vi. 18.	2	Jer. viii. 6.	8
2 Chron. xxxii. 30.	4	Ps. lxxxii. 5.	5	xxiii. 10.	8

COURT

1 בַּיִת *m.* house: Amos vii. 13, "king's court," or house of the kingdom.

2 חָצֵר *m.* a court surrounded, a vacant space open to the sky, as of the tabernacle and temple, in the midst of a house built round about it; into which the windows mostly opened, and large doors; smaller windows and a low door for entrance from the street; sometimes translated town, village, 2 Kings xx. 4 [k]. [a] חָצִיר *m.* only in Isa. xxxiv. 13. Gussetius thinks the meaning of grass or some kind of vegetation should be retained; see *Grass.* Bush renders it residence.

3 עֲזָרָה *f.* a court shut in or enclosed. Taylor makes the primary derived meaning to be, to help; and adds, The court mentioned (2 Chron. iv. and vi.) seems to have been a square work raised above the pavement, with a parapet round about it, and a door in the parapet, before the altar of burnt offerings. Upon this elevated square stood Solomon's "scaffold" or pulpit: 2 Chron. iv. 9, 9; vi. 13.

4 עִיר *f.* city: 2 Kings xx. 4 [k].

COVENANT

בְּרִית *f.* There is great probability that this word is derived from בָּרָה to eat, by which act the covenant was ratified between two parties; so it applies to the eating of the sacrifice by the party offering, being at the same time when offered the bread of God; and so it illustrates the character of the Lord's Supper as a ratification on our part of Christ's covenant by eating. See Cudworth's Discourse on the true notion of the Lord's Supper. It is derived by some from בָּרָה to choose, importing the selection of conditions of the covenant to be ratified; by some from בָּרָא to cut or strike, as in Latin we have *foedus ferire*, because in covenants it was usual to slay some animal: but Parkhurst, with some others, considers it to be deduced from בָּרַר to purify ceremonially or with sacred rites; it may however be very difficult at this time to ascertain what has really been the first origin of the word and its application, which is to be sought for in the very earliest testimonies and

customs of the people of God rather than of other nations. It is used of God's everlasting covenant of salvation; of the "new covenant" of the gospel, Jer. xxxi. 31: of any covenant of God with man, or of man with man; and also of any promise or stipulation, as also of any fixed arrangement, Jer. xxxiii. 20, or precept to be observed, Jer. xxxiv. 15. It is also put for the conditions of a covenant, as the Decalogue, Deut. iv. 13; ix. 9, 11: Isa. xxviii. 18; and for the sign of a covenant, Gen. xvii. 13. The blood of the victim slain was called the blood of the covenant, Exod. xxiv. 8, Zech. ix. 11; hence we read, Matt. xxvi. 28, of the blood of Christ as the blood of the new covenant: comp. Mark xiv. 24, Heb. xiii. 20. A covenant of salt is a perpetual stipulation of stipend or maintenance, according to some; or a perpetual covenant: see *Salt*. Gen. vi. 18, &c.

COVENANT (V)

כָּרַת to cut, to cut asunder; to make (a covenant), to covenant. KAL *pret.* 2 Chron. vii. 18, Jer. xxxiv. 13; with בְּרִית, Hag. ii. 5; *fut.* Isa. lvii. 8, *marg.* 'or, hewed it;' Gesenius, Thou didst covenant for thyself from them, *i. e.* to receive from them the price of thy whoredom. Others, Thou hast joined with thee some of them, *sc.* in covenant; Vulg. "Fœdus pepegisti cum eis, *i. e.* cum quibusdam ex eis."

COVER (See TAPESTRY)

1 אֹהֶל *m.* a tent.

2 בָּלַע to swallow down; perhaps *metaph.* to conceal or cover suddenly out of sight. But the Lxx. in Num. iv. 20, have rendered בְּבַלַּע by ἐξάπινα, *lit.* as the swallowing (of spittle): so it is an injunction not to go suddenly or hastily within sight of the holy vessels. Gussetius would render the passage, But they shall not go in to see, (for this would be) as the swallowing down of that which is sacred.

3 חָפָה to cover the head and face for sorrow, disgrace, and shame. KAL [a]*pret.* [b]*part.* Poel. NIPHAL [c]*part.*

4 חָפַף to cover by way of protection. KAL *part.* Poel.

5 טָלַל to shade; to cover over. PIEL *fut.*

6 יָעַט to clothe. KAL *pret.*

7 כָּסָה to cover, to conceal: God covers sin when he pardons it: Ps. xxxii. 1, *lit.* covered (as to) sin, Neh. iv. 5. Man covers sin, either when he cloaks and extenuates it, Prov. xxviii. 13, or when he passes it by and buries it in oblivion, Prov. xvii. 9. To cover is to obscure the understandings of men, Isa. xxix. 10. To overwhelm with confusion and calamity, Ps. cxl. 9: Prov. x. 6: Hab. ii. 17. To cover pride from man is to dispose him to humility, Job xxxiii. 17. KAL [a]*part.* Poel. [b]*part.* Paül. NIPHAL [c]*pret.* [d]*inf.* PIEL [e]*pret.* [f]*inf.* [g]*imp.* [h]*fut.* [i]*part.* PUAL [k]*pret.* [l]*fut.* [m]*part.* HITHPAEL [n]*fut.* [o]*part.* כָּסוּי [p]*m.* covering. כְּסוּת [q]*f. id.* מִכְסֶה [r]*m. id.* מְכַסֶּה [s]*m. id.*

8 כָּפַשׁ to cover over. HIPHIL *pret.* The Talmudists use it to express crowded, pressed, heaped measure; also of the

Jewish church, bowed down in ashes, covered with ashes. —*Gesenius.*

9 כָּשָׂה to cover; to be covered (with fat). KAL *pret.*

10 לָאַט to wrap around, to muffle, to cover. KAL *pret.*

11 לוֹט *m.* a covering, veil; muffler.

12 נָסַךְ to pour out a libation: to cover. KAL [a]*inf.* HOPHAL [b]*fut.* [c]מַסֵּכָה *f.* a covering. Lowth, in accordance with the Lxx. and the Syriac, renders this expression in Isa. xxx. 1, "who ratify covenants," *i. e.* make a compact; which is adopted by Rosenmüller, Gesenius, and others. Alexander, with Ewald and J. D. Michaelis, to weave a web: Gussetius, a covering for protection. [d]נֶסֶךְ *m.* libation.

13 סָכַךְ to cover, so as to secure, protect, with לְ giving the idea of an obstacle as well as of protection; also followed by two *acc.* and עַל; Hiphil *seq.* עַל and לְ: to cover the feet, an *euphemism* for to ease oneself, to satisfy a call of nature. KAL [a]*pret.* [b]*fut.* [c]*part.* Poel. HIPHIL [d]*inf.* [e]*fut.* [f]*part.* [g]מָסָךְ *m.* [h]מוּסַךְ *m.* covert. [i]כְּתִיב מֵיסַךְ [k]סֹךְ *m.* covert. [l]סֻכָּה *f.* [m]מְסֻכָּה *f.* that with which one is covered.

14 סָפַן to ceil. KAL [a]*fut.* [b]*part.* Paül.

15 סָתַר *m.* see *Hide*. [a]מִסְתּוֹר *m.* a hidingplace, refuge.

16 עוּב to be in a dark, cloudy state. HIPHIL, to cover as with a cloud: *fut.*

17 עָטָה to cover or wrap oneself up with a cloak or upper garment. It is also applied to the covering of the upper lip, or veiling the upper part of the face, which was usual in great sorrow or shame. With *inf.*, will surely cover. KAL [a]*pret.* [b]*inf.* [c]*fut.* [d]*part.* Poel. HIPHIL [e]*pret.*

18 עָטַף (see *Overwhelm*), to cover as with a garment, &c. KAL *fut.*

19 צַב *m.* litter, sedan, palanquin, as being lightly and gently borne; probably, litter-wagons.

20 צָמִיד *m.* lid, cover of a vessel, as "made fast" upon it.

21 צָפָה to be spread; to overlay. PIEL [a]*pret.* [b]*fut.* PUAL [c]*part.* [d]צִפּוּי *m.* overlaying, metal laid over statues.

22 קָרַם to draw over, to cover; *seq.* עַל. KAL [a]*pret.* [b]*fut.*

23 קְשָׂה and קַשְׂוָה *f.* covers to dishes; or, dishes, bowls for libations. Lxx. σπονδεῖα.

24 מֶרְכָּב *m.* the covering or tilt of a carriage in motion: Gesenius, a seat in a chariot or other vehicle.

25 שׁוּף to lie in wait for; to fall upon suddenly. KAL *fut.*

26 שָׂכַךְ to interweave; to cover. KAL *pret.*

Gen. vii. 19, 20.	7 l	Exod. xxiv. 15, 16.	7 h	Exod. xl. 3.	13 a
viii. 13.	7 r	xxv. 20.	13 c	xl. 19.	7 r
ix. 23.	7 h	xxv. 29, 29.	23, 12 b	xl. 21, 21.	13 g e
xx. 16.	7 q	xxvi. 7.	1	xl. 34.	7 h
xxiv. 65.	7 n	xxvi. 13.	7 f	Lev. iii. 3, 9, 14.	7 i
xxxviii. 14.	7 h	xxvi. 14, 14.	7 r	iv. 8.	7 i
xxxviii. 15.	7 h	xxviii. 42.	7 f	vii. 3.	7 i
Exod. viii. 6.	7 h	xxix. 13, 22.	7 i	ix. 19.	7 s
x. 5.	7 e	xxxiii. 22.	26	xiii. 12, 13.	7 e
x. 15.	7 h	xxxv. 11.	7 r	xiii. 45.	17 c
xiv. 28.	7 h	xxxv. 12.	13 g	xvi. 13.	7 e
xv. 5.	7 h	xxxvi. 19, 19.	7 r	xvii. 13.	7 e
xv. 10.	7 e	xxxvii. 9.	13 c	Num. iii. 25.	
xvi. 13.	7 h	xxxvii. 16, 16.	23, 12 b	iv. 5, 5.	13 g, 7 e
xxi. 33.	7 h	xxxix. 34, 34.		iv. 6, 14.	7 p
xxii. 27.	7 q	34.	7 r r, 13 g	iv. 7, 7.	23, 12 d

Num. iv. 8, 8.	7 e r	Job xxiii. 17.	7 e	Isa. xxix. 10.	7 e
iv. 9.	7 e	xxiv. 7.	7 q	xxx. 1, 1.β	12 a c
iv. 10.	7 r	xxvi. 6.	7 q	xxx. 22.	21 d
iv. 11, 11.	7 e r	xxxi. 19.α	7 q	xxxii. 2.	15
iv. 12, 12.	7 e r	xxxi. 33.	7 e	xxxvii. 1.	7 n
iv. 15.	7 f	xxxvi. 30, 32.	7 e	xxxvii. 2.	7 o
iv. 20.	2	xxxviii. 34.	7 h	l. 3.	7 q
iv. 25, 25.	7 r	xxxviii. 40.	13 l	li. 16.	7 e
vii. 3.	19	xl. 21.	15	lviii. 7.	7 e
ix. 15.	7 e	xl. 22.	13 b	lix. 6.	7 n
ix. 16.	7 h	Ps. xxxii. 1.	7 b	lx. 2, 6.	7 h
xvi. 38, 39.	21 d	xliv. 15.	7 e	lxi. 10.	6
xvi. 42.	7 e	xliv. 19.	7 h	Jer. iii. 25.	7 h
xix. 15.	20	lxi. 4.	15	xiv. 3, 4.	3 a
xxii. 5.	7 e	lxv. 13.	18	xxv. 38.	13 k
xxii. 11.	7 h	lxviii. 13.	3 b	xlvi. 8.	7 h
Deut. xxii. 12.	7 h	lxix. 7.	7 e	li. 42.	7 c
xxiii. 13.	7 e	lxxi. 13.	17 c	li. 51.	7 e
xxxii. 15.	9	lxxiii. 6.	18	Lam. ii. 1.	16
xxxiii. 12.	4	lxxx. 10.	7 k	iii. 16.	8
Josh xxiv. 7.	7 h	lxxxv. 2.	7 e	iii. 43, 44.	13 a
Judg. iii. 24.	13 f	lxxxix. 45.	17 e	Ezek. i. 11, 23, 23.	7 i
iv. 18, 19.	7 h	xci. 4.	13 e	vii. 18.	7 e
1 Sam. xii. 13.	7 h	civ. 2.	17 d	xii. 6, 12.	7 h
xxiv. 3.	13 d	civ. 6.	7 e	xvi. 8, 10, 18.	7 h
xxv. 20.	15	civ. 9.	7 f	xviii. 7.	7 h
xxviii. 14.	17 d	cvi. 39.	13 g	xviii. 16.	7 f
2 Sam. xv. 30, 30.	3 b a	cvi. 11, 17.	7 h	xxiv. 7.	7 f
xvii. 19.	13 g	cix. 19, 29.	17 c	xxiv. 8.	7 d
xix. 4.	10	cxxxix. 11.	25	xxiv. 17, 22.	17 c
1 Kings i. 1.	7 h	cxxxix. 13.	13 b	xxvi. 10.	7 h
vi. 9.	14 a	cxl. 7.	13 a	xxvi. 19.	7 h
vi. 15, 15.	21 a b	cxl. 9.	7 h	xxvii. 7.	7 s
vi. 20.	21 b	cxlvi. 8.	7 i	xxviii. 13.	13 m
vi. 35.	21 a	Prov. x. 6, 11, 12.	7 h	xxviii. 14, 16.	13 c
vii. 3, 7.	14 b	xii. 16.	7 a	xxx. 18.	7 h
vii. 18, 41, 42.	7 f	xvii. 9.	7 i	xxxi. 15.	7 e
viii. 7.	13 b	xxiv. 31.	7 k	xxxii. 7, 7.	7 e h
2 Kings xvi. 18.	13 h i	xxvi. 23.	21 c	xxxvii. 6.	22 a
xix. 1.	7 n	xxvi. 26.	7 n	xxxvii. 8.	22 b
ix. 2.	7 o	xxviii. 13.	7 h	xxxvii. 9, 16.	7 f
1 Chron. xxviii. 18.	13 c	Eccles. vi. 4.	7 l	xli. 16.	7 m
2 Chron. iv. 12, 13.	7 f	Cant. iii. 10.	24	Hos. ii. 9.	7 f
v. 8.	7 h	Isa. iv. 6.	15 a	x. 8.	7 g
Neh. iii. 15.	5	vi. 2, 2.	7 h	Obad. 10.	7 h
iv. 5.	3 b	ix. 9.	7 i	Jonah iii. 6.	7 h
Esth. vi. 12.	3 b	xiv. 11.	7 s	iii. 8.	7 s
vii. 8.	3 a	xvi. 4.	15	Micah iii. 7.	17 a
Job ix. 24.	7 h	xxii. 8.	13 g	vii. 10.	7 h
xv. 27.	7 e	xxii. 17.	17 b d	Hab. ii. 14, 17.	7 h
xvi. 18.	7 h	xxv. 7.	11	iii. 3.	7 h
xxi. 26.	7 h	xxvi. 21.	7 h	Mal. ii. 13.	7 f
xxii. 11.	7 h	xxviii. 20.	12 c	ii. 16.	7 e
xxii. 14.	15				

α lit. no covering to the poor.   β or, that pour out a libation.

COVET

1 אָוָה to desire earnestly. HITHPAEL a pret. b fut.

2 בָּצַע to cut and tear away, to plunder; to get by covetous, dishonest means. KAL a part. Poel. b בֶּצַע m. rapine, prey; any unjust gain.

3 חָמַד to desire strongly, to take delight in; used both in a good and bad sense. KAL a pret. b fut.

Exod. xviii. 21.	2 b	Prov. xxi. 26.	1 a
xx. 17, 17.	3 b	xxviii. 16.	2 b
Deut. v. 21.	1 b	Isa. lvii. 17.	2 b
Josh. vii. 21.	3 b	Jer. vi. 13.	2 b
Ps. x. 3.	2 a	viii. 10.	2 b
cxix. 36.	2 b	Jer. xxii. 17.	2 b
		li. 13.	2 b
		Ezek. xxxiii. 31.	2 b
		Micah ii. 2.	3 a
		Hab. ii. 9, 9.	2 a b

COW

1 בָּקָר com. horned cattle, most commonly at full age; collectively, herd.

2 עֶגְלָה f. a heifer: "young cow," lit. heifer of the herd.

3 פָּרָה m. heifer; also of a heifer or young cow in milk, or as bearing the yoke.

4 שׁוֹר m. an ox, bullock, so called from its strength and boldness; but without respect to sex or age.

Lev. xxii. 28.	4	Job xxi. 10.	4	Isa. xi. 7.	3
Num. xviii. 17.	4	Isa. vii. 21.	4	Ezek. iv. 15.	2, 1

CRACKLING

קֹל m. any sound, noise, voice: Eccles. vii. 6, marg. 'sound.'

CRACKNEL

נִקֻּדִים m. a kind of cake, pricked or marked with points: 1 Kings xiv. 3: according to some, roasted ears of corn. Buxtorf, biscuits. Harmer, cakes spotted with coriander and other seeds, still common in Syria and the East.

CRAFT, CRAFTSMAN

1 חָרָשׁ m. engraver, artificer. a חֶרֶשׁ m. work of an artificer.

2 עָרַם to be crafty, cunning, mostly in a bad sense. HIPHIL a fut. b עֹרֶם m. craftiness. c עָרוּם adj. crafty.

3 מִרְמָה f. deceit, fraud.

Deut. xxvii. 15.	1	Job v. 12.	2 c	Ps. lxxxiii. 3.	2 a
2 Kings xxiv. 14, 16.	1	v. 13.	2 b	Dan. viii. 25.	3
1 Chron. iv. 14.	1 a	xv. 5.	2 c	Hos. xiii. 2.	1
Neh. xi. 35.	1 a				

CRAG

שֵׁן com. tooth; sharp rock, cliff, crag: Job xxxix. 28.

CRANE

סוּס m. the swallow, a bird of passage, with a chattering querulous note: Bochart: Isa. xxxviii. 14; Jer. viii. 7, סִיס כתיב m. id., Jer. viii. 7. According to the Rabbins, a crane.

CRASHING

שֶׁבֶר m. a breaking: Zeph. i. 10.

CRAVE

אָכַף to impel, to urge: others have derived this verb from כָּפַף to bow. KAL pret. Prov. xvi. 26.

CREATE

בָּרָא to bring into being; to produce, put in form, or renew; to put in a new or happier condition. It is a word having an especial reference to God, and his operations by an infinite power. "The leading import of בָּרָא is twofold: (1) The production or effectuation of something new, rare, and wonderful; the bringing something to pass in a striking and marvellous manner, as Num. xvi. 30, Jer. xxxi. 22. (2) The act of renovating, remodelling, or reconstituting, something already in existence, Ps. li. 10, explained by the parallel clause. Isa. lxv. 17."—Bush on Gen. i. 1. KAL a pret. b inf. c imp. d fut. e part. Poel. NIPHAL f pret. g inf. h fut. i part.

Gen. i. 1.	a	Ps. civ. 30.	a	Isa. xlv. 8, 12.	h	a
i. 21.	a	cxlviii. 5.	d	xlv. 18, 18.	e, a	e, a
i. 27, 27, 27.	d, a, a	Eccles. xii. 1.	a	xlvii. 7.	f	f
ii. 3.	a	Isa. iv. 5.	a	liv. 16, 16.	a	a
ii. 4.	g	xl. 26.	a	lvii. 19.	a	b
v. 1.	b	xl. 28.	a	lxv. 17, 18, 18.	a	a
v. 2, 2.	a, g	xli. 20.	a	Jer. xxxi. 22.	a	e
vi. 7.	a	xlii. 5.	a	Ezek. xxi. 30.	a	a
Deut. iv. 32.	a	xliii. 1, 15.	a	xxviii. 13, 15.	g	f
Ps. li. 10.	c	xliii. 7.	a	Amos iv. 13.	e	g
lxxxix. 12.	i	xlv. 7, 7.	e	Mal. ii. 10.	a	e
cii. 18.	i					a

CREATURE

חַי *adj.* any living thing; usually joined with the following word; see *Life, Living :* in these passages, translated "living creature:" Ezek. i. 5, 13, 13, 14, 15, 15, 19, 19, 20, 21, 22; iii. 13 : x. 15, 17, 20.

נֶפֶשׁ *com.* soul: Gen. i. 21, *lit.* living soul, 24; ii. 19; ix. 10, 12, 15, 16 : Lev. xi. 46, 46.

CREDITOR

בַּעַל *m.* master : Deut. xv. 2, *lit.* master of the lending of his hand.

יָד *com.* hand : Deut. xv. 2.

נָשָׁה to lend on usury. KAL *part.* Poel, 2 Kings iv. 1 : Isa. l. 1. מַשָּׁה *m.* lending : Deut. xv. 2.

CREEP

1 רָמַשׂ to creep, the appropriate verb for the motion of the smaller animals which creep along the ground; both of those which have four feet or more, and also of those without feet, which glide or drag themselves upon the ground, as worms and serpents; in a wider sense, of aquatic or amphibious reptiles. KAL ᵃ*fut.* ᵇ*part.* Poel. ᶜרֶמֶשׂ *m.* reptile.

2 שָׁרַץ to creep, to crawl; to bring forth abundantly: the two senses are united in our use of the word creep; spoken of reptiles and the smaller aquatic animals. KAL ᵃ*part.* Poel. ᵇשֶׁרֶץ *m.* reptile.

Gen. i. 24, 25.	1 c	Lev. v. 2.	2 b	Deut. iv. 18.	1 b	
i. 26, 26.	1 c b	xi. 20, 21, 23, 31.	2 a	xiv. 19.	2 b	
i. 30.	1 b	xi. 29, 29.	2 b a	1 Kings iv. 33.	1 c	
vi. 7, 20.	1 c	xi. 41, 41.	2 b a	Ps. civ. 20.	1 a	
vii. 8.	1 b	xi. 42, 42.	2 b a	civ. 25.	1 c	
vii. 14, 14.	1 c b	xi. 43, 43.	2 b a	cxlviii. 10.	1 c	
vii. 21, 21.	2 b a	xi. 44, 44.	2 b, 1 b	Ezek. viii. 10.	1 c	
vii. 23.	1 c	xi. 46.	2 a	xxxviii. 20, 20.	1 c b	
viii. 17, 17.	1 c b	xx. 25.	1 a	Hos. ii. 18.	1 c	
viii. 19, 19.	1 c b	xxii. 5.	2 b	Hab. i. 14.	1 c	

CRIB

אֵבוּס *m.* a place in which cattle are fattened; a crib or stall : Job xxxix. 9 : Prov. xiv. 4 : Isa. i. 3.

CRIME

זִמָּה *f.* purpose, counsel, plan, *sc.* for evil, rarely for good; mischief, wickedness, crime, heinous crime. Specially of crimes arising from unchastity, as rape, incest : Job xxxi. 11.

מִשְׁפָּט *m.* judgment : Ezek. vii. 23, *lit.* the judgment of bloods.

CRIMSON

כַּרְמִיל *m.* crimson or deep scarlet, a colour prepared from insects inhabiting a species of oak; *coccus ilicis* of Linn. Also, crimson stuffs : 2 Chron. ii. 7, 14; iii. 14.

שָׁנִי *m.* see *Scarlet.* Jer. iv. 30.

תּוֹלָע *m.* a worm; *coccus ilicis,* Linn., or the *helix ianthina;* less permanent than scarlet as a dye, of a bluish tint, and commonly rendered 'blue :' Isa. i. 18.

CRISPING-PIN

חֲרִיטִים *m. pl.* see *Bag.* Isa. iii. 22, *i.e.* money-bags or purses, highly ornamented; probably of metal.

CROOKBACKED

גִּבֵּן *adj.* gibbous, hunchbacked : Lev. xxi. 20.

CROOKED

1 בָּרִיחַ see *Bar.* Job xxvi. 13. LXX. δράκοντα ὄφιν φεύγοντα; *alibi* ἀποστάτην. Aq. ὄφιν μοχλόν. The constellation in the heavens is undoubtedly intended by the crooked or fleeing serpent.

2 הָדַר to be tumid; to be elevated. KAL *part.* Paül.

3 עָוָה to turn awry or the wrong way; to make crooked. PIEL *pret.*

4 עָוַת to be crooked, in opposition to being straight. PIEL ᵃ*pret.* PUAL ᵇ*part.*

5 עָקֹב *adj.* a hill, acclivity.

6 עֲקַלְקַל *adj.* winding, crooked, bypaths. ᵃעֲקַלָּתוֹן *adj.* winding, tortuous, epithet of a serpent.

7 עָקַשׁ to twist, pervert, wrest. PIEL ᵃ*pret.* ᵇעִקֵּשׁ *adj.* perverse. ᶜמַעֲקַשִּׁים *m. pl.* tortuous ways.

8 פְּתַלְתֹּל *adj.* crooked, crafty, perverse.

Deut. xxxii. 5.	8	Eccles. i. 15.	4 b	Isa. xlii. 16.	7 c
Job xxvi. 13.	1	vii. 13.	4 a	xlv. 2.	2
Ps. cxxv. 5.	6	Isa. xxvii. 1.	6 a	lix. 8.	7 a
Prov. ii. 15.	7 b	xl. 4.	5	Lam. iii. 9.	3

CROP (V)

קָטַף to pluck off, to break off. KAL *pret.* Ezek. xvii. 4. *fut.* Ezek. xvii. 22.

CROP (N)

מֻרְאָה *f.* crop, craw of birds : Lev. i. 16.

CROSSWAY

פֶּרֶק *m.* a place where two ways break or separate : Obad. 14.

CROUCH

דָּכָה to be bruised, crushed. KAL *fut.* Ps. x. 10, *or,* he is crushed.

שָׁחָה to bow down. HITHPAEL *inf.* 1 Sam. ii. 36.

CROWN

1 זֵר *m.* a list or border which went about the top of the ark of the covenant, the table of shewbread, and the altar of incense.

2 כָּתַר to compass about. HIPHIL ᵃ*fut.* ᵇכֶּתֶר *m.* diadem.

3 נֵזֶר *m.* the golden plate which was fixed upon the fore part of the high priest's mitre, with this inscription upon it, "Holiness to the Lord," was a token of his eminent distinction and separation to God; therefore it has the name of separation or consecration given to it, which we translate crown. And as a crown or diadem is the badge of separation or eminent distinction from the inferior

part of mankind, so this name is also given to the crowns or diadems of kings, and to the hair of the Nazarite : Jer. vii. 29. ᵃ מְנָזְרִים *m. pl.* crowned, *i. e.* princes.

4 עָטַר to compass, to crown. PIEL ᵃ*pret.* ᵇ*fut.* ᶜ*part.* HIPHIL ᵈ*part.* ᵉ עֲטָרָה *f.* a crown, convivial or royal ; any ornament or dignity : 2 Sam. xii. 30, &c.

5 קָדְקֹד *m.* crown of the head.

No. 4 e not included.

Gen. xlix. 26.	5	2 Sam. xiv. 25.	5	Ps. cxxxii. 18.	3
Exod. xxv. 11, 24, 25.	1	2 Kings xi. 12.	5	Prov. xiv. 18.	2 a
xxix. 6.	3	2 Chron. xxiii. 11.	3	xxvii. 24.	3
xxx. 3, 4.	1	Esth. i. 11.	2 b	Cant. iii. 11.	4 e a
xxxvii. 2, 11, 12, 26,		ii. 17.	2 b	Isa. iii. 17.	5
27.	1	vi. 8.	2 b	xxiii. 8.	4 d
xxxix. 30.	3	Job ii. 7.	5	Jer. ii. 16.	5
Lev. viii. 9.	3	Ps. viii. 5.	4 b	xlviii. 45.	5
xxi. 12.	3	lxv. 11.	4 a	Nah. iii. 17.	3 a
Deut. xxxiii. 20.	5	lxxxix. 39.	3	Zech. ix. 16.	3
2 Sam. i. 10.	3	ciii. 4.	4 c		

CRUEL

1 חָמָס *m.* see *Violence.*

2 חָמֵץ to be acid ; to be violent and oppressive from a malicious heart. KAL *part.* Poel.

3 אַכְזָר *adj.* cruel and unrelenting, without regard to the sorrows and sufferings of others ; without consideration, mercy, or compassion : Jer. vi. 23. ᵇ אַכְזָרִיּ ᵃ *adj. id.* ᵇ אַכְזְרִיוּת *f.* cruelty, fierceness.

4 עֹשֶׁק *m.* oppression.

5 פֶּרֶךְ *m.* oppression, rigour, from the idea of crushing.

6 קָשָׁה to be hard, severe, vehement. KAL ᵃ*pret.* ᵇ קָשֶׁה *adj.* hard, hardened.

Gen. xlix. 5.	1	Ps. lxxi. 4.	2	Isa. xiii. 9.	3 a
xlix. 7.	6 a	lxxiv. 20.	1	xix. 4.	6 b
Exod. vi. 9.	6 b	Prov. v. 9.	3 a	Jer. vi. 23.	3 a
Deut. xxxii. 33.	3	xi. 17.	3 a	xxx. 14.	3 a
Judg. ix. 24.	1	xii. 10.	3 a	l. 42.	3 a
Job xxx. 21.	3	xvii. 11.	3 a	Lam. iv. 3.	3
Ps. xxv. 19.	1	Cant. viii. 6.	6 b	Ezek. xviii. 18.a	4
xxvii. 12.	1			xxxiv. 4.	5

a *lit.* he oppressed an oppression.

CRUSE

בַּקְבֻּק *m.* see *Bottle.* 1 Kings xiv. 3.

צְלֹחִית *f.* a dish : 2 Kings ii. 20.

צַפַּחַת *f.* a cruse, flask, for water : 1 Sam. xxvi. 11, 12, 16 : 1 Kings xvii. 12, 14, 16 ; xix. 6.

CRUSH

דָּכָא see *Break.* PIEL *inf.* Lam. iii. 34. *fut.* Job iv. 19. HITHPAEL *fut.* Job v. 4.

הָמַם to defeat, to destroy. KAL *pret.* Jer. li. 34.

זוּר to press, to squeeze together. KAL *fut.* Job xxxix. 15. וּרָה *m.* crushed : Isa. lix. 5.

כָּתַת to beat, stamp, break in pieces. KAL *part.* Paül. Lev. xxii. 24.

לָחַץ to press, squeeze. KAL *fut.* Num. xxii. 25.

רָצַץ to break, to break in or down. KAL *part.* Poel. Amos iv. 1. *part.* Paül. Deut. xxviii. 33.

שָׁבַר to break, to break in pieces. KAL *inf.* Lam. i. 15.

CRY

1 אָנַק to roar for pain or anguish ; to cry out in distress ; to groan as men do that are mortally wounded. KAL ᵃ*inf.* NIPHAL ᵇ*inf.* ᶜ*part.* ᵈ אֲנָקָה *f.* crying out.

2 זָעַק to cry out with a loud voice, chiefly from sorrow or fear ; in complaint of some great sorrow, or imploring help ; of those afflicted or oppressed by an enemy, hard pressed in battle, in danger at sea, in any great distress or strait, oppressed by hard servitude ; sometimes to call, to call together. It is used also in a religious sense, of penitents, to express their earnestness, 1 Sam. xii. 10, Joel i. 14 : it may be the cry of faith, Ps. cxlii. 5 ; a persevering cry, 1 Sam. xv. 11 ; which receives a gracious hearing from God, Ps. xxii. 5, cvii. 13, 19 ; Isa. xxx. 19 ; or does not receive, Isa. lvii. 13, Jer. xi. 11, Lam. iii. 8, Hab. i. 2. It is attributed to the heart, Isa. xv. 5, Hos. vii. 14 ; to inanimate things, Hab. ii. 11 ; a cry of destruction, Isa. xv. 5, such as men raise in any great calamity. The person to whom one cries, whom one implores, is put with אֶל, לְ, and in *acc.* the thing or cause of complaint is put after מִלִּפְנֵי, לְ, עַל, also in *acc.*, as Hab. i. 2, where both constructions are joined ; (how long) shall I cry out unto thee (because of) violence ! comp. Job xix. 7. It is once used of the intemperate or boastful language of a foolish prince, Eccles. ix. 17 ; of clamour, strife, comp. 2 Tim. ii. 23, 24. KAL ᵃ*pret.* ᵇ*inf.* ᶜ*imp.* HIPHIL ᵉ*fut.* זְעָק Ch. Pᵉʟ ᶠ*pret.* ᵍ זְעָקָה *f.* an outcry.

3 הָמָה (see *Noise*), to be clamorous. KAL *fut.*

4 יָבַב to cry aloud. PIEL *fut.* Judg. v. 28, in expectation of his triumphal approach, perhaps imitating the triumphal shout.

5 הֶמְיָה *f.* a clamorous noise : Prov. xix. 18, "for his crying." The *marg.* takes the word to be HIPHIL *inf.* of מוּת for his crying, *or*, to his destruction, *or*, to cause him to die.

6 נָתַן to give. KAL ᵃ*pret.* ᵇ*fut.*

7 עָנָה to answer, to cry responsively ; of jackals, which howl in answer to one another. KAL ᵃ*pret.* ᵇ*inf.*

8 עָרַג to look upwards ; to long for. See *Pant.* This word very beautifully expresses the natural action of animals parched with thirst and deprived of all supply of water. —Henderson in loc. According to Hebrew writers, expressive of the cry of the deer. KAL *fut.*

9 פָּעָה to cry out, to scream, of a woman in travail. KAL *fut.*

10 צָהַל is used of any clear, shrill sound ; to neigh, to cry aloud. KAL ᵃ*pret.* PIEL ᵇ*imp.*

11 צְוָחָה *f.* outcry, *e.g.* of sorrow, on account of some sudden and unexpected calamity.

12 צָעַק to cry out, especially for pain, sorrow ; in complaint and for help : it evidently implies earnestness and intensity of spirit, as well as energy of utterance : in Exod. xiv. 15 it seems to imply mental crying : *seq.* אֶל of person, and לְ. *Seq. acc.* of thing, of which one complains. With *inf.*, cry at all. KAL ᵃ*pret.* ᵇ*inf.* ᶜ*imp.*

^d *fut.* ^e *part.* Poel.　Piel ^f *part.* ^g צְעָקָה *f.* crying out, especially for aid.

13　צָרַח　to be clear; *trop.* of the voice, to cry aloud.　Kal *part.* Poel.

14　קוֹל　*m.* any sound, noise, voice.

15　קָרָא　to cry out, to call, to proclaim, to call together.　Kal ^a *pret.* ^b *inf.* ^c *imp.* ^d *fut.* ^e *part.* Poel.　Niphal ^f *pret.* Pual ^g *pret.* קְרָא Ch. P'al ^h *fut.* ⁱ *part. active.*

16　רוּעַ　to make a loud noise; to shout for joy; more rarely of a mournful cry.　Hiphil ^a *inf.* ^b *imp.* ^c *fut.*

17　רָנַן　to give forth the voice with vehemence, either in joy or sorrow.　Kal ^a *imp.* ^b *fut.* Piel ^c *fut.* ^d רִנָּה *f.* shouting for joy; a mournful cry.

18　תְּשֻׁאוֹת *f. pl.* noise, clamour.

19　שָׁוַע　to cry for help in distress.　Piel ^a *pret.* ^b *inf.* ^c *fut.* ^d *part.* ^e שׁוּעַ *m.* cry for help. ^f שׁוֹעַ *m.* ^g שַׁוְעָה *m. id.* ^h שַׁוְעָה *f. id.*

20　שָׁעַע　Our version takes this word to be of the same meaning as שָׁוַע; but according to Gesenius and others, *pr.* to stroke, to smear; to be blinded; Pilp. to delight oneself, to be delighted.　Kal ^a *imp.* Isa. xxix. 9, "and cry," *marg.* 'and riot.' Hithpalpel ^b *imp.* Isa. xxix. 9, *marg.* 'or, take your pleasure,' *i. e.* indulge yourselves, if ye will, in your delights and pleasures; but soon ye shall be blinded with astonishment at the things which shall happen. So that in this and the previous clause, verbs alike in form and different in sense are used.　See Appendix.

Gen. iv. 10.	12 e	1 Sam. iv. 14.	12 g	Neh. v. 1.	12 g	
xviii. 20.	2 g	v. 10.	2 d	v. 6.	2 g	
xviii. 21.	12 g	v. 12.	19 h	ix. 4, 28.	2 d	
xix. 13.	2 g	vii. 8.	2 b	ix. 9.	2 g	
xxvii. 34, 34.	12 d g	vii. 9.	2 d	ix. 27.	12 d	
xxix. 14, 15, 18.	15 d	viii. 18.	2 a	Esth. iv. 1, 1.	2 d g	
xli. 43.	15 d	ix. 16.	12 g	ix. 31.	2 g	
xli. 55.	12 d	xii. 8, 10.	2 d	Job xvi. 18.	2 g	
xlv. 1.	15 d	xv. 11.	2 d	xix. 7, 7.	12 d, 19 c	
Exod. ii. 23, 23.	2 d, 19 h	xvii. 8.	15 d	xxiv. 12.	19 c	
iii. 7, 9.	2 d	xx. 37, 38.	15 d	xxvii. 9.	12 g	
v. 8.	12 e	xxiv. 8.	15 d	xxix. 12.	19 d	
v. 15.	12 d	xxvi. 14, 14.	15 d a	xxx. 5.	16 c	
viii. 12.	12 d	xxviii. 12.	2 d	xxx. 20, 28.	19 c	
xi. 6.	12 g	2 Sam. xiii. 19.β	2 a	xxx. 24.γ	19 f	
xii. 30.	12 g	xviii. 25.	15 d	xxxi. 38.	2 d	
xiv. 10, 15.	12 d	xix. 4.	2 d	xxxiv. 28, 28.	12 g	
xv. 25.	12 d	xix. 28.	2 b	xxxv. 9, 9.	2 e, 19 c	
xvii. 4.	12 d	xx. 16.	15 d	xxxv. 12.	19 c	
xxii. 23, 23.	12 b d g	xxii. 7, 7.	15 d, 19 h	xxxvii. 13.	19 c	
xxii. 27.	12 d	1 Kings viii. 28.	17 d	xxxviii. 41.	19 c	
xxxii. 18.	7 b	xiii. 2, 21.	15 d	xxxix. 7.	18	
Lev. xiii. 45.	15 d	xiii. 4, 32.	15 a	Ps. iii. 4.	15 d	
Num. xi. 2.	12 d	xvii. 20, 21.	15 d	v. 2.	19 g	
xii. 13.	12 d	xviii. 27.	15 c, 14	ix. 12.	12 g	
xiv. 1. a	6 b	xviii. 28.	15 d, 14	xvii. 1.	17 d	
xvi. 34.	14	xx. 39.	12 a	xviii. 6, 6.	19 c h	
xx. 16.	12 d	xxii. 32.	2 d	xviii. 41.	19 c	
Deut. xv. 9.	15 a	2 Kings ii. 12.	12 f	xxii. 2.	15 d	
xxii. 24, 27.	12 a	iv. 1, 40.	12 a	xxii. 5.	2 a	
xxiv. 15.	15 d	vi. 5.	12 d	xxii. 24.	19 b	
xxvi. 7.	12 a	vi. 26.	12 a	xxvii. 7.	15 d	
Josh. xxiv. 7.	12 d	viii. 3.	12 b	xxviii. 1.	15 d	
Judg. iii. 9, 15.	2 d	viii. 5.	12 e	xxviii. 2.	19 b	
iv. 3.	12 d	xi. 14.	15 d	xxx. 8.	19 a	
v. 28.	4	xx. 11.	15 d	xxx. 8.	15 d	
vi. 6.	2 d	1 Chron. v. 20.	2 a	xxxi. 22.	19 b	
vii. 7.	2 a	2 Chron. v. 19.	17 d	xxxiv. 6.	15 a	
vii. 20.	15 d	xiii. 12.	16 a	xxxiv. 15.	19 h	
vii. 21.	16 c	xiii. 14.	12 d	xxxiv. 17.	12 a	
ix. 7.	15 d	xiv. 11.	15 d	xxxix. 12.	19 h	
x. 10.	2 d	xviii. 31.	2 d	xl. 1.	19 h	
x. 12.	2 d	xx. 9.	15 d	lv. 17.	3	
x. 14.	2 c	xxxii. 18.	15 d	lvi. 9.	19 c	
xviii. 23.	15 d	lvii. 2.	15 d	lvii. 2.	15 d	
1 Sam. iv. 13.	2 d	xxxii. 20.	2 d	lxi. 1.	17 d	

Ps. lxi. 2.	15 d	Isa. xxiv. 14.	10 a	Jer. xlix. 29.	1 a		
lxvi. 17.	15 a	xxvi. 17.	2 d	l. 46.	2 g		
lxix. 3.	15 b	xxix. 9, 9.δ	20 a b	li. 54.	2 g		
lxxii. 12.	19 d	xxx. 7.	15 a	Lam. ii. 18.	12 a		
lxxvii. 1.	12 d	xxxiii. 7.	19 e	ii. 19.	17 a		
lxxxiv. 2.	17 c	xxxiii. 7.	12 a	iii. 8.	2 d		
lxxxvi. 3.	15 d	xxxiv. 14.	15 d	iii. 56.	19 h		
lxxxviii. 1.	12 a	xxxvi. 13.	15 d	iv. 15.	15 a		
lxxxviii. 13.	17 d	xl. 2.	15 c	Ezek. viii. 18.	15 a		
lxxxviii. 13.	19 a	xl. 3.	15 e	ix. 1.	15 d		
lxxxix. 26.	15 d	xl. 6, 6.	15 c d	ix. 4.	1 c		
cii. 1.	19 h	xlii. 2.	12 d	ix. 8.	2 d		
cvi. 44.	17 d	xlii. 13.	16 c	xi. 13.	15 g		
cvii. 6, 28.	12 d	xlii. 14.	9	xxiv. 17.	1 b		
cvii. 13, 19.	2 d	xliii. 14.	17 d	xxvii. 15.	1 a		
cxix. 145, 146.	15 a	xlvi. 7.	12 d	xxvii. 28.	2 g		
cxix. 147.	19 c	liv. 1.	10 b	xxvii. 30.	2 d		
cxix. 169.	17 d	lvii. 13.	2 b	Dan. iii. 4.	15 i		
cxx. 1.	15 a	lviii. 1.	15 c	iii. 14.	15 i		
cxxx. 1.	15 a	lviii. 9.	19 c	v. 7.	15 h		
cxxxviii. 3.	15 a	lxv. 19.	12 d	v. 20.	2 f		
cxli. 1, 1.	15 a b	lxv. 19.	2 g	Hos. v. 8.	16 b		
cxlii. 1.	15 a	Jer. ii. 2.	15 a	vii. 14.	2 a		
cxlii. 5.	2 a	iii. 4.	15 a	viii. 2.	2 d		
cxliii. 6.	17 d	iv. 5.	15 c	Joel i. 14.	2 c		
cxlv. 19.	19 h	iv. 20.	15 f	i. 19.	15 d		
cxlvii. 9.	15 d	vii. 16.	17 d	i. 20.	8		
Prov. i. 20.	17 b	viii. 19.	19 h	Amos iii. 4.	6, 14		
i. 21.	15 d	xi. 11, 12.	2 a	Jonah i. 2.	15 c		
ii. 3.	15 d	xi. 14, 14.	17 d, 15 b	i. 5.	2 d		
viii. 1.	15 d	xii. 8.	6 a, 14	i. 14.	15 d		
viii. 3.	17 b	xiv. 2.	11	ii. 2, 2.	15 a, 19 a		
ix. 3.	15 d	xiv. 12.	17 d	iii. 4, 8.	15 d		
xxi. 18.	5	xviii. 22.	2 g	Micah iii. 4.	2 c		
xxi. 13, 13.	2 g, 15 d	xx. 8, 8.	2 d, 15 d	iii. 5.	15 a		
Eccles. ix. 17.	2 g	xx. 16.	2 g	vi. 9.	16 c		
Isa. v. 7.	12 g	xxii. 20, 20.	12 c	vi. 9.	15 d		
vi. 3.	15 a	xxv. 34.	2 c	Hab. i. 2, 2.	19 a, 2 d		
vi. 4.	15 e	xxv. 36.	12 g	ii. 11.	2 d		
viii. 4.	15 b	xxx. 15.	2 d	Zeph. i. 10.	12 g		
xii. 6.	10 b	xxxi. 6.	15 a	i. 14.	13		
xiii. 22.	7 a	xlvi. 17.	15 a	Zech. i. 4.	15 a		
xiv. 31.	2 c	xlvi. 2.	2 a	i. 14, 17.	15 c		
xv. 4, 4.	2 d, 16 c	xlviii. 3, 5.	12 g	vi. 8.	2 e.		
xv. 5, 5.	2 d g	xlviii. 4, 34.	2 g	vii. 7.	15 a		
xv. 8.	2 d	xlviii. 20.	2 c	x. 14.	15 a		
xix. 20.	12 d	xlviii. 31.	2 d	viii. 13, 13.	15 a d		
xxi. 8.	15 d	xlix. 3.	12 c	Mal. ii. 13.	1 d		
xxii. 5.	19 e	xlix. 3.	15 a				
xxiv. 11.	15 d	xlix. 21.	12 g				

^α *lit.* lifted and gave their voices.　^β *lit.* going and cried. crying is to them.　^δ *marg.* ' or, take your pleasure and riot.' 'give forth his voice.'　^γ *lit.* ^ε *marg.*

CRYSTAL

זְכוּכִית *f.* (see *Pure*), glass or crystal: Job xxviii. 17.

קֶרַח *m.* ice; crystal, as resembling ice: Ezek. i. 22.

CUBIT

אַמָּה a measure, near 22 inches, or 1.824 foot long; occurs very frequently: Gen. vi. 15, &c. אַמִּין *f. pl.* Ch. Ezra vi. 3, 3: Dan. iii. 1, 1.

גֹּמֶד *m.* a staff, rod; then a cubit: only in Judg. iii. 16.

CUCKOW

שַׁחַף *m.* according to Lxx. and Vulg. sea-mew, sea-gull; Vulg. *larus*, an aquatic bird, so called from its leanness.— *Bochart.* Dr. Shaw, in his Travels, p. 252, gave it as his opinion that it might be, agreeably to the scripture name, the saf-saf; but this is doubtful, and no sufficient reason has been given for disturbing our translation: Lev. xi. 16: Deut. xiv. 15.

CUCUMBER

קִשֻּׁאִים *m. pl.* cucumbers, or probably the water-melons, which are still an abundant article of food in Egypt, highly prized, especially by the poor, and very grateful in so hot a country: Num. xi. 5. מִקְשָׁה *f.* a garden of cucumbers: Isa. i. 8.

CUD

גֵּרָה *f.* the cud which is drawn up through the neck to be chewed again. See *Chew.* Lev. xi. 3, 4, 4, 5, 6, 7, 26: Deut. xiv. 6, 7, 7, 8.

CUMBRANCE

טֹרַח *m.* burden, trouble: Deut. i. 12.

CUMMIN

כַּמֹּן *m.* the cummin of the ancients is the *cuminum sativum* of Linnæus: Isa. xxviii. 25, 27, 27.

CUNNING

1 אָמָן *m.* an artist, faithful and trustworthy in his art: "a cunning workman."

2 בִּין to understand. See *Prudent, Skilful.* HIPHIL *part.*

3 חָכָם *adj.* wise.

4 חָשַׁב to think, to devise; to be skilful or ingenious in any work. KAL ª *part.* Poel. ᵇ מַחֲשָׁבֶת *f.* thought, device.

5 יָדַע to know. KAL ª *part.* Poel. ᵇ דַּעַת *f.* knowledge.

Gen. xxv. 27. α		5 a	Exod. xxxix. 3, 8.	4 a	2 Chron. xxvi. 15.	4 a
Exod. xxvi. 1, 31.		4 a	1 Sam. xvi. 16, 18.	5 a	Cant. vii. 1.	1
xxviii. 6, 15.		4 a	1 Kings vii. 14.	5 b	Isa. iii. 3.	3
xxxi. 4.		4 b	1 Chron. xxii. 15.	3	xl. 20.	3
xxxv. 33. β		4 b	xxv. 7.	2	Jer. ix. 17.	3
xxxv. 35, 35.		4 a b	2 Chron. ii. 7, 7, 13,		x. 9.	3
xxxvi. 8, 35.		4. a	14, 14.	3	Dan. i. 4.	5, 3
xxxviii. 23.		4. a				

α *lit.* a man understanding hunting.   β *lit.* work of invention.

CUP

גָּבִיעַ *m.* a cup or bowl: Gen. xliv. 2, 2, 12, 16, 17.

אַגָּן *m.* a cup, basin, goblet: Isa. xxii. 24.

כּוֹס *f.* a cup; the cup of consolation (Jer. xvi. 7.) seems to refer to the refreshment taken after funerals, which was sent by friends. כִּים *m.* a purse, a bag: Prov. xxiii. 31. כתיב.

מְנַקִּיּוֹת *f. pl.* see *Bowl:* Jer. lii. 19.

סַף *m.* bowl: Zech. xii. 2.

קְשָׂה *f. pl.* dishes, bowls for libations. LXX. σπονδεῖα. 1 Chron. xxviii. 17.

שָׁקָה to water, to give to drink; a cupbearer. HIPHIL *part.* 1 Kings x. 5: 2 Chron. ix. 4: Neh. i. 11.

CURDLE

קָפָא to coagulate as milk, to curdle. HIPHIL *fut.* Job x. 10.

CURE

נָהָה to thrust away, to remove either the bandages of a wound or the power of disease, and so to heal, to cure. KAL *fut.* Hos. v. 13.

תְּעָלָה *f.* an ascending, coming up, as when a wound heals: Jer. xlvi. 11, *lit.* no cure shall be unto thee.

רָפָא to heal. KAL *pret.* Jer. xxxiii. 6.   מַרְפֵּא *m.* healing: Jer. xxxiii. 6.

CURIOUS

חָשֵׁב *m.* cunning, curious work, girdle, &c.: Exod. xxviii. 8, 27,

28; xxix. 5; xxxix. 5, 20, 21: Lev. viii. 7.   מַחֲשָׁבֶת *f.* artificial work: Exod. xxxv. 32.

רָקַם to embroider. PUAL *pret.* Ps. cxxxix. 15, "curiously wrought," *lit.* embroidered.

CURRENT

עָבַר to pass: it is applied to such money as passes with merchants, approved and allowed as the precious metals were, in pieces; probably the weight was marked upon them. Coined money could hardly have been known in the days of the Patriarchs. KAL *part.* Poel, Gen. xxiii. 16.

CURSE

1 אָלָה to swear, to adjure; to bind oneself to another person by an oath; to curse. KAL ª *pret.* ᵇ אָלָה *f.* an oath; see *Swear.* ᶜ תַּאֲלָה *f.* curse, execration.

2 אָרַר to curse, mostly as to its effect; but also to wish or speak evil of any one; *comp.* Exod. xxii. 28 with Acts xxiii. 5: Job iii. 8, cursers of the day, *i. e.* a class of magicians who were thought able to render particular days unfortunate by their imprecations. KAL ª *pret.* ᵇ *inf.* ᶜ *imp.* ᵈ *fut.* ᵉ *part.* Poel. ᶠ *part.* Paül. NIPHAL ᵍ *part.* PIEL ʰ *pret.* ⁱ *part.* HOPHAL ᵏ *fut.* ˡ מְאֵרָה *f.* curse, execration, most commonly in its effect.

3 בָּרַךְ to kneel; to invoke God; to invoke blessings or evil; means sometimes to curse, by a signification which is peculiar to similar words in other languages, as in the Latin, *sacrare imprecari,* &c., and to be decided by the connection in which the word is used, or by the manner and intention of the speaker: in the same way it means sometimes to blaspheme, as well as to speak well of; see *Blaspheme.* PIEL ª *pret.* ᵇ *imp.* ᶜ *fut.*

4 חֵרֶם *m.* a devoted thing; that which is separated or appointed to destruction.

5 נָקַב to note or mark with dishonour or ignominy, to stigmatise. This primary meaning should be applied to passages in which it is rendered to curse. It is stronger in meaning than קָלַל. KAL *fut.*

6 קָבַב to curse, perhaps to pierce with words, *i. q.* נָקַב. KAL ª *pret.* ᵇ *inf.* ᶜ *imp.*

7 קָלַל to be light; to esteem lightly. In Job xxiv. 18 there is an elegant paronomasia between the words translated swift and cursed, being from the same root. PIEL, to utter violent reproaches, to imprecate evil, to curse: ª *pret.* ᵇ *inf.* ᶜ *imp.* ᵈ *fut.* ᵉ *part.* PUAL ᶠ *fut.* ᵍ *part.* ʰ קְלָלָה cursing; execration, curse. Observe the use of this word in Deut. xxvii. 13, compared with v. 15, &c.

8 שְׁבוּעָה *f.* an oath.

Gen. iii. 14, 17.	2 f	Lev. xx. 9, 9.	7 d a	Num. xxiii. 11.	6 b
iv. 11.	2 f	xxiv. 11, 15.	7 d	xxiii. 13.	6 c
v. 29.	2 h	xxiv. 14, 23.	7 e	xxiii. 25. β	5, 6 b
viii. 21. α	2 h	Num. v. 18, 19, 22, 24,		xxiii. 27.	6 a
ix. 25.	2 f	24.	2 i	xxiv. 9, 9.	2 f e
xii. 3, 3.	2 d, 7 e	v. 21, 23.	1 b	xxiv. 10.	6 b
xxvii. 12, 13.	7 h	v. 27, 27.	2 i, 1 b	Deut. vii. 26, 26.	4
xxvii. 29, 29.	2 f	xxii. 6, 6.	2 c d k	xi. 26, 28, 29.	7 h
xlix. 7.	2 f	xxii. 11, 17.	6 c	xiii. 17.	4
Exod. xxi. 17. α	7 e	xxii. 12.	2 d	xxiii. 4.	7 b
xxii. 28.	2 d	xxii. 7.	2 c	xxiii. 5.	7 b
Lev. xix. 14.	7 d	xxiii. 8, 8.	5, 6 a	xxvii. 13. γ	7 h

Deut. xxvii. 15, 16, 17,	2 Kings ii. 24.	7 d	Prov. xxx. 10, 11.	7 d
18, 19, 20, 21, 22,	ix. 34.	2 f	Eccles. vii. 21.	7 e
23, 24, 25, 26.	2 f	xxii. 19.	7 h	vii. 22.	7 a
xxviii. 15, 45.	7 h	2 Chron. xxxiv. 24.	1 b	x. 20, 20.	7 d
xxviii. 16, 16, 17, 18,		Neh. x. 29.	1 b	Isa. viii. 21.	7 a
19, 19.	2 f	xiii. 2, 2.	7 b h	xxiv. 6.	1 b
xxviii. 20.	2 l	xiii. 25.	7 d	xxxiv. 5.	4
xxix. 19, 20, 21.	1 b	Job i. 5.	3 a	xliii. 28.	8
xxix. 27.	7 h	i. 11.	3 c	lxv. 15.	8
xxx. 1, 19.	7 h	ii. 5.	3 c	Jer. xi. 3.	2 f
xxx. 7.	1 b	ii. 9.	3 b	xv. 10.	7 e
Josh. vi. 18.	4	iii. 1.	7 d	xvii. 5.	2 f
vi. 26.	2 f	iii. 8, 8.	5, 2 e	xx. 14, 15.	2 f
viii. 34.	7 h	v. 3.	5	xxiv. 9.	7 h
ix. 23.	2 f	xxiv. 18.	7 f	xxv. 18.	7 h
xxiv. 9.	7 b	xxxi. 30.	1 b	xxvi. 6.	7 h
Judg. v. 23, 23. δ	2 c, 2 b c	Ps. x. 7.	1 b	xxix. 18.	1 b
ix. 27.	7 d	xxxvii. 22.	7 g	xxix. 22.	7 h
ix. 57.	7 h	lix. 12.	1 b	xlii. 18.	7 h
xvii. 2.	1 a	lxii. 4.	7 d	xliv. 8, 12, 22.	7 h
xxi. 18.	2 f	cix. 17, 18.	7 h	xlviii. 10, 10.	2 f
1 Sam. xiv. 24, 28.	2 f	cix. 28.	7 d	xlix. 13.	7 h
xvii. 43.	7 d	cxix. 21.	2 f	Lam. iii. 65.	1 c
xxvi. 19.	2 f	Prov. xi. 26.	5	Dan. ix. 11.	1 b
2 Sam. xvi. 5.	7 e	xi. 26.	7 e	Zech. v. 3.	1 b
xvi. 7.	7 b	xx. 20.	5	viii. 13.	7 h
xvi. 9, 11, 13.	7 d	xxiv. 24.	5	Mal. i. 14.	2 f
xvi. 10, 10.	7 d c	xxvi. 2, 2.	7 h	ii. 2, 2, 2.	2 l a a
xvi. 12.	7 h	xxvii. 14.	7 h	iii. 9, 9.	2 g l
xix. 21.	7 a	xxviii. 27.	2 l	iv. 6.	4
1 Kings ii. 8, 8.	7 a h	xxix. 24.	1 b		

a *lit.* add to curse.   β *lit.* cursing curse.   γ *lit.* for a cursing.   δ *lit.* cursing curse.

CURTAIN

דֹּק *m.* a fine thin garment or curtain : Isa. xl. 22.

יְרִיעָה *f.* a curtain, from its tremulous motion : occurs frequently in Exod. xxvi. and xxxvi. and in Num. iv. 25 : 2 Sam. vii. 2 : 1 Chron. xvii. 1 : Ps. civ. 2 : Cant. i. 5 : Isa. liv. 2 : Jer. iv. 20 ; x. 20 ; xlix. 29 : Hab. iii. 7.

מָסָךְ *m.* hanging, covering : Num. iii. 26.

CUSTODY

יָד the hand : Esth. ii. 3, 8, 8, 14.

פְּקֻדָּה *f.* care, oversight : Num. iii. 36, *marg.* 'the office of the charge.'

CUSTOM

דֶּרֶךְ *com.* way : Gen. xxxi. 35.

הֲלָךְ Ch. *m.* toll : Ezra iv. 13, 20 ; vii. 24.

חֹק *m.* a statute, law, decree, ordinance : Judg. xi. 39 : Jer. xxxii. 11. חֻקָּה *f.* Lev. xviii. 30 : Jer. x. 3.

מִשְׁפָּט *m.* judgment, right, law, custom : 1 Sam. ii. 13 : Ezra iii. 4.

CUT

1 בָּצַע to cut off pieces, to divide, to separate, to snatch away. KAL a *imp.* PIEL b *fut.*

2 בָּצַר to cut off ; to strip a vineyard by gathering all the grapes in time of vintage. KAL *fut.*

3 בָּקַע to cleave. PIEL *pret.*

4 בָּרָא to hew, hew out ; to cut down, to cut off. PIEL *pret.*

5 גָּדַד to cut and hew ; to cut in, to make incisions in the flesh, *e. g.* in mourning, or as a part of idol worship. HITHPOEL a *fut.* b *part.* c גְּדוּד *m.* furrow.

6 גָּדַע to cut off, to cut asunder, to cut down, implying a degree of violence, and therefore sometimes translated to hew down, and to break down ; yet it is once used of cutting off the beard, and as this is in token of grief, it may well admit of some idea of violence, Isa. xv. 2 ; to cut asunder a rod or staff in token of breaking a covenant. KAL a *pret.* b *fut.* c *part.* Paül. NIPHAL d *pret.* PIEL e *pret.* f *fut.* PUAL g *pret.*

7 נוּן to pass away quickly ; or to be cut off. KAL *pret.*

8 גָּזַז to mow, to shear. KAL a *imp.* NIPHAL, to be cut off or slain. b *pret.*

9 גָּזַר to cut, to cut off ; to divide, to separate ; to be cut off, to fail, to perish. KAL a *pret.* b *fut.* NIPHAL c *pret.* גְּזַר Ch. ITHP'AL d *pret.*

10 גָּרַן to cut off, as with an axe. NIPHAL *pret.*

11 דָּמָה to be reduced to a state of silence ; to be laid waste, to be cut off ; applied to nations, to cities, and to men. NIPHAL a *pret.* b *inf.* c דֳּמִי *m.* quiet, rest, stillness : Isa. xxxviii. 10 ; Gesenius, in the quiet of my days.

12 דָּמַם the same. NIPHAL a *pret.* b *fut.*

13 חָטַב to fell or hew wood. KAL *fut.*

14 חָלַף to pass ; to change ; to pass on against, to assail. KAL *fut.*

15 חָצַב to hew or cut stone or wood ; *fig.* to hew with destructive judgments. HIPHIL *part.*

16 חָצַץ to cut, or divide. PUAL, to be cut off in the midst, *i. e.* finished, or ended : *pret.*

17 חֲרֹשֶׁת *f.* cutting or engraving of stones.

18 כָּחַד (see *Hide*), to cut off or demolish ; *pr.* to make to disappear. NIPHAL a *pret.* b *fut.* c *part.* HIPHIL d *pret.* e *inf.* f *fut.*

19 כָּסַח to cut down. KAL *part.* Paül.

20 כָּרַת to cut, to cut off, to root out, to destroy ; to strike, to smite ; to punish with death. With *inf.*, cut off utterly. KAL a *pret.* b *inf.* c *imp.* d *fut.* e *part.* Poel. f *part.* Paül. NIPHAL g *part.* h *inf.* i *fut.* PUAL k *part.* HIPHIL l *pret.* m *inf.* n *fut.* HOPHAL o *pret.*

21 מוּל to cut off, to circumcise ; to cut down grass ; to be cut down, as stalks of corn : so Ps. lviii. 7 may be understood, according to Gussetius, "Their arrows shall be as though they were cut down," and lie like stalks of corn in the field. POLEL a *fut.* HITHPOLEL b *fut.*

22 נָמַל the same ; to cut off a branch. KAL *fut.*

23 נָקָה to be clean, clear. Our version seems to have followed the reading of נָקַם. Cocceius takes the meaning in this passage to be, 'to be cleared away.' NIPHAL *pret.* Zech. v. 3. *marg.* 'or, every one of this *people* that stealeth holdeth *himself* guiltless.'

24 נָקַף to cut off, to clear away and open thickets in a wood. PIEL *pret.*

25 נָתַח to cut flesh in pieces, applied both to sacrifices and to the human body. PIEL a *pret.* b *fut.*

26 עֲבַד Ch. to make, do, &c. ITHP'AL *fut.*

27 עָלָה to go up ; to be taken away. KAL *inf.*

28 פָּלַח to cleave, to cut up, to cleave wood. KAL *part.* Poel.

29 צָמַת to be silent ; to make silent, to cut off, to destroy. KAL a *pret.* NIPHAL b *pret.* PILEL c *pret.* HIPHIL d *imp.* e *fut.*

30 קוּט to loathe, to nauseate, to be offensive : Gesenius, to cut off. KAL a *fut.* Job viii. 14. Taylor, "whom his hope shall

loathe or abominate," *i. e.* who shall loathe or hate the thing that he hopes for.

31 קָטַף to pluck off, to break off. KAL [a] *part.* NIPHAL [b] *fut.*

32 קָמַט to cut down; to lay fast hold of, according to Gesenius and others. PUAL *pret.* Job xxii. 16. The meaning here is probably, "who were huddled together by the waters."—*Barnes.* It is supposed in the whole of the context there is allusion to the deluge. See Good on Job.

33 קָסַס to cut off, fruit. POEL *fut.*

34 קָפַד to cut off, a weaver's web. PIEL *pret.*

35 קָצַץ to cut off, a cord, the hand, &c.; to cut up into threads; to cut away, to cut loose. KAL [a] *pret.* PIEL [b] *pret.* [c] *fut.* PUAL [d] *part.* [e] קְצַץ Ch. PAEL *pret.*

36 קָצַב to cut off or down, a tree. KAL *fut.*

37 קָצָה to cut off, hence to destroy; to cut short. KAL [a] *inf.* PIEL [b] *inf.* PIEL [c] *part.*

38 קָצַר to reap. KAL *fut.*

39 קָרַע to rend, to cut in pieces, to cut out. KAL [a] *pret.* [b] *fut.*

40 שָׂרַט to cut, to gash oneself, to make incisions in the flesh, as was customary in mourning. With *inf.*, cut in pieces. KAL [a] *inf.* NIPHAL [b] *fut.* [c] שֶׂרֶט *m.* an incision. [d] שָׂרֶטֶת *f. id.*

41 תָּזַז to cut off or away. HIPHIL *pret.*

42 שׂוּר to saw. KAL *fut.*

Gen. ix. 11.	20 i	Josh. xvii. 15, 18.	4	2 Chron. xiv. 3.	6 f
xvii. 14.	20 g	xxiii. 4.	20 l	xv. 16.	20 d
Exod. iv. 25.	20 d	Judg. i. 6.	35 c	xxii. 7.	20 m
ix. 15.	18 b	i. 7.	35 d	xxvi. 21.	9 c
xii. 15, 19.	20 g	vi. 25, 26.	20 d	xxviii. 24.	35 c
xxiii. 23.	18 d	vi. 28.	20 k	xxxi. 1.	20 l
xxix. 17.	25 b	vi. 30.	20 a	xxxii. 21.	18 f
xxx. 33, 38.	20 g	ix. 48, 49.	20 d	xxxiv. 4, 7.	6 e
xxxi. 5.	17	xx. 6.	25 d	Job iv. 7.	18 a
xxxi. 14.	20 g	xxi. 6.	6 d	vi. 9.	1 b
xxxiv. 33.	20 d	Ruth iv. 10.	20 i	viii. 12.	31 b
xxxv. 33.	17	1 Sam. ii. 31.	6 a	viii. 14.	30
xxxix. 3.	35 b	ii. 33.	20 n	xi. 10.	14
Lev. i. 6, 12.	25 a	v. 4.	20 f	xiv. 2.	20 d
vii. 20, 21, 25, 27.	20 g	xvii. 51.	20 f	xiv. 7.	20 i
viii. 20.	25 a	xx. 15, 15.	20 n m	xviii. 16.	22
xvii. 4, 9.	20 g	xxiv. 4.	20 a	xxi. 21.	16
xvii. 10.	20 l	xxiv. 5.	20 a	xxii. 16.	32
xvii. 14.	20 i	xxiv. 11.	20 b	xxii. 20.	18 a
xviii. 29.	20 g	xxiv. 21.	20 n	xxiii. 17.	29 b
xix. 8.	20 g	xxviii. 9.	20 l	xxiv. 24.	22
xix. 28.	40 c	xxxi. 9.	20 d	xxviii. 10.	1 b
xx. 3, 5, 6.	20 l	2 Sam. iv. 12.	35 c	xxx. 4.	31 a
xx. 17, 18.	20 g	vii. 9.	20 l	xxxvi. 20.	27
xxi. 5.	40 d	x. 4.	20 d	Ps. xii. 3.	20 n
xxii. 3.	20 g	xx. 22.	20 d	xxxi. 22.	10
xxii. 24.	20 f	1 Kings ix. 7. *a*	20 l	xxxiv. 16.	20 m
xxiii. 29.	20 g	xi. 16.	20 d	xxxvii. 2.	22
xxvi. 30.	20 l	xiii. 34.	18 e	xxxvii. 9, 22.	20 l
Num. iv. 18.	20 n	xiv. 10.	20 l	xxxvii. 34.	20 h
ix. 13.	20 l	xiv. 14.	20 l	xxxviii. 28, 38.	20 g
xiii. 23.	20 d	xviii. 4.	20 m	xlvi. 9.	35 b
xiii. 24.	20 a	xviii. 23, 33.	25 b	liv. 5.	29 d
xv. 30.	20 d	xviii. 28.	5 a	lviii. 7.	21 b
xv. 31.	20 h i	xxi. 21.	20 l	lxv. 10.	6 f
xix. 13, 20.	20 g	2 Kings vi. 4.	9 b	lxxvi. 12.	2
Deut. vii. 5.	6 f	vi. 6.	36	lxxx. 16.	20
xii. 29.	20 n	ix. 8.	20 l	lxxxi. 4.	18 f
xiv. 1.	5 a	x. 32. *β*	37 b	lxxxviii. 5.	9 c
xix. 1.	20 n	xvi. 17.	35 c	lxxxviii. 16.	29 c
xix. 5.	20 l	xviii. 4.	20 a	xc. 6.	21 a
xx. 19.	20 a	xviii. 16.	35 b	xc. 10.	7
xx. 20.	20 a	xix. 23.	20 d	xciv. 23, 23.	29 e
xxiii. 1.	20 f	xxiii. 14.	20 d	ci. 5.	29 e
xxiv. 19.	38	xxiv. 13.	35 c	ci. 8.	20 m
xxv. 12.	35 a	1 Chron. xvii. 8.	20 n	cvii. 16.	6 e
Josh. iii. 13.	20 i	xix. 4.	20 d	cix. 13.	20 l
iii. 16.	20 g	xx. 3.	42	cix. 15.	20 n
iv. 7, 7.	20 l	2 Chron. ii. 8.	20 b	cxxix. 4.	35 b
vii. 9.	20 l	ii. 10.	20 e	cxli. 7.	28
xi. 21.	20 n	ii. 16.	20 d	cxliii. 12.	29 e

Prov. ii. 22.	20 i	Jer. xli. 5.	5 b	Hos. x. 7.	11 a
x. 31.	20 l	xliv. 7, 8, 11.	20 m	x. 15.	11 b a
xxiii. 18.	20 i	xlvi. 23.	20 a	Joel i. 5, 16.	20 g
xxiv. 14.	20 i	xlvii. 4.	20 m	i. 9.	20 o
xxvi. 6.	37 c	xlvii. 5, 5.	11 a, 5 a	Amos i. 5, 8.	20 l
Isa. ix. 10.	6 g	xlvii. 2, 2.	20 n, 12 b	ii. 3.	20 l
ix. 14.	20 n	xlviii. 3.	20 m	iii. 14.	6 d
x. 7.	20 m	xlviii. 25.	6 d	ix. 1. γ	1 a
x. 34.	24	xlviii. 37.	5 c	Obad. 5.	11 a
xi. 13.	20 i	xlix. 26.	12 b	9.	20 i
xiv. 12.	6 d	l. 16.	20 c	10.	20 g
xiv. 22.	20 l	l. 23.	6 d	14.	20 m
xv. 2.	6 c	l. 30.	12 b	Micah v. 9.	20 i
xviii. 5, 5.	20 a, 41	li. 6.	12 b	v. 10, 11, 12, 13.	20 l
xxii. 25, 25.	6 d, 20 g	li. 62.	20 m	Nah. i. 12.	8 b
xxix. 20.	20 g	Lam. ii. 3.	6 a	i. 14.	20 n
xxxiii. 12.	19	iii. 53.	29 a	i. 15.	20 g
xxxvii. 24.	20 d	iii. 54.	9 c	ii. 13.	20 l
xxxviii. 10.	11 b	Ezek. vi. 6.	6 d	iii. 15.	20 n
xxxviii. 12, 12.	34, 1 b	xiv. 8, 13, 17.	20 l	Hab. ii. 10.	37 a
xlv. 2.	6 f	xiv. 19, 21.	20 m	Zeph. i. 3, 4.	20 l
xlviii. 9.	20 m	xvi. 4.	20 k	i. 11, 11.	11 a, 20 g
xlviii. 19.	20 i	xvii. 9.	33	iii. 6.	20 l
li. 9.	15	xvii. 17.	20 m	iii. 7.	20 i
liii. 8.	9 c	xxv. 7, 13, 16.	20 l	Zech. v. 3, 3.	23
lv. 13.	20 i	xxix. 8.	20 l	ix. 6.	20 l
lvi. 5.	20 i	xxx. 15.	20 l	ix. 10, 10.	20 l g
Jer. vii. 28.	20 g	xxxi. 12.	20 d	xi. 8.	18 f
vii. 29.	8 a	xxxv. 7.	20 l	xi. 9, 9.	18 c b
ix. 21.	20 m	xxxvii. 11.	9 c	xi. 10, 14.	6 b
x. 3.	20 a	xxxix. 10.	13	xi. 16.	18 c
xi. 19.	20 d	Dan. ii. 5.	26	iii. 8.	40 a b
xvi. 6.	5 a	ii. 34, 45.	9 d	xiii. 2.	20 n
xxii. 7.	20 a	iii. 29.	26	xiii. 8.	20 i
xxii. 14.	39 a	iv. 14.	35 e	xiv. 2.	20 l
xxv. 37.	12 a	ix. 26.	20 i	Mal. ii. 12.	20 n
xxxiv. 18.	20 a	x. 6.	20 i		
xxxvi. 23.	39 b	Hos. viii. 4.	20 i		

a lit. cut off from the face of the land. *β lit.* to cut off the ends of. *γ or,* dash them in pieces on the heads of all.

CYMBALS

צְלְצְלִים *m.* put for any tinkling, ringing, clanging instrument; cymbals which are struck together and produce a loud clanging sound: 2 Sam. vi. 5 : Ps. cl. 5, 5. מְצִלְתַּיִם *dual,* pair of cymbals : 1 Chron. xiii. 8 ; xv. 16, 19, 28; xvi. 5, 42 ; xxv. 1, 6 : 2 Chron. v. 12, 13 ; xxix. 25 : Ezra iii. 10 : Neh. xii. 27.

CYPRESS

תִּרְזָה *f.* a species of the oak, so called from its hardness and strength, much like the Latin, *robur ;* Vulg. *ilex :* Isa. xliv. 14. Its wood is fragrant, and not liable to rot or be wormeaten. The imperishable coffins of the Egyptian mummies are sometimes made of this wood.

DAGGER

חֶרֶב *f.* see *Sword.* Judg. iii. 16, 21, 22.

DAINTY

תַּאֲוָה *f.* desire : Job xxxiii. 20, *marg.* 'meat of desire.'
מַטְעַמּוֹת *f. pl.* (see *Savoury*), "dainty meats," Prov. xxiii. 3, 6.
מַנְעַמִּים *m. pl.* (see *Pleasant*), " dainties," Ps. cxli. 4.
מַעֲדָן *m.* see *Delicate.* Gen. xlix. 20.

DALE

עֵמֶק *m.* see *Valley.* Gen. xiv. 17 : 2 Sam. xviii. 18.

DAMAGE

חָמָס *m.* violence, oppression, wrong : Prov. xxvi. 6.
חֲבָל Ch. *m.* hurt : Ezra iv. 22.

נְזַק Ch. to suffer injury, damage. P'AL *part. passive*, Dan. vi.
2.   נְזַק *m.* injury, damage : Esth. vii. 4.

DAMASCUS

דַּמֶּשֶׂק Damascus is the metropolis of Damascene Syria, famous
for its silk cloth, called therefore damask. The word
may be put for such cloth, Amos iii. 12, a couch of
Damascene cloth, which may account for the change of
שׂ in the name of the place into שׁ on this occasion, to
mark a difference in the pronunciation. שׂ however is
the reading of many MSS. The margin has it, ' or, on
the bed's feet,' according to the interpretation of Ibn-
Ezra and Kimchi.

DAM

אֵם *f.* a mother : Exod. xxii. 30 : Lev. xxii. 27 : Deut. xxii.
6, 6, 7.

DAMSEL

יַלְדָּה *f.* a young woman : Gen. xxxiv. 4.

נַעֲרָה *f.* a young female unmarried : Gen. xxiv. 14, &c.

עַלְמָה *f.* a virgin : Ps. lxviii. 25.

רֶחֶם *com.* womb ; a maiden, a damsel : Judg. v. 30.   רַחֲמָה *f.*
damsel : Judg. v. 30, *lit.* two damsels.

DANCE

1   חָגַג to move with various turns and agitations in token of joy.
KAL *part.* Poel.

2   חוּל to turn, to twist ; to dance. KAL [a]*inf.* POLEL [b]*part.*
מָחוֹל *m.* dancing, perhaps with music, in distinction
from that without music. [d]מְחוֹלָה *f. id.*

3   כָּרַר to move nimbly, to dance. PILPEL *part.*

4   רָקַד to leap, to skip, to dance for joy. KAL [a]*inf.* PIEL [b]*fut.*
[c]*part.*

Exod. xv. 20.	2 d	1 Sam. xxix. 5.	2 d	Ps. cxlix. 3.	2 c
xxxii. 19.	2 d	xxx. 16.	1	cl. 4.	2 c
Judg. xi. 34.	2 d	2 Sam. vi. 14, 16.	3	Eccles. iii. 4.	4 a
xxi. 21, 21.	2 a d	1 Chron. xv. 29.	4 c	Isa. xiii. 21.	4 b
xxi. 23.	2 b	Job xxi. 11.	4 b	Jer. xxxi. 4, 13.	2 c
1 Sam. xviii. 6.	2 d	Ps. xxx. 11.	2 c	Lam. v. 15.	2 c
xxi. 11.	2 d				

DANDLED

שָׁעַע to stroke, to soothe ; to be caressed. PALPAL *fut.* Isa.
lxvi. 12.

DARK

1   אֹפֶל *m.* the setting of the sun, darkness ; *trop.* misfortune,
calamity : this word is more intense than חֹשֶׁךְ ; darkness with clouds and a tempest. [a]אֲפֵלָה *f.* thick and
intense darkness. [b]אָפֵל *adj.* obscure, dark. [c]מַאֲפֵל *m.*
darkness. [d]מַאְפֵלְיָה *f.* darkness of Jehovah, thick darkness : Jer. ii. 31, "Have I been a wilderness unto Israel ?"
without fruit ? "Have I been a land of darkness ?" without the light of joy or help !

2   חִידָה *f.* a proverb, a riddle ; "dark speeches," "dark saying,"
"dark sentences."

3   חָשַׁךְ to be dark : darkness is put for the night, Job xxiv. 16 ;
for the grave, Ps. lxxxviii. 12 ; for oblivion, Eccles. vi.

4 ; for privacy, Isa. xxix. 18, Ezek. viii. 12.   *Metaph.*
applied to all kinds of adversity and sorrow ; to death ;
to that which is unknown or obscure ; to ignorance and
error, Isa. v. 20 ; to unbelief and the pursuit of sin,
Prov. ii. 13. To darken is to obscure right principles
and truth by an ignorant representation, Job xxxviii. 2 ;
dark waters for heavy watery clouds charged with
tempests ; *comp.* 2 Sam. xxii. 12. KAL [a]*pret.* [b]*fut.*
HIPHIL [c]*pret.* [d]*fut.* [e]*part.* [f]חֹשֶׁךְ *m.* darkness ; misery,
adversity, ignorance, darkness, wickedness : Gen. ii. 4,
&c. [g]חֶשְׁכָּה *f.* darkness. [h]חָשְׁכָה *f. id.* Micah iii. 6, see
also חֹשֶׁךְ : some copies read חָשֵׁכָה, *pret.* [i]חֲשֵׁיכָה *f. id.*
[k]מַחְשָׁךְ *m. id.* [l]חֲשׁוֹךְ Ch. *m. id.*

4   חַשְׁרָה *f.* from the verb to collect or bind : 2 Sam. xxii. 12, *marg.*
' binding,' *i. e.* condensation of waters, which Schultens
thinks is designedly put for חֶשְׁכָּה darkness (of waters)
in Ps. xviii. 11.

5   כָּהָה to be blunted, dulled, repressed, abated. KAL [a]*inf.* [b]*fut.*
[c]כֵּהָה *adj. f.* applied to the darkishness of a cutaneous
eruption, in opposition to its being reddish and fiery.

6   נֶשֶׁף *m.* see *Twilight.*

7   עֵיפָה *f.* darkness ; which covers or shades.

8   עֲלָטָה *f.* the obscurity which follows the setting of the sun ; also
thick darkness.

9   עָרַב see *Evening.*   KAL *pret.*

10   עֲרָפֶל thick clouds, darkness, gloom ; gross darkness : it seems
to be made up from עָרִיף cloud, and אָפֵל to be dark.

11   עָתַם occurs only in NIPHAL *pret.* Isa. ix. 19, which according
to the Rabbins is rendered darkened : Gesenius, is consumed, burned : Lxx. συγκέκανται : Cod. Alex. συγκαυ-
θήσεται : Targ. is burned.

12   צָלַל to be darkish or shadowy. KAL *pret.*

13   קָדַר to be dirty, foul ; to be of a dusky colour, darkened.
KAL [a]*pret.* HIPHIL [b]*pret.* [c]*fut.*

14   קָפָא to be thickened, as liquids ; to be dark, foggy. KAL
[a]*fut.* כְּתִיב. [b]קִפָּאוֹן *m.* congelation, קְרִי.

No. 3 *f,* rendered *Darkness,* not included.

Gen. xv. 12.	3 i	Job xxxviii. 9.	10	Isa. xlv. 19.	3 f
xv. 17.	8	Ps. xviii. 9.	10	l. 10.	3 i
Exod. x. 15.	3 b	xviii. 11, 11..a	3 f, 3 g	lviii. 10.	1 a
xx. 21.	10	xxxv. 6.	10	lix. 9.	3 a
Lev. xiii. 6, 21, 26,		xlix. 4.	2	ix. 2, 2.	3 f, 10
28, 39, 56.	5 c	lxix. 23.	3 b	Jer. ii. 31.	1 d
Num. xii. 8.	2	lxxiv. 20.	3 k	xiii. 16, 16, 16.	3 d, 6, 10
Deut. iv. 11, 11.	3 f, 10	lxxviii. 2.	2	xxiii. 12.	1 a
v. 22.	8	lxxxi. 5.	3 i	Lam. iii. 6.	3 k
xxviii. 29.	1 a	lxxxviii. 6, 18.	8 k	Ezek. viii. 12.	3 f
Josh. ii. 5.	1 c	lxxxviii. 12.	3 f	xxx. viii.β	3 f
xxiv. 7.	1 c	xci. 6.	1	xxxii. 7.	13 b
2 Sam. xxii. 10.	10	xcvii. 2.	10	xxxii. 8, γ 8.	13 c, 3 f
xxii. 12, 12.	3 f, 4	cv. 28, 28.	3 f, 1 d	xxxiv. 12.	10
1 Kings viii. 12.	10	cxxxix. 12, 12.	3 f, 3 i	Dan. ii. 22.	3 l
2 Chron. vi. 1.	10	cxliii. 3.	3 k	viii. 23.	2
Neh. xiii. 19.	12	Prov. i. 6.	2	Joel ii. 2, 2.	3 f, 10
Job iii. 6.	1	iv. 19.	1 a	ii. 10.	13 a
iii. 9.	3 b	vii. 9.	1 a	iii. 15.	13 a
x. 22, 22, 22.	7, 1, 1	Eccles. xii. 2.	3 b	Amos iv. 13.	7
xii. 25.	3 f	xii. 3.	3 a	v. 8.	3 c
xviii. 6.	3 a	Isa. v. 30, 30.	3 b a	v. 20, 20.	3 f, 1 b
xxii. 13.	10	viii. 22, 22.	3 i, 1 a	viii. 9.	3 c
xxiii. 17, 17.	3 f, 10	ix. 19.	11	Micah iii. 6, 6.	3 a h, 13 a
xxiv. 16.	3 f	xiii. 10.	3 a	Zeph. i. 15, 15.	3 f, 10
xxviii. 3, 3.	3 f, 1	xxiv. 11.	9	Zech. xi. 17.	3 k
xxx. 26.	1	xxix. 15.	3 k	xiv. 6.	14 a, or b
xxxviii. 2.	3 f	xlii. 16.	10		

[a] *lit.* darkness of water.   [β] *marg.* ' or, restrained ;' some copies read
חֲשַׁךְ.   [γ] *lit.* I make them dark.

DARLING

יָחִיד *adj.* only : Ps. xxii. 20 ; xxxv. 17 : *marg.* 'my only one.'

DART

חֵץ *m.* an arrow : Prov. vii. 23.

מַסָּע *m.* a missile weapon, discharged with violence : Job xli. 26.

שֶׁבֶט *com.* a rod or staff, a spear, lance, as composed of a staff or rod, with an iron point : 2 Sam. xviii. 14.

שֶׁלַח *m.* a missile weapon, as sent against an enemy ; a dart, javelin, spear, &c. : 2 Chron. xxxii. 5.

תּוֹתָח *m.* a club, bludgeon : Job xli. 29 : LXX. σφῦρα ; Vulg. *malleus.* Gesenius, the ballista, stones of, understood.

DASH

1 נָגַף to strike ; to strike or dash against so as to stumble. KAL *fut.*

2 נָפַץ to dash, to break and shatter, so as to disperse and scatter abroad all the parts or pieces. PIEL [a] *pret.* [b] *fut.*

3 פּוּץ to disperse. HIPHIL *part.*

4 רָטַשׁ to smite, break, to kill by dashing children against the stones. PIEL [a] *fut.* PUAL [b] *pret.* [c] *fut.*

5 רָעַע to break, crush ; *metaph.* to harass, to oppress a people. KAL *fut.*

Exod. xv. 6.		5	Ps. cxxxvii. 9.	2 a	Hos. x. 14.	4 b
2 Kings viii. 12.		4 a	Isa. xiii. 16.	4 c	xiii. 16.	4 c
Ps. ii. 9.		2 b	xiii. 18.	4 a	Nah. ii. 1.	3
xci. 12.		1	Jer. xiii. 14.	2 a	iii. 10.	4 c

DAUB

חָמַר (see *Slime*), to daub with clay, mortar, or bitumen. KAL *fut.* Exod. ii. 3.

טוּחַ to cover, by plastering with mortar. KAL *pret.* Ezek. xiii. 12, 14 ; xxii. 28. *part.* Poel, Ezek. xiii. 10, 11, 15, 15. טִיחַ *m.* Ezek. xiii. 12.

DAUGHTER

בַּיִת *m.* house : Isa. x. 32 כְּתִיב house of.

בַּת *f.* a daughter ; properly, as yet subject to a father's authority, hence the people that dwell in a city ; the daughter of Zion and of Jerusalem, 2 Kings xix. 21, signify the inhabitants of Zion and Jerusalem : in the plural, the towns or villages adjacent to a city : very frequent : Gen. v. 4, &c.

כַּלָּה *f.* (see *Bride, Spouse*), "daughter-in-law :" Gen. xi. 31, &c.

בֵּן *m.* son : 2 Chron. xi. 18, כְּתִיב.

DAVID

דָּוִיד beloved, from דָּוַד *part. pass.* to love. David, the king of Israel ; also the son of David, the Messiah : Jer. xxx. 9 : Ezek. xxxiv. 23, 24 ; xxxvii. 24, 25 : Hos. iii. 5. Cf. Isa. lv. 3 : Acts xiii. 34.

DAWNING

נֶשֶׁף *m.* twilight : Job vii. 4 : Ps. cxix. 147.

עָלָה to ascend. KAL *inf.* Josh. vi. 15.

עַפְעַפַּיִם *m. pl.* eyelids : Job iii. 9.

פָּנָה to turn, applied to the dawning of the morning. KAL *inf.* Judg. xix. 26.

DAY, DAILY

1 אוֹר *m.* light ; the space assigned to the light, *i. e.* day ; "day and night," *lit.* light with darkness, implying the succession of day and night ; till there be no night : Isa. lx. 20 : Zech. xiv. 6, 7 : Judg. xvi. 2, "until the morning, when it is day ;" *lit.* until the light of the morning.

2 בֹּקֶר *m.* the morning : *pr.* day-break.

3 יוֹם a day ; it is frequently put for time in general, or for a long time ; a whole period under consideration, as, in the day signifieth in the time when ; in that day, at that time. Day is also put for a particular season or time when any extraordinary event happens, whether it be prosperous and joyful, or adverse and calamitous ; which day is denominated either from the Lord who appoints it, or from those who suffer in it : Job xviii. 20 : Ps. cxxxvii. 7 : Ezek. xxi. 25. "Day of the Lord," a day of visitation or of judgment. Hos. vi. 2, "two days," two seasons of calamity. All the day, all the day long, is the same as always, continually. Days are put for years : Lev. xxv. 29 : 1 Sam. xxvii. 7 : 1 Kings xvii. 15. Other peculiarities may be seen and easily accounted for in the several translations : Gen. i. 5, &c. [a] יוֹם Ch. *m.* [b] יוֹמָם *adv.*

4 יָכַח see *Reprove*, &c. HIPHIL *part.* Job ix. 33, *marg.* 'umpire.'

5 עֶרֶב *m.* evening.

6 שַׁחַר *m.* morning ; "day-spring." See *Break, Dawn.*

7 תְּמוֹל *adv.* yesterday.

8 תָּמִיד *m.* continually.

No. 3 not included, except in cases of peculiar construction.

Gen. xxxii. 24, 26. α	6	2 Sam. xiii. 4, 4.	2	Ps. lxxviii. 14.	3 b
xxxix. 10. β	3	xxi. 10.	3 b	lxxxvi. 4. φ	3
Exod. v. 13, γ 19. γ	3 b	1 Kings viii. 59.	3 b	lxxxviii. 17. φ	3
xiii. 21, 21, 22.	3 b	xvii. 15.	3 b	xci. 5.	3 b
xvi. 4, γ 5. δ	3	2 Kings xxv. 30. γ	3	cxxi. 6.	3 b
xxi. 21. ε	3 b	1 Chron. ix. 33.	3 b	Prov. viii. 30, β 34. β	3
i. 38.	3 b	vii. 37. γ	3	Isa. iv. 5, 6.	3 b
Lev. viii. 33. ζ	3	2 Chron. vi. 20.	3	xxi. 8.	3 b
viii. 35.	3 b	viii. 13, γ 14. γ	3	xxxiv. 10.	3 b
xii. 4, η 5. θ	3	xxxi. 16. γ	3	lviii. 2. β	3
xxiii. 37. γ	3	Ezra iii. 4, ρ 4. γ	3	lx. 11, 19.	3 b
xxiv. 8. ι	3	vi. 9, 9, 15.	3 a	Jer. ix. 1.	3 b
Num. vi. 16.	8	Neh. i. 6.	8	xiv. 17.	3 b
vi. 13. κ	3	iv. 9.	3 b	xv. 9. ψ	3, or 3 b
vii. 11. λ	3	v. 18. ς	3 b	xvi. 13.	3 b
vii. 72, 78. μ	3	ix. 12, 19.	3 b	xx. 7, 8. χ	3
ix. 21.	3 b	xi. 23. π	3 b	xxv. 34.	3
x. 34.	3 b	xiii. 47. τ	3 b	xxxi. 35.	3 b
xiv. 14.	3 b	Esth. ii. 11. ν	3	xxxiii. 20, 25.	3 b
xiv. 34. ν	3	lii. 34. γ	3	Lam. ii. 18.	3 b
xxviii. 3.	3	Job iii. 9.	6	Ezek. iv. 6.	3 b
xxix. 6.	3	v. 14.	8	vi. 3, 4, 7.	3 b
Deut. i. 33.	3 b	ix. 33.	4	xvi. 56.	3 b
xxviii. 66. ξ	3 b	xxiv. 16.	3 b	Dan. i. 5. γ	3
Josh. i. 8.	6	xxvi. 10.	1	ii. 28, 44.	3 a
vi. 15.	6	xxxviii. 12.	6	iv. 34.	3 a
Judg. vi. 27.	3 b	Ps. i. 2.	3 b	v. 11.	3 a
xvi. 2.	1	ii. 2.	3	vi. 7, 10, 12, 13.	3 a
xvi. 16. ο	3	xxii. 2.	3 b	vii. 9, 13, 22.	3 a
xix. 25.	6	xxxii. 4.	3 b	viii. 11, 12, 12.	3 a
xix. 26.	2	xiii. 3, 8.	3 b	viii. 14.	5, 2
1 Sam. ix. 20.	3	iii. 10. φ	3 b	ix. 31.	8
ix. 26.	6	lv. 10.	3 b	xii. 11.	8
xxi. 5. π	7	li. 8. β	3	Hos. xii. 1. χ	8
xxiii. 14. ο	3	lxxii. 15. φ	3		
xxv. 16.	3 b	lxxiv. 22 χ	3 b		

a lit. the morning riseth.   *β lit.* day, day.   *γ lit.* of a day in his day.   *δ lit.* a day, day.   *ε lit.* two days.   *η lit.* thirty days and three days.   of the fulfilling of the days of, &c.   *ζ lit.* until the days   *ι lit.* on the sabbath day, on the sabbath   *θ lit.* sixty days and six days.

day. *κ lit.* in the day of the fulfilling of the days of. *λ lit.* a prince on a day, a prince on a day. *μ lit.* on a day, the . . . . day. *ν lit.* a day for a year, a day for a year. *ξ lit.* night and day. *o lit.* all days. *π lit.* as yesterday the third (day). *ρ lit.* of a day in a day. *ς lit.* for one day. *τ lit.* the affair of the day in his day. *υ lit.* day and day. *φ lit.* all the day. *χ lit.* every day. *ψ lit.* their day.

DEAF

חָרַשׁ to be deaf, *i. e.* smitten or struck in the tongue or ears; as we still say a man is struck dumb: so in Latin, "tusus, obtusus auribus vel lingua." KAL *fut.* Micah vii. 16. חֵרֵשׁ *adj.* deaf: Exod. iv. 11: Lev. xix. 14: Ps. xxxviii. 13; lviii. 4: Isa. xxix. 18; xxxv. 5; xlii. 18, 19; xliii. 8.

DEAL, DEALING

1 דָּבָר *m.* word, &c.

2 חָלַק to divide, distribute. PIEL *fut.*

3 עָשָׂה to do; *seq.* בְּ of person, to do with, to deal with or against any one, according to one's own pleasure. KAL a *pret.* b *inf.* c *imp.* d *fut.* e *part.* Poel.

4 פָּרַם to break, to break bread to any one, to distribute. KAL *inf.*

In general, see under the word which accompanies this, as *Treacherously*, &c.

Gen. xxiv. 49.	3 e	2 Kings xxi. 6.	3 a	Isa. lviii. 7.	4
xxxiv. 31.	3 d	xxii 7.	3 e	Jer. vi. 13.	3 e
xlvii. 29.	3 a	1 Chron. xvi. 3.	2	viii. 10.	3 e
Exod. v. 15.	3 d	xx. 3.	3 d	xviii. 23.	3 c
xiv. 11.	3 a	2 Chron. ii. 3.	3 a	xxi. 2.	3 d
xxi. 9.	3 a	xix. 11.β	3 c	Ezek. viii. 18.	3 a
xxiii. 11.	3 d	xxxiii. 6.	3 a	xvi. 59.	3 a
Num. xi. 15.	3 e	Job xlii. 8.γ	3 b	xviii. 9.	3 b
Deut. vii. 5.	3 d	Ps. ciii. 10.	3 a	xxii. 7.	3 a
Josh. ii. 14.	3 a	cxix. 65.	3 a	xxii. 14.	3 a
Judg. ix. 16, 19.	3 a	cxix. 124.	3 c	xxiii. 25, 29.	3 a
xviii. 4. a	3 a	cxlvii. 20.	3 a	xxv. 12, 15.	3 a
Ruth i. 8, 8.	3 d a	Prov. x. 4.	3 e	xxxi. 11.	3 b d
1 Sam. ii. 23.	1	xii. 22.	3 e	Dan. i. 13.	3 c
xx. 8.	3 a	xiii. 16.	3 d	xi. 7.	3 a
xxiv. 18.	3 a	xiv. 17.	3 d	Joel ii. 26.	3 a
2 Sam. vi. 19.	2	xxi. 24.	3 e	Zech. i. 6.	3 a
2 Kings xii. 15.	3 e				

a lit. thus did Micah unto me.   *β lit.* take courage and do.
γ lit. that not to do.

DEAR

יָקִיר *adj.* precious: Jer. xxxi. 20.

DEARTH

בַּצֹּרֶת *f.* a cutting off (of rain): Jer. xiv. 1.

דָּבָר *m.* word, &c.: Jer. xiv. 1, *lit.* words of the dearths.

רָעָב *m.* hunger, famine: Gen. xli. 54, 54: 2 Kings iv. 38: 2 Chron. vi. 28: Neh. v. 3.

DEATH

1 יְשִׁימוֹת *f. pl.* desolations, destructions, יְשִׁיא מָוֶת קרי. כתיב, let death seize upon them: Ps. lv. 15.

2 מוּת to die, to be put to death, to cause to die. KAL a *inf.* b *fut.* c *part.* HIPHIL d *pret.* e *inf.* f *fut.* g *part.* HOPHAL h *pret.* i *fut.* k מָוֶת *m.* death. l מוֹת Ch. *m. id.* m מֻת *m. id.* n מָמוֹת *m.* deaths. o תְּמוּתָה *f.* death. See *Die.*

3 רָצַח to kill, to slay. KAL *fut.*

No. 2 k not included.

Gen. xxvi. 11. a	2 a i	Ex. xxxi. 14, a 15. a	2 a i	Lev. xxiv. 16, a 16.	2 a i i
Exod. xxi. 15. a	2 a i	xxxv. 2.	2 i	xxiv. 17. a	2 a i
xxi. 12, a 15, a 16, a		Lev. xix. 20.	2 i	xxiv. 21.	2 a i
17. a	2 a i	xx. 2, a 9, a 10, a		xxvii. 29. a	2 a i
xxi. 29.	2 i	11, a 12, a 13, a		Num. i. 51.	2 i
xxii. 19. a	2 a i	15, a 16, a 27. a	2 a i	iii. 10, 38.	2 i

Num. xv. 35. a	2 a i	Judg. xx. 13.	2 f	Ezra vii. 26.	2 l
xvi. 29.	2 k	xxi. 5. a	2 a i	Esth. iv. 11.	2 e
xviii. 7.	2 i	1 Sam. iv. 20.	2 a	Ps. xlviii. 14.	2 m
xxxv. 16, a 17, a	2 a i	xi. 12.	2 f	lv. 15.	1, 2 k
18, a 21. a		xi. 13.	2 i	cii. 20.	2 o
xxxv. 30.	3	2 Sam. viii. 2.	2 e	Isa. xxxviii. 1.	2 a
xxxv. 31, 31. a	2 a a i	xix. 21, 22.	2 i	liii. 9.	2 k
Deut. xiii. 5.	2 i	xx. 3.	2 a	Jer. xvi. 4.	2 n
xiii. 9.	2 e	xxi. 9.	2 h	xxvi. 15.	2 g
xvii. 6, 6, 6.	2 c i i	1 Kings ii. 8.	2 f	xxvi. 19.	2 e d
xvii. 7.	2 e	ii. 24.	2 i	xxvi. 21, 24.	2 f
xxi. 22, 22.	2 k h	ii. 26, 26.	2 k f	xxxviii. 4.	2 i
xxiv. 16, 16, 16.	2 i	2 Kings xiv. 6, 6, 6.	2 i	xxxviii. 15.	2 e f
Josh. i. 18.	2 i	xx. 1.	2 a	xxxviii. 16, 25.	2 f
vi. 31.	2 i	2 Chron. xv. 13.	2 i	xliii. 3.	2 e
xvi. 16.	2 a i	xxiii. 7.	2 i	lii. 27.	2 f
		xxxii. 24.	2 a i	Ezek. xviii. 8.	2 n

a lit. dying shall be caused to die.

DEBASE

שָׁפֵל to be made low; to humble. HIPHIL *fut.* Isa. lvii. 9.

DEBATE

מַצָּה *f.* strife, contention: Isa. lviii. 4.

רִיב to contend, strive, quarrel; to plead a cause. KAL *imp.* Prov. xxv. 9. *fut.* Isa. xxvii. 8.

DEBT

חוֹב *m.* debtor: Ezek. xviii. 7.

יָד *com.* hand: Neh. x. 31, *marg.* 'hand.'

נָשָׁא to lend on usury, to loan. KAL *part.* 1 Sam. xxii. 2, *marg.* 'had a creditor.' נְשִׁי *m.* debt: 2 Kings iv. 7, *marg.* 'or, creditor.' מַשָּׁאָה *f. id.* Prov. xxii. 26.

DECAY

חָרֵב to be dried up. KAL *fut.* Job xiv. 11. חָרְבָּה *f.* dryness; desolation: Isa. xliv. 26, *marg.* 'wastes.'

כָּשַׁל to be or become weak, feeble; or, to stumble and falter from weakness. KAL *pret.* Neh. iv. 10.

מוֹט to waver, to shake, to be moved; to fall into decay. KAL *pret.* Lev. xxv. 35, *marg.* 'his hand faileth.'

מָכַךְ to melt away; to decay. NIPHAL *fut.* Eccles. x. 18.

DECEASED

רְפָאִים *m. pl.* the dead beneath the earth; according to some, the apostate dead, referring to Gen. vi. 4, Isa. xxvi. 14.

DECEIVE, DECEIT

1 בָּגַד to cover, conceal; to act under a cover or pretence, to deal treacherously, faithlessly, perfidiously; to disappoint one's hope and confidence; to violate a just obligation. KAL a *pret.* b *inf.*

2 הָתַל to mock or delude, to impose upon, to cheat, deceive. PIEL a *pret.* b *inf.* c *fut.* PUAL d *pret.* e מַהֲתַלּוֹת *f. pl.* deceitful things.

3 כָּזָב *m.* a lie; deceit, fraud, guile: Prov. xxiii. 3, *lit.* meat of lies.

4 כָּחַשׁ to lie, to speak lies; to deceive, to disappoint hope or expectation, to fail; to feign, to pretend, as false prophets. PIEL *inf.*

5 נָכַל to deceive, to act deceitfully, to deal fraudulently. KAL *part.* Poel.

6 נָשָׁא to err; to seduce, to corrupt; to deceive, to impose upon any one, to lead into pernicious error; a deception of one who is led to a false judgment of that in which he is deceived, and to false hopes. See *Beguile*. With *inf.*, deceive greatly. NIPHAL [a]*pret.* HIPHIL [b]*pret.* [c]*inf.* [d]*fut.* מַשָּׁאוֹן *m.* fraud, deception.

7 עָקֹב *adj.* fraudulent, deceitful, supplanting.

8 עָשַׁק to oppress; to defraud any one, to extort from him by fraud and violence, to get deceitfully. KAL *pret.* [a]עֹשֶׁק *m.* a 'thing' deceitfully gotten.

9 עָתַר to be rich, abundant; to be multiplied: see also *Intreat*. NIPHAL *part.* Prov. xxvii. 6. The most probable interpretation of this difficult word is, " to be deprecated are the kisses of an enemy." The Niphal is applied to that which is obtained by intreaty.

10 פָּתָה to open, to be open; to let oneself be enticed, persuaded; to persuade, to delude with words. KAL [a]*fut.* NIPHAL [b]*pret.* [c]*fut.* PIEL [d]*pret.* [e]*inf.* PUAL [f]*fut.*

11 רָמָה to cast, to throw; to deceive, probably to cast down, to make fall. PIEL [a]*pret.* [b]רְמִיָה *f.* a letting fall, remissness; deceit, fraud: this word is used of a " deceitful bow," but whether on account of its missing the mark, or because of the state of the string, which may be affected by the temperature, is not agreed; the latter seems to be sanctioned by the proper meaning of this word, to be relaxed or loosened, but the former seems rather implied by the context of the passages in which the word occurs. [c]מִרְמָה *f.* fraud. [d]תַּרְמִית *f. id.*

12 שָׁגַג to wander, go astray, to err. KAL *part.* Poel.

13 שָׁגָה to wander, go astray. KAL [a]*part.* Poel. HIPHIL [b]*part.*

14 שָׁלָה to be secure. NIPHAL, to err. HIPHIL, to deceive.

15 שֶׁקֶר *m.* a lie, falsehood; deception, a vain thing, that which deceives and disappoints hope.

16 תֹּךְ *m.* oppression, violence. [a]תְּכָכִים *m. pl.* vexations, oppressions.

17 תָּעָה to go astray, to err. NIPHAL *pret.*

18 תָּעַע to mock, to scoff at. PILPEL *part.*

Gen. xxvii. 12.	18	Ps. xliii. 1.	11 c	Isa. xliv. 20.	2 d	
xxxi. 7.	2 a	l. 19.	11 c	liii. 9.	11 c	
xxxiv. 13.	11 c	lii. 2.	11 b	Jer. iv. 10.	6 c b	
Exod. viii. 29. a	2 b	lii. 4.	11 c	v. 27.	11 c	
xxi. 8.	1 b	lv. 11.	16	viii. 5.	11 d	
Lev. vi. 2.	8	lv. 23.	11 c	ix. 5.	2 c	
vi. 4.	8 a 8	lxxii. 14.	16	ix. 6, 6, 8.	11 c	
Deut. xi. 16.	10 a	lxxviii. 57.	11 b	xiv. 14.	11 d	
1 Sam. xix. 17.	11 a	ci. 7.	11 b	xvii. 9.	7	
xxviii. 12.	11 a	cix. 2.	11 b	xx. 7, 7.	10 d c	
2 Sam. iii. 25.	10 e	cxix. 118.	11 d	xxiii. 26.	11 d	
xix. 26.	11 a	cxx. 2.	11 b	xxix. 8.	6 d	
2 Kings iv. 28.	14	Prov. xi. 18.	15	xxxvii. 9.	6 d	
xviii. 29.	6 d	xii. 5, 17, 20.	11 c	xlviii. 10.	11 b	
xix. 10.	6 d	xiv. 8, 25.	11 c	xlix. 16.	6 b	
2 Chron. xxxii. 15.	6 d	xx. 1.	13 a	Lam. i. 19.	11 a	
Job vi. 15.	11 c	xx. 17.	15	Ezek. xiv. 9, 9.	10 f d	
xii. 16, 16.	12, 13 b	xxiii. 3.	3	Dan. xi. 23.	11 c	
xiii. 7.	11 b	xxiv. 28.	10 d	Hos. vii. 16.	11 b	
xv. 31.	17	xxvi. 19.	11 a	xi. 12.	11 c	
xv. 35.	11 c	xxvi. 24.	11 c	xii. 7.	11 c	
xxvii. 4.	11 b	xxvi. 26.	6 e	Amos viii. 5.	11 c	
xxxi. 5.	11 c	xxvii. 6.	9	Obad. 3, 7.	11 c	
xxxi. 9.	10 b	xxix. 13.	16 a	Micah vi. 11.	6 b	
Ps. v. 6.	11 c	xxxi. 30.	15	vi. 12.	11 b	
x. 7.	11 c	Isa. xix. 13.	6 a	Zeph. i. 9.	11 b	
xxiv. 4.	11 c	xxx. 10.	2 e	iii. 13.	11 d	
xxxv. 20.	11 c	xxxvi. 14.	6 d	Zech. xiii. 4.	4	
xxxvi. 3.	11 c	xxxvii. 10.	11 c	Mal. ii. 14.	5	
xxxviii. 12.	11 c					

[a] *lit.* add to mock.

DECIDE, DECISION

חָרַץ to cut, to cut to a point; to determine. KAL *pret.* 1 Kings xx. 40. חָרוּץ *m.* decision, judgment: Joel iii. 14, 14.

DECK

יָפָה to be bright; to be fair, beautiful, comely; to beautify, to deck: PIEL *fut.* Jer. x. 4.

כָּהַן to minister in the priest's office; as the high priest was arrayed with curious splendid garments, for glory and for beauty, hence is taken the idea of decking with extraordinary elegance and splendour. PIEL *fut.* Isa. lxi. 10, *marg.* 'decketh as a priest.'

עָדָה to pass; to cause to pass over upon; to dress in a splendid manner, to adorn. KAL *pret.* Ezek. xxiii. 40. *imp.* Job xl. 10. *fut.* Jer. iv. 30: Ezek. xvi. 11, 13: Hos. ii. 13.

עָשָׂה to do, to make, &c. KAL *fut.* Ezek. xvi. 16.

רָבַד to deck or adorn the body or a bed. KAL *pret.* Prov. vii. 16.

DECLARE (See also PEDIGREE)

1 אָמַר to speak, to say. KAL *pret.* אֲמַר Ch. P'AL *imp.*

2 בָּאַר to make plain, to shew the sense. PIEL *inf.*

3 בּוּר *i. q.* בָּרַר (see *Pure*), to make plain and manifest; Gesenius, to search out, to examine, to prove. KAL *inf.*

4 דָּבַר to speak. PIEL [a]*pret.* [b]*fut.*

5 אַחְוָה *f.* a shewing of opinion, a declaration of one's mind.

6 יָדַע to know. HIPHIL [a]*pret.* [b]*imp.*

7 נָגַד KAL, *inusit,* to be in sight; Hiphil, to bring forward, to light, Job xxi. 31; to point out, or represent, Ezek. xliii. 10; to put forward, Isa. iii. 9; but most frequently to shew, declare, or tell; Lxx. mostly ἀναγγέλλειν, ἀπαγγέλλειν. Sometimes to inform against, Jer. xx. 10; to foretell, Isa. xli. 22, &c.; to explain, Judg. xiv. 12; distinguished from מָצָא to find out, to confess, Ps. xxxviii. 18; particularly and emphatically to publish with praise, to celebrate, Ps. ix. 11, &c. HIPHIL [a]*pret.* [b]*inf.* [c]*imp.* [d]*fut.* [e]*part.* HOPHAL [f]*pret.*

8 סָפַר to number; to relate, to tell; to announce. PIEL [a]*pret.* [b]*inf.* [c]*imp.* [d]*fut.* [e]*part.* PUAL [f]*fut.*

9 פָּרַשׁ *pr.* to cleave, to divide; to separate, to distinguish; to declare distinctly. PUAL [a]*pret.* [b]פָּרָשָׁה a distinct or accurate declaration.

10 שִׂיחַ to speak, to talk, to converse; to meditate, to think. POLEL *fut.*

11 שָׁמַע to hear; to cause to hear, to announce. HIPHIL [a]*pret.* [b]*imp.* [c]*part.*

Gen. xli. 24.	7 e	Job xii. 8.	8 d	Ps. xxx. 9.	7 d	
Exod. ix. 16.	8 b	xiii. 17.	5	xxxviii. 18.	7 d	
Lev. xxiii. 14.	4 b	xv. 17.	8 d	xl. 5.	7 d	
Num. xv. 34.	9 a	xxi. 31.	7 d	xl. 10.	1 a	
Deut. i. 5.	2	xxvi. 3.	6 a	l. 6.	7 d	
iv. 13.	7 d	xxvii. 27.	8 d	l. 16.	8 b	
Josh. xx. 4.	4 a	xxxi. 37.	8 d	lxiv. 9.	7 d	
Judg. xiv. 12. a	7 b d	xxxviii. 4, 18.	7 c	lxvi. 16.	8 d	
xiv. 13.	7 d	xl. 7.	6 b	lxxi. 17.	7 d	
xiv. 15.	7 d	xli. 4.	6 b	lxxiii. 28.	8 b	
2 Sam. vix. 6.	7 a	Ps. ii. 7.	7 d	lxxv. 1.	8 a	
1 Chron. xvi. 24.	8 c	ix. 11.	7 c	lxxv. 2.	7 d	
Neh. viii. 12.	8 c	xix. 1.	8 e	lxxvii. 14.	6 a	
Esth. iv. 8.	7 b	xxii. 22.	8 d	lxxviii. 6.	8 d	
x. 2.	9 b	xxii. 31.	7 d	lxxxviii. 11.	8 f	

Ps. xcvi. 3.	8 c	Isa. xliii. 12.	7 a	Jer. xxxvi. 13.	7 d
xcvii. 6.	7 a	xliv. 7.	8 c	xxxviii. 15.	7 d
cii. 21.	8 b	xliv. 8.	7 d	xxxviii. 25.	7 c
cvii. 22.	8 d	xlv. 19.	7 a	xlii. 4, 21.	7 d
cxviii. 17.	8 d	xlv. 21.	7 e	xlii. 20.	7 c
cxix. 13, 26.	8 a	xlvi. 10.	11 a	xlvi. 14.	7 c
cxlv. 4.	7 d	xlviii. 3, 14.	7 e	l. 2.	7 c
cxlv. 6.	8 d	xlviii. 5, 6.	7 a	l. 28.	7 b
Eccles. ix. 1.	3	xlviii. 20.	7 d	li. 10.	8 d
Isa. iii. 9.	7 a	liii. 8.	7 c	Ezek. xii. 16.	8 d
xii. 4.	6 b	lvii. 12.	8	xxiii. 36.	7 c
xxi. 2.	7 f	lxvi. 19.	7 d	xl. 4.	7 c
xxi. 6.	7 d	Jer. iv. 5.	7 a	Dan. iv. 18.	7 a
xxi. 10.	7 a	iv. 15.	7 c	Hos. iv. 12.	7 c
xli. 22.	11 b	v. 20.	7 e	Amos iv. 13.	7 e
xli. 26, 26.	7 a, 11 c	xxxi. 10.	7 c	Micah i. 10.	7 d
xlii. 9.	7 d			iii. 8.	7 b
xlii. 12.	7 d			Zech. ix. 12.	7 e
xliii. 9.	7 d				

a declaring ye can declare.

DECLINE

1 נָטָה to stretch out; to turn aside, to turn away. KAL *a pret.* *b inf.* *c fut.* *d part.* Paúl. HIPHIL *e fut.*

2 סוּר to turn aside; to depart. KAL *a pret.* *b fut.*

3 שָׂטָה to turn aside from a way. KAL *fut.*

Exod. xxiii. 2.	1 b	Ps. xliv. 18.	1 c	Ps. cxix. 51, 157.	1 a
Deut. xvii. 11.	2 b	cii. 11.	1 d	Prov. iv. 5.	1 c
2 Chron. xxxiv. 2.	2 a	cix. 23.	1 b	vii. 25.	3
Job xxiii. 11.	1 e				

DECREASE

חָסֵר to grow less and less, to decrease as the ebbing tide. KAL *inf.* Gen. viii. 5, *marg.* 'were in going and decreasing.'

מָעַט to be few or little. HIPHIL *fut.* Ps. cvii. 38.

DECREE

1 מַאֲמָר *m.* commandment.

2 אֱסָר Ch. *m.* interdict, or prohibition.

3 גָּזַר to cut, to cut off; to divide, to separate; *metaph.* to decide, to cut off contention and uncertainty by a determination or decree. KAL *a fut.* NIPHAL *b pret.* *c* גְּזֵרָה Ch. *f.* decree, sentence.

4 דָּבָר a word, &c.

5 דָּת *f.* an imperial law, or edict, enforced by the highest and most absolute authority. *a* דָּת Ch. *f.* law.

6 חָקַק to grave; to ordain, to appoint; to prescribe. KAL *a part.* Poel. POEL *b fut.* *c* חֹקֵק *m.* decree, thing determined. *d* חֹק *m.* statute, law.

7 חָרַץ to decide: it implies strict and severe justice, or determined and fixed issue. KAL *part.* Paúl.

8 טַעַם *m.* taste; discernment, judgment, &c., Jonah iii. 7, by the decree, the judgment, or according to the deliberate opinion of the king and nobles, consulting together what was best to be done. *a* טְעֵם Ch. *m.* taste; sentence, royal edict: freq. with the verb שׂוּם. See *Make.*

9 פִּתְגָם *m.* rescript, decree.

10 קוּם to rise up; to confirm, to establish; *seq.* עַל to enjoin anything upon any one, *pr.* to cause to be imposed upon any one. PIEL *pret.*

2 Chron. xxx. 5.	4	Esth. ii. 1.	3 b	Esth. ix. 1, 13, 14.	5
Ezra v. 13, 17.	8 a	ii. 8.	5	ix. 31.	10
vi. 1, 3, 8, 11, 12.	8 a	iii. 15.	5	ix. 32.	1
vii. 13, 21.	8 a	iv. 3, 8.	5	Job xxii. 28.	3 a
Esth. i. 20.	9	viii. 14, 17.	5	xxviii. 26.	6 d

Job xxxviii. 10.	6 d	Isa. x. 22.	7	Dan. vi. 7, 8, 9, 12, 13,	
Ps. ii. 7.	6 d	Jer. v. 22.	6 d	15.	2
cxlviii. 6.	6 d	Dan. ii. 9, 13, 15.	5 a	vi. 26.	8 a
Prov. viii. 15.	6 b	iii. 10, 29.	8 a	Jonah iii. 7.	8
viii. 29.	6 d	iv. 6.	8 a	Micah vii. 11.	6 d
Isa. x. 1, 1.	6 a c	iv. 17, 24.	3 c	Zeph. ii. 2.	6 d

DEDICATE

1 חָנַךְ to initiate: it is applied to the first use of anything, as of a house, the temple, an altar, &c., by setting them apart in a solemn manner; to instruct. KAL *a pret.* *b fut.* *c* חֲנֻכָּה *f.* dedication. *d* חֲנֻכָּה Ch. *f. id.*

2 חֵרֶם *m.* a devoted thing: this word is stronger than the following, since anything thus devoted could not be redeemed; but that which was set apart or sanctified might be redeemed or ransomed.

3 קָדַשׁ to be holy; to sanctify; to consecrate. With *inf.*, dedicate wholly. HIPHIL *a pret.* *b inf.* *c part.* *d* קֹדֶשׁ *m.* holiness; a holy thing, sacred, consecrated to God.

Num. vii. 10, 11, 84, 88.	1 c	1 Chron. xviii. 11.	3 a	2 Chron. vii. 9.	1 c
Deut. xx. 5, 5.	1 a b	xxvi. 20.	3 d	xv. 18, 18.	3 d
Judg. xvii. 3.	3 b a	xxvi. 26, 26.	3 a d	xxiv. 7.	3 d
2 Sam. viii. 11, 11.	3 a	xxvi. 27.	3 a	xxxi. 12.	3 d
1 Kings vii. 51.	3 d	xxvi. 28, 28.	3 a c	Ezra iv. 16, 17.	1 d
viii. 63.	1 b	xxviii. 12.	3 d	Neh. xii. 27, 27.	1 c
xv. 15, 15.	3 d	2 Chron. ii. 4.	3 b	Ps. xxx. title.	1 c
2 Kings xii. 4.	3 d	v. 1.	3 d	Ezek. xliv. 29.	2
xii. 18.	3 a	vii. 5.	1 b	Dan. iii. 2, 3.	1 d

DEED

1 אוּלָם *part. adversative,* "in very deed."

2 אָמְנָם *part.* indeed, "in very deed."

3 גְּמוּלָה *f.* see *Reward.* Deeds according to their desert.

4 דָּבָר word, matter, &c.

5 חֶסֶד *m.* kindness, "good deed."

6 טוֹב *adj.* good, "good deed."

7 כֵּן to establish. NIPHAL *part.* "in very deed."

8 עֲלִילָה *f.* occasions, actions, works.

9 פֹּעַל *m.* work; deed, act, *facinus.*

10 מַעֲשֶׂה *m.* work, labour; work, deed.

Gen. xx. 9.	10	1 Chron. xvi. 8.	8	Esth. i. 17, 18.	4
xliv. 15.	10	2 Chron. vi. 18.	2	Ps. xxviii. 4.	9
Exod. xvi. 16.	1	xxxv. 27.	4	cv. 1.	8
1 Sam. xxv. 34.	1	Ezra ix. 13.	10	Isa. lix. 18.	3
xxvi. 4.	7	Neh. vi. 19.	6	Jer. v. 28.	4
2 Sam. xii. 14.	5	xiii. 14.	5	xxv. 14.	9

DEEP, DEPTH

1 מַהֲמֹרוֹת *f.* streams, whirlpools, abysses of waters: Ps. cxl. 10. The Rabbins, Symm., and Jerome understand "deep pits" of water.

2 מֶחְקָר *m.* the inmost depth, the recesses; what is known by scrutiny; as mines, &c., which occupy so much the labour of man.

3 עָמַק to be deep, *metaph.* unsearchable, *comp.* Rom. xi. 33, to make deep; often followed by an infinitive verb, Isa. vii. 11, make deep to ask, *i. e.* demand that a miracle shall come from the deep, from below. Also with a gerund, so as to be taken in an adverbial sense, Jer. xlix. 8, 30; make deep to dwell, dwell in the depths of the earth, Isa. xxix. 15; that seek deep,

that form subtle projects, to hide their counsel, Hos. ix. 9, "they have deeply corrupted themselves," not through infirmity or ignorance, but with a deep deliberate thought. Deep speech, deep lips, a language difficult to understand; see *Strange*. Things are also said to be deep which extend to a great length from the eye of the spectator; as we speak of a deep house from front to rear, so of a deep tract, deep court; see *Valley*. KAL [a] *pret.* HIPHIL [b] *pret.* [c] *imp.* [d] *part.* [e] עָמֵק *adj.* deep, deep of lip. *i. e.* using an unintelligible language. [f] עָמֹק *adj. id.* [g] עֹמֶק *m.* depth. [h] מַעֲמַקִּים *m. pl.* depths, deep places. [i] עַמִּיק Ch. *adj.* deep, *figuratively*, hidden.

4   צוּלָה *f.* depths of the sea, abyss. [a] מְצוֹלָה *f.* a depth, deep place. [b] מְצוּלָה *f. id.*

5   שָׁקַע to sink; to make deep. HIPHIL [a] *fut.* [b] מִשְׁקָע *m.* a place where water settles.

6   תְּהוֹם *m. pr.* a mass of raging waters, *spec.* the ocean, sea, the deep; more rarely of any other mass of waters, as those covering the earth at the creation, Gen. i. 2, Ps. civ. 6; or the subterranean waters, the deep, the abyss, whence spring fountains and streams, Gen. xlix. 25, Deut. xxxiii. 13; also in the description of roaring waters, Ps. xlii. 8.—Gen. i. 2, &c.

No. 6, *Deep, Depth*, not included.

Lev. xiii. 3, 4, 25, 30,		Ps. cvii. 24.	4 b	Isa. xxxiii. 19.	3 e
31, 32, 34.	3 f	cxxx. 1.	3 h	xliv. 27.	3 h
Neh. ix. 11.	4 a	cxl. 10.	1	li. 10, 10.	6, 3 h
Job xi. 8.	3 f	Prov. ix. 18.	3 e	Jer. xlix. 8, 30.δ	3 b
xii. 22.	3 f	xviii. 4.	3 f	Ezek xxiii. 32.	3 f
xli. 31.	4 b	xx. 5.	3 f	xxvii. 34.	3 h
Ps. lxiv. 6.	3 f	xxii. 14.	3 f	xxxii. 14.	5 b
lxix. 2, 2.	4 b, 3 h	xxiii. 27.	3 f	xxxiv. 18.	5 h
lxix. 14.	3 h	xxv. 3.		Dan. ii. 22.	3 i
lxix. 15.	4 b	Eccles. vii. 24.α	3 g	Hos. ix. 9.ε	3 d
lxxxviii. 6.	4 b	Isa. vii. 11.β	3 c	Jonah ii. 3.	4 b
xcii. 5.	4 a	xxix. 15.	3 d	Micah vii. 19.	4 b
xcv. 4.	2	xxx. 33.	3 b	Zech. x. 11.	4 b

α lit. and deep deep.   *β lit.* deepen thy petition.   *γ lit.* have deepened revolt.   *δ lit.* the inhabitants have deepened to dwell.   *ε lit.* they have deepened, they have corrupted.

DEFAMING

דִּבָּה *f.* slander: Jer. xx. 10.

DEFEAT

פָּרַר to break; to violate, to make vain, to frustrate. HIPHIL *pret.* 2 Sam. xv. 34; *inf.* 2 Sam. xvii. 14.

DEFEND, DEFENCE

1   בָּצַר to cut off, to cut out as metals, to cut off access, to make inaccessible. KAL [a] *part.* Paül. [b] בֶּצֶר *m.* defence; or rather ore of gold and silver. [c] מִבְצָר *m.* defence of a city, fortress.

2   גָּנַן to cover; to protect; everywhere of God as protecting men. KAL [a] *pret.* [b] *inf.* HIPHIL [c] *fut.* [d] מָגֵן *m.* shield.

3   חֻפָּה *f.* covering, protection. LXX. σκεπασθήσεται.

4   יָשַׁע to save. HIPHIL *inf.*

5   נָצַל to deliver. HIPHIL *fut.*

6   סָכַךְ to cover, to shelter, protect. KAL [a] *part.* Poel. HIPHIL [b] *fut.*

7   מְצוּדָה *f.* fortress, hold.

8   מָצוֹר *m.* bulwark.

9   צֵל *m.* shade, shelter, protection.

10   שָׂנֵב to be high. PIEL [a] *fut.* [b] מִשְׂגָּב *m.* high tower.

11   שָׁפַט to judge. KAL *imp.*

Num. xiv. 9.	9	Ps. lix. 9, 16, 17.	10 b	Isa. xxxvi. 1.	1 a
Judg. x. 1.	4	lxii. 2, 6.	10 b	xxxvii. 26.	1 a
2 Sam. xxiii. 12.	1	lxxxii. 3.	11	xxxvii. 35.	2 a
2 Kings xix. 34.	2 a	lxxxix. 18.	2 d	xxxviii. 6.	2 a
xx. 6.	2 a	xciv. 22.	10 b	Jer. i. 18.	1 c
2 Chron. xi. 5.	8	Eccles. vii. 12, 12.	9	iv. 5.	1 c
Job xxii. 25.	1 b	Isa. iv. 5.	3	viii. 14.	1 c
Ps. v. 11.	6 b	xix. 6.	8	xxxiv. 7.	1 c
vii. 10.	2	xxv. 2.	8	Ezek. xxi. 20.	1 a
xx. 1.	10 a	xxvii. 10.	1 a	Nah. ii. 5.	6 a
xxxi. 2.	7	xxi. 5, 5.	2 c b	Zech. ix. 15.	2 c
lix. 1.	10 a	xxxiii. 16.	10 b	xii. 8.	2 c

DEFER

אָחַר to come after, to delay. PIEL *pret.* Gen. xxxiv. 19. *fut.* Eccles. v. 4: Dan. ix. 19.

אָרַךְ to be long; to prolong, continue, protract. HIPHIL *pret.* Prov. xix. 11. *fut.* Isa. xlviii. 9.

מָשַׁךְ to draw, to draw out; to delay. PUAL *part.* Prov. xiii. 12.

DEFILE

1   גָּאַל to be common, profane, polluted, unclean. NIPHAL [a] *pret.* HITHPAEL [b] *fut.* [c] גֹּאַל defiling.

2   חָלַל to profane. NIPHAL [a] *pret.* PIEL [b] *pret.* [c] *inf.* [d] *part.*

3   חָנֵף to be profaned, polluted, defiled; to make profane. KAL [a] *pret.* [b] *fut.* HIPHIL [c] *fut.*

4   טָמֵא to be unclean; chiefly of Levitical uncleanness. KAL [a] *pret.* [b] *inf.* [c] *fut.* NIPHAL [d] *pret.* PIEL [e] *pret.* [f] *inf.* [g] *imp.* [h] *fut.* HITHPAEL [i] *fut.* HOTHPAEL [k] *pret.* [l] טָמֵא *adj.* impure, unclean.

5   טָמָה to be unclean, to be defiled. NIPHAL *pret.*

6   טָנַף to soil, to defile. PIEL *fut.*

7   נָחַל to inherit. PIEL *pret.*

8   עָלַל *pr.* in the primary sense, to roll, and thence to do a thing frequently: here the idea seems to be chiefly humiliation, when the horn that has been lifted up is rolled in the dust: POEL *pret.* Job xvi. 15.

9   עָנָה to oppress, to afflict, to humble; to humble or defile a woman. PIEL *fut.*

10   קָדֵשׁ to be holy; sacred; of things devoted to the sacred treasury. KAL *fut.*

Gen. xxxiv. 2.	9	Num. v.13; 14, 14, 20,		Isa. xxx. 22.	4 e
xxxiv. 5, 13, 27.	4 e	27, 28, 29.	4 d	lix. 3.	1 a
xlix. 4.	2 b	vi. 9.	4 d	Jer. ii. 7.	4 h
Exod. xxxi. 14.	2 d	vi. 12.	4 d	iii. 9.	3 b
Lev. v. 3.	4 c	ix. 6, 7.	4 l	xvi. 18.	2 b
xi. 43.	5	xix. 13, 20.	4 h	xix. 13.	4 l
xi. 44.	4 h	xxxv. 33.	3 c	xxxii. 34.	4 f
xiii. 46.	4 i	xxxv. 34.	4 h	Ezek. iv. 13.	4 l
xv. 31.	4 f	Deut. xxi. 23.	4 h	v. 11.	4 l
xv. 32.	4 b	xxii. 9.	10	vii. 22.	4 l
xviii. 20, 23,	4 b	xxiv. 4.	4 k	vii. 24.	2 a or 7
xviii. 24, 24.	4 i d	2 Kings xxiii. 8.	4 h	ix. 7.	4 g
xviii. 25, 27.	4 c	xxiii. 10, 13.	4 e	xviii. 6, 11, 15.	4 h
xviii. 28.	4 f	1 Chron. v. 1.	2 c	xx. 7, 18.	4 l
xviii. 30.	4 i	Neh. xiii. 29.	1 c	xx. 43.	4 l
xix. 31.	4 f	Job xvi. 15.	8	xxiii. 3.	4 b
xx. 3.	4 f	Ps. lxxiv. 7.	2 b	xxiii. 7.	4 a
xxi. 1, 3, 4, 11.	4 b	cvi. 39.	4 e	xxiii. 11.	4 e
xxii. 8.	4 b	Cant. v. 3.	5	xxiii. 7, 13.	4 e
Num. v. 2.	4 l	Isa. xxiv. 5.	3 a	xxiii. 17.	4 h
v. 3.	4 h			xxiii. 38.	4 e

Ezek. xxviii. 7, 18.	2 b	Ezek. xliii. 7.	4 h	Hos. v. 3.	4 d
xxxiii. 26.	4 e	xliii. 8.	4 e	vi. 10.	4 d
xxxvi. 17.	4 h	xliv. 25, 25.	4 b	Micah iv. 11.	3 b
xxxvii. 23.	4 i	Dan. i. 8, 8.	1 b		

DEFRAUD

עָשַׁק to oppress ; to extort from any one by fraud and violence, with acc., of person, also of the thing. KAL pret. 1 Sam. xii. 3, 4. fut. Lev. xix. 13.

DEFY

זָעַם to be very angry, to be indignant ; to curse, with an acc. KAL pret. Num. xxiii. 8. imp. Num. xxiii. 7. fut. Num. xxiii 8.

חָרַף to reproach, upbraid, to scorn. PIEL pret. 1 Sam. xvii. 10, 26, 36, 45. inf. 1 Sam. xvii. 25 : 2 Sam. xxiii. 9. fut. 2 Sam. xxi. 21 : 1 Chron. xx. 7.

DEGENERATE

סוּר m. turned away ; degenerate : Jer. ii. 21.

DEGREE

אָדָם m. see Man : Ps. lxii. 9, men of low degree, lit. sons of Adam.

אִישׁ see Man : Ps. lxii. 9, men of high degree, lit. sons of man.

בֵּן m. son : Ps. lxii. 9, 9.

מַעֲלָה f. steps, degrees : as prefixed to Pss. cxx.—cxxxiv., it probably means the steps of the temple on which, while ascending, the Levites sung these Psalms on some particular occasion ; unless, as Gesenius suggests, the word has reference to the rhythm, there being a peculiar construction in the composition ; the last word of a former sentence is often repeated in the beginning of the next : see Gesenius' Lexicon and Thesaurus. 2 Kings xx. 9, 9, 10, 10, 11, by which, lit. by the degrees which : 1 Chron. xvii. 17, "high degree." See High. Isa. xxxviii. 8, 8, 8, 8.

DELAY

אָחַר to tarry ; to defer. PIEL fut. Exod. xxii. 29.

בּוּשׁ to feel shame. PIEL, to cause shame, to delay beyond one's expectation. pret. Exod. xxxii. 1.

מָהַהּ to linger. HITHPALPEL : Ps. cxix. 60.

DELECTABLE

חָמַד to desire strongly. KAL part. Paül, Isa. xliv. 9.

DELICATE

1 עֵדֶן m. delight, pleasure. מַעֲדָן m. delight, delicate food.

2 עָנַג to live delicately and effeminately. PUAL part. HITHPAEL inf. עָנֹג adj. delicate, soft. תַּעֲנוּג m. delight.

3 פָּנַק to treat with great indulgence and lenity. PIEL part.

Deut. xxviii. 54.	2 c	Prov. xxix. 21.	3	Jer. li. 34.	1
xxviii. 56, 56.	2 c b	Isa. xlvii. 1.	2 c	Lam. iv. 5.	1 a
1 Sam. xv. 32.	1 a	Jer. vi. 2.	2 a	Micah i. 16. a	2 d

a lit. the children of thy delight.

DELIGHT

1 גִּיל to rejoice. KAL fut.

---

2 חָמַד to desire strongly. KAL a pret. PIEL b pret.

3 חָפֵץ the primary meaning, according to Schultens, seems to be, to bend, to bend towards ; and metaph. applied to the will, it implies entire and full inclination towards an object or person : it may simply mean what is included in the Latin velle, or it may carry with itself the notion of delight and affection : to will anything, is to purpose that in the doing of which he shall find pleasure. See Please. KAL a pret. b fut. c חָפֵץ adj. to delight in. d חֵפֶץ m. delight.

4 חָשַׁק to be attached, to desire. See Desire. KAL pret.

5 נָעֵם to be pleasant, lovely. KAL fut.

6 עָדַן HITHPAEL, to enjoy or delight oneself. a fut. b עֵדֶן m. delights. c מַעֲדָן m. delight, joy.

7 עָנַג to be delicate ; to delight in anything. HITHPAEL a pret. b imp. c fut. d עֹנֶג m. pleasure. e תַּעֲנוּג m. delight.

8 רָצָה to delight in any person or thing, to take pleasure in ; seq. acc. of person or thing, and בְּ, sometimes with עִם, giving a fulness of meaning, Job xxxiv. 9. KAL a pret. b inf. c fut. d רָצוֹן m. delight, acceptance, approbation.

9 שָׁעַע to stroke ; to delight, to rejoice ; to delight oneself, to be delighted. PILPEL a pret. b fut. HITHPALPEL c fut. d שַׁעֲשֻׁעִים m. pl. delight, pleasure.

Gen. xxxiv. 19.	3 a	Ps. xxxvii. 4.	7 b	Prov. xviii. 2.	3 b
Num. xiv. 8.	3 a	xxxvii. 11.	7 a	xix. 10.	7 e
Deut. x. 15.	4	xxxvii. 23.	3 b	xxiv. 25.	7 e
xxi. 14.	3 a	xl. 8.	3 a	xxix. 17.	6 c
1 Sam. xv. 22.	3 a	li. 16.	8 c	Eccles. ii. 8.	7 e
xviii. 22.	3 a	lxii. 4.	8 c	Cant. ii. 3.	2 b
xix. 2.	3 a	lxviii. 30.	3 b	vii. 6.	7 e
2 Sam. i. 24.	6 b	xciv. 19.	9 b	Isa. i. 11.	3 a
xv. 26.	3 a	cix. 17.	3 a	xiii. 17.	3 b
xxii. 20.	3 a	cxii. 1.	3 a	xlii. 1.	8 a
xxiv. 3.	3 a	cxix. 16, 47.	9 c	lv. 2.	7 c
1 Kings x. 9.	3 a	cxix. 24, 77, 92, 143,		lviii. 2, 2.	3 b
2 Chron. ix. 8.	3 a	174.	9 d	lviii. 13.	7 d
Neh. ix. 25.	6 a	cxix. 35.	3 a	lviii. 14.	7 c
Esth. ii. 14.	3 a	cxix. 70.	9 a	lxii. 4.	3 a
vi. 6, 6.	3 a b	cxlvii. 10.	3 b	lxv. 12.	3 a
vi. 7, 9, 9, 11.	3 a	Prov. i. 22.	2 a	lxvi. 3, 4.	3 a
Job xxii. 26.	7 c	ii. 14.	1	lxvi. 11.	7 a
xxvii. 10.	7 c	iii. 12.	8 c	Jer. vi. 10.	3 b
xxxiv. 9.	8 b	viii. 30, 31.	9 d	ix. 24.	3 a
Ps. i. 2.	3 d	xi. 1, 20.	8 d	Micah vi. 18.	3 a
xvi. 3.	3 d	xii. 22.	8 d	Mal. ii. 17.	3 a
xviii. 19.	3 a	xv. 8.	8 d	iii. 11.	3 c
xxii. 8.	3 d	xvi. 13.	8 d	iii. 12. a	3 d

a lit. a land of delight.

DELIVER

1 אָנָה to meet. PIEL, to cause to come : pret.

2 גָּאַל to recover, to retrieve ; to redeem, to deliver. KAL imp.

3 חָלַץ to draw out, to draw off gently a garment or shoe ; to withdraw, or draw aside ; to deliver out of danger with a gentle hand from the hand of an enemy : it denotes in Piel, powerful and ready liberation and rescue from the greatest troubles and miseries, from the rage of evil men, and from the most imminent danger of death ; used in opposition to צָרָה trouble out of which a person is drawn, Prov. xi. 8. Ps. vii. 4, according to Lud. de Dieu, may be translated, Yea (if) I have spoiled, i. e. stripped him that is mine enemy : see Spoil. NIPHAL a pret. b fut. PIEL c pret. d imp. e fut.

4 יְהַב Ch. to give. P'AL part. P'il.

5 יָלַד to bear, or bring forth as a mother, to be delivered. KAL a pret. b inf. c fut.

6 יָשַׁע to save. HIPHIL *a pret.* *b inf.* *c fut.* *d part.* *e* יְשׁוּעָה *f.* salvation. *f* תְּשׁוּעָה *f.* help; victory.

7 מָנַן to give up freely, fully, and largely. PIEL *a pret.* *b fut.*

8 מָלַט to be smooth, to slip away, to escape; to let escape, to deliver; to escape from some imminent danger by slipping away, or in some quick expeditious manner, without trouble or difficulty. With *inf.*, surely deliver. NIPHAL *a pret.* *b imp.* *c fut.* PIEL *d pret.* *e inf.* *f imp.* *g fut.* HIPHIL *h pret.*

9 מָסַר to separate, to deliver; or to be numbered. NIPHAL *fut.*

10 מָצָא to find; Hiphil, to make to find, or to be found in the hands of an enemy. HIPHIL *a pret.* *b part.*

11 נָטָה to turn aside, or away, *i. e.* from punishment. HIPHIL *fut.*

12 נָכַר to treat as a stranger, to estrange, to alienate. PIEL *pret.* I Sam. xxiii. 7, God, who hath hitherto favoured him, now has delivered him, alienated, and thrown him into my hand.

13 נָצַל to pluck out of the hands of an oppressor or enemy; to preserve, recover, rescue; to deliver from danger, evil, trouble; to be delivered, to escape; implying, in most cases, exertion, tumult, bursting of bonds, &c., with power and courage. With *inf.*, deliver at all, surely deliver. NIPHAL *a pret.* *b inf.* *c imp.* *d fut.* PIEL *e fut.* HIPHIL *f pret.* *g inf.* *h imp.* *i fut.* *k part.* נְצַל Ch. APHEL *l inf.* *m* הַצָּלָה *f.* deliverance.

14 נָתַן to give. With *inf.*, indeed; without fail; doubtless deliver. KAL *a pret.* *b inf.* *c imp.* *d fut.* *e part.* Poel. NIPHAL *f pret.* *g inf.* *h fut.* *i part.* HOPHAL *k fut.*

15 סָגַר to shut; Piel, to deliver, *i. e.* into the power of any one, or to shut up in the power of any one. Fürst deduces Piel and Hiphil from a distinct meaning of סָגַר to flow; to pour out, to deliver up, give over. PIEL *a pret.* *b fut.* HIPHIL *c pret.* *d inf.* *e fut.*

16 עָבַר to pass over, to pass away. KAL *fut.*

17 פָּדָה to loose or separate; to redeem: usually with reference to a price or consideration, *seq.* בְּ; or generally to set free; to redeem. KAL *a pret.* *b imp.*

18 פָּרַע to deliver, *i. q.* פָּדָה. KAL *pret.*

19 פָּלַט to slip away, to escape; to let escape, to deliver; to escape wholly, to deliver fully. PIEL *a pret.* *b fut.* *c part.* HIPHIL *d fut.* *e* פָּלֵט *m.* liberation. *f* פְּלֵיטָה *f.* escape, deliverance.

20 פָּצָה (see *Rid*), to snatch away, to deliver by breaking through impediments. KAL *part.* Poel.

21 פָּרַק to break, to let break away, to deliver, *e. g.* from the power of an enemy. KAL *part.* Poel.

22 שׁוּב to return; to cause to return. With *inf.*, in any case deliver. HIPHIL *a pret.* *b inf.* *c imp.* *d fut.*

23 שֵׁיזֵב Ch. to set free, to deliver. PEEL or PEIL *a pret.* *b inf.* *c fut.* *d part.*

24 שְׁלַם Ch. to complete; to restore. APHEL *imp.*

25 שָׁפַט to judge. KAL *fut.*

Gen. ix. 2.	14 f	Gen. xxxii. 11.	13 h
xiv. 20.	7 a	xxxii. 16.	14 d
xxv. 24.	5 b	xxxvii. 21.	13 i

Gen. xxxvii. 22.	22 b		
xl. 13.	14 a		
xlii. 34.	14 d		

Gen. xlii. 37.	14 c	1 Sam. vii. 14.	13 f	2 Chron. xxviii. 5,		
xlv. 7.	19 f	x. 18.	13 i	5.	14 d i
Exod. i. 19.	5 a	xii. 10.	13 h	xxviii. 9.	14 a
ii. 19.	13 f	xii. 11, 21.	13 i	xxviii. 11.	22 c
iii. 8.	13 d	xiv. 10, 12.	14 a	xxix. 8.	14 d
v. 18.	14 d	xiv. 37.	14 d	xxxii. 11.	13 i
v. 23.	13 g f	xiv. 48.	13 i	xxxii. 13, 14, 14.	13 g
xii. 27.	13 f	xvii. 35.	13 f	xxxii. 15, 15.	13 g i
xviii. 4, 8.	13 i	xvii. 37, 37.	13 i	xxxii. 17, 17.	13 f i
xviii. 9, 10, 10.	13 f	xvii. 46.	15 b	x · xiv. 9, 15, 17.	14 d
xxi. 13.		xxiii. 4.	14 e	Ezra v. 14.	4
xxii. 7, 10.	14 d	xxiii. 7.	12	vii. 19.	24
xxii. 26.	22 a	xxiii. 11, 12, 12.	15 e	viii. 31.	13 i
xxiii. 31.	14 d	xxiii. 14.	14 a	viii. 36.	14 d
Lev. xxvi. 25.	14 a	xxiii. 20.	15 d	ix. 7.	13 i
xxvi. 26.	22 a	xxiv. 4.	14 e	ix. 13.	19 f
Num. xxi. 2.	14 b d	xxiv. 10.	14 a	Neh. ix. 27.	13 i
xxi. 3.	14 d	xxiv. 15.	25	ix. 28.	13 i
xxi. 34.	14 a	xxiv. 18.	15 a	Esth. iv. 14.	13 m
xxxi. 5.	9	xxvi. 8.	15 a	vi. 9.	14 b
xxxv. 25.	13 f	xxvi. 23.	13 i	Job v. 4.	13 k
Deut. i. 27.	14 b	xxvi. 24.	13 i	v. 19.	13 i
ii. 30.	14 b	xxviii. 19, 19.	14 d	vi. 23.	8 f
ii. 33.	14 d	xxx. 15.	15 e	x. 7.	13 k
ii. 36.	14 d	xxx. 23.	14 d	xvi. 11.	15 e
iii. 2.	14 a	2 Sam iii. 8.	13 i	xxii. 30, 30.	8 g a
iii. 3.	14 d	iii. 14.	14 c	xxiii. 7.	19 b
v. 22.	14 d	v. 19, 19.	14 d b d	xxix. 12.	8 g
vii. 2, 23, 24.	14 a	x. 10.	14 a	xxxiii. 24.	18
vii. 16.	14 e	xii. 7.	14 c	xxxiii. 28.	17 a
ix. 10.	14 a	xiv. 7.	14 c	xxxvi. 15.	3 e
xix. 12.	14 a	xiv. 16.	13 g	xxxvi. 18.	13 i
xx. 13.	14 a	xvi. 8.	14 d	Ps. vi. 4.	3 d
xx. 10.	14 a	xvii. 28.	15 a	vii. 1.	13 h
xxiii. 14.	13 g	xix. 9.	8 d	vii. 2.	13 k
xxiii. 15.	15 e	xx. 21.	14 c	vii. 4.	19 a
xxiv. 13.	22 b d	xxi. 6.	14 k	xvii. 13.	19 a
xxxi. 11.	13 g	xxi. 9.	14 d	xviii. title.	13 f
xxxi. 9.	14 d	xxii. 1.	13 f	xviii. 2.	19 x
xxxii. 39.	13 k	xxii. 2.	13 i	xviii. 17, 48.	13 i
Josh. ii. 13.	13 f	xxii. 18, 49.	13 i	xviii. 19.	3 e
ii. 24.	14 a	xxii. 20.	3 e	xviii. 43.	13 i
vii. 7.	14 a	xxii. 44.	19 b	xviii. 48, 48.	19 c, 13 i
viii. 7.	14 i	1 Kings ii. 17.	5 c	xviii. 50.	6 e
ix. 26.	13 i	iii. 18, 18.	5 b c	xxii. 4.	19 b
x. 8, 19.	14 a	viii. 46.	14 a	xxii. 5.	8 a
x. 12.	14 b	xiii. 26.	14 d	xxii. 8, 8.	19 b, 13 i
x. 30, 32.	14 d	xv. 18.	14 d	xxii. 20.	13 h
xi. 6.	14 e	xvii. 23.	14 d	xxv. 20.	13 h
xi. 8.	14 d	xviii. 9.	14 e	xxvii. 12.	14 d
xx. 5.	15 e	xx. 5.	14 d	xxxi. 1.	19 a
xxi. 44.	14 a	xx. 13.	14 d	xxxi. 2, 15.	13 h
xxii. 31.	13 f	xx. 28.	14 a	xxxi. 7.	19 e
xxiv. 10.	13 i	xxii. 6.	14 d	xxxiii. 16.	13 d
xxiv. 11.	14 d	xxii. 12, 15.	14 a	xxxiii. 17.	8 g
Judg. i. 2.	14 a	2 Kings iii. 10, 13.	14 b	xxxiii. 19.	13 g
i. 4.	14 d	v. 1.	14 a	xxxiv. 4, 17.	13 f
ii. 14.	14 d	v. 7, 15.	14 d	xxxiv. 7.	3 e
ii. 16.	6 c	xiii. 3.	14 d	xxxiv. 19.	13 i
ii. 18.	6 a	xiii. 17, 17.	6 f	xxxv. 10.	13 k
ii. 23.	14 a	xvii. 20.	14 d	xxxvii. 40, 40.	19 b
iii. 9, 9.	6 d c	xvii. 39.	13 i	xxxix. 8.	13 h
iii. 10.	14 d	xviii. 23.	14 d	xl. 13.	13 g
iii. 15.	6 d	xviii. 29.	13 g	xl. 17.	19 c
iii. 28.	14 a	xviii. 30, 30.	13 g i, 14 h	xli. 1.	8 g
iii. 31.	6 c	xviii. 32.	13 i	xli. 2.	14 d
iv. 7, 14.	14 a	xviii. 33.	13 g f	xliii. 1.	19 b
vi. 1, 13.	14 d	xviii. 34.	13 f	xliv. 4.	6 e
vi. 9.	13 i	xviii. 35, 35.	13 f i	l. 15.	3 e
vii. 7, 9, 14, 15.	14 a	xix. 10.	14 h	l. 22.	13 k
viii. 3.	14 a	xix. 11.	13 d	li. 14.	13 h
viii 7.	14 b	xix. 12.	13 f	liv. 7.	13 f
viii. 22.	6 a	xx. 6.	14 d	lv. 18.	17 a
viii. 34.	13 k	xxii. 5, 9.	14 a	lvi. 13.	13 f
ix. 17.	13 i	xxii. 7.	14 i	lix. 1, 2.	13 h
x. 12, 14.	6 c	xxii. 10.	14 a	lix. 5.	3 b
x. 13.	6 b	1 Chron. v. 20.	14 i	lxix. 14, 14.	13 h d
x. 15.	13 h	xi. 14, 14.	13 i, 6 f	lxix. 18.	17 b
xi. 9.	14 a	xvi. 35, 35.	14 d	lxx. 1.	13 g
xi. 21, 32.	14 d	xix. 10, 10.	14 a	lxx. 5.	19 c
xi. 30.	14 b d	xvi. 7.	14 a	lxxi. 2.	13 i
xii. 2.	6 a	xvi. 35.	13 h	lxxi. 4.	19 a
xii. 3, 3.	6 d, 14 d	2 Chron. vi. 36.	14 a	lxxi. 11.	13 k
xiii. 1.	14 d	vi. 7.	19 f	lxxii. 12.	13 i
xiii. 5.	6 b	xiii. 16.	14 d	lxxiv. 19.	14 d
xv. 12.	14 b	vi. 8.	6 f	lxxviii. 42.	17 a
xv. 13.	14 a	xviii. 28.	14 a	lxxviii. 61.	14 d
xv. 18.	6 f	xviii. 11.	14 a	lxxix. 9.	13 h
xvi. 23, 24.	13 k	xviii. 14.	14 h	lxxxi. 6.	16
xviii. 28.	14 c	xviii. 31.	14 d	lxxxi. 7.	3 e
xx. 13.		xviii. 9.	14 d	lxxxii. 4.	19 a
xx. 28.		xxiv. 24.	14 a	lxxxvi. 13.	13 f
1 Sam. iv. 8.	13 i	xxv. 15.	13 f	lxxxvi. 48.	8 g
iv. 19.	5 b	xxv. 20.	14 b	xci. 3.	13 i
vii. 3.	13 i			xci. 14.	19 b

Ps. xci. 15.	3 e	Isa. xxxvi. 18, 18.	13 f	Ezek. xiii. 21, 23.	13 f
xcvii. 10.	13 i	xxxvi. 19.	13 f	xiv. 14.	13 e
cvi. 43.	13 i	xxxvi. 20, 20.	13 f i	xiv. 16, 16.	13 i d
cvii. 6.	13 i	xxxvii. 11.	13 d	xiv. 18, 18.	13 i d
cvii. 20.	8 g	xxxvii. 12.	13 f	xiv. 20, 20.	13 i
cviii. 6.	3 b	xxxviii. 12.	13 i	xvi. 21, 27.	14 d
cix. 21.	13 h	xliii. 13.	13 k	xvii. 15.	8 a
cxvi. 4.	8 f	xliv. 17.	13 h	xxi. 31.	14 a
cxvi. 8.	3 c	xliv. 20.	13 i	xxiii. 9.	14 a
cxix. 134.	17 b	xlvi. 2.	8 e	xxiii. 28.	14 e
cxix. 153.	3 d	xlvi. 4.	8 g	xxv. 4.	14 e
cxix. 154.	2	xlvii. 14.	13 i	xxv. 7.	14 a
cxix. 170.	13 h	xlix. 24, 25.	8 c	xxxi. 11.	14 d
cxx. 2.	13 h	l. 2.	13 g	xxxi. 14.	14 f
cxl. 1.	3 d	lvii. 13.	13 i	xxxii. 20.	14 f
cxlii. 6.	13 h	lxvi. 7.	8 h	xxxiii. 5.	8 d
cxliii. 9.	13 h	Jer. i. 8, 19.		xxxiii. 9.	13 f
cxliv. 2.	19 c	vii. 10.	13 a	xxxiii. 12.	13 i
cxliv. 7, 11.	13 h	xv. 9.	14 d	xxxiv. 10, 12, 27.	13 f
cxliv. 10.	20	xv. 20.	13 g	Dan. iii. 15.	23 c
Prov. ii. 12, 16.	13 g	xv. 21.	13 f	iii. 17, 17.	23 b c
iv. 9.	7 b	xviii. 21.	14 c	iii. 28.	23 a
vi. 3, 5.	13 c	xx. 5.	14 a	iii. 29.	13 l
x. 2.	13 i	xx. 13.	13 f	vi. 14, 14.	23 b, 13 l
xi. 4, 6.	13 i	xxi. 7.	14 d	vi. 16.	23 c
xi. 8.	3 a	xxi. 12.	13 h	vi. 20.	23 b
xi. 9.	3 b	xxii. 3.	13 h	vi. 27, 27.	23 d a
xi. 21.	8 a	xxiv. 9.	14 a	viii. 4, 7.	13 k
xii. 6.	13 i	xxix. 18.	14 a	xii. 1.	8 c
xiv. 25.	13 k	xxix. 21.	14 e	Hos. ii. 10.	13 i
xix. 19.	13 i	xxxii. 4.	14 g h	xi. 8.	7 b
xxiii. 14.	13 i	xxxii. 16.	14 b	Joel ii. 32, 32.	8 c, 19 f
xxiv. 11. a	13 h	xxxvi. 3.	14 f	Amos i. 6, 9.	15 d
xxviii. 26.	8 c	xxxiv. 3.	14 h	ii. 14, 15, 15.	8 g
xxxi. 24.	14 a	xxxvii. 17.	14 h	vi. 8.	15 c
Eccles. viii. 8.	8 g	xxxviii. 19, 20.	14 d	ix. 1.	8 c
ix. 15.	8 d	xxxix. 17.	13 f	Obad. 14.	15 e
Isa. v. 29.	13 k	xlii. 11.	8 e g	17.	19 f
xix. 20.	13 f	xliii. 3.	13 l	Jonah iv. 6.	13 g
xx. 6.	13 b	xliii. 3.	14 b	Micah iv. 10.	13 d
xxvi. 17.β	5 b	xlvi. 24.	14 f	v. 6.	13 f
xxvi. 18.	6 e	xlvi. 26.	14 a	v. 8.	13 k
xxix. 11.	14 d	li. 6, 45.	8 f	vi. 14, 14.	19 d b
xxix. 12.	14 f	Lam. i. 14.	14 a	Hab. ii. 9.	13 b
xxxi. 5.	13 f	v. 8.	21	Zeph. i. 18.	13 g
xxxiv. 2.	14 a	Ezek. iii. 19, 21.	13 f	Zech. ii. 7.	8 b
xxxvi. 14.	13 g	vii. 19.	13 g	xi. 6, 6.	10 b, 13 i
xxxvi. 15,	13 g	xi. 9.	14 a	Mal. iii. 15.	8 c
15.	13 g i, 14 h				

Judg. vi. 2.	5	Isa. xi. 8.	1	Dan. vi. 7, 12, 16, 17, 19, 20, 23, 23, 24, 24.	3
Job xxxvii. 8.	8	xxxii. 14.	4	Amos iii. 4.	7 a
xxxviii. 40.	7 a	Jer. vii. 11.	4	Nah. ii. 12.	7 a
Ps. x. 9.	6	ix. 11.	7		
civ. 22.	7 a	x. 22.	7		
Cant. iv. 8.	7 a				

a *lit.* deliver &c. if thou forbear.   β "the time of her delivery," *lit.* to bear.

DELUSIONS

תַּעֲלוּלִים *m. pl.* see *Act, Doing.* Isa. lxvi. 4, *marg.* ' or, devices ;' Gesenius, vexation, adversity.

DEMAND

1 אָמַר to say. KAL *inf.*

2 שָׁאַל to ask. KAL a *fut.* שְׁאֵל Ch. PA'L b *part. active.* c שְׁאֵלָא Ch. f. pr. question, petition ; anything inquired for, matter, affair.

Exod. v. 14.	1	Job xl. 7.	2 a	Dan. ii. 27.	2 b
2 Sam. xi. 7.	2 a	xlii. 4.	2 a	iv. 17.	2 c
Job xxxviii. 3.	2 a				

DEN

1 מְאוּרָה *f.* light, light-hole, by which light enters, so a den : Isa. xi. 8, Ch. pupil of the eye, with which the serpent fascinates and destroys.

2 אֹרֶב *m.* a lying in wait, a lurking-place.

3 גֹּב Ch. a pit, den, in which lions were kept.

4 מְעָרָה *f.* a cave.

5 מִנְהָרוֹת *f. pl.* fissures, or clefts, in mountains or rocks, hollowed out by the water ; such were used by the Israelites as dens, recesses, retreats.

6 סֹךְ *m.* a thicket of trees, a covert, lair or den of wild beasts.

7 מָעוֹן *m.* habitation, den of beasts. a מְעוֹנָה *f.* habitation ; a refuge.

DENOUNCE

נָגַד (see *Tell*) ; to declare solemnly. HIPHIL *pret.* Deut. xxx. 18.

DENY

כָּחַשׁ to lie, speak lies ; to deny what is true, to disavow a person or thing ; to deny or refuse to acknowledge God, his goodness, truth, or power. PIEL *pret.* Job viii. 18 ; xxxi. 28 : Prov. xxx. 9, *marg.* 'belie.' *fut.* Gen. xviii. 15 : Josh. xxiv. 27.

מָנַע to withhold, keep back. KAL *pret.* 1 Kings xx. 7, *marg.* 'kept not back from him.' *fut.* Prov. xxx. 7.

שׁוּב to return. HIPHIL *fut.* 1 Kings ii. 16, "deny me not," *marg.* ' turn not away my face.'

DEPART

1 בּוֹא to come, go, &c. KAL *fut.*

2 גָּלָה to be naked, to make naked ; to be taken away, to disappear. KAL a *pret.* b *fut.*

3 הָלַךְ to go, in opposition to בּוֹא. KAL a *pret.* b *inf.* c *part.* Poel. HITHPAEL d *fut.*

4 יָלַךְ to walk, to go. KAL a *inf.* b *imp.* c *fut.* With *inf., cf.* הָלַךְ surely depart.

5 יָצָא to go out, to go forth. KAL a *pret.* b *inf.* c *fut.*

6 יָקַע to be disjointed ; see *Alienate.* KAL *fut.*

7 לוּז to turn aside from that which is straight. Gussetius thinks that this word has the same force as παραρρύειν in Heb. ii. 1, by which LXX. have rendered it in Prov. iii. 21. KAL a *fut.* HIPHIL b *fut.*

8 מוּשׁ to give way, to recede, to depart. KAL a *pret.* b *fut.* HIPHIL c *fut.*

9 נָדַד to flee away. KAL *fut.*

10 נָסַג to remove. KAL *inf.*

11 נָסַע to pull up, to tear up, *e. g.* the tent pins or stakes, in order to take it down ; to break up a camp, to remove, to journey. KAL a *pret.* b *fut.* NIPHAL c *pret.*

12 סוּר to turn aside out of the way, to depart ; to depart from a place, from a person, for a time, &c., *seq.* מֵאַחֲרֵי, מִתּוֹךְ, מֵעַל, מִן, מֵעַם, once *seq.* בְּ: Hos. vii. 14. To remove from calamity of any kind is to escape from it, Job xv. 30 ; LXX. οὐδὲ μὴ ἐκφύγῃ τὸ σκότος ; so Prov. xiii. 14, "to escape from the snares of death." KAL a *pret.* b *inf.* c *imp.* d *fut.* e *part.* Poel. f *part.* Paül. g יָסוּר סוּר *m.* כתיב a drawing back.

13 עֲדָה Ch. to pass away. PA'L *pret.*

14 עָלָה to ascend, to go up. KAL a *fut.* NIPHAL to be brought up, to depart from, with מֵעַל. b *fut.*

15 צָפַר to go in a circle, to turn about, in order to depart. KAL *fut.*

16 שׁוּר *i.q.* סוּר to go away, to depart. KAL *inf.*

17 שָׁלַח to send away, to dismiss. PIEL ᵃ imp. ᵇ fut.

18 שָׁעָה to look, to look away from, seq. מִן. KAL fut.

Gen. xii. 4, 4.	4 c, 5 b	1 Sam. xxii. 5, 5.	4 b c	Job xxviii. 28.	12 b
xiv. 12.	4 c	xxiii. 13.	5 c	Ps. vi. 8.	12 c
xxi. 14.	4 c	xxviii. 15, 16.	12 a	xxxiv. title.	4 c
xxiv. 10.	4 c	xxix. 10.	4 b	xxxiv. 14.	12 c
xxvi. 17, 31.	4 c	xxix. 11.	4 a	xxxvii. 27.	12 c
xxxi. 40.	9	xxx. 22.	4 c	lv. 11.	8 c
xxxi. 55.	4 c	2 Sam. vi. 19.	4 c	ci. 4.	12 d
xxxv. 18. a	5 b	vii. 15.	12 d	cv. 38.	5 b
xxxvii. 17.	11 a	xi. 8.	5 c	cxix. 102.	12 a
xlii. 26.	4 c	xi. 11.	17 b	cxix. 115.	12 c
xlv. 24.	4 c	xii. 10.	12 d	cxxxix. 19.	12 c
xlix. 10.	12 d	xii. 15.	4 c	Prov. iii. 7.	12 c
Exod. viii. 11, 29.	12 a	xv. 14.	4 a	iii. 21.	7 a
xvi. 1.	5 b	xvii. 21.	4 a	iv. 21.	7 b
xviii. 27.	17 b	xix. 24.	4 a	v. 7.	12 d
xix. 2.	11 b	xx. 21.	4 c	xiii. 14, 19.	12 b
xxi. 22.	5 a	xxii. 23.	12 d	xiv. 16.	12 e
xxxiii. 1.	4 b	1 Kings xi. 21.	17 a	xiv. 27.	12 b
xxxiii. 11.	8 c	xii. 5, 5.	4 b c	xv. 24.	12 b
xxxv. 20.	5 c	xii. 16.	4 a	xvi. 6, 17.	12 b
Lev. xiii. 58.	12 a	xii. 24.	4 a	xvii. 13.	8 b
xxv. 41.	5 a	xv. 17.	4 c	xxii. 6.	12 d
Num. x. 30.	4 c	xv. 19.	14 a	xxvii. 22.	12 d
x. 33.	11 b	xix. 19.	4 c	Eccles. vi. 4.	4 c
xii. 9.	4 c	xx. 9, 38.	4 c	Isa. vii. 17.	12 b
xii. 10.	12 a	xx. 36, 36.	3 c, 4 c	xi. 13.	12 a
xiv. 9.	12 a	2 Kings i. 4.	4 c	xiv. 25, 25.	12 a d
xiv. 44.	4 c	iii. 3.	12 a	xxxvii. 8.	11 a
xvi. 26.	12 c	iii. 27.	11 b	xxxvii. 37.	11 b
xxii. 7.	4 c	v. 5, 19, 24.	4 c	xxxviii. 12.β	11 c
xxxiii. 3, 6, 8, 13, 15,		viii. 14.	4 c	lii. 11, 11.	12 c
17, 18, 19, 20, 27,		x. 12.	1	liv. 10, 10.	8 b
30, 31, 35, 41, 42,		x. 15.	4 c	lix. 13.	10
43, 44, 45, 48.	11 b	x. 29, 31.	12 a	lix. 15.	12 a
Deut. i. 19.	11 b	xiii. 2, 6, 11.	12 a	lix. 21.	8 b
iv. 9.	12 d	xiv. 24.	12 a	Jer. vi. 8.	6
ix. 7.	5 a	xv. 9, 18, 24, 28.	12 a	xvii. 5.	12 a
xxiv. 2.	5 a	xvii. 22.	12 a	xvii. 13.	12 f g
Josh. i. 8.	8 b	xviii. 6.	12 a	xxix. 2.	5 b
ii. 21.	4 c	xix. 8.	11 a	xxxi. 36.	8 b
xxii. 9.	4 c	xix. 36.	11 b	xxxii. 40.	12 b
xxiv. 28.	17 b	1 Chron. xvi. 43.	4 c	xxxvii. 5.	14 b
Judg. vi. 18.	8 b	2 Chron. viii. 15.	12 a	xxxviii. 9, 9.γ	3 b, 4 c, c
vi. 21.	3 a	x. 5.	4 c	xli. 10, 17.	4 c
vii. 3.	15	xvi. 3.	14 a	l. 3.	3 a
ix. 55.	4 c	xx. 20.	12 a	Lam. i. 6.	5 c
xvi. 20.	12 a	xxi. 20.	4 c	iv. 15, 15, 15.	12 c
xvii. 8.	4 c	xxiv. 25.	4 c	Ezek. vi. 9.	12 a
xviii. 7, 21.	4 c	xxxiv. 33.	4 a	x. 18.	5 c
xix. 5, 7, 8, 9.	4 a	xxxv. 15.	12 b	xvi. 42.	12 a
xix. 10.	4 c	Ezra viii. 31.	11 b	xxvi. 18.	5 b
xxi. 24.	3 d	Neh. ix. 19.	12 a	Dan. xi. 31.	11 c
1 Sam. iv. 21, 22.	2 a	Job vii. 19.	18	ix. 5, 11.	12 b
vi. 6.	4 a	xv. 30.	12 d	Hos. ix. 12.	16
x. 2.	4 a	xx. 28.	2 b	x. 5.	2 a
xv. 6, 6.	12 c d	xxi. 14.	12 c	Micah ii. 10.	4 b
xvi. 14, 23.	12 a	xxii. 17.	12 c	Nah. iii. 1.	8 c
xviii. 12.	12 a	xxvii. 21.	4 c	Zech. x. 11.	12 d
xx. 42.	4 c			Mal. ii. 8.	12 a
xxii. 1.	4 c				

α lit. in the going out of her soul. β lit. is being taken down.
γ lit. departing shall depart.

DEPOSE

נָחַת Ch. to come down. HOPHAL pret. Dan. v. 20, lit. caused to descend.

DEPRIVE

נָשָׁה to forget, to cause to forget. HIPHIL pret. Job xxxix. 17.

פָּקַד see To Miss. PUAL pret. Isa. xxxviii. 10, I am made to miss, to want the residue of my years.

שָׁכַל to be bereaved of children. KAL fut. Gen. xxvii. 45.

DEPUTY

נָצַב see Officer. NIPHAL part. 1 Kings xxii. 47.

פֶּחָה m. governor, captain: Esth. viii. 9; ix. 3.

DERIDE, DERISION

1 לוץ to deride, to mock any one, seq. acc.; pr. by imitating his voice or mode of speaking. HIPHIL pret.

2 לָעַג to mock, deride; pr. by imitating the stammering voice of any one in derision; of one who contemns the threats and efforts of enemies. KAL ᵃ fut. ᵇ לַעַג m. derision, mockery.

3 קֶלֶס m. scorn, derision.

4 שָׂחַק to laugh; seq. עַל to laugh at, to deride; seq. לְ to laugh at, but especially in scorn. KAL ᵃ pret. ᵇ fut. ᶜ שְׂחוֹק m. laughter, derision.

Job xxx. 1.	4 a	Ps. cxix. 51.	1	Ezek. xxiii. 24.	2 b
Ps. ii. 4.	2 a	Jer. xx. 7.	4 c	xxxv. 4.	2 b
xliv. 13.	3	xx. 8.	3	Hos. vii. 16.	2 b
lix. 8.	2 a	xlviii. 26, 27, 39.	4 c	Hab. i. 10.	4 b
lxxiv. 4.	3	Lam. ii. 14.	4 c		

DESCEND

יָרַד to go down. KAL ᵃ pret. ᵇ fut. ᶜ part. Poel.

Gen. xxviii. 12.	c	Josh. ii. 23.	b	Ps. cxxxiii. 3.	c
Exod. xix. 18.	a	xvii. 9.	a	Prov. xxx. 4.	b
xxxiii. 9.	b	xviii. 13, 16, 16, 17.	a	Isa. v. 14.	a
xxxiv. 5.	b	1 Sam. xxvi. 10.	b	Ezek. xxvi. 20.	c
Num. xxxiv. 11.	a	Ps. xlix. 17.	b	xxxi. 16.	c
Deut. ix. 21.	b				

DESCRIBE

כָּתַב to write. KAL inf. Josh. xviii. 8. imp. Josh. xviii. 8. fut. Josh. xviii. 4, 6, 9: Judg. viii. 14, marg. 'writ.'

DESCRY

תּוּר to go about; to spy out. HIPHIL fut. Judg. i. 23, "sent to descry."

DESERT

1 מִדְבָּר m. a desert, uninhabited, or but thinly inhabited; see Wilderness.

2 חָרְבָּה f. dry place, desert; desolations, ruins.

3 יְשִׁימוֹן m. a waste, a wilderness.

4 עֲרָבָה f. arid tract, sterile region, wilderness; see Plain.

5 צִיָּה f. dryness, drought; a dry land. צִיִּים m. pl. inhabitants of the desert, wild beasts.

Exod. iii. 1.	1	Ps. lxxviii. 40.	3	Isa. xlviii. 21.	2
v. 3.	1	cii. 6.	2	li. 3.	4
xix. 2.	1	cvi. 14.	1	Jer. ii. 6.	4
xxiii. 31.	1	Isa. xiii. 21.	5	xvii. 6.	4
Num. xx. 1.	1	xxi. 1, 1.	5	xxv. 24.	4
xxvii. 14.	1	xxxiv. 14.	5	l. 12.	1
xxxiii. 16.	1	xxxv. 1, 6.	4	l. 39.	5
Deut. xxxii. 10.	1	xl. 3.	1	Ezek. xiii. 4.	2
2 Chron. xxvi. 10.	1	xli. 19.	4	xlvii. 8. a	4
Job xxiv. 5.	1	xliii. 19, 20.	3		

a marg. 'or, plain.'

DESERT, DESERVING

גְּמוּל m. reward, recompense: Judg. ix. 16: Ps. xxviii. 4.

מִשְׁפָּט m. judgment: Ezek. vii. 27.

DESIRE, DESIRABLE

1 אָב our translators seem to have taken this as a particle expressive of a wish, אָבִי o si, Job xxxiv. 36; others take it as rendered in the marg. 'My father, let Job be tried,' as addressed to God.

2 אֲבִיוֹנָה f. desire, appetite or natural desire.

3 אָוָה to desire earnestly, to have a strong affection, or, to long for, the soul (which word frequently accompanies this verb) going after that which is sought, in order to

possess and enjoy it. This word differs from others of a similar import in including an idea of impulse : its opposite is קוּט to loathe, abhor. PIEL ª *pret.* ᵇ *fut.* HITHPAEL ᶜ *pret.* ᵈ *fut.* ᵉ *part.* ᶠ אַוַּת *f. constr.* desire. ᵍ מַאֲוַיִּים *m. pl.* desires. ʰ תַּאֲוָה *f.* desire, lust, delight.

4 **אָמַר** to say. KAL *fut.* 1 Sam. xx. 4, *lit.* say what is thy mind.

5 **בְּעָה** Ch. to seek, to search after. P'AL ª *pret.* ᵇ *inf.*

6 **בָּקַשׁ** to seek, to search for, to inquire after. PIEL *part.*

7 **חָמַד** to desire strongly ; to take delight in ; to covet ; as *subst.* that which is the object of desire, precious, pleasant, lovely. KAL ª *pret.* ᵇ *fut.* ᶜ *part.* Paül. NIPHAL ᵈ *part.* ᵉ חֶמֶד *m.* beauty, desirableness, pleasantness. ᶠ חֶמְדָּה desire ; object of desire, delight. "The desire of all nations," Micah ii. 7, is understood of the Messiah ; this desire, with many blessings in view, is put before a plural verb, "shall come." Dan. xi. 37, "he shall not regard...the desire of women," has been most generally considered as equivalent to the mark of Antichrist given in 1 Tim. iv. 3, "forbidding to marry." In correspondence with the Apostle's application of this mark to Antichrist, it must be observed, that the word used for women is not that which would apply to concubines or harlots, but to married women or wives ; it is therefore equivalent to the despising of marriage and the pretence of unusual chastity, which we find in the church of Rome. ᵍ מַחְמָד *m.* desire, object of desire.

8 **חָפֵץ** to favour, to take delight in ; to desire ; mostly *seq.* בְּ. KAL ª *pret.* ᵇ *fut.* ᶜ חָפֵץ *adj.* to delight in. ᵈ חֵפֶץ *m.* delight, desire, pursuit, ardour.

9 **חָשַׁק** to join, to fasten together ; to be attached to any one ; *seq.* בְּ and *inf.* KAL ª *pret.* ᵇ חֵשֶׁק *m.* desire, delight.

10 **כָּסַף** to be pale, to pine after, desire ; *seq.* לְ. KAL ª *fut.* NIPHAL ᵇ *part.* Zeph. ii. 1 ; Gesenius, not ashamed, shameless, as paleness is attributed to shame as well as blushing ; *comp.* Isa. xxix. 22.

11 **נֶפֶשׁ** *com.* animal life ; the soul, mind, as the seat of affections.

12 **נָשָׂא** to lift up. PIEL *part.*

13 **רָצוֹן** *m.* delight ; will, pleasure.

14 **שָׁאַל** to ask. KAL ª *pret.* ᵇ *fut.* ᶜ *part.* Poel. ᵈ מִשְׁאָלָה *f.* prayer, petition.

15 **שָׁאַף** to pant after ; earnestly to desire. KAL *fut.*

16 **תָּו** *m.* mark ; mark or cross as subscribed to a bill of complaint : hence subscription, *meton.* the bill itself ; charge : Job xxxi. 35, *marg.* 'or, behold my sign is that the Almighty will answer me.' The Vulg. and English version seem to have taken תָּו for תַּאֲוָה ; see above.

17 **תְּשׁוּקָה** *f.* desire, longing ; Gussetius, that affection which is drawn out towards a superior.

Gen. iii. 6.		7 d	Exod. x. 11.	6	Deut. vii. 25.		7 b
iii. 16.		17	xxxiv. 24.	7 b	xiv. 26.		14 b
iv. 7.		17	Deut. v. 21.	7 b	xviii. 6.		3 f

Deut. xviii. 16.	14 a	Job xxxi. 35.	16	Prov. xix. 22.	3 h
xxi. 11.	9 a	xxxiii. 32.	8 a	xxi. 10.	3 a
Judg. viii. 24.	14 b	xxxiv. 36.	1	xxi. 20.	7 d
1 Sam. ii. 16.	3 b	xxxvi. 20.	15	xxi. 25.	3 h
ix. 20.	7 f	Ps. x. 3, 17.	3 h	xxiii. 3, 6.	3 d
xii. 13.	14 a	xix. 10.	7 d	xxiv. 1.	3 d
xviii. 25.	8 d	xxi. 2.	3 h	Eccles. ii. 10.	14 a
xx. 4.	4	xxvii. 4.	14 a	vi. 2.	3 d
xxiii. 20.	3 f	xxxiv. 12.	8 c	vi. 9.	11
2 Sam. iii. 21.	3 b	xxxvii. 4.	14 d	xii. 5.	2
xxiii. 5.	8 d	xxxviii. 9.	3 h	Cant. vii. 10.	17
1 Kings ii. 20.	14 c	xl. 6.	8 a	Isa. i. 29.	7 a
v. 8, 9, 10.	14 d	xlv. 11.	8 a	xxvi. 8.	3 h
ix. 1.	9 b	li. 6.	8 a	xxvi. 9.	3 a
ix. 11.	8 d	li. 16.	8 d	liii. 2.	7 b
ix. 19.	9 b a	lxviii. 16.	7 a	Jer. xvii. 16.	3 c
xi. 2.	3 b	lxx. 2.	8 a	xxii. 27.	12, 11
xi. 37.	3 b	lxxiii. 25.	8 a	xlii. 22.	8 a
2 Kings iv. 28.	14 b	lxxviii. 29.	3 h	Ezek. xxiii. 6, 12, 23. β	7 e
2 Chron. viii. 6.	9 b a	cvii. 30. a	8 d	xxiv. 16, 21, 25.	7 g
vi. 12.	8 d	cxii. 10.	3 a	xxiv. 12, 11.	5 b
xi. 23.	14 b	cxxxii. 13, 14.	3 b	Dan. ii. 16, 23.	5 b
xxi. 8.	13	cxl. 8.	3 g	ii. 18.	7 f
xxi. 20.	7 f	cxlv. 16, 19.	13	xi. 37.	7 f
Neh. i. 11.	8 c	Prov. iii. 15.	8 d	Hos. vi. 6.	8 a
Esth. ii. 13.	4	viii. 11.	8 d	x. 10.	3 f
Job vii. 2.	15	x. 24.	3 h	Amos v. 18.	3 a
xiii. 3.	8 b	xi. 23.	3 h	Micah vii. 1.	3 a
xiv. 15.	10 a	xii. 12.		vii. 3.	11
xx. 20.	7 c	xiii. 4.	3 e	Hab. ii. 5.	11
xxi. 14.	8 a	xiii. 12, 19.	3 h	Hag. ii. 7.	7 f
xxiii. 13.	3 a	xviii. 1.	3 h	Zeph. ii. 1.	10 b
xxxi. 16.	8 d				

a *lit.* of their desire.   β *lit.* young men of desire.

DESOLATE

1 **אַלְמָנָה** *f.* a widow. אַלְמְנוֹת *f.* desolate houses, palaces. *i. q.* אַרְמְלוֹת. Gesenius.

2 **אָשַׁם** to be guilty ; to make desolate, to be desolate. KAL ª *fut.* NIPHAL ᵇ *pret.* ᶜ אֲשֵׁמִים *m. pl.* Isa. lix. 10. Gesenius, in fertile fields ; Jerome, in dark places ; LXX. they groan as the dying. The Chaldee renders the passage, "It is closed (*i. e.* the way) before us as the sepulchre is closed upon the dead." The derivation of the Heb. word is uncertain, but the opinions of modern critics are divided between אָשֵׁם in the sense of to be laid waste, and שָׁמֵן to be fat. Fürst prefers the former.

3 **בָּדָד** *m.* alone, solitary.

4 **בַּתּוֹת** *f.* desolation.

5 **גַּלְמוּד** *adj.* solitary, desolate ; Gesenius, sterile, barren.

6 **חָרֵב** to be dry ; to be laid waste, a desert. KAL ª *imp.* ᵇ *fut.* NIPHAL ᶜ *part.* ᵈ חָרֵב *adj.* laid waste ; destroyed. ᵉ חֹרֶב *m.* a laying waste. ᶠ חָרְבָּה *f.* a desolation, a place laid waste, ruins.

7 **יָחִיד** *adj.* one alone, only, solitary.

8 **יָצַת** to be burned up. NIPHAL *pret.*

9 **יָשֵׁם** to be waste, desolate. KAL *fut.*

10 **כָּחַד** to hide, conceal ; to cut off, destroy. NIPHAL *part.*

11 **נָקָה** to be clean ; to be vacant, empty. NIPHAL *pret.*

12 **שָׁאָה** to be laid waste or ruined by a sudden tumultuous overthrow, which beareth down all before it. NIPHAL ª *fut.* ᵇ שְׁאִיָּה *f.* כתיב a wasting tempest. ᶜ שְׁאֵת *f.* destruction. ᵈ שׁוֹאָה *f.* a storm, tempest ; sudden and irresistible destruction. ᵉ מְשׁוֹאָה *f.* waste places. ᶠ מַשּׁוּאוֹת *f. pl.* ruins, desolations.

13 **שֹׁד** *m.* devastation, waste, destruction.

14 **שָׁמֵם** to be laid waste or desolate ; see *Astonish ;* desolate

places are silent and quiet. KAL [a] *pret.* [b] *inf.* [c] *fut.* [d] *part.* Poel. NIPHAL [e] *pret.* [f] *part.* POLEL [g] *part.* HIPHIL [h] *pret.* [i] *inf.* [k] *fut.* HOPHAL [l] *inf.* HITHPOLEL [m] *fut.* [n] שָׁמֵם *adj.* wasted, desolate. [o] שְׁמָמָה *f.* astonishment, desolation.—P—שְׁמָמָה *f. id.* [q] שַׁמָּה *f.* wasting, desolation, astonishment. [r] מְשַׁמָּה *f.* astonishment, desolation.

Gen. xlvii. 19.	9	Isa. lxiv. 10.	14 o	Ezek. xxv. 3.	14 e
Exod. xxiii. 29.	14 o	Jer. ii. 12.	6 a	xxv. 13.	6 f
Lev. xxvi. 22.	14 e	iv. 7.	14 q	xxvi. 19.	6 c
xxvi. 31, 32.	14 h	iv. 27.	14 o	xxvi. 20.	6 f
xxvi. 33.	14 o	vi. 8.	14 o	xxix. 9, 10.	14 o
xxvi. 34, 35, 43.	14 l	vii. 34.β	6 f	xxix. 12,12,12.	14 o f o
Josh. viii. 28.	14 o	ix. 11.γ	14 o	xxx. 7, 7.	14 e f
2 Sam. xiii. 20.	14 d	x. 22.	14 o	xxx. 14.	14 h
2 Kings xxii. 19.	14 q	x. 25.	14 h	xxxii. 15.	14 o
2 Chron. xxx. 7.	14 q	xii. 10.	14 o	xxxiii. 28.	14 o r
xxxvi. 21.	14 l	xii. 11, 11, 11.	14 o n e	xxxiii. 28.	14 a
Ezra ix. 9.	6 f	xviii. 16.	14 q	xxxiii. 29.	14 o r
Job iii. 14.	6 f	xix. 8.	14 q	xxxv. 3.	14 o r
xv. 28.	10	xxii. 5.	6 f	xxxv. 4, 14.	14 o
xv. 34.	5	xxv. 9, 11, 18.	6 f	xxxv. 7.	14 p o
xvi. 7.	14 h	xxv. 12.	14 o	xxxv. 9.	14 p
xxx. 3, 14.	12 d	xxv. 38.	14 q	xxxv. 12.	14 a
xxxviii. 27.	12 d	xxvi. 9.	6 b	xxxv. 15, 15.	14 a o
Ps. xxv. 16.	7	xxxi. 43.	14 o	xxxvi. 3.	14 b
xxxiv. 21, 22.	2 a	xxxiii. 10, 10.	6 d, 14 f	xxxvi. 4.	14 d
xl. 15.	14 c	xxxiii. 12.	6 d	xxxvi. 34, 34.	14 o o
xlvi. 8.	14 q	xxxiv. 22.	14 o	xxxvi. 35, 35, 36.	14 f
lxix. 25.	14 f	xliv. 6.	14 o	xxxviii. 12.	6 f
lxxiii. 19.	14 q	xlvi. 19.	8	Dan. viii. 13.	14 d
lxxiv. 3.	12 f	xlviii. 9.	14 q	ix. 2.	6 f
cix. 10.	6 f	xlviii. 9.	14 q	ix. 17.	14 n
cxliii. 4.	14 m	xlix. 2, 33.	14 o	ix. 18, 26.	14 d
Prov. i. 27.	12 b or d	xlix. 13, 17.	14 q	ix. 27, 27.	14 g d
iii. 25.	12 d	xlix. 20.	14 k	xi. 31.	14 g
Isa. i. 7, 7.	14 o	l. 3, 23.	14 q	xii. 11.	14 d
iii. 26.	11	l. 13.	14 o	Hos. v. 9.	14 g
v. 9.	14 q	l. 45.	14 k	xiii. 16.	13
vi. 11.	12 a, 14 o	li. 26, 62.	14 o	Joel i. 17.	2 a
vii. 19.α	4	li. 29, 43.	14 o	i. 18.	14 e
x. 3.	12 d	Lam. i. 4, 13, 16.	14 d	ii. 3, 20.	2 b
xiii. 9.	14 q	iii. 11.	14 d	iii. 19, 19.	14 o
xiii. 22.	1	iii. 47.	12 c	Amos vii. 9.	14 o
xv. 6.	14 r	iv. 5.	14 e	Micah i. 7.	14 o
xxii. 9.	14 o	v. 18.	14 a	vi. 13.	14 i
xxiv. 6.	2 a	Ezek. vi. 4.	14 a	vi. 16.	14 q
xxiv. 12.	14 q	vi. 6, 6.	9, 2 a	vii. 13.	14 o
xxvii. 10.	3	vi. 14, 14.	14 o r	Zeph. i. 13.	14 o
xlvii. 11.	12 d	vii. 27.	14 o	i. 15.	12 e
xlix. 8, 19.	14 d	xii. 19.	9	ii. 4, 9, 13.	14 o
xlix. 21.	5	xii. 20.	14 o	ii. 14.	6 e
li. 19.	13	xiv. 15, 16.	14 o	ii. 15.	14 q
liv. 1.	14 d	xv. 8.	14 o	iii. 6.	14 o
liv. 3.	14 f	xix. 7, 7.	1, 9	Zech. vii. 14, 14.	14 e q
lix. 16.	2 c	xx. 26.	14 k	Mal. i. 4.	6 f
lxi. 4, 4.	14 d	xxiii. 33.	14 o		
lxii. 4.	14 o				

α *lit.* valleys of desolations.   β *lit.* for desolation.   γ *lit.* desolation.

DESPAIR, DESPERATE

יָאַשׁ to despond, to despair; to renounce hope, relatively, though not absolutely or totally: so Eccles. ii. 20, Job vi. 26, desperate, *i.e.* desperate afflicti, Schmid. NIPHAL *pret.* 1 Sam. xxvii. 1. *part.* Job vi. 26. PIEL *inf.* Eccles. ii. 20.

אָנַשׁ to be sick unto death. KAL *part.* Paül, Isa. xvii. 11: Jer. xvii. 9, "desperately wicked."

DESPISE

1 בּוּז to despise, contemn: this word is evidently of stronger meaning than בָּזָה; it denotes open contempt, with mockery, ἀτιμοῦν, ἐνυβρίζειν; the act of one who, full of arrogance and self-esteem, contemns others, despises their gifts, aggravates their faults and infirmities, and disdains all acts of love and kindness from them: such a one, through pride, despises precept, admonition, and wisdom. Zech. iv. 10 refers to a sinful contempt of the day of small things. Prov. vi. 30, *cf.* 32, an adulterer is more worthy of contempt (such as is implied in this word) and mockery than a thief that steals to satisfy hunger. Reproach and contempt are joined together, Ps. cxix. 22. KAL [a] *pret.* [b] *fut.* [c] *part.* Poel. [d] בּוּז *m.* contempt. [e] בּוּזָה *f. id.* hence who is contemned.

2 בָּזָה to do that which implies contempt; to slight, neglect, make little account of, to treat contemptuously and proudly; LXX. φαυλίζειν ἐξουθενεῖν; it is opposed to the act of esteeming, appreciating, or caring for; it implies sometimes only to make little account of: *cf.* Matt. vi. 24, opposed to כָּבַד, 1 Sam. ii. 30, Mal. i. 6, שָׁמַר, Prov. xix. 16. Observe the antithesis in the following passages, Prov. xiv. 2, xv. 20, and the use of this word in Gen. xxv. 34, 1 Sam. x. 27, 2 Sam. vi. 16, Esth. iii. 6: David despised God when he did not obey the will of God, but preferred to it his own lusts, 2 Sam. xii. 9, 10, *cf.* Prov. xiv. 2, *i.e.* when he did not fear God. A man despiseth his oath when he violates a covenant, Ezek. xvii. 18, 19. A man despiseth his ways who walks without fear and caution; Prov. xix. 16, "He that keepeth the commandments keepeth his own soul; but he that despiseth his ways shall die:" the antithesis would seem to have required, 'he that despiseth the commandments;' but by an elegant inversion of the train of thought he speaks of one who despiseth his ways, as he certainly does who despises the will of God, since he does not regard them with that care and attention which the word of God requires: so may be explained Acts xiii. 46; 'you judge the gospel not worthy, you despise it, and so judge yourselves unworthy of eternal life.' This word is chiefly used of man; yet it is attributed to God of man, and implies the withdrawal of his favour, care, help, &c.: negatively it betokens his favourable regard, fatherly care, and protection. KAL [a] *pret.* [b] *fut.* [c] *part.* Poel. [d] *part.* Paül. NIPHAL [e] *part.* HIPHIL [f] *inf.* [g] בָּזֹה *adj.* despised.

3 זוּל to shake off, to put aside; to account and cast away as vile. HIPHIL *pret.*

4 מָאַס to refuse, reject as vile and worthless, with disdain and aversion; see *Abhor, Reject.* KAL [a] *pret.* [b] *inf.* [c] *fut.* [d] *part.* Poel.

5 נָאַץ to treat with scorn and contumely; see *Abhor.* It is that kind of contempt which provokes to anger; as when man despises counsel, reproof, correction; and God himself, his word and ordinances. KAL [a] *pret.* [b] *fut.* PIEL [c] *pret.* [d] *part.*

6 קָלַל to be light; to be lightly esteemed; insignificant, vile; to make light of, to despise; opposed to כָּבַד. KAL [a] *fut.* HIPHIL [b] *pret.*

7 קָלָה to be light; to be treated as vile and ignominious. NIPHAL *part.*

8 שׁוּט to contemn, to despise. KAL *part.*

Gen. xvi. 4, 5.	6 a	Ps. xxii. 24.	2 a	Isa. v. 24.	5 c		
xxv. 34.	2 b	li. 17.	2 b	xxx. 12.	4 b		
Lev. xxvi. 15.	4 c	liii. 5.	4 a	xxxiii. 8.	4 a		
xxvi. 43.	4 a	lxix. 33.	2 a	xxxiii. 15.	4 d		
Num. xi. 20.	4 a	lxxiii. 20.	2 b	xxxvii. 22.	2 a		
xiv. 31.	4 a	cii. 17.	2 a	xlix. 7.	2 g		
xv. 31.	2 a	cvi. 24.	4 c	liii. 3, 3.	2 e		
Judg. ix. 38.	4 a	cxix. 141.	2 e	lx. 14.	5 d		
1 Sam. ii. 30.	2 c	Prov. i. 7.	1 a	Jer. iv. 30.	4 a		
x. 27.	2 b	i. 30.	5 a	xxii. 28.	2 e		
2 Sam. vi. 16.	2 b	iii. 11.	4 c	xxiii. 17.	5 d		
xii. 9, 10.	4 a	v. 12.	5 a	xxxiii. 24.	5 b		
xix. 43.	6 b	vi. 30.	1 b	xlix. 15.	2 d		
2 Kings xix. 21.	2 a	xi. 12.	1 c	Lam. i. 8.	3		
1 Chron. xv. 29.	2 b	xii. 8.a	1 d	ii. 6.	5 b		
2 Chron. xxxvi. 16.	2 c	xii. 9.	7	Ezek. xvi. 57.	8		
Neh. ii. 19.	2 b	xiii. 13.	1 c	xvi. 59.	2 a		
iv. 4.	1 e	xiv. 2.	2 c	xvii. 16, 18, 19.	2 a		
Esth. i. 17.	2 f	xiv. 21.	1 c	xx. 13, 16, 24.	4 a		
Job v. 17.	4 c	xv. 5.	5 b	xxii. 8.	2 a		
ix. 21.	4 c	xv. 20.	2 c	xxviii. 24, 26.	8		
x. 3.	1 d	xv. 32.	4 d	Amos ii. 4.	4 b		
xii. 5.	4 a	xix. 16.	2 c	v. 21.	4 a		
xix. 18.	4 a	xxiii. 9, 22.	1 b	Obad. 2.	2 d		
xxxi. 13.	4 c	xxx. 17.	1 b	Zech. iv. 10.	1 a		
xxxvi. 5.	4 c	Eccles. ix. 16.	2 d	Mal. i. 6, 6.	2 c a		
Ps. xxii. 6.	2 d	Cant. viii. 1.	1 b				

a *lit.* for contempt.

DESPITE

שְׁאָט *m.* contempt, *i.e.* pride and arrogance, including an eager impulse of mind ; Ezek. xxv. 6, 15 ; xxxvi. 5.

DESTITUTE

חָסֵר *adj.* wanting, lacking : Prov. xv. 21, *marg.* 'void of heart.'

עָזַב to forsake, to leave destitute. KAL *pret.* Gen. xxiv. 27.

עָרָה to make naked ; to leave destitute. PIEL *fut.* Ps. cxli. 8, *marg.* 'make not my soul bare.' Gesenius, do not empty out my life, *i.e.* let not my blood be shed ; *comp.* Isa. liii. 12. עָרָר *adj.* naked ; poor, needy : Ps. cii. 17.

שָׁמֵם to be desolate. NIPHAL *part.* Ezek. xxxii. 15, *marg.* 'desolate.'

DESTROY, DESTRUCTION

1 אָבַד to perish, to be destroyed ; to cause to perish, to destroy, or disperse. KAL a *pret.* b *inf.* c *fut.* PIEL d *pret.* e *inf.* f *fut.* g *part.* HIPHIL h *pret.* i *inf.* k *fut.* l *part.* אֲבַד Ch. APHEL m *inf.* n *fut.* HOPHAL o *pret.* אֲבֵדָה p *f.* כתיב place of destruction, Hades. אֲבַדּוֹן q *m.* place of destruction, abyss. אָבְדָן r *m.* slaughter, destruction.

2 אֵיד *m.* a heavy calamity, which oppresses and brings into straits.

3 אָסַף to gather ; to take out of the way, to destroy. KAL *fut.*

4 אָשַׁם to be guilty ; to bear one's guilt ; to make or hold guilty. HIPHIL *imp.*

5 תְּבוּסָה *f.* a treading down, destruction.

6 תַּבְלִית *f.* consumption, destruction.

7 בָּלַע to swallow up ; to cause to disappear ; to consume, to destroy. PIEL a *pret.* b *inf.* c *imp.* d *fut.* PUAL e *part.*

8 גָּרַר to saw, to drag, to sweep away as a whirlwind. KAL *fut.*

9 דָּבַר to destroy as with a pestilence ; see *Pestilence.* PIEL *fut.*

10 דָּכָא to be broken ; to break in pieces. PIEL a *fut.* HITHPAEL b *fut.* דַּכָּא c *adj.* broken very small.

11 דָּמָה to be silent ; to cause to cease, to destroy ; to cut off. KAL a *pret.* NIPHAL b *pret.* c דָּמָה *f.* laying waste, that which is laid waste.

12 הוּם to put in motion, throw into commotion, consternation. KAL a *pret.* b מְהוּמָה *f.* commotion, disturbance.

13 הָמַם to discomfit. KAL a *pret.* b *inf.* c *fut.*

14 הָרַג to kill, to slay. KAL *fut.*

15 הָרַס to pull or tear down, to destroy. KAL a *pret.* b *fut.* NIPHAL c *fut.* PIEL d *part.* e הֲרִיסוּת *f.* destruction. f הֶרֶס *m.* destruction ; some copies read חֶרֶס the sun : Isa. xix. 18. In the idiom of Isaiah, 'one of these cities shall be destroyed.'

16 חָבַל to act perversely, corruptly ; Hiph. to be destroyed ; Piel, to spoil, to destroy. The primary meaning is, to bind, to bind fast, with which, as a secondary meaning, Fürst connects to decay, to perish. NIPHAL a *fut.* PIEL b *pret.* c *inf.* d *fut.* PUAL e *pret.* חֲבָל Ch. PAEL f *inf.* g *imp.* ITHPAEL h *fut.* i חֲבָל *com.* cord ; destruction, desolation.

17 חֲלוֹף *m.* a passing away ; destruction, or destitution.

18 חָרֵב to be dried up ; to lay waste, to destroy. HIPHIL a *pret.* b *part.* חֲרֵב Ch. HOPHAL c *pret.* d חָרְבָּה *f.* desolation, a place laid waste.

19 חָרַם : the primary meaning of this word in Kal seems to involve one or other of these significations, to cut off or be cut off, to shut up, to be separated or set aside irrevocably ; hence to devote, to destroy utterly, to exterminate. With *inf.*, utterly destroy. HIPHIL a *pret.* b *inf.* c *imp.* d *fut.* HOPHAL e *fut.* f חֵרֶם *m.* the devoting of anything to utter destruction.

20 מְחִתָּה *f.* a breaking in pieces ; destruction, ruin.

21 יָנָה to be violent, raging, cruel ; to destroy in a rage. KAL *fut.*

22 יָרֵשׁ to take possession ; to dispossess, disinherit ; or repossess. HIPHIL *fut.*

23 כִּיד *m.* destruction, calamity.

24 כָּלָה to be completed, finished ; to make a full end, consume ; to destroy utterly. PIEL a *inf.* b *part.*

25 כָּרַת to cut off. KAL a *fut.* HIPHIL b *pret.* c *inf.*

26 כָּתַת to beat, to beat in pieces, to beat down. PUAL a *pret.* HIPHIL b *fut.* HOPHAL c *fut.*

27 מְגַר Ch. to cast down, to overthrow. PAEL *fut.*

28 מוּל to cut off, to circumcise ; to destroy. HIPHIL *fut.*

29 מוּת to die ; to perish, to be destroyed. HIPHIL a *inf.* b *part.*

30 מָחָה to wipe off, to wipe away ; to blot out ; to destroy men from the face of the earth. KAL a *pret.* b *fut.* NIPHAL c *fut.* HIPHIL d *inf.* According to Schultens, either a *substantive* or *part pl.*

31 נָסַח to pluck up, to tear away ; to destroy, *e.g.* a house. KAL *fut.*

32 נָקַף to cut down ; to smite in pieces ; to destroy. PIEL *pret.*

33 נָשַׁם to destroy. KAL *fut.* See also שָׁמֵם, which is the proper root.

34 נָתַץ to tear, to break down, to destroy, *e.g.* houses, buildings, walls, a city, an altar. KAL [a]*fut.*

35 נָתַשׁ to tear up, to pluck up, a plant; to tear down, to destroy cities. KAL *pret.*

36 סָפָה to scrape; to take away, to consume; to take away life, or persons from life; to destroy. KAL [a]*inf.* [b]*fut.* NIPHAL [c]*part.*

37 סָתַר Ch. to hide; to destroy, *pr.* to hide away, to remove out of sight. P'AL *pret.*

38 פִּיד *m.* calamity, misfortune.

39 פָּרִיץ *m.* violent, rapacious, oppressor, tyrant; used *pr.* of one that breaks through houses, perhaps of those who break through laws.

40 צָדָה to cut down; to lay waste, to desolate a region or a city. NIPHAL *pret.*

41 צָמַת to cut off, to take away; to cut off totally, either in reality or in imagination. HIPHIL [a]*pret.* [b]*fut.* [c]*part.*

42 קוּר to dig, to dig under; see *Break;* to destroy persons. PILPEL *pret.* It cannot be doubted that the deduced meaning, to destroy, from קוּר to dig, is somewhat forced. Schultens (see Rosenmuller *in loc.*) derives קַרְקַר from קִיר a wall, and renders it in Num. xxiv. 17, *struet, fundabit,* "he will build up all the children of Seth," *i.e.* his church, while he destroys the Moabites, or enemies of his people. Gussetius admits the meaning as better suited to the passage, but suggests that in Num. xxiv. 17 it may be derived from קָרַר to be cool, to be refreshed: so that the prediction may have reference to the times of refreshing or of restitution, Acts iii. 19, 21, to be vouchsafed by the Messiah to all his people at his second coming.

43 קֶטֶב *m.* a cutting off, destruction; specially contagion, pestilence. [a]קֶטֶב *m. id.* specially contagion, pestilence.

44 קְפָדָה *m.* destruction, with terror or horror.

45 קֶרֶץ *m.* a cutting; see *Form:* Jer. xlvi. 20.

46 רוּעַ to be evil, to become evil, to be made worse. NIPHAL *fut.*

47 שְׁאִיָּה *f.* desolation, ruins.

48 שָׁבַר to break; to break down, to destroy. KAL [a]*imp.* [b]*fut.* NIPHAL [c]*pret.* [d]*fut.* [e]שֶׁבֶר *com.* a breaking, breach, fracture. [f]שִׁבָּרוֹן *m. id.*

49 שׁוֹאָה *f.* desolation; destruction, ruin, especially sudden and unexpected. [a]שׁוֹא *m. id.* [b]מַשּׁוּאוֹת *f. pl. id.*

50 שָׁדַד to practise violence, to treat with violence, and hence to oppress, to destroy any one, a people, especially through hostile invasion; to lay waste, to desolate a land, cities. KAL [a]*pret.* [b]*fut.* [c]*part.* Poel. [d]*part.* Paül. [e]שֹׁד *m.* violence, oppression of the weak; desolation.

51 שָׁחַת to destroy, to ruin, to lay waste; applied also to the afflictive and wasting effects of divine judgments, which do not actually extinguish life. PIEL [a]*pret.* [b]*inf.* [c]*imp.* HIPHIL [d]*pret.* [e]*inf.* [f]*imp.* [g]*fut.* [h]*part.* [i]שַׁחַת *f.* pit. [k]שְׁחִית *f. id.* [l]מַשְׁחִית *f.* destruction, a destroyer. [m]מַשְׁחָת *f. id.*

52 שָׁכֹל to be bereaved of children; to bereave, to make child-

less. PIEL *fut.* Deut. xxxii. 25, abroad (in battle) the sword shall make childless, *i.e.* destroy your sons.

53 שָׁמַד to destroy, to lay waste, to cut off, to blot out, exterminate; Gr. ἐξαιρεῖν: see Vitringa on Isa. xiv. 23. With *inf.,* utterly be destroyed. NIPHAL [a]*pret.* [b]*inf.* [c]*fut.* HIPHIL [d]*pret.* [e]*inf.* [f]*imp.* [g]*fut.*

54 שָׁמֵם to be astonished, desolate; to lay waste, to make desolate. KAL [a]*fut.* HIPHIL [b]*pret.* [c]*fut.* HITHPOLEL [d]*fut.*

55 שָׁסָה to plunder, to spoil. KAL *part.* Poel.

Gen. vi. 7.	30 b	Josh. viii. 26.	19 a	2 Chron. xxii. 10.		9
vi. 13.	51 h	ix. 24.	53 e	xxiv. 23.		51 g
vi. 17.	51 b	x. 1, 37, 39.	19 d	xxv. 16.		51 e
vii. 4.	30 a	x. 28, 35, 40.	19 a	xxvi. 16.		51 e
vii. 23, a 23.	30 c	xi. 1.	19 b	xxxi. 1.		24 a
ix. 11, 15.	51 b	xi. 12, 21.	19 a	xxxii. 14.		19 a
xiii. 10.	51 b	xi. 20, 20.	19 b, 53 e	xxxiii. 9.		53 d
xviii. 23, 24.	36 b	xii. 33.	51 b	xxxiv. 11.		51 d
xviii. 28, 28, 31, 32.	51 g	xxiii. 15.	53 e	xxxv. 21.		51 g
xix. 13, 13.	51 h b	xxiv. 8.	53 g	xxxvi. 19.		51 e
xix. 14.	51 b	Judg. i. 17.	19 d	Ezra iv. 15.		18 c
xix. 29.	51 b	iv. 24.	25 b	v. 12.		37
xxxiv. 30.	53 a	vi. 4.	51 g	vi. 12, 12, 27.		16 f
Exod. viii. 9.	25 c	vi. 5.	51 b	Esth. iii. 6, 13.		53 e
x. 7.	1 a	xvi. 24.	18 b	iv. 1.		1 e
xii. 13.	51 l	xx. 21, 25, 35.	51 g	iv. 7.		1 e
xii. 23.	51 h	xx. 42.	51 h	iv. 8.		53 e
xv. 9.β	22	xxi. 11.	19 d	iv. 14.		1 c
xxii. 20.	19 e	xxi. 16.	53 a	vii. 4.		53 e
xxiii. 27.	13 a	xxi. 17.	30 c	viii. 5.		1 e
xxxiv. 13.	34	1 Sam. i. 16.	54 c	viii. 6.		1 r
Lev. xxiii. 30.	1 h	v. 9, 11.	12 b	viii. 11.		53 e
xxvi. 22.	25 b	v. 3, 8, 15, 18, 20.	19 a	ix. 5.		1 r
xxvi. 30.	53 d	xv. 6.	3	ix. 6, γ 12, 24, 24.		1 g
xxvi. 44.	24 a	xv. 9, 9.	19 b a	Job ii. 3.		7 b
Num. xxi. 2.	19 a	xv. 9, 9.	19 b a	iv. 20.		26 c
xxi. 3.	19 d	xv. 21.	19 f	v. 21, 22.		50 e
xxiv. 17.	42	xxiii. 10.	51 b	vi. 9.		10 a
xxiv. 19.	1 h	xxiv. 21.	51 g	viii. 18.		7 d
xxxii. 15.	51 a	xxvi. 15.	51 g	ix. 22.		24 b
xxxiii. 52, 52.	1 d f	xxvii. 15.	51 e	ix. 8.		7 d
Deut. i. 27.	53 e	2 Sam. i. 14.	51 b	xii. 23.		1 f
i. 44.	26 b	xi. 1.	51 g	xiv. 19.		1 h
ii. 12, 21.	53 g	xi. 11.	51 g	xv. 21.		50 c
ii. 15.	13 b	xiv. 11, 11.	51 b, 53 g	xviii. 12.		2
ii. 22, 23.	53 d	xiv. 16.	53 e	xix. 10.		34
ii. 34.	19 d	xx. 19.	29 a	xix. 26.		32
iii. 6, 6.	19 d b	xx. 20.	51 g	xxi. 17, 30.		23
iv. 3.	53 d	xxi. 5.	53 a	xxi. 20.		23
iv. 26.	53 e	xxii. 38.	53 g	xxvi. 6.		1 q
iv. 31.	51 g	xxii. 41.	41 b	xxviii. 22.		1 q
vi. 15.	53 d	xxiv. 16, 16.	51 b h	xxx. 12.		2
vii. 2.	19 b d	1 Kings ix. 21.	19 b	xxx. 24.		38
vii. 4.	53 d	xiii. 34.	53 e	xxxi. 3, 23.		2
vii. 5.	34	xv. 13.	25 a	xxxi. 12.		1 q
vii. 10.	1 i	xv. 29.	53 d	xxxi. 29.		38
vii. 20.	1 b	xvi. 12.	53 g	xxxiii. 22.		29 b
vii. 23, 23.		xx. 42.	19 f	xxxiv. 25.		10 b
23.	12 a b, 53 b	2 Kings viii. 19.	51 e	Ps. v. 6.		1 f
vii. 24, 24.	1 h, 53 e	x. 17.	53 d	v. 10.		4
viii. 20.	1 l	x. 19.	1 i	ix. 5.		1 d
ix. 3, 3.	53 g, 1 h	x. 28.	53 g	ix. 6, 6.		18 d. 35
ix. 8, 19, 20, 25.	53 e	xi. 1.	1 f	xi. 3.		15 c
ix. 14.	51 g	xiii. 7.	1 d	xvii. 4. δ		39
ix. 26.	51 g	xiii. 23.	53 d	xviii. 40.		41 b
x. 10.	51 e	xviii. 25, 25.	51 e f	xxi. 10.		1 f
xi. 4.	53 e	xix. 11.	19 b	xxviii. 5.		15 b
xii. 2.	1 e f	xix. 12.	51 a	xxxv. 8, 8.		49
xii. 3.	1 d	xix. 17.	18 a	xxxv. 17.		49 a
xii. 30.	53 b	xix. 18.	1 f	xxxvii. 38.		53 n
xiii. 15.	19 c	xxi. 9.	53 d	xl. 14.		36 a
xx. 17.	19 b d	xxi. 9.	53 d	lii. 5.		34
xx. 19, 20.	51 g	xxiv. 2.	1 i	lv. 9.		7 c
xxviii. 20, 24, 25,		1 Chron. iv. 41.	19 d	lv. 23.		51 i
61.	53 b	v. 25.	53 e	lxiii. 9.		49
xxviii. 48.	53 e	xx. 1.	15 b	lxix. 4.		41 c
xxviii. 51, 51.	53 b, 1 j	xii. 12, 12.	36 c, 51 h	lxxiii. 18.		47 a
xxviii. 63.	1 i	xxi. 15, 15, 15.	51 e e h	lxxiii. 27.		41 a
xxxi. 3.	53 g	2 Chron. xii. 7.	51 g	lxxiv. 8.		21
xxxi. 4.	53 d	xii. 12.	51 g	lxxviii. 38, 45.		51 g
xxxii. 24.	43	xiv. 13.	48 c	lxxviii. 47.		14
xxxii. 25.	52	xv. 6.	26 a	lxxxviii. 11.		1 q
xxxii. 27.	53 f	xx. 10.	53 d	xc. 3.		10 c
Josh. ii. 10.	19 a	xx. 23, 23.	53 e, 51	xci. 6.		43
vi. 21.	19 d	xxi. 7.	51 e	xcii. 7.		53 b
vii. 1.	1 i	xxii. 4.	51 l	ci. 8.		41 b
vii. 12.	53 g	xxii. 7.	5	ciii. 4.		51 i

Ps. cvi. 23, 23.	53 e, 51 e	Isa. xxxvii. 12.	51 d	Ezek. vi. 3.	1 d
cvi. 34.	53 d	xxxvii. 19.	1 f	vii. 25.	44
cvii. 20.	51 k	xlii. 14.	33, 54 a	ix. 1.	51 m
cxviii. 10, 11, 12.	28	xlviii. 19.	53 c	ix. 9.	51 h
cxix. 95.	1 e	xlix. 17.	15 d	xiv. 9.	53 d
cxxxvii. 8.	50 d	xlix. 19.	15 e	xx. 17.	51 b
cxliii. 12.	1 h	li. 13.	51 e	xxi. 31.	51 l
cxliv. 6.	13 c	li. 19.	48 e	xxii. 27.	1 e
cxlv. 20.	53 g	liv. 16.	16 c	xxii. 30.	51 b
Prov. i. 27.	2	lix. 7.	48 e	xxv. 7.	53 g
i. 32.	1 f	lx. 18.	48 e	xxv. 15.	51 l
vi. 32.	51 h	lxv. 8, 8.	51 g e	xxv. 16.	1 h
x. 14, 15, 29.	20	lxv. 25.	51 g	xxvi. 4.	51 a
xi. 3.	50 a′b or b	Jer. i. 10.	1 i	xxvi. 12.	34
xi. 9.	51 g	iii. 30.	51 h	xxvi. 17.	1 a
xiii. 3.	20	iv. 6, 20, 20.	48 e	xxvii. 32. ι	11 c
xiii. 13.	16 a	iv. 7.	51 h	xxviii. 16.	1 f
xiii. 20. ε	46	v. 10.	51 c	xxx. 8.	48 c
xiii. 23.	36 c	vi. 1.	48 e	xxx. 11.	51 b
xiv. 28.	20	vi. 5.	51 g	xxx. 13.	1 h
xv. 11.	1 q	ix. 19.	51 g	xxxii. 9.	48 e
xv. 25.	31	xii. 10.	51 a	xxxii. 12.	53 a
xvi. 18.	48 e	xii. 17.	1 e	xxxii. 13.	1 h
xvii. 19.	48 e	xiii. 14.	51 e	xxxiv. 16.	53 g
xviii. 7.	20	xv. 3.	51 e	xliii. 3.	51 b
xviii. 12.	48 e	xv. 6.	51 g	Dan. ii. 12.	1 m
xxi. 7. ζ	8	xv. 7.	1 d	ii. 24, 24.	1 m n
xxi. 15.	20	xvii. 18, 18.	48 a f	ii. 44.	16 h
xxiv. 2.	50 e	xviii. 7.	1 i	iv. 23.	16 g
xxvii. 20.	1 p′b or 1 q	xxii. 7.	51 h	vi. 26.	16 h
xxviii. 24. η	51 h	xxiii. 20.	48 c	vii. 14.	1 o
xxix. 1.	48 d	xxiii. L.	1 g	viii. 14.	16 h
xxxi. 3.	30 d	xxv. 9.	19 a	viii. 26.	1 m
xxxi. 8.	17	xxxi. 28.	1 i	viii. 24, 24.	51 g d
Eccles. v. 6.	16 b	xxxvi. 29.	51 d	viii. 25.	51 g
vii. 7.	1 f	xlvi. 1.	1 k	ix. 26.	51 g
vii. 16.	54 d	xlvi. 20.	45	xi. 26.	48 d
ix. 18.	1 f	xlviii. 3, 5.	48 e	xi. 26.	48 b
Isa. i. 28.	48 e	xlviii. 4.	48 c	xi. 44.	53 e
iii. 12.	7 a	xlviii. 8, 42.	53 a	Hos. ii. 12.	54 b
ix. 16.	7 e	xlviii. 18.	51 a	iv. 5.	11 a
x. 7.	53 e	xlix. 9.	51 d	iv. 6.	11 b
x. 25.	6	xlix. 38.	1 h	vii. 13.	50 e
x. 27.	16 e	l. 11.	55	ix. 6.	50 e
xi. 9.	51 g	l. 21.	19 b	x. 8.	53 a
xi. 15.	19 a	l. 22.	48 e	x. 9.	51 b
xiii. 6.	16 c	l. 26.	19 c	xiii. 9.	51 a
xiii. 6.	50 e	li. 1.	51 h	xiii. 14.	43 a
xiii. 9.	53 g	li. 3.	19 c	Joel i. 15.	50
xiv. 7.	15 a	li. 8.	48 d	Amos ii. 9, 9.	53 d g
xiv. 20.	51 a	li. 11.	51 e	ix. 8, 8. κ	53 d e g
xiv. 23.	53 e	li. 20.	51 d	Obad. 8.	1 b
xv. 5.	48 e	li. 25, 25.	51 l h	12.	1 b
xix. 3.	7 d	li. 54.	48 e	Micah ii. 10, 10.	16 d i
xix. 18.	15 f	li. 55.	1 d	v. 10.	1 h
xxiii. 11.	53 e	Lam. ii. 5, 6.	51 a	v. 14.	53 d
xxiv. 12.	47	ii. 8, 8.	51 e, 7 b	Zeph. ii. 5.	1 h
xxv. 7.	7 a	ii. 9.	1 d	ii. 13.	1 f
xxvi. 14.	53 g	ii. 11.	48 e	iii. 6.	40
xxviii. 2. θ	43	iii. 47, 48.	48 e	Hag. ii. 22.	53 d
xxxii. 7.	16 c	iii. 66.	53 g	Zech. xii. 9.	53 e
xxxiv. 2.	19 a	iv. 10.	48 e	xiv. 11.	19 f
xxxvi. 10, 10.	51 e f	Ezek. v. 16, 16.	51 l b	Mal. iii. 11.	51 g
xxxvii. 11.	19 b				

α *lit.* he, or, it destroyed every, &c.   β *lit.* or, repossess, *i.e.* bring them back to slavery.   γ *lit.* and to destroy.   δ or, transgressor.   ε *marg.* 'broken.'   ζ *marg.* 'will saw them,' or 'dwell with them,' from גור.   η *lit.* a man destroying.   θ *lit.* a storm of destruction.   ι or, like the desolated.   κ *lit.* destroying I will destroy.

DETAIN

עָצַר to shut up, to close; to hold back, to hinder, to detain. KAL *fut.* Judg. xiii. 15, 16. NIPHAL *part.* 1 Sam. xxi. 7.

DETERMINE, DETERMINATION

1 אָמַר to say, &c. KAL *fut.*

2 חָרַץ to be sharp and pointed; applied to the exact discrimination between justice and injustice, to that which is decreed, fully and irrevocably determined, which admits of no intercession; that which is stinted, limited, and brought to a settled point. KAL ᵃ*part.* Paül. NIPHAL ᵇ*part.*

3 חָתַךְ to cut; to decide, to determine. NIPHAL *pret.*

4 יָעַץ to deliberate, to devise. KAL ᵃ*pret.* ᵇ*part.* Poel.

5 כָּלָה to be quite done, to be finished, to be brought to an end, or conclusion; applied to a full purpose, a resolution perfectly formed in the mind. KAL ᵃ*pret.* ᵇ כָּלָה *f.* completion, perfection.

6 שׂוּם to put or set with design, care, exactness. KAL *part.* Paül.

7 מִשְׁפָּט *m.* judgment.

1 Sam. xx. 7, 9.	5 a	2 Chron. xxv. 16.	4 a	Isa. xxviii. 22.	2 b
xx. 33.	5 b	Esth. vii. 7.	5 a	Dan. ix. 24. α	3
xxv. 17.	5 a	Job xiv. 5.	2 a	ix. 26, 27.	2 b
2 Sam. xiii. 32.	6	Isa. x. 23.	2 b	xi. 36.	2 b
2 Chron. ii. 1.	1	xix. 17.	4 b	Zeph. iii. 8.	7

α *lit.* are divided; *i.e.* so as to be accurately determined.

DETEST

שָׁקַץ to be filthy; to loathe, abominate, abhor, *spec.* things unclean and idolatrous. PIEL *inf.* Deut. vii. 26, *lit.* detesting thou shalt detest; *fut.* Deut. vii. 26. שִׁקּוּץ *m.* abomination: Jer. xvi. 18: Ezek. v. 11; vii. 20; xi. 18, 21; xxxvii. 23.

DEVISE, DEVICE

1 בָּרָא to form; to feign, to invent, followed by מִלִּבּוֹ of his own heart. KAL *pret.*

2 דָּמָה to be like; Piel, to compare, to estimate by comparison; to think, to devise. PIEL *pret.*, or, from דָּמָה to be silent, &c. See *Cut.*

3 הִגָּיוֹן *m.* see *Meditate.*

4 זָמַם to meditate, to have in mind, to purpose; with its derivatives mostly used in a bad sense. KAL ᵃ*pret.* ᵇ זָמָם *m.* "wicked device." ᶜ זִמָּה *f. id.* ᵈ מְזִמָּה *f.* "mischievous, wicked devices."

5 חָרַשׁ to plough, to engrave, to work; to devise. KAL ᵃ*fut.* ᵇ*part.* Poel.

6 חָשַׁב to consider; to design; to contrive with studied thinking. KAL ᵃ*pret.* ᵇ*inf.* ᶜ*fut.* ᵈ*part.* Poel. PIEL ᵉ*fut.* ᶠ*part.* ᵍ חֶשְׁבּוֹן *m.* invention; art, device. ʰ מַחֲשָׁבָה *f.* counsel, purpose, plan. ⁱ מַחֲשֶׁבֶת *f.* that which any one meditates, &c., a counsel, project.

7 יָעַץ to deliberate, to determine. KAL ᵃ*pret.* ᵇ מוֹעֵצוֹת *f. pl.* counsels.

Exod. xxxi. 4.	6 b	Ps. xxxv. 4.	6 d	Prov. xxiv. 8.	6 f
xxxv. 32.	6 b	xxxv. 20.	6 o	Eccles. ix. 10.	6 o
xxxv. 35.	6 d	xxxvi. 4.	6 c	Isa. xxxii. 7, 7.	7 a, 4 c
2 Sam. xiv. 14.	6 a	xxxvii. 7.	4 d	xxxii. 8.	7 a
xxi. 5.	2	xli. 7.	6 c	Jer. xi. 19, 19.	6 a i
1 Kings xii. 33.	1	lii. 2.	6 c	xviii. 11, β 11.	6 d h
2 Chron. ii. 14.	6 i	cxl. 8.	4 b	xviii. 12.	6 i
Esth. viii. 3, 3.	6 i a	Prov. i. 31.	7 b	xviii. 18, 18.	6 c i
viii. 5. α	6 a	iii. 29.	5 a	xlviii. 2.	6 a
ix. 24.	6 a	vi. 14, 18.	5 b	li. 11.	4 d
ix. 25, 25.	6 i a	xii. 2.	4 d	li. 12.	4 a
Job v. 12.	6 d	xiv. 17.	6 d	Lam. ii. 17.	4 a
xxi. 27.	6 i	xiv. 22, 22.	5 b	iii. 62.	3
Ps. x. 2.	4 d	xvi. 9.	4 d	Ezek. xi. 2.	6 i
xxi. 11.	4 d	xvi. 30.	6 b	Dan. xi. 24, 25.	6 i
xxxi 13.	4 d	xix. 21.	6 i	Micah ii. 1, 3.	6 d
xxxiii. 10.	6 i				

α *lit.* the device of.   β *lit.* and (I am) devising.

DEVIL

שֵׁד *m.* idol, *pr.* lord; LXX. Vulg. δαιμόνια, *dæmonia:* Deut. xxxii. 17: Ps. cvi. 37.

שָׂעִיר *m.* see *Satyr:* Lev. xvii. 7: 2 Chron. xi. 15.

DEVOTE

חָרַם this word implies a total separation to certain respects, from which it cannot be redeemed. See *Destroy*. HIPHIL [a] *fut.* HOPHAL [b] *fut.* חֵרֶם [c] *m.* a devoted thing; accursed.

| Lev. xxvii. 21. | c | Lev. xxvii. 29, 29. | c b | Num. xviii. 14. | c |
| xxvii. 28, 28, 28. | c a c | | | | |

DEVOUR

1 אָכַל to eat, to eat up, to consume. KAL [a] *pret.* [b] *inf.* [c] *fut.* [d] *part.* Poel. NIPHAL [e] *fut.* PUAL [f] *pret.* [g] *fut.* אֲכַל Ch. P'AL [h] *imp.* [i] *fut.* [k] *part.* [l] אָכְלָה *f.* meat.

2 בָּלַע to swallow; to destroy, to abolish, to consume. KAL [a] *fut.* PIEL [b] *inf.* [c] *fut.* [d] בֶּלַע *m.* a devouring.

3 יָלַע to swallow; Gesenius, to speak rashly, to utter at random. KAL *pret.* Prov. xx. 25. Gesenius, it is the snare (destruction) of a man that he rashly utters a vow, and after the vow makes inquiry.

4 לָחַם to eat bread; consume. KAL *part.* Paül.

5 רָעָה to feed, feed on. KAL *fut.*

6 שָׁאַף to pant; to pant after, to catch at with open mouth. KAL *fut.*

Gen. xxxi. 15. α	1 c b	Isa. xxx. 27, 30.	1 d	Ezek. xxxiv. 28.	1 c
xxxvii. 20, 33.	1 a	xxxi. 8.	1 c	xxxvi. 13.	1 d
xli. 7, 24.	2 a	xxxiii. 11.	1 c	xxxvi. 14.	1 c
xlix. 27.	1 a	xxxiii. 14.	1 d	xxxix. 4.	6
Exod. xxiv. 17.	1 d	xlii. 14.	6	Dan. vii. 5.	1 h
Lev. x. 2.	1 c	lvi. 9.	1 b	vii. 7, 19.	1 k
Num. xxvi. 10.	1 b	Jer. ii. 3.	1 d	vii. 23.	i
Deut. xxxi. 17. β	1 b	iii. 30.	1 b	Hos. v. 7.	1 c
xxxii. 24.	4	iii. 24.	1 a	vii. 7, 9.	1 a
xxxii. 42.	1 c	v. 14.	1 a	viii. 14.	1 a
Judg. ix. 15, 20, 20.	1 c	viii. 16.	1 a	xi. 6.	1 a
2 Sam. ii. 26.	1 c	x. 25.	1 a	xiii. 8.	1 c
xi. 25.	1 c	xii. 9.	1 l	Joel i. 19, 20.	1 a
xviii. 8, 8.	1 b a	xii. 12.	1 d	ii. 3.	1 a
xxii. 9.	1 c	xv. 3.	1 b	ii. 5.	1 a
2 Chron. vii. 13.	1 b	xvii. 27.	1 a	Amos i. 4, 7, 10, 12, 14.	1 a
Job xviii. 13, 13.	1 c	xxi. 14.	1 a	ii. 2, 5.	1 a
Ps. xxi. 9.	1 c	xxx. 16, 16.	1 d e	iv. 9.	1 a
l. 3.	1 c	xlvi. 10, 14.	1 a	v. 6.	1 a
liii. 4.	1 c	xlviii. 45.	1 a	vii. 4.	1 a
lxxviii. 45.	2 d	l. 7, 17, 32.	1 a	Obad. 18.	1 a
lxxix. 7.	1 a	li. 34.	1 a	Nah. i. 10.	1 f
lxxx. 13.	5	Lam. ii. 3.	1 a	ii. 13.	1 c
cv. 35.	1 c	iv. 11.	1 a	iii. 13.	1 a
Prov. xix. 28. γ	2 c	Ezek. vii. 15.	1 c	iii. 15.	1 c
xx. 25.	3	xv. 4, 5.	1 a	Hab. i. 13.	2 b
xxx. 14.	1 b	xv. 7.	1 c	iii. 14.	1 b
Isa. i. 7.	1 d	xvi. 20.	1 b	Zeph. i. 18.	1 e
i. 20.	1 g	xx. 47.	1 a	iii. 8.	1 e
v. 24.	1 b	xxii. 25.	1 a	Zech. ix. 4.	1 e
ix. 12, 18.	1 c	xxiii. 25.	1 a	ix. 15.	1 a
x. 17.	1 a	xxiii. 37.	1 l	xi. 1.	1 c
xxiv. 6.	1 a	xxviii. 18.	1 a	xii. 6.	1 d
xxvi. 11.	1 c	xxxiii. 27.	1 b	Mal. iii. 11.	1 a
xxix. 6.	1 d				1 d

α lit. hath eaten even by eating.   *β lit.* be for devouring.   *γ* see *Cover*.

DEW

טַל *m.* dew, from its gently moistening the earth; or from its covering and refreshing vegetation; when the sun waxeth hot, it is exhaled and vanisheth away: Hos. vi. 4. Isa. xxvi. 19, "thy dew," *i.e.* that which is thy dew; namely, the divine influence, which shall raise thee out of the grave, is as the dew of herbs, which makes them grow and flourish: so shall thou spring out of the earth at the resurrection to life and glory (Isa. lxvi. 14), but the earth shall cast forth the impious tyrannical dead abortives, doomed to eternal death. Vegetation, beautified with its countless drops of dew, furnishes a striking figure of the abundance of the first converts to the faith of Christ: Ps. cx. 3.—— Gen. xxvii. 28, &c. טַל Ch. *m. id.* Dan. iv. 15, 23, 25, 33; v. 21.

DIADEM

צָנִיף *m.* tiara, turban, as wound round the head: Job xxix. 14: Isa. lxii. 3. צָנוֹף *m.* Isa. lxii. 3, כתיב. מִצְנֶפֶת *f.* tiara, turban of a king: Ezek. xxi. 26.

צְפִירָה *f.* a crown, diadem: Isa. xxviii. 5.

DIAL

מַעֲלָה *f.* a going up; step, stair; degree: 2 Kings xx. 11: Isa. xxxviii. 8.

DIAMOND

יַהֲלֹם *m.* a very hard precious stone: Exod. xxviii. 18; xxxix. 11: Ezek. xxviii. 13.

שָׁמִיר *m.* a sharp point; a diamond, so called from its perforating and cutting other substances; the point of the stylus was a diamond: Jer. xvii. 1.

DIE, DEAD

1 גָּוַע to breathe out one's life, to expire, to die, to perish; *Gr.* ἐκλείπειν, *comp.* fail, Luke xvi. 9; of men and of brutes; it is used also of a violent death, Num. xvii. 12; xx. 3. The Lxx. have rendered this word twice by τελευτᾶν, twice by ἀποθνήσκειν, six times by ἀπολείπειν, to depart; it would seem, therefore, to apply more generally to a gentle death. With *inf.*, surely die. KAL [a] *pret.* [b] *inf.* [c] *fut.* [d] *part.* Poel.

2 מוּת to die, to be slain; to make to die. KAL [a] *pret.* [b] *inf.* [c] *imp.* [d] *fut.* [e] *part.* HIPHIL [f] *inf.* HOPHAL [g] *fut.* [h] מָוֶת *m.* death. [i] תְּמוּתָה *f. id.*

3 נְבֵלָה *f.* see *Carcase*.

4 נָפַל to fall. KAL *pret.*

5 נֶפֶשׁ *com.* the animal life: it is used in a singular manner to signify a dead animal body; but as in some places, where this word is translated body, the *adj.* is joined, it may in other instances be understood.

6 פֶּגֶר *m.* carcase; dead body.

7 רְפָאִים *m. pl.* giants; the illustrious dead of past times in Hades, supposed to be within the earth.

8 שָׁדַד to lay waste, to destroy. KAL *part.* Paül.

Gen. ii. 17.	2 b d	Gen. xxv. 32.	2 b	Gen. xlviii. 7.	2 a
iii. 3.	2 d	xxvi. 9.	2 d	xlviii. 21.	2 e
iii. 4.	2 b d	xxvii. 4.	2 d	l. 5, 24.	2 e
v. 5, 8, 11, 14, 17, 20, 27, 31.	2 d	xxx. 1.	2 e	l. 15.	2 b
		xxxiii. 13.	2 a	l. 16.	2 h
vi. 17.	1 c	xxxv. 8, 19, 29.	2 d	l. 26.	2 d
vii. 21.	1 c	xxxv. 18.	2 a	Exod. i. 6.	2 d
vii. 22.	2 a	xxxvi. 33, 34, 35, 36, 37, 38, 39.	2 d	ii. 23.	2 d
ix. 29.	2 d	xxxviii. 11, 12.	2 d	iv. 19.	2 a
xi. 28, α 32.	2 d	xlii. 2, 20.	2 d	vii. 18.	2 d
xix. 19.	2 a	xliii. 8.	2 d	vii. 21.	2 a
xx. 3.	2 e	xliv. 9, 20, 22, 31.	2 a	viii. 13.	2 d
xx. 7.	2 b d	xlv. 28.	2 a	ix. 4.	2 d
xxiii. 2.	2 d	xlvi. 12, 30.	2 a	ix. 6, 6.	2 d a
xxiii. 3, 4, 6, 6, 8, 11, 13, 15.	2 e	xlvii. 15, 19, 19.	2 d	ix. 7, 19.	2 a
		xlvii. 29.	2 b	x. 28.	2 d
xxv. 8, 17.	2 d			xi. 5.	2 a
xxv. 18.	4			xii. 30, 33.	2 e

Exod. xiv. 11, 12.	2 b
xiv. 30.	2 e
xvi. 3.	2 b
xx. 19.	2 d
xxi. 12, 20, 28.	2 a
xxi. 14.	2 b
xxi. 18.	2 d
xxi. 34, 36.	2 e
xxi. 35, 35.	2 a e
xxii. 2, 10, 14.	2 a
xxviii. 35.	2 d
xxviii. 43.	2 a
xxx. 20, 21.	2 d
Lev. vii. 24.	3
viii. 35.	2 d
x. 2, 6, 7, 9.	2 d
xi. 31, 32.	2 h
xi. 39.	2 d
xv. 31.	2 d
xvi. 1, 2, 13.	2 d
xvii. 15.	3
xix. 28.	5
xx. 20.	2 d
xxi. 1.	5
xxi. 11.	2 e
xxii. 4.	5
xxii. 8.	3
xxii. 9.	2 a
Num. iii. 4.	2 d
iv. 15, 20.	2 a
iv. 19.	2 d
v. 2.	5
vi. 6.	2 e
vi. 7.	2 h
vi. 9. β	2 e d
vi. 11.	5
ix. 6, 7, 10.	5
xii. 12.	2 e
xiv. 2, 2.	2 a
xiv. 35, 37.	2 d
xv. 36.	2 d
xvi. 29.	2 d
xvi. 48, 49, 49.	2 e
xvii. 10.	2 d
xvii. 12.	1 a
xvii. 13, 13.	2 d, 1 b
xviii. 3, 32.	2 d
xviii. 22.	2 e
xix. 11, 16, 18.	2 e
xix. 13, 13.	2 e d
xix. 14.	2 d
xx. 1, 28.	2 d
xx. 3, 3.	1 a b
xx. 4.	2 b
xx. 26.	2 a
xx. 29.	1 a
xxi. 5.	2 b
xxi. 6.	2 d
xxiii. 10.	2 d
xxv. 9.	2 h
xxvi. 10.	2 h
xxvi. 11.	2 a
xxvi. 19, 61.	2 d
xxvi. 65.	2 b d
xxvii. 3, 3.	2 a
xxvii. 8.	2 d
xxxiii. 38.	2 d
xxxiii. 39.	2 d
xxxv. 12, 16, 17, 17.	2 d
xxxv. 18, 18, 20, 21, 23, 23.	2 d
xxxv. 30.	2 b
Deut. ii. 16.	2 b
iv. 22.	2 e
v. 25, 25.	2 d a
x. 6.	2 a
xiii. 10.	2 a
xiv. 1.	2 e
xiv. 8, 21.	3
xvii. 5, 12.	2 d
xviii. 16.	2 d
xviii. 20.	2 a
xix. 5, 11, 12.	2 a
xx. 5, 6, 7.	2 d
xxi. 21.	2 a
xxii. 21, 22, 24, 25.	2 a
xxiv. 3.	2 d
xxiv. 7.	2 a
xxv. 5, 5.	2 a e
xxv. 6.	2 a
xxvi. 14.	2 e
xxxi. 14.	2 b
xxxii. 50, 50.	2 c a
xxxiii. 6.	2 d
xxxiv. 5.	2 d
Deut. xxxiv. 7.	2 h
Josh. i. 2.	2 a
v. 4.	2 a
x. 11, 11.	2 d a
xx. 9.	2 d
xxiv. 29.	2 d
xxiv. 33.	2 a
Judg. i. 7.	2 d
ii. 8, 21.	2 d
ii. 19.	2 h
iii. 11.	2 d
iii. 25.	2 e
iv. 1.	2 a
iv. 21.	2 e
iv. 22.	2 e
v. 27.	8
vi. 23, 30.	2 d
viii. 32.	2 d
viii. 33.	2 d
ix. 49, 54.	2 d
ix. 55.	2 d
x. 2, 5.	2 d
xii. 7, 10, 12, 15.	2 d
xiii. 22.	2 b d
xv. 18.	2 e
xvi. 30, 30.	2 d e
xx. 5.	2 d
Ruth i. 3, 5, 17, 17.	2 d
i. 8.	2 e
ii. 20.	2 e
iv. 5, 5, 10, 10.	2 e
iv. 17, 19.	2 a
iv. 18.	2 d
1 Sam. ii. 33, 34.	2 d
iv. 18.	2 d
v. 11. γ	2 a
v. 12.	2 a
xii. 19.	2 d
xiv. 39.	2 b d
xiv. 43.	2 d
xiv. 44.	2 b d
xiv. 45, 45.	2 d a
xvii. 51.	2 a
xx. 2, 14.	2 h
xx. 31.	2 d
xxii. 16.	2 b d
xxiv. 14.	2 e
xxv. 1, 37, 38.	2 a
xxv. 39.	2 a
xxvi. 10.	2 a
xxvi. 16.	2 h
xxviii. 3.	2 a
xxviii. 9.	2 f
xxxi. 5, 5.	2 a d
xxxi. 6.	2 d
xxxi. 7.	2 a
2 Sam. i. 4, 4.	2 d a
i. 5.	2 d
i. 15.	2 d
ii. 7, 31.	2 a
ii. 23, 23.	2 d
iii. 27.	2 a
iii. 33, 33.	2 d h
iv. 1, 10.	2 a
iv. 7.	2 d
ix. 8.	2 e
x. 1, 18.	2 a
xi. 15, 26.	2 a
xi. 17.	2 d
xi. 21, 21.	2 d a
xi. 24, 24.	2 d a
xii. 5.	2 h
xii. 13.	2 a
xii. 14.	2 b d
xii. 18, 18, 18.	2 d a a
xii. 19, 19, 19, 21.	2 a
xiii. 32, 33, 33, 39.	2 a
xiv. 2.	2 e
xiv. 5.	2 d
xiv. 14.	2 b d
xvi. 9.	2 e
xvii. 23.	2 e
xviii. 3.	2 d
xviii. 20.	2 a
xviii. 33.	2 b
xix. 6.	2 a
xix. 23, 37.	2 d
xix. 28.	2 h
xx. 10.	2 d
xx. 15.	2 d
1 Kings i. 52.	2 a
ii. 1.	2 b
ii. 25, 30, 46.	2 d
ii. 37.	2 b d
1 Kings ii. 42.	2 b d
iii. 19.	2 d
iii. 20, 22, 22, 23, 23.	2 e
iii. 21.	2 a
xi. 21.	2 a
xii. 18.	2 a
xiii. 31.	2 b
xiv. 11, 11.	2 a
xiv. 12, 17.	2 a
xvi. 4, 4.	2 a
xvi. 18, 22.	2 a
xvii. 12.	2 a
xix. 4.	2 b
xxi. 10, 13, 14.	2 a
xxi. 15, 15.	2 d a
xxi. 16.	2 a
xxi. 24, 24.	2 e
xxii. 35, 37.	2 d
2 Kings i. 4.	2 b d
i. 6.	2 b d
i. 16.	2 b d
i. 17.	2 d
iii. 5.	2 h
iv. 1.	2 a
iv. 20.	2 a
iv. 32.	2 a
vii. 3, 4, 4, 4.	2 a
vii. 17, 20.	2 a
viii. 5. δ	2 e
viii. 10.	2 b d
viii. 15.	2 d
ix. 27.	2 a
xi. 1.	2 a
xii. 21.	2 d
xiii. 14, 20, 24.	2 d
xviii. 32.	2 d
xix. 35.	2 e
xx. 1.	2 e
xxiii. 30.	2 e
xxiii. 34.	2 e
xxv. 25.	2 d
1 Chron. i. 44, 45, 46, 47, 48, 49, 50, 51.	2 d
ii. 19, 30, 32.	2 d
ii. 24.	2 h
x. 5, 5.	2 a d
x. 6, 6.	2 d a
x. 7.	2 a
x. 13.	2 a
xiii. 10.	2 d
xix. 1.	2 d
xxiii. 22.	2 d
xxiv. 2.	2 d
xxix. 28.	2 d
2 Chron. x. 18.	2 d
xiii. 20.	2 d
xvi. 13.	2 d
xviii. 34.	2 d
xx. 24, 25.	6
xxi. 19.	2 d
xxii. 10.	2 a
xxiv. 15, 15.	2 d h
xxiv. 22.	2 h
xxiv. 25.	2 d
xxv. 4, 4, 4.	2 b
xxxii. 11.	2 b
xxxv. 24.	2 h
Esth. ii. 7.	2 d a
Job i. 19.	2 d
ii. 9.	2 d
iii. 11.	2 d
iv. 21.	2 d
xii. 2.	2 d
xiv. 8, 10, 14.	2 d
xxi. 23, 25.	2 d
xxvi. 5.	7
xxvii. 5.	1 c
xxix. 18.	1 c
xxxiv. 20.	2 d
xxxvi. 12.	1 c
xxxvi. 14.	2 d
xlii. 17.	2 d
Ps. xvii. 9.	5
xxxi. 12.	2 e
xli. 5.	2 d
xlix. 10.	2 d
xlix. 17.	2 h
lxxix. 2.	3
lxxix. 11.	2 i
lxxxii. 7.	2 d
lxxxviii. 5.	2 d
lxxxviii. 10, 10, 22.	7
lxxxviii. 15.	1 d
civ. 29.	1 c
Ps. cvi. 28.	2 e
cxv. 17.	2 e
cxviii. 17.	2 e
cxliii. 3.	2 e
Prov. ii. 18.	7
v. 23.	2 d
ix. 18.	7
x. 21.	2 d
xi. 7.	2 h
xv. 10.	2 d
xix. 16.	2 d
xxi. 16.	7
xxiii. 13.	2 d
Eccles. ii. 16.	2 d
iii. 2.	2 b
iii. 19, 19.	2 h
iv. 2, 2.	2 e a
vii. 17.	2 d
ix. 3, 4.	2 e
ix. 5, 5.	2 d e
x. 1.	2 h
Isa. vi. 1.	2 h
viii. 19.	2 e
xiv. 9.	7
xiv. 28.	2 h
xxii. 2.	2 e
xxii. 13, 14, 18.	2 d
xxvi. 14.	2 e
xxvi. 19, 19, 19.	2 e, 3, 7
xxxvii. 36.	2 e
xxxviii. 1.	2 e
l. 2.	2 d
li. 6, 12, 14.	2 d
lix. 5.	2 d
Isa. lix. 10.	2 e
lxv. 20.	2 d
lxvi. 24.	2 d
Jer. xi. 21, 22, 22.	2 d
xvi. 4.	2 d
xvi. 6.	2 a
xvi. 7.	2 a
xx. 6.	2 d
xxi. 6, 9.	2 d
xxii. 10.	2 d
xxii. 12, 26.	2 d
xxvi. 8.	2 b d
xxvi. 11, 16.	2 h
xxvi. 23.	3
xxvii. 13.	2 e
xxviii. 16.	2 e
xxviii. 17.	2 d
xxxi. 30.	2 d
xxxi. 40.	6
xxxiii. 4.	6
xxxiv. 4, 5.	2 d
xxxiv. 20.	3
xxxvi. 30.	3
xxxviii. 2, 9, 10, 24.	2 d
xxxviii. 26.	2 b
xli. 9.	6
xliii. 16, 17, 22.	2 d
xliv. 12.	2 d
Lam. iii. 6.	2 e
Ezek. iii. 18, 18.	2 b d d
iii. 19, 20, 20.	2 d
iv. 14.	3
v. 12.	2 d
Ezek. vi. 12, 12.	2 d
vii. 15.	2 d
xi. 13.	2 a
xiii. 13.	2 d
xiii. 19.	2 d
xvii. 16.	2 d
xviii. 4, 17, 20, 21, 24, 28, 31.	2 d
xviii. 13.	2 b g
xviii. 18, 32.	2 e
xviii. 23.	2 h
xviii. 26, 26.	2 a d
xxiv. 17.	2 e
xxiv. 18.	2 d
xxviii. 8.	2 a
xxviii. 10.	2 d
xxxiii. 8, 8.	2 b d d
xxxiii. 9, 11, 13, 15, 27.	2 d
xxxiii. 14.	2 b d
xxxiii. 18.	2 a
xliv. 25.	2 e
xliv. 31.	3
Hos. xiii. 1.	2 d
Amos ii. 2.	2 a
vi. 9.	2 a
vii. 11, 17.	2 d
viii. 3.	6
ix. 10.	2 d
Jonah iv. 3.	2 h
iv. 8, 8.	2 b h
Hab. i. 12.	2 d
Zech. xi. 9, 9.	2 e d
xiii. 8.	1 c

α lit. died upon the face of.   β "die very suddenly."   γ lit. destruction of death.   δ "dead body."

DIET

אָרְחָה f. see *Victuals*. Jer. lii. 34, 34.

DIFFERENCE

בָּדַל to separate, to divide; to make distinction between. HIPHIL *pret.* Lev. xx. 25: Ezek. xxii. 26; *inf.* Lev. x. 10; xi. 47.

פָּלָה to separate, to distinguish, to put a difference in a marvellous and glorious manner. HIPHIL *fut.* Exod. xi. 7; *Gr.* παραδοξάσει.

DIG

1   חָפַר to dig; to dig a deep well; to search for water, or treasure, by digging; to search and see what one can find or discover in an unknown place. KAL ᵃ*pret.* ᵇ*fut.* ᶜ*part.* Poel.

2   חָצַב to hew, cut, or engrave. KAL ᵃ*pret.* ᵇ*fut.* ᶜ*part.* Paül.

3   חָתַר to dig through; to break into a house, by digging through its mud wall. KAL ᵃ*pret.* ᵇ*imp.* ᶜ*fut.*

4   כָּרָה to dig a pit, a well, a grave; to dig (a pit understood), hence, *metaph.* to lay snares or to plot against any one: Job vi. 27, so Job xli. 6 may be understood; see *Banquet*, see also *Open*. The word has another meaning, to buy. KAL ᵃ*pret.* ᵇ*fut.* ᶜ*part.* Poel. NIPHAL ᵈ*fut.*

5   נָקַר to pierce, to dig out. PUAL *pret.*

6   עָדַר: this word, according to Taylor, imports to draw together the adjacent earth into an orderly heap about the roots of vines, with a hoe or spade. See Virgil's Georg. ii. 354: *Seminibus positis, superest deducere terram sæpius ad capita et diros jactare bidentes.* NIPH. *fut.*

7   עָקַר to pluck up, to root up; to hough horses, by cutting the principal tendon of their legs, which, with respect to

their usefulness, is the same thing as extirpating a plant. PIEL *pret.* Gen. xlix. 6, they digged down a wall, *marg.* ' *or*, houghed oxen ;' see *Wall.* But neither appears from the history ; on the contrary, they preserved and seized upon the oxen, Gen. xxxiv. 28. If the Grammar will but bear it, the best sense, I apprehend, is, " in their self-will they extirpated a prince ;" see *Prince* : they slew the subjects and extirpated the prince's family.— *Taylor.* Some, they destroyed a city.

8 קוּר to dig for water. KAL *pret.*

Gen. xxi. 30.	1 a	2 Kings xix. 24.	8	Prov. xxvi. 27.	4 c
xxvi. 15, 32.	1 a	2 Chron. xxvi. 10.	2 b	Eccles. x. 8.	1 c
xxvi. 18, a 18.	1 b a	Neh. ix. 25.	2 c	Isa. v. 6.	6
xxvi. 19, 21, 22.	1 b	Job iii. 21.	1 b	vii. 25.	6
xxvi. 25.	4 b	vi. 27.	4 b	xxxvii. 25.	8
xlix. 6.	7	xi. 18.	1 a	li. 1.	5
l. 5.	4 a	xxiv. 16.	3 a	Jer. xiii. 7.	1 b
Exod. vii. 24.	1 b	Ps. vii. 15.	1 b	xviii. 20, 22.	4 a
xxi. 33.	4 a	xxxv. 7.	3 a	Ezek. viii. 8, 8.	3 b c
Num. xxi. 18, 18.	1 a, 4 a	lvii. 6.	4 a	xii. 5.	3 b
Deut. vi. 11, 11.	2 c a	xciv. 13.	4 a	xii. 7.	3 a
viii. 9.	2 b	cxix. 85.	4 a	xii. 12.	3 c
xxiii. 13.	1 a	Prov. xvi. 27.	4 c	Amos ix. 2.	3 c

a lit. and he returned and digged.

DIGNITY

גְּדוּלָה *f.* greatness ; majesty : Esth. vi. 3.

מָרוֹם *m.* height ; high condition : Eccles. x. 6.

שְׂאֵת *f.* a lifting up ; elevation, dignity, majesty : Gen. xlix. 3, "excellency of dignity," in allusion to the honour of priesthood involved in the birthright. Hab. i. 7, *marg.* ' captivity.'

DILIGENT

1 אָדְרַזְדָּא *adv.* Ch. quickly, or carefully, exactly : Ezra vii. 23.

2 חָרוּץ sharp, or acute in business, &c.

3 יָטַב to be good ; to do good. HIPHIL *inf.*

4 יָדַע to know. KAL *fut.* Prov. xxvii. 23, *lit.* in knowing thou shalt know.

5 מְאֹד *m.* very much.

6 מָהִיר *adj.* with haste : Prov. xxii. 29.

7 מִשְׁמָר *m.* keeping ; what is guarded, kept : Prov. iv. 23, *marg.* ' above all keeping,' *i. e.* above all that is kept, above all things else.

8 קֶשֶׁב *f.* attention, heed : Isa. xxi. 7, "diligently with much heed," *lit.* hearkened with attention, with much attention.

Deut. iv. 9.	5	Ezra vii. 23.	1	Prov. xxi. 5.	2
xiii. 14.	3	Ps. cxix. 4.	5	xxii. 29.	6
xvii. 4.	3	Prov. iv. 23.	7	xxvii. 23.	4
xix. 18.	5	x. 4.	2	Isa. xxi. 7.	8
xxiv. 8.	5	xii. 24, 27.	2	Jer. ii. 10.	5
Josh. xxii. 5.	5	xiii. 4.	2		

See also the verb to which *Diligently* is joined, as *Hearken*, &c.

DIM

1 חָשַׁךְ to be dark. KAL *pret.*

2 כָּבֵד to be heavy. KAL *pret.*

3 כָּהָה to be blunted, dulled, repressed, abated. KAL *a pret.* *b fut.* *c* כֵּהָה *adj. f.* failing, weak, of eyes become dim.

4 מָעוּף *m.* darkness or dimness of sight, which either is occasioned by a vertigo or dizziness of the head, or which produces dizziness. *a* מוּעָף *m.* darkness.

---

5 עָמַם to hide, to conceal ; to be obscured, to become dim. HOPHAL *fut.*

6 קוּם to rise up ; to stand, applied to the eye when it becomes set and fixed from old age. KAL *pret.*

7 שָׁעָה to look ; also to smear, to close, to make blind. KAL *fut.*

Gen. xxvii. 1.	3 b	1 Sam. i. 15.	6	Isa. xxxii. 3.	7
xlviii. 10.	2	Job xvii. 7.	3 b	Lam. iv. 1.	5
Deut. xxxiv. 7.	3 a	Isa. viii. 22.	4	v. 17.	1
1 Sam. iii. 2.	3 c	ix. 1.	4 a		

DIMINISH

גָּרַע to lessen, to diminish ; to take from, or abate in small portions ; as by clipping, &c. ; *opp.* יָסַף, Deut. iv. 2 ; xii. 32. KAL *fut.* Exod. v. 8 ; xxi. 10. (Gr. οὐκ ἀποστερήσει, *comp.* 1 Cor. vii. 5.) Deut. iv. 2 ; xii. 32 : Jer. xxvi. 2 : Ezek. v. 11 ; xvi. 27. NIPHAL *part.* Exod. v. 11.

מָעַט to be few or little. KAL *fut.* Prov. xiii. 11 : Isa. xxi. 17 : Jer. xxix. 6. HIPHIL *pret.* Ezek. xxix. 15 ; *fut.* Lev. xxv. 16.

DINE

אָכַל to eat. KAL *fut.* Gen. xliii. 16.

DINNER

אֲרֻחָה *f.* allowance, victuals, a portion of food : Prov. xv. 17.

DIP

1 טָבַל to plunge, or dip in any liquid, to dye. This word is used of Naaman the Syrian, who had been commanded to wash (רָחַץ) ; yet they are not synonymous. KAL *a pret.* *b fut.* *c part.* Poel. NIPHAL *d pret.*

2 מָחַץ to smite ; to imbrue the hand, sword, or foot in blood. KAL *fut.*

Gen. xxxvii. 31.	1 b	Num. xix. 18.	1 a	1 Sam. xiv. 27.	1 b
Exod. xii. 22.	1 a	Deut. xxxiii. 24.	1 c	2 Kings v. 14.	1 b
Lev. iv. 6, 17.	1 a	Josh. iii. 15.	1 d	viii. 15.	1 b
ix. 9.	1 b	Ruth ii. 14.	1 a	Ps. lxviii. 23.	2
xiv. 6, 16, 51.	1 a				

DIRECT

1 בִּין to understand, to consider. KAL and HIPHIL *fut.* Prov. xxi. 29, קרי.

2 יָרָה to teach, instruct. HIPHIL *inf.*

3 יָשַׁר to be right ; to direct in the right way. PIEL *a pret.* *b fut.*

4 כּוּן (see *Establish*), to set things right, &c. ; applied to actions rightly directed. NIPHAL *a fut.* HIPHIL *b inf.* *c fut.*

5 כָּשֵׁר (see *Prosper*), to give success. HIPHIL *inf.*

6 נָתַן to give. KAL *pret.*

7 עָרַךְ to set in order, words, or prayer, as the shew-bread was set in order and presented to the Lord. KAL *a pret.* *b fut.*

8 שָׁרָה to loose, to let go free. KAL *fut.*

9 תָּכַן to make even ; to poise, to weigh ; to prove, to try. PIEL *pret.*

Gen. xlvi. 28. a	2	Prov. iii. 6.	3 b	Isa. xl. 13.	9
Job xxxii. 14.	7 a	ii. 5.	3 b	xlv. 13.	6
xxxvii. 3.	3 a, or 8	xvi. 9.	4 c	lxi. 8.	3 b
Ps. v. 3.	7 b	xxi. 29.	1, or 4 c	Jer. x. 23.	4 b
cxix. 5.	4 a	Eccles. x. 10.	5		

a or, to prepare before him.

DIRECTLY

הָגִין *adj.* convenient, commodious : Ezek. xlii. 12.

נֹכַח *m.* used as a *preposition* and *adverb;* over against, in a straight line : Num. xix. 4.

DIRT

טִיט *m.* mire, soft clay : Ps. xviii. 42 : Isa. lvii. 20.

פַּרְשְׁדֹנָה *m.* according to the Targ., Vulg., Luth., Engl., dung, dirt. But the ה paragogic implies rather the place at which anything comes out, and so it is rendered in the *marg.* Judg. iii. 22, 'or, it came out at the fundament.'

DISALLOW

נוּא to disallow, reject, refuse, having respect to the person making a vow or promise. HIPHIL *pret.* Num. xxx. 5, 5, 11. *fut.* Num. xxx. 8.

DISANNUL

כָּפַר to cover, to obliterate. PUAL *pret.* Isa. xxviii. 18.

פָּרַר to break ; to violate ; to make vain ; to annul, to abolish a vow. HIPHIL *fut.* Job xl. 8 : Isa. xiv. 27.

DISAPPOINT

פָּרַר to break ; see above. HIPHIL *inf.* Prov. xv. 22. *part.* Job v. 12.

קָדַם to go before, prevent. PIEL *imp.* Ps. xvii. 13.

DISCERN

1 בִּין to discern, to mark, to understand. KAL and HIPHIL [a] *fut.* HIPHIL [b] *inf.*

2 יָדַע to know. KAL [a] *pret.* [b] *fut.* HIPHIL [c] *fut.*

3 נָכַר to recognise. HIPHIL [a] *pret.* [b] *imp.* [c] *fut.* [d] *part.*

4 רָאָה to see. KAL *pret.*

5 שָׁמַע to hear. KAL *inf.*

Gen. xxvii. 23.	3 a	1 Kings iii. 11.	5	Prov. vii. 7.			
xxxi. 32.	3 b	xx. 41.	3 c	Eccles. viii. 5.	2 b		
xxxviii. 25.	3 b	Ezra iii. 13.	3 d	Ezek. xliv. 23.	2 c		
2 Sam. xiv. 17.	5	Job iv. 16.	3 c	Jonah iv. 11.	2 a		
xix. 35.	2 b	vi. 30.	1 a	Mal. iii. 18.	4		
1 Kings iii. 9.	1 b						

DISCHARGE

נָפַץ to break, to disperse ; of floats or rafts broken up. PIEL *pret.* 1 Kings v. 9.

מְשַׁלַּחַת *f.* a sending away : Eccles. viii. 8.

DISCIPLE

לִמּוּד *adj.* learned : Isa. viii. 16.

DISCIPLINE

מוּסָר *m.* chastisement, instruction : Job xxxvi. 10.

DISCLOSE

גָּלָה to open, uncover, reveal, discover. PIEL *pret.* Isa. xxvi. 21.

DISCOMFIT

1 הָמַם to put in commotion, consternation, to disturb, to dis- comfit, as God his enemies. KAL [a] *fut.* מְהוּמָה [b] *f.* commotion, disturbance.

2 חָלַשׁ to prostrate, to overthrow. KAL *fut.*

3 חָרַד to tremble ; to terrify. HIPHIL *pret.*

4 כָּתַת to beat down, to rout an enemy. HIPHIL *fut.*

5 מַס *m.* tribute, tribute-service ; from מָסַס to melt.

Exod. xvii. 13.	2	Judg. viii. 12.	3	2 Sam. xxii. 15.	1 a		
Num. xiv. 45.	4	1 Sam. vii. 10.	1 a	Ps. xviii. 14.	1 a		
Josh. x. 10.	1 a	xiv. 20.	1 b	Isa. xxxi. 8.	5		
Judg. iv. 15.	1 a						

DISCONTENTED

מַר *adj.* bitter ; נֶפֶשׁ *com.* soul : 1 Sam. xxii. 2.

DISCONTINUE

שָׁמַט to let fall, to let lie, to release ; *seq.* מִן to desist from anything, to discontinue. KAL *pret.* Jer. xvii. 4.

DISCORD

מָדוֹן *m.* contention, quarrel, strife : Prov. vi. 14. מְדָנִים *m. pl.* Prov. vi. 14, כתיב, 19.

DISCOVER

1 גָּלָה to make naked, to uncover. Piel, to take away a cover- ing ; in Lam. ii. 14 and iv. 22, take the *prep.* עַל ellipti- cally, implying a veil over sin not removed. NIPHAL [a] *pret.* [b] *inf.* NIPHAL [c] *fut.* PIEL [d] *pret.* [e] *fut.* [f] *part.* HITHPAEL [g] *inf.*

2 חָשַׂף to strip off, to uncover. KAL [a] *pret.* [b] *fut.*

3 יָדַע to know. NIPHAL *pret.*

4 עָרָה to be naked ; to make bare, uncover. PIEL [a] *inf.* [b] *fut.* HIPHIL [c] *pret.*

Exod. xx. 26.	1 c	Prov. xviii. 2.	1 g	Ezek. xvi. 37.	1 d		
Lev. xx. 18.	4 c	xxv. 9.	1 e	xxi. 24.	1 b		
Deut. xxii. 30.	1 e	Isa. iii. 17.	4 b	xxii. 10.	1 d		
1 Sam. xiv. 8.	1 a	xxii. 8.	1 e	xxiii. 10.	1 d		
xiv. 11.	1 c	viii. 8.	1 d	xxiii. 18, 18.	1 e		
xxii. 6.	3	Jer. xiii. 22.	1 a	xxiii. 29.	1 a		
2 Sam. xxii. 16.	1 c	xiii. 26.	2	Hos. ii. 10.	1 e		
xli. 13.	1 d	Lam. ii. 14.	1 d	vii. 1.	1 a		
Job xii. 22.	1 c	iv. 22.	1 d	Micah i. 6.	1 e		
Ps. xviii. 15.	1 c	Ezek. xiii. 14.	1 a	Nah. iii. 5.	1 d		
xxix. 9.	2 b	xvi. 36, 57.	1 c	Hab. iii. 13.	4 a		

DISCOURAGE

חָתַת see *Dismay.* NIPHAL *fut.* Deut. i. 21.

מָסַס to melt ; to faint. HIPHIL *pret.* Deut. i. 28.

נוּא to deny ; to disallow, hinder. KAL [a] *fut.* Num. xxxii. 7. (כתיב). HIPHIL *fut.* Num. xxxii. 7, 9.

קָצַר to cut off ; to be shortened. KAL *fut.* Num. xxi. 4.

רָצַץ to break, to treat with violence, to oppress. KAL *fut.* Isa. xlii. 4.

DISCREET, DISCRETION

בִּין to discern, to mark, to understand. NIPHAL *part.* Gen. xli. 33, 39. תְּבוּנָה *f.* understanding : Jer. x. 12.

מְזִמָּה *f.* meditation, thought ; device, counsel, purpose : Prov. i. 4; ii. 11; iii. 21; v. 2.

טַעַם *m.* taste, judgment, reason : Prov. xi. 22.

שֵׂכֶל *m.* intelligence, understanding, wisdom : Prov. xix. 11.

מִשְׁפָּט *m.* judgment : Ps. cxii. 5 : Isa. xxviii. 26 ; see *Instruct.*

DISDAIN

בָּזָה to despise, contemn. KAL *fut.* 1 Sam. xvii. 42.

מָאַס to reject ; to contemn, despise. KAL *pret.* Job xxx. 1.

DISEASE

1 דָּבָר *m.* word, matter, thing.

2 חָלָא to be sick. KAL ª *fut.* ᵇ תַּחֲלֻאִים *m. pl.* diseases.

3 חָלָה to be weak, to be sick. KAL ª *pret.* NIPHAL ᵇ *part.* ᶜ חֳלִי *m.* disease ; affliction, evil, calamity. ᵈ מַחֲלֶה *m.* ᵉ מַחֲלָה *f.* disease. ᶠ מַחֲלֻיִים *m. pl.* diseases.

4 מַדְוֶה *m.* sickness, disease.

Exod. xv. 26.	3 e	2 Chron. xvi. 12, 12,		2 Chron. xxiv. 25.	3 f
Deut. vii. 15.	4	12.	2 a, 3 c c	Ps. xli. 8.	1
xxviii. 60.	4	xxi. 15.	3 d	ciii. 3.	2 b
1 Kings xv. 23.	3 a	xxi. 18.	3 c	Eccles. vi. 2.	3 c
2 Kings i. 2.	3 c	xxi. 19.	2 b	Ezek. xxxiv. 4, 21.	3 b
viii. 8, 9.	3 c				

DISGRACE

נָבֵל to act foolishly ; to esteem lightly ; to disgrace. PIEL *fut.* Jer. xiv. 21.

DISGUISE

חָפַשׂ to search ; to let oneself be sought ; to disguise oneself. HITHPAEL *pret.* 2 Chron. xxxv. 22. *inf.* 1 Kings xxii. 30 : 2 Chron. xviii. 29. *fut.* 1 Sam. xxviii. 8 : 1 Kings xx. 38 ; xxii. 30 : 2 Chron. xviii. 29.

סֵתֶר *m.* secret : Job xxiv. 15, *lit.* setteth (his) face in secret.

שׂוּם to set. KAL *fut.* Job xxiv. 15.

שָׁנָה to do a second time, to change, to change oneself, *i. e.* one's garments. HITHPAEL *imp.* 1 Kings xiv. 2.

DISH

סֵפֶל *m.* a dish, a bowl : Judg. v. 25.

צַלַּחַת *f.* a dish : 2 Kings xxi. 13.

קְעָרָה *f.* a dish, bowl, charger : Exod. xxv. 29 ; xxxvii. 16 : Num. iv. 7.

DISHONOUR

כְּלִמָּה *f.* shame, reproach, contumely : Ps. xxxv. 26 ; lxix. 19 ; lxxi. 13.

נָבֵל to act foolishly ; to esteem lightly. PIEL *part.* Micah vii. 6.

עֶרְוָה Ch. *f.* shame, ignominy, disgrace : Ezra iv. 14.

קָלוֹן *m.* contempt, shame, dishonour : Prov. vi. 33.

DISINHERIT

יָרַשׁ see *Dispossess.* HIPHIL *fut.* Num. xiv. 12.

DISMAY

1 בָּהַל to be troubled, suddenly seized with fear. NIPHAL *pret.* Isa. xxi. 3, *lit.* dismayed from seeing, so that I cannot see.

2 חָתַת to be broken so as to be quite disabled ; applied to a mind daunted, broken and faint-hearted : it denotes that con-

sternation of the mind which is the reverse of the mind under the influence of joy, hope, and confidence. It is frequently joined with יָרֵא, and sometimes with בּוֹשׁ, הוֹבִישׁ. KAL ª *pret.* NIPHAL ᵇ *fut.* HIPHIL ᶜ *pret.* ᵈ חַת *m.* alarm. ᵉ מְחִתָּה *f.* consternation, alarm, terror.

3 שָׁעָה to look, to look around for help ; to look on each other, to be amazed. HITHPAEL *fut.*

Deut. xxxi. 8.	2 b	Isa. xxi. 3.	1	Jer. xlvi. 5.	2 d
Josh. i. 9.	2 b	xxxvii. 27.	2 a	xlvi. 27.	2 b
viii. 1.	2 b	xli. 10, 23.	3	xlviii. 1.	2 a
x. 25.	2 b	Jer. i. 17.	2 b	xlviii. 39.	2 e
1 Sam. xvii. 11.	2 b	viii. 9.	2 a	xlix. 37.	2 c
2 Kings xix. 26.	2 a	x. 2, 2.	2 b	l. 36.	2 a
1 Chron. xxii. 13.	2 b	xvii. 18, 18.	2 b	Ezek. ii. 6.	2 b
xxviii. 20.	2 b	xxiii. 4.	2 b	iii. 9.	2 b
2 Chron. xx. 15, 17.	2 b	xxx. 10.	2 b	Obad. 9.	2 a
xxxii. 7.	2 b				

DISMISS

פָּטַר to let loose. KAL *pret.* 2 Chron. xxiii. 8.

DISOBEY

מָרָה to rebel. KAL *pret.* 1 Kings xiii. 21, 26. HIPHIL *fut.* Neh. ix. 26.

DISPATCH

בָּרָא to cut ; to cut down, *e. g.* with a sword. PIEL *inf.* Ezek. xxiii. 47.

DISPERSE

1 זָרָה to scatter, to disperse. NIPHAL ª *fut.* PIEL ᵇ *pret.* ᶜ *inf.* ᵈ *fut.*

2 נָפַץ to dash and break in pieces, so as to disperse and scatter abroad. KAL *part.* Paül.

3 פּוּץ to break or dash in pieces ; to scatter, disperse, dissipate. KAL ª *imp.* ᵇ *fut.* ᶜ *part.* Paül. ᵈ תְּפוֹצָה *f.* dispersion.

4 פָּזַר to scatter, disperse, to distribute largely. PIEL *pret.*

5 פָּרַד to separate, or sever. PUAL *part.* Esth. iii. 8, separated in a moral sense.

6 פָּרַץ to break forth violently. KAL *fut.*

1 Sam. xiv. 34.	3 a	Prov. xv. 7.	1 d	Ezek. xxii. 15.	1 b
2 Chron. xi. 23.	6	Isa. xi. 12.	1 b	xxix. 12.	1 b
Esth. iii. 8.	5	Jer. xxv. 34.	3 d	xxx. 23, 26.	1 b
Ps. cxii. 9.	4	Ezek. xii. 15.	1 b	xxxvi. 19.	1 a
Prov. v. 16.	3 b	xx. 23.	1 c	Zeph. iii. 10.	3 c

DISPLAY

נָסַס to lift, to display. HITHPOLEL *inf.* Ps. lx. 4, or from נוּס to flee ; to betake oneself to flight.

DISPLEASE

1 אֹזֶן *m.* ear.

2 אָנַף to show oneself angry. KAL *pret.*

3 בְּאֵשׁ Ch. to be bad, evil, *seq.* עַל to displease. P'AL *pret.*

4 זָעֵף *adj.* angry ; see *Indignation.*

5 חֵמָה heat of anger, wrath, hot displeasure.

6 חָרָה to be angry, wroth. KAL ª *part.* ᵇ *fut.* ᶜ חָרוֹן *m.* wrath ; "sore displeasure."

7 יָרַע to fare ill, to be evil. KAL ª *fut.*

8 עַיִן *com.* eye.

9 עָצַב to grieve. KAL *pret.*

10 עָשָׂה to do. KAL *fut.*

11 קָצַף to break out in anger, to be wroth. KAL ᵃpret. ᵇpart.
Poel. ᶜקֶצֶף m. displeasure.

12 רָעַע to be evil. KAL ᵃpret. ᵇרַע adj. evil.

Gen. xxxi. 35.a.	6 b, 8	2 Sam. vi. 8.	6 b	Ps. xxxviii. 1.		5
xxxviii. 10.β	7 a, 8	xi. 25.β	7 a, 8	lx. 1.		2
xlviii. 17.β	7 a, 8	xi. 27.β	7 a, 8	Prov. xxiv. 18.β	12 a, 8	
Num. xi. 1.γ	12 b, 1	1 Kings i. 6.	9	Isa. lix. 15.β	7 a, 8	
xi. 10.β	12 a, 8	xx. 43.	4	Dan. vi. 14.		3
xxii. 34.β	12 a, 8	xxi. 4.	4	Jonah iv. 1.δ	7 a, 12 b	
Deut. ix. 19.	5	1 Chron. xiii. 11.	6 b	Hab. iii. 8.		6 a
Judg. xv. 3.	12 b	xxi. 7.β	7 a, 8	Zech. i. 2.		11 a c
1 Sam. viii. 6.β	7 a, 8	Ps. ii. 5.	6 c	i. 15.ε		11 a c
xviii. 8.β	7 a, 8	vi. 1.	5	i. 15.		11 b
xxix. 7.	10, 12 b, 8					

a *lit.* let it not be displeasing in the eyes of.   β *lit.* evil in the eyes of.
γ *lit.* it was evil in the ears of.   δ *lit.* displeased with great grief.   ε *lit.* I
am displeased with great displeasure.

DISPOSE, DISPOSING

שׂוּם to set, put, place. KAL *pret.* Job xxxiv. 13; *inf.* Job
xxxvii. 15.

מִשְׁפָּט judgment; right: Prov. xvi. 33.

DISPOSSESS

יָרַשׁ to take possession; Hiphil with *acc.* of *pers.* to seize upon
one's possessions, to dispossess. HIPHIL *pret.* Num.
xxxiii. 53: Judg. xi. 23. *inf.* Deut. vii. 17. *fut.* Num.
xxxii. 39.

DISPUTE

יָכַח to be right; to shew to be right. NIPHAL, to have right
demonstrated, implying submission to conviction. *part.*
Job xxiii. 7.

DISQUIET

הָמָה (see *Noise*), of internal emotion, tumult; of a mind agitated and disquieted by cares, anxiety, &c. KAL *fut.*
Ps. xxxix. 6; xlii. 5, 11; xliii. 5.

נְהָמָה f. roaring of the sea, groaning of the afflicted: Ps. xxxviii. 8.

רָגַז to be moved, disturbed, thrown into commotion. KAL *pret.*
Prov. xxx. 21. HIPHIL *pret.* 1 Sam. xxviii. 15: Jer. l.
34.

DISSEMBLE

כָּחַשׁ to fail, to deny. PIEL *pret.* Josh. vii. 11.

נָכַר to look upon, to behold; to know; not to let oneself be
known, to feign, dissemble. NIPHAL *fut.* Prov. xxvi. 24.

עָלַם to hide, conceal. NIPHAL *part.* Ps. xxvi. 4.

תָּעָה to go astray; to seduce, to use deceit. HIPHIL *pret.* Jer.
xlii. 20.

DISSOLVE

מוּג to melt, to flow down; to be dissolved with fear and terror.
NIPHAL *pret.* Isa. xiv. 31: Nah. ii. 6. *part.* Ps. lxxv. 3.
POLEL *fut.* Job xxx. 22.

מָקַק to melt, to pine away. NIPHAL *pret.* Isa. xxxiv. 4, *i. e.*
shall be melted. Vitringa supposes the figure of wax
tapers is here intended. Maurer, to pine away.

פָּרַר to break, to break in pieces. KAL *inf.* Isa. xxiv. 19,
lit. dissolving is dissolved. HITHPOLEL *pret.* Isa. xxiv.
19.

שְׁרָא Ch. to loose, to unbind, to solve, *e. g.* knotty questions.
P'AL *inf.* Dan. v. 16. PAEL *part.* Dan. v. 12.

DISTAFF

פֶּלֶךְ m. a circle; whirl of a spindle, and hence for the spindle
itself: Prov. xxxi. 19.

DISTIL

נָזַל to flow or run down; it implies the natural tendency of a
fluid to run down, and is very suitably used of speech.
KAL *fut.* Deut. xxxii. 2.

רָעַף to drop, to distil. KAL *fut.* Job xxxvi. 28.

DISTINCTLY

פָּרַשׁ to separate, to distinguish. PUAL *part.* Neh. viii. 8.

DISTRACTED

פּוּן to be perplexed, distracted. KAL *fut.* Ps. lxxxviii. 15.
LXX. ἐξηπορήθην. Vulg. "conturbatus sum." Compare
ἀδημονεῖν. St. Matt. xxvi. 37; St. Mark xiv. 33, "to be
very heavy," utterly weighed down with deepest sorrow,
causing utter perplexity, and distraction.

DISTRESS

1 יָצַר to be straitened, narrow; to be in distress, anxiety; implying a sore strait, from which there seems no way of
escape. KAL *fut.*

2 נָגַשׂ to urge, to impel, to drive; to be harassed, wearied, distressed. NIPHAL *pret.*

3 צוּק to be compressed; to distress by oppression. HIPHIL ᵃpret.
ᵇfut. ᶜpart. ᵈמָצוֹק m. distress. ᵉמְצוּקָה f. id.

4 צוּר to straiten, to press upon; to press upon in a hostile sense.
KAL *fut.*

5 צָרַר to press; to press upon, to persecute, to be hostile; to be
pressed, straitened, distressed. KAL ᵃpret. HIPHIL ᵇpret.
ᶜinf. צַר m. distress, affliction. ᵒצָרָה f. distress. מֵצַר
m. distress.

6 קוּץ to loathe, with chagrin and abhorrence; to feel irksome.
KAL *fut.*

7 רַע adj. evil.

Gen. xxii. 7.	1	1 Sam. xxx. 6.	1	Ps. cxviii. 5.	5 f
xxxv. 3.	5 e	2 Sam. i. 26.	5 a	cxx. 1.	5 e
xlii. 21.	5 e	xxii. 7.	5 d	Prov. i. 27.	5 e
Num. xxii. 3.	6	1 Kings i. 29.	5 e	Isa. xxv. 4.	5 d
Deut. ii. 9, 19.	4	2 Chron. xxviii. 20.	4	xxix. 2.	3 a
xxviii. 53, 55, 57.	3 b	xxviii. 22.	5 c	xxix. 7.	3 c
Judg. ii. 15.	1	Neh. ii. 17.	7	Jer. x. 18.	5 b
x. 9.	1	ix. 37.	5 e	Lam. i. 20.	5 a
xi. 7.	5 d	Ps. iv. 1.	5 d	Ezek. xxx. 16.	5 d
1 Sam. xiii. 6.	2	xviii. 6.	5 d	Obad. 12, 14.	5 e
xiv. 24.	2	xxv. 17.	3 e	Zeph. i. 15.	3 e
xxii. 2.	3 d	cvii. 6, 13, 19, 28.	3 e	l. 17.	5 b
xxviii. 15.	5 a				

DISTRIBUTE

חָלַק to divide, to distribute, to appropriate, especially by lot.
KAL *pret.* 2 Chron. xxiii. 18; *inf.* Neh. xiii. 13. NIPHAL
fut. 1 Chron. xxiv. 3. PIEL *fut.* Job xxi. 17.

נָתַן to give. KAL *inf.* 2 Chron. xxxi. 14.

DITCH

גֵּב m. a pit or ditch: 2 Kings iii. 16, *lit.* ditches ditches.

מִקְוָה f. gathering place for waters, pool, reservoir: Isa. xxii. 11.

שׁוּחָה f. slough, or clay-pit: Prov. xxiii. 27.

שַׁחַת *f.* corruption ; a pit ; a cistern, having mire at the bottom : Job ix. 31 : Ps. vii. 15.

DIVERS, DIVERSE

אֱנֹשׁ *m.* man : 2 Chron. xxx. 11, *lit.* men.

כִּלְאַיִם *dual,* separation, things separated, diverse : Lev. xix. 19 : Deut. xxii. 9.

שְׁנָא *Ch.* to be changed, to be different from. PA'L *fut.* Dan. vii. 23, 24 : *part.* Dan. vii. 3, 19. PAEL *part.* Dan. vii. 7.

שָׁנָה to change, to be doubled. KAL *part.* Poel, Esth. i. 7 ; iii. 8.

DIVIDE

1 בָּדַל to separate, divide, to distinguish. HIPHIL [a] *pret.* [b] *inf.* [c] *fut.* [d] *part.*

2 בָּקַע to cleave, divide. KAL [a] *pret.* [b] *imp.* [c] *part.* Poel. NIPHAL [d] *fut.*

3 בָּתַר to cut in pieces, to cut off. KAL [a] *pret.* PIEL [b] *fut.*

4 גָּזַר to cut asunder, to divide. KAL [a] *imp.* [b] *part.* Poel.

5 חָלַק to divide into parts, portions, &c., each receiving his portion ; to part, distribute, especially by lot ; to distribute oneself. KAL [a] *pret.* [b] *imp.* [c] *fut.* NIPHAL [d] *fut.* PIEL [e] *pret.* [f] *inf.* [g] *imp.* [h] *fut.* PUAL [i] *pret.* [k] *fut.* HITHP. [l] *pret.* [m] חֶלְקָה *f.* division. [n] מַחֲלֹקֶת *f.* order, course.

6 חָצַב to hew, to cut out, to divide by fissure. KAL *part.* Poel.

7 חָצָה to divide or part in two ; to share, to distribute, in parts equal or unequal. KAL [a] *pret.* [b] *fut.* NIPHAL [c] *fut.*

8 נָחַל to divide for an inheritance, or by inheritance. KAL [a] *inf.* [b] *fut.* PIEL [c] *pret.* [d] *inf.* HIPHIL [e] *inf.* [f] *fut.* HITHPAEL [g] *pret.*

9 נָפַל to fall. HIPHIL, to cast lots, to divide by lot : [a] *pret.* [b] *inf.* [c] *imp.* [d] *fut.*

10 נָתַח to cut in pieces. PIEL *fut.*

11 פְּדוּת *f.* division, distinction, from the primary sense of cutting or setting free ; also liberation, redemption.

12 פָּלַג to cleave, to divide. NIPHAL [a] *pret.* PIEL [b] *pret.* [c] *imp.* פְּלַג *Ch.* PA'L [d] *part. passive.* [e] פְּלַג *Ch. m.* half. [f] פְּלַגָּה *f.* division, class ; Gesenius, rivers, streams. [g] פְּלֻגָּה *f.* division, class. [h] פְּלֻגָּה *Ch. f. id.* [i] מִפְלַגּוֹת *f. id.*

13 פָּרַד to break off, to separate by breaking. NIPHAL *pret.*

14 פָּרַס to break, or distribute ; to divide in a certain order or proportion. HIPHIL [a] *pret.* [b] *fut.* [c] *part.* פְּרַס *Ch. id.* PA'L [d] *part. passive.*

15 פָּרַר to break, to break in pieces. POEL *pret.*

16 רָגַע to make a noise, to throw into tumultuous agitation, to shake ; to break with a noise, to burst, to divide. Others, to terrify, to make afraid ; to restrain by threats. KAL [a] *pret.* [b] *part.* Poel.

17 רוּץ to run. HIPHIL, to divide speedily : *fut.*

18 שָׁלַשׁ to divide into three parts. PIEL *pret.*

Gen. i. 4, 7.	1 c	Josh. xiii. 6.	9 c	Job xxxviii. 25.	12 b
i. 6. α	1 d	xiii. 7.	5 g	Ps. xxix. 7.	6
i. 14, 18.	1 b	xiv. 5.	5 c	lv. 9.	12 c
x. 5, 32.	13	xviii. 5.	5 l	lx. 6.	5 h
x. 25.	12 a	xviii. 10, 10.	5 h n	lxviii. 12.	5 h
xiv. 15.		xix. 49.	8 a	lxxiv. 13.	15
xv. 10, 10.	3 b a	xix. 51, 51.	8 c, 5 f	lxxviii. 13.	2 a
xxxii. 7.	7 b	xxii. 8.	5 b	lxxviii. 55.	9 d
xxxiii. 1.	7 b	xxiii. 4.	9 a	cviii. 7.	5 b
	5 h	Judg. v. 15, 16.	12 f	cxxxvi. 13.	4 b
Exod. viii. 23.	11	v. 30.	5 h	Prov. xvi. 19.	5 f
xiv. 16.	2 b	vii. 16.	7 b	Isa. ix. 3.	5 f
xiv. 21.	2 d	ix. 43.	7 b	xxxiii. 23.	5 i
xv. 9.	5 h	xix. 29.	10	xxxiv. 17.	5 e
xxi. 35, 35.	7 a b	2 Sam. i. 23.	13	liii. 12, γ 12.	5 h
xxvi. 33.	1 a	xix. 29.	5 c	lxiii. 12.	2 c
Lev. i. 17.	1 c	1 Kings iii. 25, 26.	14 a	Jer. xxxi. 35.	16 b
v. 8.	1 c	xvi. 21.	5 d	li. 15.	5 h
xi. 4, 4, 7, 26.	14 c	xviii. 6.	5 h	Lam. iv. 16.	5 a
xi. 5.	14 b	2 Kings ii. 8.	7 c	Ezek. v. 1.	5 e
xi. 6.	14 a	1 Chron. i. 19.	5 c	xvii. 22.	9 b
Num. xxvi. 53, 55, 56.	5 d	xxiii. 6.	5 d	xlv. 1.	9 b
xxxi. 27, 42.	7 a	xxiv. 1. β	5 n	xlvii. 21.	5 c
xxxiii. 54.	8 g	xxiv. 4, 5.	5 n	xlvii. 22.	9 d
xxxiv. 18.	8 a	xxvi. 1, 12, 19.	5 n	xlviii. 29.	9 d
xxxiv. 29.	8 d	2 Chron. xxxv. 5,		Dan. ii. 41.	12 d
Deut. iv. 19.	5 a	5.	12 g, 5 m	v. 28.	14 d
xiv. 7, 7.	14 c a	xxxv. 12.	12 i	vii. 25.	12 e
xiv. 8.	14 c	xxxv. 13.	17	xi. 4.	7 c
xix. 3.	18	Ezra vi. 18.	12 h	xi. 39.	5 h
xxxii. 8.	8 e	Neh. ix. 11.	2 a	Hos. x. 2.	5 a
Josh. i. 6.	8 f	ix. 22.	5 c	Amos vii. 17.	5 a
xi. 23.	5 n	xi. 36.	5 n	Micah ii. 4.	5 h
xii. 7.	5 n	Job xxvi. 12.	16 a	Zech. xiv. 1.	5 i
		xxvii. 17.	5 c		

[a] *lit.* let it be separating, *i.e.* by a continued act. [β] *lit.* unto the sons .... their divisions. [γ] *or,* assign him a portion in the many.

DIVINE

1 נָחַשׁ to take auguries, to practise divination, to divine ; in a wider sense, to divine, to prognosticate, to feel presages. PIEL [a] *inf.* [b] *fut.*

2 קָסַם to divine, to practise divination, used in the verb only of false prophets of the Hebrews, of necromancers, of prophets of the Philistines, of Balaam. KAL [a] *inf.* [b] *imp.* [c] *fut.* [d] *part.* Poel. [e] קֶסֶם *m.* divination, rewards of divination ; once in a good sense, "divine sentence." [f] מִקְסָם *m. id.*

Gen. xliv. 5. α	1 a b	Prov. xvi. 10.	2 e	Ezek. xiii. 23, 23.	2 c e
xliv. 15. α	1 a b	Isa. xliii. 25.	2 d	xxi. 21.	2 a e
Num. xxii. 7.	2 e	Jer. xiv. 14.	2 e	xxi. 22.	2 e
xxiii. 23.	2 e	xxvii. 9.	2 e	xxi. 23, 29.	2 a
Deut. xviii. 10.	2 d e	xxix. 8.	2 d	xxii. 28.	2 d
xviii. 14.	2 d	Ezek. xii. 24.	2 f	Micah iii. 6.	2 a
1 Sam. vi. 2.	2 d	xiii. 6.	2 e	iii. 7.	2 d
xxviii. 8.	2 b	xiii. 7.	2 f	iii. 11.	2 c
2 Kings xvii. 17.	2 c e	xiii. 9.	2 d	Zech. x. 2.	2 d

[a] *lit.* divining divineth.

DIVORCE

גָּרַשׁ to cast out. KAL *part.* Paül, Lev. xxi. 14 ; xxii. 13 : Num. xxx. 9.

כְּרִיתוּת *f.* cutting off : Deut. xxiv. 1, 3 : Isa. l. 1 : Jer. iii. 8.

DO

1 בַּעַל *m.* master, owner, &c.

2 בָּרָא to create ; to make ; to do. NIPHAL *pret.*

3 גָּמַל to do, shew, or cause to any one, good or evil, to deal well or ill with him, with *dupl. acc.* of person and of thing. KAL [a] *pret.* [b] *part.*

4 גָּרַע to take away ; to diminish, to do away. NIPHAL *fut.*

5 דָּבָר *m.* word, matter, &c.

6 חָטָא to sin, to do (sin). KAL *pret.*

7 טוֹב to do (good). HIPHIL *pret.*

8   יָטַב   to do (good). HIPHIL *fut.*

9   יָסַף   to add. HIPHIL *fut.*

10   כָּלָה   to be completed, perfected, finished, done. KAL ᵃ*pret.* PIEL ᵇ*pret.* ᶜ*inf.* ᵈ*fut.*

11   מָעַל   to deal covertly, to act treacherously; see *Trespass.* KAL ᵃ*inf.* ᵇ*fut.*

12   נָתַן   to give. NIPHAL *fut.*

13   עָבַד   to labour, to work, to do work; to serve. KAL ᵃ*pret.* ᵇ*inf.* ᶜ*fut.* עֲבַד Ch. id. PA'L ᵈ*pret.* ᵉ*inf.* ᶠ*fut.* ᵍ*part. active.* ITHP'AL ʰ*fut.*

14   עָבַר   to pass; to cause to pass, to do away. HIPHIL *imp.*

15   עָלַל   to roll; to do anything in repetition or with frequency; to do a deed, as with earnestness, to perform, to accomplish; to do evil to any one, to vex, to maltreat, *seq.* לְ of person; see also *Abuse, Mock, seq.* בְּ. POEL ᵃ*pret.* ᵇ*imp.* POAL ᶜ*pret.* ᵈ עֲלִילָה *f.* deed, work; deeds of men, especially in a bad sense; yet used of the doings of God in a good sense, showing the essential difference of the agent. ᵉ מַעֲלָל *m.* work; twice applied to the illustrious deeds of God, and chiefly to the evil works of men. כתיב מַעֲלִיל *m. id.*

16   עָשָׂה   to work, to labour, to do; to begin or attempt to do, Exod. viii. 18; to make, to do, to produce by labour; *emphat.* to effect, to execute, to accomplish a thing proposed, to purpose; to do, *i. e.* to perform the laws of God, his will, precepts, &c., also to do or commit wrong, &c., *seq.* לְ of person; sometimes the thing done is omitted, and to be gathered only from the context; instead of לְ is found also עִם, and אֵת. *Seq.* בְּ to do with any one, to deal with him, according to one's own pleasure, Jer. xviii. 23. Often עָשָׂה is so put as to express the simple idea of a verb of action, to do, to act, rendered definite only by the context or the circumstance. With *inf.*, do indeed, certainly. KAL ᵃ*pret.* ᵇ*inf.* ᶜ*imp.* ᵈ*fut.* ᵉ*part.* Poel. ᶠ*part.* Paül. NIPHAL ᵍ*pret.* ʰ*inf.* ⁱ*fut.* ᵏ*part.* ˡ מַעֲשֶׂה *m.* work.

17   פָּעַל   to make, to do; to practise righteousness, iniquity, &c. *Seq. acc.* and לְ of thing, and לְ of person. KAL ᵃ*pret.* ᵇ*fut.* ᶜ*part.* Poel. ᵈ פֹּעַל *m.* deed, work.

18   שׂוּם   to put, set, place. KAL ᵃ*pret.* ᵇ*inf.*

19   שָׁלוֹם   *m.* peace.

20   שָׁנָה   to do anything a second time, do again. KAL *fut.*

21   תָּמַם   to complete, to perfect, to finish. KAL ᵃ*pret.* ᵇ*inf.*

Gen. iii. 13, 14.	16 a	Gen. xxi. 1.	16 d	Gen. xxx. 26.	13 a
iv. 10.	16 a	xxi. 22.	16 e	xxx. 31.	16 d
vi. 22, 22.	16 d a	xxi. 23, 23.	16 a d	xxxi. 12.	16 e
vii. 5.	16 d	xxi. 26.	16 a	xxxi. 16.	16 c
viii. 21.	16 a	xxii. 12.	16 a	xxxi. 26.	16 a
ix. 24.	16 a	xxii. 16.	16 a	xxxi. 28, 29.	16 b
xi. 6, 6.	16 b	xxiv. 15, 22.	10 b	xxxi. 43.	16 d
xii. 18.	16 a	xxiv. 19, 19.	10 d b	xxxiv. 7.	16 a
xvi. 6.	16 c	xxiv. 45.	10 d	xxxiv. 14,β 19.	16 b
xviii. 5, 29, 30.	16 d	xxiv. 66.	16 a	xxxviii. 10.	16 e
xviii. 17.	16 e	xxvi. 10.	16 a	xxxix. 3, 22, 22, 23.	16 e
xviii. 19.	16 b	xxvi. 29, 29.	16 d a	xxxix. 9.	16 d
xviii. 21.	16 d	xxvii. 19, 45.	16 a	xxxix. 11.	16 d
xviii. 25, 25.	16 b d	xxvii. 37.	16 d	xxxix. 19.	16 a
xix. 8, 8.α	16 c d	xxviii. 15.	16 a	xl. 15.	16 b
xix. 22.β	16 b	xxix. 25.	16 a	xli. 25, 28.	16 e
xx. 5, 6, 10.	16 a	xxix. 26.	16 i	xli. 34, 55.	16 b
xx. 9, 9, 9.	16 a a i	xxix. 28.	16 d	xlii. 20, 25.	16 d

Gen. xlii. 18.	16 c	Lev. xxiii. 3, 3.	16 i d	Deut. xv. 17, 18.	16 d
xlii. 28.	16 a	xxiii. 7, 8, 21, 25, 28,		xvi. 8.	16 d
xliii. 11.	16 c	30, 31, 35, 36.	16 d	xvi. 12.	16 a
xliii. 17.	16 d	xxiv. 19, 19.	16 a i	xvii. 10, 10.	16 a b
xliv. 2.	16 d	xxiv. 20.	12	xvii. 11, 12.	16 d
xliv. 5, 15.	16 a	xxiv. 23.	16 a	xvii. 19.	16 b
xliv. 7, 17.	16 b	xxv. 18, 18.	16 a	xviii. 9.	16 b
xlv. 17, 19.	16 c	xxvi. 3.	16 a	xviii. 12.	16 e
xlv. 21.	16 a	xxvi. 14, 16.	16 d	xix. 9.	16 b
xlvii. 30.	16 b	xxvi. 15.	16 b	xix. 19, 19.	16 a b
l. 12.	16 d	Num. i. 54, 54.	16 d a	xx. 15.	16 d
l. 15, 17.	3 a	ii. 34.	16 d	xxi. 9.	16 d
Exod. i. 17, 18.	16 a	iii. 7, 8.	13 b	xxii. 3, 3, 3, 26.	16 d
ii. 4.	16 i	iii. 9.	16 b	xxii. 5.	16 e
iii. 16.	6 f	iv. 19.	16 c	xxiv. 8, 8, 18, 22.	16 b
iii. 20.	16 d	iv. 23, 30, 47.	13 b	xxiv. 9.	16 a
iii. 15, 17, 30.	16 d	v. 4, 4.	16 d a	xxv. 9.	16 i
iv. 21.	16 a	v. 6.	11 a	xxv. 16, 16.	16 e
vi. 1.	16 d	v. 7.	16 a	xxv. 17.	16 a
vii. 6, 6.	16 d a	v. 27.	11 b	xxvi. 14.	16 a
vii. 10, 11, 20, 22.	16 d	vi. 21.	16 d	xxvi. 16, 16.	16 b a
viii. 7, 13, 17, 18,		vii. 5.	13 b	xxvii. 10.	16 a
24, 31.	16 d	viii. 3, 7, 26.	16 b	xxvii. 26.	16 a
viii. 26.	16 b	viii. 19.	13 b	xxviii. 1, 13, 15, 58.	16 b
ix. 5, 6.	16 d	viii. 20, 20.	16 d a	xxviii. 20, 20.	16 d, 15 e
x. 2.	18 a	viii. 22, 22.	8 b, 16 a	xxix. 2, 24.	16 a
xi. 10.	16 a	viii. 26.	13 c	xxix. 9, 9.	16 a d
xii. 16, 16.	16 i	ix. 5.	16 a	xxix. 29.	16 b
xii. 28, 28.	16 d a	ix. 14.	16 d	xxx. 8.	16 b
xii. 35.	16 a	x. 32, 32.	8, 7	xxx. 12, 13.	16 d
xii. 50, 50.	16 d a	xiv. 22.	16 a	xxx. 14.	16 b
xiii. 8.	16 a	xiv. 28, 35.	16 d	xxxi. 4, 4, 5.	16 a
xiv. 4.	16 d	xv. 11, 34.	16 i	xxxi. 4.	16 b
xiv. 5, 31.	16 a	xv. 12, 13, 14, 14,		xxxi. 29.	16 d
xv. 11.	16 e	30.	16 d	xxxii. 27.	17 a
xv. 26.	16 a	xv. 39, 40.	16 a	xxxii. 46.	16 b
xvi. 17.	16 d	xvi. 6.	16 c	xxxiv. 9.	16 b
xvii. 4, 6, 10.	16 d	xvi. 9.	13 b	xxxiv. 11.	16 b
xviii. 1, 8, 9.	16 d	xvi. 28.	16 b	Josh. i. 7, 8.	16 b
xviii. 14, 14, 17.	16 e	xvii. 11, 11.	16 a d	i. 16.	16 d
xviii. 20, 23, 24.	16 a	xviii. 6.	13 b	ii. 10.	16 a
xix. 4.	16 d	xx. 27.	16 d	iii. 5.	16 d
xix. 8.	16 a	xxi. 34, 34.	16 a	iv. 8.	16 d
xx. 9.	16 a	xxii. 2, 28.	16 d	iv. 23.	16 a
xx. 10.	16 d	xxii. 17, 20.	16 d	v. 8.	21 a
xxi. 11.	16 a	xxii. 18, 30.	16 b	v. 15.	16 d
xxi. 30.	16 d	xxiii. 2, 19, 26, 30.	16 a	vi. 3.	16 d
xxi. 31.	16 i	xxiii. 11.	16 a	vi. 14.	16 a
xxii. 30.	16 d	xxiii. 12, 24.	16 b	vii. 19, 20.	16 a
xxiii. 12, 24.	16 d	xxiv. 14.	16 d	vii. 19, 2.	16 a
xxiii. 22.	16 a	xxiv. 18.	16 e	viii. 8.	16 d
xxiv. 3, 7.	16 d	xxiv. 23.	18 b	ix. 3, 9, 10.	16 a
xxiv. 14.γ	1	xxvii. 4.	4	ix. 20, 24, 26.	16 d
xxix. 1, 41.	16 d	xxvii. 22.	16 d	ix. 25, 25.	16 b c
xxix. 35.	16 a	xxviii. 18, 25, 26.	16 d	x. 1, 1, 28, 30, 32,	
xxxi. 11.	16 d	xxviii. 1, 7, 12, 35,		35, 37, 39, 39, 39.	16 a
xxxi. 14.	16 e	39.	16 d	x. 23, 25, 28, 30.	16 d
xxxi. 15, 15.	16 i e	xxx. 2.	16 d	xi. 9.	16 d
xxxii. 14.	16 b	xxxi. 31.	16 d	xi. 15.	16 a
xxxii. 21.	16 a	xxxii. 8.	16 a	xiv. 5.	16 a
xxxii. 28.	16 d	xxxii. 13.	16 e	xiv. 5.	16 b
xxxiii. 5, 17.	16 d	xxxii. 20, 23, 24, 25,		xxii. 5.	16 b
xxxiv. 10, 10,		31.	16 d	xxii. 24.	16 a
10.	16 d, 2, 16 e	xxxiii. 56, 56.	16 d b	xxii. 27.	13 b
xxxiv. 33.	16 d	xxxvi. 10.	16 a	xxiii. 3, 8.	16 a
xxxv. 1.	16 b	Deut. i. 14.	16 d	xxiii. 6.	16 b
xxxv. 2, 2.	16 i e	i. 18, 44.	16 d	xxiv. 5, 7, 17, 31.	16 a
xxxv. 35.	16 e	i. 30.	16 a	Judg. i. 7.	16 a
xxxvi. 2.	16 b	ii. 12, 22, 29.	16 a	ii. 2, 7, 10, 17.	16 a
xxxvi. 29.	16 a	iii. 2, 2, 6.	16 a	ii. 11.	16 d
xxxix. 32, 32.	16 d a	iii. 21, 21.	16 a d	ii. 19.	15 e
xxxix. 43, 43.	16 a	iii. 24.	16 d	iii. 7.	16 d
xl. 16, 16.	16 d a	iv. 1, 5, 14.	16 d	iii. 12, ζ 12.	16 b a
Lev. iv. 2, 2.	16 i a	iv. 3, 6, 25, 34.	16 a	iv. 1, ζ	16 b
iv. 13, 13.	16 a i	v. 1, 32.	16 b	vi. 1, 20, 40.	16 b
iv. 20, 20, 20.	16 a a d	v. 13, 27, 31.	16 a	vi. 27, 27, 27.	16 d b d
iv. 22, 22.	16 a	v. 31.	16 a	vi. 29, 29.	16 a
iv. 27, 27.	16 b i	v. 14.	16 d	vii. 17, 17, 17.	16 d
v. 17.δ	16 i	vi. 1, 3, 24, 25.	16 b	viii. 2.	16 a
vi. 3, 7.	16 d	vi. 18.	16 a	viii. 3.	16 b
viii. 4, 36.	16 d	vii. 11.	16 b	ix. 16, 16, 33, 56.	16 a
viii. 5.	16 b	vii. 12, 18.	16 a	ix. 48, 48.	16 a c
viii. 34, 34.	16 a b	vii. 19.	16 d	x. 6, ζ	16 b
ix. 6.	16 d	viii. 1.	16 b	x. 15.	16 c
x. 7.	16 d	ix. 18.	16 b	xi. 27.	16 e
xi. 32.	16 i	x. 21.	16 a	xi. 10, 39.	16 c
xvi. 15, 15.	16 a	xi. 3, 4, 5, 6, 7.	16 a	xi. 27.	16 c
xvi. 16, 29, 34.	16 d	xi. 22, 32.	16 b	xi. 36.	16 e
xviii. 3, 3, 3, 3.	16 l d, l d	xii. 1, 32.	16 b	xi. 37. ζ	16 i
xviii. 4, 5.	16 d	xii. 4, 14, 25, 28,		xiii. 1, 19.	16 b
xviii. 27.	16 a	30.	16 d	xiii. 8.	16 d
xviii. 30.	16 d	xii. 8, 8.	16 d e	xiii. 12.	16 l
xix. 15, 35.	16 d	xii. 31, 31.	16 d a	xiv. 6.	16 a
xix. 37.	16 a	xiii. 11, ε 18.	16 d	xiv. 10.	16 c
xx. 8, 22.	16 a	xiv. 29.	16 b	xv. 3.	16 e
xxii. 31.	16 a	xv. 5.	16 b		

Ezek. xx. 21, 21.	16 b d	Ezek. xliv. 14.	16 i	Amos iii. 6.	16 a
xx. 43, 44.	15 d	xlv. 20, 25.	16 d	iii. 7.	16 d
xxi. 24.	15 d	xlvi. 12.	16 d	iii. 10.	16 b
xxii. 14.	16 a	Dan. iv. 35, 35.	13 g d	iv. 12, 12.	16 d
xxiii. 30.	16 b	vi. 10.	13 g	ix. 12.	16 d
xxiii. 38, 39.	16 a	vi. 22.	13 d	Obad. 15, 15.	16 a i
xxiii. 48. φ	16 d	viii. 4.	16 a	Jonah i. 10, 14.	16 a
xxiv. 14, 14.	16 a, 15 d	viii. 27.	16 d	i. 11.	16 d
xxiv. 18.	16 d	ix. 12, 12.	16 g	iii. 10, 10.	16 b a
xxiv. 19.	16 e	ix. 14.	16 a	Micah ii. 7.	15 e
xxiv. 22, 22.	16 a	ix. 19.	16 c	iii. 4.	15 e
xxiv. 24, 24.	16 a d	xi. 3, 17, 24, 24, 28,		vi. 3.	16 a
xxv. 14.	16 a	30, 32, 39.	16 a	vi. 8.	16 b
xxxiii. 14, 16, 19.	16 a	xi. 16.	16 d	vii. 13.	15 e
xxxiii. 31.	16 d	xi. 36, 36.	16 a g	Zeph. iii. 5, 13.	16 d
xxxiii. 32.	16 e	Hos. iv. 9.	15 e	iii. 7, 11.	15 d
xxxv. 11.	16 a	v. 4.	15 e	Hag. i. 14.	16 d
xxxv. 15.	16 d	vi. 4, 4.	16 d	Zech. i. 4.	15 e
xxxvi. 17, 19.	15 d	vii. 2.	15 e	i. 6, 6.	16 b, 15 e
xxxvi. 22, 32.	16 e	ix. 5.	15 e	i. 21.	16 b
xxxvi. 27, 36.	16 a	x. 3.	15 e	viii. 16.	16 a
xxxvi. 31.	15 e	x. 15.	16 d	Mal. ii. 12, 13.	16 d
xxxvi. 37.	16 b	x. 17.	16 a	ii. 17.	16 d
xxxvii. 24.	16 a	xii. 8.	15 e	iv. 1, 3.	16 e
xxxix. 24.	16 a	Joel ii. 20, χ 21. χ	16 b		
xliii. 11, 11.	16 a				

a *lit.* do not a thing.   β *lit.* not able to do.   γ *lit.* who is a master of business.   δ *lit.* are not to be done.   ε *lit.* shall not add to do.   ζ *lit.* added to do evil.   η *lit.* doing thou shalt do.   θ *lit.* hast been evil to do.   ι *lit.* added to do.   κ *lit.* we shall do.   λ *lit.* to do.   μ *lit.* we did wickedly in doing.   ν *lit.* be doing.   ξ *lit.* is upon us to do.   ο *lit.* they returned to do evil.   π *lit.* to do.   ρ *lit.* magnified to do.   ς *lit.* thou shalt do.   τ *lit.* done ill in doing.   υ *lit.* doing will do.   φ *lit.* they shall not do.   χ *lit.* magnified to do.

DOCTRINE

מוּסָר *m.* chastisement, instruction, learning : Jer. x. 8.

לֶקַח *m.* fair speech, taking arguments ; doctrine, learning, knowledge, which one receives, perceives, learns : Deut. xxxii. 2 : Job xi. 4 : Prov. iv. 2 : Isa. xxix. 24.

שְׁמוּעָה *f.* tidings, message, news ; instruction, teaching : Isa. xxviii. 9.

DOG

כֶּלֶב *m.* a dog, so called from barking. Among the Hebrews, dogs were kept to guard houses and flocks ; but throughout the East they are mostly without masters, and wander, half-famished and fierce, in troops around the cities and villages ; whence *dogs* is often an appellation for fierce and cruel enemies. It was also a name of reproach. Exod. xi. 7, &c.

DOLEFUL

אֹחִים *m. pl. pr.* howlings, shrieks ; hence howling animals, doleful creatures : Isa. xiii. 21.

נְהִיָה *f.* lamentation : Micah ii. 4, *marg.* 'with a lamentation of lamentations.'

DOMINION

1   בָּעַל to have dominion and authority as lord and proprietor. KAL *pret.*

2   יד *com.* hand, cf. Jer. xxxiv. 1.

3   מָשַׁל to reign, to be superior in power, authority, and dominion, as a governor. KAL [a] *pret.* [b] *inf.* [c] *fut.* [d] *part.* Poel. HIPHIL [e] *inf.* [f] *fut.* [g] מֹשֵׁל *m.* dominion. [h] מִמְשָׁל *m. id.* [i] מֶמְשָׁלָה *f.* dominion, rule ; dominions, jurisdictions.

4   רָדָה to tread, to tread down ; to have dominion, to rule, to bear rule, *seq.* בְּ over any one, and *seq. acc. id.* KAL [a] *imp.* [b] *fut.* [c] *part.* Poel. PIEL [d] *fut.*

5   רוד according to the Rabbinical interpreters, of the same

meaning with the previous word, to have dominion. HIPHIL *fut.* Gen. xxvii. 40. See Bush's Notes on Genesis for other interpretations.

6   מִשְׁטָר *m.* dominion, empire.

7   שָׁלַט to rule, to have dominion. HIPHIL [a] *fut.* [b] שִׁלְטָן Ch. *m.* dominion, rule.

Gen. i. 26.	4 b	2 Chron. xxi. 8.	2	Isa. xxvi. 13.	1
i. 28.	4 a	Neh. ix. 28.	4 b	xxxix. 2.	3 i
xxvii. 40.	5	ix. 37.	3 d	Jer. xxxiv. 1.	3 i, 2
xxxvii. 8 *a*	3 b c	Job xxv. 2.	3 e	li. 28.	3 i
Num. xxiv. 19.	4 b	xxxviii. 33.	6	Dan. iv. 3, 22, 34, 34.	7 b
Judg. v. 13, 13.	4 d	Ps. viii. 6.	3 f	vi. 26, 26.	7 b
xiv. 4.	3 d	xix. 13.	3 c	vii. 6, 12, 14, 14, 14,	
1 Kings iv. 24.	4 c	xlix. 14.	4 b	26, 27, 27.	7 b
ix. 19.	3 i	lxxii. 8.	4 b	xi. 3.	3 h
2 Kings xx. 13.	3 i	ciii. 22.	3 i	xi. 4.	3 g
1 Chron. iv. 22.	1	cxiv. 2.	3 i	li. 5, 5, 5.	3 a i h
xviii. 3.	2	cxix. 133.	7 a	Micah iv. 8.	3 i
2 Chron. viii. 6.	1	cxlv. 13.	3 i	Zech. ix. 10.	3 g

a lit. having dominion shalt thou have dominion.

DOOR, DOORPOST, DOORKEEPER

1   בַּיִת *m.* house.

2   דַּל *m.* a door hanging on hinges. [a] דָּלָה *f. id.* [b] קְרִי. דֶּלֶת *f.* a door, gate, &c. ; in the *dual,* two-leaved doors.

3   סַף *m.* see *Threshold.* סָפַן *verb demon.* to stand or wait at the threshold. HITHPOEL [a] *inf.*

4   פֶּתַח *m.* an opening, entrance, doorway ; in a looser sense, door of a house, tent, ark, chamber, city, &c. : Gen. iv. 7, &c.

5   שַׁעַר *m.* gate. שׁוֹעֵר *m.* porter, doorkeeper.

6   מַשְׁקוֹף *m.* lintel, upper door-post.

No. 4 not included.

Gen. xix. 6, 9, 10.	2 b	2 Kings xii. 9.	3	Job xxxi. 32.	2 b
Exod. xii. 7.	6	xviii. 16.	2 b	xxxviii. 8, 10.	2 b
xxi. 6.	2 b	xxii. 4.	3	xxxviii. 17.	5
xxxv. 17.	5	xxiii. 4.	3	xli. 14.	2 b
Deut. xv. 7.	2 b	xxv. 18.	3	Ps. lxxviii. 23.	2 b
Josh. ii. 19.	2 b	1 Chron. xv. 23, 24.	5 a	lxxxiv. 10.	3 a
Judg. iii. 23, 24, 25.	2 b	xxii. 3.	2 b	cxli. 3.	2
xi. 31.	2 b	2 Chron. iii. 7.	2 b	Prov. xxvi. 14.	2 b
xvi. 3.	2 b	iv. 9, 9, 22, 22.	2 b	Eccles. xii. 4.	2 b
xix. 22, 27.	2 b	xxiii. 4.	3	Cant. viii. 9.	2 b
1 Sam. iii. 15.	2 b	xxviii. 24.	2 b	Isa. vi. 4.	3
xxi. 13.	2 b	xxix. 3, 7.	2 b	xxvi. 20.	2 a, or 2 b
2 Sam. xiii. 17, 18.	2 b	xxxiv. 9.	3	lvii. 8.	2 b
1 Kings vi. 31, 32, 34,		Neh. iii. 1, 3, 6, 13, 14,		Jer. xxxv. 4.	2 b
34, 34.	2 b	vi. 1, 10.	2 b	lii. 24.	3
vii. 50, 50.	2 b	vi. 1, 3.	3	Ezek. xli. 16, 16.	3
xiv. 17.	1	Esth. ii. 21.	3	xli. 23, 24, 24, 25.	2 b
2 Kings iv. 4, 5, 33.	2 b	vi. 2.	3	Zech. xi. 1.	2 b
vi. 32, 32.	2 b	vi. 2.	3	Mal. i. 10.	2 b
ix. 3, 10.	2 b	Job iii. 10.	2 b		

DOTE

יָאַל to become foolish. NIPHAL *pret.* Jer. l. 36.

עָנַב to love, of impure love ; *seq.* עַל and אֶל. KAL *pret.* Ezek. xxiii. 7, 9, 12. *fut.* Ezek. xxiii. 5, 16, 20.

DOUBLE

1   כָּפַל to fold double. KAL [a] *pret.* [b] *part.* Pail. NIPHAL [c] *fut.* [d] כֶּפֶל *m.* Job xi. 6, doubled ; manifold or the wisdom of God is double-fold, complicated, abundant.

2   לֵב *m.* the heart ; a double heart ; *Heb.* a heart and a heart, implying diversity.

3   שְׁנַיִם *adj. num.* dual, two. [a] מִשְׁנֶה *m.* second ; twofold, double, the double. שָׁנָה to do a thing a second time. NIPHAL [b] *inf.*

Gen. xli. 32.	3 b	Deut. xxi. 17.	3	Isa. xl. 2.	1 d	
xliii. 12, 15.	3 a	2 Kings ii. 9.	3	lxi. 7, 7.	3 a	
Exod. xxii. 4, 7, 9.	3	1 Chron. xii. 33.	3	xvii. 18.	3 a	
xxvi. 9.	1 a	Job xi. 6.	1 d	Jer. xvi. 18.	3 a	
xxviii. 16.	1 b	xli. 13.	1 d	Ezek. xxi. 14.	1 c	
xxxix. 9, 9.	1 b	Ps. xii. 2.	2	Zech. ix. 12.	3 a	
Deut. xv. 18.	3 a					

DOUBT, DOUBTLESS

אָמְנָם *part.* of a truth ; no doubt : Job xii. 2.

קְטַר Ch. *m.* joints ; *trop.* knotty questions : Dan. v. 12, 16.

DOUGH

בָּצֵק *m.* dough, so called from its swelling, rising ; but spoken also of that not yet fermented : Exod. xii. 34, 39 : Jer. vii. 18 : Hos. vii. 4.

עֲרִיסָה *f.* only in the *pl.*, groats, grits, coarse meal, ptisana. Lxx. and Vulg. in Num. φύραμα, *pulmentum ;* in Neh. σῖτος, *cibum.* Num. xv. 20, 21 : Neh. x. 37 : Ezek. xliv. 30.

DOVE

יוֹנָה *f.* see *Pigeon.* Gen. viii. 8, 9, 10, 11, 12 : Ps. lv. 6 ; lxviii. 13 : Cant. i. 15 ; ii. 14 ; iv. 1 ; v. 2, 12 ; vi. 9 : Isa. xxxviii. 14 ; lix. 11 ; lx. 8 : Jer. xlviii. 28 : Ezek. vii. 16 : Hos. vii. 11 ; xi. 11 : Nah. ii. 7.

DOWN, DOWNWARD

בּוֹא to come, to be down, to go down : used of the setting sun, in opposition to יָצָא. KAL *pret.* Lev. xxii. 7. *inf.* Deut. xxiii. 11 : Josh. viii. 29 : 2 Sam. iii. 35.

מַטָּה *adv.* beneath : 2 Kings xix. 30 : 2 Chron. xxxii. 30 : Eccles. iii. 21 : Isa. xxxvii. 31 : Ezek. i. 27 ; viii. 2.

DOWRY

זֶבֶד *m.* a gift, dowry : Gen. xxx. 20.

מֹהַר *m.* price paid for a bride to her parents : Gen. xxxiv. 12 : Exod. xxii. 17 : 1 Sam. xviii. 25.

DRAG

מִכְמֶרֶת a net, fish-net : Hab. i. 15, 16, *marg.* 'or, flue-net.'

DRAGON

תַּנִּין *m.* a great fish, sea monster ; a serpent ; a dragon ; a crocodile, put as the emblem of Egypt or Pharaoh : Deut. xxxii. 33 : Neh. ii. 13 : Ps. lxxiv. 13 ; xci. 13 ; cxlviii. 7 : Isa. xxvii. 1 ; li. 9 : Jer. li. 34. תַּנִּים *m. pl.* : Job xxx. 29 : Ps. xliv. 19 : Isa. xiii. 22 ; xxxiv. 13 ; xxxv. 7 ; xliii. 20 : Jer. ix. 11 ; x. 22 ; xiv. 6 ; xlix. 33 ; li. 37 : Micah i. 8. תַּנִּים *m.* a great serpent ; a sea monster : Ezek. xxix. 3. תַּנּוֹת *f. pl. id.* : Mal. i. 3.

DRAMS

אֲדַרְכֹּנִים *m. pl.* a daric, a Persian coin of pure gold, common also among the Jews while they were under the Persian dominion. The coin usually bears the image of an archer with a tiara : 1 Chron. xxix. 7 : Ezra viii. 27.

דַּרְכְּמוֹנִים *m. pl.* a daric : Ezra ii. 69 : Neh. vii. 70, 71, 72.

DRAUGHT-HOUSE

מוֹצָאוֹת *f. pl.* outgoings ; draught-house, *cloacæ :* 2 Kings x. 27.

מַחֲרָאוֹת *f. pl.* the same : 2 Kings x. 27, כתיב.

DRAW

1 אָרַךְ to prolong. HIPHIL *fut.*

2 פּוּחַ to break forth ; to bring or draw forth, *e. g.* a stream of waters. KAL *fut.* ; see *Drink.*

3 דָּלָה the primary meaning seems to be included in or expressed by, to let down, to hang down, to be pendulous, flaccid, exhausted ; to let down a pitcher into a well, and so to draw water ; to draw up or out, so to deliver. With *inf.*, draw enough. KAL ᵃ*pret.* ᵇ*inf.* ᶜ*fut.*

4 דָּרַךְ to draw a bow by treading upon it. KAL *part.* Poel.

5 חָלַץ to draw out or off ; see *Loose.* KAL *pret.*

6 חָשַׂף to make bare ; to draw off. KAL *inf.*

7 יָצָא to go forth. HIPHIL ᵃ*pret.* ᵇ*fut.*

8 לָקַח to take, to take by violence, to seize. KAL *part.* Paül.

9 מָלֵא to fill. PIEL *pret.* to draw a bow with full strength, *lit.* to fill the hand with a bow.

10 מָשָׁה to draw with a gentle hand. KAL ᵃ*pret.* HIPHIL ᵇ*fut.*

11 מָשַׁךְ to draw, to draw out, to draw after, to draw towards. To draw as beasts in the plough or wagon, Deut. xxi. 3. Figuratively, to draw iniquity along like a plough, keeping it at work, promoting and encouraging the practice of it, with cords of vanity, idle precepts, arguments, and allegations, Isa. v. 18 ; or to draw to themselves punishment with the cords of iniquity, *i. e.* by their impiety draw upon themselves vengeance with all their strength. To draw a bow, 1 Kings xxii. 34. To protract, prolong, continue, lengthen out ; so Jer. xxxi. 3 may be interpreted, "I have extended to thee lovingkindness." To draw along, as those who draw in a large body, or army, Judg. iv. 6, xx. 37. Job xxi. 33, "shall draw after him," *i. e.* shall follow him. Exod. xii. 21, "draw out and take you a lamb." To lay hold, as one drags away another to death, punishment, &c. Ps. xxviii. 3 : Job xxiv. 22 : Ezek. xxxii. 20. KAL ᵃ*pret.* ᵇ*inf.* ᶜ*imp.* ᵈ*fut.* ᵉ*part.* Poel.

12 נָגַע to reach, to extend to. HIPHIL, to draw near : ᵃ*pret.* ᵇ*fut.*

13 נָגַשׁ to come near. KAL ᵃ*imp.* ᵇ*fut.* NIPHAL ᶜ*pret.* HITHPAEL ᵈ*imp.*

14 נָדַח to thrust, to be impelled, to be seduced. NIPHAL *pret.*

15 נָטַשׁ to thrust out, to draw out. KAL *part.* Paül.

16 נָתַק to draw or pull asunder, to draw away. KAL ᵃ*pret.* NIPHAL ᵇ*fut.* HIPHIL ᶜ*inf.* HOPHAL ᵈ*pret.*

17 סָחַב to drag and tear along the ground. KAL ᵃ*pret.* ᵇ*inf.* ᶜ*fut.*

18 עָתִיק *adj.* taken away, *sc.* from the mother's breast, set free, weaned.

19 פּוּק to go out ; to give out, to furnish, to supply. HIPHIL *fut.*

20 פָּתַח to open ; to set loose, to free. KAL ᵃ*pret.* ᵇ*part.* Paül. ᶜ פְּתֻחוֹת *f. pl.* drawn swords.

21 קָרַב to draw or come near, to approach. KAL ᵃ*pret.* ᵇ*imp.* ᶜ*fut.* HIPHIL ᵈ*pret.* ᵉ*fut.* ᶠ קָרֵב *adj.* drawing near. ᵍ קְרָבָה *f.* approach, drawing near.

22   רוּק   to pour out; to draw out, the sword, &c., troops for war. HIPHIL ^a *pret.* ^b*imp.* ^c*fut.*

23   רָפָה   to be weak; of the day declining. KAL *pret.*

24   שָׁאַב   to draw water. KAL ^a*pret.* ^b*inf.* ^c*imp.* ^d*fut.* ^e*part.* Poel. ^f מַשְׁאַבִּים *m.* places of drawing water.

25   שׁוּב   to return; to draw back. HIPHIL ^a*pret.* ^b*part.*

26   שָׁלַף   to draw out or extract; to draw off or pull off. KAL ^a*pret.* ^b*imp.* ^c*fut.* ^d*part.* Poel. ^e*part.* Paül.

27   תָּאַר   to be marked out or off, to be described, as a boundary. KAL *pret.*

Gen. xviii. 23.	13 b	1 Sam. vii. 10.	13 c	Ps. lxxv. 5.	11 d
xxiv. 11.	24 e	ix. 11.	24 b	lxxxviii. 3.	12 a
xxiv. 13, 43.	24 b	ix. 18.	13 b	cvii. 18.	12 b
xxiv. 19, 44, 45.	24 d	xiv. 36.	21 c	cxix. 150.	21 a
xxiv. 20, 20.	24 b d	xiv. 38.	13 a	Prov. xx. 5.	3 c
xxxvii. 28.	11 d	xvii. 16, 40.	13 b	xxiv. 11.	8
xxxviii. 29.	25 b	xvii. 41.	21 f	Eccles. xii. 1.	12 a
xlvii. 29.	21 c	xvii. 48.	21 c	Cant. i. 4.	11 c
Exod. ii. 10.	10 a	xvii. 51.	26 c	Isa. v. 18.	11 e
ii. 16.	3 c	xxxi. 4.	26 b	v. 19.	21 c
ii. 19.α	3 b a	2 Sam. x. 13.	13 b	xii. 3.	24 a
iii. 5.	21 c	xvii. 13.	17 a	xxi. 15.	15
xii. 21.	11 c	xviii. 25.	21 f	xxvi. 17.	21 e
xiv. 10.	21 d	xxii. 17.	10 b	xxviii. 9.	18
xv. 9.	22 c	xxiii. 16.	24 d	xxix. 13.	13 c
xx. 21.	13 c	xxiv. 9.	26 d	xli. 5.	21 a
Lev. ix. 5.	21 c	1 Kings ii. 1.	21 c	xlv. 20.	13 d
xxvi. 33.	22 a	viii. 8.	1	lvii. 3.	21 b
Num. xxii. 23, 31.	26 e	xxii. 34.	11 a	lvii. 4.	1
Deut. xxi. 3.	11 a	2 Kings iii. 26.	26 d	lviii. 10.	19
xxv. 11.	21 a	ix. 24.	9	lxvi. 19.	11 e
xxix. 11.	24 e	1 Chron. x. 4.	26 d	Jer. xxii. 19.	17 b
xxx. 17.	14	xi. 18.	15 b	xxx. 21.	21 d
Josh. v. 13.	26 e	xix. 14.	7 b	xxxi. 3.	11 a
viii. 6.	16 c	xix. 36.	4	xxxviii. 13.	11 d
viii. 11.	13 b	xxi. 5, 5.	26 d	xlvi. 3.	13 a
viii. 16.	16 b	xxi. 11.	16 b	xlix. 20.	17 c
viii. 26.	25 a	2 Chron. v. 9.	1	l. 45.	17 c
ix. 21, 23, 27.	24 e	xiv. 8.	4	Lam. ii. 3.	25 a
xv. 9, 9, 11.	27	xviii. 33.	11 a	iii. 57.	21 a
xviii. 14, 17.	27	Esth. v. 2.	21 c	iv. 3.	5
Judg. iii. 22.	26 a	ix. 1.	12 a	Ezek. v. 2, 12.	22 e
iv. 6, 7.	11 a	Job xx. 25.	26 a	vii. 12.	12 a
v. 11.	24 f	xxi. 33.	11 d	ix. 1.	21 a
viii. 10.	26 d	xxiv. 22.	11 a	xii. 14.	22 c
viii. 20.	26 a	xxxiii. 22.	21 c	xxi. 3, 5.	7 a
ix. 54.	26 b	xl. 23.	2	xxi. 28.	20 b
xix. 9.	23	xli. 1.	11 d	xxii. 4.	21 e
xix. 13.	21 c	Ps. v. 9.	11 b	xxvii. 7.	22 a
xx. 2, 15, 17, 25, 35,		xviii. 16.	10 b	xxx. 11.	22 a
46.	26 d	xxviii. 3.	11 d	xxxii. 20.	11 c
xx. 31.	16 d	xxxv. 3.	22 b	Hos. xi. 4.	11 d
xx. 32.	16 a	xxxvii. 14.	20 a	Joel iii. 9.	13 b
xx. 37.	11 d	lv. 21.	20 c	Nah. iii. 14.	24 c
Ruth ii. 9.	24 d	lxix. 18.	21 b	Zeph. iii. 2.	21 a
iv. 8.	26 c	lxxii. 28.	21 g	Hag. ii. 16.	6
1 Sam. vii. 6.	24 d				

a lit. drawing he drew.

DREAD

1   אֵימָה   *f.* terror.

2   דְּחַל   Ch. to fear, to be afraid; to terrify. P'AL *part.* P'il.

3   חַת   *m.* dismay, terror, dread.

4   יָרֵא   to fear; to be feared, fearful. KAL ^a*fut.* NIPHAL ^b*part.* ^cיִרְאָה *f.* fear, terror. ^dמוֹרָא *m. id.*

5   עָרַץ   to terrify, to make afraid; to fear, to be afraid, to tremble. KAL ^a*fut.* HIPHIL ^b*part.*

6   פָּחַד   to tremble, to be in trepidation; to fear, to be afraid. פַּחַד *m.* fear, terror.

Gen. ix. 2.	3	1 Chron. xxii. 13.	4 a	Dan. vii. 7, 19.	2
xxviii. 17.	4 b	Job xiii. 11.	6	ix. 4.	4 b
Exod. xv. 16.	6	xiii. 21.	1	Hab. i. 7.	4 b
Deut. i. 29.	5 a	xv. 21.α	6	Mal. i. 6.	4 b
ii. 25.	6	Isa. viii. 13.	5 b	iv. 5.	4 b
xi. 25.	4 d	Ezek. i. 18.β	4 c		

a marg. 'a sound of fears.'   *β lit.* and fear was to them.

DREAM

1   בַּעַל   *m.* master, owner; dreamer, *lit.* master of dreams.

2   חָלַם   to dream. KAL ^a*pret.* ^b*fut.* ^c*part.* Poel. HIPHIL ^d*part.* ^eחֲלוֹם *m.* a dream. Dreams are put for follies, trifles. Gen. xx. 3, 6, &c. ^fחֵלֶם Ch. *m. id.* Dan. ii. 4, &c.

Gen. xxviii. 12.	2 b	Gen. xli. 1.	2 c	Judg. vii. 13, 13,	
xxxvii. 5, 5.	2 b e	xli. 5.	2 b	13.	2 e a e
xxxvii. 6, 6.	2 e a	xli. 11, 11, 11,		Ps. cxxvii. 1.	2 c
xxxvii. 9, 9, 9,		11.	2 b e 2 a e	Isa. xxix. 8, 8.	2 b
9.	2 b e 2 a e	xli. 15, 15, 15.	2 a e e	Jer. xxiii. 25, 25.	2 b
xxxvii. 10, 10.	2 e a	xli. 9, 9.	2 e a	xxix. 8, 8.	2 e d
xxxvii. 19.	1, 2 a	Deut. xiii. 1, 1.	2 c e	Dan. ii. 1, 1.	2 a e
xl. 5, 5, 5, 5.	2 b 2 e e e	xiii. 3, 3.	2 e a	ii. 3, 3, 3.	2 a c e
xl. 8, 8.	2 a e	xiii. 5, 5.	2 c e	Joel ii. 28, 28.	2 b e

DREGS

קֻבַּעַת   *f.* according to ancient interpreters, the dregs which subside to the bottom of the cup. Gesenius, the goblet cup, but the former meaning suits best the context, and agrees with similar expressions in the Prophets and Rev. xiv. 10. The idea of dregs is taken from the custom of mixing various substances to produce an intoxicating quality in wine: Isa. li. 17, 22.

שְׁמָרִים   *m. pl.* lees: Ps. lxxv. 8.

DRESS

1   יָטַב   to be good; to make good. HIPHIL *inf.*

2   עָבַד   to labour; to work at, to labour in anything, to till the ground, to dress a vineyard, &c. KAL ^a*pret.* ^b*inf.*

3   עָשָׂה   to work about anything, to prepare food. KAL ^a*pret.* ^b*inf.* ^c*imp.* ^d*fut.* ^e*part.* Paül, "ready dressed." NIPHAL ^f*pret.*

Gen. ii. 15.	2 b	Deut. xxviii. 39.	2 a	2 Sam. xix. 24.	3 a
xviii. 7.	3 b	1 Sam. xxv. 18.	3 e	1 Kings xvii. 12.	3 a
xviii. 8.	3 a	2 Sam. xii. 4, 4.	3 b d	xviii. 23, 26.	3 d
Exod. xxx. 7.	3 a	xiii. 5.	3 a	xviii. 25.	3 c
Lev. vii. 9.	3 f	xiii. 7.	3 c		

DRINK, DRUNKARD, DRUNKENNESS

1   גָּמָא   to absorb, to drink up eagerly, to swallow. HIPHIL *imp.*

2   סָבָא   to drink to excess, to tope; the primary idea seems to be that of sucking up, absorbing. KAL ^a*part.* Poel. ^b*part.* Paül. ^cסֹבֶא *m.* wine, a carousal.

3   עָשַׁק   to oppress, to treat with violence and injustice; to defraud and extort. KAL *fut.* Job xl. 23. But a very different sense is given to this verse by Bochart, Gesenius, Noyes, Schultens, Umbreit, Prof. Lee, and Rosenmüller. According to their interpretation, the meaning is, "The stream overfloweth and he feareth not; he is secure, even though Jordan rush forth even to his mouth." LXX. Ἐὰν γένηται πλημμύρα, κ.τ.λ.—*Bush.*

4   רָוָה   to drink to the full, to be satisfied, sated with drink. KAL ^a*pret.* HIPHIL ^b*pret.* ^cרָוֶה *adj.* satiated with drink.

5   שָׁכַר   to drink to the full, to drink to hilarity; to drink deeply, to be filled with drink, to be drunken, intoxicated; *metaph.* in the prophets, the wicked are said to be drunken when they rush, by a sort of madness, to their own destruction; *comp.* Jer. xxv. 16, 17, in which there may also be an allusion to medicated wine; see below. KAL ^a*pret.* ^b*inf.* ^c*imp.* ^d*fut.* ^e*part.* Paül.

PIEL ^{f} *inf.* ^{g} *fut.* ^{h} *part.* HIPHIL ^{i} *pret.* ^{k} *imp.* ^{l} *fut.* HITHPAEL ^{m} *fut.* ^{n} שֵׁכָר *m.* temetum, strong drink ; wine mixed with frankincense ; given to malefactors about to be executed ; any intoxicating liquor, whether wine, or an intoxicating drink resembling wine prepared or distilled from barley, honey, or dates ; it is then often distinguished from wine. ^{o} שִׁכָּרוֹן *m.* drunkenness. ^{p} שִׁכּוֹר *adj.* drunken.

6 שָׁקָה to drink ; to give to drink, to let drink ; *seq. dupl. acc.* of person and thing ; also *seq.* בְּ of thing, Ps. lxxx. 5 ; מִן of anything, Cant. viii. 2. HIPHIL ^{a} *pret.* ^{b} *inf.* ^{c} *imp.* ^{d} *fut.* ^{e} *part.* שִׁקּוּי *m.* drink. ^{g} שִׁקּוּי *m. id.* ^{h} מַשְׁקֶה *m. id.*

7 שָׁתָה to drink ; *seq. acc.* of drink, *seq.* מִן Job xxi. 20 ; *seq.* בְּ of anything, with the notion of enjoyment, Prov. ix. 5 ; also *seq.* בְּ of the vessel, Amos vi. 6. *Metaph.* Job xv. 16. "drinking in iniquity like water," *i.e.* as greedy of it as a thirsty man is of water. Good supposes there may be an allusion to the large draught of water which the camel makes. But in Prov. xxvi. 6 the same phrase is taken in a passive sense, the lame man drinketh in injury, *i.e.* must suffer it, cannot avenge it. With *inf.*, certainly, assuredly, surely. KAL ^{a} *pret.* ^{b} *inf.* ^{c} *imp.* ^{d} *fut.* ^{e} *part.* Poel. NIPHAL ^{f} *fut.* שָׁתָה Ch. *id.* P'AL ^{g} *pret.* ^{h} *fut.* ^{i} *part.* שְׁתִיָּה ^{k} *f.* a drinking, carousing. ^{l} מִשְׁתֶּה *m.* a drinking, drink, banquet. ^{m} שְׁתִי *m.* drinking, drunkenness.

Gen. ix. 21, 21.	7 d, 5 d	
xix. 32, 33, 34, 35.	6 d	
xxi. 19.	6 d	
xxiv. 14, 14,		
14.	7 d c, 6 d	
xxiv. 17.	1	
xxiv. 18, 18.	7 b, 6 d	
xxiv. 19, 19.	6 b, 7 b	
xxiv. 22.	7 d	
xxiv. 43, 45.	6 c	
xxiv. 44.	7 c	
xxiv. 46, 46, 46,		
46.	7 c, 6 d, 7 d, 6 a	
xxiv. 54.	7 d	
xxv. 34.	7 d	
xxvi. 30.	7 d	
xxvii. 25.	7 d	
xxx. 38, 38.	7 d	
xliii. 34.	7 d	
xliv. 5.	7 d	
Exod. vii. 18, 21, 24,		
24.	7 d	
xv. 23.	7 b	
xv. 24.	7 d	
xvii. 1.	7 b	
xvii. 2.	7 d	
xvii. 6.	7 a	
xxiv. 11.	7 b	
xxxii. 6.	7 b	
xxxii. 20.	7 d	
xxxiv. 28.	7 a	
Lev. x. 9, 9.	7 d, 5 n	
xi. 34, 34.	6 h, 7 f	
Num. v. 24, 27.	6 a	
v. 26.	6 d	
vi. 3, 3, 3,		
3.	5 n, 7 d, 5 n, 7 d	
vi. 20.	7 d	
xx. 5.	7 b	
xx. 8.	6 a	
xx. 11, 17, 19.	7 d	
xxi. 22.	7 d	
xxiii. 24.	7 d	
xxxiii. 14.	7 b	
Deut. ii. 6, 28.	7 a	
ix. 9, 18.	7 d	
xi. 11.	7 d	
xiv. 26.	5 n	
xxi. 20.	2 a	
xxviii. 39.	7 d	
xxix. 6, 6.	7 a, 5 n	

Deut. xxix. 19.	4 c
xxxii. 14, 38.	7 d
xxxii. 42.	5 l
Judg. iv. 19, 19.	6 c d
vii. 5, 6.	7 b
ix. 27.	7 d
xiii. 4, 4.	7 d, 5 n
xiii. 7, 7.	7 d, 5 n
xiii. 14, 14.	7 d, 5 n
xv. 19.	7 d
xix. 4, 6, 21.	7 d
Ruth ii. 9.	7 a
iii. 3.	7 b
1 Sam. i. 9.	7 b
i. 13.	5 p
i. 14.	5 m
i. 15, 15.	7 a, 5 n
xxv. 36.	5 p
xxx. 11.	6 d
xxx. 12.	7 a
xxx. 16.	7 e
2 Sam. xi. 11.	7 b
xi. 13, 13.	7 d, 5 g
xii. 3.	7 d
xvi. 2.	7 d
xix. 35.	7 d
xxiii. 15.	6 d
xxiii. 16, 17.	7 b
1 Kings i. 25.	7 b
iv. 20.	7 e
xiii. 8, 9, 16, 17, 18,	
19, 22, 22.	7 d
xiii. 23.	7 d
xvi. 9, 9.	7 e, 5 p
xvii. 4, 6, 10.	7 d
xviii. 41.	7 d
xviii. 42.	7 d
xix. 6, 8.	7 d
xx. 12.	7 d
xx. 16, 16.	7 e, 5 p
2 Kings iii. 17.	7 a
vi. 22, 23.	7 d
vii. 8.	7 d
ix. 34.	7 d
xviii. 27.	7 b
xviii. 31.	7 c
Eccles. ii. 24.	7 d
iii. 13.	7 d
v. 18.	7 d
1 Chron. xi. 17.	6 d
xi. 18.	7 b

1 Chron. xi. 19, 19.	7 d b
xii. 39.	7 e
xxix. 22.	7 d
2 Chron. ix. 20.	6 h
xxviii. 15. *a*	7 b
Ezra iii. 7.	7 l
x. 6.	7 a
Neh. viii. 10.	7 b
viii. 12.	7 b
Esth. i. 7.	7 k
i. 8.	7 k
iii. 15.	7 d
iv. 16.	7 d
Job i. 4.	7 e
i. 13, 18.	7 e
iv. 4.	7 d
xii. 25.	7 p
xv. 16.	7 d
xxi. 20.	7 d
xxii. 7.	7 d
xxxiv. 7.	7 d
xl. 23.	3
Ps. xxxvi. 8.	6 d
l. 13.	7 d
lx. 3.	6 a
lxix. 12.	7 e, 5 n
lxix. 21.	7 d
lxxv. 8.	7 d
lxxviii. 15.	7 d
lxxviii. 44.	6 d
lxxx. 5.	6 d
cii. 9.	6 f
civ. 11.	6 d
cvii. 27.	5 p
cx. 7.	7 d
Prov. iv. 17.	7 d
v. 15.	7 c
ix. 5.	5 n
xx. 1.	7 a
xxiii. 7.	7 d
xxiii. 21.	2 a
xxv. 21.	6 c
xxvi. 6.	7 e
xxxi. 4, 4.	7 b, 5 n
xxxi. 5, 7.	7 d
xxxi. 6.	5 n
Eccles. ii. 24.	7 d
iii. 13.	7 d
v. 18.	7 d
viii. 15.	7 b

Eccles. ix. 7.	7 c
x. 17.	7 m
Cant. v. 1, 1, 1.	7 a c, 5 c
viii. 2.	6 d
Isa. v. 11.	5 h
v. 22, 22.	7 b, 5 n
xix. 14.	5 p
xxi. 5.	7 b
xxii. 13, 13.	7 b
xxiv. 9, 9, 9.	7 d, 5 n, 7 e
xxiv. 20.	5 p
xxviii. 1, 3.	5 p
xxviii. 7, 7, 7.	5 n
xxix. 8.	7 e
xxix. 9, 9.	a n
xxxii. 6.	6 h
xxxvi. 12.	7 b
xxxvi. 16.	7 c
xxxvii. 25.	7 a
xliii. 20.	6 b
xliv. 12.	7 a
xlix. 26.	5 d
li. 17, 17.	7 a
li. 21.	5 e
li. 22. *β*	7 b
lvi. 12.	5 n
lxii. 8, 9.	7 d
lxiii. 6.	5 g
lxv. 13.	7 d
Jer. ii. 18, 18.	7 b
viii. 14.	6 d
ix. 15.	6 a
xiii. 13.	7 d

Jer. xvi. 7.	6 d
xvi. 8.	7 b
xxii. 15.	7 a
xxiii. 9.	5 p
xxiii. 15.	6 a
xxv. 15.	6 a
xxv. 16.	7 a
xxv. 17.	6 d
xxv. 26.	7 d
xxv. 27, 27.	7 d, 5 n, 7 e
xxv. 28, 28.	7 b, 7 b d
xxxv. 2.	6 a
xxxv. 5.	7 c
xxxv. 6, 6.	7 d
xxxv. 8.	7 b
xxxv. 14, 14.	7 b a
xlvi. 10.	4 a
xlviii. 26.	5 k
xlix. 12, 12,	
12.	7 b, 7 b d, 7 b d
li. 7, 7.	5 h, 7 a
li. 39, 57.	5 i
Lam. iv. 21.	5 d
iv. 21.	5 b
v. 4.	7 a
Ezek. iv. 11, 11, 16.	7 d
xii. 18, 19.	7 d
xxiii. 32.	7 a
xxiii. 33.	5 o
xxiii. 34.	7 a
xxv. 4.	7 d
xxxi. 14, 16.	7 e
xxxiv. 18, 19.	7 d

Ezek. xxxix. 17.	7 a
xxxix. 18.	7 d
xxxix. 19, 19.	7 a, 5 o
xliv. 21.	7 d
Dan. i. 5, 8, 10, 16.	7 l
i. 12. *γ*	7 d
v. 1, 23.	7 i
v. 2.	7 h
v. 3, 4.	7 g
Hos. ii. 5.	6 g
iv. 18.	2
Joel i. 5, 5.	5 p, 7 e
iii. 3.	7 d
Amos ii. 8.	7 d
ii. 12.	6 d
iv. 1.	7 d
iv. 8.	7 b
v. 11.	7 d
vi. 6.	7 d
ix. 14.	7 a
Obad. 16, 16, 16.	7 a d a
Jonah iii. 7.	7 d
Micah ii. 11.	5 n
vi. 15.	7 d
Nah. i. 10, 10.	2 c b
iii. 11.	5 d
Hab. ii. 15, 15.	6 e, 5 f
ii. 16.	7 c
Zeph. i. 13.	7 d
Hag. i. 6, 6.	7 b, 5 b
Zech. vii. 6, 6.	7 d e
ix. 15.	7 d

a lit. fed them and gave them drink.   *γ lit.* and we will drink.   *β lit.* thou shalt not add to drink it.

DRINK-OFFERING (See OFFERING)

DRIVE

1 בָּרַח to flee. HIPHIL, to make to flee : *pret.*

2 גָּרַשׁ to expel, drive, or cast out ; implying also violence, power, anger, or hatred in the agent ; as mire is cast up by the sea, Isa. lvii. 20 ; as our first parents were driven out of Paradise, Gen. iii. 24 ; as a son is thrust out of his father's house, Judg. xi. 2, 7 ; a wife from the house of her husband by divorce, Lev. xxi. 7, 14, &c. ; Moses and Aaron from the presence of Pharaoh, Exod. x. 11 ; Gaal and his brethren from dwelling in Sichem, Judg. ix. 41 ; inhabitants from a country or city, Zeph. ii. 4, Exod. xxxiii. 2. Hence it applies to that which is acted on by violence ; see *Troubled.* The use of the word mostly carries with it the idea of shame and disgrace, and in many cases of just execution of a sentence of banishment, Exod. xxxiv. 11. KAL ^{a} *part.* Poel. PIEL ^{b} *pret.* ^{c} *inf.* ^{d} *fut.* PUAL ^{e} *fut.*

3 דָּחָה to thrust, push, to overthrow ; to be cast down by death or irretrievable calamity : Ps. xxxvi. 12. NIPHAL *fut.*

4 הָדַף to drive away totally, so as to destroy or ruin. KAL ^{a} *pret.* ^{b} *fut.*

5 חִיל to bring forth. POLEL *fut.* Prov. xxv. 23, *marg.* ' or, bringeth forth.' This is undoubtedly the proper meaning, rather than 'drive away,' which some have deduced from חֲלִילָה *absit.*

6 טְרַד Ch. to thrust. P'AL ^{a} *part. active.* ^{b} *part. passive.*

7 יָרַשׁ to possess, to take possession, to drive another from possession. With *inf.*, utterly, without fail. KAL ^{a} *fut.* Num. xxi. 32, כתיב. HIPHIL ^{b} *pret.* ^{c} *inf.* ^{d} *fut.* ^{e} *part.*

8 נָגַשׂ see *Oppressor.* KAL *part.* Poel.

9 נָדָא to remove away. HIPHIL *fut.* כתיב.

10 נָדַח to push, to thrust with great force. NIPHAL ᵃ*pret.* ᵇ*part.* PUAL ᶜ*part.* HIPHIL ᵈ*pret.* ᵉ*inf.* ᶠ*fut.*

11 נָדַף to drive away, to disperse. KAL ᵃ*fut.* NIPHAL ᵇ*pret.* ᶜ*inf.* ᵈ*part.*

12 נָהַג to lead, to drive a cart, &c. KAL ᵃ*pret.* ᵇ*imp.* ᶜ*fut.* ᵈ*part.* Poel. PIEL ᵉ*fut.* ᶠמִנְהָג *m.* driving of a chariot.

13 נָשַׁב see *Blow.* HIPHIL *fut.*

14 נָשַׁל to cast out. PIEL *fut.*

15 נָתַר to let loose, to drive asunder. HIPHIL *fut.*

16 סָבַב to turn about, back. NIPHAL *fut.*

17 סוג to go back. NIPHAL *fut.*

18 פּוּץ to scatter. HIPHIL *pret.*

19 רָחַק to be far; to remove far away. HIPHIL *fut.*

20 רָכָב *m.* a rider, horseman; driver of a chariot.

21 שָׁבָה to take away captive. NIPHAL *pret.*

Gen. iii. 24.	2 d	Josh. xxiii. 9.	7 d	Prov. xiv. 32.	3
iv. 14.	2 b	xxiii. 13.	7 c	xxii. 15.	19
xv. 11.	13	xxiv. 12, 18.	2 d	xxv. 23.	5
Exod. ii. 17.	2 d	Judg. i. 19, 19.	7 d c	Isa. viii. 22.	10 c
vi. 1.	2 d	i. 21, 27, 29, 30, 31,		xix. 7.	11 b
x. 11.a	2 d	32, 33.	7 b	xxii. 19.	4 a
xiv. 25.	12 e	i. 28.γ	7 b c	xli. 2.	11 d
xxii. 10.	21	ii. 3.	7 d	Jer. viii. 3.	10 d
xxiii. 28, 31.	2 b	ii. 21, 23.	7 c	xvi. 15.	10 d
xxiii. 29, 30.	2 b	vi. 9.	2 d	xxiii. 2.	10 f
xxxiii. 2.	2 b	xi. 24.	7 b	xxiii. 3, 8.	10 d
xxxiv. 11.	2 a	1 Sam. xxvi. 19.	2 b	xxiii. 12.	3
Num. xxi. 32.	7 a, or. b	xx. 20.	12 a	xxiv. 9.	10 f
xxii. 6.	2 d	2 Sam. vi. 3.	12 d	xxvii. 10.	10 d
xxii. 11.	2 b	1 Kings xxii. 34.	20	xxvii. 15.	10 e
xxxii. 21.	7 c	2 Kings iv. 24.	12 b	xxix. 14, 18.	10 d
xxxiii. 52.	7 c	ix. 20, 20, 20.	12 f f c	xxxiii. 37.	10 d
xxxiii. 55.	7 d	xvii. 21.	9, or, 10 f	xl. 12.	10 a
Deut. iv. 19.	10 a	1 Chron. viii. 13.	1	xliii. 5.	10 a
iv. 38.	7 c	xiii. 7.	12 d	xlvi. 15.	4 a
ix. 3.	7 b	xvii. 21.	2 c	xlvi. 28.	10 d
ix. 4, 5.	7 e	2 Chron. xx. 7.	7 b	xlix. 5.	10 a
xi. 23.	7 b	Job vi. 13.	10 a	l. 17.	10 d
xviii. 12.	7 e	xiii. 25.	11 d	Ezek. iv. 13.	10 f
xxx. 1.	10 d	xviii. 11.	18	xxxi. 11.	2 b
xxx. 4.	10 b	xviii. 18.	4 b	xxxiv. 4, 16.	10 b
Josh. iii. 10.β	7 c d	xix. 3.	12 c	Dan. iv. 25, 32.	6 a
xiii. 6.	7 d	xxx. 5.	2 e	iv. 33.	6 b
xiv. 12.	7 b	xxxix. 7.	8	v. 21.	6 b
xv. 14.	7 d	Ps. i. 4.	11 a	ix. 7.	10 d
xv. 63.	7 b	xxxiv. title	2 d	Hos. ix. 15.	2 d
xvi. 10.	7 b	xl. 14.	17	Joel ii. 20.	10 d
xvii. 12.	7 c	xlii. 2.	2 b	Micah iv. 6.	10 b
xvii. 13.γ	7 b c	lxviii. 2, 2.	11 c a	Hab. iii. 6.	15
xvii. 18.	7 d	cxiv. 3, 5.	16	Zeph. ii. 4.	2 d
xxiii. 5.	7 b			iii. 19.	10 b

a lit. and one drove them.   *β lit.* driving he will drive out.   *γ lit.* driving he did not drive out.

DROMEDARY

בֶּכֶר *m.* and בִּכְרָה *f.* a young camel: Isa. lx. 6: Jer. ii. 23. Bochart and Gesenius.

רֶכֶשׁ *m.* a horse of a nobler and fleeter race, a steed, courser: 1 Kings iv. 28. Bochart.

רַמָּךְ *f.* a dromedary: Esth. viii. 10. According to Gesenius and others, a mare.

DROP

1 אֲגָלִים *m. pl.* drops of dew, from their globular form: Job xxxviii. 28. Gesenius, reservoirs of dew; *comp.* in ver. 22, the storehouses of the snow and hail.

2 דָּלַף to drop, to drip, to distil. KAL ᵃ*fut.* ᵇדֶּלֶף *m.* a dropping.

3 הֵלֶךְ *m.* a flowing: 1 Sam. xiv. 26, *lit.* a dropping of honey.

4 מֹר *m.* a drop, from the idea of flowing: see *Myrrh.*

5 נָזַל to flow, to run as liquids. KAL *fut.*

6 נָטַף to drop, to fall in drops, to distil; *metaph.* of discourse. KAL ᵃ*pret.* ᵇ*fut.* ᶜ*part.* Poel. HIPHIL ᵈ*pret.* ᵉ*imp.* ᶠ*fut.* ᵍנָטָף *m.* a drop.

7 נָתַךְ to be poured out. NIPHAL *pret.*

8 עָרַף to drop, distil, *metaph.* of speech. KAL *fut.*

9 רְסִיסִים *m. pl.* drops, dew-drops.

10 רָעַף to drop, distil, as clouds drop down dew. KAL ᵃ*fut.* HIPHIL ᵇ*imp.*

Deut. xxxii. 2.	8	Ps. lxv. 11, 12.	10 a	Cant. v. 5.	6 a
xxxii. 28.	8	lxviii. 8.	6 a	v. 13.	6 c
Judg. v. 4, 4.	6 a	Prov. iii. 20.	10 a	Isa. xl. 15.	4
1 Sam. xxvi. 26.	3	v. 3.	6 b	xlv. 8.	10 b
2 Sam. xxi. 10.	5	xix. 13.	2 b	Ezek. xx. 46.	6 e
Job xxix. 22.	7	xxvii. 15.	2 b	xxi. 2.	6 e
xxxvi. 27.	6 g	Eccles. x. 18.	2 a	Joel iii. 18.	6 b
xxxvi. 28.	5	Cant. iv. 11.	6 b	Amos vii. 16.	6 f
xxxviii. 28.	1	v. 2.	9	ix. 13.	6 d

DROSS

סִיג *m.* what goes off from metal, *recedanea, scoria,* dross; base metal, originally mixed with the finer, and separated from it by smelting: Ps. cxix. 119: Prov. xxv. 4; xxvi. 23: Isa. i. 22, 25: Ezek. xxii. 18, 18, 19. סוג *m. id.*: Ezek. xxii. 18, כתיב.

DROUGHT

בַּצֹּרֶת *f.* restraint: Jer. xvii. 8, *marg.* 'restraint;' *i.e.* of rain.

חֹרֶב *m.* dryness: Gen. xxxi. 40: Jer. l. 38: Hag. i. 11. חֲרָבוֹן *m. id.* heat of summer: Ps. xxxii. 4.

תַּלְאוּבָה *f. pl.* thirst; great drought: Hos. xiii. 5.

צִיָּה *f.* dryness, drought: Job xxiv. 19: Jer. ii. 6.

צִחְצָחוֹת *f.* dry places: Isa. lviii. 11.

צִמָּאוֹן *m.* a thirsty, *i.e.* dry region: Deut. viii. 15.

DROVE

מַחֲנֶה *com.* army; company: Gen. xxxiii. 8.

עֵדֶר *m.* flock: Gen. xxxii. 16, *lit.* drove, drove; 16, 16, 19.

DROWN

טָבַע to sink, to be sunk, immersed. PUAL *pret.* Exod. xv. 4.

שָׁטַף to gush or pour out abundantly; to overthrow, to overwhelm. KAL *fut.* Cant. viii. 7.

שָׁקָה to drink, to give drink. NIPHAL *pret.* Amos viii. 8, כתיב.

שָׁקַע to sink, to subside; to be submerged, overflowed, drowned. KAL *pret.* Amos ix. 5. NIPHAL *pret.* Amos viii. 8.

DROWSINESS

נוּמָה *f.* slumber, light sleep: Prov. xxiii. 21.

DRY

1 בּוּשׁ to be ashamed. KAL *fut.* Hos. xiii. 15, "with shame shall dry up." See APPENDIX, Paronomasia.

2 דָּלַל to hang down; to be slack, languid, feeble; to be brought

low. KAL *pret.* Job xxviii. 4. Gesenius, of miners letting themselves down into the pits or shafts.

3 חָרֵב to be dry; in a less degree than יָבֵשׁ, when distinguished from it, as in Gen. viii. 13, 14: it means, therefore, only the taking away of moisture in general, or from the surface; when these two words are used in connexion, חָרֵב usually precedes, and יָבֵשׁ follows, as in Job xiv. 11, Isa. xix. 5. Prov. xvii. 1, a dry morsel, not even dipped; *comp.* Lev. vii. 10. KAL ª *pret.* ᵇ *imp.* ᶜ *fut.* PUAL ᵈ *pret.* HIPHIL ᵉ *pret.* ᶠ *fut.* ᵍ *part.* ʰ חָרֵב *adj.* dry. ⁱ חֹרֶב *m.* dryness, drought. ᵏ חָרָבָה *f.* dry land.

4 חָרַר to be dry; to be so dry as to be ready to burn. NIPHAL *pret.*

5 יָבֵשׁ to dry, or be dried up: it implies more than the two former; and is used of things moist, which become withered; of rivers, &c., dried up: it is figuratively applied to the wasting of strength and vigour, Ps. xxii. 15, Num. xi. 6. With *inf.*, clean dried up. KAL ª *pret.* ᵇ *inf.* ᶜ *fut.* PIEL ᵈ *fut.* HIPHIL ᵉ *pret.* ᶠ *fut.* ᵍ יָבֵשׁ *adj.* dry, dried up. ʰ יַבָּשָׁה *f.* that which is dry, dry land. ⁱ יַבֶּשֶׁת *f. id.*

6 צִיָּה *f.* aridity, drought. ª צִיּוֹן *m.* arid land.

7 צַח *adj.* sunny, bright, serene; a warm and dry wind. ª צְחֵה *adj.* dry, with thirst. ᵇ צְחִיחָה *f.* an arid land.

8 צִמָּאוֹן *m.* thirsty land, *i. e.* dry, parched.

9 צָמַק to dry up, to be dry; of the breasts. KAL *part.* Poel.

10 קָלָה to roast, to parch ears of corn. KAL *part.* Paül.

Gen. i. 9, 10.	5 h	Job xiv. 11.	5 a	Isa. liii. 2.		6
vii. 22.	3 k	xv. 30.	5 d	lvi. 3.		5 g
viii. 7.	5 b	xviii. 16.	5 c	Jer. iv. 11.		7
viii. 13, 13.	3 a	xxviii. 4.	2	xxiii. 10.		5 a
viii. 14.	5 a	Ps. xxii. 15.	5 a	i. 12.		6
Exod. iv. 9, 9.	5 h i	lxiii. 1.	6	i. 38.		5 a
xiv. 16, 22, 29.	5 h	lxvi. 6.	5 h	li. 36, 36.	3 e, 5 e	6
xiv. 21.	3 k	lxvii. 6.	7 b	li. 43.		6
xv. 19.	5 h	lxix. 3.	4	Ezek. xvii. 24, 24.	5 e	g
Lev. ii. 14.	10	lxxiv. 15.	5 e	xix. 12.		5 a
vii. 10.	3 h	xcv. 6.	5 i	xix. 13.		6
Num. vi. 3.	5 g	cv. 41.	6	xx. 47.		5 g
xi. 6.	5 g	cvi. 9.	3 c	xxx. 12.γ		3 k
Josh. ii. 10.	5 e	cvii. 33.	8	xxxvii. 2, 4.		5 g
iii. 17, 17.	3 k	cvii. 35.α	6	xxxvii. 11.		5 a
iv. 18.	3 k	Prov. xvii. 1.	3 h	Hos. ii. 3.		6
iv. 22.	5 h	xvii. 22.	5 d	ix. 9.		9
iv. 23, 23.	5 e	Isa. v. 13.	7 a	ix. 16.		5 a
v. 1.	5 h	xix. 5.	5 a	xiii. 15, 15.	1, 3 c	5 a
ix. 5, 12.	5 a	xix. 6.	3 a	Joel i. 10, δ 12		5 e
Judg. vi. 37, 39, 40.	3 i	xxv. 5.	6 a	i. 20.		5 a
xvi. 7, 8.	3 d	xxxii. 2.	6 a	Jonah i. 9.		5 h
1 Kings xiii. 4.	5 c	xxxvii. 25.	3 f	ii. 10.		5 h
xvii. 7.	5 c	xli. 18.β	6	Nah. i. 4, 4.	5 d, 3 k	6
2 Kings iii. 8.	3 k	xliii. 15, 15.	5 f	i. 10.		5 g
xix. 24.	3 f	xliv. 3.	5 h	Zeph. ii. 13.		6
Neh. ix. 11.	5 h	xliv. 27, 27.	3 b, 5 f	Hag. ii. 6.		3 k
Job xii. 15.	5 c	i. 2.	3 f	Zech. x. 11.		6
xiii. 25.	5 g	li. 10.	3 g	xi. 17.ϵ		5 b c

a lit. ground of drought.   β *lit.* land of drought.   γ *marg.* 'drought.'   δ *marg.* 'or, ashamed.'   ϵ *lit.* in drying shall be dried up.

DRYSHOD

נַעַל *f.* shoe: Isa. xi. 15, *marg.* 'in shoes.'

DUE

בַּעַל *m.* owner: Prov. iii. 27, *marg.* 'from the owners thereof.'

דָּבָר *m.* word, matter, &c.: Neh. xi. 23.

חֹק *m.* statute, portion, due: Lev. x. 13, 13, 14, 14.

מִשְׁפָּט *m.* judgment, right: Deut. xviii. 3.

DUKE

אַלּוּף and אֶלֶף *m.* head of a family, or tribe, *i. e.* who unites its members into one body: occurs in this rendering in Gen. xxxvi., Exod. xv., and 1 Chron. i.; see also *Guide.*

נָסִיךְ *m.* see *Prince:* Josh. xiii. 21. Hengstenberg, vassals.

DULCIMER

סוּמְפֹּנְיָה Ch. *f.* Dan. iii. 5, *marg.* 'symphony, *or,* singing;' 10, 15.

סִיפֹנְיָה Ch. *f.* Dan. iii. 10, כתיב.

DUMB

אָלַם to bind, to confine; tongue-tied, dumb, silent. NIPHAL *pret.* Ps. xxxix. 2, 9: Isa. liii. 7: Ezek. iii. 26; xxxiii. 22: Dan. x. 15. *fut.* Ezek. xxiv. 27. אִלֵּם *adj.* mute, dumb: Exod. iv. 11: Ps. xxxviii. 13: Prov. xxxi. 8: Isa. xxxv. 6; lvi. 10: Hab. ii. 18.

דּוּמָם *adv.* silent: Hab. ii. 19.

DUNG

1 אַשְׁפּוֹת *m.* dung, a dunghill; *trop.* the emblem of deep and squalid poverty; as it was the retreat of the poorest beggar.

2 גָּלָל *m.* dung, from its roundness. ª גֵּלֶל *m.* dung; dried and used as fuel, giving a very offensive flavour to what is cooked. Some nations used even human dung, and cow-dung was not uncommonly employed.

3 דִּבְיוֹנִים *m. pl.* dove's dung, used in raising fruit, especially melons: 2 Kings vi. 25.

4 דֹּמֶן *m.* dung, manure. ª מַדְמֵנָה *f.* a dunghill.

5 חֲרָאִים *m. pl.* excrement, dung: קרי · חֲרִים *m. pl. id.* כתיב.

6 נְוָלוּ Ch. *f.* dunghill. ª נְוָלִי Ch. *f. id.*

7 פֶּרֶשׁ *m.* excrement, dung, so called as being separated and thrown off; dung of sacrifices.

8 צֹאָה *f.* excrement, ordure.

9 צְפִיעַ *m.* excrement of animals. ª צָפוּעַ *m. id.* כתיב.

Exod. xxix. 14.	7	Ezra vi. 11.	6	Jer. ix. 22.	4
Lev. iv. 11.	7	Neh. ii. 13.	1	xvi. 4.	4
viii. 17.	7	iii. 13, 14.	1	xxv. 33.	4
xvi. 27.	7	xii. 31.	1	Lam. iv. 5.	1
Num. xix. 5.	7	Job xx. 7.	2 a	Ezek. iv. 12.	2 a
1 Sam. ii. 8.	4	Ps. lxxxiii. 10	4	iv. 15, 15. 9, or 9 a, 2 a
1 Kings xiv. 10.	2	cxiii. 7.	1	iv. 29.	6 a
2 Kings vi. 25.	3, or 5 a	Isa. xxv. 10.	4 a	Dan. ii. 5.	6 a
ix. 37.	4	xxxvi. 12.	8, or 5	Zeph. i. 17.	2 a
xviii. 27.	8, or 5 a	Jer. viii. 2.	4	Mal. ii. 3, 3.	7

DUNGEON

בּוֹר *m.* see *Pit:* Gen. xl. 15; xli. 14: Exod. xii. 29, *lit.* house of the pit: Jer. xxxvii. 16, *lit. id.;* xxxviii. 6, 6, 7, 9, 10, 11, 13: Lam. iii. 53, 55.

בַּיִת *m.* house: Exod. xii. 29: Jer. xxxvii. 16.

DURABLE

עָתֵק *adj.* old, stable, durable: Prov. viii. 18. עָתִיק *adj.* Isa. xxiii. 18. Gesenius, splendid; others, comely. "According to the Arabic analogy, this word means 'ancient,' as an epithet of praise, and is accordingly resolved by

the modern writers into 'fine' or 'splendid.'"—*Alexander in loc.*

DURST

יָרֵא to fear. KAL *fut.* Job xxxii. 6, durst not, *lit.* feared.

DUST

אָבָק dust, small dust, *spec.* such as is fine and light, easily driven by the wind, or raised by horses running; hence distinguished from עָפָר, thick, heavy dust: Deut. xxviii. 24. *Poet.* the dust of His feet, for the clouds, as if trodden of God: Nah. i. 3. Exod. ix. 9: Isa. v. 24; xxix. 5: Ezek. xxvi. 10: Nah. i. 3.

דָּקַק to beat small, to crush, to make into powder. HIPHIL *pret.* 2 Chron. xxxiv. 4.

עָפָר *m.* dust, dry earth: put for the grave or the sepulchre, Job xx. 11, xxi. 26; hence put for the dead as about to dissolve into dust, Ps. xxx. 9, Eccles. xii. 7; to cast dust upon any one is to account him worthy of death, 2 Sam. xvi. 13, Acts xxii. 22–24; to eat dust, to lick the dust, of those who prostrate themselves in the dust; "dust and ashes," a proverbial expression for the lowness and frailty of human nature; dust also implies that which is innumerable, Num. xxiii. 10, Gen. ii. 7, &c.

שַׁחַק *m.* dust, fine dust; a cloud: Isa. xl. 15.

DUTY

דָּבָר *m.* word, matter, &c.: 2 Chron. viii. 14: Ezra iii. 4.

עוֹנָה *f.* conjugal cohabitation, "duty of marriage:" Exod. xxi. 10.

DWARF

דַּק *adj.* slender, thin, lank, withered; of a person, tabid, withered, or having a withered member: Lev. xxi. 20, *marg.* ' or, too slender.'

DWELL

1 אֹהֶל *m.* tent, tabernacle; dwelling, habitation, house.

2 גּוּר to sojourn, to dwell for a time. KAL [a] *pret.* [b] *inf.* [c] *fut.* [d] *part.* Poel. [e] מָגוּר *m.* sojourning.

3 דּוּר to remain, to dwell. KAL [a] *inf.* דּוּר Ch. P'AL [b] *fut.* [c] *part.* [d] מְדָר Ch. *m.* habitation. [e] מְדוֹר Ch. *m. id.*

4 זָבַל to dwell, to dwell with. KAL [a] *fut.* זְבוּל and זֶבֶל *m.* a dwelling, habitation. *Poetic.*

5 חָנָה to set oneself down in a place, to pitch a tent, to abide. KAL [a] *pret.* [b] *fut.*

6 יָשַׁב to sit down, to seat oneself; to remain, abide, tarry; to dwell, to dwell in, to inhabit; to dwell (together), as a family, in concord, Ps. cxxxiii. 1. KAL [a] *pret.* [b] *inf.* [c] *imp.* [d] *fut.* [e] *part.* Poel. HIPHIL [f] *pret.* [g] *imp.* [h] *fut.* [i] מוֹשָׁב *m.* habitation; dweller.

7 יְתֵב Ch. to sit. P'AL *part.*

8 מָכוֹן *m.* foundation; place; dwelling-place, fixed abode.

9 לִין to lodge all night. KAL *fut.*

10 נָוֶה *m.* seat in which one rests; habitation, dwelling. [a] נָוָה *f. id.*

11 מָעוֹן *m.* habitation, dwelling. [a] מְעוֹנָה *f. id.*

12 עָמַד to stand, to abide, continue. KAL *part.* Poel.

13 שָׁכַן to lay oneself down; to abide, to dwell; *seq.* בְּ, and *acc.* of place; also to pitch a tent, Job iii. 5. Schultens, "let the cloud pitch its tent over it." Good, "the gathered tempest pavilion over it." KAL [a] *pret.* [b] *inf.* [c] *imp.* [d] *fut.* [e] *part.* Poel. [f] *part.* Paül. PIEL [g] *pret.* [h] *inf.* [i] *fut.* HIPHIL [k] *fut.* שֶׁכֶן Ch. PAEL [l] *pret.* [m] מִשְׁכָּן *m.* tabernacle, dwelling, dwelling-place.

14 שְׁרָא Ch. to loose; to put up for the night; to lodge, to dwell. P'AL *pret.*

Gen. iv. 16.	6 d	Num. xxiv. 21.	6 i	Judg. xviii. 7.		6 e
iv. 20.	6 e	xxxi. 10.	6 e	xviii. 28.		6 d
ix. 27.	13 d	xxxii. 17.	6 a	xxi. 23.		6 d
x. 30.	6 i	xxxii. 40.	6 d	Ruth i. 4.		6 d
xi. 2, 31.	6 d	xxxiii. 40, 55.	6 e	ii. 23.		6 d
xiii. 6, 6.	6 b	xxxiii. 53.	6 a	1 Sam. iv. 4.		6 e
xiii. 7.	6 e	xxxv. 2, 3, 32.	6 b	vii. 8.		6 h
xiii. 12, 12.	6 a	xxxv. 29.	6 i	xii. 11.		6 d
xiii. 18.	6 d	xxxv. 34, 34.	13 e	xix. 18.		6 d
xiv. 7, 12.	6 e	Deut. i. 4, 4, 44.		xxii. 4.		6 d
xiv. 13.	13 e	i. 6.	6 b	xxiii. 29.		6 d
xvi. 3.	6 b	ii. 4, 8, 29, 29.	6 e	xxvii. 3, 5, 5.		6 d
xvi. 12.	13 d	ii. 10, 20.	6 a	xxvii. 7, 11.		6 d
xix. 29.	6 a	ii. 12, 12.	6 a d	xxxi. 7.		6 d
xix. 30, 30, 30.	6 d b d	ii. 21.	6 d	2 Sam. iii. 3.		6 d
xx. 1.	6 d	ii. 22, 22.	6 e d	v. 9.		6 d
xx. 15.	6 c	ii. 23, 23.	6 e d	vi. 2.		6 e
xxi. 20, 21.	6 d	iii. 2.	6 e	vii. 2, 2.		6 d
xxii. 19.	6 d	iv. 46.	6 a	vii. 5.		6 b
xxiii. 10.	6 e	viii. 12.	6 a	vii. 6.		6 a
xxiv. 3, 37, 62.	6 d	xi. 30.	6 e	vii. 10.		13 a
xxv. 11.	6 d	xi. 31.	6 a	ix. 12.		6 i
xxv. 18.	13 d	xii. 10, 10, 29.	6 a	ix. 13.		6 d
xxv. 27.	6 e	xii. 11.	13 h	xiv. 28.		6 d
xxvi. 2.	13 c	xiii. 12.	6 b	1 Kings ii. 36.		6 d
xxvi. 6, 17.	6 d	xvii. 14.	6 a	ii. 38.		6 d
xxvii. 39.	6 i	xix. 1.	6 e	iii. 17.		6 d
xxx. 20.	4 a	xxiii. 16.	6 d	iv. 25.		6 d
xxxiv. 10, 10.	6 d c	xxv. 5.	6 d	vi. 13.		13 a
xxxiv. 16.	6 a	xxvi. 1.	6 a	vii. 8.		6 d
xxxiv. 21, 23.	6 b	xxxiii. 40.	6 d	viii. 12.		13 b
xxxiv. 22.	6 b	xxix. 16.	6 a	viii. 13. β		4 b
xxxv. 1.	6 c	xxx. 20.	6 d	viii. 27.		6 d
xxxv. 22.	13 b	xxxiii. 12, 12.	13 d a	viii. 30, 39, 43, 49.		6 e
xxxvi. 7.	6 b	xxxiii. 16.	13 e	ix. 16.		6 d
xxxvi. 8.	6 d	xxxiii. 20.	13 a	xi. 24.		6 d
xxxvii. 1.	6 d	xxxiii. 28.	13 d	xii. 2, 25.		6 d
xxxviii. 11.	6 d	Josh. ii. 15.	6 e	xii. 17.		6 d
xlv. 10.	6 a	vi. 25.	6 d	xiii. 11, 25.		6 e
xlvi. 34.	6 d	vii. 7.	6 d	xv. 18.		6 e
xlvii. 4, 27.	6 d	ix. 7, 16, 22.	6 e	xv. 21.		6 d
xlvii. 6, 6.	6 g d	x. 6.	6 e	xvii. 5.		6 d
xlix. 13.	13 d	xii. 2, 4.	6 e	xvii. 9.		6 a
l. 22.	6 d	xiii. 13.	6 e	xxi. 8.		6 d
Exod. ii. 15.	6 d	xiii. 21.	6 e	2 Kings iv. 13.		6 e
ii. 21.	6 b	xiv. 4.	6 d	vi. 1.		6 e
viii. 22.	12	xv. 63.	6 d	vi. 2.		6 e
x. 23.	6 i	xvi. 10, 10.	6 e d	xiii. 5.		6 d
xii. 40.	6 a	xvii. 12.	6 b	xv. 5.		6 d
xv. 17.	6 b	xvii. 16.	6 d	xvi. 6.		6 d
xxiii. 33.	6 d	xix. 47, 50.	6 d	xvii. 24, 27, 28.		6 d
xxv. 8.	13 a	xx. 4, 6.	6 a	xvii. 25.		6 b
xxix. 45.	13 a	xxi. 2.	6 b	xvii. 29.		6 e
xxix. 46.	13 b	xxi. 43.	6 d	xix. 15.		6 e
Lev. iii. 17.	6 i	xxii. 19.	13 a	xix. 36.		6 d
vii. 26.	6 i	xxii. 33.	6 e	xxii. 14.		6 e
xiii. 46.	6 d	xxiv. 2.	6 e	xxv. 24.		6 e
xviii. 3.	6 d	xxiv. 7, 13.	6 d	1 Chron. ii. 55.	6 e a
xix. 34.	2 d	xxiv. 8, 15, 18.	6 e	iv. 23, 23.	6 d
xx. 22.	6 b	Judg. i. 9, 10.	6 e	iv. 28, 41, 43.	6 e
xxiii. 3, 14, 21, 31.	6 d	i. 16, 21, 30, 32, 33.	6 e	iv. 40.	6 e
xxiii. 42, 42.	6 d	i. 27, 35.	6 b	v. 8.	6 e
xxiii. 43.	6 f	i. 29, 29.	6 e d	v. 10, 16, 22.	6 d
xxv. 18, 19.	6 a	iii. 3.	6 e	v. 11, 23.	6 a
xxv. 29.	6 b	iii. 5.	6 a	vi. 32.	13 m
xxvi. 5.	6 a	iv. 2, 5.	6 e	vi. 54.	6 i
xxvi. 32.	6 e	vi. 10.	6 e	vii. 29.	6 a
xxvi. 35.	6 b	viii. 11.	13 f	viii. 28, 29, 32.	6 e
Num. v. 3.	13 e	viii. 29.	6 d	ix. 3, 34, 35, 38.	6 e
xiii. 18, 19, 19, 28, 29, 29, 29.	6 e	ix. 21.	6 d	ix. 16.	6 e
xiv. 25, 45.	6 e	ix. 41, 41.	6 d b	x. 7.	6 e
xiv. 30.	13 h	x. 1.	6 e	xi. 7.	6 d
xx. 15.	6 d	xi. 3.	6 d	xiii. 6.	6 e
xxi. 1, 34.	6 e	xi. 26.	6 b	xvii. 1.	6 e
xxi. 15.	6 b	xv. 8.	6 d	xvii. 4.	6 b
xxi. 25, 31.	6 d	xvii. 10.	6 d	xvii. 5.	6 a
xxiii. 9. a	13 d	xvii. 11.	6 b	xvii. 9.	13 a
		xviii. 1.	6 b	xxiii. 25.	13 d

2 Chron. ii. 3.	6 b	Ps. ci. 6.	6 b	Jer. xliv. 1, 1, 2, 13, 15, 26.	6 e
vi. 1.	13 b	ci. 7.	6 d	xliv. 8.	2 b
vi. 2, 21, 30, 33, 39.	6 b	cvii. 4.	6 i	xliv. 14.	6 b
vi. 18.	6 d	cvii. 34.	6 e	xlvi. 19.	6 e
viii. 2.	6 h	cvii. 36.	6 h	xlvii. 2.	6 e
viii. 11.	6 d	cxiii. 5.	6 b	xlviii. 9.	6 e
x. 17.	6 e	cxx. 5, 6.	13 a	xlvii. 28, 28.	6 e, 13 c
xi. 5.	6 e	cxxiii. 1.	6 e	xlix. 1.	6 a
xvi. 2.	6 e	cxxxii. 14.	6 d	xlix. 8, 30.	6 b
xix. 4.	6 d	cxxxiii. 1.	6 b	xlix. 16.	13 e
xix. 10.	6 e	cxxxv. 21.	13 e	xlix. 18.	2 c
xx. 8.	6 d	cxxxix. 9.	13 d	xlix. 31, 31.	6 e, 13 d
xxvi. 7.	6 e	cxl. 13.	6 d	xlix. 33, 33.	11, 2 c
xxvi. 21.	6 d	Prov. i. 33.	13 d	l. 3.	6 e
xxviii. 18.	6 d	ii. 21.	13 d	l. 39, 39, 39.	6 d a, 13 d
xxx. 25.	6 e	iii. 29.	6 e	l. 40.	2 c
xxx. 27.	11	viii. 12.	13 a	li. 1.	6 e
xxxi. 4, 6.	6 e	xxi. 9, 19.	6 b	li. 13.	13 e
xxxiv. 22.	6 e	xxiv. 15.	10	li. 30.	13 m
xxxvi. 15.	11	xxv. 24.	6 b	li. 37.	11
Ezra ii. 70.	6 d	Cant. viii. 13.	6 e	lii. 4.	6 d
iv. 17.	7	Isa. iv. 5.	8	Lam. i. 3.	6 a
vi. 12.	13 l	vi. 5.	6 e	iv. 21.	6 e
Neh. iii. 26.	6 e	viii. 18.	13 e	Ezek. ii. 6.	6 e
iv. 12.	6 e	ix. 2.	6 e	iii. 15.	6 e
vii. 73.	6 d	x. 24.	6 e	vi. 6.	6 i
viii. 14.	6 d	xi. 6.	2 a	vii. 7.	6 e
xi. 1, 1.	6 d b	xiii. 20.	13 d	xii. 2, 19.	6 e
xi. 2.	6 b	xiii. 21.	13 a	xvi. 46, 46.	6 e
xi. 3, 3, 4, 25.	6 a	xvi. 4.	2 c	xvii. 23, 23.	13 a d
xi. 6, 21.	6 e	xviii. 3.	13 e	xxv. 4.	13 m
xi. 30.	5 b	xviii. 4.	8	xxviii. 25, 26, 26.	6 a
xiii. 16.	6 a	xxiii. 18.	6 e	xxxi. 6.	6 a
Esth. ix. 19.	6 e	xxiv. 6.	6 e	xxxi. 17.	6 a
Job iii. 5.	13 d	xxvi. 5.	6 e	xxxii. 15.	6 a
iv. 19.	13 e	xxvi. 19.	13 e	xxxiv. 25, 28.	6 a
viii. 22.	1	xxix. 1.	5 a	xxxvi. 17.	6 a
xi. 14.	13 k	xxx. 19.	6 d	xxxvi. 28.	6 a
xv. 28.	13 d	xxxii. 16.	13 a	xxxvi. 33.	6 f
xviii. 15.	13 d	xxxii. 18, 18.	6 a, 13 m	xxxvii. 23.	6 a
xviii. 19.	2 e	xxxiii. 5.	13 e	xxxvii. 25, 25, 25.	6 a
xviii. 21.	13 m	xxxiii. 14, 14.	2 c	xxxviii. 8.	6 a
xix. 15.	2 d	xxxiii. 16.	13 d	xxxviii. 11, 11, 12.	6 e
xxi. 28.	1, 13 m	xxxiii. 24.	6 e	xxxviii. 14.	6 b
xxii. 8.	6 d	xxxiv. 11, 17.	13 d	xxxix. 6, 9.	6 e
xxix. 25.	13 d	xxxvii. 16.	6 e	xxxix. 26.	6 b
xxx. 6.	13 b	xxxvii. 37.	6 d	xliii. 7.	13 d
xxxviii. 19.	13 d	xl. 22.	6 b	xliii. 9.	13 a
xxxix. 6.	13 m	xlvii. 8.	6 e	xlviii. 15.	6 i
xxxix. 28.	13 d	xlix. 20.	6 d	Dan. ii. 11.	3 d
Ps. iv. 8.	6 h	li. 6.	6 e	ii. 22.	14
v. 4.	2 c	lvii. 15.	13 d	ii. 38.	3 c
ix. 11.γ	6 c	lviii. 12.	6 b	iv. 1.	3 c
xv. 1.	13 d	lxv. 9.	13 d	iv. 12, 21.	3 b
xxiii. 6.	6 a	Jer. ii. 6.	9	iv. 25, 32.	3 e
xxiv. 1.	6 e	iv. 29.	6 e	v. 21.	3 e
xxv. 13.	9	vii. 3.	13 i	vi. 25.	3 c
xxvi. 8.	13 m	vii. 7.	13 g	Hos. iv. 3.	6 d
xxvii. 4.	6 b	viii. 16.	6 e	ix. 3.	6 d
xxxvii. 3, 27.	13 d	ix. 19.	13 m	xii. 9.	6 h
xxxvii. 29.	13 d	ix. 26.	6 e	xiv. 7.	6 e
xlix. 11.	13 m	xii. 4.	6 e	Joel iii. 17, 21.	13 e
xlix. 14.	4 b	xx. 6.	6 e	iii. 20.	6 d
lii. 5.	1	xxiii. 6.	13 d	Amos iii. 12.	6 e
lv. 15.	2 e	xxiii. 8.	6 a	v. 11.	6 d
lxv. 4.	13 d	xxiv. 8.	6 e	viii. 8.	6 d
lxv. 8.	6 e	xxv. 5.	6 c	Obad. 3.	13 e
lxviii. 6.	13 a	xxv. 24.	13 e	Micah iv. 10.	13 a
lxviii. 10.	6 a	xxvii. 11.	6 a	vii. 13.	6 e
lxviii. 16, 16.	6 b, 13 d	xxix. 5, 28.	6 c	vii. 14.	13 e
lxviii. 18.	13 b	xxix. 16, 32.δ	6 e	Nah. i. 5.	6 e
lxix. 25.	6 e	xxx. 18.	13 m	ii. 11.	11
lxix. 35.	6 a	xxxi. 24.	6 a	iii. 18.	13 d
lxix. 36.	13 d	xxxii. 37.	6 f	Hab. i. 6.	13 m
lxxiv. 2.	13 a	xxxiii. 16.	13 d	ii. 8, 17.	6 e
lxxiv. 7.	13 m	xxxv. 7, 10, 11.	6 d	Zeph. i. 18.	6 e
lxxvi. 2.	11 a	xxxv. 9.	6 d	ii. 5.	10 a
lxxviii. 55.	13 k	xxxv. 15.	6 c	ii. 15.	6 c
lxxix. 7.	10	xxxix. 14.	6 d	iii. 7.	11
lxxx. 1.	6 e	xl. 5, 9.	6 c	Hag. i. 4.	6 b
lxxxiv. 4.	6 e	xl. 6.		Zech. ii. 6.	6 e
lxxxv. 10.	3 a	xl. 10, 10.	6 e c	ii. 10, 11.	13 a
lxxxv. 9.	13 b	xli. 17.	6 d	viii. 3, 8.	13 a
lxxxvii. 2.	13 m	xlii. 13, 14.	6 d	viii. 4.	6 d
xc. 1.	11	xliii. 4.	6 d	ix. 6.	6 a
xci. 1.	6 c	xliii. 5.	2 b	xiv. 11.	6 a
xci. 10.	1				
xciv. 17.	13 a				
xcviii. 7.					

α *lit.* dwelleth alone. β *lit.* a house of habitation. γ or, sitteth (on his throne) in Zion, as in ver. 7. δ *lit.* dwelling.

spoken especially of a bright red or scarlet colour, as of the scarlet mantle or pallium of a prince. KAL *part.* Paül, Isa. lxiii. 1.

טְבוּלִים *m. pl.* head-bands, tiaras, turbans; as dyed with different colours: Ezek. xxiii. 15.

EAGLE

נֶשֶׁר *m.* the eagle, king of birds, armed with a strong crooked beak and talons. It becomes remarkably bare in moulting time, when it casts its feathers, Micah i. 16; but appears in the beauty and gaiety of youth when they grow again, Isa. xl. 31. Its wings are very large and strong, Ezek. xvii. 3; its flight exceeding swift (Deut. xxviii. 49) and lofty, Prov. xxiii. 5; its sight very penetrating and extensive, Job xxxix. 27–29. It is said to be very affectionate to its young, assisting and supporting their flight, when they first leave their nests, with its own wings.—*Bochart.* Exod. xix. 4, &c. נְשַׁר Ch. *m. id.*

רָחָם *m.* רַחֲמָה *f.* gier-eagle: a species of the vulture, so called from its affection to its young. By the Naturalists it is called *vultur perchopterus.* There are several flocks near Cairo, which feed upon the carrion and what is thrown without the city; very harmless and inoffensive: Lev. xi. 18: Deut. xiv. 17.

EAR

1 אָזַן to ponder, to give ear, to listen: *abs.* Isa. i. 2, *seq. acc.* Gen. iv. 23; לְ, אֶל, עַל, and צַד, both of person and thing. HIPHIL [a] *pret.* [b] *imp.* [c] *fut.* [d] *part.* [e] אֹזֶן *m.* the ear; "in the ears" is expressive not only of attention on the part of the hearer, but of his laying up in his mind what he hears, Exod. xvii. 14. To hear with the ear is emphatic, Ps. xliv. 1: Job xxviii. 22. Ps. xl. 6, "mine ears hast thou opened:" some explain this phrase by an allusion to the custom of boring the ears of slaves, who vowed perpetual service to their masters; but our translation seems to prefer the meaning which we find elsewhere, of revealing the ear or uncovering it, Job xxxiii. 16: Isa. l. 4, 5: 1 Sam. xx. 2, 12, 13; xxii. 8, 8, 17. The main import of Ps. xl. 6 may be, "thou hast prepared me to be obedient;" which is according to the Lxx.; and St. Paul adopts the same, "a body hast thou prepared me," *i. e.* in which that obedience shall be fulfilled: Gen. xx. 8, &c.

2 שָׁמַע to hear, give ear. KAL *pret.*

No. 1 e not included.

Exod. xv. 26.	1 a	Ps. xxxix. 12.	1 b	Prov. xvii. 4.	1 d
Deut. i. 45.	1 a	xlix. 1.	1 b	Isa. i. 2, 10.	1 b
xxxii. 1.	1 b	liv. 2.	1 b	viii. 9.	1 b
Judg. v. 3.	1 b	lv. 1.	1 b	xxviii. 23.	1 b
2 Chron. xxiv. 19.	1 a	lxxvii. 1.	1 a	xxxii. 9.	1 b
Neh. ix. 30.	1 a	lxxviii. 1.	1 b	xlii. 23.	1 c
Job xxix. 21.	2	lxxx. 1.	1 b	li. 4.	1 b
xxxii. 11.	1 c	lxxxiv. 8.	1 b	lxiv. 4.	1 a
xxxii. 2.	1 b	lxxxvi. 6.	1 b	Jer. xiii. 15.	1 b
Ps. v. 1.	1 b	cxli. 1.	1 b	Hos. v. 1.	1 b
xvii. 1.	1 b	cxliii. 1.	1 b	Joel i. 2.	1 b

DYE

חָמֵץ to be sharp; as to the sight, colour, to be bright, dazzling,

EAR OF CORN

אָבִיב *m.* green ears of corn: Exod. ix. 31: Lev. ii. 14.

כַּרְמֶל *m.* Carmel, a fruitful field, or hill; figuratively, the fruit that grows in such a field; green ears, or the best and fullest ears of corn while green: Lev. ii. 14; xxiii. 14: 2 Kings iv. 42.

מְלִילָה *f.* ears of corn, so called because about to be cut off when reaped; therefore in Deut. xxiii. 25 to be understood of ears beginning to ripen.

שִׁבֹּלֶת *f.* an ear of grain; or perhaps the spices and stalks of standing grain, as implied in Isa. xvii. 5.——Gen. xli. 5, 6, 7, 7, 22, 23, 24, 24, 26, 27: Ruth ii. 2: Job xxiv. 24: Isa. xvii. 5, 5.

EAR (V)

חָרַשׁ to plough. KAL *inf.* 1 Sam. viii. 12. חָרִישׁ *m.* time for ploughing: Gen. xlv. 6: Exod. xxxiv. 21.

עָבַד to work, to labour: it is applied to tilling the ground. KAL *part.* Poel, Isa. xxx. 24. NIPHAL *fut.* Deut. xxi. 4.

EARLY

בֹּקֶר *m.* see *Morning.* Ps. xlvi. 5; xc. 14; ci. 8, *lit.* to the mornings.

שַׁחַר *m.* morning: Ps. lvii. 8; cviii. 2, *or,* I will awake the morning.

שָׁכַם to rise early; to get up early; *seq.* לְ to any place; see *Rise.* HIPHIL *pret.* Judg. xix. 9: 1 Sam. xxix. 10. *fut.* Gen. xix. 27: 2 Kings vi. 15: Cant. vii. 12. *part.* Ps. cxxvii. 2: Hos. vi. 4; xiii. 3.

שְׁפַרְפָּרָא Ch. *m.* dawn: Dan. vi. 19, "very early in the morning."

EARNEST

חָרָה to be hot. HIPHIL *pret.* Neh. iii. 20, *lit.* made hot to repair.

יָטַב to be good; to do well. HIPHIL *inf.* Micah vii. 3.

EAR-RING

לַחַשׁ *m.* see *Charm.* It is most probable that what is intended in Isa. iii. 20 is some kind of amulet or ornament on which charms were written, and not ear-rings. Barnes, small images of serpents, worn by oriental females. Chardin says that ear-rings had some kind of characters on them, as charms.

נֶזֶם *m.* an ornament worn by women (and also by men, Job xlii. 11) in the nose, or over it, hanging down from the forehead, Gen. xxiv. 47; such as is still worn in Ethiopia. Also an ornament for the ear, Gen. xxxv. 4, Exod. xxxii. 2. In some places it is uncertain where it was worn: Gen. xxiv. 22; xxx. 47; xxxv. 4: Exod. xxxii. 3; xxxv. 22: Judg. viii. 24, 24, 25, 26: Job xlii. 11: Prov. xxv. 12: Hos. ii. 13.

עָגִיל *m.* some ornament of a round or circular form: Num. xxxi. 50: Ezek. xvi. 12.

EARTH, EARTHEN

1 אֲדָמָה *f.* the earth, material earth, the ground; cultivated land; sometimes put for the whole earth, or world.

2 אֶרֶץ *com.* the earth in the largest sense, both the habitable and uninhabitable parts; with some accompanying word of limitation, it is used of some portion of the earth's surface, a land or country. Gussetius derives this word, the name which God himself pronounced, from אָרְצָה the future of רָצָה to love; as intended to signify God's promised benevolence to the world he had created, to which he supposes there is an allusion in Prov. viii. 31.— Gen. i. 1, &c. [a] אַרְקָא *f. emphat.* Ch. *id.* [b] אֲרַע *f.* Ch. *id.* אַרְעָא Ch. כְּתִיב.

3 חֲרַשׂ *m.* potter's clay or earth; earthen.

4 יַבֶּשֶׁת Ch. *f.* dry.

5 יָצַר to form as a potter. KAL *part.* Poel.

6 עָפָר *m.* dust, dry earth, or barren.

No. 2 not included.

Gen. i. 25, 25.	2 1	Deut. xii. 1, 19.*a*	1	Isa. xxiii. 17.		1
iv. 11.	1	xiv. 2.	1	xxiv. 21, 21.		1
iv. 14, 14.	1 2	xxvi. 2.	1	xxx. 23.		1
vi. 1, 7, 20.	1	1 Sam. iv. 12.	1	xlv. 9.		1
vii. 4, 4.	2 1	xx. 15.	1	Jer. viii. 2.		1
vii. 8.	1	2 Sam. i. 2.	1	x. 11, 11.	2 b	[a]
ix. 2, 2.	2 1	xiv. 7.	1	xvi. 4, 4.	1	[2]
xii. 3.	1	xv. 32.	1	xix. 1.		3
xxvi. 15.	6	xvii. 28.*β*	5	xxv. 26.		1
xxviii. 14, 14.	2 1	1 Kings xiii. 34.	1	xxviii. 16.		3
Exod. x. 6.	1	xvii. 14.	1	xxxii. 14.		3
xx. 24.	1	xviii. 1.	1	Lam. iv. 2.		3
xxxii. 12.	1	2 Kings v. 17.	2 b	Ezek. xxxviii. 20, 20.		4
xxxiii. 16.	1	Ezra v. 11.	1	Dan. ii. 10.		2 b
Lev. vi. 28.	3	Neh. ix. 1.	1	ii. 35, 39.		
xi. 33.	3	Job viii. 19.	6	iv. 1, 10, 11, 15, 15,		
xiv. 5, 50.	3	xix. 25.	6	20, 22, 23, 35, 35.		2 b
xv. 12.	3	xxviii. 2.	6	vi. 25, 27.		2 b
Num. v. 17.	3	xxx. 6.	6	vii. 4, 17, 23, 23.		2 b
xii. 3.	1	ii. 33.	6	xii. 2.*γ*		1, 6
xvi. 30.	1	Ps. lxxxiii. 10.	1	Amos iii. 2.		1
Deut. iv. 10, 40.	1	civ. 30.	1	iii. 5, 5.	2 1	
vi. 15.	1	cxlvi. 4.	1	ix. 8.		1
vii. 6.	1	Isa. ii. 19, 19.	6 2			

a lit. thy earth.   *β lit.* vessels of the potter.   *γ lit.* earth of dust.

EARTHQUAKE

רַעַשׁ *m.* a trembling, shaking; earthquake: 1 Kings xix. 11, 11, 12: Isa. xxix. 6: Amos i. 1: Zech. xiv. 5.

EASE, EASY

1 הָלַךְ to go. KAL *fut.,* *lit.* what goeth from me.

2 טוֹב *adj.* good.

3 יָשַׁב to sit; to ease oneself. KAL *inf.*

4 מְנוּחָה *f.* a resting; rest, quiet.

5 נָחַם to repent, to grieve; to console oneself; to avenge oneself, to take vengeance. NIPHAL *fut.*

6 נָשָׂא to lift up, to bear. KAL *fut.*

7 קָלַל to be light. NIPHAL [a]*pret.* HIPHIL [b]*imp.*

8 רָגַע to cause to tremble; to shrink for fear; to be quiet, still. HIPHIL *fut.*

9 שָׁאַן to rest, to be quiet. PILEL [a]*pret.* [b]שַׁאֲנָן *adj.* tranquil. living at ease, careless.

10 שַׁלְאֲנָן *adj.* tranquil.

11 שָׁלֵו *adj.* secure, tranquil, at rest; in a bad sense, at ease, careless.

Exod. xviii. 22.	7 b	2 Chron. x. 4, 9.	7 b	Job xvi. 12.	11
Deut. xxiii. 13.	3	Job vii. 13.	6	xxi. 23.	10
xxviii. 65.	8	xii. 5.	9 b	Ps. xxv. 13.	2
Judg. xx. 43.	4	xvi. 6.	1	cxxiii. 4.	9 b

Prov. xiv. 6.	7 a	Jer. xlvi. 27.	9 a	Amos vi. 1.	9 b
Isa. i. 24.	5	xlviii. 11.	9 a	Zech. i. 15.	9 b
xxxii. 9, 11.	9 b	Ezek. xxiii. 42.	11		

EAST, EASTWARD

1 בֵּן *m.* son: Isa. xi. 14, *marg.* 'children of the east.'

2 דֶּרֶךְ *com.* way; "eastward," *lit.* the way of the east.

3 מִזְרָח *m.* the rising of the sun.

4 חַרְסִית *f.* Jer. xix. 2, *marg.* 'the sun gate.'

5 מוֹצָא *m.* going forth, applied to the rising of the sun.

6 קֶדֶם *m.* that which is before, the east, eastern quarter. a קֵדְמָה *m. id.* with ה local. b קֵדְמָה *f. id.* c קַדְמוֹן *adj.* eastern. d קַדְמוֹנִי *adj. id.* e קָדִים the east, east wind; very violent, hot and scorching, pernicious to fruit, &c.: Gen. xli. 6, &c.

7 שֶׁמֶשׁ *com.* sun; east side, eastward: Judg. xi. 18, *lit.* rising of the sun; xxi. 19: 2 Kings x. 33.

No. 6 e not included.

Ref	Code	Ref	Code	Ref	Code
Gen. ii. 8.	6	Josh. xvi. 1, 5, 6, 6.	3	2 Chron. xxxi. 14.	3
ii. 14.	6 b	xvii. 10.	3	Neh. iii. 26, 29.	3
iii. 24.	6	xviii. 7.	3	xii. 37.	3
iv. 16.	6 b	xviii. 20.	6 a	Job i. 3.	6
x. 30.	6	xix. 12.	6 a	lxxv. 6.	3
xi. 2.	6	xix. 13. a	6 a	ciii. 12.	3
xii. 8, 8.	6	xx. 8.	6 a, 3	cvii. 12.	3
xiii. 11.	6	Judg. vi. 3, 33.	6	Isa. ii. 6.	6
xiii. 14.	6 a	vii. 12.	6	xi. 14.	1, 6
xxv. 6, 6.	6 a b	viii. 10, 11.	6	xli. 2.	3
xxviii. 14.	6 a	xi. 18.	3, 7	xliii. 5.	3
Exod. xxvii. 13, 13.	6 a, 3	xxi. 19.	3, 7	xlvi. 11.	3
xxxviii. 13, 13.	6 a, 3	1 Sam. xiii. 5.	6 b	Jer. xix. 2.	4
Lev. i. 6.	6 a	1 Kings iv. 30.	6	xxxi. 40.	3
xvi. 14.	6 a	vii. 25.	3	xlix. 28.	6
Num. ii. 3.	6 a	vii. 39.	6 a	Ezek. iv. 8.	6 a
iii. 38, 38.	6 a, 3	xvii. 3.	6 a	viii. 16, 16.	6 a
x. 5.	6 a	2 Kings x. 33.	3, 7	x. 19.	6 d
xxiii. 7.	6	xiii. 17.	6 a	xi. 1.	6 d
xxxii. 19.	3	1 Chron. iv. 39.	3	xxxix. 11.	3
xxxiv. 3, 10, 15.	6 a	v. 9, 10.	3	xl. 10. β	2, 6 e
xxxiv. 11, 11.	6, 6 a	vi. 78.	3	xlv. 7, 7.	6 a c e
xxxv. 5.	6 a	vii. 28.	3	xlvii. 8.	6 c
Deut. iii. 17, 27.	3	ix. 18, 24.	3	xlvii. 18, 18, 18.	6 e d e
iv. 49.	3	xii. 15.	3	Dan. viii. 9.	3
Josh. xvii. 19.	3	xxvi. 14, 17.	3	xi. 4, 4.	3
vii. 2.	6	2 Chron. iv. 4.	3	Joel ii. 20.	6 d
xi. 3, 9.	3	iv. 10.	6 a	Amos viii. 12.	3
xii. 1, 3, 3.	3	v. 12.	3	Zech. viii. 7.	3
xiii. 8, 27, 32.	3	xxix. 4.	3	xiv. 4.	3
xv. 15.	6 a				

a *lit.* eastward, toward the sun rising.   β *lit.* the way of the east.

EAT

1 אָכַל to eat, to eat up, to consume victuals, &c., to taste: Deut. iv. 28. *c. acc.* of food; rarely *seq.* לְ, בְּ, and מִן. To diminish, to take from: Ezek. xlii. 5: see *High.* Ps. xiv. 4, "They eat up my people as they eat bread," *i. e.* they plunder, harass, and exhaust them; *cf.* Prov. xxx. 14, Hab. iii. 14. Jer. xv. 16, "Thy words were found and I did eat them," *i. e.* I received them with great readiness, and laid them up in my heart: so we are to understand the visions of Ezekiel and John eating the roll, Ezek. ii. 8, iii. 1, &c., Rev. x. 9, 10; and this illustrates the phrase of eating the words and flesh of Christ, John vi. 32, &c. To eat means sometimes to enjoy, Job xxi. 25; as also to delight in sin, Prov. xxx. 20. To eat of the same bread is a token of friendship, Ps. xli. 9. With *inf.,* freely, indeed, in nowise at all, in plenty. KAL a *pret.* b *inf.* c *imp.* d *fut.* e *part.* Poel. NIPHAL f *inf.* g *fut.* h *part.* HIPHIL i *pret.* k *imp.* l *fut.* אֲכַל Ch. PA'L m *fut.* n אָכַל *m.* eating. o אָכְלָה *f.* food.

2 בּוֹא to enter in. KAL a *pret.* b *fut.*

3 בָּלַע to swallow down. KAL *fut.*

4 בָּעַר to burn; to eat up, to feed. PIEL a *pret.* b *inf.* HIPHIL c *fut.*

5 בָּרָה to eat a meal's meat. See *Choose.* KAL a *pret.* b *fut.* HIPHIL c *inf.*

6 חָלַל to profane; to eat as common things; see *Gather.* PIEL a *pret.* b *fut.*

7 טְעַם Ch. to taste. PA'L *fut.*

8 כָּלָה to be finished, consumed. PIEL *pret.*

9 לָחַם to eat, to devour, to consume. KAL a *pret.* b *inf.* c *imp.* c *fut.* e לֶחֶם *m.* bread. f לחום *m.* food.

10 פֶּה *m.* mouth: Gen. xxv. 28, *lit.* venison was in his mouth.

11 קֶרֶב *m.* inward.

12 רָעָה to feed. KAL *fut.*

Ref	Code	Ref	Code	Ref	Code
Gen. ii. 16.	1 b d	Exod. xxix. 34.	1 g	Deut. iv. 28.	1 d
ii. 17, 17.	1 d b	xxxii. 6.	1 b	vi. 11.	1 a
iii. 1, 2, 3, 6, 6, 12, 13, 14, 17, 17, 17,	1 a	xxxiv. 15, 28.	1 a	viii. 9, 12.	1 d
19.	1 d	xxxiv. 18.	1 d	viii. 10.	1 d
iii. 5.	1 b	Lev. iii. 17.	1 d	ix. 9, 18.	1 a
iii. 11, 11.	1 a b	vi. 16, 16, 16.	1 d g d	xi. 15.	1 a
iii. 18, 22.	1 a	vi. 18, 29.	1 d	xi. 7, 21.	1 a
vi. 21.	1 d	vi. 23, 30.	1 g	xii. 15, 15.	1 a d
ix. 4.	1 d	vi. 26, 26.	1 d g	xii. 16, 18, 24, 25, 27.	1 d
xiv. 24.	1 d	vii. 6, 6.	1 d g	xii. 17.	1 d
xviii. 8.	1 d	vii. 15, 16, 16.	1 g	xii. 20, 20, 20.	1 d b d
xix. 3.	1 d	vii. 18, 18.	1 f g e	xii. 22, 22, 22.	1 g d d
xxiv. 33, 33.	1 b d	vii. 19, 19.	1 g d	xii. 23, 23.	1 b d
xxiv. 54.	1 d	vii. 20, 23, 26, 27.	1 d	xiv. 3, 4, 6, 7, 8, 9, 9, 10, 11, 12, 20.	1 g
xxv. 28.	10	vii. 24.	1 b d	xiv. 19.	1 g
xxv. 34.	1 d	vii. 25, 25.	1 e	xiv. 23, 26, 29.	1 a
xxvi. 30.	1 d	viii. 31, 31.	1 d	xv. 20, 22, 23.	1 d
xxvii. 4, 7, 25, 25, 31, 33,	1 d	x. 12.	1 c	xvi. 3, 3, 8.	1 d
xxvii. 19.	1 a	x. 13, 17, 19.	1 a	xvi. 7.	1 d
xxvii. 20.	1 c	x. 14.	1 d	xviii. 1, 8.	1 a
xxviii. 20.	1 b	x. 18.	1 b d	xx. 6, 6.	6 a b
xxxi. 38.	1 a	xi. 2, 3, 4, 8, 9, 9, 11, 21, 22, 42.	1 d	xx. 14.	1 d
xxxi. 46.	1 d	xi. 13, 34, 41.	1 g	xx. 19.	1 d
xxxi. 54, 54.	1 b d	xi. 39.	1 o	xxiii. 24.	1 d
xxxii. 32.	1 d	xi. 40.	1 e	xxvi. 12, 14.	1 a
xxxvii. 25.	1 b	xiv. 47.	1 h g	xxvii. 7.	1 a
xxxix. 6.	1 e	xvii. 10, 10.	1 d e	xxviii. 31, 33, 39, 55, 57.	1 d
xl. 17.	1 e	xvii. 12, 12, 15.	1 d	xxviii. 51, 53.	1 a
xl. 19.	1 a	xvii. 14, 14.	1 d e	xxix. 6.	1 a
xli. 4, 20.	1 d	xix. 6, 23.	1 d	xxxi. 20.	1 d
xli. 21, 21.	2 b, 11, 2 a, 11	xix. 7. β	1 f g	xxxii. 13, 38.	1 a
xliii. 2. a	8, 1 b	xix. 25, 26.	1 e	Josh. v. 11.	1 d
xliii. 25.	1 d	xxi. 22.	1 d	v. 12, 12.	1 b d
xliii. 32, 32.	1 e b	xxii. 4, 6, 7, 8, 10, 10, 11, 12, 13, 13,	1 d	xxiv. 13.	1 e
xlv. 18.	1 c	14.	1 d	Judg. ix. 27.	1 a
xlvii. 22.	1 a	xxii. 16.	1 b	xiii. 4, 7, 14, 14, 16.	1 d
Exod. ii. 20.	1 d	xxii. 30.	1 g	xiv. 9, 9.	1 b d
x. 5, 5.	1 a	xxiii. 6, 14.	1 d	xiv. 14.	1 e
x. 12, 15.	1 a	xxiv. 9.	1 a	xix. 4, 6, 8, 21.	1 d
x. 14.	1 n	xxv. 12, 20.	1 d	Ruth ii. 14, 14.	1 a d
xii. 7, 9, 18, 20, 20, 43, 44, 45, 48.	1 d	xxv. 19.	1 a	iii. 3.	1 b
xii. 8, 8.	1 a d	xxv. 22, 22.	1 a d	iii. 7.	1 b
xii. 11, 11.	1 d a	xxvi. 5, 10, 16, 26, 38.	1 a	1 Sam. i. 7, 8, 18.	1 d
xii. 15, 15.	1 d e	xxvi. 29, 29.	1 a d	i. 9.	1 b
xii. 16, 46.	1 g	Num. vi. 3, 4.	1 d	ii. 36.	1 d
xii. 19.	1 e	ix. 11.	1 d	ix. 13, 13, 13.	1 b d d
xiii. 3, 7.	1 g	xi. 4.	1 l	ix. 19.	1 d
xiii. 6.	1 d	xi. 5, 13, 19.	1 d	ix. 24, 24.	1 c d
xvi. 3, 8.	1 d	xi. 18, 18, 18.	1 a l a	xiv. 24, 28, 32.	1 d
xvi. 12.	1 d	xi. 21.	1 a	xiv. 30.	1 a b
xvi. 15.	1 o	xiii. 32.	1 e	xiv. 33.	1 b
xvi. 16, 18, 21.	1 n	xv. 19.	1 b	xiv. 34, 34.	1 a b
xvi. 25.	1 c	xviii. 10, 10, 11, 13.	1 d	xx. 24.	1 b
xvi. 35, 35.	1 b	xviii. 31.	1 a	xx. 34.	1 a
xviii. 12.	1 b	xxiii. 24.	1 d	xxviii. 20.	1 a
xxi. 28.	1 g	xxiv. 8.	1 d	xxviii. 22.	1 c
xxii. 5.	4 c	xxv. 2.	1 d	xxviii. 23, 25.	1 d
xxii. 31.	1 d	xxviii. 17.	1 g	xxx. 11.	1 d
xxiii. 11, 11.	1 a d	Deut. ii. 6, 28.	1 a	xxx. 12, 12.	1 d a
xxiii. 15.	1 d			xxx. 16.	1 e
xxiv. 11.	1 d			2 Sam. iii. 35.	5 c d
xxix. 32.	1 a			ix. 7.	1 d
xxix. 33, 33.	1 a d				

2 Sam. ix. 10, γ 10.	1 a d	Job xxxi. 39.	1 a	Isa. lxi. 6.	1 d
ix. 11, 13.	1 e	xl. 15.	1 d	lxii. 9.	1 d
xi. 11.	1 b	xli. 11.	1 d	lxv. 4.	1 d
xi. 13.	1 d	Ps. xiv. 4, 4.	1 e a	lxv. 13, 22, 25.	1 e
xii. 3, 20, 21.	1 d	xxii. 26.	1 a	lxv. 21.	1 d
xii. 17.	5 a	xxii. 29.	1 a	lxvi. 17.	1 e
xiii. 5.	1 a	xxvii. 2.	1 b	Jer. ii. 7.	1 b
xiii. 6, 10.	5 b	xli. 9.	1 e	v.17,17,17,17.	1 a d d d
xiii. 9, 11.	1 b	liii. 4, 4.	1 c a	vii. 21.	1 d
xvi. 2.	1 b	lxix. 9.	1 a	x. 25.	1 a
xvii. 29.	1 b	lxxviii. 24.	1 a	xv. 16.	1 d
xix. 28.	1 e	lxxviii. 25.	1 a	xvi. 8.	1 b
xix. 35.	1 d	lxxviii. 29.	1 d	xix. 9, 9.	1 i d
xix. 42.	1 a b	cii. 4.	1 b	xxii. 15.	1 d
1 Kings i. 25.	1 e	cii. 9.	1 a	xxii. 22.	12
i. 41.	1 b	cv. 35.	1 d	xxiv. 2, 3, 8.	1 g
ii. 7.	1 e	cvi. 20.	1 d	xxix. 5, 28.	1 c
iv. 20.	1 e	cvi. 28.	1 d	xxix. 17.	1 g
xiii. 8, 9, 16, 17, 18, 19, 22, 22.	1 d	cxxvii. 2.	1 e	xxxi. 5.	6 a
xiii. 15.	1 c	cxxviii. 2.	1 d	xxxi. 29.	1 a
xiii. 23.	1 b	cxli. 4.	9 d	xxxi. 30.	1 e
xiii. 28.	1 a	Prov. i. 31.	1 d	xli. 1.	1 d
xiv. 11, 11.	1 d	iv. 17.	9 a	lii. 33.	1 a
xvi. 4, 4.	1 d	ix. 5.	9 c	Lam. ii. 20.	1 a
xvii. 12.	1 a	xiii. 2.	1 d	Ezek. ii. 8.	1 c
xvii. 15.	1 a	xiii. 25.	1 d	iii. 1, 1.	1 d
xviii. 19.	1 a	xviii. 21.	1 d	iii. 2.	1 l
xviii. 41.	1 c	xxiii. 1.	9 b	iii. 3, 3.	1 l d
xviii. 42.	1 b	xxiii. 6.	1 b	iv. 9, 10, 10, 12, 13.	1 d
xix. 5.	1 c	xxiii. 7.	1 c	iv. 14, 16.	1 a
xix. 6, 8, 21.	1 d	xxiii. 8.	1 a	v. 10, 10.	1 a
xxi. 4.	1 a	xxiv. 13.	1 c	xii. 18, 19.	1 d
xxi. 5.	1 e	xxv. 16.	1 c	xvi. 13.	1 a
xxi. 7.	1 c	xxv. 21.	1 k	xviii. 2.	1 d
xxi. 23, 24, 24.	1 d	xxv. 27.	1 b	xviii. 6, 11, 15.	1 a
2 Kings iv. 8, 8, 40, 40, 40.	1 b	xxvii. 18.	1 d	xxii. 9.	1 a
iv. 41, 42, 44.	1 d b	xxx. 17.	1 d	xxiv. 17, 22.	1 a
iv. 43, 43.	1 b	xxx. 20.	1 a	xxv. 4.	1 d
vi. 22, 23, 28, 28, 29, 29.	1 d	xxxi. 27.	1 d	xxxiii. 25.	1 d
vii. 2, 8, 19.	1 d	Eccles. ii. 24, 25.	1 d	xxxiv. 3.	1 d
ix. 10, 34, 36.	1 d	iii. 13.	1 d	xxxiv. 18, 19.	12
xviii. 27.	1 b	iv. 5.	1 d	xxxvii. 17, 19.	1 d
xviii. 31.	1 c	v. 11.	1 e	xxxix. 18.	1 d
xix. 29, 29.	1 b c	v. 12, 17.	1 d	xlii. 13.	1 d
xxiii. 9.	1 a	v. 18, 19.	1 d	xliv. 3.	1 b
xxv. 29.	1 a	vi. 2, 2.	1 b d	xliv. 29, 31.	1 g
1 Chron. xii. 39.	1 e	viii. 15.	1 b	xlv. 21.	1 g
xxix. 22.	1 d	ix. 7.	1 d	Dan. i. 12.	1 e
2 Chron. xxviii. 15.	1 l	x. 16, 17.	1 d	i. 13, 15.	1 e
xxx. 18.	1 a	Cant. iv. 16.	1 d	iv. 25, 32.	7
xxx. 22.	1 a	v. 1, 1.	1 a c	iv. 33.	1 m
xxxi. 10.	1 b	Isa. i. 19.	1 d	x. 3.	1 a
Ezra ii. 63.	1 d	iii. 10.	1 d	Hos. ii. 12.	1 a
vi. 21.	1 d	iii. 14.	4 a	iv. 8.	1 a
ix. 12.	1 a	iv. 1.	1 d	iv. 10.	1 a
x. 6.	1 a	v. 5.	4 b	viii. 13.	1 a
Neh. v. 2.	1 d	v. 17.	1 d	ix. 3.	1 a
v. 14.	1 a	vii. 15, 22, 22.	1 d	ix. 4.	1 e
vii. 65.	1 d	ix. 20, 20.	1 d	x. 13.	1 a
viii. 10.	1 c	xi. 7.	1 d	Joel i. 4, 4, 4.	1 a
viii. 12.	1 b	xxi. 5.	1 b	ii. 25.	1 a
ix. 25.	1 b	xxii. 13, 13.	1 b	ii. 26.	1 a b
ix. 36.	1 b	xxiii. 18.	1 b	Amos vi. 4.	1 b
Esth. iv. 16.	1 b	xxviii. 4.	3	vii. 2.	1 a
Job i. 4.	1 b	xxix. 8.	1 e	vii. 4.	1 a
i. 13, 18.	1 e	xxx. 24.	1 a	vii. 12.	1 c
iii. 24.δ	9 e	xxxvi. 12.	1 a	ix. 14.	1 a
v. 5.	1 d	xxxvi. 16.	1 a	Micah iii. 3.	1 a
vi. 6.	1 g	xxxvii. 30, 30.	1 b c	vi. 14.	1 b
xiii. 28.ε	1 a	xliv. 16, 19.	1 d	vii. 1.	1 a
xx. 23.	9 f	l. 9.	1 d	Nahum iii. 12.	1 e
xxi. 25.	1 a	li. 8, 8.	1 b	iii. 15.	1 a
xxxi. 8.	1 d	lv. 1, 2.	1 c	Hab. i. 8.	1 b
xxxi. 17, 17.	1 d a	lv. 10.	1 c	Hag. i. 6.	1 b
		lix. 5.	1 e	Zech. vii. 6, 6.	1 d e
				xi. 9, 16.	1 a

α *lit.* had made an end of eating.   β *lit.* being eaten be eaten.   γ *lit.* and he may eat it.   δ *lit.* before my bread.   ε *lit.* the moth hath eaten it.

EBONY

הָבְנִים *m. pl.* an Indian wood, very black and hard, of great value in ancient times.—*Bochart.* Ezek. xxvii. 15.

EDGE

1   פֶּה *m.* mouth; edge of the sword: Exod. xvii. 13, &c.   פִּיָּה * *f. id.*

2   פָּנִים *m. pl.* face.

---

3   צוּר *m.* rock; stone; edge, of the sword; see *Sharp.* Lxx., Vulg., Syr., Arab. understand knives of stone. Hengstenberg and others, the strength of the sword.

4   קָהָה to become dull, to be blunted; set on edge. KAL *fut.*

5   קָצֶה *f.* end, edge. ᵃ קָצֶה *f. id.* ᵇ כתיב קֵץ *m. id.*

6   שָׂפָה *f.* lip; edge.

No. 1 not included.

Exod. xiii. 20.	5 b	Exod. xxxvi. 12.	5 b	Ps. lxxix. 43.	3
xxvi. 4, 4, 10, 10.	6	xxxvi. 4.	5, or 5 a	Eccles. x. 10.	2
xxvi. 5.	5 b	Num. xxxiii. 6, 37.	5 b	Jer. xxxi. 29, 30.	4
xxviii. 7.	5	Josh. xiii. 27.	5 b	Ezek. xviii. 2.	4
xxxvi. 11, 17, 17.	6	Judg. iii. 16.	1 a	xliii. 13.	6

EFFECT

דָּבָר *m.* word, matter, &c.: Ezek. xii. 23.

עֲבוֹדָה *f.* work; effect, result: Isa. xxxii. 17.

נוֹא to deny; to disallow; to bring to nought. HIPHIL *pret.* Ps. xxxiii. 10.

עָשָׂה to do. KAL *pret.* Jer. xlviii. 30.

פָּרַר to break; to make void, to prostrate. HIPHIL *pret.* Num. xxx. 8.

צָלֵחַ to go on well, to prosper. HIPHIL *pret.* 2 Chron. vii. 11, "prosperously effected."

EGG

בֵּיצִים *f. pl.* eggs, so called from their whiteness: Deut. xxii. 6, 6: Job xxxix. 14: Isa. x. 14; lix. 5, 5.

חַלָּמוּת *f.* various interpretations are given of this word, but that most generally received is sanctioned by the Rabbins (see Gesenius), the white of an egg, as they explain the passage, the slime of a yolk, *i.e.* a tasteless, insipid food: Job vi. 6.

ELDER, ELDEST

1   אִישׁ *m.* man: Num. xi. 25, *lit.* men the elders.

2   בְּכוֹר *m.* first-born, eldest son.

3   גָּדוֹל *adj.* great.

4   זָקֵן *adj.* old, aged; elder, chief magistrate, *synon.* with ruler, governor, often without regard to age: Gen. xxiv. 2, &c.

5   יוֹם *m.* day: Job xv. 10, *lit.* more advanced in days; xxxii. 4, *marg.* 'elder for days.'

6   רִאשׁוֹן *adj.* head, highest, chief.

7   רַב *adj.* great; great in age.

8   שִׂיב Ch. to be gray, hoary. P'AL *part.*

No. 4 not included.

Gen. x. 21.	3	Num. xxvi. 5.	2	Ezra vi. 7, 8, 14.	8
xxv. 23.	7	1 Sam. xvii. 13, 14, 28.	3	Job i. 13, 18.	2
xxvii. 1, 15, 42.	3	xviii. 17.	3	xv. 10.	5
xxix. 16.	3	1 Kings ii. 22.	3	xxxii. 4.	5
xliv. 12.	3	2 Kings iii. 27.	3	Ezek. xvi. 46, 61.	3
Num. i. 20.	3	2 Chron. xxii. 1.	6	xxiii. 4.	3
xi. 25.	1, 4	Ezra v. 5, 9.	8		

ELECT

בָּחִיר *adj.* chosen, elect; of the Messiah: Isa. xlii. 1; xlv. 4; lxv. 9, 22.

ELM

אֵלָה *f.* see *Oak.* Hos. iv. 13, *lit.* and terebinth.

ELOQUENT

אִישׁ a man : Exod. iv. 10, *marg.* 'a man of words.'

בִּין to understand. NIPHAL *part.* Isa. iii. 3.

דָּבָר word : Exod. iv. 10.

לַחַשׁ *m.* see *Charm.* Isa. iii. 3, eloquent orator, does not very suitably express the meaning ; better, skilful of speech.

ELUL

אֱלוּל *m.* the sixth Hebrew month, from the new moon of September to that of October : Neh. vi. 15.

EMBALM

חָנַט to sweeten ; applied to the embalming of dead bodies with spices, by which they were sweetened and preserved from putrefaction. KAL *inf.* Gen. l. 2 ; *fut.* Gen. l. 2, 26 ; *part.* Paül, Gen. l. 3. The body lay in nitre thirty days for the purpose of drying up all its superfluous and noxious moisture, and the remaining forty were employed in anointing with gums and spices to preserve it.—*Paxton.*

EMBOLDEN

מָרַץ to be vehement, bold, powerful. HIPHIL *fut.* Job xvi. 3.

EMBRACE

חָבַק to embrace by folding the arms around. KAL *inf.* Eccles. iii. 5. *part.* Poel, 2 Kings iv. 16. PIEL *pret.* Job xxiv. 8 : Lam. iv. 5. *inf.* Eccles. iii. 5. *fut.* Gen. xxix. 13 ; xxxiii. 4 ; xlviii. 10 : Prov. iv. 8 ; v. 20 ; Cant. ii. 6 ; viii. 3.

EMBROIDER

רָקַם to deck with colours, to variegate ; to embroider with coloured figures. KAL *part.* Poel, Exod. xxxv. 35 ; xxxviii. 23.

שָׁבַץ to interweave ; to weave in checker work. PIEL *pret.* Exod. xxviii. 39.

EMERALD

נֹפֶךְ *m.* a gem, precious stone, of an uncertain kind ; Lxx., thrice ἄνθραξ, *i.e.* carbuncle : doubtful : Exod. xxviii. 18 ; xxxix. 11 : Ezek. xxvii. 16 ; xxviii. 13, *marg.* 'or, chrysoprase.' Bush : This gem is undoubtedly the same with the ancient smaragdos, or emerald, one of the most beautiful of all the precious stones. It is characterised by a bright green colour, with scarcely any mixture, though differing somewhat in degrees. The true oriental emerald is now very scarce. The best that are at present accessible are from Peru. In the time of Moses they came from India.

EMERODS

טְחוֹרִים *m. pl.* the piles, hemorrhoids : Deut. xxviii. 27 : 1 Sam. v. 6, 9, 12 ; vi. 4, 5, 11, 17.

עֹפֶל *m.* a hill ; in the *pl.* (כתיב) tumours : Deut. xxviii. 27 : 1 Sam. v. 6, 9, 12 ; vi. 4, 5.

EMINENT

גַּב *m.* something raised, "eminent place ;" a vault, *fornix, spec.* of a brothel, arched cell, in which harlots prostituted themselves : Ezek. xvi. 24, 31, 39.

תָּלַל to heap up, to make high. KAL *part.* Paül, Ezek. xvii. 22.

EMPIRE

מַלְכוּת *f.* kingdom : Esth. i. 20.

EMPLOY

בּוֹא to come. KAL *inf.* Deut. xx. 19, *marg.* 'to go from before thee ; *or, for*, O man, the tree of the field (is) to be employed in the siege.'

עָמַד to stand. KAL *pret.* Ezra x. 15.

EMPTY

1 בֹּהוּ *m.* emptiness, voidness.

2 בּוּקָה emptiness, *i.e.* desolation ; expressing the most entire desolation.

3 בָּקַק to pour out, to empty ; of a vine emptying itself, *i.e.* not bringing fruit to perfection, by spending its strength in shoots and leaves. KAL [a] *pret.* [b] *part.* Poel. With *inf.*, utterly emptied. NIPHAL [c] *inf.* [d] *fut.* POLEL [e] *fut.*

4 דָּלַל to be pendulous, to hang down ; to be languid, weak ; of shallow waters flowing languidly. KAL *pret.*

5 עָרָה to be naked ; to make naked, to empty. PIEL *fut.*

6 פָּנָה to turn ; to cause to turn and go away, to clear, to prepare. PIEL *pret.*

7 פָּקַד to visit. NIPHAL, to be missing : *fut.*

8 רוּק to pour itself out, to be emptied ; to empty. HIPHIL [a] *inf.* [b] *fut.* [c] *part.* HOPHAL [d] *pret.* רִיק [e] *adj.* empty, vain. רֵיק [f] and רַק [g] *adj. id.* רֵיקָם [g] *adv.* emptily.

9 תֹּהוּ *m.* wasteness ; emptiness, vanity.

Gen. xxiv. 20.		5	1 Sam. vi. 3.	8 g	Isa. xxxiv. 11.	1
xxxi. 42.		8 g	xx. 18, 25, 27.	7	Jer. xiv. 3.	8 g
xxxvii. 24.		8 f	2 Sam. i. 22.	8 g	xlviii. 11.	8 d
xli. 27.		8 f	2 Kings iv. 3.	8 f	xlviii. 12.	8 b
xlii. 35.		8 c	2 Chron. xxiv. 11.	5	li. 2.	3 e
Exod. iii. 21.		8 g	Neh. v. 13.	8 f	li. 34.	8 e
xxiii. 15.		8 g	Job xxii. 9.	8 g	Ezek. xxiv. 11.	8 f
xxxiv. 20.		8 g	xxvi. 7.	9	Hos. x. 1.	3 b
Lev. xiv. 36.		6	Eccles. xi. 3.	8 b	Nah. ii. 2, 2.	3 b a
Deut. xv. 13.		8 g	Isa. xix. 6.	4	ii. 10.	2
xvi. 16.		8 g	xxiv. 1.	3 b	xii. 2.	3 a
Judg. vii. 16.		8 f	xxiv. 3.	3 c d	Hab. i. 17.	8 b
Ruth i. 21.		8 g	xxix. 8.	8 f	Zech. iv. 12.	8 c
iii. 17.		8 g	xxxii. 6.	8 a		

EN-HAKKORE

עַיִן eye ; well. קָרָא to call. KAL *part.* Poel, Judg. xv. 19, *marg.* 'the well of him that called, *or*, cried.'

ENCAMP (See CAMP)

ENCHANTMENT

חֶבֶר *m.* see *Charm.* Isa. xlvii. 9, 12.

לְהָטִים *m. pl.* magic arts : Exod. vii. 11.

לַחַשׁ *m.* a charm : Eccles. x. 11.

לָט *adj.* secret, magic arts : Exod. vii. 22 ; viii. 7, 18.

נָחַשׁ to whisper, as sorcerers; to take auguries, to practise divination. PIEL *pret.* 2 Kings xxi. 6 : 2 Chron. xxxiii. 6. *fut.* Lev. xix. 26 : 2 Kings xvii. 17, *lit.* and used enchantments. *part.* Deut. xviii. 10. נַחַשׁ *m.* enchantment : Num. xxiii. 23 ; xxiv. 1.

עָנֵן to observe clouds, times ; to use sorcery. POEL *part.* Jer. xxvii. 9.

ENCOURAGE

חָזַק see *Strong.* KAL *fut.* 2 Chron. xxxi. 4. PIEL *imp.* Deut. i. 38 ; iii. 28 : 2 Sam. xi. 25. *fut.* 2 Chron. xxxv. 2 : Ps. lxiv. 5 : Isa. xli. 7. HITHPAEL *fut.* Judg. xx. 22 : 1 Sam. xxx. 6.

END

1 אַחֲרִית *f.* latter, latter end ; last end (see *Latter*); issue, event ; reward.

2 אָפֵס to end, cease, come to nought. KAL ᵃ*pret.* ᵇ אֶפֶס cessation ; end, extremity.

3 בָּלַע to swallow up. HITHPAEL *fut.*

4 גְּבֻלֹת *f.* bordering, bounding ; Gesenius, wreathen work. ᵃ מִגְבָּלֹת *f. pl. id.*

5 גָּמַר to cease, to finish. KAL *fut.*

6 דִּבְרָה *f.* manner ; cause, reason.

7 חָדַל to cease, to leave off. KAL *pret.*

8 חָנָה to incline, decline ; of day, to grow to an end. KAL *inf.*

9 חָתַם to seal up, to complete, finish. KAL *inf.* Dan. ix. 24, *marg.* ' to seal up.'

10 יָצָא to go out. KAL *inf.*

11 כָּלָה to be completed, finished ; to be over, past ; to end, to make an end of. KAL ᵃ*pret.* ᵇ*inf.* ᶜ*fut.* PIEL ᵈ*pret.* ᵉ*inf.* ᶠ*fut.* PUAL ᵍ*pret.* ʰ כָּלָה *f.* a full end, an utter end. ⁱ תַּכְלִית *f.* perfection, end.

12 כָּנָף *com.* wing ; corners or ends of the earth.

13 מָלֵא to fill ; to be filled. KAL *inf.*

14 נָלָה to complete ; to make an end. HIPHIL *inf.*

15 נֶצַח perpetual, for ever ; duration, but not without limit.

16 סוּף (see *Consume*), to have an end. KAL ᵃ*pret.* ᵇ סוֹף *m.* conclusion. ᶜ סוֹף Ch. *m. id.*

17 עַד *m.* eternity ; "world without end ;" *lit.* unto the ages of eternity.

18 עוֹלָם *m.* everlasting.

19 עָקֵב *m.* extremity, end.

20 פֵּאָה *f.* side quarter.

21 פֶּה *m.* mouth ; "from one end to another," *lit.* mouth to mouth, a phrase derived from the fulness of vessels.

22 תְּקוּפָה *f.* circuit, as of the sun ; hence the return of seasons.

23 קָצֶה *f.* uttermost part ; see *Part.* ᵃ קָצֶה *m. id.* ᵇ קֵצֶה *m. id.* ᶜ קְצוּ *m. id.* ᵈ קְצֵנָה *f. id.* ᵉ קְצָת *f. id.* ᶠ קְצָת Ch. end.

24 קֵץ *m.* extremity.

25 רֹאשׁ *m.* head.

26 שָׁלֵם to be complete, finished. KAL ᵃ*pret.* ᵇ*fut.* HIPHIL ᶜ*fut.*

27 תָּמַם to be complete, finished, to come to an end. KAL ᵃ*pret.* ᵇ*inf.* ᶜ*fut.* NIPHAL ᵈ*fut.* HIPHIL ᵉ*pret.* ᶠ*inf.*

Gen. ii. 2.	11 f	1 Kings viii. 8.	25	Isa. xxiii. 15, 17.	24
vi. 13.	24	viii. 54.	11 e	xxiv. 8.	7
viii. 3.	23 a	ix. 10.	23 a	xxvi. 15.	23 c
viii. 6.	24	2 Kings viii. 3.	23 a	xxxiii. 1.	14
xxiii. 9.	23 a	x. 21.	21	xxxviii. 12, 13.	26 c
xxvii. 30.	11 d	x. 25.	11 e	xl. 28.	23
xli. 1.	24	xviii. 10.	23 a	xli. 5, 9.	23
xli. 53.	11 c	xxi. 16.	21	xli. 22.	1
xlvii. 18.	27 c	1 Chron. xvi. 2.	11 f	xlii. 10.	23 a
xlvii. 21, 21.	23 a	2 Chron. v. 9.	25	xliii. 6.	23 a
xlix. 33.	11 f	vii. 1.	11 e	xlv. 17.	17, 18
Exod. xii. 41.	24	viii. 1.	24	xlv. 22.	2 b
xxiii. 16.	10	xx. 16.	16 b	xlvi. 10.	1
xxv. 18, 19, 19, 19.	23 a	xx. 23.	11 e	xlvii. 11.	1
xxvi. 28, 28.	23 a	xxi. 19. a	10, 24	xlviii. 20.	23 a
xxviii. 14.	4 a	xxiv. 10.	11 e	xlix. 6.	23 a
xxviii. 22.	4	xxiv. 23.	22	lii. 10.	2 b
xxviii. 23, 24, 25, 26.	23	xxix. 17.	11 d	lx. 20.	26 a
xxxi. 18.	11 e	xxix. 29.	11 e	lxii. 11.	23 a
xxxiv. 22.	22	xxxv. 34.	11 b	Jer. i. 3.	27 b
xxxvi. 33.	23 a	Ezra ix. 11.	21	iii. 5.	15
xxxvii. 7.	23	x. 17.	11 f	iv. 27.	11 h
xxxvii. 8, 8, 8.	23	Neh. iii. 21.	11 i	v. 10, 18.	11 h
xxxviii. 5.	23 d	iv. 2.	11 f	v. 31.	1
xxxix. 15.	4	Job vi. 11.	24	viii. 20.	11 a
xxxix. 16, 17, 18, 19.	23	viii. 7.	1	x. 13.	23 a
Lev. viii. 33.	13	xvi. 3.	24	xii. 4.	1
xvi. 20.	11 d	xviii. 2.	24	xii. 12, 12.	23 a
Num. iv. 15.	11 d	xxvi. 10.	11 i	xvi. 19.	2 b
xvi. 31.	11 e	xxviii. 3.	24	xvii. 11.	1
xxiii. 10.	1	xxviii. 24.	23	xxv. 31, 33, 33.	23 a
xxiv. 20.	1	xxxi. 40.	27 a	xxvi. 8.	11 e
Deut. viii. 16.	1	xxxiv. 36.	15	xxix. 11.	1
ix. 11.	24	xxxvii. 3.	12	xxx. 11, 11.	11 h
xi. 12.	1	xxxviii. 13.	12	xxxi. 17.	1
xiii. 7, 7.	23 a	xlii. 12.	1	xxxiv. 14.	24
xiv. 28.	23 a	Ps. vii. 9.	5	xliii. 1.	11 e
xv. 1.	24	ix. 6.	27 a	xliv. 27.	11 b
xx. 9.	11 e	xix. 4.	24	xlvi. 28, 28.	11 h
xxvi. 12.	11 f	xix. 6, 6.	23 a, 23	li. 13.	24
xxviii. 49, 64.	23 a	xxii. 27.	2 b	li. 16, 31.	23 a
xxxi. 10.	24	xxxvii. 37, 38.	1	li. 63.	11 e
xxxi. 24.	11 e	xxxix. 4.	24	Lam. i. 9.	24
xxxii. 20, 29.	1	xlvi. 9.	23 a	iv. 18, 18.	24
xxxii. 45.	11 f	xlviii. 10.	23 c	Ezek. iii. 16.	23 a
xxxiii. 17.	2 b	lix. 13.	2 b	iv. 8.	11 e
xxxiv. 8.	27 c	lxi. 2.	23 a	vii. 2, 3, 3, 6, 6.	23 a
Josh. viii. 24.	11 e	lxv. 5.	23 c	xi. 13.	11 h
ix. 16.	23 a	lxvii. 7.	2 b	xv. 4.	23
x. 20.	11 e	lxxii. 8.	23 a	xx. 17.	11 h
xv. 5, 8.	23 a	lxxii. 20.	11 g	xxi. 25, 29.	24
xviii. 15, 16, 19.	23 a	lxxiii. 17.	1	xxix. 13.	24
xix. 49, 51.	11 f	xcviii. 3.	2 b	xxxv. 5.	24
Judg. iii. 18.	11 d	cii. 27.	27 d	xxxix. 14.	23 a
vi. 13.	23 a	cvii. 27.	3	xli. 12.	20
xi. 39.	24	cxix. 33, 112.	19	xlii. 15.	11 d
xv. 17.	11 e	cxix. 96.	24	xliii. 23.	11 e
xix. 9.	8	cxxxv. 7.	23 a	xliii. 1.	11 e
Ruth ii. 21.	11 d	Prov. v. 4.	1	Dan. i. 5, 15, 18.	23 e
ii. 23.	11 b	xiv. 12, 13.	1	iv. 11, 22.	16 c
iii. 7.	23 a	xvi. 25.	1	iv. 29, 34.	23 f
1 Sam. ii. 10.	2 b	xvii. 24.	23 a	vi. 26.	16 c
iii. 12.	11 e	xix. 20.	1	vii. 26, 28.	16 c
ix. 27.	23 a	xx. 21.	1	viii. 17.	24
x. 13.	11 f	xxiii. 18.	1	viii. 19, 19.	1, 24
xiii. 10.	11 e	xxv. 8.	1	ix. 24.	9, or 27 f
xiv. 27, 43.	23 a	xxx. 4.	2 b	ix. 26, 26.	24
xviii. 1.	11 e	Eccles. iii. 11.	16 b	xi. 6, 27, 35, 40, 45.	24
xxiv. 16.	11 e	iv. 8, 16.	24	xii. 4, 6, 9, 13, 13.	24
2 Sam. vi. 18.	11 f	vii. 2.	16 b	xii. 8.	1
xi. 19.	11 e	vii. 8.	1	Amos iii. 15.	16 a
xiii. 36.	11 e	vii. 14.	6	vii. 2.	11 d
xiv. 26.	24	x. 13.	1	viii. 2.	24
xx. 18.	23 a	xii. 12.	24	viii. 10.	1
xxiv. 8.	27 e	Isa. ii. 7, 7.	23 b	Micah v. 4.	2 b
1 Kings i. 41.	11 d	v. 26.	23 a	Nah. i. 8, 9.	11 h
ii. 39.	24	ix. 7.	24	ii. 9.	23 b
iii. 1.	11 e	xiii. 5.	23 a	iii. 3.	23 b
vii. 40.	11 f	xvi. 4.	2 a	Hab. ii. 3.	24
vii. 51.	26 b			Zech. ix. 10.	2 b

ᵃ *lit.* at the going out of the end.

ENDAMAGE

נְזַק Ch. to suffer injury. APHEL, to endamage : *fut.* Ezra iv. 13.

ENDANGER

חוּב to be under penalty; to make liable. PIEL *pret.* Dan. i. 10.

סָכַן to bring into danger. NIPHAL *fut.* Eccles. x. 9.

ENDEAVOUR

מַעֲלָל *m.* doings: Ps. xxviii. 4.

ENDOW

מָהַר to buy or purchase with a dowry. KAL *inf.* and *fut.* Exod. xxii. 16, *lit.* endowing he shall endow.

ENDUE

זָבַד to present a gift, to give a portion or dowry with a woman when she is married. KAL *pret.* Gen. xxx. 20.

יָדַע to know. KAL *part.* Poel, 2 Chron. ii. 12, 13.

ENDURE

1 הָיָה to be. KAL *fut.*
2 יָכֹל to be able. KAL *fut.*
3 יָשַׁב to sit, to dwell. KAL *fut.*
4 לִין to lodge or stay all night. KAL *fut.*
5 עָמַד to stand. KAL a *inf.* b *fut.* c *part.* Poel.
6 לִפְנֵי before, in the presence of, as long as: Ps. lxxii. 5, *lit.* with the sun, and before the moon; 7, *lit.* till there be no moon.
7 קוּם to rise up, to stand up. KAL *fut.*
8 רֶגֶל *f.* foot; pace, ability to march: Gen. xxxiii. 14, *marg.* 'according to the foot of the work,' &c., and according to the foot of the children.

Gen. xxxiii. 14.	8	Ps. xix. 9.	5 c	Ps. cii. 12.	3
Exod. xviii. 23.	5 a	xxx. 5.	4	cii. 26.	5 b
Esth. viii. 6, 6.	2	lxxii. 5, 7.	6 1	civ. 31.	1
Job viii. 15.	7	lxxii. 17.	1	cxi. 3, 10.	5 c
xxxi. 23.	2	lxxxi. 15.	1	cxii. 3, 9.	5 c
Ps. ix. 7. a	3	lxxxix. 36.	1	Ezek. xxii. 14.	5 b

a *or,* shall sit (on his throne) for ever.

ENEMY, ENMITY

1 אֹיֵב and אוֹיֵב *m.* an enemy, adversary, oppressor, who seeks to injure, and delights in the accomplishment of it. It is used of the enemies of God, of his people, and of the Messiah; sometimes of God in respect to man, denoting his purpose to punish: Exod. xxiii. 22, Lam. ii. 5, *cf.* Isa. lxiii. 10.——Gen. xxii. 17, &c. אָיַב to be an adversary, to pursue with enmity and hostility. KAL a *pret.* b אֵיבָה *f.* enmity, differing from שִׂנְאָה, which implies only aversion, the former a desire and endeavour to injure.

2 עָר an enemy; perhaps one that watches for an opportunity of injuring; or from ערה to make destitute; as it would apply to Saul stripped of his kingdom, 1 Sam. xxviii. 16; some take the word to be similar to צַר by a change of the first letters. a עָר Ch. *m. id.*

3 צָרַר to bind up close; to afflict, distress, oppress. KAL a *part.* Poel. b צַר *m.* an adversary that distresses.
4 קוּם to rise up, to rise up against. KAL *part.*
5 שׁוּר an enemy that looks out, lies in wait.
6 שָׁרַר to observe, watch, or lay wait. KAL *part.* Poel.
7 שָׂנֵא to hate; this implies aversion, but not necessarily hostility. KAL *part.* Poel.

No. 1 not included.

Gen. iii. 15.	1 b	Esth. ix. 10, 24.	3 a	Ps. lxxviii. 42, 61, 66.	3 b
xiv. 20.	3 b	Job vi. 23.	3 b	xcii. 11.	5
Exod. i. 10.	7	xvi. 9.	3 b	xcvii. 3.	3 b
xxiii. 22, 22.	1 a, 1	xix. 11.	3 b	cv. 24.	3 b
xxxii. 25.	4	Ps. v. 8.	6	cvi. 11.	3 b
Num. x. 9, 9.	3 b, 1	vi. 7.	3 a	cvii. 2.	3 b
xxiv. 8.	3 b	vii. 4, 6.	3 a	cviii. 13.	3 b
xxxv. 21, 22.	1 b	viii. 2, 2.	3 a, 1	cxii. 8.	3 b
Deut. xxxii. 41.	3 b	x. 5.	3 a	cxix. 139, 157.	3 b
xxxiii. 7.	3 b	xxiii. 5.	3 a	cxxxvi. 24.	3 b
1 Sam. ii. 32. a	3 b	xxvii. 2, 12.	3 b	cxxxix. 20.	2
xxviii. 16.	2	xxvii. 11.	6	Prov. xxv. 21.	7
2 Sam. xix. 6.	3 b	xxxi. 11.	3 a	xxvii. 6.	7
xxiv. 13.	3 b	xlii. 10.	3 a	Isa. xxvi. 11.	3 b
1 Chron. xii. 17.	3 b	xliv. 5, 7, 10.	3 b	lix. 19.	3 b
2 Chron. i. 11.	7	liv. 5.	6	Jer. xlviii. 5.	3 b
Neh. ix. 27, 27.	3 b	lvi. 2.	6	Lam. i. 5, 5.	1, 3 b
Esth. iii. 10.	3 a	lix. 10.	6	i. 7.	3 b
vii. 6.	3 b	lx. 12.	3 b	Ezek. xxxix. 23.	3 b
viii. 1.	3 a	lxxiv. 4, 23.	3 a	Dan. iv. 19.	2 a

a *marg.* 'or, the affliction of the tabernacle for all the wealth which God would have given Israel.'

ENFLAME

חָמַם to be hot; see *Heat;* figuratively applied to the spiritual whoredom of idolaters. NIPHAL *part.* Isa. lvii. 5.

ENGAGE

עָרַב to give a pledge, to pledge or engage the heart readily and pleasantly; see *Sweet.* KAL *pret.* Jer. xxx. 21.

ENGINE

חִשְּׁבֹנוֹת *f. pl.* inventions of ingenuity: 2 Chron. xxvi. 15.

מְחִי *m.* a striking: Ezek. xxvi. 9, *lit.* the stroke of what is over against it, *i. e.* battering rams, or the like.

ENGRAVE

חָרָשׁ an engraver: Exod. xxviii. 11; xxxv. 35; xxxviii. 23.

פָּתַח to open, to grave. PIEL *fut.* Exod. xxviii. 11. *part.* Zech. iii. 9. פִּתּוּחַ *m.* Exod. xxviii. 11, 21, 36; xxxix. 14, 30.

ENJOIN

פָּקַד to visit, to appoint, to give charge over. KAL *pret.* Job xxxvi. 23.

קוּם to rise up. PIEL, to ordain, decree: *pret.* Esth. ix. 31.

ENJOY

בָּלָה to be worn out with age and use. PIEL *fut.* Isa. lxv. 22. Alexander, the work of their hands my chosen ones shall wear out, or survive. *Cum eis senescent, fruentur eo.*—Cocc. *Ad vetustatem deducere.*—Geier.

הָיָה to be. KAL *fut.* Deut. xxviii. 41, *lit.* they shall not be thine.

יָרַשׁ to possess. KAL *pret.* Josh. i. 15. *fut.* Num. xxxvi. 8.

רָאָה to see. KAL *pret.* Eccles. iii. 13. *inf.* Eccles. v. 18. *imp.* Eccles. ii. 1. HIPHIL *pret.* Eccles. ii. 24.

רָצָה to take delight in. KAL *pret.* 2 Chron. xxxvi. 21. *fut.* Lev. xxvi. 34, 43. HIPHIL *pret.* Lev. xxvi. 34.

ENLARGE

1 פָּתָה to be open, wide; open-hearted. Piel, to persuade. Hiphil, to make wide, to enlarge. HIPHIL *fut.*

2 רָבָה to multiply, increase. HIPHIL *pret.*

3 רֶוַח *m.* breath, respiration, freedom of breathing, *i. e.* largeness of space.

4 רָחַב to be large and spacious, as of a chamber; of the mouth opened wide, of the heart, by joy. Hiphil, to make large, a tent, a bed. KAL a *pret.* HIPHIL b *pret.* c *inf.* d *imp.* e *fut.* f *part.*

5 שָׂמַח to spread out, to expand. KAL *part.* Poel.

Gen. ix. 27.	1	Esth. iv. 14.	3	Isa. liv. 2.	4 d
Exod. xxxiv. 24.	4 b	Job xii. 23.	5	lvii. 8.	4 b
Deut. xii. 20.	4 e	Ps. iv. 1.	4 b	lx. 5.	4 a
xix. 8.	4 e	xviii. 36.	4 e	Ezek. xli. 7.	4 a
xxxiii. 20.	4 f	xxv. 17.	4 b	Amos i. 13.	4 c
1 Sam. ii. 1.	4 a	cxix. 32.	4 e	Micah i. 16.	4 d
2 Sam. xxii. 37.	4 e	Isa. v. 14.	4 b	Hab. ii. 5.	4 b
1 Chron. iv. 10.	2				

ENLIGHTEN

אוֹר (see *Light*), to shine, to shine upon, to be enlightened; it implies both receiving light and giving forth light; to be glorious in light : Job xxxiii. 30. KAL *pret.* 1 Sam. xiv. 29. *fut.* 1 Sam. xiv. 27, קרי. NIPHAL *inf.* Job xxxiii. 30. HIPHIL *pret.* Ps. xcvii. 4. *part.* Ps. xix. 8.

נָגַהּ to shine brightly. HIPHIL *fut.* Ps. xviii. 28.

רָאָה to see. KAL *fut.* 1 Sam. xiv. 27, כתיב.

ENOUGH

1 דַּי *m.* sufficiency : Jer. xlix. 9, "till they have enough."

2 דָּלָה to draw. KAL *inf.* and *pret.* Exod. ii. 19, *lit.* drawing he drew.

3 הוֹן *m.* riches, substance, enough.

4 יָד *com.* hand : Gen. xxxiv. 21, *lit.* large of hands, or sides.

5 כֹּל all : Gen. xxxiii. 11.

6 מָצָא to find. NIPHAL, to suffice for anything : *fut.*

7 רַב *adj.* many, much, great.

8 שָׂבַע to be satisfied. KAL a *inf.* b *fut.* c שִׂבְעָה *f.* fulness.

Gen. xxiv. 25.	7	Josh. xvii. 16.	6	Isa. lvi. 11.	8 c
xxxiii. 9.	7	2 Sam. xxiv. 16.	7	Jer. xlix. 9.	1
xxxiii. 11.	5	1 Kings xix. 4.	7	Hos. iv. 10.	8 b
xxxiv. 21.	4	1 Chron. xxi. 15.	7	Obad. 5.	1
xlv. 28.	7	2 Chron. xxxi. 10.	8 a	Nah. ii. 12.	1
Exod. ii. 19.	2	Prov. xxvii. 27.	1	Hag. i. 6.	8 c
ix. 28. a	7	xxviii. 19.	8 b	Mal. iii. 10.	1
xxxvi. 5.	1	xxx. 15, 16.	3		

a *or*, and let it be enough of the being of the voices of God, &c.—*Keil.*

ENQUIRE

1 בָּעָה to seek after with eagerness, and strong desire. KAL a *imp.* b *fut.*

2 בָּקַר to look into or after attentively, to enquire with great care and diligence; *seq.* בְּ to look at with pleasure, to behold with admiration, to admire. PIEL a *inf.* בִּקֵּר Ch. PAEL b *inf.*

3 בָּקַשׁ to seek, to enquire with a view to finding, learning; to seek the face. PIEL a *pret.* b *fut.*

4 דָּרַשׁ to seek, look for, search for; to ask about, to enquire into; to seek from any one, *seq. acc.* of person or thing about or into which one enquires; also *seq.* לְ, 2 Sam. xi. 3, עַל, 2 Chron. xxxi. 9, Eccles. i. 13. *Spec.* to enquire of any one, to ask an oracle, to consult God, *c. acc.;* also idols, magicians; *seq.* בְּ *pr.* to enquire at any one; *seq.* אֶל *pr.* to go with enquiry to any one, לְ, and מֵעַל out of the book of Jehovah, Isa. xxxiv. 16. The prophet by or through whom one enquires of God is put with מֵאֵת מֵעִם, and בְּ. It is applied to an anxious, studious enquiry. KAL a *pret.* b *inf.* c *imp.* d *fut.* NIPHAL e *inf.* f *fut.*

5 פָּנִים *m. pl.* face.

6 שָׁאַל to ask; to enquire of; to enquire of or consult; to enquire after; *seq. acc.* of person, rarely *seq.* לְ of person, to consult an oracle, mostly *seq.* בְּ; *seq.* לְ for any one. KAL a *pret.* b *inf.* c *imp.* d *fut.*

7 שָׁחַר to seek early. PIEL *pret.*

Gen. xxiv. 57.	6 d	2 Sam. xi. 3.	4 d	2 Chron. xxxii. 31.	4 b
xxv. 22.	4 b	xvi. 23.	6 d	xxxiv. 21.	4 c
Exod. xviii. 15.	4 b	xxi. 1.	3 b,-5	xxxiv. 26.	4 b
Deut. xii. 30.	4 d	1 Kings xxii. 5.	4 c	Ezra vii. 14.	2 b
xiii. 14.	4 a	xxii. 7.	4 b	Job viii. 8.	6 c
xvii. 4, 9.	4 a	xxii. 8.	4 b	x. 6.	3 b
Judg. iv. 20.	4 a	2 Kings i. 2.	4 c	Ps. xxvii. 4.	2 a
vi. 29.	4 d	i. 3, 6, 16, 16.	4 b	lxxviii. 34.	7
viii. 14.	6 d	iii. 11.	4 b	Prov. xx. 25.	2 a
xx. 27.	6 d	viii. 8.	4 a	Eccles. vii. 10.	6 a
1 Sam. ix. 9.	4 b	xvi. 15.	2 a	Isa. xxii. 12, 12.	1 b a
x. 22.	6 d	xxii. 13.	4 c	Jer. xxi. 2.	4 c
xvii. 56.	6 d	xxii. 18.	4 b	xxxvii. 7.	4 b
xxii. 10.	6 d	1 Chron. x. 13.	4 b	Ezek. xiv. 3.β	4 f e
xxii. 13, 15.	6 d	x. 14.	4 a	xiv. 7.	4 d
xxiii. 2.	6 d	xiii. 3.	4 a	xx. 1.	4 b
xxiii. 4. α	6 b	xiv. 10, 14.	4 b	xx. 3, 3.	4 b f
xxviii. 6.	6 d	xviii. 10.	6 b	xx. 31, 31.	4 f
xxviii. 7.	4 d	xxi. 30.	4 b	xxxvi. 37.	4 f
xxx. 8.	6 d	2 Chron. xviii. 4.	4 c	Dan. i. 20.	3 a
2 Sam. ii. 1.	6 d	xviii. 6.	4 d	Zeph. i. 6.	4 a
v. 19, 23.	6 d	xviii. 7.	4 d		

a *lit.* added to enquire. β *lit.* should I be enquired of to be enquired of by them?

ENRICH

עָשַׁר to be rich. HIPHIL *pret.* Ezek. xxvii. 33. *fut.* 1 Sam. xvii. 25 : Ps. lxv. 9.

ENSIGN

אוֹת *c.* a sign; memorial; also a military ensign, especially that of each particular tribe : Num. ii. 2 : Ps. lxxiv. 4.

נָסַס to lift up anything on high; to lift up an ensign. HITHPOEL *part.* Zech. ix. 16. נֵס *m.* a standard, banner, &c., placed on conspicuous situations, Isa. xxx. 17, for the purpose of calling the people together, Isa. v. 26, xi. 10, 12; to collect fugitives, or bring together forces of an army for an attack on the enemy, Isa. xviii. 3; xxxi. 9; of the Messiah, Isa. xi. 10.

ENSNARED

מוֹקֵשׁ *m.* a snare : Job xxxiv. 30, *lit.* from the snares of the people.

ENTANGLE

בּוּךְ to roll up, to involve, to entangle; to be perplexed, to wander about in perplexity. NIPHAL *part.* Exod. xiv. 3; see *Perplex.*

ENTER, ENTRANCE, ENTRY

1 אִיתוֹן *m.* entrance: Ezek. xl. 15.

2 בּוֹא to come in. KAL [a] *pret.* [b] *inf.* [c] *imp.* [d] *fut.* [e] *part.* Poel. HIPHIL [f] *pret.* [g] *part.* [h] מָבוֹא *com.* entrance. [i] בִּאָה *f.* an entrance.

3 הָלַךְ to walk, to go, &c. KAL *inf.*

4 חָדַר (see *Chamber*), to enter into an inner chamber. KAL *part.* Poel, Ezek. xxi. 14; Gesenius and Fürst, which besieges them, which besets them on every side.

5 נָחַת to come down upon, to sink deep into, to make a deep impression on the mind. KAL *fut.* Prov. xvii. 10, *marg.* 'aweth,' as from חָתַת.

6 עָבַר to pass over. KAL *inf.*

7 פֶּה *m.* a mouth.

8 פֶּתַח *m.* door; entering in; entry: Micah v. 6, *marg.* 'with her own naked swords;' see *Draw.* [a] פֶּתַח *m.* entrance.

Gen. vii. 13.	2 a	1 Chron. ix. 19.	2 h	Jer. xvii. 27.	2 b		
xii. 11.	2 b	xiii. 5.	2 b	xix. 2.	8		
xix. 3.	2 d	xix. 15.	2 d	xxi. 13.	2 d		
xix. 23.	2 a	2 Chron. iv. 22.	8	xxii. 2.	2 e		
xxxi. 33.	2 d	vii. 2, 8.	2 b	xxii. 4.	2 a		
xliii. 30.	2 d	xii. 10.	8	xxvi. 10.	8		
Exod. xxxiii. 9.	2 b	xii. 11.	2 b	xxxiv. 10.	2 a		
xxxv. 15.	8	xv. 12.	2 d	xxxvi. 10.	8		
xl. 35.	2 b	xviii. 9.	8	xxxvii. 16.	2 a		
Num. iv. 3, 23, 30, 35,		xxiii. 4.	2 e	xxxviii. 14.	2 h		
39, 43.	2 e	xxiii. 13, 15.	2 h	xli. 17.	2 b		
v. 24, 27.	2 a	xxiii. 19.	2 d	xlii. 15, 18.	2 b		
xx. 24.	2 d	xxvi. 8.	2 b	xliii. 9.	8		
xxxiv. 8.	2 b	xxvii. 2.	2 a	Lam. i. 10, 10.	2 a d		
Deut. xxiii. 1, 2, 2, 3,		xxx. 8.	2 c	iii. 13.	3 f		
3, 8.	2 d	xxxi. 16.	2 e	iv. 12.	2 d		
xxix. 12.	6	xxxii. 1.	2 d	Ezek. ii. 2.	2 d		
Josh. ii. 3.	2 a	xxxiii. 14.	2 b	iii. 24.	2 d		
viii. 19.	2 d	Neh. ii. 8, 15.	2 d	vii. 22.	2 a		
viii. 29.	8	x. 29.	2 e	viii. 5.	2 i		
x. 19.	2 b	Esth. iv. 2.	2 b	xiii. 9.	2 d		
x. 20.	2 d	Job xxii. 4.	2 d	xvi. 8.	2 d		
xiii. 5.	2 b	xxxiv. 23.	3	xx. 38.	2 d		
xx. 4.	8	xxxviii. 16, 22.	2 a	xxi. 14.	4		
Judg. i. 24, 25.	2 h	Ps. xxxvii. 15.	2 d	xxvi. 10, 10.	2 b h		
iii. 3.	2 b	xlv. 15.	2 d	xxvii. 3.	2 h		
vi. 5.	2 d	xcv. 11.	2 d	xxxvi. 20.	2 d		
ix. 35, 40, 44.	8	c. 4.	2 c	xxxvii. 5.	2 g		
ix. 46.	2 d	cxviii. 20.	2 d	xl. 11, 38, 40.	8		
xviii. 9.	2 b	cxix. 130.	8 a	xl. 15.	1		
xviii. 16, 17.	8	cxliii. 2.	2 d	xli. 6.	8		
1 Sam. xxiii. 7.	2 b	Prov. ii. 10.	2 d	xlii. 9.	2 h or 2 g		
2 Sam. x. 8.	8	iv. 14.	2 d	xlii. 12, 14.	2 b		
x. 14.	2 d	viii. 3.	7	xliv. 2, 2.	2 d a		
xi. 23.	8	xvii. 10.	5	xliv. 3, 9, 16.	2 d		
1 Kings vi. 31.	8	xviii. 6.	2 d	xliv. 5.	2 h		
viii. 65.	2 b	Isa. ii. 10.	2 d	xliv. 17, 21.	2 b		
xiv. 12.	2 b	iii. 10.	2 c	xlvi. 2.	2 a		
xviii. 46.	2 b	xxiii. 1. a	2 b	xlvi. 8.	2 b		
xix. 13.	8	xxvi. 2.	2 h	xlvi. 9, 9.	2 e		
xxii. 10.	8	xxvi. 20.	2 c	xlvi. 19.	2 h		
xxii. 30.	2 b	xxxvii. 24.	2 d	Dan. xi. 7, 24.	2 d		
2 Kings vii. 3.	8	lvii. 2.	2 d	xi. 17.	2 b		
vii. 4, 8.	2 d	lix. 14.	2 b	xi. 40, 41.	2 a		
ix. 31.	2 a	Jer. i. 15.	8	Hos. xi. 9.	2 d		
x. 8.	8	ii. 7.	2 d	Joel ii. 9.	2 d		
xi. 5.	2 e	vii. 2.	2 e	Amos v. 5.	2 b		
xiv. 25.	2 d	viii. 14.	2 d	vi. 14.	2 d		
xvi. 18.	2 h	ix. 21.	2 a	Obad. 11.	2 a		
xix. 23.	2 d	xiv. 18.	2 a	13.	2 d		
xxiii. 8.	8	xvi. 5.	2 d	Jonah iii. 4.	2 b		
xxiii. 11.	2 b	xvii. 20.	2 e	Micah v. 6.	8		
1 Chron. iv. 39.	2 h	xvii. 25.	2 a	Hab. iii. 16.	2 d		
v. 9.	2 b			Zech. v. 4.	2 a		

[a] *lit.* from entering.

ENTERPRISE

תּוּשִׁיָּה *f.* (see *Substance, Wisdom*), counsel, fixed purpose: Job v. 12, "their hands cannot perform their enterprise," *marg.* 'anything; their counsel or purpose.'

ENTICE

סוּת to urge, to stir up, to persuade, to entice. HIPHIL *fut.* Deut. xiii. 6.

פָּתָה to be open, wide; to be open-hearted, easily persuaded or enticed; Piel, to persuade, to entice. KAL *fut.* Job xxxi. 27. PIEL *imp.* Judg. xiv. 15; xvi. 5. *fut.* Exod. xxii. 16: 2 Chron. xviii. 19, 20, 21: Prov. i.10; xvi. 29. PUAL *fut.* Jer. xx. 10.

ENTREAT

פָּגַע to fall upon; to strike a league with any one, to entreat well. HIPHIL *pret.* Jer. xv. 11, *marg.* 'or, I will entreat the enemy for thee.' Gesenius, "I will cause the enemy to come as a suppliant to thee."

ENVIRON

סָבַב to compass. NIPHAL *pret.* Josh. vii. 9.

ENVY

קָנָא perhaps originally to burn or be inflamed; in Piel it is applied to the mind burning with jealousy, envy, zeal, &c. PIEL *pret.* Ps. lxxiii. 3. *fut.* Gen. xxvi. 14; xxx. 1; xxxvii. 11: Ps. xxxvii. 1; cvi. 16: Prov. iii. 31; xxiii. 17; xxiv. 1, 19: Isa. xi. 13: Ezek. xxxi. 9. *part.* Num. xi. 29. קִנְאָה *f.* ardour, ardent zeal, envy, jealousy: Job v. 2: Prov. xiv. 30; xxvii. 4: Eccles. iv. 4; ix. 6: Isa. xi. 13; xxvi. 11: Ezek. xxxv. 11.

EPHAH

אֵיפָה more rarely אֵפָה *f.* a measure, the capacity of which is not clearly ascertained; Josephus compares it to the *Attic Medimnus*, which is about 1 and $\frac{1}{12}$th of an English bushel: Exod. xvi. 36, &c.

EPHOD

אֵפוֹד and אֵפֹד *m.* אֲפֻדָּה *f.* (see *Gird*), a garment belonging to the high priest when officiating in the temple, richly embroidered with a curious variety of colours and figures. It was put on over all the other garments, and reached but a little below the middle of the body: it had no sleeves, and was fastened on each shoulder by two pieces joined together by a golden button, on which was a precious stone, engraved with the names of the twelve tribes, six on one shoulder and six on the other. A girdle of the same precious work was fastened to the ephod, as a part of it, and served to gird it over the heart or breast to the high priest's body. Ephods, or garments of the same shape with the high priest's ephod, were worn by priests and Levites. King David also wore an ephod. אֵפוֹד and אֵפֹד *m.* Exod. xxv. 7, &c. אֲפֻדָּה *f.* Exod. xxviii. 8; xxxix. 5.

EQUAL

1   דָּלָה   to hang down; to draw up, to lift up; *or*,

2   דָּלַל   to bring low; to fail, to be impoverished. KAL *pret.* Prov. xxvi. 7. It is disputed to which root this form should be referred; the meaning may be, hangs down as a useless limb, is impoverished or made useless; perhaps both meanings should be considered as belonging to the expression.

3   מֵישָׁרִים   *m. pl.* uprightness; things that are equal.

4   עָרַךְ   to set in order; to compare; to estimate. KAL ^a *fut.* ^b עֵרֶךְ *m.* order, estimation: Ps. lv. 13.

5   שָׁוָה   to be compared. KAL ^a *fut.* HIPHIL ^b *fut.*

6   שָׁלַב   (see *Ledges*); this verb seems to express the idea of parallel uniformity; equally distant. PAUL *part.*

7   תָּכַן   to weigh. NIPHAL *fut.*

Exod. xxxvi. 22.	6	Prov. xxvi. 7.	1, or 2	Ezek. xviii. 25, 25,	
Job xxviii. 17, 19.	4 a	Isa. xl. 25.	5 a	29, 29.	7
Ps. xvii. 2.	3	xlvi. 5.	5 b	xxxiii. 17, 17, 20.	7
lv. 13.	4 b	Lam. ii. 13.	5 b		

EQUITY

יָשָׁר straight, right: Micah iii. 9. יֹשֶׁר *m.* Prov. xvii. 26. מִישׁוֹר *m.* Isa. xi. 4: Mal. ii. 6. מֵישָׁרִים *m. pl.* Ps. xcviii. 9; xcix. 4: Prov. i. 3; ii. 9.

כִּשְׁרוֹן *m.* rectitude, prosperity, success: Eccles. ii. 21.

נְכֹחָה *f.* uprightness, right: Isa. lix. 14.

ERECT

נָצַב to place; to set up. HIPHIL *fut.* Gen. xxxiii. 20.

ERRAND

דָּבָר a word, &c.: Gen. xxiv. 33: Judg. iii. 19: 2 Kings ix. 5.

ERR, ERROR

1   שָׁגַג   to err from imprudence, rashness, or ignorance, but not wilfully, being deceived. KAL ^a *pret.* ^b שְׁגָגָה *f.* that which is done in ignorance, unwittingly, or unawares.

2   שָׁגָה   of the same primary meaning with the former, but implying something more or stronger in the act; it is used of those who err through wine, or under the influence of strong passions, or of those who go far astray: as implying sin, it is to be distinguished from what is done presumptuously, or with a high hand; comp. Num. xv. 22, &c., with xv. 30. Ps. cxix. 21, "the proud, who do err from thy commandments," *i.e.* leave them, not walking in them, and doing and teaching what they do not know; comp. 1 Tim. i. 7; verse 118, "that err from thy statutes;" Lxx. ἀποστατοῦντας ἀπὸ τῶν δικαιωμάτων σου. 1 Tim. iv. 1, 2 Pet. ii. 18: "one that erreth," and "the simple," are spoken of in conjunction, Ezek. xlv. 20; the former, not knowing what he saith or doeth; the latter, deceived and misled. KAL ^a *pret.* ^b *inf.* ^c *fut.* ^d *part.* Poel. ^e שְׁגִיאוֹת *f. pl.* errors. ^f מְשׁוּגָה *f.*

3   שָׁל   *m.* a fault committed inadvertently in ease or negligence of mind. ^a שָׁלוּ Ch. *f.* error, negligence.

---

4   תָּעָה   to wander, go astray; spoken of drunken persons, and of the mind as erring from the paths of virtue and piety; to be deceived, in a moral sense. KAL ^a *pret.* ^b *fut.* ^c *part.* HIPHIL ^d *pret.* ^e *fut.* ^f *part.* ^g תּוֹעָה *f.* error, impiety. ^h תַּעְתֻּעִים *m. pl.* mockery.

Lev. v. 18.	1 a	Prov. x. 17.	4 f	Isa. xxxii. 6.	4 g
Num. xv. 22.	2 c	xix. 27.	4 b	xxxv. 8.	4 b
1 Sam. xxvi. 21.	2 c	Eccles. v. 6.	1 b	lxiii. 17.	4 e
2 Sam. vi. 7.	3	v. 24.	1 b	Jer. x. 15.	4 h
2 Chron. xxxiii. 9.	4 e	Isa. iii. 12.	4 h	xxiii. 13, 32.	4 h
Job vi. 24.	2 a	ix. 16.	4 f	ll. 18.	4 h
xix. 4, 4.	2 a f	iii. 12.	4 f	Ezek. xlv. 20.	2 d
Ps. xix. 12.	2 e	xxviii. 7, 7, 7.	2 a	Dan. vi. 4.	3 a
xcv. 10.	4 c	xxix. 24.	4 b	Hos. iv. 12.	4 d
cxix. 21, 118.	2 d	xxx. 28.	4 f	Amos ii. 4.	4 e
cxix. 110.	4 a			Micah iii. 5.	4 f

ESCAPE

1   אָבַד   to perish. KAL *pret.* Job xi. 20.

2   יָצָא   to go out; to go forth as delivered from danger. KAL ^a *pret.* ^b *inf.*

3   מָלַט   to be smooth; to slip away, to escape quickly. With *inf.*, speedily escape. NIPHAL ^a *pret.* ^b *inf.* ^c *imp.* ^d *fut.* ^e *part.* HIPHIL ^f *fut.*

4   מָנוֹס   *m.* flight; see *Flee.*

5   נָצַל   to deliver with energy and power. NIPHAL ^a *fut.* HIPHIL ^b *pret.*

6   עָבַר   to pass over. KAL *fut.*

7   עַיִן   *com.* eye: 2 Sam. xx. 6.

8   פָּלַט   to escape out of danger; very similar to מָלַט. KAL ^a *pret.* PIEL ^b *fut.* ^c פֶּלֶט *m.* such as escape. ^d פַּלֵּט *m.* liberation. ^e פָּלִיט *m.* escaper, that escapeth, is escaped, &c. ^f פָּלִיט *m.* those that escape. ^g פְּלֵיטָה *f.* escape, deliverance; what has escaped. ^h מִפְלָט *m.* escape.

9   שְׁאֵרִית   *f.* remnant, remainder.

Gen. xiv. 13.	8 e	2 Kings xix. 30, 31.	8 g	Isa. lxvi. 19.	8 f
xix. 17, 17, 22.	8 c	xix. 37.	3 a	Jer. xi. 11.	2 b
xix. 19.	3 b	1 Chron. iv. 43.	8 g	xxv. 35. δ	8 g
xix. 20.	3 d	2 Chron. xvi. 7.	8 g	xxxii. 4.	3 d
xxxii. 8. a		xx. 24.	8 g	xxxiv. 3.	3 d
Exod. x. 5.	8 g	xxx. 6.	8 g	xxxviii. 18, 23.	3 d
Num. xxi. 29.	8 f	xxxvi. 20.	9	xli. 15.	3 a
Deut. xxiii. 15.	5 a	Ezra ix. 8, 14, 15.	8 g	xlii. 17. ε	8 e
Josh. viii. 22. β	8 e	Neh. i. 2.	8 g	xliv. 14, 14.	8 e c
Judg. iii. 26, 26.	8 a d	Esth. iv. 13.	3 b	xliv. 28.	8 e
iii. 29.	3 a	Job i. 15, 16, 17, 19.	8 e	xlvi. 6.	3 d
xii. 5.	8 e	xi. 20.	4, 1	xlviii. 8.	3 d
xxi. 17.	8 e	xix. 20.	3 f	xlviii. 19.	3 e
1 Sam. xiv. 41.	2 a	Ps. lv. 8.	8 h	l. 28.	8 g
xix. 10, 12, 17, 18.	3 d	lvi. 7. γ	8 d	l. 29. ζ	8 g
xxii. 1, 20.	3 d	lxxi. 2.	8 h	ll. 50.	8 e
xxiii. 13.	3 a	cxxiv. 7, 7.	3 a	Lam. ii. 22.	8 e
xxvii. 1, 1.	3 b d, a	cxli. 10.	3 d	Ezek. vi. 8, 9.	8 e
xxx. 17.	3 a	Prov. xix. 5.	3 d	vii. 16, 16.	8 e a
2 Sam. i. 3.	3 a	Eccles. vii. 26.	8 a	xvii. 15, 18.	3 d
iv. 6.	3 a	Isa. iv. 2.	8 g	xxiv. 26, 27.	3 d
xv. 14.	8 g	x. 20.	8 g	xxxiii. 21, 22.	8 e
xx. 6.	5 b, 7	xv. 9.	8 g	Dan. xi. 41.	3 d
1 Kings xviii. 40.	3 d	xx. 6.	8 d	xi. 42.	3 d
xix. 17, 17.	3 e	xxxvii. 31, 32.	8 g	Joel ii. 3.	8 g
xx. 20.	3 d	xxxvii. 38.	3 a	Amos ix. 1.	8 e
2 Kings ix. 15.	8 e	xlv. 20.	8 g	Obad. 14.	8 e
x. 24.	3 d				

a lit. shall be for an escaping.   *β lit.* a remainder, *or* escaper.   *γ lit.* shall deliverance be to them.   *δ lit.* and escaping shall perish.   *ε lit.* a remainder, *or* escaper.   *ζ lit.* there be no escaping.

ESCHEW

סוּר to turn aside out of the way. KAL *part.* Poel, Job i. 1, *lit.* turned from; 8; ii. 3.

ESPOUSE, ESPOUSAL

אָרַשׂ to betrothe. PIEL pret. 2 Sam. iii. 14.

כְּלוּלוֹת f. pl. espousals; see *Spouse*: Jer. ii. 2.

חֲתֻנָּה f. see *Marry*: Cant. iii. 11.

ESPY See SPY

ESTABLISH

1 אָמַן to support, bear. Niphal, to be supported, borne; to be faithful, firm; to be founded, stable. NIPHAL ^a*pret.* ^b*fut.* ^c*part.* ^d אֱמֶת f. truth.

2 אָמַץ to be firm, strong. PIEL, to strengthen; to set up, to build: *inf.*

3 חָזַק to be strong; see *Confirm*. KAL *pret.*

4 יָסַד to lay the foundation, to found. KAL *pret.*

5 יָצַג to set; to establish. HIPHIL *imp.*

6 יָשַׁב to sit, to dwell; to make to dwell. HIPHIL *fut.*

7 כּוּן to stand, to be erect; to stand firm, to be established; to be prepared; to be founded. NIPHAL ^a*pret.* ^b*fut.* ^c*part.* POLEL ^d*pret.* ^e*imp.* ^f*fut.* HIPHIL ^g*pret.* ^h*inf.* ⁱ*fut.* ^k*part.* HOPHAL ^l*pret.* HITHPOLEL ^m*fut.*

8 נָצַב to set, to put, to place; to fix, to establish. HIPHIL *fut.*

9 סָמַךְ to lean; to keep firm and steady, to establish. KAL *part.* Paul.

10 סָעַד to uphold, to support. KAL *inf.*

11 עָמַד to stand. HIPHIL ^a*inf.* ^b*fut.*

12 קוּם to arise; to stand firm and upright; to continue. KAL ^a*pret.* ^b*fut.* HIPHIL ^c*pret.* ^d*inf.* ^e*imp.* ^f*fut.* ^g*part.* קוּם Ch. P'AL ^h*inf.* APHEL ⁱ*fut.*

13 תְּקַן Ch. to be or become straight. HOPHAL *pret.*

Gen. vi. 18.	12 c	1 Chron. xvii. 14.	7 c	Prov. iv. 26.		7 b	
ix. 9.	12 g	xvii. 23.	1 b	viii. 28.		2	
ix. 11, 17.	12 c	xvii. 24, 24.	1 b, 7 c	xii. 3, 19.		7 b	
xvii. 7, 19.	12 c	xxii. 10.	7 g	xv. 22.		12 b	
xvii. 21.	12 f	xxviii. 7.	7 g	xv. 25.		8	
xli. 32.	7 c	2 Chron. i. 9.	1 b	xvi. 3, 12.		7 b	
Exod. vi. 4.	12 c	ix. 8.	11 a	xx. 18.		7 b	
xv. 17.	7 d	xii. 1.	7 h	xxiv. 3.		7 m	
Lev. xxv. 30.	12 a	xx. 20.	1 b	xxv. 5.		7 b	
xxvi. 9.	12 c	xxv. 3.	3	xxix. 4.		11 b	
Num. xxx. 13.	12 f	xxxii. 1.	1 d	xxix. 14.		7 b	
xxx. 14.	12 f	xxx. 5.	11 b	xxx. 4.		12 c	
Deut. viii. 18.	12 d	Job xxi. 8.	7 c	Isa. ii. 2.		7 c	
xix. 15.	12 b	xxii. 28.	12 b	vii. 9.		1 b	
xxviii. 9.	12 f	xxxvi. 7.	6	ix. 7.		10	
xxix. 13.	12 d	Ps. vii. 9.	7 f	xvi. 5.		7 l	
xxxii. 6.	7 f	xxiv. 2.	7 f	xlv. 18.		7 d	
1 Sam. i. 23.	12 f	xl. 2.	7 d	xlix. 8.		12 d	
iii. 20.	1 c	xlviii. 8.	7 f	liv. 14.		7 m	
xiii. 13.	7 g	lxxviii. 8.	12 f	lxii. 7.		7 f	
xx. 31.	7 b	lxxviii. 69.	4	Jer. x. 12.		7 k	
xxiv. 20.	12 a	lxxxvii. 5.	7 f	xxx. 20.		7 b	
2 Sam. v. 12.	7 g	lxxxix. 2, 4.	7 i	xxxiii. 2.		7 h	
vii. 12.	7 g	lxxxix. 21, 37.	7 b	li. 15.		7 k	
vii. 16, 16.	1 a, 7 c	xc. 17, 17.	7 e	Ezek. xvi. 60, 62.		12 c	
vii. 25.	12 e	xciii. 2.	7 c	Dan. iv. 36.		13	
vii. 26.	7 c	xcvi. 10.	7 b	vi. 7.		12 h	
1 Kings ii. 12.	7 b	xcix. 4.	7 d	vi. 8, 15.		12 i	
ii. 24.	7 g	cii. 28.	7 b	xi. 14.		11 a	
ii. 45.	7 c	cxii. 8.	9	Amos v. 15.		5	
ii. 46.	7 a	cxix. 90.	7 d	Micah iv. 1.		7 c	
ix. 5.	12 c	cxl. 11.	7 b	Hab. i. 12.		4	
xv. 4.	11 a	Prov. iii. 19.	7 d	Zech. v. 11.		7 l	
1 Chron. xvii. 11.	7 g						

ESTATE

גָּדַל to become great. HIPHIL, to come to great estate: *pret.* Eccles. i. 16.

דִּבְרָה f. state, condition, manner: Eccles. iii. 18.

כֵּן m. place, &c.: Dan. xi. 7, 20, 21, 38.

קַדְמָה f. antiquity; former estate, old estate: Ezek. xvi. 55, 55, 55; xxxvi. 11.

תּוֹר m. law; probably *i. q.* תּוֹרָה in the parallel place. 1 Chron. xvii. 17, "Hast regarded me according to the estate of a man of high degree, O Lord God;" rather and literally, according to the law of the man from on high, Jehovah Elohim. See C. B. Michaelis, Uberiores Annotationes *in loc.* "Thou hast spoken to me of my son and seed, so that I conclude he will be the Jehovah that shall reign," Ps. xciii. 1; xcvi. 10: the true God, Ps. xlv. 7, 8: and thy son in the divine nature, Ps. ii. 7; and my Lord, Ps. cx. 1, Matt. xxii. 43, 44. See *Manner*.

ESTEEM, ESTIMATE, ESTIMATION

1 חָשַׁב to think, intend, account; regard. KAL ^a*pret.* ^b*fut.* NIPHAL ^c*pret.* ^d*fut.*

2 יָשַׁר to be right. PIEL, to esteem right: *pret.*

3 עָרַךְ to set in order; to esteem, to estimate. KAL ^a*fut.* HIPHIL ^b*pret.* ^c*fut.* ^d עֵרֶךְ m. estimation.

4 צָפַן to hide, to lay up in store, to lay up carefully. KAL *pret.*

Lev. v. 15, 18.	3 d	Lev. xxvii. 14, 14.	3 b c	Ps. cxix. 128.	2
vi. 6.	3 d	Num. xviii. 16.	3 d	Isa. xxix. 16, 17.	1 d
xxvii. 2, 3, 3, 4, 5, 6,		Job xxiii. 12.	4	liii. 3, 4.	1 a
6, 7, 8, 13, 15, 16,		xxxvi. 19.	3 a	Lam. iv. 2.	1 c
17, 18, 19, 23, 23,		xli. 27.	1 b		
25, 27, 27.	3 d				

ESTRANGE

זוּר (see *Strange*); to be a stranger in another country, or to be estranged from the friendship and privileges of the place where one sojourns. KAL ^a*pret.* Job xix. 13: Ps. lviii. 3; lxxviii. 30. NIPHAL ^b*pret.* Ezek. xiv. 5.

נָכַר (see *Strange*); PIEL, to make strange, or reject: *fut.* Jer. xix. 4. LXX. and Vulg. ἀπηλλοτρίωσαν, *abalienarunt (mihi) hunc locum, i. e.* by consecrating it to foreign gods. Targ. and Syr., they have polluted.

ETERNAL, ETERNITY

עַד (see *Ever*); Isa. lvii. 15.

עוֹלָם ever, everlasting; duration of time that is concealed or hidden: Isa. lx. 15.

קֶדֶם m. that which is before; ancient: Deut. xxxiii. 27.

ETHANIM

אֵיתָן *adj.* constant, lasting, never failing, *perennis*, applied especially to water: 1 Kings viii. 2, *i. e.* the month of flowing brooks (otherwise called Tizri), which corresponds to part of September and part of October.

EVEN

מִישׁוֹר m. plain, even place: Ps. xxvi. 12.

צֶדֶק m. righteousness: Job xxxi. 6, *lit.* balance of righteousness.

EVEN, EVENING, EVENTIDE

יוֹם m. day: Prov. vii. 9, *marg.* 'evening of the day.'

עָרַב to be or grow dark. KAL *inf.* Judg. xix. 9. HIPHIL *inf.* 1 Sam. xvii. 16. עֶרֶב *m.* the evening, when the day begins to be obscured : Gen. i. 5, &c. עֲרָבָה *f.* desert : Jer. v. 6. עַרְבַּיִם *dual,* found only in the phrase בֵּין הָעַרְבַּיִם between the two evenings, Exod. xii. 6, Lev. xxiii. 5, Num. ix. 3, 5, 11—the paschal lamb was slain, and—according to Exod. xxix. 39, 41, Num. xxviii. 4, 8 —the daily evening offering was presented. See Ges. Lexicon.

עֵת *com.* time, season, convenient opportunity : Gen. viii. 11, *lit.* in the time of the evening ; translated *tide,* in connexion with *even,* Josh. viii. 29 : 2 Sam. xi. 2 : Isa. xvii. 14.

פָּנָה to look. KAL *inf.* Gen. xxiv. 63, "at the eventide ;" *Heb.* at the looking forth, *or,* the turn towards the even.

EVENT

מִקְרֶה *m.* that which befalleth : Eccles. ii. 14 ; ix. 2, 3.

EVER

1 אֹרֶךְ *m.* length ; for ever, *lit.* length of days, all the days.
2 דּוֹר *m.* generation ; for evermore, *lit.* to generation and generation.
3 יוֹם *m.* day ; for ever, evermore, *lit.* all days, length of days.
4 נֶצַח *m.* permanency, perpetuity, eternity ; for ever.
5 עַד *m.* time forward, in duration ; where not determined by some word accompanying, perpetuity, eternity ; "ever," "for ever," "evermore."

6 עוֹלָם *m.* everlasting ; duration of time that is concealed or hidden ; eternity ; "ever," "for ever," "evermore." Gen. iii. 22, &c. : 1 Chron. xxviii. 7, "unto for ever ;" xxix. 10, *lit.* from ever and ever. עָלַם *m.* עָלִים [α] Ch. *m.*

7 צְמִיתֻת *f.* a cutting off ; "for ever," *marg.* 'for cutting off, *or,* be quite cut off.'
8 קֶדֶם *m.* that which is before, ancient.
9 תָּמִיד *m.* continual, perpetual.

No. 6 not included.

Gen. xliii. 9.	3	Job xxxvi. 7.	4	Ps. lxxiii. 17.	5
xliv. 32.	3	Ps. ix. 5, 5.	6, 5	lxxxix. 29.	5
Exod. xv. 18, 18.	6, 5	ix. 18.	5	lxxxix. 46.	5
Lev. vi. 13.	9	x. 16, 16.	6, 5	xcii. 7.	5
xxv. 23, 30.	7	xiii. 1.	4	xciii. 1.	1, 3
Num. xxiv. 20, 24.	5	xvi. 11.	5	civ. 5. α	6, 5
Deut. iv. 40.	3	xix. 9.	5	cv. 4.	5
xviii. 5.	3	xxi. 4, 4.	6, 5	cxi. 3, 10.	5
xix. 9.	3	xxii. 26.	5	cxi. 8, 8.	5, 6
xxviii. 29.	3	xxii. 26.	5	cxii. 3, 9.	5
Josh. iv. 24.	3	xxiii. 6.	1, 3	cxix. 44, 44.	6, 5
1 Sam. ii. 32, 35.	3	xxv. 15.	9	cxxii. 12, 14.	6, 5
xxviii. 2.	3	xxxvii. 26.	3	cxxxii. 14.	5
2 Sam. ii. 26.	4	xxxvii. 29.	5	cxlv. 1, 1.	2, 5
1 Kings v. 1.	3	xliv. 23.	4	cxlv. 2, 2.	6, 5
xi. 39.	3	xlv. 6, 6.	6, 5	cxlv. 21, 21.	6, 5
xii. 7.	3	xlv. 17, 17.	6, 5	cxlviii. 6, 6.	6, 5
2 Kings xvii. 37.	3	xlviii. 14, 14.	6, 5	Prov. viii. 23. β	8
1 Chron. xxviii. 9.	3	xlix. 9.	4	xii. 19.	5
2 Chron. x. 7.	3	li. 3.	9	xxix. 14.	5
xxi. 7.	3	lii. 5.	5	Isa. xxvi. 4.	5
xxxiii. 7.	6 a	lii. 8, 8.	6, 5	xxviii. 28.	5
Job iv. 20.	3	lxi. 8.	5	xxx. 8, 8.	6, 5
xiv. 20.	4	lxviii. 16.	5	xxxiii. 20.	5
xix. 24.	4	lxxiv. 1, 10, 19.	4	xxxiv. 10, 10, 10.	6, 4, 4
xx. 7.	4	lxxvii. 8, 8.	4, 2	lxiv. 9.	5
xxiii. 7.	4	lxxix. 5.	5	lxv. 18.	5
				Jer. xxxi. 36.	5

Jer. xxxii. 39.	3	Dan. iii. 9.	6 b	Dan. xii. 3, 3.	6, 5
xxxv. 19.	3	iv. 34.	6 b	Amos i. 11.	4
l. 39.	4	v. 10.	6 b	Micah iv. 5, 5.	6, 5
Lam. v. 20.	4	vi. 6, 21, 26.	6 b	vii. 18.	5
Dan. ii. 4, 20, 20, γ 44.	6 b	vii. 18, 18, 18.	6 b		

α lit. for ever and ever.   *β lit.* from the olden times of the earth.   *γ lit.* unto ever.

EVERLASTING

יוֹם *m.* day : Micah v. 2, *marg.* 'from the days of eternity.'

עַד *m.* (see *Ever*) : Isa. ix. 6, *lit.* father of eternity ; Hab. iii. 6. Compare *Te Deum,* ver. 2.

עוֹלָם *m.* (see *Ever*) : Gen. ix. 16, &c. : Hab. iii. 6. Ps. xc. 2, 2, of time, endless and unlimited, whether past or yet to come. עָלַם Ch. *m.* Dan. iv. 3, 34 ; vii. 14, 27.

קֶדֶם *m.* that which is before, ancient : Hab. i. 12.

EVIDENCE

סֵפֶר *m.* book, register : Jer. xxxii. 10, 11, 12, 14, 14, 14, 16, 44.

EVIDENT

פָּנִים *m. pl.* face : Job vi. 28, *marg.* 'before your face.'

EVIL

1 אָוֶן *m.* vanity, misfortune, calamity : Prov. xii. 21.
2 אִישׁ *m.* a man : Ps. cxl. 11, *marg.* 'a man of tongue.'
3 דָּבָר *m.* word, matter, &c. ; "evil favouredness," *lit.* an evil thing.
4 בְּלִיַּעַל see *Wicked :* Ps. xli. 8, *marg.* 'a thing of Belial.'
5 יָרַע to be evil, wicked ; to be pernicious, hurtful. KAL *fut.*
6 לָשׁוֹן *com.* tongue : Ps. cxl. 11, *marg.* 'a man of tongue.'
7 רָעַע to break, to break in pieces ; *intrans.* to be evil, bad ; from the idea of breaking, being broken and so made worthless ; to be evil ; to do evil ; to deal ill with. It implies also displeasure, anger, sadness, envy. With *inf.,* indeed do evil. KAL [a] *pret.* HIPHIL [b] *pret.* [c] *inf.* [d] *fut.* [e] *part.* [f] רַע *adj.* Gen. ii. 9, &c. [g] רֹעַ *m.* evil, wickedness.
8 רָעָה to feed ; to consume. KAL *part.* Poel, Job xxiv. 21, *i. e.* oppresseth.

No. 7 f not included.

Gen. xliv. 5.	7 b	Ps. xli. 8.	4	Jer. xiii. 23.	7 c
Exod. v. 22, 23.	7 b	xciv. 16.	7 e	xx. 13.	7 e
Lev. v. 4.	7 c	cxix. 115.	7 e	xxi. 12.	7 g
Deut. xv. 9.	7 f	cxl. 11.	1, 6	xxiii. 2.	7 g
xvii. 1.	7 f, 3	Prov. xii. 21.	1	xxiii. 14.	7 e
xxvi. 6.	7 d	xxiv. 8.	7 c	xxiii. 22, 22.	7 f g
xxviii. 54, 56.	5	xxiv. 19.	7 e	xxiv. 3, 3, 3.	7 f f g
Josh. xxiv. 15.	7 a	Isa. i. 4.	7 e	xxiv. 8, 8.	7 f g
1 Kings xiv. 9.	7 d	i. 16, 16.	7 g c	xxv. 5, 5.	7 f f g
xvii. 20.	7	ix. 17.	7 d	xxv. 29.	7 c
1 Chron. xxi. 17.	7 c b	xiv. 20.	7 e	xxvi. 3, 3, 3.	7 f f g
Job viii. 20.	7 e	xxxi. 2, 2.	7 f e	xxix. 17.	7 g
xxiv. 21.	8	xli. 23.	7 d	xxxviii. 9.	7 b
Ps. xxvi. 5.	7 e	Jer. iv. 4.	7 g	xliv. 22.	7 g
xxxvii. 1, 9.	7 e	iv. 22.	7 e	Zeph. i. 12.	7 d
xxxvii. 8.	7 c	x. 5.	7 d		

EUNUCH

סָרִיס an eunuch ; courtier, chamberlain : 2 Kings ix. 32, *marg.* 'or, chamberlains ;' xx. 18 : Isa. xxxix. 7 : lvi. 3, 4 : Jer. xxix. 2, *marg.* 'or, chamberlains ;' xxxiv. 19 ; xxxviii. 7 ; xli. 16 ; lii. 25 : Dan. i. 3, 7, 8, 9, 10, 11, 18.

EWE   (See also YOUNG)

כִּבְשָׂה *f.* a lamb that has done sucking ; a young sheep ; ewe

לֶמֶב ; covenants were ratified by a present of seven
ewe lambs or sheep : Gen. xxi. 28, 29, 30 : Lev. xiv. 10 :
Num. vi. 14 : 2 Sam. xii. 3.

רָחֵל a female, or mother sheep : Gen. xxxi. 38 ; xxxii. 14.

שֶׂה *com.* a lamb or kid, a sheep or goat : Lev. xxii. 28, *marg.*
' *or*, she goat.'

EXACT, EXACTION

1 גְּרֻשָׁה *f.* expulsion, driving out, of persons from their possessions.

2 יָצָא to go forth. HIPHIL, to cause to come forth : *fut.*

3 נָגַשׂ to urge, drive on to labour ; to press a debtor ; to oppress.
KAL ᵃ*pret.* ᵇ*fut.* ᶜ*part.* Poel.

4 נָשָׁה to receive as usury, *or*, to exact. KAL ᵃ*part.* Poel. HI-
PHIL ᵇ*fut.* Job xi. 6, *or*, God hath caused thee to be
forgotten of thine iniquity.

5 נָשָׁא the same. KAL ᵃ*part.* HIPHIL ᵇ*fut.* ᶜ מַשָּׁא *m.* exaction.

Deut. xv. 2, 3.	3 b	Neh. v. 10, 11.	4 a	Isa. lviii. 3.	3 b
2 Kings xv. 20.	2	x. 31.	5 c	lx. 17.	3 c
xxiii. 35.	3 a	Job xi. 6.	4 b	Ezek. xlv. 9.	1
Neh. v. 7.	5 a, or 4 a	Ps. lxxxix. 22.	5 b		

EXALT

1 גָּבַהּ to be high, to be exalted. KAL ᵃ*pret.* ᵇ*fut.* HIPHIL
ᶜ*pret.* ᵈ*inf.* ᵉ*fut.* ᶠ*part.* See *Gate.*

2 נָשָׂא to lift or raise up. KAL ᵃ*pret.* NIPHAL ᵇ*fut.* ᶜ*part.*
PIEL ᵈ*pret.* HITHPAEL ᵉ*fut.* ᶠ*part.*

3 סָלַל to cast up, to oppose oneself. PILPEL ᵃ*imp.* HITHPOEL
ᵇ*part.*

4 עָלָה to ascend. NIPHAL *pret.*

5 רוּם to be high or lifted up ; to exalt oneself, *seq.* עַל to triumph
over any one : Ps. xiii. 3. KAL ᵃ*pret.* ᵇ*inf.* ᶜ*imp.* ᵈ*fut.*
POLEL ᵉ*imp.* ᶠ*fut.* POLAL ᵍ*fut.* ʰ*part.* HIPHIL ⁱ*pret.*
ᵏ*imp.* ˡ*fut.* ᵐ*part.* HITHPOLEL ⁿ*fut.*

6 רָמַם to be lifted up ; to be high. KAL ᵃ*pret.* ᵇ*part.* Poel.
NIPHAL ᶜ*fut.*

7 שָׂגַב to be raised high, as an inaccessible fortress ; as a person, in
such a place of defence. Hence in Piel, to set on high,
or out of the reach of danger. KAL ᵃ*pret.* NIPHAL
ᵇ*pret.* ᶜ*part.* HIPHIL ᵈ*fut.*

Exod. ix. 17.	3 b	Ps. xlvii. 9.	4	Isa. xii. 4.	7 c
xv. 2.	5 f	lvii. 5, 11.	5 c	xiii. 2.	5 k
Num. xxiv. 7.	5 e	lxvi. 7.	5 d	xiv. 13.	5 d or l
1 Sam. ii. 1.	5 a	lxxv. 10.	5 g	xxv. 1.	5 f
ii. 10.	5 l	lxxxi. 16, 17, 24.	5 d	xxx. 18.	5 e
2 Sam. v. 12.	2 d	lxxxix. 19.	5 i	xxxiii. 5.	7 c
xxii. 47.	5 d	xcii. 10.	5 l	xxxiii. 10.	6 i
1 Kings i. 5.	2 f	xcvii. 9.	4	xxxvii. 23.	5 i
xiv. 7.	5 i	xcix. 5, 9.	5 e	xl. 4.	2 b
xvi. 2.	5 i	cvii. 32.	5 f	xlix. 11.	5 d
2 Kings xix. 22.	5 i	cviii. 5.	5 c	lii. 13.	5 d
1 Chron. xxix. 11.	2 f	cxii. 9.	5 d	Ezek. xvii. 24.	1 c
Neh. ix. 5.	5 h	cxviii. 16.	6 b	xix. 11.	1 b
Job v. 11.	7 a	cxviii. 28.	5 f	xxi. 26.	1 d
xvii. 4.	5 f	cxl. 8.	5 d	xxix. 15.	1 c
xxiv. 24.	6 a	cxlviii. 14.	5 l	xxxi. 5.	1 a
xxxvi. 7.	1 b	Prov. iv. 8.	3 a	xxxi. 14.	1 b
xxxvi. 22.	7 d	xi. 11.	5 d	Dan. xi. 14.	5 d
Ps. xii. 8.	5 b	xiv. 29.	5 m	xi. 36.	5 n
xiii. 2.	5 d	xiv. 34.	5 f	Hos. xi. 7.	5 f
xviii. 46.	5 d	xvii. 19.	1 f	xiii. 1.	1 a
xxi. 13.	5 c	Isa. ii. 2.	2 c	xiii. 6.	5 d
xxxiv. 3.	5 f	ii. 11, 17.	7 b	Obad. 4.	1 e
xxxvii. 34.	5 f	v. 16.	1 b	Micah iv. 1.	2 c
xlvi. 10, 10.	5 d				

EXAMINE

בָּחַן to try. KAL *imp.* Ps. xxvi. 2.

דָּרַשׁ to search. PIEL *inf.* Ezra x. 16. For דָּרוֹשׁ see Gesenius'
Gram. § 8, rem. 10.

EXCEED, EXCEEDING, EXCEEDINGLY

1 אֱלֹהִים *m. pl.* God : Jonah iii. 3, *lit.* of God ; *comp.* Ps. xxxvi. 6.

2 גָּבַר to be strong, to prevail. HITHPAEL, to conduct oneself proudly, insolently : *fut.*

3 גָּדַל to be or become great. KAL ᵃ*fut.* HIPHIL ᵇ*pret.*
ᶜ גָּדוֹל *adj.* great.

4 גִּיל *m.* gladness : Job iii. 22, *lit.* rejoicing unto gladness.

5 יָסַף to add. KAL ᵃ*pret.* HIPHIL ᵇ*pret.* ᶜ*fut.*

6 יֶתֶר *m.* abundance, used adverbially. ᵃ יַתִּיר Ch. *adj. id.*

7 מְאֹד *m.* strength, force ; used also adverbially, exceedingly,
either singly, or ᵃ מְאֹד מְאֹד, or ᵇ בִּמְאֹד מְאֹד.

8 סָרַח to be superfluous, to hang over. KAL *part.* Paül.

9 רַב *adj.* many, much, &c.

10 רָבָה to multiply. HIPHIL *inf.*

11 שַׂגִּיא Ch. *adj.* many, great, much.

12 שִׂמְחָה *f.* joy, gladness.

Gen. vii. 19.	7	2 Sam. xiii. 15.	3 c, 7	Ps. lxviii. 3.	12
xiii. 13.	7	1 Kings iv. 29.	7	cxix. 96, 167.	7
xv. 1.	7	vii. 47.	7 a	cxxiii. 3, 4.	9
xvi. 10.	10	x. 7.	5 b	Jer. xlviii. 29.	7
xvii. 2, 6, 20.	7 b	x. 23.	3 a	Ezek. ix. 9.	7 b
xxvii. 33.	3 c, 7	2 Kings x. 4.	7 a	xvi. 13.	7 b
xxvii. 34.	7	1 Chron. xx. 2.	7	xxiii. 15.	8
xxx. 43.	7 a	2 Chron. xx. 6.	5 a	xxxvii. 10.	7
xlvii. 27.	7	xi. 12. a	7, 10	xlvii. 10.	7
Exod. i. 7.	7 b	xiv. 14.	9	Dan. iii. 22.	6 a
xix. 16.	7	xxxii. 27.	7	vi. 23.	11
Num. xiv. 7.	7 a	Neh. ii. 10. β	3 c	vii. 19.	6 a
Deut. xxv. 3, 3.	5 c	Esth. iv. 4.	7	viii. 9.	6
1 Sam. xx. 41.	3 b	Job iii. 22.	4	Jonah i. 10, 16.	3 c
xxvi. 21.	7, 10	xxxvi. 9.	7	iii. 3.	1
2 Sam. viii. 8.	7	xliii. 4.	5 b	iv. 1. β	12
xii. 2.	7			iv. 6.	3 c

ᵃ *lit.* and strengthened them to a multitude of strength. β *lit.* with
great grief.

EXCEL, EXCELLENT, EXCELLENCY

1 אַדִּיר *adj.* mighty, illustrious, powerful, noble. See *Glory.*

2 בָּחַר to choose. KAL *part.* Paül.

3 גָּאָה to rise up, to be raised up ; to be eminent, to excel. Applied to God, it signifies
the highest magnificence, power, and excellency
most illustriously displayed ; applied to men, it
signifies superior honour, virtue, excellence, and
lustre ; applied to waters, the sea, waves, it signifies their rising, overflowing, boisterous tossing and
roaring ; applied to plants, it denotes their growth ;
to smoke, its ascending up ; to afflictions, their increase, &c. Excellency sometimes means that which
causes elation of mind, Ezek. xxiv. 21. ᵃ גָּאוֹן *m.* sublimity, majesty ; ornament, glory, splendour ; pride,
arrogance. ᵇ גֵּאוּת *f.* a lifting up, glory. ᶜ גַּאֲוָה *f.*
magnificence, majesty.

4 גֹּבַהּ *m.* height ; majesty, magnificence.

5 גִּבּוֹר *adj.* mighty.

6 גָּדַל to become great. HIPHIL *pret.*

7 הָדָר *m.* glory, honour, majesty.

8 יָקָר *adj.* precious, costly.

9   יָתַר   to remain; to be abundant; to be more than others; to excel. HIPHIL ^a*fut.* יָתִיר ^b *m.* what exceeds bounds or measure, pre-eminence. ^c יִתְרוֹן *f.* profit. ^d יַתִּיר Ch. *adj.* very great, excellent. ^e יֶתֶר *adj.* excellent; *marg.* 'abundant.' See also תּוּר.

10   נָגִיד   *m.* a captain, ruler, noble; used also abstractly, *nobilia, honesta*; worthy of a prince or ruler.

11   נָצַח   see *Victory, Oversee.* PIEL *inf.*

12   שְׂאֵת   *f.* a rising, exaltation, dignity. ^a שִׂיא *m.* height, greatness.

13   עֲדִי   *m.* ornaments: Ezek. xvi. 7.

14   עָלָה   to ascend; *metaph.* to rise, increase, advance. KAL *pret.*

15   תִּפְאָרָה   *f.* ornament; glory, praise, honour; "excellent majesty."

16   קַר   *adj.* cold: Prov. xvii. 27, כתיב.

17   רֹאשׁ   *m.* head, the first or highest in its kind.

18   רֹב   *m.* multitude, abundance.

19   רָבָה   to be multiplied, to become great. KAL *fut.*

20   שַׂגִּיא   *adj.* great, excellent.

21   שָׂגַב   to rise, to be high, to be exalted. NIPHAL *part.*

22   שָׁלִישׁ   *m.* captain, lord; abstractly, *principalia.* שִׁלְשׁוֹם, כתיב, the day before yesterday, *i. e.* in time past. Umbreit distinctly prefers this reading and sense in Prov. xxii. 20 to the קרי, as a contrast to "day" in the former verse.

23   תּוּר   to search, explore. HIPHIL, to direct in the way: *fut.* The meaning of Prov. xii. 26, according to this root, will be, "the righteous explores or directs his way more than his neighbour; but the way of the wicked (*pl.*) seduceth them."

Gen. xlix. 3, 3.	9 b	Ps. xlvii. 4.	3 a	Cant. v. 15.	2
xlix. 4.	9 a	lxii. 4.	12	Isa. iv. 2.	3 a
Exod. xv. 7.	3 a	lxviii. 34.	3 c	xii. 5.	3 b
Deut. xxxiii. 26, 29.	3 c	lxxvi. 4.	1	xiii. 19.	3 a
1 Kings iv. 30.	19	ciii. 20.	5	xxviii. 29.	6
1 Chron. xv. 21.	11	cxli. 5.	17	xxxv. 2, 2.	7
Esth. i. 4.	15	cxlviii. 13.	21	lx. 15.	3 a
Job iv. 21.	9 b	cl. 2.	18	Ezek. xvi. 7.	13
xiii. 11.	12	Prov. viii. 6.	10	xxiv. 21.	3 a
xx. 6.	12 a	xii. 26.	9 e, or 22	Dan. ii. 31.	9 d
xxxvii. 4.	3 a	xvii. 7.	9 b	iv. 36.	9 d
xxxvii. 23.	20	xvii. 27.	8, or 16	v. 12, 14.	9 d
xl. 10.	1	xxii. 20.	22	vi. 3.	9 d
Ps. viii. 1, 9.	1	xxxi. 29.	14	Amos vi. 8.	3 a
xvi. 3.	1	Eccles. ii. 13, 13. *a*	9 c	viii. 7.	3 a
xxxvi. 7.	8	vii. 12.	9 c	Nah. ii. 2, 2.	3 a

a lit. as much as the excellence of light above darkness.

EXCHANGE

מוּר   to change, exchange. HIPHIL *fut.* Ezek. xlviii. 14.
תְּמוּרָה   *f.* exchange: Lev. xxvii. 10: Job xxviii. 17.

EXECRATION

אָלָה   *f.* an oath; imprecation, curse: Jer. xlii. 18; xliv. 12.

EXECUTE

1   דִּין   to judge. KAL *imp.*

2   עָבַד   to labour, to serve. With *inf.*, thoroughly execute. KAL ^a *inf.* עֲבַד Ch. ITHP'AL ^b *part.*

3   עָשָׂה   to make, do, act; to execute or accomplish anything. KAL ^a*pret.* ^b*inf.* ^c*imp.* ^d*fut.* ^e*part.* Poel. NIPHAL ^f*pret.* ^g*inf.*

4   שָׁפַט   to judge. KAL ^a*imp.* NIPHAL ^b*inf.*

Exod. xii. 12.	3 d	Ps. ciii. 6.	3 e	Ezek. xviii. 8.	3 d
Num. v. 30.	3 a	cxix. 84.	3 d	xviii. 17.	3 a
viii. 11.	2 a	cxlvi. 7.	3 e	xx. 24.	3 a
xxxiii. 4.	3 a	cxlix. 7, 9.	3 b	xxiii. 10.	3 a
Deut. x. 18.	3 e	Eccles. viii. 11.	3 f	xxv. 11.	3 d
xxxiii. 21.	3 a	Isa. xvi. 3.	3 c	xxv. 17.	3 a
1 Sam. xxviii. 18.	3 a	Jer. v. 1.	3 b	xxviii. 22, 26.	3 b
2 Sam. viii. 15.	3 e	vii. 5.	3 b d	xxx. 14, 19.	3 a
1 Kings vi. 12.	3 d	xxi. 12.	1	xxxix. 21.	3 a
2 Kings x. 30.	3 b	xxii. 3.	3 c	xlv. 9.	3 c
1 Chron. xviii. 14.	3 e	xxiii. 5.	3 a	Hos. xi. 9.	3 d
2 Chron. xxii. 8.	4 b	xxiii. 20.	3 b	Joel ii. 11.	3 e
xxiv. 24.	3 a	xxxiii. 15.	3 a	Micah v. 15.	3 a
Ezra vii. 26.	2 b	Ezek. v. 8, 10.	3 a	vii. 9.	3 a
Esth. ix. 1.	3 g	v. 15.	3 b	Zech. vii. 9.	3 a
Ps. ix. 16.	3 a	xi. 9, 12.	3 a	viii. 16.	4 a
xcix. 4.	3 a	xvi. 41.	3 a		

EXEMPT

נָקִי   *adj.* clear, innocent, free: 1 Kings xv. 22, *marg.* 'free.'

EXERCISE

גָּזַל   to take away by violence; to rob; to exercise (robbery). KAL *pret.* Ezek. xxii. 29.

הָלַךְ   to go. With בְּ to enter upon, engage in. PIEL *pret.* Ps. cxxxi. 1.

עָנָה   to bestow labour or toil on anything; *seq.* בְּ. KAL *inf.* Eccles. i. 13; iii. 10.

עָשָׂה   to make, do, act; to carry into effect. KAL *part.* Poel, Jer. ix. 24.

EXILE

גָּלָה   to go into captivity. KAL *part.* Poel, 2 Sam. xv. 19.

צָעָה   to wander; or, to be bent, bowed down, as a captive by fetters. KAL *part.* Poel, Isa. li. 14. Our translators have rendered this word "captive exile," but Schroeder has shown (see Rosenmüller *in loc.*) that the proper meaning is, to be bent or bowed down by bonds, as the captive in the pit, who cannot raise himself erect.

EXPECT

מַבָּט   *m.* expectation; looking out in hope, but mostly ashamed: Isa. xx. 5, 6. מֶבָט *m. id.* Zech. ix. 5.

תִּקְוָה   *f.* hope, expectation: Ps. ix. 18; lxii. 5: Prov. x. 28; xi. 7, 23; xxiii. 18; xxiv. 14: Jer. xxix. 11.

EXPEL

גָּרַשׁ   to drive out. PIEL *fut.* Judg. xi. 7.

הָדַף   to thrust away. KAL *fut.* Josh. xxiii. 5.

יָרַשׁ   to possess. HIPHIL, to dispossess: *pret.* Josh. xiii. 13. *fut.* Judg. i. 20.

נָדַח   to push, thrust out, expel. KAL *fut.* 2 Sam. xiv. 14.

EXPENSES

נִפְקָא   *f. emph.* נִפְקָתָא Ch. expense, cost, what is paid out or expended: Ezra vi. 4, 8.

EXPERIENCE

נָחַשׁ   to divine, to use enchantment in order to obtain omens; so,

to learn by experience, *or*, by close inspection. PIEL *pret.* Gen. xxx. 27, *i.e.* ascertained by close inspection.

רָאָה to see. KAL *pret.* Eccles. i. 16, *lit.* had seen much.

EXPERT

לָמַד to learn, to be instructed. PUAL *part.* Cant. iii. 8.

עָרַךְ to set in order. KAL *inf.* 1 Chron. xii. 36. *part.* Poel, 1 Chron. xii. 33, 35.

שָׂכַל to act wisely, successfully. HIPHIL *part.* Jer. i. 9, or, according to another rendering,

שָׁכַל to be bereaved. HIPHIL *part.* Jer. l. 9, *marg.* 'or, destroyer.'

EXPIRE

כָּלָה to be finished. PIEL *fut.* Ezek. xliii. 27.

מָלֵא to be full, fulfilled. KAL *pret.* 1 Sam. xviii. 26 : 1 Chron. xvii. 11. *inf.* Esth. i. 5.

תְּשׁוּבָה *f.* return ; applied to the close of one and the return of another year : 2 Sam. xi. 1 : 1 Chron. xx. 1 : 2 Chron. xxxvi. 10.

EXPOUND

נָגַד see *Declare, Show.* HIPHIL *inf.* Judg. xiv. 14. *part.* Judg. xiv. 19.

EXPRESS

אָמַר to say. KAL *inf.* 1 Sam. xx. 21, *lit.* if saying I say.

נָקַב (see *Appoint, Name*), to mark, note, or expressly to nominate a certain number of persons. NIPHAL *pret.* Num. i. 17 : 1 Chron. xii. 31 ; xvi. 41 : 2 Chron. xxviii. 15 ; xxxi. 19 : Ezra viii. 20.

EXTEND

מָשַׁךְ to draw, draw out ; to continue, lengthen out. KAL *part.* Poel, Ps. cix. 12.

נָטָה to stretch, extend, expand, (see *Turn*) : Isa. lxvi. 12, " I will extend peace to her as a river," in the abundance and perpetuity of a full large river. KAL *part.* Poel, Isa. lxvi. 12. HIPHIL *pret.* Ezra vii. 28. *fut.* Ezra ix. 9.

EXTINCT

דָּעַךְ to be extinguished, to go out, *pr.* of a light. KAL *pret.* Isa. xliii. 17.

זָעַךְ to cut off, to extinguish. NIPHAL *pret.* Job xvii. 1.

EXTOL

נָשָׂא to lift up. NIPHAL *pret.* Isa. lii. 13.

סָלַל to raise, cast up ; to esteem, to prefer, to extol. KAL *imp.* Ps. lxviii. 4 ; Gesenius, make plain (*sc.* the way).

רוּם to be lifted up. POLEL *fut.* Ps. xxx. 1 ; cxlv. 1. POLAL *pret.* Ps. lxvi. 17. רום Ch. P'AL *part.* active, Dan. iv. 37. רוֹמָם *m.* a lifting up, praise ; Ps. lxvi. 17, *comp.* Ps. cxlix. 6 ; lxvi. 17, or a verb, as above.

EXTORTION

מוּץ to force, press, squeeze ; hence, to oppress by extortion. KAL *part.* Isa. xvi. 4, *marg.* ' wringer.'

נָשָׁה to lend, to exact usury. KAL *part.* Poel, Ps. cix. 11.

עֹשֶׁק *m.* oppression, deceit, fraud : Ezek. xxii. 12.

EXTREMITY

פַּשׁ occurs but once in the Hebrew : Job xxxv. 15. It does not appear what our translators understood by the word which they have rendered *extremity.* Mercer and other older critics take it to mean multitude, abundance ; the LXX. and Vulg., transgression, as though it were the same as פֶּשַׁע. To this Gesenius leans, and Barnes, who would render the sentence, "does not take cognizance severely of transgressions."

EYE, EYELIDS, EYESIGHT

עַיִן *com.* the eye : it is put for several affections of the mind : —(1) The understanding ; Ps. xix. 8, Isa. xlii. 7, Jer. v. 21 : God's omniscience or watchful providence ; Ezra v. 5, Prov. xv. 3, Jer. xl. 4. (2) The judgment ; Deut. xvi. 19. (3) Esteem ; Prov. xvii. 8. (4) Kind regard ; Ps. ci. 6, Isa. i. 15. (5) Desire, good or bad ; Gen. xx. 16, xxxix. 7, Ps. xxv. 15, Prov. xxvii. 20. (6) Expectation ; 1 Kings i. 20. (7) Compassion ; Isa. xiii. 18. עַפְעַפִּים *m. dual,* eyelashes, or eyelids : Job xvi. 16 ; xli. 18 : Ps. xi. 4 ; cxxxii. 4 : Prov. iv. 25 ; vi. 4, 25 ; xxx. 13 : Jer. ix. 18. עַיִן Ch. eye : Ezra v. 5 ; Dan. iv. 34 ; vii. 8, 8, 20. עִין to eye. KAL *part.* Poel, 1 Sam. xviii. 9, *lit.* was eyeing.

FACE

אַף *m.* nose ; anger ; face : Gen. iii. 19 ; xix. 1 ; xxiv. 47, *lit.* her nose : xlii. 6 ; xlviii. 12 : Num. xxii. 31 : 1 Sam. xx. 41 ; xxiv. 8 ; xxv. 41 ; xxviii. 14 : 2 Sam. xiv. 4, 33 ; xviii. 28 : xxiv. 20 : 1 Kings i. 23, 31 : 1 Chron. xxi. 21 : 2 Chron. vii. 3 ; xx. 18 : Neh. viii. 6 : Isa. xlix. 23 : Ezek. xxxviii. 18. אַנְפִּין Ch. *pl. id.* Dan. ii. 46.

עַיִן *com.* the eye ; surface, appearance : Exod. x. 5, 15 ; Num. xiv. 14, 14 ; xxii. 5, 11 : 1 Kings xx. 38, 41 : 2 Kings ix. 30.

פָּנָה to turn ; to look ; to turn the face. KAL *fut.* Gen. xviii. 22. פָּנִים *m. pl.* the face, countenance, aspect ; a person ; Deut. i. 17. The presence of a person, especially of God ; Lam. ii. 19, iii. 35 ; Exod. xxv. 30. Face is put for favour or regard, 1 Kings xiii. 6, Job xxxiv. 29, Prov. xix. 6, xxix. 26, Jer. ii. 27 ; anger or displeasure, Lam. iv. 16 ; the surface of the earth or water, Gen. i. 2, 29 ; the mouth of a well, 2 Sam. xvii. 19 ; the edge of a tool, Eccles. x. 10 ; the front of an army, the forepart of a building, 1 Chron. xix. 10.——Gen. i. 2, &c.

FADE

נָבֵל to be exhausted of the natural moisture and spirits ; see *Wither :* Isa. xl. 7. It signifies the loss of spirit and courage, 2 Sam. xxii. 46, Exod. xviii. 18 ; the loss of power, wealth, honour, grandeur, happiness, Isa. xxiv. 4. KAL *pret.* Isa. xxiv. 4, 4 ; xl. 7, 8 : Jer. viii. 13. *fut.* 2 Sam. xxii. 46 : Ps. xviii. 45 : Isa. lxiv. 6 : Ezek. xlvii. 12 : Isa. lxiv. 6. *part.* Poel, Isa. i. 30 ; xxviii. 1, 4.

154 OLD TESTAMENT WORD STUDIES

FAIL

1 אָבַד to perish, *seq.* מִן to perish from, to fail. KAL *pret.*

2 אָזַל to go away, to depart, to fail. KAL *pret.*

3 אָמַן to be firm; sure. NIPHAL *pret.* that fail, *i. e.* not sure.

4 אָפֵס to cease, to have an end. KAL *pret.*

5 בָּקַק to empty; to be exhausted. NIPHAL *pret.*

6 גָּמַר to finish; to leave off; to fail. KAL *pret.*

7 גָּעַל to loathe, reject, or refuse. HIPHIL *fut.*

8 דָּלַל to hang down, to be brought low, to languish. KAL *pret.*

9 חָדַל to cease, to forsake. KAL *pret.*

10 חָסֵר to decrease (see *Lack*): it seems to be used especially of liquids, as water, oil, &c., failing. KAL ᵃ *fut.* HIPHIL ᵇ *fut.* ᶜ חָסֵר *adj.* wanting, lacking.

11 יָצָא to go forth: applied to the fainting of the soul when the spirits, as it were, go forth. KAL ᵃ *pret.* ᵇ *fut.*

12 כָּהָה to be dim: applied to faintness of the spirit, when the vigour of the mind is enfeebled or dulled. KAL *fut.*

13 כָּזַב to lie, deceive. PIEL *fut.*

14 כָּחַשׁ to waste; to deny; to deceive, to lie. KAL ᵃ *pret.* PIEL ᵇ *pret.* ᶜ *fut.*

15 כָּלָה to be quite done, spent, wasted, exhausted. KAL ᵃ *pret.* ᵇ *inf.* ᶜ *fut.* PIEL ᵈ *fut.* ᵉ כָּלֶה *adj.* pining away, of the eye. ᶠ כִּלָּיוֹן *m.* pining, wasting away.

16 כָּרַת to cut off. NIPHAL, to perish, or fail: *fut.*

17 כָּשַׁל to stumble, to fall. KAL *pret.*

18 נָפַל to fall, to fall to the ground, to fail. KAL ᵃ *pret.* ᵇ *fut.* HIPHIL ᶜ *fut.*

19 נָשַׁת to dry up, to become dry. KAL ᵃ *pret.* NIPHAL ᵇ *pret.*

20 עָבַר to pass on; to pass away, to be altered, annulled; ineffectual, disregarded. KAL *fut.*

21 עָדַר to forsake, to leave, to depart. NIPHAL, to be lacking: ᵃ *pret.* ᵇ *part.*

22 עָזַב to leave, to forsake. KAL *pret.*

23 עָטַף to cover, to be covered; see *Faint, Overwhelmed.* KAL *fut.*

24 פָּסַס to cease, fail, disappear; kindred to אָפֵס. KAL *pret.*

25 פָּרַר see *Disannul.* HIPHIL *fut.*

26 רָפָה to be slack, to slacken the hand, to desist from. HIPHIL *fut.*

27 שָׁבַת to rest, to cease. HIPHIL, to cause to cease: ᵃ *pret.* ᵇ *inf.*

28 שְׁלָה Ch. *f.* error, something done amiss so as to fail.

29 שָׁקַר to deal falsely; to lie. PIEL *fut.*

30 תָּמַם to be finished, to be ended. KAL ᵃ *pret.* ᵇ *fut.*

Gen. xlii. 28.	11 b	Josh. xxiii. 14, 14.	18 a	1 Chron. xxviii. 20.	26
xlvii. 15, 15.	30 b, 4	1 Sam. xvii. 32.	18 b	2 Chron. vi. 16.	16
xlvii. 16.	4	2 Sam. iii. 29.	16	vii. 18.	16
Deut. xxviii. 32.	15 e	1 Kings ii. 4.	16	Ezra iv. 22.	28
xxviii. 65.	15 f	viii. 25.	16	vi. 9.	28
xxxi. 6, 8.	26	viii. 56.	18 a	Esth. vi. 10.	18 c
Josh. i. 5.	26	ix. 5.	16	ix. 27, 28.	20
iii. 16.	30 a	xvii. 14.	10 a	Job xi. 20.	15 c
xxi. 45.	18 a	xvii. 16.	10 c	xiv. 11.	2

Job xvii. 5.	15 c	Prov. xxii. 8.	15 c	Isa. li. 14.	10 a
xix. 14.	9	Eccles. x. 3.	10 c	lvii. 16.	23
xxi. 10.	7	xii. 5.	25	lviii. 11.	13
xxxi. 16.	15 d	Cant. v. 6.	11 a	lix. 15.	21 b
Ps. xii. 1.	24	Isa. xv. 6.	15 a	Jer. xiv. 6.	15 a
xxxi. 10.	17	xix. 3.	5	xv. 18.	3
xxxviii. 10.	22	xix. 5.	19 b	xlviii. 33.	27 a
xl. 12.	22	xxi. 16.	15 a	li. 30.	19 a
lxix. 3.	15 a	xxxi. 3.	15 c	Lam. ii. 11.	15 a
lxxi. 9.	15 a	xxxii. 6.	15 a	iii. 22.	15 a
lxxiii. 26.	15 a	xxxii. 10.	15 a	iv. 17.	15 c
lxxvii. 8.	6	xxxiv. 16.	21 a	Ezek. xii. 22.	1
lxxxix. 33.	29	xxxviii. 14.	8	Hos. ix. 2.	14 c
cix. 24.	14 a	xl. 26.	19 a	Amos viii. 1.	27 b
cxix. 82, 123.	15 a	xli. 17.	19 a	Hab. iii. 17.	14 b
cxlii. 4.	1	xlii. 4.	12	Zeph. iii. 5.	21 a
cxliii. 7.	15 a				

FAINT

1 דָּוֶה *adj.* sick, faint, languid; sad. ᵃ דַּוָּי *adj.* sick of mind.

2 הָיָה to be. NIPHAL, to be done, finished, wearied out; like Lat. *confici:* *pret.* Dan. viii. 27.

3 יָגַע to be weary, spent with labour. KAL *pret.*

4 יָעַף to be faint and exhausted through constant laborious action; especially from running. KAL ᵃ *fut.* ᵇ יָעֵף *adj.* fatigued, wearied, tired.

5 כָּהָה to be feeble, fail in strength. PIEL *pret.*

6 כָּלָה to be quite done, exhausted; with לְ to faint, with great desire. KAL *pret.*

7 לָאָה to be weary, to sink, to be dispirited, to despair under a calamity. KAL *fut.*

8 לָהַה to be languid. KAL *fut.*

9 מוּג to flow, dissolve, melt: *metaph.* to faint, despond. KAL ᵃ *inf.* NIPHAL ᵇ *pret.*

10 מָסַס to dissolve the consistency or substance of a body; see *Melt.* KAL ᵃ *inf.* NIPHAL ᵇ *fut.*

11 עוּף to be weary, to be faint through fatigue or want of refreshment. KAL *fut.*

12 עָטַף to cover; to be covered, overwhelmed; to swoon, to be faint. KAL ᵃ *part.* Paül. HITHPAEL ᵇ *inf.* ᶜ *fut.*

13 עָיֵף *adj.* languid, faint, weary.

14 עָלַף to wrap or muffle up so as to be disguised: this seems to have been applied to fainting or swooning. PUAL ᵃ *pret.* HITHPAEL ᵇ *fut.* ᶜ עֻלְפֶּה *m.* languishing.

15 פָּנַר to be exhausted of strength and vigour. PIEL *pret.*

16 פּוּג to intermit in strength, to cease to move, to stop. KAL *fut.*

17 רָכַךְ to be tender. NIPHAL ᵃ *fut.* ᵇ מֹרֶךְ *m.* softness; fear, timidity. ᶜ רַךְ *adj.* tender.

18 רָפָה to be loose, to be weak. KAL ᵃ *fut.* HITHPAEL ᵇ *pret.*

Gen. xxv. 29, 30.	13	Ps. lxxiv. 2.	6	Jer. xlv. 3.	3
xlv. 26.	16	cvii. 5.	12 c	xlix. 23.	9 b
xlvii. 13.	8	cxix. 81.	6	li. 46.	17 a
Lev. xxvi. 36.	17 b	Prov. xxiv. 10.	18 b	Lam. i. 13.	1
Deut. xx. 3.	17 a	Isa. i. 5.	1 a	i. 22.	1 a
xx. 8, 8.	17 c, 10 b	vii. 4. a	17 a	ii. 19.	12 a
xxv. 18.	13	x. 18.	10 a	v. 17.	1
Josh. ii. 9, 24.	9 b	xiii. 7.	18 a	Ezek. xxi. 7.	5
Judg. viii. 4, 5.	13	xxix. 8.	13	xxi. 15.	9 a
1 Sam. xiv. 28, 31.	11	xl. 28, 30, 31.	4 a	xxxi. 15.	14 c
xxx. 10, 21.	15	xl. 29.	4 b	Dan. viii. 27.	2
2 Sam. xvi. 2.	4 b	xliv. 12.	4 a	Amos viii. 13.	14 b
xxi. 15.	11	li. 20.	9 b	Jonah ii. 7.	12 b
Job iv. 5.	7	Jer. viii. 18.	1 a	iv. 8.	14 b

a lit. let not thy heart be tender.

FAIR

1 זָהָב *m.* gold; the golden splendour of the firmament; see *Weather*.

2 חָנַן to be gracious. PIEL *fut.*

3 טָהוֹר *adj.* pure, clear, clean, as opposed to filthy.

4 טוֹב *adj.* good in a very extensive sense. [a] טוּב *m.* goodness.

5 יָפָה to be fair, beautiful, comely: implies internal as well as external beauty; so applied to the Messiah, Ps. xlv. 2; to the Church, Ps. xlv. 11. KAL [a] *pret.* [b] *fut.* PUAL [c] *pret.* HITHPAEL [d] *fut.* [e] יָפֶה *adj.* [f] יְפֵה־פִיָּה *adj.* very fair.

6 לֶקַח *m.* doctrine, "fair speech."

7 תִּפְאָרָה *f.* ornaments, particularly of the head; "fair jewels."

8 פּוּךְ *m.* painting, "fair colours."

9 מַרְאֶה *m.* countenance; fair, *lit.* good of countenance.

10 שַׁפִּיר Ch. *adj.* elegant, beautiful.

11 תֹּאַר *m.* the form, shape, or appearance; fair, *lit.* fair of form.

Gen. vi. 2.	4	Job xlii. 15.	5 e	Jer. iv. 30.	5 d
xii. 11, 14.	5 e	Ps. xlv. 2.	5 c	xi. 16.	5 e
xxiv. 16.	4	Prov. vii. 21.	5 e	xlvi. 20.	5 f
xxvi. 7.	4	xi. 22.	5 e	Ezek. xvi. 17, 39.	7
Judg. xv. 2.	4	xxvi. 25.	2	xxiii. 26.	7
1 Sam. xvii. 42.	5 e	Cant. i. 8, 15, 15, 16.	5 e	xxxi. 3, 9.	5 e
2 Sam. xiii. 1.	5 e	ii. 10, 13.	5 e	xxxi. 7.	5 b
xiv. 27.	5 e	iv. 1, 1, 7.	5 e	Dan. i. 15.	4
1 Kings i. 3, 4.	5 e	iv. 10.	5 a	iv. 12, 21.	10
Esth. i. 11.	5 e	v. 9.	5 e	Hos. x. 11.	4 a
ii. 2.	4, 9	vi. 1, 10.	5 e	Amos viii. 13.	5 e
ii. 3.	4, 9	vii. 6.	5 a	Zech. iii. 5, 5.	3
ii. 7.	5 e, 11	Isa. v. 9.	4		
Job xxxvii. 22.	1	liv. 11.	8		

FAIRS

עִזָּבוֹן *m.* traffic by exchange; wages, gains: Ezek. xxvii. 12, 14, 16, 19, 22, 27.

FAITH, FAITHFUL

1 אָמַן to support, bear. Niphal, to be supported, borne; to be firm, faithful. KAL [a] *part.* Paül. NIPHAL [b] *pret.* [c] *part.* אָמַן Ch. to be trusty: APHEL [d] *part.* [e] אֱמוּן *m.* faithfulness. [f] אֱמוּנָה also אֲמָנָה *f.* firmness, faithfulness in fulfilling promises. [g] אֱמֶת *f.* truth.

2 כּוּן to establish. NIPHAL *part.* Ps. v. 9, *marg.* 'or, stedfast.'

Num. xii. 7.	1 c	Ps. xii. 1.	1 a	Prov. xxv. 13.	1 c
Deut. vii. 9.	1 c	xxxi. 23.	1 a	xxvii. 6.	1 c
xxxii. 20.	1 e	xxxvi. 5.	1 f	xxviii. 20.β	1 f
1 Sam. ii. 35.	1 f	xl. 10.	1 f	xxix. 14.	1 g
xxii. 14.	1 f	lxxxviii. 11.	1 f	Isa. i. 21, 26.	1 c
xxvi. 23.	1 f	lxxxix. 1, 2, 5, 8,		viii. 2.	1 c
2 Sam. xx. 19.	1 a	24, 33.	1 f	xi. 5.	1 f
2 Kings xii. 15.	1 f	lxxxix. 37.	1 c	xxv. 1.	1 f
xxii. 7.	1 f	xcii. 2.	1 f	xlix. 7.	1 f
2 Chron. xix. 9.	1 f	ci. 6.	1 c	Jer. xxiii. 28.	1 g
xxxi. 12.	1 f	cxix. 75, 86, 90, 138.	1 f	xlii. 5.	1 f
xxxiv. 12.	1 f	cxliii. 1.	1 f	Lam. iii. 23.	1 f
Neh. vii. 2. a	1 g	Prov. xi. 13.	1 b	Dan. vi. 4.	1 d
ix. 8.	1 c	xiii. 17.	1 e	Hos. ii. 20.	1 f
xiii. 13.	1 f	xiv. 5.	1 e	xi. 12.	1 c
Ps. v. 9.	2	xx. 6.	1 e	Hab. ii. 4.	1 f

α *lit.* a man of truth.   β *lit.* a man of faithfulnesses.

FALL

1 בּוֹא to come, to go down. KAL *pret.*

2 דְּחִי *m.* (see *Thrust*), a pushing down.

3 הָיָה to be. KAL *pret.* Josh. xxii. 20.

4 חוּל see *Abide*. KAL and HIPHIL *fut.* Jer. xxiii. 19, "fall grievously;" xxx. 23, "fall with pain:" LXX., συστρεφομένη.

5 יָצָא to go out: used of a lot coming forth and falling to any one. KAL [a] *pret.* [b] *fut.*

6 יָרַד to go down. KAL [a] *inf.* [b] *fut.* HIPHIL [c] *fut.*

7 כָּרַע to bow down. KAL *fut.*

8 כָּשַׁל to stumble through weakness or want of strength: this word takes נָפַל in connexion with itself to express fully an actual falling down. With *inf.,* utterly fall. KAL [a] *pret.* [b] *inf.* [c] *fut.* כְּתִיב. [d] *part.* Poel. NIPHAL [e] *pret.* [f] *inf.* [g] *fut.* HIPHIL [h] *pret.* [i] *fut.* [k] כִּשָּׁלוֹן *m.* [l] מִכְשׁוֹל *m.* stumbling-block.

9 לָבַט to be thrown down, to fall, to perish; to be thrown down, according to the *marg.* 'in order to be beaten.' NIPHAL *fut.*

10 מוּט to move, quake, tremble. KAL [a] *pret.* Lev. xxv. 35, "fallen in decay," *lit.* his hand faileth, *or,* trembleth. [b] *part.* NIPHAL [c] *fut.*

11 מָרַט to pluck off; of hair pilled or fallen off. NIPHAL *fut.*

12 נָבֵל to fade away; to fall as withered fruit. KAL [a] *inf.* [b] *fut.* [c] *part.* Poel.

13 נָגַר to drain off a fluid, to cause blood to flow by the sword; to flow, to pour out; to deliver up, to give over. HIPHIL *fut.* Ps. lxiii. 10, *marg.* 'they shall make him run out (like water) by the hands of the sword;' rather, they shall be given up into the hands of the sword.

14 נָטַשׁ to cast or thrust down, to let fall. KAL *fut.*

15 נָפַל to fall, as a house or city; in war; to fall sick, asleep: also in the following phrases: (1) to descend, as a divine revelation; (2) with עַל to fall on any one, spoken of sleep or terror; (3) to fall away (and pass over) to any one; (4) to fall, to be cast, as a lot; (5) to fall to any one as a division, with לְ; (6) to fall before, or in comparison with any one, *i. e.* to yield or be inferior to him, with מִן and מִן; לִפְנֵי (7) to fall from one's counsel; (8) to be vain, fruitless, *irritum cadere;* as empty promises, to fall to the ground; (9) to fall or turn out; (10) to fall, sink, to be desponding, as the countenance; (11) to fall into ruin, as a house; to become lean, as the body. As expressing more of voluntary action, it means also, to fall on, to fall down, to fall upon, to attack, to encamp, &c. With *inf.,* surely fall. KAL [a] *pret.* [b] *inf.* [c] *imp.* [d] *fut.* [e] *part.* Poel. HIPHIL [f] *pret.* [g] *inf.* [h] *fut.* HITHPAEL [i] *pret.* [k] *inf.* [l] *fut.* נְפַל Ch. P'AL [m] *pret.* [n] *fut.* [o] *part.* [p] מַפֶּלֶת *f.* fall, ruin.

16 סָגַד to fall down, as in worship; *seq.* לְ used chiefly of idol-worship. KAL *fut.*

17 עָלָה to arise, to ascend, spoken of a lot rising up or coming forth from the urn. KAL *pret.*

18 פָּגַע to meet, meet with, light upon; to fall on. KAL [a] *pret.* [b] *inf.* [c] *imp.* [d] *fut.*

19 פָּשַׁט to spread out, to rush upon, attack for plunder. KAL *fut.*

20 קָרָא see *Befall.* KAL *fut.*

21 רָבַץ to lie down, to couch as an animal. KAL *fut.*

22 רָגַז to shake, to tremble; to be in great commotion. KAL *fut.* Gen. xlv. 24, be not stirred, do not fall into contentions by criminations and recriminations.

23 שָׁחָה to bow down. HITHPAEL, to fall down flat: *fut.*

24 שָׁלַל to draw out; also to take spoil: it is used in the directions given by Boaz to his reapers to afford greater opportunity to Ruth for gleaning: "Let fall .... of purpose," *or,* draw out as if stealthily some ears from the handfuls as you reap. KAL [a] *inf.* [b] *fut.*

Gen. ii. 21.	15 h
iv. 5.	15 d
iv. 6.	15 a
xiv. 10.	15 d
xv. 12, 12.	15 a e
xvii. 3, 17.	15 d
xxxiii. 4.	15 d
xliii. 18.	15 k
xliv. 14.	15 d
xlv. 14.	15 d
xlv. 24.	22
xlvi. 29.	15 d
xlix. 17.	15 d
l. 1, 18.	15 d
Exod. i. 10.	20
v. 3.	18 d
xv. 16.	15 d
xxi. 33.	15 a
xxxii. 28.	15 d
Lev. ix. 24.	15 d
xi. 32, 33, 35, 37.	15 d
xi. 38.	15 a
xiii. 40, 41.	11
xvi. 9. 10.	17
xxv. 35.	10 a
xxvi. 7, 8, 36.	15 a
xxvi. 37.	8 a
Num. xi. 9, 9.	6 a b
xi. 31.	14
xiv. 3.	15 b
xiv. 5, 29, 32.	15 d
xiv. 43.	15 a
xvi. 4, 22, 45.	15 d
xx. 6.	15 d
xxii. 27.	21
xxii. 31.	23
xxiv. 4, 16.	15 e
xxxii. 19.	1
xxxiii. 54.	5 b
xxxiv. 2.	15 d
Deut. ix. 18.	15 l
ix. 25, 25.	15 l i
xxii. 4.	15 e
xxii. 8.α	15 e d
Josh. ii. 9.	15 a
v. 14.	15 d
vi. 5.	15 a
vi. 20.	15 d
vii. 6.	15 d
viii. 24.	15 d
viii. 25.	15 e
xi. 7.	15 d
xvi. 1.	5 b
xvii. 5.	15 d
xxii. 20.	3
Judg. iii. 25.	15 e
iv. 16.	15 d
v. 27, 27, 27.	15 a
vii. 13.	15 d
viii. 10.	15 e
viii. 21.	18 c
xii. 6.	15 d
xiii. 20.	15 d
xv. 12.	18 d
xv. 18.	15 a
xvi. 30.	15 d
xviii. 1.	15 a
xix. 26.	15 d
xix. 27.	15 e
xx. 44.	15 d
xx. 46.	15 e
Ruth ii. 10.	15 d
ii. 16.	24 a b
iii. 18.	15 d
1 Sam. iii. 19.	15 f
iv. 10, 18.	15 d
v. 3, 4.	15 e
xi. 7.	15 d
xiv. 13, 45.	15 d
1 Sam. xvii. 49, 52.	15 d
xviii. 25.	15 g
xx. 41.	15 d
xxi. 13.	6 c
xxii. 17.	18 b
xxii. 18, 18.	18 c d
xxv. 23, 24.	15 d
xxvi. 12.	15 a
xxvi. 20.	15 d
xxviii. 20.	15 d
xxix. 3.	15 b
xxxi. 1, 4, 5.	15 d
xxxi. 8.	15 e
2 Sam. i. 2.	15 d
i. 4, 12, 19, 25, 27.	15 a
i. 10.	15 b
i. 15.	18 c
ii. 16.	15 d
ii. 23, 23.	15 d a
iii. 29.	15 e
iii. 34, 34.	15 b a
iii. 38.	15 a
iv. 4.	15 d
ix. 6.	15 d
xi. 17.	15 d
xiv. 4, 11, 22.	15 d
xvii. 12.	15 d
xviii. 28.	23
xix. 18.	15 a
xx. 8.	15 d
xxi. 9, 22.	15 d
xxii. 39.	15 d
xxiv. 14, 14.	15 d
1 Kings i. 52.	15 d
ii. 25, 34, 46.	18 a
ii. 29, 31.	18 c
ii. 32.	18 a
xviii. 7, 38, 39.	15 d
xx. 30.	15 d
xxii. 20.	15 d
2 Kings i. 2.	15 d
i. 13.	7
ii. 13, 14.	15 a
iv. 37.	15 d
vi. 5, 6.	15 a
vii. 4.	15 d
x. 10.	15 d
xiv. 10.	15 a
xix. 7.	15 f
xxv. 11.	15 a
1 Chron. v. 10.	15 d
v. 22.	15 a
x. 1, 4, 5.	15 d
x. 8.	15 e
xii. 19, 19.	15 a d
xii. 20.	15 a
xx. 8.	15 d
xxi. 13, 13, 14, 16.	15 d
xxvi. 14.	15 d
2 Chron. xiii. 17.	15 d
xv. 9.	15 a
xviii. 19.	15 d
xx. 18.	15 a
xx. 24.	15 e
xxi. 15.	5 b
xxi. 19.	5 a
xxv. 8.	8 i
xxv. 13.	19
xxv. 19.	15 a
xxix. 9.	15 a
Ezra ix. 5.	7
Esth. vi. 13, 13.	15 b b d
vii. 8.	15 e
viii. 3.	15 d
viii. 17.	15 a
ix. 2, 3.	15 a
Job i. 15, 19, 20.	15 d
i. 16.	15 a
i. 17.	1 g
Job iv. 4.	8 d
iv. 13.	15 b
xiii. 11.	15 d
xiv. 18.	15 e
xxxi. 22.	15 d
xxxiii. 15.	15 b
Ps. v. 10.	15 d
vii. 15.	15 d
ix. 3.	8 g
x. 10.	15 a
xvi. 6.	15 a
xviii. 38.	15 d
xx. 8.	15 a
xxvii. 2.	15 a
xxxv. 8.	15 d
xxxvi. 12.	15 a
xxxvii. 24.	15 d
xlv. 5.	15 d
lv. 4.	15 a
lvi. 13.	2
lvii. 6.	15 a
lxiii. 10.	13
lxiv. 8.	8 i
lxix. 9.	15 a
lxxii. 11.	23
lxxviii. 28.	15 h
lxxviii. 64.	15 a
lxxxii. 7.	15 d
xci. 7.	15 d
cv. 38.	15 a
cvii. 12.	8 a
cxvi. 8.	2
cxviii. 13.	15 b
cxl. 10.	10 c
cxli. 10.	15 d
cxlv. 14.	15 e
Prov. iv. 16.	8 i, or 8 c
x. 8, 10.	9
xi. 5, 14, 28.	15 d
xiii. 17.	15 d
xvi. 18.	8 k
xvii. 20.	15 d
xxii. 14.	15 d
xxiv. 16, 16.	15 d, 8 g
xxiv. 17.	15 b
xxv. 26.	10 b
xxvi. 27.	15 d
xxviii. 10, 14, 18.	15 d
xxix. 16.	15 p
Eccles. iv. 10, 10.	15 d
ix. 12.	15 d
x. 8.	15 d
xi. 3, 3.	15 d
Isa. iii. 8.	15 a
iii. 25.	15 d
viii. 15.	15 a
ix. 10.	15 a
x. 4, 34.	15 d
xiii. 15.	15 d
xiv. 12.	15 a
xvi. 9.	15 a
xxi. 9, 9.	15 a
xxii. 25.	15 a
xxiv. 18.	15 d
xxiv. 20.	15 a
xxvi. 18.	15 d
xxviii. 13.	8 a
xxx. 13.	15 e
xxx. 25.	15 b
xxxi. 3, 3.	8 a, 15 a
xxxi. 8.	15 a
xxxiv. 4, 4, 4.	12 b a c
xxxvii. 7.	15 f
xl. 30.	8 b g
xliv. 15, 17, 19.	16
xlv. 14.	23
xlvi. 6.	16
xlvii. 11.	15 d
liv. 15.	15 d
Isa. lix. 14.	8 a
Jer. iii. 12.	15 h
vi. 15, 15.	15 d e
vi. 21.	8 a
viii. 4.	15 d
viii. 12, 12.	15 d e
ix. 22.	15 a
xv. 8.	15 f
xix. 7.	15 f
xx. 4.	15 a
xxi. 9.	15 a
xxiii. 12.	15 a
xxiii. 19.	4
xxv. 27.	5 c
xxv. 34.	15 a
xxx. 23.	4
xxxvii. 13, 14.	15 e
xxxviii. 19.	15 a
xxxix. 9, 9.	15 e a
xxxix. 18.	15 d
xliv. 12.	15 d
xlvi. 6, 12.	15 a
xlvi. 16, 16.	8 d, 15 a
xlviii. 32.	15 a
xlviii. 44.	15 d
xlix. 21.	15 b
xlix. 26.	15 d
l. 15, 32.	15 a
l. 30.	15 d
li. 4, 8, 44.	15 a
li. 47.	15 d
li. 49, 49.	15 b a
lii. 15, 15.	15 e a
Lam. i. 7.	15 b
i. 14.	8 h
ii. 21.	15 a
v. 13.	8 a
Lam. v. 16.	15 a
Ezek. i. 28.	15 d
iii. 23.	15 d
v. 12.	15 d
vi. 7.	15 a
vi. 11, 12.	15 d
viii. 1.	15 d
ix. 8.	15 d
xi. 5, 10, 13.	15 d
xiii. 11, 11.	15 d
xiii. 12, 14.	15 a
xvii. 21.	15 d
xxiii. 25.	15 d
xxiv. 6.	15 a
xxiv. 21.	15 d
xxv. 13.	15 d
xxvi. 15, 18.	15 p
xxvii. 27.	15 d
xxvii. 34.	15 a
xxix. 5.	15 d
xxx. 4.	15 b
xxx. 5, 17, 25.	15 d
xxx. 6, 6.	15 a d
xxx. 22.	15 f
xxxi. 12.	15 a
xxxi. 16.	15 p
xxxii. 10.	15 p
xxxii. 12.	15 h
xxxii. 20.	15 d
xxxii. 22, 23, 24, 27.	15 e
xxxiii. 12.	8 g
xxxiii. 27.	15 d
xxxv. 8.	15 d
xxxvi. 15.	8 i
xxxviii. 20, 20.	15 a d
xxxix. 3.	15 h
xxxix. 4, 5, 23.	15 d
Ezek. xliii. 3.	15 d
xliv. 4.	15 d
xliv. 12.	8 c
xlvii. 14.	15 a
Dan. ii. 46.	15 m
iii. 5, 6, 10, 11, 15.	15 n
iii. 7.	15 o
iii. 23.	15 m
iv. 31.	15 m
vii. 20.	15 m
viii. 19.	15 d
x. 7.	15 a
xi. 14, 33.	8 e
xi. 19, 26.	15 a
xi. 34.	8 f
xi. 35.	8 g
Hos. iv. 5, 5.	8 a
iv. 14.	9
v. 5, 5.	8 g a
vii. 7.	15 a
vii. 16.	15 d
x. 8.	15 c
xiii. 16.	15 d
xiv. 1.	8 a
xiv. 9.	8 g
Joel ii. 8.	15 d
Amos iii. 5.	15 d
iii. 14.	15 a
v. 2.	15 a
vii. 17.	15 d
viii. 14.	15 a
ix. 9.	15 d
ix. 11.	15 e
Jonah i. 7.	15 d
Micah vii. 8.	15 a
Nah. iii. 12.	15 a
Zech. xi. 2.	15 a

α *lit.* one falling shall fall.

FALLOW DEER

יַחְמוּר *m.* a species of deer, of a reddish colour, with serrated horns, which are cast every year: Deut. xiv. 5: 1 Kings iv. 23.

FALSE, FALSEHOOD

1 אָוֶן *m.* iniquity: Prov. xvii. 4, *lit.* lips of iniquity.

2 חָמָס *m.* violence: Ps. xxxv. 11, *marg.* 'witnesses of wrong.'

3 כָּזָב *m.* lie: Prov. xxi. 28, *marg.* 'a witness of lies.'

4 כָּחַשׁ to lie, to deal falsely. PIEL *fut.*

5 מַעַל *m.* trespass, against God: Job xxi. 34.

6 עָוַת only in PIEL, to bend, make crooked, pervert: *inf.*

7 מִרְמָה *f.* fraud; false, *marg.* 'of deceit.' [a] רְמִיָּה *f.* deception, fraud.

8 שָׁוְא *m.* what is vain, useless, false.

9 שָׁקַר to lie, to deceive. KAL [a] *fut.* PIEL [b] *pret.* [c] שֶׁקֶר a lie, fraud, vanity; false, *lit.* of falsehood; falsely, with a preposition prefixed.

Gen. xxi. 23.	9 a
Exod. xx. 16.	9 c
xxiii. 1.	8
xxiii. 7.	9 c
Lev. vi. 3,α 5.	9 c
xix. 11.	4
xix. 12.	9 c
Deut. v. 20.	8
xix. 16.	2
xix. 18, 18.	9 c
2 Sam. xviii. 13.	9 c
2 Kings ix. 12.	9 c
Job xxi. 34.	5
xxxvi. 4.	9 c
Ps. vii. 14.	9 c
xxvii. 12.	9 c
xxxv. 11.	2
xliv. 17.	9 b
cxix. 104, 118, 128.	9 c
Ps. cxx. 3.	7 a
cxliv. 8, 11.	9 c
Prov. vi. 19.	9 c
xi. 1.	7
xii. 17.β	9 c
xiv. 5.	9 c
xvii. 4.	1
xix. 5, 9.β	9 c
xx. 23.	7
xxi. 28.	3
xxv. 14, 18.	9 c
Isa. xxviii. 15.	9 c
lvii. 4.	9 c
lix. 13.	9 c
Jer. v. 2, 31.	9 c
vi. 13.	9 c
vii. 9.	9 c
viii. 10.	9 c
x. 14.	9 c
Jer. xiii. 25.	9 c
xiv. 14.	9 c
xxiii. 32.	9 c
xxix. 9.	9 c
xxxvii. 14.	9 c
xl. 16.	9 c
xliii. 2.	9 c
li. 17.	9 c
Lam. ii. 14.	8
Ezek. xxi. 23.	8
Hos. vii. 1.	9 c
x. 4.	8
Micah ii. 11.γ	9 c
Amos viii. 5.	6
Zech. v. 4.	9 c
viii. 17.	9 c
x. 2.	8
Mal. iii. 5.	9 c

α *lit.* upon a lie. β *lit.* falsehoods. γ *marg.* '*or,* lie falsely.'

FAME

קוֹל *m.* voice: Gen. xlv. 16.

שֵׁם *m.* name: 1 Kings iv. 31: 1 Chron. xiv. 17; xxii. 5: Zeph. iii. 19.

שֵׁמַע *m.* hearing, report: Num. xiv. 15: 1 Kings x. 1: 2 Chron. ix. 1: Job xxviii. 22: Isa. lxvi. 19. שֹׁמַע *m.* Josh. vi. 27; ix. 9: Esth. ix. 4: Jer. vi. 24. שְׁמוּעָה *f.* news, tidings, report: 1 Kings x. 7: 2 Chron. ix. 6.

FAMILIAR

אוֹב *m.* a leathern bottle or skin: a necromancer (*lit.* ventriloquist, one who speaks in the hollow of his belly); a "familiar spirit," supposed so to speak; LXX. those who speak from the ground: Lev. xix. 31, xx. 6, 27, *lit.* when a spirit of divination shall be in them; Deut. xviii. 11: 1 Sam. xxviii. 3, 7, 7, 8, 9: 2 Kings xxi. 6; xxiii. 24: 1 Chron. x. 13: 2 Chron. xxxiii. 6: Isa. viii. 19; xix. 3; xxix. 4.

אִישׁ *m.* man: Ps. xli. 9, "familiar friend."

אֱנוֹשׁ *m.* man: Jer. xx. 10.

בַּעֲלָה *f.* mistress: 1 Sam. xxviii. 7, 7, *lit.* mistress of a familiar spirit.

יָדַע to know. PUAL *part.* Job xix. 14, "familiar friends."

שָׁלוֹם *m.* peace: Ps. xli. 9, Jer. xx. 10, "men of my peace."

FAMILY

אָב *m.* father: 2 Chron. xxxv. 5, *lit.* house of a father; 12, *lit.* house of fathers.

אֶלֶף *m.* thousand; family: Judg vi. 15.

בַּיִת *m.* house: 1 Chron. xiii. 14; 2 Chron. xxxv. 5, 5, 12, *lit.* of a house of fathers; Ps. lxviii. 6.

טַף *m.* (see *Little Ones*): Gen. xlvii. 12, *marg.* 'according to their little ones; or, as a little child is nourished.'

מִשְׁפָּחָה *f.* a kind or species, associated together; a tribe; a subdivision of a tribe, a family, among the Israelites: it is also applied to nations and inanimate things. It occurs very frequently, especially in Numbers and other historical books. Gen. x. 5, &c.

FAMINE, FAMISH

כָּפָן *m.* an earnest longing for food; see *Bend*. Job v. 22; xxx. 3.

רָזָה to make lean. KAL *pret.* Zeph. ii. 11.

רָעֵב to suffer hunger, to be famished. KAL *fut.* Gen. xli. 55. HIPHIL *fut.* Prov. x. 3. רָעָב *m.* famine: it occurs frequently in this rendering: Isa. v. 13. Gen. xii. 10, &c. רְעָבוֹן *m.* Gen. xlii. 19, 33: Ps. xxxvii. 19.

FAMOUS

אֱנוֹשׁ *m.* man: 1 Chron. xii. 30, *marg.* 'men of names.'

אַדִּיר *adj.* mighty, distinguished, excellent, glorious: Ps. cxxxvi. 18: Ezek. xxxii. 18.

יָדַע to know. NIPHAL *fut.* Ps. lxxiv. 5.

קָרָא to call, proclaim. KAL *imp.* Ruth iv. 11, *marg.* 'proclaim thy name.' *part.* Paül, Num. xxvi. 9, כְּתִיב. NIPHAL *fut.* Ruth iv. 14. קָרִיא *m.* called, chosen: Num. xvi. 2; xxvi. 9.

שֵׁם *m.* name: Ruth iv. 11: 1 Chron. v. 24; xii. 30: Ezek. xxiii. 10.

FAN, FANNER

זוּר to be strange. KAL *part.* Jer. li. 2. Some critics take this word in the sense of *strangers* rather than as a participle of the following word; Lee, as implying hostility: thus the paronomasia is the more striking זָרִים וְזֵרוּהָ.

זָרָה to scatter, disperse; to winnow. KAL *inf.* Jer. iv. 11. *fut.* Isa. xli. 16, Jer. xv. 7. PIEL *pret.* Jer. li. 2. מִזְרֶה *m.* Isa. xxx. 24, Jer. xv. 7.

FAR

1 מְאֹד *m.* much, exceedingly, &c.

2 רָחַק to be removed, distant; to be far, far away, far off, to flee far, get, go, keep far, to be removed far. Piel, to put far, remove far. Hiphil, to put away far, to drive far, to cast far off, to remove far, to withdraw far. With *inf.*, go very far away. KAL [a] *pret.* [b] *inf.* [c] *imp.* [d] *fut.* PIEL [e] *pret.* [f] *fut.* HIPHIL [g] *pret.* [h] *inf.* [i] *imp.* [k] *fut.* [l] *adj.* going far away. [m] רָחוֹק *adj.* far off, remote; in respect to place, time, help; arduous, difficult; precious: Deut. xiii. 7, &c. רַחִיק [p] Ch. *adj.* far off, remote. [o] מֶרְחָק *m.* at a great distance, far off, from far, far countries.

No. 2 m, far, far off, far abroad, not included.

Gen. xliv. 4.	2 g	Ps. lxxxviii. 8, 18.	2 g	Isa. xlix. 19.	2 a
Exod. viii. 28.	2 h k	xcvii. 9.	1	liv. 14.	2 o
xxiii. 7.	2 d	ciii. 12, 12.	2 b g	lviii. 9.	2 a
Deut. xii. 21.	2 d	cix. 17.	2 d	Jer. ii. 5.	2 a
xiv. 24.		cxix. 150.	2 a	iv. 16.	2 o
Josh. iii. 16.	2 k	Prov. iv. 24.	2 i	v. 15.	2 o
viii. 4.	2 k	v. 8.	2 a	vi. 20.	2 o
Judg. xix. 11.	1	xix. 7.	2 a	viii. 19.	2 o
2 Sam. xv. 17.	2 n	xxii. 5.	2 a	xxv. 26.	2 m
Ezra vi. 6.	2 n	xxii. 15.	2 k	xxvii. 10.	2 h
Job v. 4.	2 d	xxv. 25.	2 o	xlix. 30.	1
xi. 14.	2 i	xxx. 8.	2 i	Lam. i. 16.	2 a
xiii. 21.	2 d	Isa. vi. 12.	2 e	Ezek. viii. 6.	2 b
xix. 13.	2 g	viii. 9.	2 o	vi. 15.	2 c
xxi. 16.	2 d	x. 3.	2 o	xi. 16.	2 g
xxii. 18.	2 a	xiii. 5.	2 o	xliii. 40.	2 o
xxx. 10.	2 i	xvii. 13.	2 o	xliii. 9.	2 f
Ps. xxii. 11, 19.	2 d	xxvi. 15.	2 o	xliv. 10.	2 a
xxxv. 22.	2 d	xxix. 13.	2 e	Joel ii. 20.	2 k
xxxviii. 21.	2 k	xxvii.	2 o	vii. 6.	2 h
lv. 7. [a]	2 k	xxxiii. 17.	2 o	Micah vii. 11.	2 d
lxxi. 12.	2 d	xlvi. 11.	2 o	Zech. x. 9.	2 o
lxxiii. 27.	2 l	xlvi. 13.	2 d		

[a] *lit.* would I go far off by wandering?

FAR BE IT

חָלִילָה interjection; see *Forbid*. We have a remarkable form of expression in 1 Sam. xx. 9, "far be it from thee (*i. e.* to suffer this, or perhaps to think this), that I should know .....and not tell thee;" the literal meaning is, profane be it or base: Gen. xviii. 25, 25: 1 Sam. ii. 30; xx. 9; xxii. 15: 2 Sam. xx. 20, 20; xxiii. 17: Job xxxiv. 10.

FARE

שָׁלוֹם *m.* peace: 1 Sam. xvii. 18, *lit.* visit thy brethren for peace.

FARE (N)

שָׂכָר m. hire: Jonah i. 3.

FASHION

1 דְּמוּת f. likeness, or representation; comp. pattern in the same verse, 2 Kings xvi. 10.

2 יָצַר to form, fashion, or shape, as a potter the clay, &c. KAL a fut. b part. Poel. PUAL c pret.

3 כּוּן to raise up; to prepare, form, make. NIPHAL a pret. POLEL b fut. c תְּכוּנָה f. arrangement, structure.

4 עָשָׂה to do, perform, make. KAL fut.

5 צוּר to form, make. KAL fut.

6 מִשְׁפָּט m. judgment, &c., custom, usage; mode or manner.

Exod. xxvi. 30.	6	Job xxxi. 15.	3 b	Isa. xliv. 12.	2 a
xxxii. 4.	5	Ps. xxxiii. 15.	2 b	xlv. 9.	2 b
1 Kings vi. 38.	6	cxix. 73.	3 b	Ezek. xvi. 7.	3 a
2 Kings xvi. 10.	1	cxxxix. 16.	2 c	xlii. 11.	6
Job x. 8.	4	Isa. xxii. 11.	2 b	xliii. 11.	3 c

FAST

1 טְוָת Ch. adv. with fasting.

2 צוּם to fast. With inf., at all fast. KAL a pret. b inf. c imp. d fut. e part. Poel. f צוֹם m. fasting, a fast: 2 Sam. xii. 16, &c.

No. 2 f not included.

Judg. xx. 26.	2 d	2 Sam. xii. 23.	2 e	Isa. lviii. 3, 3.	2 a f
1 Sam. vii. 6.	2 d	1 Kings xxi. 27.	2 d	lviii. 4, 4.	2 d
xxxi. 13.	2 d	1 Chron. x. 12.	2 d	Jer. xiv. 12.	2 d
2 Sam. i. 12.	2 d	Ezra viii. 23.	2 d	Dan. vi. 18.	1
xii. 16.	2 d f	Neh. i. 4.	2 d	Zech. vii. 5.	2 a
xii. 21, 22.	2 d	Esth. iv. 16, 16.	2 c d	vii. 5.	2 b a

FAST, FASTEN

1 אָחַז to take hold of, to join; see Take. KAL a inf. b part. Paül. HOPHAL c part.

2 אָסְפַּרְנָא adv. Ch. carefully, diligently, speedily.

3 חָזַק to be strong, to make strong. PIEL fut.

4 טָבַע to sink. HOPHAL pret.

5 כּוּן to set up, prepare, establish. HOPHAL part.

6 מְאֹד adv. much, exceedingly.

7 נָטַע to plant. KAL part. Paül.

8 נָתַן to give; to set, place, fix. KAL a pret. b inf. c fut.

9 צָמַד to bind, fasten. PUAL part.

10 צָנַח to descend or sink. KAL fut. Judg. iv. 21, lit. it sank into the ground.

11 תָּקַע to strike, smite, to fasten by nailing. KAL a pret. b fut. c part. Paül.

Exod. xxviii. 14.	8 a	2 Sam. xx. 8.	9	Eccles. xii. 11.	7
xxviii. 25.	8 c	1 Kings vi. 6.	1 a	Isa. xxii. 23.	11 a
xxxix. 18.	8 a	1 Chron. x. 10.	11 a	xxii. 25.	11 c
xxxix. 31.	8 b	2 Chron. ix. 18.	1 c	xli. 7.	3
xl. 18.	8 c	Ezra v. 8.	2	Jer. x. 4.	3
Judg. iv. 21.	10	Esth. i. 6.	1 b	xlviii. 16.	6
xvi. 14.	11 b	Job xxxviii. 6.	4	Ezek. xl. 43.	5
1 Sam. xxxi. 10.	11 a				

FAT

1 אָבַס to fatten. KAL part. Paül.

2 בָּרָא to feed; Hiphil, to feed so as to fatten. HIPHIL a inf. b בְּרִיא adj. fattened, fat. c בְּרִי adj. fat.

3 דָּשֵׁן to be fat; metaph. to be prosperous, and abundant in temporal good things; to have comfort, peace, and joy of mind, to have a blessing in the ordinances of religion. KAL a pret. PIEL b fut. PUAL c fut. HOTHPAEL d pret. e דָּשֵׁן adj. fat; full of sap; rich. f דֶּשֶׁן m. fatness, fertility, abundance.

4 חֵלֶב m. the best, richest, and most delicious nutriment; particularly and most commonly milk, fat, marrow; the best provision or fruits of a land: Gen. xlv. 18. Metaph. the choicest and most delightful spiritual blessings; it is also expressive of great worldly prosperity, or spiritual insensibility: Gen. iv. 4, &c.

5 חָלַץ to arm, to gird the loins, to strengthen; to be active, vigorous. HIPHIL fut. Isa. lviii. 11. Our version has followed the Lxx., but the word hardly means, to be fat.

6 טָפַשׁ to be fat; to be heavy, stupid, senseless; it is used of the proud hardened in maliciousness, insensible to the authority and excellence of the law of God. KAL a pret.

7 יָקָר adj. precious: as a noun, beauty, fatness.

8 מֵחַ m. adj. fat. מֵחִים m. pl. fatlings, "fat ones."

9 מְרִיא m. fat, well fed; fatlings, fat cattle.

10 פֶּדֶר m. fat, grease.

11 מַרְבֵּק m. a place of fattening, a stall; "fat," lit. of the stall.

12 שָׁמֵן to be fat; to be dull and insensible. KAL a pret. b fut. HIPHIL c imp. d fut. e שָׁמֵן adj. fat, applied to the human body, eatables, cattle, and a fruitful soil. f שֶׁמֶן m. fatness, oil. g מִשְׁמָן m. fatness; fertile; vigorous. h מַשְׁמַנִּים m. pl. fatnesses, dainties.

13 מִשְׁנֶה m. second: 1 Sam. xv. 9, "fatlings," marg. 'or, second sort, perhaps lambs of the second birth, i.e. autumnal lambs, weaker, and of less value.'

14 מַשְׁקֶה m. moistened, well watered; fat pastures.

No. 4 not included.

Gen. xxvii. 28, 39.	12 g	Job xxxvi. 16.	3 f	Isa. xxv. 6, 6.	12 f
xli. 2, 4, 18, 20.	2 b	Ps. xxii. 29.	3 e	xxviii. 1, 4.	12 f
xlix. 20.	12 e	xxxvi. 8.	3 f	xxx. 23.	3 e
Lev. i. 8, 12.	10	xxxvii. 20.	7	xxxiv. 6, 6, 6.	3 d, 4, 4
viii. 20.	10	lxiii. 5.	3 f	xxxiv. 7, 7.	3 c, 4
Num. xiii. 20.	12 e	lxv. 11.	3 f	lv. 2.	3 f
Deut. xxxi. 20.	3 a	lxvi. 15.	8	lviii. 11.	5
xxxii. 15, 15.	12 b a	lxxviii. 31.	12 g	Jer. v. 28.	12 a
Judg. iii. 17.	2 b	xcii. 14.	3 e	xxxi. 14.	3 f
ix. 9.	3 f	cix. 24.	12 f	xlvi. 21.	11
1 Sam. ii. 29.	2 a	cxix. 70.	6	Ezek. xxxiv. 14, 16.	12 e
xv. 9.	13	Prov. xi. 25.	3 c	xxxiv. 20.	2 c
xxviii. 24.	11	xiii. 4.	3 c	xxxix. 18.	9
2 Sam. vi. 13.	9	xv. 30.	3 b	xlv. 15.	14
1 Kings i. 9, 19, 25.	9	xx. 25.	3 c	Dan. i. 15.	2 b
iv. 23, 23.	2 b, 1	Isa. v. 17.	9	xi. 24.	12 g
1 Chron. iv. 40.	12 e	vi. 10.	12 c	Amos v. 22.	9
Neh. viii. 10.	12 h	x. 16.	12 g	Hab. i. 16.	12 e
ix. 25, 25.	12 e d	xi. 6.	9	Zech. xi. 16.	2 b
ix. 35.	12 e	xvii. 4.	12 g		

FATS

יֶקֶב m. see Wine-press: Joel ii. 24; iii. 13.

FATHER

אָב m. father, progenitor, any remote ancestor: Gen. xxviii. 13: 1 Kings xv. 11. Metaph. an inventor of any art; a former or creator: Job xxxviii. 28: Isa. lxiii. 16;

lxiv. 8: Jer. ii. 27; iii. 19: Mal. ii. 10;—a benefactor or guardian, Job xxix. 16: Isa. ix. 6; xxii. 21. The Messiah is called The Everlasting Father, Isa. ix. 6. Gen. ii. 24, &c.

אָב *m.* Ch.: Ezra iv. 15; v. 12: Dan. ii. 23; v. 2, 11, 11, 11, 13, 18.

בֵּן *m.* son: Lev. xxiv. 10, *lit.* and he the son of.

FATHER-IN-LAW

חָם *m.* a woman's father-in-law: Gen. xxxviii. 13, 25: 1 Sam. iv. 19, 21.

חָתַן to marry, to join in affinity; any relation by affinity or marriage. KAL *part.* Poel, Exod. iii. 1; iv. 18; xviii. 1, 2, 5, 6, 7, 8, 12, 12, 14, 15, 17, 24, 27: Num. x. 29: Judg. i. 16; iv. 11; xix. 4, 7, 9.

FATHERLESS

אָב *m.* father: Lam. v. 3, *lit.* no fathers.

יָתוֹם *m.* an orphan; any one destitute of friends and succour: Exod. xxii. 22, 24, &c.

FAULT

אָשַׁם to be guilty. KAL *fut.* Hos. x. 2. אָשֵׁם *adj.* guilty, in fault: 2 Sam. xiv. 13.

חָטָא to sin. KAL *pret.* Exod. v. 16. חֵטְא *m.* a sin: Gen. xli. 9.

מְאוּמָה *f.* something, anything; mostly with a negative: 1 Sam. xxix. 3, *lit.* not anything.

עָוֺן *m.* iniquity: 2 Sam. iii. 8: Ps. lix. 4.

רִשְׁעָה *f.* wickedness: Deut. xxv. 2.

שְׁחַת Ch. to be corrupt. P'AL *part. passive,* Dan. vi. 4, 4.

FAVOUR

1 חָנַן to be kindly and tenderly affected toward; to shew favour, mercy, pity. KAL ᵃ*pret.* ᵇ*inf.* ᶜ*imp.* ᵈ*fut.* ᵉ*part.* Poel. POEL ᶠ*fut.* HOPHAL ᵍ*pret.* ʰ חֵן *m.* ⁱ חֲנִינָה *f.* pity or compassion. ᵏ תְּחִנָּה *f.* grace; supplication: Josh. xi. 20.

2 חֶסֶד *m.* kindness, mercy, as an inward disposition.

3 חָפֵץ see *Delight.* KAL ᵃ*pret.* ᵇ חָפֵץ *adj.* having favour.

4 טוֹב *adj.* good; "in favour," *lit.* to be good in the eyes of.

5 יָטַב to be good; to find favour. KAL *fut.*

6 עַיִן *com.* eye.

7 פָּנִים *m. pl.* face.

8 מַרְאֶה *m.* appearance; "favoured," their appearance was; "well favoured," *lit.* good of countenance.

9 רָצָה to be well pleased with, or to take delight in. KAL ᵃ*pret.* ᵇ*inf.* ᶜ*fut.* ᵈ רָצוֹן *m.* acceptance, delight, satisfaction; grace, favour, good-will.

10 שָׁלוֹם *m.* peace.

11 תֹּאַר *m.* form, beauty; favoured, *lit.* of form.

Gen. xviii. 3.		Gen. xli. 2, 3, 4, 4, 21.	8	Num. xi. 11, 15.	1 h
xxix. 17.	8	xli. 18, 19.	11	Deut. xxiv. 1.	1 h
xxx. 27.	1 h	Exod. iii. 21.	1 h	xxviii. 50.	1 d
xxxix. 6.	8	xi. 3.	1 h	xxxiii. 23.	9 d
xxxix. 21.	1 h	xii. 36.	1 h	Josh. xi. 20.	1 k

Judg. xxi. 22. *a*	1 c	Ps. xxxv. 27.	3 b	Prov. xvi. 15.	9 d
Ruth ii. 13.	1 h	xli. 11.	3 a	xviii. 22.	9 d
1 Sam. ii. 26.	4	xliv. 3.	9 a	xix. 6.	7
xvi. 22.	1 h	xlv. 12.	7	xix. 12.	9 d
xx. 29.	1 h	lxxvii. 7.	9 b	xxi. 10.	1 g
xxv. 8.	1 h	lxxxv. 1.	9 a	xxii. 1.	1 h
xxix. 6. β	4, 6	lxxxix. 17.	9 d	xxviii. 23.	1 h
2 Sam. xv. 25.	1 h	cii. 13.	1 b	xxix. 26.	7
xx. 11.	3 a	cii. 14.	1 f	xxxi. 30.	1 h
1 Kings xi. 19.	1 h	cvi. 4.	9 d	Eccles. ix. 11.	1 h
Neh. ii. 5.	5	cix. 12.	1 e	Cant. viii. 10.	10
Esth. ii. 15.	1 h	cxii. 5.	1 e	Isa. xxvi. 10.	1 g
ii. 17.	2	cxix. 58.	7	xxvii. 11.	1 d
v. 2, 8.	1 h	Prov. iii. 4.	1 h	lx. 10.	9 d
vii. 3.	1 h	viii. 35.	9 d	Jer. xvi. 13.	1 i
viii. 5.	1 h	xi. 27.	9 d	Lam. iv. 16.	1 h
Job x. 12.	2	xii. 2.	9 d	Dan. i. 4.	8
xxxiii. 26.	9 c	xiii. 15.	1 h	Nah. iii. 4. γ	1 h
Ps. v. 12.	9 d	xiv. 9, 35.	9 d		
xxx. 5, 7.	9 d				

a marg. 'gratify us in them.'   β *lit.* in the eyes of the lords thou art not good.   γ *lit.* of good favour.

FEAR

1 אֵימָה *f.* terror: the genitive which follows is often to be understood passively, as Prov. xx. 2, the fear of a king, which he causes.

2 גּוּר to turn aside; to be afraid, to turn aside through fear; it seems in some cases to have the sense of horror, terror, which men turn away from; and also of reverence with humility towards God, &c. KAL ᵃ*imp.* ᵇ*fut.* ᶜ מָגוֹר *m.* fear, terror. ᵈ מְגוֹרָה *f. id.* ᵉ מְגוּרָה *f.* fear, what is feared.

3 דְּאָגָה *f.* fear, with great anxiety and solicitude.

4 דְּחַל Ch. to be afraid; *pr.* to creep along hesitatingly and timidly. P'AL *part. active.*

5 חוּל to travail; to fear and tremble with pain and anguish of mind. KAL *imp.*

6 חֲרָדָה *f.* (see *Afraid*), fear with trembling and agitation.

7 חַת *m.* fear, with dismay; see *Afraid, Dismay.* ᵃ חִתְחַתִּים *m. pl.* terrors.

8 יָגֹר to live in fear of some evil that may befal us or others. KAL ᵃ*pret.* ᵇ*part.*

9 יָרֵא to fear from an apprehension of danger and a sense of our own weakness, joined therefore with trembling, Ps. lv. 5, Gen. xix. 30;—to be timorous; to fear, venerate, religiously reverence: hence it is put for the whole of a religious character, as fear is put for the whole of the doctrine which teaches the fear of God; to worship God. In Niphal, to be feared, fearful, dreadful, tremendous. KAL ᵃ*pret.* ᵇ*inf.* ᶜ*imp.* ᵈ*fut.* NIPHAL ᵉ*fut.* ᶠ*part.* PIEL ᵍ*inf.* ʰ*part.* ⁱ יָרֵא *adj.* fearing, reverencing. ᵏ יִרְאָה *f.* fear, terror. ˡ מוֹרָא *m.* fear, that which is feared or reverenced. ᵐ מוֹרָה *m.* terror, (כְּתִיב).

10 מָהַר to hasten. NIPHAL *part.* Isa. xxxv. 4, *marg.* 'hasty.'

11 עָרַץ to fear one on account of his power or violence; to cause fear on this account. This word is therefore used of God, who ought to be feared for his power, which none can resist; for his holiness and justice, which none can satisfy; and for his wisdom, which none can attain to. KAL ᵃ*fut.* NIPHAL ᵇ*part.* HIPHIL ᶜ*fut.*

12 פָּחַד to fear, to be under fearful apprehensions of a distant danger, which keepeth the mind either in an uneasy

suspense or in religious reverence; it implies a fear which is vehement, Exod. xv. 16, Job iv. 14; without peace, Jer. xxx. 5; caused by an enemy, Ps. lxiv. 1; or inflicted by God himself, 1 Sam. xi. 7. It is said of things which come unexpectedly, and produce a fear that is good or evil; to stand in awe of. KAL [a] *pret.* [b] *fut.* PIEL [c] *fut.* [d] *part.* [e] פַּחַד *m.* fear, terror; the object of fear and reverence. [f] פַּחְדָּה *f.* terror.

13   פַּלָּצוּת *f.* fearfulness with trembling and horror.

14   פָּנִים *m. pl.* face; for fear of, *lit.* before, from the face of, denoting true fear.

15   רֹגֶז disquiet, trouble, rage; see *Afraid.*

16   רֶטֶט *m.* fear, terror.

17   רְעָדָה *f.* trembling, fear, fearfulness.

18   שָׂעַר to shudder, shiver from fear, alarm. KAL *pret.*

Gen. ix. 2.	9 l	Judg. vi. 27.	9 a	Job xxii. 4.	9 k	
xv. 1.	9 d	vii. 3, 10.	9 i	xxii. 10.	12 e	
xix. 30.	9 a	viii. 20.	9 a	xxv. 2.	12 e	
xx. 11.	9 k	ix 21.	14	xxviii. 28.	9 k	
xxi. 17.	9 d	Ruth iii. 11.	9 d	xxxi. 34.	11 a	
xxii. 12.	9 i	1 Sam. iii. 15.	9 a	xxxvii. 24.	9 a	
xxvi. 7.	9 a	iv. 20.	9 d	xxxix. 16, 22.	12 e	
xxvi. 24.	9 d	xi. 7.	12 e	xli. 33.	7	
xxxi. 42, 53.	12 e	xii. 14, 18, 20.	9 d	Ps. ii. 11.	9 k	
xxxii. 11.	9 i	xii. 24.	9 c	v. 7.	9 k	
xxxv. 17.	9 d	xiv. 26.	9 a	ix. 20.β	9 l m	
xlii. 18.	9 i	xv. 24.	9 a	xiv. 5.	12 a e	
xliii. 23.	9 d	xxi. 10.	14	xv. 4.	9 i	
xlvi. 3.	9 d	xxii. 23.	9 d	xix. 9.	9 k	
l. 19, 21.	9 d	xxiii. 17.	9 d	xxii. 23, 23.	9 i, 2 a	
Exod. i. 17.	9 d	xxiii. 26.	14	xxii. 25.	9 i	
i. 21.	9 a	2 Sam. iii. 11.	9 b	xxiii. 4.	9 d	
ii. 14.	9 d	ix. 7.	9 d	xxv. 12, 14.	9 i	
ix. 20.	9 i	x. 19.	9 d	xxvii. 1, 3.	9 d	
ix. 30.α	9 d, 14	xii. 18.	9 d	xxxi. 11.	12 e	
xiv. 13, 31.	9 d	xiii. 28.	9 d	xxxi. 13.	2 c	
xv. 11.	9 f	xxiii. 3.	9 k	xxxi. 19.	9 i	
xv. 16.	1	1 Kings i. 50, 51.	9 a	xxxiii. 8.	9 d	
xviii. 21.	1	iii. 28.	9 d	xxxiii. 18.	9 i	
xx. 20, 20.	9 d k	viii. 40.	9 d	xxxiv. 4.	2 e	
xxiii. 27.	1	viii. 43.	9 b	xxxiv. 7.	9 i	
Lev. xix. 3.	9 d	xvii. 13.	9 d	xxxiv. 9, 9.	9 c i	
xix. 14, 32.	9 a	xviii. 3.	9 i	xxxiv. 11.	9 k	
xxv. 17, 36, 43.	9 a	xix. 12.	9 a	xxxvi. 1.	12 e	
Num. xiv. 9, 9.	9 d	2 Kings iv. 1.	9 i	xl. 3.	9 d	
xxi. 34.	9 d	vi. 16.	9 d	xlvi. 2.	9 d	
Deut. i. 21.	9 d	xvii. 7, 28, 35, 36,		xlviii. 6.	17	
ii. 25.	9 k	37, 38, 39.	9 d	xlix. 5.	9 d	
iii. 2, 22.	9 d	xvii. 25.	9 a	lii. 6.	9 d	
iv. 10.	9 b	xvii. 32, 33, 34, 41.	9 i	liii. 5, 5.	12 a e e	
v. 29.	9 b	xxv. 24.	9 d	lv. 5.	9 k	
vi. 2, 13.	9 d	1 Chron. xiv. 17.	12 e	lv. 19.	9 a	
vi. 24.	9 b	xvi. 25.	9 f	lvi. 4.	9 d	
viii. 6.	9 b	xvi. 30.	5	lx. 4.	9 i	
x. 12.	9 b	xxviii. 20.	9 d	lxi. 5.	12 e	
x. 20.	9 d	2 Chron. vi. 31.	9 d	lxiv. 1.	12 e	
xi. 25.	12 e	vi. 33.	9 b	lxiv. 4, 9.	9 d	
xiii. 4, 11.	9 d	xiv. 14.	12 e	lxvi. 16.	9 i	
xiv. 23.	9 b	xvii. 10.	12 e	lxvii. 7.	9 d	
xvii. 13.	9 d	xix. 7.	12 e	lxxii. 5.	9 d	
xvii. 19.	9 b	xix. 9.	9 a	lxxvi. 7.	9 f	
xix. 20.	9 d	xx. 3, 17.	9 d	lxxvi. 8.	9 a	
xx. 3.	9 d	xxvi. 5.	12 e	lxxvi. 11.γ	9 l	
xx. 8.	9 i	Ezra iii. 3.	1	lxxviii. 53.	12 a	
xxi. 21.	9 d	Neh. i. 11.	9 b	lxxxv. 9.	9 i	
xxv. 18.	9 i	v. 9, 15.	9 k	lxxxvi. 11.	9 b	
xxviii. 58, 58.	9 b f	vi. 14.	9 h	lxxxix. 7.	11 b	
xxviii. 66.	12 a	vi. 19.	9 g	xc. 11.	9 k	
xxviii. 67, 67.	12 e b	vii. 2.	9 a	xcvi. 4.	9 f	
xxxi. 6, 8.	9 d	Esth. iii. 17.	12 e	xcvi. 9.	5	
xxxi. 12.	9 a	ix. 2, 3.	12 e	cii. 15.	9 d	
xxxi. 13.	9 b	Job i. 1, 8.	9 i	ciii. 11, 13, 17.	9 i	
xxxii. 17.	18	i. 9.	9 a	cv. 38.	12 e	
xxxii. 27.	9 d	ii. 3.	9 a	cxi. 5.	9 i	
Josh. iv. 14, 14.	9 d a	iii. 25.	12 a e	cxi. 10.	9 k	
iv. 24.	9 a	iv. 6.	9 d	cxii. 1.	9 a	
viii. 1.	9 d	iv. 14.	12 e	cxv. 11, 13.	9 i	
x. 2, 8, 25.	9 d	vi. 14.	9 k	cxviii. 4.	9 i	
xxii. 24.	3	ix. 34.	1	cxviii. 6.	9 d	
xxii. 25.	9 d	ix. 35.	9 d	cxix. 38.	9 k	
xxiv. 14.	9 c	xi. 15.	9 d	cxix. 39.	8 a	
Judg. iv. 18.	9 d	xv. 4.	9 k	cxix. 63.	9 a	
vi. 10, 23.	9 d	xxi. 9.	12 e	cxix. 74, 79.	9 i	

Ps. cxix. 120.	12 e	Isa. viii. 12, 12.	9 d l	Jer. xxxv. 11, 11.	14
cxxviii. 1, 4.	9 i	viii. 13.	9 l	xxxvii. 11.	14
cxxx. 4.	9 e	xi. 2, 3.	9 k	xl. 9.	9 d
cxxxv. 20.	9 i	xiv. 3.	15	xli. 9.	14
cxxxix. 14.	9 f	xix. 16.	12 a	xlii. 11.	9 i
cxlv. 19.	9 i	xxi. 4, 4.	13, 6	xliv. 10.	9 a
cxlvii. 11.	9 i	xxiv. 17, 18.	12 e	xlvi. 5.	2 c
Prov. i. 7, 29.	9 k	xxv. 3.	9 d	xlvi. 27, 28.	9 d
i. 26, 27, 33.	12 e	xxix. 13.	9 k	xlviii. 43, 44.	12 e
ii. 5.	9 k	xxix. 23.	11 c	xlix. 5.	12 e
iii. 7.	9 c	xxxi. 9.	2 c	xlix. 24.	16
ii. 25.	12 e	xxxiii. 6.	9 k	xlix. 29.	2 c
viii. 13.	9 k	xxxiii. 14.	17	l. 16.	14
ix. 10.	9 i	xxxv. 4, 4.	10, 9 d	li. 46.	9 d
x. 24.	2 d	xli. 5, 10, 13, 14.	9 d	Lam. iii. 47.	12 e
x. 27.	9 i	xliii. 1, 5.	9 d	iii. 57.	9 d
xiii. 13.	9 i	xliv. 2.	9 d	Ezek. iii. 9.	9 d
xiv. 2, 16.	9 i	xliv. 8, 11.	12 b	xi. 8.	9 a
xiv. 26, 27.	9 k	l. 10.	9 i	xxx. 13.	9 k
xv. 16, 33.	9 k	li. 7.	9 k	Dan. i. 10.	9 i
xvi. 6.	9 k	li. 13.	12 c	v. 19.	4
xix. 23.	9 k	liv. 4, 14.	9 d	vi. 26.	4
xx. 2.	1	lvii. 11, 11.	9 d	x. 12, 19.	9 d
xxii. 4.	9 k	lix. 19.	9 d	Hos. iii. 5.	12 a
xxiii. 17.	9 k	lx. 5.	12 a	x. 3.	9 a
xxiv. 21.	9 c	lxiii. 17.	9 k	x. 5.	2 b
xxviii. 14.	12 d	lxvi. 4.	2 e	Joel ii. 21.	9 d
xxix. 25.	6	Jer. ii. 19.	12 f	Amos iii. 8.	9 d
xxxi. 30.	9 i	iii. 8.	9 a	Jonah i. 9.	9 i
Eccles. iii. 14.	9 d	v. 22, 24.	9 a	i. 16.ζ	9 d k
v. 7.	9 c	vi. 25.	2 c	Micah vii. 17.	9 d
vii. 18.	9 i	x. 7.	9 d	Zeph. iii. 7, 16.	9 d
viii. 12, 12.	9 i d	xx. 10.	2 c	Hag. i. 12.	9 d
viii. 13.	9 i	xxii. 25.	8 b	ii. 5.	9 d
ix. 2.	9 i	xxiii. 4.	9 d	Zech. iii. 13, 15.	9 d
xii. 5.	7 a	xxvi. 19.	9 i	ix. 5.	9 d
xii. 5.	9 c	xxx. 5.є	12 e	Mal. i. 6.	9 l
Cant. iii. 8.	12 e	xxx. 10.	9 d	ii. 5, 5.	9 l d
Isa. ii. 10, 19, 21.δ	12 e	xxxii. 39.	9 b	iii. 5.	9 a
vii. 4.	9 d	xxxii. 40.	9 k	iii. 16, 16.	9 i
vii. 25.	9 d	xxxiii. 9.	12 e	iv. 2.	9 i

[a] *lit.* fear before the Lord.   β *or,* put them into fear.   γ *lit.* unto fear.   δ *lit.* from the face of the time.   є *or,* there is fear and not peace.   ζ *lit.* feared a great fear.

FEAST

1   חָג and חַג *m.* a festival or occasion of great joy, such as holy days or religious solemnities, on which some signal instances of God's favour were celebrated with sacrificing and feasting: Exod. x. 9, &c. חָגַג to keep a feast, to hold a feast; with and without חַג. KAL [a] *pret.* [b] *inf.* [c] *imp.* [d] *fut.*

2   מוֹעֵד *m.* a time or season appointed or agreed on by the parties; see *Congregation:* see also *Set, Solemn.* [a] מוֹעֲדוֹת *f.* solemn feasts.

3   לֶחֶם *m.* bread; also the various provisions and delicacies of a feast. [a] לְחֵם Ch. *m.*

4   מָעוֹג *m.* cakes of bread baked.

5   עָשָׂה to make. KAL *pret.* Job i. 4, *lit.* made a feast.

6   מִשְׁתֶּה *m.* a drinking, a banquet, feast.

No. 1 not included.

Gen. xix. 3.	6	1 Sam. xxv. 36, 36.	6	Prov. xv. 15.	6
xxi. 8.	6	2 Sam. iii. 20.	6	Eccles. vii. 2.	6
xxvi. 30.	6	1 Kings iii. 15.	6	x. 19.	3
xxix. 22.	6	1 Chron. xxiii. 31.	2	Isa. v. 12.	6
xl. 20.	6	2 Chron. ii. 4.	2	xxv. 6, 6.	6
Exod. v. 1.	6	viii. 13.	2 a	Jer. xvi. 8.	6
xii. 14.	1 a, 1	xxx. 22.	2	li. 39.	6
xii. 14.	1 d	xxxi. 3.	2	Lam. i. 4.	2
xxiii. 14.	1 d	Ezra iii. 5.	2	ii. 6, 7.	2
Lev. xxiii. 2, 4, 37,		Neh. x. 33.	2	Ezek. xxxvi. 38.	2
44.	2	Esth. i. 3, 5, 9.	6	xlvi. 9.	2
xxiii. 39.	1 d, 1 a	ii. 18, 18.	6	Dan. v. 1.	3 a
xxiii. 41.	1 d	viii. 17.	6	Hos. ii. 11.	2
Num. xv. 3.	1 a, 1	ix. 17, 18, 19, 22.	6	xii. 9.	2
xxix. 12.	2	Job i. 4.	5, 6	Nah. i. 15.	1 c, 1
xxix. 39.	2	i. 5.	6	Zech. viii. 19.	6
Deut. xvi. 15.	1 d	Ps. xxxv. 16.	4	xiv. 16, 18, 19.	1 b, 1
Judg. xiv. 10, 12, 17.	6				

FEATHER

אֶבְרָה *f.* a wing, in which lies the strength of a bird ; or *collect.* plumage covering the sides : Ps. lxviii. 13 ; xci. 4.

כָּנָף *com.* wing ; feathered, *lit.* of wing : Ps. lxxviii. 27 : Ezek. xxxix. 17.

נוֹצָה *f.* feathers, the instruments of flying : Ezek. xvii. 3, 7 : Job xxxix. 13.

נֹצָה *f.* taking it to be the same word as the preceding, it means feathers. Fürst deduces it from יָצָה = יָצָא ; in this case it means the contents of the crop, *excrementum* : Lev. i. 16, *marg.* ' or, the filth thereof.'

FEEBLE

1 אָמַל to wither, languish. PULAL [a] *pret.* [b] אֻמְלַל *adj.* languid, feeble.

2 חָשַׁל to be weak, exhausted. NIPHAL *part.*

3 כַּבִּיר *adj.* great, much, many ; feeble, *lit.* not many.

4 כָּרַע to bow. KAL *part.* Poel.

5 כָּשַׁל to stumble. KAL [a] *part.* Poel. NIPHAL [b] *part.*

6 עָטַף to faint. KAL [a] *part.* Paül. HIPHIL [b] *inf.*

7 עָצוּם *adj.* mighty ; feeble, *lit.* not mighty.

8 פּוּג see *Faint.* NIPHAL *pret.*

9 רָפָה to be slack, hang down ; to be loosened. KAL [a] *pret.* [b] *fut.* [c] רִפְיוֹן *m.* slackness, remissness.

Gen. xxx. 42, 42.	6 b a	Ps. xxxviii. 8.	8	Jer. xlvii. 3.		9 c
Deut. xxv. 18.	2	cv. 37.	5 a	xlix. 24.		9 a
1 Sam. ii. 5.	1 a	Prov. xxx. 26.	7	l. 43.		9 a
2 Sam. iv. 1.	9 b	Isa. xvi. 14.	3	Ezek. vii. 17.		9 b
2 Chron. xxviii. 15.	5 a	xxxv. 3.	5 a	xxi. 7.		9 a
Neh. iv. 2.	1 b	Jer. vi. 24.	9 a	Zech. xii. 8.		5 b
Job iv. 4.	4					

FEED

1 אָכַל to eat, eat up, consume ; to give to eat, to feed. KAL [a] *part.* Poel. HIPHIL [b] *pret.* [c] *imp.* [d] *fut.* [e] *part.*

2 בָּעַר to feed, graze, consume by grazing. PIEL *pret.*

3 בָּרִיא *adj.* fat, fatlings, fat flock or herd.

4 זוּן to nourish. HOPHAL [a] *part.* (כתיב). זוּן Ch. ITHP'EL [b] *fut.*

5 טְעֵם Ch. to taste ; to give to taste. PA'L *fut.*

6 טָרַף to tear. HIPHIL, to cause to eat, to feed : *imp.*

7 יֵזֶן to nourish. HOPHAL *part.*

8 כּוּל to hold ; Pilpel, to support or maintain, to provide with the means of living. PILPEL [a] *pret.* [b] *inf.* [c] *fut.*

9 לָעַט to eat, particularly with greediness or daintiness. HIPHIL *imp.*

10 נָהַל to lead, guide ; to provide for ; comp. Ps. xxiii. 2, Isa. xlix. 10. PIEL *fut.*

11 רָעָה to feed (a flock), including all the care of a shepherd over his flock ; with an accusative, more rarely with בְּ. Without a case following, to wander about as a nomade ; see *Wander. Metaph.* to feed a people, *i.e.* to lead or guide them as a shepherd ; spoken, (1) of a prince, *e.g.* 2 Sam. v. 2, vii. 7 ; Jer. xxiii. 2 ; with בְּ, Ps. lxxviii. 71 ; *comp.* the Homeric phrase, ποιμένες λαῶν ; (2) of God, Ps. xxiii. 1, xxviii. 9, lxxx. 1 ; (3)

Prov. x. 21, the lips of the righteous feed or guide many ; to feed, graze, spoken of cattle ; the pasture fed upon is put in the accusative. KAL [a] *pret.* [b] *inf.* [c] *imp.* [d] *fut.* [e] *part.* Poel. HIPHIL [f] *fut.* [g] מִרְעֶה *m.* pasture, feeding-place.

12 שָׂבַע to be satiated ; to feed to the full. HIPHIL *fut.* Jer. v. 7, *or,* " when I adjured them," according to the generally received text, from שָׁבַע. But the LXX. ἐχόρτασα preserves the preferable and older Jewish reading, which is more agreeable to the whole context.

Gen. xxv. 30.	9	Ps. xxxvii. 3.	11 c	Jer. ix. 15.		1 e
xxix. 7.	11 c	xlix. 14.	11 d	xxiii. 2.		11 e
xxx. 31. a	11 d	lxxviii. 71.	11 b	xxiii. 4.		11 a
xxx. 36.	11 e	lxxviii. 72.	11 f	xxiii. 15.		1 e
xxxvi. 24.	11 b	lxxx. 5.	1 b	l. 19.		11 a
xxxvii. 2, 13, 16.	11 e	lxxxi. 16.β	1 d	Lam. iv. 5.		1 a
xxxvii. 12.	11 b	Prov. x. 21.	11 d	Ezek. xvi. 19.		1 b
xli. 2, 18.	11 d	xv. 14.	11 d	xxxiv. 2, 2.		11 e d
xlvii. 17.	10	xxx. 8.	6	xxxiv. 3, 3.		3, 11 d
xlviii. 15.	11 e	Cant. i. 7.	11 d	xxxiv. 8, 8.		11 d
Exod. xvi. 32.	1 b	i. 8.	11 c	xxxiv. 10, 10.		11 b d
xxii. 5.	2	ii. 16.	11 e	xxxiv. 13.		11 a
xxxiv. 3.	11 d	iv. 5.	11 e	xxxiv. 14, 14, 15,		
Deut. viii. 3.	1 d	vi. 2.	11 b	16.		11 a d
viii. 16.	1 e	vi. 3.	11 e	Dan. iv. 12.		4 b
1 Sam. xvii. 15.	11 b	Isa. v. 17.	11 a	v. 21.		
2 Sam. v. 2.	11 d	xi. 7.	11 d	xi. 26.		1 a
vii. 7.	11 b	xiv. 30.	11 a	Hos. iv. 16.		11 d
xix. 33.	8 a	xxvii. 10.	11 a	ix. 2.		11 d
xx. 3.	8 c	xxx. 23.	11 d	xii. 1.		11 d
1 Kings xvii. 4.	8 b	xl. 11.	11 e	Jonah iii. 7.		11 e
xviii. 4.	8 a	xliv. 20.	11 d	Micah v. 4.		11 d
xviii. 13.	8 c	xlix. 9.	11 d	vii. 14, 14.		11 c d
xxii. 27.	1 c	xlix. 26.	1 b	Nah. ii. 11.		11 g
1 Chron. xi. 2.	11 d	lviii. 14.	11 b	Zeph. ii. 7.		11 d
xvii. 6.	11 b	lxi. 5.	11 a	Zech. xi. 4.		11 c
xxvii. 29.	11 e	lxv. 25.	11 a	xi. 7, 7, 9.		11 d
2 Chron. xviii. 26.	1 c	Jer. iii. 15.	11 a	xi. 16.		8 c
xxiv. 2.	11 e	v. 7.	12			
Ps. xxviii. 9.	11 d	v. 8.	7, or 4 a			
		vi. 3.	11 a			

a lit. I will return, I will feed.   *β lit.* fed him.

FEEL

בִּין to understand, discern, perceive. KAL and HIPHIL *fut.* Ps. lviii. 9.

יָדַע to know. KAL *pret.* Job xx. 20 : Prov. xxiii. 35. *fut.* Eccles. viii. 5.

יָמֻשׁ to touch, feel. HIPHIL *imp.* Judg. xvi. 26, כתיב.

מוּשׁ *id.* KAL *fut.* Gen. xxvii. 21. HIPHIL *imp.* Judg. xvi. 26.

מָשַׁשׁ *id.* KAL *fut.* Gen. xxvii. 12, 22. HIPHIL *fut.* Exod. x. 21.

FEIGN

בָּדָא to invent a falsehood, *or,* to babble, to talk idly, to pretend. KAL *part.* Poel, Neh. vi. 8.

נָכַר (see *Know, Strange*), not to let oneself be known. HITHPAEL *part.* 1 Kings xiv. 5, 6.

מִרְמָה *f.* deceit : Ps. xvii. 1.

שֶׁקֶר *m.* a lie, falsehood, deception : Jer. iii. 10.

FELL

כָּרַת to cut off, to cut down. KAL *part.* Poel, Isa. xiv. 8.

נָפַל to fall ; to make to fall, to fell. HIPHIL *fut.* 2 Kings iii. 19, 25. *part.* 2 Kings vi. 5.

FELLOES

חִשֻּׁקִים *m. pl.* 1 Kings vii. 33. It is applied to the spokes of wheels

which run between the nave and the rim, and being inserted into both, connect them together.

FELLOW

אִישׁ *m.* man, *vir :* I Sam. xxix. 4.

אֱנוֹשׁ *m.* man, *homo :* Judg. xviii. 25.

חָבַר to join together things of the same sort; to be joined together. PUAL *fut.* Ps. xciv. 20. חָבֵר *adj.* associate, companion, fellow : Ps. xlv. 7 : Eccles. iv. 10 : Isa. xliv. 11 : Ezek. xxxvii. 19. חַבַר Ch. *m. id.* Dan. ii. 13, 18. חַבְרָה Ch. *f.* Dan. vii. 20, companion; another.

יָד hand; fellowship, *Heb.* the putting in the hand : Lev. vi. 2.

עָמִית *m.* society, companionship; equal, of the Messiah, Zech. xiii. 7.

רֵעַ *m.* a friend, companion, acquaintance, with whom one lives, has friendly intercourse : Exod. ii. 13 : Judg. vii. 13, 14, 22 : I Sam. xiv. 20 : 2 Sam. ii. 16, 16 : Isa. xxxiv. 14 : Jonah i. 7 : Zech. iii. 8. רֵעָה *f.* companion : Judg. xi. 37. רַעְיָה *f.* female friend : Judg. xi. 37, כתיב.

תְּשׂוּמֶת *f.* a placing in; with יָד a deposit : Lev. vi. 2, *marg.* ' or, in dealing.'

FEMALE

אִשָּׁה *f.* woman : Gen. vii. 2, 2.

נְקֵבָה *f.* a female of man and of beast; Gen. i. 27; v. 2; vi. 19; vii. 3, 9, 16 : Lev. iii. 1, 6; iv. 28, 32; v. 6; xii. 7; xxvii. 4, 5, 6, 7 : Num. v. 3 : Deut. iv. 16.

FEN

בִּצָּה *f.* marsh, fen : Job xl. 21.

FENCE

1 בָּצַר to cut off, to cut off access; by walls and fortifications to keep off an enemy, and to defend a town. KAL [a] *part.* Paül. [b] מִבְצָר *m.* fortification, munitions.

2 גָּדַר to fence about with hedge or wall. KAL [a] *pret.* [b] גָּדֵר *com.* wall.

3 מָלֵא to fill. NIPHAL *fut.* 2 Sam. xxiii. 7, *lit.* filled with iron, *or*, armed completely.

4 עָזַק to surround with a fence; *or*, to loosen the earth, to dig up or about. PIEL *fut.*

5 מָצוֹר *m.* fortification, fortress. [a] מְצוּרָה *f.* a bulwark, a fortified city.

6 שׂוּךְ *f.* to hedge, to hedge in or about. POLEL *fut.* Job x. 11.

Num. xxxii. 17, 36.	1 b	2 Kings xviii. 8.	1 b	2 Chron. xxxiii. 14.	1 a	
Deut. iii. 5.	1 a	xviii. 13.	1 a	Job x. 11.	6	
ix. 1.	1 a	xix. 25.	1 a	xix. 8.	2 a	
xxviii. 52.	1 a	2 Chron. viii. 5.	5	Ps. lxii. 3.	2 b	
Josh. x. 20.	1 b	xi. 10, 23.	5 a	Isa. ii. 15.	1 a	
xiv. 12.	1 a	xii. 4.	5 a	v. 2.	4	
xix. 35.	1 b	xiv. 6.	5 a	Jer. v. 17.	1 b	
1 Sam. vi. 18.	1 b	xvii. 2.	1 a	xv. 20.	1 a	
2 Sam. xx. 6.	1 b	xvii. 19.	1 b	Ezek. xxxvi. 35.	1 a	
xxiii. 7.	3	xix. 5.	1 a	Dan. xi. 15.	1 b	
2 Kings iii. 19.	1 b	xxi. 3.	1 a	Hos. viii. 14.	1 a	
x. 2.	1 b	xxxii. 1.	1 a	Zeph. i. 16.	1 a	
xvii. 9.	1 b					

FERRET

אֲנָקָה *f.* a shriek, cry, mourning; a species of reptile, probably of the lizard genus, having its name from a moaning cry; some suppose it to be the gecko : Lev. xi. 30.

FERRY-BOAT

עֲבָרָה *f.* a ferry-boat for passing a stream : 2 Sam. xix. 18.

FETCH

1 אָסַף to take away, to remove, to gather, to receive; see *Gather.* KAL *fut.*

2 בּוֹא to come. HIPHIL, to bring in, *imp.*

3 יָצָא to go out. HIPHIL, to bring out, *fut.*

4 לָקַח to take, to take away; see *Take.* KAL [a] *pret.* [b] *inf.* [c] *imp.* [d] *fut.* [e] *part.* Poel. HOPHAL [f] *fut.*

5 מָהַר to hasten. PIEL *imp.* "fetch quickly," *lit.* hasten.

6 נָשָׂא to take up; to take away. KAL [a] *pret.* [b] *fut.*

7 סָבַב to go about, to fetch about; see *Compass.* PIEL *inf.*

8 עָבַט to change, to give and borrow on pledge. KAL *inf.*

9 עָלָה to ascend, to fetch up. KAL [a] *fut.* HIPHIL [b] *imp.* [c] *fut.*

10 שׁוּב to return. HIPHIL *inf.*, "to fetch home again."

Gen. xviii. 4.	4 f	Judg. xx. 10.	4 b	1 Kings vii. 13.	4 d	
xviii. 5, 7.	4 d	ix. 28.	4 d	xvii. 10.	4 c	
xxvii. 9, 13.	4 c	vi. 21.	9 b	xvii. 11.	4 b	
xxvii. 14.	4 d	vii. 1.	9 c	2 Kings vi. 13.	4 d	
xxvii. 45.	4 a	x. 23.	4 d	xi. 4.	4 d	
xlii. 16.	4 d	xvi. 11.	4 c	2 Chron. i. 17.	9 a	
Exod. ii. 5.	4 d	xx. 31.	4 c	xii. 11.	6 a	
Num. xx. 10.	3	xxvi. 22.	4 d	xviii. 8.	5	
Deut. xix. 12.	4 a	2 Sam. iv. 6.	4 e	Neh. viii. 15.	2	
xxiv. 10.	8	ix. 5.	4 d	Job xxxvi. 3.	6 b	
xxiv. 19.	4 b	xi. 27.	1	Isa. lvi. 12.	4 d	
xxx. 4.	4 d	xiv. 2.	4 d	Jer. xxvi. 23.	3	
Judg. xi. 5.	4 b	xiv. 13.	10	xxxvi. 21.	4 b	
xviii. 18.	4 d	xiv. 20.	7			

FETTER

זִקִּים *m. pl.* bonds, fetters, chains; see *Chains :* Job xxxvi. 8.

כֶּבֶל *m.* a fetter; see *Bind :* Ps. cv. 18; cxlix. 8.

נְחֹשֶׁת *com.* brass; fetters of brass : Judg. xvi. 21 : 2 Sam. iii. 34: 2 Kings xxv. 7 : 2 Chron. xxxiii. 11; xxxvi. 6.

FEVER

קַדַּחַת *f.* burning fever : Deut. xxviii. 22.

FEW

1 אֶחָד one; in the plural joined with יוֹם *pl.* a few days : Isa. lxvi. 17, behind one (tree), *marg.* ' one after another.'

2 מִזְעָר *m.* smallness, fewness.

3 מָעַט to be few or little, relates to number, space, condition, and time. KAL [a] *inf.* [b] *fut.* PIEL [c] *pret.* HIPHIL [d] *pret.* [e] *fut.* [f] מְעָט *m.* a little.

4 מְתִים men; men in a diminutive sense, fellows; a few.

5 מִסְפָּר *m.* number; few, *lit.* a number, or of a number.

6 קָצֵר *adj.* short : Job xiv. 1, *marg.* ' short of days.'

Gen. xvii. 44.	1	Lev. xxv. 52.	3 f	Num. xxxiii. 54.	3 f	
xxix. 20.	1	xxvi. 22.	3 d	xxxv. 8, 8.	3 f e	
xxxiv. 30.	4	Num. ix. 20.	5	Deut. iv. 27.	4	
xlvii. 9.	3 f	xiii. 18.	3 f	vii. 7.	3 f	
Lev. xxv. 16.	3 a	xxvi. 54, 56.	3 f	xxvi. 5.	3 f	

Deut. xxviii. 62.	3 f	Neh. ii. 12.	3 f	Eccles. xii. 3. β	3 c	
xxxiii. 6.	5	vii. 4.	3 f	Isa. x. 7.	3 f	
Josh. vii. 3.	3 f	Job x. 20.	3 f	x. 19.	5	
1 Sam. xiv. 6.	5	xiv. 1.	6	xxiv. 6.	5	
xvii. 28.	3 f	xvi. 22.	5	Jer. xxx. 19.	3 b	
2 Kings iv. 3.α	3 e	Ps. cv. 12, 12.	4, 3 f	xlii. 2.	3 f	
1 Chron. xvi. 19.	4, 5	cix. 8.	3 f	Ezek. v. 3.	3 f	
xvi. 19.	3 f	Eccles. v. 2.	3 f	xii. 16.	5	
2 Chron. xxix. 34.	3 f	ix. 14.	3 f	Dan. xi. 20.	1	

a marg. 'or, scant not,' *i.e.* to borrow little.' *β marg.* 'because they (grind)

FIELD

1 אֶרֶץ the earth, land, ground, earth as opposed to the sea.

2 בַּר Ch. *m.* corn ; field, country.

3 חוּץ any place that lieth without a city, out-places.

4 חֶלְקָה *f.* a portion ; portion of a field, with or without שָׂדֶה.

5 יְגֵבִים *m. pl.* a field as ploughed.

6 שָׂדֶה *m.* field, country, the open field lying unenclosed and without fences or hedges, as is still the case throughout the East : Gen. ii. 5, &c. ᵃשָׂדַי *m.* field, country, but only poetic.

7 שְׁדֵמָה *f.* in *pl.* fields, especially fields of grain, or of vines, vineyards.

8 שְׁרֵמוֹת *f. pl.* fields cut up or overflowed : Jer. xxxi. 40, כתיב.

No. 6 not included.

Deut. xxxii. 13.	6 a	Ps. civ. 11.	6 a	Ezek. xxix. 5, 5.	6, 1	
xxxii. 32.	7	Prov. viii. 26.		Dan. iii. 38.	3	
2 Sam. xiv. 30, 30, 31.	4	Isa. xvi. 8.	7	iv. 12, 15, 21, 23, 23,		
2 Kings xxiii. 4.		lvi. 9.	6 a	25, 32.	2	
Job v. 10.	3	Jer. iv. 17.	6 a	Hos. x. 4.	6 a	
Ps. viii. 7.		xviii. 18.	6 a	xii. 11.	6 a	
l. 11.	6 a	xxxi. 40, 40.	7, or 8	Joel ii. 22.	6 a	
lxxx. 13.	6 a	xxxix. 10.	5	Hab. iii. 17.	7	
xcvi. 12.	6 a	Lam. iv. 9.	6 a			

FIERCE

1 חָדַד to be sharp ; to be quick, vehement, fierce. KAL *pret.* Hab. i. 8, *marg.* 'sharp ;' of the horses of the Chaldeans, more fierce than the evening wolves, when they rush forward, and attack the ranks of the enemy ; so *genus acre luporum*, Virg. Geo. iii. 246 ; *acri gaudet equo*, Aen. iv. 156.

2 חֳרִי heat, with אַף heat of anger, *i.e.* fierce anger, always including a degree of sorrow and displeasure. ᵃחָרוֹן *m.* heat, with אַף fierce anger.

3 עַז to be strong, firm, robust. NIPHAL *part.* Symmachus, ἀναιδής ; Vulg., *impudens.* ᵃעַז *adj.* strong, vehement.

4 אַכְזָר *adj.* cruel ; unrelenting ; in a good sense, bold.

5 קָשָׁה to be hard, harsh. KAL *fut.*

6 רַעַשׁ *m.* a trembling, quaking.

Gen. xlix. 7.	3 a	Ezra x. 14.	2 a	Jer. xxx. 24.	2 a	
Exod. xxxii. 12.	2 a	Job xxxix. 24.	6	xlix. 37.	2 a	
Num. xxv. 4.	2 a	xli. 10.	4	li. 45.	2 a	
xxxii. 14.	2 a	Ps. lxxviii. 49.	2 a	Lam. i. 12.	2 a	
Deut. xiii. 17.	2 a	lxxxv. 3.	2 a	ii. 3.	2	
xxviii. 50.	4	lxxxviii. 16.	2 a	iv. 11.	2 a	
Josh. vii. 11.	2 a	Isa. xiii. 4.	2	Dan. viii. 23.	3 a	
1 Sam. xx. 34.	2	xiii. 9, 13.	2 a	Hos. xi. 9.	2 a	
xxviii. 18.	2	xix. 4.	2 a	Jonah iii. 9.	2 a	
2 Sam. xix. 43.	5	xxxiii. 19.	2 a	Nah. i. 6.	2 a	
2 Kings xxiii. 26.	2 a	Jer. iv. 8, 26.	2 a	Hab. i. 8.	1	
2 Chron. xxviii. 11, 13.	2 a	xii. 13.	2 a	Zeph. ii. 2.	2 a	
xxix. 10.	2 a	xxx. 37, 38, 38.	2 a	iii. 8.	2 a	
xxx. 8.	2 a					

FIFTH

חָמַשׁ to take up the fifth part. PIEL *pret.* Gen. xli. 34.

FIG, FIG-TREE

פַּג *m.* green fig : Gesenius, unripe figs, which hang on the tree over winter : Cant. ii. 13.

תְּאֵנָה *f.* fig-tree ; also the fruit, a fig : Gen. iii. 7, &c.

FIGHT

1 לָחַם to eat, to consume ; to war against ; to eat up, to devour, seems to have been a very early mode of expressing the violence of enemies in war, and their determination to conquer, as Joshua says of the Canaanites, "they are bread for us," Num. xiv. 9 ; so also the sword is said to devour, אָכַל. *Seq.* אֵת of person, with whom, and לְ ; more usual in Niphal in a *recipr. signif.* like Gr. μάχεσθαι. The person, with whom, is put in the *accus.* also, with בְּ, עִם, אֵת, אֶל, עַל. The person, for whom, is put with לְ and עַל. With *inf.*, ever fight. KAL ᵃ*imp.* ᵇ*part.* Poel. NIPHAL ᶜ*pret.* ᵈ*inf.* ᵉ*imp.* ᶠ*fut.* ᵍ*part.* ʰמִלְחָמָה *f.* warring, fighting.

2 מַעֲרָכָה *f.* arrangement, order, array.

3 עָשָׂה to do, &c. KAL *part.* Poel, 2 Chron. xxvi. 11, *lit.* making war.

4 צָבָא to go forth to war, as a soldier, to make war. KAL ᵃ*pret.* ᵇ*inf.* ᶜ*part.* Poel.

5 צָבָה to go forth to war. KAL *part.* Poel.

Exod. i. 10.	1 c	1 Sam. xvii. 9, 33.	1 d	2 Chron. xviii. 31.	1 d	
xiv. 14.	1 f	xvii. 10.	1 g	xx. 17.	1 d	
xiv. 25.	1 g	xvii. 19.	1 g	xx. 29.	1 c	
xvii. 8.	1 f	xvii. 30.	1 c	xxii. 6.	1 d	
xvii. 9.	1 e	xvii. 32.	1 c	xxvi. 11.	3, 1 h	
xvii. 10.	1 d	xviii. 17.	1 e	xxvii. 5.	1 c	
Num. xxi. 1, 23.	1 f	xix. 8.	1 f	xxxii. 2.	1 h	
xxi. 26.	1 c	xxiii. 1.	1 g	xxxiii. 8.	1 c	
Deut. i. 30, 42.	1 f	xxiii. 5.	1 f	xxxv. 20, 22, 22.	1 d	
i. 41.	1 c	xxv. 28.	1 g	Neh. iv. 8.	1 d	
ii. 32.	1 h	xxix. 8.	1 c	iv. 14.	1 e	
iii. 22.	1 c	xxxi. 1.	1 c	iv. 20.	1 f	
xx. 4, 10.	1 d	2 Sam. ii. 28.γ	1 g	Ps. xxxv. 1, 1.	1 a b	
Josh. ix. 2.	1 d	viii. 10.	1 c	lvi. 1, 2.	1 a	
x. 14, 25, 42.	1 g	x. 17.	1 f	cix. 3.	1 f	
x. 29, 31, 34, 36, 38.	1 f	xi. 17.	1 f	cxliv. 1.	1 h	
xi. 5.	1 d	xi. 20.	1 d	Isa. xix. 2.	1 c	
xix. 47.	1 f	xii. 26, 29.	1 f	xx. 1.	1 f	
xxiii. 3, 10.	1 g	xii. 27.	1 c	xxix. 7, 7.	4 c, 5	
xxiv. 8, 11.	1 f	xxi. 15.	1 f	xxix. 8.	4 c	
Judg. i. 1, 9.	1 d	1 Kings xii. 21.	1 f	xxx. 32.	1 c	
i. 3, 5, 8.	1 f	xii. 24.	1 f	xxxi. 4.	4 b	
v. 19, 19, 20, 20.	1 c	xx. 23, 25.	1 f	lxiii. 10.	1 c	
viii. 1.	1 d	xx. 26.	1 h	Jer. i. 19.	1 c	
ix. 17, 45.	1 c	xxii. 31.	1 h	xv. 20.	1 c	
ix. 38.	1 e	xxii. 32.	1 f	xxi. 4.	1 g	
ix. 39, 52.	1 f	2 Kings iii. 21.	1 d	xxi. 5.	1 c	
x. 9, 18.	1 d	viii. 29.	1 d	xxxii. 5.	1 g	
xi. 6, 20.	1 f	ix. 15.	1 c	xxxii. 24, 29.	1 g	
xi. 8.	1 c	x. 3.	1 e	xxxiii. 5.	1 d	
xi. 9, 12, 32.	1 f	xii. 17.	1 f	xxxiv. 1, 7.	1 g	
xi. 25.α	1 d c	xiii. 12.	1 c	xxxiv. 22.	1 c	
xii. 1, 3.	1 d	xiv. 28.	1 c	xxxvii. 8.	1 c	
xii. 4.	1 c	xvi. 5.	1 c	xxxvii. 10.	1 c	
xx. 20.β	1 h	xix. 9.	1 d	xli. 12.	1 g	
1 Sam. iv. 9.	1 c	1 Chron. x. 1.	1 d	xli. 13.	1 d	
iv. 10.	1 f	xviii. 10.	1 c	Dan. x. 20.	1 c	
viii. 20.	1 f	xix. 17.	1 f	xi. 11.	1 c	
xii. 9.	1 f	2 Chron. xi. 1.	1 d	Zech. x. 5.	1 c	
xiii. 5.	1 d	xi. 4.	1 f	xiv. 3, 3.	1 c d	
xiv. 47.	1 f	xiii. 12.	1 c	xiv. 12.	4 a	
xv. 18.	1 f	xviii. 30.	1 f	xiv. 14.	1 f	

a lit. fighting did he fight. *β lit.* arrayed a battle. *γ lit.* added to fight.

FIGURE

תַּבְנִית *f.* manner of building ; model ; likeness : Isa. xliv. 13.

סֶמֶל *m.* an image, likeness, with or without a prototype : Deut. iv. 16.

מִקְלַעַת *f.* figure, that has been carved : 1 Kings vi. 29.

FILE

פֶּה *m.* mouth : 1 Sam. xiii. 21.

פְּצִירָה *f.* that which is notched : 1 Sam. xiii. 21.

FILL

1   מָלָא to be abundant and overflowing ; to fill, as anything does a vacant space with its own bulk or abundance, with an *acc.* of place ; to fill a place with anything, with two *acc.*, of the place, and of the thing filling, to fill up ; to fill the hand (see *Consecrate*); to be filled, to be full, with an *acc.* of the thing with which anything is full ; to be filled with that which takes full possession of the mind ; to be fulfilled or completed. KAL [a] *pret.* [b] *imp.* NIPHAL [c] *pret.* [d] *fut.* PIEL [e] *pret.* [f] *inf.* [g] *imp.* [h] *fut.* [i] *part.* [k] מְלָא Ch. P'AL *pret.* [l] מְלָא *adj.* [m] מְלֵא *m.*

2   סָבָא to drink to excess. KAL *fut.*

3   עָטָה to cover. KAL *fut.*

4   רָוָה to drink to the full. KAL [a] *fut.* HIPHIL [b] *pret.*

5   שָׂבַע to be satisfied, filled. KAL [a] *pret.* [b] *fut.* HIPHIL [c] *pret.* [d] *fut.* [e] שֹׂבַע *m.*

Gen. i. 22.	1 b	Job xxii. 18.	1 e	Isa. xliii. 24.	4 b
vi. 11.	1 d	xxiii. 4.	1 h	lvi. 12.	2
vi. 13.	1 a	xxxviii. 39.	1 h	lxv. 20.	1 h
xxi. 19.	1 h	xli. 7.	1 h	Jer. xiii. 12, 12.	1 d
xxiv. 16.	1 h	Ps. xvii. 14.	1 h	xiii. 13.	1 l
xxvi. 15. *a*	1 h	xxxviii. 7.	1 a	xv. 17.	1 a
xliii. 25.	1 h	lxxi. 8.	1 d	xvi. 18.	1 a
xliv. 1.	1 g	lxxii. 19.	1 d	xix. 4.	1 a
Exod. i. 7.	1 d	lxxviii. 29.	1 h	xxiii. 24.	1 a
ii. 16.	1 h	lxxx. 9.	1 h	xxxiii. 5.	1 f
x. 6.	1 a	lxxxi. 10.	1 h	xli. 9.	1 a
xvi. 12.	5 b	lxxxiii. 16.	1 g	xlvi. 12.	1 a
xvi. 32.	1 m	lxxxiv. 6.	3	li. 5.	1 a
xxviii. 3.	1 e	civ. 28.	5 b	li. 14, 34.	1 a
xxxi. 3.	1 h	cvii. 9.	1 e	Lam. iii. 15.	5 c
xxxv. 31.	1 h	cx. 6.	1 e	iii. 30.	5 b
xxxv. 35.	1 e	cxxiii. 3, 4.	5 a	Ezek. iii. 3.	1 h
xl. 34, 35.	1 a	cxxvi. 2.	1 e	vii. 19.	1 a
Lev. xxv. 19.	5 e	cxxix. 7.	1 e	viii. 17.	1 a
Num. xiv. 21.	1 d	cxlvii. 14.	1 h	ix. 7.	1 g
Deut. vi. 11.	1 e	Prov. i. 13.	1 h	x. 2.	1 g
xxiii. 24.	5 e	i. 31.	5 b	x. 3.	1 a
xxvi. 12.	5 a	iii. 10.	1 d	x. 4.	1 d
xxxi. 20.	5 a	v. 10.	5 b	xi. 6.	1 e
Josh. ix. 13.	1 e	vii. 18.	4 a	xxiii. 33.	1 d
1 Sam. xvi. 1.	1 g	viii. 21.	1 h	xxiv. 4.	1 a
1 Kings vii. 14.	1 e	xii. 21.	1 a	xxvii. 33.	5 c
viii. 10, 11.	1 a	xiv. 14.	5 b	xxviii. 16.	1 a
xviii. 33.	1 b	xviii. 20.	5 b	xxx. 11.	1 a
xviii. 35.	1 e	xx. 17.	1 d	xxxii. 4.	1 e
xx. 27.	1 e	xxiv. 4.	1 d	xxxii. 5.	1 e
2 Kings iii. 17, 20.	1 d	xxv. 16.	5 a	xxxv. 8.	1 l
iii. 25.	1 e	xxx. 16.	5 a	xxxvi. 38.	1 l
xxi. 16.	1 e	xxx. 22.	5 b	xxxix. 20.	5 a
xxiii. 14.	1 h	Eccles. i. 8.	5 b	xliii. 5.	1 a
xxiv. 4.	1 h	vi. 3.	5 b	xliv. 4.	1 a
2 Chron. v. 13, 14.	1 a	vi. 7.	1 d	Dan. ii. 35.	1 k
vii. 1, 2.	1 a	Cant. v. 2.	1 c	Hos. xiii. 6, 6.	5 b a
xvi. 14.	1 e	Isa. vi. 1.	1 l	Nah. ii. 12.	1 h
Ezra ix. 11.	1 e	vi. 4.	1 d	Hab. ii. 14.	1 d
Neh. ix. 25.	5 b	viii. 8. *β*	1 m	ii. 16.	5 a
Job iii. 15.	1 i	xiv. 21.	1 a	Hag. ii. 7.	1 a
viii. 21.	1 h	xxi. 3.	1 a	Zeph. i. 9.	1 i
ix. 18.	5 d	xxvii. 6.	1 a	Zech. ix. 13.	1 e
xv. 2.	1 h	xxxiii. 5.	1 e	ix. 15.	1 a
xx. 23.	1 f	xxxiv. 6.	1 a		

a lit. and they filled.   *β marg.* 'the fulness of the breadth of thy land shall be the stretchings out of his wings.'

FILLET

חוּט *m.* a thread : Jer. lii. 21.

חָשַׁק to join or fasten together. PIEL *pret.* Exod. xxxviii. 28. PUAL *part.* Exod. xxvii. 17 ; xxxviii. 17. חֲשֻׁקִים *m. pl.* joinings, *i. e.* poles or rods, which served to join together the tops of the columns around the court of the taber-

nacle, and from which the curtains were suspended : Exod. xxvii. 10, 11 ; xxxvi. 38 ; xxxviii. 10, 11, 12, 17, 19.

FILTHY

1   אָלַח to be rotten and fetid : Ps. xiv. 3 : LXX. ἠχρειώθησαν, useless and of no value, like a rotten tree. It is applied figuratively to the corruption and pollution of the mind, and expresses the natural depravity of man, and original sin, which makes him filthy in the sight of God. NIPHAL [a] *pret.* [b] *part.*

2   טֻמְאָה *f.* uncleanness, pollution. It denotes the highest degree of impurity and contrariety to holiness.

3   מוֹרָאָה filthy : the Rabbins refer to a fictitious verb, meaning to be foul and polluted. The *marg.* makes it the same with מֻרְאָה the crop or maw (Lev. i. 16), and gives *Heb.* maw or gluttonous. Modern critics, with less probability, deduce it from מָרָא to be perverse, rebellious. KAL *part.* Poel. There is in all probability a play on the word מֹרִיָּה Moriah, as referring to Jerusalem.

4   נִדָּה *f.* abomination, uncleanness, impurity ; menstrual defilement.

5   נְחֹשֶׁת *com.* brass : the *Heb.* interpreters seem, in Ezek. xvi. 36, to have understood the word to mean the rust of brass, or the foulness which attaches itself to a brazen pot which has been on the fire ; but Gesenius and other modern critics take it in the sense of money, as the Latin *æs* : "because thy money was poured out," *i. e.* profusely given.

6   עִדִּים *m. pl. pr.* stated times ; applied to what is menstruous.

7   צֹאָה *f.* excrement ; what is filthy, applied *metaph.* to sin. [a] צוֹא *adj.* filthy, used of garments, as a token of sorrow, and of being under accusation.

2 Chron. xxix. 5.	4	Prov. xxx. 12.	7	Ezek. xxii. 15.	2
Ezra vi. 21.	2	Isa. iv. 4.	7	xxiv. 11, 13, 13.	2
ix. 11.	4	xxviii. 8.	7	xxxvi. 25.	2
Job xv. 16.	1 b	lxiv. 6.	7	Zeph. iii. 1.	3
Ps. xiv. 3.	1 a	Lam. i. 9.	2	Zech. iii. 3, 4.	7 a
liii. 3.	1 a	Ezek. xvi. 36.	5		

FIND

1   חָקַר to search, to investigate ; to explore, to search out. NIPHAL *pret.* חֵקֶר *m.* a searching.

2   חָשַׁב to think, to consider, to devise. KAL *inf.*

3   מָצָא Michaelis considers the primary import of this word to be expressed by *pertingit*, to come to, to reach, to arrive at ; hence, to find, to attain to, &c. It is used of finding emphatically, in sufficiency, to find favour, to find evil, to find by experience, to find in possession, to find by enjoyment, &c. In Niphal, to be found is to be present. KAL [a] *pret.* [b] *inf.* [c] *imp.* [d] *fut.* [e] *part.* Poel. NIPHAL [f] *pret.* [g] *inf.* [h] *fut.* [i] *part.* HIPHIL [k] *fut.*

4   שְׁכַח Ch. to find, to acquire, obtain. ITHP'AL [a] *pret.* APHEL [b] *pret.* [c] *inf.* [d] *fut.*

Gen. ii. 20.	3 a	Gen. xi. 2.	3 d	Gen. xviii. 29, 31, 32.	3 h
iv. 14, 15.	3 e	xvi. 7.	3 d	xviii. 30, 30.	3 h d
vi. 8.	3 a	xviii. 3.	3 a	xix. 11.	3 b
viii. 9.	3 a	xviii. 26, 28.	3 d	xix. 19.	3 a

Gen. xxvi. 19. 3 d
xxvi. 32. 3 a
xxvii. 20. a 3 b
xxx. 14. 3 d
xxx. 27. 3 a
xxxi. 32. 3 d
xxxi. 33, 34, 35, 37. 3 a
xxxii. 5, 19. 3 b
xxxiii. 8. 3 b
xxxiii. 10. 3 a
xxxiii. 15. 3 d
xxxiv. 11. 3 d
xxxvi. 24. 3 a
xxxvii. 15, 17. 3 d
xxxvii. 32. 3 a
xxxviii. 20, 22, 23. 3 a
xxxix. 4. 3 d
xli. 38. 3 d
xliv. 8. 3 a
xliv. 9, 10, 12. 3 h
xliv. 16, 16. 3 a f
xliv. 17. 3 f
xlvii. 14. 3 i
xlvii. 21. 3 d
xlvii. 29. 3 a
l. 4. 3 a
Exod. v. 11. 3 d
ix. 19. 3 h
xii. 19. 3 h
xv. 22. 3 a
xvi. 25. 3 d
xvi. 27. 3 a
xxi. 16. 3 f
xxii. 2, 7, 8. 3 h
xxii. 4, 4. 3 g h
xxxiii. 12, 16, 17. 3 a
xxxiii. 13, 13. 3 a d
xxxiv. 9. 3 a
xxxv. 23, 24. 3 f
Lev. vi. 3, 4. 3 a
Num. xi. 11, 15. 3 a
xv. 32. 3 d
xv. 32. 3 e
xxxii. 5. 3 a
xxxii. 13. 3 d
xxxv. 27. 3 a
Deut. iv. 29. 3 a
xvii. 2. 3 h
xviii. 10. 3 h
xx. 11. 3 i
xxi. 1. 3 h
xxii. 3, 14, 17, 23, 27. 3 a
xxii. 20. 3 f
xxii. 22. 3 h
xxii. 25. 3 d
xxii. 28, 28. 3 d f
xxiv. 1, 1. 3 d a
xxiv. 7. 3 h
xxxii. 10. 3 a
Josh. ii. 22. 3 a
x. 17. 3 f
Judg. i. 5. 3 d
vi. 17. 3 a
ix. 33. β 3 d
xiv. 12, 18. 3 a
xv. 15. 3 d
xvii. 8, 9. 3 d
xxi. 12. 3 d
Ruth i. 9. 3 c
ii. 2, 13. 3 d
ii. 10. 3 a
1 Sam. i. 18. 3 d
vi. 8. 3 a
ix. 4, 4, 11. 3 a
ix. 13, 13. 3 d
ix. 20. 3 f
x. 2, 2. 3 a f
x. 16, 21. 3 f
xii. 5. 3 a
xiii. 19. 3 h
xiii. 22, 22. 3 f h
xiv. 30. 3 a
xvi. 22. 3 a
xx. 3, 29. 3 a
xx. 21, 36. 3 c
xxiii. 17. 3 d
xxiv. 19. 3 d
xxv. 8. 3 d
xxv. 28. 3 h
xxvii. 5. 3 a
xxix. 3, 6, 8. 3 a
xxxi. 11. 3 d
xxxi. 8. 3 d
2 Sam. vii. 27. 3 a

2 Sam. xiv. 22. 3 a
xv. 25. 3 d
xvi. 4. 3 d
xvii. 12, 13. 3 f
xvii. 20. 3 a
1 Kings i. 3. 3 d
i. 52. 3 h
vii. 47. 1 a
xi. 19, 29. 3 d
xiii. 14, 28. 3 d
xiv. 13. 3 f
xviii. 5, 10, 12. 3 d
xix. 19. 3 d
xx. 36, 37. 3 d
xxi. 20, 20. 3 a
2 Kings ii. 17. 3 a
iv. 39. 3 a
ix. 35. 3 a
xii. 5. 3 a
xii. 10, 18. 3 i
xiv. 14. 3 i
xvi. 8. 3 i
xvii. 4. 3 d
xviii. 15. 3 i
xix. 8. 3 i
xx. 13. 3 f
xxii. 8. 3 d
xxii. 9, 13. 3 i
xxiii. 2. 3 i
xxiii. 24. 3 a
xxv. 19, 19. 3 a
1 Chron. iv. 40. 3 d
iv. 41. 3 f
x. 8. 3 a
xvii. 25. 3 a
xx. 2. 3 d
xxiv. 4. 3 a
xxvi. 31. 3 h
xxviii. 9. 3 h
xxix. 8. 3 i
2 Chron. ii. 14. 2
ii. 17. 3 h
iv. 18. 1 a
v. 2, 4, 15. 3 h
xix. 3. 3 f
xx. 16. 3 a
xx. 25. 3 d
xxi. 17. 3 i
xxii. 8. 3 d
xxv. 5. 3 a
xxv. 24. 3 i
xxix. 16. 3 i
xxxii. 4. 3 a
xxxiv. 14, 15. 3 a
xxxiv. 17, 30. 3 i
xxxiv. 21. 3 f
xxxvi. 8. 3 i
Ezra ii. 62. 3 f
iv. 15. 4 d
iv. 19. 4 b
vi. 2. 4 a
vii. 16. 4 d
viii. 15. 3 a
x. 18. 3 a
Neh. v. 8. 3 a
vii. 5, 5. 3 d
vii. 64. 3 f
viii. 14. 3 d
ix. 8. 3 a
xiii. 1. 3 f
Esth. ii. 23. 3 h
v. 8. 3 a
vi. 2. 3 h
viii. 5. 3 a
Job iii. 22. 1 b
ix. 10. 1 b
xi. 7, 7. 3 d
xvii. 10. 3 d
xix. 28. 3 f
xx. 8. γ 3 d
xxiii. 3. 3 d
xxviii. 12, 13. 3 d
xxxi. 29. 3 d
xxxii. 3, 13. 3 a
xxxiii. 10. 3 a
xxxiii. 11. 3 k
xxxvii. 23. 3 a
xlii. 15. 3 f
Ps. x. 15. 3 d
xvii. 3. 3 d
xviii. 22, 22. 3 d
xxi. 8, 8. 3 d
xxiv. 14. 3 a

Ps. xxv. 16. 3 a
xxxii. 6. 3 b
xxxvi. 2. 3 b
xxxvii. 36. 3 f
lxix. 20. 3 a
lxxv. 5. 3 a
lxxxiv. 3. 3 a
lxxxix. 20. 3 a
cvii. 4. 3 a
cxvi. 3. 3 d
cxix. 162. 3 a
cxxxii. 5. 3 d
cxxxii. 6. 3 a
Prov. i. 13, 28. 3 d
ii. 5. 3 c
iii. 4. 3 c
iii. 13. 3 a
iv. 22. 3 e
vi. 31. 3 f
vii. 15. 3 d
viii. 9. 3 e
viii. 12, 17. 3 d
viii. 35, 35. 3 e a
x. 13. 3 h
xvi. 20. 3 a
xvi. 31. 3 h
xvii. 20. 3 a
xviii. 22, 22. 3 a
xix. 8. 3 b
xx. 6. 3 d
xxi. 21. 3 d
xxiv. 14. 3 a
xxv. 16. 3 a
xxviii. 23. 3 a
xxxi. 10. 3 d
Eccles. iii. 11. 3 d
vii. 14, 24. 3 d
vii. 26. 3 e
vii. 27, 27. 3 a b
vii. 28, 28, 29. 3 a
viii. 17, 17, 17. 3 b d b
ix. 10. 3 d
xi. 1. 3 a
xii. 10. 3 b
Cant. iii. 1, 2, 3, 4. 3 a
v. 6, 7. 3 a
v. 8. 3 d
viii. 1. 3 a
viii. 10. 3 e
Isa. x. 10. 3 a
x. 14. 3 d
xiii. 15. 3 i
xxii. 3. 3 i
xxx. 14. 3 h
xxxiv. 14. 3 h
xxxv. 9. 3 h
xxxvii. 8. 3 h
xxxix. 2. 3 f
xli. 12. 3 h
li. 3. 3 h
lv. 6. 3 g
lvii. 10. 3 a
lviii. 3. 3 b
lviii. 13. 3 b
lxv. 1. 3 f
lxv. 8. 3 h
Jer. ii. 5. 3 a
ii. 24. 3 d
ii. 34, 34. 3 f a
v. 1. 3 a
v. 26. 3 f
x. 18. 3 d
xi. 9. 3 f
xiv. 3. 3 d
xv. 16. 3 d
xxiii. 11. 3 f
xxix. 13. 3 a
xxix. 14. 3 a
xxxi. 2. 3 a
xli. 3, 8. 3 a
xli. 12. 3 d
xlv. 3. 3 d
xlviii. 27. 3 f
l. 7. 3 f
l. 20. 3 h
l. 24. 3 f
lii. 25, 25. 3 f i
Lam. i. 3, 6. 3 a
ii. 9, 16. 3 a
Ezek. iii. 11. 3 a
xxii. 30. 3 a
xxvi. 21. 3 h

Ezek. xxviii. 15. 3 f
Dan. i. 19. 3 f
i. 20. 3 d
ii. 25. 4 b
ii. 35. 4 a
v. 11, 12, 14, 27. 4 a
vi. 4, 4, 4. 4 c c a
vi. 5, 5. 4 b d

Dan. vi. 11. 4 b
vi. 22, 23. 4 a
xi. 19. 3 h
xii. 1. 3 i
Hos. ii. 6, 7. 3 d
v. 6. 3 d
ix. 10. 3 a
xii. 4. 3 d

Hos. xii. 8, 8. 3 a d
xiv. 8. 3 f
Amos viii. 12. 3 d
Jonah i. 3. 3 d
Micah i. 13. 3 f
Zeph. iii. 13. 3 h
Zech. x. 10. 3 h
Mal. ii. 6. 3 f

a lit. hasted to find.   β lit. so thine hand shall find.   γ lit. they shall not find him.

FINE

זָקַק to refine. KAL *fut.* Job xxviii. 1.

חֵלֶב *m.* fat : Ps. lxxxi. 16 ; cxlvii. 14, *marg.* 'fat of wheat.'

טוֹב *adj.* good : 2 Chron. iii. 5, 8 : Ezra viii. 27, *lit.* good shining. טָב Ch. *m. id.* Dan. ii. 32.

צָהַב to glitter, to shine. HOPHAL *part.* Ezra viii. 27, *marg.* 'yellow, *or,* shining brass.'

צָרַף to refine. KAL *part.* Poel, Prov. xxv. 4. מַצְרֵף *m.* fining-pot : Prov. xvii. 3 ; xxvii. 21.

שָׂרִיק *adj.* fine, *i.e.* cleansed by combing, of flax : Isa. xix. 9.

FINGER

אֶצְבַּע *f.* a finger, especially the forefinger, which is more usually dipped in anything : Exod. viii. 19, &c. אֶצְבְּעָן Ch. *f. pl.* Dan. v. 5.

FINISH

1 בָּצַע to cut, to break off ; to accomplish, to perform. PIEL *fut.*

2 יְצָא Ch. to bring to an end, to finish. SHAPHEL *pret.*

3 כָּלָא to confine, restrain, keep back, refrain, hinder. PIEL *inf.* Dan. ix. 24, *marg.* 'to restrain :' by abolishing the law as it subjects to condemnation, and by bringing in the grace of the gospel, which pardons and restores the penitent to life, our Lord has restrained or put an end, as it were, to transgression.

4 כָּלָה to be completed, perfected, finished ; to finish ; followed by an *inf.*, to cease doing anything. KAL a *pret.* b *inf.* c *fut.* PIEL d *pret.* e *inf.* f *fut.* PUAL g *fut.*

5 כְּלַל Ch. to complete, to perfect. SHAPHEL *pret.*

6 עָשָׂה to do, to make. KAL *inf.*

7 שָׁלַם to be whole ; to be completed, finished, ended. KAL a *fut.* PIEL b *pret.* שְׁלַם Ch. P'AL c *part. passive.* APHEL d *pret.*

8 תָּמַם to complete, to perfect, to finish. KAL a *inf.* b *fut.*

Gen. ii. 1. 4 g
vi. 16. 4 f
Exod. xxxix. 32. 4 f
xl. 33. 4 f
Deut. xxxi. 24. 8 a
Josh. iv. 10. 8 a
Ruth iii. 18. 4 d
1 Kings vi. 9, 14. 4 f
vi. 22. 8 a
vi. 38. 4 a
vii. 1. 4 f

1 Kings vii. 22. 8 b
ix. 1. 4 e
ix. 25. 7 b
1 Chron. xxvii. 24. 4 d
xxviii. 20. 4 a
2 Chron. iv. 11. 4 f, 6
v. 1. 7 a
vii. 11. 4 f
viii. 16. 4 a
xxiv. 14. 4 e
xxix. 28. 4 b

2 Chron. xxxi. 1. 4 e
xxxi. 7. 4 d
Ezra vi. 16. 7 c
vi. 14. 5
vi. 15. 2
Neh. vi. 15. 7 a
Dan. iv. 26. 7 d
ix. 24. 3
xii. 7. 4 c
Zech. iv. 9. 1

FINS

סַנְפִּיר *m.* fin of fishes : Lev. xi. 9, 10, 12 : Deut. xiv. 9, 10.

FIR

בְּרוֹשׁ *m.* a cypress, a tall and fruit or cone-bearing tree, con-

stituting, along with the cedar, with which it is often joined, the glory of Lebanon : 2 Sam. vi. 5, &c. בְּרוֹתִים *m. pl.* Cant. i. 17.

FIRE, FIERY

1   אוּד   *m.* see *Brand.*

2   אוֹר   (see *Light*), to shine ; Hiphil, to set on fire. HIPHIL [a]*part.* [b] אוּר *m.* light, fire, a hearth. [c] אֻרִים *pl.* fires, light, regions of light or fire, the east. Isa. xxiv. 15, *marg.* 'valleys,' according to Bochart.

3   אֵשׁ   *com.* fire, lightning ; fire for war ; *trop.* for destruction, ruin ; heat, scorching of the sun ; shining, brightness, splendour, as stones of fire : Ezek. xxviii. 14, &c.—— Gen. xix. 24, &c. [a] אִשֶּׁה *f.* fire ; made by fire, *lit.* of fire ; see also *Offering.*

4   אֶשָּׁה   *f.* fire : Jer. vi. 29, *lit.* according to כְּתִיב, of their fire.

5   בָּעַר   to burn ; PIEL, to set on fire : [a]*pret.* [b] בְּעֵרָה *f.* burning.

6   דַּי   *m.* sufficiency ; "in the fire," "in the very fire," *lit.* in the sufficiency of fire.

7   זִקִּים   *m. pl.* fetters ; firebrands : Prov. xxvi. 18. Gesenius, burning arrows, fiery darts fitted with combustibles.

8   מַחְתָּה   *f.* fire-pan, fire-shovel, censer, in which coals were taken up, and incense kindled.

9   יָצַת   to kindle, to burn, followed by בָּאֵשׁ to set on fire. HI-PHIL [a]*pret.* [b]*imp.* [c]*fut.*

10   לָהַט   to burn or be burnt, with the vehement heat of a strong penetrating flame. KAL [a]*part.* Poel, Ps. lvii. 4, " the men that are set on fire," flaming, breathing out fire. PIEL [b]*fut.*

11   לַפִּיד   *m.* lamp, torch, firebrand.

12   נוּר   Ch. *m.* fire, fiery.

13   לְשׁוֹן   *com.* tongue : Isa. v. 24, *marg.* 'the tongue of fire.'

14   שָׂרָף   *adj.* burning, fiery, fiery serpent.

No. 3 not included.

Exod. xxii. 6, 6.	3, 5 b	2 Kings xxv. 15.	8	Isa. xlvii. 14, 14.	3, 2 b
xxvii. 3.	8	Ps. lvii. 4.	10 a	Jer. vi. 29.	4
xxxviii. 3.	8	lxxxiii. 14, 14.	3, 10 b	xxxii. 29.	9 a, 3
Lev. xxii. 27.	3 a	Prov. xxvi. 18.	7	li. 58.	6
Num. xxi. 6, 8.	14	Isa. v. 24.	13, 3	lii. 19.	8
Deut. viii. 15.	14	vii. 4.	1	Ezek. v. 2.	2 b
xxxii. 22, 22.	3, 10 b	xiv. 29.	14	xxxix. 9.	5 a
Josh. viii. 8.	9 c, 3	xxiv. 15.	2 c	Dan. iii. 6, 11, 15, 17,	
viii. 19.	9 c, 3	xxvii. 11.	2 a	20, 21, 22, 23, 24,	
Judg. ix. 49.	9 c, 3	xxx. 6.	14	25, 26, 26, 27 27.	12
xv. 4, 4.	11	xxxi. 9.	2 b	vii. 9, 9, 10.	12
2 Sam. xiv. 30.	9 b, 3	xlii. 25.	10 b	Amos iv. 11.	1
xiv. 30.	9 c, 3	xliv. 16, 16.	3, 2 b	Hab. ii. 11.	6
xiv. 31.	9 a, 3				

FIRM

בָּרִיא   *adj.* fat, a new and better habit of body : Ps. lxxiii. 4.

יָצַק   to pour melted metal into a mould ; what is thus molten is solid and firm. KAL *part.* Paül, Job xli. 23, 24.

כּוּן   to be set in a firm, erect position. HIPHIL *inf.* Josh. iii. 17 ; iv. 3.

תְּקַף   Ch. to be strong. PAEL, to make firm : *inf.* Dan. vi. 7.

FIRMAMENT

רָקִיעַ   *m.* the expanse, ἐκπέτασμα, spread out over the earth, in which the stars appear as if they were fixed ; the arch or vault of heaven ; LXX. στερέωμα. Vulg. *firmamentum,* or, according to our present knowledge of the heavens, that extensive circumambient fluid, the atmosphere : Gen. i. 6, *marg.* 'expansion ;' 7, 7, 7, 8, 14, 15, 17, 20 : Ps. xix. 1 : cl. 1 : Ezek. i. 22, 23, 25, 26 ; x. 1 : Dan. xii. 3.

FIRST

1   אֶחָד   *adj.* one ; first. [a] חַד Ch. *adj. num.*

2   בָּכַר   to be first, to come, *or,* do first ; to be first born, first-ling, to bring forth first child. PIEL [a]*inf.* PUAL [b]*fut.* HIPHIL [c]*part.* [d] בְּכוֹר *m.* first-born, firstling ; used as a term of dignity and of endearment, Exod. iv. 22 ; higher than his brethren, Ps. lxxxix. 27 ; typical of Christ and true Christians ; see *Birthright.*—Gen. x. 15, &c. [e] בְּכוֹר *m.* first-fruit, first-ripe, first-ripe fig. [f] בְּכוֹרָה *f.* first-born, firstling. [g] בִּכּוּרָה *f.* first-ripe, first-ripe fruit. [h] בַּכּוּרָה *f.* first-ripe. [i] בְּכִירָה *adj. f.* first-born.

3   בֵּן   *m.* son ; of the first year, *lit.* son of a year. [a] בַּת *f. id.*

4   חָלַל   see *Begin.* HIPHIL [a]*pret.* [b] תְּחִלָּה *f.* beginning.

5   פֶּטֶר   *m.* that which first breaks forth ; firstling.

6   קַדְמַי   Ch. *adj.* before, in space.

7   רֹאשׁ   *m.* the head ; first or highest in his kind ; what is first, foremost, *i. e.* the beginning, first part, front. [a] רִאשׁוֹן *adj.* head, highest, chief ; first, in place and order ; more frequently of time, the first, former, earliest. In anti-thesis, with ordinals following, as second, third, &c. ; often the first, former, earlier, as opposed to the present time. Spoken of the time which is yet first to come, opposed to a time more remote, future time : Joel ii. 23, in the first time, *i. e.* immediately, presently.—Gen. viii. 13, &c. [b] רֵאשִׁית *f.* topmost, highest ; first in its kind. [c] רֵאשֹׁנִי *adj.* first.

7 a *First,* 2 d *First-born, Firstling* not included.

Gen. i. 5.	1	75, 77, 81, 83, 87,		2 Chron. xxix. 17.	1
ii. 11.	1	88.	3	xxxi. 5.	7 b
iv. 4.	2 f	Num. xiii. 20.	2 e	xxxvi. 22.	1
viii. 5, 13, 13.	1	xv. 20, 21.	7 b	Ezra i. 1.	1
xix. 31, 33, 34, 37.	2 i	xv. 27.	3 a	iii. 6.	1
xxix. 26.	2 i	xviii. 12.	7 b	v. 13.	1 a
xliii. 18, 20.	4 b	xviii. 13.	2 e	vi. 3.	1 a
Exod. xii. 5.	3	xxiv. 20.	7 b	vii. 9, 9.	1
xiii. 12, 13.	5	xxviii. 3, 9, 11, 19,		x. 16, 17.	1
xxiii. 16.	2 f	27.	3	Neh. i. 1.	1
xxiii. 19, 19.	7 b, 2 e	xxviii. 26.	2 e	x. 35, 35.	2 e
xxvii. 17.	1	xxix. 1.	1	x. 36.	2 f
xxix. 38.	3	xxix. 2, 8, 17, 20, 23,		x. 37.	7 b
xxxiv. 19, 20.	5	26, 29, 32, 36.	3	xii. 44.	7 b
xxxiv. 22.	2 e	xxxiii. 38.	1	xiii. 31.	2 e
xxxiv. 26, 26.	7 b, 2 e	Deut. i. 3.	1	Job xli. 14.	1
xxxix. 10.	1	xii. 6, 17.	2 f	Prov. iii. 9.	7 b
xl. 2, 17.	1	xiv. 23.	7 b	Isa. xli. 1.γ	7 a
Lev. ii. 12.	7 b	xviii. 4, 4.	7 b	Jer. ii. 3.	7 b
ii. 14, 14.	2 e	xxi. 16.	2 a	iv. 31.	2 c
ix. 3.	3	xxi. 17.	2 e	xxiv. 2.	2 h
xii. 6.	3	xxvi. 2, 10.	7 b	xxv. 1.	7 c
xiv. 10.	3 a	xxxiii. 21.	7 b	Ezek. xx. 40.	7 b
xxiii. 10.	3	Judg. i. 1.	1	xxvi. 1.	1
xxiii. 12, 18, 19.	3	xx. 18, 18.	4 b	xxix. 17.	1
xxiii. 17, 20.	2 e	1 Sam. viii. 2.a	3	xxxi. 1.	1
xxiii. 24.	1	xiv. 35.β	4 a	xxxii. 1.	1
xxvii. 26.	2 b	xiv. 49.	2 i	xliv. 30, 30,	
Num. i. 1, 18.	1	xvii. 9.	4 b	30.	7 b, 2 e, 7 b
vi. 12.	3	1 Kings xvi. 23.	1	xlv. 18.	1
vii. 14, 14.	3, 3 a	2 Kings ix. 42.	2 e	xlvi. 13.	3
vii. 15, 17, 21, 23, 27,		1 Chron. xii. 9.	7	xlviii. 14.	7 b
29, 33, 35, 39, 41,		xvi. 7.	7	Dan. i. 21.	1
45, 47, 51, 53, 57,		xxiii. 19, 20.	7	vi. 2.	1 a
59, 63, 65, 69, 71,		xxiv. 21.	7	vii. 1.	1 a

Dan. vii. 4, 8, 24.	6	Dan. xi. 1.	1	Micah vii. 1.	2 g	
viii. 1.	4 b	Hos. ix. 10, 10.	2 g, 7 b	Nah. iii. 12.	2 e	
ix. 1, 2.	1	Amos vi. 7.	7	Hag. i. 1.	1	

a *lit.* his son the first born. β *marg.* 'that altar he began to build.'
γ *lit.* at the first time.

FISH, FISH-POOL

דָּג *m.* a fish, so called as multiplying abundantly: Gen. ix. 2:
Num. xi. 22: 1 Kings iv. 33: 2 Chron. xxxiii. 14: Neh.
iii. 3; xii. 39; xiii. 16: Job xii. 8; xli. 7: Ps. viii. 8:
Eccles. ix. 12: Ezek. xxxviii. 20: Hos. iv. 3: Jonah i.
17, 17; ii. 10: Hab. i. 14: Zeph. i. 3, 10. דִּיג to fish.
KAL *pret.* Jer. xvi. 16. דַּיָּג *m.* fisher: Isa. xix. 8: Jer.
xvi. 16. דַּוָּג *m.* fisher: Jer. xvi. 16 (כתיב), Ezek. xlvii.
10. דּוּגָה *f.* fish; see *Hook:* Amos iv. 2. דָּגָה *f.* fish,
but mostly used collectively: Gen. i. 26, 28: Exod. vii.
18, 21; Num. xi. 5: Deut. iv. 18: Ps. cv. 29: Isa. l. 2:
Ezek. xxix. 4, 4, 5; xlvii. 9, 10, 10: Jonah ii. 1.

נֶפֶשׁ *com.* the animal life: it is used in a singular manner of
fish, one species of the animal creation: Isa. xix. 10,
"ponds for fish," *marg.* 'of living things.' Others render it, ponds of desire, or pleasant ponds: *stagna animœ,*
i. e. *stagna in quibus anima eorum hæret ob commodum
quod inde obtinet.*—Stock. But modern critics render
the clause, 'grieved in mind;' see *Pond.*

בְּרֵכָה *f.* see *Pool:* Cant. vii. 4.

FIST

אֶגְרוֹף *m.* fist, from גָּרַף to grasp: Exod. xxi. 18: Isa. lviii. 4.
חָפְנַיִם *dual,* see *Hand:* Prov. xxx. 4.

FIT, FITLY

אוֹפָן *m.* a wheel: Prov. xxv. 11, *marg.* 'spoken upon his wheels,'
i. e. easily, freely, and suitably; or from

אֹפֶן *m.* season: Prov. xxv. 11.

יָצָא to go out. KAL *part.* Poel, 1 Chron. vii. 11, "fit to go
out to war," *lit.* going out to war.

יָשַׁר to be right; applied to the covering of carved work with
thin plates of gold, exactly fitted and adapted to it.
PUAL *part.* 1 Kings vi. 35.

כּוּן to set right; applied to words ready and prepared on the
lips, to be used as occasion requires. NIPHAL *fut.* Prov.
xxii. 18.

מִלֵּאת *f.* fulness: Cant. v. 12, fitly set, *marg.* 'sitting in fulness,'
i. e. fitly placed, and set as a precious stone in a ring.

עָשָׂה to do, to make. KAL *fut.* Isa. xliv. 13.

עָתַד to prepare, make ready. PIEL *imp.* Prov. xxiv. 27.

עִתִּי *adj.* from עֵת time, opportune: Lev. xvi. 21, *marg.* 'a man
of opportunity.'

FITCHES

כֻּסֶּמֶת *f.* spelt, *triticum spelta:* Linn. The ζέα of the Greeks;
the *far* and *adoreum* of the Romans, a species of grain
resembling wheat with shorn ears: Ezek. iv. 9, *marg.*
'or, spelt.'

קֶצַח *m.* black cumin, *nigella melanthium,* according to the LXX.,

Vulg., and the Rabbins. See Celsii Hierobot. P. II.
p. 70, Isa. xxviii. 25, 27, 27.

FIX

כּוּן to set right. NIPHAL *part.* Ps. lvii. 7, *marg.* 'or, prepared ;' 7; cviii. 1; cxii. 7.

FLAG

אָחוּ *m.* a flag, which grows in moist places; a flaggy sort of
grass, growing near the river Nile, very grateful to
cattle, and very proper for fattening them: Cels. Hierob. P. I. p. 355, Job viii. 11; see *Meadow.*

סוּף *m.* a weed, which grows in the Red Sea, and gives it its
name: Exod. ii. 3, 5: Isa. xix. 6.

FLAGON

אֲשִׁישָׁה *f.* a vessel for holding wine; the LXX. have translated the
word πέμματα, according to Jerome, *placentœ,* a cake or
hardened syrup made of grapes: in Hos. iii. 1, mentioned
in reference to idol-worship, but in other places as a
refreshment; Cant. ii. 5, particularly on a journey;
2 Sam. vi. 19, 1 Chron. xvi. 3.

נֵבֶל *m.* a bottle; also an instrument of music; see *Viol:* Isa.
xxii. 24, *marg.* 'or, instruments of viols.'

FLAKES

מַפָּל *m.* those parts of an animal which usually fall or hang
down: Job xli. 23, *marg.* 'fallings.'

FLAME

1 אֵשׁ *com.* fire; "flaming," *lit.* with fire of. a אֶשָּׁא *f. emph.* Ch.

2 כָּלִיל *adj.* denoting universality, all, the whole, &c.: Judg. xx.
40, *marg.* 'the whole consumption,' i. e. the whole of the
city ascended up in a flame to heaven.

3 לַבָּה *f.* a contraction of לֶהָבָה.

4 לַהַב *m.* a flame as it rises to a point. a לֶהָבָה *f. id.*

5 לָהַט to burn with the vehement heat of a strong penetrating
flame, of angels as the executioners of God's vengeance.
KAL a *part.* Poel. b לַהַט *m.* flame, resembling a sword,
guarding the tree of life. c שַׁלְהֶבֶת *f.* flame, Cant.
viii. 6. שַׁלְהֶבֶתְיָה *lit.* flame of Jehovah, or lightning,
a most vehement flame.

6 מַשְׂאֵת *f.* a lifting up; smoke or flame which rises up.

7 שְׁבִיב Ch. *m.* flame.

Gen. iii. 24.	5 b	Ps. cvi. 18.	4 a	Lam. ii. 3.	4 a	
Exod. iii. 2.	3	Cant. viii. 6.	5 c	Ezek. xx. 47, 47.	4 a, 5 c	
Num. xxi. 28.	4 a	Isa. iv. 5.	4 a	Dan. iii. 22.	7	
Judg. xiii. 20, 20.	4	v. 24.	4 a	vii. 9.	7	
xx. 38.	6	x. 17.	4 a	vii. 11.	1 a	
xx. 40, 40.	6, 2	xiii. 8. a	4	xi. 33.	4 a	
Job xv. 30.	5 c	xxix. 6.	4	Hos. vii. 6.	4 a	
xli. 21.	4	xxx. 30.	4	Joel i. 19.	4 a	
Ps. xxix. 7.	4	xliii. 2.	4 a	ii. 3.	4 a	
lxxxiii. 14.	4 a	xlvii. 14.	4 a	ii. 5.	4	
civ. 4.	5 a	lxvi. 15.	4	Obad. 18.	4	
cv. 32.	4 a	Jer. xlviii. 45.	4 a	Nah. ii. 3.	1	

a *marg.* 'faces of the flames.'

FLANKS

כֶּסֶל *m.* the loins, the flanks: Lev. iii. 4, 10, 15; iv. 9; vii. 4:
Job xv. 27.

FLAT NOSE

חָרַם to shut up ; to shut in the nose, to have a flat nose. KAL *part*. Paül, Lev. xxi. 18.

FLATTER

1 חָלַק to smooth, to smooth the tongue or lips ; to flatter, to deceive. HIPHIL ᵃ *pret*. ᵇ *fut*. ᶜ *part*. ᵈ חָלָק *adj*. smooth, flattering, with deceit implied, Prov. xxvi. 28. ᵉ חֵלֶק *m*. smoothness, flattery ; portion of spoil ; portion : Job xvii. 5 ;—Gesenius, "who betrays his friends to the plunder." ᶠ חֶלְקָה *f*. smoothness, flattery. ᵍ חֲלַקּוֹת *f. pl.* flatteries. ʰ חֲלַקְלַקּוֹת *f. pl.* flatteries, blandishments.

2 כָּנָה to give titles of honour, either to those in real dignity, or by way of compliment and flattery. PIEL *fut*.

3 פָּתָה to be open ; to allure, coax, persuade by flattery, to deceive. KAL ᵃ *part*. Poel. PIEL ᵇ *fut*.

Job xvii. 5.		1 e	Prov. ii. 16.	1 a	Prov. xxviii. 23.	1 c
xxxii. 21, 22.		2	vi. 24.	1 f	xxix. 5.	1 c
Ps. v. 9.		1 b	vii. 5.	1 a	Ezek. xii. 24.	1 d
xii. 2, a 3. a		1 f	vii. 21.	1 e	Dan. xi. 21, 34.	1 h
xxxvi. 2.		1 a	xx. 19.	3 a	xi. 32.	1 g
lxxviii. 36.		3 b	xxvi. 28.	1 d		

a lit. lips of flatteries.

FLAX

פִּשְׁתָּה *f.* the common name of flax : Exod. ix. 31, 31 : Isa. xlii. 3. פֵּשֶׁת *m. id.* : Josh. ii. 6, *lit.* with flax of stalks : Judg. xv. 14 : Prov. xxxi. 13 : Isa. xix. 9 : Ezek. xl. 3 : Hos. ii. 5, 9.

FLAY

פָּשַׁט to put off ; to strip. HIPHIL *pret*. Lev. i. 6, Mic. iii. 3. *inf*. 2 Chron. xxix. 34. *part*. 2 Chron. xxxv. 11.

FLEA

פַּרְעשׁ *m.* a flea : 1 Sam. xxiv. 14 ; xxvi. 20.

FLEE, FLIGHT

1 בָּרַח to pass from one place to another ; to escape or get out of the way, implying swiftness and fear, as Jacob fled from Laban, Gen. xxxi. 22 ; David from Saul, 1 Sam. xix. 18, and on account of Absalom, 2 Sam. xv. 14 ; Moses from Pharaoh, Exod. ii. 15 ; Jonah from the presence of God, Jonah i. 3 ; as men flee to hide themselves, Dan. x. 7 ; as a shadow fleeth, Job xiv. 2. With *inf*., fain flee. KAL ᵃ *pret*. ᵇ *inf*. ᶜ *imp*. ᵈ *fut*. ᵉ *part*. Poel. HIPHIL ᶠ *fut*.

2 כָּסָה to cover ; to hide. PIEL *pret*.

3 נָדַד to shake, as birds their wings, to wander, to flee away. KAL ᵃ *pret*. ᵇ *fut*. ᶜ *part*. Poel. POAL ᵈ *pret*. HITHPOLEL ᵉ *fut*.

4 נוד *id.* KAL *imp*.

5 נוּס to flee swiftly, as upon swift horses : Isa. xxx. 16, " we will flee upon horses, therefore shall ye flee," where there is a play upon the double meaning of the word, to flee and to hasten ; it is synonymous with בָּרַח with which it is often joined, having the force of *elabi* in Latin, to make escape. It is used of soldiers fleeing when they have lost the victory, Gen. xiv. 10, Judg. iv.

17, 1 Sam. iv. 17, 2 Sam. i. 4 ;—of those who prudently avoid impending danger, as David, 1 Sam. xix. 10 ;—of the man-slayer, who flees to a city of refuge, Num. xxxv. 11, 25, Deut. iv. 42 ;—of those who flee from some groundless fear, as by panic, Prov. xxviii. 1, Lev. xxvi. 17. It is applied also to inanimate things. It is followed by מִפְּנֵי, מִן, לִפְנֵי, and once with לְ, Num. xvi. 34 ; of the place with אֶל, לְ, and the *acc*. with ה local ; with עַל of the person. With the *inf*., flee away. KAL ᵃ *pret*. ᵇ *inf*. ᶜ *imp*. ᵈ *fut*. ᵉ *part*. HIPHIL ᶠ *pret*. ᵍ *fut*. ʰ מָנוֹס *m*. flight. ᶦ מְנוּסָה *f. id*.

6 נוץ to flee, to wander about in flight. KAL *pret*.

7 נָצָא to flee away, as with wings. KAL *inf*.

8 עוּף to fly. KAL *fut*.

9 עָרַק to flee. KAL *part*. Poel, Job xxx. 3. Such is the usual interpretation of the word. The Syriac and Arabic render it, "gnawing," which is followed by most modern critics ; *i. e.* gnawing roots and herbs in the deserts. "But the verb is used by Onkelos, Gen. xvi. 6, 'she fled.' So too here Lxx. and Vulg. *fugientes*, which sense is more suited to the context which follows."—*Churton.*

10 רָדַף to pursue. KAL *fut*.

Gen. xiv. 10, 10.	5 d a	1 Sam. xix. 8.	5 d	2 Chron. xxv. 22, 27.	5 d
xvi. 6.	1 d	xix. 10.	5 a	Neh. vi. 11.	1 d
xvi. 8.	1 e	xix. 12.	1 d	xiii. 10.	1 d
xix. 20.	5 b	xix. 18.	1 a	Job ix. 25.	1 a
xxvii. 43.	1 c	xx. 1.	1 d	xiv. 2.	1 d
xxxi. 20.	1 e	xxi. 10.	1 d	xx. 24.	1 d
xxxi. 21.	1 d	xxii. 17.	1 d	xxvii. 22.	1 b d
xxxi. 22.	1 a	xxii. 20.	1 d	xxx. 3.	9
xxxi. 27.	1 b	xxiii. 6.	1 b	xli. 28.	1 f
xxxix. 12, 13, 15, 18.	5 d	xxvii. 4.	1 a	Ps. iii. title.	1 b
Exod. ii. 15.	1 d	xxx. 17.	5 d	xi. 1.	4
iv. 3.	1 d	xxxi. 1.	5 d	xxxi. 11.	3 a
ix. 20.	5 f	xxxi. 7, 7.	5 a d	lvii. title.	1 b
xiv. 5.	1 a	2 Sam. i. 4.	5 a	lxiv. 8.	3 d
xiv. 25.	5 d	iv. 3.	1 d	lxviii. 1.	3 d
xiv. 27.	5 e	iv. 4, 4.	5 d b	lxviii. 12. β	3 b
xxi. 13.	5 d	x. 13, 18.	5 d	civ. 7.	5 d
Lev. xxvi. 8.	10	x. 14, 14.	5 a d	cxiv. 3, 5.	5 d
xxvi. 17.	5 a	xiii. 29.	5 d	cxxxix. 7.	1 d
xxvi. 36, 36.	5 a h	xiii. 34.	5 d	cxliii. 9. γ	2
Num. x. 35.	5 a	xiii. 37, 38.	1 a	Prov. xxviii. 1.	5 a
xvi. 34.	5 a	xv. 14.	1 d	xxviii. 17.	5 a
xxiv. 11.	1 c	xvii. 2.	5 a	Cant. ii. 17.	5 a
xxxv. 6, a 15, 32. a	5 b	xviii. 3.	5 d b	iv. 6.	5 a
xxxv. 11, 25.	5 a	xviii. 17.	5 a	Isa. x. 3.	5 d
xxxv. 26.	5 d	xix. 3.	5 b	x. 29.	5 d
Deut. iv. 42, 42.	5 b a	xix. 8.	5 a	xiii. 14.	5 d
xix. 3.	5 b	xix. 9.	1 a	xvii. 13.	5 a
xix. 4, 5.	5 d	xxiii. 11.	5 a	xx. 6.	5 a
xix. 11.	5 a	1 Kings ii. 7.	1 b	xxi. 14.	3 c
xxviii. 7, 25.	5 a	ii. 28.	5 d	xxi. 15.	3 a
xxxii. 30.	5 a	ii. 29.	5 a	xxii. 3, 3.	3 a, 1 a
Josh. vii. 4.	5 a	xi. 17, 40.	1 d	xxiv. 18.	1 e
viii. 5.	5 a	xi. 23.	1 a	xxx. 16, 16, 17.	5 a
viii. 6, 6.	5 e a	xii. 2.	1 a	xxxi. 8.	5 a
viii. 15.	5 d	xii. 18.	5 b	xxxiii. 3.	3 a
viii. 20, 20.	5 b e	xx. 20.	5 d	xxxv. 10.	5 a
x. 11.	5 b	xx. 30, 30.	5 d a	xlviii. 20.	1 c
x. 16.	5 d	2 Kings iii. 24.	5 d	li. 11.	5 a
xx. 3, 9.	5 b	vii. 7, 7.	5 d	lii. 12.	5 h
xx. 4, 6.	5 d	viii. 21.	5 d	Jer. iv. 25.	3 a
Judg. i. 6.	5 d	ix. 3.	5 d	iv. 29.	1 e
iv. 15.	5 d	ix. 10, 23, 27, 27.	5 d	ix. 10.	3 a
iv. 17.	5 a	xiv. 12, 19.	5 d	xxv. 35.	5 h
vii. 21, 22.	5 d	1 Chron. x. 1.	5 d	xxvi. 21.	1 d
viii. 12.	5 d	x. 7, 7.	5 a d	xxxix. 4.	5 d
ix. 21.	1 d	xi. 13.	5 a	xlvi. 5.	5 a h
ix. 40, 51.	5 d	xii. 15.	1 f	xlvi. 21.	5 a
xi. 3.	1 d	xix. 14, 18.	5 d	xlviii. 6.	5 c
xx. 32, 45, 47.	5 d	xix. 15, 15.	5 a d	xlviii. 9.	7
1 Sam. iv. 10.	5 d	2 Chron. x. 2.	1 a	xlviii. 19, 45.	5 e
iv. 16, 17.	5 a	x. 18.	5 d	xlviii. 44.	5 e
xiv. 22.	5 a	xiii. 16.	5 d	xlix. 8, 30.	5 e
xvii. 24, 51.	5 d	xiv. 12.	5 d	xlix. 24.	5 b

Jer. l. 16.	5 d	Amos ii. 14.	5 h	Jonah iv. 2. δ	1 b
l. 28.	5 e	ii. 16.	5 d	Nah. ii. 8.	5 e
li. 6.	5 c	v. 19.	5 d	iii. 7.	3 b
lii. 7.	1 d	vii. 12.	1 c	iii. 16.	8
Lam. iv. 15.	6	ix. 1, 1.	5 e d	iii. 17.	3 d
Dan. x. 7.	1 d	Jonah i. 3.	1 b	Zech. ii. 6.	5 c
Hos. vii. 13.	3 a	i. 10.	1 e	xiv. 5, 5, 5.	5 a
xii. 12.	1 d				

α *lit.* for fleeing.   β *lit.* did flee, did flee.   γ *lit.* I hide me with thee.
δ *lit.* I was beforehand to flee. See *Prevent.*

FLEECE

גֵּז *m.* wool shorn off, a fleece: Deut. xviii. 4: Job xxxi. 20. גִּזָּה *f.* Judg. vi. 37, 37, 38, 38, 39, 39, 40.

FLESH

בָּשָׂר *m.* flesh, the soft muscular substance which is spread over the bones, blood-vessels, and nerves of the animal body; as differing from שְׁאֵר, it may imply flesh with all its qualities and appetites, its weakness and corruption by sin. It is put for that which is wholly carnal and sensual, of those given up to fleshly appetites and passions, Gen. vi. 3; "all flesh," all living creatures, but more especially, all men. It is used of consanguinity; "my bone and my flesh," a near relative; of the whole body, *opp.* נֶפֶשׁ; and also of the flesh of animals as meat, Exod. xvi. 12.—Gen. ii. 21, &c.: Ch. *m. id.* Dan. ii. 11; iv. 12; vii. 5.

טִבְחָה *f.* flesh of a beast slain, a feast on it: 1 Sam. xxv. 11.

לְחוּם *m.* meat: Zeph. i. 17, the flesh of sinners, so called in a passive sense, with respect to its corruptibility; or its being exposed, being fit only to be devoured by beasts and fowls.

שְׁאֵר *m* flesh, *pr.* remainder, as we say, remains of a mere body; (Forster: *quæ est reliqua pars animalis post animam*), simply flesh independent of connexion with the mind; it is used, however, of flesh for food, as well as of flesh of consanguinity, and implies flesh with its moisture as necessary to vitality: Ps. lxxiii. 26; lxxviii. 20, 27: Prov. xi. 17: Jer. li. 35: Micah iii. 2, 3.

FLINT

חַלָּמִישׁ *m.* a hard rock or stone: Deut. viii. 15; xxxii. 13: Ps. cxiv. 8: Isa. l. 7.

צֹר *m.* a rock: Ezek. iii. 9. צֹר *m.* a stone, pebble, flint: Isa. v. 28.

FLOATS

דֹּבְרוֹת *f. pl.* floats or rafts, from their being impelled or driven along: 1 Kings v. 9.

FLOCK

1 חָשֹׂף *m.* used of a flock of kids: 1 Kings xx. 27; Lxx., δύο ποίμνια αἰγῶν; Vulg., *duo parvi greges caprarum.* So also the Chaldaic Interpreter, Kimchi, and other Jewish commentators; perhaps so named as a flock, because it is naked, not folded; or because it leaves the ground uncovered in comparison with the Syrians who filled the land; or so called from being cut off, separated.

2 עֵדֶר *m.* a drove, proceeding in orderly direction; or flock feeding together, and moving as they do in one direction.

3 עַשְׁתְּרוֹת *f. pl.* flocks, as of sheep.

4 צֹאן *com.* a collective noun denoting small cattle, *i.e.* sheep and goats (the μῆλα of Homer), particularly sheep. The corresponding *nomen unitatis,* or noun expressing an individual, is שֶׂה. See Exod. xxii. 1, Ezek. xlv. 15. Sometimes goats are separately mentioned, and then צֹאן denotes sheep: 1 Sam. xxv. 2.—Gen. iv. 4, &c.

5 מִקְנֶה *m.* see *Cattle;* "flocks," *lit.* cattle of the sheep.

6 מַרְעִית *f.* pasturing, a flock.

No. 4 not included.

Gen. xxix. 2, 2, 3, 8.	2	Ps. lxxviii. 48.	5	Jer. xiii. 20, 20.	2, 4
xxx. 40, 40, 40.	4, 4, 2	lxxviii. 52.	2	xxxi. 10, 24.	2
xlvii. 17.	5, 4	Cant. i. 7.	2	li. 23.	2
Num. xxxi. 9.	5	iv. 1, 2.	2	Ezek. xxxiv. 12.	2
xxxii. 26.	5	vi. 5, 6.	2	Joel i. 18.	2
Deut. vii. 13.	3	Isa. xvii. 2.	2	Micah ii. 12.	2
xxviii. 4, 18, 51.	3	xxxii. 14.	2	iv. 8.	2
Judg. v. 16.	2	xl. 11.	2	v. 8.	2
1 Sam. xvii. 34.	2	Jer. vi. 3.	2	Zeph. ii. 14.	2
1 Kings xx. 27.	1	x. 21.	6	Zech. x. 3.	2
2 Chron. xxxii. 28.	2	xiii. 17.	2	Mal. i. 14.	2
Job xxiv. 2.	2				

FLOOD

1 זֶרֶם to flow, to pour out; with an *accus.* to overflow, to carry away as with a flood. KAL [a] *pret.* [b] זֶרֶם *m.* a shower, storm of rain.

2 יְאוֹר *m.* a river, specially the Nile; a flood. See *River.*

3 מַבּוּל *m.* a flood, from יָבַל to flow. This word is limited to the general deluge. Gr. κατακλυσμός.

4 נָהָר *m.* a stream, river, specially the Euphrates; it is also used of the currents of the sea: Jonah ii. 3: Ps. xciii. 3.

5 נָזַל to flow down, by the natural tendency of waters to do so; hence in the *part.* denoting streams. KAL *part.* Poel.

6 נַחַל *m.* a valley, brook, river: Job xxviii. 4. Gesenius, shaft or pit in a mine; rather an horizontal shaft, like a torrent valley.

7 שִׁבֹּלֶת *f.* a large and copious stream, a flood.

8 שֶׁטֶף *m.* an overflowing stream, like an inundation.

Gen. vi. 17.	3	Ps. xviii. 4.	6	Isa. xxviii. 2.	1 b
vii. 6, 7, 10, 17.	3	xxiv. 2.	4	xliv. 3.	5
ix. 11, 11, 15, 28.	3	xxix. 10.	3	lix. 19.	4
x. 1, 32.	3	xxxii. 6.	8	Jer. xlvi. 7, 8.	2
xi. 10.	3	lxvi. 6.	4	xlvii. 2.	6
Exod. xv. 8.	5	lxix. 2, 15.	7	Ezek. xxxi. 15.	6
Josh. xxiv. 2, 3, 14, 15.	4	lxxiv. 15.	6	Dan. ix. 26.	8
2 Sam. xxii. 5.	6	lxxviii. 44.	5	xi. 22.	8
Job xiv. 11.	4	xc. 5.	1 a	Amos viii. 8, 8.	2
xx. 17.	4	xciii. 3, 3, 3.	4	ix. 5, 5.	2
xxii. 16.	4	xcviii. 8.	4	Jonah ii. 3.	4
xxviii. 4.	6	Cant. viii. 7.	4	Nah. i. 8.	8
xxviii. 11.	3				

FLOOR

גֹּרֶן *m.* see *Threshing-floor:* Gen. l. 11: Deut. xv. 14: Judg. vi. 37: Ruth iii. 3, 6, 14: Isa. xxi. 10: Hos. ix. 1, 2; xiii. 3: Joel ii. 24: Micah iv. 12.

קַרְקַע *m.* ground, bottom; the floor or pavement of the temple: Num. v. 17: 1 Kings vi. 15, 15, 16, 30; vii. 7.

קָרָה see *Beams.* PIEL *inf.* 2 Chron. xxxiv. 11.

FLOTES

רַפְסֹדוֹת *f. pl.* floats or rafts, several pieces of timber fixed together : 2 Chron. ii. 16.

FLOUR

בָּצֵק *m.* see *Dough :* 2 Sam. xiii. 8, *marg.* 'or, paste.'

סֹלֶת *com.* meal, flour, fine flour : Exod. xxix. 2, 40, &c.

קֶמַח *m.* flour, boiled meal : Judg. vi. 19 : 1 Sam. i. 24 ; xxviii. 24 : 2 Sam. xvii. 28.

FLOURISH

1   נוץ to put forth flowers or blossoms. HIPHIL *fut.* "The almond tree is used as a symbol of that watchfulness with which old age is visited. Jer. i. 11 may be used as a commentary on this verse."—*Hengstenberg.*

2   פָּרַח to sprout, to blossom ; to be vigorous and strong. KAL ᵃ *pret.* ᵇ *fut.* HIPHIL ᶜ *pret.* ᵈ *fut.*

3   צוּץ to shine, hence to flourish ; words of shining are made to signify verdure and blossoming. Ps. cxxxii. 18 may be understood in the primary sense, 'shall be conspicuous,' or be bright like the high priest's frontlet, called צִיץ from its brightness. HIPHIL *fut.*

4   רַעֲנָן *adj.* green, flourishing. ᵃ רַעֲנַן Ch. *adj.* flourishing, of a person.

Ps. lxxii. 7.	2 b	Ps. xcii. 14.	4	Cant. vi. 11.	2 a
lxxii. 16.	3	ciii. 15.	3	vii. 12.	2 a
xc. 6.	3	cxxxii. 18.	3	Isa. xvii. 11.	2 d
xcii. 7.	3	Prov. xi. 28.	2 b	lxvi. 14.	2 b
xcii. 12.	2 b	xiv. 11.	2 d	Ezek. xvii. 24.	2 c
xcii. 13.	2 d	Eccles. xii. 5.	1	Dan. iv. 4.	4 a

FLOW

1   זוּב to flow (see *Gush*) ; also spoken of the person or place, in, on, or from which anything flows ; as a land flowing with milk and honey. KAL *part.* Poel, Jer. xlix. 4, *or,* thy valley floweth away (see *Pine*), or flows (with blood).

2   יָלַךְ to go. KAL *fut.*

3   נָבַע to flow and bubble as water out of a spring. KAL *part.* Poel.

4   נָגַר to flow ; Niphal, to be poured out, or drained off. NIPHAL *part.*

5   נָהַר to flow as waters in a full large river. KAL ᵃ *pret.* ᵇ *fut.*

6   נָזַל to flow down, as a flood or stream. KAL ᵃ *pret.* ᵇ *fut.* ᶜ *part.* Poel. HIPHIL ᵈ *pret.* Some deduce Isa. lxiv. 1, 3, from זָלַל to shake or be agitated. NIPHAL *pret.*

7   צוּף to flow or glide along as water, to overflow. KAL *pret.*

8   שָׁטַף to overflow with a violent stream, as an inundation. KAL *part.* Poel.

Exod. iii. 8, 17.	1	Deut. xxxi. 20.	1	Isa. lxvi. 12.	8
xiii. 5.	1	Josh. iv. 18.	2	Jer. xi. 5.	1
xxxiii. 3.	1	v. 6.	1	xviii. 14.	6 c
Lev. xx. 24.	1	Job xx. 28.	4	xxxi. 12.	5 a
Num. xiii. 27.	1	Ps. cxlvii. 18.	6 b	xxxii. 22.	1
xiv. 8.	1	Prov. xviii. 4.	3	xlix. 4.	1
xvi. 13, 14.	1	Cant. iv. 16.	6 b	li. 44.	5 b
Deut. vi. 3.	1	Isa. ii. 2.	5 a	Lam. iii. 54.	7
xi. 9.	1	xlviii. 21.	5	Ezek. xx. 6, 15.	1
xxvi. 9, 15.	1	lx. 5.	5 a	Joel iii. 18, 18.	2
xxvii. 3.	1	lxiv. 1, 3.	6 a	Micah iv. 1.	5 a

FLOWER

מִגְדָּל *m.* a tower ; Cant. v. 13, sweet flowers, *marg.* 'towers of perfumes, *or,* beds of spices.'

נִדָּה *f.* separation, menstrual uncleanness : Lev. xv. 24, 33.

נִצָּה *f.* a blossom, flower : Job xv. 33 : Isa. xviii. 5. נִצָּן *m.* a flower : Cant. ii. 12.

פֶּרַח *m.* a blossom ; also an artificial ornament : Exod. xxv. 31, 33, 33, 34 ; xxxvii. 17, 19, 19, 20 : Num. viii. 4 : 1 Kings vii. 26, 49 : 2 Chron. iv. 5, 21 ; Nah. i. 4.

צִיץ *m.* blossom, from its shining, bright appearance ; see *Flourish :* 1 Kings vi. 18, 29, 32, 35 ; Job xiv. 2 : Ps. ciii. 15 : Isa. xxviii. 1 ; xl. 6, 7, 8. צִיצָה *f.* Isa. xxviii. 4. The beauty and appropriateness of the ideal meaning of the word in all these passages is very striking.

FLUTE

מַשְׁרוֹקִיתָא Ch. *f.* a pipe, reed, flute ; from שָׁרַק to hiss, to pipe : Dan. iii. 5, 7, 10, 15.

FLUTTER

רָחַף to shake ; to hover, flutter, as an eagle over her young. PIEL *fut.* Deut. xxxii. 11.

FLY

זְבוּב *m.* fly, gadfly. Egypt abounded with flies, especially the œstri, whose distant hum is said to strike beasts with consternation, and whose bite inflicts on man and beast a torment almost insupportable. The forces of Egypt are compared to this fly for numbers and destructive effects. The idol-god of Ekron is called Baal-zebub, Lord of the fly, to whom was attributed their protection from it. This name was afterwards used as a title of the prince of evil spirits : Matt. x. 25 ; xii. 24.——Eccles. x. 1 : Isa. vii. 8. See Carpzovii Apparatus Criticus Antiq. Heb. p. 497. See Bruce's Travels for a description of the Zimb, vol. i. p. 5, v. 191.

עָרֹב (see *Swarms*), the dog-fly, which penetrates the skin and draws the blood, exceedingly troublesome and painful ; Lxx. κυνόμυια, Aqu. παμμυία. Jerome, *omne genus muscarum* (probably deriving it from עָרַב to mix). But that עָרֹב is not a general term, but the name of a definite species, is evident from Exod. viii. 29, 31 ; "divers sorts of flies," Ps. lxxviii. 45 ; cv. 31.

FLY   (See also FLEE)

1   אָבַר to mount upward. HIPHIL *fut.*

2   דָּאָה to fly, as the eagle, or bird of prey ; it is used also of the Deity, intimating his swiftness in helping the poor, and his sudden attack on their enemies. KAL *fut.*

3   יָעַף to run swiftly. HOPHAL *part.*

4   כָּנָף *com.* wing : Ps. cxlviii. 10, *marg.* 'birds of wing.'

5   עוּף to fly, as a bird ; used also of an arrow, of God's swift help ; to fly away, as a dream, as human life, as an army ; to fly upon, to fly to. KAL ᵃ *pret.* ᵇ *inf.* ᶜ *fut.* ᵈ *part.* Poel. POLEL ᵉ *fut.* ᶠ *part.* HIPHIL ᵍ *inf.* כְּתִיב. HITHPOLEL ʰ *fut.* עוֹף *m.* fowl ; applied also to reptiles.

6   עִיט to fall on or attack in a fierce and ravenous manner. KAL *fut.*

7 עָשָׂה to do, make, &c. KAL *fut.* I Sam. xiv. 32, כתיב.

8 פָּרַח to sprout ; also to fly, as in other synonymous words. KAL *part.* Poel.

Gen. i. 20. a	5 e	Ps. xviii. 10, 10.	5 c, 2	Isa. xxx. 6.		5 f
Lev. xi. 21, 23.	5 i	lv. 6.	5 c	xxxi. 5.		5 d
Deut. iv. 17.	5 c	xc. 10.	5 c	lx. 8.		5 c
xiv. 19.	5 i	xci 5.	5 c	Jer. xlviii. 40.		2
xxviii. 49.	2	cxlviii. 10.	4	xlix. 22.		2
1 Sam. xiv. 32.	6 or 7	Prov. xxiii.5.	5 c, or 5 g	Ezek. xiii. 20, 20.		8
xv. 19.	6	xxvi. 2.	5 b	Dan. ix. 21.		3
2 Sam. xxii. 11.	5 c	Isa. vi. 2.	5 e	Hos. ix. 11.		5 h
Job v. 7.	5 b	vi. 6.	5 c	Hab. i. 8.		5 c
xx. 8.	5 c	xi. 14.	5 a	Zech. v. 1, 2.		5 d
xxxix. 26.	1	xiv. 29.	5 f			

a lit. let fowl fly.

FOAL

בֵּן *m.* son: Zech. ix. 9.

עַיִר *m.* a young ass, an ass's colt: Gen. xxxii. 15 ; xlix. 11.

FOAM

קֶצֶף *m.* foam; anger, wrath: Hos. x. 7. Lxx., however, has φρύγανον, which Gesenius follows, and renders it, chips, twigs, splinters.

FODDER

בְּלִיל *m.* mingled provender: Job vi. 5.

FOE

אֹיֵב see *Enemy.* KAL *part.* Poel, Ps. xxvii. 2 ; xxx. 1.

צַר and צָר *m.* an enemy, that afflicts or oppresses: 1 Chron. xxi. 12 : Ps. lxxxix. 23.

שָׂנֵא to hate. KAL *part.* Poel, Esth. ix. 16.

FOLD

גְּדֵרָה *f.* a wall ; more frequently, a place surrounded by a wall, into which the shepherds drove their flocks by night for security against wild animals: Num. xxxii. 16, 24, 36 : Zeph. ii. 6.

דֹּבֶר *m.* a fold, pasture : Micah ii. 12.

מִכְלָה *f.* a pen, fold, to confine sheep : Ps. l. 9 ; lxxviii. 70 : Hab. iii. 17.

נָוֶה *m.* see *Habitation:* Isa. lxv. 10 : Jer. xxiii. 3 : Ezek. xxxiv. 14, 14.

רָבַץ to lie down as beasts when resting themselves ; to make their fold. HIPHIL *fut.* Isa. xiii. 20.

FOLD

גָּלִיל *adj.* turning, folding : 1 Kings vi. 34, 34.

חָבַק to embrace, to fold the arms. KAL *part.* Poel, Eccles. iv. 5. חִבֻּק *m.* a folding : Prov. vi. 10 ; xxiv. 33.

סָבַךְ to interweave, fold together. KAL *part.* Paül, Nah. i. 10.

FOLK

עַם *com.* people, nations, community : Gen. xxxiii. 15 : Prov. xxx. 26.

לְאֹם *m.* people, nation : poetic Jer. li. 58.

FOLLOW

1 אַחַר *m.* after ; as an adverb it goes with many verbs translated follow ; as a *prep.* also rendered follow, following, &c. אַחֵר *adj.* אַחֲרוֹן *adj.*

2 בּוֹא to come, to follow, *lit.* to go after. KAL *fut.* *part.* Poel.

3 דָּבַק to adhere, to follow close ; see *Cleave.* KAL *pret.* *fut.* HIPHIL *pret.* *fut.*

4 הָלַךְ to walk (after). KAL *pret.* *part.* Poel. HITHPAEL *part.*

5 יָלַךְ to go (after). KAL *inf.* *imp.* *fut.*

6 יָצָא to go out (after). KAL *fut.*

7 מָלֵא to fill, fulfil ; to follow, *lit.* to fulfil after, to show full obedience. PIEL *pret.* *fut.*

8 עָשָׂה to do ; "not followed," *marg.* 'not done.' NIPHAL *pret.*

9 רֶגֶל *f.* foot ; to follow, *lit.* to be, to walk, at the feet of.

10 רָדַף to run or follow after, to pursue. KAL *pret.* *inf.* *imp.* *fut.* *part.* Poel. *pret.* *part.*

Gen. xxiv. 5, 8.	5 a, 1	1 Sam. xv. 11.	1	2 Kings xvii. 21.	1
xxiv. 39, 61.	5 c, 1	xvii. 13, 14.	4 a, 1	xviii. 6.	1
xxxii. 19.	4 b, 1	xxiv. 1.	1	1 Chron. x. 2.	3 d
xli. 31.	1	xxv. 27.β	4 c, 9	xvii. 7.	1
xliv. 4.	10 c	xxx. 21.	5 a	2 Chron. xxiii. 14.	2 b, 1
Exod. xi. 8.	9	xxxi. 2.	1	xxv. 27.	1
xiv. 4.	10 a	2 Sam. i. 6.	3 c	xxxiv. 33.	1
xiv. 17.	2 a, 1	ii. 19, 21, 22, 26, 27,		Neh. ix. 23.	1
xxiii. 2.		30.		Ps. xxiii. 6.	10 d
Num. xiv. 24.	7 b, 1	iii. 31.	4 b, 1	xxxviii. 20.	10 b
xvi. 25.	5 c, 1	vii. 8.	1	xlv. 14.	1
xxxii. 11.	7 a, 1	xi. 8.	1	xlviii. 13.	1 b
xxxii. 12.	7 a, 1	xvii. 9.	6, 1	lxiii. 8.	3 a
Deut. i. 36. a	7 a, 1	xvii. 23.	8	lxxviii. 71.	1
iv. 3.	3 a, 1	xx. 2.	1	xciv. 15.	1
vii. 4.	1	1 Kings i. 7.	1	cix. 13.	1
xii. 30.	1	ix. 6.	1	cxix. 150.	10 e
xvi. 20.	10 d	xii. 20.	1	Prov. xii. 11.	10 g
Josh. vi. 8.	4 b, 1	xiv. 8.	4 a, 1	xv. 9.	10 g
xiv. 8, 9, 14.	7 a, 1	xvi. 21,γ 21, 22, 22.	1	xxi. 21.	10 g
xxii. 16, 18, 23, 29.	1	xviii. 18.	5 c, 1	xxviii. 19.	10 g
Judg. ii. 12.	5 c, 1	xviii. 21, 21.	5 b, 1	Isa. i. 23.	10 e
ii. 19.	5 c, 1	xix. 20.	5 c, 1	v. 11.	10 d
iii. 28.	10 c	xix. 20.	1	li. 1.	10 e
viii. 5.	9	xx. 19.	1	Jer. xvii. 16.	1
ix. 3.	1	xxi. 26.	5 a, 1	xlii. 16.	3 b
ix. 4, 49.	5 c, 1	2 Kings iii. 9.	9	Ezek. x. 11.	5 c, 1
Ruth i. 16.	1	iv. 30.	5 c, 1	xiii. 3.	4 b, 1
iii. 10.	5 a, 1	v. 21.	10 d	Hos. ii. 7.	10 f
1 Sam. xii. 14.	1	vi. 19.	5 b, 1	vi. 3.	10 d
xii. 20.	1	ix. 27.	1	xii. 1.	10 e
xiii. 7.	1	xi. 15.	2 b, 1	Amos vii. 15.	1
xiv. 22.	3 d	xiii. 2.	1		
xiv. 46.	1	xvii. 15.	5 c, 1		

a marg. 'fulfilled to go after.'   β marg. 'walked at the feet of.'
γ lit. were after.

FOOD

1 אָכַל to eat. KAL *inf.* אֹכֶל food, particularly grain, produce of the field. אָכְלָה *f. id.* מַאֲכָל *m. id.* מַכֹּלֶת *f. id.*

2 בּוּל *m.* produce.

3 לֶחֶם *m.* bread, any kind of food for men or animals.

4 צַיִד *m.* venison ; prey, booty.

5 שְׁאָר *m.* a portion of meat reserved or set apart for a particular person : Exod. xxi. 10, *i.e.* the share of food that should be reserved for her.

Gen. ii. 9.	1 d	Lev. xix. 23.	1 d	Ps. civ. 14.	3
iii. 6.	1 d	xxii. 7.	3	cxxxvi. 25.	3
vi. 21, 21.	1 d c	Deut. x. 18.	3	cxlvi. 7.	3
xli. 35, 35, 36, 48,		1 Sam. xiv. 24, 24, 28.	3	cxlvii. 9.	3
48, 48.	1 b	2 Sam. ix. 10.	3	Prov. vi. 8.	1 d
xlii. 7, 10.	1 b	1 Kings v. 9.	3	xiii. 23.	1 b
xliii. 2, 4, 20, 22.	1 b	v. 11.	1 e	xxvii. 27, 27.	3
xliv. 1, 25.	1 b	Job xxiv. 5.		xxviii. 3.	3
xlvii. 24, 24.	1 b a	xxxviii. 41.	4	xxx. 8.	3
Exod. xxi. 10.	5	xl. 20.	3	xxx. 14.	3
Lev. iii. 11, 16.	3	Ps. lxxviii. 25.	3	Ezek. xlviii. 18.	3

FOOL, FOOLISHNESS, FOLLY

1 אָוַל an obsolete root, which is supposed to imply weakness, and, applied to the mind, to include also confidence, fond expectation ; hence the notion of folly. A fool is

one who is not prudent or provident, without aim or counsel, regardless of the means or instruments he should use, most ready to form rash hopes, who carelessly commits everything to an uncertain issue ; opposed to one who walks uprightly, or straight forward ; is easily provoked, Job v. 3. Caryl on Job v. 3 has quaintly defined a fool to be one " who acts without counsel, and whose will is too hard for his understanding ; he hath no reason for what he doth, but because he hath a mind to do it." כְּסִיל a fool, to whom אִוֶּלֶת is always in Prov. assigned, is one who is not delighted with תְּבוּנָה understanding, Prov. xviii. 2 ; who trusts in his own heart or mind, xxviii. 26, xiv. 16 ; to whom confidence and a fond expectation of some good are so peculiar, that from it he receives his especial designation ; opposed to a prudent man, Prov. xii.16 ; and to a wise man, x. 14 ; it involves the charge of impiety, Job v. 3 ; but not so much as נָבָל: it is identified with sin, Ps. xxxviii. 5, lxix. 5. א אֱוִיל adj. a fool foolish. b אֱוִלִי adj. id. c אִוֶּלֶת f. folly.

2 בַּעַר m. brutish.

3 הָלַל to praise ; to boast oneself, to rave with foolish conceit ; madness. That the word is stronger than סִכְלוּת is evident from Eccles. x. 13. KAL a fut. b part. Poel. POEL c fut.

4 יָאַל to be willing, liable to impulse in mind and action ; to become foolish. NIPHAL pret.

5 כָּסַל to be fat ; applied in a good sense to strength, and in a bad sense to inertness and folly. KAL a pret. b כֶּסֶל m. the loins, the flanks ; hope, confidence ; foolishness (mostly in the Lxx. ἄφρων), stupidity ; as the loins and flanks are sometimes crowded with fat, Job xv. 27, and so attended with dull, inactive heaviness: Schultens on Prov. iii. 26, &c. The word unites with itself the idea of ungodliness or impiety, Ps. xlix. 13, Eccles. vii. 25. c כִּסְלָה f. folly. d כְּסִילוּת f. folly. e כְּסִיל m. a fool ; "obstinate in that on which he has set his heart, not to be moved by reason or counsel."—*Gussetius.*

6 נָבֵל to fade, wither ; to fall as withered fruit ; to act foolishly. KAL a pret. b נָבָל adj. stupid, foolish ; impious, abandoned, wicked. c נְבָלָה f. vice, villany, or what can be supposed in bad morals to be answerable to sapless, withered flowers, leaves, fruit.

7 סָכַל to act stupidly, absurdly, inconsistently ; to be sottish, infatuated : it denotes any deviation of the mind from what is true, good and right, wise and prudent. NIPHAL a pret. PIEL b imp. c fut. HIPHIL d pret. e סָכָל m. foolish. f סֶכֶל m. folly ; fools. g סִכְלוּת f. folly. h שִׂכְלוּת f. id.

8 פְּתִי adj. a silly, careless, ignorant, weak person, easily imposed upon ; see *Simple.*

9 תָּהֳלָה f. found only in Job iv. 18, a fault, error, defect ; Lxx. σκολιόν τι ; Vulg. *pravum quid* ; Syr. *stupor* ; Chald. *iniquitas.* So many interpreters take the meaning, but others derive it from הָלַל to shine, and render it " light," supposing it to imply perfection absolute and entire.

Job iv. 8, *marg.* ' or, nor in his angels, (in whom) he put light.'

10 תָּפֵל m. anything that is *indebite dispositum,* not rightly mixed, applied to unsavoury meats, untempered mortar, and indiscreet speeches ; in a moral or metaphorical sense, that which hath no salt of reason, righteousness, justice, or equity in it ; that which is done beside, without, or against all these. a תִּפְלָה f. unsavouriness, something silly, foolish, and even impious.

Gen. xxxi. 28.	7 d	Prov. i. 7.	1 a	Prov. xxvi. 1, 3, 6, 7,		
xxxiv. 7.	6 c	i. 22, 32.	5 e	8, 9, 10, 12.		5 e
Num. xii. 11.	4	iii. 35.	5 e	xxvi. 4, 4.		5 e, 1 c
Deut. xxii. 21.	6 c	v. 23.	1 c	xxvi. 5, 5.		5 e, 1 c
xxxii. 6, 21.	6 b	vii. 22.	1 a	xxvi. 11, 11.		5 e, 1 c
Josh. vii. 15.	6 c	viii. 5.	5 e	xxvii. 3.		1 a
Judg. xix. 23.	6 c	ix. 6.	8	xxvii. 22, 22.		1 a c
xx. 6, 10.	6 c	ix. 13.	5 d	xxviii. 26.		5 e
1 Sam. xiii. 13.	7 a	x. 1, 18, 23.	5 e	xxix. 9.		1 a
xxv. 25.	6 c	x. 8, 10, 14, 21.	1 a	xxix. 11, 20.		5 e
xxvi. 21.	7 d	xi. 29.	1 a	xxx. 22.		5 e
2 Sam. iii. 33.	6 b	xii. 15, 16.	1 a	xxx. 32.		6 a
xiii. 13.	6 c	xii. 23, 23.	5 e, 1 c	Eccles. i. 17.		7 h
xiii. 13.	6 b	xiii. 16, 16.	5 e, 1 c	ii. 3, 12, 13.		7 g
xv. 31.	7 b	xiii. 19, 20.	5 e	ii. 14, 15, 16, 16.		5 e
xxiv. 10.	7 a	xiv. 1, 17, a 18, 29.	1 c	ii. 19.		7 e
1 Chron. xxi. 8.	7 a	xiv. 3, 9.	1 a	iv. 5, 13.		5 e
2 Chron. xvi. 9.	6 c	xiv. 7, 16, 33.	5 e	v. 1, 3, 4.		5 e
Job i. 22.	10 a	xiv. 8.	1 a	vi. 8.		5 e
ii. 10.	6 b	xiv. 24, 24, 24.	1 c, 5 e, 1 c	vii. 4, 5, 6, 9.		5 e
iv. 18.	9	xv. 2, 2.	5 e, 1 c	vii. 17.		7 e
v. 2, 3.	1 a	xv. 5.	1 a	vii. 25, 25.		5 b, 7 g
xii. 17.	1 a	xv. 7, 20.	5 e	ix. 17.		5 e
xxiv. 12.	10 a	xv. 14, 14.	5 e, 1 c	x. 1, 13.		7 g
xxx. 8.	6 c	xv. 21.	1 c	x. 2, 12, 15.		5 e
xlii. 8.	6 c	xvi. 22, 22.	1 a c	x. 3, 3, 14.		7 e
Ps. v. 5.	3 b	xvii. 7.	5 e	x. 6.		7 f
xiv. 1.	6 b	xvii. 10, 16, 24,	5 e	Isa. ix. 17.		6 c
xxxviii. 5.	6 b	25.	5 e	xix. 11.		1 a
xxxix. 8.	6 b	xvii. 12, 12.	5 e, 1 c	xix. 13.		4
xlix. 10.	5 b	xvii. 21, 21.	5 e, 6 b	xxxv. 8.		1 a
xlix. 13.	5 b	xvii. 28.	1 a	xliv. 25.		7 c
liii. 1.	6 b	xviii. 2, 6, 7.	5 e	Jer. iv. 22.		1 a
lxix. 5.	1 c	xviii. 6, 7.	1 c	v. 4.		4
lxxiii. 3.	3 b	xix. 1, 10, 13, 29.	5 e	v. 21.		7 e
lxxiii. 22.	2	xix. 3.	1 c	v. 8.		5 a
lxxiv. 18, 22.	6 b	xx. 3.	1 a	xvii. 11.		6 b
lxxv. 4, 4.	3 b a	xxi. 20.	5 e	xviii. 13.		10 a
lxxxv. 8.	5 c	xxii. 15.	1 c	Lam. ii. 14.		10
xcii. 6.	5 e	xxiii. 9.	5 e	Ezek. xiii. 3.		6 b
xciv. 8.	5 e	xxiv. 7.	5 e	Hos. ix. 7.		1 a
cvii. 17.	1 a	xxiv. 9.	1 c	Zech. xi. 15.		1 b

a lit. will do foolishness.

FOOT, FOOTMAN, FOOTSTEP

1 אִישׁ m. man, with רַגְלִי footman.

2 כֵּן base, pedestal or foot, which is set firmly, fitly, and exactly, to support that which is set upon it in a true, upright, and steady position.

3 כַּף f. hand, sole of the foot : Deut. ii. 5, foot-breadth, *marg.* ' the treading of the sole of the foot.'

4 עָקֵב m. heel ; footstep.

5 פַּעַם com. an alternate stroke of the foot on the ground ; steps, footsteps, feet.

6 קַרְסֻלַּיִם dual, ankles.

7 רֶגֶל f. a foot ; feet are put for the legs, 1 Sam. xvii. 6 ; for the lower parts of the body, below the girdle, Gen. xlix. 10 : Isa. vi. 2 : Deut. xxviii. 57 : 2 Kings xviii. 27 : Isa. vii. 20. To cover the feet, to lie down to sleep in the heat of the day, Judg. iii. 24 : 1 Sam. xxiv. 3. See Patrick. To be at a person's feet, is to follow a leader, 2 Sam. xv. 18, Isa. xli. 2, "called to his foot," *i. e.* to follow, to act under his direction ; Deut. xxxiii. 3. "they sat down at," were attached to, "thy feet ;" to

follow thy guidance and directions : it is thus also applied to cattle at the owner's feet, under his management, care, and disposal; see *Follow, Possessions.* Hab. iii. 5, "went forth at his feet," *i. e.* followed him. To be under the feet, is to be in absolute subjection. To water with the foot, Deut. xi. 10, *i. e.* by transferring the water from one channel into another by the foot. In some cases, foot has obviously the sense of labour, as Isa. lviii. 13; xxxii. 20; and elsewhere equivalent to conduct, guidance, direction, 2 Sam. xv. 17: 2 Kings iii. 9: Gen. xxx. 30. We move upon the feet; hence, 1, the motions or course of life, Job xxiii. 11: Ps. cxix. 59, 101, 105: Prov. i. 15; iv. 26; v. 5;—2, actions, management, endeavours, Prov. xix. 2; xxvi. 6, "cutteth off the feet," rendereth his endeavours ineffectual, Isa. lviii. 13, "turn away thy foot," thy acting in ordinary employments and amusements, "from the sabbath ;" —3, the movements, affections, inclinations, dispositions of the mind, Job xxxi. 5 : Prov. vi. 18 : Eccles. v. 1: Isa. lii. 7, "how beautiful are the feet," the motions, the affections, and the speed, &c. We stand upon the feet, hence the standing, state, or condition of life which, when the feet stand unmoved, is prosperous, firm, secure, 1 Sam. ii. 9, Ps. xxvi. 12 ; when the feet slip or are moved, is in adversity or distress, Ps. xxxviii. 16; lxvi. 9.—Gen. viii. 9, &c. רְגַל [a] Ch. *com. id.* רַגְלִי [b] *m.* on foot, footmen ; with or without אִישׁ [c] מַרְגְּלוֹת *f. pl.* what is at one's feet.

8   רוּץ   to run. KAL *part.* "footmen," *marg.* 'runners, *or,* guard.'

No. 7 not included.

Exod. xii. 37.	7 b	1 Sam. xv. 4.	7 b	Ps. lviii. 10.	5
xxx. 18, 28.	2	xxii. 17.	8	lxxiv. 3.	5
xxxi. 9.	2	2 Sam. viii. 4.	1, 7 b	lxxvii. 19.	4
xxxv. 16.	2	x. 6.	1, 7 b	lxxxix. 51.	4
xxxviii. 8.	2	xxii. 37.	6	Prov. xxix. 5.	5
xxxix. 39.	2	1 Kings xx. 29.	7 b	Cant. i. 8.	4
xl. 11.	2	2 Kings xiii. 7.	7 b	vii. 1.	5
Lev. viii. 11.	2	xix. 24.	5	Isa. xxxvii. 25.	5
Num. xi. 21.	7 b	1 Chron. xviii. 4.	1, 7 b	Jer. xii. 5.	7 b
Deut. ii. 5.	3, 8	xix. 18.	1, 7 b	Dan. iii. 33, 34, 41, 42.	7 a
Judg. xx. 2.	1, 7 b	Ps. xvii. 5.	5	vii. 4, 7, 19.	7 a
Ruth iii. 4, 7, 8, 14.	7 c	xviii. 36.	6	x. 6.	7 c
1 Sam. iv. 10.	7 b				

FOOTSTOOL

כֶּבֶשׁ   *m.* a footstool, placed, as it were, in subjection to the feet: 2 Chron. ix. 18. See also *Stool.*

FORBEAR

1   אַף   *m.* anger; "forbearing," *lit.* by length of anger.

2   דָּמַם   to be silent, still ; to forbear. KAL *imp.*

3   חָדַל   to cease ; to let alone, not to do ; with an *inf.*, especially with לְ and an *inf.*, with an *acc.* of the noun. KAL [a] *pret.* [b] *imp.* [c] *fut.* [d] חָדֵל *adj.* ceasing.

4   חָשַׂךְ   to restrain, to keep back from. KAL *fut.*

5   כּוּל   to hold or keep together; figuratively, to suppress a passion, to keep it within the limits of the breast, without venting it in words. PILPEL *inf.*

6   מָשַׁךְ   to draw, to protract, prolong. KAL *fut.* Neh. ix. 30, *marg.* 'protract over them,' *i. e.* thy patience.

Exod. xxiii. 5.	3 a	2 Chron. xxxv. 21.	3 b
Num. ix. 13.	3 a	Neh. ix. 30.	6
Deut. xxiii. 22.	3 c	Job xvi. 6.	3 c
1 Sam. xxiii. 13.	3 c	Prov. xxiv. 11.	4
1 Kings xxii. 6, 15.	3 c	xxv. 15.	1
2 Chron. xviii. 5, 14.	3 c	Jer. xx. 9.	5
xxv. 16, 16.	3 b c	xl. 4.	3 b

Jer. xli. 8.	3 c
li. 30.	3 a
Ezek. ii. 5, 7.	3 c
iii. 11.	3 c
iii. 27, 27.	3 d c
xxiv. 17.	2
Zech. xi. 12.	3 b

FORBID

חָלִילָה   *adv.* far be it, God forbid, forbid, *lit.* base, profane ; in Lxx. μὴ γένοιτο, or μηδαμῶς; Job xxvii. 5, μὴ εἴη, with מִן and an *inf.*, or, with אִם and a finite verb, in the same sense. In each of the above constructions we sometimes find מֵיהוָה before Jehovah inserted : Gen. xliv. 7, 17: Josh. xxii. 29: xxiv. 16: 1 Sam. xii. 23; xiv. 45; xx. 2; xxiv. 6; xxvi. 11: 1 Kings xxi. 3: 1 Chron. xi. 19: Job xxvii. 5.

כָּלָא   to confine, restrain, keep back. KAL *imp.* Num. xi. 28.

עָשָׂה   to do. NIPHAL *fut.* Lev. v. 17, *lit.* are not to be done.

צָוָה   to command to do, or not to do. PIEL *pret.* Deut. ii. 37; iv. 23.

FORCE, FORCIBLE

1   אֶדְרָע   Ch. the same as דְּרָע arm.

2   אוֹן   *m.* (see *Strength*), substance, power.

3   אָפַק   to hold in by force, as the banks hold in the water, rivers, pools, &c., hence by strong resolution to restrain the passions or inclinations of the mind. HITHPAEL *fut.* 1 Sam. xiii. 12, "I forced myself therefore," I forcibly restrained my inclinations to obey, and offered a burnt-offering contrary to your orders.

4   גְּבוּרָה   *f.* strength, might, power.

5   חָזַק   to be strong, to prevail, to take strong hold. HIPHIL [a] *pret.* [b] חָזְקָה *f.* might, violence.

6   יָד   *com.* hand.

7   כָּבַשׁ   to cast and keep down, or tread down by violence. KAL *inf.*

8   כֹּחַ   *m.* strength, vigour of body.

9   לָחַץ   to press upon, so as to force out, thrust out. KAL *fut.*

10   מִיץ   *m.* a pressing, wringing, churning.

11   מָרַץ   to be vehement, strong, powerful. NIPHAL *pret.*

12   נָדַח   to push, thrust ; to drive an ox. KAL [a] *inf.* HIPHIL [b] *fut.*

13   עָנָה   to afflict, to humble in carnal intercourse. PIEL [a] *pret.* [b] *inf.* [c] *fut.*

Deut. xx. 19.	12 a	2 Sam. xiii. 32.	13 b	Prov. xxx. 33.	10
xxii. 25.	5 a	Ezra iv. 33.	1	Jer. xviii. 21.	6
Judg. i. 34.	9	Esth. vii. 8.	7	xxiii. 10.	4
xx. 5.	13 a	Job vi. 25.	11	xlviii. 45.	5
1 Sam. ii. 16.	5 b	xxx. 18.	8	Ezek. xxxiv. 4.	5 b
xiii. 12.	3	xl. 16.	8	xxxv. 5.	6
2 Sam. xiii. 12, 14.	13 c	Prov. vii. 21.	12 b	Amos ii. 14.	8
xiii. 22.	13 a				

FORCES

מַאֲמַצִּים   *m. pl.* strength, powers ; joined with כֹּחַ : Job xxxvi. 19.

חַיִל   *m.* strength, valour in war, forces, an army ; wealth : 2 Chron. xvii. 2 : Isa. lx. 5, 11, *marg.* 'or, wealth ;' Jer. xl. 7, 13 ; xli. 11, 13, 16; xlii. 1, 8; xliii. 4, 5 : Dan. xi. 10 : Obad. 11.

מָעוֹז   *m.* fortress : Dan. xi. 38, *marg.* 'mauzzim, *or,* munitions.'

FORD

מַעֲבָר m. passage over a river: Gen. xxxii. 22. מַעְבָּרָה f. id. Josh. ii. 7: Judg. iii. 28: Isa. xvi. 2.

FORECAST

חָשַׁב to think, intend, purpose; to imagine, invent, devise. KAL fut. Dan. xi. 25. PIEL fut. Dan. xi. 24.

FOREFATHER

אָב m. (see *Father*). רִאשׁוֹן adj. former: Jer. xi. 10.

FOREFRONT, FOREPART

1 מוּל m. before, over against; in combination with פָּנִים rendered forefront, forepart.

2 פָּנִים m. pl. face.

3 רֹאשׁ m. head.

4 שֵׁן com. tooth.

Exod. xxvi. 9.	1, 2	1 Sam. xiv. 5.	4	2 Chron. xx. 27.	3		
xxviii. 27.	2	2 Sam. xi. 15.	1, 2	Ezek. xl. 19, 19.	2		
xxviii. 37.	1, 2	1 Kings vi. 20.	2	xlii. 7.	2		
xxxix. 20.	2	2 Kings xvi. 14.	2	xlvii. 1.	2		
Lev. viii. 9.	1, 2						

FOREHEAD

אַף m. nose; face, countenance: Ezek. xvi. 12, *or*, nose.

מֵצַח com. forehead, brow, front: Exod. xxviii. 38, 38: 1 Sam. xvii. 49, 49: 2 Chron. xxvi. 19, 20: Jer. iii. 3: Ezek. iii. 8, 8, 9; ix. 4.

FOREIGNER

נָכְרִי adj. strange, a stranger: Deut. xv. 3, Obad. 11.

תּוֹשָׁב m. a sojourner, a stranger: Exod. xii. 45.

FOREMOST

רִאשׁוֹן adj. first, former, foremost: Gen. xxxii. 17; xxxiii. 2: 2 Sam. xviii. 27.

FORESEE

רָאָה to see. KAL *pret.* Prov. xxii. 3; xxvii. 12.

FORESKIN

עָרְלָה f. prepuce, foreskin; foreskin of the heart, its impurity: Gen. xvii. 11, 14, 23, 24, 25: Exod. iv. 25: Lev. xii. 3: Deut. x. 16: Josh. v. 3: 1 Sam. xviii. 25, 27: 2 Sam. iii. 14: Jer. iv. 4. עָרֵל to treat as uncircumcised. NIPHAL *imp.* Hab. ii. 16, "let thy foreskin be uncovered."

FOREST

חֹרֶשׁ m. a thick wood, an intricate thicket: 2 Chron. xxvii. 4.

יַעַר m. a wood, a forest; see *Wood*. Contrasted with יַעַר is כַּרְמֶל a park, garden, as the smaller with the greater, the cultivated with the wild, Isa. xxix. 17; xxxii. 15: Hos. ii. 12; but the forest of cedars in Lebanon, as being small and beautiful, is called "the forest of his park," 2 Kings xix. 23: Isa. xxxvii. 24; house of the forest, Isa. xxii. 8; or fully, house of the forest of Lebanon, 1 Kings vii. 2; x. 17; *i. e.* the armoury or arsenal of king Solomon, called also "the armoury," Neh. iii. 19. *Metaph.* a forest of enemies, Isa. xxxii. 19, comp. x. 18, 19, 34; *i. e.* an army; the glory of the forest, the princes

and nobles of it or of a nation; the briers and thorns, the common people, Isa. x. 18. Figuratively, a nation or body of men, 1 Sam. xxii. 5, &c. יַעֲרָה f. id. Ps. xxix. 9.

פַּרְדֵּס m. a garden of trees, a park for animals; a word derived from the Persian, in which it denotes the royal park; hence the Greek, παράδεισος. Neh. ii. 8.

FORFEIT

חָרַם see *Devote*. HOPHAL *fut.* Ezra x. 8, *marg.* 'devoted.'

FORGE

טָפַל to patch; *trop.* to patch up falsehood; to invent, contrive. KAL *pret.* Ps. cxix. 69. *part.* Poel, Job xiii. 4.

FORGET

1 נָשָׁה to forget, to forsake, neglect. KAL [a] *pret.* In Jer. xxiii. 39, the *inf. abs.* of נָשָׁא is added to express utter forgetfulness. NIPHAL [b] *fut.* PIEL [c] *pret.* [d] נְשִׁיָּה f. forgetfulness.

2 שָׁכַח to forget, with an *acc.*, and with מִן and an infinitive; also to leave something from forgetfulness. With *inf.*, at all forget. KAL [a] *pret.* [b] *inf.* [c] *imp.* [d] *fut.* [e] *part.* Poel. NIPHAL [f] *fut.* [g] *part.* [h] *part.* PIEL [i] *pret.* HIPHIL [k] *inf.* HITHPAEL [l] *fut.* [m] שָׁכֵחַ adj. forgetting.

Gen. xxvii. 45.	2 d	Ps. x. 12.	2 d	Isa. xliv. 21.	1 b
xl. 23.	2 d	xiii. 1.	2 d	xlix. 14.	2 a
xli. 30.	2 f	xxxi. 12.	2 f	xlix. 15, 15, 15.	2 d
xli. 51.	1 c	xlii. 9.	2 a	li. 13.	2 d
Deut. iv. 9, 23, 31.	2 d	xliv. 17, 20.	2 a	liv. 4.	2 d
vi. 12.	2 d	xliv. 24.	2 d	lxv. 11.	2 m
viii. 11.	2 d	xlv. 10.	2 c	lxv. 16.	2 f
viii. 14.	2 a	l. 22.	2 e	Jer. ii. 32, 32.	2 d a
viii. 19.	2 b d	lix. 11.	2 d	iii. 21.	2 a
ix. 7.	2 d	lxxiv. 19, 23.	2 a	xiii. 25.	2 a
xxiv. 19.	2 a	lxxvii. 9.	2 a	xviii. 15.	2 d
xxv. 19.	2 d	lxxviii. 7, 11.	2 d	xx. 11.	2 g
xxvi. 13.	2 a	lxxxviii. 12.	1 d	xxiii. 27, 27.	2 k a
xxxi. 21.	2 g	cii. 4.	2 a	xxiii. 39.	1 a
xxxii. 18.	2 d	ciii. 2.	2 d	xxiii. 40.	2 g
Judg. iii. 7.	2 d	cvi. 13, 21.	2 a	xxx. 14.	2 g
1 Sam. i. 11.	2 d	cxix. 16, 93.	2 d	xliv. 9.	2 a
xii. 9.	2 d	cxix. 61, 83, 109,		l. 5.	2 g
2 Kings xvii. 38.	2 d	139, 141, 153,		l. 6.	2 a
Job viii. 13.	2 e	176.	2 a	Lam. ii. 6.	2 i
ix. 27.	2 d	cxxxvii. 5, 5.	2 a	iii. 17.	1 a
xi. 16.	2 d	Prov. ii. 17.	2 a	v. 20.	2 d
xix. 14.	2 a	iii. 1.	2 d	Ezek. xxii. 12.	2 a
xix. 20.	2 d	iv. 5.	2 d	xxiii. 35.	2 a
xxviii. 4.	2 h	xxxi. 5, 7.	2 d	Hos. ii. 13.	2 d
xxxix. 15.	2 d	Eccles. ii. 16.	2 f	iv. 6, 6.	2 d
Ps. ix. 12.	2 a	viii. 10.	2 l	viii. 14.	2 d
ix. 17.	2 m	ix. 5.	2 f	xiii. 6.	2 a
ix. 18.	2 g	Isa. xvii. 10.	2 a	Amos viii. 7.	2 d
x. 11.	2 a	xxiii. 15, 16.	2 h		

FORGIVE

1 כָּפַר to cover; Piel, to pardon, to procure forgiveness, to make an atonement. PIEL [a] *fut.* HITHPAEL [b] *pret.*

2 נָשָׂא to bear; to take, accept; to take away guilt, to forgive. KAL [a] *pret.* [b] *imp.* [c] *fut.* [d] *part.* Poel. [e] *part.* Paül, Ps. xxxii. 1, *lit.* forgiven (as to) iniquity, *comp.* Isa. xxxiii. 24.

3 סָלַח to pardon, construed with a dative; it is used only of God, and implies the forgiveness of God offended. KAL [a] *pret.* [b] *imp.* [c] *fut.* [d] *part.* Poel. NIPHAL [e] *pret.* [f] סַלָּח m. ready to forgive. [g] סְלִיחָה f. forgiveness.

Gen. l. 17, 17.	2 b	Josh. xxiv. 19.	2 c	Ps. lxxxvi. 5.	3 f	
Exod. x. 17.	2 b	1 Sam. xxv. 28.	2 b	xcix. 8.	2 d	
xxxii. 32.	2 c	1 Kings viii. 30, 34,		ciii. 3.	3 d	
xxxiv. 7.	2 d	36, 39, 50.	3 a	cxxx. 4.	3 g	
Lev. iv. 20, 26, 31, 35.	3 e	2 Chron. vi. 21, 25,		Isa. ii. 9.	2 c	
v. 10, 13, 16, 18.	3 e	27, 30, 39.	3 a	xxxiii. 24.	2 a	
vi. 7.	3 e	vii. 14.	3 c	Jer. xviii. 23.	2 e	
xix. 22.	3 e	Ps. xxv. 18.	2 b	xxxi. 34.	1 a	
Num. xiv. 18.	2 d	xxxii. 1.	2 e	xxxvi. 3.	3 c	
xiv. 19.	2 a	xxxii. 5.	3 a	Dan. ix. 9.	3 a	
xv. 25, 26, 28.	3 e	lxxviii. 38.	3 a	ix. 19.	3 g	
xxx. 5. 8, 12.	3 e	lxxxv. 2.	2 a	Amos vii. 2.	3 b	
Deut. xxi. 8.	1 b					

FORK

קִלְּשׁוֹן *m.* a pointed or pronged instrument : 1 Sam. xiii. 21.

שְׁלוֹשׁ three : 1 Sam. xiii. 21, *lit.* and for the triple forks.

FORM

1 תַּבְנִית *f.* pattern ; form, likeness, similitude.

2 פָּנִים *m. pl.* face : 2 Sam. xiv. 20, "to fetch about this form of speech," *Heb.* to turn about the face of this speech, namely, by transferring it from the fictitious case of my sons to the real case of Absalom.

3 צוּרָה *f.* form.

4 צֶלֶם *Ch. m.* a form, image, likeness.

5 רֵו *Ch. m.* form, appearance.

6 מַרְאֶה *m.* appearance.

7 מִשְׁפָּט *m.* judgment ; manner, fashion, form.

8 תֹּאַר *m.* form, visage ; a beautiful form.

9 תֹּהוּ *m.* a vast desert, waste and barren, a void place : Gen. i. 2, "without form."

Gen. i. 2.		Isa. lii. 14.	8	Ezek. xliii. 11, 11, 11,	
1 Sam. xxviii. 14.	8	liii. 2.	8	11.	3
2 Sam. xiv. 20.	2	Jer. iv. 23.	9	Dan. ii. 31.	5
2 Chron. iv. 7.	6	Ezek. viii. 3, 10.	1	iii. 19.	4
Job iv. 16.	6	x. 8.	1	iii. 25.	5

FORM (*V*)

1 חוּל implies power going forth in action to an especial object, as of formation, creation, &c. ; see *Abide;* to travail in birth. POLEL [a] *pret.* [b] *fut.* [c] *part.*

2 יָצַר to form, fashion, or shape ; to form in the mind, to purpose ; different from עָשָׂה, Isa. xlvi. 11. Used of potters making vessels of clay, also of the formation of man, to denote the care and skill of the Almighty in the formation of the human body : Isa. xliii. 10, *marg.* ' or, nothing formed of God ; rather, there was not formed a God ;' see אַל. KAL [a] *pret.* [b] *fut.* [c] *part.* Poel. NIPHAL [d] *pret.* HOPHAL [e] *fut.*

3 קָרַץ to cut off. PUAL *pret.* Job xxxiii. 6, *marg.* ' cut :' the figure is taken from the potter, who nips off a piece of clay from the mass before he shapes it.

Gen. ii. 7, 19.	2 b	Prov. xxvi. 10.	1 c	Isa. xlix. 5.	2 c
ii. 8.	2 a	Isa. xxvii. 11.	2 c	liv. 17.	2 e
Deut. xxxii. 18.	1 c	xxxvii. 26.	2 a	Jer. i. 5.	2 b
2 Kings xix. 25.	2 a	xli. 1.	2 c	x. 16.	2 c
Job xxvi. 5.	1 b	xli i. 7, 21.	2 a	xxxiii. 2.	2 c
xxvi. 13.	1 a	xliii. 10.	2 d	li. 19.	2 c
xxxiii. 6.	3	xliv. 2, 24.	2 d	Amos iv. 13.	2 c
Ps. xc. 2.	1 b	xliv. 10, 21.	2 a	v. 1.	2 c
xciv. 9.	2 a	xlv. 7.	2 c	Zech. xii. 1.	2 c a
xcv. 5.	2 a	xlv. 18, 18.	2 c a		

FORMER

אֶמֶשׁ see *Yesternight:* Job xxx. 3, *marg.* 'yesternight.'

פָּנִים *m. pl.* face : Ruth iv. 7.

קַדְמָה *f.* origin, antiquity ; former estate : Ezek. xvi. 55, 55, 55. קַדְמוֹנִי *adj.* ancients ; east : Zech. xiv. 8 : Mal. iii. 4.

רִאשׁוֹן *adj.* first, former : Gen. xl. 13, &c. : Ps. lxxix. 8, *marg.* ' or, the iniquities of them that were before us.' רִישׁוֹן *adj.* Syriac orthography : Job viii. 8 (כתיב).

FORNICATION

זָנָה to commit fornication, to whore ; the word is applied to lewdness, fornication, or whoredom in general ; and figuratively, to idolatry, since Jehovah was regarded as the husband of his people, to whom they were under bonds of conjugal fidelity ; idolatry, therefore, was unfaithfulness to him : see Ezek. xvi. 8, 22 ; Hos. i. 2. The person with whom fornication is committed, either literally or figuratively, is put in the *accus.*, or is preceded by אֶל, or by בְּ, but most frequently by אַחֲרֵי after any one. The person sinned against is preceded by מִן, by מֵאַחֲרֵי, by מִתַּחַת, by תַּחַת, or by מֵעַל. KAL *pret.* Isa. xxiii. 17. *fut.* Ezek. xvi. 26. HIPHIL *fut.* 2 Chron. xxi. 11. תַּזְנוּת *f.* Ezek. xvi. 15, 29.

FORSAKE

1 אַלְמָן *adj.* see *Widow.*

2 חָדַל to cease, leave off, desist from, leave. KAL *pret.*

3 נָטַשׁ to be loose ; to relax the ties of an obligation, to leave in a neglected, abandoned, exposed condition, loose and open to any injuries or sufferings ; to cast off, reject, put away from one : it is used of God rejecting his people ; and of man forsaking God. KAL [a] *pret.* [b] *fut.* NIPHAL [c] *pret.* PUAL [d] *pret.*

4 נָתַשׁ to root up, to pluck ; in Niphal, used of waters dried up. NIPHAL *fut.*

5 עָזַב to leave, forsake, in a forlorn, destitute condition, without any further care, but not in the strong sense of נָטַשׁ ; to let go, in opposition to holding fast, Job xx. 13 ; so Job x. 1, I will no longer restrain my complaint ; see *Leave.* KAL [a] *pret.* [b] *inf.* [c] *imp.* [d] *fut.* [e] *part.* Poel. [f] *part.* NIPHAL [g] *pret.* [h] *fut.* [i] *part.* [k] *part.* עֲזוּבָה *f.* ruins.

6 רָפָה to be slack, loose ; Hiphil, to let lie, leave, forsake. HIPHIL *fut.*

7 שָׁלַח to send ; to throw or cast out in displeasure. PUAL *part.*

Deut. iv. 31.	6	1 Kings viii. 57.	3 b	2 Chron. xxiv. 25.	5 a	
xii. 19.	5 d	ix. 9.	5 a	Ezra viii. 22.	5 e	
xiv. 27.	5 d	xi. 33.	5 a	ix. 9, 10.	5 d	
xxviii. 20.	5 a	xii. 8, 13.	5 d	Neh. ix. 17, 19, 31.	5 a	
xxix. 25.	5 a	xviii. 18.	5 b	x. 39.	5 d	
xxxi. 6, 8.	5 d	xix. 10, 14.	5 a	xiii. 11.	5 g	
xxxi. 16, 17.	5 a	2 Kings xxi. 14.	3 a	Job vi. 14.	5 d	
xxxi. 15.	3 d	xxi. 22.	5 a	xviii. 4.	5 h	
Josh. i. 5.	5 d	xxii. 17.	5 a	xx. 13.	5 d	
xxiv. 16.	5 b	1 Chron. v. 7.	5 d	xx. 19.	5 d	
xxiv. 20.	5 d	xxviii. 9, 20.	5 a	Ps. xx. 10.	5 d	
Judg. ii. 12, 13.	5 d	2 Chron. vii. 19, 22.	5 a	xxii. 1.	5 a	
vi. 13.	3 a	x. 8, 13.	5 d	xxvii. 9.	5 a	
ix. 11.	2	xii. 1, 5.	5 d	xxvii. 10.	5 c	
x. 6.	5 a	xiii. 10, 11.	5 d	xxxvii. 8.	5 o	
x. 10, 13.	5 a	xv. 2, 2.	5 d	xxxvii. 25.	5 d	
1 Sam. viii. 8.	5 a	xxi. 10.	5 a	xxxvii. 28.	5 d	
xii. 10.	5 a	xxiv. 20, 20.	5 a d	xxxvii. 28.	5 d	
xii. 22.	3 b	xxiv. 24.	5 a	xxxviii. 21.	5 d	
xxxi. 7.	5 a	xxviii. 6.	5 b	lxxi. 9, 18.	5 d	
1 Kings vi. 13.	3 b	xxix. 6.	5 d	lxxi. 11.	5 a	
				lxxviii. 60.	3 b	

Ps. lxxxix. 30.	5 d	Isa. xxvii. 10.	7	Jer. xii. 7.	5 a
xciv. 14.	5 d	xxxii. 14.	3 d	xiv. 5.	5 b
cxix. 14.	5 d	xli. 17.	5 d	xv. 6.	3 a
cxix. 53.	5 e	xliii. 16.	5 a	xvi. 11, 11.	5 a
cxix. 87.	5 a	xlix. 14.	5 a	xvii. 13, 13.	5 e a
cxxxviii. 8.	6	liv. 6.	5 f	xviii. 14.	4
Prov. i. 8.	3 b	liv. 7.	5 a	xix. 4.	5 a
ii. 17.	5 e	lv. 7.	5 d	xxii. 9.	5 a
iii. 3.	5 d	lviii. 2.	5 a	xxiii. 33, 39.	3 a
iv. 2, 6.	5 d	lx. 15.	5 f	xxv. 38.	5 a
vi. 20.	3 b	lxii. 12.	5 i	li. 5.	1
ix. 6.	5 c	lxv. 11.	5 e	li. 9.	5 c
xv. 10.	5 e	Jer. i. 16.	5 a	Lam. v. 20.	5 d
xxvii. 10.	5 d	ii. 13.	5 a	Ezek. viii. 12.	5 a
xxviii. 4, 13.	5 e	ii. 17, 19.	5 b	xx. 8.	5 a
Isa. i. 4.	5 a	iv. 29.	5 f	xxxvi. 4.	5 a
i. 23.	5 e	v. 7, 19.	5 a	Dan. xi. 30.	5 e
ii. 6.	3 a	vii. 11.	5 a	Amos v. 2.	3 c
vi. 12.	5 k	ix. 13.	5 b	Jonah ii. 8.	5 d
vii. 16.	5 h	ix. 19.	5 a	Zeph. ii. 4.	5 f
xvii. 2, 9.	5 f				

2   הָלַךְ   to go. KAL *inf.* Gen. xxvi. 13, *lit.* went going.

3   יָעַל   to profit; to set forward, *i.e.* heighten a calamity. HIPHIL *fut.*

4   נָסַע   to break up, to remove, used of nomadic life; to journey, set, go, forward. KAL ᵃ *pret.* ᵇ *inf.* ᶜ *fut.*

5   פָּנִים   *m. pl.* face; "straight forward," *lit.* on the side of face.

6   קֶדֶם   *m.* before: Job xxviii. 8.

Gen. xxvi. 13.	2	Num. x. 5, 17, 18, 21,	4 a	1 Sam. x. 3.	1
Exod. xiv. 15.	4 c	22, 25.	4 a	xviii. 9.	1
Num. i. 51.	4 b	x. 28.	4 c	Job xxiii. 8.	6
ii. 17, 17.	4 a c	x. 35.	4 b	xxx. 13.	3
ii. 24.	4 c	xxi. 10.	4 c	Jer. vii. 24.	5
ii. 34.	4 a	xxii. 1.	4 c	Ezek. x. 22.	5
iv. 5, 15.	4 b	xxxii. 19.	1	xxxix. 22.	1
				xliii. 27.	1

FORT, FORTRESS

1   מִבְצָר   *m.* a fortified place, a fenced city, stronghold.

2   דָּיֵק   *m.* a wooden turret, used in besieging towns, to enable the enemy to approach and scale the walls.

3   מְצָד   *m.* a fortress, stronghold, castle on a mountain. ᵃ מְצוּדָה *f. id.*

4   מָעוֹז   *m.* stronghold, fortification; defence.

5   עֹפֶל   *m.* a hill, cliff.

6   מָצוֹר   *m.* a wall or bulwark against a city besieged; a fortification, fenced city. ᵃ מְצוּרָה *f. id.*

7   מִשְׂגָּב   *m.* a high tower, high fort.

2 Sam. v. 9.	3 a	Isa. xxv. 12, 12.	1, 7	Ezek. xvii. 17.	2
xxii. 2.	3 a	xxix. 3.	6 a	xxi. 22.	2
2 Kings xxv. 1.	2	xxxii. 14.	2	xxvi. 8.	2
Ps. xviii. 2.	3 a	xxxiv. 13.	1	xxxiii. 27.	3
xxxi. 3.	3 a	Jer. vi. 27.	1	Dan. xi. 7, 10, 19.	4
lxxi. 3.	3 a	x. 17.	6	Hos. x. 14.	1
xci. 2.	3 a	xvi. 19.	4	Amos v. 9.	1
cxliv. 2.	3 a	lii. 4.	1	Micah vii. 12.	6
Isa. xvii. 3.	1	Ezek. iv. 2.	2		

FORTH

בַּיִת   *m.* house: 2 Chron. xxiii. 14, *lit.* to the outside.

הָלַךְ   to go. KAL *inf.* Ps. cxxvi. 6, *lit.* going.

חוּץ   *m.* without, abroad: Gen. xxxix. 13; Judg. xix. 25.

FORTHWITH

אָסְפַּרְנָא   *adv.* Ch. carefully, diligently, speedily: Ezra vi. 8.

FORTIFY

אָמַץ   to be strong. PIEL *imp.* Nah. ii. 1.

בָּצַר   to cut off; to make inaccessible; hence to fortify. PIEL *inf.* Isa. xxii. 10. *fut.* Jer. li. 53.

חָזַק   to be strong; Piel, to strengthen, to fortify. PIEL *imp.* Nah. iii. 14. *fut.* 2 Chron. xi. 11; xxvi. 9, *marg.* ' or, repaired.'

עָזַב   to leave. KAL *fut.* Neh. iii. 8; iv. 2. Fürst, however, thinks the root has also the meaning of repairing a wall.

צוּר   to inclose for defence, as well as for siege. KAL *part.* Poel, Judg. ix. 31. מָצוּר *m.* "fortified," Micah vii. 12.

FORWARD, HENCEFORWARD

1   הָלְאָה   *adv.* to a distance, farther, beyond, forward; to space, and to time.

FOUL

חָמַר   to be red; to be made red, as the countenance with weeping. POALAL *pret.* Job xvi. 16.

רָפַשׂ   to tread with the feet, and make water turbid. KAL *fut.* Ezek. xxxii. 2; xxxiv. 18. מִרְפָּשׂ *m.* Ezek. xxxiv. 19.

FOUND, FOUNDATION

1   אֶדֶן   *m.* a base, a socket.

2   אָשִׁישׁ   *m.* foundation: Isa. xvi. 7, foundations, *i. e.* ruins of buildings destroyed to the foundations, so that those alone remain. *Comp.* Isa. lviii. 12, of ruins.

3   אֻשִּׁין   Ch. *m. pl.* foundations.

4   אָשְׁיוֹת   *m. pl.* (קרי). (כתיב אֲשֻׁיָה אֲשִׁיּוֹת) support.

5   יָסַד   to found or lay the foundation (of a building): this primary signification is more frequent in Piel, for in Kal the verb is used commonly in a metaphorical sense, as of the founding of the earth, Ps. xxiv. 2, lxxviii. 69, Job xxxviii. 4; of the heavens, Amos ix. 6; of a nation, Isa. xxiii. 13; "founded it for them that dwell in the wilderness," *i.e.* the Assyrians gave the land of Chaldea for a settlement to those who before inhabited the wilderness, and thus was the foundation laid of the Chaldean empire. KAL ᵃ *pret.* ᵇ *inf.* ᶜ *part.* NIPHAL ᵈ *inf.* ᵉ *fut.* PIEL ᶠ *pret.* ᵍ *inf.* ᵏ *part.* PUAL ⁱ *pret.* ᵏ *part.* HOPHAL ˡ *pret.* ᵐ יְסוֹד *m.* foundation, base, as of the altar, of a building. *Metaph.* used of princes, Ezek. xxx. 4. ⁿ יְסֹדָה *f.* foundation. ° מוּסָד *m. id.* ᵖ מוֹסָדָה *f.* foundation. ᑫ מוֹסָדוֹת *f. pl.* foundations. ʳ מַסָּד *m.* foundation.

6   מָכוֹן   *m.* a settled place, a foundation or base.

7   שָׁת   *m.* foundations, pillars.

Exod. ix. 18. α	5 d	Ezra vi. 3.	3	Prov. x. 25.	5 m
Deut. xxxii. 22.	5 q	Job iv. 19.	5 m	Isa. xiv. 32.	5 f
Josh. vi. 26.	5 h	xxii. 16.	5 m	xvi. 7.	2
2 Sam. xxii. 8, 16.	5 q	xxxviii. 4.	5 b	xxiii. 13.	5 a
1 Kings v. 17.	5 g	xxxviii. 6.	1	xxiv. 18.	5 g
vi. 37.	5 i	Ps. xi. 3.	7	xxviii. 16, 16.	5 f o
vii. 9.	5 r	xviii. 7, 15.	5 q	xl. 21.	5 q
vii. 10.	5 k	xxiv. 2.	5 a	xliv. 28.	5 e
xvi. 34.	5 f	lxxxii. 5.	5 q	xlviii. 13.	5 a
2 Chron. viii. 16.	5 o	lxxxix. 1.	5 n	li. 13.	5 c
xxiii. 5.	5 m	cii. 25.	5 a	li. 16.	5 b
xxxi. 7.	5 b	civ. 5.	5 a	liv. 11.	5 b
Ezra iii. 6.	5 i	cxix. 152.	5 a	lviii. 12.	5 q
iii. 10.	5 f	cxxxvii. 7.	5 m	Jer. xxxi. 37.	5 q
iii. 12.	5 b	Prov. iii. 19.	5 a	l. 15.	4
iv. 12.	3	viii. 29.	3	li. 26.	5 q
v. 16.	3			Lam. iv. 11.	5 m
				Ezek. xiii. 14.	5 m

OLD TESTAMENT WORD STUDIES

177

Ezek. xxx. 4.	5 m	Micah vi. 2.	5 q	Zech. iv. 9.	5 f
xli. 8.	5 p	Hab. iii. 13.	5 m	viii. 9.	5 i
Amos ix. 6.	5 a	Hag. ii. 18.	5 i	xii. 1.	5 c
Micah i. 6.	5 m				

a *lit.* from the day it was founded.

FOUNDER

צָרַף to melt metals, to refine. KAL *inf.* Jer. vi. 29 ; *part.* Poel, Judg. xvii. 4 : Jer. x. 9, 14 ; li. 17.

FOUNTAIN

1 בּוֹר (כתיב), בִּיר (קרי) a pit, well.

2 מַבּוּעַ *m.* spring of water.

3 עַיִן *com.* eye, also a fountain, or orifice through which water comes ; or a well, like an eye in the ground. מַעְיָן a *m. id.*

4 מָקוֹר *m.* a fountain or perpetual spring of water ; also an issue, or fountain of blood, of life, of wisdom, &c.

Gen. vii. 11.	3 a	Neh. ii. 14.	3	Prov. xiv. 27.	4
viii. 2.	3 a	iii. 15.	3	xxv. 26.	3 a
xvi. 7, 7.	3	iii. 37.	3	Eccles. xii. 6.	2
Lev. xi. 36.	3 a	Ps. xxxvi. 9.	4	Cant. iv. 12, 15.	3
xx. 18, 18.	4	lxviii. 26. a	4	Isa. xli. 18.	3
Num. xxxiii. 9.	3	lxxiv. 15.	3 a	Jer. ii. 13.	4
Deut. viii. 7.	3	cxiv. 8.	3 a	vi. 7.	1
xxxiii. 28.	3 a	Prov. v. 16.	3 a	ix. 1.	4
Josh. xv. 9.	3 a	v. 18.	4	xvii. 13.	4
1 Sam. xxix. 1.	3	viii. 24.	3 a	Hos. xiii. 15.	3 a
1 Kings xviii. 5.	3	viii. 28.	3	Joel iii. 18.	3 a
2 Chron. xxxii. 3.	3	xiii. 14.	4	Zech. xiii. 1.	4
xxxii. 4.	3				

a *marg.* 'or, ye that are of the fountain of Israel:' *comp.* Isa. xlviii. 1.

FOURSQUARE

רָבַע a verb formed from אַרְבַּע four. KAL *part.* Paül, Exod. xxvii. 1 ; xxviii. 16 ; xxx. 2 ; xxxvii. 25 ; xxxviii. 1 ; xxxix. 9. PUAL *part.* 1 Kings vii. 31 : Ezek. xl. 47.
רְבִיעִי *adj. num.* fourth : Ezek. xlviii. 20.

FOWL

בַּרְבֻּרִים *m.* fowl fatted as a great delicacy ; others, game, venison : 1 Kings iv. 23.
עוֹף *m.* bird, fowl ; also flying insects : Lev. xi. 20 : Gen. i. 20, 21, &c. עוֹף Ch. *m. id.* Dan. ii. 38 : vii. 6.
עַיִט *m.* a collective noun, birds of prey : Gen. xv. 11 : Job xxviii. 7 : Isa. xviii. 6, 6.
צִפּוֹר *com.* any small bird, a bird generally : Deut. iv. 17 : Neh. v. 18 : Ps. viii. 8 ; cxlviii. 10 : Ezek. xvii. 23 ; xxxix. 17. צְפַר Ch. *m.* Dan. iv. 12, 14, 21.

FOWLER

יָקֹשׁ to lay snares, as fowlers do. KAL *part.* Poel, Ps. cxxiv. 7.
יָקוֹשׁ *m.* a fowler : Hos. ix. 8. יְקוּשׁ *m. id.* Ps. xci. 3 : Prov. vi. 5.

FOX

שׁוּעָל *m.* Palestine so much abounded with foxes, especially if we include the jackal (see *Wild Beast*), that Samson, in three or four weeks' time, with the assistance which he, as judge or chief magistrate in Israel (Judg. xvi. 31), could command, might catch a great number of them. This creature will eat either flesh or fruits, and is parti-

cularly fond of grapes ; he feeds also on the dead and dying : Ps. lxiii. 11 ; Bochart. Judg. xv. 4 : Neh. iv. 3 : Ps. lxiii. 10 : Cant. ii. 15, 15 : Lam. v. 18 : Ezek. xiii. 4.

FRAIL

חָדֵל *adj.* frail, transitory ; or to be in a state of utter cessation, to be lifeless and dead : Ps. xxxix. 4. Gesenius, *scire cupio quando desinam esse, quando moriar.*

FRAME

מִבְנֶה *m.* a building : Ezek. xl. 2.
יָצַר to form, make, create ; to imagine, devise. KAL *part.* Poel, Ps. xciv. 20 : Isa. xxix. 16 : Jer. xviii. 11. יֵצֶר *m.* something formed by an artificer, a form, frame ; imagination, thought : Ps. ciii. 14 : Isa. xxix. 16.
כּוּן to raise up, erect ; to prepare, form, make. HIPHIL *fut.* Judg. xii. 6.
נָתַן to give. KAL *fut.* Hos. v. 4, *marg.* 'give.'
צָמַד to join together ; artfully to frame deceit. HIPHIL *fut.* Ps. l. 19.

FRANKINCENSE

לְבוֹנָה *f.* a known gum extracted from a shrub in Arabia : it burns with a bright and strong flame, not easily extinguished.—Raii Hist. Plant. tom. ii. p. 1840. It was used in the temple service, and is an emblem of prayer : Ps. cxli. 2 : Rev. viii. 3, 4. Authors give the best sort of it the epithet of pure, bright, pellucid : Exod. xxx. 34 : Lev. ii. 1, 2, 15, 16 ; v. 11 ; vi. 15 ; xxiv. 7 : Num. v. 15 : 1 Chron. ix. 29 : Neh. xiii. 5, 9 : Cant. iii. 6 ; iv. 6, 14.

FRAUD

תֹּךְ *m.* deceit ; *or,* oppression, violence : Ps. x. 7.

FRAY

חָרַד to tremble ; to put in consternation, to make afraid. HIPHIL *inf.* Zech. i. 21. *part.* Deut. xxviii. 26 : Jer. vii. 33.

FREE, FREELY, FREEDOM, FREE-WILL

1 חִנָּם *adv.* literally, for mere favour, without recompense or reward, for nothing.

2 חָפַשׁ to be in a separate, independent state, unconnected with other people and things : 2 Kings xv. 5. See Patrick's Commentary : to be free or independent of the right or authority of a master. Gesenius, to spread out loose things ; to set free, *e.g.* a slave. PUAL a *pret.* b חֻפְשָׁה *f.* freedom. חָפְשִׁי c *adj.* free, severed.

3 כָּרַת to cut off. NIPHAL *fut.* Josh. ix. 23, *marg.* 'not be cut off from you.'

4 נָדַב to be of a ready and bountiful mind, to offer freely. נְדַב Ch. ITHPAEL a *part.* Ezra vii. 13, "minded of their own freewill." b נְדָבָה *f.* free offerings, free-will offerings ; see *Offering.* נָדִיב c *adj.* willing.

5 נָקָה to be pure, free from punishment, an oath, &c. NIPHAL ᵃ *pret.* ᵇ *imp.* ᶜ נְקִי *adj.* free, clear.

6 פָּטַר to let loose, to set free, dismiss. KAL ᵃ *part.* Paül.

7 פָּתַח to open ; to let loose. PIEL *fut.* Ps. cv. 20.

Exod. xxi. 2, 5, 26,		Josh. ix. 23.	3	Ps. li. 12.	4 c
27.	2 c	1 Sam. xvii. 25.	2 c	liv. 6.	4 b
xxi. 11.	1	1 Chron. ix. 33.	6 a	lxxxviii. 5.	2 c
Lev. xix. 20, 20.	2 b a	2 Chron. xxix. 31.	4 c	cv. 20.	7
Num. v. 19.	5 b	xxxi. 14.	4 b	Isa. lviii. 6.	2 c
v. 28.	5 a	Ezra vii. 13.	4 a	Jer. xxxiv. 9, 10, 11,	
xi. 5.	1	Job iii. 19.	2 c	14.	2 c
Deut. xv. 12, 13, 18.	2 c	xxxix. 5.	2 c	Hos. xiv. 4.	4 b
xxiv. 5.	5 c				

FRESH

חָדָשׁ *adj.* new : Job xxix. 20.

לָשָׁד *m.* juice, sap ; moisture : Num. xi. 8.

רַעֲנָן *adj.* see *Green, Flourishing* ; applied to oil, which gives a fresh, blooming appearance : Ps. xcii. 10.

רֻטֲפַשׁ to be in a fresh, thriving condition, supposed to be compounded of רָטֹב to be green, and שָׁפֵשׁ to be thick, fat : *pret.* Job xxxiii. 25.

FRET

1 זָעֵף to be discomposed ; troubled, displeased. KAL *fut.*

2 חָרָה to be warm, to fume ; applied to grief and fretting. HITHPAEL *fut.*

3 מָאַר to be exasperated or to rankle ; applied to a malignant leprosy. HIPHIL *part.*

4 פְּחֶתֶת *f.* a deep-pitted fret of leprosy (in a garment infected), "fret inward."

5 קָצַף to foam, to be wroth, displeased. HITHPAEL *pret.*

6 רָגַן to be shaken or moved with a violent concussion ; to be agitated with any passion. KAL *fut.*

7 רָעַם is used of a commotion that is attended with noise ; of the inward commotion of the mind attended with moans or complaints. HIPHIL *inf.*

Lev. xiii. 51, 52.	3	1 Sam. i. 6.	7	Prov. xxiv. 19.	2
xiii. 55.	4	Ps. xxxvii. 1, 7, 8.	2	Isa. viii. 21.	5
xiv. 44.	3	Prov. xix. 3.	1	Ezek. xvi. 43.	6

FRIEND

1 אָהַב to love. KAL ᵃ *part.* Poel. PIEL ᵇ *part.*

2 אִישׁ *m.* man ; "familiar friend," *lit.* the man of my peace.

3 אַלּוּף *m.* a chief person ; a captain, a leader ; "chief friends."

4 אֱנוֹשׁ *m.* man as mortal : Jer. xxxviii. 22, *lit.* men of thy peace.

5 לֵב *m.* heart ; "friendly," to the heart.

6 מְתִים *m. pl.* men, implying fewness : Job xix. 19, "my inward friends," the men of my secret.

7 רָעָה to take delight or pleasure in ; to choose or treat as a friend. PIEL ᵃ *pret.* HITHPAEL ᵇ *fut.* ᶜ רֵעַ *m.* a companion, acquaintance, friend ; paramour : Hos. iii. 1.— Gen. xxxviii. 12, &c. ᵈ רֵעָה *m. id.* ᵉ רֵיעַ *m. id.* ᶠ מֵרֵעַ *m. id.*

8 רֵעַ *i. q.* רֵעָה. HITHPOLEL *inf.*

9 שָׁלוֹם *m.* peace ; "familiar friend," man of my peace.

No. 7 c not included.

Gen. xxvi. 26.	7 f	2 Chron. xx. 7.	1 a	Prov. xviii. 24,	
Judg. xiv. 20.	7 a	Esth. v. 10, 14.	1 a	24, 24.	7 c, 8, 1 a
xix. 3.	5	vi. 13.	1 a	xix. 7.	7 f
Ruth ii. 13.	5	Job vi. 27.	7 e	xxii. 24.	7 b
2 Sam. iii. 8.	7 f	xix. 19.	6	xxvii. 6.	1 a
xv. 37.	7 d	Ps. xli. 9.	2, 9	Isa. xli. 8.	1 a
xvi. 16.	7 d	Prov. xiv. 20.	1 a	Jer. xx. 4, 6.	1 a
xix. 6.	1 a	xvi. 28.	3	xxxviii. 22.	4, 9
1 Kings iv. 5.	7 d	xvii. 9.	3	Zech. xiii. 6.	1 b

FRINGES

גְּדִלִים *m. pl.* plaited work, twisted thread ; spoken of the sacred tufts or tassels on the four corners of the upper garment : Deut. xxii. 12.

צִיצִת *f.* flower-like, or wing-like : Num. xv. 38, 38, 39.

FROG

צְפַרְדֵּעַ *m.* frog ; used collectively in the feminine : Exod. viii. 2, 3, 4, 5, 6, 7, 8, 9, 11, 12, 13 : Ps. lxxviii. 45 ; cv. 30.

FRONT

פָּנִים *m. pl.* face : 2 Sam. x. 9 : 2 Chron. iii. 4.

FRONTIER

קָצֶה end, extremity : Ezek. xxv. 9.

FRONTLET

טוֹטָפוֹת *f. pl.* bracelets, frontlets ; especially scrolls of parchment, with passages of the Mosaic law (such as Exod. xiii. 1-10, 11-16 : Deut. vi. 4-9 ; xi. 13-21) written upon them, commanded to be worn on the forehead and left wrist : Exod. xiii. 16 : Deut. vi. 8 ; xi. 18. These were afterwards regarded as amulets. They are called by the modern Jews תְּפִלִּין, and in the N. T. φυλακτήρια, phylacteries.

FROST, FROZEN

חֲנָמָל *m.* a nipping hoar frost, or hail, which greatly injures vines : Ps. lxxviii. 47.

לָכַד to take ; to hold or adhere, as that which is frozen : HITHPAEL *fut.* Job xxxviii. 30.

קֶרַח *m.* ice : Gen. xxxi. 40 : Job xxxvii. 10 : Jer. xxxvi. 30.

FROWARD

1 הֲפַכְפַּךְ *adj.* (see *Pervert, Perverse*). ᵃ תַּהְפֻּכוֹת *f. pl.* perversity, foolishness ; deceit, fraud.

2 לוּז to decline (opposed to יָשָׁר), to turn aside from that which is even, right and just. See also *Depart.* NIPHAL *part.*

3 עִקֵּשׁ *adj.* perverse ; deceitful, false. ᵃ עִקְּשׁוּת *f.* with פֶּה perverseness of mouths, *i. e.* fraudulent, deceitful speech.

4 פָּתַל to twist ; to be perverted, false, deceitful. NIPHAL ᵃ *part.* HITHPAEL ᵇ *fut.*

5 שׁוֹבָב *adj.* backsliding, *marg.* 'turning away.'

Deut. xxii. 20. α	1 a	Prov. iii. 32.	2	Prov. xi. 20.	3
2 Sam. xxii. 27.	1 a	iv. 24.	3 a	xvi. 28, 30.	1 a
Job v. 13.	4 a	vi. 12.	3 a	xvii. 20. β	3
Ps. xviii. 26, 26.	3, 4 b	vi. 14.	1 a	xxi. 8.	1
ci. 4.	3	viii. 8.	4 a	xxii. 5.	1 a
Prov. ii. 12, 14.	1 a	viii. 13.	1 a	Isa. lvii. 17.	5
ii. 15.	2	x. 31, 32.	1 a		

α *lit.* a generation of perversities.　β *lit.* the froward of heart.

FRUIT

1 אֵב *m.* verdure, greenness. ᵃ אֵב Ch. *m. id.*

2 מַאֲכָל *m.* food : Neh. ix. 25, *lit.* tree of food.

3 תְּבוּאָה *f.* the produce of the earth ; income, revenue.

4 בָּכַר (see *First-born*), to bring forth new fruit. PIEL *fut.*

5 בֵּן *m.* son : Isa. v. 1, "a very fruitful hill."

6 זִמְרָה *f.* any choice, select thing, most praised and esteemed, "best fruits."

7 זֶרַע *m.* seed : Ezek. xvii. 5, *lit.* field of seed.

8 יְבוּל *m.* produce of the earth, for the sustenance of man or beast.

9 יֶלֶד *m.* child.

10 כֹּחַ *m.* strength.

11 כַּרְמֶל *m.* Carmel ; a fruitful field or hill ; the fruit that grows there ; by a figure, applied to the army of Sennacherib.

12 לֶחֶם *m.* bread ; any kind of victuals.

13 מְלֵאָה *f.* fulness ; it is used of the tenths or first-fruits, to be offered to the Lord ; to signify that he required only of their abundance, Exod. xxii. 29, "the first of thy ripe fruits ;" or, according to Gussetius, "the fulness of thy (floor) when the harvest was gathered in." LXX. ἀπαρχὰς ἅλωνος καὶ ληνοῦ σου.

14 נוב to bring forth fruit. KAL ᵃ *fut.* ᵇ נִיב *m.* fruit ; *fig.* any discourse (*cf.* Prov. xviii. 20 ; x. 31), but particularly the praise of God, thanksgiving ; so Isa. lvii. 19 (*cf.* Ps. xl. 3 : Hos. xiv. 2 : Heb. xiii. 15). ᶜ תְּנוּבָה *f.* fruit.

15 פָּרָה to be fruitful, to bear fruit ; to bear young. KAL ᵃ *pret.* ᵇ *imp.* ᶜ *part.* Poel. HIPHIL ᵈ *pret.* ᵉ *fut.* ᶠ *part.* ᵍ פְּרִי *m.* fruit : Gen. i. 11, &c. ʰ פָּרָא to be fruitful. HIPHIL *fut.*

16 שֶׁמֶן *com.* oil ; Isa. v. 1, "a very fruitful hill."

No. 15 g not included.

Gen. i. 22, 28.	15 b	Lev. xxvi. 9.	15 d	Isa. xxxii. 12.	15 c	
viii. 17.	15 a	Deut. xi. 17.	8	xxxii. 15, 15, 16.	11	
ix. 1, 7.	15 b	xxii. 19, b	13, 3	lvii. 19.	14 b	
xvii. 6, 20.	15 d	xxxiii. 14.	3	Jer. iv. 26.	11	
xxvi. 22.	15 a	Josh. v. 12.	3	xi. 19.	12	
xxviii. 3.	15 e	Judg. ix. 11.	14 c	xxiii. 3.	15 a	
xxxv. 11.	15 b	2 Kings viii. 6.	3	Lam. iv. 9.	14 d	
xli. 52.	15 d	Neh. ix. 25.	2	Ezek. xvii. 5.	7	
xliii. 11.	6	Job xxxi. 39.	15	xix. 10.	15 c	
xlviii. 4.	15 f	Ps. xcii. 14.	14 a	xxxvi. 11.	15 a	
xlix. 22, 22.	15 c	Prov. x. 16.	15 c	xlvii. 12, 12,		
Exod. i. 7.	15 a	x. 11.	3	12.	15 g, 4, 15 g	
xxi. 22.	9	Cant. vii. 11.	1	Dan. iv. 12, 14, 21.	1 a	
xxii. 29.	13	Isa. v. 1.a	5, 16	Hos. xiii. 15.	15 h	
xxiii. 10.	3	x. 18.	11	Hab. iii. 17.	8	
Lev. xxiii. 39.	3	xvii. 6.	15 c	Hag. i. 10.	8	
xxv. 3, 15, 16, 21, 22,	15 a	xxvii. 6.	14 d	Mal. i. 12.	14 b	
22.	3	xxix. 17, 17.	11			

β *lit.* horn of the son of oil.

FRUSTRATE

פָּרַר to break ; to break or make void. HIPHIL *inf.* Ezra iv. 5 ; *part.* Isa. xliv. 25.

FRY

רָבַךְ to fry, to bake. HOPHAL *part.* Lev. vii. 12 : 1 Chron. xxiii. 29.

מַרְחֶשֶׁת *f.* a vessel for baking or frying : Lev. ii. 7 ; vii. 9.

FUEL

אׇכְלָה *f.* meat, food, fuel, &c. : Ezek. xv. 4, 6 ; xxi. 32. מַאֲכֹלֶת *f.* meat : Isa. ix. 5, 19.

FUGITIVE

בְּרִיחַ *m.* a bar ; so gate, border, &c. ; Gesenius understands the word in the following passage of fugitives from בָּרַח to flee : Isa. xv. 5. מִנְרָה *m.* flight ; fugitive : Ezek. xvii. 21.

נוע to wander. KAL *part.* Gen. iv. 12, 14.

נָפַל to fall. KAL *part.* Poel, 2 Kings xxv. 11.

פָּלִיט *m.* one that has escaped by flight, especially from battle and slaughter : Judg. xii. 4.

FULFIL

1 בָּצַע to cut off, to bring to an end ; to accomplish, perform, finish. PIEL *pret.*

2 כָּלָה to be completed, finished, to be perfected. KAL ᵃ *inf.* PIEL ᵇ *pret.* ᶜ *imp.*

3 מָלֵא to fill, to be full ; to be complete, satisfied ; to fulfil, to fulfil a promise, &c. KAL ᵃ *pret.* ᵇ *inf.* ᶜ *fut.* NIPHAL ᵈ *fut.* PIEL ᵉ *pret.* ᶠ *inf.* ᵍ *imp.* ʰ *fut.*

4 סוּף Ch. to have an end, to be fulfilled ; of prophecy. P'AL *pret.*

5 עָשָׂה to do, &c. KAL ᵃ *pret.* ᵇ *inf.* ᶜ *fut.* ᵈ *part.* Poel.

Gen. xxv. 24.	3 c	Num. vi. 5, 13.	3 b	Job xxxix. 2.	3 h
xxix. 21.	3 a	2 Sam. vii. 12.	3 c	Ps. xx. 4, 5.	3 h
xxix. 27.	3 g	xiv. 22.	5 a	cxlv. 19.	5 c
xxix. 28.	3 h	1 Kings ii. 27.	3 f	cxlviii. 8.	5 d
1. 3, 3.	3 c	1 Chron. xxii. 13.	3 e	Jer. xliv. 25.	3 h
Exod. v. 13.	2 c	2 Chron. vi. 4, 15.	5 b	Lam. ii. 17.	3 a
v. 14.	2 b	xxxvi. 21, 21.	3 f	iv. 18.	3 a
vii. 25.	3 d	Ezra i. 1.	2 a	Ezek. v. 2.	3 b
xxiii. 26.	3 h	Job xxxvi. 17.	3 b	Dan. iv. 33.	4
Lev. xii. 4, 6.	3 b			x. 3.	3 b

FULL

1 יוֹם a day ; a full month, year, *lit.* a month, year, of days ; "three full weeks," *lit.* three weeks days : Dan. x. 2.

2 כָּלָה (see *Fulfil*), to make a full end. PIEL *inf.*

3 מָלֵא to fill, to be full ; to give in full tale, *i. e.* to make up in full number, 1 Sam. xviii. 27 ; with another verb, to do anything fully, Num. xiv. 24. KAL ᵃ *pret.* ᵇ *inf.* NIPHAL ᶜ *fut.* PIEL ᵈ *pret.* ᵉ *inf.* כְּתִיב ᶠ *fut.* מְלָא Ch. ITHP'AL ᵍ *pret.* Dan. iii. 19, *marg.* 'filled.' מָלֵא ʰ *adj.* filling, filled, full. מְלֹא ⁱ *m.* fulness ; full, *lit.* fulness of. ᵏ מְלֵאָה *f.* fulness, abundance ; see *Fruit.*

4 רַב *adj.* great, many ; abundant.

5 רָבָה to multiply. HIPHIL *fut.*

6 שָׂבַע implies abundance, hence to be satisfied, filled with abundance of anything ; properly, with food, more rarely with that which supplies thirst : it is used also of the eye, of the earth, of trees, and of the sword. The thing with which a person is filled, satisfied, or not satisfied, is put in the accusative, or is preceded by מִן, by בְּ, or is expressed by לְ before an *inf.* ; *metaph.* to be satisfied or filled with money, fornication, reproach, contempt, troubles, poverty : it is used in respect to that affluence

which produces pride, Prov. xxx. 9, Hos. xiii. 6: it also occasionally carries with it the notion of weariness and disgust, Isa. i. 11, Job vii. 4. Piel takes a double accusative of the person and thing; Hiphil also, but sometimes with מִן, and בְּ of the thing, and once with לְ of the person, Ps. cxlv. 16. KAL [a]pret. [b]inf. [c]fut. [d]שָׂבַע adj. satisfied; "full of years," lit. fully, i. e. satisfied, satiated; Targ. Jon. saturated with all good. שֹׂבַע [e] m. satiety, fulness; abundance. [f]שָׂבְעָה f. id. [g]שִׂבְעָה f. id.

7 שָׁלֵם adj. complete, finished; complete, full.

8 תָּמַם to be finished, completed. HIPHIL [a]inf. [b]תָּמִים adj. complete, whole, perfect. [c]תֹּם m. perfection: Job xxi. 23, marg. 'in his very perfection, or, to the strength of his perfection.'

Gen. xv. 16.	7	2 Kings xv. 13.	1	Eccles. x. 14.	5
xxv. 8.	6 d	1 Chron. xi. 13.	3 h	xi. 3.	3 c
xxxv. 29.	6 d	xvi. 32.	3 i	Isa. i. 11.	6 a
xli. 1.	1	xxi. 22, 24.	3 h	i. 15.	3 a
xli. 7, 22.	3 h	xxiii. 1.	6 a	i. 21.	3 h
Exod. viii. 21.	3 a	xxix. 28.	6 d	ii. 7, 7, 8.	3 c
xvi. 3.	6 e	2 Chron. xxiv. 15.	6 c	vi. 3. β	3 i
xvi. 8.	6 b	Neh. ix. 25.	3 h	viii. 8.	3 i
xvi. 33.	3 i	Esth. iii. 5.	3 c	ix. 9.	3 a
Lev. xvi. 12, 12.	3 i	v. 9.	3 c	xii. 21.	3 a
xix. 29.	3 a	Job vii. 4.	6 a	xv. 9.	3 a
xxv. 29.	1	x. 15.	6 d	xxii. 2.	3 a
xxv. 30.	8 b	xiv. 1.	6 d	xxii. 7.	3 a
xxvi. 5.	6 e	xx. 11.	3 a	xxviii. 8.	3 a
Num. vii. 1.	2	xx. 22.	3 b, or e	xxx. 27.	3 a
vii. 13, 14, 19, 20, 25,		xxi. 23.	8 c	li. 20.	3 a
26, 31, 32, 37, 38,		xxi. 24.	3 a	Jer. iv. 12.	3 h
43, 44, 49, 50, 55,		xxxiii. 18.	3 a	v. 27, 27.	3 a
56, 61, 62, 67, 68,		xxxvi. 16.	3 a	vi. 11, 11.	3 a h
73, 74, 79, 80, 86.	3 h	xlii. 17.	6 d	xxiii. 10.	3 a
xiv. 24.	3 f	Ps. x. 7.	3 a	xxviii. 3, 11.	1
xviii. 27.	3 k	xvi. 11.	6 e	xxxv. 5.	3 a
xxii. 18.	3 i	xvii. 14.	6 c	Lam. i. 1.	4
xxiv. 13.	3 i	xxiv. 1.	3 i	iii. 30.	6 c
Deut. vi. 11, 11.	3 h, 6 a	xxvi. 10.	3 a	Ezek. i. 18.	3 h
viii. 10, 12.	6 a	xxxiii. 5.	3 a	vii. 23, 23.	3 a
xi. 15.	6 a	xlviii. 10.	3 a	ix. 9, 9.	3 c a
xxi. 13.	1	l. 12.	3 i	x. 4.	3 a
xxxiii. 16.	3 i	lxv. 9.	3 a	x. 12.	3 h
xxxiii. 23.	3 h	lxxiii. 10.	3 h	xvi. 49.	6 g
xxxiv. 9.	3 h	lxxiv. 20.	3 a	xvii. 8.	3 h
Judg. vi. 38.	3 i	lxxv. 8.	3 h	xix. 7.	3 i
xvi. 27.	3 a	lxxviii. 25.	6 e	xxviii. 12.	3 i
Ruth i. 21.	3 h	lxxxviii. 3.	6 a	xxxii. 6.	3 c
ii. 12.	7	lxxxix. 11.	3 i	xxxii. 15.	3 i
1 Sam. ii. 5.	6 d	xcvi. 11.	3 i	xxxvii. 1.	3 h
xviii. 27.	3 f	xcviii. 7.	3 i	xxxix. 19. γ	6 f
xxvii. 7.	1	civ. 16.	6 c	xli. 8.	3 i
2 Sam. viii. 2.	3 i	civ. 24.	3 a	Dan. iii. 19.	3 g
xiii. 23.	1	cxix. 64.	3 a	viii. 23.	8 a
xiv. 28.	1	cxxvii. 5.	3 d	x. 2.	1
xxiii. 11.	3 h	cxliv. 13.	3 h	Joel ii. 24.	3 a
1 Kings xi. 6.	3 d	Prov. xvii. 7.	3 h	iii. 13.	3 a
2 Kings iv. 4.	3 h	xxvii. 7.	6 d	Amos ii. 13.	3 h
iv. 39.	3 b	xxvii. 20.	6 c	Nah. i. 10.	6 c
vi. 17.	3 a	xxx. 9.	6 c	iii. 1.	3 h
vii. 15.	3 h	Eccles. i. 7.	3 h	Micah iii. 8.	3 a
ix. 24. a	3 d	iv. 6.	3 i	vi. 12.	3 a
x. 21.	3 c	viii. 11.	3 a	Hab. iii. 3.	3 a
		ix. 3.	3 a	Zech. viii. 5.	3 c

α lit. filled his hand with a bow.   β lit. his glory is the fulness of the whole earth.   γ lit. unto fulness.

FULLER

כָּבַס to wash, cleanse clothes; see *Wash*. KAL *part.* 2 Kings xviii. 17: Isa. vii. 3; xxxvi. 2. PIEL *part.* Mal. iii. 2.

FURBISH

מָרַט to make smooth. KAL *inf.* Ezek. xxi. 11; *part.* Paül, Ezek. xxi. 9, 28. PUAL *part.* Ezek. xxi. 10, 11.

מָרַק to cleanse metal from rust by scouring. KAL *imp.* Jer. xlvi. 4.

FURNACE

אַתּוּן Ch. *com.* oven, furnace: Dan. iii. 6, 11, 15, 17, 19, 20, 21, 22, 23, 26.

כִּבְשָׁן *m.* a furnace, a smelting oven, which subdues metals, or in which bricks are burnt: Gen. xix. 28: Exod. ix. 8, 10; xix. 18.

כּוּר *m.* a crucible, a vessel which would bear the hottest fire, and in which metals of all sorts were refined; hence, figuratively, afflictions, considered as appointed of God to purge from the dross of sin, and to refine the mind to greater purity; the iron furnace seems to denote afflictions of the heaviest kind: Deut. iv. 20: 1 Kings viii. 51: Prov. xvii. 3; xxvii. 21: Isa. xlviii. 10: Jer. xi. 4: Ezek. xxii. 18, 20, 22.

עֲלִיל *m.* furnace, or crucible: Ps. xii. 6.

תַּנּוּר *m.* a baking oven: in the East it often consists only of a large conical pot, which is first heated, and then cakes are baked on its sides: in a similar way the κλίβανος of the Greeks seems to have been formed: Gen. xv. 17: Neh. iii. 11; xii. 38: Isa. xxxi. 9.

FURNISH, FURNITURE

כְּלִי *m.* a general name for all kinds of vessels, &c.: Exod. xxxi. 7, 8, 8, 9; xxxv. 14; xxxix. 33: Jer. xlvi. 19: Nah. ii. 9.

כַּר *m.* a camel's saddle, or camel's tent; a small tent fastened on the back of a camel, in which the women usually sit: Gen. xxxi. 34.

מָלֵא to be filled; Piel, to fill. PIEL *fut.* Isa. lxv. 11.

נָשָׂא to lift up; Piel, to assist, help, by presents especially. PIEL *pret.* 1 Kings ix. 11.

עָנַק to compass about like a chain; Hiphil, to give liberally. HIPHIL *inf.* Deut. xv. 14. *fut.* Deut. xv. 14.

עָרַךְ to set in order. KAL *pret.* Prov. ix. 2. *inf.* Ps. lxxviii. 19.

עָשָׂה to do, to make, &c. KAL *imp.* Jer. xlvi. 19.

FURROW

גְּדוּד *m.* cutting: Ps. lxv. 10.

עַיִן *com.* eye: Hos. x. 10 (כתיב), i. e. before their two eyes.

עֹונָה *f.* iniquity: Hos. x. 10 (קרי), i. e. because of their two sins, the golden calves. This meaning is now generally preferred. Taylor deduces it from עָנָה to labour, to till the ground, in the sense our translators have taken the word.

מַעֲנָה *m.* furrow: Ps. cxxix. 3 (כתיב).

מַעֲנִית *f.* furrow: Ps. cxxix. 3 (קרי).

עֲרוּגָה *f.* ridges or sunk trenches on which vines are planted: Ezek. xvii. 7, 10.

תֶּלֶם *m.* a furrow: Job xxxi. 38; xxxix. 10; Hos. x. 4; xii. 11.

FURTHER

יָסַף to add. KAL *pret.* Deut. xx. 8, *lit.* shall add to speak. HIPHIL *fut.* Num. xxii. 26, *lit.* added to pass on: Job xxxviii. 11, *lit.* but shall not add.

יוֹתֵר *m.* (see *Profit*), residue, something remaining over; more, further: Eccles. xii. 12.

נָשָׂא to bear, to lift up; Piel, to advance, to further, *pr.* to give a lift. PIEL *pret.* Ezra viii. 36.

פּוּק to go out; to give out, afford; to let or cause to be accomplished. HIPHIL *fut.* Ps. cxl. 8.

FURY

בַּעַל *m.* owner; a furious man, *lit.* master of fury: Prov. xxix. 22: Nah. i. 2.

חֵמָא *f.* heat: Dan. xi. 44. חֲמָא and חֲמָא Ch. *f.* Dan. iii. 13, 19.

חֵמָה *f.* heat, wrath, displeasure: Gen. xxvii. 44, &c.

חָרוֹן *m.* burning; fierceness: Job xx. 23.

קְצַף Ch. to be wroth: P'AL *pret.* Dan. ii. 12.

שִׁגָּעוֹן *m.* madness: 2 Kings ix. 20.

GAD

אָזַל to go away; to gad about. KAL *fut.* Jer. ii. 36.

GAIN

תְּבוּאָה *f.* increase, revenue: Prov. iii. 14.

בָּצַע (see *Covetous*), to get by dishonest means. KAL *fut.* Job xxvii. 8. PIEL *fut.* Ezek. xxii. 12. בֶּצַע *m.* prey; unjust gain: Judg. v. 19: Job xxii. 3: Prov. i. 19; xv. 27: Isa. xxxiii. 15; lvi. 11: Ezek. xxii. 13, "dishonest gain;" 27, *id.*: Micah iv. 13.

זְבַן Ch. to buy. P'AL *part.* Dan. ii. 8.

מְחִיר *m.* price: Dan. xi. 39.

תַּרְבִּית *f.* increase, exorbitant usury: Prov. xxviii. 8, "unjust gain."

GALBANUM

חֶלְבְּנָה *f.* a powerful and very fragrant gum procured from a Syrian plant. *Comp.* Celsii Hierobot. tom. I. p. 267. Exod. xxx. 34.

GALEED

גַּל *m.* heap; עֵד *m.* witness: Gen. xxxi. 47, 48.

GALL

מְרֹרָה *f.* bitterness; gall: Job xx. 14, 25. מְרֵרָה *f.* gall: Job xvi. 13.

רֹאשׁ a poisonous plant, which grows in the fields, bears fruit in clusters, and is bitter: hence its frequent connexion with wormwood. Its specific meaning cannot be determined. Perhaps, nightshade; or, according to Michaelis, darnel, *lolium temulentum;* or, according to Oedman, the poisonous *coloquintida;* or, according to Celsius (Hierob. II. 46), the *cicuta;* severe punishment, bitter suffering: Deut. xxix. 18: Ps. lxix. 21: Jer. viii. 14; ix. 15; xxiii. 15: Lam. iii. 5, 19: Amos vi. 12. רוֹשׁ *m.* Deut. xxxii. 32.

GALLANT

אַדִּיר *adj.* see *Glory:* Isa. xxxiii. 21.

GALLERY

אַתִּיק *m.* an obscure expression in architecture, but probably a gallery with pillars along the side of a building: Ezek. xli. 15, 16; xlii. 3, 3, 5. אַתִּיק *m. id.* Ezek. xli. 15 (כתיב).

רַהַט *m.* canal, trough; gallery: Cant. vii. 5.

GALLEY

אֳנִי *c.* ship; *collect.,* navy, fleet: Isa. xxxiii. 21.

GALLOWS

עֵץ *m.* wood, tree: Esth. v. 14, 14; vi. 4; vii. 9, 10; viii. 7; ix. 13, 25.

GAMMADIMS

גַּמָּדִים *m. pl.* proper name of a people, probably of Phœnicia, of whom nothing farther is known; others, bold, stout, from the Arabic, probably warriors: Ezek. xxvii. 11.

GAP

פֶּרֶץ *m.* breach: Ezek. xiii. 5, *marg.* 'or, breaches;' xxii. 30.

GAPE

פָּעַר to open the mouth wide; see *Open.* KAL *pret.* Job xvi. 10.

פָּצָה to open (the mouth); see *Open.* KAL *pret.* Ps. xxii. 13.

GARDEN

גַּן *com.* a garden (fenced in); see *Defend:* Gen. ii. 8, &c. גַּנָּה *f. id.* Num. xxiv. 6: Job viii. 16: Eccles. ii. 5: Isa. i. 29, 30; lxi. 11; lxv. 3; lxvi. 17: Jer. xxix. 5, 28: Amos iv. 9; ix. 14. גַּנָּה *f. id.* Esth. i. 5; vii. 7, 8: Cant. vi. 11.

GARLICK

שׁוּם *m.* a herb, very plenteous and much esteemed in Egypt: Num. xi. 5.

GARMENT

1 אַדֶּרֶת *f.* a garment of distinction, a robe.

2 בֶּגֶד *m.* is used of any kind of clothing that covers the body, or keeps it warm; whether ordinary or precious, for daily use or solemn occasions, common or sacred purposes, to express joy or sorrow; hence the Hebrew generally admits of some other word of designation; to be "clothed with garments of salvation," Isa. lxi. 10, is to be in a happy or joyful state, as people at festivals put on their most beautiful attire; or they may mean garments of acquittal and deliverance, *cf.* Zech. iii. 1-5. Such are called, still, in the East, Cafftan or Kalaa.—*Chardin's Voyages.* Rev. iii. 5 is also an allusion to such; and 1 Macc. x. 62. Filthy garments are the opposite to these, Zech. iii. 3, denoting the condition of one under guilt or condemnation; a similar custom prevailed with the Romans; garments of vengeance are military garments, proper for the occasion: Gen. xxxviii. 14, 19, &c.

3 כְּתֹנֶת *f.* (see *Coat*), a garment of divers colours, embroidered,

and otherwise ornamented; the dress of kings' daughters and ladies of rank.

4 תַּכְרִיךְ *m.* a wide garment.

5 לְבוּשׁ *m.* clothing. לְבֻשׁ Ch. *m. id.*

6 מִדָּה *f.* extension; garment spread out. ᵃ מְדוּ *m.* garment. ᵇ מַד *m.* garment spread out.

7 מַעֲטֶה *m.* a garment, a covering.

8 שִׂמְלָה *f.* a garment for men or women; see *Cloth.* By transposition of two letters, ᵃ שַׂלְמָה *f. id.*

9 שִׁית *m.* dress, attire.

10 שַׁעַטְנֵז *m.* a cloth made of divers threads.

No. 2 not included.

Gen. ix. 23.	8	2 Sam. xx. 8.	6 b	Ps. civ. 6.	5
xxv. 25.	1	1 Kings x. 25.	8 a	cix. 18.	6 b
xxxv. 2.	8	xi. 29, 30.	8 a	cxxxiii. 2.	6
xlix. 11.	5	1 Chron. xix. 4.	6 a	Prov. xxx. 4.	8
Lev. vi. 10.	6 b	Ezra ii. 69.	3	Cant. vi. 11.	8 a
Deut. xxii. 5.	8	Neh. vii. 70, 72.	5	Isa. ix. 5.	8
xxii. 11.	10	Esth. viii. 15.	4	lxi. 3.	7
Josh. vii. 21, 24.	1	Job xxx. 18.	5	Lam. iv. 14.	5
ix. 5. 13.	8 a	xxxviii. 9, 14.	5	Dan. iii. 21.	5 a
Judg. viii. 25.	8	xli. 13.	5	vii. 9.	5 a
1 Sam. xviii. 4.	6 b	Ps. lxix. 11.	5	Micah ii. 8.	8 a
2 Sam. x. 4.	6 a	lxxiii. 6.	9	Zech. xiii. 4.	1
xiii. 18, 19.	3	civ. 2.	8 a	Mal. ii. 16.	5

GARNER

אוֹצָר *m.* store, stores, treasure-house: Joel i. 17.

מְזָו *m.* cell, garner: Ps. cxliv. 13. מְזָוִים *m. pl.*

GARNISH

צָפָה see *Overlay.* PIEL *fut.* 2 Chron. iii. 6, *marg.* 'covered.'

שִׁפֵּר to adorn. PIEL *pret.* Job xxvi. 13, implying the making of them beautiful and pleasant to the eye; so κόσμος, the world, because of its beauty.

GARRISON

נְצִיב *m.* a military post or station: 1 Sam. x. 5; xiii. 3, 4: 2 Sam. viii. 6, 14, 14: 1 Chron. xi. 16; xviii. 13: 2 Chron. xvii. 2. מַצָּב *m. id.* 1 Sam. xiii. 23; xiv. 1, 4, 6, 11, 15: 2 Sam. xxiii. 14. מַצָּבָה *f. id.* 1 Sam. xiv. 12. מַצֵּבָה *f. id.* Ezek. xxvi. 11.

GATE

דֶּלֶת *f.* door, gate; *dual,* double doors, folding doors: Deut. iii. 5: Josh. vi. 26: 1 Sam. xxiii. 7: 1 Kings xvi. 34: 2 Chron. viii. 5; xiv. 7: Neh. xiii. 19: Ps. cvii. 16: Prov. viii. 34: Isa. xlv. 1, 2: Jer. xlix. 31: Ezek. xxvi. 2; xxxviii. 11.

סַף *m.* threshold: 1 Chron. ix. 19, 22.

פֶּתַח *m.* a door of a porch or house usually very low, to hinder the entrance of robbers; hence the import of Prov. xvii. 19.—1 Kings xvii. 10: 1 Chron. xix. 9: Esth. v. 1: Prov. xvii. 19: Cant. vii. 13: Isa. iii. 26; xiii. 2.

שַׁעַר *m.* gate of a city, in which were held markets, courts of judgment, and where the idle assembled; a gate of a palace, which, as used only by the prince, was lofty as well as magnificent, and never opened but for his use, hence the import of Ps. xxiv. 7, and of Ezek. xliv. 1, 2.

A gate is sometimes put for the people who come out of it, *i. e.* all the inhabitants of a city, Ruth iii. 11. Gen. xix. 1, &c., frequent.

תְּרַע Ch. *m.* an opening; the gate of the royal palace, over which Daniel was appointed: Dan. ii. 49.

GATHER

1 אָגַר to collect, to gather in the harvest. KAL ᵃ *pret.* ᵇ *fut.* ᶜ *part.* Poel.

2 אָסַף to take in, bring in, gather in; *seq.* אֶל, עַל, and לְ, properly connoting some place or situation to which things or persons are taken or gathered; it applies to things dispersed, or otherwise collected for preservation or destruction. To be gathered to his fathers, is a peculiar phrase deserving notice; it is distinguished from death which precedes, and from burial of the body which follows: Gen. xxv. 8; xxxv. 29: 2 Kings xxii. 20. It seems to denote the being received by his own people, or among them. We read in the N. T. of being received into Abraham's bosom, or of sitting down with Abraham, Isaac, and Jacob, in the kingdom of heaven, as at a feast; so that to be gathered to his own people, is to be with them in joy or torment in Hades. It is sometimes joined with קָבַץ, with an evident distinction of meaning; קָבַץ applying more to the collecting of that which is dispersed, and אָסַף to the assembling or bringing together those things which might be dispersed; see *Rereward.* The two words are used in Micah iv. 6. With *inf.,* generally gathered. KAL ᵃ *pret.* ᵇ *inf.* ᶜ *imp.* ᵈ *fut.* ᵉ *part.* Poel. NIPHAL ᶠ *pret.* ᵍ *inf.* ʰ *imp.* ⁱ *fut.* ᵏ *part.* PIEL ˡ *part.* PUAL ᵐ *pret.* ⁿ *part.* HITHPAEL ᵒ *inf.* ᵖ אָסִיף *m.* in-gathering. ۹ אֹסֶף *m.* collection, gathering. ʳ אֲסֵפָה *f.* a gathering together.

3 אָרָה to pluck, pluck off. KAL *pret.*

4 בָּזַז to take and carry off booty and pillage. KAL *part.* Poel.

5 בָּלַס to attend to and cultivate figs. KAL *part.* Poel, one who nips sycamore figs, which helps to ripen.

6 בָּצַר to cut off, to cut away; to gather the vintage of grapes. KAL ᵃ *fut.* ᵇ *part.* Poel, "grape gatherers."

7 גָּדַד to cut; to break in upon; to crowd in great numbers into one place. KAL ᵃ *fut.* HITHPAEL ᵇ *fut.*

8 גּוּר see *Sojourn.* The primary meaning of this word may have been to sojourn collectively, and so it comes to express the idea of being collected together, and is applied to assembling for war, to catching fish in a net, to a gathering or sweeping whirlwind, to a barn in which corn is gathered. With *inf.,* surely gather. KAL ᵃ *pret.* ᵇ *inf.* ᶜ *fut.*

9 דָּגַר to gather as a bird her eggs or young for warmth; Gesenius and others, brood or cherish, after the Vulg. *fovet.* KAL *pret.*

10 זָעַק to cry out; to gather or be gathered by proclamation. NIPHAL ᵃ *pret.* ᵇ *fut.* HIPHIL ᶜ *fut.*

11 חָלַל (see *Profane*), to apply to common uses. PIEL ᵃ *fut.* Deut. xxviii. 30, gather the grapes thereof, *marg.* 'profane, or, use it as common meat;' *i. e.* thou art at liberty to

eat it as common after the first four years, during which it was to be accounted sacred; *comp.* Deut. xx. 6.

12 יָעַד to appoint; to come together by appointment or agreement. NIPHAL [a]*pret.* [b]*part.*

13 יְקָהָה *f.* subjection, submission, ready obedience, according to all modern critics, rather than from קָוָה.

14 כָּנַס to collect, gather, heap up stones, treasures, water; to gather together persons. KAL [a]*pret.* [b]*inf.* [c]*imp.* [d]*part.* Poel. PIEL [e]*pret.* [f]*fut.*

15 כְּנַשׁ Ch. to gather together, to assemble. P'AL [a]*inf.* ITHPAEL [b]*part.*

16 לָקַט to pick up or gather things from the earth, to glean. KAL [a]*pret.* [b]*inf.* [c]*imp.* [d]*fut.* PIEL [e]*inf.* [f]*fut.* [g]*part.* PUAL [h]*fut.* HITHPAEL [i]*fut.*

17 לָקַשׁ to gather the fruits of the vineyard or field. PIEL *fut.*

18 מָלֵא to fill or be filled. Gather (Heb. fill) the shields, make them completely strong and good; *or*, fill them with your bodies, defend yourselves with them: Jer. li. 11. Hithpael, they have gathered themselves together, *i.e.* they filled up themselves, they supplied every vacancy, and rushed together against me. KAL [a]*imp.* PIEL [b]*imp.* HITHPAEL [c]*fut.*

19 מָעַט to be few or little; to make or do anything a little, or in a slight degree. HIPHIL *part.*

20 נָתַךְ to pour self out, to be poured out, to melt. HIPHIL [a]*pret.* [b]*fut.*

21 סָפַח to add; to be gathered together. PUAL *fut.*

22 סָקַל to stone, to gather out stones. PIEL [a]*imp.* [b]*fut.*

23 עוּז to flee for refuge; "to gather themselves to flee." HIPHIL [a]*pret.* [b]*imp.*

24 עָרַם to be high; to be heaped up. NIPHAL *pret.*

25 עָשָׂה to work about anything; "gathered a host," *marg.* '*or*, wrought mightily.' KAL *fut.*

26 צָבַר to heap up. KAL *fut.*

27 צָעַק to cry, to call together. NIPHAL *fut.*

28 קָבַץ to take hold of, to collect food, spoil, wealth, also persons; *fig.*, iniquity: with אֶל, אֵלָיו and עָלָיו. Piel, to gather in the arms, or bosom, Isa. xl. 11; liv. 7; to bring together, to assemble animals, men, people, especially the dispersed; to gather to oneself, to draw in, to withdraw, Joel ii. 6: Nah. ii. 10. With the *inf.*, surely gather. KAL [a]*pret.* [b]*imp.* [c]*fut.* [d]*part.* Poel. [e]*part.* Paül. NIPHAL [f]*pret.* [g]*inf.* [h]*imp.* [i]*fut.* [k]*part.* PIEL [l]*pret.* [m]*inf.* [n]*imp.* [o]*fut.* [p]*part.* PUAL [q]*part.* HITHPAEL [r]*pret.* [s]*imp.* [t]*fut.* [u]קְבֻצָה *f.* collection, heap.

29 קָהַל to call, to call together, to assemble either on a civil or religious account; see *Congregation.* NIPHAL [a]*pret.* [b]*inf.* [c]*fut.* HIPHIL [d]*pret.* [e]*inf.* [f]*imp.* [g]*fut.*

30 קָוָה to wait, to look for; Niphal, to be gathered together, as waters, or people. NIPHAL [a]*pret.* [b]*fut.* [c]מִקְוֶה *m.* a congregation, gathering together.

31 קָלָה probably for קָהַל to congregate. NIPHAL *fut.* כתיב.

32 קָשַׁשׁ to pick up straws, sticks, &c., wherever they may be found. KAL [a]*imp.* Poel. [b]*pret.* [c]*inf.* [d]*part.* HITHPOEL [e]*imp.*

33 רָבָה to multiply, to "gather much." HIPHIL *part.*

34 רָכַשׁ to get, acquire. KAL *pret.*

35 שָׁמַע to hear; to make to hear, to call together. PIEL *fut.*

Gen. i. 9.	30 b
i. 10.	30 c
vi. 21.	2 a
xii. 5.	34
xxv. 8, 17.	2 i
xxix. 3.	2 f
xxix. 7.	2 g
xxix. 8.	2 i
xxix. 22.	2 d
xxxi. 46.	16 c
xxxiv. 30.	2 f
xxxv. 29.	2 i
xli. 35, 48.	23 c
xli. 49.	26
xlvii. 14.	16 f
xlix. 1.	2 h
xlix. 2.	28 h
xlix. 10.	13
xlix. 29.	2 k
xlix. 33, 33.	2 d i
Exod. iii. 16.	2 a
iv. 29.	2 d
v. 7.	32 b
v. 12.	32 c
viii. 14.	26
ix. 19.	23 b
xv. 8.	24
xvi. 4, 22.	16 a
xvi. 5, 17, 21, 26.	16 d
xvi. 16.	16 c
xvi. 18, 18, 18.	33, 19, 16 a
xvi. 27.	16 b
xxiii. 10.	2 a
xxiii. 15.	2 p
xxiii. 16, 16.	2 p b
xxxii. 1.	29 c
xxxii. 26.	2 i
xxxiv. 22.	2 p
xxxv. 1.	29 g
Lev. viii. 3.	29 f
viii. 4.	29 c
xix. 9, 10.	16 f
xxiii. 22.	16 f
xxiii. 39.	2 b
xxv. 3.	2 a
xxv. 5, 11.	6 a
xxv. 20.	2 d
xxvi. 25.	2 f
Num. viii. 9.	29 d
x. 4.	12 a
x. 7.	29 e
xi. 8.	16 a
xi. 16.	2 c
xi. 22.	2 i
xi. 24.	2 d
xi. 32, 32, 32.	2 d, 19, 2 a
xiv. 35.	12 b
xv. 32, 33.	30 d
xvi. 3.	29 c
xvi. 11.	12 b
xvi. 19.	29 g
xvi. 42.	29 b
xix. 9.	2 a
xix. 10.	2 e
xx. 2.	29 c
xx. 8.	29 f
xx. 10.	29 g
xx. 24, 26.	2 i
xxi. 16.	2 c
xxi. 23.	2 d
xxvii. 3.	12 b
xxvii. 13, 13.	2 f
xxxi. 2.	2 i
Deut. iv. 10.	29 f
xi. 14.	2 a
xiii. 16.	28 c
xvi. 13.	2 b
xxiv. 21.	6 a
xxviii. 30.	11
xxviii. 38.	2 d
xxviii. 39.	1 b
xxx. 3.	28 l
xxx. 4.	28 o
xxxi. 12, 28.	29 f

Deut. xxxii. 50, 50.	2 h i
xxxiii. 5.	2 o
Josh. ix. 2.	28 t
x. 5.	2 i
x. 6.	28 f
xxii. 12.	29 c
xxiv. 1.	2 d
Judg. i. 7.	16 g
ii. 10.	2 f
iii. 13	2 d
iv. 13.	10 c
vi. 33.	2 f
vi. 34, 35.	10 b
vii. 23, 34.	27
ix. 6.	2 i
ix. 27.	6 a
ix. 47.	28 r
x. 17.	27
xi. 3.	16 i
xi. 20.	2 d
xii. 1.	27
xii. 4.	28 c
xvi. 23.	2 f
xviii. 22.	10 a
xx. 1.	29 c
xx. 11, 14.	2 i
Ruth ii. 7.	2 a
1 Sam. v. 8, 11.	2 d
vii. 5.	28 b
vii. 6.	28 i
vii. 7.	28 r
viii. 4.	28 t
xiii. 5.	2 f
xiii. 11.	2 k
xiv. 48.	25
xv. 4.	35
xvii. 1, 1.	2 d i
xvii. 2.	2 f
xx. 38.	16 f
xxii. 2.	28 t
xxv. 1.	28 i
xxviii. 1.	28 c
xxviii. 4, 4.	28 i c
xxix. 1.	28 c
2 Sam. ii. 25.	28 t
ii. 30.	28 c
iii. 21.	28 c
vi. 1.	2 d
x. 15.	2 i
x. 17.	2 d
xii. 28.	2 c
xii. 29.	2 d
xiv. 14.	2 i
xvii. 11.	2 g i
xx. 14.	29 c, or 31
xxi. 13.	2 d
xxiii. 9.	2 f
xxiii. 11.	2 i
1 Kings x. 26.	2 d
xi. 24.	28 c
xvii. 10, 12.	32 d
xviii. 19.	28 b
xviii. 20.	28 c
xx. 1.	28 a
xxii. 6.	28 c
2 Kings iii. 21.	27
iv. 39, 39.	16 e f
vi. 24.	28 c
x. 18.	28 c
xxii. 4.	2 a
xxii. 9.	20 a
xxii. 20, 20.	2 e f
xxiii. 1.	2 d
1 Chron. xi. 1.	28 i
xi. 13.	2 f
xiii. 2.	28 i
xiii. 5.	29 g
xv. 3.	29 g
xvi. 35.	28 n
xix. 7.	2 f
xix. 17.	2 d
xxii. 2.	14 b
xxiii. 2.	2 d
2 Chron. i. 14.	2 d
xi. 1.	29 g

2 Chron. xii. 5.	2 f
xiii. 7.	28 i
xv. 9.	28 c
xv. 10.	28 i
xviii. 5.	28 c
xx. 4.	28 i
xx. 25.	4
xxiii. 2.	28 c
xxiv. 5, 5.	28 c b
xxiv. 11.	2 d
xxv. 5.	28 c
xxviii. 24.	2 d
xxix. 4, 15, 20.	2 d
xxx. 3.	2 f
xxxii. 4.	28 i
xxxii. 6.	28 c
xxxiv. 9.	2 a
xxxiv. 17.	20 b
xxxiv. 28, 28.	2 e f
xxxiv. 29.	2 d
Ezra iii. 1.	2 i
vii. 28.	28 c
viii. 15.	28 c
x. 7.	28 g
x. 9.	28 i
Neh. i. 9.	28 o
v. 16.	28 e
vii. 5.	28 c
viii. 1.	2 i
viii. 13.	2 f
xii. 28.	2 i
xii. 44.	14 b
xiii. 11.	28 o
Esth. ii. 3.	28 c
ii. 8, 19.	28 g
iv. 16.	14 c
viii. 11.	29 b
ix. 2, 16.	29 a
ix. 15.	29 c
Job xi. 10.	29 g
xvi. 10.	18 c
xxiv. 6. *a*	17
xxvii. 19.	2 i
xxx. 7.	21
xxxiv. 14.	2 d
xxxix. 12.	2 d
Ps. xxvi. 9.	2 d
xxxiii. 7.	14 d
xxxv. 15, 15.	2 f
xxxix. 6.	2 e
xli. 6.	28 c
xlvii. 9.	2 f
l. 5.	2 c
lvi. 6.	8 c
lix. 3.	8 c
xciv. 21.	7 a
cii. 22.	28 g
civ. 22.	2 i
civ. 28.	16 d
cvi. 47.	28 n
cvii. 3.	28 l
cxl. 2.	8 c
cxlvii. 2.	14 f
Prov. vi. 8.	1 a
x. 5.	1 c
xiii. 11.	28 d
xxvii. 25.	2 f
xxviii. 8.	28 o
xxx. 4.	2 a
Eccles. ii. 8.	14 a
ii. 26.	2 b
iii. 5.	14 b
Cant. v. 1.	3
vi. 2.	16 b
Isa. v. 2.	22 b
x. 14, 14.	2 b a
x. 31.	23 a
xi. 12.	28 o
xiii. 4.	2 k
xvii. 5, 5.	2 b, 16 g
xxii. 9.	28 o
xxiv. 22, 22.	2 m r
xxvii. 12.	16 h
xxxii. 10.	2 q
xxxiii. 4, 4.	2 m q

Isa. xxxiv. 15, 15.	9, 28 f	Jer. xxxii. 37.	28 p	Hos. viii. 10.	28 o
xxxiv. 16.	28 l	xl. 10.	2 c	ix. 6.	28 o
xl. 11.	28 o	xl. 12.	2 d	x. 10.	2 m
xliii. 5.	28 o	xl. 15.	28 k	Joel i. 14.	2 c
xliii. 9.	28 f	xlix. 5.	28 p	ii. 6.	28 l
xliv. 11.	28 t	xlix. 5.	6 b	ii. 16, 16.	2 c
xlix. 5.	2 i	xlix. 14.	28 s	iii. 2.	28 l
xlix. 18.	28 f	li. 11.	18 a	iii. 11.	28 f
liv. 7.	28 o	Ezek. xi. 17.	28 l	Amos vii. 14.	5
liv. 15, 15.	8 b c a	xvi. 37, 37.	28 p l	Obad. 5.	6 b
lvi. 8, 8, 8.	2ꝫ p o k	xx. 34, 41.	28 l	Micah i. 7.	28 l
lx. 4.	28 f	xxii. 19.	28 d	ii. 12.	28 m o
lx. 7.	28 l	xxii. 20, 20.	28 u c	iv. 6.	28 o
lxii. 9.	2 l	xxii. 21.	14 e	iv. 11.	2 f
lxii. 10.	22 a	xxiv. 4.	2 c	iv. 12.	28 l
lxvi. 18.	28 m	xxviii. 25.	28 m	v. 1.	7 b
Jer. iii. 17.	30 a	xxix. 5.	28 i	vii. 1.	2 q
iv. 5.	18 b	xxix. 13.	28 o	Nah. ii. 10.	28 l
vi. 1.	23 b	xxxiv. 13.	28 l	iii. 18.	28 p
vi. 9.	6 b	xxxvi. 24.	28 l	Hab. i. 9, 15.	2 d
vii. 18.	16 g	xxxvii. 21.	28 l	ii. 5.	2 d
viii. 2.	2 i	xxxviii. 8.	28 q	Zeph. ii. 1, 1.	32 e a
ix. 22.	2 l	xxxviii. 12.	2 n	iii. 8.	2 a
x. 17.	2 c	xxxviii. 13.	29 d	iii. 18.	2 a
xxiii. 3.	28 o	xxxix. 17.	2 h	iii. 19.	28 o
xxv. 33.	2 i	xxxix. 27.	28 l	iii. 20.	28 m
xxvi. 9.	29 c	xxxix. 28.	14 e	Zech. x. 8, 10.	28 o
xxix. 14.	28 l	Dan. iii. 2.	15 a	xii. 3.	2 f
xxxi. 8.	28 l	iii. 3, 27.	15 b	xiv. 2.	2 a
xxxi. 10.	28 o	Hos. i. 11.	28 f	xiv. 14.	2 m

a or, the wicked gather the vintage.

GAZE

רָאָה   to see, look earnestly, attentively.   KAL *inf.* Exod. xix. 21.   רְאִי *m.* a sight, vision, spectacle, gazing stock : Nah. iii. 6.

GENDER

יָלַד   to beget ; to bring forth.   KAL *pret.* Job xxxviii. 29.

עָבַר   to pass ; to cause to pass, to conceive.   PIEL *pret.* Job xxi. 10, the bull (or the cow) gendereth.

רָבַע   to lie down.   HIPHIL *fut.* Lev. xix. 19.

GENEALOGY

יַחַשׂ   *m.* a genealogy or register of descent in a family by the father's side : ^a Neh. vii. 5.   Hence יָחַשׂ *verb denom.* to enrol one's name in the genealogical tables ; to be enrolled.   KAL ^b *pret.* HITHPAEL ^c *inf.* ^d *part.*

1 Chron. iv. 33.	c	1 Chron. ix. 1.	b	Ezra ii. 62.	d
v. 1, 7.	c	ix. 22.	c	viii. 1, 3.	c
v. 17.	b	2 Chron. xii. 15.	c	Neh. vii. 5, 5.	c a
vii. 5, 7, 9, 40.	c	xxxi. 16, 17, 18, 19.	c	vii. 64.	d

GENERAL

שַׂר   *m.* see *Captain*.   1 Chron. xxvii. 34.

GENERATION

דּוֹר   *m.* an age, a generation of men ; a race of men cotemporary, Gen. vi. 9, *or*, implying conformity, Prov. xxx. 10–14.   So it may be understood in that disputed passage, Isa. liii. 8, "his generation," the race conformed to the Messiah, equivalent to "the seed," verse 10 : Gen. vi. 9, &c., all, many generations, Heb. generation and generation ; every generation, Heb. *id.* דָּר *m.* Ch. *id.* Dan. iv. 3, 3, 34, 34.

תּוֹלְדוֹת   families, generations ; family history ; origin, or events in reference to the creation of the world, &c., Jarchi, sometimes order of birth : Gen. xxv. 13 : Exod. xxviii. 10.— Gen. ii. 4 ; v. 1 ; vi. 9 ; x. 1, 32 ; xi. 10, 27 ; xxv. 12, 13, 19 ; xxxvi. 1, 9 ; xxxvii. 2 : Exod. vi. 16, 19 : Num. i.

20, 22, 24, 26, 28, 30, 32, 34, 36, 38, 40, 42 ; iii. 1 : Ruth iv. 18 : 1 Chron. i. 29 ; v. 7 ; vii. 2, 4, 9 ; viii. 28 ; ix. 9, 34 ; xxvi. 31.

GENTILE

גּוֹי   *m.* a people, in the *pl.* of the other nations besides Israel : Gen. x. 5 : Judg. iv. 2, 13, 16 : Isa. xi. 10 ; xlii. 1, 6 ; xlix. 6, 22 ; liv. 3 ; lx. 3, 5, 11, 16 ; lxi. 6, 9 ; lxii. 2 ; lxvi. 12, 19 : Jer. iv. 7 ; xiv. 22 ; xvi. 19 ; xlvi. 1 : Lam. ii. 9 : Ezek. iv. 13 : Hos. viii. 8 : Joel iii. 9 : Micah v. 8 : Zech. i. 21 : Mal. i. 11.

GENTLE

אַט   slowly, softly ; gently, tenderly : 2 Sam. xviii. 5.

עָנָה   to be afflicted, to be humble.   KAL *inf.* 2 Sam. xxii. 36 ; or, עֲנָוָה *f.* gentleness, *ibid.* עֲנָוָה *f.* gentleness : Ps. xviii. 35.

GERAH

גֵּרָה   *f.* a grain, berry ; used as the smallest weight or coin of the Hebrews ; a gerah was equivalent to the twentieth part of a shekel.   Lxx., Vulg., ὀβολος, *obolus*.   Exod. xxx. 13 : Lev. xxvii. 25 : Num. iii. 47 ; xviii. 16 : Ezek. xlv. 12.

GERSHOM

גֵּרְשֹׁם   *pr. n.* from גֵּר a sojourner ; and שָׁם there ; a son of Moses : Exod. ii. 22 ; xviii. 3.

GET

1   אָסַף   to gather, to take or bring to a place, to betake oneself to.   NIPHAL *fut.*

2   בָּהַל   to be in great haste.   PUAL *part.* gotten hastily, or greedily. —Schultens.

3   בּוֹא   to come, &c.   KAL ^a *pret.* ^b *inf.* ^c *imp.* ^d *fut.*   HIPHIL ^e *fut.*

4   בָּצַע   to covet, to gain ; or to tear in pieces, to get gain.   KAL *inf.*

5   בָּקַשׁ   to search, to seek for, to try to get ; opposed to אָבַד.   PIEL *inf.*

6   גָּנַב   to steal.   HITHPAEL *fut.*

7   הָלַךְ   to walk, to go away.   KAL *pret.*

8   יָלַךְ   to go, go away.   KAL ^a *inf.* ^b *imp.* ^c *fut.*

9   יָסַף   to add, to increase, to get more.   HIPHIL *pret.*

10   יָצָא   to go out, to get away, out, forth.   KAL ^a *imp.* ^b *fut.*

11   יָרַד   to go down.   KAL ^a *pret.* ^b *imp.*

12   לָקַח   to take, to receive.   KAL ^a *pret.* ^b *imp.* ^c *part.* Poel.

13   מָלַט   see *Escape*.   NIPHAL *fut.*

14   מָצָא   to find.   KAL ^a *pret.* ^b *fut.*

15   נָגַע   to touch, to reach unto.   KAL *fut.*

16   נוּד   to wander, to flee.   KAL ^a *imp.* נוד Ch. P'AL ^b *fut.*

17   נָסַע   to remove, depart.   KAL *imp.*

18   נָשַׂג   to reach, to attain to ; with יָד "able to get," Heb. his hand can attain.   HIPHIL ^a *fut.* ^b *part.*

19 נָתַן to give. HOPHAL *fut.*

20 סוּר to turn aside out of the way. KAL *imp.*

21 עָבַר to pass over. KAL *imp.*

22 עָלָה to go up. KAL [a] *pret.* [b] *fut.* [c] *imp.* [d] *fut.* [e] *part.* Poel. NIPHAL [f] *imp.* [g] *fut.*

23 עָשָׂה to labour about anything, to acquire. KAL [a] *pret.* [b] *inf.* [c] *fut.* [d] *part.* Poel.

24 פּוּק to draw out, to obtain from. HIPHIL *fut.*

25 פֹּעַל *m.* work, getting.

26 קוּם to rise, get up. KAL *imp.*

27 קָנָה to acquire. KAL [a] *pret.* [b] *inf.* [c] *imp.* [d] *fut.* [e] *part.* Poel. קִנְיָן *m.* getting.

28 רָכַב to ride. KAL *fut.*

29 רָכַשׁ to acquire, to gain for oneself. KAL *pret.*

30 רָמַם to be high and lofty. NIPHAL *imp.*

31 שׁוּב to return. KAL [a] *imp.* [b] *fut.*

32 שׂוּם to set or place. KAL *pret.*

Gen. iv. 1.		27 a	Deut. xvii. 8.	22 a	Prov. iv. 5, 5.	27 c
xii. 1.		8 b	xxviii. 43.	22 d	iv. 7, 7, 7.	27 c f c
xii. 5.		23 a	xxxii. 49.	22 c	vi. 33.	14 b
xix. 14.		10 a	Josh. iii. 16.	8 b	ix. 7.	12 c
xxii. 2.		8 b	vii. 10.	26	xv. 32.	27 e
xxxi. 1.		23 a	viii. 15.	22 c	xvi. 16, 16.	27 b
xxxi. 13.		10 a	xxii. 4.	8 b	xvii. 16.	27 b
xxxi. 18, 18, 18.	29, 27 f, 29	Judg. vii. 9.	11 b	xviii. 15.	27 d
xxxiv. 4.		12 b	ix. 48, 51.	22 d	xix. 8.	27 e
xxxvi. 6.		29	xiv. 2, 3.	12 b	xx. 21.	2
xxxix. 12, 15.		10 b	xix. 28.	8 c	xxi. 6.	25
xlii. 2.		11 b	Ruth iii. 3.	11 a	xxii. 25.	12 a
xliv. 17.		22 c	1 Sam. ix. 13.	22 c	Eccles. i. 16.	9
xlv. 17.		3 c	xiii. 15.	22 d	ii. 7.	27 a
xlvi. 6.		29	xv. 6.	11 b	ii. 8.	23 a
Exod. i. 10.		22 a	xx. 29.	13	iii. 6.	5
v. 4.		8 b	xxii. 5.	3 a	Cant. iv. 6.	8 c
v. 11.		19 b	xxiii. 26.	8 a	Isa. xv. 7.	23 a
vii. 15.		8 b	xxiv. 22.	22 a	xxii. 15.	3 c
x. 28.		8 b	xxv. 5.	22 a	xxx. 11.	20
xi. 8.		10 a	xxvi. 12.	8 c	xxx. 22.	10 a
xii. 31.		10 a	2 Sam. iv. 7.	7	xl. 9.	22 c
xix. 24.		11 b	v. 8.	15	xlvii. 5.	3 c
xxiv. 18.		22 d	viii. 13.	23 c	Jer. v. 5.	8 c
xxxii. 7.		11 b	xiii. 20.	28	xiii. 1, 4.	27 a
Lev. xiv. 21.		22 b	xvii. 13.	1	xiii. 2.	27 d
xiv. 22, 30, 31, 32.	18 a	xvii. 23.	23 d	xvii. 11.	23 d
Num. vi. 21.		18 a	xix. 3. a	6, 3 b	xix. i.	27 a
xi. 30.		1	xx. 6.	14 a	xlvi. 4.	22 c
xiii. 17.		22 c	1 Kings i. 13.	3 c	xlviii. 9.	10 b
xiv. 25.		17	ii. 26.	8 b	xlviii. 18.	23 a
xiv. 40.		22 d	xii. 18.	22 b	xlviii. 44.	22 e
xvi. 24.		22 f	xiv. 2.	7	xlix. 30.	16 a
xvi. 27.		22 g	xiv. 12.	8 b	xlix. 31.	22 c
xvi. 45.		30	xvii. 3, 9.	8 b	Lam. iii. 7.	10 b
xxii. 13.		8 b	xviii. 41.	22 c	v. 9. β	3 e
xxii. 34.		31 b	xviii. 44.	11 b	Ezek. iii. 4, 11.	3 c
xxvii. 12.		22 c	2 Kings iii. 13.	8 b	xxii. 27.	4
xxxi. 50.		14 a	vii. 12.	3 d	xxviii. 4, 4.	23 a c
Deut. ii. 13.		21	2 Chron. x. 18.	22 b	xxxviii. 12.	23 d
iii. 27.		22 c	Neh. ix. 10.	28 c	Dan. iv. 14.	16 b
v. 30.		31 a	Job xxxviii. 15.	19	ix. 15.	23 c
viii. 17.		23 a	xxxi. 25.	14 a	Joel iii. 13.	11 b
viii. 18.		23 b	Ps. cxvi. 13.	14 a	Zeph. iii. 19.	32
ix. 12.		11 b	Prov. iii. 13.	24	Zech. vi. 7.	8 b.

a lit. stole to enter. β *lit.* upon our souls, or lives, we brought our bread.

GHOST

גָּוַע to die, to give up the ghost; the word does not strictly signify to give up the soul, though it is implied that the spirit is yielded. KAL *pret.* Lam. i. 19. *fut.* Gen. xxv. 8, 17; xxxv. 29; xlix. 33: Job iii. 11; x. 18; xiii. 19; xiv. 10. See *Die.*

נֶפֶשׁ *com.* animal life : Job xi. 20 : Jer. xv. 9.

GIANT

גִּבּוֹר *adj.* mighty : Job xvi. 14.

נְפִלִים *m. pl. pr.* fallers, apostates fallen from true religion ; and falling on men with violence and rapine, and causing them to fall ; such were also strong and robust in body, and leaders of others : Gen. vi. 4 : Num. xiii. 33, 33.

רְפָאִים a gentile noun, the Rephaim, or sons of Raphah, a Canaanitish race of giants that lived beyond Jordan, from whom Og, the giant king of Bashan, was descended. In a broader sense, it appears to have included all the giant tribes of Canaan, Deut. ii. 11, 20. In subsequent times, the sons of Raphah appear to have been men of extraordinary strength among the Philistines; see 2 Sam. xxi. 16, 18.——Deut. ii. 11, 20, 20 ; iii. 11, 13 : Josh. xii. 4 ; xiii. 12 ; xv. 8 ; xvii. 15 ; xviii. 16 : 1 Chron. xx. 4, 6, 8.

רָפָה *m.* Rapha : 2 Sam. xxi. 16, 18, 20, 22.

GIN

מוֹקֵשׁ *m.* a noose or snare, by which wild beasts are caught : Ps. cxl. 5 ; cxli. 9 : Amos iii. 5.

פַּח *m.* net, snare, perhaps what is laid on the ground and spread out : Job xviii. 9 ; Isa. viii. 14.

GIRD, GIRDLE

1 אַבְנֵט *m.* a belt or girdle to keep up the garments.

2 אָזַר to gird, gird up or about ; to gird on, to gird oneself, to apply to any business with vigour and strength ; Piel, to gird, with a double accusative of the person and thing ; to give success, Isa. xlv. 5 ; it seems to imply abundance in the sense of compassing about, Ps. xxx. 11, and strength, Ps. lxv. 6. KAL [a] *pret.* [b] *imp.* [c] *fut.* [d] *part.* Paül. NIPHAL [e] *part.* PIEL [f] *fut.* [g] *part.* HITHPAEL [h] *pret.* [i] *imp.* אֵזוֹר [k] *m.*

3 אָסַר to bind ; to bind on a sword ; to gird the loins with a girdle, Job xii. 18. Schultens understands this as a mark of captivity or servitude, apprehending that the girdle here signifies the band wherewith captives were bound ; or it may imply to bind by authority and dominion ; *cf.* Ps. cv. 22. KAL [a] *fut.* [b] *part.* Paül.

4 אָפַד to fit or tie a garment to the body with a girdle or sash ; see *Ephod.* KAL *pret.*

5 חָבַשׁ to bind, to bind on, to bind about. KAL *fut.*

6 חָגַר to gird, to gird up, to gird on, an ephod, a girdle, armour, sackcloth ; to gird the sword on the thigh is a part of the ceremony of royal inauguration, Ps. xlv. 3 ; to gird up for expedition and activity. Figuratively, it implies both restraint and abundance, or to be girded with fear, or to be girded with joy ; which may both be resolved into being beset with either. KAL [a] *pret.* [b] *inf.* [c] *imp.* [d] *fut.* [e] *part.* Poel. [f] *part.* Paül. חָגוֹר [g] *m.* binding, a girdle ; girded, clad. חֲגוֹרָה [h] *f.* girdle. מַחֲגֹרֶת [i] *f.* girdle, belt.

7 מֵזַח *m.* a girdle ; *fig.*, strength.

8 שָׁנַס to gird up. PIEL *fut.*

See also *Curious* (Girdle).

Exod. xii. 11.	6 f	1 Kings xviii. 46.	8	Isa. xi. 5, 5.	2 k
xxviii. 4, 39, 40.	1	xx. 11.	6 e	xv. 3.	6 a
xxix. 5.	4	xx. 32.	6 d	xxii. 12.	6 b
xxix. 9, 9.	6 a, 1	2 Kings i. 8, 8.	2 d k	xxii. 21.	1
xxxix. 29.	1	iv. 29.	6 c	xxii. 11.	6 h
Lev. viii. 7, 7, 7.	6 d, 1, 6 d	ix. 1.	6 c	xlv. 5.	2 f
viii. 13, 13.	6 d, 1	Neh. iv. 18.	3 b	Jer. i. 17.	2 c
xvi. 4, 4.	6 d, 1	Job xii. 18, 18.	3 a, 2 k	iv. 8.	6 c
Deut. i. 41.	6 d	xxxviii. 3.	2 b	vi. 26.	6 c
Judg. iii. 16.	6 d	xl. 7.	2 b	xiii. 1. 2, 4, 6, 7, 7,	
1 Sam. ii. 4.	2 a	Ps. xviii. 32.	2 g	10, 11.	2 k
ii. 18.	6 f	xviii. 39.	2 f	xlix. 3.	6 c
xvii. 39.	6 d	xxx. 11.	2 f	Lam. ii. 10.	6 a
xviii. 4.	6 g	xlv. 3.	6 c	Ezek. vii. 18.	6 a
xxv. 13, 13, 13.	6 c d d	lxv. 6.	2 e	xvi. 10.	5
2 Sam. iii. 31.	6 c	xciii. 1.	2 h	xxiii. 15, 15.	6 g k
vi. 14.	6 f	cix. 19, 19.	7, 6 d	xxvii. 31.	6 a
xviii. 11.	6 h	Prov. xxxi. 17.	6 a	xliv. 18.	6 d
xx. 8, 8.	6 f g	xxxi. 24.	6 g	Joel i. 8.	6 f
xxi. 16.	6 f	Isa. iii. 24, 24.	6 h i	i. 13.	6 c
xxii. 40.	2 f	v. 27.	2 k		
1 Kings ii. 5.	6 h	viii. 9, 9.	2 i		

GIRL

יַלְדָּה f. a young female: Joel iii. 3: Zech. viii. 5.

GITTITH

גִּתִּית f. supposed to be the name of an instrument of music invented at Gath, or so called from גַּת a wine-press, because used chiefly at the joyful season of vintage: Ps. viii. title; lxxxi. title; lxxxiv. title.

GIVE

1 אוֹר to be light; Hiphil, to give light (see *Light*), to give (light). HIPHIL *fut.*

2 בּוֹא to come. HIPHIL *fut.*

3 בַּעַל owner, master; "one given to," *i. e.* with the command and use of.

4 בֶּצַע to be greedy, covetous; "to be given to" (covetousness). KAL *part.* Poel.

5 בָּרָה to eat. HIPHIL *fut.* 2 Sam. xiii. 5, *lit.* cause me to eat bread.

6 גָּדַל to be great; to give great. HIPHIL *part.* Ps. xviii. 50, *lit.* magnifying salvation.

7 גְּמוּל m. recompence: Prov. xix. 17, *marg.* 'or, his deed.'

8 דָּבַר to speak; to give, *lit.* to speak, judgment. PIEL *fut.*

9 הָלַל to shine; to give light. HIPHIL *fut.*

10 הָפַךְ to turn; to give another, *lit.* to turn the, heart. KAL *fut.*

11 חָלַק to divide; to give a portion. KAL *pret.*

12 יָהַב to give, supply, contribute that which is wanting; to meet or answer anxious desires; some consider the word to mean, to desire, to be solicitous: 1 Sam. xiv. 41 is translated in the margin, "shew the innocent;" from which Gussetius remarks that Jonathan was legitimately rescued. KAL ᵃ *imp.* יְהַב Ch. P'AL ᵇ *pret.* ᶜ *imp.* ᵈ *part.* active. ᵉ *part.* P'il. ITHP'AL ᶠ *fut.* ᵍ *part.*

13 יָסַף to add. HIPHIL *fut.*

14 יָעַץ to counsel, to give counsel, to give (counsel). KAL ᵃ *pret.* ᵇ *fut.* ᶜ *part.* Poel.

15 מִנְחָה f. a present, a gift, as a mark of honour, or of subjection; the proud daughter of Tyre brings her gift to the church in token of submission to her victorious Lord, when all his enemies have been subdued, Ps. xlv. 12.

16 מָעַט to diminish; to give less, few. HIPHIL *fut.*

17 מָשַׁךְ to draw. Our translators seem to have taken the word in Eccles. ii. 3 in the sense of indulging the flesh in wine; *cf.* Hor. Ep. I. 17, 12, *"Se benignius tractare,"* cutem curare et oblectare vino. KAL *inf.* Eccles. ii. 3, *lit.* to draw my flesh with wine, *or,* to draw forth my flesh unto wine, taking wine in the sense of including all delicacy of living. This interpretation is most approved by older commentators, and suits best to the context. Solomon had tried the opposite extremes of wisdom and pleasure; then he endeavours to temper them together, wisdom duly restraining the delights of the body. So Mercer, Geier, &c.

18 נֶדֶה m. a liberal gift, as the price of prostitution.

19 נָדָן m. the same.

20 נָכָה to smite; to give (wounds). HIPHIL ᵃ *pret.* ᵇ *fut.*

21 נָפַח to breathe out. KAL ᵃ *pret.* ᵇ מַפֵּחַ m. "giving up."

22 נָשָׂא to bear, to lift up; Piel, to help, to make presents. PIEL ᵃ *pret.* ᵇ מַשְׂאֵת f. a gift. ᶜ נְשֻׂאת f. id.

23 נָתַן to give; to lay, set, place; to make, to do; the varied use of this word may be classed under these significations:—I. To give, with an *acc.* of the thing, and לְ of the person, and with אֶל, seldom with an *acc.* of the person; to give in the hand of any one בְּיַד, is to deliver up to his power, but עַל יַד, to entrust, commit, to give grace, &c., is to shew favour, but to give it in the sight of any one is to procure it for another; to give honour, praise, wish, &c., is used in the sense of satisfying, but once in a bad sense, to cause sorrow, Prov. x. 10. Under this head it bears the sense, to grant, to give forth, utter, &c., to tell, to teach, to requite. II. To set, place, with בְּ in, with אֶל unto, within, &c., with עַל upon; it is used for planting, fixing, &c. III. To make, to do; with a double *accus.* to constitute, cause to be; with כְּ to make like. KAL ᵃ *pret.* ᵇ *inf.* ᶜ *imp.* ᵈ *fut.* ᵉ *part.* Poel. ᶠ *part.* Paül. NIPHAL ᵍ *pret.* ʰ *inf.* ⁱ *fut.* ᵏ *part.* HOPHAL ˡ *fut.* נְתַן Ch. P'AL ᵐ *fut.* ⁿ מַתָּן m. a gift. ᵒ מַתְּנָא Ch. f. id. ᵖ מַתָּנָה f. a gift, present, especially a bribe. ۹ מַתַּת f. a gift.

24 סָגַר to shut up; Piel, to deliver up into another's power, so that there is no way of escape. HIPHIL ᵃ *pret.* ᵇ *fut.*

25 סָכַר to shut up; to deliver over into the hands of another. PIEL *pret.*

26 עָשָׂה to do, to make. KAL ᵃ *inf.* NIPHAL ᵇ *fut.*

27 קָרָא to call, to give a name. KAL ᵃ *fut.*

28 רָבָה to multiply; to give more. HIPHIL ᵃ *fut.*

29 רוּם to be lifted up; Hiphil, to bring, to offer. HIPHIL ᵃ *pret.* ᵇ *fut.* ᶜ תְּרוּמָה f. an offering.

30 שׁוּב to return; Hiphil, to bring again, to recompense. HIPHIL *fut.*

31 שׂוּם to put, place, set. KAL ᵃ *pret.* ᵇ *inf.* ᶜ *imp.* ᵈ *fut.* שׂוּם Ch. P'AL ᵉ *imp.* ITHP'AL ᶠ *fut.*

32 שָׁחַד to make a present, to conciliate favour, to bribe; to give a reward. KAL [a] *imp.* [b] שֹׁחַד *m.* a gift, particularly to purchase deliverance from punishment, to turn aside judgment.

33 שָׂכַר to hire; sometimes implying bribery. אֶשְׂכָּר *m.* a gift.

34 שָׁלַח to send. KAL [a] *pret.* PIEL [b] *fut.*

35 שָׁלֵם to be finished, to be at peace; Piel, to restore, make good. PIEL *fut.*

Gen. i. 29.	23 a	Exod. v. 16.	23 k	Num. xviii. 11, 11.	23 n a	Deut. xxi. 1, 23.	23 e	Ruth iv. 12,13.	23 d	2 Kings xii. 11.	23 a

Gen. i. 29. 23 a
ii. 20. 27
iii. 6. 23 d
iii. 12, 12. 23 a
ix. 3. 23 a
xii. '. 23 d
xiii. 15, 17. 23 d
xiv. 20. 23 d
xiv. 21. 23 c
xv. 2. 23 d
xv. 3, 18. 23 a
xv. 7. 23 b
xvi. 3. 23 d
xvi. 5. 23 a
xvii. 8, 16. 23 a
xviii. 7. 23 d
xx. 14. 23 d
xx. 16. 23 a
xxi. 14, 27. 23 d
xxiii. 4. 23 d
xxiii. 9, 9. 23 d
xxiii. 11, 11, 11, 13. 23 a
xxiv. 7, 32, 35, 36, 41. 23 a
xxiv. 53, 53. 23 d a
xxv. 5. 23 d
xxv. 6, 6. 23 a p
xxv. 30. 23 a
xxvi. 3. 23 d
xxvi. 4. 23 a
xxvii. 17, 28. 23 a
xxvii. 37. 23 a
xxviii. 4, 4. 23 d a
xxviii. 13, 22. 23 d
xxviii. 20. 23 a
xxix. 19, 19, 26. 23 b
xxix. 21. 12 a
xxix. 24, 27, 28, 29, 33. 23 d
xxx. 1. 12 a
xxx. 4, 6, 9, 28, 31, 31, 35. 23 d
xxx. 14, 26. 23 c
xxx. 18, 18. 23 a
xxxi. 9. 23 d
xxxiv. 8. 23 c
xxxiv. 9, 11, 21. 23 d
xxxiv. 12, 12, 12. 23 n d c
xxxiv. 14. 23 b
xxxiv. 16. 23 a
xxxv. 4. 23 d
xxxv. 12, 12, 12. 23 a d d
xxxviii. 9. 23 b
xxxviii. 14. 23 g
xxxviii. 16, 17, 18, 18. 23 d
xxxviii. 26. 23 a
xxxix. 21. 23 a
xl. 11, 21. 23 d
xli. 45. 23 a
xlii. 25, 27. 23 b
xliii. 14, 24, 24. 23 d
xliii. 23. 23 a
xlv. 18, 21, 21. 23 d
xlv. 22, 22. 23 a
xlvi. 18, 25. 23 a
xlvii. 11, 17. 23 a
xlvii. 15. 12 a
xlvii. 16. 16. 12 a, 23 d
xlvii. 19. 23 c
xlvii. 22, 24. 23 a
xlviii. a, 9, 22. 23 a
xlix. 21. 23 d
Exod. ii. 9, 21. 23 d
iii. 21. 23 a
v. 7. 13, 23 b
v. 10. 23 e

Exod. v. 16. 23 k
v. 18. 23 i
vi. 4. 23 b
vi. 8, 8. 23 b a
x. 25. 23 d
xi. 3. 23 d
xii. 25. 23 d
xii. 36. 23 a
xiii. 5. 23 b
xiii. 11. 23 a
xvi. 8. 23 b
xvi. 15. 23 a
xvi. 29, 29. 23 a e
xvii. 2. 23 c
xx. 12. 23 e
xxi. 4, 32. 23 d
xxi. 23, 30. 23 a
xxi. 54. 30
xxii. 17. 23 b
xxii. 29, 30. 23 d
xxiii. 8, 8. 32 b
xxiv. 12. 23 d
x v. 16, 21. 23 d
xxviii. 38. 23 p
xxx. 12. 23 a
xxx. 13, 14. 23 d
xxx. 15, 15, 15. 28, 16, 23 b
xxxi. 6. 23 a
xxxi. 18. 23 d
xxxii. 13, 24. 23 d
xxxiii. 1. 23 d
Lev. i. 16. 23 a
vi. 5. 23 d
vi. 17. 23 a
vii. 32, 34. 23 d
vii. 36. 23 b
x. 14. 23 g
x. 17. 23 a
xiv. 34. 23 e
xv. 14. 23 a
xvii. 11. 23 a
xix. 20. 23 g
xx. 2, 24. 23 d
xx. 3. 23 a
xx. 4. 23 b
xxii. 14. 23 a
xxiii. 10. 23 d
xxiii. 38, 38. 23 p d
xxv. 2. 23 e
xxv. 37. 23 d
xxv. 51, 52. 30
xxvi. 4, 6. 23 d
xxvii. 9. 23 d
Num. iii. 9, 9. a 23 a f f
iii. 48. 23 a
iii. 51. 23 d
v. 7. 23 d
v. 10. 23 d
vi. 26. 31 d
viii. 5, 7, 8, 9. 23 d
vii. 6. 23 d
viii. 16. a 23 f f
viii. 19, 19. 23 d f
x. 29. 23 d
xi. 13, 13. 23 b c
xi. 18. 23 a
xi. 21, 25. 23 d
xiv. 8. 23 a
xiv. 23. 23 d
xv. 21. 23 a
xv. 14. 23 a
xvii. 6. 23 d
xviii. 6, 6. 23 f p
xviii. 7, 7. 23 d p
xviii. 8, 8, 12, 19, 21, 24, 26, 28. 23 a

Num. xviii. 11, 11. 23 n a
xviii. 29. 23 p
xix. 3. 23 a
xx. 8, 12, 24. 23 a
xx. 21. 23 b
xxi. 16. 23 d
xxi. 29. 23 a
xxii. 13. 23 b
xxii. 18. 23 d
xxiv. 13. 23 d
xxv. 12. 23 e
xxvi. 54, 54, 54. 28, 16, 23 l
xxvi. 62. 23 g
xxvii. 4. 23 c
xxvii. 7. 23 b d
xxviii. 9, 10, 11, 12. 23 a
xxxi. 29, 30. 23 a
xxxi. 41, 47. 23 d
xxxii. 5. 23 l
xxxii. 7, 9, 29. 23 a
xxxii. 33, 40. 23 d
xxxii. 38. 27
xxxiii. 53. 23 a
xxxiii. 54, 54. 28, 16
xxxiv. 13. 23 b
xxxv. 2, 2. 23 a d
xxxv. 4, 6, 7, 13, 14, 14. 23 d
xxxv. 8, 8, 8, 8. 23 d, 28, 16, 23 d
xxxvi. 2, 2. 23 b
Deut. i. 18, 35. 23 b
i. 20, 25. 23 e
i. 36, 39. 23 d
ii. 5, 5. 23 d a
ii. 9, 9. 23 d a
ii. 12, 24. 23 a
ii. 19, 19. 23 d a
ii. 28. 23 d
ii. 29. 23 e
ii. 31. 23 b
iii. 12, 13, 15, 16, 18, 19. 23 a
iii. 20, 20. 23 e a
iv. 1, 21, 40. 23 e
iv. 38. 23 b
v. 16, 31. 23 e
vi. 10, 23. 23 b
vii. 3. 23 d
vii. 13. 23 b
viii. 10. 23 e
viii. 18. 23 e
ix. 6. 23 d
ix. 11, 23. 23 a
x. 4. 23 d
x. 11, 18. 23 b
xi. 9, 21. 23 b
xi. 14. 23 a
xi. 17, 31. 23 d
xii. 1, 15, 21. 23 a
xii. 9. 23 a
x ii. 11. 23 a
xiii. 12. 23 d
xiii. 17. 23 d
xv. 4, 7. 23 a
xv. 9, 14. 23 d
xv. 10, 10. 23 b d b
xvi. 5, 18, 20. 23 e
xvi. 10. 23 d
xvii. 17. 23 a
xvi. 19, 19. 32 b
xvii. 2, 14. 23 a
xviii. 3. 23 a
xviii. 4. 23 d
xviii. 9. 23 d
xix. 1, 2, 10, 14. 23 a
xix. 8, 8. 23 a b
xx. 14. 23 a
xx. 16. 23 e

Deut. xxi. 1, 23. 23 e
xxi. 17. 23 b
xxii. 14, 17. 31 a
xxii. 16, 19, 29. 23 a
xxiii. 14. 23 b
xxiv. 1, 3. 23 a
xxiv. 4. 23 e
xxiv. 15. 23 d
xxv. 15, 19. 23 e
xxvi. 1, 2. 23 b
xxvi. 3. 23 b
xxvi. 9. 23 d
xxvi. 10, 11, 12, 13, 14, 15. 23 a
xxvii. 2, 3. 23 e
xxviii. 8. 23 e
xxviii. 11, 12, 55. 23 b
xxviii. 31, 32. 23 f
xxviii. 52, 53, 65. 23 a
xxix. 4. 23 a
xxix. 8. 23 d
xxix. 26. 11
xxx. 20. 23 b
xxxi. 5. 23 b
xxxi. 7. 23 b
xxxii. 49, 52. 23 e
xxxiii. 4. 23 d
Josh. i. 2, 11. 23 e
i. 3, 13, 14. 23 a
i. 6. 23 b
i. 15, 15. 23 e a
ii. 9, 12. 23 a
ii. 14. 23 b
v. 6. 23 b
vi. 2, 16. 23 a
vii. 19. 31 c
viii. 1. 23 d
ix. 24. 23 d
xi. 23. 23 d
xii. 6, 7. 23 d
xiii. 8, 8, 14, 33. 23 d
xiii. 15, 24, 29. 23 d
xiv. 3, 3, 3. 23 a
xiv. 12. 23 c
xv. 13. 23 a
xv. 13, 16. 23 a
xv. 17. 23 d
xv. 19, 19, 19, 19. 23 c a q d
xvii. 4, 4. 23 b d
xvii. 14. 23 a
xviii. 3, 7. 23 a
xviii. 4. 12 a
xix. 49. 23 d
xix. 50. 23 a
xx. 4. 23 a
xxi. 2. 23 b
xxi. 3, 8, 9, 11, 21. 23 d
xxi. 12, 13. 23 a
xxi. 43, 43. 23 d b
xxii. 4, 7, 7. 23 a
xxiii. 13, 15, 16. 23 a
xxiv. 3, 4, 4, 8, 13. 23 d
xxiv. 33. 23 g
Judg. i. 12. 23 a
i. 13, 20. 23 d
i. 15, 15, 15, 15. 12 a, 23 a a d
iii. 6. 23 a
v. 25. 23 d
vi. 9. 23 d
vii. 2. 23 b
viii. 6, 15. 23 d
viii. 25. 23 b d b
ix. 4. 23 d
xiv. 9, 19. 23 d
xiv. 12, 13. 23 a
xv. 2, 6. 23 a
xv. 18. 23 b
xvi. 5. 23 a
xvi. 4, 10. 23 d
xviii. 10. 23 a
xx. 7. 12 a
xx. 36. 23 d
xxi. 1, 14. 23 b
xxi. 7. 23 b
xxi. 18, 18. 23 b e
xxi. 22. 23 a
Ruth i. 6. 23 b
ii. 18. 23 b
iii. 17. 23 d
iv. 7. 23 a

Ruth iv. 12,13. 23 d
iv. 17. 27
1 Sam. i. 4, 11, 11. 23 a
i. 5. 27
ii. 10, 16, 28. 23 d
ii. 15. 23 c
ii. 20. 31 d
vi. 5. 23 a
viii. 6. 23 c
viii. 14, 15. 23 a
ix. 8, 23. 23 a
x. 4. 23 a
x. 9. 10
xiv. 41. 12 a
xvii. 28. 23 a
xvii. 10. 23 c
xvii. 25, 44. 23 d
xvii. 46, 47. 23 a
xviii. 4, 17, 21, 27. 23 d
xviii. 19, β 19. 23 b g
xxi. 3, 9. 23 c
xxi. 6. 23 d
xxii. 7. 23 d
xxiii. 10, 10. 23 a
xxiii. 13. 23 b
xxv. 8. 23 c
xxv. 11, 44. 23 a
xxv. 27. 23 d
xxvii. 5, 6. 23 d
xxviii. 17. 23 d
xxx. 11, 12, 22. 23 d
xxx. 23. 23 a
2 Sam. iv. 10. 23 b
vii. 2, 6. 15
ix. 9. 23 a
xii. 8, 8, 8. 23 d d, 13
xii. 11. 23 a
xiii. 5. 23 a
xvi. 20. 12 a
xvii. 7. 14 a
xviii. 11. γ 23 a
xix. 42, 42. 22 a c
xxi. 6. 23 d
xxii. 36. 23 d
xxii. 41. 23 a
xxiv. 9. 23 a
xxiv. 24. 23 a
1 Kings i. 12. 14 b
i. 48. 23 a
ii. 17. 23 d
ii. 21. 23 l
iii. 5, 6. 23 d
iii. 9, 12, 13. 23 a
iii. 25, 26, 27. 23 c
iv. 29. 23 d
v. 6. 23 d
v. 7, 12. 23 a
v. 9. 23 b
v. 10. δ 23 e
v. 11, 11. 23 a d
viii. 32. 23 b
viii. 34, 36, 36, 39, 40, 48, 50, 56. 23 a
ix. 7, 12, 13. 23 a
ix. 11, 16. 23 a
x. 10, 10. 23 d
x. 13, 13. 23 a
xi. 11, 31, 35, 38. 23 a
xi. 13, 19, 36. 23 d
xi. 18, 18. 23 d a
xii. 8, 13. 14 a
xiii. 3, 5. 23 a
xiii. 7, 8. 23 a
xiii. 8. 23 a
xiv. 15. 23 a
xv. 4. 23 a
xv. 19. 23 a
xvii. 19. 23 c
xviii. 26. ε 23 a
xix. 21. 23 d
xxi. 2, 2, 2. 23 c d d
xxi. 3, 15. 23 b
xxi. 7. 23 d
xxi. 6, 6, 6. 23 c d d
2 Kings iv. 42, 43. 23 a
v. 1. 23 a
v. 22. 23 c
vi. 28, 29. 23 b
viii. 19. 23 b
viii. 19. 20 b
ix. 15. 20 b
ix. 15. 23 c d
x. 15, 15. 23 c d
xi. 10. 23 a

2 Kings xii. 11. 23 a
xii. 14. 23 d
xiii. 5. 23 c
xiv. 9. 23 d
xv. 19. 23 d
xv. 20. 23 b
xvii. 3. 30
xvii. 15, 16. 23 d
xxi. 8. 23 a
xxii. 5, 8. 23 a
xxiii. 11. 23 a
xxiii. 35, 35, 35. 23 a b b
xxv. 6. 8
xxv. 30. 23 g
1 Chron. ii. 35. 23 d
v. 1. 23 g
vi. 55, 64, 65, 67. 23 d
vi. 56, 57. 23 a
xvi. 39. 23 d
xvi. 28, 28, 29. 12 a
xviii. 2, 6. 15
xxi. 5, 25. 23 d
xxi. 23, 23. 23 d
xxiii. 9. 12 23 d
xxii. 18. 23 a
xxviii. 5. 23 a
xxviii. 11. 23 d
xxix. 3, 8, 14. ζ 23 a
xxix. 7. 23 d
xxix. 19. 23 c
2 Chron. i. 7, 12. 23 c
i. 10. 23 c
ii. 10, 12. 23 a
vi. 23. 23 b
vi. 25, 27, 31, 38. 23 a
vii. 20. 23 a
ix. 9, 9. 23 d a
ix. 12. 23 a
x. 8. 14 a
xi. 23. 23 d
xiii. 5. 32 a
xix. 7. 32 b
xx. 7. 23 d
xxi. 3, 3, 3. 23 d p a
xxi. 7. 23 b
xxi. 6. 20 a
xxiv. 12. 23 d
xxiv. 9, 9. 23 a b
xxv. 18. 23 c
xxvi. 4, 8, 8. 23 d, 15
xxvii. 5. 23 d
xxviii. 21. 23 d
xxx. 7. 23 d
xxx. 12. 23 b
xxx. 24, 24. 29 a
xxxii. 11. 23 b
xxxii. 23. 15
xxxii. 24, 29. 23 a
xxxiv. 10, 11. 23 d
xxxv. 18. 23 a
xxxv. 7. 29 b
xxxv. 8, 8. 29 a, 23 a
xxxv. 9. 29 a
xxxvi. 17, 23. 23 a
Ezra i. 2. 23 a
ii. 69. 23 a
iii. 7. 23 d
iv. 21, 21. 31 e f
v. 12. 12 b
vi. 4. 12 f
vi. 8, 9. 12 g
vii. 6, 11. 23 a
vii. 19. 12 g
ix. 8, 8, 9, 9. 23 b
ix. 12. 23 d
ix. 13. 23 a
x. 19. 23 d
Neh. i. 1, 7, 8, 9. 23 d
iii. 5. 23 c
vii. 70, 70, 71, 72. 23 a
viii. 8. 31 b
ix. 7. 31 a
ix. 8, 8. 23 b
ix. 13, 22, 24, 27, 30. 23 d
ix. 15, 15. 23 a b
ix. 20, 20, 35, 35, 36. 23 a
x. 29. 23 g
x. 30. 23 d
xii. 47. 23 e

Neh. xiii. 10.	23 g
xiii. 25.	23 d
Esth. i. 19, 20.	23 d
ii. 3, 9, 9.	23 b
ii. 13.	23 i
ii. 18, 18.	23 d, 22 b
iii. 10.	23 d
iii. 11.	23 f
iii. 14.	23 h
iii. 15.	23 g
iv. 8, 8.	23 a g
v. 3.	23 i
vii. 3.	23 i
viii. 1, 7.	23 a
viii. 2.	23 h
viii. 13.	23 h
viii. 14.	23 g
ix. 14.	23 i
ix. 22.	23 p
Job i. 21.	23 a
ii. 4.	23 d
iii. 20.	23 d
v. 10.	23 e
vi. 22.	32 a
ix. 24.	23 g
xi. 20.	21 b
xv. 19.	23 g
xxiv. 23.	23 d
xxxv. 7.	23 d
xxxv. 10.	23 e
xxxvi. 6, 31.	23 d
xxxvii. 10.	23 d
xxxviii. 36.	23 a
xxxix. 19.	23 d
xlii. 10.	13
xlii. 11, 15.	23 d
Ps. ii. 8.	23 d
xviii. 13, 35.	23 d
xviii. 40.	23 a
xviii. 50.	6
xxi. 2, 4.	23 a
xxviii. 4, 4.	23 c
xxix. 1, 1, 2.	12 a
xxix. 11.	23 d
xxxvii. 4.	23 d
xxxvii. 21.	23 e
xliv. 11.	23 d
xlv. 12.	15
xlix. 7.	23 d
l. 19.	34 a
li. 16.	23 d
lx. 4.	23 a
lx. 11.	12 a
lxi. 5.	23 a
lxviii. 11.	23 d
lxviii. 18. η	23 p
lxviii. 35.	23 e
lxix. 21.	23 c
lxxii. 1.	23 c
lxxii. 10.	33
lxxii. 15.	23 d
lxxiv. 14.	23 d
lxxviii. 20.	23 b
lxxviii. 24.	23 a
lxxviii. 29.	2
lxxviii. 46.	23 d
lxxviii. 48, 62.	24 b
lxxviii. 50.	24 a
lxxix. 2.	23 a
lxxxi. 12.	34 b
lxxxiv. 11.	23 d
lxxxv. 12.	23 d
lxxxvi. 16.	23 c
xcvi. 7, 7, 8.	12 a
xcix. 7.	23 a
civ. 27.	23 d
civ. 28.	23 d
cv. 11, 44.	23 a
cv. 32.	23 a
cvi. 15, 41.	23 d
cviii. 12.	12 a
cxi. 5.	23 a
cxi. 6.	23 b
cxii. 9.	23 b
cxv. 1.	23 c
cxv. 16.	23 a
cxviii. 18.	23 a
cxx. 3.	23 a
cxxiv. 6.	23 a
cxxvii. 2.	23 d
cxxxii. 4.	23 d
cxxxv. 12.	23 a
cxxxv. 21.	23 d
cxxxvi. 25.	23 e
cxliv. 10.	23 e

Ps. cxlv. 15.	23 e
cxlvi. 7.	23 e
cxlvii. 9, 16.	23 e
Prov. i. 4.	23 b
ii. 6.	23 d
iii. 28, 34.	23 d
iv. 2.	23 d
iv. 9.	23 d
v. 9.	23 d
vi. 4, 31.	23 d
vi. 35, 35.	28, 32 b
viii. 29.	31 b
ix. 9.	23 c
xiii. 15.	23 d
xv. 27.	23 p
xvii. 8, 23.	32 b
xviii. 16.	23 n
xix. 6, 6. θ	23 n
xix. 17.	7
xxi. 14.	23 n
xxi. 26.	23 d
xxii. 9.	23 a
xxii. 16.	23 e
xxiii. 2.	3
xxiii. 26.	23 c
xxiii. 31.	23 d
xxv. 14.	23 q
xxvi. 8.	23 e
xxviii. 27.	23 e
xxix. 4.	29 c
xxix. 15, 17.	23 d
xxx. 8.	23 d
xxx. 15, 15.	12 a
xxxi. 3, 15.	23 d
xxxi. 6, 31.	23 c
Eccles. i. 13, 13.	23 a
i. 17.	23 d
ii. 3.	17
ii. 26, 26, 26.	23 a
iii. 10.	23 a
iii. 13.	23 q
v. 1.	23 b
v. 18.	23 a
v. 19, 19.	23 a q
vi. 2.	23 a
vii. 7.	23 p
viii. 8.	3
viii. 15.	23 a
ix. 9.	23 a
xi. 2.	23 c
xi. 7.	23 a
xii. 11.	23 g
Cant. ii. 13.	23 a
vii. 12.	23 d
vii. 13.	23 d
viii. 7.	23 d
Isa. i. 23.	32 b
iii. 4.	23 a
iii. 11.	26 b
vii. 14.	23 d
vii. 22.	26 a
viii. 18.	23 a
ix. 6.	23 g
xiii. 10.	9
xix. 4.	25
xxx. 20, 23.	23 a
x xiii. 16.	23 k
xxxv. 2.	23 g
xxxvi. 8.	23 d
xxxvii. 10.	23 i
xl. 29.	23 e
xli. 2, 2, 27.	23 e
xl i. 5.	23 e
xlii. 6, 8.	23 d
xlii. 12.	31 d
xlii. 24.	23 d
xliii. 3, 20.	23 a
xliii. 4, 28.	23 d
xliii. 6.	23 c
xlv. 3.	23 a
xlvii. 6.	23 d
xlviii. 11.	23 a
xl x. 6.	23 a
xlix. 8.	23 a
l. 4, 6.	23 a
lv. 4.	23 a
lvi. 5, 5.	23 a d
lxi. 3.	23 b
lxii. 7, 8.	23 b
Jer. iii. 8, 19.	23 d
iii. 15.	23 a
iv. 12.	8
iv. 16.	23 e
v. 24.	23 e
vi. 13.	4

Jer. vii. 7, 14.	23 a
viii. 10, 10.	23 d, 4
viii. 13.	23 d
xi. 5.	23 b
xii. 7.	23 d
xiii. 16.	23 c
xiii. 20.	23 g
xiv. 13, 22.	23 d
xv. 9.	21 a
xv. 13.	23 d
xvi. 15.	23 a
xvii. 3.	23 d
xvii. 4.	23 a
xvii. 10.	23 b
xix. 7.	23 a
xx. 4, 5.	23 d
xxi. 10.	23 i
xxii. 13.	23 d
xxii. 25.	23 a
xxiii. 39.	23 a
xxiv. 7, 10.	23 a
xxiv. 8.	23 d
xxv. 5, 31.	23 a
xxvi. 24.	23 b
xxvii. 5, 6, 6.	23 d
xxviii. 14.	23 c
xxix. 6.	23 c
xxix. 11.	23 b
xxx. 3.	23 d
xxx. 16.	23 d
xxxi. 35.	23 e
xxxii. 3, 28.	23 d
xxxii. 12.	23 d
xxxii. 22, 22.	23 d b
xxxii. 24, 25, 43.	23 g
xxxii. 44.	23 a
xxxiv. 2.	23 e
xxxiv. 18, 20.	23 d
xxxiv. 21.	23 d
xxxv. 15.	23 d
xxxvi. 32.	23 d
xxxvii. 21.	23 b
xxxviii. 3.	23 i h
xxxviii. 16.	23 d
xxxviii. 18.	23 g
xxxix. 5.	8
xxxix. 10.	23 d
xxxix. 17.	23 i
xl. 5.	23 d
xliv. 30, 30.	23 e a
xlv. 5.	23 a
xlviii. 9.	23 c
l. 15.	23 a
lii. 19.	23 a
lii. 34.	28 g
Lam. i. 11.	23 a
ii. 7.	24 a
ii. 18.	23 d
iii. 30, 65.	23 d
v. 6.	23 a
Ezek. ii. 8.	23 a
iii. 3.	23 e
iv. 15.	23 e
vii. 21.	23 a
xi. 2.	14 c
xi. 15.	23 g
xi. 17, 19, 19.	23 a
xv. 6, ι 6.	23 a
xvi. 17, 19, 36, 38, 39, 61.	23 a
xvi. 33, 33, 33, 33.	23 d, 18, 23 a, 19
xvi. 34, 34.	23 b g
xvi. 41.	23 d
xvii. 15.	23 b
xvii. 18.	23 a
xviii. 7, 8.	23 d
xviii. 13, 16.	23 d
xx. 11.	23 d
xx. 12, 15, 25.	23 a
xx. 26, 31, 39.	23 p
xx. 28, 42.	23 d
xxi. 11, 11.	23 d b
xxi. 27.	23 a
xxii. 12.	32 b
xxiii. 31.	23 a
xxiii. 46.	23 b
xxv. 10.	23 a
xxvii. 19.	23 a
xxix. 5, 20.	23 a
xxix. 19.	23 e
xxix. 21.	23 d
xxxii. 7. κ	1
xxxiii. 15.	35

Ezek. xxxiii. 24.	23 g
xxxiii. 27.	23 a
xxxv. 12.	23 g
xxxvi. 26, 26, 28.	23 a
xxxvii. 25.	23 a
xxxix. 4.	23 a
xxxix. 11, 23.	23 d
xliii. 19.	23 a
xliv. 28, 30.	23 d
xlv. 8.	23 d
xlvi. 5, 11. λ	23 d
xlvi. 16, 16.	23 d p
xlvi. 17, 17.	23 d p
xlvii. 11.	23 g
xlvii. 14.	23 d
xlvii. 23.	23 d
Dan. i. 2, 12.	23 d
i. 7, 7.	31 d
i. 16.	23 e
i. 17.	23 a
ii. 6.	23 o

Dan. ii. 16.	23 m
ii. 21.	12 d
ii. 23, 37, 38.	12 b
ii. 48, 48.	12 b, 23 o
iv. 16.	12 f
iv. 17, 25, 32.	23 m
v. 17, 17.	23 o, 12 c
v. 18, 19.	12 b
v. 28.	12 e
vi. 2.	12 d
vii. 4, 6, 11, 14, 22.	
27.	12 e
vii. 25.	12 f
viii. 12.	23 k
viii. 13.	23 b
xi. 6.	23 k
xi. 11.	23 g
xi. 17.	23 d
xi. 21.	23 a
Hos. ii. 5.	23 a
ii. 8, 12, 15.	23 a

Hos. iv. 18.	12 a
ix. 14, 14, 14.	23 c d c
xi. 8.	23 d
xiii. 10.	23 c
xiii. 11.	23 d
Joel ii. 17.	23 d
ii. 23.	23 a
iii. 3.	23 d
Amos iv. 6.	23 a
ix. 15.	23 a
Micah i. 14.	23 d
v. 3.	23 d
vi. 7, 14.	23 d
Hag. ii. 9.	23 d
Zech. iii. 7.	23 a
viii. 12, 12, 12.	23 d
x. 1.	23 d
xi. 12.	12 a
Mal. ii. 2.	23 b
ii. 5.	23 d

a wholly given; *lit.* given, given. β *lit.* at the time of giving. γ *lit.* upon me to give. δ *lit.* was giving. ε *lit.* which he gave them. ζ *lit.* of thine hand have we given thee. η *lit.* gifts in the man. θ *lit.* to a man of gifts. ι *lit.* have given it. κ *lit.* cause her light to shine. λ *lit.* as the gift of his hand.

GLAD, GLADNESS

1 גּיל to rejoice with exultation, showing gladness by outward signs. גִּיל is frequently joined with שִׂמְחָה to express both inward and outward joy, sometimes used of inanimate things. KAL a *imp.* b *fut.* c גִּיל *m.* exultation, rejoicing.

2 חָדָה to rejoice; seems to refer chiefly to spiritual joy. PIEL, a *fut.* b חֶדְוָה *f.* joy, gladness.

3 טְאֵב Ch. to be joyful. P'AL *pret.*

4 טוֹב *adj.* good; cheerful. a טוּב *m.* with לֵב gladness, cheerfulness.

5 יָטַב to be good, to be joyful, spoken of the heart. KAL *fut.*

6 רִנָּה *f.* a rejoicing, a shout of joy.

7 שׂושׂ to have inward and fervent joy; see *Rejoice*. KAL a *pret.* b *imp.* c *fut.* d שָׂשׂוֹן *m.* joy, gladness, often coupled with שִׂמְחָה. Oil of gladness refers to the anointing used at feasts.

8 שָׂמַח to be affected with joy and delight; see *Rejoice*. It is sometimes used of the joy of the wicked. With *inf.*, to make very glad. KAL a *pret.* b *imp.* c *fut.* PIEL d *pret.* e *inf.* f *imp.* g *fut.* h שָׂמֵחַ *adj.* rejoicing, joyful. i שִׂמְחָה *f.* joy, gladness; joyful voices; joyful banquets, pleasures.

Exod. iv. 14.	8 a	Ps. xvi. 9.	8 a	Ps. xcvii. 11.	8 i		
Num. x. 10.	8 i	xxi. 6.	2 a, 8 i	c. 2.	8 i		
Deut. xxviii. 47.	4 a	xxx. 11.	8 i	civ. 15.	8 g		
Judg. xviii. 20.	5	xxxi. 7.	1 b	civ. 34.	8 c		
1 Sam. xi. 9.	8 c	xxxii. 11.	8 b	cv. 38.	8 a		
2 Sam. vi. 12.	8 i	xxxiv. 2.	8 c	cv. 43.	6		
1 Kings viii. 66.	4	xxxv. 27.	8 c	cvi. 5.	8 i		
1 Chron. xvi. 27.	2 b	xl. 16.	8 c	cvi. 30.	8 c		
xvi. 31.	8 c	xlv. 7.	7 d	cxviii. 24.	8 c		
xxix. 22.	8 i	xlv. 8.	8 d	cxix. 74.	8 c		
2 Chron. vii. 10.	8 h	xlv. 15.	8 i	cxxii. 1.	8 a		
xxix. 30.	8 i	xlvi. 4.	8 g	cxxvi. 3.	8 h		
xxx. 21, 23.	8 i	xlviii. 11.	1 b	Prov. x. 1.	8 g		
Neh. viii. 17.	8 i	li. 8.	8 i	x. 28.	8 i		
xii. 27.	8 i	liii. 6.	8 c	xii. 25.	8 g		
Esth. v. 9.	4	lxiv. 10.	8 c	xv. 20.	8 g		
viii. 15.	8 h	lxvii. 4.	8 i	xvii. 5.	8 h		
viii. 16.	8 i	lxviii. 3.	8 c	xxiii. 25.	8 c		
viii. 17.	7 d	lxix. 32.	8 c	xxiv. 17.	1 b		
ix. 17, 18, 19.	8 i	lxx. 4.	8 c	xxvii. 11.	8 f		
Job iii. 22.	7 c	xc. 14.	8 c	Cant. i. 4.	1 b		
xxii. 19.	8 i	xc. 15.	8 f	iii. 11.	8 i		
Ps. iv. 7.	8 i	xcii. 4.	8 d	Isa. xvi. 10.	8 i		
ix. 2.	8 c	xcvi. 11.	8 c	xxii. 13.	8 i		
xiv. 7.	8 c	xcvii. 1, 8.	8 c	xxv. 9.	1 b		

Isa. xxx. 29.	8 i	Jer. xx. 15.	8 d e	Dan. vi. 23.	3
xxxv. 1.	7 c	xxv. 10.	8 i	Hos. vii. 3.	8 g
xxxv. 10.	8 i	xxxi. 7.	8 i	Joel i. 16.	1 c
xxxix. 2.	8 c	xxxiii. 11.	8 i	ii. 21, 23.	1 a
li. 3.	8 i	xli. 13.	8 c	Jonah iv. 6.	8 c i
li. 11.	7 d	xlviii. 33.	10	Hab. i. 15.	1 b
lxv. 18.	7 b	l. 11.	8 c	Zeph. iii. 14.	8 b
lxvi. 10.	1 a	Lam. i. 21.	7 a	Zech. viii. 19.	8 i
Jer. vii. 34.	8 i	iv. 21.	8 b	x. 7.	8 a
xvi. 9.	8 i				

GLASS

גִּלָּיוֹן *m.* a tablet of wood, metal, &c.: in Isa. iii. 23, probably mirrors (as a female ornament, *comp.* Exod. xxxviii. 8), *lit.* metallic plates; so the Vulg. and Chald.; according to the Lxx., thin transparent garments.

GLEAN, GLEANING

לָקַט to collect, gather, especially from the ground, as ears, manna, stones, flowers. KAL *inf.* Ruth ii. 8. PIEL *pret.* Ruth ii. 16, 17, 18, 19. *inf.* Ruth ii. 15, 23. *fut.* Ruth ii. 2, 3, 7, 15, 17. לֶקֶט *m.* a gleaning: Lev. xix. 9; xxiii. 22.

עָלַל perhaps this word may mean to do anything by repetition, to persevere in doing; hence to glean grapes. POEL *inf.* Jer. vi. 9, *lit.* gleaning they shall glean. *fut.* Lev. xix. 10: Deut. xxiv. 21: Judg. xx. 45: Jer. vi. 9. עֹלֵלוֹת *f. pl.* gleaning of grapes: Judg. viii. 2: Isa. xvii. 6; xxiv. 13: Jer. xlix. 9: Micah vii. 1.

GLEDE

רָאָה *f.* a kite or glede, a bird of prey of quick and distant sight: Bochart; Deut. xiv. 13.

GLISTER, GLITTER

בָּרָק *m.* lightning: Deut. xxxii. 41, *lit.* the lightning of my sword: Job xx. 25: Ezek. xxi. 10, *lit.* have lightning, 28: Nah. iii. 3: Hab. iii. 11.

לַהַב *m.* flame: Job xxxix. 23.

פּוּךְ *m.* paint; ornament, decoration: 1 Chron. xxix. 2, stones for ornament, and of various colours. Lxx., λίθοι πολυτελεῖς καὶ ποίκιλοι.

GLOOMINESS

אֲפֵלָה *f.* darkness: Joel ii. 2: Zeph. i. 15.

GLORY, GLORIOUS, GLORIFY

1 אָדַר not found in Kal, but its primary signification seems to have been, to be wide, broad; hence to be illustrious. NIPHAL [a] *part.* [b] אַדִּיר *adj.* great, mighty, powerful; distinguished; splendid, glorious, majestic; primarily used of God, and of the Messiah, Jer. xxx. 21; also of men, as kings and princes; of the godly, Ps. xvi. 3; it is also applied to inanimate things, waters, cedars. [c] אַדֶּרֶת *f.* this word retains the primary meaning of wide, ample, and is therefore used of a robe or mantle; also of anything glorious or excellent: Zech. xi. 3, "their glory is spoiled;" which is variously interpreted, of Judea, of the temple, of the nation, or of the priesthood.

2 אוֹר (see *Light*), to shine. NIPHAL *part.*

3 נָאָה to be exalted, majestic, excellent. KAL *inf.*

4 דָּבָר *m.* word, &c.: Ps. lxxix. 9, *lit.* upon the matter of the glory.

5 הָדַר very similar to אָדַר to be wide, broad, and probably high; to adorn; to honour, respect, reverence. KAL [a] *part.* Paul. [b] הָדוּר Ch. PAEL *pret.* [c] הַדַּר *m.* ornament, honour, glory manifested, displayed, or acquired; of an active signification, and often joined with הוֹד. [d] הָדָר *m.* ornament.

6 הוֹד *m.* any good quality or endowment for which a person is admired, honoured, or celebrated; renown, glory; power, majesty; splendour, beauty: it is used of God and of the Messiah.

7 הָלַל to shine; to praise; to boast, to glory in a good sense. HITHPAEL [a] *inf.* [b] *imp.* [c] *fut.* [d] *part.*

8 טֹהַר *m.* brightness, glory; of the glory and splendour of a king: Ps. lxxxix. 44. Michaelis Suppl. 902, would translate it 'victories,' which suitably agrees with the context.

9 יְקָר Ch. *m.* costly things; honour, majesty.

10 כָּבֵד and כָּבַד to be heavy: this word is used to signify anything that renders a nation, person, or place, of weight, considerable, or respectable; as wealth, numbers, commerce, power, wisdom, promotion, superiority, dignity, authority, nobility, splendour, valour, magnificence, extraordinary privileges and advantages; or whatever instance or badge of greatness, excellency, or happiness renders a person praiseworthy, or commands esteem or veneration: this is honour and glory. The apostle alludes to the primary meaning of this word when he speaks of βάρος δόξης to express the greatness and abundance of future glory. KAL [a] *fut.* NIPHAL [b] *pret.* [c] *inf.* [d] *imp.* [e] *fut.* [f] *part.* PIEL [g] *imp.* [h] *fut.* HIPHIL [i] *pret.* [k] כָּבוֹד *m.* glory; used of the tongue, Ps. xvi. 9, *comp.* Acts ii. 26: or of the soul, or of a glorious state and condition.—Gen. xxxi. 1, &c. [l] כְּבוּדָּה *adj. f.* glorious.

11 פָּאַר to adorn, to beautify. PIEL [a] *pret.* [b] *fut.* HITHPAEL [c] *inf.* [d] *imp.* [e] *fut.* [f] תִּפְאָרָה and תִּפְאֶרֶת *f.* ornament, splendour, beauty; glory, praise, honour; often of the divine glory, the light and splendour of the divine presence.

12 צְבִי *m.* honour, majesty, glory; as of a kingdom, of a crown, of an inheritance, of the land of Israel.

13 שָׁבַח to praise, commend, to glory. HITHPAEL *fut.*

No. 10 k (*Glory*) not included.

Exod. viii. 9.	11 d	Job xxxix. 20.	6	Ps. lxxxvi. 9, 12.	10 h		
xv. 1, 21.	3	xl. 10.	6	lxxxvii. 3.	10 f		
xv. 6, 11.	1 a	Ps. viii. 1.	6	lxxxix. 17.	11 f		
Lev. x. 3.	10 e	xxii. 23.	10 g	lxxxix. 44.	8		
Deut. xxviii. 58.	10 f	xxix. 2.	10 k	xc. 16.	5 c		
xxxiii. 17.	5 c	xlv. 3.	6	xcvi. 8.	10 k		
2 Sam. vi. 20.	10 b	xlv. 13.	10 l	cv. 3.	7 b		
2 Kings xx. 10.	10 d	l. 15, 23.	10 h	cvi. 5.	7 a		
1 Chron. xvi. 10.	7 b	lxiii. 11.	7 c	cxi. 3.	5 c		
xvi. 27.	6	lxiv. 10.	7 c	cxlv. 5, 12. a	10 k		
xvi. 35.	13	lxvi. 2.	10 k	cxlviii. 13.	6		
xxii. 5.	6	lxxii. 19.	10 k	Prov. xv. 9.	11 f		
xxix. 11, 13.	11 f	lxxv. 4.	2	xvi. 31.	11 f		
Neh. ix. 5.	10 k	lxxviii. 61.	11 f	xvii. 6.	11 f		
Esth. i. 4.	10 k	lxxix. 9.	4, 10 k	xix. 11.	11 f		

Prov. xx. 29.	11 f	Isa. xlvi. 13.	11 f	Jer. xlix. 4.	7 c	
xxviii. 12.	11 f	xlix. 3.	11 e	Ezek. xx. 6, 15.	12	
Isa. ii. 10, 19, 21.	5 c	xlix. 5.	10 e	xxiv. 25.	11 f	
iv. 2.β	10 k	lv. 5.	11 a	xxv. 9.	12	
v. 14.	5 c	lx. 7, 7.	11 b f	xxvi. 20.	12	
x. 12.	11 f	lx. 9.	11 a	xxvii. 25.	10 a	
xi. 10.	10 k	lx. 13, 13.	10 k h	xxviii. 22.	10 b	
xiii. 19.	10 k	lx. 19.γ	11 f	xxxix. 13.	10 c	
xx. 5.	11 f	lx. 21.γ	11 c	Dan. ii. 27.	9	
xxii. 23.	10 k	lxi. 3.	11 c	iv. 36.	9	
xxiii. 9.	12	lxii. 3.	11 f	v. 18, 20.	5 b	
xxiv. 15.	10 g	lxiii. 1.	5 a	v. 23.	9	
xxiv. 16.	10 h	lxiii. 12, 14, 15.	11 f	vii. 14.	12	
xxiv. 23.	10 h	lxvi. 5.	10 a	xi. 16, 41, 45.	12	
xxv. 3.	10 h	Jer. iv. 2.	7 c	xi. 24.	5 d	
xxvi. 15.	10 b	ix. 23, 23, 23.	7 c	Micah ii. 9.	5 c	
xxviii. 1, 4, 5.	12	ix. 24, 24.	7 d c	Hab. iii. 3.	6	
xxx. 30.	6	xiii. 11, 18.	11 f	Hag. i. 8.	10 e	
xxxiii. 21.	1 b	xvii. 12.	10 k	Zech. vi. 13.	6	
xli. 16.	7 c	xxii. 18.	6	xi. 3.	1 c	
xliv. 23.	11 e	xxx. 19.	10 i	xii. 7, 7.	11 f	
xlv. 25.	7 c					

a *lit.* and the glory of the honour of.　　β *lit.* for glory.
γ *lit.* for glorifying.

GLUTTON

זָלַל to be prodigal, to live in luxury, to riot. KAL *part.* Poel,
Deut. xxi. 20: Prov. xxiii. 21.

GNASH

חָרַק to grate or grind the teeth through the highest degree of
indignation and spite. KAL *pret.* Job xvi. 9. *inf.* Ps.
xxxv. 16, *lit.* to gnash. *fut.* Ps. cxii. 10: Lam. ii. 16.
part. Poel, Ps. xxxvii. 12.

GNAW　(See BONE)

GO

1　אֲזַד Ch. this word is usually taken as equivalent to אֲזַל Ch. to
depart, to be gone, or passed away (*comp.* Dan. ix. 23,
Isa. xlv. 23), and in this sense it may be understood of
the king's commandment, to which many apply it, as
well as to the dream : in the latter case, it means the
dream had passed from his recollection ; in the former,
it is to be understood of the king's decree, verse 2, "the
word from me is fixed," which is the rendering given
by Aben-Ezra, comparing it with the Talmudic אֲזַדָּא,
strength : Lxx., however, has ἀπέστη. P'AL *pret.*

2　אָזַל to go away ; to disappear, quickly, suddenly ; applied to
the drying up of water, Job xiv. 11 ; to the consumption of the articles of food, 1 Sam. ix. 7 ; to the
disappearing of succour, Deut. xxxii. 36. KAL *pret.*
part. PUAL *part.* אֲזַל Ch. P'AL *pret.* *imp.*

3　אָחַד a verb, from אֶחָד one, found only in HITHPAEL *imp.*
Ezek. xxi. 16. Our translators seem to have understood it, make thyself one, either with the right hand
or with the left, "go thee one way or other :" others
have explained it, join thyself, *i. e.* sword to sword,
go forth with united strength ; or, be 'directed to one
object ; or, be one, collect thyself, so as to give attention to the work of destruction.

4　אֵין *part.* used adverbially ; not ; "was gone," *lit.* he not.

5　אָפֵס cease, fail, come to an end ; to be clean gone. KAL
pret.

6　אָרַח to travel. KAL *pret.*

7　אָשַׁר to go straight on. KAL *imp.* PIEL *fut.* אֲשֻׁר *f.* step,
going.

8　בּוֹא to come in, to enter ; to come ; more rarely to go ; to go
down, go in, go to war. KAL *pret.* *inf.* *imp.* *fut.*
part. Poel. HIPHIL *pret.* מָבוֹא *com.* entrance ;
going down of the sun, with an implied returning as
in opposition to מוֹצָא used of his rising.

9　גָּלָה to go into captivity, to go away, as into exile. KAL
pret.

10　דָּדָה to walk with a soft, slow, solemn pace. HITHPAEL *fut.*

11　דָּרַךְ to tread on ; to walk, to come, to go. KAL *part.* Poel.
HIPHIL *pret.* *imp.*

12　הוּךְ Ch. to go. P'AL *inf.* *fut.*

13　הָלַךְ to go ; applied to things both animate and inanimate ;
e.g. to the ark floating, Gen. vii. 18 ; to a boundary
extending itself, Josh. xvi. 8 ; to a report circulating,
2 Chron. xxvi. 8. The place whither is most frequently
preceded by ל or אֶל, but sometimes stands in the
accusative, Judg. xix. 18, 2 Chron. ix. 21. To depart
by death, Gen. xv. 2. The most remarkable constructions of this word are the following :—1. With
an accusative, to go through a place, Deut. i. 19, ii. 7 ;
Job xxix. 3. 2. With בְּ, to go with anything, Exod.
x. 9 ; hence to bring or carry, Hos. v. 6. 3. With עִם
or אֵת, to be conversant with, or associate with, Job
xxxiv. 8, Prov. xiii. 20, *comp.* Job xxxi. 5. 4. With
אַחֲרֵי, to go after, to follow, Gen. xxiv. 5, 8, xxxvii. 17 ;
to go after God or Baalim, *i. e.* to serve or be devoted
to them, Deut. iv. 3, 1 Kings xiv. 8, Jer. ii. 8 ; also to
pursue, persecute, Jer. xlviii. 2. To go on, continue,
last. The Hebrew writers express the continuation or
continued increase of an action by means of this verb,
in various constructions. KAL *pret.* *inf.* *imp.*
fut. *part.* Poel. *pret.* PIEL *pret.* *fut.* HITH-
PAEL *inf.* *fut.* *part.* תַּהֲלוּכָה *f.* goings, progress.
הֲלִיכָה *f. id.*

14　זוּר to be estranged. NIPHAL *pret.*

15　חָלַף to pass, to go on forward. KAL *pret.*

16　חָמַק to turn and wind about in order to elude a pursuer, to
withdraw, to go away, to wander. HITHPAEL *fut.*

17　חָתַת to be broken so as to be quite disabled, to be dismayed.
NIPHAL *fut.* See also נָחַת.

18　יָהַב (see *Give*), come. The word seems to be used, as it is
translated in the Lxx., like δεῦτε. KAL *imp.*

19　יָלַךְ to go, to go away, to go out ; to go one's way ; by a
peculiarity of idiom, often employed in the sense of
commencing or entering upon an action or enterprise :
Gen. xxxv. 22 : Deut. xxxi. 1 : Hos. iii. 1, *comp.* Eph.
ii. 17, 1 Pet. iii. 19. KAL *inf.* *imp.* *fut.* HIPHIL
imp. *fut.*

20　יָצָא to go forth ; to go abroad, to go on ; to go forth
on the affairs and business of life, usually with בּוֹא,
sometimes without ; with אֶל come out against in a
hostile manner, Judg. ix. 33, or without אֶל. KAL
pret. *inf.* *imp.* *fut.* *part.* Poel. HIPHIL *pret.*

ᵍ*imp.* ʰ*fut.* מוֹצָא *m.* a going out, coming forth, rising; place of rising; passage out, door, gate. ᵏ מוֹצָאוֹת *f.* Micah v. 2, *lit.* who his goings forth. ˡ הוֹצָאוֹת *f. pl.* a place of going out; a going forth, extremity, limit.

21 יָרַד to go down, to descend from a higher to a comparatively lower place; applied also to inanimate things, to a road, to a boundary, to the day, to a river, to a valley. KAL ᵃ*pret.* ᵇ*inf.* ᶜ*imp.* ᵈ*part.* Poel. HIPHIL ᶠ*fut.* HOPHAL ᵍ*pret.* ʰ מוֹרָד *m.* a declivity, a country abounding in declivities.

22 כָּבָה to be extinguished, as fire, or light. KAL *fut.*

23 מָדַד to measure. PIEL *pret.* Job vii. 4, *marg.* 'the evening be measured;' or, מָדַד *m.* measure, that there be a measure of the evening, *i. e.* that the evening be gone; others deduce the word from נָדַד to flee away, *lit.* the flight of the evening.

24 מוּשׁ to depart, to go back. HIPHIL *fut.*

25 נָא particle of entreaty; "go to."

26 נָגַשׁ to draw near; to advance against an enemy; go up. KAL ᵃ*inf.* ᵇ*imp.* ᶜ*fut.* NIPHAL ᵈ*pret.*

27 נְדַד Ch. to flee away. P'AL *pret.*

28 נָדַח to drive, push, thrust; Niphal, to go astray. NIPHAL *part.*

29 נוּעַ to wander. KAL ᵃ*pret.* ᵇ*fut.* HIPHIL ᶜ*fut.*

30 נָחַת to descend, come down. KAL ᵃ*fut.* See also חָתַת.

31 נָטָה to stretch, extend; to turn aside; to decline, falter, stumble. KAL ᵃ*pret.* ᵇ*inf.* ᶜ*part.* Paül.

32 נָכָה to smite. HIPHIL ᵃ*pret.* ᵇ*fut.*

33 נָסַע to pull up the stakes of a tent; to remove, to go forward, to march, to journey; peculiarly applied to a wind issuing forth, driving forward with violence, from God, Num. xi. 31; to go away. KAL ᵃ*pret.* ᵇ*inf.* ᶜ*fut.* ᵈ*part.* Poel. NIPHAL ᵉ*pret.* HIPHIL ᶠ*fut.*

34 נְפַק Ch. to go forth, proceed. P'AL *pret.*

35 נָקַף to go in a circle, to surround. HIPHIL ᵃ*pret.* ᵇ*inf.* ᶜ*imp.*

36 נָשָׂא to lift up. KAL *fut.*

37 סָבַב to move in a circle, to go about. KAL ᵃ*pret.* ᵇ*imp.* ᶜ*fut.* ᵈ*part.* Poel. NIPHAL ᵉ*pret.* ᶠ*fut.* POEL ᵍ*fut.*

38 סוּג to turn back, depart from God. KAL ᵃ*pret.* ᵇ*fut.*

39 סוּר to turn away, depart; to turn aside. KAL ᵃ*pret.* ᵇ*fut.*

40 סָחַר to go about, to travel around; to trade, make merchandize. KAL *pret.* Jer. xiv. 18, *marg.* 'or, make merchandize against a land, and men acknowledge it not.' It is foretold that the false prophets and priests should go about, huckstering their wares, *i. e.* dreams and predictions, in a strange land. *Qualiacunque voles Judæi somnia vendunt.—Juvenal.*

41 עֲבַד Ch. to make, do; Ithp'al, to be made, to be done or go on, to happen. ITHP'AL *part.*

42 עָבַר to pass; to go or pass on; to go or pass through; to pass by; to pass over; to pass away, to go on. KAL ᵃ*pret.* ᵇ*inf.* ᶜ*imp.* ᵈ*fut.* ᵉ*part.* Poel. HIPHIL ᶠ*fut.*

43 מַעְגָּלָה *f.* path; goings.

44 עָלָה to ascend, go up; to ascend as a sacrifice in burning; to vanish. With *inf.*, go up at once. KAL ᵃ*pret.* ᵇ*inf.* ᶜ*imp.* ᵈ*fut.* ᵉ*part.* Poel. NIPHAL ᶠ*pret.* HIPHIL ᵍ*fut.* ʰ עֲלִיָּה *f.* see *Chamber.* ⁱ עֹלָה *f.* step. ᵏ מַעֲלָה *f.* step. ˡ מַעֲלָה *m.* ascent.

45 עֲלַל Ch. to go in, to enter. P'AL ᵃ*pret.* Dan. ii. 16, 24; vi. 10. ᵇ מֵעָל Ch. *m.* of the setting sun, Dan. vi. 14.

46 עָשָׂה to do. KAL *part.* Poel.

47 פָּנָה to turn; to go away. KAL *pret.*

48 פַּעַם *com.* footstep.

49 פָּקַד to visit. KAL *imp.* 2 Kings ix. 34, with נָא *part.* "Go, see."

50 פָּרַע to set free, let loose. KAL *fut.*

51 פָּשַׁע to go, with בְּ to go against. KAL *fut.*

52 צָלַח to pass over. KAL *pret.*

53 צָעַד to go, proceed, move. KAL ᵃ*pret.* ᵇ*fut.* ᶜ צַעַד *m.* a step. ᵈ מִצְעָד *m. id.* ᵉ צְעָדָה *f. id.*

54 קָדַם to go before. PIEL ᵃ*pret.* ᵇ*fut.* ᶜ קַדְמוֹנִי *adj.* "that went before."

55 קָרַב to come near. KAL ᵃ*imp.* ᵇ*fut.* PIEL ᶜ*fut.*

56 רֶגֶל *f.* the foot. רָגַל TIPHEL, to teach to go: *pret.*

57 רוּם to be lifted up. KAL *fut.*

58 רָחַק to be far, to go far. KAL ᵃ*pret.* ᵇ*inf.* HIPHIL ᶜ*inf.* ᵈ*fut.*

59 רָפָה to loosen, to let go. KAL ᵃ*fut.* HIPHIL ᵇ*fut.*

60 שָׁגַג to err. KAL *part.* Poel.

61 שָׁנָה to wander about; to err. KAL ᵃ*fut.* HIPHIL ᵇ*part.*

62 שׁוּב to turn, to come or go again. With *inf.*, in any wise go back. KAL ᵃ*pret.* ᵇ*inf.* ᶜ*imp.* ᵈ*fut.*

63 שׁוּט to pass rapidly, to move with alacrity and in a hurry, to run to and fro. KAL ᵃ*pret.* ᵇ*inf.* ᶜ*imp.* ᵈ*fut.*

64 שׁוּר to see or look on with attention, to regard; to go, to travel. KAL ᵃ*fut.* Isa. lvii. 9, thou wentest, *marg.* 'or, respectedst.'

65 שָׂטָה to turn out of the way of truth, virtue, or duty. KAL ᵃ*pret.* ᵇ*fut.*

66 שָׁלַח to send, to let go. KAL ᵃ*fut.* PIEL ᵇ*pret.* ᶜ*inf.* ᵈ*imp.* ᵉ*fut.* ᶠ*part.*

67 תָּמַם to be finished, to be done and spent. KAL *inf.*

68 תָּעָה to wander, to go astray. KAL ᵃ*pret.* ᵇ*inf.* ᶜ*fut.* ᵈ*part.* Poel. HIPHIL ᵉ*pret.*

Gen. ii. 6.	44 d	Gen. viii. 7.	20 d b, 62 b	Gen. xi. 7, 7.	18, 21 d
ii. 10.	20 e	viii. 16.	20 c	xi. 31, 31.	20 d, 19 a
ii. 14.	13 e	viii. 18.	20 d	xii. 4.	19 c
iii. 14.	19 c	viii. 19.	20 a	xii. 5, 5.	20 d, 19 a
iv. 16.	20 d	ix. 10, 18.	20 e	xii. 9.	13 b, 33 b
vii. 7, 15.	8 d	ix. 23.	19 c	xii. 10.	21 d
vii. 9.		x. 11.	20 a	xii. 19.	19 b
vii. 16, 16.	8 e a	x. 19, 30.	8 b	xiii. 1.	44 d
vii. 18.	19 c	xi. 3, 4.	18	xiii. 3.	19 c

Judg. iii. 13. 19 c
iii. 22. 8 d
iii. 24. 20 a
iii. 27, 28. 21 d
iv. 6. 19 b
iv. 8, 8, 8, 8. 19 c, 13 a, 19 c c
iv. 9.ι 13 b, 19 c
iv. 9. 19 c
iv. 10, 10. 44 d
iv. 12. 44 a
iv. 14, 14. 20 a, 21 d
iv. 18. 20 d
iv. 21. 8 d
v. 4, 31. 20 b
v. 11. 21 a
vi. 14. 19 b
vi. 19. 8 a
vi. 33. 42 d
vii. 3. 25
vii. 4, 4, 4, 4, 7. 19 c
vii. 10, 10. 21 b c
vii. 11,κ 11. 21 a d
viii. 1. 13 a
viii. 8, 11. 44 d
viii. 29. 19 c
ix. 1, 6, 7, 21, 50. 19 c
ix. 5. 8 d
ix. 8.λ 13 b a
ix. 9,μ 11, 13. 13 a
ix. 26. 42 d
ix. 27, 27. 20 d, 8 d
ix. 35, 39, 42. 20 d
ix. 38. 20 c
ix. 52.ν 26 c
x. 14. 19 b
xi. 3. 20 d
xi. 5, 11, 18, 40. 19 c
xi. 8. 13 a
xi. 35. 62 b
xi. 37.ξ 19 c, 21 a
xi. 38, 38. 19 b c
xii. 1, 1. 42 d, 19 a
xii. 5. 42 d
xiii. 11. 19 c
xiii. 20. 44 b
xiv. 1, 5, 7, 10. 21 d
xiv. 3. 13 e
xiv. 9.ο 13 b, 19 c
xiv. 18. 8 d
xiv. 19, 19. 21 d, 44 d
xv. 1, 1. 8 b d
xv. 4. 19 c
xv. 5. 66 e
xv. 8, 11. 21 d
xv. 9. 44 d
xvi. 1, 1. 19 c, 8 d
xvi. 3, 14. 33 c
xvi. 17. 39 a
xvi. 19. 39 b
xvi. 20. 20 d
xvii. 9. 13 e
xvii. 10. 19 c
xv ii. 2, 6, 19. 19 b
xviii. 5, 14. 13 e
xviii. 6, 24, 26. 19 c
xviii. 9, 9. 44 d, 19 a
xviii. 10. 8 b
xviii. 11. 33 c
xviii. 12. 44 d
xviii. 17, 17. 13 e, 44 d
xviii. 18. 8 a
xviii. 20. 8 d
xviii. 26. 62 d
xix. 2, 3, 5, 17, 18, 28. 19 c
xix. 9. 13 a
xix. 14, 14. 19 c, 8 d
xix. 15, 15. 8 b d
xix. 18. 13 e
xix. 23. 20 d
xix. 25. 66 e
xix. 27, 27. 20 d, 19 a
xx. 1, 20, 25. 20 d
xx. 3. 44 a
xx. 8. 19 c
xx. 14. 20 b
xx. 18, 18, 26, 30. 44 d
xx. 23, 23, 23. 44 d, 26 a, 44 c
xx. 28, 28. 20 b, 44 c
xx. 31, 31. 20 d, 44 e
xxi. 10, 20. 19 b
xxi. 19. 44 e
xxi. 21. 13 a
Judg. xxi. 23. 19 c
xxi. 24. 20 d
Ruth i. 1, 11, 16, 16, 19. 19 c
i. 7, 7. 20 d, 19 c
i. 8, 12. 19 b
i. 13. 20 a
i. 15. 62 a
i. 18. 19 a
i. 21. 13 a
ii. 2, 2. 19 c b
ii. 3. 19 c
ii. 8, 8. 19 c, 42 d
ii. 9, 9. 13 a
ii. 18. 8 d
ii. 22. 20 d
iii. 4. 8 a
iii. 6. 21 d
iii. 7, 15, 17. 8 d
iv. 1. 44 a
iv. 13. 8 d
1 Sam. i. 3, 22. 44 a
i. 7. 44 b
i. 17. 19 b
i. 18. 19 c
i. 21. 44 d
ii. 11. 19 c
ii. 20. 13 a
iii. 3. 22
iii. 5, 6, 8. 19 c
iii. 9, 9. 19 b c
iv. 1. 20 d
v. 11. 62 d
v. 12. 44 d
vi. 6. 66 e
vi. 8. 13 a
vi. 9, 20. 44 d
vi. 12,π 12, 12. 13 a b e
vii. 7. 44 d
vii. 11. 20 d
vii. 16. 13 a
viii. 20. 20 a
viii. 22. 19 b
ix. 3. 19 b
ix. 6, 6. 19 c, 13 a
ix. 7, 10, 16. 19 c
ix. 9, 9. 19 a c
ix. 11, 11. 44 e, 20 e
ix. 13. 44 d
ix. 14, 14. 44 d b
ix. 19, 19. 44 c, 66 b
ix. 26. 20 d
ix. 27. 21 e
x. 2, 14. 13 a
x. 3, 3. 15, 44 e
x. 8. 21 a
x. 9. 19 a
x. 26, 26. 13 a, 19 c
xi. 14, 15. 19 c
xiii. 7. 42 a
xiii. 10, 23. 20 d
xiii. 20. 21 d
xiv. 1, 6. 42 d
xiv. 3, 17. 13 a
xiv. 4. 42 b
xiv. 9. 44 d
xiv. 10, 21. 44 a
xiv. 16. 19 c
xiv. 19.ρ 13 b, 19 c
xiv. 36, 37. 21 d
xiv. 46, 46. 44 d, 13 a
xv. 3, 6, 18. 19 b
xv. 12, 12. 37 f, 21 d
xv. 20. 19 c
xv. 27. 19 a
xv. 34, 34. 19 c, 44 a
xvi. 1. 19 b
xvi. 2, 13. 19 c
xvii. 4. 20 d
xvii. 7, 15. 13 e
xvii. 12. 8 a
xvii. 13, 13. 19 c, 13 a
xvii. 20, 20. 19 c, 20 e
xvii. 32. 19 c
xvii. 33, 39, 39. 19 a
xvii. 35. 20 a
xvii. 37. 19 b
xvii. 55. 20 e
xviii. 2.σ 62 b
xviii. 5, 13. 20 d
xviii. 16. 20 e
xviii. 27. 19 c
xviii. 30, 30. 20 d b
xix. 3, 8. 20 d
xix. 12, 18, 22. 19 c
1 Sam. xix. 17. 66 d
xix. 23, 23.τ 19 c, 13 b, 19 c
xx. 5. 66 b
xx. 11, 11, 35. 20 d
xx. 13. 13 a
xx. 19. 21 d
xx. 21, 22, 40. 19 b
xx. 29. 66 d
xx. 41. 8 e
xx. 42, 42. 19 b, 8 e
xxi. 10. 8 d
xxii. 1. 21 d
xxii. 3. 19 c
xxii. 14. 39 a
xxiii. 2, 2. 19 c b
xxiii. 4. 21 c
xxiii. 5, 16, 24, 25, 26, 28. 19 c
xxiii. 8. 21 b
xxiii. 13, 13, 13. 13 k k, 20 b
xxiii. 18, 23. 13 a
xxiii. 22. 19 b
xxiii. 29. 44 d
xxiv. 2, 7, 22. 19 c
xxiv. 3. 8 d
xxiv. 8. 20 d
xxiv. 19. 66 d
xxv. 1. 21 d
xxv. 5. 8 a
xxv. 12. 62 d
xxv. 13. 44 d
xxv. 19. 42 c
xxv. 35. 44 c
xxv. 37. 20 b
xxv. 42, 42. 13 e, 19 c
xxvi. 2, 6, 6. 21 d
xxvi. 11, 25. 19 c
xxvi. 13. 42 d
xxvi. 19. 19 b
xxvii. 8, 8. 44 d, 8 b
xxviii. 1. 20 d
xxviii. 7, 8, 22, 25. 19 c
xxix. 4, 4. 62 d, 21 d
xxix. 6. 20 b
xxix. 7. 19 b
xxix. 8. 8 d
xxix. 9. 44 d
xxix. 11. 44 a
xxx. 2, 9. 19 c
xxx. 10. 42 b
xxx. 21. 20 d
xxx. 22, 22. 13 a
xxx. 24. 21 e or g
xxxi. 12. 19 c
2 Sam. i. 15. 26 b
ii. 1, 1, 1. 44 d c d
ii. 2. 44 d
ii. 12. 20 d
ii. 13. 20 a
ii. 15. 42 d
ii. 19. 19 a
ii. 24. 8 a
ii. 27.υ 44 f
ii. 29, 32. 19 c
iii. 7. 8 a
iii. 16. 13 b, 19 c
iii. 16. 19 b
iii. 19, 21, 21, 22, 23. 19 c
iii. 24.φ 13 b, 19 c
iii. 25. 20 i
iv. 5. 19 c
v. 6. 19 c
v. 10.χ 19 e, 13 b
v. 17. 21 d
v. 19, 19. 44 d c
v. 23. 44 d
v. 24, 24. 53 e, 20 a
vi. 2, 12. 19 c
vi. 4. 13 e
vi. 13. 53 a
vii. 3, 5. 19 b
vii. 9, 23. 13 a
vii. 18. 8 d
viii. 3. 19 a
viii. 6, 14. 13 a
xi. 1. 20 b
xi. 8. 21 c
xi. 9, 10, 10, 13. 21 a
xi. 11. 8 d
xi. 13, 17. 20 d
xi. 21. 26 d
xi. 22. 19 c
2 Sam. xii. 16. 8 a
xii. 23. 13 e
xii. 24. 8 d
xii. 29. 19 c
xiii. 7, 15. 19 b
xiii. 8, 24, 26, 26, 37, 38. 19 b
xiii. 9. 20 d
xiii. 13. 19 e
xiii. 19.χ 19 c, 13 b
xiii. 25, 25. 19 c a
xiii. 27. 66 a
xiii. 39. 20 b
xiv. 8, 21, 30. 19 b
xiv. 23. 19 c
xv. 7, 19. 19 c
xv. 9, 9. 19 b c
xv. 11, 11. 13 a e
xv. 16, 17. 20 d
xv. 20.ψ 29 c or b, 19 a
xv. 20.ω 13 e e
xv. 22. 19 b
xv. 24. 44 d
xv. 30, 30, 30, 30, 30. 40 e e, 13 e, 44 a b
xvi. 9. 42 d
xvi. 13, 13, 13. 19 c, 13 e b
xvi. 17. 13 a
xvi. 21. 8 c
xvi. 22. 8 d
xvii. 11. 13 e
xvii. 17, 17. 13 a, 19 c
xvii. 18, 18. 19 c, 21 d
xvii. 20, 22. 42 a
xvii. 21. 19 c
xvii. 25. 8 a
xviii. 2.α 20 b d
xviii. 3, 6. 20 d
xviii. 9, 9. 8 d, 42 a
xviii. 21. 19 b
xviii. 24. 19 c
xviii. 33, 33. 44 d, 19 a
xix. 7, 7. 20 c e
xix. 15. 19 a
xix. 17. 52
xix. 18. 42 a
xix. 19. 20 a
xix. 20. 21 b
xix. 25. 13 a
xix. 26. 19 c
xix. 31, 36, 37, 38, 39. 42 d
xix. 34. 44 d
xix. 40, 40. 42 d a
xx. 2. 44 d
xx. 3. 8 a
xx. 5. 19 c
xx. 7, 7. 20 d
xx. 8, 8. 8 a, 20 a
xx. 13. 42 a
xx. 14, 14. 42 d, 8 d
xx. 22. 8 d
xxi. 12. 19 c
xxi. 15. 21 d
xxi. 17. 20 d
xxii. 9. 44 a
xxiii. 9. 44 d
xxiii. 13, 21. 21 d
xxiii. 17. 13 e
xxiii. 20. 21 a
xxiv. 1. 19 b
xxiv. 2. 63 c
xxiv. 4, 7, 20. 20 d
xxiv. 8. 63 d
xxiv. 12. 13 b
xxiv. 18. 44 c
xxiv. 19. 44 d
1 Kings i. 13, 53. 19 b
i. 15. 8 d
i. 25. 21 a
i. 38. 21 d
i. 49, 50. 19 c
ii. 2. 13 e
ii. 6. 21 f
ii. 8. 19 a
ii. 19. 8 d
ii. 29. 19 b
ii. 34. 44 d
ii. 36, 46. 20 d
ii. 37, 42. 20 b
ii. 40, 40. 19 c
ii. 41. 13 a
iii. 4. 19 c
1 Kings iii. 7. 20 b
vi. 8. 44 d
viii. 44. 20 d
viii. 66. 19 c
ix. 6. 13 a
ix. 16. 44 a
x. 5. 44 d
x. 13. 19 c
x. 16, 17. 44 g
x. 29. 20 d
xi. 2. 8 d
xi. 5, 21, 24. 19 c
xi. 10. 19 a
xi. 15. 44 b
xi. 17. 8 b
xi. 22, 22.b 19 a, 66 c e
xi. 29. 20 a
xii. 1, 30. 19 c
xii. 24. 44 d
xii. 25. 20 d
xii. 27, 27. 44 d, 62 a
xii. 28. 44 b
xiii. 8. 8 d
xiii. 10, 14, 24, 28. 19 c
xiii. 12, 12. 13 a
xiii. 16. 8 b
xiii. 17. 19 a
xiii. 19. 62 d
xiv. 3. 8 a
xiv. 4, 9. 19 c
xiv. 7. 19 b
xiv. 10. 67
xiv. 28. 8 b
xv. 17, 17. 44 d, 20 e
xvi. 10, 18. 8 d
xvi. 17. 44 d
xvi. 31. 19 c
xvii. 5, 5, 10, 11, 15. 19 c
xvii. 12. 8 a
xvii. 13. 8 c
xviii. 1, 5, 8, 11, 14. 19 b
xviii. 2, 12, 16, 16, 45. 19 c
xviii. 6, 6. 13 a
xviii. 42, 42. 44 d a
xviii. 43, 43, 43. 44 c d, 62 c
xviii. 44. 44 c
xix. 3, 8, 21. 19 c
xix. 4. 13 a
xix. 11. 20 c
xix. 13. 20 d
xix. 15. 19 b
xix. 20.c 19 b, 62 c
xx. 1, 26. 44 d
xx. 16, 17, 21, 31. 20 d
xx. 22. 19 b
xx. 27, 43. 19 c
xx. 33. 8 c
xx. 39. 20 a
xx. 40. 4
xx. 42. 66 b
xxi. 16. 21 b
xxi. 18, 18. 21 c a
xxi. 27. 13 h
xxii. 4, 49. 19 c
xxii. 6, 6. 19 c, 44 c
xxii. 12. 44 c
xxii. 13. 13 a
xxii. 15, 15. 19 c, 44 c
xxii. 20, 29. 44 d
xxii. 22, 22. 20 d c
xxii. 24, 24. 26 c, 42 a
xxii. 25, 30. 8 d
xxii. 36, 36. 42 d, 8 b
xxii. 48, 48. 19 a, 13 a
2 Kings i. 2. 19 b
i. 3, 3. 44 c, 13 e
i. 4, 16. 44 a
i. 6, 6. 19 b, 44 a
i. 9, 13. 44 d
i. 15, 15. 21 c d
ii. 1, 6, 16, 18, 25. 19 c
ii. 2. 21 d
ii. 7. 13 a
ii. 8, 14. 42 d
ii. 9. 42 b
ii. 11, d 11. 13 b e, 44 d
ii. 13. 62 d
ii. 21. 20 d
ii. 23, 23, 23, 23. 44 d e c c
iii. 6. 20 d
2 Kings iii. 7, 7, 7. 19 c c, 44 d
iii. 8. 44 d
iii. 9. 19 c
iii. 12. 21 d
iii. 24.e 32 b a
iii. 25. 37 c
iv. 3, 7, 24, 29. 19 b
iv. 5, 25. 19 c
iv. 18, 39. 20 d
iv. 21, 21. 44 d, 20 d
iv. 23. 13 e
iv. 31. 62 d
iv. 33. 8 d
iv. 34, 35. 44 d
iv. 37, 37. 8 d, 20 d
v. 2. 20 a
v. 4. 8 d
v. 5, 5. 19 b, 8 c
v. 10. 13 b
v. 11, 12. 19 c
v. 14. 21 d
v. 18. 8 b
v. 19. 19 b
v. 24. 66 e
v. 25, 25.f 8 e, 13 a
v. 26. 13 a
v. 27. 20 d
vi. 2, 2. 19 c b
vi. 3, 3. 19 b c
vi. 4, 22, 23. 19 c
vi. 13. 19 b
vi. 15. 20 d
vi. 24. 44 d
vii. 5. 8 b
vii. 8, 8, 8. 8 d, 19 c c
vii. 9. 8 d
vii. 12, 16. 20 d
vii. 14. 19 b
vii. 15. 19 c
viii. 1, 8, 10. 19 b
viii. 2, 9, 28. 19 c
viii. 3. 20 d
viii. 21. 42 d
viii. 29, 29. 62 d, 21 a
ix. 1. 19 b
ix. 2. 8 a
ix. 4, 16, 18, 35. 19 c
ix. 6. 8 d
ix. 15, 15. 20 d, 19 a
ix. 21, 21, 24. 20 d
ix. 27. 44 l
ix. 34. 49
x. 9. 20 d
x. 13. 21 d
x. 23, 24. 8 d
x. 25, 25. 8 c, 19 c
xi. 7, 9. 20 e
xi. 8. 20 b
xi. 16, 18. 8 d
xii. 17, 17. 44 d b
xii. 18. 44 d
xii. 20. 21 e
xiii. 5. 20 d
xiv. 11. 44 d
xv. 14. 44 d
xvi. 9. 44 d
xvi. 10. 19 c
xvii. 5. 44 d
xvii. 27. 19 c
xviii. 7. 20 d
xviii. 17. 44 d
xviii. 21. 8 a
xviii. 25. 44 c
xix. 1. 8 d
xix. 14. 44 d
xix. 27. 20 b
xix. 31, 35. 20 d
xix. 36. 19 c
xx. 4.g 20 a
xx. 5. 44 d
xx. 8. 44 a
xx. 9, 9. 13 a, 62 d
xx. 10. 31 b
xx. 11. 21 a
xxii. 4. 44 c
xxii. 13. 19 b
xxii. 14. 19 c
xxiii. 2. 44 d
xxiii. 29, 29. 44 a, 19 c
xxiv. 12. 20 d
xxv. 4. 19 c
1 Chron. ii. 21. 8 a
iv. 39. 19 c
iv. 42. 13 a

1 Chron. v. 18.	20 e
vi. 15.	13 a
vii. 11.	20 e
vii 23.	8 d
xi. 4.	19 c
xi. 6.	44 d
xi. 15, 23.	21 d
xi. 22.	21 a
xii. 15.	42 a
xii 17.	20 d
xii. 20.	19 a
xii. 33, 36.	20 e
xiii. 6.	44 d
xiv. 8, 8.	44 d, 20 d
xiv. 10, 10.	44 d c
xiv. 14.	44 d
xiv. 15, 15, 15.	53 e, 20 d a
xiv. 17.	13 e
xv. 25.	13 k
xvii. 4.	19 b
xvii. 11.	19 a
xvii. 21.	13 a
xviii. 3.	19 a
xviii. 6, 13.	13 a
xix. 5.	19 c
xx. 1.	20 b
xxi. 2, 10.	19 b
xxi. 4.	13 k
xxi. 18, 19.	44 d
xxi. 21.	20 d
xxi. 30.	19 a
xxvi. 16.	44 e
xxvii. 1.	20 e
xxix. 30.	42 a
2 Chron. i. 3.	19 c
i. 6.	44 g
i. 10.	20 d
vi. 34.	20 d
vii. 19.	13 a
viii. 3.	19 c
viii. 17.	13 a
viii. 18.	8 d
ix. 4.	44 d
ix. 12.	19 c
ix. 15, 16.	44 g
ix. 21.	13 e
x. 1, 16.	19 c
xi. 4, 4.	44 d, 19 a
xiv. 10.	20 d
xiv. 11.	8 a
xv. 2.	20 d
xv. 5.	20 e
xvi. 1.	19 b
xvi. 3.	37 c
xvii. 9.	
xviii. 2, 2.	21 d, 44 b
xviii. 3.	19 c
xviii. 5, 5.	19 c, 44 c
xviii. 11.	44 d
xviii. 12.	13 a
xviii. 14, 14.	19 c, 44 c
xviii. 19, 28.	44 d
xviii. 21, 21.	20 d c
xviii. 23.	42 a
xviii. 24.	8 d
xviii. 29, 29.	8 b d
xviii. 34.	8 b
xix. 2.	20 d
xix. 4. h	62 d, 20 d
xx. 16.	21 c
xx. 17.	20 c
xx. 20, 20.	20 d b
xx. 21.	20 b
xx. 27.	62 b
xx. 36, 37.	19 a
xxi. 9.	42 d
xxii. 5.	19 c
xxii. 6.	21 a
xxii. 7.	20 a
xxiii. 2.	37 c
xxiii. 6, 17.	8 d
xxiii. 7.	20 b
xxiii. 8.	20 a
xxiv. 5.	20 c
xxv. 5.	8 d
xxv. 8.	8 c
xxv. 10, 13.	19 a
xxv. 11.	19 c
xxv. 21.	44 d
xxvi. 6.	20 d
xxvi. 11.	20 e
xxvi. 16, 17.	8 d
2 Chron. xxvi. 18.	20 c
xxvi. 20.	20 b
xxviii. 9.	20 d
xxix. 16, 18.	8 d
xxix. 20.	44 d
xxxi. 1.	19 c
xxxiv. 21.	20 a
xxxiv. 22.	19 b
xxxiv. 30.	19 c
xxxv. 20.	44 d
xxxvi. 23.	20 d
Ezra i. 3.	44 d
i. 5.	44 d
ii. 1, 59.	44 b
iv. 23.	44 e
v. 8, 8.	2 d
v. 15.	2 d
vii. 6.	2 e
vii. 7.	44 a
vii. 9.	44 d
vii. 13, 13.	44 k
vii. 28.	12 a b
viii. 1.	44 b
viii. 31.	44 b
ix. 11.	19 a
x. 6.	8 e
Neh. ii. 13.	19 c
ii. 14.	20 d
ii. 15. i	42 a
ii. 16.	44 e
iii. 15.	13 a
iii. 19.	21 e
iii. 31, k 32.	44 b
iv. 3.	44 h
vi. 11, 11.	44 d
vii. 6, 61.	8 d
viii. 10.	44 e
viii. 12.	19 b
viii. 15.	19 c
viii. 15.	20 c
ix. 11.	20 d
ix. 12, 19.	42 d
ix. 15, 23.	19 c
ix. 24.	8 b
xii. 1.	44 a
xii. 31.	13 m
xii. 32.	19 c
xii. 37, 37.	44 a l
xii. 38.	13 e
Esth. i. 19.	20 d
ii. 12, 13, 15.	8 b
ii. 14.	8 e
iii. 15.	20 a
iv. 1, 6.	20 d
iv. 8.	19 b, 8 d
iv. 16, 16.	42 d
iv. 17.	20 d
v. 9.	8 c
v. 14.	20 a
vii. 8.	20 a
viii. 14, 15.	13 e
ix. 4.	13 a
Job i. 4.	35 a
i. 5.	63 b
i. 7.	20 d
i. 12.	63 b
ii. 2.	20 d
ii. 7.	33 e
iv. 21.	44 d
vi. 18.	23
vii. 4.	21 e
vii. 9.	42 d
ix. 11.	19 c
x. 21.	20 f
xv. 13.	39 b
xv. 30.	13 d
xvi. 22.	21 d
xvii. 16.	54 c
xviii. 20. l	19 c
xix. 10.	17 or 30 a
xxi. 13.	42 e
xxi. 29.	13 d
xxiii. 8.	24
xxiii. 12.	20 a
xxiv. 5.	13 g
xxiv. 10.	59 b
xxvii. 6.	29 a
xxviii. 4.	20 b
xxix. 7.	13 g
xxx. 28.	20 d
xxxi. 34.	55 c
xxxi. 37.	21 b
xxxiii. 24.	42 b
xxxiii. 28.	
Job xxxiv. 8.	6
xxxiv. 21.	53 c
xxxvii. 2.	20 d
xxxvii. 8.	8 d
xxxviii. 35.	19 c
xxxix. 4.	20 a
xxxix. 21.	20 d
xli. 19.	13 d
xli. 20, 21.	20 d
xlii. 8.	19 b
xlii. 9.	19 c
Ps. xiv. 3.	39 a
xvii. 5.	7 c
xvii. 8.	44 a
xix. 4.	20 a
xix. 6.	20 i
xxi. 29.	21 e
xxvi. 4.	8 d
xxviii. 1.	21 e
xxx. 3.	21 b
xxx. 3.	21 b or e
xxx. 9.	21 b
xxxii. 8.	19 c
xxxviii. 4.	42 a
xxxviii. 10.	4
xxxix. 13.	19 c
xl. 2.	7 c
xli. 6.	20 d
xli. 4, 4.	42 d, 10
xlii. 7.	42 a
xlii. 9.	19 c
xliii. 4.	13 k
xliii. 4.	8 d
xliv. 9.	20 d
xlvii. 5.	44 a
xlviii. 12.	35 c
l. i.	8 d
li. title.	8 a
liii. 3.	38 a
lv. 10.	37 g
lv. 15.	21 d
lviii. 3.	68 a
lix. 6, 14.	37 g
lx. 10.	20 d
lxiii. 9.	8 d
lxvi. 6.	8 a
lxvi. 12.	8 a
lxvi. 13.	8 d
lxviii. 7.	20 b
lxviii. 21.	13 l
lxviii. 24, 24.	13 n
lxviii. 25.	54 a
lxxi. 16.	8 d
lxxiii. 2.	31 a or c
lxxiii. 17.	8 d
lxxvii. 8.	5
lxxvii. 17.	13 k
lxxvii. 52.	33 f
lxxx. 18.	38 b
lxxxi. 5.	20 b
lxxxiv. 7.	19 c
lxxxv. 13.	13 h
lxxxviii. 4.	21 e
lxxxviii. 16.	42 a
lxxxix. 14.	54 b
lxxxix. 34.	20 i
xcvii. 3.	19 c
civ. 8, 8.	44 d, 21 d
civ. 19.	8 g
civ. 23.	20 d
civ. 26.	13 h
cv. 13.	13 k
cvii. 7.	19 a
cvii. 23.	21 e
cvii. 26.	21 d
cviii. 11.	20 d
cix. 23.	13 f
cxiii. 3.	8 g
cxiv. 1.	20 b
cxv. 17.	21 e
cxviii. 19.	8 d
cxix. 35.	11 c
cxix. 67.	60
cxix. 176.	68 a
cxxi. 8.	20 b
cxxii. 1.	19 c
cxxii. 4.	44 a
cxxiv. 4, 5.	19 c, 13 b
cxxvi. 6.	42 e
cxxxi. 8.	44 d
cxxxii. 3.	44 d
cxxxii. 7.	8 d
cxxxiii. 2.	21 e
Ps. cxxxix. 7.	19 c
cxl. 4.	48
cxliii. 7.	21 e
cxliv. 14.	20 e
cxlvi. 4.	20 d
Prov. i. 12.	21 e
ii. 19.	8 e
iii. 28.	19 b
iv. 12.	19 a
iv. 13.	59 b
iv. 14.	7 b
v. 21.	21 e
v. 21.	43
v. 3, 6.	61 a
vi. 22.	19 b
vi. 28.	13 i
vi. 29.	8 e
vii. 19.	53 b
vii. 22, 22.	13 e, 8 d
vii. 25.	68 c
vii. 27.	21 e
ix. 6.	7 a
xiv. 7.	19 b
xiv. 15.	7 c
xv. 12.	19 c
xviii. 8.	21 a
xx. 14.	2 b
xx. 19.	13 e
xx. 24.	53 d
xxii. 10.	20 d
xxii. 24.	8 d
xxiii. 30.	8 e
xxiv. 30.	42 a
xxv. 8.	44 a
xxvi. 7.	44 a
xxvi. 20.	22
xxvi. 22.	21 a
xxvii. 10.	8 d
xxviii. 10.	61 b
xxx. 27.	20 d
xxx. 29, o 29.	53 c, 19 a
xxxi. 18.	22
Eccles. i. 5.	13 e
i. 6.	13 e
ii. 1.	19 b
ii. 20.	37 a
iii. 20.	13 e
iii. 21, 21.	44 e, 21 e
v. 1, 16.	19 c
v. 15.	13 e
vi. 6.	13 e
vii. 2, 2.	19 a
viii. 3.	19 c
viii. 10.	13 h
ix. 7.	19 b
ix. 10.	13 e
x. 15.	19 a
xii. 5, 5.	13 e, 37 a
Cant. i. 8.	20 c
ii. 11.	13 a
iii. 2.	37 g
iii. 3.	37 d
iii. 4.	59 b
iii. 11.	20 c
v. 6.	42 a
v. 7.	37 d
vi. 1.	20 a
vi. 2, 11.	21 a
vi. 6.	44 d
vii. 8.	13 e
vii. 9.	20 d
Isa. i. 4.	14
ii. 3, 3, 3.	13 a, 44 d, 20 d
ii. 19.	8 a
ii. 21.	8 b
iii. 16.	19 c
iii. 12.	13 b
v. 24.	44 d
vi. 8.	19 c
vi. 9.	19 b
vii. 1.	44 a
vii. 3.	20 c
vii. 6.	44 d
viii. 6.	55 b
viii. 6.	13 e
viii. 7.	13 a
viii. 8.	42 a
x. 29.	42 a
xi. 15.	11 b
xiii. 2.	8 d
xiii. 10.	20 b
xiv. 19.	21 e
xv. 2.	44 a
Isa. xv. 5.	44 d
xv. 8.	35 a
xvi. 8.	42 a
xvi. 9.	19 b
xvii. 2.	19 b
xx. 2.	44 c
xxi. 2.	19 b
xxi. 6.	44 a
xxii. 1.	19 b
xxii. 15.	19 b
xxiii. 16.	37 b
xxiv. 11.	9
xxvii. 4.	51
xxviii. 13.	19 c
xxviii. 19.	42 b
xxx. 2. p	21 b
xxx. 8.	8 c
xxx. 29.	13 e
xxxi. 1.	21 e
xxxiii. 21.	19 c
xxxiv. 10.	44 d
xxxv. 9.	8 a
xxxvi. 6.	44 c
xxxvi. 10.	8 d
xxxvii. 1.	44 d
xxxvii. 14.	20 b
xxxvii. 28.	20 b
xxxvii. 32, 36.	20 d
xxxvii. 37.	19 c
xxxviii. 5.	21 a
xxxviii. 8, 8.	21 a
xxxviii. 13.	19 c
xxxviii. 15.	10
xxxviii. 18.	21 e
xxxviii. 22.	44 d
xli. 3.	8 d
xlii. 10.	21 e
xlii. 13.	20 d
xlv. 2.	19 c
xlv. 13.	16 e
xlv. 16.	13 a
xlv. 23.	20 a
xlvi. 2. q	13 a
xlviii. 3.	20 a
xlviii. 17.	19 c
xlviii. 20.	20 c
xlix. 9.	20 d
xlix. 17.	20 a
li. 5.	19 a
li. 23, 23.	44 d e
lii. 4.	21 a
lii. 11, 11.	20 c
lii. 12, 12.	
12.	20 d, 19 c, 13 e
liii. 6.	68 a
liv. 9.	42 b
lv. 11, 12.	20 d
lvii. 7.	44 a
lvii. 8.	44 d
lvii. 9.	64 a
lvii. 17.	19 c
lviii. 6.	66 e
lviii. 8, 18.	13 a
lix. 8, 8.	43, 11 a
lx. 15.	42 a
lx. 20.	8 d
lxii. 1.	20 d
lxii. 10, 10.	42 c
lxiii. 14.	21 d
lxvi. 24.	20 a
Jer. i. 7.	19 c
ii. 2, 2.	13 b, 19 a
ii. 5.	58 a
ii. 23.	13 a
ii. 25.	19 c
ii. 37.	20 d
iii. 1.	13 a
iii. 6.	13 e
iii. 8.	19 c
iii. 12.	13 b
iv. 5.	8 d
iv. 7.	20 a
iv. 29.	8 a
v. 6.	20 e
v. 10.	44 c
v. 23.	19 c
vi. 4, 4.	44 d, 47
vi. 5.	44 d
vi. 25.	20 d
vii. 12.	19 b
ix. 2.	19 c
ix. 10.	13 a
x. 5.	53 b
x. 20.	20 a
xi. 10, 12.	13 a
xiii. 1.	13 b
Jer. xiii. 4, 6.	19 b
xiii. 5, 7.	19 c
xiv. 2.	44 a
xiv. 18, 18.	20 a, 40
xv. 1, 2.	20 d
xv. 5.	39 b
xv. 6.	19 c
xv. 9.	8 a
xvi. 5.	19 c
xvi. 8.	8 d
xvii. 19, 19.	13 b, 20 d
xviii. 2.	21 a
xviii. 3.	21 d
xix. 1.	13 b
xix. 2.	20 a
xix. 10.	13 e
xx. 6.	19 c
xxi. 2.	44 d
xxi. 9.	20 d
xxii. 1.	21 c
xxii. 10.	13 e
xxii. 11.	20 a
xxii. 20.	44 c
xxii. 22.	19 c
xxiii. 15, 19.	20 a
xxv. 6.	19 c
xxv. 32.	20 e
xxvi. 21.	8 d
xxvii. 18.	8 a
xxviii. 4.	8 d
xxviii. 11.	19 c
xxviii. 13.	13 b
xxix. 12.	13 a
xxix. 16.	20 a
xxx. 16.	19 c
xxx. 23.	20 a
xxxi. 2.	13 b
xxxi. 4, 39.	20 a
xxxi. 6.	44 d
xxxi. 21.	13 a
xxxi. 22.	16
xxxi. 24.	33 a
xxxiv. 2.	13 b
xxxiv. 3.	8 d
xxxiv. 9.	66 c
xxxiv. 10, 10.	66 c c
xxxiv. 11.	66 b
xxxiv. 14, 14.	66 b e
xxxiv. 21.	44 e
xxxv. 2, 13.	13 b
xxxv. 15.	8 d
xxxvi. 3.	19 c
xxxvi. 5.	8 b
xxxvi. 6.	8 a
xxxvi. 12.	21 d
xxxvi. 19.	19 b
xxxvi. 20.	20 e
xxxvii. 4.	
xxxvii. 12, 12.	20 d, 19 a
xxxviii. 2.	20 e
xxxviii. 8, 18.	20 d
xxxviii. 11.	8 d
xxxviii. 17. r	20 b d
xxxviii. 21.	20 b
xxxix. 4, 4.	20 d
xxxix. 16.	13 b
xl. 1.	19 a b
xl. 5, 5, 5, 5.	
5.	62 d c, 19 b a, 66 e
xl. 6.	19 c
xl. 15.	19 c
xli. 6, 6.	20 d, 13 b e
xli. 10.	42 b
xli. 12, 14, 15.	19 c
xli. 17.	19 a
xlii. 14, 19.	8 d
xlii. 15.	8 a
xlii. 17, 22.	8 b
xliii. 2.	8 d
xliii. 12.	20 a
xliii. 3.	19 a
xliv. 8, 14, 28.	8 e
xliv. 12.	8 b
xliv. 17.	20 a
xlv. 5.	19 c
xlvi. 8.	44 d
xlvi. 11.	44 c
xlvi. 16.	62 d
xlviii. 5, 5, 5.	44 l d, 21 h
xlviii. 7.	20 a
xlviii. 11.	13 a
xlviii. 15, 15.	44 a, 21 a

Jer. xlviii. 32.	42 a	Ezek. xxiii. 44, 44,		Hos. ii. 5, 7, 13.	19 c
xlix. 3.	19 c	44.	8 d b a	iii. 1.	19 b
xlix. 17.	42 e	xxiv. 6.	20 a	iv. 15.	44 d
xlix. 28.	44 c	xxiv. 12.	20 d	v. 6, 13, 14, 15.	19 c
l. 4, 4.	13 b, 19 c	xxiv. 14.	50	vi. 3.	20 i
l. 6, 6.	68 e, 13 a	xxv. 3.	13 a	vi. 4.	13 e
l. 8.	20 c	xxvi. 11.	21 d	vi. 5.	20 d
l. 13.	42 e	xxvi. 20.	21 e	vii. 11.	13 a
l. 21.	44 c	xxvii. 19.	2 c	vii. 12.	19 c
l. 27.	21 d	xxvii. 33.	20 b	viii. 9.	44 a
l. 33.	66 c	xxx. 9.	20 d	ix. 6.	13 a
li. 9.	19 a	xxx. 17, 18.	19 c	ix. 10.	8 a
li. 45.	20 c	xxxi. 12.	21 d	xi. 2.	13 a
li. 50.	13 c	xxxi. 14.	21 e	xi. 3.	56
li. 59.	19 a	xxxi. 15.	21 b	Joel ii. 16.	20 d
lii. 7, 7.	20 d, 19 c	xxxi. 17.	21 a	Amos i. 15.	13 a
Lam. i. 5, 18.	13 a	xxxii. 18, 25, 29.	21 e	ii. 7.	19 c
i. 6.	19 c	xxxii. 19.	21 c	iv. 3.	20 d
iv. 18.	19 a	xxxii. 21, 27.	21 a	v. 3, 3.	20 e
Ezek. i. 9, 9.	19 a c	xxxii. 24, 24.	21 a e	v. 19.	19 a
i. 12, 12, 12,		xxxii. 30, 30.	21 a e	vi. 2, 2.	19 b, 21 c
12.	19 c a c a	xxxiii. 31.	13 e	vii. 12, 15.	19 b
i. 13, 13.	13 l, 20 e	xxxvi. 20, 20.	8 a, 20 a	viii. 5.	42 d
i. 17, 17, 17.	19 a c a	xxxvi. 21, 22. s	8 a	viii. 9.	8 f
i. 19, 19.	19 a c	xxxvii. 21.	13 a	ix. 4.	19 c
i. 20, 20, 20.	19 a c a	xxxviii. 11, 11.	44 d, 8 d	Jonah i. 2.	19 b
i. 21, 21.	19 a c	xxxix. 9.	20 a	i. 3, 3, 3,	
i. 24.	19 a	xl. 6, 22, 49.	44 d	3.	21 d, 8 e, 21 d, 8 b
iii. 1, 4, 11.	19 b	xl. 26.	44 i	i. 5.	21 a
iii. 14.	19 c	xl. 31, 34, 37	44 l	ii. 6.	21 a
iii. 22.	20 c	xl. 40.	44 e	ii. 2.	19 b
iii. 23, 25.	20 d	xli. 3.	8 a	iii. 3.	19 c
iii. 24.	8 c	xlii. 9.	8 b	iv. 5.	20 d
vii. 10.	20 d	xlii. 11.	20 i	Mic. i. 8.	19 c
vii. 14.	13 e	xlii. 14.	20 i	ii. 3.	19 c
viii. 6.	58 b	xliii. 11.	20 i	ii. 13.	20 d
viii. 9.	8 c	xliv. 3.	20 d	iii. 6.	8 a
viii. 10.	8 d	xliv. 5.	20 i	iv. 2, 2.	44 d, 20 d
viii. 11.	44 d	xliv. 10, 10.		iv. 10, 10.	20 d, 8 a
ix. 2.	8 d	10.	58 a, 68 b a	v. 2.	20 k
ix. 3.	44 f	xliv. 15.	68 b	v. 8.	42 a
ix. 4, 5.	42 c	xliv. 19.	20 b	Nah. iii. 10.	13 a
ix. 7, 7.	20 c a	xliv. 27.	20 c	iii. 14.	8 c
x. 2, 2.	8 c d	xlvi. 2.	20 a	Hab. i. 4.	20 d
x. 3.	8 b	xlvi. 8.	8 d, 20 d	iii. 5, 5.	19 c, 20 d
x. 4.	57	xlvi. 9, 9, 9.	20 d	iii. 11. t	13 h
x. 6.	8 d	xlvi. 10, 10.		iii. 13.	20 a
x. 7.	20 d	10, 10.	8 b d, 20 b d	Hag. i. 8.	44 c
x. 11, 11, 11,		xlvi. 12, 12.	20 b	Zech. ii. 2.	13 e
11.	19 a c a a	xlvii. 3.	20 b	ii. 3, 3.	20 e
x. 16, 16.	19 a c	xlvii. 8, 8.	21 a, 8 a	v. 3, 6.	20 e
x. 19.	20 b	xlvii. 15.	8 b	v. 5, 5.	20 d e
x. 22.	19 c	xlviii. 1.	8 b	vi. 5.	20 e
xi. 23, 24.	44 d	xlviii. 11, 11,		vi. 6, 6, 6.	20 e a a
xii. 4, 4.	20 d i	11.	68 a b a	vi. 7, 7.	20 a, 19 a
xii. 11.	19 c	xlviii. 30.	20 l	vi. 8.	20 e
xii. 12.	20 d	Dan. ii. 5, 8.	1	vi. 10.	20 e
xiii. 5.	44 a	ii. 13, 14.	34	viii. 10.	20 e
xiii. 20.	66 b	ii. 16.	45 a	viii. 21, 21,	
xiv. 11.	68 c	ii. 17.	2 d	21.	13 a, 19 c c
xiv. 17.	42 d	ii. 24, 24.	45 a, 2 d	viii. 23.	19 c
xv. 7.	20 a	vi. 10.	45 a	ix. 14, 14.	20 a, 13 a
xvi. 14.	20 d	vi. 14.	45 b	x. 2.	33 a
xix. 6.	13 k	vi. 18, 18.	2 d, 28	xiv. 2, 3.	20 a
xix. 14.	20 d	vi. 19.	2 d	xiv. 8.	20 d
xx. 10.	20 h	ix. 25.	20 i	xiv. 16.	44 a
xx. 16.	13 e	xi. 44.	20 a	xiv. 18.	44 d
xx. 29.	8 e	xii. 9, 13.	19 b	Mal. i. 11.	8 g
xx. 39.	19 b	Hos. i. 2.	19 b	iii. 7.	39 a
xxi. 4.	20 d	i. 3.	19 o	iv. 2.	20 a
xxi. 16.	3				

a lit. going was gone.   β lit. going thou hast gone.   γ lit. loosened from him.   δ lit. only going far ye shall not go far in going on your way.   ε lit. who and who (are) going.   ζ lit. not go out as ... go out.   η pass through and return.   θ lit. added to pass.   ι lit. going I will go.   κ lit. and thou shalt go down.   λ lit. going went.   μ see Promote.   ν lit. "went hard."   ξ marg. 'that I may go and go down.'   o lit. going went.   π lit. went going in.   ρ lit. going went.   σ "go home."   τ lit. going went.   υ marg. 'or, gone away.'   φ lit. going gone.   χ lit. went going,   ψ marg. 'make thee wander in going.'   ω lit. I go whither I am going.   a lit. going I will go forth.   b lit. letting go let me go.   c marg. 'go, return.'   d lit. going went.   e "they went forward smiting;" lit. they smote in it even smiting.   f. marg. 'went not hither or thither.'   g lit. was not gone out.   h lit. returned and went out.   i lit. was I going up.   k marg. 'or, corner chamber.'   l lit. 'or, lived with him.'   m lit. from those that go down.   n marg. 'the soul shall go.'   o lit. do well in going.   p lit. going in the descent to Egypt.   q marg. 'their soul is gone.'   r lit. going forth will go forth.   s or, ye have come.   t marg. 'or, thine arrows walked in the light.'

GOAD

דָּרְבָן m. the iron-pointed part of a goad; the wooden part, or rather the whole instrument, being called by another name; see below. "In ploughing," says Maundrell (Travels, p. 110), "they use goads eight feet long, and six inches about the thicker end: at the smaller end they are armed with a sharp prickle for driving the oxen; at the other end, with a little spade or paddle, strong and massy, for cleaning the plough from the mould which encumbers it in working:" and possibly at other times for cutting up weeds.—*Taylor*. 1 Sam. xiii. 21. דָּרְבֹנוֹת f. pl. Eccles. xii. 11.

מַלְמָד m. a goad, by which bullocks in the waggon or plough were disciplined or made accustomed to labour; a stout stick, with an iron point at one end: Judg. iii. 31.

GOAT

1 יְעֵלִים m. pl. mountain goats, which climb up and frequent the highest mountains and rocks, with large horns, which were of great value among the ancients, as they served to make curious bows and drinking cups.—*Bochart*.

2 אַקּוֹ m. the tragelaphus or goat-deer, of the bigness of an heifer of a year old.—*Shaw's Supp.* p. 76.

3 עֵז f. a goat: Gen. xv. 9, &c. עֵז Ch. f.

4 עַתּוּד m. a he-goat, as the leader of a flock.

5 צָפִיר m. a he-goat, with עֵז lit. an he-goat of the goats. צְפִירָא Ch. m.

6 שֶׂה com. one of the smaller cattle, a sheep or a goat: Deut. xiv. 4, lit. and the kid of goats.

7 שָׂעִיר m. a he-goat, from its being hairy.

8 תַּיִשׁ m. a he-goat.

No. 3 not included.

Gen. xxx. 35, 35.	8, 3	Deut. xiv. 4.	6, 3	Prov. xxvii. 26.	4
xxxii. 14, 14.	3, 8	xiv. 5.	2	xxx. 31.	8
Lev. iv. 24.	7	xxxii. 14.	4	Isa. i. 11. a	4
ix. 15.	7	1 Sam. xxiv. 2.	1	xxxiv. 6.	4
x. 16.	7	2 Chron. xvii. 11.	8	Jer. l. 8.	4
xvi. 7, 8, 9, 10, 15,		xxix. 21.	5, 3	li. 40.	4
18, 20, 21, 21, 22,		xxix. 23.	7	Ezek. xxvii. 21.	4
22, 26, 27.	7	Ezra vi. 17.	5 a, 3 a	xxxiv. 17. a	4
Num. vii. 17, 23, 29,		viii. 35.	5	xxxix. 18. a	4
35, 41, 47, 53, 59,		Job xxxix. 1.	1	xliii. 25.	7
65, 71, 77, 83, 88.	4	Ps. l. 9, 13.	4	Dan. viii. 5, 8.	5, 3
xxviii. 22.	7	lxvi. 15.	4	Zech. x. 3.	4
xxix. 22, 28, 31, 34,		civ. 18.	1		
38.	7				

a marg. 'great he-goats.'

GOBLET

אַגָּן m. bowl, cup: Cant. vii. 2.

GOD

1 אֵל m. a name of God, generally supposed to imply strength, omnipotence; particularly used in poetry, and as the language of an individual relation to God. In prose it is scarcely ever used without an attributive adjective or genitive. In poetic language it is more frequently used alone, and occurs frequently in Job, Psalms, and Isaiah, sometimes with the article הָאֵל. In the Psalms, אֵל is frequently used with the pronoun 'my' subjoined, but never with 'thy' or 'his.' Once we find the God of Israel, Ps. lxviii. 35, comp. Gen. xxxiii. 20; xlvi. 3; xlix. 25; the God of Jacob, Ps. cxlvi. 5; God of my life, Ps. xlii. 8; God of truth, Deut. xxxii. 4: Ps. xxxi.

5 ; God of Jeshurun, Deut. xxxiii. 26 ; God of glory, Ps. xxix. 3 ; God of salvation, Ps. lxxiii. 19 ; our God is the God of salvation, Ps. lxviii. 20 ; my father, my God, and the rock of my salvation, Ps. lxxxix. 26 ; God of heaven, Ps. cxxxvi. 26 ; God my salvation, Isa. xii. 2 ; a God of recompenses, Jer. li. 56. These phrases may illustrate in what sense the believer uses this name of God, when he would call Him "my God." Yet this title is also the general name of idols and false gods, of whom it is used probably with an implied reference to the true God, in whose stead idols are put by those who fall away from Jehovah ; in this sense Deut. xxxii. 21 must be understood, אֵל לֹא. This name of God is used to express whatever is pre-eminent in excellence, as cedars of God, Ps. lxxx. 6 ; mountains of God, Ps. xxxvi. 6.

אֱלָהּ a root, not in use, but believed to signify to worship, to adore, not however in the exclusive sense of divine worship ; hence אֱלוֹהַּ m. one name of God, as the Supreme Deity, assumed by Pagans to belong to their false deities : Dan. xi. 37, 38, 39 : 2 Chron. xxxii. 15. Hab. i. 11, "this his power is for a god ;" so Job xii. 6 may be translated, "who bear a god in their hands." This title is strictly denied of the idols of the Gentiles ; Ps. xviii. 31, "who is God, save the LORD" (Jehovah). It is most frequently used of the true God, and almost exclusively in the book of Job. ª אֱלֹהִים m. pl. the name more generally used of the God revealed in Scripture, as to creation and providence, in the plural intimating the three persons of the Godhead ; the second person more particularly as Creator, and communing with our first parents in paradise. In this view He is more generally referred to by this name in respect to other people, than to the professed worshippers of the God of his own people. A clear distinction may be traced by an intelligent mind in every passage of Holy Writ between this title and that of Jehovah, the revealed God of grace afterwards to be manifested in the flesh, and the discrimination is confidently recommended to all attentive readers of the Scriptures, as including much instruction and security against assumed notions of the sceptics of the day. ᵇ אֱלָהּ m. Ch. id.

3 יְהֹוָה Jehovah (see Lord), is sometimes rendered God, especially in connexion with אֲדֹנָי, but distinguished in our version by being put in small capitals. In some instances, however, this latter title seems to be rendered, as in Hab. iii. 19, " the LORD God (is) my strength ;" and in Exod. xxxiv. 23 ; and there represented by GOD, in capitals.

No. 2 not included except to distinguish it from אֱלוֹהַּ.

Gen. xiv. 18, 19, 20, 22.	1	Exod. vi. 3.	1	Deut. v. 9, 9.	2 a, 1
xvi. 13.	1	xv. 2, 2.	1, 2 a	vi. 15, 15, 15.	2 a, 1, 2 a
xvii. 1.	1	xv. 11.α	1	vii. 9, 9, 9.	2 a a, 1
xxi. ˙3.	1	xx. 5, 5.	2 a, 1	vii. 21, 21.	2 a, 1
xxviii. 3.	1	xxxiv. 6, 14, 14.	1	x. 17, 17, 17.	
xxxi. 13.	1	xxxiv. 23, 23.	3, 2 a	17.	2 a a, 1
xxxv. 1, 1.	2 a, 1	Num. xii. 13.	1	xxxii. 4, 12, 18, 21.	1
xxxv. 3.	1	xvi. 22, 22.	1	xxxii. 15.	2
xxxv. 11, 11.	2 a, 1	xxiii. 8, 19, 22, 23.	1	xxxii. 17, 17.	2, 2 a
xliii. 14.	1	xxiv. 4, 8, 16, 23.	1	xxxiii. 26.	1
xlvi. 3, 3.	1, 2 a	Deut. iii. 24.	1	Josh. xi. 10.	
xlviii. 3.	1	iv. 24, 24.	2 a, 1	xxii. 22, 22, 22.	2 b
xlix. 25.	1	iv. 31, 31.	2 a, 1	22.	1, 2 a, 1, 2 a

Josh. xxiv. 19, 19.	2 a, 1	Job xxxv. 2, 13.	1	Ps. cxxxvi. 26.	1
Judg. ix. 46.	1	xxxv. 10.	2	cxxxix. 17, 23.	2
1 Sam. ii. 3.	1	xxxvi. 2.	2	cxxxix. 19.	1
2 Sam. xxii. 31, 33, 48.	1	xxxvi. 5, 22, 26.	1	cxl. 6.	2
xxii. 32, 32.	1, 2 a	xxxvii. 5, 10, 14.	1	cxlvi. 5, 5.	1, 2 a
xxiii. 5.	1	xxxvii. 15, 22.	2	cxlix. 6.	1
2 Chron. xxii. 15,		xxxviii. 41.	1	cl. 1.	1
15.	2, 2 a	xxxix. 17.	2	Prov. xxx. 5.	2
Ezra iv. 24.	2 b	xl. 2.	2	Isa. v. 16.	1
v. 1, 2, 2, 5, 8, 11, 12,		xl. 9, 19.	1	viii. 10.	1
13, 14, 15, 16, 17.	2 b	Ps. v. 4.	1	ix. 6.	1
vi. 3, 5, 5, 7, 7, 8, 9,		vii. 11, 11.	2 a, 1	x. 21.	1
10, 12, 12, 14, 16,		x. 11, 12.	1	xii. 2.	1
17, 18.	2 b	xvi. 1.	1	xiv. 13.	1
vii. 12, 14, 15, 16,		xvii. 6.	1	xxxi. 3.	1
17, 18, 19, 19, 20,		xviii. 2, 30, 32, 47.	1	xl. 18.	1
21, 23, 23, 24, 25,		xviii. 31, 31.	2, 2 a	xlii. 5.	1
25, 26.	2 b	xix. 1.	1	xliii. 10, 12.	1
Neh. i. 5, 5.	2 a, 1	xxii. 1, 1, 10.	1	xliv. 8.	2
ix. 17.β	2	xxix. 3.	1	xliv. 10, 15, 17, 17.	1
ix. 31.	1	xxxi. 5.	1	xlv. 14, 14.	1, 2 a
ix. 32, 32.	2 a, 1	xlii. 2, 2, 2.	2 a, 1, 2 a	xlv. 15, 15.	1, 2 a
Job iii. 4, 23.	2	xliii. 8, 9.	1	xlv. 20, 22.	1
iv. 9, 17.	2	xliii. 4, 4, 4,		xlv. 21, 21.	2 a, 1
v. 8, 8.	1, 2 a	4.	2 a, 1, 2 a a	xlvi. 6.	1
v. 17.	2	xliv. 20, 20.	2 a, 1	xlvi. 9, 9.	1, 2 a
vi. 4, 8, 9.	2	l. 22.	2	Jer. x. 11.	2 b
viii. 3, 5, 13, 20.	1	lii. 1, 5.	1	xxxii. 18.	1
ix. 2.	1	lv. 19, 19.	1, 2 a	li. 56.	1
ix. 13.	2	lvii. 2, 2.	2 a, 1	Lam. iii. 41.	1
x. 2.	1	lxiii. 1, 1.	2 a, 1	Ezek. x. 5.	1
xi. 5, 6, 7.	2	lxviii. 19, 20, 20.	1	xxviii. 2, 2,	
xii. 4.	2	lxviii. 24, 24.	2 a, 1	2, 2.	1, 2 a, 1, 2 a
xii. 6, 6.	1, 2	lxviii. 35, 35,		xxviii. 9, 9.	2 b
xiii. 3, 7, 8.	1	35.	2 a, 1, 2 a	Dan. ii. 11, 18, 19, 20,
xv. 4, 11, 13, 25.	1	lxxiii. 11, 17.	1	23, 28, 37, 44, 45,
xv. 8.	1	lxxiv. 8.	1	47.	2 b
xvi. 11.	1	lxxvii. 9, 14.	1	iii. 12, 14, 15, 17, 18,
xvi. 20, 21.	1	lxxvii. 13, 13,		25, 26, 28, 28, 28,
xviii. 21.	1	13.	2 a, 1, 2 a	29, 29.	2 b
xix. 6, 21, 26.	1	lxxviii. 7, 7.	2 a, 1	iv. 2, 8, 8, 9, 18.	2 b
xix. 22.	1	lxxviii. 8, 18, 34, 41.	1	v. 3, 4, 11, 11, 14, 18,
xx. 15.	1	lxxviii. 19, 19.	2 a, 1	21, 23, 23, 26.	2 b
xx. 29, 29.	2 a, 1	lxxviii. 35, 35.	2 a, 1	vi. 5, 7, 10, 11, 12,
xxi. 9, 19.	2	lxxxi. 9, 9.	1	16, 20, 22, 23, 26,
xxi. 14, 22.	1	lxxxiii. 1, 1.	2 a, 1	26.	2 b
xxii. 2, 13, 17.	1	lxxxiv. 2.	1	ix. 4, 4.	2 a, 1
xxii. 12, 26.	2	lxxxv. 8.	1	xi. 36, 36, 36.	1
xxiii. 16.	2	lxxxvi. 15.	1	xi. 37, 37.	2 a, 2
xxiv. 12.	2	lxxxix. 7, 26.	1	xi. 38, 38, 39.	2
xxv. 4.	1	xc. 2.	1	Hos. i. 10.	1
xxvii. 2, 9, 11, 13.	1	xciv. 1, 1.	1	xi. 9, 12.	1
xxvii. 3, 8, 10.	2	xcv. 3, 3.	1, 2 a	Jonah iv. 2.	1
xxix. 2, 4.	2	xcix. 8, 8.	2 a, 1	Mic. vii. 18.	1
xxxi. 2, 6.	1	cii. 24.	1	Nah. i. 2.γ	1
xxxi. 14, 23, 28.	1	civ. 21.	1	Hab. i. 11.	2
xxxii. 13.	1	cvi. 14, 21.	1	iii. 3.	2
xxxiii. 4, 6, 14, 29.	1	cvii. 11.	1	iii. 19.	3
xxxiii. 12, 26.	2	cxiv. 7.	2	Zech. vii. 2.	1
xxxiv. 5, 10, 12, 23,		cxviii. 27.	1	Mal. i. 9.	1
31, 37.	1	cxviii. 28, 28.	1, 2 a	ii. 10, 11.	1

ª marg. ' or, mighty ones.'   β marg. ' a God of pardons.'   γ lit. the LORD is a jealous God.

GODLY

אֱלֹהִים m. pl. God ; godly seed, lit. seed of God : Mal. ii. 15.

חָסִיד adj. pious, holy, godly : one who has received grace or shews grace : the pious towards Jehovah, חָסִיד לוֹ : Ps. iv. 3 ; xii. 1 ; xxxii. 6.

GOLD

1 בֶּצֶר a precious metal, or something costly, which cannot be determined with certainty, either from etymology or from the ancient versions, or from Jewish tradition. According to David Kimchi, gold ; according to Aben-Ezra, Gesenius, and others, ore of gold and silver : Job xxii. 24. The parallel clause, ver. 24, has (gold) of Ophir ; ver. 25, treasures of silver. ª בְּצֻר m. id. the same : Job xxxvi. 19. Perhaps, in general, any precious treasure, or precious metal.

2 דְּהַב Ch. m. the same, with זָהָב Heb. gold, golden. ª מִדְהֲבָה f. found only in Isa. xiv. 4. According to the Jewish com-

mentators, exactress of gold (spoken of Babylon); others, extortion of gold, referring to the Arabic; *marg.* 'exactress of gold;' or there may be some allusion to an epithet used by the Chaldeans of their city. Schultens and others explain the word to mean, destroyer or plunderer. "J. D. Michaelis, and the later Germans, are disposed to read מְרְהֵבָה oppression, which is found in one edition, appears to be the basis of the ancient versions, and agrees well with the use of נָגַשׂ and יִרְהָבוּ in iii. 5." —*Alexander in loc.*

3 זָהָב *m.* gold. This seems to be the only word expressive of gold as a mineral. When used after numerals, shekels is to be supplied, as Gen. xxiv. 22. Figuratively, the golden splendour of the firmament, Job xxxvii. 22; golden-coloured oil, Zech. iv. 12; occurs very frequently. —Gen. ii. 11, &c.

4 חָרוּץ *m.* gold, so called, according to Fürst, from its glittering, bright appearance, from which χρυσός seems to have been derived.

5 כֶּתֶם *m.* gold, also from its brightness; or, according to others, from its being precious; hence translated 'pure gold,' 'fine gold.'

6 סְגוֹר *m.* gold laid up, precious; or gold purified, refined.

7 פָּז fine, pure gold; from פָּנַי in Piel, make solid, purify.

No. 3, *Gold, Golden*, not included.

Ezra v. 14.	2	Ps. xlv. 9.	5	Isa. xiv. 4.	2 a
vi. 5.	2	lxviii. 13.	4	Lam. iv. 1, 1.	3, 5
vii. 15, 16, 18.	2	cxix. 127, 127.	3, 7	iv. 2.	7
Job xxii. 24.	1	Prov. iii. 14.	4	Dan. ii. 32, 35, 38, 45.	2
xxviii. 15.	6	viii. 10.	4	iii. 1, 5, 7, 10, 12, 14,	
xxviii. 16, 19.	5	viii. 19, 19.	4, 7	18.	2
xxviii. 17, 17.	3, 7	xvi. 16.	4	v. 2, 3, 4, 7, 16, 23,	
xxxi. 24, 24.	3, 5	xxv. 12, 12.	3, 5	29.	2
xxxvi. 19.	1 a	Cant. v. 11. a	5, 7	x. 5.	5
Ps. xix. 10, 10.	3, 7	v. 15.	7	Zech. ix. 3.	4
xxi. 3.	7	Isa. xiii. 12, 12. β	7, 5		

a lit. gold fine gold.　　　　β "golden wedge."

GOLDSMITH

צָרַף to melt, fuse; to refine gold, &c., by fire, to separate the dross. KAL *part.* Poel, Neh. iii. 8, 32 : Isa. xl. 19; xli. 7, *marg.* 'or, founder;' xlvi. 6. צֹרְפִי *m.* perhaps a proper name : Neh. iii. 31.

GOOD

1 חָלַם to be strong, healthy; "in good liking." KAL *fut.*

2 חֶסֶד *m.* love, kindness; "good deeds;" and spoken of God, grace, mercy; beneficence, liberality. a חָסִיד *adj.* kind.

3 טוֹב This word, in its various forms, is used in a very extensive sense : of that which is good to the senses, agreeable, pleasant, and desirable; beautiful, fair, Exod. ii. 2, *comp.* Acts vii. 20, Heb. xi. 23; of that which is useful, fit, and suitable; of that which is morally good, honest, becoming, and virtuous; of that which is right. It is also applied to things prosperous and abundant; to happiness and joyfulness; to advantage and pleasure. טוֹב to be good, to go well, to please. KAL a *pret.* HIPHIL b *pret.* c *inf.* d *imp.* e *part.* f טוֹב *adj.* fitting, right, or as a thing should be, Gen. i. 10; right and true, Job xxxiv. 4; desirable, goodly, beautiful, Gen.

xlix. 15, Deut. iii. 25; valuable, Gen. xxx. 20; convenient, Exod. xviii. 17; favourable, profitable to one's advantage, Ruth ii. 22, 1 Sam. xix. 4; happy, joyful, cheerful, 1 Sam. xxv. 8, 36, Esth. i. 10, viii. 17; comfortable, Prov. xii. 25; sweet, Prov. xxiv. 13; wholesome, Prov. xxv. 27; kind, liberal, bountiful, beneficent, propitious, 2 Chron. v. 13. It occurs very frequently in this translation, and is often used as a substantive, Gen. i. 4, &c. g טָב Ch. *m. id.* Ezra v. 17. h טוּב *m.* goodness, good condition; what is good or best; goods, riches; joyfulness, prosperity, happiness; beauty, glory.

4 יָטַב as a verb, partakes of the meaning of the previous word. KAL a *fut.* HIPHIL b *pret.* c *inf.* d *imp.* e *fut.* יְטַב Ch. f *fut.*

5 יָעַל to be useful; to profit. HIPHIL *fut.*

6 יָשַׁר to be right, to seem good. KAL *pret.*

7 כִּשְׁרוֹן *m.* success; gain, advantage.

8 מְאֹד exceedingly, greatly, &c.

9 סְגֻלָּה *f.* see *Peculiar*.

10 צָלַח to go on, to prosper. KAL *fut.*

11 קוּם to stand up; to cause to stand. HIPHIL *fut.*

12 שָׁלַם to restore, requite, recompense; to make good. PIEL a *inf.* b *fut.*

13 שָׁפַר to be pleasant, acceptable. שְׁפַר Ch. P'AL *pret.*

No. 3 f, *Good, Goodness*, not included.

Gen. xxii. 12.	4 c e	2 Chron. xxxii. 32. a	2	Ps. cxxviii. 5.	3 h
xli. 37.	4 a	xxxv. 26. a	2	cxliv. 2.	2
xlv. 18, 20, 23.	3 h	Ezra v. 17.	3 g	cxlv. 7.	3 h
Exod. xxi. 34.	12 b	vii. 18.	4 f	Prov. xxii. 22.	4 e
xxii. 11, 13, 15.	12 b	ix. 12.	3 h	xx. 6.	2
xxii. 14.	12 a	Neh. ix. 25, 35, 36.	3 h	Eccles. v. 11.	7
xxxiii. 19.	3 h	xiii. 14. a	2	Isa. i. 19.	3 h
xxxiv. 6.	2	Esth. v. 4.	3 a	xli. 23.	4 e
Lev. v. 4.	4 c	Job x. 3.	3 a	lxiii. 7.	3 h
xxiv. 18.	12 b	xiii. 9.	4 a	Jer. ii. 7.	3 h
Num. x. 2, 9.	3 b	xv. 3.	5	iv. 22.	4 c
x. 29, 29.	3 b f	xxi. 16.	3 h	x. 5.	4 c
xxiii. 19.	11	xxiv. 21.	4 e	xiii. 10.	10
Deut. ii. 4.	8	xxix. 4.	1	xiii. 23.	4 c
iv. 15.	8	Ps. xxv. 7.	3 h	xviii. 4.	6
vi. 11.	3 h	xxvii. 13.	3 h	xviii. 11.	4 d
viii. 16.	4 c	xxxi. 19.	3 h	xxxi. 12, 14.	3 h
xxviii. 63.	4 c	xxxiii. 5.	2	xxxii. 40.	4 c
xxx. 5.	4 b	xxxvi. 3.	2	xxxii. 41.	3 c
Josh. xxiii. 11.	4 b	li. 18.	4 d	Dan. iv. 2.	13
xxiv. 20.	4 b	lii. 1.	2	Hos. iii. 5.	3 h
Judg. xvii. 13.	4 e	lxv. 4.	3 h	vi. 4.	2
1 Sam. xx. 12.	4 a	cvii. 8, 15, 21, 31.	2	Micah i. 7.	2 a
xxiv. 4.	4 a	cxix. 66.	3 h	vii. 2.	2 a
2 Kings xix. 9.	3 h	cxix. 68, 68.	3 f e	Zeph. i. 12.	4 e
1 Chron. xiii. 2.	3 h	cxxv. 4, 4.	3 d f	Zech. ix. 17.	3 h
xxix. 3.					

a kindnesses.

GOODLY

1 אֶדֶר *m.* glory, magnificence. a אַדֶּרֶת *f. id.* b אַדִּיר *adj.* illustrious.

2 אֵל *m.* God.

3 הָדָר *m.* see *Glory.*

4 הוֹד *m.* see *Glory.*

5 חֶמְדָּה *f.* desire. a חֲמוּדוֹת *f. pl.* desires. b מַחְמָד *m.* desire; something precious.

6 חֵסֶד desire, favour, grace.

7 טוֹב to be good. KAL a *pret.* HIPHIL b *pret.* c טוֹב *adj.* good,

8 יָפֶה *adj.* fair.

9 עָלַס to exult : this word, occurring in Job xxxix., is clearly Niphal *pret.*, whatever the rendering of our version assigns to it ; and the sentence may be translated, "The wing of the peacocks exults." See *Peacock.*

10 פְּאֵר *m.* beauty : Exod. xxxix. 28, *lit.* ornaments of bonnets.

11 צְבִי *m.* honour, glory, majesty.

12 מַרְאֶה *m.* countenance ; "goodly," *lit.* of countenance, or sight.

13 שָׁפַר to be good, fair, shining ; pleasant, acceptable. KAL ᵃ *pret.* ᵇ שֶׁפֶר beauty.

14 תֹּאַר *m.* shape, form, or appearance of a person.

Gen. xxvii. 15.	5 a	1 Sam. viii. 16.	7 c	Ps. lxxx. 10.		2
xxxix. 6.	8, 14	ix. 2, 2.	7 c	Isa. xl. 6.		6
xlix. 21.	13 b	xvi. 12.	7 c	Jer. iii. 19.		11
Exod. ii. 2.	7 c	2 Sam. xxiii. 21.	12	xi. 16.		14
xxxix. 28.	10	1 Kings i. 6.	7 c, 14	Ezek. xvii. 8. a		1 a
Lev. xxiii. 40.	3	xx. 3.	7 c	xvii. 23.		1 b
Num. xxiv. 5.	7 a	2 Chron. xxxvi. 10.	5	Hos. x. 1.		7 b
Deut. iii. 25.	7 c	xxxvi. 19.	5 b	Joel iii. 5.		7 c
vi. 10.	7 c	Job xxxix. 13.	9	Zech. x. 3.		4
viii. 12.	7 c	Ps. xvi. 6.	13 a	xi. 13. β		1
Josh. vii. 21.	7 c					

a *lit.* a vine of magnificence.   β *lit.* the magnificence of the price.

GOODMAN

אִישׁ *m.* man, husband : Prov. vii. 19.

GOODWILL

רָצוֹן *m.* see *Favour.* Deut. xxxiii. 16 : Mal. ii. 13.

GOODS

אוֹן *m.* see *Strength.* Job xx. 10.

חַיִל *m.* ability, wealth, riches : Num. xxxi. 9 : Zeph. i. 13.

טוּב *m.* good : Gen. xxiv. 10 : Neh. ix. 25 : Job xx. 21. טוֹב *adj.* Deut. xxviii. 11 : Eccles. v. 11.

מְלָאכָה *f.* work ; stuff, or subject of a man's occupation : Exod. xxii. 8, 11.

נִכְסִין Ch. *m. pl.* riches, treasures : Ezra vi. 8 : vii. 26.

קִנְיָן *m.* getting, possession : Ezek. xxxviii. 12, 13.

רְכוּשׁ *m.* substance, goods, possessions : Gen. xiv. 11, 12, 16, 16, 21 ; xxxi. 18 : xlvi. 6 : Num. xvi. 32 ; xxxv. 3 : 2 Chron. xxi. 14 : Ezra i. 4, 6.

GOPHER

גֹּפֶר *m.* found only in Gen. vi. 14, fir or pine-wood ; according to the Chaldee and the Jewish commentators, cedar ; or the cypress, with a straight, smooth stem, fit for building the ark, of a very compact and imperishable nature.

GORE

נָגַח to push, as an horned animal, to gore. KAL *fut.* Exod. xxi. 28, 31, 31.

GORGEOUSLY

מִכְלוֹל *m.* perfection, perfect beauty, complete in all the ornaments, which make a perfect appearance : Ezek. xxiii. 12.

GOURD

פַּקֻּעֹת *f. pl.* the wild cucumber, whose leaves are very much like those of the vine (whence it might take the name of the wild vine), but of an odious, poisonous bitter taste.— *Taylor.* 2 Kings iv. 39.

קִיקָיוֹן *m.* according to Jerome, Syr., the *palma christi,* a biennial plant, which shoots up to the height of a small tree, but, like all plants of a rapid growth, withers immediately from the slightest injury. According to the Lxx., the gourd.— *Gesenius.* Jonah iv. 6, 6, 7, 9, 10.

GOVERN, GOVERNOR

1 אַלֻּף *m.* a chief person, a captain, a leader.

2 חָבַשׁ to bind ; to exercise power, to rule, *imperio coercere.* KAL *fut.*

3 חָקַק to decree ; to act as a judge, or leader of the people, a law-giver. KAL ᵃ *part.* Poel. POEL ᵇ *part.*

4 מָשַׁל to rule, to be master. KAL ᵃ *part.* Poel. ᵇ מֶמְשָׁלָה *f.* government.

5 נָגִיד *m.* captain, chief governor ; see *Ruler.*

6 נָחָה to lead. HIPHIL *fut.*

7 נָשִׂיא *m.* one lifted up in power, &c., a ruler, captain, prince.

8 סְגָנִין Ch. *m. pl.* see *Ruler.*

9 עָשָׂה to do, in an emphatic sense.

10 פֶּחָה *m.* a satrap, governor, deputy, viceroy (of a province), an officer under the ancient Chaldean and Persian monarchs. Used also of the governor of Judea under the Persians. ᵃ פֶּחָה Ch. *m. id.* Now Pasha.

11 פָּקַד to set over, to appoint—governor. HIPHIL ᵃ *pret.* ᵇ פָּקִיד *m.* officer, overseer.

12 שַׁלִּיט *adj.* one that has arbitrary power.

13 שַׂר *m.* (see *Prince*), captain, commander, chief. ᵃ מִשְׂרָה *f.* government.

Gen. xlii. 6.	12	2 Chron. xxiii. 20.	4 a	Isa. ix. 6, 7.	13 a
xlv. 26.	4 a	xxviii. 7.	5	xxii. 21.	4 b
Judg. v. 9.	3 a	xxxiv. 8.	13	Jer. xx. 1.	11 b
v. 14.	3 b	Ezra v. 3, 6, 14.	10 a	xxx. 21.	4 a
1 Kings x. 15.	10	vi. 6, 7, 13.	10 a	xl. 5, 7.	11 a
xxi. 7.	9	viii. 36.	10	xli. 2, 18.	11 a
xxii. 26.	13	Neh. ii. 7, 9.	10	Dan. ii. 48.	8
2 Kings xxiii. 8.	13	iii. 7.	10	iii. 2, 3, 27.	8
xxv. 23.	11 a	v. 14, 15, 18.	10	vi. 7.	8
1 Chron. xxiv. 5, 5.	13	xii. 26.	10	Hag. i. 1, 14.	10
xxix. 22.	13	Esth. iii. 12.	10	ii. 2, 21.	10
2 Chron. i. 2.	7	Job xxxiv. 17.	2	Zech. ix. 7.	1
ix. 14.	10	Ps. xxii. 28.	4 a	xii. 5, 6.	5
xviii. 25.	13	lxvii. 4.	6	Mal. i. 8.	10

GRACE, GRACIOUS

1 חָנַן denotes a free and spontaneous willingness to bestow good on him that is destitute of it, either in a way of kindness חֶסֶד, or in a way of compassion רַחֲמִים ; hence to show favour, mercy, pity, as the act of previous goodwill. The word excludes all idea of merit or desert in the object of free favour. The will and the act are closely conjoined in this word as it is used of God, and the force and emphasis are transferred to the N. T. in the words χαρίζεσθαί τινα, and χαριτοῦν τινα, Eph. i. 6, Luke i. 28 ; so the meaning is, sometimes, to give graciously, Gen. xxxiii. 5, &c. With *inf.*, very gracious. KAL ᵃ *pret.* ᵇ *inf.* ᶜ *imp.* ᵈ *fut.* NIPHAL ᵉ *pret.* PIEL ᶠ *fut.* ᵍ חֵן *m.* grace, favour, goodwill ; also that which conciliates favour. ʰ חַנּוּן *adj.* used only of God, to express his free and tender affection to those who have no merit or deserving, on whom God bestows freely the

tokens of his love and pity, pardons their sins, and mercifully effects their deliverance from punishment, affliction, &c.; often joined with רחום merciful; Lxx., ἐλεήμων, οἰκτίρμων. ¹ תְּחִנָּה‎ *f.* grace, mercy.

2 טוֹב‎ *adj.* good, graciously.

No. 1 g, *Grace,* and 1 h, *Gracious,* not included.

Gen. xxxiii. 5, 11.	1 a	Ezra ix. 8.	1 i	Isa. xxxiii. 2.	1 c
xliii. 29.	1 d	Job xxxiii. 24.	1 d	Jer. xxii. 23.	1 e
Exod. xxxiii. 19, 19.	1 a d	Ps. lxxvii. 9.	1 b	Hos. xiv. 2.	2
Num. vi. 25.	1 d	cxix. 29.	1 c	Amos v. 15.	1 d
2 Sam. xii. 22.	1 a or f	Isa. xxx. 18.	1 b	Mal. i. 9.	1 d
2 Kings xiii. 23.	1 d	xxx. 19.	1 b d		

GRAIN

צְרוֹר‎ *m.* a bundle; a stone, hence a grain, kernel: Amos ix. 9, "least grain."

GRANT

רִשְׁיוֹן‎ *m.* a grant, permission: Ezra iii. 7.

GRANT

1 בּוֹא‎ to come; to bring. HIPHIL *fut.*

2 נָתַן‎ to give. KAL ᵃ*pret.* ᵇ*inf.* ᶜ*imp.* ᵈ*fut.* ᵉ*part.* Paül. NIPHAL ᶠ*fut.*

3 עָשָׂה‎ to do, make, &c. KAL *pret.*

Lev. xxv. 24.	2 d	Ezra vii. 6.	2 d	Esth. ix. 12, 13.	2 f
Ruth i. 9.	2 d	Neh. i. 11.	2 c	Job vi. 8.	2 d
1 Sam. i. 17.	2 d	ii. 8.	2 d	x. 12.	3
1 Chron. iv. 10.	1	Esth. v. 6.	2 f	Ps. xx. 4.	2 d
xxi. 22, 22.	2 c	v. 8.	2 b	lxxxv. 7.	2 d
2 Chron. i. 12.	2 e	vii. 2.	2 f	cxl. 8.	2 d
xii. 7.	2 a	viii. 11.	2 a	Prov. x. 24.	2 d

GRANT GRACIOUSLY (See GRACE, חָנַן‎)

GRAPE

בְּאֻשִׁים‎ *m. pl.* ill-flavoured, unripe, sour grapes; wild grapes, or a fruit resembling the grape: Isa. v. 2, 4: *comp.* 2 Kings iv. 39–41: Deut. xxxii. 32, 33.

בֹּסֶר‎ *m.* an unripe grape, which is then very sour, but afterwards ripens to great sweetness: Job xv. 33. בֹסֶר‎ *m.* sour grape: Isa. xviii. 5: Jer. xxxi. 29, 30: Ezek. xviii. 2.

סְמָדַר‎ *m.* vine-blossom; "tender grapes:" Cant. ii. 13, 15; vii. 12.

עֹלֵלוֹת‎ *f. pl.* grape gleanings: Obad. 5, *marg.* 'or, gleanings:' Micah vii. 1.

עֵנָב‎ *m.* a grape, *i. e.* the berries: Gen. xl. 10, 11, &c.

פֶּרֶט‎ *m.* what is left behind or omitted: Lev. xix. 10.

GRASS

1 דּוּשׁ‎ to tread down. KAL *part.* Poel, *f.,* with א‎ in the place of ה‎; Jer. l. 11, *triturans:* or it may be regarded as דָּשָׁא‎ *adj.*

2 דֶּשֶׁא‎ *m.* grass just springing up, "tender grass." ᵃ דְּתָא‎ Ch. *m.*

3 חָצִיר‎ *m.* grass, hay, herbage: Isa. xxxv. 7, *marg.* 'or, a court for reeds and rushes.'

4 יֶרֶק‎ *m.* greenness, herbs.

5 עֵשֶׂב‎ *m.* an herb, and, collectively, herbs, particularly for fodder, or for the table. ᵃ עֲשַׂב‎ Ch. *m. id.*

No. 3 not included.

Gen. i. 11, 12.	2	Ps. lxxii. 16.	5	Jer. xiv. 6.	5
Num. xii. 4.	4	xcii. 7.	5	l. 11.	5
Deut. xi. 15.	5	cii. 4, 11.	5	Dan. iv. 15, 15.	2 a, 5 a
xxix. 23.	5	cvi. 20.	5	iv. 23.	2 a
xxxii. 2.	5	Prov. xix. 12.	5	iv. 25, 32, 33.	5 a
2 Sam. xxiii. 4.	2	xxvii. 25.	2	v. 21.	5 a
2 Kings xix. 26.	5, 3	Isa. xv. 16.	2	Amos vii. 2.	5
Job v. 25.		xxxvii. 27, 27.	5, 3	Micah v. 7.	5
vi. 5.	2	Jer. xiv. 5.	2	Zech. x. 1.	5

GRASSHOPPER

1 אַרְבֶּה‎ *m.* see *Locust.*

2 גּוֹב‎ *m.* a locust, so called from its issuing from the earth when hatched—*Gesenius;* or from congregating together—*Fürst.* Amos vii. 1, *marg.* 'or, green worms;' Nah. iii. 17, *lit.* as the grasshopper of grasshoppers.

3 חָנָב‎ *m.* a locust, winged, and edible; so called, it is said, as covering the ground, hiding the sun, &c.—*Gesenius;* or from congregating together—*Fürst.*

Lev. xi. 22.	3	Job xxxix. 20.	1	Jer. xlvi. 23.	1
Num. xiii. 33.	3	Eccles. xii. 5.	3	Amos vii. 1.	2
Judg. vi. 5.	1	Isa. xl. 22.	3	Nah. iii. 17.	2
vii. 12.	1				

GRATE

מִכְבָּר‎ *m.* anything twisted or woven: Exod. xxvii. 4; xxxv. 16; xxxviii. 4, 5, 30; xxxix. 39.

GRAVE

בְּעִי‎ *m.* seems to have been regarded by our translators as compounded of בְּ‎ and עִי‎ a hill, grave: Job xxx. 24, *marg.* 'heap.' Others, בְּעִי לֹא‎ prayer (avails) nothing, he will send, &c.; as from עָצָה‎; see *Enquire.*

קֶבֶר‎ *m.* (see *Bury*), a grave, a sepulchre; a nation in captivity and affliction are raised out of their graves, and made to live, when restored to a prosperous condition in their own country: Ezek. xxxvii. 12, &c.: Gen. l. 5, &c. קְבוּרָה‎ *f. id.* Gen. xxxv. 20, 20: Ezek. xxxii. 23, 24.

שְׁאוֹל‎ *com.* (see *Hell*), the grave as a state distinguished from the present life; as the receptacle of the dead: Gen. xxxvii. 35; xlii. 38; xliv. 29, 31: 1 Sam. ii. 6: 1 Kings ii. 6, 9: Job vii. 9; xiv. 13; xvii. 13; xxi. 13; xxiv. 19: Ps. vi. 5; xxx. 3; xxxi. 17; xlix. 14, 14, 15; lxxxviii. 3; lxxxix. 48; cxli. 7: Prov. i. 12; xxx. 16: Eccles. ix. 10: Cant. viii. 6: Isa. xiv. 11; xxxviii. 10, 18: Ezek. xxxi. 15: Hos. xiii. 14, 14.

שַׁחַת‎ *f.* pit, corruption: Job xxxiii. 22.

GRAVE

1 חָצֵב‎ to hew, cut, or engrave (chiefly) stone. NIPHAL *fut.*

2 חָקַק‎ to engrave, a writing or picture; to portray; to dig out. KAL ᵃ*pret.* ᵇ*part.* Poel.

3 חֶרֶט‎ *m.* a graving tool, a pen, a style.

4 חָרַשׁ‎ to engrave or cut, as smiths or masons, implying force, therefore used of ploughing. KAL *part.* Paül.

5 חָרַת‎ the same as above. KAL *part.* Paül.

6 פָּסַל‎ to cut or hew wood or stone into any form, particularly

that of an image for idolatrous worship. KAL ᵃ*pret.* ᵇ פָּסֶל *m.* a graven image. ᶜ פְּסִילִים *m. pl.*

7   פָּתַח to open; Piel, to plough, furrow, *terram aperire;* to engrave wood, precious stones. PIEL ᵃ*pret.* ᵇ*inf.* ᶜ*fut.* PUAL ᵈ*part.* ᵉ פִּתּוּחַ *m.* engraving.

8   מִקְלַעַת *f.* sculpture, carved work, *sc.* in relief.

No. 6 b and c not included.

Exod. xxviii. 9, 36.	7 a	1 Kings vii. 36.	7 c	Isa. xxii. 16.	2 b
xxxii. 4.	3	2 Chron. ii. 7.β	7 b e	xlix. 16.	2 a
xxxii. 16.	5	ii. 14, 14.	7 b e	Jer. xvii. 1.	4
xxxix. 6, 6.a	7 d e	iii. 7.	7 a	Hab. ii. 18.	6 a
1 Kings vii. 31.	8	Job xix. 24.	1	Zech. iii. 9.	7 e

a *lit.* as the engravings of signets.   β *lit.* to grave gravings.

GRAVEL

חָצָץ *m.* gravel, gravel-stones, being in a divided or broken state: Prov. xx. 17: Lam. iii. 16.

מָעָה *f.* a small stone, a gravel-stone; so the ancient versions have rendered it in Isa. xlviii. 19; modern critics, however, take the word to be the same as מֵעִים bowels, and render the passage, "thy offspring should have been like (the offspring of) its bowels," *i. e.* of the sea, in allusion to the vast increase of fishes.

GRAY-HEADED

שִׂיב to be gray-headed. KAL *pret.* 1 Sam. xii. 2: *part.* Poel, Job xv. 10. שֵׂיבָה *f.* old age, gray hairs: Gen. xlii. 38; xliv. 29, 31: Deut. xxxii. 25: Ps. lxxi. 18: Prov. xx. 29: Hos. vii. 9.

GREASE

חֵלֶב *m.* see *Fat.* Ps. cxix. 70.

GREAT

1   אִישׁ *m.* man, *vir;* great man, mighty man.

2   אֵל God; great, *lit.* of God.

3   אֱלֹהִים *m.* God; great, very great, *lit.* of God.

4   אַצִּיל *m.* see *Armhole.* Ezek. xli. 8, "great cubits," *lit.* cubits reaching to the armholes, whereas the common cubit reached only to the elbow.

5   בַּעַל *m.* owner, master: Prov. xviii. 9, "a great waster," *lit.* lord of wasting; *or,* given to wasting; *i. e.* one that wastes at his own will, and wantonly. *Dominus devastationis est vastator malitiosus, qui habitum in opere isthoc pravo contraxit, qui præsentia magnoque labore parta frivole destruit aut corrumpIt.—Geier in loc.*

6   גְּבוּל *m.* border: Josh. xv. 47, *lit.* according to the כתיב, the sea of the border.

7   גָּבַר to be strong, to prevail. KAL *pret.*

8   גָּדַל to be or become great, either in quantity or quality; to account great, or to be great; to do, make great. KAL ᵃ*pret.* ᵇ*fut.* PIEL ᶜ*pret.* HIPHIL ᵈ*pret.* ᵉ*inf.* ᶠ*fut.* ᵍ*part.* גָּדֵל *adj.* growing, growing up. ʰ גִּדֻּל *m.* greatness, majesty. ᵏ גָּדוֹל *adj.* great: Gen. i. 16, &c. ˡ גְּדוּלָה and גְּדֻלָּה *f.* great things, greatness.

9   גָּלָל Ch. *m.* rolling; "great stones," *lit.* stones of rolling.

10   גָּלָל *adj.* כתיב rough, morose, stern. Theodot. μεγαλόθυμος. Michaelis renders the כתיב the lot of great wrath (is) he suffers punishment. See *Lot.*

11   הָלַךְ to go. KAL ᵃ*inf.* ᵇ*part.* Poel.

12   הָרָה *adj. f.* great with child.

13   חֲרִי *m. pl.* with אַף heat of anger.

14   כָּבֵד heavy, abundant. ᵃ כֹּבֶד *m.* heaviness, multitude, "great number."

15   מְאֹד *m.* much, very much, exceedingly, greatly. ᵃ עַד מְאֹד.

16   עָצַם to be strong, mighty. KAL ᵃ*pret.* ᵇ עָצוּם *adj.* strong, powerful.

17   רַב *adj.* much, many, numerous; great, mighty, large, vast. ᵃ רַב Ch. *adj.* great. ᵇ רַבְרַב Ch. *adj.* chief, leader. ᶜ רֹב *m.* multitude, abundance; greatness, might, "great number."

18   רָבָה to be or become many, great. KAL ᵃ*pret.* ᵇ*fut.* 2 Chron. xxiv. 27. קרי may be rendered, "and (how) was multiplied the burden." HIPHIL ᶜ*inf.*, sometimes used as an adjective, as in Gen. xv. 1. ᵈ*imp.* ᵉ*fut.* רָבָה Ch. *id.* PAEL ᶠ*pret.* ᵍ רִבּוֹ *f.* a myriad: Hos. viii. 12, רִבּוֹ Ch. *f. id.* ʰ מַרְבָּה *m.* plenty. ᵏ מַרְבִּית *f.* multitude, magnitude.

19   שַׂגִּיא *adj.* great. ᵃ שַׂגִּיא Ch. *adj. id.*

No. 8 k not included.

Gen. vi. 5.	17	1 Sam. xvii. 11.	15	Ezra v. 8, 8.	17 a, 9
vii. 11.	17	xxvi. 13.	17	v. 11.	17 a
vii. 18.	15	xxviii. 15.	17	vi. 4.	9
xii. 2, 2.	8 k d	xxx. 6.	15	x. 1.	17
xiii. 6.	17	2 Sam. iii. 22.	17	Neh. iv. 1, 19.	18 c
xv. 1.	18 c	vii. 21, 23.	8 l	ix. 17, 31, 35.	17
xviii. 20.	17	vii. 22.	8 a	xi. 14.	8 k
xix. 3.	15	x. 5.	15	xiii. 22.	17 c
xix. 13.	8 a	xiii. 5, 30.	15	Esth. i. 20, 20.	17, 8 k
xxiv. 35, 35.	15, 8 b	xxii. 36.	18 e	ix. 4, 4, δ 4.	8 k, 11, 8 k
xxvi. 13, 13.	8 b a	xxiv. 10.	15	Job i. 3, 3.	17, 8 k
xxvi. 14.	17	xxiv. 14, 14.	15, 17	ii. 13.	8 a
xxx. 8.	3	1 Kings i. 37, 47.	8 c	v. 25.	17
xxxii. 7.	15	ii. 12.	15	viii. 7.	15
xli. 40.	8 b	iii. 9.	17	xxii. 5.	15
xlviii. 19, 19.	8 b	v. 7, 7.	15, 17	xxiii. 6.	17 c
l. 9.	14	x. 2.	15	xxx. 18.	17 c
Exod. xi. 8.	13	x. 11.	15	xxxi. 25, 34.	17
xv. 7.	17 c	xi. 19.	15	xxxii. 9.	17
xix. 18.	15	xix. 7.	15	xxxiii. 12.	18 b
Num. xi. 10.	17	2 Kings vi. 14.	14	xxxv. 15.	15
xi. 33.	17	xviii. 17.	14	xxxvi. 18.	17 c
xiv. 17.	8 b	1 Chron. iv. 38.	17 c	xxxvi. 26.	19
xiv. 18.	17	ix. 9.a	11, 8 k	xxxviii. 21.	17
xiv. 19.	8 i	xii. 29.	18 k	xxxix. 11.	17
xiv. 39.	15	xxv. 25, 25.	8 k, 15	Ps. xviii. 35.	18 e
xxxii. 1.	16 b	xvii. 19, 19, 21.	8 l	xviii. 50.ε	8 g
Deut. iii. 5.	15	xix. 5.	15	xix. 11, 13.	17
iii. 24.	8 i	xxi. 8.	17	xxi. 1.	15
v. 24.	8 i	xxi. 13, 13.	15, 17	xxii. 25.	15
vii. 1.	17	xxix. 11.	8 l	xxv. 11.	17
ix. 14.	17	xxix. 12.	8 c	xxxi. 19.	17
ix. 26.	8 i	2 Chron. ii. 9.	8 k	xxxiii. 17.	17 c
xi. 2.	8 i	ix. 1.	14	xxxv. 18.	15
xvii. 17.	15	ix. 6.	18 k	xxxvi. 6, 6.	2, 17
xxxii. 21.	8 i	ix. 9.	15	xxxviii. 6.	15 a
Josh. x. 2, 2, 2.	15, 8 k k	xviii. 8, 17.	17	xl. 9, 10.	17
xi. 8.	17	xv. 5.	15	xlvii. 9.	15
xv. 47.	8 k, or 6	xvii. 12.	8 k	xlviii. 1, 1.	8 k, 15
xvii. 14, 15.	17	xx. 2, 12, 15.	15	xlviii. 2.	17
xvii. 17, 17.	17, 8 k	xxi. 3, 15.	17	lxii. 2.	17
xix. 28.	17	xxiv. 24.	15	lxv. 9.	17
Judg. ii. 15.	15	xxiv. 25.	17	lxvi. 3.	17 c
xii. 2.	15	xxiv. 27.	18 b, or 17 c	lxviii. 17.	17
xx. 38.	18 d	xxv. 10, 10.	15, 13	lxix. 16.	17
1 Sam. xi. 6, 15.	15	xxvii. 13.	17	lxxi. 21.	8 l
xii. 17.	17	xxx. 13, 24.β	17 c	lxxvii. 19.	17
xii. 18.	15	xxxii. 12.	15	lxxviii. 15.	17
xii. 24.	8 d	xxxiv. 30.γ	8 k	lxxviii. 59.	15
xiv. 15.	3	Ezra iv. 10.	17 a	lxxix. 11.	8 i
xiv. 30.	18 a			lxxxix. 7.	17
xvi. 21.	15				

Ps. xcii. 5.	8 a	Isa. xvi. 14.	17
xcvi. 4, 4.	8 k, 15	xix. 20.	17
ciii. 11.	7	xxiii. 3.	17
civ. 1.	8 a	xxx. 25.	17
cv. 24.	15	xxxii. 2.	15
cvii. 23.	17	xxxiii. 23.	15
cviii. 38.	15	xxxvi. 2.	14
cix. 30.	15	xl. 26.	18 i
cxii. 1.	15	xlvii. 9.	14
cxvi. 10.	15	li. 10.	17 c
cxvii. 2.	7	liii. 12.	15
cxix. 51.	15	liv. 13.	17
cxix. 156, 162, 165.	17	lvii. 10.	17
cxxvi. 2, 3. ζ	8 d	lxiii. 1.	17
c xxv. 10.	17	lxiii. 7.	17 c
cxxxix. 17.	16 a	Jer. v. 27.	17 c
c.liv. 7.	17	ix. 19.	8 a
cxlv. 3, 3, 3.	8 k, 15, 8 i	xiii. 9.	15
cxlv. 6.	8 l	xiii. 22.	17 c
cxlv. 7.	17	xx. 11.	17
cxlv. 8.η	8 k	xx. 17.	12
cxlvii. 5, 5.	8 k, 17	xli. 12.	17
cl. 2.	8 i	li. 55, 55.	8 k, 17
Prov. v. 23.	17 c	Lam. i. 1.	17 c
xiii. 7.	17	i. 3.	17
xiv. 29.	17	iii. 23.	17 c
xv. 16.	17	iv. 6.	8 b
xvi. 3.	17 c	Ezek. i. 24.	17
xviii. 9.	5	xvi. 7.	8 b
xix. 19.η	8 k, or 10	xvi. 26.	8 h
xxii. 1.	17	xvii. 3.η	8 k
xxvi. 10.	17	xvii. 5, 8, 17.	17
xxviii. 12, 16.	17	xx. 13.	15
Eccles. i. 16, 16.θ	8 d, 18 c	xxiv. 9.	8 f
ii. 4.ε	8 d	xxiv. 12.	17
ii. 7.	18 c	xxvi. 19.	17
ii. 9.	8 a	xxvii. 26.	17
ii. 21.	17	xxviii. 5.	17 c
viii. 6.	17	xxxi. 2, 18.	8 i
x. 6.	17	xxxi. 4.	8 c
Isa. iii. 9.	17	xxxi. 7, 7.	8 i, 17
vi. 12.	17	xii. 11.	17
xiii. 4.	17	xiv. 13.	17
		xxxi. 14.	15

Ezek. xxxviii. 4.	17	Gen. i. 30.	3 a
xli. 8.	4	ix. 3.	3 a
xlvii. 9.	17	xxx. 37.	5
Dan. ii. 6.	19 a	Exod. x. 15.	3 a
ii. 31, 31.	19 a, 17 a	Lev. ii. 14.	1 a
ii. 35, 45.	17 a	xiii. 49.	3 c
ii. 48, 48.	18 f, 17 b	xiv. 37.	3 c
iv. 3.	17 b	Deut. xii. 2.	7
iv. 10.	19 a	Judg. xvi. 7, 8.	5
iv. 22.	18 h	1 Kings xiv. 23.	7
iv. 30.	17 a	2 Kings xvi. 4.	7
v. 1.	19 a	xvii. 10.	7
v. 9.	17 a		
vii. 2.	17 a		
vii. 3, 7, 8, 11, 17, 20.	17 b		
vii. 27.	18 h		
viii. 4.	8 d		
viii. 8, 8.	8 d k		
viii. 9, 10.	8 b		
ix. 18.	17		
xi. 3, 5, 10, 11.	17		
xi. 13, 13.	17, 8 k		
Hos. viii. 12.	17 c, or 18 g		
ix. 7.	17		
Joel ii. 2, 13.	17		
ii. 11, 11.	17, 8 k		
ii. 20, 21.ζ	8 d		
iii. 13.	17		
Amos iii. 9, 15.	17		
vi. 2, 2.	17		
vii. 4.	17		
viii. 5.	8 e		
Obad. 2.	15		
Jonah iv. 2.	17		
Micah v. 4.	8 b		
Nah. iii. 3.	14 a		
Hab. iii. 15.	17		
Zeph. i. 14.	15		
Zech. ix. 3.	17		
xii. 11.	8 b		
xiv. 13.	17		
xiv. 14.	15		

2 Kings xix. 26.	3 a	Isa. xv. 6.	3 b
2 Chron. xxviii. 4.	7	xxxvii. 27.	3
Esth. i. 6.	5	lvii. 5.	7
Job viii. 12.	3 a	Jer. ii. 20.	7
viii. 16.	1 a	iii. 6, 13.	7
xv. 32.	7	xi. 16.	7
xxxix. 8.	3 b	xvii. 2, 8.	7
Ps. xxiii. 2.	7	Ezek. vi. 13.	7
xxxvii. 2.	5	xvii. 24.	5
xxxvii. 35.	7	xx. 47.	7
lii. 8.	7	Hos. xiv. 8.	7
Cant. i. 16.	7		

a lit. went going and great. β lit. to a great number. γ lit. from great to small. δ lit. going and great. ε lit. magnifying salvation. ζ lit. hath magnified to do. η lit. great of. θ lit. had seen much. ι lit. I greatened my works.

GREAVES

מִצְחָה f. from מֵצַח forehead, brow, front. The Hebrews employed the same word to express forehead, shin-bone, greaves, on account of their resemblance to each other in their external surface: 1 Sam. xvii. 6.

GREEDY

תַּאֲוָה f. desire: Prov. xxi. 26, lit. desireth a desire.

בָּצַע to get gain; to covet. KAL part. Poel, Prov. i. 19; xv. 27. PIEL fut. Ezek. xxii. 12, "hast greedily gained."

כָּסַף to pine after, to desire, to long for. KAL fut. Ps. xvii. 12.

נֶפֶשׁ com. soul: Isa. lvi. 11, lit. strong of soul, or appetite.

עַז adj. strong, mighty; hard, cruel: Isa. lvi. 11.

GREEN

1 אָב m. verdure. a אָבִיב m. green ears of corn.

2 דֶּשֶׁא m. tender grass.

3 יֶרֶק m. the verdure of herbs. a יָרָק m. greenness. b יָרוֹק m. that which is green. c יְרַקְרַק adj. greenish, of leprosy seen in garments.

4 כַּרְפַּס m. fine white linen or cotton cloth; whence carpasus, κάρπασος, a species of fine flax, which the classics speak of as brought from India and the East.

5 לַח adj. moist, green, fresh.

6 רָטֹב adj. juicy, in full green.

7 רַעֲנָן adj. green, of trees in full growth, of a leaf: Jer. xvii. 8. The verdant tree is an emblem of prosperity.

GREET

שָׁאַל to ask. KAL pret. שָׁלוֹם m. peace: 1 Sam. xxv. 5, marg. 'ask him in my name as to peace.'

GREYHOUND

זַרְזִיר adj. from זָרַר to bind; girt in the loins, which some take to be the greyhound, others a war-horse, others the horseman: Prov. xxx. 31. The war-horse is ornamented about the loins with girths and buckles, as is frequently seen in the sculptures of Persepolis.—Ges. Thes.

מָתְנַיִם m. dual, loins: Prov. xxx. 31, as above.

GRIEF, GRIEVE, GRIEVOUS, GRIEVANCE

1 אָדַב of similar import with דָּאַב; to pine away, to languish. HIPHIL inf.

2 חוּל to be in pain; to "fall grievously," see Abide. KAL a pret. KAL and HIPHIL b fut. HITHPOLEL c part. HITHPALPEL d fut.

3 חֵטְא m. sin: Lam. i. 8, lit. hath sinned a sin.

4 חָלָה to be weak, feeble; to be pained; applied to weakness of mind from great concern and grief. KAL a pret. NIPHAL b pret. c part. Jer. x. 19, of a deadly wound; Isa. xvii. 11; see Heap. HIPHIL d pret. חֳלִי m. sickness, disease, grief; תַּחֲלוּאִים m. pl. sicknesses.

5 חָמֵץ to be sour; applied to the mind soured by grief and vexation. HITHPAEL fut. Ps. lxxiii. 21, i.e. embittered; or a process of turbulent emotion may be implied, as of a mental leaven of envy, vexation, and indignation; comp. 3, 13, 14.

6 חָרָה to be warm, to fume; applied to grief and vexation. KAL fut.

7 יָגָה to be afflicted with grief and anguish. PIEL a fut. HIPHIL b pret. c יָגוֹן m. sorrow.

8 יָרַע to tremble, to fear, or to fare ill; to be ill in mind; chagrined, fretted, uneasy, displeased. KAL a pret. b fut.

9 כָּאַב to be in a state of great suffering and grief. HIPHIL a part. b כְּאֵב m. grief, with pain of body. c מַכְאוֹב m. pain and sorrow.

10 כָּאָה to be sad or faint-hearted. NIPHAL pret.

11 כָּבֵד to be heavy. KAL a pret. HIPHIL b pret. "grievously afflict." c כָּבֵד adj. heavy, grievous, burdensome. d כֹּבֶד m. heaviness.

12 כַּעַס to be under any turbulent, uneasy commotion of mind, as anger, grief, &c. KAL a pret. b כַּעַס m. vexation, grief.

ᶜ כַּעַשׂ *m. id.* Job vi. 2. This is the same word that Eliphaz uses, v. 2, there translated "wrath."

13   כְּרָא   Ch. to be pained, sorrowful. ITHP'EL *pret.*

14   לָאָה   to be weary and disgusted with the tediousness and trouble of a matter. KAL ᵃ*fut.* NIPHAL ᵇ*pret.*

15   מַעַל   *m.* a trespass; grievously, *lit.* by trespassing a trespass.

16   מָרָה   to rebel. KAL *inf.* grievously, *lit.* rebelling.

17   מָרַר   to be bitter. KAL ᵃ*pret.* PIEL ᵇ*fut.* ᶜ מֹרָה *f.* bitterness: Gen. xxvi. 35, *lit.* bitterness of spirit; or from מָרָה, according to the Lxx. ἦσαν ἐρίζουσαι. Ch. they were rebellious and stubborn against the mandate of Isaac and Rebekah.

18   מָרַץ   to be sharp, vehement, strong. NIPHAL *part.*

19   סוּר   to turn aside, depart. KAL *part.* Poel. See *Revolt.*

20   עָגַם   to be sad, sorrowful, *seq.* עַל. KAL *pret.*

21   עָמָל   wearisome labour; trouble, adversity, κάματος, πόνος; oppression, injustice.

22   עָצַב   to labour; to suffer pain, to be distressed in mind. KAL ᵃ*inf.* ᵇ*part.* Paül. NIPHAL ᶜ*pret. seq.* אֶל. ᵈ*fut.* HIPHIL ᵉ*fut.* HITHPAEL ᶠ*fut.* ᵍ עֶצֶב *m.* sorrow; grievous words, causing pain or sorrow.

23   עָתַק   to be durable, to wax old. עָתָק *adj.* hard: Ps. xxxi. 18, grievous things. It may denote a durable, obstinate, unrelenting malice; or such invectives as are intended to fix a perpetual infamy.

24   פּוּקָה   *f.* obstacle in the way, which causes one to stagger; stumbling-block.

25   קוּט   to loathe, abhor, be grieved with, tired of a thing or person; *seq.* בְּ. KAL ᵃ*fut.* HITHPOLEL ᵇ*fut.*

26   קוּץ   to loathe, abhor, to be weary of; implying mingled chagrin and abhorrence. KAL *fut.*

27   קָצַר   to be shortened; to be impatient, vexed, troubled. KAL *fut.*

28   קָשָׁה   to be hard, cruel. HIPHIL ᵃ*pret.* ᵇ קָשֶׁה *adj.* hard.

29   רַע   *adj.* evil.

Gen. vi. 6.	22 f	2 Chron. x. 4, 4.	28 a b	Isa. x. 1.	21
xii. 10.	11 c	Neh. ii. 10.β	8 b, 29	xv. 4.	8 a
xviii. 20.	11 a	viii. 11.	22 d	xvii. 11.	4 c
xxi. 11, 12.	8 b	xiii. 8.	8 b	xxi. 2.	28 b
xxvi. 35.	17 c	Esth. iv. 4.	2 d	xxi. 15.	11 d
xxxiv. 7. *a*	22 f	Job ii. 13.	9 b	liii. 3, 4.	4 e
xli. 31.	11 c	iv. 2.	14 a	liii. 10.	4 d
xlv. 5.	22 d	vi. 2.	12 c	liv. 6.	22 b
xlix. 23.	17 b	xvi. 6.	9 b	lvii. 10.	4 a
l. 11.	11 c	xxx. 25.	20	Jer. v. 3.	2 a
Exod. i. 12.	26	Ps. vi. 7.	22 b	vi. 7.	4 e
viii. 24.	11 c	x. 5.	2 b	vi. 28.	19
ix. 3, 18, 24.	11 c	xxxi. 9.	12 b	x. 19, 19.	4 c e
x. 14.	11 c	xxxi. 10.	7 c	xiv. 17.	4 c
Deut. xv. 10.	8 b	xxxi. 18.	23	xvi. 4.	4 f
Judg. x. 16.	27	lxix. 26.	9 c	xxiii. 19, 19.	2 c b
Ruth i. 13.	17 a	lxxiii. 21.	5	xxx. 12.	4 c
1 Sam. i. 8.	8 b	lxxviii. 40.	22 e	xlv. 3.	7 c
i. 16.	12 b	xcv. 10.	25 a	Lam. i. 8.	3
ii. 33.	1	cxii. 10.	12 a	i. 20.	16
xv. 11.	6	cxix. 158.	25 b	iii. 32.	7 b
xx. 3.	22 d	cxxxix. 21.	25 b	iii. 33.	7 a
xx. 34.	22 c	Prov. xv. 1.	22 g	Ezek. xiv. 13.	15
xxv. 31.	24	xv. 10.	29	xxiv. 23.	9 a
xxx. 6.	17 a	xvii. 25.	12 b	Dan. vii. 15.	13
2 Sam. xix. 2.	22 c	xxvi. 23.	14 b	xi. 30.	10
1 Kings ii. 8.	18	Eccles. i. 18.	12 b	Amos vi. 6.	4 b
xii. 4, 4.	28 a b	ii. 17.	29	Jonah iv. 6.	6
1 Chron. iv. 10.	22 a	ii. 23.	12 b	Nah. iii. 19.	4 c
2 Chron. vi. 29.	9 c	Isa. ix. 1.	11 b	Hab. i. 3.	21

a Gr. κατενύγησαν, comp. Acts ii. 37.   β *lit.* it grieved him with great grief.

GRIND

טָחַן   to grind (see *Mill*); to oppress greatly, Isa. iii. 15; the employment of grinding at a mill is expressive of the most abject slavery, Job xxxi. 10, *comp.* Exod. xi. 5, Isa. xlvii. 2. KAL *pret.* Numb. xi. 8. *inf.* Deut. ix. 21. *imp.* Isa. xlvii. 2. *fut.* Exod. xxxii. 20: Job xxxi. 10: Isa. iii. 15. *part.* Poel, Judg. xvi. 21: Eccles. xii. 3. טַחֲנָה *f.* mill, hand-mill: Eccles. xii. 4. רֵחַיִם *m. id.* Lam. v. 13.

GRISLED

בָּרֹד   *adj.* spotted, speckled, party-coloured; it differs from "speckled," by indicating spots of a larger size. Gen. xxxi. 10, 12: Zech. vi. 3, 6.

GROAN

אָנַח   to sigh. NIPHAL *part.* Joel i. 18. אֲנָחָה *f.* a sigh: Job xxiii. 2: Ps. vi. 6; xxxviii. 9; cii. 5.

אָנַק   to cry out from pain. KAL *fut.* Jer. li. 52. אֲנָקָה *f.* loud groaning: Ps. cii. 20.

נָאַק   to groan as a dying man, or as under the heaviest affliction. KAL *pret.* Ezek. xxx. 24. *fut.* Job xxiv. 12. נְאָקָה *f.* the crying out, the groan of the oppressed: Exod. ii. 24; vi. 5: Judg. ii. 18: Ezek. xxx. 24.

GROPE

גָּשַׁשׁ   to grope after, with an accusative of the thing. PIEL *fut.* Isa. lix. 10, 10.

מָשַׁשׁ   to touch, feel; to grope in darkness; to be in a dark, confused, bewildered condition. PIEL *fut.* Deut. xxviii. 29: Job v. 14; xii. 25. *part.* Deut. xxviii. 29.

GROSS   (See DARKNESS)

GROUND

אֲדָמָה   *f.* the earth, from its redness: Gen. ii. 5, 6, 7, 9, 19; iii. 17, 19, 23; iv. 2, 3, 10, 12; v. 29; vii. 23; viii. 8, 13, 21; xix. 25: Exod. iii. 5; viii. 21: Lev. xx. 25: Num. xvi. 31: Deut. iv. 18; xxviii. 4, 11: 1 Sam. xx. 31: 2 Sam. xvii. 12: 1 Kings vii. 46: 1 Chron. xxvii. 26: 2 Chron. iv. 17: Neh. x. 35, 37: Job v. 6: Ps. cv. 35: Isa. xxviii. 24; xxx. 23, 24: Jer. vii. 20; xiv. 4; xxv. 33: Hos. ii. 18: Hag. i. 11: Mal. iii. 11, *lit.* the ground.

אֶרֶץ   the earth, as opposed to heaven; the ground, in distinction from something higher; with ה local; *lit.* towards the earth: Gen. xviii. 2, &c.

חֶלְקָה   *f.* a portion, a field: 2 Sam. xxiii. 12.

חָרִישׁ   *m.* ground for tillage: 1 Sam. viii. 12.

נִיר   *m.* fallow ground: Jer. iv. 3: Hos. x. 12.

עָפָר   *m.* dust: Job xiv. 8.

שָׂדֶה   *m.* a field: Josh. xxiv. 32: 1 Sam. xiv. 25: 2 Sam. xxiii. 11: 1 Chron. xi. 13.

GROUNDED

מוּסָדָה   *f.* foundation; an institution or appointment: Isa. xxx. 32, *i. e.* the rod of correction appointed of God.

GROVE

אֵשֶׁל m. (see *Tree*), any large tree, and *collect.* trees, wood, grove: Gen. xxi. 33, *marg.* 'tree.'

אֲשֵׁרָה and אֲשִׁירָה f. This word, usually translated grove, is to be understood of the idol worshipped in groves. Gesenius endeavours to shew that it means the goddess Astarte, or Asherah, usually united with Baal, and corresponding to the Venus of Rome. The idol itself he supposes to have been a pillar of wood, like that of Hermes, and therefore so often described as burnt. The idea of an idol or image is confirmed by all the ancient versions, except the Lxx.—Exod. xxxiv. 13, &c.

GROW

1 אֲפִילָה *adj. pl.* from אֹפֶל, that which is yet concealed and in the dark, therefore applied to corn not grown up: Exod. ix. 32, *marg.* 'hidden, or, dark.'

2 גָּאָה to rise up; applied to plants, it denotes their growth. KAL *fut.*

3 גָּדַל to be or become great; to grow, to grow up. KAL a *pret.* b *fut.* PIEL c *pret.* d *inf.* PUAL e *part.* f גָּדֵל *verb. adj.* growing, growing up.

4 דָּגָה to increase, as fishes. KAL *fut.*

5 הָלַךְ to go. KAL *part.* Poel.

6 חָלַף to pass, to change; to renew, to spring or sprout afresh. KAL a *pret.* b *fut.*

7 יָלַךְ to go, go on. KAL *fut.*

8 יָצָא to go out. KAL *fut.*

9 יָצַק to pour out; to cast metal; to pour self out, to flow. KAL *inf.* See *Firm.*

10 סָפִיחַ m. grain which springs up of itself the second year after it has been sown.

11 עָלָה to ascend, to spring up, grow. KAL a *pret.* b *fut.*

12 פּוּשׁ to increase, spread out, enlarge; to grow fat; the Lxx., however, translate it by σκιρτᾶν, to gambol. KAL a *pret.* b *fut.*

13 פָּרָה to be fruitful. KAL *fut.*

14 פָּרַח to break out, to sprout, blossom. KAL a *pret.* b *fut.*

15 פָּרַץ to break forth, to increase. KAL *fut.* See *Spread.*

16 צָמַח to sprout or spring up, mostly from under the ground; of the hair in its first growth. KAL a *pret.* b *fut.* c *part.* Poel. PIEL d *pret.* e *inf.* f *fut.* HIPHIL g *fut.* h *part.* i צֶמַח m. a sprout.

17 קָמָה f. stalks, *coll.* put for standing corn.

18 רָבָה to multiply. KAL a *fut.* רְבָה Ch. P'AL b *pret.*

19 שְׂנָא Ch. to increase. P'AL *fut.*

20 שָׂנָה to increase. KAL *fut.*

21 שָׂגָן to increase. PILPEL *fut.* Isa. xvii. 11, according to Kimchi; but Gesenius and Fürst derive it from שׂוּג to hedge about.

22 שָׁלַח to send forth. PIEL *fut.* "suffer to grow long."

23 שָׁלַף to draw out; to pluck up. KAL *pret.*

See *Latter, End,* &c.

Gen. ii. 5.	16 b	1 Sam. ii. 21.	3 b	Ps. cxxix. 6.	23
ii. 9.	16 g	ii. 26. α	5, 3 f	cxliv. 12.	3 e
xix. 25.	16 i	iii. 19.	3 b	cxlvii. 8.	16 h
xxi. 8, 20.	3 b	2 Sam. x. 5.	16 f	Prov. xxiv. 31.	11 a
xxv. 27.	3 b	xii. 3.	3 b	Isa. xi. 1.	13
xxvi. 13.	3 f	xxiii. 5.	16 g	xvii. 11.	21
xxxviii. 11.	3 b	1 Kings xii. 8, 10.	3 b	xxxvii. 27.	17
xxxviii. 14.	3 a	2 Kings iv. 18.	3 b	xxxvii. 30.	10
xlvii. 27.	13	xix. 26.	17	liii. 2.	11 b
xlviii. 16.	4	xix. 29.	10	Jer. xii. 2.	7
Exod. i. 12.	15	1 Chron. xix. 5.	16 f	xxxiii. 15.	16 g
ii. 10, 11.	3 b	Ezra iv. 22.	19	l. 11. β	12 b
ix. 32.	1	iv. 6.	3 a	Ezek. xvi. 7.	16 d
x. 5.	16 c	Job viii. 11, 11.	2, 20	xvii. 6.	16 b
Lev. xiii. 27.	16 a	xiv. 19.	16 b	xvii. 10.	16 i
xiii. 39.	14 a	xiv. 19.	11	xix. 10.	22
xxv. 5, 11.	10	xxxi. 40.	8	xlvii. 12.	11 b
Num. vi. 5.	3 d	xxxviii. 38.	9	Dan. iv. 11, 20, 22, 22, 33.	18 b
Deut. xxix. 23.	11 b	xxxix. 4.	18 a	Hos. xiv. 5, 7. γ	14 b
Judg. xi. 2.	3 b	Ps. xc. 5.	6 b	Jonah iv. 10.	3 c
xiii. 24.	3 b	xc. 6.	6 a	Zech. vi. 12. δ	16 b
xvi. 22.	16 e	xcii. 12.	20	Mal. iv. 2.	12 a
Ruth i. 13.	3 b	civ. 14.	16 h		

a *lit.* going and great.   β *marg.* 'big or corpulent.'   γ *marg.* 'or, blossom.'
δ *marg.* 'or, branch up from under him.'

GRUDGE

לוּן to murmur. KAL *fut.* Ps. lix. 15, *marg.* ' or, if they be not satisfied then they will stay all night;' as if from לין.

נָטַר to keep, retain, namely אַף, anger; to bear grudge. KAL *fut.* Lev. xix. 18.

GUARD

טַבָּח m. slaughterer: executioner, one who inflicts capital punishment. This task in the East belonged to the body-guards of the king; the captain of the body-guard was also the king's chief executioner, like the captain pacha of the Ottoman Porte. Gen. xxxvii. 36. טַבָּח Ch. m. Dan. ii. 14.

רוּץ to run; in KAL *part. pl.* רָצִים and רָצִין runners, state couriers, among the Persians, who published the royal edicts in the provinces: Esth. iii. 13, 15; viii. 14. Among the Hebrews, they made a part of the royal body-guard under Saul, 1 Sam. xxii. 17, and the later kings, 2 Kings x. 25; xi. 6, &c., and correspond probably to the פְּלֵתִי under David. *Comp.* further, 1 Kings i. 5; xiv. 27: 2 Sam. xv. 1. KAL *part.* 1 Kings xiv. 27, 28, 28: 2 Kings x. 25, 25; xi. 4, 6, 11, 13, 19, 19: 2 Chron. xii. 10, 11, 11.

מִשְׁמַעַת f. obedience; put either for a privy-council, who have access to the king, or for a body-guard: 2 Sam. xxiii. 23: 1 Chron. xi. 25.

מִשְׁמָר m. a place where one keeps watch; the persons watching: Neh. iv. 22, 23: Ezek. xxxviii. 7.

GUEST

קָרָא to call. KAL *part.* Paül, 1 Kings i. 41, 49: Prov. ix. 18: Zeph. i. 7.

GUIDE

1 אַלּוּף m. head of a family or tribe, who unites and guides them; implying precedency and rule, together with fellowship and mutual confidence.

2 אָשַׁר to go; Piel, to lead or guide straight; to guide generally. PIEL *imp.*

3   דָּרַךְ   to tread, to go.   HIPHIL *fut.*

4   יָעַץ   to counsel.   KAL *fut.* Ps. xxxii. 8, *marg.* 'I will counsel (thee), mine eye (shall be) upon thee.'

5   כּוּל   to comprehend; Pilpel, to support or sustain; to provide with the means of living; to defend, sustain.   PILPEL *fut.*

6   נָהַג   to guide, lead, a flock.   PIEL *fut.*

7   נָהַל   to lead, guide gently, softly, and with care, as a shepherd guides his flock.   PIEL [a] *pret.* [b] *fut.* [c] *part.*

8   נָחָה   to lead, guide; most frequently of God, who leads men.   KAL [a] *pret.* HIPHIL [b] *fut.*

9   קָצִין   *m.* captain, ruler, prince.

Exod. xv. 13.	7 a	Ps. lv. 13.	1	Prov. xi. 3.	8 b	
2 Chron. xxxii. 22.	7 b	lxxiii. 24.	8 b	xxiii. 19.	2	
Job xxxi. 18.	8 b	lxxviii. 52.	6	Isa. xlix. 10.	7 b	
xxxviii. 32.	8 b	lxxviii. 72.	8 b	li. 18.	7 c	
Ps xxv. 9.	3	cxii. 5.	5	lviii. 11.	8 a	
xxxi. 3.	7 b	Prov. ii. 17.	1	Jer. iii. 4.	1	
xxxii. 8.	4	vi. 7.	9	Mic. vii. 5.	1	
xlviii. 14.	6					

GUILE

עָרְמָה   *f.* craft, deceit; wisdom, prudence: Exod. xxi. 14.

רָמָה   to throw; to cause to fall unexpectedly; to deceive, beguile by promising one thing and doing another. מִרְמָה *f.* fraud, hypocrisy: Ps. xxxiv. 13; lv. 11. רְמִיָּה *f. id.* Ps. xxxii. 2.

GUILT

אָשַׁם   to be guilty; see *Trespass.* KAL *pret.* Lev. iv. 13, 22, 27; v. 2, 3, 4, 17; vi. 4: Num. v. 6: Prov. xxx. 10: Ezek. xxii. 4. *fut.* Lev. v. 5; Judg. xxi. 22: Zech. xi. 5. אָשָׁם *m.* guilt: Gen. xxvi. 10. אָשֵׁם *adj.* one who has contracted guilt: Gen. xlii. 21: Ezra x. 19.

רָשָׁע   *adj.* wicked: Num. xxxv. 31, *marg.* 'faulty to die.'

GUILTLESS

נָקָה   to be clear, free, guiltless; to acquit. NIPHAL *pret.* Num. v. 31: 1 Sam. xxvi. 9. PIEL *fut.* Exod. xx. 7: Deut. v. 11: 1 Kings ii. 9. נָקִי *adj.* free from blame: Num. xxxii. 22: Josh. ii. 19: 2 Sam. iii. 28; xiv. 9.

GUSH

זוּב   to flow.   KAL *fut.* Ps. lxxviii. 20; cv. 41: Isa. xlviii. 21.

נָזַל   to melt, to drop.   KAL *fut.* Jer. ix. 18.

שָׁפַךְ   to pour out.   KAL *inf.* 1 Kings xviii. 28, *lit.* till there poured out blood upon them.

GUTTER

צִנּוֹר   *m.* gutter, waterspout: 2 Sam. v. 8. According to others, a subterraneous passage between the castle of Zion and the town.

רַהַט   *m.* watering-troughs for cattle: Gen. xxx. 38, 41.

HABERGEON

שִׁרְיָה   *f.* a coat of mail, probably so called from its glittering, to defend the neck and breast: Job xli. 26. שִׁרְיוֹן *m. id.* 2 Chron. xxvi. 14: Neh. iv. 16.

תַּחְרָא   *f.* a linen coat of mail or habergeon, θώραξ, *lorica,* a closely-woven linen garment, furnished with a coat of mail in the upper part about the neck: Exod. xxviii. 32; xxxix. 23.

HABITABLE

תֵּבֵל   *f.* the earth, as fertile and inhabited, "habitable part:" Prov. viii. 31.

HABITATION

1   גֵּרוּת   *f.* place of sojourning, habitation, encampment.

2   זְבֻל   *m.* a home or place of residence. *Poetic.*

3   טִירָה   *f.* a place surrounded by a wall, *marg.* 'palace.'

4   יָשַׁב   to sit, to dwell, to settle, remain. KAL *inf.* מוֹשָׁב *m.* a sitting down, habitation.

5   מָכוֹן   *m.* a prepared, established place, *marg.* 'establishment.'

6   מְכוּרָה   *m.* The Heb. interpreters have taken this word and the following to be מְגוּרָה habitation. Later critics most commonly understand the word to mean nativity, birth, from כּוּר to dig; *pr.* a digging out of a mine out of which metals are taken: Ezek. xxix. 14, *marg.* 'or, birth.'

7   מְכֵרָה   *f.* To this has been given the same interpretation on the same grounds. Later critics, however, derive this word also from כּוּר to pierce, and suppose it to mean a sword. But it may be deduced from מָכַר to sell, bargain, make contracts, and so may have reference both to the case of the Shechemites and that of Joseph, Gen. xxxvii. 27; see *Bush.* Others have rendered the word counsels, plots, wicked devices: Gen. xlix. 5, probably instruments of violence are their bargainings or covenants; or perhaps knives or swords (of circumcision).

8   נָאָה   *f.* seat, dwelling, habitation: Ps. lxxiv. 20: Jer. ix. 10; xxv. 37: Lam. ii. 2: Amos i. 2.

9   נָוָה   to be settled in an habitation. HIPHIL *fut.* Exod. xv. 2, "I will prepare him an habitation;" but Lxx. δοξάσω αὐτόν, which agrees with the parallel, "I will exalt him." Vulg. *glorificabo eum.* So Hier. Jon. and Syr., supposing נָוָה to be *i. q.* נָאָה to be comely, beautiful. Kimchi and Chald. understand it as in our version. Taylor translates it, "I will make him a resting-place to my soul." The noun implies a place of abode where one settles and rests satisfied, Prov. xxiv. 15: Jer. l. 7, "the Lord the habitation of justice," in whom justice constantly resides. The temple was God's habitation or resting-place, 2 Sam. xv. 25. The idea of a fold is also included in the use of the term habitation as applied to Israel, Jer. xxxiii. 12; l. 19. [a] נָוֶה *m.* a habitation; a pasture, where flocks lie down and rest; hence also, pleasant places. [b] נָוָה *f.* a seat, a habitation.

10   מָעוֹן   *m.* a dwelling, a place of residence; sometimes also considered as a place of safety. [a] מְעוֹנָה *f.* a habitation.

11 שָׁכַן to settle down ; to lie down, to abide, to dwell. KAL ᵃ*fut.* שָׁכַן Ch. P'AL ᵇ*fut.* ᶜ שְׁכַן *m.* a dwelling. ᵈ מִשְׁכָּן *m.* habitation, dwelling ; tent, tabernacle. ᵉ Ch. *m. id.*

Gen. xxxvi. 43.	4 a	Ps. xxvi. 8.	10	Isa. liv. 2.	11 d
xlix. 5.	7	xxxiii. 14.	4	lxiii. 15.	2
Exod. xii. 20.	4 a	lxviii. 5.	10	Jer. ix. 6.	4
xv. 2.	9	lxix. 25.	3	ix. 10.	8
xv. 13.	9 a	lxxi. 3.	10	x. 25.	9 a
xxxv. 3.	4 a	lxxiv. 20.	5	xiii. 13.	10 a
Lev. xiii. 46.	4 a	lxxviii. 28.	11 d	xxv. 30, 30.	10, 9 a
xxiii. 17.	4 a	lxxxix. 10.	5	xxv. 37.	8
Num. xv. 2.	4 a	xci. 9.	10	xxxi. 23.	9 a
Deut. xii. 5.	11 c	xcvii. 2.	5	xxxiii. 12.	9 a
xxvi. 15.	10	civ. 12.	11 a	xli. 17.	1
1 Sam. ii. 29, 32.	10	cvii. 7, 36.	4 a	xlix. 19, 20.	9 a
2 Sam. xv. 25.	9 a	cxxii. 5.	11 d	l. 7, 19, 44, 45.	9 a
1 Chron. iv. 33.	4 a	cxxxii. 13.	4 a	Lam. ii. 2.	8
iv. 41.	10	Prov. iii. 33.	9 a	Ezek. vi. 14.	4 a
vii. 28.	4 a	Isa. xxii. 16.	11 d	xxix. 14.	6
2 Chron. vi. 2.	2	xxvii. 10.	9 a	Dan. iv. 21.	11 b
xxix. 6.	11 d	xxxii. 18.	9 a	Amos i. 2.	8
Ezra vii. 15.	11 e	xxxiii. 20.	9 a	Obad. 3.	4
Job v. 3, 24.	9 a	xxxiv. 13.	9 a	Hab. iii. 11.	2
viii. 6.	9 b	xxxv. 7.	9 a	Zech. ii. 13.	10
xviii. 15.	9 a				

HAFT

נָצָב *m.* (*pr. part.* NIPH. נָצַב) *lit.* something fixed ; the handle of a dagger : Judg. iii. 22.

HAIL

1 בָּרַד to scatter ; to hail. KAL ᵃ*pret.* Isa. xxxii. 19, paronomasia. ᵇ בָּרָד *m.* hail, hail stones : Exod. ix. 18, &c.

2 אֶלְגָּבִישׁ *m.* hail, ice : Ezek. xiii. 11, *pr.* stones of ice ; 13 ; xxxviii. 22.

Exod. ix. 18, 19, 22, 23, 23, 24, 24, 25, 25, 26, 28, 29, 33, 34.		Job xxxviii. 22.	1 b	Isa. xxx. 30.	1 b
		Ps. xviii. 12, 13.	1 b	xxxii. 19.	1 a
		lxxviii. 47, 48.	1 b	Ezek. xiii. 11, 13.	2
	1 b	cv. 32.	1 b	xxxviii. 22.	2
x. 5, 12, 15.	1 b	cxlviii. 8.	1 b	Haggai ii. 17.	1 b
Josh. x. 11.	1 b	Isa. xxviii. 2, 17.	1 b		

HAIR

1 בַּעַל *m.* owner : 2 Kings i. 8, *lit.* a man an owner of hair, or hairy garment.

2 דַּלָּה *f.* that which hangs down ; flowing hair.

3 מָרַט to make smooth ; to pluck off the hair. KAL ᵃ*fut.* ᵇ*part.* Poel. NIPHAL, "to have the hair fallen off :" ᶜ*fut.*

4 נֵזֶר *m.* separation (see *Crown*) ; hair not shorn, of the Nazarite, the token of his separation.

5 מִקְשֶׁה *m.* turned work ; twisted or plaited hair ; "well-set hair," *lit.* the work of curling.

6 שֵׂעָר *m.* hair, for the most part collectively : Gen. xxv. 25, &c. ᵃ שְׂעַר Ch. *m. id.* ᵇ שַׂעֲרָה *f. id.* ᶜ שָׂעִיר *m.* hairy. ᵈ שַׂעַר *m.* hair.

No. 6, Hair, Hairy, not included.

Gen. xxvii. 11, 23.	6 c	Ezra ix. 3.	3 a, 6	Isa. vii. 20.	6 d
Lev. xiii. 40, 41.	3 c	Neh. xiii. 25.	3 a	l. 6.	3 b
Judg. xx. 16.	6 b	Job iv. 15.	6 b	Jer. vii. 29.	4
1 Sam. xiv. 45.	6 b	Ps. xl. 12.	6 b	Dan. iii. 27.	6 a
2 Sam. xiv. 11.	6 b	lxix. 4.	6 b	iv. 33.	6 a
1 Kings i. 52.	6 b	Cant. vii. 5.	2	vii. 9.	6 a
2 Kings i. 8.	1, 6	Isa. iii. 24.	5		

HALF

1 חָצָה to divide. KAL ᵃ*fut.* ᵇ מֶחֱצָה *f.* half. ᶜ מַחֲצִית *f. id.* ᵈ חֲצִי *m.* half : Exod. xxvi. 6, &c.

2 תָּוֶךְ *m.* the middle, the midst.

No. 1 d not included.

Exod. xxx. 13, 13, 15, 23.		Num. xxxi. 29, 30, 42, 47.	1 c	1 Kings xvi. 9.	1 c
	1 c	xxxi. 36, 43.	1 c	1 Chron. vi. 61, 61.	1 c d
xxxviii. 26.	1 c	Deut. iii. 16.	1 b	vi. 70.	1 c
Lev. vi. 20, 20.	1 c	Josh. xxi. 36.	2	Ps. lv. 23. ᵃ	1 a

ᵃ *marg.* 'shall not half their days.'

HALLOW

קָדַשׁ to be holy, sanctified ; see *Sanctify.* KAL ᵃ*pret.* ᵇ*fut.* NIPHAL ᶜ*pret.* PIEL ᵈ*pret.* ᵉ*inf.* ᶠ*imp.* ᵍ*fut.* ʰ*part.* HIPHIL ⁱ*pret.* ᵏ*fut.* ˡ*part.* ᵐ קֹדֶשׁ *m.* holy, holiness. ⁿ מִקְדָּשׁ *m.* a holy place or sanctuary ; something consecrated.

Exod. xx. 11.	g	Lev. xxii. 32, 32.	c h	1 Sam. xxi. 4, 6.	m
xxviii. 38.	k	xxv. 10.	d	1 Kings viii. 64.	d
xxix. 1.	e	Num. iii. 13.	i	ix. 3, 7.	i
xxix. 21.	a	v. 10.	m	2 Kings xii. 18, 18.	m
xl. 9.	d	vi. 11.	d	2 Chron. vii. 7.	g
Lev. xii. 4.	m	xvi. 37.	a	xxxvi. 14.	g
xvi. 19.	d	xvi. 38.	b	Jer. xvii. 22.	d
xix. 8.	m	xviii. 8.	m	xv i. 24, 27.	d
xxii. 2.	l	xviii. 29.	n	Ezek. xx. 20.	f
xxii. 3.	k	Deut. xxvi. 13.	m	xliv. 24.	g

HALT

פָּסַח to pass over ; to halt, or be lame, to waver between two opinions. KAL *part.* Poel. 1 Kings xviii. 21. Where it is spoken in derision of the fruitless dance of the priests of Baal ; the same word is used in verse 26. See *Leap.*

צָלַע to halt, limp, *lit.* to incline to one side. KAL *part.* Poel, Gen. xxxii. 31 : Micah iv. 6, 7 : Zeph. iii. 19. צֶלַע *m.* limping, fall : Ps. xxxviii. 17, *marg.* 'for halting :' Jer. xx. 10.

HAMMER

הָלַם to smite with a hammer. KAL *pret.* Judg. v. 26. הַלְמוּת *f.* hammer : Judg. v. 26.

כֵּילַפּוֹת *f. pl.* hammers or hatchets for striking : Ps. lxxiv. 6.

מַקָּבָה *f.* a hammer to pierce or strike with ; the pointed hammer of the stonecutter and smith : 1 Kings vi. 7 : Isa. xliv. 12 : Jer. x. 4. מַקֶּבֶת *f. id.* Judg. iv. 21.

פַּטִּישׁ *m.* a hammer ; *metaph.* a desolator : Isa. xli. 7 : Jer. xxiii. 29 ; l. 23.

HAMON-GOG

הָמוֹן *m.* multitude : Ezek. xxxix. 11, 15.

HAND

1 אֶכֶף *m. i. q.* כַּף, in a similar passage, Job xiii. 21, hand.

2 הָרַג to kill. KAL *inf.* "out of hand," *lit.* in killing.

3 חָפְנַיִם *dual,* the two fists ; or two hands as full of anything.

4 טֶפַח *m. pr.* the spread hand, palm, put as the measure of four fingers, a "hand-breadth." ᵃ טֹפַח *m. id.*

5 יָד *com.* the hand, *pr.* as extended ; *metaph.* power, strength, might ; *meton.* a stroke, blow ; a side, a place, a part, a monument, trophy : hand is sometimes used to denote any kind of instrumentality or ministry, as by the hand of a prophet : with a preposition following or

preceding, it takes various meanings, as also after verbs. Prov. xi. 21, *lit.* hand to hand, *i.e.* joining of hands, in making a compact or engagement. When two persons make a contract, they bring the palms of their hands into contact, and then raise them to their lips and forehead.—*Paxton.* The hand also was raised to heaven in taking an oath: Gen. xiv. 22.—Gen. iii. 22, &c. ^a יָד Ch. *com.*

6   כַּף   the palm, the hollow or curvature of the hand, the hand closed; the grasp of the hand; "to take a handful," *lit.* to fill the hand; "hands together," *lit.* hand to hand.

7   מְלֹא   *m.* fulness; handful, *lit.* the fulness of the hand.

8   עָמִיר   *m.* a handful of grain, as cut down, before it is gathered into sheaves.

9   פִּסָּה   *f.* a handful, sheaf; Gesenius, expansion, abundance.

10   צְבָתִים   *m. pl.* bundles, sheaves.

11   קָמַץ   to press together, to compress: to take a handful. KAL ^a *pret.* ^b קֹמֶץ *m.* a handful; with or without מְלֹא: Gen. xli. 47.

12   קָרַב   to come near, to be at hand. KAL ^a *pret.* ^b *fut.* PIEL ^c *pret.* ^d קָרוֹב *adj.* near.

13   שֹׁעַל   *m.* hollow hand, palm; handful.

No. 5 not included.

Gen. xx. 5.	6	2 Kings xi. 12.	6	Prov. xxii. 26.	6
xxvii. 41.	12 b	vii. 7, 7.	6	xxxi. 13, 16.	6
xxxi. 42.	6	xviii. 21.	6	xxxi. 19, 19.	5, 6
xl. 11, 11.	5, 6	xx. 6.	6	xxxi. 20, 20.	6
xl. 21.	6	1 Chron. xii. 17.	6	Eccles. iv. 6.	6, 7
xli. 47.	11 b	2 Chron. iv. 5.	4	iv. 6.	3
Exod. iv. 4, 4, 4.	5, 5, 6	vi. 12, 13, 29.	6	Isa. i. 15, 15.	6, 5
ix. 8.	7, 3	xxx. 6.	6	xiii. 6.	6
ix. 29, 33.	6	xxxii. 11.	6	xxviii. 4.	6
xxv. 25.	4 a	Ezra v. 8, 12.	5 a	xxxvi. 6.	6
xxix. 24, 24.	6	vi. 12.	5 a	xxxvii. 6.	6
xxxiii. 22, 23.	6	vii. 14, 25.	5 a	xxxviii. 6.	6
xxxvii. 12.	4 a	viii. 31, 31.	5, 6	xl. 12.	13
Lev. ii. 2.	11 b, 7	ix. 5.	6	xlix. 16.	6
v. 12.	11 b, 7	Job ix. 30.	6	lv. 12.	6
vi. 15.	11 b	x. 3.	6	lix. 3, 6.	6
viii. 27, 27, 28.	6	xi. 13.	6	lxii. 3, 3.	5, 6
ix. 17.	6	xiii. 14, 21.	6	Jer. iv. 31.	6
xiv. 16, 18, 27, 29.	6	xvi. 17.	6	ix. 22.	6
xiv. 17, 17.	6, 5	xxii. 30.	6	xii. 7.	6
xiv. 28, 28.	6, 5	xxvii. 23.	6	xv. 21, 21.	5, 6
xvi. 12.	3	xxix. 9.	6	xxiii. 23.	12 d
Num. v. 18, 18.	6, 5	xxxi. 7.	6	Lam. ii. 15, 19.	6
v. 26.	11 a	xxxiii. 7.	1	iii. 41.	6
vi. 19.	6	xli. 8.	6	Ezek. vi. 11.	6
xi. 15.	2	Ps. vii. 3.	6	x. 2.	6
xxiv. 10.	6	ix. 16.	6	x. 7, 7.	5, 2
Deut. xv. 9.	12 a	xviii. title, title.	6, 5	xii. 23.	12 a
xxv. 12.	6	xxiv. 6.	6	xiii. 19.	13
xxxii. 35.	12 d	xxvi. 6.	6	xxi. 14, 17, 24.	6
Judg. vi. 13, 14.	6	xxxix. 6.	5	xxii. 13.	6
viii. 6, 6.	6, 5	xliv. 20.	6	xxix. 7.	6
viii. 15, 15.	6, 5	xlvii. 1.	6	xxxvi. 6.	12 c
xii. 3, 3.	6, 5	lxiii. 4.	6	xl. 5, 5.	5, 4 a
xiv. 9.	6	lxxi. 4, 4.	5, 6	xl. 43.	6
Ruth ii. 16.	10	lxxii. 16.	9	xliii. 13.	4 a
1 Sam. iv. 3.	6	lxxiii. 13.	6	Dan. iii. 34,a 38, 45.a	5 a
xix. 5.	6	lxxviii. 72.	6	iii. 15, 17.	5 a
xxviii. 21.	6	lxxxi. 6.	6	iv. 35.	6
2 Sam. xiv. 16.	6	lxxxviii. 9.	6	v. 5, 5, 23, 24.	5 a
xviii. 12, 12.	6, 5	xci. 12.	6	vii. 25.	5 a
xviii. 14.	6	xcviii. 8.	6	Joel ii. 6.	12 d
xix. 9, 9.	6	cxix. 48, 109.	6	ii. 1.	12 d
xxi. 1, 1.	6	cxxviii. 2.	6	Jonah iii. 8.	6
1 Kings vii. 26.	4	cxxix. 7.	6	Micah iv. 10.	6
viii. 22, 38, 54.	6	cxxxix. 9.	6	vii. 3.	6
xvii. 12.	6, 7	cxli. 2.	6	Nah. iii. 19.	6
xviii. 44.	6	Prov. vi. 1, 3.	6	Zeph. i. 7.	6
xx. 10.	13	x. 4, 4.	6, 5	Hag. i. 11.	12 d
2 Kings iv. 34, 34.	6	xvii. 18.	6		

a marg. 'or, which, (was) not in hands.'

HANDMAID   (See MAID)

HANDLE

1   אָחַז   to take, to lay hold of. KAL *part.* Poel.

2   כַּף   hand; "to be handled," *lit.* to hold in the hand.

3   מוּשׁ   to feel, to touch. HIPHIL *fut.*

4   מָשַׁךְ   to draw; to draw, in the sense of numbering, enrolling. KAL *part.* Poel.

5   עָרַךְ   to set in order, to prepare, arrange. KAL *part.* Poel.

6   תָּפַשׂ   to lay hold of. KAL ^a *inf.* ^b *part.* Poel.

Gen. iv. 21.	6 b	Cant. v. 5.	2	Ezek. xxi. 11.	6 a, 2
Judg. v. 14.	4	Jer. ii. 8.	6 b	xxvii. 29.	6 b
1 Chron. xii. 8.	5	xlvi. 9, 9.	6 b	xxxviii. 4.	6 b
2 Chron. xxv. 5.	1	l. 16.	6 b	Amos ii. 15.	6 b
Ps. cxv. 7.	3				

HANG

1   חָנַק   to choke, suffocate, or strangle in any way. NIPHAL *fut.*

2   יָקַע   to be out of joint. Hiphil, to be hanged, because thus the joints or limbs become loose, as if disjointed. HIPHIL ^a *pret.* ^b *imp.* ^c *fut.* HOPHAL ^d *part.*

3   יָרַד   to go down; to let down. HIPHIL *pret.*

4   מְחָא   Ch. to smite, to destroy. ITHP'AL *fut.*

5   נָתַן   to give; to set, to place. KAL *pret.*

6   סָרַח   to pour forth, to spread; to be redundant. KAL ^a *fut.* ^b *part.* Paül.

7   תָּלָא   to hang up or suspend; to hang in doubt. KAL ^a *pret.* ^b *part.* Paül.

8   תָּלָה   to hang up or suspend; to hang upon a stake or cross, to crucify; a species of punishment common to the Hebrews, Egyptians, and Persians. KAL ^a *pret.* ^b *inf.* ^c *imp.* ^d *fut.* ^e *part.* Poel. ^f *part.* Paül. NIPHAL ^g *pret.* ^h *fut.* PIEL ⁱ *pret.*

Gen. xl. 19, 22.	8 a	2 Sam. iv. 12.	8 d	Esth. vii. 10.	8 d
xli. 13.	8 a	xvii. 23.	1	viii. 7.	8 d
Exod. xxvi. 12.	6 a	xviii. 10.	8 f	ix. 13.	8 d
xxvi. 13.	6 b	xxi. 6.	2 a	ix. 14, 25.	8 a
xxvi. 32, 33.	5	xxi. 9.	2 c	Job xxvi. 7.	8 e
xl. 8.	5	xxi. 12.	7 a or 8 a	Ps. cxxxvii. 2.	8 a
Num. xxv. 4.	2 b	xxi. 13.	2 d	Cant. iv. 4.	8 f
Deut. xxi. 22.	8 a	Ezra vi. 11.	4	Isa. xxii. 24.	8 a
xxi. 23.	8 f	Esth. ii. 23.	8 h	Lam. ii. 10.	3
xxviii. 66.	7 b	v. 14.	8 d	v. 12.	8 g
Josh. viii. 29.	8 a	vii. 9.	8 b	Ezek. xv. 3.	8 b
x. 26, 26.	8 d f		8 c	xxvii. 10, 11.	8 i

HANGING

1   בַּיִת   a house; "hangings," *i. e.* houses made of curtains.

2   מָסָךְ   *m.* covering; veil or curtain, hanging.

3   קְלָעִים   *m. pl.* a sling; curtain, hanging.

Exod. xxvi. 36, 37.	2	Exod. xxxvi. 37.	2	Exod. xl. 5, 8, 28, 33.	2
xxvii. 9, 11, 12, 14,		xxxvii. 9, 12, 14, 15,		Num. iii. 25, 31.	3
15.	3	16.	3	iii. 26.	3
xxvii. 16.	2	xxxviii. 18, 18.	2, 3	iv. 25.	2
xxxv. 15.	2	xxxix. 38.	2	iv. 26, 26.	3, 2
xxxv. 17, 17.	3, 2	xxxix. 40, 40.	3, 2	2 Kings xxiii. 7.	1

HAP, HAPLY, HAPPEN

1   אָנָה   to be in great sorrow; to fall in the way of, to happen, or befal; rather with reference to locality than to time. PUAL *fut.*

2 נָגַע to reach to, or come at. HIPHIL *part.*

3 קָרָא to encounter, to meet any one; to cause to happen, to befal. KAL [a] *pret.* NIPHAL [b] *pret.*

4 קָרָה to meet; to happen or befal. KAL [a] *pret.* [b] *fut.* NIPHAL [c] *pret.* [d] מִקְרֶה *m.* chance, accident; event, hap.

Ruth ii. 3.	4 d b	Esth. iv. 7.	4 a	Eccles. viii. 14, 14.	2
1 Sam. xxviii. 10.	4 b	Prov. xii. 21.	1	ix. 11.	4 b
2 Sam. i. 6.	4 c	Eccles. ii. 14.	4 b	Isa. xli. 22.	4 b
xx. 1.	3 b	ii. 15, 15.	4 b d	Jer. xliv. 23.	3 a
Esth. ii. 3.	4 b				

HAPPY

1 אָשַׁר to go straight forward; to prosper, to be happy, to call happy. PIEL [a] *part.* PUEL [b] *part.* [c] אַשְׁרֵי *m. pl. const.* with the nature and force of an interjection, having also the import of a wish, as Ps. cxxxvii. 8, 9. [d] אֶשֶׁר *m.* happiness.

2 שָׁלָה to be secure, tranquil, at rest; especially of one who enjoys quiet prosperity. KAL *pret.*

Gen. xxx. 13.	1 d	Ps. cxxviii. 2.	1 c	Prov. xiv. 21.	1 c
Deut. xxxiii. 29.	1 c	cxxxvii. 8, 9.	1 c	xvi. 20.	1 c
1 Kings x. 8, 8.	1 c	cxlvi. 15, 15.	1 c	xxviii. 14.	1 c
2 Chron. ix. 7, 7.	1 c	cxlvi. 5.	1 c	xxix. 18.	1 c
Job v. 17.	1 c	Prov. iii. 13.	1 c	Jer. xii. 1.	2
Ps. cxxvii. 5.	1 c	iii. 18.	1 b	Mal. iii. 15.	1 a

HARD

1 אֵיתָן strong like a rock, hard, rough, pernicious; Luther, what brings woe.

2 אָמַץ to be strong, resolute, and vigorous; to harden. PIEL *fut.*

3 חִידָה *f. pr.* what is sharpened; *or,* involved; hard questions. See *Riddle.* [a] אֲחִידָן Ch. *pl.* hard sentences.

4 חָזַק to brace up or tighten, in opposition to a state of relaxation: Isa. xxxv. 3; to be stout and courageous, to be confirmed and established. This is the word used of the hardness of Pharaoh's heart, and implies his strengthening himself against all fear and alarm, stoutly resisting the warnings and motives urged upon him, and the terrors of God's judgments; *comp.* Ps. xcv. 8. It is in Piel that this word is used of God's hardening his heart, when he left him to his own obstinacy and rebellion, and withdrew that favour or benevolence by which alone he might have been brought to relent. The Hebrew, in the narrative respecting Pharaoh, employs three distinct words, differing from each other by a marked diversity of import, but which are all indiscriminately rendered by "harden." The whole number of passages in which Pharaoh's heart is said to have been hardened is nineteen; in thirteen of which the term employed is חָזַק, in five כָּבֵד, and in one קָשָׁה. KAL [a] *fut.* PIEL [b] *pret.* [c] *inf.* [d] *fut.* [e] *part.* [f] חָזָק *adj.* firm; in a bad sense, hardened.

5 יָצַק to pour melted metal into a mould. KAL [a] *part.* Paül. [b] מוּצָק *m.* something poured out, cast; used of dust formed into a mass of mire.

6 כָּבֵד to be heavy. This word also is applied to the hardness of the heart of Pharaoh, and seems to point to his insensibility and want of conviction, as the same word is applied to the ear when not duly impressed with sounds, or to the eye, when it becomes dim. KAL [a] *fut.* PIEL [b] *pret.* [c] *fut.* HIPHIL [d] *pret.* [e] *inf.* [f] *fut.* [g] כָּבֵד *adj.* heavy, hard; "hard language."

7 סָלַד This word occurs but once, and has given occasion to numerous interpretations. The one most generally admitted is, to exult, to rejoice, according to the LXX. and Targ. Professor Lee defends the meaning given in our version. Fürst pleads for that assigned to it by Luther, to pray fervently; and gives the meaning of the passage, "I have yet this consolation, that in my sorrows, which spare me not, I would fervently make my supplications to God." PIEL *fut.* Job vi. 10.

8 עָזַז to strengthen. HIPHIL *pret.*

9 עָנָה to afflict; to deal hardly with. PIEL *fut.*

10 עָתָק *adj.* bold, impudent, wicked.

11 פָּלָא (see *Wonderful*), to be hard, difficult, arduous. NIPHAL *fut.*

12 קָשָׁה to be hard, harsh, severe; to be obstinate, intractable, perverse; applied to that which is very difficult and distressing. KAL [a] *fut.* NIPHAL [b] *part.* "hardly bestead." PIEL [c] *fut.* HIPHIL [d] *pret.* [e] *inf.* [f] *fut.* [g] *part.* [h] קָשֶׁה *adj.* hard.

13 קָשַׁח to be hard; to harden the heart; to treat harshly. HIPHIL [a] *pret.* [b] *fut.*

14 תְּקֵף Ch. to be strong, used of a mind become obstinate. P'AL *fut.*

Gen. xvi. 6.α	9	Exod. xiv. 17.	4 e	Job xxxix. 16.	13 a
xviii. 14.	11	xviii. 26.	12 h	xli. 24.	5
xxxv. 16.	12 c	Deut. i. 17.	12 a	Ps. lx. 3.	12 h
xxxv. 17.β	12 e	ii. 30.	12 d	xciv. 4.	10
Exod. i. 14.	12 h	xv. 7.	2	xcv. 8.	12 f
iv. 21.	4 d	xv. 18.	4 b	Prov. xviii. 15.	1
vii. 3.	12 f	xvii. 8.	11	xxi. 29.	8
vii. 13, 22.	4 a	Josh. xi. 20.	4 c	xxviii. 14.	12 g
vii. 14.	6 g	1 Sam. vi. 6, 6.	6 c b	xxix. 1.	12 g
viii. 15.	6 e	2 Sam. iii. 39.	12 h	Isa. viii. 21.	12 b
viii. 19.	4 a	xiii. 2.	11	xiv. 3.	12 h
viii. 32.	6 g	1 Kings x. 1.	3	lxiii. 17.	13 b
ix. 7.	6 a	2 Kings ii. 10.	12 d	Jer. v. 3.	4 b
ix. 12.	4 b	xvii. 14.	12 f	vii. 26.	12 f
ix. 34.	6 f	2 Chron. ix. 1.	3	xix. 15.	12 d
ix. 35.	4 a	xxxvi. 13.	2	xxxii. 17, 27.	11
x. 1.	6 d	Neh. ix. 16, 17.	12 f	Ezek. iii. 5, 6.δ	6 g
x. 20, 27.	4 d	ix. 29.	12 d	iii. 7.	12 h
xi. 10.	4 d	Job vi. 10.	7	iii. 9.	4 f
xiii. 15.γ	12 d	ix. 4.	12 d	Dan. v. 12.	3 a
xiv. 4.	4 d	xxxviii. 38.	5 b	v. 20.	14
xiv. 8.	4 d				

α *marg.* 'afflicted her;' see *Submit.* β *lit.* when she had difficulty in labour. γ *lit.* hardened himself to let us go. δ *lit.* heavy of tongue or language.

HARE

אַרְנֶבֶת *f.* the hare.—*Bochart.* Lev. xi. 6: Deut. xiv. 7.

HARLOT

1 אִשָּׁה *f.* a woman, a wife; harlot, *lit.* a woman a harlot.

2 זָנָה to play the harlot; see *Whore.* KAL [a] *pret.* [b] *fut.* [c] *part.* Poel.

3 קָדֵשׁ see *Unclean;* hence קְדֵשָׁה a harlot or prostitute.

Gen. xxxiv. 31.	2 c	Josh. ii. 1.	1, 2 c	1 Kings iii. 16.	2 c
xxxviii. 15.	2 c	vi. 17, 25.	2 c	Prov. vii. 10.	2 c
xxxviii. 21, 21, 22.	2 a	xvi. 1.	1, 2 c	Isa. i. 21.	2 c
xxxviii. 24.	2 a	Judg. xi. 1.	1, 2 c	xxiii. 15, 16.	2 c
Lev. xxi. 14.	2 c	xvi. 1.	1, 2 c	xxiii. 15, 16.	2 c

HARM

דָּבָר word, matter, &c. : 2 Kings iv. 41. Heb. evil thing.

חָטָא to sin ; "the harm that he hath done." KAL *pret.* Lev. v. 16.

יָרַע to be evil ; to displease, to do harm. KAL *fut.* 2 Sam. xx. 6.

רָעַע to break ; to be evil ; to do evil, to deal ill with any one, to afflict. HIPHIL *fut.* 1 Sam. xxvi. 21 : 1 Chron. xvi. 22 : Ps. cv. 15. רַע *adj.* bad, evil, worthless ; hurtful : Gen. xxxi. 52 : Num. xxxv. 23 : 2 Kings iv. 41 : Prov. iii. 30 : Jer. xxxix. 12.

HARNESS

אָסַר to bind ; to harness. KAL *imp.* Jer. xlvi. 4.

חֲמֻשִׁים *adj. pl.* see *Armed.* Exod. xiii. 18, *marg.* 'or, by five in a rank.'

נֶשֶׁק *m.* weapon, arms ; harness : 2 Chron. ix. 24.

שִׁרְיָן *m.* a coat of mail : 1 Kings xxii. 34 : 2 Chron. xviii. 33.

HARP

כִּנּוֹר *m.* the harp, an instrument in the use of which David excelled, 1 Sam. xvi. 23 ; used for sacred purposes, 1 Kings x. 12 : 1 Chron. xiii. 8 ; xv. 28 ; xvi. 5 ; also on common occasions, Isa. xxiii. 16 ; xxiv. 8 ; to express joy, Gen. xxxi. 27 : Isa. v. 12 : Job xxi. 12 : Ezek. xxvi. 13 ; and sorrow, Job xxx. 31 : Isa. xvi. 11 ; to accompany sacred songs, Ps. xxxiii. 2 ; xliii. 4 ; xlix. 4 ; lvii. 8 ; lxxi. 22 ; cxxxvii. 2 ; cxlix. 3 ; cl. 3.—Gen. iv. 21, &c.

קַתְרוֹם Ch. *m. i. q.* Gr. κίθαρις, *cithara :* Dan. iii. 5, 7, 10, 15. קִיתָרֹם Ch. *m.* כתיב, Dan. iii. 5, 7, 10, 15.

HARROW

חָרַץ to be sharp and pointed ; applied to sharp-pointed teeth of harrows, and such threshing instruments as were in use in those days. חָרִיץ *m.* sharpened : 2 Sam. xii. 31 : 1 Chron. xx. 3.

שָׂדַד to break the clods. PIEL *fut.* Job xxxix. 10.

HART

אַיָּל *com.* a hart, remarkable for its beauty and agility ; figuratively, the timid, and ready to flee : Lam. i. 6. Also the spouse of Christ, quick in doing his will : Cant. ii. 9, 17, *lit.* the fawn of harts ; viii. 14.——Deut. xii. 15, 22 ; xiv. 5 ; xv. 22 : 1 Kings iv. 23, *lit.* beside of the hart : Ps. xlii. 1 : Isa. xxxv. 6.

עֹפֶר a fawn, a young hind, a kid ; joined with the above, and translated "young," in Cant. ii. 9, 17 ; viii. 14.

HASTE

1 אוּץ to hasten, to urge or press one ; to urge oneself ; *seq.* מִן to

hasten from, to withdraw oneself : Jer. xvii. 16. KAL [a] *pret.* [b] *part.* HIPHIL [c] *fut. seq.* בְּ of person.

2 בָּהַל to be suddenly hurried away, by fear or otherwise ; to flee in trepidation ; to hasten after, *seq.* לְ *i.e.* anxiously. NIPHAL [a] *fut.* [b] *part.* PIEL [c] *inf.* [d] *fut.* PUAL [e] *part.* HIPHIL [f] *fut.* [g] בְּהִילוּ Ch. *f.* haste. בְּהַל Ch. ITHP'AL [h] *inf.*

3 בִּכּוּר *m.* first fruits ; hasty fruit : Isa. xxviii. 4, *i.e.* the early fig, which ripens in June.

4 בָּרַח to break away, to flee. KAL *imp.*

5 דָּחַף to urge ; to impel oneself, to make haste. KAL [a] *part.* Paül. NIPHAL [b] *pret.*

6 חוּשׁ to make great haste : it is *fig.* transferred to any great emotion of the mind, Job xx. 2 ; and so to any passions, pleasures, or lusts : Eccles. ii. 25, "Who else can hasten hereunto more than I ?" who hath indulged himself or enjoyed the pleasures of life more than I ? It differs from מָהַר in a greater degree of speed, also in the extent or distance of that speed. מָהַר may be used of every action or labour, חוּשׁ only of that which includes motion and distance. KAL [a] *pret.* [b] *inf.* [c] *imp.* [d] *fut.* HIPHIL [e] *pret.* [f] *fut.* חִישׁ KAL [g] *imp.* כתיב.

7 חָפַז to flee away in great haste or hurry, through dread of some imminent danger, or enemy threatening death. KAL [a] *inf.* [b] *fut.* NIPHAL [c] *pret.* [d] *fut.* [e] *part.* [f] חִפָּזוֹן *m.* a hasty flight.

8 חֲצַף Ch. to be sharp ; to be harsh, severe. It is twice used in Daniel of a harsh and severe mandate, Dan. ii. 15 ; iii. 22. APHEL *part.*

9 טוּשׂ to fly very swiftly ; to fly upon suddenly, as the eagle upon prey. KAL *fut.*

10 מָהַר to make haste, to be very expeditious : as to Ps. xvi. 4, Hengstenberg pleads that מָהַר has the sense of hastening only in Piel, and that here it is to be understood of buying with a dowry, as idolaters do the false gods. Michaelis includes both ideas in his Not. Uber. *in loc.,* who hasten after another (God), and honour an idol with a dowry, rejecting the free mercies of Jehovah : the idea of being married to idolatry, and so of committing spiritual adultery, is certainly included. KAL [a] *pret.* NIPHAL [b] *part.* PIEL [c] *pret.* [d] *inf.* [e] *imp.* [f] *fut.* [g] מַהֵר *adj.* hastening. [h] מַהֵר *adv.* hastily. [i] מְהֵרָה *f.* hastening, celerity. [k] מָהִיר *adj.* quick.

11 נָחַץ to urge, to press ; to require haste. KAL *part.* Paül.

12 קָצֵר *adj.* short ; impatient.

13 שָׁאַף to breathe hard, to pant. KAL *part.* Poel.

14 שָׁקַד to wake ; *seq.* עַל to watch over anything, to give attention to it. KAL *part.* Poel, Jer. i. 12, an allusion to the name of the almond-tree.

1 Sam. xxiii. 26.	7 e	Ps. xvi. 4.		Eccles. v. 2.	10 f	Ps. lxxxvi. 17.	3 e	Prov. xi. 15.	3 e	Isa. lxvi. 5.	3 e
xxiii. 27.	10 e	xxii. 19.	10 a	vii. 9.	2 d	lxxxix. 23.	3 h	xii. 1.	3 e	Jer. xii. 8.	3 a
xxv. 18, 23, 42.	10 f	xxxi. 22.	6 c	viii. 3.	2 a	xcvii. 10.	3 c	xiii. 5.	3 d	xliv. 4.	3 a
xxv. 34.	10 c	xxxviii. 22.	7 a	Cant. viii. 14.	4	ci. 3.	3 a	xiii. 24.	3 a	Ezek. xvi. 27.	3 e
xxviii. 24.	10 f	xl. 13.	6 c	Isa. v. 19.	6 f	cv. 25.	3 b	xiv. 17, 20.	3 g	xvi. 37.	3 a
2 Sam. iv. 4.γ	10 f	xlviii. 5.	7 c	xvi. 5.	10 k	cvi. 10, 41.	3 a	xv. 10, 27.	3 a	xxiii. 28.	3 a
xix. 16.	10 f	lv. 8.	6 f	xviii. 4.	3	cix. 3, 5.	3 k	xv. 17.	3 k	xxiii. 29.	3 k
1 Kings xx. 33, δ 41.	10 f	lxx. 1, 5.	6 c	xxviii. 16.	6 f	cxviii. 7.	3 a	xix. 7.	3 a	xxv. 15.	1
xxii. 9.	10 e	lxxi. 12.	6 c or g	xlix. 17.	10 c	cxix. 104, 113, 128,		xxv. 17.	3 a	xxxv. 5.	1
2 Kings vii. 15.	7 a	civ. 7.	7 d	li. 14.	10 c	163.	3 a	xxvi. 24.	3 e	xxxv. 6.	3 a
ix. 13.	10 f	cxvi. 11.	7 a	lii. 12.	7 f	cxx. 6.	3 a	xxvi. 26.	3 e	xxxv. 11.	3 k
2 Chron. xxiv. 5, 5.	10 f c	cxix. 60.	6 a	lix. 7.	6 f	cxxix. 5.	3 e	xxvi. 28.	3 d	Dan. iv. 19.	3 i
xxvi. 20.	5 b	cxli. 1.	6 c	lx. 22.	6 f	cxxxix. 21, 21.	3 d h	xxviii. 16.	3 d	Hos. vii. 8.	2 b
xxvii. 21.	2 c	Prov. i. 16.	10 f	Jer. i. 12.	14	cxxxix. 22, 22.	3 a k	xxix. 10.	3 a	ix. 15.	3 a
Ezra iv. 23.	2 g	vii. 23.	10 d	ix. 18.	10 f	Prov. i. 22.	3 d	xxix. 24.	3 a	Amos v. 10, 21.	3 a
Esth. iii. 15.	5 a	xix. 29.	12	xvii. 13.	1 a	i. 29.	3 a	Eccles. ii. 17, 18.	3 a	v. 15.	3 c
v. 5.	10 e	xx. 21.	1 b	xlviii. 16.	10 c	v. 12.	3 a	iii. 8.	3 a	Micah iii. 2.	3 e
vi. 10.	10 e	xxi. 5.	2 e	Dan. ii. 15.	8	vi. 16.	3 a	ix. 1, 6.	3 k	Zech. viii. 17.	3 a
vi. 12.	5 b	xxviii. 20.	10 h	ii. 25.	2 h	viii. 13, 13.	3 h	Isa. i. 14.	3 a	Mal. i. 3.	3 a
vi. 14.	2 f	xxviii. 22.	1 b	iv. 19.	2 h	viii. 36.	3 h	lx. 15.	3 f	ii. 16.	3 a
viii. 14.	2 e	xxix. 20.	2 h	Nah. ii. 5.	10 f	ix. 8.	3 h	lxi. 8.	3 e		
Job ix. 26.	9	Eccles. i. 5.	1 b	Zeph. i. 14.	10 g	x. 12, 18.	3 k				
xx. 2. ε	6 b	ii. 25.	13	Hab. i. 6.	10 b						
xxxi. 5.	6 d			i. 8.	6 d						
xl. 23.	7 b										

a lit. they added to hate.

a lit. and hasted to call.   *β lit.* hasted and came in.   *γ lit.* in her hastening.   *δ lit.* and they hasted and caught.   *ε lit.* my haste (is) in me.

HARVEST

קָצַר to reap. KAL *part.* Poel, reaper, harvest man : Jer. ix. 22. קָצִיר *m.* harvest : Gen. viii. 22, &c.

HAT

כַּרְבְּלָא Ch. *f.* Dan. iii. 21, *marg.* ' or, turbans.' Gesenius, mantle, pallium.

HATCH

בָּקַע to break through : see *Cleave*. When the young one is hatched, it breaks through the separated sides of the egg. KAL *pret.* Isa. xxxiv. 15. PIEL *pret.* Isa. lix. 5.

יָלַד to bring forth. KAL *pret.* Jer. xvii. 11.

HATE, HATRED

1 אֵיבָה *f.* enmity, hostile mind.

2 שָׂטַם to hate with deep and implacable malice and persecution. KAL [a] *fut.* [b] מַשְׂטֵמָה *f.* hatred, persecution.

3 שָׂנֵא to hate ; which is not always to be understood in the strongest sense, but must sometimes mean only a less degree of love and regard ; to be cold and indifferent to, to show less favour to. KAL [a] *pret.* [b] *inf.* [c] *imp.* [d] *fut.* [e] *part.* Poel. [f] *part.* Paül. NIPHAL [g] *fut.* PIEL [h] *part.* שְׂנָא Ch. *id.* P'AL [i] *part.* [k] שְׂנֵאָה *f.* hatred. [l] שְׂנִיא *adj.* hated.

Gen. xxiv. 60.	3 e	Deut. xxi. 16, 17.	3 f	Job xxxiv. 17.	3 e
xxvi. 27.	3 a	xxii. 13.	3 a	Ps. v. 5.	3 a
xxvii. 41.	2 a	xxii. 16.	3 d	ix. 13.	3 e
xxix. 31, 33.	3 f	xxiv. 3.	3 e	xi. 5.	3 e
xxxvii. 4.	3 d	xxx. 7.	3 e	xviii. 17.	3 a
xxxvii. 5, a 8.a	3 b	xxxii. 41.	3 h	xviii. 40.	3 h
xlix. 23.	2 a	xxxiii. 11.	3 h	xxi. 8.	3 e
l. 15.	2 a	Josh. xx. 5.	3 e	xxv. 19, 19.	3 a k
Exod. xviii. 21.	3 e	Judg. xi. 7.	3 a	xxvi. 5.	3 a
xx. 5.	3 e	xiv. 16.	3 a	xxxi. 6.	3 a
xxiii. 5.	3 e	xv. 2.	3 b a	xxxiv. 21.	3 e
Lev. xix. 17.	3 d	2 Sam. v. 8.	3 f	xxxv. 19.	3 e
xxvi. 17.	3 e	xiii. 15, 15, 15.	3 d k k a	xxxvi. 2.	3 b
Num. x. 35.	3 h	xiii. 22.	3 a	xxxviii. 19.	3 e
xxxv. 20.	3 h	xix. 6.	3 b	xli. 7.	3 e
Deut. i. 27.	3 k	xxii. 18.	3 e	xliv. 7, 10.	3 e
iv. 42.	3 e	xxii. 41.	3 h	xlv. 7.	3 d
v. 9.	3 e	1 Kings xxii. 8.	3 a	l. 17.	3 a
vii. 10, 10, 15.	3 e	2 Chron. xviii. 7.	3 a	lv. 3.	2 a
ix. 28.	3 k	xix. 2.	3 a	lv. 12.	3 h
xii. 31.	3 a	Esth. iii. 1, 5.	3 a	lxviii. 1.	3 h
xvi. 22.	3 a	Job viii. 22.	3 e	lxix. 4, 14.	3 e
xix. 4, 6, 11.	3 a	xvi. 9.	2 a	lxxxi. 15.	3 e
xxi. 15, 15, 15.	3 f f l	xxxi. 29.	3 h	lxxxiii. 2.	3 h

HAUGHTY

1 גַּאֲוָה *f.* exaltation, greatness ; pride, arrogance.

2 גָּבַהּ to be lifted up ; to be proud, arrogant, haughty. KAL [a] *pret.* [b] *inf.* [c] *fut.* [d] גֹּבַהּ *m.* pride. [e] גָּבֹהַּ *adj.* proud.

3 יָהִיר *adj.* proud, arrogant.

4 רוּם to be lifted up ; to be high, lofty. KAL [a] *part.* Poel. [b] רוּם *m.* elation of mind. [c] רוֹמָה *adv.* with uplifted neck. [d] מָרוֹם *m.* elation of mind.

2 Sam. xxii. 28.	4 a	Isa. ii. 11, 17.	4 b	Isa. xxiv. 4.	4 d
Ps. cxxxi. 1.	2 a	ii. 16.	2 a	Jer. xlviii. 29.	4 b
Prov. xvi. 18.	2 d	x. 33.	2 e	Ezek. xvi. 50.	2 c
xviii. 12.	2 c	xiii. 11.	1	Micah ii. 3.	4 c
xxi. 24.	3	xvi. 6.	1	Zeph. iii. 11.	2 b

HAUNT

הָלַךְ to go. HITHPAEL *pret.*, 1 Sam. xxx. 31, "wont to haunt."

יָשַׁב to dwell. KAL *part.* Poel, Ezek. xxvi. 17.

רֶגֶל *f.* foot ; haunt, where a man often goes : 1 Sam. xxiii. 22.

HAVE

בּוֹא to come. KAL *pret.* Gen. xliii. 25 : Job vi. 8, *lit.* and oh that my request would come.

בַּעַל *m.* master, owner, possessor ; any one who takes part in a matter : Exod. xxiv. 14, *lit.* who is a master of business : Prov. xvi. 22 ; xvii. 8 : Eccles. vii. 12 ; x. 20, *lit.* and the master of wings : Isa. xli. 15 : Dan. viii. 6, 20. בַּעֲלָה *f.* mistress : 1 Sam. xxviii. 7, 7.

הָוָה to be. KAL *part.* Poel, Eccles. xxi. 22, *llt.* what being to man.

חֲזָה Ch. to see. P'AL *pret.* Dan. vii. 1, *lit.* saw a dream.

יָדַע to know. KAL *pret.* Job xxxviii. 4 : Isa. lvi. 11. *fut.* Prov. xxx. 3. *part.* Poel, Prov. xvii. 27, *lit.* he that knoweth knowledge.

יָצָא to go forth. HIPHIL, to have forth, to have out. *imp.* 2 Sam. xiii. 9 : 2 Kings xi. 15 : 2 Chron. xxiii. 14.

יֵשׁ see *To Be.* Gen. xxxiii. 9, *lit.* there is to me ; 11 ; xxxix. 4, 5, 5, 8 ; xliii. 7 ; xliv. 19, 20 : Ruth i. 12 : 2 Sam. xix. 28 : 1 Kings xvii. 12 : 2 Kings iv. 2 : 1 Chron. xxix. 3 : 2 Chron. xvi. 9 ; xxv. 8 : Ezra x. 14 : Job xxxviii. 28 : Prov. iii. 28 : Eccles. iv. 9 : Isa. xliii. 8 : Jer. xli. 8 : Mal. i. 14.

מָצָא to find. Niphal *pret.* 1 Sam. ix. 8. *fut.* Deut. xxi. 17.

שׂוּם to set, or put; to produce. Kal *fut.* Ezra x. 44, *lit.* they produced children.

HAVEN

חוֹף *m.* coast, shore : Gen. xlix. 13, 13.

מָחוֹז *m.* the utmost limit or boundary : Ps. cvii. 30. Gesenius, refuge ; hence haven, harbour.

HAVOTH

חַוּוֹת *f. pl.* small towns or villages : Num. xxxii. 41 : Deut. iii. 14 : Judg. x. 4.

HAWK

נֵץ *m.* a hawk, from its flying with great swiftness : Lev. xi. 16 : Deut. xiv. 15 : Job xxxix. 26.

תַּחְמָס *m.* according to Lxx. and Vulg., the night-hawk ; Bochart, the male ostrich : Lev. xi. 16 : Deut. xiv. 15.

HAY

חָצִיר *m.* grass cut down : Prov. xxvii. 25 : Isa. xv. 6.

HAZEL

לוּז *m.* the almond-tree : Gen. xxx. 37.

HEAD

בַּרְזֶל *m.* iron axe-head : Deut. xix. 5 : 2 Kings vi. 5.

גֻּלְגֹּלֶת *f.* skull : 1 Chron. x. 10.

לַהֶבֶת *f.* flame ; glittering steel, or point of a spear : 1 Sam. xvii. 7.

קִשֻּׁרִים *m. pl.* girdles, bands, head-bands : Isa. iii. 20.

רֹאשׁ *m.* head ; whatever is highest and supreme ; sum, amount ; what is first and foremost, the beginning, commencement : Gen. ii. 10, &c. רֵאשׁ Ch. *m.* Dan. ii. 28, 32, 38 ; iii. 27 ; iv. 5, 10, 13 ; vii. 1, 6, 9, 15, 20. מְרַאֲשֹׁת *f. pl.* bolster, "at his head:" 1 Kings xix. 6. רֹאשָׁה *f.* head (stone) : Zech. iv. 7.

HEAL, HEALTH

1 אָרַךְ to prolong ; or, according to Fürst, to be suitable, convenient, well-tempered. אֲרוּכָה and אֲרֻכָה health, which is the prolongation of life, or the fitness of the functions of the body.

2 חָבַשׁ to bind up wounds, and so to heal ; see *Governor*. The Lxx. seem to have attached this meaning to the word, by rendering it ἀρχηγός. Kal *part.* Poel.

3 יְשׁוּעָה salvation, health, saving health.

4 כֵּהָה *f.* mitigation, alleviation ; applied to the assuaging the anguish of a bruise or wound.

5 נָתַן to give. Kal *inf.*

6 תְּעָלָה *f.* (see *Cure*), healing.

7 רָפָא to heal diseases of all kinds (Ps. ciii. 3), particularly wounds by outward application, and binding or sewing : Ezek. xxx. 21, to heal a distressed nation or person by restoring them to prosperous circumstances ; to heal in a moral sense, to cure the mind, to pardon the soul. Kal [a]*pret.* [b]*inf.* [c]*imp.* [d]*fut.* [e]*part.* Poel. Niphal [f]*pret.* [g]*inf.* [h]*fut.* Piel [i]*pret.* [k]*inf.* [l]*fut.* Hithpael [m]*inf.* [n]רְפָאוֹת *f.* healing, *marg.* 'medicine.' [o]רְפֻאוֹת *f. pl.* medicines. [p]מַרְפֵּא *m.* healing.

8 שָׁלוֹם *m.* health, prosperity, peace.

Gen. xx. 17.	7 d	Ps. xliii. 5.	3	Jer. viii. 15.	7 p	
xliii. 28.	8	lx. 2.	7 c	viii. 22.	1	
Exod. xv. 26.	7 e	lxvii. 2.	3	xiv. 19, 19.	7 p	
xxi. 19. a	7 k	ciii. 3.	7 e	xv. 18.	7 g	
Lev. xiii. 18, 37.	7 f	cvii. 20.	7 d	xvii. 14, 14.	7 c h	
xiv. 3, 48.	7 f	cxlvii. 3.	7 e	xxx. 13.	6	
Num. xii. 13.	7 c	Prov. iii. 8.	7 n	xxx. 17, 17.	1, 7 d	
Deut. xxviii. 27, 35.	7 g	iv. 22.	7 p	xxxviii. 16.	1	
xxxii. 39.	7 d	xii. 18.	7 p	li. 8.	7 h	
1 Sam. vi. 3.	7 h	xiii. 17.	7 p	li. 9, 9.	7 i f	
2 Sam. xx. 9.	8	xvi. 24.	7 p	Lam. ii. 13.	7 d	
2 Kings ii. 21.	7 i	Eccles. iii. 3.	7 b	Ezek. xxx. 21. γ	5, 7 o	
ii. 22.	7 h	Isa. iii. 7.	2	xxxiv. 4.	7 i	
viii. 29.	7 m	vi. 10.	7 a	xlvii. 8.	7 f	
ix. 15.	7 m	xix. 22, 22.	7 b a	xlvii. 9, 11.	7 h	
xx. 5.	7 e	xxx. 26.	7 d	Hos. v. 13.	7 b	
xx. 8.	7 f	liii. 5. β	7 f	vi. 1.	7 d	
2 Chron. vii. 14.	7 d	lvii. 18.	7 d	vii. 1.	7 d	
xxii. 6.	7 m	lvii. 19.	7 d	xi. 3.	7 a	
xxx. 20.	7 d	lviii. 8.	1	xiv. 4.	7 d	
Ps. vi. 2.	7 c	Jer. iii. 22.	7 d	Nah. iii. 19.	4	
xxx. 2.	7 d	vi. 14.	7 l	Zech. xi. 16.	7 l	
xli. 4.	7 c	viii. 11.	7 l	Mal. iv. 2.	7 p	
xliii. 11.	3					

a *lit.* healing healed.   β *lit.* it is healed to us.   γ *lit.* to give healings.

HEAP

1 גַּל *m.* a heap of stones, of ruined cities.

2 חָבַר to join or couple together things of the same sort. Hiphil *fut.* Job xvi. 4, "I could heap together, join together, vain unmeaning words as you do."

3 חֹמֶר a large quantity, a heap of anything ; see *Homer ;* also clay, mud. [a]חֲמוֹר *m.* [b]חֲמֹרָתָיִם *f. dual.* There is a singular paronomasia in Judg. xv. 16, since חֲמוֹר means both an ass and a heap : *lit.* a heap, two heaps.

4 חָתָה to take up ; to take a quantity of fire from the hearth. Kal *part.* Poel.

5 כָּנַס to gather, to crowd or heap together all that one can. Kal *inf.*

6 נוּד to be moved, agitated ; also to heap or collect together ; hence נֵד a heap or mound ; used of the waves of the sea, Ps. xxxiii. 7 ; so in Exod. xv. 8. Lxx. ὡσεὶ τεῖχος (cf. xiv. 22), Ps. lxxviii. 13 ; Virgil, Georg. iv. 361, *At illum curvata in montis faciem circumstetit unda.* Isa. xvii. 11, "the harvest shall be a heap," *or*, the heap of harvest, the gathering of it, shall be in a day of grief, &c. ; the *marg.* has it, 'the harvest shall be removed in the day of inheritance,' rendering it as if the word נֵד were derived from נוּד, to shake, move, wander. Rosenmüller translates it by "the heap of the harvest shall be inexpressible sorrow." See also *Grief.* [a]נֵד *m.* a heap.

7 סָפָה to add. Hiphil, to scrape together, to heap up, with עַל upon. *fut.* Deut. xxxii. 23. Lxx. συνάξω ; Vulg. *congregabo.*

8 עִי *m.* heap, ruin. מְעִי *m. id.*

9 עֲרֵמָה *f.* a heap of rubbish, of grain, of sheaves.

10 צָבַר to heap up dust, earth, &c. ; to heap up silver is to amass

it together insatiably without bounds. KAL ^a *fut.* ^b צְבָרִים *m. pl.* heaps.

11 קָבַץ to gather together. KAL *fut.*

12 רָבָה to multiply. HIPHIL *imp.*

13 שׂוּם to put or set with care, exactness. KAL *fut.*

14 תֵּל *m.* an eminence or heap raised by human labour; a heap of ruins raised by demolishing a town.

15 תַּמְרוּרִים high heaps; or upright columns, or mounds raised high, probably as way-marks.

Gen. xxxi. 46, 46, 48,		Neh. iv. 2.	9	Jer. ix. 11.	1
51, 52, 52, 52.	1	Job viii. 17.	1	xxvi. 18.	8
Exod. viii. 14. a	3	xv. 28.	1	xxx. 18.	14
xv. 8.	6 a	xvi. 4.	2	xxxi. 21.	15
Deut. xiii. 16.	14	xxvii. 16.	10 a	xlix. 2.	14
xxxii. 23.	7	xxxvi. 13.	13	l. 26.	9
Josh. iii. 13, 16.	6 a	Ps. xxxiii. 7.	6 a	li. 37.	9
vii. 26.	1	xxxix. 6.	10 a	Ezek. 24. 10.	12
viii. 28.	14	lxxviii. 13.	6 a	Hos. xii. 11.	1
viii. 29.	1	lxxix. 1.	8	Mic. i. 6.	8
Judg. xv. 16, 16.	3 a b	Prov. xxv. 22.	4	iii. 12.	8
Ruth iii. 7.	9	Eccles. ii. 26.	5	Hab. i. 10.	10 a
2 Sam. xviii. 17.	1	Cant. vii. 2.	9	ii. 5.	11
2 Kings x. 8.	10 b	Isa. xvii. 1.	8 a	iii. 15.	3
xix. 25.	1	xvii. 11.	6 a	Hag. ii. 16.	9
2 Chron. xxxi. 6, β 7,		xxv. 2.	1	Zech. ix. 3.	10 a
8, 9.	1	xxxvii. 26.	1		

α *lit.* heaps, heaps. β *lit.* heaps, heaps.

HEAR, HEARKEN

1 אָזַן to give ear, to hearken, to attend: when this word is joined with שָׁמַע, it implies the understanding of hidden speech. HIPHIL ^a*imp.* ^b*fut.* ^c אֹזֶן *m.* ear, audience.

2 עָנָה to answer; to hear, *lit.* to answer prayer, used particularly of God. KAL ^a*pret.* ^b*imp.* ^c*fut.* NIPHAL ^d*fut.*

3 קָשַׁב to dispose the ear or mind to ready, earnest, serious attention. KAL ^a*fut.* HIPHIL ^b*pret.* ^c*inf.* ^d*imp.* ^e*fut.* ^f*part.* ^g קֶשֶׁב *m.* attention.

4 שָׁמַע to hear, to listen, to give heed, obey. With *inf.*, hearken or hear diligently, surely, certainly, attentively, indeed. KAL ^a*pret.* ^b*inf.* ^c*imp.* ^d*fut.* ^e*part.* Poel. NIPHAL ^f*pret.* ^g*inf.* ^h*fut.* ⁱ*part.* HIPHIL ^k*pret.* ^l*inf.* ^m*imp.* ⁿ*fut.* שְׁמַע Ch. P'AL ^o*pret.* ^p*fut.* ^q*part.* שֶׁמַע *m.* hearing. מִשְׁמָע *m.* a hearing, the thing heard. ^t הַשְׁמָעוּת *i. q. inf.* of the verb, a causing to hear.

Gen. iii. 8.	4 d	Gen. xxxvii. 17.	4 a	Exod. xxii. 27.	4 a
iii. 10, 17.	4 a	xxxvii. 21.	4 d	xxiii. 13.	4 h
iv. 23, 23.	4 c, 1 a	xxxix. 10.	4 a	xxviii. 35.	4 f
xiv. 14.	4 d	xxxix. 15, 19.	4 b	xxxii. 17.	4 d
xvi. 2.	4 d	xli. 15.	4 a	xxxii. 18.	4 a
xvi. 11.	4 a	xlii. 2, 21, 22.	4 a	xxxiii. 4.	4 d
xvii. 20.	4 a	xliii. 25.	4 a	Lev. v. 1.	4 a
xviii. 10.	4 e	xlv. 2. a	4 d	x. 20.	4 d
xxi. 6.	4 e	xlv. 16.	4 f	xxiv. 14.	4 a
xxi. 12.	4 c	xlix. 2, 2.	4 c	xxvi. 14, 18, 27.	4 d
xxi. 17, 17.	4 d a	Exod. ii. 15, 24.	4 d	xxvi. 21.	4 b
xxi. 26.	4 a	iii. 7, 18.	4 a	Num. vii. 89.	4 d
xxiii. 6, 8, 11, 13,		iv. 1, 8, 9, 31.	4 d	ix. 8.	4 d
15.	4 c	vi. 5, 9.	4 a	xi. 1, 10.	4 a
xxiii. 16.	4 d	vi. 12, 12.	4 a d	xii. 2.	4 d
xxiv. 30.	4 b	vi. 30.	4 d	xii. 6.	4 a
xxiv. 52.	4 a	vii. 4.	4 d	xiv. 13, 14, 15, 22,	
xxvii. 5.	4 e	vii. 13, 16, 22.	4 a	27.	4 a
xxvii. 6.	4 a	viii. 15, 19.	4 a	xvi. 4.	4 a
xxvii. 34.	4 b	ix. 12.	4 a	xvi. 8.	4 c
xxix. 13.	4 b	xi. 9.	4 d	xvi. 10.	4 c
xxix. 33.	4 a	xv. 14.	4 a	xx. 16.	4 d
xxx. 6.	4 a	xv. 26.	4 b d	xxi. 1, β 3.	4 a
xxx. 17, 22.	4 d	xvi. 7, 8.	4 b	xxii. 36.	4 d
xxxi. 1.	4 d	xvi. 9, 12, 20.	4 a	xxiii. 18, 18.	4 c, 1 a
xxxiv. 5.	4 a	xviii. 1, 24.	4 d	xxiv. 4, 16.	4 e
xxxiv. 7.	4 b	xviii. 19.	4 c	xxx. 4, 11.	4 a
xxxiv. 17, 24.	4 d	xix. 5.	4 d	xxx. 5, 8, 12, 14, 15.	4 b
xxxv. 22.	4 d	xx. 19.	4 a	xxx. 7, 7.	4 a b
xxxvii. 6.	4 c	xxii. 23.	4 b d	xxxiii. 40.	4 d

Deut. i. 16.	4 b	1 Sam. viii. 7, 9, 22.	4 c	2 Kings vii. 1.	4 c
i. 17, 17.	4 d a	viii. 18.	2 c	vii. 6.	4 k
i. 34.	4 d	viii. 21.	4 d	ix. 30.	4 e
i. 43, 45.	4 a	xi. 6.	4 b	x. 6.	4 e
ii. 25.	4 d	xii. 1.	4 a	xi. 13.	4 d
iii. 26.	4 a	xiii. 3, 3.	4 d	xiii. 4.	4 a
iv. 1.	4 c	xiii. 4.	4 a	xiv. 11.	4 a
iv. 6, 28.	4 n	xiv. 22, 27.	4 a	xvi. 9.	4 d
iv. 10.	4 n	xv. 1.	4 c	xvii. 14, 40.	4 d
iv. 12.	4 a	xv. 14.	4 e	xviii. 12.	4 a
iv. 32.	4 f	xv. 22.	3 c	xviii. 28.	4 c
iv. 33, 33.	4 a	xvi. 2.	4 a	xviii. 31, 32.	4 d
iv. 36, 36.	4 k a	xvii. 11, 23, 28.	4 d	xix. 1.	4 b
v. 1.	4 a	xvii. 31.	4 h	xix. 4, 4.	4 d a
v. 23, 25.	4 b	xix. 6.	4 d	xix. 6, 7, 8, 11, 20,	
v. 24, 26.	4 d	xxii. 1, 6.	4 d	25.	4 a
v. 27, 27.	4 c a	xxii. 7, 12.	4 c	xix. 9.	4 d
v. 28, 28.	4 d a	xxiii. 10.	4 b a	xix. 16, 16.	4 c
vi. 3.	4 c	xxiii. 11.	4 a	xx. 5, 12.	4 a
vi. 4.	4 c	xxiii. 25.	4 d	xx. 13.	4 d
vii. 12.	4 a	xxiv. 9.	4 d	xx. 16.	4 a
ix. 1.	4 c	xxv. 4, 39.	4 d	xxi. 9.	4 a
ix. 2, 23.	4 a	xxv. 7, 35.	4 a	xxi. 1°.	4 b
ix. 19.	4 n	xxv. 24.	4 c	xxii. 1...	4 b
x. 10.	4 d	xxvi. 19.	4 d	xxii. 13, 18.	4 a
xi. 13.	4 b d	xxviii. 21, 23.	4 d	xxii. 19, 19.	4 b a
xiii. 3, 8, 11, 12, 18.	4 d	xxviii. 22.	4 c	xxv. 23.	4 d
xv. 5.	4 b d	xxx. 24.	4 d	1 Chron. x. 11.	4 d
xvii. 4.	4 a	xxxi. 11.	4 d	xiv. 8, 8.	4 d
xvii. 12.	4 c	2 Sam. iii. 28.	4 d	xiv. 15.	4 b
xvii. 13.	4 d	v. 17, 17.	4 d	xvii. 20.	4 a
xviii. 14, 15, 19.	4 a	v. 24.	4 a	xviii. 9.	4 d
xviii. 16.	4 b	vii. 22.	4 a	xix. 8.	4 d
xix. 20.	4 d	viii. 9.	4 d	xviii. 2.	4 c
xxi. 18, 21.	4 c	x. 7.	4 d	2 Chron. v. 13.	4 b
xxiii. 5.	4 b	xi. 26.	4 a	vi. 19, 20.	4 b
xxvi. 7.	4 a	xii. 18.	4 a	vi. 21, 21, 21.	4 a d a
xxvi. 14.	4 a	xiii. 14, 16.	4 a	vi. 23, 25, 27, 30,	
xxvii. 17.	4 b	xiv. 16.	4 a	33.	4 d
xxvii. 9.	4 c	xv. 3.	4 e	vi. 35, 39.	4 d
xxviii. 1.	4 b d	xv. 10.	4 d	vii. 12.	4 d
xxviii. 2, 13, 15.	4 d	xv. 35, 36.	4 d	vii. 14.	4 d
xxviii. 45.	4 a	xvi. 21.	4 a	ix. 1, 5, 6.	4 a
xxix. 4, 19.	4 b	xvii. 5.	4 d	ix. 7.	4 a
xxx. 10, 17.	4 d	xvii. 9. γ	4 e a	ix. 23.	4 b
xxx. 12, 13.	4 n	xviii. 5.	4 a	x. 15, 16.	4 a
xxxi. 11.	1 c	xviii. 12.	1 c	xiii. 2.	4 a
xxxi. 12, 13.	4 d	xix. 2.	4 a	xiii. 4.	4 d
xxxii. 1.	4 a	xix. 35.	4 a	xvi. 4.	4 b
xxxiii. 7.	4 c	xx. 16, 16.	4 d	xvi. 5.	4 b
xxxiv. 9.	4 d	xx. 17, 17.	4 c e	xviii. 18, 27.	4 c
Josh. i. 17, 17.	4 a d	xxii. 45. δ	4 b, 1 c	xx. 9.	3 d
i. 18.	4 d	1 Kings i. 11, 45.	4 a	xx. 15.	4 b
ii. 10.	4 a	i. 41, 41.	4 a	xx. 20.	4 a
ii. 11.	4 d	i. 42.	4 a	xx. 29.	4 b
iii. 9.	4 c	iii. 28.	4 d	xxiii. 12.	4 a
v. 1.	4 d	iv. 34, 34.	4 b a	xxiv. 17.	4 a
vi. 5, 20.	4 d	v. 1.	4 a	xxv. 16, 20.	4 a
vii. 9.	4 b	v. 7.	4 b	xxviii. 11.	4 c
ix. 1.	4 b	vi. 7.	4 f	xxx. 5.	4 d
ix. 3, 9.	4 a	viii. 28, 29, 52.	4 b	xxx. 20.	4 d
ix. 16.	4 d	viii. 30, 30, 30.	4 a d a	xxx. 27.	4 h
x. 1, 14.	4 b	viii. 32, 34, 36, 39,		xxxiii. 10.	3 b
xi. 1.	4 a	42, 43.	4 d	xxxiii. 13.	4 d
xiv. 12.	4 a	viii. 45, 49.	4 d	xxxiv. 19.	4 b
xxii. 11, 12, 30.	4 b	ix. 3.	4 b	xxxiv. 26.	4 a
xxiv. 10.	4 a			xxxiv. 27, 27.	4 b a
xxiv. 27.	4 a	x. 1, 8.	4 e	xxxv. 22.	4 a
Judg. ii. 17, 20.	4 a	x. 6, 7.	4 a	Ezra iii. 13.	4 f
iii. 4.	4 a	x. 24.	4 b	iv. 1.	4 d
v. 3.	4 d	xi. 21.	4 a	iv. 3.	4 b
v. 16.	4 b	xi. 38.	4 d	Neh. i. 4, 6.	4 b
vii. 11.	4 b	xii. 2, 20.	4 a	ii. 10, 19.	4 a
vii. 15.	4 b	xii. 15, 16.	4 a	iv. 1, 7, 15.	4 a
ix. 7. 7.	4 c d	xii. 24.	4 d	iv. 4.	4 c
ix. 30, 46.	4 a	xiii. 4.	4 b	iv. 20.	4 a
xi. 17, 28.	4 a	xiii. 26.	4 d	v. 6.	4 a
xiii. 9.	4 d	xiv. 6.	4 b	vi. 1.	4 f
xiv. 13.	4 a	xvi. 16.	4 d	vi. 16.	4 a
xviii. 25.	4 n	xv. 21.	4 b	viii. 2, 9.	4 b
xix. 3.	4 d	xvi. 16.	4 d	ix. 9, 16, 29, 29.	4 d
xx. 3.	4 d	xvii. 22.	4 d	ix. 27, 28.	4 d
Ruth i. 6.	4 a	xviii. 26, 37, 37.	4 b	ix. 34.	3 b
ii. 8.	4 a	xix. 13.	4 b	xii. 43.	4 h
1 Sam. i. 13.	4 h	xx. 8, 25.	4 d	xiii. 27.	4 d
ii. 22.	4 a	xx. 12.	4 b	Esth. i. 18.	4 a
ii. 23, 24.	4 e	xx. 31.	4 a	ii. 8.	4 g
ii. 25.	4 d	xxi. 15, 16, 27.	4 b	iii. 4.	4 d
iii. 9, 10, 11.	4 e	xxi. 19, 28.	4 d	Job ii. 11.	4 a
iv. 6, 14, 19.	4 a	2 Kings iii. 21.	4 a	iii. 18.	4 a
vii. 7, 7.	4 d	iv. 31.	3 g	iv. 16.	4 a
vii. 9.	2 c	vi. 30.	4 b	v. 27.	4 c

Job ix. 16. — 1 b
xiii. 1. — 4 a
xiii. 6, 6. — 4 c, 3 d
xiii. 17.ε — 4 b c
xv. 8. — 4 d
xv. 17. — 4 c
xvi. 2. — 4 a
xix. 7. — 2 d
xx. 3. — 4 d
xxi. 2.ε — 4 b c
xxii. 27. — 4 a
xxvi. 14. — 4 f
xxvii. 9. — 4 a
xxviii. 22. — 4 a
xxix. 11. — 4 a
xxx. 20. — 2 c
xxxi. 35. — 4 e
xxxii. 10. — 4 c
xxxiii. 1, 1. — 4 c, 1 a
xxxiii. 8, 8. — 1 c, 4 d
xxxiii. 31, 33. — 4 c
xxxiv. 2, 10. — 4 c
xxxiv. 16, 16. — 4 c, 1 a
xxxiv. 28. — 4 d
xxxiv. 34. — 4 e
xxxv. 13. — 4 d
xxxvii. 2. — 4 b c
xxxvii. 4. — 4 h
xxxvii. 14. — 1 a
xlii. 4. — 4 c
xlii. 5, 5. — 4 a r
Ps. iii. 4. — 2 c
iv. 1, 1. — 2 b, 4 c
iv. 3. — 4 d
v. 2. — 3 d
v. 3.ζ — 4 d
vi. 8, 9. — 4 a
x. 17, 17. — 4 a, 3 e
xiii. 3. — 2 b
xvii. 1. — 4 e
xvii. 6, 6. — 2 c, 4 c
xviii. 6. — 4 a
xviii. 44. — 4 r, 1 c
xix. 3. — 4 f
xx. 1, 6, 9. — 2 c
xxii. 2. — 2 c
xxii. 21. — 2 a
xxii. 24. — 4 c
xxvii. 7. — 4 c
xxviii. 1. — 4 c
xxviii. 6. — 4 a
xxx. 10. — 4 c
xxxi. 13, 22. — 4 a
xxxiv. 2. — 4 d
xxxiv. 4. — 2 a
xxxiv. 6, 17. — 4 a
xxxiv. 11. — 4 c
xxxviii. 13. — 4 d
xxxviii. 14. — 4 e
xxxviii. 15. — 2 c
xxxix. 12. — 4 c
xl. 1. — 4 d
xliv. 1. — 4 a
xlv. 10. — 4 c
xlviii. 8. — 4 a
xlix. 1. — 4 c
l. 7. — 4 c
li. 8. — 4 n
liv. 2. — 4 c
lv. 2. — 2 b
lv. 17, 19. — 4 d
lviii. 5. — 4 e
lix. 7. — 4 e
lx. 5. — 2 b
lxi. 1. — 4 c
lxi. 5. — 4 a
lxii. 11. — 4 a
lxiv. 1. — 4 c
lxv. 2. — 4 e
lxvi. 8. — 4 m
lxvi. 16. — 4 d
lxvi. 18. — 4 d
lxvi. 19. — 4 a
lxix. 13, 16, 17. — 2 b
lxix. 33. — 4 a
lxxvii. 8. — 4 k
lxxviii. 3, 21, 59. — 4 a
lxxxi. 5. — 4 d
lxxxi. 8, 8. — 4 c d
lxxxi. 11. — 4 a
lxxxi. 13. — 4 e
lxxxiv. 8. — 4 a
lxxxv. 8. — 4 d
lxxxvi. 1. — 4 b
xcii. 11. — 4 d

Ps. xciv. 9. — 4 d
xcv. 7. — 4 d
xcvii. 8. — 4 a
cii. 1. — 4 c
cii. 20. — 4 b
ciii. 20. — 4 b
cvi. 25. — 4 a
cvi. 44. — 4 b
cxv. 6. — 4 d
cxvi. 1. — 2 a
cxviii. 21. — 2 c
cxix. 26. — 2 b
cxix. 145. — 4 c
cxx. 1. — 2 c
cxxx. 2. — 4 c
cxxxii. 6. — 4 a
cxxxv. 17. — 1 b
cxxxviii. 4. — 4 a
cxl. 6. — 1 a
cxli. 6. — 4 a
cxliii. 1. — 4 c
cxliii. 7. — 2 b
cxliii. 8. — 4 m
cxlv. 19. — 4 d
Prov. i. 5. — 4 d
i. 8. — 4 c
i. 33. — 4 e
iv. 1, 10. — 4 c
v. 7. — 4 c
vii. 24. — 4 c
viii. 6, 32, 33. — 4 e
viii. 34. — 4 e
xii. 15. — 4 c
xiii. 1, 8. — 4 a
xv. 29. — 4 d
xv. 31, 32. — 4 e
xviii. 13. — 4 d
xix. 20. — 4 c
xix. 27. — 4 b
xx. 12. — 4 c
xxi. 13. — 4 e
xxi. 28. — 4 c
xxii. 17. — 2 d
xxiii. 19, 22. — 4 c
xxv. 10. — 4 e
xxviii. 9. — 4 b
xxix. 12. — 3 f
xxix. 24. — 4 d
Eccles. i. 8. — 4 b
v. 1. — 4 b
vii. 5, 5. — 4 b e
vii. 21. — 4 e
ix. 16, 17. — 4 i
xii. 13.η — 4 d
Cant. ii. 12. — 4 f
ii. 14. — 4 m
xiii. 13, 13. — 3 f, 4 m
Isa. i. 2, 10. — 4 c
i. 15. — 4 e
vi. 8, 10. — 4 d
vi. 9. — 4 c b
vii. 13. — 4 c
x. 30. — 3 d
xi. 3. — 4 s
xv. 4. — 4 f
xvi. 6. — 4 a
xviii. 3. — 4 d
xxi. 3. — 4 c
xxi. 7. — 3 b
xxi. 10. — 4 a
xxiv. 16. — 4 a
xxviii. 12. — 4 c
xxviii. 14. — 4 b
xxviii. 23, 23, 23. — 4 c, 3 d, 4 c
xxix. 18. — 4 c
xxx. 9, 19. — 4 b
xxx. 21. — 4 d
xxx. 30. — 4 e
xxxii. 3, 3. — 4 e, 3 a
xxxii. 9. — 4 c
xxxiii. 13. — 4 c
xxxiv. 1, 1, 1. — 4 b, 3 d, 4 d
xxxvi. 13. — 4 c
xxxvi. 16. — 4 b
xxxvii. 4, 4. — 4 d a
xxxvii. 6, 7, 8, 11, 26. —
xxxvii. 9, 9. — 4 a
xxxvii. 17, 17. — 4 c

Isa. xxxviii. 5. — 4 a
xxxix. 1. — 4 a
xxxix. 5. — 4 c
xl. 21. — 4 c
xl. 28. — 4 a
xli. 17. — 2 c
xli. 26. — 4 e
xlii. 2. — 4 n
xlii. 18. — 4 a
xlii. 20. — 4 d
xlii. 23, 23. — 3 e, 4 d
xliii. 9. — 4 d
xliv. 1. — 4 c
xlvi. 3. — 4 c
xlvi. 12. — 4 c
xlvii. 8. — 4 c
xlviii. 1, 12, 14, 16. — 4 a
xlviii. 6, 7, 8. — 4 a
xlviii. 18. — 3 d
xlix. 1. — 4 c
xlix. 8. — 2 a
l. 4. — 4 b
li. 1, 7, 21. — 4 c
li. 4. — 3 d
lii. 15. — 4 a
lv. 2. — 4 b c
lv. 3. — 4 l
lviii. 4. — 4 b
lix. 1, 2. — 4 h
lx. 18. — 4 a
lxiv. 4. — 4 a
lxv. 12. — 4 a
lxv. 19. — 4 h
lxv. 24. — 4 d
lxvi. 4, 8, 19. — 4 a
lxvi. 5. — 4 c
Jer. ii. 4. — 4 c
iii. 21. — 4 f
iv. 19, 31. — 4 a
iv. 21. — 4 d
v. 21, 21. — 4 c d
vi. 7. — 4 h
vi. 10, 10. — 4 d, 3 c
vi. 17, 17. — 3 d e
vi. 18. — 4 c
vi. 19, 19. — 4 c, 3 b
vi. 24. — 4 a
vii. 2. — 4 a
vii. 13, 24, 26. — 4 a
vii. 16. — 4 d
vii. 27. — 4 a
viii. 6, 6. — 3 b, 4 d
viii. 16. — 4 f
ix. 10. — 4 a
ix. 19. — 4 f
ix. 20. — 4 c
x. 1. — 4 c
xi. 2, 6. — 4 c
xi. 10. — 4 b
xi. 11. — 4 d
xi. 14. — 4 d
xiii. 10. — 4 b
xiii. 11. — 4 c
xiii. 15. — 4 c
xiii. 17. — 4 e
xiv. 12. — 4 e
xvi. 12. — 4 c
xvii. 20. — 4 e
xvii. 23. — 4 k
xvii. 24. — 4 b d
xvii. 27. — 4 n
xviii. 2. — 4 a
xviii. 13. — 4 a
xviii. 19. — 4 e
xviii. 22. — 4 e h
xix. 3, 3. — 4 b
xix. 15. — 4 b
xx. 1. — 4 a
xx. 10, 16. — 4 a
xxi. 11. — 4 c
xxii. 2, 29. — 4 c
xxii. 5, 21. — 4 b
xxiii. 16, 18, 18. — 4 d
xxiii. 22. — 4 a
xxiii. 25. — 4 a
xxv. 3, 7, 8. — 4 a
xxv. 4, 4. — 4 a b
xxvi. 3, 4, 7, 10, 21, 21. — 4 d
xxvi. 5. — 4 b a
xxvi. 11, 12. — 4 a
xxvi. 14, 16, 17. — 4 d
xxviii. 7, 15. — 4 d
xxix. 8. — 4 d
xxix. 12, 19, 19. — 4 a
xxix. 20. — 4 c

Jer. xxx. 5. — 4 a
xxxi. 10. — 4 c
xxxi. 15. — 4 f
xxxi. 18. — 4 b a
xxxii. 33. — 4 e
xxxiii. 9. — 4 d
xxxiii. 10. — 4 h
xxxiv. 10. — 4 c
xxxiv. 14, 17. — 4 d
xxxv. 13. — 4 b
xxxv. 14, 15, 16, 17. — 4 a
xxxvi. 3, 11. — 4 d
xxxvi. 13, 25, 31. — 4 a
xxxvi. 16. — 4 b
xxxvi. 24. — 4 e
xxxvii. 2, 14. — 4 a
xxxvii. 5. — 4 c
xxxvii. 20. — 4 c
xxxviii. 1, 7, 15, 25. — 4 d
xl. 7. — 4 d
xl. 11. — 4 d
xli. 11. — 4 d
xlii. 4. — 4 a
xlii. 15. — 4 c
xliv. 5. — 4 a
xliv. 16. — 4 e
xliv. 24, 26. — 4 c
xlvi. 12. — 4 a
xlvii. 4. — 4 k
xlviii. 5, 29. — 4 a
xlix. 2. — 4 k
xlix. 14, 23. — 4 c
xlix. 20. — 4 c
xlix. 21. — 4 f
l. 43. — 4 a
l. 45. — 4 c
l. 46. — 4 f
li. 46. — 4 i
li. 51. — 4 c
Lam. i. 18. — 4 c
i. 21, 21. — 4 a
iii. 56, 61. — 4 a
Ezek. i. 24, 28. — 4 d

Ezek. ii. 2, 5, 7. — 4 d
ii. 8. — 4 c
iii. 6, 11, 12. — 4 d
iii. 7, 7. — 4 c
iii. 10. — 4 c
iii. 17. — 4 a
iii. 27, 27. — 4 e d
vi. 3. — 4 c
viii. 18. — 4 d
ix. 5. — 1 c
x. 5. — 4 f
x. 13. — 1 c
xii. 2, 2. — 4 b a
xiii. 2. — 4 c
xiii. 19. — 4 e
xvi. 35. — 4 c
xviii. 25. — 4 c
xix. 9. — 4 h
xx. 8. — 4 b
xx. 39. — 4 e
xx. 47. — 4 c
xxiv. 26. — 4 t
xxv. 3. — 4 c
xxvi. 13. — 4 h
xxvii. 30. — 4 k
xxxiii. 4. — 4 e a
xxxiii. 5, 7, 31, 32. — 4 a
xxxiii. 30. — 4 c
xxxiv. 7, 9. — 4 c
xxxv. 12, 13. — 4 a
xxxvi. 1, 4. — 4 c
xxxvi. 5. — 4 n
xxxvii. 4. — 4 c
xl. 4. — 4 d
xliii. 6. — 4 d
xliv. 5. — 4 d
Dan. iii. 5, 10, 15. — 4 p
iii. 7. — 4 o
v. 14, 16. — 4 o
v. 23. — 4 o
vi. 14. — 4 o
viii. 13, 16. — 4 a
ix. 6. — 4 a
ix. 17, 18. — 4 a

Dan. ix. 19, 19. — 4 c, 3 d
x. 9, 9. — 4 d b
x. 12. — 4 f
xii. 7. — 4 d
xii. 8. — 4 a
Hos. ii. 21, 21, 21, 22, 22. — 2 c
iv. 1. — 4 c
v. 1, 1. — 4 c, 3 d
vii. 12. — 4 r
ix. 17. — 4 a
xiv. 8. — 2 a
Joel i. 2. — 4 c
Amos iii. 1, 13. — 4 c
iv. 1. — 4 c
v. 1. — 4 c
v. 23. — 4 d
vii. 16. — 4 c
viii. 4. — 4 c
Obad. i. — 4 a
Jonah ii. 2, 2. — 2 c, 4 a
Mic. i. 2, 2. — 4 c, 3 d
iii. 1, 9. — 4 c
iii. 4. — 2 c
v. 15. — 4 a
vi. 1, 1. — 4 c d
vi. 2, 9. — 4 d
vii. 7. — 4 d
Nah. i. 13. — 4 h
iii. 19. — 4 e
Hab. i. 2. — 4 a
iii. 2, 16. — 4 a
Zeph. ii. 8. — 4 a
Zech. i. 4, 4. — 4 a, 3 b
iii. 8. — 4 c
vii. 11, 11. — 3 c, 4 b
vii. 12. — 4 b
vii. 13, 13. — 4 a
viii. 9. — 4 e
viii. 23. — 4 a
x. 6. — 2 c
Mal. ii. 2. — 3 e, 4 d

α lit. the Egyptians heard and the house of Pharaoh heard. β "heard tell." γ lit. a hearer heareth. δ lit. at the hearing of the ear. ε lit. hearing hear. ζ or, mayest thou hear. η marg. 'hath been heard,' as if NIPHAL pret.

HEART

1   בַּל   Ch. m. heart : Dan. vi. 14.

2   לֵב   This word, in its primary meaning, is supposed to express quick and constant motion to and fro, and to be the root from which לֵב m. the heart, is deduced. The Niphal of the verb is denominative of לֵב, to be heartened, prudent, wise. In Piel the sense is much the same, to excite the heart, to enflame the heart ; which however, in our translation, has a primitive sense assigned to it. PIEL pret. Cant. iv. 9, "hath ravished," marg. 'taken away.' This may, however, be a rendering according to popular notions ; to ravish the heart, and to enflame the heart, expressing the same effect. לֵבָב and לֵב the heart ; seldom used of the material heart, or of the heart of brutes : 2 Sam. xviii. 14, &c. ; the fountain of life in the blood, and therefore put for life, or the principle of natural life ; comp. Jer. iv. 18 with 10, נֶפֶשׁ. The heart is the seat of feeling and the affections, and takes those epithets and verbs which designate the affections themselves. But the Hebrews regard it more generally as likewise the seat of intellect ; hence, (1) mind, purpose, intention ; (2) understanding, knowledge, insight ; (3) courage, spirit. With suffixes, it forms a periphrasis of the personal pronouns. In some cases, heart is used for stomach, as in the Greek καρδιαλγία. A heart and heart, is put for a double or deceitful heart, Ps. xii. 3, comp. 1 Chron. xii. 33. A man after his own heart,

1 Sam. xiii. 14, *comp.* ii. 35, Jer. iii. 15. ᶜלֵב Ch. *m. id.*
ᵈ לְבַב Ch. *m. id.* ᵉ לִבָּה *f. id.*

3 נֶפֶשׁ *com.* animal life, the soul.

4 מֵעִים *m. pl.* bowels ; *or*, the heart : Ps. xl. 8.

5 קִיר *m.* a wall : Jer. iv. 19, probably the præcordia of the heart.

6 קֶרֶב *m.* middle, inner part ; bowels ; heart, as the seat of thought and affection.

7 שֶׂכְוִי *m.* the mind ; intelligence.

No. 2 b not included.

Exod. xxiii. 9.	3	Prov. xxi. 2.	2 e	Lam. iii. 51.	3
Lev. xxvi. 16.	3	xxiii. 7.	3	Ezek. xvi. 30.	2 e
Deut. xxiv. 15.	3	xxiv. 12.	2 e	xxv. 6, 15.	3
1 Sam. ii. 33.	3	xxvii. 9.	3	xxvii. 31.	3
2 Sam. iii. 21.	3	xxviii. 25.	3	Dan. ii. 30.	2 d
Job xxxviii. 36.	7	Cant. iv. 9, 9.	2 a	iv. 16, 16.	2 d
Ps. vii. 9.	2 e	Isa. xliv. 18.	2 e	v. 20, 21, 22.	2 d
x. 3.	3	Jer. xix. 19.	5, 2 b	vi. 14.	1
xl. 8.	4	ix. 8.	6	vii. 4.	2 d
cxxv. 4.	2 e	xlii. 20.	3	vii. 28.	2 c
Prov. xv. 11.	2 e			Hos. iv. 8.	3
xvii. 3.	2 e				

HEARTH

אָח *f.* a hearth, rather a dish or vessel, such as is used in the present day in Eastern countries : Jer. xxxvi. 22, 23, 23.

יָקַד to burn, as a culinary fire. KAL *part.* Paül. Isa. xxx. 14. מוֹקֵד *m.* burning ; or hearth ; or wood burned : Ps. cii. 3.

כִּיוֹר *m.* a laver, a pan of fire : Zech. xii. 6.

HEAT, HOT

1 אֲזָא Ch. to heat. P'AL ᵃ *inf.* ᵇ *part. passive.*

2 בָּעַר to burn. KAL *part.* Poel.

3 חָמַם to be warm, and cause warmth : it is used chiefly of a corporeal substance which receives or gives out heat or warmth, and communicates it to another body of the same substance and nature ; as of a man warmed by the fire, of two lying together, of the sun causing the day to be warm. In Piel, of a bird warming and hatching its eggs, θάλπειν. When, therefore, it applies to anger, zeal, or desire of any kind, it implies that which has been cherished and enflamed. KAL ᵃ *pret.* NIPHAL ᵇ *fut.* ᶜ חָם *adj.* hot. ᵈ חֹם *m.* heat.

4 חֹרֶב drought.

5 חָרָה to be warm, to fume. KAL ᵃ *pret.* ᵇ *fut.* ᶜ חֲרִי *m.*

6 יָחַם to be hot with anger, &c. KAL ᵃ *fut.* ᵇ חַמָּה *f.* heat of the sun. ᶜ חֵמָה *f.* "hot displeasure." Anger is said to be the heat of the blood about the heart.

7 שָׁרָב *m.* heat of the sun : Isa. xlix. 10.

Gen. viii. 22.	3 d	1 Sam. xi. 9, 11.	3 d	Isa. iv. 6.	4
xviii. 1.	3 d	xxi. 6.	3 d	xviii. 4, 4.	3 d
Exod. xvi. 21.	3 a	2 Sam. iv. 5.	3 d	xxv. 4, 5.	4
xxii. 24.	5 a	1 Kings i. 1.	6 a	xlix. 10.	7
xxxii. 10, 11, 19,		i. 2. a	3 a	Jer. xvii. 8.	3 d
22.	5 b	Neh. vii. 3.	3 d	xxxvi. 30.	4
Deut. ix. 19.	6 c	Job vi. 17.	3 d	li. 39.	3 d
xix. 6.	6 a	xxiv. 19.	3 d	Ezek. iii. 14.	6 c
xxix. 24.	5 c	xxx. 30.	4	xxiv. 11.	6 a
Josh. ix. 12.	3 c	Ps. vi. 1.	6 c	Dan. iii. 19, 19.	1 a
Judg. ii. 14, 20.	5 b	xix. 6.	6 b	iii. 22.	1 b
iii. 8.	5 b	xxxviii. 1.	6 c	Hos. vii. 4.	2
vi. 39.	5 b	xxxix. 3.	3 a	vii. 7.	3 b
x. 7.	5 b	Eccles. iv. 11.	3 a		

ᵃ *lit.* heat may be to my lord.

HEATH

עַרְעָר *adj. lit.* naked. Lxx., Vulg., Chald. *myrica,* tamarisk tree ; others, juniper : Jer. xvii. 6. עֲרוֹעֵר *m. id.* Jer. xlviii. 6.

HEATHEN

גּוֹי people, nation, in the widest sense ; more especially, in the *pl.*, foreign nations, nations not Hebrew, often in the sense of enemies, barbarians : Lev. xxv. 44 ; xxvi. 33, 38, 45, &c. This is the only word translated " heathen."

HEAVE

רוּם to be lifted up ; Hiphil, to lift up, to bring as an offering, by a particular rite, to heave an offering, in presenting it to God. HIPHIL *inf.* Num. xviii. 30, 32. *fut.* Num. xv. 20. HOPHAL *pret.* Exod. xxix. 27. תְּרוּמָה *f.* an offering, a heave-offering : Exod. xxix. 27, 28, 28, 28 : Lev. vii. 14, 32, 34, *lit.* shoulder of heave-offering ; x. 14, 15 : Num. vi. 20 ; xv. 19, 20, 20, 21 ; xviii. 8, 11, 19, 24, 26, 27, 28, 28, 29 ; xxxi. 29, 41 : Deut. xii. 6, 11, 17.

HEAVEN

גַּלְגַּל *m.* that which is round ; so, as some think, the round orb of the sky ; others, a whirlwind : Ps. lxxvii. 18, " thy thunder was in the whirlwind or storm." Hengstenberg says the word is never clearly used of a whirlwind, and would render it whirled round, *lit.* in a whirl.

עֲרָבָה *f.* usually rendered, plain ; and, in Ps. lxviii. 4, may very suitably be intended to express the large expanse of the heavens, through which Jehovah rides, as it were, on the storm. Hengstenberg, in the deserts, as the context seems to require.

עֲרִיפִים *m.* droppings ; clouds, heavens ; Syr. and Vulg. darkness : Isa. v. 30 ; probably in the gloomy clouds ready to distil the rain. *Comp.* עָרַף Deut. xxxii. 2, and xxxiii. 28.

שַׁחַק *m.* dust ; clouds, the skies, heaven : Ps. lxxxix. 6, 37.

שָׁמַיִם *m.* heaven, from its height ; the air or atmosphere, the firmament : Gen. i. 9. The heaven of heavens, may be either the vast space beyond our atmosphere, or beyond all the worlds, perhaps in the centre of the universe, the supposed residence of God himself : the end or side of heaven is the horizon, where the earth and skies seem to meet : Deut. iv. 32, *lit.* from the side of heaven unto the side of heaven. Gen. i. 1, &c.

שְׁמַיִן Ch. *m. dual,* Ezra v. 11, 12 ; vi. 9, 10 ; vii. 12, 21, 23, 23 : Jer. x. 11, 11 : Dan. ii. 18, 19, 28, 37, 38, 44 ; iv. 11, 12, 13, 15, 20, 21, 22, 23, 23, 25, 26, 31, 33, 34, 35, 37 ; v. 21, 23 ; vi. 27 ; vii. 2, 13, 27.

HEAVY

1 אֲגֻדָּה *f.* a collection, a bunch. See *Burden.*

2 תַּאֲנִיָּה *f.* mourning, sadness, sorrow.

3 דְּאָנָה *f.* fearful, anxious solicitude.

4 תּוּגָה *f.* grief and anguish, which gall and tear the heart, and give most painful sorrow.

5   כָּבֵד   to be heavy ; this is the primary and proper sense, as applied to sand, Job vi. 3 ; and to a chain, Lam. iii. 7 : it is also used of sin, Gen. xviii. 20 ; of the hand of a conqueror, Judg. i. 35 ; of the hand of God punishing, Ps. xxxii. 4, 1 Sam. v. 11, *comp.* Job xxiii. 2.   It implies sometimes trouble, riches, number, vehemence. As things heavy are not easily moved, so it is used of dulness in the senses, Gen. xlviii. 10 ; and of hardness of heart, Exod. ix. 7 ; of that which is troublesome, Prov. xxvii. 3, *comp.* Sir. xxii. 15 ; of that which is difficult, Exod. xviii. 18, Num. xi. 14. KAL [a] *pret.* [b] *fut.* HIPHIL [c] *pret.* [d] *imp.* [e] כָּבֵד *adj.* [f] כֹּבֶד *m.* heaviness, vehemence. [g] כְּבֵדָת *f. id.*

6   כֵּהָה   *adj. f.* blunted ; applied to faintness of the spirit, when the vigour of the mind is dulled and enfeebled.

7   מַר   *adj.* bitter : Prov. xxxi. 6.

8   מוֹטָה   *f.* a yoke : Isa. lviii. 6, " heavy burdens," *marg.* ' bundles of the yoke.' It does not seem very clear which translation was intended for this word, heavy or burden.

9   נָשׁ   to be sick ; from which comes νόσος νοῦσος. KAL *fut.*

10   סַר   *adj.* discontented, displeased, sullen.

11   תַּעֲנִית   *f.* self-humiliation, mortification, fasting.

12   פָּנִים   *m. pl.* face, aspect : Job ix. 27.

13   קָדַר   to be black, dark-coloured ; to mourn. KAL *part.* Poel.

14   קָשֶׁה   *adj.* hard, rough.

15   רַע   *adj.* wicked, evil ; applied to a mind broken or shattered with grief or vexation.

Exod. xiv. 25.	a	2 Chron. x. 10, 14.	5 c	Prov. xiv. 13.		4
xvii. 12.	5 e	Ezra ix. 5.	11	xxv. 20.		15
xviii. 18.	5 e	Neh. ix. 5.	5 e	xxvii. 3, 3.		5 f e
Num. xi. 14.	5 e	Job vi. 3.	5 b	xxix. 6.		7
1 Sam. iv. 18.	5 a	ix. 27.	12	Isa. vi. 10.		5 d
v. 6.	5 b	xxiii. 2.	5 a	xxiv. 20.		5 a
v. 11.	5 a	xxxiii. 7.	5 b	xxix. 2.		2
2 Sam. xiv. 26.	5 a	Ps. xxxii. 4.	5 b	xxx. 27.		5 f
1 Kings xii. 4, 11.	5 e	xxxv. 14.	13	xlvii. 6.		5 c
xii. 10, 14.	5 c	xxxviii. 4, 4.	5 e b	lviii. 6.		8, 1
xiv. 6.	14	lxix. 20.	9	lix. 1.		5 a
xx. 43.	10	cxix. 28.	4	lix. 3.		6
xxi. 4.	10	Prov. x. 1.	4	Lam. iii. 7.		5 c
2 Chron. x. 4, 11.	5 e	xii. 25.	3			

a lit. with heaviness.

HEDGE

1   גָּדַר   to fence, to wall up ; the word refers rather to a stone wall, as it is translated in Isa. v. 5, than to a thorn hedge, which is the meaning of מְשׂוּכָה. KAL [a] *pret.* [b] גָּדֵר *com.* a wall. [c] גְּדֵרָה *f.* wall, place fortified by a wall, a fold.

2   סָכַךְ   to cover, to protect. HIPHIL *fut.*

3   שׂוּךְ   to hedge in, to hedge about ; either in a way of protection or to prevent escape. KAL [a] *pret.* [b] *part.* [c] מְשׂוּכָה *f.* a hedge of briers and thorns. [d] *f. id.*

1 Chron. iv. 23.	1 c	Prov. xv. 19.	3 c	Ezek. xiii. 5.	1 b
Job i. 10.	3 a	Eccles. x. 8.	1 b	xxii. 30.	1 b
iii. 23.	2	Isa. v. 5.	3 c	Hos. ii. 6.	3 b
Ps. lxxx. 12.	1 b	Jer. xlix. 3.	1 c	Micah vii. 4.	3 d
lxxxix. 40.	1 c	Lam. iii. 7.	1 a	Nah. iii. 17.	1 c

HEED

1   אָזַן   to weigh, to balance, to examine ; or as a denominative from אֹזֶן the ear ; to give ear, to listen attentively ; to give good heed. PIEL *pret.*

2   זָהַר   Ch. to take heed. P'AL *part.*

3   לֵב   *m.* heart : Eccles. vii. 21, *marg.* ' give not thine heart.'

4   סָכַת   to be silent, to attend. HIPHIL *imp.*

5   קָשַׁב   to dispose the ear, or mind, to ready, earnest, serious attention ; to give heed. HIPHIL [a] *imp.* [b] *fut.* [c] *part.* [d] קֶשֶׁב *m.* attention.

6   רָאָה   to see ; to take heed. KAL *imp.*

7   שָׁמַר   to keep watch, guard ; to watch, mark, observe ; to take heed, beware. KAL [a] *pret.* [b] *inf.* [c] *imp.* [d] *fut.* NIPHAL [e] *pret.* [f] *imp.*

Gen. xxxi. 24, 29.	7 f	1 Sam. xix. 2.	7 f	Ps. xxxix. 1.	7 d
Exod. x. 28.	7 f	2 Sam. xx. 10.	7 e	cxix. 9.	7 b
xix. 12.	7 f	1 Kings ii. 4.	7 d	Prov. xvii. 4.	5 c
xxxiv. 12.	7 f	viii. 25.	7 d	Eccles. vii. 21.	3
Num. xxiii. 12.	7 d	2 Kings x. 31.	7 a	xii. 9.	1
Deut. ii. 4.	7 e	1 Chron. xxii. 13.	7 d	Isa. vii. 4.	7 f
iv. 9, 23.	7 f	xxviii. 10.	6	xxi. 7.	5 d
iv. 15.	7 e	2 Chron. vi. 16.	7 d	Jer. ix. 4.	7 f
xi. 16.	7 f	xix. 6.	6	xvii. 21.	7 f
xii. 13, 19, 30.	7 f	xix. 7.	7 c	xviii. 18.	5 b
xxiv. 8.	7 f	xxxiii. 8.	7 d	xviii. 19.	5 a
xxvii. 9.	7 d	Ezra iv. 22.	2	Hos. iv. 10.	7 b
Josh. xxii. 5.	7 c	Job xxxvi. 21.	7 f	Mal. ii. 15, 16.	7 e
xxiii. 11.	7 e				

HEEL

עָקֵב   *m.* the heel : Gen. iii. 15 ; xxv. 26 ; xlix. 17 : Job xviii. 9 : Ps. xli. 9 ; xlix. 5 : Jer. xiii. 22. עָקַב to take by the heel. KAL *pret.* Hos. xii. 3.

שֹׁרֶשׁ   *m.* a root ; the lowest part of anything, the sole of the foot : Job xiii. 27.

HEIFER

בָּקָר   *com.* cattle (most commonly) at full age ; *collect.* herd : Deut. xxi. 3, *lit.* an heifer of the herd : 1 Sam. xvi. 2, *lit. id.*

עֶגְלָה   *f.* a steer ; a bullock ; a heifer : Gen. xv. 9 : Deut. xxi. 3, 4, 4, 6 : Judg. xiv. 18 : 1 Sam. xvi. 2 : Isa. xv. 5 : Jer. xlvi. 20 : xlviii. 34 : l. 11 : Hos. x. 11.

פָּרָה   *f.* a young cow, or heifer : Num. xix. 2, 5, 6, 9, 10 : Hos. iv. 16.

HEIGHT

1   בָּמָה   *f.* a high place.

2   גָּבַהּ   to be high ; to raise up a great height ; to exalt. HIPHIL [a] *inf.* [b] *fut.* [c] גֹּבַהּ *m.* height. [d] גָּבֹהַּ *adj.* high, lofty.

3   קוֹמָה   *f.* height : Gen. vi. 15, &c.

4   רֹאשׁ   *m.* head ; first in order ; summit.

5   רוּם   *m.* height. [a] רוּם Ch. *id.* [b] רָמוּת *f.* a heap, pile. [c] מָרוֹם *m.* height ; a lofty, fortified place.

No. 3 not included.

1 Sam. xvi. 7.	2 d	Prov. xxv. 3.	5	Ezek. xx. 40.	5 c
xvii. 4.	2 c	Isa. vii. 11. a	2 a	xxxi. 10, 10.	3, 2 c
2 Kings xix. 23.	5 a	xiv. 14.	1	xxxi. 14, 14.	3, 2 c
2 Chron. iii. 4.	2 c	xxxvii. 24, 24.	5 c	xxxii. 5.	5 b
xxxiii. 14.	5 a	Jer. xxxi. 12.	5 c	xli. 8.	2 c
Ezra vi. 3.	5 a	xlix. 16.	5 c	Dan. iii. 1.	5 a
Job xxii. 12, 12.	2 c, 4	li. 53.	5 c	iv. 10, 11, 20.	5 a
Ps. cii. 19.	5 c	Ezek. xvii. 23.	5 c	Amos ii. 9, 9.	2 c
cxlviii. 1.	5 c	xix. 11.	2 c		

a or, to exalt ; *inf. abs., lit.* making high to above.

HEIR

יָרַשׁ to possess, either by inheritance, gift, or violence, what belongs to others; to be heir. KAL *pret.* Jer. xlix. 2. *fut.* Gen. xv. 4, 4; xxi. 10: Prov. xxx. 23. *part.* Poel, Gen. xv. 3: 2 Sam. xiv. 7: Jer. xlix. 1, 2: Micah i. 15.

HELKATH-HAZZURIM.

חֶלְקָה *f.* a field. צוּר *m.* a rock: 2 Sam. ii. 16, *marg.* 'the field of strong men.'

HELL

שְׁאוֹל *com.* Whatever be the derivation of this word, there can be no doubt of the scriptural application of it to the state and abode of the dead; hence the grave in which the body rests, and the invisible world, to which the souls of men depart in death. Poetically, this state is said to have gates, which shews that something more than the grave is meant, although the sepulchres of Palestine appear to have had commonly gates or doors, opening along grooves or on hinges. We have also, Job xi. 8, "Deeper than hell what canst thou know?" It is the invisible state, not the grave, which has a depth that cannot be known: Deut. xxxii. 22: 2 Sam. xxii. 6: Job xi. 8; xxvi. 6: Ps. ix. 17; xvi. 10; xviii. 5; lv. 15; lxxxvi. 13; cxvi. 3; cxxxix. 8: Prov. v. 5; vii. 27; ix. 18; xv. 11, 24; xxiii. 14; xxvii. 20: Isa. v. 14; xiv. 9, 15; xxviii. 15, 18; lvii. 9: Ezek. xxxi. 16, 17; xxxii. 21, 27: Amos ix. 2: Jonah ii. 2: Hab. ii. 5.

HELMET

כּוֹבַע *m.* a helmet, of a round form, rising a little on the top of the head, as may be seen in the ancient sculptures, especially those lately discovered at Nineveh: 1 Sam. xvii. 5: 2 Chron. xxvi. 14: Isa. lix. 17: Jer. xlvi. 4: Ezek. xxvii. 10; xxxviii. 5.

קוֹבַע *m. id.* 1 Sam. xvii. 38: Ezek. xxiii. 24.

HELP

1 זְרוֹעַ *com.* arm: Ps. lxxxiii. 8, *marg.* 'they have been an arm to.'

2 חָזַק to be strong, to prevail. PIEL [a] *fut.* HIPHIL [b] *fut.*

3 יָד *com.* hand: Job viii. 20, *lit.* take by the hand.

4 יָשַׁע to save. HIPHIL [a] *pret.* [b] *inf.* [c] *imp.* [d] *fut.* [e] יְשׁוּעָה *f.* deliverance. [f] תְּשׁוּעָה *f.* deliverance, salvation.

5 נָשָׂא to bear; in Piel implying advantageous action, to help, assist. PIEL [a] *part.* [b] *fut.*

6 סְעַד Ch. to help, aid, assist. APHEL *part.*

7 עָזַב to leave. KAL [a] *inf.* Exod. xxiii. 5, *lit.* thou shalt forbear to leave to him, *i. e.* to the owner alone; 5. [b] *fut.* Exod. xxiii. 5, *lit.* thou shalt surely leave with him, *i. e.* not leave without helping him.

8 עָזַר to help, aid, assist; as one succours the miserable and destitute, Job xxvi. 2, xxix. 12: especially of God: as allies assist in war, 1 Kings xx. 16. KAL [a] *pret.* [b] *inf.* [c] *imp.* [d] *fut.* [e] *part.* Poel. [f] *part.* Paül. NIPHAL [g] *pret.* [h] *inf.* [i] *fut.* HIPHIL [k] *part.* [l] עֵזֶר *m.* aid, help. [m] עֶזְרָה *f. id.*

9 קוּם to rise up, to raise up. HIPHIL [a] *inf.* Deut. xxii. 4, *lit.* raising up thou shalt raise up with him. [b] *fut.*

10 קָרָא to meet. KAL *inf.*

Gen. ii. 18, 20.	8 l	2 Chron. xxix. 34.	2 a	Ps. lxxxvi. 17.	8 a
xlix. 25.	8 d	xxxii. 8.	8 b	lxxxix. 19.	8 l
Exod. ii. 17.	4 d	Ezra i. 4.	5 b	xciv. 17.	8 m
xviii. 4.	8 l	v. 2.	6	cvii. 12.	8 e
xxiii. 5, 5, 5.	7 a a b	viii. 22.	8 a	cviii. 12, 12.	8 m, 4 f
Deut. xxii. 4, 4.	9 a b	x. 15.	8 a	cix. 26.	8 c
xxxii. 38.	8 d	Esth. ix. 3.	5 a	cxv. 9, 10, 11.	8 l
xxxiii. 7, 26, 29.	8 a	Job vi. 13.	8 m	cxvi. 6.	4 d
Josh. i. 14.	8 a	viii. 20.	2 b, 3	cxviii. 7.	8 a
x. 4, 6.	8 c	ix. 13.	8 e	cxviii. 13.	8 a
x. 33.	8 b	xxvi. 2.	8 a	cxix. 86.	8 c
Judg. v. 23, 23.	8 m	xxix. 12.	8 a	cxix. 173.	8 b
1 Sam. vii. 12.	8 a	xxx. 13.	8 e	cxix. 175.	8 d
xi. 9.	4 f	xxxi. 21.	8 m	cxxi. 1, 2.	8 l
2 Sam. x. 11, 11.	4 e b	Ps. iii. 2.	4 e	cxxiv. 8.	8 l
x. 19.	4 c	x. 14.	8 e	cxlvi. 3.	4 f
xiv. 4.	4 c	xii. 1.	4 c	cxlvi. 5.	8 l
1 Kings i. 7.	8 d	xxii. 1.	8 b	Eccles. iv. 10.	9 a
xx. 16.	8 b	xxii. 11.	8 e	Isa. x. 3.	8 m
2 Kings vi. 26.	4 c	xxii. 19.	8 m	xx. 6.	8 m
vi. 27, 27.	4 d	xxvii. 9.	8 m	xxx. 5.	8 l
xiv. 26.	8 e	xxviii. 7.	8 g	xxx. 7.	8 d
1 Chron. v. 20.	8 i	xxx. 10.	8 e	xxxi. 1, 2.	8 m
xii. 1.	8 e	xxxiii. 20.	8 l	xxxi. 3, 3.	8 e f
xii. 17, 22.	8 b	xxxv. 2.	8 m	xli. 6.	8 e
xii. 18, 18.	8 e a	xxxvii. 40.	8 d	xli. 10, 13, 14.	8 a
xii. 19, 21.	8 a	xxxviii. 22.	8 m	xlii. 2.	8 d
xv. 26.	8 b	xl. 13, 17.	8 m	xlix. 8.	8 d
xviii. 5.	8 b	xlii. 5.γ	4 e	l. 7, 9.	8 d
xix. 12, 12.	4 f a	xliv. 26.	8 m	lxiii. 5.	8 e
xix. 19.	4 b	xlvi. 1.	8 m	Jer. xxxvii. 7.	8 m
xxii. 17.	8 b	xlvi. 5.	8 d	xlvii. 4.	8 e
2 Chron. xiv. 11, 11.	8 b c	liv. 4.	8 e	Lam. i. 7.	8 e
xviii. 31.	8 a	lix. 4.	10	iv. 17.	8 m
xix. 2.	8 b	lx. 11, 11.	8 m, 4 f	Ezek. xii. 14.	8 l
xx. 9.	4 d	lxiii. 7.	8 m	xxx. 8.	8 e
xx. 23.	8 a	lxx. 1.	8 m	xxxii. 21.	8 e
xxv. 8.	8 b	lxx. 5.	8 l	Dan. x. 13.	8 b
xxvi. 7.	8 d	lxxii. 12.	8 m	xi. 34, 34.	8 i l
xxvi. 13. α	8 b	lxxix. 9.	8 e	xi. 45.	8 m
xxvi. 15.	8 h	lxxxiii. 8.	1	Hos. xiii. 9.	8 l
xxviii. 16.	8 b			Nah. iii. 9.	8 l
xxviii. 21. β	8 m			Zech. i. 15.	8 m, 8 a
xxviii. 23, 23.	8 k d				

α *lit.* he marvelled to be helpen. β *lit.* was not for a help to him. γ *or*, his presence is salvation.

HELVE

עֵץ *m.* tree, wood: Deut. xix. 5.

HEM

שׁוּל *m.* the skirts of a garment: Exod. xxviii. 33, 33, 34; xxxix. 24, 25, 26.

HEMLOCK

לַעֲנָה *f.* see *Wormwood.* Amos vi. 12.

רֹאשׁ *m.* a poisonous plant, Deut. xxix. 18; which grows in fields, Hos. x. 4; bears fruit in clusters, Deut. xxxii. 32 (unless this verse fall under the general signification of poison); and is bitter, Ps. lxix. 21, Lam. iii. 5; see *Gall.* —Hos. x. 4.

HENCEFORTH

יָסַף to add. HIPHIL *fut.* Gen. iv. 12, *lit.* it shall not add to give: Judg. xxi. 21, *lit.* will not add to drive out.

HEPHZIBAH

חֵפֶץ *m.* delight: Isa. lxii. 4, *marg.* 'my delight is in her.'

HERALD

כָּרוֹז Ch. *m.* one that makes proclamation: Dan. iii. 4.

HERB

1 אוֹר light: Isa. xviii. 4. Most critics render אוֹר herbs; the Rabbins, rain; but Henderson, sunshine; comp. Hab. iii. 4. [a] אוֹרֹת f. pl. herbs. In the Shemitish languages, the ideas of sprouting, being green, flourishing, are connected in many words with that of shining; see *Flower*.

2 דֶּשֶׁא m. grass, tender herb.

3 חָצִיר m. grass.

4 יֶרֶק m. green.

5 עֵשֶׂב m. green herbs.

Gen. i. 11, 12, 29, 30.	5	1 Kings xxi. 2.	4	Prov. xv. 17.	4
ii. 5.	5	2 Kings iv. 39.	1 a	xxvii. 25.	5
iii. 18.	5	xix. 26.	2	Isa. xviii. 4.	1
ix. 3.	5	Job viii. 12.	3	xxvi. 19.	1 a
Exod. ix. 22, 25.	5	xxxviii. 27.	2	xxxvii. 27.	2
x. 12, 15, 15.	5	Ps. xxxvii. 2.	2	xlii. 15.	5
Deut. xi. 10.	4	civ. 14.	5	lxvi. 14.	5
xxxii. 2.	2	cv. 35.	5	Jer. xii. 4.	5

HERD

בָּקָר com. horned cattle (most commonly), at full age, when fit for the plough; *collect.* cattle, herd: Gen. xiii. 5, &c. בּוֹקֵר m. a herdman: Amos vii. 14.

נֹקֵד m. see *Sheep-master*; or, more particularly, keeper of a peculiar breed of sheep and goats, small and stunted: Amos i. 1.

עֵדֶר m. an orderly collection of cattle; flocks, herds: Prov. xxvii. 23: Joel i. 18.

מִקְנֶה m. cattle, as a possession: Gen. xlvii. 18.

רָעָה to feed cattle. KAL *part.* Poel, feeder, herdman: Gen. xiii. 7, 7, 8, 8; xxvi. 20, 20: 1 Sam. xxi. 7.

HERE

זָרַק to sprinkle. KAL *pret.* Hos. vii. 9, "are here and there," *marg.* 'sprinkled.'

מָצָא to find. NIPHAL *part.* Gen. xix. 15, "which are here," *marg.* 'are found.' Ch. which are found faithful with thee.

HERITAGE

1 יְרֻשָּׁה f. possession, inheritance. [a] מוֹרָשָׁה f. id.

2 נָחַל to inherit. KAL [a] *pret.* [b] נַחֲלָה f. inheritance. [c] נַחֲלָה f.id.

Exod. vi. 8.	1 a	Ps. cxxvii. 3.	2 b	Jer. xii. 7, 8, 9, 15.	2 b
Job xx. 29.	2 b	cxxxv. 12, 12.	2 b	xvii. 4.	2 b
xxvii. 13.	2 b	cxxxvi. 21, 22.	2 b	l. 11.	2 b
Ps. xxvi. 6.	2 c	Isa. xlix. 8.	2 b	Joel ii. 17.	2 b
lxi. 5.	1	liv. 17.	2 b	iii. 2.	2 b
xciv. 5.	2 b	lviii. 14.	2 b	Micah ii. 2.	2 b
cxi. 6.	2 b	Jer. ii. 7.	2 b	vii. 14, 18.	2 b
cxix. 111.	2 a	iii. 19.	2 b	Mal. i. 3.	2 b

HERON

אֲנָפָה f. an unclean bird of several species: Lev. xi. 19: Deut. xiv. 18.

HEW

1 גְּדַד Ch. to cut, to hew down. P'AL *imp.*

2 גָּדַע to cut; to hew down; to break in pieces, to root out. KAL [a] *part.* Paül. PIEL [b] *fut.*

3 גָּזִית f. hewn stones; *lit.* stones of hewing, אַבְנֵי understood, except in 1 Kings v. 17, Ezek. xl. 42.

4 חָטַב to hew wood. KAL [a] *inf.* [b] *part.* Poel.

5 חָצַב to hew, to hew out, especially stones. KAL [a] *pret.* [b] *inf.* [c] *part.* Poel. PUAL [d] *pret.* [e] מֶחְצָב m. hewing.

6 כָּרַת to cut, to cut off, to hew down. KAL [a] *inf.* [b] *imp.* [c] *fut.*

7 נָתַח to cut in pieces. PIEL *fut.*

8 פָּסַל to cut or hew out of stone. KAL [a] *imp.* [b] *fut.*

9 קָמַל to languish, to wither. KAL *pret.*

10 שָׂסַף to hew in pieces. PIEL *fut.*

Exod. xx. 25.	3	1 Kings v. 18.	8 b	Isa. x. 33.	2 a
xxxiv. 1.	8 a	vi. 36.	3	xxii. 16, 16.	5 a c
xxxiv. 4.	8 b	vii. 9, 11, 12.	3	xxxiii. 9.	3
Deut. x. 1.	8 a	2 Kings xii. 12, 12.	5 c e	xliv. 14.	6 a
x. 3.	8 b	xxii. 6.	5 e	li. 1.	5 d
xii. 3.	2 b	1 Chron. xxii. 2.	5 b	Jer. ii. 13.	5 b
xix. 5.	4 a	xxii. 15.	5 c	vi. 6.	6 b
xxix. 11.	4 b	2 Chron. ii. 2, 18.	5 c	xlvi. 22.	4 b
Josh. ix. 21, 23, 27.	4 b	ii. 10.	4 b	Lam. iii. 9.	3
1 Sam. xi. 7.	7	xxxiv. 11.	5 e	Ezek. xl. 42.	3
xv. 33.	10	Prov. ix. 1.	5 a	Dan. iv. 14, 23.	1
1 Kings v. 6, 6.	6 c a	Isa. ix. 10.	3	Hos. vi. 5.	5 a
v. 15.	5 c	x. 15.	5 c	Amos v. 11.	3
v. 17.	3				

HIDE

1 חָבָא to hide, to withdraw from the sight or violence of another; to hide or conceal oneself; generally for the sake of security; from fear of anger, Gen. iii. 8, 10; from respect, Job xxix. 8, 10; from modesty, 1 Sam. x. 22; for insidious purposes, 2 Kings vii. 12; *meton.* from calumny and insult, Job v. 21, Isa. xlix. 2. NIPHAL [a] *pret.* [b] *inf.* [c] *fut.* [d] *part.* PUAL [e] *pret.* HIPHIL [f] *pret.* [g] *fut.* HOPHAL [h] *pret.* HITHPAEL [i] *pret.* [k] *fut.* [l] *part.* [m] מַחֲבָא hiding-place.

2 חָבָה *i. q.* חָבָא to hide oneself. KAL [a] *imp.* Isa. xxvi. 20. NIPHAL [b] *pret.* [c] *inf.* [d] חֶבְיוֹן m. covering. Cocceius thinks this is an allusion to the fire which was the symbol of the divine presence, hidden in the cloud in which it was involved, so that the Israelites did not see the fulness of his glory, yet some rays of it burst through the cloud.

3 חָפַשׂ to search for; to be sought; to be hidden. PUAL *fut.*

4 חָשַׁךְ to be dark. HIPHIL *fut.*

5 טָמַן to hide, chiefly by covering up in the earth, &c. KAL [a] *pret.* [b] *inf.* [c] *imp.* [d] *fut.* [e] *part.* Paül. NIPHAL [f] *imp.* HIPHIL [g] *fut.* [h] מַטְמוֹן m. treasure, hidden treasures, riches.

6 כָּחַד to cover; to hide, to conceal, with *acc.* and מִן of person: *opp.* יָדַע Hos. v. 3. NIPHAL [a] *pret.* [b] *fut.* PIEL [c] *pret.* [d] *fut.* HIPHIL [e] *fut.*

7 כָּסָה to cover, to cover over. PIEL [a] *pret.* [b] *fut.* [c] *part.*

8 נוּס to flee for one's life in imminent danger. HIPHIL *inf.*

9 נָצַר to keep, hide, conceal, in a safe, secret, secure place. KAL *part.* Paül.

10 סָתַם to stop up; to be secret. KAL *part.* Paül.

11 סָתַר to hide; to be hidden, to lie hid, to hide oneself. Hiphil, to cover over, especially the face: Isa. liii. 3, *marg.* 'Heb. as an hiding of faces from him, *or*, from us.' Gesenius, as one from whom they hide the face, *i. e.* from whom they turn their eyes as from something disgusting and abominable. Jehovah is said to hide his face when he does not regard human affairs, or when it denotes

displeasure ; to conceal something from any one ; to guard, defend. KAL [a] *fut.* כתיב. NIPHAL [b] *pret.* [c] *inf.* [d] *imp.* [e] *fut.* [f] *part.* PIEL [g] *imp.* HIPHIL [h] *pret.* [i] *inf.* [k] *imp.* [l] *fut.* [m] *part.* HITHPAEL [n] *fut.* [o] *part.* סֵתֶר [p] *m.* secret place.

12 עָטַף to cover, as with a garment, to conceal. KAL *fut.*

13 עָלַם to cover, conceal ; to be hidden, to lie hid ; Hiphil, *seq.* מִן to hide from the eyes, in neglect, or refusing aid, sometimes in connivance. NIPHAL [a] *pret.* [b] *part.* HIPHIL [c] *pret.* [d] *inf.* [e] *fut.* [f] *part.* HITHPAEL [g] *pret.* [h] *inf.* [i] *fut.* [k] תַּעֲלֻמָה *f.* what is hid or concealed.

14 עָמַם to be obscure ; to be hidden, concealed : figuratively, to surpass : Ezek. xxxi. 8. KAL *pret.*

15 פָּלָא see *Wonderful.* NIPHAL *part.*

16 צָפַן to conceal, particularly in order to protect ; to hide oneself, to lie in wait ; to lay up, to restrain, or deny to any one, *seq.* מִן ; to be hidden, as unknown to, or as destined for any one, *seq.* לְ. KAL [a] *pret.* [b] *fut.* [c] *part.* Poel. [d] *part.* Paul. NIPHAL [e] *pret.* HIPHIL [f] *inf.* [g] *fut.* [h] מַצְפֻּנִים *m. pl.* hidden places.

Gen. iii. 8.	1 k	2 Chron. ix. 2.	13 a	Ps. lxxxiii. 3.	16 d	
iii. 10.	1 c	xviii. 24.	1 b	lxxxviii. 14.	11 l	
iv. 14.	11 e	xxii. 9, 12.	1 l	lxxxix. 46.	11 e	
xviii. 17.	7 c	xxii. 11.	11 l	cii. 2.	11 l	
xxxv. 4.	5 d	Job iii. 10.	11 l	civ. 29.	11 l	
xlvii. 18.	6 d	iii. 16.	5 e	cxix. 11.	16 a	
Exod. ii. 2.	16 b	iii. 21.	5 h	cxix. 19.	11 l	
ii. 3.	16 f	iii. 23.	11 b	cxix. 114.	11 p	
ii. 12.	5 d	v. 21.	1 c	cxxxix. 12.	4	
iii. 6.	11 l	vi. 16.	13 i	cxxxix. 15.	6 a	
Lev. iv. 13.	13 a	x. 13.	16 a	cxl. 5.	5 a	
v. 2, 3, 4.	13 a	xiii. 20.	11 e	cxliii. 7.	11 l	
xx. 4.	13 d e	xiii. 24.	11 l	cxliii. 9. *a*	7 a	
Num. v. 13.	13 a	xiv. 13.	16 g	Prov. ii. 1.	16 b	
Deut. vii. 20.	11 f	xv. 18.	6 c	ii. 4.	5 h	
xxii. 1, 4.	13 g	xv. 20.	16 e	x. 18.	7 c	
xxii. 3.	13 h	xvii. 4.	16 a	xix. 24.	5 h	
xxx. 11.	15	xx. 12.	6 e	xxii. 3.	11 b or a	
xxxi. 17.	11 h	xx. 26.	5 e	xxvi. 15.	5 a	
xxxi. 18.	11 i l	xxiii. 9.	12	xxvii. 12.	11 b	
xxxii. 20.	11 l	xxiv. 1.	16 e	xxvii. 16, 16.	16 c a	
xxxiii. 19.	5 e	xxiv. 4.	1 e	xxvii. 12.	3	
Josh. iv. 4.	16 b	xxvii. 11.	13 k	xxviii. 27.	13 f	
ii. 6.	5 d	xxviii. 21.	13 a	xxviii. 28.	11 e	
ii. 16.	2 b	xxix. 8.	1 a	Isa. i. 15.	13 e	
vi. 17, 25.	1 f	xxxi. 33.	5 b	ii. 10.	5 f	
vii. 19.	6 d	xxxiii. 17.	7 b	iii. 9.	6 c	
vii. 21, 22.	5 e	xxxiv. 22.	11 c	viii. 17.	11 m	
x. 16.	1 c	xxxiv. 29.	11 l	xvi. 3.	11 g	
x. 17.	1 d	xxxviii. 30.	1 k	xxvi. 20.	2 a	
x. 27.	1 a	xl. 13.	5 c	xxviii. 15.	11 b	
Judg. vi. 11.	8	xli. 3.	13 f	xxviii. 17.	11 p	
ix. 5.	1 a	Ps. ix. 16.	5 a	xxix. 14.	11 n	
1 Sam. iii. 17, 17.	6 d	x. 1.	13 e	xxix. 15.	11 i	
iii. 18.	6 c	x. 11.	11 h	xxxii. 2.	1 m	
x. 22.	1 d	xiii. 1.	11 l	xl. 27.	11 b	
xiii. 6.	1 k	xvii. 8.	11 l	xlii. 22.	1 h	
xiv. 11.	1 i	xvii. 14.	16 d	xlv. 3.	5 h	
xiv. 22.	1 l	xix. 6.	11 f	xlv. 15.	11 o 9	
xix. 2.	1 a	xxii. 24.	11 h	xlviii. 6.	3	
xx. 2.	11 l	xxvii. 5, 5.	16 b, 11 l	xlix. 2, 2.	1 f, 11 h	
xx. 5, 19.	11 b	xxvii. 9.	11 l	l. 6.	11 h	
xx. 24.	11 e	xxx. 7.	11 h	liii. 3.	11 m	
xxiii. 19.	11 o	xxxi. 20.	11 l	liv. 8.	11 h	
xxiii. 23.	1 k	xxxii. 5.	7 a	lvii. 17.	11 i	
xxvi. 1.	11 o	xxxii. 7.	11 p	lviii. 7.	13 i	
2 Sam. xiv. 18.	6 d	xxxv. 7, 8.	5 b	lix. 2.	11 h	
xvii. 9.	1 d	xxxviii. 9.	11 b	lxiv. 7.	11 h	
xviii. 13.	6 b	xl. 10.	7 a	lxv. 16.	11 b	
1 Kings x. 3.	13 b	xliv. 24.	11 l	Jer. xiii. 4.	5 c	
xvii. 3.	11 b	li. 6.	11 l	xiii. 5.	5 d	
xviii. 4, 13.	1 g	li. 9.	11 k	xiii. 6.	5 b	
xxii. 25.	2 c	liv. title.	11 o	xiii. 7.	5 b	
2 Kings iv. 27.	13 c	lv. 1.	13 i	xvi. 17, 17.	11 b, 16 e	
vi. 29.	1 g	lv. 12.	11 h	xviii. 22.	5 a	
vii. 8, 8.	5 g	lvi. 6.	16 b	xxiii. 24.	11 e	
xi. 2.	11 l	lxiv. 2.	11 l	xxxiii. 15.	11 e	
xi. 3.	1 l	lxix. 5.	6 a	xxxvi. 19.	11 d	
1 Chron. xxi. 20.	1 l	lxix. 17.	11 l	xxxvi. 26.	11 l	
		lxxviii. 4.	6 d	xxxviii. 14, 25.	6 d	

Jer. xliii. 9, 10.	5 a	Ezek. xxxix. 23, 24,	
xlix. 10.	2 c	29.	11 l
Lam. iii. 56.	13 e	Dan. x. 7.	1 b
Ezek. xxii. 26.	13 c	Hos. v. 3.	6 a
xxviii. 3.	14	xiii. 12.	16 d
xxxi. 8.	14	xiii. 14.	11 e

Amos ix. 3, 3.	1 c, 11 e		
Obad. 6.	16 h		
Mic. iii. 4.	11 l		
Nah. iii. 11.	13 b		
Hab. iii. 4.	2 d		
Zeph. ii. 3.	11 l		

a lit. I hide me with thee.

HIDE

עוֹר *m.* skin of men, or hide of animals, when taken off : Lev. viii. 17 ; ix. 11.

HIGGAION

הִגָּיוֹן *m.* meditation ; or a poem, a song : Ps. ix. 16, *marg.* 'that is meditation.' Lxx. ᾠδὴ διαψάλματος, an interlude chorus. So Symm., Aqu., Vulg. According to others, it denotes a musical instrument.

HIGH, HIGHWAY

1 אִישׁ *m.* man ; sons of men, is used *emph.* for the noble, the high ; *opp.* to בְּנֵי אָדָם ; see *Low.*

2 אָכַל to eat ; to eat off ; *i. e.* to take from, to diminish. KAL *fut.* Ezek. xlii. 5, *i. e.* occupied part of the space.

3 אֹרַח *com.* way, path, road ; highway.

4 אָרֹךְ *adj.* long.

5 בָּמָה *f.* what is high and lofty ; an eminence ; high place ; particularly the hills where chapels and altars were erected to idols, and sometimes, though contrary to law, to the true God : Lev. xxvi. 30, &c.

6 בֵּן *m.* son : Ps. xlix. 2 ; lxii. 9.

7 גַּאֲוָה *f.* elevation, exaltation ; pride, haughtiness, insolence.

8 גַּב *m.* back or upper part of an altar.

9 גָּבַהּ to be high, lofty, tall ; to be elevated. KAL [a] *pret.* [b] *inf.* [c] *fut.* HIPHIL [d] *fut.* [e] *part.* [f] גֹּבַהּ *m.* height ; pride. [g] גָּבֹהַ and גָּבֹהּ [h] גֶּבֶהּ *adj.* high, lofty, proud.

10 גְּבַנֻּנִים *m.* heights, summits.

11 גָּדוֹל *adj.* great.

12 גַּף *m.* back : Prov. ix. 3, "upon the high places ;" *lit.* upon the back of the high places, *or,* pinnacles of the high places.

13 דֶּרֶךְ *com.* a way, path, in which one treads.

14 חוּץ *m.* the outside ; abroad, without, highways.

15 נָשָׂא to lift up. NIPHAL [a] *part.* [b] שְׂאֵת *f.* a lifting up.

16 מְסִלָּה *f.* a raised way, highway. מַסְלוּל *m. id.*

17 עַל *m.* height, summit ; high, most high. עֲלִי Ch. *adj.* [b] עֶלְיוֹן *adj.* high, higher, upper ; most high, of the Messiah, Ps. xlvii. 2, *comp.* ver. 6 ; supreme ; once of a thing in an elevated place as an example of punishment, corresponding to the Greek παραδειγματί(ε)σθαι : 1 Kings ix. 8. Vulg. *et domus hæc erit in exemplum.* [c] עֶלְיוֹן Ch. *adj.* מַעֲלָה *f.* a going up ; an elevated place, high degree, excellence : 1 Chron. xvii. 17, in evident allusion to the Messiah foretold as the descendant of David, God-man. See *Estate, Manner.*

18 פָּלָא to be wonderful, "too high." NIPHAL *part.*

19 צַחִיחַ *m.* sunny, hence dry, parched.

20 צַמֶּרֶת *f.* foliage of trees, *i. e.* the extreme tender branches, which may be compared to wool or a fleece.

21 צָרִיחַ *m.* a high building, which may be seen far, *e. g.* a tower, a watch-tower.

22 קוֹמָה *f.* height, stature.

23 רֹאשׁ *m.* head; "on high among," *lit.* on the top of the people.

24 רוּם to lift up oneself, to be high, lofty; *metaph.* of those conspicuous in power and dignity; to lift up, to raise, to make high. KAL a *pret.* b *fut.* c *part.* Poel. HIPHIL d *fut.* e רוּם *m.* height, elevation; "high look," *marg.* 'haughtiness of eyes.' f רוֹם *adv.* g רוֹמָם *m.* a lifting up, praise, "high praises." h רָמָה *f.* a lofty place. i מָרוֹם *m.* height, what is high, lofty; pride.

25 שָׂגַב to be high, inaccessible; to be high, as a city, a wall. NIPHAL a *pret.* b *part.* PIEL, see *Set.*

26 שָׁפָה this verb evidently implies something bare, bald, and naked; it is therefore used of mountains and high places, not covered with wood, open to view. NIPHAL a *part.* b שְׁפִי *m.* a naked hill.

No. 5, *high place,* No. 17 b, *most high,* not included.

Gen. vii. 19.	9 g	Job xxxi. 2.	24 i	Isa. xxvi. 5.	24 i
xxix. 7.	11	xxxi. 23.	15 b	xxx. 13.	25 b
Exod. xiv. 8.	24 c	xxxv. 5.	9 a	xxx. 25, 25.	9 g,15 a
Lev. xxi. 10.	11	xxxviii. 15.	24 c	xxxii. 15.	24 i
Num. xx. 19.	16	xxxix. 18.	24 i	xxxiii. 5, 16.	24 i
xxiii. 3.	26 b	xxxix. 27.	24 d	xxxiii. 3.	16
xxiv. 7.	24 b	xli. 39.	9 g	xxxv. 8.	16 a
xxxiii. 3.	24 c	Ps. vii. 7.	24 i	xxxvi. 2.	16
xxxv. 25, 28, 28.	11	xviii. 13.	17 b	xxxvii. 23.	24 i
Deut. ii. 27.a	13	xviii. 27.	24 c	xl. 3.	16
iii. 5.	9 g	xlix. 2.	1, 6	xl. 9.	9 g
vii. 18, 22, 25, 27.	17 c	lii. 13.	9 a	xl. 26.	24 i
xii. 2.	24 c	lv. 9, 9.	9 a	xl. 18.	26 b
xxvi. 19.	17 b	lvi. 2.	24 i	xlix. 9.	26 b
xxviii. 1.	17 b	lxi. 2.	24 b	xlix. 11.	16
xxviii. 52.	9 g	lxii. 9.	1, 6	lii. 13.	9 a
xxxii. 27.	24 a	lxviii. 15, 16.	10	lv. 9, 9.	9 a
Josh. xx. 6.	11	lxviii. 18.	24 i	lvii. 7.	15 a
Judg. v. 6.	3	lxxi. 19.	24 i	lvii. 15, 15.	24 c i
v. 18.	24 i	lxxv. 5.	24 i	lviii. 4.	24 i
xx. 31, 32, 45.	16	lxxviii. 35.	17 b	lxii. 10.	16
xxi. 19.	16	lxxviii. 69.	24 c	Jer. ii. 20.	9 g
1 Sam. vi. 12.β	16	lxxxvii. 6.	17 b	iii. 2, 21.	26 b
ix. 2.	9 g	lxxxix. 13.	24 b	iii. 6.	9 g
x. 23.	9 c	lxxxix. 27.	17 b	iv. 11.	26 b
xiii. 6.	21	xcii. 11.	24 i	vii. 29.	26 b
2 Sam. xx. 12, 12, 13.	16	xciii. 4.	24 i	xii. 12.	26 b
xxiii. 1.	17	xcvii. 9.	17 b	xiv. 6.	26 b
1 Kings vi. 10, 23.	22	xcix. 2.	24 a	xvii. 2.	9 g
vii. 15, 35.	22	ci. 5.	9 h	xvii. 12.	24 i
ix. 8.	17 b	ciii. 11.	9 b	xx. 2.	17 b
xiv. 23, 23.	5, 9 g	cxiii. 4.	9 g	xxx. 30.	24 i
xxi. 9, 12.	23	cxiii. 4.	24 c	xxxi. 21.	16
2 Kings xix. 10.	11	cxiii. 5.	9 e	xxxvi. 10.	17 b
xv. 35, 35, 35.	5, 5, 17 b	cxxxi. 1.	18	xlix. 16.	9 d
xvii. 10.	9 g	cxxxviii. 6.	24 c	li. 58.	9 g
xviii. 17.	16	cxxxix. 6.	25 a	Ezek. i. 18.	9 f
xix. 22.	24 i	cxlix. 6.	24 g	vi. 13.	24 c
xxii. 4, 8.	11	Prov. viii. 2.	24 i	ix. 2.	17 b
xxiii. 4.	11	viii. 26.	23	xvi. 24, 25, 31, 39.	24 h
1 Chron. xvii. 17.	17 d	ix. 3.	12, 24 i	xvii. 3.	20
2 Chron. iii. 15.	4	ix. 14.	24 i	xvii. 22, 22,	
vi. 13.	22	xvi. 17.	16	22.	20, 24 c, 9 g
vii. 21.	17 b	xviii. 11.	25 b	xvii. 24.	9 g
xxiii. 20.	17 b	xxi. 4.	24 e	xx. 28.	24 c
xxiv. 11.	23	xxiv. 7.	24 c	xxi. 26.	9 g
xxvii. 3.	17 b	Eccles. v. 8, 8, 8.	9 g	xxxi. 3.	9 h
xxxiv. 9.	11	xii. 5.	9 g	xxxiv. 6.	24 c
Neh. iii. 1, 20.	11	Isa. ii. 13, 14.	24 c	xxxiv. 14.	24 i
iii. 25.	17 b	ii. 15.	9 g	xl. 2.	9 g
iv. 19.	19	vi. 1.	24 c	xl. 42.	9 f
xiii. 28.	11	vii. 3.	16	xli. 7.	17 b
Esth. v. 14.	9 g	x. 12.	24 e	xli. 22.	9 g
vii. 9.	9 g	x. 33.	24 c	xlii. 5.	2
Job v. 11.	24 i	xiii. 2.	26 a	xlii. 13.	8
xi. 8.	9 f	xiii. 3.	7	Dan. iii. 26.	17 a
xvi. 19.	24 i	xix. 23.	16	iv. 2, 17, 24, 25,	
xxi. 22.	24 c	xxii. 16.	24 i	34.	17 a
xxii. 12.	24 a	xxiv. 18, 21, 21.	24 i	v. 18, 21.	17 a
xxv. 2.	24 i			vii. 18, 22, 27.	17 c

Dan. vii. 25, 25.	17 a c	Obad. 3.	24 i	Hag. i. 1, 12, 14.	11
viii. 3, 3, 3.	9 g	Mic. vi. 6.	24 i	ii. 2, 4.	11
Hos. vii. 16.	17	Hab. ii. 9.	24 i	Zech. iii. 1, 8.	11
xi. 7.	17	iii. 10.	24 f	vi. 11.	11
Amos v. 16.	17	Zeph. i. 16.	9 g		

a *lit.* by the way, by the way.   β *lit.* in one path.

HILL.

1 גִּבְעָה *f.* a hill: Gen. xlix. 26, &c.

2 הַר *m.* a mountain, "hill country." a הָרָר *m. id.*

3 מַעֲלֶה *m.* a going up: 1 Sam. ix. 11, *lit.* in the ascent of.

4 קֶרֶן *f.* horn; the sharp point of a hill, a hill: Isa. v. 1, "a very fruitful hill;" *marg.* 'the horn of the son of oil.'

No. 1 not included.

Gen. vii. 19.	2	Judg. xvi. 3.	2	Ps. xxiv. 3.	2
Exod. xxiv. 4.	2	1 Sam. ix. 11.	3	xlii. 3.	2
Num. xiv. 44, 45.	2	xxv. 20.	2	xliii. 3.	2
Deut. i. 7, 41, 43.	2	xxvi. 13.	2	l. 10.	2 a
viii. 7.	2	2 Sam. xiii. 34.	2	lxviii. 15, 15, 15,	
viii. 9.	2 a	xvi. 13.	2	16, 16.	2
xi. 11.	2	xxi. 9.	2	lxxx. 10.	2
Josh. ix. 1.	2	1 Kings xi. 7.	2	xcv. 4.	2
x. 40.	2	xvi. 24, 24, 24.	2	xcvii. 5.	2
xi. 16.	2	xx. 23, 28.	2	xcviii. 8.	2
xiii. 6.	2	xxii. 17.	2	xcix. 9.	2
xv. 9.	2	2 Kings i. 9.	2	civ. 10, 13, 18, 32.	2
xvii. 16.	2	iv. 27.	2	cxxi. 1.	2
xviii. 13, 14.	2	Ps. ii. 6.	2	Isa. v. 1.	4
xxi. 11.	2	iii. 4.	2	v. 25.	2
xxiv. 30.	2	xv. 1.	2	vii. 25.	2
Judg. ii. 9.	2	xviii. 7.	2		

HIN

הִין *m.* a measure of liquids containing the seventh part of a bath, *i. e.* twelve Roman sextarii, according to Josephus. Exod. xxix. 40, &c.

HIND

אַיָּלָה *f.* a hind, female deer, and perhaps also *caprea,* wild she-goat—Gesenius: Gen. xlix. 21: 2 Sam. xxii. 34: Job xxxix. 1: Ps. xviii. 33; xxix. 9: Cant. ii. 7; iii. 5: Hab. iii. 19. אַיֶּלֶת *f.* a hind, as a term of endearment towards a female: Prov. v. 19: Jer. xiv. 5.

HINDER, HINDERMOST, HINDMOST

1 אַחַר *m.* after, hinder part. a אָחוֹר *m.* back parts. b אַחֲרוֹן *adj.* hinder, latter. c אַחֲרִית *f.* latter part.

2 זָנָב *m.* the tail; hence the *denom. verb* זָנַב to hurt or cut off the tail, to smite the rear of an army. PIEL a *pret.* b *fut.*

3 סוֹף Ch. *m.* end; of the rear of an army.

Gen. xxxiii. 2.	1 b	2 Sam. ii. 23.	1	Jer. l. 12.	1 c
Num. ii. 31.	1 b	1 Kings vii. 25.	1 a	Joel ii. 20.	3
Deut. xxv. 18.	2 b	2 Chron. iv. 4.	1 a	Zech. xiv. 8.	1 b
Josh. x. 19.	2 a	Ps. lxxviii. 66.	1 a		

HINDER (V)

1 אָחַר to delay, retard, hinder. PIEL *fut.*

2 בְּטֵל Ch. to cease. P'AL *inf.*

3 חָשַׂךְ to hold back, to restrain; to spare, to use tenderly. KAL *pret.*

4 מָנַע to withhold. NIPHAL *fut.*

5 עָשָׂה to do. KAL *inf.*

6 שׁוּב to return. HIPHIL *fut.* Perhaps in one or both cases it may be rendered, "who shall cause him to restore."

7 תּוֹעָה *f.* error in respect to things of religion, impiety, wickedness.

Gen. xxiv. 56.	1	Neh. iv. 8. β	5, 7	Job xi. 10. δ	6
Num. xxii. 16. α	4	Job ix. 12. γ	6	Isa. xiv. 6.	3
Ezra vi. 8.	2				

α *marg.* 'Be not thou letted.' β *marg.* 'to make an error to it.'
γ *marg.* 'turn him away.' δ *marg. id.*

HINGE

פֹּת *m.* hinges : 1 Kings vii. 50.

צִיר *m.* hinge of a door : Prov. xxvi. 14.

HIP

שׁוֹק *m.* the leg from the knee to the foot : Judg. xv. 8, "hip and thigh" is a proverbial expression, the primary meaning of which it is difficult to ascertain, but probably pointing out the peculiar wounds given to an enemy in flight.

HIRE

1 מְחִיר *m.* price.

2 שָׂכַר to hire. KAL *part.* Poel.

3 שָׁחַד to give, to make a present, especially to be free from punishment, to bribe. KAL *fut.*

4 שָׂכַר to hire; sometimes to bribe. KAL ᵃ*pret.* ᵇ*inf.* ᶜ*fut.* ᵈ*part.* Poel. ᵉ*part.* Paül. NIPHAL ᶠ*pret.* ᵍ שָׂכָר *m.* hire, wages, reward. ʰ שָׂכִיר *m.* one hired, hireling, hired labourer. שְׂכִירָה *f.* a hiring.

5 תָּנָה to give presents, to distribute gifts; especially to hire any one. KAL ᵃ*fut.* HIPHIL ᵇ*pret.* ᶜ אֶתְנָן *m.* a gift, hire, *e.g.* of a harlot; *metaph.* of fruits and produce of the fields, regarded by idolaters as gifts from the idols.

Gen. xxx. 16. α	4 b a	1 Sam. ii. 5.	4 f	Isa. vii. 20.	4 i		
xxx. 18, 32, 33.	4 g	2 Sam. x. 6.	4 g	xvi. 14.	4 h		
xxxi. 8.	4 g	1 Kings v. 6.	4 g	xxi. 16.	4 h		
Exod. xii. 45.	4 h	2 Kings vii. 6.	4 a	xxiii. 17, 18.	5 c		
xxii. 15, 15.	4 h g	1 Chron. xix. 6.	4 b	xlvi. 6.	4 h		
Lev. xix. 13.	4 h	xix. 7.	4 c	Jer. xlvi. 21.	4 h		
xxii. 10.	4 h	2 Chron. xxiv. 12. β	4 c	Ezek. xvi. 31, 41.	5 c		
xxv. 6, 40, 50, 53.	4 h	xxv. 6.	4 c	xvi. 33.	3		
Deut. xv. 18.	4 h	Ezra iv. 5.	2	Hos. viii. 9.	4 h		
xxiii. 4.	4 a	Neh. vi. 12.	4 h	viii. 10.	5 a		
xxiii. 18.	5 c	vi. 13.	4 e	Micah i. 7, 7, 7.	5 c		
xxiv. 14.	4 h	xiii. 11.	1				
xxiv. 15.	4 g	Job vii. 1, 2.	4 h	Zech. viii. 10, 10.	4 g		
Judg. ix. 4.	4 c	xiv. 6.	4 h	Mal. iii. 5.	4 h		
xviii. 4.	4 c						

α *lit.* hiring I have hired. β *lit.* and were hiring.

HISS

שָׁרַק to hiss, to whistle; *seq.* לְ to hiss or whistle for any one, to call by a hiss or whistle, *e.g.* bees, flies, in the manner of bee-keepers; to hiss in scorn and derision. KAL *pret.* 1 Kings ix. 8 : Isa. v. 26 : Lam. ii. 15, 16 : Ezek. xxvii. 36. *fut.* Job xxvii. 23 : Isa. vii. 18 : Jer. xix. 8 ; xlix. 17 ; l. 13 : Zeph. ii. 15 : Zech. x. 8. שְׁרֵקָה *f.* hissing, derision : 2 Chron. xxix. 8 : Jer. xix. 8 ; xxv. 9, 18 ; xxix. 18 ; li. 37 : Micah vi. 16. שְׁרוּקת *f. pl.* hissings, derisions : Jer. xviii. 16, כתיב. שְׁרִיקות *f. pl. id.* Jer. xviii. 16, קרי.

HIT

מָצָא to find. KAL *fut.* 1 Sam. xxxi. 3 : 1 Chron. x. 3.

HOAR-FROST, HAIRS, HEAD

כְּפוֹר *m.* hoar-frost, so called because it covers the ground : Exod. xvi. 14 : Job xxxviii. 29 : Ps. cxlvii. 16.

שֵׂיבָה *f.* grayness of hair, hoariness : Lev. xix. 32 : 1 Kings ii. 6, 9 : Job xli. 32 : Prov. xvi. 31 : Isa. xlvi. 4.

HOLD

1 מְצָד *m.* a fastness, castle, stronghold, on a hill or mountain, so called as a place of lying in wait and watching; coupled with caverns : Judg. vi. 2 : Ezek. xxxiii. 27. ᵃ מְצוּדָה *f.* fortress. ᵇ מְצוּדָה *f.* top of a mountain; fortress.

2 צָרִיחַ *m.* a high building, which may be seen far and wide, *e.g.* a tower, or castle, a watch-tower.

Judg. vi. 2.	1	1 Sam. xxiv. 22.	1 b	1 Chron. xii. 8, 16.	1		
ix. 46, 49, 49.	2	2 Sam. v. 7, 17.	1 b	Jer. xlviii. 41.	1		
1 Sam. xxii. 4, 5.	1 b	xxiii. 14.	1 b	li. 30.	1		
xxiii. 14, 19, 29.	1	1 Chron. xi. 16.	1 b	Ezek. xix. 9.	1 a		

HOLD

1 אָחַז to lay hold of, to take, to seize, especially with the hand, to take hold ; see *Take ;* to hold, to hold fast that which one has taken hold of ; to hold or fasten together, to join : Ezek. xli. 6. KAL ᵃ*pret.* ᵇ*inf.* ᶜ*imp.* ᵈ*fut.* ᵉ*part.* Paül. PIEL ᶠ*part.*

2 אָסַר to bind. KAL *part.* Paül.

3 בָּלַם to bind together, to shut fast, to stop, specially the mouth with a bit or muzzle. KAL *inf.*

4 דָּמַם to be silent, to hold one's peace. KAL *fut.*

5 הָסָה to keep silence, to hold one's peace, hold one's tongue, PIEL *imp.*

6 חָבָא to hide, to conceal. NIPHAL *pret.*

7 חָזַק to bind fast, to lay hold, to hold fast to anything ; to make firm, strong ; to strengthen. HIPHIL ᵃ*pret.* ᵇ*imp.* ᶜ*fut.* ᵈ*part.* HITHPAEL ᵉ*part.*

8 חָרֵשׁ (see *Silent*), to hold one's peace ; implying, rather, voluntary silence, and refraining from action. KAL ᵃ*fut.* HIPHIL ᵇ*pret.* ᶜ*inf.* rendered "altogether," *lit.* in holding peace. ᵈ*imp.* ᵉ*fut.* ᶠ*part.*

9 חָשַׁב to think, to count. KAL *fut.*

10 חָשָׁה to cease ; to keep silence ; to hold one's peace. KAL ᵃ*fut.* HIPHIL ᵇ*pret.* ᶜ*imp.* ᵈ*part.*

11 חָשַׂךְ to hold back, to restrain. KAL *pret.*

12 יָשַׁט to hold out, to extend. HIPHIL *fut.*

13 כּוּל to hold, contain ; to hold up, endure. HIPHIL ᵃ*inf.* ᵇ*fut.*

14 לָחַץ to press ; to crowd upon so as to thrust forth, or hold fast out. KAL *pret.*

15 לָכַד to take fast hold. NIPHAL *fut.*

16 נָשָׂא to lift up, hold up. KAL *fut.*

17 סָמַךְ to sustain, uphold. NIPHAL *pret.*

18 סָעַד to prop, to uphold, to support ; to sustain, to aid, to strengthen. KAL ᵃ*imp.* ᵇ*fut.*

19 עָשָׂה to do, to make, to hold a feast. KAL ᵃ*fut.* NIPHAL ᵇ*pret.*

20 קָבַל to take ; take hold. HIPHIL *part.*

21 קוֹל *m.* voice.

22 קוּם to rise, to stand firm, to withstand. KAL *fut.*

23 רוּם to be high ; to lift up, to hold up. HIPHIL *fut.*

24 שׂוּם to put. KAL *part.* Poel.

25 תָּמַךְ to take fast hold ; to support. KAL ᵃ*pret.* ᵇ*inf.* ᶜ*fut.* ᵈ*part.* Poel. NIPHAL ᵉ*fut.*

26 תָּפַשׂ to lay hold of, to hold. KAL ᵃ*pret.* ᵇ*inf.* ᶜ*imp.* ᵈ*part.* Poel.

Gen. xix. 16.	7 c	Neh. viii. 11.	5	Prov. v. 22.	25 e
xxi. 18. *a*	7 b	Esth. iv. 11.	12	xi. 12.	8 e
xxiv. 21.	8 f	iv. 14.	8 c e	xvii. 28.	8 f
xxxiv. 5.	8 b	v. 2.	12	xxxi. 19.	25 a
xlviii. 17.	25 c	vii. 4.	8 b	Eccles. ii. 3.	1 b
Exod. ix. 2.	7 d	viii. 4.	12	Cant. iii. 4.	1 a
xiv. 14.	8 e	Job ii. 3.	7 d	iii. 8.	1 e
xvii. 11.	23	vi. 24.	8 e	vii. 5.	2
xxxvi. 12.	20	viii. 15.	7 c	Isa. v. 29.	1 d
Lev. x. 3.	4	xi. 3.	8 e	xxxiii. 15.	25 b
Num. xxx. 4, 7, 11.	8 b	xiii. 5.	8 c e	xxxvi. 21.	8 e
xxx. 14, 14.	8 c e b	xiii. 13.	8 d	xli. 13.	7 d
Deut. xxi. 19.	26 a	xiii. 19.	8 e	xlii. 6.	7 c
xxii. 28.	26 a	xiii. 24.	9	xlii. 14.	10 b
Judg. vii. 20.	7 c	xvii. 9.	1 d	xlv. 1.	2
xvi. 26.	7 d	xxiii. 11.	1 a	lvi. 2.	7 c
xviii. 19.	8 d	xxvi. 9.	1 f	lvii. 11.	10 d
xix. 29.	7 c	xxvii. 6.	7 a	lxii. 1, 6.	10 a
Ruth iii. 15, 15.	1 c d	xxix. 10.	21, 6	lxiv. 12.	10 a
1 Sam. x. 27.	8 f	xxxiii. 31, 33.	8 d	Jer. ii. 13.	13 b
xv. 27.	7 c	xxxvi. 8.	15	iv. 19.	8 e
2 Sam. ii. 21.	1 c	xli. 26.	22	vi. 11.	13 a
ii. 22.	16	Ps. xvii. 5.	25 b	vi. 23.	7 c
xiii. 20.	8 d	xvii. 35.	18 b	viii. 5.	7 a
xviii. 16.	11	xxxii. 9.	3	xlix. 16.	26 d
1 Kings viii. 65.	19	xxxix. 2.	10 b	l. 33.	7 a
xiii. 4.	26 c	xxxix. 12.	8 a	l. 42.	7 c
2 Kings ii. 3, 5.	10 c	lxvi. 9.	24	Ezek. xxx. 21.	26 b
vi. 32.	14	lxxi. 6.	17	xli. 6, 6.	1 e
vii. 9.	10 d	lxxiii. 23.	1 a	Dan. x. 21.	7 e
xviii. 36.	8 b	lxxvii. 4.	1 a	xii. 7.	23
xxiii. 22, 23.	19 b	lxxxiii. 1.	8 a	Amos i. 5, 8.	25 d
1 Chron. xiii. 9.	1 b	xciv. 18.	18 b	vi. 10.	5
2 Chron. iv. 5.	13 b	cix. 1.	8 a	Hab. i. 3.	8 e
vii. 22.	7 c	cxix. 117.	18 a	Zeph. i. 7.	5
Neh. iv. 16, 17, 21.	7 d	cxxxix. 10.	1 d	Zech. xiv. 13.	7 a
v. 8.	8 e	Prov. iii. 18.	7 d		

a lit. strengthen thy hand upon him.

HOLE

1 בָּחוּר *m.* 'young man,' according to the *marg.* of Isa. xlii. 22.

2 חוֹר *m.* a hole, spoken of a window, Cant. v. 4 ; of the socket of the eye, of a cave. ᵃ חוּר *m.* hole of a viper ; also a narrow and filthy subterranean prison.

3 נָקַב to pierce. KAL ᵃ*part.* Paül. ᵇ מַקֶּבֶת *f.* a hammer ; a quarry, figurative of extraction and descent.

4 נָקִיק *m.* cleft of a rock.

5 מִסְגֶּרֶת *f.* close places, *i.e.* fortified places.

6 מְעָרָה *f.* cave.

7 פֶּה *m.* mouth.

8 פַּחַת *m.* pit.

Exod. xxviii. 32, 32, 32.	7	Isa. vii. 19.	4	Jer. xlviii. 28.	8
xxxix. 23, 23, 23.	7	xi. 8.	2 a	Ezek. viii. 7.	2
1 Sam. xiv. 11.	2	xlii. 22.	2 a, or 1	Micah vii. 17.	5
2 Kings xii. 9.	2	li. 1.	3 b	Nah. ii. 12.	2
Cant. v. 4.	2	Jer. xiii. 4.	4	Hag. i. 6.	3 a
Isa. ii. 19.	6	xvi. 16.	4	Zech. xiv. 12.	2

HOLLOW

כַּף *f.* the hollow of the hand : Gen. xxxii. 25, 25, 32, 32.

מַכְתֵּשׁ *m.* a mortar : in Judg. xv. 19, probably socket of a tooth. Lat. *mortariolum*, Gr. ὅλμίσκος : *or*, a place similar in form that was in Lehi.

נָבַב to hollow out. KAL *part.* Paül, Exod. xxvii. 8 ; xxxviii. 7 : Jer. lii. 21.

שְׁקַעֲרוּרֹת *f.* sunken places, hollows in a wall. Lxx. κοιλάδες,

Vulg. *valliculæ.* Lev. xiv. 37, an effect on the walls through leprosy, which may be described by the word " pitted."

שֹׁעַל *m.* the hand contracted and made hollow, to hold water : Isa. xl. 12.

HOLY

1 חָגַג to keep a festival, holy day. KAL *part.* Poel.

2 חָסִיד *adj.* kind, merciful ; or of one who has received mercy or favour in the Messiah : Ps. lxxxvi. 2. Of God, good, merciful, gracious.

3 קָדַשׁ to be pure, clean ; to be holy, sacred ; to be regarded as holy, to pronounce holy. KAL ᵃ*pret.* ᵇ*fut.* PIEL ᶜ*inf.* ᵈ*part.* ᵉ קֹדֶשׁ *m.* holiness, sanctity ; most frequently in the genitive after another noun, instead of an adjective, and rendered, holy ; ascribed to all those things which in any way pertain to God, or his worship ; rarely only, and in doubtful cases, is it to be taken as *abstr.* holiness : Amos iv. 2 : Ps. lx. 8 : cviii. 8 ; perhaps more correctly rendered, sanctuary ; *concr.* a holy thing, something sacred, consecrated to God, *opp.* חֹל profane ; a holy place, sanctuary : most holy, קֹדֶשׁ הַקֳּדָשִׁים *lit.* holy of holies, *or*, holiness of holinesses, is used of the Messiah, Dan. ix. 24, of things, of men, and of places. ᶠ קָדוֹשׁ *adj.* holy, sacred ; free from the defilement of vice, idolatry, and other impure and profane things ; *opp.* is חָנֵף impure, profane. In a higher sense, and somewhat varied, it is applied to God, usually translated the Holy One. ᵍ קַדִּישׁ Ch. *adj.* ʰ מִקְדָּשׁ *m.* sanctuary, holy place, " holy place for the sanctuary."

No. 3 e, *Holy,* and No. 3 f, *Holy One,* not included.

Exod. xix. 6.	3 f	Deut. xiv. 2, 21.	3 f	Ps. cxi. 9.	3 f
xx. 8.	3 c	xxiii. 14.	3 f	cxlv. 17.	2
xxix. 31.	3 f	xxvi. 19.	3 f	Prov. ix. 10.	3 f
xxix. 37.	3 b	xxvii. 9.	3 f	xxx. 3.	3 f
xxx. 29.	3 b	xxxiii. 8.	2	Eccles. viii. 10.	3 f
Lev. vi. 16, 26.	3 f	Josh. xxiv. 19.	3 f	Isa. iv. 3.	3 f
vi. 18.	3 b	1 Sam. ii. 2.	3 f	v. 16.	3 f
vi. 27, 27.	3 b f	vi. 20.	3 f	vi. 3, 3, 3.	3 f
vii. 6.	3 f	2 Kings iv. 9.	3 f	lvii. 15, 15.	3 f
x. 13.	3 f	2 Chron. xxxv. 3.	3 f	lviii. 13.	3 f
xi. 44, 44, 45, 45.	3 f	Neh. viii. 9, 10, 11.	3 f	lxv. 5.	3 a
xvi. 24.	3 f	Ps. xvi. 10.	2	Ezek. vii. 24.	3 d
xix. 2, 2.	3 f	xxii. 3.	3 f	xxi. 2.	3 h
xx. 7, 26, 26.	3 f	xlii. 4.	1	xlii. 13.	3 h
xxi. 6, 7, 8, 8.	3 f	xlvi. 4.	3 f	Dan. iv. 8, 13, 17,	
xxiv. 9.	3 f	lxv. 4.	3 f	18, 23.	3 h
Num. v. 17.	3 f	lxviii. 35.	3 h	v. 11.	3 g
vi. 5, 8.	3 f	lxxxvi. 2.	2	viii. 24.	3 f
xv. 40.	3 f	lxxxix. 19.	3 f	Hag. ii. 12.	3 b
xvi. 3, 5, 7.	3 f	xcix. 3, 5, 9.	3 f		
Deut. vii. 6.	3 f				

HOME

אֹהֶל *m.* tent : Judg. xix. 9, *marg.* ' to thy tent.'

בַּיִת *m.* house ; " home " to his house ; " long home," Eccles. xii. 5, *lit.* the house of ages. Gen. xxxix. 16, &c.

נָוָה to be settled in a habitation. KAL *fut.* Hab. ii. 5, *i.e.* confines not himself to a peaceable settlement in his own dominions.

מָקוֹם *com.* place : 1 Sam. ii. 20 : 2 Chron. xxv. 10, 10.

HOME-BORN (See BORN)

HOMER

חֹמֶר *m.* a heap; homer (κόρος, St. Luke xvi. 7), the largest measure of things dry, containing ten baths : Lev. xxvii. 16 : Num. xi. 32 : Isa. v. 10 : Ezek. xlv. 11, 11, 11, 13, 13, 14, 14 : Hos. iii. 2.

לֶתֶךְ *m.* a half-homer, a measure for grain: Hos. iii. 2.

HONEY, HONEYCOMB

דְּבַשׁ *m.* common honey, also palm-honey; Gesenius, honey of grapes, syrup, the juice of grapes boiled down : Gen. xliii. 11, &c.

יַעַר *m.* comb; wood-honey, in hot weather running down the tree; honeycomb : Cant. v. 1. יַעְרָה *f.* 1 Sam. xiv. 27. With דְּבַשׁ honeycomb.

נֹפֶת *f.* a sprinkling, dropping; with צוּפִים, Ps. xix. 10, dropping of the honeycombs, *i. e.* honey dropping from the combs; and also alone, Prov. v. 3; xxiv. 13; xxvii. 7: Cant. iv. 11.

צוּף honey spontaneously flowing from the comb; or comb, honeycomb, from which it flows : Ps. xix. 10 : Prov. xvi. 24. With דְּבַשׁ honeycomb.

HONOUR, HONOURABLE

1 אָדַר to be powerful, noble, glorious. HIPHIL, to make honourable : *fut.*

2 הָדַר this word includes the ideas of glory, honour, majesty, splendour, beauty; also implying an object of reverence. KAL [a] *pret.* [b] *fut.* NIPHAL [c] *pret.* הֲדַר Ch. PAEL [d] *pret.* [e] *part.* [f] הָדָר *m.* ornament, majesty, honour. [g] הֲדַר Ch. *id.* [h] הֲדָרָה *f.* ornament.

3 הוֹד any good quality or endowment for which a person is admired, honoured, praised.

4 יָקָר *adj.* heavy; precious, honourable. [a] יְקָר *m.* preciousness, honour. [b] יְקָר Ch. *m. id.*

5 כָּבֵד to be heavy: to come to honour, to get honour, and glory, in opposition to קָלַל to be light, despised. Piel, to regard, treat, or practically declare one as worthy of honour : Exod. xx. 12, compare its opposite, Deut. xxvii. 16. Isa. v. 13, honourable men, opposed to הָמוֹן multitude. KAL [a] *fut.* NIPHAL [b] *pret.* [c] *inf.* [d] *fut.* [e] *part.* PIEL, to promote to honour, [f] *pret.* [g] *inf.* [h] *imp.* [i] *fut.* [k] *part.* PUAL [l] *fut.* [m] *part.* HITHPAEL [n] *part.* [o] כָּבוֹד *f.* glory.

6 נָשָׂא to lift up; with פָּנִים to accept the person of any one. KAL *part.* Paül.

7 תִּפְאָרָה *f.* ornament, beauty; splendour, magnificence, glory; often of the divine glory; honour, glory, in a moral sense.

Gen. xxiv. 19.	5 e	Num. xxii. 37.	5 g	1 Sam. ii. 30, 30.	5 k i		
xlix. 6.	5 o	xxiv. 11,a 11.	5 g i o	ix. 6.	5 e		
Exod. xiv. 4, 17.	5 d	xxvii. 20.	3	xv. 30.	5 h		
xiv. 18.	5 c	Deut. v. 16.	5 h	xxii. 14.	5 e		
xx. 12.	5 h	xxvi. 19.	7	2 Sam. vi. 22.	5 d		
Lev. xix. 15.	2 b	Judg. iv. 9.	5 i	x. 3.	5 k		
xix. 32.	2 a	ix. 9.	5 i	xxiii. 19, 23.	5 e		
Num. xxii. 15.	5 e	xiii. 17.	5 f	1 Kings iii. 13.	5 o		
xxii. 17.a	5 g i	1 Sam. ii. 29.	5 i	2 Kings v. 1.	6		

1 Chron. iv. 9.	5 e	Ps. xcvi. 6.	3	Eccles. vi. 2.	5 o
xi. 21, 25.	5 e	civ. 1.	3	x. 1.	5 o
xvi. 27.	2 f	cxi. 3.	3	Isa. iii. 3.	5 o
xvii. 18.	5 o	cxii. 9.	5 o	iii. 5.	5 6
xix. 3.	5 k	cxlv. 5.	2 f	v. 13.	5 o
xxix. 12, 28.	5 o	cxlix. 9.	2 f	ix. 15.	6
2 Chron. i. 11, 12.	5 o	Prov. iii. 9.	5 h	xxiii. 8, 9.	5 o
xvii. 5.	5 o	iii. 16.	5 o	xxix. 13.	5 f
xviii. 1.	5 o	iv. 8.	5 i	xlii. 21.	5 l
xxvi. 18.	5 o	v. 9.	3	xliii. 4.	5 b
xxxii. 27, 33.	5 o	viii. 18.	5 o	xliii. 20.	5 i
Esth. i. 4, 20.	4 a	xi. 16.	5 o	xliii. 23.	5 f
vi. 3, 6, 6, 7, 9, 9, 11.	4 a	xii. 9.	5 n	lviii. 13, 13.	5 m f
viii. 16.	4 a	xiii. 18.	5 l	Jer. xxxiii. 9.	7
Job xiv. 21.	5 a	xiv. 28.	2 h	Lam. i. 8.	5 k
xxii. 8.	6	xiv. 31.	5 k	v. 12.	2 c
Ps. vii. 5.	5 o	xv. 33.	5 o	Dan. ii. 6.	4 b
viii. 5.	2 f	xviii. 12.	5 o	iv. 30.	4 b
xv. 4.	5 i	xx. 3.	5 o	iv. 34.	2 d
xxi. 5.	3	xxi. 21.	5 o	iv. 36.	2 g
xxvi. 8.	5 c	xxii. 4.	5 o	iv. 37.	2 g
xlv. 9.	4	xxv. 2.	5 o	v. 18.	2 g
xlix. 12, 20.	4 a	xxvi. 1, 8.	5 o	xi. 21.	3
lxvi. 2.	5 o	xxvii. 18.	5 l	xi. 38, 38.	5 i
lxxi. 8.	7	xxix. 23.	5 o	Nah. iii. 10.	5 o
xci. 15.	5 i	xxxi. 25.	2 f	Mal. i. 6, 6.	5 i o

a honouring I will honour thee.

HOOD

צָנִיף *m.* tiara, turban, as wound around the head of men or women : Isa. iii. 23.

HOOF

עָקֵב *m.* heel; hoof of a horse : Judg. v. 22.

פָּרַס to break, to divide, to cleave. HIPHIL *part.* Ps. lxix. 31, having .... hoofs. פַּרְסָה *f.* cleft, cloven foot, hoof : Exod. x. 26, &c.

HOOK

1 אַגְמוֹן a rush; a hook bent like the top of a rush; Gesenius, a rope made of reeds.

2 וָו hooks like tenter-hooks; or like those on which doors turn; for the curtains and vails of the tabernacle.

3 מַזְלֵג *m.* a flesh-hook. [a] מִזְלָגוֹת *f. pl. id.*

4 חָח a hook or ring inserted in the nostrils of animals, to which a cord was fastened, to drag them about, subdue, or tame them.

5 סִיר *com.* thorn; hook.

6 חַכָּה a hook with a bait to catch fish.

7 צִנָּה a thorn, a hook, a fish-hook.

8 שְׁפַתַּיִם *m. dual*, places in the court of the temple where the victims were fastened, *marg.* ' or, end-irons, or two hearth-stones;' see *Pots.*

Exod. xxvi. 32, 37.	2	Num. iv. 14.	3 a	Job xli. 2.	1
xxvii. 3.	3 a	1 Sam. ii. 13, 14.	3	Isa. xxxvii. 29.	4
xxvii. 10, 11, 17.	2	2 Kings xix. 28.	4	Ezek. xxix. 4.	4
xxxvi. 36, 38.	2	1 Chron. xxviii. 17.	3 a	xxxviii. 4.	4
xxxviii. 3.	3 a	2 Chron. iv. 16.	3 a	xl. 43.	8
xxxviii. 10, 11, 12, 17, 19, 28.	2	Job xli. 1.	6	Amos iv. 2, 2.	5, 7

HOPE

1 בָּטַח to trust, confide in; see *Trust.* KAL [a] *pret.* HIPHIL [b] *part.* [c] בֶּטַח *m.* confidence. [d] בִּטָּחוֹן *m. id.* [e] מִבְטָח *m.* sure and firm hope.

2 חָסָה to trust in for safety and protection; see *Trust.* KAL [a] *part.* Poel. [b] מַחְסֶה *m.* a refuge, shelter.

3 יָאַשׁ to despair. NIPHAL *part.* " there is no hope," implying the rejection of counsel.

4 יָחַל to wait, to hope; importing, properly, a long and patient waiting; a lingering hope, still expecting and earnestly desiring, though hitherto exercised with delay and disappointment. PIEL [a] *pret.* [b] *imp.* [c] *fut.* [d] *part.* HIPHIL [e] *pret.* [f] *imp.* [g] *fut.* [h] יָחִיל *adj.* waiting, hoping. תּוֹחֶלֶת *f.* expectation, hope.

5 כֶּסֶל the loins, the flank: hence, hope, confidence, what a man depends on, as the loins are the strength and firmness of the body.

6 קָוָה to hope strongly; to stretch out the mind in a straight direction towards an object of hope or expectation; to expect earnestly; to hope that a thing will be effected, and to wait steadily and patiently till it is effected. תִּקְוָה [a] *f.* expectation, hope. מִקְוֶה [b] *m. id.*

7 שָׂבַר to look attentively in expectation; to hope, seq. לְ. PIEL [a] *pret.* [b] *fut.* שֵׂבֶר *m.* hope.

Ruth i. 12.	6 a	Ps. xxxviii. 15.	4 e	Prov. xxix. 20.	6 a			
Ezra x. 2.	6 b	xxxix. 7.	4 i	Eccles. ix. 4.	1 d			
Esth. ix. 1.	7 a	xlii. 5, 11.	4 f	Isa. xxxviii. 18.	7 b			
Job iv. 6.	6 a	xliii. 5.	4 f	lvii. 10.	3			
v. 16.	6 a	lxxi. 5.	4 a	Jer. ii. 25.				
vi. 11.	4 c	lxxi. 14.	4 c	xiv. 8.	6 b			
vi. 20.	1 a	lxxviii. 7.	5	xvii. 7.	6 b			
vii. 6.	6 a	cxix. 43, 49, 74, 81,		xvii. 13.	6 b			
viii. 13.	6 a	114, 147.	4 a	xvii. 17.	2 b			
viii. 14.	6 a	cxix. 116.	7 c	xviii. 12.	3			
xi. 18, 20.	6 a	cxix. 166.	7 a	xxxi. 17.	6 b			
xiv. 7, 19.	6 a	cxx. 5.	4 e	l. 7.	6 b			
xvii. 15, 15.	6 a	cxxx. 7.	4 b	Lam. iii. 18.	4 i			
xix. 10.	6 a	cxxxi. 3.	4 b	iii. 21, 24.	4 g			
xxvii. 8.	6 a	cxlvi. 5.	7 c	iii. 26.	4 h			
xxxi. 24.	5	cxlvii. 11.	4 d	iii. 29.	4 a			
xli. 9.	4 i	Prov. x. 28.	4 i	Ezek. xiii. 6.	4 a			
Ps. xvi. 9.	1 c	xi. 7.	4 i	xix. 5.	6 a			
xxii. 9.	1 b	xiii. 12.	4 i	xxxvii. 11.	6 a			
xxxi. 24.	4 d	xiv. 32.	2 a	Hos. ii. 15.	4 a			
xxxiii. 18.	4 d	xix. 18.	6 a	Joel iii. 16.	2 b			
xxxiii. 22.	4 a	xxvi. 12.	6 a	Zech. ix. 12.	6 a			

HORN

קֶרֶן *f.* a horn, as of an ox, ram; also an artificial horn: *metaph.* horn is put as the symbol of strength, might, power, the image being drawn from the bull and other animals, which push with their horns; so, to exalt, to lift up the horn of any one, is to strengthen any one, to increase his power or dignity; in a bad sense, to lift up one's horn, to be proud, Ps. lxxv. 5, 6, *comp.* Lat. *cornua sumere*, of those who place too much confidence in their own strength, and thus become overbearing; also Hor. Od. iii. 21, 18, "*addis cornua pauperi.*" In prophetic vision, horns are put for kings, powerful princes; both Alexander and the Seleucidæ are represented on coins with horns. From resemblance to a horn, it is used of a wind instrument, cornet, Josh. vi. 5; of elephants' teeth, called horns of ivory, Ezek. xxvii. 15; so Plin. "*cornua elephanti;*" of horns of the altar, projecting points on the four corners of the altar; *dual, i. q.* rays of light, splendour: Hab. iii. 4: Gen. xxiii. 13, &c. קְרֶן Ch. *f.* Dan. vii. 7, 8, 8, 8, 8, 11, 20, 20, 21, 24. קָרַן to have horns. HIPHIL *part.* Ps. lxix. 31.

HORNET

צִרְעָה *f.* according to the ancient versions and Rabbins, a hornet, with the article collective, hornets, wasps, so called from their striking or stinging; hornets and wasps in warm countries are accustomed to attack travellers, coming in large swarms. Exod. xxiii. 28: Deut. vii. 20: Josh. xxiv. 12.

HORROR, HORRIBLE

1 אֵימָה *f.* terror, dread.

2 זַלְעָפָה *f.* a scorching, blasting wind; to be in a scorched, blasted state, without life or spirit.

3 פַּלָּצוּת *f.* trembling, horror.

4 שָׁאוֹן *m.* noise, uproar, tumult; *or,* desolation.

5 שָׂעַר to shudder, to be horribly afraid. KAL [a] *imp.* [b] שַׂעַר *m.* horror.

6 שַׁעֲרוּר *adj.* something horrible, vile. [a] שַׁעֲרוּרִי *adj. id.*

Gen. xv. 12.		1	Ps. cxix. 53.	2	Jer. xxiii. 14.	6
Ps. xi. 6.		2	Jer. ii. 12.	5 a	Ezek. vii. 18.	3
xl. 2.		4	v. 30.	6	xxxii. 10. a	5 b
lv. 5.		3	xviii. 13.	6 a	Hos. vi. 10.	6 a

a lit. afraid with horror.

HORSE, HORSEBACK, HORSEMAN

בַּעַל *m.* owner, master, lord: 2 Sam. i. 6, *lit.* and masters of the horsemen.

סוּס *m.* a horse, so called from his leaping; *sing.* often *collect.* horses, war-horses, cavalry: Exod. xiv. 9, 23: Deut. xvii. 16: 1 Kings xviii. 5, &c. The war-horse is described, Job xxxix. 19, &c. סוּסָה *f.* a mare: Cant. i. 9. Lxx. ἡ ἵππος, which the Vulg. renders as a collective *equitatus.*

פָּרָשׁ *m.* horseman, rider, *eques;* it is always translated horseman, but is thought sometimes to mean horses for riding, steeds, as it is evidently to be distinguished from סוּסִים common horses for chariots: 1 Kings iv. 26: Ezek. xxvii. 14: Joel ii. 4: 2 Sam. i. 6, *lit.* masters of the horsemen, &c. Gen. i. 9, &c.

רָכַב to ride. KAL *part.* Poel, 2 Kings ix. 18, *lit.* riding on a horse; 19. HIPHIL *pret.* Esth. vi. 9. *fut.* Esth. vi. 11, brought on horseback. רַכָּב rider, horseman: 2 Kings ix. 17.

HORSELEACH

עֲלוּקָה *f. pr.* leech, bloodsucker; only occurs in Prov. xxx. 15.

HOSEN

פַּטִּישׁ *m.* Ch. tunics, under garments: Dan. iii. 21 (כתיב). פְּטָשׁ Ch. *m.* Dan. iii. 21 (קרי).

HOST

1 חַיִל *m.* strength, might, valour; forces, army, host. [a] חֵיל *m. id.*

2 מַחֲנֶה *com.* an encampment; an army, host.

3 צָבָא *m.* war, warfare; an army, host; specially of angels, and of the heavenly bodies; one of all the earth contains, Gen. ii. 1. Jehovah, God of hosts, *i. e.* of the celestial armies, is a very usual appellation of the Most High God, especially in Isaiah, Jeremiah, Zechariah, and Malachi, but does not occur in the Pentateuch, in the

books of Joshua and Judges, nor in Ezekiel, Job, and the writings of Solomon. Gen. ii. 1, &c.

No. 3 not included.

Gen. xxxii. 2.	2	1 Sam. xi. 11.	2	2 Kings xi. 15.	1		
Exod. xiv. 4, 17, 28.	1	xiv. 15, 19.	2	xviii. 17.	1 a		
xiv. 24, 24.	2	xiv. 48.	1	xxv. 1.	1		
xv. 4.	1	xvii. 20.	1	1 Chron. ix. 19.	2		
xvi. 13.	2	xviii. 46.	2	xi. 15, 18.	2		
Num. xxxi. 14.	1	xxviii. 5, 19.	2	xii. 22, 22.	2		
Deut. ii. 14, 15.	2	xxix. 6.	2	xiv. 15, 16.	2		
xxiii. 9.	2	2 Sam. v. 24.	2	xviii. 9.	1		
Josh. i. 11.	2	viii. 9.	1	2 Chron. xiv. 9.	2		
iii. 2.	2	xxiii. 16.	2	xiv. 13.	1		
viii. 13.	2	xxiv. 2, 4, 4.	1	xvi. 7, 8.	1		
x. 5.	2	1 Kings xv. 20.	1	xviii. 33.	2		
xi. 4.	2	xx. 1.	1	xxiii. 14.	1		
xviii. 9.	2	xxii. 34, 36.	2	xxiv. 23, 24.	1		
Judg. iv. 15, 16, 16.	2	2 Kings iii. 9.	2	xxvi. 11.	1		
vii. 1, 8, 9, 10, 11,		vi. 14, 15.	1	Ps. xxvii. 3.	2		
11, 13, 14, 15, 15,		vi. 24.	1	xxxiii. 16.	1		
21, 22, 22.	2	vii. 4, 14.	2	cxxxvi. 15.	1		
viii. 10, 10, 11, 11,		vii. 6, 6.	2, 1	Ezek. i. 24.	2		
12.	2	ix. 5.	1	Obad. 20.	1 a		

HOSTAGE

בֵּן *m.* son : 2 Kings xiv. 14, *lit.* sons of pledges : 2 Chron. xxv. 24, *lit. id.*

תַּעֲרוּבָה *f.* suretyship : 2 Kings xiv. 14, *lit.* as above ; 2 Chron. xxv. 24, *lit. id.*

HOT

אֵשׁ *com.* fire : Lev. xiii. 24, *marg.* 'burning of fire.'

חָזָק *adj.* strong, applied to war : 2 Sam. xi. 15.

HOUGH

עָקַר to pluck up, to root out ; Piel, to hamstring a horse, *i. e.* to cut the sinews of the hind leg, by which the animal is rendered wholly useless. PIEL *pret.* Josh. xi. 9. *fut.* Josh. xi. 6 : 2 Sam. viii. 4 : 1 Chron. xviii. 4.

HOUR

שָׁעָה *Ch. f.* moment of time : Dan. iii. 6, 15 ; iv. 19, 33 ; v. 5.

HOUSE, HOUSEHOLD

נָאוֹת *f. pl.* pleasant places, pastures, habitations : Ps. lxxxiii. 12.

בַּיִת *m.* a house built by man's industry and labour, in which he dwells and abides, his fixed home ; sometimes translated household, family : to build, to make a house, is to give a numerous posterity. This word is applied to temples, as " the house of God," the " house of Jehovah," 1 Kings vi. 37 ; vii. 12 : Isa. lxvi. 1 ; also to temples of idols, Isa. xxxvii. 38 ; xliv. 13 : 1 Sam. v. 2, 5. It is used of royal houses, palaces, and fortresses ; of royal and adorned sepulchres, Isa. xiv. 18, *cf.* xxii. 16 ; very suitably rendered in Eccles. xii. 5, man's "long home." It is in a peculiar manner applied to receptacles or places for inanimate things ; see *Contain, Place, Tablet :* and to that which is within, the inner part ; see *Within.*—Gen. vii. 1, &c. בַּיִת *Chald. m. id.* Ezra iv. 24, &c.

עֲבֹדָה service ; household : Job i. 3, *marg.* ' *or,* husbandry.'

HOUSETOP

גַּג *m.* see *Roof.* Housetops were accessible from one to

another : Isa. xxii. 1.—2 Kings xix. 26 : Ps. cii. 7 ; cxxix. 6 : Prov. xxi. 9 ; xxv. 24 : Isa. xxii. 1 ; xxxvii. 27 : Jer. xlviii. 38 : Zeph. i. 5.

HOWL

יָלַל to cry out or shriek as a woman in labour ; to wail and lament as persons in distress. Applied to wild beasts, it is to howl or yell. HIPHIL *pret.* b *imp.* c *fut.* d יֵלֵל *m.* yelling or howling. e יְלָלָה *f. id.*

Deut. xxxii. 10.	d	Jer. iv. 8.	b	Ezek. xxx. 2.	b
Isa. xiii. 6.	b	xxv. 34.	b	Hos. vii. 14.	c
xiv. 31.	b	xxv. 36.	b	Joel i. 5, 11, 13.	b
xv. 2, 3.	c	xlvii. 2.	a	Amos viii. 3.	a
xv. 8, 8.	c	xlviii. 20, 39.	b	Micah i. 8.	c
xvi. 7, 7.	c	xlviii. 31.	c	Zeph. i. 10.	b
xxiii. 1, 6, 14.	c	xlix. 3.	c	Zech. xi. 2, 2.	b
iii. 5.	c	li. 8.	b	xi. 3.	e
lxv. 14.	b	Ezek. xxi. 12.	b		

HUGE

רֹב *m.* multitude, abundance : 2 Chron. xvi. 8.

HUMBLE

1 דָּכָא to bruise ; to be in distress ; penitent, submissive to the will of God. PUAL *pret.*

2 כָּנַע to be bowed down ; applied to the humbling or mortifying the proud ; to a wicked person being humbled for his sins by repentance. NIPHAL a *pret.* b *inf.* c *fut.*

3 עַיִן the eye : Job xxii. 29.

4 עָנָה (see *Afflict*), to humble by oppression, by carnal intercourse. NIPHAL a *inf.* PIEL b *pret.* c *inf.* d *imp.* e *fut.* f עָנָו *adj.* humble, meek. g עֲנָוָה *f.* a lowly mind.

5 צָנַע to be lowly, submissive, modest ; to act submissively, modestly. HIPHIL *inf.*

6 רָכַס to trample ; to let oneself be trampled upon, to humble oneself. HITHPAEL *imp.*

7 שׁוּחַ to sink down, to be bowed down. HIPHIL *fut.*

8 שָׁחָה to bow the head ; to beseech humbly, *lit.* to do obeisance. HITHPAEL *pret.*

9 שָׁחַח to be bowed down, to be depressed. KAL a *fut.* b שַׁח *adj.* cast down.

10 שָׁפֵל to be low in situation, in mind, in condition, or in any other respect. KAL a *pret.* b *fut.* HIPHIL c *imp.* d *part.* שְׁפַל *Ch.* APHEL e *pret.* f שָׁפָל *adj.* low.

Exod. x. 3.	4 a	2 Chron. xxxiii. 12.	2 c	Prov. xv. 33.	4 g		
Lev. xxvi. 41.	2 c	xxxiii. 19.	2 b	xvi. 19.	10 f		
Deut. viii. 2, 16.	2 c	xxxiii. 23, 23.	2 a b	xviii. 12.	4 g		
viii. 3.	4	xxxiv. 27, 27.	2 c	xxii. 4.	4 g		
xxi. 14.	4 b	xxxvi. 12.	2 a	xxix. 23.	10 f		
xxii. 24, 29.	4 b	Job xxii. 29.	9 b, 3	Isa. ii. 9.	10 b		
Judg. xix. 24.	4 d	Ps. ix. 12.	4 f	ii. 11.	10 a		
2 Sam. xvi. 4.	8	ix. 12.	4 f	v. 15, 15.	10 b		
1 Kings xxi. 29, 29.	2 a	x. 10.	9 a	x. 33.	10 b		
2 Kings xxii. 19.	2 c	x. 12, 17.	4 f	lviii. 15, 15.	10 f		
2 Chron. vii. 14.	2 c	x. 12.	4 h	Jer. xiii. 18.	10 c		
xii. 6.	2 c	xxxiv. 2.	4 f	xliv. 10.	1		
xii. 7, 7.	2 a	xxxv. 13.	4 f	Lam. iii. 20.	7		
xii. 12.	2 b	lxix. 32.	4 f	Ezek. xxii. 10, 11.	4 b		
xxx. 11.	2 b	cxiii. 6.	10 d	Dan. v. 22.	10 e		
xxxii. 26.	2 c	Prov. vi. 3.	6	Micah vi. 8.	5		

HUNGER

רָעֵב to hunger, to be hungry, of individuals or of a whole

country. KAL [a]pret. [b]fut. HIPHIL [c]fut. [d] רָעֵב m. hunger, famine. [e] רָעֵב adj. hungry, hunger-bitten.

Exod. xvi. 3.	d	Ps. xxxiv. 10.		Isa. xxxii. 6.	e
Deut. viii. 3.	c	l. 12.	a	xliv. 12.	b
xxviii. 48.	d	cvii. 5, 9, 36.	e	xlix. 10.	e
xxxii. 24.	d	cxlvi. 7.	e	lviii. 7, 10.	b
1 Sam. ii. 5.	e	Prov. vi. 30.	e	lxv. 13.	b
2 Sam. xvii. 29.	e	xix. 15.	b	Jer. xxxviii. 9.	d
2 Kings vii. 12.	e	xxv. 21.	e	xlii. 14.	b
Neh. ix. 15.	d	xxvii. 7.	e	Lam. ii. 19.	d
Job v. 5.	e	Isa. viii. 21, 21.	e b	iv. 9.	d
xviii. 12.	e	ix. 20.	e	Ezek. xviii. 7, 16.	d e
xxii. 7.	e	xxix. 8.	e	xxxiv. 29.	d
xxiv. 10.	e				

HUNT

1 צָדָה to lie in wait, to hunt after; seq. acc. KAL part. Poel.

2 צוּד to lie in wait; seq. acc. to hunt wild beasts, to catch birds. KAL [a]pret. [b]inf. [c]fut. POEL [d]inf. [e]fut. [f]part. [g] מְצוֹדָה f. capture, prey. [h] צַיִד m. hunting, the chase. [i] צַיָד m. hunter.

3 רָדַף to pursue after, to chase. KAL fut.

Gen. x. 9, 9.α	2 h	1 Sam. xxvi. 20.	3	Jer. xvi. 16, 16.	2 i a
xxv. 27.β	2 h	Job x. 16.	2 c	Lam. iv. 18.	2 c
xxvii. 5.	2 b	xxxviii. 39.	2 c	Ezek. xiii. 18, 18.	2 d e
xxvii. 30.	2 c	Ps. cxl. 11.	2 c	xiii. 20, 20.	2 f
Lev. xvii. 13.γ	2 c h	Prov. vi. 26.	2 c	xiii. 21.	2 g
1 Sam. xxiv. 11.	1	xii. 27.	2 h	Micah vii. 2.	2 c

α lit. mighty of hunting.   β lit. skilful of hunting.
γ lit. which hunteth a hunting.

HURL

שָׁלַךְ to cast, to throw. HIPHIL pret. Num. xxxv. 20.

שָׂעַר to shudder. PIEL, to sweep away in a storm, seq. מִן: fut. Job xxvii. 21.

HURT

1 דָּבָר m. word, matter, business, &c.

2 חֲבַל Ch. to hurt, to harm. PAEL [a]pret. [b] חֲבַל Ch. m. injury. [c] חֲבַל Ch. m. damage. [d] חֲבוּלָה Ch. f. a wicked action.

3 חַבּוּרָה f. a stripe, weal, bruise.

4 כָּלַם (see Ashamed), to hurt or injure to another's shame. HIPHIL [a]pret. HOPHAL [b]pret.

5 נָגַף to smite. KAL [a]pret. [b]fut.

6 נְזַק Ch. to suffer loss, detriment. APHEL [a]inf. [b]part.

7 עָנָה see Afflict. PIEL pret.

8 עָצַב to be grieved; to be pained, to hurt oneself, seq. בְּ with anything. NIPHAL fut.

9 פָּקַד to visit; with עַל to visit upon, i. e. to inflict. KAL fut.

10 רָעַע to be evil; to do evil. HIPHIL [a]pret. [b]inf. [c]fut. [d] רַע adj. evil.

11 שָׁבַר to break. NIPHAL [a]pret. HOPHAL [b]pret. [c] שֶׁבֶר m. breaking, destruction.

Gen. iv. 23.	3	1 Sam. xxiv. 9.	10 d	Ps. xv. 4.	10 b
xxvi. 29.	10 d	xxv. 7.	4 a	xxxv. 4, 26.	10 d
xxxi. 7.	10 b	xxv. 15.	4 b	xxxviii. 12.	10 d
xxxi. 29.	10 d	xxv. 34.	10 b	xli. 7.	10 d
Exod. xxi. 22.	5 a	2 Sam. xviii. 32.	10 d	lxx. 2.	10 d
xxi. 35.	5 b	2 Kings xiv. 10.	10 b	lxxi. 13, 24.	10 d
xxii. 10, 14.	11 a	2 Chron. xxv. 19.	10 d	cv. 18.	7
Num. xvi. 15.	10 a	Ezra iv. 15.	6 b	cxliv. 10.	10 d
Josh. xxiv. 20.	10 a	iv. 22.	6 a	Eccles. v. 13.	10 d
1 Sam. xx. 21.	1	Esth. ix. 2.	10 d	viii. 9.	10 d

Eccles. x. 9.	8	Jer. viii. 11.	11 c	Jer. xxv. 7.	10 d
Isa. xi. 9.	10 c	viii. 21, 21.	11 c b	xxxviii. 4.	10 d
xxvii. 3.	9	x. 19.	11 c	Dan. iii. 25.	2 b
lxv. 25.	10 c	xxiv. 9.	10 d	vi. 22, 22.	2 a d
Jer. vi. 14.	11 c	xxv. 6.	10 c	vi. 23.	2 c
vii. 6.	10 d				

HUSBAND

1 אִישׁ m. man, husband: Gen. iii. 6, &c.

2 אֱנוֹשׁ m. man.

3 בָּעַל to be lord and master over anything; to become the husband of any one. KAL [a]pret. [b]part. Poel. [c] בַּעַל m. master, husband.

4 חָתָן m. one who marries the daughter of any one; hence in respect to the bride, a bridegroom, spouse: Exod. iv. 25, 26. These words, "a bloody husband," are commonly understood as applied to Moses, but by some they are referred to the infant, now espoused to God by the seal of circumcision. Aben-Ezra remarks, "It is the custom of women to call a son, when he is circumcised, a spouse." Kimchi concurs in this view, and it is adopted by Schindler, Spencer, Mede, and others. The context however, as Abendana points out, evidently refers them to Moses.

5 רֵעַ m. companion, friend, neighbour.

No. 1 not included.

Exod. iv. 25, 26.	4	2 Sam. xi. 26, 26.	1, 3 c	Jer. iii. 20.	5
xxi. 22.	3 c	Esth. i. 17, 20.	3 c	xxix. 6.	2
Deut. xxi. 13.	3 a	Prov. xii. 4.	3 c	xxxi. 32.	3 a
xxii. 22.	3 c	xxxi. 11, 23, 28.	3 c	Ezek. xvi. 45, 45.	1, 2
xxiv. 4.	3 c	Isa. liv. 5.	3 b	Joel i. 8.	3 c
Ruth i. 11.	2				

HUSBANDMAN, HUSBANDRY

1 אֲדָמָה f. ground.

2 אִישׁ m. man.

3 אִכָּר m. a digger, a husbandman.

4 נוּב to dig, to plough. KAL part. (כתיב).

5 יָנַב to cut, to plough. KAL part. Poel.

6 עָבַד to labour, to work; to till the ground. KAL part. Poel.

Gen. ix. 20.α	2, 1	Jer. xxxi. 24.	3	Joel i. 11.	3
2 Kings xxv. 12.	5 or 4	li. 23.	3	Amos v. 16.	3
2 Chron. xxvi. 10, 10.	3, 1	lii. 16.	5	Zech. xiii. 5.β	2, 6, 1

α lit. a man of the ground.   β lit. a man a tiller of the ground.

HUSK

זָג m. the skin of a grape, husk, as being transparent: Num. vi. 4.

צִקְלוֹן m. sack, bag, scrip, from being drawn up and tied: 2 Kings iv. 42.

HYPOCRITE

אָדָם m. man; "hypocrite," lit. profane man: Job xxxiv. 30.

חָנֵף adj. (see Defile), one defiled in mind and conscience, yet concealing it, and pretending to be outwardly what he is not inwardly; to have zeal and affection towards God, when his heart is far from him; or dividing his heart between God and the world; opp. to the innocent, who has a good conscience, Job xvii. 8; one that causes to

dissemble by flatteries, Dan. xi. 32. Hypocrites are distinguished from sinners, Isa. xxxiii. 14; the latter being more fully declared by their opposite in the former part of verse 15, and the former by the opposite in the remainder of verse 15. Lxx. ἀσεβής, ἄνομος, παράνομος, only twice ὑποκριτής. Job viii. 13; xiii. 16; xv. 34; xvii. 8; xx. 5; xxvii. 8; xxxiv. 30; xxxvi. 13: Ps. xxxv. 16: Prov. xi. 9: Isa. ix. 17; x. 6; xxxiii. 14. חֹנֵף m. hypocrisy: Isa. xxxii. 6.

HYSSOP

אֵזוֹב m. a herb of a bitter taste, growing on the mountains near Jerusalem, as well as on the walls round the city and in the Sinai desert; much used by the Hebrews in their sacred purifications and sprinklings, for which it was well adapted, as it literally grows in bunches. The emblem of spiritual purification, Ps. li. 7. Under this name, the Hebrews appear to have comprised not only the common hyssop of the shops, but also other aromatic plants, especially mint, wild marjoram, &c.: Exod. xii. 22: Lev. xiv. 4, 6, 49, 51, 52: Num. xix. 6, 18: 1 Kings iv. 33: Ps. li. 7.

ICE

קֶרַח m. ice, so called from its smoothness; see *Bald*. Job vi. 16; xxxviii. 29. קְרַח m. id. Ps. cxlvii. 17. Some copies read קָרְחוֹ from the preceding word; *poet.* for hail.—Gesenius.

IDLE

עַצְלוּת f. sloth, indolence: Prov. xxxi. 27.

רְמִיָּה f. a letting fall of the hand, *i. e.* remissness, sloth: Prov. xix. 15.

רָפָה to be relaxed; to be slack, *i. e.* remiss, idle. NIPHAL *part.* Exod. v. 8, 17, 17.

שִׁפְלוּת f. a letting down, *e. g.* of the hands: Eccles. x. 18.

שָׁקַט to rest, to keep quiet, secure. HIPHIL *inf.* Ezek. xvi. 49.

IDOL, IDOLATRY

1 אָוֶן m. nothingness, vanity; specially of the nothingness of idols and of everything pertaining to idolatry, and so put for an idol.

2 אֵימָה f. terror, dread; *pl.* idols, so called from the terror with which they impress their worshippers, as the opposite of peace enjoyed by a true worshipper of Jehovah.

3 אֵל m. God; also a general name for a supposed divinity; see *God*. Isa. lvii. 5, *marg.* 'among the oaks;' as from אוּל, *pl.* אֵלִים.

4 אֱלִיל m. or *adj.* nought, empty, vain, worthless.

5 גִּלּוּלִים m. *pl.* trunks, logs, blocks, which are rolled; hence, in derision, idols: others derive this word from גָּלַל dung, *i. e.* detestable and contemptible; chiefly used in Ezekiel. Lev. xxvi. 30, &c.

6 חַמָּנִים m. images, images of the sun.

7 מִפְלֶצֶת f. horror, terror; an idol, as inspiring terror.

8 סֶמֶל m. likeness, image.

9 עֶצֶב m. image, idol; either because it is wrought and laboured; *or*, because the service of idols is laborious; *or*, because it causes grief and trouble. ᵃ עָצָב m. id. ᵇ עֹצֶב m. id.

10 צִיר m. form, shape; see *Fashion*.

11 שִׁקּוּץ m. abomination, "abominable idols."

12 תְּרָפִים m. (see *Teraphim*), idols, "idolatry."

No. 5 not included.

Lev. xix. 4.	4	Ps. xcvii. 7.	4	Isa. lxvi. 3.	1
xxvi. 1.		cvi. 36, 38.	9	Jer. xxii. 28.	9 a
1 Sam. xv. 23.	4	cxv. 4.	9	l. 2.	9
xxxi. 9.	12	cxxxv. 15.	9	l. 38.	2
1 Kings xv. 13, 13.	9	Isa. ii. 8, 18, 20, 20.	4	Hos. iv. 17.	9
1 Chron. x. 9.	7	x. 10. a	4	xiii. 2.	9
xvi. 26.	9	x. 11, 11.	4, 9	xiv. 8.	9
2 Chron. xv. 8.	11	xix. 1, 3.	4	Micah i. 7.	9
xv. 16, 16.	7	xxxi. 7, 7.	4	Hab. ii. 18.	4
xxiv. 18.		xlv. 16.	10	Zech. x. 2.	12
xxxiii. 7, 15.	8	xlvi. 1.	9	xi. 17.	4
xxxiv. 7.	6	xlvii. 15.	9 b	xiii. 2.	9
Ps. xcvi. 5.	4	lvii. 5.	3		

a lit. idol.

IGNOMINY

קָלוֹן m. contempt, shame, dishonour: Prov. xviii. 3.

IGNORANCE

יָדַע to know. KAL *pret.* Isa. lvi. 10, *lit.* they know not; lxiii. 16, *lit.* know us not. *fut.* Ps. lxxiii. 22, *marg.* 'I knew not.' דַּעַת f. knowledge; ignorantly, *lit.* without knowledge: Deut. xix. 4.

שָׁגַג to err; to sin ignorantly. KAL *part.* Poel, Num. xv. 28. שְׁגָגָה f. an error, mistake, transgression through ignorance or inadvertence: Lev. iv. 2, 22, 27; v. 15, 18: Num. xv. 24, 25, 25, 26, 27, 28, 29.

ILL, ILL-FAVOURED

רָעַע to be evil, bad. KAL *pret.* Jer. xl. 4. HIPHIL *pret.* Gen. xliii. 6: Mic. iii. 4. רַע *adj.* evil: Gen. xli. 3, 4, 19, 20, 21, 27: Deut. xv. 21: Isa. iii. 11. יָרַע to go ill. KAL *fut.* Job xx. 26: Ps. cvi. 32.

IMAGE

1 אֱלִיל m. an idol. See *Idol*.

2 גִּלּוּלִים m. idols. See *Idol*.

3 חַמָּנִים m. an idol. *Marg.* 'sun images.'

4 מַצֵּבָה f. anything set upright; statues or pillars.

5 תְּמוּנָה f. appearance, form, shape.

6 סֶמֶל m. likeness, image.

7 עֶצֶב m. an idol. See *Idol*.

8 צֶלֶם m. image, likeness, shadowing forth anything; splendour, or whatever makes man remarkable or procures respect. Amos v. 26. Lxx. τύπους. צְלֵם Ch. m.

9 צַעֲצֻעִים m. *pl.* sculptured work: 2 Chron. iii. 10, *marg.* 'or (as some think), of moveable work.'

10 מַשְׂכִּית m. image, figure: Ezek. viii. 12, chambers of imagery, the walls painted with figures of idols; Lev. xxvi. 1, "a standing image." See Layard's Nineveh.

11 תְּרָפִים m. *pl.* See *Teraphim*.

Gen. i. 26, 27, 27.	8	2 Kings xi. 18.	8	Ezek. vi. 4, 6.	3
v. 3.	8	xvii. 10.	4	vii. 20.	8
ix. 6.	8	xviii. 4.	4	viii. 3, 5.	6
xxxi. 19, 34, 35.	11	xxiii. 14.	4	viii. 12.	10
Exod. xxiii. 24.	4	xxiii. 24.	11	xvi. 17.	8
xxxiv. 13.	4	2 Chron. iii. 10.	9	xxi. 21.	11
Lev. xxvi. 1, 1.	4, 10	xiv. 3.	4	xxiii. 14.	8
xxvi. 30.	3	xiv. 5.	3	xxx. 13.	1
Num. xxxiii. 52.	4	xxiii. 17.	8	Dan. ii. 31, 31, 32, 34,	
Deut. vii. 5.	4	xxxi. 1.	4	35.	8 a
xvi. 22.	4	xxxiv. 4.	4	iii. 1, 2, 3, 5, 7, 10,	
1 Sam. vi. 5, 5, 11.	8	Job iv. 16.	5	12, 14, 15, 18.	8 a
xix. 13, 16.	11	Ps. lxxiii. 20.	8	Hos. iii. 4.	4
2 Sam. v. 21.	7	Isa. xvii. 8.	3	x. 1, 2.	4
1 Kings xiv. 23.	4	xxvii. 9.	3	Amos v. 26.	8
2 Kings iii. 2.	4	Jer. xliii. 13.	4	Micah v. 13.	4
x. 26, 27.	4	l. 2.	2		

IMAGINE

1　הָגָה　to meditate.　KAL *fut.*

2　זָמַם　to devise ; to purpose.　KAL *fut.*

3　חָרַשׁ　to fabricate ; to devise.　KAL *part.* Poel.

4　חָשַׁב　to think ; to design, to contrive, to purpose.　KAL [a] *pret.* [b] *fut.* [c] *part.* Poel.　PIEL [d] *fut.* [e] מַחֲשֶׁבֶת *f.* imagination.

5　יֵצֶר　*m.* frame ; meditation, thought : Gen. vi. 5, *marg.* ' or, the whole imagination.'　"The Hebrew word signifieth not only the imagination, but also purposes and desires."

6　שְׁרִירוּת　*f.*　Our version seems to have derived the meaning of this word from שׁוּר to contemplate, or שָׁרַר to lie in wait, to observe ; whence imagination, evil device ; but it is now more commonly referred to שָׁרַר to be firm, hard ; hence hardness, stubbornness, as in the margin of our version.

Gen. vi. 5.	5	Ps. xxi. 11.	4 a	Jer. xvi. 12.	6
viii. 21.	5	xxxviii. 12.	1	xviii. 12.	6
xi. 6.	2	cxl. 2.	4 a	xxiii. 17.	6
Deut. xxix. 19.	6	Prov. vi. 18.	4 e	Lam. iii. 60, 61.	4 e
xxxi. 21.	5	xii. 20.	3	Hos. vii. 15.	4 d
1 Chron. xxviii. 9.	5	Jer. iii. 17.	6	Nah. i. 9.	4 d
xxix. 18.	5	vii. 24.	6	i. 11.	4 c
Job vi. 26.	4 b	ix. 14.	6	Zech. vii. 10.	4 b
Ps. ii. 1.	1	xi. 8.	6	viii. 17.	4 b
x. 2.	4 a	xiii. 10.	6		

IMMANUEL

עִמָּנוּאֵל　*lit.* God with us : a name in anticipation of the Incarnation of the only-begotten Son of God, the Word made flesh : Isa. vii. 14 ; viii. 8.

IMPART

חָלַק　to divide, *seq.* בְּ of the thing.　KAL *pret.* Job xxxix. 17.

IMPERIOUS

שַׁלֶּטֶת　*adj. f.* hard, vehement, imperious : Ezek. xvi. 30.

IMPOSE

רְמָה　Ch. to cast, to set ; to impose tribute.　P'AL *inf.* Ezra vii. 24.

IMPOVERISH

דָּלַל　to hang down ; to bring low ; to enfeeble.　NIPHAL *fut.* Judg. vi. 6.

סָכַן　to be poor and needy ; to be dangerously impoverished.　PUAL *part.* Isa. xl. 20, *marg.* ' is poor of oblation.'

רוּשׁ　to be poor ; or רָשַׁשׁ to break down.　POEL *fut.* Jer. v. 17.　PUAL *pret.* Mal. i. 4.

IMPRISONMENT

אֱסוּר　Ch. band : Ezra vii. 26.

IMPUDENT

חָזָק　*adj.* strong. מֵצַח *com.* forehead : Ezek. iii. 7, *lit.* stiff of forehead.

עָזַז　to strengthen.　HIPHIL *pret.* Prov. vii. 13, *marg.* ' she strengthened her face :' this implies that her face was unveiled, after the manner of harlots.

קָשֶׁה　*adj.* hard. פָּנִים *m. pl.* face : Ezek. ii. 4, *lit.* hard of face.

IMPUTE

חָשַׁב　to think, to account, to lay to one's charge, to put to account.　KAL *fut.* 2 Sam. xix. 19 : Ps. xxxii. 2.　NIPHAL *fut.* Lev. vii. 18 ; xvii. 4.

שׂוּם　to set, put, place.　KAL *fut.* 1 Sam. xxii. 15.

INCENSE

לְבוֹנָה　*f.* frankincense : Isa. xliii. 23 ; lx. 6 ; lxvi. 3 ; Jer. vi. 20 ; xvii. 26 ; xli. 5.

קָטַר　to burn incense ; see *Burn.*　HOPHAL *part.* Mal. i. 11. קִטֵּר *m.* Jer. xliv. 21. קְטֹרֶת *f.* incense, fat : Exod. xxv. 6, &c. קְטוֹרָה *f. id.* Deut. xxxiii. 10.

INCENSE (V)

חָרָה　to wax hot.　NIPHAL *part.* Isa. xli. 11 ; xlv. 24.

INCLINE

1　נָטָה　the word imports the action or motion of stretching or extending, expanding.　It is applied to the stretching out or extending the heart towards an object in regard, favour, mercy, compassion.　KAL [a] *pret.* [b] *fut.* HIPHIL [c] *pret.* [d] *inf.* [e] *imp.* [f] *fut.*

2　קָשַׁב　to attend to anything, to hearken.　HIPHIL *inf.*

3　שׁוּחַ　to sink down, to settle down.　KAL *pret.*

Josh. xxiv. 23.	1 e	Ps. cii. 2.	1 e	Isa. lv. 3.	1 e
Judg. ix. 3.	1 b	cxvi. 2.	1 c	Jer. vii. 24, 26.	1 c
1 Kings viii. 58.	1 d	cxix. 36.	1 e	xi. 8.	1 c
Ps. xvii. 6.	1 e	cxix. 112.	1 a	xvii. 23.	1 c
xl. 1.	1 b	cxli. 4.	1 f	xxv. 4.	1 c
xlv. 10.	1 e	Prov. ii. 2.	2	xxxiv. 14.	1 c
xlix. 4.	1 f	ii. 18.	3	xxxv. 15.	1 c
lxxi. 2.	1 e	iv. 20.	1 e	xliv. 5.	1 c
lxxviii. 1.	1 e	v. 13.	1 c	Dan. ix. 18.	1 e
lxxxviii. 2.	1 e	Isa. xxxvii. 17.	1 e		

INCLOSE, INCLOSING

1　גָּדַר　to fence, to fence up, to inclose.　KAL *pret.*

2　כָּתַר　to compass about as a crown compasseth the head.　PIEL *pret.*

3　מִלֻּאָה　*f.* filling, *i. e.* setting of gems.

4　נָעַל　to make a door fast, or a place secure with bolts and bars.　KAL *part.* Paül.

5　נָקַף　to move in a circle, to surround.　HIPHIL *pret.*

6　סָבַב　to compass, surround.　HOPHAL *part.*

7　סָגַר　to shut, to close.　KAL *pret.*

8　צוּר　to bind, to press ; *seq. acc.* and עַל to press one thing upon another.　KAL *fut.*

Exod. xxviii. 20.	3	Judg. xx. 43.	2	Cant. iv. 12.	4
xxxix. 6.	6	Ps. xvii. 10.	7	viii. 9.	8
xxxix. 13, 13.	6, 3	xxii. 16.	5	Lam. iii. 9.	1

INCREASE

1 אָמַץ to be strong, resolute, and vigorous. PIEL, to make strong, to increase (strength): *part.*

2 תְּבוּאָה *f.* produce, increase of the earth; gain, profit; *trop.* result, consequence: Prov. xviii. 20.

3 גָּאָה to rise up; to exalt self. KAL *fut.* Job x. 16. There may be implied figuratively, as the aggravation of his affliction, pride and arrogance, with insult.

4 גָּדַל to become great. HIPHIL *pret.*

5 יְבוּל *m.* the produce of the earth, or what it *brings* in for sustenance of man or beast.

6 יָסַף to add, *seq. acc.* and עַל; to add to, to increase, to augment, *seq.* עַל, אֶל, לְ, and *acc.* KAL *a pret.* NIPHAL *b part.* HIPHIL *c pret.* *d inf.* *e fut.*

7 נוּב to bring forth fruit. KAL *a fut.* Ps. lxii. 10, "if riches increase," *i. e.* as fruit from the land, in opposition to increase by oppression and robbery. *b* תְּנוּבָה *f.* produce.

8 עָלָה to ascend, to rise, to increase: of a battle, of tumult, of a building. KAL *a fut.* *b part.* Poel.

9 עָצַם to bind; to be strong, mighty; to be strong in number. KAL *pret.*

10 פָּרָה to bear; to be fruitful. KAL *a pret.* *b fut.* HIPHIL *c fut.*

11 פָּרַץ to break, to break out or forth; to spread abroad; usually employed to signify a vast and sudden increase.—*Bush.* KAL *a pret.* *b fut.*

12 רָבַב to become much, or many, to multiply. KAL *a pret.* *b* רֹב *m.* multitude, abundance. *c* רַב *adj.*

13 רָבָה to be multiplied, increased; to increase. KAL *a pret.* *b inf.* *c imp.* *d fut.* PIEL *e pret.* *f imp.* HIPHIL *g pret.* *h inf.* *i fut.* *k part.* *l* תַּרְבּוּת *f. pr.* a growth, *i. e.* a brood, progeny, in contempt. *m* תַּרְבִּית *f.* interest, usury. *n* מַרְבֶּה *m.* enlargement. *o* מַרְבִּית *f.* greatness.

14 שָׂנָא to be or become great, to grow. HIPHIL *part.*

15 שָׂנָה *id.* KAL *a fut.* HIPHIL *b part.*

16 שֶׁגֶר *m.* that which is cast forth, as at birth; young, offspring.

17 שָׁרַץ to bring forth abundantly. KAL *fut.*

Gen. vii. 17, 18.	13 d	1 Chron. iv. 38.	11 a	Ps. cvii. 37.		2
xxx. 30, 43.	11 b	v. 23.	13 a	cxv. 14.		6 e
xlvii. 24.	2	xxvii. 23.	13 h	Prov. i. 5.		2
Exod. i. 7.	17	2 Chron. xviii. 34.	8 a	iii. 9.		2
xxiii. 30.	10 b	xxxi. 5.	2	ix. 9, 11.		6 e
Lev. xix. 25.	2	xxxii. 28.	2	xi. 24.		6 b
xxv. 7, 12, 20.	2	Ezra ix. 6.	13 a	xiii. 11.		13 i
xxv. 16.	13 i	x. 10.	6 d	xiv. 4.		2
xxv. 36.	13 m	Neh. ix. 37.	2	xvi. 21.		6 e
xxv. 37.	13 o	Job i. 10.	11 a	xviii. 20.		2
xxvi. 4, 20.	5	viii. 7.	15 a	xxii. 16.		13 h
Num. xviii. 30, 30.	2	x. 16.	3	xxiii. 28.		6 e
xxxii. 14.	13 l	x. 17.	13 i	xxiv. 5.		2
Deut. vi. 3.	13 d	xii. 23.	14	xxviii. 8.		13 k
vii. 13.	16	xx. 28.	5	xxviii. 28.		13 d
vii. 22.	13 d	xxxi. 12.	2	xxix. 16.		13 d
xiv. 22, 28.	2	Ps. iii. 1.	12 a	Eccles. i. 18, 18.		6 e
xvi. 15.	2	iv. 7.	12 a	ii. 9.		6 c
xxvi. 12.	2	xliv. 12.	2	v. 10.		2
xxviii. 4, 18, 51.	16	xlix. 16.	13 d	v. 11, 11.	13 b, 12 a	
xxxii. 13.	7 b	lxii. 10.	7 a	vi. 11.		13 k
xxxii. 22.	5	lxvii. 6.	2	Isa. ix. 3.		4
Judg. vi. 4.	13 f	lxxi. 21.	2	ix. 7.		13 n
ix. 29.	13 f	lxxiii. 12.	15 b	xxvi. 15, 15.		6 a
1 Sam. ii. 33.	13 o	lxxviii. 46.	8 b	xxix. 19.		6 a
xiv. 19.	12 c	lxxviii. 12.	5	xxx. 23.		2
2 Sam. xv. 12.	12 c	lxxxv. 12.	5	xl. 29.		13 i
1 Kings xxii. 35.	8 a	cv. 24.	10 c	li. 2.		13 i

Isa. lvii. 9.	13 i	Ezek. xvi. 26.	13 i	Ezek. xlviii. 18.	2
Jer. ii. 3.	2	xviii. 8, 13, 17.	13 m	Dan. xi. 39.	13 i
iii. 16.	10 a	xxii. 12.	13 m	xii. 4.	13 d
v. 6.	9	xxiii. 14.	6 e	Hos. iv. 7.	12 b
xv. 8.	9	xxviii. 5.	13 g	iv. 10.	11 b
xxiii. 3.	13 a	xxxiv. 27.	5	x. 1.	13 g
xxix. 6.	13 c	xxxvi. 11.	13 a	xii. 1.	13 i
xxx. 14, 15.	9	xxxvi. 29.	13 g	Amos iv. 9.	13 h
Lam. ii. 5.	13 i	xxxvi. 30.	7 b	Hab. ii. 6.	13 k
Ezek. v. 16.	6 e	xxxvi. 37.	13 i	Zech. viii. 12.	5
xvi. 7.	13 d	xli. 7.	8 a	x. 8, 8.	13 a

INCURABLE

אָנַשׁ to be sick unto death; to be in very great distress, in a desperate, incurable condition, past all relief; mortal, fatal. KAL *part.* Paûl, Job xxxiv. 6: Jer. xv. 18; xxx. 12, 15: Micah i. 9, *marg.* '(she is) grievously sick of her wounds.'

מַרְפֵּא *m.* healing, cure: 2 Chron. xxi. 18, *lit.* no curing.

INDIGNATION

1 זַעַם Schultens, upon Prov. xxiv. 24, affirms, from the Arabic, that the original force of this word is to foam at the mouth, favoured by Isa. xxx. 27, which may be so rendered. Hence, to be in great wrath and indignation, the indignation of one who has been injured, and is enraged, and seeketh vengeance; to express in bitter language the highest detestation, to defy. It is used in conjunction with אָרַר, and קָבַב, and set in opposition to blessing: Prov. xxiv. 24, 25. It denotes great severity in affection, purpose, words, and actions. In Jer. xv. 17 it may imply the sorrow of indignation, or the feeling it calls forth. The word is used in the Old Testament of the severity of God under that dispensation, of his chastisement of the Jews by the Assyrians, and their present dispersion, (*cf.* Isa. liv. 7, 8): Isa. x. 25: Dan. xi. 36; viii. 19. In Daniel, the time of indignation is primarily the time of the persecution of Antiochus. KAL *a pret.* *b* זַעַם *m.* anger, indignation, wrath; especially of God.

2 זָעַף Though this word seems very similar in meaning to זַעַם, yet, probably, the primary sense may be different. As זַעַם is properly to foam at the mouth, so זָעַף may be the quick breathing of one greatly displeased and discomposed; hence it applies to one of a sad countenance. Cocceius has defined the force of the word by, *affectus displicentiæ excitatus, prævalens et recalcitrans; cf.* Lam. ii. 6, and Isa. xxx. 30. Each rendered 'the indignation of his anger;' the latter word, 'anger,' being the same in each, אַף. The former implies severity of anger, which no consideration can induce (he despiseth king and priest) to forego his determination to punish; the latter implies rather displeasure of anger, called out by impenitence, and roused to take vengeance. So Micah vii. 9 is to be understood rather of displeasure than severity. *a* זַעַף *m.* anger, rage.

3 חֵמָה *f.* heat, wrath, anger.

4 כַּעַס to be under any turbulent, uneasy commotion of mind; to take indignation. KAL *a fut.* *b* כַּעַשׂ *m.* vexation.

5 קֶצֶף *m.* wrath.

Deut. xxix. 28.	5	Esth. v. 9.	3	Ps. lxxviii. 49.	1 b
2 Kings iii. 27.	5	Job x. 17.	4 b	cii. 10.	1 b
Neh. iv. 1.	4 a	Ps. lxix. 24.	1 b	Isa. x. 5, 25.	1 b

Isa. xiii. 5.	1 b	Jer. xv. 17.	1 b	Dan. xi. 36.	1 b
xxvi. 20.	1 b	l. 25.	1 b	Micah vii. 9.	2 a
xxx. 27.	1 b	Lam. ii. 6.	1 b	Nah. i. 6.	1 b
xxx. 30.	2 a	Ezek. xxi. 31.	1 b	Hab. iii. 12.	1 b
xxiv. 2.	5	xxii. 24, 31.	1 b	Zeph. iii. 8.	1 b
lxvi. 14. a	1 a	Dan. viii. 19.	1 b	Zech. i. 12.	1 a
Jer. x. 10.	1 b	xi. 30.	1 a	Mal. i. 4.	1 a

a lit. and he shall be angry.

INDITING

רָחַשׁ to boil up or over, as a fountain or boiling water: Ps. xlv. 1.

INDUSTRIOUS

עָשָׂה to do, to work, to labour. KAL *part.* Poel, 1 Kings xi. 28, with מְלָאכָה *f.* work.

INFAMY

דִּבָּה *f.* a slander, an infamous report: Prov. xxv. 10: Ezek. xxxvi. 3.

טָמֵא *adj.* unclean. שֵׁם *m.* name: Ezek. xxii. 5.

INFANT

עוּל *m.* sucking child, infant: Isa. lxv. 20. עוֹלֵל *m.* a boy, child, infant: 1 Sam. xv. 3, *lit.* from infant: Job iii. 16: Hos. xiii. 16.

INFERIOR

נָפַל to fall. KAL *part.* Poel, Job xii. 3; xiii. 2.

אֲרַע *f.* Ch. the earth: Dan. ii. 39.

INFINITE

מִסְפָּר *m.* number: Ps. cxlvii. 5, *marg.* 'no number.'

קֵץ *m.* end: Job xxii. 5, *lit.* no end to thine iniquities. קֵצָה *m.* end: Nah. iii. 9, *lit.* no end.

INFIRMITY

דָּוֶה see *Sick.* KAL *inf.* Lev. xii. 2.

חָלָה to wear, waste, weaken. PIEL *inf.* Ps. lxxvii. 10. מַחֲלֶה *m.* disease, or some disease which extends its influence through the whole system: Prov. xviii. 14.

INFLAME

דָּלַק to burn, kindle, inflame; to pursue hotly. HIPHIL *fut.* Isa. v. 11. דַּלֶּקֶת *f.* burning fever: Deut. xxviii. 22.

צָרֶבֶת *f.* burning; Gesenius, scar, cicatrix, as Lxx., Vulg., Chald., whether from a burn, or as left by a sore: Lev. xiii. 28.

INFLUENCES

מַעֲדַנּוֹת delights, pleasures: used of the constellation Pleiades, as introducing the delights of spring: Job xxxviii. 31. "Canst thou bind the sweet influences of Pleiades," *i. e.* as they are bound up by Orion, which draws in the rigours of winter.

INFOLDING

לָקַח to take; to take hold. HITHPAEL *part.* Ezek. i. 4, *marg.* 'catching itself;' *i. e.* holding together, continuous; or, implying a motion inward into itself, as if it were in the act of devouring something, bursting out into a flame, and then drawing itself in, as one may see in a conflagration: a fearful symbol of divine wrath.

INFORM

בִּין to consider; to make to understand. KAL and HIPHIL *fut.* Dan. ix. 22.

יָרָה to teach. HIPHIL *fut.* Deut. xvii. 10.

INHABIT

1   גּוּר to dwell, to abide in a place. KAL *part.* Poel, Job xxviii. 4. Gesenius, from where men dwell, *i. e.* from the surface of the ground as the abode of man. Taylor supposes נָר to be from נָגַר to drain off a fluid, and that it means a subterraneous canal, or drain, passing from the bottom of the mine or pit, where the ore of metal is found, under the mountain, to a proper outlet by which water is drained away; and so renders the whole passage, "a brook issueth (out of the mine) through the drain (even waters), disregarded by the foot (of travellers, because they lie deep in the earth); they are emptied (or dried up) from the men (from the miners); they pass away." Rosenmüller, however, has elegantly translated this verse as follows:—*Cuniculos effodiunt consueto se subducturi consortio, en oblivioni dantur remoti ab iis qui supra ambulant, penduli demittuntur, relictis hominibus huc illuc se vibrant:* where he interprets, מֵעִם־נָר, *ex loco quo versatur homo.* For a fuller account of interpretations of this most obscure passage, see Rosenmüller, Good, and Barnes.

2   גְּזֵרָה *f.* a being cut off: Lev. xvi. 22, *marg.* 'of separation,' *i. e.* from the use and habitation of man.

3   דּוּר Ch. to dwell. P'AL *part.*

4   יָשַׁב to sit down; to dwell, dwell in, inhabit. KAL ᵃ*pret.* ᵇ*inf.* ᶜ*fut.* ᵈ*part.* Poel, Gen. xix. 25, &c., frequent. Isa. x. 13, Gesenius understands the word of kings sitting on thrones. NIPHAL ᵉ*pret.* ᶠ*part.* HIPHIL ᵍ*fut.* HOPHAL ʰ*fut.* מוֹשָׁב ⁱ*m.* habitation. תּוֹשָׁב ᵏ*m.* sojourner.

5   שָׁכַן to dwell; to abide. KAL ᵃ*pret.* ᵇ*fut.* ᶜ*part.* Poel. שָׁכֵן ᵈ*adj.* inhabitant.

No. 4 d, *Inhabitant,* not included.

Gen. xxxvi. 20.	4 d	Isa. xlv. 18.	4 b	Ezek. xxix. 11.	4 c
Exod. xvi. 35.	4 f	liv. 3.	4 g	xxxiii. 24.	4 d
Lev. xvi. 22.	2	lvii. 15.	5 c	xxxiv. 13.	4 i
Num. xxxv. 34.	4 d	lxv. 21.	4 a	xxxvi. 10.	4 e
Judg. i. 17, 21.	4 d	lxv. 22.	4 c	xxxvi. 35.	4 a
1 Kings xvii. 1.	4 k	Jer. vi. 8.	4 e	xxxviii. 12.	4 f
1 Chron. v. 9.	4 a	xvii. 6, 6.	5 a, 4 a	Dan. iv. 35, 35.	3
Job xv. 28.	4 c	xix. 6.	4 e	Hos. x. 5.	5 d
xxvi. 5.	5 c	xlvi. 26.	5 b	Amos xiv. 14.	4 a
xxviii. 4.	1	xlviii. 18.	4 d	Zeph. i. 13.	4 c
Ps. xxii. 3.	4 c	l. 13, 39.	4 c	Zech. ii. 4.	4 c
Prov. x. 30.	5 b	Ezek. xii. 20.	4 f	vii. 7, 7.	4 d
Isa. xiii. 20.	4 c	xxvi. 17.	4 f	ix. 5.	4 c
xxxiii. 24.	5 d	xxvi. 19.	4 e	xii. 6.	4 a
xlii. 11.	4 c	xxvi. 20.	4 c	xiv. 10, 11.	4 a
xliv. 26.	4 d				

INHERIT

1   חָלַל see *Profane.* NIPHAL *pret.* Ezek. xxii. 16, *marg.* 'or, be profaned.'

2   חֵלֶק *m.* a portion.

3 יָרַשׁ to possess by inheritance. KAL ᵃ*pret.* ᵇ*inf.* ᶜ*fut.* ᵈ*part.* Poel. HIPHIL ᵉ*pret.* ᶠיְרֵשָׁה *f.* inheritance. ᵍמוֹרָשָׁה *f.* possession.

4 נָחַל to take possession of, specially by inheritance. Piel, to give to possess, to distribute, or divide an inheritance. Hiphil, to cause to possess. Hithpael, to receive for one's own use, to possess. KAL ᵃ*pret.* ᵇ*inf.* ᶜ*fut.* PIEL ᵈ*pret.* ᵉ*inf.* HIPHIL ᶠ*pret.* ᵍ*inf.* ʰ*fut.* ⁱ*part.* HITHPAEL ᵏ*pret.* ˡ*inf.* ᵐ*fut.* נַחֲלָה *f.* inheritance: Gen. xxxi. 14, &c.

No 4 n, *Inheritance*, not in general included.

Gen. xv. 7.	3 b	Deut. xix. 3.	4 h	Ps. lxxxii. 8.	4 c
xv. 8.	3 c	xix. 14, 14.	4 n c	cv. 44.	3 c
xxviii. 4.	3 b	xix. 16.	4 g	Prov. iii. 35.	4 c
Exod. xxiii. 30.	4 a	xxi. 7.	4 h	viii. 21.	4 g
xxxii. 13.	4 a	xxxii. 8.	4 a	xi. 29.	4 c
xxxiv. 9.	4 a	xxxiii. 4.	3 g	xiii. 22.	4 h
Lev. xx. 24.	3 c	Josh. i. 6.	4 h	xiv. 18.	4 a
xxv. 46, 46.	4 k, 3 b	xiii. 32.	4 d	Isa. xlix. 8.	4 g
Num. xviii. 20, 20.	4 c n	xiv. 1, 1.	4 a d	liv. 3.	3 c
xviii. 23.	4 c n	xvi. 4.	4 c	lvii. 13.	3 c
xviii. 24, 24.	4 n c n	xvii. 14.	4 h	lx. 21.	3 c
xxvi. 55.	4 c	xix. 9, 9, 9.	4 n c n	lxv. 9, 9.	3 d a
xxxii. 18, 18.	4 c n	xix. 49, 49.	4 b n	Jer. iii. 18.	4 n
xxxii. 19, 19.	4 c n	xix. 51, 51.	4 n d	viii. 10.	3 d
xxxiii. 54, 54, 54, 54.	4 k n n m	Judg. xi. 2.	4 c	xii. 14, 14.	4 n f
xxxiv. 13.	4 m	xxi. 17.	3 f	xvi. 19.	4 a
xxxiv. 18.	4 b	1 Sam. i. 8.	4 h	xxxii. 8.	3 d
xxxiv. 29.	4 e	1 Chron. xxviii. 8.	4 f	xlix. 1.	3 a
xxxv. 8, 8.	4 n c	2 Chron. xx. 11.	3 e	Ezek. xxii. 16.	4 d or l
Deut. i. 38.	4 h	Ezra ix. 12.	3 e	xxxiii. 24, 24.	3 c g
ii. 31.	3 b	Ps. xvi. 5.	2	xlvi. 18, 18.	4 n h
iii. 28.	4 h	xxv. 13.	3 c	xlvii. 13.	4 m
xii. 10.	4 i	xxxvii. 9, 11, 22, 29.	3 c	xlvii. 14, 14.	4 a n
xvi. 20.	3 a	xxxvii. 34.	3 b	Zech. ii. 12.	4 a
		lxix. 36.	4 c		

INIQUITY

1 אָוֶן *m.* iniquity, vanity, trouble: this word seems to have an especial reference to the nature and consequences of sin (see *Wicked*), especially idolatry; and it stands in opposition to the solid good and happiness which attends on true religion; "the punishment of iniquity." To plough iniquity, to reap, to conceive, and to bring forth, have respect to the consequences of a man's ways upon himself. Some derive this word from אָוָה to desire, taken in a bad sense, and apply it to wickedness, as the working of corrupt desires; hence also it expresses grief, trouble, sorrow, &c.

2 דָּבָר *m.* word, thing, or matter: Ps. lxv. 3.

3 הַוָּה *f.* see *Wickedness, Calamity.* Ps. xciv. 20.

4 עָוָה to turn awry, or the wrong way: applied to the distortion of the heart or actions, from that which is right to that which is wrong; to commit iniquity: Ps. xxxviii. 6 is supposed to express its primary meaning, *i. e.* of the body distorted by pain; see *Trouble.* Comp. Isa. xxi. 3, "I was bowed down." KAL ᵃ*pret.* HIPHIL ᵇ*pret.* ᶜ*inf.* ᵈעָוֹן *m.* perverseness; sin, guilt, iniquity; a crime; also punishment for sin. 2 Sam. vii. 14 may be rendered, "in punishing I will chasten him;" as also Ps. xxxii. 5; xl. 12. Lxx. ἁμαρτία, ἁμάρτημα, ἀδικία; frequently joined with חַטָּא, Exod. xxxiv. 9. עֲוֹן קֵן iniquity, which hath brought destruction, Ezek. xxi. 25, 29; xxxv. 5: comp. Gen. xv. 16. Cocceius has well defined it, *Pravitas ἀμετανόητος post multas admonitiones et castigationes, et exempla judicii, et longam tolerantiam est pravitas finis.* The word, as well as חָמָא, Ps. li. 7,

applies to the original pravity of man, by which he is turned aside from the image of God, and the love of holiness, Ps. li. 5, as well as that which is acquired and actual: most commonly translated iniquity, and occurs frequently, Gen. xv. 16, &c. ᵉעֲוָיָא Ch. *f.* perverseness.

5 עָוַל to act in a deceitful, tricking, insidious manner; bad, dishonest dealing in secret (Ainsworth on Ps. vii. 3), or under some cover; unfair usage; unrighteousness in judgment, and injustice in ordinary dealings with men: sometimes the word seems to be used of a remarkable accumulation of wickedness, perverseness, and lawlessness: Ps. liii. 1: Ezek. xviii. 24: xxxiii. 15. ᵃעָוֶל *m.* wickedness, depravity. ᵇעַוְלָה *f. id.* ᶜעוֹלָה *f. id.* ᵈעַלְוָה *f.* by transposition for עֲוֹלָה evil, wickedness.

6 עָמָל *m.* labour, toil; iniquity, fault, implying sorrow.

7 רֶשַׁע *m.* wickedness.

No 4 d not included.

Num. xxiii. 21.	1	Ps. liii. 1.	5 a	Isa. xxix. 20.	1
Deut. xxxii. 4.	5 a	liii. 4.	1	xxxi. 2.	1
1 Sam. xv. 23.	1	lv. 3.	1	xxxii. 6.	1
2 Sam. vii. 14.	4 c	lvi. 7.	1	lix. 4, 6, 7.	1
2 Chron. xix. 7.	5 b	lix. 2.	1	Jer. ii. 5.	5 b
Job iv. 8.	1	lxiv. 2.	1	ix. 5.	4 c
v. 16.	5 c	lxiv. 6.	5 c	Ezek. iii. 20.	5 a
vi. 29, 30.	1	lxv. 3.	4 d	xviii. 8, 24, 26, 26.	5 b
xi. 14.	1	lxvi. 18.	1	xxviii. 15.	5 b
xv. 16.	1	xcii. 7, 9.	1	xxviii. 18, 18.	4 d, 5 a
xxi. 19.	1	xciv. 4, 16, 23.	1	xxxiii. 13, 15, 15.	5 b
xxii. 23.	5	xciv. 20.	3	28.	5 a
xxxi. 3.	1	cvi. 6.	4 b	Dan. iv. 27.	4 e
xxxiv. 8, 22.	1	cvii. 42.	5 b	Hos. vi. 8.	5 a
xxxiv. 10, 32.	5 a	cxix. 3.	1	x. 9.	5 d
xxxvi. 10, 21.	1	cxix. 133.	1	x. 13.	5 b
xxxvi. 23.	5 b	cxxv. 3.	5 b	xii. 11.	1
Ps. v. 5.	1	cxxv. 5.	1	Micah ii. 1.	1
vi. 8.	1	cxli. 4, 9.	1	iii. 10.	5 b
vii. 3.	5 a	Prov. x. 29.	1	Hab. i. 3.	1
vii. 14.	1	xix. 28.	1	i. 13.	6
xiv. 4.	1	xxi. 15.	1	ii. 12.	5 b
xxviii. 3.	1	xxii. 8.	5 b	Zeph. iii. 5, 13.	5 b
xxxvi. 3, 12.	1	Eccles. iii. 16.	7	Mal. ii. 6, 6.	4 d, 5 b
xxxvii. 1.	5 b	Isa. i. 13.a			
xli. 6.	1				

a marg. 'or, grief.'

INJUSTICE

חָמָס *m.* violence: Job xvi. 17.

INK

דִּיוֹ *m.* Jer. xxxvi. 18, made of lamp-black or powdered charcoal, prepared with gum and water, of a jet black colour, and remains without fading, but may be washed out or off; see *Blot*.

INK-HORN

קֶסֶת The ink-horns described by Dr. Shaw (Travels, p. 293) were of brass, and square, with a lid to clasp over them: to this square piece, which held the ink, was affixed a long, hollow, flat shaft, which served both for a pen-case and to stick the ink-horn into the girdle, where the writers and secretaries wear them as a badge of their office. And in this manner, as now, so the writers in Ezekiel's time seem to have carried their ink-horns by their sides, *Heb.* loins. Ezek. ix. 2, 3, 11.

INN

מָלוֹן *m.* a lodging-place; particularly the place where the cara-

vans rest, whether it be covered or not : Gen. xlii. 27 ; xliii. 21 : Exod. iv. 24.

INNER

חֶדֶר *m.* (see *Chamber*), innermost, inward parts, the heart and affections, &c. of man : Prov. xviii. 8 ; xxvi. 22.

פְּנִים *adv.* within, inner part : 2 Chron. xxix. 16. פְּנִימִי *adj.* inner : 1 Kings vi. 27, &c.

INNOCENT

1 דָּם *m.* blood : Deut. xxvii. 25, *lit.* a soul of innocent blood.

2 זַכּוּ *Ch. f.* just, pure, innocent.

3 חִנָּם *adv.* without a cause.

4 חַף *adj.* pure, in a moral sense : Job xxxiii. 9.

5 נָקָה to be clean, blameless ; see *Clear.* NIPHAL [a] *pret.* [b] *fut.* PIEL. to hold innocent : [c] *fut.* [d] נָקִי *adj.* [e] נָקִיא *adj.* נִקָּיוֹן [f] *m.* (כתיב).

Gen. xx. 5.	5 f	Job xxii. 19, 30.	5 d	Prov. xxviii. 20.	5 b
Exod. xxiii. 7.	5 d	xxvii. 17.	5 d	Isa. lix. 7.	5 d
Deut. xix. 10, 13.	5 d	xxxiii. 9.	4	Jer. ii. 34.	5 d
xxi. 8, 9.	5 d	Ps. x. 8.	5 d	ii. 35.	5 a
xxvii. 25.	5 d, 1	xv. 5.	5 d	vii. 6.	5 d
1 Sam. xix. 5.	5 d	xix. 13.	5 a	xix. 4.	5 d
1 Kings ii. 31.	3	xxvi. 6.	5 f	xxii. 3, 17.	5 d
2 Kings xxi. 16.	5 d	lxxiii. 13.	5 f	xxvi. 15.	5 d
xxiv. 4, 4.	5 d	xciv. 21.	5 d	Dan. vi. 22.	2
Job iv. 7.	5 d	cvi. 38.	5 d	Hos. viii. 5.	5 f
ix. 23.	5 d	Prov. i. 11.	5 d	Joel iii. 19.	5 d
ix. 28.	5 c	vi. 17.	5 d	Jonah i. 14.	5 d or e
xvii. 8.		vi. 29.	5 b		

INNUMERABLE

מִסְפָּר number ; innumerable, *Heb.* without number. Job xxi. 33 : Ps. xl. 12 ; civ. 25 : Jer. xlvi. 23.

INQUISITION

בָּקַשׁ to seek. PUAL *fut.* Esth. ii. 23, "inquisition was made."

דָּרַשׁ to search after anything. KAL *pret.* Deut. xix. 18. *part.* Poel, Ps. ix. 12.

INSIDE

בַּיִת *m.* house : 1 Kings vi. 15.

INSPIRATION

נְשָׁמָה *f.* breath : Job xxxii. 8.

INSTANT

פֶּתַע *m.* opening of the eyes, wink ; moment ; as an *adv.* in a moment : Isa. xxix. 5 ; xxx. 13.

רֶגַע *m.* moment : Jer. xviii. 7, 9.

INSTRUCT

1 בִּין to understand, to give heed to. KAL and HIPHIL [a] *fut.* POLEL, the context seems to fix the meaning of giving heed to the nation of Israel in the wilderness. Syr. loved him. [b] *fut.*

2 יָדַע to know. NIPHAL *inf.*

3 יָסַד to lay a foundation. HOPHAL *pret.*

4 יָסַר to bind, to correct ; by instruction to correct and reform.

KAL [a] *inf.* NIPHAL [b] *imp.* PIEL [c] *pret.* [d] *inf.* יִסּוֹר [e] *m.* מוּסָר [f] *m.* מֻסָּר [g] *m.*

5 יָרָה to adjust, to direct ; to teach. HIPHIL *pret.*

6 לָטַשׁ to sharpen or whet a tool ; figuratively, it is elegantly used to signify the whetting or polishing, that is, instructing the mind in the art of working brass and iron. KAL *part.* Paül.

7 לָמַד to teach. PIEL [a] *fut.* [b] *part.* PUAL [c] *part.*

8 שָׂכַל (see *Wise*), implies maturity of understanding. HIPHIL [a] *inf.* [b] *fut.*

Gen. iv. 22.	6	Ps. l. 17.	4 f	Prov. xxiii. 12, 23.	4 f
Deut. iv. 36.	4 d	Prov. i. 2, 3, 7, 8.	4 f	xxiv. 32.	4 f
xxxii. 10.	1 b	iv. 1, 13.	4 f	Cant. viii. 2.	7 a
2 Kings xii. 2.	5	v. 12, 23.	4 f	Isa. viii. 11.	4 c
1 Chron. xv. 22.	4 a	v. 13.	7 b	xxviii. 26.	4 c
xxv. 7.	5	viii. 10, 33.	4 f	xl. 14.	1 a
2 Chron. iii. 3.	3	x. 17.	4 f	Jer. vi. 8.	4 b
Neh. ix. 20.	8 a	xii. 1.	4 f	xvii. 23.	4 f
Job iv. 3.	4 c	xiii. 1, 18.	4 f	xxxii. 19.	2
xl. 16.	4 g	xv. 5, 32, 33.	4 f	xxxii. 33.	4 f
xl. 2. a	4 e	xvi. 22.	4 f	xxxv. 13.	4 f
Ps. ii. 10.	4 b	xix. 20, 27.	4 f	Ezek. v. 15.	4 f
xvi. 7.	4 c	xxi. 11.	8 a	Dan. xi. 33.	1 a
xxxii. 8.	8 b			Zeph. iii. 7.	4 f

a *or, lit.* be a reprover.

INSTRUMENT

רִחַן *Ch. f. pl.* according to the Rabbins, instruments of music : Dan. vi. 18, perhaps, *lit.* concubines ; which seems to supply the best meaning for the context.

יָד *com.* a hand : 2 Chron. xxix. 27, *marg.* 'hands of instruments.'

כְּלִי *m.* a general name for all kinds of vessels, tools, &c. : Gen. xlix. 5, &c.

מִנִּים *m. pl.* kinds : Ps. cl. 4. *Heb.* in kinds, *i. e.* in various kinds of music mixed together in symphony.

נְגִינָה *f.* stringed instrument ; see *Sing, Play.* Hab. iii. 19.

שִׁדָּה *f.* This exceedingly obscure word is more generally referred to mean musical symphony, and supposed to mean either musical instruments or singers. Eccles. ii. 8.

שָׁלִישׁ *m.* supposed to mean either three-stringed instruments or triangles, an instrument struck in concert with drums, as in modern military music : 1 Sam. xviii. 6.

INSURRECTION

נְשָׂא *Ch.* to lift up oneself, to rise up against any one, *seq.* עַל ITHPAEL *part.* Ezra iv. 19.

רִגְשָׁה *f.* a noisy crowd, running together : Ps. lxiv. 2.

INTEGRITY

תֹּם *m.* wholeness, entireness ; integrity of mind, uprightness, innocence ; put for that simplicity which is remote from mischief or ill design : Gen. xx. 5, *marg.* ' or, simplicity, or, sincerity,' 6 : 1 Kings ix. 4 : Ps. vii. 8 ; xxv. 21 ; xxvi. 1, 11 ; xli. 12 ; lxxviii. 72 : Prov. xix. 1 ; xx. 7. תֻּמָּה *f.* Job ii. 3, 9 ; xxvii. 5 ; xxxi. 6 : Prov. xi. 3.

INTELLIGENCE

בִּין to understand ; to have intelligence. KAL and HIPHIL *fut.* Dan. xi. 30.

INTEND

אָמַר to say. KAL *pret.* Josh. xxii. 33. *part.* Poel, Exod. ii. 14: 2 Chron. xxviii. 13.

נָטָה to stretch out; to spread out over. KAL *pret.* Ps. xxi. 11.

INTENT

מְזִמָּה see *Device.* Jer. xxx. 24.

דִּבְרָה *f. Ch.* cause, reason: Dan. iv. 17.

INTERCESSION

פָּגַע to intreat. KAL *fut.* Jer. vii. 16; xxvii. 18. HIPHIL *pret.* Jer. xxxvi. 25. *fut.* Isa. liii. 12. *part.* Isa. lix. 16.

INTERMEDDLE

גָּלַע see *Meddle.* HITHPAEL *fut.* Prov. xviii. 1.

עָרַב to interweave; to mingle; to intermeddle. HITHPAEL *fut.* Prov. xiv. 10.

INTERMISSION

הֲפֻגוֹת *f. pl.* remission, cessation: Lam. iii. 49.

INTERPRET

1 לוּץ to speak unintelligibly, in a foreign language, *pr.* to stammer like another, hence to mock; to act as interpreter. HIPHIL ᵃ*part.* ᵇ מְלִיצָה *f.* what needs interpretation.

2 פְּשַׁר *Ch.* to explain, to interpret, to make interpretations. P'AL ᵃ*inf.* PAEL ᵇ*part.* ᶜ פְּשַׁר *Ch. m.* interpretation. ᵈ פֵּשֶׁר *m. id.*

3 פָּתַר to interpret a dream. KAL ᵃ*pret.* ᵇ*inf.* ᶜ*fut.* ᵈ*part.* Poel.ᵉ פִּתְרוֹן *m.* interpretation.

4 שֵׁבֶר *m.* breaking; solution, interpretation.

5 תִּרְגֵּם to translate from one language into another: *part. passive.*

Gen. xl. 5, 12, 18.	3 d	Gen. xlii. 23.	1 a	Dan. ii. 30, 36, 45.	2 c
xl. 8, 8.	3 d e	Judg. vii. 15.	4	iv. 6, 7, 9, 18, 18, 19,	
xl. 16, 22.	3 a	Ezra iv. 7.	5	19, 24.	2 c
xli. 8.	3 d	Job xxxiii. 23.	1 a	v. 7, 8, 15, 15, 16, 16,	
xli. 11.	3 e	Prov. i. 6.	1 b	17, 26.	2 c
xli. 12, 12.	3 c a	Eccles. viii. 1.	2 d	v. 12, 12.	2 b c
xli. 13.	3 a	Dan. ii. 4, 5, 6, 6, 7, 9,		v. 16, 16.	2 a c c
xli. 15, 15.	3 d b	16, 24, 25, 26.	2 c	vii. 16.	2 c

INTREAT

1 חָלָה (see *Pray*), to beseech, implying humble submission, supplication, or deprecation. PIEL ᵃ*pret.* ᵇ*imp.* ᶜ*fut.*

2 חָנַן to shew favour; to pray or supplicate for favour. KAL ᵃ*pret.* HITHPAEL ᵇ*fut.* ᶜ תַּחֲנוּנִים *m. pl.* supplications.

3 עָתַר to pray as a suppliant, to supplicate God, powerfully, abundantly, or successfully; being generally used in Niph. of intreaty that prevails with God. KAL ᵃ*fut.* NIPHAL ᵇ*pret.* ᶜ*inf.* ᵈ*fut.* HIPHIL ᵉ*pret.* ᶠ*imp.* ᵍ*fut.*

4 פָּגַע to fall upon, to light upon; to assail with petitions, to urge, to intreat any one, *seq.* בְּ, also *seq.* לְ of him for whom one asks or intercedes. KAL ᵃ*imp.* ᵇ*fut.*

5 פָּלַל to pray. HITHPAEL *fut.*

Gen. xxiii. 8.	4 a	Exod. viii. 9.	3 g	Exod. ix. 28.	3 f
xxv. 21, 21.	3 a d	viii. 29.	3 e	x. 17.	3 f
Exod. viii. 8, 28.	3 f	viii. 30.	3 a	x. 18.	3 a

Judg. xiii. 8.	3 a	1 Chron. v. 20.	3 c	Ps. xlv. 12.	1 c
Ruth i. 16.	4 b	2 Chron. xxxiii. 13.	3 d	lxiv. 6.	1 a
1 Sam. ii. 25.	5	xxxiii. 19.	3 c	Prov. xviii. 23.	2 c
2 Sam. xxi. 14.	3 d	Ezra viii. 23.	3 d	xix. 6.	1 c
xxiv. 25.	3 d	Job xix. 16.	2 b	Isa. xix. 22.	3 b
1 Kings xiii. 6.	1 b	xix. 17.ᵃ	2 a		

a or, though I have a tender affection for her.

INVADE

בּוֹא to come; *seq.* בְּ to invade. KAL *inf.* 2 Chron. xx. 10. *fut.* 2 Kings xiii. 20.

גּוּד to press or crowd upon any one. KAL *fut.* Hab. iii. 16.

פָּשַׁט to spread oneself out, used of hostile troops, &c.; *seq.* עַל of a land or people, to invade. KAL *pret.* 1 Sam. xxiii. 27; xxx. 1, 14: 2 Chron. xxviii. 18. *fut.* 1 Sam. xxvii. 8.

INVENT

חָשַׁב to think, to meditate, to purpose; *seq. acc.* to think out, to invent, devise. KAL *pret.* Amos vi. 5. חִשְּׁבֹנוֹת *f. pl.* arts, devices: Eccles. vii. 29. מַחֲשֶׁבֶת *f.* 2 Chron. xxvi. 15, *lit.* the invention of.

מְזִמָּה *f.* thought, counsel, purpose; machination, device, plot; "witty inventions:" Prov. viii. 12.

עֲלִילָה *f.* work, deed, doing: Ps. xcix. 8. מַעֲלָל *m.* work, deed: Ps. cvi. 29, 39.

INVITE

קָרָא to call. KAL *pret.* 1 Sam. ix. 24. *fut.* 2 Sam. xiii. 23. *part.* Paül, Esth. v. 12.

INWARD

1 בַּיִת *m.* house. בַּיְתָה inward.

2 חֶדֶר *m.* chamber; inward parts.

3 טֻחוֹת *f. pl.* the reins, according to Hebrew interpreters, so called because overspread with fat; put for the seat of the mind, feelings, intellect, and affections.

4 סוֹד *m.* circle of persons sitting together; assembly; familiar converse, intimacy.

5 פְּנִים *adv.* within. פְּנִימִי *adj. id.*

6 קֶרֶב *m.* the midst, middle, inner part; interior of the body or of the mind.

Exod. xxviii. 26.	1	2 Sam. v. 9.	1	Ps. lxii. 4.	6
xxix. 13, 17, 22.	6	1 Kings vii. 25.	1	lxiv. 6.	2
xxxix. 19.	1	2 Chron. iii. 13.	1	Prov. xx. 27, 30.	6
Lev. i. 9, 13.	6	iv. 4.	6	Isa. xvi. 11.	6
iii. 3, 3, 9, 9, 14, 14.	6	Job xix. 19.	4	Jer. xxxi. 33.	6
iv. 8, 8, 11.	6	xxxviii. 36.	3	Ezek. xl. 9.	1
vii. 3.	6	Ps. v. 9.	6	xl. 16.	5
viii. 16, 21, 25.	6	xlix. 11.	4	xli. 3.	5
ix. 14.	6	li. 6.	3	xlii. 4.	5 a

IRON

בַּרְזֶל *m.* iron; often put as the symbol of hardness and firmness, as Ps. ii. 9, a sceptre of iron for stern dominion; Isa. xlviii. 4, "a sinew of iron is thy neck," in allusion to the perverse obstinacy of a people.—Gen. iv. 22, &c.

פַּרְזֶל *Ch. m.* iron: Dan. ii. 33, 33, 34, 35, 40, 40, 40, 41, 41, 41, 42, 43, 43, 45; iv. 15, 23; v. 4, 23; vii. 7, 19.

THAT WHICH IS

תּוּשִׁיָּה *f. pr.* a setting upright, uprightness; hence help, deliver-

ance ; purpose, undertaking, enterprise ; counsel, wisdom, understanding : Job xi. 6, "double to that which is," or the double of understanding ; Job xxvi. 3.

ISH-ISHI

אִישׁ *m.* man, husband : Hos. ii. 16.

ISLAND, ISLE

אִי *m. pr.* habitable ground, dry land, opposed to water, the sea, rivers : Isa. xlii. 15, "I will make the rivers dry lands ;" *comp.* xliii. 19, l. 2 ; *terra maritima*, land adjacent to the sea, sea-coast, whether on the shore of a mainland, or an island ; specially the coast, the sea-coast : Isa. xx. 6, xxiii. 2, 6 ; Ezek. xxvii. 7, "the coast of Elishah," *i.e.* of Peloponnesus or Greece ; an island, Jer. xlvii. 4, "the country of Caphtor," *marg.* 'isles ;' Ezek. xxvii. 6, "the isles of Chittim ;" Jer. ii. 10. The *pl.* is put very often for coasts, maritime regions, especially beyond sea, as in Jer. xxv. 22, *marg.* 'region by the sea-side ;' hence generally of coasts and islands far remote, Isa. xxiv. 15, xl. 15, xli. 1, 5, xlii. 4, 10, 12, xlix. 1, li. 5, especially those of the Mediterranean : Ps. lxxii. 10 : Dan. xi. 18 ; Isa. xi. 11 : Gen. x. 5 : Zeph. ii. 11. In Ezek. xxvii. 15 the Indian Archipelago is to be understood.—*Gesenius.* Esth. x. 1 : Job xxii. 30 : Ps. xcvii. 1 : Isa. lix. 18 ; lx. 9 ; lxvi. 19 : Jer. xxxi. 10 : Ezek. xxvi. 15, 18, 18 ; xxvii. 3, 35 ; xxxix. 6. See also *Wild Beasts.*

ISSUE

1　זוּב to flow, as water, to have an issue, *lit.* to run a running, to have a running issue. KAL [a] *fut.* [b] *part.* Poel. [c] זוּב *m.* a flowing.

2　זִרְמָה *f.* a flowing, emission of seed.

3　מוֹלֶדֶת *f.* birth, nativity : offspring, progeny.

4　יָצָא to go forth. KAL [a] *pret.* [b] *fut.* [c] *part.* Poel [d] תּוֹצָאוֹת *f. pl.* goings forth.

5　נְגַד Ch. to flow. PAEL *part.*

6　צִפְעוֹת *f. pl.* progeny.

7　מָקוֹר *m.* fountain.

Gen. xlviii. 6.	3	Lev. xv. 19, α 19.	1 b c	Job xxxviii. 8.	4 b
Lev. xii. 7.	7	xv. 25, β 25.	1 a c c	Ps. lxviii. 20.	4 d
xv. 2, 2.	1 a c	xv. 33.	1 b c	Prov. iv. 23.	4 d
xv. 3, 3, 3, 15, 26,		xxii. 4.	1 b	Isa. xxii. 24.	6
28, 30.	1 c	Num. v. 2.	1 b	xxxix. 7.	4 b
xv. 4, 6, 7, 8, 9, 11,		Josh. viii. 22.	4 a	Ezek. xxxi. 20, 20.	2
12, 32.	1 b	2 Sam. iii. 29.	1 b	xlvii. 1, 8, 12.	4 c
xv. 13, 13.	1 b c	2 Kings xx. 18.	1 b	Dan. vii. 10.	5

α *lit.* be having.　　β *lit.* shall run a running.

ITCH

חֶרֶם *m.* itch, from its causing scratching : Deut. xxviii. 27.

IVORY

שֵׁן *com.* tooth, ivory : 1 Kings x. 18 ; xxii. 39 : 2 Chron. ix. 17 : Ps. xlv. 8 : Cant. v. 14 ; vii. 4 : Ezek. xxvii. 6, 15 : Amos iii. 15 ; vi. 4.

שֶׁנְהַבִּים *m. pl.* elephant's teeth, according to the LXX. and Targ. : 1 Kings x. 22 : 2 Chron. ix. 21.

JAREB

רִיב to plead. KAL *fut.* Hos. v. 13 ; x. 6.

JASHER

יָשָׁר *adj.* right : Josh. x. 13 : 2 Sam. i. 18.

JASHUB

שׁוּב to return. KAL *fut.* Isa. vii. 3.

JASPER

יָשְׁפֵה *m.* a precious stone of various colours, but mostly green : Exod. xxviii. 20 ; xxxix. 13 : Ezek. xxviii. 13.

JAVELIN

חֲנִית *f.* a spear, lance, so called as being flexible : 1 Sam. xviii. 10, 11 ; xix. 9, 10, 10 ; xx. 33.

רֹמַח *m.* lance, spear, used by heavy-armed troops : Num. xxv. 7.

JAW, JAW-BONE, JAW-TEETH

לְחִי cheek ; jaw-bone : Judg. xv. 15, 16, 16, 17, 19, *marg.* ' or, in Lehi :' Job xli. 2 : Isa. xxx. 28 : Ezek. xxix. 4 ; xxxviii. 4 : Hos. xi. 4.

מַלְקוֹחַ *m.* prey, booty ; *dual,* the two jaws with which food is taken : Ps. xxii. 15.

מְתַלְּעוֹת *f. pl.* biters, grinders : Job xxix. 17 : Prov. xxx. 14.

JEALOUS

קָנָא to be inflamed, to be red.—*Schultens.* Applied to a warm, violent affection of the mind, either for or against any one, in the following cases :—(1) To be jealous of a rival's sharing in our honours or enjoyments : thus, a man is jealous of his wife, Num. v. 14 ; God is moved to jealousy when the honour due to him is given to idols, Deut. xxxii. 21 : 1 Kings xiv. 22 : Ezek. viii. 3 ; xxiii. 25 ; and he moved his people, the Jews, to jealousy, by transferring their honours to other nations, Deut. xxxii. 21. (2) To be warmly concerned to vindicate injured honour, Exod. xx. 5. "I am a jealous God," moved with hot indignation when robbed of my honour, Deut. iv. 24 : 1 Kings xix. 10 : Ezek. xxxvi. 5 : Joel ii. 18. "The Lord will be jealous for his land," zealous for the honour and prosperity of his land, Nah. i. 2 : Zech. i. 14 ; viii. 2. PIEL [a] *pret.* [b] *inf.* [c] *fut.* HIPHIL [d] *fut.* [e] קַנָּא *adj.* [f] קִנְאָה *f.* [g] קַנּוֹא *adj.* [h] קָנָה to buy ; to let be bought, to sell. HIPHIL *part.* Ezek. viii. 3, "where was the seat of the image of jealousy," (הַקִּנְאָה) *i.e.* the idol provoking the divine vengeance) which selleth (הַמַּקְנֶה) *sc.* Israel to his enemies, *i.e.* which delivers Israel even as a slave into the power of his enemies. Note the paronomasia, according to this rendering, which seems to be the true one.

Exod. xx. 5.	1 e	Num. v. 15, 18, 25,		Deut. iv. 24.	1 e
xxxiv. 14, 14.	1 e	29.	1 f	v. 9.	1 e
Num. v. 14, 14, 14,		v. 30, 30.	1 f a	vi. 15.	1 e
14.	1 f a f a	xxv. 11.	1 f	xxix. 20.	1 f

JEGAR-SAHADUTHA

יְגַר Ch. *m.* a hill or heap of stones. שָׂהֲדוּתָא Ch. *f.* emphatically, testimony: Gen. xxxi. 47.

JEHOVAH

יְהֹוָה Jehovah, a name applied to God, and rendered LORD in our version, seems to have an especial reference to the purpose of redemption revealed to our first parents after the fall. The promise that "the seed of the woman should bruise the serpent's head" led to the expectation of a Redeemer to come. Eve gave expression to her faith in this promise on the birth of her first-born in saying, "I have gotten a man Jehovah," using the future tense of the verb הָוָה to be, Jahveh, or Jehovah; which term became the name used by the Church in future ages of their hope in the promised Saviour. Jehovah in the Lxx. is rendered Κύριος, the title subsequently used of Christ in the New Testament.—Gen. ii. 4, &c.

JEHOVAH-JIREH, JEHOVAH-NISSI, JEHOVAH-SHALOM

רָאָה to look; *seq.* לְ to look out anything for oneself, to provide, to choose. KAL *fut.* Gen. xxii. 14. מָרְאִיָה, *contr.* מֹרִיָה, *Moriah.*

נֵם *m.* an ensign: Exod. xvii. 15.

שָׁלוֹם *m.* peace: Judg. vi. 24.

JEOPARD

חָרַף to reproach, to scorn; *seq.* נֶפֶשׁ to scorn one's life, *i. q.* to lightly esteem, to abandon, to expose one's life to great and pressing danger, especially in battle, παραβάλλεσθαι. PIEL *pret.* Judg. v. 18.

נֶפֶשׁ *com.* life, soul: 2 Sam. xxiii. 17, with בְּ *lit.* with their souls: 1 Chron. xi. 19.

JESHIMON

יְשִׁימֹן *m.* a waste, desert: Num. xxi. 20; xxiii. 28: 1 Sam. xxiii. 19, 24; xxvi. 1, 3.

JEW

יָהַד a secondary verb. *denom.* from יְהוּד Judah; to make oneself a Jew, to become a Jew. HITHPAEL *part.* Esth. viii. 17.

JEWEL

חֲלִי *m.* necklace, trinket; so called as being polished: Cant. vii. 1. חֶלְיָה *f. id.* Hos. ii. 13.

כְּלִי *m.* apparatus, implement, equipment, &c., vessels, valuable effects: Gen. xxiv. 53, 53, &c.

נֶזֶם *m.* ring; a nose-ring: Prov. xi. 22: Isa. iii. 21: Ezek. xvi. 12.

סְגֻלָּה *f.* see *Peculiar.* Mal. iii. 17. LXX. εἰς περιποίησιν.

JOIN, JOINT

1 בָּחַר to choose. PUAL *fut.* Eccles. ix. 4. (כְּתִיב.)

2 דָּבַק to cleave, or adhere to; to adhere in affection, &c.; see *Cleave.* KAL [a] *pret.* PUAL [b] *fut.* [c] דָּבֵק *adj.* adhering. [d] דֶּבֶק *m.* joining.

3 חָבַר to couple together things of the same sort; to be joined, to adhere. KAL [a] *pret.* [b] *part.* Poel. [c] *part.* Paül. PIEL [d] *fut.* PUAL [e] *pret.* [f] *fut.* HITHPAEL [g] *pret.* [h] *inf.* [i] *fut.* [k] מְחַבְּרוֹת *f. pl.* cramps, or hooks of iron.

4 חָדָה to rejoice. KAL *fut.* Job iii. 6.

5 חוּט Ch. to sew, to sew together. APHEL *fut.*

6 חַמּוּק *m.* that which is circular.

7 יָחַד to be joined in society. KAL *fut.*

8 יָסַף to add. NIPHAL *pret.*

9 יָקַע to be out of joint. KAL *fut.*

10 לָוָה to be joined, connected together, in various senses; perhaps *pr.* to wreathe or infold itself. NIPHAL [a] *pret.* [b] *fut.* [c] *part.*

11 מֻעָרֶדֶת *adj. f.* wavering, unsteady; out of joint.

12 נָגַע to reach, to extend to; applied to simple extension. HIPHIL *part.*

13 נָטַשׁ see *Spread.* KAL *fut.* 1 Sam. iv. 2; the battle was let loose when the signal was given.

14 סָפָה to add, to augment. NIPHAL *part.* Selig Newman, to be gathered together as in a besieged city.

15 סָכַךְ to cover; to mingle. PILPEL *fut.*

16 עָרַךְ to set in order. KAL *fut.*

17 פָּרַד to separate; to be out of joint. HITHPAEL *pret.*

18 צָמַד to join to, to fasten, to couple together. NIPHAL [a] *fut.* [b] *part.*

19 קָטַר to bind, to tie; and hence to shut, to close. KAL [a] *part.* Paül, Ezek. xlvi. 22, *marg.* 'or, made with chimneys.' Gesenius, courts shut up, *i.e.* surrounded by a wall and closed with doors; referring to the smaller courts in the four corners of the great court, which served as kitchens, verse 24. [b] קְטַר Ch. *m.* joints: Dan. v. 6.

20 קָרַב to be near. KAL [a] *fut.* PIEL [b] *imp.*

21 קָשַׁר to bind, to tie. NIPHAL *fut.*

JOURNEY

1   דֶּרֶךְ   *com.* a way, a track, a road, a journey.

2   מַהֲלָךְ   *m.* a way, journey.

3   נָסַע   to move a camp, to remove, to journey. KAL [a] *pret.* [b] *inf.* [c] *imp.* [d] *fut.* [e] *part.* Poel. [f] מַסַּע *m.* a removing. Deut. x. 11, *lit.* go in journeying.

4   נָשָׂא   to lift up. KAL *fut.* Gen. xxix. 1.

5   עָשָׂה   to do, &c. KAL *inf.* Judg. xvii. 8.

6   רֶגֶל   *f.* foot.

Gen. xi. 2.	3 b	Exod. xvii. 1, 1.	3 d f	Num. xxxiii. 12, 22.	3 d
xii. 9.	3 d	xl. 36, 38.	3 f	Deut. i. 7, 40.	3 c
xiii. 3.	3 f	xl. 37.	3 d	ii. 1.	3 c
xiii. 11.	3 d	Num. ix. 10, 13.	1	ii. 24.	3 c
xx. 1.	3 d	ix. 17, 18, 19, 20,		x. 6, 7.	3 a
xxiv. 21.	1	22, 22, 23.	3 d	x. 11.	3 f
xxix. 1.	4, 6	ix. 21, 21.	3 a	Josh. ix. 11, 13.	1
xxx. 36.	1	x. 2, 12, 28.	3 f	ix. 17.	3 d
xxxi. 23.	1	x. 6, 6.	3 a f	Judg. iv. 9.	1
xxxiii. 12.	3 d	x. 13.	3 d	xvii. 8.	5, 1
xxxiii. 17.	3 a	x. 29.	3 e	1 Sam. xv. 18.	1
xxxv. 5, 16, 21.	3 d	x. 33, 33.	1	2 Sam. xi. 10.	1
xlvi. 1.	3 d	xi. 31, 31.	1	1 Kings xviii. 27.	1
Exod. iii. 18.	1	xi. 35.	3 a	xix. 4, 7.	1
v. 3.	1	xii. 15.	3 a	2 Kings iii. 9.	1
viii. 27.	3 d	xx. 22.	3 d	Neh. ii. 6.	2
xii. 37.	3 d	xxi. 4, 11.	3 d	Prov. vii. 19.	1
xiii. 20.	3 d	xxxiii. 1, 2, 2.	3 f	Jonah iii. 3, 4.	2
xvi. 1.	3 d	xxxiii. 8.	1		

JOY

1   גִּיל   to rejoice: it is that joy which expresses itself in the gestures of the body. KAL [a] *imp.* [b] *fut.* [c] גִּיל *m.* joy. [d] גִּילָה *f. id.*

2   דּוּץ   to leap and move with life and spirits; "to be turned into joy." KAL *fut.*

3   חֶדְוָה   *f.* joy, gladness. [a] חֶדְוָה Ch. *f. id.*

4   טוֹב   *adj.* good, joyful. [a] טוּב *m.* goodness.

5   עָלַז   to exult, to triumph; probably primarily of a cry or shout of exultation. KAL [a] *fut.* [b] עָלִיז *adj.* joyous.

6   עָלַץ   to exult, rejoice; to be joyful. KAL *fut.* In Ps. v. 11 three synonymous words are used, of which this seems in gradation the strongest.

7   רָאָה   to see; to live joyfully, *lit.* see life. KAL *imp.*

8   רוּעַ   to make a loud noise; to shout for joy. HIPHIL [a] *imp.* [b] *fut.* HITHPOLEL [c] *fut.* [d] תְּרוּעָה *f.* a joyful noise.

9   רָנַן   to sing; to shout for joy, to be joyful. KAL [a] *fut.* PIEL [b] *inf.* [c] *fut.* HIPHIL [d] *imp.* [e] *fut.* [f] רִנָּה *f.* shout of joy; singing. [g] רְנָנָה *f.* cry of joy.

10   שׂוּשׂ   and שִׂישׂ to exult, to be glad, to rejoice. KAL [a] *pret.* [b] שָׂשׂוֹן *m.* joy, gladness. [c] מָשׂוֹשׂ *m. id.*

11   שָׂמַח   to rejoice, to be joyful, to be glad. The primary idea seems to be that of a smiling, cheerful, merry countenance; see *Rejoice.* KAL [a] *pret.* [b] *fut.* PIEL [c] *pret.* [d] שָׂמֵחַ *adj.* joyful. [e] שִׂמְחָה *f.* joy.

Deut. xxviii. 47.	11 e	Ezra iii. 12, 13.	11 e	Job iii. 7.	9 g
1 Sam. xviii. 6.	11 e	vi. 16.	3 a	viii. 19.	10 c
1 Kings i. 40.	11 e	Neh. viii. 10.	11 e c	xx. 5.	11 e
viii. 66.	11 d	Neh. viii. 10.	3	xxix. 13.	9 e
1 Chron. xii. 40.	11 e	xii. 43, 43.	11 e	xxxiii. 26.	8 b
xv. 16, 25.	11 e	Esth. v. 9.	11 d	xxxviii. 7.	11 a
xxix. 9, 17.	11 e	vii. 16.	11 e	xli. 22.	2
2 Chron. xx. 27.	11 e	viii. 17.	11 e	Ps. v. 11, 11.	9 c, 6
xxx. 26.	11 e	ix. 22, 22.	11 e	xvi. 11. a	11 e

Ps. xxi. 1.	11 b	Ps. cxlix. 5.	5 a	Isa. li. 11, 11.	11 e
xxvii. 6.	8 d	Prov. xii. 20.	11 e	lv. 12.	11 e
xxx. 5.	9 f	xiv. 10.	11 e	lvi. 7.	11 c
xxxii. 11.	9 d	xv. 21, 23.	11 e	lx. 15.	10 c
xxxv. 9.	1 b	xvii. 21.	11 b	lxi. 3.	10 b
xxxv. 27.	9 a	xxi. 15.	11 e	lxi. 7.	11 e
xlii. 4.	1	xxiii. 24.	11 b	lxi. 10.	1 b
xliii. 4.	11 e, 1 c	Eccles. ii. 10, 26.	11 e	lxv. 14.	4 a
xlviii. 2.	10 c	v. 20.	11 e	lxv. 18.	10 c
li. 8, 12.	10 b	vii. 14.	4	lxv. 19.	10 a
lxiii. 5.	9 g	ix. 7.	11 e	lxvi. 5.	11 e
lxv. 13.	8 c	ix. 9.	7	lxvi. 10.	10 c
lxvi. 1.	8 a	Isa. ix. 3, 3, 3.	11 e a e	Jer. xv. 16.	10 b
lxvii. 4.	9 c	ix. 17.	11 b	xxxi. 13.	10 b
lxxxi. 1.	8 a	xii. 3.	10 b	xxxiii. 9, 11.	10 b
lxxxix. 15.	8 d	xvi. 10.	1 c	xlviii. 33.	11 e
xcv. 1, 2.	8 b	xxii. 2.	5 b	xlix. 25.	10 c
xcvi. 12.	5 a	xxii. 13.	10 b	Lam. ii. 15.	10 c
xcviii. 4, 6.	8 a	xxiv. 7.	5 b	v. 15.	10 c
xcviii. 8.	9 c	xxiv. 8.	10 c	Ezek. xxiv. 25.	10 c
c. 1.	8 a	xxix. 19.	11 e	xxxvi. 5.	11 e
cv. 43.	10 b	xxix. 19.	11 e	Hos. ix. 1.	1 c
cxiii. 9.	11 d	xxxii. 13, 13.	10 c, 5 b	Joel i. 12.	10 b
cxxvi. 5.	9 f	xxxii. 14.	10 c	i. 16.	11 e
cxxii. 5.	9 c	xxxv. 2.	1	Hab. iii. 18.	1
cxxxii. 16.β	9 b c	xxxv. 10, 10.	11 e, 10 b	Zeph. iii. 17, 17.	11 e, 1 b
cxxxvii. 6.	11 e	xlix. 13.	1 a	Zech. viii. 19.	10 b
cxlix. 2.	1 b	li. 3.	11 e		

α *lit.* joys.   β *lit.* shouting shall shout.

JUBILEE

יוֹבֵל   *com.* an onomato-poetic word, signifying a cry of joy, joyful shout, and then transferred to the sound or clangour of trumpets, trumpet-signal, or alarm. The year of jubilee was so called from the sounding of trumpets on the tenth day of the seventh month, by which it was announced to the people: Lev. xxv. 9. It occurred every fiftieth year, Lev. xxv. 10, 11: Jos. Ant. 3, 12, 3, not, as some suppose, in the forty-ninth; and according to the Mosaic law, in this year all lands which had been sold returned to their first possessor, all slaves were to be set free, and the ground lay untilled. Lxx. ἔτος ἀφέσεως, ἄφεσις. Lev. xxv. 10, 11, 12, 13, 15, 28, 28, 30, 31, 33, 40, 50, 52, 54; xxvii. 17, 18, 18, 21, 23, 24: Num. xxxvi. 4.

תְּרוּעָה   *f.* shout: Lev. xxv. 9, *lit.* of loud sound.

JUDGE

1   אֲדַרְגָּזְרַיָּא   Ch. *pl.* chief judges.

2   אֱלֹהִים   *m. pl.* a name of God; given also to magistrates, because they represent God, and act by his authority.

3   דָּבָר   *m.* word, matter, &c.; "in judgment," *lit.* in the matter of judgment.

4   דִּין   to judge; to sit in judgment, and take cognizance of a cause; to vindicate or right the injured; to execute judgment, or punish the guilty; to plead, debate; to strive, to contend, to wrangle. KAL [a] *pret.* [b] *inf.* [c] *fut.* [d] *part.* Poel. דִּין Ch. P'AL [e] *part. active.* [f] דִּין *m.* judgment. [g] דִּין Ch. *m. id.* [h] דַּיָּן *m. id.* [i] דַּיָּן Ch. *m. id.* [k] דּוּן *m. id.*

5   טַעַם   *m.* taste, discernment, good taste, discretion.

6   יָכַח   to be right; to set right, to decide, to judge. HIPHIL *fut.*

7   מִדִין   in Judg. v. 10 rendered judgment; later critics understand the word of carpets, coverings, or large outer garments.

8   פָּלַל   to judge; *or,* to arbitrate. PIEL [a] *pret.* [b] *fut.* [c] פָּלִיל *m.* a judge. [d] פְּלִילָה *f.* right, judgment. [e] פְּלִילִי *adj.*

judicial. In Ezek. xxviii. 23, נְכְלָל, as rendered in our version, is NIPHAL *pret.* of פָּלַל, but usually given by critics as PILEL *pret.* of נָפַל to fall.

9 פָּקַד to visit; to punish, to avenge. KAL *pret.*

10 שָׁפַט to judge; to bring matters to the rule of right; to administer justice, as a magistrate or governor. There is a considerable difference between this word and דִּין, the former being much more general. Jer. x. 24, "correct me, but with judgment," as a just as well as a considerate judge. The latter rather implies a settlement of right between two persons, as to what is due to one or both; if Jeremiah had used this word, he would have prayed God to correct him according to his deserts. With *inf.*, needs be a judge. KAL ᵃ *pret.* ᵇ *inf.* ᶜ *imp.* ᵈ *fut.* ᵉ *part.* Poel. NIPHAL ᶠ *inf.* ᵍ *fut.* POEL ʰ *part.* שָׁפוֹט *m.* judgment, penalty. ᵏ שְׁפָטִים *m. pl.* judgments, punishments. ˡ מִשְׁפָּט *m.* judgment, ordinance, statute.

Gen. xv. 14.	4 d
xvi. 5.	10 d
xviii. 19.	10 l
xviii. 25.	10 e
xix. 9. a	10 b d
xxx. 6.	4 a
xxxi. 37.	6
xxxi. 53.	10 d
xlix. 16.	4 c
Exod. ii. 14.	10 e
v. 21.	10 d
vi. 6.	10 k
vii. 4.	10 k
xii. 12.	10 k
xviii. 13.	10 b
xviii. 16.	10 a
xviii. 22, 22.	10 a d
xviii. 26, 26.	10 a d
xxi. 1, 31.	10 l
xxi. 6.	2
xxi. 22.	8 c
xxii. 8, 9, 9.	2
xxiii. 6.	10 l
xxiv. 3.	10 l
xxviii. 15, 29, 30. 30.	10 l
Lev. xviii. 4, 5, 26.	10 l
xix. 15, 15.	10 l d
xix. 35.	10 l
xx. 22.	10 l
xxv. 18.	10 l
xxvi. 15, 43, 46.	10 l
Num. xxv. 5.	10 e
xxvii. 11, 21.	10 l
xxxiii. 4.	10 k
xxxv. 12, 29.	10 l
xxxv. 24, 24.	10 a l
xxxvi. 13.	10 l
Deut. i. 16, 16.	10 e a
i. 17, 17.	10 l
iv. 1, 5, 8, 14, 45.	10 l
v. 1, 31.	10 l
vi. 1, 20.	10 l
vii. 11, 12.	10 l
viii. 11.	10 l
x. 18.	10 l
xi. 1, 32.	10 l
xii. 1.	10 l
xvi. 18, 18, 18.	10 e a l
xvi. 19.	10 l
xvii. 8, 11.	10 l
xvii. 9, 9.	10 e l
xvii. 12.	10 e
xix. 17, 18.	10 e
xxi. 2.	10 e
xxiv. 17.	10 l
xxv. 1, 1.	10 l a
xxv. 2.	10 l
xxvi. 16, 17.	10 l
xxvii. 19.	10 l
xxx. 16.	10 l
xxxii. 4, 41.	10 l
xxxii. 31.	8 c
xxxii. 36.	4 c
Deut. xxxiii. 10, 21.	10 l
Josh. viii. 33.	10 e
xx. 6.	10 e
xxiii. 14.	10 e
xxiv. 1.	10 e
Judg. ii. 16, 17, 18, 18, 18, 19.	10 e
iii. 10.	10 d
iv. 4.	10 e
iv. 5.	10 l
v. 2, 3.	10 e
v. 10.	7
1 Sam. ii. 10.	4 c
ii. 25, 25.	2, 8 a
iii. 13.	10 e
iv. 18.	10 e
vii. 6, 15.	10 a
vii. 16, 17.	10 a
viii. 1, 2.	10 e
viii. 3.	10 l
viii. 5, 6.	10 b
viii. 20.	10 a
xxiv. 12.	10 d
xxiv. 15, β 15.	4 h, 10 a
2 Sam. vii. 11.	10 e
viii. 15.	10 l
xv. 2, 6.	10 l
xv. 4.	10 e
xxiii. 3.	10 l
1 Kings ii. 3.	10 l
iii. 9, 9.	10 b
iii. 11.	10 l
iii. 28, 28, 28.	10 a l
vi. 12.	10 l
vii. 7, 7.	10 d l
viii. 32.	10 a
ix. 4.	10 l
x. 9.	10 l
xi. 33.	10 l
xx. 40.	10 e
2 Kings xv. 5.	10 e
xxiii. 22, 22.	10 e a
xxv. 6.	10 l
1 Chron. xvi. 12, 14.	10 l
xvi. 33.	10 b
xvii. 6, 10.	10 l
xviii. 14.	10 l
xxii. 13.	10 l
xxiii. 4.	10 e
xxvi. 29.	10 e
xxviii. 7.	10 l
2 Chron. i. 2.	10 l
i. 10, 11.	10 d
vi. 23.	10 a
ix. 8.	10 l
xix. 5.	10 e
2 Chron. xix. 6, 6.	10 e d
xix. 6.	3, 10 l
xix. 8, 10.	10 l
xx. 9.	10 l
xx. 12.	10 d
xxii. 8.	10 f
xxiv. 24.	10 k
xxxi. 21.	10 e
Ezra vii. 10.	10 l
vii. 25, 25.	4 i e
vii. 26.	4 g
Neh. i. 7.	10 l
ix. 13, 29.	10 l
x. 29.	10 l
Esth. i. 13.	4 f
Job viii. 3.	10 l
ix. 15.	10 h
ix. 19, 32.	10 l
ix. 24.	10 e
xii. 17.	10 e
xiv. 3.	10 l
xix. 7.	10 l
xix. 29.	4 k
xxi. 22.	10 d
xxii. 4.	10 l
xxii. 13.	10 d
xxiii. 7.	10 e
xxvii. 2.	10 l
xxix. 14.	10 l
xxxi. 11.	8 c
xxxi. 28.	8 e
xxxii. 9.	10 l
xxxiv. 4, 5, 12, 23.	10 l
xxxv. 14.	4 f
xxxvi. 17, 17.	4 f
xxxvi. 31.	4 c
xxxvii. 23.	10 l
xl. 8.	10 l
Ps. i. 5.	10 l
ii. 10.	10 e
vii. 6.	10 l
vii. 8, 8.	4 c, 10 c
vii. 11.	10 e
ix. 4.	10 e
ix. 7, 16.	10 l
ix. 8, 8.	10 d, 4 c
ix. 19.	10 g
x. 5.	10 l
x. 18.	10 b
xviii. 22.	10 l
xix. 9.	10 l
xxv. 9.	10 l
xxvi. 1.	10 c
xxxiii. 5.	10 l
xxxv. 23.	10 l
xxxv. 24.	10 c
xxxvi. 6.	10 l
xxxvii. 6, 28, 30.	10 l
xxxvii. 33.	10 f
xliii. 1.	10 l
xlviii. 11.	10 l
l. 4.	4 b
l. 6.	10 e
Ps. li. 4.	10 b
liv. 1.	4 c
lviii. 1.	10 d
lviii. 11.	10 d
lxvii. 4.	10 d
lxviii. 5.	4 h
lxxii. 1.	10 l
lxxii. 2, 2.	4 c, 10 l
lxxii. 4.	10 l
lxxv. 2.	10 e
lxxv. 7.	10 e
lxxvi. 8.	4 f
lxxvi. 9.	10 l
lxxxii. 1, 2.	10 d
lxxxii. 8.	10 c
lxxxix. 14, 30.	10 l
xciv. 2.	10 e
xciv. 15.	10 l
xcvi. 10.	4 c
xcvi. 13, 13.	10 b d
xcvii. 2, 8.	10 l
xcviii. 9, 9.	10 b d
xcix. 4, 4.	10 l
ci. 1.	10 l
ciii. 6.	10 l
cv. 5, 7.	10 l
cvi. 3.	10 l
cvi. 30.	8 b
cix. 7.	10 l
cx. 6.	4 c
cxix. 7, 13, 20, 30, 39, 43, 52, 62, 75, 84, 102, 106, 108, 120, 121, 137, 149, 156, 160, 164, 175.	10 l
cxix. 66.	5
cxxii. 5.	10 l
cxxxv. 14.	4 c
cxli. 6.	10 e
cxliii. 2.	10 e
cxlvi. 7.	10 l
cxlvii. 19, 20.	10 l
cxlviii. 11.	10 e
cxlix. 9.	10 l
Prov. i. 3.	10 l
ii. 8, 9.	10 l
viii. 16.	10 e
viii. 20.	10 l
xiii. 23.	10 l
xvi. 10.	10 l
xvii. 23.	10 l
xviii. 5.	10 l
xix. 28.	10 l
xix. 29.	10 k
xx. 8.	10 l
xxi. 3, 7, 15.	10 l
xxiv. 23.	10 l
xxviii. 5.	10 l
xxix. 4, 26.	10 l
xxix. 14.	10 e
xxxi. 5.	4 f
xxxi. 9.	10 c
Eccles. iii. 16.	10 l
iii. 17.	10 d
v. 8.	10 l
Eccles. viii. 5, 6.	10 l
xi. 9.	10 l
xii. 14.	10 l
Isa. i. 17, 17.	10 l c
i. 21, 27.	10 l
i. 26.	10 e
ii. 4.	10 a
iii. 2.	10 a
iii. 13.	4 b
iii. 14.	10 e
iv. 4.	10 l
v. 3.	10 c
v. 7, 16.	10 l
ix. 7.	10 l
x. 2.	4 f
xi. 4.	10 a
xvi. 3.	8 d
xvi. 5, 5.	10 e l
xxvi. 8, 9.	10 l
xxviii. 6, 6, 17.	10 l
xxviii. 7.	8 e
xxviii. 18.	10 l
xxx. 18.	10 e
xxxii. 1, 16.	10 l
xxxiii. 5.	10 l
xxxiii. 22.	10 l
xxxiv. 5.	10 e
xl. 14, 27.	10 l
xl. 23.	10 e
xli. 1.	10 l
xli. 3.	10 l
xlii. 1, 3, 4.	10 l
xlix. 4.	10 l
li. 4.	14 l
li. 5.	10 d
liii. 8.	10 l
liv. 17.	10 l
lvi. 1.	10 l
lix. 8, 9, 11, 14, 15.	10 l
lxi. 8.	10 l
Jer. i. 16.	10 l
iv. 2.	10 l
v. 1, 4, 5.	13 l
vii. 5.	10 l
viii. 7.	10 l
ix. 24.	10 l
x. 24.	10 l
xi. 20.	10 e
xii. 1.	10 l
xxi. 12.	10 l
xxii. 3, 15.	10 l
xxiii. 5.	10 l
xxv. 31.	10 e
xxx. 11.	10 l
xxxiii. 15.	10 l
xxxix. 5.	10 b
xlviii. 21, 47.	10 l
xlix. 12.	10 l
li. 9.	10 l
li. 47, 52.	9
liii. 9.	10 l
Lam. iii. 59.	10 l
Ezek. v. 6, 7, 7, 8.	10 l
v. 10, 15.	10 k
vii. 3, 8.	10 a
vii. 27.	10 d
Ezek. xi. 9.	10 k
xi. 10, 11.	10 d
xi. 12.	10 d
xiv. 21.	10 k
xvi. 38, 38.	10 a l
xvi. 41.	10 k
xvi. 52.	8 a
xviii. 8, 9, 17.	10 l
xviii. 30.	10 l
xx. 4, 4.	10 d
xx. 11, 13, 16, 18, 19, 21, 24, 25.	10 l
xxi. 30.	10 d
xxii. 2, 2.	10 d
xxiii. 10.	10 l
xxiii. 24, 24, 24.	10 l a l
xxiii. 36, 45.	10 l
xxiv. 14.	10 a
xxv. 11.	10 l
xxviii. 22, 26.	10 k
xxviii. 23.	8 f
xxx. 14, 19.	10 k
xxxiii. 20.	10 l
xxxiv. 16.	10 l
xxxiv. 17.	10 l
xxxiv. 20, 22.	10 a
xxxv. 11.	10 l
xxxvi. 19.	10 a
xxxvi. 27.	10 l
xxxvii. 24.	10 l
xxxix. 21.	10 l
xliv. 24, 24, 24.	10 l d l
xlv. 9.	10 l
Dan. iii. 2, 3.	1
iv. 37.	4 g
iv. 10, 22, 26.	4 g
ix. 5.	10 l
ix. 12, 12.	10 e a
Hos. ii. 19.	10 l
v. 1, 11.	10 l
v. 5.	10 l
x. 4.	10 l
xi. 6.	10 l
xiii. 10.	10 e
Joel iii. 12.	10 b
Amos ii. 3.	10 e
v. 7, 15, 24.	10 l
vi. 12.	10 l
Obad. 21.	10 b
Micah iii. 1, 8, 9.	10 l
iii. 11.	10 d
iv. 3.	10 a
v. 1.	10 e
vii. 3.	10 e
vii. 9.	10 l
Hab. i. 4, 4, 7, 12.	10 l
Zeph. ii. 3.	10 l
iii. 8.	10 e
iii. 15.	10 l
Zech. iii. 7.	4 c
vii. 9.	10 l
viii. 16. γ	10 l
Mal. ii. 17.	10 l
iii. 5.	10 l
iv. 4.	10 l

a lit. judging he will judge.   *β lit.* for a judge.   *γ lit.* truth and the judgment of peace.

JUICE

עֲסִיס *m.* new wine; also juice of pomegranates: Cant. viii. 2.

JUMP

רָקַד to leap, to spring; of a chariot driven rapidly over rough ways. PIEL *part.* Nah. iii. 2.

JUNIPER

רֹתֶם *com.* according to Hebrew interpreters and Jerome, the juniper. Gesenius, the genista, or broom, growing in the deserts of Arabia, the roots of which make the best charcoal: 1 Kings xix. 4, 5: Job xxx. 4: Ps. cxx. 4.

JUST, JUSTICE, JUSTIFY

1 יָשָׁר *adj.* right: Prov. xxix. 10.

2 צָדַק to be just, righteous. KAL [a] *pret.* [b] *fut.* PIEL [c] *pret.* [d] *inf.* [e] *fut.* HIPHIL [f] *pret.* [g] *inf.* [h] *imp.* [i] *fut.* [k] *part.* [l] צֶדֶק *m.* just, *lit.* of righteousness. [m] צְדָקָה *f.* right. [n] צַדִּיק *adj.* just : Gen. vi. 9, &c.

3 שָׁלֵם *adj.* perfect ; a just weight, *marg.* ' perfect stone.'

4 מִשְׁפָּט *m.* judgment ; just weight, *lit.* weight of judgment.

No. 2 n, *Just,* not included.

Gen. xviii. 19.	2 m	Job xxv. 4.	2 b	Isa. v. 23.	2 k
Exod. xxiii. 7.	2 i	xxvii. 5.	2 i	ix. 7.	2 m
Lev. xix. 36, 36, 36, 36.	2 l	xxxii. 2.	2 d	xliii. 9, 26.	2 b
Deut. xvi. 18, 20. a	2 l	xxxiii. 12.	2 a	xlv. 25.	2 b
xxv. 1.	2 f	xxxiii. 32.	2 d	l. 8.	2 k
xxv. 15, 15.	2 l	xxxvi. 17.	4	liii. 11.	2 i
xxxiii. 21.	2 b	xxxvii. 23.	2 m	lvi. 1.	2 m
2 Sam. viii. 15.	2 m	Ps. li. 4.	2 b	lviii. 2.	2 l
xv. 4.	2 f	lxxii. 3.	2 h	lix. 4.	2 l
1 Kings viii. 32.	2 g	cxix. 121.	2 l	lix. 9, 14.	2 m
x. 9.	2 m	cxliii. 2.	2 b	Jer. iii. 11.	2 c
1 Chron. xviii. 14.	2 m	Prov. i. 3.	2 l	xxii. 15.	2 m
2 Chron. vi. 23.	2 g	viii. 15.	2 l	xxiii. 5.	2 l
ix. 8.	2 m	xi. 1.	3	xxxi. 23.	2 l
Job iv. 17.	2 b	xvi. 11.	4	l. 7.	2 l
viii. 3.	2 l	xvii. 15, 15.	2 k n	Ezek. xvi. 51.	2 e
ix. 2, 20.	2 b	xxi. 3.	2 m	xvi. 52.	2 d
xi. 2.	2 b	xxix. 10.	1	xlv. 9.	2 m
xiii. 18.	2 b	Eccles. v. 8.	2 l	xlv. 10, 10, 10.	2 l
				Micah vi. 8.	4

a marg. ' justice justice.'

JUSTLE

שָׁקַק to run to and fro. HITHPALPEL *fut.* Nah. ii. 4.

KEEP

1 אָסַר to bind. NIPHAL *imp.*

2 אָצַל to separate, to reserve. KAL *pret.*

3 גָּרַע to lessen ; to subtract, abate, take from, to keep back. NIPHAL *fut.*

4 דָּבַק (see *Cleave*), to adhere to. KAL *fut.*

5 חָשַׂךְ (see *Withhold*), to restrain, to keep back from. KAL [a] *pret.* [b] *imp.* [c] *fut.*

6 יָשַׁב to dwell ; to make to dwell. HIPHIL *part.*

7 כָּבַשׁ to cast and keep down, or tread down, by violence ; to subdue, to keep under. KAL *inf.*

8 כָּלָא to confine, restrain, keep back, refrain, hinder. KAL [a] *pret.* [b] *fut.*

9 מָנַע to withhold, to keep back. KAL [a] *pret.* [b] *fut.* [c] *part.* Poel.

10 נָטַר to keep the eye intently fixed, as upon an object of care, &c. KAL [a] *pret.* [b] *fut.* [c] *part.* Poel. נְטַר Ch. P'AL [d] *pret.*

11 נָפַל to fall, to lie upon (a bed). KAL *pret.*

12 נָצַר to keep in a safe, secret place ; to guard ; to look after ; see *Observe.* KAL [a] *pret.* [b] *inf.* [c] *imp.* [d] *fut.* [e] *part.* Poel.

13 עָבַד to serve, to keep. KAL [a] *pret.* עֲבַד Ch. P'AL [b] *pret.*

14 עָדַר to set in array. KAL [a] *inf.* [b] *part.* Poel.

15 עָצַר to shut up, to close ; to hold back. KAL [a] *inf.* [b] *part.* Paül.

16 עָשָׂה to do, make, &c., to observe ; see *Observe.* KAL [a] *pret.* [b] *inf.* [c] *imp.* [d] *fut.* [e] *part.* Poel. NIPHAL [f] *pret.* [g] *part.*

17 פָּקַד see *Oversight.* HOPHAL, to be delivered to keep : [a] *pret.* [b] פִּקָּדוֹן *m.* a deposit.

18 קָדַשׁ to keep holy ; to celebrate. PIEL [a] *inf.* HITHPAEL [b] *inf.*

19 קָנָה to get, acquire ; to buy. HIPHIL *pret.* Zech. xiii. 5, "taught me to keep cattle," probably, bought or hired me.

20 רָעָה to feed a flock. KAL *part.* Poel.

21 שַׂר *m.* a prefect, master, chief.

22 שָׁבַח to soothe, to still, to restrain. PIEL *fut.*

23 שָׁבַת to rest, to keep a holiday, sabbath, &c. KAL *pret.*

24 שָׁמַר to keep, to watch, to guard ; to keep safe, to protect, to preserve ; to retain, to reserve ; to observe ; to regard. With *inf.,* keep diligently. KAL [a] *pret.* [b] *inf.* [c] *imp.* [d] *fut.* [e] *part.* Poel. [f] *part.* Paül. NIPHAL [g] *pret.* HITHPAEL [h] *fut.* [i] מִשְׁמֶרֶת *f.* a keeping.

Gen. ii. 15.	24 b	Deut. vi. 2.	24 b	1 Kings xx. 39.	24 c
iii. 24.	24 b	vi. 17. β	24 d d	2 Kings ix. 14.	24 e
iv. 2.	20	vii. 8.	24 b	xi. 5.	24 e
iv. 9.	24 e	vii. 9, 9.	24 e	xi. 6, 7.	24 a
xvii. 9, 10.	24 a	vii. 10, 11, 12, 12.	24 a	xii. 9.	24 e
xviii. 19.	24 a	viii. 2.	24 d	xvii. 13.	24 c
xxvi. 5.	24 d	viii. 6.	24 b	xvii. 19.	24 a
xxviii. 15, 20.	24 b	viii. 11.	24 b	xviii. 6.	24 d
xxix. 9.	20	x. 13.	24 b	xxii. 4, 14.	24 b
xxx. 31.	24 d	xi. 1, 8.	24 a	xxiii. 3.	24 b
xxxix. 9.	5 a	xi. 22. β	24 b d	xxiii. 4.	24 e
xxxix. 21, 22, 23.	21	xiii. 4.	24 a	xxiii. 21.	16 c
xli. 35.	24 a	xiii. 18.	24 b	xxv. 18.	24 e
xlii. 16.	1	xvi. 1, 10.	16 a	1 Chron. iv. 10.	16 a
Exod. iii. 1.	20	xvii. 19.	24 b	ix. 19, 19.	24 e
xii. 6.	24 i	xix. 9.	24 d	x. 13.	24 a
xii. 25.	24 a	xxiii. 9.	24 g	xii. 1.	15 b
xii. 47.	16 d	xxiii. 23.	24 b	xii. 29.	24 e
xii. 48, 48.	16 a b	xxvi. 16.	24 a	xii. 33.	14 a
xiii. 5.	13 a	xxvi. 17, 18.	24 b	xii. 38.	14 b
xiii. 10.	24 a	xxvii. 1.	24 b	xxii. 12.	24 b
xv. 26.	24 a	xxvii. 9.	24 d	xxiii. 19.	24 b
xvi. 23, 32, 33, 34.	24 i	xxviii. 45.	24 b	xxviii. 8.	24 c
xvi. 28.	24 b	xxix. 9.	24 a	xxix. 18.	24 a
xix. 5.	24 a	xxx. 10, 16.	24 b	xxix. 19.	24 b
xx. 6.	24 e	xxxii. 10.	12 d	2 Chron. vi. 14.	24 a
xx. 8.	18 a	xxxiii. 9.	12 d	vi. 15.	24 a
xxi. 18.	11	Josh. v. 10.	16 d	vi. 16.	24 c
xxi. 29, 36.	24 d	vi. 18.	24 c	vii. 8.	16 d
xxii. 7, 10.	24 d	x. 18.	24 a	vii. 9.	16 a
xxiii. 15.	24 d	xxii. 2, 3.	24 a	xii. 10.	24 c
xxiii. 20.	24 a	xxii. 5.	24 b	xiii. 11.	24 a
xxxi. 13.	24 d	xxiii. 6.	24 b	xxii. 9.	15 a
xxxi. 14, 16.	24 a	Judg. ii. 22, 22.	24 e a	xxiii. 6.	24 d
xxxiv. 7.	12 e	Ruth ii. 21, 23.	4	xxviii. 10.	7
xxxiv. 18.	24 d	1 Sam. ii. 9.	24 d	xxx. 1, 2, 3, 5, 13.	16 b
Lev. vi. 2.	17 b	vii. 1.	24 b	xxx. 21.	16 d
vi. 4. a	17 b a	ix. 24.	24 f	xxx. 23, 23.	16 b d
viii. 35.	24 d	xiii. 13, 14.	24 a	xxxiv. 9, 22.	24 a
xviii. 4.	24 d	xvi. 11.	20	xxxiv. 21.	24 a
xviii. 5, 26, 30.	24 d	xvii. 20, 22.	24 e	xxxiv. 31.	24 a
xix. 3, 19, 30.	24 d	xvii. 34.	20	xxxv. 1, 17.	16 d
xx. 8, 22.	24 a	xxi. 4.	24 g	xxxv. 16.	16 b
xxii. 9, 31.	24 a	xxi. 5.	15 b	xxxv. 18, 18,	
xxv. 2.	23	xxv. 16.	20	18.	16 f a a
xxv. 18.	24 d	xxv. 21.	24 a	xxxv. 19.	16 f
xxvi. 2, 3.	24 b	xxv. 33.	8 a	Ezra iii. 4.	16 d
Num. i. 53.	24 a	xxv. 34.	9 a	vi. 16.	13 b
iii. 7, 8.	24 a	xxv. 39.	5 a	vi. 19, 22.	16 d
iii. 28, 32, 38.	24 e	xxvi. 15, 16.	24 a	viii. 29.	24 c
vi. 24.	24 a	xxviii. 2.	24 e	Neh. i. 5.	24 a
viii. 26.	24 b	2 Sam. xv. 16.	24 b	i. 7, 9.	24 a
ix. 2, 3, 3, 5, 11, 12.	16 d	xvi. 21.	24 b	ii. 8.	24 e
ix. 4, 6, 13.	16 b	xx. 3.	24 b	iii. 29.	24 e
ix. 7.	3	xxii. 22.	24 a	viii. 18.	16 d
ix. 10, 14.	16 a	xxii. 24.	24 h	ix. 32.	24 e
ix. 19, 23.	24 a	xxii. 44.	24 f	ix. 34.	16 a
xvii. 10.	24 i	1 Kings ii. 3, 3.	24 a b	xi. 19.	24 e
xviii. 3, 4, 5.	24 a	ii. 43.	24 a	xii. 25.	24 e
xviii. 7.	24 d	iii. 6.	24 a	xii. 27.	16 b
xix. 9.	24 i	iii. 14.	24 b	xii. 45.	24 d
xxiv. 11.	9 a	vi. 12.	24 a	xiii. 22.	24 e
xxxi. 30, 47.	24 e	viii. 24.	24 e	Esth. ii. 3, 8, 14, 15,	
xxxvi. 7, 9.	4	viii. 25.	24 c	21.	24 e
Deut. iv. 2.	24 b	viii. 58, 61.	24 b	iii. 8.	16 e
iv. 6, 40.	24 a	ix. 4, 6.	24 d	vi. 2.	24 e
iv. 9.	24 c	xi. 10, 11, 34.	24 a	ix. 21, 27.	16 e
v. 1.	24 a	xi. 38.	24 b	ix. 28.	16 g
v. 10.	24 a	xiii. 21.	24 a	Job xx. 13.	9 b
v. 12, 29.	24 b	xiv. 8.	24 a	xxiii. 11.	24 a
v. 15.	16 b	xiv. 27.	24 e	xxvii. 18.	12 e
				xxxiii. 18.	5 c

Ps. xii. 7.	24 d	Prov. ii. 20.	24 d	Isa. xlii. 6.	12 d		
xvii. 4.	24 a	iii. 1.	12 d	xliii. 6.	8 b		
xvii. 8.	24 a	iii. 21.	12 c	lvi. 1.	24 c		
xviii. 21.	24 a	iii. 26.	24 a	lvi. 2, 2, 6.	24 c		
xviii. 23.	24 h	iv. 4, 21.	24 c	lvi. 4.	24 d		
xix. 11.	24 b	iv. 6.	12 d	Jer. iii. 5.	24 d		
xix. 13.	5 b	iv. 13, 23.	12 c	iii. 12.	10 b		
xxv. 10.	12 e	v. 2.	12 d	iv. 17.	24 c		
xxv. 20.	24 c	vi. 20.	12 c	xvi. 11.	24 e		
xxxiv. 13.	12 c	vi. 22.	24 d	xxxi. 10.	24 b		
xxxiv. 20.	24 c	vi. 24.	24 c	xxxv. 4.	24 c		
xxxvii. 34.	24 c	vii. 1, 2.	24 c	xxxv. 18.	24 e		
xxxix. 1.	24 d	vii. 5.	24 d	xlii. 4.	9 b		
lxxviii. 12	12 d	viii. 32.	24 d	xlviii. 10.	9 c		
lxxviii. 10, 56.	24 a	x. 17.	24 e	lii. 24.	24 c		
lxxxix. 28, 31.	24 d	xiii. 6.	12 d	Ezek. v. 7.	16 a		
xci. 11.	24 b	xiii. 3, 3,	12 e, 24 e	xi. 20.	24 d		
xcix. 7.	24 a	xvi. 17.	12 e	xvii. 14.	24 b		
ciii. 9.	10 b	xix. 8, 16, 16.	24 e	xviii. 9, 19, 21.	24 c		
ciii. 18.	24 e	xxi. 23, 23.	24 e	xx. 19.	24 c		
cv. 45.	12 d	xxii. 5.	24 e	xx. 21.	24 a		
cvi. 3.	24 e	xxii. 18.	24 d	xxxvi. 27.	24 d		
cxiii. 9.	6	xxiv. 12.	12 e	xl. 45, 46.	24 d		
cxix. 2.	12 e	xxvii. 18.	12 e	xliii. 11.	24 d		
cxix. 4, 5, 57, 60, 106		xxviii. 4.	24 e	xliv. 8, 8.	24 e		
cxix. 8, 17, 44, 55, 88, 101, 134, 146.	24 b	xxviii. 7.	12 e	xliv. 14.	24 e		
		xxix. 11.	22	xliv. 15, 16.	24 a		
cxix. 22, 56, 100, 129.	24 d	xxix. 18.	24 e	xliv. 24.	24 d		
		Eccles. ii. 10.	2	xlvii. 11.	24 a		
cxix. 33, 34, 69, 115, 145.	12 a	iii. 6.	24 b	Dan. vii. 28.	10 d		
		v. 1.	24 f	ix. 4, 4.	24 b		
cxix. 63.	12 d	v. 13.	24 f	Hos. xii. 6.	24 c		
cxix. 67, 136, 158, 167, 168.	24 e	viii. 2.δ	24 e	xii. 12.	24 e		
		viii. 5.	24 e	Amos i. 11.	24 a		
cxxi. 3, 4, 5.	24 a	xii. 3.	24 e	ii. 4.	24 a		
		xii. 13.	24 c	Micah vi. 16.	24 h		
cxxvii. 1.	24 d	Cant. i. 6, 6.	10 c a	vii. 5.	24 c		
cxxxii. 12.	24 d	v. 7.	24 e	Nah. ii. 1.	12 b		
cxl. 4.	24 e	viii. 11, 12.	10 c	Zech. iii. 7, 7.	24 d		
cxli. 3.	12 c	Isa. xxvi. 2.	24 e	xiii. 5.	19		
cxli. 9.	24 c	xxvi. 33.	12 d	Mal. ii. 7.	24 d		
cxlvi. 6.	24 e	xxvii. 3, 3.	12 e d	ii. 9.	24 e		
Prov. ii. 8.γ	12 b	xxx. 29.	18 b	iii. 7, 14.	24 a		
ii. 11.	12 d						

α *lit.* the deposit which was deposited with him.   β *lit.* keeping shall keep.   γ *lit.* to keep.   δ *lit.* keep. אֲבִי standing alone, is as much as, I counsel thee : שָׁמַר being rendered as if in the *inf.*

KERCHIEFS

מִסְפָּחוֹת *f. pl.* cushions, quilts, mattresses, so called from being spread : Ezek. xiii. 18, 21.

KERNEI·

חַרְצַנִּים *m. pl.* The Talmudists understand grape-kernels, grape-stones, so called from their acrid taste : Num. vi. 4.

KETTLE

דּוּד *m.* a pot, caldron : 1 Sam. ii. 14.

KEY

מַפְתֵּחַ *m.* opening ; a key : Judg. iii. 25 : Isa. xxii. 22.

KIBROTH-HATTAAVAH

קֶבֶר *m.* a grave, *or,* burying-place. תַּאֲוָה *f.* lust : Num. xi. 34, 35 ; xxxiii. 16, 17 : Deut. ix. 22.

KICK

בָּעַט to tread down, to trample under foot ; *metaph.* to contemn, neglect ; to kick, as an ox, *trop.* of obstinacy and rebellion against God. KAL *fut.* Deut. xxxii.15 : 1 Sam. ii. 29.

KID

1   בֵּן *m.* son, lambs, *lit.* sons of goats.

2   גְּדִי *m.* a kid, so called from cropping the herbage ; esteemed a great delicacy in the East. ^a גְּדִיָּה *f.* a she-kid.

3   עֵז *f.* goat, a kid, not separated from the flock.

4   שָׂעִיר *m.* he-goat, buck. ^a שְׂעִירָה *f.* a female-goat.

Gen. xxvii. 9, 16.	2	Lev. xxiii. 19.	4	Judg. xiii. 19.	2, 3
xxxvii. 31.	4	Num. vii. 16, 22, 28,		xiv. 6.	2
xxxviii. 17.	2, 3	34, 40, 46, 52, 58,		xv. 1.	2, 3
xxxviii. 20.	2, 3	64, 70, 76, 82, 87.	4	1 Sam. x. 3.	2
xxxviii. 23.	2	xv. 11.	3	xvi. 20.	2, 3
Exod. xxiii. 19.	2	xv. 24.	4	1 Kings xx. 27.	3
xxxiv. 26.	2	xxviii. 15, 30.	4	2 Chron. xxxv. 7.	1, 3
Lev. iv. 23.	4	xxix. 5, 11, 16, 19,		Cant. i. 8.	2 a
iv. 28.	4	25.	4	Isa. xi. 6.	2
v. 6.	4 a	Deut. xiv. 21.	2	Ezek. xliii. 22.	4
ix. 3.	4	Judg. vi. 19.	2, 3	xlv. 23.	4
xvi. 5.	4	xiii. 15.	2, 3		

KIDNEY

כְּלָיוֹת *f. pl.* reins : Exod. xxix. 13, 22 : Lev. iii. 4, 4, 10, 10, 15, 15 ; iv. 9, 9 ; vii. 4, 4 ; viii. 16, 25 ; ix. 10, 19 : Deut. xxxii. 14 : Isa. xxxiv. 6.

KILL

1   הָרַג to kill, or slay, in general, either justly or unjustly ; the most proper term to designate legally to kill ; see *Slay.* With *inf.,* kill out of hand, surely. KAL ^a *pret.* ^b *inf.* ^c *imp.* ^d *fut.* ^e *part.* Poel. PUAL ^f *pret.*

2   זָבַח to kill, or slay, in general, or as a sacrifice. KAL ^a *pret.* ^b *fut.*

3   חָלָל *adj.* pierced through, wounded, or slain.

4   טָבַח to slay, slaughter, or butcher cattle ; to kill or slaughter men. KAL *pret.*

5   מוּת to die, to be slain ; to make to die, to slay. HIPHIL ^a *pret.* ^b *inf.* ^c *fut.* ^d *part.*

6   נָכָה to smite ; to strike deep, so as to wound or kill ; with נֶפֶשׁ, *lit.* to smite the life of. HIPHIL ^a *pret.* ^b *inf.* ^c *fut.* ^d *part.*

7   נָקַף to smite, to cut ; applied, in Isa. xxix. 1, to the slaying of a sacrifice ; but חַג means, mostly, a feast, and נָקַף to go round ; modern critics translate it, let the festivals go their round. KAL *fut.*

8   קָטַל to kill, to slay ; a poetic word. KAL *fut.*

9   רָצַח to break or dash in pieces ; to kill, to slay, in a violent, unjust manner ; to murder ; never applied to the slaying of brute beasts. KAL ^a *pret.* ^b *inf.* ^c *fut.*

10   שָׁחַט to kill animals, to slaughter ; to kill persons, to slay. KAL ^a *pret.* ^b *inf.* ^c *imp.* ^d *fut.* ^e *part.* Poel. ^f *part.* Paül. NIPHAL ^g *fut.* ^h שְׁחִיטָה *f.* slaying.

Gen. iv. 15.	6 b	Lev. i. 5, 11.	10 a	Num. xi. 15.	1 c b
xii. 12.	1 a	iii. 2, 8, 13.	10 a	xiv. 15.	5 b
xxvi. 7.	1 d	iv. 4, 15.	10 a	xvi. 13.	5 b
xxvii. 42.	1 b	iv. 24, 24.	10 a d	xvi. 41.	5 a
xxxvii. 21.	1 b	iv. 33.	10 a	xxii. 29.	1 a
xxxvii. 31.	10 d	vi. 25, 25.	10 g	xxxi. 17, 17.	1 c
Exod. i. 16.	5 a	vii. 2, 2.	10 d	xxxi. 19.	1 e
ii. 14, 14.	1 a b	viii. 19.	10 a	xxxv. 11, 15, 30.	6 d
iv. 24.	5 a	xiv. 5, 25, 50.	10 a	xxxv. 27.	9 a
xii. 6.	10 a	xiv. 13, 19.	10 f	Deut. iv. 42.	9 c
xii. 21.	10 c	xiv. 19.	10 d	v. 17.	9 c
xvi. 3.	5 b	xvi. 11, 15.	10 d	xii. 15.	2 b
xvii. 3.	5 a	xvii. 3, 3.	10 a	xii. 21.	2 a
xx. 13.	9 a	xvii. 4.	10 a	xix. 4.	6 c
xxi. 29.	5 a	xx. 16.	1 a	xix. 6.	6 c
xxii. 1.	1 a	xxii. 28.	10 d	xxxii. 39.	6 c
xxii. 24.	1 a	xxiv. 17.	6 c	Josh. xx. 3, 9.	6 d
xxix. 11, 20.	10 a	xxiv. 18, 21, 21.	6 d	Judg. ix. 24.	1 b

Judg. xiii. 23.	5 b	2 Sam. xxi. 4.	5 b	2 Chron. xxxv. 1, 11.	10 d	
xv. 13.	5 b c	xxi. 17.	5 c	xxxv. 6.	10 c	
xvi. 2.	1 a	1 Kings xi. 40.	5 b	Ezra vi. 20.	10 d	
xx. 31, 39.	3	xii. 27.	1 a	Esth. iii. 13.	1 b	
1 Sam. ii. 6.	5 d	xvi. 7.	6 a	Job v. 2.	1 d	
xvi. 2.	1 a	xvi. 10.	5 c	xxiv. 14.	8	
xvii. 9, 9.	6 a	xxi. 19.	9 a	Ps. xliv. 22.	1 f	
xvii. 25, 26, 27.	6 c	2 Kings v. 7.	5 b	lix. title.	5 b	
xix. 1, 2.	5 b	vii. 4.	5 c	Prov. ix. 2.	4	
xix. 17.	5 c	xi. 15.	5 b	xxi. 25.	5 c	
xxiv. 10.	1 b	xv. 25.	5 b	Eccles. iii. 3.	1 b	
xxiv. 11, 18.	1 a	1 Chron. xix. 18.	5 a	Isa. xiv. 30.	5 a	
xxv. 11.	4	2 Chron. xviii. 2.	2 b	xiii. 13.	10 b	
xxviii. 24.	2 b	xxv. 3.	6 d	xxix. 1.	7	
xxx. 15.	5 c	xxix. 22, 22, 22,		lxvi. 3.	10 e	
2 Sam. xii. 9.	6 a	24.	10 d	Lam. ii. 21.	4	
xiii. 28.	5 a	xxx. 15.	10 d	Ezek. xxxiv. 3.	2 b	
xiv. 7.	5 c	xxx. 17.	10 h	Hos. iv. 2.	9 b	
xiv. 32.	5 a					

KIN, KIND

בָּשָׂר   *m.* flesh : Lev. xviii. 6 ; xxv. 49 : Job xii. 10, *lit.* flesh of man.

קָרוֹב   *adj.* near, near of kin : Lev. xxv. 25, *lit.* his kinsman that is near unto him : Ruth ii. 20 : 2 Sam. xix. 42.

שְׁאֵר   *m.* flesh ; *pr.* remainder, used with בָּשָׂר *lit.* remainder of his flesh, so intimately united, or rather identified, that the one was, as it were, the remainder of the other : Lev. xviii. 6 ; xx. 19 ; xxi. 2 ; xxv. 49.

KIND (N)

זַן   *m.* form, sort, kind, manner ; divers kinds : 2 Chron. xvi. 14. זַן Ch. *m.* Dan. iii. 5, 7, 10, 15.

מִין   *m.* species, form, kind, sort : Gen. i. 11, &c.

מִשְׁפָּחָה   *f.* genus, kind ; tribe, clan ; family : Gen. viii. 19 : Jer. xv. 3.

KIND, KINDNESS

1   חֶסֶד   *m.*   The general import of this word seems to be, the full flow of natural affection, corresponding to στοργή in Greek ; hence חֲסִידָה *f.* the stork, so remarkable for affection to her young. The corresponding word in Arabic is used of the flowing of the mother's milk to the breasts, so nearly connected with affection for her offspring ; hence has been derived, probably, the phrase, "full of the milk of human kindness." It is used of the goodness and abundant grace of God to his own people, his free favour and faithfulness ; in man, it is expressive of kindness and gratitude in a high degree, also of piety towards God ; holiness, and zealous affection towards all that is good, and truly desirable.

2   טוֹב   *adj.* good ; "kindly," *lit.* good things.

3   לֵב   *m.* the heart ; kindly, *lit.* to the heart of.

Gen. xx. 13.	1	1 Sam. xx. 8, 14, 15.	1	2 Chron. xxiv. 22.	1
xxi. 23.	1	2 Sam. ii. 5.	1	Neh. ix. 17.	1
xxiv. 12, 14, 49.	1	ii. 6, 6.	1, 2	Esth. ii. 9.	1
xxxiv. 3.	3	iii. 8.	1	Ps. xxxi. 21.	1
xl. 14.	1	ix. 1, 3, 7.	1	cxli. 5.	1
xlvii. 29.	1	x. 2, 2.	1	Prov. xix. 22.	1
l. 21.	3	xvi. 17.	1	xxxi. 26.	1
Josh. ii. 12, 12, 14.	1	1 Kings ii. 7.	1	Isa. liv. 8, 10.	1
Judg. viii. 35.	1	iii. 6.	1	Jer. ii. 2.	1
Ruth i. 8.	1	2 Kings xxv. 28.	2	lii. 32.	2
ii. 20.	1	1 Chron. xix. 2, 2.	1	Joel ii. 13.	1
iii. 10.	1	2 Chron. i. 7.	1	Jonah iv. 2.	1
1 Sam. xv. 6.	1				

KINDLE

1   אוֹר   to shine ; to cause to shine, of an altar, to kindle fire on. HIPHIL *fut.*

2   בָּעַר   see *Burn.* KAL [a] *pret.* [b] *fut.* [c] *part.* Poel. PIEL [d] *pret.* [e] *fut.* [f] *part.* HIPHIL [g] *part.*

3   דָּלַק   to burn, kindle, or inflame. KAL [a] *pret.* [b] *part.* HIPHIL [c] *inf.*

4   חָרָה   to burn, to be kindled ; often used in connexion with wrath. KAL [a] *pret.* [b] *inf.* [c] *fut.* HIPHIL [d] *fut.*

5   חָרַר   to be burned to a red-hot coal ; figuratively applied to the inflaming of strife. PILPEL *inf.*

6   יָצַת   to burn with a destructive conflagration. KAL [a] *fut.* NIPHAL [b] *pret.* HIPHIL [c] *pret.* [d] *fut.* [e] *part.*

7   יָקַד   to burn as a common culinary fire, which burns slow and steady, but may spread wide, consume much, and continue long. KAL *fut.*

8   כָּמַר   to be heated like an oven. NIPHAL *pret.*

9   לָהַט   to burn, or to be burnt with the vehement heat of a strong penetrating flame. PIEL *fut.*

10   נָשַׂק   to kindle a fire, to set on fire. NIPHAL [a] *pret.* HIPHIL [b] *fut.*

11   קָדַח   to kindle fire. KAL [a] *pret.* [b] *part.* Poel.

12   קָטַר   to burn incense. HIPHIL *part.*

13   שָׂרַף   to burn up, to consume with fire. KAL *pret.*

Gen. xxx. 2.	4 c	2 Sam. vi. 7.	4 c	Isa. xxx. 33.	2 c
xxxix. 19.	4 c	xii. 5.	4 c	xliii. 2.	2 b
Exod. iv. 14.	4 c	xxii. 9, 13.	2 a	xliv. 15.	10 b
xxii. 6.	2 g	xxiv. 1.	4 b	l. 11, 11.	11 b, 2
xxxv. 3.	2 e	2 Kings xiii. 3.	4 c	Jer. vii. 18.	2 f
Lev. x. 6.	13	xxii. 13, 17.	6 b	xi. 16.	6 c
Num. xi. 1, 10.	4 a	xxiii. 26.	4 a	xv. 14.	11 a
xi. 33.	4 a	1 Chron. xiii. 10.	4 c	xvii. 4.	11 a
xvi. 9.	4 a	2 Chron. xxv. 10, 15.	4 c	xvii. 27.	6 c
xxii. 22, 27.	4 c	Job xix. 11.	4 d	xxi. 14.	6 c
xxiv. 10.	4 c	xxxii. 2, 2.	4 a	xxxiii. 18.	12
xxv. 3.	4 c	xxxii. 3.	4 a	xliii. 12.	6 c
xxxii. 10, 13.	4 c	xxxii. 5.	4 c	xliv. 6.	2 b
Deut. vi. 15.	4 a	xli. 21.	9	xlix. 27.	6 c
vii. 4.	4 a	xlii. 7.	4 a	l. 32.	6 c
xi. 17.	4 a	Ps. ii. 12.	2 b	Lam. iv. 11.	6 d
xxix. 27.	4 a	viii. 8.	2 a	Ezek. xx. 47.	6 e
xxxi. 17.	4 a	lxxviii. 21.	10 a	xx. 48.	2 d
xxxii. 22.	11 a	cvi. 18.	2 b	xxiv. 10.	3 c
xxxiii. 16.	4 a	cvi. 40.	4 a	Hos. viii. 5.	4 a
Josh. vii. 1.	4 c	cxxiv. 3.	4 b	vi. 8.	8
vii. 19.	4 c	Prov. xxvi. 21.	5	Amos i. 14.	6 c
xiv. 14.	4 c	Isa. v. 25.	4 a	Obad. 18.	3 a
1 Sam. xi. 6.	4 c	ix. 18.	6 a	Zech. x. 3.	4 a
xvii. 28.	4 c	x. 16.	7	Mal. i. 10.	1
xx. 30.	4 c				

KINDRED

1   אָח   *m.* a brother, relation, or friend.

2   גְּאֻלָּה   *f.* redemption.

3   מוֹדַעַת   *f.* a known person, relative, acquaintance.

4   מוֹלֶדֶת   *f.* kindred, family.

5   מִשְׁפָּחָה   *f.* genus, kind ; tribe, clan, family.

Gen. xii. 1.	4	Num. x. 30.	4	Esth. ii. 10, 20.	4
xxiv. 4, 7.	4	Josh. vi. 23.	5	viii. 6.	4
xxiv. 38, 40, 41.	5	Ruth ii. 3.	5	Job xxxii. 2.	5
xxxi. 3, 13.	4	iii. 2.	5	Ps. xxii. 27.	5
xxxii. 9.	4	1 Chron. xii. 29.	5	xcvi. 7.	5
xliii. 7.	4	xvi. 28.	5	Ezek. xi. 15.	2

KINE

אֶלֶף   a bull, beeve, or ox : Deut. vii. 13 ; xxviii. 4, 18, 51.

בָּקָר   *com.* horned cattle ; see *Herd.* Deut. xxxii. 14 : 2 Sam. xvii. 29.

פָּרָה *f.* heifer: Gen. xxxii. 15; xli. 2, 3, 3, 4, 4, 18, 19, 20, 20, 26, 27: 1 Sam. vi. 7, 7, 10, 12, 14: Amos iv. 1.

KING, KINGLY, KINGDOM

מָלַךְ to reign, to be a king; Hiphil, to make, to set up a king, with or without מֶלֶךְ. KAL [a] *pret.* [b] *inf.* [c] *fut.* HIPHIL [d] *pret.* [e] *inf.* [f] *fut.* [g] *part.* HOPHAL [h] *pret.* [i] מֶלֶךְ *m.* a king; very frequent; used often of the Messiah, Ps. ii. 6, xlvii. 3, &c. [k] מֶלֶךְ *m.* Ch. מַלְכוּ [l] Ch. *f.* a kingdom. [m] מַלְכוּת *f.* a kingdom: a word of later date, found chiefly in the Chronicles, Esther, and Daniel; seldom in the more ancient books, Num. xxiv. 7, 1 Sam. xx. 31, 1 Kings ii. 12; it occurs in Psalms of uncertain date, Ps. xlv. 6, ciii. 19, cxlv. 11, 12, 13, 13. [n] מַמְלָכָה *f.* a kingdom. [o] מַמְלָכוּת *f.* a kingdom: a word belonging to the earlier age of the Hebrew language, though found in the later books occasionally. [p] מְלוּכָה *f.* usually the kingdom.

Not including i, k, l, m, n, o, p.

Judg. ix. 6, 6.	f i	1 Kings xvi. 21.	e	2 Chron. xi. 22.	e
ix. 16. 18.		2 Kings viii. 20.	f i	xxi. 8.	f i
1 Sam. viii. 22.	d i	ix. 13.	a	xxii. 1.	f
xi. 15.	f	x. 5.	f	xxiii. 1.	f
xii. 1.	f i	xi. 12.	f	xxvi. 1.	f
xv. 11.	d i	xiv. 21.	f	xxxiii. 25.	f
xv. 35.	f	xvii. 21.	f	xxxvi. 1, 4, 10.	f
xxiii. 17.	c	xxi. 24.	f	Isa. vii. 6.	f i
xxiv. 20, 20.	c b	xxiii. 30, 34.	f	Jer. xxxvii. 1, 1, 1.	i i f
2 Sam. ii. 9.	f	xxiv. 17.	f	Ezek. xvii. 13. α	p
xi. 1.	f	1 Chron. xi. 10.	c	Dan. i. 3. α	p
1 Kings i. 5, 35.	c	xii. 31, 38, 38.	f	v. 20.	g
i. 43, 43.	c d	xxiii. 1.	f	ix. 1.	h
iii. 7.	f	xviii. 4.	e	Hos. viii. 4.	d
xii. 1.	e	xxix. 22.	f	Amos vii. 13. β	n
xii. 20.	f	2 Chron. i. 9, 11.	d		
xvi. 16.	f	x. 1.	f		

α *lit.* the seed of the kingdom.   β *lit.* house of the kingdom.

KINSMAN, KINSFOLK, KINSWOMAN

1   גָּאַל to redeem, to do the part of a kinsman. KAL [a] *pret.* [b] *inf.* [c] *fut.* [d] *part.* Poel.

2   יָדַע to know. PUAL [a] *part.* [b] מוֹדָע *m.* familiarity; a friend, acquaintance.

3   קָרוֹב *adj.* near.

4   שְׁאֵר see *Kin.* [a] שַׁאֲרָה *f. id.*

Lev. xviii. 12, 13.	4	Ruth ii. 1.	2 b	Ruth iv. 1, 3, 6, 8,	1 d
xviii. 17.	4 a	ii. 20.	1 d	14.	
Num. v. 8.	1 d	iii. 9, 12, 12.	1 d	Job xix. 14.	3
xxvii. 11.	4	iii. 13, 13, 13,		Ps. xxxviii. 11.	3
1 Kings xvi. 11.	1 a	13.	1 c c b a	Prov. vii. 4.	2 b
2 Kings x. 11.	2 a				

KISS

נָשַׁק to be joined; to kiss, by joining the mouth to the mouth or hand of another, in token of the friendly, affectionate union of hearts, or of reverence and subjection. A kiss was the last token of affection to the dead, Gen. l. 1. KAL [a] *pret.* [b] *inf.* [c] *imp.* [d] *fut.* PIEL [e] *inf.* [f] *imp.* [g] *fut.* [h] נְשִׁיקָה *f.*

Gen. xxvii. 26.	c	Exod. iv. 27.	d	1 Kings xix. 20.	d
xxvii. 27.	d	xviii. 7.	d	Job xxxi. 27.	d
xxix. 11.	d	Ruth i. 9, 14.	d	Ps. ii. 12.	f
xxix. 13.	g	1 Sam. x. 1.	d	lxxxv. 10.	a
xxxi. 28.	e	xx. 41.	d	Prov. vii. 13.	a
xxxi. 55.	g	2 Sam. xiv. 33.	d	xxiv. 26.	d
xxxiii. 4.	d	xv. 5.	d	Cant. i. 2, 2.	d h
xlv. 15.	g	xix. 39.	d	viii. 1.	h
xlviii. 10.	d	xx. 9.	d	Hos. xiii. 2.	a
l. 1.	d	1 Kings xix. 18.	a		

KITE

אַיָּה *f.* a fowl of the hawk kind, called by the English a merlin boch: Lev. xi. 14: Deut. xiv. 13.

KNEAD

לוּשׁ to knead. KAL *inf.* Hos. vii. 4.   *imp.* Gen. xviii. 6. *fut.* 1 Sam. xxviii. 24: 2 Sam. xiii. 8. *part.* Poel, Jer. vii. 18.

KNEADING-TROUGH

מִשְׁאֶרֶת *f.* a kneading-trough or bowl, in which the dough swells: Exod. viii. 3; xii. 34.

KNEE, KNEEL

אַרְכֻּבָה Ch. *f.* the knees: Dan. v. 6.

בָּרַךְ to bow the knee: this seems to be the original and proper meaning of the word, as it is the only term for the knee in the Hebrew. KAL *fut.* 2 Chron. vi. 13: Ps. xcv. 6. HIPHIL *fut.* Gen. xxiv. 11. בְּרַךְ Ch. P'AL *part.* Dan. vi. 10. בֶּרֶךְ *f.* the knee: Gen. xxx. 3, &c. בְּרֵךְ Ch. *f.* Dan. vi. 10.

כָּרַע to bow the knee. KAL *inf.* 1 Kings viii. 54.

KNIFE

מַאֲכֶלֶת *f.* a knife to eat with; or any other knife: Gen. xxii. 6, 10: Judg. xix. 29: Prov. xxx. 14.

מַחֲלָפִים *m. pl.* (see *Pass Through*), knives, so called because they pass through the flesh in slaying sacrifices: Ezra i. 9.

חֶרֶב *f.* (see *Sword*), also a knife: Josh. v. 2, 3: 1 Kings xviii. 28: Ezek. v. 1, 2.

שַׂכִּין *m.* a knife: Prov. xxiii. 2.

KNIT

חָבֵר *adj.* see *Join, Couple.* Judg. xx. 11, *marg.* 'fellows.'

יַחַד *m.* (see *Unite*), joined, in heart and affection: 1 Chron. xii. 17.

קָשַׁר to bind. NIPHAL *pret.* 1 Sam. xviii. 1.

KNOCK

דָּפַק to force forward; to push against. KAL *part.* Poel, Cant. v. 2.

KNOP

כַּפְתּוֹר *m.* a device in architecture, and in the golden candlestick in the temple, bearing a resemblance to round apples or pomegranates: Exod. xxv. 31, 33, 33, 34, 35, 35, 35, 36; xxxvii. 17, 19, 19, 20, 21, 21, 21, 22.

KNOPS

פְּקָעִים *m. pl.* (see *Gourds*), an architectural ornament: 1 Kings vi. 18; vii. 24, 24.

KNOW

1   בִּין to consider. KAL and HIPHIL [a] *fut.* [b] בִּינָה *f.* knowledge. [c] בִּינָה Ch. *f. id.*

2   יָדַע Gesenius considers the primary meaning to be, to see;

and gives the following order of significations : (1.) To perceive, to be sensible of, by sight, Isa. vi. 9 ; by touch, Gen. xix. 33 ; but chiefly in the mind ; hence to understand, observe, Judg. xiii. 21 ; to consider ; to mark and observe with a purpose ; that which comes unexpectedly or suddenly, men are said not to know, Job ix. 5, &c. (see *Unawares*); to see to. (2.) To come to the knowledge of, by seeing, by hearing, and by experience : in this sense, it has an especial reference to threatenings and judgments, Hos. ix. 7, Job xxi. 19. (3.) To know, as that which was not known before. (4.) To know, to be acquainted with. (5.) To know, to understand, to know how. (6.) Absolutely, to know, to be wise. In Hebrew words of knowledge imply also the exercise of the affections : Ps. i. 6 ; xxxi. 7 : Prov. xxiv. 23 : Job xxxiv. 19 ; to know implies faith, Job xix. 25, *cf.* John xvii. 3. With *inf.*, know certainly, of a surety, for a certainty, for certain, diligent to know   KAL [a]*pret.* [b]*inf.* [c]*imp.* [d]*fut.* [e]*part.* Poel. [f]*part.* Paül. NIPHAL [g]*pret.* [h]*fut.* [i]*part.* PIEL [k]*pret.* PUAL [l]*part.* HIPHIL [m]*pret.* [n]*inf.* [o]*imp.* [p]*fut.* [q]*part.* HOPHAL [r]*pret.* [s]*part.* HITHPAEL [t]*inf.* [u]*fut.* יָדַע Ch. P'AL [v]*pret.* [x]*imp.* [y]*fut.* [z]*part. active.* APHEL [bb]*pret.* [cc]*inf.* [dd]*fut.* [ee]*part.* [ff] דֵּעַ *m.* what one knows. [gg] דֵּעָה *f.* knowledge. [hh] דַּעַת *f.* knowing, knowledge, intelligence : Gen. ii. 9, 17, &c. [ii] מַדָּע *m.* knowledge, mind. [kk] מַנְדַּע Ch. *m.* knowledge, understanding.

3   נָכַר   according to Taylor, to be distinguished from other things or persons by some particular discriminating mark or appearance ; to know, to acknowledge, to own as an acquaintance or friend, Job vii. 10, Ps. cxli. 4 ; to treat as an acquaintance, to distinguish, to difference by favour, Ruth ii. 19 ; to distinguish one thing or person from another by peculiar marks or known appearances, Job xxi. 29, "do ye not know," discern, their tokens ? or the distinguishing appearances of the prosperity of the wicked, which in every country are visible to everybody ; or rather, as Coccejus thinks, Have you not observed, discerned, distinguished by their apparent marks, the pompous sepulchral monuments of great wicked men placed by the side of the roads, which shew that they died in peace and splendour ? *Namque sepulchrum Incipit apparere Bianoris*, saith one traveller to another, Virg. Eclog. ix. Job xxiv. 13, "they know not," discern, distinguish not the marks, characters, and excellencies of the ways thereof. NIPHAL [a]*pret.* PIEL [b]*fut.* HIPHIL [c]*pret.* [d]*inf.* [e]*imp.* [f]*fut.* [g]*part.* HITHPAEL [h]*fut.*

4   עַיִן   the eye : Num. xv. 24. Heb. from the eyes.

5   שֵׂכֶל   *m.* understanding, wisdom.

No. 2 hh, *Knowledge*, not included.

Gen. iii. 5, 5.	2 e	Gen. xviii. 19.	2 a	Gen. xxviii. 16.	2 a
iii. 7.	2 d	xviii. 21.	2 d	xxix. 5, 5.	2 a
iii. 22.	2 b	xix. 5.	2 d	xxx. 26, 29.	2 a
iv. 1, 9.	2 a	xix. 8.	2 a	xxxi. 6, 32.	2 a
iv. 17, 25.	2 d	xx. 6.	2 a	xxxvii. 13.	2 c
viii. 11.	2 d	xxii. 12.	2 a	xxxvii. 32.	3 e
ix. 24.	2 d	xxiv. 14.	2 d	xxxvii. 33.	3 f
xii. 11.	2 a	xxiv. 16.	2 a	xxxviii. 9.	2 d
xv. 8.	2 d	xxvii. 2.	2 a	xxxviii. 16.	2 a
xv. 13.	2 d b			xxxviii. 26.	2 b

Gen. xxxix. 6.	2 a	Judg. vi. 37.	2 a	2 Kings ix. 11.	2 a
xli. 21.	2 g	xi. 39.	2 a	x. 10.	2 c
xli. 31.	2 h	xiii. 16, 21.	2 a	xvii. 26, 26.	2 a e
xlii. 7, 7.	3 f	xiv. 4.	2 a	xix. 19.	2 d
xlii. 8, 8.	3 f c	xv. 11.	2 a	xix. 27.	2 d
xlii. 23.	2 a	xvi. 9.	2 g	1 Chron. xii. 32.	2 b
xlii. 33, 34.	2 a	xvii. 13.	2 a	xvi. 8.	2 o
xliii. 7, 7.	2 b d	xviii. 3.	3 c	xvii. 18.	2 a
xliv. 27.	2 a	xviii. 5.	2 d	xvii. 19.	2 n
xlv. 1.	2 t	xviii. 14.	2 a	xxi. 2.	2 d
xlvii. 6.	2 a	xix. 22, 25.	2 a	xxviii. 9.	2 c
xlviii. 19, 19.	2 a	xx. 34.	2 a	xxix. 17.	2 a
Exod. i. 8.	2 a	xxi. 12.	2 a	2 Chron. i. 10, 11, 12.	2 ii
ii. 14.	2 g	Ruth ii. 10.	3 d	ii. 8.	2 a
iii. 7.	2 d	ii. 11.	2 a	vi. 29.	2 d
iv. 14.	2 a	ii. 19.	3 g	vi. 30, 30.	2 d a
v. 2.	2 a	iii. 3.	2 h	vi. 33, 33.	2 d b
vi. 3.	2 g	iii. 11.	2 e	viii. 18.	2 e
vi. 7.	2 a	iii. 14, 14.	3 f, 2 h	xii. 8.	2 d
vii. 5.	2 a	iii. 18.	2 d	xiii. 5.	2 b
vii. 17.	2 d	iv. 4.	2 d	xx. 12.	2 d
viii. 10, 22.	2 d	1 Sam. i. 19.	2 d	xxv. 16.	2 a
ix. 14, 29.	2 d	ii. 3.	2 gg	xxx. 22.	5
ix. 30.	2 a	ii. 12.	2 a	xxxii. 13.	2 d
x. 2.	2 a	iii. 7, 13.	2 a	xxxii. 31.	2 b
x. 7, 26.	2 d	iii. 20.	2 d	xxxiii. 13.	2 d
xi. 7.	2 d	vi. 3.	2 g	Ezra iv. 12, 13.	2 aa
xiv. 4, 18.	2 a	vi. 9.	2 a	iv. 15.	2 y
xvi. 6, 12.	2 a	x. 11.	2 e	v. 8.	2 aa
xviii. 11.	2 a	xiv. 38.	2 c	vii. 25, 25.	2 z
xviii. 16.	2 m	xvii. 46, 47.	2 d	Neh. ii. 16.	2 a
xxi. 36.	2 g	xviii. 28.	2 d	iv. 11.	2 d
xxiii. 9.	2 a	xx. 3.	2 b a	iv. 15.	2 g
xxix. 46.	2 a	xx. 9, 33.	2 d	ix. 10.	2 a
xxxi. 13.	2 b	xx. 30, 39, 39.	2 d	ix. 14.	2 m
xxxii. 22.	2 a	xxi. 2.	2 d	x. 28.	2 e
xxxiii. 5, 13, 17.	2 d	xxii. 3.	2 d	Esth. i. 13, 13.	2 e
xxxiii. 12, 12.	2 m a	xxii. 15, 17, 22.	2 a	ii. 11.	2 b
xxxiii. 16.	2 h	xxiii. 9.	2 d	ii. 22.	2 h
xxxvi. 1.	2 b	xxiii. 17.	2 e	iv. 5.	2 b
Lev. iv. 14.	2 g	xxiii. 22, 23.	2 c	iv. 11, 14.	2 e
iv. 23, 28.	2 r	xxiv. 11.	2 a	Job i. 12.	2 a
v. 1, 3, 4.	2 a	xxiv. 20.	2 a	v. 24, 25.	2 a
xxiii. 43.	2 d	xxv. 11.	2 a	v. 27.	2 a
Num. x. 31.	2 a	xxv. 17.	2 c	vii. 10.	3 f
xi. 16.	2 a	xxvi. 12.	2 e	viii. 9.	2 d
xii. 6.	2 u	xxvii.	3 f	ix. 2, 5, 28.	2 d
xiv. 31, 34.	2 a	xxviii. 1, 2.	2 a	ix. 21.	2 d
xv. 24.	4	xxviii. 9.	2 a	x. 7.	2 hh
xvi. 28.	2 d	xxviii. 15.	2 a	x. 13.	2 a
xx. 14.	2 a	xxix. 9.	2 a	xi. 6.	2 c
xxii. 19.	2 a	2 Sam. i. 5.	2 a	xi. 8.	2 a
xxii. 34.	2 a	ii. 26.	2 a	xi. 11.	2 a
xxiv. 16.	2 e hh	iii. 25, 25, 25.	2 a b b	xii. 9.	2 a
xxxi. 17.	2 c	iii. 26.	2 a	xiii. 2.γ	2 hh
xxxi. 18, 35.	2 a	iii. 38.	2 d	xiii. 2, 18.	2 a
Deut. i. 13, 15.	2 f	vii. 20.	2 a	xiii. 23.	2 c
i. 39.	2 a	vii. 21.	2 n	xiv. 21.	2 d
ii. 7.	2 a	xi. 16, 20.	2 a	xv. 9, 9.	2 a d
iii. 19.	2 a	xiv. 20.	2 a	xv. 23.	2 a
iv. 35.	2 b	xiv. 22.	2 a	xviii. 21.	2 a
iv. 39.	2 a	xv. 11.	2 a	xix. 6.	2 c
vii. 9, 15.	2 a	xvii. 8.	2 a	xix. 25.	2 a
viii. 2.	2 b	xvii. 10.	2 e	xix. 29.	2 a
viii. 3, 3, 3.	2 a a n	xvii. 19.	2 g	xx. 4.	2 a
viii. 16.	2 a	xviii. 29.	2 a	xxi. 19.	2 a
ix. 2.	2 a	xix. 20, 22.	2 a	xxi. 27.	2 a
ix. 24.	2 b	xix. 44.	2 a	xxi. 29.	3 b
xi. 2, 2, 28.	2 a	xxiv. 2.	2 a	xxii. 13.	2 a
xiii. 2, 6, 13.	2 a	1 Kings i. 4, 11, 18.	2 a	xxiii. 3, 10.	2 a
xiii. 3.	2 b	ii. 5, 9, 15, 32, 44.	2 a	xxiii. 5.	2 d
xviii. 21.	2 d	ii. 37, 42.	2 d	xxiv. 1.	2 e
xx. 20.	2 d	iii. 7.	2 d	xxiv. 13.	3 c
xxi. 1.	2 g	v. 3, 6.	2 a	xxiv. 16.	2 a
xxii. 2.	2 a	viii. 38.	2 d	xxiv. 17.	3 f
xxvii. 33, 36, 64. a	2 d	viii. 39, 39.	2 d a	xxvii. 7, 13, 23.	2 a
xxix. 6.	2 d	viii. 43, 43.	2 d b	xxix. 16.	2 a
xxix. 16, 26.	2 a	viii. 60.	2 b	xxxi. 6.	2 d
xxxi. 13, 21, 27, 29.	2 a	ix. 27.	2 e	xxxii. 22.	2 c
xxxii. 17.	2 a	xiv. 2.β	2 e	xxxiv. 2.	2 e
xxxiii. 9.	2 a	xvii. 24.	2 d	xxxiv. 4.	2 d
xxxiv. 6, 10.	2 a	xviii. 12, 37.	2 d	xxxiv. 25.	3 f
Josh. ii. 9.	2 a	xviii. 36.	2 h	xxxv. 15.	2 a
iii. 4, 7, 10.	2 d	xx. 13, 28.	2 d	xxxvi. 3.	2 ff
iv. 22.	2 m	xxii. 3.	2 a	xxxvi. 4.	2 gg
iv. 24.	2 a	2 Kings ii. 3, 3, 5, 5.	2 a	xxxvii. 7.	2 b
xiv. 6.	2 a	iv. 1, 39.	2 a	xxxvii. 16, 16.	2 d f
xxii. 22, 22.	2 c d	v. 8.	2 a	xxxviii. 5.	2 d
xxiii. 13.	2 d	v. 15.	2 a	xxxviii. 12.	2 d
xxiv. 31.	2 a	vii. 12.	2 a	xxxviii. 18, 21, 33.	2 a
Judg. ii. 10.	2 a	viii. 12.	2 a	xxxviii. 20.	1 a
iii. 1.	2 a				
iii. 2, 2.	2 b a				
iii. 4.	2 b				

Job xxxix. 1. 2.	2 a
xlii. 2.	2 a
xlii. 3.	2 d
Ps. i. 6.	2 e
iv. 3.	2 c
ix. 10.	2 e
ix. 16.	2 g
ix. 20.	2 d
xiv. 4.	2 a
xviii. 43.	2 a
xx. 6.	2 a
xxxi. 7.	2 a
xxxv. 11, 15.	2 a
xxxvi. 10.	2 e
xxxvii. 18.	2 e
xxxix. 4, 4.	2 o d
xxxix. 6.	2 d
xl. 9.	2 a
xli. 11.	2 a
xliv. 21.	2 e
xlvi. 10.	2 c
xlviii. 3.	2 g
l. 11.	2 a
li. 6.	2 p
lii. i.	2 a
lvi. 9.	2 a
lix. 13.	2 d
lxvii. 2.	2 b
lxix. 5, 19.	2 a
lxxi. 15.	2 a
lxxii. 11, 11.	2 a gg
lxxiii. 16.	2 b
lxxiv. 9.	2 e
lxxvi. 1.	2 i
lxxvii. 19.	2 g
lxxviii. 3, 6.	2 d
lxxviii. 5.	2 n
lxxix. 6.	2 a
lxxix. 10.	2 h
lxxxii. 5.	2 a
lxxxiii. 18.	2 d
lxxxvii. 4.	2 e
lxxxix. 12.	2 h
lxxxix. 1.	2 p
lxxxix. 15.	2 e
xc. 11.	2 a
xci. 14.	2 a
xcii. 6.	2 d
xciv. 11.	2 e
xcv. 10.	2 a
xcviii. 2.	2 m
c. 3.	2 c
ci. 4.	2 d
ciii. 7.	2 p
ciii. 14.	2 a
ciii. 16.	3 f
civ. 19.	2 a
cv. 1.	2 o
cvi. 8.	2 n
cix. 27.	2 d
cxix. 75.	2 a
cxix. 79.	2 e
cxix. 125.	2 d
cxix. 152.	2 a
cxxxv. 5.	2 a
cxxxviii. 6.	2 d
cxxxix. 1.	2 d
cxxxix. 2, 4.	2 a
cxxxix. 14.	2 e
cxxxix. 23, 23.	2 c
cxl. 12.	2 a
cxlii. 3.	2 a
cxlii. 3.	3 g
cxliii. 8.	2 o
cxliv. 3.	2 d
cxlv. 12.	2 n
cxlvii. 20.	2 a
Prov. i. 2.	2 b
i. 23.	2 p
ii. 3.	1 b
iv. 1.	2 b
iv. 19.	2 a
v. 6.	2 d
vii. 23.	2 a
ix. 13, 18.	2 a
x. 9.	2 h
x. 32.	2 d
xii. 16.	2 h
xiv. 10.	2 e
xiv. 33.	2 n
xvii. 27.	2 e hh
xx. 11.	3 h
xxii. 19.	2 m
xxii. 21.	2 n
xxiv. 12, 12.	2 a d
Prov. xxiv. 14. δ	2 c
xxiv. 22.	2 e
xxvii. 1.	2 d
xxvii. 23.	2 b
xxviii. 2.	2 e
xxix. 7.	2 b h
xxx. 3. ε	2 d hh
xxx. 18.	2 a
xxxi. 23.	2 i
Eccles. i. 17.	2 e
ii. 19.	2 e
iii. 12, 14.	2 e
iii. 21.	2 e
iv. 5.	2 a
vi. 8, 12.	2 a
vi. 10.	2 i
vii. 22.	2 a
vii. 25, 25.	2 b
viii. 1, 7, 12.	2 e
viii. 16, 17.	2 b
ix. 1, 5, 5.	2 a
ix. 12.	2 d
x. 15.	2 a
xi. 2.	2 d
xi. 5, 5.	2 e d
xi. 6.	2 e
xi. 9.	2 c
Cant. i. 8.	2 d
Isa. i. 3, 3.	2 a
v. 19.	2 d
vii. 15.	2 d
vii. 16.	2 d
viii. 4.	2 d
ix. 9.	2 a
xi. 9.	2 gg
xii. 5.	2 s, or l
xix. 12.	2 d
xix. 21, 21.	2 g d
xxviii. 9.	2 gg
xxix. 15.	2 e
xxxvii. 20.	2 d
xxxvii. 28.	2 a
xxxvii. 19.	2 p
xl. 21.	2 a
xl. 28.	2 a
xli. 20, 22, 23, 26.	2 a
xlii. 16, 16, 25.	2 a
xliii. 10, 19.	2 d
xliv. 8, 18.	2 a
xliv. 9.	2 d
xlv. 3, 6.	2 d
xlv. 4, 5, 20.	2 a
xlvii. 8, 11, 11.	2 d
xlviii. 4.	2 hh
xlviii. 6, 7, 8, 8.	2 a
xlix. 23, 26.	2 a
l. 4.	2 b
l. 7.	2 d
li. 7.	2 e
lii. 6.	2 a
liii. 11. ζ	2 hh
lv. 5, 5.	2 d a
lviii. 2.	2 hh
lviii. 3.	2 d
lix. 8, 8, 12.	2 a
lx. 16.	2 a
lxi. 9.	2 g
lxiv. 2.	2 n
lxvi. 14.	2 g
Jer. i. 5.	2 a
ii. 8.	2 a
ii. 19, 23.	2 c
iii. 15.	2 gg
iv. 22, 22.	2 a
v. 1.	2 c
v. 4, 5.	2 a
v. 15.	2 d
vi. 18.	2 c
vi. 27.	2 d
vii. 9.	2 a
viii. 7, 7.	2 a
ix. 3, 16.	2 a
ix. 6, 24.	2 a
x. 14.	2 a
x. 23, 25.	2 a
xi. 18, 18.	2 m d
xi. 19.	2 a
xii. 3.	2 a
xiii. 12.	2 a
xiv. 18.	2 a
xv. 14.	2 a
xv. 15, 15.	2 a c
xvi. 13.	2 a
xvi. 21, 21, 21.	2 q p a
xvii. 4, 16.	2 a
Jer. xvii. 9.	2 d
xviii. 23.	2 a
xix. 4.	2 a
xxi. 29.	3 b
xxii. 16.	2 hh
xxiii. 28.	2 a
xxiv. 7.	2 b
xxvi. 15.	2 b
xxviii. 9.	2 h
xxix. 11.	2 a
xxix. 23.	2 e
xxxi. 34, 34.	2 c d
xxxii. 8.	2 a
xxxiii. 3.	2 a
xxxvi. 19.	2 d
xxxviii. 24.	2 d
xl. 14, 15.	2 d
xli. 4.	2 a
xlii. 19, 22.	2 d
xliv. 3, 28.	2 d
xlv. 15.	2 d
xliv. 29.	2 d
xlviii. 17.	2 a
xlviii. 30.	2 a
Lam. iv. 8.	3 a
Ezek. ii. 5.	2 a
v. 13.	2 a
vi. 7, 10, 13, 14.	2 a
vii. 4, 9, 27.	2 a
x. 20.	2 d
xi. 5, 10, 12.	2 a
xii. 15, 16, 20.	2 a
xiii. 9, 14, 21, 23.	2 a
xiv. 8, 23.	2 a
xv. 7.	2 a
xvi. 2.	2 o
xvi. 62.	2 a
xvii. 12, 21, 24.	2 a
xix. 7.	2 o
xx. 4.	2 o
xx. 5.	2 a
xx. 9.	2 h
xx. 12, 20.	2 b
xx. 26.	2 a
xx. 38, 42, 44.	2 a
xxi. 5.	2 a
xxii. 16, 22.	2 a
xxiii. 49.	2 a
xxiv. 24, 27.	2 a
xxv. 5, 7, 11, 14, 17.	2 a
xxvi. 6.	2 a
xxviii. 19.	2 a
xxviii. 22, 23, 24, 26.	2 a
xxix. 6, 9, 16, 21.	2 a
xxx. 8, 19, 25, 26.	2 a
xxxii. 9, 15.	2 a
xxxiii. 29, 33.	2 a
xxxiv. 27, 30.	2 a
xxxv. 4, 9, 12, 15.	2 a
xxxv. 11.	2 g
xxxvi. 11, 23, 36, 38.	2 a
xxxvi. 32.	2 h
xxxvii. 3, 6, 13, 14, 28.	2 a
xxxviii. 14.	2 d
xxxviii. 16.	2 b
xxxviii. 23, 23.	2 a
xxxix. 6, 22, 23, 28.	2 a
xxxix. 7, 7.	2 a
Dan. i. 17.	2 ii
ii. 3.	2 a
ii. 5, 25.	2 a
ii. 8, 22.	2 z
ii. 9, 9.	2 d d y
ii. 15, 17, 23, 23, 28, 29, 45.	2 bb
ii. 21, 21.	2 kk z
ii. 26.	2 cc
ii. 30, 30.	2 dd y
iii. 18.	2 na
iv. 6.	2 dd
iv. 7.	2 ee
iv. 9.	2 v
iv. 17, 25, 26, 32.	2 v
iv. 18.	2 cc
v. 8, 15, 16.	2 cc
v. 12.	2 kk
v. 17.	2 dd
v. 21, 22.	2 v
v. 23.	2 z
vi. 10.	2 v
vi. 15.	2 v
vii. 16.	2 dd
viii. 19.	2 q
ix. 25.	2 d
Dan. x. 20.	2 a
xi. 32.	2 e
xi. 38.	2 a
Hos. ii. 8, 20.	2 a
v. 3, 4.	2 a
v. 9.	2 m
vi. 3, 3.	2 a
vii. 9, 9.	2 a
viii. 2, 4.	2 a
ix. 7.	2 a
xi. 3.	2 a
xiii. 4.	2 d
xiii. 5.	2 b

α *lit.* thou hast not known nor thy fathers. β *lit.* they may not know thee. γ *lit.* as your knowledge. δ *lit.* know that such is wisdom. ε *marg.* 'the knowledge.' ζ *lit.* by the knowledge of him. η *lit.* to know.

Hos. xiv. 9.	2 d
Joel ii. 14.	2 e
ii. 27.	2 e
iii. 17.	2 a
Amos iii. 2, 10.	2 a
v. 12.	2 a
Jonah i. 7.	2 a
i. 10.	2 a
i. 12.	2 a
iv. 2.	2 d
Micah iii. 1.	2 a
iv. 12.	2 a
Nah. i. 7.	2 e
iii. 17.	2 g
Hab. ii. 14. η	2 a
iii. 2.	2 p
Zeph. iii. 5.	2 e
Zech. ii. 9, 11.	2 a
iv. 5, 9, 13.	2 a
vi. 15.	2 a
vii. 14.	2 d
xi. 11.	2 a
xiv. 7.	2 h
Mal. ii. 4.	2 a

LABOUR

1 אוּץ to hasten, to urge, to press on. HIPHIL *fut.*

2 יָגַע to be fatigued, weary; quite exhausted and spent with labour, or in any other way; to work hard, to take great pains; laborious, fatiguing work, weariness. KAL ᵃ *pret.* ᵇ *fut.* PIEL ᶜ *fut.* ᵈ יְגִיעַ *m.* labour. ᵉ יָגִיעַ *m. id.* ᶠ יָגֵעַ *adj.* weary.

3 יָד the hand: Prov. xiii. 11, *marg.* 'with the hand.'

4 יָלַד to labour in parturition. KAL *inf. lit.* she had difficulty in her labour.

5 מְלָאכָה *f.* any work, business, or affair.

6 עָבַד to work, to labour. KAL ᵃ *fut.* ᵇ *part.* Poel. ᶜ עֲבוֹדָה *f.* service, bondage.

7 עָמַל to labour, with the idea of effort and exhaustion; to toil; with עָמָל to take labour. KAL ᵃ *pret.* ᵇ *fut.* ᶜ עָמָל *m.* labour, toil; trouble, vexation, sorrow. ᵈ עָמֵל *adj.* labouring.

8 עֶצֶב *m.* labour; grief: Isa. lviii. 3, *marg.* 'griefs, *or,* things wherewith you grieve others.' ᵃ עֶצֶב *m.* labour, hard and painful toil; sorrow, pain.

9 עָשָׂה to do, to make, &c. KAL ᵃ *inf.* ᵇ *fut.* ᶜ *part.* Poel. ᵈ מַעֲשֶׂה *m.* work.

10 פְּעֻלָּה *f.* labour, work, occupation.

11 שְׁדַר Ch. to exert oneself, to strive to do anything. ITHPAEL *part.*

Gen. xxxi. 42.	2 e
xxxv. 16, 17.	4
Exod. v. 9.	9 b
xx. 9.	6 a
xxiii. 16, 16.	9 d
Deut. v. 13.	6 a
xxvi. 7.	7 c
xxviii. 33.	2 e
Josh. vii. 3.	2 c
xxiv. 13.	2 a
Neh. iv. 21.	5
iv. 22.	5
v. 13.	2 z
Job ix. 29.	2 b
xx. 18.	2 b
xxxix. 11, 16.	2 e
Ps. lxxviii. 46.	2 e
xc. 10.	7 c
civ. 23.	6 c
cv. 44.	7 c
cvii. 12.	7 c
cix. 11.	2 e
cxxvii. 1.	7 a
cxxix. 2.	7 a
Prov. v. 10.	8 a
Prov. x. 16.	10
xiii. 11.	3
xiv. 23.	8 a
xvi. 26, 26.	7 d a
xxi. 25.	9 a
xxiii. 4.	2 b
Eccles. i. 3.	7 c b
i. 8.	2 f
ii. 10, 10, 20, 24.	7 c
ii. 11, 11.	9 c
ii. 18.	7 c b
ii. 19, 19.	7 c a
ii. 20.	7 c a
ii. 21, 21.	7 c a
ii. 22, 22.	7 d c
iii. 9.	7 d
iii. 13.	7 c
iv. 8, 8.	7 c d
iv. 9.	7 c
v. 12.	6 b
v. 15, 19.	7 c
v. 16.	7 c
v. 18.	7 c d
vi. 7.	7 c
viii. 15.	7 c
Eccles. viii. 17.	7 b
ix. 9.	7 c d
x. 15.	7 c
Isa. xxii. 4.	1
xlv. 14.	2 e
xlvii. 12, 15.	2 a
xlix. 4.	2 a
lv. 2.	2 e
lviii. 3.	8
lxii. 8.	3 a
lxv. 23.	2 b
Jer. iii. 24.	2 e
xx. 5.	7 c
xx. 18.	7 c
li. 58.	2 b
Lam. v. 5.	2 e
Ezek. xxiii. 29.	2 e
xxix. 20.	10
Dan. vi. 14.	11
Hos. xii. 8.	2 e
Jonah iv. 10.	7 a
Hab. iii. 13.	2 b
iii. 17.	9 d
Hag. i. 11.	9 d

LACE

פָּתִיל *m.* a thread, line, cord; lace; Exod. xxviii. 28, 37; xxxix. 21, 31.

LACK

1 חָסֵר to be diminished, to fail ; to want, to lack. KAL ᵃ*pret.* ᵇ*fut.* HIPHIL ᶜ*pret.* ᵈ חָסֵר *adj.* wanting. ᵉ מַחְסוֹר *m.* want.

2 עָדַר to miss, to find lacking. NIPHAL ᵃ*pret.* PIEL ᵇ*fut.*

3 פָּקַד to visit, to look after, to look after that which is missing, to miss ; to be lacking. NIPHAL ᵃ*pret.* ᵇ*inf.* ᶜ*fut.*

4 קָלַט to contract, to draw together. KAL *part.* Paül, "lacking in his parts."

5 רוּשׁ to be poor, to suffer want. KAL *pret.*

6 שָׁבַת to cease. HIPHIL *fut.*

Gen. xviii. 28.	1 b	Judg. xxiii. 4.	3 c	Neh. ix. 21.	1 a
Exod. xvi. 18.	1 c	1 Sam. xxx. 19.	2 a	Ps. xxxiv. 10.	5
Lev. ii. 13.	6	2 Sam. ii. 30.	3 c	Prov. vi. 32.	1 d
xxii. 23.	4	iii. 29.	1 d	xii. 9.	1 d
Num. xxxi. 49.	3 a	xvii. 22.		xxviii. 27.β	1 e
Deut. ii. 7.	1 a	1 Kings iv. 27.α	2 b	Eccles. ix. 8.	1 b
viii. 9.	1 b	xi. 22.	1 d	Jer. xxiii. 4.	3 c
Judg. xxi. 3.	3 b				

α *lit.* suffered nothing to be wanting.   β *lit.* shall not have want.

LAD

נַעַר *m.* boy, youth, young man, servant : Gen. xxi. 12, &c.

LADDER

סֻלָּם *m.* a staircase, ladder : Gen. xxviii. 12. It is doubtful to what root we should refer this word, or that it means an ordinary ladder. It is commonly referred to סָלַל, which means, to raise up in a pile, to heap up ; see *Cast up.* Bush, therefore, understands it to mean, in this passage, a towering elevation, as of mountains heaped together, having also ledges serving as steps. So interpreted by Jewish commentators ; see Bush *in loc.*

LADE, LOADEN

1 טָעַן to lade beasts of burden. KAL *imp.*

2 כָּבַד to be heavy ; to make heavy. HIPHIL ᵃ*part.* ᵇ כָּבֵד *adj.*

3 נָשָׂא to bear ; "laden with," *lit.* carrying. KAL ᵃ*fut.* ᵇ*part.* Poel.

4 עָמַס to take up, to take up and place upon a beast, to load. KAL ᵃ*fut.* ᵇ*part.* Poel. ᶜ*part.* Paül. HIPHIL ᵈ*pret.* עָמֵשׂ *id.* KAL ᵉ*part.* Poel.

Gen. xlii. 26.	3 a	1 Kings xii. 11.	4 d	Isa. i. 4.	2 b
xliv. 13.	4 a	Neh. iv. 17.	4 e	xlvi. 1.	4 c
xlv. 17.	1	xiii. 15.	4 b	Hab. ii. 6.	2 a
xlv. 23, 23.	3 b	Ps. lxviii. 19.	4 a		

LADY

גְּבֶרֶת *f.* mistress : Isa. xlvii. 5, 7.

שָׂרָה *f.* princess, noble lady : Judg. v. 29 : Esth. i. 18.

LAMB

1 אִמְּרִין Ch. *pl.* lambs.

2 בֶּן *m.* son ; lambs, *lit.* the sons of sheep.

3 טְלָאִים *m. pl.* young sucking-lambs, which, by natural instinct, join themselves to their dams. ᵃ טָלֶה *m. id.*

4 כֶּבֶשׂ *m.* a lamb that has done sucking, a young sheep of a year old, and till it reaches the third ; esteemed a great delicacy in the East. Exod. xxix. 38, &c. ᵃ כִּבְשָׂה ᵇ *f.* ewe-lambs.

5 כַּר *m.* a pasture ; a lamb well fed.

6 כֶּשֶׂב *m.* the same as כֶּבֶשׂ. ᵃ כִּשְׂבָּה ᵇ *f.*

7 צֹאן *com.* small cattle, sheep and goats.

8 שֶׂה *com.* one of a flock, a sheep, a goat ; a lamb.

No. 4 not included.

Gen. xxi. 28, 29, 30.	4 a	Lev. xvii. 3.	6	Ps. cxiv. 4.	2, 7
xxii. 7, 8.	8	xxii. 23.	8	cxiv. 6.	2, 7
xxx. 40.	6	Num. vi. 14, 14.	4, 4 a	Isa. xvi. 1.	5
Exod. xii. 3, 3, 4, 4, 5.	8	xv. 11.α	4, 8	xxxiv. 6.	5
xii. 21.	7	Deut. xxxii. 14.	6	xl. 11.	3
xiii. 13.	8	1 Sam. vii. 9.	3 a	liii. 7.	8
xxxiv. 40.	8	xv. 9.	5	lxv. 25.	3 a
Lev. iii. 7.	6	xvii. 34.	8	lxvi. 3.	8
iv. 35.	6	2 Sam. xiii. 3, 4, 6.	4 a	Jer. li. 40.	5
v. 6.	6 a	2 Kings iii. 4.	5	Ezek. xxvii. 21.	5
v. 7.	8	Ezra vi. 9, 17.	1	xxxix. 18.	5
xii. 8.	8	vii. 17.	1	xlv. 15.	8
xiv. 10, 10.	4, 4 a	Ps. xxxvii. 20.	5	Amos vi. 4.	5

α *lit.* a lamb of the sheep or of the goats.

LAME

נָכֶה *adj.* lame, *i. e.* smitten : 2 Sam. iv. 4 ; ix. 3.

פָּסַח to halt, to become lame. NIPHAL *fut.* 2 Sam. iv. 4. פִּסֵּחַ *adj.* lame : Lev. xxi. 18 : Deut. xv. 21 : 2 Sam. v. 6, 8, 8 ; ix. 13 ; xix. 26 : Job xxix. 15 : Prov. xxvi. 7 : Isa. xxxiii. 23 ; xxxv. 6 : Jer. xxxi. 8 : Mal. i. 8, 13.

LAMENT

1 אָבַל to mourn. KAL ᵃ*pret.* HIPHIL ᵇ*fut.* HITHPAEL ᶜ*fut.*

2 אָלָה to lament aloud, with invocations of the Deity. KAL *imp.*

3 אָנָה to be in great sorrow ; to mourn. KAL ᵃ*pret.* ᵇ אֲנִיָּה *f.* Lam. ii. 5, mourning and mourning, *i. e.* a continual mourning without intermission.

4 בָּכָה to weep. KAL *fut.*

5 נָהָה to wail. KAL ᵃ*pret.* NIPHAL ᵇ*fut.* ᶜ נְהִי *m.* lamentation.

6 סָפַד to mourn. KAL ᵃ*inf.* ᵇ*imp.* ᶜ*fut.* ᵈ*part.* Poel. NIPHAL ᵉ*fut.* ᶠ מִסְפֵּד *m.* wailing, lamentation.

7 עֲצַב Ch. to be grieved, afflicted. P'AL *part.*

8 קוּן to chant a mournful song ; to lament. POLEL ᵃ*pret.* ᵇ*fut.* ᶜ קִינָה *f.* a mournful song.

9 תָּנָה to rehearse ; to talk with or of ; to celebrate. PIEL *inf.*

Gen. l. 10.	6 f	Jer. vi. 26.	6 f	Ezek. xix. 1, 14, 14.	8 c
Judg. xi. 40.	9	vii. 29.	8 c	xxvi. 17.	8 c
1 Sam. vi. 19.	1 c	ix. 10, 20.	8 c	xxvii. 2.	8 c
vii. 2.	5 b	xvi. 4.	6 e	xxvii. 32, 32.	8 c a
xxv. 1.	6 c	xvi. 5.	6 a	xxviii. 12.	8 c
xxviii. 3.	6 c	xvi. 6.	6 c	xxxii. 2.	8 c
2 Sam. i. 17, 17.	8 b c	xxiii. 18, 18.	6 c	xxxii. 16, 16, 16,	
iii. 33.	8 b	xxv. 33.	6 e	16.	8 c a b b
2 Chron. xxxv. 25,		xxxi. 15.	8 c	Dan. vi. 20.	7
25, 25.	8 b c c	xxxiv. 5.	6 c	Joel i. 8.	2
Ps. lxxviii. 64.	4	xlviii. 38.	6 f	i. 13.	6 b
Isa. iii. 26.	3 a	xlix. 3.	6 b	Amos v. 1.	8 c
xix. 8.	1 a	Lam. ii. 5.	3 b	v. 16.	5 c
xxxii. 12.	6 d	ii. 8.	1 b	viii. 10.	5 c
Jer. iv. 8.	6 b	Ezek. ii. 10.	8 c	Micah ii. 4, 4.	5 a c

LAMP

1 לַפִּיד *m.* a burning lamp or torch. In the East, a lamp or flame is appealed to in confirmation of a covenant, which is thought to explain Gen. xv. 17. Job xii. 5, a lamp or torch, despised, *i. e.* burning dimly, or thrown aside,

having ceased to burn : *delapsa fax in cineres*, Hor. *Cf.* Isa. vii. 4.

2 נֵר *m.* a lamp, a candle, light ; often used of the lamps of the holy candlestick, constantly burning in the sanctuary ; or of the candlestick itself. It is figuratively used of happiness, glory, and of instruction. Job xviii. 6 is in allusion to the lamp suspended in the tent. Lamps, in the East, were kept burning all night, and are still reckoned one of the most refined comforts the Orientals can enjoy, and for which they would make any sacrifice. The origin of the custom may have been to preserve themselves from serpents and other noxious reptiles ; hence the putting out of a light is a figure of great danger, as the light is the symbol of prosperity. See *Candle.* Exod. xxv. 37, &c. נִיר a *m. id.* נִיר b *m. id.*

Gen. xv. 17.	1	Num. viii. 3.	2	Job xii. 5.	1
Exod. xxv. 37, 37.	2	Judg. vii. 16, 20.	1	xli. 19.	1
xxvii. 20.	2	1 Sam. iii. 3.	2	Ps. cxix. 105.	2
xxx. 7, 8.	2	2 Sam. xxii. 29.	2 a	cxxxii. 17.	2
xxxv. 14.	2	1 Kings vii. 49.	2	Prov. vi. 23.	2
xxxvii. 23.	2	xv. 4.	2 b	xiii. 9.	2
xxxix. 37, 37.	2	1 Chron. xxviii. 15,		xx. 20.	2
xl. 4, 25.	2	15, 15.	2	Isa. lxii. 1.	1
Lev. xxiv. 2, 4.	2	2 Chron. iv. 20, 21.	2	Ezek. i. 13.	1
Num. iv. 9.		xiii. 11.	2	Dan. x. 6.	1
viii. 2, 2.	2	xxix. 7.	2	Zech. iv. 2, 2.	1

LANCE

כִּידוֹן *m.* spear : Jer. l. 42. See *Spear.*

LANCET

רֹמַח *m.* spear, used by heavy-armed troops ; sometimes an iron point, lance-head : 1 Kings xviii. 28.

LAND

1 אֲדָמָה *f.* the earth, the ground ; a land or country.

2 אֶרֶץ *com.* the earth ; a land, a country : Gen. ii. 11, &c.

3 שָׂדֶה *m.* field ; country.

No. 2 not included.

Gen. xxviii. 15.	1	2 Sam. xix. 29.	3	Jer. xxv. 5.	1
xlvii. 18, 19, 19,		1 Kings viii. 34, 40.	1	xxvii. 10, 11.	1
19, 22, 22, 23, 23,		ix. 7.	1	xxxv. 7, 15.	1
26, 26.	1	xiv. 15.	1	xlii. 12.	1
xlvii. 20, 20.	1, 2	2 Kings viii. 3, 3.	2, 3	lii. 27, 27.	2, 1
Exod. xx. 12.	1	viii. 5.	3	Ezek. vii. 2, 2.	1, 2
xxiii. 19.	1	xvii. 23.	1	xi. 17.	1
xxxiv. 26.	1	xxi. 8.	1	xii. 19, 19, 19.	2, 1, 2
Lev. xx. 24.	1, 2	xxv. 21, 21.	2, 1	xii. 22.	1
Num. xi. 12.	1	2 Chron. vi. 25, 31.	1	xiii. 9.	1
xxxii. 11.	1	vii. 20.	1	xviii. 2.	1
Deut. v. 16.	1	xxxiii. 8.	1	xx. 38, 42.	1
vii. 13, 13.	1	Neh. v. 3, 4, 5, 11, 16.	3	xxi. 2, 3.	1
xi. 9, 9.	1, 2	ix. 25.	1	xxv. 3, 6.	1
xi. 17, 17.	1, 2	Job xxxi. 38.	1	xxvii. 26.	1
xi. 21.	1	Ps. xlix. 11.	1	xxxiii. 24, 24, 24.	1, 2, 2
xxi. 1, 23.	1	cxxxviii. 4.	1	xxxiv. 13, 27.	1
xxv. 15.	1	Prov. xii. 11.	1	xxxvi. 6, 17, 24.	1
xxvi. 10.	1	xxxiii. 19.	1	xxxvii. 12, 14, 21.	1
xxvi. 15, 15.	1, 2	Isa. i. 7.	1	xxxviii. 18, 19.	1
xxviii. 11, 18, 21, 33,		vi. 11.	1	xxxix. 26, 28.	1
42, 51, 63.	1	vii. 16.	1	Dan. xi. 9, 39.	1
xxix. 28, 28.	1, 2	xiv. 1, 2.	1	Joel i. 10.	1
xxx. 9, 18, 20.	2	xv. 9.	1	ii. 21.	1
xxxi. 13, 20.	1	xix. 17.	1	Amos v. 2.	1
xxxii. 43, 47.	1	xxxii. 13.	1	vii. 11, 17, 17, 17.	1
Josh. xxiii. 13, 15.	1	Jer. xii. 14.	1	xi. 15, 15.	1
1 Sam. xiv. 14.	3	xvi. 15, 15, 15.	2, 2, 1	Zeph. i. 2, 3.	1
2 Sam. ix. 7.	3	xxiii. 8.	1	Zech. ii. 12.	1
ix. 10.	1	xxiv. 10.	1	ix. 16.	1

LANDMARK

נְבוּל *m.* border, bounds : Deut. xix. 14 ; xxvii. 17 : Prov. xxii. 28 ; xxiii. 10. גְּבוּלָה *f.* border, margin : Job xxiv. 2.

LANGUAGE

1 דָּבָר a word, speech.

2 לָעַז to speak in a strange language. KAL *part.* Poel.

3 לָשׁוֹן *com.* the tongue, language. a לְשָׁן Ch. *com.*

4 שָׂפָה *f.* lip ; speech.

Gen. xi. 1, 6, 7, 9.	4	Ps. lxxxi. 5.	4	Dan. iv. 1.	3 a
Neh. xiii. 24.	3	cxiv. 1.	2	v. 19.	3 a
Esth. i. 22, 22.	3	Isa. xix. 18.	4	vi. 25.	3 a
iii. 12.	3	Jer. v. 15.	3	vii. 14.	3 a
viii. 9, 9.	3	Ezek. iii. 5, 6.	3	Zeph. iii. 9.	4
Ps. xix. 3.	1	Dan. iii. 4, 7, 29.	3 a	Zech. viii. 23.	3

LANGUISH

אָמַל (see *Feeble*), to wither, to be in extremity of weakness and decay ; also to be sorrowful. PULAL *pret.* Isa. xvi. 8 ; xix. 8 ; xxiv. 4, 4, 7 ; xxxiii. 9 : Jer. xiv. 2 ; xv. 9 : Lam. ii. 8 : Hos. iv. 3 : Joel i. 10, 12 : Nah. i. 4, 4.

דְּוַי *m.* (see *Faint*), sorrowful, languid : Ps. xli. 3.

LAP

בֶּגֶד *m.* an outer garment, robe : 2 Kings iv. 39, *i. e.* in the fold of his outer garment.

חֵיק *m.* the bosom : Prov. xvi. 33

חֹצֶן *m.* the bosom of a garment : Neh. v. 13, "I shook my lap," as a solemn form of execration. He opened the fold of his garment, in which they were accustomed to carry things, and shook it, to signify its being empty.

LAP (V)

לָקַק to lick, or lap, as a dog. KAL *fut.* Judg. vii. 5, 5. PIEL *part.* Judg. vii. 6, 7.

LAPWING

דּוּכִיפַת *f.* a bird about as large as a lapwing or pewet, which has a beautiful crest, consisting of a double row of small feathers, and reaching from the bill quite to the back of the neck, which it can erect or drop at pleasure.— *Shaw's Supp.* p. 72 ; *Rait Synops. Avium*, p. 48.—Lev. xi. 19 : Deut. xiv. 18.

LARGE

1 יָד *com.* hand ; large, *lit.* broad of hands, or spaces.

2 רָוַח to breathe, to be enlarged. PUAL *part.*

3 רָחַב to be or become wide, large, spacious. NIPHAL a *part.* HIPHIL b *pret.* רָחָב c *adj.* d רֹחַב *m.* breadth. e מֶרְחָב *m.* broad space.

Gen. xxxiv. 21.	3 c	Neh. vii. 4.	3 c, 1	Isa. xxx. 23.	3 a
Exod. iii. 8.	3 c	ix. 35.	3 c	xxx. 33.	3 b
Judg. xviii. 10.	3 c, 1	Ps. xviii. 19.	3 e	Jer. xxii. 14.	2
2 Sam. xxii. 20.	3 e	xxxi. 8.	3 e	Ezek. xxiii. 32.	3 c
1 Kings iv. 29.	3 d	cxviii. 5.	3 e	Hos. iv. 16.	3 e
Neh. xix. 19.	3 c	Isa. xxii. 18.	3 c, 1		

LAST

1 אַחֲרוֹן *adj.* hinder, hindermost, latter, opposed to foremost. a אַחֲרֵין Ch. *adv.* preceded by עַד, at last. b אַחֲרִית *f.* the last or extreme part, uttermost part ; oftener of time, the end of a period, the end or event of any course ;

aftertime, the future, especially in the prophetic formula, in the last days.

2 עוֹלָם *m.* perpetual; everlasting.

3 עָקֵב *m.* heel; end, last.

Gen. xlix. 1. *a*	1 b	2 Chron. xx. 34.	1	Isa. xliv. 6.	1
xlix. 19.	3	xxv. 26.	1	xlviii. 12.	1
Num. xxiii. 10.	1 b	xxvi. 22.	1	Jer. xii. 4.	1 b
Deut. xxxiii. 15.	2	xxviii. 26.	1	l. 17.	1
2 Sam. xix. 11, 12.	1	xxxv. 27.	1	Lam. i. 9.	1 b
xxiii. 1.	1	Ezra viii. 13.	1	Dan. iv. 8.	1 a
1 Chron. xxiii. 27.	1	Neh. viii. 18.	1	viii. 3.	1
xxix. 29.	1	Prov. v. 11. β	1 b	viii. 19.	1 b
2 Chron. ix. 29.	1	xxiii. 32.	1	Amos ix. 1.	1 b
xii. 15.	1	Isa. ii. 2.	1 b	Micah iv. 1.	1 b
xvi. 11.	1	xli. 4.	1		

a *lit.* in the end of the days.   β *lit.* at thy last.

LATCHET

שְׂרוֹךְ *m.* a shoe-latchet, sandal-thong, which fastens a shoe or sandal, so called from lacing and binding together; proverbially, for anything of little value: Gen. xiv. 23: Isa. v. 27.

LATE

אָחַר to delay. PIEL *part.* Ps. cxxvii. 2.

אֶתְמוֹל see *Yesterday.* Micah ii. 8.

LATTER

אַחֲרוֹן *adj.* see *Last.* Exod. iv. 8: Deut. xxiv. 3, 3; Ruth iii. 10: 2 Sam. ii. 26: Job xix. 25: Dan. xi. 29: Hag. ii. 9. אַחֲרִית *f.* Num. xxiv. 14, 20: Deut. iv. 30; viii. 16; xxxi. 29; xxxii. 29: Job viii. 7; xlii. 12: Prov. xix. 20: Isa. xli. 22; xlvii. 7: Jer. xxiii. 20; xxx. 24; xlviii. 47; xlix. 39; Ezek. xxxviii. 8, 16: Dan. viii. 23; x. 14: Hos. iii. 5. אַחֲרִית Ch. *f.* Dan. ii. 28.

לֶקֶשׁ *m.* latter grass, aftermath; latter growth: Amos vii. 1, 1. See also *Rain.*

LATTICE

אֶשְׁנָב *m.* a lattice, *i. e.* a latticed window, through which the cool breeze passes: Judg. v. 28.

חֲרַכִּים *m. pl.* lattices of windows, properly a net, net-work: Cant. ii. 9.

שְׂבָכָה *f.* net; lattice, lattice-work; before a window or balcony, to protect persons from falling: 2 Kings i. 2.

LAUGH

1 לָעַג to mock, deride. KAL *pret.* See also *Scorn.*

2 צָחַק to laugh; to play, to sport, to jest; to laugh may imply admiration and joy, or unbelief and mistrust: see Gen. xvii. 17 and xviii. 12. KAL [a] *pret.* [b] *fut.* [c] צְחֹק *m.* laughter.

3 שָׂחַק to laugh; *seq.* אֶל to laugh or smile upon; *seq.* עַל to laugh at, deride; *seq.* לְ *id.*, but especially in contempt to laugh at in scorn, to scorn, especially of powerless threats; *seq.* בְּ to mock, to rejoice in others' calamities; to jest, to sport, to play. KAL [a] *pret.* [b] *inf.* [c] *fut.* HIPHIL [d] *part.* שְׂחוֹק *m.* laughter, derision.

Gen. xvii. 17.	2 b	2 Chron. xxx. 10.	3 d	Job xii. 4.	3 e
xviii. 12.	2 b	Job v. 22.	3 c	xxix. 24.	3 c
xviii. 13, 15, 15.	2 a	viii. 21.	3 e	xli. 29.	3 c
xxi. 6, *a* 6.	2 c b	ix. 23.	1	Ps. ii. 4.	3 c

Ps. xxxvii. 13.	3 c	Prov. i. 26.	3 c	Eccles. iii. 4.	3 b
lii. 6.	3 c	xiv. 13.	3 e	vii. 3, 6.	3 e
lix. 8.	3 c	xxix. 9.	3 a	x. 19.	3 e
lxxx. 6.	1	Eccles. ii. 2.	3 e	Ezek. xxiii. 32.	2 c
cxxvi. 2.	3 e				

a *lit.* made laughter to me.

LAVER

כִּיּוֹר *m.* a large vessel of brass, which held water for washing the hands and feet of the priests: Exod. xxx. 18, &c.

LAVISH

זוּל to shake out, to pour out. KAL *part.* Isa. xlvi. 6.

LAW

1 דָּת *f.* a mandate of a king, edict, decree; law, statute. [a] דָּת Ch. *f. id.*

2 חָקַק to prescribe, decree. POEL [a] *part.* lawgiver, collectively for teachers of the law, according to Chald. Jerus. Targ. and Targ. Jon. PUAL [b] *part.* [c] חֹק *m.* appointed law.

3 תּוֹרָה *f.* instruction, precept: Job xxii. 22, human, as of parents, Prov. i. 8; iii. 1; iv. 2; vi. 20; vii. 2: divine through the prophets, Isa. i. 10, &c.: Gen. xxvi. 5, &c.

4 צַדִּיק *adj.* just, righteous, lawful: Isa. xlix. 24.

5 מִצְוָה *f.* commandment.

6 שַׁלִּיט Ch. *adj.* one that has power; *seq.* לְ, with *inf.* there is power to do, *i. e.* it is permitted, *licet.*

7 מִשְׁפָּט *m.* judgment; right, rectitude, justice; "manner of law." No. 3 not included.

Gen. xlvii. 26.	2 c	Esth. i. 8, 13.	1	Prov. xxxi. 5.	2 b
xlix. 10.	2 a	i. 15, 19.	1	Isa. xxxiii. 22.	2 a
Lev. xxiv. 22.	7	iii. 8, 8.	1	xlix. 24.	4
Num. xxi. 18.	2 a	iv. 11, 16.	1	Jer. xxxii. 11.	5
Deut. xxxiii. 2.	1	Ps. lx. 7.	2 a	Ezek. xviii. 5, 19, 21,	
xxxiii. 21.	2 a	lxxxi. 4.	7	27.	7
1 Chron. xvi. 17.	2 c	xciv. 20.	2 c	xxxiii. 14, 16, 19.	7
Ezra vii. 12, 14, 21, 25,		cv. 10.	2 c	Dan. vi. 5, 8, 12, 15.	1 a
26, 26.	1 a	cviii. 8.	2 a	vii. 25.	1 a
vii. 24.	6				

LAY

1 אָחַז to lay hold; to take, to seize. KAL [a] *inf.* [b] *imp.* [c] *fut.*

2 אָצַר to lay up in store. KAL *pret.*

3 בּוֹא to come in, to enter. KAL *pret.* Ps. cv. 18, Heb. his soul came into iron.

4 חָזַק to hold fast to anything, to keep strong fast hold. HIPHIL [a] *prct.* [b] *fut.* [c] *part.*

5 חָלָה to be sick, to make sick. PIEL *pret.* See *Sick.*

6 חָסַן Schultens, on Prov. xv. 6, says this root imports strength entire and inviolable; riches laid up untouched and well secured.—*Taylor.* NIPHAL *fut.*

7 טָמַן to hide, to lay privily. KAL [a] *pret.* [b] *inf.* [c] *part.* Paül.

8 יְהַב Ch. see *Give.* P'AL *pret.*

9 יָנַח to set or lay a thing down, or to lay it up, and leave it to be or lie there. HIPHIL [a] *pret.* [b] *imp.* [c] *fut.*

10 יָסַד to lay the foundation of a house; see *Foundation.*

11 יָצָא to go out; to make to go out, to lay out. KAL [a] *fut.* HIPHIL [b] *fut.*

12 יָצַע to spread clothes, to lay under. HOPHAL *fut.*

13 יָצַק to pour out. HIPHIL *fut.*

14   יָקֹשׁ   to lay snares ; see *Snares*.

15   יָרָה   to set right, as stones in a building ; see *Cast*.   KAL *pret.*

16   כָּבֵד   to be heavy.   KAL ᵃ *fut.*   HIPHIL ᵇ *pret.*

17   כָּמַס   to lay up in store.   KAL *part.* Paül.

18   מָלַט   to slip away ; to let slip, to deliver ; hence to lay eggs.   PIEL *fut.*

19   נָגַע   to touch ; to cause to touch.   HIPHIL *fut.*

20   נוּחַ   to rest ; to cause to rest.   HIPHIL *fut.*

21   נְחַת   Ch. to come down.   APHEL *part.*

22   נָטָה   to stretch out ; to extend.   HIPHIL *fut.*

23   נָצַב   to set, to place ; to set up.   HIPHIL *fut.*

24   נָשָׂא   to bear ; to impose, require.   KAL ᵃ *pret.* ᵇ *fut.*

25   נָשַׂג   to reach ; to attain to ; *seq. dupl. acc.* to lay at one with a sword.   HIPHIL *part.*

26   נָתַן   to give.   KAL ᵃ *pret.* ᵇ *inf.* ᶜ *fut.* ᵈ *part.* Poel. NIPHAL ᵉ *pret.*

27   סְבַל   Ch. to bear a burden, implying strength ; hence strongly laid, of a foundation.   POAL *part.*

28   סוּר   to turn aside out of the way ; to lay away, to lay by.   HIPHIL ᵃ *pret.* ᵇ *fut.*

29   סָמַךְ   to place or lay upon anything ; to impose, so as to rest or be supported upon anything.   KAL ᵃ *pret.* ᵇ *fut.*

30   עָבַר   to pass ; to make to pass.   HIPHIL *fut.*

31   עָלָה   to ascend, to go up, to be put or laid upon.   KAL *inf.*

32   פָּגַע   to strike, to fall upon, to meet.   HIPHIL *pret.*

33   פָּקַד   to look after, to lay up in a secure place.   HIPHIL ᵃ *pret.* ᵇ *fut.* ᶜ פְּקֻדָּה *f.* that which is laid up and guarded.

34   פָּרַשׂ   to spread, to lay open.   KAL *fut.*

35   צָבַר   to heap up, to lay up.   KAL *fut.*

36   צָפַן   to hide.   KAL ᵃ *pret.* ᵇ *fut.* ᶜ *part.* Paül.

37   קָרַב   to be near ; to make to be near.   HIPHIL *fut.*

38   שָׁוָה   to be made even ; to put, set, place.   PIEL ᵃ *pret.* ᵇ *fut.*

39   שׂוּם   to set, place ; to put, to place, to lay things, sometimes persons, so that they may remain in a recumbent posture.   KAL ᵃ *pret.* ᵇ *inf.* ᶜ *imp.* ᵈ *fut.* ᵉ *part.* Poel. שׂוּם Ch. P'AL ᶠ *part. passive.* ITHP'AL ᵍ *part.*

40   שִׁית   of the same meaning : to lay the hand upon any one in protection, or as an arbiter or mediator.   KAL ᵃ *pret.* ᵇ *inf.* ᶜ *fut.*   HOPHAL ᵈ *fut.*

41   שָׁכַב   to lie.   HIPHIL, to lay : ᵃ *pret.* ᵇ *fut.*   HOPHAL ᶜ *pret.* ᵈ *imp.* ᵉ *part.*

42   שָׁכַן   to dwell ; to cause to dwell.   HIPHIL *fut.*

43   שָׁלַח   to send, to stretch out.   KAL ᵃ *pret.* ᵇ *inf.* ᶜ *fut.*   PIEL ᵈ *pret.* ᵉ מִשְׁלוֹחַ *m.* a sending ; the thing upon which the hand is sent.

44   שָׁתַת   to set, to place.   KAL *pret.*

45   תָּפַשׂ   to lay hold ; see *Hold* ; to make fast in gold or silver, to overlay.   KAL *part.* Paül.

See also *Lie* ; and *Foundation, Snare, Wait.*

Gen. ix. 23.	39 d	Gen. xxxvii. 22.	43 c	Exod. ii. 3.	39 d
xv. 10.	26 c	xxxviii. 19.	28 b	v. 8.	39 d
xix. 16.	4 b	xxxix. 16.	9 c	v. 9.	16 a
xxiii. 6, 9.	39 d	xli. 35.	35	vii. 4.	26 a
xxii. 12.	43 c	xli. 48, 48.	26 c a	xvi. 23, 33.	9 b
xxx. 41.	39 a	xlviii. 14, 17.	40 c	xvi. 24, 34.	9 c

Exod. xix. 7.		2 Kings xx. 7.	39 d	Isa. v. 8.	37
xxi. 22.	40 c	xx. 17.	2	v. 29.	1 c
xxi. 30, 30.	40 d	2 Chron. vi. 22.	24 a	vi. 7.	19
xxii. 25.	39 d	vii. 22.	4 b	x. 28.	33 b
xxiv. 11.	43 a	xvi. 14.	41 b	xi. 14.	39 b
Lev. ii. 15.	39 d	xxiii. 15.	39 d	xiii. 19.	39 b
iii. 2, 8, 13.	29 a	xxix. 23.	29 b	xv. 7.	33 c
iv. 4, 15, 24, 29, 33.	29 a	xxxi. 6.	26 c	xxii. 22.	26 a
viii. 14, 18, 22.	29 b	Ezra v. 8.	39 f	xxiii. 18.	6
xvi. 21.	29 a	v. 16.	8	xxviii. 17.	39 a
xxiv. 14.	29 a	vi. 1.	21	xxx. 32.	20
Num. viii. 12.	29 b	vi. 3.	27	xxxiv. 15.	18
xi. 11.	39 b	Neh. xiii. 5.	26 d	xxxix. 6.	2
xii. 11.	40 c	xiii. 21.	43 c	xlii. 25.	39 d
xvi. 18.	39 d	Esth. ii. 21.	43 c	xlvii. 6.	16 b
xvii. 4.	9 a	iii. 6.	43 b	xlvii. 7.	39 a
xvii. 7.	9 c	iv. 3.	12	li. 23.	39 d
xix. 9.	9 a	vi. 2.	43 b	liii. 6.	32
xxvii. 18.	9 a	viii. 7.	43 b	lvi. 2.	4 b
xxvii. 23.	29 b	ix. 2.	43 b	lvii. 1.	39 e
Deut. vii. 15.	26 a	ix. 10, 15, 16.	43 a	lvii. 11.	39 a
xi. 18.	39 a	x. 1.	39 d	Jer. vi. 21.	26 d
xi. 25.	26 c	Job vi. 2.	24 b	vi. 3.	4 b
xiv. 28.	9 a	ix. 33.	40 c	ix. 8.	39 d
xxvi. 6.	26 c	xvii. 3.	39 d	xii. 11.	39 e
xxix. 22.	5	xviii. 10.	7 c	xxxvi. 20.	33 a
xxxii. 34.	17	xxi. 5.	39 c	Ezek. iii. 20.	26 a
xxxiv. 9.	29 a	xxi. 19.	36 b	iv. 1, 2, 5, 8.	26 a
Josh. iv. 8.	9 c	xxi. 22.	26 a	iv. 4.	39 a
vii. 23.	13	xxii. 24.	40 b	iv. 5.	39 a
viii. 2.	39 d	xxiv. 12.	39 d	xi. 7.	39 a
Judg. vi. 20.	9 b	xxix. 9.	39 d	xxv. 14.	39 a
ix. 24.	39 b	xxxiv. 23.	39 d	xxv. 17.	26 a
ix. 48.	39 d	xxxviii. 5.	39 a	xxvi. 12.	39 d
xviii. 19.	39 c	xxxviii. 6.	15	xxvi. 16.	28 a
xix. 29.	4 b	xl. 4.	39 a	xxviii. 17.	26 a
Ruth iii. 15.	40 c	xli. 8.	39 c	xxxii. 5.	39 d
iv. 16.	40 c	Ps. vii. 6.	42	xxxii. 19.	41 d
1 Sam. vi. 8.	26 a	xxi. 5.	38 b	xxxii. 27.	26 c
vi. 11.	39 d	xxxi. 4.	7 a	xxxii. 32.	41 c
x. 25.	9 c	xxxi. 19.	36 a	xxxiii. 28.	26 a
xi. 2.	39 a	xlix. 14.	26 d	xxxiii. 29.	26 b
xv. 2.	39 a	lxii. 9.	44	xxxv. 4.	39 d
xv. 27.	4 b	lxiv. 5.	31	xxxvi. 29.	26 c
xix. 13.	39 d	lxvi. 5.	7 b	xxxvii. 6.	26 a
xxi. 12.	39 d	lxvi. 11.	39 a	xxxix. 21.	39 a
xxv. 18.	39 d	lxxix. 1.	39 a	xl. 42.	9 c
2 Sam. ii. 21.	1 b	lxxxiv. 3.	40 a	xlii. 13, 14.	39 a
xiii. 19.	39 d	lxxxviii. 6.	40 a	xliv. 19.	9 a
xviii. 17.	23	lxxxix. 19.	38 a	Dan. vi. 17.	39 f
1 Kings iii. 20, 20.	41 b a	cv. 18.	3	Hos. xi. 4.	22
viii. 31.	24 a	cxix. 30.	38 a	Joel i. 7.	39 a
xiii. 29, 30.	9 c	cxix. 110.	26 a	Amos ii. 8.	22
xiii. 31.	9 b	cxxxix. 5.	40 c	Obad. 7.	39 d
xvii. 19.	41 b	cxli. 3.	7 a	13.	43 c
xviii. 23, 23.	39 d, 26 a	Prov. ii. 7.	36 b	Jonah i. 14.	26 c
xviii. 33.	39 d	iii. 18.	4 c	15.	6
2 Kings iv. 21.	41 b	vii. 1.	36 b	Micah i. 7.	39 d
iv. 29.	39 a	x. 14.	36 b	v. 1.	39 a
iv. 31.	39 d	xiii. 16.	34	vii. 16.	39 d
iv. 32.	41 e	xiii. 22.	36 c	Hab. ii. 19.	45
v. 23.	26 c	xxvi. 24.	40 c	Hag. ii. 15.	39 b
ix. 25.	24 a	xxix. 19.	43 d	Zech. iii. 9.	26 a
x. 8.	39 c	Eccles. ii. 3.	1 a	vii. 14.	39 d
xi. 16.	39 d	vii. 2.	26 c	xiv. 13.	4 a
xii. 11.	11 b	Cant. vii. 13.	36 a	Mal. i. 3.	39 d
xii. 12.	11 a	Isa. v. 6.	40 c	ii. 2, 2.	39 d e

LEAD

עוֹפֶרֶת   *f.* lead, so called from its whitish colour.—*Gesenius.*   Exod. xv. 10 : Num. xxxi. 22 : Job xix. 24 : Jer. vi. 29 : Ezek. xxii. 18, 20 ; xxvii. 12 : Zech. v. 7, 8.

LEAD

1   אָשַׁר   to go straight ; to guide or lead ; to pronounce blessed.   PIEL ᵃ *part.*   PUAL ᵇ *part.*

2   בּוֹא   to come.   HIPHIL ᵃ *pret.* ᵇ *fut.*

3   דָּרַךְ   to walk, to go ; to lead.   HIPHIL ᵃ *pret.* ᵇ *imp.* ᶜ *fut.* ᵈ *part.*

4   הָלַךְ   to walk, to go.   PIEL *fut.*

5   יָבַל   to bring, to lead along, gently and uniformly ; see *Bring.*   HIPHIL ᵃ *fut.*   HOPHAL ᵇ *fut.*

6   יָלַךְ   to go, to walk.   HIPHIL ᵃ *pret.* ᵇ *fut.* ᶜ *part.*

7 יָצָא to go out; to make to go out. HIPHIL ᵃ*fut.* ᵇ*part.*

8 נָגִיד a captain ; of the Messiah, Isa. lv. 4 ; see *Ruler.*

9 נָהַג to lead, to guide, to conduct. KAL ᵃ*pret.* ᵇ*fut.* ᶜ*part.* Poel. PIEL ᵈ*pret.* ᵉ*fut.* ᶠ*part.*

10 נָהַל to lead flocks with gentleness and care. PIEL ᵃ*fut.* HITH-PAEL ᵇ*fut.*

11 נָחָה to lead, guide, conduct. Lxx. mostly ὁδηγέω, καθηγέω, sometimes ἄγω, ἐπάγω. KAL ᵃ*pret.* ᵇ*imp.* HIPHIL ᶜ*pret.* ᵈ*inf.* ᵉ*fut.*

12 סָבַב to compass ; to lead about, or compass about in a way of protection. POEL ᵃ*fut.* HIPHIL ᵇ*fut.*

13 רֹאשׁ *m.* head : Deut. xx. 9, *marg.* '(to be) in the head of.'

Gen. xxiv. 27.	11 a	2 Chron. xxxii. 21.	8	Prov. viii. 20.	4
xxiv. 48.	11 c	Neh. ix. 12.	11 c	xvi. 29.	6 a
xxxiii. 14.	10 b	ix. 19.	11 d	Cant. viii. 2.	9 b
Exod. iii. 1.	9 b	Job xii. 17, 19.	6 c	Isa. iii. 12.	1 a
xiii. 17.	11 a	Ps. v. 8.	11 b	ix. 16, a 16.β	1 a b
xiii. 18.	12 b	xiii. 2.	10 a	xi. 8.	9 c
xiii. 21.	11 d	xxiii. 3.	11 e	xx. 4.	9 b
xv. 13.	11 a	xxv. 5.	3 b	xl. 11.	10 a
xxxii. 34.	11 b	xxvii. 11.	11 b	xli. 16.	3 c
Num. xxvii.17.	7 a	xxxi. 3.	11 e	xlvii. 17.	3 d
Deut. iv. 27.	9 e	xliii. 3.	11 e	xlviii. 21.	6 a
viii. 2.	6 a	lx. 9.	11 a	xlix. 10.	9 e
viii. 15.	6 c	lxi. 2.	11 e	lv. 4.	8
xx. 9.	13	lxxvii. 20.	11 e	lv. 12.	5 b
xxviii. 37.	9 e	lxxviii. 14, 53.	11 e	lvii. 18.	11 e
xxix. 5.	6 b	lxxx. 1.	9 c	lxiii. 12, 13.	6 c
xxxii. 10.	12 a	cvi. 9.	6 b	lxiii. 14.	9 d
xxxii. 12.	11 e	cvii. 7.	3 c	Jer. ii. 6, 17.	6 c
Josh. xxiv. 3.	6 b	cviii. 10.	11 a	xiii. 8.	2 a
1 Sam. xxx. 22.	9 b	cxxv. 5.	6 b	xxxi. 9.	5 a
2 Sam. v. 2.	7 b	cxxxvi. 16.	6 c	xxxii. 5.	6 b
2 Kings vi. 19.	6 b	cxxxix. 10.	11 a	Lam. iii. 2.	9 a
1 Chron. xi. 2.	7 b	cxxxix. 24.	11 b	Ezek. xvii. 12.	2 b
xii. 27.	8	cxliii. 10.	11 e	xlvii. 2.	12 b
xiii. 1.	8	Prov. iv. 11.	3 a	Amos ii. 10.	6 b
xx. 1.	9 b	vi. 22.	11 e	Nah. ii. 7.	9 f
2 Chron. xxv. 11.	9 b				

a marg. 'or, they that call them blessed.' *β marg.* 'or, they that are called blessed of them.'

LEAF

טָרָף *m.* leaf ; properly, freshly plucked off : Ezek. xvii. 9.

עָלֶה *m.* leaf, green and flourishing, the emblem of prosperity ; collectively, leaves, foliage : Gen. iii. 7 ; viii. 11 : Lev. xxvi. 36 : Job xiii. 25 : Ps. i. 3 : Isa. i. 30 ; xxxiv. 4 ; lxiv. 6 : Jer. viii. 13 : xvii. 8 : Ezek. xlvii. 12, 12.

עֳפִי *Ch. m.* boughs, foliage of trees : Dan. iv. 12, 14, 21.

צֶלַע *f.* rib, side ; leaf of a door : 1 Kings vi. 34.

LEAGUE

בְּרִית *f.* covenant : Josh. ix. 6, &c.

חָבַר to be joined together. HITHPAEL *inf.* Dan. xi. 23.

כָּרַת to cut ; to strike a league, to make a covenant. KAL *inf.* 1 Sam. xxii. 8 ; see *Make.*

LEAN

1 דַּל *adj.* weak, feeble, lean, thin.

2 דַּק *adj.* slender, thin, lank, withered.

3 כַּחַשׁ *m.* (see *Fail*), pining away, leanness.

4 רָזָה to make thin and lean. NIPHAL ᵃ*fut.* ᵇרָזֶה *m.* lean. ᶜרָזוֹן *m.* leanness, also destruction, disease ; diminution by pestilence, in Isa. x. 16. ᵈרְזִי *m.* leanness, or woe.

5 רַק *adj.* thin, lean.

Gen. xli. 3, 4.	2	Job xvi. 8.	3	Isa. xvii. 4.	4 a
xli. 19, 20.	5	Ps. cvi. 15.	4 c	xxiv. 16, 16.	4 d
Num. xiii. 20.	4 b	Isa. x. 16.	4 c	Ezek. xxxiv. 20.	4 b
2 Sam. xiii. 4.	1				

LEAN (V)

1 חָזַק to take and keep strong hold. HIPHIL *part.*

2 סָמַךְ to place or lay upon anything. KAL ᵃ*pret.* NIPHAL ᵇ*fut.*

3 רָפַק to lean upon. HITHPAEL *part.*

4 שָׁעַן to lean upon, to rest upon ; said of kings, who lean upon their officers and attendants in public ; to rely upon, to trust in. NIPHAL ᵃ*inf.* ᵇ*fut.* ᶜ*part.*

Judg. xvi. 26.	4 b	2 Kings xviii. 21.	2 b	Isa. xxxvi. 6.	2 b
2 Sam. i. 6.	4 c	Job viii. 15.	4 b	Ezek. xxix. 7.	4 a
iii. 29.	1	Prov. iii. 5.	4 b	Amos v. 19.	2 a
2 Kings v. 18.	4 c	Cant. viii. 5.	3	Micah iii. 11.	4 b
vii. 2, 17.	4 c				

LEANNOTH

עֲנָה to be afflicted ; to afflict. PIEL *inf.* Ps. lxxxviii. title. Hengstenberg, "upon the distress of oppression."

LEAP

1 דָּלַג to leap, to spring. KAL ᵃ*part.* Poel. PIEL ᵇ*fut.* ᶜ*part.*

2 זָנַק to leap, to spring forth with violence. PIEL *fut.*

3 מָלַט to escape ; to be delivered. HITHPAEL *fut.*

4 נָתַר to spring up and down, to leap, to move by leaps, as the locust. PIEL *inf.*

5 עָלָה to ascend, to leap upon. KAL *part.* Poel.

6 פָּזַז to be strong ; to leap, probably with great agility. PIEL *part.*

7 פָּסַח to pass over ; to leap, to dance ; dancing was customary at some sacrifices ; see 2 Sam. vi. 16. PIEL *fut.*

8 רָצַד to leap, according to ancient interpreters, by a change of one letter for the following. PIEL ᵃ*fut.* Ps. lxviii. 16. Gesenius, Fürst, and others, to look askance, to watch insidiously.

9 רָקַד to leap, to skip for joy, to dance. PIEL *fut.*

Gen. xxxi. 10, 12.	5	1 Kings xviii. 26.	7	Cant. ii. 8.	1 c
Lev. xi. 21.	4	Job xli. 19.	3	Isa. xxxv. 6.	1 b
Deut. xxxiii. 22.	2	Ps. xviii. 29.	1 b	Joel ii. 5.	9
2 Sam. vi. 16.	6	lxviii. 16.	8	Zeph. i. 9.	1 a
xxii. 30.	1 b				

LEARN

1 אָלַף to learn, from the notion of accustoming, training. KAL *fut.*

2 יָדַע to know ; "not learned," *lit.* know not a book. KAL ᵃ*pret.* ᵇ*part.* Poel.

3 לָמַד to teach, to train, to discipline ; to be trained, taught, *i. e.* to learn. KAL ᵃ*pret.* ᵇ*inf.* ᶜ*imp.* ᵈ*fut.* ᵉלִמּוּד *adj.* one taught, a disciple.

4 לֶקַח *m.* learning, doctrine, instruction, worthy to be received.

5 סֵפֶר *m.* writing ; a book.

Deut. iv. 10.	3 d	Deut. xxxi. 13.	3 a	Prov. xvi. 21, 23.	4
v. 1.	3 a	Ps. cvi. 35.	3 d	xxii. 25.	1
xiv. 23.	3 d	cxix. 7.	3 b	xxx. 3.	3 a
xvii. 19.	3 d	cxix. 71, 73.	3 d	Isa. i. 17.	3 c
xviii. 9.	3 d	Prov. i. 5.	4	ii. 4.	3 d
xxxi. 12.	3 d	ix. 9.	4	xxvi. 9, 10.	3 a

Isa. xxix. 11.	2 b, 5	Isa. l. 4, 4.	3 e	Ezek. xix. 3, 6.	3 d
xxix. 12.	2 a, 5	Jer. x. 2.	3 d	Dan. i. 4, 17.	5
xxix. 12.	2 a, 5	xii. 16.	3 b d	Micah iv. 3.	3 d
xxix. 24.	3 d				

LEASING

כָּזָב m. lie, falsehood ; deceit, fraud, guile : Ps. iv. 2 ; v. 6.

LEAST

צָעִיר small ; ignoble, mean, least ; young : Judg. vi. 15 : 1 Sam. ix. 21 : Jer. xlix. 20 ; l. 45.

קָטֹן adj. little, small : Jer. viii. 10 ; xlii. 1, 8 ; xliv. 12. קָטָן adj. id. : 2 Kings xviii. 24 : 1 Chron. xii. 14 : Isa. xxxvi. 9 : Jer. vi. 13 ; xxxi. 34 : Jonah iii. 5.

LEATHER

עוֹר m. skin : 2 Kings i. 8, probably a garment made of hair ; comp. Matt. iii. 4.

LEAVE

1 חָדַל to leave off, cease, desist ; to cease from any person or thing ; to leave undone, to let alone, to forbear, not to do. KAL [a] pret. [b] fut.

2 חָרֵשׁ to be silent, to leave off speaking. HIPHIL fut.

3 יָנַח to set or lay down ; to lay up ; to leave that which remains where left ; to leave behind ; rather from נוּחַ to rest ; to cause to rest. HIPHIL [a] pret. [b] inf. [c] imp. [d] fut. HOPHAL [e] part.

4 יָצַג to set, to place ; to let stand, i. e. to leave. HIPHIL fut.

5 יָרַשׁ to possess ; to cause to possess ; to leave for an inheritance. HIPHIL pret.

6 יָתַר to be over and above ; to be left, to remain. NIPHAL [a] pret. [b] fut. [c] part. HIPHIL [d] pret. [e] inf. [f] fut. [g] יֶתֶר m. remainder, rest, residue.

7 כָּלָה to be completed, perfected, finished ; to finish, to leave off. PIEL [a] pret. [b] fut.

8 לִין to remain all night. KAL fut.

9 מָצָא to find. NIPHAL part. The passive participle is often used to denote what is present in a certain place, or, more generally, what is extant, in existence, or forthcoming. The meaning left is suggested wholly by the noun, with which the participle here agrees.—Alexander on 2 Kings xix. 4.

10 נָחַל to inherit ; to cause to inherit. HIPHIL [a] pret. [b] fut.

11 נָטַשׁ to thrust out, cast off, reject, scq. to עַל to cast upon any one, to commit to any one. KAL [a] pret. [b] inf. [c] fut.

12 נָתַן to give. KAL [a] pret. [b] fut.

13 עָזַב to leave, relinquish, desert a place, God, a law, a covenant ; opp. to עָצַר ; to let go, to dismiss, to leave destitute ; to leave in the hand of any one, to commit, entrust ; to leave an inheritance to another ; to leave without restraint, to itself. KAL [a] pret. [b] inf. [d] imp. [d] fut. [e] part. Poel [f] part. Paül. NIPHAL [g] fut. [h] part. PUAL [i] pret.

14 עָמַד to stand, to stand still, to cease. KAL [a] pret. [b] fut.

15 עָתַק to remove. HIPHIL pret.

16 רָפָה to slacken, to let go, to leave off. HIPHIL fut.

17 שָׁאַל to ask ; to ask leave, to obtain leave. NIPHAL pret.

18 שָׁאַר to be left over, to remain. NIPHAL [a] pret. [b] fut. [c] part. HIPHIL [d] pret. [e] inf. [f] fut. [g] שְׁאֵרִית f. remnant.

19 שְׁבַק Ch. to leave. P'AL [a] inf. [b] imp. ITHPAEL [c] fut.

20 שָׁבַת to cease, to rest. HIPHIL pret. Ruth iv. 14.

21 שׂוּם to set, put, place. KAL inf.

22 שָׁלַח to send ; to be sent away, to be let go, dismissed. PUAL part.

23 שָׂרִיד m. one left, escaped from a slaughter, a survivor.

Gen. ii. 24.	13 d	1 Sam. ix. 5.	1 b	Neh. vi. 3.	16
xi. 8.	1 b	ix. 24.	18 c	ix. 28.	13 d
xvii. 22.	7 b	x. 2.	11 a	x. 31.	11 c
xviii. 33.	7 a	xi. 11.	18 a	xiii. 6.	17
xxiv. 27.	13 a	xiv. 36.	18 f	Job ix. 27.	13 d
xxviii. 15.	13 d	xvii. 20, 22.	11 c	x. 1.	13 d
xxix. 35.	14 b	xvii. 28.	11 a	xx. 21, 26.	23
xxx. 9.	14 a	xxv. 22.	18 f	xxxii. 15.	15
xxxii. 8.	18 c	xxv. 34.	6 a	xxxix. 11, 14.	13 d
xxxii. 24.	6 b	xxx. 9.	6 c	Ps. xvi. 10.	13 d
xxxiii. 15.	4	xxx. 13.	13 d	xvii. 14.	3 a
xxxix. 6, 12, 15, 18.	13 d	2 Sam. v. 21.	13 d	xxvii. 9.	11 c
xxxix. 13.	13 a	ix. 1.	6 a	xxxvi. 3.	1 a
xli. 49.	1 a	xiii. 30.	6 a	xxxvii. 33.	13 d
xlii. 33.	3 c	xiv. 7, 7.	18 a, 21	xlix. 10.	13 a
xlii. 38.	18 a	xv. 16.	13 d	cvi. 11.	6 a
xliv. 12.	7 a	xvi. 21.	3 a	cxix. 121.	3 d
xliv. 20.	6 b	xviii. 14.	13 d	Prov. ii. 13.	13 e
xliv. 22, 22.	13 b a	xx. 3.	3 a	xiii. 22.	10 b
xlvii. 18.	18 a	1 Kings vii. 47.	3 d	xvii. 14.	11 b
l. 8.	13 a	viii. 57.	13 d	xxix. 15.	22
Exod. ii. 20.	13 a	ix. 20.	6 c	Eccles. ii. 18.	3 d
ix. 21.	13 d	ix. 21.	6 a	ii. 21.	12 b
x. 12.	18 d	xiv. 10.	13 f	x. 4.	3 d
x. 15.	6 d	xv. 18.	6 c	Isa. i. 8.	6 a
x. 26.	18 b	xv. 29.	18 d	i. 9.	6 d
xvi. 19, 20.	6 f	xvi. 11.	18 d	iv. 3.	18 c
xxiii. 11.	6 g	xvi. 21.	13 d	vii. 22.	6 c
xxxiv. 25.	8	xvii. 17.	6 a	x. 3.	13 d
Lev. ii. 10.	6 c	xix. 3.	3 d	x. 14.	13 f
vii. 15.	3 d	xix. 3, 10, 14.	6 b	xi. 11, 16.	18 b
x. 12, 16.	6 c	xix. 18.	6 c	xvii. 6.	18 a
xvi. 23.	3 a	xix. 20.	13 d	xvii. 9.	13 a
xix. 10.	13 d	xx. 30.	6 c	xviii. 6.	13 g
xxii. 30.	6 f	xxi. 21.	13 f	xxiv. 6, 12.	18 a
xxiii. 22.	13 d	2 Kings ii. 2, 4, 6.	13 d	xxvii. 10.	13 h
xxvi. 36, 39.	18 c	iv. 30.	18 d	xxx. 17.	6 a
xxvi. 43.	13 g	iv. 43.	13 d	xxxii. 14.	13 i
Num. ix. 12.	18 f	iv. 44.	6 e	xxxvii. 4.	9
x. 31.	13 d	vii. 7.	13 d	xxxix. 6.	6 b
xxi. 35.	18 d	vii. 13, 13.	18 a	xlix. 21.	18 a
xxvi. 65.	6 a	viii. 6.	13 b	lxv. 15.	3 a
xxxii. 15.	3 b	ix. 8.	13 f	Jer. ii. 2.	13 d
Deut. ii. 34.	18 d	x. 11, 14.	18 a	xii. 7.	11 a
iii. 3.	18 d	x. 21.	18 a	xiv. 9.	3 d
iv. 27.	18 a	viii. 7.	18 d	xvii. 11.	13 d
vii. 20.	18 c	xiv. 26.	13 f	xviii. 14.	13 d
xxviii. 51.	18 f	vvi. 16.	18 d	xxi. 7.	18 c
xxviii. 54.	6 f	xvii. 18.	18 a	xxvii. 18.	6 c
xxviii. 55.	18 a	xix. 4.	9	xxxi. 2.	23
xxviii. 62.	18 f	xx. 17.	6 b	xxxiv. 7.	6 c
xxxii. 36.	13 f	xxv. 11.	18 c	xxxviii. 22.	18 a
Josh. iv. 3.	3 a	xxv. 12, 22.	18 d	xxxviii. 27.	2
vi. 23.	3 d	1 Chron. vi. 61.	6 c	xxxix. 10.	18 d
viii. 17, 17.	18 a, 13 d	xiii. 2.	18 c	xl. 6.	18 c
x. 33, 37, 39, 40.	18 d	xiv. 12.	13 d	xl. 11.	12 a
xi. 8, 14.	18 d	xvi. 37.	13 d	xlii. 2.	18 a
xi. 11, 22.	6 a	xxviii. 8.	10 a	xliii. 6.	3 a
xxii. 3.	13 a	2 Chron. viii. 7.	6 c	xliv. 7.	6 e
Judg. ii. 21.	13 a	viii. 8.	6 a	xliv. 18.	1 a
ii. 23.	3 d	xi. 14.	13 a	xlviii. 28.	13 c
iii. 1.	3 a	xii. 5.	13 a	xlix. 9.	18 f
iv. 16.	18 a	xvi. 5.	1 b	xlix. 11.	13 f
vi. 4.	18 f	xxi. 17.	18 a	xlix. 25.	13 i
viii. 10.	6 c	xxiv. 18.	13 d	l. 26.	18 g
ix. 5.	6 b	xxiv. 25.	13 a	lii. 16.	18 d
ix. 9, 13.	1 a	xxviii. 14.	18 a	Ezek. vi. 8. a	6 d
Ruth i. 3, 5.	18 b	xxxi. 10, 10.	6 e c	ix. 8.	18 c
i. 16.	13 b	xxxii. 31.	13 a	xii. 16.	6 d
i. 18.	1 b	xxxiv. 21.	18 c	xiv. 22.	18 a
ii. 11.	13 d	Ezra iv. 8.	18 e	xvi. 39.	18 a
ii. 14.	6 f	ix. 12.	5	xxii. 20.	3 a
ii. 16, 20.	13 a	Neh. i. 2, 3.	18 a	xxiii. 8, 25.	13 a
iii. 14.	20	v. 10.	13 d	xxiv. 21.	13 c
1 Sam. ii. 36.	6 a	vi. 1.	6 a	xxix. 5.	11 a
v. 4.	18 a			xxxi. 12, 12.	11 c

Ezek. xxxii. 4.	11 a	Dan. x. 8, 17.	18 a	Obad. 5.	18 f
xxxvi. 36.	18 b	Hos. iv. 10.	13 a	Zeph. iii. 12.	18 d
xxxix. 28.	6 f	xii. 14.	11 c	Hag. ii. 3.	18 c
xli. 9, 11, 11.	3 e	Joel i. 4, 4, 4.	6 g	Zech. xi. 17.	13 e
xlviii. 15.	6 c	ii. 14.	18 d	xiii. 8.	6 b
Dan. ii. 44.	19 c	Amos v. 3, 3.	18 f	xiv. 16.	6 c
iv. 26.	19 a	v. 7.	3 a	Mal. iv. 1.	13 d
iv. 15, 23.	19 b				

a "leave a remnant."

LEAVEN

1 חָמֵץ   to be sharp, sour, leavened. KAL a pret. b inf. c fut. HIPHIL d part. e חָמֵץ m. leaven, leavened bread.

2 מַצָּה   f. sweetness; not fermented, unleavened; "without leaven."

3 שְׂאֹר   m. leaven, sour dough; properly, leaving or remainder.

Exod. xii. 15, 15.	3, 1 e	Exod. xiii. 7, 7.	1 e, 3	Lev. x. 12.	2
xii. 19, 19.	3, 1 d	xxiii. 18.	1 e	xxiii. 17.	1 e
xii. 20.	1 d	xxxiv. 25.	1 e	Deut. xvi. 3.	1 e
xii. 34.	1 c	Lev. ii. 11, 11.	1 e, 3	xvi. 4.	3
xii. 39.	1 a	vi. 17.	1 e	Hos. vii. 4.	1 b
xiii. 3.	1 e	vii. 11.	1 e	Amos iv. 5.	1 e

LEAVES

דֶּלֶת   f. door, gate; leaves of a gate: Isa. xlv. 1, two-leaved gates; the columns or chapters of a roll, Jer. xxxvi. 23. Ezek. xli. 24, 24, 24.

קְלָעִים   m. pl. curtains, hangings; leaves of a door: 1 Kings vi. 34.

LEDGE

יָד   com. hand, side: 1 Kings vii. 35, 36.

שְׁלַבִּים   m. pl. joinings, joints, e.g. at the corners of a base or pedestal; their ledges or borders covering these joints or joinings: 1 Kings vii. 28, 29, 29.

LEEK

חָצִיר   m. grass; especially leek, collectively leeks: Num. xi. 5.

LEES

שְׁמָרִים   m. pl. lees of wine, so called because wine is kept, preserved in strength and colour, by letting it stand on the lees: Jer. xlviii. 11, Zeph. i. 12, to rest upon one's lees, is, to live a life of quiet indifference; Isa. xxv. 6, 6, "wines on the lees well refined," i. e. generous old wine purified from the lees.

LEFT

אָטֵר   adj. shut up, bound, i. e. impeded: Judg. iii. 15; xx. 16. With יָמִין bound of the right hand.

שׂוּם   to set, place. HIPHIL imp. Ezek. xxi. 16, "on the left," marg. 'set thyself, take the left hand.'

שְׂמֹאל   to use the left hand; to turn to the left. HIPHIL inf. 2 Sam. xiv. 19. imp. Ezek. xxi. 16, marg. 'set thyself, take the left hand.' fut. Gen. xiii. 9: Isa. xxx. 21. part. 1 Chron. xii. 2. שְׂמֹאול m. the left hand, to the left: Gen. xiii. 9, &c. שְׂמָאלִי adj. left: Lev. xiv. 15, 16, 26, 27: 1 Kings vii. 21: 2 Kings xi. 11: 2 Chron. iii. 17; xxiii. 10: Ezek. iv. 4.

LEG

1 כְּרָעַיִם   f. the legs, from the knee to the ankle, so called as being bent under, in sitting, kneeling, or lying down; of the locusts' feet for leaping.

2 רֶגֶל   f. foot.

3 שֹׁבֶל   m. The primary meaning of this word seems to be, that which stretcheth itself forward, or in length; hence a flood, a leg; or perhaps to flow, hence some have rendered this use of it, a lock of hair; Gesenius and others, a flowing robe or train, which, when gathered up, makes bare the leg: Isa. xlvii. 2.

4 שׁוֹק   m. the leg from the knee to the foot. שָׁק Ch. m. id.

Exod. xii. 9.	1	Lev. ix. 14.	1	Prov. xxvi. 7.	4
xxix. 17.	1	xi. 21.	1	Cant. v. 15.	4
i. 9, 13.	1	Deut. xxviii. 35.	1	Isa. xlvii. 2.	3
iv. 11.	1	1 Sam. xvii. 6.	2	Dan. ii. 33.	4 a
viii. 21.	1	Ps. cxlvii. 10.	1	Amos iii. 12.	1

LEND

1 לָוָה   to be joined, to be connected together; to make to be joined by lending. HIPHIL a pret. b fut. c part.

2 נָשָׁה   to lend on usury, including the idea of exaction. KAL a pret. b part. Poel. HIPHIL c fut. d מַשָּׁאָה debt, loan.

3 נָתַן   to give. KAL fut.

4 עָבַט   to turn about, to make property turn or change sides, to lend upon a pledge; seq. acc. of person to whom, Deut. xv. 6; seq. dupl. acc. of person and thing, 48. HIPHIL a pret. b inf. c fut.

5 שָׁאַל   to ask, to ask as a loan, seq. לְ to lend, or, according to the margin, to return that which has been obtained by petition. KAL a pret. b part Paül. HIPHIL c pret. d fut.

Exod. xii. 36.	5 d	Deut. xxiv. 10.	2 c d	Ps. xxxvii. 26.	1 c
xxii. 25.	1 b	xxiv. 11.	2 b	cxii. 5.	1 c
Lev. xxv. 37.	3	xxviii. 12.	1 a	Prov. xix. 17.	1 c
Deut. xv. 2.	2 c	xxviii. 44, 44.	1 b	xxii. 7.	1 c
xv. 6.	4 a	1 Sam. i. 28, 28.	5 c b	Isa. xxiv. 2.	1 c
xv. 8.	4 b c	ii. 20.	5 a	Jer. xv. 10, 10.	2 a

LENGTH

אַחֲרִית   f. see End. Prov. xxix. 21, Heb. at his end.

אָרַךְ   to prolong, continue, protract, lengthen. HIPHIL pret. 1 Kings iii. 14. imp. Isa. liv. 2. fut. Deut. xxv. 15. אֹרֶךְ m. length: Gen. vi. 15, &c.

אַרְכָּא   Ch. f. Dan. iv. 27, marg. 'an healing of thine error.'

LENTILES

עֲדָשִׁים   m. pl. lentiles, a kind of pulse resembling small beans, used chiefly by the poor, ground into meal, and made into a red kind of pottage: Gen. xxv. 34: 2 Sam. xvii. 28; xxiii. 11: Ezek. iv. 9.

LEOPARD

נָמֵר   m. panther, leopard, so called from his spots. This animal is remarkable for swiftness and for watching his prey; cannot be tamed. Not improbably the tiger was also comprised under this name, as the Hebrews had no specific name for that animal: Cant. iv. 8: Isa. xi. 6; Jer. v. 6; xiii. 23: Hos. xiii. 7: Hab. i. 8. נְמַר Ch. m. Dan. vii. 6.

LEPER

צָרַע   to smite heavily, to strike; hence, a leprous person,

probably smitten, scourged of God, since the leprosy was regarded as a special divine infliction. KAL *part.* Paül, Lev. xiii. 44, 45 ; xiv. 3 ; xxii. 4 : Num. v. 2. PUAL *part.* Exod. iv. 6 : Lev. xiv. 2 : Num. xii. 10, 10 : 2 Sam. iii. 29 : 2 Kings v. 1, 11, 27; vii. 3, 8 ; xv. 5 : 2 Chron. xxvi. 20, 21, 21, 23. צָרַעַת *f.* leprosy, of persons, *i. e.* the white leprosy. The black leprosy is the elephantiasis ; see *Boil.* Also of houses, and of garments : Lev. xiii. 2, &c.

LESS

מַטָּה *adv.* beneath : Ezra ix. 13.

מָעַט to be little, few. HIPHIL, to diminish. *fut.* Exod. xxx. 15 : Num. xxvi. 54 ; xxxiii. 54. *part.* Exod. xvi. 17.

קָטֹן *adj.* little, small : Num. xxii. 18 : Ezek. xliii. 14. קָטֹן *adj.* Gen. i. 16 : 1 Sam. xxii. 15 ; xxv. 36.

LET

1 חָדַל to cease, to leave off, to desist ; to let alone. KAL *imp.*
2 יָלַךְ to go, to go down. KAL *fut.*
3 יָנַח to leave things or persons in any condition, disposition, or situation, undisturbed, unmeddled with, uninterrupted, unassisted ; to let alone, to desist ; to let remain. HIPHIL [a] *pret.* [b] *imp.*
4 יָרַד to descend, to go down. HIPHIL [a] *pret.* [b] *fut.*
5 מָלַט to escape ; to let escape. PIEL [a] *fut.* NIPHAL [b] *fut.*
6 נוּחַ to rest ; to let down. HIPHIL *fut.*
7 נָטָה to incline ; to let down. HIPHIL *imp.*
8 נָתַן to give. KAL [a] *pret.* [b] *inf.* [c] *fut.*
9 פָּטַר to let loose, to let out. KAL *part.* Poel.
10 פָּרַע to let go loose ; to dismiss. HIPHIL *fut.*
11 רָפָה to be slackened ; to let down, to let go ; dismiss ; to let alone. KAL [a] *fut.* PIEL [b] *fut.* HIPHIL [c] *imp.* [d] *fut.*
12 שָׁאַר to leave. HIPHIL *pret.*
13 שְׁבַק Ch. to leave, let alone. P'AL *imp.*
14 שׁוּב to return. HIPHIL *fut.*
15 שִׁית to set, put, or place, so as to remain ; so *seq.* מִן to withdraw, *sc.* the hand ; to let alone. KAL *imp.*
16 שָׁלַח to send ; to let down ; let go ; see *Go.* PIEL *fut.*
17 שָׁקַע to drown. HIPHIL *fut.*

Gen. xxiv. 14.	7	Josh. x. 28, 30.	12	Job vii. 19.	11 d	
xxiv. 18, 46.	4 b	Judg. xi. 37.	11 c	x. 20.	15	
Exod. iii. 19.	8 c	1 Sam. xviii. 2.	8 a	xxviii. 6.	11 d	
iv. 26.	11 a	xix. 12.	4 b	xli. 1.	17	
v. 4.	10	xx. 29.	5 b	Prov. iv. 13.	9	
xiv. 12.	1	2 Sam. xvi. 11.	3 b	xvii. 14.	11 d	
xvii. 11.	6	2 Kings iv. 27.	11 c	Cant. iii. 4.	11 d	
xxxii. 10.	3 b	xiii. 21.	2	viii. 11.	8 a	
Lev. xviii. 21.	8 c	xxiii. 18, 18.	3 b, 5 a	Isa. xliii. 13.	14	
Deut. ix. 14.	11 c	2 Chron. xvi. 1.	8 b	Jer. xvii. 11.	3 a	
Josh. ii. 15.	4 b	xx. 10.	8 a	xxxviii. 6, 11.	16	
ii. 18.	4 a	Ezra vi. 7.	13	Ezek. i. 24, 25.	11 b	
viii. 22.*a*	12	Job vii. 16.	1	Hos. iv. 17.	3 b	

a lit. left no remainder, *or,* escaper.

LETTER

1 אִגֶּרֶת *f.* a letter, to convey intelligence. [a] אִגְּרָא *f.* Ch. *id.*
2 נִשְׁתְּוָן *m. Heb.* and *Chald.* an epistle, letter.
3 סֵפֶר *m.* writing, book : 2 Sam. xi. 14, &c.
4 פִּתְגָּם Ch. *m.* a word, letter ; decree.

2 Sam. xi. 14, 15.	3	Ezra iv. 7.	2	Esth. i. 22.	3
1 Kings xxi. 8, 8, 9, 11.	3	iv. 8, 11.	1 a	iii. 13.	3
2 Kings v. 5, 6, 6, 7.	3	iv. 18, 23.	3	viii. 5, 10.	3
x. 1, 2, 6, 7.	3	v. 5.	2	ix. 20, 25, 30.	3
xix. 14.	3	v. 6.	1 a	ix. 26, 29.	1
xx. 12.	3	v. 7.	2	Isa. xxxvii. 14.	4
2 Chron. xxx. 1, 6.	1	vii. 11.	3	xxxix. 1.	3
xxxii. 17.	3	Neh. ii. 7, 8, 9.	1	Jer. xxix. 1, 25, 29.	3
		vi. 5, 17, 19.	1		

LEVIATHAN

לִוְיָתָן *pr.* an animal wreathed, gathering itself in folds ; a serpent ; the crocodile. See *Mourning.* So Isa. xxvii. 1, as the symbol of the hostile kingdom of Babylon ; the crocodile, Job xli. 1 ; a sea monster, Ps. civ. 26 ; *trop.* for a cruel enemy, Ps. lxxiv. 14.

LEVY

מַס *m.* see *Tribute.* 1 Kings v. 13, 13, 14 ; ix. 15.

עָלָה to ascend ; to raise a levy, to levy. HIPHIL *fut.* 1 Kings ix. 21.

רוּם to lift up. HIPHIL *pret.* Num. xxxi. 28.

LEWD

זִמָּה *f.* see *Wickedness.* Judg. xx. 6 : Jer. xiii. 27 : Ezek. xvi. 27, 43, 58 ; xxii. 9, 11 ; xxiii. 21, 27, 29, 35, 44, 48, 48, 49 ; xxiv. 13 : Hos. vi. 9. מְזִמָּה *f.* Jer. xi. 15.

נַבְלוּת *f.* see *Folly.* Hos. ii. 10.

LIBERAL

בְּרָכָה *f.* a blessing : Prov. xi. 25, *lit.* the soul of blessing.

נָדִיב *adj.* willing, voluntary, ready, prompt : Isa. xxxii. 5, 8, 8, 8.

עָנַק to adorn with a collar, with gifts ; to give liberally. HIPHIL *inf.* Deut. xv. 14. *fut.* Deut. xv. 14.

LIBERTY

דְּרוֹר *m.* a letting go free ; freedom, liberty : Lev. xxv. 10 : Isa. lxi. 1 : Jer. xxxiv. 8, 15, 17, 17 : Ezek. xlvi. 17.

חָפְשִׁי *adj.* free, as opposed to a slave or captive : Jer. xxxiv. 16.

רָחָב *adj.* broad, wide : Ps. cxix. 45.

LICE

כֵּן *m.* lice, from כּוּן, to establish, alluding to the steadiness with which they adhere to the human body : Exod. viii. 16, 17, 18 : Ps. cv. 31. Others suppose it to be the Egyptian gnat, as also

כִּנָּם *f.* gnats, which is now generally admitted by interpreters : Exod. viii. 17, 18. Gr. σκνῖφες. Yet lice are exceedingly numerous and troublesome in Egypt.

LICK

לָחַךְ to lick up ; *metaph.* to devour a country. KAL *inf.* Num. xxii. 4. PIEL *pret.* 1 Kings xviii. 38. *fut.* Num. xxii. 4 : Ps. lxxii. 9 : Isa. xlix. 23 ; Micah vii. 17.

לָקַק to lap or lick as a dog. KAL *pret.* 1 Kings xxi. 19. *fut.* 1 Kings xxi. 19 ; xxii. 38.

LID

דֶּלֶת *f.* a door, gates of a town, lid of a box : 2 Kings xii. 9.

LIE

1 חָנָה to encamp. KAL *part.* Poel.

2 יָדַע to know. KAL *part.* Poel, Judg. xxi. 11, *lit.* that knoweth the lying with man.

3 יָצָא to go forth; to lie out. KAL *part.* Poel.

4 יָצַע to spread down, to make one's bed. HOPHAL *fut.*

5 שִׁיבָה *f.* lying, dwelling.

6 לִין to lodge, to lay all night. KAL [a] *pret.* [b] *imp.* [c] *fut.*

7 נָטָה to stretch out; to stretch out one's members on a couch. HIPHIL *fut.*

8 נָטַשׁ to let go, to let alone, to let rest. KAL *pret.*

9 נָפַל to fall, to lie along; to cause to lie down. KAL [a] *pret.* [b] *fut.* [c] *part.* Poel. HIPHIL [d] *pret.*

10 נָתַן to give; "to lie with," *lit.* to give his lying. KAL *fut.*

11 סָמַךְ to place or lay upon anything; to lean or rest upon anything, to lie hard. KAL *pret.*

12 פָּנָה to turn. HOPHAL *part.*

13 צוּק to straiten; to press upon; to lie sore upon. HIPHIL *pret.*

14 רָבַע to lie down. KAL [a] *inf.* [b] רֶבַע *m.* lying down.

15 רָבַץ to lie down, to recline, as beasts and animals; also of a beast of prey: *trop.* of men dwelling in security, of waters reposing in the bosom of the earth, of a curse which rests upon any one. KAL [a] *pret.* [b] *fut.* [c] *part.* Poel. HIPHIL [d] *fut.* [e] *part.* [f] רִבֵץ *m.* a place to lie down in. [g] מַרְבֵּץ *m. id.*

16 שָׁכַל to lie with a woman. KAL [a] *fut.* כתיב. PUAL [b] *pret.* כתיב.

17 שׁוּב to return. KAL *imp.* "lie down again," *lit.* return, lie down.

18 שָׁכַב to lie down, to lie, to sleep; to lay down to sleep, &c. KAL [a] *pret.* [b] *inf.* [c] *imp.* [d] *fut.* [e] *part.* Poel. PUAL [f] *pret.* HIPHIL [g] *pret.* [h] שְׁכָבָה *f.* lying. [i] שְׁכֹבֶת *f. id.* [j] מִשְׁכָּב *m. id.* a bed, "laying with," "lying of."

19 שָׁעַן to lean. NIPHAL *pret.*

Gen. iv. 7.	15 c	Lev. xx. 15.	10, 18 i	Ruth iii. 7, 7.	18 b d		
xix. 4, 32.	18 d	xx. 16.	14 a	iii. 8.	18 e		
xix. 33, 33.	18 d b	xxvi. 6.	18 a	iii. 13.	18 c		
xix. 34, 34.	18 a c	Num. v. 13, 19.	18 a	iii. 14.	18 d		
xix. 35, 35.	18 d b	v. 20.	10, 18 i	1 Sam. ii. 22.	18 d		
xxvi. 10.	18 a	x. 5, 6.	1	iii. 2, 3.	18 e		
xxviii. 13.	18 e	xxi. 15.	19	iii. 5.	18 c, 17		
xxix. 2.	15 c	xxiii. 24.	18 d	iii. 5.	18 d		
xxx. 15, 16.	18 d	xxiv. 9.	18 a	iii. 6.	18 c, 17		
xxxiv. 2.	18 d	xxvii. 17, 18, 35.	18 k	iii. 9, 9.	18 c d		
xxxiv. 7.	18 b	Deut. vi. 7.	18 b	iii. 15.	18 d		
xxxv. 22.	18 d	xi. 19.	18 b	xix. 24.	18 e		
xxxix. 7, 12.	18 c	xxi. 1.	9 c	xxvi. 5, 5.	18 a e		
xxxix. 10, 14.	18 b	xxii. 22, 22, 29.	18 e	xxvii. 7, 7.	18 e		
xlvii. 30.	18 a	xxii. 23, 25, 25, 28.	18 a	2 Sam. iv. 5, 7.	18 e		
xlix. 25.	18 a	xxv. 2.	9 d	xi. 4.	18 d		
Exod. xvi. 13, 14. α	18 h	xxvii. 20, 21, 22,		xi. 11, 13.	18 b		
xxii. 16.	18 a	23.	18 e	xiii. 3, 24.	18 d		
xxii. 19.	18 e	xxviii. 30.	18 d, or 16 a	xii. 11.	18 a		
xxiii. 5.	15 c	xxix. 20.	15 a	xii. 16. β	6 a, 18 a		
xxiii. 11.	8	Josh. ii. 8.	18 d	xiii. 5, 11.	18 c		
Lev. xiv. 47.	18 e	vii. 10.	9 c	xiii. 6, 14, 31.	18 d		
xv. 4, 18, 20, 26,		Judg. iv. 22.	9 c	xiii. 8.	18 e		
33.	18 d	v. 27.	18 a	xix. 32.	5		
xv. 24, 24.	18 d k d	vii. 12.	9 c	1 Kings i. 2.	18 a		
xviii. 20.	10, 18 i	vii. 13.	9 a	xix. 5, 6. γ	18 d		
xviii. 22.	18 d	viii. 17.	13	xxi. 4, 27.	18 d		
xviii. 23.	10, 18 i	xvi. 3.	18 d	2 Kings iv. 11, 34.	18 d		
xviii. 23.	14 a	xxi. 11.	2, 18 k	ix. 16.	18 d		
xix. 20.	18 d	xxi. 12.	2, 18 k	Neh. iii. 25, 26, 27.	3		
xx. 11, 12, 18, 20.	18 d	xxi. 15.	19	Esth. iv. 3.	4		
xx. 13, 13.	18 d k	Ruth iii. 4, 4, 4.	18 b d a	Job iii. 13.	18 a		

Job vii. 4.	18 a	Cant. i. 13.	6 c	Ezek. ix. 2.	12		
xi. 19.	15 a	Isa. xi. 6, 7.	15 b	xix. 2.	15 a		
xiv. 12.	18 a	xiii. 21.	15 a	xxiii. 8.	18 a		
xx. 11.	18 d	xiv. 8, 18.	18 a	xxix. 3.	15 c		
xxi. 26.	18 d	xiv. 30.	15 b	xxxi. 18.	18 d		
xxvii. 19.	18 d	xvii. 2.	15 a	xxxii. 21.	18 a		
xxix. 19.	6 c	xvii. 10.	15 b	xxxii. 27, 28, 29,			
xl. 21.	15 f	xxxv. 7.	15 f	30.	18 d		
Ps. iii. 5.	18 a	xliii. 17.	18 d	xxxiv. 14.	15 b		
iv. 8.	18 d	l. 11.	18 d	xxxiv. 15.	15 d		
xxiii. 2.	15 d	li. 20.	18 a	Hos. ii. 18.	18 g		
xli. 8.	18 a	liv. 11.	15 e	Joel i. 13.	6 b		
lvii. 4.	18 d	lvi. 10.	18 d	Amos ii. 8.	7		
lxviii. 13.	15 a	lxv. 10.	15 f	vi. 4.	18 e		
lxxxviii. 5.	18 e	Jer. iii. 2.	18 f, or 16 b	Jonah i. 5.	18 d		
lxxxviii. 7.	11	iii. 25.	18 a	Micah vii. 5.	18 e		
civ. 22.	15 b	xxxiii. 12.	15 e	Zeph. ii. 7.	15 b		
cxxxix. 3.	14 b	Lam. ii. 21.	18 a	ii. 14.	15 a		
Prov. iii. 24, 24.	18 d a	Ezek. iv. 4, 4.	18 c d	ii. 15.	15 g		
xxiii. 34, 34.	18 e	iv. 6.	18 a	iii. 13.	15 a		
Eccles. iv. 11.	18 e	iv. 9.	18 a				

α *lit.* the lying of the dew.　　β *lit.* and lodged all night and lay.　　γ *lit.* returned and laid down.

LIE, LIAR, BELIE

1 אָוֶן *m.* iniquity, vanity. תְאָנִים *m. pl.* vain toil, weariness; or equivalent to *frustra:* Ezek. xxiv. 12, *or,* she hath wearied me with lies, or vain labour.

2 אִישׁ *m.* a man: Prov. xix. 22. Heb. a man of lies.

3 בַּד *m.* empty talk, lies, vain boasting. See also *Staff, Bar.*

4 דָּבָר *m.* word.

5 כְּדַב Ch. *f.* a lie, falsehood.

6 כָּזַב in KAL occurring only once, to fail or disappoint; in PIEL to impose upon or deceive, in affirming, assuring, promising; of those who flatter sinners, and promise them life; or in professing regard. HIPHIL, to reprove of lying, to convict of falsehood. KAL [a] *part.* Poel. NIPHAL [b] *pret.* PIEL [c] *pret.* [d] *inf.* [e] *fut.* HIPHIL [f] *fut.* [g] כָּזָב *m.* knavish lies, intended to deceive and cheat; hence what deceives and disappoints expectation. [h] אַכְזָב *adj.* lying, false.

7 כָּחַשׁ to fail; to deny, conceal, or dissemble the truth; to feign to flatter; most commonly used of the vanquished pretending subjection and love towards a victor. NIPHAL [a] *fut.* PIEL [b] *pret.* [c] *inf.* [d] כַּחַשׁ *m.* falsehood, fraud, deception. [e] כְּחָשִׁים *m. pl.* lying.

8 שָׁוְא *m.* evil, falsehood, a lie.

9 שָׁקַר to lie, to tell lies. PIEL [a] *fut.* [b] שֶׁקֶר *m.* a lie; fraud, vanity.

Lev. vi. 2, 3.	7 b	Ps. cxvi. 11.	6 a	Isa. lix. 4.	8		
xix. 11.	9 a	cxix. 29, 69, 163.	9 b	lix. 13.	7 c		
Num. xxx. 19.	6 a	cxx. 2.	3	lxiii. 8.	9 a		
Deut. xxxiii. 29.	7 a	Prov. vi. 17.	9 b	Jer. v. 12. β	7 b		
Judg. xvi. 10, 13.	6 g	vi. 19.	9 b	vii. 4, 8.	9 b		
1 Sam. xv. 29.	6 g	x. 18.	9 b	ix. 3, 5.	9 b		
1 Kings xiii. 18.	9 b	xii. 19, 22.	9 b	xiv. 14.	9 b		
xxii. 22, 23.	9 b	xiii. 5.	4, 9 b	xvi. 19.	6 h		
2 Kings iv. 16.	6 e	xiv. 5, 5.	6 e g	xvi. 19.	9 b		
2 Chron. xviii. 21, 22.	9 b	xiv. 25.	6 g	xx. 6.	9 b		
Job vi. 28.	6 e	xvii. 4, 7.	9 b	xxiii. 14, 25, 26, 32.	9 b		
xi. 3.	3	xix. 5, 9.	6 e	xxvii. 10, 14, 15, 16.	9 b		
xiii. 4.	9 b	xix. 22.	2, 6 g	xxviii. 15.	9 b		
xxiv. 25.	6 f	xxv. 18.	9 b	xxix. 21, 23, 31.	9 b		
xxxiv. 6.	6 e	xxvi. 28.	9 b	xlviii. 30.	9 b		
Ps. xxxi. 6.	8	xxx. 12. α	4, 9 b	l. 36.	3		
xxxi. 18.	9 b	xxx. 6.	6 b	Ezek. xiii. 6, 7, 8, 9.	6 g		
xl. 4.	6 e	xxx. 6.	4, 6 g	xiii. 19, 19.	6 g d		
lii. 3.	9 b	Isa. ix. 15.	6 b	xiii. 22.	9 b		
lviii. 3.	8	xvi. 6.	3	xxi. 29.	6 g		
lix. 12.	7 d	xxviii. 15, 17.	6 g	xxii. 28.	6 g		
lxii. 4, 9.	6 g	xxx. 9.	7 d	xxiv. 12.	1		
lxiii. 11.	9 b	xxxii. 7.	6 g	Dan. ii. 9.	6 g		
lxxviii. 36.	6 e	xliv. 20.	9 b	xi. 27.	6 g		
lxxix. 35.	6 e	xliv. 25.	3	Hos. iv. 2.	7 d		
ci. 7.	9 b	lvii. 11.	6 e	vii. 3.	7 d		
cix. 2.	9 b	lix. 3.	9 b	vii. 13.	6 g		

Hos. x. 13.	7 d	Micah i. 14.	6 h	Hab. ii. 18.	9 b
xi. 12.	7 d	ii. 11.	6 c	Zeph. iii. 13.	6 g
xii. 1.	6 g	vi. 12.	9 b	Zech. x. 2.	9 b
Amos ii. 4.	6 g	Nah. iii. 1.	7 d	xiii. 3.	9 b
Jonah ii. 8.	8	Hab. ii. 3.	6 e		

α *lit.* the word of a lie.   β *lit.* lied against.

LIEUTENANTS

אֲחַשְׁדַּרְפְּנִים *m. pl.* satraps, the governors or the viceroys of the large provinces among the ancient Persians, possessing both civil and military power, and being in the provinces the representatives of the sovereign, whose state and splendour they also rivalled. Single parts or subdivisions of these provinces were under procurators or prefects, פֶּחוֹת; the satraps governed only whole provinces. Ezra viii. 36: Esth. iii. 12; viii. 9; ix. 3.

LIFE, LIVE, ALIVE

1 חָיָה to live; to be happy, Neh. ix. 29; to be happy for ever, Ps. cxxxiii. 3; to revive, applied to the restoring to life, 2 Kings viii. 1; to the recovery of health, 2 Kings viii. 10; to keep alive, Ps. xxii. 29; to save alive in a slaughter, Judg. xxi. 14. KAL ᵃ*pret.* ᵇ*inf.* ᶜ*imp.* ᵈ*fut.* PIEL, to save, preserve, &c., alive: ᵉ*pret.* ᶠ*inf.* ᵍ*fut.* ʰ*part.* HIPHIL ⁱ*pret.* ᵏ*inf.* ˡ*imp.*

2 חַי to live. KAL ᵃ*pret.* ᵇ חַי *adj.* alive, living, lively; vigorous, having vital energy; life. ᶜ מִחְיָה *f.* preservation of life. ᵈ חָיָה *adj.* lively. ᵉ חַיּוּת *f.* life. and חַיָּא Ch. P'AL ᶠ*imp.* APHEL ᵍ*part.* חַי Ch. *adj.* alive, living.

3 חָצָה to divide; to live out half (their days). KAL *fut.*

4 יוֹם *m.* a day; long life, *lit.* many days, length of days.

5 מוּת to die. KAL *inf.*

6 נֶפֶשׁ *com.* the animal life, or that principle by which every animal, according to its kind, lives; Gen. i. 20, every moving creature that hath (the soul) of life; ver. 24, let the earth bring forth the living creature, the soul of life; ver. 30, every beast, fowl, &c., wherein there is life, the soul of life, Lev. xi. 46; which animal life, so far as we know anything of its existence, or so far as the Scripture leads our thoughts, consists in the breath; Job xxxi. 39, to lose life, to breathe out the soul; Lev. xvii. 11, 14, the life, the soul of the flesh, is in the blood. Hence the following senses:—(1) Life: Gen. ix. 5: Exod. xxi. 30: 1 Kings xvii. 21: Prov. xii. 10, and in many other places, where it is translated soul. (2) That which supports life: Deut. xxiv. 6, he taketh a man's life, he taketh a soul, to pledge. To restore, convert, relieve, refresh, the life or soul, is the same phrase in the original. He put his life in his hand, 1 Sam. xix. 5; he hazarded it, put it into a desperate, hopeless situation, where it might easily have been dashed out of his hand. Put my life in my hand, Job xiii. 14; account it to be in a desperate, hopeless condition.

7 עֶצֶם *f.* bone.

8 רוּחַ *com.* breath, spirit: "of life," *lit.* of the spirit of life.

9 שָׂרִיד *m.* a survivor.

Gen. i. 20. α	2 b, 6	Deut. xii. 23, 23.	6	1 Kings xviii. 5. ε	1 g
i. 21, 24, 28.	2 b	xvi. 3.	2 b	xviii. 10, 15.	2 b
i. 30. α	2 b, 6	xvi. 20.	1 d	xix. 2, 3, 4, 10,	
ii. 7, 7, 9, 19.	2 b	vii. 19.	2 b	14.	6
iii. 14, 17, 20, 24.	2 b	xix. 4, 5.	2 a	xx. 18, 18.	2 b
iii. 22, 22.	2 b a	xix. 21, 21.	6	xx. 31, 39, 39, 42,	
v. 3, 6, 7, 9, 10, 12,		xx. 16.	1 g	42.	6
13, 15, 16, 18, 19,		xxv. 6.	6	xx. 32, ς 32.	1 d, 2 b
21, 25, 26, 28, 30.	1 d	xxviii. 66, 66.	2 b	xxi. 15.	6
v. 5.	2 a	xxx. 6, γ 15, 20.	2 b	xxii. 14.	2 b
vi. 17.	2 b	xxx. 16.	1 a	2 Kings i. 13, 13, 14.	6
vi. 19, 19.	2 b, 1 k	xxx. 19, 19,		ii. 2, 4, 6, 6.	2 b
vi. 20.	1 k	19.	2 b b, 1 d	iii. 14.	2 b
vii. 3.	1 f	xxxi. 13, 27.	2 b	iv. 7.	6
vii. 11, 15.	2 b	xxxii. 39.	1 g	iv. 16, 17, 30, 30.	2 b
vii. 22.	8, 2 b	xxxii. 40, 47.	2 b	v. 7.	1 k
viii. 1, 17, 21.	2 b	xxxiii. 6.	1 d	v. 16, 20.	2 b
ix. 3, 10, 12, 15, 16.	2 b	xxxiv. 14.	1 e	vii. 4, 4.	1 g d
ix. 4, 5, 5.	6	Josh. i. 5.	2 b	vii. 7.	6
ix. 28.	1 d	ii. 13, 13.	1 i, 6	vii. 12.	2 b
xi. 11, 13, 15, 16,		ii. 14. δ	6, 5	viii. 1, 5, 5.	1 i
17, 18, 19, 20, 21,		iii. 10.	2 b	x. 14, 14.	2 b
22, 23, 24, 25, 26.	1 d	iv. 25.	1 d	x. 19.	1 d
xi. 12, 14.	2 a	vi. 25.	1 d	x. 24, 24.	6
xii. 12.	1 g	viii. 23.	2 b	xiv. 17.	1 d
xii. 13.	1 a	ix. 15.	1 f	xviii. 32.	1 c
xvii. 18.	1 d	ix. 20.	1 k	xix. 4, 16.	2 b
xviii. 10, 14.	2 b	ix. 21.	1 d	xx. 1.	1 d
xix. 17, 19.	2 b	ix. 21 b.	6		
xix. 20.	1 d	xiv. 10.	1 i	1 Chron. xi. 19, 19.	6
xix. 7.	1 c	Judg. v. 18.	6, 1	2 Chron. i. 11, 11.	6, 4
xxiii. 1.	2 b	viii. 19, 19.	2 b, 1 i	vi. 31.	2 b
xxv. 6, 17.	2 b	ix. 17.	6	x. 6.	2 b
xxv. 7, 7.	2 b a	xii. 3.	6	xviii. 13.	2 b
xxvii. 40.	1 d	xvi. 30.	2 b	xxv. 12.	2 b
xxvii. 46, 46.	2 b	xviii. 25, 25.	6	xxv. 25.	1 d
xxxi. 32.	1 d	xxi. 14.	1 e	Ezra iv. 10.	2 h
xxxii. 30.	6	Ruth ii. 20.	2 b	Neh. ii. 3.	1 d
xlii. 2.		iii. 13.	2 b	v. 2.	1 d
xlii. 15, 16.	2 b	iv. 15.	6	vi. 11.	2 a
xlii. 18.	1 c	1 Sam. i. 11, 26.	2 b	ix. 29.	1 a
xliii. 7, 27, 28.	2 b	ii. 6.	1 h	Esth. iv. 11.	6
xliii. 8.	1 d	vii. 15.	2 b	vii. 3, 7.	6
xliv. 30, 30. β	6	xiv. 39, 45.	2 b	viii. 11.	6
xlv. 3, 26, 28.	2 b	xv. 8.	2 b	ix. 16.	6
xlv. 5.	2 c	xvii. 26, 36, 55.	6	Job ii. 4, 6.	6
xlv. 7.	1 k	xviii. 18.	2 b	iii. 20.	2 b
xlvi. 30.	2 b	xix. 5, 11.	2 b	vi. 11.	6
xlvii. 9, 9.	2 b	xix. 6.	2 b	vii. 7.	2 b
xlvii. 19, 28.	1 d	xx. 1.	6	vii. 15.	7
xlvii. 25.	1 d	xx. 3, 3, 14, 21.	2 b	vii. 16.	1 d
l. 20.	1 k	xx. 31.	2 a	ix. 21.	2 b
l. 22.	2 b	xxii. 23, 23.	6	x. 1, 12.	2 b
Exod. i. 14.	2 b	xxiii. 15.	6	xii. 10.	2 b
i. 16.	2 b	xxv. 6, 26, 26, 29,		xiii. 14.	6
i. 17, 18, 22.	1 g	34.	2 b	xix. 25. η	1 d
i. 19.	2 d	xxvi. 10, 16.	2 b	xxi. 7.	1 d
iv. 18.	2 b	xxvi. 24, 24.	6	xxvii. 22.	2 b
iv. 19.	6	xxvii. 9, 11.	1 g	xxvii. 2.	2 b
vi. 16, 18, 20.	2 b	xxviii. 9, 21.	2 b	xxviii. 13, 21.	2 b
xix. 13.	1 d	xxviii. 10.	2 b	xxx. 23.	2 b
xxi. 23, 23, 30.	2 b	xxix. 6.	2 b	xxxi. 39.	6
xxi. 35.	2 b	2 Sam. i. 9.	6	xxxiii. 4.	1 g
xxii. 4.	2 b	i. 10.	1 d	xxxiii. 18, 20, 22,	
xxii. 18.	1 g	i. 23.	2 b	28, 30.	2 b
xxxiii. 20.	2 b	iv. 8.	6	xxxvi. 6.	1 g
Lev. xi. 10, 46.	2 b	iv. 9.	6	xxxvi. 14.	2 b
xiv. 4, 6, 6, 7, 51,		viii. 2.	1 k	xlii. 16.	1 d
52, 53.	2 b	xii. 22.	2 b	Ps. xvi. 11.	2 b
xvi. 10, 20, 21.	2 b	xiv. 11, 11.	2 b	xvii. 14. θ	2 b
xvii. 11, 14, 14.	6	xii. 5, 18, 21, 22, 22.	2 b	xviii. 46.	2 b
xviii. 5.	2 a	xiv. 7.	6	xxi. 4.	2 b
xviii. 18.	2 b	xiv. 11, 19.	2 b	xxii. 26.	1 e
xxv. 35, 36.	2 b	xv. 21, 21, 21.	2 b	xxii. 29.	6
Num. iv. 19.	1 a	xvi. 11.	6	xxiii. 6.	2 b
xxi. 28.	2 b	xviii. 14, 18.	2 b	xxvii. 9.	2 b
xiv. 38.	6	xix. 5, 5, 5, 5.	6	xxx. 1, 4, 13.	2 b
xvi. 33, 48.	2 b	xix. 6, 34.	2 b	xxx. 3.	1 e
xxi. 8, 9.	2 b	xx. 3.	2 e	xxx. 5.	2 b
xxi. 35.	9	xxi. 47.	2 b	xxx. 10.	2 b
xxii. 33.	1 i	xxiii. 17.	6	xxxiii. 19.	1 f
xxiv. 23.	1 d	1 Kings i. 12, 12.	6	xxxiv. 12.	6
xxxi. 15.	1 e	i. 29.	2 b	xxxvi. 9.	2 b
xxxi. 18.	1 l	i. 31.	1 d	xxxviii. 12.	6
xxxv. 31.	6	ii. 23.	2 b	xxxviii. 19.	2 b
Deut. iv. 1, 33.	1 d	ii. 24.	2 b	xli. 2.	1 g
iv. 9, 10.	2 b	iii. 11, 11.	4, 6	xlii. 2, 8.	2 b
iv. 42.	2 a	iii. 22, 22, 23, 23,		xlix. 9.	2 b
v. 3.	6	25, 26, 26, 27.	2 b	xlix. 18.	2 b
v. 24.	2 a	iv. 21.	2 b	lii. 5.	3
v. 26, 26.	2 b, d	viii. 40.	2 b	lv. 23.	6
v. 33.	1 d	xi. 34.	2 b	lvi. 13.	2 b
vi. 2.	2 b	xii. 6.	2 b	lviii. 9.	2 b
vi. 24.	1 f	xv. 5, 6.	2 b		
viii. 1, 3, 3.	1 d	xvii. 1, 12, 23.	2 b		
xii. 1.	2 b				

Ps. lxi. 6.	4
lxiii. 3, 4.	2 b
lxiv. 1.	2 b
lxvi. 9.	2 b
lxix. 28.	2 b
lxix. 32.	1 d
lxxii. 15.	1 d
lxxviii. 50.	2 b
lxxxiv. 2.	2 b
lxxxviii. 3.	2 b
lxxxix. 48.	1 d
xci. 16.	4
ciii. 4.	2 b
civ. 33.	2 b
cxvi. 9.	2 b
cxviii. 17.	1 d
cxix. 17, 77, 116, 144, 175.	1 d
cxxviii. 5.	2 b
cxxxiii. 3.	2 b
cxlii. 5.	2 b
cxliii. 2, 3.	2 b
cxlv. 16.	2 b
cxlvi. 2.	2 b
Prov. i. 12.	2 b
i. 18, 19.	6
ii. 19.	2 b
iii. 2, 18, 22.	2 b
iv. 4.	1 c
iv. 10, 13, 22, 23.	2 b
v. 6.	2 b
vi. 23.	2 b
vi. 26.	6
vii. 2.	1 c
vii. 23.	6
viii. 35.	2 b
ix. 6.	1 c
ix. 11.	2 b
x. 11, 16, 17.	2 b
xi. 19, 30.	2 b
xii. 10.	6
xii. 28.	2 b
xiii. 3, 8.	6
xiii. 12, 14.	2 b
xiv. 27, 30.	2 b
xv. 4, 24, 31.	2 b
xv. 27.	1 d
xvi. 15, 22.	2 b
xviii. 21.	2 b
xix. 23.	2 b
xxi. 21.	2 b
xxii. 4.	2 b
xxxi. 12.	2 b
Eccles. ii. 3, 17.	2 b
iii. 12.	2 b
iv. 2, 2, 15.	2 b
v. 18, 20.	2 b
vi. 3.	1 d
vi. 6.	1 a
vi. 8, 12, 12.	2 b
vii. 2.	2 b
vii. 12.	1 g
viii. 15.	2 b
ix. 3, 4, 4, 5, 9, 9, 9.	2 b
ix. 8.	1 d

Cant. iv. 15.	2 b
Isa. iv. 3.	2 b
viii. 19.	2 b
xv. 4.	6
xxvi. 14, 19.	1 d
xxxviii. 4, 17.	2 b
xxxviii. 1.	1 d
xxxviii. 11, 12, 19, 19, 20.	2 b
xxxviii. 16, 16, 16.	1 d, 2 b, 1 l
xliii. 4.	6
xlix. 18.	2 b
liii. 8.	2 b
lv. 3.	1 d
lvii. 10.	2 b
Jer. ii. 13.	2 b
iv. 2.	2 b
iv. 30.	6
v. 2.	2 b
viii. 3.	2 b
x. 10.	2 b
xi. 19.	6
xi. 21.	6
xii. 16.	2 b
xvi. 14, 15.	2 b
xvii. 13.	2 b
xix. 7, 9.	6
xxi. 7.	6
xxi. 8.	2 b
xxi. 9, 9.	1 d, 6
xxii. 24.	2 b
xxii. 25.	6
xxiii. 7, 8, 36.	2 b
xxvii. 12, 17.	1 c
xxxiv. 20, 21.	6
xxxv. 7.	1 d
xxxvii. 2, 2, 2, 2.	1 d, 6, 2 a
xxxviii. 16, 16.	2 b, 6
xxxviii. 17, 17.	1 a
xxxviii. 20.	1 d
xxxix. 18.	6
xliv. 26.	2 b
xliv. 30, 30.	6
xlv. 5.	6
xlvi. 18.	2 b
xlvi. 26.	6
xlviii. 6.	6
xlix. 11.	1 g
xlix. 37.	6
lii. 33, 34.	2 b
Lam. ii. 19.	6
iii. 39, 53, 58.	2 b
iv. 20.	1 d
v. 9.	6
Ezek. i. 5, 13, 13, 14, 15, 15, 19, 19, 20, 21, 22.	2 b
iii. 13.	2 b
iii. 18.	1 f
iii. 21.	1 b d
v. 11.	2 b
vii. 13, 13.	2 b
x. 15, 17, 20.	2 b

Ezek. xiii. 18.	1 g
xiii. 19, 19.	1 f d
xiii. 22.	1 k
xiv. 16, 18, 20.	2 b
xvi. 6, 6.	1 c
xvi. 48.	2 b
xvii. 16, 19.	2 b
xviii. 3.	2 b
xviii. 9.	1 b d
xviii. 13, 13.	2 a, 1 d
xviii. 17.	1 b d
xviii. 19.	1 b d
xviii. 21.	1 b d
xviii. 22.	1 d
xviii. 23.	1 a
xviii. 24.	2 a
xviii. 27.	1 g
xviii. 28.	1 b d
xviii. 32.	1 c
xx. 3, 31, 33.	2 b
xx. 11, 13, 21.	2 a
xx. 25.	1 d
xxvi. 20.	2 b
xxxii. 10.	6
xxxii. 23, 24, 25, 26, 27, 32.	2 b
xxxiii. 10, 19.	1 d
xxxiii. 11, 11.	2 b, 1 a
xxxiii. 12.	1 b
xxxiii. 13.	1 b d
xxxiii. 15, 15.	2 b, 1 b d
xxxiii. 16.	1 b d
xxxiii. 27.	2 b
xxxiv. 8.	2 b
xxxv. 6, 11.	2 b
xxxvii. 3, 9, 10.	1 d
xxxvii. 5, 6, 14.	1 a
xlvii. 9, 9, 9.	2 b a, 1 d
Dan. ii. 4.	2 f
ii. 30.	2 h
iii. 9.	2 f
iv. 17, 34.	2 h
v. 10.	2 h
v. 19.	2 g
vi. 6, 21.	2 f
vi. 20, 26.	2 h
vii. 12.	2 h
xii. 2, 7.	2 b
Hos. i. 10.	2 b
iv. 15.	2 b
vi. 1.	1 d
Amos v. 4, 6.	1 c
v. 14.	1 d
viii. 14, 14.	2 b
Jonah i. 14.	6
ii. 6.	2 b
iv. 3, 3.	6, 2 b
iv. 8.	2 b
Hab. ii. 4.	1 d
Zeph. ii. 9.	2 b
Zech. i. 5.	1 d
x. 9.	1 a
xiii. 3.	1 d
xiv. 8.	2 b
Mal. ii. 5.	2 b

7 נוּף to lift up, as if about to strike; to move up and down, to wave. HIPHIL [a]pret. [b]fut.

8 נָטַל Ch. to lift up. P'AL [a]pret. P'IL [b]pret.

9 נָשָׂא to take up, to receive. To lift up the hand in swearing, Deut. xxxii. 40 (compare similar expressions, Gen. xiv. 22, Dan. xii. 7); also in offering violence, 2 Sam. xx. 21; in taking punishment, Ps. x. 12; in prayer and adoration, Ps. xxviii. 2, lxiii. 4, cxxxiv. 2 (cf. Lam. iii. 41); in beckoning, Isa. xlix. 22, cf. xiii. 2. To lift up the head, is said of one who is glad and happy, Job x. 15, Zech. i. 21; of one who becomes powerful or wealthy, Judg. viii. 28, Ps. lxxxiii. 2; but to lift up the head of any one out of prison, is to bring him up from it, being generally under ground, 2 Kings xxv. 27, Gen. xl. 13, 20; to lift up the face, to be cheerful, confident, and satisfied, Job xi. 15, ellipt. Gen. iv. 7; to lift up the eyes on, to look with attention, care, and affection, Ps. cxxiii. 1, Ezek. xviii. 12; to lift up the soul in earnest desire, especially to God; to lift up the voice in prayer, &c.; to lift up the head from off a person, to take away his life. To lift up the voice in the streets, Isa. xlii. 2, is an allusion to the custom of talking loud in the streets prevalent in the East. KAL [a]pret. [b]inf. [c]imp. [d]fut. [e]part. Poel. NIPHAL [f]pret. [g]inf. [h]imp. [i]fut. [k]part. PIEL [l]imp. HITHPAEL [m]inf. [n]fut. [o]מַשָּׂא f. a lifting up.

10 נָתַן to give. KAL [a]imp. [b]fut.

11 נָתַק to draw asunder, to pluck up. NIPHAL pret.

12 עוּד (see Witness, Relieve), to set up again, to restore, confirm. PILEL part.

13 עוּר to awake; to raise up, to lift up. POLEL [a]pret. HITHPOLEL [b]pret.

14 עָלָה to go up. HIPHIL [a]fut. [b]part. HITHPAEL [c]fut. [d]מַעַל m. lifting up.

15 עָנָה to chant, to sing; to cry aloud, to shout. KAL pret.

16 עָפַל to swell, to become tumid; to be inflated, elated, proud. PUAL pret.

17 צָהַל to cry aloud. PIEL imp.

18 קוּם to rise up. HIPHIL [a]pret. [b]inf. [c]fut.

19 רָאַם to be high. KAL pret.

20 רוּם to lift up oneself, to rise, to be lifted or raised up. KAL [a]pret. [b]inf. [c]fut. POLEL [d]fut. [e]part. HIPHIL [f]pret. [g]inf. [h]imp. [i]fut. [k]part. רוּם Ch. P'AL [l]part. passive. HITHPOLEL [m]pret.

21 רָמַם to be high, to be lifted up, exalted. NIPHAL [a]fut. רְמִמֹת f. a lifting up.

α lit. a living soul. β lit. in his life. γ lit. on account of thy life. δ our life for yours, lit. our life instead of you to die. ε lit. and we shall save alive. ζ lit. let my soul live. η lit. living; Lxx. ἀέννaος, eternus. θ lit. whose portion is in life. ι lit. every soul of life.

LIFT

1 בּוֹא to come. HIPHIL, to cause to come: part.

2 גֵּוָה f. a lifting up. [a]גֵּאוּת f. id.

3 גָּבַהּ to be high, tall, lofty; to be lifted up is used in a good sense, 2 Chron. xvii. 6; or in a bad sense, 2 Chron. xxvi. 16. KAL [a]pret. [b]fut.

4 גָּדַל to be, or to become great. HIPHIL pret.

5 דָּלָה (see Draw), to raise or lift up. PIEL pret.

6 מָרָא to raise up. HIPHIL fut. Job xxxix. 18, she lifteth up herself (on high), to run away; see Schultens; she lasheth herself with her wings, like the rider his horse, into full speed.

Gen. vii. 17.	20 c	Gen. xxxvii. 25.	9 d	Num. xvi. 3.	9 n
xiii. 10.	9 d	xxxvii. 28.	14 a	xx. 11.	20 i
xiii. 14.	9 c	xxxix. 15.	20 f	xxiii. 24.	9 n
xiv. 22.	20 f	xxxix. 18.	20 g	xxiv. 2.	9 d
xviii. 2.	9 d	xl. 13, 19, 20.	9 d	Deut. iii. 27.	9 c
xxi. 16.	9 d	xli. 44.	20 i	iv. 19.	9 d
xxi. 18.	9 c	xliii. 29.	9 d	viii. 14.	20 a
xxii. 4, 13.	9 d	Exod. vii. 20.	20 i	xvii. 20.	20 b
xxiv. 63, 64.	9 d	xiv. 10.	9 d	iv. 4. [a]	18 b a
xxvii. 38.	9 d	xiv. 16.	20 h	xxvii. 5.	7 b
xxix. 11.	9 d	xx. 25.	7 a	xxxii. 40.	9 d
xxxi. 10.	9 d	Lev. ix. 22.	9 d	Josh. iv. 18.	11
xxxi. 12.	9 c	Num. vi. 26.	9 c	v. 13.	9 d
xxxiii. 1, 5.	9 d	xiv. 1.	9 d	viii. 31.	7 a

Judg. ii. 4.	9 d	Ps. xxv. 1.	9 d	Jer. iii. 2.	9 c	
viii. 28. β	9 b	xxvii. 6.	20 c	vii. 16.	9 d	
ix. 7.	9 d	xxviii. 2.	9 b	xi. 14.	9 d	
xix. 17.	9 d	xxviii. 9.	9 l	xiii. 20.	9 c	
xxi. 2.	9 d	xxx. 1.	1	xxii. 20.	10 a	
Ruth i. 9, 14.	9 d	xli. 9.	4	li. 3.	14 c	
1 Sam. ii. 7.	20 e	lxiii. 4.	9 d	li. 9.	9 f	
ii. 8.	20 i	lxxiv. 3.	20 h	li. 14.	15	
vi. 13.	9 d	lxxiv. 5.	1	li. 31.	9 a	
xi. 4.	9 d	lxxv. 4, 5.	20 i	Lam. ii. 19.	9 c	
xxiv. 16.	9 d	lxxxiii. 2.	9 a	iii. 41.	9 d	
xxx. 4.	9 d	lxxxvi. 4.	9 d	Ezek. i. 19, 19.	9 i	
2 Sam. iii. 32.	9 d	xciii. 3, 3, 3.	9 a a d	i. 20.	9 i	
xiii. 34, 36.	9 d	xciv. 2.	9 h	i. 21, 21.	9 g i	
xviii. 24.	9 d	cii. 10.	9 a	iii. 14.	9 a	
xviii. 28.	9 a	cvi. 26.	9 d	viii. 3.	9 d	
xx. 21.	9 a	cvii. 25.	20 d	viii. 5, 5.	9 c d	
xxii. 49.	20 d	cx. 7.	20 i	x. 15.	21 a	
xxiii. 18.	13 a	cxiii. 7.	20 i	x. 16.	9 b	
1 Kings xi. 26.	20 i	cxix. 48.	9 d	x. 17, 17.	20 b, 21 a	
xi. 27.	20 f	cxxi. 1.	9 a	x. 19.	9 d	
2 Kings ix. 32.	9 a	cxxiii. 1.	9 a	xi. 1, 1.	9 d	
xiv. 10.	9 a	cxxxiv. 2.	9 c	xvii. 14.	9 m	
xix. 4.	9 a	cxli. 2.	9 o	xviii. 6, 12, 15.	9 a	
xix. 22.	9 d	cxliii. 8.	9 a	xx. 5, 5,	9 d	
xxv. 27.	9 a	cxlv.i. 6.	2	xx. 6, 15, 23, 28, 42.	9 a	
1 Chron. xi. 11, 20.	13 a	Prov. ii. 3.	10 b	xxi. 22.	20 g	
xiv. 2.	9 f	xxx. 13.	9 i	xxiii. 27.	9 d	
xv. 16.	20 g	xxx. 32.	9 m	xxvi. 8.	18 a	
xxi. 16.	9 a	Eccles. iv. 10.	18 c	xxviii. 2, 17.	3 a	
xxv. 5.	20 g	Isa. ii. 4.	9 d	xxviii. 5.	3 b	
2 Chron. v. 13.	20 g	ii. 12, 13, 14.	9 k	xxxi. 10, 10.	3 a, 20 a	
xvii. 6.	3 b	v. 26.	9 d	xxxiii. 25.	9 d	
xxv. 19.	9 a	vi. 1.	9 k	xxxvi. 7.	9 a	
xxvi. 16.	3 a	ix. 18.	2 a	xliv. 12.	9 a	
xxxii. 25.	3 a	x. 15, 15.	20 g k	xlvii. 14.	9 a	
Ezra ix. 6.	20 g	x. 24.	9 d	Dan. iv. 34.	8 a	
Neh. viii. 6.	14 d	x. 30.	17	v. 20.	20 l	
Job ii. 12, 12.	9 d	xiii. 2.	9 c	v. 23.	20 m	
x. 15.	9 d	xviii. 3.	9 b	vii. 4.	8 b	
xi. 15.	9 d	xxiv. 14.	9 d	vii. 9.	9 d	
xxii. 26.	9 d	xxvi. 11.	20 a	x. 5.	9 d	
xxii. 29.	2	xxxiii. 3.	21 b	xi. 12.	20 a	
xxx. 22.	9 d	xxxiii. 10.	9 i	Micah iv. 3.	9 d	
xxxi. 21.	7 a	xxxvii. 4.	9 a	v. 9.	20 c	
xxxi. 29.	13 b	xxxvii. 23.	9 d	Nah. iii. 3.	14 b	
xxxviii. 34.	20 i	xl. 9, 9.	20 h	Hab. ii. 4.	16	
xxxix. 18.	6	xl. 26.	9 c	iii. 10.	9 a	
Ps. iii. 3.	20 k	xlii. 2, 11.	9 d	Zech. i. 18.	9 d	
iv. 6.	9 c	xlix. 18.	9 c	i. 21, 21.	9 a e	
vii. 6.	9 h	xlix. 22.	9 h	ii. 1.	9 d	
ix. 13.	20 e	li. 6.	9 c	v. 1, 9, 9.	9 c	
x. 12.	9 c	lii. 8.	9 a	v. 5.	9 c	
xviii. 48.	20 d	lviii. 1.	20 h	v. 7.	9 f	
xxiv. 4.	9 a	lx. 4.	9 c	vi. 1.	9 d	
xxiv. 7, 7.	9 c h	lxii. 10.	20 h	xiv. 10.	19	
xxiv. 9, 9.	9 c					

a lit. raising up thou shalt raise up with him.   *β lit.* added not to lift up.

LIGHT, LIGHTNING

1 אוֹר to shine, shine upon, enlighten : light is that subtle fluid, called into existence the first day of creation ; as this material element of nature was created before the sun, so it appears to subsist independent of that body (see Job xxxviii. 19, 24), to which it is attracted as a centre, and flows back in powerful agency through the solar system to every planet included in it. When the sun and moon were formed the word is עָשָׂה not בָּרָא. Parkhurst derives this word from an obsolete verb, אָר to flow ; whence the noun, a river, a flood, Amos viii. 8. Light is put for life, natural, Job iii. 20 ; natural and spiritual, Ps. lvi. 13. Light is sometimes put for day. By an elegant figure, light signifies prosperity, honour, joy, &c., and all manner of happiness in this world and the next, Esth. viii. 16: Job xviii. 6 : Ps. xlix. 19 ; xcvii. 11 ; cxviii. 27. Light in darkness is encouragement, comfort, or good hope in adversity, Ps. cxii. 4. The light of the countenance is kind and favourable regard, Job xxix. 24, "if I laughed on them, they believed it not ;" and "the light of my countenance," my

cheerful aspect, they did not cast down, did not oblige me to change it into severe looks : Schultens ; Ps. xliv. 3 : Prov. xvi. 15. The light of the Lord is his favour, blessing, and illumination, Job xxix. 3 : Ps. xxxvi. 9 ; xliii. 3 : Isa. ii. 5. Deliverance from captivity, Micah vii. 9 ; salutary counsel, Job xii. 25 ; the light of conscience, Job xxiv. 13. Light, in a spiritual sense, attributed to God, Ps. xxvii. 1 ; to Christ, Isa. ix. 2 ; x. 17 ; xlii. 6 ; xlix. 6 ; lx. 1, 19, 20 ; and, according to R. Salomo, Ps. xliii. 3, *cf.* Ps. cxxxii. 17 ; hence, the saving knowledge of God and of Christ, Ps. lxxxix. 15 : Isa. ii. 5 ; attributed to the Word of God, Ps. xxxvi. 9 ; cxix. 105 : Prov. vi. 23 : Isa. v. 20. KAL ᵃ*pret.* HIPHIL ᵇ*pret.* ᶜ*inf.* ᵈ*imp.* ᵉ*fut.* ᶠ*part.* ᵍ אוֹר *m.* light: Gen. i. 3, &c. ʰ אוּר *m. id.* ⁱ אוֹרָה *f. id.* ᵏ מָאוֹר light, of the sun and moon.

2 בָּזָק *m.* lightning, flash of lightning.

3 בָּרָק *m.* lightning.

4 חָזִיז *m.* lightning, which is usually followed with thunder and rain.

5 חָזָה to see ; to introduce light into a building. מֶחֱזָה *f.* a window-light.

6 יָפַע to shine bright and full, as the sun in his meridian splendour. HIPHIL *fut.*

7 לַפִּיד *m.* a burning lamp or torch.

8 נָגַהּ to shine. HIPHIL ᵃ*fut.* ᵇ נֹגַהּ *f.* light.

9 נָהַר to flow as waters in a full large river ; to flow as light from the sun. KAL ᵃ*pret.* ᵇ נְהָרָה *f.* the light of day. ᶜ נְהוֹר Ch. *m.* light. ᵈ נַהִירוּ Ch. *f. id.*

10 נֵר *m.* a lamp ; figuratively used of David, the lamp of Israel. ᵃ נִיר *m. id.*

11 עָלָה to go up ; to cause to go up, to light a lamp. HIPHIL ᵃ*pret.* ᵇ*inf.* ᶜ*fut.*

12 שַׁחַר *m.* morning.

13 שְׁקֻפִים *m. pl.* See *Windows.*

No. 1 g not included.

Gen. i. 14, 16, 16, 16.	1 k	1 Kings vi. 4.	13	Ps. cxviii. 27.	1 e
i. 15, 15.	1 k c	vii. 4, 4, 5, 5.	5	cxix. 130.	1 e
i. 17.	1 c	xi. 36.	10 a	cxxxv. 7.	3
xliv. 3.	1 a	2 Kings viii. 19.	10 a	cxxxix. 12. β	1 i
Exod. xiii. 21.	1 c	2 Chron. xxi. 7.	10 a	cxliv. 6.	3
xiv. 20.	1 e	Ezra iv. 8.	1 c	Prov. xv. 30.	1 k
xix. 16.	3	Neh. ix. 12, 19.	1 c	xxix. 13.	1 f
xx. 18.	3	Esth. viii. 16.	1	Isa. viii. 20.	12
xxv. 6.	1 k	Job iii. 4.	9 b	i. 10.	8 b
xxv. 37, 37.	11 a, 1 b	x. 22.	6	l. 11.	1 h
xxvii. 20.	1 k	xxviii. 26.	4	lx. 19, 19, 19.	1 g e g
xxx. 8.	11 b	xxxvii. 3.	1 g	Jer. iv. 23. γ	1 g
xxxv. 8, 14, 14, 28.	1 k	xxxvii. 15.	4	x. 13.	3
xxxix. 37.	1 k	xxxviii. 35.	3	li. 16.	3
xl. 4.	11 a	Ps. xiii. 3.	1 d	Ezek. i. 13.	3
xl. 25.	11 c	xviii. 14.	3	i. 14.	2
Lev. xxiv. 2.	1 k	xviii. 28.	1 e	xxxii. 7.	1 e g
Num. iv. 9, 16.	1 k	xxxiv. 5. α	9 a	xxxii. 8. δ	1 k g
viii. 2, 2.	11 b, 1 a	lxxiv. 16.	1 k	Dan. ii. 22.	9 c
viii. 3.	11 a	lxxvii. 18, 18.	3 1 b	v. 11, 14.	9 d
1 Sam. xxix. 10.	1 a	xc. 8.	1 k	v. 14.	3
2 Sam. xxi. 17.	10	xcvii. 4.	3	Nah. ii. 4.	3
xxii. 15.	3	cv. 39.	1 c	Zech. ix. 14.	3
xxii. 29.	8 a				

a marg. 'they flowed.'   *β lit.* as darkness as light.   *γ lit.* not their light.   *δ marg.* 'lights of the light in heaven.'

LIGHT, ALIGHT

1 יָרַד to descend ; to light down. KAL *fut.*

2   מָצָא   to find, to light on.   KAL ^a *pret.* ^b *fut.*

3   נַחַת   *m.* a descending or letting down, from נָחַת; or a resting, from נוּחַ: Isa. xxx. 30, of the heavy and abiding strokes of the arm of divine justice.

4   נָפַל   to fall, to light down.   KAL ^a *pret.* ^b *fut.*

5   פָּגַע   to reach, to fall upon.   KAL *fut.*

6   צָנַח   to let oneself down, to descend, to alight.   KAL *fut.*

7   קָרָה   to happen.   KAL ^a *fut.* ^b מִקְרֶה *m.* accident.

Gen. xxiv. 64.	4 b	Judg. i. 14.	6	2 Kings v. 21.	4 b
xxviii. 11.	5	iv. 15.	2	x. 15.	2 b
Deut. xix. 5.	2 a	Ruth ii. 3.	7 a b	Isa. ix. 8.	4 a
Josh. xv. 18.	6	1 Sam. xxv. 23.	1	xxx. 30.	3

LIGHTLY, LIGHTNESS

1   מְעַט   few or little, with ל prefixed, nearly, "lightly."

2   נָבֵל   to be foolish.   PIEL to esteem lightly : *fut.*

3   פָּחַז   to leap, to spring ; to be proud, vain-glorious ; to be light, wanton, lewd ; see *Unstable.* KAL ^a *part.* Poel. ^b פַּחֲזוּת *f.* pride, boasting.

4   קָלָה   to be light ; to make light of ; to be made light of.   NIPHAL ^a *part.* HIPHIL ^b *part.*

5   קָלַל   to be light ; to be lightly esteemed ; to make light, lighten ; to make light of.   KAL ^a *fut.* ^b *inf.* NIPHAL ^c *pret.* HIPHIL ^d *pret.* ^e *inf.* ^f *imp.* ^g *fut.* HITHPALPEL ^h *pret.* ⁱ קַלְקֵל *adj.* despicable. ^k קַל *adj.* light.

6   קוֹל   *m.* voice, rumour.

Gen. xxvi. 10.	1	2 Sam. ii. 18.	5 k	Isa. xlix. 6.	5 c
Num. xxi. 5.	5 i	1 Kings xii. 4, α 9,	9	Jer. iii. 9.	6
Deut. xxvii. 16.	4 b	10.	5 f	iv. 24.	5 h
xxxii. 15.	2	xvi. 31.	5 c	xxiii. 32.	3 b
Judg. ix. 4.	3 a	2 Kings iii. 18.	5 c	Ezek. viii. 17.	5 c
1 Sam. iii. 30.	5 a	xx. 19.	5 c	xxii. 7.γ	5 d
vi. 5.	5 g	2 Chron. x. 10.	5 f	Jonah i. 5.	5 e
xviii. 23, 23.	5 c, 4 a	Isa. ix. 1.β	3	Zeph. iii. 4.	3 a

a lit. lighten from the service.   β "lightly afflicted."   γ "set light."

LIGURE

  לֶשֶׁם   *m.* a species of gem, of doubtful colour, but generally supposed to be nearly related to the hyacinth, *i.e.* a red, strongly tinged with orange yellow. Exod. xxviii. 19 ; xxxix. 12.

LIKE, ALIKE

1   אָח   *m.* brother.

2   בַּד   *m.* a part.

3   תַּבְנִית   *f.* structure, model, likeness.

4   דָּמָה   to be like ; to liken ; to compare ; also to cut off.   KAL ^a *pret.* ^b *imp.* ^c *fut.* ^d *part.* Poel. NIPHAL ^e *pret.* PIEL ^f *fut.* HITHPAEL ^g *fut.* דְּמֵה Ch. P'AL ^h *part. active.* ⁱ דְּמוּת *f.* likeness, representation, image. ^k דִּמְיוֹן *m. id.*

5   תְּמוּנָה   *f.* appearance, form, or representation of that which is not visible : in Exod. xx. 4, it is evidently to be taken in this sense ; see *Similitude.* Likeness does not convey the correct meaning of the word, and the second Commandment undoubtedly forbids all representations or symbols of heavenly objects for worship. See *Image.*

6   מָשַׁל   to be superior ; a parable or proverb ; hence, as the simile or comparison was the proper and common form

of מָשָׁל an eminent saying, the word may have come to signify to compare, to liken.   NIPHAL ^a *pret.* HITHPAEL ^b *fut.* ^c מָשָׁל *m.* a proverb. ^d מֹשֶׁל *m.* similitude.

7   שָׁוָה   to be made even, level ; to be equal, like in value, *seq.* בְּ ; to resemble, *seq.* לְ. KAL ^a *fut.* PIEL ^b *part.* NITHPAEL ^c *pret.* שְׁוָה Ch. PAEL ^d *pret.*

Gen. i. 26.	4 i	Ps. xlix. 12, 20.	6 a	Isa. xl. 18, 18.	4 f i
v. 1, 3.	4 i	lviii. 4.δ	4 i	xl. 25.	4 f
Exod. xx. 4.	5	lxxxix. 6.	4 c	xlvi. 5, 5.	4 f c
xxx. 34.	2	cii. 6.	4 a	Jer. vi. 2.	4 a
Deut. iv. 16, 17, 17,	3	cxliii. 7.	6 a	Lam. ii. 13.	4 f
18, 18.	3	cxliv. 4.	4 a	Ezek. i. 5, 5, 10, 13,	
iv. 23, 25.	5	Prov. xxvi. 4.	7 a	16, 22, 26, 26,	
v. 8.	5	xxvii. 15.	7 c	26, 28.	4 i
2 Sam. xxii. 34.	7 b	Cant. ii. 9.	4 d	viii. 2.	4 i
Job xiii. 12. a	6 c	ii. 17.	4 b	x. 1, 10, 21, 22.	4 i
xxx. 19.	6 b	vii. 7.	4 a	xviii. 10.	1
xli. 33.	6 d	viii. 14.	4 b	xxxi. 2, 8, 8, 18.	4 a
Ps. xvii. 12.β	4 k	Isa. i. 9.	4 a	xxxii. 2.	4 d
xvii. 15.γ	5	xiii. 4.	4 i	Dan. iii. 25.	4 h
xviii. 33.	7 b	xiv. 10.	4 a	v. 21.	7 d
xxviii. 1.	6 a	xiv. 14.	4 g	vii. 5.	4 h

a lit. are parables of ashes.   β *marg.* 'the likeness of him (that is, of every one of them) is as a lion.'   γ *or,* image.   δ *marg.* 'according to the likeness of.'

LIKE (*V*)

  אָהַב   to love.   KAL *pret.* Amos iv. 5, *marg.* 'ye love.'

  חָפֵץ   see *Delight.* KAL *pret.* Deut. xxv. 8. *fut.* Deut. xxv. 7.

  חָשַׁב   to think, imagine, purpose ; used of things inanimate. PIEL *pret.* Jonah i. 4.

  טוֹב   *adj.* good : Deut. xxiii. 16, *marg.* 'is good for him ;' Esth. viii. 8, *lit.* as is good in your eyes.

  רָצָה   to delight in ; *seq.* בְּ. KAL *pret.* 1 Chron. xxviii. 4.

LIKING   See GOOD, WORSE

LILY

  שׁוֹשָׁן   *m.* a lily, especially white ; having six leaves, six petals, and six stamina. The snowy whiteness of its petals, its lofty stature reaching sometimes to four feet and a half, the delicacy of its form, and the uncommon elegance of all its parts, cannot but strike with admiration every attentive observer. It was one of the ornaments of the temple and its furniture ; the brim of the molten sea was wrought with flowers of lilies, the chapiters were of lily-work, and the tops of the pillars. It was worn on festive occasions, especially nuptial, and the title of Ps. xlv., Shoshannim, may have this reference. 1 Kings vii. 22, 26 : Cant. ii. 16 ; iv. 5 ; v. 13 ; vi. 2, 3 ; vii. 2. שׁוֹשָׁן *m. id.* 1 Kings vii. 19. שׁוֹשַׁנָּה *f. id.* 2 Chron. iv. 5 ; Cant. ii. 1, 2 : Hos. xiv. 5.

LIME

  שִׂיד   *m.* lime, plaster : Isa. xxxiii. 12 : Amos ii. 1.

LIMIT

  גְּבוּל   *m.* border, coast : Ezek. xliii. 12.

  תָּוָה   to mark, to point out the boundaries by marks, to limit. HIPHIL *pret.* Ps. lxxviii. 41. Gesenius, to grieve, to afflict. Hengstenberg, to dishonour.

LINE

  חֶבֶל   *com.* cord, rope ; measuring-line : 2 Sam. viii. 2, 2, 2 : Ps. xvi. 6 ; lxxviii. 55 : Amos vii. 17 : Zech. ii. 1.

חוּט *m.* a thread : 1 Kings vii. 15.

פָּתִיל *m.* a thread, line, cord : Ezek. xl. 3.

קָו *m.* a cord, line, employed in measuring or building, Job xxxviii. 5 : Ezek. xlvii. 3 ; and sometimes in setting out the limits of an intended destruction, Lam. ii. 8. It is also applied to lines in a book, Isa. xxviii. 10 : Ps. xix. 4, *marg.* 'rule or direction.' 1 Kings vii. 23, &c. תִּקְוָה *f. id.* Josh. ii. 18, 21.

שֶׂרֶד *m.* Lowth renders this word "red-ochre;" so Kimchi ; which a carpenter uses on a line to mark out his work. But according to Gesenius, an awl ; a stylus or engraver, with which the artist sketches the outlines of a figure to be sculptured. Isa. xliv. 13.

LINEN

1 אֵטוּן *m.* thread, yarn, of linen or cotton ; once, Prov. vii. 16, tapestry, coverings of Egyptian yarn, which was distinguished for its firmness and beauty.—*Celsii Hierob.* I. 89.

2 בַּד *m.* thread, yarn, especially of linen ; hence, fine white linen, linen garments.

3 בּוּץ *m.* byssus, cloth of byssus, fine white linen ; as worn by kings, priests, and persons of high rank or honour. See Wilkinson's Manners and Customs of the Ancient Egyptians, III. p. 115.

4 סָדִין *m. indusium,* shirt, a wide under-garment of linen worn next the body.

5 פִּשְׁתָּה *m.* flax, linen, the material.

6 מִקְוֵא *m.* linen yarn. Interpreters, however, differ very widely as to the meaning of this word ; Gesenius, a band, company of men and animals, *e. g.* of horses, a caravan.

7 שַׁעַטְנֵז *m.* a kind of cloth or garment, made of different threads ; linen and woollen woven together.

8 שֵׁשׁ *m.* something white, *or,* whiteness ; byssus, *i. e.* fine cotton, so called from its whiteness : Gen. xli. 42, &c. שְׁשִׁי *m.* Ezek. xvi. 13, כְּתִיב.

No. 8 not included.

Exod. xxviii. 42.	2	1 Kings x. 28, 28.	6	Prov. xxxi. 24.	4
xxxix. 28.	2	1 Chron. iv. 21.	3	Isa. iii. 23.	4
Lev. vi. 10, 10.	2	xv. 27, 27.	3, 2	Jer. xiii. 1.	5
xiii. 47, 48, 52, 59.	5	2 Chron. i. 16, 16.	6	Ezek. ix. 2, 3, 11.	2
xvi. 4, 4, 4, 4, 23, 32.	6	ii. 14.	3	x. 2, 6, 7.	2
xix. 19.	7	iii. 14.	3	xxvii. 16.	3
Deut. xxii. 11.	5	v. 12.	3	xliv. 17, 18, 18.	5
1 Sam. ii. 18.	2	Esth. i. 6.	3	Dan. x. 5.	2
xxii. 18.	2	viii. 15.	3	xii. 6, 7.	2
2 Sam. vi. 14.	2	Prov. vii. 16.	1		

LINGER

מָהַהּ to deny, to refuse ; to delay, linger, in distraction. HITHPALPEL *pret.* Gen. xliii. 10. *fut.* Gen. xix. 16.

LINTEL

אַיִל *m.* ram ; see *Post :* 1 Kings vi. 31.

כַּפְתּוֹר *m.* see *Knop.* Such devices, mixed with flowers, being usual upon the lintels in doorsteads, hence the word is used to signify a lintel : Amos ix. 1, *marg.* 'or, chapiter, *or,* knop :' Zeph. ii. 14, *marg. id.* Gesenius, the capital of a column.

מַשְׁקוֹף *m.* lintel, the upper part of a doorway : Exod. xii. 22, 23.

LION

1 אֲרִי *m.* a general name for a lion, from אָרָה to tear, the chief of tearing and devouring beasts ; symbolical of David's reign. Gussetius thinks this name of a lion is deduced from to pluck or crop the herbs largely, which the lion may have done in a primitive state ; and it is twice foretold that it shall eat straw like the ox : Isa. xi. 7 ; lxv. 25. Gen. xlix. 9, &c. אֲרִיאֵל *m.* ariel, a lion of God, a great lion, lionlike men. אַרְיֵה *m.* Ch.

2 כְּפִיר *m.* a young lion, old enough to roar, going forth for prey, ferocious and bloodthirsty in his youthful strength. How it differs from a whelp, see Ezek. xix. 2, 3. *Trop.* of cruel and bloodthirsty enemies ; of the young princes or warriors of a state : Ezek. xxxviii. 13, *comp.* Nah. ii. 13.

3 לָבִיא *com.* a lion, lioness, so called from roaring ; a lioness is stronger and fiercer than a lion after she has whelped : Gen. xlix. 9, symbolical of Solomon's reign. לְבִיָּא *f.* a lioness. לְבָאוֹת *f. pl. id.* לְבָאִים *m. pl.* lions.

4 לַיִשׁ *m.* a lion of the strongest and bravest kind.

5 שַׁחַל *m.* a fierce, roaring lion ; or, according to Bochart, the swarthy lion of Syria ; or an old lion, which becomes more formidable to inhabited places, ceasing to hunt.

All the above names of a lion occur in Job iv. 10, 11. Kimchi enumerates these names of a lion, leaving out the last two, and places them in the following order as to strength, &c. 1. גּוּר a whelp : 2. כְּפִיר. 3. אַרְיֵה. 4. לָבִיא. 5. לַיִשׁ.

6 שַׁחַץ *m.* elation, pride : Job xxviii. 8, *lit.* sons of pride ; *i. e.* the larger beasts of prey, as the lion, so called from his proud gait.

No. 1 not included.

Gen. xlix. 9, 9, 9.	1, 1, 3	Ps. xci. 13, 13.	5, 2	Ezek. xxxii. 2.	2
Num. xxiii. 24, 24.	3, 1	civ. 21.	2	xxxviii. 13.	2
xxiv. 9, 9.	1, 3	Prov. xix. 12.	2	xli. 19.	2
Deut. xxxiii. 20.	3	xx. 2.	2	Dan. vi. 7, 12, 16, 19,	
Judg. xiv. 5. *a*	2, 1	xxvi. 13, 13.	5, 1	20, 22, 24, 27.	1 b
2 Sam. xxiii. 20, 20.	1 a, 1	xxviii. 1.	2	vii. 4.	1 b
1 Chron. xi. 22.	1 a	xxx. 30.	4	Hos. v. 14, 14.	5, 2
Job ix. 10, 10, 10.	1, 5, 2	Isa. v. 29, 29.	3, 2	xiii. 7.	5
iv. 11, 11.	4, 3	xi. 6.	2	xiii. 8.	3
x. 16.	3	xxx. 6.	3, 4	Joel i. 6, 6.	5, 3
xxviii. 8, 8.	5, 6	xxxi. 4, 4.	1, 2	Amos iii. 4.	1, 2
xxxviii. 39, 39.	3, 2	Jer. ii. 15.	2	Micah v. 8, 8.	1, 2
Ps. xvii. 12, 12.	1, 2	xxv. 38.	2	Nah. ii. 11, 11,	
xxxiv. 10.	2	li. 38, 38.	4, 2	11, 11, 11.	1, 2, 1, 3, 1
xxxv. 17.	2	Ezek. xix. 2, 2, 2.	3 a, 1, 2	ii. 12, 12.	1, 3 b
lvii. 4.	3 c	xix. 3, 5.	2	ii. 13.	2
lviii. 6.	2	xix. 6, 6.	1, 2	Zech. xi. 3.	2

a lit. a whelp of lions.

LIP

שָׂפָה *f.* lip, of the organ of speech, also of language : Exod. vi. 12, &c. "Words of the lips," Ps. lix. 12, vain and sinful words, here put in connexion with "sin of their mouth." Comp. Prov. xiv. 23.

שָׂפָם *m. pr.* lip-beard, upper lip : Lev. xiii. 45 : Ezek. xxiv. 17, 22 ; Micah iii. 7, *marg.* 'upper lip.'

LIQUOR

דֶּמַע *m.* tear, tears of olives and grapes, *i. e.* wine and oil : Exod. xxii. 29.

מֶזֶג *m.* wine, as mixed, *i. e.* spiced wine : Cant. vii. 2.

מִשְׁרָה *f.* maceration, steeping : Num. vi. 3, the steeping of grapes, *i. e.* a drink prepared from macerated grapes.

LISTEN

שָׁמַע to hear. KAL *imp.* Isa. xlix. 1.

LITTER

צָב a litter, sedan, palanquin : Isa. lxvi. 20, *marg.* ' or, coaches.'

LITTLE

1 דַּק *adj.* (see *Small*), a very little thing.

2 זְעֵיר *m.* a few, a little ; either of men, things, or time. זְעֵירᵃ Ch. *adj.*

3 טַף *m.* little ones, or children, while they are in the hands and under the care of the women ; in conjunction with whom they are commonly mentioned ; and, therefore, putting the part for the whole, when little ones only are named, both women and children are often, if not always, included. The word is rightly translated 'families,' Gen. xlvii. 12. The Lxx. have rendered the word λαός, Judg. xxi. 10 ; ὄχλος, 2 Sam. xv. 22 ; οἰκία, Gen. l. 21 ; συγγένεια, Gen. l. 8.—Gen. xxxiv. 29, &c.

4 כִּבְרָה *f.* length, or measure of distance ; a little way, *lit.* and *marg.* ' a little piece of ground.'

5 מָעַט to be few or little ; the sense is nearly uniform, and relates to number, space, condition, and time : Ps. ii. 12, "when his wrath is kindled but a little," *Heb.* for his anger will burn very soon. KAL ᵃ *fut.* HIPHIL ᵇ *part.* ᶜ מְעַט and מְעַט ᵈ *m.* Gen. xviii. 4, &c.

6 עוֹלֵל *m.* see *Young.* ᵃ עֲוִיל *m.* a suckling.

7 צָעַר to be small. KAL ᵃ *part.* Poel. ᵇ צָעִיר *adj.* small. ᶜ מִצְעָר *m.* something small, little. ᵈ מִצְעִירָה *adj. f.* something smallish, little.

8 קוּט to loathe. KAL *pret.* Ezek. xvi. 47, "as (if that were) a very little (thing)," *marg.* ' or, that was loathed as a small (thing) ;' where, however, both the reading and the interpretation are doubtful. All the ancient versions read קָט ; others make it, according to the Arabic only, *duntaxat ;* see Thesaur. p. 1202 ; so our version seems to take it. Or קָט may be a noun, loathing.

9 קָטָן *adj.* little, small. ᵃ קָטֹן *adj. id.*

10 שֵׁמֶץ *m.* a transient sound, rapidly uttered and swiftly dying away. Gesenius, a whisper.

11 שֶׁצֶף *m.* This word occurs only in Isa. liv. 8, and has given occasion to many conjectures as to its true meaning. It is from the context that it has been supposed to imply a short time, or a little quantity. The Vulgate renders the phrase, "in a moment of indignation ;" but the Syriac, "in great wrath." The most probable solution of the difficulty is, that שֶׁצֶף is used instead of שֶׁטֶף, for the sake of a paronomasia, שֶׁצֶף קֶצֶף, and that the meaning may be the same, *i. e.* overflowing ; as Rosenmüller and Gesenius have translated it, "in thy overflowing wrath ;" or, according to Alexander, "in a gush of wrath." This paronomasia has been attempted to be transferred into versions—by Gesenius (*in der Fluth der Zorngluth*)—by Hitzig (*in derber Herbe*)—by Ewald (*als der Groll war voll*).

No. 3, *Little ones, Little children,* and No. 5 c, not included.

Gen. xix. 20, 20.	7 c	2 Kings ii. 23.	9	Cant. viii. 8.	9
xxxv. 16.	4	iv. 10.	9	Isa. xi. 6.	9 a
xliv. 20.	9	v. 2.	9	xxviii. 10, 10, 13, 13.	2
xlviii. 7.	9	v. 14.	9 a	xl. 15.	1
Exod. xii. 4.	5 a	v. 19.	4	liv. 8.	11
xvi. 18. α	5 b	2 Chron. x. 10.	9	lx. 22.	9 a
1 Sam. ii. 19.	9 a	Neh. ix. 32. β	5 a	lxiii. 18.	7 c
xv. 17.	9 a	Job iv. 12.	10	Jer. xiv. 3.	7 b
xx. 35.	9 a	xxi. 11.	6 a	xlviii. 4.	7 b
2 Sam. xii. 3.	9	xxvi. 14.	10	Ezek. xvi. 47. γ	5 c, 8
1 Kings iii. 7.	9 a	xxxvi. 2.	2	Dan. vii. 8.	2 a
viii. 64.	9 a	Ps. lxviii. 27.	7 b	viii. 9.	7 d
xi. 17.	9 a	cxxxvii. 9.	6	Amos vi. 11.	9 a
xii. 10.	9 a	Prov. xxx. 24.	9	Micah v. 2.	7 b
xvii. 13.	9	Eccles. ix. 14.	9	Zech. xiii. 7.	7 a
xviii. 44.	9	Cant. ii. 15.	9		

α "gathered little."   β "seem little."   γ *marg.* ' or, that was loathed as a small thing.'

LIVER

כָּבֵד *m.* liver, the heaviest of all the bowels. So the lungs, the lightest of the bowels, are in our language called the lights. Exod. xxix. 13, 22 : Lev. iii. 4, 10, 15 ; iv. 9 ; vii. 4 ; viii. 16, 25 ; ix. 10, 19 : Prov. vii. 23 : Lam. ii. 11 : Ezek. xxi. 21.

LIZARD

לְטָאָה *f.* a kind of lizard, which Shaw, in his Travels, p. 250, supposes to be the chameleon, living upon flies and insects, which it catches with its tongue, darted out with incredible swiftness. Lev. xi. 30.

LO

רָאָה to see. KAL *imp.* 1 Chron. xxi. 23 : Eccles. vii. 29 : Ezek. iv. 15.

הִנֵּה *part. interj.* lo, behold : Gen. xviii. 10, &c.

LOAD (See **LADE**)

LOAF

כִּכָּר *f.* what is in a round flat form, as a cake or loaf of bread : Exod. xxix. 23 : Judg. viii. 5 : 1 Sam. x. 3 : 1 Chron. xvi. 3.

לֶחֶם *m.* bread : Lev. xxiii. 17 : 1 Sam. xvii. 17 ; xxv. 18 : 1 Kings xiv. 3 : 2 Kings iv. 42.

LOAN

שְׁאֵלָה *f.* an asking ; loan, thing lent : 1 Sam. ii. 20.

LOCK

מַחְלְפוֹת *f. pl.* braids, plaits of hair : Judg. xvi. 13, 19.

פֶּרַע hair, locks, as being shorn : Num. vi. 5 : Ezek. xliv. 20.

צִיצִת *f.* fringe or tassel ; lock of hair, forelock : Ezek. viii. 3.

צַמָּה *f.* braided hair ; or, according to modern critics, a veil : Cant. iv. 1, 3 ; vi. 7 : Isa. xlvii. 2.

קְוֻצּוֹת *f. pl.* locks of hair, forelocks, so called from being cut, shorn : Cant. v. 2, 11.

LOCK (V)

נָעַל to make a door fast, or a place secure, by bolts and bars. KAL *pret.* Judg. iii. 23. *part.* Paül, Judg. iii. 24. מַנְעוּל *m.* lock : Neh. iii. 3, 6, 13, 14, 15 : Cant. v. 5.

LOCUST

אַרְבֶּה *m.* a locust, an insect which increases prodigiously, from רָבָה to multiply. There are various species of them, which consequently have different names. Exod. x. 4, &c. See Dr. Pusey on Joel ii. 2-11.

גֹּב *m.* another name for the locust, perhaps that kind described by Pliny, xi. 29, s. 35 : *Hæ pariunt, in terram demisso spinæ caule, ova condensa autumni tempore. Ea durant hieme sub terra. Subsequente anno exitu veris emittunt parvas . . . . . siceo vere major proventus.* Arist. Hist. Anim. v. 28, et Bocharti Hieroz. II. p. 443. Gesenius. Isa. xxxiii. 4.

חָנָב *m.* a species of the locust, whose name is taken from an Arabic root, importing their veiling the sun, or clouding the light : 2 Chron. vii. 13.

סָלְעָם *m.* the bald locust; the name is of Chaldean origin, importing their devouring the fruits of the earth: Lev. xi. 22.

צְלָצַל *m.* put for a stridulous insect, which gives forth a tinkling or clanging sound, *e.g.* grasshopper, a cricket : Deut. xxviii. 42.

LODGE

1 לִין to lodge, to stay all night, to continue in a settled state. KAL ᵃ*pret.* ᵇ*inf.* ᶜ*imp.* ᵈ*fut.* ᵉ*part.* HIPHIL ᶠ*fut.* ᵍ מָלוֹן *m.* an inn. ʰ מְלוּנָה *f.*

2 שָׁכַב to lie down. KAL *fut.*

Gen. xxiv. 23, 25.	1 b	Judg. xix. 9.	1 c	Job xxiv. 7.	1 f
xxxii. 13.	1 d	xix. 13.β	1 a	xxxi. 32.	1 b
xxxii. 21.	1 a	xix. 15, 15.	1 b	Cant. vii. 11.	1 d
Num. xxii. 8.	1 c	xx. 4.	1 b	Isa. i. 8.	1 h
Josh. ii. 1.	2	Ruth i. 16, 16.	1 d	i. 21.	1 d
iii. 1.	1 d	2 Sam. xvii. 8, 16.	1 d	x. 29.	1 g
iv. 3, 3.	1 g d	1 Kings xix. 9.	1 d	xxi. 13.	1 g
iv. 8.	1 g	2 Kings xix. 23.	1 g	lxv. 4.	1 g
vi. 11.	1 g	1 Chron. ix. 27.	1 d	Jer. iv. 14.γ	1 f
viii. 9.	1 d	Neh. iv. 22.	1 d	ix. 2.	1 g
Judg. xviii. 2.	1 d	xiii. 20.	1 d	Zeph. ii. 14.	1 d
xix. 4, 7, a 11, 20.	1 d	xiii. 21.	1 e		

a lit. he returned and lodged. *β lit.* and we will lodge.
γ or, how long wilt thou harbour vain thoughts.

LOFT

עֲלִיָּה *f.* upper chamber : 1 Kings xvii. 19.

LOFTY

1 גֹּבַהּ *m.* height. ᵃ גַּבְהוּת *f.* pride. ᵇ גָּבֹהַּ *adj.* high, lofty; proud, arrogant.

2 נָשָׂא to lift up, to be lifted up. NIPHAL *part.*

3 רוּם to lift up oneself. KAL ᵃ*pret.* ᵇ*part.* Poel. ᶜ מָרוֹם *m.* height.

4 שָׂגַב to lift oneself up ; to be high. NIPHAL *part.*

Ps. lxxiii. 8.	3 c	Isa. ii. 12.	3 b	Isa. lvii. 7.	1 b
cxxxi. 1.	3 a	v. 15.	1 b	lvii. 15.	2
Prov. xxx. 13.	3 a	xxvi. 5.	4	Jer. xlviii. 29.	1
Isa. ii. 11, 17.	1 a				

LOG

לֹג *m.* the smallest measure of liquid things ; a measure, the twenty-second part of an ephah, containing three-quarters of a pint. According to the Rabbins, the twelfth part of a hin, equal to the contents of six eggs.—*Gesenius.* Lev. xiv. 10, 12, 15, 21, 24.

LOINS

חֲלָצַיִם *f. dual.* the loins, where one girds himself for strength, vigour, alacrity : Gen. xxxv. 11 : 1 Kings viii. 19 : 2 Chron. vi. 9 : Job xxxi. 20 ; xxxviii. 3 ; xl. 7 : Isa. v. 27 ; xxxii. 11 : Jer. xxx. 6.

חֲרַץ Ch. *f. id.* Dan. v. 6.

יָרֵךְ *f.* the thigh of man or beast; the part from the loins : Gen. xlvi. 26 : Exod. i. 5.

כֶּסֶל *m.* the flanks ; *pl.* the internal muscles of the loins, the inward parts : Ps. xxxviii. 7.

מָתְנַיִם *dual. m.* the loins ; the seat of strength or of weakness ; burdens are borne on the loins, Ps. lxvi. 11 ; the seat of pain ; to smite through, or to crush the loins, is to crush a man wholly ; shaking loins are a sign of weakness. Gen. xxxvii. 34, &c.

LONG, LONG SUFFERING

1 אָרַךְ to prolong, to lengthen ; to be long, to make long; it is applied both to time and space. KAL ᵃ*pret.* ᵇ*fut.* HIPHIL ᶜ*pret.* ᵈ*inf.* ᵉ*fut.* ᶠ אָרֵךְ *adj.* long ; slow ; with אַף "long suffering ;" slow to anger. ᵍ אֹרֶךְ *m.* length ; long life, long time, *lit.* length of days. ʰ אֲרֻכָּה *f. adj.* long.

2 בּוּשׁ to feel shame ; to cause shame ; to delay beyond one's expectation. PIEL *pret.*

3 גָּדוֹל *adj.* great.

4 הָלַךְ to go. KAL *part.* Poel, Exod. xix. 19, sounded long, *lit.* going and mighty.

5 יוֹם day ; "as long as," *lit.* all the days of.

6 יָסַף to add. HIPHIL *fut.* Exod. ix. 28, *lit.* ye shall not add to stay.

7 מָשַׁךְ to draw out ; to make long, to sound long. KAL *inf.*

8 עוֹלָם *m.* time long past ; *or,* time to come, future, for ever.

9 עֵת *com.* time, season.

10 פָּנִים *m. pl.* "as long as," *lit.* before.

11 רֹב *m.* multitude. רַבָּה *adj.* רָבָה to be multiplied. KAL ᵇ*fut.*

12 רָחוֹק *adj.* afar off, "long ago."

13 שָׁנָה *f.* year ; see *Life.*

Gen. xxvi. 8. a	1 a	1 Sam. i. 28.	5	Ps. cxx. 6.	11 a
Exod. ix. 28.	6	vii. 2.	11 b	cxxix. 3.	1 e
xix. 13.	7	xx. 31.	5	cxli. 3.	8
xix. 19.	4	xxv. 15.	5	Prov. iii. 2.	13
xx. 12.	1 e	xxix. 8.	5	vii. 19.	12
xxvii. 1, 9, 11.	1 g	2 Sam. iii. 1.	1 h	xxv. 15.	1 g
xxxiv. 6.	1 f	xiv. 2.	11 a	Eccles. xii. 5.γ	8
Lev. xxvi. 34, 35.	5	xix. 34.	5	Isa. xlviii. 11.	12
Num. ix. 18.	5	1 Kings iii. 11.β	11 a	xxxvii. 26.	12
ix. 19.	1 d	2 Kings xix. 25.	12	xlii. 14.	7
xiv. 18.	1 f	2 Chron. i. 11.	11 a	Jer. xv. 15.	1 f
xx. 15.	11 a	iii. 11.	5	xxix. 28.	1 h
Deut. i. 6.	11 a	vi. 13.	1 g	Lam. v. 20.	1 g
ii. 3.	11 a	vi. 31.	5	Ezek. xvii. 3.	1 f
xii. 19.	5	xv. 3.	5	xxxi. 5.	1 b
xiv. 24.	11 b	xxvi. 5.	5	xliii. 13.	7
xix. 6.	11 a	xxx. 5.	11	xl. 7, 29, 30, 33, 42,	1 g
xx. 19.	11 a	xxxvi. 21.	5	47.	1 g
xxxi. 13.	11 a	Esth. viii. 3.	9	xli. 13, 13.	1 g
Josh. vi. 5.	7	Job xi. 9.	1 h	xlii. 11, 20.	1 g
ix. 13.	11	xxvii. 8.	13	xliii. 16, 17.	1 g
xi. 18.β	11 a	Ps. lxxii. 17.	10	xlv. 6.	1 g
xiii. 1.	11 a	lxxxvi. 15.	1 f	xlv. 1, 2.	1 g
xxiv. 7.	11 a	xci. 16.	1 g	Dan. x. 1.	3
Judg. v. 28.	2	cxvi. 2.	5	Hos. xiii. 13.	9

a lit. days were prolonged to him. *β lit.* many days. *γ lit.* the house of ages.

LONG (V)

1 אָוָה to desire earnestly, to have a strong affection, or to long for. PIEL [a] *pret.* HITHPAEL [b] *fut.*

2 חָכָה to wait in hope and expectation of some benefit or advantage. PIEL *part.*

3 חָשַׁק to love, to delight in, to desire, *seq.* לְ; expressive of intense affection. KAL *pret.*

4 יָאַב earnestly to desire and long after. KAL *pret.*

5 כָּלָה to be quite done, effected; to be consumed. PIEL *fut.*

6 כָּמַהּ to pine with longing. KAL *pret.*

7 כָּסַף Schultens, upon Job, says that this word in Arabic signifies to be pale, and as paleness is the effect of earnest longing and desire, hence it is used to signify vehemently to desire or long for a thing. NIPHAL [a] *pret.* [b] *inf.*

8 תִּקְוָה *f.* expectation, hope.

9 שָׁקַק to run up and down; to be eager for. KAL *part.* Poel.

10 תָּאַב to desire, to long after. KAL [a] *pret.* [b] תַּאֲבָה *f.* desire, longing.

Gen. xxxi. 30.	7 b a	1 Chron. xi. 17.	1 b	Ps. cvii. 9.	9
xxxiv. 8.	3	Job iii. 21.	2	cxix. 20.	10 b
Deut. xii. 20.	1 a	vi. 8.	8	cxix. 40, 174.	10 a
2 Sam. xiii. 39.	5	Ps. lxiii. 1.	6	cxix. 131.	4
xxiii. 15.	1 b	lxxxiv. 2.	7 a		

LOOK

1 בִּין to distinguish, to attend to, to look well to, *seq.* לְ. KAL and HIPHIL *fut.*

2 חוּל *i. q.* יָחַל to wait, to expect, to abide. KAL and HIPHIL *fut.*

3 חָזָה to look, to behold, *seq.* בְּ; to see, so as to be happy in or pleased with what we see; to contemplate with delight. KAL [a] *imp.* [b] *fut.* [c] חֲזוּ Ch. *m.* look, appearance.

4 לֵב *m.* the heart; "look well," *lit.* set thy heart.

5 נָבַט to look, with attention and observation, with pleasure, with hope and expectation, with favour, respect, and regard, with concern, with fear, with consideration and compassion, with indignation. Lot's wife looked back on Sodom with a look of affection to the place, of regret to leave it, and of unbelief and distrust of its threatened destruction. The same word is used of the prohibition to Lot in Gen xix. 17. PIEL [a] *pret.* HIPHIL [b] *pret.* [c] *inf.* [d] *imp.* [e] *fut.* [f] *part.*

6 עַיִן *com.* the eye; "look well," *lit.* set thine eye upon.

7 פָּנָה to turn oneself; to turn in order to look at anything. KAL [a] *pret.* [b] *inf.* [c] *imp.* [d] *fut.* [e] *part.* Poel. HIPHIL [f] *pret.* [g] *part.* [h] פָּנִים *m. pl.* face.

8 פָּקַד to go to see, to visit; to look after, to take care of. KAL *fut.*

9 צָפָה to look out, to view from a distance or from a watch-tower; to look out for, to watch. KAL [a] *part.* Poel. PIEL [b] *fut.*

10 קָוָה to wait, expect, hope for. PIEL [a] *pret.* [b] *inf.* [c] *fut.*

11 רָאָה to see. KAL [a] *pret.* [b] *inf.* [c] *imp.* [d] *fut.* [e] *part.* Poel. NIPHAL [f] *fut.* HITHPAEL [g] *fut.* [h] רְאִי *m.* looking-glass.

[i] רְאִי *m.* appearance. [k] מַרְאָה *f.* vision; looking-glass.
[l] מַרְאֶה *m.* appearance.

12 שָׁנַח to look, to see, to behold; to look narrowly. HIPHIL [a] *pret.* [b] *fut.* [c] *part.*

13 שׂוּם to set, put, place. KAL [a] *imp.* [b] *fut.*

14 שָׁזַף to look upon, to scan. KAL *pret.*

15 שׁוּר to look round or about. KAL *fut.*

16 שִׁית to set, or place. KAL *imp.*

17 שָׁמַר to keep watch; to observe. KAL *fut.*

18 שָׁעָה to look, to have respect to; to look, expecting help, *seq.* אֶל, עַל, and בְּ. KAL [a] *pret.* [b] *imp.* [c] *fut.*

19 שָׁקַף to project over, to bend forward; to look forth or abroad, as from a window, &c. NIPHAL [a] *pret.* [b] *part.* HIPHIL [c] *pret.* [d] *imp.* [e] *fut.*

Gen. vi. 12.	11 d	1 Sam. ix. 16.	11 a	Ps. lxxx. 14.	5 d
viii. 13.	11 d	xiii. 18.	19 b	lxxxiv. 9.	5 d
ix. 16.	11 a	xiv. 16.	11 d	lxxxv. 11.	19 a
xii. 11.	11 l	xvi. 6.	11 d	ci. 5.γ	6
xiii. 14.	11 c	xvi. 7,7,7.	5 e, 11 d d	cii. 19.	19 c
xv. 5.	5 d	xvi. 12.	11 i	civ. 32.	5 f
xvi. 13.	11 a	xvii. 18.	8	cix. 25.	11 d
xviii. 2.	11 d	xvii. 42.	5 e	cxix. 132.	7 c
xviii. 16.	19 e	xxiv. 8.	5 e	cxli. 4.	5 d
xix. 17, 26.	5 e	2 Sam. i. 7.	7 d	Prov. iv. 25.	5 e
xx. 28.	19 e	ii. 20.	7 d	vi. 17.	5 e
xxii. 13.	11 d	vi. 16.	19 a	vii. 6.	19 a
xxiv. 16.	11 l	ix. 8.	7 a	vii. 18.	1 k
xxvi. 7.	11 l	xi. 2.	11 l	xv. 15.	l
xxvi. 8.	19 e	xiii. 34.	11 d	xxi. 4.	6
xxix. 2.	11 d	xvi. 12.	18 c	xxiii. 31.	11 d
xxix. 32.	11 a	xviii. 24.	11 d	xxiv. 32.	11 a
xxxiii. 1.	11 d	xxii. 42.	18 c	xxvii. 23.	16, 4
xxxvii. 25.	11 d	xxiv. 20.	19 e	Eccles. ii. 11.	7 a
xxxix. 23.	11 e	1 Kings vii. 25, 25,		iii. 3.	7 a
xl. 6.	11 d	25, 25.	7 e	xii. 3.	19 c
xl. 7.	7 h	xviii. 43, 43.	5 d e	Cant. i. 6, 6.	11 d, 14
xli. 33.	11 d	xix. 6.	5 e	ii. 9.	12 c
xlii. 1.	11 g	2 Kings ii. 24.	11 d	iv. 8.	15
Exod. ii. 11, 25.	11 d	iii. 14.	5 e	vi. 10.	19 b
ii. 12.	7 d	vi. 30.	11 d	vi. 13.	3 b
iii. 2.	11 d	vi. 32.	11 c	vii. 4.	9 a
iii. 6.	5 c	ix. 2.	11 c	Isa. ii. 11.	6
iv. 31.	11 a	ix. 30, 32.	19 e	v. 2, 7.	10 c
v. 21.	11 d	x. 3.	11 a	v. 4.	10 a
x. 10.	11 c	x. 23.	11 c	v. 30.	5 a
xiv. 24.	19 e	xi. 14.	11 d	viii. 17.	10 a
xvi. 10.	7 d	xv. 8, 11.	11 g	viii. 21.	7 a
xxv. 40.	11 c	1 Chron. xii. 17.	11 d	viii. 22.	5 e
xxxiii. 8.	5 b	xv. 29.	19 a	x. 12.	6
xxxviii. 8.	11 k	xxi. 21.	5 e	xvi. 9.	12 b
xxxix. 43.	11 d	2 Chron. iv. 4, 4, 4, 4.	7 e	xvii. 7, 8.	18 c
Lev. xiii. 3, 5, 6,		xiii. 14.	7 d	xxii. 4.	18 b
25, 27, 32, 34,		xx. 24.	7 d	xxii. 8.	5 e
36, 39, 43, 50,		xxiii. 13.	11 d	xxii. 11.	5 e
51, 55, 56.	11 a	xxiv. 22.	11 d	xxviii. 4.	11 e
xiii. 12.α	11 l, 6	xxvi. 20.	7 d	xxxi. 1.	18 a
xiii. 21, 26, 31, 53.	11 d	Neh. iv. 14.	11 d	xxxiii. 20.	3 a
xiv. 3, 37, 39, 44,		Esth. i. 11.	11 l	xlii. 18.	5 d
48.	11 a	ii. 15.	11 e	xlv. 22.	7 c
Num. xii. 10.	7 d	Job iii. 9.	10 c	li. 1, 2, 6.	5 d
xv. 39.	11 a	vi. 19.	5 b	lvi. 11.	7 a
xvi. 42.	19 e	vii. 2.	7 c	lix. 11.	10 c
xvii. 9.	11 d	vii. 2.	10 c	lxiii. 5.	5 e
xxi. 8.	11 a	viii. 27.	17	lxiii. 15.	5 d
xxi. 20.	19 a	xx. 21.	2	lxiv. 3.	10 c
xxiii. 28.	19 b	xxvii. 24.	5 e	lxvi. 2.	5 e
xxiv. 20, 21.	11 d	xxx. 26.	10 a	lxvi. 24.	11 a
Deut. ix. 16.	11 d	xxxiii. 27.	15	Jer. viii. 15.	10 b
ix. 27.	7 d	xxxv. 5.	5 d	xiii. 16.	10 a
xxvi. 7.	11 d	xxxvii. 18.	11 h	xiv. 19.	10 b
xxvi. 15.	19 d	xl. 12.	11 c	xxxix. 12.	13 a, 6
xxviii. 32.	11 e	Ps. v. 3.	9 b	xl. 4.	13 b, 6
Josh. v. 13.	11 d	xiv. 2.	19 c	xlvi. 5.	7 f
viii. 20.	7 d	xviii. 27.β	18 b	xlvii. 3.	7 f
xv. 2, 7.	7 e	xxii. 17.	5 e	Lam. ii. 16.	10 a
Judg. v. 28.	19 a	xxv. 18.	11 c	iii. 50.	19 e
vi. 14.	7 d	xxxiii. 13.	5 b	Ezek. i. 4.	11 d
vii. 17.	11 d	xxxiii. 14.	12 a	ii. 6.	7 h
ix. 43.	11 d	xxxiv. 5.	5 b	iii. 9.	11 d
xiii. 19, 20.	11 e	xxxv. 17.	11 d	iii. 9.	7 h
xx. 40.	7 d	xl. 12.	11 b	viii. 3.	7 e
1 Sam. i. 11.	11 b d	liii. 2.	19 c	viii. 7.	11 d
vi. 19.	11 a	lxix. 20.	10 c	x. 1, 9.	11 d

Ezek. x. 11.	7 d	Ezek. xlvi. 1, 12, 19.	7 e	Nah. ii. 8.		7 g
xi. 1.	7 e	xlvii. 2.	7 e	iii. 7.		11 e
xvi. 8.	11 d	Dan. i. 13.	11 f	Hab. i. 13, 13.		5 c e
xxi. 21.	11 a	vii. 20.	3 c	ii. 15.		5 c
xxiii. 15.	11 l	x. 5.	11 d	Hag. i. 9.		7 b
xxix. 16.	7 b	xii. 5.	11 a	Zech. ii. 1.		11 d
xl. 6, 20, 22.	7 h	Hos. iii. 1.	7 e	iv. 2.		11 a
xliii. 1.	7 e	Obad. 12, 13.	11 d	v. 1, 9.		11 d
xliii. 17.	7 b	Jonah ii. 4.	5 c	vi. 1.		11 d
xliv. 1.	7 e	Micah iv. 11.	3 b	xii. 10.		5 b
xliv. 4.	11 d	vii. 7.	9 b			

α *lit.* to all the sight of the eyes of the priest. β *lit.* lofty eyes.
γ *lit.* that is lofty of eyes.

LOOPS

לֻלָאֹת *f. pl.* loops into which the hooks were put in the curtains of the holy tabernacle : Exod. xxvi. 4, &c.

LOOSE

1 זָחַח to move oneself, to be taken off, displaced ; to be removed. NIPHAL *fut.*

2 חָלַץ to draw off gently, to put off. KAL ᵃ *pret.* ᵇ *part.* Paül.

3 מָסַס to dissolve, to melt. NIPHAL *fut.*

4 נָטַשׁ to be loose; to forsake. NIPHAL *pret.* Isa. xxxiii. 23, *marg.* 'or, they have forsaken thy tacklings.' Gesenius, are broken in pieces. LXX. ἐρράγησαν. Symm. ἐξερρίφη.

5 נָשַׁל to draw out or off. KAL *imp.*

6 נָתַר to move with a sudden springing motion ; to leap, to let loose. HIPHIL ᵃ *fut.* ᵇ *part.*

7 פָּתַח to open, to let loose, to set free. NIPHAL ᵃ *pret.* ᵇ *inf.* PIEL ᶜ *pret.* ᵈ *inf.* ᵉ *fut.* HITHPAEL ᶠ *imp.*

8 רָחַק to be far away, to put far away. NIPHAL *fut.* כתיב.

9 רָתַק to bind. NIPHAL (in a contrary signification) *fut.* Eccles. xii. 6, קרי.

10 שָׁלַח to send, to send away. KAL ᵃ *part.* Paül. PIEL ᵇ *pret.*

11 שְׁרָא Ch. to loose, to unbind, to solve. P'AL ᵃ *part.* ITHPAEL ᵇ *part.*

Gen. xlix. 21.	10 a	Job xxx. 11, 11.	7 c, 10 b	Isa. xx. 2.		7 c
Exod. xxviii. 28.	1	xxxviii. 31.	7 e	xxxiii. 23.		4
xxxix. 21.	1	xxxix. 5.	7 c	xlv. 1.		7 e
Lev. xiv. 7.	10 b	Ps. cii. 20.	7 d	li. 14.		7 b
Deut. xxv. 9.	2 a	cv. 20.	6 a	lii. 2.		7 f
xxv. 10.	2 b	cxvi. 16.	7 c	lviii. 6.		7 d
Josh. v. 15.	5	cxlvi. 7.	6 b	Jer. xl. 4.		7 c
Judg. xv. 14.	3	Eccles. xii. 6.	9, or 8	Dan. iii. 25.		11 a
Job vi. 9.	6 a	Isa. v. 27.	7 a	v. 6.		11 b
xii. 18.	7 c					

LOP

סָעֵף to divide ; to cut off branches. PIEL *part.* Isa. x. 33.

LORD, Lord, lord

1 אָדוֹן *m.* lord, master, as owner or ruler: Gen. xviii. 12, &c., (mostly without a capital, thus, "lord ;" with a capital, thus, "Lord," in the index.) אֲדֹנָי the Lord, used only of God: Gen. xv. 2, &c. (distinguished by a capital, thus, "Lord.")

2 אַדִּיר *adj.* excellent, noble, lordly.

3 בַּעַל *m.* owner, master.

4 גְּבִיר *m.* lord, from the idea of power: Gen. xxvii. 29, 37.

5 יְהֹוָה Jehovah, the divinely communicated name of the Supreme God ; that "glorious and fearful name" by which he is known to his church and people. It expresses the eternity and immutability of the divine nature, and the faithfulness of God to all his purposes and promises. (In our version it is distinguished by "LORD" in small capitals. See also *Jehovah*.)

6 יָהּ supposed to be an abbreviation of the former, or another name derived from the same root, to express his essential attribute of self-existence.—*Gussetius.*

7 מָרֵא Ch. *m.* lord.

8 סֶרֶן *m.* a prince, used only of the five princes of the Philistines.

9 רַב Ch. *adj.* great, master, lord.

10 רוּד to have dominion. KAL *pret.*

11 רַבְרְבָן Ch. great, chief, leader, prince.

12 שַׂר *m.* leader, prince.

13 שָׁלִישׁ *m.* see *Captain.*

No. 5, LORD, No. 1 a, Lord, No. 1, lord, not included.

Gen. xix. 18.	1	Ps. lxxvii. 11.	6	Ps. cxlvii. 5.	1
xxvii. 29, 37.	4	lxxxix. 8, 8.	5, 6	cxlviii. 1, 1.	6, 5
xxxiii. 13.	1	xciv. 7, 12.	6	cxlviii. 14.	6
Exod. xv. 2.	1	xcvii. 5, 5.	5, 1	cxlix. 1, 1.	6, 5
xvii. 16, 16.	6, 5	cii. 18.	6	cxlix. 9.	6
xxii. 17.	1	civ. 35, 35.	5, 6	cl. 1, 6, 6.	6
xxxiv. 23.	1	cv. 45.	6	Isa. i. 24.	1
Num. xxi. 28.	3	cvi. 1, 1.	1	x. 16, 16.	1, 1 a
Deut. x. 17, 17.	1	cvi. 48, 48.	5, 6	x. 33, 33.	1, 5
Josh. iii. 11, 13.	8	cx. 1, 1.	1	xvi. 1.	1
xiii. 3.	8	cxi. 1, 1.	6, 5	xix. 4, β	1
Judg. iii. 3.	8	cxii. 1, 1.	1	xxi. 8.	1 a
v. 25. α	2	cxiii. 1, 1.	6, 5	xxviii. 2.	1
vi. 13.	1	cxiii. 9.	6	li. 22.	1
xvi. 5, 8, 18, 18, 23,		cxiv. 7.	1	J-r. ii. 31.	10
27, 30.	8	cxv. 17, 18, 18.	8	Ezek. xxiii. 23.	13
1 Sam. v. 8, 11.	8	cxvi. 19, 19.	5, 6	Dan. ii. 10.	9
vi. 4, 4, 12, 16, 18.	8	cxvii. 2, 2.	5, 6	ii. 47.	7
vii. 7.	8	cxviii. 5, 5, 14, 17,		iv. 19, 24.	7
xxiv. 8.	1	18, 19.	6	iv. 36.	11
xxix. 2, 6, 7.	8	cxxii. 4, 4.	6	v. 1, 9, 10.	11
2 Sam. xix. 9.	1	cxxx. 3, 3.	6, 5	v. 23, 23.	7, 11
2 Kings vii. 2, 17, 19.	13	cxxxv. 1, 1.	6, 5	vi. 17.	11
1 Chron. xii. 19.	8	cxxxv. 3, 3.	6, 5	vii. 18.	11
Ezra vii. 25.	12	cxxxv. 4.	6	viii. 8.	1
x. 3.	1 a	cxxxv. 5.	1	Hos. xii. 14.	1
Neh. iii. 5.	1	cxxxv. 21, 21.	5, 6	Micah iv. 13.	1
viii. 10.	1	cxxxvi. 3, 3.	1	Zech. iv. 14.	1
x. 29.	1	cxli. 1, 1.	1	vi. 5.	1
Ps. viii. 1, 1.	5, 1	cxlvi. 10, 10.	6, 5	Mal. iii. 1.	1
xlv. 11.	1	cxlvii. 1, 20.	6		

α *lit.* a dish or bowl of princes. β *lit.* lords.

LOSE

1 אָבַד to perish ; to be lost, as for a time ; to have gone astray; *comp.* ἀπολωλός in the N. T., Matt. xviii. 11, Luke xix. 10 ; in Eccles. iii. 6, *opp.* בָּקַשׁ. KAL ᵃ *pret.* ᵇ *fut.* ᶜ *part.* Poel. PIEL ᵈ *inf.* ᵉ אֲבֵדָה *f.* lost thing.

2 אָסַף to take away, as things gathered into the same bundle for that purpose. KAL *pret.*

3 חָטָא to sin, to suffer for sin, to bear the loss, as if guilty. PIEL *fut.*

4 כָּרַת to cut off. HIPHIL *fut.* 1 Kings xviii. 5. In the authorized edition of 1611, it is translated, "that we leese not," *marg.* 'that we cut not off ourselves from the beasts.'

5 נָפַח to breathe, to cause to breathe out. HIPHIL *pret.* Job xxxi. 39.

6 נָפַל to fall. KAL ᵃ *fut.* ᵇ *part.* Poel.

7 שֶׁבֶת *m.* ceasing ; "loss of time."

8 שָׁחַת to be corrupt. PIEL *pret.*

9 שָׁכַל to be bereaved, to lose children. KAL [a] *part.* Paül.
    [b] שְׁכֻלִים *m. pl.* bereavement. [c] שִׁכּוּל *m. id.*

Gen. xxxi. 39.	3	1 Sam. ix. 3.	1 b	Isa. xlvii. 8, 9.	9 c
Exod. xxi. 19.	7	ix. 20.	1 c	xlix. 20. a	9 b
xxii. 4.	1 e	1 Kings xviii. 5.	4	xlix. 21.	9 a
Lev. vi. 3, 4.	1 e	xx. 25.	6 b	Jer. l. 6.	1 c
Num. vi. 12.	6 a	Job xxxi. 39.	5	Ezek. xix. 5.	1 a
Deut. xxii. 3.	1 e	Ps. cxix. 176.	1 c	xxxiv. 4, 16.	1 a
xxii. 3, 16.	1 e b	Prov. xxiii. 8.	8	xxxvii. 11.	1 a
Judg. xviii. 25.	2	Eccles. iii. 6.	1 d		

a lit. of thy bereavement.

LOT

1 גּוֹרָל a lot, primarily a stone, which is cast or drawn in doubtful or equal cases, as when several persons are to have each a share, to determine which share each shall have ; the share or portion so allotted ; any portion or possession assigned by God's providence : Lev. xvi. 8, &c.

2 חֶבֶל *com.* a cord, a measuring-line ; a plot, lot, or tract of land, measured or laid out.

3 נָפַל to fall ; to fall, as an estate or inheritance falls to a man ; to divide by lot. HIPHIL [a] *pret.* [b] *inf.* [c] *imp.* [d] *fut.*

No. 1 not included.

Deut. xxxii. 9.	2	1 Chron. xvi. 18.	2	Ezek. xlvii. 22.	3 d
Josh. xiii. 6.	3 c	Ps. cv. 11.	2	xlviii. 29.	3 d
xxiii. 4.	3 a	Ezek. xlv. 1.	3 b		

LOTHE, OR LOATHE

1 בָּאַשׁ to stink, to be loathsome and odious ; see *Abhor.* HIPHIL *fut.*

2 בּוּס to tread under foot, to despise. KAL *fut.*

3 גָּעַל to loathe, reject with aversion, or throw away ; see *Abhor.* KAL [a] *pret.* [b] *part.* Poel. [c] גֹּעַל *m.* loathing.

4 זָרָא *f.* that which is forced out or vomited up as being loathsome to the stomach.

5 לָאָה to be tired and disgusted with the tediousness and trouble of an affair ; to loathe, to have an aversion to. NIPHAL *pret.*

6 מָאַס to reject with contempt and disdain as hateful, greatly disagreeable, and not worth our regard ; see *Abhor, Despise.* KAL [a] *pret.* NIPHAL [b] *fut.* Job vii. 5, see *Melt.* Here it is applied to a wound running with fetid matter ; "my wound breaks through the skin, and runs with loathsome matter."

7 קוּט to loathe, to nauseate. NIPHAL *pret.*, seq. בִּפְנֵי.

8 קוּץ to feel disgusting, to abhor. KAL *pret.*

9 קָלָה to be light, loathsome ; to be dried up. NIPHAL *part.*

10 קָצַר to be shortened. KAL *fut.* Zech. xi. 8, *marg.* 'was straitened for them ;' *lit.* my soul is short ; *i.e.* I am impatient.

Exod. vii. 18.	5	Ps. xxxviii. 7.	9	Ezek. xvi. 5.	3 c
Num. xi. 20.	4	Prov. xiii. 5.	1	xvi. 45, 45.	3 b a
xxi. 5.	8	xxvii. 7.	2	xx. 43.	7
Job vii. 5.	6 b	Jer. xiv. 19.	3 a	xxxvi. 31.	7
vii. 16.	6 a	Ezek. vi. 9.	7	Zech. xi. 8.	10

LOUD

1 גָּדוֹל *adj.* great ; applied to sound.

---

2 הָמָה to rage, to roar, to make a great noise ; see *Noise.* KAL *part.* Poel.

3 חָזָק *adj.* strong in a prevailing degree. [a] חָזָק *adj.*

4 עֹז *m.* strength ; "loud instruments."

5 מְאֹד *m.* much, exceeding ; louder and louder.

6 רוּם to be lifted up. KAL *part.* Poel.

7 שָׁמַע to hear ; to make to be heard. HIPHIL [a] *fut.* [b] שֵׁמַע *m.* hearing.

Gen. xxxix. 14.	1	2 Chron. xv. 14.	1	Esth. iv. 1.	1
Exod. xix. 16.	3	xx. 19.	1	Ps. cl. 5.	7 b
xix. 19, 19. a	3 a, 5	xxx. 21.	4	Prov. vii. 11.	2
Deut. xxvii. 14.	6	xxxii. 18.	1	xxvii. 14.	1
1 Sam. xxviii. 12.	1	Ezra iii. 12, 13.	1	Isa. xxxvi. 13.	1
2 Sam. xv. 23.	1	x. 12.	1	Ezek. viii. 18.	1
xix. 4.	1	Neh. ix. 4.	1	ix. 1.	1
1 Kings viii. 55.	1	xii. 42.	7 a	xi. 13.	1
2 Kings xviii. 28.	1				

a lit. going and strengthening exceedingly.

LOVE

1 אָהַב and אָהֵב to love that in which a man delights, or which he earnestly desires ; it implies ardent and vehement inclination of the mind, at the same time tenderness and fulness of affection, and is to be taken in the same extensive sense as the English word "love ;" and is used of the unspeakable love and tender mercies of God in covenant with his people. *Seq. acc.*, rarely *c.* לְ and בְּ ; *seq. inf. c.* לְ. *Contr.* שָׁנָא. KAL [a] *pret.* [b] *inf.* [c] *imp.* [d] *fut.* [e] *part.* Poel. NIPHAL [f] *part.* PIEL [g] *part.* a lover, but only in a bad sense. [h] אַהֲבָה *f.* love. [i] אֲהָבִים *m. pl.* of אַהַב [k] אֳהָבִים *m. pl.* of אֹהַב.

2 דּוֹד *m.* love, only used in the plural, דֹּדִים.

3 חָבַב to cherish with tender love, to hide in the bosom, to love fervently, and so to protect. KAL *part.* Deut. xxxiii. 3.

4 מַחְמָד *m.* that which is the object of desire, lovely.

5 חֶסֶד kindness, mercy, loving-kindness.

6 חָשַׁק to connect or join together. It signifies that connexion of heart with any object which inclines us to love it, to delight in it, to desire and long for it ; to set one's love on. KAL *pret.*

7 טוֹב *adj.* good, loving.

8 יָדִיד *adj. const.* : see *Beloved.*

9 עָגַב to be charmed, to be greatly delighted ; of impure love ; see *Dote.* KAL [a] *part.* Poel. [b] עֲגָבָה *f.* "inordinate love." [c] עֲגָבִים *m. pl.*

10 רָחַם to be tender ; to have compassion. KAL [a] *fut.* [b] רַחֲמִים *m. pl.* bowels, mercy ; tender love.

11 רֵעַ *m.* friend ; lover. [a] רֵעְיָה *f.* friend, companion ; one beloved, love.

Gen. xxii. 2.	1 a	Lev. xix. 18, 34.	1 a	Deut. xi. 1.	1 a
xxiv. 67.	1 d	Deut. iv. 37.	1 a	xi. 13, 22.	1 b
xxv. 28, 28.	1 d e	v. 10.	1 e	xiii. 3.	1 e
xxvii. 4, 9, 14.	1 a	vi. 5.	1 a	xv. 16.	1 a
xxix. 18, 30, 32.	1 d	vii. 7.	1	xix. 9.	1 b
xxix. 20.	1 d	vii. 8.	1 h	xxiii. 5.	1 a
xxxiv. 3.	1 d	vii. 9.	1 e	xxx. 6, 16, 20.	1 a
xxxvii. 3, 4.	1 a	vii. 13.	1 a	xxxiii. 3.	3
xliv. 20.	1 d	x. 12, 15.	1 a	Josh. xxii. 5.	1 a
Exod. xx. 6.	1 a	x. 18.	1 e	xxiii. 11.	1 a
xxi. 5.	1 a	x. 19.	1 a	Judg. v. 31.	1 e

9 צָנַע to depress; to be submissive, humble, modest. KAL part. Paül.

10 צָעַר to be small; to be low and despised, to be brought low. KAL fut.

11 קָצֶה f. end.

12 שָׁחַח to bow down. KAL [a] fut. NIPHAL [b] fut.

13 שָׁפֵל to be brought low, depressed, cast down, e.g. a mountain, lofty trees, a city; metaph. to be made low, of persons who fall from a high state of dignity, of the voice, of the spirit. KAL [a] pret. [b] fut. HIPHIL [c] pret. [d] inf. [e] fut. [f] part. שָׁפָל adj. low. [h] שֵׁפֶל m. low estate, low place. [i] שִׁפְלָה f. id. [k] שְׁפֵלָה f. low plain, low country.

14 תַּחְתּוֹן adj. what is underneath, lower. [a] תַּחְתִּי adj. lower part.

a marg. '*or*, impoverished, *or*, weakened.'

LOW

נָעָה to low as an ox or cow. KAL *inf.* 1 Sam. vi. 12; *fut.* Job vi. 5.

קוֹל m. voice: 1 Sam. xv. 14.

LUCIFER

הֵילֵל m. according to Lxx., Vulg., Targ., Rabbin., Luth., brilliant star, i.e. Lucifer, the morning star. This suits best with the context and parallelism. Isa. xiv. 12.

LUCRE

בֶּצַע m. profit, gain: 1 Sam. viii. 3.

LUMP

דְּבֵלָה f. a lump of figs; see *Cake.* 2 Kings xx. 7: Isa. xxxviii. 21.

LURK

מַאֲרָב m. ambush; lurking-places: Ps. x. 8.

מַחֲבֹאִים m. pl. hiding-places: 1 Sam. xxiii. 23.

יָשַׁב to sit; to lie in ambush, to lurk. KAL part. Poel, Ps. xvii. 12, marg. 'sitting.'

צָפַן to hide, conceal; to conceal oneself, to lurk in ambush. KAL fut. Prov. i. 11, 18.

LUST

1 אָוָה to desire, implying with impulse and vehemence; see

LOW

1 אָדָם m. see *Man.* בֵּן m. son: Ps. xlix. 2, low and high, lit. sons of אָדָם, and sons of אִישׁ; lxii. 9, men of low degree, lit. sons of Adam.

2 דָּלַל to hang down; to be feeble, weak. KAL pret.

3 חָסֵר to be diminished; to want. PIEL fut. Ps. viii. 5, "a little lower" in condition than angels; comp. Phil. ii. 7.

4 כָּנַע to bow the knee; to be low, depressed. HIPHIL [a] pret.

5 כָּרַע to bow the knee; to be in a feeble, afflicted condition. HIPHIL [a] pret. [b] inf.

6 מַטָּה adv. beneath; "very low," lit. low, low.

7 מָכַךְ to decay, to be brought low. KAL [a] fut. HOPHAL [b] pret.

8 עָנָה to afflict. KAL [a] fut. [b] עָנִי adj. (see *Meek*), lowly. [c] עָנִי adj. afflicted, poor, used of the Messiah, Zech. ix. 9. Matt. xxi. 5, rendered "meek."

Desire. PIEL ᵃ *fut.* HITHPAEL ᵇ *pret.* ᶜ *fut.* ᵈ *part.* ᵉ אַוָּת *f.* desire. ᶠ תַּאֲוָה *f.* lust.

2 חָמַד to desire ; to delight in ; to covet. KAL *fut.*

3 נֶפֶשׁ *com.* animal life, soul ; affections of the soul.

4 שְׁרִירוּת *f.* hardness, stubbornness, coupled with לֵב and רַע לֵב hardness of heart, stubbornness ; common translation, imagination, lust.

Exod. xv. 9.	3	Deut. xiv. 26.	1 a	Ps. lxxxi. 12.	4
Num. xi. 4. ᵃ	1 b f	Ps. lxxviii. 18.	3	cvi. 14. ᵃ	1 a f
xi. 34.	1 d	lxxviii. 30.	1 f	Prov. vi. 25.	2
Deut. xii. 15, 20, 21. β	1 e				

a marg. 'lusted a lust.'   *β lit.* in all the desire of thy soul.

LUSTY

שָׁמֵן *adj. fat* : Judg. iii. 29, of a strong, lusty man.

MAD

1 הָלַל to shine ; to make oneself shine, to boast of oneself, to be foolish ; to be puffed up with vain glory, to vaunt, to rave with foolish conceit ; hence, to be mad, to rage. POEL ᵃ *fut.* ᵇ *part.* HITHPOEL ᶜ *imp.* ᵈ *fut.* ᵉ הוֹלֵלָה *f.* madness, implies so great a departure from wisdom, that the mind, without any control, rushes on with a blind fury, μανία. ᶠ הוֹלֵלוּת *f. id.*

2 לָהַהּ to faint with thirst ; in Hithpalpel the word may seem to express the quick breathing of a dog or of man, exhausted by running or the heat of the sun ; hence, rabid or mad. HITHPALPEL *part.*

3 שָׁגַע *m.* Pual, spoken of one raving, frenzied, furious, as if inspired, of false prophets ; also of true prophets in contempt. PUAL ᵃ *part.* HITHPAEL ᵇ *inf.* ᶜ *part.* ᵈ שִׁגָּעוֹן *m.* madness.

Deut. xxviii. 28.	3 d	Eccles. i. 17.	1 e	Isa. xliv. 25.	1 a
xxviii. 34.	3 a	ii. 2.	1 b	Jer. xxv. 16.	1 c
1 Sam. xxi. 13.	1 d	ii. 12.	1 e	xxix. 26.	3 a
xxi. 14.	3 c	vii. 7.	1 a	l. 38.	1 d
xxi. 15, 15.	3 a b	vii. 15.	1 e	li. 7.	1 d
2 Kings ix. 11.	3 a	ix. 3.	1 e	Hos. ix. 7.	3 a
Ps. cii. 8.	1 b	x. 13.	1 f	Zech. xii. 4.	3 d
Prov. xxvi. 18.					

MAGICIAN

חַרְטֻמִּים *m. pl.* men in the early ages of the world pretending to profound learning, Gr. ἐξηγηταί, science, and curious arts ; so called, perhaps, from חֶרֶט a style, or graving-tool, as they might portray their pretended science and schemes in mysterious hieroglyphical figures upon stone, brass, &c, Gen. xli. 8, &c. חַרְטֹם Ch. *m. id.* Dan. ii. 10, 27 ; iv. 7, 9 ; v. 11.

MAGISTRATE

יָרַשׁ to possess. KAL *part.* Poel, Judg. xviii. 7. עָצַר *m.* restraint, rule, authority : Judg. xviii. 7, *marg.* 'possessor, *or*, heir of restraint.'

שְׁפַט Ch. to judge. P'AL *part. active,* Ezra vii. 25.

MAGNIFY

1 גָּדַל to be or become great. KAL ᵃ *fut.* PIEL ᵇ *pret.* ᶜ *inf.* ᵈ *imp.* ᵉ *fut.* HIPHIL ᶠ *pret.* ᵍ *inf.* ʰ *fut.* ⁱ *part.* HITHPAEL ᵏ *pret.* ˡ *fut.*

2 נָשָׂא to lift up. NIPHAL *fut.*

3 שָׂנָא to be or become great ; to magnify ; to extol with praise. HIPHIL *fut.*

Gen. xix. 19.	1 h	Job xxxvi. 24.	3	Isa. xlii. 21.	1 h
Josh. iii. 7.	1 c	Ps. xxxiv. 3.	1 d	Jer. xlviii. 26, 42.	1 f
iv. 14.	1 b	xxxv. 26.	1 i	Lam. i. 9.	1 f
2 Sam. vii. 26.	1 a	xxxv. 27.	1 a	Ezek. xxxviii. 23.	1 k
1 Chron. xvii. 24.	1 f	xxxviii. 16.	1 f	Dan. viii. 11.	1 f
xxii. 5.	1 g	xl. 16.	1 a	viii. 25.	1 h
xxix. 25.	1 f	lv. 12.	1 f	xi. 36, 37.	1 l
2 Chron. i. 1.	1 e	lxix. 30.	1 e	Zech. xii. 7.	1 a
xxxii. 23.	1 f	lxx. 4.	1 b	Zeph. ii. 8, 10.	1 h
Job vii. 17.	1 e	cxxxviii. 2.	1 f	Mal. i. 5.	1 a
xix. 5.	1 h	Isa. x. 15.	1 l		

MAHALATH

מַחֲלַת *m.* a stringed instrument, lute or guitar, accompanied by the voice : Ps. liii. title, lxxxviii. title.

MAID

1 אָמָה *f.* maid-servant, bond-servant ; hand-maid, bond-maid : Gen. xx. 17, &c. The son of a hand-maid is a home-born slave, belonging of right to the master, though the father go out free, Exod. xxi. 4 ; used to denote the people of God as of his family.

2 בְּתוּלָה a marriageable virgin. ᵃ בְּתוּלִים *m. pl.* virginity.

3 נַעַר a young person, male or female, probably from the agility and vigour with which they act. נַעֲרָה *f.*

4 נְקֵבָה *f.* a female ; maid-child.

5 עַלְמָה *f.* virgin.

6 שִׁפְחָה *f.* one of the family, family servant, maid-servant, hand-maid ; for the difference between it and אָמָה, see 1 Sam. xxv. 41.

No. 1 not included.

Gen. xii. 16.	6	1 Sam. i. 18.	6	Prov. ix. 3.	3
xvi. 1, 2, 3, 5, 6, 8.	6	viii. 16.	6	xxvii. 27.	3
xxiv. 35.	6	ix. 11.	3	xxx. 19.	5
xxv. 12.	6	xxv. 27.	6	xxx. 23.	6
xxix. 24, 24, 29.	6	xxviii. 21, 22.	6	xxxi. 15.	3
xxx. 4, 7, 9, 10, 12, 18, 43.	6	2 Sam. vi. 6, 7, 12, 15, 17, 19.	6	Eccles. ii. 7.	6
xxxiii. 1, 2, 6.	6	2 Kings iv. 2, 16.	3	Isa. xiv. 2.	6
xxxv. 25, 26.	6	v. 2, 4.	3	xxiv. 2.	6
Exod. ii. 5, 5.	3, 1	v. 26.	2	Jer. ii. 32.	2
ii. 8.	3	2 Chron. xxxvi. 17.	2	xxxiv. 9, 10, 11, 11, 16, 16.	6
xi. 5.	6	Esth. ii. 4, 7, 8, 9, 9, 9, 12, 13.	3	li. 22.	2
xxii. 16.	2	iv. 4, 16.	3	Lam. v. 11.	2
Lev. xii. 5.	4	Job xxxi. 1.	2	Ezek. ix. 6.	2
Deut. xxii. 14, 17.	2 a	xli. 5.	3	xliv. 22.	2
Judg. xix. 24.	2	Ps. lxxviii. 63.	6	Joel iii. 2.	6
Ruth ii. 8, 22, 23.	3	cxxiii. 2.	6	Amos ii. 7.	6
ii. 13, 13.	6	cxlviii. 12.	6	Zech. ix. 17.	2
iii. 2.	3				

MAIL

קַשְׂקֶשֶׂת *f.* scales ; mail, a coat of mail, consisting of small plates like scales : 1 Sam. xvii. 5.

MAIMED

חָרַץ to be sharp or pointed, lacerated. KAL *part.* Paūl, Lev. xxii. 22.

MAINTAIN, MAINTENANCE

1 חָזַק to make firm, strong, to strengthen, repair. PIEL *inf.*

2 חַי *adj.* living, life.

3 יָכַח to shew, to prove, in order to convince or refute by reasons, arguments, or actions. HIPHIL *fut.*

4 מְלַח Ch. *m.* salt. ᵃ מְלַח Ch. P'AL *pret.*

5 עָשָׂה to do, to make; to complete, or execute. KAL [a] *pret.* [b] *inf.* [c] *fut.*

6 תָּמַךְ to take hold of. KAL *part.* Poel.

1 Kings viii. 45, 49.	5 a	Ezra iv. 14. a	4, 4 a	Ps. xvi. 5.		6
viii. 59.	5 b	Job xiii. 15.	3	cxl. 12.		5 c
1 Chron. xxvi. 27.	3	Ps. ix. 4.	5 a	Prov. xxvii. 27.		2
2 Chron. vi. 35, 39.	5 a					

a *marg.* 'we are salted with the salt of the palace;' *or,* Gesenius, *lit.* because we have eaten the salt of, &c.

MAJESTY

1 גָּאוֹן *m.* sublimity, majesty; glory; see *Excel.* [a] גֵּאוּת *f.* a lifting up, majesty.

2 גְּדוּלָה *f.* greatness.

3 הָדָר *m.* glory, honour, majesty, splendour, beauty; "full of majesty," *marg.* 'in majesty.' [a] הֲדַר Ch. *id.*

4 הוֹד *m.* any good quality or endowment for which a person is admired, honoured, and celebrated; power, majesty.

5 רְבוּ Ch. *f.* greatness.

Esth. i. 4.		2	Ps. xciii. 1.	1 a	Isa. xxvi. 10.	1 a
1 Chron. xxix. 11, 25.	4	xcvi. 6.	3	Ezek. vii. 20.	1
Job xxxvii. 22.	4	civ. 1.	3	Dan. iv. 30.	3 a
xl. 10.	1	cxlv. 5.	4	iv. 36.	5
Ps. xxi. 5.	3	cxlv. 12.	3	v. 18, 19.	5
xxix. 4.	3	Isa. ii. 10, 19, 21.	1	Micah v. 4.	1
xlv. 3, 4.	3	xxiv. 14.	3		

MAKE

1 אֲרוּכָה *f.* healing.

2 בָּנָה to build. KAL [a] *pret.* [b] *fut.* בְּנָה Ch. P'AL [c] *part.*

3 בְּעָה Ch. to desire, to ask. P'AL *part.*

4 בָּרָא to create; to be distinguished from עָשָׂה. KAL [a] *pret.* [b] *fut.*

5 גָּדַר to hedge. KAL [a] *pret.* [b] *fut.* [c] *part.* Poel.

6 הָפַךְ to turn; to turn or make a bed. KAL *pret.*

7 הָרַג to slay. NIPHAL *inf.*

8 חוּל to bring forth, to produce; see *Form.* PULAL *pret.*

9 חָנַן to supplicate, to make (supplication). HITHPAEL *pret.*

10 חָצַב to hew, to dig. KAL *pret.*

11 חָרַם to destroy utterly; utterly to make away. HIPHIL *inf.*

12 חָרָשׁ *m.* an engraver, a worker.

13 יָסַף to add; to make more, to make. HIPHIL *fut.*

14 יָצַג to put or place persons or things in any situation. HIPHIL *pret.*

15 יָצַר to form, fashion, or shape. KAL [a] *pret.* [b] *part.* Poel.

16 כְּלִי *m.* vessels, instruments, &c.; "that is made."

17 כְּלַל Ch. to set up, to finish. SHAPHEL *inf.*

18 כָּרָה to prepare, make ready, to provide; to dig. KAL *pret.*

19 כָּרַת to cut off; to cut a sacrificed bullock in twain (Jer. xxxiv. 18), a solemn ancient rite in confirming a grant of blessings, or a compact. The parts of the animal cut in two were laid on each side at a distance, and either the party granting, or both parties contracting, passed between them: Gen. xv. 9, 10, 17; the Shechinah, or token of the divine presence, passed between the pieces. It is observable, that the next verse is the first place in Scripture where כָּרַת is applied to the cutting or making a covenant. Hence, the proper force of the word seems to be, in this case, solemnly to ratify a grant or agreement. KAL [a] *pret.* [b] *inf.* [c] *imp.* [d] *fut.* [e] *part.* Poel.

20 לָבַב (see *Cake*), to make cakes. PIEL *fut.*

21 לָבֵן to make brick. KAL [a] *inf.* [b] *fut.*

22 מְלָאכָה *f.* work: Lev. xiii. 48, *marg.* 'any work of skin.'

23 מָלַךְ to reign. HIPHIL, to make (a king): [a] *pret.* [b] *fut.*

24 נָדַר to vow. KAL *fut.*

25 נָכָה to smite, to make (a slaughter). HIPHIL *pret.*

26 נָתַן to give, to place, to make, to account one thing in the place of another, or like it; to appoint. KAL [a] *pret.* [b] *inf.* [c] *imp.* [d] *fut.* [e] *part.* Poel. NIPHAL [f] *fut.*

27 נָתַר to break; to undo, let loose. HIPHIL *fut.*

28 עֲבַד Ch. to make, to do, *i.q.* Heb. עָשָׂה. P'AL [a] *pret.* [b] *part. active.* ITHP'AL [c] *fut.* [d] *part.*

29 עָלָה to ascend. KAL *pret.*

30 עָמַד to stand; to make to stand. HIPHIL *fut.*

31 עָצַב to work, to form, to fashion, with labour and toil; to suffer pain. PIEL *pret.*

32 עָשָׂה to work, to labour, to do; to make, to do, to produce by labour; specially to make, *i.q.* to form, to construct, to prepare, to build; (to make a house, see *Build,* בָּנָה); *seq.* עַל and לְ to make upon or unto, with a double *acc.* of the material, sometimes with לְ of the thing made; to create; to produce, or yield; to make, *i.e.* to get by labour, to acquire; to make ready, to prepare, to dress; to prepare a victim, to offer; to make unto, to cause to become anything, *seq. dupl. acc.* or *seq. acc.*, and לְ, hence *i.q.* to constitute, appoint; to make war, peace, covenant; emphatically, to effect, to execute, to accomplish a thing proposed, purpose; to keep any stated day, to hold, to celebrate; to do; often עָשָׂה is so put as to express the simple idea of a verb of action, to do, to act, rendered definite only by the context or the circumstance. KAL [a] *pret.* [b] *inf.* [c] *imp.* [d] *fut.* [e] *part.* Poel. [f] *part.* Paül. NIPHAL [g] *pret.* [h] *inf.* [i] *fut.* PUAL [k] *pret.* [l] מַעֲשֶׂה *m.* work.

33 פָּלַל to pray; to make (prayer). HITHPAEL *fut.*

34 פָּלַס to weigh; to make level. PIEL *fut.*

35 פָּעַל to make, to do, implying a rational agent; *seq. acc.* and לְ of thing. KAL [a] *pret.* [b] *fut.* [c] *part.* Poel. [d] פֹּעַל *m.* work.

36 פָּקַד see *Appoint.* KAL [a] *pret.* HIPHIL [b] *pret.* [c] *fut.*

37 פָּרַץ to break forth. KAL *pret.*

38 פְּשַׁר Ch. to interpret. P'AL *inf.*

39 קוּם to rise, to stand up; to make to stand, to make to stand still. HIPHIL [a] *fut.* קוּם Ch. APHEL [b] *pret.*

40 קָרַח see *Bald.* KAL *fut.*

41 קָשַׁר to conspire. KAL [a] *pret.* [b] *fut.*

42 רָפַד to strew, to spread, a bed. PIEL *pret.*

43   רָקַח   to compound ointment.   KAL *part.* Poel.

44   שָׁוָה   Ch. to put, to set, to make.   ITHPAEL *fut.*

45   שׂוּם   to put, set, place.   KAL [a]*pret.* [b]*inf.* [c]*imp.* [d]*fut.* [e]*part.* Poel.   שׂוּם Ch. P'AL [f]*pret.* [g]*part. passive.* ITHP'AL [h]*fut.*

46   שִׁית   to set, to put, to place ; to set as, *i. e.* to make, to render ; *seq. dupl. acc., seq. acc.,* and לְ, *seq. acc.* and בְּ ; rarely *simpl.* to make, to do ; *seq. dat.* to make or prepare for any one, *i. q.* to give.   KAL [a]*pret.* [b]*imp.* [c]*fut.*

47   שָׁמֵם   to be desolate ; to make desolate.   HIPHIL *pret.*

48   שָׂרַט   to cut, to gash.   KAL *fut.*

49   שָׂרַף   to burn.   KAL *fut.*

Gen. i. 7, 16, 25, 26.	32 d	Exod. xxv. 9, 39.	32 d	Lev. ii. 7, 8, 11.	32 i	Judg. vi. 2.	32 a	2 Kings iv. 10.	32 d	2 Chron. xxviii. 24.	32 d
i. 31.	32 a	xxv. 18, 18.	32 a	vi. 21.	32 i	vi. 19.	32 d	vi. 2.	32 d	xxix. 10.	19 b
ii. 2, 2.	32 a	xxv. 19, 19.	32 c d	xiii. 48.	22	viii. 27.	32 d	vii. 2, 19.	32 e	xxxi. 5.	32 d
ii. 3, 4.	32 b	xxv. 29, 29.	32 a d	xiii. 51.	32 i	viii. 33.	45 d	viii. 20.	23 b	xxxii. 27.	32 a
ii. 18.	32 d	xxv. 31, 31.	32 a i	xix. 4.	32 d	ix. 6.	23 b	ix. 9.	26 a	xxxiii. 3.	32 d
ii. 22.	2 b	xxv. 40.	32 c	xix. 28.	26 d	ix. 27.	32 d	x. 27.	45 d	xxxiii. 7, 22.	32 a
iii. 1.	32 a	xxvi. 1, 1, 5, 5, 17,		xxi. 5, 5.	40, 48	xi. 11.	45 d	xi. 4, 17.	19 d	xxxiv. 31.	19 d
iii. 7, 21.	32 d	19, 22, 23, 29.	32 a d	xxii. 22.	26 d	xiii. 15.	32 d	xii. 13.	32 i	xxxv. 25.	26 d
v. 1.	32 a	xxvi. 4, 4.	32 a d	xxii. 24.	32 d	xiv. 10.	32 d	xii. 20.	41 b	Ezra iv. 19.	28 d
vi. 6, 7.	32 a	xxvi. 6, 10, 11, 14,		xxvi. 1.	32 d	xvii. 3.	32 b	xiii. 7.	45 d	v. 3, 9.	17
vi. 14, 14.	32 c d	15, 18, 26, 36,		xxvi. 19, 31, 46.	26 a	xvii. 4, 5.	32 d	xiv. 9.	41 b	v. 4.	2 c
vi. 15, 16, 16.	32 d	37.	32 a d	Num. iv. 26.	32	xviii. 3.	32 e	xv. 15.	41 a	v. 13, 14.	45 f
vii. 4.	32 a	xxvi. 7, 7.	32 a d	v. 21, 21.	26 d b	xviii. 24, 27, 31.	32 a	xv. 30.	41 b	v. 17.	45 g
viii. 6.	32 a	xxvi. 31, 31.	32 a d	vi. 4.	32 i	xxi. 15.	32 a	xvi. 11.	32 a	vi. 1, 3, 12.	45 f
ix. 6.	32 a	xxvii. 1, 2, 4, 4, 6,		viii. 4.	32 a	Ruth iv. 11.	26 d	xvii. 8, 19, 30, 30,		vi. 8.	45 d
ix. 12.	26 e	9.	32 a	x. 2, 2.	32 c d	1 Sam. ii. 19.	32 d	30, 31.	32 a	vi. 11, 11.	45 g, 28 c
xi. 3.	21 b	xxvii. 3, 3.	32 a d	xi. 8.	26 d	vi. 5.	32 a	xvii. 13, 21.ε	45 g
xi. 4.	32 d	xxvii. 8, 8.	32 d	xiv. 4.	26 d	vi. 7.	32 c	xvii. 14, 16, 32.	32 d	vii. 13, 21.ε	45 g
xii. 2.	32 d	xxviii. 2, 3, 6, 13,		xiv. 12.	32 d	viii. 1.	45 d	xvii. 29,β 29.	32 e a	x. 3.	19 d
xiii. 4.	32 a	22, 23, 26, 27,		xv. 3, 3.	32 a b	viii. 5.	45 c	xvii. 35.	19 d	x. 11.	26 c
xiii. 16.	45 a	31, 33, 36.	32 a	xv. 38.	32 a	viii. 12.	32 b	xviii. 4.	32 a	Neh. iii. 16.	32 f
xiv. 2.	32 a	xxviii. 4, 4.	32 a d	xvi. 30.	4 b	viii. 22.	23 a	xviii. 31.	32 c	iv. 7.ζ	1, 29
xv. 18.	19 a	xxviii. 11, 14.	32 d	xvi. 38.	32 a	ix. 22.	26 d	xix. 15.	32 a	viii. 4.	52 a
xvii. 2.	26 d	xxviii. 15, 15,		xxi. 8.	32 c	xi. 1.	19 c	xx. 20.	32 a	viii. 12, 15.	32 b
xvii. 5, 6, 20.	26 a	15.	32 a d d	xxi. 9.	32 d	xi. 2.	19 d	xxi. 3.	32 d	viii. 16, 17.	32 d
xviii. 6.	32 c	xxviii. 39, 39.	32 a d	xxxi. 20.α	16	xii. 1.	23 b	xxi. 7.	32 a	ix. 6, 18.	32 a
xix. 3.	32 d	xxviii. 40, 40.		Deut. i. 11.	13	xii. 22.	32 b	xxiii. 3.	19 d	ix. 8.	19 b
xxi. 6.	32 a	40.	32 d a d	i. 13.	45 d	xiii. 19.	32 d	xxiii. 4.	32 d	ix. 38.	19 e
xxi. 8.	32 d	xxviii. 42.	32 c	i. 15.	26 d	xiv. 14.	25	xxiii. 12, 12, 15, 19.	32 a	x. 32.	30 a
xxi. 13, 18.	45 d	xxix. 2.	32 d	iv. 16, 25.	32 a	xvii. 25.	32 d	xxiv. 13.	32 a	xiii. 26.	26 d
xxi. 27, 32.	19 d	xxx. 1, 1.	32 d	iv. 23, 23.	19 a, 32 a	xviii. 3.	19 d	xxv. 16.	32 a	Esth. i. 3, 5, 9.	32 a
xxvi. 28.	19 d	xxx. 3, 5, 18, 25,		v. 2, 3.	19 a	xviii. 13.	45 d	1 Chron. v. 10.	32 a	i. 20.	32 d
xxvi. 30.	32 d	35.	32 a	v. 8.	32 d	xx. 16.	19 d	v. 19.	32 d	ii. 18, 18.	32 a d
xxvii. 4, 7.	32 c	xxx. 4, 4, 32, 37,		vii. 2.	19 d	xxii. 7.	45 d	ix. 30.	43	v. 14, 14.	32 d
xxvii. ε, 14, 31.	32 d	37, 38.	32 d	ix. 9.	19 a	xxiii. 18.	19 d	ix. 31.	32 l	ix. 17, 18, 22.	32 b
xxvii. 37.	45 a	xxxi. 6, 17.	32 a	ix. 12, 16, 21.	32 a	xxv. 28.	32 b d	xi. 3.	19 d	ix. 19.	32 e
xxix. 22.	32 d	xxxii. 1, 23.	32 f	ix. 14.	32 d	xxx. 25.	45 d	xii. 18.	26 d	Job i. 17.	45 a
xxxi. 44.	19 d	xxxii. 4, 10, 31.	32 d	x. 1, 5.	32 a	2 Sam. iii. 12.	19 c	xvii. 11.	26 d	iv. 9.	17 e
xxxi. 46.	32 d	xxxii. 8, 20, 35, 35.	32 a	x. 3.	32 d	iii. 13, 21.	19 d	xv. 1.	32 d	ix. 9.	32 e
xxxii. 12.	45 a	xxxiv. 10.	19 e	x. 22.	45 a	iii. 20.	32 d	xvi. 16.	19 a	x. 8.	31
xxxiii. 17.	32 a	xxxiv. 12, 15.	19 d	xiv. 1.	32 d	v. 3.	19 d	xvi. 26.	32 a	x. 9.	32 a
xxxv. 1.	32 c	xxxiv. 17.	32 d	xv. 1.	32 d	vi. 8.	37	xvii. 8.	32 a	xv. 7.	8
xxxv. 3.	32 d	xxxiv. 27.	19 a	xvi. 18.	26 d	vii. 9.	32 a	xvii. 21.	45 b	xv. 27.	32 d
xxxvii. 3.	32 a	xxxv. 10.	32 d	xvi. 21.	32 d	vii. 11.	32 d	xvii. 22.	26 d	xvii. 6.	14
xl. 20.	32 d	xxxv. 29, 33.	32 b	xx. 9.	36 a	vii. 23.	45 b	xviii. 8.	32 a	xvii. 13.	42
xli. 43.	26 b	xxxv. 3, 5, 7.	32 b	xx. 12.	32 a	viii. 6.	20	xix. 3.	13	xviii. 2.	45 d
xlv. 8.	45 d	xxxv. 4.	32 d	xx. 20.	32 e	viii. 10.	32 a	xxi. 29.	32 a	xxiv. 25.	45 d
xlv. 9.	45 a	xxxvi. 6, 13, 18, 19,		xxii. 8.	32 a	xiii. 6.	32 a	xxiii. 8.	32 a	xxv. 2.	32 a
xlvi. 3.	45 d	20, 23, 31, 33, 36,		xxii. 12.	32 a	xiii. 10.	32 a	xxiii. 5.	32 a	xxvii. 18.	32 a
xlvii. 6.	45 a	37.	32 d	xxvi. 19, 19.	26 b, 32 a	xv. 4.	45 d	xxvi. 10.	45 d	xxviii. 25, 26.	32 b
xlvii. 26.	45 a	xxxvi. 8, 8.	32 d a	xxvii. 15.	32 d	xvii. 25.	45 a	2 Chron. i. 3, 5.		xxxi. 1.	19 a
xlviii. 4.	26 a	xxxvi. 11, 11.	32 d a	xxviii. 13.	26 a	xxii. 12.	46 c	i. 15, 15.	26 d a	xxxi. 15, 15.	32 e a
xlviii. 20.	45 d	xxxvi. 12, 12, 22,		xxviii. 24.	26 d	xxii. 33.	27	ii. 11.	26 a	xxxii. 22.	45 a
l. 10.	32 d	24, 25, 27, 28,		xxix. 1, 1.	19 b a	xxiii. 5.	45 a	ii. 12.	32 a	xxxiii. 4.	32 a
Exod. i. 21.	32 d	34.	32 a	xxix. 12, 14.	19 a	1 Kings ii. 24.	32 a	iii. 8, 10, 14, 15, 16,		xxxv. 10.	32 e
ii. 14.	45 a	xxxvi. 14, 14.	32 d a	xxix. 25.	19 a	iii. 15.	32 d	16.	32 d	xxxvi. 3.	35 c
iv. 11, 11.	45 a d	xxxvi. 17, 17.	32 d a	xxxi. 16.	19 a	v. 12.	19 d	iv. 1, 2, 6, 7, 8, 8,		xxxviii. 9.	45 b
v. 7, 14.	21 a	xxxvii. 1, 2, 4, 6,		xxxi. 6, 15.	32 a	vi. 4, 5, 23.	32 d	9, 18, 19.	32 d	xxxix. 6.	45 a
v. 8.	32 e	10, 11, 12, 12,		Josh. v. 2.	32 c	vi. 6.	26 a	iv. 11, 11.	32 d a	xl. 15.	32 a
v. 16.	32 c	15, 16, 23, 25,		v. 3.	32 d	vi. 31, 33.	32 a	iv. 14, 14, 16.	32 a	xl. 19.	32 e
vii. 1.	26 a	26, 28, 29.	32 d	vi. 18.	45 a	vii. 6, 7, 16, 37, 45,		v. 1.	32 a	xli. 4.	19 d
xiv. 21.	45 d	xxxvii. 7, 7.	32 d a	vii. 19.	26 c	51.	32 a	v. 10.	19 a	xli. 31.	45 d
xv. 17.	35 a	xxxvii. 8, 24, 27.	32 a	viii. 28.	45 d	vii. 8, 18, 23, 27,		vi. 11.	19 a	xli. 33.	32 f
xv. 25.	26 d	xxxvii. 17, 17.	32 a d	ix. 6, 11.	19 c	38, 48.	32 d a	vi. 13.	32 a	Ps. iv. 15, 15.	18, 35 b
xviii. 25.		xxxv-ii. 1, 2, 4, 6,		ix. 7.	19 d	vii. 40, 40.	32 d a	vii. 6, 7.	32 a	ix. 15.	32 a
xx. 4, 23, 23, 24,		8, 9, 30.	32 d	ix. 15, 15.	32 d, 19 d	viii. 9, 21.	19 a	vii. 11.	32 b	xviii. 11.	46 c
25.	32 d	xxxviii. 7, 22, 28.	32 a	ix. 16.	19 a	viii. 29.	33	vii. 11.	32 b	xviii. 32.	26 d
xx. 11.	32 a	xxxviii. 27.	32 d	ix. 27.	26 d	ix. 3.	9	viii. 9.	26 a	xviii. 43.	45 d
xxiii. 27.	26 a	xxxviii. 28.	32 a	xi. 18.	32 a	ix. 22.	26 a	viii. 9.	26 a	xxi. 6, 9, 12.	46 c
xxiii. 22.	19 d	xxxix. 2, 8, 15, 16,		xxii. 28.	32 a	ix. 26.	32 a	ix. 11, 15, 17.	32 d	xxxiii. 6.	32 g
xxiv. 8.	19 a	19, 20, 22, 24,		xxii. 28.	32 a	x. 9.	45 d	ix. 8.	26 d	xxxv. 5.	26 a
xxv. 8, 10, 11, 13,		25, 27, 30.	32 d	xxiv. 25.	19 d	x. 12, 16, 18.	32 d	ix. 19.	32 g	xxxix. 8.	45 d
17, 23, 24, 25,		Judg. ii. 2.	19 d	Judg. ii. 2.	19 d	x. 20.	32 d	ix. 27, 27.	26 d a	xl. 4.	45 a
25, 26, 28, 37.	32 a	xxxix. 4, 9, 42.	32 a	iii. 16.	32 b	2 Kings iii. 2.	32 a	xi. 15.	32 a	xli. 3.	6
										xliv. 13, 14.	45 d
										xlv. 1.	32 l
										xlvi. 16.	46 c
										xlvi. 8.	45 a
										l. 5.	19 e
										lii. 7.	45 d
										lxix. 2.	45 c
										lxix. 11.	26 d
										lxxiv. 17.	15 a
										lxxviii. 50.	34
										lxxx. 6.	45 d
										lxxxiii. 11, 13.	46 b
										lxxxiii. 16.	46 c
										lxxxvi. 9.	32 a
										lxxxviii. 8.	46 a
										lxxxix. 3.	19 a
										lxxxix. 27.	26 d
										lxxxix. 29.	45 a
										lxxxix. 47.	4 a
										xci. 9.	45 a
										xcv. 5.	32 a

Ps. xcv. 6.	32 e
xcvi. 5.	32 a
c. 3.	32 a
civ. 3.	45 e
civ. 4.	32 e
civ. 20.	46 c
civ. 24.	32 a
civ. 26.	15 a
cv. 9.	19 a
cv. 21.	45 a
cvi. 19.	32 d
cvi. 46.	26 d
cvii. 29.	39 a
cvii. 41.	45 d
cx. 1.	46 c
cxi. 4.	32 a
cxv. 8, 15.	32 e
cxviii. 24.	32 a
cxix. 73.	32 a
cxxi. 2.	32 e
cxxiv. 8.	32 e
cxxxiv. 3.	32 e
cxxxv. 7.	32 a
cxxxv. 18.	32 e
cxxxvi. 5, 7.	32 e
cxxxix. 15.	32 k
cxlvi. 6.	32 e
cxlvii. 14.	45 e
cxlviii. 5.	26 a
cxlix. 2.	32 e
Prov. viii. 26.	32 a
xiv. 31.	32 e
xvi. 4.	35 a
xvii. 5.	32 e
xix. 4.	13
xx. 12.	32 a
xx. 18.	32 c
xxii. 2.	32 e
xxiii. 5.	32 b d
xxiv. 6.	32 d
xxx. 26.	45 d
xxxi. 22, 24.	32 a
Eccles. ii. 5, 6.	32 a
iii. 11, 11.	32 a
vii. 29.	32 a
x. 19.η	32 e
xi. 5.	32 d
xii. 12.	32 b
Cant. i. 6.	45 a
i. 11.	32 d
iii. 9, 10.	32 a
vi. 12.	45 a
Isa. i. 31.	35 d
ii. 8, 20.	32 a
iii. 7.	45 d
v. 2.	10
x. 23.	32 e
xiv. 17, 23.	45 a
xvi. 3.	46 b
xvii. 7.	32 e
xvii. 8.	32 a
xix. 10.	32 e
xxii. 11, 11.	32 a e
xxv. 2.	45 a
xxv. 6.	32 a
xxvii. 5, 5.	32 d
xxvii. 9.	45 b
xxvii. 11.	32 e
xxviii. 15, 15.	19 a, 45 a
xxix. 16, 16.	32 e a
xxxi. 7.	32 a
xxxvi. 16.	32 c
xxxvii. 16.	32 a
xl. 23.	32 a
xli. 15, 15.	45 a d
xli. 18.	45 d
xlii. 15.	45 a
xliii. 15.	45 d
xliii. 16.	32 a
xliii. 19.	45 d
xliv. 2, 24.	32 e
xliv. 9.	15 b
xliv. 13, 19.	32 d
xliv. 15, 15.	35 b, 32 a
xliv. 17.	32 e
xlv. 7, 18.	32 e
xlv. 9, 9.	15 b, 32 d
xlv. 11.	15 b
xlv. 12.	32 a
xlvi. 4.	32 a
xlvi. 6.	32 a
xlix. 2, 2.	45 d
xlix. 11.	45 a
l. 2, 3.	45 d

Isa. li. 3.	45 d
li. 10.	45 a
li. 12.	26 f
li. 13.	32 e
liii. 9.θ	26 d
liii. 10.ι	45 d
liv. 5.	32 e
liv. 12.	45 a
lv. 3.	19 d
lvii. 8.	19 d
lvii. 16.	32 a
lx. 15, 17.	45 a
lxi. 8.	19 d
lxii. 7.	45 d
lxiii. 12, 14.	32 b
lxvi. 2.	32 a
lxvi. 22.	32 e
Jer. i. 18.	26 a
ii. 7.	45 a
ii. 15.	46 c
ii. 28.	32 a
iv. 7.	45 d
iv. 27.	32 d
v. 10, 18.	32 d
v. 14.	26 e
vi. 8.	45 d
vi. 26.	32 c
viii. 8.	32 a
ix. 11, 11.	26 a d
x. 11.	28 a
x. 13.	32 e
x. 13.	32 a
xi. 10.	45 b
xii. 10.	32 a
xii. 11.	45 a
xiii. 16.	46 b
xiv. 22.	32 a
xv. 20.	26 a
xvi. 18.	32 e
xvii. 5.	45 a
xviii. 4, 4, κ 4.	32 e d b
xviii. 16.	45 b
xix. 8.	45 a
xix. 12.	45 a
xx. 4.	26 e
xxv. 9, 12.	45 a
xxv. 18.	26 b
xxvi. 6, 6.	26 a d
xxvii. 2.	32 c
xxvii. 5.	32 a
xxviii. 13.	32 a
xxix. 17, 26.	26 a
xxix. 22.	45 d
xxx. 11, 11.	32 d
xxxi. 21.	45 c
xxxi. 31, 32.	19 a
xxxi. 33.	19 d
xxxii. 17.	32 a
xxxii. 20.	32 d
xxxii. 40.	19 a
xxxiii. 2.	32 e
xxxiv. 8.	19 b
xxxiv. 13, 18.	19 a
xxxiv. 15.	19 d
xxxiv. 17.	26 a
xxxiv. 22.	26 d
xxxvii. 16.	32 a
xxxviii. 16.	32 a
xli. 18.	32 a
xliv. 19.	32 a
xlvi. 28, 28.	32 d
xlix. 15.	26 a
l. 3.	46 c
li. 15.	32 a
li. 16.	32 a
li. 25.	32 a
li. 29.	45 b
li. 34.	32 a
li. 39.	46 c
lii. 20.	32 a
Lam. i. 13.	26 a
ii. 7.	26 a
iii. 11.	45 a
iii. 45.	45 d
Ezek. iii. 8, 9, 17.	26 a
iv. 9.	32 a
v. 14.	26 d
vi. 14.	26 a
vii. 20.	45 a
vii. 23.	32 c
xi. 13.	32 a
xiii. 5.	5 b
xiii. 18.	32 e

Ezek. xiv. 8.λ	47
xv. 8.	26 a
xvi. 17, 24.	32 d
xvi. 31.	32 a
xvii. 13.	19 d
xvii. 17.	32 e
xviii. 31.	32 c
xix. 5.	45 a
xx. 17.	32 a
xx. 28.	45 d
xxi. 15.	32 f
xxii. 3, 13.	32 a
xxii. 4, 4.	32 a, 26 a
xxii. 30.	5 c
xxiv. 17.	32 d
xxv. 4, 5, 15.	26 a
xxvi. 4, 8, 14.	26 a
xxvi. 15.	7
xxvi. 19.	26 b
xxvi. 21.	26 d
xxvii. 5, 5.	2 a, 32 d
xxvii. 6, 6.	32 a
xxvii. 16, 18.	32 l
xxix. 3, 9.	32 a
xxix. 10, 12.	26 a
xxx. 12.	32 a
xxxi. 9.	32 a
xxxii. 15.	26 b
xxxiv. 25.	19 a
xxxiv. 26.	26 a
xxxv. 3, 7.	26 a
xxxv. 9.	26 d
xxxv. 14.	32 a
xxxvii. 19, 22.	32 a
xxxvii. 26.	19 a
xl. 14.	32 d
xl. 17.	32 d
xli. 18, 19, 20, 25, 25.	32 f
xliii. 18.	32 h
xliii. 27.	32 d
xliv. 14.	26 a
xlvi. 23.	32 f
Dan. ii. 5.	45 h
i. 1, 15.	28 a
iii. 10.	45 f
iii. 29,μ 29.	45 g, 44
iv. 6.	45 g
v. 1.	28 a
v. 11.	39 b
v. 16.	38
vi. 13.	3
vi. 26.ν	45 g
vii. 21.	28 a
xi. 6.	32 b
xi. 44.	11
Hos. iii. 3, 12.	45 a
ii. 6.	5 a
ii. 18.	19 a
viii. 4, 6.	32 a
viii. 14.	32 e
x. 4.	19 b
xi. 8.	26 d
xii. 1.	19 d
xiii. 2.	32 d
Joel iii. 19.	26 d
Amos iv. 13.	32 e
v. 8.	32 e
v. 26.	32 a
viii. 10.	45 a
ix. 14.	32 a
Obad. 2.	26 a
Jonah i. 9.	32 a
i. 16.	24
iv. 5.	32 d
Micah i. 6.	45 a
i. 8.	32 d
iv. 7.	45 a
iv. 13, 13.	45 d
vi. 16.	26 b
Nah. i. 8.	32 d
i. 9.	32 e
i. 14.	45 d
Hab. i. 14.	32 d
ii. 18, 18, 18.	32 a
18.	15 b b, 32 b
Zeph. i. 18.	45 d
ii. 13.	45 d
iii. 20.	26 d
Zech. vi. 11.	45 a
vii. 12.	45 a
ix. 13.	32 e
x. 1.	32 e
x. 3.	45 a

Zech. xi. 10.	19 a
xii. 2.	45 e
Zech. xii. 3, 6.	45 d
Mal. ii. 9.	26 a
Mal. ii. 15.	32 a
iii. 17.	32 e

α lit. vessels of skins. *β lit.* were making. *γ lit.* and they made it. *δ lit.* have we given thee to be. *ε lit.* by me is made. *ζ lit.* the healing went up to the walls. *η lit.* men make a feast. *θ lit.* there was given to him. *ι or,* put, equivalent to τίθημι in N.T. *κ lit.* he turned and made it. *λ lit.* make him desolate for a sign. *μ lit.* a decree is made by me. *ν lit.* from before me a decree is made.

MALE

אִישׁ see *Man.* Gen. vii. 2, 2.

זָכַר to remember; to be remembered; applied to a male child, because the memory of the father was thereby preserved in the genealogy of the family; which genealogy was confined wholly to males. NIPHAL *fut.* Exod. xxxiv. 19. זָכָר *m.* a male, both of men and animals: Gen. i. 27, &c. זָכוּר *m. id.* Exod. xxiii. 17: Deut. xvi. 16; xx. 13.

MALLOWS

מַלּוּחַ *m.* (see *Salt*), halimus or common sea purslane, an herb very grateful to camels.—*Schult. in Job.* Any mean bitter herb the miserably poor might use to satisfy hunger: Job xxx. 4.

MAN, MANKIND

1 אָדָם *m.* man, as *homo* in Latin; collectively, men, mankind; other men, in opposition to some already named; common men, in opposition to better men; or more noble, אִישׁ: Isa. ii. 9; v. 15; to שָׂרִים, Ps. lxxii. 7; *cf.* Isa. xxix. 19: Ps. xlix. 2, "both low and high," *lit.* sons of אָדָם, and sons of אִישׁ, Prov. viii. 4: Job xxxv. 8: Isa. xxxi. 8: lii. 14: Micah v. 7: Ps. lxii. 9: 2 Kings vii. 10: of the Messiah, 2 Sam. vii. 19: also son of man, Ps. viii. 4: once used of slaves, Num. xvi. 32: of soldiers, Isa. xxii. 6.

2 אִישׁ *m.* man, as *vir* in Latin; Schindler derives it from אוּשׁ, which is of the same meaning with אָשַׁשׁ to be firm, or strong; as *vir*, in Latin, implies strength and vigour (*vires*) of mind and body; of the Messiah, Zech. vi. 12. אָדָם and אִישׁ are often opposed to each other: Ps. xxii. 6; xlix. 2; lxii. 9: Isa. ii. 9, 11; v. 15; lii. 14. The former is man simply, the latter is man with some degree or kind of pre-eminence; the former implies weakness, and insufficiency, and folly, Eccles. vi. 10, Isa. xxxi. 3, Ps. lxxii. 7: yet used once of an infant, Isa. lxvi. 13, "as one." As weakness is the property of man, so that which man may bear, which is suited to his impotency, is called human; the "cords of a man," and "the rod of men," which are suited to human nature: Hos. xi. 4: 2 Sam. vii. 14. We have πειρασμὸς ἀνθρώπινος, 1 Cor. x. 13, temptation or trial which does not exceed human strength; "any man, whosoever," &c., *lit.* a man a man; "every one," *lit. id.* Gen. ii. 23, &c. אִישׁ: HITHPALEL *imp.* Isa. xlvi. 8, "shew yourselves men;" *i.e.* be wise, cast away the childish trifles of idolaters.

3 אָנַשׁ to be sick unto death; to be in very great distress, in a desperate, incurable condition, past all relief; mortal, fatal: man in this condition, and according to nature.

As אָדָם is the common name of man in regard to his earthly origin, so אֱנוֹשׁ is the common name of man in regard to his being heir to corruption and weakness: not used of man before the fall, occurs first in Gen. vi. 4 : used of the Messiah, Ps. viii. 4. It is rendered "men of the common sort," Ps. lxxiii. 5 : so Isa. viii. 1, "with the pen of a man," *i. e.* in the writing with which they are familiar, and can easily read ; *cf.* Hab. ii. 2. ᵃ אֱנַשׁ Ch. *id.* ᵇ אֲנַשׁ Ch. *id.*

4   בֵּן *m.* son ; followed by a genitive, denoting virtue, vice, or condition of life, which is rendered an adjective : "man," *lit.* son of man, frequently.

5   בַּעַל master, having dominion : inhabitants or rulers of a city.

6   גֶּבֶר *m.* (see *Prevail*), a man in regard to his strength and superiority ; used of a male child unborn, Job iii. 3 ; of the Messiah conceived of a virgin, Jer. xxxi. 22 ; of a mighty or honourable man, Isa. xxii. 17 ; of a king, Jer. xxii. 30 ; of the Messiah suffering, Zech. xiii. 7 ; of man, in distinction from his wife, Prov. vi. 34 ; of man distinct from the deity, Job xxii. 2. ᵃ גְּבַר *m. id.* ᵇ גְּבַר Ch. *m. id.* ᶜ גִּבּוֹר *adj.* see *Mighty.*

7   גֻּלְגֹּלֶת *f.* the poll ; " for every man." *marg.* ' by the poll, *or*, head.'

8   זָכָר (see *Male*), man-child. ᵃ זָכוּר *m. id.*

9   נַעַר *m.* boy, young man.

10   נֶפֶשׁ *com.* animal life, a person.

No. 2 not included.

Gen. i. 26, 27.	1	Exod. xii. 12.	1	Num. xxv. 5.	3	Judg. ix. 49, 49, 49.	2, 3, 2	1 Kings ix. 22, 27.	3	Job xi. 12, 12.	2, 1

Gen. i. 26, 27. — 1
ii. 5, 7, 7, 8, 15, 16, 18, 22, 22, 25. — 1
iii. 12, 22, 24. — 1
v. 1. — 1
vi. 1, 2, 3, 5, 6. ᵃ — 1
vi. 4, 4, 4. — 1, 6 c, 3
vi. 7, 7. — 1
vii. 21, 23. β — 1
viii. 21, 21. — 1
ix. 5, 5, 5. — 1, 2, 1
ix. 6, 6, 6. — 1
xi. 5. — 1
xii. 20. — 3
xiii. 13. — 3
xiv. 24. — 1
xvi. 12. — 1
xvii. 10, 12, 14. — 8
xvii. 23, 27. — 3
xviii. 2, 16, 22. — 3
xix. 4, 4, 5, 8, 10, 11, 12, 16. — 3
xx. 3. — 5
xx. 8. — 3
xxiv. 13, 54, 59. — 3
xxiv. 32, 32. — 2, 3
xxvi. 7, 7. — 3
xxix. 22. — 3
xxxii. 28. — 3
xxxiv. 7, 20, 21, 22. — 3
xxxviii. 21, 22. — 3
xxxix. 11. γ — 3
xxxix. 14. — 3
xliii. 15, 16, 16, 18, 33. — 3
xliii. 17, 17, 17. — 2, 2, 3
xliii. 24, 24. — 2, 3
xliv. 1, 1. — 3, 2
xliv. 3, 4. — 3
xlvi. 32. — 3
xlvii. 2, 6. — 3
Exod. ii. 13. — 3
iv. 11. δ — 3
iv. 19. — 3
v. 9. — 3
viii. 17, 18. — 1
ix. 9, 10, 19, 22, 25. — 3
x. 7. — 3
x. 11. — 6

Exod. xii. 12. — 1
xii. 16. — 10
xii. 37. — 6
xiii. 2, 13, 15. — 1
xvi. 16. — 7
xvii. 9. — 1
xviii. 21, 21, 25. — 3
xxi. 18, 22. — 3
xxii. 31. — 1
xxx. 32. — 1
xxxiii. 20. — 8 a
xxxiv. 23. — 1
xxxv. 22, 22. — 3, 2
xxxviii. 26. — 7
Lev. i. 2. — 1
v. 3, 4. — 1
vi. 3. — 1
vii. 11. — 1
xii. 2. — 1
xiii. 2, 9. — 1
xv. 33. — 1
xvi. 17. — 1
xviii. 5. — 1
xviii. 22. — 8
xviii. 27. — 3
xx. 13. — 8
xxi. 4. — 5
xxii. 5. — 1
xxiv. 17, 20, 21. — 1
xxvii. 28, 28. — 2, 1
xxvii. 29. — 3
Num. i. 5, 17. — 1
iii. 13. — 1
v. 6, 6. — 2, 1
viii. 17. ε — 1
ix. 6, 6. — 3, 1
ix. 7, 7. — 3, 1
xi. 26. — 1
xii. 3, 3. — 2, 1
xiii. 2, 2. ζ — 3
xiii. 3, 16, 31, 32. — 3
xiv. 22, 36, 37, 38. — 1
xvi. 2, 14, 26, 30. — 3
xvi. 29, 29, 32. — 1
xviii. 15, 15. — 1
xix. 11, 13, 14, 16. — 1
xxii. 9, 20, 35. — 2, 1
xxiii. 19, 19. — 1
xxiv. 3, 15. — 6

Num. xxv. 5. — 3
xxxi. 11, 26, 47. — 1
xxxi. 18, 35. — 8
xxxi. 21, 28, 42, 53. — 3
xxxi. 49, 49. — 3, 2
xxxii. 11, 14. — 3
xxxiv. 17, 19. — 3
Deut. i. 13, 15, 22, 23, 35. — 3
ii. 14, 16. — 3
iv. 28, 32. — 1
v. 24. — 1
viii. 3, 3. — 1
xiii. 13. — 1
xix. 17. — 1
xx. 19. — 1
xxi. 21. — 6
xxii. 5, 5. — 3
xxii. 21. — 1
xxv. 1, 11. — 3
xxxi. 12. — 1
xxxii. 26. — 3
Josh. ii. 1, 2, 3, 4, 4, 5, 5, 7, 9, 14, 17, 23. — 3
iv. 2, 2. ς — 3, 2
v. 4, 6. — 3
vi. 3, 22. — 1
vii. 2, 2. — 1
vii. 4, 4. — 2, 3
vii. 5, 5, 5. — 3, 2
vii. 14, 14, 17, 17, 18, 18. — 6
viii. 14, 20, 21. — 1
viii. 25, η 25. — 2, 3
ix. 14. — 3
x. 2, 6, 18, 24. — 3
xi. 14. — 1
xiv. 15. — 1
xviii. 4, 8, 9. — 3
xxiv. 11. — 5
Judg. v. 30. — 6
vi. 27, 27, 28, 30. — 3
viii. 5, 8, 8, 9, 15, 15, 16, 17, 18. — 3
viii. 14, 14, 14. — 9, 3, 2
ix. 2, 3, 6, 7, 1C, 20, 20, 23, 23, 24, 25, 26, 39, 46, 47. — 5
ix. 9, 13, 28, 36, 51, 57. — 3

Judg. ix. 49, 49, 49. — 2, 3, 2
xi. 3. — 3
xii. 4, 4, 5. — 3
xiv. 18. — 3
xvi. 7, 11, 17. — 3
xvi. 27, 27. — 3, 2
xviii. 2, 2. — 3, 3, 4
xviii. 7, 7. — 3, 1
xviii. 14, 22. — 3
xviii. 17, 17. — 3, 2
xviii. 28. — 1
xix. 16, 16. — 2, 3
xix. 22, 22. — 3, 2
xx. 5. — 5
xx. 10, 12, 13, 44. — 2, 3
xx. 46, 46. — 2, 3
xxi. 11. — 8
Ruth iv. 2. — 3
1 Sam. i. 11. — 3
ii. 17, 26. — 3
iv. 9, 9. — 3
v. 7, 9, 12. — 3
vi. 10, 15, 20. — 3
vi. 19, 19. — 3, 2
vii. 1, 11. — 3
viii. 22, 22. — 3, 2
x. 2, 3. — 3
ix. 1, 5, 10, 12, 15. — 3
xi. 9, 9. — 2, 3
xiv. 8, 12. — 3
xiv. 52, 52. θ — 2, 4
xv. 29. — 1
xvi. 7, 7. — 3
xvii. 12, 28, 52. — 3
xvii. 26, 26. — 8, 2
xvii. 32. — 3
xviii. 5. — 3
xix. 27, 27. — 3, 2
xxii. 6. — 3
xxiii. 3, 5, 8, 13, 24, 25, 26, 26, 26. — 3
xxiii. 11. — 5
xxiii. 12, 12. — 5, 3
xxiv. 2, 2. — 2, 3
xxiv. 3, 4, 6, 22. — 3
xxiv. 9. — 1
xxv. 11, 15, 20. — 3
xxv. 13, 13, 13, 13. — 3, 2, 2
xxv. 29. — 1
xxvi. 19. — 1
xxvii. 3, 3. — 3
xxvii. 8. — 3
xxviii. 1, 8. — 3
xxix. 2, 4, 11. — 3
xxx. 1, 3, 21, 31. — 3
xxxi. 1, 6, 7, 7. — 3
2 Sam. i. 11. — 3
ii. 3, 3. — 3, 2
ii. 4, 4, 5, 17, 29, 32. — 3
ii. 31, 31. — 3, 2
iii. 20, 20, 39. — 3
iii. 34. — 4
iv. 2, 11. — 3
v. 6, 21. — 3
vii. 14, 14. — 3, 1
vii. 19. — 3
x. 5. — 3
xi. 16, 17, 23. — 3
xii. 1. — 3
xv. 6, 22. — 3
xvi. 13. — 3
xvii. 8, 8. — 4
xvii. 10. — 3
xvii. 12. — 3
xviii. 28. — 3
xix. 28. — 3
xix. 41, 41, 41. — 2, 2, 3
xx. 7. — 3
xx. 11. ι — 2, 9
xxi. 6, 17. — 3
xxi. 12. — 3
xxii. 26. — 6 c
xxiii. 1. — 1
xxiii. 3. — 3
xxiii. 17. — 3
xxiv. 14. — 3
1 Kings ix. 9. — 4
i. 52. κ — 3
ii. 32. — 1
iv. 31. — 3
viii. 38, 38. — 1, 2
viii. 39, 39. — 2, 1
viii. 46. — 1

1 Kings ix. 22, 27. — 3
x. 8, 15. — 3
xi. 18, 24. — 3
xiii. 2. — 1
xiii. 25. — 3
xx. 17, 33. — 3
xxi. 10, 11, 13, 13. — 3
2 Kings i. 8. — 2
ii. 16. λ — 3, 4
ii. 19. — 3
iv. 40, 40. — 3, 2
v. 24. — 3
vii. 3. — 3
vii. 10, 10. — 2, 1
x. 6. — 3
x. 24, 24. — 2, 3
xi. 9, 9. — 2, 3
xii. 4, 4. — 10, 2
xii. 15. — 3
xvii. 30, 30, 30. — 3
xviii. 27. — 3
xix. 18. — 3
xx. 14. — 3
xxiii. 14, 20. — 3
xxiii. 17, 17. — 3, 2
xxiv. 16. — 3
xxv. 4, 23, 23, 24, 25. — 3
xxv. 19, 19, 19. — 3, 3, 2
1 Chron. iv. 12, 22, 42. — 3
v. 18, 18. — 3, 4
v. 21. — 10, 1
v. 24, 24. — 3
vii. 21, 40. — 3
viii. 40. — 3
ix. 9. — 3
ix. 13. — 6 c
xi. 19. — 3
xii. 8, 8. — 6 c, 3
xii. 38. — 3
xvii. 17. — 1
xix. 5, 5. — 3
xxi. 13. — 1
xxiii. 3, 3. — 6
xxiv. 4. — 3
xxv. 1. — 3
xxvi. 7, 9, 30, 32. — 4
xxvi. 12. — 3
xxviii. 1. — 6 c
xxix. 1. — 3
2 Chron. vi. 18, 29, 36. — 1
vi. 30, 30. — 2, 1
viii. 9. — 3
ix. 7, 14. — 3
xiii. 3, 3, 3, 3. — 6 c, 2, 2, 6 c
xiii. 7. — 3
xiv. 11. — 3
xvii. 13. — 3
xix. 6. — 3
xxiii. 8, 8. — 2, 3
xxiv. 24. — 3
xxvi. 17. — 4
xxvii. 6. — 4
xxviii. 15. — 3
xxxi. 19. — 3
xxxii. 19. — 3
xxxiv. 12. — 3
Ezra i. 4. — 3
ii. 2, 22, 23, 27, 28. — 3 a
iv. 11. — 6 b
iv. 21. — 3
v. 4, 10. — 6 b
vi. 8. — 6 b
x. 1, 9, 17. — 3
Neh. i. 2. — 3
ii. 10. — 1
ii. 12, 12. — 3, 1
iii. 2, 7, 22. — 3
iv. 23. — 3
vii. 7, 26, 27, 28, 29, 30, 31, 32, 33. — 3
viii. 3. — 3
ix. 29. — 3
Job i. 3, 3. — 2, 4
iii. 3, 23. — 6
iv. 13. — 3
iv. 17, μ 17. — 3, 6
v. 7. — 3
v. 17. — 3
vii. 1, 17. — 3
vii. 20. — 3
ix. 2. — 3
x. 4. — 3
x. 5, 5. — 3, 6

Job xi. 12, 12. — 2, 1
xii. 10. ν — 2
xiv. 1. — 3
xiv. 10, 10. — 6, 1
xiv. 14. — 6
xiv. 19. — 3
xv. 7. — 3
xv. 14. — 3
xvi. 21. — 3
xvi. 21. — 4, 1
xx. 4, 29. — 3
xxi. 4, 33. — 1
xxii. 2. — 6
xxv. 4. — 3
xxv. 6, 6. — 3, 1
xxvii. 13. — 3
xxviii. 4, 13. — 3
xxviii. 28. — 3
xxxii. 1, 5, 8. — 3
xxxiii. 12, 15, 16, 26, 27. — 3
xxxiii. 17, 17. — 1, 6
xxxiii. 23. — 1
xxxiii. 29. — 6
xxxiv. 7, 9, 34. — 3
xxxiv. 8, 10, 34, 36. — 3
xxxiv. 11, 11. — 1, 2
xxxiv. 15, 29. — 3
xxxv. 8, 8. — 2, 1
xxxv. 24, 25. — 3
xxxvi. 25, 28. — 1
xxxvii. 7, 7. — 1, 3
xxxvii. 24. — 3
xxxviii. 3. — 6
xxxviii. 26, 26. — 2, 1
xl. 7. — 6
Ps. viii. 4, 4. — 3, 1
ix. 19, 20. — 3
x. 18. — 3
xi. 4. — 1
xii. 1. — 3
xii. 8. — 4, 1
xiv. 2. — 1
xvii. 4. — 1
xviii. 25. — 6 a
xxi. 10. — 3
xxx. 6, 6. — 2, 1
xxvi. 9. — 3
xxxi. 19. — 3
xxxii. 2. — 3
xxxiii. 13. — 3
xxxiv. 8. — 3
xxxvi. 6, 7. — 3
xxxvii. 23. — 1
xxxix. 5. — 1
xxxix. 11, 11. — 3, 3
xl. 4. — 1
xlv. 2. — 3
xlix. 12, 20. — 1
lii. 7. — 3
liii. 2. — 1
lv. 13, 23. — 3
lvi. 1. — 1
lvi. 11. — 3
lvii. 4. — 1
lviii. 1, 11. — 3
lix. 2. — 1
lx. 11. — 3
lxii. 9. ξ — 4, 1
lxii. 9. — 4, 2
lxiv. 9. — 1
lxvi. 5. — 3
lxvi. 12. — 1
lxviii. 18. — 1
lxxiii. 5, 5. π — 3, 1
lxxvi. 12. — 1
lxxviii. 60. — 1
lxxx. 17, 17. — 2, 1
lxxxii. 7. — 3
lxxxiv. 5, 12. — 1
lxxxvii. 4. — 6
lxxxix. 47. — 6
lxxxix. 48. — 1
xc. 3, 3. — 3, 1
xciv. 10, 11. — 3
xciv. 12. — 1
ciii. 15. — 3
civ. 14, 23. — 3
civ. 15, 15. — 3, 1
cvi. 8. — 1
cvii. 8, 15, 21, 31. — 3
cviii. 12. — 1
cxv. 4, 16. — 3

Ps. cxvi. 11.	1	Isa. xlv. 14.	3	Ezek. xvi. 17.	8	
cxviii. 6, 8.	1	xlvi. 8.	2 a	xvii. 2.	1	
cxix. 134.	1	xlvii. 3.	1	xix. 3, 6.	1	
cxxiv. 2.	1	xlix. 7.σ	10	xx. 3, 4, 11, 13, 21,		
cxxvii. 5.	6	li. 7.	3	27, 46.	1	
cxxviii. 4.	5	li. 12, 12.	3, 1	xxi. 2, 6, 9, 12, 14,		
cxxxv. 8, 15.	1	lii. 14, 14.	2, 1	19, 28.	1	
cxxxix. 19.	3	lvi. 2, 2.	3, 1	xxi. 31.	3	
cxl. 1, 1.	1, 2	lvii. 1, 1.	2, 3	xxii. 2, 18, 24.	3	
cxliv. 3, 3.	1, 3	lviii. 5.	1	xxii. 9.	3	
cxliv. 4.	1	lxvi. 7.	8	xxiii. 2, 36.	3	
cxlv. 12.	1	lxvi. 24.	3	xxiii. 14, 40, 42, 45.	3	
cxlvi. 3.	1	Jer. ii. 6, 6.	2, 1	xxiv. 2, 16, 25.	3	
Prov. iii. 4, 13, 13, 30.	1	iv. 25.	1	xxiv. 17, 22.	3	
vi. 34.	6	v. 26.	3	xxv. 2, 13.	3	
viii. 4, 4.	2, 1	vii. 10.	1	xxv. 4, 10.	3	
viii. 31, 34.	1	ix. 22.	1	xxvi. 2.	1	
xi. 7.	1	x. 14.	3	xxvii. 2, 13.	3	
xii. 3, 23, 27.	1	x. 23,τ 23.	1, 2	xxvii. 10, 27.	3	
xii. 14, 14.	2, 1	xi. 21, 23.	3	xxvii. 11, 15.	3	
xv. 11, 20.	1	xvi. 20.	1	xxviii. 2, 2, 9, 12, 21.	1	
xvi. 1, 9.	1	xvii. 5, 5.	6, 1	xxix. 2, 8, 11, 18.	1	
xvii. 18.	1	xvii. 7.	6	xxx. 2, 21.	5	
xviii. 16.	1	xviii. 21.	3	xxx. 5.	4	
xix. 3, 11, 22.	1	xix. 10.	3	xxxi. 2, 14.	1	
xx. 6, 6.	1, 2	xx. 15, 15.	2, 8	xxxii. 2, 13, 18.	3	
xx. 24, 24.	6, 1	xxi. 6.	1	xxxiii. 2, 2.	1, 2	
xx. 25, 27.	1	xxii. 30, 30, 30.	2, 6, 2	xxxiii. 7, 10, 12, 24, 30.	1	
xxi. 16, 20.	1	xxiii. 9, 9.	2, 6	xxxiv. 2, 31.	1	
xxii. 24, 24.	5, 2	xxvi. 22, 22.	3	xxxv. 2.		
xxiii. 2.	5	xxvii. 5.	3	xxxvi. 1, 10, 11, 12,		
xxiii. 28.	1	xxx. 6, 6.	8, 6	13, 14, 17, 37, 38.	1	
xxiv. 1.	1	xxxi. 22.	6	xxxvii. 3, 9, 11, 16.	1	
xxiv. 5, 5.	6, 2	xxxi. 27, 30.	1	xxxviii. 2, 14, 20.	1	
xxiv. 9, 12, 30.	1	xxxii. 19, 20, 43.	3	xxxix. 1, 15, 17.	3	
xxv. 1.	3	xxxiii. 5, 10, 10, 12.	3	xxxix. 14.	3	
xxv. 5.	6	xxxiv. 18.	3	xl. 4, 4.	2, 1	
xxvii. 19, 19, 20.	3	xxxvi. 29.	1	xli. 19.	1	
xxviii. 2, 12, 14, 17,		xxxvii. 10, 10.	3, 2	xliii. 7, 10, 18.	1	
23, 28.	1	xxxvii. 4, 4, 4.	2, 3, 2	xliv. 7.	1	
xxviii. 3, 21.	6	xxxviii. 9, 10, 11,		xlvi. 6.	1	
xxviii. 5.	1	16.	3	Dan. ii. 10.	3 b	
xxix. 5.	6	xxxix. 4, 17.	3	ii. 38, 43.	3 a	
xxix. 8.	1	xl. 7, 7, 8, 9.	3	ii. 25.	6 b	
xxix. 22, 22.	2, 5	xli. 1, 2, 3, 7, 8, 9,		iii. 10.	3 a	
xxix. 23, 25.	1	12, 15, 16.	3	iii. 12, 13, 20, 21,		
xxx. 1, 19.	6	xlii. 17.	3	22, 23, 24, 25, 27.	6 b	
xxx. 2, 14.	1	xliii. 2, 9.	3	iv. 16, 17, 17, 25,		
Eccles. i. 3, 13.	1	xliii. 6.	6	25, 32, 32, 33.	3 a	
ii. 3, 8, 12, 18, 21, 21,		xliv. 15, 19.	3	v. 5, 21, 21.	3 a	
22, 24, 26.	1	xliv. 20.	6	v. 11.	6 b	
iii. 10, 11, 13, 18, 19,		xlvii. 2.	1	vi. 5, 11, 15, 24.	6 b	
19, 22.	1	xlviii. 14, 31, 36.	3	vi. 7, 12, 12.	3 a	
iii. 21.	4, 1	xlix. 15.	1	vii. 4, 4, 8, 13.	3 a	
v. 19.	1	xlix. 18, 18.	2, 1	viii. 15.	1	
vi. 1, 7, 10, 11, 12,		xlix. 26.	3	viii. 16, 17.	6	
12.	1	xlix. 28.	4	x. 7.	3	
vii. 2, 14, 20, 28, 29.	1	xlix. 33, 33.	2, 1	x. 16, 18.	3	
viii. 1, 6, 8, 9, 11, 15,		l. 3.	1	Hos. vi. 7.	1	
17, 17.	1	l. 30.	3	ix. 12.	1	
ix. 1, 3, 12, 12.	1	l. 40, 40.	2, 1	xi. 4.	1	
ix. 14.	1	li. 14, 17, 62.	1	xiii. 2.	3	
ix. 15, 15, 15.	2, 1, 2	li. 32.	3	Joel i. 12.	1	
x. 14.	1	li. 43, 43.	2, 1	ii. 7.	3	
xi. 8.	1	li. 7.	3	iii. 9.	1	
xii. 3.	3	lii. 25, 25, 25.	3, 3, 2	Amos iv. 13.	3	
xii. 5, 13.	1	Lam. iii. 1, 27, 35.	6	vi. 9.	1	
Isa. ii. 9, 9.ρ	1, 2	iii. 36.	1	Obad. 7, 7.	3	
ii. 11, 11.	1, 3	iii. 39, 39.	1, 6	Jonah i. 10, 10, 13, 16.	3	
ii. 17, 17.	1, 3	Ezek. i. 5, 8, 10, 26.	1	iii. 7, 8.	3	
ii. 20, 22.	1	ii. 1, 3, 6, 8.	1	Micah ii. 2, 2.	6, 2	
v. 15.	1	iii. 1, 3, 4, 10, 17,		ii. 12.	1	
v. 22.	1	25.	1	v. 5.	1	
vi. 11, 12.	1	iv. 1, 12, 15, 16.	1	v. 7, 7.	2, 1	
vii. 13.	3	v. 1.	1	vi. 8.	1	
viii. 1.	3	vii. 2.	1	vii. 2.	1, 2	
xiii. 7.	3	viii. 5, 6, 8, 15, 17.	1	vii. 6, 6.	2, 3	
xiii. 12, 12.	3, 1	viii. 12, 12.	1, 2	Nah. ii. 3.	3	
xvii. 7.	1	ix. 2, 2, 2.	3, 2, 2	Hab. i. 14.	1	
xxii. 6.	1	ix. 4, 6.	3	ii. 5.	6	
xxiv. 6.	1	x. 8, 14, 21.	1	ii. 8, 17.	1	
xxviii. 14.	3	xi. 2, 2.	1, 3	Zeph. i. 3, 3, 17.	1	
xxix. 13.	3	xi. 4.	1	i. 12.	3	
xxix. 19, 21.	1	xi. 15, 15.	1, 3	Hag. i. 11.	1	
xxxi. 3.	1	xii. 2, 3, 9, 18, 22,		Zech. ii. 4.	1	
xxxi. 8, 8.	2, 1	27.	1	iii. 8.	1	
xxxiii. 8.	3	xii. 16.	3	viii. 10, 10.	1	
xxxvi. 12.	3	xiii. 2, 17.	1	viii. 23.	3	
xxxvii. 19.	3	xiv. 3, 3.	1, 3	ix. 1.	1	
xxxviii. 11.	3	xiv. 13, 13, 17, 19,		ix. 6.	3	
xxxix. 3.	3	21.	1	xii. 1.	1	
xliii. 4.	1	xiv. 14, 16, 18.	3	xiii. 5.	6	
xliv. 11, 15.	1	xv. 2.	3	xiii. 7.	1	
xliv. 13, 13.	2, 1	xvi. 2.	1	Mal. iii. 8.	1	
xlv. 12.	1					

α *lit.* the man.   β *lit.* from man unto.   γ *lit.* not a man of the men.
δ *lit.* mouth to man.   ε *lit.* in man.   ζ *lit.* one man one man for a tribe.
η *lit.* from man.   θ *lit.* son of valour.   ι *lit.* a man of the young men
of Joab.   κ *lit.* if he shall be for a son of valour.   λ *lit.* men sons of
strength.   μ "mortal man."   ν *lit.* flesh of man.   ξ *lit.* sons of Adam.
ο *lit.* sons of men.   π *lit.* with other men.   ρ *lit.* "mean man," "great
man."   σ *marg.* 'or, despised in soul.'   τ *lit.* not to man is his way.

MANDRAKES

דּוּדַי *m.* some lovely fruit or flower. Celsus is persuaded it is
the fruit of the lote-tree, the *lotus cyrenaica*, called in
Africa and Asia, sidia and nobak : a small tree like the
acacia, with leaves and flowers resembling those of
jujub, bearing little round aromatic apples, in flavour
and taste so delicious that they are fit only for the table
of princes. The Turks suppose it was one of the trees in
Paradise. It grows in Judea and Syria, and bears fruit
both in spring and autumn ; but the spring fruit seldom
comes to perfection, by reason of the latter rains falling
in April. One of the old Rabbis says this fruit is the
dudaim Rachel was so fond of ; and the Talmudists
were acquainted with it under the name of rimin. See
divers accounts of it, ancient and modern, in Olav. Cels.
Hierobot. Pt. i. p. 20, &c.; Homer, Odyss. ix. l. 94;
Hiller. Hierophyt. i. 268.—Gen. xxx. 14, 14, 15, 15, 16:
Cant. vii. 13.

MANEH

מָנֶה *m.* see *Pound.* Gesenius. Another, and somewhat obscure,
signification is given, Ezek. xlv. 12, twenty shekels,
twenty-five shekels, fifteen shekels, shall be your mina ;
spoken either of a treble mina, of twenty, twenty-five,
and fifteen shekels ; or of a single mina of sixty shekels
distributed into three parts, fifteen, twenty, twenty-five.
The latter is best.

MANIFEST

בָּרַר to separate. Kal *inf.* Eccles. iii. 18, to search out, to
prove. Hengstenberg, that God may purify them : Dan.
xi. 35.

MANNA

מָן *Quid?* Exod. xvi. 15, "It is manna," Heb. what is it?
See Noldius ; or,

מָנָה to number ; a certain measure, part, or portion, assigned
or allotted ; but this does not ascertain the derivation
of manna, which depends on the meaning of the expression, מָן הוּא, which the Israelites used when they
first saw it. If it means, "what is it," then manna is
but the Chaldee particle, מַן, turned into a noun ; but
if it means, "it is a portion," something that God has
appointed for us, then it belongs to this root. מָן *m.*
Exod. xvi. 15, "It (is) manna," 31, 33, 35, 35 : Num.
xi. 6, 7, 9 : Deut. viii. 3, 16 : Josh. v. 12, 12 : Neh. ix.
20 : Ps. lxxviii. 24.

MANNER

1   אֹרַח *com.* a way, a path ; manner, what is customary or incident to.

2   דָּבָר *m.* word, matter, thing spoken of, what is said of it.   דְּבָר א
m. rather, pasture ; see *Fold.*

3   דְּמוּת   *f.* likeness.

4   דֶּרֶךְ   *com.* way, path.

5   דָּת   *f.* law.

6   חֻקָּה   *f.* see *Ordinance, Statute.*

7   מִשְׁפָּט   *m.* judgment; justice; manner, custom, prescription; manner, fashion, sort, kind; manner of law; ordinance.

8   תּוֹרָה   *f.* law; custom, manner : 2 Sam. vii. 19, *marg.* 'law.' As this is the only place in which תּוֹרָה seems to have the meaning of manner, custom, and is more properly law, or precept, often implying the revealed law of God, and as הָאָדָם is with the ה emphatic, the sentence is conceived by many to have reference to the Man whose coming was a part of the revealed will of God; and may be translated, ' and this is the revealed law of, *or,* with respect to, the Man.' Michaelis, however, with Gussetius, thinks that תּוֹרָה may imply the order of succession of men in which the Messiah should at length appear.

9   זַן   *m.* form, sort, kind, manner : Ps. cxliv. 14, "all manner of store," *lit.* from sort to sort.

Gen. xviii. 11. α	1	Judg. xviii. 7.	7	2 Chron. iv. 20.	7
xviii. 25.	2	1 Sam. viii. 9, 11.	7	xxx. 16.	7
xix. 31.	4	x. 25.	7	Neh. iv. 4, 5.	2
xxxii. 19.	2	xvii. 27, 30, 30.	2	viii. 18.	7
xxxix. 19.	2	xxviii. 24.	2	Esth. i. 13.	2
xl. 13.	7	xxi. 5.	7	ii. 12.	5
Exod. xxi. 9.	7	xxvii. 11.	7	Ps. cxliv. 13.	9
xxii. 9.	2	2 Sam. vii. 19.	8	Isa. v. 17.	2 a
Lev. v. 10.	7	xiv. 3.	2	x. 24, 26.	4
ix. 16.	7	xv. 6.	2	Jer. xxii. 21.	4
xx. 23.	6	xvii. 6.	7	xxx. 18.	7
xxiv. 22.	7	1 Kings xviii. 28.	7	Ezek. xi. 12.	7
Num. ix. 14.	7	2 Kings i. 7.	7	xx. 30.	4
xv. 16, 24.	2	xi. 14.	7	xxiii. 15.	3
xxix. 6, 18, 21, 24,		xvii. 26, 26, 27, 33,		xxiii. 45, 45.	7
27, 30, 33, 37.	7	34, 40.	7	Amos iv. 10.	4
Deut. xv. 2.	2	1 Chron. xxiv. 19.	7	viii. 14.	4
Josh. vi. 15.	7				

α *lit.* the way as of women.

MAN-SERVANT

עֶבֶד   *m.* see *Serve, Servant.* Gen. xii. 16, &c.

MAN-SLAYER

רָצַח   to kill, to slay. KAL *part.* Poel, Num. xxxv. 6, 12.

MANTLE

אַדֶּרֶת   *f.* a wide cloak, mantle, pallium : 1 Kings xix. 13, 19; 2 Kings ii. 8, 13, 14.

מְעִיל   *m.* an upper garment, large and without sleeves; see *Robe.* 1 Sam. xv. 27; xxviii. 14 : Ezra ix. 3, 5 : Job i. 20, *marg.* ' or, robe;' ii. 12 : Ps. cix. 29.

מַעֲטָפוֹת   *f. pl.* a larger tunic, worn over the common one, with sleeves, and reaching down to the feet : Isa. iii. 23.

שְׂמִיכָה   *f.* a quilt, coverlet : Judg. iv. 18, *marg.* ' or, rug, *or,* blanket.'

MANY, MANIFOLD

1   הָמוֹן   noise; "many," *lit.* multitude of.

2   כָּבֵד   to be heavy; this root seems to imply number as well as weight; see Nah. iii. 3, and its use as an *adj.* HITHPAEL *imp.*

3   רָבַב   to become much or many, to multiply. KAL ᵃ *pret.*

רָבָה the same. KAL ᵇ *pret.* ᶜ *fut.* HIPHIL ᵈ *pret.* ᵉ *inf.* ᶠ *imp.* ᵍ *fut.* ʰ *part.* רַב ⁱ *adj.* many, equivalent to πολλοὶ in N. T., Rom. v. 15 : Gen. xxi. 34, &c. רֹב ᵏ *m.* multitude. רְבָבָה ˡ *f.* myriad.

4   שַׂגִּיא   Ch. *adj.* great, much, many.

No. 3 i, *Many,* not included.

Gen. xvii. 4, 5.	1	2 Chron. xvi. 8.	3 e	Isa. i. 15.	3 g
Num. x. 36.	3 l	Ezra v. 11.	4	xxii. 9.	3 a
xxxv. 8, 8. α	3 i g	x. 13, 13.	3 i d	xxiii. 16. δ	3 f
Deut. iii. 5.	3 e	Neh. vi. 17.	3 h	xxiv. 22.	3 k
Judg. xvi. 24.	3 d	Job xli. 3. β	3 g	lxvi. 16.	3 a
1 Sam. xvi. 24.	3 a	Ps. xxv. 19.	3 a	Jer. v. 6.	3 a
2 Sam. i. 4.	3 e	lxxviii. 38. γ	3 d	xiv. 7.	3 a
xii. 2.	3 e	civ. 24.	3 a	xlii. 2.	3 e
1 Kings vii. 47.	3 k	Prov. iv. 10.	3 c	xlvi. 11, ε 16.	3 d
1 Chron. vii. 4.	3 d	Eccles. v. 7.	3 e	Ezek. xxii. 25.	3 d
viii. 40.	3 h	vi. 11.	3 e	Dan. ii. 48.	4
xxiii. 11.	3 d	xi. 1.	3 k	Hos. viii. 11.	3 d
xxiii. 17.	3 b	xi. 8, 8.	3 e	Amos v. 12.	3 i
2 Chron. xi. 23.	1	xi. 9, 12.	3 e	Nah. iii. 15, 15.	2

α "give many."   β "make many."   γ *lit.* multiplied to turn.
δ *lit.* multiply the song.   ε "use many."

MAR

כָּאַב   to grieve, to afflict, to destroy. HIPHIL *fut.* 2 Kings iii. 19, make it useless and sterile by casting stones upon it; *comp.* Isa. v. 2, Job v. 23. LXX. ἀχρειώσατε.

נָתַם   to tear up, to break up, to destroy. KAL *pret.* Job xxx. 13.

שָׁחַת   to corrupt, to destroy. NIPHAL *pret.* Jer. xiii. 7; xviii. 4. PIEL *pret.* Nah. ii. 2. HIPHIL *fut.* Lev. xix. 27: Ruth iv. 6 : Jer. xiii. 9. *part.* 1 Sam. vi. 5. מִשְׁחָת *m.* something marred : Isa. lii. 14.

MARA

מַר   *adj.* bitter : Exod. xv. 23 : Ruth i. 20.

MARBLE

שַׁיִשׁ   *m.* white marble, alabaster : 1 Chron. xxix. 2. שֵׁשׁ *m. id.* Esth. i. 6 : Cant. v. 15.

MARCH

הָלַךְ   to go, to walk. KAL *part.* Poel, Hab. i. 6.

יָלַךְ   to go, to walk. KAL *fut.* Jer. xlvi. 22 : Joel ii. 7.

נָסַע   to journey. KAL *part.* Poel, Exod. xiv. 10.

צָעַד   to step, to move slowly, in a solemn manner. KAL *inf.* Judg. v. 4 : Ps. lxviii. 7. *fut.* Hab. iii. 12.

MARINER

מַלָּח   *m.* seamen : Ezek. xxvii. 9, 27, 29 : Jonah i. 5.

שׁוּט   to row. KAL *part.* Ezek. xxvii. 8.

MARISH

גֶּבֶא   *m.* pit, marsh, pool : Ezek. xlvii. 11.

MARK

1   אוֹת   *com.* a sign : Gen. iv. 15, or gave a sign to Cain; see *Sign.*

2   בִּין   to discern, perceive; to mark, attend, give heed to. KAL and HIPHIL *fut.*

3 חָתַם to seal. PIEL *pret.*

4 מְגַמָּה *f.* scope, aim ; mark. סַפְרָא *a* *f. id.*

5 יָדַע to know. KAL *a pret. b imp.*

6 כְּתֹבֶת *f.* writing, mark : Lev. xix. 28, *lit.* an inscription of a mark.

7 כָּתַם to cut, engrave. NIPHAL *part.*

8 מִפְגָּע *m.* attack, assault ; object of assault, mark.

9 פָּנָה to look ; with אֶל to mark. KAL *imp.*

10 קַעֲקַע *m.* a stigma, mark, cut or burnt.

11 קָשַׁב to hearken. HIPHIL *a pret. b imp.*

12 רָאָה to see, look on. KAL *imp.*

13 שׂוּם to set, with לֵב to mark, *lit.* to set the heart. KAL *a pret. b imp.*

14 שִׁית to put, to set, with לֵב, as above. KAL *imp.*

15 שָׁמַר to keep, to watch, to guard ; to keep in view, to observe, to mark. KAL *a pret. b imp. c fut. d part.* Poel.

16 תָּאַר to be marked out or off, to be described ; to delineate. PIEL *fut.*

17 תָּו *m.* a mark impressed on the person.

Gen. iv. 15.	1	Job xvi. 12.	4	Ps. xlviii. 13.	14
Lev. xix. 28.	6, 10	xviii. 2.	2	lvi. 6.	15 d
Ruth iii. 4.	5 a	xxi. 5.	9	cxxx. 3.	15 d
1 Sam. i. 12.	15 d	xxii. 15.	15 c	Isa. xliv. 13, 13.	16
xx. 20.	4	xxiv. 16.	3	Jer. ii. 22.	7
2 Sam. xiii. 28.	12	xxxiii. 11.	15 c	xxiii. 18.	11 a
1 Kings xx. 7, 22.	5 b	xxxiii. 31.	11 b	Lam. iii. 12.	4 a
Job vii. 20.	8	xxxix. 1.	15 c	Ezek. ix. 4, 6.	17
x. 14.	15 a	Ps. xxxvii. 37.	15 b	xliv. 5, 5.	13 b a

MARKET

מַעֲרָב *m.* merchandise : Ezek. xxvii. 13, 17, 19, 25.

MARROW

חֵלֶב *m.* fatness, fat of the inwards : Ps. lxiii. 5.

מָחָה to be fat. PUAL *part.* Isa. xxv. 6. מֹחַ *m.* fat : Job xxi. 24.

שִׁקּוּי *m.* a watering, moistening of the bones : Prov. iii. 8.

MARRY

1 בָּעַל to be master ; to become a husband. KAL *a pret. b fut. c part.* Paül. NIPHAL *d fut. e* בַּעַל *m.* Exod. xxi. 3, *lit.* husband of a wife.

2 הָלַל to praise. PUAL *pret.* Ps. lxxviii. 63, "were not given to marriage," *marg.* 'praised,' *i.e.* in nuptial songs.

3 חָתַן to join in affinity, to make marriages. HITHPAEL *a pret. b imp. c fut.*

4 יָבָם *m.* husband's brother. יָבַם to marry a brother's widow. PIEL *a imp.*

5 יָשַׁב to dwell. Hiphil, to let dwell, to cohabit. HIPHIL *a pret. b inf.*

6 לָקַח to take. KAL *a pret. b part.* Poel.

7 נָשָׂא to bear ; to take a wife. KAL *fut.*

8 נָשִׁים *f. pl.* wives ; married, Heb. for wives.

9 עֹנָה *f.* living together, duty of marriage.

Gen. xix. 14.	6 b	Deut. vii. 3.	3 c	Ps. lxxviii. 63.	2
xxiv. 9.	3 b	xxii. 22.	1 c	Prov. xxx. 23.	1 d
xxxviii. 8.	4	xxiv. 1.	1 a	Isa. liv. 1.	1 d
Exod. xxi. 3.	1 e	Josh. xxiii. 12.	3 a	lxii. 4.	1 d
xxi. 10.	9	1 Chron. ii. 21.*α*	1 a	lxii. 5, 5.	1 b
Num. xii. 1, 1.	6 a	2 Chron. xiii. 21.*β*	7	Jer. iii. 14.	1 a
xxxvi. 3, 6, 6, 11,	8	Neh. xiii. 23.	5 a	Mal. ii. 11.	1 a
12.	8	xiii. 27.	5 b		

a lit. and he took her.   *β lit.* took to him.

MART

סְחַר *m.* merchandise : Isa. xxiii. 3.

MARVEL

1 פָּלָא to separate, to distinguish ; to make distinguished, extraordinary, wonderful. NIPHAL *a pret. b fut. c part.* HIPHIL *d pret. e inf.* HITHPAEL *f fut. g* פֶּלֶא *m.* wonder. פָּלָה *i. q.* פָּלָא. HIPHIL *h imp.*

2 תָּמַהּ to be astonished, to wonder. KAL *a pret. b imp. c fut.*

Gen. xliii. 33.	2 c	Ps. xvii. 7.	1 h	Ps. cxxxix. 14.	1 c
Exod. xxxiv. 10.	1 c	xxxi. 21.*β*	1 d	Eccles. v. 8.	2 c
1 Chron. xvi. 12, 24.	1 c	xlviii. 5.	2 a	Isa. xxix. 14, 14.	1 e
2 Chron. xxvi. 15.	1 d	lxxviii. 12.	1 g	Dan. xi. 36.	1 c
Job v. 9.	1 d	xcviii. 1.	1 c	Micah vii. 15.	1 c
x. 16.*a*	1 f	cv. 5.	1 c	Hab. i. 5.	2 b
xxxvii. 5.	1 c	cxviii. 23.	1 a	Zech. viii. 6, 6.	1 b
Ps. ix. 1.	1 c				

a lit. he hath marvellously shewed his kindness.   *β lit.* thou returnest, thou shewest thyself, &c.

MASCHIL

שָׂכַל to be prudent, wise ; Hiphil, to become wise, intelligent ; to make wise, to teach, instruct ; in the title of Psalms of instruction. HIPHIL *part.* Ps. xxxii. title ; xlii. title ; xliv. title ; xlv. title ; lii. title ; liii. title ; liv. title ; lv. title ; lxxiv. title ; lxxviii. title ; lxxxviii. title ; lxxxix. title ; cxlii. title.

MASON

1 אֶבֶן *f.* stone.

2 גָּדַר to build a wall. KAL *part.* Poel.

3 חָצַב to hew. KAL *part.* Poel.

4 חָרָשׁ *m.* engraver, workman, workers of stone or of wall.

5 קִיר *m.* wall ; masons, *lit.* hewers of the stone of the wall.

2 Sam. v. 11.	4, 1, 5	1 Chron. xiv. 1.	4, 5	2 Chron. xxiv. 12.	3
2 Kings xii. 12.	2	xxii. 2.	3	Ezra iii. 7.	3
xxii. 6.	2				

MASSAH

מַסָּה *f.* temptation : Exod. xvii. 7 : Deut. vi. 16 ; ix. 22 ; xxxiii. 8.

MAST

חֶבֶל the mast of a ship, so called from the ropes and stays by which it is fastened : Prov. xxiii. 34.

תֹּרֶן a pine, a mast of a ship : Isa. xxxiii. 23 : Ezek. xxvii.

MASTER, MASTERY

1 אָדוֹן *m.* master, as owner, or as ruler : Gen. xxiv. 9, &c.

2 אִישׁ *m.* man.

3 בַּעַל *m.* lord, master, possessor, owner.

4 גְּבוּרָה *f.* might, mastery.

5 עוּר to awake. KAL *part.* Poel.

6   רַב *adj.* much ; great, in age or skill.   רַב Ch. *adj. id.*

7   שַׂר *m.* a prefect, leader ; master, chief.

8   שְׁלֵט Ch. to rule, to have dominion ; *seq.* בְּ to get the mastery of, *i. e.* to rush or fall upon. P'AL *pret.*

No. 1 not included.

Exod. i. 11.		7	Eccles. xii. 11.	3	Dan. v. 11.	6 a
xxii. 8.		3	Isa. i. 3.	3	vi. 24.	8
xxxii. 18.		4	Dan. i. 3.	6	Jonah i. 6.	6
Judg. xix. 22.	1, 3		iv. 9.	6 a	Mal. ii. 12.	5
xix. 23.		3				

MATE

רְעוּת *f.* female companion : Isa. xxxiv. 15, 16.

MATRIX

רֶחֶם *m.* womb : Exod. xiii. 12, 15 ; xxxiv. 19 : Num. iii. 12 ; xviii. 15.

MATTER

בַּעַל *m.* master : Exod. xxiv. 14, *lit.* who is a master of business.

דָּבָר *m.* word, thing, matter : Gen. xxiv. 9, &c.

חֵפֶץ *m.* desire, will, purpose : Eccles. v. 8.

טַעַם Ch. *m.* commandment, decree : Ezra v. 5.

מִלָּה *f.* word ; speech, discourse : Job xxxii. 18.   מִלָּה Ch. *f.* Dan. ii. 10, 23 ; vii. 1, 28, 28.

פִּתְגָּם Ch. *m.* word ; decree : Dan. iii. 16 ; iv. 17.

MATTOCK

חֶרֶב *f.* sword ; tool : 2 Chron. xxxiv. 6, *marg.* 'or, mauls.'

מַחֲרֵשָׁה *f.* ploughshare, coulter : 1 Sam. xiii. 20, 21.

מַעְדֵּר *m.* (see *Dig*), mattock, probably a hoe or spade : Isa. vii. 25.

MAUL

מֵפִיץ *m.* a mallet, maul, war-club, that breaketh in pieces : Prov. xxv. 18.

MAW

קֵבָה *f.* maw, ventricle, *i. e.* the rough prickly stomach of ruminating animals : Deut. xviii. 3.

MAY

יָכֹל to be able. KAL *fut.* Gen. xliii. 32 : xliv. 26 : Deut. vii. 22 ; xii. 17 ; xvi. 5 ; xvii. 15 ; xxi. 16 ; xxii. 3, 19, 29 ; xxiv. 4 : Josh. ix. 19 : Judg. xxi. 18 : 2 Sam. xvii. 17 : 1 Kings xiii. 16 : xx. 9 : Eccles. vi. 10 : Jer. xiii. 23.

MAZZAROTH

מַזָּרוֹת *f. pl.* (see *Planets*), the twelve signs of the Zodiac : Job xxxviii. 32.

ME

נֶפֶשׁ soul, animal life ; " me," *lit.* my soul, or my life : Num. xxiii. 10 : Judg. xvi. 30 : 1 Kings xx. 32.

MEADOW

אָחוּ *m.* marsh-grass, reeds, bulrushes, sedge, everything green which grows in wet grounds. Jerome says it is an Egyptian or Coptic word. Gen. xli. 2, 18.

מַעֲרֶה *m.* naked place, *i. e.* a field or plain without trees or dwelling : Judg. xx. 33.

MEAL

אֹכֶל *m.* food : Ruth ii. 14.

סֹלֶת *f.* very fine flour ; with קֶמַח Gen. xviii. 6, " fine meal."

קֶמַח *m.* meal, flour : Gen. xviii. 6 : Num. v. 15 : 1 Kings iv. 22 ; xvii. 12, 14, 16 : 2 Kings iv. 41 : 1 Chron. xii. 40 : Isa. xlvii. 2 : Hos. viii. 7.

MEAN

אָדָם *m.* man ; common men, in opposition to those of higher rank and better character : Isa. ii. 9 ; v. 15 ; xxxi. 8.

חָשֹׁךְ *adj.* dark ; obscure, mean : Prov. xxii. 29.

MEAN   (V.)

בִּינָה *f.* understanding : Dan. viii. 15.

דָּמָה to be like ; Piel, to liken in the mind, to imagine, think. PIEL *fut.* Isa. x. 7.

חָשַׁב to think, devise, purpose. KAL *pret.* Gen. l. 20.

MEANS

יָד *com.* hand : 1 Kings x. 29 : 2 Chron. i. 17 : Jer. v. 31 : Mal. i. 9.

מַחֲשֶׁבֶת *f.* thoughts, device, purpose, invention : 2 Sam. xiv. 14.

MEASURE

1   אֵיפָה *f.* an ephah ; " divers measures," an ephah and an ephah.

2   אַמָּה *f.* a cubit.

3   חֹק *m.* portion ; an appointed bound, limit.

4   כֹּר *m.* cor, a measure both of things dry and liquid.   כּוֹרִין Ch. *m. pl. id.*

5   מָדַד to extend ; to mete, to measure ; also of hollow measures as well as of length ; figuratively applied to the proportioning of God's judgments to the wickedness of man. KAL ᵃ *pret.* ᵇ*inf.* ᶜ*fut.* NIPHAL ᵈ*fut.* PIEL ᵉ*fut.* POLEL ᶠ*fut.* מִדָּה ᵍ measure. ʰ מַד *m. id.* מִמַּדִּים ᶦ *m. pl. id.*

6   מְשׂוּרָה *f.* measure, *i. e.* of liquids.

7   סְאָה *f.* a certain measure for grain, seah ; according to the Rabbins, the third part of an ephah ; and according to Jerome, a modius and a half.   סָאסְאָה *f.* with prefix בְּ for בְּ. בְּסַאסְאָה. Isa. xxvii. 8, by measure and measure, according to measure, *i. e.* with moderation.

8   שָׁלִישׁ *m.* a third ; probably a third part of an ephah.

9   מִשְׁפָּט *m.* judgment ; right, rectitude, justice.

10   תֹּכֶן *m.* task ; a measure.   מַתְכֹּנֶת ᵃ *f. id.*

No. 5 g not included.

Gen. xviii. 6.	7	Ruth iii. 15.	5 c	1 Kings xviii. 32.	7
Lev. xix. 35.	6	1 Sam. xxv. 18.	5	2 Kings vii. 1, 1, 16,	
Num. xxxv. 5.	5 a	2 Sam. viii. 2, 2.	5 e	16, 18, 18.	7
Deut. xxi. 2.	5 a	1 Kings iv. 22, 22.	4	1 Chron. xxiii. 29.	6
xxv. 14, 15.	1	v. 11, 11.	4	2 Chron. ii. 10, 10.	4

2 Chron. xxvii. 5.	4	Jer. xlvi. 28.	9	Ezek. xlii. 16, 16, 16.	5 a g g
Ezra vii. 22.	4 a	li. 13.	2	xlii. 17, 17.	5 a g
Job xi. 9.	5 h	Ezek. iv. 11, 16.	6	xlii. 18, 18.	5 a g
xxxviii. 5.	5 i	xl. 5, 5.	5 g c	xlii. 19, 19.	5 a g
Ps. lxxx. 5.	8	xl. 6, 8, 9, 11, 13, 19, 23, 27, 47, 48.	5 c	xlii. 20.	5 a
Prov. xx. 10.	1	xl. 20.	5 a	xliii. 10.	5 a
Isa. v. 14.	3	xl. 24, 24.	5 a g	xlv. 3.	5 a
xxvii. 8.	7 a	xl. 28, 28.	5 c g	xlv. 11, 11.	10, 10 a
xl. 12, 12.	5 a, 8	xl. 32, 32.	5 c g	xlvii. 3, 4, 4, 5, 18.	5 c
lxv. 7.	5 a	xl. 35, 35.	5 c g	Hos. i. 10.	5 d
Jer. xiii. 25.	5 h	xli. 13, 15.	5 a	Micah vi. 10.	1
xxx. 11.	9	xlii. 15, 15.	5 g a	Hab. iii. 6.	1 f
xxxi. 37.	5 d			Zech. ii. 2.	5 b
xxxiii. 22.	5 d				

MEAT

1 אָכַל to eat. KAL a *inf.* HIPHIL b *fut.* אֹכֶל m. food. d אָכְלָה f. id. e אֲכִילָה f. id. f מַאֲכָל m. id.: Gen. xl. 17, *lit.* meat of Pharaoh, the work of a baker.

2 בָּרָה to eat. PIEL a *inf.* בָּרוּת f. food. b בִּרְיָה f. id.

3 מָזוֹן m. food, as nutriment. a מָזוֹן Ch. m. id.

4 טֶרֶף m. prey.

5 לֶחֶם m. bread, food, meat, both for men and animals.

6 פַּת f. morsel.

7 מִנְחָה f. a present, gift, meat-offering, rather meal or flour-offering, with oil and frankincense, the only word so rendered: Exod. xxix. 41, &c.; in Lev. ii. 1, joined with קָרְבָּן. a מִנְחָה Ch. f. id.

8 פַּתְבַּג m. delicate food, dainties, of the king's table; "provision, portion, of meat."

9 צֵידָה f. see *Victual.*

No. 1 f not included; *Meat offering*, No. 7, not included.

Gen. i. 29, 30.	1 d	Job xii. 11.	1 c	Prov. xxiii. 3.	5
ix. 3.	1 d	xx. 14.	5	xxx. 22, 25.	5
xlv. 23.	3	xx. 21.	5	xxxi. 15.	4
Lev. xi. 34.	1 c	xxx. 4.	5	Isa. lxv. 25.	5
xxii. 11, 13.	5	xxxiv. 3.	5	Lam. i. 11, 19.	1 c
xxv. 6.	1 d	xxxvi. 31.	1 a	iv. 10.	2 a
xxv. 7.	1 a	xxxviii. 41.	1 c	Ezek. xvi. 19.	5
Num. xxviii. 24.	5	Ps. xlii. 3.	5	xxix. 5.	1 d
Deut. ii. 6, 28.	1 c	lix. 15.	5	xxxiv. 5, 8, 10.	1 d
1 Sam. xx. 5.	1 a	lxix. 21.	1 a	Dan. i. 5, 8, 13, 15, 16.	8
xx. 24, 27, 34.	5	lxxviii. 18, 30.	1 c	iv. 12, 21.	3 a
2 Sam. iii. 35.	5	lxxviii. 25.	5	xi. 26.	8
xii. 3.	5	civ. 21, 27.	1 c	Hos. xi. 4.	1 b
xiii. 5, 5.	5, 2 c	cvii. 18.	1 c	Joel i. 16.	1 c
xiii. 7, 10.	2 c	cxi. 5.	4	Hab. iii. 17.	1 c
1 Kings xix. 8.	1 e	cxlv. 15.	1 c	Mal. i. 12.	1 c
Ezra vii. 17.	7 a	Prov. vi. 8.	1 c	iii. 10.	4
Job vi. 7.	5				

MEDDLE

גָּלַע to be mingled with, to intermeddle. HITHPAEL *pret.* Prov. xvii. 14. *fut.* Prov. xx. 3. Gesenius, to become angry, to grow warm, to be irritated.

גָּרָה to stir up, to contend with, *seq.* ב. HITHPAEL *fut.* Deut. ii. 5, 19: 2 Kings xiv. 10: 2 Chron. xxv. 19.

עָבַר to pass; Hithp. to pass bounds, to be enraged. HITHPAEL *part.* Prov. xxvi. 17.

עָרַב to mingle; Hithp. to mingle oneself, to intermeddle. HITHPAEL *fut.* Prov. xx. 19; xxiv. 21.

MEDICINE

גֵּהָה f. healing, cure; see *Cure.* Prov. xvii. 22.

רְפֻאוֹת f. pl. healing, health; medicines for wounds: Jer. xxx. 13; xlvi. 11.

תְּרוּפָה f. medicine: Ezek. xlvii. 12.

MEDITATE

1 הָגִיג of the same import with the following; hence הָגִיג m. meditation.

2 הָגָה to murmur, to mutter; to make sound with the mouth; it is thus generally applied to the roaring of the lion when he has got his prey, Isa. xxxi. 4; to soft thunder, Job xxxvii. 2; to the muttering of charmers, Isa. viii. 19; to the sound of the harp, Ps. ix. 16, xcii. 3; to the mourning of the dove, Isa. xxxviii. 14, lix. 11; to the groaning and sighing of men, Isa. xvi. 7, Jer. xlviii. 31. It is from the palate, Prov. viii. 7; the throat, Ps. cxv. 7; or the tongue, Ps. xxxv. 28. When understood, therefore, of meditation, it implies what we express by one talking to himself. KAL a *pret.* b *fut.* c הָגוּת f. meditation. d הִגָּיוֹן m. id.

3 שׂוּחַ to meditate. KAL *inf.*

4 שִׂיחַ to speak, to talk, to converse; to talk with oneself, to meditate. KAL a *inf.* b *fut.* c שִׂיחַ m. meditation. d שִׂיחָה f. id.

Gen. xxiv. 63.	3	Ps. xlix. 3.	2 c	Ps. cxix. 97, 99.	4 d
Josh. i. 8.	2 a	lxiii. 6.	2 b	cxix. 148.	4 a
Ps. i. 2.	2 b	lxxvii. 12.	2 a	cxliii. 5.	2 a
v. 1.	1	civ. 34.	2 c	Isa. xxxiii. 18.	2 b
xix. 14.	1 d	cxix. 15, 23, 48, 78.	4 b		

MEEK

עָנָו adj. oppressed, afflicted, wretched, but everywhere with the accessory idea of humility, meekness, *i.e.* the humble, the meek, who prefer to suffer wrong rather than do wrong, and who therefore enjoy God's favour. Cocceius has drawn a distinction between עָנִי and עָנָו, that the former is applied to those who patiently suffer without resistance; the latter to those who willingly endure with submission what they might escape from.—*Cocceius* on Gen. xvi. 6. Ps. xxii. 26; xxv. 9, 9; xxxvii. 11; lxxvi. 9; cxlvii. 6; cxlix. 4: Isa. xi. 4; xxix. 19; lxi. 1: Amos ii. 7: Zeph. ii. 3. עֲנָוָה f. a lowly mind: Zeph. ii. 3. עֲנָוָה f. id. Ps. xlv. 4. עָנָיו adj. id. Num. xii. 3.

MEET

1 אֲרַךְ Ch. to make long; to fit, adapt. P'AL *part.*

2 בֵּן m. son; "meet for the war," *lit.* sons of valour.

3 יָשַׁר to be right. KAL a *pret.* "it seemed meet." b יָשָׁר *adj.* right. c יֹשֶׁר m. what is just and meet.

4 כּוּן to be set up, made to stand; to be right, fit, proper, appointed, ordained. NIPHAL *part.*

5 נֶגֶד before כְּנֶגֶד *lit.* as over against, corresponding to, suitable for, meet: Gen. ii. 18, 20.

6 עָשָׂה to do. NIPHAL a *pret.* b *fut.*

7 צָלַח to prosper. KAL *fut.*

8 רָאָה to see. KAL *part.* Paûl, which made a suitable appearance.

Gen. ii. 18, 20.	5	Ezra iv. 14.	1	Jer. xxvii. 5.	3 a
Exod. viii. 26.	4	Esth. ii. 9.	8	Ezek. xv. 4.	7
Deut. iii. 18.	2	Prov. xi. 24.	3 c	xv. 5, 5.	6 b a
2 Kings x. 3.	3 b	Jer. xxvi. 14.	3 b		

MEET (V)

1 יָעַד to appoint; Niph. *reflex.* to meet with any one at an

appointed place; *recipr.* to meet together at an appointed time and place by appointment; generally to come together, to assemble. NIPHAL ᵃ*pret.* ᵇ*fut.*

2 מָצָא to find. KAL ᵃ*pret.* ᵇ*fut.*

3 פָּגַע to come upon, to reach to, to overtake; to come upon with a hostile intention; to come up with as a friend or helper; to light upon accidentally. KAL ᵃ*pret.* ᵇ*imp.* ᶜ*fut.*

4 פָּגַשׁ to meet, as one person meets another on the road, and in a hostile manner. KAL ᵃ*pret.* ᵇ*inf.* ᶜ*fut.* NIPHAL ᵈ*pret.* PIEL ᵉ*fut.*

5 פָּנִים *m. pl.* face.

6 קָדַם to be before, to prevent; to give assistance unasked, freely. PIEL *pret.*

7 קָרָא to encounter, to meet any one. KAL ᵃ*inf.* NIPHAL ᵇ*pret.* ᶜ*fut.*

8 קָרָה to meet, to go or come to meet any one, in a hostile sense, *seq. acc.* Exod. iii. 18, *comp.* v. 3. Niph., to meet or fall in with, to light upon any one, *seq.* אֶל, Num. xxiii. 4, 16, *seq.* לִקְרַאת, v. 3. KAL ᵃ*pret.* NIPHAL ᵇ*pret.* Exod. iii. 18, in allusion to the divine appearance at Mount Sinai. ᶜ*fut.*

Gen. xiv. 17.	7 a	Josh. iv. 5.	1 b	2 Kings iv. 26, 31.	7 a
xviii. 2.	7 a	ix. 11.	1 b	iv. 29.	2 b
xix. 1.	7 a	xi. 5.	1 b	v. 21, 26.	7 a
xxiv. 17, 65.	7 a	xvii. 10.	3 c	viii. 8, 9.	7 a
xxix. 13.	7 a	Judg. iv. 18, 22.	7 a	ix. 17, 18.	7 a
xxx. 16.	7 a	vi. 35.	7 a	ix. 21.	2 b
xxxii. 1.	3 c	xi. 31, 34.	7 a	x. 13.	7 a
xxxii. 6.	7 a	xix. 3.	7 a	x. 15.	7 a
xxxii. 17.	4 c	Ruth ii. 22.	3 c	ix. 10.	7 n
xxxiii. 4.	7 a	1 Sam. x. 3.	2 a	1 Chron. xii. 17.	5
xxxiii. 8.	4 a	x. 5.	3 a	xix. 5.	7 a
xlvi. 29.	7 a	x. 10.	3 a	2 Chron. xv. 2.	5
Exod. iii. 18.	8 b	xiii. 10.	7 a	xix. 2.	5
iv. 14.	7 a	xv. 12.	7 a	Neh. vi. 2, 10.	1 b
iv. 24.	7 a	xvii. 48, 48.	7 a	xiii. 2.	6
iv. 27, 27.	7 a, 4 c	xviii. 6.	7 a	Job v. 14.	4 e
v. 3.	7 b	xxi. 1.	7 a	xxxix. 21.	7 a
v. 20.	3 c	xxv. 20.	4 c	Ps. lxxxv. 10.	4 d
xviii. 7.	7 a	xxv. 32, 34.	7 a	Prov. vii. 10, 15.	4 b
xix. 17.	7 a	xxx. 20, 21.	7 a	xvii. 12.	4 b
xxiii. 4.	3 c	2 Sam. ii. 13.	4 c	xxii. 2.	4 c
xxiv. 22.	1 a	vi. 20.	7 a	xxix. 13.	4 d
xxix. 42.	1 a	x. 5.	7 a	Isa. vii. 3.	7 a
xxix. 43.	1 a	xv. 32.	7 a	xiv. 9.	7 a
xxx. 6, 36.	1 b	xvi. 1.	7 a	xxxiv. 14.	4 a
Num. xvii. 4.	1 b	xviii. 9.	7 c	xlvii. 3.	3 c
xxii. 36.	7 a	xix. 15, 16, 24, 25.	7 a	lxiv. 5.	3 a
xxiii. 3.	7 a	1 Kings ii. 8, 19.	7 a	Jer. xli. 6, 6.	7 a, 4 b
xxiii. 4, 15, 16.	8 c	xiii. 24.	2 b	li. 31, 31.	4 c
xxxi. 13.	7 a	xviii. 7, 16, 16.	7 a	Hos. xiii. 8.	4 c
xxxv. 19, 21.	3 b	xxi. 18.	7 a	Amos iv. 12.	7 a
Deut. xxiii. 4.	6	2 Kings i. 3, 6, 7.	7 a	v. 19.	7 a
xxv 18.	8 a	ii. 15.	7 a	Zech. ii. 3.	7 a
Josh. ii. 16.	3 c				

MELODY

זִמְרָה *f.* song, music: Isa. li. 3: Amos v. 23.

נָגַן to play upon, and sing to, stringed musical instruments. PIEL *inf.* Isa. xxiii. 16, *lit.* be good to play.

MELONS

אֲבַטִּחִים *m. pl.* Num. xi. 5.

MELT

1 דָּלַף to drop, to drip, to distil. KAL *pret.*

2 הֲמָסִים *m. pl.* This confessedly difficult word may be deduced from a root which imports that light noise which is made by persons walking; or by small boughs or brushwood, thrown together and breaking with a crackling sound; or by stubble, when trodden on or burnt; Isa. lxiv. 2, perhaps, *lit.* brushwood or stubble.

3 יָצַק to pour; to cast. KAL ᵃ*part.* Paül. HOPHAL ᵇ*part.*

4 מָאַס *i. q.* מָסַס to melt, to melt away, to run. NIPHAL *fut.*

5 מוּג to melt, to flow down; *trop.* to melt, to be dissolved with fear and terror. KAL ᵃ*fut.* NIPHAL ᵇ*pret.* HITHPOLEL ᶜ*pret.* ᵈ*fut.*

6 מָסָה *i. q.* מָסַס to melt, to flow down. HIPHIL ᵃ*pret.* ᵇ*fut.*

7 מָסַס to melt, to flow down; to have the consistency, firmness, substance, dissolved, as of manna in the heat of the sun, Exod. xvi. 21; wax in the heat of the fire, Ps. lxviii. 2; as a snail consumes away, Ps. lviii. 8; as water evaporates and wastes, Ps. lviii. 7; applied to the wasting of disease, to the fainting of fear, grief, or sorrow. NIPHAL ᵃ*pret.* ᵇ*inf.* ᶜ*fut.* ᵈ תָּמֶס *m.* a melting. ᵉ הַמָּסִים *m. pl.* meltings: Isa. lxiv. 2, *marg.* 'fire of meltings.'

8 נָזַל to flow, to run down. KAL *pret.* Judg. v. 5, *marg.* 'flowed.' Modern critics, however, deduce the word in this passage from זָלַל to shake; see *Flow down.* Lxx. have ἐσαλεύθησαν (the root זָלַל corresponding in etymology, also, with σάλος σαλεύω), and the same is expressed by Chald. and Arab. Polyglot. Arab., to shake the earth, earthquake.

9 נָסַךְ to pour out; to cast, to found. KAL ᵃ*pret.* ᵇ מַסֵּכָה *f.* a pouring out what is molten, a molten image: Exod. xxxii. 4, &c. ᶜ נֶסֶךְ *m.* molten image.

10 נָתַךְ to pour out, be poured out; to flow, to be melted. NIPHAL ᵃ*pret.* HIPHIL ᵇ*pret.* ᶜ*inf.* HOPHAL ᵈ*fut.* ᵉ הִתּוּךְ melting.

11 צוּק to pour out, to cast. KAL *fut.*

12 צָרַף to melt gold or silver, in order to refine them, and separate the dross. KAL ᵃ*pret.* ᵇ*part.* Poel.

No. 9 b, *Molten, Molten image,* not included.

Exod. xv. 15.	5 b	Ps. xlvi. 6.	5 a	Isa. xlviii. 5.	9 c
xvi. 21.	7 a	lviii. 7.	4	lxiv. 2.	2, or 7 e
Josh. ii. 11.	7 c	lviii. 8.	7 d	Jer. vi. 29.	12 a
v. 1.	7 c	lxviii. 2.	7 a	ix. 7.	12 b
vii. 5.	7 c	xcvii. 5.	7 a	li. 17.	9 c
viii. 8.	6 a	cvii. 26.	5 d	Ezek. xxi. 7.	7 a
Judg. v. 5.	8	cxii. 10.	7 a	xxii. 20, 20.	10 c b
1 Sam. xiv. 16.	5 b	cxix. 28.	1	xxii. 11.	10 a
2 Sam. xvii. 10.	7 b c	cxlvii. 18.	6 b	xxii. 22, a 22.	10 e d
1 Kings vii. 16, 23, 33.	3 b	Isa. xiii. 7.	7 c	xxiv. 11.	10 a
vii. 30.	3 a	xix. 1.	7 c	Amos ix. 5.	5 a
2 Chron. iv. 2.	3 b	xxxiv. 3.	7 a	ix. 13.	5 d
Job xxviii. 2.	11	xl. 19.	9 c	Micah i. 4.	7 a
xxxvii. 18.	3 b	xli. 29.	9 c	Nah. i. 5.	5 c
Ps. xxii. 14.	7 a	xliv. 10.	9 c	ii. 10.	7 a

a lit. as the melting of silver.

MELZAR

מֶלְצַר *m.* with the *art.* ה the name of an office in the Babylonian court, probably Persian, master of wine, chief butler: Dan. i. 11, 16.

MEMBER

יְצָרִים *m. pl. pr.* things formed, forms; members, as the Vulg., imagination, thought. Others understand lineaments of the face: Job xvii. 7.

MEMORIAL, MEMORY

זֵכֶר and זֶכֶר *m.* remembrance, memory; memorial: Exod. iii. 15: Esth. ix. 28: Ps. ix. 6; cix. 15; cxxxv. 13; cxlv. 7: Prov. x. 7: Eccles. ix. 5: Isa. xxvi. 14: Hos. xii. 5. זִכָּרוֹן *m.* remembrance, memorial; a memento, record; a day of memorial, a celebration festival: Lev. xxiii. 24.— Exod. xii. 14; xiii. 9; xvii. 14; xxviii. 12, 12, 29; xxx. 16; xxxix. 7: Lev. xxiii. 24: Num. v. 15, 18; x. 10; xvi. 40; xxxi. 54: Josh. iv. 7: Neh. ii. 20: Zech. vi. 14. אַזְכָּרָה *f.* memorial, remembrance, offering: Lev. ii. 2, 9, 16; v. 12; vi. 15; xxiv. 7: Num. v. 26.

MEN

מְתִים *m. pl.* men, in a diminutive sense, or as opposed to women, children, &c., frequently with a genitive following; see *Few, Inward, Number.* Vitringa thinks the word to be much the same as mortal, and derived from מוּת, though the Masoretic punctuation is against this derivation. Deut. ii. 34; iii. 6; xxxiii. 6: Job xi. 3, 11; xxii. 15; xxiv. 12; xxxi. 31: Ps. xvii. 14, 14; cv. 12: Isa. iii. 25; v. 13; xli. 14, *marg.* 'or, few men:' this seems elliptical for such expression as we find in Ps. cv. 12. מְתֹם *m. id.* Judg. xx. 48.

אָדָם *m.* see *Man.*

חָזַק to be strong, to play the men. HITHPAEL *fut.* 2 Sam. x. 12.

עַם *com.* people; men in opposition to leaders; servants, attendants: Num. xxxi. 32.

MEND

חָזַק to be strong, to strengthen, repair. PIEL *inf.* 2 Chron. xxiv. 12.

MENE

מְנָה Ch. to number. P'AL *part. passive,* Dan. v. 25, 25, *i. e.* hath numbered the years of thy reign. Is there not an allusion to the idol Meni? See *Number.*

MENSTRUOUS

דָּוֶה sick, faint; especially of women in the monthly courses; a menstruous cloth: Isa. xxx. 22.

נִדָּה uncleanness; separation; menstrual discharge: Lam. i. 17; Ezek. xviii. 6.

MENTION

1 בּוֹא to come. KAL *part.* Poel, 1 Chron. iv. 38, *marg.* 'coming;' *comp.* Job iii. 6.

2 זָכַר to remember, to recollect, to call to mind; to mention, make mention of; in Hiphil importing frequently praise. KAL [a]*fut.* NIPHAL [b]*fut.* HIPHIL [c]*pret.* [d]*inf.* [e]*imp.* [f]*fut.* [g]*part.,* Isa. lxii. 6, *marg.* 'or, ye that are the Lord's remembrancers.' Some think it refers to the watchmen, whose custom it was to use some pious sentiment, including the name of Jehovah, as a watchword. See Paxton.

3 עָלָה to ascend. HOPHAL, to be put on record. *pret.*

4 קָרָא to call. KAL *fut.*

5 שְׁמוּעָה *f.* hearing, report.

Gen. xl. 14.	2 c	Ps. lxxi. 16.	2 f	Isa. lxiii. 7.	2 f		
Exod. xxiii. 13.	2 f	lxxxvii. 4.	2 f	Jer. iv. 16.	2 e		
Josh. xxi. 9.	4	Isa. xii. 4.	2 e	xx. 9.	2 a		
xxiii. 7.	2 f	xix. 17.	2 f	xxiii. 36.	2 a		
1 Sam. iv. 18.	2 d	xxvi. 13.	2 f	Ezek. xvi. 56. β	5		
1 Chron. iv. 38.	1	xlviii. 1.	2 f	xviii. 22, 24.	2 b		
2 Chron. xx. 34.	3	xlix. 1.	2 c	xxxiii. 16.	2 b		
Job xxviii. 18. a	2 b	lxii. 6.	2 g	Amos vi. 10.	2 d		

a lit. shall not be remembered.   *β marg.* 'for a report, *or,* hearing.'

MEONENIM

עָנַן to observe times. POEL *part.* Judg. ix. 37.

MERATHAIM

מְרָתַיִם *f. dual, pr.* double rebellion, a symbolical name for Babylon: Jer. l. 21.

MERCHANT, MERCHANDISE

1 כְּנַעַן *m.* the Canaanites were commonly merchants, hence the name of a merchant. [a] כְּנַעֲנִי *m.*

2 סָחַר to travel about, to traverse countries as a merchant in order to buy or sell. KAL [a]*part.* Poel. [b] סָחַר *m.* merchandise. [c] סַחַר *m.* trading, gain. [d] סְחֹרָה *f.* traffic.

3 עָמַר to gather up; to make gain. HITHPAEL [a]*pret.* [b]*fut.*

4 מַעֲרָב *m.* a mixing together for the purpose of trade; a market; merchandise.

5 רָכַל to go about for traffic as a dealer. KAL [a]*part.* Poel. [b] רְכֻלָּה *f.* traffic. [c] מַרְכֹּלֶת *f.* merchandise bought in one place and sold in another.

6 תּוּר to go or travel about; to go for traffic. KAL *part.* Poel.

Gen. xxiii. 16.	2 a	Prov. xxxi. 14.	2 a	Ezek. xxvii. 9, 27, 27,	
xxxvii. 28.	2 a	xxxi. 18.	2 c	33, 34.	4
Deut. xxi. 14.	3 b	xxxi. 24.	1 a	xxvii. 12, 16, 18.	2 a
xxiv. 7.	3 a	Isa. xxiii. 2, 8.	2 a	xxvii. 15, 15.	5 a
1 Kings x. 15, 15.	6, 5 a	xxiii. 11.	1	xxvii. 21, 36.	2 a
x. 28.	2 a	xxiii. 18, 18.	2 c	xxvii. 24, 24.	5 a
2 Chron. i. 16.	2 a	xlv. 14.	2 b	xxviii. 16.	5 b
ix. 14.	2 a	xlvii. 15.	2 a	xxxviii. 13.	2 a
Neh. iii. 31, 32.	5 a	Ezek. xvii. 4.	2 a	Hos. xii. 7.	5 b
xiii. 20.	5 a	xxvi. 12.	5 b	Nah. iii. 16.	5 a
Job xli. 6.	1 a	xxvii. 3, 13, 17, 20,		Zeph. i. 11.	1
Cant. iii. 6.	5 a	22, 22, 23, 23.	5 a		
Prov. iii. 14, 14.	2 c b				

MERCY, MERCIFUL

1 חֶמְלָה *f.* mercy, gentleness. Gen. xix. 16, *lit.* in the mercy of Jehovah upon him.

2 חָנַן to be kindly and tenderly affected towards; to shew favour, mercy, pity. KAL [a]*imp.* [b]*fut.* [c]*part.* Poel. POEL [d]*part.* חָנַן Ch. P'AL [e]*inf.*

3 חָסַד that which is abundant, extraordinary, or uncommon; goodness, kindness, and beneficence; see *Kind.* HITHPAEL [a]*fut.* [b] חֶסֶד *m.* grace, favour, mercy: sure mercies of David, *i. e.* of Christ so called, Isa. iv. 3: Gen. xix. 19, &c. [c] חָסִיד *adj.* kind, merciful.

4 כָּפַר to cover, to make atonement, to propitiate. PIEL [a]*pret.* [b]*imp.* כַּפֹּרֶת the mercy-seat or cover of the ark of the covenant.

5 רָחַם to love tenderly; to have mercy, compassion upon any one, to pity; applied to God's mercy and tender pity for his people. PIEL [a]*pret.* [b]*imp.* [c]*fut.* [d]*part.* PUAL [e]*pret.* [f]*fut.* [g] רָחוּם *adj.* merciful. [h] רַחֲמִים *m. pl.* tender mercies. [i] רַחֲמִין Ch. *m. pl.*

No. 3 b, *Mercy*, not included.

Gen. xix. 16.	1	Ps. xxv. 16.	2 a	Isa. xxx. 18.	5 b
xliii. 14.	5 h	xxvi. 11.	2 a	xlvii. 6.	5 h
Exod. xxv. 17, 18, 19,		xxvii. 7.	2 a	xlix. 10.	5 d
20, 20, 21, 22.	4 c	xxx. 10.	2 a	xlix. 13.	5 c
xxvi. 34.	4 c	xxxi. 9.	2 a	liv. 7.	5 a
xxx. 6.	4 c	xxxvii. 21, 26.	2 c	liv. 8.	5 a
xxxi. 7.	4 c	xl. 11.	5 h	liv. 10.	5 d
xxxiii. 19, 19.	5 a c	xli. 4, 10.	2 a	lv. 7.	5 c
xxxiv. 6.	5 g	li. 1, 1.	2 a, 5 h	lvii. 1.	3 b
xxxv. 12.	4 c	lvi. 1.	2 a	lx. 10.	5 a
xxxvii. 6, 7, 8, 9, 9.	4 c	lvii. 1, 1.	2 a	lxiii. 7, 15.	5 h
xxxix. 35.	4 c	lix. 5.	2 b	Jer. iii. 12.	3 c
xl. 20.	4 c	lxvii. 1.	2 b	vi. 14.	5 c
Lev. xvi. 2, 2, 13, 14,		lxix. 16.	5 h	xiii. 14.	5 c
14, 15, 15.	4 c	lxxvii. 9.	5 h	xvi. 5.	5 h
Num. vii. 89.	4 c	lxxix. 8.	5 h	xxi. 7.	5 c
Deut. iv. 31.	5 g	lxxxi. 3, 16.	2 a	xxx. 18.	5 c
vii. 2.	2 b	cii. 13.	5 c	xxxi. 20.	5 b c
xiii. 17.	5 h	ciii. 4.	5 h	xxxiii. 26.	5 h
xxi. 8.	4 b	ciii. 8, 8.	5 g, 3 b	xlii. 12, 12.	5 h a
xxxii. 43.	5 h	cxvi. 5.	5 d	l. 42.	5 a
2 Sam. xxii. 26, 26.	3 c a	cxvii. 2.	3 b	Ezek. xxxix. 25.	5 a
xxiv. 14.	5 h	cxix. 58, 132.	2 a	Dan. ii. 18.	5 i
1 Kings xx. 31.	3 b	cxix. 76.	3 b	iv. 27.	2 e
1 Chron. xxi. 13.	5 h	cxix. 77, 156.	5 h	ix. 9, 18.	5 h
xxviii. 11.	4 c	cxxiii. 2.	2 b	Hos. i. 6, 7.	5 c
2 Chron. xxx. 9.	5 g	cxxiii. 3, 3.	2 a	ii. 4.	5 c
Neh. i. 11.	5 h	cxlv. 9.	5 h	ii.19.	5 h
ix. 17.	5 g	Prov. xi. 17.	3 b	ii. 23, 23.	5 a e
ix. 19, 27, 28.	5 h	xii. 10.	5 h	xiv. 3.	5 f
ix. 31, 31.	5 h g	xiv. 21.	2 d	Joel ii. 13.	5 g
Ps. iv. 1.	2 a	xiv. 31.	2 c	Jonah iv. 2.	5 g
vi. 2.	2 a	xxviii. 13.	5 f	Hab. iii. 2.	5 b
ix. 13.	2 a	Isa. xiv. 17.	5 c	Zech. i. 12.	5 c
xviii. 25, 25.	3 c a	xiv. 1.	5 c	i. 16.	5 h
xxv. 6.	5 h	xxvii. 11.	5 c	x. 6.	5 a

MERIBAH

מְרִיבָה *f.* strife, contention: Exod. xvii. 7: Num. xx. 13, 24; xxvii. 14: Deut. xxxii. 51; xxxiii. 8: Ps. lxxxi. 7.

MERRY

1   הִלּוּלִים *m. pl.* praises.

2   חַי *adj.* living, life.

3   טוֹב *adj.* good.

4   יָטַב to be good, well. KAL ᵃ*fut.* HIPHIL ᵇ*part.*

5   שָׂחַק to laugh, make sport. PIEL *part.*

6   שָׁכַר to drink plentifully. KAL *fut.*

7   שָׂמַח to rejoice, to be glad. KAL ᵃ*inf.* PIEL ᵇ*fut.* ᶜשָׂמֵחַ *adj.* joyful.

Gen. xliii. 34.	6	1 Kings iv. 20.	7 c	Prov. xvii. 22.	7 c
Judg. ix. 27.	1	xxi. 7.	4 a	Eccles. viii. 15.	7 a
xvi. 25.	3	2 Chron. vii. 10.	3	ix. 7.	3
xix. 6, 9.	4 a	Esth. i. 10.	3	x. 19. *a*	7 b, 2
xix. 22.	4 b	v. 14.	7 c	Isa. xxiv. 7.	7 c
Ruth iii. 7.	4 a	Prov. xv. 13.	7 c	Jer. xxx. 19.	5
1 Sam. xxv. 36.	3	xv. 15.	3	xxxi. 4.	5
2 Sam. xiii. 28.	3				

a lit. maketh glad the life.

MESS

מַשְׂאֵת *f.* a gift, a present; a mess of meat sent as a present: Gen. xliii. 34, 34, *lit.* than the messes of all; 2 Sam. xi. 8.

MESSAGE

דָּבָר *m.* word: Judg. iii. 20: 1 Kings xx. 12: Prov. xxvi. 6.

מַלְאֲכוּת *f. const.* a message sent: Hag. i. 13.

MESSENGER

בָּשַׂר to bring or publish, generally good tidings. PIEL *part.* 1 Sam. iv. 17.

מַלְאָךְ *m.* a messenger or angel sent and commissioned to transact any affair whatever; a messenger of death, one who is commissioned to put to death on the spot: Prov. xvi. 14: 2 Kings vi. 32.—Gen. xxxii. 3, 6, &c.

נָגַד to tell, to shew, to declare. HIPHIL *part.* 2 Sam. xv. 13: Jer. li. 31, *lit.* and messenger to meet messenger.

צָוָה to command. PIEL *fut.* Gen. l. 16, "sent a messenger."

צִיר *m.* ambassador, messenger: Prov. xxv. 13: Isa. lvii. 9.

MESSIAH

מָשִׁיחַ *adj. m.* anointed: Dan. ix. 25, 26.

METE

מָדַד to measure. KAL *fut.* Exod. xvi. 18. PIEL *fut.* Ps. lx. 6; cviii. 7. מִדָּה *f.* meteyard: Lev. xix. 35.

קָו *m.* a line: Isa. xviii. 2, 7, *lit.* a nation of a line a line. Michaelis, a nation measured by a line, *i.e.* whose land had been divided by victors.

תָּכַן to weigh, to measure. PIEL *pret.* Isa. xl. 12.

METHINKETH

רָאָה to see. KAL *part.* Poel, 2 Sam. xviii. 27, *marg.* 'I see.'

MICHTAM

מִכְתָּם *m.* a writing, as if *i. q.* מִכְתָּב poem, psalm; or from כָּתַם gold, *i.e.* a golden psalm, precious: found only in the titles of Ps. xvi, lvi, lvii, lviii, lix, and lx. Hengstenberg, a secret, a song with a deep import.

MID, MIDDLE, MIDS, MIDST, MIDDAY

1   גַּו Ch. *m.* middle, midst.

2   חֵיק *m.* bosom.

3   חָצָה to divide; to reach to the midst. KAL ᵃ*fut.* ᵇחֲצוֹת middle, mid, mid*night*. ᶜמַחֲצִית *f.* half, mid, mid*night*. ᵈחֲצִי *m.* mid*night*.

4   חָצַץ to divide. PUAL *pret.* See *Cut*.

5   טַבּוּר *m.* the navel; the middle or highest part of the country.

6   כַּף *f.* the hollow of the hand; the hollow of a sling.

7   לֵב *m.* the heart, the middle or midst of anything. ᵃלֵבָב *m. id.*

8   צֹהַר *m.* clearest light; noonday, midday.

9   קֶרֶב *m.* what is nearest, inward; middle, centre.

10   תָּוֶךְ *m.* middle or midst of anything; it seems sometimes to be used emphatically; see Ezek. xxx. 7.—Gen. i. 6, &c. 1 Kings iii. 20, "mid*night*." ᵃתִּיכוֹן *adj. id.*

No. 10 not included.

Gen. xlviii. 16.	9	Josh. vii. 13.	9	Job xxxiv. 20.	3 b
Exod. iii. 20.	9	x. 13.	9	Ps. xlvi. 2.	7
viii. 22.	9	Judg. vii. 19.	10 a	xlvi. 5.	9
xi. 4, 4.	3 b, 9	ix. 37.	5	xlviii. 9.	9
xii. 29.	3 d	xvi. 3, 3.	3 d	lv. 10, 11.	9
xxiii. 25.	9	xviii. 20.	9	lxxiv. 4, 12.	9
xxvi. 28, 28.	10 a, 10	Ruth iii. 8.	3 d	lxxviii. 28.	9
xxvii. 5.	3 d	1 Sam. xvi. 13.	9	cii. 24.	3 d
xxxiii. 3, 5.	9	xxv. 29.	10, 6	cx. 2.	9
xxxiv. 12.	9	2 Sam. x. 4.	3 d	cxix. 62.	3 b
xxxvi. 33.	10 a	xviii. 14.	7	cxxxviii. 7.	9
xxxviii. 4.	3 d	1 Kings vi. 6, 8, 8.	10 a	Prov. xiv. 33.	9
Deut. iv. 11.	7	xviii. 29.	8	xxiii. 34.	7
iv. 34.	9	xx. 39.	9	xxx. 19.	9
xi. 6.	9	xxii. 35.	2	Isa. iv. 4.	9
xiii. 5.	9	2 Kings xx. 4.	10 a	v. 8, 25.	9
xvii. 20.	9	1 Chron. xix. 4.	3 d	vi. 12.	9
xviii. 15.	9	Neh. viii. 3.	3 c	x. 23.	9
xxiii. 14.	9	Job xxi. 21.	4	xii. 6.	9

MIDWIFE

יָלַד to bring forth. PIEL, to do the office of midwife: inf. Exod. i. 16. part. Gen. xxxv. 17; xxxviii. 28: Exod. i. 15, 17, 18, 19, 19, 20, 21.

MIGHT, MIGHTY

1 אַבִּיר adj. strong; valiant, a hero, illustrious, chief, noble; of bulls, &c.; of a horse only in Jeremiah. ᵃ אָבִיר m. const. of God, infinitely powerful protector.

2 אַדִּיר adj. great, mighty, powerful, noble.

3 אֵלֵי m. pl. constr. of אֵילִים: the mighty, the powerful, the nobles of a state. ᵃ אוּל m. (כתיב). ᵇ אֵל m. God, the God of gods, superior to and stronger than all other beings; pr. mighty, strong; might, strength, power.

4 אוֹן m. strength.

5 אִישׁ m. man.

6 אֵיתָן m. firmness, strength.

7 אֱלֹהִים m. pl. God; mighty, lit. of God.

8 אַמִּיץ adj. strong, resolute, and vigorous.

9 אָפִיק strong in resolution and courage.

10 בֵּן m. son: Ps. xxix. 1, marg. 'sons of the mighty.'

11 בָּצַר to fence, to fortify; to be inaccessible. KAL part. Paül, Jer. xxxiii. 3. Gesenius, difficult to be understood.

12 גָּבַר to be or become strong, mighty; to prevail. KAL ᵃ pret. ᵇ גֶּבֶר m. man, so called from his strength. ᶜ גְּבַר Ch. m. ᵈ גִּבּוֹר adj. mighty and powerful, especially in war or in dominion, Gen. x. 8; also in any undertaking, 1 Kings xi. 28, Neh. xi. 14; in derision of them that are mighty to drink wine, Isa. v. 22. It is applied to Jehovah victorious over his enemies, Deut. x. 17; and to the Messiah, Ps. xxiv. 8. It is seldom used in a bad sense of the proud and tyrannical, Ps. lii. 1. Schmidt thinks that it means one that is strenuous in his undertakings, strong in his own conscious integrity, without pretence or hypocrisy. Most commonly translated, a mighty man: Gen. vi. 4, &c. ᵉ גְּבוּרָה f. might, physical strength, courage. ᶠ גְּבוּרָה Ch. f. id.

13 גָּדוֹל adj. great.

14 חָזַק to be strong. HITHPAEL ᵃ fut. ᵇ חָזָק adj. firm, strong, vigorous. ᶜ חָזְקָה f. might, violence.

15 זְרוֹעַ com. arm; it sometimes implies strength or violence.

16 חַיִל m. strength, might, valour; army. ᵃ חַיִל Ch. m. id.

17 כַּבִּיר adj. to be strong, as the wind or a flood of waters, or mighty as God, denoting a combination of power.

18 כֹּחַ m. strength and vigour of body; in opposition to a dry, withered, and consequently languid state.

19 מְאֹד m. might, ability on the stretch; a strong vehement endeavouring. Always, except here (Deut. vi. 5), used adverbially.

20 עֹז m. strength, might, power, of God, of men, of animals; also vehemence, violence, as of rain, thunder, &c. ᵃ עֱזוּז m. strength. ᵇ עַז adj. powerful.

21 עֵים m. strength: Isa. xi. 15, lit. with the strength of his wind. LXX. ἐν πνεύματι βιαίῳ; Vulg. in fortitudine spiritus sui.

22 עָצַם to be strong, mighty, powerful; to be strong in a prevailing degree, which is capable of bearing down all opposition: Ps. lxix. 4, "mighty," and therefore able to destroy me. KAL ᵃ pret. ᵇ fut. ᶜ עֹצֶם m. strength. ᵈ עָצוּם adj. strong, &c., of a people, of kings, of waters; warriors, heroes; strong in number, numerous: Amos v. 12.

23 עָרִיץ adj. terrible, inspiring terror by their strength.

24 צוּר m. a rock; the mighty God.

25 צָלַח to prosper, to come mightily. KAL fut.

26 רַב adj. much; large, great, vast, i.q. mighty, powerful.

27 שַׁלִּיט powerful, mighty, i.e. having power over any one.

28 תַּקִּיף adj. one that has superior, overbearing strength. ᵃ תַּקִּיף Ch. adj. id. ᵇ תְּקֹף Ch. m. strength.

Ezek. xvii. 13.	3	Dan. iv. 3.	28 a	Jonah iii. 8.	14 c
xvii. 17.	13	iv. 30.	28 b	Micah iii. 8.	12 e
xx. 33, 34.	14 b	viii. 24, 24.	22 a d	vii. 16.	12 e
xxxi. 11.	3 b	ix. 15.	14 b	Nah. ii. 1.	19
xxxii. 29, 30.	12 e	xi. 25.	22 d	Hab. i. 12.	24
xxxviii. 15.	26	Amos v. 12.	22 d	Zech. iv. 6.	16
Dan. ii. 20, 23.	12 f	v. 24.	6	xi. 2.	2
iii. 20.	12 c, 16 a	Jonah i. 4.	13		

a *lit.* mighty men of valour.   β *lit.* of God.   γ *lit.* an arm with might.   δ *lit.* with the strength of his wind.

MILCH

יָנַל to suck; to give suck. HIPHIL *part.* Gen. xxxii. 15.

עוּל to give suck. KAL *part.* Poel, 1 Sam. vi. 7, 10.

MILDEW

יֵרָקוֹן *m.* paleness; yellowness, mildew: Deut. xxviii. 22: 1 Kings viii. 37: 2 Chron. vi. 28: Amos iv. 9: Hag. ii. 17.

MILK

חָלָב *m.* milk, *i.e.* new milk, so called from its fatness; or coagulated sour milk, still used in the East, and called leban; see Paxton. A land of milk and honey, *i.e.* abounding in all the products necessary to life and agreeable to the taste. Gen. xviii. 8, &c.

מָצַץ to suck out, implying sweetness. KAL *fut.* Isa. lxvi. 11.

MILL, MILLSTONES

רֵחַיִם *dual,* a hand-mill, millstones; with which families in the East grind their wheat, at which women were employed, frequently two for each mill. The sound of millstones, generally used every morning, and very great in a large city, is on that account expressive of prosperity: Jer. xxv. 10.—Exod. xi. 5: Num. xi. 8: Isa. xlvii. 2: Jer. xxv. 10: the nether or lower millstone, Deut. xxiv. 6.

רֶכֶב *com.* chariot; the rider, the upper millstone was so called because it revolved on the lower one: used alone in Deut. xxiv. 6, Judg. ix. 53; but with פֶּלַח in 2 Sam. xi. 21; see *Piece.*

MILLET

דֹּחַן *m.* a species of millet, used chiefly for making coarse bread or pottage: Ezek. iv. 9.

MILLION

רְבָבָה *f.* a myriad, ten thousand; and often a great indefinite number: Gen. xxiv. 60.

MINCING

טָפַף to take short and quick steps, to trip, of the walk of children; also of the affected gait of coquettish females. KAL *inf.* Isa. iii. 16.

MIND

1 יֵצֶר *m.* imagination; thought.

2 לֵב *m.* heart. a לְבָב *m. id.* "minded," *lit.* in the heart of.

3 נֶפֶשׁ *com.* soul.

4 פֶּה *m.* the mouth.

5 רוּחַ *com.* spirit. a רוּחַ Ch. *com. id.*

Gen. xxiii. 8.	3	1 Chron. xxviii. 9.	3	Jer. xliv. 21.	2
xxvi. 35.	5	2 Chron. xxiv. 4.	2	li. 50.	2 a
Lev. xxiv. 12.	4	Neh. iv. 6.	2	Lam. iii. 21.	2
Num. xvi. 28.	2	Ps. xxxi. 12.	2	Ezek. xi. 5.	5
xxiv. 13.	2	Prov. xxix. 11.	5	xx. 32.	5
Deut. xviii. 6.	3	Isa. xxvi. 3.	1	xxiii. 17, 18, 18, 22,	
xxviii. 65.	3	xlvi. 8.	2	28.	3
xxx. 1.	2 a	lxv. 17.	2	xxiv. 25. a	3
1 Sam. ii. 35.	3	Jer. iii. 16.	2	xxxvi. 5.	3
ix. 20.	3	xv. 1.	2	xxxviii. 10.	2 a
2 Sam. xvii. 8.	3	xix. 5.	2	Dan. v. 20.	5 a
2 Kings ix. 15.	3	xxxii. 35.	2	Hab. i. 11.	5
1 Chron. xxii. 7.	2 a				

a *lit.* the lifting up of their soul.

MINDFUL

זָכַר to remember. KAL *pret.* Neh. ix. 17: Ps. cxv. 12: Isa. xvii. 10. *imp.* 1 Chron. xvi. 15. *fut.* Ps. viii. 4; cxi. 5.

MINGLE

1 בָּלַל to flow, to be mingled, to confound by mixing different things together. KAL *part.* Paül.

2 כִּלְאַיִם *dual, pr.* separation from כָּלָא to shut up, to shut out; things separated, diverse; found only in the *dual,* two things of diverse kinds, heterogeneous.

3 לָקַח to take. HITHPAEL *part.* Exod. ix. 24, taking hold on itself, infolding, with the hail.

4 מָסַךְ to mix in due proportion. KAL a *pret.* b *inf.*

5 עָרַב to interweave. Hith. to mingle oneself, to intermeddle. HITHPAEL a *pret.* b *fut.* עֲרַב Ch. ITHPAEL c *part.* d עֲרָב *m.* mixture; mingled people.

Exod. ix. 24.	3	Num. vii. 13, 19, 25, 31,		Ps. cii. 9.	4 a
xxix. 40.	1	37, 43, 49, 55, 61,		cvi. 35.	5 b
Lev. ii. 4, 5.	1	67, 73, 79.	1	Prov. ix. 2, 5.	4 a
vii. 10, 12, 12.	1	viii. 8.	1	Isa. v. 22.	4 b
ix. 4.	1	xv. 4, 6, 9.	1	xix. 14.	4 a
xiv. 10, 21.	1	xxviii. 5, 9, 12, 12,		Jer. xxv. 20, 24.	5 d
xix. 19, 19.	2	13, 20, 28.	1	l. 37.	5 d
xxiii. 13.	1	xxix. 3, 9, 14.	1	Ezek. xxx. 5.	5 d
Num. vi. 15.	1	Ezra i. 4.	5 a	Dan. ii. 43.	5 c

MINISH

גָּרַע to diminish. KAL *fut.* Exod. v. 19.

מָעַט to be few or little, to be made few or little. KAL *fut.* Ps. cvii. 39.

MINISTER

1 דִּין to judge, to minister judgment. KAL *fut.*

2 יָד *com.* hand, "ministry."

3 עֲבוֹדָה *f.* service; ministry, "ministering," *lit.* of service.

4 פְּלַח Ch. to serve. P'AL *part.*

5 שַׁמָּשׁ to minister, to wait upon. PAEL *fut.*

6 שָׁרַת to wait upon, to serve, to minister unto; with an *acc.* of *pers.,* implying rather honorary attendance than servile office. PIEL a *pret.* b *inf.* c *fut.* d *part.* e שָׁרֵת *m.* ministry.

Exod. xxiv. 13.	6 d	Num. xvi. 9.	6 b	1 Kings i. 15.	6 d
xxviii. 35, 43.	6 b	xviii. 2.	6 c	viii. 11.	6 b
xxix. 30.	6 b	Deut. x. 8.	6 b	x. 5.	6 c
xxx. 20.	6 b	xvii. 12.	6 b	xxi. 21.	6 c
xxxix. 26.	6 b	xviii. 5.	6 b	2 Kings xxv. 14.	6 c
Num. i. 50.	6 c	xviii. 7.	6 a	1 Chron. vi. 32.	6 d
iii. 6.	6 a	xxi. 5.	6 b	ix. 28.	3
iii. 31.	6 c	Josh. i. 1.	6 d	xv. 2.	6 b
iv. 9, 12.	6 c	1 Sam. ii. 11, 18.	6 d	xvi. 4.	6 b
iv. 12, 12.	6 e c	iii. 1.	6 d	xvi. 37.	6 b
iv. 47.	3	2 Sam. xiii. 17.	6 d	xxiii. 13.	6 b
viii. 26.	6 a	1 Kings i. 4.	6 c	xxvi. 12.	6 b

1 Chron. xxviii. 1.	6 d	Neh. x. 36, 39.	6 d	Ezek. xliii. 19.	6 b
2 Chron. v. 14.	6 b	Esth. ii. 2.	6 d	xliv. 11, 11, 11.	6 d d b
vii. 6.	6 d	vi. 3.	6 d	xliv. 12.	6 c
viii. 14.	6 b	Ps. ix. 8.	1	xliv. 15, 16, 17, 27.	6 b
ix. 4.	6 d	ciii. 21.	6 d	xliv. 19.	6 c
xiii. 10.	6 d	civ. 4.	6 d	xlv. 4, 4.	6 d b
xxii. 8.	6 d	Isa. lx. 7, 10.	6 c	xlv. 5.	6 c
xxiii. 6.	6 d	lxi. 6.	6 d	xlvi. 24.	6 d
xxiv. 14.	6 e	Jer. xxxiii. 21, 22.	6 d	Dan. vii. 10.	5
xxix. 11.	6 d	lii. 18.	6 c	Hos. xii. 10.	2
xxxi. 2.	6 b	Ezek. xl. 46.	6 b	Joel i. 9, 13, 13.	6 d
Ezra vii. 24.	4	xlii. 14.	6 c	ii. 17.	6 d
viii. 17.	6 d				

MINSTREL

נָגַן to play upon, and sing to, any stringed musical instrument. PIEL part. 2 Kings iii. 15, 15.

MIRACLE

אוֹת c. see *Sign*. Num. xiv. 22: Deut. xi. 3.

מוֹפֵת m. see *Wonder*. Exod. vii. 9: Deut. xxix. 3.

פָּלָא to be distinguished, marvellous, wondrous. NIPHAL part. Judg. vi. 13.

MIRE

1 בֹּץ mire, mud. ᵃ בִּצָּה f. id.

2 חֹמֶר m. clay, loam, potter's clay.

3 טִיט m. mud, mire, of streets, very abundant in Eastern cities, from the wasting of mud walls; in a cistern or subterraneous prison, on the banks of the Nile; *trop.* deep calamity: Ps. lxix. 14. ᵃ טִין Ch. m. id.

4 יָוֵן m. mud, mire; probably *pr.* dregs, fœces; "miry clay."

5 רֶפֶשׁ m. the mire of troubled water.

2 Sam. xxii. 43.	3	Ps. lxix. 14.	3	Ezek. xlvii. 11.	1 a
Job viii. 11.	1 a	Isa. x. 6.	2	Dan. ii. 41, 43.	3 a
xxx. 19.	3	lvii. 20.	3	Micah vii. 10.	3
xli. 30.	3	Jer. xxxviii. 6, 6.	3	Zech. ix. 3.	3
Ps. xl. 2.	4	xxxviii. 22.	1	x. 5.	3
lxix. 2.	4				

MIRTH

שׂוּשׂ to rejoice, to make mirth. KAL fut. Ezek. xxi. 10. שָׂשׂוֹן m. joy, gladness: Jer. vii. 34; xvi. 9; xxv. 10. מָשׂוֹשׂ m. id. Isa. xxiv. 8, 11: Hos. ii. 11.

שִׂמְחָה f. gladness: Gen. xxxi. 27: Neh. viii. 12: Ps. cxxxvii. 3: Prov. xiv. 13: Eccles. ii. 1, 2; vii. 4; viii. 15.

MISCARRY

שָׁכֵל to be bereaved of children, to cast the young. HIPHIL part. Hos. ix. 14, *marg.* 'that casteth the fruit.'

MISCHIEF

1 אָוֶן m. nothingness, vanity; nothingness as to worth, wickedness, iniquity.

2 אָסוֹן m. hurt, harm, violence, done to any one.

3 הַוָּה f. wickedness, calamity; calamity prepared for others. ᵃ הֹוָה f. calamity.

4 הָתַת to talk or prate mischievously; to imagine mischief. POEL fut. Ps. lxii. 3. Gesenius, how long will ye break in upon a man? *i.e.* set upon him. Lxx. ἐπιτίθεσθε. Vulg. *irruitis*.

5 זִמָּה f. purpose, mischief, wickedness, crime; specially of crimes arising from unchastity. ᵃ מְזִמָּה f. devices, mischievous device.

6 עָוֹן m. perverseness, wrong; punishment of sin, calamity, misery.

7 עָמָל m. labour, toil; trouble, vexation, sorrow.

8 רָעַע to be evil; to do evil, to do wickedly. HIPHIL ᵃ fut. רַע ᵇ adj. evil, wicked.

Gen. xlii. 4, 38.	2	Ps. xxvi. 10.	5	Prov. xii. 21.	8 b
xliv. 29.	2	xxviii. 3.	8 b	xiii. 17.	8 b
Exod. xxi. 22, 23.	2	xxxvi. 4.	1	xvii. 20.	8 b
xxxii. 12, 22.	8 b	xxxviii. 12.	3	xxiv. 2.	7
Deut. xxxii. 23.	8 b	lii. 1.	8 b	xxiv. 8.	5 a
1 Sam. xxiii. 9.	8 b	lii. 2.	3	xxiv. 16.	8 b
2 Sam. xvi. 8.	8 b	lxii. 3.	1	xxviii. 14.	8 b
1 Kings xi. 25.	8 b	lxii. 3.	4	Eccles. x. 13.	8 b
xx. 7.	8 b	xciv. 20.	7	Isa. xlvii. 11.	3 a
2 Kings vii. 9.	6	cxix. 150.	5	lix. 4.	7
Neh. vi. 2.	8 b	cxl. 2.	7	Ezek. vii. 26, 26.	3 a
Esth. viii. 3.	8 b	cxl. 9.	7	xi. 2.	3
Job xv. 35.	7	Prov. vi. 16.	8 a	Dan. xi. 27.	8 b
Ps. vii. 14, 16.	7	vi. 14, 18.	3	Hos. vii. 15.	8 b
x. 7, 14.	7	x. 23.	5	Micah vii. 3.	3
xxi. 11.	5 a	xi. 27.	8 b		

MISERY

עָמָל m. labour, toil; trouble, vexation, sorrow; often coupled with synonymous words: Judg. x. 16: Job xi. 16; xvi. 2: Prov. xxxi. 7. עָמֵל adj. labouring; sorrowful: Job iii. 10.

מָרוּד m. wandering; the condition of a person driven from home, and wandering about destitute and afflicted: Lam. i. 7; iii. 19.

רַע adj. evil: Eccles. viii. 6.

MISS

חָטָא to miss the mark. HIPHIL fut. Judg. xx. 16.

פָּקַד to go to see, to visit, to look after; to muster, number; to miss in mustering or numbering, to miss, implying looking after something. KAL pret. 1 Sam. xxv. 15. inf. 1 Sam. xx. 6, lit. missing shall miss me. fut. 1 Sam. xx. 6. NIPHAL pret. 1 Sam. xx. 18; xxv. 7, 21. inf. 1 Kings xx. 39, lit. if missing he be missed. fut. 1 Kings xx. 39.

MIST

אֵד m. vapour, mist, rising from the earth and forming clouds, so called because it surrounds the earth like a veil or covering: Gen. ii. 6.

MISTRESS

בַּעֲלָה f. a mistress, a possessor of anything: 1 Kings xvii. 17; Nah. iii. 4.

גְּבֶרֶת f. mistress, opposed to maid-servant: Gen. xvi. 4, 8, 9: 2 Kings v. 3: Ps. cxxiii. 2: Prov. xxx. 23: Isa. xxiv. 2.

MISUSE

תָּעַע to mock, to scoff. HITHPALPEL part. 2 Chron. xxxvi. 16.

MITRE

צָנִיף m. a tiara, turban, worn by the high priest: Zech. iii. 5, 5. מִצְנֶפֶת f. id. Exod. xxviii. 4, 37, 37, 39; xxix. 6, 6; xxxix. 28, 31: Lev. viii. 9, 9; xvi. 4.

MIX

בָּלַל see *Mingle*. HITHPOEL *fut.* Hos. vii. 8.

מָהַל to cut off, prune; to adulterate, to mix wine. KAL *part.* Paül, Isa. i. 22.

עֲרַב Ch. see *Mingle*. PAEL *part.* Dan. ii. 41, 43. ITHPAEL *part.* Dan. ii. 43. עֵרֶב *m.* what is mixed, Exod. xii. 38: Neh. xiii. 3, "mixed multitude."

MIXTURE

מֶסֶךְ *m.* mixed wine, *i.e.* spiced: Ps. lxxv. 8.

MOCK

1 הָתַל to deceive, *seq.* בְּ to mock, to deride. PIEL [a] *pret.* [b] *inf.* [c] *fut.* [d] הֲתֻלִים *m. pl.* mockings; *poet.* mockers.

2 לִיץ (see *Scorn*), to deride, to mock at any one. KAL [a] *part.* HIPHIL [b] *fut.* HITHPALPEL [c] *fut.*

3 לָעַב to jest at, to mock. HIPHIL *part.*

4 לָעַג to mock, to deride; *pr.* by imitating the voice of any one in derision, used also of the eye: Prov. xxx. 17. KAL [a] *fut.* [b] *part.* Poel. HIPHIL [c] *fut.* [d] *part.* [e] לָעֵג *adj.* mocker.

5 עָלַל not used in Kal, which seems to have had the general signification to do, perform, be occupied in, a bad sense being implied. Hithp. *seq.* בְּ to vex, to maltreat, to use with indignity, insolence, and scorn; Gesenius, to gratify or indulge oneself in vexing, abusing, deriding any one; LXX. ἐμπαίζω; Vulg. *illudo.* HITHPAEL *pret.*

6 צָחַק to laugh, to laugh in sport, in contempt, to ridicule, sneer, banter. PIEL [a] *inf.* [b] *part.*

7 קָלַס to scoff at, to scorn, to deride. HITHPAEL [a] *fut.* [b] קַלָּסָה *f.* scorn.

8 שָׂחַק to laugh, sport, make merry; to deride, scorn: see *Laugh*. KAL [a] *pret.* [b] *fut.* PIEL [c] *part.* [d] שְׂחוֹק *m.* derision.

Gen. xix. 14.	6 b	Job xi. 3.	4 a	Prov. xx. 1.			2 a
xxi. 9.	6 b	xii. 4.	8 d	xxx. 17.			4 a
xxxix. 14, 17.	6 a	xiii. 9,a 9.	1 b c	Isa. xxviii. 22.			2 c
Num. xxii. 29.	5	xvii. 2.	1 d	Jer. xv. 17.			8 c
Judg. xvi. 10, 13, 15.	1 a	xxi. 3.	4 c	xx. 7.			4 b
1 Kings xviii. 27.	1 c	xxix. 22.	8 b	xxxviii. 19.			5
2 Kings ii. 23.	7 a	Ps. xxxv. 16.	4 e	Lam. i. 7.			8 a
2 Chron. xxx. 10.	4 d	Prov. i. 26.	4 a	Ezek. xxii. 4.			7 b
xxxvi. 16.	3	xiv. 9.	2 b	xxii. 5.			7 a
Neh. iv. 1.	4 c	xvii. 5.	4 b				

[a] *lit.* as the mocking at a man.

MODERATELY

צְדָקָה *f.* righteousness: Joel ii. 23, *lit.* according to righteousness.

MOIST

לַח *adj.* moist, hence green, fresh: Num. vi. 3.

לְשַׁד *m.* juice, sap; vital moisture, life-blood, vigour: Ps. xxxii. 4.

שָׁקָה to drink; to water, to moisten. PUAL *fut.* Job xxi. 24.

MOLE

חֲפַרְפָּרָה *f.* according to Jerome, the mole, from its digging holes and burrowing in the ground: Isa. ii. 20, *or*, according to the reading, which makes two words, "into the digging of rats."

תִּנְשֶׁמֶת *f.* an unclean animal; Lxx. and Vulg. *talpa*, mole. Bochart classes it with the species of lizard, and supposes it to be the chameleon. Lev. xi. 30.

MOLLIFIED

רָכַךְ to be tender; to be softened, mollified as a wound with ointment. PUAL *pret.* Isa. i. 6.

MOLOCH

מֹלֶךְ *m.* king; *pr. n.* of an idol of the Ammonites; to whose image, in the latter days of the commonwealth, the Hebrews sacrificed children.

MOMENT

רֶגַע *m.* the shortest possible space of time, from רָגַע to divide; the twinkling of an eye, a moment: Exod. xxxiii. 5: Num. xvi. 21, 45: Job vii. 18; xx. 5; xxi. 13; xxxiv. 20: Ps. xxx. 5; lxxiii. 19: Isa. xxvi. 20; xxvii. 3; xlvii. 9; liv. 7, 8: Jer. iv. 20: Lam. iv. 6: Ezek. xxvi. 16; xxxii. 10. Hence רָגַע in HIPHIL *fut.* Prov. xii. 19, seems to be *denom.* verb.

MONEY

כֶּסֶף silver; money, which originally consisted only of bars of pieces of silver not coined: Gen. xvii. 12, &c. כְּסַף Ch. *m.* Ezra vii. 17.

קִנְיָן *m.* getting: Lev. xxii. 11, *lit.* the purchase of his money.

קְשִׂיטָה *f.* something weighed out; hence as the name of a certain weight, kesitah, especially of gold and silver, by which, as also by the shekel, money was estimated in the time of the Patriarchs: it was heavier than the shekel, and contained about four shekels, as appears from a comparison of the passages Gen. xxxiii. 19 and xxiii. 16. Most of the ancient interpreters understand by it a lamb, a sense which has no support either from etymology or the kindred dialects; nor is it in accordance with the patriarchal usages, since, in their age, merchandise was no longer usually exchanged, but actual sales were common for money either by weight or by tale; *comp.* Gen. xxiii. 16, xlvii. 16.—*Genesius.* Gen. xxxiii. 19, *marg.* ' or, lambs;' Job xlii. 11.

MONSTER (SEA)

תַּנִּין *m.* a great fish, sea monster; see *Whale*. Lam. iv. 3.

MONTH, MOON

1 חֹדֶשׁ *m.* the new moon, day of the new moon, the first day of the lunar month, which was a festival to the Hebrews; a month, *i.e.* a lunar month, beginning at the new moon: Gen. vii. 11, &c.

2 יָרֵחַ *m.* moon, so called from its paleness. [a] יֶרַח *m.* month. [b] יְרַח Ch. *id.*

3 לְבָנָה *f.* the moon, from its whiteness.

No. 1 not included.

Gen. xxxvii. 9.	2	Job xxv. 5.	2	Isa. xiii. 10.	2
Exod. ii. 2.	2 a	xxix. 2.	2 a	xxiv. 23.	3
Deut. iv. 19.	2	xxxi. 26.	2	xxx. 26.	3
xvii. 3.	2	xxxix. 2.	2	lx. 19.	2
xxi. 13.	2 a	Ps. viii. 3.	2	lx. 20.	2 a
xxxiii. 14.	2 a	lxxii. 5, 7.	2	Jer. viii. 2.	2
Josh. x. 12, 13.	2	lxxix. 37.	2	xxxi. 35.	2
1 Kings vi. 37, 38.	2 a	civ. 19.	2	Ezek. xxxii. 7.	2
viii. 2.	2 a	cxxi. 6.	2	Dan. iv. 29.	2 b
2 Kings xv. 13.	2 a	cxxxvi. 9.	2	Joel ii. 10, 31.	2
xxiii. 5.	2	cxlviii. 3.	2	iii. 15.	2
Ezra vi. 15.	2 b	Eccles. xii. 2.	2	Hab. iii. 11.	2
Job iii. 6.	2 a	Cant. vi. 10.	3	Zech. xi. 8.	2 a
vii. 3.	2 a				

MONUMENTS

נָצַר to keep, to watch, to guard; to keep from view, to hide. KAL *part.* Paül. Isa. lxv. 4. Gesenius, they lodge in secret places, perhaps the recesses of heathen temples, *or,* with the LXX., sepulchral caverns, parallel with sepulchres.

MORE

1 גָּדוֹל *adj.* great.

2 הָלַךְ to go. KAL *part.* Poel.

3 יָסַף to add; in conjunction with another verb often translated more, as, "I will punish you .... more," *lit.* I will add to punish, to do more, &c. KAL a *pret.* b *part.* Poel. NIPHAL c *part.* HIPHIL d *pret.* e *fut.*

4 יוֹתֵר *m.* what is over and above.

5 עָבַר to pass. KAL *pret.* "to have more," *lit.* to pass the thoughts, &c.

6 עָדַף to remain, to be over and above. KAL *part.* Poel.

7 עָצַם to be strong, strong in number. KAL *pret.*

8 רָבַב to be many, to be multiplied. KAL a *pret.* b רַב *adj.* many. c רֹב *m.* multitude; "more in number."

9 רָבָה to multiply. KAL a *fut.* HIPHIL b *pret.* c *inf.* d *fut.* HIPHIL e *part.* "some more," *lit.* multiplying.

10 שְׁאָר Ch. *m.* rest, residue.

11 שׁוּב to return. KAL *fut.*

12 שֵׁנִי *adj. ord.* second, second time.

Gen. xxxvi. 7.	8 b	Judg. x. 13.	3 e	1 Chron. xxiv. 4.	8 b
xxxvii. 5, 8.	3 e	xiii. 21.	3 a	2 Chron. xxv. 9.	9 c
xliv. 23.	3 e	xvi. 30.	8 b	xxviii. 22.	8 b
Exod. i. 9.	8 b	Ruth i. 17.β	3 e	xxxii. 7.	8 b
v. 7.	3 e	1 Sam. ii. 3.γ	9 d	xxxii. 23.	3 e
viii. 29.	3 e	iii. 17.β	3 e	xxxiii. 23.ζ	9 b
ix. 34.	3 e	vii. 13.	3 a	Ezra vii. 20	10
x. 28.	3 e	xiv. 44.β	3 e	Esth. vi. 6.	4
xi. 6.	3 e	xv. 35.	3 a	Job vii. 7.	11
xvi. 17.	9 e	xviii. 29.	3 e	xx. 9.	3 e
xxxvi. 5.α	3 e	xx. 13.β	3 e	xxxiv. 32.	3 e
Lev. xi. 42.	9 e	xxii. 15.	1	xli. 8.	3 e
xiii. 5, 33, 54.	12	xxv. 22.β	3 e	Ps. x. 18.	7
xxvi. 18.	3 a	xxv. 36.	1	xl. 5, 12.	7
Num. iii. 46.	6	xxvii. 14.	3 a	xli. 8.	3 e
xxii. 15.	8 b	2 Sam. ii. 28.	3 a	lix. 4.	8 a
xxii. 18.	1	iii. 9.	3 e	lxi. 14.	3 d
xxii. 19.	3 e	iii. 35.β	3 e	lxxiii. 7.	5
xxxiii. 54.	8 b	vii. 10, 20.	3 e	lxxvii. 7.	3 e
Deut. iii. 26.	3 e	xiv. 10.	3 e	lxxviii. 17.	3 e
v. 25.	3 b	xiv. 11.δ	9 c	cxxxix. 18.	9 a
vii. 7.	3 e	xviii. 8.ε	9 d	Prov. iv. 18.η	2
vii. 17.	8 b	xix. 13.β	3 e	Eccles. ii. 15.	4
xiii. 11.	3 e	1 Kings ii. 23.β	3 e	vi. 8.	4
xvii. 16.	3 e	xvi. 33.	3 e	xii. 9.	4
xix. 20.	3 e	xix. 2.β	3 e	Isa. i. 5, 13.	3 e
xx. 1.	8 b	xx. 10.β	3 e	x. 20.	3 e
xxviii. 68.	3 e	2 Kings vi. 16.	8 b	xv. 2.θ	3 e
Josh. vii. 12.	3 e	vi. 23.	3 a	xxiii. 12.	3 e
x. 11.	8 b	vi. 31.	3 e	xlvii. 1, 5.	3 e
xxiii. 13.	3 a	xxi. 8.	3 e	li. 22.	3 e
Judg. viii. 28.	3 a	1 Chron. xvii. 9, 18.	3 e	lii. 1.	3 e

Isa. liv. 1.	8 b	Ezek. xxxvi. 12.	3 e	Amos v. 2.	3 e
lvi. 12.	1	Hos. i. 6.	3 e	Jonah iv. 11.	9 c
Jer. xxxi. 12.	3 e	ix. 15.	3 e	Nah. i. 15.	3 e
xlvi. 23.	8 a	xiii. 2.	3 e	Zeph. iii. 11.	3 e
Lam. iv. 15, 16, 22.	3 e	Joel ii. 2.	3 e		

a *lit.* multiply in bringing. β "and more also;" *lit.* so may he add. γ "talk no more;" *lit.* multiply not; talk not high high. δ *lit.* multiply to destroy. ε *lit.* multiplied to devour. ζ *lit.* multiplied trespass. η *lit.* going and shining. θ *lit.* additions.

MORNING

1 אוֹר *m.* light.

2 בֹּקֶר *m.* the first breaking forth of light; dawn of prosperity and happiness; "every morning," *lit.* in the morning in the morning: also, to the mornings. Gen. i. 5, &c.

3 נֹגַהּ Ch. *f.* morning light, dawn, day-break.

4 צְפִירָה *f.* a circle, cycle; put for the vicissitude or term of human things, which return in the same succession as if in a circle.

5 שַׁחַר *m.* aurora, dawn, morning. a מִשְׁחָר *m. id.*

6 שָׁכָה to roam about, to wander. HIPHIL *part.*

7 שָׁכַם to rise up early. HIPHIL a *inf.* b *part.*

No. 2 not included.

Gen. xix. 15.	5	Ps. cxxxix. 9.	5	Dan. vi. 19.	3
1 Sam. xvii. 16.	7 a	Cant. vi. 10.	5	Hos. vi. 3.	5
Neh. iv. 21.	5	Isa. xiv. 12.	5	x. 15.	5
viii. 3.	1	lviii. 8.	5	Joel ii. 2.	5
Job xli. 18.	5	Jer. v. 8.	6, or 7 b	Amos iv. 13.	5
Ps. cx. 3.	5 a	Ezek. vii. 7, 10.	4	Jonah iv. 7.	

MORROW

1 בֹּקֶר *m.* morning.

2 מָחָר *m.* to-morrow, the morrow: Exod. viii. 10, &c. מָחֳרָת a *f. id.*

No. 2 not included.

Gen. xix. 34.	2 a	Num. xxii. 41.	1	1 Sam. xx. 27.	2 a
Exod. vi. 6.	2 a	xxxiii. 3.	2 a	xxxi. 8.	2 a
xviii. 13.	2 a	Josh. v. 11, 12.	2 a	2 Sam. xi. 12.	2 a
xxxii. 6, 30.	2 a	Judg. vi. 38.	2 a	2 Kings viii. 15.	2 a
Lev. vii. 16.	2 a	ix. 42.	2 a	1 Chron. x. 8.	2 a
xix. 6.	2 a	xxi. 4.	2 a	Esth. ii. 14.	1
xxii. 30.	1	1 Sam. v. 3, 4.	2 a	v. 14.	1
xxiii. 11, 15, 16.	2 a	xi. 19.	1	Jer. xx. 3.	2 a
Num. xvi. 5.	1	xi. 11.	2 a	Zeph. iii. 3.	1
xvi. 41.	2 a	xviii. 10.	1		
xvii. 8.	2 a				

MORSEL

בִּכָּר *f.* a circle: 1 Sam. ii. 36, *lit.* a round of bread.

פַּת *f.* a bit, crumb, morsel: Gen. xviii. 5: Judg. xix. 5: Ruth ii. 14: 1 Sam. xxviii. 22: 1 Kings xvii. 11: Job xxxi. 17: Ps. cxlvii. 17: Prov. xvii. 1; xxiii. 8.

MORTAL

אֱנוֹשׁ *m.* man as mortal; mortal man: Job iv. 17.

נֶפֶשׁ *com.* soul, life: Deut. xix. 11, *marg.* 'in life.'

MORTAR

מְדֹכָה *f.* a mortar, in which things are beaten or bruised: Num. xi. 8.

מַכְתֵּשׁ *m.* a mortar for pounding; it seems also to have been a capital punishment, as it is in Turkey still, to pound in a mortar. Prov. xxvii. 22.

MORTER

חֹמֶר *m.* clay, cement or morter: Gen. xi. 3: Exod. i. 14: Isa. xli. 25: Nah. iii. 14.

עָפָר *m.* dust: Lev. xiv. 42, 45.

MORTGAGE

עָרַב to become surety; to pledge. KAL *part.* Poel, Neh. v. 3.

MOST

חַיִל Ch. power: Dan. iii. 20, "most mighty," *lit.* mighty of strength.

כַּבִּיר *adj.* great, vast, mighty: Job xxxiv. 17.

כֶּתֶם *m.* pure gold: Cant. v. 11, "most fine gold," *lit.* gold fine gold.

רֹב *m.* multitude: Prov. xx. 6.

MOTH

עָשׁ *m.* a moth, which consumes garments: Job iv. 19; xiii. 28; xxvii. 18: Ps. xxxix. 11: Isa. l. 9; li. 8: Hos. v. 12.

MOTHER

אֵם *f.* mother; "mother's children," are to be understood of children by the same mother in distinction from the children of another wife to the same father: Gen. ii. 24, &c.

חָמוֹת *f.* mother-in-law; Ruth i. 14; ii. 11, 18, 19, 19, 23; iii. 1, 6, 16, 17: Micah vii. 6.

חָתַן to contract affinity. KAL *part.* Poel, Deut. xxvii. 23.

MOULDY

נִקֻּדִים *m. pl.* bread spotted with mould: Josh. ix. 5, 12.

MOUNT, MOUNTAIN

1 הַר *m.* a mountain, a mount; often with a proper name, as mount Sinai, mount Tabor, and mount Lebanon; further, the mountain of God, *t. e.* Sinai, as the place where the law was given, Exod. iii. 1; iv. 27; xviii. 5: Zion, Ps. xxiv. 3: Isa. ii. 3, which also is often called God's holy mountain; mountain of Bashan, which is very high compared with lesser hills westward, Ps. lxviii. 15; *m. pl.* the holy land Palestine, as being mountainous, the mountains of God, Isa. xiv. 25; xlix. 11; lxv. 9; collectively, mountains, mountainous region, Josh. xiv. 12, *e. gr.* mountains of Seir, mountains of Judah, Josh. xv. 48; with the *art.* הָהָר the mountains; the high mountainous tract extending nearly through Palestine, between the plain on the sea coast and the valley of the Jordan, Gen. xii. 8, *lit.* mountainwards, *i. e.* towards the mountainous district, Josh. ix. 1; the mountains of Judah, *i. e.* the same tract south of Jerusalem, (ἡ ὀρεινή, Luke i. 39,) Num. xiii. 29, Deut. i. 2; the mountainous region east of the Dead Sea, Gen. xiv. 10; xix. 17, 19, 30.—Gen. vii. 20, &c.

2 הָרָר *m.* a mountain.

3 טוּר Ch. *m.* a rock, a mountain.

4 מַצָּב *m.* station of troops; post.

5 סֹלְלָה *f.* a bank; a mound, rampart, especially a mound thrown up by besiegers against a city.

No. 1 not included.

Gen. xiv. 6.	2	Ps. xxxvi. 6.	2	Cant. iv. 8.	2
Num. xxiii. 7.	2	lxxvi. 4.	2	Isa. xxix. 3.	4
Deut. xxxiii. 15.	2	lxxxvii. 1.	2	Jer. vi. 6.	5
Ps. xxx. 7.	2	cxxxiii. 3.	2	xvii. 3.	2

Jer. xxxii. 24.	5	Ezek. xvii. 17.	5	Dan. ii. 35, 45.	3
xxxiii. 4.	5	xxi. 22.	5	xi. 15.	5
Ezek. iv. 2.	5	xxvi. 8.	5	Hab. iii. 6.	2

MOUNT (V)

1 אָבַךְ to roll; to roll itself together; to be carried up as dust or smoke. HITHPAEL *fut.*

2 גָּבַהּ to be lifted up. HIPHIL *fut.*

3 עָלָה to go up, ascend. KAL ᵃ*fut.* ᵇ מַעֲלֶה *m.* going up.

4 רוּם to be high. KAL *inf.*

5 רָמַם to be high. NIPHAL *fut.*

Job xx. 6.	3 a	Isa. ix. 18.	1	Jer. li. 53.	3 a
xxxix. 27.	2	xv. 5.	3 b	Ezek. x. 16.	4
Ps. cvii. 26.	3 a	xl. 31.	3 a	x. 19.	5

MOURN

1 אָבַל to mourn, *seq.* עַל over anything; figuratively of things inanimate. KAL ᵃ*pret.* ᵇ*fut.* HITHPAEL ᵈ*pret.* ᵉ*imp.* ᶠ*fut.* ᵍ*part.* ʰ אָבֵל *adj.* mourning. ⁱ אֵבֶל *m.* this is used of the loud wailing customary in the East at the time of burial and for thirty days after, during which they abstained from the ordinary occupations and comforts of life.

2 אָוֶן vanity; evil, trouble, sorrow.

3 אָנָה to sigh, to groan internally. KAL ᵃ*pret.* ᵇ תַּאֲנִיָּה *f.* heaviness, mourning.

4 אָנַח to sigh. NIPHAL ᵃ*fut.* ᵇ אֲנָחָה *f.* sigh.

5 בָּכָה to weep. KAL ᵃ*fut.* ᵇ בְּכִית *f.* weeping.

6 דָּאַב to be sorrowful; *or,* to pine away, to languish. KAL *pret.*

7 הָגָה to meditate; to mourn in a low muttering voice. KAL ᵃ*inf.* ᵇ*fut.* ᶜ הֶגֶה *m.* sighing.

8 הָמָה to roar; to mourn with a loud voice; of a company mourning. KAL *part.* Poel.

9 לִוְיָתָן see *Leviathan*: as this word nowhere else bears this meaning of mourning, it is rather to be understood of some large serpent or crocodile, which some professed to have control over; or some evil power symbolized by this name, and supposed to be raised by those who professed to be able to do so in order to curse. Job iii. 8.

10 נָהַם to roar like a lion, or as the sea; to lament; to groan under great pain and sorrow. KAL *pret.*

11 נוּד see *Bemoan*. KAL *inf.*

12 סָפַד to beat the breast, as a sign of mourning; hence to lament, to mourn, chiefly for the dead, *seq.* לְ, עַל, לִפְנֵי, and *abs.*; also for a public calamity; mourning for the dead was done at the door of their tent or house: Gen. xxiii. 2. KAL ᵃ*pret.* ᵇ*inf.* ᶜ*imp.* ᵈ*fut.* ᵉ*part.* Poel. ᶠ מִסְפֵּד *m.* wailing.

13 קָדַר to be black, dark; to go about in filthy garments, as mourners, to mourn; to be afflicted. KAL ᵃ*part.* Poel. HIPHIL ᵇ*fut.* ᶜ קְדֹרַנִּית *adv.* in mourning dress.

14 קוּן to chant a mournful song, to lament. Hence in Ireland to keen, *i. e.* to make a wailing for the dead. POLEL *part.*, of hired mourners.

15 רוּד to wander about; to give up oneself to. HIPHIL *fut.*

16 מִזְרָח *m.* the primary meaning is thought to be any great outcry for joy or for sorrow.

Gen. xxiii. 2.	12 b	Job iii. 8.	9	Jer. xii. 11.	1 a	Prov. v. 3.	2	Cant. v. 16.	2	Dan. vi. 17, 22.	5

Gen. xxiii. 2.	12 b	Job iii. 8.	9	Jer. xii. 11.	1 a
xxvii. 41.	1 i	v. 11.	13 a	xiv. 2.	1 a
xxxvii. 34.	1 f	xiv. 22.	1 b	xvi. 5.	16
xxxvii. 35.	1 h	xxix. 25.	1 h	xvi. 7.	1 i
l. 3.	5 a	xxx. 28.	13 a	xxiii. 10.	1 a
l. 4.	5 b	xxx. 31.	1 i	xxxi. 13.	1 i
l. 10, 10.	12 d, 1 i	Ps. xxx. 11.	12 f	xlviii. 31.	7 b
l. 11, 11.	1 i	xxxv. 14.	1 h	Lam. i. 4.	1 h
Exod. xxxiii. 4.	1 f	xxxviii. 6.	13 a	ii. 5.	3 b
Num. xiv. 39.	1 f	xlii. 9.	13 a	v. 15.	1 i
xx. 29.	5 a	xliii. 2.	13 a	Ezek. ii. 10.	7 c
Deut. xxvi. 14.	2	lv. 2.	15	vii. 12, 27.	1 f
xxxiv. 8.	1 i	lxxxviii. 9.	6	vii. 16.	8
1 Sam. xv. 35.	1 d	Prov. v. 11.	10	xxiv. 16.	12 d
xvi. 1.	1 g	xxix. 2.	4 a	xxiv. 17.	1 i
2 Sam. i. 12.	12 d	Eccles. iii. 4.	12 b	xxiv. 23, 23.	12 d, 10
iii. 31.	12 c	vii. 2, 4.	1 i	xxxi. 15, 15.	1 c, 13 b
xi. 26.	12 d	xii. 5.	12 e	Dan. x. 2.	1 g
xi. 27.	1 i	Isa. iii. 26.	1 a	Hos. iv. 3.	1 b
xiii. 37.	1 f	xvi. 7.	7 b	ix. 4.	2
xiv. 2, 2, 2.	1 e i g	xix. 8.	3 a	x. 5.	1 a
xix. 1.	1 f	xxiv. 4, 7.	1 a	Joel i. 9, 10.	1 a
xix. 2.	1 i	xxxiii. 9.	1 a	ii. 12.	12 f
1 Kings xiii. 29.	12 b	xxxviii. 14.	7 b	Amos i. 2.	1 a
xiii. 30.	12 d	li. 11.	1 a	v. 16.	1 i
xiv. 13.	12 a	lvii. 18.	1 h	viii. 8.	1 a
xiv. 18.	12 d	lix. 11.	7 a b	viii. 10, 10.	1 a
1 Chron. vii. 22.	1 f	lx. 20.	1 i	ix. 5.	1 a
2 Chron. xxxv. 24.	1 g	lxi. 2.	1 i	Micah i. 8.	1 i
Ezra x. 6.	1 g	lxi. 3, 3.	1 h i	i. 11.	12 f
Neh. i. 4.	1 f	lxvi. 10.	1 g	Zech. vii. 5.	12 b
viii. 9.	1 f	Jer. iv. 28.	1 b	xii. 10, 10.	12 a f
Esth. iv. 3.	1 i	vi. 26.	1 i	xii. 11, 11.	12 f
vi. 12.	1 h	ix. 17.	14	xii. 12.	12 a
ix. 22.	1 i	xii. 4.	1 b	Mal. iii. 14.	13 c
Job ii. 11.	11				

Prov. v. 3.	2	Cant. v. 16.	2	Dan. vi. 17, 22.	5
viii. 7.	2	Dan. iii. 26.	2	vii. 5, 8, 20.	5
xv. 14.	4, or 6	iv. 31.	2	Hos. viii. 1.	2

MOUSE

עַכְבָּר *m.* a mouse; especially a field-mouse, which is said to be very destructive to the harvest: Lev. xi. 29: 1 Sam. vi. 4, 5, 11, 18: Isa. lxvi. 17.

MOUTH

1 גָּרוֹן *m.* throat.

2 חֵךְ *m.* palate, roof of the mouth.

3 עֲדִי *m.* ornament; supposed also to mean cheek, or mouth; but the first signification is preferred by modern critics in Ps. xxxii. 9, *or,* whose ornaments are bit and bridle for restraint; in ciii. 5 it is supposed to have the meaning of age; by some, soul.

4 פֶּה *m.* mouth, so called from breathing and blowing. Spoken of the mouth of man and beast; as an instrument of speech, so of eating, tasting, &c. To speak with one mouth to mouth, *i. e.* in person, without mediator or interpreter. That which is spoken is said to be upon the mouth, as we say upon the lips; rendered 'appointment' in Num. iv. 27, 2 Sam. xiii. 32. The mouth is also put by *meton.* for a speaker, a spokesman: Exod. iv. 16, *comp.* vii. 1: Jer. xv. 19. Aperture, orifice, entrance, of a sack, a well, &c. Mouth of the sword, *i. e.* the edge, as biting and devouring like the mouth. The mouth of a lion was very formidable: Rev. xiii. 2.—Gen. iv. 11, &c.

5 פֻּם Ch. *m.* mouth, aperture, entrance.

6 פָּנִים *m. pl.* face: Prov. xv. 14, כתיב.

7 תְּרַע Ch. *m.* gate, door, of a furnace or oven.

No. 4 not included.

2 Sam. xvii. 19.	6	Job xxxi. 30.	2	Ps. xxxii. 9.	3
Job xii. 11.	2	xxxiii. 24.	2	ciii. 5.	3
xx. 13.	2	xxxiv. 3.	2	cxlix. 6.	1

MOVE

1 גָּעַשׁ to shake by a sudden impulse; to be moved violently to and fro. HITHPAEL [a] *fut.* HITHPOEL [b] *pret.* [c] *fut.*

2 הוּם to put in motion, to throw into commotion, consternation; to be agitated. NIPHAL *fut.*

3 הָלַךְ to walk, to go. HITHPAEL *fut.*

4 הָמָה to make a great noise. KAL *pret.*

5 זוּעַ to shake, to be agitated from fear or reverence. KAL *pret.*

6 חָפַץ to bend. KAL *fut.*

7 חָרַץ to cut; to sharpen, *pr.* to point. KAL [a] *pret.* [b] *fut.*

8 מוֹט to waver, be moved; it is used of things that ought to be firm and fixed, and therefore it implies a very great agitation, as of mountains, kingdoms, &c.; in Kal and Niphal, implying motion which causes ruin or injury. KAL [a] *pret.* [b] *inf.* NIPHAL [c] *fut.* HITHPAEL [d] *pret.* [e] מוֹט *m.* a being moved, of the foot.

9 נָדַד to move; to move oneself, to flit. KAL *part.* Poel.

10 נוּד to nod; to move, to be shaken, to wander; with a *dat.* to pity, to commiserate. HIPHIL [a] *inf.* [b] נִיר *m.* moving, pity, comfort.

11 נוּט to be moved, to quake, *i.q.* מוֹט. KAL *fut.* Ps. xcix. 1, *marg.* 'stagger.' LXX. σαλευθήτω ἡ γῆ, Vulg. *moveatur terra;* and so Syr. and Chald.

12 נוּעַ to nod, to waver, to reel; to move to and fro unsteadily; to wander; of the lips in speaking. KAL [a] *pret.* [b] *inf.* [c] *fut.* [d] *part.* HIPHIL [e] *fut.*

13 נוּף *m.* to wave, to move to and fro with agility. HIPHIL *fut.*

14 נָתַר to tremble, of the heart, to palpitate. KAL *fut.*

15 סוּת to stir up, to persuade. HIPHIL *fut.*

16 עֲבַד Ch. to do, to perform; to make. P'AL *part. active.*

17 פּוּק to move to and fro, to be unsteady. HIPHIL *fut.*

18 פָּעַם to strike; to impel, to urge. KAL *inf.*

19 קָלַל to be light. HITHPALPEL, to move lightly: *pret.*

20 קָרַץ to wink; to compress, from the idea of pinching; Vulg. to bite the lips, as significative of a malicious purpose formed in the mind. KAL *part.* Poel.

21 רָגַז to be moved, disturbed; to be thrown into commotion by any passion. KAL [a] *pret.* [b] *fut.*

22 רָחַף to brood over; or to hover with a gentle wavering or fluttering motion, as of a bird over her young, see Deut. xxxii. 11. PIEL *part.*

23 רָמַשׂ to creep. KAL [a] *fut.* [b] *part.* Poel. [c] רֶמֶשׂ *m.* a reptile, or any animal moving (birds excepted).

24 רָעַשׁ to tremble, to shake violently. KAL [a] *pret.* NIPHAL [b] *fut.*

25 שָׁרַץ to creep, to swarm; used especially of multitudinous life in motion. KAL [a] *fut.* [b] שֶׁרֶץ reptile, or any moving creature, especially produced in great multitudes.

Gen. i. 2.	22	2 Chron. xviii. 31.	15	Ps. cxii. 6.	8 c
i. 20.	25 b	Ezra iv. 15.	16	cxxi. 3.	8 e
i. 21, 28.	23 b	Esth. v. 9.	5	Prov. v. 6.	12 a
vii. 21.	23 b	Job ii. 3.	15	xii. 3.	8 c
ix. 2.	23 a	xvi. 5.	10 b	xvi. 30.	2 b
ix. 3.	23 c	xxxvii. 1.	14	xxiii. 31.	3
Exod. xi. 7.	7 b	xl. 17.	6	Cant. iv. 4.	4
Lev. xi. 10.	25 b	xli. 23.	8 c	Isa. vi. 4.	12 c
xi. 46.	23 b	Ps. x. 6.	8 c	vii. 2, 2.	12 c b
Deut. xxiii. 25.	13	xiii. 4.	8 c	x. 14.	9
Josh. x. 21.	7 a	xv. 5.	8 c	xiv. 9.	21 a
xv. 18.	15	xvi. 8.	8 c	xix. 1.	12 a
Judg. i. 14.	15	xviii. 7.	21 b	xxiv. 19.	8 b d
xiii. 25.	18	xxi. 7.	8 c	xl. 20.	8 c
Ruth i. 19.	2	xxx. 6.	8 c	xli. 7.	8 c
1 Sam. i. 13.	12 d	xlvi. 5.	8 c	Jer. iv. 24.	19
2 Sam. vii. 10.	21 b	xlvi. 6.	8 a	x. 4.	17
xviii. 33.	21 b	lv. 22.	8 b	xxv. 16.	1 b
xxii. 8.	4	lxii. 2, 6.	8 c	xlvi. 7.	1 a
xxiv. 1.	15	lxvi. 9.	8 e	xlvi. 8.	1 c
2 Kings xxi. 8.	10 a	lxix. 34.	23 b	xlix. 21.	24 a
xxiii. 18.	12 e	xciii. 1.	8 c	l. 46.	24 b
1 Chron. xvi. 30.	8 c	xcvi. 10.	8 c	Ezek. xlvii. 9.	25 a
xvii. 9.	21 b	xcix. 1.	11	Micah vii. 17.	21 b

MOW

גֵּז *m.* mowing; mown grass, *or,* mown meadow: Ps. lxxii. 6: Amos vii. 1.

קָצַר to cut off or down; to reap, to mow. KAL *part.* Poel, Ps. cxxix. 7.

MUCH

1   דַּי sufficiency; too much.

2   יָתַר to be over and above, to be left. HIPHIL *inf.*

3   כָּבֵד *adj.* heavy; much, numerous, great.

4   כַּבִּיר *adj.* strong, much, many. See also *Mighty.*

5   מְאֹד *adv.* mightily: Isa. lvi. 12, *lit.* very great.

6   עָצוּם strong, mighty.

7   רָבָה to multiply. KAL ᵃ *fut.* HIPHIL ᵇ *pret.,* much, very, *lit.* he multiplied, *seq. inf.* ᶜ *imp.* ᵈ *inf.* ᵉ רַב *adj.* much, many, great, large: Gen. xxx. 43, &c. ᶠ רֹב *m.* multitude. ᵍ מִרְבָּה *f.* amplitude, fulness.

8   שַׂגִּיא Ch. *adj.* great; many.

No. 7 e not included.

Gen. xxvi. 16.	5	2 Kings xxi. 16.	5	Prov. xiii. 23.	7 f
xxxiv. 12. a	7 c, 5	1 Chron. xx. 2.	5	xiv. 4.	7 f
xli. 49.	7 d	2 Chron. xiii. 3.	7 d	xxv. 27.	7 f
xliii. 34.	7 a	xxv. 9.	5	Eccles. i. 18, 18.	7 f
Exod. xii. 38.	3	xxvii. 3.	7 f	v. 12, 17, 20.	7 d
xxxvi. 7.	2	xxxii. 27.	5	vii. 16, 17.	7 d
Num. xx. 20.	3	xxxiii. 6.	7 b	ix. 18.	7 d
Josh. xiii. 1.	7 d	xxxvi. 14.	7 b	xii. 12.	7 d
xxii. 8, 8, 8.	7 e e d	Neh. iv. 10.	7 d	Isa. xxx. 33.	7 d
Ruth i. 13.	5	vi. 16.	5	lvi. 12.	5
1 Sam. xviii. 30.	5	Esth. i. 18.	1	Jer. ii. 36.	5
xix. 2.	5	Job xv. 10.	4	xl. 12.	7 d
2 Sam. viii. 8.	7 d	xxxi. 25.	5	Ezek. xxii. 32.	7 g
xiv. 25.	5	Ps. xxxiii. 16.	7 f	Dan. iv. 12.	8
1 Kings iv. 29.	7 d	xxxv. 18.	6	vii. 5, 28.	8
xxi. 6.	7 b	cxix. 107.	5	Hag. i. 6, 9.	7 d
2 Kings x. 18.	7 d	Prov. vii. 21.	7 f		

a lit. multiply upon me very much.

MUFFLERS

רְעָלָה *m.* female ornaments, so called from their tremulous or fluttering motion: Isa. iii. 19, *marg.* 'or, spangled ornaments.' Gesenius, veils.

MULBERRY

בָּכָא *m.* the name of a certain tree, so called from its weeping, *i. e.* distilling an odoriferous gum: 2 Sam. v. 23, 24:
1 Chron. xiv. 14, 15. There is great uncertainty what tree is intended; some think a kind of poplar.

MULE

יֵמִם This is one of the words of most doubtful meaning in all Scripture. The Jewish commentators most generally render it by mule, which is adopted in our version. It tends somewhat to the confirmation of the Rabbinical interpretation, that Anah seems to be mentioned with a note of reprobation, since, if he discovered and adopted the mode of producing mules, it was contrary to the Mosaic law: Lev. xix. 19. Others translate it Emim, a gigantic people, Gen. xiv. 5, 6, Deut. ii. 10, 11, whom Anah conquered; so מָצָא may be explained. See Taylor, Bochart, Poli. Synops., Celsii Hierobot. Modern critics, following the Vulg., understand it of warm springs; see Gesenius, Bush *in loc.,* Fürst. Gen. xxxvi. 24.

פֶּרֶד *m.* a mule, so called because of his being solitary or separate as to producing its same species: 2 Sam. xiii. 29; xviii. 9, 9, 9: 1 Kings x. 25; xviii. 5: 2 Kings v. 17: 1 Chron. xii. 40: 2 Chron. ix. 24: Ezra ii. 66: Neh. vii. 68: Ps. xxxii. 9: Isa. lxvi. 20: Ezek. xxvii. 14: Zech. xiv. 15. פִּרְדָּה *f.* 1 Kings i. 33, 38, 44.

רֶכֶשׁ *m. pr.* a swift beast, as a horse, as a young horse, or mule, a steed, or courser: Esth. viii. 10, 14.

MULTIPLY

1   הָמָה to make a noise, to rage. KAL *inf.* Ezek. v. 7; or, הָמוֹן *i. q.* הָמוֹן noise, multitude; hence, perhaps, our version has "multiplied;" but most critics agree in supposing that tumultuous rage against God is implied.

2   כָּבַר to be great, much, many; to make many. HIPHIL *fut.*

3   עָתַר to be rich, abundant. HIPHIL *pret.*

4   רָבַב to become much, or many. KAL ᵃ *pret.* ᵇ *inf.* ᶜ רַב *adj.* many. ᵈ רְבָבָה *f.* myriad.

5   רָבָה to become much or many, to multiply, to increase. KAL ᵃ *pret.* ᵇ *inf.* ᶜ *imp.* ᵈ *fut.* HIPHIL ᵉ *pret.* ᶠ *inf.* ᵍ *imp.* ʰ *fut.*

6   שְׂגָא Ch. to be or become great. P'AL *fut.*

Gen. i. 22, 22.	5 c d	Deut. viii. 1.	5 a	Prov. xxix. 16.	5 b
i. 28.	5 c	viii. 13, 13, 13.	5 d	Isa. ix. 3.	5 b
iii. 16.	5 h f	xi. 21.	5 d	lix. 12.	4 a
vi. 1.	4 b	xiii. 17.	5 e	Jer. iii. 16.	5 d
viii. 17.	5 a	xvii. 16, 16.	5 d	xxx. 19.	5 e
ix. 1, 7, 7.	5 c	xvii. 17, 17.	5 h	xxxiii. 22.	5 h
xvi. 10.	5 h f	xxviii. 63.	5 f	Ezek. v. 7.	1
xvii. 2.	5 h	xxx. 5.	5 e	xi. 6.	4 d
xvii. 20.	5 e	xxx. 16.	5 e	xvi. 25, 29, 51.	5 h
xxii. 17, 17.	5 h f	Josh. xxiv. 3.	5 h	xxi. 15.	5 f
xxvi. 4, 24.	5 e	1 Chron. iv. 27.	5 e	xxiii. 19.	5 h
xxviii. 3.	5 h	v. 9.	5 e	xxxi. 5.	5 d
xxxv. 11.	5 c	Neh. ix. 23.	5 e	xxxv. 13.	3
xlvii. 27.	5 e	Job xiv. 17.	5 e	xxxvi. 10, 11, 30.	3 e
xlviii. 4.	5 e	xxix. 18.	5 d	xxxvii. 26.	5 e
Exod. i. 7, 10, 12, 20.	5 d	xxxiv. 37.	5 h	Dan. iv. 1.	6
vii. 3.	5 e	xxxv. 6.	4	Hos. ii. 8.	5 e
xi. 9.	5 b	xxxv. 16.	2	viii. 11.	5 e
xxiii. 29.	4 c	Ps. xvi. 4.	5 e	xii. 10.	5 e
xxxii. 13.	5 e	xxxviii. 19.	4 a	Amos iv. 4.	5 g
Lev. xxvi. 9.	5 e	cvii. 38.	5 d	Nah. iii. 16.	5 e
Deut. i. 10.	5 e	Prov. ix. 11.	5 d		
vii. 13.	5 e				

MULTITUDE

1 אָמוֹן *i.q.* הָמוֹן *m.* a multitude ; *or,* a proper name: Jer. xlvi. 25, *marg.* 'Amon, *or,* nourisher;' see *Nurse.*

2 אֲסַפְסֻף *m. pr.* collected, a mixed multitude, rabble, following the camp of the Israelites.

3 הָמוֹן *m.* a multitude, a concourse of people, including the idea of noise and tumult.

4 חַי *adj.* living ; beast ; company : Ps. lxxiv. 19, wild beasts is more generally taken to be the meaning here.

5 עֵדָה *f.* an appointed meeting, assembly ; any assembly, multitude.

6 מָלֵא *adj.* full. ᵃ מְלֹא *m.* Gen. xlviii. 19, *marg.* 'fulness,' *comp.* Rom. xi. 25, "fulness of the Gentiles."

7 סָךְ *m.* a multitude, *i. e.* a dense crowd, like a thicket of trees.

8 עֵרֶב *m.* mixture ; mixed, mixed multitude.

9 קָהָל *m.* an assembly or convocation of the people for civil or religious purposes ; in a wider sense, any assembly or multitude of men.

10 רַב *adj.* much, many. ᵃ רֹב *m.* multitude, abundance ; equivalent to, the whole : Gen. xvi. 10, &c.

11 מַרְבִּית *f.* greatness, multitude.

12 רִיב *m.* strife : Job xxxiii. 19, כתיב.

13 רֶכֶב *com.* chariot : 2 Kings xix. 23, כתיב.

14 שִׁפְעָה *f.* abundance.

No. 10 a not included.

Gen. xxviii. 3.	9	2 Chron. xxxii. 7.	3	Jer. x. 13.	3
xlviii. 4.	9	Neh. xiii. 3.	8	xii. 6.	6
xlviii. 19.	6 a	Job xxxi. 34.	3	xliv. 15.	9
Exod. xii. 38.a	10	xxxiii. 19.	12, or 10 a	xlvi. 25.	1
xxiii. 2.	10	xxxix. 7.	3	xlix. 32.	3
Num. xi. 4.	2	Ps. xlii. 4, 4.	7, 3	li. 16, 42.	3
xxxii. 1.	10	lxviii. 30.	5	lii. 15.	1
Judg. iv. 7.	3	lxxiv. 19.	4	Ezek. vii. 11, 12, 13, 14.	3
1 Sam. xiv. 16.	3	xcvii. 1.	10	xxiii. 42.	3
2 Sam. vi. 19.	3	cix. 30.	10	xxix. 19.	3
1 Kings xx. 13, 28.	3	Isa. v. 13, 14.	3	xxx. 4, 10, 15.	3
2 Kings vii. 13, 13.	3	xiii. 4.	3	xxxi. 2, 18.	3
xix. 23.	10 a, or 13	xvi. 14.	3	xxxi. 5.	10
xxv. 11.	3	xvii. 12.	3	xxxii. 12, 16, 18, 20,	3
2 Chron. i. 9.β	10	xxix. 5, 5, 7, 8.	3	24, 25, 26, 31, 32.	3
xiii. 8.	3	xxxi. 4.	6 a	xxxix. 11.	3
xiv. 11.	3	xxxii. 14.	3	Dan. x. 6.	3
xx. 2, 15, 24.	3	lx. 6.	14	xi. 10, 11, 11, 12, 13.	3
xxx. 18.	11	Jer. iii. 23.	3	Joel iii. 14, 14.	3

a lit. a great mixture. *β lit.* much as dust of the earth.

MUNITION

מְצוֹדָה *f.* a fortress, castle, stronghold : Isa. xxix. 7. מְצָד see *Hold* : Isa. xxxiii. 16.

מְצוּרָה *f.* fortress, fortified city : Nah. ii. 1.

MURDER

הָרַג to kill or slay, in general. KAL *fut.* Ps. x. 8. *part.* Poel, Jer. iv. 31 : Hos. ix. 13.

נָכָה to smite. HIPHIL *part.* 2 Kings xiv. 6.

רָצַח to kill, to slay. KAL *inf.* Jer. vii. 9. *part.* Poel, Num. xxxv. 16, 16, 17, 17, 18, 18, 19, 21, 21, 30, 31 : Job xxiv. 14. PIEL *fut.* Ps. xciv. 6 : Hos. vi. 9. *part.* 2 Kings vi. 32 : Isa. i. 21.

MURMUR

1 לוּן to pass the night ; to remain ; Niph. to shew oneself obstinate, to be stubborn, from the idea of remaining

and persisting, taken in a bad sense ; hence to murmur, to complain. NIPHAL ᵃ *fut.* HIPHIL ᵇ *pret.* ᶜ *fut.* ᵈ *part.* ᵉ תְּלֻנּוֹת *f. pl.* murmuring.

2 רָגַן to murmur ; to be contumacious, to rebel. KAL ᵃ *part.* Paül. NIPHAL ᵇ *fut.*

Exod. xv. 24.	1 a	Num. xiv. 2.	1 a	Num. xvii. 5, 5.	1 e d
xvi. 2.	1 a	xiv. 27, 27, 27.	1 d e d	xvii. 10.	1 e
xvi. 7, 7.	1 e c	xiv. 29.	1 c	Deut. i. 27.	2 b
xvi. 8, 8, 8.	1 e d e	xiv. 36.	1 c	Josh. ix. 18.	1 a
xvi. 9, 12.	1 e	xvi. 11.	1 c	Ps. cvi. 25.	2 b
xvii. 3.	1 c	xvi. 41.	1 a	Isa. xxix. 24.	2 a

MURRAIN

דֶּבֶר *m.* pestilence : Exod. ix. 3.

MUSE

הָגִיג *m.* meditation : Ps. xxxix. 3.

שִׂיחַ to speak, to talk, to converse ; to talk with oneself, to meditate. POLEL *fut.* Ps. cxliii. 5.

MUSIC

זְמָר Ch. *m.* music of instruments : Dan. iii. 5, 7, 10, 15.

נְגִינָה *f.* music of stringed instruments : Lam. v. 14. מַנְגִּינָה *f.* a song : Lam. iii. 63.

שִׁיר *m.* a song, music ; musical, *lit.* of song : 1 Chron. xv. 16 ; xvi. 42 : 2 Chron. v. 13 ; vii. 6 ; xxiii. 13 ; xxxiv. 12 : Neh. xii. 36 : Eccles. xii. 4 : Amos vi. 5.

MUSTER

פָּקַד see *Number.* PIEL *part.* Isa. xiii. 4.

צָבָא to go forth to war ; to levy, to muster. HIPHIL *part.* 2 Kings xxv. 19 : Jer. lii. 25.

MUTTER

הָגָה to murmur, to mutter, to utter a low indistinct sound. KAL *fut.* Isa. lix. 3. HIPHIL *part.* Isa. viii. 19.

MUZZLE

חָסַם to muzzle an ox. KAL *fut.* Deut. xxv. 4.

MYRRH

לֹט *m.* a fragrant resinous gum, which is gathered from the leaves of a shrub growing in the island of Crete, Arabia, and Africa ; κίστος, *Cistus ladanifera* : Gen. xxxvii. 25 ; xliii. 11.

מֹר *m.* myrrh, so called from its flowing, distilling in tears from a tree growing in Arabia, resembling the Egyptian thorn : these tears then harden into a bitter aromatic gum, which was highly prized, and used in incense, perfumes, unguents, and among the Greeks for strengthening wine : Mar. xv. 23, 36. Cant. i. 13, a bag of myrrh, worn for the sake of its odour, suspended from the neck of a female : Exod. xxx. 23 : Esth. ii. 12 : Ps. xlv. 8 : Prov. vii. 17 : Cant. i. 13 ; iii. 6 ; iv. 6, 14 ; v. 1, 5, 5, 13.

MYRTLE

הֲדַס the myrtle : Neh. viii. 15 : Isa. xli. 19 ; lv. 13 : Zech. i. 8, 10, 11.

NAIL

טְפַר Ch. *m.* nail of a man, Dan. iv. 33 ; hoof of an animal, vii. 19.

יָתֵד a peg, pin, nail, as driven into the wall, or fastened in some secure manner in the houses of the East, often of mud ; specially a tent-pin driven into the earth to fasten the tent ; hence to drive a pin, to fasten a nail, is to the Hebrews the image of a fixed dwelling, a firm and stable abode, Isa. xxii. 23 ; for which also יָתֵד is put alone, Ezra ix. 8. Further, a nail, pin, is put metaphorically for a prince, on whom the care and welfare of the state depends, Zech. x. 4 ; where the same person is also called פִּנָּה corner-stone, on whom the state is founded : Judg. iv. 21, 21, 22 ; v. 26 : Ezra ix. 8, *marg.* ' or, a pin :' Isa. xxii. 23, 25 : Zech. x. 4.

מַסְמֵר *m.* nail, from its being pointed : 1 Chron. xxii. 3 : 2 Chron. iii. 9 : Isa. xli. 7 : Jer. x. 4.

צִפֹּרֶן *m.* nail of the finger : Deut. xxi. 12.

מַשְׂמְרוֹת *f. pl.* nails : Eccles. xii. 11.

NAKED

1　בָּשָׂר *m.* flesh ; " their nakedness," *lit.* flesh of their nakedness.

2　עוּר to be naked. NIPHAL [a] *fut.* Hab. iii. 9, *lit.* in nakedness is thy bow made naked, *i. e.* drawn forth from its sheath ; *comp.* Isa. xxii. 6. מָעוֹר [b] *m.* nakedness.

3　עָרָה to be naked ; to uncover nakedness, what is shameful or weak, what is indecent or improper to be seen ; to be destitute, exposed. HITHPAEL [a] *fut.* עֶרְוָה [b] *f.* nakedness : Gen. ix. 22, &c. עֶרְיָה [c] *f.* bare. מַעַר [d] *m.* nakedness.

4　עָרוֹם *adj.* naked, either as without clothing or stripped of the outer or peculiar garment designating rank or office. עֵירֹם [a] *adj.* naked. מַעֲרֻמִּים [b] *m. pl.* nakedness ; the naked.

5　פָּרַע to let go loose ; to uncover, by loosening the garments, &c. Gesenius, to let go loose, unbridled, unchecked, which is the meaning he gives to the following passages. KAL [a] *pret.* [b] *part.* Paül. HIPHIL [c] *pret.*

No. 3 b not included.

Gen. ii. 25.	4	Job xxii. 6.	4	Ezek. xxiii. 29,
iii. 7, 10, 11.	4 a	xxiv. 7, 10.	4	29. 4 a, 3 b
Exod. xxviii. 42.	1, 3 b	xxvi. 6.	4	Hos. ii. 3. 4
xxxii. 25, 25.	5 b a	Eccles. v. 15.	4	Amos ii. 16. 4
Deut. xxviii. 48.	4 a	Isa. xx. 2, 3, 4.	4	Micah i. 8. 4
1 Sam. xix. 24.	4	lviii. 7.	4	i. 11. 3 c
2 Chron. xxviii. 15.	4 b	Lam. iv. 21.	3 a	Nah. iii. 5. 3 d
xxviii. 19.	5 c	Ezek. xvi. 7, 22, 39.	4 a	Hab. ii. 15. 2 b
Job i. 21, 21.	4	xviii. 7, 16.	4 a	iii. 9. 2 a, 3 e

NAME

1　אָמַר to say. KAL [a] *fut.* [b] *part.* Paül.

2　דָּבַר to speak. PIEL *pret.*

3　נָקַב to note or mark : to separate or distinguish, to declare distinctly. KAL [a] *fut.* [b] *part.* Paül.

4　קָרָא to call. KAL [a] *pret.* [b] *fut.* NIPHAL [c] *pret.* [d] *fut.* [e] *part.*

5　שׂוּם to put. KAL [a] *pret.* שׂוּם Ch. P'AL [b] *pret.*

6　שֵׁם Schultens, upon Job i. 1, derives שֵׁם a name, from the Arabic שָׁמָא to be high, elevated, eminent ; therefore, according to him, the primary and proper notion of שֵׁם is a mark or sign, standing out, raised up, or exposed

to open view ; a standing mark or title of distinction or eminence : Gen. xi. 4, " and let us," say the heads or leaders, " make us a name," a monument or token of superiority and eminence ; to denote and to signify to all succeeding generations that they were the true original governors, to whom all mankind ought to be in subjection. More particularly it is applied—I. To the memory, memorial, or remembrance of a person in the world : Exod. iii. 15 : Deut. xxix. 20 : Job xviii. 17 : Prov. x. 7. II. To the character, good or bad, by which persons are marked, distinguished, or known in the world : Deut. xxii. 14 : 2 Sam. vii. 9 ; viii. 13 : 1 Kings i. 47 : Eccles. vii. 1. III. To the name or title given to a person, place, city, animal, &c., by which it is marked and distinguished from others. And thus the great God is distinguished and known by several names and titles in Scripture, as Jehovah, Jah, Lord God, Lord of hosts, &c. : Exod. vi. 3. By my name Jehovah (as giving being to my promises in the execution of them) was I not known, experimentally, to them : Deut. xxviii. 58 : Ps. lxxxiii. 18 : Isa. x. 16. *Obs.*— (1.) The name is supposed to correspond to the nature of a person or thing ; or to express some qualities or circumstances relating to them : Gen. xvi. 13 ; xxii. 14 ; xxvi. 20, 33 ; xli. 45, 51, 52, &c. Hence the name of God sometimes signifies the nature, and properties, and attributes of God, as his power, wisdom, goodness, majesty, holiness, justice, and truth : Exod. xxiii. 21, " my name is in him," *lit.* in the midst of him ; *comp.* 1 Kings iii. 28. Thus, also, to be called by a name is frequently, in Scripture, the same as to be what a person or thing is called or named : Isa. i. 26 ; ix. 26 ; lxii. 4 : Matt. v. 19 : Luke i. 76 : 1 John iii. 1. (2.) To be called by the name of a person, denotes the standing in a peculiar relation to him, or the being his property, his people, city, house : Gen. xlviii. 16 : Isa. xliv. 5 : 2 Chron. vii. 14 : Jer. vii. 10 ; xxv. 29 : Amos ix. 12. (3.) To act in a person's name, is to act by his commission or authority, real or feigned. (4.) To call by name is to single out and appoint a person for any work, as eminently qualified for it, or as the object of special favour : Exod. xxxi. 2 : Esth. ii. 14 : Isa. xlv. 3, 4. So God knew Moses by name, as he was very high in God's favour : Exod. xxxiii. 12, 17. (5.) To call the heavenly bodies by names imports absolute dominion over them, as having all and every one of them at command with respect to their stations and motions : Isa. xl. 26. שֵׁם [a] Ch. *m. id.*

No. 6 not included.

Gen. xxiii. 16.	2	2 Kings xvii. 34. α	5 a	Jer. xliv. 26, 26,	
xxvii. 36.	6, 4 a	1 Chron. xxiii. 14.	4 d	26.	6, 6, 4 e
xlviii. 16.	6, 4 d, 6	Ezra v. 1, 4, 10, 10,		Dan. ii. 20, 26.	6 a
Ruth iv. 17.	3 b	14.	6, 4 a	iv. 8, 8, 19.	6 a
1 Sam. iv. 21.	4 b	Eccles. vi. 10. β	6, 4 c	v. 12. γ	5 b, 6 a
xvi. 3.	1 a	Isa. lxi. 6.	4 a	Amos vi. 1.	3 b
xxviii. 8.	1 a	lxii. 2, 2.	6, 3 a	Micah ii. 7.	1 b

a lit. whose name he put Israel. β *lit.* its name is called. γ *lit.* put his name.

NARROW

אוּץ to press on, to press close, *i. e.* to be straight, narrow. KAL *pret.* Josh. xvii. 15.

אָטַם to shut, to close, to stop, *e. g.* the mouth, the ears ; to be straight or narrow. KAL *part.* 1 Kings vi. 4, Ezek. xl. 16. Gesenius, closed with bar or lattices, which, being let into the walls or beams, could not be opened and shut at pleasure. Lxx. θυρίδες δικτυωταί : Symm. τοξικαί. xli. 16, 26.

מִגְרָעוֹת *f.* contractions, drawings in of the wall, offsets, rests : 1 Kings vi. 6, *marg.* 'narrowings, *or,* rebatements.'

יָצַר to be straitened. KAL *fut.* Isa. xlix. 19.

צָרַר to press upon ; to be pressed, straitened, distressed. KAL *pret.* Isa. xxviii. 20. צַר *adj.* Num. xxii. 26 : Prov. xxiii. 27.

NATION

1 אֻמָּה *f.* a people, nation, tribe, as if from one mother ; found only in the *pl.* אֻמּוֹת *f. pl.* ᵃ אֻמָּה *f.* Ch. *id.*

2 אֶרֶץ *com.* the earth ; land ; a country, nation.

3 גּוֹי *com.* a general word spoken of nations universally, and also of the Israelites, as a nation separated from the other nations. The plural, however, is used especially of nations other than Israel, foreign nations ; see *Heathen :* Neh. v. 8. Often with the accessory notion of hostile and barbarous : Ps. ii. 1, 8 ; ix. 5, 15, 19, 20 ; x. 16 ; lix. 5, 8 ; lxxix. 6, 10 ; cvi. 47 : or also as profane, aliens from the true God, *i.e.* Gentiles, heathen, Jer. xxxi. 10 : Ezek. xxiii. 30 ; xxx. 11 : Ps. cxxxv. 15. Sometimes *opp.* to עַם, הָעָם, by which the Israelites usually spoke of themselves : Isa. xlii. 6 : Deut. xxvi. 18, 19 ; xxxii. 43. Very rarely found *seq. gen.* or a *suff.* The Lxx. commonly render עַם by λαός, and גּוֹי by ἔθνος, Vulg. *gens ;* whence, also, in the N. T. τὰ ἔθνη are opposed to τῷ λαῷ Θεοῦ Ἰσραήλ, Luke ii. 32.—Gesenius. It implies nations according to their locality, 1 Cor. xvi. 20 ; or, as under a form of government their own, Exod. ix. 24. Gen. x. 5, &c.

4 אֶזְרָח *m.* (see *Born*), "any of your own nation."

5 לְאֹם *m.* a people, nation.

6 עַם *com.* a people, nation, so called from their being a multitude congregated together, or from their common interests, &c. ; community, commonwealth.

No. 3 not included.

Gen. xxv. 16.	1	2 Chron. vii. 20.	6	Prov. xxiv. 24.	5
xxvii. 29.	5	xiii. 9.	6	Isa. xvii. 12, 13.	5
Exod. xxi. 8.	6	Ezra iv. 10.	1 a	xxxvii. 18.	2
Lev. xviii. 26.	4	Neh. i. 8.	6	li. 4.	6
Deut. ii. 25.	6	ix. 22.	6	Ezek. xxxviii. 8.	6
iv. 6, 6.	6, 3	Ps. xlvii. 3.	6	Dan. iii. 4, 7, 29.	1 a
iv. 19, 27.	6	lvii. 9.	5	iv. 1.	1 a
xiv. 2.	6	lxvii. 4, 4.	5	v. 19.	1 a
xxviii. 33, 37.	6	xcvi. 5.	5	vi. 25.	1 a
xxx. 3.	6	cvi. 34.	6	vii. 14.	1 a
1 Chron. xvi. 24.	6	cviii. 3.	5		

NATIVE, NATIVITY

מוֹלֶדֶת *f.* birth, nativity : Gen. xi. 28 : Ruth ii. 11 : Jer. xxii. 10 ; xlvi. 16 : Ezek. xvi. 3, 4 ; xxiii. 15.

מְכוּרָה *f.* see *Birth.* Ezek. xxi. 30.

NATURAL

לֵחַ *m.* green, fresh, moisture ; or freshness, vigour ; "natural force :" Deut. xxxiv. 7.

NAUGHTY

בְּלִיַּעַל *m.* (see *Belial*), wicked : Prov. vi. 12.

הַוָּה *f.* (see *Calamity*), wickedness : Prov. xi. 6 ; xvii. 4.

רַע *adj.* evil : 2 Kings ii. 19 : Prov. xx. 14, 14 : Jer. xxiv. 2. רֹצ *m.* evil, badness : 1 Sam. xvii. 28.

NAVE

נַב *m.* something convex, arched ; the rim of a wheel, circumference, felloes : 1 Kings vii. 33.

NAVEL

שֹׁרֶר *m.* the navel, the region around the navel, the belly : Cant. vii. 2. שָׁרִיר *m.* firm, hard : Job xl. 16. Gesenius, the nerves, sinews, brawn. שֹׁר *m.* navel ; nerve, muscle : Gesenius : Prov. iii. 8 : Ezek. xvi. 4.

NAVY

אֳנִי *c.* a ship, or rather, collectively, ships, navy : 1 Kings ix. 26, 27 ; x. 11, 22, 22, 22.

NAZARITE

נָזִיר *m.* one that is separate ; Nazarites, who bound themselves by a vow to abstain from certain things (see the law, Num. vi. 2, &c.) : Num. vi. 2, 13, 18, 19, 20, 21 : Judg. xiii. 5, 7 ; xvi. 17 : Lam. iv. 7 : Amos ii. 11, 12.

NEAR

1 אֵצֶל side ; by the side of.

2 יָד *com.* hand : Josh. xv. 46, *marg.* 'by the place of.'

3 נָגַע to touch, to come, draw near. KAL ᵃ *part.* Poel. HIPHIL ᵇ *pret.* ᶜ *fut.*

4 נָגַשׁ to come near, draw near ; see *Come, Draw* ; to be near. KAL *fut.*

5 קָרַב to come near : to be near. KAL ᵃ *pret.* ᵇ קָרוֹב *adj.* near : Gen. xix. 20, &c.

6 רָאָה to see. KAL *part.* Poel, Jer. lii. 25, "were near the king's person," *lit.* of them that saw the face of the king.

7 שְׁאָר *m.* see *Kin.*

No. 5 b not included.

Lev. xviii. 6, 12, 13.	7	2 Chron. xxi. 16.		Jer. lii. 25.	6	
xx. 19.	7	Esth. ix. 1.	3 b	Lam. iv. 18.	5 a	
Deut. xvi. 21.	1	Job xli. 16.	4	Ezek. vii. 12.	3 b	
Josh. xv. 46.	2	Ps. cvii. 18.	3 c	Dan. viii. 17.	1	
Judg. xx. 34.	3 a	Prov. vii. 8.	1			

NECESSARY

חֹק *m.* portion : Job xxiii. 12, *marg.* 'appointed portion.'

NECK   See also STIFF

1 גָּרוֹן *m.* throat.

2 גַּרְגְּרוֹת *f. pl.* throat, gullet, neck, externally.

3 עֹרֶף *m.* the back part of the neck. עָרַף *v. denom.* to break the neck. KAL ᵃ *pret.* ᵇ *part.* Poel.

4 מַפְרֶקֶת *f.* the neck, the joint or vertebra of the neck.

5 צַוָּאר *m.* the neck ; the derivation of this word is very doubtful ; Gesenius thinks it means the nape of the neck, and is so called from bearing, as it is used in connexion with bearing burdens, ornaments, the feet of the conqueror,

&c. Sometimes the neck generally is to be understood, and once it is put for the headless trunk, Ezek. xxi. 34.—Gen. xxvii. 16, &c. ᵃ צַוָּאר Ch. *m. id.* ᵇ צַוְרוֹן neck, with a diminutive termination, used lovingly.

No. 5 not included.

Gen. xlix. 8.	3	2 Chron. xxxvi. 13.	3	Isa. iii. 16.		1
Exod. xiii. 13.	3 a	Neh. ix. 16, 17, 29.	3	xlviii. 4.		3
xxxiv. 20.	3 a	Job xvi. 12.	3	lxvi. 3.		3 b
Lev. v. 8.	3	Ps. xviii. 40.	3	Jer. vii. 26.		3
Deut. xxi. 4.	3 a	Prov. i. 9.	2	xvii. 23.		3
xxxi. 27.	3	iii. 3, 22.	2	xix. 15.		3
1 Sam. iv. 18.	4	vi. 21.	2	Ezek. xvi. 11.		1
2 Sam. xxii. 41.	3	xxix. 1.	2	Dan. v. 7, 16, 29.		5 a
2 Kings xvii. 14, 14.	3	Cant. iv. 9.	5 b			

NECROMANCER

דָּרַשׁ to seek, to inquire. KAL *part.* Poel, Deut. xviii. 11, *lit.* one that inquireth of the dead.

מוּת to die. KAL *part.* Deut. xviii. 11, *lit.* as above.

NEED

חָסַר to lack, want. KAL *fut.* Prov. xxxi. 11. חָסֵר *adj.* wanting : 1 Sam. xxi. 15. מַחְסוֹר *m.* want of anything : Deut. xv. 8.

חֲשַׁח Ch. to be needed, necessary. P'AL *part.* Ezra vi. 9. חַשְׁחוּת *f.* what is needful : Ezra vii. 20.

צֹרֶךְ *m.* need : 2 Chron. ii. 16.

NEEDLEWORK

רָקַם to work with the needle divers colours of embroidery. KAL *part.* Poel, Exod. xxvi. 36 ; xxvii. 16 ; xxviii. 39 ; xxxvi. 37 ; xxxviii. 18 ; xxxix. 29. רִקְמָה *f.* Judg. v. 30, 30, needlework on both sides ; Ps. xlv. 14, raiment of needlework.

מַעֲשֶׂה *m.* work ; makes a part in some of the passages above, as in Exod. xxvi. 36 ; xxvii. 16 ; xxviii. 39 ; xxxvi. 37 ; xxxviii. 18 ; xxxix. 29.

NEEDY

אֶבְיוֹן *adj.* needy, poor, afflicted : Deut. xv. 11, &c.

דַּל *adj.* (see *Poor*), Isa. x. 2 ; xxvi. 6.

רוּשׁ to lack, to be poor, to suffer want. KAL *part.* Poel, Ps. lxxxii. 3.

NEESING

עֲטִישָׁה *f.* sneezing : Job xli. 18.

NEGINAH, NEGINOTH

נְגִינָה *f.* a stringed instrument : in the titles of Psalms iv, vi, liv, lv, lxi, lxvii, lxxvi.

NEGLIGENT

שָׁלָה to be secure, to sin from ignorance or inadvertence. NI-PHAL *fut.* 2 Chron. xxix. 11.

NEHILOTH

נְחִילוֹת *f. pl.* an instrument of music, probably *tibiæ*, pipes, flutes : Ps. v. title, or inheritances, possessions, lots ; referring to the twofold destiny of the righteous and of the wicked set forth in this Psalm.—Hengstenberg.

NEHUSHTAN

נְחֻשְׁתָּן *adj.* the serpent of brass erected by Moses, and broken in pieces by Hezekiah because the Israelites worshipped it : 2 Kings xviii. 4.

NEIGH

צָהַל to shine ; *trop.* of a clear loud voice ; hence, to neigh, of a horse. KAL *fut.* Jer. v. 8. מִצְהֲלוֹת *f. pl.* neighings : Jer. viii. 16 ; xiii. 27.

NEIGHBOUR

1   עָמִית *m.* companionship ; neighbours, fellow man, not confined to one of the same city or nation.

2   קָרוֹב *adj.* one that is near.

3   רֵעַ *m.* a friend, companion, acquaintance ; neighbour : Exod. xi. 2, &c. רְעוּת *f.* a female companion.

4   שָׁכֵן *adj.* a dweller, an inhabitant ; one who dwells near, an inhabitant.

No. 3 not included.

Exod. iii. 22.	4	Josh. ix. 16.	2	Prov. xxvii. 10.	4
xi. 2, 2.	3, 3 a	Ruth iv. 17.	4	Jer. vi. 21.	4
xii. 4.	4	2 Kings iv. 3.	4	ix. 20.	3 a
xxxii. 27.	2	Ps. xv. 3, 3.	3, 2	xlix. 10, 18.	4
Lev. vi. 2, 2.	1	xxxi. 11.	4	l. 40.	4
xviii. 20.	1	xliv. 13.	4	Ezek. xvi. 46.	4
xix. 15, 17.	1	lxxix. 4, 12.	4	xxiii. 5, 12.	2
xxiv. 19.	1	lxxx. 6.	4		
xxv. 14, 14, 15.	1	lxxxix. 41.	4		

NEPHEW

בֵּן *m.* son : Judg. xii. 14, employed in other and wider senses.

נֶכֶד *m.* progeny : Job xviii. 19 : Isa. xiv. 22.

NEST

קֵן *m.* a nest : Num. xxiv. 21 : Deut. xxii. 6 ; xxxii. 11 : Job xxix. 18 ; xxxix. 27 : Ps. lxxxiv. 3 : Prov. xxvii. 8 : Isa. x. 14 ; xvi. 2 : Jer. xlix. 16 : Obad. 4 : Hab. ii. 9. קָנַן *v. denom.* to make a nest. PIEL *pret.* Isa. xxxiv. 15 : Ezek. xxxi. 6. *fut.* Ps. civ. 17 : Jer. xlviii. 28. PUAL *part.* Jer. xxii. 23.

NET

1   חֵרֶם *m.* a net for fishing or fowling, so called from its shutting in the prey.

2   מַכְמֹר *m.* a net, hunter's net. ᵃ מִכְמָר *m. id.* ᵇ מִכְמֶרֶת *f.* fish-net.

3   מָצוֹד *m.* hunter's net. ᵃ מָצוּד *m. id.* ᵇ מְצוֹדָה *f. id.* ᶜ מְצוּדָה *f. id.*

4   רֶשֶׁת *f.* a net for taking prey.

5   שְׂבָךְ *m.* a net, from its being interwoven.

Exod. xxvii. 4, 4, 5.	4	Ps. lxvi. 11.	3 c	Ezek. xii. 13.	4
xxxviii. 4.	4	cxl. 5.	4	xvii. 20.	4
1 Kings vii. 17.	5	cxli. 10.	2	xix. 8.	1
Job xviii. 8.	4	Prov. i. 17.	4	xxvi. 5, 14.	1
xix. 6.	3 a	xii. 12.	3	xxxii. 3, 3.	4, 1
Ps. ix. 15.	4	xxix. 5.	4	xlvii. 10.	4
x. 9.	4	Eccles. vii. 26.	1	Hos. v. 1.	4
xxv. 15.	4	ix. 12.	3 b	vii. 12.	4
xxxi. 4.	4	Isa. xix. 8.	2 b	Micah vii. 2.	1
xxxv. 7, 8.	4	li. 20.	2 a	Hab. i. 15, 16, 17.	1
lvii. 6.	4	Lam. i. 13.	4		

NET-WORK

חוֹר net-work, from its being full of holes ; or white linen, cloths of linen or byssus : Isa. xix. 9.

מַעֲשֶׂה *f.* work ; joined with רֶשֶׁת, see above : Exod. xxvii. 4 ; xxxviii. 4.

שְׂבָכָה *f.* checker ; net-work : 1 Kings vii. 18, 20, 41, 42, 42 : Jer. lii. 22, 23.

NETHER, NETHERMOST

תַּחְתּוֹן *adj.* lower, lowest : Josh. xvi. 3 ; xviii. 13 : 1 Kings vi. 6 ; ix. 17 : 1 Chron. vii. 24 : 2 Chron. viii. 5. תַּחְתִּי *adj.* lower, lowest ; nether part : Exod. xix. 17 : Josh. xv. 19 : Judg. i. 15 : Job xli. 24 : Ezek. xxxi. 14, *lit.* lower, 16, 18 ; xxxii. 18, 24.

NETHINIMS

נְתִינִים *m. pl.* the given, the devoted, as the name of the Hebrew ἱερόδουλοι, or servants of the temple, temple-slaves, who were under the Levites in the ministry of the temple. For the origin of the word, *comp.* Num. viii. 19.—1 Chron. ix. 2 : Ezra ii. 43, 58, 70 ; vii. 7 ; viii. 17, 20, 20 : Neh. iii. 26, 31 ; vii. 46, 60, 73 ; x. 28 ; xi. 3, 21, 21. נְתִינִים *m.* Ezra viii. 17, כְּתִיב. נְתִינִין Ch. *m. pl.* Ezra vii. 24.

NETTLE

חָרוּל *m.* a thorny shrub, growing sometimes to a considerable height, in desert uncultivated ground : Celsii Hierobot. tom. ii. p.166 : Job xxx. 7 : Prov. xxiv. 31 : Zeph. ii. 9.

קִמּוֹשׁ and קִימוֹשׁ *m.* a prickly weed, *e.g.* nettle, thistle : Celsii Hierobot. tom. ii. p. 206 : Kimchi, thorns : Isa. xxxiv. 13 : Hos. ix. 6.

NEVER

דּוֹר *m.* generation : Ps. x. 6, *marg.* 'unto generation and generation.'

נֶצַח *m.* (see *Ever*), for ever ; never, *lit.* not for ever : Ps. x.11 ; xlix. 19 : Isa. xiii. 20 : Amos viii. 7 : Hab. i. 4.

עוֹלָם *m.* (see *Ever*), everlasting ; never, *lit.* not for ever : Judg. ii. 1 : 2 Sam. xii. 10 : Ps. xv. 5 ; xxx. 6 ; xxxi. 1 ; lv. 22 ; lxxi. 1 ; cxix. 93 : Prov. x. 30 : Isa. xiv. 20 ; xxv. 2 ; lxiii. 19 : Ezek. xxvi. 21 : Joel ii. 26, 27. עָלַם Ch. *m. id.* Dan. ii. 44.

תָּמִיד *m.* (see *Ever*), always, continually : Isa. lxii. 6, *lit.* not ever.

NEW

בְּרִיאָה *f.* a creation, a thing created or formed of God, especially new and unheard of : Num. xvi. 30.

חָדָשׁ *adj.* new ; fresh, unheard of ; new moon, see *Moon* ; new king : Exod. i. 8, *i.e.* of another race or dynasty, probably the shepherd kings : of the birth of the Messiah, Jer. xxxi. 22 : Exod. i. 8, &c. חֲדַת Ch. *adj.* Ezra vi. 4.

טָרִי *adj.* new, fresh, as a wound, or a bone, not yet dried : Judg. xv. 15, *marg.* 'moist.'

קָרוֹב *adj.* near : Deut. xxxii. 17, *lit.* from near.

NEWS

שְׁמוּעָה *f.* tidings, message, news : Prov. xxv. 25.

NEXT

אַחֵר *adj.* after, hinder, following, next following, *gen.* another : Gen. xvii. 21 : 2 Kings vi. 29, *marg.* 'other.'

מָחֳרָת *f.* morrow ; next day, next : Num. xi. 32 : 1 Sam. xxx. 17, *marg.* 'their morrow :' Jonah iv. 7.

מִשְׁנֶה *m.* second : 1 Sam. xvii. 13 ; xxiii. 17 : 1 Chron. v. 12 ; xvi. 5 : 2 Chron. xxviii. 7, *marg.* 'the second ;' xxxi. 12 : Esth. x. 3.

קָרוֹב *adj.* near : Exod. xii. 4 : Num. xxvii. 11 : Deut. xxi. 3, 6 : Esth. i. 14.

NIGH

קָרוֹב *adj.* near : Lev. x. 3 ; xxi. 3 : Num. xxiv. 17 : Deut. iv. 7 ; xiii. 7 ; xxii. 2 ; xxx. 14 : 1 Kings viii. 59 : 1 Chron. xii. 40 : Esth. ix. 20 : Ps. xxxiv. 18 ; lxxxv. 9 ; cxlv. 18 : Joel ii. 1.

שְׁאֵר *m.* (see *Kin*) : Lev. xxv. 49.

שָׁכֵן *adj.* (see *Neighbour*) : Deut. i. 7, *lit.* all his neighbours.

NIGHT

בּוּת Ch. to pass the night. P'AL *pret.* Dan. vi. 18.

בֵּן *m.* son : Jonah iv. 10, "in a night," *lit.* son of a night.

חֹשֶׁךְ *m.* darkness : Job xxvi. 10.

לַיִל *m.* night ; figuratively, a state of distress, of blindness, or ignorance : Gen. i. 5, &c. לֵילְיָא Ch. *f.* Dan. ii. 19 ; v. 30 ; vii. 2, 7, 13.

נֶשֶׁף *m.* the evening twilight, when cooling breezes blow ; put for the evening, darkness, night : Isa. v. 11 ; xxi. 4 ; lix. 10.

עֶרֶב *m.* evening : Gen. xlix. 27 : Lev. vi. 20 : Job vii. 4, *marg.* 'evening be measured :' Ps. xxx. 5, *marg.* 'in the evening.'

NIGHT-HAWK

תַּחְמָס *m.* an unclean bird, so called from its violence and cruelty ; according to Bochart, Hieroz. ii. p. 232, the male ostrich : Lev. xi. 16 : Deut. xiv. 15.

NISAN

נִיסָן *m.* the first month of the Hebrew year, so called as being the month in which the military standards were brought out, and kings went forth to battle, 2 Sam. xi. 1 ; corresponding to the Roman Martius. Is named in the Pentateuch, Abib. Neh. ii. 1 : Esth. iii. 7.

NITRE

נֶתֶר *m.* the natron of the moderns, or Egyptian nitre, a mineral alkali (differing from בְּרִית, vegetable alkali), which, mingled with oil, is still used as soap : Jer. ii. 22. With an acid, it effervesces and loses its strength, hence Prov. xxv. 20.

NOBLE

1 אַדִּיר *adj.* mighty, powerful, noble, excellent ; of God, of the Messiah, in Jer. xxx. 21, *lit.* noble one. See *Glory*.

2 אֵילִים *m. pl.* (see *Chief*).

3 בְּרִיחַ *m.* a bar ; *metaph.* bars, bolts for princes as aiding to protect and defend a state ; *comp.* בַּר, Hos. xi. 6.

4 גָּדוֹל *adj.* great.

5 חוֹרִים *m. pl.* freeborn, noble ; or *pr.* pure, referring to noble birth, high born, illustrious.

6 יַקִּיר Ch. *adj.* precious ; honoured, mighty, powerful.

7 כָּבֵד see *Honourable*. NIPHAL *part.*

8 נָגִיד see *Ruler*.

9 נָדִיב *adj.* willing ; generous, noble-minded ; of noble birth, noble.

10 פַּרְתְּמִים *m. pl.* nobles, princes ; a Persian word.

Exod. xxiv. 11.	2	Neh. vi. 17.	5	Eccles. x. 17.	5
Num. xxi. 18.	9	vii. 5.	5	Isa. xiii. 2.	9
Judg. v. 13.	1	x. 29.	1	xxxiv. 12.	5
1 Kings xxi. 8, 11.	5	xiii. 17.	5	xliii. 14.	3
2 Chron. xxiii. 20.	1	Esth. i. 3.	10	Jer. xiv. 3.	1
Ezra iv. 10.	6	vi. 9.	10	xxvii. 20.	5
Neh. ii. 16.	5	Job xxix. 10.	8	xxx. 21.	1
iii. 5.	1	Ps. lxxxiii. 11.	9	xxxix. 6.	5
iv. 14, 19.	5	cxlix. 8.	7	Jonah iii. 7.	4
v. 7.	5	Prov. viii. 16.	9	Nah. iii. 18.	1

NOISE

1 הוּם to put in motion ; to make commotion, to make a noise ; of an unquiet mind, internal commotion. HIPHIL *fut.*

2 הָמָה to make a noise ; applied to some animals, as the bear, Isa. lix. 11 ; the howling of a dog, Ps. lix. 6, 14 ; the mourning of a dove, Ezek. vii. 16 ; applied also to the sighing of men, Ps. lv. 17, lxxvii. 3, which is compared to the noise of bears and doves, Ezek. vii. 16, Isa. lix. 11. This word is also used of the sound of the harp, Isa. xvi. 11, *comp.* xiv. 11, and of other musical instruments, Jer. xlviii. 36 ; of rain, 1 Kings xviii. 41 ; of waves, Ps. xlvi. 3, Isa. li. 15, Jer. v. 22, xxxi. 35, li. 55 ; of a tumultuous people, Ps. xlvi. 6, lix. 6, lxxxviii. 2, 1 Kings i. 41 ; often compared to the tumult of waves, Isa. xvii. 12, Jer. vi. 23, l. 42 ; of a tumultuous city, Isa. xxii. 2 ; place of concourse, Prov. i. 21. It is applied to the tumult of the mind, Jer. iv. 19 ; see *Disquiet, Trouble,* &c. KAL ᵃ *pret.* ᵇ *inf.* ᶜ *fut.* ᵈ *part.* Poel. ᵉ הָמוֹן noise, especially of a multitude. ᶠ הֶמְיָה *f.* sound of a harp.

3 פָּצַח to break forth ; to make a loud noise. KAL *imp.*

4 קוֹל *m.* any sound, noise, voice ; applied to the noise locusts make in browsing, Joel ii. 5, which may be heard at a great distance, and resembles the rattling of hail, or the noise of an army foraging in secret.—*Paxton.* Exod. xx. 18, &c.

5 רֹגֶן *m.* tumult, wild commotion ; noise of thunder.

6 רַע *m.* outcry, noise, of approaching rain, or of thunder : Job xxxvi. 33. ᵃ תְּרוּעָה *f.* loud noise, tumult ; sound.

7 רַעַשׁ *m.* trembling, shaking, as of a spear ; a tumult of war ; confused noise.

8 שָׁאוֹן *m.* noise, uproar, tumult ; *e.g.* of waters, of a crowd or multitude of men, of war, of outcry, clamour. ᵃ תְּשֻׁאוֹת *f. pl.* noise, crashing.

9 שָׁמַע to hear. HIPHIL ᵃ *fut.* ᵇ *part.*

No. 4 not included.

Josh. vi. 10.	9 a	Ps. lxv. 7, 7.	8	Jer. iv. 19.	2 d
1 Sam. xiv. 19.	2 e	xcviii. 4.	3	xxv. 31.	8
1 Chron. xv. 28.	9 b	Isa. ix. 5.	7	xlvi. 17.	8
Job xxxvi. 29.	8 a	xiv. 11.	2 f	li. 55.	8
xxxvi. 33.	6	xvii. 12.	2 c b	Ezek. xxvi. 13.	2 e
xxxvii. 2.	5	xxiv. 8.	8	Amos v. 23.	2 e
Ps. xxxiii. 3.	6 a	xxv. 5.	8	Micah ii. 12.	2 e
lv. 2.	1	xxxi. 4.	2 e	Zech. ix. 15.	2 a
lix. 6, 14.	2 c	lxvi. 6.	8		

NOISOME

הַוָּה *f.* see *Calamity.* Ps. xci. 3, *i. e.* fatal.

רַע *adj.* evil : Ezek. xiv. 15, 21.

NONE

אִישׁ *m.* man ; with no, not, "none :" Gen. xxiii. 6, *lit.* a man shall not : Exod. xii. 22, *lit.* no man : Lev. xviii. 6, *lit.* a man, a man shall not, &c.

NOON

צֹהַר *m.* the clearest light, noon, noon-day, noontide : Gen. xliii. 16, 25, &c.

NORTH

מְזָרִים *m. pl. lit.* the scattering ; *poet.* for the north winds, which scatter the clouds, and bring severe cold : Job xxxvii. 9. Some make the word the twelve signs of the Zodiac ; (see *Mazzaroth*).

צָפוֹן *com. pr.* the hidden, the dark, the northern part of the heavens ; the ancients regarded the north as the seat of gloom and darkness, while they supposed the south to be clear and illuminated by the sun (see *South*) : Gen. xiii. 14, &c. צְפוֹנִי *adj.* Joel ii. 20.

NOSE, NOSTRIL

אַף *m.* nose ; אַפַּיִם *dual*, nostrils : Gen. ii. 7, &c.

נַחַר *m.* a snorting : Job xxxix. 20. נְחִירִים *m. pl.* nostrils : Job xli. 20.

NOTABLE

חָזוּת *f.* vision : Dan. viii. 5, *marg.* 'a horn of sight,' 8.

NOTE

חָקַק to cut in, to engrave ; on a tablet. KAL *imp.* Isa. xxx. 8.

רָשַׁם to write down, to record. KAL *part.* Paül, Dan. x. 21.

NOTHING

אֶפֶס *m. pr.* cessation, nothing : Isa. xxxiv. 12 ; xl. 17 ; xli. 29.

בְּלִימָה compounded of בְּלִי and מָה, not any thing, nothing : Job xxvi. 7.

חִנָּם *adv.* for nothing : Exod. xxi. 2.

מָעַט to be few, little ; to make few, diminish. HIPHIL *fut.* Jer. x. 24.

תֹּהוּ *m.* wasteness, desolation ; *trop.* emptiness, vanity ; a vain thing, worthless ; nothing : Job vi. 18.

NOTICE

נָכַר to know; to acknowledge. HIPHIL *pret.* 2 Sam. iii. 36.

NOUGHT

1 אָוֶן *m.* nothingness, vanity: Amos v. 5, *lit.* shall be Aven, in allusion to Beth-aven.

2 אֱלִיל *m.* nought, empty, vain.

3 אָפֵס to fail. KAL [a] *pret.* [b] אֶפֶס *m.* cessation, nothing.

4 אֶפַע *m.* supposed to be for אֶפֶס, but rendered by the Rabbins as in *marg.* 'worse than of a viper.'

5 הוֹן *m.* riches; "for nought," *lit.* without riches.

6 חִנָּם *adv.* for nought; to no purpose, in vain.

7 מְאוּמָה *f.* anything, something; nought, *lit.* not anything.

8 נָבֵל to fade away, to come to nought. KAL *fut.*

9 פּוּר to break, to break in pieces. HIPHIL *pret.*

10 פָּרַע to let go loose, to dismiss; to set at nought, refuse. KAL *fut.*

11 פָּרַר to break; to make vain, to bring to nought, to frustrate. HIPHIL [a] *fut.* HOPHAL [b] *fut.*

12 שָׁמַד to destroy; to bring to nought. HIPHIL *inf.*

13 תֹּהוּ *m.* (see *Nothing*), "a thing of nought."

Gen. xxix. 15.	6	Ps. xxxiii. 10.	9	Isa. xli. 24.			4
Deut. xiii. 17.	7	xliv. 12.	5				13
xxviii. 63.	12	Prov. i. 25.	10	iii. 3, 5.			6
Neh. iv. 15.	11 a	Isa. viii. 10.	11 b	Jer. xiv. 14.			2
Job i. 9.	6	xxix. 20.	3 a	Amos v. 5.			1
xiv. 18.	8	xxix. 21.	13	Mal. i. 10.			6
xxii. 6.	6	xli. 12.	3 b				

NOURISH

1 גָּדַל to be or become great; to bring up. PIEL [a] *pret.* [b] *inf.* [c] *part.*

2 חָיָה to live; to keep alive. PIEL *fut.*

3 כּוּל to hold; to sustain, to nourish: in Gen. xlvii. 12, the Lxx. render it by ἐσιτρομέτρει, comp. σιτρομέτριον of Luke xii. 42, where allusion is made probably to this account. —*Bush.* PILPEL [a] *pret.* [b] *inf.* [c] *fut.*

4 רָבָה to increase, to grow up. PIEL *pret.*

Gen. xlv. 11.	3 a	Ruth iv. 15.	3 b	Isa. xliv. 14.	1 c
xlvii. 12.	3 c	Isa. i. 2.	1 a	Ezek. xix. 2.	4
l. 21.	3 c	vii. 21.	2	Dan. i. 5.	1 b
2 Sam. xii. 3.	2	xxiii. 4.	1 a		

NOW

יוֹם *m.* day: Deut. xxxi. 21: 1 Sam. ix. 9: Neh. i. 6, *lit.* this day: Jer. xxxiv. 15, *marg.* 'to-day.'

כְּבָר *adv.* (see *Already*): Eccles. ii. 16; iii. 15; ix. 6, 7.

פַּעַם this time, in this thing; now, now indeed: Gen. ii. 23; xxix. 35; xxx. 20; xlvi. 30: Prov. vii. 12, 12.

NUMBER

1 הֵקֶר *m.* searching, without number, *lit.* without searching, *i.e.* innumerable.

2 כֹּבֶד *m.* heaviness; a great number.

3 מִכְסָה *f.* a number or share counted and assigned for a particular purpose.

4 מָנָה to divide out, to measure out; to allot, to appoint; to

---

number out, to count. KAL [a] *pret.* [b] *inf.* [c] *imp.* [d] *fut.* NIPHAL [e] *pret.* [f] *inf.* [g] *fut.* מְנָה Ch. P AL [h] *pret.* [i] מְנִי *m.* Gesenius, fate, fortune; with the *art.* הַמְּנִי as the name of an idol which the Jews in Babylonia worshipped along with Gad, (see *Troop*). Probably the planet Venus is intended. Gussetius takes this word in its literal meaning, as referring to a prescribed number of cups fixed by the ruler of the feast. [k] מִנְיָן Ch. *m.* number.

5 סָפַר to number, to count; to recount, to narrate, to tell, to declare. KAL [a] *pret.* [b] *inf.* [c] *imp.* [d] *fut.* NIPHAL [e] *fut.* PIEL [f] *inf.* [g] *fut.* [h] סֵפֶר *m.* numbering. [i] סְפֹרָה number. [k] מִסְפָּר *m.* number; seems to imply a number that can easily be reckoned, used, therefore, with numerals; and the phrase 'without number' is therefore equivalent to innumerable; and, on the contrary, 'men of number' means few, easy to be numbered: Gen. xxxiv. 30, &c.

6 עָדַף to remain; that which remaineth over and above. KAL *part.* Poel. "odd number."

7 פָּקַד to visit; to visit for the sake of reviewing, inspecting; hence to number. KAL [a] *pret.* [b] *inf.* [c] *imp.* [d] *fut.* [e] *part.* Paül. HITHPAEL [f] *pret.* [g] *fut.* HOTHPAEL [h] *pret.* [i] פְּקֻדָה *f.* enumeration. [k] מִפְקָד *m.* numbering.

No. 5 k not included.

Gen. xiii. 16, 16.	4 b g	Num. iv.23,29,30,34.	7 d	1 Kings xx.15,15.	7 d a
xv. 5.	5	iv. 36, 38, 40, 42,		xx. 25.	4 d
xvi. 10.	5 e	44, 48.	7 e	xx. 26.	7 d
xxxii. 12.	5 e	iv. 37, 37.	7 e a	xx. 27.	7 h
xli. 49, 49.	5 b k	iv. 41, 41.	7 e a	2 Kings iii. 6.	7 d
Exod. iv. 4.	3	iv. 45, 45.	7 e a	1 Chron. xxi. 1, 17.a	4 b
xxx. 12, 12, 12.	7 e b b	iv. 46, 46.	7 e a	xxi. 2.	5 k
xxx. 13, 14.	7 e	iv. 49, 49.	7 a e	xxi. 5.	7
xxxviii. 25, 26.	7 e	vii. 2.	7 e	xxiii. 3, 3.	5 e k
Lev. xv. 13, 28.	5 d	xiv. 29, 29.	7 e, 5 k	xxvii. 24.	4 b, 5 k
xxiii. 16.	5 d	xxvi. 7, 18, 22, 25,		2 Chron. ii.17,17,	
xxv. 8.	5 a	27, 34, 37, 41, 43,		17.	5 d h a
Num. i. 3, 19, 49.	7 d	47, 50, 51, 54, 57.	7 e	v. 6.	4 g
i. 21, 23, 25, 27, 29,		xxvi. 62, 62.	7 e h	xvii. 14.	7 i
31, 33, 35, 37, 39,		xxvi. 63, 63.	7 e a	xxv. 5.	7 d
41, 43, 45, 46.	7 e	xxvi. 64, 64.	7 e a	Ezra i. 8.	5 d
i. 22, 22.	7 c, 5 k	Deut. xxv. 9, 9.	7 e a	Job xiv. 16.	5 d
i. 44, 44.	7 e a	Josh. viii. 10.	7 d	xxxiv. 24.	1
i. 47.	7 h	Judg. xx. 15, 15.	7 g f	xxxviii. 37.	5 g
ii. 4, 6, 8, 9, 11, 13,		xx. 17.	7 f	xxxix. 2.	5 d
15, 16, 19, 21, 23,		xxi. 9.	7 g	Ps. xl. 5.	5 f
24, 26, 28, 30, 31,		1 Sam. xi. 8.	7 d	lxxi. 15.	5 i
32, 32.	7 e	xiv. 17, 17.	7 c d	xc. 12.	4 b
ii. 33.	7 h	xv. 4.	7 d	Eccles. i. 15.	4 f
iii. 15, 15.	7 d	2 Sam. xviii. 1.	7 d	Isa. xxii. 10.	5 a
iii. 16, 42.	7 c d	xxiv. 1.	7 e	liii. 12.	4 i
iii. 22, 22,		xxiv. 2, 2.	7 c, 5 k	lxv. 11.	4 i
22.	7 e, 5 k, 7 e	xxiv. 4.	7 b	lxv. 12.	4 a
iii. 39, 39.	7 e a	xxiv. 9.	7 k	Jer. xxxiii. 22.	5 e
iii. 40, 40.	7 c, 5 k	xxiv. 10.	5 a	Dan. v. 26.	4 h
iii. 43, 43.	5 k, 7 e	1 Kings iii. 8.	4 g	Hos. i. 10.	5 k e
iii. 48.	6	viii. 5.	4 g	Nah. iii. 1.	2

a lit. to number the people.

NURSE

1 אִשָּׁה *f.* a woman; "nurse," *lit.* nursing woman.

2 אָמַן to stay, support, to bear; also, to be faithful, as nurses were to their charge; and in this it is distinguished from a nurse who gives milk. KAL [a] *part.* Poel. NIPHAL [b] *fut.*

3 יָנַק to suck; to give suck. HIPHIL [a] *imp.* [b] *fut.* [c] *part.*

4 נוּק to suck; to give suck. HIPHIL *fut.*

Gen. xxiv. 59.	3 c	Exod. ii. 9, 9.	3 a, 4	2 Kings xi. 2.	3 c
xxxv. 8.	3 c	Num. xi. 12.*a*	2 a	2 Chron. xxii. 11.	3 c
Exod. ii. 7.	3 c, 1	Ruth iv. 16.	2 a	Isa. xlix. 23, 23.	2 a, 3 c
ii. 7.	3 b	2 Sam. iv. 4.	2 a	lx. 4.	2 b

a "nursing father."

NUT

אֱגוֹז *m.* the walnut; this tree, both for shade and fruit, was in much esteem in the East; and probably among other gardens (Eccles. ii. 5) Solomon had planted one principally consisting of walnut-trees, but intermixed with vines and pomegranates.—Olav. Cels. Part I. p. 28; Taylor. Cant. vi. 11. The Church compared to a garden of nuts.—Dillherr, note *in loc.*

בָּטְנִים *m. pl.* pistacia nuts; pistachios, which are the produce of Syria and Palestine, but are not known to grow in Egypt.—Olav. Cels. Hierobot. p. 27; Taylor. Gen. xliii. 11.

O THAT

אַחֲלַי *part.* of wishing: Ps. cxix. 5.

נָתַן to give. KAL *fut.* "o that," *lit.* who will give. Job vi. 8; xi. 5; xiii. 5; xiv. 13; xix. 23, 23; xxiii. 3; xxix. 2; xxxi. 31, 35: Ps. xiv. 7; liii. 6; lv. 6: Cant. viii. 1; Jer. ix. 1, 2.

OAK

אַיִל *m.* strong, mighty; applied to a tree, specially the oak, terebinth, and sometimes the palm: Isa. i. 29. אֵלָה *f.* oak; the tree under the shade of which Abraham sat is now supposed to be the terebinth, described by Dr. Robinson as very shady, and living to a very great age. —Bibl. Researches, III. 15. Gen. xxxv. 4: Judg. vi. 11, 19: 2 Sam. xviii. 9, 9, 10, 14: 1 Kings xiii. 14: 1 Chron. x. 12: Isa. i. 30: Ezek. vi. 13. אַלָּה *f. id.* Josh. xxiv. 26.

אַלּוֹן *m.* noun collective, a strong and hardy tree, especially the oak: Gen. xxxv. 8: Isa. ii. 13; vi. 13; xliv. 14: Ezek. xxvii. 6: Hos. iv. 13: Amos ii. 9: Zech. xi. 2.

OAR

שַׁיִט *m.* an oar; see *Rower:* Isa. xxxiii. 21. מָשׁוֹט *m.* an oar: Ezek. xxvii. 29. מִשּׁוֹט *m. id.* Ezek. xxvii. 6.

OATH

1 אָלָה *f.* an oath, an oath of cursing; a covenant confirmed by an oath.

2 שָׁבַע to swear; Hiph. to charge with an oath; to take an oath of. HIPHIL ᵃ *pret.* ᵇ *inf.* ᶜ *fut.* ᵈ שְׁבוּעָה *f.* an oath, an oath sworn in making a covenant, an oath of execration: Gen. xxiv. 8, &c.

No. 2 d not included.

Gen. xxiv. 41, 41.	1	1 Sam. xiv. 27.	2 b	2 Chron. vi. 22, 22.	1
xxvi. 28.	1	xiv. 28.	2 a	Neh. v. 12.	2 c
l. 25.	2 c	1 Kings viii. 31, 31.	1	Ezek. xvi. 59.	1
Num. v. 19.	2 a	xviii. 10.	2 a	xvii. 13, 16, 18, 19.	1
Deut. xxix. 12, 14.	1	2 Kings xi. 4.	2 c		

OBEISANCE

שָׁחָה to bow down even to the ground; to do obeisance. HITHPAEL *inf.* 2 Sam. xv. 5. *fut.* Gen. xxxvii. 7; xliii. 28, *lit.* bowed themselves: Exod. xviii. 7: 2 Sam. i. 2; xiv. 4: 1 Kings i. 16: 2 Chron. xxiv. 17. *part.* Gen. xxxvii. 9.

OBEY

1 יִקְּהָה *f.* subjection, submission, ready obedience.

2 שָׁמַע to hear, to hear and to obey. With *inf.*, obey indeed diligently. KAL ᵃ *pret.* ᵇ *inf.* ᶜ *imp.* ᵈ *fut.* ᵉ *part.* Poel. NIPHAL ᶠ *fut.* שָׁמַע Ch. ITHPAEL ᵍ *fut.* ʰ מִשְׁמַעַת *f.* obedience, obedient ones.

Gen. xxii. 18.	2 a	1 Sam. xii. 14.	2 a	Jer. xi. 3.	2 d
xxvi. 5.	2 a	xii. 15.	2 d	xi. 4, 7.	2 c
xxvii. 8, 13, 43.	2 d	xv. 19, 20.	2 a	xi. 8.	2 d
xxviii. 7.	2 d	xv. 22, 22.	2 b	xii. 17.	2 d
Exod. v. 2.	2 a	xv. 24.	2 a	xvii. 23.	2 d
xix. 5.	2 b d	xxviii. 18, 21.	2 a	xviii. 10.	2 b
xxiii. 21.	2 c	2 Sam. xxii. 45.	2 f	xxii. 21.	2 d
xxiii. 22.	2 b d	1 Kings xx. 36.	2 a	xxvi. 13.	2 c
xxiv. 7.	2 d	2 Kings xviii. 12.	2 a	xxxii. 23.	2 a
Num. xxvii. 20.	2 d	1 Chron. xxix. 23.	2 a	xxxiv. 10.	2 d
Deut. iv. 30.	2 d	2 Chron. xi. 4.	2 d	xxxv. 8, 10.	2 d
viii. 20.	2 d	Neh. ix. 17.	2 b	xxxv. 14, 18.	2 d
xi. 27, 28.	2 d	Job xxxvi. 11, 12.	2 d	xxxviii. 20.	2 c
xiii. 4.	2 d	Ps. xviii. 44.	2 f	xl. 3.	2 a
xxi. 18, 20.	2 a	Prov. v. 13.	2 a	xlii. 13, 16.	2 d
xxvii. 10.	2 a	xxv. 12.	2 e	xlii. 13.	2 a
xxviii. 62.	2 d	xxx. 17.	1	xlii. 21.	2 d
xxx. 2, 8.	2 a	Isa. i. 19.	2 a	xliii. 4, 7.	2 a
xxx. 20.	2 b	xi. 14.	2 h	xliv. 23.	2 a
Josh. v. 6.	2 a	xliii. 24.	2 a	Dan. vii. 27.	2 g
iii. 2.	2 a	l. 10.	2 e	ix. 10, 14.	2 a
xxiv. 24.	2 d	Jer. iii. 13, 25.	2 a	ix. 11.	2 b
Judg. ii. 2.	2 a	vii. 23.	2 c	Zeph. iii. 2.	2 a
ii. 17.	2 a	vii. 28.	2 a	Hag. i. 12.	2 d
vi. 10.	2 a	ix. 13.	2 a	Zech. vi. 15.	2 b d
1 Sam. viii. 19.	2 b				

OBLATION

1 מִנְחָה *f.* a gift, present; an offering to God, any offering that is not a bloody sacrifice, a meat-offering. ᵃ מִנְחָה Ch. *f. id.*

2 קָרְבָּן *m.* an offering, oblation, sacrifice.

3 תְּרוּמָה *f.* an offering, a heave-offering. תְּרוּמִיָּה *f. id.*

4 מַשְׂאֵת *f.* a lifting up; a gift, present.

Lev. ii. 4, 5, 7, 12, 13.	2	Isa. i. 13.	1	Ezek. xlv. 1, 6, 7, 7,	
iii. 1.	2	xix. 21.	1	13, 16.	3
vii. 14, 29, 38.	2	xl. 20.	3	xlviii. 9, 10, 18, 18,	
xxii. 18.	2	lxvi. 3.	1	20, 20, 21, 21, 21.	3
Num. xviii. 9.	2	Jer. xiv. 12.	1	xlviii. 12.	3 a
xxxi. 50.	2	Ezek. xx. 40.	4	Dan. ii. 46.	1 a
2 Chron. xxxi. 14.	3	xliv. 30, 30.	3	ix. 21, 27.	1

OBSCURE

אִישׁוֹן *m.* the apple or pupil of the eye: Prov. xx. 20 (כְּתִיב). Gesenius, *metaph.* the midst or middle of anything, in the very eyeball of darkness: אֶשׁוּן *m.* darkness: Prov. xx. 20 (קְרִי), darkness, obscurity.

אֹפֶל *m.* thick darkness: Isa. xxix. 18.

חֹשֶׁךְ *m.* darkness: Isa. lviii. 10; lix. 9.

OBSERVE

1 נָחַשׁ to divine; in a wider sense, to prognosticate, to observe diligently. PIEL *fut.* 1 Kings xx. 33, *i. e.* the men took as a good omen, *sc.* the words of Ahab in verse 32.

2 נָצַר to keep; to observe diligently; to keep, observe, as a covenant, a law, the ways of righteousness, a father's commands, the commandments of God, good counsel. KAL *fut.*

3 עָנַן this word is derived from עָנָן a cloud, and refers to some kind of observation of auguries; hence commonly rendered, to observe times. POEL ᵃ *pret.* ᵇ *fut.* ᶜ *part.*

4 עָשָׂה to do ; to observe the sabbath, &c., implies those active duties required on the sabbath. KAL [a] *inf.* [b] *fut.*

5 רָצָה to be favourable to. KAL *fut.* Prov. xxiii. 26, כתיב.

6 שׁוּר to look around ; to look after. KAL *fut.*

7 שָׁמַר to keep, to watch, to guard ; to keep in view, to observe, to mark ; to observe, *i. e.* not to violate, a covenant, a precept, the sabbath, a promise. KAL [a] *pret.* [b] *inf.* [c] *imp.* [d] *fut.* [e] *part.* Poel. PIEL [f] *part.* [g] שָׁמְרִים *m. pl.* observation, celebration of a feast.

Gen. xxxvii. 11.	7 a	Deut. xvi. 1.	7 b	2 Kings xxi. 8.		7 d
Exod. xii. 17, 17, 24.	7 a	xvi. 12.	7 a	2 Chron. vii. 17.		7 d
xii. 42. 42.	7 g	xvi. 13.	4 b	xxxiii. 6.		3 a
xxxi. 16.	4 a	xvii. 10.	7 a	Neh. i. 5.		7 e
xxxiv. 11.	7 c	xviii. 10, 14.	3 c	x. 29.		7 b
xxxiv. 22.	4 b	xxiv. 8, 8.	7 b d	Ps. cv. 45.		7 d
Lev. xix. 26.	3 b	xxviii. 1, 13, 15.	7 b	cvii. 43.		7 d
xix. 37.	7 a	xxviii. 58.	7 d	cxix. 34.		7 d
Num. xv. 22.	4 b	xxxi. 12.	7 a	Prov. xxiii. 26.	5, or 2
xxviii. 2.	7 d	xxxii. 46.	7 b	Eccles. xi. 4.		7 e
Deut. v. 32.	7 a	Josh. i. 7.	7 b	Isa. xlii. 20.		7 d
vi. 3.	7 d	i. 8.	7 d	Jer. viii. 7.		7 a
vi. 25.	7 d	Judg. xiii. 14.	7 d	Ezek. xx. 18.		7 d
viii. 1.	7 d	2 Sam. xi. 16.	7 b	xxxvii. 24.		7 d
xi. 1.	7 a	1 Kings xx. 33.	1	Hos. xiii. 7.		6
xii. 1, 32.	7 d	2 Kings xvii. 37.	7 d	xiv. 8.		6
xii. 28.	7 c	xxi. 6.	3 a	Jonah ii. 8.		7 f
xv. 5.	7 b					

OBSTINATE

אָמֵץ to be strong, resolute, and vigorous. PIEL *pret.* Deut. ii. 30.

קָשָׁה *adj.* hard, stiff: Isa. xlviii. 4.

OBTAIN

חָזַק to take fast hold. HIPHIL *pret.* Dan. xi. 21.

נָשָׂא to take, to bear. KAL *pret.* Esth. v. 2. *fut.* Esth. ii. 9, 17. *part.* Poel, Esth. ii. 15.

נָשַׂג to reach, to attain. HIPHIL *fut.* Isa. xxxv. 10; li. 11.

פּוּק to draw, to bring out for use. HIPHIL *fut.* Prov. viii. 35; xii. 2; xviii. 22.

OCCASION

1 תְּאֵנָה *f.* a coming together. [a] תֹּאֲנָה *f.* see *Happen.*

2 מָצָא to find. KAL *fut. lit.* as thine hand shall find.

3 תְּנוּאָה *f.* a holding back, alienation, enmity, or occasion of enmity.

4 נָפַל Ch. to fall, to fall out, to happen. P'AL *fut.*

5 סָבַב to turn, to go about anything, to bring about, to be the cause of. KAL *pret.* Vulg. *ego sum reus omnium animarum.*

6 עִלָּה Ch. *f.* cause, occasion, pretext.

7 עֲלִילָה *f.* work ; of the actions of men in a bad sense.

Deut. xxii. 14, 17.	7	1 Sam. x. 7.	2	Job xxxiii. 10.	3
Judg. ix. 33.	2	xxii. 22.	5	Jer. ii. 24.	1
xiv. 4.	1 a	Ezra vii. 20.	4	Dan. vi. 4, 4, 5.	6

OCCUPY, OCCUPATION

מְלָאכָה *f.* work: Judg. xvi. 11: Jonah i. 8, "occupation."

נָתַן to give. KAL *pret.* Ezek. xxvii. 16, 19, 22, *lit.* they gave, *i. e.* produced, contributed, exposed for sale.

סָחַר see *Merchant.* KAL *part.* Poel, Ezek. xxvii. 21.

עָרַב to mix, to interchange, &c. KAL *inf.* Ezek. xxvii. 9. *part.* Poel, Ezek. xxvii. 27.

עָשָׂה to do. KAL *part.* Paül, Exod. xxxviii. 24. NIPHAL *pret.* Judg. xvi. 11: מַעֲשֶׂה *m.* that which any one makes or does, business: Gen. xlvi. 33; xlvii. 3.

OCCURRENT

פֶּגַע *m.* what lights upon any one, incident, event, chance: 1 Kings v. 4.

ODIOUS

בָּאַשׁ to stink, to be loathsome. HITHPAEL *pret.* 1 Chron. xix. 6.

שָׂנֵא to hate. KAL *part.* Paül, Prov. xxx. 23.

ODOUR (See SWEET)

OFFEND

1 אָשַׁם to trespass, to be guilty. With *inf.,* to offend greatly. KAL [a] *pret.* [b] *inf.* [c] *fut.* [d] אַשְׁמָה *f.* offence.

2 בָּגַד to transgress, deal treacherously. KAL *pret.*

3 חָבַל to deal corruptly. KAL *fut.*

4 חָטָא to sin. KAL [a] *pret.* HIPHIL [b] *part.* [c] חֵטְא *m.* sin, fault. [d] חֹטֵא *m.* one who bears blame.

5 מִכְשׁוֹל *m.* stumbling-block, *lit.* have no stumbling-block.

6 פָּשַׁע to break with any one, rebel, revolt. NIPHAL *part.*

Gen. xx. 9.	4 a	Ps. lxxiii. 15.	2	Jer. xxxvii. 18.	4 a
xl. 1.	4 a	cxix. 165.	5	l. 7.	1 c
1 Sam. xxv. 31.	5	Prov. xviii. 19.	6	Ezek. xxv. 12.	1 c b
1 Kings i. 21.	4 d	Ec:les. x. 4.	4 c	Hos. iv. 15.	1 c
2 Kings xvii. 14.	4 a	Isa. viii. 14.	5	v. 15.β	1 c
2 Chron. xxviii. 13. a	1 d	xxix. 21.	4 b	xiii. 1.	1 c
Job xxxiv. 31.		Jer. ii. 3.	1 c	Hab. i. 11.	1 a

a lit. for to the offence of the Lord upon us.   β "acknowledge their offence;" *marg.* ' be guilty.'

OFFER

1 אִשֶּׁה *f.* an "offering made by fire;" spoken of every kind of sacrifice and offering, once even of those not burned : Lev. xxiv. 7, 9.—Exod. xxix. 18, &c.

2 אָשָׁם a sacrifice for fault or guilt, a trespass-offering ; in the Mosaic law these sacrifices for fault are carefully distinguished from sacrifices for sin, or sin-offerings (חַטָּאוֹת). Not only were the rites and ceremonies of each different (see Lev. v. 1-26, or 1-19, and vi. 1-7, vii. 1-7, *comp.* iv. 1-35, vi. 17-23, or 24-30), but the different victims pertaining to each were sometimes conjoined in one and the same offering (as Lev. xiv. 10 *sq.,* Num. vi. 12 *sq., comp.* Lev. v. 7-10), and the particular faults or sins are carefully enumerated by the lawgiver, which were to be expiated by this or that rite: Lev. v. ; xiv. 12, 24; xix. 20-22 : Num. vi. 11, 12. Still the precise point of distinction between the two kinds of faults or sins has hitherto been sought in vain. Bush, in his Notes on Leviticus, observes that the class of offences for which the trespass-offering was to be brought included those which, though not amounting to wilful and presumptuous acts, were yet usually committed against knowledge, and were therefore of a higher grade of guilt than the sins of mere ignorance and infirmity which were con-

templated by the sin-offerings. The blood sprinkled in the most holy place was not the blood of this offering, but only of the sin-offering, חַטָּאת Lev. v. 6, &c. ᵃ אַשְׁמָה f. trespass, trespass-offering.

3   דְּבַח Ch. to sacrifice, to offer sacrifice. P'AL part. active.

4   הַבְהָבִים m. pl. gifts, sacrificial offerings.

5   זָבַח to kill and slay in general; to slay and offer up a beast in a religious manner, as an act of worship; to sacrifice, to render thanksgiving to God. It is not used of priests slaying sacrifices, but of private persons offering sacrifices at their own cost. KAL ᵃ pret. ᵇ inf. ᶜ imp. ᵈ fut. ᵉ part. Poel. PIEL ᶠ part. ᵍ זֶבַח m. see Sacrifice.

6   חָטָא to sin; Piel, to offer as a sin-offering, as a sacrifice of atonement or expiation. PIEL ᵃ fut. ᵇ part. ᶜ חַטָּאָה f. sin-offering. ᵈ חַטָּאָה Ch. f. sin-offering. ᵉ חַטָּאת f. sin-offering: Exod. xxix. 14, &c.

7   מִנְחָה f. a gift, present; an offering to God, a sacrifice; spoken especially of a bloodless offering, meat-offering, opposed to זֶבַח a bloody sacrifice; a small part was burned on the altar, and the remainder was eaten by Aaron and his sons, with salt, Lev. ii. 1, 9, 13; usually translated meat-offering. ᵃ מִנְחָה Ch. f. id.

8   מִמְסָךְ m. mixed wine, spiced wine; a drink-offering.

9   נָגַשׁ to come near; to bring near. HIPHIL ᵃ pret. ᵇ fut. ᶜ part. HOPHAL ᵈ part.

10   נָדַב to act willingly and generously. A free-will offering was such as the offerer was not obliged to by any law, but which he presented of his own choice. HITHPAEL ᵃ pret. ᵇ inf. ᶜ fut. ᵈ part. נְדַב Ch. ITHPAEL ᵉ pret. ᶠ inf. ᵍ part. ʰ נְדָבָה f. free-will offering: Lev. xxii. 18, &c.

11   נוּף to lift up; to lift up repeatedly, to wave to and fro, to shake, to wave, from side to side; specially of a certain ceremony in sacrifices by which portions of the victims or offerings, before being placed on the altar, were waved to and fro, as if to show them on every side; joined also with the right of elevating, or the heave-offering; between which rites the Rabbins justly distinguish thus, viz. that the heave-offering is presented with a motion up and down, and the wave-offering with a motion from side to side; see Carpzov. p. 709 sq. In the case of living victims, and in the consecration of the Levites, the waving would seem to consist in leading them about to and fro, Num. viii. 11–21. Among the Romans the porrectio was a similar rite; as also the elevation of the host (monstratio) in the Latin Church: Gesenius. HIPHIL ᵃ pret. ᵇ fut. ᶜ תְּנוּפָה f. a wave-offering: Exod. xxix. 24, &c.

12   נָטָה to stretch out, to offer, to hold out for choice. KAL part. Poel.

13   נָטַל to lay upon, to impose upon. KAL part. Poel.

14   נָסַךְ to pour out, as water and wine are solemnly poured out in drink-offering. KAL ᵃ fut. HIPHIL ᵇ fut. נְסַךְ Ch. PAEL ᶜ inf. ᵈ נֵסֶךְ and נֶסֶךְ m. a libation, a drink-offering: Gen. xxxv. 14, &c. ᵉ נְסִיךְ m. id. נְסַךְ Ch. m.

15   נָשָׂא to lift up. KAL inf.

16   נָתַן to give. KAL ᵃ pret. ᵇ fut.

17   עָלָה to ascend; to make to ascend. KAL ᵃ inf. ᵇ fut. HIPHIL ᶜ pret. ᵈ inf. ᵉ imp. ᶠ fut. ᵍ part. HOPHAL ʰ pret. ⁱ עֹלָה f. a burnt-offering, holocaust, a sacrifice to be wholly consumed; so called as being carried up and laid on the altar; usually translated, burnt-offering. ᵏ עֲלָה Ch. f. id.

18   עָשָׂה to do, to make; to make ready, prepare; to dress or prepare a victim for sacrifice; hence to offer. KAL ᵃ pret. ᵇ inf. ᶜ imp. ᵈ fut. NIPHAL ᵉ fut. ᶠ מַעֲשֶׂה m. work.

19   פֶּסַח m. passover, passover-offering.

20   קָטַר to burn incense. PIEL ᵃ pret. ᵇ inf. ᶜ part. HIPHIL ᵈ inf. ᵉ part.

21   קָרַב to come near; to bring near, to offer. KAL ᵃ inf. HIPHIL ᵇ pret. ᶜ inf. ᵈ imp. ᵉ fut. ᶠ part. קְרֵב Ch. PAEL ᵍ fut. APHEL ʰ pret. ⁱ part. ᵏ קָרְבָּן m. offering: Lev. i. 20, &c. ˡ קֻרְבָּן m. id.

22   רוּם to be lifted up; to offer up. HIPHIL ᵃ pret. ᵇ fut. ᶜ part. ᵈ תְּרוּמָה f. oblation, heave-offering: Exod. xxix. 27, &c.

23   שָׁחַט to kill, slay, especially victims for sacrifice. KAL fut.

24   שֶׁלֶם m. thanks, thank-offering; usually translated peace-offering, but sometimes taking זֶבַח with it: Exod. xx. 24, &c.

No. 1, *Offering made by fire*, not included; No. 2, *Trespass-offering*, ditto; No. 6 e, *Sin-offering*, ditto; No. 7, *Meat-offering*, ditto; No. 10 h, *Free-will offering*, ditto; No. 11 c, *Wave-offering*, ditto; No. 14 d, *Drink-offering*, ditto; No. 17 i, *Burnt-offering*, ditto; No. 21 k, *Offering*, ditto; No. 22 d, *Heave-offering*, ditto; No. 24, *Peace-offering*, ditto.

Gen. iv. 3, 4, 5.	7
viii. 20.	17 f
xxii. 2.	17 e
xxii. 13.	17 f
xxxi. 54.	5 d
xlvi. 1.	5 d
Exod. xxiii. 18.	5 d
xxiv. 5, 5.	17 f, 5 g
xxv. 2, 2, 3.	17 e
xxix. 36, 38, 39, 39, 41.	18 d
xxx. 9.	17 f
xxx. 13, 14, 15.	22 d
xxxii. 6.	17 f
xxxiv. 25.	23
xxxv. 5, 5, 21.	22 d
xxxv. 22, 22.	11 a c
xxxv. 24, 24, 24.	22 c d d
xxxv. 29.	10 h
xxxvi. 3, 3.	22 d, 17 f
xxxvi. 6.	22 d
xxxviii. 24, 29.	11 c
xl. 29.	17 f
Lev. i. 3, 3.	17 f
ii. 1, 1.	21 e, 7
ii. 12, 13, 14, 14.	21 e
ii. 1, 1.	21 f e
iii. 3, 9, 12, 14.	21 b
iii. 6.	21 e
iii. 7, 7.	21 f b
iv. 14.	21 b
v. 8.	21 b
v. 10.	18 d
vi. 5.	2 a
vi. 14.	21 d
vi. 20, 21.	21 e
vi. 22.	18 d
vi. 26.	6 b
vii. 3, 11, 13, 25.	21 b
vii. 8, 8.	21 f b
vii. 9, 18, 29, 33.	21 f
vii. 12, 12.	21 e b
vii. 14.	21 b

Lev. vii. 15.	21 k
vii. 16, 16.	10 h, 21 c
vii. 38.	21 c
ix. 2.	21 d
ix. 7, 7.	18 c
ix. 15.	6 a
ix. 16.	18 d
ix. 22.	18 b
x. 1.	21 e
x. 19.	21 b
xiv. 12.	21 b
xiv. 19, 30.	18 a
xiv. 20.	17 c
xv. 15, 30.	18 a
xvi. 1.	21 a
xvi. 6.	21 b
xvi. 9, 24.	18 a
xvii. 5, 5, 5.	5 e a g
xvii. 7.	5 b
xvii. 8.	17 f
xvii. 9.	18 b
xix. 5, 5.	5 d
xix. 6, 8.	5 g
xxi. 6, 8.	21 f
xxi. 17, 21, 21.	21 c
xxii. 12.	22 d
xxii. 15.	22 b
xxiii. 18, 18, 20, 21, 22, 24, 25.	21 e
xxiii. 23.	18 d
xxiii. 29, 29.	5 d
xxiii. 8, 16, 18, 25, 27.	21 b
xxiii. 12.	18 a
xxiii. 36, 36.	21 e b
xxiii. 37.	21 c
xxvii. 11.	21 e
Num. iv. 3.	
v. 9.	21 a
v. 15, 15, 18, 18, 26.	7
v. 25, 25, 25.	7, 7, 21 b
vi. 11, 16.	18 a

Num. vi. 14.	21 b
vi. 17, 17.	18 d a
vii. 2, 10, 10, 11.	21 e
vii. 12.	21 f
vii. 18, 19.	21 b
viii. 11, 11.	11 a c
viii. 12.	18 a
viii. 13, 13.	11 a c
viii. 21, 21.	11 b c
ix. 7.	21 c
xv. 4.	21 f
xv. 7.	21 e
xv. 13.	21 c
xv. 14, 24.	18 a
xv. 19, 20.	22 b
xvi. 15.	7
xvi. 35.	21 f
xvi. 38, 39.	21 b
xvi. 40.	20 d
xviii. 19, 24, 28, 29.	22 b
xviii. 26.	22 d
xxii. 40.	5 d
xxiii. 2, 4, 14, 30.	17 f
xxvi. 61.	21 c
xxviii. 2.	21 c
xxviii. 3, 11.	21 e
xxviii. 4, 4, 8, 8, 20, 21, 23, 31.	18 d
xxviii. 15.	18 e
xxviii. 19, 27.	21 b
xxviii. 24, 24.	18 d e
xxix. 2.	18 a
xxix. 8, 13, 36.	18 a
xxxi. 52, 52.	22 d a
Deut. xii. 13, 14.	17 f
xii. 27.	18 a
xviii. 3.	5 e
xxvii. 6.	17 c
xxvii. 7.	5 a
xxxii. 38.	14 e
xxxiii. 19.	5 d

Josh. viii. 31.	17 f	1 Chron. xxi. 26.	17 f	Ps. li. 19.	17 f
xxii. 23, 23,		xxiii. 31.	17 d	lxvi. 15, 15.	17 f, 18 d
23.	17 d, 18 b, 5 g	xxix. 6.	10 c	lxxii. 10.	21 e
Judg. iii. 18.	21 c	xxix. 9, 9.	10 b a	xcvi. 8.	7
v. 2.	10 b	xxix. 14.	10 b	cxvi. 17.	5 d
v. 9.	10 d	xxix. 17, 17.	10 a b	Prov. vii. 14.	5 g
vi. 16.	17 c	xxix. 21.	17 f	Isa. xliii. 23.	7
vi. 28.	17 h	2 Chron. i. 6.	17 f	liii. 10.	2
xi. 31.	17 c	iv. 6.β	18 f, 17 c	lvii. 6.	17 c
xiii. 16, 16.	18 d, 17 f	vii. 4.	5 e	lvii. 7.	5 b
xiii. 19.	17 b	vii. 5.	17 d	lxiii. 10.	2
xvi. 23.	5 b	vii. 7.	18 a	lxv. 11.	8
xx. 26.	17 f	viii. 12.	17 c	lxvi. 3.	17 g
xxi. 4.	17 f	viii. 13.	17 d	lxvi. 20, 20.	7
1 Sam. i. 4.	5 d	xv. 11.	5 d	Jer. xi. 12.	20 c
i. 21.	5 b	xvii. 16.	10 d	xi. 17.	20 b
ii. 13.	5 e	xxiii. 18.	17 d	xiv. 12.	17 f
ii. 17, 29, 29.	7	xxiv. 14, 14.	17 d g	xxxii. 29.	20 a
ii. 19.	5 b	xxix. 7.	17 c	xxxiii. 18.	17 g
ii. 28, 28.	17 a, 1	xxix. 21, 27, 29.	17 c	xli. 5.	7
iii. 14.	7	xxx. 22, 22.	5 f g	xlviii. 35.	17 g
vi. 14, 15.	17 c	xxxi. 10, 12.	22 d	Ezek. vi. 13.	16 a
vii. 9.	17 f	xxxiii. 16.	5 g	vii. 17.	21 e
vii. 10.	17 g	xxxv. 7, 8, 9.	19	xx. 28.	5 d
x. 8.	17 d	xxxv. 12.	21 c	xx. 31.	15
xiii. 9, 12.	17 f	xxxv. 14, 16.	17 d	xx. 40.	22 d
xiii. 10.	17 d	Ezra i. 6.	10 b	xliii. 18.	17 d
xxvi. 19.	7	ii. 68.	10 a	xliii. 22, 23.	21 e
2 Sam. i. 21.	22 d	iii. 2, 6.	17 d	xliii. 24, 24.	21 b, 17 c
vi. 17.	17 f	iii. 3.	17 d	xliv. 7, 15.	21 c
vi. 18.	17 d	iii. 5.	10 d	xliv. 27.	21 e
xv. 12.	5 b	vi. 3.	3	xlv. 1, 13.	22 b
xxiv. 12.	13	vi. 9.	17 k	xlvi. 4.	21 e
xxiv. 22, 24, 25.	17 f	vi. 10.γ	17 e	xlviii. 8, 8.	22 d b
1 Kings iii. 4.	17 f	vi. 17, 17.	21 h, 6 d	xlviii. 9, 20.	22 b
iii. 15, 15.	17 f, 18 d	vii. 15.	10 d	xlviii. 12.	22 d
viii. 62.	5 e	vii. 16, 16.	10 f g	Dan. ii. 46.	14 c
viii. 63, 63.	5 d a	vii. 17, 17.	7 a, 21 g	Hos. viii. 13.	4
viii. 64.	18 a	viii. 25, 25.	22 d a	ix. 4.	14 a
ix. 25.	17 c	viii. 35.	21 b	Amos iv. 5, 5.	20 b, 10 h
xii. 32, 33, 33.	17 f	Neh. x. 34.	21 l	v. 22.	17 f
xiii. 2.	5 a	x. 37, 39.	22 d	v. 25, 25.	9 a, 7
xviii. 29, 36.	17 a	xi. 2.	10 d	Jonah i. 8.	1
xxii. 43.	5 f	xii. 43.	5 d	i. 16.	5 d
2 Kings iii. 20.	17 a	xii. 44.	22 d	Zeph. iii. 10.	7
iii. 27.	17 f	xiii. 22.	22 d	Hag. ii. 14.	21 e
v. 17.	18 d	xiii. 31.	21 l	Mal. i. 7.	9 c
x. 24, 25.	18 b	Job i. 5.	17 c	i. 8, 8, 8.	9 b b, 21 d
xvi. 12.	17 f	i. 8.	17 f	i. 10, 13.	7
1 Chron. vi. 49.	20 e	Ps. iv. 5.	5 c	i. 11, 11.	9 d, 7
xv. 26.	5 d	xvi. 4.	14 b	ii. 12, 12.	9 c, 7
xvi. 1.	21 e	xx. 3.	7	ii. 13.	7
xvi. 2, 40.	17 d	xxvii. 6.	5 d	iii. 3, 3.	9 c, 7
xvi. 29.	7	xl. 6, 6.	7, 6 c	iii. 4.	7
xxi. 10.	12	l. 14.	5 c	iii. 8.	22 d
xxi. 24.	17 d	l. 23.	5 e		

α *lit.* in the day of your sacrifice. β *marg.* 'the work of burnt-offerings.'
γ *lit.* may be offering.

OFFICE

1 אֱמוּנָה *f.* truth, faithfulness; "set office."
2 בֵּן *m.* place, station in life, office.
3 עֲבוֹדָה *f.* service.
4 מַעֲמָד *m.* standing.
5 פְּקֻדָּה *f.* oversight, charge.
6 מִשְׁמָר *m.* ward, *marg.* 'or, observations.' a מִשְׁמֶרֶת *f.* charge.

Gen. xli. 13.	2	1 Chron. xxiii. 28.	4	2 Chron. xxiv. 11.	5
Num. iv. 47.	5	xxiv. 3.	5	xxxi. 15, 18.	1
1 Chron. vi. 32.	3	2 Chron. vii. 6.	6 a	Neh. xiii. 14.	6
ix. 22, 26, 31.	1	xxiii. 18.	5	Ps. cix. 8.	5

OFFICER

1 מְלָאכָה *f.* work: Esth. ix. 3, *marg.* 'those which did the business that belonged to the king.'

2 נָצַב to set; to be set; to place or station oneself. NIPHAL a *part.* b נְצִיב *m.* one set over.

3 סָרִים *m.* an eunuch: Isa. lvi. 3, 4. Such persons Oriental monarchs were accustomed to set over their harems, and also to employ them in various offices of the court. So Dan. i. 3, the chief of the eunuchs had charge of the king's sons, as at the present day in Turkey the Kislar Aga has charge of the Sultan's children. Hence, according to some, generally a minister of court, a court-officer.—*Gesenius.* But the word signifies not only eunuchs, but also chamberlains, courtiers, and officers.

4 עָשָׂה to do. KAL *part.* Poel.
5 פָּקַד to visit; to set over, to give the oversight of, to appoint. KAL a *part.* Poel. b פְּקֻדָּה *f.* care, oversight, office, officers. c פָּקִיד *m.* officer.
6 רַב *adj.* much, great; a great man, chief, a leader.
7 שֹׁטֵר *m.* a writer, scribe; an overseer, in whose office was combined various duties, including enrolments, orders, &c., also genealogies; a magistrate, prefect, leader of the people; especially the leaders, officers of the Israelites in Egypt and in the desert, *i. q.* the seventy elders; magistrates in the cities and towns of Palestine.

Gen. xxxvii. 36.	3	Josh. viii. 33.	7	1 Chron. xxiii. 4.	7
xxxix. 1.	3	xxiii. 2.	7	xxvi. 29.	7
xl. 2, 7.	3	xxiv. 1.	7	xxvi. 30.	5 b
xli. 34.	5 c	Judg. ix. 28.	5 c	xxvii. 1.	7
Exod. v. 6, 10, 14, 15.	3	1 Sam. viii. 15.	3	xxviii. 1.	3
19.	7	1 Kings iv. 5, 7, 27.	2 a	2 Chron. xviii. 10.	2 a
Num. xi. 16.	7	iv. 19.	2 b	xviii. 8.	3
xxxi. 14, 48.	5 a	v. 16.	2 a	xix. 11.	7
Deut. i. 15.	7	ix. 23.	2 a	xxiv. 11.	5 c
xvi. 18.	7	2 Kings viii. 6.	3	xxvi. 13.	7
xx. 5, 8, 9.	7	xi. 15.	5	Esth. i. 8.	6
xxix. 10.	7	xi. 18.	5 a, or b	ii. 3.	5 c
xxxi. 28.	7	xxiv. 12, 15.	3	ix. 3.	4, 1
Josh. i. 10.	7	xxv. 19.	3	Isa. lx. 17.	5 b
iii. 2.	7			Jer. xxix. 26.	5 c

OFF-SCOURING

סְחִי *m.* sweepings; *trop.* for anything worthless: Lam. iii. 45.

OFFSPRING

צֶאֱצָאִים *m. pl.* shoots; offspring, children; descendants: Job v. 25; xxi. 8; xxvii. 14; xxxi. 8: Isa. xxii. 24; xliv. 3; xlviii. 19; lxi. 9; lxv. 23.

OFTENTIMES

פַּעַם step, tread; with numerals &c. translated 'times:' Job xxxiii. 29, *lit.* twice (and) thrice: Eccles. vii. 22.

רַב *adj.* much, many: Eccles. vii. 22.

שָׁלוֹשׁ three: Job xxxiii. 29, *lit.* twice (and) thrice.

OIL, OINTMENT

1 יִצְהָר *m.* oil, from its brightness; especially that which was new, of the same year's growth. a צָהַר *verb denom.* to make oil. HIPHIL *fut.*

2 מִשְׁחָה *f.* anointing. a מְשַׁח Ch. *m.*

3 רֹקַח *m.* ointment, perfume. a מִרְקָחָה *f.* a pot of ointment. b מִרְקַחַת *f.* ointment.

4 שֶׁמֶן *com.* fatness; oil; spiced oil, ointment, with which on joyous occasions they were wont to anoint the head, hence the oil or ointment of joy or gladness: Ps. xlvii. 2.—Gen. xxviii. 18, &c.

No. 4 not included.

Exod. xxx. 25,		Deut. xi. 14.	1	Deut. xxviii. 51.	1
25, 25, 25.	4, 2, 3, 4	xii. 17.	1	2 Kings xviii. 32.	1
Num. xviii. 12.	1	xiv. 23.	1	1 Chron. ix. 30.	2 b
Deut. vii. 13.	1	xviii. 4.	1	2 Chron. xxxi. 5.	1

2 Chron. xxxii. 28.	1	Neh. xiii. 5, 12.	1	Hos. ii. 8, 22.	1
Ezra vi. 9.	2 a	Job xxiv. 11.	1 a	Joel i. 10.	1
vii. 22.	2 a	xli. 31.	3 a	ii. 19, 24.	1
Neh. v. 11.	1	Jer. xxxi. 12.	1	Hag. i. 11.	1
x. 37, 39.	1				

OLD

1   בָּלָה to waste by use and age; of garments, to decay; to be worn out, to wax old; also *trop.* of the heavens. KAL *a pret.* *b inf.* *c fut.* PIEL *d pret.* *e* בָּלָה *adj.* worn out with use and age. *f* בְּלוֹא *m.* rags of worn-out clothes.

2   בֵּן *m.* son; age is expressed by the phrase, son of, as Gen. v. 32, *lit.* was son of five hundred years. *a* בַּת *f.* daughter. *b* בַּר Ch. *m.* son.

3   זָקֵן to be or become old. KAL *a pret.* *b fut.* HIPHIL *c fut.* *d* זָקֵן *adj.* old. *e* זִקְנָה *f.* old age; "when .... was old," *lit.* in the time of the old age of. *f* זְקֻנִים *m. pl. id.*

4   חַי *adj.* living.

5   יוֹם *m.* day.

6   יָשִׁישׁ *m.* a very old man, grey-headed.

7   יָשֵׁן to fall asleep; to be old. NIPHAL *a part.* "old store." *b* יָשָׁן *adj.* old, not new.

8   עַד *m.* see *Ever.*

9   עוֹלָם *m.* ever; everlasting, perpetual; also of time long past, "ever of old." עָלַם Ch. *m. id.*

10   עָתַק to be removed; to grow old. KAL *pret.*

11   פָּנִים *m. pl.* face; לְפָנֵי "of old time," *lit.* before.

12   קֶדֶם *m.* that which is before, ancient. *a* קַדְמָה *f.* old estate. *b* קַדְמֹנִי *adj.* ancient.

13   רִאשׁוֹן *adj.* head, highest, chief; first in order, and also in time.

14   רָחוֹק *adj.* afar off.

15   שֵׂיבָה *f.* old age, hoary and grey-headed.

16   שָׁנָה *f.* year.

17   אֶתְמוֹל aforetime, of old; yesterday.

No. 3 d not included.

Gen. v. 32.	2	Num. i. 3, 18, 20, 22, 24,		1 Sam. xii. 2.	3 a
vi. 4.	9	26, 28, 30, 32, 34,	2	xvii. 12.	3 a
vii. 6.	2	36, 38, 40, 42, 45,	2	xxvii. 8.	9
xi. 10.	2	iii. 15, 22, 28, 34, 39,		2 Sam. ii. 10.	2
xii. 4.	2	40, 43.	2	iv. 4.	2
xv. 15.	15	iv. 3, 3, 23, 23, 30,		v. 4.	2
xvi. 16.	2	30, 35, 35, 39, 39,		xix. 32, 35.	2
xvii. 1, 12, 24, 25.	2	43, 43, 47, 47.	2	xx. 18.	13
xvii. 17, 17.	2, 2 a	viii. 24.	2	1 Kings i. 1, 15.	3 a
xviii. 12, 12.	1 b, 3 a	xiv. 29.	2	xi. 4, γ	3 a
xviii. 13.	3 a	xviii. 16.	2	xiv. 21.	2
xix. 31.	3 a	xxvi. 2, 4, 62.	2	xv. 23.	3 e
xxi. 2, 7.	3 f	xxxii. 11.	2	2 Kings iv. 14.	3 a
xxi. 4, 5.	2	xxxiii. 39.	2	viii. 17.	2
xxiii. 1. *α*	4	Deut. ii. 20.	11	viii. 26.	2
xxiv. 1.	3 a	viii. 4.	1 a	xi. 21.	2
xxiv. 36. *β*	2	xix. 14.	13	xiv. 2, 21.	2
xxv. 8, 8.	15, 3 d	xxix. 5, 5.	1 a	xv. 2, 33.	2
xxv. 20, 26.	2	xxxi. 2.	2	xvi. 2.	2
xxvi. 34.	2	xxxii. 7.	2	xviii. 2.	2
xxvii. 1, 2.	3 a	xxxiv. 7.	2	xxi. 1, 19.	2
xxxvii. 2.	2	Josh. ix. 4, 4, 5, 5.	1 e	xxii. 1.	2
xxxviii. 3.	3 f	ix. 13.	1 a	xxiii. 31, 36.	2
xli. 46.	2	xiii. 1, 1.	3 a	xxiv. 8, 18.	2
xliv. 20, 20.	3 d f	xiv. 7, 10.	2	1 Chron. ii. 21.	2
xlvii. 8.	5, 16, 4	xxiii. 1, 2.	3 a	iv. 40.	11
l. 26.	2	xxiv. 2.	2	xxiii. 1.	3 a
Exod. vii. 7, 7.	2	xxiv. 29.	2	xxiii. 27.	2
xxx. 14.	2	Judg. ii. 8.	2	xxvii. 23.	15
xxxviii. 26.	2	iii. 32.	15	xxix. 28.	15
Lev. xiii. 11.	7 a	Ruth i. 12.	3 a	2 Chron. xii. 13.	2
xxv. 22, 22.	2	1 Sam. ii. 22.	3 a	xx. 31.	2
xxvi. 10.	7 b a	iv. 15.	15	xxi. 5, 20.	2
xxvi. 10.	7 b	iv. 15.	2	xxii. 2.	2
xxvii. 3, 3, 5, 5, 6,		iv. 18.	3 a	xxiv. 1.	2
6, 7.	2	viii. 1, 5.	3 a		

2 Chron. xxiv. 15,		Ps. lxviii. 33.	12	Isa. lxiii. 9, 11.	9
15.	3 b, 2	lxxi. 9, 18.	3 e	lxv. 20, 20, 20.	3 d, 2, 2
xxv. 1, 5.	2	lxxiv. 2, 12.	12	Jer. ii. 20.	9
xxvi. 1, 3.	2	lxxvii. 5, 11.	12	vi. 16.	9
xxvii. 1, 8.	2	lxxviii. 2.	12	xxviii. 8.	9
xxviii. 1.	2	xcii. 14.	15	xxxi. 3.	14
xxix. 1.	2	cii. 25.	11	xxxviii. 11, 11, 12.	1 f
xxxi. 16, 17.	2	cii. 26.	1 c	xlvi. 26.	12
xxxiii. 1, 21.	2	cxix. 52.	9	lii. 1.	2
xxxiv. 1.	2	cxix. 152.	12	Lam. i. 7.	12
xxxvi. 2, 5, 9, 11.	2	Prov. xxii. 6.	3 c	ii. 17.	12
Ezra iii. 8.	2	xxiii. 10.	12	iii. 4.	1 d
iv. 15, 19. *δ*	9 a	xxiii. 22.	2	iii. 6.	9
ix. 21.	1 a	Eccles. i. 10.	9	v. 21.	12
xii. 39.	7 b	Cant. vii. 13.	7 b	Ezek. xxiii. 43.	1 e
iii. 46.	12	Isa. xxii. 11.	7 b	xxv. 15.	9
Job xiv. 8.	3 c	xxv. 1.	12	xxvi. 20, 20.	9
xx. 4.	8	xxx. 33.	17	xxxvi. 11.	12 a
xli. 7.	10	xli. 18.	12 b	xxxviii. 17.	12 b
xxii. 15.	9	xlvi. 4.	3 e	Dan. v. 31.	2 b
xxxii. 6.	6	xlvi. 9.	9	Amos ix. 11.	9
Ps. vi. 7.	10	l. 9.	9	Micah v. 2.	12
xxv. 6.	9	li. 9.	1 c	vi. 6.	2
xxxii. 3.	1 a	li. 9.	9	vii. 14.	9
xxxvii. 25.	3 a	lvii. 11.	9	vii. 20.	12
xliv. 1.	12	lviii. 12.	12	Nah. ii. 8.	5
lv. 19.	9	lxi. 4.	9	Mal. iii. 4.	9

a lit. the life of Sarah was.   *β lit.* after her old age.   *γ lit.* in the time of the old age of.   *δ lit.* from the days of age.

OLIVE

זַיִת *m.* an olive, both tree and fruit; the tree is remarkable for easily casting its flower, Job xv. 33, and for the spread of its branches, Hos. xiv. 6; an olive-yard; mount Olivet, or (mount of) Olives: Gen. viii. 11, &c.

שֶׁמֶן *com.* oil: 1 Kings vi. 23, *lit.* trees of oil, 31, 32, 33.

OMER

עֹמֶר *m.* a handful of grain, a sheaf; a measure, the tenth part of an ephah, containing near three wine quarts, which might be about the quantity of grain which a sheaf of corn yielded: Exod. xvi. 16, 18, 22, 32, 33, 36.

ONION

בֶּצֶל *m.* an onion, of which there was great plenty, excellent in kind, in Egypt: Num. xi. 5.

ONLY

אֶחָד *adj.* one, one only: Josh. xvii. 17: 1 Kings iv. 19: Cant. vi. 9: Ezek. vii. 5.

בָּדָד *m.* alone: Ps. iv. 8.

יַחַד a being one, oneness, union; it connects two or more nouns more closely by the idea of equality, likeness, together, alike, in like manner: Job xxxiv. 29. יָחִיד *adj unicus,* one alone, only, only child: Gen. xxii. 2, 12, 16: Judg. xi. 34: Prov. iv. 3: Jer. vi. 26: Amos viii. 10: Zech. xii. 10.

ONYCHA

שְׁחֵלֶת *f. pr.* a shell, or, according to the Hebrew interpreters, ὄνυξ, *unguis odoratus,* the blatta byzantina of the shops: Exod. xxx. 34. It consists of the shell or cover of a species of muscle found in the lakes of India, where the nard grows; when burned it emits a musky odour.

ONYX

שֹׁהַם *m.* a species of gem; according to many, sardonyx or onyx, so called from its resemblance to the human nail: Gen. ii. 12: Exod. xxv. 7; xxviii. 9, 20; xxxv. 9, 27;

xxxix. 6, 13 : 1 Chron. xxix. 2 : Job xxviii. 16 : Ezek. xxviii. 13.

OPEN

1 גָּלָה to make naked, to uncover; and then, to disclose, to reveal; especially in the phrase, to make bare or uncover the ear of any one by removing the overhanging locks, as is done in whispering a secret to another; in a slightly different sense spoken of God: Job xxxvi. 10, "he openeth their ear to discipline," to instruction, *i.e.* causeth them to hear. KAL ᵃ *fut.* ᵇ *part.* Paül. NIPHAL ᶜ *pret.* PIEL ᵈ *pret.* ᵉ *imp.* ᶠ *fut.* PUAL ᵍ *part.*

2 כָּרָה to dig. KAL *pret.* Ps. xl. 6, *marg.* ' digged ;' in allusion to the custom prescribed in Exod. xxi. 2, &c. ; Deut. xv. 16, &c., in token of perpetual servitude; implying the willing and pledged obedience of the Messiah in his body.

3 עַיִן *com.* eye.

4 פָּטַר to let loose, to open what was pent up : Num. iii. 12. Applied to the openings of flowers from the bud. KAL ᵃ *part.* Paül. ᵇ פֶּטֶר *m.* that which first breaks forth. ᶜ פִּטְרָה *f. id.*

5 פָּנִים *m. pl.* face ; "open," *lit.* the face of.

6 פָּעַר to open wide, to gape ; *trop.* it signifies an enlarged earnest desire of receiving instruction or a blessing. KAL *pret.*

7 פָּצָה to tear apart, to rend ; to open wide. KAL ᵃ *pret.* ᵇ *imp.* ᶜ *fut.* ᵈ *part.* Poel.

8 פָּקַח to open the eyes, once used of the ears. KAL ᵃ *pret.* ᵇ *inf.* ᶜ *imp.* ᵈ *fut.* ᵉ *part.* Poel. ᶠ *part.* Paül. NIPHAL ᵍ *pret.* ʰ *fut.* ⁱ פְּקַח־קוֹחַ *m.* opening of the prison; see *Prison.*

9 פָּרַץ to break forth, to spread abroad. NIPHAL *part.*

10 פָּרַשׂ to spread out, to lay open. KAL *fut.*

11 פָּשַׂק to open wide. KAL ᵃ *part.* Poel. PIEL ᵇ *fut.*

12 פָּתַח to open a door, a house, the mouth, the ear, the eyes, the grave, the clods of the earth by ploughing ; to open or loosen, *i. e.* to draw out the sword ; to open as a bud, Cant. vii. 12 ; to open wheat, *i.e.* to expose it to sale, Amos viii. 5. KAL ᵃ *pret.* ᵇ *inf.* ᶜ *imp.* ᵈ *fut.* ᵉ *part.* Poel. ᶠ *part.* Paül. NIPHAL ᵍ *pret.* ʰ *fut.* ⁱ *part.* PIEL ᵏ *pret.* ˡ *fut.* פָּתַח Ch. Pˈɪʟ ᵐ *pret.* ⁿ *part.* ᵒ פֶּתַח *m.* opening, door. ᵖ פִּתְחוֹן *m.* opening. ᑫ מַפְתֵּחַ *m. id.* ʳ מִפְתָּח *m. id.*

13 מָקוֹם *com.* place.

14 רָחַב to be wide ; to make wide, to open wide. HIPHIL ᵃ *imp.* ᵇ *fut.*

15 שָׁתַם to unclose, to open. Gesenius, to shut, to close, in sleep for receiving visions. KAL *part.* Paül, *marg.* ' who had his eyes shut, but now opened.' Hengstenberg retains the ordinary meaning of this verb, and would render the passage, " the man with closed eyes," *i. e.* in an ecstasy.

Gen. i. 20.	5	Gen. xxi. 19.	8 d	Gen. xlii. 27.	12 d
iii. 6.	8 g	xxix. 31.	12 d	xliii. 21.	12 d
iii. 7.	8 h	xxx. 22.	12 d	xliv. 11.	12 d
iv. 11.	7 a	xxxviii. 14.	12 o, 3	Exod. ii. 6.	12 d
vii. 11.	12 g	xxxviii. 21.	3	xiii. 2, 12, 15.	4 b
viii. 6.	12 d	xli. 56.	12 d	xxi. 33.	12 d

Exod. xxxiv. 19.	4 b	Job xiv. 3.	8 a	Isa. xxxvii. 17.	8 c
Lev. xiv. 7, 53.	5	xxvii. 19.	8 a	xli. 18.	12 d
xvii. 5.	5	xxix. 23.	6	xlii. 7, 20.	8 b
Num. iii. 12.	4 b	xxxi. 32.	12 d	xlv. 1.	12 b
viii. 16.	4 c	xxxii. 20.	12 d	xlv. 8.	12 d
xvi. 30.	7 a	xxxiii. 2.	12 a	xlviii. 8.	12 k
xvi. 32.	12 d	xxxiii. 16.	1 a	l. 5.	12 a
xviii. 15.	4 b	xxxiv. 26.	13	liii. 7, 7.	12 d
xix. 15.	12 f	xxxv. 16.	7 c	lx. 11.	12 k
xix. 16.	5	xxxvi. 10, 15.	1 a	lxi. 1.	8 i
xxii. 28.	12 d	xxxviii. 17.	1 c	Jer. v. 16.	12 f
xxii. 31.	1 f	xli. 14.	12 k	ix. 22.	5
xxiv. 3, 15.	15	Ps. v. 9.	12 f	xiii. 19.	12 e
xxiv. 4, 16.	1 b	xxxv. 21.	14 b	xx. 12.	1 d
xxvi. 10.	12 d	xxxviii. 13.	12 d	xxxii. 11, 14.	1 b
Deut. xi. 6.	7 a	xxxix. 9.	12 d	xxxii. 19.	8 f
xv. 8.ᵃ	12 b d	xl. 6.	2	l. 25.	12 a
xv. 11.ᵃ	12 b d	xlix. 4.	12 c	l. 26.	12 c
xx. 11.	12 a	li. 15.	12 d	Lam. ii. 16.	7 a
xxviii. 12.	12 d	lxxviii. 2.	12 d	iii. 46.	7 a
Josh. iii. 17.	12 f	lxxix. 23.	12 a	Ezek. i. 1.	12 g
x. 22.	12 c	lxxxi. 10.	14 a	ii. 8.	7 b
Judg. iii. 25, 25.	12 e d	xcviii. 2.	1 d	iii. 2, 27.	12 d
iv. 19.	12 d	civ. 28.	12 d	xvi. 5.	5
xi. 35, 36.	7 a	cv. 41.	12 a	xvi. 25.	11 b
xix. 27.	12 d	cvi. 17.	12 d	xvi. 63.β	12 p
1 Sam. iii. 1.	9	cix. 2.	12 a	xx. 26.	4 b
iii. 15.	12 d	cxviii. 19.	12 c	xxi. 22.	12 b
2 Sam. xi. 11.	5	cxix. 18.	1 e	xxiv. 27.	12 h
1 Kings vi. 18, 29, 32,		cxix. 131.	6	xxv. 9.	12 e
35.	4 a	cxlv. 16.	12 e	xxix. 5.	5
viii. 29, 52.	12 f	cxlvi. 8.	8 e	xxix. 21.	12 p
2 Kings iv. 35.	8 d	Prov. i. 21.	12 o	xxxii. 4.	5
vi. 17, 17.	8 c d	viii. 6.	12 r	xxxiii. 22, 22.	12 d h
vi. 20, 20.	8 c d	xiii. 3.	11 a	xxxiii. 27.	5
ix. 3.	12 a	xiii. 16.	10	xxxvii. 2.	5
ix. 10.	12 d	xx. 13.	8 c	xxxvii. 12.	12 e
xiii. 17, 17.	12 c d	xxiv. 7.	12 d	xxxvii. 13.	12 b
xv. 16.	12 a	xxvii. 5.	1 g	xxxix. 5.	5
xix. 16.	8 c	xxxi. 8, 9.	12 c	xliv. 2.	12 h
1 Chron. ix. 27.	12 q	xxxi. 26.	12 a	xlvi. 1, 1.	12 h
2 Chron. vi. 20, 40.	12 f	Cant. v. 2.	12 b	xlvi. 12.	12 a
vii. 15.	12 f	v. 5.	12 b	Dan. vi. 10.	12 n
xxix. 3.	12 a	v. 6.	12 a	vii. 10.	12 m
Neh. i. 6.	12 f	Isa. v. 14.	6	ix. 18.	12 d
vi. 5.	12 f	x. 14.	7 d	x. 16.	12 d
vii. 3.	12 h	xiv. 17.	12 a	Nah. ii. 6.	12 g
viii. 5, 5.	12 d b	xxii. 22, 22.	12 a e	iii. 13.	12 g b
xiii. 19.	12 d	xxiv. 18.	12 g	Zech. xi. 1.	12 c
Job iii. 1.	12 a	xxvi. 2.	12 c	vii. 4.	8 d
xi. 5.	12 d	xxviii. 24.	12 l	xiii. 1.	12 i
xii. 14.	12 h	xxxv. 5.	8 h	Mal. iii. 10.	12 d

a lit. opening thou shalt open. *β lit.* opening of the mouth may not be to thee.

OPERATION

מַעֲשֶׂה *m.* work, deed : Ps. xxviii. 5: Isa. v. 12.

OPHEL

עֹפֶל *m.* a hill, tumulus ; specially with the *art.* הָ *pr. n.* of a hill or ridge on the east of Mount Zion, surrounded and fortified by a separate wall ; see Robinson's Palestine, I. p. 394 : 2 Chron. xxvii. 3 ; xxxiii. 14 : Neh. iii. 26, 27 ; xi. 21.

OPINION

דֵּעַ *m.* what one knows, opinion, knowledge : Job xxxii. 6, 10, 17.

סְעִפִּים *f. pl.* divided opinions, parties : 1 Kings xviii. 21. Vulg. *usquequo claudicatis in duas partes.*

OPPOSE

שָׂטַם to lie in wait for any one, to persecute ; see *Hate.* KAL *fut.* Job xxx. 21.

OPPRESS

1 אִישׁ *m.* man : Prov. iii. 31, *marg.* ' a man of violence.'

2 דָּכָא to break in pieces, to crush. PIEL *fut.*

3   דַּךְ *adj.* from a root of similar meaning.

4   חָמָס *m.* violence : Prov. iii. 31, *marg.* 'man of violence.'

5   חָמוֹץ *m.* one who suffers violence : Isa. i. 17. Gesenius, oppressor ; who, with many others, takes the word in an *active* sense.

6   יָנָה *m.* to act violently ; to treat violently, to oppress, chiefly of the rich and noble towards the poor, widows, orphans, and strangers ; of fraud and over-reaching in buying and selling, Lev. xxv. 14, 17, with an *acc.* of the person, and מִן to thrust out of a possession by violence, Ezek. xlvi. 18. KAL [a] *part.* Poel. HIPHIL [b] *pret.* [c] *inf.* [d] *fut.* [e] *part.*

7   לָחַץ to press or squeeze very hard ; LXX. θλίβω, Num. xxii. 25 : to oppress, distress persons, a people, by laying them under heavy contributions, or such like constraints or restraints. KAL [a] *pret.* [b] *fut.* [c] *part.* [d] לַחַץ *m.* oppression, troubling of a people ; calamities, distresses.

8   נָגַשׂ to urge, impel, to drive ; to exact tribute, &c. KAL [a] *part.* Poel. NIPHAL [b] *pret.*

9   עֹצֶר *m.* a shutting up ; constraint, oppression, vexation.

10   עָקָה *f.* the primary idea seems to lie in pressing heavily down ; oppression.

11   עָרַץ to terrify, to make afraid. KAL [a] *inf.* [b] עָרִיץ *adj.* violent, fierce.

12   עָשַׁק to treat with violence and injustice, to load with hard, injurious usage ; to bear hard upon a person, in opposition to showing mercy : Prov. xiv. 31, to oppress by violence or fraud : in Micah ii. 2, it seems to include both senses of oppression and fraud. KAL [a] *pret.* [b] *inf.* [c] *fut.* [d] *part.* Poel. [e] *part.* Paül. PUAL [f] *part.* [g] עֹשֶׁק *m.* violence and calumny ; something taken away by force or fraud, unjust gain ; anguish. [h] עָשְׁקָה *f.* anguish, distress. [i] עָשׁוֹק *m.* an oppressor. [k] עֲשׁוּקִים *m. pl.* oppressions, injuries.—[l] מַעֲשַׁקּוֹת *f. pl.* oppressions, forcible exactions.

13   צוּק to be straitened ; to straiten, press upon, distress any one. HIPHIL *part.*

14   צָרַר to press ; to press upon, *i.e.* to persecute, to vex, as a rival. KAL *part.* Poel.

15   רָמַס to tread down. KAL *part.* Poel.

16   רָצַץ to break, to break in or down ; to treat with violence, to vex ; to be shattered, bruised, or crushed. KAL [a] *pret.* [b] *part.* Paül. PIEL [c] *pret.* [d] *fut.* Poel [e] *fut.*

17   שָׁדַד to practise violence, to treat with violence, hence to oppress, to destroy. KAL [a] *pret.* [b] שֹׁד *m.* destruction, oppression.

18   מִשְׂפָּח *m.* a doubtful word, occurring but once : Isa. v. 7, *marg.* 'a scab.' In the Hebrew there is a double and elegant paronomasia, which has probably caused a change of one letter in this word, and makes it likely that it stands for מִסְפָּחַ. LXX. and Jerome, ἀνομίαν ; Chald. oppression ; Kimchi and Aben-Ezra, a scab ; Gesenius, shedding of blood.

Exod. iii. 9, 9.	7 d c	Ps. lv. 3.	10	Isa. xlix. 26.	6 e
xxii. 21.	7 b	lvi. 1.	7 b	li. 13, 13.	13
xxiii. 9.	7 b	lxii. 10.	12 g	lii. 4.	12 a
Lev. xxv. 14, 17.	6 d	lxxi . 4.	12 d	liii. 7.	8 b
Num. x. 9.	14	lxxii. 8.	12 g	liv. 14.	12 g
Deut. xxiii. 16.	6 d	lxxiv. 21.	3	lviii. 6.	16 b
xxiv. 14.	12 c	ciii. 6.	12 e	lix. 13.	12 g
xxvi. 7.	7 d	cvi. 42.	7 b	Jer. vi. 6.	12 g
xxviii. 29, 33.	7 a	cvii. 39.	9	vii. 6.	12 c
Judg. ii. 18.	7 c	cxix. 121.	12 d	xxi. 12.	12 d
iv. 3.	7 a	cxix. 122.	12 c	xxii. 3.	12 i
vi. 9.	7 c	cxix. 134.	12 g	xxii. 17.	12 g
x. 8.	16 e	cxix. 7.	12 e	xxv. 38.	6 a
x. 12.	7 a	Prov. iii. 31.	1, 4	xxx. 20.	7 c
1 Sam. x. 18.	7 c	xiv. 31.	12 d	xlvi. 16.	6 a
xii. 3, 4.	16 a	xxii. 16.	12 d	l. 16.	6 a
2 Kings xiii. 4, 4.	7 d a	xxii. 22.	2	l. 33.	12 e
xiii. 22.	7 a	xxviii. 3.	12 d	Ezek. xviii. 7.	6 b
2 Chron. xvi. 10.	16 d	xxviii. 16.	12 l	xviii. 12, 16.	6 b
Job iii. 18.	8 a	Eccles. iv. 1, 1, 1.	12 k e d	xviii. 18.	12 a
x. 3.	12 c	v. 8.	12 g	xxii. 7.	12 g
xv. 20.	11 b	vii. 7.	12 g	xxii. 29, 29.	12 g a
xx. 19.	16 c	Isa. i. 17.	5	xlv. 8.	6 d
xxvii. 13.	11 b	iii. 5.	8 b	xlv. 18.	6 c
xxxv. 9.	12 k	iii. 12.	8 a	Hos. v. 11.	12 e
xxxvi. 15.	7 d	v. 7.	18	x i. 7.	12 a
Ps. ix. 9.	3	ix. 4.	8 a	Amos iii. 9.	12 k
x. 18, 18.	3, 11 a	xiv. 2, 4.	8 a	iv. 1.	12 d
xii. 5.	17 b	xvi. 4.	15	Micah ii. 2.	12 a
xvii. 9.	17 a	xix. 20.	7 c	Zeph. iii. 1.	6 a
xlii. 9.	7 d	xxiii. 12.	12 f	Zech. vii. 10.	12 c
xliii. 2.	7 d	xxx. 12.	12 g	ix. 8.	8 a
xliv. 24.	7 d	xxxiii. 15. a	12 l	x. 4.	8 a
liv. 3.	11 b	xxxviii. 14.	12 h	Mal. iii. 5.	12 d

a. lit. oppression to me.

ORACLE

דָּבָר word : 2 Sam. xvi. 23, *marg.* 'word.' דְּבִיר *m.* the inner sanctuary of the Mosaic tabernacle and of Solomon's temple, called also the holy of holies : 1 Kings vi. 5, 16, 19, 20, 21, 22, 23, 31 ; vii. 49 ; viii. 6, 8 : 2 Chron. iii. 16 ; iv. 20 ; v. 7, 9 : Ps. xxviii. 2.

ORATOR

לַחַשׁ *m.* whispering, prayer, incantation, charm ; persuasive speech : Isa. iii. 3, *marg.* 'skilful of speech.'

ORCHARD

פַּרְדֵּס *m.* park, pleasure-grounds, place planted with trees. It corresponds to the Gr. παράδεισος, a word applied to the pleasure-gardens and parks, with wild animals, around the residence of the Persian monarchs. Eccles. ii. 5 : Cant. iv. 13.

ORDAIN

1   יָסַד to set, to place, to appoint, to ordain. PIEL *pret.*

2   כּוּן to set upright ; to form ; to fix, to settle. POLEL *pret.*

3   מְנָה Ch. to number ; to constitute, to appoint. PAEL *pret.*

4   נָתַן to give. KAL *pret.*

5   עָמַד to stand, to make to stand, to appoint, establish. HIPHIL *fut.*

6   עָרַךְ to set in successive order, to appoint. KAL [a] *pret.* [b] *part.* Paül.

7   עָשָׂה to make, to constitute, appoint. KAL [a] *fut.* [b] *part.* Paül.

8   פָּעַל to work (emphatical), with attention, to make ready. KAL *fut.*

9   קוּם to rise up ; Piel *sq.* עַל to enjoin upon any one, *pr.* to cause to be imposed upon. PIEL *pret.*

10 שׂוּם to set, put, place ; to establish, to appoint, to make a law ; Gr. νόμον τιθέναι. KAL *pret.*

11 שָׁפַת to set, to put, to place, in an even steady position. KAL *fut.*

Num. xxviii. 6.	7 b	Esth. ix. 27.	9	Isa. xxvi. 12.	11
1 Kings xii. 32, 33.	7 a	Ps. vii. 13.	8	xxx. 33.	6 b
2 Kings xxiii. 5.	4	viii. 2.	1	Jer. i. 5.	4
1 Chron. ix. 22.	1	viii. 3.	2	Dan. ii. 24.	3
xvii. 9.	10	lxxi. 5.	10	Hab. i. 12.	10
2 Chron. xi. 15.	5	cxxxii. 17.	6 a		

ORDER

1 אָסַר to bind, to bind on, to join ; applied to battle, to join battle, to begin the fight. KAL *fut.*

2 דִּבְרָה f. manner, mode : Ps. cx. 4, Lxx. κατὰ τὴν τάξιν ; Heb. vii. 15, κατὰ τὴν ὁμοιότητα.

3 יָד *com.* hand.

4 כּוּן to stand upright ; to set upright, to adjust, direct ; to set right or in good order. NIPHAL [a]*fut.* PULAL [b]*pret.* HIPHIL [c]*inf.* [d]*imp.*

5 סְדָרִים *m. pl.* order, of things arranged in order : Job x. 22, *comp.* Ovid on Chaos, "*Unus chaos, rudis indigestaque moles.*"

6 עָרַךְ to place in a row, to put in order, to arrange ; to prepare, to put battle in array, to set in order words, to set in order a cause. KAL [a]*pret.* [b]*inf.* [c]*imp.* [d]*fut.* [e]*part.* Paül. [f]עֶרֶךְ *m.* row, pile ; preparation, equipment. [g]מַעֲרָכָה f. arrangement, disposition, order.

7 פְּקֻדָּה f. oversight, office, charge.

8 פַּעַם *com.* step, foot, time, or turns.

9 צָוָה to command. PIEL [a]*imp.* [b]*fut.*

10 מִשְׁפָּט *m.* judgment, ordinance.

11 שׂוּם to set, put, or place. KAL *pret.*

12 שָׁלַב to notch into each other, to join by tenon and mortise. PUAL *part.* Exod. xxvi. 17, *i.e.* two tenons to each board, joined one to another, perhaps by transverse pieces of wood under the sockets ; verse 19, or fitted (corresponding) one to another. But Lxx. ἀντιπίπτοντας ἕτερον τῷ ἑτέρῳ, opposite one to another.

13 תָּקַן to be straight, to set in right order, to compose. PIEL *pret.*

Gen. xxii. 9.	6 d	1 Kings xviii. 33.	6 d	Job xxxvii. 19.	6 d
Exod. xxvi. 17.	12	xx. 14.	1	Ps. xxxvii. 23.	4 b
xxvii. 21.	6 d	2 Kings xx. 1.	9 a	xl. 5.	6 b
xxxix. 37.	6 g	1 Chron. vi. 32.	10	l. 21.	6 d
xl. 4, 4.	6 a f	xv. 13.	10	l. 23.	11
xl. 23, 23.	6 d f	xxiii. 31.	6 a	cx. 4.	2
Lev. i. 7, 8, 12.	6 a	xxiv. 19.	7	cxix. 133.	4 d
vi. 12.	6 a	xxv. 2, 6.	3	Eccles. xii. 9.	13
xxiv. 3, 4, 8.	6 d	2 Chron. viii. 14.	10	Isa. ix. 7.	4 c
Josh. ii. 6.	6 e	xxix. 35.	4 a	xxxviii. 1.	9 a
Judg. vi. 26.	6 g	Job x. 22.	5	xliv. 7.	6 d
xiii. 12.	10	xiii. 18.	6 a	Jer. xlvi. 3.	6 c
2 Sam. xvii. 23.	9 b	xxiii. 4.	6 d	Ezek. xli. 6.	8
xxiii. 5.	6 e	xxxiii. 5.	6 c		

ORDINANCE

1 חֹק *m.* something decreed, prescribed, appointed ; statute, ordinance, law. [a]חֻקָּה f. *id.*

2 יָד *com.* hand ; *lit.* at the hands of, under his guidance.

3 מִצְוָה f. commandment.

4 מִשְׁמֶרֶת f. charge.

5 מִשְׁפָּט *m.* judgment.

Exod. xii. 14, 17, 43.	1 a	Num. xxxi. 21.	1 a	Isa. xxiv. 5.	1
xii. 24.	1 a	Josh. xxiv. 25.	1	lviii. 2, 2.	5
xiii. 10.	1 a	1 Sam. xxx. 25.	5	Jer. xxxi. 35.	1 a
xv. 25.	5	2 Kings xvii. 34, 37.	5	xxxi. 36.	1
xviii. 20.	1	2 Chron. xxxiii. 8.	5	xxxiii. 25.	1 a
Lev. xviii. 3, 4.	1 a	xxxv. 13.	5	Ezek. xi. 20.	5
xviii. 30.	4	xxxv. 25.	1	xliii. 11, 11, 18.	5
xxii. 9.	4	Ezra iii. 10.	2	xliv. 5.	1
Num. ix. 12, 14, 14.	1 a	Neh. x. 32.	3	xlv. 14.	1
x. 8.	1 a	Job xxxviii. 33.	1 a	xlvi. 14.	1
xv. 15, 15.	1 a	Ps. xcix. 7.	1	Mal. iii. 7.	1 a
xviii. 8.	1	cxix. 91.	5	iii. 14.	4
xix. 2.	1 a				

ORDINARY

חֹק *m.* something prescribed, appointed : Ezek. xvi. 27.

ORGAN

עוּגָב a wind instrument, pipe, reed ; or one consisting of many pipes : Gen. iv. 21 : Job xxi. 12 ; xxx. 31 : Ps. cl. 4.

ORION

כְּסִיל *m.* as the name of a constellation, according to most of the ancient interpreters, the constellation Orion, which the Orientals call the giant : Job ix. 9 ; xxxviii. 31 : Amos v. 8.

ORNAMENT

1 אֲפֻדָּה f. ephod : Isa. xxx. 22, or the covering overlaying a statue with gold : idols or wood were often thus overlaid with plates of gold or silver.—*Gesenius.*

2 חֲלִי *m.* a jewel or some ornament belonging to women ; so called, perhaps, from its being polished.

3 לִוְיָה f. something added : an ornament forming a graceful addition to the head-dress, perhaps a wreath or garland.

4 עֲדִי *m.* ornament ; collective, ornaments.

5 עֶכֶס *m.* ankle-band, common among Eastern nations ; tinkling ornaments.

6 פְּאֵר *m.* head-dress, tire, turban.

7 צָעָדָה f. ornaments of the legs ; step-chains, attached to the ankle-band, which compelled females to take short and measured steps, or to walk in a stately manner.

8 שַׂהֲרֹנִים *m. pl.* crescents, ornaments like the moon worn on the necks of men, women, and camels.

Exod. xxxiii. 4, 5, 6.	1	Isa. iii. 18.	5	Jer. ii. 32.	4
Judg. viii. 21, 26.	8	iii. 20.	7	iv. 30.	4
2 Sam. i. 24.	4	xxx. 22.	1	Ezek. vii. 20.	4
Prov. i. 9.	3	xlix. 18.	4	xvi. 7, 11.	4
iv. 9.	3	lxi. 10.	6	xxiii. 40.	4
xxv. 12.	2				

ORPHAN

יָתוֹם *m.* fatherless : Lam. v. 3.

OSPRAY

עָזְנִיָּה f. a species of eagle : Lev. xi. 13 : Deut. xiv. 12.

OSSIFRAGE

פֶּרֶס *m.* a species of eagle : Lev. xi. 13 : Deut. xiv. 12.

OSTRICH

יְעֵנִים *m. pl.* ostriches; so called from their greediness and gluttony: Lam. iv. 3.

חֲסִידָה *f.* the stork: Job xxxix. 13. As our translation of this extremely difficult verse stands, the rendering of ostrich must be assigned to this word; but, as Bochart has elaborately shewn, since the whole context (ver. 13–18) refers to the ostrich only, this sentence may very suitably to this reason be rendered, 'even the wings and feathers of the stork,' *i. e.* to the ostrich, as peacock may be translated. This is the interpretation of J. D. Michaelis. The *marg.* takes נוֹצָה to mean an ostrich; or, the feathers of the stork and ostrich.

נוֹצָה *f.* It is doubted whether this word means an ostrich, which is by most modern critics understood to be the proper meaning of רְנָנִים in the former part of the verse; see *Goodly*: it is therefore otherwise rendered 'feathers;' 'pinion' by Gesenius. Job xxxix. 13, *marg.* 'or, feathers of the stork and ostrich.'

OTHER

1 אָח *m.* brother: Gen. xiii. 11.

2 אֶחָד *adj.* one.

3 אָחוֹת *f.* sister.

4 אַחֵר *adj. pr.* after, hinder, following, specially next following, next, second; hence generally, another, other: Gen. viii. 10, &c., frequent. [a] אַחֲרֵי Ch. *adj.* [b] אָחֳרָן Ch. *adj.*

5 רֵעַ *m.* companion.

6 שְׁאָר *m.* rest, residue.

7 שֵׁנִי *adj. ordinal*, second.

No. 4 not included.

Gen. iv. 19.	7	Lev. xiv. 22, 31.	2	1 Kings xviii. 23.	2
xiii. 11.	1	xv. 15, 30.	2	2 Chron. iii. 12, 17.	2
Exod. i. 15.	7	xvi. 8.	2	Neh. iii. 11, 20.	7
xvii. 12.	2	Num. vi. 11.	2	iv. 17.	2
xviii. 4.	2	viii. 12.	2	iii. 38.	7
xviii. 7.	5	xi. 26.	7	Esth. ix. 16.	6
xxv. 12, 32.	7	xxviii. 4, 8.	7	Jer. xxiv. 2.	2
xxv. 19, 33.	2	Judg. xx. 31.	2	xxxvi. 16.	5
xxvi. 27.	7	Ruth i. 4.	7	Ezek. i. 23.	3
xxvii. 15.	7	1 Sam. i. 2.	7	xl. 6.	
xxviii. 10.	7	xv. 4, 5, 40.	2	Dan. ii. 11, 44.	4 b
xxix. 19, 39, 41.	7	2 Sam. iv. 2.	7	iii. 29.	4 b
xxxvi. 25, 32.	7	xii. 1.	2	vii. 20.	4 a
xxxvii. 3, 18.	7	xiv. 6.	2	viii. 3.	7
xxxviii. 15.	7	1 Kings iii. 25.	2	xii. 5.	2
Lev. v. 7.	2	vi. 24, 25, 26, 27, 27, 34.	7	Zech. iii. 3.	2
viii. 22.	7	vii. 16, 17, 18, 20.	7	xi. 7.	2
xii. 8.	2	xii. 29.	2	xi. 14.	7

OUCHES

מִשְׁבְּצוֹת *f. pl.* textures; settings, bezels, in which gems are set: Exod. xxviii. 11, 13, 14, 25; xxxix. 6, 13, 16, 18.

OUGHT

דָּבָר *m.* word, matter, &c.: Exod. v. 11: Josh. xxi. 45.

מְאוּמָה *f.* whatever, something, anything: Gen. xxxix. 6: 1 Sam. xii. 4, 5; xxv. 7: 2 Sam. iii. 35.

מִמְכָּר *m.* a selling: Lev. xxv. 14, *lit.* sell a selling.

OUT, OUTER, OUTMOST, OUTSIDE, OUTWARD

1 חוּץ *m.* without. [a] חִיצוֹן *adj.*

2 קָצֶה *m.* end, extremity, that which is utmost.

3 קִיצוֹן *adj.* uttermost.

Gen. xxiv. 29.	1	Num. xxxiv. 3.	2	Neh. xi. 16.	1 a
xxxix. 12, 15, 18.	1	xxxv. 4.	1	xiii. 8.	1
Exod. xxvi. 10.	3	Judg. vii. 11, 17, 19.	2	Esth. vi. 4.	1 a
Lev. x. 4, 5.	1	2 Sam. xiii. 17, 18.	1	Ezek. x. 5.	1 a
xiv. 3, 45, 53.	1	1 Kings vii. 9.	1	xl. 5.	1
xvii. 3.	1	xxi. 13.	1	xl. 17, 20, 34.	1 a
xxiv. 23.	1	1 Chron. xxvi. 29.	1 a	xliv. 1.	1 a
Num. xii. 14, 15.	1	2 Chron. xxxiii. 15.	1		

OUTCAST

דָּחָה to thrust, to push or knock down. See *Drive, Cast.* NIPHAL *part.* Ps. cxlvii. 2: Isa. xi. 12; lvi. 8.

נָדַח to thrust, to impel; to thrust out. NIPHAL *part.* Isa. xvi. 3, 4; xxvii. 13: Jer. xxx. 17; xlix. 36.

OUTGOING

מוֹצָא *m.* a going out: Ps. lxv. 8. תּוֹצָאוֹת *f. pl.* goings out: Josh. xvii. 9, 18; xviii. 19; xix. 14, 22, 29, 33.

OUTLANDISH

נָכְרִי *adj.* stranger: Neh. xiii. 26.

OUTLIVE

אָרַךְ to be long, to prolong. HIPHIL *pret.* Judg. ii. 7. With יוֹם *m.* day, and אַחַר. *marg.* 'prolonged days after.'

OUTRAGEOUS

שֶׁטֶף *m.* a gushing out, an outpouring: Prov. xxvii. 4.

OUTSTRETCHED

נָטָה to spread out, extend. KAL *part.* Paül, Deut. xxvi. 8: Jer. xxi. 5; xxvii. 5.

OVEN

תַּנּוּר *m.* fire-oven, oven, furnace, for baking bread, was made in the ground, and when heated the cakes were fixed to the sides, and very soon baked: Exod. viii. 3: Lev. ii. 4; vii. 9; xi. 35; xxvi. 26: Ps. xxi. 9: Lam. v. 10: Hos. vii. 4, 6, 7: Mal. iv. 1.

OVER

1 חָלַף to glide along, to pass by. KAL *pret.*

2 יוֹתֵר *m.* what is over and above, rest, residue.

3 עָדַף to be redundant; to be more than enough, to remain over, overplus. KAL [a] *part.* Poel. HIPHIL [b] *pret.*

4 עָמַד to stand. KAL *part.* Poel.

5 רָבָה to multiply. HIPHIL *inf.* "over much."

Exod. xvi. 18.	3 b	Num. vii. 2.	4	Eccles. vii. 17.	5
Lev. xxv. 27.	3 a	Eccles. vii. 16, 16.	4, 2	Cant. ii. 11.	1
Num. iii. 49.	3 a				

OVERCOME

1 נוּד to press or crowd upon any one. KAL *fut.*

2 הָלַם to beat, to strike, to smite. KAL *part.* Paül, overcome with wine, *lit.* smitten; as in Gr. οἰνοπλήξ; Lat. *percussus tempora Baccho.*—Tibull.

3 חֲלֻשָׁה *f.* overthrow, defeat.

4 יָכֹל to be able. KAL *inf.*

5 לָחַם to eat; to fight. NIPHAL *inf. lit.* in fighting.

6 עָבַר to pass over. KAL *pret.*

7 רָהַב to be high-spirited, fierce, full of courage; to press upon greatly, to attack. HIPHIL *pret.*

Gen. xlix. 19, 19.	1	Num. xxii. 11.	5	Isa. xxviii. 1.	2
Exod. xxxii. 18.	3	2 Kings xvi. 5.	5	Jer. xxiii. 9.	6
Num. xiii. 30.	4	Cant. vi. 5.	7		

OVERDRIVE

דָּפַק to thrust, to beat; to drive hard. KAL *pret.* Gen. xxxiii. 13.

OVERFLOW

1 בְּכִי *m.* weeping; applied to the trickling of water in mines.

2 זֶרֶם *m.* shower, storm of rain, storm.

3 יָצַק to pour out. HOPHAL *fut.*

4 מָלֵא to be full. KAL *a pret.* PIEL *b part.*

5 צוּף to flow, to overflow. HIPHIL *pret.*

6 שׁוּק to run over, to overflow. HIPHIL *pret.*

7 שָׁטַף to gush or pour out; to overflow with a violent stream, as an inundation; applied to the inroads of an invader, to heavy loads of affliction, to the rushing of a horse into battle. KAL *a pret.* *b fut.* *c part.* Poel. NIPHAL *d fut.* שֶׁטֶף *m.* outpouring of rain.

Deut. xi. 4.		Ps. lxxviii. 20.	7 b	Ezek. xiii. 11, 13.	7 c
Josh. iii. 15.	4 a	Isa. viii. 8.	7 a	xxxviii. 22.	7 c
1 Chron. xii. 15.	4 b	x. 22.	7 c	Dan. xi. 10, 40.	7 a
Job xxii. 16.	3	xxviii. 2, 15, 18.	7 c	xi. 22.	7 d
xxviii. 11.	1	xxviii. 17.	7 b	xi. 26.	7 b
xxxvii. 25.	7 e	xxx. 28.	7 c	Joel ii. 24.	6
Ps. lxix. 2.	7 a	xliii. 2.	7 b	iii. 13.	6
lxix. 15.	7 b	Jer. xlvii. 2, 2.	7 c b	Hab. iii. 10.	2

OVERLAY

1 חָפָה to cover; to overlay with gold, silver, &c. PIEL *a pret.* *b fut.*

2 טוּחַ to spread over, to daub, to plaster. KAL *inf.*

3 עָלַף to cover, to wrap up; to be covered over. PUAL *part.*

4 צָפָה to cover, or spread over with metal or boards; to gild, to overlay, to wainscot. PIEL *a pret.* *b fut.* PUAL *c part.* *d* צִפּוּי *m.* overlaying, metal laid over.

5 שָׁכַב to lie down. KAL *pret.*

Exod. xxv. 11, 11.	4 a b	Exod. xxvi. 38.	4 a	1 Kings x. 18.	4 b
xxv. 13, 24, 28.	4 a	xxxvii. 2, 4, 11, 15,		2 Kings xviii. 16.	4 a
xxvi. 29, 29.	4 b a	26, 28.	4 a b	1 Chron. xxix. 4.	2
xxvi. 32.	4 c	xxxviii. 2, 6.	4 b	2 Chron. iii. 4, 10.	4 b
xxvi. 37.	4 a	xxxviii. 17, 19.	4 d	iii. 5, 7, 8.	1 b
xxvii. 2, 6.	4 a	xxxviii. 28.	4 a	iii. 9.	1 a
xxx. 3, 5.	4 a	1 Kings iii. 19.	5	iv. 9.	4 a
xxxvi. 34, 34.	4 a b	vi. 20, 21, 21, 28.	4 b	ix. 17.	4 a
xxxvi. 36.	4 b	vi. 22, 22, 30, 32.	4 a	Cant. v. 14.	3

OVERLIVE

אָרַךְ to prolong. HIPHIL *pret.* Josh. xxiv. 31, *lit.* prolonged their days after.

OVERPASS

עָבַר to pass over. KAL *pret.* Jer. v. 28. *fut.* Ps. lvii. 1: Isa. xxvi. 20.

OVERPLUS (See OVER)

OVERRUN

עָבַר to pass over. KAL *fut.* 2 Sam. xviii. 23, *lit.* passed. *part.* Poel, Nah. i. 8.

OVERSEE

1 נָצַח to be strong, powerful, valiant; to superintend. PIEL *part.*

2 נָתַן to give. KAL *part.* Paül, Neh. xiii. 4.

3 פָּקַד to go to see; to set over, to make overseer. KAL *a part.* Paül, כתיב. HIPHIL *b pret.* *c fut.* HOPHAL *d part.* *e* פְּקֻדָּה *f.* charge, oversight. *f* פָּקִיד *m.* an officer.

4 מִשְׁגֶּה *m.* error, oversight.

5 שָׁמַר see *Officer.* KAL *part.* Poel.

Gen. xxxix. 4.	3 c	2 Kings xii. 11.	3 d, or 3 a	2 Chron. xxxiv. 13.	1
xxxix. 5.	3 b	xxii. 5, 9.	3 d	Neh. xi. 9, 14, 22.	3 f
xliii. 12.	4	2 Chron. ii. 2, 18.	1	xii. 42.	3 f
Num. iii. 32.	3 e	xxxi. 13.	3 f	xiii. 4.	2
iv. 16.	3 e	xxxiv. 10, 12, 17.	3 d	Prov. vi. 7.	5

OVERSPREAD

כָּנָף *com.* wing; the forces of a great king or state: Dan. ix. 27, *lit.* the army of abominations. Gesenius interprets it, of the highest point, battlement, or pinnacle of the temple; and would translate it, *super fastigio abominationis erit vastator;* or, *super fastigio (templi collocatæ erunt) abominationes vastatoris, sc. idola Antiochi.* Comp. πτερύγιον τοῦ ἱεροῦ, Matt. iv. 5.

נָפַץ see *Scatter;* of a people, to disperse themselves. KAL *pret.* Gen. ix. 19, *lit.* from these the whole earth dispersed itself.

OVERTAKE

1 דָּבַק to cleave, to adhere; to come upon, to overtake. HIPHIL *a pret.* *b fut.*

2 נָגַשׁ to come near. NIPHAL *a pret.* HIPHIL *b fut.*

3 נָשַׂג to reach, to extend unto; to come up with; to reach, so as to seize, take hold of; applied to blessings or calamities coming on a person. HIPHIL *a pret.* *b inf.* *c fut.* *d part.*

Gen. xxxi. 23.	1 b	Judg. xviii. 22.	1 b	Jer. xxxix. 5.	3 c
xxxi. 25.	3 c	xx. 42.	1 a	xlii. 16.	3 c
xliv. 4.	3 a	1 Sam. xxx. 8, 8.	3 c b c	lii. 8.	3 c
xliv. 6.	3 c	2 Sam. xv. 14.	3 a	Lam. i. 3.	3 a
Exod. xiv. 9.	3 a	2 Kings xxv. 5.	3 a	Hos. ii. 7.	3 c
xv. 9.	3 d	1 Chron. xxi. 12.	3 d	x. 9.	3 c
Deut. xix. 6.	3 a	Ps. xviii. 37.	3 c	Amos ix. 10.	2 b
xxviii. 2, 15, 45.	3 a	Isa. lix. 9.	3 c	ix. 13.	2 a
Josh. ii. 5.	3 c				

OVERTHROW

1 דָּחָה to thrust, to push down. KAL *inf.*

2   מִדְחֲפֹת   *f. pl.* thrustings, impulses, *sc.* in order to a fall; hence overthrow, ruin.

3   הָפַךְ   to turn, turn over; overturn, overthrow; see *Overturn*. KAL [a] *pret.* [b] *inf.* [c] *fut.* [d] *part.* Paül. NIPHAL [e] *part.* הַסֵּכָה [f] *f.* overturning. [g] מַהְפֵּכָה *f.* overturning when rendered as a verb, *lit.* as the overthrow of.

4   הָרַס   to throw down. KAL [a] *imp.* [b] *fut.* NIPHAL [c] *fut.* PIEL [d] *inf.* [e] *fut.*

5   כָּשַׁל   to be weak, to falter, to stumble. NIPHAL [a] *fut.* HOPHAL [b] *part.*

6   נָטָה   to stretch out, to turn aside; to turn away, to thrust out, *sc.* from a way. HIPHIL *inf.*

7   נָעַר   to shake, to shake off. PIEL [a] *pret.* [b] *fut.*

8   נָפַל   to fall. KAL [a] *inf.* [b] *fut.* HIPHIL [c] *inf.*

9   נָתַץ   to tear or break down. PIEL *pret.*

10   סָלַף   to pervert, to wrest; to subvert, to overthrow. PIEL [a] *fut.* [b] *part.*

11   עָוַת   to be crooked; to bend, to pervert, subvert. PIEL *pret.*

12   שָׁמַד   to destroy. NIPHAL *fut.*

13   שָׁמַט   to thrust, to cast down. NIPHAL *pret.*

Gen. xix. 21.	3 b	Job xii. 19.	10 a	Prov. xxii. 12.	10 a		
xix. 25.	3 c	xix. 6.	11	xxix. 4.	4 b		
xix. 29, 29.	3 b f	Ps. cvi. 26, 27.	8 c	Isa. i. 7.	3 g		
Exod. xiv. 27.	7 b	cxxxvi. 15.	7 a	xiii. 19.	3 g		
xv. 7.	4 b	cxl. 4.	1	Jer. xviii. 23.	5		
xxiii. 24.	4 d e	cxl. 11.	2	xx. 16.	3 a		
Deut. xii. 3.	9	cxli. 6.	13	xlix. 18.	3 g		
xxix. 23, 23.	3 g a	Prov. xi. 11.	4 c	l. 40.	3 g		
Judg. ix. 40.	8 b	xii. 7.	3 b	Lam. iv. 6.	3 d		
2 Sam. x. 3.	3 b	xiii. 6.	10 a	Dan. xi. 41.	5 a		
xi. 25.	4 a	xiv. 11.	12	Amos iv. 11, 11.	3 a g		
xvii. 9.	8 a	xviii. 5.	6	Jonah iii. 4.	3 e		
1 Chron. xix. 3.	3 b	xxi. 12.	10 b	Hag. ii. 22, 22.	3 a		
2 Chron. xiv. 13.	8 b						

OVERTURN

1   הָפַךְ   to turn; to overturn, a chariot, a tent, cities, a land, mountains, men. LXX. καταστρέφω. KAL [a] *pret.* [b] *fut.*

2   עֵוָה   *f.* overturning, overthrow.

3   שׂוּם   to set, place. KAL *fut.*

Judg. vii. 13.	1 b	Job xxviii. 9.	1 a	Ezek. xxi. 27, 27,	
Job ix. 5.	1 a	xxxiv. 25.	1 a	27. a	2, 2, 2, 3
xii. 15.	1 b				

a lit. perverted, perverted, perverted, will I set it.

OVERWHELM

1   כָּסָה   to cover, conceal. PIEL [a] *pret.* [b] *fut.*

2   נָפַל   to fall. HIPHIL *fut.*

3   עָטַף   to put on, to be covered; to the mind covered or muffled up with sorrow; see *Faint*. KAL [a] *inf.* [b] *fut.* HITHPAEL [c] *inf.* [d] *fut.*

4   שָׁטַף   to overflow. KAL *pret.*

Job vi. 27.	2	Ps. lxxvii. 3.	3 d	Ps. cxxiv. 4.	4
Ps. lv. 5.	1 b	lxxviii. 53.	1 a	cxlii. 3.	3 c
lxi. 2.	3 a	cii. title.	3 b	cxliii. 4.	3 d

OWL

1   בַּת   *f.* daughter.

2   יַעֲנָה   *f.* (see *Ostrich*), the female ostrich: Bochart, Hieroz. II. 230.

3   כּוֹס   *f.* a species of unclean bird, living among ruins. The ancient versions render it owl, but against the etymology. Bochart more correctly, Hieroz. II. p. 267, understands the pelican or cormorant, so called from the receptacle or pouch under the throat.

4   לִילִית   *f.* screech-owl; a bird of the owl kind, frequenting ruined buildings: Isa. xxxiv. 14, *marg.* 'or, night monster;' probably from לַיְל night.

5   יַנְשׁוּף   *m.* an unclean bird, probably a water or marsh-fowl, frequenting deserts or marshes. Lxx. and Vulg. render it Ibis, *i. e.* the Egyptian heron; Chald. and Syr. the owl, which also Bochart adopts, Hieroz. II. 281, and supposes it to be derived from נֶשֶׁף twilight. Most probably some species of heron or crane is to be understood, whose cry resembles the blowing of a horn or trumpet, as the ardea stellaris or bittern, the ardea agami or trumpeter bird, or the common crane, &c., and this is supported by the etymology from נָשַׁף to blow. In the list of unclean birds, Lev. xi, this is followed by the תִּנְשֶׁמֶת, derived from a similar verb, נָשַׁם.—*Gesenius.*

6   קִפּוֹז   *m.* great owl: Isa. xxxiv. 15, or, *serpens jaculus*, arrowsnake, from its darting suddenly upon a man, and inevitably killing him; it abounds only in desolate places.—*Bochart, Hieroz.* II. 408.

Lev. xi. 16.	1, 2	Ps. cii. 6.	3	Isa. xxxiv. 15.	6
xi. 17, 17.	3, 5	Isa. xiii. 21.	1, 2	xliii. 20.	1, 2
Deut. xiv. 15.	1, 2	xxxiv. 11.	5	Jer. l. 39.	1, 2
xiv. 16, 16.	3, 5	xxxiv. 13.	1, 2	Micah i. 8.	1, 2
Job xxx. 29.	1, 2	xxxiv. 14.	3		

OWNER

אָדוֹן   *m.* master, lord, *dominus;* of an owner, and of a ruler: 1 Kings xvi. 24.

בַּעַל   *m.* lord, master, possessor, owner: Exod. xxi. 28, 29, 29, 34, 34, 36; xxii. 11, 12, 14, 15: Job xxxi. 39: Prov. i. 19: Eccles. v. 11, 13.

קָנָה   to get, gain, obtain; to own, to possess. KAL *part.* Poel, Isa. i. 3.

OX

1   אֶלֶף   *m.* an ox or cow; *pl.* cattle, oxen; *lit.* herd, collection of cattle. [a] אַלּוּף and אַלֻּף *m.* oxen, cattle, *i. e.* beasts that are confined, tamed.

2   בָּקָר   *com.* a beeve, Lat. *bos*, male or female, ox or cow, so called as used for ploughing; collectively oxen, cattle, herd of neat cattle.

3   פַּר   and פָּר   *m.* bull, young bullock.

4   שׁוֹר   *m.* an ox, bullock, so called from its strength, boldness: Gen. xxxii. 5, &c.

5   תְּאוֹ   *m.* wild ox; or rather a species of antelope or mountain goat, so called from its swiftness; see *Bull*.

6   תּוֹר   Ch. bullocks.

No. 4 not included.

Gen. xii. 16.	2	Exod. xxiv. 5.	3	Deut. xiv. 26.	2
xx. 14.	2	Num. vii. 3, 6, 7, 8,		Judg. iii. 31.	2
xxi. 27.	2	17, 23, 29, 35, 41,		1 Sam. xi. 7, 7.	2
xxxiv. 28.	2	47, 53, 59, 65, 71,		xiv. 32.	2
Exod. ix. 3.	2	77, 83, 87, 88.	2	xv. 9, 14, 15, 21.	2
xx. 24.	2	xxii. 40.	2	xxvii. 9.	2
xxii. 1, 1, 1.	4, 2, 4	xxiii. 1.		2 Sam. vi. 6.	2
xxiv. 3, 3.	2, 4	Deut. xiv. 5.	5	xxiv. 22, 22, 24.	2

1 Kings i. 9.	2	2 Chron. v. 6.	2	Ps. viii. 7.	1		
iv. 23, 23.	2	vii. 5.	2	cxliv. 14.	1 a		
vii. 25, 29, 29, 44.	2	xv. 11.	2	Prov. xiv. 4, 4.	1, 4		
viii. 5, 63.	2	xviii. 2.	2	Isa. xi. 7.	2		
xix. 20, 21, 21.	2	xxix. 33.	2	xxii. 13.	2		
2 Kings v. 26.	2	xxxi. 6.	2	xxx. 24.	1		
xvi. 17.	2	xxxv. 8, 9, 12.	2	Jer. xi. 19.	1 a		
1 Chron. xii. 40, 40.	2	Job i. 3, 14.	2	Dan. iv. 25, 32, 33.	6		
xiii. 9.	2	xl. 15.	2	v. 21.	6		
xxi. 23.	2	xlii. 12.	2	Amos vi. 12.	2		
2 Chron. iv. 3, 3, 4, 15.	2						

PACE

צַעַד *m.* step : 2 Sam. vi. 13.

PACIFY

יָנַח see *Leave*; or from נוּחַ to cause to rest, to quiet. HI-PHIL *fut.* Eccles. x. 4.

כָּפָה to bend, to bow; to tame, to subdue. KAL *fut.* Prov. xxi. 14. LXX. ἀνατρέπει ὀργάς, and so Syr., *contr.* Symmachus σβέσει ὀργήν. Vulg. *extinguit iras.*

כָּפַר to make atonement, to reconcile. PIEL *inf.* Ezek. xvi. 63. *fut.* Prov. xvi. 14.

שָׁכַךְ to subside, to still; to be appeased. KAL *pret.* Esth. vii. 10.

PADDLE

יָתֵד *f.* a pin, nail; a little spade, paddle : Deut. xxiii. 13.

PAIN

1 חֵבֶל *com.* mostly in the plural, writhings, pains, pangs.

2 חוּל to twist oneself with pain, to writhe, to be in pain. KAL [a] *pret.* [b] *inf.* [c] *imp.* KAL and HIPHIL [d] *fut.* HITH-POLEL [e] *part.* [f] חִיל *m.* pain. [g] חַלְחָלָה *f.* great pain.

3 חָלָה to be weak, sick; to be wearied. NIPHAL *pret.*

4 יָחַל the same as חוּל, to be in pain. HIPHIL *fut.*

5 כָּאַב to be in great pain; very sore in body, which seems the primary meaning in Gen. xxxiv. 25; applied also to the mind, and by a figure to a dead body. KAL [a] *fut.* [b] כְּאֵב *m.* pain, sorrow. מַכְאוֹב [b] *m. id.*

6 עָמָל *m.* labour.

7 צִיר *m.* writhings, throes, pains.

8 מֵצַר *m.* straitness, distress.

1 Sam. iv. 19.	7	Isa. xiii. 8.	2 d	Jer. xv. 18.	5 b
Job xiv. 22.	5 a	xxi. 3.	2 g	xxii. 23.	2 f
xv. 20.	2 e	xxiii. 5.	2 d	xxiii. 23.	2 d
xxxiii. 19.	5 c	xxvi. 17.	2 d	li. 8.	5 c
Ps. xxv. 18.	6	xxvi. 18.	2 a	Ezek. xxx. 4, 9.	2 d
xlviii. 6.	2 f	lxvi. 7.	1	xxx. 16.β	2 b d
lv. 4.	2 d	Jer. iv. 19.	4, or 2 d	Joel ii. 6.	2 d
lxxiii. 16.a	6	vi. 24.	2 f	Micah iv. 10.	2 c
cxvi. 3.	8	xii. 13.	3	Nah. ii. 10.	2 g

a marg. 'it was labour in mine eyes.'   β *lit.* in having pain shall have pain.

PAINT

כָּחַל to paint the eyes with stibium. KAL *pret.* Ezek. xxiii. 40. See פּוּךְ below.

מָשַׁח to spread over with anything, to anoint; to paint. KAL *inf.* Jer. xxii. 14.

פּוּךְ *m.* paint used by the Hebrew women, a powder producing a black colour, commonly prepared from antimony, or from lead ore and zinc, which they mixed with water, and spread upon the eyelids in such a way that the white of the eyes might appear more white by being surrounded by a black margin : 2 Kings ix. 30, *marg.* 'put her eyes in painting :' Jer. iv. 30.

שׂוּם to put or set. KAL *fut.* 2 Kings ix. 30, *marg.* 'as above,' *i. e.* adjusted or set off her eyes.

PALACE

1 אַרְמוֹן *m.* a fortress, castle, palace, so called from its height : 1 Kings xvi. 18, the fortress of the king's house, the innermost part as the highest and strongest, the citadel. Spoken of the citadel of a hostile metropolis, Isa. xxv. 2. — 1 Kings xvi. 18, &c.: Ezek. xix. 7. See *Desolate.* [a] הַרְמוֹן *m. id.*

2 בִּירָה *f.* a fortress, castle, fortified palace. [a] בִּירָה Ch. *f. id.*

3 בַּיִת *m.* house. [a] בִּיתָן *m.* great house.

4 הֵיכָל *com.* a large building, edifice, a palace. [a] הֵיכָל Ch.

5 טִירָה *f.* a tower, castle, palace; surrounded by a wall, inclosed.

6 אַפֶּדֶן *m.* a palace.

No. 1 not included.

1 Kings xxi. 1.	4	Esth. ii. 3, 5, 8.	2	Isa. xxxix. 7.	4
2 Kings xx. 18.	4	iii. 15.	2	Ezek. xxv. 4.	5
1 Chron. xxix. 1, 19.	2	vii. 7, 8.	3 a	Dan. i. 4.	4
2 Chron. ix. 11.	3	viii. 14.	2	iv. 4, 29.a	4 a
Ezra iv. 14.	4 a	ix. 6, 11, 12.	2	v. 5.	4 a
vi. 2.	2 a	Ps. xlv. 8, 15.	4	vi. 18.	4 a
Neh. i. 1.	2	cxliv. 12.	4	viii. 2.	2
ii. 8.	2	Prov. xxx. 28.	4	xi. 45.	6
vii. 2.	2	Cant. viii. 9.	5	Amos iv. 3.	1 a
Esth. i. 2.	2	Isa. xiii. 22.	4	Nah. ii. 6.	4
i. 5, 5.	2, 3 a				

a or, upon the palace, *i. e.* on the flat roof.

PALE

חָוַר to become white; of the face, to wax pale, *sc.* for shame. KAL *fut.* Isa. xxix. 22.

יֵרָקוֹן *m.* of persons, it implies paleness of countenance, that ghastly greenish yellow tinge which arises from sudden and overwhelming affright.—*Gesenius.* Jer. xxx. 6.

PALM

כַּף *f.* the hollow of the hand : Lev. xiv. 15, 26 : 1 Sam. v. 4 : 2 Kings ix. 35 : Isa. xlix. 16 : Dan. x. 10.

PALM-TREE

תָּמָר *m.* the palm-tree, whose trunk is large, round, strait, and lofty, having no branches; covered with a rough thick bark, rising all the way with several scaly knots, by which a person with a loose bandage about his body and the tree, may readily climb to the top of it, slipping the bandage still upwards as he ascends. Cant. vii. 8. The top is crowned with a large tuft of spiring leaves, from ten to eighteen feet long : the whole is very beautiful. At the bottom of the leaves the fruit called dates grows in clusters, like grapes, sweet and agreeable to the palate.—*Poinet.* p. 136; *Cels. Hierobot.* The palm-tree, as Dr. Shaw was informed (Travels, p. 244), is in its greatest vigour about thirty years after it is planted, and continues in full vigour about seventy years longer; bearing all this while every year about three or four hundred pounds weight of dates. Ps. xcii. 12, 13, 14. This tree, though now rare in the Holy Land, abounded

there of old, especially in the southern part, where several places were named after it (Deut. xxxiv. 3, 2 Chron.
xx. 2). Hence it appears on Roman coins as the symbol
of Judea.—*Alexander.* The palm-tree yields a kind of
honey, which comes under the general name of דְּבַשׁ,
which ferments and becomes intoxicating; being distilled, yields an agreeable spirit, supposed to be the
strong drink of Scripture: Num. xxviii. 7: Isa. v. 11.—
Exod. xv. 27: Lev. xxiii. 40: Num. xxxiii. 9: Deut.
xxxiv. 3: Judg. i. 16; iii. 13: 2 Chron. xxviii. 15: Neh.
viii. 15: Ps. xcii. 12: Cant. vii. 7, 8: Joel i. 12. תֹּמֶר *m.*
palm-tree, or column: Judg. iv. 5: Jer. x. 5. תִּמֹרָה *f.*
palm-tree, *i. e.* artificial, as an architectural ornament:
1 Kings vi. 29, 32, 32, 35; vii. 36: 2 Chron. iii. 5: Ezek.
xl. 16, 22, 26, 31, 34, 37; xli. 18, 18, 19, 19, 20, 25, 26.

PALMER-WORM

גָּזָם   *m.* eruca; a species of locust, so called from its cutting
the bark and tender branches of trees, not yet winged:
Joel i. 4; ii. 25: Amos iv. 9.

PAN

כִּיּוֹר   *m.* a small basin, fire-pot, fire-pan, for boiling or roasting:
1 Sam. ii. 14.

חֲבִתִּים   *m. pl.* things cooked or fried: 1 Chron. ix. 31. מַחֲבַת *f.*
a pan, a frying-pan, or flat iron plate for baking cakes:
Lev. ii. 5, *marg.* 'or, on a flat plate, *or,* slice:' vi. 21,
vii. 9, *marg. id.*; 1 Chron. xxiii. 29, *marg.* 'or, flat plate;'
Ezek. iv. 3, *marg.* 'or, a flat plate, *or,* slice.'

מַשְׂרֵת   *f.* a frying-pan: 2 Sam. xiii. 9.

סִיר   *com.* pot for boiling: see *Pot:* Exod. xxvii. 3.

פָּרוּר   *m.* pot for boiling: Num. xi. 8.

צֵלָחָה   *f.* a dish or platter, into which things are poured for being
served up: 2 Chron. xxxv. 13.

PANG

חֵבֶל   *com.* mostly in the plural, writhings, pains, pangs: Isa.
xxvi. 17: Jer. xxii. 23.

חִיל   *m.* pain, pang, especially of childbirth: Jer. l. 43; Micah
iv. 9.

צִיר   *m.* writhing, pain: Isa. xiii. 8; xxi. 3, 3.

צָרַר   to be in distress. HIPHIL *part.* Jer. xlviii. 41; xlix. 22.

PANNAG

פַּנַּג   *m.* perhaps a kind of pastry or sweet cake.—*Gesenius.*
Ezek. xxvii. 17.

PANT

סָחַר   to go about; Pilp. to move about rapidly, *e. g.* of the
heart, to palpitate strongly. PILPEL *pret.* Ps. xxxviii.
10.

עָרַג   to cry, to long for, according to the Rabbins, who say that
it refers to the cry of the stag; but the rendering of
Gesenius, drawn from the Arabic, seems more suitable,
to rise, ascend; *seq.* עַל and אֶל to look up towards, to long
for; Gr. ὀρέγω. KAL *fut.* Ps. xlii. 1, *marg.* 'brayeth,'
1, "after the water-brooks," may be translated 'by' or

'beside the water-brooks,' intended to represent the deer
standing on the brink of the channels in which water
usually flowed, but which had become dry.

שָׁאַף   to breathe hard, to pant, to pant after. KAL *fut.* Ps. cxix.
131. *part.* Poel, Amos ii. 7.

תָּעָה   to go astray, to wander. KAL *pret.* Isa. xxi. 4, *marg.* 'or,
thy mind wandered.' It is also used of drunken per-
sons, see Isa. xxviii. 7, and hence *trop.* of the mind;
my heart reeleth, is seized with giddiness.—*Gesenius.*

PAP

שַׁד   *m.* breasts: Ezek. xxiii. 21.

PAPER-REED

עָרוֹת   *f. pl.* This is a word of difficult interpretation; it probably means green pastures, or fields and meadows, that
were beside the brooks or along the banks of the Nile:
Isa. xix. 7.

PARABLE

מָשָׁל   *m.* a similitude, parable; see *Proverb:* Num. xxiii. 7, 18;
xxiv. 3, 15, 20, 21, 23: Job xxvii. 1; xxix. 1: Ps. xlix.
4; lxxviii. 2: Prov. xxvi. 7, 9: Ezek. xvii. 2; xx. 49:
xxiv. 3: Micah ii. 4: Hab. ii. 6.

PARAMOUR

פִּלֶגֶשׁ   *f.* concubine: Ezek. xxiii. 20.

PARBAR

פַּרְבָּר   *m.* Targ. and Talm. make this word to mean suburb; Gesenius, probably the open porticoes surrounding the
courts of the temple, from which was the entrance to
the cells or chambers: 1 Chron. xxvi. 18, 18.

PARCEL

חֶלְקָה   *f.* portion, part: Gen. xxxiii. 19: Josh. xxiv. 32: Ruth
iv. 3: 1 Chron. xi. 13, 14.

PARCH

חֲרֵרִים   *m. pl.* arid places, parched or burnt by the sun: Jer.
xvii. 6.

קָלָה   to roast, to parch, as ears of corn or pulse. KAL *part.*
Paül, Josh. v. 11. קָלִי and קָלִיא *m.* parched corn or
pulse: Lev. xxiii. 14: Ruth ii. 14: 1 Sam. xvii. 17; xxv.
18: 2 Sam. xvii. 28, 28.

שָׁרָב   *m.* heat of the sun; the Serab, or Mirage, having the
appearance of a sea or lake: hence the beauty of the
following passage, Isa. xxxv. 7, the mirage shall become a lake; the deceitful appearance of a lake shall
become a real lake.

PARDON

1   כָּפַר   to cover; to make atonement; to be reconciled. PIEL *fut.*

2   נָשָׂא   to lift up, to bear; to take away sin, guilt, to forgive. KAL
ᵃ*imp.* ᵇ*fut.* ᶜ*part.* Poel.

3   סָלַח   to forgive, to pardon; used only of God when offended.
KAL ᵃ*pret.* ᵇ*inf.* ᶜ*imp.* ᵈ*fut.* ᵉ סְלִיחָה *f.* pardon.

4   רָצָה   to delight in; to receive graciously; to satisfy or be satis-

fied, as one to whom expiation has been made. NIPHAL *pret.*

Exod. xxiii. 21.	2 b	2 Kings xxiv. 4.	3 b	Isa. lv. 7.β	3 b
xxxiv. 9.	3 a	2 Chron. xxx. 18.	1	Jer. v. 1, 7.	3 d
Num. xiv. 19.	3 c	Neh. ix. 17.α	3 e	xxxiii. 8.	3 a
xiv. 20.	3 a	Job vii. 21.	2 b	l. 20.	3 d
1 Sam. xv. 25.	2 a	Ps. xxv. 11.	3 a	Lam. iii. 42.	3 a
2 Kings v. 18, 18.	3 d	Isa. xl. 2.	4	Micah vii. 18.	2 c

α marg. 'a God of pardons.' *β marg.* 'he will multiply to pardon.'

PARE

עָשָׂה to do. KAL *pret.* Deut. xxi. 12, *marg.* 'make, dress, or suffer to grow.'

PARLOUR

חֶדֶר *m.* an apartment, chamber, especially an inner one : 1 Chron. xxviii. 11.

לִשְׁכָּה *f.* (see *Chamber*), once of Solomon's hall for eating : 1 Sam. ix. 22.

עֲלִיָּה *f.* an upper chamber (see *Chamber*); which being separate from the rest of the house facilitated the escape of Ehud : Judg. iii. 20, 23, 24, 25.

PART, PARTNER

1. בַּד *m.* separation, a part.
2. בֶּתֶר *m.* a piece, part, of a victim as cut up.
3. גֶּזֶר *m.* piece, part.
4. דָּבָר *m.* word, thing, matter, &c.
5. חָלַק to divide into parts, to part. KAL a*fut.* b*part.* Poel. NIPHAL c*fut.* PIEL d*pret.* e*fut.* f חֵלֶק *m.* a portion; Num. xviii. 20, &c. g חֶלְקָה *f. id.*
6. חָצָה to divide, especially into two parts. KAL a*fut.* NIPHAL b*fut.* c חֲצִי *m.* a half.
7. יָד *com.* the hand. Gesenius, perhaps *pr.* a handful.
8. יַרְכָּה *f.* side.
9. מְנָה *f.* portion. מְן Ch. part of anything.
10. נָצַל to deliver. HIPHIL *part.*
11. נֵתַח *m.* piece cut off.
12. פֵּאָה *f.* side, extreme part.
13. פֶּה *m.* mouth ; portion, part.
14. פֶּלֶךְ *m.* circle, circuit, district.
15. פָּרַד to break off, to break in pieces, to separate by breaking. NIPHAL a*fut.* HIPHIL b*fut.*
16. פַּס Ch. *m.* palm of the hand.
17. פָּרַס to break, to cleave, to divide. HIPHIL *part.*
18. פָּתַת to break, to break in pieces. KAL *inf.*
19. קָצֶה *m.* the end or extremity of a thing ; there is a twofold extremity, that which is utmost and that which is nearest. The word takes in both in one text, Ps. xix. 6. In Job xxvi. 14 we are to understand it of the nearest extremity, implying that there are many and glorious things not to be reached. a קָצֶה *f. id.* b קְצָת Ch. *f. id.* "partly," *lit.* of part.

No. 5 f not included.

Gen. ii. 10.	15 a	Lev. ii. 6.	18	Lev. xiii. 41.	12
xlvii. 24.	7	vii. 33.	9	Deut. xiv. 6.	17
Exod. xxix. 26.	9	viii. 29.	9	Ruth i. 17.	15 b
Lev. i. 8.	11	xi. 3.	17	ii. 3.	5 g

1 Sam. xxx. 24, 24, 24.	5 f f a	Neh. xi. 1.	7	Jer. xxxiv. 18, 19.	2
2 Sam. xiv. 6.α	10	Job xxvi. 14.	19	Ezek. xxxviii. 15.	8
		xxxviii. 24.	5 c	xxxix. 2.	8
		xix. 43.	7	Dan. i. 2.	19 a
1 Kings vi. 38.	4	xli. 12.	6 a	ii. 33, 33, 41, 41,	
xvi. 21.	1	Ps. xxii. 18.	5 e	42, 42.	9 a
2 Kings ii. 11.	15 b	cxxxvi. 13.	3	ii. 42, 42.	19 b, 9 a
ii. 14.	6 b	Prov. xvii. 2.	5 a	v. 5, 24.	16
xi. 7.	7	xviii. 18.	15 b	Joel iii. 2.	5 d
Neh. iii. 9, 12, 14, 15, 16, 17, 17, 18.	14	xxix. 24.	5 b	Zech. xiii. 8.	13
		Isa. xliv. 16, 16, 19.	6 c		

α marg. 'no deliverer between them.'

PARTAKER

חֵלֶק *m.* portion : Ps. l. 18, *marg.* 'thy portion was with.'

PARTIAL

נָשָׂא to lift up, to accept. KAL *part.* Poel, Mal. ii. 9, *marg.* 'accepted faces, *or,* lifted up the face against.'

PARTING

אֵם *f.* mother : Ezek. xxi. 21, *marg.* 'at the mother of the way.'

PARTITION

עָבַר to pass; to make to pass, *e. g.* a bar or bolt, hence to shut up or close with bolts. PIEL *fut.* 1 Kings vi. 21, and he closed up with golden chains (instead of bars or bolts) before the holy of holies.

PARTRIDGE

קֹרֵא *m.* a partridge; *pr.* the crier, caller; as in other languages. In Jer. xvii. 11 there is an allusion to the idea of ancient naturalists, that the partridge steals the eggs of other birds, and sits upon them ; the allusion, however, is evidently to the uncertainty in the hatching of eggs, in consequence of the nest being on the ground. The Arabs catch partridges by hunting them down. 1 Sam. xxvi. 20 : Jer. xvii. 11.

PASS, PASSAGE, PASSENGER, PASSOVER

1. גָּדַל to be or become great. KAL *fut.*
2. דֶּרֶךְ *com.* way ; passengers, *lit.* passers of the way.
3. הָלַךְ to walk, to go. KAL a*fut.* b*part.* Poel.
4. חָלַף to slip, glide, spoken of the swift motion of anything smooth ; hence to pass by, to pass on, to pass away; to pass through, &c. KAL a*pret.* b*inf.* c*fut.* חֲלַף Ch. P'AL d*fut.*
5. עָבַר to pass over, to pass through, to pass beyond, to pass by, to pass along or away ; to pass through fire in consecration to some idol ; or to be destroyed by fire. KAL a*pret.* b*inf.* c*imp.* d*fut.* e*part.* Poel. NIPHAL f*fut.* HIPHIL g*pret.* h*inf.* i*fut.* k*part.* l עֵבֶר *m.* passage. m מַעֲבָר *m.* a passing over ; a pass of the mountain. n מַעְבָּרָה *f. id.*
6. עָדָה to pass, to pass over or by. KAL a*pret.* עֲדָה Ch. *id.* P'AL b*pret.* c*fut.*
7. פָּנָה to turn, to turn away, to pass away. KAL *pret.*
8. פָּסַח to leap over, to pass over ; more specifically, to ward off

a blow, to bend or spring forward, as bending or kneeling on one knee (compare פָּסַח to go halting, lame of one limb, as Jacob) in act and posture to ward off either a stroke, or to oppose the threatened entrance of an enemy. KAL [a] *pret.* [b] *inf.* [c] פֶּסַח *m.* a passing over, sparing, deliverance from punishment and calamity; hence the sacrifice instituted on account of the immunity of the Israelites, the paschal lamb, the passover, described Exod. xii. 27, the sacrifice of sparing (*pr.* of passing-over) is this to Jehovah, &c.; the festival of the passover, paschal-day, *i. e.* the fourteenth day of the month Nisan, Lev. xxiii. 5, which was followed by the seven days' festival of unleavened bread: Exod. xii. 11, &c.

No. 8 c, *Passover*, not included.

Gen. viii. 1.	5 i	Josh. xxii. 11.	5 l	Job ix. 26.	4 a	
xii. 6.	5 d	xxii. 19.	5 c	xi. 16.	5 a	
xv. 17.	5 a	xxiv. 17.	5 a	xiv. 5.	5 d	
xviii. 3, 5.	5 d	Judg. iii. 26.	5 a	xv. 20.	3 a	
xxx. 32.	5 d	iii. 28.	5 b	xv. 19.	5 a	
xxxi. 21, 52, 52.	5 d	viii. 4.	5 e	xvii. 11.	5 a	
xxxii. 10, 31.	5 a	x. 9.	5 d	xix. 8.	5 a	
xxxii. 16.	5 c	xi. 17, 19, 32.	5 d	xviii. 8.	6 a	
xxxii. 22.	5 d	xi. 20.	5 b	xxx. 16.	5 a	
xxxiii. 3.	5 a	xi. 29, 29, 29.	5 d d a	xxxiv. 20.	5 a	
xxxiii. 14.	5 d	xii. 11.	5 a	xxxvii. 21.	5 a	
xxxvii. 28.	5 d	xii. 3.	5 a	Ps. viii. 8.	5 e	
l. 4.	5 d	xii. 5, 6.	5 n	xviii. 12.	5 a	
Exod. xii. 12.	5 a	xviii. 13.	5 a	xxxvii. 36.	5 d	
xii. 13, 27.	8 a	xix. 12.	5 a	xlviii. 4.	5 a	
xii. 23, 23.	5 a, 8 a	xix. 14.	5 d	lviii. 8.	3 a	
xv. 16, 16.	5 d	xix. 18.	5 e	lxxviii. 13.	5 i	
xxx. 13, 14.	5 e	1 Sam. ix. 4, 4, 4, 4,		lxxviii. 39.	3 b	
xxxiii. 19.	5 i	27, 27.	5 d	lxxx. 12.	5 e	
xxxiii. 22, 22.	5 b	xiii. 23.	5 m	lxxxiv. 6.	5 d	
xxxiv. 6.	5 d	xiv. 4.	5 n	lxxxix. 41.	5 e	
Lev. xviii. 21.	5 h	xiv. 8.	5 a	xc. 4.	5 d	
xxvii. 32.	5 d	xiv. 23.	5 a	xc. 9.	7	
Num. xiv. 7.	5 a	xv. 12.	5 d	ciii. 16.	5 a	
xx. 17, 17, 17, 18.	5 d	xvi. 8, 9, 10.	5 i	civ. 9.	5 d	
xx. 21.	5 b	xxvii. 2.	5 d	cxxxvi. 14.	5 g	
xxi. 22, 22.	5 d	xxix. 2, 2.	5 e	cxliv. 4.	5 e	
xxi. 23.	5 b	2 Sam. ii. 29.	5 d	cxlviii. 6.	5 d	
xxvii. 7, 8.	5 g	x. 17.	5 d	Prov. iv. 15, 15.	5 c d	
xxxii. 27, 29, 30, 32.	5 d	xi. 27.	5 d	vii. 8.	5 e	
xxxiii. 8.	5 e	xii. 31.	5 g	viii. 29.	5 d	
xxxiii. 51.	5 e	xv. 18, 18, 23, 23,		ix. 15.	5 e, 2	
xxxiv. 4, 4.	5 a	23.	5 e	x. 25.	5 b	
Deut. ii. 4, 18.	5 e	xv. 22, 22.	5 c d	xix. 11.	5 a	
ii. 8, 8, 27, 28, 29.	5 d	xv. 24.	5 b	xxii. 3.	5 a	
ii. 24.	5 c	xv. 33.	5 a	xxvi. 17.	5 e	
ii. 30.	5 h	xvi. 1.	5 a	xxvii. 12.	5 a	
iii. 18.	5 d	xvii. 16.β	5 b d	Eccles. i. 4.	3 b	
iii. 21.	5 e	xvii. 21.	5 c	Cant. ii. 11.	5 a	
ix. 1.	5 e	xvii. 22.	5 d	iii. 4.	5 a	
xi. 31.	5 e	xvii. 24.	5 a	Isa. viii. 8.	4 a	
xviii. 10.	5 k	xxiv. 5.	5 d	viii. 21.	5 a	
xxvii. 2.	5 d	1 Kings ii. 37.	5 a	x. 28.	5 a	
xxvii. 3.	5 b	ix. 8.	5 d	x. 29.	5 n	
xxix. 16.	5 a	viii. 25.	5 e	xxi. 1.	4 b	
xxx. 18.	5 e	xviii. 6, 29.	5 b	xxiii. 2.	5 e	
Josh. i. 11, 11.	5 c e	xix. 11.	5 e	xxiii. 6, 10, 12.	5 c	
i. 14.	5 d	xix. 19.	5 d	xxviii. 15, 18, 19.	5 d	
ii. 23.	5 d	xx. 39.	5 e	xxix. 5.	5 e	
iii. 1.	5 d	2 Kings iv. 8, 8.	5 d b	xxx. 32.	5 m	
iii. 4, 16.	5 a	iv. 9.	5 e	xxxi. 5.	8 b	
iii. 6.	5 c	iv. 31.	5 e	xxxi. 9.	5 d	
iii. 11.	5 e	iv. 9.	5 a	xxxiii. 21.	5 a	
iii. 14.	5 b	vi. 26, 30.	5 e	xxxiv. 10.	5 e	
iii. 17, 17.	5 e b	xii. 4.	5 d	xxxv. 8.	5 d	
iv. 1, 7, 23.	5 b	xiv. 9.	5 a	xl. 27.	5 d	
iv. 5.	5 c	xvi. 3.	5 d	xli. 3.	5 e	
iv. 10, 12.	5 d	xvii. 17.	5 i	xliii. 2.	5 d	
iv. 11, 11.	5 d b	xxii. 14.	5 g	xlvii. 2.	5 d	
iv. 13.	5 a	xxiii. 10.	5 h	li. 10.	5 b	
v. 14.	5 b	1 Chron. xix. 17.	5 d	Jer. ii. 6.	5 a	
vi. 7, 7.	5 d c	2 Chron. vii. 21.	5 a	ii. 10.	5 c	
vi. 8.	5 a	ix. 22.	1	v. 22, 22.	5 d	
x. 29, 31, 34.	5 a	xxv. 18.	5 d	viii. 13.	5 d	
xv. 3, 3, 4, 6, 7, 10,		xxx. 10.	5 e	viii. 20.	5 a	
10, 11.	5 a	xxxiii. 6.	5 g	ix. 10, γ 12.	5 e	
xvi. 2, 6.	5 a	Neh. ii. 14.	5 b	xi. 15.	5 a	
xviii. 9.	5 d	Job iv. 15.	4 c	xiii. 24.	5 a	
xviii. 18, 19.	5 a	vi. 15.	4 a	xv. 14.	5 g	
xix. 13.	5 a	ix. 11.	4 c	xviii. 16.	5 e	

Jer. xix. 8.	5 e	Ezek. xx. 26, 31.	5 h	Amos vii. 8.δ	5 b	
xxii. 8.	5 a	xx. 37.	5 g	viii. 2.δ	5 b	
xxii. 20.	5 l	xxiii. 37.	5 g	Jonah ii. 3.	5 a	
xxxii. 35.	5 h	xxix. 11, 11.	5 d	Micah i. 11.	5 c	
xxxiii. 13.	5 d	xxxiii. 28.	5 e	ii. 8.	5 e	
xxxiv. 18.	5 d	xxxv. 7.	5 e	ii. 13, 13.	5 d	
xxxiv. 19.	5 e	xxxvi. 34.	5 e	vii. 18.	5 e	
xlvi. 17.	5 g	xxxvii. 2.	5 g	Nah. i. 12.	5 b	
li. 32.	5 n	xxxix. 11, 11, 14, 14.	5 e	i. 15.	5 b	
li. 43.	5 d	xxxix. 15, 15.	5 e a	iii. 19.	5 a	
Lam. i. 12	5 e, 2	xlvi. 21.	5 i	Hab. i. 11.	5 d	
ii. 15.	5 e, 2	xlvii. 5, 5.	5 b f	iii. 10.	5 a	
iii. 44.	5 b	Dan. iii. 27.	6 b	Zeph. ii. 2.	5 a	
iv. 21.	5 d	iv. 16, 23, 25, 32.	4 d	ii. 15.	5 e	
Ezek. v. 1.	5 g	vii. 14.	6 c	ii. 6.	5 e	
v. 14.	5 e	xi. 10, 40.	5 a	Zech. iii. 4.	5 g	
v. 17.	5 d	Hos. x. 11.	5 a	vii. 14.	5 a	
xiv. 15, 15.	5 i e	xiii. 3.	3 b	ix. 8, 8.	5 e d	
xvi. 6, 8.	5 d	Joel iii. 17.	5 d	x. 11.	5 a	
xvi. 15, 25.	5 e	Amos v. 5, 17.	5 d	xiii. 2.	5 i	
xvi. 21.	5 h	vi. 2.	5 c			

α *lit.* according to קְרִי they were passed over.   β *lit.* passing pass over.   γ *lit.* without a man passing.   δ *lit.* not add to pass.

PAST

סוּר to turn aside. KAL *pret.* 1 Sam. xv. 32, *lit.* turned aside.

קֶדֶם *m.* ancient, of old: Job xxix. 2.

רִאשׁוֹן *adj.* first, former: Deut. iv. 32.

רָדַף to pursue, drive away, or persecute. NIPHAL *part.* Eccles. iii. 15.

שׁוּב to return. KAL *inf.* Job xiv. 13, *lit.* return, *i. e.* from me.

PASTOR

רָעָה to feed. KAL *part.* Poel, Jer. ii. 8; iii. 15; x. 21; xii. 10; xvii. 16; xxii. 22; xxiii. 1, 2.

PASTURE

1 כַּר *m.* a lamb; a pasture for lambs. This word was also adopted by the Ionians in the sense both of lamb and pasture.—*Gesenius.*

2 נָאָה *f.* only in the *pl. const.* seats, dwellings, habitations; pastures, in which flocks lie down and rest.

3 רְעִי *m.* pasture. [a] מִרְעֶה *m.* pasture, *i. e.* place of feeding; also feed for cattle. [b] מַרְעִית *f.* a pasturing.

Gen. xlvii. 4.	3 a	Ps. lxxix. 13.	3 b	Lam. i. 6.	3 a
1 Kings iv. 23.	3 a	xcv. 7.	3 b	Ezek. xxxiv. 14, 14,	
1 Chron. iv. 39, 40, 41.	3 a	c. 3.	3 b	18, 18.	3 a
Job xxxix. 8.	3 a	Isa. xxx. 23.	1	xxxiv. 31.	3 b
Ps. xxiii. 2.	2	xxxii. 14.	3 a	Hos. xiii. 6.	3 b
lxv. 12.	2	xlix. 9.	3 b	Joel i. 18.	3 a
lxv. 13.	1	Jer. xxiii. 1.	3 b	i. 19, 20.	2
lxxiv. 1.	3 b	xxv. 36.	3 b	ii. 22.	2

PATE

קָדְקֹד *m.* crown of the head: Ps. vii. 16.

PATH

1 אֹרַח *com.* a way, path, road: Gen. xlix. 17, &c.

2 מְסִלָּה *f.* highway.

3 מַעְגָּל *m.* a track, rut, in which wheels go; a way, path. [a] מַעְגָּלָה *f. id.*

4 מִשְׁעוֹל *m.* narrow path, hollow way.

5 נָתִיב *m.* trodden, a trodden way, beaten path; a foot-path, by-way. [a] נְתִיבָה *f. id.* with דֶּרֶךְ.

6 שְׁבִיל *m.* way, path: Ps. lxxvii. 19: Jer. xviii. 15.

No. 1 not included.

Num. xxii. 24.	4	Ps. cxix. 35.	5	Isa. xxvi. 7.	3	
Job xix. 8.	5 a	cxix. 105.	5 a	xlii. 16.	5 a	
xxiv. 13.	5 a	cxlii. 3.	5 a	xliii. 16.	5 a	
xxviii. 7.	5	Prov. i. 15.	5 a	lviii. 12.	5	
xxx. 13.	5 a	ii. 9.	3	lix. 7.	5	
xxxviii. 20.	5 a	ii. 15, 18.	3 a	lix. 8.	2	
xli. 32.	5	iii. 17.	5 a	Jer. vi. 16.	5 a	
Ps. xvii. 5.	3 a	iv. 11, 26.	5	xviii. 15, 15.	6, 5 a	
xxiii. 3.	3	vii. 25.	5 a	Lam. iii. 9.	5 a	
lxv. 11.	3	viii. 2, 20.	5 a	Hos. ii. 6.	5 a	
lxxvii. 19.	6	xii. 28.	5 a	Joel ii. 8.	2	

PATIENT

אָרֵךְ *adj.* long; tardy, slow: Eccles. vii. 8.

קָוָה to wait. PIEL *inf.* Ps. xl. 1, in waiting I wait.

PATRIMONY

אָב *m.* father: Deut. xviii. 8.

PATTERN

תַּבְנִית *f.* structure, mode of building; model, pattern after which anything is built; or the pattern of what has been built: Josh. xxii. 28: Exod. xxv. 40. LXX. τύπος. Exod. xxv. 9, 9, 40: Josh. xxii. 28: 2 Kings xvi. 10: 1 Chron. xxviii. 11, 12, 18, 19.

תַּבְנִית *f.* measure, structure, arrangement: Ezek. xliii. 10, *marg.* 'or, sum, or, number.'

מַרְאֶה *m.* sight; appearance, form: Num. viii. 4.

PAVED, PAVEMENT

לִבְנָה *f.* from לְבֵנָה a brick, supposed to mean a pavement, as if laid in curious bricks; but Gesenius and others render it whiteness, clearness, transparency: Exod. xxiv. 10.

רָצַף to range stones artificially, *e. gr.* in a pavement or tesselated work. KAL *part.* Paül, Cant. iii. 10. רִצְפָּה *f.* a tesselated pavement: 2 Chron. vii. 3: Esth. i. 6: Ezek. xl. 17, 17, 18, 18; xlii. 3. מַרְצֶפֶת *f. id.* 2 Kings xvi. 17.

PAVILION

סֹךְ *m.* a booth, hut; *poet.* for a tabernacle, dwelling: Ps. xxvii. 5. סֻכָּה *f. id.* 2 Sam. xxii. 12: 1 Kings xx. 12, *marg.* 'tents,' 16: Ps. xviii. 11; xxxi. 20.

PAW

חָפַר to dig; applied to the pawing of a mettlesome horse. KAL *fut.* Job xxxix. 21, *marg.* 'or, his feet dig.'

יָד *com.* hand: 1 Sam. xvii. 37, 37.

כַּף *f.* hand, used of the foot with its toes: Lev. xi. 27.

PAY

1 יְהַב Ch. to give. ITHP'AL *part.*

2 מֶכֶר *m.* price: Num. xx. 19, *lit.* I will give the price of them.

3 נָתַן to give. KAL [a] *pret.* [b] *fut.* נְתַן Ch. P'AL [c] *fut.*

4 עָלָה to ascend. HIPHIL *fut.*

5 שׁוּב to return; to cause to return. HIPHIL *pret.*

6 שָׁלַם to be whole; to make whole, make good, recompense. PIEL [a] *pret.* [b] *inf.* [c] *imp.* [d] *fut.*

7 שָׁקַל to weigh money, either in receiving or paying. KAL [a] *inf.* [b] *fut.*

Exod. xxi. 19.	3 b	2 Chron. viii. 8.	4	Ps. lxvi. 13.	6 d
xxi. 22.	3 a	xxvii. 14.	5	lxxvi. 11.	6 c
xxi. 36.	6 b d	Ezra iv. 13.	3 c	cxvi. 14, 18.	6 d
xxii. 7, 9.	6 d	iv. 20.	1	Prov. vii. 14.	6 a
xxii. 17.	7 b	Esth. iii. 9.	7 b	xix. 17.	6 d
Num. xx. 19.	3 a, 2	iv. 7.	7 a	xxii. 27.	6 b
Deut. xxiii. 21.	6 b	Job xxxiv. 27.	6 d	Eccles. v. 4, 4.	6 b c
2 Sam. xv. 7.	6 d	Ps. xxii. 25.	6 d	v. 5.	6 d
1 Kings xx. 39.	7 b	xxxvii. 21.	6 d	Jonah i. 3.	3 b
2 Kings iv. 7.	6 c	i. 14.	6 d	ii. 9.	6 d

PEACE

1 שָׁלֵו *adj.* secure, tranquil, at rest. [a] שַׁלְוָה *f.* tranquillity, security, mostly in a bad sense.

2 שָׁלַם to be whole, complete; to be at peace, in friendship with any one. KAL [a] *imp.* [b] *part.* Poel. [c] *part.* Paül. HIPHIL [d] *pret.* [e] *fut.* HOPHAL [f] *pret.* [g] שָׁלוֹם *m.* health, welfare, peace; concord, friendship: Gen. xv. 15, &c. [h] שְׁלָם Ch. *m. id.* [i] שָׁלֵם *adj.* [k] שֶׁלֶם *m.* requital; thanks, thank-offering, sacrifice offered to God, with praise and thanksgiving; peace-offerings; usually rendered peace-offering, but sometimes taking זֶבַח with it; see *Offering.* Exod. xx. 24, &c.

No. 2 g, Peace, and 2 k, Peace-offering, not included.

Gen. xxxiv. 21.	2 i	1 Kings ii. 13.γ	2 g	Ps. vii. 4.	2 b
xxxvii. 4. α	2 g	ii. 13.δ	2 g	lv. 20.ζ	2 g
Exod. xxiv. 5.	2 g	xxii. 44.	2 e	Prov. vii. 14.	2 g
Lev. xvii. 5.	2 g	2 Kings ix. 18, 19.ε	2 g	xvi. 7.	2 e
Deut. xx. 12.	2 e	1 Chron. iv. 40.	1	Isa. xxvi. 3.η	2 g
Josh. i. 4.	2 d	xii. 17.α	1 g	xxxii. 18.θ	2 g
xi. 19.	2 d	xix. 19.	2 g	Jer. ix. 8.δ	2 g
Judg. xi. 13.β	2 g	2 Chron. xxx. 22.	2 g	xxv. 37.θ	2 g
xxi. 13.	2 g	xxxiii. 16.	2 g	Dan. iv. 11.	2 h
1 Sam. xvi. 4.γ	2 g	Ezra iv. 17.	2 h	vi. 25.	2 h
xvi. 5.δ	2 g	v. 7.	2 h	viii. 25.	1 a
2 Sam. x. 19.	2 e	Job v. 23.	2 f	xi. 21, 24.	1 a
xx. 19.	2 c	xxi. 21.	2 a	Obad. 7.	2 g

α *lit.* to peace.   β *lit.* in peace.   γ *lit.* peace of thy coming.
δ *lit.* peace.   ε *lit.* what to thee and to peace.   ζ *lit.* (the men) of
his peace.   η "perfect peace," *lit.* peace, peace.   θ *lit.* of peace.

PEACOCK

תֻּכִּיִּים *m. pl.* 1 Kings x. 22, and תֻּכִּיִּים, 2 Chron. ix. 21, peacocks, according to the Targ., Syr. (with the Arab.), Jerome, and the Hebrew interpreters.—*Gesenius.*

רְנָנִים *m. pl.*: on the authority of Kimchi this has been rendered peacocks, but it is now agreed among critics that it means ostriches, from the cry they make: Job xxxix. 13; see *Goodly.*

PEARL

גָּבִישׁ *m. pr.* ice; see *Hail: trop.* crystal, which resembles ice, and was in fact supposed to be ice: Plin. H. N. 37, 2; *comp.* Gr. κρύσταλλος.—*Gesenius.* Job xxviii. 18.

PECULIAR

סְגֻלָּה *f.* property, wealth, private property, which is laid up or reserved; the leading idea is that of select, precious, endeared; something exceedingly prized and sedulously preserved; answering to περιούσιος and εἰς περιποίησιν,

in the N.T., and to the Latin term *peculium*. Exod. xix. 5 : Deut. xiv. 2 ; xxvi. 18 : Ps. cxxxv. 4 : Eccles. ii. 8.

PEDIGREE

יָלַד to beget ; Hithp. to declare one's pedigree, descent, or birth ; to give one's name to be enrolled in genealogical tables : *fut.* Num. i. 18.

PEELED

מָרַט to make smooth ; to make bald, bare. KAL *part.* Paül, Ezek. xxix. 18. PUAL *part.* Isa. xviii. 2, 7.

PEEP

צָפַף only in Pilp. an onomatopoietic verb, to peep, to chirp as a small bird. Like the Gr. τρίζω, it is transferred to the voice of the manes or shades, which the wizards professed to imitate ; to the same the Latin poets apply the epithet *stridor.—Gesenius.* PILPEL *part.* Isa. viii. 19 ; x. 14.

PEKOD

פְּקוֹד *m.* visitation, *i. e.* punishment, put allegorically as a name for Babylon : Jer. l. 21 : Ezek. xxiii. 23.

PELETHITES

פְּלֵתִי *m.* the king's messengers, everywhere coupled with כְּרֵתִי Cherethites : 2 Sam. viii. 18 ; xv. 18 ; xx. 7, 23 : 1 Kings i. 38, 44 : 1 Chron. xviii. 17.

PELICAN

קָאַת *f.* the vomiter, a water-fowl, inhabiting also desert places ; according to the ancient versions, the pelican : Targ., Syr., Arab., Lxx., πελεκάν. So called from its vomiting the shells and other things which it has voraciously swallowed. Lev. xi. 18 : Deut. xiv. 17 : Ps. cii. 6.

PEN

חֶרֶט *m.* a graving tool ; also a style, with which letters were written or inscribed on wood or stone ; hence *poet.* of a manner of writing, Isa. viii. 1, with a man's style, *i. e.* with the common letters, so as to be read without difficulty by the common people.—*Gesenius.*

עֵט *m. stylus*, style, *i. e.* a writer's style, reed, *calamus* : Jer. viii. 8 : Ps. xlv. 1. Also of iron, for inscribing letters upon stone or metal : Job xix. 24 : Jer. xvii. 1.

סָפַר to write. KAL *part.* Poel, Jer. xxxvi. 23, penknife, *lit.* knife of a writer.

שֵׁבֶט *com.* a rod, staff, or wand ; it nowhere else means pen, and ought probably to be understood here of the numbering rod of the shepherd, see *Rod* ; *metaph.* applied to the levying of a certain number out of the tribe : Judg. v. 14.

תַּעַר *m.* razor, sharp knife ; writer's knife, with which he sharpens the *calamus*, penknife : Jer. xxxvi. 23, *lit.* with the knife of a writer.

PENURY

מַחְסוֹר *m.* poverty, need, want : Prov. xiv. 23.

PEOPLE

1 אִישׁ *m.* man.

2 אֻמָּה *f.* family, tribe, people ; found only in the plural. אֻמּוֹת [a] and אֻמִּים [b] *m.*

3 אֱנוֹשׁ *m.* man, men collectively.

4 בֵּן *m.* a son.

5 גּוֹי *m.* a nation, a people ; *pl.* Gentiles, heathen.

6 לְאֹם *m.* a people, nation ; mostly in the plural.

7 עֵדָה *f.* assembly, congregation.

8 עַם and עָם *com.* people, considered as associated in a country, town, army, or company : Gen. xxxiv. 22, "to be one people." Sometimes it seems to be used of a smaller number, even when not especially connected : 1 Sam. ix. 24, *comp.* ver. 22.—Gen. xi. 6, &c. עַם Ch. *m. id.*

No. 8 not included.

Gen. xxv. 23, 23, 23.	6	Esth. i. 22.	8	Isa. xlix. 1.	6
xxix. 1.	4	iii. 12, 12.	8	lv. 4, 4.	6
Lev. x. 6.	7	viii. 9.	8	lx. 2.	6
xx. 17.	4, 8	Ps. ii. 1.	6	Jer. li. 58.	6
Num. xxv. 15.	2 a	vii. 7.	6	Dan. ii. 44.	8 a
Josh. iii. 17.	5	ix. 8.	6	iii. 4, 7, 7, 29.	8 a
iv. 1.	5	xliv. 2, 14.	6	iv. 1.	8 a
v. 6, 8.	5	lxvii. 4.	6	v. 19.	8 a
x. 13.	5	cv. 44.	6	vi. 25.	8 a
Judg. ii. 20.	5	cxvii. 1.	2 b	vii. 14, 27.	8 a
2 Sam. xx. 13.	1	cxlviii. 11.	6	viii. 24.	8
2 Kings vi. 18.	5	cxlix. 7.	6	xi. 23.	5
2 Chron. xxxv. 5, 7, 12, 13.	5, 7	Prov. xi. 26.	6	Joel iii. 8.	5
	4, 8	xiv. 28, 34.	6	Jonah iii. 5.	6
Ezra v. 12.	8 a	Isa. xxxiv. 1.	6	Hab. ii. 13.	6
vi. 12.	8 a	xli. 1.	6	Zeph. ii. 9.	5
vii. 13, 16, 25.	8 a	xliii. 4, 9.	6	Zech. xii. 3.	5
Neh. xiii. 24.	8				

PERAZIM

פֶּרֶץ a breach : 2 Sam. v. 20, 20 : 1 Chron. xiv. 11, 11 : Isa. xxviii. 21.

PERCEIVE

1 אָזַן to hear, hearken, give ear, perceive by the ear. HIPHIL *pret.*

2 בִּין to perceive, observe. KAL and HIPHIL [a] *fut.* HIPHIL [b] *inf.* HITHPOLEL [c] *pret.*

3 טָעַם to taste. KAL *pret.*

4 יָדַע to know ; to see, perceive, discern. KAL [a] *pret.* [b] *inf.* [c] *imp.* [d] *fut.*

5 נָכַר KAL not used ; HIPHIL, to discern, to acknowledge by certain tokens : *fut.*

6 רָאָה to see, with clearness and evidence. KAL [a] *pret.* [b] *inf.* [c] *fut.*

7 שׁוּר to look with attention and earnestness, to discover. KAL *fut.*

8 שָׁמַע to hear ; to understand, to have a right discernment of. KAL [a] *inf.* NIPHAL [b] *pret.*

Gen. xix. 33, 35.	4 a	2 Kings iv. 9.	4 a	Prov. i. 2.	2 b
Deut. xxix. 4.	4 b	1 Chron. xiv. 2.	4 d	xiv. 7.	4 a
Josh. xxii. 31.	4 a	2 Chron. xviii. 32.	6 b	xxxi. 18.	3
Judg. vi. 22.	6 c	Neh. vi. 12.	5	Eccles. i. 17.	4 a
1 Sam. iii. 8.	2 a	vi. 16.	4 d	ii. 14.	4 a
xii. 17.	4 c	xiii. 10.	4 d	iii. 22.	4 a
xxviii. 14.	4 d	Esth. iv. 1.	4 a	Isa. vi. 9.	4 d
2 Sam. v. 12.	4 a	Job ix. 11.	2 a	xxxiii. 19.	4 a
xii. 19.	2 a	xiv. 21.	2 a	lxiv. 4.	1
xiv. 1.	4 a	xxxiii. 14.	7	Jer. xxiii. 18.	6 c
xix. 6.	4 a	xxxviii. 18.	2 c	xxxviii. 27.	8 b
1 Kings xxii. 33.	6 b				

PERES

פְּרַס Ch. to divide. P'AL *part. passive*, Dan. v. 28; the same word translated also in the same verse, "is divided."

PEREZ

פֶּרֶץ *m.* breach: 2 Sam. vi. 8: 1 Chron. xiii. 11.

PERFECT

1 אֲרוּכָה *f.* health.

2 בִּינָה *f.* understanding.

3 גָּמַר to finish, accomplish, execute. KAL ᵃ *fut.* גְּמַר Ch. P'AL ᵇ *part. passive.*

4 כּוּן see *Establish.* NIPHAL *part.* Prov. iv. 18, *firmum, sc. stabile diei; i.e.* mid-day, when the sun seems to be stationary for a time, having attained the highest point in the heavens.

5 כָּלַל to complete, make perfect. KAL ᵃ *pret.* ᵇ כָּלִיל *adj.* perfect, complete. מִכְלָל ᶜ *m.* that which is perfect.

6 כָּלָה to be completed, finished. תִּכְלָה ᵃ *f.* perfection. תַּכְלִית *f.* perfection, completion. ᵇ מִכְלוֹת *f. pl.* perfections.

7 נָלָה to complete, to attain. מִנְלֶה *m.* translated perfection. Job xv. 29; probably possession, prosperous condition. —*Gesenius.*

8 עָלָה to go up. KAL *fut.*

9 שָׁלַם to be complete, perfect, entire: it applies to quantity, Deut. xxv. 15; to the mind and heart; to the outward state and circumstances; to the completely finishing or perfecting of a work, or to the doing anything in a full and complete manner. PUAL ᵃ *part.* ᵇ שָׁלֵם *adj.* whole, perfect. ᶜ שָׁלוֹם *m.* peace.

10 תָּמַם to complete, to make full, perfect, or entire; to finish. KAL ᵃ *inf.* HIPHIL ᵇ *fut.* ᶜ תָּמִים *adj.* complete, whole; without blemish, sound, uninjured; perfect. ᵈ תָּם *adj.* blameless, upright, righteous; the proper notion is that of simplicity, sincerity, absence from guile or evil intention; implying completeness of parts rather than of degrees. ᵉ תֹּם *m.* integrity.

Gen. vi. 9.	10 c	2 Chron. xxiv. 13.	1, 8	Ps. ci. 6.	10 e
xvii. 1.	10 c	xxv. 2.	9 b	cxix. 96.	6
Lev. xxii. 21.	10 c	Ezra vii. 12.	3 b	cxxxviii. 8.	3 a
Deut. xviii. 13.	10 c	Job i. 1, 8.	10 d	cxxxix. 22.	6 a
xxv. 15, 15.	9 b	ii. 3.	10 d	Prov. ii. 21.	10 c
xxxii. 4.	10 c	viii. 20.		iv. 18.	4
1 Sam. xiv. 41.	10 c	ix. 20, 21, 22.	10 d	xi. 5.	10 c
2 Sam. xxii. 31, 33.	10 c	xi. 7.	6 a	Isa. xviii. 15.	10 a
1 Kings viii. 61.	9 b	xv. 29.	7	xxvi. 3.	9 c
xi. 4.	9 b	xxii. 3.	10 d	xxxvii. 3.	9 c
xv. 3, 14.	9 b	xxviii. 3.	6 a	xlii. 19.	9 a
2 Kings xx. 3.	9 b	xxxvi. 4.	10 e	xlvii. 9.	10 e
1 Chron. xii. 38.	9 b	xxxvii. 16.	10 c	Jer. xxiii. 20.β	2
xxviii. 9.	9 b	Ps. xviii. 30, 32.	10 d	Lam. ii. 15.	5 b
xxix. 9, 19.	9 b	xix. 7.	10 c	Ezek. xvi. 14.	5 b
2 Chron. iv. 21.	6 b	xxxvii. 37.	10 d	xxvii. 3.	5 b
viii. 16.	9 b	l. 2.	5 c	xxvii. 4, 11.	5 a
xv. 17.	9 b	lxiv. 4.	10 d	xxviii. 12.	5 b
xvi. 9.	9 b	ci. 2, 2.α	10 c e	xxviii. 15.	10 c
xix. 9.	9 b				

ᵃ *lit.* in the integrity of my heart.   β *lit.* with understanding.

PERFORM

1 בָּצַע to cut or break off, as a workman when he has completed his intended work; to accomplish, perform, finish. PIEL *fut.*

2 גָּמַר to finish, accomplish, execute. KAL *part.* Poel.

3 נָתַן to give. KAL *fut.*

4 עָשָׂה to make, do, act; to labour in; to execute or accomplish. KAL ᵃ *pret.* ᵇ *inf.* ᶜ *fut.* NIPHAL ᵈ *fut.*

5 פָּלָא to separate in a distinguishing manner. PIEL *inf.*

6 צָבָא to go forth, or march out to war, to carry on war. KAL *inf. lit.* to war the warfare.

7 קוּם to arise; to stand, to be performed. KAL ᵃ *pret.* PIEL ᵇ *fut.* HIPHIL ᶜ *pret.* ᵈ *inf.* ᵉ *fut.* HOPHAL ᶠ *pret.*

8 שָׁלַם to be complete, perfect, entire. PIEL ᵃ *pret.* ᵇ *inf.* ᶜ *imp.* PUAL ᵈ *fut.* HIPHIL ᵉ *fut.*

Gen. xxvi. 3.	7 c	Neh. v. 13.	7 e	Jer. i. 12.	4 b
Exod. xviii. 18.	4 b	ix. 8.	7 e	xi. 5.	7 d
Num. iv. 23.	6	Esth. i. 15.	4 a	xxiii. 20.	7 d
xv. 3.	5	v. 6.	4 d	xxviii. 6.	7 e
Deut. iv. 13.	4 b	v. 8.	4 b	xxix. 10.	7 c
ix. 5.	7 d	vii. 2.	4 c	xxx. 24.	7 d
xxiii. 23.	4 a	Job v. 17.	4 c	xxxiii. 14.	7 c
1 Sam. iii. 12.	7 e	xxiii. 14.	8 e	xxxv. 18.	7 c
xv. 11, 13.	7 c	Ps. lvii. 2.	2	xxxv. 14.	7 f
2 Sam. xiv. 15.	4 c	lxi. 1.	8 b	xxxv. 16.	7 c
xxi. 14.	4 d	lxv. 1.	8 d	xliv. 25.	4 b c
1 Kings vi. 12.	7 c	cxix. 106.	7 b	xliv. 25.	4 b c
viii. 20.	7 c	cxix. 112.	4 b	li. 29.	7 a
xii. 15.	7 c	Isa. xix. 7.		Ezek. xii. 12.	4 a
2 Kings xxiii. 3, 24.	7 d	x. 12.	1	xxxvii. 14.	4 a
2 Chron. vi. 10.	7 e	xix. 21.	8 b	Micah vii. 20.	8
x. 15.	7 d	xliv. 26, 28.	8 e	Nah. i. 15.	8 c
xxxiv. 31.	4 b				

PERFUME

נוּף to wave, to move to and fro; to sprinkle. KAL *pret.* Prov. vii. 17.

קָטַר to burn incense; to be perfumed. PUAL *part.* Cant. iii. 6. קְטֹרֶת *f.* incense: Exod. xxx. 35, 37: Prov. xxvii. 9.

רְקָחִים *m. pl.* perfumes mixed and compounded: Isa. lvii. 9.

PERISH

1 אָבַד to perish in reality, in apprehension, or relatively; to be lost or gone; to pass away or cease to be, to die. There seems to be a cognate meaning between this root and בָּדַד to be separated, from which probably it is formed. Applied to the death of men and animals; to land and houses laid waste; to the disappearance of rivers, Job vi. 18; to the destruction of weapons of war, 2 Sam. i. 27; to the loss or failure of a harvest, Joel i. 11; to the losing of wealth, Eccles. v. 14; of hope, Ezek. xix. 5; of courage, Jer. iv. 9; of truth, Jer. vii. 28; of knowledge, counsel, Jer. xlix. 7; of flight and refuge, Job xi. 20, Ps. cxli. 4; to a prophecy not fulfilled, Ezek. xii. 22; to the extinction of wisdom in a people, Isa. xxix. 14; of a person's name and memory, Ps. xli. 5, Job xviii. 17. It is opposed to עָמַד, Ps. cii. 26. KAL ᵃ *pret.* ᵇ *inf.* ᶜ *fut.* ᵈ *part.* Poel. PIEL ᵉ *inf.* ᶠ *fut.* HIPHIL ᵍ *pret.* אֲבַד Ch. P'AL ʰ *fut.* APHEL ⁱ *fut.* אֲבַד ᵏ *m.* destruction.

2 גָּוַע to die. KAL ᵃ *pret.* ᵇ *fut.*

3 דָּמָה to be silent; to cause to cease, to destroy, to cut off. KAL ᵃ *fut.*

4 כָּרַת to cut off. NIPHAL *fut.* Gen. xli. 36, *marg.* 'be not cut off.'

5 נָפַל to fall, to fall in battle, &c. KAL *pret.*

6 סוּף to have an end. KAL *fut.*

7 סָפָה to consume. NIPHAL ᵃ *pret.* ᵇ *fut.*

8 עָבַר to pass, to pass away. KAL [a] *inf.* [b] *fut.*

9 פָּרַע to throw off, to let loose; hence to uncover, to make naked; or, according to some, to give the reins. NIPHAL *fut.* Prov. xxix. 18, *marg.* 'or, is made naked, stripped of their honour and defence.' Gesenius, however, translates it *effrenatus factus*, as he also understands Exod. xxxii. 25. See *Naked.*

10 שָׁחַת to corrupt, to destroy. PIEL *pret.*

11 שָׁמַד to destroy, to ruin, to undo. NIPHAL *pret.*

Gen. xxv. 18.	5	Job xviii. 17.	1 a	Eccles. v. 14.	1 a
xli. 36.	4	xx. 7.	1 c	vii. 15.	1 d
Exod. xix. 21.	5	xxix. 13.	1 d	ix. 6.	1 f
xxi. 26.	10	xxx. 2.	1 a	Isa. xxvi. 14.	1 d
Lev. xxvi. 38.	1 a	xxxi. 19.	1 d	xxvii. 13.	1 a
Num. xvi. 33.	1 c	xxxiii. 18.	8 a	xxix. 14.	1 a
xvii. 12, 12.	1 a	xxxiv. 15.	2 b	xli. 11.	1 c
xxi. 30.	1 a	xxxvi. 12.	8 b	lvii. 1.	1 a
xxiv. 20, 24.	1 k	Ps. i. 6.	1 c	lx. 12.	1 a
Deut. iv. 26.	1 b c	ii. 12.	1 c	Jer. iv. 9.	1 c
viii. 19.	1 b c	ix. 3, 18.	1 a	vi. 21.	1 a
viii. 20.	1 c	ix. 6.	1 a	vii. 28.	1 a
xi. 17.	1 a	x. 16.	1 a	ix. 12.	1 h
xxvi. 5.	1 d	xxxvii. 20.	1 a	x. 11.	1 c
xxviii. 20, α 22. β	1 b	xli. 5.	1 c	x. 15.	1 c
xxx. 18.	1 b c	xlix. 10.	1 a	xviii. 18.	1 c
Josh. xxii. 20.	2 a	xlix. 12, 20.	3 a	xxvii. 10, 15.	1 a
xxiii. 13.	1 b	lxvii. 2.	1 c	xl. 15.	1 a
xxiii. 16.	1 a	lxxiii. 27.	1 c	xlviii. 8, 36, 46.	1 a
Judg. v. 31.	1 c	lxxx. 16.	11	xlix. 7.	1 a
1 Sam. xxvi. 10.	7 a	lxxxiii. 10.	1 c	li. 18.	1 a
xxvii. 1.	7 b	lxxxiii. 17.	1 c	Lam. iii. 18.	1 a
2 Sam. i. 27.	1 c	xcii. 9.	1 c	Ezek. vi. 26.	1 g
2 Kings ix. 8.	1 a	cii. 26.	1 c	xxv. 7.	1 a
Esth. iii. 13.	1 e	cxii. 10.	1 c	Dan. xi. 18.	1 a
iv. 16, 16.	1 a	cxix. 92.	1 a	Joel i. 11.	1 a
vii. 4.	1 e	cxlvi. 4.	1 a	Amos i. 8.	1 a
viii. 11.	1 e	Prov. x. 28.	1 c a	ii. 14.	1 a
ix. 28.	6	xi. 7, 7.	1 b	iii. 15.	1 c
Job iii. 3.	1 a	xi. 10.	1 c	Jonah i. 6, 14.	1 c
iv. 7.	1 a	xix. 9.	1 c	iii. 9.	1 c
iv. 9, 20.	1 c	xxviii. 28.	1 c	iv. 10.	1 a
iv. 11.	1 d	xxix. 18.	1 c	Micah iv. 9.	1 b
vi. 18.	1 c	xxxi. 6.	1 d	Zech. ix. 5.	1 a
viii. 13.	1 c				

a lit. even to destruction.   *β lit.* to destruction.

PERPETUAL

1 יוֹם *m.* day; perpetually, *Heb.* all the days.

2 נֶצַח *m.* strength, victory; eternity, for ever. [a] נִצְחָ *adj.* according to Fürst, perpetual, total. LXX. ἀναιδής.

3 עַד *m.* duration in time.

4 עוֹלָם *m.* duration of time, which is concealed, as being of an unknown or great length, with respect to time either past or to come.

5 תָּמִיד *m.* always, continually.

Gen. ix. 12.	4	2 Chron. vii. 16.	1	Jer. xxv. 9, 12.	4
Exod. xxix. 9.	4	Ps. ix. 6. a	2	xlix. 13.	2
xxx. 8.	4	lxxiv. 3.	4	l. 5.	4
xxxi. 16.	4	lxxviii. 66.	4	li. 39, 57.	4
Lev. iii. 17.	4	Jer. v. 22.	4	Ezek. xxxv. 5, 9.	4
vi. 20.	5	xv. 5.	2 a	xlvi. 14.	4
xxiv. 9.	4	xv. 18.	2	Amos i. 11.	3
xxv. 34.	4	xviii. 16.	4	Hab. iii. 6.	4
Num. xix. 21.	4	xxiii. 40.	4	Zeph. ii. 9.	4
1 Kings ix. 3.	1				

a lit. completed for ever.

PERPLEX

בּוּךְ to be in perplexity, not knowing what to do; a metaphor taken from thick entangled boughs. NIPHAL *pret.* Joel i. 18. *part.* Esth. iii. 15. מְבוּכָה *f.* perplexity: Isa. xxii. 5, Micah vii. 4.

PERSECUTE

1 אַחַר *m.* after: Jer. xxix. 18, *lit.* pursue after them.

2 דָּלַק to burn; to pursue or persecute with a hot malicious mind. KAL [a] *fut.* [b] *part.*

3 רָדַף to follow after in order to overtake; to pursue, to persecute. KAL [a] *pret.* [b] *imp.* [c] *fut.* [d] *part.* Poel. NIPHAL [e] *pret.* PIEL [f] *fut.* [g] מִרְדָּף *m.* persecution.

Deut. xxx. 7.	3 a	Ps. lxix. 26.	3 a	Jer. xv. 15.	3 d
Neh. ix. 11.	3 d	lxxi. 11.	3 b	xvii. 18.	3 d
Job xix. 22, 28.	3 c	lxxiii. 15.	3 c	xx. 11.	3 d
Ps. vii. 1.	3 d	cix. 16.	3 c	xxix. 18.	3 a, 1
vii. 5.	3 f	cxix. 84, 157.	3 d	Lam. i. 3.	3 d
vii. 13.	2 b	cxix. 86, 161.	3 a	iii. 43, 66.	3 c
x. 2.	2 a	cxliv. 6.	3 d	iv. 19.	3 d
xxxi. 15.	3 d	cxliii. 3.	3 a	v. 5.	3 e
xxxv. 3, 6.	3 d	Isa. xiv. 6.	3 g		

PERSON

1 אָדָם *m.* man; persons, sometimes *lit.* soul of man.

2 אִישׁ *m.* man.

3 אֱנוֹשׁ *m.* man.

4 בַּעַל *m.* owner, master: Prov. xxiv. 8, *lit.* a mischief master.

5 מְתִים *m. pl.* see *Men.*

6 נֶפֶשׁ *com.* animal life, soul.

7 פָּנִים *m. pl.* the face; presence of a person.

Gen. xiv. 21.	6	Deut. xxviii. 50.	7	Prov. vi. 12.	1
xxxvi. 6.	6	Josh. xx. 3, 9.	6	xviii. 5.	7
Exod. xvi. 16.	6	Judg. ix. 2, 5, 18.	2	xxiv. 8.	4
Lev. xix. 15, 15.	6	ix. 4.	3	xxiv. 23.	7
xxvii. 2.	6	xx. 39.	2	xxviii. 17.	7
Num. v. 6.	6	1 Sam. ix. 2, 22.	7	xxviii. 21.	7
xix. 18, 18.	2, 6	xvi. 18.	2	Jer. xliii. 6.	6
xxxi. 19.	6	xxii. 18.	2	lii. 25.	6
xxxi. 28, 30.	1	xxii. 22.	2	lii. 29.	6
xxxi. 35. α	6, 1	xxv. 35.	2	lii. 30, 30.	6
xxxi. 40. β	6	2 Sam. iv. 11.	2	Lam. iv. 16.	7
xxxi. 40.	6	xiv. 14.	6	Ezek. xvi. 5.	6
xxxi. 46.	6, 1	xvii. 11.	7	xvii. 17.	6
xxxv. 11, 15, 30, 30.	6	2 Kings x. 6, 7.	2	xvii. 13.	6
Deut. i. 17.	7	2 Chron. xxx. 7.	7	xxxiii. 6.	6
x. 17.	7	Job xiii. 8, 10.	7	xliv. 25.	6
x. 22.	6	xxxii. 19, 21.	7	Jonah iv. 11.	1
xvi. 19.	7	Ps. xxvi. 4.	2	Zeph. iii. 4.	3
xxvii. 25.	6	lxxii. 2.	7	Mal. i. 8, 9.	7

a lit. and the soul of man were thirty-two thousand souls.   *β lit.* and the soul of man.

PERSUADE

סוּת to excite, to instigate, to put upon doing a thing, to stir up. HIPHIL *fut.* 2 Kings xviii. 32, *marg.* 'or, deceiveth;' 2 Chron. xviii. 2; xxxii. 15: Isa. xxxvi. 18. *part.* 2 Chron. xxxii. 11.

פָּתָה to allure, entice; to persuade by flattery. PIEL *fut.* 1 Kings xxii. 20, 21, 22. PUAL *fut.* Prov. xxv. 15.

PERTAIN

הָיָה to be. KAL *pret.* 1 Sam. xxvii. 6: 2 Sam. ix. 9.

כְּלִי vessels, instruments, &c.: Deut. xxii. 5.

PERVERT

1 גֶּזֶל *m.* a taking away by violence.

2 הַוָּה *f.* calamity, wickedness.

3 הָפַךְ to turn; to overturn, to change. KAL [a] *pret.* NIPHAL [b] *pret.* תַּהְפֻּכוֹת *f. pl.* forwardness.

4 יָרַט to turn out of the right road. KAL *pret.*

5 **סוּר** The sense of this word is opposite to that of יָשַׁר, and means, to decline, to turn aside from that which is straight, even, and direct, or right, true, and just. See *Depart.* NIPHAL [a] *part.* [b] לוּזוּת *f.* perverseness.

6 **נָטָה** to stretch out ; to decline, to turn aside, to pervert. HIPHIL [a] *inf.* [b] *fut.* [c] *part.* [d] מֻטֶּה *m.* a turning aside, or wresting of judgment.

7 **סָלַף** is not used in Kal, which probably means, to be slippery ; hence, Piel, to place in a slippery condition, to overthrow. PIEL [a] *fut.* [b] סֶלֶף *m.* smoothness, slipperiness, hence flattery ; perhaps, generally, whatever is contrary to simplicity and integrity.

8 **עָוָה** to bend, to turn awry, to act perversely. NIPHAL [a] *part.* HIPHIL [b] *pret.* [c] עִוְּעִים *m. pl.* depravities, perversities. Alexander, subversion, confusion. Vulg. *spiritus vertiginis.* Gussetius, *imprudentia.*

9 **עַוְלָה** *f.* wickedness, iniquity.

10 **עָוַת** not used in Kal ; Piel, to bend, to make crooked, pervert ; to pervert judgment, &c. PIEL [a] *pret.* [b] *fut.*

11 **עָמָל** *m.* labour, toil, sorrow, trouble ; hence, whatsoever is grievous and vexatious, mischief, wickedness.

12 **עִקֵּשׁ** "This word expresseth the character of a man who walketh in a double way, and doth not keep steadily to the end and rule of upright conduct ; who windeth this or that way as best suiteth his own selfish bad views, and maketh virtue itself subservient to vice. This is the account Cocceius giveth of this word."—*Taylor.* Caryl, on Job ix. 20, has given the following exposition of Prov. xxviii. 18, "Whoso walketh uprightly," having the frame of his inward man right, "he shall be saved :" "but he that is perverse in his ways," having a wandering vagrant mind, going sometime this way, sometime that, holding somewhat of this, somewhat of that, but nothing to purpose, or steadily of anything, this man "shall fall at once ;" a man of an uncertain spirit shall have a certain downfall. KAL [a] *fut.* NIPHAL [b] *part.* PIEL [c] *fut.* [d] *part.* [e] עִקֵּשׁ *adj.* perverse, deceitful, false.

13 **שׁוּב** to turn : to cause to turn away. POLEL *pret.*

14 **שָׁנָה** to double ; to do a thing over again, to do it in a different manner ; to change, to alter. PIEL *fut.*

Exod. xxiii. 8.		7 a	Job xxxiii. 27.	8 b	Prov. xxiii. 33.	3 c
Num. xxii. 32.		4	xxxiv. 12.	10 b	xxviii. 6.	12 e
xxiii. 21.		11	Ps. cxix. 78.	10 a	xxviii. 18.	12 b
Deut. xvi. 19.		7 a	Prov. iv. 24.		xxxi. 5.	14
xxiv. 17.		6 b	viii. 8.	12 e	Eccles. v. 8.	1
xxvii. 19.		6 c	x. 9.	12 d	Isa. xix. 14.	8 c
xxxii. 5.		12 e	xi. 3.		xxx. 12.	5 a
1 Sam. viii. 3.		6 b	xii. 8.	7 b	xlvii. 10.	13
xx. 30.		8 b	xv. 2.	8 a	lix. 3.	9
2 Sam. xix. 19.		8 b	xv. 4.	5 a	Jer. iii. 21.	7 b
1 Kings viii. 47.		8 b	xvii. 20. a	7 b	xxiii. 36.	8 a
Job vi. 30.		2	xvii. 23.	3 b	Ezek. ix. 9.	3 a
viii. 3, 3.		10 b	xix. 1.	6 a	Micah iii. 9.	6 d
ix. 20.		12 a	xix. 3.	12 e		12 c
				7 a		

a lit. he that is turned in his tongue.

PESTILENCE

דֶּבֶר *m.* (see *Destroy*), pestilence, murrain ; often translated in the LXX. by θάνατος, death ; which word, in the N. T., may therefore mean violent death ; Rev. ii. 28, &c.— Exod. v. 3, &c.

PESTLE

עֱלִי *m.* a pestle, from its motion in the use, ascending up in order to bruise : Prov. xxvii. 22.

PETITION

שְׁאֵלָה *f.* a request : 1 Sam. i. 17, 27 : 1 Kings ii. 16, 20 : Esth. v. 6, 7, 8 ; vii. 2, 3 ; ix. 12. מִשְׁאָלָה *f.* prayer, petition : Ps. xx. 5.

בְּעָה to desire, to ask, with בָּעוּ to make a petition. P'AL *part.* Dan. vi. 13. בָּעוּ Ch. *f.* a petition, request, prayer : Dan. vi. 7, 13.

PHYSICIAN

רָפָא to heal. KAL *part.* Poel, Gen. l. 2, 2 ; 2 Chron. xvi. 12 : Job xiii. 4 : Jer. viii. 22.

PICK

נָקַר to thrust out ; to dig out. KAL *fut.* Prov. xxx. 17.

PICTURE

שְׂכִיָּה *f.* a sight, picture : Isa. ii. 16, or, sights. It appears to be a general expression embracing all the preceding particulars in verses 13-16.—*Gesenius.* מַשְׂכִּית *f.* an image, figure, picture : Num. xxxiii. 52 : Prov. xxv. 11.

PIECE

1 **אֲגוֹרָה** *f.* name of a small coin, such as was usually given to beggars.

2 **בָּדָל** *m.* a piece or part separated.

3 **בֶּתֶר** *m.* a piece cut off, spoken of the parts of a sacrificial victim.

4 **גֶּזֶר** *m.* a part divided.

5 **הַדָּם** Ch. *m.* piece, in reference to the capital punishment, common in several ancient nations, to hew in pieces, or to dismember (μέλη ποιεῖν, 2 Macc. i. 16).

6 **חֶלְקָה** *f.* part, portion.

7 **כִּכָּר** *f.* what is in a round flat form, a cake, or loaf.

8 **מִדָּה** *f.* measure, size.

9 **נֵתַח** *m.* a piece cut off, particularly of flesh.

10 **פֶּלַח** *m.* a piece or slice cut off.

11 **פַּת** *f.* a morsel. [a] פתות *m. id.*

12 **קְרָעִים** *m. pl.* pieces of a garment, rags, rent or torn.

13 **מִקְשָׁה** *f.* beaten work.

14 **רֵץ** *m.* shattered pieces.

15 **שְׁבָבִים** *m. pl.* small pieces.

16 **אַשְׁפָּר** *m.* "a good piece of flesh." The etymology is very doubtful ; our translation derives it from שָׁפַר to be beautiful. Vulg., a roasting of beef, deriving it, perhaps, from אֵשׁ fire, and פַּר. Syr. and Chaldee, a piece of flesh.

Gen. xv. 10.	3	Lev. viii. 20, 20.	9	1 Sam. xxx. 12.	10
xv. 17.	4	ix. 13.	9	2 Sam. vi. 19.	16
Exod. xxix. 17, 17.	9	Num. x. 2.	13	xi. 21.	10
Lev. i. 6, 12.	9	Judg. ix. 53.	10	xxiii. 11.	6
ii. 6.	11	xix. 29.	9	1 Kings xi. 30, 31.	12
vi. 21.	11	1 Sam. ii. 36, 36.	1, 11	2 Kings ii. 12.	12

2 Kings iii. 19, 25.	6	Prov. vi. 26.	7	Ezek. xxiv. 4, 4, 6, 6.	9
1 Chron. xvi. 3.	16	xxviii. 21.	11	Dan. ii. 5.	5
Neh. iii. 11, 19, 20, 21,		Cant. iv. 3.	10	iii. 29.	5
24, 27, 30.	8	vi. 7.	10	Hos. viii. 6.	15
Job xli. 24.	10	Jer. xxxvii. 21.	7	Amos iii. 12.	2
Ps. lxviii. 30.	14	Ezek. xiii. 19.	11 a	iv. 7, 7.	6

PIERCE

1 אֲרִי *m.* a lion : Ps. xxii. 16, *lit.* like a lion. According to the reading of the Hebrew printed copies כָּאֲרִי ; but, according to Masora, כָּארוּ for כָּרוּ.

2 בָּרִיחַ *m.* This word is variously interpreted ; it may mean swift, see *Flee ;* or straight, see *Bar ;* see also *Crooked.* Isa. xxvii. 1, *marg.* ' *or,* crossing like a bar.' The word here refers to that which is extended, flying, tortuous, and is used to represent the vast extent of the power of the king of Babylon.—*Barnes.*

3 דָּקַר to stab or thrust through with a sword. KAL ᵃ *pret.* ᵇ מַדְקָרוֹת *f. pl.* piercings.

4 כָּרָה to dig. KAL *pret.*

5 מָחַץ to give a deep and deadly wound ; see *Smite.* KAL ᵃ *pret.* ᵇ *fut.*

6 נָקַב to bore. KAL ᵃ *pret.* ᵇ *fut.*

7 נָקַר to bore, pierce ; to bore out, dig out ; Niph. to be pierced with sharp pain. PIEL *pret.*

Num. xxiv. 8.	5 b	Job xl. 24.	6 b	Isa. xxvii. 1.	2
Judg. v. 26.	5 a	Ps. xxii. 16.	1, or 4	xxxvi. 1.	6 a
2 Kings xviii. 21.	6 a	Prov. xii. 18.	3 b	Zech. xii. 10.	3 a
Job xxx. 17.	7				

PIGEON

יוֹנָה *f.* a pigeon, a dove ; they build in various situations, according to their different kinds, as stock-doves, turtle-doves, wild pigeons, &c.: they were found in great numbers in Canaan, and were very cheap. Lev. i. 14 ; v. 7, 11 ; xii. 6, 8 ; xiv. 22, 30 ; xv. 14, 29 : Num. vi. 10.

PILE

מְדוּרָה *f.* a pile of wood ; literally, the place of a pile of wood : Isa. xxx. 33 : Ezek. xxiv. 9.

PILGRIMAGE

מָגוּר *m.* sojourning : Gen. xlvii. 9, 9 : Exod. vi. 4 : Ps. cxix. 54.

PILLAR

1 אֹמְנוֹת *f. pl.* pillars, from their firmness.

2 נָצַב to set, to put, to place. HOPHAL ᵃ *part.* ᵇ נְצִיב *m.* something placed or set, a statue. ᶜ מַצֵּבָה *f.* a statue or image ; a pillar or monument, for religious purposes, for the remembrance of the dead, &c. It is not improbable that the word means also a heap of stones piled up as a memorial. ᵈ מַצֶּבֶת *f. id.*

3 מִסְעָד *m.* a support.

4 עַמּוּד *m.* a column, a pillar ; the pillar of cloud, the pillar of fire ; the pillars of heaven, Job xxvi. 11 ; of the earth, Job ix. 6 ; it is used frequently : 1 Kings vii. 15, *lit.* eighteen cubits was the height of one pillar, 15, *lit.* the second pillar ; Jer. i. 18, *lit.* for an iron pillar, lii. 22, *lit.* and like these was to the second pillar.—Exod. xiii. 21, &c.

5 מְצֻק *m.* that which is set fast : 1 Sam. ii. 8, perhaps the foundations of the earth.

6 תִּימָרוֹת *f. pl.* found only in the expression, " pillars of smoke ;" perhaps from their resemblance to the palm-tree.

No. 4 not included.

Gen. xix. 26.	2 b	Exod. xxiv. 4.	2 c	1 Kings x. 12.	3
xxviii. 18, 22.	2 c	Deut. xii. 3.	2 c	2 Kings xviii. 16.	1
xxxi. 13, 45, 51,		Judg. ix. 6.	2 a	Cant. iii. 6.	6
52, 52.	2 c	1 Sam. ii. 8.	5	Isa. xix. 19.	2 c
xxxv. 14, 14.	2 c d	2 Sam. xviii. 18, 18.	2 d	Joel ii. 30.	6
xxxv. 20, 20.	2 c d				

PILLED

פָּצַל to take off the bark in strakes : found only in PIEL. *pret.* Gen. xxx. 38. *fut.* Gen. xxx. 37.

PILLOW

כָּבִיר something twisted or platted, a quilt : compare the similar expressions under net, sieve, grate, thick cloth : 1 Sam. xix. 13, 16.

כְּסָתוֹת *f. pl.* a cushion, pillow : Ezek. xiii. 18, 20.

מְרַאֲשֹׁת *f. pl.* place of or about the head (*comp.* מַרְגְּלוֹת, the place of the feet ; see *Feet*) : Gen. xxviii. 11, 18.

PILOT

חֹבֵל *m.* (see *Shipmaster*) : Ezek. xxvii. 8, 27, 28, 29.

PIN

יָתֵד *f.* a peg or pin, to be driven into a wall, Ezek. xv. 3 ; but especially a tent-pin : Exod. xxvii. 19, 19 ; xxxv. 18, 18 ; xxxviii. 20, 31, 31 ; xxxix. 40 : Num. iii. 37 ; iv. 32 : Judg. xvi. 14, 14 : Ezek. xv. 3.

PINE

תִּדְהָר *m.* a tree which grew upon Mount Lebanon, of what kind is uncertain ; the ancient translators fluctuate between the beech, pine, cypress, larch, &c. Isa. xli. 19 ; lx. 13.

עֵץ *m.* tree, trees ; Neh. viii. 15, *lit.* oil trees.

שֶׁמֶן *com.* oil : Neh. viii. 15, *lit.* branches of trees of oil.

PINE (V)

דַּלָּה *f.* pining sickness : or fine threads, from דָּלַל to be dried, or to hang down ; see *Hair ;* or to be slender. Isa. xxxviii. 12, *marg.* ' *or,* from the thrum.'

זוּב to flow out ; see *Issue.* KAL *fut.* Lam. iv. 9, *marg.* ' flow out.'

מָקַק to putrify ; to waste away, as from putrid sores. NIPHAL *pret.* Ezek. xxiv. 23. *fut.* Lev. xxvi. 39, 39. *part.* Ezek. xxxiii. 10.

PIPE

חָלִיל *m.* a flute or pipe : 1 Sam. x. 5 : 1 Kings i. 40, *marg.* ' *or,* flutes ;' Isa. v. 12 ; xxx. 29 : Jer. xlviii. 36, 36. חָלַל PIEL *part.* 1 Kings i. 40.

מוּצֶקֶת *f.* pipes through which the oil was poured : Zech. iv. 2.

נֶקֶב *m.* a pipe bored through : Ezek. xxviii. 13.

צַנְתְּרוֹת *f. pl.* tubes, pipes, through which the oil ran from the vessel to the lamps : Zech. iv. 12.

PISS

מַיִם *m. dual*, water : 2 Kings xviii. 27 : Isa. xxxvi. 12, *lit.* water of their feet.

רֶגֶל *f.* foot : 2 Kings xviii. 27 : Isa. xxxvi. 12, *lit.* the water of their feet.

שֵׁינִים *m. pl.* כתיב urine : 2 Kings xviii. 27 : Isa. xxxvi. 12.

שָׁתַן found only in HIPHIL *part.*, and it seems to be used by way of contempt : 1 Sam. xxv. 22, 34 : 1 Kings xiv. 10 ; xvi. 11 ; xxi. 21 : 2 Kings ix. 8.

PIT

1 בְּאֵר *f.* a well, a pit of springing water ; a deep pit, in which a person may be swallowed up and drowned : Gen. xiv. 10, full of pits ; *lit.* pits, pits.

2 בּוֹר *m.* a pit for receiving rain water, a cistern ; a dry pit, sometimes used as a dungeon ; the grave : Gen. xxxvii. 20, &c.

3 גֵּב *m.* pit or well.

4 גֵּבֶא *m.* a pit, pond, or pool ; a marsh, in which water is collected.

5 גּוּמָץ *m.* a pit in which water is collected.

6 מַהֲמֹרוֹת *f. pl.* deep pits ; the etymology is unknown.

7 מְכֵרָה *m.* a pit which has been prepared.

8 פַּחַת *m.* a pit dug out. As representing destruction, it is joined, by way of paronomasia, with פַּחַד and פַּח in Isa. xxiv. 17, Jer. xlviii. 43. See APPENDIX.

9 שְׁאוֹל *com.* the grave, hell, destruction.

10 שׁוּחָה *f.* a slough or clay-pit. ᵃ שִׁיחָה *f. id.* ᵇ שׁוּחוֹת *f. id.* ᶜ שְׁחִית *f. id.*

11 שַׁחַת *f.* corruption ; a pit ; a pitfall, to entrap wild beasts.

No. 2 not included.

Gen. xiv. 10.	1	Ps. lxix. 15.	1	Isa. xxxviii. 17.	11
Num. xvi. 30, 33.	9	xciv. 13.	11	li. 14.	11
2 Sam. xvii. 9.	8	cxix. 85.	10 a	Jer. ii. 6.	10
xviii. 17.	8	cxl. 10.	6	xiv. 3.	3
Job xvii. 16.	9	Prov. xxii. 14.	1	xviii. 20.	10
xxxiii. 18, 24, 28, 30.	11	xxiii. 27.	1	xviii. 22.	10, or 10 a
Ps. ix. 15.	11	xxvi. 27.	11	xlviii. 43, 44, 44.	8
xxx. 9.	11	xxviii. 10.	10 b	Lam. iv. 20.	10 c
xxxv. 7.	11	Eccles. x. 8.	5	Ezek. xix. 4, 8.	11
lv. 23.	1	Isa. xxiv. 17, 18, 18.	8	xxviii. 8.	11
lvii. 6.	10 a	xxx. 14.	4	Zeph. ii. 9.	7

PITCH

זֶפֶת *f.* pitch, or kind of bitumen : Exod. ii. 3, Isa. xxxiv. 9, 9.

כָּפַר to cover, to overlay, to pitch. KAL *pret.* Gen. vi. 14. כֹּפֶר *m.* Gen. vi. 14.

PITCH

1 חָנָה to set oneself down in any place ; to encamp, to pitch a tent, to pitch. KAL ᵃ *pret.* ᵇ *inf.* ᶜ *fut.* ᵈ *part.* Poel.

2 נָטָה to stretch out, to pitch a tent. KAL ᵃ *pret.* ᵇ *fut.*

3 קוּם to rise. HIPHIL, to set up : *pret.*

4 תָּקַע to strike ; to pitch a tent by driving in the tent pins. KAL *pret.*

See also *Tent.*

Gen. xii. 8.	2 b	Gen. xxxiii. 18.	1 c	Num. i. 51.	1 b
xxvi. 17.	1 c	Exod. xxxiii. 1.	1 c	i. 52.	1 a
xxvi. 25.	2 b	xix. 2.	1 c	i. 53.	1 c
xxxi. 25, 25.	4	xxxiii. 7.	2 a	ii. 2, 2.	1 c

PITCHER

כַּד *f.* a great earthern vessel to hold water, meal, &c. : Gen. xxiv. 14, 15, 16, 17, 18, 20, 43, 45, 46 : Judg. vii. 16, 16, 19, 20 : Eccles. xii. 6.

נֵבֶל *m.* (see *Bottle*) : Lam. iv. 2.

PITY

1 חוּס to have a favourable tender regard to ; and for that reason to spare, to exempt from punishment, to be loath to part with ; because compassion and sympathy are awakened by the sight, it is often joined with עַיִן the eye. KAL ᵃ *pret.* ᵇ *fut.*

2 חָמַל to be soft and tender ; to treat with tenderness, humanity, and clemency ; to show favour and indulgence ; to be loath to lose or destroy ; to pity, to spare ; see *Spare.* KAL ᵃ *pret.* ᵇ *fut.* חֶמְלָה ᶜ *f.* mercy, gentleness. ᵈ מַחְמָל *m.* the object of pity, sympathy ; then of love and affection, a delight : Ezek. xxiv. 21, *marg.* 'the pity of your soul ;' this word seems to have been used by paronomasia with מַחְמָד ; see *Desire ;* comp. verse 25.

3 חָנַן to be kindly and tenderly affected towards ; to show favour, mercy, pity. KAL ᵃ *imp.* ᵇ *part.* Poel.

4 חֶסֶד *m.* see *Kindness.*

5 נוּד see *Bemoan.* KAL *inf.*

6 רָחַם this word implies the tenderest love, affection, pity, compassion. PIEL ᵃ *pret.* ᵇ *inf.* ᶜ *fut.* ᵈ רַחֲמִים *m. pl.* bowels ; pity, grace, favour. ᵉ רַחֲמָנִי *adj.* merciful, compassionate.

Deut. vii. 16.	1 b	Prov. xxviii. 8.	3 b	Ezek. vii. 4, 9.	2 b
xiii. 8.	1 b	Isa. xiii. 18.	6 c	viii. 18.	2 b
xix. 13, 21.	1 b	xiii. 9.	2 c	ix. 5, 10.	2 b
xxv. 12.	1 b	Jer. xiii. 14.	2 b	xvi. 5.	1 d
2 Sam. xii. 6.	2 a	xv. 5.	2 b	xxiv. 21.	2 d
Job vi. 14.	4	xxi. 7.	2 b	xxxvi. 21.	2 b
xix. 21, 21.	3 a	Lam. ii. 2, 17, 21.	2 a	Joel ii. 18.	2 b
Ps. lxix. 20.	5	iii. 43.	2 a	Amos i. 11.	6 d
ciii. 13, 13.	6 b d	iv. 10.	6 e	Jonah iv. 10.	1 a
cvi. 46.	6 d	Ezek. v. 11.	2 b	Zech. xi. 5, 6.	2 b
Prov. xix. 17.	3 b				

PLACE

1 אֹהֶל *m.* tent : Job xxi. 28, "dwelling-places," *marg.* 'the tent of the tabernacles ;' see *Tabernacle.*

2 אֲתַר Ch. *m.* place.

3 בַּיִת *m.* house ; a place of habitation ; a place or that in which anything lieth, is contained, or is laid up.

4 גְּבוּלָה *f.* border.

5 זוּר see *Stranger.* KAL *part.* "that come from another place."

Num. ii. 3, 5, 12.	1 d	Josh. iv. 20.	3	1 Sam. xxviii. 4, 4.	1 c
ii. 34.	1 a	viii. 11.	1 c	xxix. 1.	1 d
iii. 23, 29, 35.	1 c	xi. 5.	1 c	2 Sam. vi. 17.	2 a
ix. 17, 18.	1 c	Judg. iv. 11.	2 b	xvii. 26.	1 c
xii. 16.	1 c	vi. 33.	1 c	xxiii. 13.	1 d
xxi. 10, 11, 12, 13.	1 c	vii. 1.	1 c	xxiv. 5.	1 c
xxii. 1.	1 c	xi. 18, 20.	1 c	1 Kings xx. 27, 29.	1 c
xxiii. 5, 6, 7, 8, 9,		xv. 9.	1 c	2 Kings xxv. 1.	1 c
15, 16, 18, 19, 20,		xviii. 12.	1 c	1 Chron. xv. 1.	2 b
21, 22, 23, 25, 27,		1 Sam. iv. 1, 1.	1 c a	xvi. 1.	2 a
28, 29, 31, 33, 36,		xiii. 5.	1 c	xix. 7.	1 c
37, 41, 42, 43, 44,		xvii. 1, 2.	1 c	2 Chron. i. 4.	2 a
45, 47, 48, 49.	1 c	xxvi. 3.	1 c	Jer. vi. 3.	4
Deut. i. 33.	1 b	xxvi. 5, 5.	1 a d	lii. 4.	1 c

6   יָד *com.* hand. Gesenius thinks that in 2 Sam. xviii. 18 it means a monument or trophy on which was sculptured a hand.

7   כֵּן *m.* a place ; a frame, stand, basis.

8   מָכוֹן *m.* a place ; foundation ; settled place, dwelling-place.

9   נָגַשׁ to draw near ; it is used apparently in the sense of receding in KAL *imp.* Isa. xlix. 20 ; LXX. ποίησόν μοι τόπον. Hieron. *fac mihi spatium.*

10   מְעוֹנָה *m.* habitation, dwelling-place, refuge.

11   עֹמֶד *m.* standing.

12   מַעֲמָד *m.* standing, station.

13   מָקוֹם *com.* a station, a standing, a place, where anything is situated, or person resides ; a country or town ; a place upon the human body, as we use the word place in English : 2 Kings v. 11.—Gen. i. 9, &c.

14   פֶּתַח *m.* door : Gen. xxxviii. 14, *marg.* ' in the door of eyes, *or,* of Enajim.'

15   יָשַׁב to dwell. KAL *inf.*

No. 13 not included.

Gen. xxxviii. 14.	14	1 Chron. xxviii. 11.	3	Job viii. 17.	3
xl. 13.	7	2 Chron. vi. 2, 30, 33,		xxi. 28.	1
Exod. xv. 17.	8	39.	8	xxxvii. 8.	10
xxv. 27.	3	xxx. 16.	11	Ps. xxxiii. 14.	8
xxvi. 29.	3	xxxiv. 31.	11	cxli. 6.	6
xxx. 4.	3	xxxv. 10.	11	Prov. viii. 2.	3
xxxvi. 34.	3	xxxv. 15.	12	Isa. xxviii. 25.	4
xxxvii. 14, 27.	3	Ezra ii. 68.	8	xlix. 20, 20.	13, 9
xxxviii. 5.	3	v. 15.	2	lvii. 8.	6
Num. ii. 17.	6	vi. 3, 5, 7.	2	Jer. vi. 3.	6
Deut. ii. 37.	6	Neh. ii. 3.	3	xviii. 14.	5
xxiii. 12.	6	iii. 3.	3	Ezek. xxi. 19.	6
1 Sam. xv. 12.	6	viii. 7.	11	xli. 9.	3
2 Sam. xv. 17.	3	ix. 31.	11	xlvi. 24.	3
xviii. 18.	6	xiii. 11.	11	Dan. ii. 35.	2
xxiii. 7.	15	Esth. vii. 8.	3	viii. 11.	8
1 Kings viii.13, 39, 43, 49.	8				

PLACE (V)

1   יָנַח to set or put down ; to leave ; to place a people in their own country. HIPHIL ᵃ*pret.* ᵇ*fut.*

2   יָשַׁב to dwell ; HIPHIL, to cause to dwell : ᵃ*pret.* ᵇ*fut.* HOPHAL ᶜ*pret.*

3   לָקַח to take, to bring. KAL *pret.*

4   נְחַת Ch. to come down. APHEL *fut.*

5   נָתַן to give. KAL ᵃ*pret.* ᵇ*fut.*

6   עָמַד to stand. HIPHIL *pret.*

7   שׂוּם to put or set. KAL ᵃ*pret.* ᵇ*inf.*

8   שָׁכַן to dwell. PIEL ᵃ*pret.* ᵇ*inf.* HIPHIL ᶜ*fut.*

Gen. iii. 24.	8 c	2 Chron. i. 14.	1 b	Jer. v. 22.	7 a
xlvii. 11.	2 b	iv. 8.	1 b	Ezek. xvii. 5.	3
Exod. xviii. 21.	7 a	xvii. 2.	5 b	xxxvii. 14.	1 a
Deut. xiv. 23.	8 b	Ezra vi. 5.	4	xxxvii. 26.	5 a
xvi. 2, 6, 11.	8 b	Job xx. 4.	7 b	Dan. xi. 31.	5 a
xxvi. 2.	8 b	Ps. lxxviii. 60.	8 a	Hos. xi. 11.	2 a
1 Kings xii. 32.	6	Isa. v. 8.	2 c	Zech. x. 6.	2 a
2 Kings xvii. 6, 24, 26.	2 b	xlvi. 13.	5 a		

PLAGUE

1   דֶּבֶר *m.* (see *Pestilence*) : Hos. xiii. 14, or, according to a different pointing, where are thy plagues? as in our N. T. translation, and the LXX. ποῦ ἡ δίκη σου.

2   נָגַע to touch ; to smite ; to inflict, or to be afflicted with any distress, calamity, plague, by the hand of God. KAL ᵃ*part.* Paül. PIEL ᵇ*fut.* PUAL ᶜ*fut.* ᵈ נֶגַע *m.* any affliction, calamity, sorrow.—Gen. xii. 17, &c. Especially the plague of leprosy, in Lev. xiii. and xiv.

3   נָגַף to smite. KAL ᵃ*fut.* ᵇ נֶגֶף *m.* a plague or destructive calamity sent by God. ᶜ מַגֵּפָה *f.* slaughter, discomfiture ; a plague sent by God.

4   מַכָּה *f.* a smiting ; slaughter ; wounds, &c.

No. 2 d not included.

Gen. xii. 17, 17.	2 b d	Num. xxvi. 1.	3 c	2 Chron. xxi. 14.	3 c
Exod. ix. 14.	3 c	xxxi. 16.	3 c	Ps. lxxiii. 5.	2 c
xii. 13.	3 b	Deut. xxviii. 59, 59,		lxxiii. 14.	2 a
xxx. 12.	3 b	59, 61,	4	lxxxix. 23.	3 a
xxxii. 35.	3 a	xxix. 22.	4	cvi. 29, 30.	3 c
Lev. xxvi. 21.	4	Josh. xxii. 17.	3 b	Jer. xix. 8.	4
Num. viii. 19.	3 b	xxiv. 5.	3 b	xlix. 17.	4
xi. 33.	4	1 Sam. iv. 8.	4	l. 13.	4
xiv. 37.	3 c	vi. 4.	3 c	Hos. xiii. 14.	1
xvi. 46, 47.	3 b	2 Sam. xxiv. 21, 25.	3 c	Zech. xiv. 12, 15, 15,	
xvi. 48, 49, 50.	3 c	1 Chron. xxi. 17, *a* 22.	3 c	18.	3 c
xxv. 8, 9, 18.	3 c				

a lit. for plague.

PLAIN

בָּאַר to dig ; to explain ; see *Declare.* PIEL *imp.* Deut. xxvii. 8 : Hab. ii. 2.

יָטַב to be well. HIPHIL *inf.* Deut. xxvii. 8, *lit.* by declaring well.

מִישׁוֹר *m.* plain, plainness : Ps. xxvii. 11, *marg.* ' way of plainness.'

נָכֹחַ *adj.* right : Prov. viii. 9.

סָלַל to cast up a road ; to make plain. KAL *part.* Paül, Prov. xv. 19, *marg.* ' raised up as a causey.'

פְּרַשׁ Ch. to distinguish. PAEL *part. passive,* Ezra iv. 18, *i.e.* distinctly, accurately, word for word.

שָׁוָה to be level and even ; PIEL, to make plain : *pret.* Isa. xxviii. 25.

צַח *adj.* white, bright, clear : Isa. xxxii. 4, *marg.* ' or, elegantly.'

תָּם *adj.* perfect ; plain, simple, sincere : Gen. xxv. 27.

A PLAIN

1   אָבֵל *f.* a grassy place, meadow ; also the name of several places.

2   אַלּוֹן *m.* an oak, or any strong durable tree ; *collect.* oaks, &c., or a plain of oaks.

3   בִּקְעָה *f.* valley, low plain. Gussetius, a way opened through obstacles, as in rough places : Isa. xl. 4. ᵃ בִּקְעָא Ch. *f. id.*

4   מִישׁוֹר *m.* plain, plainness.

5   עֲבָרָה *f.* passage over : 2 Sam. xv. 28, and xvii. 16, כְּתִיב.

6   עֲרָבָה *f.* a plain ; particularly a waste, desert ; when joined with the article הָעֲרָבָה by way of eminence, the country between the Dead Sea and the Elanitic Gulf, Deut. i. 1 ; ii. 8 : Josh. xii. 1 ; whence the Dead Sea is called the Sea of the Plain : Deut. iv. 49 : Josh. iii. 19.—Num. xxii. 1, &c.

7   כִּכָּר circle ; circuit, surrounding country.

8 שְׁפֵלָה *f.* a low place, a valley, a low plain.

No. 6 not included.

Gen. xi. 2.	3	Judg. ix. 6, 37.	2	Neh. vi. 2.	3
xii. 6.	2	xi. 33.	1	xii. 28.	7
xiii. 10, 11, 12.	7	1 Sam. x. 3.	2	Isa. xl. 4.	8
xiii. 18.	2	2 Sam. xv. 28.	6, or 5	Jer. xvii. 26.	8
xiv. 13.	2	xvii. 16.	6, or 5	xxi. 13.	4
xviii. 1.	2	xviii. 23.	7	xlviii. 8, 21.	4
xix. 17, 25, 28, 29.	7	1 Kings vii. 46.	2	Ezek. iii. 22, 23.	7
Deut. iii. 10.	4	xx. 23, 25.	4	viii. 4.	8
iv. 43.	4	1 Chron. xxvii. 28.	8	Dan. iii. 1.	3 a
xi. 30.	2	2 Chron. iv. 17.	7	Amos i. 5.	8
xxxiv. 3.	7	ix. 27.	8	Obad. 19.	8
Josh. xiii. 9, 16, 17, 21.	4	xxvi. 10.	4	Zech. iv. 7.	4
xx. 8.	4	Neh. iii. 22.	7	vii. 7.	8
Judg. iv. 11.	2				

PLANES

מַקְצֻעוֹת *f. pl.* a plane or some similar instrument : Isa. xliv. 13.

PLANETS

מַזָּלוֹת *f. pl.* This word is most generally supposed to mean the constellations of the Zodiac, and various opinions are given as to the derivation, yet Fürst adheres to our translation, supposing that נָזַל may mean to wander as well as to flow : 2 Kings xxiii. 5, *marg.* 'or, twelve signs, or constellations.'

PLANK

עַב *m.* thick planks ; according to Gesenius, an architectural term, probably a threshold forming the entrance to a colonnade or temple. Ezek. xli. 26.

עֵץ *m.* a tree, wood : Ezek. xli. 25.

צֵלָע *f.* a rib, a board : 1 Kings vi. 15.

PLANT

1 יוֹנֵק *m.* a twig or young tender branch, deriving its nutriment from the tree.

2 נָטַע to plant, to set with plants ; *metaph.* to plant, settle, establish (a people) ; to drive in (a nail) ; to set up (an image), Deut. xvi. 21 ; to pitch or erect (a tent), *tentorium figere*, from the driving in of the tent pins, Dan. xi. 45 ; hence applied to the tent of heaven, Isa. li. 16. KAL ^a*pret.* ^b*inf.* ^c*imp.* ^d*fut.* ^e*part.* Poel. ^f*part.* Paül. NIPHAL ^g*pret.* ^h נֵטַע *m.* a plant, a planting, a place planted. ⁱ נְטִעִים *m. pl.* plants. ^k מַטָּע *m.* a plantation, place of plants.

3 נְטִישׁוֹת *f. pl.* branches that spread out.

4 נָתַן to give. KAL *fut.*

5 שִׂיחַ *m.* a plant, shrub, or bush.

6 שֶׁלַח *m.* a sprout, a shoot.

7 שְׁרוּקִים *m. pl.* noble shoots or tendrils of the vine, "principal plants :" Isa. xvi. 8.

8 שָׁתַל to plant ; Geier, to transplant ; more frequently, *figur.* to settle in a habitation. KAL ^a*pret.* ^b*fut.* ^c*part.* Paül. ^d שְׁתִל *m.* a plant, a shoot.

Gen. ii. 5.	5	Num. xxiv. 6.	2 a	2 Sam. vii. 10.	2 a
ii. 8.	2 d	Deut. vi. 11.	2 a	2 Kings xix. 29.	2 c
ix. 20.	2 d	xvi. 21.	2 d	1 Chron. iv. 23.	2 h
xxi. 33.	2 d	xx. 6.	2 a	xvii. 9.	2 h
Exod. xv. 17.	2 d	xxviii. 30, 39.	2 d	Job xiv. 9.	2 h
Lev. xix. 23.	2 a	Josh. xxiv. 13.	2 a	Ps. i. 3.	8 c

Ps. xliv. 2. | lxxx. 8. etc.

Ps. xliv. 2.	2 d	Isa. xli. 19.	4	Jer. xlii. 10.	2 a
lxxx. 8.	2 d	xliv. 14.	2 a	xlv. 4.	3
lxxx. 15.	2 a	li. 16.	2 b	xlviii. 32.	3
xcii. 13.	8 c	Ezek. xvii. 5.	4	
xciv. 9.	2 e	lx. 21.	2 i	xvii. 7.	2 i
civ. 16.	2 a	lxi. 3.	2 i	xvii. 8, 10.	8 c
cvii. 37.	2 d	lxv. 21.	2 a	xvii. 22.	8 a
cxxviii. 3.	8 d	lxv. 22.	2 a	xvii. 23.	8 b
cxliv. 12.	2 i	Jer. i. 10.	2 b	xix. 10, 13.	8 c
Prov. xxxi. 16.	2 a	i. 21.	2 a	xxxii. 26.	2 a
Eccles. ii. 4, 5.	2 a	xi. 17.	2 e	xxxi. 4.	2 i
ii. 2, 2.	2 b f	xviii. 9.	2 b	xxxiv. 29.	2 a
Cant. iv. 13.	6	xxiv. 6.	2 a	xxxvi. 36.	2 a
Isa. v. 2.	2 h	xxix. 5, 28.	2 c	Hos. ix. 13.	8 c
v. 7.	2 h	xxxi. 5, 5, 5.	2 d e a	Amos v. 11.	2 a
xvi. 8.	7	xxxi. 28.	2 a	ix. 14, 15.	2 a
xvii. 10, 10.	2 d h	xxxii. 41.	2 a	Micah i. 6.	2 i
xvii. 11.	2 h	xxxv. 7.	2 d	Zeph. i. 13.	2 a
xxxvii. 30.	2 c				
xl. 24.	2 g				

PLASTER

גִּיר Ch. *m.* chalk, plaster : Dan. v. 5.

טוּחַ to cover, overlay, to plaster. KAL *pret.* Lev. xiv. 42. NIPHAL *inf.* Lev. xiv. 43, 48.

מָרַח to rub or bruise, and so to prepare a plaster for a sore or wound. KAL *fut.* Isa. xxxviii. 21, LXX. καὶ τρίψον καὶ καταπλάσαι ; Vulg. *et cataplasmarent super vulnus.*

שִׂיד *m.* lime, plaster : Deut. xxvii. 2, 4. שִׂיד to cover with lime. KAL *pret.* Deut. xxvii. 2, 4.

PLAT

חֶלְקָה *f.* (see *Portion*) : 2 Kings ix. 26, *marg.* 'or, portion,' 26.

PLATE

לוּחַ *m.* a tablet of stone or wood : 1 Kings vii. 36.

סֶרֶן an axle-tree, which in ancient times, especially in waggons, were fastened to the wheels, and went round with them. —*Gesenius.* 1 Kings vii. 30.

פַּח a gin or snare ; thin plates : Exod. xxxix. 3 : Num. xvi. 38.

צִיץ *m.* something shining, especially the gold plate which the high-priest wore on his forehead : Exod. xxviii. 36 ; xxxix. 30 : Lev. viii. 9.

רָקַע to beat, to spread out, to make broad ; PUAL, to spread into plates : *part.* Jer. x. 9.

PLAY

1 חָלִיל *m.* a flute or pipe. חָלַל *denom.* to blow the flute or pipe. KAL *part.* Poel, "players on instruments."

2 טוֹב to be good. HIPHIL, to play well : *part.*

3 נָגַן to play upon and to sing to stringed instruments. KAL ^a*part.* Poel. PIEL ^b*pret.* ^c*inf.* ^d*part.*

4 צָחַק to laugh. Piel, to play, or sport, with singing, leaping, dancing. PIEL *inf.* Exod. xxxii. 6 ; it seems to imply wantonness, *comp.* Num. xxv. 1, 2.

5 שָׂחַק to laugh, to sport, to mock, to make merry. PIEL ^a*pret.* ^b*inf.* ^c*fut.* ^d*part.*

6 שָׁעַע to take pleasure in, to delight oneself. PILPEL *pret.*

Exod. xxxii. 6.	4	2 Sam. vi. 5.	5 d	Ps. xxxiii. 3.	3 c
1 Sam. xvi. 16, 16.	3 b d	vi. 21.	5 a	lxviii. 25.	3 a
xvi. 17, 18.	3 c	2 Kings iii. 15.	3 c	lxxxvii. 7.	1
xvi. 23.	3 b	1 Chron. xiii. 8.	5 d	civ. 26.	5 b
xviii. 7.	5 d	xv. 29.	5 d	Isa. xi. 8.	5 d
xviii. 10.	3 d	Job xl. 20.	5 c	Ezek. xxxiii. 32.	3 c, 2
xix. 9.	3 d	xli. 5.	5 c	Zech. viii. 5.	5 d
2 Sam. ii. 14.	5 c				

PLEA, PLEAD

1   דִּין to judge, to plead a cause. KAL ^a imp. ^b part. Poel. ^c דִּין m. judgment.

2   יָכַח to show, prove; to judge, decide; to contend with any one. HIPHIL ^a fut. HITHPAEL ^b fut.

3   רִיב to strive, to contend; to maintain a cause before a judge, seq. acc. of the person whose cause one sustains, to defend; to prove guilt, or discover the weakness of a cause. KAL ^a pret. ^b inf. ^c imp. ^d fut. ^e part. ^f רִיב m. strife, contention; a forensic cause.

4   שָׁפַט to judge; to do justice to any one, spoken of a judge; to plead for any one, spoken of an advocate; Niphal, to be judged, to contend with a person, construed usually with אֵת. NIPHAL ^a pret. ^b fut. ^c part.

Deut. xvii. 8, 8.	1 c	Ps. cxix. 154.	3 c	Jer. xxv. 31.	4 c	
Judg. vi. 31, 31, 31,		xxii. 23.	3 d	xxx. 13.	1 b	
32.	3 d	xxiii. 11.	3 d	l. 34.	3 b d	
1 Sam. xxiv. 15.	3 d	xxxi. 9.	1 a	li. 36.	3 e	
xxv. 39.	3 a	Isa. i. 17.	3 c	Lam. iii. 58.	3 a	
Job xiii. 6.	3 f	iii. 13.	3 b	Ezek. xvii. 20.	4 a	
xiii. 19.	3 d	xliii. 26.	4 b	xx. 35.	4 a	
xvi. 21.	2 a	li. 22.	3 d	xx. 36, 36.	4 a b	
xix. 5.	2 a	lix. 4.	4 c	xxxviii. 22.	4 a	
xxiii. 6.	3 d	lxvi. 16.	4 b	Hos. ii. 2, 2.	4 c	
Ps. xxxv. 1.	3 c	Jer. ii. 9, 9, 29.	3 d	Joel iii. 2.	4 a	
xliii. 1.	3 c	ii. 35.	4 c	Micah vi. 2.	2 b	
lxxiv. 22.	3 c	xii. 1.	3 d	vii. 9.	3 d	

PLEASE, PLEASANT, PLEASURE

1   אַוַּת f. earnest desire, strong affection. ^a תַּאֲוָה f. desire; object of desire.

2   חָמַד to desire strongly; to take delight in; to covet. NIPHAL ^a part. ^b חֶמֶד m. desirableness, the object of desire. ^c חֶמְדָּה f. a desiring, object of desire; pleasantness, preciousness. ^d חֲמֻדוֹת f. pl. id. ^e מַחְמָד m. desire, the object of desire. ^f מַחֲמַדִּים m. pl. id. Lam. i. 11, כְּתִיב.

3   חֵן m. grace, favour: Prov. v. 19, lit. roe of favour.

4   חֵפֶץ (see Delight), to will that in which one has great delight when accomplished; joined, therefore, with a negative, it implies very great aversion and dislike: Ezek. xviii. 3, "have I any pleasure," do I desire so as to have pleasure and satisfaction in the death of the wicked. KAL ^a pret. ^b inf. ^c fut. ^d חָפֵץ adj. having a delight in. ^e חֵפֶץ m. delight; that which is precious as an object of delight; Gesenius, pursuit, ardour; hence affair, matter.

5   חֵשֶׁק m. desire, delight.

6   טוֹב to be good, to seem good; with עַיִן to please, lit. to be good in the eyes of. KAL ^a pret. ^b טוֹב adj.

7   יָאַל to be willing, implying a force on the will; to yield, not to refuse; to be content, to consent. HIPHIL ^a pret. ^b imp. ^c fut.

8   יָטַב to be good; with עַיִן as טוֹב. KAL ^a fut. HIPHIL ^b fut.

9   יָפֶה adj. fair, beautiful.

10   יָשַׁר to be right; to please, Heb. to be right in the eyes of. KAL ^a pret. ^b fut. ^c יָשָׁר adj. right.

11   מֶגֶד m. costly or precious gifts, especially of nature.

12   נָאָה f. (see Pasture, Habitation), pleasant places.

13   נָוֶה m. (see Habitation).

14   נָעֵם to be pleasant, lovely; spoken of a country, of one beloved, of a friend. KAL ^a pret. ^b fut. ^c נֹעַם m. pleasantness, loveliness. ^d נְעָמִים m. pl. pleasantnesses. ^e נָעִים adj. pleasant, lovely.

15   נֶפֶשׁ com. soul; faculties and affections of the mind.

16   עֵדֶן m. delight, pleasure. ^a עֶדְנָה f. pleasure. ^b עָדִין adj. given to pleasure.

17   עַיִן com. eye.

18   עֹנֶג delights, delicate life. ^a תַּעֲנֻג m. id.

19   עָרֵב to mix; to be well mixed, to be sweet, pleasant. KAL ^a pret. ^b fut.

20   פָּנִים m. pl. face: "pleased," lit. was good before.

21   צְבִי m. glory, loveliness, beauty.

22   קֳדָם Ch. prep. Dan. vi. 1, lit. it was seemly before.

23   רַע adj. evil.

24   רְעוּת Ch. f. will, pleasure.

25   רָצָה to be well pleased with, to take delight in. KAL ^a pret. ^b inf. ^c imp. ^d fut. ^e part. Poel. PIEL ^f fut. ^g רָצוֹן m. delight, satisfaction.

26   שִׂמְחָה f. joy, gladness, mirth.

27   שָׂפַק to clap the hands, in primary meaning supposed to be similar to סָפַק to smite; hence to be pleased; or, to strike a covenant, make leagues; or, to abound. HIPHIL fut. Isa. ii. 6, marg. 'or, abound with;' see Suffice. Gesenius supposes the meaning may be either they make covenants, or they trade with the children of strangers, in which sense the word strike may be used.

28   שְׁפַר Ch. to be seemly. P'AL pret.

29   שַׁעֲשֻׁעִים m. pl. pleasure, delight, also an object of delight.

Gen. ii. 9.	2 a	Ezra v. 17.	24	Ps. cxlvii. 10.	25 d
iii. 6.		x. 11.	25 g	cxlvii. 11.	25 e
xvi. 6.	6 b, 17	Neh. ii. 5, 7.	6 a	cxlix. 4.	25 e
xviii. 12.	16 a	ii. 6.	8 a	Prov. ii. 10.	14 b
xx. 15.	6 b, 17	ix. 37.	25 g	iii. 17.	14 c
xxviii. 8.	23, 17	Esth. i. 8.	25 g	v. 19.	3
xxxiii. 10.	25 d	i. 19.	6 a	ix. 17.	14 b
xxxiv. 18.	8 a, 17	i. 21.	8 a, 17	xv. 26.	14 c
xlv. 16.	8 a, 17	ii. 4.	8 a, 17	xvi. 7.	25 b
xlix. 15.	14 a	ii. 4.	8 a, 17	xvi. 24.	14 c
Exod. xxi. 8.	23, 17	ii. 9.	8 a, 17	xxi. 17.	26
Num. xxiii. 27.	10 b, 17	iii. 9.	9	xxii. 18.	14 e
xxiv. 1.	6 a, 17	v. 8.	6 a	xxiv. 4.	14 e
Deut. i. 23.	8 a, 17	v. 14.	8 a, 20	Eccles. ii. 1.	6 b
xxiii. 24.	15	vii. 3.	6 a	v. 4.	6 b
Josh. xxii. 30.	8 a, 17	viii. 5, 5.	6 b	vii. 26.	6 b, 20
xxii. 33.	8 a, 17	ix. 13.	6 b	viii. 3.	4 c
Judg. xiii. 23.	4 a	Job iv. 9.	7 c	xi. 7.	6 b
xiv. 3.	10 a, 17	xx. 10. a	25 f	xii. 1.	4 e
xiv. 7.	10 b, 17	xxi. 21.	4 e	Cant. i. 16.	14 e
1 Sam. xii. 22.	7 a	xxi. 25.	6 b	ii. 7.	4 c
xviii. 20.	10 b, 17	xxii. 3.	4 e	iii. 5.	4 c
xviii. 26.	10 b, 17	xxxvi. 11.	14 e	iv. 13, 16.	11
xx. 13.	8 b	Ps. v. 4.	4 d	vi. 9.	14 a
2 Sam. i. 23.	14 e	xvi. 6, 11.	14 e	vii. 13.	11
i. 26.	14 a	xxxv. 27.	4 d	viii. 4.	4 c
iii. 36.	6 b, 17	xxxvi. 8.	16	Isa. ii. 6.	27
iii. 36.	6 b, 17	xl. 13.	25 c	ii. 16.	2 c
vii. 29.	7 a	li. 18.	25 g	v. 7.	29
xvii. 4.	10 b, 17, 17	li. 19.	4 c	xiii. 22.	18
xix. 6.	10 b, 17	lxix. 31.	8 a	xvii. 10.	14 d
1 Kings iii. 10.	8 a, 17	lxxxi. 2.	14 e	xxi. 4.	5
ix. 1.	4 a	cii. 14.	25 a	xxxii. 12.	2 b
ix. 12.	10 a, 17	ciii. 21.	25 g	xlii. 21.	3 a
xx. 6.	2 a	cv. 22.	15	xliv. 28.	4 e
xxi. 6.	4 d	cvi. 24.	2 c	xlvi. 10.	4 e
2 Kings ix. 19.	4 e	cxi. 2.	29	xlvii. 8.	16 b
1 Chron. xvii. 27.	7 a	cxv. 3.	4 a	xlviii. 14.	4 e
xxix. 17.	25 d	cxxxiii. 12.	4 a	liii. 10, 10.	4 a e
2 Chron. x. 7.	25 a	cxxxv. 3.	14 e	liv. 12.	21
xxx. 4.	10 b, 17, 17	cxxxv. 6.	4 a	lv. 11.	4 e
xxxii. 27.	2 c	cxlvii. 1.	14 e	lvi. 4.	4 a

Isa. lviii. 3, 13, 13.	4 e	Ezek. xvi. 37.	19 a	Hos. ix. 13.	13
lxiv. 11.	2 e	xviii. 23.	4 b c	xiii. 15.	2 c
Jer. ii. 24.	1, 15	xxvi. 12.	4 c	Joel iii. 5.	2 e
iii. 19.	2 c	xxxiii. 11.	4 c	Amos v. 11.	2 b
xii. 10.	2 c	xxxiii. 32.	9	Jonah i. 14.	4 a
xxii. 28.	4 e	Dan. vi. 1.	28, 22	Micah ii. 9.	18 a
xxiii. 10.	12	viii. 9.	21	vi. 7.	25 d
xxv. 34.	2 c	x. 3.	29	Nah. ii. 9.	2 c
xxxi. 20.	29	xi. 38.	2 d	Hag. i. 8.	25 d
xxxiv. 16.	15	Hos. viii. 8.	2 d	Zech. vii. 14.	2 c
xlviii. 38.	2 f	ix. 4.	4 e	Mal. i. 8.	25 d
Lam. i. 7.	2 f	ix. 6.	19 b	i. 10.	4 e
i. 10, 11.	2 e		2 e	iii. 4.	19 a
ii. 4.	2 e				

a marg. ' or, the poor shall oppress his children,' as if from רָצַץ.

PLEDGE

1 חָבַל to tie with a cord, to twist, to bind; to take a pledge of any one, to bind him by a pledge; to take anything as a pledge. KAL ᵃ inf. ᵇ imp. ᶜ fut. ᵈ part. Poel. ᵉ part. Paül. ᶠ חֲבֹל m. a pledge. ᵍ חֲבֹלָה f. id.

2 עֲבוֹט m. a pledge or security for what is lent.

3 עָרַב to mix, to exchange, to stand in the place of any one (see Surety), to pledge, to give as a pledge. HITHPAEL ᵃ imp. ᵇ עֲרֻבָּה f. a pledge. ᶜ עֵרָבוֹן m. id.

Gen. xxxviii. 17, 18,		1 Sam. xvii. 18.	3 b	Isa. xxxvi. 8.	3 a
20.	3 c	2 Kings xviii. 23.	3 a	Ezek. xviii. 7.	1 g
Exod. xxii. 26.	1 a c	Job xxii. 6.	1 c	xii. 12, 16.	1 f
Deut. x i.v. 6, 6.	1 c d	xxiv. 3, 9.	1 c	xxxiii. 15.	1 f
xxiv. 17.	1 c	Prov. xxvii. 16.	1 b	Amos ii. 8.	1 e
xxiv. 10, 11, 12, 13.	2	xxvii. 13.	1 b		

PLEIADES

כִּימָה f. the seven stars called Pleiades; *lit.* a heap or collection: Job ix. 9; xxxviii. 31.

PLENTY

1 אָכַל to eat. KAL inf. "in plenty," *lit.* to eat.

2 בָּרִיא adj. fat, dainty.

3 תּוֹעֲפוֹת f. pl. weariness, wearisome labour; hence probably possession, substance, treasure: Job xxii. 25, marg. 'silver of strength, or, silver of treasures,' *i. e.* treasures of silver. So the word is derived from יָעַף to be weary: others consider the root to be, by a transposition of letters, יָפַע to shine, or, according to the Arabic, to be high, and would explain the passage, silver of heaps, or heaps of silver; see Strength.

4 יָתַר to remain, to be left; Hiphil, to make to abound, with an accusative of the person, and בְּ of the thing. HIPHIL ᵃ pret. ᵇ יֶתֶר m. remnant, abundance; with עַל plentifully. ᶜ מוֹתָר m. pre-eminence, abundance.

5 כַּרְמֶל m. fruitful field; Carmel.

6 נְדָבָה f. free-will; a free-will offering; copiousness.

7 מִקְוֶה m. a gathering together.

8 רַב adj. much, many, numerous. ᵇ רֹב m. multitude.

9 רָבָה to be numerous, great. HIPHIL inf.

10 שָׂבַע to be satisfied, satiated, filled, to have plenty. KAL ᵃ fut. ᵇ שָׂבָע plenty, abundance.

11 שָׁמֵן adj. fat.

Gen. xvii. 28.	8 a	Lev. xi. 36.	7	1 Kings x. 11.	9
xli. 29, 30, 31, 34,		Deut. xxviii. 11.	4 a	2 Chron. xxxi. 10.	8 a
47, 53.	10 b	xxx. 9.	4 a	Job xxii. 25.	3

Job xxvi. 3.	8 a	Ps. cxxx. 7.	9	Jer. ii. 7.	5
xxxvii. 23.	8 a	Prov. iii. 10.	10 b	xliv. 17.	10 a
Ps. xxxi. 23.	4 b	xxi. 5.	4 c	xlviii. 33.	5
lxvii. 9.	6	xxviii. 19.	10 a	Hab. i. 16.	1
lxxxvi. 5, 15.	8	Isa. xvi. 10.	5		2
ciii. 8.	8	xxx. 23.	11		

PLOT

זָמַם see *Devise.* KAL *part.* Poel, Ps. xxxvii. 12, marg. ' or, practiseth.'

PLOUGH, PLOW

1 אִכָּר m. one that tills or plows.

2 אֵת m. a tool used in digging the ground; a coulter, hoe, or mattock.

3 חָרַשׁ to cut, engrave; to plow, till. KAL ᵃ pret. ᵇ fut. ᶜ part. Poel. NIPHAL ᵈ fut.

4 נִר m. from נוּר to shine, whence נִיר land first broken up for tillage, from its bright appearance: so נוּר means also to plow: our translators have given this interpretation; others render it 'light.'

Deut. xxii. 10.	3 b	Prov. xxi. 4.	4	Hos. x. 13.	3 a
Judg. xiv. 18.	3 a	Isa. ii. 4.	3 a	Joel iii. 10.	3 b
1 Kings xix. 19.	3 c	xxviii. 24, 24.	3 c b	Amos vi. 12.	3 b
Job i. 14.	3 c	lxi. 5.	1	ix. 13.	3 c
iv. 8.	3 c	Jer. xiv. 4.	1	Micah iii. 12.	3 d
Ps. cxxix. 3, 3.	3 c a	xxvi. 18.	3 d	iv. 3.	2
Prov. xx. 4.	3	Hos. x. 11.	3 b		

PLUCK

1 אָרָה to pluck, crop off. KAL pret.

2 גָּזַל to tear away anything, to take away by violence; with an accusative of the person, to rob, or plunder. KAL ᵃ fut. ᵇ part. Poel.

3 הָרַס to tear down, demolish; to destroy. KAL fut.

4 טָרֵף adj. newly plucked or torn off.

5 יָצָא to go out; to cause to go out. HIPHIL fut.

6 כָּלָה to be completed or finished; Piel, to accomplish, finish. PIEL imp. Ps. lxxiv. 11. The rendering given in this verse is rather the implied meaning drawn from the former part of the verse, and therefore more is to be included: draw thy hand out of thy bosom, and complete the overthrow of our enemies. Hengst. recompense out of thy bosom.

7 מָרַט to make smooth by pulling or rubbing off the hair, &c.; to pluck off the hair, or beard, which was considered the greatest indignity. KAL ᵃ fut. ᵇ part. Poel. ᶜ מָרַט Ch. to pluck. P'IL pret.

8 נָסַח to tear down, to tear from one's dwelling or country. KAL ᵃ fut. NIPHAL ᵇ pret.

9 נָצַל to take, to take away. HOPHAL part.

10 מַשָּׂאַת f. a lifting up, a plucking up by the roots: Ezek. xvii. 9. According to Gesenius, מַשָּׂאוֹת in this passage is the Aram. inf. from נָשָׂא.

11 נָתַק to pluck or tear off, to draw off (from a place). KAL ᵃ fut. NIPHAL ᵇ pret. PIEL ᶜ fut.

12 נָתַשׁ to root out, strictly plants, hence to destroy, e. g. cities, idols; fig. to drive out of a country. KAL ᵃ pret. ᵇ inf. ᶜ fut. ᵈ part. Poel. NIPHAL ᵉ fut. HOPHAL ᶠ fut.

13 סוּר to turn aside, to depart; to make to depart. HIPHIL pret.

14 עָקַר to root out, to pluck up anything planted. KAL [a] inf. עֲקַר Ch. id. ITHP'AL [b] fut.

15 קָטַף to pluck off or crop, a branch, or ears of corn. KAL pret.

16 שָׁלַךְ see Cast. HIPHIL fut.

17 שָׁלַף to draw off, a shoe. KAL pret.

18 שָׁמַד to destroy, to pluck down. HIPHIL fut.

Gen. viii. 11.	4	Ps. xxv. 15.	5	Jer. xxxi. 28.	12 b
Exod. iv. 7.	5	lii. 5.	8 a	xxxi. 40.	12 e
Lev. i. 16.	13	lxxiv. 11.	6	xlii. 10.	12 c
Num. xxxiii. 52.	18	lxxx. 12.	1	xlv. 4.	12 d
Deut. xxiii. 25.	15	Prov. xiv. 1.	3	Ezek. xvii. 9.	10
xxviii. 63.	8 b	Eccles. iii. 2.	14 a	xix. 12.	12 e
Ruth iv. 7.	17	Isa. l. 6.	7 b	xxiii. 34.	11 c
2 Sam. xxiii. 21.	2 a	Jer. vi. 29.	11 b	Dan. vii. 4.	7 c
1 Chron. xi. 23.	2 a	xii. 14, 14.	12 d c	vii. 8.	14 b
2 Chron. vii. 20.	12 a	xii. 15.	12 b	ix. 4.	12 e
Ezra ix. 3.	7 a	xii. 17.	12 b a	Amos iv. 11.	9
Neh. xiii. 25.	7 a	xviii. 7.	12 b	Micah iii. 2.	2 b
Job xxiv. 9.	2 a	xxii. 24.	11 a	v. 14.	12 a
xxix. 17.	16	xxiv. 6.	12 c	Zech. iii. 2.	9

PLUMBLINE

אֲנָךְ m. lead; hence a plumb, plummet: Amos vii. 7, 7, 8, 8, "I will set a plumbline in the midst of my people," i. e. I will destroy all as by rule and line: cf. Isa. xxxiv. 11 : 2 Kings xxi. 13.

PLUMMET

אֶבֶן f. stone: Zech. iv. 10, marg. 'stone of tin.'

בְּדִיל m. tin: Zech. iv. 10.

מִשְׁקָל m. a weight. מִשְׁקֶלֶת f. plummet: Isa. xxviii. 17. f. id. 2 Kings xxi. 13.

PLUNGE

טָבַל to dip in, with בְּ. KAL fut. Job ix. 31.

POINT

אִבְחָה f. found only in Ezek. xxi. 15, point of the sword, marg. 'or, glittering, or, fear.' Probably the threatening of the sword, i. e. the threatening sword. It may also be rendered, sword of punishment. According to others, the destruction of the sword, i. e. the destroying sword. Gesenius, turning of the sword, or more probably i. q. מִבְחַת slaughter of the sword.

הָלַךְ to go. KAL part. Poel, Gen. xxv. 32, marg. 'going to die.'

עֻמָּה prep. secundum, juxta; near, answerable, corresponding to: Eccles. v. 16, "in all points as he came, so," &c., i. e. answerably in all respects as he came, so, &c.

צִפֹּרֶן m. a nail, a claw; fig. the (diamond) point of a style, lit. its nail: Jer. xvii. 1. Comp. Plin. N. H. xxxvii. ch. 4. A diamond was used for writing on tablets of brass.

POINT OUT

תָּאָה probably of the same signification as תָּוָה to mark out or describe. PIEL fut. Num. xxxiv. 7, 8, 10. Grammarians, however, observe that, in verse 10, the pointing requires that the word be referred to the HITHPAEL pret. of אָוָה; and Professor Lee proposes to translate it, "and claim for yourselves." See Lex.

POISON

חֵמָה f. wrath, fury, hot displeasure; poison, from its hot burning nature: Deut. xxxii. 24, 33 : Job vi. 4 : Ps. lviii. 4, 4 ; cxl. 3.

רֹאשׁ m. (see Hemlock): Job xx. 16.

POLE

נֵס m. anything lifted up so as to be seen afar off: Num. xxi. 8, 9. LXX. ἐπὶ σημείον: Vulg. pro signo.

POLICY

שֵׂכֶל m. understanding, wisdom, prudence: Dan. viii. 25.

POLISH

בָּרַר to separate; to cleanse, purify; to burnish or sharpen an arrow. KAL part. Paül, Isa. xlix. 2.

גָּזַר to cut; to divide; to separate; hence גִּזְרָה f. which our translators have rendered polishing, in Lam. iv. 7. Gesenius, body, breast. Fürst, forma, figura, species. According to the meaning given by others, appearance; as we find קֶצֶב appearance, form, from קָצַב to cut; and in French, taille.

חָטַב to hew wood, to form by hewing. PUAL part. Ps. cxliv. 12, marg. 'cut.'

קָלַל adj. (see Burnished), whet, make bright: Dan. x. 6.

POLL (N)

גֻּלְגֹּלֶת f. the skull or head of a man, used therefore to express an individual person: Num. i. 2, 18, 20, 22 ; iii. 47 : 1 Chron. xxiii. 3, 24.

POLL (V)

גָּזַז to shear, to shave the head; or, pluck off the hair in great sorrow. KAL imp. Micah i. 16.

גָּלַח to shave, either the beard or the hair of the head; the accusative which follows the verb may be either the hair, 2 Sam. xiv. 26, or the head, Num. vi. 9. PIEL pret. 2 Sam. xiv. 26. inf. 2 Sam. xiv. 26. fut. 2 Sam. xiv. 26.

כָּסַם to shear, ears of corn; to poll or cut the hair of the head. KAL inf. Ezek. xliv. 20, lit. in polling they shall poll. fut. Ezek. xliv. 20.

POLLUTE

1 בּוּס to tread or trample upon; to tread under foot; Hithpolel, to be exposed to be trodden under foot: part. Ezek. xvi. 6, 22. The allusion is to an infant exposed after its birth.

2 גָּאַל if the primary and general meaning, according to Fürst, be to set free, deliver, &c., it is obvious how it may have

come to be applied to things made common and open to all, profane, and so polluted or defiled : in this sense, however, it does not occur in Kal. It is used of things ceremonially unclean, of garments stained with blood, of Jerusalem polluted by sin : Zeph. iii. 1. NIPHAL [a] *pret.* [b] *part.* PIEL [c] *pret.* PUAL [d] *fut.* [e] *part.*

3 חָלַל (see *Profane*), to make common or unclean that which is sacred, holy, or dignified ; to apply anything to a use for which it was not designed. NIPHAL [a] *inf.* [b] *fut.* PIEL [c] *pret.* [d] *inf.* [e] *fut.* HIPHIL [f] *fut.*

4 חָנֵף (see *Defile*), it is here used only of land being defiled, and refers to a concealed stain, which at length brings down the judgments of God. KAL [a] *inf.* [b] *fut.* HIPHIL [c] *fut.*

5 טָמֵא to be unclean, impure, polluted ; either morally or ceremonially ; it denotes a great degree of defilement ; see *Unclean.* KAL [a] *inf.* [b] *fut.* NIPHAL [c] *pret.* [d] *part.* PIEL [e] *pret.* [f] *inf.* [g] *fut.* PUAL [h] *part.* HITHPAEL [i] *fut.* [k] טָמֵא *adj.* impure.

6 עָקֹב *adj.* crooked, deceitful : Hos. vi. 8, *marg.* 'cunning for blood ;' *i. e.* Gilead is a land in which the inhabitants lay wait for, and it is defiled by blood. Our version may imply that so much blood is shed that it is recklessly trampled under foot by the inhabitants, and so the land is defiled.

Exod. xx. 25.	3 e	Jer. xxxiv. 16.	3 e	Ezek. xxiii. 17.	5 b
Num. xviii. 32.	3 e	Lam. ii. 2.	3 c	xxiii. 30.	5 c
xxxv. 33.	4 c	iv. 14.	2 a	xxxvi. 18.	5 e
2 Kings xxiii. 16.	5 g	Ezek. iv. 14.	5 h	xxxix. 7.	3 f
2 Chron. xxxvi. 14.	5 g	vii. 21, 22.	3 c	xliv. 7.	3 d
Ezra ii. 62.	2 d	xiii. 19.	3 e	Dan. xi. 31.	3 c
Neh. vii. 64.	2 d	xiv. 11.	5 i	Hos. vi. 8.	6
Ps. cvi. 39.	4 b	xvi. 6, 22.	1	ix. 4.	5 i
Isa. xlvii. 6.	3 c	xx. 9, 14, 22.	3 a	Amos vii. 17.	5 k
xlviii. 11.	3 b	xx. 13, 16, 21, 24.	3 c	Micah ii. 10.	5 a
lvi. 2, 6.	3 d	xx. 26.	5 g	Zeph. iii. 1.	2 b
Jer. ii. 23.	5 c	xx. 30, 31.	5 d	iii. 4.	3 c
iii. 1.	4 a b	xx. 39.	3 e	Mal. i. 7, 7.	2 e c
iii. 2.	4 c	xxii. 10.	5 k	i. 12.	2 e
vii. 30.	5 f				

POMEGRANATE

רִמּוֹן *m.* the pomegranate, both tree and fruit. The tree, or rather shrub, is but low ; the boughs slender, armed with prickles ; the leaves like those of the common myrtle ; the blossoms of bright red or scarlet, resembling the pyrus japonica ; the fruit, the glory of the land of Canaan, as big as a large apple, quite round, but compressed a little at the top and bottom ; the rind hard but brittle, of a light red, at first smooth, afterwards wrinkled ; the whole form so beautiful that it was honoured with a place among the bells at the bottom of the high-priest's robe, and was the principal ornament of the stately columns of Solomon's temple. A section of the apple gives a fine resemblance of a beautiful cheek : Cant. iv. 3. The inside is full of small kernels, replenished with a generous liquor ; in short, there is scarcely any part of the pomegranate which doth not wonderfully delight and recreate the senses. Large numbers of this beautiful fruit tree, in general growth and form often resembling the lilac, are still grown on the Mount of Olives around Bethany, and in many other more cultivated parts of Palestine.—*Celsii Hierob.* part i. p. 272 ; *Raii Hist. Plant.* tom. ii. p. 1462 ; *Taylor.* Exod. xxviii. 33, &c.

POMMEL

גֻּלָּה *f.* anything round ; in architecture, the name of some part of the chapiter of a pillar, the bowl : 2 Chron. iv. 12, 12, 13.

POMP

גָּאוֹן *m.* exaltation ; pride ; that of which any one is proud : Isa. xiv. 11 : Ezek. vii. 24 : xxx. 18 ; xxxii. 12 ; xxxiii. 28.

שָׁאוֹן *m.* (see *Tumult*), the bustle or tumult of a multitude of people, or display made in war or victory : Isa. v. 14.

POND, POOL

1 אֲגַם *m.* a collection of water, standing water ; pond or pool ; *metaph.* abundance of divine blessings through Christ. In Isa. xix. 10, אַגְמֵי is taken by modern critics to be an *adj.*, meaning afflicted, parallel to מְדֻכָּאִים, broken in the former clause, and rendered grieved in mind.

2 בְּרֵכָה *f.* a blessing ; pools, so called because of their importance in Eastern countries ; according to some, because camels were accustomed to kneel down to them to drink : Gen. xxiv. 11. [a] בְּרֵכָה *f.* a pool.

3 מִקְוֶה a gathering together, collection—of waters, &c.

Exod. vii. 19, 19.	1, 3	Neh. ii. 14.	2 a	Isa. xix. 10.	1
viii. 5.	1	iii. 15, 16.	2 a	xxii. 9, 11.	2 a
2 Sam. ii. 13, 13, 13.	2 a	Ps. lxxxiv. 6.	2	xxxv. 7.	1
iv. 12.	2 a	Eccles. ii. 6.	2 a	xxxvi. 2.	2 a
1 Kings xxii. 38.	2 a	Cant. vii. 4.	2 a	xli. 18.	1
2 Kings xviii. 17.	2 a	Isa. vii. 3.	2 a	xlii. 15.	1
xx. 20.	2 a	xiv. 23.	1	Nah. ii. 8.	2 a

PONDER

פָּלַס in Piel, to make straight, smooth, even ; to weigh, observe, ponder ; the former is adopted by Fürst as the meaning of the verb. PIEL *imp.* Prov. iv. 26. *fut.* Prov. v. 6. *part.* Prov. v. 21.

תָּכַן to weigh, measure, or adjust with accuracy. KAL *part.* Poel, Prov. xxi. 2 ; xxiv. 12.

POOR, POVERTY

1 אֶבְיוֹן *adj.* a poor man who is seeking support or relief, being *desirous* of help ; one who is content and humble in a destitute condition, in the lowest condition of poverty driven to express his desire of relief ; also the afflicted in want of protection ; the spiritually poor, who know their need of spiritual blessings, or are in spiritual distress. It is also applied to the Messiah.

2 דַּל *adj.* one that has become exhausted, low, wasted, and weak in substance or natural strength ; opposed to גָּדוֹל in Lev. xix. 15 : it implies one that is miserable, helpless, and despised. [a] דַּלָּה *f.* lowness, poverty ; low or poor people.

3 חֶלְכָּה *adj.* poor, unfortunate. This may be a quadrilateral compound word from חָלָה to be weak, sick, and כָּאָה to be sorrowful ; hence in the *pl.* חֵלְכָּאִים.

4   חַיִל   host: Ps. x. 10, *lit.* the host of the miserable.

5   חֶסֶר   *m.* want, poverty. ᵃ מַחְסוֹר *m.* want, poverty; a poor man, *lit.* a man of want, *i. e.* very poor.

6   יָרֵשׁ   to possess; to take possession, hence to dispossess; Niph. to become poor. NIPHAL ᵃ *fut.* HIPHIL ᵇ *part.*

7   כָּאִים   the sad, desponding, or afflicted: Ps. x. 10, *lit.* the host of the afflicted; but the translators have followed the כתיב.

8   מוּךְ   *adj.* to be reduced in circumstances, to become poor. KAL ᵃ *fut.* ᵇ *part.* Poel.

9   מִסְכֵּן   *adj.* poor, unfortunate; not able to profit others.—*Plantavitius.*

10   עָנָה   see *Afflict.* עֲנָה Ch. P'AL ᵃ *part.* ᵇ עָנִי *adj.* depressed, afflicted in circumstances, mind, and body; humble, pious, gentle, and meek: Exod. xxii. 25, &c. ᶜ עָנָו *adj.* this word is more commonly translated meek, humble, implying patient submission to suffering and trouble; sometimes כתיב for עָנִי.

11   רֹשׁ   to be very poor, in want. KAL ᵃ *part.* Poel. HITHPOLEL ᵇ *part.* ᶜ רֵישׁ *m.* poverty. ᵈ רָאשׁ *m. id.* ᵉ רִישׁ *m. id.*

No. 10 b not included.

Gen. xli. 19.	2 a	Ps. xli. 1.	2	Prov. xxviii. 6, 27.	11 a
xlv. 11.	6 a	xlix. 2.	1	xxviii. 8, 11, 15.	2
Exod. xxiii. 3.	2	lix. 33.	1	xxviii. 19.	11 e
xxiii. 6, 11.	1	lxxii. 13.	2	xxviii. 22.	5
xxx. 15.	2	lxxxii. 3, 4.	2	xxix. 7, 14.	2
Lev. xiv. 21.	2	cvii. 41.	1	xxix. 13.	11 a
xix. 15.	2	cix. 31.	1	xxx. 8.	11 d
xxv. 25, 35, 39.	8 a	cxiii. 9.	1	xxx. 9.	6 a
xxv. 47.	2	cxiii. 7.	2	xxxi. 7.	11 e
xxvii. 8.	8 b	cxxxii. 15.	1	Eccles. iv. 13.	9
Deut. xv. 4, 7, 7, 9.	1	cxl. 12.	1	iv. 14.	11 a
xv. 11, 11.	1, 10 b	Prov. vi. 11.	11 d	v. 8.	11 a
Judg. vi. 15.	2	x. 4.	11 a	ix. 15, 15, 16.	9
Ruth iii. 10.	2	x. 15, 15.	2, 11 c	Isa. xi. 4.	2
1 Sam. ii. 7.	6 b	xi. 24.	5 a	xiv. 30.	2
ii. 8.	1	xiii. 7.	11 b	xxv. 4.	2
xviii. 23.	11 a	xiii. 8, 23.	11 a	xxix. 19.	1
2 Sam. xii. 1, 3, 4.	11 a	xiii. 18.	11 c	xxxii. 7.	10 c, or b
2 Kings xxiv. 14.	2 a	xiv. 20.	11 a	Jer. ii. 34.	1
xxv. 12.	2 a	xiv. 21.	10 c, or b	v. 4.	2
Esth. ix. 22.	1	xiv. 31, 31.	2, 1	xx. 13.	2
Job v. 15.	1	xvii. 5.	11 a	xxxix. 10.	2
v. 16. a	2	xviii. 23.	11 a	xl. 7.	2 a
xx. 10, 19.	2	xix. 1, 7, 22.	11 a	lii. 15, 16.	2 a
xxiv. 4.	10 b or c	xix. 4, 17.	2	Dan. iv. 27.	10 a
xxix. 16.	1	xx. 13.	6 a	Amos ii. 6.	2
xxx. 25.	1	xxi. 13.	2	ii. 7.	2
xxxi. 16.	2	xxi. 17.	5 a	iv. 1.	2
xxxi. 19.	1	xxii. 2, 7.	11 a	v. 11.	2
xxxiv. 19, 28.	2	xxii. 9, 16, 22, 22.	2	v. 12.	1
Ps. ix. 18.	10 b or c	xxiii. 21.	6 a	viii. 4.	10 b, or c
x. 8, 14.	3	xxiv. 34.	11 c	viii. 6.	2
x. 10.	4, or 3, 7	xxviii. 3, 3.	11 a, 2	Zeph. iii. 12.	2

a lit. to the poor is hope.

POPLAR

לִבְנֶה   *m.* the white poplar (according to the Lxx. in Hosea, and the Vulg. in Genesis), growing on mountains as well as in low grounds, much celebrated for its shade, and still frequent by the streams on the lower slopes of Lebanon. The Lxx. and the Arabic version in Genesis render it styrax, the storax tree. See Celsii Hierob. part i. p. 292; *comp.* J. D. Michaelis Supplem. p. 1404. Gen. xxx. 37: Hos. iv. 13.

POPULOUS

אָמוֹן   *m. i. q.* הָמוֹן a multitude of people: Nah. iii. 8.

רַב   *adj.* many: Deut. xxvi. 5.

PORCH

אוּלָם or אֵלָם   *m.* a porch, a gallery, an arch which is bound to or connected with the main building, especially the vestibule of the temple (ὁ πρόναος), before which was the altar of burnt-offering (1 Kings vi. 3; 2 Chron. iii. 4, viii. 12, xxix. 7), called the porch of the Lord (2 Chron. xv. 8, xxix. 17); hence, "between the porch and the altar," where prayer was made, Joel ii. 17.—Ezek. viii. 16, &c.

מִסְדְּרוֹן   *m.* a piazza, cloister, or large porch, admitting the full light of the day, in which they might sit or walk. Judg. iii. 23.

PORT, PORTER

שַׁעַר   *m.* gate: 1 Chron. xvi. 42, *marg.* 'for the gate:' Neh. ii. 13. שׁוֹעֵר *m.* porter: 2 Sam. xviii. 26, &c.

תְּרַע   Ch. *m.* door-keeper: Ezra vii. 24.

PORTION

1   אֶחָד   *adj.* one: "a portion for," *lit.* one.

2   אָחַז   to take; to take out or away, *i. e.* from a larger number. KAL *part.* Paül, *lit.* taken out, from a lot or portion.

3   אֲמָנָה   *f.* a firm covenant, a fixed task, or stated allowance.

4   דָּבָר   word, matter, business, &c.

5   חֶבֶל   *com.* a line, measuring-line, a portion of land measured out and assigned to any one by lot.

6   חָלַק   to divide, to divide out as a spoil, to take away a portion. KAL ᵃ *pret.* ᵇ חֵלֶק *m.* a part or portion taken from a whole, as of meat, prey, land, inheritance; that which is given to man by God for his enjoyment: Eccles. ii. 10; iii. 22; v. 18, 19. It is used by those who refuse subjection to David; "what portion have we in David?" meaning that they are no part of his kingdom, or that they have no communion with him: 1 Kings xii. 16. The lot or punishment of the wicked: Job xx. 29; xxvii. 13: Isa. xi. 14. God is the portion of his people, not only for his care of them, and their receiving of blessings from him, but for their confidence in him: Gen. xiv. 24, &c. ᶜ חֶלְקָה *f. id.* ᵈ חֲלָק Ch. *m. id.* ᵉ מַחֲלֹקֶת *f.* divisions, courses.

7   חֹק   *m.* something fixed and appointed; a man's right, that which lies within the bounds of his property, or is assigned to him as his share or due.

8   מָנָה   *f.* a part, portion, particularly of food; lot, destiny. ᵃ מְנָת *f.* a part, portion.

9   פֶּה   *m.* a mouth; a part.

10   פַּתְבַּג   *m.* Heb. and Chald. a division or portion of food; Gesenius, costly food, delicacies, supposed to have been offered or consecrated to an idol, which would more especially account for Daniel's rejection of this provision; and the consideration of this meaning may add to the emphasis of its use in Dan. xi. 26. It was undoubtedly contrary to the law of Moses and of

religion to eat of things offered to idols; *comp.* Exod. xxxiv. 15, Ps. xvi. 4, Hos. ix. 3, Ezek. iv. 13, 14.

11 קֹדֶשׁ *m.* what is holy or sacred; "a holy portion."

12 שֶׁכֶם *m.* shoulder; a part, portion; so the ancient versions render it, and the connexion seems to require: Gen. xlviii. 22. Ikenius, Dissert. Philol.-Theol. part i. diss. iv. p. 38, refers the sentence to Sichem, by allusion or paronomasia, which, however, he supposes to mean a remuneration, *donum pro dono*, and that this gift was the country around Sichem, which at length became the possession of the tribe of Ephraim, and Joseph's bones were laid there. Rosenmüller accedes to this view.— Scholia in Gen. *loc.*

No 6 b not included.

Gen. xlvii. 22, 22.	7	2 Chron. xxxi. 16.	4	Ps. lxiii. 10.	8 a
xlviii. 22.	12	xxxi. 19.	8	Prov. xxxi. 15.	7
Num. xxxi. 30, 47.	2	Ezra iv. 16. *a*	6 d	Jer. xii. 10, 10.	6 c
Deut. xxi. 17.	9	Neh. viii. 10, 12.	8	xiii. 25.	8
xxxiii. 21.	6 c	xi. 23.	5	lii. 34.	4
Josh. xvii. 5, 14.	5	xii. 44.	8 a	Ezek. xlv. 1.	11
xix. 9.	5	xiii. 47, 47.	8 a, 4	xlvii. 13.	5
1 Sam. i. 4, 5.	3	xiii. 10.	8 a	xlviii. 1, 2, 3, 4, 5, 6, 7,	
ix. 23.	8	Esth. ix. 19, 22.	8	23, 24, 25, 26, 27.	1
2 Kings ii. 9.	5	Job xxiv. 18.	6 c	xlviii. 29.	6 e
ix. 21, 25.	6 a	xxvi. 14.	4	iv. 15, 23.	6 d
2 Chron. xxviii. 21.	6 a	Ps. xi. 6.	8 a	xi. 26.	10
xxxi. 3, 4.	8 a	xvi. 5.	8		

a lit. there shall be to thee no portion.

POSSESS

1 אָחַז to seize, to hold fast; to make oneself possessor of anything, to take or have possession. NIPHAL a*pret.* b*imp.* c*fut.* d אֲחֻזָּה *f.* possession, especially of land, fields, &c. Gen. xvii. 8, &c.

2 חֲסַן Ch. to have in possession, implying strength. APHEL a*pret.* b*fut.*

3 יָרֵשׁ to take into possession either by inheritance, gift, or violence, what belongs to others; in which sense there are two objective words belonging to this verb, one of the thing, and one of the person from whom it passes; to possess or enjoy what is one's own, see *Enjoy;* thus a possession is any valuable enjoyment which is in our own power, or we have the use of; so the law of Moses was a possession to the congregation of Jacob, Deut. xxxiii. 4. Job xiii. 26, "thou makest me to possess," thou entailest upon me the iniquities of my youth by continued punishment of them. KAL a*pret.* b*inf.* c*imp.* d*fut.* e*part.* Poel. HIPHIL f*fut.* g יְרֵשָׁה *f.* a possession. h יְרֵשָׁה *f. id.* i מוֹרָשׁ *m. id.* k מוֹרָשָׁה *f. id.*

4 נָחַל to inherit, to acquire possession. KAL a*fut.* HIPHIL b*pret.* HOPHAL c*pret.* HITHPAEL d*pret.* e נַחֲלָה *f.* inheritance.

5 מַעֲשֶׂה *m.* work, marg. 'business.'

6 קָנָה to get, gain, acquire; to buy; to redeem; to obtain for a possession; to possess. KAL a*pret.* b*part.* Poel. NIPHAL c*fut.* d מִקְנֶה *m.* possession, but used only of cattle, which, among nomadic tribes, is the principal and almost the only property; see *Cattle.* e מִקְנָה *f.* a purchase, a possession.

7 רֶגֶל *f.* foot; "in their possession," *lit.* at their feet.

No. 1 d, *Possession*, not included.

Gen. xiv. 19, 22.	6 b	Deut. xv. 4.	3 b	Ezra ix. 11.	3 b
xxii. 17.	3 d	xvii. 14.	3 a	Neh. ix. 15, 23.	3 b
xxiii. 18.	6 e	xviii. 14.	3 e	ix. 22, 24, 25.	3 d
xxiv. 60.	3 b	xix. 2, 14.	3 b	Job vii. 3.	4 c
xxvi. 14, 14.	6 d	xxi. 1.	3 b	xiii. 26.	3 f
xxxiv. 10.	1 b	xxiii. 20.	3 d	Ps. xliv. 3.	3 a
xlvii. 27.	1 c	xxv. 19.	3 a	lxix. 35.	3 a
Lev. xx. 24.		xxvi. 1.	3 a	lxxxiii. 12.	3 d
Num. xiii. 30.	3 a	xxvii. 21, 63.	3 b	cxxxix. 13.	6 a
xxiv.	3 f	xxx. 5, 5.	3 a	Prov. viii. 22.	6 a
xxi. 24, 35.	3 d	xxx. 16, 18.	3 a	xxviii. 10.	4 a
xxiv. 18, 18.	3 g	xxxi. 3.	3 b	Eccles. ii. 7.	6 d
xxvi. 56.	4 e	xxxi. 13.	3 b	Isa. xiv. 2.	4 d
xxvii. 11.	3 d	xxxii. 47.	3 b	xiv. 21.	3 a
xxxii. 30.	1 a	xxxiii. 23.	3 c	xiv. 23.	3 i
xxxiii. 53.	3 b	Josh. i. 11, 11.	3 a	xxxiv. 11.	3 a
xxxvi. 8.	3 e	i. 15, 15.	3 a h	xxxiv. 17.	3 d
Deut. i. 8, 21.	3 b	xii. 6, 7.	3 h	lvii. 13.	4 a
i. 39.	3 d	xiii. 1.	3 d	lxi. 7.	3 a
ii. 5, 9, 9, 12, 19, 19.	3 h	xviii. 3.	3 a	lxxi. 18.	3 a
ii. 24, 31.	3 c	xix. 47.	3 d	Jer. xxx. 3.	6 c
iii. 12.	3 d	xxi. 43.	3 d	xxxii. 23.	3 c
iii. 18.	3 b	xxii. 9.	3	xxxii. 23.	3 c
iii. 20, 20.	3 a h	xxii. 19, 19, 19.	1 d d b	Ezek. vii. 24.	3 a
iv. 1, 22.	3 b	xxiii. 5.	3 a	xi. 15.	3 k
v. 14, 26.	3 d	xxiv. 4.	3 d	xxv. 4, 10.	3 k
iv. 47.	3 b	xxiv. 8.	3 d	xxxiii. 25, 26.	3 d
v. 31.	3 d	Judg. ii. 6.	3 d	xxxv. 10.	3 a
v. 33.	3 d	iii. 13.	3 b	xxxvi. 2, 3, 4.	3 k
vi. 1.	3 b	ii. 21, 22, 23.	3 d	xxxvi. 12.	3 k
vi. 18.	3 b	ii. 24, 24, 24.	3 d f d	Dan. viii. 18.	2 a
vii. 1.	3 b	iii. 18, 9.	3 b	vii. 22.	2 a
viii. 1.	3 b	1 Sam. xxv. 2.	5	Hos. ix. 6.	3 b
ix. 1, 4, 5, 6.	3 b	1 Kings xxi. 15.	3 b	Amos ii. 10.	3 b
ix. 23.	3 c	xxi. 16, 18.	3 b	ix. 12.	3 b
x. 11.	3 b	xxi. 19.	3 a	Obad. 17, 17.	3 a i
x. 6.	7	2 Kings xvii. 24.	3 d	19, 19.	3 b
xi. 8, 8.	3 a b	2 Chron. xxviii. 1.	6 d	20.	3 b
xi. 10, 11, 29.	3 a	xxviii. 8.	6 d	Hab. i. 6.	3 b
xi. 23.	3 a	2 Chron. xx. 11.	3 h	Zeph. ii. 9.	4 a
xi. 31, 31.	3 b a	xxxii. 22.	6 d	Zech. viii. 12.	3 b
xii. 1, 29.	3 b			xi. 5.	6 b
xii. 2.	3 e				

POST

אַיִל *m.* a ram, from his strength; it is used also as a technical expression in architecture, the meaning of which it is difficult to trace. The passages in which it occurs in Ezekiel will have the clearest sense if we render the word pillars or pilasters, with which the doors and wall of the temple were ornamented: it is found in Ezek. xl., and twice in xli. 1, 3.

אַמָּה *f.* cubit; posts, the angle which they make with the threshold being like an elbow. Gesenius would translate Isa. vi. 4, the mothers, *i.e.* the foundations, of the thresholds. The word occurs in this sense in the Arabic and in the Talmud.

מְזוּזָה *f.* a door-post, on which the door turns or is moved; side post: Exod. xii. 7, 22, 23; xxi. 6: Deut. vi. 9; xi. 20; Judg. xvi. 3: 1 Sam. i. 9: 1 Kings vi. 31, 33; vii. 5: Prov. viii. 34: Isa. lvii. 8: Ezek. xli. 21, *marg.* 'post;' xliii. 8, 8; xlv. 19, 19; xlvi. 2.

סַף *m.* door, threshold, gate: 2 Chron. iii. 7: Ezek. xli. 16: Amos ix. 1.

מַשְׁקוֹף *m.* the upper door-post, the timber over the door-posts: Exod. xii. 7.

POSTS

רוּץ to run; *part. pl.* רָצִים and רָצִין runners, state couriers, among the Persians, who published the royal edicts in the provinces, Esth. iii. 13, 15; viii. 14. Among the Hebrews they made a part of the royal body-guard under Saul, 2 Kings x. 25, xi. 6, &c., and correspond probably to the פְּלֵתִי under David; *comp.* further, 1 Kings i. 5;

xiv. 27 : 2 Sam. xv. 1. KAL *part.* 2 Chron. xxx. 6, *lit.* runners, 10 ; Esth. iii. 13, 15 ; viii. 10, 14 : Job ix. 25 : Jer. li. 31, *lit.* post shall run to meet post.

POSTERITY

אַחַר   *m.* after : 1 Kings xvi. 3, 3 ; xxi. 21 : Ps. xlix. 13.   אַחֲרִית *f.* Ps. cix. 13 : Dan. xi. 4 : Amos iv. 2.

דּוֹר   *m.* generation : Num. ix. 10.

שְׁאֵרִית   *f.* a remnant of people : Gen. xlv. 7, *marg.* ' to put for you a remnant.'

POT

1   גָּבִיעַ   *m.* a cup or bowl ; in Jer. xxxv. 5 it appears to denote a larger drinking vessel, a goblet, crater, and כּוֹס, a smaller one, wine-glass, cyathus, into which they drew from the other.

2   דּוּד   *m.* kettle, caldron, seething pot. Gesenius, a labourer's basket.

3   כְּלִי   *m.* a general name for all kinds of tools, vessels, &c.

4   אָסוּךְ   *m.* ointment-bottle, oil-vessel.

5   סִיר   *com.* a pot, kettle, caldron : Exod. xvi. 3, &c.

6   פָּרוּר   *m.* pan, pot, or kettle.

7   צִנְצֶנֶת   *f.* a pot or basket to keep things in.

8   מֶרְקָחָה   *f.* ointment, or spices : a pot of ointment.

9   שְׁפַתַּיִם   *m. dual.* This word, as a noun, being always in the dual number, seems to signify any two things placed over against each other. In Ps. lxviii. 13 it is usually understood to apply to two stones, or end-irons, set upon a hearth to support a pot in which meat is boiled : "Though ye have lien among the pots," or, rather, pot-ranges, where the suttlers or scullions dressed victuals for the camp ; and where the strolling followers of the camp, who were not provided with tents, probably used to lodge, for the sake of the warmth, and so were in a dirty condition, which is here used to signify being in a low contemptible state. Fürst, Gesenius, and others, suppose the word means folds for cattle, particularly the open summer stalls, in which cattle in warmer climates pass the whole summer, from שָׁפַת to place, like *stabula* from stare. See *Burden, Hook.*

No. 5 not included.

Exod. xvi. 33.	7	2 Kings iv. 2.	4	Ps. lxviii. 13.	9
Lev. vi. 28.	3	Job xli. 31, 31.	5, 8	lxxxi. 6.	2
Judg. vi. 19.	6	xli. 20.	2	Jer. xxxv. 5.	1
1 Sam. ii. 14.	6				

POTSHERD

חֶרֶשׂ   *m.* fragment of an earthen vessel : Job ii. 8 : Ps. xxii. 15 : Prov. xxvi. 23 : Isa. xlv. 9, 9.

POTTAGE

נָזִיד   *m.* pottage ; any boiled dish or food : supposed to have been lentiles, whose meal made pottage of a chocolate colour : Gen. xxv. 29, 34 : 2 Kings iv. 38, 39, 40 : Hag. ii. 12.

POTTER

יָצַר   to form, fashion, and shape, as the potter the clay. KAL *part.* Poel, 1 Chron. iv. 23 : Ps. ii. 9 : Isa. xxix. 16 ; xxx. 14 ; xli. 25 ; lxiv. 8 : Jer. xviii. 2, 3, 4, 4, 6, 6 ; xix. 1, 11 : Lam. iv. 2 : Zech. xi. 13, 13.

פֶּחָר   Ch. *m.* potter : Dan. ii. 41.

POUND

מָנֶה   *m.* a Hebrew weight, which, according to 1 Kings x. 17, comp. 2 Chron. ix. 16, contained a hundred shekels ; see *Maneh:* 1 Kings x. 17 : Ezra ii. 69 : Neh. vii. 71, 72.

POUR

1   דָּלַף   to drip, to have drops falling from ; to weep, spoken of the eye. KAL *pret.*

2   זָקַק   to pour out : to filter, to refine. KAL *fut.*

3   זָרַם   to flow, to pour out. POAL *pret.*

4   יִסַּךְ   to be poured out. KAL *fut.*

5   יָצַק   to pour out water or oil, &c. ; to cast ; figuratively to pour out is to bestow and communicate spiritual gifts and graces ; to pour water on the hands is to serve any one. KAL ᵃ*pret.* ᵇ*imp.* ᶜ*fut.* HOPHAL ᵈ*pret.* ᵉ*fut.* ᶠ*part.*

6   נָבַע   to spring, to flow ; Hiph. to let flow out, especially to pour forth words ; it is used emphatically of God's pouring forth his spirit in rich profusion and continued fulness, as a well-spring of wisdom ; comp. Prov. xviii. 4. HIPHIL ᵃ*fut.*

7   נָגַר   to flow down, as tears from the eyes, as water spilt on the ground, as goods that disappear. HIPHIL ᵃ*pret.* ᵇ*imp.* HOPHAL ᶜ*part.*

8   נָזַל   to flow, as water, as speech, as fragrant odours. KAL *fut.*

9   נָסַךְ   to pour out in a deliberate careful manner, as water and wine are solemnly poured out in a drink-offering to God ; as oil is poured out in anointing kings and rulers ; as a founder pours out liquid metal when he casts an image in a mould. KAL ᵃ*pret.* ᵇ*fut.* PIEL ᶜ*fut.* HIPHIL ᵈ*pret.* ᵉ*inf.* ᶠ*imp.* ᵍ*fut.*

10   נָתַךְ   to flow, with an implied force or power, as of heavy rain, of metal or any thing dissolved by violent heat, of the wrath of God poured out on a wicked people ; figuratively, as of the roarings of a man in pain. KAL ᵃ*fut.* NIPHAL ᵇ*pret.* ᶜ*part.* HIPHIL ᵈ*fut.*

11   נָתַן   to give. KAL *fut.*

12   עָרָה   to be emptied ; Piel, to empty, to pour out abundantly. NIPHAL ᵃ*fut.* HIPHIL ᵇ*pret.*

13   צוּק   to pour out. KAL ᵃ*pret.* ᵇ*fut.*

14   רוּק   to be empty ; Hiphil, to pour out plentifully, to empty out. HIPHIL ᵃ*pret.* HOPHAL ᵇ*fut.*

15   שָׁפַךְ   to pour out, properly liquids, but also other things, as dust, ashes, earth, stones ; figuratively the soul, thoughts, anger, contempt, the steps, so that they slip ; Niphal, to be poured out is to be weakened and exhausted of strength, to be wasted ; the soul is poured out in a lingering painful death, or the anticipation of it ; Ps. xlii. 4, "I pour out my soul in me," Heb. upon myself, in solitude, without any friend to open my mind to ; to pour their own wickedness upon persons is to punish

them severely in a manner which is suitable to their wickedness; this word is used of God's pouring out his Spirit. KAL [a] *pret.* [b] *inf.* [c] *imp.* [d] *fut.* [e] *part.* Poel. [f] *part.* Paül. NIPHAL [g] *pret.* [h] *inf.* [i] *fut.* PUAL [k] *pret.* HITHPAEL [l] *inf.* [m] *fut.* שֶׁפֶךְ *m.* a pouring out.

Gen. xviii. 18.	5 c	2 Kings ix. 6.	5 b	Jer. xviii. 21.	7 b	
xxxv. 14, 14.	9 g, 5 c	xvi. 13.	9 g	xix. 13.	9 e	
Exod. iv. 9.	15 a	1 Chron. xi. 18.	9 e	xxxii. 29.	9 d	
ix. 33.	10 b	2 Chron. xii. 7.	10 a	xlii. 18, 18.	10 b a	
xxix. 7.	5 a	xxxiv. 21.	10 b	xliv. 6.	10 a	
xxix. 12.	15 d	xxxiv. 25.	10 a	xliv. 17, 18, 19, 19, 25.	9 e	
xxx. 9.	9 b	Job iii. 24.	10 a	Lam. ii. 4.	15 a	
xxx. 32.	4	x. 10.	10 d	ii. 11.	15 g	
Lev. ii. 1, 6.	5 a	xii. 21.	15 e	ii. 12.	15 l	
iv. 7, 18, 25, 30, 34.	15 d	xvi. 13.	15 d	ii. 19.	15 c	
iv. 12, a 12. a	15 n	xvi. 20.	1	iv. 1.	15 m	
viii. 12.	5 c	xxix. 6.	13 b	iv. 11.	15 a	
viii. 15.	5 a	xxx. 16.	15 m	Ezek. vii. 8.	15 d	
ix. 9.	5 a	xxxvi. 27.	2	ix. 8.	15 b	
xiv. 15.	5 a	Ps. xxii. 14.	15 g	xiv. 19.	15 a	
xiv. 18.	11	xlii. 4.	15 d	xvi. 15.	15 d	
xiv. 26.	5 c	xlv. 2.	5 d	xvi. 36.	15 h	
xiv. 41.	15 a	lxii. 8.	15 c	xx. 8, 13, 21.	15 b	
xvii. 13.	5 a	lxix. 24.	15 c	xx. 28.	9 g	
xxi. 10.	5 e	lxxv. 8.	7 b	xx. 33, 34.	15 f	
Num. v. 15.	5 c	lxxvii. 17.	3	xxi. 31.	15 a	
xxiv. 7.	8	lxxix. 6.	15 c	xxiii. 22.	15 a	
xxviii. 7.	9 f	cii. title.	15 d	xxiii. 8.	15 d	
Deut. xii. 16, 24.	15 d	cvii. 40.	15 e	xxiv. 3.	5 b	
xii. 27.	15 i	cxlii. 2.	15 d	xxiv. 7.	15 a	
xv. 23.	15 d	Prov. i. 23.	6	xxx. 15.	15 a	
Judg. vi. 20.	15 c	v. 2, 28.	6	xxxvi. 18.	15 d	
1 Sam. i. 15.	15 d	Cant. i. 3.	14 b	xxxix. 29.	15 a	
vii. 6.	15 d	Isa. xxvi. 16.	13 a	Dan. ix. 11, 27.	10 a	
x. 1.	5	xxix. 10.	9 a	Hos. v. 10.	15 d	
2 Sam. xiii. 9.	5 c	xxxii. 15.	12 a	Joel ii. 28, 29.	15 d	
xxiii. 16.	9 g	xlii. 25.	15 d	Amos v. 8.	15 d	
1 Kings xiii. 3.	15 g	xliv. 3, 3.	5 c	ix. 6.	15 d	
xiii. 5.	15 i	xlv. 8.	8	ix. 4.		
xviii. 33.	5 b	liii. 12.	12 b	Micah i. 4.	7 c	
2 Kings iii. 11.	5 a	lvii. 6.	15 a	i. 6.	7 a	
iv. 4.	5 a	Jer. vi. 11.	15 b	Nah. i. 6.	10 b	
iv. 5.	5 f	vii. 18.	9 e	Zeph. i. 17.	15 k	
iv. 40.	5 c	vii. 20.	10 c	iii. 8.	15 b	
iv. 41.	5 b	x. 25.	15 c	Zech. xii. 10.	15 a	
ix. 3.	5 a	xiv. 16.	15 a	Mal. iii. 10.	14 a	

a lit. at the pouring out of.

POURTRAY

חָקָה to engrave, to mark out sculpture, which may afterwards have been painted; see Layard's Nineveh. PUAL *part.* Ezek. viii. 10; xxiii. 14.

חָקַק to engrave a writing or picture. KAL *pret.* Ezek. iv. 1. *part.* Paül, Ezek. xxiii. 14.

POWDER

אָבָק *m.* dust, small dust; *meton.* great drought, which produces dust: Deut. xxviii. 24.

אֲבָקַת *f. const.* Cant. iii. 6, *i.e.* aromatic dust.

דָּקַק to beat small. KAL *pret.* Exod. xxxii. 20, *lit.* till that it was made small. HIPHIL *inf.* 2 Chron. xxxiv. 7, *marg.* 'to make powder.'

עָפָר *m.* any dust, ashes, or powder; the dust of the earth: 2 Kings xxiii. 6, 6, 15.

POWER

1   אֵל *m.* strength; faculty, ability, power.

2   גְּבוּרָה *f.* strength, might, power.

3   דָּבָר word, Job xli. 12, *lit.* word of his powers, *i. e.* what is to be said of his powers or strength.

4   זְרוֹעַ *com.* arm; *fig.* power, strength.

5   חַיִל *m.* power, strength, courage; substance, riches, wealth. [a] חַיִל Ch. *m. id.*

6   חֹסֶן Ch. *m.* might, power.

7   יָד *com.* hand; power, ability, agency, dominion, &c. [a] יַד Ch. *com. id.*

8   יְכֹל to be able. KAL [a] *inf.* [b] *fut.*

9   כֹּחַ *m.* vigour, alacrity; power, strength: Gen. xxxi. 6, &c.

10   כַּף *f.* the palm of the hand.

11   מָשַׁל to rule, to govern; with בְּ to rule over, govern; with עַל to domineer, tyrannise over; with לְ and an *inf.* to have power to do. KAL [a] *pret.* [b] *fut.* [c] מֶמְשָׁלָה *f.*

12   עַז *adj.* strong, firm, hard, mighty: spoken of a nation, of the wind, of waves, of anger; "the excellency of power," in respect to the right of dominion belonging to the birth-right. [a] עֹז *m.* strength, might, power of God or man, of kings also. [b] עִזּוּז *adj.* strong; *coll.* strong ones.

13   תַּעֲצֻמוֹת *f. pl.* might.

14   עָרִיץ *adj.* terrible in strength and violence.

15   תְּקוּמָה *f.* a withstanding, resisting; "power to stand."

16   שׂוּר to reign; to contend, struggle. KAL *fut.*

17   שָׁלַט to rule over; to be master of; construed with בְּ and עַל. KAL [a] *inf.* HIPHIL [b] *pret.* [c] *fut.* שְׁלֵט Ch. P'AL [d] *pret.* [e] שִׁלְטוֹן *m.* mighty. [f] שַׁלִּיט *adj.* "having power over."

18   שָׂרָה to rule; to be a leader, prince, chief; "as a prince to have power," to contend, to struggle with. KAL *pret.*

19   תֹּקֶף *m.* power, authority.

No. 9 not included.

Gen. xxxi. 29.	1	Job xxvi. 14.	2	Eccles. v. 19.	17 b
xxxii. 28.	18	xli. 12. β	3, 2	vi. 2.	17 c
xlix. 3.	12	xlix. 15.	2	viii. 4.	17 e
Exod. xxi. 8.	11 b	xxii. 20.	7	viii. 8, 8.	17 f e
Lev. xxvi. 19.	12 a	xxxvii. 35.	14	Isa. xxxvii. 27.	7
xxvi. 37.	15	xlix. 15.	7	xliii. 17.	12 b
Num. xxii. 38.	8 a b	lix. 11.	5	xlvii. 14.	7
Deut. xxxii. 36.	7	lix. 16.	12 a	Ezek. xvii. 9.	4
Josh. viii. 20.	7	lxiii. 2.	12 a	xxii. 6.	4
1 Sam. ix. 1.	5	lxv. 6.	2	xxx. 6.	12 a
2 Sam. xxii. 33.	5	lxvi. 8.	2	Dan. ii. 37.	6
2 Kings xix. 26.	7	lxvi. 7.	2	iii. 2.	17 d
1 Chron. xx. 1.	5	lxviii. 35.	13	iii. 27.	18 d
xxix. 11.	2	lxxi. 18.	2	iv. 30.	6
2 Chron. xxxii. 9.	11 c	lxxviii. 26.	12 a	vi. 27.	7 a
Ezra iv. 23.	5	lxxix. 11.	4	xi. 43.	11 a
viii. 22.	12 a	xc. 11.	12 a	xii. 7.	7
Neh. v. 5. a	1, 7	cvi. 8.	2	Hos. xii. 3.	18
Esth. i. 3.	5	cx. 3.	2	xii. 4.	16
viii. 11.	5	cxlv. 11.	2	xii. 4.	7
ix. 1.	17 a	cl. 1.	2	Micah ii. 1.	1
x. 2.	19	cl. 1.	12 a	Hab. iii. 9.	10
Job i. 12.	7	Prov. iii. 27.	1	iii. 4.	12 a
v. 20.	7	xviii. 21.	7	Zech. ix. 4.	5
xxi. 7.	5				

a lit. in the power of our hand.   β *lit.* the word of his powers.

PRACTISE

חָרַשׁ to work, labour; Hiphil, to "secretly practise," combining with the leading idea of the verb the other meaning, which also belongs to it, to be silent. HIPHIL *part.* 1 Sam. xxiii. 9.

עָלַל to do or perform. HITHPOEL *inf.* Ps. cxli. 4.

עָשָׂה to make, do, act; to labour in anything, to be busied therein; *constr.* with בְּ. KAL *pret.* Dan. viii. 12, 24. *inf.* Isa. xxxii. 6. *fut.* Micah ii. 1.

PRAISE

1   בָּרַךְ   to kneel ; to worship God, implying all for which men kneel before him ; to praise. PIEL *a imp.* *b fut.*

2   הָלַל   to shine, to make to shine ; to give forth a clear and distinct sound. This twofold meaning may be combined in the signification to praise, which, as relating to God, is often described as done with a loud voice ; the word is usually explained, to make illustrious, glorious, to celebrate, &c. PIEL *a pret.* *b inf.* *c imp.* *d fut.* *e part.* PUAL *f part.* HITHPAEL *g fut.* הַלּוּלִים *h m. pl.* תְּהִלָּה *i f.* praise : Exod. xv. 11, &c. מַהֲלָל *k m.* praise.

3   זָמַר   to sing in set composition of words and music, to sing praises, to sing psalms in honour of God ; construed with a dative of the person sung or celebrated, or with an accusative. PIEL *a inf.* *b imp.* *c fut.*

4   יָדָה   to confess, to praise. HIPHIL *a inf.* *b imp.* *c fut.* תּוֹדָה *d f.* thanksgiving, "sacrifice of praise."

5   יָסַף   to add. HIPH. *pret. seq.* עַל, Ps. lxxi. 14, *lit.* I will add unto all thy praise ; *i.e.* praise thee again and yet again. The idea seems to be the finding still fresh material for praise beyond all past praises.

6   שָׁבַח   to commend, to pronounce happy. PIEL *a imp.* *b fut.* *c part.* שְׁבַח Ch. PAEL *d pret.* *e part.*

No. 2 i not included.

Gen. xxix. 35.	4 c	Ps. xlix. 18.	4 c	Ps. cxix. 164.	2 a
xlix. 8.	4 c	l. 23.	4 d	cxix. 175.	2 d
Lev. xix. 24.	2 h	lii. 9.	4 c	cxxviii. 1, 3, 4.	4 c
Judg. v. 2.	1 a	liv. 6.	4 c	cxxxv. 1, 1, 1, 21.	2 c
v. 3.	3 c	lvi. 4, 10, 10.	2 d	cxxxv. 3, 3.	2 c, 3 b
xvi. 24.	2 d	lvi. 12.	4 d	cxxxviii. 1, 1.	4 c, 3 c
2 Sam. xiv. 25.	2 b	lvii. 7.	3 c	cxxxviii. 2, 4.	4 c
xxii. 4.	2 f	lix. 9.	4 c	cxxxix. 14.	4 c
xxii. 50.	4 c	lxi. 8.	3 c	cxli. 7.	4 a
1 Chron. xvi. 4, 36.	2 b	lxiii. 3.	6 b	cxliv. 9.	3 c
xvi. 25.	2 f	lxiii. 5.	2 d	cxlv. 3.	2 d
xxiii. 5, 5.	2 e b	lxvii. 3, 3, 5, 5.	4 c	cxlv. 3.	2 f
xxiii. 30.	2 b	lxviii. 4, 32.	3 b	cxlv. 4.	6 b
xxv. 3.	2 b	lxix. 30, 34.	3 d	cxlv. 10.	4 c
xxv. 13.	2 e	lxxi. 14.		cxlvi. 1, 1, 10.	2 c
2 Chron. v. 13, 13.	2 e	lxxi. 22.	4 c	cxlvi. 2, 2.	2 d, 3 c
vii. 3.	4 a	lxxii. 15. a	1 b	cxlvii. 1, 1.	2 c, 3 a
vii. 6, 6.	4 a, 2 b	lxxiv. 21.	2 d	cxlvii. 7.	3 b
viii. 14.	2 b	lxxv. 9.	3 c	cxlvii. 12, 12.	6 a, 2 c
xx. 19.	2 b	lxxvi. 10.	3 c	cxlvii. 20.	2 c
xx. 21, 21.	2 e, 4 b	lxxxiv. 4.	2 d	cxlviii. 1, 1, 1, 2, 2,	
xxiii. 12.	2 b	lxxxvi. 12.	4 c	3, 3, 4, 7, 14.	2 c
xxiii. 13.	2 b	lxxxviii. 10.	4 c	cxlviii. 5, 13.	2 d
xxix. 30, 30.	2 b d	lxxxix. 5.	4 c	cxlix. 1, 9.	2 c
xxx. 21.	2 e	xcii. 1.	3 a	cxlix. 3, 3.	2 d, 3 c
xxxi. 2.	2 b	xcvi. 4.	2 f	cl. 1, 1, 1, 2, 2, 3,	
Ezra iii. 10, 11, 11.	2 b	xcviii. 4.	3 b	3, 4, 4, 5, 5.	2 c
Neh. v. 13.	2 d	xcix. 3.	4 c	cl. 6, 6.	2 d c
xii. 24.	2 b	c. title.	4 d	Prov. xxvii. 2.	2 d
Ps. vii. 17, 17.	4 c, 3 c	cii. 18.	2 d	xxvii. 21.β	2 k
ix. 1.	4 c	civ. 33.	3 c	xxviii. 4.	2 d
ix. 2.	3 c	civ. 35.	2 c	xxxi. 30.	2 g
ix. 11.	3 b	cv. 45.	2 c	xxxi. 28, 31.	2 d
xviii. 3.	2 f	cvi. 1, 48.	2 c	Eccles. iv. 2.	6 c
xviii. 49.	3 c	cvii. 8, 15, 21, 31.	4 c	Cant. vi. 9.	2 d
xxi. 13.	3 c	cvii. 32.	2 c	Isa. xii. 1.	4 b
xxii. 22, 26.	2 d	cviii. 1.	3 c	xii. 4.	4 b
xxii. 23.	2 c	cviii. 3, 3.	4 c, 3 c	xxv. 1.	4 c
xxvii. 6.	3 c	cix. 30, 30.	4 c, 2 d	xxxviii. 18, 19.	4 c
xxviii. 7.	4 c	cxi. 1, 1.	2 c, 4 c	lxii. 9.	2 a
xxx. 9.	4 c	cxi. 1.	2 c	lxiv. 11.	2 a
xxx. 12.	3 c	cxiii. 1, 1, 1, 9.	2 c	Jer. xvii. 26.	4 d
xxxiii. 2.	4 b	cxiii. 3.	2 f	xx. 13.	2 c
xxxv. 18.	2 d	cxv. 17.	2 d	xxxi. 7.	2 c
xlii. 4.	4 d	cxv. 18.	2 c	xxxiii. 11, 11.	4 b d
xlii. 5, 11.	4 c	cxvi. 19.	2 c	Dan. ii. 23.	6 d
xliii. 4, 5.	4 c	cxvii. 1, 1.	2 c, 6 a	iv. 34.	6 d
xliv. 8.	2 d	cxvii. 2.	2 c	iv. 37.	6 d
xlv. 17.	4 c	cxviii. 19, 21, 28.	4 c	v. 4, 23.	6 d
xlviii. 6, 6, 6, 6, 7.	3 b	cxix. 7.	4 c	Joel ii. 26.	2 a
xlviii. 1.	2 f				

a lit. shall one bless him.   *β lit.* to the mouth of his praise.

PRANSE

דָּהַר   to pursue, chase ; move quickly. KAL *part.* Poel, Nah. iii. 2. דַּהֲרָה *f.* pursuit, rapid movement, haste : Judg. v. 22, 22, *marg.* 'tramplings, *or*, plungings.' See Bocharti Hieroz. part i. p. 97 ; Michaelis Supplem. p. 401.

PRATING

שָׂפָה   *f.* lip : Prov. x. 8, 10, "prating fool," *marg.* 'a fool of lips.'

PRAY

1   אָנָּא   an interjection of intreating.

2   בְּעָה   Ch. to seek, to request. P'AL *part.*

3   חָלָה   in Piel, with פְּנֵי following, this verb signifies (1) to flatter or caress ; see *Intreat, Beseech;* (2) to supplicate any one, to ask his favour. Gesenius supposes it to be the same with the Arabic or Syr., meaning to be sweet, pleasant, acceptable ; hence literally, in Piel, to make the face of any one serene, to make him friendly. PIEL *a pret.* *b inf.*

4   חָנַן   to be gracious ; Hithpael, to supplicate for pity, to intreat ; see *Beseech.* HITHPAEL *pret.*

5   לַחַשׁ   *m.* a whispering ; incantation ; *marg.* 'secret speech.'

6   נָא   a primitive particle expressive of respectful intreaty or exhortation.

7   עָתַר   to intreat, to make earnest and fervent prayer, which ascends like incense before God ; see *Intreat.* Others think the primary meaning of the word implies power and abundance as well as sweet odour. KAL *a fut.* HIPHIL *b fut.*

8   פָּנַע   to meet ; to address with a supplication, to urge, supplicate, intreat. KAL *fut.*

9   פָּלַל   the sense of this word seems to correspond with that of *arbitror* in Latin, only it extends somewhat further ; in Kal, to decide ; in Piel, to judge ; in Hithpael, to pray. The deity to whom a person prays is preceded by לְ, Gen. xx. 17, Num. xi. 2. The person for whom one prays is preceded by בְּעַד, Deut. ix. 20, 1 Sam. vii. 5 ; by עַל, Job xlii. 8 ; by לְ, 1 Sam. ii. 25. The thing about which one prays is preceded by אֶל, 1 Sam. i. 27. HITHPAEL *a pret.* *b inf.* *c imp.* *d fut.* *e part.* *f* תְּפִלָּה *f.* prayer, in a somewhat large sense, being the title of several Psalms. 2 Sam. vii. 27, &c.

10   צְלָא   Ch. to pray. PAEL *part.*

11   שָׁאַל   to ask, to give. KAL *imp.*

12   שִׂיחַ   to meditate, to commune with oneself, to complain. KAL *a fut.* שִׂיַח *m.* meditation. שִׂיחָה *b f. id.*

No. 9 f, *Prayer*, and No. 6, *I pray you*, not included.

Gen. xii. 13.	6	1 Sam. i. 27.	9 a	1 Kings viii. 54.	9 b
xviii. 4.	6	ii. 1.	9 d	xiii. 6.	9 c
xx. 7, 17.	9 d	vii. 5.	9 d	2 Kings iv. 33.	9 d
l. 17.	1	viii. 6.	9 d	vi. 17, 18.	9 d
Num. xi. 2.	9 d	xii. 19.	9 c	xix. 15.	9 d
xxi. 7, 7.	9 c d	xii. 23.	9 b	xix. 20.	9 a
Deut. ix. 20, 26.	9 d	2 Sam. vii. 27.	9 b	xx. 2.	9 d
Judg. ix. 38.	6	1 Kings viii. 28.	9 e	1 Chron. xvii. 25.	9 b
1 Sam. i. 10.	9 d	viii. 30.	9 d	2 Chron. vi. 19.	9 e
i. 12, 26.	9 d	viii. 33, 35, 42, 44, 48.	9 a	vi. 20.	9 d

2 Chron. vi. 24, 26, 32, 34, 38.	9 a	Job xlii. 8.	9 d	Jer. xiv. 11.	9 d
vi. 37.	4	xlii. 10.	9 b	xxix. 7.	9 c
vii. 1.	9 b	Ps. v. 2.	9 d	xxix. 12.	9 a
vii. 14.	9 d	xxxii. 6.	9 d	xxxii. 16.	9 d
xxx. 18.	9 a	lv. 17.	12 a	xxxvii. 3.	9 c
xxxii. 20, 24.	9 d	lxiv. 1.	12 b	xlii. 2, 20.	9 c
xxxiii. 13.	9 d	lxxii. 15.	9 d	xlii. 4.	9 e
Ezra vi. 10.	10	cxxii. 6.	11	Dan. vi. 10.	10
x. 1.	9 b	Isa. xvi. 12.	9 b	vi. 11.	2
Neh. i. 4, 6.	9 e	xxvi. 16.	5	ix. 4.	9 d
ii. 4.	9 d	xxxvii. 15.	9 d	ix. 13.	3 a
iv. 9.	9 d	xxxvii. 21.	9 a	ix. 20.	9 e
Job xv. 4.	12 c	xxxviii. 2.	9 d	Jonah ii. 1.	9 d
xxi. 15.	8	xliv. 17.	9 d	iv. 2, 2.	9 d, 1
xxii. 27.	7 b	xlv. 20.	9 e	Zech. vii. 2.	3 b
xxxiii. 26.	7 a	Jer. vii. 16.	9 d	viii. 21, 22.	3 b
		xi. 14.	9 d		

PREACH

בִּשַּׂר to bring or preach (generally) good tidings. PIEL *pret.* Ps. xl. 9. *inf.* Isa. lxi. 1.

קֹהֶלֶת *m.* Koheleth, the proper name by which Solomon is distinguished in the book of Ecclesiastes; once with the article, Eccles. xii. 8, "the Preacher;" so called from his delivering his lectures of wisdom in the assembly or congregation of the people. Eccles. i. 1, 2, 12; vii. 27; xii. 8, 9, 10.

קָרָא to call, to proclaim. KAL *inf.* Neh. vi. 7. *imp.* Jonah iii. 2. קְרִיאָה *f.* preaching: Jonah iii. 2.

PRECEPT

פִּקּוּדִים *m. pl.* what are committed to one to be observed; statutes, commandments: Ps. cxix. 4, 15, 27, 40, 45, 56, 63, 69, 78, 87, 93, 94, 100, 104, 110, 128, 134, 141, 159, 168, 173.

צִוָּה to command. צַו and צָו *m.* precept: Isa. xxviii. 10, 10, 10, 10, 13, 13, 13, 13. מִצְוָה *f.* commandment: Neh. ix. 14: Isa. xxix. 13: Jer. xxxv. 18: Dan. ix. 5.

PRECIOUS

1 חָמַד to desire strongly. חֶמְדָּה *f.* a desiring, longing; object of desire. [a] חֲמוּדוֹת *f. pl.* preciousness, precious things.

2 חֵן *m.* grace, favour.

3 חֹפֶשׁ *m.* freedom; *or*, a spreading out; Gesenius, clothes spread out for riding or driving.

4 טוֹב *adj.* good.

5 יָקַר to be heavy, difficult; to be dear, costly, precious. KAL [a] *pret.* [b] *fut.* HIPHIL [c] *fut.* [d] יָקָר *adj.* 1 Sam. iii. 1, &c. [e] יְקָר *m.* preciousness.

6 מֶגֶד *m.* costly and delicious productions of the earth, as fruits, metals, gems, &c. [a] מִגְדָּנוֹת *f. pl. id.*

7 מֶשֶׁךְ *m.* drawing forth, of seed, *i.e.* the scattering of it along: *comp.* Amos ix. 13; others take the word to mean the basket out of which the sower draws his seed.

8 נְכֹת *m.* probably treasure-house, as it is rendered by the Syr., Chald., and Arab., although no philological support can be found for it. Aqu., Sym., Vulg. house of spicery; see *Spicery*.

No. 5 d not included.

Gen. xxiv. 53.	6 a	1 Sam. xxvi. 21.	5 a	2 Chron. xx. 25.	1 a
Deut. xxxiii. 13, 14, 14, 15, 16.	6	2 Kings i. 13, 14.	5 b	xxi. 3.	6 a
		xx. 13, 13.	8, 4	Ezra i. 6.	6 a
Ezra viii. 27.	1 a	Ps. cxxxix. 17.	5 a	Isa. xliii. 4.	5 a
Job xxviii. 10.	5 e	Prov. xvii. 8.	2	Jer. xx. 5.	5 e
Ps. xlix. 8.	5 b	xx. 15.	5 e	Ezek. xxii. 25.	5 e
lxxii. 14.	5 b	Eccles. vii. 1.	4	xxvii. 20.	3
cxxvi. 6.	7	Isa. xiii. 12.	5 c	Dan. xi. 8.	1
cxxxiii. 2.	4	xxxix. 2, 2.	8, 4	xi. 43.	1 a

PRE-EMINENCE

מוֹתָר *m.* pre-eminence, abundance: Eccles. iii. 19.

PREFER

נְצַח Ch. to conquer, surpass. ITHPAEL *part.* Dan. vi. 3.

עָלָה to ascend; Hiphil, to make to ascend, to exalt. HIPHIL *fut.* Ps. cxxxvii. 6, "if I prefer not Jerusalem above my chief joy," *marg.* 'the head of my joy.'

שָׁנָה to alter, change; to remove, change the place of a thing. PIEL *fut.* Esth. ii. 9.

PREPARE

1 אָסַר to bind; to harness a chariot. KAL *imp.*

2 חָלַץ see *Armed.* KAL *part.* Paül.

3 זְמַן Ch. Pael, to appoint, prepare; Ithpael, to agree, to concert: Dan. ii. 9, קרי, ye have agreed; *comp.* Amos iii. 3. The כתיב is in Aphel.

4 כּוּן to stand up; to be placed upright, to establish, confirm; these significations run through all the conjugations; in Hiphil, mostly translated prepare; to prepare, in the widest sense. NIPHAL [a] *pret.* [b] *imp.* [c] *fut.* [d] *part.* POLEL [e] *pret.* [f] *imp.* [g] *fut.* PULAL [h] *pret.* HIPHIL [i] *pret.* [k] *inf.* [l] *imp.* [m] *fut.* [n] *part.* HOPHAL [o] *pret.* [p] *part.* HITHPOLEL [q] *fut.*

5 כָּרָה to make ready, to provide; applied to provision for a feast. KAL *fut.*

6 מָנָה to number, to appoint; to assign. PIEL [a] *imp.* [b] *fut.*

7 עָרַךְ to set in array, to arrange, prepare. KAL [a] *pret.* [b] *inf.* [c] *fut.* [d] *part.* Poel. [e] *part.* Paül. [f] מַעֲרָךְ *m.* arrangement, purpose: Prov. xvi. 1, *marg.* 'disposings,' *lit.* to man the purposes of the heart, but from Jehovah the answer of the tongue; which in this sense, so understood by Geier, may be illustrated by the case of Balaam, the purpose of whose heart was covetousness, but God overruled the answer of his tongue.

8 עָשָׂה to work, to labour, to do; to make ready. KAL [a] *pret.* [b] *inf.* [c] *imp.* [d] *fut.* NIPHAL [e] *pret.* [f] *part.*

9 פָּנָה to turn, to turn away; Piel, to clear, empty, prepare. PIEL [a] *pret.* [b] *imp.*

10 קָדַשׁ to be sacred; to set apart, sanctify, appoint, proclaim. PIEL [a] *pret.* [b] *imp.* HIPHIL [c] *imp.*

11 רָקַח to spice, season; to compound as an apothecary. PUAL *part.*

See also *Habitation.*

Gen. xxiv. 31.	9 a	Num. xxiii. 1, 29.	4 l	1 Sam. vii. 3.	4 l
xxvii. 17.	8 a	xxiii. 4.	7 a	xxiii. 22.	4 l
Exod. xii. 39.	8 a	Deut. xix. 3.	4 m	2 Sam. xv. 1.	8 d
xvi. 5.	4 i	Josh. i. 11.	4 l	1 Kings i. 5.	8 d
xxiii. 20.	4 i	iv. 4.	4 i	v. 18.	4 m
Num. xv. 5, 6, 8, 12.	8 d	iv. 13. *a*	2	vi. 19.	4 i
xxi. 27.	4 q	xxii. 26.	8 d	xviii. 44.	1

2 Kings vi. 23.	5	Esth. vi. 14.	8 a	Isa. lxii. 10.	9 b	
1 Chron. ix. 32.	4 k	vii. 10.	4 i	lxiv. 4.	8 d	
xii. 39.	4 i	Job viii. 8.	4 f	lxv. 11.	7 d	
xv. 1.	4 m	xi. 13.	4 i	Jer. vi. 4.	10 b	
xv. 3, 12.	4 i	xv. 35.	4 m	xii. 3.	10 c	
xxii. 3, 14, 14.	4 i	xxvii. 16, 17.	4 m	xxii. 7.	10 a	
xxii. 5, 5.	4 m	xxviii. 27.	4 i	xlvi. 14.	4 l	
xxix. 2, 3, 16.	4 i	xxix. 7.	4 m	li. 12.	4 l	
xxix. 18.	4 l	Ps. viii. 13.	4 i	li. 27, 28.	10 b	
2 Chron. i. 4.	4 k	ix. 7.	4 e	Ezek. iv. 15.	8 a	
ii. 9.	4 k	x. 17.	4 m	xii. 3.	8 c	
iii. 1.	4 i	xxiii. 5.	7 c	xxiii. 41.	7 e	
viii. 16.	4 c	lvii. 6.	4 i	xxviii. 13.	4 h	
xii. 14.	4 i	lix. 4.	4 q	xxxv. 6.	8 d	
xvi. 14.	11	lxi. 7.	6 a	xxxviii. 7, 7.	4 b l	
xvii. 18.	2	lxv. 9.	4 m	xliii. 25, 25.	8 d	
xix. 3.	4 i	lxviii. 10.	4 m	xlv. 17, 23, 24.	8 d	
xx. 33.	4 i	lxxiv. 16.	4 i	xlv. 22.	8 a	
xxvi. 14.	4 m	lxxx. 9.	9 a	xlvi. 2.	4 i	
xxviii. 6.	4 i	ciii. 19.	4 i	xlvi. 7, 13, 13, 14.	8 d	
xxix. 19, 36.	4 i	cvii. 36.	4 g	xlvi. 12, 12.	8 d a	
xxx. 19.	4 i	cxlvii. 8.	4 n	xlvi. 15.	8 d	
xxxi. 11, 11.	4 k m	Prov. viii. 27.	4 k	Dan. ii. 9.	3	
xxxv. 4.	4 l	xvi. 1.	7 f	Hos. ii. 8. β	8 a	
xxxv. 6.	4 l	xix. 29.	4 a	vi. 3.	4 d	
xxxv. 10, 16.	4 c	xxi. 31.	4 p	Joel iii. 9. γ	10 b	
xxxv. 14, 15, 20.	4 i	xxiv. 27.	4 l	Amos iv. 12.	4 b	
Ezra vii. 10.	4 i	xxx. 25.	4 m	Jonah i. 17.	6 b	
Neh. v. 18, 18.	8 f e	Isa. xiv. 21.	4 l	iv. 6, 7, 8.	6 b	
viii. 10.	4 d	xxi. 5.	7 b	Micah iii. 5.	10 a	
xiii. 5.	8 d	xxx. 33.	4 o	Nah. ii. 3.	4 k	
xiii. 7.	8 b	xl. 3.	9 b	ii. 5.	4 o	
Esth. v. 4, 5, 12.	8 a	xl. 20.	4 k	Zeph. i. 7.	4 i	
v. 8.	8 d	lvii. 14.	9 b	Mal. iii. 1.	9 a	
vi. 4.	4 i					

a marg. 'ready armed.'   *β marg.* 'or, wherewith they made Baal.'   *γ marg.* 'sanctify.'

PRESCRIBE

כָּתַב to write; to describe, to ordain. PIEL *pret.* Isa. x. 1, *marg.* 'or, to the writers that write grievousness.' כְּתָב *m.* a writing: Ch. Ezra vii. 22. The manner of making decrees in the East is, to write the decree first, which the magistrate afterwards authenticates or annuls. See Barnes on Isa. x. 1, and Harmer.

PRESENCE, PRESENT

1 כּוּל to comprehend; to sustain, support. POLPAL *pret.* 1 Kings xx. 27, *marg.* 'or, victualled.' Our translators seem to have referred this expression to כָּלַל to be perfect, complete, they were all present. Gussetius conceives that the primary meaning of כּוּל may have been, 'to be sufficient,' from which all the other senses given to the several forms were deduced.

2 מָצָא to find, to find emphatically; see *Find*. Ps. xlvi. 1, "a very present," *lit.* much found, *i. e.* most sufficient; see *Suffice*. NIPHAL ᵃ *pret.* ᵇ *part.*

3 עַיִן *com.* the eye.

4 עָמַד to stand. KAL *imp.*

5 פָּנִים *m. pl.* face: Gen. iii. 8, &c.

6 קֳדָם Ch. *pr.* before.

7 רָאָה to see. KAL ᵃ *part.* Poel.

No. 5 not included.

Gen. xxiii. 11, 18.	3	1 Chron. xxix. 17.	2 a	Ezra viii. 25.	2 b	
Deut. xxv. 9.	3	2 Chron. v. 11.	2 b	Esth. i. 5.	2 b	
1 Sam. xiii. 15, 16.	2 b	xxix. 29.	2 b	iv. 16.	2 b	
xxi. 3.	2 b	xxx. 21.	2 b	Ps. xlvi. 1.	2	
2 Sam. xx. 4.	4	xxxi. 1.	2 b	Jer. xviii. 1, 5, 5, 11.	3	
1 Kings xx. 27.	1	xxxiv. 32, 33.	2 b	xxxii. 12.	2 b	
2 Kings xxv. 19. α	7 a, 5	xxxv. 7, 17, 18.	2 b	Dan. ii. 27.	6	

a marg. 'of them that saw the king's face.'

PRESENT

1 בְּרָכָה *f.* a blessing: Isa. xxxvi. 16, *marg.* 'blessing,' *i. e.* make with me peace that we may speak friendly to each other, *or,* that you may have the benefit of my clemency, and receive my favour as a blessing.

2 מִגְדָּנוֹת *f.* costly or precious things.

3 מִנְחָה *f.* an offering: Gen. xxxii. 13, &c.

4 תְּשׁוּרָה *f.* a present made for admission into the presence of a person of eminence.

5 שֹׁחַד *m.* a gift or bribe.

6 שַׁי *m.* a present, so called from its being brought.

7 אֶשְׁכָּר *m.* a gift for hire or reward.

8 שִׁלּוּחִים *m. pl.* that which is sent as a present.

No. 3 not included.

1 Sam. ix. 7.	4	2 Kings xviii. 31.	1	Isa. xviii. 7.	6
xxx. 26.	1	2 Chron. xxxii. 23.	2	xxxvi. 16.	1
1 Kings ix. 16.	8	Ps. lxviii. 29.	6	Ezek. xxvii. 15.	7
xv. 19.	5	lxxvi. 11.	6	Micah i. 14.	8
2 Kings xvi. 8.	5				

PRESENT (V)

1 יָצַב to place; to present oneself. HITHPAEL ᵃ *inf.* ᵇ *imp.* ᶜ *fut.*

2 יָצַן to cause to stand, to place, set. HIPHIL *fut.*

3 מָצָא to find. HIPHIL ᵃ *pret.* ᵇ *fut.*

4 נָגַשׁ to come near. HIPHIL *fut.*

5 נָפַל to fall; used of presenting a petition. KAL ᵃ *fut.* HIPHIL ᵇ *inf.* ᶜ *part.*

6 נָצַב to place, to present oneself. NIPHAL *pret.*

7 נָתַן to give. KAL *fut.*

8 עָמַד to stand; to cause to stand. HIPHIL ᵃ *pret.* HOPHAL ᵇ *fut.*

9 קָרַב to come near. HIPHIL *pret.*

10 רָאָה to see. NIPHAL *fut.*

Gen. xlvi. 29.	10	Lev. xvi. 10.	8 b	1 Sam. xvii. 16.	1 c
xlvii. 2.	2	xxvii. 8, 11.	8 a	Job i. 6.	1 a
Exod. xxxiv. 2.	6	Num. iii. 6.	8 a	ii. 1, 1.	1 a
Lev. ii. 8.	9	Deut. xxxi. 14, 14.	1 b c	Jer. xxxvi. 7. α	5 a
vii. 35.	9	Josh. xxiv. 1.	1 c	xxxviii. 26.	5 c
ix. 12, 18.	3 b	Judg. vi. 19.	4	xlii. 9.	5 b
ix. 13.	3 a	xx. 2.	1 c	Ezek. xx. 28.	7
xiv. 11.	8 a	1 Sam. x. 19.	1 b	Dan. ix. 18, 20.	5 c
xvi. 7.	8 a				

a marg. 'their supplication shall fall.'

PRESENTLY

יוֹם *m.* day: 1 Sam. ii. 16, *marg.* 'as on the day:' Prov. xii. 16, *marg.* 'in that day.'

PRESERVE

1 חָיָה to live. PIEL, to save alive: ᵃ *inf.* ᵇ *fut.* ᶜ *part.* ᵈ מִחְיָה *f.* preservation of life.

2 יָשַׁע to save, deliver. HIPHIL *fut.*

3 יָתַר to remain, to be left. HIPHIL, to preserve or exempt from death: *imp.*

4 מָלַט to escape; to save, to deliver. HIPHIL *pret.*

5 נָצַר to keep in a safe place; to guard or secure from enemies,

dangers, &c., Ps. xxxi. 23 ; to observe, inspect the conduct of men, Job vii. 20. KAL ᵃ*pret.* ᵇ*fut.* ᶜ*part.* Poel. ᵈ*part.* Paül. ᵉנָצִיר *m.* preserved.

6 נָצַל to deliver. NIPHAL *fut.*

7 שׂוּם to put. KAL *inf.*

8 שָׁמַר to keep, guard, preserve. KAL ᵃ*pret.* ᵇ*imp.* ᶜ*fut.* ᵈ*part.* Poel. NIPHAL ᵉ*pret.*

Gen. xix. 32, 34.	1 b	Ps. xvi. 1.	8 b	Ps. cxl. 1, 4.	5 b
xxxii. 30.	6	xxv. 21.	5 b	cxlv. 20.	8 d
xlv. 5.	1 d	xxxi. 23.	5 c	cxlvi. 9.	8 c
xlv. 7.	7	xxxii. 7.	5 b	Prov. ii. 8, 11.	8 c
Deut. vi. 24.	8 c	xxxvi. 6.	2	iv. 6.	8 c
Josh. xxiv. 17.	8 c	xxxvii. 28.	8 e	xiv. 3.	8 c
1 Sam. xxx. 23.	8 c	xl. 11.	8 c	xvi. 17.	8 d
2 Sam. viii. 6, 14.	2	xli. 2.	8 c	xx. 28.	5 b
1 Chron. xviii. 6, 13.	2	lxi. 7.	5 b	xxii. 12.	5 a
Neh. ix. 6.	1 c	lxiv. 1.	5 b	Isa. xxxi. 5.	4
Job vii. 20.	5 c	lxxix. 11.a	3	xlix. 6.	5 d, or e
x. 12.	8 a	lxxxvi. 2.	8 b	xlix. 8.	
xxix. 2.	8 c	xcvii. 10.	8 d	Jer. xlix. 11.	1 b
xxxvi. 6.	1 b	cxvi. 6.	8 d	Hos. xii. 13.	8 e
Ps. xii. 7.	5 b	cxxi. 7, 7, 8.	8 c		

a marg. 'reserve the children of death.'

PRESIDENTS

סָרְכִין Ch. *m. pl.* overseer, prefects : Dan. vi. 2, 3, 4, 6, 7.

PRESS

גַּת *f.* wine-press: Joel iii. 13.

יֶקֶב *m.* wine-press, or reservoir for receiving the must : Prov. iii. 10 : Isa. xvi. 10 : Hag. ii. 16, "pressfat."

פּוּרָה *f.* wine-press in which the grapes are broken : Hag. ii. 16.

PRESS (*V.*)

1 דָּחַף to press on, to hasten. KAL *part.* Paül.

2 מָעַךְ to cause to sink down by pressing. PUAL *pret.*

3 נָחַת to come down ; to press down. KAL *fut.*

4 עוּק to be bowed down by hard pressure ; to be oppressed. HIPHIL ᵃ*fut.* ᵇ*part.*

5 פָּצַר to press or urge any one with entreaties, with a degree of violence or importunity ; Gr. καταβιάζεσθαι ; *comp.* Luke xxiv. 29. KAL *fut.*

6 פָּרַץ to break forth ; to urge strongly in order to break through resolution, stubbornness, &c. KAL *fut.*

7 צוּק to be straitened, pressed ; to be urged to do a thing contrary to inclination.

8 שָׁחַט to crush. KAL *fut.*

Gen. xix. 3, 9.	5	2 Sam. xiii. 25, 27.	6	Ezek. xxiii. 3.	2
xl. 11.	8	Esth. viii. 14.	1	Amos ii. 13, 13.	4 b a
Judg. xvi. 16.	7	Ps. xxxviii. 2.	3		

PRESUME, PRESUMPTUOUS

1 זוּד to act proudly, rashly ; to be disobedient to God ; applied to the person who sins not ignorantly or inadvertently, but wilfully, knowingly, of set purpose ; to deal wickedly with any one. HIPHIL ᵃ*fut.* ᵇזֵד *adj.* proud. ᶜזָדוֹן *m.* swelling, pride, haughtiness.

2 יָד *com.* hand ; "presumptuously," *lit.* with a high hand.

3 מָלֵא to be full, to fill ; a man's heart filleth him to do a thing,

when it giveth him full resolution and confidence to do it. KAL *pret.*

4 עָפַל to be lifted up in vain confidence or presumptuous dependence. HIPHIL *fut.*

5 רוּם to be high. KAL *part.* Poel.

Exod. xxi. 14.	1 a	Deut. xvii. 12.	1 b	Deut. xviii. 22.	1 b
Num. xiv. 44.	4	xvii. 13.	1 a	Esth. vii. 5.	3
xv. 30.	5, 2	xviii. 20.	1 a	Ps. xix. 13.	1 b
Deut. i. 43.a	1 a				

a marg. 'ye were presumptuous and went up.'

PREVAIL

1 אָמַץ to be strong, resolute, and vigorous ; to act with great spirit and undaunted courage. KAL *fut.*

2 גָּבַר to prevail, to exceed or excel ; to be superior or mighty in valour, strength, power, or authority ; to strengthen, establish, or confirm ; it is used of an enemy prevailing, Jer. ix. 3, Lam. i. 16, Exod. xvii. 11, *comp.* 1 Sam. ii. 9 ; of waters, Gen. vii. 18, &c. ; of power, Job xxi. 7 ; of divine favour, Ps. ciii. 11, cxvii. 2. With מִן to be stronger than, 2 Sam. i. 23, Ps. lxv. 4 ; with עַל, Gen. xlix. 26 ; with בְּ to be strongest among, 1 Chron. v. 2. KAL ᵃ*pret.* ᵇ*fut.* HIPHIL ᶜ*fut.* HITHPAEL ᵈ*fut.*

3 חָזַק to be strong in a prevailing degree. KAL ᵃ*pret.* ᵇ*fut.* HIPHIL ᶜ*pret.* ᵈ*fut.*

4 יָכֹל to be able. KAL ᵃ*pret.* ᵇ*inf.* ᶜ*fut.* יְכֵל Ch. P'AL ᵈ*part.*

5 כָּבֵד to be heavy. KAL *fut.* Judg. i. 35, *marg.* 'was heavy ;' as the hand of one who has conquered over his fallen foe.

6 לָחַם to fight, war. NIPHAL *inf.*

7 עָזַז to be or show oneself strong or mighty. KAL *fut.*

8 עָצַר to restrain ; to rule. KAL *fut.*

9 עָרַץ to fear, to make afraid. KAL *fut.* Isa. xlvii. 12, or, according to others, to resist ; "if so be thou mayest resist," *or*, terrify.

10 קָשֶׁה *adj.* hard, rough.

11 רָדָה to have dominion. KAL *fut.*

12 תָּקַף to prevail over or oppress. KAL *fut.*

Gen. vii. 18, 24.	2 b	2 Sam. xxiv. 4.	3 b	Ps. lxv. 4.	2 a
vii. 19, 20.	2 a	1 Kings xvi. 22.	3 b	cxxix. 2.	4 a
xxx. 8.	4 a	xxii. 22.	4 c	Eccles. iv. 12.	12
xxxii. 25.	4 a	2 Kings xxv. 3.	3 b	Isa. vii. 1.	
xxxii. 28.	4 c	1 Chron. v. 2.	2 a	xvi. 12.	4 c
xlvii. 20.	3 a	xxi. 4.	3 a	xlii. 13.	2 d
xlix. 26.	2 a	2 Chron. viii. 3.	3 b	xlvii. 12.	9
Exod. xvii. 11, 11.	2 a	xiii. 18.	3	Jer. i. 19.	
Num. xxii. 6.	4 c	xiv. 11.	8	v. 22.	4 c
Judg. i. 35.	5	xvii. 21.	4 c	xx. 7, 10, 11.	4 c
iii. 10.	7	xxvii. 5.	3 b	xxxviii. 22.	4 a
iv. 24.	10	Esth. vi. 13.	4	Lam. i. 13.	11
vi. 2.	7	Job xiv. 20.	12	i. 16.	2
xvi. 5.	7	xv. 24.	12	Dan. vii. 21.	4 d
1 Sam. ii. 9.	2 b	xviii. 9.	3 d	xi. 7.	3 c
xvii. 9.	4 c	Ps. ix. 19.	7	Hos. xii. 4.	4 c
xvii. 50.	3 b	xi. 4.	2 c	Obad. 7.	4 a
xxvi. 25.	4 b	xiii. 4.	4 a		
2 Sam. xi. 23.	2 a				

PREVENT

קָדַם to go before ; to be beforehand, to anticipate ; Hiphil, to be first in doing a service, gratuitously and unobliged. PIEL *pret.* 2 Sam. xxii. 6 : Job iii. 12 ; xxx. 27 : Ps. xviii. 5 ; cxix. 147, 148 : Isa. xxi. 14. *fut.* 2 Sam. xxii.

19 : Ps. xviii. 18 ; xxi. 3 ; lix. 10 ; lxxix. 8 ; lxxxviii. 13.
HIPHIL *pret.* Job xli. 11. *fut.* Amos ix. 10.

PREY

1   אֹכֶל   *m.* food.

2   בָּזַז   to spoil, plunder ; to take for a prey. KAL [a] *pret.* [b] *inf.*
[c] *fut.* [d] *part.* Poel. [e] בַּז and בֵּז *m.* prey, spoil. [f] בִּזָּה *f. id.*

3   חֵטֶף   *m.* prey, spoil ; see *Take.*

4   טָרַף   to tear in pieces as wild beasts tear their prey. KAL
[a] *inf.* [b] טֶרֶף *m.* prey : Gen. xlix. 9, &c.

5   מַלְקוֹחַ   *m.* prey, spoil, or booty, taken by violence.

6   עַד   *m.* a prey, booty ; from עָדָה to pass on or away ; Hiphil,
to make to pass away, to take away by violence.

7   שָׁלַל   to draw out, to strip, to spoil, to plunder ; Hithpolel, to
make himself a prey. HITHPOLEL [a] *part.* Isa. lix. 15,
marg. ' or, is accounted mad,' on the authority of the
Lxx. and Jarchi, without foundation in etymology or
usage. The usual rendering is assented to by most
modern critics. Scheidius in Spec. Obss. proposes to
render the word 'withdraweth himself,' which suits well
the context. [b] שָׁלָל *m.* spoil.

No. 4 b not included.

Gen. xlix. 27.	6	Esth. iii. 13.	2 b	Jer. xxi. 9.		7 b
Num. xiv. 3, 31.	2 e	viii. 11.	2 b	xxx. 16, 16.	2 d e	
xxxi. 11, 12, 26, 27.	5	ix. 15, 16.	2 f	xxxviii. 2.		7 b
xxxi. 32.	2 e	Job ix. 26.	1	xxxix. 18.		7 b
Deut. i. 39.	2 e	xxxix. 29.	1	xlv. 5.		7 b
ii. 35.	2 a	Ps. xvii. 12.	4 a	Ezek. vii. 21.		2 e
iii. 7.	2 a	Prov. xxiii. 28.	3	xxvi. 12.		2 a
Josh. viii. 2.	2 c	Isa. x. 2.	7 b	xxix. 19.		2 e
viii. 27.	2 a	x. 6.	2 e	xxxiv. 8, 22, 28.		2 e
xi. 14.	2 a	xxxiii. 23, 23.	6, 2 e	xxxvi. 4, 5.		2 e
Judg. v. 30, 30, 30.	7 b	xlii. 22.	2 e	xxxviii. 12, 13.		2 e
viii. 24, 25.	7 b	xlix. 24, 25	5	Dan. xi. 24.		2 f
2 Kings xxi. 14.	2 e	lix. 15.	7 a	Zeph. iii. 8.		6
Neh. iv. 4.	2 f					

PRICE

יְקָר   *m.* an honorary price or value set upon a person : Zech.
xi. 13.

גְּאֻלָּה   *f.* price of redemption : Lev. xxv. 51, 52.

כֶּסֶף   *m.* silver, money, price : Lev. xxv. 50 : 1 Chron. xxi. 22, 24.

מְחִיר   *m.* worth, price : Deut. xxiii. 18, &c.

מֶכֶר   *m.* price, in sale : Prov. xxxi. 10.

מֶשֶׁךְ   *m.* the acquisition : Job xxviii. 18.

עֵרֶךְ   *m.* estimation, value : Job xxviii. 13.

מִקְנָה   *f.* that which is bought, possession ; price : Lev. xxv.
16, 16.

שָׂכָר   *m.* hire, gain, profit, or advantage arising from labour,
wages : Zech. xi. 12, 12.

PRICK

מָאַר   to be exasperated, to rankle ; applied to the deep tearing
scratch of the brier, which festers, and is very painful.
HIPHIL *part.* Ezek. xxviii. 24.

שָׁנַן   to whet, sharpen. HITHPOLEL *fut.* Ps. lxxiii. 21.

שֵׂךְ   *m.* a thorn : Num. xxxiii. 55.

PRIDE, PROUD

1   גָּאָה   to be lifted up, to rise ; to be exalted, excellent, &c.

[a] גֵּאֶה *adj.* elated, proud, arrogant, bold, violent, wicked ;
applied to Moab, Isa. xvi. 6 ; to the enemies of David,
who laid snares for him, Ps. cxl. 5 ; to the enemies of
the Church, Ps. xciv. 2 ; in opposition to the humble,
Prov. xvi. 19. [b] גֵּא *adj. id.* [c] גֵּאָה *f.* pride, arrogance.
[d] גַּאֲוָה *f.* exaltation, majesty, greatness ; pride, arrogance, violence. [e] גָּאוֹן *m. id.* [f] גֵּאוּת *f. id.* [g] גַּאֲיוֹן *adj.*
proud, arrogant. [h] גֵּוָה *f.* lifting up, pride. [i] גֵּוָה Ch. *f.*
pride.

2   גָּבַהּ   to be high ; proud, arrogant. KAL [a] *fut.* [b] גָּבֹהַּ *adj.* lofty,
high. [c] גֹּבַהּ *m.* height, pride, arrogance. [d] גַּבְהוּת *adj.*
high, proud, "exceeding proudly," *lit.* high high.

3   גָּדַל   to be great. HIPHIL, to magnify : [a] *fut.* Obad. 12, shouldest
thou have spoken proudly, *marg.* 'shouldest thou have
magnified thy mouth.' [b] גָּדוֹל *adj.* great ; proud.

4   זוּד   to boil as water ; hence, in Hiphil, to cook ; see *Sod;* it
is transferred to the mind under the influence of pride,
arrogance, wantonness, rashness and insolence, urging
to violence and presumptuousness, though unprovoked ;
so of the pride and violence of the Egyptians to the
Israelites, Exod. xviii. 11, Neh. ix. 10 ; of the Israelites
acting stubbornly and presumptuously against God, Deut.
xvii. 13, Neh. ix. 16, 29, Jer. l. 29 ; especially when,
with presumption, rashness, and impetuosity, they went
up to the mount, against the will of God, to fight with
their enemies, Deut. i. 43 ; of one who settled purpose slays another, Exod. xxi. 14 ; of a prophet who
rashly and wantonly speaks in the name of the Lord,
Deut. xviii. 20. As an adjective, the word is applied
to those who, with this kind of presumption, and without reverence of God, or regard to the duty they owe
him, proudly despise and persecute others. This pride
is attended by wrath, Prov. xxi. 24 ; by contempt and
shame, Prov. xi. 2 ; stubbornness, Deut. xvii. 12 ; contention, Prov. xiii. 10 ; bold confidence in teaching, Deut.
xviii. 22 ; boasting, Jer. xlix. 16, Obad. 1, 3. It was the
especial character of Babylon, Jer. l. 31, 32 ; charged
on David as his motive in coming to see the battle,
1 Sam. xvii. 28. KAL [a] *pret.* HIPHIL [b] *pret.* זוּד Ch.
APHEL [c] *inf.* [d] זֵד *adj.* proud, with the connected idea
of insolence and impiety. [e] זָדוֹן *m.* pride, haughtiness.
[f] זֵידוֹן *adj.* overflowing of water.

5   יָהִיר   *adj.* elated, proud, arrogant.

6   יָנָה   to exercise violence ; to oppress. KAL *part.* Poel, Ps.
cxxiii. 4, קְרִי, in two words, proud oppressors.

7   רָהַב   to be high spirited, fierce, full of courage : to rage, or to
press upon ; *seq.* בְּ. [a] רָהָב *adj.* proud, haughty. [b] רַהַב *m.*
rage, insolence, pride.

8   רוּם   to be lifted up, high. KAL *part.* Poel.

9   רָחָב   *adj.* wide, broad, large ; puffed up, proud, arrogant, synonymous with a high look.

10   לִכֶם   *m.* (see *Rough*), rough, proud, untractable, vexatious in
temper or action, which are, in life, what rugged knobs
are in a road.

11   שַׁחַץ   *m.* majesty, pride ; spoken also of beasts of prey, a lion.

Exod. xviii. 11.	4 a	Ps. cxix. 21, 51, 69,		Isa. xxviii. 1, 3.	1 f
Lev. xxvi. 19.	1 e	78, 85, 122.	4 d	Jer. xiii. 9, 9.	1 e
1 Sam. ii. 3.	2 d	cxxiii. 4.	1 g, or 1 a, 6	xiii. 15.	2 a
xvii. 28.	4 e	cxxiv. 5.	4 f	xiii. 17.	1 h
2 Chron. xxxii. 26.	2 c	cxxxviii. 6.	2 d	xliii. 2.	4 d
Neh. ix. 10, 16, 29.	4 b	cxl. 5.	1 a	xlviii. 29, 29, 29.	1 e a d
Job ix. 13.	7 b	Prov. vi. 17.	8	xlix. 16.	4 e
xxvi. 12.	7 b	viii. 13.	1 c	l. 29.	4 a
xxxiii. 17.	1 h	xi. 2.	4 e	l. 31, 32.	4 e
xxxv. 12.	1 e	xiii. 10.	4 e	Ezek. vii. 10.	4 e
xxxviii. 11.	1 e	xiv. 3.	1 d	xvi. 49, 56.	1 e
xl. 11, 12.	1 a	xv. 25.	1 a	xxx. 6.	1 e
xli. 15.	1 d	xvi. 5.	2 b	Dan. iv. 37.	1 i
xli. 34.	11	xvi. 18.	1 e	Hos. v. 5.	4 c
Ps. x. 2.	1 d	xvi. 19.	1 a	vii. 10.	1 e
x. 4.	2 c	xxi. 4.	9	Obad. 3.	4 e
xii. 3.	3 b	xxi. 24, 24.β	4 d e	12.	3 a
xvii. 10. a	1 f	xxviii. 25.	9	Hab. ii. 5.	5
xxxi. 18, 23.	1 d	xxix. 23.	1 d	Zeph. ii. 10.	1 e
xxxi. 20.	10	Eccles. vii. 8.	1 b	iii. 11.	1 d
xxxvi. 11.	1 d	Isa. ii. 12.	1 a	Zech. ix. 6.	1 e
xl. 4.	7 a	iii. 5.	7	x. 11.	1 e
lix. 12.	1 e	ix. 9.	1 d	xi. 3.	1 e
lxxiii. 6.	1 d	xiii. 11.	1 d	Mal. iii. 15.	4 d
lxxxvi. 14.	4 d	xvi. 6, 6, 6.	1 e b e	iv. 1.	4 d
xciv. 2.	1 a	xxiii. 9.	1 e		
ci. 5.	9	xxv. 11.	1 d		

a *lit.* with pride.   β *marg.* 'the wrath of pride.'

PRIEST

1 כֹּהֵן *m.* a priest, with respect to God; of the Messiah, Zech. vi. 13, Ps. cx. 4; a prince, in respect to a king: the name appears to be synonymous with קָרוֹב or ἐγγίζων, Lev. x. 3, and to mean one who attends upon God, to administer in things pertaining to the service of God: Gen. xiv. 18, &c. כָּהַן *v. denom.* to minister in the priest's office. PIEL a *pret.* b *inf.* c *fut.* d כְּהֻנָּה *f.* the priest's office, priesthood. e כָּהֵן *Ch. m.*

2 כְּמָרִים *m. pl.* idolatrous priests, perhaps of Baal.

No. 1 not included.

Exod. xxviii. 1, 3, 4.	1 b	Lev. xvi. 32, 32.	1, 1 b	1 Chron. vi. 10.	1 a
xxviii. 41.	1 a	Num. iii. 3, 3.	1, 1 b	xxiv. 2.	1 c
xxix. 1, 44.	1 b	iii. 4.	1 c	2 Chron. xi. 14.	1 b
xxix. 9.	1 b	iii. 10.	1 d	Ezra ii. 62.	1 d
xxx. 30.	1 d	xvi. 10.	1 d	vi. 9, 16, 18.	1 e
xxxi. 10, 10.	1, 1 b	xviii. 1, 7, 7.	1 d	vii.12,13,16,21,24.	1 d
xxxv. 19.	1 b	xxv. 13.	1 d	Neh. vii. 64.	1 d
xxxix. 41, 41.	1, 1 b	Deut. x. 6.	1 c	xiii. 29, 29.	1 d
xl. 13.	1 a	Josh. xviii. 7.	1 d	Ezek. xliv. 13.	1 b
xl. 15, 15.	1 a d	1 Sam. ii. 36.	1 d	Hos. iv. 6.	1 b
Lev. vii. 35.	1 b	2 Kings xxiii. 5.	2	x. 5.	2

PRINCE

1 אֲחַשְׁדַּרְפְּנַיָּא *Ch. m. pl. emph.* high satraps, chief governors, Persian officers nearly analogous to the present Turkish pachas. These satraps, or high satraps, had the civil and military jurisdiction over several smaller provinces, each of which had its own פֶּחָה or governor.

2 אִישׁ *m.* man.

3 חַשְׁמַנִּים *m. pl.* according to the Rabbins; others render it as a Gentile noun, Chasmoneans, a province of Egypt.

4 כֹּהֵן *m.* see *Priest.*

5 נָגִיד *m.* a captain, a person raised, eminent, and conspicuous, one that goes before, directs and guards others; of the Messiah, Dan. ix. 25; see *Ruler.*

6 נָדִיב *adj.* willing, free, liberal; so Prov. xix. 6 may be understood; applied to character, see *Liberal;* so Prov. xvii. 7, 26 may be rendered in opposition to נָבָל; applied to rank and station. Twice the word appears to be used in a bad sense, Job xxi. 28 (Isa. xiii. 2, nobles). This word is synonymous with נָגִיד, but a difference must be observed in the order of signification: the former is transferred from the character of a liberal mind to rank and nobility; the latter, originating in the notion of a leader, is transferred to those virtues which belong to rank.

7 נָסִיךְ *m.* one anointed, rather one formed, invested, appointed; see *Set.*

8 נָשִׂיא *m.* one lifted up—in esteem, honour, &c.; Messiah, a Prince, Ezek. xxxiv. 24; a prince, a king, the princes of the tribes of Judah, or of the Ishmaelites: among the Israelites there were also princes of the congregation; see *Chief.*

9 סְגָנִים *m. pl.* see *Ruler.*

10 פַּרְתְּמִים *m. pl.* princes, nobles.

11 קָצִין *m.* a judge, magistrate, ruler; a leader in war, a general, a captain; a prince, chief.

12 רַב *adj.* much; great, mighty; as a *subst.* a chief, captain, leader, prince. a רַבְרְבָן *Ch. m.* a noble.

13 רָזַן to deliberate upon weighty and important affairs, to weigh or to poize counsel as standing near the king. KAL a *part.* Poel. b רוֹזֵן *m. id.*

14 שׂוּר to exercise dominion, to rule. HIPHIL *pret.*

15 שָׂרַר to bear rule. HITHPAEL a *inf.* b *fut.* c שַׂר *m.* a captain, commander, chief; Prince of Peace, the Messiah, Isa. ix. 6; a chief, prince, courtier; an archangel, or one of the seven principal angels which surround the throne of God, and act as patrons of particular nations in the heavenly court, οἱ ἑπτὰ ἄγγελοι, οἱ ἐνώπιον τοῦ Θεοῦ ἑστήκασι (Rev. viii. 2); Dan. x. 13, 20.—Gen. xii. 15, &c. d שָׂרָה *f.* princess. שָׂרָה to have power as a prince. KAL e *prct.*

16 שָׁלִישׁ *m.* see *Captain, Lord.*

No. 15 c not included.

Gen. xvii. 20.	8	1 Chron. ii. 10.	8	Ezek. vii. 27.	8
xxiii. 6.	8	iv. 38.	8	xii. 10, 12.	8
xxv. 16.	8	vii. 40.	8	xix. 1.	8
xxxii. 28.	15 e	Ezra i. 8.	8	xxi. 12, 25.	8
xxxiv. 2.	8	Job xii. 19.	4	xxii. 6.	8
Exod. ii. 14.	2	xii. 21.	6	xxiii. 15.	16
Num. i. 16, 44.	8	xxi. 28.	6	xxvi. 16.	8
vii. 2, 3, 3, 10, 10, 11,		xxxi. 37.	5	xxvii. 21.	8
18, 24, 30, 36, 42,		xxxiv. 18.	6	xxviii. 2.	8
48, 54, 60, 66, 72,		Ps. xlvii. 9.	6	xxx. 13.	8
78, 84.	8	lxviii. 31.	6	xxxii. 29.	8
x. 4.	8	lxxvi. 12.	5	xxxii. 30.	7
xvi. 2.	8	lxxxiii. 11.	7	xxxiv. 24.	8
xvi. 13.	15 a b	cvii. 40.	6	xxxvii. 25.	8
xvii. 2, 6, 6.	8	cxiii. 8, 8.	6	xxxviii. 2, 3.	8
xxv. 14, 18.	8	cxviii. 9.	6	xxxix. 1, 18.	8
xxvii. 2.	8	cxlvi. 3.	6	xliv. 3, 3.	8
xxxi. 13.	8	Prov. viii. 15.	13 a	xlv. 7, 8, 9, 16, 17, 22.	8
xxxii. 2.	8	xiv. 28.	13 b	xlvi. 2, 4, 8, 10, 12, 16,	
xxxiv. 18, 22, 23, 24,		xvii. 7, 26.	6	17, 18.	8
25, 26, 27, 28.	8	xix. 6.	6	xlviii. 21, 21, 22, 22.	8
xxxvi. 1.	8	xxv. 7.	6	Dan. i. 3.	10
Josh. ix. 15, 18, 18, 19,		xxv. 15.	11	iii. 2, 3, 27.	3
21, 21.	8	xxviii. 16.	5	v. 2, 3.	12 a
xiii. 21.	8	xxxi. 4.	13 a	vi. 1, 2, 3, 4, 6, 7.	1
xvii. 4.	8	Cant. vii. 1.	6	ix. 25, 26.	5
xxii. 14, 14, 30, 32.	8	Isa. xxi. 23.	13 a	ix. 8.	7
Judg. v. 3.	13	xli. 25.	9	xi. 18.	11
1 Sam. ii. 8.	6	Jer. xxxix. 13.	12	xi. 22.	5
1 Kings xi. 3.	15 d	xli. 1.	12	Hos. viii. 4.	14
xi. 34.	8	Lam. i. 1.	15 d	Micah iii. 1, 9.	11
xiv. 7.	5			Hab. i. 10.	13 a
xvi. 2.	8				

PRINCIPAL

1 אָב *m.* father; "principal household," *marg.* 'house of the fathers.'

2 אַדִּיר *adj.* great, mighty; distinguished, chief.

3 כֹּהֵן *m.* (see *Priest*), principal officer.

4 נָסִיךְ *m.* prince.

5 רֹאשׁ head. ᵃ רֵאשִׁית *f.* beginning. ᵇ מַרְאֹשׁת *f. pl.* principalities.

6 שׂוֹרָה *f.* from שָׂרָה to rule, "principal wheat:" Isa. xxviii. 25, *marg.* 'or, the wheat in the principal (place).' *Vulg. per ordinem*, in its proper order, place, proportion. Lowth, in due measure. Gesenius, in rows, from שָׂרָה to set in order.

7 שַׂר *m.* prince.

Exod. xxx. 23.	5	1 Chron. xxiv. 6.	1	Jer. xiii. 18.	5 b
Lev. vi. 5.	5	xxiv. 31.	5	xxv. 34, 35, 36.	2
Num. v.7.	5	Neh. xi. 17.	5	lii. 25.	7
1 Kings iv. 5.	3	Prov. iv. 7.	5 a	Micah v. 5.	4
2 Kings xxv. 19.	7	Isa. xxviii. 25.	6		

PRINT

חָקָה to engrave, to mark out. HITHPAEL *fut.* Job xiii. 27, thou settest a print upon my heels, about my feet thou drawest a mark, *i. e.* thou markest out for my feet how far they should go.

חָקַק to grave, to pourtray. HOPHAL *fut.* Job xix. 23.

נָתַן to give. KAL *fut.* Lev. xix. 28.

PRISED

יָקַר to be precious. KAL *pret.* Zech. xi. 13.

PRISON

1 אָסַר to bind. KAL ᵃ *part.* Paül. ᵇ אֵסוּר *m.* band, prison. ᶜ אָסִיר *m.* prisoner. ᵈ אַסִּיר *m.* prisoner.

2 בַּיִת *f.* house; "prison," *lit.* house of the prison.

3 מַהְפֶּכֶת *f.* a wooden frame, in which the feet, perhaps also the hands and head, of prisoners were confined; shackles, stocks, pillory, *nervus, cippus.*

4 כֶּלֶא *m.* a shutting up, restraint, "prison," *lit.* house of restraint. קרי כְּלוּא ᵇ *m.* כתיב כְּלִיא ᵃ *m.*, restraint.

5 מַטָּרָה *f.* a prison or place where a person is placed in custody or watched.

6 מַסְגֵּר *m.* that which encloses, a place of confinement, a prison.

7 סֹהַר *m.* castle, fortress, tower.

8 עֹצֶר *m.* oppression, or the being shut up.

9 פְּקֻדָּה *f.* ward, "prison," *marg.* 'house of the wards.'

10 קוֹחַ *m.* has been supposed to mean a prison, or separate place. Isa. lxi. 1; it is better, however, to consider פְּקַחְקוֹחַ as one word instead of two, the common reading, the two last letters of the root repeated for an increase of signification, complete deliverance; but as פָּקַח is generally applied to opening the eyes, the Lxx. have translated it "and sight to the blind," as it is quoted by St. Luke, we may take the Hebrew to have a general meaning which admits this signification, or we may understand the expression with Alexander, of the entire illumination of the spiritually blind, *lit.* open opening.

11 מִשְׁמָר *m.* ward.

12 שְׁבִי *m.* (also *adj.*) captive.

Gen. xxxix. 20.	2, 7	2 Chron. xviii. 26.	2, 4	Isa. liii. 8.	8
xxxix. 20.	1 c	Neh. iii. 25.	5	lxi. 1.	10
xxxix. 20.	2, 7	xii. 39.	5	Jer. xxix. 26.	3
xxxix. 21.	2, 7	Job iii. 18.	1 c	xxxii. 2, 8, 12.	5
xxxix. 22.	2, 7	Ps. lxix. 33.	1 c	xxxiii. 1.	5
xxxix. 22.	1 c	lxxix. 11.	1 c	xxxvii. 4.	2, 4 a, or b
xxxix. 22.	2, 7	cii. 20.	1 c	xxxvii. 15.	2, 1 b
xxxix. 23.	2, 7	cxlii. 7.	6	xxxvii. 15.	2, 4
xl. 3.	2, 7	cxlvi. 7.	1 a	xxxvii. 18.	2, 4
xl. 5.	2, 7	Eccles. iv. 14.	2, 1 a	xxxvii. 21, 21.	5
xli. 19.	11	Isa. x. 4.	1 d	xxxviii. 6, 13, 28.	5
Num. xxi. 1.	12	xiv. 17.	1 c	xxxix. 14, 15.	5
Judg. xvi. 21, 25.	1 a	xx. 4.	12	lii. 11.	2, 9
1 Kings xxii. 27.	2, 4	xxiv. 22, 22.	1 d, 6	lii. 31.	2, 4 a, or b
2 Kings xvii. 4.	2, 4	xlii. 7, 7, 7.	1 d, 6, 4	lii. 33.	4
xxv. 27.	2, 4	xlii. 22.	4	Lam. iii. 34.	1 c
xxv. 29.	2, 4	xlix. 9.	1 a	Zech. ix. 11, 12.	1 c
2 Chron. xvi. 10.	3				

PRIVILY

אֹפֶל *m.* thick darkness: Ps. xi. 2, *marg.* 'in darkness.'

לָט *adj.* softly, secretly: 1 Sam. xxiv. 4.

סֵתֶר *m.* secretly: Ps. ci. 5.

צָפַן to hide, conceal, to lurk privily, to be set privily. KAL *fut.* Ps. x. 8, *marg.* 'hide themselves;' Prov. i. 11, 18.

תָּרְמָה *f.* deceit: Judg. ix. 31, *marg.* 'craftily, or, to Tormah.'

PRIVY

חָדַר to enter into a privy chamber. KAL *part.* Poel, Ezek. xxi. 14.

יָדַע to know. KAL *pret.* 1 Kings ii. 44.

שָׁפְכָה *f.* the privy member: Deut. xxiii. 1.

PROCEED

1 יָסַף to add. KAL ᵃ *part.* Poel. HIPHIL ᵇ *fut.*

2 יָצָא to go out. KAL ᵃ *pret.* ᵇ *fut.* ᶜ *part.* Poel. ᵈ מוֹצָא *m.* that which goes out, proceeds from.

Gen. xxiv. 50.	2 a	Judg. xi. 36.	2 a	Isa. li. 4.	2 b
Exod. xxv. 35.	2 c	1 Sam. xxiv. 13.	2 b	Jer. ix. 3.	2 a
Num. xxx. 2.	2 d	2 Sam. vii. 12.	2 b	xxx. 19.	2 b
xxx. 12.	2 d	Job xxxvi. 1.	1 b	xxx. 21.	2 b
xxxii. 24.	2 c	xl. 5.	1 b	Lam. iii. 38.	2 b
Deut. viii. 3.	2 d	Eccles. x. 5.	2 c	Hab. i. 4, 7.	2 b
Josh. vi. 10.	2 b	Isa. xxix. 14.	1 a		

PROCESS

יוֹם *m.* day: Gen. xxxviii. 12, *lit.* the days were multiplied: Judg. xi. 4, *lit.* after days: 2 Chron. xxi. 19, *lit.* to days from days.

קֵץ *m.* end: Gen. iv. 3, *marg.* 'at the end of days.'

רַב *adj.* much, many: Exod. ii. 23, *lit.* in those many days.

רָבָה to multiply. KAL *fut.* Gen. xxxviii. 12, *marg.* 'and the days were multiplied.'

PROCLAIM

1 זָעַק to shout, to cry out. HIPHIL *fut.*

2 כְּרַז to cry out publicly, to make proclamation. APHEL *pret.*

3 עָבַר to pass, with קוֹל to make the voice to pass, *i. e.* to proclaim. HIPHIL ᵃ *inf.* ᵇ *fut.*

4 קָדַשׁ to set apart, to prepare, to sanctify. PIEL *imp.*

5 קוֹל *m.* a voice.

6 קָרָא to call. KAL ᵃ *pret.* ᵇ *inf.* ᶜ *imp.* ᵈ *fut.* ᵉ *part.* Poel.

7 רִנָּה *f.* a cry; a shout of joy.

8 שָׁמַע to hear, to cause to hear, to proclaim. HIPHIL *pret.*

Exod. xxxii. 5.	6 d	2 Kings xxiii. 16, 16.	6 a	Isa. lxi. 1, 2.	6 b
xxxiii. 19.	6 a	xxiii. 17.	6 d	lxii. 11.	8
xxxiv. 5, 6.	6 d	2 Chron. xx. 3.	6 d	Jer. iii. 12.	6 a
xxxvi. 6.	3 b, 5	xxiv. 9.	5	vii. 2.	6 a
Lev. xxiii. 2, 4, 37.	6 d	xxx. 5.	3 a, 5	xi. 6.	6 c
xxiii. 21.	6 a	xxxvi. 22.	3 b, 5	xix. 2.	6 a
xxv. 10.	6 a	Ezra i. 1.	3 b, 5	xxxiv. 8, 15.	6 b
Deut. xx. 10.	6 a	viii. 21.	6 d	xxxiv. 17, 17.	6 b e
Judg. vii. 3.	6 c	x. 7.	3 b, 5	xxxvi. 9.	6 a
1 Kings xv. 22.	8	Neh. viii. 15.	3 b, 5	Dan. v. 29.	2
xxi. 9.	6 c	Esth. vi. 9.	6 a	Joel iii. 9.	6 c
xxi. 12.	6 a	vi. 11.	6 d	Amos iv. 5.	6 c
xxii. 36.	7	Prov. xii. 23.	6 d	Jonah iii. 5.	6 d
2 Kings x. 20, 20.	4, 6 d	xx. 6.	6 d	iii. 7.	1

PROCURE

בָּקַשׁ to seek. PIEL *fut.* Prov. xi. 27.

עָשָׂה to do. KAL *pret.* Jer. iv. 18. *fut.* Jer. ii. 17. *part.* Poel, Jer. xxvi. 19 ; xxxiii. 9.

PRODUCE

קָרַב to come near, to bring near. PIEL *imp.* Isa. xli. 21, *marg.* 'cause to come near.'

PROFANE

1 חָלַל to penetrate, wound, or stab ; to open, violate, or dissolve ; Piel, to profane sacred things, a temple, a thing hallowed, the sabbath, the name of God, the priests, the family of the priesthood, the holy land, the Jewish commonwealth as being holy, divine laws, the covenant, the father's bed ; applied also to the staining of what is beautiful and glorious, Isa. xxiii. 9, Ezek. xxviii. 7, *comp.* Ps. lxxxix. 39, and to that which comes into common use after being sacred ; see *Gather.* NIPHAL ᵃ *pret.* ᵇ *inf.* ᶜ *fut.* PIEL ᵈ *pret.* ᵉ *inf.* ᶠ *fut.* ᵍ *part.* PUAL ʰ *part.* ⁱ חָלָל *adj.* profane. ᵏ חֹל *adj.* profane, unholy, common.

2 חָנֵף to be defiled. KAL ᵃ *pret.* ᵇ חֲנֻפָּה *f.* see *Hypocrisy.*

Lev. xviii. 21.	1 f	Isa. xliii. 28.	1 f	Ezek. xxxvi. 20.	1 f
xix. 8, 12.	1 d	Jer. xxiii. 11.	2 ℓ	xxxvi. 21, 22.	1 d
xx. 3.	1 e	xxiii. 15.	2 b	xxxvi. 23, 23.	1 h d
xxi. 4.	1 b	Ezek. xxi. 25.	1 i	xlii. 10.	1 k
xxi. 6, 12, 15, 23.	1 f	xxii. 8.	1 d	xliv. 23.	1 k
xxi. 7, 14.	1 i	xxii. 26, 26, 26.	1 f k c	xlviii. 15.	1 k
xxi. 9, 9.	1 c g	xxiii. 38.	1 d	Amos ii. 7.	1 e
xxii. 2, 9, 15, 32.	1 f	xxiii. 39.	1 e	Mal. i. 12.	1 g
Neh. xiii. 17.	1 g	xxiv. 21.	1 g	ii. 10.	1 e
xiii. 18.	1 e	xxv. 3.	1 a	ii. 11.	1 d
Ps. lxxxix. 39.	1 d	xxviii. 16.	1 f		

PROFESS

נָגַד HIPHIL, to declare, show, make known : *pret.* Deut. xxvi. 3.

PROFIT

1 בֶּצַע *m.* covetousness, gain ; gain in general.

2 יָעַל to be useful. HIPHIL, to profit, to receive profit, to gain : ᵃ *pret.* ᵇ *inf.* ᶜ *fut.* ᵈ *part.*

3 יִתְרוֹן *f.* excellence ; advantage, profit. יוֹתֵר ᵃ *m.* (see *More*), gain ; pre-eminence, advantage. מוֹתָר ᵇ *m.* pre-eminence, abundance.

4 סָכַן to be useful, profitable ; to receive profit. KAL *fut.*

5 צָלֵחַ to go on, to advance forward, to succeed, prosper. KAL *fut.*

6 שָׁוָה to be equal, equivalent ; useful, serviceable, profitable. KAL ᵃ *pret.* ᵇ *part.* Poel.

PROFOUND

עָמַק to be deep ; applied to formed, meditated, deep schemes. HIPHIL *pret.* Hos. v. 2.

PROGENITORS

הָרָה to bring forth children. KAL *part.* Poel, Gen. xlix. 26. The plural is used of both parents.

PROGNOSTICATOR

יָדַע to know. HIPHIL *part.* Isa. xlvii. 13, *marg.* 'that give knowledge concerning the months.'

PROLONG

1 אָרַךְ to be or grow long ; to prolong, continue, protract. KAL ᵃ *fut.* HIPHIL ᵇ *pret.* ᶜ *fut.* ᵈ *part.* ᵉ אֲרֻכָה *f.* Ch. length.

2 יְהַב Ch. to give. P'AL *part.* P'il.

3 יָסַף to add. HIPHIL *fut.*

4 נָטָה to stretch, extend. KAL *fut.*

5 מָשַׁךְ to draw out. NIPHAL *fut.*

Deut. iv. 26, 40.	1 c	Deut. xxxii. 47.	1 c	Eccles. viii. 12.	1 d
v. 16.	1 c	Job vi. 11.	1 c	viii. 13.	1 c
v. 33.	1 b	xv. 29.	4	Isa. xiii. 22.	5
vi. 2.	1 c	Ps. lxi. 6. α	3	Ezek. xii. 22.	1 a
xi. 9.	1 c	Prov. x. 27.	3	xii. 25, 28.	5
xvii. 20.	1 c	xxviii. 2, 16.	1 c	Dan. vii. 12.β	1 e, 2
xxii. 7.	1 b	Eccles. vii. 15.	1 d		
xxx. 18.	1 c				

α *marg.* 'thou shalt add days to the days of the king.' β *lit.* a prolonging in life was given them.

PROMISE

1 אָמַר to say, speak, &c. KAL ᵃ *pret.* ᵇ *fut.* ᶜ אֹמֶר *m.* word, speech, thing.

2 דָּבַר to speak. KAL ᵃ *part.* Poel. PIEL ᵇ *pret.* ᶜ *fut.* ᵈ דָּבָר *m.* word ; promise.

3 חָיָה to live, to keep alive, to promise life. HIPHIL *inf.*

Exod. xii. 25.	2 b	Josh. ix. 21.	2 b	2 Chron. vi. 10, 15, 16.	2 b
Num. xiv. 40.	1 a	xxii. 4.	2 b		
Deut. i. 11.	2 b	xxii. 5, 10, 15.	2 b	xxi. 7.	1 a
vi. 3.	2 b	2 Sam. vii. 28.	2 c	Neh. v. 12, 13, 13.	2 d
ix. 28.	2 b	1 Kings ii. 24.	2 b	ix. 15.	1 b
x. 9.	2 b	v. 12.	2 b	ix. 23.	1 a
xii. 20.	2 b	viii. 20, 24, 25.	2 b	Esth. iv. 7.	1 a
xv. 6.	2 b	viii. 56, 56, 56.	2 b d b	Ps. lxxvii. 8.	1 c
xix. 8.	2 b	v. 5.	2 b	cv. 42.	2 d
xxiii. 23.	2 b	2 Kings viii. 19.	1 a	Jer. xxxii. 42.	2 a
xxvi. 18.	2 b	1 Chron. xvii. 26.	2 c	xxxiii. 14.	2 b
xxvii. 3.	2 b	2 Chron. i. 9.	2 d	Ezek. xiii. 22. α	3

α *marg.* 'quickening him.'

PROMOTE

1 גָּדַל to be or become great. PIEL *pret.*

2 הַר *m.* that which is high, a mountain : Ps. lxxv. 6. Hengstenberg renders this verse in the order of the original,

"For not from the rising of the sun, not from the going down of the sun, and not from the wilderness of mountains;" verse 6 is to be supplemented from verse 7, "it is not from the east," &c., but the decision is hence that God judgeth, &c.

3 כָּבַד to be heavy. PIEL, to honour; to promote to honour: a inf. b fut.

4 נוּע to move or be moved; it may be understood of the cares and vicissitudes of government. KAL inf.

5 צְלַח Ch. to bless, prosper, promote. APHEL pret.

6 רוּם to be lifted up. POLEL a fut. HIPHIL b inf. c part.

Num. xxii. 17.	3 a b	Esth. iii. 1.	1	Prov. iii. 35.	6 c
xxii. 37.	3 a	v. 11.	1	iv. 8.	6 a
xxiv. 11.	3 a b	Ps. lxxv. 6.	6 b, or 2	Dan. iii. 30.	5
Judg. ix. 9, 11, 13.	4				

PRONOUNCE

בָּטָה to speak or declare a thing inconsiderately or rashly. PIEL inf. Lev. v. 4. fut. Lev. v. 4.

דָּבַר to speak, &c. PIEL pret. Neh. vi. 12 ; Jer. xi. 17 ; xvi. 10 ; xviii. 8 ; xix. 15 ; xxv. 13 ; xxvi. 13, 19 ; xxxiv. 5 ; xxxv. 17 ; xxxvi. 7, 31 ; xl. 2. inf. Judg. xii. 6.

קָרָא to call. KAL fut. Jer. xxxvi. 18.

PROPHET, PROPHESY

1 אִישׁ m. a man: Judg. vi. 8. אִשָּׁה f. a woman: Judg. iv. 4.

2 חָזָה to see; vision, seer. KAL a imp. b fut. c חֹזֶה m. seer.

3 נָבָא to announce, to show, to deliver an oracle from God, to speak as God's ambassador; to foretell future events; to sing songs or hymns: each implying divine inspiration. In Hithpael, often to prophesy falsely, to feign being a prophet. NIPHAL a pret. b inf. c imp. d fut. e part. HITHPAEL f pret. g inf. h fut. i part. נְבָא Ch. ITHPAAL k pret. נְבוּאָה f. prophecy. m נְבוּאָה Ch. f. id. נָבִיא n m. a prophet, interpres Dei, one commissioned by God to make known his will to man. This signification is illustrated by Exod. vii. 1, thou shalt, in reference to Pharaoh, i. e. in conversation with him, be the God, i. e. the sovereign director, and Aaron, thy brother, shall be thine interpreter; comp. iv. 16, and he shall be thy mouth; also Jer. xv. 19, Deut. xviii. 18. (In Greek, προφήτης, ὑποφήτης, strictly an interpreter of the divine oracles.) Hence a friend of God, spoken of Abraham, Gen. xx. 7; of the patriarchs generally, Ps. cv. 15; of Moses, Deut. xxxiv. 10; of the Messiah, Deut. xviii. 15, 18; a prophet, one inspired of God to foretell future events, Deut. xiii. 2; used also in reference to false gods. Those educated as prophets were called sons of the prophets, i. e. their disciples: Gen. xx. 7, &c. o נְבִיא Ch. m. id. p נְבִיאָה f. a prophetess, a prophet's wife.

4 נָטַף to drop, as rain from the clouds, &c.; to let flow out, as words; to speak, to prophesy. HIPHIL a fut. b part.

5 מַשָּׂא m. a burden, a prophecy, containing things of eminence, weight, and importance, taught by man or revealed by God.

No. 3 n not included.

Exod. xv. 20.	3 p	Prov. xxx. 1.	5	Ezek. xi. 13.	3 b
Num. xi. 25, 26.	3 h	xxxi. 1.	5	xii. 27.	3 a
xi. 27.	3 i	Isa. viii. 3.	3 p	xiii. 2, 2, 2, 2.	3 c n e n
Judg. iv. 4.	1 a, 3 p	xxx. 10, 10, 10.	2 c a b	xiii. 16.	3 e
vi. 8.	1, 3 n	Jer. ii. 8.	3 a	xiii. 17, 17.	3 i c
1 Sam. x. 5.	3 i	v. 31.	3 a	xx. 46.	3 c
x. 6.	3 f	xi. 21.	3 d	xxi. 2, 9, 14, 28.	3 c
x. 10.	3 h	xiv. 14, 14.	3 e i	xxv. 2.	3 c
x. 11.	3 a	xiv. 15, 16.	3 e	xxviii. 21.	3 c
x. 13.	3 g	xix. 14.	3 e	xxix. 2.	3 c
xviii. 10.	3 h	xx. 1, 6.	3 a	xxx. 2.	3 c
xix. 20, 20, 20.	3 n e h	xxiii. 13.	3 f	xxxiv. 2, 2.	3 c
xix. 21, 21, 23, 24.	3 h	xxiii. 16, 25, 26, 32.	3 e	xxxv. 2.	3 c
1 Kings xviii. 29.	3 h	xxiii. 21.	3 a	xxxvi. 1, 3, 6.	3 c
xxii. 8, 18.	3 h	xxv. 13.	3 a	xxxvii. 4, 9, 9, 12.	3 c
xxii. 10.	3 i	xxv. 30.	3 d	xxxvii. 7, 7.	3 a b
xxii. 12.	3 i	xxvi. 9, 11.	3 a	xxxvii. 10.	3 f
2 Kings xxii. 14.	3 p	xxvi. 12.	3 b	xxxviii. 2, 14.	3 c
1 Chron. xxv. 1.	3 e	xxvi. 18. a	3 e	xxxviii. 17.	3 c
xxv. 2, 3.	3 a	xxvi. 20, 20.	3 d i	xxxix. 1.	3 c
2 Chron. ix. 29.	3 l	xxvii. 10, 14, 15,		Dan. ix. 24.	3 n
xv. 8.	3 l	15, 16, 16.	3 e	Joel ii. 28.	3 a
xviii. 7, 9.	3 i	xxviii. 6.	3 a	Amos ii. 12.	3 d
xviii. 11.	3 e	xxviii. 8, 9.	3 d	iii. 8.	3 d
xviii. 17.	3 e	xxix. 9, 21.	3 a	vii. 12, 16.	3 d
xx. 37.	3 h	xxix. 26, 27.	3 i	vii. 13.	3 b
xxxiv. 22.	3 h	xxix. 31.	3 a	vii. 15.	3 d
Ezra v. 1, 1, 1.	3 o o k	xxxii. 3.	3 e	Micah ii. 6, 6, 6, 11.	4 a
v. 2.	3 a	xxxvii. 19.	3 a	ii. 11.	4 b
vi. 14, 14.	3 m o	Ezek. iv. 7.	3 a	Zech. xiii. 3, 3.	3 d b
Neh. vi. 12.	3 l	vi. 2.	3 c	xiii. 4.	3 b
vi. 14.	3 p	xi. 4, 4.	3 c		

a lit. was prophesying.

PROPORTION

מַעַר m. nakedness; empty room: 1 Kings vii. 36, marg. 'nakedness;' i. e. according to the room of each.

עֵרֶךְ m. order, row, pile, arrangement; used of the scaly covering or armature of the crocodile: Job xli. 12.

PROSPECT

פָּנִים m. pl. face: Ezek. xl. 44, 44, 45, 46; xlii. 15; xliii. 4.

PROSPER

1 הָלַךְ to go. KAL inf.

2 טוֹב adj. good.

3 יָלַךְ to go. KAL fut.

4 כָּשֵׁר to be well and rightly adjusted for its proper end and purpose. KAL fut.

5 צָלַח to go through; to prosper; to accomplish successfully: it may always have a transitive signification, as in Deut. xxviii. 29, lit. thou shalt not make thy ways to go through, i. e. to reach the goal. KAL a pret. b imp. c fut. HIPHIL d pret. e imp. f fut. g part. צְלַח Ch. id. APHEL h pret. i part.

6 שָׂכַל to act wisely, prudently; to prosper. HIPHIL a pret. b fut.

7 שָׁלָה to be in quiet, to enjoy undisturbed prosperity. This word does not carry the idea of good, but with some other word to imply it.—Gussetius. KAL a pret. b fut. c שָׁלֵו adj. safe, secure. d שַׁלְוָה m. security. e שַׁלְוָה f. id.

8 שָׁלַם to be whole, sound, safe. KAL a fut. PIEL b pret. c שָׁלוֹם m. peace, lit. of the peace of the war.

Gen. xxiv. 21, 40, 56.	5 d	Num. xiv. 41.	5 c	Deut. xxix. 9.	6 b
xxiv. 42.	5 g	Deut. xxiii. 6.	2	Josh. i. 7.	6 b
xxxix. 2, 3, 23.	5 g	xxviii. 29.	5 f	i. 8.	5 f

Judg. iv. 24.	1, 3	Job viii. 6.	8 b	Isa. lv. 11.	5 d
xviii. 5.	5 f	ix. 4.	8 a	Jer. ii. 37.	5 f
2 Sam. xi. 7.	8 c	xii. 3.	7 b	v. 28.	5 f
1 Kings ii. 3.	6 b	xv. 21.	8 c	x. 21.	6 a
x. 7.		xxxvi. 11.	2	xii. 1.	5 f
xxii. 12, 15.	5 e	Ps. i. 3.		xx. 11.	6 a
2 Kings xviii. 7.	6 b	xxx. 6.	7 d	xxii. 21.	5 c
1 Chron. xxii. 11.	5 d	xxxv. 27.	8 c	xxii. 30, 30.	5 f
xxii. 13.	5 f	xxxvii. 7.	5 g	xxiii. 5.β	5 b
xxix. 23.	5 f	xlv. 4.	5 b	xxxii. 5.	8 c
2 Chron. vii. 11.	5 d	lxxiii. 3.	5 f	xxxiii. 9.	7 c
xiii. 12.	5 f	lxxiii. 12.	5 f	Lam. i. 5.	5 e
xiv. 7.	5 f	cxviii. 25.	5 e	iii. 17.	7 b
xviii. 11, 14.	5 e	cx. vi. 6.	5 e	Ezek. xvi. 13.	7 e
xx. 20.	5 e	Prov. i. 32.	5 f	xvii. 9, 10, 15.	7 c
xxiv. 20.	5 f	xvii. 8.	5 d	Dan. vi. 28.	5 h
xxvi. 5.	5 d	xxviii. 13.	5 f	viii. 12, 24, 25.	5 b
xxxi. 21.	5 d	Eccles. vii. 14.α	5 f	xi. 27.	5 f
xxxii. 30.	5 f	xi. 6.	5 i	xi. 36.	2
Ezra v. 8.	5 i	Isa. xlviii. 15.	5 i	Zech. i. 17.	4
vi. 14.	5 i	liii. 10.	5 d	vii. 7.	7 c
Neh. i. 11.	5 e	liv. 17.	5 c	viii. 12.	8 c
ii. 20.	5 f				

α *lit.* in the day of good be in good. β *or*, act wisely.

PROSTITUTE

חָלַל see *Profane*. PIEL *fut*. Lev. xix. 29.

PROTECTION

סִתְרָה *m.* a hiding-place. Deut. xxxii. 38.

PROTEST

עוּד see *Testify*. HIPHIL *pret.* Gen. xliii. 3 : Jer. xi. 7. *inf.* Gen. xliii. 3 : 1 Sam. viii. 9 : Jer. xi. 7, 7. *fut.* 1 Sam. viii. 9 : 1 Kings ii. 42 : Zech. iii. 6.

PROVE

1 בָּחַן to try, to prove, as one examines and purifies metals in the fire ; used also of men tempting God : Mal. iii. 10, 15. KAL [a] *pret.* [b] *imp.* [c] *fut.* NIPHAL [d] *fut.*

2 נָסָה to try, tempt, or put to the test ; spoken of God, who tries men by afflictions ; of men who tempt God by unbelief or despondency ; see *Tempt.* PIEL [a] *pret.* [b] *inf.* [c] *imp.* [d] *fut.* [e] *part.*

Gen. xlii. 15, 16.	1 d	Judg. iii. 1, 4.	2 b	Ps. lxxxi. 7.	1 c
Exod. xv. 25.	2 a	vi. 39.	2 d	xcv. 9.	1 a
xvi. 4.	2 d	1 Sam. xvii. 39, 39.	2 a	Eccles. ii. 1.	2 d
xx. 20.	2 b	1 Kings x. 1.	2 b	vii. 23.	2 a
Deut. viii. 2, 16.	2 b	2 Chron. ix. 1.	2 b	Dan. i. 12.	2 c
xiii. 3.	2 e	Ps. xvii. 3.	1 a	i. 14.	2 d
xxxiii. 8.	2 a	xxvi. 2.	2 c	Mal. iii. 10.	1 b
Judg. ii. 22.	2 b	lxvi. 10.	1 a		

PROVENDER

בָּלַל to mingle, to give provender. KAL *fut.* Judg. xix. 21. בְּלִיל *m.* Isa. xxx. 24.

מִסְפּוֹא *m.* fodder, provender for cattle : Gen. xxiv. 25, 32 : xlii. 27 ; xliii. 24 : Judg. xix. 19.

PROVERB

חִידָה *f.* (see *Riddle*), a parable, or proverbial expression : Hab. ii. 6.

מָשָׁל *m.* a comparison, similitude, parable ; a sentiment, maxim ; a proverb, by-word, satire : Deut. xxviii. 37, &c. מָשַׁל to utter a proverb : with the idea of speaking with authority, so as to command reverence ; hence the meaning of parable or proverb ; *comp.* Prov. viii. 6.

See *Excellent.* KAL *fut.* Ezek. xii. 23 ; xvi. 44. *part.* Poel, Num. xxi. 27 : Ezek. xvi. 44.

PROVIDE

1 חָזָה to see, to look out, choose, select. KAL *fut.*

2 כּוּן to prepare ; provide, make provision. HIPHIL [a] *pret.* [b] *fut.*

3 עָשָׂה to do, make, &c. KAL [a] *pret.* [b] *fut.*

4 רָאָה to see. KAL [a] *pret.* [b] *imp.* [c] *fut.*

Gen. xxii. 8.	4 c	1 Sam. xvi. 1.	4 a	Job xxxviii. 41.	2 b
xxx. 30.	3 b	xvi. 17.	4 b	Ps. lxv. 9.	2 b
Exod. xviii. 21.	1	2 Chron. ii. 7.	2 a	lxxviii. 20.	2 b
Deut. xxxiii. 21.	4 c	xxxii. 29.	3 a	Prov. vi. 8.	2 b

PROVINCE

מְדִינָה *f. lit.* a jurisdiction ; a province ; a land, country : 1 Kings xx. 14, &c., "every province," *lit.* in province and province. מְדִינָה Ch. *f.* Ezra iv. 15 ; v. 8 ; vi. 2 ; vii. 16 : Dan. ii. 48, 49 ; iii. 1, 2, 3, 12, 30.

PROVISION

דָּבָר *m.* word, matter, &c. : Dan. i. 5.

כּוּל to sustain, to nourish ; to make provision. PILPEL *inf.* 1 Kings iv. 7.

כּוּן to make provision. HIPHIL *pret.* 1 Chron. xxix. 19.

כֵּרָה *f.* a feast, banquet : 2 Kings vi. 23.

לֶחֶם *m.* bread : 1 Kings iv. 22, *marg.* ' bread.'

צוּד to hunt, to take provision for a journey. HITHPAEL *pret.* Josh. ix. 12. צַיִד *m.* food : Josh. ix. 5 : Ps. cxxxii. 15. צֵידָה *f.* provision for a journey : Gen. xlii. 25 ; xlv. 21.

PROVOKE, PROVOCATION

1 אַף *m.* anger ; with עַל a provocation of mine anger : Jer. xxxii. 31, *lit.* for my anger ; *i. e.* the object of my anger.

2 כָּעַס to be grieved. PIEL, to provoke to anger : [a] *pret.* HIPHIL [b] *pret.* [c] *inf.* [d] *fut.* [e] *part.* [f] כַּעַס *m.* this and the verb are generally used of men's provocation of God by the worship of idols ; mostly in the Lxx. rendered by ὀργή, θυμός.

3 מָרָה to rebel. HIPHIL [a] *pret.* [b] *inf.* [c] *fut.*

4 מָרַר to be bitter ; to make bitter. HIPHIL *fut.*

5 נָאַץ to treat with scorn and contumely ; to be provoked to anger by such treatment ; the word implies contempt, joined with hatred and malignity. PIEL [a] *pret.* [b] *fut.* [c] *part.* [d] נָאָצוֹת *f. pl.* reproaches.

6 סוּת to stir up, excite, instigate. HIPHIL *fut.* See *Move*.

7 עָבַר to pass, to go beyond. HITHPAEL, to be wroth ; to provoke to anger : *part*

8 רָגַז to tremble. HIPHIL, to disquiet : [a] *part.* רְגַז Ch. APHEL [b] *pret.*

9 מְרִיבָה *f.* see *Strife*.

Exod. xxiii. 21.	4	Deut. iv. 25.	2 c	Deut. xxxii. 16.	2 d
Num. xiv. 11.	5 b	ix. 18.	2 c	xxxii. 19.	2 f
xiv. 23.	5 a	xxxii. 20.	5 a	xxxii. 21, 21.	2 a d
xvi. 30.	5 a	xxxi. 29.	2 c	Judg. ii. 12.	2 d

1 Sam. i. 6.	2 a	2 Chron. xxxiii. 6.	2 c	Isa. iii. 8.	3 b
i. 7.	2 d	xxxiv. 25.	2 c	lxv. 3.	2 e
1 Kings xiv. 9.	2 c	Ezra v. 12.	8 b	Jer. vii. 18.	2 e
xiv. 15.	2 e	Neh. iv. 5.	2 b	vii. 19.	2 e
xv. 30, 30.	2 f b	ix. 18, 26.	5 d	viii. 19.	2 b
xvi. 2, 7, 13, 26, 33.	2 c	Job xii. 6.	8 a	xi. 17.	2 c
xxi. 22, 22.	2 f b	xvii. 2.	3 b	xxv. 6.	2 d
xxii. 53.	2 d	Ps. lxxviii. 17.	3 b	xxv. 7.	2 c
2 Kings xvii. 11, 17.	2 c	lxxviii. 40, 56.	3 c	xxxii. 29, 32.	2 c
xxi. 6.	2 c	lxxviii. 58.	2 d	xxxii. 30.	2 e
xxi. 15.	2 e	xcv. 8.	9	xxxii. 31.	1
xxii. 17.	2 c	cvi. 7, 43.	3 c	xliv. 3, 8.	2 c
xxiii. 19.	2 c	cvi. 29.	2 d	Ezek. viii. 17.	2 c
xxiii. 26, 26.	2 f b	cvi. 33.	3 a	xvi. 26.	2 c
1 Chron. xxi. 1.	6	Prov. xiv. 2.	7	xx. 28.	2 f
2 Chron. xxviii. 25.	2 d	Isa. i. 4.	5 a	Hos. xii. 14.	2 b

PRUDENCE, PRUDENT

1 בִּין to consider, to balance, to weigh things in the mind; to form a judgment; to have judgment and discretion. KAL ᵃ part. NIPHAL ᵇ pret. ᶜ part.

2 עָרַם to be crafty, prudent. HIPHIL ᵃ fut. ᵇ עָרוּם adj. crafty, cautious. ᶜ עָרְמָה f. craftiness.

3 קָסַם to divine. KAL part. Poel.

4 שָׂכַל to behave wisely, prudently; to prosper. HIPHIL ᵃ fut. ᵇ part. ᶜ שֵׂכֶל m. intelligence.

1 Sam. xvi. 18.	1 c	Prov. xvi. 21.	1 c	Isa. x. 13.	1 b
2 Chron. ii. 12.	4 c	xviii. 15.	1 c	xxix. 14.	1 c
Prov. viii. 12.	2 c	xix. 14.	4 b	lii. 13.	4 a
xii. 16, 23.	2 b	xxii. 3.	2 b	Jer. xlix. 7.	1 a
xiii. 16.	2 b	xxvii. 12.	2 b	Hos. xiv. 9.	1 c
xiv. 8, 15, 18.	2 b	Isa. iii. 2.	3	Amos v. 13.	4 b
xv. 5.	2 a	v. 21.	1 c		

PRUNE

זָמַר to prune. KAL fut. Lev. xxv. 3, 4. NIPHAL fut. Isa. v. 6. מַזְמֵרוֹת f. pl. pruning-hooks, or any instrument to cut with: Isa. ii. 4, marg. 'scythes,' xviii. 5: Joel iii. 10, marg. id.: Micah iv. 3.

PSALM

זָמַר to sing, to sing praises, to sing psalms. PIEL imp. 1 Chron. xvi. 9: Ps. cv. 2. זִמְרָה f. psalm, melody: Ps. lxxxi. 2; xcviii. 5. זָמִיר m. song, hymn: 2 Sam. xxiii. 1, "sweet psalmist," lit. of psalms: Ps. xcv. 2. מִזְמוֹר m. a song or psalm; used only in the superscription of the psalms.

PSALTERY

1 נֵבֶל m. the name of a musical instrument, a kind of harp or lyre; in Greek, νάβλα; in Latin, nablium. Josephus (Antiq. Jud. vii. 10) represents it as having twelve strings, which were played on by the hand. Jerome gives it the form of an inverted delta (∇). The wine vessels or bottles were usually in this form, which may have given a name to this instrument.

2 כְּלִי m. instruments, &c.; in two instances joined with the previous word.

3 פְּסַנְתֵּרִין Ch. m. pl. psaltery. ᵃ פְּסַנְתֵּרִין Ch. m. pl. id. Gr. ψαλτήριον.

1 Sam. x. 5.	1	2 Chron. ix. 11.	1	Ps. lxxxi. 2.	1
2 Sam. vi. 5.	1	xx. 28.	1	xcii. 3.	1
1 Kings x. 12.	1	xxix. 25.	1	cviii. 2.	1
1 Chron. xiii. 8.	1	Neh. xii. 27.	1	cxliv. 9.	1
xv. 16, 20, 28.	1	Ps. xxxiii. 2.	1	cl. 3.	1
xvi. 5.	1, 2	lvii. 8.	1	Dan. iii. 5, 10, 15.	3 a
xxv. 1, 6.	1	lxxi. 22.	1, 2	iii. 7.	3
2 Chron. v. 12.	1				

PUBLISH

1 אָמַר to say, &c. KAL fut.

2 בָּשַׂר to bring or publish (generally) good tidings. PIEL ᵃ inf. ᵇ fut. ᶜ part.

3 גָּלָה to open, reveal, discover. KAL part. Paül.

4 דָּבַר to speak, &c. PIEL part.

5 קָרָא to call. KAL fut.

6 שָׁמַע to hear. NIPHAL ᵃ pret. HIPHIL ᵇ inf. ᶜ imp. ᵈ fut. ᵉ part.

Deut. xxxii. 3.	5	Esth. viii. 13.	3	Jer. xxxi. 7.	6 c
1 Sam. xxxi. 9.	2 a	Ps. xxvi. 7.	6 b	xlvi. 14.	6 c
2 Sam. i. 20.	2 b	lxviii. 11.	2 c	l. 2, 2.	6 c
Neh. viii. 15.	6 d	Isa. lii. 7, 7.	6 e	Amos iii. 9.	6 c
Esth. i. 20.	6 a	Jer. iv. 5, 16.	6 c	iv. 5.	6 c
i. 22.	4	iv. 15.	6 e	Jonah iii. 7.	1
iii. 14.	3	v. 20.	6 c	Nah. i. 15.	6 e

PUFF

פּוּחַ to breathe, blow. HIPHIL fut. Ps. x. 5; xii. 5, marg. 'or, would ensnare him;' see Snare.

PULL

1 בּוֹא to come; to cause to come, to pull in. HIPHIL fut.

2 הָרַס (see Throw down), to pull down from his station; to drive from their habitation. KAL fut.

3 יָצָא to go out; to make to go out. HIPHIL fut.

4 נְסַח Ch. to pluck or tear away. ITHP'AL fut.

5 נָתַן to give. KAL fut.

6 נָתַץ to break down, to demolish. KAL inf.

7 נָתַק to draw or pluck asunder. PIEL ᵃ fut. HIPHIL ᵇ imp.

8 נָתַשׁ to extirpate, dig up, pull up by the roots. NIPHAL fut.

9 סָרַר (see To Backslide, to Rebel), to withdraw. KAL part. Poel, Zech. vii. 11, marg. 'gave a backsliding shoulder.'

10 פָּשַׁח to tear in pieces, only in PIEL fut.

11 פָּשַׁט to put off; to pull off. HIPHIL fut.

12 שׁוּב to return; to cause to return, to pull in again. HIPHIL inf.

Gen. viii. 9.	1	Jer. i. 10.	6	Lam. iii. 11.	10
xix. 10.	1	xii. 3.	7 b	Ezek. xvii. 9.	7 a
1 Kings xiii. 4.	12	xviii. 7.	6	Amos ix. 15.	8 a
Ezra vi. 11.	4	xxiv. 6.	2	Micah ii. 8.	11
Ps. xxxi. 4.	3	xlii. 10.	2	Zech. vii. 11.	5, 9
Isa. xxii. 19.	2				

PULPIT

מִגְדָּל m. something raised high, a tower: Neh. viii. 4. Lxx. βῆμα; Vulg. gradus; probably the same which is afterwards called stairs, ix. 4.

PULSE

זֵרֹעִים m. pl. seed, pulse: Dan. i. 12. זֵרְעֹנִים m. pl. id. Dan. i. 16.

PUNISH

1 חֵטְא m. sin; punishment of sin. חַטָּאת f. id.

2 חָשַׂךְ to withhold, to spare. KAL pret. Ezra ix. 13, marg. 'withheld beneath our iniquities,' i.e. in punishing.

3 תּוֹכֵחָה f. rebuke.

4 יָסַף to add. KAL pret.

5 יָסַר to discipline, to correct, chastise. PIEL inf.

6 נָכָה to smite. HIPHIL pret.

7 נָקַם to revenge; to punish with severity; see *Avenge*. KAL ᵃ*inf.* NIPHAL ᵇ*fut.* HOPHAL ᶜ*fut.*

8 עָוֹן *lit.* perverseness; sin, guilt, iniquity; more rarely "punishment of iniquity." Gussetius supposes this word to mean primarily, physical and moral evil, hence affliction; suffering for sin.

9 עָנַשׁ to amerce. KAL ᵃ*inf.* NIPHAL ᵇ*pret.* ᶜ*fut.* ᵈ עֹנֶשׁ *m.* fine.

10 פָּקַד to visit; to punish, *animadvertere in;* the crime punished is put in the accusative; the person punished is generally preceded by עַל, also by אֶל, and sometimes put in the accusative. This verb is most frequently construed with an accusative of the crime, and with עַל of the person; once with בְּ of the person. KAL ᵃ*pret.* ᵇ*inf.* ᶜ*fut.* ᵈ*part.* Poel.

11 רָעַע to do evil; to bring evil upon. HIPHIL *inf.*

Gen. iv. 13.	8	Isa. xiii. 11.	10 a	Jer. xlvi. 25.	10 d
Exod. xxi. 20.	7 a b	xxiv. 21.	10 c	l. 18, 18.	10 d a
xxi. 21.	7 c	xxvi. 21.	10 b	li. 44.	10 a
xxii. 22.	9 a c	xxvii. 1.	10 c	Lam. iii. 39.	1
Lev. xxvi. 18.	4, 5	Jer. ix. 25.	10 a	iv. 6, 6.	8, 1 a
xxvi. 24.	6	xi. 22.	10 d	iv. 22.	10
xxvi. 41, 43.	8	xiii. 21.	10 c	Ezek. xiv. 10, 10, 10.	8
1 Sam. xxviii. 10.	8	xxi. 14.	10 a	Hos. iv. 9.	10 a
Ezra ix. 13.	8	xxiii. 34.	10 a	iv. 14.	10 c
Job xix. 29.	8	xxv. 12.	10 c	xii. 2.	10 b
Ps. cxlix. 7.	8	xxvii. 8.	10 c	Amos iii. 2.	10 c
Prov. xvii. 26.	9 a	xxix. 32.	10 d	Zeph. i. 8, 9, 12.	10 a
xix. 19.	9 d	xxx. 20.	10 a	iii. 7.	10 a
xxi. 11.	9 a	xxxvi. 31.	10 a	Zech. viii. 14.	11
xxiii. 1.	9 b	xliv. 13, 13.	10 a	x. 3.	10 c
xxvii. 12.	9 b	xliv. 29.	10 d	xix. 19, 19.	1 a
Isa. x. 12.	10 c				

PUR

פּוּר *m.* lot, a die, a Persian word, explained Esth. iii. 7, by גּוֹרָל; applied to the festival of Purim, celebrated by the Jews in memory of the events recorded in the book of Esther, on the 14th and the 15th days of the month Adar: Esth. iii. 7; ix. 24, 26, 26, *marg.* 'that is, lot,' 28, 29, 31, 32.

PURCHASE

גָּאַל to redeem. KAL *fut.* Lev. xxv. 33, *marg.* 'or, (one) of the Levites redeem them.'

קָנָה to buy, purchase, or procure as an addition to a man's possessions. KAL *pret.* Gen. xxv. 10: Exod. xv. 16: Ruth iv. 10: Ps. lxxiv. 2; lxxviii. 54. מִקְנָה *m.* purchase: Gen. xlix. 32. מִקְנָה *f. id.* Jer. xxxii. 11, 12, 12, 14, 16.

PURE, PURGE, PURIFY

1 בָּרַר to separate; to separate that which is impure or drossy; to make clean, pure, clear and bright by washing, rubbing, polishing, &c.; to be clean, pure, clear: Zeph. iii. 9, "I will turn to the people a pure language," a language agreeable to the genius of true religion, free from all impure mixture of profaneness, idolatry, &c. KAL ᵃ*pret.* ᵇ*part.* Paül. NIPHAL ᶜ*part.* PIEL ᵈ*inf.* HITHPAEL ᵉ*fut.* בַּר ᶠ *adj.* clear, pure. ᵍ בֹּר *m.* purity.

2 דּוּחַ to cast out; to wash, purge out. HIPHIL *fut.*

3 דְּרוֹר *m.* liberty; applied to myrrh which flows of its own accord without an incision, and reckoned the purest.

4 זָכַךְ to be pure in a physical sense, and also in a moral sense; it signifies also to shine or glisten as glass or crystal, noting that purity in our lives shines as light: Matt. v. 16. The works of the holy should be pure as crystal. The word is used, Lam. iv. 7, to set forth the exactest beauty. The oil, Lev. xxiv. 2, and the frankincense, Exod. xxx. 34, appointed for the use of the sanctuary, were pure, shining, pellucid; they were a type of the purity of those who had communion with God in holy things. KAL ᵃ*pret.* ᵇ זַךְ *adj.* pure. זָכָה to be pure morally. KAL ᶜ*fut.*

5 זָקַק to purge and refine from impure mixtures, as metals and wines are refined. PIEL ᵃ*pret.* PUAL ᵇ*part.*

6 חָטָא to sin; Piel, to suffer punishment for sin, to make a sin-offering, to purify, to cleanse. In Ps. li. 7 the word is applied to a spiritual purification, as in murder and adultery there was no sin-offering provided: so in Job xli. 25, they purify themselves, *i. e.* spiritually, by confessing their sins and seeking peace of conscience. PIEL ᵃ*pret.* ᵇ*fut.* HITHPAEL ᶜ*fut.* ᵈ חַטָּאת *f.* sin, also rendered purification for sin.

7 חֶמֶר *m.* wine, as being fermented.

8 טָהֵר *m.* to be clear, bright, and shining; to be pure, unmixed, refined from that which debases or sullies metals; to be ceremonially clean, clear, or purged from moral pollution; to be cleared from the penal consequences of sin. KAL ᵃ*pret.* ᵇ*fut.* PIEL ᶜ*pret.* ᵈ*inf.* ᵉ*fut.* ᶠ*part.* HITHPAEL ᵍ*pret.* ʰ*fut.* ⁱ*part.* ᵏ טָהֹר *m.* purity. ˡ טֹהַר *m. id.* ᵐ טָהֳרָה *f.* purity, purification. ⁿ טָהוֹר *adj.* Exod. xxv. 11, &c., chiefly used of gold.

9 כָּפַר to make atonement, to purify. PIEL ᵃ*pret.* ᵇ*imp.* ᶜ*fut.* PUAL ᵈ*fut.* HITHPAEL ᵉ*fut.*

10 כָּתִית see *Beaten.*

11 מְרוּקִים *m. pl.* purification, cleansing. The maidens received into the harem of the Persian king underwent a course of purification and anointing with perfumes for twelve months. ᵃ תַּמְרוּק *m.* purification, ointments for purification.

12 נְקֵא Ch. *adj.* pure; see *Clear.*

13 סָגַר to shut; to lay up, hence costly, of gold. KAL *part.* Paül.

14 צָרַף to melt gold or silver, in order to refine them by separating the dross; to refine the mind by afflictions, or such trials as God may be pleased to employ for that end. KAL ᵃ*fut.* ᵇ*part.* Paül.

15 קָדַשׁ to sanctify by setting apart. HITHPAEL *part.*

No. 8 n, *Pure (gold),* not included.

Exod. xxvii. 20.	4 b	Num. xxxi. 19, 20, 23.	6 c	Neh. xii. 30, 30.	8 h e
xxx. 23.	3	Deut. xxxii. 14.	7	xii. 45.	8 m
xxx. 34.	4 b	1 Sam. iii. 14.	9 e	Esth. ii. 3, 9.	11 a
xxxi. 8.	8 n	2 Sam. xi. 4.	15	ii. 12, 12.	11, 11 a
xxxix. 37.	8 n	xxii. 27, 27.	8 n	Job iv. 17.	8 b
Lev. viii. 15.	6 b	1 Kings v. 11.	1 c	viii. 6.	4 b
ii. 4, 4.	8 m l	vi. 20, 21.	13	xi. 4.	8 b
xii. 5.	8 m	vii. 49, 50.	13	xvi. 17.	4 b
xii. 6.	8 l	x. 21.	13	xxii. 30.	1 g
xxiv. 2, 7.	4 b	1 Chron. xxiii. 28.	8 m	xxv. 5.	4 a
Num. viii. 7.	6 d	2 Chron. iv. 20, 22.	13	xxv. 26.	4 c
viii. 21.	6 d	ix. 20.	13	Ps. xii. 6, 6.	8 n, 5 b
xix. 9, 17.	6 d	xiii. 11.	8 n	xviii. 26, 26.	1 c e
xix. 12, 12, 13, 20.	6 c	xxx. 19.	8 m	xix. 8.	1 f
xix. 19.	6 a	xxxiv. 3, 8.	8 d	xxiv. 4.	1 f
		Ezra vi. 20, 20.	8 g n	li. 7.	6 b

Ps. lxv. 3.	9 c	Prov. xxx. 12.	8 n	Ezek. xliii. 20.	9 a
lxxix. 9.	9 b	Isa. i. 25, 25.	1 g, 14 a	xliii. 26, 26.	9 c, 8 c
cxix. 140.	14 b	iv. 4.	2	Dan. vii. 9.	12
Prov. xv. 26.	8 n	vi. 7.	9 d	xi. 35.	1 d
xvi. 6.	9 d	xxii. 14.	9 d	xii. 10.	1 e
xx. 9.	8 a	xxvii. 9.	9 d	Micah vi. 11.	4 c
xx. 11.	4 b	lxvi. 17.	8 i	Hab. i. 13.	8 n
xxi. 8.	4 b	Lam. iv. 7.	4 a	Zeph. iii. 9.	1 b
xxii. 11.	8 k	Ezek. xx. 38.	1 g	Mal. i. 11.	8 n
xxx. 5.	14 b	xxiv. 13,13,13.	8 c a b	iii. 3, 3.	8 f c, 5 a

PURPLE

אַרְגָּן *m.* purple : 2 Chron. ii. 7 ; supposed to be the same with

אַרְגְּמָן *m.* purple, reddish purple, a precious colour, the art of which is now lost, obtained from certain species of shell-fish or muscles found on the coasts of the Mediterranean. Gr. πορφύρα ; Lat. *purpura.* Exod. xxv. 4, &c.

PURPOSE

1 אָמַר to say, speak, &c. KAL *part.* Poel.

2 דָּבָר *m.* word, matter, &c.

3 זָמַם to tie fast, to tie up ; it is applied to the mind, and signifies a fixed deliberate purpose, to which the mind is, as it were, tied up by a course or series of thoughts, and which is so fixed and settled in the heart that it will not be loosed from it. KAL ᵃ *pret.* ᵇ *inf.* ᶜ וְזַמָּה *f.* counsel.

4 חֵפֶץ *m.* pleasure, delight ; desire ; matter, concern, business.

5 חָשַׁב to think, intend, purpose. KAL ᵃ *pret.* ᵇ *part.* Poel. ᶜ מַחֲשָׁבָה *f.* counsel, purpose, plan. ᵈ מַחֲשֶׁבֶת *f. id.*

6 יָעַץ to advise, to give advice ; to take counsel, to purpose. KAL ᵃ *pret.* ᵇ *part.* Paül. ᶜ עֵצָה *f.* counsel.

7 יָצַר to form, &c., to imagine, devise. KAL *pret.*

8 מַעֲשֶׂה *m.* a deed, action, concern, business.

9 פָּנִים *m. pl.* face.

10 צְבוּ Ch. *f.* will, purpose.

11 רִיק *adj.* in vain, to no purpose.

12 שׂוּם to set, place, put ; to settle, resolve. KAL *fut.*

13 שָׁת *m.* foundation. Gesenius, columns, pillars : Isa. xix. 10, *marg.* 'foundations,' *i. e.* the nobles of the state ; *opp.* hired labourers, *i. e.* the vulgar. Barnes, banks or dykes. Alexander : The simplest exposition of the verse is that proposed by Gesenius and adopted by most succeeding writers, which regards this as a general description extending to the two great classes of society, the pillars or chief men, and the labourers or commonalty.

1 Kings v. 5.	1	Prov. xx. 18.	5 d	Jer. iv. 28.	3 a
2 Chron. xxviii. 10.	1	Eccles. iii. 1, 17. γ	4	xxvi. 3.	5 b
xxxii. 2. α	9	viii. 6.	4	xxxvi. 3.	5 b
Ezra iv. 5.	6 c	Isa. xiv. 24, 27.	6 a	xlix. 20, 20.	5 d a
Neh. viii. 4.	2	xiv. 26, 26.	6 c b	xlix. 30.	5 c
Job xvii. 11.	3 c	xix. 10.	13	l. 45, 45.	5 d a
xxxiii. 17.	8	xix. 12.	6 a	li. 29.	5 d
Ps. xvii. 3. β	3 b	xxiii. 9.	6 a	Lam. ii. 8.	5 a
cxl. 4.	5 a	xxx. 7.	11	Dan. i. 8.	12
Prov. xv. 22.	5 d	xlvi. 11.	7	vi. 17.	10

    α *lit.* his face was to.   β *lit.* my purpose.   γ *or,* desire.

PURSE

כִּיס a bag for money or weights (see *Cup*): Prov. i. 14.

PURSUE

1 אַחַר after ; "from pursuing him," *lit.* from after him.

---

2 דָּבַק to adhere, to follow close, to pursue hard. HIPHIL *fut.*

3 דָּלַק to burn ; to pursue or persecute with a hot, malicious mind. KAL *pret.*

4 יָלַךְ to go (after). KAL *fut.*

5 שִׂיג from נָשַׂג to overtake ; a pursuit. Cocceius derives it from סוּג to go back, and translates it, 'he is gone backward, retired ; or, is in his private retirement.'

6 רָדַף to run or follow after, in order to overtake ; to persecute ; to infest, to stick to, to accompany wherever one goes, Deut. xxviii. 22, 45 ; to follow, to apply the mind to, to be addicted to, to practise, to endeavour to procure, Ps. xxxiv. 14 ; to pursue with words, to be instant, pressing, Prov. xix. 7. KAL ᵃ *pret.* ᵇ *inf.* ᶜ *imp.* ᵈ *fut.* ᵉ *part.* Poel. PIEL ᶠ *fut.* ᵍ *part.*

Gen. xiv. 14, 15.	6 d	Judg. viii. 4, 5.	6 e	2 Kings xxv. 5.	6 d
xxxi. 23.	6 d	viii. 12.	6 d	2 Chron. xiii. 19.	6 d
xxxi. 36.	3	xx. 45.	2	xiv. 13.	6 d
xxxv. 5.	6 a	1 Sam. vii. 11.	6 d	xviii. 32.	1
Exod. xiv. 8, 9, 23.	6 d	xvii. 52.	6 d	Job xiii. 25.	6 d
xv. 9.	6 d	xxiii. 25.	6 d	xxx. 15.	6 d
Lev. xxvi. 17, 36, 37.	6 d	xxiii. 28.	6 b	Ps. xviii. 37.	6 d
Deut. xi. 4.	6 b	xxiv. 14.	6 e	xxxiv. 14.	6 d
xix. 6.	6 d	xxv. 29.	6 b	Prov. xi. 19.	6 g
xxviii. 22, 45.	6 a	xxvi. 18.	6 e	xiii. 21.	6 f
Josh. ii. 5.	6 c	xxx. 8, 8.	6 d c	xix. 7.	6 g
ii. 7, 7.	6 a e	xxx. 10.	6 d	xxviii. 1.	6 e
ii. 16, 16, 22, 22.	6 e	2 Sam. ii. 19, 24, 28.	6 d	Isa. xxx. 16.	6 d
viii. 16, 16.	6 b d	xvii. 1.	6 d	xli. 3.	6 d
viii. 17.	6 e	xviii. 16.	6 b	Jer. xxxix. 5.	6 d
viii. 20.	6 c	xx. 6.	6 d	xlviii. 2.	4
x. 19.	6 c	xx. 7, 13.	6 b	lii. 8.	6 d
xx. 5.	6 d	xx. 10.	6 a	Lam. i. 6.	6 e
xxiv. 6.	6 d	xxii. 38.	6 d	iv. 19.	3
Judg. i. 6.	6 a	xxii. 13.	6 e	Ezek. xxxv. 6, 6.	6 d
iv. 16.	6 a	1 Kings xviii. 27.	5	Hos. viii. 3.	6 d
iv. 22.	6 e	xx. 20.	6 d	Amos i. 11.	6 b
vii. 23, 25.	6 d	xxii. 33.	1	Nah. i. 8.	6 f

PURTENANCE

קֶרֶב *m.* inwards : Exod. xii. 9.

PUSH

נָגַח to thrust or push with the horns, **as a horned animal.** KAL *fut.* Exod. xxi. 32. PIEL *fut.* Deut. xxxiii. 17 : 1 Kings xxii. 11 : 2 Chron. xviii. 10 : Ps. xliv. 5 : Ezek. xxxiv. 21. *part.* Dan. viii. 4. HITHPAEL *fut.* Dan. xi. 40. נַגָּח *adj.* wont to push : Exod. xxi. 29, 36.

שָׁלַח to send ; to send away. PIEL *pret.* Job xxx. 12.

PUT

1 אָסַף to gather, to put together, to put up. KAL ᵃ *fut.* NIPHAL ᵇ *imp.*

2 בּוֹא to come in ; to bring in, to put. HIPHIL ᵃ *pret.* ᵇ *imp.* ᶜ *fut.* HOPHAL ᵈ *pret.* ᵉ *fut.*

3 בָּעַר to burn, in order to clear away briers, &c. ; to put away what is corrupt and pernicious ; it applies also, as a formula, to the punishment of death. PIEL ᵃ *pret.* ᵇ *fut.*

4 גָּבַר to be strong ; to strengthen ; with חַיִל to put to more strength. PIEL *fut.*

5 גָּרַשׁ to drive out ; to put away. KAL ᵃ *part.* Paül. ᵇ גֶּרֶשׁ *m.* what is put forth, produce.

6 דָּעַךְ to be extinguished. KAL *fut.*

7 הָדָה to stretch out the hand. KAL *pret.*

8 הָדַר to be tumid, to swell, to show oneself proud, to put forth oneself. HITHPAEL *fut.*

9 הָרַג to slay. KAL *part.* Paül, *lit.* the slain (of death).

10 חָבַשׁ to bind, to put on a head-dress. KAL a*pret.* b*fut.*

11 חָגַר to gird. KAL *part.* Poel.

12 חוּד to put forth (a riddle). KAL a*pret.* b*imp.* c*fut.*

13 חָלַץ to draw off (a shoe), to put off. KAL *fut.*

14 חָנַט to ripen, to mature. KAL *pret.*

15 יָנַח to lay or set down, to make to stay or abide. HIPHIL a*pret.* b*fut.*

16 יָסַף to add, to put more. KAL a*pret.* NIPHAL b*pret.* HIPHIL c*inf.* d*fut.*

17 יָצָא to go out ; to bring forth, to put away. HIPHIL *inf.*

18 יָצַג to cause to stand. HIPHIL a*fut.* b*part.*

19 יָרַד to go down ; to put down, off. HIPHIL a*imp.* b*fut.*

20 יֻשַׂם to be set, placed. KAL *fut.*

21 כָּבָה to be quenched, to be put out. KAL a*fut.* PIEL b*inf.* c*fut.*

22 כָּפַר to cover ; to make atonement. PIEL *inf.*

23 לָבַשׁ to put on (garments). KAL a*pret.* b*inf.* c*imp.* d*fut.* PUAL e*part.* HIPHIL f*pret.* g*fut.* h*לְבוּשׁ m.* a garment, clothing ; garment put on.

24 לָקַח to take. KAL *fut.*

25 מָחָה to wipe off, to blot out. KAL a*pret.* b*inf.* c*fut.* NIPHAL d*fut.*

26 נָגַשׁ to come near, to bring near, unto. HOPHAL *pret.*

27 נָדָה to recede ; to remove, to put far away. PIEL a*part.* b נִדָּה *f.* separation, put apart.

28 נָחָה to lead ; to bring into. HIPHIL *fut.*

29 נָטָה to stretch out ; to put away. HIPHIL *fut.*

30 נָקַר to pierce, bore, dig out. PIEL *fut.*

31 נָשַׂג to overtake, to reach unto. HIPHIL *part.*

32 נָשַׁל to put off (a shoe), to cast out. KAL a*pret.* b*imp.*

33 נָתַן to give ; to put, set, place. KAL a*pret.* b*inf.* c*imp.* d*fut.* e*part.* Poel. NIPHAL f*pret.* g*fut.* HOPHAL h*fut.*

34 סוּר to turn away ; to put away. HIPHIL a*pret.* b*imp.* c*fut.*

35 סָמַךְ to lay or place upon something. KAL *pret.*

36 סָפָה to add. KAL *imp.* Jer. vii. 21, or from יָסַף.

37 סָפַח to add, to join oneself, associate. KAL a*imp.* PIEL b*part.*

38 עָבַר to pass ; to cause to pass, to put away. HIPHIL a*pret.* b*inf.* c*imp.* d*fut.*

39 עָוַר to blind the eyes by digging them out. PIEL *pret.*

40 עָטָה to cover, to clothe oneself. KAL *fut.*

41 עָלָה to ascend ; to put on. KAL a*pret.* HIPHIL b*fut.* c*part.*

42 עָמַס to lade. HIPHIL *pret.*

43 עָשָׂה to do, &c. KAL *pret.*

44 פָּשַׁט to put off (garments). KAL a*pret.* b*fut.* c*part.* Poel.

45 פָּתַח to open, loose. PIEL a*pret.* b*part.*

46 צוּר to bind up, to put up in bags. KAL *fut.*

47 רָחַק to be far, to put far away, to put away. PIEL a*fut.* HIPHIL b*pret.* c*imp.* d*fut.*

48 רָכַב to ride, to make to ride. HIPHIL a*imp.* b*fut.*

49 שָׁבַת to cease ; to cause to cease, to put down. HIPHIL a*pret.* b*fut.*

50 שׁוּב to return ; to cause to return, to put again. HIPHIL a*pret.* b*imp.* c*fut.*

51 שׂוּם to put, set, place. KAL a*pret.* b*inf.* c*imp.* d*fut.* e*part.* Poel.

52 שִׁית to lay, put, set, place ; to put the hand with any one is to join hands with him in doing anything. KAL a*pret.* b*imp.* c*fut.*

53 שָׁלַח to send ; to send out, to stretch out, frequently followed by יָד the hand, with עַל ; with בְּ, to put the hand to anything with force, or to purloin ; with אֶל, to lay hands upon any one ; sometimes יָד is omitted. KAL a*pret.* b*inf.* c*imp.* d*fut.* e*part.* Poel. PIEL f*pret.* g*inf.* h*fut.* PUAL i*pret.* שָׁלַח Ch. P'AL k*fut.* l מִשְׁלָח *m.* that to which the hand is put, business. m שֶׁלַח *m.* weapon.

54 שָׁפֵל to be made low ; to put down. HIPHIL a*inf.* b*fut.* שְׁפַל Ch. APHEL c*part.*

Gen. ii. 8.	51 d	Exod. xxiv. 6.	51 d	Lev. viii. 9, 26.	51 d
ii. 15.	15 b	xxv. 12, 16, 26.	33 a	viii. 13, 13.	23 g, 10 b
iii. 15.	52 c	xxv. 14.	2 a	ix. 9.	33 d
iii. 22.	53 d	xxv. 21, 21.	33 a d	ix. 20.	51 d
viii. 9.	53 d	xxvi. 11.	34 a	x. 1, 1.	33 d, 51 d
xix. 10.	53 d	xxvi. 34.	33 a	xi. 32.	2 e
xxi. 14.	51 a	xxvi. 35.	33 a	xi. 38.	33 h
xxiv. 2.	51 c	xxvii. 5.	33 a	xiv. 14, 25, 28, 34.	33 a
xxiv. 9, 47.	51 d	xxvii. 7.	2 d	xiv. 17, 29.	33 d
xxvii. 15.	23 g	xxviii. 12, 26, 37.	51 a	xiv. 42.	2 a
xxvii. 16.	23 f	xxviii. 23, 24, 25,		xv. 19.	27 b
xxviii. 11.	51 d	27, 30.	33 a	xvi. 4, 4.	23 d a
xxviii. 18.	51 a	xxviii. 41.	23 f	xvi. 13, 18, 21. a	33 a
xxviii. 20.	23 b	xxix. 3, 6, 12, 17,		xvi. 23, 23.	44 a, 23 a
xxix. 3.	50 a	20.	33 a	xvi. 24, 32.	23 a
xxx. 40, 40.	52 c a	xxix. 5, 8.	23 f	xix. 14.	33 d
xxx. 42.	51 d	xxix. 6, 24.	51 a	xxi. 7.	5 a
xxxi. 34.	51 d	xxix. 9.	10 a	xxi. 10.	23 b
xxxiii. 16.	51 d	xxix. 10, 15.	35	xxii. 14.	16 a
xxxiii. 2.	51 d	xxix. 30.	23 d	xxiv. 7.	33 a
xxxv. 2.	34 b	xxx. 6, 18, 18, 36.	33 a	xxiv. 12.	15 b
xxxvii. 34.	51 d	xxx. 33.	33 d	Num. iv. 6, 6.	51 a
xxxviii. 14.	34 c	xxxi. 6.	33 a	iv. 7, 10, 10, 12, 12.	33 a
xxxviii. 19.	23 d	xxxii. 27.	51 c	v. 2, 3, 3, 4.	53 h
xxxviii. 28.	33 d	xxxiii. 4.	52 a	v. 15.	33 d
xxxix. 4.	33 a	xxxiii. 5.	19 a	v. 17, 18.	33 a
xxxix. 20.	33 d	xxxiii. 22.	51 a	vi. 18, 19.	33 a
xl. 3.	33 d	xxxiv. 33.	33 d	vi. 27.	51 a
xl. 15.	51 a	xxxiv. 35.	50 a	viii. 10.	35
xli. 10.	33 d	xxxv. 34.	33 a	viii. 11.	51 a
xli. 42, 42.	33 d, 51 d	xxxvi. 1, 2.	33 d	viii. 14, 14.	51 a, 33 a
xlii. 17.	1 a	xxxvii. 5.	2 c	xi. 17.	51 a
xliii. 22.	51 a	xxxvii. 13.	33 d	xi. 29.	33 d
xliv. 1.	51 c	xxxviii. 7.	2 c	xv. 34.	15 b
xliv. 2.	51 d	xxxix. 7, 19.	51 d	xv. 38.	33 a
xlvi. 4.	52 c	xxxix. 16, 17, 18,		xvi. 7, 7.	33 c, 51 c
xlvii. 29.	51 c	20, 25.	33 d	xvi. 14.	30
xlviii. 18.	51 c	xl. 3, 5, 29.	51 a	xvi. 17.	33 a
i. 26.	20	xl. 7.	33 a	xvi. 18, 47.	33 d
Exod. ii. 3.	51 d	xl. 13.	23 f	xvi. 46, 46.	33 c, 51 c
iii. 5.	32 b	xl. 18, 20, 20, 22,		xix. 17.	33 a
iii. 22.	51 a	30.	33 d	xx. 26.	23 f
iv. 4, 4.	53 c d	Lev. i. 4.	35	xx. 28.	23 g
iv. 6, 6.	2 b c	ii. 1, 15.	33 a	xxi. 9.	51 d
iv. 7, 7.	50 b c	iv. 7, 25, 30, 34.	33 a	xxiii. 38.	51 d
iv. 15, 21.	51 a	iv. 18.	33 a	xxiv. 21.	51 d
v. 21.	33 b	v. 11, 11.	51 d, 33 d	xxvii. 20.	33 a
viii. 23.	51 a	vi. 10, 10,		xxxvi. 3, 4.	16 b
xii. 15.	49 b	10.	23 a d, 51 a	Deut. ii. 25.	33 d
xv. 26.	51 d	vi. 11, 11.	44 a, 23 a	vii. 15.	51 d
xvi. 33.	33 d	viii. 10.	21 a	vii. 22.	32 a
xvii. 12.	51 d	vii. 7, 7, 15, 23,		x. 2.	51 d
xvii. 14.	25 b c	24, 27.	33 d	xi. 29.	33 a
xxii. 5.	53 f	viii. 7, 7.	23 c	xii. 5, 21.	51 b
xxii. 8, 11.	53 a				
xxiii. 1.	52 c	viii. 8, 8.	51 d, 33 d		

Deut. xii. 7, β 18.β	53 l
viii. 5.	3 a
xv. 10.	53 l
xvi. 7, 12.	3 a
xviii. 18.	33 a
xix. 13, 19.	3 a
xxi. 9.	3 b
xxi. 13.γ	34 a
xxi. 21.	3 a
xxii. 5.	23 d
xxii. 19, 29.	53 g
xxii. 21, 22, 24.	3 a
xxiii. 24.	33 d
xxiv. 7.	3 a
xxv. 6.	25 d
xxv. 11.	53 a
xxvi. 2.	51 a
xxvii. 15.	51 a
xxviii. 48.	33 a
xxx. 7.	33 a
xxxi. 19.	51 c
xxxi. 26.	51 a
xxxiii. 10.	51 d
xxxiii. 14.	5 b
Josh. vi. 24.	33 a
vii. 6.	41 b
vii. 11.	51 a
x. 24, 24.	51 c d
xvii. 13.	33 d
xxiv. 7.	51 d
xxiv. 14, 23.	34 b
Judg. i. 28.	51 d
iii. 21.	53 d
v. 26.	53 d
vi. 19, 19.	51 a
vi. 21.	53 d
vi. 37.	18 b
vii. 16.	33 b
viii. 27.	18 a
ix. 49.	51 d
x. 16.	34 c
xii. 3.	51 d
xiv. 2.	12 c
xiv. 12, 13.	12 b
xiv. 16.	12 a
xv. 4.	51 d
xv. 15.	53 d
xvi. 3.	51 d
xvi. 21.	30
xviii. 21.	51 d
xx. 13.	3 b
Ruth iii. 3.	51 a
1 Sam. i. 14.	34 b
ii. 36.	37 a
vi. 8, 15.	51 d
vii. 3.	34 b
vii. 4.	34 c
viii. 16.	43
xi. 11.	51 d
xiv. 26.	31
xiv. 27, 27.	53 d, 50 c
xvii. 38.	33 a
xvii. 39.	34 c
xvii. 40.	51 d
xvii. 49.	53 d
xvii. 54.	51 a
xix. 5.	51 d
xix. 13.	51 a
xxi. 6.	51 b
xxii. 17.	53 b
xxiv. 10.	53 d
xxviii. 3.	34 a
xxviii. 8.	23 d
xxviii. 21.	51 d
xxxi. 10.	51 d
2 Sam. i. 24.	41 c
iii. 34.	26
vi. 6.	53 d
vii. 15.	34 a
viii. 6.	51 d
viii. 14, 14.	51 d a
xii. 13.	38 a
xii. 31.	51 d
xiii. 17.	53 c
xiii. 19.	24
xiv. 2.	23 c
xiv. 3.	51 d
xiv. 19.	51 a
xv. 5.	53 a
xviii. 12.	53 d
xx. 3.	33 d
xx. 8.	23 h
1 Kings ii. 5.	33 d
ii. 35, 35.	33 d a
v. 3.	33 b
vii. 39.	33 d
1 Kings vii. 51.	33 a
viii. 9.	15 a
ix. 3.	51 b
x. 17.	33 d
x. 24.	33 a
xi. 36.	51 b
xii. 4, 9, 29.	33 a
xiii. 4, 4.	53 d a
xiv. 21.	51 b
xviii. 23, 23, 25, 42.	51 d
xx. 6, 31.	51 d
xx. 11.	45 b
xx. 24.	51 c
xx. 27.	51 d
xxii. 10.	23 e
xxii. 23.	33 a
xxii. 27.	51 c
xxii. 30.	23 c
2 Kings ii. 20.	51 c
iii. 2.	34 c
iii. 21.	11
iv. 34.	51 d
v. 7.	53 d
vi. 7.	53 d
x. 13.	51 d
xi. 12.	51 d
xii. 9.	33 a
xii. 10.	46
xiii. 16, 16, 16.	48 a b, 51 d
xvi. 14, 17.	33 d
xvii. 19.	15 b
xviii. 11.	28
xviii. 14.	33 d
xix. 28.	51 a
xxi. 4, 7.	51 d
xxiii. 7.	49 a
xxiii. 24.	3 a
xxiii. 33.	33 d
1 Chron. x. 10.	51 d
xiii. 9.	53 d
xiii. 10.	53 a
xviii. 6, 13.	51 d
xxi. 27.	50 c
xxvii. 24.δ	41 a
2 Chron. i. 5.	51 a
ii. 14.	33 g
iii. 16, 16.	33 d
iv. 6.	33 d
v. 1, 10.	33 a
vi. 11.	51 d
vi. 20.	51 b
ix. 16.	33 d
ix. 23.	33 a
x. 4, 9.	33 a
x. 11.	33 d
xii. 13.	51 b
xv. 8.	38 d
xvi. 10.	33 d
xvii. 19.	33 a
xviii. 22.	33 a
xviii. 26.	51 c
xviii. 29.	23 c
xxii. 11.	33 d
xxix. 7.	21 c
xxxiii. 7, 10.	51 d
xxxv. 3.	33 c
xxxv. 24.	48 b
xxxvi. 3.	34 c
xxxvi. 7.	33 d
Ezra i. 7.	33 d
vi. 12.	53 k
vii. 27.	33 a
x. 3, 19.	17
Neh. ii. 12.	33 e
iii. 5.	33 d
iv. 23, 23.ε	44 c, 53 m
vii. 5.	33 d
Esth. iv. 1.	23 d
v. 1.	23 d
viii. 3.	38 b
Job i. 11.	53 c
i. 12.	51 d
ii. 5.	53 c
xi. 14.	47 c
xiii. 14, 27.	51 d
xvi. 11, 12.	6
xvii. 14.	51 a
xvii. 2.	12 b
xix. 13.	47 b
xxi. 17.	6
xxii. 23.	47 d
xxiv. 17.	51 d
xxvi. 16.	44 b
Job xxvii. 17.	23 d
xxviii. 9.	53 a
xxix. 14.	23 a
xxxiii. 11.	51 d
xxxviii. 36.	52 a
xli. 2.	51 b
Ps. iv. 7.	33 a
viii. 6.	52 a
ix. 5.	25 a
ix. 20.	52 b
xv. 5.	33 a
xviii. 22.	34 c
xxvii. 9.	29
xxx. 11.	45 a
xl. 3.	33 d
lv. 20.	53 a
lvi. 8.	51 c
lxxiii. 28.	52 a
lxxv. 7.	54 b
lxxviii. 66.	47 b
lxxxiii. 9, 18.	49 a
cxv. 3.	33 d
cxix. 119.	53 d
Prov. iv. 24, 24.	34 b, 47 c
viii. 1.	33 d
xiii. 9.	6
xx. 20.	6
xxiii. 2.	51 a
xxiv. 20.	6
xxv. 6.	8
xxv. 7.	54 a
Eccles. iii. 14.	16 c
x. 10.	4
xi. 10.	38 c
Cant. ii. 13.	14
v. 3, 3.	44 a, 23 d
v. 4.	53 a
Isa. i. 16.	34 b
v. 20, 20.	51 a
x. 13.	19 b
xi. 8.	7
xx. 2.	13
xxxvii. 29.	51 a
xlii. 1.	33 a
xlvii. 10.	22
l. 1, 1.	53 f i
li. 9.	23 c
li. 16.	51 d
li. 23.	51 a
lii. 1, 1.	23 c
lviii. 9.	53 b
lix. 17, 17.	23 d
lix. 21.	51 a
lxiii. 11.	51 e
Jer. i. 9, 9.	53 d, 33 a
iii. 1.	53 h
iii. 8.	53 f
iii. 19.	52 c
iv. 1.	34 c
vii. 21.	36
xiii. 1, 1.	51 a, 2 c
xiii. 2.	51 d
xviii. 21.	9
xx. 2.	33 d
xxvii. 2.	33 a
xxvii. 8.	33 d
xxviii. 14.	33 a
xxix. 26.	33 a
xxxi. 33.	33 a
xxxii. 14.	33 a
xxxii. 40.	33 a
xxxviii. 4, 15, 18.	33 a
xxxviii. 7.	33 a
xxxviii. 12.	51 c
xxxix. 7.	39
xl. 10.	51 c
xliii. 12.	40
xlvi. 4.	23 c
xlvii. 6.	1 b
lii. 11, 11.	39, 33 d
Ezek. iii. 25.	33 d
iv. 9.	33 a
viii. 3.	53 a
viii. 17.	53 e
x. 7.	33 d
xi. 19.	33 d
xiv. 3.	33 d
xiv. 4, 7.	51 d
xvi. 11, 12.	51 a
xvii. 14.	12 b
xvii. 2.	33 d
xix. 9.	33 d
xxiii. 42.	33 d
xxiv. 17.	51 d
xxvi. 16.	44 b
Ezek. xxix. 4.	33 a
xxx. 13, 24.	33 a
xxx. 21.	33 b
xxx. 25.	33 b
xxxii. 7.	21 b
xxxii. 25.	33 f
xxxvi. 26, 27.	33 d
xxxvii. 6, 14, 19.	33 a
Dan. v. 19.	33 a
Ezek. xxxviii. 4.	33 a
xlii. 14.	23 a
xliii. 9.	47 a
xliii. 20.	33 a
xliv. 19, 19.	44 b, 23 a
xliv. 22.	5 a
xlv. 19.	33 a
Dan. v. 19.	54 c
Hos. ii. 2.	34 c
Joel iii. 13.	53 c
Amos vi. 3.	27 a
Jonah iii. 5.	23 d
Micah iii. 12.	51 d
iii. 5.	33 d
Hab. ii. 15.	37 b
Mal. ii. 16.	53 g

α *lit.* and he shall put.   β *lit.* in all putting of the hand unto.   γ *lit.* remove.   δ *comp.* 2 Chron. xx. 34.   ε *marg.* 'or, every one (went) with his weapon for water.'

PUTRIFYING

טְרִי *adj.* recent, fresh, green; applied to a wound which cannot be healed: Isa. i. 6.

PYGARG

דִּישׁוֹן *m.* a species of gazelle or antelope, so called from its leaping or springing: Deut. xiv. 5, *marg.* 'dishon, *or,* bison.'

QUAILS

(קרי) שְׂלָיו (כתיב) שֶׁלָו *m.* coturnix, a quail, so called from its fatness: Exod. xvi. 13: Num. xi. 31, 32: Ps. cv. 40.

QUAKE

חָרַד see *Tremble.* KAL *fut.* Exod. xix. 18. חֲרָדָה *f.* terror, fear: Dan. x. 7.

רָגַז see *Tremble.* KAL *pret.* Joel ii. 10. *fut.* 1 Sam. xiv. 15.

רָעַשׁ see *Tremble.* KAL *pret.* Nah. i. 5. רַעַשׁ *m.* trembling: Ezek. xii. 18.

QUARREL

נָקָם *m.* vengeance: Lev. xxvi. 25.

אָנָה to befal; to seek occasion against any one, to seek a quarrel. HITHPAEL *part.* 2 Kings v. 7.

QUARRY

פְּסִילִים *m.* graven images; quarries: Judg. iii. 19, *marg.* 'or, graven images;' 26, perhaps hewn stones.

QUARTER

גְּבוּל *m.* (see *Border*): Exod. xiii. 7.

יְרֵכָה *f.* side; coast or border of a country: Ezek. xxxviii. 6.

כָּנָף *com.* wing: Deut. xxii. 12.

עֵבֶר *m.* region or country beyond: Isa. xlvii. 15.

פֵּאָה *f.* the extremity or remotest parts of a country: Num. xxxiv. 3: Josh. xv. 5: xviii. 14, 15.

קָצֶה *f.* end, extremity: Jer. xlix. 36. קָצֶה *m.* Gen. xix. 4: Isa. lvi. 11.

רוּחַ *com.* wind: 1 Chron. ix. 24, *lit.* winds.

QUEEN

גְּבִירָה *f.* mistress, female ruler, reigning queen: 1 Kings xi. 19; xv. 13: 2 Kings x. 13: 2 Chron. xv. 16: Jer. xiii. 18; xxix. 2.

מָלַךְ to reign. KAL *fut.* Esth. ii. 4. HIPHIL *fut.* Esth. ii. 17. מַלְכָּה *f.* 1 Kings x. 1, 4, 10, 13: 2 Chron. ix. 1, 3, 9, 12: Esth. i. 9, 11, 12, 15, 16, 17, 17, 18; ii. 22; iv. 4; v. 2, 3, 12; vii. 1, 2, 3, 5, 6, 7, 8; viii. 1, 7; ix. 12,

29, 31 : Cant. vi. 8, 9. מַלְכָּה Ch. *f.* Dan. v. 10, 10. מְלֶאכֶת *f.* Jer. vii. 18, *marg.* ʽor, frame, or workmanship ;ʼ as if for מְלֶאכֶת ; xliv. 17, *marg.* ʽframe ;ʼ 18, 19, 25.

שָׂרָה *f.* lady, princess : Isa. xlix. 23.

שֵׁגַל *f.* wife : Neh. ii. 6 : Ps. xlv. 9.

QUENCH

דָּעַךְ to be extinct. PUAL *pret.* Ps. cxviii. 12.

כָּבָה to go out, to be extinguished ; as fire, light, the anger of God. KAL *pret.* Isa. xliii. 17. *fut.* 2 Kings xxii. 17 : 2 Chron. xxxiv. 25 : Isa. xxxiv. 10 ; lxvi. 24 : Jer. vii. 20 ; xvii. 27 : Ezek. xx. 47, 48. PIEL *pret.* 2 Sam. xiv. 7. *inf.* Cant. viii. 7. *fut.* 2 Sam. xxi. 17 : Isa. xlii. 3. *part.* Isa. i. 31 : Jer. iv. 4 ; xxi. 12 : Amos v. 6.

שָׁבַר to break. KAL *fut.* Ps. civ. 11.

שָׁקַע to sink. KAL *fut.* Num. xi. 2.

QUESTION

דָּבָר *m.* word, matter, &c. : 1 Kings x. 3, *marg.* ʽwords ;ʼ 2 Chron. ix. 2.

דָּרַשׁ to seek, inquire. KAL *fut.* 2 Chron. xxxi. 9.

חִידָה *f.* riddle, hard question : 1 Kings x. 1 : 2 Chron. ix. 1.

QUICK, QUICKEN

חָיָה to live ; to save alive, quicken. PIEL *pret.* Ps. cxix. 50, 93. *imp.* Ps. cxix. 25, 37, 40, 88, 107, 149, 154, 156, 159. *fut.* Ps. lxxi. 20, *lit.* shall return, shall quicken me ; lxxx. 18 ; cxliii. 11. חַי *adj.* life, living : Num. xvi. 30 : Ps. lv. 15 ; cxxiv. 3. מִחְיָה *f.* Lev. xiii. 10, *marg.* ʽ the quickening of living flesh ;ʼ 24.

QUICKLY

מְאֹד *m.* much, greatly : 1 Sam. xx. 19, *marg.* ʽgreatly, *or,* diligently.ʼ

מָהַר to hasten. PIEL *pret.* Gen. xxvii. 20, *lit.* that thou hast hasted to find. *imp.* Gen. xviii. 6, "make ready quickly," *marg.* ʽhasten ;ʼ 2 Chron. xviii. 8, "fetch quickly," *marg.* ʽhasten.ʼ מַהֵר *adv.* hastening : Exod. xxxii. 8 : Deut. ix. 3, 12, 16 ; xxviii. 20 : Josh. ii. 5 : Judg. ii. 17. מְהֵרָה *f.* hastening : Num. xvi. 46 : Deut. xi. 17 : Josh. viii. 19 ; x. 6 ; xxiii. 16 : 2 Sam. xvii. 16, 18, 21 : 2 Kings i. 11 : Eccles. iv. 12.

QUIET

1 דָּמַם to be quiet, to be still ; to compose oneself. POAL *pret.* דּוּמָם [a] *adv.* silently, "quietly wait."

2 חָרַשׁ see *Silence.* HITHPAEL *fut.*

3 נוּחַ to rest. KAL [a]*pret.* HIPHIL [b]*pret.* [c]מְנוּחָה *f.* rest, repose. [d]נַחַת *m.* rest, quietness, opposite עָמָל travail.

4 רָגַע *adj.* see *Rest.*

5 שָׁאַן to be in profound tranquillity, at ease, undisturbed. PILEL [a]*pret.* [b]שַׁאֲנָן *adj.* tranquil ; living at ease.

6 שָׁלָה to enjoy uninterrupted prosperity. [a]שָׁלֵו and שָׁלֵיו safe, secure. [b]שַׁלְוָה *f.* security. [c]שְׁלִי *m.* tranquillity.

7 שָׁלֵם *adj.* peaceable.

8 שָׁקַט to rest, to have repose ; of one who is never infested, harassed, troubled ; and of one who has no fear or dread ; also of those who trouble no one. KAL [a]*pret.* [b]*fut.* [c]*part.* Poel. HIPHIL [d]*inf.* [e]*imp.* [f]*fut.* [g]שֶׁקֶט [s] *m.* rest, quiet.

9 שָׁתַק to be still or quiet after disturbance or vehement tossings. KAL *fut.*

Judg. viii. 28.	8 b	Job xx. 20.	6 a	Isa. xxx. 15.	8 d
xvi. 2.	2	xxi. 23.	6 a	xxxii. 17.	8 d
xviii. 7. 27.	8 c	xxxiv. 29.	8 f	xxxii. 18.	5 b
2 Sam. iii. 27.	6 c	xxxvii. 17.	8 d	xxxiii. 20.	5 b
2 Kings xi. 20.	8 a	Ps. xxxv. 20.		Jer. xxx. 10.	5 a
1 Chron. iv. 40.	8 c	cvii. 30.	9	xlvii. 6, 7.	8 b
xxii. 9.	8 g	cxxxi. 2.	1	xlix. 23.	8 d
2 Chron. xiv. 1.	8 a	Prov. i. 33.	5 a	li. 59.	8 c
xiv. 5.	8 b	Eccles. iv. 6.	6 b	Lam. iii. 26.	1 a
xx. 30.	8 b	ix. 17.	3 d	Ezek. xvi. 42.	8 a
xxiii. 21.	8 a	Isa. vii. 4.	3 d	Nah. i. 12.	7
Job iii. 13.	8 b	xiv. 7.	8 e	Zech. vi. 8.	3 b
iii. 26.	3 a		8 a		

QUIT

נָקָה to be clear, blameless, innocent ; to be free from punishment. NIPHAL *pret.* Exod. xxi. 19. נָקִי *adj.* free from blame : Exod. xxi. 28 : Josh. ii. 20.

QUIT (*V*)

הָיָה to be. KAL *imp.* 1 Sam. iv. 9, 9, *lit.* be ye for men.

QUIVER

אַשְׁפָּה *f.* a case for arrows : Job xxxix. 23 : Ps. cxxvii. 5 : Isa. xxii. 6 ; xlix. 2 : Jer. v. 16 : Lam. iii. 13.

תְּלִי a quiver, so called from its being suspended from the back : Gen. xxvii. 3.

QUIVER (*V.*)

צָלַל to tingle ; of the lips, to chatter, to quiver. KAL *pret.* Hab. iii. 16.

RACE

אֹרַח *com.* a way, path, road ; the course of the sun : Ps. xix. 5.

מֵרוֹץ *m.* a race, running : Eccles. ix. 11.

RAFTER

רָהִיט *m.* carved or fretted ceiling, so called from the hollows in it resembling troughs or channels : Cant. i. 17, *marg.* ʽ or, galleries.ʼ

רָחִיט *m.* the same : Cant. i. 17, כתיב.

RAG

בֶּגֶד *m.* garment, cloth : Isa. lxiv. 6.

מְלָחִים *m. pl.* old clothes, worn-out garments, "rotten rags :" Jer. xxxviii. 11, 12.

קְרָעִים *m. pl.* pieces : Prov. xxiii. 21.

RAGE

1 גֵּאוּת *f.* rising up, and tossing, applied to waves of the sea.

2   הָלַל   see *Mad.* HITHPOEL [a] *imp.* [b] *fut.*

3   הָמָה   to rage, to roar, to make a great noise; see *Noise.* KAL [a] *pret.* [b] *part.* Poel.

4   זַעַם   anger, indignation.

5   זַעַף   *m.* wrath, indignation; applied also to the sea.

6   חֵמָה   *f.* wrath, fury.

7   עָבַר   to pass. HITHPAEL, to be wroth: [a] *part.* [b] עֶבְרָה *f.* wrath: or the effect of wrath, or blows.

8   רָגַז   to be shaken or moved with a violent commotion. KAL [a] *pret.* HITHPAEL [b] *inf.* [c] רֹגֶז *m.* tumult, anger. [d] רְגַז Ch. *m.* anger.

9   רָגַשׁ   to rage, tumultuate. KAL *pret.*

2 Kings v. 12.		6	Ps. vii. 6.	7 b	Isa. xxxvii. 28, 29.	8 b
xx. 27, 28.	8 b		xlvi. 6.	3 a	Jer. xlvi. 9.	2 a
2 Chron. xvi. 10.		5	lxxxix. 9.	1	Dan. iii. 13.	8 d
xxvii. 9.		5	Prov. vi. 34.	6	Hos. vii. 16.	4
Job xxxix. 24.	8 c		xiv. 16.	7 a	Jonah i. 15.	5
xl. 11.	7 b		xx. 1.	3 b	Nah. ii. 4.	2 b
Ps. ii. 1.		9	xxix. 9.	8 a		

RAHAB

רַהַב   *m.* pride: Ps. lxxxvii. 4, *lit.* pride; lxxxix. 10: Isa. li. 9.

RAIL

חָרַף   to reproach; to disparage, to vilify. PIEL *inf.* 2 Chron. xxxii. 17.

עִיט   to fly upon, as a ravenous bird. KAL *fut.* 1 Sam. xxv. 14.

RAIMENT

1   בֶּגֶד   *m.* garment, especially any outward covering. In Gen. xxvii. 15 the Gr. has τὴν στολὴν τὴν καλήν, evidently referring to some particular garment, which was probably similar to what was afterwards worn by the priests (Exod. xxviii. 2–4), and may have been at this time the badge of birthright, and the stole of the priesthood going with it.

2   מַחֲלָצוֹת   *f. pl.* raiment gently drawn off and changed, worn only out of the house.

3   כְּסוּת   *f.* a covering.

4   לְבֻשׁ   *m.* clothing. [a] מַלְבּוּשׁ *m.* a garment.

5   מַד   *m.* an upper garment, which extends over, and as it were measures, the whole body.

6   רִקְמָה   *f.* embroidered work; raiment of needlework.

7   שַׂלְמָה   *f.* by transposition for the following.

8   שִׂמְלָה   *f.* a garment both of men and women, especially the wide outer garment or mantle in which a person wrapped himself at night.

Gen. xxiv. 53.	1	Num. xxxi. 20.	1	1 Sam. xxviii. 8.	1
xxvii. 15, 27.	1	Deut. viii. 4.	8	2 Kings v. 5.	1
xxviii. 20.	1	x. 18.	8	vii. 8.	1
xli. 14.	8	xxi. 13.	8	2 Chron. ix. 24.	7
xlv. 22, 22.	8	xxii. 3.	8	Esth. iv. 4.	1
Exod. xxii. 22.	8	xxiv. 13.	7	Job xxvii. 16.	4 a
xii. 35.	8	xxiv. 17.	1	Ps. xlv. 14.	6
xxi. 10.	3	Josh. xxii. 8.	8	Isa. xiv. 19.	4
xxii. 9, 26.	7	Judg. iii. 16.	5	lxiii. 3.	4
xxii. 27.	8	viii. 26.	1	Ezek. xvi. 13.	4 a
Lev. xi. 32.	1	Ruth iii. 3.	8	Zech. iii. 4.	2

RAIN

1   גֶּשֶׁם   *m.* rain; more particularly that which is abundant, in distinction from the more general word מָטָר (yet frequently used for rain in general), as of the deluge, Gen. vii. 12, viii. 2; as of the rain that fell after the drought in the days of Elijah, 1 Kings xviii. 41, 44, 45; the autumnal and winter rains, Lev. xxvi. 4, *lit.* your rain; Ezra x. 13, *lit.* rains; Isa. lv. 10; Jer. v. 24. *Metaph.* divine blessings, as of the spirit, Ps. lxviii. 9; and the preaching of the gospel (Ezek. xxxiv. 26, 26), Zech. x. 1; divine punishment (Ezek. xiii. 11, 13). נָשַׁם to rain with violence. HIPHIL [a] *part.* [b] גֶּשֶׁם *m.* rain.

2   יָרָה   to cast forth, shoot, sprinkle: these are the meanings usually attached to this word, but it becomes matter of doubt how the rendering 'former rain' is deduced from these primary significations. Most modern critics suppose the idea is that of sprinkling the earth after the seed is sown; Fürst, that of irrigating, and so of impregnating the soil with the seed; Cocceius has a similar interpretation, that it implies the settling and placing of the seed in the ground in order to germination. But since the latter rain seems to have been denominated the rain of gathering (see below), it is more probable that the former rain is *lit.* the rain of shooting, being preparatory to and necessary for the shooting of the seed; as the latter rain is preparatory to the gathering in of harvest: this is the interpretation which Professor Lee gives to Hos. vi. 3, considering the *part.* KAL to be equivalent to HIPHIL, causing the earth to send forth or shoot out. The former rain fell about the end of October, and continued through November and December. During the summer season the land was seldom refreshed with rain, 1 Sam. xii. 17. If the rain was seasonable and moderate, the land was fruitful; if it failed, a dearth ensued, and the drought, like fire, devoured the pastures, &c.; if it fell immoderately, the grain rotted under the clods, Joel i. 19, 17.—*Ainsworth* on Deut. xii. 14. KAL [a] *part.* Poel, Hos. vi. 3, perhaps as the latter rain, sprinkling, irrigating the earth, or causing it to shoot out when the seed germinates. HIPHIL [b] *fut.* Hos. x. 12, or, teach righteousness; see *Teach.* [c] יוֹרֶה *m.* first, former, rain. [d] מוֹרֶה former rain: Joel ii. 23, *marg.* 'or, a teacher of righteousness,' 23.

3   מַלְקוֹשׁ   *m.* the latter rain, usually in March or early in April, before the gathering of the harvest, which was greatly beneficial in filling the grain.

4   מָטַר   to rain; to cause to rain; applied also to the sending of hail, lightning, manna; as immoderate rain was very injurious, so the word is used of sending heavy and severe judgments, Ps. xi. 6, Ezek. xxxviii. 22, perhaps in allusion to the destruction of the cities of the plain; *comp.* Job xx. 23. NIPHAL [a] *fut.* HIPHIL [b] *pret.* [c] *inf.* [d] *fut.* [e] *part.* [f] מָטָר *m.* rain, "small rain," "great rain," *lit.* shower of, showers of, rain.

5   סַגְרִיר   *m.* a heavy rain, which shuts up and confines people to their houses.

6 שְׂעִירִים *m. pl.* small rain, which in falling resembles hairs.

Gen. ii. 5.	4 b	Ezra x. 9, 13.	1	Eccles. xii. 2.	1
vii. 4.	4 e	Job v. 10.	4 f	Cant. ii. 11.	1
vii. 12.	1	xx. 23.	4 d	Isa. iv. 6.	
viii. 2.	1	xxviii. 26.	4 f	v. 6, 6.	4 c f
xix. 24.	4 b	xxix. 23, 23.	4 f, 3	xxx. 23.	4 f
Exod. ix. 18.	4 e	xxxvi. 27.	4 f	xliv. 14.	1
ix. 23.	4 d	xxxvii. 6.	1, 4 f	lv. 10.	1
ix. 33, 34.	4 f	xxxviii. 6.	1, 4 f	Jer. iii. 3.	1
xvi. 4.	4 e	xxxviii. 26.	4 c	v. 24.	1, 2 c, 3
Lev. xxvi. 4.	4 f	xxxviii. 28.a	4 f	x. 13.	1
Deut. xi. 11, 17.	4 f	Ps. xi. 6.	4 d	xiv. 4.	1
xi. 14, 14, 14.	4 f, 2 c, 3	lxviii. 9.	1	xiv. 22.	1 a
xxviii. 12, 24.	4 f	lxxii. 6.	4 d	li. 16.	1
xxxii. 2, 2.	4 f, 6	lxxviii. 24, 27.	4 d	Ezek. i. 28.	1 b
1 Sam. xii. 17, 18.	4 f	lxxxiv. 6.	4 d	xxii. 24.	1
2 Sam. i. 21.	4 f	cv. 32.	1	xxxviii. 22, 22.	4 d, 1
xxiii. 4.	4 f	cxxxv. 7.	4 f	Hos. vi. 3, 3.	1, 3, 2 a
1 Kings viii. 35, 36.	4 f	cxlvii. 8.	4 f	x. 12.	2 b
xvii. 1.	4 f	Prov. xvi. 15.	1	Joel ii. 23, 23,	
xvii. 7, 14.	1	xxv. 14, 23.	1	23, 23.	2 d, 1, 2 d, 3
xviii. 1.	1	xxvi. 1.	4 f	Amos iv. 7, 7.	
xviii. 41, 44, 45.	1	xxvii. 15.	5	7, 7, 7.	1, 4 b d a d
2 Kings iii. 17.	1	xxviii. 3.	4 f	Zech. x. 1, 1, 1.	4 f, 3, 4 f
2 Chron. vi. 26, 27.	4 f	Eccles. xi. 3.	1	xiv. 17.	1
vii. 13.	4 f				

a *lit.* is there to the rain a father?

RAISE

1 גָּבַהּ to be high; "to raise up a great height." HIPHIL *fut.*

2 זָקַף to raise up and comfort those that are in affliction. KAL *part.* Poel.

3 נָגַשׂ to exact. KAL *part.* Poel.

4 נָשָׂא to bear, to take up, to utter, speak, declare; to raise a false report may imply both the origination and propagation of it. KAL a *fut.* b שְׂאֵת *f.* raising up.

5 סָלַל to raise or cast up. KAL *fut.*

6 עָבַר to pass over. HIPHIL *fut.*

7 עוּר to awake out of sleep; to excite or call forth; to be raised up. NIPHAL a *pret.* b *fut.* POLEL c *pret.* d *inf.* e *fut.* HIPHIL f *pret.* g *part.*

8 עִיר if a verb, to awake, raise. KAL *inf.* Hos. vii. 4, *marg.* 'or, waking.' Gesenius and Fürst make it a noun, and render it 'from heating.'

9 עָלָה to ascend. HIPHIL a *pret.* b *fut.*

10 עָמַד to stand. HIPHIL a *pret.* b *fut.*

11 עָרַר *i.q.* עוּר, or to be naked, to lay naked; or to wake, raise up. POEL *pret.* Isa. xxiii. 13. Gesenius, demolished, rased.

12 קוּם to rise; to make to stand. POLEL a *fut.* HIPHIL b *pret.* c *inf.* d *imp.* e *fut.* f *part.* HOPHAL g *pret.* קוּם Ch. *id.* APHEL h *pret.*

Gen. xxxviii. 8.	12 d	2 Chron. xxxii. 5.	9 b	Isa. xlix. 6.	12 c
Exod. ix. 16.	10 a	xxxiii. 14.	1	lviii. 12.	12 a
xxiii. 1.	4 a	Ezra i. 5.	7 f	lxi. 4.	12 a
Deut. xviii. 15, 18.	12 e	Job iii. 8.	7 d	Jer. vi. 22.	7 b
xxv. 7.	12 e	xiv. 12.	7 b	xxiii. 5.	12 b
Josh. v. 7.	12 b	xix. 12.	5	xxv. 32.	12 b
vii. 26.	12 e	xxx. 12.	5	xxix. 15.	12 b
viii. 29.	12 e	xli. 25.	4 b	xxx. 9.	12 a
Judg. ii. 16.	12 e	Ps. xli. 10.	12 d	l. 9.	7 g
ii. 18.	12 b	cvii. 25.	10 b	l. 32.	12 f
iii. 9, 15.	12 e	cxiii. 7.	12 f	l. 41.	7 b
Ruth iv. 5, 10.	12 c	cxlv. 14.	2	li. 1.	7 g
1 Sam. ii. 8.	12 b	cxlvi. 8.	2	li. 11.	7 f
ii. 35.	12 b	Cant. viii. 5.	7 c	Ezek. xiii. 22.	7 g
2 Sam. xii. 11.	12 f	Isa. xiv. 9.	12 b	xxxiv. 29.	12 b
xii. 17.	12 c	xv. 9.	7 e	Dan. vii. 5.	12 h
xxiii. 1.	12 g	xxiii. 13.	11	xi. 20.a	6, 3
1 Kings v. 13.	9 b	xli. 2, 25.	12 b	Hos. vi. 2.	12 b
ix. 15.	9 a	xliv. 26.	12 a	vii. 4.	8
xiv. 14.	12 b	xlv. 13.	7 f	Joel iii. 7.	7 g
1 Chron. xvii. 11.	12 b			Amos ii. 11.	12 e

Amos v. 2.	12 f	Micah v. 5.	12 b	Zech. ii. 13.	7 a
vi. 14.	12 f	Hab. i. 3.	4 a	ix. 13.	7 c
ix. 11, 11.	12 e	i. 6.	12 f	xi. 16.	12 f

a *marg.* 'or, one that causeth an exactor to pass over.'

RAISINS

צִמּוּקִים *m. pl.* dried grapes, raisins, bunches of raisins: 1 Sam. xxv. 18; xxx. 12: 2 Sam. xvi. 1: 1 Chron. xii. 40.

RAM

אַיִל *m.* a ram or stag, the principal of the flock, or leader; see *Strength*: Gen. xv. 9, &c.

דְּכַר Ch. *m.* a male, a ram: Ezra vi. 9, 17; vii. 17.

יוֹבֵל *com.* (see *Jubilee*): the ram's horn was used apparently as an early and simple form of trumpet. Thus its sound might serve to remind the Israelite of Abraham's substituted sacrifice on Mount Moriah, Gen. xxii. 13.— Josh. vi. 4, 5, 6, 8, 13.

כַּר *m.* (see *Lamb*), a battering-ram; *metaph.* captain or chief leader: Ezek. iv. 2; xxi. 22.

עַתּוּד *m.* he-goat, as leader of the flock: Gen. xxxi. 10, 12.

RAMPART

חֵיל *m.* (see *Trench*): Lam. ii. 8: Nah. iii. 8.

RANGE

יָתוּר *m.* a wide place where there is room to range about in quest of food: Job xxxix. 8.

שְׂדֵרָה *f.* row, rank, of soldiers: 2 Kings xi. 8, 15: 2 Chron. xxiii. 14.

RANGE (V.)

שָׁקַק to run to and fro. KAL *part.* Poel, Prov. xxviii. 15.

RANGES

כִּירַיִם *m. dual,* a cooking-furnace, ranges for pots: Lev. xi. 35.

RANK

בְּרִיא *adj.* fat: Gen. xli. 5, *marg.* 'fat,' 7.

RANK

אֹרַח *com.* a way or road: Joel ii. 7, *lit.* shall not change their course.

עָרַד to arrange, put in order. KAL *inf.* 1 Chron. xii. 33, keep rank, *marg.* 'or, set the battle in array.'

מַעֲרָכָה *f.* army set in order: 1 Chron. xii. 38.

פַּעַם *com.* applied to situation, it signifies a row, rank, order: 1 Kings vii. 4, 5.

RANSOM

גָּאַל to redeem. KAL *pret.* Jer. xxxi. 11. *part.* Paül, Isa. li. 10.

כֹּפֶר *m.* price of expiation or redemption: Exod. xxx. 12: Job xxxiii. 24, *marg.* 'or, atonement;' xxxvi. 18: Ps. xlix. 7: Prov. vi. 35; xiii. 8; xxi. 18: Isa. xliii. 3.

פָּדָה to redeem; to set free. KAL *fut.* Hos. xiii. 14. *part.* Paül, Isa. xxxv. 10. פִּדְיוֹן *m.* price of redemption: Exod. xxi. 30.

RARE

יַקִּיר Ch. *adj.* precious: Dan. ii. 11.

RASE

עָרָה to uncover; to lay bare the foundation of an edifice, *i. e.* to demolish, to rase. PIEL *imp.* Ps. cxxxvii. 7, 7.

RASH

בָּהַל to be in trepidation, to hasten; to do anything rashly. PIEL *fut.* Eccles. v. 2.

מָהַר to make haste. NIPHAL *part.* Isa. xxxii. 4.

RASOR

מוֹרָה *m.* a razor, as drawn over the skin: Judg. xiii. 5; xvi. 17: 1 Sam. i. 11.

תַּעַר *m.* a razor, sharp knife, as making bare the skin: Num. vi. 5: Ps. lii. 2: Isa. vii. 20: Ezek. v. 1.

RATE

דָּבָר *m.* word, matter, &c.: Exod. xvi. 4: 1 Kings x. 25: 2 Kings xxv. 30: 2 Chron. viii. 13; ix. 24.

RATHER

בָּחַר to choose. KAL *pret.* Ps. lxxxiv. 10, *seq.* מִן, implying preference, *marg.* 'I would choose rather to sit at the threshold.'

RATTLE

רִנָּה a word which applies either to the rattling of the arrows in the quiver, or to the whizzing of the arrows in passing through the air: KAL *fut.* Job xxxix. 23.

רַעַשׁ *m.* quaking, shaking: Nah. iii. 2.

RAVEN

עֹרֵב *m.* a raven, so called from its black colour, perhaps comprehending kindred species of birds, especially the crow: Gen. viii. 7: Lev. xi. 15: Deut. xiv. 14: 1 Kings xvii. 4, 6: Job xxxviii. 41: Ps. cxlvii. 9: Prov. xxx. 17: Cant. v. 11: Isa. xxxiv. 11.

RAVENOUS

עַיִט *m.* a ravenous beast or bird rushing on his prey: Isa. xlvi. 11: Ezek. xxxix. 4.

פָּרִיץ *m.* violent, rapacious: Isa. xxxv. 9.

RAVIN

טָרַף to tear in pieces. KAL *fut.* Gen. xlix. 27. *part.* Poel, Ps. xxii. 13, Ezek. xxii. 25, 27. טְרֵפָה *f.* that which has been torn: Nah. ii. 12.

RAVISH (See HEART)

עָנָה see *Humble.* PIEL *pret.* Lam. v. 11.

שָׁגָה to err, to be seduced. KAL *fut.* Prov. v. 19, 20.

שָׁגַל to lie with a woman. NIPHAL *fut.* Isa. xiii. 16, כתיב; Zech. xiv. 2, כתיב.

שָׁכַב to lie with. NIPHAL *fut.* Isa. xiii. 16: Zech. xiv. 2.

RAW

חַי *adj.* living: Lev. xiii. 10, *marg.* 'the quickening of living flesh;' 14, 15, 15, 16: 1 Sam. ii. 15.

נָא *adj.* that which is new, fresh, raw; used of meat raw or half-cooked: Exod. xii. 9.

REACH

1   בָּרַח to pass through, to reach across. HIPHIL *part.*

2   מְטָא Ch. to come to. P'AL [a] *pret.* [b] *fut.*

3   מָחָה to wipe off; to strike, to strike upon, geographically, to reach unto, to extend to as a boundary. KAL *pret.*

4   נָגַע to touch, to reach unto. KAL [a] *pret.* HIPHIL [b] *pret.* [c] *fut.* [d] *part.*

5   נָשַׂג to overtake, attain. HIPHIL [a] *pret.* [b] *fut.*

6   פָּגַע to meet, meet with, light upon; to reach to, border on, be contiguous, spoken of a territory. KAL *pret.*

7   צָבַט to reach out to any one, *seq. dat.* KAL *fut.*

8   שָׁלַח to send; to reach forth. PIEL *pret.*

Gen. xxviii. 12.	4 d	Ruth ii. 14.	7	Jer. iv. 10, 18.	4 a
Exod. xxvi. 28.	1	2 Chron. iii. 11, 11, 12.	4 d	xlviii. 32.	4 a
Lev. xxvi. 5, 5.	5 a b	xxviii. 9.	4 b	li. 9.	4 a
Num. xxiv. 11.	3	Job xx. 6.	4 c	Dan. iv. 11, 20.	2 b
Josh. xix. 11, 11, 22,		Prov. xxxi. 20.	8	iv. 22.	2 a
26, 27, 34, 34.	6	Isa. viii. 8.	4 c	Zech. xiv. 5.	4 c

READ

קָרָא to call, to read. KAL [a] *pret.* [b] *inf.* [c] *imp.* [d] *fut.* [e] *part.* Poel. NIPHAL [f] *pret.* [g] *part.* קְרָא Ch. P'AL [h] *inf.* [i] *fut.* [k] *part. active.* [l] *part. passive.* [m] מִקְרָא *m.* reading.

Exod. xxiv. 7.	d	Ezra iv. 18, 23.	l	Jer. xxxvi. 8, 13, 23.	b
Deut. xvii. 19.	a	Neh. viii. 3, 18.	d	xxxvi. 10, 21.	d
xxxi. 11.	d	viii. 8, 8.	d m	xxxvi. 14.	a
Josh. viii. 34, 35.	a	ix. 3.	d	xxxvi. 15, 15.	c d
2 Kings v. 7.	b	xiii. 1.	f	li. 61.	a
xix. 14.	d	Esth. vi. 1.	g	li. 63.	b
xxii. 8, 10.	d	Isa. xxix. 11, 12.	c	Dan. v. 7.	k
xxii. 16.	d	xxxiv. 16.	c	v. 8, 16.	h
xxiii. 2.	d	xxxvii. 14.	d	v. 15, 17.	i
2 Chron. xxxiv. 18, 30.	d	Jer. xxix. 29.	d	Hab. ii. 2.	e
xxxiv. 24.	a	xxxvi. 6, 6.	a d		

READY

1   אָסַר to bind, to make ready a chariot. KAL [a] *imp.* [b] *fut.*

2   הוּן to act rashly, inconsiderately, with an implied contempt of a divine command and presumption; *comp.* Num. xiv. 44: Deut. i. 43. HIPHIL *fut.*

3   חוּשׁ to make great haste. KAL *part.* Paûl.

4   טוֹב *adj.* good.

5   כּוּן to raise up, erect; to prepare. NIPHAL [a] *part.* POLEL [b] *pret.* [c] *fut.* HIPHIL [d] *pret.* [e] *inf.* [f] *imp.* [g] *fut.*

6   מָהַר to make haste, to be expeditious. PIEL [a] *imp.* [b] *fut.* [c] מָהִיר *adj.* quick.

7   מוֹט to be moved, to totter, to be on the very brink of. KAL *part.*

8   מָצָא to find. KAL *part.* Poel.

9   עָתַד to be ready, prepared; practised, skilful. HITHPAEL [a] *pret.* [b] עָתוּד *adj.* ready, prepared, כתיב [c] עָתִיד *adj. id.* [d] עֲתִיד Ch. *adj. id.*

10   קָרַב to approach, to draw near. PIEL [a] *pret.* [b] קָרוֹב *adj.* near.

11 שָׁלֵם *adj.* completed, finished.

Gen. xviii. 6.		1 Chron. xxviii. 2.	5 d	Ps. xi. 2.		5 b
xliii. 16.	6 a	2 Chron. xxviii. 14.	5 d	xxi. 12.		5 c
xliii. 25.	5 f	Ezra vii. 6.	6 c	xxxviii. 17.		5 a
xlvi. 29.	5 g	Esth. iii. 14.	9 c	xlv. 1.		6 c
Exod. xiv. 6.	1 b	viii. 13.	9 b, or c	Prov. xxiv. 11.		7
xix. 11, 15.	1 b	Job iii. 8.	9 c	Eccles. v. 1.		10 b
xxxiv. 2.	5 a	xii. 5.	5 a	Isa. xxxii. 4.		6 b
Num. xxxii. 17.	5 a	xv. 23.	5 a	xli. 7.		4
Deut. i. 41.	3	xv. 24.	9 c	li. 13.		5 a
Josh. viii. 4.		xv. 28.	9 a	Ezek. vii. 14.		5 e
2 Sam. xviii. 22.	8	xviii. 12.	5 a	Dan. iii. 15.		9 d
1 Kings vi. 7.	11	Ps. vii. 12.	5 c	Hos. vii. 6.		10 a
2 Kings ix. 21, 21.	1 a b					

REALM

מַלְכוּת *f.* kingdom : 2 Chron. xx. 30 : Dan. i. 20 ; ix. 1 ; xi. 2.
מַלְכוּ Ch. *f. id.* Ezra vii. 13, 23 : Dan. vi. 3.

REAP

1 כָּלָה to be quite done, to make a clean riddance, as in reaping a field. PIEL *fut.*

2 קָצַר to cut off or down. KAL [a] *pret.* [b] *inf.* [c] *imp.* [d] *fut.* [e] *part.* Poel. HIPHIL [f] *fut.* כָתִיב.

Lev. xix. 9.	2 b	1 Sam. viii. 12.	2 b	Isa. xvii. 5.	2 d
xix. 9.a	1, 2 b	2 Kings iv. 18.	2 e	xxxvii. 30.	2 c
xxiii. 10.	2 a	xix. 29.	2 c	Jer. xii. 13.	2 a
xxiii. 22, 22.	2 b	Job iv. 8.	2 d	Hos. viii. 7.	2 d
xxv. 5, 11.	2 d	xxiv. 6.	2 d, or f	x. 12.	2 c
Ruth ii. 3, 4, 5, 6, 7, 14.	2 e	Ps. cxxvi. 5.	2 d	xiii. 3.	2 a
ii. 9.	2 d	Prov. xxii. 8.	2 d	Amos ix. 13.	2 e
1 Sam. vi. 13.	2 e	Eccles. ix. 4.	2 d	Micah vi. 15.	2 d

a lit. finish to reap.

REAR

1 נָצַב to place. HIPHIL *fut.*

2 קוּם to stand or get up, to rise. HIPHIL [a] *pret.* [b] *inf.* [c] *imp.* [d] *fut.* HOPHAL [e] *pret.*

Exod. xxvi. 30.	2 a	Num. ix. 15.	2 b	2 Kings xxi. 3.	2 d
xl. 17.	2 e	2 Sam. xviii. 18.	1	2 Chron. iii. 17.	2 d
xl. 18, 18, 33.	2 d	xxiv. 18.	2 c	xxxiii. 3.	2 d
Lev. xxvi. 1.	2 d	1 Kings xvi. 32.	2 d		

REASON

דָּבָר *m.* word, reason, *lit.* word concerning : 1 Kings ix. 15.

תְּבוּנָה *f.* understanding : Job xxxii. 11, *marg.* 'understandings.'

חֶשְׁבּוֹן *m.* reason, cause, or ground of things, as they are the object of thought and study : Eccles. vii. 25.

טַעַם *m.* taste, understanding, judgment : Prov. xxvi. 16.

מַנְדַּע Ch. *m.* knowledge, understanding : Dan. iv. 36.

REASON (V)

יָכַח to be right ; to reason, to demonstrate what is right and true. NIPHAL *fut.* Isa. i. 18. HIPHIL *inf.* Job xiii. 3 ; xv. 3. תּוֹכַחַת *f.* act of proving, proof, demonstration : Job xiii. 6.

פָּנִים *m. pl.* face, &c., with *prep.* לְ rendered 'by reason of:' Gen. xli. 31, &c.

שָׁפַט to judge. NIPHAL *fut.* 1 Sam. xii. 7 ; see *Plead.*

REBEL

1 בֵּן *m.* son : Num. xvii. 10, *marg.* 'children of rebellion.'

2 מָרַד to revolt from the government of a lawful sovereign, and

of subjects to become enemies ; to rebel against the light is to hate it, and declare war against it : Job xxiv. 13. This verb is construed with בְּ, more rarely with עַל. KAL [a] *pret.* [b] *inf.* [c] *fut.* [d] *part.* Poel. [e] מְרַד Ch. *m.* rebellion. מֶרֶד [f] *m. id.* [g] מָרָד Ch. *adj.* rebellious. מַרְדוּת [h] *f.* contumacy : 1 Sam. xx. 30, *marg.* 'son of perverse rebellion, *or*, thou perverse rebel.'

3 מָרָה to be refractory, perverse, rebellious ; with an *accus.* of the person or thing against which any one is refractory ; also with בְּ ; Hiphil, to contend with, to be rebellious ; with an *accus.* with בְּ, and with עִם. KAL [a] *pret.* [b] *inf.* [c] *part.* Poel. HIPHIL [d] *pret.* [e] *fut.* [f] *part.* [g] מְרִי *m.* contumacy.

4 סוּר to turn aside, to depart, *seq.* בְּ. KAL [a] *fut.* [b] סָרָה *f.* departure from Jehovah, *marg.* 'revolt.'

5 סָרַר to be refractory, rebellious, perverse ; see *Backsliding* : said of man, it implies the perfidy of one who is bound to subjection and submission ; used of a son in relation to his parent, of a wife to her husband, of his people to God. It applies particularly to the Jews, see Isa. lxv. 2, *comp.* Rom. x. 20, 21. KAL *part.* Poel.

6 פָּשַׁע to fall away, revolt, rebel, with בְּ from or against any one ; to rebel against God, to apostatize from him, to sin against him, with עַל. KAL [a] *pret.* [b] *fut.* [c] פֶּשַׁע *m.* transgression.

Gen. xiv. 4.	2 a	2 Kings xxiv. 1, 20.	2 c	Isa. l. 5.	3 a
Num. xiv. 9.	2 c	2 Chron. x. 19.	6 b	lxiii. 10.	3 a
xvii. 10.	1, 3 g	xiii. 6.	2 a	lxv. 2.	5
xx. 10.	3 c	xxxvi. 13.	2 a	Jer. iv. 17.	3 c
xx. 24.	3 a	Ezra iv. 12, 15.	2 g	v. 23.	5
xxvii. 14.	3 a	iv. 19.	2 e	xxviii. 16.	4 b
Deut. i. 26, 43.	3 e	Neh. ii. 19.	2 d	xxix. 32.	4 b
ix. 7, 24.	3 f	vi. 6.	2 b	lii. 3.	2 a
ix. 23.	3 e	ix. 17.	3 g	Lam. i. 18.	3 a
xxi. 18, 20.	3 c	ix. 26.	5	i. 20.a	3 b a
xxxi. 27, 27.	3 g f	Job xxiv. 13.	2 c	iii. 42.	3 b
Josh. i. 18.	3 e	xxxiv. 37.	6 c	Ezek. ii. 3, 3.	2 d a
xxii. 16, 29.	2 b	Ps. v. 10.	3 a	ii. 5, 6, 7, 8, 8.	3 g
xxii. 18, 19, 19.	2 c	lxvi. 7.	5	iii. 9, 26, 27.	3 g
xxii. 22.	2 f	lxviii. 6, 18.	3 a	xii. 2, 2, 3, 9, 25.	3 g
1 Sam. xii. 14.	3 e	lxxviii. 8.	3 c	xvii. 15.	2 c
xii. 15.	3 a	cv. 28.	3 d	xvii. 15.	3 g
xv. 23.	3 g	cvii. 11.	3 a	xx. 8, 13, 21.	3 e
xx. 30.	2 h	Prov. xvii. 11.	3 g	xx. 38.	2 d
1 Kings xii. 19.	6 b	Isa. i. 2.	3 g	xxiv. 3.	3 g
2 Kings i. 1.	6 b	i. 20.	6 a	xliv. 6.	3 g
iii. 5.	6 b	i. 23.	5	Dan. ix. 5, 9.	2 a
iii. 7.	6 a	xxx. 1.	5	Hos. vii. 14.	4 a
xviii. 7.	2 c	xxx. 9.	3 g	xiii. 16.	3 a
xviii. 20.	2 a	xxxvi. 5.	2 a		

a lit. rebelling I have rebelled.

REBUKE

1 נָּעַר to reprove, as a father his son, Gen. xxxvii. 10 ; to rebuke with severity either of words or deeds ; to check, curb, chastise the insolent and unruly. KAL [a] *pret.* [b] *inf.* [c] *imp.* [d] *fut.* [e] *part.* Poel. [f] גְּעָרָה *f.* rebuke, reproof. [g] מִגְעֶרֶת *f.* the rebuke of God.

2 חֶרְפָּה *f.* reproach.

3 מוּסָר *m.* correction, instruction.

4 יָכַח to show, prove ; to correct, reprove, convince, refute ; to rebuke, reproach, censure ; to punish ; see *Reprove.* HIPHIL [a] *pret.* [b] *inf.* [c] *imp.* [d] *fut.* [e] *part.* [f] תּוֹכֵחָה *f.* rebuke. [g] תּוֹכַחַת *f. id.*

5 רִיב to strive, to plead, to chide. KAL *fut.*

Gen. xxxi. 42.	4 d	Ps. lxxx. 16.	1 f	Isa. xxxvii. 3.	4 f
xxxvii. 10.	1 d	civ. 7.	1 d	l. 2.	1 f
Lev. xix. 17.	4 b d	cvi. 9.	1 d	li. 20.	1 f
Deut. xxviii. 20.	1 g	cxix. 21.	1 d	liv. 9.	1 b
Ruth ii. 16.	1 d	Prov. ix. 7.	4 e	lxvi. 15.	1 f
2 Sam. xxii. 16.	1 f	ix. 8.	4 c	Jer. xv. 15.	1 f
2 Kings xix. 3.	4 f	xiii. 1, 8.	1 f	Ezek. v. 15.	4 g
1 Chron. xii. 17.	4 d	xxiv. 25.	4 e	xxv. 17.	4 g
Neh. v. 7.	5	xxviii. 23.	4 e	v. 9.	4 f
Ps. vi. 1.	4 d	Eccles. vii. 5.	1 f	Amos v. 10.	1 f
ix. 5.	1 a	Isa. ii. 4.	4 a	Micah iv. 3.	4 a
xviii. 15.	1 f	xvii. 13.	1 a	Nah. i. 4.	1 e
xxxviii. 1.	4 b	xxv. 8.	2	Zech. iii. 2, 2.	1 d
xxxix. 11.	4 g	xxx. 17, 17.	1 f	Mal. iii. 11.	1 a
lxviii. 30.	1 c				
lxxvi. 6.	1 f				

RECALL

שׁוּב to return. HIPHIL *fut.* Lam. iii. 21, *marg.* 'make to return to my heart.'

RECEIVE

1   אָסַף to gather, to receive to common privileges. NIPHAL [a] *fut.* PIEL [b] *part.*

2   חָזַק to take hold : to receive, to take in, to hold. HIPHIL *part.*

3   חָלַק to divide ; to receive a share, inheritance, &c. KAL *pret.*

4   כּוּל to contain. HIPHIL *inf.*

5   לָקַח to take ; to receive, take what is given, 2 Kings v. 26 ; to receive, take, so as to obey or improve instruction, a law, a commandment, Prov. xxiv. 32 ; to receive, take, as a charge, to be instated in power or authority, Ps. lxxv. 2 ; or in a possession or heritage, Job xxvii. 13 ; to receive as good, pleasing, and acceptable, Ps. l. 9 : Isa. xl. 2 : Zeph. iii. 2. KAL [a] *pret.* [b] *inf.* [c] *imp.* [d] *fut.*

6   מָצָא to find. KAL *fut.*

7   נָשָׂא to bear, to take, to receive. KAL *fut.*

8   קָבַל to take hold ; *fig.* to take hold of what is sent, proposed, enjoined ; to receive, accept, admit, consent ; to take upon one. PIEL [a] *pret.* [b] *imp.* [c] *fut.* קָבַל Ch. PAEL [d] *fut.*

9   שָׁקַל to weigh ; to receive money by weighing. KAL *part.* Poel.

Gen. iv. 11.	5 b	2 Kings v. 20, 26, 26.	5 b	Prov. x. 8.	5 d
xxvi. 12.	6	xii. 7.	5 d	xix. 20.	8 b
xxxiii. 10.	5 b	xii. 8.	5 b	xxi. 11.	5 d
xxxviii. 20.	5 b	xix. 14.	5 d	xxiv. 32.	5 a
Exod. xxix. 25.	5 d	1 Chron. xii. 18.	8 c	Isa. xxxiii. 18.	9
xxxii. 4.	5 d	2 Chron. i. 16.	5 d	xxxvii. 14.	5 a
xxxvi. 3.	5 d	iv. 5.	2	xl. 2.	5 a
Num. xii. 14.	1 a	vii. 7.	4	Jer. ii. 30.	5 a
xviii. 28.	5 d	xxix. 22.	8 c	v. 3.	5 b
xxiii. 20.	5 a	Esth. iv. 4.	8 a	vii. 28.	5 b
xxxiv. 14, 14, 15.	5 a	Job ii. 10, 10.	8 c	ix. 20.	5 d
Deut. ix. 9.	5 b	iv. 12.	5 d	xvii. 23.	5 b
xxxiii. 3.	7	xxii. 22.	5 c	xxxii. 33.	5 b
Josh. xiii. 8.	5 a	xxvii. 13.	5 d	xxxv. 13.	5 b
xviii. 2.	3	xxxv. 7.	5 d	Ezek. iii. 10.	5 d
xviii. 7.	5 a	Ps. vi. 9.	5 d	xvi. 61.	5 a
Judg. xiii. 23.	5 a	xxiv. 5.	5 d	xviii. 17.	5 a
xix. 18.	1 b	xlix. 15.	7	xxxvi. 30.	5 d
1 Sam. x. 4.	5 a	lxviii. 18.	5 a	Dan. ii. 6.	8 d
xii. 3.	5 a	lxxiii. 24.	5 d	Hos. x. 6.	5 a
xxv. 35.	5 d	lxxv. 2.	5 d	xiv. 2.	5 c
2 Sam. xviii. 12.	9	Prov. i. 3.	5 b	Micah i. 11.	5 d
1 Kings v. 9.	7	ii. 1.	5 a	Zeph. iii. 2.	5 a
viii. 64.	5 d	iv. 10.	5 d	iii. 7.	5 b
x. 28.	5 d	viii. 10.	5 c	Mal. ii. 13.	5 b
2 Kings v. 16.	5 d				

RECKON

1   חָשַׁב to think ; to account to be ; to count or number ; to reckon with a person in pecuniary matters ; to put to one's account. NIPHAL [a] *pret.* [b] *fut.* PIEL [c] *pret.* [d] *fut.* HITHPAEL [e] *fut.*

2   סָפַר to number. KAL *fut.*

3   פָּקַד to look after, to take an account of, to number or muster an army. KAL [a] *fut.* [b] פְּקֻדָּה *f.* muster, enumeration.

4   שָׁוָה to be equal ; to make plain, even ; to quiet, compose the mind ; see *Behave.* PIEL *pret.*

Lev. xxv. 50.	1 c	Num. xxiii. 9.	1 e	1 Chron. xxiii. 11.	3 b
xxvii. 18, 23.	1 c	2 Sam. iv. 2.	1 b	Isa. xxxviii. 13.	4
Num. iv. 32.	3 a	2 Kings xii. 15.	1 d	Ezek. xliv. 26.	2
xviii. 27.	1 a	xxii. 7.	1 b		

RECOMPENCE, RECOMPENSE

1   גָּמַל to make returns of any kind to others ; see *Reward.* KAL [a] *fut.* [b] *part.* Poel. גְּמוּל [c] *m.* retribution, recompence. גְּמוּלָה [d] *f. id.*

2   תְּמוּרָה *f.* exchange.

3   נָתַן to give ; to set or place (upon), to impute guilt : Ezek. vii. 3, "will recompense upon thee," or will lay upon thee, so as to require the punishment of, "all thine abominations." KAL [a] *pret.* [b] *inf.* [c] *fut.*

4   שׁוּב to return ; to cause to return. HIPHIL [a] *pret.* [b] *inf.* [c] *fut.* HOPHAL [d] *part.*

5   שָׁלַם to be ended ; finished ; Piel, to complete, to restore, make good, to recompense, requite, reward. PIEL [a] *pret.* [b] *imp.* [c] *fut.* [d] *part.* PUAL [e] *fut.* [f] שִׁלֵּם *m.* retribution, remuneration, reward. [g] שִׁלּוּם *m. id.*

Num. v. 7.	4 a	Isa. xxxiv. 8.	5 g	Ezek. vii. 3, 8.	3 a
v. 8, 8.	4 b d	xxxv. 4.	5 d	vii. 4, 9.	3 a
Deut. xxxii. 35.	5 f	lix. 18, 18.	1 c	ix. 10.	3 a
Ruth ii. 12.	5 d	lxv. 6, 6.	5 a	xi. 21.	3 a
2 Sam. xix. 36.	1 a	lxvi. 6.	1 c	xvi. 43.	3 a
xxii. 21, 25.	4 c	Jer. xvi. 18.	5 a	xvii. 19.	3 a
2 Chron. vi. 23.	3 b	xviii. 20.	5 e	xxii. 31.	3 a
xxxiv. 33.	5 c	xxv. 14.	5 a	xxiii. 49.	3 a
Job xv. 31.	2	xxxii. 18.	5 d	Hos. ix. 7.	5 g
Ps. xviii. 20, 24.	4 c	l. 29.	5 b	xii. 2.	4 c
Prov. xi. 31.	5 e	li. 6.	1 c	Joel iii. 4, 4, 4.	1 c b c
xii. 14.	1 c	li. 56.	1 d	iii. 7.	1 c
xx. 22.	5 c	Lam. iii. 64.	1 c		

RECONCILE

חָטָא to sin ; Piel, to cleanse, purify. PIEL *fut.* 2 Chron. xxix. 24.

כָּפַר to cover, to make atonement. PIEL *pret.* Ezek. xlv. 20. *inf.* Lev. vi. 30 ; viii. 15 ; xvi. 20 : Ezek. xlv. 15, 17 : Dan. ix. 24.

רָצָה to have a favour to. HITHPAEL *fut.* 1 Sam. xxix. 4.

RECORD

1   דְּכַן Ch. *m.* record, memoir. [a] דִּכְרוֹן Ch. *m. id.*

2   זָכַר to remember ; to bring to remembrance, to record. HIPHIL [a] *inf.* [b] *fut.* [c] *part.* [d] זִכָּרוֹן *m.* memorial.

3   כָּתַב to write. KAL *part.* Paül.

4   עוּד (see *Testify*), to call to record. HIPHIL [a] *pret.* [b] *fut.*

5   שָׂהֵד *m.* an eye-witness.

Exod. xx. 24.	2 b	2 Kings xviii. 18, 37.	2 c	Neh. xii. 22.	3
Deut. xxx. 19.	4 a	1 Chron. xvi. 4.	2 a	Esth. vi. 1.	2 d
xxxi. 28.	4 a	xviii. 15.	2 c	Job xix. 19.	5
2 Sam. viii. 16.	2 c	2 Chron. xxxiv. 8.	2 c	Isa. viii. 2.	4 c
xx. 24.	2 c	Ezra iv. 15, 15.	1	xxxvi. 3, 22.	2 c
1 Kings iv. 3.	2 c	vi. 2.	1 a		

RECOUNT

זָכַר to remember. KAL *fut.* Nah. ii. 5.

RECOVER

1 אָסַף to gather; to take to oneself, to receive; to receive one from leprosy; *i.e.* to restore a leprous person so that he is again received into the society and intercourse of others. KAL ^a*pret.* ^b*inf.* ^c*fut.*

2 בָּלַג to take comfort, to recover strength. HIPHIL *fut.*

3 חָזַק to be strong. KAL *fut.*

4 חָיָה to live. KAL ^a*inf.* ^b*fut.* מִחְיָה^c *f.* preserving of life.

5 חָלַם to be fat, sound; to heal, to let recover. HIPHIL *fut.*

6 נָצַל to take away; to snatch from danger, to deliver. HIPHIL ^a*pret.* ^b*fut.* ^c*inf.*

7 עָלָה to ascend; to go up, *i.e.* to heal. KAL *pret.*

8 עָצַר to shut up; to hold back; to retain. KAL *pret.*

9 קָנָה to buy; to redeem, to recover from captivity. KAL *inf.*

10 שׁוּב to return. HIPHIL ^a*pret.* ^b*inf.* ^c*fut.*

Judg. xi. 26.	6 a	2 Kings viii. 8.	4 b a	2 Chron. xiv. 13.	4 c
1 Sam. xxx. 8.	6 c b	viii. 9.	4 b	Ps. xxxix. 13.	2
xxx. 18.	6 b	viii. 10.	4 b a	Isa. xi. 11.	9
xxx. 19.	10 a	viii. 14.	4 b a	xxxviii. 9, 21.	4 b
xxx. 22.	6 b	xiii. 25.	10 c	xxxviii. 16.	5
2 Sam. viii. 3.	10 b	xiv. 28.	10 a	xxxix. 1.	3
2 Kings i. 2.	4 b	xvi. 6.	10 a	Jer. viii. 22.	7
v. 3.	1 c	xx. 7.	4 b	xli. 16.	10 a
v. 6, 11.	1 a	2 Chron. xiii. 20.	8	Hos. ii. 9.	6 a
v. 7.	1 b				

RED

1 אָדַם to be red, ruddy. KAL ^a*pret.* PUAL, to be dyed red: ^b*part.* HIPHIL ^c*fut.* HITHPAEL ^d*fut.* אָדֹם ^e*adj.* red, ruddy: Gen. xxv. 30, &c. אֲדַמְדָּם ^f*adj.* reddish. אַדְמֹנִי ^g and אַדְמֹנִי *adj.* red, ruddy.

2 בַּהַט *m.* a species of marble used for pavement.

3 חַכְלִילִי *adj.* red, as the effect of wine on the eyes; Gesenius, dim, dark; חַכְלִלוּת in Prov. xxiii. 29, the effect of the abuse of wine; but in Gen. xlix. 12, merely implying plenty of wine.

4 חָמַר to be red, from the idea of boiling, foaming, becoming heated or inflamed. KAL ^a*pret.* חֶמֶר^b *m.* wine, "red wine," or, as fermented: Isa. xxvii. 2. Some copies read חֶמֶד pleasantness, beauty, beloved.

No. 1 e not included.

Gen. xxv. 25.	1 g	Lev. xiii. 19, 24, 42,		Prov. xxiii. 29.	3
xlix. 12.	3	43, 49.	1 f	xxiii. 31.	1 d
Exod. xxv. 5.	1 b	xiv. 37.	1 f	Isa. i. 18.	1 c
xxvi. 14.	1 b	1 Sam. xvi. 12.	1 g	xxvii. 2.	4 b
xxxv. 7, 23.	1 b	xvii. 42.	1 g	Lam. iv. 7.	1 a
xxxvi. 19.	1 b	Esth. i. 6.	2	Nah. ii. 3.	1 b
xxxix. 34.	1 b	Ps. lxxv. 8.	4 a		

RED SEA

סוּף *m.* rush, reed, sedge; sea-weed, sedge; hence sea of sedge, or red sea, which abounds in sea-weed: Exod. x. 19, *lit.* sea of suph, *or*, of weeds: &c.

REDEEM

1 גָּאַל to demand back one's property; hence, (1) to repurchase, buy again an estate which had been sold, Lev. xxv. 25,

comp. Ruth iv. 4, 6; (2) to redeem what has been vowed or is otherwise due to the service of God, Lev. xxvii. 13, 15, 19, 20; (3) to require satisfaction for blood shed, to avenge the blood of one slain, *sanguinem repetere*, found only in *part.* גֹּאֵל הַדָּם an avenger of blood. Num. xxxv. 19, &c., and without הַדָּם. To redeem, ransom, Lev. xxv. 49; hence, in general, to deliver, set free, Gen. xlviii. 16, Exod. vi. 6. Frequently spoken of God in the Psalms and Prophets; because the right of repurchase, and of redemption, as well as of the avenging of blood, pertained, by the Jewish law, only to the nearest of kin. the participle comes to signify the nearest of kin. KAL ^a*pret.* ^b*inf.* ^c*imp.* ^d*fut.* ^e*part.* Poel, lit. a redeemer. ^f*part.* Paül. NIPHAL ^g*pret.* ^h*fut.* גְּאֻלָּהⁱ *f.* redemption, the price of redemption.

2 פָּדָה to loose, or separate; to redeem, ransom; *seq.* בְּ of price; to set free, deliver, without reference to price, *seq.* מִן, from servitude, death, &c.; it is used of redemption out of Egypt. KAL ^a*pret.* ^b*inf.* ^c*imp.* ^d*fut.* ^e*part.* Poel. ^f*part.* Paül. NIPHAL ^g*pret.* ^h*fut.* HIPHIL ⁱ*pret.* HOPHAL ^k*inf.* פְּדוּיִם^l *m. pl.* price of redemption. פְּדוּת^m *f.* liberation. פִּדְיוֹםⁿ *m.* price of redemption, פִּדְיוֹן כְּתִיב *m. id.*

3 פָּרַק to break by rending; to pull or rescue out of the hands of an enemy. KAL *fut.*

4 קָנָה to purchase. KAL *pret.*

Gen. xlviii. 16.	1 e	Ruth iv. 4, 4,		Ps. cxxxvi. 24.	3	
Exod. vi. 6.	1 a	4, 4, 4.	1 d c d b d	Prov. xxiii. 11.	1 e	
xiii. 13, 13, 13, 15.	2 d	iv. 6, 6, 6.	1 b c b	Isa. i. 27.	2 h	
xv. 13.	2 d	iv. 7.	1 i	xxix. 22.	2 a	
xxi. 8.	2 i	2 Sam. iv. 9.	2 a	xxxv. 9.	1 f	
xxxiv. 20, 20, 20.	2 d	vii. 23, 23.	2 b a	xli. 14.	2 a	
Lev. xix. 20.	2 k g	1 Kings i. 29.	2 a	xliii. 1.	1 a	
xxv. 24, 29, a 29, a		1 Chron. xvii. 21,		xliii. 14.	1 a	
31, 32, 51, 52.	1 i	21.	2 b a	xliv. 6, 24.	1 a	
xxv. 25, β 25.	1 e a	Neh. i. 10.	2	xliv. 22, 23.	1 a	
xxv. 26, 26.	1 e i	v. 8.	4	xlvii. 4.	1 a	
xxv. 30, 54.	1 h	Job v. 20.	2 d	xlvii. 17.	1 a	
xxv. 48, 48.	1 i d	vi. 23.	2 d	xlviii. 20.	1 a	
xxv. 49, 49,		xix. 25.	1 e	xlix. 7, 26.	1 a	
49.	1 d d g	Ps. xix. 14.	2 e	l. 2.	2 m	
xxvii. 13.	1 b d	xxv. 22.	2 c	li. 11.	2 f	
xxvii. 15.	1 d	xxvi. 11.	2 c	lii. 3.	1 h	
xxvii. 19.	1 b d	xxxi. 5.	2 a	lii. 9.	1 a	
xxvii. 20, 20.	1 d h	xxxiv. 22.	2 a	liv. 5, 8.	1 e	
xxvii. 27, 27.	2 a, 1 a	xliv. 26.	2 c	lix. 20.	1 e	
xxvii. 28, 33.	1 h	xlix. 7.	2 b d	lx. 16.	1 a	
xxvii. 29.	2 h	xlix. 8.	2 o	lxii. 12.	1 f	
xxvii. 31.	1 b d	xlix. 15.	2 d	lxiii. 4.	1 f	
Num. iii. 46, 48.	2 l	lxix. 18.	1 c	lxiii. 9.	1 a	
iii. 49, 49.	2 n l	lxxi. 23.	2 a	lxiii. 16. γ	1 a	
iii. 51.	2 l or n	lxxii. 14.	1 d	Jer. xv. 21.	2 a	
xviii. 15.	2 b d	lxxiv. 2.	1 a	xxxi. 11.	2 a	
xviii. 15, 17.	2 d	lxxvii. 15.	1 a	xxxii. 7, 8.	1 l	
xviii. 16, 16.	2 f d	lxxviii. 35.	1 e	l. 34.	1 a	
Deut. vii. 8.	2 d	ciii. 4.	1 e	Lam. iii. 58.	1 e	
ix. 26.	2 a	cvi. 10.	2 e	Hos. vii. 13.	2 d	
xiii. 5.	2 e	cvii. 2, 2.	1 f a	xiii. 14.	2 d	
xv. 15.	2 d	cxi. 9.	2 m	Micah iv. 10.	1 d	
xxi. 8.	2 a	cxxx. 7.	2 m	vi. 4.	2 a	
xxiv. 18.	2 d	cxxx. 8.	2 d	Zech. x. 8.	2 a	

a lit. the redemption thereof shall be to him. *β lit.* the redeemer thereof that is near unto him shall come. *γ marg.* 'or, our redeemer from everlasting (is) thy name.'

REED

אֲגַם a pool; a rush, a reed: Jer. li. 32.

קָנֶה *m.* a reed, both the small sort, which grows in our rivers and ponds, and the much larger sort, which grows in the Eastern countries; see also *Cane:* 1 Kings xiv. 15: 2 Kings xviii. 21: Job xl. 21: Isa. xix. 6; xxxv. 7;

xxxvi. 6 ; xlii. 3 : Ezek. xxix. 6 ; xl. 3, 5, 5, 5, 6, 6, 7, 7, 7, 8 ; xli. 8 ; xlii. 16, 16, 16, 17, 17, 18, 18, 19, 19.

REEL

חָגַג   to move round in a circle ; to dance ; to reel, to be giddy, to stagger. KAL *fut.* Ps. cvii. 27.

נוּע   to move to and fro unsteadily. KAL *inf.* and *fut.* Isa. xxiv. 20, reeling it shall reel.

REFINE

זָקַק   to strain, to filter, *e.g.* wine ; *trop.* metals. PUAL *part.* I Chron. xxviii. 18 ; xxix. 4 : Isa. xxv. 6.

צָרַף   to melt ; to try, to purify by fire. KAL *pret.* Isa. xlviii. 10 : Zech. xiii. 9. *inf.* Zech. xiii. 9. PIEL *part.* Mal. iii. 2, 3.

REFORM

יָסַר   to chasten, to correct. NIPHAL *fut.* Lev. xxvi. 23.

REFRAIN

1   אָפַק   to hold ; to contain oneself, to refrain from giving way, *e.g.* to affection, to anger, to conscience. HITHPAEL ª *inf.* ᵇ *fut.*

2   חָטַם   to muzzle an animal in order to subdue or tame ; to refrain oneself.

3   חָשַׂךְ   to hold back, to restrain. KAL ª *pret.* ᵇ *fut.* ᶜ *part.* Poel.

4   כָּלָא   to close, to shut up ; to withhold, to restrain. KAL ª *pret.* ᵇ *fut.*

5   מָנַע   to keep back, to withhold, to restrain. KAL *imp.*

6   עָצַר   to shut up ; to hold back, detain. KAL *pret.*

7   רָחַק   to be far. KAL *inf.*

Gen. xliii. 31.	1 b	Ps. xl. 9.	4 b	Isa. xlii. 14.	1 b
xlv. 1.	1 a	cxix. 101.	4 a	xlviii. 9.	2
Esth. v. 10.	1 b	Prov. i. 15.	5	lxiv. 12.	1 b
Job vii. 11.	3 b	x. 19.	3 c	Jer. xiv. 10.	3 a
xxix. 9.	6	Eccles. iii. 5.	7	xxxi. 16.	5

REFRESH

1   נָפַשׁ   to breathe ; to take breath, to be refreshed. NIPHAL *fut.*

2   סָעַד   to uphold, sustain ; to refresh with food. KAL *imp.*

3   רָוַח   to breathe, to breathe freely, to be refreshed. KAL ª *pret.* ᵇ *fut.*

4   שׁוּב   to return. HIPHIL *fut.*

5   מַרְגֵּעָה   *f.* rest, quiet.

Exod. xxiii. 12.	1	2 Sam. xvi. 14.	1	Prov. xxv. 13.	4
xxxi. 17.	1	1 Kings xiii. 7.	2	Isa. xxviii. 12.	5
1 Sam. xvi. 23.	3 a	Job xxxii. 20.	3 b		

REFUGE

1   חָסָה   to flee, to take refuge ; to trust. KAL ª *fut.* ᵇ מַחְסֶה *m.* a refuge, shelter.

2   מָנוֹס   *m.* escape for life, or from imminent danger.

3   מְעוֹנָה   *f.* a dwelling, a place of residence ; sometimes also considered as a place of safety.

4   מִקְלָט   *m.* a place of reception, yet of contracted, abridged habitation, in which the manslayer was secured, while he remained within its limits, from the avenger.

5   מִשְׂגָּב   *m.* an inaccessible impregnable situation ; a high place or tower.

Num. xxxv. 6, 11, 12,		Ps. xiv. 6.	1 b	Ps. xciv. 22.	1 b
13, 14, 15, 25, 26,		xlvi. 1.	1 b	civ. 18.	1 b
27, 28, 32.	4	xlvi. 7, 11.	5	cxlii. 4.	2
Deut. xxxiii. 27.	3	xlviii. 3.	5	cxlii. 5.	1 b
Josh. xx. 2, 3.	3	lvii. 1.	1 a	Prov. xiv. 26.	1 b
xxi. 13, 21, 27, 32, 38.	4	lix. 16.	2	Isa. iv. 6.	1 b
2 Sam. xxii. 3.	2	lxii. 7, 8.	5	xxv. 4.	5
1 Chron. vi. 57, 67.	4	lxxi. 7.	1 b	xxviii. 15, 17.	1 b
Ps. ix. 9, 9.	5	xci. 2, 9.	1 b	Jer. xvi. 19.	2

REFUSE

1   מָאֵן   to refuse with a resolved mind, which cannot be prevailed on by the means that have been used ; figuratively applied to a wound that admits of no cure, Jer. xv. 18. PIEL ª *pret.* ᵇ *inf.* ᶜ *fut.* ᵈ מָאֵן *adj.* unwilling. ᵉ מָאֲנִים *adj. pl.* pertinaciously refusing.

2   מָאַס   see *Despise, Abhor.* KAL ª *pret.* ᵇ *inf.* ᶜ *fut.* NIPHAL ᵈ *fut.*

3   מָסַס   to melt, dissolve ; of diseased flocks. NIPHAL *pret.*

4   מְפֻל   *m.* the refuse of the wheat which falls through the sieve.

5   עָזַב   to forsake. KAL *part.* Poel.

6   פָּרַע   to let go loose, to dismiss ; to break loose from. KAL ª *fut.* ᵇ *part.* Poel.

Gen. xxxvii. 35.	1 c	2 Sam. xiii. 9.	1 c	Isa. vii. 15, 16.	2 b
xxxix. 8.	1 c	1 Kings xx. 35.	1 c	viii. 6.	2 a
xlviii. 19.	1 c	xxi. 15.	1 a	liv. 6.	2 d
Exod. iv. 23.	1 c	2 Kings v. 16.	1 c	Jer. iii. 3.	1 a
vii. 14.	1 a	Neh. ix. 17.	1 c	v. 3, 3.	1 a
viii. 2.	1 d	Esth. i. 12.	1 c	viii. 5.	1 a
ix. 2.	1 d	Job vi. 7.	1 a	ix. 6.	1 a
x. 3.	1 a	xxxiv. 33.	2 a	xi. 10.	1 a
x. 4.	1 d	Ps. lxxvii. 2.	2 a	xiii. 10.	1 e
xvi. 28.	1 a	lxxviii. 10.	1 c	xv. 18.	1 a
xxii. 17.	1 b c	lxxviii. 67.	2 c	xxv. 28.	1 a
Num. xx. 21.	1 c	cxviii. 22.	2 a	xxxi. 15.	1 a
xxii. 13, 14.	1 a	Prov. i. 24.	1 c	xxxviii. 21.	1 d
Deut. xxv. 7.	1 c	viii. 33.	6 a	l. 33.	1 d
1 Sam. viii. 19.	1 c	x. 17.	5	Lam. iii. 45.	2 b
xv. 9.	5	xiii. 18.	6 b	Ezek. v. 6.	2 a
xvi. 7.	2 a	xv. 32.	6 b	Hos. xi. 3.	1 a
xxviii. 23.	1 c	xxi. 7, 25.	1 a	Amos viii. 6.	4
2 Sam. ii. 23.	1 c	Isa. i. 20.	1 c	Zech. vii. 11.	1 c

REGARD

1   בִּין   to understand. KAL and HIPHIL ª *fut.* HITHPOLEL ᵇ *fut.*

2   דִּבְרָה   *f.* manner, mode ; cause, reason.

3   דָּרַשׁ   to seek or search after anything. KAL *fut.*

4   חוּס   to have a favourable regard to, and for that reason to spare ; to be loth to part with. KAL *fut.*

5   חָשַׁב   to think, to consider, to reflect upon ; to regard, to value. KAL ª *pret.* ᵇ *fut.*

6   יָדַע   to know. KAL *part.* Poel.

7   טָעַם   Ch. *m.* taste ; intelligence, reason.

8   לֵב   *m.* heart ; following שׂוּם or שִׁית, to regard.

9   נָבַט   to look, behold, have respect to. HIPHIL ª *inf.* ᵇ *imp.* ᶜ *fut.*

10   נָכַר   to look upon ; to regard with partiality. PIEL *pret.*

11   נָשָׂא   see *Accept.* KAL ª *fut.* Deut. x. 17 : Gr. οὐ θαυμάζει πρόσωπον, comp. Jude 16. ᵇ *part.* Poel.

12   עַיִן   *com.* eye : Gen. xlv. 20, *marg.* 'let not your eye spare.'

13   פָּנָה   to turn towards ; to look with a favourable aspect. KAL ª *pret.* ᵇ *inf.* ᶜ *fut.* ᵈ פָּנִים *m. pl.* face.

14   קָשַׁב   to hearken. HIPHIL ª *part.* ᵇ קֶשֶׁב *m.* attention.

15 רָאָה to see, to look upon. KAL ᵃ*pret.* ᵇ*fut.* ᶜ*part.* Poel.

16 שׂוּם to set, put, or place; with מְעָם or לֵב to regard. KAL ᵃ*pret.* ᵇ*fut.* HIPHIL ᶜ*part.* שׂוּם Ch. *id.* P'AL ᵈ*pret.*

17 שׁוּר to see, behold, view. KAL *fut.*

18 שִׁית to set, with לֵב to regard. KAL ᵃ*pret.* ᵇ*fut.* 2 Sam. xiii. 20, *i.e.* lay not this matter on thy heart.

19 שָׁמַע to hear. KAL *fut.*

20 שָׁמַר to keep, observe. KAL ᵃ*inf.* ᵇ*part.* Poel.

21 שָׁעָה to have respect; *seq.* בְּ to meditate upon anything, to be occupied in it: such is the sense given in all versions of Exod. v. 9. KAL *fut.*

Gen. xlv. 20.	12, 4	Job xxxv. 13.	17	Prov. xxix. 7.	1 a
Exod. v. 9.	21	xxxvi. 21.	13 c	Eccles. v. 8.	20 b
ix. 21.	16 a, 8	xxxix. 7.	19	viii. 2.	2
Lev. xix. 31.	13 c	Ps. xxviii. 5.	1 a	xi. 4.	15 c
Deut. x. 17.	11 a	xxxi. 6.	20 b	Isa. v. 12.	9 c
xxviii. 50.	11 a	lxvi. 18.	15 a	xiii. 17.	5 b
1 Sam. iv. 20.	18 a, 8	xciv. 7.	1 a	xxxiii. 8.	5 a
xxv. 25.	16 b, 8	cii. 17.	13 a	Lam. iv. 16.	9 a
2 Sam. xiii. 20.	18 b, 8	cvi. 44.	15 b	Dan. iii. 12.	16 d, 7
1 Kings xviii. 29.	14 b	Prov. i. 24.	14 a	vi. 13.	16 d, 7
2 Kings iii. 17.	11 b	v. 2.	20 a	xi. 37, 37.	1 a
1 Chron. xvii. 17.	15 a	vi. 25. α	13 d	Amos v. 22.	9 c
Job iii. 4.	3	vi. 35.	9 c	Hab. i. 5.	9 b
iv. 20.	16 c	xii. 10.	11 a	Mal. i. 9.	11 a
xxx. 20.	1 b	xiii. 18.	20 b	ii. 13.	13 b
xxxiv. 19.	10	xv. 5.	20 b		

a marg. 'he will not accept the face of.'

REGION

חֶבֶל *com.* a cord; a measuring-line; a portion measured out; also, generally, a tract, region, country: Deut. iii. 4, 13: 1 Kings iv. 13.

נָפָה *f.* high place, height: 1 Kings iv. 11.

REGISTER

כְּתָב *m.* writing; book, decree, register of names: Ezra ii. 62, Neh. vii. 64.

סֵפֶר *m.* writing, a book, or roll: Neh. vii. 5.

REHEARSE

דָּבַר to speak. PIEL *fut.* 1 Sam. viii. 21.

נָגַד to show, to tell, declare, announce. HIPHIL *fut.* 1 Sam. xvii. 31.

שׂוּם to put, place. KAL *imp.* Exod. xvii. 14.

תָּנָה to praise, to celebrate. PIEL *fut.* Judg. v. 11.

REIGN

1 מָלַךְ to reign, to be king; to be made king, to begin to reign. KAL ᵃ*pret.* ᵇ*inf.* ᶜ*imp.* ᵈ*fut.* ᵉ*part.* Poel. HIPHIL ᶠ*pret.* ᵍמְלֻךְ Ch. *f.* reign, dominion; realm. ʰמַלְכוּת *f.* ᵢמַמְלָכָה *f.* ᵏמַמְלָכוּת.

2 מָשַׁל to rule. KAL ᵃ*pret.* ᵇ*inf.* ᶜ*fut.* ᵈ*part.* Poel.

3 עָצַר to restrain; to rule. KAL *fut.* 1 Sam. ix. 17.

4 רָדָה to have dominion, to rule, with בְּ over. KAL *pret.*

5 שׂוּר to be prince, to have dominion. KAL *fut.*

Gen. xxxvi. 31, 31.	1 a b	Deut. xv. 6, 6.	2 a c	Judg. ix. 22.	5
xxxvi. 32, 33, 34, 35, 36, 37, 38, 39.	1 d	Josh. xii. 5.	2 d	1 Sam. viii. 7.	1 b
xxxvii. 8.	1 b d	xiii. 10, 12, 21.	1 a	viii. 9, 11.	1 d
Exod. xv. 18.	1 d	Judg. iv. 2.	1 a	ix. 17. a	3
Lev. xxvi. 17.	4	ix. 2, 2.	2 b	xi. 12.	1 d
		ix. 8, 10, 12, 14.	1 c	xii. 12.	1 d

1 Sam. xii. 14.	1 a	2 Kings xvi. 1.	1 a	2 Chron. xxvii. 8, 8.	1 b a
xiii. 1, β 1.	1 b a	xvi. 2, 2.	1 b a	xxvii. 9.	1 d
xvi. 1.	1 b	xvi. 20.	1 d	xxviii. 1, 1.	1 b a
2 Sam. ii. 10, 10.	1 b a	xvii. 1.	1 a	xxviii. 27.	1 d
iii. 21.	1 a	xviii. 1.	1 a	xxix. 1, 1.	1 a
v. 4, 4.	1 b a	xviii. 2, 2.	1 b a	xxix. 3.	1 b
v. 5, 5.	1 a	xix. 37.	1 d	xxix. 19.	1 h
viii. 15.	1 a	xx. 21.	1 d	xxxii. 33.	1 d
x. 1.	1 d	xxi. 1, 1.	1 b a	xxxiii. 1, 1.	1 b a
xv. 10.	1 a	xxi. 18, 26.	1 d	xxxiii. 20.	1 d
xvi. 8.	1 a	xxi. 19, 19.	1 b a	xxxiii. 21, 21.	1 b a
1 Kings i. 11, 18.	1 a	xxii. 1, 1.	1 b a	xxxiv. 1, 1.	1 b a
i. 13, 13.	1 d a	xxiii. 31, 31.	1 b a	xxxiv. 3, 8.	1 b
i. 17, 24, 30.	1 d	xxiii. 33.	1 b	xxxv. 19.	1 h
ii. 11, 11, 11.	1 a	xxiii. 36, 36.	1 b a	xxxvi. 2, 2.	1 b a
ii. 15.	1 b	xxiv. 6.	1 d	xxxvi. 5, 5.	1 b a
iv. 21.	2 d	xxiv. 12.	1 b	xxxvi. 8.	1 d
vi. 1.	1 b	xxiv. 18, 18.	1 b a	xxxvi. 9, 9.	1 b a
xi. 24, 25, 43.	1 d	xxv. 1, 27.	1 b	xxxvi. 11, 11.	1 b a
xi. 37, 42.	1 a	1 Chron. i. 43, 43.	1 a b	xxxvi. 20.	1 d
xii. 17.	1 d	i. 44, 45, 46, 47, 48, 49, 50.	1 b a	Ezra iv. 5, 6, 6.	1 h
xiv. 19.	1 a	iii. 4, 4.	1 d a	iv. 24.	1 g
xiv. 20, 20.	1 a	iv. 31.	1 b	vi. 15.	1 h
xiv. 21, 21, 21.	1 a b a	xvi. 31.	1 a	vii. 1.	1 h
xv. 1, 2, 9, 10, 33.	1 a	xviii. 14.	1 d	viii. 1.	1 h
xv. 8, 24, 28.	1 a d	xix. 1.	1 d	Neh. xii. 22.	1 h
xv. 25, 25.	1 a d	xxvi. 31.	1 h	Esth. i. 1.	1 e
xv. 29.	1 b	xxix. 12.	2 d	i. 3.	1 b
xvi. 6, 10, 22, 28.	1 a	xxix. 26, 27, 27, 27.	1 a	ii. 16.	1 h
xvi. 8, 15, 23, 23.	1 a	xxix. 28.	1 d	Job xxxiv. 30.	1 b
xvi. 11.	1 b	xxix. 30.	1 h	Ps. xlvii. 8.	1 a
xvi. 29, 29.	1 a d	2 Chron. i. 8.	1 f	xciii. 1.	1 a
xxii. 40, 50.	1 d	i. 13.	1 d	xcvi. 10.	1 a
xxii. 41.	1 a	iii. 2.	1 h	xcvii. 1.	1 a
xxii. 42, 42.	1 b a	ix. 26.	2 d	xcix. 1.	1 a
xxii. 51, 51.	1 a d	ix. 30, 31.	1 d	cxlvi. 10.	1 d
2 Kings i. 17.	1 d	x. 17.	1 d	Prov. viii. 15.	1 d
iii. 1, 1.	1 a d	xii. 13, 13, 13.	1 d b a	xxx. 22.	1 d
iii. 27.	1 d	xii. 16.	1 d	Eccles. iv. 14.	1 d
viii. 15, 24.	1 d	xiii. 1.	1 a	Isa. xxiv. 23.	1 a
viii. 16, 25.	1 a	xiii. 2.	1 a	xxxii. 1.	1 d
viii. 17, 17.	1 b a	xiv. 1.	1 b	xxxvii. 38.	1 d
viii. 26, 26.	1 b a	xv. 10.	1 h	lii. 7.	1 a
ix. 29.	1 a	xvi. 1, 12.	1 a	Jer. i. 2.	1 b
x. 35.	1 d	xvi. 13.	1 b	xxii. 11.	1 b
x. 36.	1 a	xvii. 1.	1 a	xxii. 15.	1 a
xi. 3.	1 e	xvii. 7.	1 b	xxiii. 5.	1 a
xi. 21.	1 b	xx. 31, 31, 31.	1 d b a	xxvi. 1.	1 k
xii. 1, 1.	1 a	xxi. 1.	1 d	xxvii. 1.	1 i
xii. 21.	1 d	xxi. 5, 5.	1 b a	xxxiii. 21.	1 e
xiii. 1, 10.	1 a	xxi. 20, 20.	1 b a	xxxvii. 1.	1 d
xiii. 9, 24.	1 d	xxii. 1.	1 a	xlix. 34.	1 h
xiv. 1, 23.	1 a	xxii. 2, 2.	1 b a	li. 59.	1 d
xiv. 2, 2.	1 b a	xxii. 12.	1 e	lii. 1, 1.	1 b a
xiv. 16, 29.	1 d	xxiii. 3.	1 b	lii. 4.	1 b
xv. 1, 8, 17, 23, 27, 32.	1 a	xxiv. 1, 1.	1 b a	lii. 31.	1 b
xv. 2, 2.	1 b a	xxiv. 27.	1 d	Dan. i. 1.	1 h
xv. 7, 10, 14, 22, 25, 30, 38.	1 d	xxv. 1, 1.	1 b a	ii. 1.	1 h
xv. 13, 13.	1 b a	xxvi. 3, 3.	1 b a	vi. 28, 28.	1 g
xv. 33, 33.	1 b a	xxvi. 23.	1 d	viii. 1.	1 h
		xxvii. 1, 1.	1 b a	ix. 2.	1 b
				Micah iv. 7.	1 a

a marg. 'restrain in.'   *β marg.* 'one year in his reigning.'

REINS

חֲלָצַיִם *f. dual*, loins: Isa. xi. 5.

כְּלָיוֹת *f. pl.* the kidneys or reins, the innermost part of the frame; as the heart לֵב, with which it is often joined, is figuratively used to signify the temper and disposition, so the reins by the sympathetic nervous system closely connected with the heart, signify close thought and reflection of the mind: the reins are sometimes put for the seat of joy, Prov. xxiii. 16; of severe grief, Ps. lxxiii. 21. The fat of kidneys, being considered the most delicate, is used as an epithet to signify the best and most nourishing wheat: Job xvi. 13; xix. 27: Ps. vii. 9; xvi. 7; xxvi. 2; lxxiii. 21; cxxxix. 13: Prov. xxiii. 16: Jer. xi. 20; xii. 2; xvii. 10; xx. 12: Lam. iii. 13.

REJECT

1 חָדֵל *adj.* ceasing; left, destitute; forsaken: Isa. liii. 3, *comp.* Job xix. 14.

2 מָאַס to reject with contempt and disdain ; see *Abhor.* KAL ^a *pret.* ^b *inf.* ^c *fut.*

1 Sam. viii. 7, 7.	2 a	2 Kings xvii. 15, 20. 2 c	Jer. vii. 29. 2 a
x. 19.	2 a	Isa. liii. 3. 1	viii. 9. 2 a
xv. 23, 23.	2 a c	Jer. ii. 37. 2 a	vi. 19. 2 b a
xv. 26, 26.	2 a c	vi. 19. 2 c	Lam. v. 22. 2 b a
xvi. 1.	2 a	vi. 30. 2 a	Hos. iv. 6, 6. 2 a c

REJOICE

1 נּגִל or גִּיל to be joyful, to be very glad ; to rejoice with a joy which expresses itself in the gestures of the body. This joy is attributed to the soul, Ps. xvi. 9, Isa. lxi. 10, since it expresses that joy which excites the affections ; it is attributed to the bones, Ps. li. 10, and to things inanimate, Ps. xcvi. 11 : Isa. xxxv. 1 : 1 Chron. xvi. 31. KAL ^a *pret.* ^b *imp.* ^c *fut.* ^d גִּיל *m.* exultation, rejoicing. ^e גִּילָה *f. id.*

2 חָגַר to gird. KAL *fut.* "rejoice on every side," *marg.* 'are girded with joy.'

3 חָדָה to be glad, to rejoice. KAL *fut.*

4 עָלַז to rejoice with exultation, to triumph ; sometimes in a bad sense, of those who exult in their prosperity, and become insolent and wicked. KAL ^a *inf.* ^b *imp.* ^c *fut.* ^d עָלֵז *adj.* exulting, rejoicing. ^e עָלִיז *adj.* exulting, joyful.

5 עָלַס to exult, to rejoice with corresponding gestures of body or signs of joy. KAL *fut.*

6 עָלַץ to rejoice with exultation ; see עָלַז. KAL ^a *pret.* ^b *inf.* ^c *fut.* ^d עָלִיצוּת *f.* exultation, rejoicing.

7 צָהַל to shine ; *fig.* of a clear shrill tone of voice, to cry aloud for joy. KAL *pret.*

8 תְּרוּעָה *f.* loud noise ; "a joyful noise," *marg.* 'shouting for joy.'

9 רָנַן to utter cries of joy ; to praise with rejoicing. KAL ^a *fut.* PIEL ^b *imp.* ^c *fut.* HIPHIL ^d *imp.* ^e *fut.* ^f רִנָּה *f.* a shouting for joy.

10 שׂוּשׂ and שִׂישׂ to exult, to be glad, to rejoice ; the primary idea is that of springing, leaping ; with עַל and בְּ. KAL ^a *pret.* ^b *inf.* ^c *imp.* ^d *fut.* ^e *part.* ^f מָשׂוֹשׂ *m.* gladness, joy. ^g שָׂשׂוֹן *m. id.*

11 שָׂחַק to laugh, to smile upon ; see *Laugh.* KAL ^a *fut.* PIEL ^b *part.*

12 שָׂמַח to rejoice, to be joyful, to be glad : the primary idea seems to be that of a smiling, cheerful, merry countenance, free from care ; sometimes of a louder joy, to be or make merry, spoken of persons feasting ; hence to rejoice before Jehovah, spoken of the sacred festivities held in the courts of the sanctuary, Lev. xxiii. 40, &c., Neh. xii. 43 ; *comp.* Isa. ix. 2 : of singing and dancing, Job xxi. 12 ; ascribed to the heart, to inanimate things, as the heavens, to Mount Zion, once to light, Prov. xiii. 9 ; the candle of the righteous rejoiceth, *i. e.* shines with a cheerful light ; with בְּ in or at, עַל *id.*, rarely with מִן ; for the idea of rejoicing over the calamities or destruction of any one, with לְ, rarely with בְּ ; the same idea in Piel, with לְ, עַל, and מִן. KAL ^a *pret.* ^b *inf.* ^c *imp.* ^d *fut.* PIEL ^e *pret.* ^f *imp.* ^g *fut.* ^h *part.* HIPHIL ⁱ *pret.* ^k שָׂמֵחַ *adj.* rejoicing, joyful. ^l שִׂמְחָה *f.* joy, gladness.

Exod. xviii. 9.	3	Ps. xxxiii. 21.	12 d	Prov. xxix. 3.	12 g
Lev. xxiii. 40.	12 a	xxxv. 9.	10 d	xxix. 6.	12 k
Deut. xii. 7, 12, 18.	12 a	xxxv. 15.	12 a	xxxi. 25.	11 a
xiv. 26.	12 a	xxxv. 19, 24.	12 a	Eccles. ii. 10.	12 k
xvi. 11, 14.	12 a	xxxv. 26.	12 k	iii. 12.	12 d
xvi. 15. α	12 k	xxxviii. 16.	12 a	iii. 22.	12 d
xxvi. 11.	12 a	xl. 16.	10 d	iv. 16.	12 d
xxvii. 7.	12 a	xlv. 15.	1 d	v. 19.	12 b
xxviii. 63, 63.	10 a d	xlviii. 11.	12 d	xi. 8.	12 d
xxx. 9, β 9.	10 b a	li. 8.	1 c	xi. 9.	12 c
xxxii. 43.	9 d	liii. 6.	1 c	Cant. i. 4.	12 d
xxxiii. 18.	12 c	lviii. 10.	12 d	Isa. v. 14.	4 d
Judg. ix. 19, 19.	12 c d	lx. 6.	4 c	viii. 6.	10 f
xvi. 23.	12 l	lxiii. 7.	9 c	ix. 3.	1 c
xix. 3.	12 a	lxiii. 11.	12 d	xiii. 3.	12 a
1 Sam. ii. 1, 1.	6 a, 12 a	lxv. 8.	9 e	xiv. 8.	12 a
vi. 13.	12 d	lxv. 12.	2, 1 d	xiv. 29.	12 d
xi. 15.	12 d	lxvi. 6.	12 d	xxiii. 12. ζ	4 a
xix. 5.	12 d	lxviii. 3.	6 c	xxiv. 8.	4 e
2 Sam. i. 20.	12 d	lxviii. 3.	10 d, 12 l	xxv. 9.	12 d
1 Kings i. 40, 45.	12 k	lxviii. 4.	4 b	xxix. 19.	1 c
v. 7.	12 d	lxx. 4.	10 d	xxxv. 1, 2.	1 c
2 Kings ix. 14.	12 k	lxxi. 23.	9 c	xli. 16.	1 c
xi. 20.	12 d	lxxxv. 6.	12 d	lxi. 7.	9 a
1 Chron. xvi. 10.	12 d	lxxxvi. 4.	12 f	lxi. 10.	10 b d
xvi. 31.	1 c	lxxxix. 12.	9 c	lxii. 5, 5.	10 f d
xvi. 32.	6 c	lxxxix. 16.	1 c	lxiv. 5.	10 e
xxix. 9, 9.	12 d a	lxxxix. 42.	12 i	lxv. 13.	12 d
2 Chron. vi. 41.	12 d	xc. 14.	9 c	lxv. 18, 18.	1 b e
xv. 15.	12 d	xcvi. 11.	12 d	lxv. 19.	1 a
xx. 27.	12 e	xcvi. 12.	9 c	lxvi. 10, 10.	12 c, 10 c
xxiii. 13.	12 k	xcvii. 1, 8.	1 c	lxvi. 14.	10 a
xxiii. 18.	12 l	xcvii. 12.	12 c	Jer. xi. 15.	4 c
xxiii. 21.	12 d	xcviii. 4.	9 b	xv. 16.	12 l
xxiv. 10.	12 d	civ. 31.	12 d	xv. 17.	4 c
xxix. 36.	12 d	cv. 3.	12 d	xxxi. 13, 13.	12 d e
xxx. 25.	12 d	cvi. 5.	12 b	xxxii. 41.	10 a
Neh. xii. 43, 43, 43.	12 d e a	cvii. 22.	9 f	l. 11.	4 c
xii. 44. γ	12 l	cvii. 42.	12 d	li. 39.	4 c
Esth. viii. 15.	7	cviii. 7.	4 c	Lam. i. 17.	12 g
viii. 21.	5	cix. 28.	12 d	iv. 21.	10 c
Job iii. 22. δ	12 k	cxviii. 15.	9 f	Ezek. vii. 12.	12 d
xx. 18.	5	cxviii. 24.	1 c	xxv. 6.	12 d
xxi. 12.	12 d	cxix. 14.	10 a	xxxv. 14.	12 d
xxxi. 25, 29.	12 d	cxix. 111.	10 g	xxxv. 15.	12 l
xxxix. 21.	10 d	cxix. 162.	10 e	Hos. ix. 1.	12 d
Ps. ii. 11.	1 b	cxxvi. 6.	9 f	x. 5.	1 c
v. 11.	12 d	cxlix. 2.	12 d	Joel ii. 21, 23.	12 c
ix. 2.	6 c	Prov. ii. 14.	12 k	Amos vi. 13.	12 k
xiii. 4, 5.	1 c	v. 18.	12 d	Obad. 12.	12 d
xiv. 7.	1 c	viii. 30, 31.	11 b	Micah vii. 8.	12 d
xvi. 9.	1 c	xi. 10.	6 c	Hab. i. 15.	12 d
xix. 5.	10 d	xiii. 9.	12 d	iii. 14.	6 d
xix. 8.	12 h	xv. 30.	12 g	iii. 18.	4 c
xx. 5.	9 c	xxiii. 15.	12 d	Zeph. ii. 15.	4 e
xx. 1.	1 c	xxiii. 16.	4 c	iii. 11.	4 e
xxviii. 7.	4 c	xxiii. 24. ε	1 c d	iii. 14.	4 b
xxx. 1.	12 e	xxiii. 25.	1 c	iii. 17.	10 d
xxxi. 7.	12 d	xxiv. 17.	12 d	Zech. ii. 10.	12 c
xxxii. 11.	1 b	xxvii. 9.	12 g	iv. 10.	12 a
xxxiii. 1.	9 b	xxviii. 12.	12 d	ix. 9.	1 b
		xxix. 2.	12 d	x. 7, 7.	12 a, 1 c

a lit. thou shalt be joyful.   *β lit.* will return to rejoice.   *γ lit.* the joy of Judah.   *δ lit.* rejoicing unto gladness.   *ε lit.* shall rejoice joy.   *ζ lit.* add to rejoice.

RELEASE

הֲנָחָה *f.* permission of rest, rest, quietness: Esth. ii. 18.

שָׁמַט to strike, to throw down ; to let fall, let lie, to remit, release. KAL *inf.* Deut. xv. 2. HIPHIL *fut.* Deut. xv. 3. שְׁמִטָּה *f.* remission, release : Deut. xv. 1, 2, 2, 9 ; xxxi. 10.

RELIEVE

אָשַׁר to be right ; to righten. PIEL *imp.* Isa. i. 17, *marg.* 'righten,' *i. e.* restore the oppressed to that which is right and just. Lxx. ῥύσασθε ἀδικούμενον. Vulg. subvenite oppresso.

חָזַק to bind fast ; to make strong, strengthen. HIPHIL *pret.* Lev. xxv. 35.

עוּד see *Witness.* PILEL, to set up again, restore, confirm : *fut.* Ps. cxlvi. 9.

שׁוּב to return. HIPHIL *inf.* Lam. i. 11. *fut.* Lam. i. 19. *part.* Lam. i. 16.

RELY

שָׁעַן to lean upon, to rely upon, to trust in. NIPHAL *pret.* 2 Chron. xiii. 18 ; xvi. 7. *inf.* 2 Chron. xvi. 7, 8.

REMAIN

1 גּוּר to sojourn, to dwell for a time. KAL ᵃ*fut.* Judg. v. 17, *i. e.* why dwells he listless on the coasts of the sea ? as aptly Lxx., Vulg., Luth.

2 יוֹם *m.* day : Gen. viii. 22, *lit.* as yet all the days of the earth.

3 יָצֵב to set, put, place ; to set or place oneself, to take a stand. HITHPAEL *inf.*

4 יָנַח to leave ; to let remain. HIPHIL *pret.*

5 יָשַׁב to sit ; to remain, abide, tarry. KAL ᵃ*pret.* ᵇ*inf.* ᶜ*imp.* ᵈ*fut.* ᵉ*part* Poel.

6 יָשֵׁן to be old ; of one who has dwelt long in a country. NIPHAL *pret.*

7 יָתַר to be abundant ; to remain. NIPHAL ᵃ*pret.* ᵇ*fut.* ᶜ*part.* HIPHIL ᵈ*fut.*

8 לִין to pass the night ; to abide, remain, dwell. KAL ᵃ*pret.* ᵇ*fut.*

9 נוּח to rest ; to set oneself down, to settle down in any place for rest. KAL *fut.*

10 עָדַף to be redundant, abundant, either in number or quantity ; of garments. KAL *part.* Poel.

11 עָמַד to stand, to continue, to remain. KAL ᵃ*pret.* ᵇ*inf.* ᶜ*fut.* ᵈ*part.* Poel.

12 קוּם to rise up ; to set oneself, to stand. KAL *pret.*

13 שָׁאַר to be abundant, redundant ; to be left over, to remain. KAL ᵃ*pret.* NIPHAL ᵇ*pret.* ᶜ*fut.* ᵈ*part.* ᵉ שְׁאֵרִית *f.* remaining part : Ps. lxxvi. 10, the remainder of wrath thou didst gird on, *comp.* Deut. xxxii. 23 : the remainder of wrath here is God's extreme wrath, reserved for extreme cases, opposed to the less degree of wrath manifested on less aggravated occasions.

14 שָׁכַן to settle down ; to abide, dwell. KAL ᵃ*inf.* ᵇ*fut.* ᶜ*part.* Poel. HIPHIL ᵈ*pret.*

15 שָׁקַד to watch. KAL *fut.*

16 שָׂרַד to flee, to escape ; to remain or be left after a common slaughter, or any destruction. KAL ᵃ*pret.* ᵇ שָׂרִיד *m.*

Gen. vii. 23.	13 c	Num. xi. 26.	13 c	Josh. xxiii. 4, 7, 12.	13 d		
viii. 22.	2	xxiv. 19.	16 b	Judg. v. 13.	16 b		
xiv. 10.	13 d	xxxiii. 55.	7 d	v. 17.	1		
xxxviii. 11.	5 c	xxxv. 28.	5 d	vii. 3.	13 b		
Exod. viii. 9, 11.	13 c	Deut. ii. 34.	16 b	xxi. 7, 16.	7 c		
viii. 31.	13 b	iii. 3.	16 b	1 Sam. xi. 11.	13 d		
x. 5.	13 d	iii. 11.	13 b	xvi. 11.	13 a		
x. 15.	7 a	iv. 25.	6	xx. 19.	5 a		
x. 19.	13 b	xvi. 4.	8 b	xxiii. 14.	5 a		
xii. 10, 10.	7 d c	xix. 20.	13 d	xxiv. 3.	5 e		
xiv. 28.	13 b	xxi. 13.	5 a	2 Sam. xiii. 20.	5 d		
xvi. 23.	10	xxi. 23.	8 b	xiv. 7.	13 e		
xxiii. 18.	8 b	Josh. i. 14.	5 d	xiv. 5.	3		
xxvi. 12, 12, 13.	10	i. 11.	12	1 Kings xi. 16.	5 a		
xxix. 34, 34.	7 b c	viii. 11.	16 b	xviii. 22.	7 a		
Lev. vi. 16.	7 c	x. 20.	16 a	xxii. 46.	13 b		
vii. 16, 17.	7 c	x. 28, 30, 33, 37, 39,		2 Kings viii. 13.	13 d		
viii. 32.	7 c	40.	16 b	x. 11, 11.	13 d, 16 b		
x. 12.	7 c	xi. 8.	16 b	x. 17.	13 d		
xvi. 16.	14 c	xi. 22.	13 b	xiii. 6.	11 a		
xix. 6.	7 c	xiii. 1, 12.	13 b	xxiv. 14.	13 b		
xxv. 52.	13 b	xiii. 2.	13 d	xxv. 22.	13 d		
xxvii. 18.	7 c	xviii. 2.	7 b	1 Chron. xiii. 14.	5 d		
Num. ix. 22.	14 a	xxi. 20, 26, 40.	7 c	Ezra i. 4.	13 d		

Ezra ix. 15.	13 b	Jer. xvii. 25.	5 a	Jer. li. 62.	5 e
Job xviii. 19.	16 b	xxiv. 8.	13 d	lii. 15.	13 b
xix. 4.	8 b	xxvii. 11.	4	Lam. ii. 22.	16 b
xxi. 32.	15	xxvii. 19, 21.	7 c	v. 19.	5 d
xxi. 34.	13 b	xxx. 18.	5 d	Ezek. iii. 15.	5 d
xxvii. 15.	16 b	xxxiv. 7.	13 b	vi. 12.	13 d
xxxvii. 8.	14 b	xxxvii. 10.	13 b	xvii. 21.	13 d
xli. 22.	8 b	xxxvii. 16, 21.	5 d	xxxi. 13.	14 b
Ps. lv. 7.	8 b	xxxviii. 2.	5 e	xxxii. 4.	14 d
lxxvi. 10.	13 e	xxxviii. 4.	13 d	xxxix. 14.	7 c
Prov. ii. 21.	7 b	xxxviii. 13.	5 d	Dan. x. 8.	13 b
xxi. 16.	9	xxxix. 9, 9.	13 d	x. 13.	7 a
Eccles. ii. 9.	11 a	xli. 10.	13 d	x. 17.	11 c
Isa. iv. 3.	7 c	xlii. 17.	16 b	Amos vi. 9.	7 b
x. 32.	11 b	xliv. 7. α	13 e	Obad. 14, 18.	16 b
xxxii. 16.	5 d	xliv. 14.	16 b	Hag. ii. 5.	11 d
xliv. 13.	5 b	xlvii. 4.	16 b	Zech. v. 4.	8 a
lxv. 4.	5 e	xlviii. 11.	11 a	ix. 7.	13 b
lxvi. 22, 22.	11 d c	li. 30.	5 a	xii. 14.	13 d
Jer. viii. 3, 3.	13 d				

ᵃ *lit.* no remnant.

REMEDY

מַרְפֵּא *m.* healing ; cure of diseases, means of cure ; help, deliverance from calamity : 2 Chron. xxxvi. 16 : Prov. vi. 15 ; xxix. 1.

REMEMBER

1 זָכַר to remember, to recollect, to call to mind ; mostly with an accusative, more rarely with לְ and בְּ ; with a dative of the person and an accusative of the thing. to or for any one, *i. e.* to bear it in mind either to his advantage or disadvantage ; *e. g.* for good, Neh. v. 19 ; for evil, Neh. vi. 14 ; xiii. 29 ; to mention, to make mention of ; it has also respect to things future, as the Latin phrases, *respice finem*, *memento mori* : Lam. i. 9 : Isa. xlvii. 7 : Eccles. xi. 8. It connotes frequently the affection of the mind and the action which accompanies recollection ; to remember by actual celebration, to commemorate, as applied to the sabbath, &c. KAL ᵃ*pret.* ᵇ*inf.* ᶜ*imp.* ᵈ*fut.* ᵉ*part.* Poel. ᶠ*part.* Paül. NIPHAL ᵍ*pret.* ʰ*inf.* ⁱ*fut.* ᵏ*part.* HIPHIL ˡ*inf.* ᵐ*imp.* ⁿ*fut.* ᵒ*part.* ᵖ זֵכֶר *m.* remembrance, memory. ᵠ זִכָּרוֹן *m.* memorial, in Job xiii. 12, perhaps memorable saying.

2 פָּקַד to go to see, to visit, to call to remembrance. KAL ᵃ*pret.* ᵇ*fut.*

Gen. viii. 1.	1 d	Deut. xxv. 17.	1 b	Job xiv. 13.	1 d
ix. 15.	1 a	xxv. 19.	1 p	xviii. 17.	1 p
ix. 16.	1 b	xxxii. 7.	1 c	xxi. 6.	1 a
xix. 29.	1 d	xxxii. 26.	1 p	xxiv. 20.	1 i
xxx. 22.	1 d	Josh. i. 13.	1 b	xxxvi. 24.	1 c
xl. 23.	1 a	Judg. viii. 34.	1 a	xli. 8.	1 c
xli. 9.	1 o	ix. 2.	1 a	Ps. vi. 5.	1 p
xiii. 9.	1 d	xvi. 28.	1 d	ix. 12.	1 a
Exod. ii. 24.	1 d	1 Sam. i. 11.	1 a	xx. 3.	1 d
vi. 5.	1 d	i. 19.	1 d	xx. 7.	1 n
xiii. 3.	1 b	vv. 2.	2 a	xxii. 27.	1 d
xvii. 14.	1 p	xxv. 31.	1 a	xxv. 6.	1 c
xxxii. 13.	1 c	2 Sam. xiv. 11.	1 l	xxv. 7, 7.	1 d c
Lev. xxvi. 42, 42,		xviii. 18.	1 l	xxx. 4.	1 p
42.	1 a d d	xix. 19.	1 d	xxxiv. 16.	1 p
xxvi. 45.	1 a	1 Kings xvii. 18.	1 l	xxxviii. title.	1 l
Num. v. 15.	1 o	2 Kings ix. 25.	1 c	xlii. 4, 6.	1 d
x. 9.	1 g	xx. 3.	1 c	xlv. 17.	1 n
xi. 5.	1 a	1 Chron. xvi. 12.	1 c	lxiii. 6.	1 a
xv. 39.	1 a	2 Chron. vi. 42.	1 c	lxx. title.	1 c
v. 40.	1 a	xxiv. 22.	1 a	lxxiv. 2, 18, 22.	1 c
Deut. v. 15.	1 a	Neh. i. 8.	1 c	lxxvii. 3, 6, 11, 11.	1 d
vii. 18.	1 b d	iv. 14.	1 c	lxxviii. 35, 39.	1 d
viii. 2, 18.	1 a	xiii. 14, 22, 29, 31.	1 c	lxxviii. 42.	1 c
ix. 7, 27.	1 c	Esth. ii. 1.	1 a	lxxix. 8.	1 d
xv. 15.	1 a	ix. 28.	1 k	lxxxiii. 4.	1 l
xvi. 3.	1 d	Job iv. 7.	1 c	lxxxviii. 5. α	1 a
xvi. 12.	1 c	vii. 7.	1 l	lxxxix. 47, 50.	1 c
xxiv. 9.	1 b	x. 9.	1 a	xcvii. 12. β	1 p
xxiv. 18, 22.	1 a	xi. 16.	1 d	xcviii. 3.	1 a
		xiii. 12.	1 q	cii. 12.	1 p

Ps. ciii. 14.	1 f	Isa. xxxviii. 3.	1 c	Lam. v. 1.	1 c
ciii. 18.	1 e	xliii. 18, 25.	1 d	Ezek. iii. 20.	1 i
cv. 5.	1 c	xliii. 26.	1 m	iv. 9.	1 a
cv. 8, 42.	1 a	xliv. 21.	1 a	xvi. 22, 43, 60, 61.	1 a
cvi. 4.	1 c	xlvi. 8, 9.	1 c	xvi. 63.	1 d
cvi. 7.	1 a	xlvii. 7.	1 a	xx. 43.	1 a
cvi. 45.	1 d	liv. 4.	1 d	xxi. 23.	1 c
cix. 14.	1 i	lvii. 8.	1 q	xxi. 24, 24.	1 1 h
cix. 16.	1 a	lviii. 11.	1 d	xxi. 32.	1 i
cxi. 4. γ	1 p	lxiii. 11.	1 d	xxiii. 19.	1 b
cxii. 6.	1 p	lxiv. 5, 9.	1 d	xxiii. 22.	2 b
cxix. 49.	1 c	lxv. 17.	1 i	xxiii. 27.	1 d
cxix. 52, 55.	1 a	Jer. ii. 2.	1 a	xxv. 10.	1 n
cxxxii. 1.	1 c	iii. 16.	1 d	xxix. 16.	1 o
cxxxvi. 23.	1 a	xi. 19.	1 i	xxxiii. 13.	1 a
cxxxvii. 1.	1 b	xiv. 10.	1 d	xxxvi. 31.	1 a
cxxxvii. 6.	1 d	xiv. 21.	1 a	Hos. iii. 17.	1 i
cxxxvii. 7.	1 c	xv. 15.	1 c	vii. 2.	1 a
cxliii. 5.	1 a	xvii. 2.	1 b	viii. 13.	1 d
Prov. xxxi. 7.	1 d	xviii. 20.	1 c	ix. 9.	1 d
Eccles. i. 11, 11.	1 q	xxxi. 20.	1 b d	Amos i. 8.	1 a
ii. 16.	1 q	xxxi. 34.	1 d	Jonah ii. 7.	1 a
v. 20.	1 q	xliv. 21.	1 a	Micah vi. 5.	1 c
ix. 15.	1 a	li. 50.	1 c	Hab. iii. 2.	1 d
xi. 8.	1 d	Lam. i. 7, 9.	1 a	Zech. x. 9.	1 d
xii. 1.	1 c	ii. 1.	1 a	xiii. 2.	1 i
Cant. i. 4.	1 n	iii. 19.	1 c	Mal. iii. 16.	1 q
Isa. xxiii. 16.	1 i	iii. 20.	1 b d	iv. 4.	1 c
xxvi. 8.	1 p				

a lit. rememberest them.   *β lit.* to the memorial.
γ lit. a memorial for his, &c.

REMNANT

1   אַחַר   after ; posterity. ᵃ אַחֲרִית *f.* end, uttermost part.

2   יָתַר   see *Remain*. NIPHAL ᵃ *part.* HIPHIL ᵇ *pret.*, to leave a remnant. ᶜ יֶתֶר *m.* remainder, rest, residue.

3   סֶרַח   *m.* redundant, superfluous, remainder.

4   פְּלֵיטָה   *f.* see *Escape.*

5   שָׁאַר   see *Remain*. NIPHAL ᵃ *part.* HIPHIL ᵇ *inf.*, to "leave a remnant." ᶜ שְׁאָר *m.* rest, residue. ᵈ שְׁאֵרִית *f.* remaining part : 2 Kings xix. 4, &c.

6   שָׂרִיד   *m.* see *Remain.*

7   שָׁרָה   to loose, to let go free. PIEL *pret.*, *lit.* I make thee free for good, קרי.

8   שֵׁרוּת   *f.* remnant : Jer. xv. 11, כתיב.

No. 5 d not included.

Exod. xxvi. 12.	3	2 Kings xxv. 11.	2 c	Isa. xvii. 3.	5 c
Lev. ii. 3.	2 a	1 Chron. vi. 70.	2 a	xxxvii. 31.	5 a
xiv. 18.	2 a	2 Chron. xxx. 6.	5 a	Jer. xv. 11.	7, or 8
Deut. iii. 11.	2 c	Ezra iii. 8.	5 c	xxxix. 9.	2 c
xxviii. 54.	2 c	ix. 8.	5 b	Ezek. vi. 8.	2 b
Josh. xii. 4.	2 c	Neh. i. 3.	5 a	xiv. 22.	4
xiii. 12.	2 c	Job xxii. 20.	2 c	xxiii. 25.	1 a
xxiii. 12.	2 c	Isa. i. 9.	6	Joel ii. 32.	6
2 Sam. xxi. 2.	2 c	x. 20, 21, 21, 22.	5 c	Micah v. 3.	2 c
1 Kings xii. 23.	2 c	xi. 11, 16.	5 c	Hab. ii. 8.	2 c
xiv. 10.	1	xiv. 22.	5 a	Zeph. i. 4.	5 c
xxii. 46.	5 a	xvi. 14.	5 c	ii. 9.	2 c
2 Kings xix. 30. *a*	5 a				

a marg. 'the escaping that remaineth.'

REMOVE

1   גָּלָה   the general meaning is to uncover, from what primary sense is uncertain. Vitringa, on Isa. xxxviii. 12, thinks the word properly means, to clear away, to roll away, and hence the force of the figure, " removed as a tent," when in haste and fear the canvas is suddenly rolled up and cleared away, which may be done in a very short space of time. If the primary meaning be, to be bare, uncovered, it will equally apply to the cases in which it is translated "removed," conveying the idea of a country cleared of its inhabitants. KAL ᵃ *pret.* ᵇ *imp.* NIPHAL ᶜ *pret.* HIPHIL ᵈ *pret.* ᵉ *fut.* ᶠ גּוֹלָה *f.* captivity, a removing into.

2   גָּלַל   to roll, *seq.* מֵעַל to roll off or away from one. KAL *imp.*

3   זְוָעָה   *f.* agitation, *i. e.* disquiet, maltreatment ; see *Vex* ; כתיב, *marg.* 'for removing, or vexation.' ᵃ זַעֲוָה *f.* by transposition for זְוָעָה.

4   זָנַח   to cast off ; see *Cast; seq.* מִן to thrust away, to repulse from. KAL *fut.* Lam. iii. 17, thou hast thrust me far away from peace or prosperity, hast destroyed my welfare.

5   יָנָה   to be separated, apart. HIPHIL *pret.*

6   כָּנַף   to cover, to protect. NIPHAL *fut.* Isa. xxx. 20, shall no longer hide themselves, *i. e.* they shall come forth openly, and no longer be vexed by persecutors.

7   מוֹט   to waver, to shake, to totter ; see *Move*. KAL ᵃ *fut.* NIPHAL ᵇ *fut.*

8   מוּר   to change, to perish. HIPHIL *inf.*

9   מוּשׁ   to give way, recede, depart. KAL ᵃ *pret.* ᵇ *fut.* HIPHIL ᶜ *fut.*

10   נָדַד   to shake as a bird its wings ; to flee away. KAL *pret.*

11   נִדָּה   *f.* (see *Separation*) : Ezek. vii. 19 ; xxxvi. 17, "a removed woman."

12   נוּד   to be moved, to wander. KAL ᵃ *pret.* ᵇ *imp.* ᶜ *fut.* HIPHIL ᵈ *fut.* HITHPOLEL ᵉ *pret.* ᶠ נִידָה *f.* exile.

13   נוּעַ   to waver, to reel ; to wander about, to remove in a confused and hurried manner ; used of mental and bodily disturbance or agitation, as in Exod. xx. 18 ; since they were already far off. KAL *fut.*

14   נָסַג   to remove a thing out of the place where it has long been, or where of right it ought to be. HIPHIL ᵃ *fut.* ᵇ *part.*

15   נָסַע   to pull up, out, away, *e. g.* a peg or pin from the wall, Judg. xvi. 14 ; the posts of a gate, 3 ; oftener the tent-pins or stakes, in order to take down a tent for removing ; hence to remove, journey, migrate. KAL ᵃ *pret.* ᵇ *inf.* ᶜ *fut.* HIPHIL ᵈ *fut.* ᵉ *part.*

16   נָשַׂג   to reach, to extend to. HIPHIL *fut.* Job xxiv. 2, or שׁ is put for ס, and the root סוג to draw back.

17   סָבַב   to turn, to go about. NIPHAL ᵃ *fut.* HIPHIL ᵇ *fut.*

18   סוּר   to go off, turn away or aside, to depart. KAL ᵃ *pret.* ᵇ *fut.* ᶜ *part.* Paül. HIPHIL ᵈ *pret.* ᵉ *inf.* ᶠ *imp.* ᵍ *fut.* ʰ *part.*

19   סוּת   to excite, instigate, *seq.* מִן to entice away from a person or place. HIPHIL *pret.* Job xxxvi. 16, *i. e.* would have led thee away persuasively out of the strait.

20   עָבַר   to pass over. HIPHIL *pret.*

21   עֲדָה   Ch. to pass. APHEL *part.*

22   עָתַק   to be taken away, removed ; to grow old. KAL ᵃ *fut.* HIPHIL ᵇ *fut.* ᶜ *part.*

23   רָעַשׁ   to tremble, to quake ; to move with quickness and rapidity. KAL *fut.*

24   רָחַק   to be far ; to remove far. KAL ᵃ *fut.* PIEL ᵇ *pret.* HIPHIL ᶜ *pret.* ᵈ *inf.* ᵉ *imp.* ᶠ *fut.*

Gen. viii. 13.	18 g	Gen. xxx. 35.	18 g	Exod. xiv. 19.	15 c
xii. 8.	22 b	xlvii. 21.	20	xx. 18.	13
xxvi. 22.	22 b	xlviii. 17.	18 e	Num. xii. 16.	15 a
xxx. 32.	18 e	Exod. viii. 31.	18 g	xxi. 12, 13.	15 a

Num. xxxiii. 5, 7, 9, 10, 11, 14, 16, 21, 24, 25, 26, 28, 32, 34, 36, 37, 46, 47.	15 c
xxxvi. 7, 9.	17 a
Deut. xix. 14.	14 a
xxvii. 17.	14 b
xxviii. 25.	3 a
Josh. iii. 1, 3.	15 c
iii. 14.	15 b
Judg. ix. 29.	18 g
1 Sam. vi. 3.	18 b
xviii. 13.	18 g
2 Sam. vi. 10.	18 e
xx. 12.	17 b
xx. 13.	5
1 Kings xv. 12, 13.	18 g
xv. 14.	18 a
2 Kings xv. 4, 35.	18 a
xvi. 17.	18 g
xvii. 18.	18 g
xvii. 23.	18 d
xvii. 26.	1 d
xviii. 4.	18 e
xviii. 27, 27.	18 d g
xxiv. 3.	18 e
1 Chron. viii. 6.	1 e
viii. 7.	1 d
2 Chron. xv. 16.	18 d
xxxiii. 8.	18 e
xxxv. 12.	18 g
Job ix. 5.	22 c
xii. 20.	18 h

Job xiv. 18.	22 a
xviii. 4.	22 a
xix. 10.	15 d
xxiv. 2.	16
xxvii. 5.	18 g
xxxvi. 16.	19
Ps. xxxvi. 11.	12 d
xxxix. 10.	18 f
xlvi. 2.	8
lxxxi. 6.	18 d
ciii. 12.	24 c
civ. 5.	7 b
cxix. 22.	2
cxix. 29.	18 f
cxxv. 1.	7 b
Prov. iv. 27.	18 f
v. 8.	24 e
x. 30.	7 b
xxi. 28.	14 a
xxiii. 10.	14 a
xxx. 8.	24 e
Eccles. x. 9.	15 e
xi. 10.	18 f
Isa. viii. 12.	24 b
x. 13.	18 g
xiii. 13.	23
xxii. 15.	9 b
xxiv. 20.	12 e
xxvi. 15.	24 b
xxix. 13.	24 b
xxx. 20.	6

Isa. xxxiii. 20.	15 c
xxxviii. 12.	1 c
xlvi. 7.	9 c
xlix. 21.	18 c
liv. 10, 10.	7 a
Jer. iv. 1.	12 c
xv. 4.	3, or 3 a
xvi. 9.	3, or 3 a
xxvii. 10.	24 d
xxxv. 18.	3, or 3 a
xxxii. 31.	18 e
xxxiv. 17.	3, or 3 a
l. 3.	12 a
l. 8.	12 b
Lam. i. 8.	12 f
iii. 17.	4
Ezek. vii. 19.	11
ix. 3, 3, 3.	1 f b a
xii. 4, 11. a	1 f
xxi. 26.	18 f
xxiii. 46.	3 a
xxxvi. 17.	11
xlv. 9.	18 f
Dan. ii. 21.	21
Hos. v. 10.	14 b
ix. 3.	10
Joel iii. 4.	24 f
iii. 6.	24 c
Amos vi. 7.	18 a
Micah ii. 3, 4.	9 c
vii. 11.	24 a
Zech. iii. 9.	9 a
xiv. 4.	9 a

a lit. in removing go into captivity.

REND, RENT

1 בָּקַע to cleave asunder, to rend, to divide; to rend a city, *i.e.* to break open its walls, to take by storm; the earth is rent when it is violently shaken. KAL ^a *pret.* NIPHAL ^b *pret.* ^c *inf.* ^d *fut.* PIEL ^e *pret.* ^f *fut.* PUAL ^g *part.* HITHPAEL ^h *pret.*

2 טָרַף to tear in pieces. KAL ^a *inf.* POAL ^b *pret.*

3 נִקְפָּה *f.* (see *Cut*), round: Isa. iii. 24, perhaps *lit.* a rope, bound round a female slave or captive, instead of a girdle or zone. LXX. σχοινίον. Vulg. *funiculus.*

4 פָּרַם to rend garments. KAL ^a *fut.* ^b *part.* Paül.

5 פָּרַק to break off by violent rending, as a strong wind the mountains; to break or rend in pieces. KAL ^a *part.* Poel. PIEL ^b *part.*

6 קָרַע to rend, to rend asunder. KAL ^a *pret.* ^b *inf.* ^c *imp.* ^d *fut.* ^e *part.* Poel. ^f *part.* Paül. NIPHAL ^g *pret.* ^h *fut.*

7 שָׁסַע to cleave, split, divide; so as that the parts torn are not totally separated. PIEL ^a *inf.* ^b *fut.*

Gen. xxxvii. 29, 34.	6 d
xxxvii. 33. a	2 a b
xliv. 13.	6 d
Exod. xxviii. 32.	6 h
xxxix. 23.	6 h
Lev. x. 6.	4 a
xiii. 45.	4 b
xiii. 56.	6 a
xxi. 10.	4 a
Num. xiv. 6.	6 a
Josh. vii. 6.	6 d
ix. 4.	1 g
ix. 13.	1 h
Judg. xi. 35.	6 d
xiv. 6, 6.	7 b a
1 Sam. iv. 12.	6 f
xv. 27.	6 h
xv. 28.	6 a
xxviii. 17.	6 d
2 Sam. i. 2.	6 f
i. 11.	6 d
iii. 31.	6 c

2 Sam. xiii. 19.	6 a
xiii. 31.	6 f
xv. 32.	6 f
1 Kings i. 40.	1 d
xi. 11.	6 b d
xi. 12, 13, 30.	6 d
xi. 31.	6 e
xiii. 3, 5.	6 g
xiv. 8.	6 d
xix. 11.	5 b
xxi. 27.	6 d
2 Kings ii. 12.	6 d
v. 7.	6 d
v. 8, 8.	6 a
vi. 30.	6 d
xi. 14.	6 d
xvii. 21.	6 a
xviii. 37.	6 d
xix. 1.	6 d
xxii. 11, 19.	6 d
2 Chron. xxiii. 13.	6 d
xxxiv. 19, 27.	6 d

Ezra ix. 3.	6 a
ix. 5.	6 b
Esth. iv. 1.	6 d
Job i. 20.	6 d
ii. 12.	6 d
xxvi. 8.	1 b
Ps. vii. 2.	5 a
Eccles. iii. 7.	6 b
Isa. iii. 24.	3
xxxvi. 22.	6 f
xxxvii. 1.	6 d
lxiv. 1.	6 a
Jer. iv. 30.	6 d
xxxvi. 24.	6 a
xli. 5.	6 f
Ezek. xiii. 11.	1 f
xiii. 13.	1 e
xxix. 7.	2
xxx. 16. β	1 c
Hos. xiii. 8.	6 d
Joel ii. 13.	6 c

a lit. in rending is rent in pieces.   β *lit.* to be rent.

RENDER

1 נָתַן to give. KAL *pret.*

2 שׁוּב to return; to cause to return. KAL ^a *fut.* HIPHIL ^b *pret.* ^c *inf.* ^d *imp.* ^e *fut.* ^f *part.*

3 שָׁלַם to be whole, sound, safe; Piel, to make good, to requite, restore. PIEL ^a *pret.* ^b *fut.* ^c *part.*

Num. xviii. 9.	2 e	Ps. xxviii. 4.	2 d	Prov. xxvi. 16.	2 f
Deut. xxxii. 41, 43.	2 e	xxxviii. 20.	3 c	Isa. lxvi. 6.	3 c
Judg. ix. 56.	2 e	lvi. 12.	3 b	lxvi. 15.	3 c
ix. 57.	2 b	lxii. 12.	3 b	Jer. li. 6.	3 a
1 Sam. xxvi. 23.	2 e	lxxix. 12.	2 d	li. 24.	3 a
2 Kings iii. 4.	2 b	xciv. 2.	2 d	Lam. iii. 64.	2 e
2 Chron. vi. 30.	1	cxvi. 12.	2 e	Hos. xiv. 2.	3 b
xxxii. 25.	2 b	Prov. xii. 14.	2 e, or a	Joel iii. 4.	3 c
Job xxxiii. 26.	2 b	xxiv. 12.	2 b	Zech. ix. 12.	2 e
xxxiv. 11.	3 b	xxiv. 29.	2 e		

RENEW

חָדַשׁ to be new; to make anew, repair, restore. PIEL *imp.* Ps. li. 10: Lam. v. 21. *fut.* 1 Sam. xi. 14: 2 Chron. xv. 8: Job x. 17: Ps. civ. 30. HITHPAEL *fut.* Ps. ciii. 5.

חָלַף to pass; to pass from one state to another, to change; to renew. HIPHIL *fut.* Job xxix. 20: Isa. xl. 31; xli. 1.

RENOWN

שֵׁם *m.* name: Gen. vi. 4: Num. xvi. 2: Ezek. xvi. 14, 15; xxxiv. 29; xxxix. 13: Dan. ix. 15.

הָלַל see *Praise.* PUAL *part.* Ezek. xxvi. 17.

קָרָא to call; to publish; a published person is one that is renowned or of eminent character. KAL *part.* Paül, Num. i. 16: Ezek. xxiii. 23. NIPHAL *fut.* Isa. xiv. 20. קָרִיא *m.* called, chosen: Num. i. 16, כתיב קריא.

REPAIR

1 בָּדַק to repair a breach. KAL *inf.*

2 בָּנָה to build or repair a house or town. KAL *fut.*

3 גָּדַר to fence. KAL *part.* Poel.

4 חָדַשׁ to be new; to make anew, to restore. PIEL ^a *pret.* ^b *inf.*

5 חָזַק to bind fast, to make firm, strong, strengthen. PIEL ^a *pret.* ^b *inf.* ^c *fut.* ^d *part.* HIPHIL ^e *pret.* ^f חָזְקָה *f. a* strengthening, repairing.

6 חָיָה to live; to make to live, revive. PIEL *fut.*

7 יְסוֹד *m.* foundation.

8 סָגַר to shut, to close. KAL *pret.*

9 עָמַד to stand; to make to stand. HIPHIL *inf.*

10 רָפָא to heal. PIEL *fut.*

Judg. xxi. 23.	2	2 Chron. xxiv. 4, 12.	4 b	Neh. iii. 4, 4, 4, 5, 6, 7, 8, 8, 9, 10, 10, 11, 12, 13, 14, 15, 16, 17, 17, 18, 20, 21, 22, 23, 23, 24, 27, 28, 29, 29, 30, 30, 31, 32.	5 e
1 Kings xi. 27.	8	xxiv. 5.	5 b	iii. 19.	5 c
xviii. 30.	10	xxiv. 27.	7	Isa. lviii. 12.	3
2 Kings xii. 5.	5 c	xxix. 3.	5 c	lxi. 4.	4 a
vi. 14.	5 a	xxxii. 5.	5 c		
xii. 7.	5 d	xxxiii. 16.	5 d		
xii. 8.	5 b	xxxiv. 4.	2		
xii. 12, 12.	5 b f	xxxiv. 10.	5 b		
xxii. 5, 6.	5 b	Ezra ix. 9.	9		
1 Chron. xi. 8.	6				

REPAY

שָׁלַם to be whole; to make whole, to make good; to requite,

to recompense. PIEL *fut.* Deut. vii. 10 : Job xxi. 31 ; xli. 11 : Prov. xiii. 21 : Isa. lix. 18, 18. *part.* Deut. vii. 10.

REPEAT

שָׁנָה to do again, the second time. KAL *part.* Poel, Prov. xvii. 9.

REPENT

1   נָחַם Niphal, in regard to others, to pity, to have compassion, *abs. seq.* עַל, אֶל, מִן ; in regard to one's own doings, to lament, grieve ; hence to repent, English, to rue ; often of one who repents, grieves, for the evil he has brought upon another, *seq.* עַל and אֶל. NIPHAL [a] *pret.* [b] *inf.* [c] *imp.* [d] *fut.* [e] *part.* HITHPAEL [f] *fut.* [g] נֹחַם *m.* repentance. [h] נְחוּמִים *m. pl.* pity, mercy.

2   שׁוּב to return, to turn again. KAL [a] *pret.* [b] *imp.*

Gen. vi. 6.		1 d	1 Chron. xxi. 15.	1 d	Jer. xlii. 10.		1 a
vi. 7.		1 a	Job xlii. 6.	1 a	Ezek. xiv. 6.		2 b
Exod. xiii. 17.		1 d	Ps. xc. 13.	1 c	xviii. 30.		2 b
xxxii. 12.		1 c	cvi. 45.	1 d	xxiv. 14.		1 d
xxxii. 14.		1 d	cx. 4.	1 d	Hos. xi. 8.		1 h
Num. xxiii. 19.		1 f	cxxxv. 14.	1 f	xiii. 14.		1 g
Deut. xxxii. 36.		1 f	Jer. iv. 28.	1 d	Joel ii. 13.		1 a
Judg. ii. 18.		1 d	viii. 6.	1 e	ii. 14.		1 a
xxi. 6.		1 d	xv. 6. α	1 a	Amos vii. 3, 6.		1 a
xxi. 15.		1 e	xviii. 8, 10.	1 a	Jonah iii. 9.		1 a
1 Sam. xv. 11, 35.		1 a	xx. 16.	1 a	iii. 10.		1 d
xv. 29, 29.	1 d b		xxvi. 3.	1 a	iv. 2.		1 e
2 Sam. xxiv. 16.		1 d	xxvi. 13, 19.	1 a	Zech. viii. 14.		1 a
1 Kings viii. 47.		2 a	xxxi. 19.	1 a			

a or, I am weary of having compassion.

REPHAIM

רְפָאִים *m.* an ancient Canaanitish tribe beyond Jordan, celebrated for their gigantic stature : Gen. xiv. 5 ; xv. 20 : 2 Sam. v. 18, 22 ; xxiii. 13 : 1 Chron. xi. 15 ; xiv. 9 : Isa. xvii. 5.

REPLENISH

מָלֵא to fill ; to be filled. KAL *pret.* Isa. ii. 6. *imp.* Gen. i. 28 ; ix. 1. NIPHAL *fut.* Ezek. xxvi. 2 ; xxvii. 25. PIEL *pret.* Isa. xxiii. 2 : Jer. xxxi. 25.

REPORT

1   אָמַר to say, &c. KAL [a] *inf.* [b] *part.* Poel.

2   דִּבָּה *f.* slander, an evil report ; the genitive which follows is either active, *i. e.* of the slanderer, or passive, *i. e.* of the person or things slandered.

3   דָּבָר *m.* word ; thing, matter, properly, thing spoken of.

4   נָגַד to show, to tell, to declare, to announce. HIPHIL [a] *imp.* [b] *fut.*

5   שׁוּב to return. HIPHIL *part.*

6   שֵׁם *m.* name.

7   שָׁמַע to hear. NIPHAL [a] *pret.* [b] *fut.* [c] שֵׁמַע *m.* fame, rumour, report. [d] שְׁמוּעָה *f.* message, tidings ; instruction, doctrine.

Gen. xxxvii. 2.		2	2 Chron. ix. 5.	3	Isa. xxiii. 5, 5.	7 c
Exod. xxiii. 1.	7 c		Neh. vi. 6.	7 a	xxviii. 19.	7 d
Num. xiii. 32.		2	vi. 7.	7 b	liii. 1.	7 d
xiv. 37.		2	vi. 13.	6	Jer. xx. 10, 10.	4 a b
Deut. ii. 25.	7 c		vi. 19.	1 b	l. 43.	7 c
1 Sam. ii. 24.	7 d		Esth. i. 17.	1 a	Ezek. ix. 11.	5
1 Kings x. 6.		3	Prov. xv. 30.	7 d		

REPROACH

1   גָּדַף to blaspheme ; to revile ; words beginning with גד imply more or less to cut, and it gives a peculiar meaning to this root of cutting and insolent revilings ; the verb is always used of blasphemy against God. PIEL [a] *part.* [b] גִּדּוּף *m.* reproaches.

2   דָּבָר *m.* word, matter, thing.

3   חֶסֶד *m.* zeal towards any one, kindness, &c. ; it is used also in a bad sense, zeal against any one, envy, &c., hence odium, reproach, disgrace.

4   חָפֵר to be ashamed, confounded. HIPHIL *part.*

5   חָרַף to pluck or strip off ; to disparage, to vilify a man's character, reputation, honour ; to reproach, to rail on, blaspheme. KAL [a] *fut.* [b] *part.* Poel. PIEL [c] *pret.* [d] *inf.* [e] *fut.* [f] *part.* [g] חֶרְפָּה *f.* reproach, as it respects the subject, the agent, or the matter of reproach : Ps. xxxix. 8 and Josh. v. 9 must be taken in reference to the agent. Gen. xxx. 23, &c., "a reproach," frequently *lit.* for a reproach.

6   כָּלַם to be ashamed, disgraced, dishonoured. HIPHIL [a] *fut.* [b] כְּלִמָּה *f.* shame, reproach.

7   קָלוֹן *m.* contempt, shame, dishonour ; reproach in words.

No. 5 g not included.

Num. xv. 30.	1 a	Ps. lvii. 3.	5 c	Prov. xiv. 34.		3
Ruth ii. 15.	6 a	lxix. 9.	5 b	xvii. 5.		5 c
2 Kings xix. 4, 16.	5 d	lxxiv. 10.	5 e	xix. 26.		4
xix. 22, 23.	5 d	lxxiv. 18.	5 c	xxii. 10.		7
Neh. vi. 13.	5 e	lxxiv. 22. α	5 g	xxvii. 11. β	5 b, 2
Job xix. 3.	6 a	lxxix. 12.	5 d	Isa. xxxvii. 4, 17.		5 d
xx. 3.	6 b	lxxxix. 51, 51.	5 c	xxxvii. 23, 24.		5 c
xxvii. 6.	5 a	cii. 8.	5 c	xliii. 28.		1 b
Ps. xlii. 10.	5 c	cxix. 42. β	5 b, 2	Jer. xx. 8. γ		5 g
xliv. 16.	5 f	Prov. xiv. 31.	5 c	Zeph. ii. 8, 10.		5 c
lv. 12.	5 e					

a lit. thy reproach from the foolish man.   *β or,* answer him that reproacheth me in a thing.   *γ lit.* was for a reproach.

REPROBATE

מָאַס to despise, reject, refuse. NIPHAL *part.* Jer. vi. 30.

REPROVE

1   אִישׁ *m.* man.

2   גָּעַר to rebuke with severity either of words or deeds. KAL [a] *pret.* [b] גְּעָרָה *f.* rebuke.

3   יָכַח to be right, straight, direct ; to be right before the eyes, to be clear, manifest. Hiphil, to make right, to decide, judge ; to show to be right, to justify, to prove ; to set right from error, &c., to admonish, to warn ; also to confute, to convict, to show to be wrong, often with the idea of censure, *i. q.* to reprove, to rebuke, to chide ; to set right by punishment, *i. q.* to correct, to chasten, to punish. This word does not necessarily imply censure of punishment, though usually rendered 'reprove,' as in Isa. xi. 4, Prov. xix. 25, but rather conviction, &c. NIPHAL [a] *part.* Gen. xx. 16: Buxtorf considers וְנֹכַחַת a substantive, and joined with כְּסוּת by the copulative, *lit.* and a reproof. HIPHIL [b] *pret.* [c] *inf.* [d] *fut.* [e] *part.* [f] תּוֹכַחַת *f.* the act of arguing, showing and maintaining the right ; rebuke, correction, by-words.

4   יָסַר to chastise : this word has rather respect to the agent and

matter of reproof, the preceding to the efficacy on the person reproved. KAL *part.* Poel.

Gen. xx. 16.	3 a	Ps. cxli. 5.	3 d	Prov. xxv. 12.	3 e	
xxi. 25.	3 b	Prov. i. 23, 25, 30.	3 f	xxix. 1, 15.	3 f	
2 Kings xix. 4.	3 b	v. 12.	3 f	xxx. 6.	3 d	
1 Chron. xvi. 21.	3 d	vi. 23.	3 f	Isa. xi. 3.	3 d	
Job vi. 25.	3 d	ix. 7.	4	xi. 4.	3 e	
vi. 26.	3 c	ix. 8.	3 d	xxix. 21.	3 d	
xiii. 10.	3 c d	x. 17.	3 f	xxxvii. 4.	3 b	
xxii. 4.	3 d	xii. 1.	3 f	Jer. ii. 19.	3 d	
xxvi. 11.	2 b	xiii. 18.	3 f	xxix. 27.	3 a	
xl. 2.	3 e	xv. 5, 10, 31, 32.	3 f	Ezek. iii. 26.	1, 3 e	
Ps. xxxviii. 14.	3 f	xv. 12.	3 c	Hos. iv. 4.	3 d	
l. 8, 21.	3 d	xvii. 10.	2 b	Hab. ii. 1.	3 f	
cv. 14.	3 d	xix. 25.	3 b			

REPUTE

חֲשַׁב Ch. P'AL *part. pass.* Dan. iv. 35.

REPUTATION

יָקָר *adj.* precious : Eccles. x. 1.

REQUEST

1 אֲרֶשֶׁת *f.* desire, longing; only in Ps. xxi. 2; LXX. δέησις : Vulg. *voluntas.*

2 בְּעָה Ch. to desire. P'AL *pret.*

3 בָּקֵשׁ to seek, to seek from any one, to ask. PIEL ᵃ *inf.* ᵇ *fut.* ᶜ *part.* ᵈ בַּקָּשָׁה *f.* a petition.

4 דָּבָר *m.* word, matter, &c.

5 שָׁאַל to ask, to ask for. KAL ᵃ *pret.* ᵇ *fut.* ᶜ שְׁאֵלָה *f.* request, petition, prayer.

Judg. viii. 24.	5 c	Neh. ii. 4.	3 c	Job vi. 8. a	5 d
viii. 26.	5 a	Esth. iv. 8.	3 a	Ps. xxi. 2.	1
2 Sam. xiv. 15, 22.	4	v. 3, 6, 7, 8.	3 d	cvi. 15.	5 d
1 Kings xix. 4.	5 b	vii. 2, 3.	3 d	Dan. i. 8.	3 b
1 Chron. iv. 10.	5 a	vii. 7.	3 a	ii. 49.	2
Ezra vii. 6.	3 d	ix. 12.	3 d		

a lit. Oh that my request would come!

REQUIRE

1 אָמַר to say. KAL *fut.*

2 בָּחַר to choose, to prefer. KAL *fut.* 2 Sam. xix. 38, *marg.* 'choose;' *seq.* עַל of person, *i. e.* chose [to lay] upon me.

3 בָּקֵשׁ to seek; to seek a thing, person, or blood, at the hand of any one, is to look to him for it, to expect that he should make it good, or be punished for it. PIEL ᵃ *pret.* ᵇ *fut.*

4 דָּרַשׁ to seek, to search for; to inquire; to demand, to require, to require or demand back; hence to avenge, to punish. KAL ᵃ *pret.* ᵇ *inf.* ᶜ *fut.* ᵈ *part.* Poel. NIPHAL ᵉ *pret.*

5 יוֹם *m.* day; with דְּבַר, "as every day required," *lit.* the matter of a day in his day.

6 שָׁאַל to ask, to ask for. KAL ᵃ *pret.* ᵇ *inf.* ᶜ *fut.* ᵈ *part.* Poel. שְׁאַל Ch. P'AL ᵉ *fut.* ᶠ *part. active.*

Gen. ix. 5, 5, 5.	4 c	2 Sam. xix. 38.	2	Ps. x. 13.	4 c
xxxi. 39.	3 b	1 Kings viii. 59.	5	xl. 6.	6 a
xlii. 22.	4 e	1 Chron. xvi. 37.	5	cxxxvii. 3.	6 a
xliii. 9.	3 b	xxi. 3.	3 b	Prov. xxx. 7.	6 a
Deut. x. 12.	6 d	2 Chron. viii. 14.	5	Eccles. iii. 15.	3 a
xviii. 19.	4 c	xxiv. 6.	4 a	Isa. i. 12.	3 b
xxiii. 21.	4 b c	xxiv. 22.	4 c	Ezek. iii. 18, 20.	3 b
Josh. xxii. 23.	3 b	Ezra iii. 4.	5	xx. 40.	3 b
Ruth ii. 11.	1	vii. 21.	6 e	xxxiii. 6.	4 c
1 Sam. xx. 16.	3 a	viii. 22.	6 b	xxxiii. 8.	3 b
2 Sam. iii. 13.	6 d	Neh. v. 12.	3 b	xxxiv. 10.	4 a
iv. 11.	3 b	v. 18.	3 a	Dan. ii. 11.	6 f
xii. 20.	6 c	Esth. ii. 15.	3 a	Micah vi. 8.	4 d

REQUITE

1 גָּמַל see *Reward.* KAL *fut.*

2 נָתַן to give. KAL *inf.*

3 עָשָׂה to do. KAL *fut.*

4 שׁוּב to return, to cause to return. HIPHIL ᵃ *pret.* ᵇ *inf.* ᶜ *fut.*

5 שָׁלַם to be complete; to make good or whole, to restore, requite, recompense. PIEL ᵃ *pret.* ᵇ *inf.* ᶜ *fut.*

Gen. l. 15.	4 b c	2 Sam. ii. 6.	3	Ps. x. 14.	2
Deut. xxxii. 6.	1	xvi. 12.	4 a	xli. 10.	5 c
Judg. i. 7.	5 a	2 Kings ix. 26.	5 a	Jer. li. 56.	5 b c
1 Sam. xxv. 21.	4 c	2 Chron. vi. 23.	4 b		

REREWARD

אַחֲרוֹן *adj.* hindermost : 1 Sam. xxix. 2.

אָסַף to gather : it is applied to the gathering up of the scattered rear of an army, or the keeping it from straggling, and defending it from the attacks of an enemy. KAL *fut.* Isa. lviii. 8. PIEL *part.* Num. x. 25 : Josh. vi. 9, 13 : Isa. lii. 12.

RESCUE

יָשַׁע to save. HIPHIL *part.* Deut. xxviii. 31, *lit.* no saviour.

נָצַל to draw out, to take away, to snatch away; to deliver. HIPHIL *pret.* 1 Sam. xxx. 18. *part.* Hos. v. 14. נְצַל Ch. APHEL *part.* Dan. vi. 27.

פָּרָה to loose, to set free, implying some degree of force; *pr.* to cut or break away; see Mutinghe, in Diss. Lugdd. p. 1154. KAL *fut.* 1 Sam. xiv. 45.

שׁוּב to return. HIPHIL *imp.* Ps. xxxv. 17.

RESEMBLE, RESEMBLANCE

עַיִן *f.* the eye; look, aspect, appearance : Zech. v. 6, in this and some other passages it is thought that עַיִן is confounded with עָוֹן sin, and that the passage may be translated with the LXX. and Syr., 'this is their sin,' *i. e.* that in which they sin, false measure.

תֹּאַר *m.* form, shape, or appearance of a person : Judg. viii. 18, *marg.* 'according to the form of.'

RESERVE

1 אָצַל to put aside, to separate; to reserve for any one, *seq.* לְ. KAL *pret.*

2 חָשַׂךְ to keep back, withhold, reserve. KAL ᵃ *pret.* NIPHAL ᵇ *fut.*

3 יָתַר to be over and above, to remain. HIPHIL ᵃ *pret.* ᵇ *fut.*

4 לָקַח to take. KAL *pret.*

5 נָטַר to guard, to keep. KAL ᵃ *fut.* ᵇ *part.* Poel.

6 שָׁאַר to remain. HIPHIL *fut.*

7 שָׁמַר to watch, to guard. KAL *fut.*

Gen. xxvii. 36.	1	1 Chron. xviii. 4.	3 b	Jer. v. 24.	7
Judg. xxi. 22.	4	Job xxi. 30.	2 b	l. 20.	6
Ruth ii. 18.	3 a	xxxviii. 23.	2 a	Nah. i. 2.	5 b
2 Sam. viii. 4.	3 b	Jer. iii. 5.	5 a		

RESIDUE

1 אַחֲרִית *adj.* latter end, remnant.

2 יָתַר to be over and above. NIPHAL ᵃ *part.* ᵇ יֶתֶר *m.* remainder, residue.

3 שְׁאָר m. rest, remnant. ᵃ שְׁאָר Ch. ᵇ שְׁאֵרִית f. remainder.

Exod. x. 5.	2 b	Jer. xxiv. 8.	3 b	Ezek. xxxvi. 3, 4, 5.	3 b
Neh. xi. 20.	3	xxvii. 19.	2 b	xlviii. 18, 21.	2 a
Isa. xxi. 17.	3	xxix. 1.	2 b	Dan. vii. 7, 19.	3 a
xxviii. 5.	3	xxxix. 3.	3 b	Zeph. ii. 9.	3 b
xxxviii. 10.	2 b	xli. 10.	3 b	Hag. ii. 2.	3 b
xliv. 17.	3 b	lii. 15.	2 b	Zech. viii. 11.	3 b
xliv. 19.	2 b	Ezek. ix. 8.	3 b	xiv. 2.	2 b
Jer. viii. 3.	3 b	xxiii. 25.	1	Mal. ii. 15. a	3
xv. 9.	3 b	xxxiv. 18, 18.	2 b a		

a marg. 'or, excellency.'

RESIST

שָׂטַן to be an adversary. KAL *inf.* Zech. iii. 1.

RESORT

בּוֹא to come. KAL *inf.* Ps. lxxi. 3.

יָצַב to set or place; to take one's stand; to attend upon a prince, &c. HITHPAEL *pret.* 2 Chron. xi. 13.

קָבַץ to gather or assemble. NIPHAL *fut.* Neh. iv. 20.

RESPECT

1 יָדַע to know. KAL *fut.*

2 נָבַט to look; to regard. HIPHIL ᵃ*inf.* ᵇ*imp.* ᶜ*fut.*

3 נָכַר to know, acknowledge. HIPHIL ᵃ*inf.* ᵇ*fut.*

4 נָשָׂא to bear; to accept the person of any one, see *Accept;* to revere. KAL ᵃ*pret.* ᵇ*fut.* ᶜ מַשּׂוֹא m. respect (of persons).

5 פָּנָה to turn, to turn in order to look, to regard. KAL ᵃ*pret.* ᵇ*fut.*

6 רָאָה to see; connoting also the affection or disposition of the mind with which an object is seen; to behold, to regard, to have respect to. KAL ᵃ*pret.* ᵇ*fut.*

7 שָׁעָה to turn the eyes either to or from an object, which is to be understood according to the current sense of the passage. KAL ᵃ*pret.* ᵇ*fut.*

Gen. iv. 4.	7 b	1 Kings viii. 28.	5 a	Ps. cxix. 15.	2 c
iv. 5.	7 a	2 Kings xiii. 23.	5 b	cxix. 117.	7 b
Exod. ii. 25.	1	2 Chron. vi. 19.	5 a	cxxxviii. 6.	6 b
Lev. xix. 15.	4 b	xix. 7.	4 c	Prov. xxiv. 23.	3 a
xxvi. 9.	5 a	Job xxxvii. 24.	6 b	xxviii. 21.	3 a
Num. xvi. 15.	5 b	Ps. xl. 4.	5 a	Isa. xvii. 7, 8.	6 b
Deut. i. 17.	3 b	lxxiv. 20.	2 b	xxii. 11.	6 a
xvi. 19.	3 b	cxix. 6.	2 a	Lam. iv. 16.	4 a
2 Sam. xiv. 14.	4 b				

RESPITE

רְוָחָה f. enlargement, relief; *lit.* breathing: Exod. viii. 15.

רָפָה to slacken: to let alone, *seq.* לְ of person, to give respite to. HIPHIL *imp.* 1 Sam. xi. 3, *marg.* 'forbear us.'

REST

1 אָחַז to take hold of, as when one part of a building takes hold of, or rests upon another. KAL *fut.*

2 דָּמַם to be silent, to be still; to forbear, rest, cease, stand still; it is applied to speech, work, or motion; to wait with silent patience and submission. KAL ᵃ*pret.* ᵇ*imp.* ᶜ דֳּמִי m. silence.

3 חָדַל to cease. KAL *fut.* Job xiv. i.e. from trouble.

4 חוּל see *Abide.* KAL and HIPHIL *fut.*

5 חָנָה to pitch a tent; to rest in a tent. KAL *fut.*

6 חָרַשׁ see *Silent.* HIPHIL *fut.*

7 נוּחַ to rest, i.e. to set oneself down, to settle down in any place; to rest, to be at rest, of men and beasts, of God, of the earth; so of the rest of death; especially to rest from labour, from vexation and calamities, to abide, so of the divine spirit which rests or abides on (עַל) any one (Isa. xi. 2, that which Isaiah expresses by this verb, St. John gives us in the force of the word μένειν, John i. 32, 33, xiv. 16, 17), and of God's hand; to rest or cease from speaking. Hiphil, to make to rest on, to give rest to, as God gave rest and quiet possession to his people in Canaan, Josh. i. 13, 15, Deut. iii. 20. (LXX. καταπαύω, and so κατάπαυσις, Heb. iii. 11; iv. 8.) *Metaph.* to allay one's anger, i.e. to satiate it on any one, Ezek. v. 13; xvi. 42; xxiv. 13: Zech. vi. 8. KAL ᵃ*pret.* ᵇ*inf.* ᶜ*fut.* HIPHIL ᵈ*pret.* ᵉ*inf.* ᶠ*imp.* ᵍ*fut.* ʰ*part.* HOPHAL ⁱ*pret.* ᵏ נוֹחַ m. ˡ מָנוֹחַ m. rest, place of rest. ᵐ מְנוּחָה f. condition of rest, place of rest. ⁿ נַחַת m. rest.

8 סָמַךְ to lean, or stay on. NIPHAL *fut.*

9 פּוּגָה f. remission, pause; not entire cessation; *comp.* Job xiv. 9.

10 רָגַע to be afraid, terrified, to shrink together for fear; hence to be still, quiet. NIPHAL ᵃ*imp.* HIPHIL ᵇ*pret.* ᶜ*inf.* ᵈ*fut.* ᵉ מַרְגּוֹעַ m. rest.

11 רָבַץ to lie down, as beasts when resting themselves. HIPHIL ᵃ*fut.* ᵇ רֵבֶץ m. resting-place.

12 שָׁאַן to be in profound tranquillity, at ease, undisturbed. PILEL *pret.*

13 שָׁבַת to rest from labour. KAL ᵃ*pret.* ᵇ*fut.* HIPHIL ᶜ*pret.* ᵈ שַׁבָּתוֹן m. sabbatical rest.

14 שָׁכַב to lie down, to take rest. KAL ᵃ*pret.* ᵇ*fut.*

15 שָׁכַן to dwell, to be settled in a place, to rest after motion; to be at ease, to remain in a state of inactivity. KAL *fut.*

16 שְׁלָה Ch. to be secure, to be at rest. P'AL *part. pass.*

17 שָׁלוֹם m. peace.

18 שָׁמַט to let fall, to let go, to release. KAL *fut.*

19 שָׁעַן to lean on, to rely, as upon a staff or support. NIPHAL ᵃ*pret.* ᵇ*imp.* ᶜ*fut.*

20 שָׁקַט to rest, to have quiet; of one who is never infested, harassed, troubled; also of one who troubles or harasses no one, Judg. xviii. 7, 27; which sometimes arises from fear, Ps. lxxvi. 9; of one who does nothing, remains inactive; hence of God, as not affording aid, Ps. lxxxiii. 2. KAL ᵃ*pret.* ᵇ*fut.* ᶜ*part.* Poel. HIPHIL ᵈ*inf.*

Gen. ii. 2.	13 b	Lev. xvi. 31.	13 d	Josh. i. 15.	7 g
ii. 3.	13 a	xxiii. 3, 32.	13 d	iii. 13.	7 b
viii. 4.	7 c	xxv. 4, 5.	13 d	xi. 23.	20 a
viii. 9.	7 l	xxvi. 34.	13 b	xiv. 15.	20 a
xviii. 4.	19 b	xxvi. 35, 35.	13 b a	xxi. 44.	7 c
xlix. 15.	7 m	Num. ix. 18, 23.	5	xxii. 4.	7 d
Exod. v. 5.	13 c	x. 12.		xxiii. 1.	7 d
x. 14.	7 c	x. 33.	7 m	Judg. iii. 11, 30.	20 b
xvi. 23.	13 d	x. 36.	7 b	v. 31.	20 b
xvi. 30.	13 b	xi. 25.	7 b	Ruth i. 9.	7 m
xx. 11.	7 c	xi. 26.	7 c	iii. 1.	7 l
xxiii. 11.	18	Deut. iii. 20.	7 g	iii. 18.	20 b
xxiii. 12, 12.	13 b, 2	v. 14.	7 c	2 Sam. iii. 29.	18
xxxi. 15.	13 d	xii. 9.	7 m	vii. 1, 11.	7 d
xxxi. 17.	13 d	xii. 10.	7 d	xxi. 10.	7 b
xxxiii. 14.	7 g	xxv. 19.	7 e	1 Kings v. 4.	7 d
xxxiv. 21, 21.	13 b	xxviii. 65.	7 l	vi. 10.	7 d
xxxv. 2.	13 d	Josh. i. 13.	7 h	viii. 56.	7 m

Ref	Code	Ref	Code	Ref	Code
2 Kings ii. 15.	7 a	Ps. xciv. 13.	20 d	Jsa. lxii. 1.	20 b
1 Chron. vi. 31.	7 l	xcv. 11.	7 m	lxii. 7.	2 c
xxii. 9, 9.	7 m d	cxvi. 7.	7 l	lxiii. 14.	7 g
xxii. 18.	7 d	cxxv. 3.	7 c	lxvi. 1.	7 m
xxiii. 25.	7 d	cxxxii. 8, 14.	7 m	Jer. vi. 16.	10 e
xxviii. 2.	7 m	Prov. xiv. 33.	7 c	xxx. 10.	20 a
2 Chron. vi. 41.	7 k	xxiv. 15.	11 b	xxxi. 2.	10 c
xiv. 6, 6.	20 a, 7 d	xxix. 9.	7 n	vii. 9.	7 n
xiv. 7.	7 c	xxix. 17.	7 g	xlvi. 27.	20 a
xiv. 11.	19 a	Eccles. ii. 23.	14 a	xlviii. 6.	10 a
xv. 15.	7 c	vi. 5.	7 n	l. 6.	11 b
xx. 30.	7 c	vii. 9.	7 c	l. 34.	10 b
xxxii. 8.	8	Cant. i. 7.	11 a	Lam. i. 3.	7 l
Neh. ix. 28.	7 b	Isa. vii. 19.	7 a	ii. 18.	7 i
Esth. ix. 16, 17, 18.	7 k	xi. 2.	7 a	v. 5.	7 i
ix. 22.	7 a	xi. 10.	7 m	Ezek. v. 13.	7 d
Job iii. 13, a 17.	7 c	xiv. 3.	7 e	xvi. 42.	7 d
iii. 18.	12	xiv. 7.	7 a	xxi. 17.	7 a
iii. 26.	20 a	xviii. 4.	20 b	xxiv. 13.	7 e
xi. 18.	14 b	xxiii. 12. β	7 c	xxxviii. 11.	7 e
xiv. 6.	3	xxv. 10.	7 c	xliv. 30.	7 e
xvii. 16.	7 n	xxviii. 12, 12.	7 m f	Dan. iv. 4.	16
xxiv. 23.	19 c	xxx. 15.	7 n	xii. 13.	7 c
xxx. 17.	14 b	xxxii. 18.	7 m	Micah ii. 10.	7 m
xxx. 27.	2 a	xxxiv. 14, 14.	7 l, 10 b	Hab. iii. 16.	7 c
Ps. xvi. 9.	15	li. 4.	10 d	Zeph. iii. 17.	6
xxxvii. 7.	2 b	lvii. 2.	7 c	Zech. i. 11.	20 c
xxxviii. 3.	17	lvii. 20.	20 d	ix. 1.	7 m
lv. 6.	15				

a *lit.* it had rested to me.   β *lit.* that no rest be to thee.

REST

1 יָתַר to be over and above. KAL a *part.* Poel. NIPHAL b *part.* c יֶתֶר *m.* remainder, rest, residue.

2 שָׁאַר to be full, abundant; to be left, to remain. NIPHAL a *part.* b שְׁאָר *m.* rest, residue, remnant. c שְׁאָר *m. id.* d שְׁאֵרִית *f.* remaining part.

3 שָׂרִיד *m.* one left, one escaped.

Ref	Code	Ref	Code	Ref	Code
Gen. xxx. 36.	1 b	2 Kings x. 34.	1 c	2 Chron. xxvii. 7.	1 c
Exod. xxviii. 10.	1 b	xii. 19.	1 c	xxviii. 26.	1 c
Lev. v. 9.	2 a	xiii. 8, 12.	1 c	xxxii. 32.	1 c
xiv. 17.	1 c	xiv. 15, 18, 28.	1 c	xxxiii. 18.	1 c
xiv. 29.	1 b	xv. 6, 11, 15, 21, 26, 31, 36.	1 c	xxxv. 26.	1 c
Num. xxxi. 32.	1 c	xvi. 19.	1 c	xxxvi. 8.	1 c
Deut. iii. 11.	1 c	xx. 20.	1 c	Ezra iv. 3, 7.	1 c
Josh. x. 20.	3	xxi. 17, 25.	1 c	iv. 9, 10, 10, 17, 17.	2 c
xiii. 27.	1 b	xxiii. 28.	1 c	vi. 16.	2 c
xvii. 2, 6.	1 b	xxiv. 5.	1 c	vii. 18.	2 c
xxi. 5, 34.	1 b	xxv. 11.	1 c	Neh. i. 6.	1 c
Judg. vii. 6.	1 c	1 Chron. iv. 43.	2 d	iv. 14, 19.	1 c
1 Sam. xiii. 2.	1 c	vi. 77.	1 b	vi. 1, 14.	1 c
xv. 15.	1 a	xi. 8.	2 b	vii. 72.	2 d
2 Sam. x. 10.	1 c	xii. 38.	2 d	x. 28.	2 b
xii. 28.	1 c	xvi. 41.	2 b	xi. 1.	2 b
1 Kings xi. 41.	1 c	xix. 11.	1 c	Esth. ix. 12.	2 b
xiv. 19, 29.	1 c	xxiv. 20.	1 b	Ps. xvii. 14.	1 c
xv. 7, 23, 31.	1 c	2 Chron. ix. 29.	2 b	Isa. x. 19.	2 b
xvi. 5, 14, 20, 27.	1 c	xiii. 22.	1 c	Jer. xxxix. 9.	1 c
xx. 30.	1 b	xx. 34.	1 c	lii. 15.	1 c
xxii. 39, 45.	1 b	xxiv. 14.	2 b	Ezek. xlviii. 23.	1 c
2 Kings i. 18.	1 c	xxv. 26.	1 c	Dan. ii. 18.	2 c
iv. 7.	1 b	xxvi. 22.	1 c	vii. 12.	2 c
viii. 23.	1 c			Zech. xi. 9.	2 a

RESTITUTION

תְּמוּרָה *f.* exchange: Job xx. 18, *marg.* 'his exchange.'

שָׁלֵם to make whole, to recompense, requite, &c. PIEL *inf.* Exod. xxii. 3, *lit.* paying make restitution; 6, *lit. id. fut.* Exod. xxii. 3, 5, 6, 12.

RESTORE

1 חָיָה to live; to restore to life. HIPHIL *pret.*

2 נָתַן to give. KAL *pret.*

3 עָלָה to ascend. HIPHIL *fut.*

4 שׁוּב to return; to cause to return, to restore to a former condition. KAL a *fut.* POLEL b *fut.* c *part.* HIPHIL d *pret.* e *inf.* f *imp.* g *fut.* h *part.* HOPHAL i *pret.*

5 שָׁלַם to make whole, to repay, &c. PIEL a *pret.* b *fut.*

6 תּוּב Ch. to return. APHEL *fut.*

Ref	Code	Ref	Code	Ref	Code
Gen. xx. 7, 7.	4 f h	Ruth iv. 15.	4 h	Job xx. 10.	4 g
xx. 14.	4 g	1 Sam. vii. 14.	4 a	xx. 18.	4 h
xl. 13.	4 d	xii. 3.	4 g	Ps. xxiii. 3.	4 b
xl. 21.	4 g	2 Sam. ix. 7.	4 d	li. 12.	4 f
xli. 13.	4 d	xii. 6.	5 b	lxix. 4.	4 g
xlii. 25.	4 e	xvi. 3.	4 g	Prov. vi. 31.	5 b
xlii. 28.	4 e	1 Kings xiii. 6, 6.	4 a	Isa. i. 26.	4 g
Exod. xxii. 1, 4.	4 i	xx. 34.	4 g	xlii. 22.	4 f
Lev. vi. 4.	4 d	2 Kings viii. 1, 5, 5, 5.	1	xlix. 6.	4 e
vi. 5.	5 a	viii. 6.	4 f	lvii. 18.	5 b
xxiv. 21.	5 b	xiv. 22.	4 g	lviii. 12.	4 c
xxv. 27.	4 d	xiv. 25.	4 d	Jer. xxvii. 22.	4 d
xxv. 28.	4 e	2 Chron. viii. 2.	2	xxxvii. 3.	3
Num. xxxv. 25.	4 d	xxvi. 2.	4 g	Ezek. xviii. 7, 12.	4 g
Deut. xxxv. 2.	4 d	Ezra vi. 5.	6	xxxiii. 15.	4 g
xxviii. 31.	4 a	Neh. v. 11.	4 f	Dan. ix. 25.	4 e
Judg. xii. 13.	4 f	v. 12.	4 g	Joel ii. 25.	5 a
xvii. 3, 3, 4.	4 g				

RESTRAIN

1 אָפַק to hold in by force; to refrain or constrain oneself. HITHPAEL *pret.*

2 בָּצַר to cut off, to cut off access, to restrain, prevent. Niphal, inaccessible, difficult. NIPHAL *fut.* Gen. xi. 6, *i. e.* nothing will be too hard for them, whatever they may purpose to do.

3 גָּרַע to take away, to detract, to withhold; *seq. acc.* to diminish, *i. e.* to take away or withhold from, Job xv. 4; *seq.* אֶל to take to or for oneself, *i. e.* to reserve, to keep, to lay up for oneself. KAL *fut.*

4 חָגַר to gird; figuratively, to restrain from doing mischief. KAL *fut.*

5 כָּהָה to be dim; to make the face dim, to frown. PIEL *pret.* 1 Sam. iii. 13, *marg.* 'frowned not upon them.'

6 כָּלָא to shut up; to withhold, to restrain. NIPHAL *fut.*

7 מָנַע to keep back, withhold, restrain, *i. e.* to stop a body in motion. KAL *fut.*

8 עָצַר to shut up, to close; to hold back, hinder, detain. KAL a *pret.* b מַעְצוֹר *m.* restraint, hindrance.

Ref	Code	Ref	Code	Ref	Code
Gen. viii. 2.	6	1 Sam. iii. 13.	5	Ps. lxxvi. 10.	4
xi. 6.	2	xiv. 6.	8 b	Isa. lxiii. 15.	1
xvi. 2.	8 a	Job xv. 4, 8.	3	Ezek. xxxi. 15.	7
Exod. xxxvi. 6.	6				

RETAIN

חָזַק to hold fast. HIPHIL *pret.* Judg. vii. 8: Micah vii. 18. *fut.* Judg. xix. 4. *part.* Job ii. 9.

כָּלָא to shut up, withhold, restrain. KAL *inf.* Eccles. viii. 8.

עָצַר to shut up, to close; to hold back, hinder, detain. KAL *pret.* Dan. x. 8, 16. *fut.* Dan. xi. 6.

תָּמַךְ to take hold of, to obtain, acquire; to hold fast; to hold up, to support. KAL *fut.* Prov. iv. 4; xi. 16, 16. *part.* Poel, Prov. iii. 18.

RETIRE

הָפַךְ to turn. KAL *fut.* Judg. xx. 39.

עוּז to flee for refuge; to gather together for this purpose. HIPHIL *imp.* Jer. iv. 6, *marg.* 'or, strengthen.'

פּוּץ to be dispersed. KAL *fut.* 2 Sam. xx. 22.

שׁוּב to return. KAL *pret.* 2 Sam. xi. 15, *lit.* turn back.

RETURN

1   יָלַךְ to go. KAL *inf.* Eccles. i. 7, *marg.* 'return to go.'

2   יָסַף to add. KAL [a] *pret.* HIPHIL [b] *fut.*

3   יָשַׁב to dwell. KAL *fut.* Ezek. xxxv. 9 (כתיב).

4   סָבַב to go about. NIPHAL *fut.*

5   פָּנָה to turn. KAL *imp.*

6   שׁוּב to turn about, to turn back, to return; for the use of this verb in conjunction with another, see *Again.* KAL [a] *pret.* [b] *inf.* [c] *imp.* [d] *fut.* [e] *part.* Poel. HIPHIL [f] *pret.* [g] *inf.* [h] *imp.* [i] *fut.* [k] שׁוּבָה *f.* return, *metaph.* conversion. [l] תְּשׁוּבָה *f.* return.

7   שָׁנָה to do a thing a second time. KAL *part.* Poel.

8   תּוּב Ch. to return back. P'AL [a] *fut.* APHEL [b] *pret.* [c] *fut.*

Ref	Code	Ref	Code	Ref	Code
Gen. iii. 19, 19.	6 b d	Judg. vii. 3, 3, 15.	6 d	2 Kings v. 15.	6 d
viii. 3. a	6 b d	viii. 13.	6 d	vii. 15.	6 d
viii. 9.	6 d	x. 31.	6 d	viii. 3.	6 b
viii. 12. β	2 a, 6 b	xi. 39.	6 d	ix. 15.	6 d
xiv. 7.	6 d	xiv. 8.	6 d	x.v. 14.	6 d
xiv. 17.	6 b	xxi. 23.	6 d	xviii. 14.	6 c
xvi. 9.	6 c	Ruth i. 6, 10.	6 d	xix. 7.	6 a
xviii. 10.	6 b d	i. 7, 16.	6 b	xix. 8, 33, 36.	6 d
xviii. 14.	6 d	i. 8, 15.	6 d	xx. 10.	6 d
xviii. ?3.	6 a	i. 22, 22.	6 d a	xxiii. 20.	6 d
xxi. 32.	6 d	1 Sam. i. 19.	6 d	1 Chron. xvi. 43.	4
xxii. 19.	6 d	vi. 3.	6 g i	xix. 5.	6 a
xxxi. 3. 13.	6 c	vi. 4.	6 i	xx. 3.	6 d
xxxi. 55.	6 d	vi. 8, 17.	6 f	2 Chron. vi. 24, 38.	6 a
xxxii. 6.	6 d	vi. 16.	6 d	x. 2.	6 d
xxxii. 9.	6 c	vii. 3.	6 e	x. 6.	6 g
xxxiii. 16.	6 d	vii. 17.	6 l	x. 9.	6 d
xxxvii. 29, 30.	6 d	ix. 5.	6 d	xi. 4, 4.	6 c d
xxxviii. 22.	6 d	xv. 26.	6 d	xiv. 15.	6 d
xlii. 24.	6 d	xvii. 15.	6 e	xviii. 16.	6 d
xliii. 10.	6 a	xvii. 53.	6 d	xviii. 26.	6 b
xliii. 18.	6 e	xvii. 57.	6 b	xviii. 27.	6 b d
x.iv. 13.	6 d	xviii. 6.	6 d	xix. 1, 8.	6 d
l. 14.	6 d	xxiii. 28.	6 d	xx. 27.	6 d
Exod. iv. 18, 18, 20.	6 d	xxiv. 1.	6 a	xxii. 6.	6 d
iv. 19.	6 c	xxv. 39.	6 f	xxv. 10, 24.	6 d
iv. 21.	6 b	xxvi. 21.	6 c	xxviii. 15.	6 d
v. 22.	6 d	xxvi. 25.	6 d	xxxi. 1.	6 d
xiii 17.	6 d	xxvii. 9.	6 d	xxxii. 21.	6 d
xiv. 27, 28.	6 d	xxix. 4.	6 h	xxxv. 7, 9.	6 d
xix. 8.	6 i	xxix. 7.	6 c	Ezra v. 5.	8 c
xxxii. 31.	6 d	xxix. 11.	6 b	v. 11.	8 b
xxxiv. 31.	6 d	2 Sam. i. 1.	6 a	Neh. ii. 6, 15.	6 d
Lev. xxii. 13.	6 a	i. 22.	6 d	iv. 12, 15.	6 d
xxv. 10, 10.	6 a d	ii. 26.	6 a	ix. 17.	6 b
xxv. 13.	6 d	ii. 30.	6 a	ix. 28.	6 d
xxv. 27, 28.	6 a d	iii. 16, 16.	6 c d	Esth. ii. 14.	6 e
xxv. 41, 41.	6 a d	iii. 27.	6 d	iv. 15.	6 g
xxvii. 24.	6 a d	vi. 20.	6 d	vii. 8.	6 a
Num. x. 36.	6 c	viii. 13.	6 b	ix. 25.	6 a
xiii. 25.	6 d	x. 5.	6 a	Job i. 21.	6 d
xiv. 3.	6 b	x. 14.	6 d	vi. 29, 29.	6 c
xiv. 4, 36.	6 d	xi. 4.	6 d	vii. 10.	6 d
xvi. 50.	6 d	xii. 23, 31.	6 d	x. 21.	6 d
xxiii. 5.	6 c	xiv. 24.	4	xv. 22.	6 d
xxiii. 6.	6 d	xv. 19, 20, 27.	6 c	xvi. 22.	6 d
xxiv. 25.	6 d	xv. 34.	6 d	xvii. 10.	6 d
xxxii. 18, 22.	6 d	xvi. 8.	6 f	xxii. 23.	6 d
xxxv. 28.	6 d	xvii. 3.	6 b	xxxiii. 25.	6 d
Deut. i. 45.	6 d	xvii. 20.	6 d	xxxvi. 10.	6 d
iii. 20.	6 a	xviii. 16.	6 c	xxxix. 4.	6 a
xvii. 16.	6 d	xix. 15, 39.	6 d	Ps. vi. 4.	6 c
xvii. 16. γ	2 b, 6 b	xx. 22.	6 d	vi. 10. δ	6 c
xx. 5, 6, 7, 8.	6 a	xxiii. 10.	6 a	vii 7.	6 c
xxx. 2, 3.	6 a	xxiv. 13.	6 i	vii. 16.	6 d
xxx. 8.	6 d	1 Kings ii. 32, 44.	6 f	xxxv. 13.	6 d
Josh. i. 15.	6 a	ii. 33.	6 a	lix. 6, 14.	6 d
ii. 16.	6 b	viii. 48.	6 a	lx. title.	6 d
ii. 22.	6 a	xii. 24, 24.	6 c d	lxxiii. 10.	6 d
ii. 23.	6 d	xii. 26.	6 d	lxxiv. 21.	6 d
iv. 18.	6 d	xiii. 10, 33.	6 d	lxxviii. 34.	6 a
vi. 14.	6 d	xiii. 16.	6 b	lxxx. 14.	6 c
vii. 3.	6 d	xix. 15.	6 c	xc. 3, 13.	6 d
viii. 24.	6 d	xix. 21.	6 d	xciv. 15.	6 d
x. 15, 21, 38, 43.	6 d	xx. 22, 26.	6 i	civ. 29.	6 d
xx. 6.	6 d	xxii. 17.	6 d	cvi. 7.	6 d
xxii. 4.	5	xxii. 28.	6 b d	cxvi. 7.	6 d
xxii. 8.	6 c	2 Kings ii. 25.	6 a	cxlvi. 4.	6 d
xxii. 9, 32.	6 d	ii. 27.	6 d	Prov. ii. 19.	6 d
Judg. ii. 19.	6 d	iv. 35.	6 d	xxvi. 11, 11.	6 a, 7
v. 29.	6 i			xxvi. 27.	6 d

Ref	Code	Ref	Code	Ref	Code
Eccles. i. 6.	6 a	Jer. xxiii. 20.	6 d	Ezek. xlvi. 17.	6 a
i. 7.	6 e, 1	xxiv. 7.	6 d	xlvii. 6.	6 i
iv. 1, 7.	6 a	xxix. 10.	6 g	xlvii. 7.	6 b
v. 15.	6 d	xxx. 3.	6 f	Dan. iv. 34, 36, 36.	8 a
ix. 11.	6 a	xxx. 10.	6 a	x. 20.	6 d
xii. 2.	6 a	xxx. 24.	6 d	xi. 9, 13. 30, 30.	6 d
xii. 7, 7.	6 a	xxxi. 8.	6 d	xi. 10, 29.	6 d
Cant. vi. 13, 13, 13, 13.	6 c	xxxii. 44.	6 i	xi. 28, 28.	6 d a
Isa. vi. 13.	6 a	xxxiii. 7.	6 f	Hos. ii. 7, 9.	6 d
x. 21, 22.	6 d	xxxiii. 11, 26.	6 d	iii. 5.	6 d
xix. 22.	6 a	xxxiv. 11, 16.	6 i	v. 15.	6 d
xxi. 12.	6 c	xxxiv. 22.	6 f	vi. 11.	6 b
xxx. 15.	6 d	xxxv. 15.	6 c	vii. 10.	6 d
xxxv. 10.	6 k	xxxvi. 3, 7.	6 d	viii. 13.	6 d
xxxvii. 7.	6 a	xxxvii. 7.	6 a	ix. 3.	6 d
xxxvii. 8, 34, 37.	6 d	xxxvii. 20.	6 i	xi. 5, 5.	6 d b
xxxviii. 8.	6 d	xxxviii. 26.	6 d	xii. 6.	6 d
xliv. 22.	6 c	xl. 12.	6 d	xii. 14.	6 i
xlv. 23.	6 d	xli. 14.	6 d	xiv. 1.	6 c
li 11.	6 d	xli. 12.	6 f	xiv. 7.	6 c
lv. 7, 10, 11.	6 c	xliii. 5.	6 a	Joel ii. 14.	6 d
lxiii. 17.	6 c	xliv. 14, 14, 14.	6 b b d	iii. 1.	6 d
Jer. iii. 1, 1.	6 d b	xlvi. 28.	6 d	iii. 7.	6 f
iii. 7.	6 a	l. 9.	6 d	Amos iv. 6, 8, 9, 10, 11.	6 a
iii. 12, 22.	6 c	Ezek. i. 14.	6 b	Obad. 15.	6 d
iv. 1, 1.	6 d	vii. 13, 13.	6 d	Micah i. 7.	6 d
v. 3.	6 b	viii. 17.	6 d	v. 3.	6 d
viii. 4.	6 b	xiii. 22.	6 b	Zech. i. 6.	6 d
viii. 5.	6 b	xvi. 55, 55, 55.	6 d	i. 16.	6 e
xiv. 15.	6 a	xviii. 23.	6 b	vi. 8.	6 e
xiv. 3.	6 a	xxi. 5.	6 d	viii. 3.	6 e
xv. 19, 19, 19.	6 d	xxi. 30.	6 h	ix. 8.	6 e
xviii. 11.	6 d	xxix. 14.	6 f	Mal. i. 4.	6 d
xxii. 10, 11.	6 d	xxxv. 7.	6 e	iii. 7, 7, 7.	6 c d d
xxii. 27, 27.	6 d, or 3	xxxv. 9.	6 d, or 3	iii. 18.	6 d
xxiii. 14.	6 a	xlvi. 9.	6 d		

a returned continually, *lit.* returned in going and returning.   β *lit.* added not to return.   γ *lit.* ye shall not add to return.   δ or, turn away *from me.*

REVEAL

1   אֹזֶן *m.* the ear: 2 Sam. vii. 27, *marg.* 'hast opened the ear of.'

2   גָּלָה see *Open.* KAL [a] *pret.* [b] *part.* Poel. NIPHAL [c] *pret.* [d] *inf.* [e] *fut.* [f] *part.* PIEL [g] *pret.* [h] *fut.* [i] *part.* גְּלָה Ch. P'AL [k] *inf.* [l] *part. active.* [m] *part. passive.*

Ref	Code	Ref	Code	Ref	Code
Deut. xxix. 29.	2 f	Isa. xxii. 14.	2 c	Jer. xxxiii. 6.	2 g
1 Sam. iii. 7.	2 e	xxiii. 1.	2 c	Dan. ii. 19, 30.	2 m
iii. 21.	2 c	xl. 5.	2 c	ii. 22, 28, 29.	2 l
2 Sam. vii. 27.	2 a, 1	liii. 1.	2 c	ii. 47, 47.	2 l k
Job xx. 27.	2 h	lvi. 1.	2 d	x. 1.	2 c
Prov. xi. 13.	2 i	Jer. xi. 20.	2 g	Amos iii. 7.	2 a
xx. 19.	2 b				

REVENGE

גָּאַל to redeem, ransom; to avenge, vindicate. KAL *part.* Poel, Num. xxxv. 19, 21, 24, 25, 27, 27: 2 Sam. xiv. 11.

נָקַם to avenge, to punish with severity. KAL *part.* Poel, Nah. i. 2, 2. NIPHAL *pret.* Ezek. xxv. 12. *imp.* Jer. xv. 15. נְקָמָה *f.* vengeance, revenge: Ps. lxxix. 10: Jer. xx. 10: Ezek. xxv. 15.

פְּרָעוֹת *f. pl.* (see *Avenge*): Deut. xxxii. 42.

REVENUE

אַפְּתֹם Ch. Aben-Ezra and others, by conjecture from the context, render it 'revenue (of the kings):' Ezra iv. 13, *marg.* 'strength.' Gesenius thinks it is an *adv. in the end,* and would render the passage, "and so at length bring damage to the kings."

תְּבוּאָה *f.* produce, fruits, increase: Prov. viii. 19; xv. 6; xvi. 8: Isa. xxiii. 3: Jer. xii. 13.

REVERENCE

יָרֵא to fear, to venerate, religiously to reverence. KAL *fut.*

Lev. xix. 30; xxvi. 2. NIPHAL *part.* Ps. lxxxix. 7; cxi. 9.

שָׁחָה to bow down the head or body in token of reverence; see *Worship.* HITHPAEL *fut.* 2 Sam. ix. 6: 1 Kings i. 31: Esth. iii. 2. *part.* Esth. iii. 2, 5.

REVERSE

שׁוּב to return. HIPHIL *inf.* Esth. viii. 5, 8. *fut.* Num. xxiii. 20.

REVILE

גִּדּוּף *m.* reproach, blaspheming; the verb is always used of blasphemy against God: Isa. li. 7: Zeph. ii. 8.

קָלַל to be light, lightly esteemed; to vilify. PIEL *fut.* Exod. xxii. 28.

REVIVE

חָיָה to live, to revive. KAL *fut.* Gen. xlv. 27: Judg. xv. 19: 1 Kings xvii. 22: 2 Kings xiii. 21. PIEL *imp.* Hab. iii. 2. *fut.* Neh. iv. 2: Ps. lxxxv. 6, *lit.* wilt thou not return? wilt thou revive us? cxxxviii. 7: Hos. vi. 2: xiv. 7. HIPHIL *inf.* Isa. lvii. 15, 15. מִחְיָה *f.* quickening: Ezra ix. 8, 9.

REVOLT

1 סוּר to turn aside; revolt, rebellion is wilfully turning aside from duty and obedience; see *Depart, Turn aside.* KAL [a] *pret.* [b] סָרָה *f.* a departing, withdrawing.

2 סָרַר to be refractory, rebellious, intractable; properly of refractory and unruly animals. KAL *part.* Poel.

3 פָּשַׁע to break with any one, *i. e.* one's covenant, allegiance; to fall away, to revolt, rebel. KAL [a] *pret.* [b] *fut.*

4 שָׂטָה to turn out of the way of truth, virtue, and duty. שֵׂט *m.* deviations from what is right.

2 Kings viii. 20.	3 a	Isa. i. 5.	1 b	Jer. vi. 28.	2
viii. 22, 22.	3 b	xxxi. 6. α	1 b	Hos. v. 2.	4
2 Chron. xxi. 8.	3 a	lix. 13.	1 b	ix. 15.	2
xxi. 10, 10.	3 b	Jer. v. 23, 23.	2, 1 a		

a lit. deepened revolt.

REWARD

1 אַחֲרִית *f.* end; event, latter state, final lot.

2 בְּשׂוֹרָה *f.* tidings, reward for tidings.

3 גָּמַל to make returns of any kind, whether good or evil: where the word is used of evil, there is always a silent contrast in respect to some good which should have been given: 1 Sam. xxiv. 17; *comp.* also Gen. l. 15, 17: 2 Chron. xx. 11: Isa. iii. 9. KAL [a] *pret.* [b] *fut.* [c] *part.* Poel. [d] גְּמוּל *m.* retribution, recompense. The word does not necessarily imply recompense, except by inference and connexion. [e] גְּמוּלָה *f. id.*

4 נִדְבָּה Ch. *f.* a gift, present, bounty.

5 מַשְׂאֵת *f.* a gift; see *Give.*

6 מַתָּת *f.* a gift.

7 עֵקֶב *m.* the end, the last of anything; hence recompense, reward, wages, as the end of labour.

8 פְּעֻלָּה *f.* work, wages for work.

9 פְּרִי *m.* fruit.

10 קֶסֶם *m.* divination; reward of divination.

11 שׁוּב to return. HIPHIL [a] *fut.* [b] *part.*

12 שׂוּם to put, place. KAL *fut.*

13 שָׁחַד to make a present, to conciliate favour, to avoid punishment, or to bribe or influence a judge. KAL [a] *imp.* [b] שֹׁחַד *m.* a bribing reward, which makes the giver and receiver one, as if compounded of חַד one.

14 שָׂכַר to hire. KAL [a] *part.* Poel. [b] שָׂכָר *m.* wages, reward. [c] שֶׂכֶר *m. id.* [d] מַשְׂכֹּרֶת *f.* wages.

15 שָׁלַם to make whole, to repay, recompense. PIEL [a] *pret.* [b] *fut.* [c] *part.* PUAL [d] *fut.* שִׁלֻּמָה *f.* retribution, penalty. [f] שַׁלְמֹנִים *m. pl.* gifts, bribes. [g] שִׁלּוּם *m.* retribution.

16 אֶתְנַן *m.* a gift or reward, especially to a harlot. [a] אֶתְנָה *f. id.*

Gen. xv. 1.	14 b	Ps. xviii. 20.	3 b	Prov. xxvi. 10, 10.	14 a
xliv. 4.	15 a	xix. 11.	7	Eccles. iv. 9.	14 b
Num. xviii. 31.	14 b	xxxi. 23.	15 c	ix. 5.	14 b
xxii. 7.	10	xxxv. 42.	15 b	Isa. i. 23.	15 f
Deut. x. 17.	13 b	xl. 15.	7	iii. 9.	3 a
xxvii. 25.	13 b	liv. 5.	11 a	iii. 11.	3 d
xxxii. 41.	15 b	lviii. 11.	9	v. 23.	13 b
Ruth ii. 12. a	14 d	lxx. 3.	7	xl. 10.	14 b
1 Sam. xxiv. 17, 17.	3 a	xci. 8.	15 e	xlv. 13.	13 b
xxiv. 19.	15 b	xciv. 2.	3 d	lxii. 11.	14 b
2 Sam. iii. 39.	15 b	ciii. 10.	3 a	Jer. xxxi. 16. δ	14 b
iv. 10.	2	cix. 5. γ	12	xl. 5.	5
xix. 36.	3 e	cix. 20.	3 d	Ezek. xvi. 34, 34.	16
xxii. 21.	3 b	cxxvii. 3.	14 b	Dan. ii. 6.	4
1 Kings xiii. 7. β	6	cxxxviii. 8.	15 b	v. 17.	4
2 Chron. xv. 7.	14 b	Prov. xi. 18.	14 c	Hos. ii. 12.	16 a
xx. 11.	3 d	xiii. 13.	15 d	iv. 9.	11 a
Job vi. 22.	13 a	xvii. 13.	11 b	ix. 1.	16
xxi. 19.	15 b	xxi. 14.	13 b	Obad. 15.	3 d
Ps. vii. 4.	3 a	xxiv. 14, 20.	1	Micah iii. 11.	13 b
xv. 5.	13 b	xxv. 22.	15 b	vii. 3.	15 g

a lit. let thy reward be full.   *β lit.* a reward shall be to thy work.   *γ lit.* and put upon me.   *δ lit.* a reward shall be to thy work.

RIB

צֵלָע *f.* a rib: Gen. ii. 21, 22. עֲלַע Ch. *com. id.* Dan. vii. 5.

RIBBAND

פָּתִיל *m.* a thread, line, cord: Num. xv. 38.

RICH

1 גָּדוֹל *adj.* great: Dan. xi. 2, far richer, *lit.* shall be rich great riches above.

2 הוֹן *m.* substance, wealth, riches.

3 הָמוֹן *m.* multitude, abundance; riches, wealth.

4 חַיִל strength, &c., wealth, riches.

5 חֹסֶן *m.* strength entire and inviolable; riches laid up untouched and well secured.

6 מַטְמוֹן *m.* hid treasure, hidden riches.

7 יָד *com.* hand: Lev. xxv. 47, *lit.* the hand of a stranger gain.

8 יִתְרָה *f.* abundance.

9 כָּבַד to be heavy, abundant. KAL *pret.*

10 נְכָסִים *m. pl.* wealth accumulated.

11 נָשַׂג to reach so as to take hold of, to attain, overtake. HIPHIL *fut.*

12 עָשַׁר to be rich. KAL [a] *pret.* [b] *fut.* HIPHIL [c] *pret.* [d] *inf.* [e] *fut.* [f] *part.* HITHPAEL [g] *part.* [h] עֹשֶׁר *m.* riches. [i] עָשִׁיר *m.* rich.

13 קִנְיָן *m.* getting, possession.

14 רְכֻשׁ *m.* possessions, property, substance.

15 שׁוֹעַ *m.* rich, opulent, liberal. שׁוּעַ *m.* riches.

No.12 h, *Riches*, and No.12 i, *Rich*, not included.

Gen. xiii. 2.	9	Ps. civ. 24.	13	Isa. x. 14.	4
xiv. 23.	12 c	cxix. 14.	2	xxx. 6.	4
xxxvi. 7.	14	Prov. viii. 18, 18.	12 h, 2	xlv. 3.	6
Lev. xxv. 47. a	7, 11	x. 4, 22.	12 e	lxi. 6.	4
Josh. xxii. 8.	10	xi. 4.	2	Jer. v. 27.	12 e
1 Sam. ii. 7.	12 f	xiii. 7, 7.	12 g, 2	xlviii. 36.	8
2 Chron. xx. 25.	14	xix. 14.	2	Ezek. xxvi. 12.	4
Job xv. 29.	12 b	xxi. 17.	12 e	xxvii. 12, 18, 27, 33.	2
xx. 15.	4	xxiii. 4.	12 d	xxviii. 4, 5, 5.	4
xxxiv. 19.	15	xxiv. 4.	2	Dan. xi. 2,	
xxxvi. 19.	15 a	xxvii. 24.	5	2. 12 e, 1, 12 h, 12 h	
Ps. xxxvii. 16.	3	xxviii. 20.	12 d	xi. 13. 24, 28.	14
xlix. 16.	12 e	xxviii. 22.	2	Hos. xii. 8.	12 a
lxii. 10.	4	Isa. viii. 4.	4	Zech. xi. 5.	12 e
lxxiii. 12.	4				

a marg. 'his hand obtain.'

RID

נָצַל to pluck out of the hands of an oppressor or enemy. HI-
PHIL *pret.* Exod. vi. 6. *inf.* Gen. xxxvii. 22. *imp.* Ps.
lxxxii. 4.

פָּצָה to tear apart, to rend ; to snatch away, to deliver by
breaking through all impediments. KAL *imp.* Ps. cxliv.
7, 11.

שָׁבַת to rest. HIPHIL *pret.* Lev. xxvi. 6, *marg.* 'cause to cease.'

RIDDANCE

כָּלָה to be quite done ; to make a clean riddance or full end.
PIEL *fut.* Lev. xxiii. 22. כָּלָה *f.* a full end : Zeph. i. 18.

RIDDLE

חִידָה *f.* a difficult problem, a covert obscure way of speaking,
which couches the sense and meaning under figurative
expressions : wise sayings involving important truths :
Judg. xiv. 12, 13, 14, 15, 16, 17, 18, 19 : Ezek. xvii. 2.

RIDE

רָכַב to ride on horseback or in a chariot : to ride is a mark of
power and dignity, Hos. x. 11 : Ps. xlv. 4. God made
the Israelites to ride on the high places of the earth,
when he brought them in a triumphant manner to
possess a noble country, where they lived in high life
and in great honour, Deut. xxxii. 13 ; but God caused
men to ride over their heads, when they were reduced
to a state of vile servitude, Ps. lxvi. 12. To ride upon
the wind (Job xxx. 22) is to be tossed about by it like a
straw, meaning that he was violently shaken by his
afflictions. God rideth in supreme majesty upon the
clouds, or upon a cherub, the most perfect and powerful
of superior beings ; his chariots are thousands of angels,
Ps. lxviii. 17 ; or when he executes speedily his judgments for the deliverance of his people, Hab. iii. 8. He
rideth, sitteth as supreme sovereign, on the heavens ;
but on earth, his chariot was the cherubim in the temple, 1 Chron. xxxviii. 18. KAL a *pret.* b *inf.* c *imp.* d *fut.*
e *part.* Poel. HIPHIL f *pret.* g *fut.*

Gen. xxiv. 61.	d	Num. xxii. 22.	e	Judg. x. 4.	e
xli. 43.	g	xxii. 30.	e	xii. 14.	e
xlix. 17.	e	Deut. xxxii. 13.	g	1 Sam. xxv. 20.	e
Exod. xv. 1, 21.	e	xxxiii. 26.	e	xxv. 42.	d
Lev. xv. 9.	d	Judg. v. 10.		xxx. 17.	a

2 Sam. xvi. 2.	b	Esth. vi. 8.	a	Jer. xxii. 4.	e
xviii. 9.	e	viii. 10, 14.	e	l. 42.	d
xix. 26.	d	Job xxx. 22.	g	li. 21, 21.	d
xxii. 11.	e	xxxix. 18.	e	Ezek. xxiii. 6, 12, 23.	e
1 Kings i. 33.	f	Ps. xviii. 10.	d	xxxviii. 15.	e
i. 38, 44.	g	xlv. 4.	g	Hos. x. 11.	g
xiii. 13.	d	lxvi. 12.	f	xiv. 3.	f
xviii. 45.	d	lxviii. 4, 33.	d	Amos ii. 15.	d
2 Kings iv. 24.	b	Isa. xix. 1.	e	Hab. iii. 8.	d
ix. 16.	e	xxx. 16.	e	Hag. ii. 22, 22.	e
ix. 25.	e	xxxvi. 8.	e	Zech. i. 8.	
x. 16.	e	lviii. 14.	e	ix. 9.	e
xxiii. 23.	e	Jer. vi. 23.	e	x. 5.	d
Neh. ii. 12.		xvii. 25.	e	xii. 4.	e

RIDGE

תֶּלֶם *m.* a furrow : Ps. lxv. 10.

RIE

כֻּסֶּמֶת *f.* a species of grain like wheat, with a smooth or bald ear,
as if shorn ; Lat. *far adoreum;* Gr. ζέα, ὄλυρά; the
modern spelt, *triticum spelta.*—Linn. Exod. ix. 32 :
Isa. xxviii. 25, *marg.* ' or, spelt.'

RIFLE

שָׁסַס to plunder, to spoil. NIPHAL *pret.* Zech. xiv. 2.

RIGHT

1 אָמַן HIPHIL, to turn to the right : a *fut.* b אֱמֶת *f.* truth,
faithfulness, assurance, fidelity.

2 גְּאֻלָּה *f.* redemption.

3 יָמַן to use the right hand ; to turn to the right. HIPHIL
a *inf.* b *imp.* c *fut.* d *part.* e יָמִין *m.* right hand, right
side, right : Gen. xiii. 9, &c. f יְמָנִי *adj. id.*

4 יָשַׁר to be straight as a road, even (1 Sam. vi. 12, see *Straight*) ;
to be right in the eyes, *i. e.* pleasing ; *metaph.* of an even
mind, tranquil, composed ; *opp.* to be inflated, proud.
KAL a *pret.* PIEL b *pret.* c *part.* d יָשָׁר *adj.* straight,
right, *prop.* of a way ; Lxx. εὐθύς, ὀρθός, Ezek. i. 7, 23,
opp. to crooked, Job xxxii. 27, Micah iii. 9. It is
applied to God, to the word of God, and its precepts ;
to the judgments and to the ways of God. It is also
applied to man, and to the ways of man. e יֹשֶׁר *m.*
what is right. f מִישׁוֹר *m.* uprightness. g מֵישָׁרִים *m.*
pl. that which is just.

5 כֻּן to stand upright ; Niph. to be right, true. NIPHAL
a *part.* b כֵּן *part.* rightly, well.

6 כָּשֵׁר to be well and rightly adjusted for its proper end and
purpose ; to be right and fit, suitable and convenient.
KAL a *pret.* b כִּשְׁרוֹן *m.* skill, activity ; success, prosperity.

7 נָכַח to be in front, before the eyes ; to go straight forward ;
whence נֹכַח *m.* used as an *adv.,* right on. a נָכֹחַ *adj.*
straight, right.

8 פָּנָה to turn. KAL *inf.* "right early," לִפְנוֹת בֹּקֶר, *marg.*
' when the morning appeareth.' a פָּנִים *m. pl.* face.
לְפָנָיו " right forth."

9 צֶדֶק *m.* righteousness. a צְדָקָה *f. id.*

10 מִשְׁפָּט *m.* judgment ; right, rectitude, justice.

No. 3 e, Right hand, Right side, Right, not included.

Gen. xiii. 9, 9.	3 c e	2 Kings xxii. 2, 2.	4 d, 3 e	Ps. cxix. 128.	4 b
xviii. 25.	10	1 Chron. xii. 2.	3 d	cxl. 12.	10
xxiv. 48.	1 b	xiii. 4.	4 a	Prov. iv. 11.	4 e
Exod. xv. 26.	4 d	2 Chron. iii. 17.	3 e	iv. 25.	7
xxix. 20, 20, 20.	3 f	iii. 17.	3 f, or g	viii. 6.	4 g
Lev. viii. 23, 23, 23,		iv. 10.	3 f	viii. 9.	4 d
24, 24, 24.	3 f	xiv. 2.	4 d	ix. 15.	4 c
xiv. 14, 14, 14, 16,		xx 32.	4 d	xii. 5.	10
17, 17, 17, 25, 25,		xxiii. 10.	3 f	xii. 15.	4 d
25, 27, 28, 28, 28.	3 f	xxiv. 2.	4 d	xiv. 12.	4 d
Num. xxvii. 7.	5 b	xxv. 2.	4 d	xvi. 8.	10
Deut. vi. 18.	4 d	xxvi. 4.	4 d	xvi. 13, 25.	4 d
xii. 8, 25, 28.	4 d	xxvii. 2.	4 d	xx. 11.	4 d
xiii. 18.	4 d	xxviii. 1.	4 d	xxi. 2, 8.	4 d
xxi. 9.	4 d	xxix. 2.	4 d	xxiii. 16.	4 g
xxi. 17.	10	xxxi. 20.	4 d	xxiv. 26.	7
xxxii. 4.	4 d	xxxiv. 2, 2.	4 d, 3 e	Eccles. iv. 4.	6 b
Josh. ix. 25.	4 d	Ezra viii. 21.	4 d	Isa. x. 2.	10
Judg. xvii. 6.	4 d	Neh. ii. 20.	9 a	xxx. 10.	7 a
xxi. 25.	4 d	ix. 13.	4 d	xxx. 21.	10
Ruth iv. 6.	2	ix. 33.	1 b	xxxii. 7.	10
1 Sam. xii. 23.	4 d	Esth. viii. 5.	6 a	xlv. 19.	4 g
2 Sam. xiv. 19.	3 a	Job vi. 25.	4 e	Jer. ii. 21. α	1 b
xv. 3.	7 a	xxxiii. 27.	4 d	v. 28.	10
xix. 28.	9 a	xxxiv. 6, 17.	10	xvii. 11.	10
1 Kings vi. 8.	3 f	xxxv. 2.	10	xvii. 16.	7
vii. 21.	3 f	xxxvi. 6.	10	xxii. 7, 8.	10
vii. 39, 39.	3 e f	xlii. 7, 8.	5 a	xxxiv. 16.	4 d
xi. 33, 38.	4 d	Ps. x. 4, 4.	10, 9	xlix. 5.	8 a
xiv. 8.	4 d	xvii. 1.	9	Lam. iii. 35.	10
xv. 5, 11.	4 d	xix. 8.	4 d	Ezek. iv. 6.	3 f, or g
xxii. 43.	4 d	xxxiii. 4.	4 d	xviii. 5, 19, 21, 27.	9 a
2 Kings x. 15, 30.	4 d	xli. 5.	4 f	xxi. 16.	3 b
xi. 11.	4 d	xlvi. 5.	8	xxi. 27.	10
xii. 2.	4 d	li. 10.	5 a	xxxiii. 14, 16, 19.	9 a
xiv. 3.	4 d	lxxviii. 37.	5 a	xlvii. 1, 2.	3 f
xv. 3, 34.	4 d	cvii. 7.	4 d	Hos. xiv. 9.	4 d
xvi. 2.	4 d	cxix. 75.	9	Amos iii. 10.	7 a
xviii. 3.	4 d				

a lit. seed of truth.

RIGHTEOUS

1 יָשָׁר *adj.* see *Right.* מִישׁוֹר *m.* מֵישָׁרִים *m. pl.*

2 צָדַק to be right, straight; to be just, righteous, in dispensing justice; to have a just cause, to be in the right; *opp.* רָשַׁע to have an unjust cause, to be in the wrong; to be righteous, upright. KAL [a]*pret.* [b]*fut.* HIPHIL [c]*part.* [d] צֶדֶק *m.* rightness, straightness; rectitude, right, just; justice, of a judge, of a king, of God; hence righteousness, uprightness, integrity. [e] צְדָקָה *f.* rectitude, right; justice, of a king, of God, exhibited in punishing the wicked, or in avenging, delivering, rewarding the righteous. *Plur.* acts of justice, *i.e.* benignant or gracious deeds, Ps. xi. 7, ciii. 6. Judg. v. 11, the righteous acts of his rule in Israel, *i.e.* the aid which he gave them, the triumph, victory, which he bestowed upon them. In private persons, righteousness, integrity, virtue, piety. [f] צְדָקָה Ch. *f.* [g] צַדִּיק *adj.* just, righteous, *i.e.* doing justice, spoken of a judge or king who dispenses justice and defends the right: 2 Sam. xxiii. 3. Hence very often of God as a righteous judge, in punishing, or rewarding, or fulfilling his promises; just in one's cause, right; of a private person, just toward other men, Prov. xxix. 7; obedient to divine laws, hence righteous, upright, virtuous, pious, often coupled with תָּמִים, Job xii. 4; נָקִי, Exod. xxiii. 7; and as often put in opposition with רָשָׁע, Prov. x. 3, 6, 7, &c.

No. 2 g, Righteous, and No. 2 e, Righteousness, not included.

Gen. xxviii. 26.	2 a	Judg. v. 11, 11. a	2 e	Job ix. 15.	2 a
Lev. xix. 15.	2 d	1 Sam. xii. 7. a	2 e	x. 15.	2 a
Num. xxiii. 10.	1	Job iv. 7. a	1	xv. 14.	2 b
Deut. i. 16.	2 d	vi. 29.	2 d	xxii. 3.	2 b
xxxiii. 19.	2 d	viii. 6.	2 d	xxiii. 7.	1

Ref	Code	Ref	Code	Ref	Code
Job xxix. 14.	2 d	Ps. lxxxv. 10, 11, 13.	2 d	Isa. i. 21, 26.	2 d
xxxiv. 5.	2 a	xciv. 15.	2 d	xi. 4, 5.	2 d
xxxv. 2.	2 d	xcvi. 10.	1 b	xvi. 5.	2 d
xxxv. 7.	2 a	xcvi. 13.	2 d	xxvi. 9, 10.	2 d
xxxvi. 3.	2 a	xcvii. 2, 6.	2 d	xxxii. 1.	2 d
xl. 8.	2 b	xcviii. 9.	2 d	xxxiii. 15. β	2 e
Ps. iv. 1, 5.	2 d	cvii. 42.	1	xli. 2, 10.	2 d
vii. 8, 17.	2 d	cxviii. 19.	2 d	xlii. 6, 21.	2 d
ix. 8.	2 d	cxix. 7, 62, 106, 123,		xlv. 8, 8.	2 d e
xv. 2.	2 d	138, 144, 160, 164,		xlv. 13, 19.	2 d
xvii. 15.	2 a	172.	2 d	li. 1, 5, 7.	2 d
xviii. 20, 24.	2 d	cxix. 142, 142.	2 e d	lviii. 8.	2 d
xix. 9.	2 a	cxxxii. 9.	2 d	lxi. 3.	2 d
xxiii. 3.	2 d	Prov. ii. 7.	1	lxii. 1, 2.	2 d
xxxv. 24, 27, 28.	2 d	ii. 9.	2 d	lxiv. 5.	2 d
xxxvii. 6.	2 d	iii. 32.	1	Jer. xi. 20.	2 d
xl. 9.	2 d	viii. 8.	2 d	xxiii. 6.	2 d
xlv. 4, 7.	2 d	xii. 17.	2 d	xxxiii. 16.	2 d
xlviii. 10.	2 d	xiv. 9.	1	Ezek. iii. 20, 20.	2 d e
l. 6.	2 d	xv. 19.	1	xvi. 52.	2 b
li. 19.	2 d	xvi. 13.	2 d	Dan. iv. 27.	2 f
lii. 3.	2 d	xxv. 5.	2 d	ix. 24.	2 c
lviii. 1.	2 d	xxviii. 10.	1	iv. 3.	2 d
lxv. 5.	2 d	xxxi. 9.	2 d	Hos. ii. 19.	2 d
lxvii. 4.	1 a	Eccles. iii. 16.	2 d	x. 12, 12.	2 e d
lxxii. 2.	2 d	vii. 15.	2 d	Zeph. ii. 3.	2 d

α *marg.* 'righteousnesses.'   β *marg.* 'in righteousnesses.'

RIGOUR

פֶּרֶךְ *m.* fierceness, oppression, rigour, from the idea of crushing: Exod. i. 13, 14: Lev. xxv. 43, 46, 53.

RING (V)

הוּם to put in motion; to make a great noise. NIPHAL *fut.* 1 Sam. iv. 5: 1 Kings i. 45.

RING (N)

גַּב *m.* back, &c., the rim of a wheel, the circumference, felloes: Ezek. i. 18, 18, *marg.* 'strakes.'

גָּלִיל *adj.* rolling, turning; *subst.* a ring: Esth. i. 6: Cant. v. 14. The fingers, when covered, are like gold rings, and the nails, dyed with henna or the like, resemble gems.

טַבַּעַת *f.* a seal, signet-ring, worn by the Hebrews on the right hand; a ring of any kind: Gen. xli. 42, &c.

RINGSTRAKED

עָקֹד *adj.* banded, *i.e.* marked with bands or stripes, striped, ringstraked, especially on the feet. Gussetius thinks there is an allusion to the tying of sheep by the four legs when about to be sacrificed (see *Bind*), and that this word implies that Jacob's sheep were marked by a ring round the legs in like form. Gen. xxx. 35, 39, 40; xxxi. 8, 8, 10, 12.

RINSE

שָׁטַף to overflow; to wash or rinse copiously. KAL *pret.* Lev. xv. 11. NIPHAL *fut.* Lev. xv. 12. PUAL *pret.* Lev. vi. 28.

RIOTOUS

זָלַל see *Glutton.* KAL *part.* Poel, Prov. xxiii. 20, riotous eaters of flesh; xxviii. 7, *marg.* 'or, feedeth gluttons.'

RIP

בָּקַע to cleave asunder, to rend, to divide. KAL *inf.* Amos i. 13, *marg.* 'or, divided the mountains.' PIEL *pret.* 2 Kings xv. 16. *fut.* 2 Kings viii. 12. PUAL *fut.* Hos. xiii. 16.

RIPE

בָּשַׁל to be cooked or ripened. KAL *pret.* Joel iii. 13. HIPHIL *pret.* Gen. xl. 10, "brought forth ripe."

נָמַל to wean a child; the same idea seems to have applied to fruit ready to be detached from the tree. KAL *part.* Poel, Isa. xviii. 5, *i.e.* when the flower is becoming a ripening grape.

RISE

1 אַלְקוּם a word compounded, according to the Hebrew interpreters, of אַל *part. of negation,* and קוּם to rise up: Prov. xxx. 31, "a king, against whom there is no rising up," *i.e.* who cannot be resisted.

2 נָאָה to lift up oneself, to rise, to increase. KAL *pret.*

3 זָרַח to rise or spring up; spoken of light, of the sun, of the majesty of the appearance of God, Deut. xxxiii. 2, see *Come;* of the glory of the gospel at the coming of Christ, Isa. lx. 1, 2; of the appearance of the leprosy on the skin. KAL [a] *pret.* [b] *fut.* [c] זֶרַח *m.* a rising. [d] מִזְרָח *m.* the rising of the sun, "sunrising."

4 יָצָא to go forth. KAL *pret.* Gen. xix. 23, *marg.* 'gone forth,' *lit.* the sun rose or went forth on the earth, and Lot entered Sodom.

5 שְׂאֵת *f.* elevation, rising up; a swelling in the skin.

6 עָלָה to go or come up, to ascend, to mount. KAL [a] *pret.* [b] *inf.* [c] *fut.* [d] *part.* Poel. HIPHIL [e] *inf.*

7 קוּם to rise up, *e.g.* from the ground, or from a bed; so of one who rises in the morning; who had fallen down, or was upon his knees, or was sitting, *e.g.* on a seat or at a table; so to rise up from fasting, Ezek. ix. 5, since in fasting, as connected with mourning, they sat on the ground; *comp.* ver. 3, 4, 2 Sam. xii. 16, Job ii. 13; to rise up to or before any one, in token of respect and reverence. Very often it stands before verbs of going, departing, and the like, Gen. xxii. 3, &c. Also, these being omitted, קוּם itself is *i. q.* to rise up and go, to set off, Gen. xxxi. 17, &c. Sometimes קוּם marks the doing or undertaking anything impetuously, 2 Sam. xxiii. 10, &c. Sometimes it implies a doing again after an interval, Josh. vi. 26, Deut. xxxi. 16. In a few cases it is pleonastic, or marks a verbose style, Num. xi. 32, Exod. ii. 17. Hence *imp.* rise up! arise! as a word of incitement, either to go or to do anything; with ה *parag. intens.* especially to Jehovah, that he may help, Ps. iii. 8, &c. To rise up against any one in a hostile manner; *seq.* אֶל, עַל, לִפְנֵי בְּ; also as a witness; Ps. xxxv. 11; *seq.* בְּ, *seq.* עַל as enemies. To arise, come forth, to appear, *e.g.* a new king after his predecessor, a leader, a prophet, a new generation. To rise up out of calamity, Jer. li. 64; also to rise in prosperity, wealth, Prov. xxviii. 12. Of God, as rising up for judgment, to punish the wicked. To rise up, to rise again, as the dead returning to life; also to arise up out of sleep; to rise up from sickness. To sit down and rise up, put for the general course of life and conduct, Ps. cxxxix. 2; so Deut. vi. 7, xi. 19. KAL [a] *pret.* [b] *inf.* [c] *imp.* [d] *fut.* [e] *part.* POLEL [f] *fut.* HITHPAEL [g] *part.* קוּם Ch. P'AL [h] *pret.* [i] *fut.* [k] קִימָה *f.* an arising. [l] תְּקוֹמֵם *m.* one who rises up against, an adversary.

8 שָׁחַר to seek early; to rise betimes. PIEL [a] *part.* [b] שַׁחַר *m.* morning.

9 שָׁכַם to rise early in the morning; to do anything with earnestness, to urge earnestly. HIPHIL [a] *pret.* [b] *inf.* [c] *imp.* [d] *fut.* [e] *part.*

Gen. iv. 8.	7 d	Judg. vii. 1.	9 d	Ps. liv. 3.	7 a
xviii. 16.	7 d	viii. 21.	7 c	lix. 1.	7 g
xix. 1.	7 d	ix. 18.	7 a	lxxiv. 23.	7 e
xix. 2.	9 a	ix. 33.	7 a	lxxxvi. 14.	7 a
xix. 23.	4	ix. 34, 35, 43.	7 d	xcii. 11.	7 e
xx. 8.	9 d	xix. 5, 7, 9, 10, 27, 28.	7 d	xciv. 16.	7 d
xxi. 14.	9 d	xx. 5, 19.	9 d	cxiii. 3.	3 d
xxi. 32.	7 d	xx. 33.	7 a	cxix. 62.	7 d
xxii. 3, 3.	9 d, 7 d	xx. 38.	6 e	cxxiv. 2.	7 b
xxii. 19.	7 d	xx. 43.	3 d	cxxvii. 2.	7 b
xxiv. 54.	7 d	Ruth ii. 15.	7 d	cxxxix. 21.	7 l
xxv. 34.	7 d	iii. 14.	7 d	cxl. 10.	7 d
xxvi. 31.	9 d	1 Sam. i. 9.	7 d	Prov. xxiv. 16.	7 a
xxxi. 17, 21.	7 d	i. 19.	9 d	xxiv. 22.	9 b
xxxi. 35.	7 d	xv. 12.	9 d	xxvii. 14.	9 b
xxxi. 55.	9 d	xvi. 13.	7 d	xxviii. 12, 28.	7 b
xxxii. 22.	7 d	xvii. 20.	9 d	xxx. 31.	1
xxxii. 31.	3 b	xxii. 13.	7 d	xxxi. 15.	7 d
xxxvii. 35.	7 d	xxiv. 7, 7.	7 b a	Eccles. x. 4.	6 c
xliii. 15.	7 d	xxv. 29.	7 d	xii. 4.	7 d
xlvi. 5.	7 d	xxviii. 25.	7 d	Cant. ii. 10.	7 c
Exod. viii. 20.	9 c	xxix. 10.	9 d	iii. 2.	7 d
ix. 13.	9 c	xxix. 11.	9 d	v. 5.	7 a
x. 23.	7 a	2 Sam. xii. 21.	7 a	Isa. v. 11.	9 e
xii. 30.	7 d	xiv. 7.	7 a	xiv. 21.	7 d
xii. 31.	7 c	xv. 2.	9 a	xiv. 22.	7 b
xv. 7.	7 d	xv. 31.	7 e	xxiv. 20. γ	7 b
xxi. 19.	7 d	xviii. 31.	7 e	xxvi. 14.	7 d
xxii. 3.	3 a	xix. 32.	7 e	xxviii. 21.	7 d
xxiv. 4.	9 d	xxiii. 40, 49.	7 e	xxxii. 9.	7 c
xxiv. 13.	7 d	1 Kings i. 49.	7 d	xxxiii. 10.	7 d
xxxii. 6, 6.	9 d, 7 d	ii. 19.	7 d	xli. 25.	7 d
xxxiii. 8.	7 d	iii. 21.	7 d	xliii. 17.	7 d
xxxiii. 10.	7 e	viii. 20.	7 d	xlv. 6.	3 d
xxxiv. 4.	9 d	xxi. 16.	7 d	xlvii. 11.	7 b
Lev. xiii. 2, 10, 10, 19, 28, 43.	5	2 Kings iii. 22.	9 d	liv. 17.	7 a
xiv. 56.	5	vi. 15. a	7 b	lviii. 10.	3 a
xix. 32.	3 d	vii. 5.	7 a	lix. 19.	3 d
Num. ii. 3.	3 d	viii. 21.	7 a	lx. 1.	3 a
x. 35.	7 c	2 Chron. vi. 10.	7 d	lx. 3.	3 c
xiv. 40.	9 d	xiii. 6.	7 d	Jer. vii. 13, 25.	9 b
xvi. 2, 25.	7 d	xx. 20.	9 d	xi. 7.	9 b
xxi. 11.	3 d	xxi. 4.	7 a	xxv. 3, 4.	9 b
xxii. 13, 14, 21.	7 d	xxi. 9.	7 a	xxv. 27.	7 d
xxii. 20.	7 c	xxvi. 19.	3 b	xxvi. 5.	9 b
xxiii. 18.	7 c	xxviii. 15.	7 d	xxvi. 17.	7 d
xxiii. 24.	7 d	xxix. 20.	7 d	xxix. 19.	9 b
xxiv. 17.	7 a	xxxvi. 15.	9 b	xxxii. 33.	9 b
xxiv. 25.	7 d	Ezra i. 5.	7 d	xxxv. 14, 15.	9 b
xxv. 7.	7 d	v. 2.	7 h	xxxvii. 10.	7 d
xxxii. 14.	3 d	x. 6.	7 d	xliv. 4.	9 b
xxxiv. 15.	3 d	Neh. ii. 18.	7 d	xlvi. 8.	6 c
Deut. ii. 13, 24.	7 d	iii. 1.	7 d	xlix. 14.	6 d
iv. 41, 47.	3 d	iv. 21.	6 b	li. 1.	7 c
vi. 7.	7 d	Job i. 5.	9 a	li. 64.	7 d
xi. 19.	7 b	ix. 7.	3 b	Lam. i. 14.	7 d
xix. 11.	7 a	xiv. 12.	7 d	iii. 62.	7 d
xix. 15, 16.	7 d	xvi. 8.	7 d	iii. 63.	7 k
xxii. 26.	7 d	xx. 27.	7 g	Ezek. vii. 11.	7 a
xxviii. 7.	7 e	xxiv. 14, 22.	7 d	xlvii. 5.	2
xxix. 22.	7 d	xxvii. 7.	7 g	Dan. iii. 24.	7 h
xxxi. 16.	7 d	xxx. 12.	7 d	vii. 24.	7 i
xxxii. 38.	7 d	xxxi. 14.	7 d	viii. 27.	7 d
xxxiii. 2.	3 a	Ps. iii. 1.	7 d	Amos v. 2. γ	7 d
xxxiii. 11, 11.	7 e d	xvii. 17.	7 g	vii. 9.	7 d
Josh. i. 15.	3 d	xviii. 38.	7 d	viii. 8.	6 a
iii. 1.	9 d	xviii. 39, 48.	7 e	viii. 14.	7 d
iii. 16.	7 d	xx. 8.	7 d	ix. 5.	6 a
vi. 12, 15.	9 d	xxvii. 3.	7 d	Obad. 1.	7 d
vi. 26.	7 d	xxvii. 12.	7 d	Jonah i. 3.	7 d
vii. 16.	9 d	xxxv. 11.	7 d	iv. 7.	6 b
viii. 7.	7 d	xxxvi. 12.	7 b	Micah ii. 8.	7 f
viii. 10, 14.	9 d	xli. 8. β	7 b	vii. 6.	
xii. 1.	3 d	xliv. 5.	7 e	Nah. i. 9.	7 d
xiii. 5.	3 d	l. 1.		Hab. i. 7.	
xviii. 4.	7 d			Zeph. iii. 7.	9 a
xix. 12, 27, 34.	3 d			iii. 8.	7 d
Judg. vi. 21.	6 c			Zech. xiv. 13.	6 a
vi. 38.	7 e			Mal. i. 11.	3 d

a *lit.* was early to rise.　β *lit.* not add to rise up.　γ *lit.* not add to rise.

RITE

חֻקָּה *f.* a statute, an ordinance : Num. ix. 3.

RIVER

1 אָפִיק *m.* channel, stream ; a channel with or without water.

2 יְאוֹר *m.* a fosse, channel, canal, Isa. xxxiii. 21, where it is the fosse of a fortified city ; Lxx. διῶρυξ ; a channel, *sc.* shaft of a mine, Job xxviii. 10 ; a river, κατ' ἐξοχήν, the river of Egypt, the Nile. In one place only spoken of another river, Dan. xii. 5, 6, 7 ; *plur.* rivers of Egypt, *i.e.* the branches and canals of the Nile.

3 יוּבַל *m.* a river or stream. אוּבָל or אָבָל *m. id.*

4 יָד *com.* hand : Jer. xlvi. 6, *lit.* by the side of the river Euphrates.

5 נָהָר *m.* a stream, current, flood ; a stream, river, *seq. gen.* of region, Gen. xv. 18, &c. ; with the *art.* ה the river κατ' ἐξοχήν so called, *i.e.* the Euphrates, Gen. xv. 18. Once the context requires נָהָר to be taken as the Nile, Isa. xix. 5. In Ps. xlvi. 5, many understand Siloam, and not unaptly, since נָהָר is also used of smaller streams, as the waters of Damascus, 2 Kings v. 12, especially Job xxviii. 11 ; but Gussetius takes the term mystically. Put as the emblem of abundance and prosperity, Isa. xlviii. 18.—Gen. ii. 10, &c. ᵃ נְהַר Ch.

6 נַחַל *m.* a stream, brook, torrent, so called from its flowing. Most of the streams of Palestine are torrents flowing only in winter, χείμαρροι, and such an one is meant in Job vi. 15, my brethren are deceitful like the torrent, which dries up unexpectedly, and so disappoints the traveller. ᵃ נַחֲלָה *f. id.*

7 פֶּלֶג *m.* the water of a brook or river divided into canals and rivulets, that it may be conveyed into any part of grounds when it is wanted. ᵃ פְּלַגָּה *f. id.*

8 תְּעָלָה *f.* trench, conduit : Ezek. xxxi. 4, "little rivers," *marg.* ' or, conduits.'

No. 5 not included.

Gen. xli. 1, 2, 3, 3, 17,		2 Kings x. 33.	6	Jer. xxxi. 9.	6
18.	2	xix. 24.	2	xlvi. 6.	4, 5
Exod. i. 22.	2	xxiv. 7, 7.	6, 5	Lam. ii. 18.	6
ii. 3, 5, 5.	2	2 Chron. vii. 8.	6	iii. 48.	7
iv. 9, 9.	2	Ezra iv. 10, 11, 16, 17,		Ezek. vi. 3.	1
vii. 15, 17, 18, 18, 18,		20.	5 a	xxix. 3, 3, 4, 4, 4, 5,	
19, 20, 20, 21, 21,		v. 3, 6, 6.	5 a	9, 10.	2
21, 24, 24, 25.	2	vi. 6, 6, 8, 13.	5 a	xxx. 12.	2
viii. 3, 5, 9, 11.	2	vii. 21, 25.	5 a	xxxi. 4.	8
xvii. 5.	2	Job xx. 17.	7 a	xxxi. 12.	1
Lev. xi. 9, 10.	6	xxviii. 10.	2	xxxii. 6.	1
Num. xxxiv. 5.	6	xxix. 6.	7	xxxiv. 13.	1
Deut. ii. 24, 36, 36, 37.	6	Ps. i. 3.	7	xxxv. 8.	1
iii. 8, 12, 16, 16.	6	xxxvi. 8.	6	xxxvi. 4, 6.	1
iv. 48.	6	lxv. 9.	6	xlvii. 5, 5, 6, 7, 9, 9,	
x. 7.	6	lxxviii. 44.	6	12.	6
Josh. xii. 1, 2, 2.	6	cxix. 136.	7	xlvii. 19.	6 a
xiii. 9, 9, 16, 16.	6	Prov. v. 16.	7	xlviii. 28.	6 a
xv. 4, 7, 47.	6	xxi. 1.	7	Dan. viii. 2, 3, 6.	3
xvi. 8.	6	Eccles. i. 7, 7.	6	xii. 5, 5, 6, 7.	2
xvii. 9, 9, 9.	6	Cant. v. 12.	2	Joel i. 20.	1
xix. 11.	6	Isa. vii. 18.	2	iii. 18.	1
Judg. iv. 7, 13.	6	xxiii. 3, 10.	2	Amos vi. 14.	2
v. 21, 21, 21.	6	xxx. 25.	7	Micah vi. 7.	6
2 Sam. xvii. 13.	6	xxxii. 2.	7	Nah. iii. 8.	2
xxiv. 5.	6	xxxvii. 25.	2	Zech. x. 11.	2
1 Kings viii. 65.	6	Jer. xvii. 8.	2		

ROAD

פָּשַׁט to invade for the purpose of driving off booty. KAL *pret.* 1 Sam. xxvii. 10.

ROAR

1 הָגָה to murmur, to mutter, to growl, *pr.* to utter a low rumbling sound, nearly the same as the next word ; spoken of the growling of the lion over his prey, distinct from the roaring before he seizes it. Gr. ὑποβρυχάομαι ; to roar is שָׁאַג βρυχάομαι. KAL *fut.*

2 הָמָה onomatopoetic, like English ' to hum ;' spoken of any murmuring, confused noise or sound ; of the sounds uttered by certain animals, *e.g.* a bear, a dog, a dove, *fig.* of the sighing, moaning of men, which is also compared with the growling of bears, Isa. lix. 11, and the cooing of doves, Ezek. vii. 16 ; of various sounds and noises, of rain, of waves, also of a tumultuous crowd. KAL ᵃ *pret.* ᵇ *fut.*

3 נָהַם to growl, to snarl, the usual word applied to the noise of the young lion, distinguished from שָׁאַג, although sometimes also attributed to the full-grown lion, Prov. xxviii. 15. The root is onomatopoetic. *Trop.* of the roaring of the sea, Isa. v. 30. KAL ᵃ *fut.* ᵇ *part.* Poel. ᶜ נַהַם *m.* growl, of a young lion. ᵈ נְהָמָה *f.* the roaring of the sea.

4 צָרַח to be clear, manifest ; of the voice, to cry aloud. HIPHIL *fut.*

5 רָעַם to be moved, agitated, to tremble ; especially of the sea, to be troubled, tossed, to rage. KAL *fut.*

6 שָׁאַג to roar ; spoken chiefly of the lion, of thunder, of raging warriors ; also of persons in extreme pain. KAL ᵃ *pret.* ᵇ *inf.* ᶜ *fut.* ᵈ *part.* Poel. ᵉ שְׁאָנָה *f.* roaring of a lion ; a cry wrung forth by grief.

Judg. xiv. 5.	6 d	Prov. xix. 12.	3 c	Jer. xxxi. 35.	2 b
1 Chron. xvi. 32.	5	xx. 2.	3 c	l. 42.	2 b
Job iii. 24.	6 e	xxviii. 15.	3 b	li. 38.	6 c
iv. 10.	6 e	Isa. v. 29, 29, 29.	6 e c, 3 a	li. 55.	6 a
xxxvii. 4.	6 c	v. 30, 30.	3 a d	Ezek. xix. 7.	6 e
Ps. xxii. 1.	6 e	xxxi. 4.	1	xxii. 25.	6 d
xxii. 13.	6 d	xlii. 13.	4	Hos. xi. 10, 10.	6 c
xxxii. 3.	6 e	li. 15.	2 b	Joel iii. 16.	6 c
xxxviii. 8.	6 a	Jer. ii. 15.	6 c	Amos i. 2.	6 c
xlvi. 3.	2 b	v. 22.	2 a	iii. 4.	6 c
lxxiv. 4.	6 a	vi. 23.	2 b	iii. 8.	6 a
xcvi. 11.	5	xxv. 30.	6 d	iii. 28.	6 a
xcviii. 7.	5	xxv. 30.	6 b c	Zeph. iii. 3.	6 d
civ. 21.	6 d			Zech. xi. 3.	6 e

ROAST

1 בָּשַׁל to be cooked. PIEL ᵃ *pret.* ᵇ *fut.*

2 חָרַךְ to burn, to scorch, to singe ; perhaps referring to the hasty way in which game was cooked after being taken. KAL *fut.*

3 צָלָה to roast. KAL ᵃ *inf.* ᵇ *fut.* ᶜ צָלִי *adj.* something roasted.

4 קָלָה to roast, to parch, as ears of corn, also the body in a way of torture. KAL *pret.*

Exod. xii. 8, 9.	3 c	2 Chron. xxxv. 13.	1 b	Isa. xliv. 19.	3 b
Deut. xvi. 7.	1 a	Prov. xii. 27.	2	Jer. xxix. 22.	4
1 Sam. ii. 15.	3 a	Isa. xliv. 16, 16.	3 b c		

ROB

1 בָּזַז to plunder, spoil, or rob ; to take and carry off the booty or pillage. KAL ᵃ *pret.* ᵇ *fut.* ᶜ *part.* Poel. ᵈ *part.* Paül. PUAL ᵉ *pret.*

2 בֵּן *m.* son : Dan. xi. 14, *marg.* ' the children of robbers.'

3 גָּזַל to pluck off, or away, to tear away, to take by force ; espe-

cially of the rich and powerful who seize upon the possessions of the poor by fraud and violence. KAL [a] *pret.* [b] *fut.* [c] *part.* Poel. [d] גֵּזֶל *m.* robbery. [e] גְּזֵלָה *f. id.*

4 עוּד *perhaps in this instance a derivation from* עַד *a prey.* PIEL *pret.* Ps. cxix. 61. Gesenius would translate it, "surrounded me," from the primary meaning, to do a thing again and again. Gussetius, "or from עוּד to witness, and in this case implying false witness, fabrication of testimony."

5 פָּרִיץ *m.* violent, rapacious, from the idea of breaking through; an oppressor, tyrant.

6 פֶּרֶק *m.* violence, rapine, from the idea of breaking in upon.

7 צַמִּים *m.* a snare, noose; *metaph.* destruction: Job v. 5. Vulg. the thirsty, taking it to be the same as צְמֵאִים, which suits better to the parallelism.

8 קָבַע to cover, to hide; hence to defraud, to rob any one covertly. KAL [a] *pret.* [b] *fut.* [c] *part.* Poel.

9 שָׁדַד to practise violence; to oppress, to destroy any one; to lay waste, to make desolate. KAL [a] *part.* Poel. [b] שֹׁד *m.* violence, oppression.

10 שָׁכֹל to be bereaved of children. PIEL [a] *pret.* [b] שַׁכּוּל *adj.* bereaved.

11 שָׁסָה to plunder, to spoil. KAL [a] *part.* Poel. POEL [b] *pret.*

Lev. xix. 13.	3 b	Prov. xxi. 7.	9 b	Ezek. vii. 22.	5
xxvi. 22.	10 a	xxii. 22.	3 b	xviii. 10.	
Judg. ix. 25.	3 b	xxviii. 24.	3 c	xxii. 29. *a*	3 a d
1 Sam. xxiii. 1.	11 a	Isa. x. 2.	1 b	xxxiii. 15.	3 e
2 Sam. xvii. 8.	10 b	x. 13.	11 b	xxxix. 10, 10.	1 a c
Job v. 5.	7	xvii. 14.	1 c	Dan. xi. 14.	2, 5
xii. 6.	9 a	xlii. 22.	1 d	Amos iii. 10.	9 b
xviii. 9.	7	xlii. 24.	1 c	Obad. 5.	9 a
Ps. lxii. 10.	3 d	lxi. 8.	3 d	Nah. iii. 1.	6
cxix. 61.	4	Jer. vii. 11.	5	Mal. iii. 8, 8, 8.	8 b c a
Prov. xvii. 12.	10 b	l. 37.	1 e	iii. 9.	8 c

a "exercised robbery."

ROBE

אֶדֶר *m.* a garment of distinction, splendour and majesty: Micah ii. 8. אַדֶּרֶת *f. id.* Jonah iii. 6.

בֶּגֶד *m.* any garment, or clothing (see *Garment*): 1 Kings xxii. 10, 30: 2 Chron. xviii. 9, 29.

כֻּתֹּנֶת *f.* a coat: Isa. xxii. 21.

מְעִיל *m.* upper garment, robe, especially an exterior tunic, fuller and larger than the common one, but without sleeves; see 2 Sam. xiii. 18. It was worn by women, 2 Sam. xiii. 18; by men of birth and rank, Job i. 20: ii. 12: by kings and princes, 1 Sam. xviii. 4; xxiv. 5, 12; by priests, xxviii. 14: Ezra ix. 3, 5: and by the high priest under the ephod, Exod. xxviii. 31; xxxix. 22, *comp.* Exod. xxviii. 32, &c., Lev. viii. 7.—Exod. xxviii. 4, &c.

ROCK

1 חַלָּמִישׁ *m.* flint: Job xxviii. 9, *marg.* 'or, flint.'

2 כֵּפִים *m. pl.* rocks, hollow or arched.

3 סֶלַע *m.* a rock; sometimes having a fortress on the top fixed in the ground, large and immovable, from which any one precipitated would be killed, in which also there might be caverns for wild beasts: Isa. xxxi. 9, xxxiii. 16: hence *metaph.* of God as a refuge, Ps. xviii. 2, &c.

4 מָעוֹז *m.* a strong or fortified place.

5 צוּר *m.* a rock, generally sharp and precipitous; *metaph.* of a place where one is secure from his enemies; *comp.* Ps. xxvii. 5; lxi. 2: hence a refuge, shelter, especially of God, affording refuge and protection to Israel; of the Messiah, "a rock of offence," Isa. viii. 14; of any tutelary deity, Deut. xxxii. 31: 1 Sam. ii. 2. By another metaphor, drawn from a quarry, צוּר is put for the founder of a people, Isa. li. 1.—Exod. xvii. 6, &c.

No. 5 not included.

Num. xx. 8, 8, 10, 10,		Neh. ix. 15.	3	Isa. xxxii. 2.	3
11.	3	Job xxviii. 9.	1	xxxiii. 16.	3
xxiv. 21.	3	xxx. 6.	2	xlii. 11.	3
Deut. xxxii. 13, 13.	3, 5	xxxix. 1, 28, 28.	3	lvii. 5.	3
Judg. i. 36.	3	Ps. xviii. 2.	3	Jer. iv. 29.	2
vi. 20.	3	xxvii. 3.	3	v. 3.	3
vi. 26.	4	xl. 2.	3	xiii. 4.	3
xv. 8, 11, 13.	3	xlii. 9.	3	xvi. 16.	3
xx. 45, 47, 47.	3	lxxi. 3.	3	xxiii. 29.	3
xxi. 13.	3	lxxviii. 16.	3	xlviii. 28.	3
1 Sam. xiii. 6.	3	civ. 18.	3	xlix. 16.	3
xiv. 4, 4.	3	Prov. xxx. 26.	3	li. 25.	3
xxiii. 25.	3	Cant. ii. 14.	3	Ezek. xxiv. 7, 8.	3
2 Sam. xxii. 2.	3	Isa. ii. 21, 21.	5, 3	xxvi. 4, 14.	3
1 Kings xix. 11.	3	vii. 19.	3	Amos vi. 12.	3
2 Chron. xxv. 12, 12.	3	xxii. 16.	3	Obad. 3.	3

ROD

1 חֹטֶר *m.* a rod, *i. e.* slender and flexible; a shoot, a twig.

2 מַקֵּל *m.* a shoot, rod; then a staff, which one carries in his hand, with which an animal is beaten, the crook of a shepherd, a spear or javelin; of a divining rod, ῥαβδομαντεία, Hos. iv. 13.

3 מַטֶּה *com.* a branch, bough, shoot, Ezek. xix. 11, so called from its stretching or extending itself; a rod or staff for walking, with which grain is beaten, Isa. xxviii. 27; especially for chastisement, Isa. x. 5, &c.; Ezek. vii. 11, a rod of wickedness, *i. e.* to chastise it; ver. 10, the rod hath blossomed, *sc.* for your chastisement; Micah vi. 9, "hear ye the rod," the chastisement, punishment; a sceptre of a king, Ps. cx. 2, hence an emblem of power, empire; a shepherd's rod or crook used in tending his flocks, Exod. iv. 2; a spear, lance, 1 Sam. xiv. 27.

4 שֵׁבֶט *m.* a stick, rod, staff; a rod or staff for chastising; hence rod of correction, Prov. xxii. 15; the rod of God, with which he corrects men, Job xxi. 9, Isa. x. 5, xi. 4; the rod of his mouth, *i. e.* his severe sentence, stern decree; also for beating out pulse, Isa. xxviii. 27; a staff on which one leans, Ps. xxiii. 4; the crook of a shepherd, Lev. xxvii. 32, with which also he numbered his flock, and marked the tenth; *trop.* Ezek. xx. 37, Micah vii. 14. Staff of office, hence sceptre of a king, *trop.* for rule and administration, of unjust rule, Ps. cxxv. 3.—Exod. xxi. 20, &c.

No. 4 not included.

Gen. xxx. 37, 37, 38,		Exod. xiv. 16.	3	Prov. xiv. 3.	1
39, 41, 41.	2	xvii. 5, 9.	3	Isa. x. 26.	3
Exod. iv. 2, 4, 17, 20,	3	Num. xvii. 2, 2, 2, 3,		xi. 1.	1
vii. 9, 10, 12, 12, 12,		3, 5, 6, 6, 6, 6, 7,		Jer. i. 11.	2
15, 17, 19, 20.	3	8, 9, 9, 10.	3	xlviii. 17.	2
viii. 5, 16, 17.	3	xx. 8, 9, 11.	3	Ezek. vii. 10, 11.	3
ix. 23.	3	1 Sam. xiv. 27, 43.	3	xix. 11, 12, 14, 14.	3
x. 13.	3	Ps. cx. 2.	3	Micah vi. 9.	3

ROE

יַעֲלָה *f.* the wild female goat, ibex: Prov. v. 19, the "pleasant

roe," or graceful ibex; an epithet for a beautiful woman.

צְבִי *m.* roe, antelope, Gr. δορκάς: it is very timid and fleet, and the flesh was, and is, regarded as a delicacy. Bochart thinks it is to be referred to the whole genus of the roe, and not to a particular species. To their fleetness pertains Cant. ii. 9, *comp.* ver. 8; 2 Sam. i. 19. The roe or antelope is highly prized by the Orientals for its elegance, and they even obtest by it, Cant. ii. 7, iii. 5.—Deut. xii. 15, 22; xiv. 5; xv. 22: 2 Sam. ii. 18, *marg.* 'one of the roes that is in the field;' 1 Kings iv. 23: 1 Chron. xii. 8: Prov. vi. 5: Cant. ii. 7, 9, 17; iii. 5; viii. 14: Isa. xiii. 14. צְבִיָּה *f.* female roe: Cant. iv. 5; vii. 3.

ROLL

1 גָּלַל to roll; it is variously used and applied: to roll along as wheels and great stones are rolled; to roll away, *metaph.* to take away or free from a reproach; to roll down from a rock or precipice; to run down as water from a spring, in rills or streams; to roll together, as parchment is rolled up; to roll upon, *metaph.* to roll upon a person is to assault him violently; to devolve guilt upon him; to take advantage against him, Gen. xliii. 12; to roll oneself, ways, works upon God, to trust him, see *Trust, Commit:* to wallow. It is applied to anything round, as heaps, &c. KAL [a]*pret.* [b]*imp.* [c]*part.* POEL. NIPHAL [d]*pret.* POAL [e]*part.* HIPHIL [f]*fut.* PILPEL [g]*pret.* HITHPALPEL [h]*pret.* [i]מְגִלָּה *f.* volume, roll, *i.e.* a book. [k]Ch. *f. id.* [l]גַּלְגַּל *m.* rolling thing.

2 גִּלָּיוֹן *m.* a table, tablet of wood, stone, or metal, on which to write or inscribe anything, *i. q.* לוּחַ, so called as being smooth, bare, naked, or empty, Isa. viii. 1. In Talmudic, גִּלָּיוֹן is the empty margin of a page or volume, roll.—*Gesenius.*

3 חִתּוּל *m.* a bandage, roller, for binding up a wound.

4 סְפַר Ch. *m.* book.

5 פָּלַשׁ to roll, to make revolve; to roll oneself, in token of great sorrow. HITHPAEL [a]*pret.* [b]*imp.*

Gen. xxix. 3, 8.	1 a	Prov. xxvi. 27.	1 c	Jer. xxxvi. 32.	1 i
xxix. 10.	1 f	Isa. viii. 1.	2	li. 25.	1 g
Josh. v. 9.	1 a	ix. 5.	1 e	Ezek. ii. 9.	1 i
x. 18.	1 b	xvii. 13.	1 l	iii. 1, 2, 3.	1 i
1 Sam. xiv. 33.	1 b	xxxiv. 4.	1 d	xxx. 21.	1 d
Ezra vi. 1.	4	Jer. xxxvi. 2, 4, 6,		Micah i. 10.	5 b, or a
vi. 2.	1 k	14, 14, 20, 21, 23,		Zech. v. 1, 2.	1 i
Job xxx. 14.	1 h	25, 27, 28, 28, 29.	1 i		

ROOF

גַּג *m.* the flat roof of the Oriental houses, on which they walked, and sometimes slept: Deut. xxii. 8: Josh. ii. 6, 6, 8: Judg. xvi. 27: 2 Sam. xi. 2, 2; xviii. 24: Neh. viii. 16: Jer. xix. 13, *lit.* which upon their roofs; xxxii. 29: Ezek. xl. 13, 13.

קוֹרָה *f.* a beam, joist, or cross-beam, translated once 'roof,' and put *synecd.* for house: Gen. xix. 8.

חֵךְ *m.* the palate, together with the corresponding lower part of the mouth, the inside mouth; "the roof of the mouth:" Job xxix. 10: Ps. cxxxvii. 6: Cant. vii. 9: Lam. iv. 4: Ezek. iii. 26.

ROOM

מָקוֹם *com.* (see *Place*): Gen. xxiv. 23, 25, 31.

קֵן *m.* nest: Gen. vi. 14, *marg.* 'nests,' *i. e.* cells, small apartments; Ch. mansions.

רָחַב to be enlarged; Hiphil, to make room: *pret.* Gen. xxvi. 22. *fut.* Prov. xviii. 16, *lit.* enlargeth. מֶרְחָב *m.* large room: Ps. xxxi. 8.

ROOT

1 נָסַח to pluck out, to tear away, to extirpate. KAL *fut.*

2 נָתַק to tear away; to pluck off. NIPHAL *fut.*

3 נָתַשׁ to tear up, to pluck up a plant. KAL [a]*pret.* [b]*inf.* [c]*fut.*

4 עָקַר to pluck up, to root out. NIPHAL [a]*fut.*

5 שֹׁרֶשׁ *m.* a root, Job xxx. 4, Jer. xvii. 8; *trop.* for the bottom or lowest part of anything, of a mountain, &c.; hence Job xix. 8, the root of controversy, *i. e.* the cause, ground of strife; root, *poet.* for fixed dwelling, abode, Judg. v. 14; just as nations taking up their abode in a land are said to be planted in it, to take root in it; a shoot, sprout, springing from the root, Isa. liii. 2; *metaph.* Isa. xi. 10, sprout of Jesse, *i. e.* the Messiah; *comp.* ῥίζα Δαβίδ, Rev. v. 5; but in Isa. xiv. 30, the root itself is meant, the metaphor being transferred from plants to a people. —Deut. xxix. 18, &c. שָׁרַשׁ a derivative verb from the above. PIEL, to root out: [a]*pret.* [b]*fut.* PUAL [c]*fut.* POEL, to take root: [d]*pret.* POAL [e]*pret.* HIPHIL [f]*fut.* [g]*part.* [h]שֹׁרֶשׁ Ch. *m.*

No. 5 not included.

Deut. xxix. 28.	3 c	Job xxxi. 12.	5 b	Isa. xl. 24.	5 d
1 Kings xiv. 15.	3 a	Ps. lii. 5.	5 a	Jer. i. 10.	3 b
Job v. 3.	5 g	lxxx. 9. a	5 f, 5	xii. 2.	5 e
xviii. 14.	2	Prov. ii. 22.	1	Dan. iv. 15, 23, 26.	5 h
xxxi. 8.	5 c	Isa. xxvii. 6.	5 f	Zeph. ii. 4.	4

[a] *lit.* didst cause its roots to take root.

ROPE

חֶבֶל a cord, a rope: 2 Sam. xvii. 13: 1 Kings xx. 31, 32.

עֲבֹת *com.* a rope well twisted together: Judg. xvi. 11, 12: Isa. v. 18.

ROSE

חֲבַצֶּלֶת *f.* a flower growing in meadows and pastures, which the ancient versions render sometimes the lily, and sometimes the narcissus; more accurately, however, the Syriac translator, who uses the same word, which, according to the Syriac lexicographers (cited in full in Ges. Commentary on Isa. xxxv. 1), signifies the *colchicum autumnale* (Linn.), or meadow saffron, an autumnal flower similar to saffron, springing from poisonous bulbous roots, and of a white and violet colour. This is favoured by the etymology, the word being compounded from חָמַץ acid, acrid, and בֶּצֶל bulb.—*Gesenius.* Cant. ii. 1: Isa. xxxv. 1. Others, the red and white cistus, which abounds even yet in the plain of Sharon.— *Wilde's Travels.*

ROT

1 מְלָחִים *m. pl.* old clothes, worn-out garments, rotten rags.

2   מַק   *m.* rottenness, putridity.

3   נָפַל   to fall; of limbs which fall away and become emaciated. KAL [a] *pret.* [b] *part.* Poel. HIPHIL [c] *inf.*

4   עָבַשׁ   to die, spoken of seed which loses its germinating power, and dies in the ground from the effects of too great heat. KAL *pret.*

5   רָקַב   to be carious, worm-eaten, or rotten as wood. KAL [a] *fut.* [b] רָקָב *m.* caries, rottenness of the bones; *metaph.* of terror striking through all one's bones. [c] רִקָּבוֹן *m.* rottenness of wood.

Num. v. 21.	3 b	Prov. x. 7.	5 a	Jer. xxxviii. 11, 12.	1
v. 22.	3 c	xii. 4.	5 b	Hos. v. 12.	5 b
v. 27.	3 a	xiv. 30.	5 b	Joel i. 17.	4
Job xiii. 28.	5 b	Isa. v. 24.	2	Hab. iii. 16.	5 b
xli. 27.	5 c	xl. 20.	5 a		

ROUGH

1   אֵיתָן   *m.* strong, hard; but, according to Gesenius, a perennial brook.

2   סָמָר   *adj.* bristling.

3   עַז   *adj.* strong, fierce.

4   קָשֶׁה   *adj.* hard, harsh; firm, rigid.

5   רְכָסִים   *m. pl.* bound-up places, *i. e.* rough, rugged, difficult to pass. Jarchi, mountain-ranges, chains of mountains.

6   שֵׂעָר   *m.* hair. [a] שָׂעִיר hairy.

Gen. xlii. 7, 30.	4	2 Chron. x. 13.	4	Jer. li. 27.	2
Deut. xxi. 4.	1	Prov. xviii. 23.	3	Dan. viii. 21.	6 a
1 Sam. xx. 10.	4	Isa. xxvii. 8.	4	Zech. xiii. 4.	6
1 Kings xii. 13.	4	xl. 4.	5		

ROUND

חַסְפַּס   *part. passive* of חָסַף to scale or peel off: Exod. xvi. 14. Gesenius, something scaled off like scales. Gussetius, something compact and cohering like clay; see *Clay*. Michaelis in Supp. ad Lex. Heb., something gathering together like flakes of snow.

דּוּר   *m.* (see *Ball*): Isa. xxix. 3.

נָקַף   (see *Compass*), to go round about; to round. HIPHIL *fut.* Lev. xix. 27.

סָבִיב   *m.* circuit; used frequently as a *subs., adv.,* and *prep.,* mostly translated "round about," and frequently doubled, *lit.* round about, round about: Gen. xxiii. 17, &c.: Ezek. xl. 5, &c. מֵסַב *m.* used also as an *adv.* and *prep.*: 1 Kings vi. 29: 2 Kings xxiii. 5: Job xxxvii. 12.

סַהַר   *m.* roundness: Cant. vii. 2.

עָגֹל   *adj.* round, rounded: 1 Kings vii. 23, 31, 31, 35; x. 19: 2 Chron. iv. 2.

שַׂהֲרֹנִים   *m. pl. dimin.* crescents like moons worn as an ornament on the necks of men, women, and camels, "round tires like the moon:" Isa. iii. 18.

ROUSE

קוּם   to rise; to make to rise. HIPHIL *fut.* Gen. xlix. 9.

ROW

טוּר   *m.* a regular course or series in which stones are laid, or columns set in a building; a row, range, as of gems: Exod. xxviii. 17, &c. טִירָה *f.* a wall round about: Ezek. xlvi. 23.

נִדְבָּךְ   Ch. *m.* layer of stones, from the idea of joining; or, wall, *i. e.* side of a room or house: it has both these significations in the Targums: Ezra vi. 4, 4.

מַעֲרָכָה   *f.* arrangement, disposition, order: Lev. xxiv. 6. מַעֲרֶכֶת *f.* a row, pile, arranged in order, as of the shew-bread or loaves set out in rows before Jehovah in the temple: Lev. xxiv. 6, 7.

תּוֹר   *m.* order, turn; a row or string of pearls, or of gold and silver beads, as an ornament for the head: Cant. i. 10.

ROW   (*V*)

חָתַר   to break through a wall, *metaph.* to break through or cleave the waves by rowing. KAL *fut.* Jonah i. 13.

שׁוּט   to whip, to scourge, to lash; to lash the sea with oars. KAL *part.* Ezek. xxvii. 26.

ROYAL

1   מֶלֶךְ   *m.* king; "royal," *lit.* of a king. [a] מְלַךְ Ch. *m.* [b] מְלוּכָה *f.* kingdom; "royal," *lit.* of the kingdom. [c] מַלְכוּת *f.* kingdom; "royal," *lit.* of the kingdom; "royal estate." [d] מַמְלָכָה *f.* kingdom.

2   (קרי) שַׁפְרִיר and (כתיב) שַׁפְרוּר   *m.* throne-ornament, tapestry with which a throne is hung.

Gen. xlix. 20.	1	1 Chron. xxix. 25.	1 e	Esth. vi. 8, 8.	1 c
Josh. x. 2.	1 d	2 Chron. xxii. 10.	1 d	viii. 15.	1 c
1 Sam. xxvii. 5.	1 d	Esth. i. 7, 9, 11, 19,		Isa. lxii. 3.	1 b
2 Sam. xii. 26.	1 b	19.	1 c	Jer. xli. 1.	1 b
1 Kings v. 13.	1	ii. 16, 17.	1 c	xliii. 10.	2
2 Kings xi. 1.	1 d	v. 1, 1, 1.	1 c	Dan. vi. 7.	1 a
xxv. 25.	1 b				

RUBBISH

עָפָר   dust, ashes, &c.: Neh. iv. 2, 10.

RUBIES

פְּנִינִים   *m. pl.* pearls, Bochart. Precious stones cut into several little square faces, and exquisitely polished so as to reflect beautifully at every point.—Schultens. Job xxviii. 18: Prov. iii. 15; viii. 11; xx. 15; xxxi. 10: Lam. iv. 7. פְּנִיִּים *m. pl.* Prov. iii. 15, כתיב.

RUDDY

אָדֹם   *adj.* red: Cant. v. 10: see also *Red*.

RUHAMAH

רָחַם   to love, to show mercy, to obtain mercy. PUAL *pret.* Hos. i. 6, *marg.* 'having obtained mercy;' 8; ii. 1.

RUIN

1   מִדְחֶה   *m.* overthrow, ruin.

2   הָרַס   to pull down, overthrow, demolish. NIPHAL [a] *part.* [b] הֲרִיסָה *f.* that which is destroyed.

3   מְחִתָּה   *f.* destruction; see *Break*.

4   כָּשַׁל   to faint, falter, stumble; see *Fall*. KAL [a] *pret.* HIPHIL [b] *inf.* [c] מִכְשֵׁלָה *f.* ruin. [d] מִכְשׁוֹל *m.* cause of falling.

5   מַפָּלָה   *f.* fallen buildings, ruin. [a] מַפֵּלָה *f. id.* [b] מַפֶּלֶת *f.* fall, ruin.

6   נָצָה   to be laid waste, desolate.   NIPHAL *part.*

7   פִּיד   m. calamity, misfortune.

2 Kings xix. 25.	6	Isa. iii. 8.	4 a	Ezek. xxi. 15.	4 d		
2 Chron. xxviii. 23.	4 b	xvii. 1. α	5	xxvii. 27.	5 b		
Ps. lxxxix. 40.	3	xxiii. 13.	5 a	xxxi. 13.	5 b		
Prov. xxiv. 22.	7	xxv. 2.	5 a	xxxvi. 35, 36.	2 a		
xxvi. 28.	1	xxxvii. 26.	6	Amos ix. 11.	2 b		
Isa. iii. 6.	4 c	Ezek. xviii. 30. β	4 d				

a lit. a heap of ruins.   β *lit.* shall not be for a stumbling-block to you.

RULE

1   מָגֵן   m. shield.

2   מָלַךְ   to reign as a king.   KAL *fut.*

3   מָשַׁל   to rule, to have dominion; of more general import than the former, including all superior authority, of kings over other kings, &c., of the Messiah, a ruler in Israel: Micah v. 2 : Matt. ii. 6.   KAL ^a*pret.* ^b*inf.* ^c*imp.* ^d*fut.* ^e*part.* Poel. HIPHIL ^f*pret.* ^g מִמְשָׁל *m.* dominion. ^h מֶמְשָׁלָה *f. id.*

4   נָגִיד   m. pr. the foremost, hence leader, prefect, prince, &c.; of any prefect, overseer, *e. g.* of the treasury, of the temple, of the priests, of the palace, of military affairs, leader, chief; absolutely, prince of a people, a general word comprehending also the royal dignity; Dan. ix. 25, the anointed prince, *i. e.* the Messiah; Dan. xi. 22, prince of the covenant.

5   נָשִׂיא   m. see *Prince.*

6   נָשַׁק   to kiss, as a token of fidelity and homage. KAL *fut.* Gen. xli. 40, *marg.* 'be armed, *or,* kiss,' *i.e.* all my people shall render to thee homage and obedience.

7   סְגָנִים   m. pl. prefects, governors, rulers; spoken of Babylonian magistrates, prefects of the provinces; of the chiefs and rulers of the people of Jerusalem in the time of Ezra and Nehemiah.

8   מַעְצָר   m. restraint; power of restraint.

9   פָּקַד   Hiphil, to set over, to make overseer, to appoint, to charge with, make ruler.   HIPHIL *fut.*

10   קַו   m. line; rule, law.

11   קָצִין   m. a judge, magistrate; a leader, chief, in war; a prince.

12   רֹאשׁ   m. head.

13   רָדָה   to hold in a low state, to have dominion over. KAL ^a*pret.* ^b*inf.* ^c*imp.* ^d*fut.* ^e*part.* Poel. HIPHIL ^f*fut.*

14   רוּד   *i. q.* רָדָה to rule.   KAL *pret.*

15   רָזַן   to be weighty, august, honoured, *poet.* for prince, king. KAL *part.* Poel.

16   שַׂר   m. a prefect, leader, master, chief; a prince, noble, chief: Gen. xlvii. 6, &c.

17   שֹׁטֵר   m. see *Officer.*

18   שָׁלַט   to rule, to have dominion; to obtain power over any one, to get the mastery. KAL ^a*pret.* ^b*fut.* שְׁלֵט Ch. P'AL ^c*fut.* APHEL ^d*pret.* ^e שִׁלְטוֹן Ch. *m.* magistrate. ^f שַׁלִּיט *adj.* having power over. ^g שַׁלִּיט Ch. *adj. id.*

19   שָׁפַט   to judge, to govern. KAL *inf.*

20   שָׂרַר   to have dominion, to rule, to be a prince. KAL ^a*fut.* ^b*part.* Poel.

See also *Chief,* כֹּהֲנִים chief ruler.

No. 16, *Ruler,* not included.

Gen. i. 16, 16.	3 h	2 Chron. xxvi. 11.	17	Isa. iii. 6, 7.		11
i. 18.	3 b	xxxi. 12, 13.	4	iii. 12.		3 a
iii. 16.	3 d	xxxv. 8.	4	xiv. 2.		13 a
iv. 7.	3 d	Ezra iv. 20.	18 g	xiv. 5.		3 e
xxiv. 2.	3 e	ix. 2.	7	xiv. 6.		13 e
xli. 40.	6	Neh. ii. 16, 16.	7	xvi. 1.		3 e
xlv. 8.	3 e	iv. 14, 19.	7	xix. 4.		3 d
Exod. xvi. 22.	5	v. 7, 17.	7	xxiii. 3.		11
xxii. 28.	5	v. 15.	18 a	xxviii. 14.		3 e
xxxiv. 31.	5	vii. 5.	7	xxix. 10.		12
xxxv. 27.	5	xi. 11.	4	xxxii. 1.		20 a
Lev. iv. 22.	5	xii. 20.	7	xl. 10.		3 e
xxv. 43, 46, 53.	13 d	xiii. 11.	7	xli. 2.		13 f
Num xiii. 2.	5	Esth. i. 22.	20 b	xliv. 13.		10
Deut. i. 13.	12	ix. 1.	18 b	xlix. 7.		3 e
Josh. xii. 2.	2	Ps. ii. 2.	15	lii. 5.		3 e
Judg. viii. 22.	3 c	lix. 13.	3 e	lxiii. 19.		3 a
viii. 23, 23, 23.	3 d	lxvi. 7.	3 e	Jer. v. 31.		13 d
xv. 11.	19	lxviii. 27.	13 e	xxii. 30.		3 e
Ruth i. 1.	19	lxxxix. 9.	3 e	xxxiii. 26.		3 e
1 Sam. xxv. 30.	4	ciii. 19.	3 e	li. 23, 28, 57.		7
2 Sam. vi. 21.	4	cv. 20, 21.	3 e	li. 46, 46.		3 e
vii. 8.	4	cvi. 41.	3 e	Lam. v. 8.		3 a
xxiii. 3, 3.	3 e	cx. 2.	13 c	Ezek. xix. 11.		3 a
1 Kings i. 35.	4	cxxxvi. 8, 9.	3 h	xix. 14.		3 b
v. 16.	13 e	Prov. vi. 7.	3 e	xx. 33.		3
ix. 23.	13 e	viii. 16.	20 a	xxiii. 6, 12, 23.		7
xi. 28.	4	xii. 24.	3 d	xxix. 15.		13 b
2 Kings xxv. 22.	9	xvi 32.	3 d	xxxiv. 4.		13 a
1 Chron. v. 2.	4	xvii. 2.	3 d	Dan. ii. 10.		18 g
ix. 11, 20.	4	xix. 10.	3 b	ii. 38, 48.		18 d
xi. 2.	4	xxii. 7.	3 d	iii. 2, 3.		18 e
xvii. 7.	4	xxiii. 1.	4	iv. 17, 25, 26, 32.		18 g
xxvi. 6.	3 g	xxv. 28.	8	v. 7, 16.		18 c
xxvi. 24.	9	xxviii. 15.	3 e	v. 21, 29.		18 g
xxvi. 32.	9	xxix. 2.	4	xi. 3, 4.		3 a
xxvii. 4, 16.	9	xxix. 12, 26.	3 e	xi. 39.		3 f
xxviii. 4.	9	Eccles. ii. 19.	18 b	Hos. iv. 18.		1
2 Chron. vi. 5.	4	viii. 9.	18 a	xi. 12.		14
vii. 18.	3 e	ix. 17.	3 e	x. 4.		3 e
viii. 10.	3 e	x. 4.	3 e	Joel ii. 17.		3 b
xi. 22.	4	x. 5.	18 f	Micah v. 2.		3 e
xix. 11.	4	Isa. i. 10.	11	Hab. i. 14.		3 a
xx. 6.	3 e	iii. 4.	3 d	Zech. vi. 13.		3 a

RUMBLING

הָמוֹן   noise; rumbling of wheels : Jer. xlvii. 3.

RUMOUR

שְׁמוּעָה   *f.* report, tidings, &c.: 2 Kings xix. 7; Isa. xxxvii. 7: Jer. xlix. 14; li. 46, 46, 46: Ezek. vii. 26, 26: Obad. 1.

RUMP

אַלְיָה   *f.* the fat tail of a common species of Oriental sheep (*ovis laticaudia,* Linn.), the smallest of which, according to Golius, himself an eye-witness, weighed ten or twelve pounds. Exod. xxix. 22 : Lev. iii. 9; vii. 3; viii. 25; ix. 19.

RUN

1   בּוֹא   to come, in an extensive sense. KAL ^a*fut.* ^b*part.* Poel.

2   בָּרַח   to flee. KAL *fut.*

3   גָּלַל   to roll. NIPHAL *fut.*

4   הָלַךְ   to go, to walk. KAL ^a*pret.* ^b*fut.* ^c*part.* Poel. PIEL ^d*fut.* HITHPAEL ^e*fut.*

5   זוּב   to flow. KAL *fut.* See *Issue.*

6   חַי   *adj.* living, running water.

7   יָלַךְ   to go. KAL ^a*fut.* HIPHIL ^b*fut.*

8   יָצַק   to pour, to pour out. KAL *fut.*

9   יָרַד   to go down, to descend. KAL ^a*pret.* ^b*fut.* ^c*part.* Poel. HIPHIL ^d*imp.* ^e*fut.*

10   נָגַר to flow as water. NIPHAL *pret., or,* is stretched out ; see *Sore.*

11   נָזַל to flow, to run, as liquids. KAL *part.* Poel.

12   נוּס to flee swiftly. KAL *fut.*

13   פָּגַע to strike upon or against ; to come up to a man violently. KAL *fut.*

14   פָּכָה to drop, to distil, to flow forth. PIEL *part.*

15   פָּשַׁט to invade with a design to spoil. KAL *pret.*

16   צָעַד to go on, to advance forward in order. KAL *pret.*

17   רָוָיה *f.* abundant drink, abundance.

18   רוּץ to run ; *seq.* אֶל and עַל to run or rush upon any one ; *seq.* בְּ to run to any one for refuge. KAL [a] *pret.* [b] *inf.* [c] *imp.* [d] *fut.* [e] *part.* POLEL [f] *fut.* HIPHIL [g] *imp.* [h] *fut.* [i] מְרוּצָה *f.* course, race.

19   רָצָא *i. q.* רוּץ. KAL *inf.*

20   רוּר to run with ; as the flesh in consequence of a sore. KAL *pret.*

21   שׁוּט to lash ; Polel, to run to and fro ; see *Go.* POLEL [a] *imp.* [b] *fut.* [c] *part.* HITHPOLEL [d] *imp.*

22   שָׁטַף to overflow. KAL *part.* Poel.

23   שָׁקַק to run to and fro, spoken of those who eagerly seek anything. KAL [a] *fut.* [b] *part.* Poel. [c] מַשָּׁק *m.* running about.

Gen. xviii. 2.	18 d	2 Sam. xviii. 27, 27.	18 i	Eccles. i. 7.		4 c
xviii. 7.	18 a	xxii. 30.	18 d	Cant. i. 4.		18 d
xxiv. 17, 20, 28,		1 Kings i. 5.	18 e	Isa. xxxiii. 4, 4.		23 c b
29.	18 d	ii. 39.	2	xl. 31.		18 d
xxix. 12, 13.	18 d	xviii. 35.	7 a	lv. 5.		18 d
xxxiii. 4.	18 d	xviii. 46.	18 d	lix. 7.		18 d
xlix. 22.	16	xix. 20.	18 d	Jer. v. 1.		21 a
Exod. ix. 23.	4 b	xxii. 35.	8	ix. 18.		9 b
Lev. xiv. 5, 6, 50, 51,		2 Kings iv. 22.	18 d	xii. 5.		18 a
52.	6	iv. 26.	18 c	xiii. 17.		9 b
xv. 3.	20	v. 20.	18 a	xv. 17.		9 b
xv. 13.	6	v. 21.	18 e	xxiii. 21.		18 a
xv. 25.	5	2 Chron. xvi. 9.	21 c	xlix. 3.		21 d
Num. xi. 27.	18 d	xxiii. 12.	18 e	xlix. 19.		18 h
xvi. 47.	18 d	xxxii. 4.	22	l. 44.		18 h
xix. 17.	6	Ezra viii. 15.	16	li. 31.		18 d
Josh. vii. 22.	18 d	Job xvi. 26.	18 d	Lam. i. 16.		9 c
viii. 19.	18 d	xvi. 14.	18 d	ii. 18.		9 d
Judg. vii. 21.	18 d	Ps. xviii. 29.	18 d	iv. 18.		9 b
ix. 21.	12	xix. 5.	18 b	Ezek. i. 14.		19
ix. 44.	15	xxiii. 5.	17	xxiv. 16.		1 a
xiii. 10.	18 d	lviii. 7.	4 e	xxxi. 4.		4 c
xviii. 25.	13	lix. 4.	18 d	xxxii. 14.		7 b
1 Sam. iii. 5.	18 d	lxxvii. 2.	10	xlvii. 2.		14
iv. 12.	18 d	lxxviii. 16.	9 e	Dan. viii. 6.		18 d
viii. 11.	18 a	civ. 10.	4 d	xii. 4.		21 b
x. 23.	18 d	cv. 41.	4 a	Joel ii. 4, 7.		18 d
xvii. 17.	18 g	cxix. 32.	18 d	ii. 9, 9.	23 a,	18 d
xvii. 22, 48, 51.	18 d	cxix. 136.	9 a	Amos v. 24.		3
xx. 6.	18 b	cxxxiii. 2.	9 c	vi. 12.		18 d
xx. 36, 36.	18 c e	cxlvii. 15.	18 d	viii. 12.		21 b
2 Sam. xv. 1.	18 e	Prov. i. 16.	18 d	Nah. ii. 4.		18 f
xviii. 19, 21.	18 d	iv. 12.	18 d	Hab. ii. 2.		18 d
xviii. 22, 22.	18 e d	v. 15.	11	Hag. i. 9.		18 e
xviii. 23, 23, 23.	18 d c d	vi. 18.	18 b	Zech. ii. 4.		18 c
xviii. 24, 26, 26.	18 e	xviii. 10.	18 d	iv. 10.		21 c

RUSH

גֹּמֶא   *m.* a bulrush, specially the Egyptian *papyrus Nilotica,* so called from its imbibing much water ; it grows in moist places near the Nile, four or five yards in height ; under the bark it consisted of thin skins, which, being separated and spread out, were applied to divers uses ; of these they made boxes and chests, and even boats, smearing them over with pitch ; being properly prepared, these skins served also for paper, till a much

better way of making it was invented.—*Celsii Hierob.* part ii. p. 144. Job viii. 11 : Isa. xxxv. 7.

אַגְמוֹן   *m.* a reed, bulrush, growing in marshes ; a man of low and humble condition : Isa. ix. 14 ; xix. 15.

RUSH (V)

פָּשַׁט to invade with an intention to plunder ; to rush upon. KAL *pret.* Judg. ix. 44. *fut.* Judg. xx. 37.

רַעַשׁ *m.* a trembling, shaking ; leaping, bounding ; tumult, noise : Jer. xlvii. 3 : Ezek. iii. 12, 13.

שָׁאָה to make a noise, to rage, to roar ; to crash, to fall with a crash. NIPHAL *fut.* Isa. xvii. 12, 13. שָׁאוֹן *m.* noise, tumult : Isa. xvii. 12, 12, 13.

שָׁטַף to overflow. KAL *part.* Poel, Jer. viii. 6.

SABBATH

שָׁבַת to rest from labour, to keep a sabbath. KAL *pret.* 2 Chron. xxxvi. 21. שַׁבָּת *com.* sabbath, or any day of rest, at the beginning or close of the great Jewish festivals : Exod. xvi. 23, &c. שַׁבָּתוֹן *m.* rest : Lev. xxiii. 24, 39, 39. מִשְׁבַּתִּים *m. pl.* Lam. i. 7, *lit.* cessations, *i. e.* of all joy, sabbaths, &c.

SABEANS

סָבָא to drink to excess. KAL *part.* Poel, Ezek. xxiii. 42 (כתיב). סָבָא *m.* Ezek. xxiii. 42, *marg.* 'or, drunkards.'

SACK

כְּלִי *m.* instruments, vessels, &c. : Gen. xlii. 25.

אַמְתַּחַת *f.* a sack, from its being stretched out or expanded when filled : Gen. xlii. 27, 28 ; xliii. 12, 18, 21, 21, 22, 23 ; xliv. 1, 1, 2, 8, 11, 11, 12.

שַׂק *m.* sacking, sackcloth, especially as made of hair, used for sieves and strainers, also for sacks to hold grain, and for mourning garments ; *pr.* a close and rough garment of sackcloth (Isa. iii. 24, Job xvi. 15, *comp.* Rev. vi. 12) worn upon the naked body, 1 Kings xxi. 27, 2 Kings vi. 30, Job xvi. 15, and not laid aside at night, 1 Kings xxi. 27, Joel i. 13 : also to put on sackcloth and ashes as a mourner, Esth. iv. 1, *comp.* Isa. lviii. 5. Spoken of the garment of ascetics and prophets, Isa. xx. 2. Translated sack, Gen. xlii. 25, 27, 35, 35, Lev. xi. 32, Josh. ix. 4 ; sackcloth, Gen. xxxvii. 34, &c.

SACKBUT

סַבְּכָא Ch. *f.* a stringed instrument of music having four strings, similar to the nablium, the harp or lyre : Dan. iii. 5. שַׂבְּכָא Ch. *f.* the same : Dan. iii. 7, 10, 15.

SACRIFICE

1   אִשֶּׁה an offering made by fire.

2   דְּבַח Ch. *m.* sacrifice.

3   זָבַח to slaughter, to kill animals for eating ; especially to kill for sacrifice, to sacrifice, to immolate victims. This verb

is not used of the priests as slaughtering victims in sacrifices, but of private persons offering sacrifices at their own cost. KAL ᵃ*pret.* ᵇ*inf.* ᶜ*imp.* ᵈ*fut.* ᵉ*part.* Poel. PIEL ᶠ*pret.* ᵍ*inf.* ʰ*fut.* ⁱ*part.* ᵏ זֶבַח *m. pr.* slaughtering of men, Isa. xxxiv. 6, Zeph. i. 7; of beasts, and then *meton.* their flesh, repast, banquet, Gen. xxxi. 54, Ezek. xxxix. 17. Prov. xvii. 1, banquets of strife, quarrelsome feasts; a sacrifice, *i.e.* the act of sacrificing, also the thing sacrificed, *opp.* both to מִנְחָה a bloodless offering, 1 Sam. ii. 29, Ps. xl. 6, and to עֹלָה burnt-offering; so that זֶבַח denotes a sacrifice which was only in part consumed by fire, such as were the sin and trespass-offerings, the thank-offerings, &c. Spoken also generally of any great and solemn sacrifice and of sacrificial feasts, a yearly sacrifice, 1 Sam. i. 21; xx. 6: a family sacrifice, xx. 29, *comp.* ix. 12, 13; xvi. 3.—Gen. xxxi. 54, &c.

4   חַג   *m.* a feast; or festival sacrifice.

5   תּוֹדָה   *f.* confession, thanksgiving, sacrifice of praise.

6   מִנְחָה   *f.* a gift, a present; an offering to God, a sacrifice; spoken especially of a bloodless offering, a meat-offering.

7   עָשָׂה   to do, in an extensive sense. KAL ᵃ*pret.* ᵇ*part.* Poel.

8   קָטַר   to burn, burn incense, or fat on the altar; generally, to offer by burning. PIEL ᵃ*inf.* HIPHIL ᵇ*inf.*

9   קָרְבָּן   *m.* offering.

No. 3 k not included.

Exod. iii. 18.	3 d	1 Sam. i. 3.	3 b	2 Chron. xxxiv. 4.	3 e
v. 3, 8, 17.	3 d	ii. 15.	3 e	Ezra iv. 2.	3 e
viii. 8, 26, 26.	3 d	vi. 15, 15.	3 d k	vi. 3.	2
viii. 25.	3 c	x. 8, 8.	3 b k	ix. 4, 5.	3 d
viii. 27, 28.	3 a	xi. 15, 15.	3 d k	Neh. iv. 2.	3 d
viii. 29.	3 b	xv. 15, 21.	3 b	Ps. liv. 6.	3 d
x. 25, 25.	3 k, 7 a	xvi. 2.	3 d	cvi. 37.	3 d
xiii. 15.	3 b	xvi. 5, 5, 5.	3 b k k	cvi. 38.	3 d
xx. 24.	3 a	2 Sam. vi. 13.	3 d	cvii. 22, 22.	3 d k
xxii. 20.	3 e	1 Kings iii. 2, 3.	3 d	cxviii. 27.	4
xxiii. 18, 18.	3 k, 4	iii. 4.	3 i	cxli. 2.	4
xxiv. 5.	3 d	viii. 5.	3 b	Eccles. ix. 2, 2.	3 b
xxxii. 8.	3 d	xi. 8.	3 i	Isa. xxix. 1.	4
xxxiv. 15, 15.	3 a k	xii. 32.	3 i	lxv. 3.	3 e
Lev. ix. 4.	3 b	xviii. 29, 36.	3 g	lxvi. 3.	3 e
x. 13.	1	2 Kings xii. 3.	3 i	Jer. xvii. 26, 26.	3 k, 5
xxiii. 19, 19.	7 a, 3 k	xiv. 4.	3 i	xxxiii. 11.	5
xxvii. 11.	9	xv. 4, 35.	3 i	Ezek. xvi. 20.	3 d
Num. xv. 25.		xvi. 4.	3 h	xxxix. 17, 17, 17.	3 k e k
xxviii. 2, 6, 8, 13, 19,		xvii. 32.	7 b	xxxix. 19, 19.	3 k a
24.	1	xvii. 35, 36.	3 d	Hos. iv. 13, 14.	3 h
xxix. 6, 13, 26.	1	1 Chron. xxi. 28.	3 d	viii. 13, 13.	3 d k
Deut. xv. 21.	3 d	xxix. 21, 21, 21.	3 d k k	xi. 2.	3 h
xvi. 2.	3 a	2 Chron. ii. 6.	8 b	xii. 11.	3 h
xvi. 4, 6.	3 d	v. 6.	3 i	xiii. 2.	3 h
xvi. 5.	3 b	xi. 16.	3 b	Amos iv. 5.	8 a
xvii. 1.	3 b	xxviii. 4.	3 h	Jonah ii. 9.	3 d
xxxii. 17.	3 d	xxvii. 23, 23.	3 d h	Hab. i. 16.	3 d
Josh. viii. 31.	3 d	xxxiii. 16.	3 d	Zech. xiv. 21.	3 e
xiii. 14.	1	xxxiii. 17.	3 e	Mal. i. 8.	3 b
Judg. ii. 5.	3 d	xxxiii. 22.	3 f	i. 14.	3 e

SAD

זָעֵף   to be angry; to be morose, gloomy, sad. KAL *part.* Poel, Gen. xl. 6, *comp.* ver. 7. Theod. aptly σκυθρωπός, comp. Matt. vi. 16.

יָרַע   to be displeased. KAL *fut.* Neh. ii. 3.

כָּאַב   to have pain, to be sore; to grieve, to be sad. HIPHIL *pret.* Ezek. xiii. 22.

כָּאָה   to rebuke; Hiphil, to afflict, to make sad. HIPHIL *inf.* Ezek. xiii. 22.

סַר   *adj.* (see *Heavy*): 1 Kings xxi. 5.

רַע   *adj.* evil; sad, sorrowful: Gen. xl. 7, *marg.* 'are your faces evil?' Neh. ii. 1, 2. רֹעַ *m.* sadness: Eccles. vii. 3.

SADDLE

1   חָבַשׁ   to bind, to bind on. KAL ᵃ*imp.* ᵇ*fut.* ᶜ*part.* Paül.

2   מֶרְכָּב   *m.* a chariot; a saddle or seat.

Gen. xxii. 3.	1 b	2 Sam. xvi. 1.	1 c	1 Kings xiii. 13, 13.	1 a b
Lev. xv. 9.	2	xvii. 23.		xiii. 23.	1 b
Num. xxii. 21.	1 b	xix. 26.	1 b	xiii. 27, 27.	1 a b
Judg. xix. 10.	1 c	1 Kings ii. 40.	1 b	2 Kings iv. 24.	1 b

SAFE

1   בֶּטַח   *m.* trust, confidence; security, fearlessness.

2   יָשַׁע   to save. NIPHAL ᵃ*fut.* ᵇ יֶשַׁע *m.* salvation; safety. ᶜ תְּשׁוּעָה *f.* deliverance.

3   פָּלַט   to escape out of danger; to deliver. HIPHIL *fut.*

4   שָׂגַב   to be high; to set on high. NIPHAL ᵃ*pret.* PUAL ᵇ*fut.*

5   שָׁלָה   to be secure, tranquil, at rest. KAL *pret.*

6   שָׁלוֹם   *m.* peace.

Lev. xxv. 18, 19.	1	Ps. iv. 8.	1	Isa. v. 29.	3
xxvi. 5.	1	xii. 5.	2 b	xiv. 30.	1
Deut. xii. 10.	1	xxxiii. 17.	2 b	xli. 3.	6
xxxiii. 12, 28.	1	lxxviii. 53.	1	Jer. xxiii. 6.	1
1 Sam. xii. 11.	1	cxix. 117.	2 a	xxxii. 37.	1
2 Sam. xviii. 29, 32.	6	Prov. i. 33.	1	xxxiii. 16.	1
1 Kings iv. 25. α	5	iii. 23.	1	Ezek. xxviii. 26. β	1
Job iii. 26.	5	xi. 14.	2 c	xxxiv. 25, 27, 28.	1
v. 4, 11.	2 b	viii. 10.	4 a	xxxviii. 8, 11, a 14.	1
xi. 18.	1	xxi. 31.	2 c	xxxix. 26.	1
xxi. 9.	6	xxiv. 6.	2 c	Hos. ii. 18.	1
xxiv. 23.	1	xxix. 25.	4 b	Zech. xiv. 11.	1

α *marg.* 'confidently.'   β *marg.* 'with confidence.'

SAFEGUARD

מִשְׁמֶרֶת   *f.* watch, guard, custody; keeping: 1 Sam. xxii. 23.

SAFFRON

כַּרְכֹּם   *m.* crocus, saffron, both the common plant and also crocus Indicus, or Indian saffron: Cant. iv. 14.

SAIL

נֵס   *m.* something lifted up; standard or flag; sail: Isa. xxxiii. 23: Ezek. xxvii. 7.

SAINT

חָסִיד   *adj.* kind, merciful, benevolent; pious toward God, godly; the word is thought also to signify such as are the objects of divine favour, holy and pious, zealous in the pursuit of good, and in doing good: 1 Sam. ii. 9: 2 Chron. vi. 41: Ps. xxx. 4; xxxi. 23; xxxvii. 28; l. 5; lii. 9; lxxix. 2; lxxxv. 8; xcvii. 10; cxvi. 15; cxxxii. 9, 16; cxlv. 10; cxlviii. 14; cxlix. 1, 5, 9: Prov. ii. 8.

קֹדֶשׁ   *m.* holiness; that which is consecrated: Deut. xxxiii. 2. קָדוֹשׁ *adj.* holy: Deut. xxxiii. 3: Job v. 1; xv. 15: Ps. xvi. 3; xxxiv. 9; lxxxix. 5, 7; cvi. 16: Dan. xiv. 13, 13: Hos. xi. 12, *marg.* 'or, most holy;' Zech. xiv. 5. קַדִּישׁ Ch. *adj.* Dan. vii. 18, 21, 22, 22, 25, 27.

SAKE

קִנְאָה   *f.* zeal: Num. xxv. 11, *lit.* with my zeal.

SALE

מִמְכָּר *m.* selling; thing sold; that which is for sale: Lev. xxv. 27, 50: Deut. xviii. 8, *marg.* 'his sales by the fathers.'

SALT

מֶלַח *m.* salt; the salt sea, *i.e.* the Dead Sea, the waters of which are very strongly impregnated with salt, and often deposit it in the marshy places along the shores; valley of salt near the Dead Sea: see Robinson's Palest. ii. pp. 223-226, 483. Covenant of salt, 2 Chron. xiii. 5, *i.e.* a league for ever sacred and inviolable, Num. xviii. 19. This formula arose from the circumstance that salt, as preserving from decay, is a symbol of duration and perpetuity; see Philo, Opp. ii. p. 225. Hence Arabs are said to eat bread and salt together in making a covenant; at any rate they have the phrase, "there is salt between us," *i.e.* a covenant: hence we may understand why the offerings of the Hebrews were to be seasoned with salt, Lev. ii. 13; because salt is the symbol of the perpetual covenant between God and Israel, which he thus daily renews and confirms. With other nations, too, salt was a symbol of friendship, and was added to their sacrifices: see Sykes' Essay on Sacrifices; Rosenm. Schol. ad Lev. ii. 13. Further, Gen. xix. 26, pillar of salt, *i.e.* statue of fossil salt, bearing the appearance of a pillar or cippus; see, for the fossil salt at the south end of the Dead Sea, Robinson's Palest. ii. p. 482 sq.; and for the legends of the Arabs respecting Lot's wife, see ibid. p. 589, Ges.; see also Bush's Notes on the above passages.—Gen. xiv. 3, &c. מֶלַח Ch. *m. id.*, Ezra vi. 9; vii. 22. מִלְחָה *f. id.*, Jer. xvii. 6. מָלַח to season with salt: new-born infants were sprinkled with salt, to make the flesh more firm. HOPHAL *pret.* Ezek. xvi. 4. *inf.* Ezek. xvi. 4, *lit.* being salted thou wast not salted.

SALUTE

1 בָּרַךְ to bless. KAL [a] *inf.* PIEL [b] *inf.* [c] *fut.*

2 שָׁאַל to ask, to inquire; with שָׁלוֹם to salute, *lit.* to inquire of peace. KAL [a] *pret.* [b] *inf.* [c] *fut.*

3 שָׁלוֹם peace.

Judg. xviii. 15.	2 c, 3	1 Sam. xxv. 14.	1 b	2 Kings iv. 29, 29.	1 c
1 Sam. x. 4.	2 a, 3	xxx. 21.	2 c, 3	x. 13.	3
xiii. 10.	1 a	2 Sam. viii. 10.	2 b, 3	x. 15.	1 c
xvii. 22.	2 c, 3				

SALVATION

יָשַׁע to save; to bring salvation. NIPHAL [a] *part.* HIPHIL [b] *fut.* יֶשַׁע [c] and יֵשַׁע *m.* deliverance, help; safety, welfare, prosperity. יְשׁוּעָה [d] *f.* deliverance, safety; help, aid, hence victory; welfare, prosperity. This word is used of the saving grace of God, and of God himself, the author of salvation. Gen. xlix. 18, &c. מוֹשָׁעוֹת [e] *f. pl. id.* תְּשׁוּעָה [f] *f. id.*

1 Sam. xi. 13.	f	Ps. xxvii. 1, 9.	c	Ps. lxviii. 20.	e
xix. 5.	c	xxxvii. 39.	f	lxix. 13.	c
2 Sam. xxii. 3, 36, 47.	c	xxxviii. 22.	f	lxxi. 15.	f
xxiii. 5.	c	xl. 10, 16.	f	lxxix. 9.	c
1 Chron. xvi. 35.	c	l. 23.	e	lxxxv. 4, 7, 9.	c
2 Chron. vi. 41.	f	li. 12.	c	xcv. 1.	c
Ps. xviii. 2, 35, 46.	c	li. 14.	c	cxix. 41, 81.	f
xxiv. 5.	c	lxii. 7.	f	cxxxii. 16.	c
xxv. 5.	c	lxv. 5.	c	cxliv. 10.	c

Isa. xvii. 10.	c	Isa. lix. 16.	b	Lam. iii. 26.	f
xlv. 8.	c	lxi. 10.	c	Micah vii. 7.	c
xlv. 17.	f	lxii. 11.	c	Hab. iii. 13, 13, 18.	c
xlvi. 13, 13.	f	lxiii. 5.	b	Zech. ix. 9.	a
li. 5.	c	Jer. iii. 23.	f		

SANCTIFY

קָדַשׁ to be holy, sacred, *sanctus*; of persons consecrated to God, of things destined for sacred uses; Niphal, to be regarded and treated as holy, to be hallowed, sanctified; also to show oneself holy, glorious, in bestowing favours or inflicting judgments, to be consecrated; Piel, to make holy, to sanctify, to hallow, *i.e.* to regard and treat as holy, to keep holy; to pronounce holy, to sanctify, to appoint a fast, &c.; to consecrate a priest, &c.; to sanctify with solemn rites, to inaugurate war; to prepare, begin: Hithp. to cleanse or purify oneself by sacred ablutions, observances. The meaning usually given to this word is rather implied than included in the proper meaning. It is used of being set apart, appointed to any office or work, Isa. xiii. 3, "my sanctified ones," of the Chaldeans, whom God had inaugurated for the war. KAL [a] *fut.* NIPHAL [b] *pret.* [c] *inf.* [d] *fut.* PIEL [e] *pret.* [f] *inf.* [g] *imp.* [h] *fut.* [i] *part.* PUAL [k] *part.* HIPHIL [l] *pret.* [m] *inf.* [n] *fut.* [o] *part.* HITHPAEL [p] *pret.* [q] *inf.* [r] *imp.* [s] *fut.* [t] *part.*

Gen. ii. 3.	h	Num. viii. 17.	l	2 Chron. xxx. 17, 17.	p m
Exod. xiii. 2.	g	xi. 18.	r	xxxi. 18.	s
xix. 10, 23.	e	xx. 12.	m	xxxv. 6.	r
xix. 14.	h	xx. 13.	d	Neh. iii. 1, 1.	o
xix. 22.	s	xxvii. 14.	m	xii. 47, 47.	o
xxviii. 41.	f	Deut. v. 12.	f	xiii. 22.	f
xxix. 27, 37.	e	xv. 19.	n	Job i. 5.	h
xxix. 33, 36.	f	xxxii. 51.	e	Isa. v. 16.	b
xxix. 43.	b	Josh. iii. 5.	r	viii. 13.	h
xxix. 44, 44.	e h	vii. 13, 13.	g r	xiii. 3.	k
xxx. 29.	e	1 Sam. vii. 1.	e	xxix. 23, 23.	n l
xxxi. 13.	i	xvi. 5, 5.	r h	xxx. 29.	i
xl. 10, 11, 13.	e	xxi. 5.	a	Jer. i. 5.	l
Lev. viii. 10, 15, 30.	h	1 Chron. xv. 12.	s	Ezek. xx. 12.	b
viii. 11, 12.	f	xv. 14.	s	xx. 41.	b
x. 3.	d	xxiii. 13.	n	xxviii. 22, 25.	b
xi. 44.	p	2 Chron. v. 11.	p	xxxvi. 23, 23.	e c
xx. 7.	p	vii. 16, 20.	l	xxxvii. 28.	i
xx. 8.	i	xxix. 5, 5.	r g	xxxviii. 16.	c
xxi. 8, 8.	e i	xxix. 15, 34.	e	xxxviii. 23.	i
xxi. 15, 23.	i	xxix. 17, 17.	f h	xxxix. 27.	p
xxii. 9, 16.	i	xxix. 19.	l	xliv. 19.	h
xxvii. 14, 16, 17, 18, 22, 26.	n	xxix. 34.	q	xlvi. 20.	f
xxvii. 15, 19.	o	xxx. 3.	p	xlviii. 11.	k
Num. vii. 1, 1.	h	xxx. 8.	r	Joel i. 14.	g
		xxx. 15, 24.	s	ii. 15, 16.	g

SANCTUARY

קֹדֶשׁ *m.* holiness; a holy place: Exod. xxx. 13, &c. מִקְדָּשׁ *m.* a place consecrated: Exod. xv. 17; xxv. 8: Lev. xii. 4; xvi. 33; xix. 30; xx. 3; xxi. 12, 12, 23; xxvi. 2, 31: Num. iii. 38; x. 21; xviii. 1; xix. 20: Josh. xxiv. 26: 1 Chron. xxii. 19; xxviii. 10: 2 Chron. xx. 8; xxvi. 18; xxix. 21; xxx. 8; xxxvi. 17: Neh. x. 39: Ps. lxxiii. 17; lxxiv. 7; lxxviii. 69; xcvi. 6: Isa. viii. 14; xvi. 12; lx. 13; lxiii. 18: Jer. xvii. 12; li. 51: Lam. i. 10; ii. 7, 20: Ezek. v. 11; viii. 6; ix. 6; xi. 16; xxiii. 38, 39; xxiv. 21; xxv. 3; xxviii. 18; xxxvii. 26, 28; xliii. 21; xliv. 1, 5, 7, 8, 9, 11, 15, 16; xlv. 3, 4, 4, 18; xlvii. 12; xlviii. 8, 10, 21: Dan. viii. 11; ix. 17; xi. 31: Amos vii. 9.

SAND

חוֹל sand, from its rolling and sliding motion. The sand of the sea is very often put as the image of abundance, Gen.

xxxii. 13, xli. 49; of extent or capacity, as being immeasurable, Jer. xxxiii. 22; also of weight, Job vi. 3, Prov. xxvii. 3. Sand is the frequent emblem of numerous days, Job xxix. 18.—Gen. xxii. 17, &c.

SAPPHIRE

סַפִּיר *m.* sapphire, a species of gem, so called from its beauty and splendour : Exod. xxiv. 10, &c.

SARDIUS

אֹדֶם *m.* a gem of a red colour, perhaps a ruby, so rendered in the margin of our translation : Exod. xxviii. 17; xxxix. 10 : Ezek. xxviii. 13.

SATAN

שָׂטָן an adversary; with the *art.* the adversary, κατ' ἐξοχήν, it assumes the nature of a proper name, *i.e.* Satan, ὁ διάβολος, the devil, the evil spirit, who seduces men to evil, 1 Chron. xxi. 1 (where alone the *art.* is wanting, *comp.* 2 Sam. xxiv. 1), and accuses and calumniates them before God, Zech. iii. 1, 2, Job i. 6, 9, ii. 1, &c., *comp.* Rev. xii. 10.—1 Chron. xxi. 1 : Job i. 6, 7, 7, 8, 9, 12, 12; ii. 1, 2, 2, 3, 4, 6, 7 : Ps. cix. 6 : Zech. iii. 1, 2, 2.

SATIATE, SATISFY, SATISFACTION

1 כֹּפֶר *m.* a ransom.

2 מָלֵא to fill. to be filled. KAL [a] *fut.* PIEL [b] *inf.*

3 רָוָה to drink to the full, to be satisfied, sated with drink, as שָׂבַע to be satisfied with food; once with fatness, which is drunk rather than eaten, Ps. xxxvi. 8. Poetically of the sword as drinking up blood, Jer. xlvi. 10; also of persons satiated with forbidden pleasures, Prov. vii. 18. KAL [a] *fut.* PIEL [b] *pret.* [c] *fut.* HIPHIL [d] *pret.*

4 שָׂבַע and שָׂבֵעַ to be or to become satisfied, satiated, filled with food, rarely with drink; *metaph.* to be satisfied with wealth, Eccles. v. 10; to be filled with reproach, Lam. iii. 30, Hab. ii. 16; with contempt, Ps. cxxiii. 3; with calamity, Ps. lxxxviii. 3; with poverty, Prov. xxviii. 19; with one's own devices, *i. e.* to reap the full reward of them, Prov. i. 31, xviii. 20. KAL [a] *pret.* [b] *inf.* [c] *imp.* [d] *fut.* PIEL [e] *imp.* [f] *fut.* HIPHIL [g] *pret.* [h] *inf.* [i] *fut.* [k] *part.* [l] שָׂבֵעַ *adj.* satisfied. [m] שֹׂבַע *m.* abundance, satisfying. [n] שִׂבְעָה *f. id.*

SATYR

שָׂעִיר *m.* he-goat : the idolatrous Hebrews are supposed either in Egypt, where the he-goat was worshipped, or afterwards, to have honoured this idol; the same word is translated "devil" in Lev. xvii. 7, 2 Chron. xi. 15. The *pl.* is used of satyrs, wood-demons, half men and half goats, fancied deities, supposed to live in deserts, especially about Babylon in ruins; LXX. δαιμόνια. See, on these popular superstitions, the Commentaries of Vitringa, Gesenius, Barnes, Bush. The last writer has a singular quotation from Dr. Wolffe, of a race who imitate these satyrs, and dance in honour of them on a particular night in the year. Isa. xiii. 21; xxxiv. 14.

SAVE

1 חָיָה to live; Piel and Hiphil, to save, to save alive. KAL [a] *fut.* God save, *lit.* let—live. PIEL [b] *pret.* [c] *inf.* [d] *fut.* HIPHIL [e] *pret.* [f] *inf.*

2 חָיַי to live. KAL *pret.*

3 יָשַׁע to save, implying in the largest sense, deliverance, help, and victory; it comprehends either the removal of evil and misery, or the restoration of good and former happiness. It is most commonly used of God, sometimes of men, and also of the Messiah; hence it has reference to that deliverance, spiritually, which he was to effect, having paid the price of our redemption : Isa. xxxv. 4 : Zech. ix. 9, *comp.* Ps. cxviii. 25. It is applied to his victory over death and the grave, as our surety : Ps. xcviii. 1, *comp.* Isa. lxiii. 1, 5. NIPHAL [a] *pret.* [b] *imp.* [c] *fut.* [d] *part.* HIPHIL [e] *pret.* [f] *inf.* [g] *imp.* [h] *fut.* [i] *part.* [k] יֶשַׁע *m.* salvation. [l] יְשׁוּעָה *f. id.*

4 מָלַט to save oneself, to escape from some imminent danger by slipping away, fleeing, or by some quick expeditious method; Piel, to let escape, to save from danger, to deliver; see *Deliver.* PIEL [a] *imp.* [b] *fut.* [c] *part.*

5 נָצַל to deliver, to rescue; to snatch from danger, to preserve, to save. HIPHIL *pret.*

6 שָׁמַר to keep, to guard, to preserve. KAL [a] *imp.* NIPHAL [b] *pret.*

Exod. xv. 9.	2 a	Ps. ciii. 5.	4 k	Isa. xliv. 16.	4 d	1 Sam. vii. 8.	3 h	2 Kings vii. 4.	1 d
Lev. xxvi. 26.	4 d	civ. 13.	4 d	liii. 11.	4 d	ix. 16.	3 e	xi. 12.	1 a
Num. xxxv. 31, 32.	1	cv. 40.	4 i	lv. 2.	4 n	x. 19.	3 i	xiii. 5.	3 i
Deut. xiv. 29.	4 a	cvii. 9.	4 g	lviii. 10.	4 i	x. 24.	1 a	xiv. 27.	3 h
xxxiii. 23.	4 l	cxxxii. 15.	4 l	lviii. 11.	4 g	xi. 3.	3 i	xvii. 7.	3 g
Job xix. 22.	4 d	cxlv. 16.	4 k	lxvi. 11.	4 a	xiv. 6.	3 f	xix. 19.	3 g
xxvii. 14.	4 d	Prov. v. 19.	3 c	Jer. xxxi. 14, 14.	3 a, 4 d	xiv. 23.	3 h	xix. 34.	3 f
xxxi. 31.	4 d	vi. 30.	2 b	xxxi. 25.	3 d	xiv. 39.	3 i	1 Chron. xi. 14.	3 h
xxxviii. 27.	4 h	xii. 11, 14.	4 d	xlvi. 10.	4 a	xvii. 47.	3 h	xvi. 35.	3 g
Ps. xvii. 15.	4 d	xiii. 25.	4 m	l. 10, 19.	4 d	Deut. xx. 4.	3 f	2 Chron. xxiii. 11.	1 a
xxii. 26.	4 d	xviii. 20.	4 d	Lam. iv. 6.	4 b	xix. 11.β	4 c	xxxii. 22.	3 h
xxxvi. 8.	3 a	xix. 23.	4 l	Ezek. vii. 19.	4 f	xxiii. 2.	3 e	Neh. vi. 1 b.γ	2
xxxvii. 19.	4 d	xx. 13.	4 c	xvi. 4.	4 a	xxiii. 5.	3 h	ix. 27, 27.	3 i h
lix. 15.	4 d	xxvii. 20.	4 d	Joel ii. 19.	4 d	xxvii. 11.	1 d	Job ii. 6.	6 a
lxiii. 5.	4 d	Eccles. i. 8.	4 d	ii. 26.	4 d	2 Sam. iii. 18.	3 f	v. 15.	3 h
lxv. 4.	4 d	iv. 8.	4 d	Amos iv. 8.	4 d	xvi. 16, 16.	1 a	xx. 20.	4 b
lxxxi. 16.	4 i	v. 10.	4 d	Micah vi. 14.	4 d	xix. 5.	4 c	xxii. 29.	3 h
xc. 14.	4 e	Isa. ix. 20.	4 a	Hab. ii. 5.	4 d	xix. 9.	5	xxvi. 2.	3 h
xci. 16.	4 i					xxii. 3, 3.	3 i h	xl. 14.	3 h
						xxii. 4.	3 c	Ps. iii. 7.	3 g
						xxii. 28.	3 h	vi. 4.	3 h
						xxii. 42.	3 h	vii. 1.	3 g
						1 Kings i. 12.	4 a	vii. 10.	3 i
						i. 25, 34, 39.	1 a	xvii. 7.	3 i
						xviii. 5.	1 d	xviii. 3.	3 c
						xx. 31.	1 b	xviii. 27.	3 h
1 Sam. iv. 3.	3 h					2 Kings vi. 10.	6 b	xviii. 41.	3 i

Ps. xx. 6, 6.	3 e k	Ps. cxviii. 25.	3 g	Jer. xi. 12.	3 f h
xx. 9.	3 g	cxix. 94, 146.	3 g	xiv. 8.	3 i
xxii. 21.	3 g	cxxxviii. 7.	3 h	xiv. 9.	3 f
xxviii. 8.	3 l	cxlv. 19.	3 h	xv. 20.	3 f
xxviii. 9.	3 g	Prov. xx. 22.	3 h	xvii. 14, 14.	3 g c
xxxi. 2.	3 f	xxviii. 18.	3 c	xxiii. 6.	3 c
xxxi. 16.	3 g	Isa. xix. 20.	3 h	xxx. 7.	3 c
xxxiii. 16.	3 d	xxv. 9.	3 h	xxx. 10.	3 i
xxxiv. 6.	3 e	xxx. 15.	3 c	xxx. 11.	3 f
xxxiv. 18.	3 h	xxxiii. 22.	3 h	xxxi. 7.	3 c
xxxvii. 40.	3 h	xxxv. 4.	3 h	xxxiii. 16.	3 c
xliv. 3, 7.	3 e	xxxvii. 20.	3 f	xlii. 11.	3 f
xliv. 6.	3 h	xxxvii. 35.	3 f	xlvi. 27.	3 i
liv. 1.	3 g	xxxviii. 20.	3 f	lviii. 6.	4 a
lv. 16.	3 h	xliii. 3, 11.	3 i	Lam. iv. 17.	3 h
lvii. 3.	3 h	xliii. 12.	3 e	Ezek. iii. 18.	1 c
lix. 2.	3 g	xlv. 15, 21.	3 i	xiii. 18.	1 d
lx. 5.	3 g	xlv. 17.	3 a	xiii. 19.	1 c
lxvii. 2.δ	3 l	xlv. 20.	3 h	xviii. 27.	1 d
lxix. 1.	3 g	xlv. 22.	3 b	xxxiv. 22.	3 e
lxix. 35.	3 h	xlvi. 7.	3 h	xxxvi. 29.	3 e
lxxi. 2.	3 g	xlviii. 13.	3 h	xxxvii. 23.	3 e
lxxi. 3.	3 h	xlviii. 15.	3 h	Hos. i. 7, 7.	3 e h
lxxii. 4, 13.	3 h	xlix. 25.	3 h	xiii. 4.	3 i
lxxvi. 9.	3 h	xlix. 26.	3 i	xiii. 10.	3 h
lxxx. 2.	3 l	lix. 1.	3 f	xiv. 3.	3 h
lxxx. 3, 7, 19.	3 c	lx. 16.	3 i	Obad. 21.	3 i
lxxxvi. 2, 16.	3 g	lxiii. 1.	3 f	Hab. i. 2.	3 h
cvi. 8, 10.	3 h	lxiii. 8.ε	3 f	Zeph. iii. 17.	3 h
cvi. 21.	3 i	lxiii. 9.	3 e	iii. 19.	3 e
cvi. 47.	3 g	lxiv. 5.	3 h	Zech. viii. 7.	3 h
cvii. 13, 19.	3 h	Jer. ii. 27.	3 g	viii. 13.	3 h
cviii. 6.	3 g	ii. 28.	3 g	ix. 16.	3 h
cix. 26.	3 g	iv. 14.	3 c	x. 6.	3 h
cix. 31.	3 f	viii. 20.	3 a	xii. 7.	3 e

α *lit.* if thou wilt be saving.   β *lit.* art not saving.   γ *lit.* and live.
δ "saving health."   ε *lit.* for a saviour to them.

SAVOUR

מַטְעַמִּים *m. pl.* dainties, savoury dishes; especially such as were made of the flesh of animals taken in hunting: Gen. xxvii. 4, 7, 9, 14, 17, 31.

נִיחוֹחַ Ch. sweet odours, incense; also a figure for a good name or repute: Exod. v. 21: Ezra vi. 10.

צַחֲנָה *f.* stench: Joel ii. 20.

רֵיחַ *m.* scent, odour: Gen. viii. 21, &c.

SAW

גָּרַר to draw, to draw to oneself, hence to saw, to cut in two. POAL *part.* 1 Kings vii. 9. מְגֵרָה *f.* a saw: 2 Sam. xii. 31: 1 Kings vii. 9: 1 Chron. xx. 3.

מַשּׂוֹר *m.* a saw: Isa. x. 15.

SAY

1 אָמַר to say: the primary idea is to bear forth, to bring out to light, hence to utter, to say: it differs from דִּבֶּר to speak, in that דִּבֶּר is put absolutely, while אָמַר is followed by the words spoken, *e.g.* Lev. i. 2: Exod. vi. 1, &c. The person *to* whom another speaks is preceded by אֶל and לְ; yet both these are sometimes used in the sense of *concerning;* followed by עַל to speak *against.* Specially to say to or of anything this or that, *i.q.* to call it so, to name, Isa. v. 20, viii. 12, Eccles. ii. 2; to say is sometimes to exhort, Job xxxvi. 10; to promise, 2 Chron. xxxii. 24; to tell, to declare, Exod. xix. 25; and hence to declare any one, *i.q.* to proclaim, to laud, Ps. xl. 10, Isa. iii. 10. Such examples are for the most part readily determined by the context. This word applies to inward thought as well as to outward expression, *i.e.* to speak within, to purpose, Gen. xvii. 17, Ps. x. 6, 11, 13, xiv. 1,

Isa. xlvii. 8. It also means to command, to say authoritatively. In order to shorten the very numerous references this root affords, say and saith, the common translation of the *pret.*, are omitted, as also saying, of the *inf.*, and said, of the *fut.*, so that these tenses of say, not found in any of the references of this and the following roots, may be assumed to be of such respective tenses. KAL ᵃ*pret.* ᵇ*inf.* ᶜ*imp.* ᵈ*fut.* ᵉ*part.* Poel. NIPHAL ᶠ*inf.* ᵍ*fut.* אָמַר Ch. P'AL ʰ*pret.* ⁱ*inf.* ᵏ*fut.* ˡ*part.* ᵐ אֲמַר words, sayings.

2 דָּבַר the primary meaning of this root seems to be, to put forth in order, hence to discourse, as the Latins say, *sermones serere;* to speak, sometimes emphatically, to speak well, Exod. iv. 14, Jer. i. 6. Rarely it is immediately followed by the words spoken, and לֵאמֹר is to be mentally supplied: Gen. xli. 17: Exod. xxxii. 7. See *Speak.* KAL ᵃ*part.* Poel. PIEL ᵇ*pret.* ᶜ*inf.* ᵈ*imp.* ᵉ*fut.* ᶠ*part.* ᵍ דָּבָר *m.* word, saying.

3 חִידָה *f.* (see *Riddle*), dark sayings.

4 מָלַל to speak, to talk; to talk in conversation, to tell, to relate, seem best to agree with this root as differing from those above; see *Speak.* PIEL ᵃ*pret.* Gen. xxi. 7, "who would have said," *i.e.* in common talk, in conversation, to Abraham. מְלַל Ch. P'AL ᵇ*pret.* ᶜ מִלָּה *f.* word.

5 נְאָם to say or speak with the greatest assurance of the truth of what is spoken. It is a term generally used by prophets speaking in God's name and behalf, importing a divine commission and inspiration, Jer. xxiii. 31, that "say, He saith," *i.e.* that pretend a divine commission, and use the expression that denotes it. When pronounced by God himself, it imports solemn assurance of what is delivered or asserted, Gen. xxii. 16. KAL ᵃ*fut.* ᵇ*part.* Paül (by some considered a noun) used as a noun followed by a genitive.

6 עָנָה to answer; see *Speak.* KAL *pret.*

7 פֶּה *m.* mouth.

8 פָּנִים *m. pl.* face; "to say one nay," *lit.* to turn away his face.

9 קָרָא to call. KAL *pret.*

10 שׁוּב to return; to cause to return. HIPHIL ᵃ*fut.*

No. 1 a, *Say* and *Saith;* No. 1 b, *Saying;* No. 1 d, *Said,* not included.

Gen. iii. 1, 3, 16, 17.	1 a	Gen. xxxiv. 11, 12.	1 d	Exod. iv. 1, 23.	1 d
x. 9.	1 g	xxxiv. 13.	2 e	iv. 12.	2 e
xii. 13.	1 c	xxxvii. 11.	2 g	iv. 26.	1 a
xii. 19.	1 a	xxxvii. 17.	1 e	v. 16, 17.	1 b
xiii. 14.	1 a	xxxviii. 11, 22.	1 a	v. 19.	1 b
xiv. 23.	1 d	xli. 15.	1 b	vi. 6.	1 c
xvi. 13.	1 a	xli. 17.	2 e	vi. 26.	1 a
xvii. 23.	2 b	xli. 54.	1 a	vi. 29.	2 a
xviii. 5.	2 b	xli. 55.	1 d	vii. 13, 22.	2 b
viii. 17.	1 a	xlii. 4.	1 a	vii. 19.	1 c
xx. 5, 5, 16.	1 a	xliii. 5.	1 a	viii. 5, 16.	1 c
xx. 13.	1 c	xliii. 7.	1 d	viii. 15, 19.	2 b
xxi. 1, 16.	1 a	xliv. 4.	1 a	xi. 1.γ	1 d
xxi. 7.	4 a	xliv. 7.	2 e	xii. 26.	1 d
xxii. 14.	1 g	xliv. 16, 16.	1 d	xii. 31, 31.	1 d, 2 c
xxii. 16.		xlv. 17.	1 c	xii. 32.	2 b
xxiv. 14, 14.	1 d a	xlv. 27.	2 b	xii. 33.	1 a
xxvi. 7.	1 b	xlvi. 31.	1 d	xiii. 17.	1 a
xxvi. 9, 9.	1 a	xlvii. 15.	1 b	xv. 9.	1 a
xxix. 32.		xlvii. 30.β	2 g	xvi. 9.	1 c
xxx. 24.		l. 17.	1 a	xvi. 23.	2 b
xxxi. 16, 31,α 49.	1 a	Exod. ii. 22.	1 a	xvii. 10.	1 a
xxxii. 9.	1 e	iii. 13, 13, 13.	1 a a d	xviii. 3, 24.	1 a
xxxii. 12, 20.	1 a	iii. 14, 15.	1 d	xix. 3.	1 d

Exod. xx. 22. 1 d
xxi. 5. 1 b d
xxiii. 13. 1 a
xxiv. 1, 14. 1 a
xxiv. 3, 7. 2 b
xxxii. 7, 13. 2 e
xxxii. 12. 1 d
xxxiii. 1. 2 e
xxxiii. 5. 1 c
xxxiii. 12, 12, 12. 1 d e a
Lev. x. 5. 2 b
x. 19. 2 e
xiv. 35. 2 b
xvi. 40. 2 b
xvii. 8. 1 d
xvii. 12. 1 a
xx. 2. 1 d
xxii. 3. 1 c
xxv. 20. 1 d
xxxii. 31. 2 b
Num. x. 29. 1 a
xi. 12, 18. 1 d
xi. 21. 1 a
xiii. 31. 1 a
xiv. 28, 28. 1 c, 5 b
xiv. 31. 1 a
xiv. 39. 2 g
xvi. 34. 1 a
xviii. 24. 1 a
xxi. 14. 1 g
xxi. 27. 1 d
xxii. 17. 1 d
xxii. 19, 38. 2 c
xxii. 20. 2 e
xxiii. 16. 2 e
xxiii. 19, 30. 1 a
xxiii. 23. 1 g
xxiv. 3, 3, 4, 15, 15, 16. 5 b
xxiv. 13. 2 e
xxv. 12. 1 c
xxvi. 65. 1 a
xxxii. 27. 2 a
xxxvi. 5. 2 a
Deut. i. 21. 2 b
i. 23. 2 g
i. 39. 1 a
i. 42. 1 c
iv. 10. 1 b
v. 27. 1 d
v. 30. 1 c
vii. 17. 1 d
ix. 3. 2 b
ix. 25. 1 a
ix. 28. 1 d
x. 1. 1 a
xi. 25. 2 b
xv. 16. 1 d
xvii. 16. 1 a
xviii. 2. 2 b
xviii. 21. 1 d
xxviii. 67, 67. 1 d
xxix. 13. 2 b
xxx. 12, 13. 1 b
xxxi. 2. 1 a
xxxi. 3. 2 b
xxxii. 26. 1 a
xxxii. 27. 1 d
xxxiii. 8, 12, 13, 18, 20, 22, 23, 24. 1 a
xxxiii. 9. 1 e
xxxiii. 27. 1 d
Josh. i. 3. 2 b
v. 2. 1 a
v. 14. 2 f
vi. 22. 1 a
vii. 8. 1 d
viii. 6. 1 d
xi. 23. 2 b
xiii. 14, 33. 2 b
xiv. 6, 10, 12. 2 b
xxii. 11. 1 b
xxii. 21. 2 e
xxii. 27, 28. 1 d
Judg. i. 20. 1 d
ii. 3. 1 a
ii. 15. 2 b
v. 23. 1 a
vi. 27. 2 b
vi. 36, 37. 1 d, 2 b
vii. 4, 4. 1 d
vii. 11. 2 e
viii. 3.δ 2 c
ix. 3. 1 a
ix. 54. 1 d
xii. 4. 1 a
Judg. xii. 6. 1 c
xiii. 13. 1 a
xiii. 17. 2 g
xvi. 15. 1 d
xvi. 24. 1 a
xviii. 24. 1 d
xix. 30. 1 a
xx. 32, 39. 1 a
xxxvi. 27. 2 b
Ruth ii. 21. 1 a
iii. 5. 1 d
iii. 17. 1 a
1 Sam. i. 22. 1 a
ii. 15, 20. 1 a
ii. 30. 5 b
ii. 30. 1 b a
ii. 30. 5 b
iii. 17, 17. 2 b
iv. 7. 1 a
iv. 20. 2 e
v. 7. 1 a
vii. 12. 1 d
viii. 6. 1 a
viii. 7. 1 d
ix. 5, 23, 27. 1 a
ix. 6. 2 e
ix. 10.ε 2 g
ix. 17. 6
ix. 24. 1 b
x. 15, 27. 1 a
xi. 9. 1 d
xi. 12. 1 e
xii. 1. 1 a
xiii. 4. 1 b
xiii. 19. 1 a
xiv. 9, 10. 1 d
xv. 16, 16, 16, 16. 1 d, 2 b, 1 d, 2 d
xvii. 55, 55. 1 a d
xviii. 8. 2 g
xviii. 17, 17. 1 d a
xviii. 22. 1 b
xviii. 25, 25. 1 d
xix. 17, 17. 1 d a
xix. 24. 1 d
xx. 3, 3, 7, 22. 1 d
xx. 21. 1 b d
xxiv. 4, 4. 1 d a
xxiv. 13. 1 d
xxv. 12. 2 g
xxv. 21, 35. 1 a
xxix. 9. 1 a
2 Sam. ii. 22. 1 b
vii. 8. 1 d
vii. 20. 2 c
vii. 25. 2 b
xi. 25, 25. 1 d
xii. 18. 1 a
xii. 22, 22. 1 d a
xiii. 35.ζ 2 g
xiv. 10, 10. 1 d, 2 f
xiv. 12. 2 d
xiv. 32. 1 b
xv. 26. 1 d
xvi. 3, 3, 3. 1 d d a
xvi. 7. 1 a
xvi. 10, 10, 10. 1 d a d
xvii. 4, 6. 2 g
xvii. 5. 7
xvii. 29. 1 a
xviii. 18, 19, 33. 1 a
xix. 2. 1 b
xix. 13. 1 d
xix. 26. 1 a
xix. 29, 29. 1 d a
xx. 16. 1 c
xxi. 4. 1 e
xxiii. 1, 1. 5 b
xxiii. 3. 1 a
xxiv. 1. 1 a
xxiv. 12, 12. 2 b a
xxiv. 19. 2 g
1 Kings i. 24, 24. 1 d a
i. 25, 36, 36. 1 d
i. 48. 1 a
ii. 4. 1 b
ii. 14, 14. 2 g d
ii. 16. 2 d
ii. 17.η 10 a, 8
ii. 20.η 10 a, 8
ii. 20. 10 a, 8
ii. 26. 1 a
ii. 30, 30, 30, 30, 30. 1 d a d b, 2 b
ii. 31, 31. 2 b, 1 d
ii. 38, 38, 38. 1 d, 2 b g
1 Kings iii. 22, 22. 1 d e
iii. 23, 23, 23. 1 d e e
iii. 26, 26. 1 d e
viii. 12. 1 a
viii. 29. 1 a
xi. 2. 1 a
xii. 6. 1 b
xii. 10. 2 e
xii. 15. 2 g
xiii. 4, 17, 32. 2 g
xiii. 7, 12. 2 e
xiii. 22. 2 b
xiv. 5, 5. 1 a, 2 e
xv. 29. 2 g
xvi. 16. 1 b
xvii. 13, 13. 1 a, 2 g
xvii. 15. 2 g
xviii. 10. 1 a
xviii. 11, 14. 1 e
xviii. 44. 1 c
xx. 4. 2 g
xx. 13, 13. 1 d a
xx. 23, 35. 1 a
xx. 28, 28, 28. 1 d a a
xxi. 5. 2 e
xxi. 6, 6. 2 e, 1 d
xxii. 8, 8, 8, 14, 14. 1 d
xxii. 20, 20, 20. 1 d d e
xxii. 32, 49. 1 a
2 Kings i. 3, 3. 2 b d
i. 6, 6, 6, 6. 2 d d b, 1 a
i. 7, 10, 12, 13, 15. 2 e
i. 9. 2 b
i. 11, 11. 2 e, 1 a
i. 16, 16. 2 e, 1 a
ii. 9, 9. 1 a d
ii. 22. 2 g
iv. 13, 13. 1 d c
iv. 17. 2 b
iv. 26. 1 c
v. 4. 2 b
v. 14. 2 g
vi. 28, 28. 1 d a
vi. 32. 1 a
vii. 17. 2 b
viii. 2. 2 b
viii. 10, 10. 1 d c
viii. 14, 14. 1 d a
ix. 13, 37. 1 d
ix. 17, 17, 17. 1 d
ix. 26, 26. 5 b
x. 17. 2 g
xi. 15, 15. 1 d a
xiv. 27. 2 b
xvii. 12. 1 a
xvii. 23. 2 b
xviii. 22, 22, 28. 1 d
xviii. 25. 1 a
xix. 6, 6, 6. 1 d d a
xix. 9, 9. 1 b
xix. 33. 5 b
xx. 14, 14, 14. 1 d a d
xxi. 4, 7. 1 a
xxii. 18, 18. 1 d a
xxii. 19. 5 b
xxiii. 27, 27. 1 d a
xxiv. 13. 2 b
1 Chron. xv. 2. 1 a
xvi. 31. 1 d
xvi. 35. 1 c
xvii. 7, 7. 1 d a
xvii. 23. 2 b
xxi. 18. 1 b
xxi. 19. 2 g
xxii. 11. 2 b
xxiii. 25. 1 a
xxvii. 23. 1 a
xxviii. 3. 1 a
2 Chron. vi. 1, 1, 20. 1 a
viii. 11. 1 a
x. 10. 1 d
xiii. 22. 2 g
xviii. 7, 13. 1 d
xviii. 15, 15. 1 d, 2 e
xviii. 19, 19, 19. 1 d e e
xviii. 31. 1 a
xx. 21. 1 e
xxii. 9. 1 a
xxiii. 3, 3. 1 d, 2 b
xxiii. 14, 14. 1 d a
xxiv. 22. 1 a
xxvi. 23. 1 a
xxxiii. 4, 7. 1 a
xxxiii. 19. 2 g
xxxiv. 26, 26. 1 d a
xxxiv. 27. 5 b
Ezra v. 3. 1 l
v. 4, 9, 15. 1 h
v. 11. 1 i
viii. 17.θ 2 g, 7, 2 c
ix. 10. 1 d
x. 12, 12.ι 1 d, 2 g
Neh. iv. 22. 1 a
v. 2, 3, 4. 1 e
v. 12, 12. 1 d e
vi. 6. 1 e
vi. 8, 8. 1 b e
Esth. i. 18. 1 d
i. 21. 2 g
v. 5,κ 8.λ 2 g
vi. 10, 10. 1 d, 2 b
Job i. 5. 1 a
iii. 3. 1 a
ix. 12. 1 d
ix. 22. 1 a
ix. 27. 1 b
x. 2. 1 d
xvii. 14. 9
xix. 28. 1 d
xx. 7. 1 d
xxi. 14, 28. 1 d
xxii. 17. 1 e
xxii. 29. 1 d
xxiii. 5. 1 d
xxxi. 24, 31. 1 a
xxxii. 7, 10. 1 a
xxxii. 11. 4 c
xxxii. 13. 1 d
xxxiii. 24, 27. 1 d
xxxiii. 32. 4 c
xxxiv. 5, 9. 1 a
xxxiv. 18. 1 b
xxxiv. 31. 1 f
xxxv. 2. 1 a
xxxv. 14. 1 d
xxxvii. 6, 19. 1 d
xxxviii. 35. 1 d
xxxix. 25. 1 d
Ps. ii. 7. 1 a
iii. 2.μ 1 e
iv. 6. 1 e
x. 6, 11, 13. 1 a
xi. 1. 1 d
xii. 4. 1 a
xii. 5. 1 d
xiii. 4. 1 d
xiv. 1. 1 a
xvi. 2. 1 a
xxvii. 8. 1 a
xxx. 6. 1 a
xxxi. 14, 22. 1 a
xxxii. 5. 1 a
xxxv. 3. 1 c
xxxv. 10, 27. 1 d
xxxv. 21. 1 a
xxxv. 25, 25. 1 d
xxxvi. 1. 5 b
xxxviii. 16. 1 a
xxxix. 1. 1 a
xl. 7. 1 a
xl. 15. 1 e
xl. 16. 1 d
xli. 4. 1 a
xlii. 3, 10. 1 b
xlii. 9. 1 d
xlix. 4. 3
xlix. 13. 7
liii. 1. 1 a
lviii. 11. 1 d
lxvi. 3. 1 c
lxviii. 22. 1 a
lxx. 3. 1 e
lxx. 4. 1 d
lxxiv. 8. 1 a
lxxv. 4. 1 a
lxxviii. 2. 3
lxxviii. 19. 1 a
lxxix. 10. 1 d
lxxxii. 6. 1 a
lxxxiii. 4, 12. 1 a
lxxxvii. 5. 1 g
lxxxix. 2. 1 a
xc. 3. 1 d
xci. 2. 1 d
xciv. 7. 1 d
xciv. 18. 1 a
xcvi. 10. 1 c
cvii. 2. 1 d
cx. 1. 5 b
cxv. 2. 1 d
cxvi. 11. 1 a
cxviii. 2, 3, 4. 1 d
Ps. cxix. 57. 1 a
cxxii. 1. 1 e
cxxii. 8. 2 e
cxxiv. 1. 1 d
cxxix. 1. 1 d
cxxxvii. 7. 1 e
cxxxix. 11. 1 d
cxl. 6. 1 a
cxlii. 5. 1 a
Prov. i. 6. 3
i. 11. 1 d
iii. 28. 1 d
iv. 10, 20. 1 m
vii. 4. 1 c
xx. 9, 14, 22. 1 d
xxiii. 7. 1 d
xxiv. 12, 29. 1 d
xxiv. 24. 1 e
xxv. 7. 1 b
xxviii. 24. 1 e
Eccles. ii. 1, 2. 1 a
ii. 15, 15. 1 a, 2 b
iii. 17, 18. 1 a
v. 6. 1 d
vii. 10. 1 d
vii. 23. 1 a
viii. 4. 1 d
viii. 14. 1 a
ix. 16. 1 a
xii. 1. 1 d
Cant. ii. 10. 1 a
vii. 8. 1 a
Isa. i. 11, 18. 1 d
i. 24. 5 b
iii. 10. 1 c
iii. 15. 5 b
iii. 16. 1 d
v. 19. 1 e
vi. 3. 1 a
vi. 8, 8. 1 d e
viii. 12, 12, 19. 1 d
ix. 9. 1 b
x. 8. 1 d
xiv. 10. 1 d
xiv. 13. 1 a
xiv. 22, 22, 23. 5 b
xvii. 3, 6. 5 b
xviii. 4. 1 a
xix. 4. 5 b
xix. 11. 1 d
xxi. 6, 12, 16. 1 a
xxii. 4. 1 a
xxii. 25. 5 b
xxv. 9. 1 a
xxviii. 12, 15. 1 a
xxix. 15. 1 d
xxix. 16, 16. 1 d a
xxx. 1. 5 b
xxx. 22. 1 d
xxxi. 9. 5 b
xxxii. 5. 1 g
xxxiii. 10, 24. 1 d
xxxv. 4. 1 c
xxxvi. 4, 4, 4. 1 d c a
xxxvi. 7, 7. 1 d
xxxvi. 10. 1 a
xxxvii. 6, 6, 6. 1 d d a
xxxvii. 9, 9. 1 b
xxxvii. 34. 5 b
xxxviii. 10, 11. 1 a
xxxviii. 15. 2 e
xxxix. 3, 3, 3. 1 d a d
xl. 1, 25, 27. 1 d
xl. 6, 6. 1 e a
xl. 9. 1 c
xli. 7, 13. 1 e
xli. 14. 5 b
xli. 21, 21, 26. 1 d
xlii. 17, 22. 1 e
xliii. 6, 9. 1 d
xliii. 10, 12. 5 b
xliv. 5, 16, 17, 20. 1 d
xliv. 19. 1 b
xliv. 26, 27. 1 e
xliv. 28, 28. 1 e b
xlv. 9. 1 d
xlv. 10. 1 e
xlv. 19. 1 a
xlvi. 10. 1 e
xlvii. 8. 1 e
xlvii. 10, 10. 1 a d
xlviii. 5, 7. 1 d
xlviii. 20. 1 c
xlix. 4. 1 a
xlix. 9. 1 b
xlix. 18. 5 b
Isa. xlix. 20. 1 d
li. 16. 1 b
li. 23. 1 a
lii. 5, 5. 5 b
lii. 7. 1 e
liv. 17. 5 b
lv. 8. 5 b
lvi. 3, 3. 1 b d
lvi. 8. 5 b
lvii. 10. 1 a
lviii. 9. 1 d
lix. 20. 5 b
lxii. 11. 1 c
lxv. 1. 1 a
lxv. 5. 1 e
lxvi. 2, 17, 22. 5 b
lxvi. 5. 1 a
lxvi. 9, 9. 1 d a
Jer. i. 7. 1 d
i. 8, 15, 19. 5 b
ii. 3, 9, 12, 19, 22, 29. 5 b
ii. 6, 8. 1 a
ii. 23. 1 d
ii. 27, 27. 1 e d
ii. 35, 35. 1 d b
iii. 1, 1. 1 b, 5 b
iii. 10, 12, 12, 13, 14. 5 b
iii. 16, 16. 5 b, 1 d
iii. 19, 19. 1 a d
iii. 20. 5 b
iv. 1, 9, 17. 5 b
iv. 5, 5. 1 c
iv. 11. 1 g
iv. 27. 1 a
v. 2, 19. 1 d
v. 4. 1 a
v. 9, 11, 18, 22, 29. 5 b
v. 15, 15. 5 b, 2 e
vi. 6. 1 a
vi. 12. 5 b
vii. 11, 13, 19, 30, 32. 5 b
viii. 1, 3, 13, 17. 5 b
viii. 8. 1 d
viii. 18. 1 d
ix. 3, 6, 9, 22, 24, 25. 5 b
ix. 13. 1 d
x. 11. 1 k
x. 19. 1 a
xii. 4. 1 a
xii. 17. 5 b
xiii. 11, 14, 25. 5 b
xiii. 18. 1 c
xiii. 21, 22. 1 d
xiv. 13, 13. 1 d e
xiv. 15. 1 e
xv. 2. 1 d
xv. 3, 6, 9, 20. 5 b
xv. 11. 1 a
xvi. 5, 11, 16. 5 b
xvi. 14, 14. 5 b, 1 g
xvi. 19. 1 d
xvii. 15. 1 e
xvii. 19. 1 a
xvii. 24. 5 b
xviii. 6. 5 b
xviii. 10, 12. 1 a
xix. 6, 12. 5 b
xx. 9. 1 a
xxi. 3, 3, 8. 1 d
xxi. 7, 10, 14. 5 b
xxi. 8. 1 d
xxi. 13, 13. 5 b, 1 e
xxii. 5, 16, 24. 5 b
xxii. 14. 1 e
xxii. 21. 1 a
xxiii. 1, 2, 4, 5, 11, 12. 5 b
xxiii. 7, 7. 5 b, 1 d
xxiii. 17. 1 b e
xxiii. 17. 2 b
xxiii. 23, 24, 24, 28, 29, 30, 32, 32, 33. 5 b
xxiii. 25. 1 a
xxiii. 31, 31, 31. 5 b a b
xxiii. 34, 35, 37. 1 d
xxiii. 38, 38, 38, 38, 38. 1 d a b b d
xxv. 5. 1 b
xxv. 7, 9, 12, 29, 31. 5 b
xxvii. 4. 1 b
xxvii. 4. 1 d

α *or,* I thought. (continuation of x. 29.)   β *lit.* as thy word.   γ *or,* had said: (xi. 4 is the continuation of x. 29.)   δ *lit.* said this thing.   ε *lit.* thy word is good.   ζ *lit.* according to the word of thy servant.   η *lit.* he will not turn away thy face.   θ *lit.* I put words in their mouth to say.   ι *lit.* according to this word.   κ *lit.* the word of.   λ according to the word of.   μ *or,* to my soul.

SCAB

גָּרָב *m.* scab, scurf, scurvy; supposed to have been a malignant discharging disease: Deut. xxviii. 27.

יַלֶּפֶת *f.* a sort of itching scab, scurf, tetter; so called from its sticking fast: Lev. xxi. 20; xxii. 22.

סַפַּחַת *f.* scurf, scab, mange; so called from its adhering, or (according to Gesenius) from the flowing out, *i.e.* falling off of the hair: Lev. xiii. 2; xiv. 56. מִסְפַּחַת *f.* Lev. xiii. 6, 7, 8. שָׂפַח to smite with a scab. PIEL *pret.* Isa. iii. 17, *i.e.* make bald.

SCABBARD

תַּעַר *m.* the sheath of a sword: Jer. xlvii. 6.

SCAFFOLD

כִּיּוֹר *m.* a platform or pulpit, *suggestus,* for speaking in public, so called from its likeness to a basin: 2 Chron. vi. 13.

SCALE (V)

עָלָה to ascend. KAL *pret.* Prov. xxi. 22.

SCALES

אָפִיק *m.* strong, mighty: Job xli. 15, "scales are his pride," *marg.* 'strong pieces of shields.'

מָגֵן *m.* shield: Job xli. 15, *marg.* 'strong pieces of shield are his pride.'

קַשְׂקֶשֶׂת *f.* scales: Lev. xi. 9, 10, 12: Deut. xiv. 9, 10: Ezek. xxix. 4, 4.

SCALES

פֶּלֶס *m.* balance, so called from being even, level; the beam of a pair of scales, or rather the steelyard: Isa. xl. 12.

SCALL

נֶתֶק *m.* a scall, mange, scab, in the head and beard, which tears out the hair: Lev. xiii. 30, 31, 31, 32, 32, 33, 33, 34, 34, 35, 36, 37, 37; xiv. 54.

SCALP

קָדְקֹד *m.* the top of the head: Ps. lxviii. 21.

SCANT

רָזוֹן *m.* leanness: Micah vi. 10, *marg.* 'measure of leanness.'

SCAPEGOAT

עֲזָאזֵל It could not accord with the nature of this undertaking to enumerate even a portion of the conjectures which have been offered on the meaning of this word, but the most common interpretation is that sanctioned by our translation, that it is compounded of עֵז a goat, and אָזַל to go away; yet the strongest objection to this explanation is the manifest antithesis in Lev. xvi. 8 between לַיהֹוָה and לַעֲזָאזֵל, for Jehovah and for Azazel. This has led critics to regard the latter as a person, but in the designation of that person I cannot acquiesce in any statement I have yet seen. Perhaps this may be allowed to remain a difficulty if we admit that in some sense a person is intended, and can establish a general typical

import in assigning a goat for Azazel as well as for Jehovah. The goat for Jehovah is destined to make satisfaction for sin, the goat for Azazel to carry away sin, to remove it out of sight ; so that the day of atonement taught these two great blessings of redemption, sin atoned and sin remitted, at the same time, one suffering for sin, another set at liberty ; the same inferences might seem to receive illustration from Jesus crucified and Barabbas released. Beyond this no certainty seems to attach itself to the many different interpretations given by critics. We have probably lost the original import of the expression "for Azazel." It occurs only in Lev. xvi. 8, *marg.* 'Azazel,' 10, 10, 26.

SCARCE

יָצָא to go out. KAL *inf.* Gen. xxvii. 30, was "scarce gone out," *lit.* going was gone.

SCARCENESS

מִסְכֵּנֻת *f.* poverty, misery : Deut. viii. 9.

SCARE

חָתַת see *Dismay.* PIEL *pret.* Job vii. 14.

SCARLET

אַרְגְּוָנָא Ch. *m. emph.* (see *Purple*): Dan. v. 7, *marg.* ' or, purple,' 16, 29.

שָׁנִי *m. pr.* a bright colour ; crimson or deep scarlet, the colour obtained from a certain insect ; a scarlet thread : Gen. xxxviii. 28, 30 : Josh. ii. 18, 21 : 2 Sam. i. 24 : Prov. xxxi. 21, *marg.* ' or, with double garments :' Cant. iv. 3 : Isa. i. 18 ; but it usually occurs in connexion with תּוֹלַעַת *m. coccus,* worm or insect, *coccus ilicis,* Linn.; in the form of תּוֹלַעַת שָׁנִי : Exod. xxv. 4 ; xxvi. 1, 31, 36 ; xxvii. 16 ; xxviii. 5, 6, 8, 15, 33 ; xxxv. 6, 23, 25, 35 ; xxxvi. 8, 35, 37 ; xxxviii. 18, 23 ; xxxix. 1, 2, 3, 5, 8, 24, 29 : Num. iv. 8 : or of שָׁנִי תּוֹלַעַת, Lev. xiv. 4, 6, 49, 51, 52 : Num. xix. 6.

תּוֹלָע *m.* (see *Crimson*): Lam. iv. 5, hence *v. denom.* תָּלַע PUAL *part.* Nah. ii. 3, "in scarlet."

SCATTER

1 בְּדַר Ch. to scatter. PAEL *pret.*

2 בָּזַר to scatter, to disperse, to dissipate. KAL ^a *fut.* PIEL ^b *pret.*

3 זָרָה to scatter by strawing, dispersing, or ventilating ; in Piel, the force of the word is increased, and it is applied to a violent dispersion, as of the Israelites to distant countries, Lev. xxvi. 33 ; to the dissolution and dissipation of that which is compact ; so to a king who scatters evil by diminishing the number of the wicked and the growth of vice, Prov. xx. 8, 26 ; to the diligent communication of knowledge, Prov. xv. 7. The word is used of the dispersion and overthrow of the wicked, who are hurried away with vehemence and rapidity like chaff before the wind ; see *Fan.* In Ps. cxxxix. 3, to try or prove, as that which is ventilated or shaken to

be examined. KAL ^a *imp.* ^b *fut.* NIPHAL ^c *inf.* PIEL ^d *pret.* ^e *inf.* ^f *fut.* ^g *part.* PUAL ^h *fut.*

4 זָרַק to sprinkle. KAL ^a *imp.* ^b *fut.*

5 מָשַׁךְ to draw out. PUAL *part.* Isa. xviii. 2, 7. LXX. ἔθνος μετέωρον, a lofty nation, as the Ethiopians are described, Isa. xlv. 14. The Chaldee, " a people suffering violence." The Syriac, " a nation distorted." The Vulgate, " a people convulsed and lacerated." Vitringa understands it of a people spread out or drawn out over a country of considerable length but narrow. See Barnes' Notes, *in loc.* Yet the expression may be regarded as prophetically descriptive of the Jews in the mixed and opposite circumstances of oppression and aggrandisement.

6 נוּעַ to wander in agitation; to cause to wander. HIPHIL *imp.*

7 נָפַץ to break, to dash in pieces; to disperse, to scatter as a flock, a people. KAL ^a *pret.* PIEL ^b *inf.* ^c נֶפֶץ *m.* scattering.

8 פָּאָה from פֵּאָה a corner, to scatter into corners. HIPHIL *fut.* Deut. xxxii. 26. LXX. διασπερῶ αὐτούς. Gr. *Venet.* ἐξυριῶ σφᾶς. Gesenius would translate it, "I will blow them away, scatter them as with a wind."

9 פּוּץ to scatter, to disperse what was before united, collected together, *e.g.* by a whirlwind ; to cast abroad fitches, as stubble, Jer. xiii. 24 ; as sheep, Jer. xxiii. 1, Zech. xiii. 7 ; as the nations over the whole earth, Gen. xi. 9 ; as an army disperses, 1 Sam. xiii. 8 ; as the unbelieving Jews among all nations, Deut. iv. 27, xxviii. 64, xxx. 3, Ezek. xxii. 15, xi. 17, Jer. ix. 16, xiii. 24 ; Egyptians, Ezek. xxix. 12 ; enemies fleeing before a conqueror, Ps. xviii. 14, comp. Ps. lxviii. 2. KAL ^a *fut.* NIPHAL ^b *pret.* ^c *part.* HIPHIL ^d *pret.* ^e *inf.* ^f *fut.* ^g *part.* HITHPAEL ^h *fut.*

10 פּוּשׁ to be scattered, dispersed. NIPHAL *pret.*

11 פָּזַר to scatter, disperse. KAL ^a *part.* NIPHAL ^b *pret.* PIEL ^c *pret.* ^d *fut.* ^e *part.* PUAL ^f *part.*

12 פָּרַד to separate ; to be dispersed. HITHPAEL *fut.*

13 פָּרַץ to break ; to break, or rend asunder, *i.e.* to disperse, to scatter. KAL *pret.*

14 פָּרַשׂ to break ; to spread out or abroad. NIPHAL ^a *fut.* PIEL ^b *inf.*

15 פָּרַשׁ to separate ; to be dispersed. NIPHAL *part.*

Gen. xi. 4.	9 a	Job iv. 11.	12	Isa. xxx. 30.	7 c	
xi. 8.	9 f	xviii. 15.	3 h	xxxiii. 3.	7 a	
xi. 9.	9 d	xxxvii. 11.	9 f	xli. 16.	9 f	
xlix. 7.	9 f	xxxviii. 24.	9 f	Jer. iii. 13.	11 d	
Exod. v. 12.	9 f	Ps. xviii. 14.	9 f	ix. 16.	9 d	
Lev. xxvi. 33.	3 f	xliv. 11.	3 d	x. 21.	9 b	
Num. x. 35.	9 a	liii. 5.	11 c	xiii. 24.	9 f	
xvi. 37.	3 a	lix. 11.	6	xviii. 17.	9 f	
Deut. iv. 27.	9 d	lx. 1.	13	xxiii. 1.	9 g	
xxviii. 64.	9 d	lxviii. 1.	9 a	xxiii. 2.	9 d	
xxx. 3.	9 d	lxviii. 14.	14 b	xxx. 11.	9 d	
xxxii. 26.	8	lxviii. 30.	2 b	xxxi. 10.	3 g	
1 Sam. xi. 11.	9 a	lxxxix. 10.	11 c	xl. 15.	9 b	
xiii. 8.	9 f	xcii. 9.	12	xlix. 32, 36.	3 d	
xiii. 15.	7 a	cvi. 27.	3 e	l. 17.	11 a	
2 Sam. xviii. 8.	8 c	cxli. 7.	11 b	lii. 8.	9 b	
xxii. 15.	9 f	cxliv. 6.	9 f	Ezek. v. 2.	3 b	
1 Kings xiv. 15.	3 d	cxlvii. 16.	11 d	v. 10.	3 d	
xxii. 17.	3 c	Prov. xxi. 24.	11 e	v. 12.	3 f	
2 Kings xxv. 5.	9 b	xx. 8, 26.	3 g	vi. 5.	3 d	
2 Chron. xviii. 16.	3 c	Isa. xviii. 2, 7. a	5	vi. 8.	3 c	
Neh. i. 8.	9 f	xxiv. 1.	9 d	x. 2.	4 a	
Esth. iii. 8.	11 f	xxviii. 25.	4 b	xi. 16.	9 d	

Ezek. xi. 17.	9 b	Ezek. xxix. 13.	9 b	Dan. xi. 24.	2 a	
xii. 14.	3 f	xxx. 23, 26.	9 d	xii. 7.	7 b	
xii. 15.	9 e	xxxiv. 5, 5.	9 a	Joel iii. 2.	11 c	
xvii. 21.	14 a	xxxiv. 6.	9 b	Nah. iii. 18.	10	
xx. 23.	9 e	xxxiv. 12, 12.	15, 9 b	Hab. iii. 6.	9 h	
xx. 34, 41.	9 b	xxxiv. 21.	9 d	iii. 14.	9 e	
xxii. 15.	9 d	xxxvi. 19.	9 f	Zech. i. 19.	3 d	
xxviii. 25.	9 b	xlvi. 18.	9 a	i. 21, 21.	3 d e	
xxix. 12.	9 d	Dan. iv. 14.	1	xiii. 7.	9 a	

a *marg.* ' *or*, outspread and polished.'

SCENT

זֵכֶר *m.* (see *Memorial*): Hos. xiv. 7, *marg.* '*or*, memorial.'

רֵיחַ *m.* savour: Job xiv. 9: Jer. xlviii. 11.

SCEPTRE

שֵׁבֶט *com.* a rod or staff; a staff of office and authority, hence sceptre: Gen. xlix. 10: Num. xxiv. 17: Ps. xlv. 6, 6: Isa. xiv. 5: Ezek. xix. 11, 14: Amos i. 5, 8: Zech. x. 11.

שַׁרְבִיט *m.* for שֵׁבֶט a form of the later Hebrew: Esth. iv. 11; v. 2, 2; viii. 4.

SCHOLAR

תַּלְמִיד *m.* a disciple, scholar: 1 Chron. xxv. 8.

עָנָה to answer. KAL *part.* Poel, Mal. ii. 12, *marg.* '*or*, him that waketh, and him that answereth.'

SCIENCE

מַדָּע *m.* knowledge: Dan. i. 4.

SCOFF

קָלַס see *Scorn*. HITHPAEL *fut.* Hab. i. 10.

SCORN

1   בָּזָה to despise. KAL *fut.*

2   לוּץ to deride, or to mock any one; a mocker, scoffer, scorner, *i.e.* a frivolous and impudent person, who sets at nought and scoffs at the most sacred precepts and duties of religion, piety, and morals. KAL a*pret.* b*part.* HIPHIL c*fut.* d*part.* e לָצוֹן *m.*

3   לָצַץ to mock. KAL *part.* Poel.

4   לָעַג to mock, to deride; properly by imitating the stammering voice of any one in derision; specially of those who mock at others in distress, Job xxii. 19; of a scoffer who mocks at God and religion, Job xi. 3; of one who contemns the threats and efforts of his enemies, Isa. xxxvii. 22. KAL a*pret.* b*fut.* HIPHIL c*fut.* d לַעַג *m.* scorning.

5   צְחֹק *m.* laughter in contempt, laughing to scorn.

6   שָׂחַק to laugh; *seq.* לְ to laugh at, to deride, to scorn, especially powerless threats. KAL a*fut.* b שְׂחוֹק *m.* laughing to scorn. c מִשְׂחָק *m. id.*

7   קָלַס to scoff at, to scorn, to deride. PIEL *inf.*

2 Kings xix. 21.	4 a	Ps. lxxix. 4.	4 d	Prov. xxi. 11, 24.	2 b		
Neh. ii. 19.	4 c	cxxiii. 4.	4 d	xxii. 10.	2 b		
Esth. iii. 6. a	1	Prov. i. 22, 22.	2 b e	xxiv. 9.	2 b		
Job xii. 4.	6 b	iii. 34, 34.	2 c b	xxix. 8.	2 e		
xvi. 20. β	2 d	ix. 7, 8.	2 b	Isa. xxviii. 14.	2 e		
xxii. 19.	4 b	ix. 12.	4 a	xxix. 20.	2 b		
xxxiv. 7.	4 d	xiii. 1.	2 a	xxxvii. 22.	4 a		
xxxix. 7, 18.	6 a	xiv. 6.	2 b	Ezek. xvi. 31.	7		
Ps. i. 1.		xv. 12.	2 b	xxiii. 32.	5		
xxii. 7.	4 c	xix. 25, 29.	2 b	Hos. vii. 5.	3		
xliv. 13.	4 d	xix. 28.	2 c	Hab. i. 10.	6 c		

a *lit.* and despised in his eyes.   β *marg.* 'are my scorners.'

SCORPION

עַקְרָב *m.* a poisonous reptile, whose body is in the form of an egg, very close to which the head is placed; it has claws like a lobster, and a tail with several joints, in the extremity of which its deadly sting is lodged.— *Bochart.* Celsius conjectures that in 1 Kings xii. 11, 14, 2 Chron. x. 11, 14, Ezek. ii. 6, it signifies a thorn whose prickles are of a venomous nature, called by the Arabians *spina scorpionis:* Deut. viii. 15. Used in a figurative sense for wicked, malicious, and crafty men: Ezek. ii. 6.

SCOUR

מָרַק to rub, to polish, to scour: PUAL *pret.* Lev. vi. 28.

SCOURGE

בִּקֹּרֶת *f.* animadversion, *i.e.* punishment, chastisement: Lev. xix. 20, from בָּקַר, Piel, to look after carefully.

שׁוֹט *m.* whip, scourge: Job v. 21, *marg.* '*or*, when the tongue scourgeth;' ix. 23: Isa. x. 26; xxviii. 15, 18. שֶׁמֶט *m.* a scourge: Josh. xxiii. 13. שַׁיִט *m. id.* Isa. xxviii. 15, כתיב.

SCRABBLE

תָּוָה to mark, to make marks; of David, feigning madness. PIEL *fut.* 1 Sam. xxi. 13, *marg.* '*or*, made marks.'

SCRAPE

גָּרַד Hithp. to scrape oneself, *e.g.* with a shell or sherd to allay itching. HITHPAEL *inf.* Job ii. 8.

סָחָה to sweep away, to wipe off. PIEL *pret.* Ezek. xxvi. 4.

קָצָה to cut off, to scrape off or away. HIPHIL *pret.* Lev. xiv. 41. *inf.* Lev. xiv. 43, *lit.* after scraping.

קָצַע to cut, to cut off, to scrape, to strip off. HIPHIL *fut.* Lev. xiv. 41.

SCRIBE

סָפַר to write; the king's scribe or secretary, an officer of state, who writes the royal edicts; also a military scribe or tribune, who had charge of the conscription and muster-rolls, muster-master: 2 Kings xxv. 19: Jer. lii. 25: 2 Chron. xxvi. 11: Isa. xxxiii. 18: so probably Jer. xxxvii. 15, a having charge of the public prison. Generally of a military leader, chief: Judg. v. 14. In later books, a scribe, *i.e.* one skilled in the sacred books and in the law. KAL *part.* Poel, 2 Sam. viii. 17, *marg.* '*or*, secretary;' xx. 25: 1 Kings iv. 3, *marg.* '*or*, secretaries:' 2 Kings xii. 10, *marg.* '*or*, secretary;' xviii. 18 and 37, *marg. id.;* xix. 2; xxii. 3, 8, 9, 10, 12; xxv. 19: 1 Chron. ii. 55; xviii. 16; xxiv. 6; xxvii. 32, *marg.* '*or*, secretary:' 2 Chron. xxiv. 11; xxvi. 11; xxxiv. 13, 15, 18, 20: Ezra vii. 6, 11, 11: Neh. viii. 1, 4, 9, 13; xii. 26, 36; xiii. 13: Esth. iii. 12 and viii. 9, *marg.* '*or*, secretaries:' Isa. xxxiii. 18; xxxvi. 3, 22, *marg.* '*or*, secretary;' xxxvii. 2: Jer. viii. 8; xxxvi. 10, 12, 12, 20, 21, 26, 32; xxxvii. 15, 20; lii. 25. סְפַר Ch. *m.* Ezra iv. 8, *marg.* '*or*, secretary,' 9, 17, 23; vii. 12, 21.

SCRIP

יַלְקוּט *m.* a sack, pouch, scrip, from לָקַט to gather : 1 Sam. xvii. 40.

SCRIPTURE

כְּתָב *m.* writing : Dan. x. 21.

SCROLL

סֵפֶר *m.* book : Isa. xxxiv. 4.

SCULL

גֻּלְגֹּלֶת *f.* scull, cranium, from its roundness : Judg. ix. 53 : 2 Kings ix. 35.

SCUM

חֶלְאָה *f.* the rust and filthiness which adheres to the side of a pot in which meat is boiled, and which is not washed and kept clean : Ezek. xxiv. 6, 6, 11, 12, 12.

SCURVY

גָּרָב *m.* (see *Scab*) : Lev. xxi. 20 ; xxii. 22.

SEA

יָם a sea or any collection of waters, a lake, a large river : Job xiv. 11. Various parts of the ocean, and also several lakes, are denoted by special names. The Mediterranean is designated in the following passages, Deut. xi. 24 ; Joel ii. 20 ; Exod. xxiii. 31 ; Num. xxxiv. 6, 7 ; Josh. i. 4 ; ix. 1 ; Ezek. xlvii. 10 : the sea of Galilee or lake of Tiberias, Num. xxxiv. 11 : the Dead Sea, Gen. xiv. 3 ; Deut. iv. 49 ; Joel ii. 20 ; Zech. xiv. 8 : the Red Sea, Ps. cvi. 7, 9, 22 ; Isa. xi. 15. *Absol.* הַיָּם, according to the context, is put for the Mediterranean, Josh. xv. 47 : the lake of Galilee, Isa. ix. 1 : the Red Sea, Isa. x. 26 : the Dead Sea, without *art.*, Isa. xvi. 8. *Poet.* the sea is put for maritime regions ; princes of the sea, *i.e.* of countries around and beyond the sea, Ezek. xxvi. 16 ; Isa. lx. 5 ; Deut. xxxiii. 19 : so Isa. xxiii. 4 is to be understood of Tyre : Isa. xi. 9, "as the waters cover the sea," *i.e.* fill its depths : Amos viii. 12, "from sea to sea," from the Mediterranean to the Persian Gulf or Indian Sea ; also Zech. ix. 10 ; Ps. lxxii. 8 ; *comp.* Micah vii. 12. The word יָם is transferred : to a great river, *e.g.* the Nile, Isa. xviii. 2 ; xix. 5 ; Nah. iii. 8 ; Job xli. 23 : the Euphrates, Isa. xxvii. 1 (*prob.* xxi. 1) ; Jer. li. 36 : the branches of the Nile, Ezek. xxxii. 2. By hyperbole, to a large vase or basin, the sea of brass, brasen sea, *i.e.* the great laver in the court of the priests before Solomon's temple, 2 Kings xxv. 13 ; 1 Kings vii. 23, &c. : to the western quarter, the west ; see *West*. The sea is put for a great multitude of people, or of inundating enemies, Isa. lvii. 20 ; Jer. vi. 23 ; l. 42, *comp.* Ps. lxv. 8 ; Ezek. xxvi. 3.—Gen. i. 10, &c. ; sea-faring men, Ezek. xxvi. 17, *marg.* 'the seas.' יָם Ch. *m.* Dan. vii. 2, 3.

SEAL

חָתַם to seal, to seal up, to close by a seal ; to seal for confirmation or for secrecy ; to complete, to finish, as sealing a letter, &c., implies its being finished : Ezek. xxviii. 12, *comp.* Dan. ix. 24, where it is applied to the cer-

tainty of the vision being assured according to the fulness of the prophecy. But in the other portion of the same passage, "to make an end of sins," is to be understood of sealing up sin so that it may not come into view, being fully pardoned by the atoning sacrifice of the Holy One. This meaning of hiding out of sight belongs to other passages, as Job ix. 7 ; Isa. viii. 16 (*comp.* Dan. viii. 26) ; xii. 4, 9. To seal up, *i.e.* to hinder, Job xxxvii. 7 ; to keep secure, as a treasure, Deut. xxxii. 34. KAL ᵃ*inf.* ᵇ*imp.* ᶜ*fut.* ᵈ*part.* Poel. ᵉ*part.* Paül. NIPHAL ᶠ*pret.* ᵍ*part.* חָתַם Ch. P'AL ʰ*pret.* ⁱ חוֹתָם *m.* seal or signet.

Deut. xxxii. 34.	e	Job xxxiii. 16.	c	Jer. xxxii. 10.	c
1 Kings xxi. 8, 8.	c, i	xxxvii. 7.	c	xxxii. 11, 14.	c
Neh. ix. 38. *a*	e	xxxviii. 14.	i	xxxii. 44.	i
x. 1. *β*	e	xli. 15.	e	Ezek. xxviii. 12.	a
Esth. iii. 12.	f	Cant. iv. 12.	f	Dan. vi. 17.	h
viii. 8, 8.	b, g	viii. 6, 6.	e	ix. 24.	b
viii. 10.	c	Isa. viii. 16.	b	xii. 4.	b
Job ix. 7.	e	xxix. 11, 11.	e	xii. 9.	e
xiv. 17.	e				

a marg. 'are at the sealing, *or*, sealed.' *β marg.* 'at the sealings.'

SEARCH

1 בָּקַר to search into, to inquire ; to inspect carefully. PIEL ᵃ*fut.* בְּקַר Ch. PAEL ᵇ*pret.* ᶜ*fut.* ITHPAEL ᵈ*fut.*

2 דָּרַשׁ to seek, to search for, to inquire. KAL ᵃ*pret.* ᵇ*fut.* ᶜ*part.* Poel.

3 חָפַר to dig, to dig out, to explore. KAL ᵃ*inf.* ᵇ*fut.*

4 חָפַשׂ to dig ; only used *trop.* to seek, to search after, to find out. KAL ᵃ*fut.* ᵇ*part.* Poel. NIPHAL ᶜ*pret.* PIEL ᵈ*pret.* ᵉ*imp.* ᶠ*fut.* PUAL ᵍ*part.* ʰ חֵפֶשׂ *m.* search.

5 חָקַר to search, to search out, to examine ; properly, the interior of the earth, spoken of mining, Job xxviii. 3 ; to search out, to explore, *e.g.* a land, Judg. xviii. 2 ; food and drink, *i.q.* to taste and try, Prov. xxiii. 30 ; wisdom, Job xxviii. 27 ; the mind or heart of any one, 1 Sam. xx. 12 : Ps. cxxxix. 1 : Prov. xxviii. 11. The general import seems to be, to examine with pains, care, and accuracy, in order to make a full and clear discovery, or a complete, exact calculation, Jer. xlvi. 23 ; so as to become fully acquainted with, Ps. xliv. 21 ; "great searchings of heart," seems to mean deep deliberation, or reflection, Judg. v. 16. KAL ᵃ*pret.* ᵇ*inf.* ᶜ*imp.* ᵈ*fut.* ᵉ*part.* Poel. NIPHAL ᶠ*fut.* ᵍ חֵקֶר *m.* searching.

6 מַחְתֶּרֶת *f.* (see *Dig*), "secret search."

7 מָשַׁשׁ to feel, to grope, in the dark ; to feel out, to explore with the hand. PIEL ᵃ*pret.* ᵇ*fut.*

8 רָגַל to spy out. PIEL *fut.*

9 תּוּר to go about, to travel ; to go about in searching, to endeavour to descry or find out ; to spy out, to reconnoitre a land ; to search out, to find out anything. *Metaph.* to investigate by the mind, to deliberate how to do anything, Eccles. ii. 3 ; to try thoroughly, to test ; taken strictly, it signifies to follow the trace of things.— *Hengstenberg.* KAL ᵃ*pret.* ᵇ*inf.* ᶜ*fut.* ᵈ*part.* Poel.

Gen. xxxi. 34.		7 b	Lev. xxvii. 33.	1 a	Num. xiii. 32, 32.	9 a b
xxxi. 35.		4 f	Num. x. 33.	9 b	xiv. 6.	9 d
xxxi. 37.		7 a	xiii. 2, 21.	9 c	xiv. 7, 36, 38.	9 b
xliv. 12.		4 f	xiii. 25.	9 b	xiv. 34.	9 a

Deut. i. 22.	3 b	Job x. 6.	2 b	Prov. xxv. 2.	5 b	1 Kings x. 19.	1 a	Job xxix. 7.	1 b	Ezek. viii. 3.	1 b
i. 24.	8	xi. 7.	5 g	xxv. 27.	5 g	Esth. iii. 1.	3	Ps. i. 1.	1 b	xxviii. 2.	1 b
i. 33.	9 b	xiii. 9.	5 d	xxviii. 11.	5 d	Job xxiii. 3.	2	Prov. ix. 14.	3	Amos vi. 3. a	1 a
xiii. 14.	5 a	xxviii. 3.	5 e	Eccles. i. 13.	9 b					
Josh. ii. 2, 3.	3 a	xxviii. 27.	5 a	vii. 25.	9 b					
Judg. v. 16.	5 g	xxix. 16.	5 d	Isa. xl. 28.	5 g					
xviii. 2, 2.	5 b c	xxxii. 11.	5 d	Jer. ii. 34.	6					
1 Sam. xxiii. 23.	4 d	xxxvi. 26.	5 g	xvii. 10.	5 e					
2 Sam. x. 3.	5 b	xxxviii. 16.	5 g	xxix. 13.	2 b					
1 Kings xx. 6.	4 d	xxxix. 8.	2 b	xxxi. 37.	5 f					
2 Kings x. 23.	4 e	Ps. xlvi. 21.	5 d	xlvi. 25.	5 f					
1 Chron. xix. 3.	5 b	lxiv. 6.	4 a	Lam. iii. 40.	4 a					
xxviii. 9.	2 c	lxiv. 6. a	4 g h	Ezek. xxxiv. 25.	2 c					
Ezra iv. 15.	1 c	lxxvii. 6.	4 f	xxxiv. 8, 11.	2 a					
iv. 19.	1 b	cxxxix. 1.	5 a	xxxix. 14.	5 d					
v. 17.	1 d	cxxxix. 23.	5 c	Amos ix. 3.	4 f					
vi. 1.	1 b	Prov. ii. 4.	4 a	Obad. 6.	4 c					
Job v. 27.	5 a	xviii. 17.	5 a	Zeph. i. 12.	4 f					
viii. 8.	5 g	xx. 27.	4 b							

a marg. 'a search searched.'

^a marg. ' or, habitation.'

SEBAT

שְׁבָט *m.* the eleventh month of the Hebrew year, from the new moon of February to the new moon of March : Zech. i. 7.

SEASON

1 זְמָן *m.* time, especially an appointed time, season, answering to 'when;' Eccles. iii. 1, to everything a stated time, *i.e.* everything remains but for a time, all things are frail and fleeting. ^a זְמָן Ch. *m. id.*

2 יוֹם *m.* day; also put for a particular season or time, when any extraordinary event happens.

3 מוֹעֵד *m.* appointment of time : 2 Sam. xxiv. 15, a time of appointment, *i.e.* appointed time, hence a set time, appointed season ; see *Appointed.*

4 עֵת *com.* time, in general ; time of the year, season, Gr. ὥρα ; a fit time, proper season, like Gr. καιρός ; a set time, certain season, which will have an end, answering to 'how long.' עוה to speak (a word) in season, to succour (the weary) with a word. KAL ^a *inf.*

SECOND

1 שָׁנָה to do a second time, to repeat. KAL ^a *imp.* ^b *fut.* ^c שֵׁנִי *adj. ordinal,* second, usually so translated, Gen. i. 8, &c. ^d שְׁנַיִם *adj. numeral dual.* ^e מִשְׁנֶה *m.* second rank, second place, in order, dignity, honour, &c., the next.

2 תִּנְיָן Ch. ^a *adj. ord.*   תִּרֵן Ch. ^b *adj. num.*

No. 1 c not included.

Gen. i. 14.	3	Josh. xxiv. 7. a	4	Prov. xv. 23. γ	4
xl. 4.	2	2 Kings iv. 16. β	3	Eccles. iii. 1.	1
Exod. xiii. 10.	3	iv. 17.	3	x. 17.	4
xviii. 22, 26.	3	1 Chron. xxi. 29.	3	Isa. l. 4.	4 a
Lev. xxiii. 4.	3	2 Chron. xx. 3.	2	Jer. v. 24.	4
xxvi. 4.	3	Job v. 26.	4	xxxiii. 20.	4
Num. ix. 2, 3, 7, 13.	3	xxxviii. 32.	4	Ezek. xxxiv. 26.	4
xxviii. 2.	3	Ps. i. 3.	4	Dan. ii. 21.	1 a
Deut. xi. 14.	4	civ. 19.	3	vii. 12.	1 a
xvi. 6.	3	civ. 27.	4	Hos. ii. 9.	3
xxviii. 12.	4	cxlv. 15.	4		

a lit. many days.   β marg. 'set time.'   γ marg. 'in his season.'

Gen. xli. 43.	1 e	2 Kings xv. 32.	1 d	Jer. lii. 24.	1 e
1 Sam. viii. 2.	1 e	xxiii. 4.	1 e	Dan. ii. 1.	1 d
xxvi. 8.	1 b	xxv. 18.	1 e	vii. 5.	2 a
2 Sam. iii. 3.	1 e	1 Chron. xv. 18.	1 e	Zeph. i. 10.	1 e
1 Kings xv. 25.	1 d	2 Chron. xxxv. 24.	1 e	Hag. i. 1, 15.	1 d
xviii. 34, 1a b	1 a b	Ezra i. 10.	1 e	ii. 10.	1 d
2 Kings i. 17.	1 d	iv. 24.	2 b	Zech. i. 1, 7.	1 d
xiv. 1.	1 d	Neh. xi. 9, 17.	1 e		

SEASON

מָלַח to salt. KAL *fut.* Lev. ii. 13, *lit.* thou shalt salt.

SEAT

1 יָשַׁב to sit. KAL ^a *inf.* ^b מוֹשָׁב *m.* habitation.

2 תְּכוּנָה *f.* a fixed prepared place.

3 כִּסֵּא *m.* throne ; the elevated seat or cathedra of the high priest ; any seat.

4 סָפַן to cover, to cover over, to ciel, to preserve : of the very numerous meanings which have been given to this word in Deut. xxxiii. 21, that found in Ainsworth, and supported by other critics, seems the most satisfactory. KAL *part.* Paül, Deut. xxxiii. 21, *marg.* 'cieled' in a portion of, *i.e.* assigned him by, the lawgiver was he seated, or rather protected, secured, *i.e.* as to his possessions and families, while they went to war before their brethren.

SECRET

1 מְבֻשִׁים *m. pl. pudenda.*

2 גָּנַב to steal, to take away by stealth, secretly. PUAL *fut.*

3 חָבָא to hide. NIPHAL *pret.*

4 חָפָא to cover, to do covertly, secretly. PIEL *fut.* 2 Kings xvii. 9. Hengstenberg, they covered words that were not so, *i.e.* they ventured by a number of perversions and false interpretations of his word to veil its true form.

5 חָרַשׁ to devise ; to practise secretly. HIPHIL ^a *part.* ^b חָרָשׁ *m.* craft.

6 טָמַן to hide, conceal. KAL *part.* Paül.

7 לָאַט to wrap around, to muffle, to cover : *adj.* Job xv. 11, "are the consolations of God small with thee ? is there any secret thing with thee ?" Numerous interpretations of this difficult passage have been given. See those of Mercer, Beza, Junius, Vulgate, Rab. Abr., collected by Caryl, *in loc.* Our translators, I think, have followed Beza : " Is there any secret thing (*reconditum delitescat*) with thee ? any secret ground of consolation, of confidence, or secret conceit of wisdom, which induces thee to reject the consolations of God which we offer to thy acceptance ?" Others : "Doth anything hide them with thee, as prejudice, pride, or anger, against thy friends for their intended faithfulness ?" Buxtorf and modern critics refer the word to אט a going softly, and with ל used adverbially. Gesenius, "and words gently (spoken) to thee." Professor Lee, in his Lexicon, translates the sentence, "and a matter (is) for gentleness with thee," *i.e.* thy circumstances are easy ; which, I confess, appears forced and unsuitable to the genius of the Hebrew language, as well as to the situation of Job at the time. Yet, in his Com. on Job, he has translated the sentence, "(is His) word unavailing with thee ?" There is no sufficient warrant for considering דָּבָר to mean here the word of God ; and if we regard the consolations of God to be

Num. xxii. 26.	4	Judg. iii. 20.	3	1 Sam. xx. 18, 25, 25.	1 b
Deut. xxxiii. 21.	4	1 Sam. i. 9.	3	2 Sam. xxiii. 8.	1 b
Josh. i. 14.	4	iv. 13, 18.	3	1 Kings ii. 19.	3

those which Job's friends presented to him, then דָּבָר must have respect to them also, according to the usage of parallelism, and the sentence must be interpreted accordingly. In Syr. and Chald. "the word which with tender pity we speak with thee," which corresponds with the rendering of Gesenius. לָאט softly, privily.

8 סוֹד *m.* a sitting together in some secret council on some affair of great importance, see *Assembly* ; hence the matter of consultation, secret counsel, that which God communicates to his friends and prophets ; a secret about which two have deliberated.

9 סָתַם to seal, to seal up. KAL *part.* Paül.

10 סָתַר to hide. NIPHAL [a] *part.* PUAL [b] *part.* HIPHIL [c] *fut.* סְתַר Ch. PAEL [d] *part.* סֵתֶר [e] *m.* secresy. [f] מִסְתָּר [m.] secret place.

11 עָלַם to hide, conceal ; the primitive idea is perhaps that of wrapping up. KAL [a] *part.* Paül. NIPHAL [b] *part.* תַּעֲלֻמָה [c] *f.* that which is hid.

12 פֹּת *m.* hinges ; the hips as the hinges of the body.

13 פִּלְאִי *adj.* wonderful, spoken of something supernatural ; כְּתִיב. פְּלִי [a] *adj. id.*

14 צָפַן to hide, conceal ; to lay up in store as a treasure ; to lay up carefully and safely ; to lay up in reserve. KAL [a] *fut.* [b] *part.* Paül.

15 רָז Ch. *m.* a secret.

16 שָׂתַר to hide ; be hid. NIPHAL *fut.*

Gen. xxxi. 27.a	3	Job xv. 11.	7	Prov. xxi. 14.	10 e	
xlix. 6.	8	xx. 26.	14 b	xxv. 9.θ	8	
Exod. xii. 14.	11 b	xxix. 4.		xxvii. 5.	10 b	
Deut. xiii. 6.	10 e	xxxi. 27.	10 e	Cant. ii. 14.	10 e	
xxv. 11.	1	xl. 13.	6	Isa. iii. 17.	12	
xxvii. 15, 24.	10 e	Ps. x. 8, 9.ζ	10 f	xlv. 3.	10 f	
xxviii. 57.	10 e	xvii. 12.	10 f	xlv. 19.	10 e	
xxix. 29.	10 a	xviii. 11.	10 e	xlviii. 16.	10 e	
Josh. ii. 1.	5 b	xix. 12.	10 a	Jer. xiii. 17.	10 f	
Judg. iii. 19.β	10 e	xxv. 14.	8	xxiii. 24.	10 f	
xiii. 18.γ	13 a	xxvii. 15.	10	xxxvii. 17.	10 e	
xiii. 18.	13	xxxi. 20, 20.	10 e, 14 a	xxxviii. 16.	10 e	
1 Sam. v. 9.δ	16	xliv. 21.	11 c	xl. 15.	10 e	
xviii. 22.	7 a	lxiv. 2.	10	xlix. 10.	10 f	
xix. 2.	10 e	lxiv. 4.	10 f	Lam. iii. 10.	10 f	
xxiii. 9.	5 a	lxxxi. 7.	10 e	Ezek. vii. 22.	14 b	
2 Sam. xii. 12.	10 e	xc. 8.	11 a	xxviii. 3.	9	
2 Kings xvii. 9.	4	xci. 1.	10 e	Dan. ii. 18, 19, 27, 28,		
Job iv. 12.ε		cxxxix. 15.	10 e	29, 30, 47, 47.	15	
xi. 6.	11 a	Prov. iii. 32.	8	ii. 22.	10 d	
xiii. 10.	10 e	ix. 17.η	10 e	iv. 9.	15	
xiv. 13.	10 c	xi. 13.	8	Amos iii. 7.	8	
xv. 8.	8	xx. 19.	8	Hab. iii. 14.	10 f	

a *lit.* wherefore didst thou hide thyself to flee away ? β *lit.* errand of secresy. γ *marg.* 'or, wonderful.' δ *lit.* and there were in secret, &c. ε *marg.* 'by stealth.' ζ *marg.* 'in the secret places.' η *marg.* 'of secrecies.' θ *lit.* the secret of another.

SECURE

בָּטַח to trust, to confide in, to rely upon ; to be confident, *i. e.* secure, without fear ; in a good sense of the trust and security of the righteous, Isa. xii. 2, Prov. xxviii. 1, Job xi. 18 ; in a bad sense of those who place trust and confidence in the things of this world, and have no fear of God or of his punishments : Isa. xxxix. 2, 10, 11 : Prov. xiv. 16. KAL *pret.* Job xi. 18. *part.* Poel, Judg. xviii. 7, 10, 27. בֶּטַח *m.* Judg. viii. 11 : Prov. iii. 29 : Micah ii. 8. בַּטֻּחוֹת *f. pl.* Job xii. 6.

SEDITION

אֶשְׁתַּדּוּר Ch. *m.* rebellion : Ezra iv. 15, 19.

SEDUCE

טָעָה to go astray, to wander. HIPHIL *pret.* Ezek. xiii. 10. LXX. ἐπλάνησαν.

תָּעָה to go out of the way, to wander. HIPHIL *pret.* Isa. xix. 13. *fut.* 2 Kings xxi. 9 : Prov. xii. 26.

SEE

1 חָזָה to see mentally ; differing from רָאָה to see, as an act of the senses. To see God, sometimes of the actual vision of the divine presence, Exod. xxiv. 11, Job xix. 26 ; elsewhere spoken of those who worship in the temple, Ps. lxiii. 2 ; so to behold the face of God, is, *metaph. i. q.* to enjoy his favour, to find him propitious, the figure being drawn from the practice of kings, who admit to their presence only those whom they favour, Ps. xi. 7, xvii. 15. Spoken especially and as the usual word for what is presented by a divine influence to the prophet's mind, either in visions properly so called (see one instance of a vision, 2 Sam. vii. 4–17), or in revelations, oracles : Hab. i. 1, the oracle which Habbakuk saw, *i.e.* which was divinely presented to his mental vision, revealed to him ; Isa. i. 1, ii. 1, xiii. 1, Num. xxiv. 4, Amos i. 1 ; Dan. vii. 1, saw a dream ; they behold lies, false revelations, Ezek. xiii. 6, Zech. x. 2 ; *seq.* לְ to announce or declare visions or revelations to any one, Lam. ii. 14, Isa. xxx. 10. To look upon, to gaze upon, to contemplate, *seq.* בְּ, Isa. xlvii. 13 ; especially with pleasure, to delight in beholding, to feast the eye upon, Ps. xxvii. 4, Cant. vi. 13, Job xxxvi. 25, Micah iv. 11. With an *accus.* to look upon with favour, to care for, Ps. xvii. 2 ; also, to look out for oneself, to choose, select, Exod. xviii. 21, Isa. lvii. 8, *comp.* רָאָה לֹו, Gen. xxii. 8. *Trop.* to see, *i.e.* to perceive, to experience, to feel, mentally, Job xv. 17, xxiv. 1, xxvii. 12, xxxiv. 32 ; by a bold metaphor, ascribed to the roots of a plant, which feel the stones, *i.e.* meet with and strike upon the stones, Job viii. 17. KAL [a] *pret.* [b] *inf.* [c] *imp.* [d] *fut.* [e] *part.* Poel. חָזָה and חֲזָא Ch. P'AL [f] *pret.* [g] *inf.* [h] *part. active.* [i] חֹזֶה *m.* seer.

2 יָרֵא to fear. KAL *fut.*

3 נָבַט to look, to behold. HIPHIL [a] *pret.* [b] *imp.* [c] *fut.*

4 פָּקֵחַ *adj.* open-eyed, seeing.

5 רָאָה to see, to look, generally : Ps. xl. 3, many saw (my deliverance) and feared, is a paronomasia ; יְרְאוּ רַבִּים וַיִּירָאוּ ; *comp.* the same *paronom.* Ps. lii. 6, Job vi. 21 ; often ascribed to the eye, Job xiii. 1, xxviii. 10, Isa. xxix. 18, xxxiii. 20, &c. *Absol.* to see is put for 'to enjoy the light,' 'to live,' Gr. βλέπειν ; more fully, to see the sun, Eccles. vii. 11 ; to see light, Ps. xlix. 19 ; in the same sense, to see Jehovah in the land of the living, Isa. xxxviii. 11 ; thus, also, is to be understood the difficult passage in Gen. xvi. 13, do I then here see (*i. e.* live) after the vision of God ? *i.e.* after having seen God. To see in vision, *i.e.* to be taught of God in visions as the

prophets, Isa. xxx. 10, *comp.* xxix. 10. To see, *i.e.* to look at, to view, to behold, with intention, purposely ; specially to see with delight, to look upon with pleasure ; contrariwise, to see with pain, to behold anything painful or afflictive ; to look upon with disdain, to look down upon any one, *comp.* καταφρονέω, to contemn, Job xli. 34, Cant. i. 6 ; to behold, to regard, to have respect to, Isa. xxvi. 10 ; especially of God as looking on affliction to remove it, Exod. iv. 31, &c. ; to see to anything, to look after, to take care of, 1 Kings xii. 16 ; to look out anything for oneself, *i.e.* to provide, to choose ; to go to see, to visit any one, in order to pay one's respects and salutations, 2 Sam. xiii. 5, 2 Kings viii. 29, 2 Chron. xxii. 6 ; *seq.* אֶל to look unto any one, as expecting help from him, Isa. xvii. 7 ; *seq.* עַל to look upon any one, as about to consider and judge his case, Exod. v. 21 ; *seq.* כְּ to look upon as, to regard as anything, Judg. ix. 36 ; *seq.* מִן of persons, to see and learn from, Judg. vii. 17 ; *trop.* to look at anything, *i.e.* to have in view, to aim at, Gen. xx. 10. Not unfrequently the Hebrews, like the Greeks and others, employ the word to see (רָאָה) of things which we perceive, not by the eyes, but in some other way, viz. by the other senses ; of what we perceive, experience, enjoy, through the medium of the vital principle, the animal spirit, life, *anima ; vice versâ,* to see affliction, &c. ; of what we perceive with the mind, rational soul, *animus,* בְּלֵב, hence *i.q.* to perceive, to understand, to learn, to know. Niphal, to be seen, to appear, to be provided for, cared for, Gen. xxii. 14 ; this would seem to have become a proverbial expression ; in Mount Moriah God provides for men and brings them help, as formerly to Abraham, so now; alluding to the etymology of the name, מֹרִיָּה, *Moriah.* KAL ᵃ*pret.* ᵇ*inf.* ᶜ*imp.* ᵈ*fut.* ᵉ*part.* Poel. NIPHAL ᶠ*pret.* ᵍ*inf.* ʰ*fut.* PUAL ⁱ*pret.* HIPHIL ᵏ*pret.* ˡ*imp.* ᵐ*fut.* HITHPAEL ⁿ*fut.* ᵒ רָאָה *adj.* seeing. P ᵃ רָאִי *m.* vision. ᵠ מַרְאֶה *m.* sight, aspect, view.

6   שׁוּר to look around, or about ; of one lying in wait, in the sense of to care for, to regard, *i.e.* to look upon or after, Job xxiv. 15 ; simply to look upon, to behold. KAL *fut.*

7   שָׁזַף to scorch, to burn, as the sun ; *poet.* of the eye, as casting its glances on anything, *i.e.* to look upon, to scan. KAL *pret.*

8   פָּקַד to visit. KAL *imp.*

Gen. i. 4, 10, 12, 18, 21, 25, 31.	5 d	Gen. xxi. 9, 16, 19.	5 d	Gen. xxxii. 20, 25.	5 d

ii. 19.	5 b	xxii. 4.	5 d	xxxiii. 5.	5 d
iii. 6.	5 d	xxii. 14.	5 h	xxxiii. 10, 10.	5 a b
vi. 2, 5.	5 d	xxiv. 30.	5 b	xxxiv. 1.	5 b
vii. 1.	5 a	xxiv. 63, 64.	5 d	xxxiv. 2.	5 d
viii. 5.	5 f	xxvi. 8.	5 d	xxxvii. 4, 18, 20.	5 d
viii. 8.	5 d	xxvi. 28.	5 b a	xxxvii. 14.	5 c
ix. 14.	5 f	xxvii. 1.	5 b	xxxviii. 2, 15.	5 d
ix. 22.	5 d	xxvii. 27.	5 c	xxxviii. 14.	5 d
ix. 23.	5 a	xxviii. 6, 8.	5 d	xxxix. 3.	5 d
xi. 5.	5 b	xxix. 10.	5 d	xxxix. 13.	5 d
xii. 12, 15.	5 d	xxix. 31.	5 d	xxxix. 14.	5 c
xiii. 15.	5 e	xxx. 1, 9.	5 d	xl. 16.	5 d
xvi. 4, 5.	5 d	xxxi. 5, 43.	5 e	xli. 19.	5 a
xvi. 13,ᵃ 13.	5 p	xxxi. 10.	5 d	xli. 22.	5 d
xviii. 2, 21.	5 d	xxxi. 12, 12.	5 c a	xli. 41.	5 c
xix. 1.	5 d	xxxi. 42.	5 a	xlii. 1, 7, 35.	5 d
xx. 10.	5 a	xxxi. 50.	5 c	xlii. 9, 12.	5 b
		xxxii. 2, 30.	5 a	xlii. 21.	5 a

Gen. xliii. 3, 5, 16, 29.	5 d	Deut. xii. 13.	5 d	2 Sam. i. 7.	5 d
xliv. 23, 26, 31.	5 b	xvi. 4.	5 h	iii. 13, 13.	5 d b
xliv. 28.	5 a	xviii. 16.	5 d	vi. 16.	5 d
xliv. 34.	5 d	xx. 1.	5 a	vii. 2.	5 c
xlv. 12.	5 e	xxi. 7, 11.	5 d	x. 6, 9, 15, 19.	5 a
xlv. 13.	5 d	xxii. 1, 4.	5 d	x. 14.	5 a
xlv. 27, 28.	5 d	xxiii. 14.	5 d	xi. 2.	5 d
xlvi. 30.	5 b	xxviii. 10.	5 a	xii. 19.	5 d
xlviii. 10, 11.	5 d	xxviii. 34, 67.	5 d	xiii. 5, 5.	5 d b
xlviii. 17.	5 d	xxviii. 68.	5 b	xiii. 6.	5 b
xlix. 15.	5 d	xxix. 2, 3, 22.	5 a	xiv. 24, 24.	5 d a
l. 11, 15, 23.	5 d	xxix. 4.	5 b	xiv. 28.	5 a
Exod. i. 16.	5 a	xxix. 17.	5 d	xiv. 30.	5 c
ii. 2, 5, 6, 12.	5 d	xxx. 15.	5 c	xiv. 32.	5 d
iii. 3.	5 d	xxxii. 19, 20, 36, 52.	5 d	xv. 3, 28.	5 e
iii. 4, 4.	5 d b	xxxii. 39.	5 c	xv. 27.	5 e
iii. 7.	5 b a	xxxiii. 9.	5 a	xvii. 17.	5 g
iii. 9.	5 d	xxxiv. 4.	5 k	xvii. 18.	5 d
iv. 11.	4	Josh. iii. 3.	5 c	xvii. 23.	5 d
iv. 14.	5 d	vi. 2.	5 c	xviii. 10, 10.	5 d a
iv. 18.	5 d	vii. 21.	5 d	xviii. 11, 21, 29.	5 a
iv. 21.	5 d	viii. 1, 8.	5 c	xviii. 26.	5 d
v. 19.	5 d	viii. 14.	5 b	xx. 12, 12.	5 d a
vi. 1.	5 d	viii. 20.	5 d	xxii. 11.	5 h
vii. 1.	5 c	viii. 21.	5 a	xxiv. 3.	5 c
viii. 15.	5 d	xxii. 10.	5 q	xxiv. 11.	1 i
ix. 34.	5 d	xxiii. 3.	5 a	xxiv. 13.	5 c
x. 5, 28, 28, 29.	5 b	xxiv. 7.	5 d	xxiv. 17.	5 b
x. 6, 23.	5 d	Judg. i. 24.	5 d	xxiv. 20.	5 e
xii. 13, 23.	5 a	ii. 7.	5 a	1 Kings i. 48.	5 e
xiii. 7, 7.	5 h	iii. 24.	5 d	i. 28.	5 a
xiii. 17.	5 b	v. 8.	5 h	vi. 18.	5 f
xiv. 13, 13, 13.	5 c a b	vi. 22.	5 a	viii. 8, 8.	5 h
xiv. 30, 31.	5 d	ix. 36, 36.	5 d e	ix. 12.	5 d
xvi. 7.	5 d	ix. 48.	5 a	x. 4, 7.	5 d
xvi. 15, 32.	5 d	ix. 55.	5 b	x. 12.	5 f
xvi. 29.	5 d	xi. 35.	5 b	xi. 28.	5 d
xviii. 14.	5 a	xii. 3.	5 d	xii. 16, 16.	5 d c
xix. 4.	5 a	xiii. 22.	5 a	xiii. 12, 25.	5 d
xx. 18, 18.	5 e d	xiv. 1.	5 d	xiv. 4.	5 b
xx. 22.	5 d	xiv. 8, 11.	5 b	xvi. 18.	5 b
xxii. 10.	5 e	xiv. 1, 18, 24.	5 d	xvii. 23.	5 c
xxiii. 5.	5 d	xvi. 5.	5 c	xviii. 17.	5 b
xxiv. 10.	5 d	xviii. 7, 26.	5 b	xviii. 39.	5 d
xxiv. 11.	1 d	xviii. 9.	5 a	xix. 3.	5 d
xxxi. 2.	5 c	xix. 3, 17.	5 d	xx. 7, 22.	5 c
xxxii. 1, 5, 19, 25.	5 d	xix. 30, 30.	5 e f	xx. 13.	5 a
xxxii. 9.	5 a	xix. 36.	5 a	xxi. 29.	5 a
xxxiii. 10.	5 a	xx. 41.	5 a	xxii. 17, 19.	5 a
xxxiii. 12.	5 c	xxi. 21.	5 a	xxii. 25.	5 d
xxxiii. 20, 20.	5 b d	Ruth i. 18.	5 d	xxii. 32.	5 b
xxxiii. 23, 23.	5 a h	ii. 18.	5 d	2 Kings ii. 10, 15.	5 d
xxxiv. 3.	5 h	1 Sam. ii. 32.	3 a	ii. 12, 12.	5 e a
xxxix. 10, 35.	5 a	iii. 2.	3 b	ii. 19.	5 b
xxxiv. 30.	5 d	iv. 15.	5 b	iii. 14, 17, 17, 22, 26.	5 d
xxxv. 30.	5 c	v. 7.	5 b	iv. 25.	5 b
Lev. v. 1.	5 a	vi. 9, 16.	5 a	v. 7.	5 c
ix. 24.	5 d	vi. 13, 13.	5 d b	v. 21.	5 d
xiii. 7, 7.	5 g f	ix. 9, 9, 11, 18, 19.	5 e	vi. 17, 17, 20, 20.	5 b
xiii. 8, 10, 15, 17, 20, 30.	5 a	ix. 17.	5 a	vi. 21.	5 b
xiv. 36, 36.	5 b	x. 11, 14.	5 a	vi. 32.	5 e
xx. 17, 17.	5 a d	x. 24.	5 a	vii. 2, 19.	5 e
Num. iv. 20.	5 b	xii. 12.	5 d	vii. 13.	5 d
xi. 15, 23.	5 d	xii. 16, 17.	5 a	vii. 14.	5 c
xiii. 18, 28, 32, 33.	5 a	xiii. 6, 11.	5 a	vii. 19.	5 b
xiv. 14.	5 f	xiv. 17, 29, 38.	5 c	ix. 16, 22.	5 b
xiv. 22.	5 e	xiv. 52.	5 a	ix. 17.	5 e
xiv. 23, 23.	5 d	xv. 35.	5 d	ix. 26, 27.	5 c
xx. 29.	5 d	xvi. 7.	5 d	ix. 34.	8
xxii. 2, 23, 25, 27, 31, 33, 41.	5 d	xvi. 18.	5 a	x. 16.	5 c
xxiii. 9, 13, 13, 13.	5 d	xvii. 24, 28, 55.	5 b	xi. 1.	5 b
xxiii. 21.	5 a	xvii. 25.	5 d	xi. 10.	5 b
xxiv. 1, 2, 17.	5 d	xvii. 42, 51.	5 a	xiii. 4.	5 a
xxiv. 4, 16.	1 d	xviii. 15, 28.	5 a	xiv. 26.	5 a
xxv. 7.	5 d	ix. 3, 5.	5 a	xvi. 10, 10.	5 d
xxvii. 12.	5 c	xix. 15.	5 b	xvii. 13.	1 i
xxvii. 13.	5 c	xix. 20.	5 c	xix. 16.	5 c
xxxii. 1, 9, 11.	5 a	xx. 29.	5 d	xx. 5, 15, 15.	5 d
xxxii. 8.	5 b	xxi. 14.	5 a	xxii. 20.	5 d
xxxv. 23.	5 d	xxii. 9.	5 a	xxiii. 17.	5 b
Deut. i. 19, 28, 31.	5 d	xxiii. 15.	5 a	xxiii. 29.	5 b
i. 35, 36.	5 a	xxiii. 22, 22.	5 c a	xxv. 19.	5 c
iii. 21.	5 e	xxiii. 23.	5 c	1 Chron. ix. 22.	5 e
iii. 25, 28.	5 d	xxiv. 10.	5 a	x. 5, 7.	5 d
iv. 3, 12.	5 a	xxiv. 11, 11, 11.	5 d	xix. 6, 10, 16, 19.	5 d
iv. 9, 15, 19.	5 c	xxiv. 15.	5 d	xix. 15.	5 a
iv. 28.	5 e	xxv. 23.	5 d	xxi.·9.	1 i
v. 24.	5 a	xxv. 35.	5 c	xxi. 16, 20, 21.	5 d
vii. 19.	5 a	xxvi. 3.	5 a	xxi. 28.	5 a
ix. 13.	5 a	xxvi. 12.	5 c	xxv. 5.	1 i
x. 21.	5 a	xxvi. 16.	5 c	xxvi. 28.	5 a
xi. 2.	5 d	xxviii. 5, 12, 21.	5 d	xxix. 17.	5 e
xi. 7.	5 e	xxviii. 13, 13.	5 d	xxix. 29, 29.	5 e, 1 l
		xxxi. 5, 7.	5 d	2 Chron. v. 9, 9.	5 h
				vii. 3.	5 e

2 Chron. ix. 3, 6.	5 d
ix. 11.	5 f
ix. 29.	1 i
x. 16, 16.	5 a c
xii. 7.	5 b
xii. 15.	1 i
xv. 9.	5 b
xvi. 7, 10.	5 e
xviii. 16, 18.	5 a
xviii. 24.	5 e
xviii. 31.	5 b
xix. 2.	1 i
xx. 17.	5 c
xxii. 6.	5 b
xxii. 10.	5 a
xxiv. 11.	5 a
xxv. 17, 21.	5 n
xxix. 8.	5 e
xxix. 25, 30.	1 i
xxx. 7.	5 e
xxxi. 8.	5 d
xxxii. 2.	5 d
xxxiii. 18, 19.	1 i
xxxiv. 28.	5 a
xxxv. 15.	1 i
Ezra iii. 12.	5 a
iv. 14.	1 g
Neh. ii. 17.	5 e
iv. 11.	5 d
vi. 16.	5 d
ix. 9.	5 d
xiii. 15, 23.	5 a
Esth. i. 14.	5 e
iii. 4.	5 b
iii. 5.	5 d
v. 2, 9.	5 b
v. 13.	5 e
vii. 7.	5 a
viii. 6, 6.	5 a
ix. 26.	5 a
Job ii. 13.	5 a
iii. 9.	5 d
iii. 16.	5 a
iv. 8.	5 a
v. 3.	5 a
vi. 21.	5 d
vii. 7.	5 b
vii. 8, 8.	5 p, 6
viii. 17.	1 d
viii. 18.	5 a
ix. 11.	5 d
ix. 25.	5 a
x. 4, 4.	5 b d
x. 15.	5 c or o
x. 18.	5 d
xi. 11.	5 d
xiii. 1.	5 a
xv. 11.	1 a
xvii. 15.	6
xix. 26, 27.	1 d
xx. 7.	5 e
xx. 17.	7
xx. 17.	5 d
xxi. 20.	5 d
xxii. 11, 14, 19.	5 d
xxiii. 9.	5 d
xxiv. 1.	1 a
xxiv. 15.	6
xxvii. 12.	1 a
xxvii. 7.	7
xxviii. 10, 27.	5 a
xxviii. 24.	5 d
xxix. 8, 11.	5 a
xxxi. 4, 19, 21.	5 a
xxxii. 5.	5 d
xxxiii. 21, 21.	5 p i
xxxiii. 26, 28.	5 d
xxxiv. 21.	5 d
xxxiv. 32.	1 d
xxxv. 5.	5 c
xxxv. 14.	6
xxxvi. 25.	1 a
xxxvii. 21.	5 a
xxxviii. 17, 22.	5 d
xlii. 5.	5 a
xlii. 16.	5 d
Ps. x. 2, 11, 14.	5 a
xiv. 2.	5 a
xvi. 10.	5 b
xviii. 15.	5 h
xxii. 7.	5 e
xxvii. 13.	5 b
xxxi. 11.	5 e
xxxiv. 8.	5 c
xxxiv. 12.	5 b
xxxv. 21, 22.	5 a
Ps. xxxvi. 9.	5 d
xxxvii. 13, 25, 35.	5 d
xxxvii. 34.	5 d
xl. 3.	5 d
xli. 6.	5 b
xlvii. 5, 8.	5 a
xlix. 9, 10, 19.	5 a
l. 18.	5 a
lii. 6.	5 d
liii. 2.	5 b
liv. 7.	5 a
lv. 9.	5 a
lviii. 8, 10.	1 a
lix. 10.	5 m
lxiii. 2, 2.	5 b, 1 a
lxiv. 5.	5 a
lxiv. 8.	5 e
lxvi. 5.	5 c
lxviii. 24.	5 a
lxix. 23.	5 b
lxix. 32.	5 a
lxxiv. 9.	5 a
lxxvii. 16, 16.	5 a
lxxxvi. 17.	5 d
lxxxix. 48.	5 d
xc. 15.	5 a
xci. 8.	5 d
xcii. 11.	3 c
xciv. 7.	5 d
xciv. 9.	3 c
xcv. 9.	5 a
xcvii. 4, 6.	5 a
xcviii. 3.	5 a
cvi. 5.	5 b
cvii. 24.	5 a
cvii. 42.	5 b
cxii. 8, 10.	5 d
cxiv. 3.	5 a
cxv. 5.	5 d
cxvii. 7.	5 d
cxix. 74.	5 d
cxix. 96.	5 a
cxxviii. 5, 6.	5 c
cxxxv. 16.	5 d
cxxxix. 16.	5 a
cxxxix. 24.	5 c
Prov. xx. 12.	5 e
xxii. 29.	1 a
xxiv. 18.	5 d
xxiv. 32.	1 d
xxv. 7.	5 a
xxvi. 12.	5 a
xxix. 16.	5 a
xxix. 20.	1 a
Eccles. i. 8.	5 b
i. 10.	5 c
i. 14.	5 a
ii. 3.	5 d
ii. 13, 24.	5 a
iii. 10, 16.	5 a
iii. 18, 22.	5 b
iv. 3.	5 a
iv. 7.	5 d
v. 8.	5 a
v. 13, 18.	5 a
vi. 1, 5, 6.	5 a
vii. 11.	5 a
vii. 15.	5 a
viii. 9, 10.	5 a
viii. 16, 16.	5 b e
ix. 11.	5 b
ix. 13.	5 a
x. 5, 7.	5 a
Cant. ii. 14.	5 l
iii. 3.	5 a
vi. 9.	5 a
vi. 11, 11.	5 b
vi. 13.	1 d
vii. 12.	5 d
Isa. i. 1.	1 a
ii. 1.	1 a
v. 19.	5 d
vi. 1, 10.	5 d
vi. 5.	5 a
vi. 9.	5 b c
ix. 2.	5 a
xiii. 1.	1 a
xiv. 16.	5 e
xvi. 12.	5 f
xviii. 3.	5 a
xxi. 3.	5 b
xxi. 6.	5 d
xxi. 7.	5 a
xxii. 9.	5 a
xxvi. 11, 11.	1 d
Isa. xxviii. 4.	5 d
xxix. 10.	1 i
xxix. 15.	5 e
xxix. 18.	5 d
xxix. 23.	5 b
xxx. 10, 10.	5 e d
xxx. 20.	5 e
xxxii. 3.	5 e
xxxiii. 15.	5 b
xxxiii. 17.	5 d
xxxiii. 19, 20.	5 d
xxxv. 2.	5 d
xxxvii. 17.	5 c
xxxviii. 5.	5 a
xxxviii. 11.	5 a
xxxix. 4, 4.	5 a
xl. 5.	5 a
xli. 5.	5 a
xli. 20.	5 a
xlii. 18, 20.	5 d
xliv. 9.	5 a
xliv. 16.	5 a
xliv. 18.	5 a
xlvii. 3.	5 h
xlvii. 10.	5 a
xlviii. 6.	1 c
xlix. 7.	5 d
lii. 8.	5 d
lii. 10, 15.	5 a
liii. 2, 10, 11.	5 d
lvii. 8.	1 a
lvii. 18.	5 a
lviii. 3.	5 a
lviii. 7.	5 a
lix. 15, 16.	5 d
lx. 2.	5 h
lx. 4.	5 c
lx. 5, 5.	5 d, or 2
lxi. 9.	5 a
lxii. 2.	5 a
lxiv. 4.	5 a
lxiv. 9.	3 b
lxvi. 8, 14, 18, 19.	5 c
Jer. i. 10.	5 c
i. 11, 11, 13, 13.	5 b
i. 12. β	5 b
ii. 10, 10, 19, 23, 31.	5 c
iii. 2.	5 c
iii. 6.	5 a
iii. 7, 8.	5 a
iv. 21.	5 a
v. 1.	5 a
v. 12, 21.	5 a
vi. 16.	5 a
vii. 11.	5 a
vii. 12.	5 c
vii. 17.	5 a
xi. 20.	5 d
xii. 3, 4.	5 d,
xiii. 27.	5 d.
xiv. 13.	5 a.
xvii. 6, 8.	5 a
xx. 12, 12.	5 e d
xx. 18.	5 d
xxii. 10.	5 a
xxii. 12.	5 d
xxiii. 13, 14.	5 a
xxiii. 24.	5 a
xxiv. 3.	5 e
xxx. 6, 6.	5 c a
xxxii. 24.	5 a
xxxix. 4.	5 d
xli. 13.	5 b
xliii. 14, 18.	5 d
xliv. 2, 17.	5 a
xlvi. 5.	5 a
li. 61.	5 a
Lam. i. 7, 8, 10.	5 a
i. 11, 12.	5 c
ii. 14, 14.	1 a d
ii. 16.	5 a
iii. 1, 59, 60.	5 a
iii. 63.	5 b
Ezek. i. 1, 28.	5 d
i. 27, 27.	5 d a
iii. 23.	5 a
viii. 4, 17.	5 a
viii. 6, 6.	5 e d
viii. 10, 13.	5 d
viii. 12, 12.	5 a
viii. 15, 16.	5 a d
ix. 9.	5 e
x. 15, 20, 22.	5 e
xi. 1.	5 d
xi. 24.	5 e
xii. 2, 2.	5 b a
xii. 6, 12, 13.	5 d
Ezek. xii. 27.	1 e
xiii. 3.	5 d
xiii. 6, 7, 8.	1 i
xiii. 9, 16.	1 i
xiii. 23.	1 d
xiv. 22.	5 a
xiv. 23.	5 a
xvi. 37, 50.	5 d
xviii. 14.	5 d
xix. 5.	5 a
xx. 28.	5 d
xx. 48.	5 a
xxi. 29.	1 i
xxii. 28.	1 i
xxiii. 11, 13, 14.	5 d
xxiii. 16.	5 q
xxxii. 31.	5 d
xxxiii. 3.	5 a
xxxiii. 6.	5 a
xxxix. 15, 21.	5 a
xl. 4.	5 e
xli. 8.	5 a
xliii. 3, 3, 3.	5 a
xlvii. 6.	5 a
Dan. i. 10, 13.	5 d
ii. 8, 26.	1 f
Dan. ii. 31, 34.	1 h
ii. 41, 41, 43, 45.	1 f
iii. 25, 27.	1 h
iv. 5, 9, 18, 20, 23.	1 f
iv. 10, 13.	1 d
v. 5, 23.	1 h
vii. 2, 7, 13.	1 h
viii. 2, 2, 2.	5 b d b
viii. 3.	5 d
viii. 4, 6, 7, 20.	5 a
viii. 15.	5 d
ix. 21.	5 a
x. 7, 7.	5 a
x. 8.	5 d
Hos. v. 5.	5 d
v. 13.	5 a
vi. 10.	5 a
ix. 5.	5 a
ix. 10, 13.	5 a
ix. 14.	5 a
x. 2.	1 a
x. 11.	5 a
Joel ii. 28.	5 d
Amos i. 1.	1 a
vi. 2.	5 c
vii. 8.	5 e
Amos vii. 12.	1 i
viii. 2.	5 e
ix. 1.	5 a
Jonah iii. 10.	5 d
iv. 5.	5 a
Micah i. 1.	1 a
iii. 7.	1 i
vi. 9.	5 d
vii. 10, 16.	5 d
Hab. i. 1.	1 a
iii. 1.	1 a
iii. 7, 10.	5 a
Zeph. iii. 15.	5 d
Hag. ii. 3, 3.	5 a e
Zech. i. 8.	5 a
i. 18.	5 d
ii. 2.	5 d
iv. 2.	5 e
iv. 10.	5 a
v. 2, 2.	5 e
v. 5.	5 d
ix. 5.	5 a
ix. 14.	5 h
x. 2.	1 a
x. 7.	5 d
Mal. i. 5.	5 d

α *lit.* thou the God of vision.   β *lit.* thou hast done well in seeing.

SEED

זֶרַע *m.* a sowing, seed time, time of sowing, *i. e.* late in autumn in Palestine; seed which is scattered, sown, whether of plants, trees, or grain; *meton.* of what springs from seed sown, field of grain, harvest, 1 Sam. viii. 15; crop, produce of the fields, Job xxxix. 12, Isa. xxiii. 3; *semen virile*, hence children, offspring, posterity; spoken also of one child when an only one, Gen. iv. 25, 1 Sam. i. 11; a race, stock, family, Ps. xxii. 23; seed royal, 2 Kings xi. 1, 14; a race or class of men, Isa. vi. 13; in a bad sense, breed, brood, Isa. i. 4, lvii. 4, *comp.* Gr. γέννημα, Matt. iii. 7; a planting, Isa. xvii. 11; also a sprout, shoot, Ezek. xvii. 5.—Gen. i. 11, &c. זֶרַע Ch. *m.* Dan. ii. 43.

פְּרֻדוֹת *f.* grains, kernels of grains scattered in the ground as seed: Joel i. 17.

שִׁכְבָה *f.* lying: Lev. xv. 32, *lit.* lying of seed; xxii. 4, *lit. id.*

SEEK

1 אָנָה see *Befall.* HITHPAEL to seek occasion against any one, *seq.* לְ: part.

2 בָּעָה to seek, to search after. NIPHAL a *pret.* בְּעָה Ch. P'AL b *pret.* c *fut.*

3 בָּקַר to search into, to inquire; to seek something known and determinate; to inspect carefully. PIEL a *pret.* b *fut.* c בְּקָרָה *f.* a looking after, care.

4 בָּקַשׁ to seek, to search; to seek that which is uncertain and doubtful, with desire of obtaining, and with care and attention; *seq.* לְ *opp.* מָצָא. Piel to seek, to search for, to inquire after; *seq.* לְ, to search or inquire into a thing, Job x. 6; different is Gen. xliii. 30, "he sought where to weep," *i. e.* a place where; specially to seek the face, presence of a king; to seek the face of Jehovah, properly to turn to him, to draw near to him, especially in prayer and supplication, 2 Sam. xii. 16, Ps. xxiv. 6, xxvii. 8, cv. 3; or, to inquire of him, to seek an oracle, 2 Sam. xxi. 1; or, in order to appease his anger, Hos. v. 15; to seek, to strive after, to try to gain, to

require, to demand, especially blood, *i.e.* to exact or inflict punishment for blood shed, 2 Sam. iv. 11, &c.; to seek from any one, *i.e.* to ask, to request. PIEL [a] *pret.* [b] *inf.* [c] *imp.* [d] *fut.* [e] *part.* PUAL [f] *fut.*

5   גָּלַל   to roll, to roll upon another, to rush or fall upon him. HITHPOEL *inf.*

6   דָּרַשׁ   *pr.* to tread a place, *i.e.* to go or come to it, to frequent, with *acc.*, 2 Chron. i. 5, Amos v. 5; *seq.* אֶל, Deut. xii. 5; *part. pass.* דְּרוּשָׁה a city frequented, celebrated, Isa. lxii. 12. The signification of going or coming to a place or person is also transferred to express the ideas of seeking, inquiring, demanding, and also caring for; hence, to seek, to search for, chiefly in the phrase to seek Jehovah, *i.e.* to seek unto him, to have recourse to him, by prayer, 2 Chron. xvi. 12, Deut. iv. 29, &c. Often of the pious, who habitually invoke God, to worship, to adore; spoken also rarely of false gods, of whom their followers implore aid; *part. pass.*, Ps. cxi. 2. The works of the Lord are great, sought out of all those delighting therein, *i.e.* sought and obtained by prayers; to apply oneself unto, to regard, to follow, to practise, justice, the divine law, &c. KAL [a] *pret.* [b] *inf.* [c] *imp.* [d] *fut.* [e] *part.* Poel. [f] *part.* Paül. NIPHAL [g] *pret.*

7   חָפַר   to dig; to search out, to explore, to espy, as the eagle his prey from a high place. KAL *pret.*

8   חָקַר   to search; to search out, food and drink, *i.e.* to taste, to try. KAL [a] *inf.* PIEL [b] *pret.*

9   קָרָא   to encounter, to meet, to fall in with. KAL *inf.*

10   שָׁחַר   to break, to break in, to pry into, hence to seek; the word is applied to the breaking in of day, and therefore to do anything early, to seek early and diligently. KAL [a] *part.* Poel. PIEL [b] *pret.* [c] *inf.* [d] *fut.* [e] *part.*

11   תּוּר   to go about in searching. KAL [a] *pret.* [b] *fut.*

Gen. xxxvii. 15.	4 d	1 Sam. xxiv. 2.	4 b	2 Chron. ix. 23.	4 e		
xxxvii. 16.	4 e	xxiv. 9.	4 e	xi. 16.	4 b		
xliii. 18.α	5	xxv. 26.	4 e	xii. 14.	6 b		
xliii. 30.	4 d	xxv. 29.	4 b	xiv. 4.	6 b		
Exod. ii. 15.	4 d	xxvi. 2, 20.	4 b	xiv. 7, 7.	6 a		
iv. 19.	4 e	xxvii. 1, 4.	4 b	xv. 2, 13.	6 d		
iv. 24.	4 d	xxviii. 7.	4 c	xv. 4.	4 d		
xxxiii. 7.	4 e	2 Sam. iii. 17.	4 e	xv. 12.	6 b		
Lev. x. 16.	6 b a	iv. 8.	4 a	xv. 15.	4 a		
xiii. 36.	3 b	v. 17.	4 b	xvi. 12.	6 a		
xix. 31.	4 d	xvi. 11.	4 e	xvii. 3, 4.	6 a		
Num. xv. 39.	11 b	xvii. 3.	4 e	xix. 3.	6 b		
xvi. 10.	4 a	xvii. 20.	4 d	xx. 3.	6 b		
xxiv. 1.	9	xx. 19.	4 e	xx. 4.	4 b		
xxxv. 23.	4 e	xxi. 2.	4 d	xxii. 9, 9.	4 d, 6 a		
Deut. iv. 29, 29.	4 a, 6 d	1 Kings i. 2, 3.	4 d	xxv. 15, 20.	6 a		
xii. 5.	6 d	ii. 40.	4 b	xxvi. 5, γ 5. δ	6 b		
xiii. 10.	4 a	x. 24.β	4 e	xxx. 19.	6 b		
xxii. 2.	6 b	xi. 22.	4 e	xxxi. 21.	6 b		
xxiii. 6.	6 d	xi. 40.	4 d	xxxiv. 3.	6 b		
Josh. ii. 22.	4 d	xviii. 10.	4 b	Ezra ii. 62.	4 a		
Judg. iv. 22.	4 e	xix. 10, 14.	4 e	iv. 2.	6 d		
xiv. 4.	4 e	xx. 7.	4 e	vi. 21.	6 b		
xviii. 1.	4 e	2 Kings ii. 16, 17.	4 d	vii. 10.	6 b		
Ruth iii. 1.	4 d	v. 7.	1	viii. 21.	4 b		
1 Sam. ix. 3.	4 c	vi. 19.	4 d	viii. 22.	4 e		
x. 2, 14.	4 b	1 Chron. iv. 39.	4 b	ix. 12.	6 d		
x. 21.	4 d	xiv. 8.	4 b	Neh. ii. 10.	4 b		
xiii. 14.	4 a	xv. 13.	6 a	vii. 64.	4 b		
xiv. 4.	4 a	xv. 15.	4 a	xii. 27.	4 a		
xvi. 16.	4 d	xvi. 10.	4 e	Esth. ii. 2, 21.	4 d		
xix. 2.	4 e	xvi. 11, 11.	6 c, 4 c	iii. 6.	4 d		
xix. 10.	4 d	xxii. 19.	6 b	vi. 2.	4 a		
xx. 1.	4 e	xxvi. 31.	6 g	ix. 2.	4 d		
xxii. 23, 23.	4 d	xxviii. 8.	6 c	x. 3.	6 e		
xxiii. 10.	4 e	xxviii. 9.	6 d	Job v. 8.	4 d		
xxiii. 14.	4 d	2 Chron. i. 5.	6 d	vii. 21.	10 b		
xxiii. 15, 25.	4 b	vii. 14.	4 d	viii. 5.	10 d		

Job xxix. 29.	7	Prov. xxi. 6.	4 e	Jer. xxix. 13.	4 a
Ps. iv. 2.	4 d	xxiii. 30.	8 a	xxx. 14.	6 d
ix. 10.	6 e	xxiii. 35.	4 b	xxx. 17.	4 e
x. 4, 15.	6 d	xxviii. 5.	4 e	xxxiv. 20, 21.	4 e
xiv. 2.	6 e	xxix. 10.	4 e	xxxviii. 4.	4 e
xxii. 26.	6 e	xxix. 26.	4 e	xxxviii. 16.	4 e
xxiv. 6, 6.	6 e, 4 e	xxxi. 13.	6 a	xliv. 30, 30.	4 d
xxvii. 4.	4 d	Eccles. i. 13.	6 b	xlv. 5, 5.	4 d
xxvii. 8, 8.	4 c d	ii. 3.	11 a	xlvi. 21.	4 e
xxxiv. 4.	6 a	vii. 25.	4 b	xlix. 37.	4 e
xxxiv. 10.	6 e	vii. 28, 29.	4 b	l. 20.	4 f
xxxiv. 14.	4 c	viii. 17.	4 b	Lam. i. 11.	4 a
xxxv. 4.	6 e	xii. 9.	8 b	i. 19.	4 a
xxxvii. 32.	4 e	xii. 10.	4 a	iii. 25.	6 d
xxxvii. 36.	6 d	Cant. iii. 1, 1.	4 a	Ezek. vii. 25, 26.	4 a
xxxviii. 12, 12.	4 e, 6 e	iii. 2, 2.	4 d a	xiv. 10.	6 e
xl. 14, 16.	4 e	v. 6.	4 a	xxii. 30.	4 d
liii. 2.	6 e	vi. 1.	4 a	xxvi. 21.	4 f
liv. 3.	4 a	Isa. i. 17.	6 c	xxxiv. 4.	4 d
lxiii. 1.	10 d	viii. 19, 19.	6 c d	xxxiv. 6.	4 d
lxiii. 1.	4 e	ix. 13.	6 a	xxxiv. 11.	3 a
lxix. 6.	4 e	xi. 10.	6 d	xxxiv. 12, 12.	3 c b
lxix. 32.	4 e	xvi. 5.	6 d	xxxiv. 16.	4 d
lxx. 2, 4.	4 e	xix. 3.	6 a	Dan. ii. 13.	2 b
lxxi. 13, 24.	4 e	xxv. 9.	10 d	i. 36.	2 c
lxxvii. 2.	6 a	xxxi. 1.	6 a	vi. 4.	2 d
lxxviii. 34.	6 a	xxxiv. 16.	6 c	viii. 15.	4 d
lxxxiii. 16.	4 d	xl. 20.	4 d	ix. 3.	4 b
lxxxvi. 14.	4 a	xli. 12.	4 d	Hos. ii. 7.	4 a
civ. 21.	4 e	xli. 17.	4 a	iii. 5.	4 a
cv. 3.	4 b	xlv. 19.	4 c	v. 6.	4 b
cv. 4, 4.	6 c, 4 c	li. 1.	4 e	v. 15, 15.	4 a, 10 d
cix. 10.	6 a	lv. 6.	6 c	vii. 10.	4 a
cxi. 2.	6 f	lviii. 2.	6 d	x. 12.	6 b
cxix. 2.	6 d	lxii. 12.	6 f	Amos v. 4, 6, 14.	6 c
cxix. 10, 45, 94,		lxv. 1, 1.	6 g, 4 a	v. 5.	6 d
155.	6 a	lxv. 10.	4 e	v. 8.	4 d
cxix. 176.	4 e	Jer. ii. 24.	6 e	Obad. 6.	2 a
cxxii. 9.	4 d	ii. 33.	4 b	Nah. iii. 7, 11.	4 d
Prov. i. 28.	10 d	iv. 30.	4 d	Zeph. i. 6.	4 a
ii. 4.	4 d	v. 1, 1.	4 c e	ii. 3, 3, 3.	4 a
vii. 15.	10 c	viii. 2.	6 a	Zech. vi. 7.	4 d
viii. 17.	10 e	x. 21.	6 a	viii. 21, 22.	4 b
xi. 27, 27.	10 a, 6 e	xi. 21.	4 e	xi. 16.	4 b
xiv. 6.	4 a	xix. 7, 9.	4 e	xii. 9.	4 d
xv. 14.	6 e	xxi. 7.	4 e	Mal. ii. 7.	4 d
xvii. 9, 19.	4 e	xxii. 25.	4 e	ii. 15.	4 e
xvii. 11.	4 d	xxvi. 21.	4 e	iii. 1.	4 e
xviii. 1, 15.	4 d	xxix. 7.	6 c		

α *marg.* 'roll himself upon us.'   β *marg.* 'sought the face of.'
γ *lit.* he was to seek.   δ *lit.* in the day of his seeking.

SEEM, SEEMLY

עַיִן   *com.* eye; Heb. to be in the eyes of, or simply, in the eyes of: Gen. xix. 14; xxvii. 12; xxix. 20: Josh. ix. 25; xxiv. 15: Judg. x. 15; xix. 24: 1 Sam. i. 23; iii. 18; xi. 10; xiv. 36, 40; xviii. 23; xxiv. 4: 2 Sam. iii. 19, 19; x. 12; xv. 26; xviii. 4; xix. 37, 38; xxiv. 22: 1 Kings xxi. 2: Esth. iii. 11: Jer. xviii. 4; xxvi. 14; xxvii. 5; xl. 4, 4.

רָאָה   to see. NIPHAL *pret.* Lev. xiv. 35. מַרְאֶה *m.* appearance: Nah. ii. 4, *marg.* 'their show.'

נָאוֶה   *adj.* (see *Become*): Prov. xix. 10; xxvi. 1.

SEETHE

בָּשַׁל   to be cooked. KAL *pret.* Ezek. xxiv. 5. PIEL *pret.* Exod. xxix. 31: Zech. xiv. 21. *inf.* 1 Sam. ii. 13. *imp.* Exod. xvi. 23: 2 Kings iv. 38. *fut.* Exod. xvi. 23; xxiii. 19; xxxiv. 26: Deut. xiv. 21.

נָפַח   to blow, to blow up a fire. KAL *part.* Paül, Job xli. 20: Jer. i. 13, "a seething-pot," *i.e.* under which one blows the fire.

SEIZE

חָזַק   to take or hold fast anything. HIPHIL *pret.* Jer. xlix. 24.

יָרַשׁ   to possess; Hiphil, to dispossess. HIPHIL *pret.* Josh. viii. 7.

לָקַח to take. KAL *fut.* Job iii. 6.

נָשָׁא to deceive. HIPHIL *fut.* Ps. lv. 15, *seq.* עַל in a pregnant sense, to surprise and destroy suddenly.

SELA AND SELAH

סֶלַע *m.* a rock : 1 Sam. xxiii. 28, *marg.* ' *i. e.* the rock of divisions ;' 2 Kings xiv. 7, *marg.* ' or, the rock ;' Isa. xvi. 1, *marg.* ' a rock, or, Petra,' *pr. n.* of the capital of the Idumeans, situated between the Dead Sea and the Elanitic Gulf, in a valley shut in by lofty rocks. Perhaps Isa. xlii. 11 refers to the same. It was subdued by the Romans under Trajan, and restored by Adrian. Its remains still exist, consisting of splendid sepulchres and temples excavated in the rock, an amphitheatre, &c. They were first visited by Burckhardt in 1812.

SELAH

סֶלָה *m.* a musical word, found seventy-three times in the Psalms, elsewhere only in Hab. iii. 3, 9, 13 ; supposed to mean silence, pause : its use seems to have been, in chanting the words of the Psalm, to direct the singer to be silent, to pause a little, while the instruments played an interlude or symphony ; see Gesenius' Lexicon by Bagster, and Ges. Thesaurus. It can either be taken as a noun, rest, pause, or, with Gesenius, as the imperative, with ה *parag.* Primarily, indeed, it is a music mark, but it generally appears where a pause is quite suitable. Some have supposed it to be a mark of repetition. The right view of this word was substantially given by Luther. The selah, says he, tells us "to pause and carefully reflect on the words of the Psalm, for they require a peaceful and meditative soul, which can apprehend and receive what the Holy Spirit there cogitates and propounds."—*Hengstenberg.*

SELF

בָּשָׂר *m.* flesh : Eccles. ii. 3, *marg.* ' draw myself.'

נֶפֶשׁ *com.* soul : Lev. xi. 43, *marg.* ' your souls ;' 44 ; Deut. iv. 15 ; Josh. xxiii. 11 ; 1 Kings xix. 4, *lit.* his soul ; Esth. iv. 13, ix. 31, *marg.* ' their souls ;' Job xviii. 4, *marg.* ' his soul ;' xxxii. 2, *marg. id.* ; Ps. cxxxi. 2, *marg.* ' my soul ;' Isa. v. 14, xlvi. 2, *marg.* ' their soul ;' xlvii. 14, *marg.* ' their souls ;' Jer. iii. 11, xvii. 21, xxxvii. 9, *marg.* ' your souls ;' li. 14, *marg.* ' his soul ;' Amos ii. 14, *marg. id.* ; 15, vi. 8 ; Jonah iv. 8.

SELFSAME

עֶצֶם *m.* a bone, a body ; *seq. genit.* it is used instead of the pronoun, self, selfsame, *ipse* : Gen. vii. 13 ; xvii. 23, 26 : Exod. xii. 17, 41, 51 : Lev. xxiii. 14, 21, 28, 29, 30 : Deut. xxxii. 48 : Josh. v. 11 : Ezek. xxiv. 2, 2 ; xl. 1.

SELL

1 בּוֹא to come. KAL *fut.*

2 מָכַר to sell things, or persons, as slaves ; hence, figuratively, God sells a person or nation when he delivers them by

his providence as slaves into the power of a conqueror, Judg. iv. 2, 9 ; a man sells himself to work wickedness when he is wholly addicted and enslaved to sin, 1 Kings xxi. 25 ; a nation sell themselves when for their iniquities they become slaves to a foreign power, Isa. l. 1 ; a father sells his daughter when he gives her in marriage for a price, Gen. xxxi. 15, Exod. xxi. 7. KAL [a]*pret.* [b]*inf.* [c]*imp.* [d]*fut.* [e]*part.* Poel. NIPHAL [f]*pret.* [g]*inf.* [h]*fut.* [i]*part.* HITHPAEL [k]*pret.* [l]*inf.* [m]*fut.* מִמְכָּר [n] *m.* a selling. מִמְכֶּרֶת [o] *f. id.*

3 מְחִיר *m.* price.

4 שָׁבַר a denominative, from שֶׁבֶר corn, to buy or sell grain. KAL [a]*fut.* HIPHIL [b]*fut.* [c]*part.*

Gen. xxv. 31.	2 c	Lev. xxv. 42.	2 h o	Neh. x. 31.	2 b
xxv. 33.	2 d	xxv. 50.	2 g	xiii. 15.	2 b
xxxi. 15.	2 a	xxvii. 20.	2 a	xiii. 16, 20.	2 e
xxxvii. 27, 28.	2 d	xxvii. 27.	2 f	Esth. vii. 4, 4.	2 f
xxxvii. 36.	2 a	xxvii. 28.	2 h	Ps. xliv. 12.	2 d
xli. 56.	4 a	Deut. ii. 28.	4 b	cv. 17.	2 f
xlii. 6.	4 c	xiv. 21.	2 b	Prov. xi. 26.	4 c
xlv. 4, 5.	2 a	xv. 12.	2 h	xxiii. 23.	2 d
xlvii. 20, 22.	2 d	xxi. 14.	2 b d	xxxi. 24.	2 d
Exod. xxi. 7.	2 d	xxiv. 7.	2 a	Isa. xxiv. 2.	2 e
xxi. 8.	2 b	xxviii. 68.	2 k	l. 1, 1.	2 a f
xxi. 16, 35.	2 a	xxxii. 30.	2 a	lii. 3.	2 f
xxii. 1.	2 a	Judg. ii. 14.	2 d	Jer. xxxiv. 14.	2 h
xxii. 3.	2 f	iii. 8.	2 d	Lam. v. 4.	1, 3
Lev. xxv. 14.a	2 d n	iv. 2, 9.	2 d	Ezek. vii. 12.	2 e
xxv. 15.	2 d	x. 7.	2 d	vii. 13, 13.	2 e n
xxv. 16.	2 e	Ruth iv. 3.	2 a	xxx. 12.	2 a
xxv. 23, 34.	2 h	1 Sam. xii. 9.	2 a	xlviii. 14.	2 d
xxv. 25.	2 a n	1 Kings xxi. 20.	2 l	Joel iii. 3, 6, 7, 8, 8.	2 a
xxv. 27.	2 a	xxi. 25.	2 k	Amos ii. 6.	2 a
xxv. 28, 33.	2 n	2 Kings iv. 7.	2 c	viii. 5, 6.	4 b
xxv. 29.	2 d n	xvii. 17.	2 m	Nah. iii. 4.	2 a
xxv. 39, 47, 48.	2 f	Neh. v. 8, 8, 8.	2 i d f	Zech. xi. 5.	2 e

a lit. sell a selling.

SELVEDGE

קָצָה *f.* end, edge : Exod. xxvi. 4 ; xxxvi. 11.

SENATORS

זָקֵן *adj.* elder : Ps. cv. 22.

SEND

1 בּוֹא to come ; to cause to come. HIPHIL *pret.*

2 הָלַךְ to go. KAL *part.* Poel, Neh. vi. 17, *marg.* ' multiplied their letters passing to.'

3 טוּל to cast forth. HIPHIL *pret.*

4 יָצָא to go forth. HIPHIL *fut.* Ezra viii. 17, *lit.* according to כְּתִיב, and I brought them.

5 לָקַח to take. KAL *fut.*

6 נָבַע to flow, to pour out. HIPHIL *fut.*

7 נוּף to shake. HIPHIL *fut.*

8 נָתַן to give. KAL [a]*pret.* [b]*inf.* [c]*fut.* [d]*part.* Poel.

9 עָבַר to pass over ; to cause to pass over. HIPHIL *fut.*

10 פָּרַץ to break forth. KAL *fut.*

11 צָוָה to command, to send with commandment. PIEL *fut.*

12 קָרָה to meet, to cause to fall in the way. HIPHIL *imp.*

13 שׁוּב to return. HIPHIL *pret.*

14 שָׁלַח to send, to send away, to let go, to send out or forth ; Piel, to send in a stronger sense, to cast, to throw, to

shoot. KAL ^a*pret.* ^b*inf.* ^c*imp.* ^d*fut.* ^e*part.* Poel.
^f*part.* Paül. NIPHAL ^g*inf.* PIEL ^h*pret.* ⁱ*inf.* ^k*imp.*
^l*fut.* ^m*part.* PUAL ⁿ*pret.* ^o*fut.* HIPHIL ^p*pret.* ^q*inf.*
^r*part.* שָׁלַח Ch. P'AL ^s*pret.* ^t*fut.* ^u*part.* מִשְׁלוֹחַ *m.*
^w*m.* מִשְׁלַחַת ^x *f.* שִׁלּוּחִים *m.* a sending away.

15 תּוּר to go about from place to place. HIPHIL *fut.*

Gen. iii. 23.	14 l	Deut. ii. 26.	14 d	2 Sam. iii. 12, 14, 15,
viii. 7, 8, 12.	14 l	vii. 20.	14 l	26.	14 d
viii. 10. α	14 i	ix. 23.	14 b	iii. 21, 23.	14 l
xii. 20.	14 l	xi. 15.	8 a	iii. 22, 24.	14 h
xix. 13, 29.	14 l	xv. 13.	14 l	v. 11.	14 d
xx. 2.	14 d	xv. 18.	14 i	viii. 10.	14 a
xxi. 14.	14 l	xix. 12.	14 a	ix. 5.	14 d
xxiv. 7, 40.	14 d	xxiv. 1, 3, 4.	14 h	x. 2, 5, 6, 7, 16.	14 d
xxiv. 12. β	12	xxviii. 20, 48.	14 l	x. 3, 3.	14 a
xxiv. 54, 56.	14 k	xxxii. 24.	14 l	xi. 1.	14 l
xxiv. 59.	14 l	xxxiv. 11.	14 a	xi. 1, 3, 4, 5, 14,
xxv. 6.	14 l	Josh. i. 16.	14 d	18, 27.	14 d
xxvi. 27, 29, 31.	14 l	ii. 1, 3.	14 d	ii. 6, 6, 6.	14 d c d
xxvii. 42.	14 d	ii. 21.	14 l	xii. 22.	14 a
xxvii. 45.	14 a	vi. 17, 25.	14 l	xiii. 1, 25, 27.	14 a
xxviii. 5.	14 d	vii. 2, 22.	14 d	xiii. 7.	14 d
xxviii. 6.	14 h	viii. 3, 9.	14 d	xiii. 16.	14 i
xxx. 25.	14 k	x. 3, 6.	14 d	xiv. 2.	14 d
xxxi. 4.	14 l	xi. 1.	14 d	xiv. 29, 29, 29.	14 d b d
xxxi. 27.	14 l	xiv. 7, 11.	14 b	xiv. 32, 32.	14 a d
xxxi. 42.	14 h	xviii. 4.	14 l	xv. 10, 12.	14 d
xxxii. 3, 5.	14 d	xxii. 6.	14 l	xv. 36.	14 a
xxxii. 18.	14 f	xxii. 7.	14 h	xvii. 16.	14 c
xxxii. 23, 23.	9	xxiii. 2.	14 d	xviii. 2.	14 l
xxxvii. 13, 14.	14 d	xxiv. 5, 9, 12.	14 d	xviii. 29.	14 b
xxxvii. 32.	14 l	Judg. i. 23.	15	xix. 11.	14 a
xxxviii. 17, 17.	14 l b	iii. 15.	14 d	xix. 14.	14 d
xxxviii. 20.	14 d	iii. 18.	14 l	xxii. 15, 17.	14 d
xxxviii. 23, 25.	14 a	iv. 6.	14 n	xxiv. 13.	14 e
xli. 8, 14.	14 d	v. 15.	14 a	xxiv. 15.	8 c
xlii. 4.	14 a	vi. 8.	14 d	1 Kings i. 44, 53.	14 d
xlii. 16.	14 c	vi. 14, 35, 35.	14 a	ii. 25, 29, 36, 42.	14 d
xliii. 4, 5.	14 m	vii. 8.	14 h	v. 1, 2, 14.	14 d
xliii. 8.	14 c	vii. 24.	14 h	v. 8, 8.	14 d a
xliii. 14.	14 h	ix. 23, 31.	14 d	vii. 13.	14 d
xliv. 3.	14 n	xi. 12, 14, 19, 38.	14 d	viii. 44.	14 h
xlv. 5, 8, 23, 27.	14 a	xi. 17, 17.	14 d a	viii. 66.	14 h
xlv. 7.	14 d	xi. 28.	14 a	ix. 14, 27.	14 a
xlv. 24.	14 l	xii. 9.	14 h	xii. 3, 18, 20.	14 d
xlvi. 5, 28.	14 a	xiii. 8.	14 d	xiv. 6.	14 f
Exod. ii. 5.	14 d	xvi. 18.	14 d	xv. 18, 20.	14 a
iii. 10.	14 d	xviii. 24.	14 d	xv. 19.	14 a
iii. 12, 13, 14, 15.	14 a	xix. 29.	14 l	xvii. 14.	8 b
iv. 13, 13.	14 c d	xx. 6.	14 l	xviii. 1.	8 c
iv. 28.	14 a	xx. 12.	14 d	xviii. 10.	14 a
v. 22.	14 a	xxi. 10, 13.	14 d	xviii. 10.	14 c
vii. 2. γ	14 h	1 Sam. iv. 4.	14 d	xviii. 20.	14 d
vii. 16.	14 a	v. 10.	14 l	xix. 2.	14 a
viii. 21.	14 r	v. 11, 11.	14 d k	xx. 2, 6, 10, 17.	14 d
ix. 7, 27.	14 d	vi. 2.	14 l	xx. 5, 7, 9.	14 a
ix. 14.	14 e	vi. 3, 3.	14 a	xxi. 34, 34.	14 l
ix. 19.	14 c	vi. 8.	14 m l	xxi. 8, 14.	14 d
ix. 23.	8 a	vi. 8.	14 h	xxi. 11, 11.	14 h
xii. 33.	14 i	vi. 21.	14 d	2 Kings i. 2, 9, 11, ε
xv. 7.	14 l	ix. 16.	14 d	13. ε	14 d
xviii. 27.	14 y	ix. 26.	14 l	i. 6, 6.	14 a e
xxiii. 20.	14 e	x. 25.	14 l	i. 16.	14 a
xxiii. 27.	14 a	xi. 3.	14 d	ii. 2, 4, 6.	14 a
xxiii. 28.	14 a	xi. 7.	14 l	ii. 16.	14 d
xxiv. 5.	14 d	xii. 8, 11.	14 d	ii. 17, 17.	14 c d
xxxiii. 2.	14 a	xii. 17, 18.	8 c	iii. 7.	14 c
xxxiii. 12.	14 d	xiii. 2.	14 h	iv. 22.	14 c
Lev. xvi. 21.	14 h	xv. 1, 20.	14 a	v. 5, 8, 10.	14 d
xxvi. 22.	14 p	xv. 18.	14 d	v. 6, 22.	14 d
xxvi. 25.	14 h	xvi. 1, 12.	14 d	v. 7.	14 e
xxvi. 36.	14 l	xvi. 11.	14 l	vi. 9, 10, 13, 14.	14 d
Num. xiii. 2, 2.	14 c d	xvi. 19, 19.	14 d c	vi. 23.	14 l
xiii. 3, 17.	14 d	xvi. 20, 22.	14 d	vi. 32, 32.	14 d a
xiii. 16, 27.	14 a	xvii. 31.	5	vii. 13, 14.	14 a
xiv. 36.	14 a	xviii. 5.	14 d	viii. 9.	14 a
xvi. 12.	14 d	xix. 11, 14, 15.	14 d	ix. 17.	14 c
xvi. 28, 29.	14 a	xix. 17.	14 l	ix. 19.	14 d
xx. 14, 16.	14 a	xix. 20, 21, 21.	14 d	x. 1, 5, 7, 21.	14 d
xxi. 6.	14 l	xx. 12, 21.	14 d	xi. 4.	14 a
xxi. 32.	14 d	xx. 13, 22.	14 h	xii. 18.	14 a
xxii. 5.	14 d	xx. 31.	14 c	xiv. 8.	14 a
xxii. 10.	14 a	xxi. 2.	14 e	xiv. 9, 9.	14 d a
xxii. 15. δ	14 b	xxii. 11.	14 d	xiv. 19.	14 d
xxii. 37.	14 b a	xxv. 5, 39.	14 d	xv. 37.	14 q
xxii. 40.	14 l	xxv. 14, 25, 32, 40.	14 a	xvi. 7, 8, 10.	14 a
xxiv. 12.	14 a	xxvi. 4.	14 d	xvi. 11.	14 a
xxxi. 4, 6.	14 l	xxx. 26.	14 l	xvii. 4, 13.	14 a
xxxii. 8.	14 b	xxxi. 9.	14 a	xvii. 25, 26.	14 l
Deut. i. 22.	14 d	2 Sam. ii. 5.	14 d	xviii. 14, 17.	14 d

2 Kings xviii. 27.	14 a	Job xiv. 20.	14 l	Jer. xxvi. 5, 5.	14 e b
xix. 2, 9, ζ 20.	14 d	xxi. 11.	14 l	xxvi. 12, 15.	14 a
xix. 4, 16.	14 a	xxii. 9.	14 h	xxvi. 22.	14 d
xx. 7.	8 d	xxxviii. 35.	14 l	xxvii. 3.	14 h
xx. 12.	14 a	xxxix. 5.	14 h	xxvii. 15.	14 a
xxii. 3, 15.	14 a	Ps. xviii. 14, 16.	14 d	xxviii. 9, 15.	14 a
xxii. 18.	14 e	xx. 2.	14 d	xxix. 1, 3, 9.	14 a
i. 16.	14 l	xliii. 3.	14 c	xxix. 17.	14 m
xxiv. 2, 2.	14 l	lvii. 3, 3.	14 d d	xxix. 19, 19.	14 a b
1 Chron. viii. 8.	14 h	lix. title.	14 b	xxix. 20.	14 h
x. 9.	14 l	lxviii. 9.	7	xxix. 31, 31.	14 c a
xii. 19.	14 h	lxviii. 33.	8 c	xxxv. 15, 15.	14 d b
xiii. 2.	10, 14 d	lxxvii. 17.	8 a	xxxvi. 14, 21.	14 d
xiv. 1.	14 d	lxxviii. 25.	14 a	xxxvii. 3, 17.	14 d
xviii. 10.	14 d	lxxviii. 45.	14 l	xxxvii. 7.	14 e
xix. 2, 5, 6, 8, 16.	14 d	lxxviii. 49.	14 x	xxxviii. 14.	14 e
xix. 3.	14 a	lxxx. 11.	14 l	xxxix. 13, 14.	14 d
xix. 4.	14 l	civ. 10.	14 m	xl. 14.	14 a
xxi. 12.	14 e	civ. 30.	14 o	xlii. 5.	14 d
xxi. 14.	8 c	cv. 17, 20, 26, 28.	14 a	xlii. 6.	14 e
xxi. 15.	14 d	cvi. 15.	14 l	xlii. 9, 20, 21.	14 a
2 Chron. ii. 3, 3, 11,		cvii. 20.	14 d	xliii. 1, 2.	14 a
15.	14 d	cx. 2.	14 d	xliii. 10.	14 a
ii. 7, 8.	14 c	cxi. 9.	14 a	xliv. 4, 4.	14 d b
ii. 13.	14 a	cxxxv. 9.	14 d	xlviii. 12.	14 h
vi. 27.	8 a	cxliv. 7.	14 c	xlix. 14.	14 f
vi. 34.	14 d	cxlvii. 15.	14 e	xlix. 37.	14 h
vii. 10.	14 h	cxlvii. 18.	14 d	li. 2.	14 h
vii. 13.	14 l	Prov. ix. 3.	14 a	li. 9.	14 h
viii. 18.	14 d	x. 26.	14 e	Lam. i. 13.	14 a
x. 3, 18.	14 d	xvii. 11.	14 o	Ezek. ii. 3, 4.	14 e
xvi. 2, 4.	14 d	xxii. 21.	14 e	ii. 9.	14 f
xvi. 3.	14 a	xxv. 13.	14 e	iii. 5.	14 f
xvii. 7.	14 a	xxvi. 6.	14 e	iii. 6.	14 a
xxiv. 19.	14 d	Eccles. x. 1.	6	v. 16, 16.	14 l i
xxiv. 23.	14 h	Cant. i. 12.	8 a	v. 17.	14 h
xxv. 13.	13	Isa. vi. 8, 8.	14 d c	vii. 3.	14 h
xxv. 15, 17, 27.	14 d	vii. 25.	14 w	xiii. 6.	14 a
xxv. 18, 18.	14 d a	ix. 8.	14 a	xiv. 13.	14 p
xxviii. 16.	14 a	x. 6, 16.	14 l	xiv. 19.	14 h
xxx. 1.	14 d	xvi. 1.	14 c	xiv. 21.	14 h
xxxii. 9.	14 a	xviii. 2.	14 e	xvii. 15.	14 b
xxxii. 21.	14 d	xix. 20.	14 d	xxiii. 16.	14 h
xxxii. 31.	14 m	xx. 1.	14 b	xxiii. 40, 40.	14 d f
xxxiv. 8, 23.	14 a	xxxii. 20.	14 m	xxvii. 23.	14 h
xxxiv. 26.	14 e	xxxv. 2.	14 a	xxxi. 4.	14 h
xxxiv. 29.	14 d	xxxvi. 12.	14 a	xxxi. 6.	14 h
xxxv. 21.	14 d	xxxvii. 2, 9, 21.	14 d	Dan. iii. 2, 28.	14 s
xxxvi. 10.	14 d	xxxvii. 4, 17.	14 a	v. 24.	14 u
xxxvi. 15, 15.	14 d b	xxxvii. 7.	8 d	vi. 22.	14 u
Ezra iv. 11, 14, 17,		xxxix. 1.	14 a	x. 11.	14 n
18.	14 s	xlii. 19.	14 d	Hos. v. 13.	14 d
v. 6, 7.	14 s	xliii. 14.	14 h	viii. 14.	14 h
v. 17.	14 t	xlviii. 16.	14 a	Joel ii. 19.	14 e
vi. 13.	14 s	lv. 11.	14 a	ii. 25.	14 h
vii. 14.	14 u	lvii. 9.	14 l	Amos i. 4; 7; 10, 12.	14 h
viii. 16.	14 d	lxi. 1.	14 a	ii. 2, 5.	14 h
viii. 17. η	11, or 4	lxvi. 19.	14 h	iv. 10.	14 d
Neh. ii. 5, 6, θ 9.	14 d	Jer. i. 7.	14 d	vii. 10.	14 d
vi. 2, 3, 4, 5, 8.	14 d	ii. 10.	14 c	viii. 11.	14 p
vi. 12, 19.	14 a	vii. 25, 25.	14 d b	Obad. 1.	14 n
vi. 17.	2	viii. 17.	14 m	Jonah i. 4.	3
viii. 10.	14 c	ix. 16.	14 h	Micah vi. 4.	14 d
viii. 12.	14 e	ix. 17.	14 c	Hag. i. 12.	14 a
Esth. i. 22.	14 d	xiv. 3, 14, 15.	14 a	Zech. i. 10.	14 a
iii. 13.	14 g	xvi. 16, 16.	14 e d	ii. 8, 9, 11.	14 a
iv. 4.	14 d	xix. 14.	14 a	iv. 9.	14 a
v. 10.	14 d	xxi. 1.	14 b	vi. 15.	14 a
viii. 10.	14 d	xxiii. 21, 32.	14 d	vii. 2.	14 a
ix. 19, 22.	14 v	xxiii. 38.	14 d	vii. 12.	14 a
ix. 20, 30.	14 h	xxiv. 5, 10.	14 h	ix. 11.	14 a
Job i. 4.	14 a	xxv. 4, 4.	14 a b	Mal. ii. 2, 4.	14 h
i. 5.	14 d	xxv. 9, 15, 16, 27.	14 a	iii. 1.	14 a
v. 10.	14 d	xxv. 17.	14 a	iv. 5.	14 e
xii. 15.	14 l				

α *lit.* he added to send forth.   β *lit.* bring to pass before me.   γ *lit.*
and so he will send.   δ *lit.* added to send.   ε *lit.* returned and
sent.   ζ *lit.* returned and sent.   η *lit.* according to כְּתִיב, and I
brought them.   θ *lit.* and he sent me.

SENSE

שֶׂכֶל *m.* understanding, knowledge : Neh. viii. 8.

SENTENCE

דָּבָר *m.* word, matter, &c.: Deut. xvii. 9, 10, *lit.* the mouth of
the word; 11.

פֶּה *m.* mouth: Deut. xvii. 10, 11, *lit.* the mouth of the law.

פִּתְגָּם *m.* word, in later Heb. from the Chald. specially rescript, decree: Eccles. viii. 11.

קֶסֶם *m.* divination: Prov. xvi. 10.

מִשְׁפָּט *m.* judgment: Ps. xvii. 2: Jer. iv. 12.

SEPARATE

1 בָּדַל to separate; Hiphil with מִן to divide; to distinguish; to select, to choose out; to shut out, as separated from. NIPHAL [a] *pret.* [b] *imp.* [c] *fut.* [d] *part.* HIPHIL [e] *pret.* [f] *inf.* [g] *fut.* [h] *part.* מִבְדָּלוֹת *f. pl.* separations, *i.e.* separate places, of cities separately assigned.

2 גְּזֵרָה *f.* a place cut off, a separate place.

3 חָלַק to divide. HIPHIL *inf.* Jer. xxxvii. 12, *marg.* 'or, slip away;' to obtain from thence his portion, his inheritance: so Vulg., Targum; but Kimchi, that he might slip away from thence, a signification which might easily come from that of smoothness.—*Gesenius.* See *Smooth.*

4 נִדָּה *f.* uncleanness, impurity; especially such ceremonial uncleanness as obliged either man or woman to live separate from all society, Lev. xv. 25, &c. The water of separation, Num. xix. 9, was the water used in cleansing those persons who, for their pollution, were separated from the congregation, and those things which, being defiled, had for some time been disused. The word means, also, any abomination.

5 נָזַר to separate; to be separated or devoted in a religious sense; to separate oneself from the common enjoyments of life for fasting and humiliation: Zech. vii. 3; see *Nazarite.* NIPHAL [a] *inf.* [b] *fut.* HIPHIL [c] *pret.* [d] *inf.* [e] *fut.* [f] נָזִיר *m.* a Nazarite. [g] נֵזֶר *m.* state of separation.

6 פָּלָא the primary idea seems to be, to separate, to distinguish. HIPHIL *fut.*

7 פָּלָה to separate, to distinguish, in a glorious manner. NIPHAL [a] *pret.* Gr. ἐνδοξασθήσομαι.

8 פָּרַד to break off, to separate by breaking: this root sometimes implies extinction of friendship, and strife between those who are separated. NIPHAL [a] *inf.* [b] *imp.* [c] *fut.* [d] *part.* PIEL [e] *fut.* HIPHIL [f] *pret.* [g] *inf.* [h] *part.*

Gen. xiii. 9.	8 b	Num. viii. 14.	1 e	Ezra x. 8, 16.	1 c	
xiii. 11.	8 c	xvi. 9.	1 e	x. 11.	1 b	
xiii. 14.	8 a	xvi. 21.	1 b	Neh. iv. 19.	8 d	
xxv. 23.	8 c	xix. 9, 13, 20, 21,		ix. 2.	1 c	
xxx. 40.	8 f	21.	4	x. 28.	1 d	
xlix. 26.	5 f	xxxi. 23.	4	xiii. 3.	1 g	
Exod. xxxiii. 16.	7 a	Deut. x. 8.	1 e	Prov. xvi. 28.	8 h	
Lev. xii. 2, 5.	4	xix. 2, 7.	1 g	xvii. 9.	8 h	
xv. 20, 25, 25, 25,		xxix. 21.	1 e	xviii. 1.	8 d	
26, 26.	4	xxxii. 8.	8 g	xix. 4.	8 c	
xv. 31.	5 c	xxxiii. 16.	5 f	Isa. lvi. 3.	1 f g	
xx. 24, 25.	1 e	Josh. xvi. 9.	1 i	lix. 2.	1 h	
xxii. 2.	5 b	1 Kings viii. 53.	1 e	Jer. xxxvii. 12.	3	
Num. vi. 2, 2.	6, 5 d	1 Chron. xii. 8.	1 a	Ezek. xiv. 7.	5 b	
vi. 3.	5 e	xxiii. 13.	1 c	xli. 12, 13, 14, 15.	2	
vi. 5, 5.	5 g c	xxv. 1.	1 g	xli. 1, 10, 13.	2	
vi. 6.	5 d	2 Chron. xxv. 10.	1 g	xlii. 20.	1 f	
vi. 4, 8, 12, 12, 13,		Ezra vi. 21.	1 d	Hos. iv. 14.	8 e	
18, 18, 19, 21,		viii. 24.	1 g	ix. 10.	5 b	
21.	5 g	ix. 1.	1 a	Zech. vii. 3.	5 a	

SEPULCHRE

קֶבֶר *m.* place of burial, sepulchre, grave: Gen. xxiii. 6, 6: Judg. viii. 32: 2 Sam. ii. 32; iv. 12; xvii. 23; xxi. 14:

1 Kings xiii. 22, 31: 2 Kings xiii. 21; xxiii. 16, 16, 17: 2 Chron. xvi. 14; xxi. 20; xxiv. 25; xxviii. 27; xxxii. 33; xxxv. 24: Neh. ii. 3, 5; iii. 16: Ps. v. 9: Isa. xxii. 16, 16: Jer. v. 16. קְבוּרָה *f.* burial, sepulchre: Deut. xxxiv. 6: 1 Sam. x. 2: 2 Kings ix. 28; xxi. 26; xxiii. 30.

SERAPHIM

שָׂרָף *m.* see *Serpent.* Seraphim, seraphs, are thought to be an order of angels and ministers of God, who stand around his throne, each having six wings, also hands and feet, and praising God with their voice: they were therefore of human form, and furnished with wings as the swift messengers of God, like the cherubim, though by no means identical with these, as some have supposed: they are so called as being of elevated rank, princes; as in Daniel the archangels are also called princes, Dan. x. 13, comp. viii. 25. Other proposed etymologies see in Thesaurus, p. 1341, *seq.* Gesenius. Isa. vi. 2, 6.

SERPENT

זָחַל to creep, to crawl, as serpents or worms. KAL *part.* Deut. xxxii. 24.

נָחָשׁ *m.* a serpent, so called from its hissing.—*Gesenius.* Frequent mention is made of its deadly bite, Num. xxi. 17, &c.; also of its cunning, Gen. iii. 1, &c., *comp.* Matt. x. 16, Bochart. Put for the constellation of the serpent or dragon in the northern quarter of the heavens, Job xxvi. 13; see also תַּנִּין below.—Gen. iii. 1, 2, 4, 13, 14; xlix. 17: Exod. iv. 3; vii. 15: Num. xxi. 6, 7, 9, 9, 9: Deut. viii. 15: 2 Kings xviii. 4: Job xxvi. 13: Ps. lviii. 4; cxl. 3: Prov. xxiii. 32; xxx. 19: Eccles. x. 8, 11: Isa. xiv. 29; xxvii. 1, 1; lxv. 25: Jer. viii. 17; xlvi. 22: Amos v. 19; ix. 3: Micah vii. 17.

שָׂרָף *adj.* burning, fiery; then poisonous, venomous, deadly, as an attribute of a serpent, from the burning inflammation caused by its bite. So Num. xxi. 6, Lxx. τοὺς ὄφεις τοὺς θανατοῦντας: Vulg. *ignitos serpentes.* Deut. viii. 15, Lxx. ὄφις δάκνων: Vulg. *serpens flatu adurens.* In Isa. xiv. 29, a venomous flying serpent, ascribed to the Arabian desert. It is now known that no species of flying serpent exists, but this ancient opinion probably rested upon a species of flying lizard (*draco volans,* Linn.) found in Africa and Asia, which, in its general appearance, resembles a serpent, but is not venomous.—*Gesenius.* Rather, a serpent which darts from one tree to another, as described by travellers. Num. xxi. 8: Isa. xiv. 29; xxx. 6.

תַּנִּין *m.* (see *Dragon*): Exod. vii. 9, 10, 12; probably here the crocodile, the monster of the Nile, is meant, so that נָחָשׁ (see above) is used for the same in Exod. iv. 3.

SERVE, SERVILE, &c.

1 אֱנוֹשׁ *m.* man.

2 בֵּן *m.* son: Eccles. ii. 7, *marg.* 'and sons of my house.'

3 גָּמַל to recompense. KAL [a] *pret.* Ps. cxxxvii. 8, *marg.* 'thy deed which thou didst to us, *or,* thy recompense which thou hast recompensed to us.' [b] גְּמוּל *m.* recompense.

4 דָּבָר *m.* word, matter, thing.

5 יָד *com.* hand: 1 Chron. vi. 31, "the service," properly the side, by the side of the singing.—*Gesenius.*

6 מָצָא to find. KAL *fut.* 1 Sam. x. 7, "as occasion serve thee," *marg.* 'thine hand shall find.'

7 נַעַר *m.* a boy, a young person; a servant.

8 עָבַד to labour, to work, to do work; to serve another; to serve in a religious sense; to be subject to a conqueror; with בְּ to impose service on any one, Jer. xxxiv. 9, 10. KAL ᵃ *pret.* ᵇ *inf.* ᶜ *imp.* ᵈ *fut.* ᵉ *part.* Poel. NIPHAL ᶠ *pret.* PUAL ᵍ *pret.* HIPHIL ʰ *pret.* ⁱ *fut.* HOPHAL ᵏ *fut.* ¹ עֶבֶד *m.* a servant; sometimes a title of office, with an idea of subordinate ruling; so of a king, his ministers, officers, &c.; synonymous with elder; of the Messiah, servant of Jehovah, Isa. xlv. 1, &c.—Gen. ix. 25, &c. ᵐ עֲבַד Ch. *m.* ⁿ עֲבֻדָּה *f.* store of servants, *marg.* 'or, husbandry.' ᵒ עֲבוֹדָה *f.* service, when so translated the reference is not given: Gen. xxix. 27, &c. ᵖ עֲבִידָה Ch. *f.*

9 עָמַד to stand, with לִפְנֵי to serve, *lit.* to stand before. KAL ᵃ *pret.* ᵇ *inf.*

10 עָשָׂה to do. KAL ᵃ *pret.* Judg. viii. 1, *marg.* 'what thing is this thou hast done unto us?'

11 פְּלַח Ch. to labour, to serve; especially to serve God. P'AL ᵃ *fut.* ᵇ *part.* ᶜ פְּלְחָן Ch. *m.*

12 פָּנִים *m. pl.* face, presence. לִפְנֵי before.

13 צָבָא *m.* host, army; warfare: Num. iv. 23, *marg.* 'war the warfare;' 30, *marg.* 'warfare;' 35, *id.*; 39, *id.*; 43, *id.*; viii. 24, *id.*

14 שִׁפְחָה *f.* maid-servant.

15 שָׂרָד *m.* a species of cloth or stuff resembling mail or network, wrought of threads by means of needles, of which the curtains of the tabernacle were made. Lxx. incorrectly, στολαὶ λειτουργικαί, as if for בנדי שרת, which the Samar. actually exhibits; but the sense requires curtains, tapestry, not garments.

16 שָׁרַת to wait upon, to serve, to minister unto. PIEL ᵃ *inf.* ᵇ *fut.* ᶜ *part.*

No. 8 l, *Servant,* and No. 8 o, *Service,* not included.

Gen. xiv. 4.	8 a	Exod. xxi. 6.	8 a	Deut. iv. 19, 28.	8 a
xv. 13.	8 d	xxiii. 24.	8 k	v. 9.	8 k
xv. 14.	8 d	xxiii. 25.	8 a	vi. 13.	8 d
xxv. 23.	8 d	xxiii. 33.	8 d	vii. 4.	8 a
xxvi. 14.	8 n	xxxi. 10.	15	vii. 16.	8 d
xxvii. 29, 40.	8 d	xxxiii. 11.	16 c	viii. 19.	8 d
xxix. 15, 25.	8 d	xxxv. 19, 19.	15, 16 a	x. 12.	8 b
xxix. 18, 20, 27, 30.	8 d	xxxix. 1, 1.	15, 16 a	x. 20.	8 d
xxx. 26, 29.	8 d	xxxix. 41, 41.	15, 16 a	xi. 13.	8 a
xxxi. 6, 41.	8 a	Lev. xxiii. 7, 8, 21,		xi. 16.	8 a
xxxix. 4.	16 b	25, 35, 36.	8 o	xii. 2.	8 a
xl. 4.	16 b	xxv. 40.	8 o	xii. 30.	8 d
xlix. 15.	8 e	Num. iii. 36.	8 o	xiii. 2.	8 k
Exod. i. 13.	8 i	iv. 23.	13	xiii. 4, 6, 13.	8 d
i. 14.	8 a	iv. 24.	8 b	v. 12, 18.γ	8 a
iii. 12.	8 a	iv. 26.	13	xvii. 3.	8 d
iv. 23.	8 d	iv. 30, 35, 39, 43.	13	xx. 11.	8 a
vii. 16.	8 d	iv. 37, 41.	8 e	xxviii. 14.	8 b
viii. 1, 20.	8 d	iv. 47, 47. a	8 o	xxviii. 36, 47, 48,	
ix. 1, 13.	8 d	viii. 15.	8 b	64.	8 b
x. 3, 7.	8 d	viii. 24.	13	xxix. 18.	8 b
x. 8, 11, 24.	8 d	viii. 25.	8 d	xxix. 26.	8 a
x. 26, 26.	8 b d	xi. 28.	16 c	xxx. 17.	8 a
xii. 31.	8 d	xviii. 7, 23.	8 a	xxxi. 20.	8 b
xiv. 5.	8 a	xviii. 21.	8 e	Josh. xvi. 10.δ	8 e
xiv. 12, 12.	8 d b	xxviii. 18, 25, 26.	7	xxii. 5.	8 b
xx. 5.	8 k	xxix. 1, 12, 35.β	8 o	xxiii. 7.	8 d
xxi. 2.	8 d			xxiii. 16.	8 d

Josh. xxiv. 2.	8 d	2 Kings iv. 43.	16 c	Prov. xxix. 12.	16 c
xxiv. 14, 14, 14.	8 c a c	v. 20, 23.	7	Eccles. ii. 7, 7.	8 l, 2
xxiv. 15, 15.		vi. 15, 15.	16 c, 7	v. 9.	8 f
15, 15.	8 b d a d	viii. 4.	7	Isa. xiv. 3.η	8 g
xxiv. 16, 19, 22.	8 b	x. 18, 18.	8 d a	xix. 23.	7
xxiv. 20.	8 a	x. 19.	8 e	xxxvii. 6.	7
xxiv. 18, 21, 24, 31.	8 d	xvii. 12, 16, 35.	8 d	xliii. 23, 24.	8 h
Judg. ii. 7, 11, 13.	8 a	xvii. 33, 41.	8 e	liii. 11.θ	8 l
ii. 19.	8 d	xviii. 7.	8 d	lvi. 6.	16 a
iii. 6, 7, 8, 14.	8 d	xix. 6.	7	lx. 12.	8 d
vii. 10, 11.	7	xix. 3.	8 d	Jer. v. 19, 19.	8 a
viii. 1.	10 a, 4	xxi. 21, 21.	8 d a	viii. 2.	8 a
ix. 28, 28, 28.	8 d c d	xxv. 24.	8 c	x. 10.	8 b
ix. 38.	8 d	1 Chron. vi. 31.	5	xiii. 10.	8 b
x. 6, 6.	8 a	vi. 49.	8 d	xvi. 11.	8 d
x. 10, 13, 16.	8 d	xxvii. 1.	16 c	xvii. 13.	8 a
xx. 3, 9, 11, 13.	7	xxviii. 9.	7	xvii. 4.	8 a
Ruth ii. 5, 6.	7	xxviii. 14, 14.ζ	8 o	xxii. 9, 13.	8 d
1 Sam. ii. 13, 15.	7	xxix. 5.	5	xxv. 6.	8 b
iv. 9.ε	8 d a	2 Chron. vii. 19.	8 a	xxv. 11, 14.	8 b
vii. 3.	8 c	viii. 14.	8 d	xxvii. 6.	8 d
vii. 4.	8 c	x. 4, 4.	8 o d	xxvii. 7, 7, 11.	8 b
viii. 8.	8 d	xxiv. 18.	8 d	xxvii. 8, 9, 13, 14.	8 d
ix. 3, 5, 7, 8, 10,		xxix. 11.	16 a	xxviii. 12, 17.	8 c
22, 27.	7	xxx. 8.	8 c	xxviii. 14, 14.	8 b a
x. 7.	7	xxxiii. 3, 22.	8 d	xxx. 8.	8 d
x. 14.	7	xxxiii. 16.	8 b	xxx. 9.	8 a
xi. 1.	7	xxxiv. 13.ζ	8 o	xxxiv. 9, 10.	8 b
xii. 10, 10.	8 d	xxxiv. 33, 33.	8 i b	xxxiv. 14.	8 a
xii. 14, 20, 24.	8 d	xxxv. 3.	8 c	xxxv. 15.	8 b
xvi. 18.	7	Ezra iv. 11.	8 m	xl. 9, 9.	8 b c
xvii. 9.	8 d	v. 11.	8 m	xl. 10.	9 b
xxi. 2.	7	vi. 18.	8 p	xliv. 3.	8 b
xxiv. 7.	1	vii. 19.	11 c	lii. 12.	9 a
xxv. 19.	7	Neh. iv. 16, 22, 23.	7	Lam. i. 3.	8 o
xxv. 41.	14	v. 10, 15, 16.	7	Ezek. xx. 32.	16 a
xxvi. 19.	8 c	vi. 5.	7	xx. 39.	8 c
2 Sam. ix. 9.	7	ix. 35.	8 d	xx. 40.	8 d
x. 19.	8 d	xiii. 19.	7	xxix. 18, 18.	8 h a
xiii. 17, 28, 29.	7	Esth. i. 10.	16 c	xxix. 20.	8 e
xiii. 18.	16 c	ii. 2.	7	xxxiv. 27.	8 e
xv. 8.	8 a	iv. 3, 5.	7	xlviii. 18.	8 e
xvi. 1.	7	Job i. 15, 16, 17.	7	xlviii. 19, 19.	8 e d
xvii. 19, 19.	8 d a	xxi. 15.	8 d	Dan. ii. 4, 7.	8 m
xix. 17.	7	xxxvi. 11.	8 d	iii. 12, 14, 17, 18.	11 b
xxii. 44.	8 d	xxxix. 9.	8 b	iii. 26.	8 m
1 Kings iv. 21.	8 e	Ps. ii. 11.	8 c	iii. 28, 28.	8 m, 11 a
ix. 6.	8 a	xviii. 43.	8 d	vi. 16.	11 b
ix. 9.	8 a	xxii. 30.	8 d	vi. 20, 20.	8 m, 11 b
xii. 4.	8 d	lxxii. 11.	8 d	vii. 14, 27.	11 a
xii. 7.	8 d	xcvii. 7.	8 e	Hos. xii. 12.	8 d
xvi. 31.	8 d	c. 2.	8 e	Zeph. iii. 9.	8 b
xviii. 43.	7	ci. 6.	16 b	Zech. ii. 9.	8 e
xix. 3.	7	cii. 22.	8 b	Mal. iii. 14.	8 b
xxii. 53.	8 d	cvi. 36.	8 d	iii. 17.	8 e
2 Kings iv. 12, 24,		cxxxvii. 8.	3 b a	iii. 18, 18.	8 e a
25, 38.	7				

α "service of the ministry." *β lit.* work of service. *γ lit.* he hath served thee. *δ lit.* were serving. *ε lit.* as they have served you. *ζ lit.* of service and service. *η lit.* which was served on thee. *θ lit.* the righteous one my servant.

SET

1 אֲמוּנָה *f.* firmness, stability, faithfulness; "set office," *marg.* 'trust.'

2 בָּנָה to build, to set up, implying prosperity; see *Build.* KAL ᵃ *pret.* NIPHAL ᵇ *pret.*

3 בּוֹא to come, to go down, as the sun sets. KAL *pret.*

4 בָּעַר to burn, to cause to burn. PIEL ᵃ *pret.* HIPHIL ᵇ *fut.*

5 גָּבַל to set bounds, to set. KAL ᵃ *pret.* HIPHIL ᵇ *pret.* ᶜ *imp.*

6 גָּדַל to be or become great, to be much set by. KAL ᵃ *pret.* ᵇ *fut.*

7 זְקַף Ch. to raise up, a criminal on a stake or cross. P'AL *part. pass.*

8 זָרַע to sow, to set. KAL *fut.*

9 חָקַק to grave; to ordain, to appoint. KAL ᵃ *inf.* ᵇ חֹק *m.* something decreed, prescribed, an appointed time.

10 יָהַב to give, set, put. KAL *imp.*

11 יָנַח to set or lay a thing down, or to lay it up, and leave it to be there; to set down and leave as a present; to set

and leave persons in any particular situation. HIPHIL [a] *pret.* [b] *fut.* HOPHAL [c] *pret.*

12 יָסַד to set, to place ; to set, *i.e.* to place, put, lay a foundation. PUAL *part.*

13 יָסַף to add. HIPHIL *fut.*

14 יָעַד to appoint, to fix upon, with לְ. HIPHIL [a] *fut.* HOPHAL [b] *part.* [c] מוֹעֵד *m.* set time, feast, &c.

15 יָצַב Hithp. to set or place oneself, to take a stand ; with בְּ and עַל of place. HITHPAEL [a] *imp.* [b] *fut.*

16 יָצַג to set, put, or place persons or things in any situation. HIPHIL [a] *pret.* [b] *inf.* [c] *fut.*

17 יָצַק to pour out ; Hiph. to set or lay out, to place ; to set down. HIPHIL *fut.*

18 יָצַת to set (on fire), to kindle. HIPHIL [a] *pret.* [b] *imp.* [c] *fut.*

19 יָקַר to be precious. KAL *fut.*

20 יָשַׁב to sit ; to set, settle, to be fixed, firm, and sure ; Hiph. to make to dwell, to set. KAL [a] *pret.* [b] *fut.* [c] *part.* Poel. PIEL [d] *pret.* HIPHIL [e] *pret.* [f] *inf.* [g] *imp.* [h] *fut.* [i] *part.*

21 יָשַׂם to put, place. KAL *fut* כתיב.

22 יְתַב Ch. to sit. P'AL [a] *pret.* APHEL [b] *pret.*

23 כּוּן to be set in a firm erect position, set fast, Ps. lxv. 6 ; to set things right or in good order ; to dispose in a right, sure, and proper manner (connoting truth, exactness, stability), applied to prayer rightly performed, Ps. cxli. 2, "set forth," set right, directed as incense, so as to answer that emblem of acceptable prayer ; to setting the face right or directly towards an object, Ezek. iv. 7. NIPHAL [a] *fut.* HIPHIL [b] *pret.* [c] *fut.* [d] *part.*

24 כְּלַל Ch. to complete, to finish. SHAPHEL [a] *pret.* ISTHTAPHEL [b] *fut.* (כתיב).

25 מָלֵא to fill, to make full, be filled ; to be fully set, *i.e.* to be filled with boldness : Eccles. viii. 11, comp. Acts ii. 5. Piel, to fill in, *i.e.* to set in sockets. KAL [a] PIEL [b] *pret.* [c] *inf.* [d] *fut.* PUAL [e] *part.* [f] מִלֵּאָה *f.* that which is filled by the insertion of gems. [g] מִלֻּאִים *m. pl.* set.

26 מָנָה to number out, to allot, to appoint. PIEL [a] *pret.* מְנָה Ch. PAEL [b] *pret.* PAEL [c] *imp.*

27 נוּחַ to rest ; to cause to rest. HIPHIL [a] *fut.* [b] נַחַת *m.* "that which should be set on," *marg.* 'the rest of.'

28 נוּעַ to be agitated, shaken. HIPHIL *fut.* "which set me," *i.e.* by violent agitation fixed me on my hands and knees.

29 נָסַךְ to pour out ; to form, to invest, to appoint ; this meaning seems preferable to that of anointing.—*Gussetius, Hengstenberg.* KAL [a] *pret.* NIPHAL [b] *pret.*

30 נָסַע to journey, to set forward (see *Forward*), to set forth. KAL [a] *fut.* HIPHIL [b] *fut.* "set aside," *i.e.* put away ; see *Remove.*

31 נָצַב to set, put, place ; to be set over ; to stand, to stand firmly ; to be fixed, settled. NIPHAL [a] *part.* HIPHIL [b] *pret.* [c] *imp.* [d] *fut.* [e] *part.* HOPHAL [f] *part.* Gen. xxviii. 12, or, was firmly fixed ; see *Ladder ;* which may with great propriety be so rendered, if the subject be, as Bush supposes, symbolical of the kingdom of Christ.

32 נָצַח to be strong, to prevail ; to urge on a work, or "to set forward," to see it done. PIEL *inf.*

33 נָשָׂא to bear, to lift up ; to lift up upon, to set upon. KAL [a] *pret.* [b] *imp.* [c] *fut.* [d] *part.* Poel. [e] מַשָּׂא *m.* lifting up, burden.

34 נָתַן to give ; to place, to fix, to plant ; to place a building, to found it : Ps. viii. 1 may be thus explained, "which glory plant thou above the heavens," *i.e.* let thy glory thus manifested here on earth (verse 2) be acknowledged and celebrated throughout the whole universe ; to appoint, to constitute. KAL [a] *pret.* [b] *inf.* [c] *imp.* [d] *fut.* [e] *part.* Poel. NIPHAL [f] *pret.*

35 סָבַב to compass about. HOPH. *part.* inclosed.

36 סוּג to hedge about, to inclose. KAL *part.* Paül.

37 סוּת to stir up, to set on. HIPHIL [a] *pret.* [b] *part.*

38 סָכַךְ to interweave, to knit together. PILPEL *pret.* Isa. xix. 2, *marg.* 'mingle.' Gesenius, however, makes the Pilpel to mean, to inflame, to incite, to arouse ; which corresponds with our translation.

39 סָמַךְ to lean or rest on anything ; to fix a firm steady resolution in the mind to engage in and go through with an affair. KAL *pret.*

40 עָבַר to pass over. HIPHIL, "to set apart :" *pret.*

41 עוּף to fly. KAL [a] *fut.* כתיב. HIPHIL [b] *fut.*

42 עָלָה to ascend. KAL [a] *fut.* HIPHIL [b] *pret.* [c] *fut.*

43 עָמַד to stand. HIPHIL [a] *pret.* [b] *inf.* [c] *imp.* [d] *fut.*

44 עֶרֶךְ *m.* estimation ; "set at," *marg.* 'of his estimation.'

45 עָשָׂה to do. KAL [a] *pret.* [b] *fut.*

46 פָּלָה to separate, set apart ; to distinguish in an honourable and glorious manner. HIPHIL *pret.*

47 פָּקַד to visit ; to cause to visit ; to appoint. KAL [a] *fut.* HIPHIL [b] *pret.* [c] *imp.* [d] פָּקִיד *m.* officer, overseer.

48 פָּשַׁט to invade, to fall upon. KAL *pret.*

49 פָּתַח to open. KAL *fut.*

50 קָהָה to be blunted ; teeth set on edge. KAL *fut.*

51 קוּם to arise. KAL [a] *pret.* HIPHIL [b] *pret.* [c] *inf.* [d] *imp.* [e] *fut.* [f] *part.* קוּם Ch. APHEL [g] *pret.* [h] *inf.* [i] *fut.* [k] *part.*

52 רוּם to be lifted up ; to bring up. POLEL [a] *pret.* [b] *inf.* [c] *fut.* HIPHIL [d] *pret.* [e] *fut.* רוּם Ch. APHEL [f] *part.*

53 רָכַב to ride ; to make to ride. HIPHIL *fut.*

54 שָׁבַץ to embroider. PUAL *part.*

55 שָׂנֵב to set on high. PIEL *fut.*

56 שׁוּב to return ; to cause to return ; to set again. HIPHIL *fut.*

57 שָׁוָה to be level ; Piel, to set in an even level position, so as to be all in the full view of the eye. PIEL *pret.*

58 שׂוּם to put or set with design, care, exactness ; to put or set in a place, hence to set or plant ; to set a boundary or limit ; to set, to apply the heart to an object ; to set, put, or give a name ; to put or set in a proper order ; to set, settle, order, establish ; to frame and fit for some special use. KAL [a] *pret.* [b] *inf.* [c] *imp.* [d] *fut.* [e] *part.* Poel. HOPHAL [f] *fut.* שׂוּם Ch. P'AL [g] *pret.*

59 שׁית to set, to place, to put; *seq.* בְּ *adnumerare, seq.* עִם *componere, seq.* עַל *imponere adjicere, seq.* מִן *detrahere.*— Fürst. KAL [a] *pret.* [b] *inf.* [c] *imp.* [d] *fut.*

60 שׁכך to incline oneself or stoop down, which a fowler does when setting snares. KAL *inf.*

61 שׁכן to dwell; to make to dwell. PIEL [a] *pret.* [b] *inf.* HIPHIL [c] *fut.*

62 שׁלח to send, to send away, to send to or on. PIEL [a] *pret.* [b] *fut.* [c] מִשְׁלַח *m.* a sending forth, putting forth (of the hand).

63 שׁפת to set, to put, to place, a pot on its supporters on the hearth. KAL *imp.*

64 שׁתת to set, to place, to set the mouth in heaven, *i. e.* to claim divine authority for what they say.

65 תוה to make marks. HIPHIL *pret.*

Gen. i. 17.	34 d	Num. viii. 13.	43 a	1 Sam. xv. 12.	31 e	2 Chron. iii. 5.	42 c	Ps. lxxv. 7.	52 e
iv. 15.	58 d	x. 21.	51 b	xviii. 5.	58 d	iv. 7.	34 d	lxxviii. 7.	58 d
vi. 16.	58 d	xi. 24.	43 d	xviii. 30.	19	iv. 10.	34 a	lxxviii. 8.	23 b
ix. 13.	34 a	xxi. 8.	58 c	xxii. 9.	31 a	vi. 10.	20 b	lxxv. 13.	58 d
xvii. 21.	14 c	xxiv. 1.	59 d	xxvi. 24, 24.	6 a b	vi. 13.	34 d	lxxxvi. 14.	58 a
xviii. 8.	34 d	xxvii. 16.	47 a	xxvii. 22.	58 d	vii. 19.	34 a	lxxxix. 25.	58 a
xix. 16.	11 b	xxvii. 19.	43 a	2 Sam. iii. 10.	51 c	ix. 8.	34 b	lxxxix. 42.	52 d
xxi. 2.	14 c	xxvii. 22.	43 d	vi. 3.	53	xi. 16.	34 e	xc. 8.	59 a
xxi. 28.	31 d	xxix. 39.	14 c	vi. 17.	16 c	xvii. 12.	34 d	xci. 14.	55
xxi. 29.	31 d	Deut. i. 8, 21.	34 a	vii. 12.	51 b	xix. 5.	43 d	ci. 3.	59 d
xxiv. 33.	58 f, or 21	iv. 8.	34 e	xi. 15.	10	xix. 8.	43 a	cii. 13.	14 c
xxviii. 11.	3	iv. 44.	58 a	xii. 20.	58 d	xx. 3.	34 d	civ. 9.	58 a
xxviii. 12.	31 f	xi. 26, 32.	34 e	xiv. 30, 30.	18 b c	xx. 17.	15 a	cvii. 41.	55
xxviii. 18.	58 d	xiv. 24.	58 b	xiv. 31.	18 a	xx. 22.	34 a	cix. 6.	47 c
xxviii. 22.	58 a	xvi. 22.	51 e	xv. 24.	17	xxiii. 10, 19.	43 d	cxiii. 8.	20 f
xxx. 36.	58 d	xvii. 14.	58 a	xviii. 1.	58 d	xxiii. 20.	20 h	cxxii. 5.	20 a
xxx. 38.	16 c	xvii. 15.	58 b d	xviii. 13.	15 b	xxiv. 8.	34 d	cxxxii. 11.	59 d
xxx. 40.	34 d	xvii. 15, 15.	58 d, 34 b	xix. 28.	59 d	xxiv. 25.	43 d	cxl. 5.	59 a
xxxi. 17.	33 c	xix. 14.	5 a	xx. 5.	14 c	xxv. 14.	43 d	cxli. 2.	23
xxxi. 21.	58 d	xxiii. 20.	62 c	xxii. 34.	43 d	xxix. 25.	43 d	cxli. 3.	59 c
xxxi. 37.	58 c	xxiv. 15.	33 d	xxiii. 23.	58 d	xxxi. 3.	14 c	Prov. viii. 23.	29 b
xxxi. 45.	52 e	xxvi. 4, 10.	11 a	1 Kings ii. 15.	58 a	xxxi. 15, 18.	1	viii. 27.	9 a
xxxv. 14, 20.	31 d	xxvii. 2.	51 b	ii. 19.	58 d	xxxii. 6.	34 d	xxii. 28.	45 a
xli. 33.	59 d	xxvii. 4.	51 e	ii. 24.	20 h	xxxiii. 7.	58 d	cxxxii. 5.	41 b, or a
xli. 41.	34 a	xxviii. 1.	34 a	v. 5.	34 d	xxxiii. 19.	43 a	Eccles. iii. 11.	34 a
xliii. 9.	16 a	xxviii. 8, 20.	62 c	vi. 19.	34 b	xxxiv. 12.	32	vii. 14.	45 a
xliii. 31.	58 c	xxviii. 36.	51 e	vi. 27.	34 d	xxxv. 2.	43 d	viii. 11.	25 a
xliii. 32.	58 d	xxviii. 56.	16 b	vii. 16.	34 b	Ezra ii. 68.	43 b	x. 6.	34 f
xliv. 21.	58 d	xxx. 1, 15, 19.	34 a	vii. 21, 21, 21.	51 e	iii. 3.	23 c	xiii. 25.	34 a
xlvii. 7.	43 d	xxxii. 8.	31 d	vii. 39.	34 a	iii. 5.	14 c	xxiii. 41.	58 a
xlviii. 20.	58 d	xxxii. 46.	58 c	viii. 21.	58 d	iii. 8, 9.	32	xxiv. 2.	39
Exod. i. 11.	58 d	Josh. iv. 9.	51 b	ix. 6.	34 a	iii. 10.	43 d	xxiv. 3, 3.	63
iv. 20.	53	vi. 26.	31 d	x. 9.	34 b	iv. 10.	22 b	xxiv. 7.	58 a
vii. 23.	59 a	viii. 8, 19.	18 c	xii. 29.	58 d	iv. 12.	24 a, or b	xxiv. 8.	34 a
ix. 5.	14 c	viii. 12, 13.	58 d	xiv. 4.	51 a	iv. 13, 16.	24 b	xxiv. 11.	43 b
xiii. 12.	40	x. 18.	47 c	xv. 4.	51 c	v. 11.	24 a	xxiv. 25.	33 e
xix. 12.	5 b	xviii. 1.	61 c	xvi. 34.	58 d	vi. 11.	7	xxv. 2.	58 c
xix. 23.	5 c	xxiv. 25.	58 d	xx. 12, 12.	58 c d	vii. 18.	51 g	xxv. 4.	20 d
xxi. 1.	58 d	xxiv. 26.	51 e	xx. 9, 10.	20 g	vii. 25.	26 c	xxvi. 9.	34 d
xxiii. 31.	59 a	Judg. i. 8.	62 a	xxi. 12.	20 e	ix. 9.	52 b	xxvi. 20, 20.	20 e, 34 a
xxv. 7.	25 g	vi. 18.	11 a	2 Kings iv. 4.	30 b	Neh. i. 9.	61 b	xxvii. 10.	58 d
xxv. 30.	34 a	vii. 5.	16 c	iv. 10.	58 d	ii. 6.	34 d	xxviii. 2.	34 b
xxvi. 35.	58 a	vii. 19. α	51 b c	iv. 38.	63	iii. 1, 3, 6, 13, 14, 15.	43 d	xxviii. 6.	34 b
xxviii. 11.	35	vii. 22.	58 d	iv. 43, 44.	34 d	iv. 9, 13, 13.	34 a	xxviii. 14.	34 a
xxviii. 17, 17.	25 b f	ix. 25.	58 d	vi. 22.	58 c	v. 7.	43 a	xxviii. 21.	58 c
xxviii. 20.	54	ix. 33.	48	vii. 3.	62 b	vi. 1.	43 d	xxix. 2.	58 c
xxxi. 5.	25 c	ix. 49.	18 c	x. 3.	58 a	vii. 1.	43 d	xxx. 8.	34 b
xxxv. 9, 27.	25 g	xv. 5.	4 b	xii. 9.	44	ix. 37.	34 a	xxx. 14, 16.	34 a
xxxv. 33.	25 c	xvi. 25.	43 d	xii. 9.	34 d	x. 33.	14 c	xxxii. 4.	52 a
xxxix. 10.	25 d	xviii. 31.	58 d	xvii. 10.	58 d	xiii. 11.	43 d	xxxii. 8.	34 b
xl. 2.	51 e	xx. 22.	13	xvii. 23.	34 b	xiii. 19.	43 a	xxxii. 23.	34 f
xl. 5, 6, 7.	34 a	xx. 29.	58 d	xxi. 7.	58 d	Esth. ii. 17.	58 d	xxxii. 25.	34 a
xl. 8.	58 a	xx. 36.	58 a	xxiv. 19.	47 d	iii. 1.	48	xxxiii. 2, 7.	34 a
xl. 18, 20, 21, 28, 30.	58 d	xx. 48.	62 a	xxv. 28.	34 d	iii. 6.	34 f	xxxiv. 23.	51 b
xl. 33.	34 d	Ruth ii. 5, 6.	34 d	1 Chron. vi. 31.	43 a	viii. 2.	58 d	xxxv. 2.	58 c
Lev. xvii. 10.	34 a	1 Sam. ii. 8, 8.	59 d, 20 f	ix. 22, 26, 31.	1	Job v. 11.	58 b	xxxvii. 1.	27 a
xx. 3.	34 d	v. 2.	16 c	ix. 14.	15 b	vii. 12.	58 d	xxxvii. 26.	34 a
xx. 5.	58 a	v. 3.	56	xi. 25.	58 d	vii. 17.	59 d	xxxvii. 2.	58 c
xx. 6.	34 a	vi. 18.	11 a	xi. 1.	16 c	vii. 20.	58 a	xxxix. 9.	4 a
xxiv. 6.	58 a	vii. 12.	58 d	xxi. 18.	51 c	ix. 19.	14 a	xxxix. 15.	2 a
xxvi. 1.	34 d	ix. 20.	58 d	xxii. 2.	43 d	xiv. 13.	9 b	xxxix. 21.	34 a
xxvi. 11, 17.	34 a	ix. 23.	58 c	xxii. 19.	34 c	xvi. 12.	51 e	xl. 2.	27 a
Num. i. 51.	51 e	ix. 24, 24.	58 d c	xxiii. 4.	32	xix. 8.	58 a	xl. 4.	58 c
ii. 9, 16.	30 a	x. 19.	58 d	xxiii. 4.	14 c	x. 20.	51 f	xliii. 8.	34 b
v. 16, 18, 30.	43 a	xii. 13.	34 a	xxiii. 31.	25 g	xi. 13.	58 a	xliv. 8.	58 d
vii. 1.	51 c	xiii. 8.	14 c	2 Chron. ii. 18.	45 b	xxi. 8.	34 e	Dan. i. 11.	26 a

Lam. iii. 12.	31 d
Ezek. ii. 2.	43 d
iii. 24.	43 d
iv. 2, 2.	34 a, 58 c
iv. 3, 3.	34 a, 23 b
iv. 7.	23 c
v. 5.	58 a
vi. 2.	58 c
vii. 20, 20.	58 a, 34 a
ix. 4.	65
xii. 6.	34 a
xiii. 17.	58 c
xiv. 3.	42 b
xiv. 4.	42 c
xiv. 7.	42 a
xiv. 8.	34 a
xv. 7, 7.	34 a, 58 b
xvi. 18, 19.	34 a
xvii. 4, 5.	58 a
xvii. 22.	34 a
xviii. 2.	50
xx. 8.	34 d
xx. 46.	58 c
xxi. 2.	58 c
xxi. 15.	34 a
xxi. 16.	14 b
xxiii. 24, 24.	58 d, 34 a
xxiii. 25.	34 a
xxiii. 41.	58 a
xxiv. 2.	39
xxiv. 3, 3.	63
xxiv. 7.	58 a
xxiv. 8.	34 a
xxiv. 11.	43 b
xxiv. 25.	33 e
xxv. 2.	58 c
xxv. 4.	20 d
xxvi. 9.	34 d
xxvi. 20, 20.	20 e, 34 a
xxvii. 10.	58 d
xxviii. 2.	34 b
xxviii. 6.	34 b
xxviii. 14.	34 a
xxviii. 21.	58 c
xxix. 2.	58 c
xxx. 8.	34 b
xxx. 14, 16.	34 a
xxxii. 4.	52 a
xxxii. 8.	34 b
xxxii. 23.	34 f
xxxii. 25.	34 a
xxxiii. 2, 7.	34 a
xxxiv. 23.	51 b
xxxv. 2.	58 c
xxxvii. 1.	27 a
xxxvii. 26.	34 a
xxxvii. 2.	58 c
xxxix. 9.	4 a
xxxix. 15.	2 a
xxxix. 21.	34 a
xl. 2.	27 a
xl. 4.	58 c
xliii. 8.	34 b
xliv. 8.	58 d
Dan. i. 11.	26 a
ii. 21.	51 k
ii. 44.	51 i
ii. 49.	58 c
iii. 1, 2, 3, 3, 5, 7, 14, 18.	51 g
iii. 12, 12.	26 b, 51 g
v. 19.	52 f
vi. 1.	51 g
vi. 3.	51 h
vii. 14.	58 g
vii. 10.	22 a
viii. 18.	43 d
ix. 3.	34 d
x. 10.	34 a
x. 12, 15.	34 a
xi. 11, 13.	43 a
xi. 17.	58 d
xii. 11.	34 b
Hos. iii. 3, 3.	16 a, 59 a
iv. 8.	33 c
vi. 11.	59 a
xi. 8.	58 d
Amos vii. 8.	58 c
viii. 5.	49
ix. 4.	58 a
Obad. 4.	58 b
Nah. iii. 6.	58 a
Hab. ii. 1.	15 b

Hab. ii. 9.	58 b	Zech. v. 11.	11 c	Zech. viii. 10.	62 b
Zech. iii. 5, 5.	58 d	vi. 11.	58 a	Mal. iii. 15.	2 b

a lit. setting they had set.   *β see Fitly.*

SETTLE

טָבַע to sink so as to be set fast; applied to the mountains of Chaos settling on their firm foundations. HOPHAL *pret.* Prov. viii. 25.

יָשַׁב to sit, to dwell. HIPHIL *pret.* Ezek. xxxvi. 11.

מָכוֹן place of dwelling, settled place: 1 Kings viii. 13.

נָחַת to go or come down, to descend. PIEL *inf.* Ps. lxv. 10.

נָצַב to stand firm and fixed. NIPHAL *part.* Ps. cxix. 89.

עָמַד to stand. HIPHIL *pret.* 1 Chron. xvii. 14. *fut.* 2 Kings viii. 11.

קָפָא (see *Curdle*) to thicken. KAL *part.* Poel, Zeph. i. 12.

שָׁקַט to be at rest, quiet. KAL *part.* Poel, Jer. xlviii. 11.

SETTLE (N.)

עֲזָרָה *f.* see *Court;* also a ledge or benching round the altar of burnt-offering, upon which the priests stood when attending to the sacrifices, and might take its name from the help or advantage it gave to them in their work: Ezek. xliii. 14, 14, 14, 17, 20; xlv. 19.

SEVEN

שֶׁבַע and שִׁבְעָה *m. adj. num.* cardinal; either a definite number, or sometimes indefinite, to denote abundance or sufficiency; see also *Six;* seven and eight are used in the same sense: 1 Sam. ii. 5: Ruth iv. 15: Jer. xv. 9. שָׁבוּעַ *com.* Ezek. xlv. 21. The festival of sevens of days is the passover, as being celebrated each time during seven whole days. "By sevens" stands in the original "seven seven."

SEVEN STARS

כִּימָה *f.* (see *Pleiades*): Amos v. 8.

SEVENTY

שִׁבְעִים *adj.* seventy, threescore and ten; often put for a large round number.

SEVER

בָּדַל to separate, divide; to select, choose. HIPHIL *fut.* Lev. xx. 26: Deut. iv. 41: Ezek. xxxix. 14.

פָּלָה to separate in a distinguishing marvellous manner. HIPHIL *pret.* Exod. viii. 22, Gr. παραδοξάσω, ix. 4, Gr. *id.;* comp. Wisd. xviii. 8.

פָּרַד to break off; to separate oneself; see *Separate.* NIPHAL *part.* Judg. iv. 11.

SEVERAL

חָפְשׁוּת *f.* (see *Free*): 2 Chron. xxvi. 21, *marg.* 'free;' a sick-house, infirmary, hospital.—*Gesenius.* חָפְשִׁית *f.* 2 Kings xv. 5: 2 Chron. xxvi. 21.

SEW

טָפַל to patch; to sew. KAL *fut.* Job xiv. 17, to sew up, *i.e.* for security and preservation.

תָּפַר to sew together, or, rather, to tie, fasten, fit, adjust. KAL *pret.* Job xvi. 15. *inf.* Eccles. iii. 7. *fut.* Gen. iii. 7. PIEL *part.* Ezek. xiii. 18.

SHADE, SHADOW, SHADY

1 טְלַל Ch. to shade, to overshadow. APHEL *fut.*

2 צֶאֱלִים *m. pl.* supposed to be another form for צְלָלִים shades, *i.e.* shady trees; rendered by Abulwalid, Schultens, and others, *loti sylvestres,* lotus bushes.—*Gesenius.*

3 צָלַל to be shady, dark, obscure. HIPHIL *a part.* *b* צֵלֶל *m.* a shadow. *c* צֵל *m.* shade; also as affording shelter, protection: Gen. xix. 8, &c. *d* צְלָצַל *m.* Isa. xviii. 1, *i.e.* protected by nature and art; and affording protection.

4 צַלְמָוֶת *f.* shadow of death, darkness of death, *i.e.* such as is poured on the eyelids on the approach of death, Job xvi. 16; compounded of צֵל shadow, darkness, מָוֶת death. Hence thickest darkness, *pr.* of that of Sheol, Job x. 21, &c., and *gen. i.q.* חֹשֶׁךְ, but stronger, Job iii. 5, &c., Amos v. 8; of a prison, Ps. cvii. 10, 14. *Metaph.* of evil and calamity, Ps. xliv. 19, Isa. ix. 2; of distress, Job xvi. 16. The desert, as being pathless, is also called the land of the shadow of death, Jer. ii. 6.

No. 3 c not included.

Job iii. 5.	4	Job xl. 21.	2	Isa. xviii. 1.	3 d
x. 21, 22.	4	xli. 22, 22.	2, 3 b	Jer. ii. 6.	4
xii. 22.	4	Ps. xxiii. 4.	4	vi. 4.	3 b
xvi. 16.	4	xliv. 19.	4	xiii. 16.	4
xxiv. 17, 17.	4	cvii. 10, 14.	4	Ezek. xxxi. 3.	3 a
xxviii. 3.	4	Cant. ii. 17.	3 b	Dan. iv. 12.	1
xxxiv. 22.	4	iv. 6.	3 b	Amos v. 8.	4
xxxviii. 17.	4	Isa. ix. 2.	4		

SHAFT

חֵץ *m.* arrow or dart; the shaft of a spear: Isa. xlix. 2.

יָרֵךְ *f.* thigh; the shaft of the golden candlestick: Exod. xxv. 31; xxxvii. 17: Num. viii. 4.

SHAHAR

שַׁחַר *m.* morning: Ps. xxii. title.

SHAKE

1 גָּעַשׁ to push, to thrust, to shake by a sudden impulse; to be shaken, to be moved violently to and fro; to quake; so also once in Kal, Ps. xviii. 7. In the parallel passage, 2 Sam. xxii. 8, Hithpael is read, which is more frequent in this signification; yet in the Psalm the writer seems to have employed Kal intransitively for the sake of a paronomasia in the words תִּגְעַשׁ וַתִּרְעַשׁ. KAL *a fut.* HITHPAEL *b fut.*

2 חִיל see *Tremble.* KAL and HIPHIL *fut.*

3 חָמַס to do violence; to tear off with violence, to shake off. KAL *fut.*

4 מוֹט to move, to shake, to totter; see *Move.* KAL *pret.*

5 מָעַד to waver, to be unsteady, to totter. HIPHIL *imp.*

6 נָדַף to drive away. NIPHAL *part.*

7 נוּד see *Remove.* KAL *a fut.* *b* מָנוֹד *m.* nodding of the head in token of derision.

8 נוּעַ to move to and fro; to shake the head, a gesture of scorn,

insult, contumely ; probably not the shaking the head, the usual token of denial, refusal, but a continued nodding to any one, which, although a usual sign of assent or approval, may also imply assent and joy in one's adversity and calamity ; just as the clapping of hands assent and approbation, but also scorn ; *comp.* Lakemacher, Observ., vii. p. 56, *sq. ;* Ges. Thesaurus, p. 865. NIPHAL [a] *fut.* HIPHIL [b] *pret.* [c] *fut.*

9 נוּף to lift up the hand repeatedly, to move or wave the hand up and down, to shake. POLEL [a] *fut.* HIPHIL [b] *pret.* [c] *inf.* [d] *imp.* [e] *part.* [f] תְּנוּפָה *f.* lifting up the hand.

10 נָעַר to move with agility and vigour ; to toss away, to shake off violently and vehemently. KAL [a] *pret.* [b] *part.* Poel. [c] *part.* Paül. NIPHAL [d] *fut.* PIEL [e] *fut.* HITHPAEL [f] *imp.*

11 נֹקֶף *m.* the beating of an olive-tree, in distinction from the first gathering ; the second was left to the poor.

12 נְתַר Ch. to fall off. APHEL *imp.*

13 עָרַץ to terrify, to make afraid ; to shake terribly. KAL *inf.*

14 פּוּץ to break in pieces ; to scatter. PILPEL *fut.*

15 פָּחַד to fear. HIPHIL *pret.*

16 רָגַז to be moved, thrown into commotion, to tremble. HIPHIL [a] *pret.* [b] *fut.* [c] *part.*

17 רָחַף according to the ancient versions, to tremble, to shake. KAL *pret.* Jer. xxiii. 9. Gesenius, all my bones are relaxed, from terror.

18 רָעַל to be violently shaken ; to be giddy, to reel. HOPHAL *pret.*

19 רָעַשׁ to shake violently, as the quick vibration of a spear, Job xli. 29. It is most commonly applied to the concussion or violent shaking of the earth, the heavens, the sea, the mountains, nations, kingdoms ; and sometimes, at least, signifieth such a shaking as produceth an alteration, and putteth things into a new state ; see Hag. ii. 6, 7, and Heb. xii. 26, 27. KAL [a] *pret.* [b] *fut.* HIPHIL [c] *pret.* [d] *part.* [e] רַעַשׁ *m.* shaking.

20 שָׁמַט to stumble. KAL *pret.*

Lev. xxvi. 36.	6	Ps. xlvi. 3.	19 b	Isa. xxx. 32.	9 f		
Judg. xvi. 20.	10 d	lx. 2.	4	xxxiii. 9, 15.	10 b		
2 Sam. vi. 6.	20	lxviii. 8.	19 a	xxxvii. 22.	8 b		
xxii. 8, 8.	1 b	lxx. 23.	5	lii. 2.	10 f		
1 Kings xiv. 15.	7 a	lxxii. 16.	19 b	Jer. xxiii. 9.	17		
2 Kings xix. 21.	8 b	lxxvii. 18.	19 b	Ezek. xxvi. 10, 15.	19 b		
Neh. v. 13, 13,		cix. 25.	8 c	xxvii. 28.	19 b		
13.	10 a e c	Isa. ii. 19, 21.	13	xxxi. 16.	19 c		
Job iv. 14.	15	x. 15, 15.	9 e c	xxxvii. 7.	19 e		
ix. 6.	16 c	x. 32.	9 a	xxxviii. 19.	19 e		
xv. 33.	3	xiii. 2.	9 b	xxxviii. 20.	19 a		
xvi. 4.	8 c	xiii. 2.	9 d	Dan. iv. 14.	12		
xvi. 12.	14	xiii. 13.	16 b	Joel iii. 16.	19 a		
xxxviii. 13.	10 d	xiv. 16.	19 d	Amos ix. 1.	19 b		
xli. 29.	19 e	xvii. 6.	11	Nah. ii. 3.	18		
Ps. xviii. 7, 7.	1 a b	xix. 16, 16.	9 f e	iii. 12.	8 a		
xxii. 1.	8 c	xxiii. 11.	16 a	Hag. ii. 6, 21.	19 d		
xxix. 8, 8.	2	xxiv. 13.	11	ii. 7.	19 c		
xliv. 14.	7 b	xxiv. 18.	19 b	Zech. ii. 9.	9 e		

SHAME

1 בּוּז *m.* contempt ; see *Despise.*

2 בּוֹשׁ see *Ashamed.* KAL [a] *pret.* HIPHIL [b] *pret.* [c] *fut.* [d] *part.* [e] בּוּשָׁה *f.* shame, ignominy. [f] בֹּשֶׁת *f.* shame ; disgrace, ignominy ; in Ps. xl. 15 to be understood actively. [g] בָּשְׁנָה *f.* shame.

3 גָּלָה to uncover. NIPHAL *inf.,* "shamelessly," *marg.* 'or, openly.'

4 חָסַד the primary idea seems to be that of strong feeling, zeal, and ardour, which shows itself either in kindness or reproach ; it means, therefore, not only to show kindness, but to treat with reproach ; see *Mercy, Kind.* PIEL *fut.*

5 יָבֵשׁ see *Ashamed.* HIPHIL *pret.*

6 חָפֵר see *Ashamed.* It applies to being frustrated and disappointed of one's plans and expectations. KAL [a] *pret.* [b] *fut.* HIPHIL [c] *fut.*

7 חֶרְפָּה *f.* reproach, contempt.

8 כָּלַם see *Ashamed.* This is a stronger word than its *synon.* בּוֹשׁ. NIPHAL [a] *fut.* HIPHIL [b] *pret.* [c] *inf.* [d] *fut.* [e] *part.* [f] כְּלִמָּה *f.* shame, ignominy ; usually in a passive sense, yet in Ezek. xxxvi. 6, 15, of the shame caused by the heathen. [g] כְּלִמּוּת *f.* state of shame.

9 עֶרְוָה *f.* nakedness.

10 קָלוֹן *m.* contempt, shame, dishonour ; shameful deed.

11 שִׁמְצָה *f.* the Hebrew and other ancient interpreters give the meaning of this word, ill-fame, reproach, comparing it with שֵׁמַע, fame, the letters צ and ע being interchanged ; but Gesenius says that rout, overthrow of enemies, is the only correct meaning.

Gen. xxxviii. 23.	1	Ps. cxix. 31.	2 c	Jer. xiii. 26.	10
Exod. xxxii. 25.	11	cxxxii. 18.	2 f	xx. 18.	2 f
Judg. xviii. 7.	8 e	Prov. iii. 35.	10	xxiii. 40.	8 g
1 Sam. xx. 34.	8 b	ix. 7.	10 b	xlvii. 12.	10
2 Sam. vi. 20.	3	x. 5.	2 d	xlviii. 39.	2 a
xiii. 13.	7	xi. 2.	10	li. 51.	8 f
xix. 5.	5	xii. 16.	10	Ezek. vii. 18.	2 e
2 Chron. xxxii. 21.	2 f	xiii. 5.	6 c c	xvi. 52, 52, 54, 63.	8 f
Job viii. 22.	2 f	xiii. 18.	10	xxxii. 24, 25, 30.	8 f
Ps. iv. 2.	2 f	xiv. 31.	10	xxxiv. 29.	8 f
xiv. 6.	2 c	xvii. 2.	2 d	xxxvi. 6, 7, 15.	8 f
xxxv. 4.	8 a	xviii. 13.	8 f	xxxix. 26.	8 f
xxxv. 26.	2 f	xix. 26.	2 d	xliv. 13.	8 f
xl. 14.	8 a	xxv. 8.	8 c	Dan. iii. 2.	7
xl. 15.	2 f	xxv. 10.	4	Hos. ii. 5.	5
xliv. 7.	2 b	xxviii. 7.	8 d	iv. 7, 18.	10
xliv. 9.	8 d	xxix. 15.	2 d	ix. 10.	2 f
xliv. 15.	2 f	Isa. xx. 4.	9	x. 6.	2 g
liii. 5.	2 b	xxii. 18.	10	Obad. 10.	2 e
lxix. 7.	8 f	xxx. 3, 5.	2 f	Micah i. 11.	2 f
lxix. 19.	2 f	xlvii. 3.	7	vii. 10.	8 f
lxx. 3.	8 f	l. 6.	8 f	vii. 10.	2 e
lxxi. 24.	6 a	liv. 4, 4.	6 c, 2 f	Nah. iii. 5.	10
lxxxiii. 16.	10	lxi. 7.	2 f	Hab. ii. 10.	2 f
lxxxiii. 17.	6 b	Jer. iii. 24, 25.	2 f	ii. 16.	10
lxxxix. 45.	2 e	xi. 13.	2 f	Zeph. iii. 5, 19.	2 f
cix. 29.	8 f				

SHAPEN

חוּל to travail in childbirth ; to bring forth. PULAL *pret.* Ps. li. 5.

SHARE

מַחֲרֶשֶׁת *f.* ploughshare : 1 Sam. xiii. 20.

SHARP

1 חָדַד to be sharp ; to sharpen. KAL [a] *fut.* HIPHIL [b] *fut.* HOPHAL [c] *pret.* [d] חַדּוּדִים *m. pl.* sharpness, a point : Job xli. 30, *marg.* ' sharp pieces of a potsherd' are under him, *i. e.* his skin is so hard that he feels them not, even when they are his bed. [e] חַד *adj.* sharp.

2 חָזְקָה *f.* strength, force.

3 חָרוּץ *m.* sharpened, pointed.

4 לָטַשׁ to sharpen, to whet a tool : Job xiv. 9, "mine enemy sharpeneth his eyes upon me," beholds me with a stern and threatening look. KAL [a] *inf.* [b] *fut.* PUAL [c] *part.*

5 נָצַב to stand, to set. HIPHIL *inf.*

6 צוּר *m.* a rock ; a sharp stone used as a knife. צֹר [a] *m. id.*

7 שָׁנַן to whet. KAL [a] *pret.* [b] *part.* Poel. [c] שֵׁן *com.* the ridge of a rock.

Exod. iv. 25.	6 a	Job xli. 30, 30.	1 d, 3	Prov. xxv. 18.	7 b
Josh. v. 2, 3.	6	Ps. xlv. 5.	7 b	xxvii. 17, 17.	1 a b
Judg. viii. 1.	2	lii. 2.	c	Isa. v. 28.	7 b
1 Sam. xiii. 20.	4 a	lvii. 4.	1 e	xli. 15.	3
xiii. 21.	5	cxx. 4.	7 b	xlix. 2.	1 c
xiv. 4, 4.	7 c	cxl. 3.	7 a	Ezek. v. 1.	1 e
Job xvi. 9.	4 b	Prov. v. 4.	1 e	xxi. 9, 10, 11.	1 c

SHAVE

1 גָּזַז to shear. KAL *fut.*

2 גָּלַח to make bare, bald ; to shave the head or beard, which was a token of servitude and indignity. PIEL [a] *pret.* [b] *fut.* PUAL [c] *pret.* [d] *part.* HITHPAEL [e] *pret.* [f] *inf.*

3 עָבַר to pass. HIPHIL, to cause (a razor) to pass over : *pret.*

4 תַּעַר *m.* razor.

Gen. xli. 14.	2 b	Num. vi. 18.	2 a	2 Sam. x. 4.	2 b
Lev. xiii. 33, 33.	2 e b	vi. 19.	2 f	1 Chron. xix. 4.	2 b
xiv. 8.	2 a	viii. 7.	3, 4	Job i. 20.	1
xiv. 9, 9.	2 b	Deut. xxi. 12.	4	Isa. vii. 20.	2 b
xxi. 5.	2 b	Judg. xvi. 17, 22.	2 c	Jer. xli. 5.	2 d
Num. vi. 9, 9.	2 a b	xvi. 19.	2 b	Ezek. xliv. 20.	2 b

SHEAF

אֲלֻמָּה *f.* a bundle, sheaf, of grain : Gen. xxxvii. 7, 7, 7, 7 : Ps. cxxvi. 6.

עֹמֶר *m.* a handful of grain, a sheaf : Lev. xxiii. 10, *marg.* 'omer, *or*, handful,' 11, 12, 15 : Deut. xxiv. 19 : Ruth ii. 7, 15 : Job xxiv. 10. עָמִיר *m.* Amos ii. 13 : Micah iv. 12 : Zech. xii. 6.

עֲרֵמָה *f.* a heap of corn, &c. : Neh. xiii. 15.

SHEAR

1 גָּזַז to cut, to mow, to shear a flock ; it was, however, the most ancient custom to pluck off the fleece, according to Varro ; see Paxton, i. p. 84. KAL [a] *inf.* [b] *fut.* [c] *part.* Poel.

2 רָעָה to feed. KAL *part.* Poel.

3 עָקַד to binding of sheep in the four legs for shearing or for sacrifice : see Bochart.

4 קָצַב to cut down. KAL *part.* Paül.

Gen. xxxi. 19.	1 a	1 Sam. xxv. 2.	1 a	2 Kings x. 14.	3
xxxviii. 12.	1 c	xxv. 4, 7, 11.	1 c	Cant. iv. 2.	4
xxxviii. 13.	1 a	2 Sam. xiii. 23, 24.	1 c	Isa. liii. 7.	1 c
Deut. xv. 19.	1 b	2 Kings x. 12.	2, 3		

SHEAR-JASHUB

שְׁאָר *m.* remnant. שׁוּב to return. KAL *fut.* Isa. vii. 3.

SHEATH

נָדָן *m.* sheath of a sword : 1 Chron. xxi. 27.

תַּעַר *m.* razor ; also a sheath, of a sword, perhaps as being made empty : 1 Sam. xvii. 51 : 2 Sam. xx. 8 : Ezek. xxi. 3, 4, 5, 30.

SHED

1 נָגַר to flow ; to pour out ; with דָּם understood ; or, *trop.* to deliver up, to give over. HIPHIL *fut.*

2 שׂוּם to put, set, place. KAL *fut.*

3 שָׁפַךְ to pour out, to shed. KAL [a] *pret.* [b] *inf.* [c] *fut.* [d] *part.* Poel. [e] *part.* Paül. NIPHAL [f] *fut.* PUAL [g] *pret.*

Gen. ix. 6, 6.	3 d f	1 Chron. xxii. 8, 8.	3 a	Lam. iv. 13.	3 d
xxxvii. 22.	3 c	xxviii. 3.	3 a	Ezek. xvi. 38.	3 d
Lev. xvii. 4.	3 a	Ps. lxxix. 3.	3 a	xviii. 10.	3 d
Num. xxxv. 33, 33.	3 g d	lxxix. 10.	3 e	xxii. 3.	3 d
Deut. xix. 10.	3 f	cvi. 38.	3 e	xxii. 6, 9, 12, 27.	3 b
xxi. 7.	3 a	Prov. i. 16.	3 b	xxiii. 45.	3 d
1 Sam. xxv. 31.	3 b	vi. 17.	3 b	xxxiii. 25.	3 c
2 Sam. xx. 10.	3 c	Isa. lix. 7.	3 b	xxxv. 5.	1
1 Kings ii. 5.	2	Jer. vii. 6.	3 b	xxxvi. 18.	3 a
ii. 31.	3 a	xxii. 3.	3 c	Joel iii. 19.	3 a
2 Kings xxi. 16.	3 b	xxii. 17.	3 b		
xxiv. 4.	3 a				

SHEEP

1 כֶּבֶשׂ *m.* a he-lamb, a young ram.

2 כֶּשֶׂב *m.* the same, by a transposition of letters.

3 צֹאן *com.* flock, flocks, *i. e.* small cattle, sheep, and goats : Gen. iv. 2, &c. צֹאון *com.* (כתיב).

4 צֹנֵא *com.* flocks, small cattle, especially sheep. [a] צֹנֶה *com.* *marg.* 'flocks.'

5 רָחֵל *f.* a sheep, an ewe.

6 שֶׂה *com.* one of a flock, *i. e.* a sheep or goat ; a noun of unity corresponding to the *collect.* צֹאן a flock of sheep or goats : Deut. xiv. 4, one of the sheep and one of the goats.

No. 3 not included.

Gen. xxx. 32, 33, 35.	2	Num. xviii. 17.	2	1 Sam. xv. 3.	6
Exod. xii. 5.	1	xxxii. 24.	4	xxii. 19.	6
xxii. 1, 1, 1.	6, 3, 6	Deut. xiv. 4. a	6, 2	Job xxxi. 20.	1
xxii. 4, 9, 10.	6	xvii. 1.	6	Ps. viii. 7.	4 a
xxxiv. 19.	6	xviii. 3.	6	cxix. 176.	6
Lev. i. 10.	2	xxii. 1.	6	cxliv. 13.	3, 3 a
vii. 23.	2	Josh. vi. 21.	6	Cant. vi. 6.	5
xxii. 19, 27.	2	Judg. vi. 4.	6	Isa. liii. 7.	6
xxvii. 26.	6	1 Sam. xiv. 34.	6	Jer. l. 17.	6

a lit. the lamb of sheep.

SHEEPCOTE

נָוֶה *m.* habitation ; a pasture, where flocks and herds remain, lie down and rest : 2 Sam. vii. 8 : 1 Chron. xvii. 7.

SHEEPFOLD

מִשְׁפְּתַיִם *dual,* folds, enclosures, open above, often made of hurdles, in which in the summer months the flocks are kept by night. The Hebrews seem to have used the dual form on account of the folds of this kind being divided into two parts for the different kinds of flocks. 'To lie down among the folds' seems to be spoken proverbially of shepherds and husbandmen living in leisure and quiet. Judg. v. 16.

SHEEPMASTER

נֹקֵד *m.* a sheep-owner : 2 Kings iii. 4.

SHEEPSHEARER (See SHEAR)

SHEET

סָדִין *m.* a shirt, or wide under garment of linen worn next the body : Judg. xiv. 12, 13. There is no reason for thinking what we call sheets were meant ; see Paxton.

SHEKEL

בֶּקַע *m.* a part, half ; specially half a shekel : Gen. xxiv. 22.

שֶׁקֶל *m.* shekel, *siclus*, a definite weight of gold or silver, containing twenty gerahs, *i.e.* grains, perhaps kernels, beans, Exod. xxx. 13 ; and this being weighed out passed as current money among the Hebrews. Two kinds of shekel are distinguished—the shekel of the sanctuary, Exod. xxx. 13, and the king's shekel, 2 Sam. xiv. 26 ; but which of these was the heaviest cannot be known. Gen. xxiii. 15, &c.

SHELTER

מַחְסֶה *m.* refuge : Job xxiv. 8 : Ps. lxi. 3.

SHEMINITH

שְׁמִינִית *adj. ord.* eighth ; an octave in music, a word denoting the lowest and gravest notes of the scale sung by men, the modern bass.—*Gesenius.* 1 Chron. xv. 21 : Ps. vi. title ; xii. title.

SHEPHERD

צֹאן *com.* sheep or goats : Gen. xlvi. 32, 34 ; xlvii. 3.

רָעָה to feed. KAL *part.* Poel, Gen. xlvi. 32, *lit.* feeders of sheep, 34, &c. Shepherd is a title given to kings, Isa. xliv. 28 ; also to the Messiah, Zech. xiii. 7. רֹעִי *m.* Isa. xxxviii. 12 : Zech. xi. 17.

SHERD

חֶרֶשׂ *m.* potsherd : Isa. xxx. 14 : Ezek. xxiii. 34.

SHERIFFS

תִּפְתָּיֵא Ch. *m. pl.* persons learned in the law, lawyers : Dan. iii. 2, 3.

SHEW

הַכָּרָה *f.* a beholding : Isa. iii. 9, shew, *i.e.* aspect, air, implying pride.

צֶלֶם *m.* image : Ps. xxxix. 6, *marg.* 'an image,' *i.e.* a shadow, a faint sketch or resemblance, no substance.

SHEW, SHEW-BREAD

מַעֲרֶכֶת *f.* a row, pile, ranged in order, as of the shew-bread or loaves set out in rows before Jehovah in the temple : 1 Chron. ix. 32 ; xxiii. 29 ; xxviii. 16 : 2 Chron. ii. 4 ; xiii. 11 ; xxix. 18 : Neh. x. 33.

פָּנִים *m. pl.* face, presence ; the shew-bread was twelve loaves set out in the holy place every sabbath, representing the spiritual food provided in the family of God. See Bush on Exod. xxv. 30. Exod. xxv. 30, *lit.* bread of faces ; xxxv. 13, *lit. id. ;* xxxix. 36 : Num. iv. 7, *lit.* table of faces : 1 Sam. xxi. 6, *lit.* bread of faces : 1 Kings vii. 48 : 2 Chron. iv. 19.

SHEW

1 אֹזֶן *m.* the ear ; to shew to one, *lit.* to uncover the ear.

2 בָּשַׂר to bring good tidings ; to shew forth. PIEL [a] *imp.* [b] *fut.*

3 גָּלָה to make naked, to uncover, and then to disclose, to reveal ; especially in the phrase, to make bare or uncover the ear of any one, by removing the overhanging locks, in whispering a secret to another ; hence to tell to any one, to disclose, to shew ; also in a slightly different sense spoken of God, Job xxxvi. 10 ; see *Open.* KAL [a] *pret.* [b] *fut.* [c] *part.* Poel. NIPHAL [d] *imp.* [e] *fut.* PIEL [f] *pret.*

4 חָוָה to breathe ; to breathe out, to declare, to shew. PIEL [a] *inf.* [b] *fut.* חֲוָה Ch. PAEL [c] *fut.* APHEL [d] *inf.* [e] *imp.* [f] *fut.* [g] אַחֲוָיָה Ch. shewing, argument.

5 יָדַע to know ; to make to know. HIPHIL [a] *pret.* [b] *inf.* [c] *imp.* [d] *fut.*

6 יָטַב to be good, to do good. HIPHIL *pret.*

7 יָפַע to shine forth. HIPHIL *imp.*

8 יָרָה to cast ; to cast out, *e. g.* the hand to shew. HIPHIL *fut.*

9 נָגַד to bring to light ; to shew, to exhibit before any one, to shew openly ; to shew, to tell, to declare, to announce. HIPHIL [a] *pret.* [b] *inf.* [c] *imp.* [d] *fut.* [e] *part.* HOPHAL [f] *pret.* [g] *inf.*

10 נָטָה to stretch out, to extend. KAL *fut.*

11 נָתַן to give. KAL [a] *pret.* [b] *imp.* [c] *fut.*

12 סָפַר to number ; to tell, to declare, to explain, to preach. PIEL [a] *fut.* [b] *part.*

13 עָשָׂה to do, &c. KAL [a] *pret.* [b] *inf.* [c] *imp.* [d] *fut.* [e] *part.* Poel.

14 פָּרַשׁ to separate, distinguish ; to declare distinctly. KAL *inf.*

15 צוּץ to glitter, to flourish ; Hiphil, to glitter, to sparkle, hence to glance, to look by stealth. HIPHIL *part.*

16 רָאָה to see. KAL [a] *fut.* NIPHAL [b] *pret.* [c] *inf.* [d] *imp.* [e] *fut.* HIPHIL [f] *pret.* [g] *inf.* [h] *imp.* [i] *fut.* [k] *part.* HOPHAL [l] *pret.* [m] *part.*

17 שׂוּם to set, put, place. KAL *pret.*

18 שִׂית to set, place. KAL *inf.*

19 שָׁמַע to hear, to make to hear. HIPHIL [a] *pret.* [b] *fut.*

Gen. xii. 1.	16 i	Exod. xv. 25.	8	Deut. iii. 24.	16 g
xix. 19.	13 a	xviii. 20.	5 a	iv. 35.	16 l
xx. 13.	13 d	xx. 6.	13 e	iv. 36.	16 f
xxiv. 12.	13 c	xxv. 9.	16 k	v. 5.	9 b
xxiv. 14.	13 a	xxv. 40.	16 m	v. 10.	13 e
xxxii. 10.	13 a	xxvi. 30.	16 l	v. 24.	16 f
xxxix. 21.	10	xxvii. 8.	16 f	vii. 22.	11 c
xl. 14.	13 a	xxxiii. 18.	5 c	xiii. 17.	11 a
xli. 25.	9 a	xxxiii. 18.	16 h	xvii. 9.	9 a
xli. 28.	16 f	Lev. xiii. 19.	16 b	xvii. 10, 11.	9 d
xli. 39.	5 b	xiii. 49.	16 l	xxxii. 7.	9 d
xlvi. 31.	9 d	xxiv. 12.	14	xxxiv. 1.	16 i
xlviii. 11.	16 f	Num. iv. 7.	16 f	xxxiv. 12.	13 a
Exod. vii. 9.	11 b	xiii. 26.	16 i	Josh. ii. 12, 12.	13 a
ix. 16.	16 g	xiv. 11.	13 a	v. 6.	16 g
x. 1.	18	xvi. 5.	5 d	Judg. i. 24, 24.	16 h, 13 a
xiii. 8.	9 a	xxiii. 3.	16 i	i. 25.	16 i
xiv. 13.	13 d	Deut. i. 33.	16 g	iv. 12.	9 d

Judg. iv. 22.	16 i	2 Chron. vii. 10.	13 a	Isa. xli. 22, 22.	9 d c
vi. 17.	13 a	Ezra ii. 59.	9 b	xli. 23.	9 c
viii. 35, 35.	13 a	Neh. vii. 61.	9 b	xli. 26.	9 e
xiii. 10.	9 d	ix. 10.	11 c	xliii. 9.	19 b
xiii. 23.	16 f	Esth. i. 4, 11.	16 g	xliii. 12.	19 a
xvi. 18.	9 a	ii. 10, 10.	9 a d	xliii. 21.	12 a
Ruth ii. 11.	9 g f	ii. 20.	9 e	xliv. 7.	9 d
ii. 19.	9 d	iii. 6.	9 a	xlvi. 6.	17
iii. 10. α	6	iv. 8.	16 g	xlviii. 3.	19 b
1 Sam. iii. 15.	9 b	Job x. 2.	5 c	xlviii. 5, 6.	19 a
viii. 9.	9 a	xi. 6.	9 d	xlix. 9.	3 d
ix. 6.	9 d	xv. 17.	9 d	lviii. 1.	9 c
ix. 27.	19 b	xxxii. 6. β	4 a	lx. 6.	2 b
x. 8.	5 a	xxxii. 10, 17.	4 b	Jer. xi. 18.	16 f
xi. 9.	9 d	xxxiii. 23.	9 b	xvi. 10.	9 d
xiv. 12.	5 d	xxxvi. 2.	4 b	xvi. 21.	11 c
xv. 6.	13 a	xxxvi. 9, 33.	9 d	xviii. 17. γ	16 a
xvi. 3.	5 d	Ps. iv. 6.	16 i	xxiv. 1.	16 f
xix. 7.	9 d	ix. 1, 14.	12 a	xxxii. 18.	13 e
xx. 2.	3 b, 1	xvi. 11.	5 d	xxxiii. 3.	9 d
xx. 12.	3 a, 1	xviii. 50.	13 e	xxxviii. 21.	16 f
xx. 13.	3 a, 1	xix. 1.	9 e	xli. 3.	9 d
xx. 14.	13 d	xix. 2.	4 b	xli. 12.	11 c
xxii. 8, 8.	3 c, 1	xxv. 4.	5 c	Ezek. xi. 25.	9 b
xxii. 17.	3 a, 1	xxv. 14.	5 b	xx. 11.	5 a
xxii. 22.	9 d	l. 23.	16 i	xxii. 2.	5 a
xxiv. 18.	9 a	li. 15.	9 d	xxii. 26.	5 a
xxv. 8.	9 d	lx. 3.	16 f	xxxiii. 31.	13 e
2 Sam. ii. 5.	13 a	lxxi. 15.	12 a	xxxvii. 18.	9 d
ii. 6.	13 d	lxxi. 18.	9 d	xl. 4, 4.	16 k g
iii. 8.	13 d	lxxi. 20.	16 f	xliii. 10.	9 c
ix. 1, 3.	13 d	lxxviii. 4.	12 b	xliii. 11.	9 c
ix. 7.	13 b d	lxxviii. 11.	16 f	Dan. ii. 2.	9 d
x. 2, 2.	13 d a	lxxix. 13.	12 a	ii. 4, 11, 24.	4 c
xi. 22.	9 d	lxxxv. 7.	16 h	ii. 6, 6.	4 f e
xv. 25.	16 f	lxxxvi. 17.	13 c	ii. 7, 9.	4 f
xxii. 51.	13 e	lxxxviii. 10.	13 d	ii. 10, 16, 27.	4 d
1 Kings i. 27.	5 a	xci. 16.	16 i	iv. 2.	4 d
ii. 7.	13 d	xcii. 2, 15.	9 b	v. 7.	4 c
iii. 6.	13 a	xciv. 1.	7	v. 12, 12.	4 g f
xvi. 27.	13 a	xcvi. 3.	2 a	v. 15.	4 d
xviii. 1.	16 d	xcviii. 2.	3 f	ix. 23.	9 b
xviii. 2.	16 c	cv. 27.	17	x. 21.	9 d
xviii. 15.	16 e	cvi. 2.	19 b	xi. 2.	9 d
xxii. 45.	13 a	cix. 16.	13 b	Joel ii. 30.	11 a
2 Kings vi. 6.	16 i	cxi. 6.	9 a	Amos vii. 1, 4, 7.	16 f
vi. 11.	9 d	cxi. 6.	9 d	viii. 1.	16 f
vii. 12.	9 d	cxiii. 2.	9 e	Micah vi. 8.	9 a
viii. 10, 13.	16 f	cxlvii. 19.	9 e	vii. 15.	16 i
xi. 4.	16 i	Prov. xii. 17.	9 d	Nah. iii. 5.	16 f
xx. 13, 13.	16 i f	xxvi. 26.	3 e	Hab. iii. 3.	16 i
xx. 15.	16 f	xxvii. 25.	16 b	Zech. i. 9, 20.	16 i
xxii. 10.	9 d	Cant. ii. 9.	15	iii. 1.	16 i
1 Chron. xvi. 23.	2 a	Isa. xxx. 30.	16 i	vii. 9.	13 c
xx. 2, 2.	13 d a	xxxix. 2, 2.	16 i f		
2 Chron. i. 8.	13 a	xl. 14.	5 d		

α *lit.* thou hast made good thy kindness. β *lit.* was afraid from shewing.
γ *lit.* I will look on them (with) the back and not the face.

No. 1 not included.

1 Sam. xvii. 7, 41.	3	2 Chron. xi. 12.	3	Ps. xci. 4.	3
xvii. 45.	2	xxiii. 9.	2	Cant. iv. 4.	3
2 Sam. viii. 7.	4	xxv. 5.	2	Jer. xlvi. 3.	3
1 Kings xi. 10.	4	Job xxxix. 23.	2	li. 11.	4
1 Chron. xii. 8, 24, 34.	3	Ps. v. 12.	4	Ezek. xxvii. 11.	4
xviii. 7.	4				

SHIGGAION, SHIGIONOTH

שִׁגָּיוֹן *m.* song, psalm, hymn, Gesenius; others a wandering song, or song of errors, having respect to the errors and transgressions of the wicked, Hengstenberg: Ps. vii. title: Hab. iii. 1. Vulg. a prayer for ignorance.

SHILOH

שִׁילֹה The most approved derivation of this most difficult word, in Gen. xlix. 13, is that which deduces it from שָׁלָה, to be at rest, to be in peace and prosperity; and so שׁילה is the Pacificator, or Prince of peace, the promised seed of the woman, who should destroy the rule and dominion of Satan, and establish peace in the world in the place of the tyranny of evil. "It signifies one, quiet, prosperous, peaceable, happy, honourable; a conqueror, to whom all things succeed well and happily."—*Mercer.* There can be no doubt that Shiloh is a name of the Messiah, so understood by the ancient Jewish interpreters, though variously explained by them. It does not fall within the province of this work to enumerate this variety; the reader is referred to Pfeifferi Dubia Vexata, pp. 106, &c., and 575, &c. The ancient versions seem to have given the meaning, "whose it is," to this word, as if it were compounded of שֶׁ *i.q.* אֲשֶׁר and לה *i.q.* לוֹ to him. Lxx. ᾧ καθήκει; in several MSS. τὰ ἀποκείμενα αὐτῷ, which are laid up for him; in others (with Symm.) ᾧ ἀπόκειται, for whom it is laid up. Syr. Saad. *is cujus est.* Targ. Onkel. *Messias, cujus regnum est; comp.* Ezek. xxi. 32.

SHIBBOLETH

שִׁבֹּלֶת *f.* an ear of corn: Judg. xii. 6.

SHIELD

1 מָגֵן *m.* a shield of less size and weight than the צִנָּה; see 1 Kings x. 16, 17, 2 Chron. ix. 16. Shields were anointed, whether made of a hide or of brass, to preserve them, and to make weapons more easily glance from them. *Metaph.* of God as a protector, and of princes, chiefs, protecting by their valour: Ps. xlvii. 10: Hos. iv. 18.—Gen. xv. 1, &c.

2 כִּידוֹן *m.* spear or lance; see *Target.*

3 צִנָּה *f.* a shield of the largest size, covering the whole body, θυρεὸς; from the middle rose a large boss, surmounted by a dagger or sharp-pointed protuberance, offensive as well as defensive.

4 שֶׁלֶט *m.* apparently so called from being hard, or perhaps tough; 2 Sam. viii. 7, "shields of gold;" mostly spoken of shields suspended for ornament on walls.

SHINE

1 אָהַל to shine; to give light. Hiphil *fut.* Job xxv. 5, "it shineth not," *i.e.* is not bright, pure, in the sight of God.

2 אוֹר (see *Light*), to be or become light, to shine, or to be bright; of the eyes of one fainting when he recovers; to lighten, to make light, to illuminate; to make light one's countenance, to cause it to shine, *i.e.* to cheer, to enliven; spoken especially of God, as regarding men with serene and propitious countenance. Kal [a]*pret.* [b]*imp.* Hiphil [c]*pret.* [d]*imp.* [e]*fut.*

3 הָלַל to be clear, bright, to shine. Kal [a]*inf.* Hiphil [b]*fut.*

4 זָהַר to be bright; to cause to shine, to give shine. Hiphil *fut.*

5 זָרַח to rise as the sun, so of light, to shine. Kal *pret.*

6 יָפַע to be bright; to shine forth, especially of Jehovah, as appearing in light and splendour. Hiphil [a]*pret.* [b]*imp.* [c]*fut.*

7 נָגַהּ to shine as the sun, moon, stars, &c. Kal [a]*pret.* [b]*fut.* Hiphil [c]*fut.* [d] נֹגַהּ *f.* dawn, light.

8 עוּף to fly; to be dark. Kal *fut.* Job xi. 17, rendered, however, in our version, "thou shalt shine forth," giving the

import of the sentence rather than the actual translation, "thou art now in darkness, but thou shalt be as the morning."

9 עָשַׁת to shine, to be bright, smooth : this word seems to import the advanced, improved state of anything, wherein it is raised above or exceeds itself or other things of the same sort. KAL *pret.*

10 צָהַל to be clear ; to cause to shine. HIPHIL *inf.*

11 קָרַן *denom.* from קֶרֶן a horn, to emit rays like horns, to shine, *e.g.* the face of Moses. KAL *pret.*

Exod. xxxiv. 29, 30,		Job xxxi. 26.	3 b	Eccles. viii. 1.	2 e
35.	11	xxxvii. 15.	6 a	Isa. iv. 5.	7 d
Num. vi. 25.	2 e	xli. 18.	3 b	ix. 2.	7 a
Deut. xxxiii. 2.	6 a	xli. 32.	2 e	xiii. 10.	7 c
2 Sam. xxiii. 4.	7 d	Ps. xxxi. 16.	2 d	lx. 1.	2 b
2 Kings iii. 22.	5	l. 2.	6 a	Jer. v. 28.	9
Job iii. 4.	6 c	lxvii. 1.	2 e	Ezek. xliii. 2.	2 c
x. 3.	6 a	lxxx. 1.	6 b	Dan. ix. 15.	2 d
xi. 17.	8	lxxx. 3, 7, 19.	2 d	xii. 3.	4
xviii. 5.	7 b	civ. 15.	10	Joel ii. 10.	7 d
xxii. 28.	7 a	cxix. 135.	2 d	iii. 15.	7 d
xxv. 5.	1	cxxxix. 12.	2 e	Hab. iii. 11.	7 d
xxix. 3. α	3 a	Prov. iv. 18, 18. β	7 d, 2 a		

α *lit.* in its shining.   β *lit.* that goeth on and shineth.

SHIP

אֳנִיָּה *f.* noun of unity corresponding to *collect.* אֳנִי, see *Navy.* Gen. xlix. 13, &c. אֳנִיּוֹת *f. pl.* (כתיב) for 2 Chron. viii. 18.

סְפִינָה *f.* a ship, specially with a deck : Jonah i. 5.

צִי *m.* a ship, so called as being set up, built : Num. xxiv. 24 : Isa. xxxiii. 21 : Ezek. xxx. 9 : Dan. xi. 30.

SHIPMASTER

חֹבֵל pilot ; רַב *adj.* great : Jonah i. 6, *lit.* the great pilot.

SHITTAH, SHITTIM

שִׁטָּה *f.* acacia, the *Spina Egyptiaca* of the ancients (*Mimosa Nilotica*, Linn.). It is a large tree growing in Egypt and Arabia, from which is obtained the gum arabic ; its bark is covered with large black thorns ; the wood is exceedingly hard, and when old resembles ebony. Exod. xxv. 5, &c.: Deut. x. 3 : Isa. xli. 19.

SHOCK

בָּדִישׁ *m.* a heap of sheaves in the field, a stack of grain : Judg. xv. 5 : Job v. 26.

SHOE, SHOD

נָעַל to bolt, fasten with bolt or bar ; to shoe, to put on sandals, which is done by confining, shutting in the foot with thongs. KAL *fut.* Ezek. xvi. 10. HIPHIL *fut.* 2 Chron. xxviii. 15. נַעַל *f.* a shoe, sandal, sometimes beautifully ornamented, inwrought with lines of gold, silver, or silk, and not seldom embroidered with jewels : Cant. vii. 1. In transferring a possession or domain, it was customary to deliver a shoe (Ruth iv. 7), as in the middle ages a glove ; hence the action of throwing down a shoe upon a region or territory was a symbol of occupancy, Ps. lx. 8. "Over Edom will I cast out my shoe," *i. e.* I will take possession, claim it as my own, Ps. cviii. 9. So in Ruth iv. 7, 8, the delivery of a shoe implied that the

next of kin gave up a sacred obligation, and he was therefore called חֲלוּץ נַעַל. Elsewhere a shoe-latchet, shoe-thong, Gen. xiv. 23, or a pair of shoes, Amos ii. 6, viii. 6, is put for anything of little value, worthless. Gen. xiv. 23, &c. מִנְעָל *m. id.* Deut. xxxiii. 25.

SHOOT

1 בָּרַח to pass through, to reach across. KAL *inf.*

2 דָּרַךְ to tread, to tread the bow ; to shoot. KAL *part.* Poel.

3 מָתַח to extend, stretch, to draw the bow. PIEL *part.* archers: Gen. xxi. 16, "bowshot."

4 יָדָה to throw, to cast. KAL *imp.*

5 יָצָא to come forth. KAL *fut.*

6 יָרָה to throw, to cast. KAL [a] *pret.* [b] *inf.* [c] *imp.* [d] *fut.* NIPHAL [e] *fut.* HIPHIL [f] *fut.* [g] *part.* יָרָא *id.* KAL [h] *inf.* HIPHIL [i] *fut.* [k] *part.*

7 נָתַן to give. KAL *fut.*

8 עָלָה to go up, ascend. KAL [a] *pret.* [b] *inf.*

9 פָּטַר to let loose. HIPHIL *fut.* Ps. xxii. 7, *marg.* 'open, *or,* they thrust out the lip, make mouths by way of sneer or contempt.'

10 רָבַב to shoot arrows in great number, so as to discharge a shower of arrows. KAL *pret.*

11 שָׁחַט to slay, to kill. KAL *part.* Paül, Jer. ix. 8, with an active signification, *lit.* an arrow slaying.

12 שָׁלַח to send, to send out ; to cast, to throw, to shoot. KAL [a] *imp.* [b] *pret.* PIEL [c] *inf.* [d] *fut.*

Gen. xxi. 16.	3	2 Kings xiii. 17, 17.	6 c f	Ps. cxliv. 6.	12 a
xl. 10.	8 a	xix. 32.	6 f	Isa. xxvii. 8. β	12 c
xlix. 23.	10	1 Chron. v. 18.	2	xxxvii. 33.	6 f
Exod. xix. 13. α	6 b e	2 Chron. xxvi. 15.	6 h	Jer. ix. 8.	11
xxxvi. 33.	1	xxxv. 23.	6 f	l. 14.	4
Num. xxi. 30.	6 d	Job viii. 16.	5	Ezek. xvii. 6.	12 a
1 Sam. xx. 20, 20.	12 c, 6 f	Ps. xi. 2.	6 b	xvii. 7.	12 b
xx. 36, 36.	6 g a	xviii. 14.	10	xxxi. 5.	12 c
xx. 37.	6 a	xxii. 7.	9	xxxi. 10, 14.	7
2 Sam. xi. 20.	6 f	lxiv. 4, 4.	6 b f	xxxvi. 8.	7
xi. 24, 24.	6 k i	lxiv. 7.	6 f	Amos vii. 1.	8 b

α *lit.* shooting shall be shot.   β *marg.* 'or, when thou sendest it forth.'

SHORE

חוֹף *m.* a coast, or shore, as washed by the sea : Judg. v. 17, *marg.* 'or, port ;' Jer. xlvii. 7.

קָצֶה *m.* an end, extremity : Josh. xv. 2.

שָׂפָה *f.* lip ; edge, border, margin : Gen. xxii. 17 : Exod. xiv. 30 : Josh. xi. 4 : 1 Sam. xiii. 5 : 1 Kings iv. 29 ; ix. 26.

SHORT

1 חֶלֶד *m.* life, as fleeting and transient.

2 מָהַר to hasten. PIEL [a] *part.* [b] מְהֵרָה *f.* speedily.

3 קָצַר to cut off, or shorten ; to be short. KAL [a] *pret.* [b] *inf.* [c] *fut.* [d] *part.* Paül. PIEL [e] *pret.* HIPHIL [f] *pret.*

4 קָרוֹב *adj.* near.

Gen. xli. 32. α	2 a	Ps. lxxxix. 47. γ	1	Isa. lix. 1.	3 a
Num. xi. 23.	3 c	cii. 23.	3 e	Jer. xxvii. 16.	2 b
Job xvii. 12.	4	Prov. x. 27.	3 c	Ezek. vii. 8.	4
xx. 5. β		Isa. xxviii. 20.	3 b	xlii. 5.	3 d
Ps. lxxxix. 45.	3 f	l. 2.	3 b a		

α *lit.* and hastening to.   β *marg.* 'from near.'
γ *lit.* how transitory I am.

SHOSHANNIM, SHOSHANNIM-EDUTH

שׁוֹשָׁן *m.* a lily: Ps. xlv. title; lxix. title; lxxx. title. Shoshannim-eduth, a musical instrument, probably so called from its resemblance to a lily. To the common lily several kinds of trumpets and pipes may be said to have a resemblance; but to the Martagon lily, or Turk's cap, the cymbal approaches nearest, and, indeed, the name of cymbal was at a later period sometimes given to this flower. Hence שׁוֹשַׁנִּים עֵדוּת may be rendered, pipes of song.—*Gesenius.* עֵדוּת *f.* precept, revelation, a Psalm revealed.

SHOULDER

1 זְרוֹעַ *com.* arm; in animals, the fore-leg, shoulder.

2 כָּתֵף *f.* shoulder; *trop.* of inanimate things, the side of a building, country, &c., hence *poet.*, Deut. xxxiii. 12, "shall dwell between his shoulders," *sc.* Jehovah's, *i.e.* between the sacred mountains, Zion and Moriah. Isa. xi. 14, "fly upon the shoulders of the Philistines," *i.e.* rush upon their borders, the figure being taken from birds of prey; *pl.* shoulder-pieces of the high priest's ephod; shoulders of an axle.

3 שׁוֹק *m.* the leg; in animals, the shoulder.

4 שְׁכֶם *m.* shoulder, or, as Simonis has well remarked, the shoulder-blades, *i.e.* the part where these approach each other behind, the upper part of the back next beneath the neck, called in English, indifferently, the shoulders or the back. Hence found only in the singular, and different from כָּתֵף; as Job xxxi. 32, *lit.* my shoulder fall from its shoulder-blade, *i.e.* from the back to which it is joined; specially the part on which burdens are borne, Job xxxi. 36, Isa. v. 9, xxii. 22; the part on which blows are inflicted, Isa. ix. 3; some ensign of office was usually borne on the shoulder, Isa. ix. 6.—Gen. ix. 23, &c. שִׁכְמָה *f.* shoulder-blade.

No. 4 not included.

Exod. xxviii. 7, 12, 12, 25.		Num. vii. 9.	2	Job xxxi. 22.		4 a
xxix. 22, 27.	2	xviii. 18.	3	Isa. xi. 14.		2
xxxix. 4, 7, 18.	2	Deut. xviii. 3.	1	xxx. 6.		2
Lev. vii. 32, 33, 34.	2	xxxiii. 12.	2	xlvi. 7.		2
viii. 25, 26.	3	Judg. xvi. 3.	2	xlix. 22.		2
ix. 21.	3	1 Sam. ix. 24.	3	Ezek. xii. 6, 7, 12.		2
x. 14, 15.	3	xvii. 6.		xxiv. 4.		2
Num. vi. 19.	1	1 Chron. xv. 15.	2	xxix. 7, 18.		2
vi. 20.	3	2 Chron. xxxv. 3.	2	xxxvii. 21.		2
		Neh. ix. 29.	2	Zech. vii. 11.		2

SHOUT

1 הֵידָד *m.* shout of joy, joyful acclamation, *e.g.* of vintagers treading the grapes, vintage-shout, Jer. xxv. 30, xlviii. 33, 33, 33; of soldiers rushing to battle, battle-shout, when they encourage one another, Jer. li. 14, Isa. xvi. 9, *marg.* 'or, the alarm,' &c., 10, where these two senses are put in antithesis; verse 9, the shouting of enemies, not of reapers; verse 10, made thy (vintage) shouting to cease.

2 עָנָה to sing; to cry aloud, to shout, which is often expressed by words implying singing: Exod. xxxii. 18, where the same root is translated shout, cry, sing; hence it appears that the signification to sing belongs more to

Piel. KAL [a] *inf.* [b] *fut.* Jer. xxv. 30, "he shall give a shout as they that tread the grapes." God's executing dreadful judgments on his enemies is compared to treading grapes in the wine-press, Isa. lxiii. 2, 3; and here he is said to shout, as was usual with the treaders of grapes by way of encouragement.

3 צָהַל used of a clear, shrill sound, hence to shout, to sing, to cry aloud for joy. PIEL *imp.*

4 צָוַח to cry out loudly, either in joy or distress. KAL *fut.*

5 קוֹל *m.* voice: Ezra iii. 12. See *Aloud.*

6 רוּעַ to make a loud noise; to cry with a loud voice, to shout; *seq.* עַל over, against; to shout for joy in triumph, in jubilee, over a vanquished enemy, *seq. dat.* in honour of any one; of warlike shouts, outcries, Josh. vi. 16, &c.; more rarely of a mourning cry. POLAL [a] *fut.* HIPHIL [b] *pret.* [c] *inf.* [d] *imp.* [e] *fut.* [f] *part.* HITHPOLEL [g] *fut.* [h] רֵעַ *m.* shouting. [i] תְּרוּעָה *f.* shout of joy, of battle, of a trumpet.

7 רָנַן to give forth a tremulous or shrill sound; to utter cries of joy, to shout, to exert the voice with vehemence in joy, praise, sometimes in sorrow. KAL [a] *imp.* [b] *fut.* PIEL [c] *inf.* [d] *fut.* HIPHIL [e] *imp.* HITHPOLEL [f] *part.* [g] רִנָּה *f.* shout of joy.

8 שָׁוַע to cry for aid. PIEL *fut.*

9 תְּשֻׁאוֹת *f. pl.* noise.

Exod. xxii. 17.	6 h	2 Chron. xv. 14.	6 i	Isa. xvi. 9.		1
xxxii. 18.	2 a	Ezra iii. 11, 11.	6 b i	xvi. 10, 10.		6 a, 1
Lev. ix. 24.	7 b	iii. 12. *a*	5, 6 i	xlii. 11.		4
Num. xxiii. 21.	6 i	iii. 13, 13, 13.	6 i f i	xliv. 23.		6 d
Josh. vi. 5, 5.	6 e i	Job xxxviii. 7.	6 i	Jer. xx. 16.		6 i
vi. 10, 10, 10.	6 e b d	xxxviii. 25.	6 i	xxv. 30.		2 b, 1
vi. 16.	6 d	Ps. v. 11.	7 d	xxxi. 7.		3
vi. 20, 20, 20.	6 e e i	xxxii. 11.	7 e	xlviii. 33, 33, 33.		1
Judg. xv. 14.	6 b	xxxv. 27.	7 b	l. 15.		6 d
1 Sam. iv. 5, 5.	6 e i	xlvii. 1.	6 d	li. 14.		1
iv. 6, 6.	6 i	xlvii. 5.	6 i	Lam. iii. 8.		8
x. 24.	6 e	lxv. 13.	6 g	Ezek. xxi. 22.		6 i
xvii. 20.	6 b	lxxviii. 65.	7 f	Amos i. 14.		6 i
xvii. 52.	6 e	cxxxii. 9.	7 d	ii. 2.		6 i
2 Sam. vi. 15.	6 i	cxxxii. 16.	7 c d	Zeph. iii. 14.		6 d
1 Chron. xv. 28.	6 i	Prov. xi. 10.	7 g	Zech. iv. 7.		9
2 Chron. xiii. 15, 15.	6 e c	Isa. xii. 6.	7 a	ix. 9.		6 d

a lit. unto shouting for joy by lifting up the voice.

SHOVEL

יָעִים *m. pl.* shovels for removing ashes: Exod. xxvii. 3; xxxviii. 3: Num. iv. 14: 1 Kings vii. 40, 45: 2 Kings xxv. 14: 2 Chron. iv. 11, 16: Jer. lii. 18.

רַחַת *f.* a winnowing-fork or shovel, a fan: Isa. xxx. 24.

SHOWER

גֶּשֶׁם *m.* (see *Rain*) violent rain, heavy shower: Ezek. xiii. 11, 13; xxxiv. 26, 26: Zech. x. 1.

זֶרֶם *m.* a pouring rain, violent shower, storm: Job xxiv. 8.

רְבִיבִים *m. pl.* rain, shower, from the multitude of drops: Deut. xxxii. 2: Ps. lxv. 10; lxxii. 6: Jer. iii. 3; xiv. 22: Micah v. 7.

SHRANK

נָשֶׁה *adj.* that which is dried up, relaxed, or strained, transferred to torpor of the members, of the nerve or tendon

in the leg and thigh, in Jacob: Gen. xxxii. 32, 32. Gr. the sinew that was benumbed, or waxed feeble. See Fürst, *in voce*.

SHRED

פָּלַח to cleave, to cut. PIEL *fut.* 2 Kings iv. 39.

SHROUD

חֹרֶשׁ *m.* a thick wood, thicket, forest: Ezek. xxxi. 3.

SHRUB

שִׂיחַ *m.* bush, shrub: Gen. xxi. 15.

SHUSHAN-EDUTH

שׁוּשַׁן *m.* lily. עֵדוּת *f. pl.* precepts, law; revelation, and hence a song or Psalm revealed: Ps. lx. title, *comp.* verse 6.

SHUT

1 אָטַם to shut, to close, to stop. KAL *part.*

2 אָטַר to shut, to close. KAL *fut.* Ps. lxix. 15. Michaelis, on this verse, observes that the Arabs form their pits of water with so much ingenuity that they can be closed so that no one can discover the opening; and that if any one chance to fall in, death is inevitable, the opening probably closing again: or the expression may refer to pits for taking wild beasts.

3 גּוּף to shut or close a door or gate; properly, to cause anything to be, or be, concealed, within. HIPHIL *fut.*

4 טוּחַ to daub. KAL *pret.* Supposed to be an allusion to the manner in which the eyes of criminals are sometimes sealed up in the East.

5 כָּלָא to close, and so to enclose, to shut up; to restrain. KAL [a] *pret.* [b] *part.* Paül.

6 נָעַל to bolt. KAL *part.* Paül.

7 סָגַר to shut, to close, as a door, a gate, the womb, a breach in a wall; *seq.* עַל to shut in, to shut up over; absolutely, without the object expressed. Isa. xxii. 22, Josh. vi. 1, where Kal refers to the closing of the gates, and Pual as *intens.* to their being fastened with bolts and bars. Vulg. *Jericho autem clausa erat atque munita.* Chald. *et Jericho erat clausa foribus ferreis et roborata vectibus æneis.* KAL [a] *pret.* [b] *inf.* [c] *imp.* [d] *fut.* [e] *part.* Poel. [f] *part.* Paül. NIPHAL [g] *pret.* [h] *imp.* [i] *fut.* PUAL [k] *pret.* [l] *part.* HIPHIL [m] *pret.* [n] *fut.* סָגַר Ch. P'AL [o] *pret.*

8 סָכַךְ to cover; to hedge in, to fence around. HIPHIL *fut.*

9 סָתַם to stop, to obstruct, as fountains; to stop or intercept the passage of prayer, to refuse to hear it: Lam. iii. 8. To stop or shut up a prophecy may signify not to divulge or publish it, to conceal it from common understandings; or to let it remain in its present obscurity without further explanation. KAL *imp.*

10 עָצָה to make fast, firm; hence to close, to shut, *e.g.* the eyes. KAL *part.* Poel.

11 עָצַם to bind, to bind up, to bind fast, *e.g.* the eyes; to be strong. KAL *part.* Poel.

12 עָצַר to shut up, to close; the primary idea lies in surrounding, enclosing, with a fence, wall. KAL [a] *pret.* [b] *fut.* [c] *part.* Paül. NIPHAL [d] *inf.*

13 צָרַר to bind up, to bind together. KAL *part.* Paül.

14 קָפַץ to draw together, to contract, *e.g.* the hand, the mouth, one's compassion. KAL [a] *pret.* [b] *fut.*

15 שָׁתַם the same with סָתַם. KAL *pret.*

16 שָׁעַע to overspread, to smear. HIPHIL *imp.*

Gen. vii. 16. *a*	7 d	2 Kings vi. 32.	7 c	Isa. xxiv. 10, 22.	7 k
xix. 6, 10.	7 a	ix. 8.	12 c	xxvi. 20.	7 c
Exod. xiv. 3.	7 a	xiv. 26.	12 c	xxxiii. 15.	11
Lev. xiii. 4, 5, 21, 26,		xvii. 4.	12 b	xliv. 18.	4
31, 33, 50, 54.	7 m	2 Chron. vi. 26.	12 d	xlv. 1.	7 l
xiii. 11.	7 n	vii. 13.	12 b	lii. 15.	14 b
xiv. 38, 46.	7 m	xxviii. 24.	7 d	lx. 11.	7 i
Num. xii. 14, 15.	7 i	xxix. 7.	7 a	lxvi. 9.	12 a
Deut. xi. 17.	12 a	Neh. vi. 10, 10.	12 c, 7 d	Jer. xiii. 19.	7 k
xv. 7.	14 b	vii. 3.	7 a	xx. 9.	12 c
xxxii. 30.	7 m	xiii. 19.	7 i	xxxii. 2.	5 b
xxxii. 36.	12 c	Job xii. 10.	7 a	xxxii. 3.	5 a
Josh. ii. 5.	7 b	xi. 10.	7 n	xxxiii. 11.	12 c
ii. 7.	7 a	xii. 14.	7 d	xxxvi. 5.	12 c
vi. 1.	7 e l	xxxviii. 8.	8	xxxix. 15.	12 c
Judg. iii. 23.	7 d	xli. 15.	7 f	Lam. iii. 8.	15
ix. 51.	7 d	Ps. xxxi. 8.	7 m	Ezek. iii. 24.	7 h
1 Sam. i. 5, 6.	7 a	lxix. 15.	2	xliv. 1, 2, 2.	7 f
vi. 10.	5 a	lxxvii. 10.	14 a	xlvi. 1.	7 f
xxiii. 7.	7 g	lxxxviii. 8.	5 b	xlvi. 2.	7 f
2 Sam. xx. 3.	13	Prov. xvi. 30.	10	xlvi. 12.	7 a
1 Kings viii. 35.	12 d	xvii. 28.	1	Dan. vi. 22.	7 o
xiv. 10.	12 c	Eccles. xii. 4.	7 k	viii. 26.	9
xxi. 21.	12 c	Cant. iv. 12.	6	xii. 4.	9
2 Kings iv. 4.	7 a	Isa. vi. 10.	16	Mal. i. 10.	7 d
iv. 5, 21, 33.	7 d	xxii. 22, 22.	7 e a		

a or, shut the door after him; some, round him.

SHUTTLE

אֶרֶג *m.* a weaver's shuttle: Job vii. 6.

SIBBOLETH

סִבֹּלֶת *f.* in the dialect of the Ephraimites, *i. q.* with שִׁבֹּלֶת an ear of grain: Judg. xii. 6.

SICK

1 אָנַשׁ to be very sick; incurable, unto death. NIPHAL *fut.*

2 דָּוֶה *adj.* languid, faint, especially of women.

3 דַּלָּה *f.* (see *Pining*) pining sickness: Isa. xxxviii. 12, *marg.* ' or, from the thrum,' as if from דָּלָה to hang down.

4 חָלָה to be worn down in strength, to be weak; to be sick, diseased. KAL [a] *pret.* [b] *inf.* [c] *fut.* [d] *part.* Poel. NIPHAL [e] *pret.* HIPHIL [f] *pret.* [g] *part.* HITHPAEL [h] *inf.* [i] *imp.* [k] *fut.* חֳלִי [l] *m.* sickness. [m] מַחֲלֶה *f. id.* [n] תַּחֲלֻאִים *m. pl.* diseases: Deut. xxix. 22, *lit.* the sicknesses thereof, wherewith the Lord hath made it sick.

Gen. xlviii. 1.	4 d	1 Kings xvii. 17,		Cant. ii. 5.	4 d
Exod. xxiii. 25.	4 m	17.	4 a l	v. 8.	4 d
Lev. xv. 33.	2	2 Kings i. 2.	4 c	Isa. i. 5.	4 l
xx. 18.	2	viii. 7, 29.	4 d	xxxiii. 24.	4 l
Deut. vii. 15.	4 l	xiii. 14, 14.	4 a l	xxxviii. 1.	4 a
xxviii. 59, 61.	4 l	xx. 1, 12.	4 a	xxxviii. 9, 9.	4 b l
xxix. 22.	4 n	2 Chron. vi. 28.	4 m	xxxviii. 12.	3
1 Sam. xix. 14.	4 d	xxi. 15, 15, 19.	4 l	xxxix. 1.	4 a
xxx. 13.	4 a	xxii. 6.	4 d	Jer. xiv. 18.	4 n
2 Sam. xii. 15.	1	xxxii. 24.	4 a	Ezek. xxxiv. 4, 16.	4 d
xiii. 2.	4 h	Neh. ii. 2.	4 d	Dan. viii. 27.	4 e
xiii. 5.	4 i	Ps. xxxv. 13.	4 b	Hos. v. 13.	4 l
xiii. 6.	4 k	xli. 3.	4 l	vii. 5.	4 f
1 Kings viii. 37.	4 m	Prov. xiii. 12.	4 g	Micah vi. 13.	4 f
xiv. 1.	4 a	xxiii. 35.	4 a	Mal. i. 8, 13.	4 d
xiv. 5.	4 d	Eccles. v. 17.	4 l		

SICKLE

חֶרְמֵשׁ *m.* a sickle or reaping-hook : Deut. xvi. 9 ; xxiii. 25.

מַגָּל *m.* sickle or scythe : Jer. l. 16 : Joel iii. 13, *or,* a knife to cut off ripe grapes.

SIDE

1 חוֹף *m.* shore.

2 יָד *com.* hand ; beside, *lit.* at the hand of.

3 יָרֵךְ *f.* thigh ; side. ᵃ יַרְכָה *f.* the hinder part, hinder side, rear ; the innermost recesses, the most distant sides of a house, cave, sepulchre, &c., the inmost recesses of Lebanon, &c., hence very remote regions. Isa. xiv. 13, "in the sides of the north," *i. e.* near the altar, between God, dwelling in the temple, and the people, as a mediator to them and vicar of God ; a prophecy of antichrist.

4 כָּתֵף *f.* shoulder ; side of a building, country, &c.

5 מָתְנַיִם *dual, m.* loins.

6 סָבַב to compass. NIPHAL ᵃ *fut.* ᵇ סָבִיב *m.* round about, on every side.

7 עֶבֶד *m.* servant : 1 Kings iv. 24, from or by means of all his servants, according to some copies.

8 עֵבֶר *m.* region, or country beyond, on the other side of a river or sea, which one must pass ; a region opposite, the other or opposite side ; with prefixes it often becomes a preposition : Exod. xxviii. 26, &c. עֲבַר Ch. *m.*

9 פֵּאָה *f.* side, quarter, region ; extremity, the remotest part of a building.

10 צַד *m.* side.

11 צֵלָע *f.* rib ; side.

12 קִיר *m.* a wall.

13 קָצֶה *m.* end, extremity.

14 רֶבַע *m.* one of four sides.

15 רוּחַ *m.* breath, wind ; east side, &c., *lit.* winds.

16 שָׂפָה *f.* lip ; edge, border, margin.

17 שְׂטַר Ch. *m.* side.

No. 8 not included.

Gen. vi. 16.	10	Exod. xxxviii. 9, 11,		Judg. xix. 1, 18.	3 a
Exod. ii. 5.	2	12, 13.	9	Ruth ii. 14.	10
xxv. 12, 12, 14.	10	xxxviii. 14, 15.	4	1 Sam. iv. 13, 18.	2
xxv. 32, 32, 32.	10	xxxix. 20.	4	vi. 8.	10
xxvi. 13.	10	xl. 22, 24.	3	xii. 11.	6 b
xxvi. 18.	9	Lev. i. 11.	3	xiv. 47.	6 b
xxvi. 20, 20.	11, 9	i. 15.	12	xix. 9.	2
xxvi. 22, 23.	3 a	v. 9.	12	xx. 20, 25.	10
xxvi. 26.	11	Num. iii. 29, 35.	3	xxiii. 26, 26.	10
xxvi. 27, 27,		xvi. 27.	6 b	xxiv. 3.	10
27.	11, 11, 3 a	xxxiii. 55.	10	2 Sam. ii. 16.	10
xxvi. 35, 35.	11	xxxiv. 11.	4	xiii. 34.	10
xxvii. 7.	11	xxxv. 5, 5, 5, 5.	9	xv. 2, 18.β	2
xxvii. 9, 9, 11, 12, 13.	9	Deut. i. 7.	1	xvi. 13.	11
xxvii. 14, 15.	4	iv. 32.α	13	xviii. 4.	2
xxviii. 27.	4	xxxi. 26.	10	1 Kings xvi. 24,	
xxx. 3.	12	xxxiii. 12.	4	24, 24.	8, 8, 8, or 7
xxx. 4.	10	Josh. iii. 16.	10	v. 4.	6 b
xxxii. 27.	3	xii. 9.	10	vi. 8.	4
xxxvi. 11.	16	xv. 8, 10, 11.	4	vi. 16.	3 a
xxxvi. 25, 31.	11	xviii. 12, 12.	9, 4	vii. 39, 39, 39.	4
xxxvi. 27, 28.	3 a	xviii. 13, 16, 18, 19.	4	2 Kings xvi. 14.	3
xxxvi. 32, 32.	11, 3 a	xviii. 20.	9	xix. 23.	3 a
xxxvii. 8, 8, 5.	11	xxiii. 10.	3	1 Chron. xxii. 18.	6 b
xxxvii. 18, 18, 18, 27.	10	Judg. ii. 3.	3	2 Chron. iv. 10.	4
xxxvii. 26.	12	vii. 12.	16	viii. 17.	16
xxxviii. 7.	11	vii. 18.	6 b	xiv. 7.	6 b
		vii. 34.		xxiii. 10, 10.	4

2 Chron. xxxii. 22.	6 b	Isa. lxvi. 12.	10	Ezek. xli. 2, 26.	4
Ezra iv. 10, 11, 16.	8 a	xli. 5, 10.	3 a	xli. 5, 10.	6 b
v. 3, 6, 6.	8 a	vi. 25.	6 b	xlii. 16, 17, 18, 19,	
vi. 13.	8 a	xx. 10.	6 b	20.	15
Neh. iv. 18.	5	xlix. 29.	6 b	xlv. 7, 7.	9
Job i. 10.	6 b	liii. 23.	15	xlvi. 19, 19.	4, 3 a
i. 14.γ	2	Ezek. i. 8, 17.	14	xlvii. 1, 2.	4
xviii. 11.	6 b	iv. 4, 6, 8, 9.	10	xlvi. 15, 17, 18, 18,	
xviii. 12.	11	ix. 2, 3, 11.	5	19, 19, 20, 20.	9
xix. 10.	14	x. 11.	14	xlviii. 1, 2, 2, 3, 3,	
Ps. xii. 8.	6 b	xvi. 33.	6 b	4, 4, 5, 5, 6, 6, 7, 7,	
xxxi. 13.	6 b	xix. 8.	3 a	8, 8, 8, 8, 16, 16,	
xlviii. 2.	3 a	xxiii. 22.	6 b	16, 16, 23, 23, 24,	
lxxi. 21.δ	6 a	xxv. 9.	4	24, 25, 25, 26, 26,	
xci. 7.	10	xxviii. 23.	6 b	27, 27, 28, 30, 32,	
cxxviii. 3.	3 a	xxxii. 23.	3 a	33, 34.	9
cxl. 5.	2	xxxiv. 21.	10	Dan. vii. 5.	17
Eccles. iv. 1.	2	xxxvi. 3.	6 b	x. 4.	2
Isa. xiv. 13, 15.	3 a	xxxvii. 21.	6 b	Amos vi. 10.	6 b
xxxvii. 24.	3 a	xxxix. 17.	6 b	Jonah i. 5.	3 a
lx. 4.	10	xl. 18, 40, 40, 41, 44, 44.	4		

ᵃ *lit.* from side unto side. β *lit.* at his hand. γ *lit.* at their hands. δ *lit.* and shall go about and comfort me.

SIEGE

צוּר to bind, to press ; to lay siege, *seq.* עַל. KAL *pret.* Isa. xxix. 3 : Ezek. iv. 3. *part.* Poel, 1 Kings xv. 27. מָצוֹר *m.* siege : Deut. xx. 19 ; xxviii. 53, 55, 57 : 2 Chron. xxxii. 10 : Jer. xix. 9 : Ezek. iv. 2, 7, 8 ; v. 2 : Micah v. 1 : Nah. iii. 14 : Zech. xii. 2.

SIEVE, SIFT

כְּבָרָה *f.* a sieve : Amos ix. 9.

נוּעַ to shake ; to move to and fro. NIPHAL *fut.* Amos ix. 9. HIPHIL *pret.* Amos ix. 9.

נוּף to lift up, to shake. HIPHIL *inf.* Isa. xxx. 28. נָפָה *f.* a sieve, fan, for winnowing : Isa. xxx. 28.

SIGH

1 אָנַח to sigh, to groan, in respect of some evil either present or to come. NIPHAL ᵃ *pret.* ᵇ *imp.* ᶜ *fut.* ᵈ *part.* ᵉ אֲנָחָה *f.* sighing, sobbing.

2 אֲנָקָה *f.* a shriek, cry, mourning.

Exod. ii. 23.	1 e	Isa. xxi. 2.	1 e	Lam. i. 8.	1 a
Job iii. 24.	1 e	xxiv. 7.	1 a	i. 22.	1 e
Ps. xii. 5.	2	xxxv. 10.	1 e	Ezek. ix. 4.	1 d
xxxi. 10.	1 e	Jer. xlv. 3.	1 e	xxi. 6, 6.	1 b c
lxxix. 11.	2	Lam. i. 4, 11, 21.	1 d	xxi. 7.	1 d

SIGHT

1 חֲזוֹת Ch. *f.* sight, view, prospect.

2 עַיִן *com.* eye : Gen. xviii. 3, &c.

3 פָּנִים *m. pl.* face.

4 רָאָה to see ; behold. KAL *part.* Poel. ᵃ מַרְאֶה *m.* sight, aspect, view.

No. 2 not included.

Gen. ii. 9.	4 a	2 Kings xxiii. 27.	3	Prov. iv. 3.	3
xxiii. 4, 8.	3	xxiv. 3.	3	Eccles. ii. 26.	3
xlvii. 18.	3	1 Chron. xxii. 8.	3	vi. 9.	4 a
Exod. iii. 3.	4 a	2 Chron. vi. 16.	3	viii. 3.	3
xxiv. 17.	4 a	vii. 20.	3	xi. 9.	4 a
Lev. xiii. 3, 4, 20, 25,		Ezra ix. 9.	3	Isa. v. 21.	3
30, 31, 32, 34.	4 a	Neh. i. 11.	3	xi. 3.	4 a
xiv. 37.	4	ii. 5.	3	xviii. 23.	3
Num. iii. 4.	3	Esth. ii. 17.	3	Jer. iv. 1.	3
Deut. xiv. 37.	3	Job xxi. 8.	3	vii. 15.	3
xxviii. 34, 67.	4 a	xxiv. 26.	3	xv. 1.	3
Josh. xxiii. 5.	3	xli. 9.	4 a	xviii. 23.	3
2 Sam. vii. 9.	3	Ps. xix. 19.	3	Ezek. xx. 43.	3
1 Kings viii. 25.	3	xix. 14.	3	xxxvi. 31.	3
ix. 7.	3	lxxvi. 7.	3	Dan. iv. 11, 20.	1
2 Kings xvii. 18, 20, 23.	3	cxliii. 2.	3	Hos. ii. 2.	3
				vi. 2.	3

SIGN

1 אוֹת *c.* a sign, mark, or token, which brings to mind, shews, or confirms anything either past, present, or to come; which excites attention or consideration; which distinguishes one thing from another; or is an inducement to believe what is affirmed, professed, or promised. The prophets were accustomed to afford tokens of some more distant event foretold; or as a proof and test of some great and important event to add to the prophecy some other prediction having a nearer issue, the fulfilment of which should be a token or sign of the accomplishment of the more distant. See Exod. iii. 12: Deut. xiii. 2, 3: 1 Sam. ii. 27–34; x. 7–9: 2 Kings xix. 29; xx. 8, 9: Isa. vii. 11–14; xxxviii. 7, 22: Jer. xliv. 29, 30—in the N. T., Mark xiii. 4: Luke i. 18; ii. 12. Gen. iv. 15 may be explained according to this idea: God gave Cain a sign to confirm his promise, that no one should slay him. See Pfeifferi Dubia Vexata, p. 44. It does not appear to have been a sign upon Cain, but given to him. The expression in the original is לָקֵן, not בְּקֵן; and שׂוּם אוֹת means to show or make manifest a sign; see Exod. x. 1, 2; Isa. lxvi. 19. The performing a miracle is expressed by עָשָׂה אוֹת, Num. xiv. 22. A sign or miracle from heaven, to prove the divine power and faithfulness of him in whose name a prophet speaks, is often joined with מוֹפֵת a wonder, Deut. iv. 34, vi. 32, Jer. x. 2, &c.; or sign of dominion or of political relation, Ps. lxxiv. 4.—Gen. i. 14, &c. [a] אָתִין Ch. *m. pl.* wonders, prodigies; miracles: Dan. iv. 2, 3; vi. 27.

2 דָּבָר *m.* word, matter, &c.: Ps. cv. 27.

3 מוֹפֵת *m.* miracle, prodigy; see *Wonder*. Kimchi distinguishes between this word and אוֹת, that it means something more special, and אוֹת generally a sign. That which arrests the attention, for whatever object it is wrought, is מוֹפֵת; that which is given by one who speaks in the name of God, in witness of some disputed truth, or as a token of some future event, is אוֹת.

4 נֵס *n.* something lifted up, as on the top of a spear, for a signal; a standard: Num. xxvi. 10, "they became a sign," *sc.* of admonition; always implying the benefit of those for whom it is set up to be a sign.

5 מַשְׂאֵת *f.* a lifting up; a sign, signal, given by fire.

6 צִיּוּן *m.* a pillar, column, as being set up, sepulchral.

7 רְשַׁם Ch. to write, to record; to subscribe, to sign. P'AL [a] *pret.* [b] *fut.* [c] *part. pass.*

No. 1 not included.

Num. xxvi. 10.	4	Ezek. xii. 6, 11.	3	Dan. vi. 8.	7 b
1 Kings xiii. 3, 3, 5.	3	xxiv. 24. 27.	3	vi. 9, 12, 13.	7 a
2 Chron. xxxii. 24.	3	xxxix. 15.	6	vi. 10.	7 c
Ps. cv. 27.	2, 1	Dan. iv. 2, 3.	1 a	vi. 27.	1 a
Jer. vi. 1.	5				

SIGNET

חוֹתָם *m.* a seal, signet ring. The Hebrews, like the Persians of the present day, sometimes wore the signet ring suspended on the breast by a string, Gen. xxxviii. 18; to which allusion is made, Cant. viii. 6.—Gen. xxxviii. 18:

Exod. xxviii. 11, 21, 36; xxxix. 6, 14, 30: Jer. xxii. 24: Hag. ii. 23. חֹתֶמֶת *f. id.*, Gen. xxxviii. 25.

עִזְקָא Ch. *f.* a signet ring: Dan. vi. 17, 17.

SILENCE

1 אָלַם to be dumb. NIPHAL *fut.*

2 דּוּמָה *f.* silence, land of silence, *poet.* for Sheol, the region of the dead. [a] דּוּמִיָּה *f.* silent, mute; silence, quiet, trust, confidence. [b] דּוּמָם *adv.*

3 דָּמָה to be dumb, silent, still; to cause to cease, to make an end of. NIPHAL [a] *pret.* [b] דֳּמִי *m.* silence, rest.

4 דָּמַם to be dumb, silent, still; *seq.* לְ to be silent to any one, *i. e.* to listen to him in silence, Job xxix. 21; to be silent towards Jehovah, *i. e.* to wait in silent faith and confidence for his help, Ps. xxxvii. 7, lxii. 6.—Jer. viii. 14, "let us be silent there," *i. e.* remain quiet, for Jehovah hath put us to silence, hath brought us to such a state that we cannot resist; to be astonished, amazed; to rest, to cease, to leave off. KAL [a] *fut.* NIPHAL [b] *fut.* HIPHIL [c] *pret.* [d] דְּמָמָה *f.* Job iv. 16, *marg.* ' or, I heard a still voice.' The Lxx. render it, "I heard a gentle breeze," αὖραν, "and a voice," καὶ φωνήν.

5 הָסָה to be silent; an onomatopoetic word. PIEL *imp.* Amos viii. 3, *lit.* be silent; *comp.* vi. 10.

6 חָרַשׁ to be smitten in the tongue, to be dumb, to keep silence: it appears, from its use, to refer rather to voluntary silence, and so differs from אָלַם, which refers to that which is involuntary: often spoken of God as not listening to and answering the prayers of men (*opp.* עָנָה), and ceasing to remain inactive: Ps. xxxv. 22, xxxix. 12, lxxxiii. 1, cix. 1; *seq.* מִן, *prægn.* Ps. xxviii. 1, keep not silence from me, *i. e.* turn not away from me in silence. Others deduce this meaning thus: to dig or plough; to meditate, devise; to keep silence, as one that is musing. KAL [a] *fut.* HIPHIL [b] *pret.* [c] *imp.*

7 חָשָׁה to be hush, silent, still. KAL [a] *inf.* [b] *fut.*

Judg. iii. 19.	5	Ps. xxxv. 22.	6 a	Isa. xlvii. 5.	2 b	
1 Sam. ii. 9.	4 b	xxxix. 2.	2 a	lxii. 6.β	3 b	
Job iv. 16.	4 d	l. 3.	6 a	lxv. 6.	7 b	
xxix. 21.	4 a	l. 21.	6 b	Jer. viii. 14, 14.	4 b c	
xxxi. 34.	4 a	lxxxiii. 1.α	3 b	Lam. ii. 10.	4 a	
Ps. xxii. 2.		xciv. 17.	2	iii. 28.	4 a	
xxviii. 1, 1.	6 a, 7 a	cxv. 17.		Amos v. 13.	4 a	
xxx. 12.	4 a	Eccles. iii. 7.	7 a	viii. 3.	5	
xxxi. 17.	4 a	Isa. xv. 1.	3 a	Hab. ii. 20.	5	
xxxi. 18.	1	xli. 1.	6 c	Zech. ii. 13.	5	
xxxii. 3.	6 b					

α *lit.* not silence to thee.   β *lit.* not silence to you.

SILK

מֶשִׁי *m.* according to the Hebrew interpreters, silk, garment of silk; Jerome, "a garment so fine as to seem equal to the finest hair:" from the root מָשָׁה to draw, silk of the finest drawn thread. Ezek. xvi. 10, 13.

שֵׁשׁ *m.* fine linen: Prov. xxxi. 22.

SILLY

פָּתָה to allure, entice, deceive; to let oneself be enticed. KAL *part.* Poel, Job v. 2: Hos. vii. 11.

SILVER

כֶּסֶף *m.* silver, from its paleness, as Gr. ἄργυρος from ἀργός, white, as gold from its yellow colour: shekels of silver, Gen. xxiii. 15; often with the word 'shekels' omitted: Gen. xx. 16; see *Money*. *Metaph.* to purify silver, *i.e.* to cleanse a people from their sins, Mal. iii. 3, *comp.* ver. 2; Isa. i. 25.—Gen. xiii. 2, &c. כְּסַף Ch. *m.* Ezra v. 14, &c.

קְשִׂיטָה *f.* (see *Money*): Josh. xxiv. 32, *marg.* 'or, lambs.'

SIMILITUDE

תַּבְנִית *f.* structure, mode of building; model, pattern; image, form, likeness: Ps. cvi. 20; cxliv. 12.

דָּמָה to be like; to use similitudes. PIEL *fut.* Hos. xii. 10. דְּמוּת *f.* likeness, representation, picture, image: 2 Chron. iv. 3: Dan. x. 16.

תְּמוּנָה *f.* appearance, form; an image, likeness: Deut. iv. 16: in Num. xii. 8, Deut. iv. 12, 15, it should rather be understood of some general appearance which does not imply likeness.

SIMPLE

פֶּתִי *adj.* simple, foolish, easily enticed and seduced, credulous, inexperienced: Ps. xix. 7; cxvi. 6; cxix. 130: Prov. i. 4, 22, 22, 32; vii. 7; viii. 5; ix. 4, 16; xiv. 15, 18; xix. 25; xxi. 11; xxii. 3; xxvii. 12: Ezek. xlv. 20. פְּתַיּוּת *f.* folly: Prov. ix. 13.

תֹּם *m.* integrity; put for that simplicity of mind which is remote from mischief or ill design: 2 Sam. xv. 11 (*comp.* 1 Kings xxii. 34).

SIN

1 אָשָׁם *m.* fault, blame, guilt: see *Trespass:* an offering for sin; it seems to imply a lighter fault than the following word, though usually translated trespass. Vid. Buddei Hist. Eccles. tom. i. sect. i. p. 576. ᵃ אַשְׁמָה *f.* guilt, trespass.

2 חָטָא to miss, not to hit the mark, spoken of an archer, slinger, Judg. xx. 16; also of the feet, to miss, to make a false step, to stumble and fall, Prov. xix. 2; to sin, *i.e.* to err from the path of duty and right; to sin away anything, *i.e.* to forfeit by sinning, to incur as penalty, *seq. acc.* Lev. v. 7, *comp.* ver. 11, Prov. xx. 2; he forfeiteth his own life, *i.e.* exposes it to danger, *comp.* Hab. ii. 10, Gen. xliii. 9. Piel, to bear the blame or loss of anything, to atone for, *seq. acc.* Gen. xxxi. 39; hence to offer as a sin-offering, as a sacrifice of atonement or expiation. KAL ᵃ*pret.* ᵇ*inf.* ᶜ*fut.* ᵈ*part.* Poel. HIPHIL ᵉ*pret.* ᶠ*inf.* ᵍ*fut.* ʰ חֵטְא *m.* sin, penalty for sin. ⁱ חַטָּא *m.* sinner: this word designates the wicked in respect to the lengthened series of sinful acts which proceed from them. — *Hengstenberg.* ᵏ חַטָּאָה *f.* sin. ˡ חַטָּאָה *f.* *id.* ᵐ חַטָּאת *f.* sin, sin-offering. Gen. iv. 7, &c. ⁿ חֲטִי Ch. *id.*

3 עָוֹן *m.* see *Iniquity.*

4 עָשָׂה to do. KAL *part.* Poel.

5 פֶּשַׁע revolt, transgression, sin.

6 שָׁגַג to err, to do wrong through ignorance or inadvertence. KAL *part.* Poel.

7 שָׁגָה to wander, to err, through ignorance. KAL *fut.*

No. 2 m not included.

Gen. xiii. 13.	2 i	1 Sam. xxiv. 11.	2 a	Ps. cxix. 11.	2 c
xx. 6.	2 b	xxvi. 21.	2 a	Prov. i. 10.	2 i
xx. 9.	2 l	2 Sam. xii. 13.	2 a	x. 12, 19.	5
xxxix. 9.	2 a	xix. 20.	2 a	xi. 31.	2 d
xlii. 22.	2 c	xxiv. 10, 17.	2 a	xiii. 6.	2 m
Exod. ix. 27.	2 a	1 Kings viii. 33, 35,		xiii. 21.	2 i
ix. 34. *a*	2 b	46. 46.	2 c	xiii. 22.	2 i
x. 16.	2 a	viii. 47, 50.	2 a	xiv. 9.	2 l
xx. 20.	2 c	xv. 16, 16.	2 a e	xiv. 21.	2 d
xxiii. 33.	2 g	xv. 26, 34.	2 e	xx. 2.	2 a
xxxii. 21.	2 l	xv. 30, 30.	2 a e	xxiii. 17.	2 i
xxxii. 30, 30, 30.	2 a l m	xvi. 2.	2 g	xxviii. 13.	2 d
xxxii. 31, 31.	2 a l	xvi. 13, 13.	2 a e	Eccles. ii. 26.	2 d
xxxii. 33.	2 a	xvi. 19.	2 a f	v. 6.	2 f
xxxiv. 7.	2 c	xvi. 26.	2 e	vii. 20.	2 c
Lev. iv. 2.	2 c	xvii. 18.	3	viii. 12.	2 d
iv. 3, 3, 3, 3. {	2 c, 1 a, / 2 m a	xviii. 9.	2 a	ix. 2, 18.	2 d
iv. 13.	7	xxi. 22.	2 e	Isa. i. 4.	2 d
iv. 14.	2 a	xxii. 52.	2 e	i. 18.	2 i
iv. 22, 27.	2 a	2 Kings iii. 3.	2 e	i. 28.	2 i
iv. 23, 28, 28.	2 a	x. 29, 29.	2 h e	xiii. 9.	2 k
v. 1, 17.	2 c	x. 31.	2 e	xxxi. 7.	2 h
v. 5, 6, 10, 11, 13,		xiii. 2, 6, 11.	2 e	xxxiii. 14.	2 i
15.	2 a	xiv. 6.	2 h	xxxviii. 17.	2 a
vi. 2, 4.	2 c	xv. 9, 18, 24, 28.	2 e	xlii. 24.	2 a
vi. 3.	2 b	xvii. 7.	2 a	xliii. 27.	2 a
xix. 17.	2 h	xvii. 21, 21.	2 e l	liii. 10.	2 c
xx. 20.	2 h	xxi. 11.	2 g	liii. 12.	2 c
xxii. 9.	2 h	xxi. 16.	2 a	lxiv. 5.	2 h
xxiv. 15.	2 h	xxi. 17.	2 a	lxv. 20.	2 d
Num. vi. 11.	2 a	xxiii. 15.	2 e	Jer. ii. 35.	2 a
ix. 13.	2 h	1 Chron. xxi. 8, 17.	2 a	iii. 25.	2 a
xii. 11.	2 a	2 Chron. vi. 22, 24, 26,		viii. 14.	2 a
xiv. 40.	2 a	36, 36.	2 c	xiv. 7, 20.	2 a
xv. 27.	2 a	vi. 37, 39.	2 a	xxxii. 35.	2 f
xv. 28, 28.	6, 2 b	xxv. 4.	2 h	xxxiii. 8, 8.	2 a
xv. 29.	4	xxviii. 10.	1 a	xl. 3.	2 a
xvi. 22.	2 c	Neh. i. 6, 6.	2 a	xliv. 23.	2 a
xvi. 38.	2 i	i. 13.	2 a	l. 7, 14.	2 a
xviii. 22, 32.	2 h	ix. 29.	2 a	li. 5.	1
xxii. 7.	2 a	xiii. 26, 26.	2 a e	Lam. i. 8. δ	2 a h
xxii. 34.	2 a	Job i. 5, 22.	2 a e	v. 7, 16.	2 b a
xxvii. 3.	2 h	ii. 10.	2 a	Ezek. iii. 21, 21.	2 c
xxxii. 14.	2 i	v. 24.	2 c	xiv. 13.	2 c
xxxii. 23.	2 a	vii. 20.	2 a	xviii. 4, 20.	2 d
Deut. i. 41.	2 a	viii. 4.	2 a	xviii. 24.	2 a
ix. 16, 18.	2 a	x. 14.	2 a	xxiii. 49.	2 h
xv. 9.	2 h	xxiv. 19.	2 a	xxviii. 16.	2 c
xix. 15, 15, 15.	2 m h c	xxxi. 30.	2 b	xxxiii. 12.	2 b
xx. 18.	2 a	xxxiii. 27.	2 a	xxxvii. 23.	2 b
xxi. 22.	2 a	xxxv. 6.	2 a	Dan. iv. 27.	2 a
xxii. 26.	2 h	Ps. i. 1, 5.	2 i	ix. 5, 8, 11, 15.	2 a
xxiii. 21, 22.	2 h	iv. 4.	2 c	ix. 16.	2 h
xxiv. 4.	2 g	xxv. 8.	2 i	Hos. iv. 7.	2 a
xxiv. 15, 16.	2 h	xxvi. 9.	2 i	viii. 11, 11.	2 b
Josh. vii. 11, 20.	2 a	xxxii. 1.	2 l	x. 9.	2 a
Judg. x. 10, 15.	2 a	xxxix. 1.	2 b	xii. 8.	2 h
xi. 27.	2 c	xli. 4.	2 a	xiii. 2.	2 b
1 Sam. ii. 25, 25.	2 c	li. 4.	2 a	Amos viii. 14.	1 a
vii. 6.	2 a	li. 5, 9.	2 a	ix. 8.	2 k
xii. 10.	2 a	li. 13.	2 i	ix. 10.	2 k
xii. 23. β	2 b	lxix. 5.	2 i	Micah vii. 19.	2 a
xiv. 33.	2 d	lxxviii. 17. γ	1 a	Hab. ii. 10.	2 d
xiv. 34.	2 c	lxxviii. 32.	2 a	Zeph. i. 17.	2 a
xv. 18.	2 i	ciii. 10.	2 h		
xv. 24, 30.	2 a	civ. 35.	2 i		
xix. 4, 4.	2 c a	cvi. 6.	2 a		
xix. 5.	2 c	cix. 7.	2 l		

a lit. added to sin. β *lit.* from sinning. γ *lit.* added to sin. δ *lit.* hath sinned a sin.

SIN-OFFERING (See OFFER)

SINCERITY, SINCERELY

תָּמִים *adj.* complete, perfect; whole-minded, upright, blameless: Josh. xxiv. 14: Judg. ix. 16, 19.

SINEW

גִּיד *m.* cord, thong, band; a nerve, sinew, tendon: Gen. xxxii. 32, 32: Job x. 11; xl. 17: Isa. xlviii. 4: Ezek. xxxvii. 6, 8.

עֹרֶק *m.* sinew, artery: Job xxx. 17.

SING, SONG

1　דָּבָר　*m.* word.

2　זָמַר　to sing in set composition of words and music; to sing praises, psalms. PIEL [a]*imp.* [b]*fut.* [c]זָמִיר *m.* song, hymn. [d]זָמִיר *m.* Cant. ii. 12; by our translators applied to the singing-time of birds, but (according to Gesenius) contrary to the usage of the verb זָמַר, and to the analogy of nouns of the form of קָמִיר; rather the pruning-time, *sc.* for vines. LXX. καιρὸς τῆς τομῆς; Symm. κ. τῆς κλαδεύσεως; Vulg. *tempus putationis.* [e]זַמָּר Ch. *m.* a singer. [f]זִמְרָה *f.* song.

3　נָגַן　to play on a stringed instrument. PIEL [a]*fut.* [b]נְגִינָה *f.* a song, psalm to be sung with the accompaniment of stringed instruments, Ps. lxxvii. 6, Isa. xxxviii. 20; a song of derision, satire, Job xxx. 9, Ps. lxix. 12, Lam. iii. 14.

4　נָצַח　see *Chief.* PIEL *part.*

5　מַשָּׂא　*m.* lifting up, of the voice: 1 Chron. xv. 22, 22, *marg.* 'lifting up.'

6　נָתַן　to give. KAL *fut.* Ps. civ. 12, *marg.* 'give a voice.'

7　עָנָה　Whatever be the primary meaning of this word, it is evident that it bears the sense of singing or chanting, probably in alternate courses. KAL [a]*pret.* [b]*imp.* [c]*fut.* PIEL [d]*inf.* [e]*imp.*

8　קוֹל　*m.* any sound, noise, voice.

9　רָבָה　to multiply. HIPHIL *imp.*

10　רָנַן　to utter cries of joy; to shout, to sing aloud. KAL [a]*inf.* [b]*imp.* [c]*fut.* PIEL [d]*pret.* [e]*inf.* [f]*imp.* [g]*fut.* PUAL [h]*fut.* HIPHIL [i]*imp.* [k]*fut.* [l]רִנָּה *f.* singing. [m]רֹן *m.* song. [n]רִנָּה *f.* shout of joy; as also a mournful cry.

11　שׁוּר　to sing; see שִׁיר. KAL *part.* Poel.

12　שִׁיר　to sing; *seq. acc.* of the song; also *seq. acc.* of the person or thing celebrated; *seq.* לְ to sing unto any one in his honour, to celebrate in song, also to sing of or concerning anything, Isa. v. 1; *seq.* בְּ to sing of, Ps. cxxxviii. 5; *seq.* עַל of him whom one addresses in song, before whom one sings, Prov. xxv. 20. But to sing is also sometimes put for, to declaim, to recite with a loud voice. KAL [a]*pret.* [b]*inf.* [c]*imp.* [d]*fut.* [e]*part.* Poel. POLEL [f]*fut.* [g]*part.* HOPHAL [h]*fut.* שִׁיר *m.* song, singing; a song, hymn, *e.g.* psalm; also not sacred, especially a song of joy: Gen. xxxi. 27, &c. "A new song" implies some remarkable manifestation of divine judgments, or revelation of divine grace: Ps. xcv. 1, 10. [k]שִׁירָה *f.* a song.

No. 12 i, *Song,* not included.

Exod. xv. 1, 1, 1.	12 d k d	1 Chron. vi. 32.	12 i	Ezra ii. 41, 65, 65, 70.	12 g		
xv. 2.	2 f	vi. 33.	12 g	iii. 11.	7 c		
xv. 21.	12 c	ix. 33.	12 g	vii. 7.	12 g		
xxxii. 18.	7 d	xiii. 8.	12 i	vii. 24.	12 g		
Num. xxi. 17,		xv. 16, 19, 27, 27.	12 g	x. 24.	12 g		
17, 17.	12 d k, 7 b	xv. 22, 22, 27.	5	Neh. vii. 1, 44, 67,			
Deut. xxxi. 19, 19,		xvi. 9, 23.	12 c	67, 73.	12 g		
21, 22, 30.	12 k	xvi. 33.	10 g	x. 28, 39.	12 g		
xxxii. 44.	12 k	2 Chron. v. 12, 13.	12 g	xi. 22, 23.	12 g		
Judg. v. 1.		ix. 11.	12 e	xii. 27.	12 i		
v. 3, 3.	12 d, 2 b	xx. 21.	12 g	xii. 28, 29, 42, 45,			
1 Sam. xviii. 6.	12 b	xx. 22.	10 n	46, 47.	12 g		
xxi. 11.	7 c	xxiii. 13.	12 g	xiii. 5, 10.	12 g		
xxix. 5.	7 c	xxiii. 18.	12 i	Job xxix. 13.	10 k		
2 Sam. xix. 35, 35.	12 e	xxix. 28, 28.α	12 i g	xxx. 9.	3 b		
xxii. 1.	12 k	xxxv. 15.	12 g	xxxv. 10.	2 c		
1 Kings x. 12.	12 e	xxxv. 25, 25.	12 e	xxxviii. 7.	10 a		

Ps. vii. title.	12 a	Ps. civ. 12.	6, 8	Isa. xxvi. 19.	10 f
xiii. 6.	12 d	civ. 33.	12 d	xxvii. 2.	7 e
xviii. title.	12 k	cv. 2.	12 c	xxxv. 2.	10 e
xxi. 13.	12 d	cvi. 12.	12 d	xxxv. 6.	10 c
xxvii. 6.	12 d	cviii. 1.	12 d	xxxv. 10.	10 n
xxx. 4.	2 a	cxviii. 14.	2 f	xxxviii. 20.	3 b
xxxii. 7.	10 m	cxix. 54.	2 c	xlii. 10.	12 c
xxxiii. 2.	2 a	cxxvi. 2.	10 n	xlii. 11.	10 c
xxxiii. 3.	12 c	cxxxvii. 3.	1, 12 i	xliv. 23, 23.	10 b n
lii. 14.	10 g	cxxxvii. 3, 3.	12 c i	xlviii. 20.	10 n
lvii. 7.	12 d	cxxxvii. 5.	12 d	xlix. 13, 13.	10 b n
lvii. 9.	2 b	cxxxviii. 5.	12 d	li. 11.	10 n
lix. 16, 16.	12 d, 10 g	cxliv. 9.	12 d	lii. 8.	10 g
lix. 17.	2 b	cxlv. 7.	10 g	lii. 9.	10 f
lxv. 13.	12 d	cxlvii. 7.	7 b	liv. 1, 1.	10 b n
lxvi. 2.	2 a	cxlix. 1.	12 c	lv. 12.	10 g
lxvi. 4, 4.	2 b	cxlix. 5.	10 g	lxv. 14.	10 c
lxvii. 4.	10 g	Prov. xxv. 20.	12 e	Jer. xx. 13.	12 c
lxviii. 4, 32.	12 c	xxix. 6.	12 e	xxxi. 7.	10 b
lxviii. 25.	12 e	Eccles. ii. 8, 8.	12 e	xxxi. 12.	10 d
lxix. 12.	3 b	Cant. ii. 12.	2 d	xl. 48.	10 d
lxxvii. 6.	3 b	Isa. v. 1, 1.	12 d k	Lam. iii. 14.	3 b
lxxxi. 1.	10 i	xii. 2.	2 f	Ezek. xxvii. 25.	11
lxxxvii. 7.	12 e	xiv. 7.	10 n	xl. 44.	12 e
lxxxix. 1.	12 d	xvi. 10.	10 h	Amos viii. 3.	12 k
xcv. 1.	10 g	xxiii. 15.	12 k	Hos. ii. 15.	7 a
xcvi. 1, 1, 2.	12 c	xxiii. 16.β	9, 12 i	Hab. iii. 19.	4
xcviii. 1.	12 c	xxiv. 14.	10 c	Zeph. ii. 14.	12 f
xcviii. 5.	2 a	xxiv. 16.	2 c	iii. 14.	10 b
c. 2.	2 b	xxvi. 1.	12 h	iii. 17.	10 n
ci. 1, 1.	12 d, 2 b			Zech. ii. 10.	10 b

α *lit.* and the song was sung.　　β *lit.* multiply the song.

SINGE

חֲרַךְ　Ch. to burn, to scorch, to singe. ITHPAEL *pret.* Dan. iii. 27.

SINGULAR

פָּלָא　to separate, distinguish; to consecrate, accomplish, pay. HIPHIL *fut.* Lev. xxvii. 2.

SINK

טָבַע　to sink; to be sunk, immersed. KAL *pret.* Ps. ix. 15; lxix. 2: Lam. ii. 9. *fut.* 1 Sam. xvii. 49: Ps. lxix. 14: Jer. xxxviii. 6. HOPHAL *pret.* Jer. xxxviii. 22.

יָרַד　to go down. KAL *pret.* Exod. xv. 5.

כָּרַע　to bow down. KAL *fut.* 2 Kings ix. 24, *marg.* 'bowed.'

צָלַל　to sink in the water. KAL *pret.* Exod. xv. 10.

שָׁקַע　to sink down, to subside. KAL *fut.* Jer. li. 64.

SIR

אָדוֹן　lord, master: Gen. xliii. 20.

SISTER-IN-LAW, FATHER'S SISTER.

אָחוֹת　sister; properly a sister of full blood, *i.e.* of both the same father and mother; but spoken also less accurately of a half-sister, *e.g.* one born to the same father but of a different mother, ὁμοπάτρια, Gen. xx. 12, 2 Sam. xiii. 2, 5; or one born of the same mother by a different father, ὁμομήτρια, Lev. xviii. 9, 11; xx. 17. The word sister is also employed by the Hebrews in other wider senses, *e.g.* a relative, kinswoman, Job xlii. 11: Gen. xxiv. 60, where the mother and brother say to Rebecca, "thou art our sister;" a countrywoman, one of the same tribe or country, *popularis,* Num. xxv. 18; an ally, a confederate city or state, Ezek. xvi. 46, xxiii. 31; one—the other; *metaph.* sister is said of anything with which we are intimately connected, Prov. vii. 4, Job xvii. 14; as a

term of endearment addressed to a spouse, Cant. iv. 9, &c.

יְבֶמֶת *f.* sister-in-law, a brother's wife; also the wife of a husband's brother: Ruth i. 15, 15.

דּוֹדָה *f.* aunt, father's sister: Exod. vi. 20.

SIT

1 דָּגַר to brood, to sit upon, as a bird her eggs or young; Lxx. συνήγαγεν; Vulg. *fovere.* KAL *pret.*

2 יָשַׁב to sit down, to seat oneself: to sit is a sign of supremacy or government: Ps. xxix. 10: Isa. xvi. 5: Ps. cx. 11: Matt. xxiii. 2. Specially it is spoken—of judges, who sit to dispense justice, hence the seat of violence, *i. e.* unjust judgment;—of kings, sitting as judges or on the throne;—of those who sit in ambush, to lie in wait, to lurk;—of mourners who sit upon the ground, or solitary, or who are said simply to sit; as of a widow, Gen. xxxviii. 11; Isa. xlvii. 8;—of those who sit still, who are quiet, idle, *opp.* to those who go out to war or to hunt, Jer. viii. 14, Isa. xxx. 7, Gen. xxv. 27; sitting in tents, *i. e.* remaining at home, occupied in domestic affairs; Ps. cxxxix. 2, "downsitting and uprising," of the common actions of life;—of an army, which sits down in a place, holds it, 1 Sam. xiii. 16;—to sit with any one, to have intercourse, to associate with him, Ps. xxvi. 4, 5, i. 1, Jer. xv. 17;—to sit at the king's right hand; see *Right Hand.* It is used also of inanimate things which elsewhere are said to be set, put, placed. KAL [a] *pret.* [b] *inf.* [c] *imp.* [d] *fut.* [e] *part.* Poel. מוֹשָׁב *m.* act of sitting.

3 יְתֵב Ch. to sit. P'AL *pret.*

4 נָתַן to give. KAL *fut.* 1 Sam. ix. 22, *lit.* gave them a place.

5 סָבַב to compass. KAL *fut.* 1 Sam. xvi. 11, *marg.* 'sit round.'

6 רָבַץ to couch, to lie down; to sit as a bird on her young. KAL *part.* Poel.

7 תָּכָה to lie down. PUAL *pret.* Deut. xxxiii. 3, *i. e.* encamped, *sc.* at the foot of Mount Sinai.

Gen. xviii. 1.	2 e	Ruth ii. 14.	2 d	1 Kings xxii. 10, 19.	2 e
xix. 1.	2 e	iii. 18.	2 c	2 Kings i. 9.	2 d
xxi. 16, 16.	2 d	iv. 1, 1, 1.	2 d c d	iv. 20.	2 d
xxvii. 19.	2 c	iv. 2, 2.	2 c d	iv. 38.	2 e
xxxi. 34.	2 d	1 Sam. i. 9.	2 e	vi. 32, 32.	2 e
xxxvii. 25.	2 d	iv. 13.	2 e	vii. 3.	2 e
xxxviii. 14.	2 d	ix. 22. α	4	vii. 4.	2 a
xliii. 33.	2 d	xvi. 11.	5	ix. 5.	2 e
xlviii. 2.	2 d	xix. 9.	2 e	x. 30.	2 e
Exod. ii. 15.	2 d	xx. 5.	2 b d	xi. 19.	2 d
xi. 5.	2 e	xx. 24, 25, 25.	2 d	xiii. 13.	2 a
xii. 29.	2 e	xxviii. 23.	2 d	xv. 12.	2 d
xvi. 3.	2 b	2 Sam. ii. 13.	2 d	xviii. 27.	2 e
xvii. 12.	2 d	vii. 1.	2 a	1 Chron. xvii. 1.	2 a
xviii. 13.	2 d	vii. 18.	2 d	xvii. 16.	2 a
xviii. 14.	2 b	xviii. 24.	2 d	xxviii. 5.	2 b
xxxii. 6.	2 d	xix. 8, 8.	2 d e	xxix. 23.	2 d
Lev. xv. 4, 20, 22, 26.	2 d	1 Kings i. 13, 17, 20,	2 e	2 Chron. vi. 16.	2 d
xv. 6, 6.	2 e d	24, 27, 30.	2 d	ix. 4.	2 f
xv. 23.	2 e	i. 35, 46.	2 a	ix. 18.	2 b
Num. xxxii. 6.	2 b	i. 48. β	2 e	xviii. 9, 9, 18.	2 b
Deut. vi. 7.	2 b	ii. 12.	2 a	Ezra ix. 3.	2 d
xi. 19.	2 b	ii. 19, 19.	2 d	ix. 4.	2 e
xvii. 18.	2 b	iii. 6.	2 e	x. 9, 16.	2 d
xxii. 6.	6	viii. 20.	2 d	Neh. i. 4.	2 e
xxxiii. 3.	7	viii. 25. β	2 e	ii. 6.	2 e
Judg. iii. 20.	2 e	x. 5.	2 f	viii. 17.	2 e
v. 10.	2 e	xiii. 14, 20.	2 d	Esth. i. 2.	2 b
vi. 11.	2 d	xvi. 13.	2 b	i. 14.	2 b
xiii. 18.	2 e	xix. 4.	2 d	ii. 19, 21.	2 e
xix. 6, 15.	2 e	xxi. 13.	2 d	iii. 15.	2 e
xx. 26.	2 d			v. 1, 13.	2 e

Esth. vi. 10.	2 e	Isa. iii. 26.	2 d	Jer. xxxviii. 7.	2 e
Job ii. 8.	2 e	vi. 1.	2 e	xxxix. 3.	2 d
ii. 13.	2 d	xiv. 13.	2 d	xlviii. 18.	2 c
xxix. 25.	2 d	xvi. 5.	2 d	Lam. i. 1.	2 e
Ps. i. 1.	2 a	xxviii. 6.	2 a	ii. 10.	2 d
ii. 4.	2 e	xxxvi. 12.	2 e	iii. 28.	2 d
ix. 4.	2 a	xl. 22.	2 e	iii. 63.	2 b
x. 8.	2 d	xlii. 7.	2 e	Ezek. iii. 15, 15.	2 d e
xxvi. 4.	2 a	xlvii. 1, 1, 5.	2 d	viii. 1, 1, 14.	2 e
xxvi. 5.	2 e	xlviii. 8.	2 d	xiv. 1.	2 e
xxix. 10, 10.	2 a d	xlvii. 14.	2 a	xx. 1.	2 e
xlvii. 8.	2 d	lii. 2.	2 c	xxiii. 41.	2 a
l. 20.	2 e	Jer. i. 8.	2 e	xxvi. 16.	2 d
lxix. 12.	2 e	viii. 14.	2 e	xxviii. 2.	2 d
xcix. 1.	2 e	xiii. 13. γ	2 e	xxxiii. 31.	2 d
cvii. 10.	2 e	xiii. 18.	2 e	xliv. 3.	2 d
cxix. 23.	2 a	xv. 17, 17.	2 e	Dan. ix. 26.	3
cxxvii. 2.	2 d	xvi. 8.	2 b	Joel iii. 12.	2 d
cxxxii. 12.	2 d	xvii. 11.	1	Jonah iii. 6.	2 d
cxxxvii. 1.	2 e	xvii. 25.	2 d	iv. 5, 5.	2 d
cxxxix. 2.	2 b	xxii. 2, 4, 30.	2 d	Micah iv. 4.	2 d
Prov. ix. 14.	2 a	xxvi. 10.	2 d	vii. 8.	2 d
xx. 8.	2 e	xxix. 16.	2 d	Zech. i. 11.	2 d
xxiii. 1.	2 d	xxxii. 12.	2 d	iii. 8.	2 c
xxxi. 23.	2 d	xxxiii. 17. δ	2 d	v. 7.	2 e
Eccles. x. 6.	2 b	xxxvi. 12, 22, 30. δ	2 d	vi. 13.	2 e
Cant. ii. 3.	2 a	xxxvi. 15.	2 c	Mal. iii. 3.	2 a

α lit. and gave them a place. *β lit.* sitting. *γ lit.* sit for David upon his throne. *δ lit.* sitting.

SITUATE

יָשַׁב to sit; to be set, placed. KAL *part.* Poel, Ezek. xxvii. 3, Nah. iii. 8. מוֹשָׁב *m.* seat, situation: 2 Kings ii. 19.

נוֹף *m.* elevation, height: Ps. xlviii. 2, beautiful for elevation is Mount Zion, *i. e.* it rises gracefully.

מָצוּק *m.* pillar; *trop.* of a rock or cliff isolated like a column: 1 Sam. xiv. 5, the one crag, a column over against Michmash: see Robinson's Palestine, ii. p. 216.

SIVAN

סִיוָן *m.* the third month of the Hebrew year, from the new moon of June to the new moon of July: Esth. viii. 9.

SIX

שֵׁשׁ *m. num. adj.* The number six denotes perfection or completeness; it seems also to be used for an indefinite number, as in Job v. 19, where seven is also added to give a greater idea of an unlimited number; see three and four so applied in Amos i. 3, &c.

שָׁשָׁא a doubtful root, found only once, Ezek. xxxix. 2: it has been usually supposed to mean, to divide into six parts, but this does not suit the context. Lxx. has καθωδήγησω σε, but Compt. κατάξω σε. Targ. *errare te faciam.* Vulg. *seducam te.* The signification of leading seems also implied in the context; Gesenius therefore gives PIEL *pret.* Ezek. xxxix. 2, I will turn again, and will lead thee, and will bring thee up, &c.; but in *marg.* we find, 'or, strike thee with six plagues; or, draw thee back with an hook of six teeth, as xxxviii. 4.'

שִׁשָּׁה to divide into six parts; and so to give a sixth part. PIEL *pret.* Ezek. xlv. 13.

SIZE

מִדָּה *f.* extension, length; measure: Exod. xxxvi. 9, 15: 1 Chron. xxiii. 29.

קֶצֶב *m.* cut, *i. e.* form, shape: 1 Kings vi. 25; vii. 37.

SKILL

1   בִּין   to discern, perceive ; to be knowing, skilful. HIPHIL [a]part. [b]תְּבוּנָה f. understanding.

2   חָכְמָה f. skill in any art, dexterity ; wisdom.

3   חָרָשׁ m. workman, artificer.

4   יָדַע to know. KAL part. Poel.

5   יָטַב to be good ; to do good. HIPHIL imp.

6   לָמַד to learn. KAL part. Paül.

7   שָׂכַל to view; to be prudent, circumspect, wise. HIPHIL [a]inf. [b]part.

1 Kings v. 6.	4	2 Chron. xxxiv. 12.	1 a	Dan. i. 4.	8 b
1 Chron. v. 18.	6	Ps. xxxiii. 3.β	5	i. 17.	7 a
xv. 22.	1 a	lxxviii. 72.	1 b	ix. 22.	7 a
xxviii. 21.α	2	Eccles. ix. 11.	4	Amos v. 16.	4
2 Chron. ii. 7, 8, 14.	4	Ezek. xxi. 31.γ	3		

α lit. in wisdom.   β lit. do good to play.
γ lit. artificers of destruction.

SKIN

בָּשָׂר m. flesh : Ps. cii. 5, marg. 'flesh.'

גֶּלֶד m. the human skin as smooth and polished : Job xvi. 15.

עוֹר the skin of a man, from its nudity ; the hide or skin of an animal : Gen. iii. 21, &c.

SKIP

נוּד to be moved, as the body is agitated in expressing great joy. HITHPOLEL fut. Jer. xlviii. 27.

קָפַץ to draw together, e.g. the limbs in order to make a spring. PIEL part. Cant. ii. 8.

רָקַד to leap, to skip, e.g. for joy, to dance. KAL pret. Ps. cxiv. 4. fut. Ps. cxiv. 6. HIPHIL fut. Ps. xxix. 6.

SKIRT

כָּנָף m. wing; extremity, corner, e.g. of a garment, skirt, flap ; as the outer garment was also used by the Orientals to wrap themselves in at night, hence it is also put for the extremity or corner of a bed-covering or coverlet : Deut. xxii. 30 ; xxvii. 20 : Ruth iii. 9 : 1 Sam. xv. 27; xxiv. 4, 5, 11, 11 : Jer. ii. 34 : Ezek. v. 3; xvi. 8 : Hag. ii. 12, 12 : Zech. viii. 23.

פֶּה m. mouth ; aperture, orifice, entrance, of a garment surrounding the neck, the collar of Aaron's ephod : Ps. cxxxiii. 2.

שׁוּל m. train, flowing skirts of a robe ; hem of a garment : Jer. xiii. 22, 26 : Lam. i. 9 : Nah. iii. 5.

SKY

שַׁחַק m. dust ; clouds ; firmament, sky, the heavens : Deut. xxxiii. 26 : 2 Sam. xxii. 12 : Job xxxvii. 18 : Ps. xviii. 11 ; lxxvii. 17 : Isa. xlv. 8 : Jer. li. 9.

SLACK

אָחַר to defer. PIEL fut. Deut. vii. 10 ; xxiii. 21.

עָצַר to restrain. KAL fut. 2 Kings iv. 24.

פּוּג to be cold ; torpid, sluggish, slack. KAL fut. Hab. i. 4.

רְמִיָּה f. a letting fall of the hands, remissness, sloth : Prov. x. 4, i.e. suffering a diminution of its authority.

רָפָה to be relaxed, slackened. KAL fut. Zeph. iii. 16, marg. ' or, faint.' HIPHIL fut. Josh. x. 6. HITHPAEL part. Josh. xviii. 3.

SLANDER

דִּבָּה f. calumnious, clandestine, and malicious report : Num. xiv. 36 : Ps. xxxi. 13 : Prov. x. 18.

הֲפִי m. a stumbling-block, cause of falling. Lxx. σκάνδαλον ; Vulg. offendiculum. Ps. l. 20, lit. thou wilt give slander, or stumbling-block, against.

נָתַן to give. KAL fut. Ps. l. 20.

לָשׁוֹן to tongue, i.e. to use the tongue freely, and by implication, to slander. PIEL part. Ps. ci. 5. POEL part. (כתיב) Ps. ci. 5.

רָגַל see Backbite. PIEL fut. 2 Sam. xix. 27.

רָכִיל m. tale-bearing, detraction : Jer. vi. 28 ; ix. 4.

SLAY, SLAUGHTER

1   הָרַג to slay, as one man slays another, or enemies in battle ; of any slaughter, 1 Kings xix. 10, &c., with a sword or with stones. It is used also of pestilence, Jer. xviii. 2, comp. Ps. lxxviii. 34 ; of the viper, Job xx. 16 ; of grief, Job v. 2 ; of a violent death, opp. to death by disease, Isa. xiv. 30 ; of the slaying of beasts, Isa. xxii. 13, xxvii. 1. Metaph. to destroy vines, Ps. lxxviii. 47, comp. מות, Isa. xiv. 8. Lxx. mostly ἀποκτείνω, seldom ἀναιρέω, θανατόω, φονεύω. KAL [a]pret. [b]inf. [c]imp. [d]fut. [e]part. Poel. [f]part. Paül. NIPHAL [g]fut. [h]inf. PUAL [i]pret. [k]הֶרֶג m. slaughter. [l]הֲרֵנָה f. id.

2   זָבַח to slaughter or kill animals for eating or for sacrifice. KAL fut.

3   חָלַל to wound. PIEL [a]part. PUAL [b]part. [c]חָלָל adj. pierced, wounded, i.e. mortally ; often also killed, slain in a private feud, oftener in battle.

4   חָרַב to be drained ; to be dried up, wasted, blood drained by being stabbed with a sword. KAL [a]imp. NIPHAL [b]pret. HOPHAL [c]inf.

5   חָרַם to destroy utterly ; see Destroy. HIPHIL inf.

6   טָבַח to slaughter, to kill, especially animals for eating ; to kill men. KAL [a]inf. [b]part. Paül. [c]טֶבַח m. slaughter. [d]מִבְחָה f. id. [e]מַטְבֵּחַ m. id.

7   מוּת to die. KAL [a]pret. POLEL [b]pret. [c]inf. [d]imp. [e]fut. [f]part. HIPHIL [g]pret. [h]inf. [i]imp. [k]fut. [l]part. HOPHAL [m]pret. [n]fut. [o]part. [p]מָוֶת m. death.

8   נָגַף to smite, as by Jehovah. NIPHAL [a]pret. [b]fut. [c]מַגֵּפָה f. a plague sent from God ; slaughter in battle.

9   נָכָה to strike, to smite ; to smite fatally, to kill, to slay. HIPHIL [a]pret. [b]inf. [c]imp. [d]fut. [e]part. HOPHAL [f]pret. [g]part. [h]מַכָּה f. smiting ; defeat, slaughter.

10   נָפַל to fall. HIPHIL pret.

11   מַפָּץ m. a smiting in pieces.

12   נֶפֶשׁ m. soul.

13 קָטַל to kill, to slay. KAL [a] *fut.* [b] קְטַל Ch. P'AL *part. active.* [c] *part. passive.* PAEL [d] *pret.* [e] *inf.* ITHP'AL [f] *inf.* ITH-PAEL [g] *part.* [h] קַטֵּל *m.*

14 רָצַח to break, or dash in pieces; to kill, to slay. KAL [a] *pret.* [b] *part.* Poel. [c] *fut.* [d] *part.* PUAL [e] *fut.* [f] רֶצַח *m.* slaughter: Ezek. xxi. 22, according to Gesenius, out-break of the voice, outcry, clamour.

15 שָׁחַט to kill animals, to slaughter, especially victims for sacrifice; Hos. v. 2, in the slaughtering (of victims) they make deep their transgressions. KAL [a] *pret.* [b] *inf.* [c] *fut.* [d] *part.* Poel. [e] *part.* Paül. NIPHAL [f] *fut.*

Gen. iv. 8, 14.	1 d	Judg. i. 4, 5, 10, 17.	9 d	2 Sam. xiii. 32.	7 g	
iv. 15.	1 e	iii. 29, 31.	9 d	xiv. 6.	7 k	
iv. 23, 25. a	1 a	vii. 25, 25.	1 d a	xiv. 7.	1 a	
xiv. 17.	9 b	viii. 17, 21.	1 d	xvii. 9.	8 c	
xviii. 25.	7 h	viii. 18, 19.	1 c	xviii. 7, 7.	8 b c	
xx. 4.	1 d	viii. 20.	1 c	xviii. 15.	7 k	
xx. 11.	1 a	ix. 5, 18.	1 d	xxi. 1.	7 g	
xxii. 10.	15 b	ix. 24, 45.	1 a	xxi. 2, 12, 16.	9 d	
xxvii. 41.	1 d	ix. 44.	9 d	xxi. 18.	9 d	
xxxiv. 25.	1 d	ix. 54, 54.	7 d, 1 a	xxi. 19, 21.	9 d	
xxxiv. 26.	1 a	ix. 56.	1 a	xxiii. 8, 18.	9 d	
xxxiv. 27.	3 c	xi. 33.	9 h	xxiii. 12.	9 d	
xxxiv. 30.	9 a	xii. 6.	15 c	xxiii. 20, 20.	9 a	
xxxvii. 18.	7 h	xiv. 19.	9 d	xxiii. 21, 21.	9 a, 1 d	
xxxvii. 20, 26.	1 d	xv. 8.	9 h	1 Kings i. 9, 19, 25.	2	
xxxviii. 7, 10.	7 k	xv. 15.	9 d	i. 51.	7 k	
xlii. 37.	7 k	xv. 16.	9 a	ii. 5, 32.	1 d	
xliii. 16.	6 a c	xvi. 24.	3 c	ii. 34.	7 k	
xlix. 6.	1 a	xvi. 30, 30.	7 g	iii. 26.	7 h k	
Exod. ii. 12.	9 d	xx. 4.	14 d	iii. 27.	7 h k	
ii. 15.	1 b	xx. 5.	1 b	ix. 16.	1 a	
iv. 23.	1 e	xx. 45.	9 d	xi. 15.	3 c	
v. 21.	1 b	1 Sam. i. 25.	15 c	xi. 24.	1 d	
xiii. 15.	1 d	ii. 25.	7 h	xiii. 24, 26.	7 k	
xxi. 14.	1 b	iv. 2.	9 d	xv. 28.	7 k	
xxiii. 7.	1 d	iv. 10.	9 h	xvi. 11, 16.	7 k	
xxix. 16.	15 a	iv. 11.	7 a	xvii. 18, 20.	7 h	
xxxii. 12.	1 b	iv. 17.	8 c	xviii. 9.	1 a	
xxxii. 27.	1 c	v. 10.	7 h	xviii. 12, 14.	1 a	
Lev. iv. 29, 33.	15 a	v. 11.	7 k	xviii. 13.	1 a	
viii. 15, 23.	15 c	vi. 19.	9 h	xviii. 40.	15 c	
ix. 8, 12, 15, 18.	15 c	xi. 11.	9 d	xix. 1, 10, 14.	1 a	
xiv. 13.	15 a	xiv. 13.	7 f	xix. 17, 17.	7 k	
xiv. 51.	15 c	xiv. 14.	9 h a	xix. 21.	2	
xx. 15.	1 d	xiv. 32.	9 h	xx. 20, 29.	9 d	
xxvi. 17.	8 a	xiv. 34, 34.	15 c	xx. 21, 21.	9 a h	
Num. xi. 22.	15 f	xv. 3.	7 g	xx. 36, 36.	9 a d	
xiv. 16.	15 c	xvii. 35.	7 g	2 Kings iii. 23. γ	4 c b	
xix. 3.	15 a	xvii. 36.	9 a	viii. 12.	1 d	
xix. 16, 18.	3 c	xvii. 50.	7 k	ix. 31.	1 e	
xxii. 33.	1 a	xvii. 51.	7 e	x. 7, 14.	15 c	
xxiii. 24.	3 c	xvii. 57.	9 b	x. 9, 9.	1 d, 9 a	
xxv. 5.	1 c	xviii. 6.	9 b	x. 11, 17.	9 d	
xxv. 14, 14.	9 g f	xviii. 7.	9 a	x. 25.	9 d	
xxv. 15, 18.	9 g	xviii. 27.	9 d	xi. 2, 2.	7 o m	
xxxi. 7.	1 d	xix. 5, 5.	9 d, 7 h	xi. 8, 15, 16.	7 n	
xxxi. 8, 8.		xix. 6.	7 n	xi. 18.	1 a	
8.	1 a, 3 c, 1 a	xix. 8, 8.	9 d h	xi. 20.	7 g	
xxxi. 19.	3 c	xix. 11, 11.	7 h o	xii. 20.	9 d	
xxxv. 11, 25, 26,		xix. 15.	7 i	xiv. 5, 5.	9 d e	
27, 28.	14 b	xx. 8.	7 i	xiv. 6.	7 g	
xxxv. 19, 19, 21.	7 k	xx. 32.	1 a	xiv. 7.	7 g	
xxxv. 24.	9 e	xx. 33.	7 h	xiv. 19.	7 k	
Deut. i. 4.	1 a	xxi. 9, 11.	9 a	xv. 10, 14, 30.	7 k	
iv. 42.	14 b	xxii. 17.	7 i	xvi. 9.	7 g	
ix. 28.	7 h	xxii. 18.	7 k	xvii. 25. δ	7 g	
xix. 3, 4.	14 b	xxii. 21.	1 a	xvii. 26.	7 k	
xix. 6, 6.	14 b, 9 a	xxiii. 21.	9 h	xxi. 23.	7 k	
xxi. 1, 1.	3 c, 9 a, 12	xxiii. 5.	9 a	xxi. 24.	9 a	
xxi. 2, 3, 6.	3 c	xxix. 5.	9 a	xxiii. 20.	2	
xxii. 26.β	14 a, 12	xxx. 2.	7 g	xxiii. 20.	9 a	
xxvii. 25.	9 b	xxxi. 1, 8.	3 c	xxv. 7.	15 a	
xxxi. 31.	6 b	xxxi. 2.	9 d	xxv. 21.	7 k	
xxxii. 42.	3 c	2 Sam. i. 1.	9 b	1 Chron. ii. 3.	3 c	
Josh. viii. 21.	9 d	i. 9.	7 d	v. 22.	3 c	
viii. 24.	1 b	i. 10.	7 e	vii. 21.	9 d	
ix. 26.	1 a	i. 16.	7 b	x. 1.	3 c	
x. 10, 10.	9 d h	i. 19, 22, 25.	3 c	x. 2.	9 d	
x. 11.	1 a	iii. 30, 30.	1 a, 7 g	x. 8.	3 c	
x. 20, 20.	9 b h	iii. 37.	7 h	x. 14.	7 k	
x. 26.	7 k	iv. 7.	7 k	xi. 11, 20.	3 c	
xi. 6.	3 c	iv. 10, 12.	1 d	xi. 14.	9 d	
xi. 17.	7 k	iv. 11.	1 a	xii. 22, 22.	9 d	
xiii. 22, 22.	1 a, 3 c	viii. 5.	9 d	xii. 23, 23.	9 a, 1 a	
xx. 3, 5, 6.	14 b	x. 18.	1 d	xviii. 5.	9 d	
xxi. 13, 21, 27, 32,		xii. 9.	1 a	xviii. 12.	1 a	
38.	14 b	xiii. 30.	9 a	xix. 18.	1 d	

1 Chron. xx. 4.	9 a	Prov. i. 32.	1 d	Lam. ii. 20.	1 g		
xx. 5, 7.	9 d	vii. 22.	6 c	ii. 21.	1 a		
2 Chron. xiii. 17,		vii. 26.	1 f	iii. 43.	1 a		
17, 17.	9 d h, 3 c	xxii. 13.	14 c	iv. 9, 9.	3 c		
xx. 23.	5	xxiv. 11.	1 k	Ezek. iv. 4, 7, 13.	3 c		
xxi. 4.	1 d	Isa. x. 4.	1 f	ix. 2.	11		
xxi. 13.	1 a	i. 26.	9 h	ix. 6.	1 d		
xxii. 8.	1 d	xi. 4.	7 k	ix. 7, 7.	3 c, 9 a		
xxii. 9.	7 k	xiv. 19.	1 f	ix. 8.	3 c		
xxii. 11, 11.	7 o g	xiv. 20.	1 a	xi. 6, 6, 7.	3 c		
xxiii. 14, 14.	7 n k	xiv. 30.	1 d	xiii. 19.	7 h		
xxiii. 15.	1 a	xxii. 2, 2.	1 d	xvi. 21.	15 c		
xxiii. 17.	3 c	xxii. 13.	1 b	xxi. 10.ζ	6 a c		
xxiii. 21.	1 a	xxvi. 21.	1 f	xxi. 14, 14, 29.	3 d		
xxiv. 22, 25.	1 d	xxvii. 1.	1 a	xxi. 15, 28.	6 c		
xxv. 3.	1 d	xxvii. 7, 7, 7.ε	1 i k f	xxi. 22.	14 f		
xxv. 4.	7 g	xxx. 25.	1 k	xxiii. 10.	1 a		
xxv. 14.	9 b	xxxiv. 2, 6.	6 c	xxiii. 39.	15 b		
xxv. 27.	7 k	xxxiv. 5.	3 c	xxiii. 47.	1 d		
xxviii. 5.	9 h	lii. 7.	6 d	xxvi. 6.	1 g		
xxviii. 6, 7, 9.	3 c	lvii. 5.	15 d	xxvi. 8, 11.	1 g		
xxxii. 21.	1 d	lvi. 12.	6 c	xxvi. 15.η	1 k h		
xxxiii. 24.	7 k	lxv. 15.	7 g	xxviii. 8.	3 c		
xxxiii. 25.	9 d	lxvi. 3.	9 e	xxviii. 9, 9.	1 e, 3 a		
xxxvi. 17.	1 d	lxvi. 16.	3 c	xxx. 4, 11.	3 c		
Neh. iv. 6.	1 a	Jer. v. 6.	9 a	xxxi. 17, 18.	3 c		
vi. 10, 10.	1 b	vii. 9.	1 l	xxxii. 20, 21, 22,			
ix. 26.	1 a	xi. 19.	3 c	23, 24, 25, 25,			
Esth. vii. 4.	1 b	xi. 3, 3.	6 d, 1 l	25, 28, 29, 30,			
viii. 11.	1 b	xiv. 18.	3 c	30, 31, 32.	3 c		
ix. 5.	1 k	xv. 3.	1 c	xxxii. 26.	3 b		
ix. 6, 10, 12.	1 a	xviii. 21.	9 b	xxxv. 8, 8.	3 c		
ix. 11.	1 f	xviii. 23.	7 l	xl. 39.	1 f		
ix. 16.	1 b	xix. 6.	1 l	xl. 41, 42.	15 c		
Job i. 15, 17.	1 d	xix. 7.	1 a	xliv. 11.	15 c		
v. 2.	7 k	xx. 17.	9 a	Dan. ii. 13, 13.	13 f g		
ix. 23.	7 k	xxv. 33.	3 c	ii. 14.	13 e		
xiii. 15.	13 a	xxvi. 23.	6 a	iii. 22.	13 d		
xx. 16.	1 d	xxvi. 23.	9 d	v. 19.θ	13 b		
xxxix. 30.	7 e	xxix. 21.	7 e	v. 30.	13 c		
Ps. xxxiv. 21.	7 e	xxxiii. 5.	9 a	vii. 11.	13 c		
xxxvii. 14.	6 a	xl. 14.	9 b, 12	Hos. ii. 3.	7 g		
xxxvii. 32.	7 h	xl. 15, 15.	9 d	vi. 2.	15 b		
xliv. 22.	6 d	xli. 2.	7 k	vi. 5.	1 a		
lix. 11.	1 d	xli. 3, 16, 18.	9 a	vi. 16.	7 g		
lxii. 3.	14 e	xli. 7.	7 h	Amos ii. 3.	1 a		
lxxviii. 31.	1 d	xli. 7.	15 c	iv. 10.	1 a		
lxxviii. 34.	1 l	xli. 8, 8.	7 k g	ix. 1.	1 d		
lxxxviii. 5.	3 c	xli. 9.	9 a, 3 c	ix. 4.	1 a		
lxxxix. 10.	3 c	xlviii. 15.	6 c	Obad. 9.	13 h		
xciv. 6.	1 d	cv. 29.	7 k	Nah. iii. 3.	3 c		
cix. 16.	7 c	li. 4, 47, 49, 49.	3 c	Hab. i. 17.	1 b		
cxxxv. 10.	1 a	li. 40.	6 a	Zeph. ii. 12.	3 c		
cxxxvi. 18.	1 d	lii. 10, 10.	15 c a	Zech. xi. 4, 7.	1 l		
cxxxix. 19.	13 a	Lam. i. 4.	1 d	xi. 5.	1 d		

[a] *lit.* for Cain slew him. [β] *lit.* smiteth him (as to) the soul. [γ] *marg.* 'destroyed,' or, *lit.* slain are slain. [δ] *lit.* were slayers. [ε] *lit.* according to the slaying of his slain. [ζ] *lit.* to slay a slaughter. [η] *lit.* when the slaughter is slaughtered. [θ] *lit.* he was slaying.

SLEEP

1 הָזָה to dream, to talk in one's dreams. KAL *part.* Poel, Isa. lvi. 10, *marg.* 'or, dreaming, or, talking in their sleep.' The primary idea seems to be that of nocturnal vision.

2 יָשֵׁן to be languid, lax, weary; to fall asleep, to go to sleep. KAL [a] *pret.* [b] *inf.* [c] *fut.* PIEL [d] *fut.* [e] יָשֵׁן *adj.* sleepy. [f] שֵׁנָה *f.* sleep. [g] שֵׁנָה Ch. *f. id.* [h] שֵׁנָא *f. id.* [i] שְׁנָת *f. id.*

3 נוּם to slumber from weariness and lassitude. The primary idea seems to be that of nodding, like Gr. νυστάζω, which the Lxx. put for it. KAL *pret.*

4 רָדַם to lie in a deep sleep. NIPHAL [a] *pret.* [b] *fut.* [c] *part.* [d] תַּרְדֵּמָה *f.* deep sleep; deep sloth, sluggishness.

5 שָׁכַב to lie down, to lie to sleep. KAL [a] *pret.* [b] *inf.* [c] *fut.*

Gen. ii. 21.	4 d, 2 c	Deut. xxiv. 12.	5 c	1 Sam. xxvi. 12,			
xv. 12.	4 d	xxiv. 13.	5 c	12.	2 e, 4 d		
xxviii. 11.	5 c	xxxi. 16.	5 d	2 Sam. vii. 12.	5 a		
xxviii. 16.	2 f	Judg. iv. 21.	4 a	xi. 9.	5 d		
xxxi. 40.	2 f	xvi. 14, 20.	2 f	1 Kings i. 21.	5 b		
xli. 5.	2 c	xvi. 19.	4 a	ii. 10.	5 a		
Exod. xxii. 27.	5 c	1 Sam. xxvi. 7.	2 e	iii. 20.	2 e		

1 Kings xi. 21.	5 a	2 Chron. xxviii. 27.	5 c	Prov. vi. 22.	5 b
xi. 43.	5 c	xxxii. 33.	5 c	x. 5.	4 c
xiv. 20, 31.	5 c	xxxiii. 20.	5 c	xix. 15.	4 d
xv. 8, 24.	5 c	Esth. vi. 1.α	2 f	xx. 13.	2 f
xvi. 6, 28.	5 c	Job iii. 13.	2 a	xxiv. 33, 33.β	2 f, 5 b
xviii. 27.	2 e	iv. 13.	4 d	Eccles. v. 12, 12.	2 f, 2 b
xix. 5.	2 c	vii. 21.	5 c	viii. 16.	2 f
xxii. 40, 50.	5 c	xiv. 12.	2 f	Cant. v. 2.	2 e
2 Kings viii. 24.	5 c	xxxiii. 15.	4 d	vii. 9.	2 e
x. 35.	5 c	Ps. iii. 5.	2 c	Isa. v. 27.	2 c
xiii. 9, 13.	5 c	iv. 8.	2 c	xxix. 10.	4 d
xiv. 16, 29.	5 c	xiii. 3.	2 c	lvi. 10.	1
xiv. 22.	5 b	xliv. 23.	2 c	Jer. xxxi. 26.	2 f
xv. 7, 22, 38.	5 c	lxxvi. 5, 5.	3, 2 f	li. 39, 39.	2 a, 2 f
xvi. 20.	5 c	lxxvi. 6.	4 c	li. 57, 57.	2 a, 2 f
xx. 21.	5 c	lxxviii. 65.	2 e	Ezek. xxxiv. 25.	2 a
xxi. 18.	5 c	xc. 5.	2 f	Dan. ii. 1.	2 f
xxiv. 6.	5 c	cxxi. 4.	2 c	vi. 18.	2 g
2 Chron. ix. 31.	5 c	cxxvii. 2.	2 h	viii. 18.	4 a
xii. 16.	5 c	cxxxii. 4.	2 i	x. 9.	4 c
xiv. 1.	5 c	Prov. iii. 24.	2 f	x. 12.	2 e
xvi. 13.	5 c	iv. 16, 16.	2 c, 2 f	Hos. vii. 6.	2 e
xxi. 1.	5 c	vi. 4.	2 f	Jonah i. 5.	4 b
xxvi. 2.	5 b	vi. 9, 9.	5 c, 2 f	i. 6.	4 c
xxvi. 23.	5 c	vi. 10, 10.β	2 f, 5 b	Zech. iv. 1.	2 f
xxvii. 9.	5 c				

α marg. 'the king's sleep fled away.'   β lit. for lying down.

SLIDE

מוט to waver, to shake, to totter; of the foot. KAL fut. Deut. xxxii. 35.

מעד to waver, to be unsteady, to totter. KAL fut. Ps. xxvi. 1; xxxvii. 31.

סרר to slide back; to be refractory, rebellious, intractable. KAL pret. Hos. iv. 16.

שוב to return, to turn from God. POLEL pret. Jer. viii. 5.

SLIGHTLY

קלל to be light. NIPHAL pret. Jer. vi. 14; viii. 11.

SLIME

חמר m. ἄσφαλτος, asphaltus, bitumen, which boils up in the manner of boiling oil or pitch, from subterranean fountains not far from Babylon, also from the bottom of the Dead Sea, which is thence called Lacus Asphaltites; it hardens in the sun, and is gathered on the surface of the waters. Comp. Robinson's Palestine, ii. p. 228, &c. It is so called either from its boiling up, or from its redness.—Gen. xi. 3; xiv. 10: Exod. ii. 3.

SLING

1 קלע to sling, to throw with a sling; trop. to sling out; i.e. to cast out a people from a land. KAL ᵃ part. Poel. PIEL ᵇ fut. ᶜ קלע m. The sling was a weapon used with great effect by the Greeks; they discharged bullets of various kinds, arrows, stones, and plummets of lead, which nothing could resist. By long practice they took so nice an aim that they were sure to hit their enemies, not only on the head, but on any part of the face they chose; comp. Judg. xx. 16. The men of Benjamin could use both the right hand and the left: 1 Chron. xii. 2. ᵈ קלע m. slinger.

2 מרגמה f. from רגם to cast stones, a sling; but Gesenius and others rather take it to mean a heap of stones: Prov. xxvi. 8, marg. 'or, putteth a precious stone in an heap of stones.' Kimchi, as the binding of a common stone on a purple (royal) garment. Gesenius, as a bag of gems in a heap of stones, a proverbial expression similar to that in Matt. vii. 6. Lxx. a sling, from רגם to throw stones; hence the version, ὃς ἀποδεσμεύει λίθον ἐν σφενδόνῃ.

Judg. xx. 16.	1 a	2 Kings iii. 25.	1 d	Prov. xxvi. 8.	2
1 Sam. xvii. 40, 50.	1 c	2 Chron. xxvi. 14.α	1 c	Jer. x. 18.	1 a
xvii. 49.	1 b	Job xli. 28.	1 c	Zech. ix. 15.	1 c
xxv. 29, 29.	1 b c				

α marg. 'stones of slings.'

SLIP (N)

זמורה f. a branch: Isa. xvii. 10.

SLIP (V), SLIPPERY

1 חלקה f. smoothness; slippery places. ᵃ חלקלקות f. pl.

2 מוט to waver, to shake, to totter. KAL ᵃ pret. ᵇ inf. NIPHAL ᶜ pret.

3 מעד to waver, to be unsteady, to totter, ready to slip. KAL ᵃ pret. ᵇ part. Poel.

4 נשל to put off; to slip off. KAL pret.

5 פטר to let go, to dismiss. KAL fut.

6 שפך to pour out; Pual, to be poured, i.e. one's steps, to slip, to fall. PUAL pret.

Deut. xix. 5.	4	Ps. xvii. 5.	2 c	Ps. lxxiii. 2.	6
1 Sam. xix. 10.	3 a	xviii. 36.	3 a	lxxiii. 18.	1
2 Sam. xxii. 37.	3 a	xxxv. 6.	1 a	xciv. 18.	2 a
Job xii. 5.α	3 b	xxxviii. 16.	2 b	Jer. xxiii. 12.	1 a

α lit. to those that slip.

SLOTHFUL, SLUGGARD

1 עצל to be at leisure, idle. NIPHAL ᵃ fut. ᵇ עצל adj. sluggard. ᶜ עצלה f. sloth, dual, much slothfulness.

2 רמיה f. a letting fall of the hands, remissness; deceit.

3 רפה to be relaxed, slackened. HITHPAEL part.

Judg. xviii. 9.	1 a	Prov. xv. 19.	1 b	Prov. xxi. 25.	1 b
Prov. vi. 6, 9.	1 b	xviii. 9.	3	xxii. 13.	1 b
x. 26.	1 b	xix. 15.	1 c	xxiv. 30.β	1 b
xii. 24, α 27.	1 b	xix. 24.	2	xxvi. 13, 14, 15, 16.	1 b
xiii. 4.	1 b	xx. 4.	1 b	Eccles. x. 18.	1 c

α marg. 'or, deceitful.'   β lit. slothful man.

SLOW

ארך adj. long, tardy, slow to: Neh. ix. 17: Ps. ciii. 8; cxlv. 8: Prov. xiv. 29; xv. 18; xvi. 32: Joel ii. 13: Jonah iv. 2: Nah. i. 3.

כבד adj. heavy; dull, slow, sluggish: Exod. iv. 10, 10.

SLUICES

שכר m. sluices, as if from סכר to shut up, to enclose; Gesenius and others from שכר to hire: Isa. xix. 10, i.e. those that make hire, that seek a livelihood by labour, as opp. to nobles; see Purposes.

SLUMBER

נום see Sleep. KAL pret. Nah. iii. 18. inf. Isa. lvi. 10. fut. Ps. cxxi. 3, 4: Isa. v. 27: תנומה f. sleep, slumber: Job xxxiii. 15: Ps. cxxxii. 4: Prov. vi. 4, 10; xxiv. 33.

SMALL

1 פרע see Diminish. PIEL fut.

2 דָּקַק to beat small. KAL [a] *pret.* [b] *fut.* HIPHIL [c] *pret.* [d] *inf.* [e] *fut.* [f] דַּק *adj.* small, thin.

3 מִזְעָר *adv.* a little, of time or number.

4 יָטַב to be good. HIPHIL *inf.* used adverbially.

5 מְעַט a little; small, few.

6 מְתִים *m. pl.* see Men.

7 צָעַר to be small. KAL [a] *fut.* [b] צָעִיר *adj.* small, in number, in estimation and value. [c] מִצְעָר *m.* little, small.

8 צַר *adj.* strait, narrow, compressed.

9 קָטֹן to be small; the primary idea seems to be that of cutting off, and so making shorter and smaller, *pr.* to be docked. KAL [a] *fut.* HIPHIL [b] *inf.* [c] קָטָן *adj.* small in size, quantity, or importance. [d] קָטֹן *adj.* little, small, opp. גָּדוֹל.

10 קָצֵר *adj.* short; "of small power," *lit.* short of hand.

Gen. xix. 11.	9 d	2 Kings xxiii. 15.	2 c	Isa. i. 9.	5
xxx. 15.	9 d	xxv. 26.	9 d	vii. 15.	5
Exod. xvi. 14, 14.	2 f	1 Chron. xvii. 17.	9 a	xvi. 14. a	5, 3
xviii. 22, 26.	9 d	xxv. 8.	9 d	xxii. 24.	9 c
xxx. 36.	2 d	xxvi. 13.	9 d	xxix. 5.	2 f
Lev. xvi. 12.	2 f	2 Chron. xv. 13.	9 d	xxxvii. 27.	10
Num. xvi. 9, 13.	9 d	xviii. 30.	9 d	xli. 15.	2 b
Deut. i. 17.	9 d	xxiv. 24.	7 c	liv. 7.	9 d
ix. 21, 21.	4, 2 a	xxxi. 15.	9 c	lx. 22.	7 b
xxv. 13, 14.	9 c	xxxiv. 30.	9 c	Jer. xvi. 6.	9 c
1 Sam. v. 9.	9 d	xxx. 19.	9 c	xxx. 19.	7 a
ix. 21.	9 c	Esth. i. 5, 20.	9 d	xliv. 28. β	6
xx. 2.	9 d	Job iii. 19.	9 d	xlix. 15.	9 d
xxx. 2, 19.	9 d	viii. 7.	7 c	Ezek. xvi. 20.	5
2 Sam. xix. 1.	9 a	xv. 11.	5	xxxv. 18.	5
1 Kings ii. 20.	9 c	xxxvi. 27.	1	Dan. xi. 23.	5
xix. 12.	2 f	Ps. civ. 25.	9 d	Amos vi. 2, 5.	9 d
xxii. 31.	9 d	cxv. 13.	9 c	viii. 5.	9 b
2 Kings xix. 26.	10	cxix. 141.	7 b	Obad. 2.	9 d
xxiii. 2.	9 d	Prov. xxiv. 10.	8	Zech. iv. 10.	9 c
xxiii. 6.	2 e				

[a] *lit.* little small.   β *lit.* men of number.

SMART

רוּעַ to be evil. NIPHAL *fut.* Prov. xi. 15. רַע *adj.* evil: Prov. xi. 15, *marg.* 'be sore broken.' Here the noun is in the manner of an *inf. absol.*

SMELL

1 בֹּשֶׂם *m.* aromatic odour, fragrance; "sweet smell."

2 עָבַר to pass. KAL *part.* Poel, "sweet smelling," *marg.* 'passing, *or,* running about.'

3 רוּחַ to breathe; to smell; to perceive by smell; to presage; to enjoy the odour of anything. In the passages of Genesis the smell is probably that of perfume in which the goodly raiment had been laid aside when not used; scent, odour. HIPHIL [a] *inf.* [b] *fut.* [c] רֵיחַ *m.* odour, smell: [d] רֵיחַ Ch. *m. id.*

Gen. viii. 21.	3 b	Job xxxix. 25.	3 b	Cant. vii. 8, 13.	3 c
xxvii. 27, 27, 27, 27.	3 b c c c	Ps. cxv. 6.	3 b	Isa. iii. 24.	1
		Cant. i. 12.	3 c	Dan. iii. 27.	3 d
Exod. xxx. 38.	3 a	ii. 13.	3 c	Hos. xiv. 6.	3 c
Lev. xxvi. 31.	3 b	iv. 10, 11, 11.	3 c	Amos v. 21.	3 b
Deut. iv. 28.	3 b	v. 5, 13.	2		

SMITE

1 דָּכָא to be broken in pieces, beaten small, crushed. PIEL *pret.*

2 הָלַם to beat, to strike, to smite, as with a hammer. KAL [a] *pret.* [b] *fut.* [c] *part.* Poel.

3 כָּרַע to bend; to bring low; to smite down. HIPHIL *pret.*

4 כָּתַת to beat; to smite a land, to lay waste. PIEL [a] *pret.* HOPHAL [b] *fut.*

5 מְחָא Ch. to strike, to smite. P'AL *pret.*

6 מָחַץ to smite through and through, *sc.* with a shock, to dash in pieces, to crush. KAL [a] *pret.* [b] *imp.*

7 מָחַק to smite through, to crush. KAL *pret.*

8 נָגַע to strike, to smite, *seq.* בְּ to smite upon: Gen. xxxii. 26, of God, to smite with plagues; *trop.* of the wind, to smite, to blast. KAL [a] *pret.* [b] *fut.* PIEL [c] *pret.* [d] *fut.*

9 נָגַף to smite, usually of Jehovah, as inflicting judgments upon men; to plague, Exod. viii. 2, mostly with some fatal disease or death. In another sense God is said to smite a people before their enemies, *i. e.* to give them up to defeat and slaughter, 1 Sam. iv. 3, &c. KAL [a] *pret.* [b] *inf.* [c] *fut.* [d] *part.* Poel. NIPHAL [e] *pret.* [f] *inf.* [g] *fut.* [h] *part.*

10 נָכָה to strike, to smite: to strike home, to strike deep, so as to wound or kill; or as plants are smitten when they begin to wither, Ps. cii. 4. NIPHAL [a] *pret.* PUAL [b] *pret.* HIPHIL [c] *pret.* [d] *inf.* [e] *imp.* [f] *fut.* [g] *part.* HOPHAL [h] *pret.* [i] *part.* [k] מַכָּה *f.* stroke.

11 נָפַל to fall; to cause to fall. HIPHIL *fut.*

12 נְקַשׁ Ch. to smite, to strike, to knock. P'AL *part.*

13 סָפַק to strike, to smite with the hands so as to make a noise; to smite upon the thigh in indignation and mourning; to smite the hands together in indignation or in derision; to smite in chastisement, spoken of God, Job xxxiv. 26. KAL [a] *pret.* [b] *imp.* [c] *fut.*

14 פִּיק *m.* wavering, tottering of the knees.

15 שָׁפַח to smite with a scab. PIEL *pret.*

16 תָּקַע to smite; to strike or drive, to fasten. KAL *fut.*

Smite the hindmost; see *Hindmost.*

Gen. viii. 21.	10 d	Num. xxv. 17.	10 c	Judg. vi. 16.	10 c
xiv. 5, 7, 15.	10 f	xxxii. 4.	10 c	vii. 13.	10 f
xix. 11.	10 c	xxxiii. 4.	10 c	viii. 11.	10 f
xxxii. 8, 11.	10 c	xxxv. 16, 17, 18.	10 c	ix. 43.	10 f
xxxvi. 35.	10 f	xxxv. 21, 21.	10 c g	xi. 21, 33.	10 f
Exod. ii. 11.	10 g	Deut. i. 42.	9 g	xii. 4.	10 f
ii. 13.	10 f	ii. 33.	10 f	xv. 8.	10 f
iii. 20.	10 c	iii. 3.	10 f	xviii. 27.	10 f
vii. 17.	10 f	iv. 46.	10 c	xx. 31.	10 f
vii. 20.	10 f	vii. 2.	10 c	xx. 32.	9 h
vii. 25.	10 f	xiii. 15.	10 d f	xx. 35.	9 c
viii. 2.	9 d	xix. 11.	10 c	xx. 36.	9 e
viii. 16.	10 e	xx. 13.	10 c	xx. 37, 48.	10 f
viii. 17.	10 f	xxv. 11.	10 g	xx. 39, 39.	10 d, 9 f h
ix. 15.	10 f	xxvii. 24.	10 g	xx. 16.	10 c
ix. 25, 25.	10 f c	xxviii. 7, 25.	9 h	1 Sam. iv. 2, 10.	9 g
ix. 31, 32.	10 b	xxviii. 22, 27, 28, 35.	10 c	iv. 3.	9 a
xii. 12, 29.	10 d	xxix. 7.	10 f	v. 6, 9.	10 f
xii. 13.	10 d	xxxiii. 11.	6 b	v. 12.	10 h
xii. 23, 23, 27.	9 b	Josh. vii. 3, 5, 5.	10 c	vi. 9.	8 a
xvii. 5, 6.	10 c	viii. 22, 24.	10 f	vi. 19, 19, 19.	10 f f c
xxi. 12, 15, 19.	10 g	ix. 18.	10 c	vii. 10.	9 g
xxi. 18.	10 c	x. 4, 10, 26, 28, 30, 32, 33, 35, 37, 39, 40, 41.	10 f	vii. 11.	10 f
xxi. 20, 26.	10 f			xiii. 3.	10 f
xxi. 27.	11			xiii. 4.	10 c
xxii. 2.	10 h	x. 8, 8, 11, 12, 17.	10 f	xiv. 31, 48.	10 c
Num. iii. 13.	10 d	xi. 10, 14.	10 c	xv. 3.	10 c
viii. 17.	10 f	xiii. 12, 15, 16.	10 f	xv. 7.	10 c
xi. 33.	10 f	xiii. 21.	10 c	xvii. 35, 35, 46.	10 f
xiv. 12, 45.	10 f	xv. 16.	10 f	xvii. 49, 50.	10 f
xiv. 42.	9 g	xix. 47.	10 c	xviii. 11.	10 f
xx. 11.	10 f	Judg. i. 8, 12, 25.	10 f	xix. 10, 10.	10 d f
xxi. 24, 35.	10 f	ii. 14.	10 c	xx. 33.	10 f
xxii. 6, 23, 27.	10 f	iii. 13.	10 f	xxii. 19.	10 c
xxii. 28, 32.	10 c	iii. 29.	10 f	xxiii. 2, 2.	10 c
xxiv. 10.	13 c	iv. 21.	16	xxiii. 5.	10 c
xxiv. 17.	6 a	v. 26, 26.	2 a, 7	xxiv. 5.	10 f

1 Sam. xxv. 38.	9 c	2 Kings xv. 10, 14,		Isa. xxiv. 12.	4 b
xxvi. 8.	10 f	16, 16, 25, 30.	10 f	xxvii. 7, 7, γ 7.	10 c k g
xxvi. 10.	9 c	xviii. 8.	10 c	xxx. 31.	10 f
xxvii. 9.	10 c	xix. 35.	10 c	xxxvii. 36.	10 f
xxx. 1, 17.	10 c	xix. 37.	10 c	xxxvii. 38.	10 c
2 Sam. i. 15.	10 f	xxv. 21, 25.	10 f	xli. 7.	2 c
ii. 22. 23.	10 f	1 Chron. i. 46.	10 g	xlix. 10.	10 f
ii. 3 .	10 c	iv. 41, 43.	10 f	l. 6.	10 g
iii. 27.	10 f	xi. 6.	10 g	liii. 4.	10 i
iv. 6, 7.	10 f	xiii. 10.	10 g	lvii. 17.	10 i
v. 8.	10 g	xiv. 11, 16.	10 f	lviii. 4.	10 d
v. 20, 25.	10 f	xiv. 15.	10 d	lx. 10.	10 c
v. 24.	10 d	xviii. 1, 2, 3, 10.	10 f	Jer. ii. 30.	10 c
vi. 7.	10 f	xviii. 9.	10 c	xiv. 19.	10 c
viii. 1, 2, 3, 10.	10 f	xx. 1.	10 f	xviii. 18.	10 f
viii. 9.	10 c	xxi. 7.	10 f	xx. 2.	10 f
viii. 13.	10 d	2 Chron. xiii. 15.	9 a	xxi. 6, 7.	10 c
x. 15, 19.	9 e	xiv. 12.	9 c	xxxi. 19.	13 a
x. 18.	10 f	xiv. 14.	10 f	xxxvii. 10, 15.	10 c
xi. 15.	10 a	xiv. 15.	10 f	xli. 2.	10 f
xi. 21.	10 c	xvi. 4.	10 f	xliii. 11.	10 c
xiii. 28.	10 e	xviii. 23, 33.	10 f	xlvi. 2.	10 c
xiv. 6.	10 f	xx. 22.β	9 g	xlvi. 13.	10 d
xiv. 7.	10 g	xxi. 9.	10 f	xlvii. 1.	10 f
xv. 14.	10 c	xxi. 14.	9 d	xlix. 28.	10 c
xvii. 2.	10 c	xxii. 18.	9 a	lii. 27.	10 f
xviii. 11.	10 c	xxii. 5.	10 f	Lam. iii. 30.	10 g
xviii. 15.	10 f	xxv. 11, 13, 16.	10 f	Ezek. v. 2.	10 f
xx. 10.	10 f	xxv. 19.	10 c	vi. 11.	10 g
xxi. 17.	10 f	xxvi. 20.	8 c	vii. 9.	10 g
xxiii. 10.	10 f	xxviii. 5, 5, 17.	10 f	ix. 5.	10 g
xxiv. 10.	10 f	xxviii. 23.	10 g	xxi. 12.	13 b
xxiv. 17.	10 g	Neh. xiii. 25.	10 f	xxi. 14.	10 c
1 Kings viii. 33.	9 f	Esth. ix. 5.	10 f	xxi. 17.	10 f
xi. 15.	10 f	Job i. 19.	8 b	xxii. 13.	10 f
xiv. 15.	10 f	ii. 7.	10 c	xxxii. 15.	10 f
xv. 20, 27.	10 f	xvi. 10.	10 f	xxxiii. 21.	10 h
xv. 29.	10 f	xxvi. 12.	6 a	xxxix. 3.	10 h
xvi. 10.	10 f	Ps. iii. 7.	10 c	xl. 1.	10 h
xx. 21.	10 f	lx. title.	10 c	Dan. ii. 34, 35.	5
xx. 35, 35.	10 e d	lxix. 26.	10 c	v. 6.	12
xx. 37, 37, 37.	10 e f d	lxxviii. 20.	10 c	Hos. vi. 1.	10 f
xxii. 24, 34.	10 f	lxxviii. 31.	3	vi. 11.	10 h
2 Kings ii. 8, 14, 14.	10 f	lxxviii. 51, 66.	10 f	Amos iii. 15.	10 c
iii. 19.	10 c	cii. 4.	10 h	iv. 9.	10 c
iii. 23, 24, 25.	10 f	cv. 33, 36.	10 f	vi. 11.	10 c
iii. 24.α	10 d f	cxxi. 6.	10 f	ix. 1.	10 c
vi. 18, 18.	10 e f	cxxxv. 8, 10.	10 c	Jonah iv. 7.	10 f
vi. 21, 21.	10 f	cxxxvi. 10, 17.	10 g	Micah v. 1.	10 f
vi. 22, 22.	10 f g	cxli. 5.	2 b	vi. 13.	10 d
viii. 21.	10 f	cxliii. 3.	1	Nah. ii. 10.δ	14
ix. 7.	10 c	Prov. xix. 25.	10 f	Hag. ii. 17.	10 c
ix. 24.	10 c	Cant. v. 7.	10 c	Zech. ix. 4.	10 c
ix. 27.	10 e	viii. iii. 17.	15	x. 11.	10 c
x. 25, 32.	10 c	v. 25.	10 c	xi. 6.	4 a
xii. 21.	10 c	ix. 13.	10 g	xi. 4. 4.	10 f
xiii. 17.	10 f	x. 20.	10 g	xiii. 7.	10 e
xiii. 18, 18.	10 e f	x. 24.	10 f	xiv. 12, 18.	10 c
xiii. 19, 19, 19.	10 d c f	xi. 4, 15.	10 c	xiv. 18.	9 c
xiv. 10.	10 d c	xiv. 6, 29.	10 g	Mal. iv. 6.	10 c
xv. 5.	8 d	xix. 22, 22.	9 a b		

α *marg.* 'they smote it even to smiting.'   β *marg.* ' or, they smote one another.'   γ *marg.* 'according to the stroke of.'   δ *lit.* the smiting together of the knees.

SMITH

בַּרְזֶל *m.* iron: Isa. xliv. 12, *lit.* artificer of iron.

חָרָשׁ *m.* a workman: 1 Sam. xiii. 19: Isa. xliv. 12: liv. 16.

מַסְגֵּר *m.* one who shuts up, closes, &c., a locksmith, smith, artisan: 2 Kings xxiv. 14, 16: Jer. xxiv. 1: xxix. 2.

SMOKE

1   כֵּהֶה *adj. f.* weak, feeble, faint; specially of the dimly burning wick of a lamp just about to go out.

2   עָשַׁן to smoke, spoken chiefly of mountains; *trop.* of anger; vapour from the nostrils of an enraged animal, used therefore generally of the signs of anger; also the clouds of smoke that show an army, or which accompany the bride in her way to her husband's house. KAL ^a*pret.* [a]*pret.* ^b*fut.* [b]*fut.* עָשֵׁן ^c*adj.* smoking. ^d עָשָׁן *m.* smoke: Gen. xv. 17, &c.

3   קִיטוֹר *m.* smoke; vapour, cloud.

No. 2 d not included.

Gen. xix. 28, 28.	3	Deut. xxix. 20.	2 b	Ps. cxliv. 5.	2 b
Exod. xix. 18, 18.		Ps. lxxiv. 1.	2 b	Isa. vii. 4.	2 c
18.	2 a d d	civ. 32.	2 b	xlii. 3.	1
xx. 18.	2 c	cxix. 83.	3		

SMOOTH

חָלַק to be smooth. KAL *pret.* Ps. lv. 21. HIPHIL *part.* Isa. xli. 7. חָלָק *adj.* Gen. xxvii. 11 : Prov. v. 3. חֵלֶק *adj.* 1 Sam. xvii. 40. *m.* smoothness: Isa. lvii. 6, "among the smooth (stones) of the torrent is thy portion; these, these are thy lot;" *i. e.* with idols formed of smooth stones set up (*comp.* 1 Sam. xvii. 40) is thy intercourse, these are thy gods; as immediately follows, "even to them hast thou poured a drink-offering," &c. חֶלְקָה *f.* smoothness: Gen. xxvii. 16 : Isa. xxx. 10.

SNAIL

חֹמֶט *m.* some unclean animal; or a kind of lizard, which lies in the sand.—*Bochart.* LXX. σαύρα; Vulg. *lacerta.* Lev. xi. 30.

שַׁבְּלוּל *m.* a snail, especially without the shell, so called from its slime and moisture: Ps. lviii. 8, of the wicked, let them melt away—as the snail which melteth as it goeth, *i. e.* which leaveth a slimy trail as it goes, and thus wastes away more and more the further it advances, until at length it dies.—*Gesenius.*

SNARE

1   חֶבֶל *com.* cord; toil, net, or snare, made of cords.

2   יָד *com.* hand.

3   יָקֹשׁ to lay snares; to be snared. KAL ^a*pret.* [a]*pret.* NIPHAL ^b*pret.* [b]*pret.* ^c*fut.* [c]*fut.* HOPHAL ^d*part.* [d]*part.* יָקוֹשׁ *m.* fowler. ^f מוֹקֵשׁ *m.* noose, snare, by which beasts and birds are taken; once of a hair-ring in the nostrils of a beast, Job xl. 24. *Metaph.* fatal dangers, Ps. xviii. 5. So of sins, as causing destruction, Prov. xiii. 14 : xiv. 27. Also of a person or thing as a cause of ruin, destruction to any one, 1 Sam. xviii. 21, &c.

4   נָקַשׁ to snare, to be snared; to lay snares. Ps. ix. 16 should rather be referred to this root, and rendered actively, "he snareth the wicked," &c. KAL ^a*pret.* [a]*pret.* NIPHAL ^b*fut.* [b]*fut.* PIEL ^c*fut.* [c]*fut.* HITHPAEL ^d*part.* [d]*part.*

5   פּוּחַ to blow upon; or from פַּח a snare, to lay a snare; but Gesenius says that with בְּ it means to blow into a flame, to kindle up a fire, Ezek. xxi. 31; and *trop. seq. acc.*, Prov. xxix. 8, to kindle up a city, *i. e.* to excite sedition. HIPHIL *fut.*

6   פַּח *m.* a plate; a net, snare, trap-net; LXX. παγίς; especially of a fowler; also such a one as seizes and holds beasts or men by the foot, Job xviii. 9, Jer. xviii. 22. They were set in the path, Prov. vii. 23, xxii. 5; and hidden on or in the ground. The form of this trap-net appears from two passages, Amos iii. 5 and Ps. lxix. 22; and it was in two parts, which when set were spread out on the ground and slightly fastened with a stick (trap-stick), so that as soon as a bird or beast

touched the stick the parts flew up and enclosed the bird in the net, or caught the foot of the animal, Job xviii. 9. פָּחַח to snare. HIPHIL [a] *inf.*

7 פַּחַת *m.* a pit, often as the emblem of destruction.

8 מָצוֹד *m.* net, *sc.* of a hunter. [a] מְצוּדָה *f.* net; fortress, &c.

9 קֹשׁ to lay snares. KAL *fut.*

10 שְׂבָכָה *f.* checker, net-work; a net.

No. 3 f not included.

Deut. vii. 25.	3 c	Ps. cxxiv. 7, 7.	6	Isa. xxviii. 13.	3 b
xii. 30.	4 b	cxl. 5.	6	xxix. 21.	9
Josh. xxiii. 13.	6	cxl. 9.β	2, 6	xlii. 22.	6 a
1 Sam. xxviii. 9.	4 d	cxli. 3.	6	Jer. v. 26.	3 e
Job xviii. 8.	10	Prov. vi. 2.	3 b	xviii. 22.	6
xviii. 10.	6	vii. 23.	6	xlviii. 43, 44.	6
xxii. 10.	6	xii. 13.	3 f	l. 24.	3 a
Ps. ix. 16.	3 b or 4 a	xxii. 5.	6	Lam. iii. 47.	7
xi. 6.α	6	xxix. 8.	5	Ezek. xii. 13.	8 a
xxxviii. 12.	4 c	Eccles. vii. 26.	8	xvii. 20.	8 a
lxix. 22.	6	ix. 12, 12.	6, 3 d	Hos. v. 1.	6
xci. 3.	6	Isa. viii. 15.	3 b	ix. 8.	6
cxix. 110.	6	xxiv. 17, 18.	6	Amos iii. 5, 5.	6

a marg. 'or, quick burning coals.' β *lit.* from the hands of the snare.

SNATCH

גָּזַר to cut; to eat, to devour; from the idea probably of gnawing. KAL *fut.* Isa. ix. 20, *marg.* 'cut;' denoting a condition of internal anarchy and strife.—*Barnes.*

SNEEZE

זָרַר to scatter; to sneeze. POEL *fut.* 2 Kings iv. 35.

SNORT

נַחֲרָה *f.* snorting, *e.g.* of a horse: Jer. viii. 16.

SNOUT

אַף the nose: Prov. xi. 22.

SNOW

שֶׁלֶג *m.* snow; sometimes brought from Lebanon to be mixed with wine in the heat of summer: Exod. iv. 6, &c.: 1 Chron. xi. 22, *lit.* in a day of snow. שָׁלַג to be white as snow. HIPHIL *fut.* Ps. lxviii. 14, "when the Almighty scattered kings in it (the land), it was snow white, like snow, in Salmon," *sc.* with the bones of the slain; or, implying the brightness of joy, or imputed purity. Compare verse 13, and Isa. i. 18.

תְּלַג Ch. *m.* snow: Dan. vii. 9.

SNUFF

נָפַח to puff, to blow, to breathe; to blow away, *metaph.* to esteem lightly, to contemn. HIPHIL *pret.* Mal. i. 13, *marg.* 'or, whereas ye might have blown it away.'

שָׁאַף to breathe hard; to pant after, to snuff in the air. KAL *pret.* Jer. ii. 24; xiv. 6.

SNUFFER

מְזַמְּרוֹת *f. pl.* snuffers: 1 Kings vii. 50: 2 Kings xii. 13; xxv. 14: 2 Chron. iv. 22: Jer. lii. 18.

SNUFF-DISH

מַחְתָּה *f.* fire-pan, censer; snuff-dishes, in which the snuffings of the lamps were put: Exod. xxv. 38; xxxvii. 23: Num. iv. 9.

מַלְקָחַיִם *m. dual,* tongs for the fire; small tongs for the lamps: Exod. xxxvii. 23.

SOAKED

רָוָה to drink to the full; to be satiated. PIEL *pret.* Isa. xxxiv. 7.

SOCKET

אֶדֶן *m.* a foundation, *e.g.* of a column, base, pedestal: Exod. xxvi. 19, &c.—Cant. v. 15.

SOD

1 בָּשַׁל to be cooked; to boil. PIEL [a] *pret.* PUAL [b] *pret.* [c] *fut.* [d] *part.* [e] בָּשֵׁל *adj.* cooked.

2 זוּד to boil. HIPHIL *fut.*

Gen. xxv. 29.	2	Num. vi. 19.	1 e	2 Chron. xxxv. 13.	1 a
Exod. xii. 9.α	1 d a	1 Sam. ii. 15.	1 d	Lam. iv. 10.	1 a
Lev. vi. 28, 28.	1 c b				

a lit. boiled sodden.

SODER

דֶּבֶק *m.* sodering or welding of metals: Isa. xli. 7, *marg.* 'or, of the soder, It is good.'

SODOMITE

קָדֵשׁ *m.* sacred, consecrated; male prostitute, so called as consecrated to the service of Astarte or Venus. Deut. xxiii. 17: 1 Kings xiv. 24; xv. 12; xxii. 46: 2 Kings xxiii. 7.

SOFT

1 אַט *m.* a going softly, gentle motion; whence, adverbially with לְ, softly, gently, slowly, *e.g.* of the still slow gait of a mourner, 1 Kings xxi. 27; of water gently flowing, Isa. viii. 6. לְאִטִּי *pr.* in my slow gait, at my convenience, gradually.

2 דָּדָה to go softly. HITHPAEL *fut.*

3 לָאַט *m.* softly, gently.

4 לָט *adj.* covertly, secretly, softly.

5 מוּג to dissolve. POLEL *fut.*

6 רָכַךְ to be tender, soft, delicate. KAL [a] *pret.* HIPHIL [b] *pret.* [c] רַךְ *adj.* tender.

Gen. xxxiii. 14.	1 a	Job xxiii. 16.	6 b	Prov. xv. 1.	6 c
Judg. iv. 21.α	3	xli. 3.	6 c	xxv. 15.	6 c
Ruth iii. 7.	4	Ps. lv. 21.	6 a	Isa. viii. 6.	1
1 Kings xxi. 27.	1	lxv. 10.β	5	xxxviii. 15.	2

a lit. with secresy. β *marg.* 'dissolved it.'

SOIL

שְׂדֵה *m.* field; a field as ploughed and tilled, but not enclosed: Ezek. xvii. 8.

SOJOURN

1 גּוּר The primary meaning seems to be, to turn aside, and so to dwell in a place to which one removes after leaving his

first habitation ; to reside in a country not one's own, to sojourn as a stranger or guest ; it may be said of persons or of nations ; also of brutes, "the wolf shall dwell," as a guest, "with the lamb," Isa. xi. 6. KAL ^a*pret.* ^b*inf.* ^c*imp.* ^d*fut.* ^e*part.* Poel. HITHPOLEL ^f*part.* גֵּר *m.* sojourner. ^hמָגוּר *m.* sojourning.

2 תּוֹשָׁב *m.* habitation ; *concr.* an inhabitant, dweller, usually a sojourner, stranger, living in another country without the rights of a citizen. ^aמוֹשָׁב *m.* time of sojourning.

Gen. xii. 10.	1 b	Lev. xx. 2.	1 e	1 Kings xvii. 20.	1 f
xix. 9.	1 b	xxii. 10.	2	2 Kings viii. 1, 1.	1 c d
xx. 1.	1 d	xxv. 6, 45.	1 e	viii. 2.	1 d
xxi. 23.	1 a	xxv. 23, 35, 40.	2	1 Chron. xxix. 15.	2
xxi. 34.	1 d	xxv. 47, 47.	1 g, 2	Ezra i. 4.	1 e
xxiii. 4.	2	Num. ix. 14.	1 d	Ps. xxxix. 12.	2
xxvi. 3.	1 c	xv. 14.	1 d	cv. 23.	1 a
xxxii. 4.	1 a	xv. 15, 16, 26, 29.	1 e	cxx. 5.	1 a
xxxv. 27.	1 a	xix. 10.	1 e	Isa. xxiii. 7.	1 b
xlvii. 4.	1 b	xxxv. 15.	2	lii. 4.	1 b
Exod. iii. 22.	1 e	Deut. xviii. 6.	1 d	Jer. xlii. 15, 17, 22.	1 b
xii. 40.	2 a	xxvi. 5.	1 d	xliii. 2.	1 b
xii. 48.	1 d	Josh. xx. 9.	1 e	xliv. 12, 14, 28.	1 b
xii. 49.	1 e	Judg. xvii. 7	1 a	Lam. iv. 15.	1 b
Lev. xvi. 29.	1 e	xvii. 8, 9.	1 b	Ezek. xiv. 7.	1 b
xvii. 8.	1 d	xix. 1.	1 d	xx. 38.	1 h
xvii. 10, 12, 13.	1 e	xix. 16.	1 a	xlvii. 22.	1 e
xviii. 26.	1 e	Ruth i. 1.	1 b	xlvii. 23.	1 a
xix. 33.	1 d	2 Sam. iv. 3.	1 e		

SOLACE

עָלַם to exult, rejoice ; rejoice oneself. HITHPAEL *fut.* Prov. vii. 18.

SOLDIER

בֵּן *m.* son : 2 Chron. xxv. 13, *marg.* ' the sons of the band.'

חַיִל *m.* an army, a band of soldiers : Ezra viii. 22.

חָלָץ see *Arm.* KAL *part.* Paül, armed soldiers, Isa. xv. 4.

צָבָא *m.* army, host : 1 Chron. vii. 4.

SOLE

כַּף *f.* the hollow hand, palm ; sole, of the foot : Gen. viii. 9, &c.

SOLEMN, SOLEMNITY

1 חַג *m.* feast, festival, solemn feast, solemnity.

2 מוֹעֵד *m.* appointment of time ; set time, appointed season ; specially, festival day, solemn feast ; see *Feast, Assembly.* מוֹעֲדִים is applied in Scripture only to the sabbath, passover, pentecost, day of atonement, and feast of tabernacles.—*Hengst. in Christol.* ^aמוֹעֲדוֹת *f. pl.* solemn feasts.

3 עֲצָרָה *f.* (see *Assembly*), usually assembly, congregation of the people for closing or concluding festivals, πανήγυρις ; especially as held on the seventh day of the passover, and on the eighth day of the festival of tabernacles ; solemn meeting, solemn assembly, *lit.* (day of) restraint ; see *Assembly.* ^aעֲצֶרֶת *f.* solemn assembly ; see *Assembly.*

Lev. xxiii. 36.	3 a	Neh. viii. 18.	3 a	Hos. ii. 11.	2
Num. x. 10.	2	Ps. lxxxi. 3.	1	ix. 5.	2
xv. 3.	2	Isa. i. 13.	3	xii. 9.	2
xxix. 35.	3 a	xxx. 29.	1	Joel i. 14.	3
Deut. xvi. 8.	3 a	xxxiii. 20.	2	ii. 15.	3
xxxi. 10.	2	Lam. i. 4.	2	Amos v. 21.	3 a
2 Kings x. 20.	3	ii. 6, 7, 22.	2	Nah. i. 15.	1
2 Chron. ii. 4.	2	Ezek. xxxvi. 38.	2	Zeph. iii. 18.	2
vii. 9.	3	xlv. 17.	2	Mal. ii. 3.	1
viii. 13.	2 a	xlvi. 9, 11.	2		

SOLITARY

בָּדָד *m.* alone, solitary : Lam. i. 1 : Micah vii. 14.

גַּלְמוּד *adj.* hard ; sterile, barren ; of a night in which none are born, a night of loneliness and desolation : Job iii. 7. Also lean, famished, emaciated with hunger ; Job xxx. 3, *marg.* ' or, dark as the night.'

יָחִיד *adj.* only : Ps. lxviii. 6.

יְשִׁימוֹן *m.* desert : Ps. cvii. 4, *lit.* in the solitude of the way.

צִיָּה *f.* drought ; wilderness : Isa. xxxv. 1.

SOME

אָחָד *adj.* one, some one ; some.

אִישׁ *m.* man ; one, some one, any one.

אֱנוֹשׁ *m.* man ; some.

דָּבָר *m.* word, matter : Deut. xxiv. 1, *lit.* nakedness of anything ; 1 Kings ii. 14, "somewhat to say."

מְאוּמָה *f.* something, anything : 2 Kings v. 20.

מְעַט *m.* a little : 2 Chron. xii. 7, *marg.* ' or, a little while ;' Neh. ii. 12.

קָצֶה *m.* end, extremity ; a part, a cutting off : Gen. xlvii. 2. קָצָת *f.* Neh. vii. 70.

SON

1 בֵּן *m.* a son by whom parents are built up and families increased ; also a son by adoption, Exod. ii. 10 ; by creation and preservation, as the angels, Job i. 6, ii. 1, xxxviii. 7 ; by regeneration, as the faithful, Ps. lxxiii. 15, Prov. xiv. 26 ; who are loved, sanctified, and blessed of God as their Father, Exod. iv. 22, Deut. xiv. 1, Isa. i. 2, Jer. iii. 19, Hos. xi. 1. The young of any creature. *Metaph.* the branch is a son with respect to the tree, Ps. lxxx. 15 ; the scholar with respect to his master (sons of the prophets), an arrow with respect to the bow or quiver, Job xli. 28 ; corn with respect to the threshing-floor, Isa. xxi. 10 ; a hill is the son of oil with respect to its fertility, Isa. v. 1 ; a wicked person is a son of Belial or wickedness ; a person guilty of a capital crime is a son of death, 1 Sam. xx. 31. Any man is said to be a son in respect to the years of his age, a son of two, &c., Gen. iv. 17, &c. בֵּן Ch. *m.*

2 בַּר *m.* a son, from the idea of begetting, being born ; the common word for son in the Chaldee, but in Hebrew only poetic. בַּר Ch. *m. id.*

3 חָתַן to make affinity by marriage. HITHPAEL ^a*inf.* to be son-in-law. ^b*imp.* ^c*fut.* ^dחָתָן *m.* son-in-law.

4 יָלַד to beget ; to bear. NIPHAL ^a*pret.* ^bיָלֵד *m.* a child. ^cיָלִיד *adj.* verbal ; born.

5 נִין *m.* progeny, offspring. מָנוֹן *m.* condition of a son.

6 נֶכֶד *m.* posterity, "son's son."

No. 1 not included.

Gen. xix. 12, 12.	3 d, 1	Judg. xv. 6.	3 d	1 Sam. xviii. 22.	3 b
xix. 14, 14.	3 d	xix. 5.	3 d	xviii. 23, 26, 27.	3 a
xxi. 23, 23.	5, 6	Ruth i. 5.	4 b	xxii. 14.	3 d
xxxii. 22.	4 b	1 Sam. xviii. 18.	3 d	2 Sam. xxi. 16, 18.	4 c
Josh. xv. 14.	4 c	xviii. 21.	3 c	2 Kings iv. 1.	1, 4 b

2 Kings viii. 27.	3 d	Neh. vi. 18.	3 d	Isa. xiv. 22.	5
1 Chron. xx. 6.	4 a	xiii. 28.	3 d	Dan. iii. 25.	2 a
Ezra v. 1, 2, 2.	2 a	Job xviii. 19.	5	v. 21.	1 a
vi. 10.	1 a	Ps. ii. 12.	2	v. 22.	2 a
vi. 14.	2 a	Prov. xxix. 21.	5	vii. 13.	2 a
vii. 23.	1 a	xxxi. 2, 2, 2.	2		

SOON

חִישׁ *adv.* (see *Haste*) : Ps. xc. 10.

מָהַר to hasten. PIEL *pret.* Exod. ii. 18, *lit.* ye have hastened to come ; Ps. cvi. 13, *marg.* 'they made haste, they forgat.' מַהֵר *adv.* quickly: Deut. iv. 26. מְהֵרָה *f. id.* Ps. xxxvii. 2.

מְעַט *m.* a little : Job xxxii. 22 : Ps. lxxxi. 14.

מַרְאֶה *m.* sight, aspect, view: Ezek. xxiii. 16, "as soon as," *marg.* 'at the sight of her eyes.'

קָצֵר *adj.* short : Prov. xiv. 17, *lit.* short of nostrils.

SOOTHSAYER

גְּזַר Ch. to cut, to cut off; to decide, to determine, to decree, specially of fate, destiny ; *part. pl.* deciders, determiners, put for the Chaldean astrologers, diviners, who by casting nativities from the place of the stars at one's birth, and by various acts of computing and divining, foretold the fortunes and destinies of individuals. P'AL *part.* Dan. ii. 27; iv. 7; v. 7, 11.

עָנַן to observe the clouds for the purpose of augury. POEL *part.* Isa. ii. 6 : Micah v. 12.

קָסַם to divine. KAL *part.* Poel, Josh. xiii. 22.

SOPE

בֹּרִית *f.* that which cleanses, anything used for cleansing and scouring, specially salt of lye, vegetable salt, alkali (that from minerals is called נֶתֶר nitre), obtained from the ashes of various plants of a saltish and soapy nature. The ancients made use of this along with oil for washing and scouring garments, instead of sope, Jer. ii. 22 ; and also in refining metals, Mal. iii. 2.

SORCERY

כָּשַׁף to practise magic arts, sorcery, charms, with an intent to do mischief to men or beasts ; or to delude and pervert the mind. LXX. φαρμακός, φαρμακεύεσθαι. Vulg. *maleficus, maleficis artibus inservire.* PIEL *part.* Exod. vii. 11 : Dan. ii. 2 : Mal. iii. 5. כַּשָּׁף *m.* magician : Jer. xxvii. 9. כְּשָׁפִים *m. pl.* magical rites : Isa. xlvii. 9, 12.

עָנַן see *Soothsayer.* POEL *part.* Isa. lvii. 3.

SORE

1 בָּכָה *m.* weeping ; "very sore," *marg.* 'a great weeping.' בְּכִי *m.* weeping sore.

2 גָּדוֹל *adj.* great ; see *Weep, Displease.*

3 חָלָה to be sick. KAL *part.* Poel, Eccles. v. 13, 16, "a sore evil," sickly evil, *i. e.* scarcely curable, or which occasions great anxiety and grief.

4 חָזַק to prevail, to be strong. KAL *pret.* *fut.* חָזָק *adj.* strong.

5 טֶבַח *m.* slaughter.

6 יָד *com.* hand ; in Ps. lxxvii. 2, taken to mean a wound, *or,* my hand is stretched out.

7 כָּאַב to have pain, to be sore ; *trop.* of the mind ; to make sore either mind or body. KAL *part.* Poel. HIPHIL *fut.*

8 כָּבֵד to be heavy. KAL *pret.* *fut.* כָּבֵר *adj.* heavy, sore.

9 כַּעַס *m.* vexation, trouble, grief.

10 מְאֹד *m.* much, very much, exceeding, greatly.

11 מַעַל *m.* transgression.

12 נֶגַע *m.* plague.

13 מַכָּה *m.* a beating ; a sore.

14 מָרַץ to be sharp, active, vehement. NIPHAL *part.*

15 קֶצֶף *m.* wrath ; "sore," *lit.* with displeasure.

16 קָשָׁה to be hard. KAL *pret.* קָשֶׁה *adj.* hard.

17 רָבָה to be many. HIPHIL *inf.* used adverbially.

18 רַע *adj.* evil.

19 שַׂגִּיא Ch. *adj.* great.

20 שַׂעַר *m.* horror.

Gen. xix. 9.	10	1 Sam. xxi. 12.	10	Ps. vi. 3, 10.	10
xx. 8.	10	xxviii. 15, 20, 21.	10	xxxviii. 8.	10
xxxiv. 25.	7 a	xxxi. 3, 3.	8 b, 10	xxxviii. 11.θ	10
xli. 56.	4 b	xxxi. 4.	16 b	lxxi. 20.	18
xli. 57.	4 a	2 Sam. ii. 17.	16 b	lxxvii. 2.	6
xliii. 1.	8 c	xiii. 36.δ	2, 1 a	Eccles. i. 13.	18
xlvii. 4, 13.	8 c	1 Kings xvii. 17.	10, 4 c	iv. 8.	18
i. 10.	8 c	xviii. 2.	4 c	v. 13, 16.	3
Exod. xiv. 10.	10	2 Kings iii. 26.	4 a	Isa. i. 6.	12
Lev. xiii. 42, 43.	12	xx. 3.ε	2, 1 a	xxvii. 1.	16 b
Num. xxii. 3.	18	1 Chron. x. 3.	8 b	xxxviii. 1.ι	2, 1 a
Deut. vi. 22.a	18	x. 4.	16	lxiv. 9, 12.	10
xxviii. 35, 59.	18	2 Chron. vi. 28, 29.	18	Jer. l. 36.	10
Josh. ix. 24.	10	xxi. 19.	18	lii. 6.	4 b
Judg. x. 9.	10	xxviii. 19.ζ	11	Ezek. xiv. 21.	18
xv. 18.	10	xxxv. 23.	10	xxi. 10.κ	5
xx. 34.	8 a	Ezra x. 1.	17, 1	xxvii. 35.λ	20
xxi. 2.β	2, 1 a	Neh. ii. 2.	17	Dan. vi. 14.	10
1 Sam. i. 6.γ		xiii. 8.	10	Micah ii. 10.	14
v. 7.	16 a	Job ii. 7.	10	Zech. i. 2.μ	15
xiv. 52.	4 c	v. 18.	7 b	i. 15.ν	15, 2
xvii. 24.	10				

a marg. 'evil.'   *β lit.* a great weeping.   *γ lit.* provoked her even to vexation.   *δ marg.* 'with a great weeping greatly.'   *ε marg.* 'with a great weeping.'   *ζ lit.* transgressed a transgression.   *η marg.* 'a great weeping.'   *θ marg.* 'stroke.'   *ι marg.* 'with great weeping.'   *κ lit.* to slay a slaughter.   *λ lit.* afraid with horror.   *μ marg.* 'with displeasure.'   *ν marg.* 'with great displeasure.'

SORROW, SORRY

1 אֲבוֹי *n. m.* want, poverty, wretchedness : Prov. xxiii. 29. Kimchi, who is followed by most interpreters, makes it an exclamation of pain, O ! wo !—*Gesenius.*

2 אָוֶן *m.* nothingness, vanity ; toil, trouble, evil, calamity, as the consequence of sin.

3 אֲנָיָה *f.* sighing, sorrow, mourning.

4 מְנִנָּה *f.* covering : Lam. iii. 65, *marg.* 'or, obstinacy ; obduracy, stubbornness,' *comp.* κάλυμμα ἐπὶ τὴν καρδίαν, 2 Chron. iii. 15. Kimchi also properly compares fatness of heart, Isa. vi. 10.

5 דָּאַב to melt away ; to pine away, to languish. KAL *pret.* *inf.* דְּאָבָה *f.* pining away. דְּאָבוֹן *m.* extreme languor.

6 דָּאַג to melt, to become liquid ; *trop.* of fear and terror, with solicitude as to the issue. KAL *pret.* *fut.* דְּאָגָה *f.* anxiety, alarm.

7 דּוּב to pine away, to languish. HIPHIL *part.*

8   דְּוַי   *m.* languor, sickness; hence spoken of anything sickening, *i.e.* insipid, loathsome.

9   חֶבֶל   *com.* cord; great pain, affliction, or sorrow, as that which binds a sufferer; or, according to Gesenius, gins, snares.

10   חוּל   (see *Travail*), to be in great pain and anguish. KAL and HIPHIL ᵃ*fut.* ᵇחִיל *m.* pain. ᶜחִילָה *f. id.*

11   חָלַל   to be wounded (see *Wound*). HIPHIL *fut.* Hos. viii. 10, marg. 'or, begin,' which is the usual translation of the Hiphil. See, on both renderings, Pusey, *Commentary on the Minor Prophets*, who adduces 2 Kings xv. 19, 20.

12   חָלָה   to be weak, sick, to be pained, concerned, anxious, grieved. KAL *part.* Poel.

13   יָגָה   to grieve. NIPHAL ᵃ*part.* ᵇיָגוֹן *m.* affliction, grief. ᶜתּוּגָה *f.* grief, sorrow, vexation.

14   כָּאַב   to have pain, to be sore; also of the mind. KAL ᵃ*fut.* ᵇ*part.* Poel. ᶜכְּאֵב *m.* pain. ᵈמַכְאוֹב *m. id.*

15   כָּעַס   to be vexed, grieved, troubled. KAL ᵃ*pret.* ᵇכַּעַס *m.* vexation, sadness.

16   כַּעַשׂ   *m.* grief, vexation; anger.

17   נוּד   to bemoan. KAL *fut.*

18   עָמָל   *ᵃm.* labour, toil; trouble, vexation, sorrow.

19   עָצַב   to grieve. NIPHAL ᵃ*fut.* ᵇעֶצֶב *m.* labour, toil; pain, sorrow of travail. ᶜעֹצֶב *m. id.* ᵈעִצָּבוֹן *m.* labour; trouble, sorrow, pain: Gen. iii. 16, thy trouble and thy pregnancy; Hendiadys, for the troubles, sorrows of thy pregnancy; 17. ᵉעַצֶּבֶת *f.* pain of body or of mind. ᶠמַעֲצֵבָה *f.* labour, affliction.

20   צִיר   *m.* pain of childbirth; *metaph.* of terror, which is often compared with the pains and trembling of childbirth.

21   צַר   *m.* straitness; distress.

22   קָשֶׁה   *adj.* hard; "of a sorrowful spirit," *marg.* 'hard of spirit.'

23   רַע   *adj.* evil. ᵇרֹעַ *m.* evil condition.

Gen. iii. 16, 16.	19 d b	Ps. xviii. 4, 5.	9	Isa. xxix. 2.	3
iii. 17.	19 d	xxxii. 10.	14 d	xxxv. 10.	13 b
xlii. 38.	13 b	xxxvii. 17.	14 d	l. 11.β	19 f
xliv. 29.	23	xxxviii. 18.	6 b	li. 11.	13 b
xliv. 31.	13 b	xxxix. 2.	14 c	li. 19.	17
Exod. iii. 7.	14 d	lv. 10.	18	liii. 3, 4.	14 d
xv. 14.	10 b	lxix. 29.	14 b	lxv. 14.	14 c
Lev. xxvi. 16.	7	xc. 10.	2	Jer. viii. 18.	13 b
Deut. xxviii. 65.	5 d	cvii. 39.	19 b	xiii. 21.	9
1 Sam. i. 15.	22	cxvi. 3, 3.	9, 13 b	xx. 18.	13 b
x. 2.	6 a	cxxvii. 2.	19 b	xxx. 15.	14 d
xxii. 8.	12	Prov. x. 10.	19 e	xxxi. 12.	5 b
2 Sam. xxii. 6.	9	x. 22.	19 b	xxxi. 13.	13 b
1 Chron. iv. 9.	19 c	xiv. 13.	14 a	xxxi. 25.	5 a
Neh. ii. 2.	23 a	xv. 13.	19 e	xlv. 3.	14 d
viii. 10.	19 a	xvii. 21.	13 c	xlix. 23.	6 c
Esth. ix. 22.	13 b	xxiii. 29.	1	xlix. 24.	9
Job iii. 10.	18	Eccles. i. 18.	14 d	li. 29.	10 a
vi. 7.	8	ii. 23.	14 d	Lam. i. 12, 12, 18.	14 d
vi. 10.	10 c	v. 17.	15 a	iii. 65.	4
ix. 28.	19 e	vii. 3.	15 b	Ezek. xxiii. 33.	13 b
xvii. 7.	16	xi. 10.	15 b	Dan. x. 16.	20
xxi. 17.	9	Isa. v. 30.	21	Hos. viii. 10.	11
xxxix. 3.	9	xiii. 8.	9	xiii. 13.	9
xli. 22. a	5 c	xiv. 3.	19·c	Zeph. iii. 18.	13 a
Ps. xiii. 2.	13 b	xvii. 11.	14 c	Zech. ix. 5.	10 a
xvi. 4.	19 e				

α *lit.* add to sorrow.   β *lit.* to or for sorrow.

SORT

גִּיל   *m.* circle, circuit; an age: Dan. i. 10.

דָּבָר   *m.* word, or matter: Neh. vi. 4.

מִכְלוֹל   *m.* perfection, *sc.* in beauty, splendour: Ezek. xxxviii. 4, clothed in perfection, *i.e.* splendidly, gorgeously. מַכְלֻלִים *m. pl.* perfections, beautiful things; hence costly merchandize, especially splendid garments: Ezek. xxvii. 24, marg. 'or, excellent things.'

כָּנָף   *com.* wing; "of every sort:" Gen. vii. 14: Ezek. xxxix. 4.

SOTTISH

סָכָל   *m.* foolish: Jer. iv. 22.

SOUL

נְדִיבָה   *f.* nobility; *trop.* elevated and happy state, excellency: Job xxx. 15, marg. 'my principal one.'

נֶפֶשׁ   *com.* the animal life, or that principle by which every animal, according to its kind, lives; hence life, vital principle, animal spirit, which is often translated soul, or spirit, Gen. xxxv. 18: 1 Kings xvii. 21, 22: Deut. xix. 21: Ps. lxix. 2, *comp.* cxxiv. 4, and Jer. iv. 10. This life, spirit, *anima*, is said to live, Gen. xii. 13: Ps. cxix. 175; and to die, Judg. xvi. 30; to be poured out, as if along with the blood, Lam. ii. 12: Isa. liii. 12; hence it is very frequent in phrases which have respect to the losing or preserving life, Jer. xliv. 7. Further, also, in many expressions which have respect to the sustinence of life by food and drink, and the contrary. Thus, the spirit, *anima*, is said to be satiated with food and drink, Prov. xxvii. 7, Isa. lv. 2; to be made fat, Prov. xi. 25, xiii. 4; also to fill, *i.e.* to satisfy one's spirit, Prov. vi. 30; so the opposite, my spirit hungers, Prov. x. 3, xxvii. 7; thirsts, Prov. xxv. 25; pines, Ps. xxxi. 9; fasts, Ps. lxix. 10; is polluted by certain kinds of food, Ezek. iv. 14; also the spirit is weary, loathes, Num. xxi.: Job vi. 7: x. 1: Zech. xi. 8; is empty, *i.e.* hungry, Isa. xxix. 8; is dried away, *i.e.* thirsty, Num. xi. 6; to open wide the life, spirit, *i.e. trop.* for the jaws, throat, Isa. v. 14, Hab. ii. 5. *Trop.* נֶפֶשׁ is also put for that which supports life, aliment, Isa. lviii. 10, *comp.* Deut. xxiv. 6. The rational soul, mind, *animus*, as the seat of the feelings, affections, emotions of various kinds. Words, also, which express feelings of the mind, or soul, are often thus used in connexion with נֶפֶשׁ; it is said to weep, Ps. cxix. 128; to be poured out in tears, Job xxx. 16; to cry for vengeance, Job xxiv. 12; and also to invoke blessings, Gen. xxvii. 4, 25; but more commonly in this connexion it is rendered mind. *Concr.* animal, Josh. x. 28, &c., every animate or living creature; living soul, often *lit.* animal of life, Gen. ii. 17, &c. Specially put for man, person, mostly in certain fixed phrases, where also in English we may use soul: Exod. i. 5; xvi. 16, &c. With suffixes it is often equivalent to I myself, thou thyself, &c. Where put for the personal pronoun, it is in cases where life is said or implied to be in danger: Ps. iii. 2, xi. 1, &c. With נָשָׂא to lift up the soul or mind, to desire: Ps. xxv. 1; Jer. xxii. 27; xliv. 14.

נְשָׁמָה   *f.* breath, spirit; the vital spirit: Isa. lvii. 16.

SOUND

1 הֶגֶה *f.* muttering; applied to the rumbling of thunder. הִגָּיֹון ‎ *m.* murmur, sound of the harp or cithara.

2 הֵד *m.* shout of joy, rejoicing: *Comp.* Isa. xvi. 9, 10.

3 הָלַךְ to go. KAL *part.* Poel.

4 הָמָה to sound, to make a noise. KAL ᵃ *fut.* ᵇ הָמֹון noise; multitude; disquietude: Isa. lxiii. 15, *marg.* 'or, the multitude,' perhaps the moaning of thy bowels, *i. e.* thy compassion.

5 חָצַר to blow a trumpet. HIPHIL *part.*

6 חַצֹּצֵר *id.* כתיב. PIEL *part.*

7 חַצְרֵר *id.* PIEL *part.* כתיב.

8 חָקַר to search. KAL *fut.*

9 עָבַר to pass. HIPHIL ᵃ *pret.* ᵇ *fut.*

10 פֶּה *m.* mouth.

11 קֹול *m.* the voice; sound: Exod. xxviii. 35, &c. קָל Ch. *m. id.*

12 רוּעַ to cry with a loud voice, to spout; to sound a trumpet, specially to sound an alarm, by blowing loud and long upon the trumpet, or perhaps with broken harsh notes, as a notice for breaking up an encampment; different from תָּקַע to blow a trumpet (once) in order to convoke an assembly; see *Alarm.* תְּרוּעָה *f.* joyful sound.

13 שָׁמַע to hear; to cause to be heard. HIPHIL ᵃ *inf.* ᵇ *part.*

14 תָּקַע to strike; to strike or clang the trumpet, *i. e.* to give one blast, to blow the trumpet once, as a signal; see רוּעַ above. KAL ᵃ *part.* Poel. ᵇ תֶּקַע *m.* blast with a trumpet.

No. 11 not included.

Exod. xix. 19. *a*	3	2 Chron. xiii. 12.	12	Ps. cl. 3.	14 b
Lev. xxv. 9, 9.	9 a b	xiii. 14.	5, or 6	cl. 5.	12
1 Sam. xx. 12.	8	xxiii. 13.	14 a	Isa. xvi. 11.	4 a
1 Chron. xv. 16.	13 b	xxix. 28.	5, or 6	lxiii. 15.	4 b
xv. 19.	13 a	Neh. iv. 18.	14 a	Jer. xlviii. 36, 36.	4 a
xvi. 5, 42.	13 b	Job xxxvii. 2.	1	Ezek. vii. 7. β	2
2 Chron. v. 12.	5, or 7	Ps. lxxxix. 15.	12	Dan. iii. 5, 7, 10, 15.	11 a
vii. 6.	5, or 6	xcii. 3.	1 a	Amos vi. 5.	10

a lit. going and strengthening exceedingly. β marg. 'or, echo.'

SOUND (ADJ.), SOUNDNESS

מַרְפֵּא *m.* healing, remedy: tranquillity, placidness of mind: Prov. xiv. 30.

תָּמִים *adj.* perfect: Ps. cxix. 80. מְתֹם *m.* wholeness, soundness: Ps. xxxviii. 3, 7: Isa. i. 6.

SOUR

סוּר to turn aside. KAL *pret.* Hos. iv. 18, *marg.* 'gone.'

SOUTH

1 מִדְבָּר *m.* desert.

2 דָּרֹום *m. pr.* bright, sunny region, hence the south, the southern quarter.

3 חֶדֶר *m.* chamber; chambers of the south, the remotest recesses of the south.

4 יָם *m.* the sea; see *West.* In Ps. cvii. 3 it is supposed to mean the south, because connected with the north, צָפֹון.

5 יָמִין *m.* the right; the Hebrews always considered themselves looking towards the east when they spoke of the points of the compass; hence the right was the south. תֵּימָן *com. id.*

6 נֶגֶב the south; the desert sandy countries which lay to the south of Judea were very dry and without water: Ps. cxxvi. 4. Turn again our captivity, O Lord, as streams in the south, brought by thy power and goodness; or, turn our captivity, and it shall be as grateful to us, and bring as many blessings, as streams in a desert: Josh. xv. 19. Thou hast given me a south land, a dry and barren land, give me also springs of water: Gen. xii. 9, &c.

No. 6 not included.

Exod. xxvi. 18, 18.	6, 5 a	1 Sam. xxiii. 19.	5	Isa. xliii. 6.	5 a
xxvi. 35.	5 a	xxiii. 24.	6	Ezek. xx. 46.	
xxvii. 9, 9.	6, 5 a	Job ix. 9.	5 a	46, 46.	5 a, 2, 6
xxxvi. 23, 23.	6, 5 a	xxxvii. 9.	3	xl. 24, 24, 27, 27,	
xxxviii. 9, 9.	6, 5 a	xxxvii. 17.	2	28, 28, 44, 45.	2
Num. ii. 10.	5 a	xxxix. 26.	5 a	xli. 11.	2
iii. 29.	5 a	Ps. lxxv. 6.	1	xliii. 12, 13, 18.	2
x. 6.	5 a	lxxviii. 26.	5 a	xlvii. 19, 19,	
Deut. iii. 27.	5 a	lxxxix. 12.	5	19, 19.	6, 5 a, 6
xxxiii. 23.	2	cvii. 3.	4	xlviii. 28, 28.	6, 5 a
Josh. iii. 3.	5 a	Eccles. i. 6.	2	Zech. vi. 6.	5 a
xiii. 4.	5 a	xi. 3.	2	ix. 14.	5 a
xv. 1, 1.	6, 5 a	Cant. iv. 16.	5 a		

SOW

1 זָרַע to scatter seed, to sow; with an *accus.* of the seed sown, and of the field; also, to plant, set. To scatter its seed is said of a seed-bearing plant or tree, Gen. i. 29. *Metaph.* to sow righteousness, iniquity, mischief, the wind, is *gener.* to prepare for oneself the rewards or punishments of good or evil actions, which, in the same connexion, are also said to be reaped, harvested; *comp.* Gal. vi. 7, 8. In another construction, Hos. x. 12, sow for yourselves in righteousness, and reap in mercy, according to mercy or piety. *Trop.* Nah. i. 14, "that no more of thy name be sown," thy name shall no longer be propagated. KAL ᵃ *pret.* ᵇ *inf.* ᶜ *imp.* ᵈ *fut.* ᵉ *part.* Poel. ᶠ *part.* Paül. NIPHAL ᵍ *pret.* ʰ *fut.* PUAL ⁱ *pret.* ᵏ זֵרֻעַ *m.* sown, to be sown. ˡ זֶרַע *m.* seed, sowing time. ᵐ מִזְרָע *m.* place sown: Isa. xix. 7, of sown fields of the Nile, *i. e.* watered by the Nile.

2 מָשַׁךְ to draw, to draw out the seed, *i. e.* to scatter it regularly along the furrows. KAL *part.* Poel. See *Precious.*

3 שָׁלַח to send; Piel, to send in a stronger sense, *i. e.* to cast, to throw, to shoot. PIEL ᵃ *fut.* ᵇ *part.*

Gen. xxvi. 12.	1 d	Job xxxi. 8.	1 d	Isa. lv. 10.	1 e
xlvii. 23.	1 a	Ps. xcvii. 11.	1 f	lxi. 11.	1 k
Exod. xxiii. 10, 16.	1 d	cvii. 37.	1 d	Jer. ii. 2.	1 f
Lev. xi. 37, 37.	1 k h	cxxvi. 5.	1 e	iv. 3.	1 d
xix. 19.	1 d	Prov. vi. 14.	3 a	xii. 13.	1 a
xxv. 3, 4, 11, 20.	1 d	vi. 19.	3 b	xxxi. 27.	1 d
xxv. 22.	1 a	xi. 18.	1 e	xxxv. 7.	1 d
xxvi. 5.	1 l	xvi. 28.	3 a	l. 16.	1 d
xxvi. 16.	1 a	xxii. 8.	1 e	Ezek. xxxvi. 9.	1 g
Deut. xi. 10.	1 d	Eccles. xi. 4.	1 d	Hos. ii. 23.	1 a
xxi. 4.	1 h	xi. 6.	1 c	viii. 7.	1 d
xxii. 9, 9.	1 d	Isa. xix. 7.	1 m	x. 12.	1 c
xxix. 23.	1 h	xxviii. 24.	1 b	Amos ix. 13.	2
Judg. vi. 3.	1 a	xxx. 23.	1 d	Micah vi. 15.	1 d
ix. 45.	1 d	xxxii. 20.	1 e	Nah. i. 14.	1 h
2 Kings xix. 29.	1 c	xxxvii. 30.	1 c	Hag. i. 6.	1 a
Job iv. 8.	1 e	xl. 24.	1 i	Zech. x. 9.	1 d

SPACE

גְּבוּל *m.* border: Ezek. xl. 12, *marg.* 'limit, or, bound;' 12.

יוֹם *m.* day: Gen. xxix. 14, *marg.* 'a month of days:' Lev. xxv. 8 : Deut. ii. 14.

מָלָא to fill, to make full. KAL *inf.* Lev. xxv. 30, *lit.* the fulfilling of a whole year.

מָקוֹם *com.* place: 1 Sam. xxvi. 13.

רֶגַע *m.* moment: Ezra ix. 8.

רְוַח *m.* enlargement; space, width: Gen. xxxii. 16, *pr.* breathing space.

רָחוֹק *adj.* far off, distant, remote: Josh. iii. 4.

SPAN

זֶרֶת *f.* a span. The longer span was half a cubit, almost eleven inches; the lesser span was a third part of a cubit, something more than seven inches and a quarter. Exod. xxviii. 16, 16 ; xxxix. 9, 9 : 1 Sam. xvii. 4 : Isa. xl. 12 : Ezek. xliii. 13.

טָפַח to spread out, to expand. PIEL *pret.* Isa. xlviii. 13. מִפְּחִים *m. pl.* Lam. ii. 20, *marg.* 'or, swaddled with their hands ;' see *Swaddle*.

SPARE

1 חוּס to pity, to have compassion on ; to spare, to treat with pity ; *seq.* עַל. In connexion with this root it is to be observed that the ideas both of pity and of sparing are attributed more frequently to the eye than to the person himself; as elsewhere weakness and strength to the hands ; longing or pining also to the eye. Hence we may gather that the primary idea of the verb is that of a gentle and humane countenance. KAL [a]*imp.* [b]*fut.*

2 חָמַל to be mild, gentle, clement; the primary idea is that of softness; hence, to pity, to have sympathy, compassion, *seq.* עַל of the person ; to spare, to treat with pity, *seq.* עַל and אֶל; also of things, to spare, to use sparingly, *seq.* אֶל, לְ, and עַל; Ezek. xxxvi. 21, I will spare my holy name, *i.e.* consult for its honour. KAL [a]*pret.* [b]*fut.*

3 חָשַׂךְ to keep back, to restrain ; to spare, *i.e.* things, to keep back, not to give out freely ; *seq.* לְ to spare for anything, *i.e.* to reserve for future use ; to spare men, to use tenderly, to treat with pity. KAL [a]*pret.* [b]*fut.* [c]*part.* Poel.

4 נָשָׂא to take up, to lift up, to raise ; to take, to take away, to forgive, to forbear, to spare. KAL [a]*pret.* [b]*fut.* Prov. xix. 18, "let not thy soul spare," or, *lit.* lift not up thy soul to spare his crying ; see *Cry*.

5 סָלַח to forgive, to pardon ; the primary idea seems to be that of lifting up, taking away. KAL *inf.*

6 שָׁעָה to look ; to look away from, to spare. HIPHIL *imp.*

Gen. xviii. 24.	4 b	Job vi. 10.	2 b	Prov. xix. 18.	4 b		
xviii. 26.	4 a	xvi. 13.	2 b	xxi. 26.	3 b		
Deut. xiii. 8.	2 b	xx. 13.	2 b	Isa. ix. 19.	2 b		
xxix. 20.	5	xxvii. 22.	2 b	xiii. 18.	1 b		
1 Sam. xv. 3, 9.	2 b	xxx. 10. *a*	3 a	xxx. 14.	2 b		
xv. 15.	2 a	Ps. xxxix. 13.	6	liv. 2.	3 b		
xxiv. 10.	1 b	lxxii. 13.	1 b	lviii. 1.	3 b		
2 Sam. xii. 4.	2 b	lxxviii. 50.	3 a	Jer. xiii. 14.	1 b		
xxi. 7.	2 b	Prov. vi. 34.	2 b	xxi. 7.	1 b		
2 Kings v. 20.	3 a	xiii. 24.	3 c	l. 14.	2 b		
Neh. xiii. 22.	1 a	xvii. 27.	3 c	li. 3.	2 b		

Ezek. v. 11.	1 b	Ezek. xx. 17.	1 b	Jonah iv. 11.	1 b
vii. 4, 9.	1 b	xxiv. 14.	1 b	Hab. i. 17.	2 b
viii. 18.	1 b	Joel ii. 17.	1 a	Mal. iii. 17, 17.	a b
ix. 5, 10.	1 b				

a lit. and from my face spare not.

SPARK

בֵּן *m.* son: Job v. 7.

זִיקוֹת *f. pl.* according to Gesenius, burning arrows, fiery darts ; but by others, flames and sparks ; see Fürst : Isa. l. 11, 11.

כִּידוֹד *m.* a spark: Job xli. 19.

נָצַץ to sparkle. KAL *part.* Poel, Ezek. i. 7. נִיצוֹץ *m.* spark: Isa. i. 31.

רֶשֶׁף *m.* flame ; lightning ; a quick brandishing motion, as of a violent flame : Job v. 7, *marg.* 'the sons of the burning coal.' Gesenius, birds of prey, which fly swift as the lightning. Others, arrows ; others, sparks.

שָׁבִיב *m.* a flame, bursting forth ; a bright flame : Job xviii. 5.

SPARROW

צִפּוֹר *com.* a small bird, so called from its chirping, twittering, specially a sparrow : Ps. lxxxiv. 3 ; cii. 7.

SPEAK, SPEECH

1 אִישׁ *m.* a man.

2 אָמַר see *To say.* KAL [a]*pret.* [b]*inf.* [c]*imp.* [d]*fut.* [e]*part.* Poel. אֲמַר Ch. P'AL [f]*inf.* [g]*fut.* [h]*part.* [i]אָמָר *m.* speech. [k]אֹמֶר *m.* saying. [l]אִמְרָה *f.* discourse.

3 בָּטָא to babble ; to talk idly, unadvisedly. KAL [a]*part.* Poel. PIEL [b]*fut.*

4 גָּדַל to be great. HIPHIL *fut.*

5 רָגַל to prate, to tattle, to blab. Gesenius, to creep about, as a slanderer, tale-bearer ; to slander, to disparage. KAL *part.* Poel.

6 דָּבַר to say, to speak, to tell, to promise, to utter, to talk, to converse, to name, to command, to tell, to bid, to pronounce, to teach, to declare, to discourse.—*Taylor.* The primary meaning of this root seems to be, to put forth in order ; hence, to discourse ; or, as the Latins say, *sermones serere.* דָּבַר differs from אָמַר in that it may be used absolutely ; the latter implies the subject of speech, and words conveying it to follow ; the former takes a higher range, and may imply eloquence, promises, declaration of good or evil, commands, kindness of address, pronouncing of sentence, singing to set music ; construed *abs.* sometimes *emphat.* to speak well ; often with אָמַר, with the *acc.* of that which one utters. Rarely it is immediately followed by the words spoken, and לֵאמֹר is to be mentally supplied. The person to or with whom we speak is commonly preceded by אֶל, לְ, &c., but בְּ, דִּבֶּר, used of God, implies the making known by revelation: Zech. i. 9, 14 ; ii. 2, 7 ; iv. 1, 4 ; v. 5: Hab. ii. 1 : Jer. xxxi. 20 : Num. xii. 6, 8. With בְּ sometimes to speak against, Num. xii. 1, 8, Job xix. 18, Ps. l. 20 ; with אֶל and עַל in the same application, the former implying that which is unjust, the latter what

may be true. This word seems to have a meaning of speaking insidiously, to plot against, to destroy; see *Destroy, Say*; so may Ps. cxxvii. 5 be understood, "and shall speak with their enemies," *marg.* 'or, subdue.' In Pual it occurs only twice; Cant. viii. 8, Ps. lxxxvii. 3, are spoken, or pronounced, *i. e.* promised or decreed of thee: it is most frequent in Piel, and, for brevity, the following renderings are not included in the references: *pret.* spoken, *inf.* to speak, *imp.* speak, *fut.* spake. KAL ᵃ *inf.* ᵇ *part.* Poel. ᶜ *part.* Paül. NIPHAL ᵈ *pret.* PIEL ᵉ *pret.* ᶠ *inf.* ᵍ *fut.* ʰ *part.* PUAL ⁱ *fut.* ᵏ *part.* HITHPAEL ˡ *part.* דָּבָר ᵐ *m.* word; collectively words, discourse. מִדְבָּר ⁿ *m.* speech, address.

7 הָגָה see *Meditate*; *poet.* to speak, to sing. KAL *fut.*

8 הֲמֻלָּה *f.* noise, sound.

9 חָרֵשׁ to be silent. HIPHIL ᵃ *fut.* ᵇ *part.*

10 לָשׁוֹן *com.* tongue.

11 לֶקַח *m.* taking arts, fair speech, by which the mind of any one is captivated.

12 מָלַל to speak; onomatopoetic word, like λαλέω in Greek. KAL ᵃ *part.* Poel. PIEL ᵇ *fut.* מִלַּל Ch. PAEL ᶜ *fut.* ᵈ *part.* מִלָּה ᵉ *f.* word, words; speech, discourse.

13 מָשַׁל to rule, to have power; to liken, to use proverbs, which are to be considered either as comparisons or as weighty important sayings. KAL ᵃ *imp.* PIEL ᵇ *part.*

14 נָאַם to speak oracularly. KAL *part.* Paül.

15 נָגַד to show, to tell, to declare, to announce. HIPHIL *fut.* Job xvii. 5; see *Flattery*. Most interpreters agree in substance with the Vulg., "he promises spoil to his companions," but the construction rather favours the rendering of Gesenius, "he betrays his friends to plunder."

16 סָפַר to number, to recount, to declare. PIEL *fut.*

17 עוּת to speak a word in season; see *Season*. KAL *inf.*

18 עָנָה to answer; is often employed when one commences a discourse, even though no question has preceded, somewhat in the sense of replying to a subject, or of speaking to a case, where a question might appropriately be asked, as in many of the following passages; ἀποκρίνομαι is frequently so used in the New Testament. KAL ᵃ *pret.* ᵇ *fut.* עֲנָה Ch. P'AL ᶜ *pret.* ᵈ *part.*

19 פֶּה *m.* mouth; "to speak proudly," to magnify the mouth.

20 פּוּחַ to breathe forth with a degree of vehemence, to utter with audacity, also in a good sense to speak. HIPHIL *fut.*

21 קוֹל *m.* voice; "speaketh fair;" see *Fair.*

22 שִׂיחַ to speak, to talk, to converse; to meditate: according to some, including the idea of expatiating. KAL ᵃ *imp.* ᵇ *fut.*

23 שֵׁמַע *m.* hearing, report.

24 שָׁנָה to do anything a second time. KAL *fut.*

25 שָׂפָה *f.* lip.

No. 6 e, *Spoken*; No. 6 f, *To Speak*; imp. *Speak*; No. 6 g, fut. *Spake*; not included.

Gen. iv. 23.	2 l	Num. xxvi. 1.	2 d	2 Sam. xiv. 4.	2 d	
ix. 8.	2 d	xxvii. 6.	2 d	xiv. 12, 15, 18.	6 g	
xi. 1. a	6 m	xxvii. 7.	6 b	xiv. 13.	6 l	
xi. 7.	25	xxvii. 8.	6 g	xv. 20.	6 m	
xvi. 13.	6 b	xxxi. 25.	2 d	xvii. 6.	2 d	
xviii. 29.	6 f	xxxii. 2, 25.	2 d	xix. 10.η	9 b	
xviii. 30, 32.	6 g	Deut. i. 1, 3, 6.	6 e	xix. 11.	6 m	
xxi. 22.	2 d	i. 9.	2 d	xix. 29.	6 g	
xxii. 7.	2 d	ii. 1.	2 d	xx. 16.	6 e	
xxiv. 7, 30.	6 d	ii. 2.	2 d	xx. 18, 18.θ	2 d, 6 f g	
xxiv. 15, 45, 50.	6 f	iii. 26.δ	2 d	xxii. 2, 3.	6 g	
xxvii. 5.	6 f	iv. 15.	6 f	xxiv. 17.	2 d	
xxvii. 6, 6.	2 a, 6 h	iv. 33.	6 h	1 Kings i. 11.	2 d	
xxix. 9.	6 h	iv. 45.	6 e	i. 42.	6 h	
xxxi. 11.	2 d	v. 1.	2 d	ii. 4, 27.	6 e	
xxxi. 24.	6 g	v. 22.	6 b	ii. 17.	2 c	
xxxi. 29, 29.	2 a, 6 f	v. 27, 27, 31.	6 g	ii. 18.	6 g	
xxxii. 4.	2 d	v. 28.	6 f	iii. 10.	6 m	
xxxii. 19.	6 g	ix. 4, 13.	2 d	iii. 26.	2 d	
xxxiv. 4.	2 d	ix. 10.	6 e	v. 5.	6 e	
xxxv. 15.	6 e	xi. 19.	6 f	vi. 12.	6 e	
xxxvii. 4.	6 f	xiii. 2.	6 e	viii. 12.	2 a	
xxxix. 14.	6 f	xviii. 18.	6 e	viii. 15, 20, 26, 53.	6 e	
xxxix. 14.	2 d	xviii. 19, 20, 22.	6 g	xii. 7, 15.	6 e	
xxxix. 19.	6 e	xx. 2, 5.	6 e	xii. 10, 10.	2 d, 6 e	
xlii. 14, 30.	6 e	xx. 8.ε	6 f	xii. 23.	2 c	
xlii. 22.	2 a	xx. 9.	6 f	xiii. 18, 26.	6 d	
xlii. 37.	2 d	xxii. 14, 17.	6 m	xiii. 31.	6 d	
xliii. 27, 29.	2 a	xxiv. 8.	6 e	xiv. 18.	6 e	
xliv. 16, 18.	2 d	xxvi. 5.	18 a	xv. 29.	6 e	
xlv. 12.	6 h	xxvii. 14.	18 a	xvi. 12, 34.	6 e	
xlvi. 2.	2 d	xxviii. 68.	2 a	xvii. 16.	6 e	
xlvii. 5.	2 d	xxxi. 28.	6 e	xviii. 24.	6 m	
xlix. 28.	6 e	xxxii. 1.	6 g	xx. 5.	2 d	
l. 17.	6 f	xxxii. 1.	6 e	xx. 28.	2 d	
Exod. i. 15.	6 e	xxxii. 2.	6 f	xx. 19, 19, 23.	6 e	
iv. 10, 10.	6 f, 19	xxxii. 45.	6 f	xxii. 13, 13, 28.	6 e	
iv. 14.β	6 f g	Josh. i. 1.	2 d	2 Kings ii. 22.	6 e	
iv. 15, 16.γ	6 e	i. 12.	2 d	iii. 13.	6 f	
v. 10.	2 d	iii. 6.	2 d	vi. 12.	6 g	
vi. 27.	6 h	iv. 9, 1, 15, 21.	2 d	vii. 17.	6 f	
vi. 28.	2 d	iv. 8, 12.	2 d	vii. 18.	6 f	
vii. 2, 2, 9.	6 g	vi. 8.	2 d	viii. 1.	6 e	
vii. 7.	6 g	vii. 2.	2 d	ix. 12.	2 a	
vii. 8, 19.	2 d	ix. 11.	2 d	ix. 36.	6 e	
viii. 1, 5.	2 d	xiv. 10, 12.	6 e	x. 10, 10, 17.	6 e	
xii. 1.	2 d	xvii. 17.	6 f	xiv. 25.	6 e	
xv. 1.	2 d	xx. 2.	6 e	xv. 12.	6 e	
xvi. 9.	2 d	xxii. 8, 24.	2 d	xvii. 26.	2 d	
xvi. 10.	6 f	xxii. 30.	6 e	xviii. 19.	6 e	
xix. 6.	6 g	xxiii. 14.	6 f	xix. 10.	2 d	
xix. 9.	6 f	xxiv. 27.	6 e	xxii. 19.	6 e	
xix. 25.	2 d	Judg. ii. 4.	6 e	xxiv. 2.	6 e	
xx. 19.	6 g	v. 10.	22 a	1 Chron. xv. 16.	2 d	
xxiii. 2.	18 b	vi. 39.	6 g	xvii. 6, 15.	6 e	
xxiii. 22.	6 g	viii. 9.	2 d	xvii. 17.	6 g	
xxviii. 3.	6 g	ix. 37.	6 f	xxi. 19.	6 e	
xxx. 31.	6 g	xiii. 11.	6 e	2 Chron. i. 2.	2 d	
xxxi. 12.	2 d	xv. 13.	2 d	ii. 15.	2 a	
xxxii. 12.	2 d	xv. 17.	2 d	vi. 4.	6 e	
xxxii. 12.	6 f	xvii. 2.	6 f	x. 7, 10, 15.	6 e	
xxxiii. 11, 11.	6 e g	xix. 22.	2 a	xi. 3.	2 d	
xxxiv. 33.	6 f	xxi. 13.ζ	6 g	xviii. 12, 12.	6 e	
xxxiv. 34.	6 e d	Ruth i. 18.	2 d	xviii. 13.	6 g	
xxxv. 4.	2 d	iv. 1.	6 e	xviii. 19.	2 d	
xxxvi. 5.	2 d	1 Sam. i. 13.	6 h	xxxii. 16.	6 e	
Lev. ix. 3.	6 g	vii. 3.	2 d	xxxii. 17.	2 b	
x. 3.	6 e	ix. 9, 17.	2 a	xxxii. 24.	2 d	
xxi. 1.	2 c	ix. 21.	6 e	xxxiii. 18.	6 h	
xxiv. 15.	6 g	x. 16.	2 d	xxxv. 25.	2 d	
Num. i. 48.	6 g	xvi. 4.	6 e	Ezra viii. 22.	2 a	
iii. 1.	6 g	xvii. 26, 30.	2 d	Neh. ii. 18.	2 d	
v. 4.	2 d	xvii. 28.	6 f	iv. 2.	2 d	
vii. 4.	2 d	xvii. 31.	6 f	viii. 1.	2 d	
vii. 89.	6 l	xviii. 1.	6 f	ix. 13.	2 d	
xii. 4.	2 d	xviii. 24.	6 e	xiii. 24, 24.	6 h f	
xii. 6, 8.	6 g	xx. 26.	6 e	Esth. iii. 4.	2 b	
xiv. 7.	6 f	xxiv. 16.	6 f	iv. 10.	2 d	
xiv. 15.	2 a	xxv. 17.	6 e	v. 14.	2 c	
xv. 37.	2 d	xxv. 24.	2 d	vi. 4.	2 b	
xvi. 31.	6 f	xxviii. 12.	6 g	viii. 3.	6 b	
xvi. 37.	6 e	xxviii. 17, 21.	6 e	Job i. 16, 17, 18.	6 h	
xvii. 12.	2 d	xxx. 6.	6 e	ii. 10, 10.	6 h f	
xviii. 20.	6 g	2 Sam. iii. 18.	2 a	ii. 13.	6 d	
xviii. 26.	6 g	v. 1, 6.	2 a	iii. 2.	18 b	
xx. 3, 12, 23.	2 d	vi. 22.	2 a	iv. 2.	12 e	
xx. 8.	6 e	vii. 7, 17.	6 g	vi. 26.	2 i	
xxi. 16.	2 a	vii. 19.	6 g	vii. 11.	6 g	
xxii. 8, 35, 35, 38.	6 g	xii. 18.	2 d	viii. 2.	12 b	
xxiii. 5, 26.	6 g	xiii. 22.	6 e	viii. 2.	6 g	
xxiv. 12.	6 e	xiii. 36.	6 e	ix. 35.	6 g	
xxiv. 13.	6 g	xiv. 3.	6 e	x. 1.	6 g	

Job xi. 5.	6 f
xii. 8.	22 a
xii. 20.	25
xiii. 3, 7, 13, 22.	6 g
xiii. 17.	12 e
xv. 3.	12 e
xvi. 4, 6.	6 g
xvii. 5.	15
xviii. 2.	6 g
xxi. 2.	12 e
xxi. 3, 3.	6 g f
xxiv. 25.	12 e
xxvii. 4.	6 g
xxix. 22, 22.	24, 12 e
xxxii. 4.	6 m
xxxii. 7, 20.	6 g
xxxii. 14.	2 i
xxxii. 15.	12 e
xxxiii. 1.	12 e
xxxiii. 8.	2 a
xxxiii. 14, 31.	6 g
xxxiv. 35.	6 g
xxxv. 1.	18 b
xxxvi. 2.	12 e
xxxvii. 20, 20.	6 g, 2 a
xli. 3.	6 g
xlii. 4.	6 g
Ps. ii. 5.	6 g
v. 6.	6 b
xii. 2, 2.	6 g
xii. 3.	6 h
xv. 2.	6 b
xvii. 6.	2 l
xvii. 10.	6 e
xviii. title.	6 e
xix. 2, 3.	2 k
xxviii. 3.	6 b
xxix. 9.	2 e
xxxi. 18.	6 e
xxxiii. 9.	2 a
xxxiv. 20.	6 f
xxxv. 20.	6 g
xxxv. 28.	7
xxxvii. 30.	7
xxxviii. 12.	6 e
xxxix. 3.	6 e
xl. 5.	6 g
xli. 5.	2 d
xli. 6.	6 g
xlv. 1.	2 e
xlix. 3.	6 g
l. 7, 20.	6 g
li. 4.	6 a
lviii. 1.	6 g
lviii. 3.	6 b
lix. 12.	16
lxiii. 11.	6 b
lxix. 12.	22 b
lxxi. 10.	2 a
lxxiii. 8, 8.	6 g
lxxiii. 15.	16
lxxv. 5.	6 g
lxxvii. 4.	6 g
lxxxv. 8, 8.	6 g
lxxxvii. 3.	6 k
lxxxix. 19.	6 e
xciv. 4.	6 g
cv. 31, 34.	2 a
cvi. 33.	3 b
cix. 20.	6 b
cxv. 5.	6 g
cxv. 7.	7
cxvi. 10.	6 g
cxix. 23.	6 d
cxix. 46.	6 g
cxix. 172.	18 b
cxx. 7.	6 g
cxxvii. 5.	6 g
cxxxv. 16.	6 g
cxxxix. 20.	2 d
cxl. 11. κ	1, 10
cxliv. 8, 11.	6 e
cxlv. 5.	22 b
cxlv. 6, 11.	2 d
cxlv. 21.	6 g
Prov. i. 12.	6 h
vi. 13.	12 a
vi. 19.	20
vii. 21.	11
viii. 6.	6 g
viii. 7.	7
xii. 17.	20
xii. 18.	3 a

Prov. xiv. 25.	20
xvi. 13.	6 b
xvii. 7.	25
xix. 5, 9.	20
xxi. 28.	6 g
xxiii. 9.	6 g
xxiii. 16.	6 f
xxv. 11.	6 c
xxvi. 25.	21
xxx. 1.	14 a
Eccles. vii. 21.	6 g
Cant. ii. 10.	18 a
iv. 3.	6 n
v. 6.	6 f
vii. 9.	5
viii. 8.	6 i
Isa. vii. 10.	6 f
viii. 5. λ	6 f
viii. 11.	2 a
viii. 20.	2 d
ix. 17.	6 b
xiv. 10.	18 b
xix. 18.	6 h
xx. 2.	6 e
xxiii. 4.	2 a
xxviii. 11.	6 g
xxviii. 23.	2 l
xxix. 4, 4, 4.	6 g, 21, 21
xxxi. 4.	2 a
xxxii. 6.	6 g
xxxii. 7.	6 f
xxxii. 9.	2 l
xxxiii. 15.	6 b
xxxiii. 19.	25
xxxvi. 11.	6 g
xxxvii. 10.	2 d
xxxviii. 15.	2 a
xl. 27.	6 g
xli. 1.	6 g
xlv. 19.	6 b
l. 4.	17
lii. 6.	6 h
lvi. 3.	2 d
lviii. 9, 13.	6 f
lix. 4, 13.	6 f
lxiii. 1.	6 h
lxv. 12.	6 e
lxv. 24.	6 h
lxvi. 4.	6 e
Jer. i. 6. μ	6 f
i. 7.	6 g
i. 17.	6 e
v. 5.	6 g
v. 14.	6 g
vi. 10.	6 g
vii. 13.	6 f
vii. 22, 27.	6 e
ix. 5.	6 g
x. 1.	6 e
x. 5.	6 e
xi. 2.	6 g
xii. 6.	6 g
xiii. 12.	2 a
xiv. 14.	6 e
xviii. 7, 9.	6 g
xviii. 11.	2 c
xix. 5.	6 e
xx. 9.	6 g
xxii. 1, 21.	6 e
xxiii. 16, 28.	6 g
xxv. 2.	6 e
xxv. 3, 3.	6 g f
xxvi. 7.	6 h
xxvi. 8, 8.	6 f
xxvi. 11, 12, 17, 18.	6 f
xxvii. 9, 14.	2 e
xxvii. 12, 16.	6 e
xxviii. 1, 2.	2 a
xxviii. 7.	6 b
xxviii. 11.	2 d
xxix. 23.	6 g
xxix. 24.	2 d
xxix. 25.	2 a
xxx. 2.	2 a
xxx. 4.	6 e
xxxi. 20.	6 f
xxxi. 23.	6 m
xxxii. 4.	6 e
xxxiv. 2.	6 e
xxxiv. 3.	6 g

Jer. xxxv. 2.	6 e
xxxv. 14.	6 f
xxxvi. 2, 2.	6 e
xxxvii. 2.	6 e
xxxviii. 1.	6 h
xxxviii. 4.	6 f
xxxviii. 20.	6 b
xxxviii. 27.	9 a
xxxix. 16.	2 a
xl. 15.	2 a
xl. 16.	6 b
xliii. 1.	6 f
xliii. 2, 2.	2 d, 6 h
xliv. 25.	6 e
xlvi. 13.	6 e
xlviii. 8.	2 a
xlviii. 27. ν	6 m
l. 1.	6 e
li. 12.	6 e
Ezek. i. 24.	8
i. 28.	6 h
ii. 1.	6 g
ii. 2, 2.	6 e l
ii. 7.	6 e
iii. 4, 11, 18.	6 e
iii. 5, 6.	25
iii. 10.	6 g
iii. 27.	6 f
x. 2.	2 d
x. 5.	6 f
xi. 5.	2 c
xi. 25, 25, 28.	6 g
xiii. 7.	2 a
xiii. 8.	6 f
xvii. 2.	13 a
xx. 49.	13 b
xxiv. 21.	2 c
xxiv. 27.	6 g
xxxi. 2.	2 c
xxxii. 21.	6 g
xxxiii. 8, 30.	6 e
xxxiii. 10, 10.	2 c a
xxxiii. 24.	2 e
xxxv. 12.	2 a
xxxvii. 18.	2 d
xxxix. 17.	2 c
xliii. 6.	6 l
Dan. i. 3.	2 d
ii. 9.	2 f
iii. 9.	18 c
iii. 14, 19, 24, 26, 28.	18 d
iii. 29.	2 g
v. 10.	18 c
iv. 19, 30.	18 d
iv. 31. o	2 h
v. 7, 13.	18 d
vi. 12.	2 h
vi. 16, 20.	18 d
vii. 2.	18 d
vii. 8, 11, 20.	12 d
vii. 25.	12 c
viii. 13, 13.	6 h
viii. 18.	6 f
ix. 6, 12.	6 e
ix. 20, 21.	6 h
x. 11, 11.	6 b f
x. 15.	2 a
x. 19, 19.	6 f g
xi. 27, 36.	6 e
Hos. ii. 14.	6 e
xiii. 1.	6 e
Amos v. 10.	6 b
v. 14.	2 a
Obad. 12.	4, 19
Jonah ii. 10.	2 d
Hab. ii. 3.	20
iii. 2.	23
Zeph. iii. 13.	6 g
Hag. i. 2.	2 a
i. 13.	2 d
ii. 2, 21.	2 c
Zech. i. 21.	2 d
iii. 4.	2 d
iv. 4, 6.	2 d
vi. 12.	2 c
vii. 3.	2 b
vii. 9.	2 a
ix. 10.	6 e
xiii. 3.	6 e
Mal. iii. 13, 16.	6 d

will speak." γ *lit.* he shall speak for thee. δ *lit.* add not to speak. ε *lit.* shall add to speak. ζ *lit.* and spake to, &c. η *marg.* 'are ye silent?'—rather, remiss, negligent; *comp.* verse 11. θ *marg.* 'or, they plainly spake in the beginning.' ι *lit.* added and spake. κ *lit.* a man of tongue. λ *lit.* added to speak. μ *lit.* I know not to speak. ν *lit.* from thy words. o *lit.* to thee they are speaking.

SPEAR

1　חֲנִית *f.* a spear, so called as being flexible; sometimes so fragile that they commonly broke when thrown, and could not be taken up and used by the enemy; a camp-spear, or javelin, such as soldiers use; such a spear held in the hand, or stuck in the ground near, was a mark of authority: 1 Sam. xiii. 19, &c.

2　כִּידוֹן *m.* a javelin, spear, smaller kind of lance, different from חֲנִית (1 Sam. xvii. 6, 7, 45, Job xxxix. 23), borne by soldiers, suspended from the shoulder, 1 Sam. xvii. 6; and thrown after brandishing, Job xli. 29; common among the Babylonians and Persians, Jer. vi. 23, l. 42; and so made as to be conspicuous when lifted up, Josh. viii. 18, *comp.* 26; being probably decorated with a flag, like the lances of the modern Polish lancers or Uhlans. So Kimchi, this is the spear on which there is a flag. Bochart aptly derives it from כִּיד destruction, or weapon of war.

3　צִלְצָל *m.* (see *Cymbal*), a fish-spear, harpoon, used by the ancient Egyptians for hunting the hippopotamus and crocodile. See Wilkinson's Manners and Customs of the Ancient Egyptians, iii. pp. 72, 73.

4　קַיִן *m.* a lance, spear.

5　קָנֶה *m.* reed, cane: Ps. lxviii. 30, *marg.* 'or, the beasts of the reeds,' *i.e.* the crocodile, or hippopotamus.

6　רֹמַח *m.* lance, spear, used by heavy-armed troops; sometimes the iron point, lance-head.

No. 1 not included.

Josh. viii. 18, 18, 26.	2	2 Chron. xxv. 5.	6	Ps. lxviii. 30.	5
Judg. v. 8.	6	xxvi. 14.	6	Jer. vi. 23.	2
2 Sam. xxi. 16.	4	Neh. iv. 13, 16, 21.	6	xlvi. 4.	6
1 Chron. xii. 24.	6	Job xli. 7.	3	Ezek. xxxix. 9.	6
2 Chron. xi. 12.	6	xli. 29.	2	Joel iii. 10.	6
xiv. 8.	6				

SPECIAL

סְגֻלָּה *f.* (see *Peculiar*): Deut. vii. 6.

SPECKLED

נָקֹד *adj.* marked with spots, speckled, spotted, of sheep and goats: Gen. xxx. 32, 32, 33, 35, 39; xxxi. 8, 8, 10, 12.

צָבוּעַ *m.* (see *Colours*): Jer. xii. 9. Lxx. ὕαινα. Others generally, beasts of prey; *comp.* Talmud, צְבוֹעִים ravenous beasts.

שָׂרֹק *adj.* reddish, bay, fox-coloured: Zech. i. 8.

SPEED

1　אָסְפַּרְנָא *adv.* Ch. diligently, carefully, speedily.

2　אָמַץ to be strong; to act with great and undaunted courage. HITHPAEL *pret.*

3　בָּהַל to be in great trepidation; to do anything in a hurried or speedy manner. NIPHAL a *part.* PIEL b *fut.*

4　הָלַךְ to go. KAL *inf.*

α *lit.* the same words.　β *lit.* speaking he will speak. The force and import of this idiom is well given by Keil, *Comm. in loc.*: "He both can and

5   מָהַר   to hasten. PIEL [a] *imp.* [b] *fut.* מַהֵר [c] *adv.* quickly. [d] מְהֵרָה *f. id.*

6   מָלַט   to escape. NIPHAL *inf.*

7   מָצָא   to find; emphatically, to find in sufficiency. KAL *fut.*

8   עָבַר   to pass. KAL *inf.*

9   קָרָה   to meet; to cause to meet. HIPHIL *imp.* Gen. xxiv. 12, *lit.* let occur to me this day, *sc.* what I seek, send me good speed.

10   רוּץ   to run. HIPHIL *fut.*

Gen. xxiv. 12.	9	2 Chron. xxxv. 13.	10	Ps. cxliii. 7.	5 c
xliv. 11. a	5 b	Ezra vi. 12, 13.	1	Eccles. viii. 11.	5 d
Judg. v. 30.	7	vii. 17, 21, 26.	1	Isa. v. 19.	5 b
1 Sam. xx. 38.	5 d	Esth. ii. 9.	3 b	v. 26.	5 d
xxvii. 1. β	6	Ps. xxxi. 2.	5 d	lviii. 8.	5 d
2 Sam. xv. 14.	5 a	lxix. 17.	5 c	Joel iii. 4.	5 d
xvii. 16. γ	8	lxxix. 8.	5 c	Zeph. i. 18.	3 a
1 Kings xii. 18.	2 a	cii. 2.	5 c	Zech. viii. 21.	4
2 Chron. x. 18.	2 a				

a *lit.* and they hasted and took down.   β *lit.* escaping I should escape.
γ *lit.* passing pass over.

SPEND

1   אָבַד   to perish; to destroy, to waste. PIEL *fut.*

2   אָזַל   to go away, to depart. KAL *pret.*

3   בָּלָה   to fall away, to decay; to consume. PIEL *fut.* כתיב.

4   בָּלַע   to swallow; to consume, destroy. PIEL *fut.*

5   כָּלָה   to be completed, perfected, finished; to be ended, spent, consumed. KAL [a] *pret.* [b] *fut.* PIEL [c] *pret.* [d] *fut.*

6   עָשָׂה   to do. KAL *fut.*

7   רָדַד   to tread down. KAL *pret.*

8   שָׁקַל   to weigh, to pay. KAL *fut.*

9   תָּמַם   to be complete; to be ended, consumed. KAL [a] *pret.* [b] *inf.*

Gen. xxi. 15.	5 b	Job vii. 6.	5 b	Prov. xxix. 3.	1
xlvii. 18.	9 a	xxi. 13.	5 d, or 3	Eccles. vi. 12.	6
Lev. xxvi. 20.	9 a	xxxvi. 11.	5 d	Isa. xlix. 4.	5 c
Deut. xxxii. 23.	5 d	Ps. xxxi. 10.	5 d	lv. 2.	8
Judg. xix. 11.	7	xc. 9.	5 c	Jer. xxxvii. 21.	9 b
1 Sam. ix. 7.	2	Prov. xxi. 20.	4		

SPICE

1   בֶּשֶׂם   *m.* balsam, balsam-plant, frequent in the gardens of the Hebrews. [a] בֶּשֶׂם *m.* aromatic odour, fragrance, especially as diffused by spices; spice itself, spicery. [b] בֹּשֶׂם *m. id.*

2   נְכֹאת   *f. pr.* contusion, a breaking in pieces; hence aromatic powder, and then this general name seems to have been transferred to some certain kind of spice or aromatic substance.

3   רָקַח   to season, to spice, *e.g.* oil for making ointments; to perfume. HIPHIL [a] *inf.* [b] רֶקַח *m.* spice. [c] מִרְקָחָה *f.* spicing.

Gen. xxxvii. 25.	2	1 Kings x. 25.	1 a	Cant. v. 1.	1
xliii. 11.	2	2 Kings xx. 13.	1 a	v. 13.	1 b
Exod. xxv. 6.	1 a	1 Chron. ix. 29, 30.	1 a	vi. 2.	1 b
xxx. 23.	1 a	2 Chron. ix. 1.	1 a	viii. 2.	3 b
xxxv. 8.	1 a	ix. 9, 9.	1 a b	viii. 14.	1 a
xxxv. 28.	1 b	ix. 24.	1 a	Isa. xxxix. 2.	1 a
1 Kings x. 2.	1 a	xxxii. 27.	1 a	Ezek. xxiv. 10. a	3 a c
x. 10, 10.	1 a b	Cant. iv. 10, 14, 16.	1 a	xxvii. 22.	1 b

a *lit.* season it with a seasoning of spices.

SPIDER

עַכָּבִישׁ   *m.* a spider (Bochart); occurs only in the description of a wicked man or hypocrite: Job viii. 14: Isa. lix. 5.

שְׂמָמִית   *f.* a small sort of lizard, poisonous, from its spots called *stellio*, a very crafty creature, whose fore-feet are like the hands of a man, with which it takes hold even of flat ceilings, and there goes in pursuit of its prey.— *Bochart.* Such a small creature may happen to be in kings' palaces, and so may the spider too, whose legs, considering the use he makes of them, may elegantly be called hands.—*Taylor.* Kirby, in his Bridgewater Treatise, thinks the spider is intended in this passage: Prov. xxx. 28.

SPIKENARD

נֵרְדְּ   *m.* nardus, a plant which grows in India; no more of it is brought to us than the root and the leaves that grow out of it, resembling a bunch of ears of corn, whence it is called *spica nardi*, or spikenard. Of this the ancients made an ointment, a very delicious and costly perfume. See Celsii Hierob. tom. ii. p. 1, &c.; Sir W. Jones on the Spikenard of the Ancients, in Asiatic Researches, vol. iv. Cant. i. 12; iv. 13, 14.

SPILL

נָגַר   to flow; to be poured out. NIPHAL *part.* 2 Sam. xiv. 14.

שָׁחַת   to destroy. PIEL *pret.* Gen. xxxviii. 9.

SPIN

טָוָה   to spin. KAL *pret.* Exod. xxxv. 25, 26. מַטְוֶה *m.* yarn: Exod. xxxv. 25.

SPINDLE

כִּישׁוֹר   *m. pr.* righter, director, *sc.* of a spindle, *i.e.* the whirl or twirl of a spindle, fixed upon its lower end for this purpose: Prov. xxxi. 19. So Kimchi. In the East the spindle is held in the hand, often perpendicularly; and is twirled with one hand while the other draws out the thread.

SPIRIT

נְשָׁמָה   *f.* breath, spirit; mind, intellect: Job xxvi. 4: Prov. xx. 27.

רוּחַ   *com.* breath, air, wind; the vital spirit, life, both of men and beasts; the rational soul, mind, spirit, as the seat of the affections, emotions, and passions of various kinds, in reference to the disposition, mode of feeling and acting, in which sense one is said to have firmness of mind, a firm spirit, &c., of will, counsel, purpose, more rarely of the understanding; *abs.* spirit, courage; the spirit of God; any spirit or ghost: Hos. ix. 7, "spiritual man," *marg.* 'man of the spirit.' Gen. i. 2, &c. רוּחַ Ch. Dan. iv. 8, 9, 18; v. 11, 12, 14; vi. 3; vii. 15.

SPIT, SPITTLE

יָרַק   to spit, expressive of great contempt. KAL *pret.* Num.

xii. 14 : Deut. xxv. 9. *inf.* Num. xii. 14, *lit.* spitting had spit.

רִיר *m.* spittle, slaver : 1 Sam. xxi. 13.

רָקַק to spit, to spit out ; to spit upon. KAL *fut.* Lev. xv. 8. רֹק *m.* spittle : Job vii. 19 ; xxx. 10, *marg.* ‘ withhold spittle from :’ Isa. l. 6.

SPITE

כַּעַס *m.* vexation, trouble, grief ; anger : Ps. x. 14.

SPOIL

1 אַרְבוֹת *f. pl.* according to the primary meaning of the root, to weave ; plots, devices, ambuscades : Isa. xxv. 11, God will humble his (Moab’s) pride, together with the devices of his hands, *i. e.* the plots which his own hands will weave.—*Gesenius.*

2 בַּג *m.* a Persian word signifying food ; *comp.* φαγεῖν, and Phryg. βεκός, bread : Herodot. ii. 2 : Ezek. xxv. 7, כתיב. The Keri has לְבַז for a spoil, which also the ancient versions express ; and this is likewise supported by the similar passages, Jer. xv. 13 and xvii. 3, and especially Ezek. xxvi. 5, xxxiv. 28.

3 בָּזָא probably the same as בָּזַז. KAL *pret.* Isa. xviii. 2, 7, *marg.* ‘ despise,’ as *i. q.* בָּזָה. According to Gesenius, to break up into parts, to divide up. The allusion is to Ethiopia, according to some ; to Judea, according to others. Vitringa supposes this clause to refer to the annual overflowing of the Nile ; and the one before it, to the Egyptian practice of treading the grain into the soil when softened by the inundation.—*Alexander.*

4 בָּזַז to prey, to spoil ; to seize as prey, to plunder ; the primary notion seems to be that of pulling in pieces, scattering. KAL ᵃ*pret.* ᵇ*imp.* ᶜ*fut.* NIPHAL ᵈ*pret.* ᵉ*inf.* ᶠ*fut.* בַּז *m.* prey, spoil, booty ; spoken of men and beasts, carried away in war, and also of goods or property plundered by an enemy. ʰ בִּזָּה *f. id.*

5 גָּזַל to strip off ; to pluck off or away, to tear away, to take by force ; to strip, to spoil, to rob any one. KAL ᵃ*pret.* ᵇ*fut.* ᶜ*part.* Poel. ᵈ*part.* Paül. ᵉ גְּזֵלָה *f.* rapine, plunder.

6 חָבַל to bend, to twist ; to lay waste. PIEL *part.*

7 חֲלִיצָה *f.* spoil, booty, stripped from the dead bodies of the slain, *exuviæ.*

8 טֶרֶף *m.* prey of a wild beast, *pr.* an animal torn in pieces.

9 נָצַל to draw out, to take away, to snatch away ; to strip off, to spoil any one with power and courage. PIEL ᵃ*pret.* ᵇ*fut.*

10 פָּשַׁט to spread out, to expand ; to put off a garment, to strip, to plunder. KAL ᵃ*pret.* PIEL ᵇ*inf.*

11 קָבַע to defraud, to rob any one covertly ; *seq. dupl. acc.* to rob one of anything, to spoil. KAL ᵃ*pret.* ᵇ*part.* Poel.

12 שָׁדַד to lay waste, to desolate ; to oppress, to destroy. KAL ᵃ*pret.* ᵇ*inf.* ᶜ*imp.* ᵈ*fut.* ᵉ*part.* Poel. ᶠ*part.* Paül.

NIPHAL ᵍ*pret.* PIEL ʰ*fut.* PUAL ⁱ*pret.* POEL ᵏ*fut.* HOPHAL ˡ*fut.* שֹׁד *m.* violence, oppression ; desolation, destruction.

13 שָׁחַת to corrupt, to destroy, to mar, to spoil, to make good for nothing, anything, or in any way. HIPHIL *part.*

14 שָׁכֹל to bereave. PIEL ᵃ*pret.* שְׁכוֹל *m.* destitution.

15 שָׁלַל to strip, to plunder, to spoil. KAL ᵃ*pret.* ᵇ*fut.* ᶜ*part.* Poel. HITHPOLEL ᵈ*fut.* ᵉ שָׁלָל *m.* spoil, plunder, booty ; gain, profit. ᶠ שׁוֹלָל *m.* spoiled.

16 שָׁסָה to plunder, to rifle. KAL ᵃ*pret.* ᵇ*fut.* ᶜ*part.* Poel. ᵈ*part.* Paül.

17 שָׁסַס to plunder, to rifle. KAL ᵃ*pret.* ᵇ*fut.* ᶜ*part.* Poel. NIPHAL ᵈ*fut.* ᵉ מְשִׁסָּה *f.* prey. כתיב. מְשׁוּסָה *f.*

No. 15 e not included.

Gen. xxxiv. 27, 29.	4 c	Isa. iii. 14.	5 e	Jer. xlviii. 1, 15, 20.	12 i
Exod. iii. 22.	9 a	xi. 14.	4 c	xlviii. 3.	12 m
xii. 36.	9 b	xiii. 16.	17 d	xlviii. 8, 18, 32.	12 e
Num. xxxi. 9, 53.	4 a	xvi. 4, 4.	12 e m	xlix. 3, 10.	12 i
Deut. xxviii. 29.	5 d	xvii. 14.	16 c	xlix. 28.	12 c
Judg. ii. 14, 14.	16 c, 17 b	xviii. 2, 7.	3	l. 10, 10.	15 e c
ii. 16.	16 c	xxi. 2, 2.	12 e	li. 48, 53, 55, 56.	12 e
xiv. 19.	7	xxii. 4.	12 m	Ezek. xiv. 15.	14 a
1 Sam. xiii. 17.	13	xxiv. 3, β	4 e f	xviii. 7.	5 b
xiv. 15.	13	xxv. 11.	1	xviii. 12, 16, 18.	5 a
xiv. 36.	4 c	xxxiii. 1, γ 1,		xxiii. 46. δ	4 g
xiv. 48.	16 c	l. 1, γ	12 e f e l	xxv. 7.	4 g, or 2
xvii. 53.	17 b	xlii. 22, 22.	16 d, 17 e	xxvi. 5.	4 g
2 Sam. xxiii. 10.	10 b	xlii. 24.	17 e	xxxii. 12.	15 a
2 Kings vii. 16.	4 c	Jer. ii. 14.	4 g	xxxix. 10, 10.	15 a c
xvii. 20.	16 c	iv. 13, 20, 20.	12 i	xlv. 9.	12 m
xxi. 14.	17 e	iv. 30.	12 f	Dan. xi. 33.	4 h
2 Chron. xiv. 14,		v. 6.	12 d	Hos. vii. 1.	10 a
14.	4 c h	vi. 7.	12 m	x. 2.	12 k
xxv. 13. a	4 c h	vi. 19.	12 e	x. 14, 14.	12 l m
xxviii. 14.	4 h	ix. 19.	12 i	xiii. 15.	16 b
Ezra ix. 7.	4 h	x. 20.	12 i	Amos iii. 11.	4 d
Esth. ix. 10.	4 h	xii. 12.	12 e	v. 9, 9.	12 m
Job xii. 17, 19.	15 f	xv. 8.	12 e	Micah ii. 4.	12 b g
xxix. 17.	8	xv. 13.	4 g	Nah. ii. 9, 9.	4 b
Ps. xxxv. 10.	5 c	xvii. 3.	4 g	iii. 16.	10 a
xxxv. 12.	14 b	xx. 5.	4 a	Hab. i. 3.	12 m
xliv. 10.	16 a	xx. 8.	12 m	ii. 8, 8.	15 a b
lxxvi. 5.	15 d	xxi. 12.	5 d	ii. 17.	12 m
lxxxix. 41.	17 a	xxii. 3.	5 d	Zeph. ii. 9.	. 4 c
cix. 11.	4 c	xxv. 36.	12 e	Zech. ii. 8.	15 c
Prov. xxii. 23, 23.	11 a b	xxx. 16, 16.	17 c e	xi. 2, 3, 3.	12 i
xxiv. 15.	12 h	xlvii. 4, 4.	12 b e		
Cant. ii. 15.	6				

a lit. and spoiled much spoil.　　*β lit.* and in being spoiled shall be spoiled.　　*γ lit.* spoiling.　　*δ lit.* and for spoil.

SPOKE

חִשֻּׁרִים *m. pl.* the nave of a wheel into which the spokes are gathered : 1 Kings vii. 33.

SPOKESMAN (See SPEAK)

SPOON

כַּף *f.* the hollow of the hand ; a hollow vessel : Exod. xxv. 29, &c.

SPORT

1 עָנַג (see *Delight*), in a bad sense, to sport over any one, *i. e.* to mock, deride, *seq.* עַל. HITHPAEL *fut.*

2 צָחַק to laugh ; to mock ; to play, to jest. PIEL ᵃ*fut.* ᵇ*part.*

3 שָׂחַק to laugh ; to jest, to sport, to play ; to deride. KAL ᵃ*inf.* PIEL ᵇ*fut.* ᶜ*part.* ᵈ שְׂחוֹק *m.* laughter.

Gen. xxvi. 8.	2 b	Judg. xvi. 27.	3 a	Prov. xxvi. 19.	3 c
Judg. xvi. 25, 25.	3 b, 2 a	Prov. x. 23.	3 d	Isa. lvii. 4.	1

SPOT

1 בֹּהַק *m.* vitiligo alba, white scurf, morphew, an efflorescence on the skin, not uncommon in the East, consisting of spots of a palish white, resembling the leprosy, but harmless, and neither contagious nor hereditary; "freckled spot."

2 בַּהֶרֶת *f.* brightness, *i.e.* a spot in the skin for the most part white. When such a spot is lower than the rest of the skin, and has in it white hairs, it is a symptom of the Oriental leprosy; otherwise it is harmless, whether it be a scar, or arise from a burning, or from the morphew; see above.

3 חֲבַרְבֻּרוֹת *f. pl.* variegated spots of the panther; or, rather, stripes, streaks of the tiger.

4 טָלָא to patch, to mend. KAL *part.* Paül, patched, *i.e.* spotted, having large spots like patches set on.

5 מוּם *m.* see *Blemish, Blot.*

6 תָּמִים *adj.* perfect, without blemish.

Gen. xxx. 32, 32, 33,		Lev. xiii. 39, 39.	2, 1	Deut. xxxii. 5.	5
35, 35, 39.	4	xiv. 56.	2	Job xi. 15.	5
Lev. xiii. 2, 4, 19, 23,		Num. xix. 2.	6	Cant iv. 7.	5
24, 25, 26, 28, 38,		xxviii. 3, 9, 11.	6	Jer. xiii. 23.	3
38, 39.	2	xxix. 17, 26.	6		

SPOUSE

כַּלָּה *f.* a bride, spouse, so called from her bridal chaplet, *r.* כָּלַל to deck: Cant. iv. 8, 9, 10, 11, 12; v. 1: Hos. iv. 13, or daughters-in-law, 14 *id.*

SPREAD

1 זָרָה see *Scatter.* PIEL [a] *pret.* PUAL [b] *part.*

2 יָלַךְ to go. KAL *fut.*

3 יָצָא to go forth. KAL *fut.*

4 יָצַע to spread down, or underneath, as a bed. HIPHIL [a] *fut.* HOPHAL [b] *fut.*

5 מָתַח to stretch, to extend, as a tent. KAL *fut.*

6 נָטָה to stretch, spread out, expand. KAL [a] *pret.* [b] *fut.* [c] *part.* Poel. NIPHAL [d] *pret.* HIPHIL [e] *fut.*

7 נָטַשׁ to leave, let loose; or, to cast off, thrust out, to reject; to be dispersed, scattered, as left to themselves. KAL [a] *part.* Paül. NIPHAL [b] *fut.*

8 נָסַךְ to cover. KAL *part.* Paül.

9 סָרַח to pour forth, to spread. KAL *part.* Poel.

10 עָרָה to pour out; to pour oneself out, to spread oneself abroad, of a flourishing vine, or other tree growing luxuriantly. HITHPAEL *part.*

11 פּוּץ to disperse. KAL [a] *fut.* NIPHAL [b] *pret.*

12 פּוּשׁ to spread oneself, to overflow; to be dispersed. KAL *pret.*

13 פָּרַח to break out, or forth. KAL *part.* Poel.

14 פָּרַץ to break forth with violence; to be diffused, increased in number or prosperity. KAL *pret.*

15 פָּרַשׂ to spread out or abroad, to expand. KAL [a] *pret.* [b] *fut.* [c] *part.* Poel. [d] *part.* Paül. PIEL [e] *pret.* [f] *inf.* [g] *fut.* [h] מִפְרָשׂ *m.* expansions of.

16 פָּרְשֶׁז to spread out, to expand. KAL *pret.*

17 פָּשָׂה to spread, as a sore on the body, or as the leprosy. KAL [a] *pret.* [b] *inf.* [c] *fut.*

18 פָּשַׁט to spread out, to expand; *intr.* to spread oneself out. KAL *fut.*

19 פָּתַח to open. KAL *part.* Paül.

20 רָדַד to tread down; to spread out, to expand, as if by treading, stamping; to overlay. HIPHIL *fut.*

21 רָפַד to strew, to spread. KAL *fut.*

22 רָקַע to beat, to beat out, *i.e.* to spread out or expand by beating; *simpl.* to spread out, to expand. KAL [a] *fut.* [b] *part.* Poel. PIEL [c] *fut.* PUAL [d] *part.* HIPHIL [e] *fut.*

23 שָׂטַח to spread out, to expand. KAL [a] *pret.* [b] *inf.* [c] *fut.* [d] מִשְׁטוֹחַ *m.* place for spreading nets. [e] מִשְׁטַח *m. id.*

24 שָׁלַח to send, to send out or forth. PIEL *fut.*

Gen. x. 18.	11 b	1 Kings viii. 22.	15 b	Isa. xl. 19.	22 c
xxviii. 14.	14	viii. 38.	15 a	xl. 22.	5
xxxiii. 19.	6 a	viii. 54.	15 d	xlii. 15.	22 b
xxxv. 21.	6 b	2 Kings viii. 15.	15 b	xliv. 24.	22 b
Exod. ix. 29, 33.	15 b	xix. 14.	15 b	lviii. 5.	4 a
xxxvii. 9.	15 c	1 Chron. xiv. 9, 13.	18	lxv. 2.	15 e
xl. 19.	15 b	2 Chron. iii. 13.	15 c	Jer. iv. 31.	15 g
Lev. xiii. 5, 6, 8, 23,		v. 8.	15 c	viii. 2.	23 a
28, 32, 34, 36, 51,		vi. 12, 13.	15 b	x. 9.	22 d
53, 55.	17 a	vi. 29.	15 c	xvii. 8.	24
xiii. 7.	17 b c	xxvi. 8.	2	xlviii. 40.	6 a
xiii. 22.	17 b c	xxvi. 15.	3	xlix. 22.	15 b
xiii. 27.	17 b c	Ezra ix. 5.	15 b	Lam. i. 10, 13.	15 e
xiii. 35.	17 b c	Job ix. 8.	6 c	i. 17.	15 e
xiii. 57.	13	xxvi. 9.	16	Ezek. ii. 10.	15 b
xiv. 39, 44, 48.	17 a	xxix. 19.	19	xii. 13.	15 a
Num. iv. 6, 8.	15 a	xxxvi. 29.	15 h	xvi. 8.	15 b
iv. 7, 11.	15 b	xxxvii. 30.	15 a	xvii. 6.	9
iv. 13.	15 b	xxxvii. 18.	22 e	xvii. 20.	15 a
xi. 32.	23 b c	xli. 30.	21	xix. 8.	15 b
xxiv. 6.	6 d	Ps. xxxvii. 35.	10	xxvi. 5, 14.	23 e
Deut. xxii. 17.	15 a	cv. 39.	15 a	xxvii. 7.	15 h
xxxii. 11.	15 b	cxl. 5.	15 a	xxviii. 3.	15 a
Judg. viii. 25.	15 b	Prov. i. 17.	1 b	xlvii. 10.	23 d
xv. 9.	7 b	xxix. 5.	15 a	Hos. v. 1.	15 d
Ruth iii. 9.	15 a	Isa. i. 15.	15 f	vii. 12.	15 b
1 Sam. xxx. 16.	15 b	xiv. 11.	4 b	vii. 6.	2
xvi. 22.		xix. 8.	15 c	Joel ii. 2.	15 d
xvii. 19, 19.	15 b, 23 c	xxv. 7.	8	Hab. i. 8.	12
xxi. 10.	6 e	xxv. 11, 11.	15 g e	Zech. i. 17.	11 a
xxii. 43.	22 a	xxxiii. 23.	15 a	ii. 6.	15 e
1 Kings vi. 32.	20	xxxvii. 14.	15 b	Mal. ii. 3.	1 a
viii. 7.	15 c				

SPRIG

זַלְזַלִּים *m. pl.* shoots, twigs of a vine, so called from their waving and tremulous motion; see *Flow;* or from their luxuriant growth: Isa. xviii. 5.

פֹּארָה *f.* green branches: Ezek. xvii. 6.

SPRING (*Noun and Verb*)

1 אֲשֵׁדָה *f.* outpouring of torrents, a low place or ravine at the foot of a mountain where a torrent flows down.

2 גַּל *m.* a fountain, spring, so called from the rolling or welling up of the waters. [a] גֻּלָּה *f. id.*

3 דָּשָׁא to sprout, to spring up. KAL *pret.*

4 חַי *adj.* living.

5 יָצָא to go out, to go forth. KAL [a] *part.* Poel. [b] מוֹצָא *m.* place of outgoing.

6 נֶבֶךְ *m.* fountain.

7 מַבּוּע *m.* fountain.

8 סָחִישׁ *m.* 2 Kings xix. 29, for which in the parallel passage, Isa.

xxxvii. 30, is found שָׁחִים, that which grows of itself the third year after sowing.

9   מַעְיָן   m. well, fountain.

10   עָלָה   to ascend. KAL ᵃ*inf.* ᵇ*imp.*

11   פָּרַח   to break forth; to grow. KAL ᵃ*pret.* ᵇ*inf.* ᶜ*part.* Poel.

12   מָקוֹר   m. fountain, *pr.* opened by digging; a perpetual spring.

13   צָמַח   to sprout, to spring up, as plants. KAL ᵃ*pret.* ᵇ*fut.* ᶜ*part.* Poel. HIPHIL ᵈ*inf.* ᵉ*fut.* ᶠ צֶמַח m. shooting.

14   שָׁחִים   m. i. q. סָחִישׁ, that which springeth of itself the third year after sowing, Isa. xxxvii. 30. This would seem to be the primitive form, and to signify *pr.* sprout, shoot.

Gen. xxvi. 19.	4	2 Kings xix. 29.	8	Isa. xli. 18.	5 b
xli. 6, 23.	13 c	Job v. 6.	13 b	xlii. 9.	13 b
Lev. xiii. 42.	11 c	xxxviii. 16.	6	xliii. 19.	13 b
Num. xxi. 17.	10 b	xxxviii. 27.	13 d	xliv. 4.	13 a
Deut. iv. 49.	1 a	Ps. lxv. 10.	13 f	xlv. 8.	13 e
viii. 7.	5 a	lxxxv. 11.	13 b	xlix. 10.	7
Josh. x. 40.	1 a	lxxxvi. 7.	9	lviii. 8.	13 b
xii. 8.	1 a	xcii. 7.	11 b	lviii. 11.	5 b
xv. 19, 19, 19.	2 a	civ. 10.	9	lxi. 11, 11.	13 e
Judg. i. 15, 15, 15.	2 a	cvii. 33, 35.	5 b	Jer. li. 36.	12
xix. 25.	10 a	Prov. xxv. 26.	12	Ezek. xvii. 9.	13 f
1 Sam. ix. 26.	10 a	Cant. iv. 12.	2	Hos. x. 4.	11 a
1 Kings iv. 33.	5 a	Isa. xxxv. 7.	7	xiii. 15.	12
2 Kings ii. 21.	5 b	xxxvii. 30.	14	Joel ii. 22.	3

SPRINKLE

1   זָרַק   to scatter, to sprinkle; of things dry, as dust, &c.; often of things liquid, as water, blood. KAL ᵃ*pret.* ᵇ*inf.* ᶜ*fut.* ᵈ*part.* Poel. PUAL ᵉ*pret.*

2   נָזָה   to be sprinkled; Hiphil, to sprinkle. On the various interpretations which have been given of this word, see Barnes and Alexander on Isa. lii. 15. The uniform use of the word in the sense of sprinkling with blood, in order to purify, establishes a most important application of this passage to the virtue of the Messiah's atonement. KAL ᵃ*fut.* HIPHIL ᵇ*pret.* ᶜ*imp.* ᵈ*fut.* ᵉ*part.*

Exod. ix. 8.	1 a	Lev. vii. 14.	1 d	Num. xix. 21.	2 e
ix. 10.	1 c	viii. 11, 30.	2 d	2 Kings xix. 33.	2 a
xxiv. 6.	1 a	viii. 19, 24.	1 c	xvi. 13, 15.	1 c
xxiv. 8.	1 c	ix. 12, 18.	1 c	2 Chron. xxix. 22, 22, 22.	1 c
xxix. 16, 20.	1 a	xiv. 7, 16, 27, 51.	2 b	xxx. 16.	1 d
xxix. 21.	2 b	xvi. 14, 14.	2 b d	xxxv. 11.	1 c
Lev. i. 5, 11.	1 a	xvi. 15, 19.	2 b	Job ii. 12.	1 c
iii. 2, 8, 13.	1 a	xvii. 6.	1 a	Isa. lii. 15.	2 d
iv. 6, 17.	2 b	Num. viii. 7.	2 c	lxiii. 3.	2 a
v. 9.	2 b	xviii. 17.	1 c	Ezek. xxxvi. 25.	1 a
vi. 27, 27.	2 a	xix. 4, 8, 19.	2 b	xliii. 18.	1 b
vii. 2.	1 c	xix. 13, 20.	1 d		

SPROUT

חָלַף   to pass; to pass from one degree, condition, or station, to another; hence to change, to renew, revive, flourish again. HIPHIL *fut.* Job xiv. 7.

SPUE

קוֹא   to spue out, to vomit forth. KAL *pret.* Lev. xviii. 28. HIPHIL *fut.* Lev. xviii. 28, xx. 22.

קָיָה   the same. KAL *imp.* Jer. xxv. 27.

קִיקָלוֹן   m. from קִי, for קִיא a vomit, and קָלוֹן ignominy: Hab. ii. 16.

SPY, ESPY

1   צָפָה   see *Watch.* PIEL ᵃ*imp.*

2   רָאָה   to see, to look. KAL ᵃ*pret.* ᵇ*imp.* ᶜ*fut.* NIPHAL ᵈ*pret.*

3   רָגַל   to go about; to go about tale-bearing, and for the sake of reconnoitring, to search, to spy out, *seq. acc.* PIEL ᵃ*inf.* ᵇ*part.*

4   שָׁמַר   to keep, to watch, to guard; to observe. KAL *part.* Poel.

5   תּוּר   to go about for the sake of traffic, for the sake of inquiry. KAL ᵃ*pret.* ᵇ*inf.* ᶜ אַחָרִים m. pl. spies, or the name of a place.

Gen. xlii. 9, 11, 14.	3 b	Josh. vi. 22, 23.	3 b	2 Kings vi. 13.	2 b
16.	3 b	vi. 25.	3 a	ix. 17.	2 c
xlii. 27.	3 c	xiv. 7.	3 a	xiii. 21.	2 a
xlii. 30, 31, 34.	3 b	Judg. i. 24.	4	xxiii. 16.	2 c
Exod. ii. 11.	2 c	xviii. 2, 14, 17.	3 a	xxiii. 24.	2 d
Num. xiii. 16, 17.	5 b	1 Sam. xxvi. 4.	3 b	1 Chron. xix. 3.	3 a
xxi. 1.	5 c	2 Sam. x. 3.	3 a	Jer. xlviii. 19.	1 a
xxi. 32.	3 a	xv. 10.	3 b	Ezek. xx. 6.	5 a
Josh. ii. 1.	3 b				

SQUARE

רָבַע   *verb. denom.* from רֶבַע i. q. אַרְבַּע four; to be quadrate or four-square, square. KAL *part.* Paül, 1 Kings vii. 5: Ezek. xli. 21: xliii. 16. PUAL *part.* Ezek. xlv. 2. רֹבַע m. one of four sides: Ezek. xliii. 16, 17 (*comp.* i. 17).

STABLE, STABLISH, STABILITY

אֱמוּנָה   f. firmness, stability; security; faithfulness: Isa. xxxiii. 6.

כּוּן   to stand upright; to be established. NIPHAL *fut.* 1 Chron. xvi. 30: Ps. xciii. 1. POLEL *pret.* 2 Sam. vii. 13: 1 Chron. xvii. 12: Hab. ii. 12. HIPHIL *fut.* 2 Chron. xvii. 5.

קוּם   to rise; to raise up. PIEL *inf.* Esth. ix. 21. HIPHIL *pret.* 2 Chron. vii. 18. *fut.* Ps. cxlviii. 6. *imp.* Ps. cxix. 38.

נָצַב   to set, to put, to place. HIPHIL *inf.* 1 Chron. xviii. 3.

STABLE

נָוֶה   m. a habitation, fold: Ezek. xxv. 5.

STACK

גָּדִישׁ   m. a heap of sheaves in the field: Exod. xxii. 6.

STACTE

נָטָף   m. a drop; an aromatic gum or resin, used for incense, so called from its flowing out in drops, distilling: Exod. xxx. 34. LXX. στακτή, *i. e.* myrrh flowing spontaneously; the Rabbins, opobalsam.

STAFF, STAVES

1   בַּדִּים   m. pl. branch; hence staves, poles, bars for bearing anything.

2   חֵץ   m. arrow; 1 Sam. xvii. 7, "staff." In Keri and the similar passages, 2 Sam. xxi. 19, 1 Chron. xx. 5, the reading is עֵץ wood, i. e. the handle or shaft of a spear; and so this word has been translated 'shaft,' which best suits the context; according to כתיב, Gesenius would render it the iron point of a spear.

3   מוֹט   m. a staff, pole or bar, so called from the unsteady motion, when bearing anything on the shoulder. ᵃ מוֹטָה f. a bar for the yoke or collar.

4   מַטֶּה   *com.* a branch, &c.; a rod, staff for walking, supporting oneself; with which grain is beaten out; a rod for chastisement: Isa. ix. 4.

5 מַקֵּל *m.* a shoot, a rod; then a staff, which one carries in his hand, Gen. xxxii. 10, Exod. xii. 11, 1 Sam. xvii. 40, 43; with which an animal is beaten, Num. xxii. 27; the crook of a shepherd, Zech. xi. 7, 10, 14; a spear or javelin, Ezek. xxxix. 9, with יָד handstaves. Hos. iv.12, this may allude to some sort of divination by staves as by arrows.

6 עֵץ *m.* tree, wood.

7 פֶּלֶךְ *m.* (see *Distaff*) a spindle; a round staff; a crutch.

8 שֵׁבֶט *com.* a stick, rod, or staff; a rod or staff for chastising; a staff on which one leans; staff of office.

9 מִשְׁעֵנָה *f.* stay or staff. ᵃ מִשְׁעֶנֶת *f. id.*

Gen. xxxii. 10.	5	Num. xxii. 27.	5	Isa. iii. 1.	9
xxxviii. 18, 25.	4	Judg. vi. 21.	9	iv. 4.	4
Exod. xii. 11.		1 Sam. xvii. 7.	2, or 6	x. 5, 15, 24.	4
xxi. 19.	9 a	xvii. 40, 43.	5	xvii. 19.	4
xxv. 13,14,15,27, 28.	1	2 Sam. iii. 29.	9	xxviii. 27.	4
xxvii. 6, 6, 7, 7.	1	xxi. 19.	6	xxx. 32.	4
xxx. 4, 5.	1	xxiii. 7.	4	xxxvi. 6.	9 a
xxxv. 12, 13, 15, 16.	1	xxiii. 21.	8	Jer. xlviii. 17.	4
xxxvii. 4, 5, 14, 15,		1 Kings viii. 7, 8, 8.	1	Ezek. iv. 16.	4
27, 28.	1	2 Kings ix. 29, 31.	9 a	v. 16.	4
xxxviii. 5, 6, 7.	1	xviii. 21.	9 a	xiv. 13.	4
xxxix. 35, 39.	1	1 Chron. xi. 23.	8	xxix. 6.	9 a
xl. 20.	1	xv. 15.	3 a	xxxix. 9.	5
Lev. xxvi. 26.	4	xx. 5.	6	Hos. iv. 12.	5
Num. iv. 6, 8, 11, 14.	4	2 Chron. v. 8, 9, 9.	4	Hab. iii. 14.	4
xiii. 23.	1	Ps. xxiii. 4.	9 a	Zech. viii. 4.	9 a
xxi. 18.	9 a	cv. 14.	4	xi. 7, 10, 14.	5

STAGGER

נוּעַ to nod, to waver, to reel; of drunken persons. KAL *pret.* Isa. xxix. 9; *fut.* Ps. cvii. 27.

תָּעָה to go astray, to wander, to err. NIPHAL *inf.* Isa. xix. 14. HIPHIL *fut.* Job xii. 25.

STAIN

גָּאַל to redeem, to ransom; also to defile. KAL *fut.* Job iii. 5, *marg.* 'or, challenge.' This is said by Job in cursing his natal day, "let darkness and death-shade redeem it for themselves," *i. e.* recover it and again take possession of it; or, in the sense of our translation, "let clouds and storms cover it, and make it dark and dismal." HIPHIL *pret.* Isa. lxiii. 3.

חָלַל (see *Profane*) to pollute. PIEL *inf.* Isa. xxiii. 9.

STAIR

מַדְרֵגָה *f.* a steep mountain, precipice, which can only be ascended by steps or stairs: Cant. ii. 14.

לוּלִים *m. pl.* winding stairs: 1 Kings vi. 8.

מַעֲלָה *f.* a going up; a step, stair, by which one ascends: 2 Kings ix. 13: Neh. iii. 15; xii. 37: Ezek. xl. 6; xliii. 17. מַעֲלֶה *m. id.*: Neh. ix. 4, *marg.* 'or, scaffold;' a platform, *suggestus* for speaking.

STAKE

יָתֵד *f.* a peg, pin, nail, as driven into the wall; specially a tent-pin, driven into the earth to fasten a tent; *fig.* of the stability of a nation: Isa. xxxiii. 20; liv. 2.

STALK

עֵץ *m.* tree, wood; stalk: Josh. ii. 6.

קָמָה stalk of grain: Hos. viii. 7, *marg.* 'or, standing corn.'

קָנֶה *m.* reed, cane; stalk of grain: Gen. xli. 5, 22.

STALL

אָבַס to fodder, to feed largely, to fatten. KAL *part.* Paúl, Prov. xv. 17.

אֻרְוָה *f.* a crib, manger, rack, whence cattle in a stall pull out their fodder; see *Pluck*; a stall of horses, *i. e.* a certain number which usually stood in one stall, or were harnessed to one vehicle; perhaps two, as this was the number harnessed to a chariot; a pair, team: 1 Kings iv. 26: 2 Chron. ix. 25; xxxii. 28.

מַרְבֵּק *m.* stall, stable, in which cattle are tied: Amos vi. 4: Mal. iv. 2.

רְפָתִים *m. pl.* stalls, according to the Hebrew interpreters: Hab. iii. 17. LXX. Vulg. *præsepia.*

STAMMER

לָעַג to speak in a barbarous or foreign tongue; to mock. NIPHAL *part.* Isa. xxxiii. 19. לָעֵג *adj.* stammerer: Isa. xxviii. 11.

עִלֵּג *adj.* evidently the same as above: Isa. xxxii. 4.

STAMP

1 דָּקַק to beat small, by stamping, pounding, &c. HIPHIL ᵃ*pret.* ᵇ *fut.*

2 כָּתַת to beat, to beat in pieces, to break. KAL *fut.*

3 רָמַס to tread down, to trample under feet. KAL *fut.*

4 רְפַס Ch. to trample down, to stamp upon. P'AL *part. active.*

5 רָקַע to beat, to smite the earth with the feet, to stamp, either in indignation or in exultation. KAL ᵃ *inf.* ᵇ *imp.*

6 שַׁעֲטָה *f.* a stamping, *e.g.* of horses advancing in warlike array.

Deut. ix. 21.	2	2 Chron. xv. 16.	1 b	Ezek. xxv. 6.	5 a
2 Sam. xxii. 43.	1 b	Jer. xlvii. 3.	6	Dan. vii. 7, 19.	4
2 Kings xxiii. 6.	1 b	Ezek. vi. 11.	5 b	viii. 7, 10.	3
xxiii. 15.	1 a				

STAND

1 אֲגַם *m.* stagnant water, a pool, marsh.

2 אָמַן to be firm, stable; to be durable, lasting, permanent. NIPHAL *part.* Ps. lxxxix. 28, *comp.* ver. 37.

3 יָצָא to go forth, to stand out. KAL *pret.*

4 יָצַב to set, to put, to place; Hithp. to set or place oneself, to take a stand, to stand; *seq.* בְּ and עַל of place; other constructions are, with עַל of person, to stand before; with עִם to stand with, near any one; with לִפְנֵי, see *Present;* to stand forth, Job xxxviii. 14; to stand firm, to endure, *sc.* before any one, either as victor before an enemy, or as upright and innocent before a judge; to stand up for any one, to stand by him, *seq.* לְ of person. HITHPAEL ᵃ*pret.* ᵇ *inf.* ᶜ *imp.* ᵈ *fut.*

5 כֻּן to stand upright. NIPHAL *part.*

6 נָגַשׁ to come near: it is used in a peculiar sense in KAL *imp.* Gen. xix. 9, stand (back). LXX. ἀπόστα ἐκεῖ. Vulg. *recede illuc,* advance further off, to some other place;

or it may mean, advance nearer to us, and further from the door, for Lot stood with his back to the door to prevent their opening it. In many languages, ancient as well as modern, there is an apparent inaccuracy in the use of words signifying approach and departure, so that they are often used of the contrary motion. See also *Place*.

7 נָצַב to set, to put, to place; to place or station oneself, to take one's stand, of God rising up for judgment, Isa. iii. 13, Ps. lxxxii. 1; to stand, to stand firm; *seq.* עַל to stand upon a thing, to be firmly fixed, settled, established, Gen. xxviii. 13; Gr. ἐστηριγμένη; to stand with or by a person. Specially, to stand firmly; also to stand still, *i. e.* to lag behind from weariness and disease, Zech. xi. 16. NIPHAL ᵃ*pret.* ᵇ*part.* HIPHIL ᶜ*fut.* ᵈ מַצָּב *m.* station, place where one stands. ᵉ מַצֵּבָה *f.* standing image.

8 סָבַב to compass. KAL *fut.*

9 סָמַךְ to sustain; to be established. KAL *part.* Paül.

10 סָמַר to stand erect, as hair of a person affrighted. PIEL *fut.*

11 עוּד to continue, to endure; to set up again, to restore, relieve; to set up oneself, to stand erect. HITHPALEL *fut.*

12 עָמַד to stand: it implies not only that one already stands in a place, but also that he comes to stand there, *q. d.* to take a stand, or place oneself. The place in or upon which one stands is put with בְּ, oftener with עַל to stand upon, or near; to stand by or for, *i. e.* to succour or defend, to stand over, to be set over, to stand upon, *i. e.* to confide in. To stand before, usually to serve, to minister, *e. g.* to a king or minister; so to stand before Jehovah is said of the priests and Levites, and of prophets. To stand, *i. e.* to stand firm, to persist, to endure, *opp.* to fall, to perish; to continue; to stand before any one, to bear up against him, to resist him; *seq.* בְּ to persist, to persevere in anything; once with *acc.* Ezek. xvii. 14, to stand to it, *comp.* Esth. iii. 4, "whether Mordecai's matters would stand," *i. e.* whether he would persist in that course. To stand, *i. e.* to stand still, to stop, *opp.* to go on, to proceed; to stay, to remain in a place, *seq.* בְּ, עַל, אֵת and *abs.* in any state and condition, *seq.* בְּ. To stand, *i. e.* to stand up, to rise up, to arise; Lxx. ἀνίστημι: *seq.* עַל to rise up against any one. Once this word occurs of doubtful signification in Ezek. xxix. 7. Our translation is according to the Hebrew text, yet the Lxx. has συνέκλασας, which meaning may be obtained by a transposition of the letters וְהִמְעַדְתָּ (for וְהַעֲמַדְתָּ), thou breakest, or madest all their loins to tremble. KAL ᵃ*pret.* ᵇ*inf.* ᶜ*imp.* ᵈ*fut.* ᵉ*part.* Poel. HIPHIL ᶠ*pret.* ᵍ*fut.* ʰ עֹמֶד *m.* standing. ⁱ עֳמָד *m.* standing. ᵏ עָמְדָה *f. id.*

13 קוּם to rise up; to set oneself, to stand; *trop.* to stand firm, to be established, to stand out, to endure; to stand out before, to resist any one; to remain, *seq.* לְ to any one; *seq.* לְ of person, to stand up for any one, in his behalf, to stand by him. KAL ᵃ*pret.* ᵇ*inf.* ᶜ*imp.* ᵈ*fut.* HIPHIL ᵉ*pret.* קוּם Ch. P'AL ᶠ*fut.* ᵍ*part.* HOPHAL ʰ*pret.*

ⁱ קָמָה *f.* stalk of grain, *collect.* stalks, for standing grain.

ᵏ תְּקוּמָה *f.* power of standing: Lev. xxvi. 37.

14 קָרַב to draw near. KAL *imp.*

Gen. xviii. 2.	7 b	Josh. iii. 8, 13, 16,		2 Chron. iv. 4.	12 e
xviii. 8, 22.	12 e	17.	12 d	v. 12.	12 e
xix. 9.	6	iv. 3, 9.	7 d	v. 14.	12 b
xix. 27.	12 a	iv. 10.	12 e	vi. 3.	12 e
xxiii. 3, 7.	13 d	v. 13, 15.	12 e	vi. 12, 13.	12 d
xxiv. 13, 43.	7 b	vii. 12, 13.	13 b	vii. 6.	12 e
xxiv. 30.	12 e	viii. 33.	12 d	ix. 7, 18, 19.	12 e
xxiv. 31.	12 d	x. 8, 13.	12 d	x. 6.	12 e
xxviii. 13.	7 b	xi. 13.	12 e	x. 8.	12 d
xxxvii. 7, 7.	7 a, 8	xx. 4.	12 d	xiii. 4.	13 d
xli. 1, 17.	12 e	xx. 6, 9.	12 b	xviii. 18.	12 d
xli. 3.	12 d	xxi. 44.	12 a	xviii. 20.	12 d
xli. 46.	12 b	xxiii. 9.	12 a	xx. 5, 9, 23.	12 d
xliii. 15.	7 b	Judg. ii. 14.	12 e	xx. 13.	12 d
xlv. 1, 1.	7 b, 12 a	iii. 19.	12 e	xx. 17.	12 c
Exod. ii. 4.	4 d	iv. 20.	12 d	xx. 19.	12 d
ii. 17.	13 d	vi. 31.	12 a	xx. 20.	12 a
iii. 5.	12 e	vii. 21.	12 d	xxiii. 13.	12 d
v. 20.	7 b	ix. 7, 35, 44.	12 d	xxiv. 20.	13 d
vii. 15.	12 e	xv. 5, 5.	13 i	xxviii. 12.	12 b
viii. 20.	4 c	xvi. 26, 29.	5	xxix. 11.	12 b
ix. 10.	12 d	xvi. 16, 17.	5	xxix. 26.	12 d
ix. 11.	12 b	xx. 28.	12 e	xxx. 16.	12 d
ix. 13.	4 c	1 Sam. i. 26.	12 e	xxxiv. 31.	12 d
xiv. 13.	4 c	iii. 10.	4 d	xxxiv. 32.	12 g
xiv. 19.	12 d	iv. 20.	7 b	xxxv. 5.	12 d
xv. 8.	7 a	vi. 14.	12 d	xxxv. 10.	12 d
xvii. 6.	12 e	vi. 20.	12 b	Ezra ii. 63.	12 b
xvii. 9.	7 b	ix. 27.β	12 c	iii. 2.	13 d
xviii. 13.	12 d	x. 23.	4 d	iii. 9.	12 d
xviii. 14.	7 b	xii. 7, 16.	4 d	ix. 15.	12 b
xix. 17.	4 d	xiv. 9.	12 a	x. 10.	13 d
xx. 18, 21.	12 d	xvi. 21, 22.	12 a	x. 13.	12 d
xxii. 6.	13 i	xvii. 3, 3, 26.	12 e	x. 14.	12 b
xxvi. 15.	12 e	xvii. 8, 51.	12 d	Neh. vii. 3.	12 b
xxxii. 26.	12 d	xx. 3.	12 a	vii. 65.	12 b
xxxiii. 8, 21.	7 a	xx. 20.	12 e	viii. 4, 4.	12 'a
xxxiii. 9.	12 a	xxii. 6, 7, 17.	7 b	viii. 5.	12 'a
xxxiii. 10.	12 e	xxvi. 13.	12 d	ix. 2.	13 d
xxxiv. 5.	4 d	2 Sam. i. 9.	12 c	ix. 3, 4.	13 d
xxxvi. 20.	12 d	i. 10.	12 d	ix. 4.	12 a
Lev. ix. 5.	12 d	ii. 23, 25, 28.	12 d	xii. 39.	12 a
xviii. 23.	12 d	xiii. 31.	7 b	xii. 40.	12 d
xix. 16.	12 d	xv. 2.	12 a	Esth. iii. 4.	12 d
xxvi. 1.	7 e	xviii. 4.	12 d	v. 1.	12 e
xxvi. 37.	13 k	xviii. 30, 30.	4 c, 12 d	v. 2.	12 e
xxvii. 14, 17.	13 d	xx. 11, 12, 12.	12 d	v. 9.	13 a
Num. i. 5.	12 d	xx. 15.	12 d	vii. 7.	12 e
ix. 8.	12 c	xxiii. 12.	4 d	vii. 9.	12 d
xi. 16.	4 a	1 Kings i. 2.	12 a	viii. 4.	12 e
xi. 32.	13 d	i. 28.	12 d	viii. 11.	12 b
xii. 5.	12 d	iii. 15, 16.	12 d	Job iv. 15.	10
xiv. 14.	12 e	vii. 25.	12 d	iv. 16.	12 d
xvi. 9.	12 b	viii. 11.	12 b	viii. 15.	12 d
xvi. 18, 48.	12 d	viii. 14.	12 e	viii. 22, 55.	12 d	xix. 25.	13 d
xvi. 27.	7 b	viii. 22, 55.	12 d	xxix. 8.	12 e
xxii. 22.	4 d	x. 8, 19, 20.	12 e	xxx. 20.	12 d
xxii. 23, 31, 34.	7 b	x. 6, 8.	12 e	xxx. 28.	12 a
xxii. 24, 26.	12 d	xiii. 1, 24, 24, 25, 28.	12 e	xxxii. 16.	12 a
xxiii. 3, 15.	4 c	xvii. 1.	12 a	xxxiii. 5.	4 c
xxiii. 6, 17.	7 b	xvii. 15.	12 a	xxxvii. 14.	12 c
xxvii. 2, 21.	12 d	xix. 11.	12 a	xxxviii. 14.	4 d
xxx. 4, 4.	13 a d	xix. 13.	12 d	xli. 10.a	4 d
xxx. 5, 9.	13 d	xxii. 19.	12 e	Ps. i. 1.	12 a
xxx. 7, 7.	13 a d	2 Kings ii. 7, 7.	12 d a	i. 5.	13 d
xxx. 11, 11.	13 a d	ii. 13.	12 d	v. 5.	4 d
xxx. 12.	13 d	iii. 14.	12 a	x. 1.	12 d
Deut. i. 38.	12 e	iv. 6.	12 d	xx. 8.	11
iv. 10.	12 d	iv. 12, 15.	12 d	xxiv. 3.	13 d
iv. 11.	12 d	v. 9, 15, 25.	12 d	xxvi. 12.	12 a
v. 5.	12 e	v. 11, 16.	12 a	xxx. 7.	12 f
v. 31.	12 c	vi. 31.	12 d	xxxiii. 9, 11.	12 d
vii. 24.a	4 d	viii. 9.	12 d	xxxv. 2.	13 c
ix. 2.	7 b	ix. 17.	12 d	xxxviii. 11, 11.	12 d a
x. 8.	12 e	x. 4, 4.	12 a d	xlv. 9.	7 a
xi. 25.a	4 d	x. 9.	12 a	lxix. 2.	12 i
xvii. 12.	12 e	xi. 11.	12 b	lxxiii. 7.	3
xviii. 5.	12 b	xi. 14.	12 a	lxxvi. 7.	12 d
xviii. 7.	12 e	xiii. 21.	13 d	lxxvii. 13.	7 b
xix. 17.	12 a	xviii. 17, 28.	12 b	lxxxii. 1.	7 b
xxiii. 25, 25.	13 i	xviii. 18.	12 d	lxxxiii. 28.	2
xxiv. 11.	12 d	xviii. 19.	12 a	lxxxix. 43.	13 e
xxv. 8.	12 a	1 Chron. vi. 39.	12 e	xciv. 16.	4 d
xxvii. 12, 13.	12 a	xxi. 1.	12 d	civ. 6.	12 d
xxix. 10.	7 b	xxi. 15, 16.	12 d	cvi. 23.	12 a
xxix. 15.	12 d	xxiii. 30.	12 d	cvi. 30.	12 d
xxxi. 15.	12 d	xxviii. 2.	13 d	cvii. 25.	12 d
Josh. i. 5.a	4 d	2 Chron. iii. 13.	12 e	cvii. 35.γ	1

Ps. cix. 6, 31.	12 d	Jer. xviii. 20.	12 b	Dan. ii. 2.	12 d
cxi. 8.	9	xix. 14.	12 d	ii. 31.	13 g
cxiv. 8.γ	1	xxiii. 18, 22.	12 d	ii. 44.	13 f
cxxii. 2.	12 e	xxvi. 2.	12 c	iii. 3.	13 g
cxxx. 3.	12 d	xxviii. 5.	12 d	vii. 10.	13 h
cxxxiv. 1.	12 e	xxxv. 19.	12 e	vii. 16.	13 f
cxxxv. 2.	12 e	xxxvi. 21.	12 e	viii. 3, 6, 15.	12 e
cxlvii. 17.	12 d	xliv. 15.	12 e	viii. 4, 22, 22, 23,	
Prov. viii. 2.	7 a	xliv. 29.	13 d	25.	12 d
xii. 7.	12 d	xlvi. 4, 14.	13 b d	viii. 7.	12 b
xix. 21.	13 d	xlvi. 15, 21.	4 c	viii. 17.	12 h
xxii. 29, 29.	4 d	xlvii. 19.	12 a	x. 11, 11.	12 c a
xxv. 6.	12 d	xlviii. 45.	12 c	x. 16.	12 e
xxvii. 4.α	12 a	xlix. 19.	12 d	xi. 1.	12 h
Eccles. iv. 15.	12 d	l. 44.	12 d	xi. 2.	12 e
viii. 3.	12 a	li. 50.	12 d	xi. 3, 7, 20, 21.	12 a
Cant. ii. 9.	12 e	Lam. ii. 4.	7 b	xi. 4.	12 b
Isa. iii. 13, 13.	7 b, 12 e	Ezek. i. 21, 21.	12 b d	xi. 6, 14, 17, 25,	
vi. 2.	12 e	i. 24, 25.	12 b	31.	12 d
vii. 7.	13 d	ii. 1.	12 c	xi. 16, 16.	12 e d
viii. 10.	13 d	iii. 23.	12 d	xii. 1, 1.	12 d e
xi. 10.	12 e	viii. 11, 11.	12 e	xii. 5.	12 e
xiv. 24.	13 d	ix. 2.	12 d	xii. 13.	12 d
xxi. 8.	12 e	x. 3.	12 e	Hos. x. 9.	12 a
xxvii. 9.	13 d	x. 6.	12 d	Amos ii. 15.	12 d
xxviii. 18.	13 d	x. 17, 17.	12 b d	vii. 7.	7 b
xxxii. 8.	13 d	x. 18, 19.	12 d	ix. 1.	12 b
xxxvi. 2, 13.	12 d	xi. 23.	12 d	Obad. 11.	12 b
xl. 8.	13 d	xiii. 5, 6.	12 b	14.	12 d
xliv. 11.	12 d	xvii. 14.	12 b	Micah i. 11.	12 k
xlvi. 7.	12 d	xxi. 21.	12 a	v. 4.	12 a
xlvi. 10.	13 d	xxii. 30.	12 e	v. 13.	7 e
xlvii. 12.	12 c	xxvii. 29.	12 d	Nah. i. 5.	12 d
xlvii. 13.	12 d	xxix. 7.	12 f	ii. 8, 8.	12 c
xlviii. 13.	12 d	xxxi. 14.	12 e	Hab. ii. 1.	12 d
l. 8.	12 d	xxxiii. 26.	12 a	iii. 6, 11.	12 a
li. 17.	13 c	xxxvii. 10.	12 d	Zech. i. 8, 10, 11.	12 e
lix. 14.	12 d	xl. 3.	12 e	iii. 1, 3, 4, 5, 7.	12 e
lxi. 5.	12 a	xliii. 6.δ	12 e	iv. 1.	12 e
lxv. 5.	14	xliv. 11, 24.	12 d	vi. 5.	4 b
Jer. vi. 16.	12 c	xliv. 15.	12 a	xi. 16.	7 b
vii. 2.	12 c	xlvi. 2.	12 a	xiv. 4.	12 e
vii. 10.	12 a	xlvii. 10.	12 a	xiv. 12.	12 e
xiv. 6.	12 a	Dan. i. 4.	12 b	Mal. iii. 2.	12 e
xv. 1, 19.	12 d	i. 5, 19.	12 d		
xvii. 19.	12 a				

α "able to stand." β lit. stand still a day. γ lit. a pool of water.
δ lit. was standing.

STANDARD

דֶּגֶל m. a flag, banner, standard, i.e. of a larger kind, carried about with the army, which may be seen afar off glistening and waving in the air; serving for three tribes together; the smaller flags being called אתות: Num. i. 52; ii. 2, 3, 10, 17, 18, 25, 31, 34; x. 14, 18, 22, 25.

נֵס m. something lifted up, a lofty signal; a standard, signal, planted on high mountains, chiefly on the irruption of an enemy, in order to point out to the people a place of rendezvous: Isa. xlix. 22; lxii. 10: Jer. iv. 6, 21; l. 2; li. 12, 27.

נָסַס to lift up on high, to lift up a standard. KAL part. Poel, Isa. x. 18. See APPENDIX. POLEL pret. Isa. lix. 19, marg. 'put him to flight,' as from נוס to flee. There has been a great variety in the rendering of this passage, and our translation differs from all the ancient versions, and nearly all the modern expositions. Lowth renders it, "When he shall come like a river straitened in his course, which a strong wind driveth along," which agrees nearly with the Lxx., Vulg., Chald., and Syriac. See Barnes' Notes. It is most probable, however, that the text-rendering of our authorized version is correct, giving a personal meaning to רוּחַ, which best agrees with the verse following; and also taking the meaning of standard-raising which suits best with the passage, Isa. x. 18. I believe it refers to the final overthrow of all Christ's enemies. See the application of ver. 20 to Rom. xi. 26.

STAR

כּוֹכָב m. star; metaph. an illustrious prince: Num. xxiv. 17, &c.

STARE

רָאָה to look. KAL fut. Ps. xxii. 17.

STARGAZER

חֹזֶה m. seer, and כּוֹכָב m. star: Isa. xlvii. 13.

STATE, STATELY, STATION

יָד com. hand: Esth. i. 7; ii. 18.

כְּבוּדָּה adj. f. splendid, magnificent: Ezek. xxiii. 41.

בֵּן see Estate. Prov. xxviii. 2.

מַעֲמָד m. station, post: Isa. xxii. 19.

מַצָּב m. station, place, or office: Isa. xxii. 19.

נָצַב to set; to be set, to stand firmly, "in his best state," Ps. xxxix. 5.

פָּנִים m. pl. face: Prov. xxvii. 23.

מַתְכֻּנָּה f. measure: 2 Chron. xxiv. 13, or, according to its former measure.—Gesenius.

STATURE

מַד m. a measure: 2 Sam. xxi. 20 (כתיב). מִדָּה f. measure: Num. xiii. 32, "of a great stature," marg. 'of statures;' 1 Chron. xi. 23, marg. 'of measure,' xx. 6; Isa. xlv. 14. מָדוֹן m. height: 2 Sam. xxi. 20.

קוֹמָה f. height: 1 Sam. xvi. 7: Cant. vii. 7: Isa. x. 33: Ezek. xiii. 18; xvii. 6; xix. 11; xxxi. 3.

STATUTE

חֹק m. something decreed, prescribed; a statute, ordinance, law; usually applied to the positive statutes appointed by Moses, the institutions of his religion and civil polity: Exod. xv. 25, &c. חֻקָּה f. id. Gen. xxvi. 5, &c.

פִּקּוּדִים m. pl. precepts: Ps. xix. 8.

קְיָם Ch. m. statute, edict: Dan. vi. 7, 15.

STAY

1 אָחַר to be after, to stay behind. KAL fut.

2 הָנָה to separate, to take away. KAL pret.

3 חוּל see Abide. KAL ᵃpret. KAL and HIPHIL ᵇfut.

4 יָד com. hand.

5 יָחַל to wait. NIPHAL fut.

6 יָצַע to set, place; to let stand, i.e. to let stay, to leave. HOPHAL fut.

7 כָּלָא to close, to withhold, to restrain. KAL ᵃpret. NIPHAL ᵇfut.

8 מָהַהּ to deny, to refuse; to delay, to linger. HITHPALPEL imp.

9 מְחָא Ch. to smite; seq. בְּיַד to smite upon one's hand, i.e. to stay his hand, to restrain. PAEL fut.

10 סָמַךּ to place or lay upon anything, to impose so as to rest or be supported upon anything. KAL ᵃpart. Paül. NIPHAL ᵇpret. PIEL ᶜimp.

11 עָצַם to shut oneself up, to remain shut up. NIPHAL fut. Ruth i. 13, "would ye therefore remain shut up?" i.e. so as not

to marry. Lxx. κατασχεθήσεσθε. According to Kimchi Talmud. עגונה is a woman who shuts herself up at home, and lives without a husband.

12 עָמַד to stand; to stand still, to stay, to remain. Kal *a* *pret.* *b* *inf.* *c* *fut.* *d* *part.* Poel. Hiphil *e* *part.* Hophal *f* *part.*

13 עָצַר to shut up, to close; to be restrained, hindered, stayed. Niphal *a* *pret.* *b* *fut.*

14 עָקַב to take by the heel; to hold back, to retard. Piel *fut.*

15 פִּנָּה *f.* corner; *metaph.* a prince, chief of a people, on whom as a corner-stone the burden of the state rests.

16 רָפָה to be relaxed; to slacken one's hand, to desist. Hiphil *imp.*

17 שִׁית to set, to put, to place; to set a bound. Kal *fut.* Job xxxviii. 11, here let one set (bounds) to thy proud waves.

18 שָׁכַב to lie down. Hiphil *fut.* Job xxxviii. 37, *marg.* 'cause to lie down;' Gesenius, to lay down, or incline a vessel, hence to pour out, to empty.

19 שָׁסַע to cleave, divide, interrupt, intercept in their intention. Piel *fut.*

20 שָׁעַן to lean upon, to rest upon; to rely upon, to trust in, *seq.* עַל and בְּ. Niphal *a* *pret.* *b* *inf.* *c* *fut.* *d* מִשְׁעָן *m.* support. מַשְׁעֵן *m. id.*

21 תָּמַךְ to take hold of; to hold up, support; *seq.* בְּ. Kal *a* *pret.* *b* *fut.*

Gen. viii. 10.	3 b	1 Sam. xxx. 9.	12 a	Prov. xviii. 17.	21 b
viii. 12.	5	2 Sam. xvii. 17.	12 d	Cant. ii. 5.	10 c
xix. 17.	12 c	xxii. 19.	20 d	Isa. iii. 1, 1, 1.	20 e d d
xxxii. 4.	1	xxiv. 16.	16	x. 20, 20.	20 b a
Exod. ix. 28.	12 b	xxiv. 21, 25.	13 b	xix. 13.	15
x. 24.	6	1 Kings x. 19, 19.	4	xxvi. 3.	10 a
xvii. 12.	21 a	xi. 35.	12 f	xxvii. 8.	2
Lev. xiii. 5, 37.	12 a	2 Kings iv. 6.	12 c	xxix. 9.	8
xiii. 23, 28.	12 c	xiii. 18.	12 c	xxx. 12.	20 c
Num. xvi. 48.	13 b	xv. 20.	12 a	xxxi. 1.	20 c
xvi. 50.	13 a	1 Chron. xxi. 15.	16	xlviii. 2.	10 b
xxv. 8.	13 b	2 Chron. ix. 18, 18.	4	l. 10.	20 c
Deut. x. 10.	12 a	xviii. 34.	12 e	Jer. iv. 6.	12 c
Josh. x. 13.	12 a	Job xxxvii. 4.	14	Lam. iv. 6.	3 a
x. 19.	12 c	xxxviii. 11.	17	Ezek. xxxi. 15.	7 b
Ruth i. 13.	11	xxxviii. 37.	18	Dan. iv. 35.	3
1 Sam. xv. 16.	16	Ps. xviii. 18.	20 d	Hos. xiii. 13.	12 c
xx. 38.	12 c	cvi. 30.	13 b	Hag. i. 10, 10.	7 a
xxiv. 7.	19				

a lit. was staying.

STEADFAST

אָמַן to prop, to stay, to support; be supported. Niphal *pret.* Ps. lxxviii. 8, 37.

אָמֵץ to be active, firm: to be strong. Hithpael *part.* Ruth i. 18.

יָצַק to pour out; to be cast or molten; firm, steadfast. Hophal *part.* Job xi. 15.

קַיָּם Ch. enduring, sure: Dan. vi. 26.

שׂוּם to set or put with care. Kal *fut.* 2 Kings viii. 11, *marg.* 'and set it.'

STEADY

אֱמוּנָה *f.* firmness, stability; faithfulness: Exod. xvii. 12.

STEAL

גָּנַב to steal, to take away by stealth, secretly; *seq. acc.* of the person, to deceive, like Gr. κλέπτειν, especially *seq.* לֵב to deceive the heart or mind of any one, as κλέπτειν νόον,

Hom. Il. xiv. 217, to conduct or demean oneself in such a way as to produce a false impression as to a matter of fact; see *Unawares.* Kal *a* *pret.* *b* *inf.* *c* *fut.* *d* *part.* Poel. *e* *part.* Paül. Niphal *f* *fut.* Piel *g* *fut.* *h* *part.* Pual *i* *pret.* *k* *inf.* Hithpael *l* *fut.*

Gen. xxx. 33.	e	Exod. xxii. 12. a	b f	2 Chron. xxii. 11.	c
xxxi. 19, 20, 26, 27.	c	Lev. xix. 11.	c	Job xxvii. 20.	c
xxxi. 30, 32.	a	Deut. v. 19.	c	Prov. vi. 30.	a
xxxi. 39, 39.	e	xxiv. 7.	d	ix. 17.	c
xl. 15.	k i	Josh. vii. 11.	a	xxx. 9.	e
xliv. 15.	c	2 Sam. xv. 6.	g	Jer. vii. 9.	a
Exod. xx. 15.	c	xix. 3, 3.	l	xxiii. 30.	b
xxi. 16.	d	xix. 41.	a	Hos. iv. 2.	b
xxii. 1.	c	xxi. 12.	a	Obad. 5.	c
xxii. 7.	i	2 Kings xi. 2.	c	Zech. v. 3.	d

a lit. stealing it be stolen.

STEEL

נְחֹשֶׁת *com.* brass: Jer. xv. 12. נְחוּשָׁה *f.* brass: 2 Sam. xxii. 35: Job xx. 24: Ps. xviii. 34.

STEEP

מַדְרֵגָה *f.* a steep mountain, precipice: Ezek. xxxviii. 20, *marg.* ' or, towers, or, stairs.'

מוֹרָד *m.* a going down: Micah i. 4, *marg.* ' a descent.'

STEM

גֶּזַע *m.* a trunk, stock, stem: Isa. xi. 1: see *Stock.*

STEP

1 אַשֻּׁר *f.* a step, a going. *a* אַשֻּׁר *f. id.*

2 הָלִיךְ *m.* a going, step.

3 עָקֵב *m.* heel.

4 מַעֲלָה *f.* a going up; step, stair.

5 פַּעַם *com.* a striking with the foot, a step.

6 פֶּשַׂע *m.* stride, step.

7 צַעַד *m.* a slow and stately step. *a* מִצְעָד *m. id.*

Exod. xx. 26.	4	Job xxxi. 7.	1	Ps. cxix. 133.	5
1 Sam. xx. 3.	6	Ps. xvii. 11.	1	Prov. iv. 12.	7
2 Sam. xxii. 37.	7	xviii. 36.	7	v. 5.	7
1 Kings x. 19, 20.	4	xxxvii. 23.	7 a	xvi. 9.	7
2 Chron. ix. 18, 19.	4	xxxvii. 31.	1 a	Isa. xxvi. 6.	5
Job xiv. 16.	7	xliv. 18.	1 a	Jer. x. 23.	7
xviii. 7.	7	lvi. 6.	3	Lam. iv. 18.	7
xxiii. 11.	1 a	lvii. 6.	5	Ezek. xl. 22, 26, 31, 34, 37, 49.	4
xxix. 6.	2	lxxiii. 2.	1 a	Dan. xi. 43.	7 a
xxxi. 4, 37.	7	lxxv. 13.	5		

STEWARD

אִישׁ *m.* man: Gen. xliii. 19, *lit.* the man over.

בַּיִת *m.* house: Gen. xliv. 4, *lit.* was over his house: 1 Kings xvi. 9, *lit. id.*

בֶּן *m.* son: Gen. xv. 2, *lit.* the son of the possession.

מֶשֶׁק *m.* possession: Gen. xv. 2. The interpretation of this difficult passage may be thus presented: "and the son of possession," *i. e.* the possessor of my house or of my domestic property, will be Eliezer of Damascus.

שַׂר *m.* a prefect, leader, master, chief: 1 Chron. xxviii. 1.

STICK

1 דָּבַק to cleave. Kal *a* *pret.* *b* *fut.* Hiphil *c* *pret.* *d* דָּבֵק *adj.* adhering.

2 לָכַד to lay fast hold. HITHPAEL *fut.*

3 מָעַךְ to press, compress; to fix. KAL *part.* Paül, 1 Sam. xxvi. 7, of Saul's spear stuck in the ground while he slept, as a mark of their leader. See Hom. Il. x. 151.

4 נָחַת to go or come down. NIPHAL [a] *pret.*

5 שָׁפָה to stand out, as a mountain, or as bones in a body that has been emaciated. PUAL [a] *pret.*, the true reading according to Hengstenberg. [b] שָׁפִי *m. pl.* כתיב.

1 Sam. xxvi. 7.		3	Ps. xxxviii. 2. a		4 a	Prov. xviii. 24.		1 d
Job xxxiii. 21.	5 a, or 5 b		cxix. 31.		1 a	Ezek. xxix. 4, 4.		1 c b
xli. 17.		2						

a lit. come down upon me, pierce me.

STICK (N)

עֵץ *m.* a tree, wood; stick: Num. xv. 32, &c.

STIFF

חָזָק *adj.* firm, strong, vigorous: Ezek. ii. 4.

עָתָק *adj.* bold, impudent, wicked: Ps. lxxv. 5.

קָשָׁה to be hard, firm, rigid. HIPHIL *fut.* Deut. x. 16: 2 Chron. xxx. 8, *marg.* 'harden not your necks;' xxxvi. 13: Jer. xvii. 23. קָשֶׁה *adj.* hard, with עֹרֶף neck, stiff-necked: Exod. xxxii. 9; xxxiii. 3, 5; xxxiv. 9: Deut. ix. 6, 13; xxxi. 27.

STILL

1 דָּמַם to be dumb, silent, still; to rest, to cease, to leave off; to wait with silent expectation and submission. KAL [a] *imp.* [b] *fut.* [c] דְּמָמָה *f.* silence.

2 הָסָה to be silent. HIPHIL *fut.*

3 חָרַשׁ to be silent. HIPHIL *fut.*

4 חָשָׁה to be hush, silent, still. KAL [a] *fut.* HIPHIL [b] *part.*

5 מְנוּחָה *f.* rest.

6 נָסַע to journey. KAL *inf.*

7 רָפָה to be relaxed, to slacken; to desist; to let alone, or allow to any one, *abs.* HIPHIL *imp.*

8 שָׁבַח to soothe, to still, to restrain. PIEL [a] *fut.* HIPHIL [b] *part.*

9 שָׁבַת to rest; to cease, desist from. HIPHIL [a] *inf.* [b] שֶׁבֶת *m.* ceasing.

10 שָׁקַט to have rest, to be quiet; properly to lie down, to recline; to cease from troubling, from affording aid. KAL [a] *pret.* [b] *fut.*

Gen. xii. 9. a		6	Neh. viii. 11.		4 b	Ps. lxxiii. 1.		10 b
Exod. xv. 16.		1 b	Ps. iv. 4.		1 a	lxxxix. 9.		8 a
Num. xiii. 30.		2	viii. 2. β		9 a	cvii. 29.		4 a
Josh. x. 12.		1 a	xxiii. 2.		5	Isa. xxiii. 2.		1 a
x. 13.		1 b	xlvi. 10.		7	xxx. 7.		9 b
Judg. xviii. 9.		4 b	lxv. 7.		8 b	xlii. 14.		3
1 Kings xix. 12.		1 c	lxxvi. 8.		10 a	Jer. xlvii. 6.		1 a
xxii. 3.		1 b						

a "going on still," *marg.* 'in going and journeying.' *β lit.* cause to cease.

STING

פָּרַשׁ to separate, to distinguish. HIPHIL, to puncture, to sting, to wound: *fut.* Prov. xxiii. 32.

STINK

1 בָּאַשׁ to have a bad smell, to stink; see *Abhor.* KAL [a] *pret.* [b] *fut.* NIPHAL [c] *pret.* HIPHIL [d] *pret.* [e] *inf.* [f] *fut.* [g] בָּאֹשׁ *m.* stench.

---

2 מַק *m.* rottenness, putridity; the fœtor of putrid ulcers, or of decomposed bodies.

Gen. xxxiv. 30.		1 e	Exod. xvi. 24.		1 d	Isa. xxxiv. 3.		1 g
Exod. vii. 18.		1 a	2 Sam. x. 6.		1 c	l. 2.		1 b
vii. 21.		1 b	Ps. xxxviii. 5.		1 d	Joel ii. 20.		1 g
viii. 14.		1 b	Eccles. x. 1.		1 f	Amos iv. 10.		1 g
xvi. 20.		1 b	Isa. iii. 24.		2			

STIR

1 פָּרָה to excite, stir up; to contend. PIEL [a] *fut.* HITHPAEL [b] *fut.*

2 נָשָׂא to lift up. KAL *pret.*

3 סוּת to stimulate, to incite, by persuasion. HIPHIL [a] *pret.*

4 עוּר to wake; to rouse to action, attention. KAL [a] *fut.* POLEL [b] *pret.* [c] *imp.* [d] *fut.* HIPHIL [e] *pret.* [f] *imp.* [g] *fut.* [h] *part.* HITHPOLEL [i] *fut.* [k] *part.*

5 עָכַר to trouble. NIPHAL *pret.*

6 עָלָה to ascend. HIPHIL *fut.*

7 קוּם to rise. HIPHIL [a] *pret.* [b] *fut.*

תְּשֻׁאוֹת *f. pl.* noise, tumult of a multitude.

Exod. xxxv. 21, 26.		2	Job xvii. 8.		4 i	Cant. iii. 5.		4 g
xxxvi. 2.			xli. 10.		4 a	viii. 4.		4 g
Num. xxiv. 9.		7 b	Ps. xxxv. 23.		4 f	Isa. x. 26.		4 g
Deut. xxxii. 11.		4 g	xxxix. 2. a		5	xiii. 17.		4 h
1 Sam. xxii. 8.		7 a	lxxviii. 38.		4 g	xiv. 9.		4 b
xxvi. 19.		3 a	lxxx. 2.		7	xxii. 2.		8
1 Kings xi. 14, 23.		7 b	Prov. x. 12.		4 c	xli. 13.		4 g
xxi. 25.		3 a	xv. 1.		6	lxiv. 7.		4 k
1 Chron. v. 26.		4 g	xv. 18.		4 a	Dan. xi. 2.		4 g
2 Chron. xxi. 16.		4 g	xxviii. 25.		4 a	xi. 10, 10.		1 b
xxxvi. 22.			xxix. 22.		1 a	xi. 25, 25.		4 g, 1 b
Ezra i. 1.		4 e	Cant. ii. 7.		4 g	Hag. i. 14.		4 g

a marg. 'troubled.'

STOCK

בֻּל *m.* produce, increase: Isa. xliv. 19, "stock of a tree," *marg.* 'that which comes of a tree.'

גֶּזַע *m.* the trunk of a tree cut down, including that which is below the surface, as well as that which remains above: Job xiv. 8: Isa. xl. 24.

מַהְפֶּכֶת *f. pr.* torsion, distorsion, hence a wrench, stocks; Lat. *nervus,* a wooden frame in which the feet, hands, and neck of a person were so fastened that his body was held bent: Jer. xx. 2, 3.

סַד *m.* stocks, *nervus,* in which the feet of a person were shut up: Job xiii. 27; xxxiii. 11.

עֶכֶס *m.* a fetter, ancle-band: Prov. vii. 22, as fetters for the punishment of the wicked; or we may take עֶכֶס for אִישׁ עֶכֶס, as one bound in fetters (goeth) to the punishment of the fool, *i. e.* of folly or crime. See, however, Hunt's Diss. on this passage, who would render it, "as a hart boundeth to the toils, till a dart strike through his liver."

עֵץ *m.* a tree, wood, &c.: Jer. ii. 27; iii. 9; x. 8: Hos. iv. 12.

עָקַר *m. pr.* a rooting up; a plant rooted up and transferred to another soil; hence, *metaph.* of a person sprung from a foreign family resident in the Hebrew territory: Lev. xxv. 47.

צִינֹק *m.* Jer. xxix. 26. Lxx. and Vulg. a prison; better, stocks, as confining the hands and feet; so Symm. and the Heb. Interpreters.

STOMACHER

פְּתִיגִיל *m.* a kind of costly raiment, perhaps an embroidered holy-day garment, or girdle worn round the breast.—*Gesenius.* Isa. iii. 24. Gussetius, a wide or flowing garment.

STONE

1 אֶבֶן *m.* a stone of any kind, whether rough or polished, large or small, from its use in constructing or building; as if from בָּנָה; stone, gem, or finer kinds of stones for building, as marble: Ezek. xxviii. 13. *Meton.* anything made of stone: vessels, Exod. vii. 19; an idol, Jer. ii. 25, iii. 9; a weight, a plummet, Isa. xxxiv. 11, Zech. iv. 10; though of lead, Zech. v. 8. *Metaph.* Christ, Ps. cxviii. 22, Isa. xxviii. 16, Zech. iii. 9, Isa. viii. 14; a rock, Gen. xlix. 24, for refuge or defence, 1 Sam. xxv. 37; hardness of heart, Ezek. xi. 19, xxxvi. 26; hail-stones, Josh. x. 11; *comp.* Isa. xxx. 30.—Gen. ii. 12, &c. אֶבֶן a Ch. *f. id.*

2 גְּבְלִי *m.* a workman who hews stones into their proper form and dimensions for building: 1 Kings v. 18. But what we translate "stone-squarers," should possibly rather be "Giblites," a people of Syria, living near Mount Lebanon. See Maund. Travels, p. 34.

3 דַּכָּה *f.* a crushing; Deut. xxiii. 1, *lit.* wounded by bruising, *i. e.* in order to produce emasculation.

4 חֶרֶשׂ *m.* potsherd: Job xli. 30. *marg.* 'pieces of potsherd.'

5 סֶלַע *m.* a rock; Ps. cxli. 6, *lit.* by the sides of the rock.

6 פַּחַד *m.* thigh, *testiculi.*

7 צוּר *m.* rock.

8 צֹר *m. pr.* flint, a knife made of flint. צְרוֹר a *m.* a small stone.

9 אֶשֶׁךְ *m.* testicle.

10 סָקַל to stone, to pelt with stones, a species of capital punishment among the Hebrews, as to which see the decisions of the Rabbins in C. D. Michaeli's Dissert. de Judiciis Pœnisque Capitalibus, § 5, in Pott. Syll. iv. p. 185. KAL a *pret.* b *inf.* c *imp.* d *fut.* NIPHAL e *fut.* PUAL f *pret.*

11 רָגַם to heap or pile up; specially to heap up stones upon any one; hence to throw stones at any one, to stone. KAL a *pret.* b *inf.* c *fut.*

No. 1 not included.

Exod. iv. 25.	8	Deut. xvii. 5.	10 a	Ezra v. 8.	1 a
viii. 26.	10 d	xxi. 21.	11 a	vi. 4.	1 a
xvii. 4. α	10 a	xxii. 21, 24.	10 a	Job xxii. 24.	7
xix. 13. β	10 b e	xxiii. 1. δ	3	xl. 17.	6
xxi. 28. β	10 b e	Josh. vii. 25, 25.	11 c, 10 d	xli. 30.	4
xxix. 29, 32.	10 e	1 Sam. xxx. 6.	10 b	Ps. cxxxvii. 9.	5
Lev. xx. 2, 27.	11 c	2 Sam. xvii. 13.	8 a	cxli. 6.	5
xxi. 20.	9	1 Kings v. 18.	2	Ezek. xi. 19. e	1
xxiv. 14.	11 b c	xii. 18.	11 c	xvi. 40.	11 a
xxiv. 16. γ	11 b c	xxi. 10.	10 c	xxiii. 47.	11 a
xxiv. 23.	11 c	xxi. 13.	10 d	xxxvi. 26. e	1
Num. xiv. 10.	11 b	xxi. 14, 15.	10 f	Dan. ii. 34, 35, 45.	1 a
xv. 35.	11 b	2 Chron. x. 18.	11 c	v. 4, 23.	1 a
xv. 36.	11 c	xxiv. 21.	11 c	vi. 17.	1 a
Deut. xiii. 10.	10 a				

α *lit.* yet a little while and they will stone me. β *lit.* stoning he shall be stoned. γ *lit.* stoning shall stone him. δ *lit.* wounded by bruising. e *lit.* heart of stone.

STOOL

אֹבֶן found only in *dual*, אָבְנָיִם, Exod. i. 16, properly a pair of stones, spoken of a low seat, stool on which workmen sat; made, as Gesenius thinks, of a block of wood, and frequently represented on Egyptian monuments. Some interpret the word as implying a seat convenient for women in labour. Gesenius, in his Thesaur., thinks it means the trough in which new-born infants were washed; but, in his later Lexicon, he takes it to be the seat used by the midwife while assisting a woman in labour: "When ye do the office of a midwife to the Hebrew women, then shall ye see (while yet) upon the stool whether it be a boy," &c.; and in this case the midwives were instructed to kill the infant, and so diminish the number of males.

הֲדֹם *m.* a stool, a footstool, everywhere *seq.* רַגְלַיִם: 1 Chron. xxviii. 2: Ps. xcix. 5; cx. 1; cxxxii. 7: Isa. lxvi. 1: Lam. ii. 1.

כִּסֵּא *m.* a throne, a seat: 2 Kings iv. 10.

STOOP

יָשֵׁשׁ *m.* aged, "to stoop for age:" 2 Chron. xxxvi. 17.

כָּרַע to bend, to bow, spoken of the knees. KAL *pret.* Gen. xlix. 9.

קָדַד to bow the head. KAL *fut.* 1 Sam. xxiv. 8; xxviii. 14.

קָרַס to bend, to bow down; hence to sink together, to collapse; *i. q.* כָּרַע in the other member, in Isa. xlvi. 1. Lxx. συνετρίβη; Vulg. *contritus est.* KAL *pret.* Isa. xlvi. 2. *part.* Poel, Isa. xlvi. 1.

שָׁחָה to bow down, to incline oneself; to sink down, to be depressed. HIPHIL *fut.* Prov. xii. 25.

שָׁחַח to bow down, to incline oneself; to be depressed. KAL *pret.* Job ix. 13.

STOP

1 אָטַם to shut, to close, to stop. KAL a *part.* HIPHIL b *fut.*

2 חָסַם to muzzle an ox; to stop the nostrils. KAL *part.* Poel, Ezek. xxxix. 11, shall stop the nostrils of them that pass by, *i. e.* by its stench. Unless we prefer to render with the Syriac, "it shall stop the way of them that pass by," *sc.* from the multitude of the slain.

3 חָתַם to seal. HIPHIL *pret.*

4 כָּבֵד to be heavy; to make heavy. HIPHIL *pret.*

5 סָגַר to shut, to close. KAL *imp.*

6 סָכַר to shut up, to close; to stop the flowing of water, and the calumnies of a lying mouth. NIPHAL *fut.*

7 סָתַם to stop, to obstruct, as fountains, the current of a brook, a breach in a wall. KAL a *pret.* b *inf.* c *fut.* NIPHAL d *inf.* PIEL e *pret.* f *fut.*

8 עָצַר to restrain. KAL *fut.*

9 קָפַץ to draw together, to contract, to shut. KAL *pret.*

10 תָּפַשׂ to take. NIPHAL *pret.*

Gen. viii. 2.	6	2 Chron. xxxii. 4.	7 c	Ps. cvii. 42.	9	Job xxi. 18.	2
xxvi. 15.	7 e	xxxii. 30.	7 a	Prov. xxi. 13.	1 a	xxvii. 21.	6 a
xxvi. 18.	7 f	Neh. iv. 7.	7 d	Isa. xxxiii. 15.	1 a	Ps. lv. 8.	3
Lev. xv. 3.	3	Job v. 16.	9	Jer. li. 32.	10	lxxxiii. 15.	2
1 Kings xviii. 44.	8	Ps. xxxv. 3.	5	Ezek. xxxix. 11.	2	cvii. 25, 29.	4
2 Kings iii. 19, 25.	7 c	lviii. 4.		Zech. vii. 11.	4		
2 Chron. xxxii. 3.	7 b	lxiii. 11.	6				

Ps. cxlviii. 8.	4	Isa. xxix. 6.	2
Isa. iv. 6.	1	Ezek. xiii. 11, 13.	4
xxv. 4, 4.	1	xxxviii. 9.	5
xxviii. 2.	6 b	Nah. i. 3.	6 c

STORE, STOREHOUSE

1 מַאֲבוּס *m.* (see *Crib*) granaries, in which were laid up what was there thrashed for fattening cattle: Jer. l. 26, figuratively, the cities, &c., into which the Babylonians betook themselves for protection, but out of which they should be brought as corn to be thrashed, *i. e.* to be destroyed; see Schmid. in *loc.*

2 אֲסָמִים *m. pl.* storehouses in which fruits, &c., are laid up.

3 אָצַר to lay up, to store, to treasure. KAL ᵃ *pret.* ᵇ *part.* Poel. ᶜ אוֹצָר *m.* treasure.

4 הָמוֹן *m.* multitude, abundance.

5 תְּכוּנָה *f.* something laid up in readiness.

6 כָּמַס to lay up, to hide away, to lay up in store. KAL *part.* Paül.

7 מִסְכְּנוֹת *f. pl.* stores, magazines, or cities where provisions are laid up.

8 פִּקָּדוֹן *m.* something laid up, deposited with any one.

9 רָבָה to multiply. HIPHIL *inf.*

10 מִשְׁאֶרֶת *f.* a kneading trough; store.

Gen. xli. 36.	8	1 Chron. xxvii. 25.	3 c	Neh. v. 18.	9
Deut. xxviii. 5.	10	xxix. 16.	4	Ps. xxxiii. 7.	3 c
xxviii. 8.	2	2 Chron. viii. 4, 6.	7	Isa. xxxix. 6.	3 a
xxviii. 17.	10	xi. 11.	3 c	Jer. l. 26.	1
xxxii. 34.	6	xvi. 4.		Amos iii. 10.	3 b
1 Kings ix. 19.	7	xvii. 12.	7	Nah. ii. 9.	1
x. 10.	9	xxxi. 10.	7	Mal. iii. 10.	3 c
2 Kings xx. 17.	3 a	xxxii. 28.	7		

STORK

חֲסִידָה *f.* the stork, properly the pious, *avis pia*, so called from its affection and tenderness towards its parents and its young, for which it was celebrated in antiquity; see Plin. H. N. x. 23; Ælian. Hist. An. iii. 23, ib. x. 16. So, on the contrary, the Arabs call the male ostrich the impious, ungodly, on account of its neglect and cruelty towards its young; *comp.* Job xxxix. 13, &c. —Lev. xi. 19: Deut. xiv. 18: Ps. civ. 17: Jer. viii. 7: Zech. v. 9.

STORM

1 זֶרֶם *m.* a pouring rain, violent shower, storm.

2 סוּפָה *f.* whirlwind, hurricane, tempest, which sweeps away all before it; see *Consume.*

3 סָעָה to rush forth; peculiarly applied to a wind issuing forth, driving forward with violence from God. KAL *part.*

4 סְעָרָה *f.* a whirlwind, a tempest.

5 שׁוֹאָה *f.* a storm, tempest, so called from the noise, roaring, crashing.

6 שָׂעַר to shudder, to shiver; spoken of the sudden commotion and rage of a tempest; to hurl away with a storm. PIEL ᵃ *fut.* ᵇ שַׂעַר *m.* storm. ᶜ שְׂעָרָה *f. id.*

STORY

מִדְרָשׁ *m.* a commentary; historical journal: 2 Chron. xiii. 22; xxiv. 27.

מַעֲלָה *f.* ascent: Amos ix. 6, *marg.* 'ascensions, *or,* spheres.'

שְׁלִשִׁים three stories, *lit.* their three.

STOUT

אַבִּיר *adj.* see *Mighty;* joined with לֵב, strong of heart: Ps. lxxvi. 5: Isa. xlvi. 12.

גֹּדֶל *m.* greatness: Isa. ix. 9; x. 12.

חָזַק to be strong. KAL *pret.* Mal. iii. 13, here applied to insolent obstinate language.

רַב Ch. *adj.* great: Dan. vii. 20.

STRAIGHT, STRAIGHTWAY

1 יָשַׁר to be straight, right; especially of a way; to take the straight way. KAL ᵃ *fut.* PIEL ᵇ *imp.* ᶜ *fut.* HIPHIL ᵈ *imp.* ᵉ *fut.* ᶠ יָשָׁר *adj.* right. ᵍ מִישׁוֹר *m.* a plain.

2 מָהַר to hasten, implying perturbation: 1 Sam. xxviii. 20, *marg.* 'made haste and fell with the fulness of his stature.' PIEL *fut.*

3 עֵבֶר *m.* side; "straight forward," with פָּנִים, *lit.* on the side of their face.

4 פִּתְאֹם *adv.* in a moment, suddenly.

5 תָּקַן to be or made straight. KAL ᵃ *inf.* PIEL ᵇ *inf.*

1 Sam. vi. 12.	1 a	Eccles. i. 15.	5 a	Jer. xxxi. 9.	1 f
xxviii. 20.	2	vii. 13.	5 b	Ezek. i. 7.	1 f
2 Chron. xxxii. 30.	1 c	Isa. xl. 3.	1 b	i. 9.	3
Ps. v. 8.	1 d	xl. 4.	1 g	i. 12.	3
Prov. iv. 25.	1 e	xliii. 16.	1 g	i. 23.	1 f
vii. 22.	4	xlv. 2.	1 b	x. 22.	3

STRAIT, STRAITEN, STRAITNESS

1 אָצַל to separate. NIPHAL, to be drawn in, contracted: *pret.*

2 יָצַר to be straitened, narrow, scanty. KAL *fut.*

3 נָחָה to lead, to conduct, to guide; to lead out or away, to carry away to any place. HIPHIL *fut.*

4 סָגַר to shut, to close. KAL *part.* Poel.

5 צוּק to be narrow, straitened, compressed; Hiphil, to straiten, to press upon, to distress any one, *seq. dat.* HIPHIL ᵃ *fut.* ᵇ מוּצָק *m.* something narrow, scanty, *opp.* רחֹב. ᶜ מָצוֹק *m.* straitness, distress.

6 צָרַר to press, to compress; to be pressed, straitened, distressed; to press upon, to straiten. KAL ᵃ *pret.* ᵇ צַר *m.* strait, narrow; straitness, narrowness. ᶜ מֵצַר *m.* restraint.

7 קָצַר to cut off or down; to be cut off or shortened. KAL *pret.*

8 שָׁאַל to ask. KAL *inf.*

9 שָׁבַע to swear. HIPHIL *inf.*

Gen. xliii. 7.	8	2 Sam. xxiv. 14.	6 a	Job xxxvii. 10. β	5 b
Exod. xix. 19. a		1 Chron. xxi. 13.	6 a	Prov. iv. 12.	2
Deut. xviii. 53, 55, 57.	5 c	2 Kings vi. 1.	6 b	Isa. xlix. 20.	6 b
Josh. vi. 1.		Job xii. 23.	3	Jer. xix. 9, 9.	5 c a
1 Sam. xiii. 6.	6 a	vii. 7.	2	Lam. i. 3.	6 c
xiv. 28. a	9	xx. 22.		Ezek. xlii. 6.	1
		xxxvi. 16, 16.	6 b, 5 b	Micah ii. 7.	7

a lit. causing to swear he had caused to swear. *β lit.* in straitness.

STRAKES

פְּצָלוֹת *f. pl.* pilled spots or streaks: Gen. xxx. 37.

שְׁקַעֲרוּרֹת *f. pl.* sunken places, hollows in a wall. LXX. κοιλάδες; Vulg. *valliculæ.* Lev. xiv. 37.

STRANGE, STRANGER

1   אַחֵר   *adj.* another : Judg. xi. 2.

2   אִישׁ   *m.* man, stranger, *lit.* a man a stranger.

3   אֱנוֹשׁ   *m.* man : 2 Chron. ii. 17, *marg.* 'the men the strangers.'

4   בֵּן   *m.* son ; stranger, *lit.* son, or children of the stranger.

5   גּוּר   to sojourn. KAL [a] *pret.* [b] *part.* Poel. [c] גֵּר *m.* one sojourning in another country, frequently joined with תּוֹשָׁב, one without possessions of his own ; *opp.* אֶזְרָח a native, and אָח a brother : often found in connexion with the fatherless and widow, whom the Israelites are cautioned not to oppress, Exod. xxiii. 9, &c. גֵּרִים strangers, Isa. v. 17, seem to be those wandering shepherds, who lead about their flocks from one place to another, as the Hebrews once did, and as the Rechabites in the time of Jeremiah. As human life is called a pilgrimage (Gen. xlvii. 9), so individual men are strangers or pilgrims on earth : Ps. xxxix. 12 : 1 Chron. xxix. 15. Thy, his, stranger, one living in thy, his, country (not in the house) : Gen. xv. 13, &c. [d] גֵּיר *m. id.* מָגוּר *m.* sojournings.

6   הָכַר   to be stiff or rigid ; to oppress. HIPHIL *fut.*

7   וָזָר   *m.* laden with guilt, guilty : Prov. xxi. 8. Gesenius, *lit.* the way of a guilty man is froward. The English version renders it as זָר, with וְ copulative. Probably the best rendering is, 'a man perverse in his way (is) also strange,' *i.e.* alienated from that which is good. There is an evident antithesis between זָר and זַךְ.

8   זוּר   to turn aside, to recede ; see *Estrange ;* to be alien, as of another people, a stranger, including frequently the notion of an enemy or barbarian, Isa. i. 7, 7 ; of another family, *opp.* to a relation, Deut. xxv. 5 ; to the father of a family, Job xix. 15, *comp.* 1 Kings iii. 18 ; to a husband, Jer. ii. 25, iii. 15, Ezek. xvi. 32 ; so a strange woman, Prov. ii. 16, vii. 5 ; for an adulteress is one that recedes from conjugal fidelity. Hos. v. 7, strange children, children of adultery. Sometimes generally of any other person, Prov. xi. 15, xiv. 10, &c. As *opp.* to that which is holy and legitimate, it means profane or unlawful. It is used also of that which is new or unheard of, Isa. xxviii. 21. Job xix. 17, my breath, or mind agitated and troubled, *i.e.* my complaint is strange to my wife, and my entreaties to the children of mine own body. KAL [a] *pret.* [b] *part.* HOPHAL [c] *part.*

9   תּוֹשָׁב   *m.* a sojourner, *i.e.* a proselyte of the gate that was allowed to dwell among the Israelites.

10   נָכַר   to know and not to know, seem both included in the meaning of this word, as is the case in other languages with certain words in common and general use. Various explanations have been given of these apparently contrary significations ; see *Estrange ;* to behave strangely,

to make strange. PIEL [a] *fut.* HITHPAEL [b] *fut.* נֵכָר [c] *m.* strangeness ; stranger, foreigner : Gen. xvii. 12, &c. [d] נֶכֶר *m.* strange fate, calamity. [e] נֵכָר *m. id.* [f] נָכְרִי *adj.* unknown, strange, foreign ; spoken of one from another land and people, of a people, a land, a city, a vine, a garment ; of one from another family, not of one's own household, *opp.* to a son and legal heir, Eccles. vi. 2. A strange woman, *opp.* to a wife, spoken usually in respect to illicit intercourse, and hence, *i. q.* an adulteress, harlot ; of another's house, Prov. v. 10 ; another, not oneself, Prov. xxvii. 2 ; strange, unheard of, exciting wonder, Isa. xxviii. 21.

11   עָמֵק   *adj.* deep.

No. 5 c, *Stranger*, not included.

Gen. xvii. 8.	5 e	1 Kings iii. 18.	8 b	Prov. xxiii. 33.	8 b
xvii. 12.	4, 10 c	viii. 41, 43.	10 f	xxvii. 2.	10 f
xvii. 27.	4, 10 c	xi. 1, 8.	10 f	xxvii. 13, 13.	8 b, 10 f
xxviii. 4.	5 e	2 Kings xix. 24.	10 f	Eccles. vi. 2.	2, 10 f
xxxi. 15.	10 f	1 Chron. xix. 19.	5 b	Isa. i. 7, 7.	8 b
xxxv. 2, 4.	10 c	2 Chron. ii. 17.	3, 5 d	ii. 6.	10 f
xxxvi. 7.	5 e	vi. 32, 33.	10 f	v. 17.	5 b
xxxvii. 1.	5 e	xv. 9.	5 b	xvii. 10.	8 b
xlii. 7.	10 b	xxxiii. 15.	10 c	xxv. 2, 5.	8 b
Exod. ii. 22.	10 f			xxviii. 21.	8 b, 10 f
vi. 4.	5 a	Ezra x. 2, 10, 11, 14,		xxix. 5.	8 b
xii. 43.	4, 10 c	17, 18, 44.	10 f	xliii. 12.	8 b
xviii. 3.	10 f	Neh. ix. 2.	4, 10 c	lvi. 3, 6.	10 c
xxi. 8.	10 f	xiii. 27.	10 f	lx. 10.	10 c
xxix. 33.	8 b	xiii. 30.	10 c	lxi. 5.	8 b
xxx. 9, 33.	8 b	Job xv. 19.	8 b	lxii. 8.	10 c
Lev. x. 1.	8 b	xix. 3.	6	Jer. ii. 21.	10 f
xxii. 10.	8 b	xix. 15.	8 b	ii. 25.	8 b
xxii. 12.	2, 8 b	xix. 17.	8 a	iii. 13.	8 b
xxii. 13.	8 b	xxxi. 3.	10 d	v. 19, 19.	10 c, 8 b
xxii. 25.	4, 10 c	Ps. xviii. 44.	4, 10 c	viii. 19.	8 b
xxv. 6, 45, 47.	9	xviii. 45.	4, 10 c	xxx. 8.	8 b
Num. i. 51.	8 b	xliv. 20.	8 b	xxxv. 7.	5 b
iii. 4, 10, 38.	8 b	liv. 3.	8 b	li. 51.	8 b
xvi. 40.	2, 8 b	lxix. 8.	8 c	Lam. v. 2.	8 b
xviii. 4, 7.	8 b	lxxxi. 9, 9.	8 b, 10 c	Ezek. iii. 5.	11
xvii. 61.	8 b	cv. 12.	5 b	iii. 6.	11
Deut. xvii. 15.	2, 10 f	cix. 11.	8 b	vii. 21.	8 b
xxiii. 20.	10 f	cxxxvii. 4.	10 c	xi. 9.	8 b
xxv. 5.	2, 8 b	cxliv. 7, 11.	10 c	xvi. 32.	8 b
xxix. 22.	10 f	Prov. ii. 16, 16.	8 b, 10 f	xxviii. 7, 10.	8 b
xxxi. 16.	10 c	v. 3.	8 b	xxx. 12.	8 b
xxxii. 12.	10 c	v. 10, 10.	8 b	xxxi. 12.	8 b
xxxii. 16.	8 b	v. 17.	8 b	xliv. 7.	4, 8 b
xxxii. 27.	10 a	vi. 20, 20.	8 b	xliv. 9, 9.	4, 10 c
Josh. xxiv. 20, 23.	10 c	vii. 1.	8 b	Dan. xi. 39.	10 c
Judg. x. 16.	10 c	vii. 24.	10 f	Hos. v. 7.	8 b
xi. 2.	1	vii. 5, 5.	8 b, 10 f	vii. 9.	8 b
xix. 12.	10 f	xi. 15.	8 b	viii. 7, 12.	8 b
Ruth ii. 10.	10 f	xiv. 10.	8 b	Joel iii. 17.	8 b
1 Sam. vii. 3.	10 c	xx. 16, 16.	8 b, 10 f	Obad. 11.	8 b
2 Sam. i. 13.	2, 5 c	xxi. 8.	7, or 8 b	12.	10 e
xv. 19.	10 f	xxii. 14.	8 b	Zeph. i. 8.	10 f
xxii. 45.	4, 10 c	xxiii. 27.	10 f	Mal. ii. 11.	10 c
xxii. 46.	4, 10 c				

STRANGLE

חָנַק   to be narrow, strait, close ; to strangle. PIEL *part.* Nah. ii. 12. מַחֲנָק *m.* Job vii. 15, *parall.* מָוֶת.

STRAW

תֶּבֶן   *m.* straw, as broken up by thrashing, short straw, chaff: Gen. xxiv. 25, 32 : Exod. v. 7, 7, 10, 11, 12, 13, 16, 18 : Judg. xix. 19 : 1 Kings iv. 28 : Job xli. 27 : Isa. xi. 7 ; lxv. 25. מַתְבֵּן *m. collect.* straw, heap of straw : Isa. xxv. 10.

STREAM

1   אָפִיק   *m.* a channel, bed of a brook or stream.

2   אֶשֶׁד   *m.* an outpouring : Num. xxi. 15, *i.e.* places where the

torrents from the mountains are poured out or flow down into the valleys or plains below, ravines.

3 יְאֹר m. see *River*.

4 יָבָל m. a river, stream, watercourse.

5 נָהָר m. river. נְהַר Ch. m. *id.*

6 נָזַל to flow. KAL *part.* Poel.

7 נַחַל m. a river or brook flowing in constant succession. נַחֲלָה w. *id.*

8 פֶּלֶג m. the water of a brook or river distributed into small streams, that it may be conveyed to any part of grounds where it is wanted.

Exod. vii. 19.	5	Ps. cxxiv. 4.	7 a	Isa. xxxiii. 21.	3
viii. 5.	5	cxxvi. 4.	1	xxxiv. 9.	7
Num. xxi. 15.	2	Cant. iv. 15.	6	xxxv. 6.	7
Job vi. 15.	1	Isa. xi. 15.	7	lvii. 6.	7
Ps. xlvi. 4.	4	xxx. 12.	7	lxvi. 12.	7
lxxvii. 16.	6	xxx. 25.	4	Dan. vii. 10.	5 a
lxxviii. 20.	5	xxx. 28, 33.	7	Amos v. 24.	7

STREET

1 חוּץ m. that which is without: Josh. ii. 19, &c.

2 פָּנִים m. pl. face: Job xviii. 17, *lit.* upon the face of the street.

3 רְחוֹב f. wide, broad, large; a broad way, any public place, capable of many meeting together.

4 שׁוּק m. a street in which one moves to and fro.

No. 1 not included.

Gen. xix. 2.	3	Ps. lv. 11.	3	Isa. lix. 14.	3
Deut. xiii. 16.	3	cxliv. 14.	3	Jer. ix. 21.	3
Judg. xix. 15, 17, 20.	3	Prov. i. 20.	3	xlviii. 38.	3
2 Sam. xxi. 12.	3	v. 16.	3	xlix. 26.	3
2 Chron. xxix. 4.	3	vii. 8.	3	l. 30.	3
xxxii. 6.	3	vii. 12.	3	Lam. ii. 11, 12.	3
Ezra x. 9.	3	xxii. 13.	3	iv. 18.	3
Neh. viii. 1, 3, 16, 16.	3	xxvi. 13.	3	Ezek. xvi. 24, 31.	3
Esth. iv. 6.	3	Eccles. xii. 4, 5.	3	Dan. ix. 25.	3
vi. 9, 11.	3	Cant. iii. 2.	4	Amos v. 16.	3
Job xviii. 17.	2, 3	Isa. xv. 3, 3.	1, 3	Zech. viii. 4, 5, 5.	3
xxix. 7.					

STRETCH

1 נָהַר to bow oneself down, to prostrate oneself with the head bowed down, near to or touching the knees. KAL *fut.*

2 מָדַד to measure. HITHPOLEL *fut.*

3 מָשַׁךְ to draw. KAL *pret.* Hos. vii. 5, he stretcheth out, draweth his hand with scorners; he joins and encourages the profane.

4 נָטָה to stretch out, to extend, the hand, &c. KAL a *pret.* b *inf.* c *imp.* d *fut.* e *part.* Poel. f *part.* Paül. NIPHAL g *fut.* HIPHIL h *fut.* i מָטוֹת f. pl. a spreading out.

5 נָטַשׁ to cast out, to disperse, to scatter; to be spread, also to be loosed. NIPHAL *pret.*

6 סָרַח to pour forth, to diffuse, to spread; *trop.* extended, stretched on a couch; to be superfluous, redundant. KAL *part.* Paül.

7 פָּרַד to separate by breaking; to spread out. KAL *part.* Paül.

8 פָּרַשׂ to separate, to distinguish; to spread out, to extend. KAL a *pret.* b *fut.* c *part.* Poel. PIEL d *pret.*

9 רוּץ to run; Hiph. to cause to run up, to let make haste. HIPHIL *fut.* Ps. lxviii. 31, *i. e.* shall let her hands make haste unto God in adoration or with oblations.

10 רָקַע to beat out, to spread out; to expand. KAL *part.* Poel.

11 שָׂטַח to spread out. PIEL *pret.*

12 שָׁלַח to send, to send out or forth, to stretch forth (the hand). KAL a *pret.* b *inf.* c *fut.*

13 שָׂרַע to stretch out. HITHPAEL *inf.*

Gen. xxii. 10.	12 c	2 Kings iv. 34, 35.	1	Isa. xliv. 13.	4 a
xlviii. 14.	12 c	xvii. 36.	4 f	xliv. 24.	4 a
Exod. iii. 20.	12 a	xxi. 13.	4 a	xlv. 12.	4 a
vi. 6.	4 f	1 Chron. xxi. 16.	4 a	li. 13.	4 e
vii. 5.	4 b	2 Chron. vi. 32.	4 f	lii. 2.	4 h
vii. 19.	4 c	Job xi. 13.	8 a	Jer. vi. 4.	4 g
viii. 5, 16.	4 a	xv. 25.	4 a	vi. 12.	4 h
viii. 6, 17.	4 d	xxvi. 7.	4 e	x. 12.	4 h
ix. 15.	4 a	xxx. 24.	12 c	x. 20.	4 h
ix. 22.	4 c	xxxviii. 5.	4 a	xxi. 5.	4 h
ix. 23.	4 a	xxxix. 26.	8 a	xxvii. 5.	4 f
x. 12, 21.	4 c	Ps. xliv. 20.	8 b	xxxii. 17, 21.	4 f
x. 13, 22.	4 a	lxviii. 31.	9	xlviii. 17.	4 a
xiv. 16, 26.	4 d	lxxxviii. 9.	11	li. 15, 25.	4 a
xiv. 21, 27.	4 d	civ. 2.	4 e	lv. 13.	4 a
xv. 12.	4 a	cxxxvi. 12.	10	Ezek. i. 11.	7
xxv. 20.	8 c	cxxxvi. 12.	8 a	i. 22.	4 f
Deut. iv. 34.	4 f	cxxxviii. 7.	12 c	vi. 14.	4 a
v. 15.	4 f	cxliii. 6.	8 d	x. 7.	12 c
vii. 19.	4 f	Prov. i. 24.	4 a	xvi. 9, 13.	4 a
ix. 29.	4 f	ii. 2.	8 a	xvi. 27.	4 a
xi. 2.	4 f	Isa. iii. 16.	4 f	xx. 33, 34.	4 f
xxvi. 8.	4 f	v. 25, 25.	4 d f	xxv. 7, 13.	4 a
Josh. viii. 18, 18.	4 c d	viii. 8.	4 i	xxv. 16.	4 a
viii. 19.	4 b	ix. 12, 17, 21.	4 f	xxv. 25.	4 a
viii. 26.	4 a	x. 4.	4 a	Dan. xi. 42.	12 c
1 Sam. xxiv. 6.	12 b	xiv. 26, 27.	4 f	Hos. vii. 5.	3
xxvi. 9.	12 a	xvi. 8.	5	Amos vi. 4.	6
xxvi. 11, 23.	12 b	xxiii. 11.	4 a	vi. 7.	6
2 Sam. i. 14.	12 b	xxviii. 20.	13	Zeph. i. 4.	4 a
xxiv. 16.	12 c	xxxi. 3.	4 h	Zech. i. 16.	4 g
1 Kings vi. 27.	8 b	xxxix. 11.	4 a	xii. 1.	4 e
viii. 42.	4 f	xl. 22.	4 e		
xvii. 21.	4 e	xlii. 5.	4 e		

STREW

זָרָה to scatter, to cast loosely about. KAL *fut.* Exod. xxxii. 20.

זָרַק to sprinkle. KAL *fut.* 2 Chron. xxxiv. 4.

STRIKE, STRICKEN, STROKE

1 בּוֹא to come, go, advance. KAL a *pret.* b *part.* Poel.

2 דָּקַר to thrust through, to pierce, to stab. PUAL *part.*

3 מַהֲלֻמוֹת f. pl. strokes, blows, as with a hammer.

4 חָלַף to pass, to pass through; to pierce, to transfix. KAL a *pret.* b *fut.*

5 יָד *com.* hand.

6 מָחַץ to smite through and through, sc. with a shock, to give a deep and deadly wound. KAL a *pret.* b מַחַץ m. bruise.

7 נָגַע to strike, to smite; see *Smite.* KAL a *part.* Paül. HIPHIL b *pret.* c נֶגַע m. stroke, blow; specially of judgments, calamities, which God sends upon men.

8 נָגַף to smite, usually of Jehovah as inflicting judgments upon men, mostly with some fatal disease or death. KAL a *fut.* b מַגֵּפָה f. plague.

9 נָדָה to thrust, to impel; to fetch a stroke. NIPHAL *pret.*

10 נוּף to shake, to wave; of the hand, as applied for soothing, healing, seq. אֶל. HIPHIL *pret.*

11 נָכָא *adj.* smitten, afflicted.

12 נָכָה to strike, to smite; see *Smite.* HIPHIL a *pret.* b *inf.* HOPHAL c *fut.* d מַכָּה f. stroke.

13 נָקַב to pierce or strike through. KAL *pret.*

14 נָתַן to give. KAL *pret.*

15 סָפַק to smite, to strike with the hand, so as to make a noise. Schultens supposes that it denotes a sudden repeated stroke; it is used of the chastisement of the wicked. KAL *pret.*

16 עָרַף to neck, to strike off the neck. KAL *pret.*

17 פָּלַח to cut, to cleave. PIEL *fut.*

18 שָׁנָה to do a thing a second time. KAL *pret.*

19 שֶׂפֶק *m.* the same with סָפַק above; stroke of chastisement.

20 תָּקַע to strike, specially the hands in rejoicing, or as a pledge of suretyship, with לְ for or with any one. KAL [a] *pret.* [b] *part.* Poel. NIPHAL [c] *fut.*

Gen. xviii. 11.	1 b	1 Kings i. 1.	1 a	Prov. xvii. 26.	12 b
xxiv. 1.	1 a	2 Kings v. 11.	10	xviii. 6.	3
Exod. xii. 7.	14	2 Chron. xiii. 20.	8 a	xxii. 26.	20 b
xii. 22.	7 b	Esth. ix. 5.	12 d	xxxiii. 35.	12 a
Deut. xvii. 8, 8.	7 c	Job xvii. 3.	20 c	Isa. i. 5.	12 c
xix. 5.	9	xx. 24.	4 b	xiv. 6.	12 d
xxi. 4.	16	xxiii. 2.	5	xvi. 7.	11
xxi. 5.	7 c	xxxiv. 26.	15	xxx. 26.	6 b
Josh. xiii. 1, 1. α	1 a	xxxvi. 18.	19	liii. 4.	7 a
xxiii. 1.	1 a	Ps. xxxix. 10.	7 c	liii. 8.	7 c
xxiii. 2. β	1 a	cx. 5.	6 a	Jer. v. 3.	12 a
Judg. v. 26.	4 a	Prov. vi. 1.	20 a	Lam. iv. 9.	2
1 Sam. ii. 14.	12 a	vii. 13.	17	Ezek. xxiv. 16.	8 b
2 Sam. xii. 15.	8 a	xvii. 18.	20 b	Hab. iii. 14.	13
xx. 10. γ	18				

α *lit.* gone in years.   β *lit.* I am gone in days.
γ *lit.* he doubled not to him.

STRING

יֶתֶר *m.* cord, string of a bow: Ps. xi. 2. מֵיתָר *m.* cord: Ps. xxi. 12.

מֵן *m.* part, portion; *pl.* מִנִּים strings of an instrument, probably slender threads, from their being divided: Ps. cl. 4.

עָשׂוֹר *m.* ten, a decad; of the cords or strings of an instrument; hence, for a ten-stringed instrument, decachord: Ps. xxxiii. 2; xcii. 3; cxliv. 9.

STRIP

1 נָצַל to spoil, to strip. PIEL [a] *fut.* HITHPAEL [b] *fut.*

2 פָּשַׁט to put off a garment; to strip, to plunder; to cause to put off. KAL [a] *inf.* [b] *fut.* PIEL [c] *inf.* HIPHIL [d] *pret.* [e] *imp.* [f] *fut.* HITHPAEL [g] *fut.*

3 שׁוֹלָל *m.* spoiled, stripped. שֵׁילָל *m.* כתיב.

Gen. xxxvii. 23.	2 f	1 Sam. xxxi. 8.	2 c	Job xxii. 6.	2 f
Exod. xxxiii. 6.	1 b	xxxi. 9.	2 f	Isa. xxxii. 11.	2 a
Num. xx. 26.	2 e	1 Chron. x. 8.	2 c	Ezek. xvi. 39.	2 d
xx. 28.	2 f	x. 9.	2 f	xxiii. 26.	2 d
1 Sam. xviii. 4.	2 g	2 Chron. xx. 25.	1 a	Hos. ii. 3.	2 f
xix. 24.	2 b	Job xix. 9.	2 d	Micah i. 8.	3

STRIPE

1 מַהֲלֻמּוֹת *f.* strokes, blows, as with a hammer.

2 חַבּוּרָה *f.* stripe, weal, bruise, *i.e.* the mark or print of blows in the skin. חֲבוּרָה *f.* bruise.

3 נֶגַע *m.* (see *Strike, Smite*) plague.

4 נָכָה to smite, to scourge; to strike home. HIPHIL [a] *inf.* [b] *fut.* מַכָּה [c] *f.* stroke, blow.

Exod. xxi. 25, 25.	3	Ps. lxxxix. 32.	3	Prov. xx. 30.	4 c
Deut. xxv. 3, 3.	4 b c	Prov. xvii. 10.	4 a	Isa. liii. 5.	2 a
2 Sam. vii. 14.	3	xix. 29.	1		

STRIPLING

עֶלֶם *m.* a young man: 1 Sam. xvii. 56.

STRIVE, STRIFE

1 אִישׁ *m.* man.

2 נִיחַ or נּוּחַ Ch. to break forth, to rush forth, *e.g.* the winds, as if to battle. APHEL *part.*

3 גָּרָה to excite, to stir up strife; to make war, to contend with, *seq.* בְּ. HITHPAEL *pret.*

4 דוּן This word has usually and most probably been considered as the same with דִּין to judge, contend, to be at strife. Most of the ancient versions give it the sense of remaining or dwelling; LXX. οὐ μὴ καταμείνῃ τὸ πνεῦμά μου, κ.τ.λ. Vulg. *non permanebit.* Syr., Arab. shall not dwell. Gesenius gives to דוּן the sense of to be low, depressed, humbled, whence he supposes may have been derived דִּין to subject to oneself, to rule, to judge. In accordance with this meaning, Gen. vi. 3 may be translated, My spirit shall not always be despised by man, *i.e.* I will not suffer my spirit, admonishing them and pleading with them by the prophets, to be perpetually neglected, I will punish them. KAL *fut.*

5 דִּין to judge; to contend together, properly before a judge; to be at strife. NIPHAL [a] *part.* [b] דִּין *m.* judgment, controversy, strife. [c] מָדוֹן *m.* contention, quarrel, strife. [d] מִדְיָנִים *m. pl.* strifes, disputes.

6 נָצָה to strive, to quarrel; to contend with blows or words, as the two Egyptians, Exod. ii. 13; two Israelites, Lev. xxiv. 10; as the two brothers, where one was slain, 2 Sam. xiv. 6. NIPHAL [a] *fut.* [b] *part.* HIPHIL [c] *pret.* [d] *inf.* [e] מַצָּה *f.* quarrel, strife.

7 עָשַׂק to strive with, *seq.* עִם. HIPHAEL *pret.*

8 רִיב to contend, to strive, to quarrel; Gr. λοιδορεῖν; rarely of those who contend by blows, &c., Deut. xxxiii. 7; oftener of those who strive in words, *seq.* עִם, אֵת, אֶל, and בְּ; also with *acc.* of him with whom one contends, Job x. 2, Isa. xxvii. 8. *Seq.* לְ of him for whom one contends, עַל of that about which one contends; to contend before a judge, to plead a cause. KAL [a] *pret.* [b] *inf.* [c] *fut.* [d] *part.* HIPHIL [e] *part.* [f] רִיב *m.* quarrel, strife. [g] יָרִיב *m.* an adversary. [h] מְרִיבָה *f.* strife.

Gen. vi. 3. α	4	2 Sam. xiv. 6.	6 a	Prov. xx. 3.	8 f
xiii. 7.	8 f	xix. 9.	5 a	xxii. 10.	5 b
xiii. 8.	8 h	xxii. 44.	8 f	xxv. 8.	8 b
xxvi. 20, 20.	8 c, 7	Job xxxiii. 13.	8 a	xxvi. 17, 21.	8 f
xxvi. 21.	8 c	Ps. xviii. 43.	8 f	xxvi. 20.	5 c
xxvi. 22.	8 a	xxxi. 20.	8 f	xxviii. 25.	5 c
Exod. ii. 13.	6 b	xxxv. 1.	8 g	xxix. 22.	5 c
xxi. 18.	8 c	lv. 9.	8 f	xxx. 33.	8 f
xxi. 22.	6 a	lx. title.	6 d	Isa. xli. 11.	8 f
Lev. xxiv. 10.	6 a	lxxx. 6.	5 c	xlv. 9.	8 d
Num. xx. 13.	8 h	cvi. 32.	8 h	lviii. 4.	8 f
xxvi. 9, 9.	6 c d	Prov. iii. 30.	8 h	Jer. xv. 10.	8 f
xxvii. 14.	8 h	x. 12.	1. 24.	3
Deut. i. 12.	8 f	xv. 18, 18.	5 c, 8 f	Ezek. xlvii. 19.	8 h
xxv. 11.	6 a	xvi. 28.	5 c	xlviii. 28.	8 h
xxxiii. 8.	8 c	xviii. 1. δ	8 f	Dan. vii. 2.	2
Judg. xi. 25. β	8 b a	xviii. 14.	5 c	Hos. iv. 4, 4.	8 c e
xii. 2. γ	1, 8 f	xvii. 19.	6 e	Hab. i. 3.	8 f

α *lit.* shall not judge, *i.e.* contend in judgment, *comp.* Eccles. vi. 10.   β *lit.* striving did he strive.   γ *lit.* a man of strife was I and my people.   δ *lit.* sacrifices of strife.

STRONG, STRENGTH, STRENGTHEN

1 אַבִּיר *adj.* strong, mighty; spoken of persons and of animals; often as *subst.* one strong, a mighty one.

2 אוּל strength, power. ᵃ אֱיָל *m. id.* ᵇ אֱיָלוּת *f. id.* ᶜ אֵל *m.* might, power.

3 אוֹן *m.* faculty, ability; strength, power, specially manly vigour.

4 אֵיתָן and אֶתָן *m.* perennity, perpetuity; firmness, strength. Gesenius, mighty, irresistible, violent (men and things), impregnable (place); might, irresistibility; constancy, pertinacity.

5 אָמֵץ to be alert, active, firm; properly spoken of the feet, to be strong in the feet, swift-footed; *trop.* of activity and alertness of mind, a firm and undaunted spirit; *seq.* מִן to be stronger than, to prevail over any one; Piel, to make firm, strengthen, properly feeble knees, faltering feet; to harden. KAL ᵃ*pret.* ᵇ*fut.* PIEL ᶜ*pret.* ᵈ*imp.* ᵉ*fut.* HIPHIL ᶠ*fut.* HITHPAEL ᵍ*fut.* ʰ אֹמֶץ *m.* vigour, properly strength of knees, so that one cannot be thrown down by another. ⁱ אַמְצָה *f.* strength. ᵏ אַמִּיץ *adj.* strong, prevailing.

6 אָפִיק *adj.* strong, mighty; "strong pieces:" Job xl. 18, *i.e.* scales; *comp.* Job xli. 7.

7 בַּדִּים *m. pl.* staves, bars.

8 בָּלַג to comfort, to take comfort, to recover strength. HIPHIL ᵃ*fut.* ᵇ*part.*

9 בָּצַר to fence. KAL ᵃ*part.* Paül. ᵇ בִּצָּרוֹן *m.* fortress. ᶜ מִבְצָר *m.* fortress.

10 גָּבַר to be or become strong, mighty, to prevail; Hithp. to show oneself strong, to conduct oneself proudly, insolently, ὑβρίζειν, *seq.* אֶל against any one. KAL ᵃ*pret.* PIEL ᵇ*pret.* HITHPAEL ᶜ*fut.* ᵈ גִּבּוֹר *adj.* mighty. ᵉ גְּבוּרָה *f.* power, courage, strength of dominion: Prov. viii. 14.

11 גֶּרֶם *m.* a bone; anything strong and firm.

12 דֹּבֶא *m.* Most ancient versions and interpreters render this word, which occurs but once, by strength; others, by old age; "as the days of thy youth, so shall be thy days of old age;" of the more modern, Hottinger supposes it to mean wealth; Pfeiffer and Rosenmüller, rest: and Gesenius, by rest, understands death to be figuratively intended. I see not that we are called to depart from the ancient interpretation that has given to this verse the force of a most gracious promise of strength according to the season of trial, *i.e.* of duty.

13 זְרוֹעַ *com.* arm, *fig.* strength.

14 חָזַק to bind fast; to hold fast to; to make firm, strong, to strengthen. Verbs of binding, binding together, girding, are thus transferred also to the idea of strength, because things are made firmer and stronger by girding or binding together. Mostly *intrans.* to be or become strong, applied to God's almighty power, Prov. xxiii. 11; to famine, sickness; to war, to a king or kingdom; to insolent, obstinate language; to an obstinate heart resolved not to comply, Exod. vii. 13, *comp.* Mal. iii. 13;

to a mind determined to act with resolution, firmness, intrepidity, steadiness and constancy, in opposition to being timorous, faint-hearted, careless, remiss and indifferent; to the sound of a trumpet; to earnest prayer, Jonah iii. 8; to severe chiding, Judg. viii. 1; to speaking earnestly and emphatically, Isa. viii. 11; to recover health, strength, &c.; to take and keep strong fast hold. KAL ᵃ*pret.* ᵇ*inf.* ᶜ*imp.* ᵈ*fut.* PIEL ᵉ*pret.* ᶠ*inf.* ᵍ*imp.* ʰ*fut.* HIPHIL ⁱ*pret.* ᵏ*imp.* ˡ*fut.* ᵐ*part.* HITHPAEL ⁿ*pret.* ᵒ*inf.* ᵖ*imp.* ᑫ*imp.* ʳ*part.* ˢ חָזָק *adj.* strong, mighty. ᵗ חָזֵק *adj.* powerful, waxing strong. ᵘ חֵזֶק *m.* help, aid. ᵂ חֹזֶק *m.* properly strength of hand for taking and retaining anything. ˣ חָזְקָה *f. id.*

15 חַיִל *m.* strength, might, valour; ability of body or of mind; wealth, riches; the strength or fertile vigour of a tree.

16 חָסֹן *adj.* Schultens says the root implies strength entire and inviolable. ᵃ חֹסֶן *m.* strength, power. ᵇ חָסִין *adj.* mighty.

17 יָד *com.* hand.

18 יָסַף to add. HIPHIL *fut.*

19 תּוֹעָפוֹת *f. pl.* labours, toils; product of labours, treasures, wealth: Ps. xcv. 4, *marg.* 'heights;' treasures of the mountains obtained by toil; strength equal to great labour.

20 כַּבִּיר *adj.* great, vast, mighty; much, many.

21 כֹּחַ *m.* strength, might, power, both to act and endure; vital strength of body, in opposition to a dry and languid state of the system; might and energy in business. In a bad sense, violence, Eccles. iv. 1. *Trop.* ability, *i.e.* wealth, riches; strength of the earth, its fruit, produce.

22 מֶזַח *m.* girdle, *trop.* strength, fortitude. ᵃ מָזִיחַ *m.* girdle, strength.

23 מָצָד *m.* fastness, castle, stronghold. ᵃ מְצוּדָה *f. id.*

24 נֶצַח *m.* superiority, glory; sincerity, truth; perpetuity, eternity; some assume also the signification of perfection, completeness. ᵃ נֵצַח *m.* see *Blood.*

25 נִצְבָּה Ch. *f.* hardness, firmness.

26 סָבַל to bear, to carry, *sc.* heavy burdens. PUAL *part.* "strong to labour."

27 סֶלַע *m.* rock, stronghold.

28 סָעַד to uphold, support. KAL *fut.*

29 עָזַז to strengthen, to make strong and firm; *seq.* לְ to give strength to any one, to make secure, to protect: Eccles. vii. 19, "wisdom strengthens the wise man more than ten chiefs," *i.e.* protects him more and better than ten leaders. *Intrans.* to be made strong. KAL ᵃ*inf.* ᵇ*imp.* ᶜ*fut.* ᵈ עִזּוּז *adj.* mighty. ᵉ עֱזוּז *m.* might. ᶠ מָעוֹז *m.* a strong or fortified place. ᵍ עַז *adj.* strong, vehement, fierce, *e.g.* a lion, an enemy, wind, waves, anger, appetite; mighty, powerful, so a people, king; fortified, guarded; harsh, hard, stern. ʰ עֹז *m.* strength, might, power of God, of men, of animals; prevailing strength by which dominion is usually obtained; also vehemence, violence, as of rain, thunder, anger; *concr.* strong ones, heroes, Judg. v. 21, *comp.* Isa. xliii. 17; strength from fortification, hence *trop.* defence, refuge, protection; in a bad sense, hardness, boldness, Eccles. viii. 1; shame-

less pride, Ezek. xxiv. 21; your strong pride, that in which you proudly trust. Splendour, majesty, glory, as the usual concomitants of might and power, with which כָּבוֹד is often coupled; Ps. xcvi. 6, splendour and majesty; Ps. cxxxii. 8, the ark (seat) of thy majesty, *i. e.* the ark of the covenant (2 Chron. vi. 41); for which *poet.* עֹז alone, Ps. lxxviii. 61, *comp.* 1 Sam. iv. 21, 22.

30 עֹפֶל *m.* hill; as a situation for a fortress.

31 עָצַם to bind up, to bind fast, to tie up; hence *intrans.* to be strong, mighty, powerful; to be strong in number. KAL [a] *pret.* [b] *inf.* HIPHIL [c] *fut.* [d] עֶצֶם *f.* bone: Job xxi. 23, "in his full strength;" see *Full: i. e.* in the height of his prosperity.—*Taylor.* [e] עֹצֶם *m.* strength. [f] עָצְמָה *f.* strength, number, multitude. [g] עֲצֻמוֹת *f.* strong defence, bulwarks, *trop.* of arguments with which disputants defend their cause. [h] עָצוּם *adj.* strong, great.

32 עָרִיץ *adj.* terrible.

33 פָּז to be hard, pure, solid, as pure gold. KAL [a] *fut.* Gen. xlix. 24; according to some Jewish critics, made golden or gilded, in allusion to the ornaments of gold put on the arms of Joseph by Pharoah, Gen. xli. 42.

34 צוּר *m.* a rock, a refuge. [a] מָצוֹר fortified place. [b] מְצוּדָה *f.* fortress.

35 קוּם to rise; to make to rise. PIEL *imp.*

36 קָשַׁר to bind; to be bound, *i. e.* firm, compact, strong. KAL [a] *part.* Paül. PUAL [b] *part.*

37 רָהַב to be violent; to make fierce, courageous, to embolden. HIPHIL [a] *fut.* [b] רַהַב *m.* violence, insolence, pride, Rahab (sea-monster) as an appellative for Egypt. Allusion is made to the origin of the name in Isa. xxx. 7. [c] רֹהַב *m.* pride, that of which one is proud: Ps. xc. 10. Taylor suggests that it should be read רחבם their enlargement is but labour and sorrow.

38 שָׂגַב to be high, inaccessible, strong. KAL *pret.*

39 תֵּל *m.* hill: Josh. xi. 13, *marg.* 'on their heap.'

40 תְּקֵף Ch. to be or become great, strong, powerful. P'AL [a] *pret.* [b] *fut.* [c] תְּקָף *m.* might, power. [d] תְּקָף Ch. *m. id.* [e] תַּקִּיף Ch. *adj.* strong, powerful.

Gen. iv. 12.	21	Deut. xxxi. 6, 7, 23.	14 c	1 Sam. xv. 29.	24	
xxv. 23.	5 b	xxxiii. 25.	12	xxiii. 14, 19, 29.	23	
xxx. 41.	36 b	Josh. i. 6, 7, 9, 18.	14 c	xxiii. 16.	14 h	
xxx. 42.	36 a	x. 25.	14 c	xxviii. 20, 22.	21	
xlviii. 2.	14 q	xi. 13.	39	2 Sam. i. 23.	10 a	
xlix. 3.	8	xiv. 11, 11,		ii. 7.	14 d	
xlix. 14.	11	11.	14 s, 21, 21	iii. 1.α	14 t	
xlix. 24, 24.	4, 33	xvii. 13.	14 a	iii. 6.β	14 r	
Exod. vi. 1, 1.	14 s	xvii. 18.	14 a	v. 7.	34 b	
x. 19.	14 s	xix. 29.	9 c	x. 11, 11.	14 d	
xiii. 3, 14, 16.	14w	xxiii. 9.	31 h	xi. 25.	14 k	
xiii. 9.	14 s	Judg. i. 28.	14 a	xiii. 14.	14 d	
xiv. 21.	29 g	iii. 12.	14 h	xv. 12.	5 k	
xiv. 27.	4	v. 21.	29 h	xvi. 21.	14 a	
xv. 2, 13.	29 h	vi. 2.	23	xxii. 18, 18.	29 g, 5 a	
Lev. xxvi. 20.	21	vii. 11.	14 d	xxii. 33.	29 f	
Num. xiii. 18, 31.	14 s	viii. 21.	10 e	xxii. 40.	15	
xiii. 19.	9 c	ix. 51.	29 h	xxiv. 7.	9 c	
xiii. 28.	29 g	xiv. 14, 18.	29 g	1 Kings vi. 2.	14 a	
xx. 20.	14 s	xvi. 5, 6, 9, 15, 17,		viii. 42.	14 s	
xxi. 24.	29 g	19.	21	xix. 8.	21	
xxiii. 22.	19	xvi. 28.	14 g	xix. 11.	14 s	
xxiv. 8.	19	xviii. 26.	14 s	xx. 22.	14 p	
xxiv. 21.	4	1 Sam. ii. 4.	15	xx. 23, 23.	14 a d	
Deut. ii. 36.	38	ii. 9.	21	xx. 25.	14 d	
iii. 28.	5 d	ii. 10.	29 h	2 Kings ii. 16.	15	
xi. 8.	14 d	iv. 9.	14 p	viii. 12.	9 c	
xxi. 17.	3	xiv. 52.	10 d	ix. 24.	17	

2 Kings xviii. 20.	10 e	Ps. xxxi. 24.	5 f	Isa. i. 31.	16	
xix. 3.	21	xxxiii. 16.	21	v. 22.	15	
xxiv. 16.	10 d	xxxiii. 17.	15	viii. 7.	31 h	
1 Chron. xi. 10.	14 r	xxxv. 10.	14 s	viii. 11.	14 x	
xvi. 11, 27, 28.	29 h	xxxvii. 39.	29 f	x. 13.	21	
xix. 12, 12.	14 d	xxxviii. 10.	21	xii. 2.	29 h	
xxii. 13.	14 c	xxxviii. 19.	31 a	xvii. 9.δ	29 f	
xxvi. 7, 9.	15	xxxix. 13.	8 a	xvii. 10.	29 f	
xxvi. 8.	21	xli. 3.	28	xxii. 21.	14 h	
xxviii. 10, 20.	14 c	xliii. 2.	29 f	xxiii. 4, 11, 14.	29 f	
xxix. 12.	14 f	xlvi. 1.	29 h	xxiii. 10.	22	
2 Chron. i. 1.	14 g	lii. 7, 7.	29 f c	xxv. 3.	29 g	
vi. 41.	29 h	liv. 1.	10 e	xxv. 4, 4.	29 f	
xi. 11.	34 b	lix. 9, 17.	29 h	xxvi. 1.	29 h	
xi. 12.	14 h	lx. 7.	21	xxvi. 4.	34	
xi. 17, 17.	14 h, 5 e	lx. 9.	34 a	xxvii. 1.	29 h	
xii. 1.	14 x	lxi. 3.	29 h	xxvii. 5.	29 h	
xii. 13.	14 q	lxii. 7.	29 h	xxviii. 2.	5 k	
xiii. 7.	5 g	lxv. 6.	21	xxviii. 6.	10 e	
xiii. 20.	21	lxviii. 28, 28.	29 h b	xxviii. 22.	14 d	
xv. 7.	21	lxviii. 34, 34, 35.	29 h	xxx. 2, 2.	29 a f	
xvi. 9.	14 o	lxxi. 3.	34	xxx. 3.	29 f	
xvii. 1.	14 q	lxxi. 7.	29 h	xxx. 7.	37 b	
xxi. 4.	14 q	lxxi. 9.	21	xxx. 15.	10 e	
xxiii. 1.	14 n	lxxi. 16.	10 e	xxxi. 1.	31 a	
xxiv. 13.	5 e	lxxi. 18.	13	xxxi. 9.	27	
xxv. 8.	14 n	lxxiii. 4.	2	xxxiii. 6.	16 a	
xxv. 11.	14 n	lxxiii. 26.	34	xxxiii. 23.	14 h	
xxvi. 8.	14 i	lxxiv. 13.	29 h	xxxv. 3.	14 g	
xxvi. 15.	14 a	lxxvii. 14.	29 h	xxxv. 4.	14 s	
xxvi. 16.	14 x	lxxvii. 4.	29 e	xxxvi. 5.	10 e	
xxviii. 20.	14 x	lxxviii. 51.	3	xxxvii. 3.	21	
xxxii. 5.	14 q	lxxviii. 61.	29 h	xl. 9, 31.	21	
xxxii. 7.	14 c	lxxx. 2.	10 e	xl. 10.	14 s	
Ezra i. 6.	14 f	lxxxi. 1.	29 h	xl. 26.	5 k	
vi. 22.	14 f	lxxxi. 1.	29 h	xl. 29.	31 f	
vii. 28.	14 n	lxxxiv. 5.		xli. 1.	21	
ix. 12.	14 d	lxxxiv. 7, 7.	15	xli. 10.	5 c	
Neh. i. 10.	14 s	lxxxvi. 16.	29 h	xli. 21.	31 g	
ii. 18.	14 h	lxxxviii. 4.	2 a	xlii. 25.	29 e	
iv. 10.	21	lxxxix. 8.	16 b	xliv. 12, e 12.ζ	21	
vi. 9.	14 g	lxxxix. 10, 17.	23 h	xliv. 14.	14 s	
viii. 10.	29 f	lxxxix. 13.	29 c	xlv. 24.	29 h	
ix. 25.	9 a	lxxxix. 21.	5 e	xlix. 4.	21	
Job iv. 3.	14 h	lxxxix. 40.	9 c	xlix. 5.	29 h	
iv. 4.	5 e	xc. 10, 10.	10 e, 37 e	li. 9.	29 h	
vi. 11, 12, 12.	21	xciii. 1.	29 h	lii. 1.	29 h	
viii. 2.	20	xcv. 4.	19	liii. 12.	31 h	
ix. 4.	21	xcvi. 6, 7.	29 h	liv. 2.	14 g	
ix. 19, 19.	21, 5 k	xcix. 4.	29 h	lx. 22.	31 h	
xii. 13.	10 e	cii. 23.	21	lxii. 8.	29 h	
xii. 20.	29 h	ciii. 20.	21	lxiii. 1.	21	
xii. 21.	22 a	civ. 15.	28	lxiii. 6.	24 a	
xv. 25.	10 c	cv. 4.	29 h	lxiii. 15.	10 e	
xvi. 5.	5 e	cv. 24.	31 c	Jer. viii. 16.	1	
xvii. 9, 9.γ	18, 5 h	cv. 36.	3	xvi. 19.	29 h	
xviii. 7, 12.	3	cviii. 8.	29 f	xx. 5.	16 a	
xviii. 13, 13.	7	cviii. 10.	9 c	xx. 7.	14 a	
xxi. 23.	31 d	cx. 2.	29 h	xxi. 5.	14 s	
xxvi. 2.	29 h	cxviii. 14.	29 h	xxiii. 14.	14 e	
xxx. 2.	21	cxix. 28.	35	xxxi. 11.	14 s	
xxx. 21.	31 e	cxxxii. 8.	29 h	xxxii. 21.	14 s	
xxxiii. 19.	4	cxxxvi. 12.	14 s	xlvii. 3.	1	
xxxvi. 5, 19.	21	cxxxviii. 3, 3.	37 a, 29 h	xlviii. 14.	15	
xxxvii. 6.	29 h	cxl. 7.	29 h	xlviii. 17.	15	
xxxvii. 18.	14 s	cxlii. 6.	5 a	xlviii. 18.	9 c	
xxxix. 11, 21.	21	cxliv. 2.	14	xlviii. 41.	23	
xxxix. 19.	10 e	cxliv. 14.	26	xlix. 19.	4	
xxxix. 28.	23 a	cxlvii. 10.	10 e	l. 34.	14 s	
xl. 16.	21	cxlvii. 13.	14 e	l. 44.	4	
xl. 18.	6	Prov. vii. 26.	31 h	li. 12.	14 k	
xli. 22.	29 h	viii. 14.	10 e	li. 53.	29 h	
Ps. viii. 2.	29 h	viii. 28.	21	Lam. i. 6, 14.	21	
x. 10.	31 h	x. 15.	29 h	ii. 2, 5.	9 c	
xviii. 1.	14 u	x. 29.	29 f	iii. 18.	24	
xviii. 2.	34	xi. 16.	32	Ezek. iii. 8, 8.	29 h	
xviii. 17, 17.	29 g, 5 a	xiv. 4.	21	iii. 14.	14 a	
xviii. 32, 39.	15	xiv. 26.	29 h	vii. 13.	14 q	
xix. 5.	10 d	xviii. 10, 11, 19.	29 h	vii. 24.	29 g	
xix. 14.	34	xx. 29.	21	xiii. 22.	14 f	
xx. 2.	29 h	xxi. 14.	29 g	xvi. 49.	14 i	
xx. 6.	10 e	xxi. 22.	29 h	xix. 11, 12, 14.	29 h	
xxi. 1, 13.	29 h	xxiv. 5, 5.	29 h, 21	xxii. 14.	14 d	
xxii. 12.	1	xxiv. 10.	21	xxiv. 25.	29 f	
xxii. 15.	21	xxx. 25.	29 g	xxiv. 25.	29 f	
xxii. 19.	2 b	xxx. 30.	10 d	xxvi. 11.	14 s	
xxiv. 8.	29 h	xxxi. 3.	15	xxvi. 17.	14 s	
xxvii. 1.	29 f	xxxi. 17, 17.	29 h, 5 e	xxx. 18.	21	
xxvii. 14.	5 f	xxxi. 25.	29 h	xxx. 21.	14 b	
xxviii. 7, 8.	29 h	Eccles. vii. 19.	29 h	xxx. 22.	14 s	
xxviii. 8.	29 h f	ix. 11.	10 e	xxx. 24.	14 s	
xxix. 1, 11.	29 h	ix. 16.	10 e	xxx. 25.	14 i	
xxx. 7.	29 h	x. 10.	15	xxxii. 21.	2 c	
xxxi. 2, 4.	29 f	x. 17.	10 e	xxxiii. 28.	29 h	
xxxi. 10.	21	xii. 3.	15	xxxiv. 4.	14 e	
xxxi. 21.	34 a	Cant. viii. 6.	29 g			

Ezek. xxxiv. 16, 16.	14 h s	Dan. xi. 24.	9 c	Micah v. 4.	29 h
Dan. ii. 37.	40 d	xi. 31.	29 f	v. 11.	9 c
ii. 40, 42.	40 e	xi. 32.	14 l	vi. 2.	4
ii. 41.	40 e	xi. 39.	29 f, 9 c	Nah. i. 7.	29 f
ii. 41.	25	Hos. vii. 9.	21	ii. 1.	14 g
iv. 11, 20.	40 a	vii. 15.	14 e	iii. 9.	31 f
iv. 22.	40 b	xii. 3.	3	iii. 11.	29 f
vii. 7.	40 c	Joel i. 6.	31 h	iii. 12.	9 c
viii. 8.	31 b	ii. 2, 5, 11.	31 h	iii. 14, 14.	9 c, 14 k
x. 8, 8, 16, 17.	21	ii. 22.	15	Hab. i. 10.	9 c
x. 18.	14 h	iii. 10.	10 d	iii. 19.	15
x. 19, 19, 19, 19.	}14 c c n e	iii. 16.	29 f	Hag. ii. 4, 4, 4.	14 c
xi. 1.	29 f	Amos ii. 9.	16	ii. 22.	14 w
xi. 2.	14 x	ii. 14, 14.	14 s, 5 e	Zech. viii. 9, 13.	14 d
xi. 5, 5.	14 d	iii. 11.	29 h	viii. 22.	31 h
xi. 6.	14 m	v. 9, 9.	8 b, 29 g	ix. 3.	34 a
xi. 12.	29 c	vi. 13.	14 w	ix. 12.	9 b
xi. 15.	21	Micah iv. 3, 7.	31 h	x. 6, 12.	10 b
xi. 17.	40 c	iv. 8.	30	xii. 5.	5 i
xi. 23.	31 a				

α *lit.* was going and strong. β *lit.* was making himself strong. γ *lit.* shall add strength. δ *lit.* the cities of his strength. ε *lit.* with the arm of his strength. ζ *lit.* no strength.

STRUGGLE

רָצַץ to break; to oppress; to dash one another, to struggle. HITHPOEL *fut.*, Gen. xxv. 22.

STUBBLE

קַשׁ *m.* straw, the dry haum of grain, partly as left standing in the fields, stubble; which then was sometimes burnt over; as partly as broken up in treading out the grain, and so separated by ventilation, draff: Exod. v. 12; xv. 7: Job xiii. 25; xli. 28, 29: Ps. lxxxiii. 13: Isa. v. 24; xxxiii. 11; xl. 24; xlii. 2; xlvii. 14: Jer. xiii. 24; Joel ii. 5; Obad. 18; Nah. i. 10; Mal. iv. 1.

תֶּבֶן *m.* straw as broken up by thrashing: Job xxi. 18.

STUBBORN

סָרַר to be refractory, rebellious, intractable. KAL *part.* Poel. Deut. xxi. 18, 20: Ps. lxxviii. 8; Prov. vii. 11.

פָּצַר to be obtuse, dull, stubborn. HIPHIL *inf.* 1 Sam. xv. 23.

קָשֶׁה *adj.* hard: Judg. ii. 19. קְשִׁי *m.* Deut. ix. 27.

STUDS

נְקֻדּוֹת *f. pl.* points, studs, *e.g.* of silver for ornament: Cant. i. 11.

STUDY

הָגָה to meditate. KAL *fut.* Prov. xv. 28; xxiv. 2.

לַהַג *m.* study, *sc.* of letters, learning, as Aben-Ezra well: Eccles. xii. 12, *marg.* 'reading.'

STUFF

כְּלִי a word of general import, furniture, implement, equipment: Gen. xxxi. 37, 37; xlv. 20: Exod. xxii. 7: Josh. vii. 11: 1 Sam. x. 22; xxv. 13; xxx. 24: Neh. xiii. 8: Ezek. xii. 3, *marg.* 'instruments,' 4, 4, 7, 7.

מְלָאכָה *f.* work, labour, business: Exod. xxxvi. 7, *i.e.* on which labour is bestowed.

STUMBLE

1 כָּשַׁל to be feeble; to falter; to stumble, as accompanying a faint and faltering gait. KAL ᵃ *pret.* ᵇ *part.* Poel. NIPHAL ᶜ *pret.* ᵈ *inf.* ᵉ *fut.* ᶠ *part.* HIPHIL ᵍ *pret.* ʰ *fut.* ⁱ מִכְשׁוֹל *m.* stumbling-block. ᵏ מַכְשֵׁלָה *f.* fall, ruin: Zeph. i. 3, *i.e.* idols, and their services.

---

2 נָגַף to smite; to strike against with the foot. KAL ᵃ *fut.* HITHPAEL ᵇ *fut.* ᶜ נֶגֶף *m.* act of stumbling.

3 פּוּק to move to and fro, to waver, as weak and ready to fall. KAL *pret.*

4 שָׁמַט to smite; to throw down; to shake. KAL *pret.*

Lev. xix. 14.	1 i	Isa. xxviii. 7.	3	Jer. l. 32.	1 a
1 Sam. ii. 4.	1 f	lvii. 14.	1 i	Ezek. iii. 20.	1 i
1 Chron. xiii. 9.	4	lix. 10.	1 a	vii. 19.	1 i
Ps. xxvii. 2.	1 a	lxiii. 10.	1 e	xiv. 3, 4, 7.	1 i
Prov. iii. 23.	2 a	Jer. vi. 21.	1 i	Dan. xi. 19.	1 c
iv. 12, 19.	1 a	xiii. 16.	2 b	Nah. ii. 5.	1 e
xxiv. 17.	1 d	xviii. 15.	1 h	iii. 3.	1 e
Isa. v. 27.	1 a	xx. 11.	1 e	Zeph. i. 3.	1 k
viii. 14.	2 c	xxxi. 9.	1 e	Mal. ii. 8.	1 g
viii. 15.	1 a	xlvi. 6, 12.	1 a		

STUMP

עִקַּר Ch. *m.* stump, trunk: Dan. iv. 15, 23, 26.

SUBDUE, SUBJECT

1 דָּבַר to set in order; to lead, to guide, to drive; to reduce to order, to subdue. HIPHIL *fut.*

2 חֲשַׁל Ch. to crush. P'AL *part. active.*

3 יָרַד to come down. KAL *inf.*

4 כָּבַשׁ to tread upon; to subdue, to bring into subjection. KAL ᵃ *pret.* ᵇ *imp.* ᶜ *fut.* NIPHAL ᵈ *pret.* PIEL ᵉ *pret.*

5 כָּנַע to be bowed down, to be low; to bow down, to bring low, to humble. NIPHAL ᵃ *fut.* HIPHIL ᵇ *pret.* ᶜ *fut.*

6 כָּרַע to bend, to bow; to cast down, to prostrate. HIPHIL *fut.*

7 רָדַד to tread down. KAL ᵃ *inf.* ᵇ *part.* Poel.

8 שָׁפַל Ch. to humble. APHEL *fut.*

Gen. i. 28.	4 b	2 Sam. viii. 11.	4 e	Ps. lxxxi. 14.	5 c
Num. xxxii. 22, 29.	4 d	xxii. 40.	6	cvi. 42.	5 a
Deut. xx. 20.	3	1 Chron. xvii. 10.	5 b	cxliv. 2.	7 b
Josh. xviii. 1.	4 d	xviii. 1.	5 c	Isa. xlv. 1.	7 a
Judg. i. 30.	5 c	xx. 4.	5 a	Jer. xxxiv. 11.	4 c
iv. 23.	5 c	xxii. 18.	4 d	xxxiv. 16.	4 c
viii. 28.	5 a	Neh. ix. 24.	4 a	Dan. ii. 40.	2
xi. 33.	5 a	Ps. xviii. 39.	5 a	vii. 24.	5 a
1 Sam. vii. 13.	5 a	xviii. 47.	5 a	Micah vii. 19.	4 c
2 Sam. viii. 1.	1	xlvii. 3.	1	Zech. ix. 15.	4 a

SUBMIT

יָד *com.* hand: 1 Chron. xxix. 24, "submitted," *lit.* gave the hand under.

כָּחַשׁ to lie; to feign, to flatter, to fawn upon, chiefly of the vanquished, who profess devotedness and love towards their victors, with לְ: to give feigned obedience. PIEL *fut.* Ps. xviii. 44; lxvi. 3; lxxxi. 15. HITHPAEL *fut.* 2 Sam. xxii. 45.

נָתַן to give. KAL *pret.* 1 Chron. xxix. 24.

עָנָה to afflict; to humble oneself. HITHPAEL *imp.* Gen. xvi. 9, *lit.* afflict thyself; (the same word translated "dealt hardly," verse 6), *comp.* 1 Pet. v. 6.

רָפַס to trample upon; to let oneself be trampled upon. HITHPAEL *part.* Ps. lxviii. 30.

SUBSCRIBE

כָּתַב to write; to write upon, to inscribe: Isa. xliv. 5, he

inscribes his hand—I am Jehovah's, *i. e.* he writes this upon his hand (LXX. ἐπιγράφει χειρὶ αὐτοῦ· τοῦ Θεοῦ εἰμι), in allusion to the ancient custom by which servants bore the names of their masters, soldiers those of their generals, idolaters those of their idols, cut or burnt in on the forehead, hand, wrist; see Rev. xiii. 16.—*Spencer, de Legib. Heb. Ritual.* § 135, 1, note 3. KAL *inf.* Jer. xxxii. 44. *fut.* Isa. xliv. 5: Jer. xxxii. 10. *part.* Poel, Jer. xxxii. 12.

Gen. vii. 4, 23.	11 a	2 Chron. xxxv. 7.	13	Prov. iii. 9.	4
xii. 5.	13	Ezra viii. 21.	13	vi. 31.	4
xiii. 6.	13	x. 8.	13	viii. 21.	7
xv. 14.	13	Job i. 3, 19.	12 a	x. 3.	3
xxxiv. 23.	12	v. 5.	5	xii. 27.	4
xxxvi. 6.	12	vi. 22.	9	xxviii. 8.	4
Deut. xi. 6.	11 a	xv. 29.	5	xxix. 3.	4
xxxiii. 11.	5	xx. 18.	5	Cant. viii. 7.	4
Josh. xiv. 4.	12	xxii. 20.	11	Isa. vi. 13, 13.	6
1 Chron. xxvii. 31.	13	xxx. 22.	8, or 14	Jer. xv. 13.	5
xxviii. 1.	13	Ps. cv. 21.	12	xvii. 3.	5
2 Chron. xxi. 17.	13	cxxix. 15.	10	Hos. xii. 8.	5
xxxi. 3.	13	cxxix. 16.	2	Obad. 13.	1
xxxii. 29.	13	Prov. i. 13.	4	Micah iv. 13.	5

SUBSTANCE

1 אוֹן *m.* faculty, ability; strength, power, wealth, substance.

2 גֹּלֶם *m.* anything rolled or wrapped together; hence an unformed mass, substance, not yet wrought, the parts of which are not yet unfolded nor developed, spoken of the embryo fœtus, Ps. cxxxix. 16, "my substance, yet being unperfect." Often, in the Talmud, for anything not yet wrought, elaborated, perfected; see Chelim, 12, § 6; also *trop.* of an unformed, unlettered man, Pirke Aboth, 5, § 7.—*Gesenius.*

3 הַוָּה *f.* desire, cupidity: Prov. x. 3, *marg.* 'or, wicked (for their) wickedness.' Gesenius, he thrusteth away the desire of the wicked; *parall.* נֶפֶשׁ צַדִּיק the soul of the righteous.

4 הוֹן *m.* riches, wealth, substance.

5 חַיִל strength; ability, wealth, riches.

6 מַצֶּבֶת *f.* anything set upright; trunk or stem of a tree.

7 יֵשׁ *pr.* τὸ εἶναι, being, existence; then what is, what exists, there is: Prov. viii. 21 may be translated, "there is to me that which I may cause them to inherit who love me;" as it is translated in 2 Chron. xxv. 9, "the Lord is able to give," &c., *i. e.* there is to Jehovah to give, &c. This word comes from

8 יָשָׁה a root not in use, *pr.* to stand, to stand out, to stand upright, and hence to be : תּוּשִׁיָּה *f. pr.* a setting upright, uprightness; hence help, deliverance; Job xxx. 22 (קרי), *marg.* 'wisdom.' Thou dissolvest my substance (or my help).

9 כֹּחַ *m.* strength and vigour of body; ability, wealth.

10 עֶצֶם *m.* strength, body, answering to German *gebein.*

11 קִים *m.* a rising up against any one in a hostile sense, hence adversary, enemy. יְקוּם *m.* whatever lives on the earth, living thing.

12 קִנְיָן *m.* a getting; possession, substance. The wealth of nomadic tribes consisted mostly in flocks and herds, hence the word signifies almost exclusively property in cattle. מִקְנֶה *m.* possession, always used of cattle.

13 רְכוּשׁ *m. pr.* what one has, possessions, property, substance; in the most general sense, fields, &c.; in a sense less general, moveable property, flocks, &c.; in the strictest sense, household goods, baggage, not including precious things, gold or silver.

14 שָׁוָה to fear. PIEL *fut.* Job xxx. 22, *lit.* according to כתיב, thou terrifiest.

SUBTIL

1 חָכָם *adj.* wise; sagacious, shrewd; in a good or bad sense.

2 נָכַל to deceive, to act deceitfully, to contrive insidiously. HITHPAEL *inf.*

3 נָצַר to keep; to keep from view, hide. KAL *part.* Paül.

4 עָקְבָּה *f.* fraud, craft, subtilty.

5 עָרַם to be naked; to be crafty, cunning. KAL ᵃ*inf.* HIPHIL ᵇ*fut.* ᶜ עָרוּם *adj.* cunning. It is observable that our first parents, before they sinned, are called (Gen. ii. 25) *naked*, and the serpent in the very next verse is called *subtil*, by one and the same word. ᵈ עָרְמָה *f.* cunning.

6 מִרְמָה *f.* deceit, fraud.

Gen. iii. 1.	5 c	2 Sam. xiii. 3.	1	Prov. i. 4.	5 d
xxvii. 35.	6	2 Kings x. 19.	4	vii. 10.	3
1 Sam. xxiii. 22.	5 a b	Ps. cv. 25.	2		

SUBURBS

מִגְרָשׁ *m.* a place whither herds are driven to graze, a pasture; spoken especially of the open country set apart for pasture around the Levitical cities: Lev. xxv. 34: Num. xxxv. 2, &c.: Josh. xiv. 4; xxi. 2, &c. An open space, area around a city or building: Ezek. xxvii. 28: xlv. 2; xlviii. 15, 17: 1 Chron. v. 16; vi. 55, &c.: 2 Chron. xi. 14; xxxi. 19.

פַּרְוָר *m.* according to the Targ. and Talm. suburbs or places adjoining to the city: 2 Kings xxiii. 11.

SUBVERT

עָוַת to be crooked; to make crooked, to pervert, to subvert. PIEL *inf.* Lam. iii. 36.

SUCCEED, SUCCESS

יָרַשׁ to take possession, with *acc.* of person, to seize upon his possession; to inherit. KAL *pret.* Deut. xii. 29; xix. 1. *fut.* Deut. ii. 12, 21, 22.

קוּם to rise, to stand up; to stand upon the name of any one, *i. e.* in the public registers to be enrolled in one's place, to succeed to the name and estate of any one. KAL *fut.* Deut. xxv. 6.

שָׂכַל to prosper, to have good success. HIPHIL *fut.* Josh. i. 8.

SUCCOTH

סֻכָּה *f.* a tabernacle, a booth: Gen. xxxiii. 17.

SUCCOUR

עָזַר to help. KAL *inf.* 2 Sam. viii. 5 ; xviii. 3, *marg.* 'be to succour.' *fut.* 2 Sam. xxi. 17. HIPHIL *inf.* 2 Sam. xviii. 3 (כתיב).

SUCH

פְּלֹנִי some one, a certain one, Gr. ὁ δεῖνα, properly one distinct, definite, whom one points out as with the finger and not by name. Everywhere joined with אַלְמֹנִי *pr.* one concealed, nameless. So of persons in Ruth iv. 1. Gr. ὁ οὗτος. Of things, 1 Sam. xxi. 2, *i.q.* to a certain place not named, 2 Kings vi. 8.

SUCK

1 חָלָב *m.* milk ; "sucking," *lit.* of milk.
2 יָנַק to suck. KAL ᵃ *pret.* ᵇ *fut.* ᶜ *part.* Poel. HIPHIL ᵈ *pret.* ᵉ *inf.* ᶠ *fut.*
3 מָצָה to suck, to suck out, to drink out greedily. KAL *pret.*
4 עוּל *m.* infant, sucking child.
5 עָלַע to sip up, to suck up. PIEL *fut.*

Gen. xxi. 7.	2 d	1 Kings iii. 21.	2 e	Isa. lxvi. 11.	2 b
Num. xi. 12.	2 c	Job iii. 12.	2 b	lxvi. 12.	2 a
Deut. xxxii. 13.	2 f	xx. 16.	2 b	Jer. xliv. 7.	2 a
xxxii. 25.	2 c	xxxix. 30.	5	Lam. ii. 11.	2 c
xxxiii. 19.	2 b	Ps. viii. 2.	2 c	iv. 3.	2 d
1 Sam. i. 23.	2 f	Cant. viii. 1.	1	iv. 4.	2 d
vii. 9.	2 c	Isa. xi. 8.	2 c	Ezek. xxiii. 34.	2 c
xv. 3.	2 c	xlix. 15.	2 c	Joel ii. 16.	2 c
xxii. 19.	2 c	lx. 16, 16.	2 a b		

SUDDEN

1 מָהַר to hasten. PIEL ᵃ *fut.* ᵇ מַהֵר *adv.* quickly.
2 מוּת to die. KAL *part.*
3 פִּתְאֹם *adv.* in a moment, suddenly.
4 פֶּתַע *m.* a moment.
5 רָגַע to tremble ; to wink with the eyes, to do suddenly. HIPHIL ᵃ *fut.* ᵇ רֶגַע *m.* moment.

Num. vi. 9. ᵃ	2, 4, 3	Ps. vi. 10.	5 b	Isa. xlviii. 3.	3
xii. 4.	4	lxiv. 4, 7.	3	Jer. iv. 20.	3
xxxv. 22.	4	Prov. iii. 25.	3	vi. 26.	3
Deut. vii. 4.	1 b	vi. 15, 15.	3, 4	xv. 8.	3
Josh. x. 9.	3	xxiv. 22.	4	xviii. 22.	3
xi. 7.	3	xxix. 1.	3	xlix. 19. γ	5 a
2 Sam. xv. 14. β	1 a	Eccles. ix. 12.	3	l. 44.	5 a
2 Chron. xxix. 36.	3	Isa. xxix. 5.	3	li. 8.	3
Job v. 3.	3	xxx. 13.	3	Hab. ii. 7.	3
ix. 23.	3	xlvii. 11.	3	Mal. iii. 1.	3
xxii. 10.	3				

ᵃ *lit.* dying in a moment, suddenly.   β *lit.* lest he make haste and overtake us.   γ *or, lit.* I will wink, I will cause him to run, *i.e.* at my wink he shall run.

SUFFER

1 חָיָה to live ; to save alive. PIEL *fut.*
2 יָכֹל to be able. KAL *fut.*
3 יָנַח to set or lay a thing down, or to lay it up and leave it to be or lie there ; to let alone. HIPHIL ᵃ *pret.* ᵇ *inf.* ᶜ *imp.* ᵈ *part.*
4 כָּתַר to surround ; to wait. PIEL *imp.* Job xxxvi. 2, wait for me, or suffer to go on a little.
5 נָטַשׁ to leave ; to leave to do anything. KAL *pret.*

6 נָשָׂא to lift up ; to take upon oneself, to bear, endure sorrow reproach ; to permit, to suffer. KAL ᵃ *pret.* ᵇ *inf.* ᶜ *imp.* ᵈ *fut.* ᵉ *part.* Poel.
7 נָתַן to give. KAL ᵃ *pret.* ᵇ *inf.* ᶜ *fut.*

Gen. xx. 6.	7 a	Judg. xv. 1.	7 a	Ps. xvi. 10.	7 c
xxxi. 7.	7 a	xvi. 26.	5	lv. 22.	7 c
xxxi. 28.	5	1 Sam. xxiv. 7.	7 a	lxvi. 9.	7 a
xxii. 18. ᵃ	7 c	1 Kings xv. 17.	7 b	lxxxviii. 15.	6 a
Exod. xii. 23.	1	1 Chron. xvi. 21.	7 b	ci. 5.	2
Lev. xix. 17. β	6	Esth. iii. 8.	3 b	cv. 14.	3 a
Num. xxi. 23.	7 a	Job ix. 18.	7 a	cxxi. 3.	7 c
Deut. xviii. 14.	7 a	xxi. 3.	6 c	Prov. xix. 19.	6 c
Josh. x. 19.	7 c	xxxi. 30.	7 a	Eccles. v. 6.	7 c
Judg. i. 34.	7 c	xxxvi. 2.	4	v. 12.	7 c
iii. 28.	7 a			Jer. xv. 15.	7 d

ᵃ "suffer to live."   β *marg.* 'or, that thou bear not sin for him.'

SUFFICE, SUFFICIENT

1 דַּי *m.* sufficiency, the full ability of a person, the full quantity, space, or quality of a thing. מִדַּי *adv.* sufficiently.
2 מָצָא to find ; to find emphatically, to find in sufficiency, to find all that is wanted, or can be found in any particular respect. KAL *pret.*
3 סֵפֶק *m.* sufficiency, abundance.
4 רַב *adj.* much.
5 שָׂבַע to be filled to one's content, to be satisfied, to have enough. KAL ᵃ *fut.* ᵇ שֹׂבַע *m.* abundance : Ruth ii. 18. ᶜ שִׂבְעָה *f. id.*, Isa. xxiii. 18.
6 שָׂפַק to be enough, to suffice. KAL ᵃ *fut.* ᵇ שֶׂפֶק *m.* sufficiency : Job xx. 22.

Exod. xxxvi. 7.	1	1 Kings xx. 10.	6 a	Prov. xxv. 16.	1
Num. xi. 22, 22. ᵃ	2	2 Chron. xxx. 3. γ	1	Isa. xxiii. 18.	5 c
Deut. iii. 26.	4	Ruth ii. 14.	5 a	xl. 16, 16.	1
xv. 8.	1	ii. 18.	5 b	Ezek. xliv. 6.	4
xxxiii. 7.	2	Job xx. 22.	3, or 6 b	xlv. 9.	4
Judg. xxi. 14. β	2				

ᵃ *lit.* and find, *i.e.* and afford a full supply for them.   β *lit.* they found so not for them.   γ lit. to what enough. (for לְמַה־דַּי and for מַה־דַּי)

SUIT (See also CHANGE)

עֵרֶךְ *m. pr.* a setting in order, apparatus, equipment : Judg. xvii. 10, *marg.* 'an order of garments ;' *i.e.* as much as would serve to be worn on different occasions, some for common use, some for religious assemblies.

חָלָה to beseech. PIEL *pret.* Job xi. 19, *marg.* 'intreat thy face.'

רִיב *m.* strife ; cause, suit, before a judge : 2 Sam. xv. 4.

SUM

כֹּפֶר *m.* ransom : Exod. xxi. 30, "sum of money."

מִסְפָּר *m.* number, with מִפְקָד *m.* "the sum of the number :" 2 Sam. xxiv. 9, 1 Chron. xxi. 5.

פָּקַד to number. KAL *part.* Patil, Exod. xxxviii. 21.

פָּרָשָׁה *f.* a specified, precise sum of money : Esth. iv. 7.

רֹאשׁ *m.* head ; sum total of a large number of men : Exod. xxx. 12 : Num. i. 2, 49 ; iv. 2, 22 ; xxvi. 2 ; xxxi. 26, 49 : Ps. cxxxix. 17. רֵאשׁ *m.* Ch. Dan. vii. 1.

תָּכְנִית *f.* measure ; structure, arrangement : Ezek. xxviii. 12.

תָּמַם to be complete. HIPHIL, to sum : *fut.* 2 Kings xxii. 4.

SUMMER

קַיִץ *m. pr.* the cutting off, of fruits, harvest, harvest of figs,

especially at midsummer, the hottest season. Sometimes it seems to include the spring, as חֹרֶף includes autumn and winter; fruit, especially figs. Jerome, *poma*, which is a general word including figs. Gen. viii. 22 : 2 Sam. xvi. 1, or, *ellipt.* a hundred cakes of figs, 2 : Ps. xxxii. 4 ; lxxiv. 17 : Prov. vi. 8 ; x. 5 ; xxvi. 1 ; xxx. 25 : Isa. xvi. 9 ; xxviii. 4 : Jer. viii. 20 ; xl. 10, 12 ; xlviii. 32 : Amos iii. 15 ; viii. 1, 2 : Micah vii. 1 : Zech. xiv. 8. קַיִם Ch. *id.*, Dan. ii. 35. קוץ *denom.* to summer. KAL *pret.* Isa. xviii. 6.

מְקֵרָה *f.* cooling, refreshing : Judg. iii. 20, 24.

SUN

אוֹר *m.* light : Job xxxi. 26, *marg.* 'light.'

חַמָּה *f.* warmth, heat ; the sun : Job xxx. 28 : Cant. vi. 10 : Isa. xxiv. 23 ; xxx. 26, 26. On this last passage, Cocceius has the following observations : *Lux Lunæ et solis diversimode in mysterio considerari possunt : 1, ut lux solis sit cognitio veritatis, lux Lunæ consolatio in cruce, quæ ratio videtur aptissima Apoc. viii. 12 ; 2, ut vice versa lux Lunæ sit cognitio veritatis, quæ imperfecta est in hac vita : solis sit lux Spiritus Sancti radians in cordibus nostris ad ea consolandum et calefaciendum quod est initium vitæ æternæ ; 3, ut duplex ordo in ecclesia sit, eorum, qui lucem aliis immittunt, et qui eam recipiunt ; doctores et fideles auditores : conf. Dan. xii. 3. Not. Lex.*

חֶרֶס *m.* the sun, probably denoting heat : Judg. viii. 13 ; xiv. 18 : Job ix. 7.

שֶׁמֶשׁ *com.* the sun : Gen. xv. 12, &c. שְׁמָשׁ Ch. *com.* Dan. vi. 14.

SUNDER

פָּרַד to separate. HITHPAEL *fut.* Job xli. 17.

SUNRISING

מִזְרָח *m.* rising (of the sun), sunrising : Num. xxxiv. 15.

SUP

מִנַּמָּה *f.* from the root נָמַם, which our translators have thought to be of the same meaning with נָמָא to drink in, to sup up : Hab. i. 9, *lit.* the supping up of their faces (as) the east wind. See various interpretations of this difficult passage in Henderson *in loc.*

SUPERFLUOUS

שָׂרַע to stretch out. KAL *part.* Paül, Lev. xxi. 18, xxii. 23.

SUPPLANT

עָקַב to take or seize by the heel ; to circumvent, deceive, defraud. KAL *inf.* Jer. ix. 4, *lit.* in supplanting will supplant. *fut.* Gen. xxvii. 36, Jer. ix. 4.

SUPPLE

מָשְׁעִי *m.* occurs only in Ezek. xvi. 4, *marg.* 'or, when I looked (upon thee),' of a new-born infant. It is referred by Abulwalid and many others to שָׁעַע to cleanse ; nor wast thou washed to cleansing, *i.e.* clean. I would rather refer it to the root שָׁעָה to look, and then the sense

would be, " nor wast thou washed for looking upon," *i.e.* for presenting to thy parents and others, which is not done until after the infant is washed and swathed.— *Gesenius.*

SUPPLIANT, SUPPLICATION

1 חָלָה (see *Intreat, Beseech*), to supplicate. PIEL *pret.*

2 חָנַן to be gracious ; to implore favour, mercy, *i.e.* to intreat, to make supplication. HITHPAEL ᵃ *pret.* ᵇ *inf.* ᶜ *fut.* חָנַן Ch. ITHPAEL ᵈ *part.* ᵉ תְּחִנָּה *f. pr.* cry for mercy. ᶠתַּחֲנוּנִים *m. pl.* prayers for mercy. ᵍ תַּחֲנוּת *f. pl. id.*

3 עָתָר *m.* (see *Intreat*), suppliant, worshipper of God.

4 פָּלַל to pray. HITHPAEL *fut.*

1 Sam. xiii. 12.	1	Job xli. 3.	2 f	Isa. xlv. 14.	4
1 Kings viii. 28, 30, 38,		Ps. vi. 9.	2 e	Jer. iii. 21.	2 f
45, 49, 52, 52, 54.	2 e	xxviii. 2, 6.	2 f	xxxi. 9.	2 f
viii. 33, 47, 59.	2 a	xxx. 8.	2 c	xxxvi. 7.	2 e
ix. 3.	2 a	xxxi. 22.		xxxvii. 20.	2 e
2 Chron. vi. 19.	2 e	lv. 1.	2 e	xxxviii. 26.	2 e
vi. 21.	2 f	lxxxvi. 6.	2 g	xlii. 2, 9.	2 e
vi. 24.	2 e	cxvi. 1.		Dan. vi. 11.	2 d
vi. 29, 35, 39.	2 e	cxix. 170.	2 e	ix. 3, 17, 18, 23.	2 f
xxxiii. 13.	2 e	cxxx. 2.	2 f	ix. 20.	2 f
Esth. iv. 8.	2 b	cxl. 6.	2 f	Hos. xii. 4.	2 c
Job viii. 5.	2 c	cxliii. 1.	2 c	Zeph. iii. 10.	3
ix. 15.	2 c	cxliii. 1.	2 f	Zech. xii. 10.	2 f

SUPPOSE

אָמַר to say. KAL *fut.* 2 Sam. xiii. 32.

SURE, SURELY, SURETY, SURETYSHIP

1 אָסַף to gather, to take away. KAL *inf., lit.* in gathering.

2 אָמַן to be firm, stable, such as one may safely lean upon ; to be sure, certain, true, of persons, and of any other thing remaining in its proper state, unalterably ; a sure place, in Isa. xxii. 23, is emphatic, considering the insecurity of Oriental houses. NIPHAL ᵃ *pret.* ᵇ *part.* HIPHIL ᶜ *fut.* אָמַן Ch. APHEL ᵈ *part.* ᵉ אֲמָנָה *f.* confirmation, surety. ᶠ אָמְנָם *adj.* verily, truly. ᵍ אֻמְנָם *adv. id.* ʰ אֱמֶת *f.* firmness, stability, perpetuity ; faithfulness, fidelity, truth.

3 בָּטַח to trust ; to be secure, without fear. KAL ᵃ *part.* Poel. ᵇ בֶּטַח *m.* trust, confidence ; security, fearlessness. ᶜ מִבְטָח *pr. id.*

4 חָזַק to hold fast to anything, to cleave, to adhere firmly ; *seq.* לְ *c. inf.* to persist in anything, to be constant, diligent in it. KAL *imp.*

5 יָדַע to know. KAL ᵃ *pret.* ᵇ *inf.* ᶜ *imp.*

6 יָסַד to found. HOPHAL *part.*

7 עָרַב to exchange ; to become surety for any one, *seq. acc.* of person, properly to exchange with him, to stand in his place ; to become surety for one's life, to pledge oneself for the life of another ; for another's debt, to give security for the payment. KAL ᵃ *pret.* ᵇ *imp.* ᶜ *fut.* ᵈ *part.* Poel. ᵉ עֲרֻבָּה *f.* pledge, surety.

8 קוּם to rise up ; to set oneself, to stand, to be confirmed, established, as we say a bargain stands. KAL ᵃ *fut.* ᵇ קַיָּם Ch. *adj.*

9 רָהַב to press or urge strongly ; *seq. acc.* of person. KAL *imp.*

10 שָׁמַר to watch, to keep, to look after. KAL *part.* Paül.

11 תָּקַע to strike ; to strike hands as a pledge of suretyship. KAL *part*. Poel.

Gen. xv. 13.	5 b	1 Kings xi. 38.	2 b	Prov. xi. 18. α	2 h
xviii. 13.	2 g	Neh. ix. 38.	2 e	xvii. 18.	7 e
xxiii. 17, 20.	8 a	Job xvii. 3.	7 b	xx. 16.	7 a
xliii. 9.	7 c	xxiv. 22.	2 c	xxii. 26.	7 d
xliv. 32.	7 a	xxxiv. 12.	2 f	xxvii. 13.	7 a
Exod. iii. 19.	5 a	Ps. xix. 7.	2 b	Isa. xxii. 23, 25.	2 b
Num. xxxii. 23.	5 c	xciii. 5.	2 a	xxviii. 16. β	6
Deut. xii. 23.	4	cxi. 7.	2 b	xxxii. 18.	3 c
xii. 23.	5 c	cxix. 122.	7 b	xxxiii. 16.	2 b
1 Sam. ii. 35.	2 b	Prov. vi. 1.	7 a	lv. 3.	2 b
xx. 7.	5 c	vi. 3.	9	Jer. viii. 13.	1
xxv. 28.	2 b	x. 9.	3 b	Dan. ii. 45.	1 d
2 Sam. i. 10.	5 a	xi. 15.	7 a	iv. 26.	8 b
xxiii. 5.	10	xi. 15, 15.	11, 3 a	Hos. v. 9.	2 b

α *lit.* reward of truth.   β a founded foundation.

SURNAME

כָּנָה to address kindly, to call kindly ; to flatter. PIEL *fut.* Isa. xliv. 5, xlv. 4.

SURPRISE

אָחַז to lay hold of, to take, to seize. KAL *pret.* Isa. xxxiii. 14.

תָּפַשׂ to lay hold of, to take in war. NIPHAL *pret.* Jer. xlviii. 41. *fut.* Jer. li. 41.

SUSTAIN, SUSTENANCE

מִחְיָה *f.* preservation of life ; means of life, sustenance : Judg. vi. 4.

כּוּל to hold, to contain ; to hold up, to sustain ; to sustain, to nourish, to furnish with the means of living. PILPEL *pret.* 2 Sam. xix. 32 : Neh. ix. 21. *inf.* 1 Kings xvii. 9. *fut.* Ps. lv. 22 : Prov. xviii. 14.

סָמַךְ to uphold, to sustain, to help, properly to let lean upon. KAL *pret.* Gen. xxvii. 37 : Isa. lix. 16. *fut.* Ps. iii. 5.

SWADDLE

חָתַל to wrap in bandages ; to swathe, to swaddle a new-born infant. PUAL *pret.* Ezek. xvi. 4, *lit.* in swaddling thou wast not swaddled. HOPHAL *inf.* Ezek. xvi. 4. חֲתֻלָּה *f.* bondage : Job xxxviii. 9.

טָפַח to spread out, extend, specially with the hand ; see *Span.* PIEL *pret.* Lam. ii. 22.

SWALLOW

דְּרוֹר *m. pr.* a swift flight, wheeling, gyration ; hence, *concr.* for a bird which flies in circles, wheels in gyrations ; according to the Hebrew Interpreters, a swallow ; according to Bochart and the ancient versions, a turtle dove, which is less suited to the context. Ps. lxxxiv. 3 : Prov. xxvi. 2.

עָגוּר *m.* chattering, twittering ; as an epithet of the swallow, Isa. xxxviii. 14, as the twittering swallow, see *Crane;* poet. for a species of the swallow itself : Jer. viii. 7.

SWALLOW (V)

1 בָּלַע to swallow down and receive into the stomach, as the whale swallowed Jonah, chap. ii. 1 ; or as one swallows what he eats, Isa. xxviii. 4 ; it is used of those who eat greedily ; hence to destroy, to abolish, to consume. In Piel the signification is still stronger, and implies entire destruction. KAL ᵃ*pret.* ᵇ*inf.* ᶜ*fut.* NIPHAL ᵈ*pret.*

PIEL ᵉ*pret.* ᶠ*fut.* ᵍ*part.* PUAL ʰ*fut.* ⁱ בֻּלָע *m.* a swallowing up.

2 גָּמָא to absorb, to drink up, to swallow ; *poet.* of the horse swallowing as it were the ground in his eagerness and fleetness. PIEL *fut.*

3 לָעַע to swallow greedily, to suck down. KAL *pret., i. e.* I want words to express my grief.

4 שָׁאַף to breathe hard, to pant ; to pant or gape after any one, is to thirst for his blood, the metaphor being taken from wild beasts. KAL ᵃ*pret.* ᵇ*inf.* ᶜ*part.* Poel.

Exod. vii. 12.	1 c	Job xx. 18.	1 c	Isa. xxv. 8.	1 e
xv. 12.	1 c	xxvii. 20.	1 h	xxviii. 7.	1 d
Num. xvi. 30.	1 a	xxxix. 24.	1 c	xlix. 19.	1 g
xvi. 32, 34.	1 c	Ps. xxi. 9.	1 f	Jer. li. 34.	1 a
xxvi. 10.	1 c	xxxv. 25.	1 e	li. 44.	1 c
Deut. xi. 6.	1 c	lvi. 1, 2.	4 a	Lam. ii. 2, 5, 5, 16.	1 e
2 Sam. xvii. 16.	1 h	lvii. 3.	4 c	Ezek. xxxvi. 3.	4 b
xx. 19, 20.	1 f	lxix. 15.	1 c	Hos. viii. 7.	1 c
Job v. 5.	4 a	cvi. 17.	1 c	viii. 8.	1 c
vi. 3.	3	cxxiv. 3.	1 a	Amos viii. 4.	4 c
vii. 19.	1 b	Prov. i. 12.	1 a	Obad. 16.	3
xx. 15.	1 a	Eccles. x. 12.	1 f	Jonah i. 17.	1 b

SWAN

תִּנְשֶׁמֶת *f.* an unclean animal classed with other species of lizards ; according to Bochart, the chameleon ; according to the opinion of the ancients, Lxx. and Vulg. *talpa*, mole ; Saad. lizard : Lev. xi. 30. Also an unclean aquatic bird, probably the pelican, *pelecanus onocrotalus*, so called from its pouch, which it can extend by inflation. Lxx. πορφυρίων, *i. e.* the crested purple heron, *ardea purpurea*, Linn. ; Vulg. *cygnus*, swan. Lev. xi. 18 : Deut. xiv. 16.—*Robinson's Ges. Lex.*

SWARM

עֵדָה. *f.* assembly, congregation, community ; of bees, a swarm : Judg. xiv. 8.

עָרֹב mixture : Exod. viii. 21, *marg. 'or*, a mixture of noisome beasts, &c.,' 21, 22, 24, 24, 29, 31 ; see *Fly.* If the previous plague was that of gnats (see *Lice*), this word may mean a mixed swarm of flies. Some have supposed it might be the beetle peculiar to Egypt, and held to be sacred.

SWEAR

1 אָלָה to swear, properly to call on God as a witness, to affirm by God ; to curse. KAL ᵃ*inf.* HIPHIL ᵇ*inf.* ᶜ אָלָה *f.* an oath, an imprecation.

2 בַּעַל *m.* master.

3 יָד *com.* hand.

4 כֵּס *m.* supposed to be, *i. q.* כִּסֵּא *m.* throne : Exod. xvii. 16, *lit.* because *the* hand on *the* throne of Jehovah, war to Jehovah with, &c. ; *i. e.* because Jehovah hath sworn there shall be war with Amalek in continuance. This is the simplest rendering, whatever various meanings may be suggested.

5 נָשָׂא to lift up ; to lift up the hand, in taking an oath. KAL ᵃ*pret.* ᵇ*fut.*

6 שָׁבַע to swear ; *denom.* from שֶׁבַע seven, since seven was a sacred number, and oaths were confirmed either by

seven victims offered in sacrifice, Gen. ii. 28, *sq.*, or by seven witnesses and pledges; see Herod. iii. 8; Hom. Il. xix. 243; *seq.* בְּ of that by which one swears; but, further, to swear by Jehovah is sometimes, *i. q.* to worship him, since one swears by the divinity he worships. Sometimes it is taken in a bad sense, to swear rashly, Eccles. ix. 2, Zech. v. 3, *comp.* 4. KAL [a]*part.* Paül. NIPHAL [b]*pret.* [c]*inf.* [d]*imp.* [e]*fut.* [f]*part.* HIPHIL [g]*pret.* [h]*inf.* [i]*fut.* שְׁבוּעָה [k] *f.* oath.

Gen. xxi. 23.	6 d	Deut. xxvi. 3, 15.	6 b	Neh. xiii. 25.	6 i
xxi. 24.	6 e	xxviii. 9, 11.	6 b	Ps. xv. 4.	6 b
xxi. 31.	6 b	xxix. 13.	6 b	xxiv. 4.	6 b
xxii. 16.	6 b	xxx. 20.	6 b	lxiii. 11.	6 f
xxiv. 3, 37.	6 i	xxxi. 7, 20, 21, 23.	6 b	lxxxix. 3, 35, 49.	6 b
xxiv. 7.	6 b	xxxiv. 4.		xcv. 11.	6 b
xxiv. 9.	6 e	Josh. i. 6.	6 d	cii. 8.	6 b
xxv. 33, 33.	6 d e	ii. 12.	6 b	cix. 106.	6 b
xxvi. 3.	6 b	ii. 17, 20.	6 g	cxix. 106.	6 b
xxvi. 31.	6 'e	v. 6, 6.	6 b	cxxxii. 2, 11.	6 b
xxxi. 53.	6 e	vi. 22.	6 e	Eccles. ix. 2.	6 f
xlvii. 31, 31.	6 d e	ix. 15.	6 e	Isa. iii. 7.	5 b
l. 5, 6.	6 g	ix. 18, 19, 20.	6 e	xiv. 24.	6 b
l. 24.	6 b	xiv. 9.	6 e	xix. 18.	6 b
Exod. vi. 8.	5 a, 3	xxi. 43, 44.	6 b	xlv. 23, 23.	6 b e
xiii. 5, 11.	6 b	xxiii. 7.	6 i	xlviii. 1.	6 f
xiii. 19. a	6 h g	Judg. ii. 1, 15.	6 b	liv. 9, 9.	6 b
xvii. 16.	3, 4	xv. 12.	6 d	lxii. 8.	6 b
xxxii. 13.	6 b	xxi. 1, 7, 18.	6 b	lxv. 16, 16.	6 f e
xxxiii. 1.	6 b	1 Sam. iii. 14.	6 b	Jer. iv. 2.	6 e
Lev. v. 1.	1 c	xix. 6.	6 e	v. 2, 7.	6 c
v. 4.	6 e	xx. 3.	6 e	vii. 9.	6 c
vi. 3.	6 e	xx. 17.	6 e	xi. 5.	6 e
vi. 5.	6 e	xx. 42.	6 b	xii. 16, 16.	6 b
xix. 12.	6 e	xxiv. 21.	6 e	xxii. 5.	6 b
Num. xi. 12.	6 b	xxiv. 22.	6 e	xxiii. 10.	1 c
xiv. 16, 23.	6 b	xxviii. 10.	6 e	xxxii. 22.	6 b
xiv. 30.	5 a, 3	xxx. 15.	6 d	xxxviii. 16.	6 e
xxx. 2.	6 c	2 Sam. iii. 9.	6 b	xl. 9.	6 e
xxxii. 10.	6 e	iii. 35.	6 e	xliv. 26.	6 b
xxxii. 11.	6 e	xix. 7.	6 e	xlix. 13.	6 b
Deut. i. 8, 35.	6 b	xix. 23.	6 e	li. 14.	6 b
ii. 14.	6 b	xxi. 2, 17.	6 b	Ezek. xvi. 8.	6 e
iv. 21.	6 b	1 Kings i. 13, 17, 30.	6 b	xxi. 23.	6 a
iv. 31.	6 b	i. 29, 51.	6 e	Dan. xii. 7.	6 e
vi. 10, 18, 23.	6 b	ii. 8, 23.	6 e	Hos. iv. 2.	1 a
vi. 13.	6 e	ii. 42.	6 g	iv. 15.	6 e
vii. 8, 12, 13.	6 b	viii. 31.	1 b	x. 4.	1 a
viii. 1, 18.	6 b	2 Kings viii. 24.	6 e	Amos iv. 2.	6 b
ix. 5.	6 b	2 Chron. vi. 22.	1 b	vi. 8.	6 b
x. 11.	6 b	xv. 14.	6 e	viii. 7.	6 b
x. 20.	6 e	xv. 15.	6 e	viii. 14.	6 b
xi. 9, 21.	6 b	xxxvi. 13.	6 e	Micah iv. 20.	6 b
xiii. 17.	6 b	Ezra x. 5, 5.	6 i e	Zeph. i. 5, 5.	6 b
xix. 8.	6 b	Neh. vi. 18.β	2, 6 k	Zech. v. 3, 4.	6 f
		ix. 15.	5 a, 3	Mal. iii. 5.	6 f

[a] *lit.* causing to swear he hath caused to swear.   β *lit.* were masters of oath.

SWEAT

יֶזַע *m.* sweat, "that which causeth sweat:" Ezek. xliv. 18, *marg.* 'in, *or,* with sweat; *or,* in sweating (places).' וְזֵעָה *f.* sweat: Gen. iii. 19.

SWEEP

גָּרַף to snatch or hurry away, to drag off, to pluck off. KAL *pret.* Judg. v. 21. Lxx. ἐξέσυρεν; Vulg. *traxit cadavera eorum.*

טוּא to remove mud or dirt. PILPEL *pret.* Isa. xiv. 23, I will sweep her (Babylon) away with the besom of destruction, *i. e.* will wholly destroy her, so that her site shall be as a place swept clean.

יָעָה to snatch away, to sweep away. KAL *pret.* Isa. xxviii. 17. Vulg. *subvertet;* Saad. *abripiet.*

סָחַף to scrape, to scrape away, to sweep away with violence, as a rain which sweeps all before it. KAL *part.* Poel,

---

Prov. xxviii. 3. NIPHAL *pret.* Jer. xlvi. 15. Gesenius, 'prostrated.'

SWEET

1   בֶּשֶׂם *m.* aromatic odour, fragrance; spice, spicery. [a] בֹּשֶׂם *m. id.*

2   טוֹב *adj.* good.

3   יָטַב to be good; to make good, or sweet. HIPHIL *imp.*

4   מֵישָׁרִים *m. pl.* straightness, rightness.

5   מָלַץ to be smooth. NIPHAL *pret.* Ps. cxix. 103. Gesenius, how smooth to my palate are thy words, *i. e.* pleasant, sweet.

6   מָתַק to suck as a child; hence to feed upon with relish, Job xxiv. 20; to be or become sweet, Job xxi. 33; sweet to him are the clods of the valley, the earth is light upon him. KAL [a]*pret.* [b]*fut.* HIPHIL [c]*fut.* [d]מֶתֶק *m.* sweetness. [e]מֹתֶק *m. id.* [f]מָתוֹק *adj.* sweet. [g]מַמְתַקִּים *m. pl.* sweetness.

7   נִיחוֹחַ *m.* rest, acquiescence; sweetness, pleasantness, delight. Found only in the phrase 'odour of delight,' or of 'rest;' to the Mosaic precepts concerning sacrifices is very often added, "a sweet odour to Jehovah." [a] נִיחוֹחַ Ch. *m.*

8   נָעֵם to be sweet; to be pleasant, lovely. KAL [a]*pret.* [b]נָעִים *adj.* pleasant.

9   סַמִּים *m. pl.* aromatics, fragrant spices; spices, sweet spices, mostly joined with incense; *lit.* incense of sweet spices.

10   עָבַר to pass; to overflow. KAL *part.* Poel.

11   עָרֵב to mingle; to be sweet, pleasant (perhaps well-tempered, well-mixed), *seq.* לְ of person, *e. g.* sleep, a desire accomplished, sacrifices, gifts, *seq.* עַל, Ps. civ. 34, Ezek. xvi. 37. KAL [a]*pret.* [b]*fut.* עָרֵב [c] *adj.* agreeable, sweet.

12   מֶרְקָחִים *m. pl.* aromatic herbs.

Gen. viii. 21.	7	Num. xviii. 17.	7	Prov. xvi. 24.	6 f
Exod. xv. 25.	6 b	xxviii. 2, 6, 8, 13,	7	xx. 17.	11 c
xxv. 6.	9	24, 27.	7	xxiii. 8.	8 b
xxix. 18, 25, 41.	7	xxix. 2, 6, 8, 13, 36.	7	xxiv. 13.	6 f
xxx. 7.	7	Judg. ix. 11.	6 e	xxvii. 7.	6 f
xxx. 23, 23.	1, 1 a	xiv. 14, 18.	6 f	xxvii. 9.	6 d
xxx. 34, 34.	9	2 Sam. xxiii. 1.	8 b	Eccles. v. 12.	6 f
xxxi. 11.	9	2 Chron. ii. 4.	9	xi. 7.	6 f
xxxv. 8, 15, 28.	9	xiii. 11.	9	Cant. ii. 3.	6 f
xxxvii. 29.	9	xvi. 14.	9	ii. 14.	11 c
xxxix. 38.	9	Ezra vi. 10.	7 a	v. 5.	10
xl. 27.	9	Neh. viii. 10.	6 g	v. 13.	12
Lev. i. 9, 13, 17.	7	Esth. ii. 12.	9	v. 13.	10
ii. 2, 9, 12.	7	Job xx. 12.	6 c	v. 16.	6 g
iii. 5, 16.	7	xxi. 33.	6 a	vi. 2.	9
iv. 7.	7	xxiv. 20.	6 a	Isa. iii. 24.	1 a
iv. 31.	7	Ps. xix. 10.	6 f	xx. 20, 20.	4
vi. 15, 21.	7	lv. 14.	6 c	xxiii. 16.	3
viii. 21, 28.	9	cxix. 103.	11 b	Jer. vi. 20, 20.	2, 11 a
xvi. 12.	9	cxix. 103.	5	xxxi. 26.	11 a
xvii. 6.	7	cxli. 6.	8 a	Ezek. iii. 3.	6 f
xxiii. 13, 18.	9	Prov. iii. 24.	11 a	vi. 13.	7
xxvi. 31.	7	ix. 17.	6 b	xvi. 19.	7
Num. iv. 16.	9	xiii. 19.	11 b	xx. 28, 41.	7
xv. 3, 7, 10, 13, 14,	7	xvi. 21.	6 d	Dan. ii. 46. a	7 a
24.					

[a] "sweet odours."

SWELL

בָּעָה to make swell, to cause to boil, as water. NIPHAL *part.* Isa. xxx. 13.

בָּצֵק to swell; hence spoken of the foot as unshod, to become callous, to have callous spots or tumours. KAL *pret.* Deut. viii. 4: Neh. ix. 21.

גַּאֲוָה *f.* pride ; *trop.* used of the swelling of the sea : Ps. xlvi. 3 (*comp.* Job xxxviii. 11). גָּאוֹן *m.* of the swelling of Jordan : Jer. xii. 5 ; xlix. 19 ; l. 44.

צָבָה to go forth ; to project, to be prominent. KAL *pret.* Num. v. 27. HIPHIL *inf.* Num. v. 22. צָבֶה *adj.* swelling : Num. v. 21.

SWIFT

1 אֵבֶה *m.* desire : Job ix. 26, *marg.* 'ships of desire, *or*, of Ebeh.' Symm. ναυσὶ σπευδούσαις. Gesenius, אֵבֶה *m.* reed, bulrush, papyrus ; from the notion of a bulrush with its head inclined, bowed down, *comp.* Isa. lviii. 5. Boats or skiffs, made of the papyrus of the Nile, were in common use among the Egyptians and Ethiopians, and famous for their lightness and swiftness, used when great expedition was necessary, especially to carry messages. See Isa. xviii. 2, "vessels of bulrushes."

2 יָעֵף *m.* weariness, fatigue from a swift course.

3 כִּרְכָּרוֹת *f. pl.* dromedaries, swift camels. Gesenius, so called from their bounding motion, their speed being also sometimes accelerated by musical instruments. According to others, multitude of circling wheels or cars.

4 מָהַר to hasten. PIEL *a inf. b part. c* מְהֵרָה *f.* quick, ready, speedy.

5 קָלַל to be light ; to be swift, fleet ; *comp.* κοῦφος, light, swift, ἐλαφρός, ἔλαφος, light ; swift. KAL *a pret.* NIPHAL *b fut. c* קַל *adj.* light ; swift.

6 רֶכֶשׁ *m.* a horse of a nobler and fleeter race, a steed, courser ; distinguished from סוּסִים, Esth. viii. 10, 14.—Micah i. 13, swift beasts.

2 Sam. i. 23.		5 a	Eccles. ix. 11.	5 c	Jer. xlvi. 6.	5 c
1 Chron. xii. 8.		4 a	Isa. v. 26.	5 c	Lam. iv. 19.	5 c
Job vii. 6.		5 a	xviii. 2.	5 c	Dan. ix. 21.	2
ix. 25.		5 a	xix. 1.	5 c	Joel iii. 4.	5 c
ix. 26.		1	xxx. 16, 16.	5 c b	Amos ii. 14, 15.	5 c
xxiv. 18. a		5 c	lxvi. 20.	3	Micah i. 13.	5 c
Ps. cxlvii. 15.		4 c	Jer. i. 23.	5 c	Hab. i. 8.	5 a
Prov. vi. 18.		4 b	iv. 13.	5 a	Mal. iii. 5.	4 b

a lit. he is light upon the face of the waters.

SWIM

צוּף to flow ; to cause to flow, to swim. HIPHIL *fut.* 2 Kings vi. 6. צָפָה *f.* Ezek. xxxii. 6. Gesenius, inundation.

שָׂחָה to swim ; to make to swim, to inundate. KAL *inf.* Isa. xxv. 11. *part.* Poel, Isa. xxv. 11. HIPHIL *fut.* Ps. vi. 6. שָׂחוּ *m.* swimming : Ezek. xlvii. 5.

SWINE

חֲזִיר *m.* a swine : Lev. xi. 7 : Deut. xiv. 8 : Prov. xi. 22 : Isa. lxv. 4 ; lxvi. 3, 17.

SWOON

עָטַף to cover ; to be covered with darkness, to languish, to faint. NIPHAL *inf.* Lam. ii. 11. HITHPAEL *inf.* Lam. ii. 12.

SWORD

בָּרָק *m.* lightning ; *trop.* of the brightness or glittering of a sword : Deut. xxxii. 41, *lit.* the lightning of my sword ; *poet.* " for a glittering sword ;" Job xx. 25.

חֶרֶב *f.* a sword, as laying waste ; straight, tapering, with two edges, fitted both for slashing and thrusting ; *metaph.* the keen and piercing words of an enemy : Gen. iii. 24, &c.

רֶצַח *m.* a slaying : Ps. xlii. 10. Gesenius, with a breaking of my bones, *i.e.* causing me the severest pain.

שֶׁלַח *m.* a missile, weapon, *sc.* of death : Job xxxiii. 18 ; xxxvi. 12 : Joel ii. 8.

SYCOMORE

שִׁקְמָה *f.* a sycomore-tree, very frequent in the level parts of Palestine, resembling the mulberry-tree in its leaves and general appearance, with fruit similar to the fig growing directly from the stem and larger boughs, and very difficult of digestion.—*Dioscorid.* i. 182. The fruit is used only by the poorest classes ; see *Gather,* בָּלַם. See Celsii Hierob. i. p. 310. It is of an insipid taste ; the wood is remarkably coarse and spongy in its texture. —*Shaw's Travels, Suppl.* p. 96. 1 Kings x. 27 : 1 Chron. xxvii. 28 : 2 Chron. i. 15 ; ix. 27 : Ps. lxxviii. 47 : Isa. ix. 10 : Amos vii. 14.

SYNAGOGUE

מוֹעֵד congregation ; place of assembly, *sc.* as appointed : Ps. lxxiv. 8. Gesenius, all the sacred places of assembly in the land, *i.e.* other places in a certain sense sacred, as Ramah, Bethel, Gilgal, &c., distinguished as seats of the prophets and as high places.

TABER (See TABRET)

TABERAH

תַּבְעֵרָה *f.* burning : Num. xi. 3 : Deut. ix. 22.

TABERNACLE

1 אֹהֶל *m.* a tent, tabernacle ; tabernacle of the congregation or assembly, *comm.* tabernacle of the covenant, *i. e.* the portable and moveable sanctuary of the Israelites in the desert, described Exod. xxvi., *comp.* xxxvi. As to the distinction in the tabernacle between אֹהֶל and מִשְׁכָּן, the former denoted the exterior covering, consisting of twelve curtains of goat's-hair, which was placed over the proper dwelling (מִשְׁכָּן the inclosed), commonly rendered 'tabernacle ;' yet, when מִשְׁכָּן occurs in the same verse, mostly rendered in this case 'tent.'—Exod. xxvi. 9, &c.

2 סֻכָּה *f.* booth, hut, formed of green branches interwoven ; in which a Jewish festival was kept. *a* סֻכּוּת *f.* tent, tabernacle, which the idolatrous Israelites constructed in the desert, like the tabernacle of the covenant in honour of Jehovah ; *comp.* the σκηνὴ ἱερά of the Carthaginians, Diod. Sic. 20, 65. *b* סֹךְ *m.* booth, hut ; *poet.* for a tabernacle, dwelling.

3 שַׂךְ *m.* a booth, hut, tabernacle, dwelling ; *or*, fence.

4   מִשְׁכָּן   *m.* a habitation, dwelling; specially a tent, tabernacle; often of the sacred tabernacle of the Israelites.

No. 1 not included.

Exod. xxv. 9.	4	Num. iii. 7, 7.	1, 4	2 Sam. vii. 6.	4
xxvi. 1, 6, 7, 12, 13,		iii. 8, 8.	1, 4	1 Chron. vi. 48.	4
15, 17, 18, 20, 22,		iii. 23.	4	xvi. 39.	4
23, 26, 27, 27, 30,		iii. 25, 25, 25.	1, 4, 1	xvii. 5.	4
35.	4	iii. 26, 29, 35, 36.	4	xxi. 29.	4
xxvii. 9, 19.	4	iii. 38, 38.	4, 1	xxiii. 26.	4
xxxv. 11, 15, 18.	4	iv. 16.	4	2 Chron. i. 5.	4
xxxvi. 8, 13, 14, 20,		iv. 25, 25, 25.	4, 1, 1	viii. 13.	2
22, 23, 25, 27, 28,		iv. 26.	4	Ezra iii. 4.	2
31, 32, 32.	4	iv. 31, 31.	1, 4	Job xxxvi. 29.	4
xxxviii. 20, 21, 21, 31.	4	v. 17.	4	Ps. xliii. 3.	4
xxxix. 32, 33, 40.	4	vii. 1, 3.	4	xlvi. 4.	4
xl. 2, 5, 6, 9, 17, 18,		ix. 15, 15, 15, 18, 19,		lxxvi. 2.	2 b
19, 21, 22, 24, 28,		20, 22.	4	lxxviii. 60.	4
29, 33, 34, 35, 36,		x. 11, 17, 17, 21.	4	lxxxiv. 1.	4
38.	4	xvi. 9, 24, 27.	4	cxxxii. 7.	4
Lev. viii. 10.	4	xvii. 13.	4	Isa. iv. 6.	2
xv. 31.	4	xix. 13.	4	Lam. ii. 6.	3
xvii. 4, 4.	4, 1	xxiv. 5.	4	Ezek. xxxvii. 27.	4
xxiii. 34.	2	xxxi. 30, 47.	4	Amos v. 26.	2 a
xxvi. 11.	4	xxxi. 10.	2	ix. 11.	2
Num. i. 50, 50, 50, 51,		Deut. xvi. 13, 16.	2	Zech. xiv. 16, 18, 19.	2
51, 53, 53.	4	Josh. xxii. 19, 29.	4		

TABLE, TABLET

בַּיִת   *m.* house: Isa. iii. 20, *marg.* 'houses of the soul.' Gesenius, receptacles for perfume.

כּוּמָז   *m.* a globe, globule of gold, perhaps *collect.* globules, drops, or rather a string of gold drops like beads worn around the neck or arm by the Israelites in the desert of the Midianites, probably heathen and idolatrous ornaments. Exod. xxxv. 22 : Num. xxxi. 50.

לוּחַ   *m.* a tablet, of stone, on which anything is inscribed or cut in; of wood, a board; sculptured; so of tablets for writing, covered perhaps with wax: Isa. xxx. 8 : Hab. ii. 2. *Trop.* Prov. iii. 3, upon the tablet of thy heart, *comp.* Jer. xvii. 1, 2 Cor. iii. 3, and the δέλτοι φρενῶν of Æschylus. Exod. xxiv. 12 : xxxi. 18, 18 : xxxii. 15, 15, 16, 16, 19 : xxxiv. 1, 1, 1, 4, 4, 28, 29 : Deut. iv. 13 ; v. 22; ix. 9, 10, 10, 11, 11, 15, 17; x. 1, 2, 2, 3, 3, 4, 5 : 1 Kings viii. 9 : 2 Chron. v. 10 : Prov. iii. 3 ; vii. 3 : Isa. xxx. 8 : Jer. xvii. 1 : Hab. ii. 2.

נֶפֶשׁ   *com.* breath, life, soul; perfume, especially that which is sweet: Isa. iii. 20. Vulg. *olfactoriola*, which women suspended from their neck; *v.* Schroeder de Vestitu, pp. 142, *seq.*

מֵסַב   *consessus, triclinium,* divan of the Orientals, arranged round about a room: Cant. i. 12.

שֻׁלְחָן   *m.* a table, so called from its being extended, spread out: Exod. xxv. 23, &c.

TABRET, TABRING

תָּפַף   to strike, to beat, especially the tabret; to beat, to smite upon the breast, *seq.* עַל. POEL *part.* Nah. ii. 7. תֹּף *m.* a drum, tabret, timbrel; an instrument of joy, which may have taken its name from the sound. It is used very elegantly in Nah. ii. 7, "tabering upon their breasts," *i. e.* beating their breasts from sorrow, instead of beating the tabret or drum, as formerly, for joy or mirth. In the East it consists of a thin wooden rim covered with membrane, and hung around with brass bells or rattles; it is used chiefly by dancing females.

Gen. xxxi. 27 : 1 Sam. x. 5; xviii. 6 : Isa. v. 12; xxiv. 8; xxx. 32 : Jer. xxxi. 4, *marg.* 'or, timbrels;' Ezek. xxviii. 13. תֹּפֶת *m. id.,* or from the obsolete word תּוּף to spit out; an object of contempt: Job xvii. 6.

TACHES

קְרָסִים   *m. pl. pr.* curves, joints; a hook, tache, to which a loop or eye is fixed, used for the curtains of the tabernacle: Exod. xxvi. 6, 6, 11, 11, 33; xxxv. 11; xxxvi. 13, 13, 18; xxxix. 33.

TACKLING

חֶבֶל   *m.* cord, tackling of a vessel: Isa. xxxiii. 23.

TAIL

זָנָב   *m.* tail of an animal; end, extremity; put also for something small, mean, contemptible, mostly in *opp.* to רֹאשׁ: Exod. iv. 4 : Deut. xxviii. 13, 44 : Judg. xv. 4, 4, 4 : Job xl. 17 : Isa. vii. 4; ix. 14, 15; xix. 15.

TAKE

1   אָבַד   to perish; to cause to perish. HIPHIL *pret.*

2   אָחַז   to lay hold of, to take, to seize, especially with the hand; *constr. c. acc.* of the person or thing; often also *seq.* בְּ. Permanent holding is expressed by בְּ after this verb; momentary seizing sometimes with בְּ sometimes without; of any disease or affection of the mind always without.—*Gussetius. Metaph.* ascribed also to terror, fear; but also, *vice versâ,* one is said, as in English, to take fright, see *Affright ;* to take, to catch, *e. g.* in hunting; to hold, to hold fast, that which one has taken hold of, *seq.* בְּ and *acc.* ; to take out, or away, from a larger number, whence *part. passive,* taken out, taken, *sc.* from a lot or portion: Num. xxxi. 3, &c. KAL [a] *pret.* [b] *inf.* [c] *imp.* [d] *fut.* [e] *part.* Poel. [f] *part.* Paül. NIPHAL [g] *imp.* [h] *part.*

3   אָסַף   to collect, to gather; to take to oneself, to receive, especially to one's hospitality and protection; to take back or away, especially that which one has formerly given. KAL [a] *pret.* [b] *imp.* [c] *fut.* NIPHAL [d] *pret.* [e] *fut.* [f] *part.* PIEL [g] *part.*

4   אָצַל   *pr.* to put aside; hence *seq.* מִן to take from or of anything. KAL [a] *pret.* HIPHIL [b] *fut.*

5   בּוֹא   to come; to bring in. HIPHIL [a] *pret.* [b] *imp.* [c] *fut.*

6   בָּזַז   to prey, to spoil, *i. e.* to seize as prey, to plunder; *abs.* with an *acc.* of the prey, to seize as prey, to carry off as spoil; and with an *acc.* of a city, country, person; see *Spoil.* KAL [a] *pret.* [b] *inf.* [c] *fut.*

7   בָּעַר   to consume; to take or put away, to remove, to destroy. PIEL [a] *pret.* [b] *fut.* HIPHIL [c] *part.*

8   גָּזָה   to cut off; to pluck out or extract. KAL *part.* Poel, Ps. lxxi. 6, *excisor meus.* This is the interpretation of more ancient critics, supposed to be an allusion to the cutting of the umbilical cord; probably it is to be preferred to the many modern renderings of this difficult word.

9 גָּזַל to pluck off or away, to tear away, to take by force; by open violence; oftener by fraud or injustice of any kind, e.g. the property or possessions of others, to seize upon or to take by force, to claim as one's own, especially of the rich and powerful who seize upon the possessions of the poor by fraud and violence. KAL [a] *pret.* [b] *inf.* [c] *fut.* [d] *part.* Paül. NIPHAL [e] *pret.* [f] גָּזֵל *m.* rapine.

10 גִּיחַ to break forth; to bring forth. KAL *part.*

11 גָּרַע to take off; to take away, to detract, to withhold. KAL [a] *inf.* NIPHAL [b] *pret.* [c] *fut.*

12 דָּבַק to cleave; to come upon, to overtake, befall. KAL *fut.*

13 הָנָה to separate, take away. KAL *inf.* for *imp.* Prov. xxv. 4, 5. Symm. κάθαιρε. Vulg. *aufer.*

14 הָלַךְ to go. KAL *part.* Poel.

15 חָזַק to hold fast; to lay hold of, to take, to seize, a person or thing, *seq.* בְּ of person or thing, also *seq.* לְ and עַל. HIPHIL [a] *pret.* [b] *inf.* [c] *imp.* [d] *part.*

16 חָלַץ to draw out, to take away. PIEL *fut.*

17 חָשַׂף to lay bare; applied to the scooping or scraping of a small quantity of water that remains at the bottom of a pit or cistern, with a thin potsherd. KAL *inf.*

18 חָתָה to lay hold, to seize; to take up. KAL [a] *inf.* [b] *fut.*

19 חָתַף to catch, to seize, in the manner of a lion. KAL *fut.*

20 יָאַל to will, to desire; see *Will, Content.* HIPHIL *pret.*

21 יָהַב to give, to set, to put. KAL *imp.*

22 יָלַךְ to go. KAL [a] *imp.* HIPHIL [b] *imp.*

23 יָעַץ to counsel; to give or take (counsel): see *Counsel.*

24 יָצָא to go out; to take out. HIPHIL *fut.*

25 יָרַד to go down; to take down. HIPHIL [a] *pret.* [b] *fut.* HOPHAL [c] *pret.*

26 יָרַשׁ to take possession of. KAL *inf.*

27 יָשַׁב to dwell; to make to dwell, to marry, to take wives. HIPHIL [a] *pret.* [b] *fut.*

28 כָּלָה to be finished, brought to an end; to be quite taken away. PIEL *fut.*

29 לָכַד to take by force or strength, by skill or stratagem; to catch, *sc.* animals, *e.g.* in a net, snares, &c., to take, or seize possession of, to take captive in war; to take a city by assault; to take or occupy; to take, to choose any one by lot. KAL [a] *pret.* [b] *inf.* [c] *imp.* [d] *fut.* [e] *part.* Poel. NIPHAL [f] *pret.* [g] *fut.* [h] *part.* [i] לָכַד *m.* a being taken, capture.

30 לָפַת to bend, to turn, to fold; to enfold, to embrace, to clasp, or to gather up oneself for exertion of strength; see *Turn.* KAL *fut.* Judg. xvi. 29. LXX. περιέλαβε. Vulg. *apprehendens.*

31 לָקַח (1) to take, *i. q.* λαμβάνω; properly to take with the hand, to lay hold of; *seq. acc.* of the person, and בְּ of the member or part; rarely *seq.* לְ of person, Jer. xl. 2; then, *i. q.* to take to oneself, to assume, *c. acc.* of thing or person, Gen. ii. 15, 21, &c. In these and similar examples לקח appears as if pleonastic, though it strictly serves to place the action more fully and vividly before the eyes. In Jer. xxiii. 31 it seems to signify that the false prophets misused their tongues. To the object is often prefixed מִן partitive, to take of a thing. Specially to take a wife; to take away, sometimes with violence and force; to take possession, to capture, to seize upon, also to take or captivate any one with blandishments, wisdom, &c.; to take a person anywhere, to lead, to bring; to take and bring to any one, to fetch, often to fetch by another, to let come. (2) to take, *i. q.* δέχομαι, to accept, to receive; to take in, to receive; to receive, *i. e.* to get, to obtain; to perceive, *sc.* with the ears. This word has frequently an implied meaning, as to take and bring, to take and give, to take and offer. KAL [a] *pret.* [b] *inf.* [c] *imp.* [d] *fut.* [e] *part.* Poel. NIPHAL [f] *pret.* [g] *inf.* [h] *fut.* PUAL [i] *pret.* HOPHAL [k] *fut.* [l] מִקָּח *m.* accepting (of gifts).

32 מוּשׁ to depart. HIPHIL *fut.*

33 מָלָא to fill. PIEL *fut.*

34 מָצָא to find. KAL *pret.*

35 נָטָה to stretch out; to turn, to take aside. HIPHIL *fut.*

36 נָטַל to take up, to lift up. KAL *fut.* Isa. xl. 15. See Vitringa *in loc.*

37 נָסַג to shrink back; to remove a boundary. KAL [a] *fut.* HIPHIL [b] *fut.*

38 נְסַק Ch. to ascend; to cause to go up. APHEL [a] *pret.* [b] *inf.* HOPHAL [c] *pret.*

39 נְפַק Ch. to go forth; to take out. APHEL *pret.*

40 נָצַל to deliver, to rescue; to take away, with power and great exertion out of tumult and difficulty, to take as from an enemy: a term answering to ῥῦσαι in the Lord's Prayer. Matt. vi. 13: Luke xi. 4. NIPHAL [a] *fut.* HIPHIL [b] *pret.* [c] *fut.*

41 נָקַם to avenge; to take (vengeance). KAL [a] *inf.* NIPHAL [b] *fut.* PIEL [c] *pret.*

42 נָשָׂא to take up, to lift up, to raise; also simply to take or receive; to lift up anything with the voice, *e.g.* to take up the name of God, *i.e.* on the lips, to take up a parable, *i.e.* to pronounce with earnestness; to utter, to declare; to take, to take away. KAL [a] *pret.* [b] *inf.* [c] *imp.* [d] *fut.* [e] *part.* Poel. NIPHAL [f] *pret.* PIEL [g] *pret.* נְשָׂא Ch. P'AL [h] *imp.*

43 נָשַׂג to overtake; to take hold of. HIPHIL [a] *pret.* [b] *fut.*

44 נָתַן to give; to put, place. KAL [a] *fut.* HOPHAL [b] *fut.*

45 סוּר to depart; to turn aside or away. KAL [a] *pret.* [b] *fut.* HIPHIL [c] *pret.* [d] *inf.* [e] *imp.* [f] *fut.* [g] *part.* HOPHAL [h] *pret.* [i] *fut.* [k] *part.*

46 סוּת to incite, to impel, to move, often in a bad sense; to seduce. HIPHIL *fut.* Job xxxvi. 18. There is great difficulty in this passage, but usually rendered, " if there be anger (from God) beware lest he lead thee forth (drive thee out) with chastisement ; then great ransom cannot turn thee away," *sc.* from punishment.

47 עָבַר to pass; to cause to pass. HIPHIL [a] *pret.* [b] *imp.* [c] *fut.*

48 עָדָה to pass, to depart; to cause to pass, to remove. HIPHIL [a] *part.* עֲדָה Ch. APHEL [b] *pret.* [c] *fut.*

49 עוּד to testify; to cause to testify, to call as witness. HIPHIL ᵃ inf. ᵇ imp. ᶜ fut.

50 עוּץ to consult, to take counsel. KAL imp.

51 עָלָה to ascend; to take up. KAL ᵃ fut. NIPHAL ᵇ pret. ᶜ inf. ᵈ fut. HIPHIL ᵉ pret. ᶠ inf. ᵍ fut.

52 עִמָּדִי part. prep. Job xxiii. 10, "the way that I take," marg. ' (is) with me.'

53 עָמַל to labour. KAL ᵃ pret. ᵇ fut. ᶜ עָמֵל adj. labouring.

54 עָשָׂה to do. KAL ᵃ pret. ᵇ inf.

55 פּוּר to break; to make void. HIPHIL fut.

56 צוּד to hunt. KAL ᵃ imp. ᵇ part. HITHPAEL ᶜ pret. ᵈ צַיִד m. taken in hunting.

57 צָעַן to load upon beasts of burden; hence to remove, to migrate, as nomades. KAL fut.

58 קָבַל to be before. PIEL pr. to let come to oneself, to receive, to take. PIEL ᵃ pret. ᵇ fut. HIPHIL ᶜ part. ᵈ קְבֵל Ch. PAEL pret. ᵉ fut.

59 קָבַץ to take or grasp in the hand; to take or fold in the arms. PIEL part.

60 קָמַץ to press together; to take with the hand. KAL pret.

61 קָפַץ to draw together, to contract, to shut up; in some sense this seems to be applied to death, in which men draw together their limbs; or rather as a general term for being gathered to the dead, or taken away from this world. NIPHAL fut.

62 קָרַב to come near. HIPHIL imp.

63 רָבָה to multiply, to take much. HIPHIL fut.

64 רָדָה to tread down, to break; to break off, to take out or away. KAL ᵃ pret. ᵇ fut.

65 רוּם to lift up; to take up or away. HIPHIL ᵃ pret. Dan. viii. 11, כְּתִיב, lit. according to כ, "he took away the daily sacrifice." ᵇ imp. ᶜ fut. ᵈ part. HOPHAL ᵉ pret. ᶠ fut.

66 שָׁבָה to take captive; see Captive. KAL ᵃ pret. ᵇ fut. ᶜ שְׁבִי m. captivity.

67 שָׁבַת to cease; to cause to cease. HIPHIL fut.

68 שׁוּב to return. HIPHIL ᵃ pret. ᵇ inf. ᶜ imp.

69 שׂוּם to put or place. KAL ᵃ imp. ᵇ fut.

70 שִׁית to set, put, place; seq. בְּ. KAL fut.

71 שָׁלַל to take spoil; see Spoil. KAL ᵃ pret. ᵇ inf.

72 שָׁלָה to draw out. KAL fut. Job xxvii. 8, when God shall draw out his spirit, sc. from his body as a sheath, i. e. shall take away his soul; so Chald. and Syr.

73 תָּמַךְ to take hold of. KAL pret.

74 תָּפַשׂ to lay hold of any one, to seize, seq. acc. and בְּ of things; seq. בְּ, to lay hold of any one by way of entreaty. Trop. to lay hold upon the name of Jehovah, Prov. xxx. 9, i. e. unlawfully and unwarrantably to do violence to the name of God by falsehood and perjury; comp. deny in the preceding member. Hence to take in war, to capture men, cities. To hold, to have in possession; trop. to practise war, Num. xxxi. 27. KAL ᵃ pret. ᵇ inf. ᶜ imp. ᵈ fut. ᵉ part. Poel. NIPHAL ᶠ pret. ᵍ inf. ʰ fut. PIEL ⁱ fut.

Gen.		Exod.		Num.	
ii. 15, 21.	31 d	vii. 15.	31 d	i. 51.	25 b
ii. 22.	31 a	viii. 8.	45 f	iii. 12, 41, 50.	31 a
ii. 23.	3 i	ix. 8.	31 c	iii. 40.	42 c
iii. 6.	31 d	ix. 10.	31 d	iii. 45.	31 c
iii. 19, 23.	31 i	x. 17.	45 f	iii. 47, 47.	31 a d
iii. 22.	31 a	x. 19.	42 d	iii. 49.	31 d
iv. 19.	31 d	x. 26.	31 d	iv. 2, 22.	42 b
v. 24.	31 a	xii. 3, 5.	31 a	iv. 5.	25 a
vi. 2.	31 d	xii. 4, 7, 22.	31 a	iv. 9, 12.	31 a
vi. 21.	31 c	xii. 21, 32.	31 c	v. 13.	74 f
vii. 2.	31 d	xii. 34.	42 d	v. 17, 17.	31 a d
viii. 9, 20.	31 d	xiii. 19.	31 d	v. 25.	31 a
ix. 23.	31 d	xiii. 22.	32	v. 26.	60
xi. 29, 31.	31 d	xiv. 6, 11.	31 a	vi. 18, 19.	31 a
xii. 5.	31 d	xiv. 7.	31 d	vii. 5.	31 c
xii. 15.	31 k	xiv. 25.	45 f	vii. 6.	31 d
xii. 19, 19.	31 d c	xv. 14. a	2 a	viii. 6.	31 c
xiv. 11, 12, 23, 24.	31 d	xv. 15.	2 d	viii. 8, 8.	31 a d
xiv. 21.	31 c	xv. 20.	31 d	viii. 16.	31 a
xv. 9.	31 c	xvi. 16.	31 d	viii. 18.	31 d
xv. 10.	31 d	xvi. 33.	31 c	ix. 17, 22.	51 c
xvi. 3.	31 d	xvii. 5, 5.	31 c	ix. 21, 21.	51 b
xvii. 23.	31 d	xvii. 12.	31 d	x. 11.	51 b
xviii. 8.	31 d	xviii. 2, 12.	31 d	x. 17.	25 c
xviii. 27, 31.	20	xx. 7, 7.	42 d	xi. 17.	4 a
xix. 15.	31 c	xx. 10, 14.	31 d	xi. 25.	4 b
xix. 19.	12	xxiii. 8.	31 d	xvi. 1, 18, 39, 47.	31 d
xx. 2, 14.	31 d	xxiii. 25.	45 c	xvi. 6, 17, 46.	31 c
xx. 3.	31 a	xxiv. 6, 7, 8.	31 d	xvi. 15.	42 a
xxi. 14, 21, 27, 30.	31 d	xxv. 2, 3.	31 a	xvi. 37.	65 c
xxi. 25.	9 a	xxv. 15.	45 b	xvii. 2.	31 c
xxii. 2.	31 c	xxvi. 5.	58 c	xvii. 9.	31 d
xxii. 3, 6, 6, 10, 13.	31 d	xxviii. 1.	62	xvii. 10.	28
xxiii. 13.	31 c	xxviii. 5.	31 a	xviii. 6.	31 a
xxiv. 3, 10, 22, 37, 61, 65, 67.	31 d	xxviii. 9.	31 a	xviii. 26.	61 d
xxiv. 4, 7, 7, 38, 40.	31 a	xxix. 1.	31 d	xix. 4, 6, 17, 18.	31 d
xxiv. 4C.	31 b	xxix. 5, 7, 12, 13, 16, 19, 20, 21, 22, 26.	31 a	xix. 8, 25.	31 c
xxiv. 51.	31 c			xx. 9.	31 d
xxv. 1.	31 d	xxix. 15, 31.	31 d	xxi. 1.	66 b
xxv. 20.	31 b	xxx. 12.	42 d	xxi. 7.	45 f
xxv. 26.	2 e	xxx. 16.	31 d	xxi. 25, 26.	31 d
xxvi. 34.	31 d	xxx. 23, 34.	31 c	xxi. 32.	29 d
xxvii. 3, 3.	42 c, 56 a	xxxii. 20.	31 d	xxii. 41.	31 d
xxvii. 15, 35.	31 d	xxxii. 7.	31 d	xxiii. 7, 18.	42 d
xxvii. 33.	56 b	xxxiii. 23.	45 c	xxiii. 11.	31 a
xxvii. 36, 36.	31 a	xxxiv. 4.	31 d	xxiv. 3, 15, 20, 21, 23.	42 d
xxvii. 46.	31 e	xxxiv. 16.	31 a	xxv. 4.	31 c
xxviii. 1, 9, 11, 18.	31 d	xxxiv. 34.	45 f	xxv. 7.	31 d
xxviii. 2.	31 c	xxxv. 5.	31 c	xxvi. 2.	42 c
xxviii. 6, 6.	31 b d	xl. 9.	31 d	xxvii. 18.	31 c
xxix. 23.	31 d	xl. 20.	31 d	xxvii. 22.	31 d
xxx. 9, 37.	31 d	xl. 36.	51 c	xxxi. 11, 29, 30, 47, 51, 54.	31 d
xxx. 15, 15.	31 b	xl. 37, 37.	51 d c	xxxi. 26, 26.	42 c, 66 c
xxx. 23.	3 a	Lev. ii. 2.	60	xxxi. 27.	74 e
xxxi. 1, 34.	31 a	ii. 9.	45 f	xxxi. 49.	42 a
xxxi. 9.	40 c	iii. 4, 9, 10, 15.	45 f	xxxii. 39, 41, 42.	29 d
xxxi. 16.	40 b	iv. 5, 25, 30, 34.	31 a	xxxiv. 18.	31 d
xxxi. 23, 45, 46, 50.	31 d	iv. 8, 19.	65 c	xxxv. 31, 32.	31 d
xxxi. 31.	9 c	iv. 9.	45 c	xxxvi. 3, 3.	11 b c
xxxi. 32.	31 c	iv. 10.	65 f	xxxvi. 4.	11 c
xxxii. 13, 22, 23.	31 d	iv. 31, 31.	45 f h	Deut. i. 13.	21
xxxiii. 11, 11.	31 c d	iv. 35, 35.	45 f i	i. 15, 23, 25.	31 d
xxxiv. 2, 9, 16, 21, 25, 26.	31 d	v. 12.	60	ii. 34.	29 d
xxxiv. 17, 28.	31 a	vi. 2.	9 f	iii. 35, 35.	6 a, 29 a
xxxvi. 2.	31 a	vi. 4.	9 a	iii. 4, 4.	29 d, 31 a
xxxvi. 6.	31 d	vi. 10, 15.	65 a	iii. 8.	31 d
xxxvii. 24, 31.	31 d	vii. 4.	45 f	iii. 14.	31 a
xxxvii. 2, 6, 23, 28.	31 d	vii. 34.	31 a	iv. 20.	31 a
xxxix. 20.	31 d	viii. 2.	31 c	iv. 34.	31 b
xl. 11.	31 d	viii. 10, 15, 16, 23, 25, 28, 29, 30.	31 d	v. 11, 11.	42 d
xli. 42.	45 f	ix. 2, 3.	31 c	vii. 3.	31 d
xlii. 24, 36.	31 d	ix. 15.	31 d	vii. 15.	45 c
xlii. 30.	31 c	ix. 17.	33	ix. 25.	31 a
xlii. 33.	31 c	x. 1.	31 d	ix. 17.	74 d
xliii. 11, 12, 13.	31 d	x. 12.	31 c	ix. 21.	31 a
xliii. 15, 15.	31 d a	xiv. 4, β 12, 14, 15, 21, 24, 25, 42, 49, 51.		x. 11.	22 a
xliii. 18.	31 b			x. 17.	31 d
xliii. 34.	42 d		31 a	xii. 26.	42 d
xliv. 11.	25 b	xiv. 6, 10.	31 d	xv. 17.	31 a
xliv. 29.	31 a	xiv. 40, 43.	16	xvi. 19.	31 d
xlv. 18, 19.	31 c	xiv. 42, 42.	31 a d	xx. 7, 7.	31 a d
xlvi. 6.	31 c	xv. 14, 29.	31 d	xx. 14.	46 c
xlvii. 2.	31 d	xvi. 5.	31 d	xx. 19.	74 b
xlviii. 1, 13.	31 d	xvi. 7, 12, 14, 18.	31 a	xxi. 3.	31 a
xlviii. 22.	31 a	xvi. 7, 12, 14, 18.	31 a	xxi. 10.	66 a
Exod. ii. 1, 3.	31 d	xviii. 17, 18.	31 d	xxii. 6, 7, 13, 30.	31 d
ii. 9, 9.	22 b, 31 d	xx. 14, 17, 21.	31 d	xxiii. 14, 15, 18.	31 a
iv. 4.	2 c	xxi. 7, 7, 13, 14, 14.	31 d	xxiv. 1.	31 a
iv. 6.	24	xxiii. 40.	31 a	xxiv. 3.	31 a
iv. 9, 9.	31 d	xxiv. 5.	31 a	xxiv. 4.	31 a
iv. 17, 20, 20, 25.	31 d	xxiv. 36.	31 d	xxiv. 5, 5.	31 d a
vi. 7, 25.	31 d	Num. i. 2.	42 c	xxv. 5.	31 a
vi. 20, 23.	31 d	i. 17.	31 d	xxv. 7, 8.	31 b
vii. 9, 19.	31 c	i. 49.	42 d	xxv. 11.	15 a

Jer. xv. 15.	31 d	Jer. lii. 9.	74 d	Ezek. xlv. 18.	31 d	Exod. v. 8.	6 a
xv. 19.	24	lii. 18, 19, 25.	31 a	xlv. 19.	31 a	v. 18.	6
xvi. 2.	31 d	lii. 24, 26.	31 d	xlvi. 18.	31 d	Lev. xix. 16.	5
xvi. 5.	3 a	Lam. iv. 20.	29 f	Dan. i. 16.	42 e	1 Chron. ix. 28.	3
xviii. 22.	29 b	v. 31.	42 a	iii. 22.	38 a	Ps. xc. 9.	1
xx. 5.	31 a	Ezek. iii. 12.	42 d	v. 2, 3.	39	Prov. xi. 13.	2, 5
xx. 10.	31 d	iii. 14.	31 d	v. 20.	48 b	xviii. 8.	4
xxv. 9.	31 a	iv. 1, 3, 9.	31 c	v. 31.	58 d	Prov. xx. 19.	5
xxv. 10.	1	v. 1, 1, 1.	31 c d a	vi. 23, 23.	28 b c	xxvi. 20, 22.	4
xxv. 15.	31 c	v. 2, 3.	31 a	vii. 12.	48 b	Ezek. xxii. 9.	5
xxv. 17.	31 d	v. 4.	31 d	vii. 18.	58 e		
xxv. 28.	31 b	viii. 3.	31 d	vii. 26.	48 c		
xxvi. 8.	74 d	x. 6.	31 c	viii. 11.	65 e, or a		
xxvii. 20.	31 a	x. 7, 7.	42 d, 31 d	xi. 12.	42 f		
xxviii. 3.	31 a	xi. 18, 19.	45 c	xi. 15, 18.	29 a		
xxviii. 10.	31 d	xi. 24.	42 a	xi. 31.	45 c		
xxix. 6, 6.	31 c	xii. 13.	74 f	xii. 11.	45 h		
xxix. 22.	31 i	xv. 3, 3.	31 k d	Hos. i. 2.	31 c		
xxxi. 32.	15 b	xvi. 16, 17, 18,		i. 6.	42 b d		
xxxii. 3, 28.	29 a	20, 32.	31 d	ii. 9.	31 a		
xxxii. 10.	49 c	xvi. 39.	31 a	ii. 17.	45 c		
xxxii. 11.	31 d	xvi. 50.	45 f	iv. 3.	3 e		
xxxii. 14.	31 b	xvii. 3, 5, 12.	31 d	iv. 11.	31 d		
xxxii. 24.	29 b	13.	31 d	v. 14.	42 d		
xxxii. 25.	49 b	xvii. 20.	74 f	xi. 3.	31 b		
xxxii. 44.	49 a	xvii. 22.	31 a	xi. 4.	65 d		
xxxiii. 26.	31 b	xviii. 8.	31 d	xiii. 11.	31 d		
xxxiv. 3.	74 b h	xviii. 13.	31 a	xiv. 2, 2.	31 e, 42 d		
xxxiv. 22.	29 a	xviii. 17.	68 a	Joel iii. 5.	31 a		
xxxv. 3.	31 d	xix. 1.	42 c	Amos iii. 4.	29 a		
xxxvi. 2, 28. θ	31 c	xix. 4, 8.	74 f	iii. 5.	51 a		
xxxvi. 14, 14.	31 c d	xix. 5.	31 d	iii. 5.	29 b d		
xxxvi. 21.	31 d	xxi. 21.	74 a	iii. 12, 12.	40 c a		
xxxvi. 26.	31 b	xxi. 24.	74 h	iv. 2.	42 g		
xxxvi. 32.	31 a	xxi. 26.	65 b	iv. 10.	66 c		
xxxvii. 8.	29 a	xxii. 12, 12.	31 a	v. 1.	42 e		
xxxvii. 13, 14.	74 d	xxii. 25.	31 d	v. 11.	31 d		
xxxvii. 17.	31 d	xxiii. 10, 26, 29.	31 a	v. 12.	31 e		
xxxviii. 3.	29 a	xxiii. 25, 25.	45 f, 31 d	v. 23.	45 e		
xxxviii. 6, 11, 11,		xxiv. 5, 25.	31 b	vi. 10.	42 a		
14.	31 d	xxiv. 8.	41 a	vi. 13.	31 a		
xxxviii. 10, 10.	31 c, 51 e	xxiv. 16.	31 e	vii. 15.	31 a		
xxxviii. 13.	51 g	xxv. 12.	41 a	ix. 2.	31 a		
xxxviii. 23.	74 h	xxv. 15.	41 b	ix. 3.	31 a		
xxxviii. 28, 28.	29 f	xxvi. 17.	42 a	Jonah i. 12.	42 c		
xxxix. 5, 14.	31 d	xxvii. 2.	42 c	i. 15.	42 d		
xxxix. 12.	31 c	xxvii. 5.	31 a	i. 15.	31 c		
xl. 1.	31 b	xxvii. 32.	42 a	Micah ii. 2, 2.	9 a, 42 a		
xl. 2.	31 d	xxviii. 12.	42 a	ii. 4.	42 d		
xl. 10.	74 a	xxix. 7.	74 b	ii. 6.	37 a		
xli. 12, 16.	31 d	xxix. 19, 19, 19. {	42 a, 71 a	ii. 9.	31 d		
xliii. 5.	31 d	xxx. 4.	31 a	iv. 9.	15 a		
xliii. 9.	31 c	xxxi. 2.	42 c	iv. 10.	37 b		
xliii. 10.	31 a	xxxiii. 2.	31 a	Hab. i. 10.	29 d		
xliv. 12.	31 a	xxxiii. 6, 6.	31 d f	i. 15.	51 e		
xlvi. 11.	31 c	xxxvi. 3.	51 d	ii. 6.	42 d		
xlviii. 1, 41.	29 f	xxxvi. 24.	31 a	Zeph. iii. 11.	45 f		
xlviii. 7, 44.	29 g	xxxvi. 26.	45 c	iii. 15.	45 c		
xlviii. 33.	3 d	xxxvii. 16, 16.	31 c	Hag. ii. 23.	31 d		
xlviii. 46.	31 i	xxxvii. 19, 21.	31 c	Zech. i. 6.	43 a		
xlix. 20, 30.	23	xxxviii. 12, 12.	71 b, 6 b	v. 8.	45 e		
xlix. 24.	2 a	xxxviii. 13, {	71 b, 6 b,	vi. 10.	31 b		
xlix. 29, 29.	31 d, 42 d	13, 13, 13. {	31 b, 71 b	vi. 11.	31 a		
l. 2, 24.	29	xxxix. 10.	42 d	viii. 23, 23.	15 d a		
l. 9.	29 g	xliii. 5.	42 d	ix. 7.	45 c		
l. 43.	15 a	xliii. 20, 21.	31 a	x. 7, 10, 13.	31 d		
l. 45.	23	xliv. 22, 22.	31 d	xi. 15.	31 c		
l. 46.	74 f	xlv. 9.	65 b	xiv. 2.	29 f		
li. 8.	31 c			xiv. 21.	31 a		
li. 26.	31 d			Mal. ii. 3.	42 a		
li. 31, 41, 56.	29 f						
li. 36.	41 c						

α or, has taken hold.   β lit. and take.   γ "we took (for) our provision." δ i.e. suspended between, &c.   ε lit. returned and took.   ζ lit. taken, taken for Ithamar.   η lit. to take away.   θ lit. return take thee.   ι lit. take to them for wives.

TALE, TALE-BEARER

1   הֶגֶה   m. meditation, thought.

2   הָלַךְ   to walk. KAL part. Poel.

3   מִסְפָּר   m. narration; number.

4   נִרְגָּן   m. garrulous; whisperer, tale-bearer, calumniator.

5   רָכִיל   m. a tale-bearer, slanderer, defamer; properly, one who goes about for slander.

6   תֹּכֶן   m. a task as weighed or measured out. a מַתְכֹּנֶת f. measure; daily task or tale.

TALENT

כִּכָּר f. a talent, from its round, flat form, a weight equal to 3,000 shekels of the sanctuary, as appears from Exod. xxxviii. 25, 26; of silver, equal to about £350 of our money; of gold, about £5,075.—Exod. xxv. 39, &c. כַּכְּרִין Ch. f. pl. Ezra vii. 22.

TALK

1   אָמַר   to say. KAL fut.

2   דָּבַר   to speak. KAL a part. Poel. NIPHAL b part. PIEL c pret. d inf. e fut. f part. g דָּבָר m. word; "talk of the lips," inconsiderate speech. Comp. ῥῆμα ἀργόν, St. Matt. xii. 36.

3   הָגָה   to meditate; to speak of. KAL fut.

4   לָשׁוֹן   com. tongue.

5   מִלָּה   word, speech, discourse.

6   סָפַר   to number, recount; to tell, declare. PIEL fut.

7   פֶּה   m. mouth.

8   שִׂיחַ   to speak, to talk, to converse largely. KAL a imp. b fut. c שִׂיחַ m. speech.

9   שָׂפָה   f. lip; "a man full of talk," marg. 'a man of lips.'

Gen. iv. 8.	1	1 Kings i. 14, 22.	2 f	Ps. cxix. 27.	8 b
xvii. 3.	2 e	xviii. 27.	8 c	cxlv. 11.	2 e
xvii. 22.	2 d	2 Kings ii. 11.	2 d	Prov. vi. 22.	8 b
xxxv. 13, 14.	2 e	vi. 33.	2 f	xiv. 23.	2 g
xlv. 15.	2 c	viii. 4.	2 c	xxiv. 2.	2 e
Exod. xx. 22.	2 c	xviii. 26.	2 e	Eccles. x. 13.	7
xxxiii. 9.	2 c	1 Chron. xvi. 9.	8 a	Jer. xii. 1.	2 c
xxxiv. 29.	2 d	2 Chron. xxv. 16.	2 d	xxxviii. 25.	2 c
xxxiv. 31.	2 c	Esth. vi. 14.	2 f	xxxiii. 30.	2 b
Num. xi. 17.	2 c	Job xi. 2.	9	Dan. ix. 22.	3
Deut. v. 4.	2 e	xiii. 7.	2 c	x. 17.	2 d
v. 24.	2 e	xv. 3.	2 g	Zech. i. 9, 13, 19.	2 a
vi. 7.	2 d	xxxi. 9.	5	iii. 3.	2 a
Judg. vi. 17.	2 f	Ps. xxxvii. 30.	2 e	iv. 1, 4, 5.	2 a
xiv. 7.	2 e	lxix. 26.	6	v. 5, 10.	2 a
1 Sam. ii. 3.	2 e	lxxi. 24.	3	vi. 4.	2 a
xiv. 19.	2 e	lxxvii. 12.	8 b		
xvii. 23.	2 f	cv. 2.	8 a		

TALL

קוֹמָה f. stature; height: 2 Kings xix. 23: Isa. xxxvii. 24.

רוּם to be lifted up; to be tall. KAL part. Poel, Deut. i. 28; ii. 10, 21; ix. 2.

TAPESTRY

מַרְבַדִּים m. pl. coverlets, "coverings of tapestry:" Prov. vii. 16; xxxi. 22.

TARGET

כִּידוֹן m. a small shield; rather, a spear; see Spear: 1 Sam. xvii. 6, marg. 'or, gorget.'

צִנָּה f. a shield of a large size, covering the whole body; θυρεός: 1 Kings x. 16, 16: 2 Chron. ix. 15, 15; xiv. 8.

TARRY

1   אָחַר   to be after, to stay behind, to tarry beyond a due time; to hinder, to linger, to stay long, to tarry late in or by

anything, *seq.* עַל. KAL ^a*fut.* (קרי). PIEL ^b*pret.* ^c*fut.* ^d*part.*

2 אָרַךְ to be long; to prolong. HIPHIL *inf.*

3 דָּמַם to be dumb, silent, still; to rest, to cease, to leave off. KAL *imp.*

4 חגל see *Abide.* KAL and HIPHIL *fut.*

5 חָכָה to look; to look for, to tarry. PIEL ^a*pret.* ^b*fut.*

6 יָחַל to stay, to delay, to wait in hope or expectation of some benefit or advantage. NIPHAL ^a*fut.* (כתיב). HIPHIL ^b*fut.*

7 יָחַר to tarry, to delay. KAL *fut.* (כתיב).

8 יָשַׁב to sit down; to remain, to abide, to tarry. KAL ^a*pret.* ^b*inf.* ^c*imp.* ^d*fut.* ^e*part.* Poel.

9 כּוּן to set; to be established. NIPHAL *fut.*

10 לִין to pass the night, to remain over night; to abide, remain, dwell. KAL ^a*inf.* ^b*imp.* ^c*fut.*

11 מָהַהּ to linger, to tarry, *pr.* asking, what? what? like our shall I? shall I? HITHPALPEL ^a*pret.* ^b*inf.* ^c*fut.* ^d*part.*

12 נָוֶה *f.* inhabiting, properly of a wife remaining at home, in *opp.* to the husband going abroad in his occupation, and to the unchaste woman; Gr. οἰκουρός, *custos domi;* comp. Tit. ii. 5.

13 עָמַד to stand; to stand still. KAL *fut.*

14 קָוָה to wait. PIEL *fut.*

15 שָׂבַר to look; to expect, to wait for. PIEL *fut.*

Gen. xix. 2.	10 b	Ruth i. 13.	15	2 Sam. xx. 5.	1 a, or 7	
xxiv. 54.	10 c	ii. 7.	8 b	2 Kings ii. 2, 4, 6.	8 c	
xxvii. 44.	8 a	iii. 13.	10 b	ii. 18.	8 e	
xxviii. 11.	10 c	1 Sam. i. 23.	8 c	vii. 9.	5 a	
xxxi. 54.	10 c	x. 8.	8 c	ix. 3.	5 b	
xlv. 9.	13	xiii. 13.	6 a, or b	xiv. 10.	8 c	
Exod. xii. 39.	11 b	xiv. 2.	8 e	1 Chron. xix. 5.	8 c	
xxiv. 14.	8 c	xiv. 9.	3	xx. 1.	8 c	
Lev. xiv. 8.	8 a	xxx. 24.	8 e	Ps. xl. 17.	1 c	
Num. ix. 19, 22.	2	2 Sam. x. 5.	8 c	lxviii. 12. a	12	
xxii. 19.	8 c	xi. 1.	8 e	lxx. 5.	1 c	
Judg. iii. 25.	4	xi. 12.	8 c	ci. 7.	1 c	
iii. 26.	11 b	xv. 17.	13	Prov. xxiii. 30.	1 d	
v. 28.	1 b	xv. 28.	11 d	Isa. xlvi. 13.	1 c	
vi. 18.	8 d	xv. 29.	8 d	Jer. xiv. 8.	10 a	
xix. 6, 9.	10 b	xviii. 14.	6 b	Micah v. 7.	14	
xix. 8.	11 a	xix. 7.	10 c	Hab. ii. 3, 3.	11 c, 1 c	
xix. 10.	10 a					

a lit. the inhabitress of the house.

TASK

1 דָּבָר *m.* word, matter.

2 חֹק *m.* an appointed portion of labour.

3 מַס *m.* tribute; burden, onerous service; imposed in the place of tribute; "taskmasters," *lit.* princes of tribute.

4 נָגַשׂ to exact. KAL *part.* Poel.

Exod. i. 11.		3	Exod. v. 6, 10.	4	Exod. v. 14, 14.	4, 2
iii. 7.		4	v. 13, 13.	4, 1	v. 19.	1

TASTE

1 חֵךְ *m.* the palate; the organ of taste.

2 טָעַם to taste, *i.e.* to try the flavour, to eat a little, to have the sense of taste, to perceive the flavour. In Dan. v. 2 a larger use seems implied. Vulg. *temulentus.* KAL ^a*pret.* ^b*inf.* ^c*imp.* ^d*fut.* ^eטַעַם *m.* taste. ^fטְעֵם Ch. *m. id.*

Exod. xvi. 31.	2 e	Job vi. 6.	2 e	Prov. xxiv. 13.	1	
Num. xi. 8, 8.	2 e	vi. 30.	1	Cant. ii. 3.	1	
1 Sam. xiv. 24, 29.	2 a	xii. 11.	2 d	Jer. xlviii. 11.	2 e	
xiv. 43.	2 b a	xxxiv. 3.	2 d	Dan. v. 2.	2 f	
2 Sam. iii. 35.	2 d	Ps. xxxiv. 8.	2 c	Jonah iii. 7.	2 d	
xix. 35.	2 d	cxix. 103.	1			

TAUNT

גְּדוּפָה *f.* reproach, reviling; the verb is always used of blasphemy against God: Ezek. v. 15.

מְלִיצָה *f.* an interpretation; a song of derision: Hab. ii. 6.

שְׁנִינָה *f.* a sharp, pointed saying; hence mockery, derision: Jer. xxiv. 9.

TAX

נָגַשׂ to exact. KAL *part.* Poel, Dan. xi. 20, "raiser of taxes," *marg.* 'one that causeth an exactor to pass over.'

עָרַךְ to set in order, to compare, to estimate, to value. HIPHIL *pret.* 2 Kings xxiii. 35. עֵרֶךְ *m.* estimation: 2 Kings xxiii. 35.

TEACH

1 אָלַף to learn; to cause to learn. PIEL ^a*fut.* ^b*part.*

2 בִּין to understand; to make to understand. HIPHIL ^a*part.* ^bמְבוֹנִים *m. pl.* wisdom, for *concr.* wise teachers (כתיב).

3 דָּבַר to speak. PIEL *pret.*

4 זָהַר to shine; to cause to shine, to enlighten, to teach, to admonish. HIPHIL *pret.*

5 חָכַם to be wise; to teach wisdom. PIEL *fut.*

6 יָדַע to know; to cause to know. HIPHIL ^a*pret.* ^b*imp.* ^c*fut.* ^d*part.* יְדַע Ch. APHEL ^e*fut.*

7 יָסַר to chasten, with strokes or words; to set right, to instruct. NITHPAEL ^a*pret.* PIEL ^b*pret.*

8 יָרָה to cast; to guide, direct, or instruct in a right way or course of action. HIPHIL ^a*pret.* ^b*inf.* ^c*imp.* ^d*fut.* ^e*part.*

9 לִיץ see *Interpret.* HIPHIL *part.*

10 לָמַד to teach. PIEL ^a*pret.* ^b*inf.* ^c*imp.* ^d*fut.* ^e*part.* PUAL ^f*part.* ^gלִמּוּד *adj.* trained, taught.

11 שָׂכַל to act wisely; to make to understand, implying maturity of understanding. HIPHIL ^a*fut.* ^b*part.*

12 שָׁנַן to whet, to sharpen; to teach diligently. PIEL *pret.*

Exod. iv. 12, 15.	8 a	2 Sam. i. 18.	10 b	Job xxxvi. 22.	8 e	
xviii. 20.	4	xxii. 35.	10 e	xxxvii. 19.	6 b	
xxiv. 12.	8 b	1 Kings viii. 36.	8 d	Ps. xviii. 34.	10 e	
xxxv. 34.	8 b	2 Kings xvii. 27.	8 d	xxv. 4, 5.	10 c	
Lev. x. 11.	8 b	xvii. 28. a	8 e	xxv. 8, 12.	8 d	
xiv. 57.	8 b	1 Chron. xv. 8.	4	xxv. 9.	10 d	
Deut. iv. 1.	10 e	2 Chron. vi. 27.	8 d	xxvii. 11.	8 c	
iv. 5.	10 a	xv. 3.	8 b	xxxii. 8.	8 c	
iv. 9.	6 a	xvii. 7.	10 b	xxxiv. 11.	10 d	
iv. 10.	10 d	xvii. 9, 9.	10 d	xlv. 4.	8 d	
iv. 14.	10 b	xxiii. 13.	6 d	li. 13.	10 d	
v. 31.	10 d	xxx. 22.	2	lx. title.	10 b	
vi. 1.	10 b	xxxv. 3, 3.	2 a, or b	lxxi. 17.	10 a	
xi. 19.	12	Ezra vii. 10.	10 b	lxxxvi. 11.	8 c	
xvii. 11.	10 d	vii. 25.	6 a	xc. 12.	6 b	
xx. 18.	10 d	Neh. viii. 9.	2 a	xciv. 10.	6 c	
xxiv. 8.	8 d	Job vi. 24.	8 d	xciv. 12.	10 d	
xxxi. 19.	10 c	xii. 7, 8.	8 d	cv. 22.	5	
xxxi. 22.	10 d	xxi. 22.	10 d	cxix. 12, 26, 64, 66, 68, 108, 124, 135.	10 c	
xxxiii. 10.	8 d	xxvii. 11.	8 d	cxix. 33.	8 c	
Judg. iii. 2.	10 b	xxxii. 7.	6 c	cxix. 99.	10 c	
viii. 16.	6 c	xxxiii. 18.	1 a	cxix. 102.	8 a	
xiii. 8.	8 d	xxxiv. 32.	8 c	cxix. 171.	8 c	
1 Sam. xii. 23.	8 a	xxxv. 11.	1 b	cxxxii. 12.	10 d	

Ps. cxliii. 10.	10 e	Isa. xxix. 13.	10 f	Jer. xxviii. 16.	3
cxliv. 1.	10 e	xxx. 20, 20.	8 e	xxix. 32.	3
Prov. iv. 4.	8 d	xl. 13.	6 c	xxxi. 34.	10 d
iv. 11.	8 a	xl. 14, 14.	10 d	xxxii. 33, 33.	10 b
v. 13.	8 e	xliii. 27.	9	Ezek. xxiii. 48.	7 a
vi. 13.	8 e	xlviii. 17.	10 e	xliv. 13.	8 d
ix. 9.	6 b	liv. 13.	10 g	Dan. i. 4.	10 b
xvi. 23.	11 a	Jer. ii. 33.	10 a	Hos. x. 11.	10 f
xxxi. 1.	7 b	ix. 5, 14.	10 a	Micah iii. 11.	8 d
Eccles. xii. 9.	10 a	ix. 20.	10 c	iv. 2.	8 d
Isa. ii. 3.	8 d	xii. 16.	10 a	Hab. ii. 18.	8 e
ix. 15.	8 e	xiii. 21.	10 a	ii. 19.	8 d
xxviii. 9, 26.	8 d				

a lit. was teaching.

TEAR

1 בָּקַע to cleave asunder, to rend, to divide. PIEL *fut.*

2 גָּזַל to pluck off or away, to tear away. KAL *part.* Patil.

3 דּוּשׁ to thresh. KAL *pret.*

4 טָרַף to pull or pluck off; to pull or tear in pieces. KAL a *pret.* b *inf.* c *fut.* d *part.* Poel. NIPHAL e *fut.* POAL f *pret.* g טְרֵפָה f. anything torn.

5 סָחַב to drag along the ground; to pull or tear in pieces. KAL *inf.*

6 סוּחָה f. that which is swept away, as filth, dung, &c. Comp. I Cor. iv. 13, περικάθαρμα περίψημα.

7 פָּרַס to break; to cleave, divide. KAL *fut.* See *marg.*

8 פָּרַק to break by rending, to tear off. PIEL *fut.*

9 קָרַע to rend. KAL a *pret.* b *fut.*

10 שָׁבַר to break. KAL a *pret.* b *fut.*

Gen. xxxi. 39.	4 g	1 Kings xiii. 28.	10 a	Ezek. iv. 14.	4 g
xliv. 28. a	4 b f	2 Kings ii. 24.	1	xiii. 20, 21.	9 a
Exod. xxii. 13. a	4 b e	Job xvi. 9.	4 a	xliv. 31.	4 g
xxii. 13, 31.	4 g	xviii. 4.	4 d	Hos. v. 14.	4 c
Lev. xvii. 15.	4 g	Ps. vii. 2.	4 c	vi. 1.	4 a
xvii. 15.	4 g	xxxv. 15.	9 a	xiii. 8.	1
xxii. 8.	4 g	l. 22.	4 c	Amos i. 11.	4 c
Deut. xxxiii. 20.	4 a	Isa. v. 25.	6	Micah v. 8.	4 a
Judg. viii. 7.	3	Jer. v. 6.	4 a	Nah. ii. 12.	4 d
2 Sam. xiii. 31.	9 b	xv. 3.	5	Zech. xi. 16.	8
1 Kings xiii. 26.	10 b	xvi. 7.	7	Mal. i. 13.	2

a lit. in rending is rent in pieces.

TEARS

בָּכָה to weep. KAL *fut.* Esth. viii. 3, *marg.* 'and she wept and besought him.'

דִּמְעָה f. tear, *collect.* tears: 2 Kings xx. 5, &c.

TEATS

דַּד m. breast, teat: Ezek. xxiii. 3, 21.

שַׁד m. breast, teat, both of man and animal: Isa. xxxii. 12.

TEBETH

טֵבֵת the tenth Hebrew month, from the new moon of January to that of February: Esth. ii. 16. But the Egyptian month here mentioned extended from the twentieth day of December to the twentieth day of January.—*Gesenius.*

TEETH

בַּעַל m. owner; master: Isa. xli. 15, having teeth, *lit.* master or owner of teeth, *marg.* 'mouths.'

מַלְתָּעוֹת f. pl. grinders, great teeth: Ps. lviii. 6. מְתַלְּעוֹת f. pl. *id.,* the letters being transposed: Prov. xxx. 14, "jaw-teeth;" Joel i. 6, "cheek-teeth."

פִּיפִיּוֹת f. pl. edges: in Isa. xli. 15, of a threshing dray, having (many) edges, *i.e.* teeth, points.

שֵׁן com. tooth, ivory: Gen. xlix. 12, &c. שֵׁן Ch. m. Dan. vii. 5, 7, 19.

TEIL-TREE

אֵלָה f. an oak: Isa. vi. 13. This, however, is thought to be the best translation of the word so often rendered 'oak.'

TEKEL

תְּקֵל Ch. to weigh. P'AL *part. pass.* Dan. v. 25, 27.

TELL

1 אֹזֶן m. ear.

2 אָמַר to say. KAL a *pret.* b *imp.* c *fut.* NIPHAL d *pret.* e *fut.* אֲמַר Ch. P'AL f *pret.* g *imp.* h *fut.* i *part.*

3 גָּלָה (see *Reveal*) with אֹזֶן to tell, *lit.* to reveal the ear of. KAL *pret.*

4 דָּבַר to speak. KAL a *part.* Poel. PIEL b *pret.* c *inf.* d *imp.* e *fut.*

5 יָדַע to know. KAL a *pret.* b *fut.* c *part.* Poel. HIPHIL d *imp.* e *fut.*

6 מָנָה to number. KAL a *fut.* b *part.* Poel.

7 נָגַד to be in front, to be in sight, to be clear, manifest. Hiph. to bring to light; hence, to show, to tell, to declare, to announce. LXX. ἀναγγέλλω, ἀπαγγέλλω: with *acc.,* with עַל to tell of anything; more particularly it signifies, to show, manifest, demonstrate by facts, 1 Sam. xxiv. 18, 2 Sam. xix. 6, Ps. xix. 1, xcii. 15, xcvii. 6; to prove by evidence, Neh. vii. 61; to acknowledge openly, Deut. xxvi. 3; to declare solemnly, Deut. xxx. 18; to avow publicly, Isa. iii. 9; to divulge, Josh. ii. 20; to explain things secret, abstruse, and obscure, Gen. xli. 24, Judg. xiv. 16, Isa. xlii. 9, Dan. ii. 2; to tell as news, 2 Sam. i. 5, iv. 10, xviii. 11. HIPHIL a *pret.* b *inf.* c *imp.* d *fut.* e *part.* HOPHAL f *pret.* g *inf.* h *fut.*

8 סָפַר to number; to recount, narrate, tell, declare. KAL a *pret.* b *imp.* c *fut.* NIPHAL d *fut.* PIEL e *pret.* f *inf.* g *imp.* h *fut.* i *part.* PUAL k *pret.* l *fut.* m מִסְפָּר m. number, narrative.

9 פֶּה m. mouth: Ezra viii. 17, "I told them what they should say," *marg.* 'I put words in their mouth.'

10 שׂוּם to put. KAL *fut.*

11 שָׁמַע to hear; to cause to hear. HIPHIL a *pret.* b *imp.* c *fut.*

12 תָּכַן to weigh. PUAL *part.*

Gen. iii. 11.	7 a	Gen. xxix. 12, 12.	7 d	Gen. xliii. 7.	7 d
ix. 22.	7 d	xxix. 13.	8 h	xliii. 22.	5 a
xii. 18.	7 a	xxix. 15.	7 c	xliv. 24.	7 d
xiv. 13.	7 d	xxxi. 20, 27.	7 a	xlv. 26.	7 a
xv. 5.	8 b	xxxi. 22.	7 h	xlv. 26.	7 d
xx. 8.	4 e	xxxii. 5.	7 b	xlvii. 1.	4 e
xxi. 26.	7 a	xxxii. 29.	7 c	xlvii. 1.	7 d
xxii. 2.	2 c	xxxvii. 5.	7 d	xlviii. 2.	7 d
xxii. 3, 9.	2 a	xxxvii. 9, 10.	8 h	xlix. 1.	7 d
xxii. 20.	7 h	xxxvii. 16.	7 c	Exod. iv. 28.	7 d
xxiv. 23, 49, 49.	7 c	xxxviii. 13, 24.	7 h	iv. 8.	8 g
xxiv. 28.	7 d	xl. 8.	8 g	ix. 1.	4 b
xxiv. 33.	4 b	xl. 9.	8 h	xiv. 5.	2 a
xxvi. 2.	2 c	xli. 8, 12.	8 h	xiv. 5.	8 h
xxvi. 32.	7 d	xli. 24.	2 c	xiv. 12.	4 b
xxvii. 42.	7 h	xliii. 6.	7 b	xvi. 22.	7 d

Exod. xviii. 8.	8 h	2 Sam. iii. 23.	7 d	2 Chron. ix. 6.	7 f
xix. 3, 9.	7 d	iv. 10.	7 e	xviii. 17.	2 a
xxiv. 3.	8 h	vi. 12.	7 h	xx. 2.	7 d
Lev. xiv. 35.	7 a	vii. 5.	2 a	xxxiv. 18.	2 b
xxi. 24.	4 e	vii. 11.	7 a	xxxiv. 23.	2 b
Num. xi. 24.	4 e	x. 5.	7 d	Ezra viii. 17.	10, 9
xi. 27.	7 d	xi. 19.	4 c	Neh. ii. 12, 16.	7 d
xiii. 27.	8 h	xii. 18, 18.	7 b, 2	ii. 18.	7 a
xiv. 14.	2 a	xii. 22.	5 c	Esth. ii. 22.	7 d
xiv. 39.	4 e	xiv. 33.	7 d	iii. 4, 4.	7 d a
xxiii. 3.	2 c	xv. 31.	7 a	iv. 4, 7, 9, 12.	7 d
xxiii. 26.	4 b	xv. 35.	7 d	v. 11.	8 h
xxix. 40.	2 c	xvii. 16.	7 c	vi. 2.	7 d
Deut. xvii. 4.	7 f	xvii. 17, 17.	7 a	vi. 13.	8 h
xvii. 11.	2 c	xvii. 18, 21.	7 d	viii. 1.	7 a
xxxii. 7.	2 c	xviii. 10, 25.	7 d	Job i. 15, 16, 17, 19.	7 b
Josh. ii. 2.	2 a	xviii. 11.	7 c	viii. 10.	2 c
ii. 23.	8 h	xviii. 21.	7 c	xii. 7.	7 d
vii. 19.	7 c	xix. 1.	7 h	xv. 18.	2 c
ix. 24.	7 g f	xix. 8.	7 a	xxxiv. 34.	2 c
x. 17.	7 h	xxiv. 13.	7 d	xxxvii. 20.	8 l
Judg. vi. 13.	8 e	1 Kings i. 20.	7 b	Ps. xxii. 17.	8 h
vii. 13.	7 d	i. 23.	7 a	xxvi. 7.	8 f
vii. 15.	8 m	i. 51.	7 h	xli. 6.	4 e
ix. 7, 42.	7 d	ii. 29, 41.	7 h	xlii. 9.	11 c
ix. 25, 47.	7 a	ii. 39.	7 d	xliv. 1.	8 e
xiii. 6, 6.	2 c, 7 a	viii. 5.	8 d	xlviii. 12.	8 b
xiii. 23.	11 a	ix. 3, 3.	7 d a	xlviii. 13.	8 h
xiv. 2, 17, 17.	7 d	x. 7.	7 f	l. 12.	2 a
xiv. 6, 9.	7 a	xiii. 11, 11.	8 h	lii. title.	7 d
xiv. 16, 16, 16.	7 a a d	xiii. 25.	4 e	lvi. 8.	7 d
xvi. 6.	7 c	xiv. 2.	2 a	lxxviii. 3.	8 e
xvi. 10, 10.	4 e, 7 c	xiv. 3.	7 d	ci. 7.	4 a
xvi. 13, 13.	4 e, 7 c	xiv. 7.	2 b	cxlvii. 4.	6 b
xvi. 15, 18.	7 d	xviii. 8, 11, 14.	2 b	Prov. xxx. 4.	5 b
xvi. 17.	7 d	xviii. 12.	7 b	Eccles. vi. 12.	7 d
xx. 3.	4 d	xviii. 13.	7 f	viii. 7.	7 d
Ruth iii. 4, 16.	7 d	xviii. 16.	7 d	x. 14, 14.	5 b, 7 d
iv. 4.	7 c	xix. 1.	7 d	Cant. i. 7.	7 c
1 Sam. iii. 13.	7 a	xx. 9.	2 b	v. 8.	7 d
iii. 18.	7 a	xx. 11.	4 d	Isa. v. 5.	5 e
iv. 13. a	7 b	xx. 17.	7 d	vi. 9.	2 a
iv. 14.	7 a	xxii. 18.	4 e	vii. 2.	7 h
vi. 2.	5 d	xxii. 18.	2 a	xix. 12.	7 d
viii. 10.	7 a	2 Kings i. 7.	4 e	xxxvi. 22.	7 d
ix. 8. β	7 a	iv. 2.	7 c	xl. 21.	7 f
ix. 15.	3, 1	iv. 7, 31.	7 d	xlii. 9.	11 c
ix. 18.	7 c	iv. 27.	2 a	xliv. 8.	11 a
ix. 19.	7 d	v. 4.	7 a	xlv. 21, 21.	7 c a
x. 15.	7 c	vi. 10.	2 a	xlviii. 20.	11 b
x. 16.	7 b a	vi. 12.	7 d	lii. 15.	8 k
x. 16.	7 a	vi. 13.	7 h	Jer. xv. 2.	2 a
x. 25.	4 e	vii. 9, 10, 11, 15.	7 d	xix. 2.	4 e
xi. 4.	4 e	viii. 4.	8 i	xxiii. 27, 28, 32.	8 h
xi. 5.	8 h	viii. 5.	8 i	xxviii. 13.	2 a
xiv. 1.	7 a	viii. 6.	7 d	xxxiii. 13.	6 b
xiv. 33.	7 a	viii. 7.	7 h	xxxiv. 2.	2 a
xiv. 43, 43.	7 c d	viii. 14.	2 a	xxxv. 13.	2 a
xv. 12.	7 h	ix. 12.	7 c	xxxvi. 17.	7 c
xv. 16.	7 d	ix. 15.	7 b	xxxvi. 20.	7 d
xvii. 55. γ	5 a	ix. 18, 20, 36.	7 d	xxxviii. 27.	7 d
xviii. 20, 24, 26.	7 d	x. 8.	7 d	xlviii. 20.	7 c
xix. 2, 11, 18, 21.	7 d	xii. 10.	6 a	Ezek. iii. 11.	2 a
xix. 3.	7 a	xii. 11.	12	xii. 23.	2 b
xix. 19.	7 h	xviii. 37.	7 d	xvii. 12.	7 d
xx. 9, 10.	7 h	xx. 5.	2 a	xix. 19.	7 d
xxii. 22.	7 b d	xxii. 15.	2 b	Dan. ii. 4, 9.	2 g
xxiii. 1, 25.	7 d	xxii. 20.	2 c	ii. 7, 36.	2 h
xxiii. 7.	7 h	1 Chron. xvii. 4.	2 a	iv. 7.	2 i
xxiii. 11.	7 c	xvii. 10.	7 d	iv. 8.	2 f
xxiii. 13.	7 f	xvii. 25.	3, 1	iv. 9.	2 g
xxiii. 22.	2 a	xix. 5.	7 d	vii. 1, 16.	2 f
xxiv. 1.	7 d	xix. 17.	7 h	viii. 26.	7 d
xxv. 12, 37.	7 d	xxi. 10.	4 b	Joel i. 3.	8 g
xxv. 14, 19, 36.	7 a	2 Chron. ii. 2.	8 c	Jonah i. 8.	7 a
xxvii. 4.	7 h	v. 6.	8 c	i. 10.	7 a
xxvii. 11.	7 d	ix. 2, 2.	7 d a	iii. 9.	7 d
2 Sam. i. 4.	7 c			Hab. i. 5.	8 l
i. 5, 6, 13.	7 e			Zech. x. 2.	4 e
i. 20.	7 d				
ii. 4.	7 d				

α *lit.* to tell. β *lit.* and he will tell us. γ *lit.* if I know.

TEMAN

תֵּימָן *com.* the south: Hab. iii. 3, *marg.* 'or, the south.'

TEMPER

בָּלַל see *Mingle.* KAL *part.* Paül, Exod. xxix. 2.

מָלַח to salt. PUAL *part.* Exod. xxx. 35.

רָסַס to sprinkle, to moisten. KAL *inf.* Ezek. xlvi. 14.

TEMPEST

זֶרֶם *m.* a pouring rain, violent shower, storm: Isa. xxviii. 2; xxx. 30; xxxii. 2.

סוּפָה *f.* whirlwind, hurricane, tempest, which sweeps all before it: Job xxvii. 20.

סָעַר to be violently agitated, tossed, as by a tempest. KAL *part.* Poel, Isa. liv. 11: Jonah i. 11, 13. סַעַר *m.* storm, tempest: Ps. lv. 8; lxxxiii. 15: Amos i. 14: Jonah i. 4, 12. סְעָרָה *f. id.* Isa. xxix. 6.

רוּחַ *com.* wind: Ps. xi. 6.

שָׂעַר to shiver; to sweep away in a storm; to rush on like a tempest. NIPHAL *pret.* Ps. l. 3. שְׂעָרָה *f.* Job ix. 17.

TEMPLE

בַּיִת *m.* house; 2 Kings xi. 10, 11, 11, 11, 13: 1 Chron. vi. 10; x. 10: 2 Chron. xxiii. 10, 10, 10; xxxv. 20.

הֵיכָל *com.* a large building, edifice, a palace; palace of Jehovah, *i.e.* the temple or tabernacle; *poet.* the heavens; specially for a part of the temple at Jerusalem, corresponding to the body or nave of modern cathedrals, between the entrance and the most holy place: 1 Kings vi. 5, 17; vii. 50. But הֵיכָל does not stand for the most holy place: 1 Sam. i. 9, &c. הֵיכָל Ch. *id.* Ezra v. 14, 14, 14, 15; vi. 5, 5: Dan. v. 2, 3.

TEMPLES

רַקָּה *f. pr.* thinness; the temples, a part of the head thin of flesh; but Cant. iv. 3 seems to be used of the cheeks. Judg. iv. 21, 22; v. 26: Cant. iv. 3; vi. 7.

TEMPT (See also PROVE)

1 בָּחַן to try, to prove, to examine, as metals. KAL *pret.*

2 נָסָה to smell, to try by the smell, to try; it differs therefore in its primary idea from בָּחַן to examine by the touch, to try by the touchstone; to prove any one, to put him to the test. Men are said to prove or tempt God by doubting, not confiding, in his power or aid. PIEL a *pret.* b *inf.* c *fut.* d מַסָּה *f.* temptation.

Gen. xxii. 1.	2 a	Deut. vi. 16, 16.	2 c a	Ps. xcv. 9.	2 a
Exod. xvii. 2.	2 c	vii. 19.	2 d	cvi. 14.	2 c
xvii. 7.	2 b	xxix. 3.	2 d	Isa. vii. 12.	2 c
Num. xiv. 22.	2 c	Ps. lxxviii. 18, 41, 56.	2 c	Mal. iii. 15.	1
Deut. iv. 34.	2 d	xcv. 8.	2 d		

TEN

עָשׂוֹר *m.* ten, a decad; an instrument of ten strings: Gen. xxiv. 55: Ps. xxxii. 2; xcii. 3; cxliv. 9.

רְבָבָה *f.* a myriad, ten thousand; often put for any great indefinite number: Lev. xxvi. 8: Deut. xxxii. 30; xxxiii. 2, 17: Judg. xx. 10: 1 Sam. xviii. 7, 8; xxi. 11; xxix. 5: Ps. iii. 6; xci. 7: Cant. v. 10: Micah vi. 7. רָבַב *denom.,* PUAL *part.* Ps. cxliv. 13.

רִבּוֹ and רִבּוֹא *f.* a myriad, ten thousand: 1 Chron. xxix. 7: Dan. xi. 12. רִבּוֹ Ch. *f.* ten thousand ten thousand: Dan. vii. 10, 10.

TENDER

רָכַךְ to be tender. KAL *pret.* 2 Kings xxii. 19: 2 Chron. xxxiv. 27. רַךְ *adj.* tender; soft, not hard; gentle, bland; weak, feeble: Gen. xviii. 7; xxix. 17; xxxiii. 13: Deut. xxviii. 54, 56: 1 Chron. xxii. 5; xxix. 1: 2 Chron. xiii. 7: Prov. iv. 3: Isa. xlvii. 1: Ezek. xvii. 22. רֹךְ *m.* tenderness: Deut. xxviii. 56.

TENON

יָד *com.* hand: Exod. xxvi. 17, 19, 19; xxxvi. 22, 24, 24.

TENOR

פֶּה *m.* mouth: Gen. xliii. 7: Exod. xxxiv. 27.

TENT　(See also PITCH)

אֹהֶל *m.* (see *Tabernacle*) dwelling, habitation, house: Gen. iv. 20, &c. אָהַל *denom.* to pitch or remove a tent. KAL *fut.* Gen. xiii. 12, 18. PIEL *fut.* Isa. xiii. 20.

חָנָה to pitch a tent. KAL *pret.* Num. i. 52. *inf.* Deut. i. 33. *fut.* Gen. xxvi. 17; xxxiii. 18: Num. ix. 17. מַחֲנֶה *com.* encampment; camp: Num. xiii. 19: 1 Sam. xvii. 53: 2 Kings vii. 16: 2 Chron. xxxi. 2: Zech. xiv. 15.

סֻכָּה *f.* booth: 2 Sam. xi. 11.

קֻבָּה *f.* tent. Gesenius, high and rounded like a dome, a vaulted pleasure-tent, devoted to the impure worship of Baalpeor: Num. xxv. 8.

מִשְׁכָּן *m.* tabernacle: Cant. i. 8.

TENTH

עָשַׂר to take the tenth part of anything, to take tithe; to pay the tenth part. KAL *fut.* 1 Sam. viii. 15, 17. PIEL *inf.* Gen. xxviii. 22, *lit.* giving the tenth I will give the tenth: *fut.* Gen. xxviii. 22. עָשׂוֹר *m.* ten, a decad; also for the last day of the ten, *i.e.* the tenth: Exod. xii. 3: Lev. xvi. 29; xxiii. 27; xxv. 9: Num. xxix. 7: Josh. iv. 19: 2 Kings xxv. 1: Jer. lii. 4, 12: Ezek. xx. 1; xxiv. 1; xl. 1. עֲשִׂירִי *adj. ord.* Gen. viii. 5, 5, &c. עִשָּׂרוֹן *m.* a tenth, tenth part, a measure of things dry, especially of grain and meal; always rendered tenth deal: Exod. xxix. 40, &c. מַעֲשֵׂר *m.* a tenth part, tithe: Num. xviii. 21, 26: Ezek. xlv. 11, 14.

TERAPHIM

תְּרָפִים *m. pl.* family gods, domestic idols; the Penates of the Hebrews: they seem to have had the human form and stature, and to have been consulted as oracles: from the Syriac, to inquire: Ezek. xxi. 21: Zech. x. 2. Jurieu suggests that it may come from רָפָא to heal or cure, and that they were gods worshipped or consulted with a view to health. Probably they may be regarded as divining images, and used for some purpose similar to that of the ephod. See Jurieu's Hist. of Doct. and Worsh. of the Church, vol. ii. p. 77.—*Bush.* Judg. xvii. 5; xviii. 14, 17, 18, 20: Hos. iii. 4.

TERMED

אָמַר to say. NIPHAL *fut.* Isa. lxii. 4, 4.

TERRACE

מְסִלָּה *f.* high way: 2 Chron. ix. 11, *marg.* 'high ways, or, stairs.'

TERROR, TERRIBLE, TERRIFY

1　אֹים *adj.* terrible, formidable. אֵימָה *f.* fear, terror, dread; that which tends to destruction: Deut. xxxii. 25.

2　בֶּהָלָה *f.* trouble, attended with confusion and consternation.

3　בַּלָּהָה *f.* terror, with great trouble of mind; sudden destruction; always in *pl.*

4　בָּעַת to make afraid, to terrify, with great consternation of mind. PIEL *fut.* בְּעוּתִים *m. pl.* terrors.

5　מָגוֹר *m.* see *Fear*.

6　דְּחַל Ch. to fear, to be afraid. P'AL *part.* P'il.

7　זַלְעָפָה *f.* see *Horror*.

8　חָפָּא *f.* vertigo (see *Reel*); consternation, terror.

9　חָתַת to be broken; to be broken down with fear; to be dismayed, terrified, confounded. HIPHIL *fut.* חִתָּה *f.* fear. חִתִּית *f. id.* מְחִתָּה *f.* destruction; consternation, terror.

10　יָרֵא to fear. NIPHAL *part.* מוֹרָא *m.* fear, reverence.

11　מָנַר to fall, to be cast down. KAL *part.* Paül.

12　אֶמְתָנִי Ch. *adj.* strong, mighty.

13　עָרַץ to terrify, make afraid, by violent and oppressive practices. KAL *inf. fut.* עָרִיץ *adj.* terrible. מַעֲרָצָה *m.* fearfulness.

14　פַּחַד *m.* fear.

15　תִּפְלֶצֶת *f.* terror, fear; see *Tremble*.

Gen. xxxv. 5.	9 b	Job xxxi. 34.	9 a	Isa. xlix. 25.	13 c	
Exod. xxxiv. 10.	10 a	xxxiii. 7.	1 a	liv. 14.	9 d	
Lev. xxvi. 16.	2	xxxvii. 22.	10 a	lxiv. 3.	10 a	
Deut. i. 19.	10 a	xxxix. 20.	1 a	Jer. xv. 8.	2	
iv. 34.	10 b	xli. 14.	1 a	xv. 21.	13 c	
vii. 21.	10 a	Ps. xlv. 4.	10 a	xvii. 17.	9 d	
viii. 15.	10 a	xlvii. 2.	10 a	xx. 4.	5	
x. 17, 21.	10 a	lv. 4.	1 a	xx. 11.	13 c	
xx. 3.	13 b	lxv. 5.	10 a	xxxii. 21.	10 b	
xxvi. 8.	10 b	lxvi. 3, 5.	10 a	xlix. 16.	15	
xxxii. 25.	1 a	lxviii. 35.	10 a	Lam. ii. 22.	5	
xxxiv. 12.	10 b	lxxiii. 19.	3	v. 10.	7	
Josh. ii. 9.	1 a	lxxvi. 12.	10 a	Ezek. i. 22.	10 a	
Judg. xiii. 6.	10 a	lxxxviii. 15.	1 a	xxi. 12.	11, or 5	
2 Sam. vii. 23.	10 a	lxxxviii. 16.	4 b	xxvi. 17.	9 c	
1 Chron. xvii. 21.	10 a	xci. 5.	14	xxvi. 21.	3	
Neh. i. 5.	10 a	xcix. 3.	10 a	xxvii. 36.	3	
iv. 14.	10 a	cvi. 22.	10 a	xxviii. 7.	13 c	
ix. 32.	10 a	cxlv. 6.	10 a	xxxii. 19.	3	
Job iii. 5.	4 a	Cant. vi. 4, 10.	1	xxx. 11.	13 c	
vi. 4.	4 b	Isa. ii. 19, 21. a	13 a	xxxii. 12.	13 c	
vii. 14.	4 a	x. 33.	13 d	xxxii. 12.	13 c	
ix. 34.	4 a	xviii. 2, 7.	13 c	xxxii. 23, 24, 25, 26,		
xviii. 11, 14.	3	xix. 17.	10 a	27, 30, 32.	9 c	
xx. 25.	3 a	xxi. 1.	10 a	Dan. ii. 31.	6	
xxiv. 17.	3	xxi. 4.	3	vii. 7.	12	
xxvii. 20.	3	xxv. 3, 4, 5.	13 c	Joel ii. 11, 31.	10 a	
xxx. 15.	3	xxix. 5, 20.	13 c	Hab. i. 7.	1	
xxxi. 23.	14	xxxiii. 18.	1 a	Zeph. ii. 11.	10 a	

a "to shake terribly."

TESTIFY, TESTIMONY

1　עוּד to say again and again; hence to affirm, and specially to testify, to exhort. Hiph. of a witness, to testify, to bear witness, *abs. seq. acc.* against any one, but also in favour of or for any one, *i.e.* to laud him, Job xxix. 11, *comp.* μαρτυρέω, Luke iv. 22: to obtest, *i.e.* to protest; to exhort solemnly, to admonish, *seq. acc.* of person, בְּ and עַל, also to chide, to upbraid, to enjoin solemnly

upon any one, *e.g.* a precept, law, and hence of the divine legislation, testimonies. HIPHIL [a] *pret.* [b] *imp.* [c] *fut.* [d] *part.* HOPHAL [e] *pret.* [f] עֵדָה *f.* witness. [g] עֵדוּת *f.* precept of God: Ps. xix. 7, lxx. 5, lxxxi. 5, cxxii. 4, "whither the tribes go up," according to the precept, to Israel. *Collect.* precepts, law, specially the decalogue. Exod. xvi. 34, &c. [h] תְּעוּדָה *f.* custom; law.

2 עָנָה to answer. KAL [a] *pret.* [b] *inf.* [c] *imp.* [d] *fut.*

No. 1 g, *Testimony*, not included.

Exod. xxi. 29.	1 e	2 Kings xvii. 15.	1 a	Ps. cxix. 2, 22, 24, 46,	
Num. xxxv. 30.	2 d	2 Chron. xxiv. 19.	1 c	59, 79, 95, 119,	
Deut. iv. 45.	1 f	Neh. ix. 26, 34.	1 c	125, 138, 146,	
vi. 17, 20.	1 f	ix. 29, 30.	1 c	152, 167, 168.	1 f
viii. 19.	1 a	xiii. 15, 21.	1 c	cxxxii. 12.	1 f
xix. 16.	2 b	Job xv. 6.	2 d	Isa. viii. 16, 20.	1 h
xix. 18.	2 a	Ps. xxv. 10.	1 f	lix. 12.	2 a
xxxi. 21.	2 a	l. 7.	1 c	Jer. xiv. 7.	2 a
xxxii. 46.	1 d	lxxviii. 56.	1 f	Hos. v. 5.	2 a
Ruth i. 21.	2 a	lxxxi. 8.	1 c	vii. 10.	2 a
iv. 7.	1 h	xciii. 5.	1 f	Amos iii. 13.	1 b
2 Sam. i. 16.	2 a	xcix. 7.	1 f	Micah vi. 3.	2 c
2 Kings xvii. 13.	1 c				

THANK

1 בָּרַךְ to bless, to salute, to thank. PIEL *fut.*

2 יְדָא Ch. to praise God. APHEL *part.*

3 יָדָה to confess; to give thanks, to praise, to celebrate, since the acknowledgment (confession) of benefits is naturally followed by thanksgiving and praise, *seq. acc.* also לְ of person. HIPHIL [a] *pret.* [b] *inf.* [c] *imp.* [d] *fut.* [e] *part.* [f] הְיָדוֹת *f. pl.* praises. [g] תּוֹדָה *f.* thanksgiving, thank-offering, thanks.

Lev. vii. 12, 12, 13, 15.	3 g	Neh. xii. 24, 46.	3 b	Ps. cvi. 1.	3 c
xxii. 29.	3 g	xii. 27, 31, 38, 40.	3 g	cvi. 47.	3 b
xxii. 50.	3 d	Ps. vi. 5.	3 d	cvii. 1.	3 c
1 Chron. xvi. 4, 7,		xviii. 49.	3 d	cvii. 22.	3 g
35, 41.	3 b	xxvi. 7.	3 g	cxvi. 17.	3 c
xvi. 8, 34.	3 c	xxx. 4.	3 c	cxviii. 1, 29.	3 c
xxiii. 30.	3 b	xxx. 12.	3 d	cxix. 62.	3 b
xxv. 3.	3 b	xxxv. 18.	3 d	cxxii. 4.	3 b
xxix. 13.	3 e	l. 14.	3 g	cxxxvi. 1, 2, 3, 26.	3 c
2 Chron. v. 13.	3 b	lxix. 30.	3 g	cxl. 13.	3 d
xxix. 31, 31.	3 g	lxxv. 1, 1.	3 a	cxlvii. 7.	3 g
xxxi. 2.	3 b	xcii. 1.	3 b	Isa. li. 3.	3 g
xxxiii. 16.	3 g	xcv. 2.	3 g	Jer. xxx. 19.	3 g
Ezra iii. 11.	3 b	xcvii. 12.	3 c	Dan. ii. 23.	2
Neh. xi. 17.a	3 d	c. 4, 4.	3 g c	vi. 10.	2
xii. 8.	3 f	cv. 1.	3 c	Amos iv. 5.	3 g
				Jonah ii. 9.	3 g

a lit. he shall give thanks.

THICK, THICKET

1 אֲפֵלָה *f.* darkness, thickness of darkness.

2 חוֹחַ *m.* thorn, thorn-bush, thicket.

3 כָּבֵד *adj.* heavy.

4 מַכְבֵּר *m.* cloth of a coarse texture.

5 סְבָךְ *m.* branches interwoven, a thicket. [a] סֹבֶךְ *m.* thicket.

6 עָב *m.* thick, thick beam. Gesenius, a term of architecture, a threshold, step, *i.e.* a projection, offset, perhaps *collect.* forming the ascent into a portico; *pl.* עָבִּים Ezek. xli. 26, as if from a singular עֹב *m.* Targ. in both passages, thresholds; Vulg. *epistylium*, architrave; against the context in both places. [a] עָב *com.* darkness, chiefly of clouds; a cloud; dark thicket of a wood.

7 עָבָה to be thick, fat. KAL [a] *pret.* [b] עָבִי *m.* עֲבִי *m.*

8 עָבֹת *adj.* interwoven, interlaced. [a] עֲבֹת *com.* a cord; braid, wreath; a branch with foliage, a thick-leaved bough.

9 עָתָר *m.* abundance. Gesenius, incense, fragrant vapour: Ezek. viii. 11. So, correctly, Lxx., Vulg., Syr.

10 רֹחַב *m.* breadth.

Gen. xxii. 13.	5	2 Kings viii. 15.	4	Jer. lii. 21.	7 c
Exod. x. 22.	1	2 Chron. iv. 5.	7 c	Ezek. vi. 13.	8
xix. 9.a	6 a	x. 10.	7 a	viii. 11.	9
xix. 16.	3	Neh. viii. 15.	8	xix. 11.	8 a
Lev. xxiii. 40.	8	Job xv. 26.	7 b	xx. 28.	8
Deut. xxxii. 15.	7 a	Ps. lxxiv. 5.	5	xxxi. 3, 10, 14.	8 a
1 Sam. xiii. 6.	2	Isa. ix. 18.	5	xli. 9, 12.	10
1 Kings vii. 6.	6	x. 34.	5	xli. 25, 26.	6
vii. 26.β	7 c	Jer. iv. 7.	5 a	xlii. 10.	10
xii. 10.	7 a	iv. 29.	6 a		

a lit. in the thickness of a cloud. *β lit.* and its thickness was a hand-breadth.

THIEF, THEFT

גַּנָּב *m.* thief: Exod. xxii. 2, &c. גְּנֵבָה *f.* theft, thing stolen: Exod. xxii. 3, 4.

THIGH

יָרֵךְ *f.* the thigh, so called from its softness; how far it differs from the loins is apparent from Exod. xxviii. 42. The hollow or socket of the thigh, by which the thigh is connected with the pelvis; on or at the thigh where the sword is worn; to smite the thigh, a gesture of mourning or indignation; also to put the hand under the thigh as an accompaniment of an oath, probably in some connexion with the sacredness of circumcision; in animals, the thigh, haunch, or ham: Gen. xxiv. 2, 9, &c. יַרְכָה Ch. *f.* Dan. ii. 32.

שׁוֹק *m.* the leg, from the knee to the foot, as that with which one runs or walks: Isa. xlvii. 2.

THIN

דָּלַל to be enfeebled, to be brought low. NIPHAL *fut.* Isa. xvii. 4.

דַּק *adj.* beaten small; slender, thin, lank, withered: Gen. xli. 6, 7, 23, 24: Lev. xiii. 30.

מוֹרָד *m.* hanging down, hanging work, festoons: 1 Kings vii. 29.

רַק *adj.* lean, thin of flesh: Gen. xli. 27.

THING

1 אֹמֶר *m.* word; matter, thing.

2 דָּבָר *m.* word; thing, matter, affair, business; properly, thing spoken of: Gen. xv. 1, &c.

3 כְּלִי *m.* a word of general import.

4 מְאוּמָה *f.* anything; mostly with a negative particle.

5 מְלָאכָה *f.* work, service, goods, &c.

6 מִלָּה Ch. *f.* word; matter.

7 נֶפֶשׁ *com.* soul; "everything that liveth," *lit.* every soul of life.

8 מַשָּׁאָה *f.* loan.

9 עֹשֶׁק *m.* anything extorted, gotten by fraud and violence.

No. 2 not included.

Gen. xxii. 12.	4	Num. xxxv. 22.	3	Eccles. v. 14, 15.	4
xxx. 31, 31.	4, 2	Deut. xxiv. 10.	8, 4	vii. 14.	4
xxxix. 9, 23.	4	Judg. xiv. 6.	4	ix. 5.	4
xl. 15.	4	1 Sam. xv. 9.	5	Jer. xxxix. 10.	4
Lev. vi. 4.	9	xx. 26, 39.	4	Ezek. xlvii. 9.	7
xi. 10.	7	xxi. 2.	4	Dan. ii. 5, 8, 10, 11,	
xiii. 48.	5	xxv. 15, 21.	4	15, 17.	6
xiii. 49, 52, 53, 57,		2 Sam. xiii. 2.	4	iv. 33.	6
58, 59.	4	1 Kings x. 21.	4	v. 15, 26.	6
xv. 4, 6, 22, 23.	3	xviii. 43.	4	vi. 12.	6
Num. xxii. 38.	4	2 Chron. ix. 20.	4	vii. 16.	6
xxxi. 20.	3	Job xxii. 28.	1	Jonah iii. 7.	4

THINK

1 אָמַר to say. KAL *a pret. b inf. c fut. d part.* Poel.

2 בִּין to understand, to consider. HITHPOLEL *fut.*

3 דָאַג to fear, to take thought ; *seq.* לְ of person. KAL *pret.*

4 דָּבַר to speak. PIEL *a pret. b* דָּבָר *m.* word.

5 דָּמָה to be like ; to liken, to liken in one's mind, to imagine ; to purpose, to meditate, to do anything ; to think upon. PIEL *a pret. b fut.*

6 הַרְהֹר Ch. *m.* conception, thought.

7 זָכַר to remember, to think on. KAL *a pret. b imp.*

8 חֵקֶק *m.* resolve : Judg. v. 15, *marg.* 'impressions.' It corresponds to a similar word in verse 16. See *Searchings.*

9 חָשַׁב to think, to meditate, to purpose ; applied to the making of curious works. Piel, to think upon with great care and exactness. KAL *a pret. b fut. c part.* Poel. PIEL *d pret. e fut. f* מַחֲשֶׁבֶת *f.* counsel, purpose, plan, what one meditates or has devised ; specially of wicked counsels, devices, machinations.

10 זָמַם to meditate, to have in mind, to purpose. KAL *a pret. b* זִמָּה *f.* intention for evil. *c* מְזִמָּה *f.* meditation, counsel, purpose.

11 מַדָּע *m.* knowledge.

12 מוֹרָשׁ *m.* possession : Job xvii. 11, *marg.* 'the possessions,' *i.e.* my delights, my pleasing hopes, possessed and cherished in the bottom of my heart.

13 סְבַר Ch. to hope, to trust ; also to think, to deem. P'AL *a fut.* Dan. vii. 25. Vulg. *putabit quod possit mutare.* As to the sense, Theod., well, ὑπονοήσει τοῦ ἀλλοιῶσαι. —*Gesenius.*

14 סְעַפִּים *m. pl.* thoughts which branch off ; as a verbal adjective in Ps. cxix. 113, divided, *i.e.* a man of divided mind, a free thinker, who has no sure faith in regard to divine things, but is driven hither and thither, a doubter, sceptic, σκεπτικός. In the above passage, such thinkers are opposed to those who receive the law, *comp.* Eccles. vii. ult.

15 עַיִן *com.* eye ; to think, *lit.* to be good, &c., in the eyes of.

16 עָשַׁת to shine ; to make shining, hence to work, to forge, to form ; *trop.* of the mind, which forms, fashions, moulds anything by revolving it ; to think upon, to recall to mind, *recogitare*, as Vulg. well, *seq.* לְ. HITHPAEL *a fut.* עֲשֵׁת Ch. to think, to have in mind, to purpose. P'AL *b pret. c* עַשְׁתּוּת *f. pl.* thought. *d* עֶשְׁתֹּנֹת *f. pl.* devices.

17 פָּלַל to judge ; to think, to suppose. PIEL *pret.*

18 קְדָם Ch. *prep.* before.

19 רָאָה to see. KAL *part.* Poel.

20 רֵעַ *m.* thoughts or agitations of the mind devising or contriving for the best, which may also admit the notion of care and solicitude.—*Schult.* Gesenius, thought, will, desire. *a* רַעְיוֹן Ch. *m.* thought, cogitation.

21 שְׂעִפִּים *m. pl.* thoughts, cogitations which divide and distract the mind.

22 שַׂרְעַפִּים *m. pl.* the same with ר inserted.

23 שִׂחַ *m.* meditation, thought.

24 שָׁעַר to divide ; to estimate, to fix the value of anything. KAL *pret.*

Gen. vi. 5.	9 f	2 Chron. xxxii. 1.	1 c	Prov. xvi. 3.	9 f
xx. 11.	1 a	Neh. v. 19.	7 b	xxi. 5.	9 f
xxxviii. 15.	9 b	v. 2, 6.	9 c	xxiii. 7.	24
xl. 14.	7 a	vi. 14.	7 b	xxiv. 9.	10 b
xlviii. 11.	17	Esth. iii. 6.	15	xxx. 32.	10 a
l. 20.	9 a	iv. 13.	5 b	Eccles. viii. 17.	1 c
Exod. xxxii. 14.	4 a	vi. 6.	1 c	x. 20.	11
Num. xxiv. 11.	1 a	Job iv. 13.	21	Isa. x. 7.	9 b
xxxiii. 56.	9	xii. 5.	6 c	xiv. 24.	5 a
xxxvi. 6.	15	xvii. 11.	12	lv. 7, 8, 8, 9, 9.	9 f
Deut. xv. 9.	4 b	xx. 2.	21	lix. 7, 7.	9 f
xix. 19.	10 a	xxi. 27.	9 f	lxv. 2.	9 f
Judg. v. 15.	8	xxxi. 1.	2	lxvi. 18.	9 f
xv. 2.	1 b a	xxxv. 2.	9 a	Jer. iv. 14.	9 f
xx. 5.	9	xli. 32.	9 b	vi. 19.	9 f
Ruth iv. 4.	1 a	xlii. 2.	10 c	xviii. 8.	9 a
1 Sam. i. 13.	9 b	Ps. x. 4.	10 c	xxiii. 20.	10 c
ix. 5.	3	xxxiii. 11.	9 f	xxiii. 27.	9 c
xviii. 25.	9 a	xl. 5.	9 f	xxix. 11, 11, 11.	9 f c f
xx. 26.	1 a	xl. 17.	9 b	Ezek. xxxviii. 10, 10.	9 a f
2 Sam. iv. 10.	15	xlviii. 9.	5 a	Dan. ii. 29, 30.	20 a
v. 6.	1 b	l. 21.	9 f	iv. 5.	18
x. 3.	15	lvi. 5.	9 f	iv. 5.	6
xiii. 2.	15	lxxiii. 16.	9 e	iv. 19.	20 a
xiii. 33.	1 b	xcii. 5.	9 f	v. 6, 10.	20 a
xiv. 13.	9 a	xciv. 11.	9 f	vi. 3.	16 b
xviii. 27.	19	xciv. 19.	21	vii. 25.	13 a
xix. 18.	15	cxix. 59.	9 d	Amos iv. 13.	23
xxi. 16.	1 c	cxix. 113.	14	Jonah i. 6.	16 a
2 Kings v. 11.	1 a	cxxxix. 2, 17.	20	Micah iv. 12.	9 f
1 Chron. xix. 3.	15	cxxxix. 23.	22	Zech. i. 6.	10 a
xxviii. 9.	9 f	Prov. xii. 5.	9 f	viii. 14, 15.	10 a
xxix. 18.	9 f	xv. 26.	9 f	xi. 12.	15
2 Chron. xiii. 8.	1 d			Mal. iii. 16.	9 c

THIRD

שָׁלוֹשׁ *m.* and שְׁלוֹשָׁה *f. adj. num.* three, third : Exod. xix. 15 ; 1 Kings xv. 28, 33 : 2 Kings xviii. 1 ; 1 Chron. xxvi. 11 : 2 Chron. xvii. 7 : Esth. i. 3 : Dan. i. 1 ; viii. 1 ; x. 1. שְׁלִישִׁי *adj. ord.* third : Gen. i. 13, &c. שְׁלֵשִׁים *m. pl.* descendants of third generation : Gen. l. 23 : Exod. xx. 5 ; xxxiv. 7 : Num. xiv. 18 : Deut. v. 9. שִׁלֵּשׁ *denom.* to divide into three parts ; to do the third time ; to do on the third day. PIEL *imp.* 1 Kings xviii. 34. *fut.* 1 Kings xviii. 34.

תְּלָת Ch. *adj. num.* three : Ezra vi. 15. תְּלָת Ch. *adj. ord.* third : Dan. v. 16, 29. תַּלְתִּי Ch. *adj. ord.* Dan. v. 7. תְּלִיתַי Ch. *adj. ord.* Dan. ii. 39.

THIRST, THIRSTY

1 עָיֵף *adj.* faint, weary, thirsty.

2 צָמָא to thirst. KAL *a pret. b fut. c* צָמָא *m.* thirst. *d* צָמָה *f. id. e* צָמֵא *adj.* thirsty. *f* צִמְאָה *f.* thirst. *g* צִמָּאוֹן *m.* thirsty land.

Exod. xvii. 3, 3.	2 b c	Ps. lxix. 21.	2 c	Isa. xliv. 3.	2 e
Deut. xxviii. 48.	2 c	civ. 11.	2 c	xlviii. 21.	2 a
xxix. 19.	2 e	cvii. 5.	2 e	xlix. 10.	2 b
Judg. iv. 19.	2 a	cxliii. 6.	2 a	l. 2.	2 c
xv. 18, 18.	2 b c	Prov. xxv. 21.	1	lv. 1.	2 e
Ruth ii. 9.	2 a	xxv. 25.	2 e	lxv. 13.	2 b
2 Sam. xvii. 29.	2 e	Isa. v. 13.	2 d	Jer. ii. 25.	2 f
2 Chron. xxxii. 11.	2 e	xxi. 14.	2 e	xlviii. 18.	2 c
Neh. ix. 15, 20.	2 c	xxix. 8.	2 e	Lam. iv. 4.	2 c
Job xxiv. 11.	2 b	xxxii. 6.	2 e	Ezek. xix. 13.	2 c
Ps. xlii. 2.	2 a	xxxv. 7.	2 g	Hos. ii. 3.	2 c
lxiii. 1, 1.	2 a, 1	xli. 17.	2 c	Amos viii. 11, 13.	2 c

THISTLE

דַּרְדַּר *m.* a plant growing luxuriously and worthless, *collect.* weeds : Gen. iii. 18 : Hos. x. 8.

חוֹחַ *m.* a thorn, thorn-bush : any plant or shrub that hath prickles or thorns that hook those that touch them, or whose branches are entangled and grow thick : 2 Kings xiv. 9, 9 : 2 Chron. xxv. 18, 18 : Job xxxi. 40.

THORN

1   אָטָד   *m.* the southern buckthorn, Christ's thorn, *Rhamnus paliurus*, Linn., so called from the firmness of its roots. Gesenius, easily taking fire.

2   חוֹחַ   *m.* thorn, thorn-bush ; see *Thistle.*

3   חֶדֶק   *m.* a species of thorn.

4   נַעֲצוּץ   *m.* a thorn-hedge, thicket of thorns, *vepretum, senticetum.*

5   מְסוּכָה   *f.* a hedge, thorn-hedge.

6   סִיר   *com.* a thorn, briar, so called from the idea of springing up with the luxuriant and abundant growth of wild plants ; see also *Pot*, and the paronomasia in Eccles. vii. 6. A thicket of thorns and briars is an emblem of wickedness, Nah. i. 10.

7   סַלּוֹנִים   *m. pl.* thorns, prickles ; properly, such as are found on the shoots and twigs of the palm-tree. *Metaph.* of wicked men.

8   צֵן   *m.* thorn, prickle.   ᵃ צְנִינִים *m. pl. id.*

9   קוֹץ   *m.* a thorn ; *collect.* thorns, thorn-bush, briars.

10   קִמָּשׂוֹן   *m.* a prickle, a thorn.

11   שַׁיִת   *m.* a thorn ; *collect.* thorns.

Gen. iii. 18.	9	Prov. xxii. 5.	8	Isa. xxxiii. 12.	9
Exod. xxii. 6.	9	xxiv. 31.	10	xxxiv. 13.	6
Num. xxxiii. 55.	8 a	xxvi. 9.	2	lv. 13.	4
Josh. xxiii. 13.	8 a	Eccles. vii. 6.	6	Jer. iv. 3.	9
Judg. viii. 7, 16.	9	Cant. ii. 2.	2	xii. 13.	9
2 Sam. xxiii. 6.	2	Isa. v. 6.	11	Ezek. ii. 6.	7
2 Chron. xxxiii. 11.	2	vii. 19.	4	xxviii. 24.	9
Job v. 5.	8	vii. 23, 24, 25.	11	Hos. ii. 6.	6
xli. 2.	2	ix. 18.	11	ix. 6.	2
Ps. lviii. 9.	1	x. 17.	11	x. 8.	9
cxviii. 12.	9	xxvii. 4.	11	Micah vii. 4.	5
Prov. xv. 19.	3	xxxii. 13.	11	Nah. i. 10.	6

THOROUGHLY

יָטַב to be good ; to do well. HIPHIL *inf.* 2 Kings xi. 18.

THOUSAND

אֶלֶף *m.* a thousand ; not unfrequently it is put for a large round number : Job ix. 3 ; xxxiii. 23 : Ps. l. 10 : put also for an indefinitely large round number : Gen. xxiv. 60. אָלַף *denom.* to bring forth thousands. HIPHIL *part.* Ps. cxliv. 13. אֶלֶף and אֲלַף Ch. *m.* Dan. v. 1, 1 ; vii. 10, 10.

THREAD

חוּט *m.* a thread ; *collect.* thread ; proverbially, Gen. xiv. 23, from a thread to a shoelatchet, *i.e.* neither a thread nor a sandal thong, not the least thing.—Gen. xiv. 23 : Josh. ii. 18 : Judg. xvi. 12 : Cant. iv. 3.

פָּתִיל *m.* thread, line, cord : Judg. xvi. 9.

THREE

שָׁלוֹשׁ *m.* שְׁלֹשָׁה *f. adj. num.* Gen. v. 22, &c. The number three seems to express sometimes a great or complete number ; three witnesses were complete or perfect evidence ; two were the least that could be admitted, Deut. xvii. 6 ; so we say thrice happy to express perfect happiness. It may be used also of an indefinite number, and followed by four still more indefinite ; see Amos i. 3, &c. שְׁלוֹשִׁים *pl. adj. num.* thirty : 2 Sam. xxiii. 13, "three of the thirty," *lit.* according to the כְּתִיב, thirty of the thirty. שְׁלִישִׁי *adj. ord.* third : 2 Sam. xxiii. 18 ; כְּתִיב, Isa. xv. 5 : Jer. xlviii. 34 : Ezek. xlii. 3. שָׁלַשׁ *denom.* to divide into three parts. PIEL *pret.* Deut. xix. 3 : 1 Sam. xx. 19. PUAL *part.* Gen. xv. 9, 9, 9 : Eccles. iv. 12 : Ezek. xlii. 6. שִׁלְשׁוֹם *adv.* three days ago, the day before yesterday : 1 Sam. xxi. 5, *lit.* as yesterday the third day.

תְּלָת Ch. *adj. num.* Ezra vi. 4 : Dan. iii. 23, 24 ; vi. 3, 10, 13 ; vii. 5, 8, 20, 24.

THREESCORE

רִבּוֹ *f.* a myriad, ten thousand : Ezra ii. 69, *lit.* six ten thousand.

שִׁבְעִים *adj. num.* seventy ; often translated threescore and ten : Gen. xxv. 7, &c.

שִׁשִּׁים *adj. num. pl.* sixty : Gen. xxv. 26, &c.

שִׁתִּין Ch. *adj. num. pl.* sixty : Ezra vi. 3, 3 : Dan. iii. 1 ; v. 31.

THRESH

1   אִדַּר   Ch. *m. pr.* a wide open space ; area, threshing-floor.

2   אָדַשׁ   to thresh. KAL *inf.*

3   גֹּרֶן   *m.* a place made level, an area ; mostly spoken of the area in which grain is trodden out or threshed in the open field, a threshing-floor or place ; Num. xviii. 30, the produce of the threshing-floor, *i.e.* grain ; Isa. xxi. 10, son of my floor, *i.e.* O my country, my people, now broken and trodden down as grain upon a threshing-floor, *parall.* my threshing ; *comp.* Micah iv. 12, 13. Or, as they are the words of the prophet himself, beaten and threshed with the repeated strokes and warnings of my prophesying. Compare a similar expression, Hos. vi. 5.

4   דּוּשׁ   to tread, to tread out grain, to thresh, *sc.* by driving cattle round upon the grain ; *trop.* of a cruel punishment inflicted by the Hebrews on captives, by crushing them with threshing-drays, like grain on the threshing-floor, Amos i. 3. KAL ᵃ *pret.* ᵇ *inf.* ᶜ *imp.* ᵈ *fut.* HOPHAL ᵉ *fut.* ᶠ דַּיִשׁ *m.* time of threshing out corn. ᵍ מְדֻשָׁה *f.* treading out : Isa. xxi. 10. In this place evidently the language of tenderness used of the afflictions of the people of God in Babylon.

5 דָּרַךְ to tread ; to tread the threshing-floor. HIPHIL *inf.*

6 חָבַט to beat out or off ; to beat out grain with a stick or staff, to thresh. KAL *part.* Poel.

7 חָרוּץ *m.* that which is sharpened and pointed ; a threshing-sledge.

8 מוֹרַג *m.* a threshing-sledge, a rustic instrument for rubbing or beating out grain upon the threshing-floor. It is of two kinds : the one is a sledge of thick planks, having the bottom fixed full of sharp stones or irons, and dragged about by oxen over the grain ; see Robinson's Palest. iii. p. 143 ; the other consists of three or four rollers of wood, iron, or stone, made rough, and joined together in the form of a sledge or dray, drawn in like manner by oxen over the grain. Of these the former is properly the Hebrew מוֹרַג, the latter is called עֲגָלָה : Isa. xxviii. 27.

Gen. l. 10.	3	2 Sam. xxiv. 22.	8	Isa. xxviii. 27, 27.	4 e, 7
Lev. xxvi. 5.	4 f	2 Kings xiii. 7.	4 b	xxviii. 28, 28. a	2, 4 d
Num. xv. 20.	3	1 Chron. xiii. 9.	3	xli. 15.	8
xviii. 27, 30.	3	xxi. 20.	4 a	xli. 15.	4 d
Judg. vi. 11.	6	xxi. 15, 18, 21, 22,		Jer. li. 33, 33.	3, 5
Ruth iii. 2.	3	28.	3	Dan. ii. 35.	1
1 Sam. xxiii. 1.	3	xxi. 23.	8	Amos i. 3, 3.	4 b, 7
2 Sam. vi. 6.	3	2 Chron. iii. 1.	3	Micah iv. 13.	4 c
xxiv. 16, 18, 21, 24.	3	Isa. xxi. 10.	4 g	Hab. iii. 12.	4 d

a lit. in the threshing he will not ever thresh it.

THRESHOLD

אֲסֻפִּים *m. pl.* collections, *i.e.* stores, storehouses, or chambers : Neh. xii. 25, *marg.* 'treasuries, *or,* assemblies.'

סַף *m.* sill, threshold ; it may seem to take in all that is before a door (see *Door, Post*) : Judg. xix. 27 : 1 Kings xiv. 17 : Ezek. xl. 6, 8 : xliii. 8 : Zeph. ii. 14.

מִפְתָּן *m.* sill, threshold : 1 Sam. v. 4, 5 ; Ezek. ix. 3 ; x. 4, 18 ; xlvi. 2 ; xlvii. 1 : Zeph. i. 9, *or,* over the threshold.

THRICE

פַּעַם *com.* (see *Time*) : once, twice, thrice : Exod. xxxiv. 23, *lit.* three times ; 24, *id.* : 2 Kings xiii. 18, *id.*; 19, *id.*

שָׁלֹשׁ *m.* and שְׁלוֹשָׁה *f. adj. num.* three : Exod. xxxiv. 23, *lit.* three times ; 24, *id.* : 2 Kings xiii. 18, *id.*; 19, *id.*

THROAT

גָּרוֹן *m.* the throat, so called as giving forth rough, harsh, hoarse sounds ; spoken of as the instrument of speech : Ps. cxv. 7. Ps. v. 9, " their throat is an open sepulchre," *i.e.* they utter smooth speeches while, like an open sepulchre, they meditate destruction.—Ps. v. 9 ; lxix. 3 ; cxv. 7 : Jer. ii. 25.

לֹעַ *m.* gullet, throat ; see *Swallow :* Prov. xxiii. 2.

THRONE

כִּסֵּא *m.* a throne, a seat, a royal throne, a kingdom ; the high priest's seat, 1 Sam. i. 9, iv. 13 ; the tribunal of judges, Ps. cxxii. 5 (*comp.* Dan. vii. 9), xciv. 20 ; of jurisdiction, Neh. iii. 7 ; of a military tribunal, Jer. i. 15. Also of any seat, 2 Kings iv. 10, Prov. ix. 14 ; especially that which is honourable, 1 Sam. ii. 8. *Metaph.* Isa. xxii. 23, *i. e.* through him all his kindred shall be honoured. Gen. xli. 40, &c.

כִּסֵּה *m.* the same : 1 Kings x. 19, 19 : Job xxvi. 9.

כָּרְסֵא Ch. *i. q.* כִּסֵּא *m.* a throne : Dan. v. 20 ; vii. 9, 9.

THROUGH, THROUGHLY

דֶּרֶךְ *com.* way : 2 Sam. iv. 7.

רָבָה to multiply. HIPHIL *imp.* Ps. li. 2, *lit.* multiply wash me.

שְׂרֵפָה *f.* a burning : Gen. xi. 3, *marg.* 'to a burning.'

THROW

1 הָרַס to pull or tear down, to destroy, *e. g.* a wall, building, city, state, or kingdom. KAL *a pret.* *b inf.* *c fut.* NIPHAL *d pret.* *e fut.*

2 יָד *com.* hand : Num. xxxv. 17, *lit.* a stone of the hand.

3 נָפַל to fall ; to cause to fall. HIPHIL *inf.*

4 נָתַץ to tear or break down, or totally demolish, a building, an altar, &c. KAL *a pret.* *b fut.* *c part.* Paül. NIPHAL *d pret.* PIEL *e fut.*

5 סָקַל to stone, to pelt with stones. PIEL *fut.*

6 רָמָה to cast, to throw. KAL *pret.*

7 שָׁלַךְ to cast, to throw. HIPHIL *a pret.* HOPHAL *b part.*

8 שָׁמַט to thrust, to cast, to throw down. KAL *a imp.* *b fut.*

Exod. xv. 1, 21.	6	1 Kings xix. 10, 14.	1 a	Jer. l. 15.	1 d
Num. xxxv. 17.		2 Kings xix. 33, 33.	8 a b	Lam. ii. 2, 17.	1 a
Judg. ii. 2.	4 b	2 Chron. xxxi. 1.	4 e	Ezek. xvi. 39.	1 d
vi. 25.	1 a	Neh. xi. 11.	1 b	xxxviii. 20.	1 d
vi. 32.	4 a	Jer. i. 10.	1 b	Micah v. 11.	1 a
2 Sam. xvi. 13.	5	xxxi. 28.	1 b	Nah. i. 6.	4 d
xx. 15.	3	xxxi. 40.	1 e	Mal. i. 4.	1 c
xx. 21.	7 b	xxxiii. 4.	4 c		

THRUST (See also OPPRESS)

1 בָּהַל to be troubled ; to hasten ; to drive out in haste, to thrust out. HIPHIL *fut.*

2 בָּתַק to thrust through with a sword. Gesenius, to hew in pieces with a sword. PIEL *pret.*

3 גָּרֵשׁ to drive, to cast out, to expel. PIEL *a inf.* *b fut.* PUAL *c pret.*

4 דָּחָה to thrust, to push, to knock down, to overthrow ; it is used of enemies rushing on David, Ps. cxl. 4 ; on the Messiah, Ps. cxviii. 13 ; of the angel rushing on the enemies of the Messiah, Ps. xxxv. 5, *comp.* xxxvi. 13. KAL *a pret.* *b inf.*

5 דָּחַק to thrust, push, press upon, as is done in a great crowd. KAL *a fut.*

6 דָּקַר to thrust through, to pierce, to stab, as with a sword or spear. KAL *a pret.* *b imp.* *c fut.* NIPHAL *d fut.* PUAL *e part.*

7 הָדַף to thrust, to push, to smite ; *seq.* מִן to thrust away. KAL *a pret.* *b inf.* *c fut.*

8 זוּר to press together, to press out. KAL *fut.*

9 טָעַן to thrust through with a sword. PUAL *part.*

10 לָחַץ to press. LXX. θλίβειν. NIPHAL *fut.*

11 נָדַד to flee ; to put to flight, to chase. HOPHAL *part.*

12 נָדַח to thrust, to impel, *sc.* forwards, from oneself ; hence to thrust out, forth. HIPHIL *inf.*

13 נָדַף to thrust, to push ; to drive away. KAL *fut.*

14 נָקַר to bore, to pierce ; to put out. KAL *inf.*

15 נָתַן to give. KAL *pret.*

16 תָּקַע to strike ; to drive a thing into another. KAL *fut.*

Exod. xi. 1.	3 a b	Judg. ix. 41.	3 b	2 Chron. xxvi. 20.	1
xii. 39.	3 c	ix. 54.	6 c	Job xxxii. 13.	13
Num. xxii. 25.	10	xi. 2.	3 b	Ps. cxviii. 13.	4 b a
xxv. 8.	6 c	1 Sam. xi. 2.	14	Isa. xiii. 15.	6 d
xxxv. 20.	7 c	xxxi. 4, 4.	6 b a	xiv. 19.	9
xxxv. 22.	7 a	2 Sam. xviii. 14.	16	Jer. li. 14.	6 e
Deut. xiii. 5, 10.	12	xxiii. 6.	11	Ezek. xvi. 40.	2
xv. 17.	15	1 Kings ii. 27.	3 b	xxxiv. 21.	7 c
xxxiii. 27.	3 b	2 Kings iv. 27.	7 b	Joel ii. 8.	5 a
Judg. iii. 21.	16	1 Chron. x. 4.	6 b	Zech. xiii. 3.	6 a
vi. 38.	8				

THUMB

בֹּהֶן *m.* the thumb, so called as shutting and covering the hand ; the great toe : Exod. xxix. 20 : Lev. viii. 23, 24 ; xiv. 14, 17, 25, 28 : Judg. i. 6, *lit.* thumbs of his hands and feet ; 7, *lit. id.*

יָד *com.* hand : Judg. i. 6, 7.

THUMMIM

תֹּם *m.* wholeness, entireness ; *pl.* תֻּמִּים perfections. Lxx. ἀλήθεια. Gesenius would render it truth, *i.e.* Urim and Thummim, Revelation and Truth ; see *Urim :* Exod. xxviii. 30 : Lev. viii. 8 : Deut. xxxiii. 8 : Ezra ii. 63 : Neh. vii. 65.

THUNDER

קוֹל *m.* voice ; any sound, as of thunder : Exod. ix. 23, 28, 29, 33, 34 ; xix. 16 ; xx. 18 : 1 Sam. vii. 10 ; xii. 17, 18 : Job xxviii. 26 ; xxxviii. 25.

רָעַם to be moved, agitated, to tremble ; to roar. HIPHIL *pret.* Ps. xxix. 3. *fut.* 1 Sam. ii. 10 ; vii. 10 : 2 Sam. xxii. 14 : Job xxxvii. 4, 5 ; xl. 9 : Ps. xviii. 13. רַעַם *m.* thunder ; hence of a thundering voice, as of warlike leaders shouting their orders, Job xxxix. 25. *Metaph.* Job xxvi. 14, "The thunder of his power who can understand ?" *i.e.* the whole compass of divine power, all the mighty deeds which can be predicated of God.—Job xxvi. 14 ; xxxix. 25 : Ps. lxxvii. 18 ; lxxxi. 7 ; civ. 7 : Isa. xxix. 6. רְעָמָה *f.* thunder. Gesenius, a trembling, quivering, shuddering ; *poet.* for the mane of a horse, probably as erect from excitement and waving or streaming in the wind ; Job xxxix. 19, hast thou clothed his neck with shuddering ? *i.e.* a waving mane ; *comp.* Gr. φόβη, mane, from φόβος.

רֶשֶׁף *m.* flame, lightning : Ps. lxxviii. 48.

TIDE

עֵת *com.* time : Josh. viii. 29 : 2 Sam. xi. 2 : Isa. xvii. 14 : Jer. xx. 16.

TIDINGS

1 בָּשַׂר to bring, bear, &c., good tidings ; used of the Messiah, Isa. xli. 27, Glassii Opusc. ; rarely more generally to bear tidings. PIEL *pret.* *inf.* *fut.* *part.* HITHPAEL *fut.* בְּשׂוֹרָה *f.* glad tidings ; reward for tidings.

2 דָּבָר *m.* word, matter.

3 שֵׁמַע *m.* something heard ; report, fame, tidings. שְׁמוּעָה *f.* what is heard ; tidings, message, news.

Gen. xxix. 13.	3	2 Sam. xviii. 22, 25,		Isa. xli. 27.	1 d
Exod. xxiii. 4.	3	27.	1 f	lii. 7, 7.	1 b
1 Sam. iv. 19.	3 a	xviii. 26.	1 d	lxi. 1.	1 b
xi. 4, 5, 6.	2	xviii. 31.	1 e	Jer. xx. 15.	1 a
2 Sam. iv. 4.	3 a	1 Kings i. 42.	1 c	xxxvii. 5.	3
iv. 10, 10.	1 d f	ii. 28.	3 a	xlix. 23.	3
xiii. 30.	3 a	2 Kings vii. 9.	1 f	Ezek. xxi. 7.	3 a
xviii. 19.	1 f	1 Chron. x. 9.	3 b	Dan. xi. 44.	3 a
xviii. 20.	1 f	Ps. cxii. 7.	3 b	Nah. i. 15.	1 d
xviii. 20, 20.	1 a c	Isa. xl. 9, 9.	1 d		

TIE

אָסַר to bind. KAL *pret.* 1 Sam. vi. 7. *fut.* 1 Sam. vi. 10. *part.* Paül, 2 Kings vii. 10, 10.

נָתַן to give. KAL *fut.* Exod. xxxix. 31.

עָנַד to bind on. KAL *imp.* Prov. vi. 21.

TILE

לְבֵנָה *f.* brick : Ezek. iv. 1.

TILL

1 נִיר *m.* (see *Break up*) fallow ground, a field recently broken up ; see *Light.*

2 עָבַד to labour, to do work ; especially labouring in the earth, tilling. KAL *pret.* *inf.* *fut.* *part.* Poel. NIPHAL *pret.* *fut.* עֲבוֹדָה *f.* tillage.

Gen. ii. 5.	2 b	1 Chron. xxvii. 26.	2 g	Prov. xxviii. 19.	2 d
iii. 23.	2 b	Neh. x. 37.	2 g	Jer. xxvii. 11.	2 e
iv. 2.	2 d	Prov. xii. 11.	2 d	Ezek. xxxvi. 9.	2 e
iv. 12.	2 c	xiii. 23.	1	xxxvi. 34.	2 f
2 Sam. ix. 10.	2 a				

TIMBER

אָע Ch. *m.* wood : Ezra v. 8 ; vi. 4, 11.

עֵץ *m.* a tree, wood ; the timber-work of a house, Hab. ii. 11 : Exod. xxxi. 5 : Lev. xiv. 45 : 1 Kings v. 6, 8, 8, 18 ; vi. 10 ; xv. 22 : 2 Kings xii. 12 ; xxii. 6 : 1 Chron. xiv. 1 ; xxii. 14, 15 : 2 Chron. ii. 8, 9, 10, 14 ; xvi. 6 ; xxxiv. 11 : Neh. ii. 8 : Ezek. xxvi. 12 : Hab. ii. 11 : Zech. v. 4.

TIMBREL

תֹּף a drum, tabret, timbrel (see *Tabret*) : Exod. xv. 20, 20 : Judg. xi. 34 : 2 Sam. vi. 5 : 1 Chron. xiii. 8 : Job xxi. 12 : Ps. lxxxi. 2 ; cxlix. 3 ; cl. 4. תָּפַף to play on the timbrel. KAL *part.* Poel, Ps. lxviii. 25.

TIME

1 אֱדַיִן *adv.* Ch. then.

2 אֶמֶשׁ *adv. pr.* the past night.

3 זְמָן *m.* time, an appointed time, season ; answering to 'when.' זְמָן Ch.

4 יָד *com.* hand.

5 יוֹם *m.* day. יוֹם Ch. *m. id.*

6 מוֹעֵד *m.* set time, appointed season ; see *Set.*

7 מָנִים *m. pl.* times, from מָנָה to number.

8 מִסְפָּר *m.* number.

9 עִדָּן Ch. *m.* time ; specially in prophetic language, a year.

10 עוֹלָם *m. pr.* occult, hidden ; hidden time, that which is uncertain or indefinite in future or past ; "at any time," "long time."

11   עֵת *com.* time in general, season or convenient opportunity; answering to 'how long;' frequently joined with prepositions: Gen. xviii. 10, 14, &c.

12   פַּעַם *com.* successive strokes of the foot; used also for successive turns or times.

13   רֶגֶל *f.* foot; step, beat; times.

14   שִׁלְשׁוֹם *adv.* three days ago, the day before yesterday; with תְּמוֹל "time past," *lit.* from yesterday the third day.

15   תְּמוֹל *adv.* yesterday. ᵃ אֶתְמוֹל *id.*

No. 11 not included.

Gen. iv. 3.	5	Judg. xi. 4.	5	1 Chron. xxix. 27.	5
xxvi. 8.	5	xiv. 8.	5	2 Chron. viii. 13.	12
xxvii. 36.	12	xv. 1.	5	xv. 11.	5
xxix. 34.	5	xvi. 15, 20.γ	12	xviii. 15.	12
xxx. 33. a	5	xviii. 31.	5	xxi. 19.ζ	5
xxxi. 7, 41.	7	xx. 15.	5	xxx. 26.	5
xxxiii. 3.	12	xx. 30,γ 31.γ	12	Ezra iv. 15, 19.	5 a
xxxviii. 12.	5	1 Sam. i. 4, 20.	5	v. 3.	3 a
xxxix. 11.	5	iii. 2.	5	v. 16.	1
xliii. 10.	12	iii. 10.γ	12	Neh. ii. 6.	3
xliii. 34.	4	iv. 13.	5	iv. 12.	12
xlvii. 29.	5	ix. 24.	6	iv. 16.	5
Exod. ii. 23.	5	x. 11.	15 a, 14	v. 14.	5
viii. 32.	12	xiv. 18.	5	vi. 4, 5.	12
ix. 14, 27.	12	xiv. 21.	15 a, 14	ix. 32.	5
xxi. 29.	15, 14	xviii. 10.	5	xii. 44.	5
xxi. 36.	15, 14	xx. 25, γ 41.	12	Esth. ix. 27, 31.	3
xxiii. 14.	13	xxx. 3.	5	Job xix. 3.η	12
xxiii. 17.	12	2 Sam. ii. 11.	8, 5	xix. 3.	5
xxxiv. 18.	6	iii. 17.	15 a, 14	xxx. 3.	2
Lev. iv. 6, 17.	12	v. 2.	5	Ps. xxvii. 5.	5
viii. 11.	12	vii. 14, 19.	5	xli. 1.	5
xiv. 7, 16, 27, 51.	12	xiv. 2.	5	xliv. 1.	5
xvi. 14, 19.	12	xvii. 7.	12	lvi. 3.	5
xxv. 8.	12	xxiii. 8.	5	cvi. 43.	12
xxv. 32.	10	xxiii. 20.	5	Prov. xxv. 13, 19.	5
Num. xiii. 20, 20.	5	1 Kings i. 6.	5	xxxi. 25.	5
xiv. 22.	12	ii. 26.	5	Isa. xxx. 8.	5
xix. 4.	12	viii. 59.	5	xxxvii. 26.	5
xx. 15.β	5	ix. 25.	12	xlii. 14.	10
xxii. 28, 32, 33.	13	xi. 42.	5	Jer. xxxix. 10.	5
xxiv. 1, γ 10.	12	xvii. 21.	12	Ezek. xxxviii. 10, 17, 18.ι	5
xxxii. 10.	5	xviii. 43.	12	Dan. i. 20.	4
Deut. i. 11.	12	xix. 16.	12	ii. 8, 9, 21.	9
iv. 42.	15, 14	2 Kings iii. 6.	5	iii. 5, 15.	9
ix. 19.	5	iv. 35.	12	iii. 7, 8.	3 a
x. 10, 10.	5, 12	v. 10, 14.	12	iv. 16, 23, 25, 32.	9
xvi. 16.	12	x. 36.	5	iv. 36.	3 a
xix. 4.	15, 14	xiii. 5.	15, 14	vi. 10, 13.	3 a
xix. 6.	15, 14	xiii. 19, 25.	12	vii. 12.	9
xx. 19.	5	xix. 25.	5	vii. 25, 25, 25,	3 a, 9, 9, 9
Josh. iii. 15.	5	1 Chron. xi. 2.	15, 14	25.	6
vi. 4, 15, 15, 16.	12	xi. 11.	12	vii. 7, 7.	12
x. 42.	12	xvii. 10.	12	Nah. i. 9.	12
xi. 18.β	5	xxi. 3.	12		
xx. 5.	15, 14				
xxiii. 1.δ	5				

a lit. in the day of to-morrow.   β lit. many days.   γ lit. as a time, in a time.   δ lit. after many days.   ε lit. the days were multiplied.   ζ lit. to days from days.   η lit. in not his day.   θ lit. to the length of days.   ι lit. in that day, the day.

TIN

בְּדִיל *m.* stannum of the ancients; alloy of lead, tin, or other inferior metals, combined in the ore, and separated from it by smelting; tin, *plumbum album:* Num. xxxi. 22: Isa. i. 25: Ezek. xxii. 18, 20; xxvii. 12.

TINGLE

צָלַל to tinkle: of the ears, to tingle with astonishment and terror. KAL *fut.* 1 Sam. iii. 11: 2 Kings xxi. 12: Jer. xix. 3.

TINKLE

עֶכֶס *m.* fetter, ancle-band: as an ornament of showy females, fastened upon the ancles: Isa. iii. 18. עָכַס *denom.* to put on anklets as an ornament, or rather to make a tinkling with them, like females desirous of attracting notice. PIEL *fut.* Isa. iii. 16.

TIP

תָּנוּךְ *m.* end, extremity: Exod. xxix. 20, 20: Lev. viii. 23, 24; xiv. 14, 17, 25, 28.

TIRE

יָטַב to be well; to make well, comely, to adorn. HIPHIL *fut.* 2 Kings ix. 30.

פָּאַר *m.* ornament: Ezek. xxiv. 17, 23.

TIRSHATHA

תִּרְשָׁתָא *m.* always with the *art.* The tirshatha, the title of the Persian governor of Judea, *q. d.* your severity; Germ. gestrenger Herr, a title formerly given to the magistrates of the free and imperial cities of Germany. Ezra ii. 63: Neh. vii. 65, 70; viii. 9; x. 1.

TITHE

עָשַׂר to take the tenth part of anything, to tithe; to give the tenth part, to pay tithe. PIEL ᵃ*inf.* ᵇ*fut.* ᶜ*part.* HIPHIL ᵈ*inf.* ᵉ מַעֲשֵׂר *m.* a tenth part, tithe: Deut. xxvi. 12, year of tithing or tithe year, every third year in which the tithes were to be applied in giving entertainments at home.

Gen. xiv. 20.	e	Deut. xiv. 22.	a b	Neh. x. 38, 38, 38.	d e e
Lev. xxvii. 30, 31, 32.	e	xiv. 23, 28.	e	xii. 44.	e
Num. xviii. 24, 26, 26, 28.	e	xxvi. 12, 12, 12.	d e e	xiii. 5, 12.	e
Deut. xii. 6, 11, 17.	e	2 Chron. xxxi. 5, 6, 6, 12.	e	Amos iv. 4.	e
		Neh. x. 37, 37.	e c	Mal. iii. 8, 10.	e

TITLE

צִיּוּן *m.* a pillar, *cippus,* a short column or slab, as being set up; either sepulchral or as a way-mark: 2 Kings xxiii. 17.

TOE

בֹּהֶן *m.* the thumb, the great toe of the foot: Exod. xxix. 20: Lev. viii. 23, 24; xiv. 14, 17, 25, 28: Judg. i. 6, *lit.* thumbs of his hands and his feet; 7.

אֶצְבַּע *f.* finger or toe: 2 Sam. xxi. 20, *lit.* and the fingers of his hands and the fingers of his feet, six and six: 1 Chron. xx. 6, *lit.* and his fingers were twenty-four, six and six. אֶצְבְּעָן Ch. *f. pl.* Dan. ii. 41, 42.

רֶגֶל *f.* foot: Judg. i. 6, *lit.* thumbs of the feet; 7, *marg. id.*

TOGETHER

1   אֶחָד *adj.* one; "together," *lit.* as one. ᵃ חַד Ch. *adj. num.*

2   אָחוֹת *f.* sister; after אִשָּׁה one, the other; "together."

3   אֲסֵפָה *f.* a gathering: Isa. xxiv. 22, *lit.* they are gathered with a gathering, *i. e.* in one gathering, all at once.

4   אִשָּׁה *f.* a woman; *seq.* אָחוֹת, or רְעוּת, one another, "together."

5   יַחַד *m.* a being one, oneness, union; hence as an *adv.* in union, conjointly, together. ᵃ Of united action, together; so after verbs of contending together. ᵇ As to place, together, in one place. ᶜ As to time, together, at the

same time; sometimes sameness of time and place is combined: 2 Sam. xiv. 16; xxi. 9. ᵈ It connects two or more nouns more closely by the idea of equality, likeness, together, alike, in like manner: Ps. xlix. 2 (comp. ver. 11); so also as connecting verbs, Isa. xliv. 11, i.e. shall both alike fear and be ashamed. ᵉ With nouns or pronouns it implies oneness, a whole, all, all as one; also after כֹּל, all together, all as one, wholly. ᶠ With כֹּל implied, altogether, all as one, wholly, poet. for כֹּל itself; so without a noun as referring to a single thing, i.q. כֹּל altogether, wholly: Job x. 8. יַחְדָּו pr. in his unions, connexions. ᵍ Of united action; so with reciprocal verbs; also with verbs of contending. ʰ As to place, together, in one place. ⁱ As to time, together, at the same time; with the idea of equality, likeness, alike, in like manner. ᵏ In this way it often connects more closely two nouns, also verbs. ˡ Put with a plural, as if comprising many in one, all, all as one; with כֹּל implied, altogether, all; so without a noun, they all. ᵐ יַחְדָּיו id.

6 צֶמֶד m. a pair: 2 Kings ix. 25, i.e. in pairs.

Gen. xiii. 6.	5 h	Job ix. 32.	5 h	Isa. xli. 1.	5 g
xiii. 6.	5	x. 8.	5 f	xli. 19.	5 k
xxii. 6, 8, 19.	5 h	xvi. 10.	5 f	xli. 20.	5
xxxvi. 7.	5 h	xvii. 16.	5 f	xli. 23.	5 g
Exod. xix. 8.	5	xix. 12.	5 f	xliii. 9.	5 i
xxvi. 6.	4, 2	xxii. 4.	5 f	xliii. 17.	5 a
xxvi. 24.	5	xxxiv. 15.	5 e	xliii. 26.	5 a
xxxvi. 29.	5	xxxviii. 7.	5	xliv. 11.	5 d
Deut. xxii. 10, 11.	5 h	xl. 13.	5 e	xlv. 8.	5 c
xxv. 5.	5 h	Ps. ii. 2.	5 a	xlv. 16.	5 l
xxv. 11.	5	xiv. 3.	5 l	xlv. 20.	5
xxxiii. 11.	5 f	xxxi. 4.	5 a	xlvi. 2.	5 g
xxxiii. 17.	5 l	xxxiv. 3.	5 g	xlvi. 2.	5 k
Josh. ix. 2.	5 h	xxxv. 26.	5 k	xlviii. 13.	5 l
xi. 5.	5	xxxvii. 38.	5 l	l. 8.	5 a
Judg. vi. 33.	5 h	xl. 14.	5 d	lii. 8, 9.	5
xix. 6.	5 h	xli. 7.	5	lx. 13.	5 k
1 Sam. xi. 11.	5 b	xlviii. 4.	5 l	lxv. 7.	5 i
xvii. 10.	5	xlix. 2.	5 d	lxv. 25.	5
xxxi. 6.	5 i	lv. 14.	5 g	lxvi. 17.	5 i
2 Sam. ii. 13.	5	lxxi. 10.	5	Jer. iii. 18.	5
ii. 16.	5 i	lxxiv. 8.	5 e	vi. 11, 12, 21.	5 k
x. 15.	5 b	lxxxiii. 5.	5 g	xiii. 14.	5 k
xii. 3.	5	lxxxviii. 17.	5	xxxi. 8, 13.	5 l
xiv. 16.	5 c	xcviii. 8.	5	xxxi. 24.	5 l
xxi. 9.	5 c	cii. 22.	5 h	xli. 1.	5 h
1 Kings iii. 18.	5	cxxii. 3.	5	xlvi. 12, 21.	5 m
2 Kings ix. 25.	6	cxxxiii. 1. a	5 b	xlviii. 7.	5
1 Chron. vi. 6.	5 i	Isa. i. 28.	5	xlix. 3.	5 m
Ezra ii. 64.	1	i. 31.	5 i	l. 4, 33.	5 l
iii. 9.	1	ix. 21.	5	li. 38.	5 l
iv. 3.	5 a	xi. 6, 7.	5	Lam. ii. 8.	5
vi. 20.	5	xi. 14.	5 g	Dan. ii. 35.	1 a
Neh. iv. 8.	5	xviii. 6.	5 l	Hos. i. 11.	5
vi. 2, 7.	5	xxii. 3, 3.	5 e, 5	xi. 8.	5
vii. 66.	1	xxiv. 22.	5	Amos i. 15.	5
Job ii. 11.	5 g	xxvii. 4.	3	iii. 3.	5
iii. 18.	5 f	xxxi. 3.	5 l	Micah ii. 12.	5
vi. 2.	5 c	xl. 5.	5	Zech. x. 4.	5

a lit. even together in unity.

TOIL

עָמָל m. labour, toil; trouble, vexation: Gen. xli. 51.

עִצָּבוֹן m. labour, hard and painful toil, travail: Gen. v. 29.

TOKEN

אוֹת c. (see Sign): Gen. ix. 12, 13, 17; xvii. 11: Exod. iii. 12; xii. 13; xiii. 16: Num. xvii. 10: Josh. ii. 12: Job xxi. 29: Ps. lxv. 8; lxxxvi. 17; cxxxv. 9: Isa. xliv. 25.

TOLL

מִדָּה f. tribute: Ezra iv. 20. מִנְדָּה Ch. f. id. Ezra iv. 13; vii. 24.

TOMB

גָּדִישׁ m. stack of corn in the field; a tomb, tumulus, sepulchral mound: Job xxi. 32, marg. 'watch in the heap.'

TONGS

מֶלְקָחַיִם m. dual, tongs for the fire: 1 Kings vii. 49: 2 Chron. iv. 21: Isa. vi. 6; thus מַלְקָחַיִם m. dual, Exod. xxv. 38: Num. iv. 9.

מַעֲצָד m. axe; tongs: Isa. xliv. 12.

TONGUE

לָשׁוֹן com. tongue, both of men and animals; spoken of the human tongue as the instrument of speech, with the following exceptions: Ps. xxii. 15, Lam. iv. 4, Isa. lvii. 4, Job xx. 16; thus Job xxxiii. 2, Ps. xii. 3, xlv. 1, xxxix. 3, cix. 2. The words which one has in his mouth ready to be uttered are said to be upon the tongue, בְּ, Job vi. 30, Ps. cxxxix. 4; עַל, 2 Sam. xxiii. 2, Prov. xxxi. 26, comp. Cant. iv. 11; which phrases seem not greatly to differ in meaning; comp. "upon the lips," Ps. xvi. 4, and "under the lips," Ps. cxl. 3. Seq. genit. a lying tongue, Prov. vi. 17. (Meton. for a lying person, c. masc. Prov. xxvi. 28); Ps. lii. 4, Prov. x. 31. Also κατ᾽ ἐξοχήν, for a spiteful, malignant tongue (comp. Ecclus. xxviii. 15), whence, Ps. cxl. 11, a man of tongue, i.e. a slanderer. (But the "master of tongue," Eccles. x. 11, babbler, or enchanter, charmer); Jer. xviii. 18, "Come, let us smite him with the tongue," i.e. as Chald. Well, let us bear false witness against him; Job v. 21, "scourge of the tongue," comp. the like figure in Germ. klatschen, Eng. lash, Fr. coup de langue; Ezek. xxxvi. 3, ye go upon the lips of the (slanderer's) tongue, i.e. are traduced in men's mouths. Meton. for speech, Job xv. 5, Prov. xvi. 1; for idiom, dialect, Dan. i. 4, Gen. x. 5, Deut. xxviii. 49, lit. who its tongue, Isa. xxviii. 11.— Gen. x. 5, &c., Prov. xvii. 20, lit. he that is perverse in his tongue.

TOOL

חֶרֶב f. sword; graver, chisel: Exod. xx. 25.

כְּלִי m. a general name for all kinds of furniture, vessels, &c.: 1 Kings vi. 7.

TOP

1 גַּג m. (see Roof) top of a house, or of an altar, &c.

2 עֶצֶם m. bone; the substance of anything, i.q. self, ipse; like עֶצֶם, 2 Kings ix. 13, i.e. on the very steps.

3 סָעִיף m. (see Branch) top. Gesenius, cleft, fissure.

4 צְחִיחַ m. the top of a rock, from its bright shining appearance, or from its being dry and parched.

5 צַמֶּרֶת f. foliage; fleece or locks of a tree.

6 קָדְקֹד m. vertex, top, crown of the head, so called because there the hair divides itself.

7 רֹאשׁ m. head, highest, chief: Gen. viii. 5, &c.

No. 7 not included.

Exod. xxx. 3.	1	Judg. xv. 8, 11.	1	Isa. ii. 21.	3		3
xxxvii. 26.	1	1 Sam. ix. 25, 26.	1	xv. 3.	1		1
Deut. xxviii. 35.	6	2 Sam. xvi. 22.	6	Ezek. xxiv. 7, 8.	1		4
xxxiii. 16.	6	2 Kings ix. 13. a	6	xxvi. 4, 14.	2		4
Judg. ix. 51.	1	xxiii. 12.	1	xxxi. 3, 10, 14.	1		5

a i.e. on the very steps.

TOPAZ

פִּטְדָה *f.* a species of gem found in Ethiopia; according to most of the ancient versions, the topaz, a pale yellowish gem, found on an island in the Red Sea, Plin. H. N. xxxvii. 8. Exod. xxviii. 17; xxxix. 10: Job xxviii. 19: Ezek. xxviii. 13.

TORCH

לַפִּיד *m.* flame; lamp, a lamp-torch: Nah. ii. 4: Zech. xii. 6.

פְּלָדָה *f.* supposed by our translators to be the same as above by a transposition of the letters, but rather iron, or scythes, attached to war-chariots: Nah. ii. 3.

TORTOISE

צָב *m.* a kind of lizard: Lev. xi. 29.

TOSS

גָּעַשׁ to shake. HITHPAEL *fut.* Jer. v. 22, i.e. shall be agitated.

נְדֻדִים *m. pl.* uneasy motions, tossings, of a sleepless person on his bed: Job vii. 4.

נָדַף to drive away. NIPHAL *part.* Prov. xxi. 6.

נָעַר to shake; to be shaken out. NIPHAL *pret.* Ps. cix. 23, i.e. cast out of the land.

צְנֵפָה *f.* (see *Turn*): Isa. xxii. 18, *lit.* with turning.

TOTTERING

דָּחָה to thrust, to overthrow. KAL *part.* Paül, Ps. lxii. 3.

TOUCH

1   נָגַע to smite, to strike; *seq.* בְּ to smite upon, Gen. xxxii. 6, 33. Hence, of God, to smite with plagues, Job xix. 21. *Trop.* of the wind, to smite, to blast, Ezek. xvii. 10. To touch, Lxx. ἅπτεσθαι, construed very often with בְּ, *q. d.* to touch upon: Gen. iii. 3; Lev. v. 3, vi. 18, xi. 24; Dan. viii. 5; *seq.* עַל, Isa. vi. 7; and אֶל, Num. iv. 15, Hag. ii. 12; *seq.* עַד, Job iv. 5; also *c. accus.* Isa. lii. 11, Job vi. 7. Specially, to touch any one is to do him harm or violence, Gen. xxvi. 11, 29, Josh. ix. 19; to touch a woman, to lie with her, *seq.* בְּ, Prov. vi. 29; *seq.* אֶל, Gen. xx. 6. So ἅπτεσθαι γυναικός, 1 Cor. vii. 1; to touch the heart, *i.e.* to move, to affect the mind of any one, 1 Sam. x. 26. In a local sense, to touch, to come in contact with, to reach to anything, *seq.* בְּ, 1 Kings vi. 27, Hos. iv. 2; עַד, Micah i. 9, Isa. xvi. 8; אֶל, Jer. li. 9; עַל, Judg. xx. 34, 41. KAL ᵃ *pret.* ᵇ *inf.* ᶜ *imp.* ᵈ *fut.* ᵉ *part.* Poel. HIPHIL ᶠ *fut.*

2   נָשַׁק to kiss. HIPHIL *part.* Ezek. iii. 13, *marg.* 'kissed,' *i.e.* of which one reached to and touched another.

3   רוּחַ to smell. HIPHIL *inf.*

Gen. iii. 3.	1 d	Num. xvi. 26.	1 d	Job vi. 7.	1 b
xx. 6.	1 b	xix. 11, 13, 18, 21.	1 d	xix. 21.	1 a
xxvi. 11.	1 e	xix. 16.	1 d	Ps. civ. 32.	1 d
xxvi. 29.	1 d	xix. 22, 22.	1 d e	cv. 15.	1 d
xxxii. 25.	1 d	xxxi. 19.	1 e	cxliv. 5.	1 c
xxxii. 32.	1 d	Deut. xiv. 8.	1 d	Prov. vi. 29.	1 d
Exod. xix. 12, 12.	1 b e	Josh. ix. 19.	1 b	Isa. vi. 7.	1 a
xix. 13.	1 d	Judg. vi. 21.	1 e	lii. 11.	1 d
xxix. 37.	1 e	xvi. 9.	3	Jer. i. 9.	1 f
xxx. 29.	1 d	Ruth ii. 9.	1 d	xii. 14.	1 d
Lev. v. 2, 3.	1 d	1 Sam. x. 26.	1 a	Lam. iv. 14, 15.	1 d
vi. 18, 27.	1 d	2 Sam. xiv. 10.	1 b	Ezek. iii. 13.	2
vii. 19, 21.	1 d	xxiii. 7.	1 d	xvii. 10.	1 d
xi. 8.	1 d	1 Kings vi. 27. a	1 e	Dan. viii. 5. β	1 d
xi. 24, 26, 27, 31, 36, 39.	1 e	vi. 27, 27.	1 d	viii. 18.	1 d
xii. 4.	1 d	xix. 5.	1 e	ix. 21.	1 a
xv. 5, 11, 12.	1 d	xix. 7.	1 d	x. 10.	1 d
xv. 7, 10, 19, 21, 22, 27.	1 e	2 Kings xiii. 21.	1 d	x. 16.	1 d
xv. 23.	1 b	1 Chron. xvi. 22.	1 d	x. 18.	1 d
xxii. 4.	1 e	Esth. v. 2.	1 d	Hos. iv. 2.	1 a
xxii. 5, 6.	1 d	Job i. 11.	1 c	Amos ix. 5.	1 a
Num. iv. 15.	1 d	ii. 5.	1 c	Hag. ii. 12.	1 a
		v. 19.	1 d	ii. 13.	1 d
				Zech. ii. 8, 8.	1 e

a lit. touched wing to wing.   *β marg.* 'or, none touched him in the earth.'

TOW

נְעֹרֶת *f.* tow, as being shaken or beaten off from flax: Judg. xvi. 9: Isa. i. 31.

פִּשְׁתָּה *m.* flax: Isa. xliii. 17, *or,* a wick, made of linen.

TOWARD

דֶּרֶךְ *com.* way: 1 Kings viii. 44, 48; xviii. 43: 2 Kings xxv. 4, "the way toward:" 2 Chron. vi. 34, 38: Ezek. xx. 46; xl. 6, 20, 22, 24, 24, 27, 27, 32, 44, 44, 45, 46; xli. 11, 12; xlii. 1, *lit.* the way, the way of; 7, 10, 11, 12, 12, 15, 15; xliii. 1, 4.

מוּל *m.* forepart, front: Exod. xviii. 19; xxviii. 27; xxxix. 20.

פָּנִים *m. pl.* Gen. xviii. 16, *lit.* on the face of; xix. 28, *lit.* toward the face of; 28, *lit. id.*; Num. xxi. 20, *lit.* upon the face of; xxiii. 28, *lit. id.*; 2 Sam. xv. 23, *lit. id.*

TOWER

1   בַּחַן a watch-tower, tower: Isa. xxxii. 14. Gesenius, the hill (Ophel) and the tower upon it; probably the tower upon the hill Ophel, mentioned in Neh. iii. 26, 27. ᵃ בָּחוּן *m.* a watch-tower built by a besieging army. ᵇ בָּחוֹן *adj.* Jer. vi. 27. Gesenius, a trier of metals, assayer; see *Try.*

2   גָּדַל to be or become great; to magnify. HIPHIL ᵃ *part.* 2 Sam. xxii. 51 (כתיב). ᵇ מִגְדָּל *m.* a tower, a great high building, chiefly belonging to fortified towns and castles, Judg. ix. 47, &c.; in this sense God is a strong tower, Ps. lxi. 3, Prov. xviii. 10; it is also used of a watch-tower, 2 Kings ix. 17, xvii. 9, xviii. 8; and of the tower of a vineyard, Gr. πύργος, Isa. v. 2, comp. Matt. xxi. 33, which Lowth, on Isa. v. 2, thinks was a building of a permanent nature, for all the purposes of making wine; also of the tower and temple of Babel, Gen. xi. 4, 5; *fig.* of powerful and proud men, Isa. xxx. 25, ii. 15. In Isa. v. 2 Aben Ezra supposes to be meant the temple; Luther, the worship of God; Schmidt includes both in one. Gen. xi. 4, 5, &c. ᶜ מִגְדֹּל *m. id.*

3 עֹפֶל *m.* a hill, *tumulus;* an advantageous situation for a fortress.

4 פִּנָּה *f.* corner, corner-stone, the strongest part of the building; put for towers or very strong buildings.

5 מָצוֹר *m.* fortress.

6 מִשְׂגָּב *m.* height, rock, crag, affording security and refuge.

No. 2 b not included.

2 Sam. xxii. 3.	6	Isa. xxiii. 13.	1 a	Ezek. xxx. 6. β	2 c
xxii. 51.	2 a, or 2 c	xxxii. 14.	6	Hab. ii. 1. γ	5
2 Kings v. 24. α	3	Jer. vi. 27.	1 b	Zeph. i. 16.	4
Ps. xviii. 2.	6	Ezek. xxix. 10. β	2 c	iii. 6. δ	4
cxliv. 2.	6				

α *marg.* ' *or,* secret place.'   β *marg.* ' *or,* from Migdol to Syene.'
γ *marg.* ' fenced place.'   δ *marg.* ' *or,* corners.'

TOWN

1 בַּת *f.* daughter; the daughters of a city are the small towns and villages lying around it and dependent on its jurisdiction.

2 חַוּוֹת *f. pl.* small towns, a village, nomadic encampment: properly, a place where one lives, dwells.

3 חָצֵר *m.* a court; village, hamlet; see *Village.*

4 עִיר *f.* see *City.*

5 פְּרָזוֹת *f. pl.* country regions, open country; towns or villages without walls.

6 קִיר *m.* side, wall; wall of a house (*e.g.* exterior); wall side: Josh. ii. 15 (and so probably 2 Kings iv. 10, a little wall chamber, built against the side of the house).

Gen. xxv. 16.	3	Judg. xi. 26, 26.	1	1 Chron. viii. 12.	1
Num. xxxii. 41.	2	1 Sam. xvi. 4.	4	xviii. 1.	1
Deut. iii. 5.	4	xxiii. 7.	4	2 Chron. xiii. 19, 19,	
Josh. ii. 15.	6	xxvii. 5. α	4	19.	1
xiii. 30.	2	1 Kings iv. 13.	2	Esth. ix. 19.	4
xv. 45, 47, 47.	1	1 Chron. ii. 23, 23.	2, 1	Jer. xix. 15.	4
xvii. 11, 11, 11, 11,		v. 16.	1	Hab. ii. 12.	4
11, 11, 16.	1	vii. 28, 28, 28, 28,		Zech. ii. 4.	5
Judg. i. 27, 27, 27, 27.	1	29, 29, 29, 29.	1		

a lit. in one of the cities of.

TRADE, TRAFFIC

אֱנוֹשׁ *m.* man: Gen. xlvi. 32, *marg.* ' they are men of cattle;' 34, *lit.* have been men of cattle.

כְּנַעַן *m.* Canaan; a merchant; traffic: Isa. xxiii. 8: Ezek. xvii. 4.

נָתַן to give. KAL *pret.* Ezek. xxvii. 12, 13, 14, 17.

סָחַר to go about; to traverse countries as a merchant, in order to buy or sell; hence with an accusative of the country. KAL *pret.* Gen. xxxiv. 10. *fut.* Gen. xxxiv. 21, xlii. 34. מִסְחָר *m.* traffic: 1 Kings x. 15.

רְכֻלָּה *f.* trade, traffic: Ezek. xxviii. 5, 18.

TRAIN

חַיִל *m.* host, army; a train or company that escorts and attends princes: 1 Kings x. 2.

חָנַךְ to imbue; to initiate; applied to the first instruction or direction given to children. KAL *imp.* Prov. xxii. 6, *marg.* ' *or,* catechise.' חָנִיךְ *adj.* Gen. xiv. 14, *marg.* ' instructed.'

שׁוּל *m.* the lower part or skirts of a garment; Isa. vi. 1: it may here signify the rays of glory issuing from his lofty throne.

TRAMPLE

רָמַס to tread upon, to trample under feet. KAL *fut.* Ps. xci. 13: Isa. lxiii. 3.

TRANQUILLITY

שְׁלֵוָה *Ch. f.* security, safety, quiet, *or,* careless security: Dan. iv. 27, *marg.* ' *or,* an healing of thine error.'

TRANSGRESS

1 בָּגַד to act covertly, deceitfully; to deal falsely, faithlessly, hypocritically; transgressors, *sc.* hypocritical dealers towards God, the ungodly, wicked. LXX. παρανομοι Stock, *denegare officia.* KAL ᵃ*pret.* ᵇ*part.* Poel.

2 מָעַל to cover; to act covertly, treacherously, to be faithless, chiefly against God; *seq.* בְּ of person, to deal treacherously, traitorously with any one; *seq.* בְּ of thing, to take by stealth, to steal. KAL ᵃ*pret.* ᵇ*inf.* ᶜ*fut.* ᵈ מַעַל *m.* perverseness, transgression.

3 עָבַד to serve. KAL *fut.* Jer. ii. 20 (כתיב).

4 עָבַר to pass over. *Metaph.* to transgress. LXX. παραβαινω, *e.g.* the commandment of God, or of the king, a covenant, a law. KAL ᵃ*pret.* ᵇ*inf.* ᶜ*fut.* ᵈ*part.* Poel. HIPHIL ᵉ*part.*

5 פָּשַׁע to revolt, rebel, to be contumacious; to refuse allegiance and duty to whom they are due; knowingly to refuse subjection to rightful authority, or obedience to a law which we ought to observe; to rebel against Jehovah, to apostatize from him. KAL ᵃ*pret.* ᵇ*inf.* ᶜ*imp.* ᵈ*fut.* ᵉ*part.* Poel. ᶠ פֶּשַׁע *m.* Exod. xxiii. 21, &c.

No. 5 f, *Transgression,* not included.

Num. xiv. 41.	4 d	Ezra x. 10.	2 a	Isa. xlvi. 8.	5 e
Deut. xvii. 2.	4 a	x. 13.	5 b	xlviii. 8.	5 e
xxvi. 13.	4 a	Neh. i. 8.	2 c	liii. 12, 12.	5 e
Josh. vii. 11, 15.	4 a	xiii. 27.	2 b	lix. 13.	5 b
xxii. 22.	2 d	Esth. iii. 3.	4 d	lxvi. 24.	5 e
xxiii. 16.	4 b	Ps. xvii. 3.	4 c	Jer. ii. 8, 29.	5 a
Judg. ii. 20.	4 a	xxv. 3.	1 b	ii. 20.	4 c, or 3
1 Sam. ii. 24.	4 e	xxxvii. 38.	5 e	iii. 13.	5 a
xiv. 33.	1 a	li. 13.	5 e	xxxiii. 8.	5 a
xv. 24.	4 a	lix. 5.	1 b	xxxiv. 18.	4 d
1 Kings viii. 50.	5 a	cxix. 158.	1 b	Lam. iii. 42.	5 a
2 Kings xviii. 12.	4 c	Prov. ii. 22.	1 b	Ezek. ii. 3.	5 a
1 Chron. ii. 7.	2 a	xi. 3, 6.	1 b	viii. 31.	5 a
v. 25.	2 c	xii. 2, 15.	1 b	xx. 38.	5 e
ix. 1.	2 d	xvii. 19.	2 c	Dan. viii. 23.	4 e
x. 13.	2 d	xxi. 18.	1 b	ix. 11.	4 a
2 Chron. xii. 2.	4 d	xxiii. 28.	1 b	Hos. vi. 7.	4 a
xxiv. 20.	4 d	xxvi. 10.	4 d	vii. 13.	5 a
xxvi. 16.	2 d	xxviii. 21.	5 d	viii. 1.	4 d
xxviii. 19. α	2 b d	Isa. i. 28.	5 e	xiv. 9.	5 e
xxix. 19.	2 d	xxiv. 5.	5 b	Amos iv. 4, 4.	5 c b
xxxvi. 14. β	2 b d	xliii. 27.	5 a	Hab. i. 5. γ	1 b
Ezra ix. 4.	2 d			Zeph. iii. 11.	5 a
x. 6.	2 d				

a lit. transgressed a transgression.   β *lit.* multiplied to transgress transgression.   γ *lit.* is transgressing.

TRANSLATE

עָבַר to pass; to cause to pass. HIPHIL *inf.* 2 Sam. iii. 10.

TRAP

מוֹקֵשׁ *m.* noose, snare, by which beasts and birds are taken: Josh. xxiii. 13: Ps. lxix. 22.

מַלְכֹּדֶת *f.* noose, snare for taking prey : Job xviii. 10.

מַשְׁחִית *f.* destruction ; a trap : Jer. v. 26.

TRAVEL, TRAVAIL

1   חָבַל   to bind ; to be in pain, to travail. PIEL *fut.*

2   חוּל   to be in pain ; to travail. KAL [a] *pret.* HIPHIL [b] *fut.*
HITHPOLEL [c] *part.*

3   חָלָה   to be sick, in great pain. KAL *part.* Poel.

4   יָלַד   to bear children. KAL [a] *inf.* [b] *fut.* [c] *part.* Poel.

5   תְּלָאָה   *f.* travail, toil, distress, the extremity of which brings a
man to despair, not knowing what to do.

6   עָמָל   labour, toil ; trouble, vexation, sorrow.

7   עִנְיָן   *m.* labour, toil ; events which occasion much trouble and
fatigue.

Gen. xxxv. 16.	4 b	Eccles. iv. 8.	7	Jer. vi. 24.	4 c
xxxviii. 27, 28.	4 a	v. 14.	7	xiii. 21.	4 a
Exod. xviii. 8.	5	Isa. xiii. 8.	4 c	xxii. 23.	4 c
Num. xx. 14.	5	xxi. 3.	4 c	xxx. 6, 6.	4 c
1 Sam. iv. 19.	4 b	xxiii. 4.	2 a	xxxi. 8.	4 a
Job xv. 20.	2 c	xlii. 14.	4 c	xlix. 24.	4 c
Ps. vii. 14.	1	liii. 11.		l. 43.	4 c
xlviii. 6.	4 c	liv. 1.	2 a	Lam. iii. 5.	5
Eccles. i. 13.	7	lxvi. 7.	2 b	Hos. xiii. 13.	4 c
ii. 23, 26.	7	lxvi. 8.	2 a	Micah iv. 9, 10.	4 c
i.i. 10.	7	Jer. iv. 31.	3	v. 3.	4 c
iv. 4, 6.	6				

TRAVEL

אָרַח   to be on the way. KAL *part.* Poel, Isa. xxi. 13, "travelling companies," *i.e.* of merchants, a caravan. אֹרַח *com.*
way ; wayfaring man : Job xxxi. 32, *marg.* 'way.'

הָלַךְ   to go, to walk, to go forth. KAL *part.* Poel, Judg. v. 6,
marg. 'and the walkers of paths.' PIEL *part.* Prov. vi.
11. HITHPAEL *part.* Prov. xxiv. 34. הֶלֶךְ *m.* going,
travel : 2 Sam. xii. 4.

נְתִיבָה   *f.* a trodden way, a beaten path : Judg. v. 6.

צָעָה   to turn on one side ; to incline, bend. Taylor observes,
" It seems plain to me that this word, in Isa. lxiii. 1,
hath relation to the actions, the superb mein or manner,
of a triumphant prince returning from a battle, in which
he hath got complete victory over his enemies." KAL
part. Poel, Isa. lxiii. 1.

TRAVERSE

שָׂרַךְ   to interweave, to entangle. PIEL *part.* Jer. ii. 23, entan-
gling her ways, *i.e.* running about wild in her season.

TREACHEROUS

1   בָּגַד   (see *Transgress*), to deal treacherously or hypocritically ;
to oppress, spoil, pillage ; mostly *seq.* בְּ ; *seq.* מִן to depart treacherously. KAL [a] *pret.* [b] *inf.* [c] *fut.* [d] *part.*
Poel. בֶּגֶד *m.* treachery. בֹּגְדוֹת [f] *f. pl.* great perfidy or
hypocrisy. [g] בָּגוֹד *adj.* perfidious.

2   מִרְמָה   *f.* deceit, fraud.

Judg. ix. 23.	1 c	Jer. iii. 7, 10.	1 g	Lam. i. 2.	1 a
2 Kings ix. 23.	2	iii. 8, 11.	1 d	Hos. v. 7.	1 a
Isa. xxi. 2, 2.	1 d d	iii. 20, 20.	1 d	vi. 7.	1 a
xxiv. 16, 16.	1 d a	v. 11.	1 b a	Hab. i. 13.	1 d
xxiv. 16, 16.α	1 e d a	ix. 2.	1 d	Zeph. iii. 4.γ	1 a
xxxiii. 1, 1, 1, 1.	1 d a b c	xii. 1.	1 d e	Mal. ii. 10, 15, 16.	1 c
xlviii. 8.β	1 b c	xii. 6.	1 a	ii. 11, 14.	1 a

α by treachery deceiving they have deceived.   β *lit.* dealing treacherously
wouldest deal, &c.   γ *lit.* men of treachery.

TREAD

1   בּוּם   to tread down, to trample under foot ; also to trample in
pieces, to stamp upon enemies, *i.e.* utterly to subdue
them ; to tread down a place, land, *i.e.* to lay waste,
with the accessory idea of pollution, profanation ; *comp.*
καταπατεῖν, *i. q.* βεβηλοῦν ; used of treading the sanctuary
by profane persons, 1 Macc. iii. 45, 51 : Rev. xi. 2 : Dan.
viii. 13. KAL [a] *pret.* [b] *part.* Poel. POLEL [c] *pret.* HO-
PHAL [d] *part.* [e] מוּבָסָה *f.* treading upon.

2   בָּשַׁם   to tread down, to trample upon, *seq.* עַל. POEL *inf.*

3   דּוּשׁ   to beat, to bruise in pieces, especially by treading ; to
tread, to trample, to crush ; to tread out grain. KAL
[a] *inf.* NIPHAL [b] *pret.* [c] *inf.* [d] דּוּשׁ Ch. P'AL *fut.*

4   דִּישׁ   to tread out grain. KAL *inf.*

5   דָּרַךְ   to tread, to trample with the feet ; especially to tread the
wine-press in order to break the fruit and express the
wine or oil ; to tread the grapes ; *metaph.* of enemies
trodden down as grapes : Isa. lxiii. 3, Judg. v. 21 ; to
tread a bow, *i.e.* to bend it ; to tread a way or place, by
going and walking upon it, entering into it, *seq.* בְּ. KAL
[a] *pret.* [b] *fut.* [c] *part.* Poel. HIPHIL [d] *pret.*

6   הָדַךְ   to tread down to the ground, to trample under foot. KAL
imp.

7   סָלָה   to trample upon, or cast down. KAL [a] *pret.* PIEL [b] *pret.*

8   עָסַם   to tread down, to tread in pieces. KAL *pret.*

9   רָמַס   to tread with the feet, *e.g.* a potter the clay, also persons
so as to destroy life, a lion his prey ; *part.* an oppressor ;
also to tread down streets with horses' hoofs : Isa. i. 12,
to trample my courts, to profane them, *comp.* Rev. xi. 2,
1 Macc. iii. 45. KAL [a] *pret.* [b] *inf.* [c] *imp.* [d] *fut.* NI-
PHAL [e] *fut.* [f] מִרְמָס *m.* a treading down, something trodden under foot.

10   שׂוּם   to set, put, lay. KAL *inf.*

Deut. i. 36.	5 a	Ps. lx. 12.	1 a	Isa. lxiii. 18.	1 c
xi. 24, 25.	5 b	xci. 13.	5 b	Jer. xii. 10.	1 c
xxv. 4.	4	cviii. 13.	1 a	xxv. 30.	5 c
xxxiii. 29.	5 b	cxix. 118.	7 a	xlviii. 33.	5 b
Josh. i. 3.	5 b	Isa. i. 12.	9 b	Lam. i. 15, 15.	7 b, 5 a
xiv. 9.	5 a	v. 5.	9 f	Ezek. xxvi. 11.	9 d
Judg. v. 21.	5 b	vii. 25.	9 f	xxxiv. 18.	9 d
ix. 27.	5 b	x. 6.	10, 9 f	xxxiv. 19.	9 f
xx. 43.	5 d	xiv. 19.	1 d	Dan. vii. 23.	3 d
1 Sam. v. 5.	5 b	xiv. 25.	1 a	viii. 13.	9 f
2 Kings vii. 17, 20.	9 d	xvi. 10, 10.	5 c b	Hos. x. 11.	3 a
ix. 33.	9 d	xviii. 2, 7.	1 e	Amos iv. 13.	2 a
xxii. 5.	9 d	xxii. 5.	1 e	v. 11.	5 a
2 Chron. xxv. 18.	9 d	xxv. 10.	3 b	ix. 13.	5 a
Neh. xiii. 15.	5 c	xxv. 10.	3 c	Micah i. 3.	5 b
Job ix. 8.	5 c	xxvi. 6.	9 d	v. 5, 6.	5 b
xxii. 15.	5 a	xxviii. 3.	9 e	vi. 8.	5 b
xxiv. 11.	5 b	xxviii. 18.	9 f	vi. 15.	5 b
xxviii. 8.	5 d	xli. 25.	9 d	vii. 10.	9 f
xl. 12.	6	lxiii. 3.	5 c	Nah. iii. 14.	5 c
Ps. vii. 5.	9 d	lxiii. 3, 3.	5 b a	Zech. x. 5.	1 b
xliv. 5.	1 a	lxiii. 6.	1 a	Mal. iv. 3.	8

TREASON

קֶשֶׁר   *m.* conspiracy : 1 Kings xvi. 20 : 2 Kings xi. 14, 14 : 2 Chron.
xxiii. 13, 13.

TREASURE

1   אָצַר   to lay up, to store, to treasure up. KAL [a] *fut.* NIPHAL
[b] *fut.* [c] אוֹצָר *m. pr.* what is laid up, a store, stock, *e.g.*
of fruits, produce, provision ; especially of gold, silver,

and other precious things ; treasure, *e.g.* of the treasures of the temple, of the king : Deut. xxviii. 12, &c.

2 גִּזְבָּרִין Ch. *m. pl.* treasurer.

3 גִּזְבָּר *m.* the keeper of the royal treasures among the Persians. ᵃ Ch. *m. id.*

4 גְּנָזִים *m. pl.* treasures. ᵃ גִּנְזִין Ch. *m. pl.* ᵇ גַּנְזַךְ *m.* treasury of the temple.

5 חֹסֶן *m.* riches, wealth ; treasure, abundance ; riches laid up untouched and secure.

6 מַטְמוֹן *m.* hidden stores, hid treasure, *sc.* underground.

7 מִכְמַנִּים *m. pl.* hidden treasures.

8 מִסְכְּנוֹת *f. pl.* stores, magazines, where provisions are laid up : Exod. i. 11, comp. 2 Chron. xvi. 4. Gr. fortified cities.

9 סָכַן to dwell with ; to be familiar with ; to be an associate, or to be entrusted with, as a steward, treasurer, &c. KAL *part.* Poel.

10 עָתוּד *adj.* ready ; things laid up in store ready for use.

11 שָׁפַן to cover. KAL *part.* Paül.

No. 1 c not included.

Gen. xliii. 23.		6	Ezra vii. 21.	3 a	Isa. x. 13.	10
Exod. i. 11.		8	Neh. xiii. 13.	1 a	xxii. 15.	9
Deut. xxxiii. 19.		11	Esth. iii. 9.	4	xxiii. 18.	1 b
1 Chron. xxviii. 11.	4 b		iv. 7.	4	Jer. xli. 8.	6
Ezra i. 8.		3 a	Job iii. 21.	6	Ezek. xxii. 25.	5
v. 17.		4 a	Prov. ii. 4.	6	Dan. iii. 2, 3.	2
vi. 1.		4 a	xv. 6.	5	xi. 43.	7
vii. 20.		4 a				

TREE

1 אֵילִים *m. pl.* strong, stout, mighty trees. ᵃ אִילָן Ch. *m. id.*

2 אֵשֶׁל *m.* a tamarisk, *myrica, tamarix orientalis,* Linn. Then perhaps any large tree, and *collect.* trees, a wood, a grove.

3 עֵץ *m.* a tree ; often *collect.* trees : Gen. i. 11, &c. Figuratively, trees represent men, green trees the righteous, dry trees the wicked, Ezek. xx. 47 ; xvii. 24, all the trees of the field, all men, the high tree the lofty and powerful, the low tree the weak and contemptible. ᵃ עֵצָה *f.* wood.

4 צֶאֱלִים *m. pl.* shady trees.

No. 3 not included.

1 Sam. xxii. 6. a	2	Isa. lxi. 3.	1	Dan. iv. 10, 11, 14,
xxxi. 13.	2	Jer. vi. 6.	3 a	20, 23, 26. 1 a
Job xl. 21, 22.	4	Ezek. xxxi. 14, 14.	3, 1	

a marg. ' or, grove in a high place.'

TREMBLE

1 זוּעַ to shake, to agitate ; to be shaken ; to quake, to tremble. KAL ᵃ*fut.* זוּעַ Ch. Pʻᴀʟ ᵇ*part.*

2 חִיל to be in great pain ; to fear and tremble as in anguish and horror of mind. KAL ᵃ*imp.* HIPHIL ᵇ*fut.*

3 חָפַז see *Haste.* KAL *fut.*

4 חָרַד to tremble, to be in trepidation, to be terrified ; ascribed to the heart ; *seq.* לְ of cause, Job xxxvii. 1. *Prægn.* to follow trembling, 1 Sam. xiii. 7 ; *seq.* לִקְרַאה to tremble at meeting any one, to meet him trembling. *Trop.* to come trembling, to hasten (comp. Lat. *trepidare,* Virg. Æn. ix. 14) ; *seq.* מִן from a place, Hos. xi. 10, 11. KAL

ᵃ*pret.* ᵇ*imp.* ᶜ*fut.* ᵈ חָרֵד *adj.* fearful, anxious. ᵉ חֲרָדָה *f.* trembling.

5 סָמַר used of a person in terror, to shudder. KAL *pret.*

6 פָּלַץ to tremble, to be shaken ; of pillars so as to be in danger of breaking. HITHPAEL ᵃ*fut.* ᵇ פַּלָּצוּת *f.* trembling, horror.

7 רָגַז to be moved or thrown into great commotion, to be moved by fear, as by a violent concussion, to tremble. KAL ᵃ*pret.* ᵇ*fut.* HIPHIL ᶜ*part.* ᵈ רַגָּז *adj.* trembling. ᵉ רָגְזָה *f.* perturbation.

8 רוּף Polel, to be moved as by a stroke or blow. POLEL *fut.*

9 רָעַד to tremble or quake, as the earth, or persons. KAL ᵃ*fut.* HIPHIL ᵇ*part.* ᶜ רַעַד *m.* trembling, awe. ᵈ רְעָדָה *f. id.*

10 רַעַל *m.* a reeling from intoxication. ᵃ תַּרְעֵלָה *f.* reeling, drunkenness.

11 רָעַשׁ to tremble, to quake ; specially for fear, terror, *e.g.* the earth, the heavens, mountains, islands, the foundations of the earth, walls, door-posts, &c. KAL ᵃ*pret.* ᵇ*fut.* ᶜ*part.* HIPHIL ᵈ*pret.*

12 רֶתֶת *m.* terror ; a trembling, stricken and humbled state.

Gen. xxvii. 33. α	4 c e	Job xxxvii. 1.	4 c	Jer. viii. 16.	11 a
Exod. xv. 15.	9 c	Ps. ii. 11.	9 d	x. 10.	11 b
xix. 16.	4 c	xviii. 7.	11 b	xxx. 5.	4 e
Deut. ii. 25.	7 a	lv. 5.	9 c	xxxiii. 9.	7 a
xx. 3.	3	lx. 2.	11 d	li. 29.	11 b
xxviii. 65.	7 d	lxxvii. 18.	7 a	Ezek. xii. 18.	7 e
Judg. v. 4.	7 d	xcvii. 4.	2 b	xxvi. 16, 16.	4 e a
1 Sam. iv. 13.	4 d	xcix. 1.	7 b	xxvi. 18.	4 c
xiii. 7.	4 a	civ. 32.	9 a	xxxii. 10.	4 a
xiv. 15, 15, 15.	4 e a e	cxiv. 7.	2 a	Dan. v. 19. β	1 b
xvi. 4.	4 c	cxix. 120.	5	vi. 26.	1 b
xxviii. 5.	4 c	Eccles. xii. 3.	1 a	x. 11.	9 b
2 Sam. xxii. 8.	11 b	Isa. v. 25.	7 b	Hos. xi. 10, 11.	4 c
Ezra ix. 4.	4 d	xiv. 16.	7 c	xiii. 1.	12
x. 3.	4 d	xxxii. 11.	4 b	Joel ii. 1.	7 b
x. 9.	9 b	li. 17, 22.	10 a	ii. 10.	11 a
Job iv. 14.	9 d	lxiv. 2.	7 b	Amos viii. 8.	7 b
ix. 6.	6 a	lxvi. 2, 5.	4 d	Hab. iii. 10.	2 b
xxi. 6.	6 b	Jer. iv. 24.	11 c	iii. 7, 16, 16.	7 b
xxvi. 11.	8	v. 22.	2 b	Zech. xii. 2.	10

a marg. 'trembled with a great trembling greatly.'   *β lit.* were trembling.

TRENCH

חֵיל *m.* host ; fortification, entrenchment, especially the exterior low wall or breastwork which surrounds and covers the trench : 2 Sam. xx. 15, *marg.* ' or, against the outmost wall.'

מַעְגָּל *m.* track, rut ; (from עֲגָלָה a waggon), a waggon-rampart, a bulwark formed of the waggons and other vehicles of the army : 1 Sam. xxvi. 5, 7. מַעְגָּלָה *f.* 1 Sam. xvii. 20, *marg.* ' or, place of the carriage.'

תְּעָלָה *f.* a channel, trench, in which water goes up from a stream to water or inundate the fields : 1 Kings xviii. 32, 35, 38.

TRESPASS

1 אָשַׁם to fail in duty, to transgress, to be guilty, to trespass. The person towards whom one fails in duty is put with לְ, that in which one is guilty with לְ and בְּ. KAL ᵃ*pret.* ᵇ*inf.* ᶜ*fut.* ᵈ אָשָׁם *m.* fault, blame, guilt ; *meton.* that through which guilt is contracted, thing trespassed ; a sacrifice for fault or guilt, a trespass-offering ; see

Offering. • אַשְׁמָה *f.* a being in fault, trespassing; fault, blame, guilt, trespass.

2 חָטָא to sin; see *Sin.* KAL *fut.*

3 מָעַל to act covertly, treacherously, to be faithless; with מַעַל and בְּ of person or thing, to deal treacherously with. KAL [a] *pret.* [b] *inf.* [c] *fut.* [d] מַעַל *m.* treachery against God, transgression, sin.

4 פָּשַׁע see *Transgress.* KAL [a] *pret.* [b] פֶּשַׁע *m.*

Gen. xxxi. 36.	4 b	Deut. xxxii. 51.	3 a	2 Chron. xxxiii. 23. δ	1 e
l. 17, 17.	4 b	Josh. vii. 1.	3 d	Ezra ix. 2.	3 d
Exod. xxii. 9.	4 b	xxii. 16, 20, 31.	3 d	ix. 6, 7, 13, 15.	1 e
Lev. v. 7.	1 d	1 Sam. xxv. 28.	4 b	x. 2.	3 a
v. 15, 15.	3 d, 1 d	1 Kings viii. 31.	2	x. 10, 19.	1 e
v. 19. a	1 b a	2 Kings xii. 16.	1 d	Ps. lxvii. 21.	1 d
vi. 2.	3 d	1 Chron. xxi. 3.	1 e	Ezek. xiv. 13.	3 b
vi. 7.	3 d	2 Chron. xix. 10, 10.	1 c	xv. 8.	3 d
xxii. 16.	1 e	xxiv. 18.	3 a	xvii. 20, 20.	3 d a
xxvi. 40, 40.	3 d a	xxvi. 18.	3 a	xx. 24, 24.	3 d a
Num. v. 6.	3 b d	xxviii. 13, 13.	1 e	xx. 27.	3 d
v. 7, 7.	1 d	xxviii. 22. γ	3 b	xxxix. 23.	3 d a
v. 8, 8.	1 d	xxix. 6.	3 a	xxxix. 26, 26.	3 d a
v. 12.	3 d	xxx. 7.	3 a	Dan. ix. 7.	3 d a
v. 27. β	3 c d	xxxiii. 19.	3 d	Hos. viii. 1.	4 a
xxxi. 16.	3 d				

[a] *lit.* trespassing he hath trespassed.   β *lit.* and have trespassed trespass.   γ *lit.* did he add to trespass.   δ *lit.* multiplied trespass.

TRIBE

1 מַטֶּה *com.* a branch; a rod, staff; a tribe of Israel, because as a branch from the same stem.

2 שֵׁבֶט *com.* a rod; a tribe, especially of the children of Israel. The expression, according to Gesenius, is metaphorical, and is derived from a plant from whose root there spring up several sprouts, shoots, stems; thus the founder of a whole race is compared to a root (Isa. xi. 1), while the ancestors of the several subdivisions or tribes are called stems (Gen. xlix. 28), as also the tribes themselves; yet it is more probable that it is to be deduced from a rod being the symbol of a tribe, Num. xvii. 2, 3, &c. It differs from מִשְׁפָּחָה, family, which is strictly a part of a tribe (Deut. xxix. 18, Judg. xviii. 19, xxi. 24); yet it is sometimes used in a narrower sense for the families of a tribe, *e. g.* of the Kohathites, Num. iv. 18; of Dan, Judg. xviii. 1, *comp.* 2; of Benjamin, Judg. xx. 12, 1 Sam. ix. 21. *Vice versa* it is also put for the whole people of Israel, called a tribe (race), the possession of Jehovah, his own peculiar people, Jer. x. 16, li. 19, Ps. lxxiv. 2, *comp. pl.* Isa. lxiii. 17; once of the Egyptian tribes, Isa. xix. 13. 2 Sam. vii. 7, "spake I a word with any of the tribes," *marg.* 'judges;' in the parallel, 1 Chron. xvii. 6, it is שֹׁפְטֵי.—Gen. xlix. 16, &c. [a] שְׁבַט Ch. *com.*

No. 2 not included.

Exod. xxxi. 2, 6.	1	Num. xiii. 2, 4, 5, 6, 7,		Num. xxxvi. 3, 3.	1, 2
xxxv. 30, 34.	1	8, 9, 10, 11, 11, 12,		xxxvi. 4, 4, 5, 6, 7, 7,	
xxxviii. 22, 23.	1	13, 14, 15.	1	7, 8, 8, 9, 9, 9, 12.	1
Lev. xxiv. 11.	1	xviii. 2, 2.	1, 2	Josh. vii. 1, 18.	
Num. i. 4. a 16, 21, 23,		xxvi. 55.	1	xiii. 15, 24, 29.	2
25, 27, 29, 31, 33,		xxx. 1.	1	xiii. 29.	2
35, 37, 39, 41, 43,	1	xxxi. 4. β	1	xiv. 1, 2, 3, 3, 4.	1
ii. 5, 7, 12, 14, 20, 22,		xxxi. 4, 5, 6.	1	xv. 1, 20, 21.	1
27, 29.	1	xxxii. 28.	1	xvi. 8.	1
iii. 6.	1	xxxiii. 54.	1	xvii. 1.	1
vii. 2, 12.	1	xxxiv. 13, 13, 14, 14,		xviii. 11, 21.	1
x. 15, 16, 19, 20, 23,		14, 15, 15, 18, 19,		xix. 1, 8, 23, 24, 31,	
24, 26, 27.	1	20, 21, 22, 23, 24,		39, 40, 48, 51.	1
		25, 26, 27, 28.	1	xx. 8, 8, 8.	1

Josh. xxi. 1, 4, 4, 4, 5,		1 Kings vii. 14.	1	1 Chron. vi. 76, 77, 78,	
5, 5, 6, 6, 6, 6, 6, 7,		viii. 1.	1	80.	1
7, 7, 9, 9, 17, 20,		1 Chron. vi. 60, 61, 61,		xii. 31.	1
23, 25, 27, 28, 30,		62, 62, 62, 62, 63,		2 Chron. v. 2.	1
32, 34, 38.	1	63, 63, 65, 65, 65,		Ezra vi. 17.	2 a
xxii. 1, 14.	1	66, 70, 71, 72, 74.	1	Hab. iii. 9.	1

[a] *lit.* a man, a man for a tribe.   β *marg.* 'a thousand of a tribe, a thousand of a tribe.'

TRIBULATION

צַר *m.* straitness, narrowness of place; *trop.* straits, distress, affliction: Deut. iv. 30. צָרָה *f. id.* Judg. x. 14: 1 Sam. x. 19; xxvi. 24.

TRIBUTE, TRIBUTARY

1 בְּלוֹ Ch. *m.* a species of tribute, probably a tax on articles consumed.

2 מֶכֶס *m.* portion, tribute assigned to the Lord; the computed value and worth of anything.

3 מִדָּה *f.* a tribute, as if measured out to each person.

4 מַס *m.* tribute; almost everywhere spoken of tribute to be rendered in service, tribute-service, fully מַס עֹבֵד (tribute of one serving). [a] מִסָּה *f. id.*

5 מַשָּׂא *m.* burden.

6 עֹנֶשׁ *m.* fine, mulct, exacted from any one.

Gen. xlix. 15.	4	2 Sam. xx. 24.	4	Ezra iv. 13, 20.	1
Num. xxxi. 28, 37, 38,		1 Kings iv. 6.	4	vi. 8.	3
39, 40, 41.	2	ix. 21.	4	vii. 24.	3
Deut. xii. 10.	4 a	xii. 18.	4	Neh. v. 4.	8
xx. 11.		2 Kings xxiii. 33.	6	Esth. x. 1.	4
Josh. xvi. 10.	4	2 Chron. viii. 8.	4	Prov. xii. 24.	4
xvii. 13.		x. 18.	4	Lam. i. 1.	4
Judg. i. 28, 30, 33, 35.	4	xvii. 11.	5		

TRICKLE

נָגַר to flow, of tears trickling down. NIPHAL *pret.* Lam. iii. 49.

TRIM

יָטַב to be good, to make good, to make comely. HIPHIL *fut.* Jer. ii. 33, *i. e.* walk or run gracefully.

עָשָׂה to do, implying action to be understood according to the case to which it applies. KAL *pret.* 2 Sam. xix. 24, of the beard.

TRIUMPH

1 גָּאָה to lift up oneself; to be exalted, majestic, glorious. KAL *pret.* Exod. xv. 1, 21, *i. e.* hath shewn himself powerful and magnificent. LXX. ἐνδόξως γὰρ δεδόξασται.

2 עָלַז to rejoice with exultation. KAL *fut.*

3 עָלַץ to exult; *seq.* לְ to exult over any one, to triumph. KAL *fut.*

4 רוּעַ to make a loud noise, to shout for joy, to triumph. HIPHIL [a] *fut.* HITHPOLEL [b] *imp.* [c] *fut.*

5 רָנַן to utter cries of joy, to shout; *seq.* בְּ in, or over. PIEL [a] *fut.* [b] רִנָּה *f.* shout of joy. [c] רְנָנָה *f. id.*

6 שָׁבַח to praise. Hithp. *seq.* בְּ to laud oneself, to glory in anything. HITHPAEL *inf.*

Exod. xv. 1, 21.	1	Ps. xli. 11.	4 a	Ps. xciv. 3.	2
2 Sam. i. 20.	6	xlvii. 1.	5 b	cvi. 47.	6
Job xx. 5.	5 b	lx. 8. a	4 b	cviii. 9.	4 c
Ps. xxv. 2.	3	xcii. 4.	5 a		

[a] *marg.* 'or, triumph thou over me (by an irony).' See Ps. cviii. 10.

TROOP

1 אֲגֻדָּה *f.* a band, a band of men, a troop.

2 אֹרַח *com.* a caravan or company of travellers.

3 גָּדַד to press or crowd upon; to assemble in troops to invade or plunder. HITHPOEL ^a*fut.* ^bגַּד *m.* Gen. xxx. 11, Isa. lxv. 11, *marg.* 'Gad, an idol, supposed to be the sun.' Gussetius is unwilling to allow this to be any allusion to an idol, but supposes that it means a troop of comrades for whom the table is prepared; see also *Number.* ^cגְּדוּד *m.* a troop, band of warriors; mostly of light-armed troops engaged in plundering and predatory excursions; Gen. xlix. 19, Gad, a troop shall press upon him, *i. e.* bands of wandering Arabs from the neighbouring desert; hosts of calamities inflicted by Jehovah, Job xix. 12; "troops of robbers," Hos. vi. 9, vii. 1.

4 חַי *adj.* living, life.

Gen. xxx. 11.	3 b	2 Sam. xxiii. 11.	4	Jer. v. 7.	3 a
xlix. 19.	3 c	xxiii. 13.	4	viii. 22.	3 c
1 Sam. xxx. 8.	3 c	Job vi. 19.	2	Hos. vi. 9.	3 c
2 Sam. ii. 25.	1	xix. 12.	3 c	vii. 1.	3 c
iii. 22.	3 c	Ps. xviii. 29.	3 c	Amos ix. 6.	1
xxii. 30.	3 c	Isa. lxv. 11.	3 b	Micah v. 1, 1.	3 a c

TROUBLE

1 אֲנַס Ch. to urge, to press. P'AL *part.*

2 בָּהַל to be in great perturbation of mind, as by the intelligence of some unexpected calamity; to be suddenly seized with fear, to be amazed and confounded. NIPHAL ^a*pret.* ^b*fut.* ^c*part.* PIEL ^d*inf.* ^e*fut.* ^f*part.* HIPHIL ^g*pret.* בְּהַל Ch. PUAL ^h*fut.* ITHP'AL ⁱ*part.* ^kבֶּהָלָה *f.* fear, terror, ruin.

3 בְּלָהּ to tremble; to terrify. PIEL ^a*part.* Ezra iv. 4 (כתיב). ^bבַּלָּהָה *f.* terror.

4 בָּעַת to be greatly terrified and perplexed in mind by sudden fear. PIEL ^a*pret.* ^b*part.* ^cבְּעָתָה *f.* terror.

5 גָּעַשׁ to shake by a sudden impulse; to be moved. PUAL *fut.* Job xxxiv. 20, shall be moved and pass away, *i. e.* be troubled, reel, and perish.

6 גָּרַשׁ to drive; to be violently acted upon. NIPHAL *part.*

7 דָּלַח to trouble water with the feet, to make turbid. KAL *fut.*

8 מְהוּמָה *f.* confusion, consternation; tumult.

9 הָמָה to sound, to make a noise; to be disquieted. KAL ^a*pret.* ^b*fut.*

10 הָמַם to agitate, to put to the rout, to discomfit. KAL *fut.*

11 זְוָעָה *f.* agitation, *i. e.* disquiet, maltreatment (כתיב). ^aזַעֲוָה the same, by transposition (קרי).

12 חָמַר to boil up, to ferment, to foam; applied to hurries and discomposure of the mind. KAL ^a*fut.* POALAL ^b*pret.*

13 טֹרַח *m.* a burden, trouble; an oppressive load, producing weariness in bearing it.

14 יוֹם *m.* day; "in trouble," *marg.* 'hard of day.'

15 תְּלָאָה *f.* travail, toil, distress.

16 סָעַר to be tossed with a tempest; applied to violent agitation of the mind. NIPHAL *fut.*

17 עָוָה to bend; to be bent down, bowed, depressed with calamities. NIPHAL *pret.*

18 עָכַר to trouble water, to disturb, to put into confusion; to throw affairs which were easy, happy, and prosperous, or which might have been so, into confusion, perplexity, and distress; implying also danger as the cause of trouble or fear; see Prov. xv. 27. KAL ^a*pret.* ^b*fut.* ^c*part.* Poel. NIPHAL ^d*part.*

19 עָמָל *m.* labouring, toiling, with severe effort and exhaustion.

20 עָנָה to answer; to be afflicted. KAL ^a*fut.* ^bעֳנִי *m.* affliction.

21 פָּעַם to beat, to strike; to impel, to urge, to move. NIPHAL ^a*pret.* ^b*fut.* HITHPAEL ^c*fut.*

22 צוֹק *m.* distress, trouble of the times.

23 צָרַר to press; to be pressed, straitened, distressed. KAL ^a*pret.* ^bצַר *m.* straitness, narrowness of place; straits, distress, affliction; an enemy that distresses or troubles. ^cצָרָה *f.* distress.

24 קָצַר to cut off; to be shortened, short, grieved. KAL *fut.*

25 קָשֶׁה *adj.* hard; "in trouble," *marg.* 'hard of day.'

26 רָגַן to be moved, troubled. KAL ^a*imp.* ^b*fut.* ^cרֹגֶן *m.* commotion; restlessness, tumult, disquiet, trouble.

27 רַע *adj.* see *Evil.*

28 רָעַם to be moved, agitated, to tremble. KAL *pret.*

29 רָפַשׂ to tread, to trample, especially of water made turbid; to foul. NIPHAL *part.*

30 רָשַׁע to do wickedly. HIPHIL *fut.*

Gen. xxxiv. 30.	18 a	Ps. xx. 1.	23 c	Prov. xi. 8.	23 c
xli. 8.	21 b	xxii. 11.	23 c	xi. 17, 29.	18 c
xlv. 3.	2 a	xxv. 17, 22.	23 c	xii. 13.	23 c
Exod. xiv. 24.	10	xxvii. 5.	27	xv. 6.	18 d
Deut. xxxi. 17, 21.	23 c	xxx. 7.	2 c	xv. 16.	8
Josh. vi. 18.	18 a	xxxi. 7.	20 b	xv. 27.	18 c
vi. 25.	18 a	xxxi. 9.	23 a	xxi. 23.	23 c
vii. 25.	18 b	xxxi. 17.	23 b	xxv. 19.	23 c
Judg. xi. 35.	18 c	xxxiv. 6, 17.	23 c	xxv. 26.	29
1 Sam. xiv. 29.	18 a	xxxviii. 39.	23 c	Isa. i. 14.	13
xvi. 14.	4 a	xli. 1.	27	viii. 22.	23 c
xvi. 15.	4 b	xlvi. 1.	23 c	xvii. 14.	3 b
xxviii. 21.	2 a	xlvi. 1.	23 c	xxii. 5.	8
2 Sam. iv. 1.	2 a	xlvii. 3.	12 a	xxvi. 16.	23 b
1 Kings xviii. 17.	18 c	xlviii. 5.	2 a	xxx. 6.	23 c
xviii. 18.	18 a	l. 15.	23 c	xxxii. 10.	26 b
2 Kings vi. 11.	16	liv. 7.	23 c	xxxii. 11.	26 a
xix. 3.	23 c	lix. 16.	23 c	xxxiii. 2.	23 c
1 Chron. ii. 7.	18 c	lx. 11.	23 b	xxxvii. 3.	23 c
xxii. 14.	20 b	lxi. 14.	23 b	xlvi. 7.	23 c
2 Chron. xv. 4.	23 b	lxix. 17.	23 a	lvii. 20.	6
xxix. 8.	11, or 11 a	lxix. 17.	23 c	lxv. 16.	23 c
xxxii. 18.	2 d	lxxiii. 5.	19	lxv. 23.	2 k
Ezra iv. 4.	2 f, or 3 a	lxxvii. 3.	23 c	Jer. ii. 27, 28.	27
Neh. ix. 27.	23 c	lxxvii. 3.	9 b	viii. 15.	4 c
ix. 32.	15	lxxvii. 16.	21 a	xi. 12, 14.	27
Job iii. 17, 26.	26 c	lxxvii. 16.	26 b	xiv. 8.	23 c
iv. 5.	2 b	lxxviii. 49.	23 c	xiv. 19.	4 c
v. 6, 7.	19	lxxxi. 7.	23 c	xxx. 7.	23 c
v. 19.	23 c	lxxxi. 7.	2 b	xxxi. 20.	9 a
xiv. 1.	26 c	lxxxvi. 7.	23 c	l. 2.	27
xv. 24.	23 b	lxxxvi. 7.	23 c	Lam. i. 20.	12 b
xxi. 4.	24	lxxxviii. 3.	27	i. 21.	27
xxii. 10.	2 e	xc. 7.	2 a	ii. 11.	12 b
xxiii. 15.	2 b	xci. 15.	23 c	Ezek. vii. 7.	8
xxiii. 16.	2 g	cii. 2.	23 b	vii. 27.	2 b
xxvii. 9.	23 c	civ. 29.	2 b	xxvi. 18.	2 a
xxx. 25.	25, 14	cvii. 6, 13, 19.	23 b	xxvii. 35.	28
xxxiv. 20.	5	cvii. 26.	27	xxxii. 2, 13, 13.	7
xxxiv. 29.a	30	cvii. 28.	23 b	Dan. ii. 1.	21 c
xxxviii. 23.	23 b	cviii. 12.	23 b	ii. 3.	21 b
Ps. iii. 1.	23 b	cxvi. 11.	23 c	iv. 5.	2 h
ix. 9.	23 c	cxix. 143.	23 c	iv. 9.	1
ix. 13.	20 b	cxxxviii. 7.	23 b	iv. 19, 19.	2 h
x. 1.	23 c	cxli. 2.	23 c	v. 6, 10.	2 h
xiii. 4.	23 b	cxliii. 11.	23 c	v. 9.	2 i

Dan. vii. 15, 28.	2 h	Dan. xii. 1.	23 c	Zeph. i. 15.	23 c
ix. 25.	22	Nah. i. 7.	23 c	Zech. x. 2.	20 a
xi. 44.	2 e	Hab. iii. 16.	23 c		

a or, condemn.

TROUGH

רַהַט <i>m.</i> canals or troughs for watering cattle : Exod. ii. 16.

שֹׁקֶת <i>f.</i> watering-troughs, made of wood or stone, for watering cattle : Gen. xxiv. 20 ; xxx. 38.

TRUE, TRUTH

1 אָמֵן <i>m.</i> faithful, faithfulness, fidelity, as impiled in the word Amen. ^a אֹמֶן <i>m.</i> faith. ^b אָמְנָם <i>part.</i> verily, truly, indeed. ^c אֱמֶת <i>f.</i> firmness, stability, perpetuity ; faithfulness, fidelity, truth, <i>i. e.</i> firmness and constancy in oneself in keeping and executing one's promise, &c., so to do or show truth, Gen. xxxii. 10, <i>comp.</i> John iii. 21, 1 John i. 6, Micah vii. 20 ; ascribed to a people, to a king, to God, to Messiah ; see <i>Amen.</i> Very frequently joined with חֶסֶד, all which passages, by ἓν διὰ δυοῖν, are to be understood of the faithful and constant goodness of God. Truth, as opposed to falsehood ; ascribed to the word of God, to prophecies, to the servant of God ; hence the truth of Jehovah is often put for his true doctrine, the true religion, the word of the Gospel, by which Messiah carries on his conquests in the world, Ps. xlv. 4. Good faith, uprightness, integrity ; opposed to רֶשַׁע, Prov. viii. 7 ; specially of a judge, uprightness, justice ; also sincerity, opposed to hypocrisy, Gen. xxiv. 49, &c. ^d אָמוּן <i>m.</i> faithful, true, sincere. ^e אֱמֻנָה <i>f.</i> faithfulness.

2 יָצַב Ch. to be firm, certain ; to speak the truth with certainty ; to know the truth. PAEL ^a <i>inf.</i> ^b יַצִּיב Ch. <i>adj.</i> firm, fixed, settled.

3 כֵּנִים <i>adj. pl. m.</i> upright, erect ; honest.

4 צְדָא Ch. <i>m.</i> purpose, design.

5 קֹשְׁט <i>m.</i> exact, precise truth ; weighed, as it were, in the evenest balance.—<i>Schultens.</i> ^a קְשֹׁט <i>m. id.</i> ^b קוֹשְׁט Ch. <i>m. id.</i>

No. 1 c omitted when rendered Truth.

Gen. xxiv. 49.	1 c	Ps. xix. 9.	1 c	Jer. vii. 28.	1 e
xlii. 11, 19, 31, 33, 34.	3	xxxiii. 4.	1 e	ix. 3.	1 e
xlvii. 29.	1 c	lx. 4.	5 a	x. 10.	1 c
Deut. xvii. 4.	1 c	lxxxix. 49.	1 e	xxviii. 9.	1 c
xxii. 20.	1 e	xcvi. 13.	1 e	xlii. 5. β	1 c
xxxii. 4.	1 c	xcviii. 3.	1 e	Ezek. xviii. 8.	1 c
Josh. ii. 12.	1 c	c. 5.	1 e	xviii. 9.	1 c
ii. 14.	1 c	cxix. 30.	1 e	Dan. ii. 47.	5 b
Judg. ix. 16, 19.	1 c	cxix. 160.	1 e	iii. 14.	4
Ruth iii. 12.	1 b	Prov. xii. 17, 22.	1 e	iii. 24.	2 b
2 Sam. vii. 28.	1 c	xiv. 25.	1 c	iv. 37.	5 b
1 Kings x. 6.	1 c	xxi. 21.	5	vi. 12.	2 b
xxii. 16.	1 c	Isa. xxv. 1.	1 a	vii. 16.	2 b
2 Kings xix. 17.	1 b	xxvi. 2. α	1 b	vii. 19.	2 a
2 Chron. ix. 5.	1 c	xxxvii. 18.	1 b	viii. 26. γ	1 c
xv. 3.	1 c	lix. 4.	1 e	x. 21.	1 c
Neh. ix. 13.	1 c	lxv. 16, 16.	1	Micah vii. 20.	1 c
Job ix. 2.	1 b	Jer. v. 1, 3.	1 e	Zech. vii. 9. β	1 c
xxxvi. 4.	1 b				

a lit. truths.   β lit. of truth.   γ lit. truth.

TRUMPET

1 חֲצֹצְרָה <i>f.</i> a straight trumpet. חָצַר <i>denom.</i> PIEL ^a <i>part.</i>   חָצֵר PIEL ^b <i>part.</i>

2 יוֹבֵל <i>com.</i> jubilee ; <i>ellipt.</i> horn of jubilee.

3 שׁוֹפָר <i>m.</i> a trumpet, horn, <i>lituus</i>, so called from its clear and shrill sound ; <i>comp.</i> Eng. clarion ; either made of horn or similar to a horn, and crooked : Exod. xix. 16, &c.

4 תְּקוֹעַ <i>m.</i> the blast of a trumpet.

No. 3 not included.

Exod. xix. 13.	2	1 Chron. xvi. 6, 42.	1	2 Chron. xxix. 26, 27,	
Num. x. 2, 8, 9, 10.	1	2 Chron. v. 12, 13.	1	28.	1
xxxi. 6.	1	v. 13, 13.	1 a, or b	Ezra iii. 10.	1
2 Kings xi. 14, 14.	1	xiii. 12, 14.	1	Neh. xii. 35, 41.	1
xii. 13.	1	xv. 14.	1	Ps. xcviii. 6.	1
1 Chron. xiii. 8.	1	xx. 28.	1	Ezek. vii. 14.	4
xv. 24, 28.	1	xxiii. 13, 13.	1	Hos. v. 8.	1

TRUST

1 אָמַן to stay, support ; to be faithful. Hiph. to trust, to confide in. NIPHAL ^a <i>part.</i> "trusty," <i>marg.</i> 'faithful.' HIPHIL ^b <i>pret.</i> ^c <i>fut.</i>

2 בָּטַח to trust, to confide, to place hope and confidence in any one ; <i>seq.</i> בְּ, עַל, and אֶל ; sometimes <i>c. dat. pleon.</i> Jer. vii. 4, 8, 2 Kings xviii. 21 ; rarely in this sense <i>abs.</i> Job vi. 20, but often <i>abs.</i> to be confident, <i>i. e.</i> to be secure without fear. Jer. xii. 5, Job xl. 23, he feareth not, though Jordan break forth over his mouth, <i>i. q.</i> Eng. over his head. In a good sense, of the trust and security of the righteous ; in a bad sense, see <i>Careless.</i> KAL ^a <i>pret.</i> ^b <i>inf.</i> ^c <i>imp.</i> ^d <i>fut.</i> ^e <i>part.</i> Poel. ^f <i>part.</i> Paül. HIPHIL ^g <i>pret.</i> ^h <i>fut.</i> ⁱ מִבְטָח <i>m.</i> trust, confidence, firm and certain ; <i>meton.</i> of a person or thing in which confidence is placed.

3 גָּלַל to roll ; <i>seq.</i> אֶל to roll from oneself to or upon another ; <i>ellipt.</i> Ps. xxii. 8, where the Psalmist introduces his enemies as deriding his confidence in God, and saying, let him devolve (his matters) upon Jehovah ; he (forsooth) will deliver him. KAL <i>inf.</i>

4 חֹגֵל <i>m.</i> stay, tarry ; to wait for. POLEL <i>fut.</i>

5 חָסָה to flee to a place, <i>i. e.</i> to take refuge or shelter, <i>seq.</i> בְּ of place ; to put trust in any one, to trust, to confide, especially in God, <i>seq.</i> בְּ. KAL ^a <i>pret.</i> ^b <i>inf.</i> ^c <i>imp.</i> ^d <i>fut.</i> ^e <i>part.</i> Poel. חָסוּת ^f refuge. ^g מַחְסֶה <i>m.</i> refuge, shelter.

6 יָחַל to wait ; especially with hope, confidence. PIEL <i>fut.</i>

7 רְחַץ Ch. to trust, <i>seq.</i> עַל on or in anything. HITHP'IL <i>pret.</i>

Deut. xxviii. 52.	2 e	Job xxxix. 11.	2 d	Ps. xxxii. 10.	2 e
xxxii. 37.	5 a	xl. 23.	2 d	xxxiii. 21.	2 a
Judg. ix. 15.	5 c	Ps. ii. 12.	5 e	xxxiv. 8.	5 d
xi. 20.	2 d	iv. 5.	2 a	xxxiv. 22.	5 e
xx. 36.	2 a	v. 11.	5 e	xxxvi. 7.	5 e
Ruth ii. 12.	5 b	vii. 1.	5 a	xxxvii. 3, 5.	2 d
2 Sam. xxii. 3.	5 d	ix. 10.	2 d	xxxvii. 40.	5 a
xxii. 31.	5 e	xi. 1.	5 a	xl. 3.	2 d
2 Kings xviii. 5, 19,		xiii. 5.	2 a	xl. 4.	2 i
20, 22.	2 a	xvi. 1.	5 a	xli. 9.	2 d
xviii. 21. α	2 a	xvii. 7.	5 e	xliv. 6.	2 d
xviii. 21.	2 d	xviii. 2.	5 d	xlix. 6.	2 d
xviii. 24.	2 d	xviii. 30.	5 e	lii. 7.	2 d
xviii. 30.	2 h	xxii. 4, 4, 5.	2 e	lii. 8.	2 a
xix. 10.	2 e	xxii. 8.	3	lv. 23.	2 d
1 Chron. v. 20.	2 a	xxv. 2.	2 a	lvi. 3.	2 d
2 Chron. xxxii. 10.	2 e	xxv. 20.	5 e	lvi. 4, 11.	2 d
Job iv. 18.	2 e	xxvi. 1.	2 a	lvii. 1.	5 e
viii. 14.	2 a	xxvii. 7.	6	lxi. 4.	5 e
xii. 20.	1 c	xxxi. 1.	5 a	lxii. 8.	2 a
xiii. 15.	2 i	xxxi. 6, 14.	2 d	lxiii. 10.	2 e
xv. 15, 31.	1 a	xxxi. 19.	5 e	lxiv. 10.	5 a
xxxv. 14.	6			lxxi. 1.	5 a

Ps. lxxi. 5.	2 i	Prov. xxix. 25.	2 e	Jer. vii. 4.	2 d	
lxxiii. 28.	5 g	xxx. 5.	5 e	vii. 8, 14.	2 d	
lxxviii. 22.	2 a	xxxi. 11.	2 a	ix. 4.	2 d	
lxxxiv. 12.	2 e	Isa. xii. 2.		xii. 5.	2 d	
lxxxvi. 2.	2 d	xiv. 32.	5 d	xiii. 25.	2 d	
xci. 2.	2 d	xxvi. 3.	2 f	xvii. 5, 7.	2 d	
xci. 4.	5 d	xxvi. 4.	2 c	xxviii. 15.	2 d	
cxii. 7.	2 f	xxx. 2.	5 b	xxix. 31.	2 a	
cxv. 8.	2 e	xxx. 3.	5 f	xxxix. 18.	2 a	
cxv. 9, 10, 11.	2 c	xxx. 12.	2 e	xlvi. 25.	2 e	
cxviii. 8, 9.	5 b	xxxi. 1.	2 d	xlviii. 7.	2 b	
cxix. 42.	2 a	xxxvi. 4, 5, 7.	2 a	xlix. 4.	2 b	
cxxv. 1.	2 e	xxxvi. 6, 6.	2 a e	xlix. 11.	2 d	
cxxxv. 18.	2 e	xxxvi. 9.		Ezek. xvi. 15.	2 d	
cxli. 8.	5 a	xxxvi. 15.	2 h	xxxiii. 13.	2 h	
cxliii. 2.	2 a	xxxvii. 10.	2 e	Dan. iii. 28.	7	
cxliv. 2.	5 a	xlii. 17.	2 e	Hos. x. 13.	2 d	
cxlvi. 3.	2 d	xlvii. 10.	2 d	Amos vi. 1.	2 e	
Prov. iii. 5.	2 e	l. 10.	2 d	Micah vii. 5.	1 c	
xi. 28.	2 e	li. 5.	6	Nah. i. 7.	2 e	
xvi. 20.	2 e	lvii. 13.	5 e	Hab. ii. 18.	2 a	
xxii. 19.	2 e	lix. 4.	2 b	Zeph. iii. 2.	2 a	
xxviii. 25, 26.	2 e	Jer. v. 17.	2 e	iii. 12.	5 a	

TRY, TRIAL

1 בָּחַן to try, to prove, especially metals; often of God, as trying the hearts or minds of men, especially by sending calamities upon them; of men, as proving or tempting God, by doubt, unbelief. KAL ᵃ*pret.* ᵇ*inf.* ᶜ*imp.* ᵈ*fut.* ᵉ*part.* Poel. NIPHAL ᶠ*fut.* PUAL ᵍ*pret.* ʰבֹּחַן *m.* trial, proof: Isa. xxviii. 16, *lit.* a stone of trial, *or,* of proof, *i.e.* proved and found suitable for a foundation-stone.

2 חָקַר to search out, to explore. KAL *fut.*

3 נָסָה to try by the smell; to try, to prove any one. PIEL ᵃ*inf.* ᵇמַסָּה *f.* tentation or trial.

4 צָרַף to melt, to smelt metals: specially of gold and silver, to purify with fire, and thus separate from scoria; *metaph.* to try, to prove any one, δοκιμάζειν. KAL ᵃ*pret.* ᵇ*inf.* ᶜ*imp.* ᵈ*fut.* ᵉ*part.* Paül. NIPHAL ᶠ*fut.*

Judg. vii. 4.	4 d	Ps. xi. 4, 5.	1 d	Jer. ix. 7.	1 a	
2 Sam. xxii. 31.	4 e	xii. 6.	4 e	xi. 20.	1 e	
1 Chron. xxix. 17.	1 e	xvii. 3.	4 a	xii. 3.	1 a	
2 Chron. xxxii. 31.	3 a	xviii. 30.	4 e	xvii. 10.	1 e	
Job vii. 18.	1 d	xxvi. 2.	4 c	xx. 12.	1 e	
ix. 23.	3 b	lxvi. 10, 10.	4 a b	Lam. iii. 40.	1 e 2	
xii. 11.	1 d	cv. 19.	4 a	Ezek. xxi. 13. a	1 g	
xxiii. 10.	1 a	cxxxix. 23.	1 c	Dan. xi. 35.	4 b	
xxxiv. 3.	1 d	Prov. xvii. 3.	1 e	xii. 10.	4 d	
xxxiv. 36.	1 f	Isa. xxviii. 16.	1 h	Zech. xiii. 9, 9.	1 a b	
Ps. vii. 9.	1 e	Jer. vi. 27.	1 a			

TUMBLE

הָפַךְ to turn; to turn or roll oneself, to tumble. HITHPAEL *part.* Judg. vii. 13.

TUMULT

1 בֵּן *m.* son; "tumultuous ones," *marg.* 'children of noise.'

2 מְהוּמָה *f.* confusion, consternation; tumult.

3 הָמָה to rage, to make a noise, to make a tumult. KAL ᵃ*fut.* ᵇ*part.* Poel. ᶜהָמוֹן noise, sound; multitude, crowd of men.

4 הֲמֻלָּה *f.* noise, sound; as of a great company speaking high and all at once.

5 שָׁאוֹן *m.* noise, uproar, tumult, *e.g.* of waters, of a crowd or multitude of men, of war, of outcry, clamour.

6 שַׁאֲנָן *adj.* quiet, careless, proud; *subst.* pride, arrogance.

1 Sam. iv. 14.	3 c	Isa. xiii. 4.	5	Jer. xlviii. 45.	1, 5	
2 Sam. xviii. 29.	3 c	xxii. 2.	3 b	Hos. x. 14.	5	
2 Kings xix. 28.	3 c	xxxiii. 3.	3 c	Amos ii. 2.	5	
Ps. lxv. 7.		xxxvii. 29.	6	iii. 9.	2	
lxxiv. 23.	3 a	Jer. xi. 16.	4	Zech. xiv. 13.	2	
lxxxiii. 2.	3 a					

TURN

1 הָפַךְ to turn, *e.g.* a cake, a dish, the hand or side, *i.e.* to turn about, return; but with בְּ, on one, *i.e.* to strike; to turn the neck before one, *i.e.* to flee from him. *Intrans.* to turn about, to return, also to turn back; to flee; 2 Kings v. 26, "turned again," *i.e.* after he had descended from his chariot, ver. 21. To change, to convert, LXX. μετα-στρέφω, μεταβάλλω,- Ps. cv. 25, *seq.* לְ, to turn into anything; *seq.* אֶל, Zeph. iii. 9, "I will turn to the people a pure language" (for an impure, mixed and manifold). *Intrans.* to be turned, changed, *seq. acc.* into anything, Lev. xiii. 3, &c.; to pervert, Isa. xxix. 16. Niphal, to turn about, to turn back; *seq.* בְּ to turn against one, Job xix. 19; עַל to any one, also *seq.* אֶל and לְ; to be turned, to be changed. Hithpa. to turn oneself: Gen. iii. 24, a sword continually turning itself, *i.e.* brandished, glittering; of a cloud moving about on the sky, Job xxxvii. 12; of the entire change of the earth in the restoration of all things, Job xxxviii. 14; see Schmidt *in loc.* KAL ᵃ*pret.* ᵇ*inf.* ᶜ*imp.* ᵈ*fut.* ᵉ*part.* Poel. ᶠ*part.* Paül. NIPHAL ᵍ*pret.* ʰ*inf.* ⁱ*fut.* HOPHAL ᵏ*pret.* HITHPAEL ˡ*fut.* ᵐ*part.*

2 זָנַח to remove far away; see *Cast.* HIPHIL *pret.*

3 יָרַט to turn out of the right road of action or of happiness. KAL *pret.* Job xvi. 11, God hath turned me over into, or, upon the hands of the wicked, *i.e.* out of the way of safety and peace into a road where I am fallen into the hands of the wicked. LXX. ἔρριψέ με. Vulg. *tradidit me.*

4 לָפַת to bend, to turn; to bend oneself, to turn oneself; or to gather up or contract oneself into a narrow compass, to shrink; to gather up oneself for strength. NIPHAL *fut.*

5 נָטָה to stretch out, to extend; to incline, to bow; to turn, to turn away, to deflect, *i.e.* to make tend to one side, *intrans.* to turn away, to decline; *seq.* אֶל to any one, מִן and מֵעַם from any one, from a way; *seq.* אַחֲרֵי to turn away after, *i.e.* to the party of any one; to go away, to go. KAL ᵃ*pret.* ᵇ*inf.* ᶜ*imp.* ᵈ*fut.* HIPHIL ᵉ*pret.* ᶠ*inf.* ᵍ*imp.* ʰ*fut.* ⁱ*part.*

6 נָסַג see *Remove.* HOPHAL *pret.*

7 נָתַן to give. KAL ᵃ*pret.* ᵇ*fut.*

8 סָבַב to turn oneself, *i.e.* to turn, *intrans.* as a door on the hinges. The place to which one turns is put with אֶל, עַל, לְ; that from which one turns is put with מֵעַל, מִן, מִפְּנֵי; *seq.* אֶל אַחֲרֵי to turn back after any one, so as to follow him, and *abs.* to return. Spoken of things, to turn to any place, *i.e.* to be brought, carried, transferred, to that place or person (see *Carry*): Hab. ii. 16, *comp.* 1 Kings ii. 15. *Trop.* to turn about, *i.e.* to change; *seq.* בְּ to become like anything, Zech. xiv. 10; to turn, or

apply to action; to turn aside. KAL [a]pret. [b]imp. [c]part. Poel. NIPHAL [d]pret. [e]fut. HIPHIL [f]pret. [g]inf. [h]imp. [i]fut. [k]part. HOPHAL [l]fut. [m]imp.

9 סוּג to go off from, to draw back, to depart, especially from God. Niph. to be turned back, of a defeated enemy, of ineffectual struggles, of disappointed hope. NIPHAL [a]pret. [b]fut. [c]part.

10 סוּר to go off, to turn aside or away, to depart, seq. מֵעַל, מִן, מֵאַחֲרֵי, מֵעָם; e.gr. from a place, especially from a way; from a person, seq. מֵאַחֲרֵי to turn aside from after any one, to desist from following him; to turn away from God, to depart, i.e. to fall away from his worship, to apostatize; to depart from the law or the divine precepts, as from the right way; to depart from evil, to avoid it by doing right, often joined with the fear of God. With a preposition, implying motion, away into a place, to turn aside to a place or person, sc. from the way; seq. הָ‍ local: Judg. xviii. 15. KAL [a]pret. [b]inf. [c]imp. [d]fut. POLEL [e]pret. HIPHIL [f]pret. [g]fut. [h]part. [i]סָרָה f. see Revolt.

11 סֵטִים m. pl. deviations from the right way, i.e. transgressions, sins.

12 עָבַר to pass. HIPHIL imp.

13 עָוָה to make crooked; to act perversely; to subvert, to turn upside down, i.e. to destroy. PIEL pret.

14 עָוַת to bend, to make crooked; to subvert the way of any one, i.e. to thrust him down to destruction. PIEL fut.

15 עָטָה to cover; to cover oneself; to turn aside. KAL part. Poel, Cant. i. 7, marg. 'or, is veiled.' Gesenius, Why should I be as one veiled by the flocks of my companions? i.e. let me not wander in search of thee among the shepherds like a harlot; comp. Gen. xxxviii. 15. LXX. περιβαλλομένη.—Taylor. It is applied to the covering of the upper lip, or veiling of the upper part of the face, which was usual in great sorrow or shame; "as one that turneth aside," as one ashamed, under disgrace; or a veiled, mourning widow.

16 פָּנָה to turn; mostly intrans. to turn oneself, i.e. (1) in order to go anywhere, to go away, hence to turn to or towards any place, to betake oneself in any direction, seq. עַל, אֶל, ל, and acc. Also seq. אֶל of person, to turn unto any one, to go to him for response or for aid, especially God, angels, idols, diviners; seq. אֶל of thing, to turn unto, e.g. iniquity; אַחֲרֵי to turn after any one, to incline to his side or party; to turn away from any one, seq. מִמֶּ; (2) in order to look at anything, hence i.q. to turn the eyes, to look at anything, seq. אֶל, בְּ, &c. Metaph. to look upon, to regard, to have respect to any person or thing, especially of God, as hearing and regarding men with favour; of a king. KAL [a]pret. [b]inf. [c]imp. [d]fut. [e]part. Poel. HIPHIL [f]pret. [g]inf. [h]fut. HOPHAL [i]pret.

17 צָדֵק to be righteous; to make righteous, to turn others to righteousness. HIPHIL part.

18 צָנַף to roll or wind around, as a turban about the head; to roll, as a ball is rolled together. KAL [a]inf. [b]fut. Isa. xxii. 18. Lowth, "He will whirl thee round and round,

and cast thee away," referring to the action of throwing a stone with a sling.

19 מִקְצוֹעַ m. corner; turning (of a wall).

20 שׁוּב to turn about, to turn back, to return; seq. מִן from, out of any place; seq. מֵאַחֲרֵי from after a person whom one has followed or pursued; seq. אֶל to a person, or to a place, though the place is oftener put with ל, also sec. acc. of a place. Followed by another verb, e.g. to return and do, or, to return to the doing of anything, it is i.q. to do again, to do a second time. Trop. to turn, to return to any person or thing, i.e. to convert, be converted, e.g. to Jehovah, seq. אֶל and ל, עַד, and עַל, and בְּ; also abs.; seq. מִן to turn from, i.e. to cease from, to leave off, e.g. an evil way, sin, evil, anger, justice; seq. מֵעַל and מֵאַחֲרֵי to turn away from any one, especially from Jehovah; from idols. To return into the possession of anything, i.e. to recover it, seq. אֶל and ל: generally to turn oneself any whither, even where one has not been before, Ps. lxxiii. 10. Hiph. to turn back, to repulse; specially to turn away the face of any one, i.e. to repulse him, deny him access, not grant his petition; to withdraw, i.e. to appease anger, to calm it; seq. מִן from any one; once with עַל in a good sense. KAL [a]pret. [b]inf. [c]imp. [d]fut. [e]part. Poel. POLEL [f]pret. [g]inf. [h]fut. HIPHIL [i]pret. [k]inf. [l]imp. [m]fut. [n]part. שׁוֹבָב adj. [p]מְשׁוּבָה f. backsliding.

21 שׂוּג to go off from, to draw back. NIPHAL pret.

22 שׂוּט to go or turn away, to turn aside to anything. KAL part. Poel.

23 שׂוּם to put, set, or place, to set in a place or condition, hence to turn or change the condition. KAL [a]pret. [b]fut.

24 שָׂטָה to go aside. KAL imp.

25 שָׁעָה to look; seq. מֵעַל to look away from, to turn away the eyes from. KAL imp.

26 תּוֹר m. a row, order, turn, especially of what goes round in a circle.

Gen. iii. 24. a	1 m	Num. xxi. 22.	5 d	Deut. xxx. 3.	20 a
xviii. 22.	16 d	xxi. 33.	16 d	xxx. 10.	20 d
xix. 2.	10 c	xxii. 23, 23.	5 d f	xxx. 17.	16 d
xix. 3.	10 d	xxii. 26.	5 b	xxxi. 18, 20.	16 a
xxiv. 49.	16 d	xxiii. 33, 33.	5 f d	xxxi. 29.	10 a
xxvii. 44.	20 a	xxv. 4.	20 d	Josh. i. 7.	10 d
xxvii. 45.	20 b	xxv. 11.	20 i	vii. 8.	1 a
xxxviii. 1, 16.	5 d	xxxii. 15.	20 d	vii. 12.	16 d
xlii. 24.	8 e	xxxiii. 7.	20 d	vii. 26.	20 d
Exod. iii. 3.	10 d	xxxiv. 4.	8 d	viii. 20.	1 g
iii. 4.	10 a	Deut. i. 7, 40.	16 c	viii. 21.	20 d
iv. 7.	20 a	i. 24.	16 d	xi. 10.	20 d
vii. 15, 17.	1 g	ii. 1, 8.	16 d	xix. 12, 27, 29, 29, 34.	20 a
vii. 20.	1 i	ii. 3.	16 c	xxii. 16, 23, 29.	20 d
vii. 23.	16 d	ii. 27.	10 d	xxii. 18.	20 d
x. 6.	16 d	iii. 1.	16 d	xxiii. 6.	10 b
x. 19.	1 d	iv. 30.	20 a	xxiii. 20.	20 a
xiv. 2.	20 d	v. 32.	10 d	xxiv. 20.	20 a
xiv. 5.	1 i	vii. 4.	10 g	Judg. ii. 17.	10 a
xxxii. 8.	10 a	ix. 12, 16.	10 a	iii. 19.	20 a
xxxii. 12.	20 c	ix. 15.	16 d	iv. 18, 18, 18.	10 c c d
xxxii. 15.	16 d	x. 5.	20 d	viii. 33.	20 d
xxxiii. 11.	20 a	xi. 16, 28.	10 d	xi. 8.	20 a
Lev. xiii. 3, 4, 10, 13, 20.	1 a	xiii. 5.	10 i	xiv. 8.	10 d
xiii. 16.	20 d	xiii. 17.	20 d	xv. 4.	16 h
xiii. 17, 25.	1 g	xvi. 7.	16 a	xviii. 3, 15.	10 d
xix. 4.	16 d	xvii. 17.	10 d	xviii. 21, 26.	16 d
xx. 6.	16 c	xvii. 20.	10 b	xix. 11, 12, 15.	10 d
Num. xiv. 25.	16 c	xxiii. 6.	1 d	xx. 8.	10 d
xiv. 43.	20 a	xxiii. 13, 14.	20 a	xx. 41.	1 a
xx. 17, 21.	5 d	xxix. 18.	16 e	xx. 42, 45, 47.	16 d

Judg. xx. 48.	20 a
Ruth i. 11, 12.	20 c
iii. 8.	4
iv. 1, 1.	10 c d
1 Sam. vi. 12.	10 a
viii. 3.	5 d
x. 6.	1 g
x. 9.	16 g
xii. 20, 21.	10 d
xiii. 17, 18, 18.	16 d
xiv. 7.	5 c
xiv. 47.	16 d
xv. 11.	20 a
xv. 25, 30.	20 c
xv. 31.	8 e
xvii. 30.	20 d
xxii. 17, 18.	8 e
xxii. 18.	8 b
xxv. 12.	8 e
2 Sam. i. 22.	1 d
ii. 19.	21
ii. 21, 21.	5 c, 10 b
ii. 22.	10 c
ii. 23.	10 b
xiv. 24.	8 e
xviii. 30, 30.	8 b e
xix. 37.	20 d
xxii. 38.	20 d
1 Kings ii. 3.	16 d
ii. 15.	8 e
ii. 28, 38.	5 a
viii. 14.	8 i
viii. 33.	20 a
viii. 35.	20 d
ix. 6.	20 d
x. 13.	16 d
xi. 2, 3.	5 h
xi. 4.	5 e
xi. 9.	5 a
xii. 27.	20 a
xiii. 9, 17.	20 d
xv. 5.	10 a
xvii. 3.	16 a
xviii. 37.	8 f
xx. 39.	10 a
xxi. 4.	8 i
xxii. 32.	10 d
xxii. 33.	20 d
xxii. 34.	1 c
xxii. 43.	10 a
2 Kings i. 5, 5.	20 d a
i. 6.	20 c
ii. 24.	16 d
iv. 8, 10, 11.	10 d
v. 12.	16 d
v. 26.	1 a
ix. 18, 19.	8 b
ix. 23.	1 d
xv. 20.	20 d
xvi. 18.	8 f
xvii. 13.	20 c
xviii. 24.	20 m
xix. 28.	20 i
xx. 2.	8 i
xx. 5.	20 c
xxi. 13.	1 a
xxii. 2.	10 a
xxiii. 16.	16 d
xxiii. 25, 26.	20 a
xxiii. 34.	8 i
xxiv. 1.	20 d
1 Chron. x. 14.	8 i
xii. 12.	8 g
xiv. 14.	8 h
xxi. 20.	20 d
2 Chron. vi. 3.	8 i
vi. 26.	20 d
vi. 37.	20 a
vi. 42.	20 m
vii. 14, 19.	20 d
ix. 16.	1 d
xii. 12.	20 a
xv. 4.	20 d
xviii. 32.	20 d
xviii. 33.	1 c
xx. 10.	10 a
xxv. 27.	20 d
xxvi. 9.	19
xxix. 6, 6. β	8 i, 7 b
xxix. 10.	16 c
xxx. 6.	20 c
xxx. 8.	20 d
xxx. 9, 9.	20 b, 10 g
xxxv. 22.	8 f
xxxvi. 4.	8 i
2 Chron. xxxvi. 13.	20 b
Ezra vi. 22.	8 f
x. 14.	20 k
Neh. i. 9.	20 a
ii. 15.	20 d
iii. 19, 20, 24, 25.	19
iv. 4.	20 l
ix. 26.	20 k
ix. 35.	20 a
xiii. 2.	1 d
Esth. ii. 12, 15.	26
ix. 1.	1 h
ix. 22.	1 g
Job v. 1.	16 d
vi. 18.	4
xiv. 6.	20 d
xv. 13.	20 m
xvi. 11.	3
xix. 19.	1 g
xx. 14.	1 g
xxiii. 13.	20 m
xxiv. 4.	5 h
xxviii. 5.	1 g
xxx. 15.	1 k
xxxi. 7.	5 d
xxxiv. 15.	20 d
xxxiv. 27.	10 a
xxxvii. 12.	1 m
xxxviii. 14.	1 l
xxxix. 22.	20 d
xli. 28.	1 g
xlii. 10.	20 a
Ps. vii. 12.	20 d
ix. 3.	20 b
ix. 17.	20 d
xviii. 37.	20 d
xxii. 27.	20 d
xxv. 16.	16 c
xxxii. 4.	1 a
xxxv. 4.	9 b
xl. 3.	20 m
xliv. 10.	20 m
xliv. 18.	9 a
lvi. 9.	20 d
lx. 1.	20 h
lxvi. 6.	1 a
lxvi. 20.	10 f
lxix. 16.	16 c
lxx. 2.	9 b
lxx. 3.	20 d
lxxviii. 9.	1 a
lxxviii. 38.	20 k
lxxviii. 41.	20 d
lxxviii. 44.	1 d
lxxviii. 57, 57.	9 b, 1 g
lxxx. 3, 7, 19.	20 l
lxxxi. 14.	20 m
lxxxv. 3.	20 m
lxxxv. 4.	20 c
lxxxv. 8.	20 d
lxxxvi. 16.	16 c
lxxxix. 43.	20 m
xc. 3.	20 m
ci. 3.	11
civ. 9.	20 d
cv. 25, 29.	1 a
cvi. 23.	20 k
cvii. 33, 35.	23 b
cxiv. 8.	1 e
cxix. 37, 39.	12
cxix. 59.	20 m
cxix. 79.	20 d
cxxv. 5.	5 i
cxxvi. 1. γ	20 b
cxxvi. 4.	20 c
cxxix. 5.	9 b
cxxxii. 11.	20 m
cxxxii. 11.	20 d
cxlvi. 9.	14
Prov. i. 23.	20 d
i. 32.	20 p
iv. 15.	24
iv. 27.	5 d
iv. 4, 16.	10 d
xv. 1.	20 m
xvii. 8.	16 d
xxi. 1.	5 h
xxiv. 18.	20 i
xxv. 10.	20 d
xxvi. 14.	20 b
xxviii. 9.	10 h
xxix. 8.	20 m
xxx. 30.	20 d
Eccles. i. 6.	8 c
ii. 12.	16 a
Eccles. iii. 20.	20 a
Cant. i. 7.	15
ii. 17.	8 b
vi. 1.	16 a
iv. 5.	8 h
Isa. i. 25.	20 m
v. 25.	20 a
ix. 12, 13, 17, 21.	20 a
x. 2.	5 f
x. 4.	20 a
xii. 1.	20 a
xiii. 14.	16 d
xiv. 27.	20 m
xix. 6.	2
xxi. 4.	23 a
xxiii. 18. δ	18 b a
xxiii. 17.	20 a
xxiv. 1.	13
xxviii. 6.	20 n
xxix. 16.	1 b
xxix. 17.	20 a
xxix. 21.	5 h
xxx. 11.	5 g
xxxiv. 9.	20 c
xxxvi. 9.	1 g
xxxvii. 29.	20 l
xxxviii. 8.	20 i
xlii. 17.	9 a
xliv. 20.	5 e
xliv. 25.	20 n
l. 5.	9 a
liii. 6.	16 a
lviii. 13.	20 m
lix. 14.	6
lix. 20.	20 e
lxiii. 10.	1 i
Jer. ii. 21.	1 g
ii. 24.	20 m
ii. 27.	16 a
ii. 35.	20 a
iii. 7, 19.	20 d
iii. 10.	20 a
iii. 14.	20 c
iv. 8.	20 d
iv. 28.	20 d
v. 25.	5 e
vi. 9.	20 l
vi. 12.	8 d
viii. 4.	20 a
viii. 6.	20 a
x. 10.	20 a
xiii. 16.	23 a
xiv. 8.	8 a
xviii. 8.	20 k
xviii. 20.	8 k
xxi. 4.	8 k
xxiii. 22.	20 c
xxv. 5.	20 c
xxvi. 3.	20 d
xxix. 14.	20 a
xxx. 6.	1 g
xxxi. 13.	1 a
xxxi. 18, 18.	20 l d
xxxi. 19.	20 c
xxxi. 21, 21.	20 c
xxxii. 33.	16 d
xxxii. 40.	20 d
xxxiv. 11, 15, 16.	20 d
xxxviii. 22.	9 a
xliv. 5.	20 b
xlvi. 5.	9 c
xlviii. 39.	16 i
xlix. 8. ε	16 i
xlix. 24.	16 i
l. 6. ζ	20 f, or o
l. 16.	16 d
Lam. i. 8.	20 i
i. 13.	20 i
i. 20.	1 g
ii. 14.	20 d, 1 d
iii. 3, 3.	20 d, 1 d
iii. 11.	10 e
iii. 35.	5 f
v. 2, 15.	20 d
v. 21, 21.	20 l d
Ezek. i. 9, 12, 17.	20 a
iii. 19.	20 a
iii. 20.	20 b
iv. 8.	1 i
vii. 13.	8 f
viii. 6, 13, 15.	20 d
x. 11, 11, 16.	20 d
xiv. 6, 6.	20 l
Ezek. xvii. 6.	16 b
xviii. 21.	20 d
xviii. 24, 26, 27.	20 b
xviii. 28.	20 d
xviii. 30, 32.	20 l
xxvi. 2.	8 d
xxxiii. 9, 9.	20 b a
xxxiii. 11, 11, 11.	20 b c c
xxxiii. 12.	20 b
xxxiii. 14.	20 a
xxxiii. 18, 19.	20 b
xxxvi. 9.	16 a
xxxvii. 4.	20 f
xxxviii. 12.	20 k
xxxix. 2.	20 f
xli. 24.	8 m
xlii. 19.	8 a
ix. 16.	20 d
x. 8, 16.	1 g
Dan. ix. 13.	20 b
Dan. xi. 18.	23 b, or 20 m
xi. 18, 19.	20 m
xii. 3.	17
Hos. v. 4.	20 b
vii. 8.	1 f
x. 2.	8 d
xii. 6.	20 d
xiv. 4.	20 a
Joel ii. 12, 13.	20 d
ii. 31.	1 i
Amos i. 3, 3, 6, 9, 11, 13.	20 m
i. 8.	20 i
ii. 1, 4, 6.	20 m
ii. 7.	5 h
v. 7, 8.	1 e
v. 12.	5 h
vi. 12.	1 a
Jonah iii. 8.	1 a
Jonah iii. 9, 9.	20 d a
iii. 10.	20 a
Micah ii. 4. η	20 g
iii. 19.	20 d
vii. 19.	20 d
Nah. ii. 2.	20 a
Hab. ii. 16.	8 e
Zeph. i. 6.	9 c
ii. 7.	20 a
iii. 9.	1 d
iii. 20.	20 b
Zech. i. 3, 3.	20 c d
i. 4.	20 c
v. 1.	20 d
ix. 12.	20 c
ix. 19.	20 a
xiii. 7.	20 i
xiv. 10.	8 e
Mal. i. 6.	20 i
iii. 5.	5 i
iii. 20.	20 l

a lit. the flame of a sword turning itself. *β marg.* 'given the neck.' *γ marg.* 'returned the returning of Zion.' *δ lit.* violently turning he will violently turn. *ε marg.* ' or, they are turned back.' *ζ lit.* backsliding. *η marg.* 'or, instead of restoring.'

TURTLE, TURTLE-DOVE

תּוֹר *m.* turtle-dove, an onomatopoetic and primitive word. As a name of endearment to one beloved, Cant. ii. 12; of the people of Israel, Ps. lxxiv. 19, "thy turtle-dove," *i.e.* the people dear to thee and now affrighted: Gen. xv. 9: Lev. i. 14; v. 7, 11; xii. 6, 8; xiv. 22, 30; xv. 14, 29: Num. vi. 10: Ps. lxxiv. 19: Cant. ii. 12: Jer. viii. 7.

TWICE, TWAIN

פַּעַם *com.* step, *dual,* twice: Gen. xli. 32: Num. xx. 11: 1 Sam. xviii. 11: 1 Kings xi. 9: Eccles vi. 6.

שְׁנַיִם *adj. num. dual,* two, twain, twice: 2 Kings iv. 33: vi. 10: Neh. xiii. 20: Job xxxiii. 14: xl. 5: Ps. lxii. 11: Isa. vi. 2, 2, 2: Jer. xxxiv. 18: Ezek. xxi. 19. מִשְׁנֶה *m.* second, double; "twice as much:" Exod. xvi. 5, 22: Job xlii. 10.

TWIG

יוֹנֶקֶת *f.* sucker, branch, young twig: Ezek. xvii. 22. יְנִיקוֹת *f. pl.* Ezek. xvii. 4.

TWILIGHT

נֶשֶׁף *m. pr.* a breathing, hence, the evening twilight, when cooling breezes blow; the morning twilight, dawn; from a like reason, the cooling wind arising in the East an hour or two after sunrise: 1 Sam. xxx. 17: 2 Kings vii. 5, 7: Job iii. 9; xxiv. 15: Prov. vii. 9.

עֲלָטָה *f.* thick darkness: Ezek. xii. 6, 7, 12.

TWIN

תָּאַם to be double, twain; to bear twins. HIPHIL *part.* Cant. iv. 2: vi. 6. תְּאוֹמִים *m. pl.* twins: Gen. xxv. 24; xxxviii. 27: Cant. iv. 5, *lit.* twins of a roe; vii. 3, *lit. id.*

TWINED

שָׁזַר to twist a thread. HOPHAL *part.* twisted (byssus): Exod. xxvi. 1, 31, 36; xxvii. 9, 16, 18; xxviii. 6, 8, 15; xxxvi. 8, 35, 37; xxxviii. 9, 16, 18; xxxix. 2, 5, 8, 24, 28, 29.

TWO

חֲצִי‎ *m.* half, half part ; two parts : 1 Kings xvi. 21.

פֶּה‎ *m.* mouth, edge : Prov. v. 4, *lit.* a sword of edges. פִּימִיוֹת‎ *f. pl.* edges, that is, two or more : Ps. cxlix. 6, *lit.* a sword of edges.

צֶמֶד‎ *m.* a pair, yoke : Judg. xix. 10 : 2 Kings v. 17.

UNACCUSTOMED

לָמַד‎ to learn ; to teach, to accustom. PUAL *pret.* Jer. **xxxi.** 18.

UNAWARES

יָדַע‎ to know. KAL *fut.* Ps. xxxv. 8. דַּעַת‎ *f.* knowledge : Deut. iv. 42, *lit.* without knowledge.

לֵב‎ *m.* heart : Gen. xxxi. 20, *marg.* 'the heart of Laban.' לְבָב‎ *m.* Gen. xxxi. 26, *lit.* stolen from my heart, *or,* stolen away my heart, *i. e.* departed without my consent and privity.

שְׁגָגָה‎ *f.* error, mistake, transgression through ignorance or inadvertence : Num. xxxv. 11, 15 : Josh. xx. 3, 9.

UNCIRCUMCISED

עָרֵל‎ *adj.* that which is superfluous ; one having a foreskin, uncircumcised. Often spoken of other nations in contempt, and with the idea of profaneness, uncleanness, as the Philistines and other Gentiles. *Metaph.* of uncircumcised lips, *i. e.* dull of speech ; Chald. of a heavy speech ; Gr. ἄλογος, *i. e.* a person wanting eloquence ; Syr. mine is a stammering tongue. Uncircumcised ear, *i. e.* an ear closed by a foreskin, that cannot hearken. An uncircumcised heart that will not understand and learn its duty, precepts of religion cannot penetrate.—*Bush.* Gen. xvii. 14 : Exod. vi. 12, 30 ; xii. 48 : Lev. xix. 23 ; xxvi. 41 : Josh. v. 7 : Judg. xiv. 3 ; xv. 18 : 1 Sam. xiv. 6 ; xvii. 26, 36 ; xxxi. 4 : 2 Sam. i. 20 : 1 Chron. x. 4 : Isa. lii. 1 : Jer. vi. 10 ; ix. 26, 26 : Ezek. xxviii. 10 ; xxxi. 18 ; xxxii. 19, 21, 24, 25, 26, 27, 28, 29, 30, 32 ; xliv. 7, 7, 9, 9. עָרְלָה‎ *f.* foreskin ; *trop.* foreskin of a tree, *i. e.* the fruit of the first three years, which by the law was to be regarded as unclean : Gen. xxxiv. 14, *lit.* one that hath a foreskin ; Lev. xix. 23, *lit.* ye shall count as uncircumcised the uncircumcision thereof, the fruit thereof ; Jer. ix. 25. עָרֵל‎ *v. denom.* to count uncircumcised. KAL *pret.* Lev. xix. 23.

UNCLE

דּוֹד‎ *m.* love ; friend ; specially, the father's brother ; uncle, called the friend of the family : Lev. x. 4 ; xx. 20 ; xxv. 49, 49 : 1 Sam. x. 14, 15, 16 ; xiv. 50 : 1 Chron. xxvii. 32 : Esth. ii. 7, 15 : Jer. xxxii. 7, 8, 9, 12 : Amos vi. 10, *lit.* his uncle. דּוֹדָה‎ *f.* uncle's wife : Lev. xx. 20.

UNCLEAN, UNCLEANNESS

1   דָּבָר‎ *m.* word, matter, thing.

2   טָמֵא‎ to be or become unclean, impure ; to be defiled, polluted. Chiefly spoken of Levitical uncleanness, both of persons and animals (*i. e.* animals not to be eaten, see Lev. xi. 1-31) ; and also of buildings, vessels, &c., *opp.* טָהֵר‎, Lev. xi. 24, &c. ; *seq.* בְּ‎ to be defiled with anything ; to pronounce unclean, *e.g.* as a priest, Lev. xiii. 3, &c. KAL *ᵃpret.* *ᵇfut.* PIEL *ᶜpret.* *ᵈinf.* *ᵉfut.* HIPHPAEL *ᶠfut.* *ᵍ* טָמֵא‎ *adj.* unclean, impure ; in a Levitical and moral sense. It speaks the greatest pollution, the sordidness and filthiness of habit, the gore of blood, the muddiness of water, whatsoever is loathsome or unlovely, noisome or unsightly, all these meet in and make up the meaning of this word.—*Caryl* on Job xiv. 4. It implies unsuitableness or contrariety to communion with him that is holy.—*Cocc.* Lev. v. 2, &c. *ʰ* טֻמְאָה‎ *f.* Lev. v. 3, &c.

3   נִדָּה‎ *f.* abomination ; uncleanness, impurity ; see *Separation.*

4   עֶרְוָה‎ *f.* nakedness ; that which causes shame.

5   קָדֵשׁ‎ *adj. pr.* sacred, consecrated ; such as are habitually addicted to any pursuit or object : Job xxxvi. 14, *i.e.* among those who are addicted, and, as it were, consecrated, to all manner of impurity and wickedness. So *auri sacra fames,* a fixed avarice, wholly addicted to the love and pursuit of wealth without any regard to justice.—*Virgil. Ego sum sacer, scelestus.*—*Plautus.*

6   קָרֶה‎ *m.* hap, chance, accident.

No. 2 g not included ; and 2 h, *Uncleanness.*

Lev. xi. 24, 24.	2 f b	Lev. xiii. 59.	2 d	Lev. xxii. 6.	2 a
xi. 25, 28, 32, 40, 40.	2 a	xiv. 36, 46.	2 b	Num. vi. 7.	2 f
xi. 26, 27, 31, 32,		xv. 4, 4, 9, 19, 20,		xix. 7, 8, 10, 11.	2 b
33, 34, 34, 35, 36,		20, 23.	2 b	xix. 14, 16, 20, 21,	
39.	2 b	xv. 5, 6, 7, 8, 11, 16,		22, 22.	2 b
xi. 2, 2.	2 a b	17, 18, 21, 22.	2 a	Deut. xxiii. 10.	6
xii. 2, 2.	2 a b	xv. 10, 10.	2 a b	xxiii. 14.	4
xii. 5.	2 a	xv. 24, 24.	2 a b	xxiv. 1.	1, 4
xiii. 3, 8, 11, 15, 20,		xv. 27, 27.	2 b a	Ezra ix. 11.	3, 2 h
22, 25, 27, 30.	2 c	xvii. 15.	2 a	Job xxxvi. 14.	5
xiii. 14.	2 b	xx. 21.	3	Hag. ii. 13, 13.	2 g b b
xiii. 44.	2 g	xx. 25.	2 d	Zech. xiii. 1.	3
xiii. 44.	2 d e	xxii. 5, 5.	2 b		

UNCOVER

1   גָּלָה‎ to make naked, to uncover ; to uncover the nakedness of a woman, *i. e.* to have carnal intercourse with her ; so to uncover the nakedness of a man, is to have unlawful intercourse with his wife, as is explained by Lev. xviii. 8 ; and in the same sense is used the father's skirt or coverlet, Deut. xxii. 30, xxvii. 20. NIPHAL *ᵃpret.* *ᵇinf.* *ᶜfut.* PIEL *ᵈpret.* *ᵉinf.* *ᶠimp.* *ᵍfut.* HITHPAEL *ʰfut.*

2   חָשַׂף‎ to strip off, to make naked. KAL *part.* Paül.

3   עָרָה‎ to be naked ; to make naked, to uncover ; *e.g.* a shield from its covering, *i.e.* to prepare for war. PIEL *ᵃpret.* HIPHIL *ᵇpret.*

4   פָּרַע‎ to let loose ; to make naked, to uncover, by loosing the garments, &c., *e. g.* the head, specially by cutting off the hair. KAL *ᵃpret.* *ᵇfut.*

Gen. ix. 21.	1 h	Lev. xviii. 7, 7, 8, 9,		Lev. xviii. 17, 17.	1 g e
Lev. x. 6.	4 b	10, 11, 12, 13, 14,		xx. 11, 17, 18, 18,	
xviii. 6, 18, 19.	1 e	15, 16.	1 g	20, 21.	1 d

Lev. xx. 19, 19.	1 g, 3 b	Ruth iii. 7.	1 g	Isa. xlvii. 3.	1 c
xxi. 10.	4 b	2 Sam. vi. 20, 20.	1 a b	Jer. xlix. 10.	1 d
Num. v. 18.	4 a	Isa. xx. 4.	2	Ezek. iv. 7.	2
Deut. xxvii. 20.	1 d	xxii. 6.	3 a	Zeph. ii. 14. β	3 a
Ruth iii. 4. a	1 d	xlvii. 2, 2.	1 f		

a marg. 'or, lift up the clothes that are on his feet.' β marg. 'or, when he hath uncovered, i.e. have torn off the ceilings of cedar, and made naked the walls.'

UNDEFILED

תָּם *adj.* whole, perfect, upright; probably a term of endearment for one beloved: Cant. v. 2; vi. 9. תָּמִים *adj.* Ps. cxix. 1.

UNDERSETTERS

כָּתֵף *f.* shoulder; side: 1 Kings vii. 30, 30, 34, 34.

UNDERSTAND

1 בִּין *pr.* to separate, to distinguish; hence, to discern, to mark, to understand, all which depend on the power of separating, distinguishing, discriminating; specially, to discern, perceive; to discern mentally, to understand. KAL a *pret.* b *imp.* KAL and HIPHIL c *fut.* NIPHAL d *part.* HIPHIL e *pret.* f *inf.* g *imp.* h *part.* HITHPOLEL i *fut.* k בִּינָה *f.* understanding, *i.e.* the act; understanding, *i.e.* the faculty of insight, intelligence; specially, of skill in any art or science. l תָּבוּן *m.* insight, understanding. תְּבוּנָה *f.* תּוּבְנָה *f.* insight (כתיב). בִּינָה ○ Ch. *f. id.*

2 טַעַם *m.* taste; intellectual taste, *i.e.* judgment, discernment, understanding, comp. Lat. *sapere, sapiens, sapientia.*

3 יָדַע to know. KAL a *pret.* b *fut.* c *part.* Poel. d מַנְדַּע Ch. *m.* knowledge, understanding, intellect.

4 לֵב *m.* heart; to the heart is ascribed understanding, intelligence, wisdom. לֵבָב *m. id.*

5 רוּחַ to smell; to delight in smelling, to take delight in. HIPHIL *inf.*

6 שָׂכַל to look at; to be prudent, circumspect; to act prudently, to be intelligent. HIPHIL a *pret.* b *inf.* c *fut.* d *part.* שֶׂכֶל *m.* intelligence, understanding, wisdom, success. שָׂכְלְתָנוּ Ch. *f.*

7 שָׁמַע to hear; to understand. KAL a *fut.* b *part.* Poel.

Gen. xi. 7.	7 a	2 Chron. ii. 12, 13.	1 k	Job xxxvi. 29.	1 c
xli. 15. a	7 a	xxvi. 5.	1 h	xxxviii. 4. ε	3 a, 1 k
xlii. 23.	7 b	Ezra viii. 16.	1 h	xxxviii. 36.	1 k
Exod. xxxi. 3.	1 m	viii. 18.	6 e	xxxix. 17.	1 k
xxxv. 31.	1 m	Neh. viii. 2. γ	1 h	xlii. 3.	1 c
xxxvi. 1.	1 m	viii. 3, 7.	1 h	Ps. xiv. 2.	6 d
Num. xvi. 30.	3 a	viii. 8.	1 c	xix. 12.	1 c
Deut. i. 13.	1 d	viii. 12.	1 e	xxxii. 9.	1 f
iv. 6, 6.	1 k d	viii. 13. δ	6 b	xlvii. 7. ζ	6 d
ix. 3, 6.	3 a	x. 28.	1 h	xlix. 3.	1 m
xxviii. 49.	7 a	xiii. 7.	1 c	xlix. 20.	1 c
xxxii. 28.	1 m	Job vi. 24.	1 g	liii. 2.	6 d
xxxii. 29.	6 c	xii. 3.	4 a	lxxiii. 17.	1 c
1 Sam. iv. 6.	3 b	xii. 12, 13.	1 m	lxxxi. 5.	3 a
xxv. 3.	6 e	xii. 20.	2	lxxxii. 5.	1 c
xxvi. 4.	3 b	xiii. 1.	1 c	xcii. 6.	1 c
2 Sam. iii. 37.	3 b	xv. 9.	1 c	xciv. 8.	1 b
1 Kings iii. 9.	7 b	xvii. 4.	6 e	cvi. 7.	1 c
iii. 11.	1 f	xx. 3.	1 k	cvii. 43.	1 b
iii. 12.	1 d	xxiii. 5.	1 c	cxi. 10.	1 i
iv. 29.	1 m	xxvi. 12.	1 m, or n	cxix. 27, 34, 73.	6 g
vii. 14.	1 m	xxvi. 14.	1 i	cxix. 99.	1 c
2 Kings xviii. 26.	1 m	xxviii. 12, 20, 28.	1 k	cxix. 100, 104.	6 i
1 Chron. xii. 32. β	3 c, 1 k	xxviii. 23.	1 e	cxix. 125, 144, 169.	1 h
xxii. 12.	1 k	xxxii. 8, 9.	1 c	cxix. 130.	1 h
xxviii. 9.	1 h	xxxiv. 10, 34.	4 a	cxxxix. 2.	1 m
xxviii. 19.	6 a	xxxiv. 16.	1 k	cxlvii. 5.	1 m

Prov. i. 2.	1 k	Prov. xvii. 27.	1 m	Isa. xliv. 19.	1 m
i. 5.	1 d	xvii. 28.	1 d	lvi. 11. κ	3 a, 1 f
i. 6.	1 f	xviii. 2.	1 m	Jer. iii. 15.	6 b
ii. 2, 3, 6, 11.	1 m	xix. 8.	1 f	iv. 22.	1 d
ii. 5, 9.	1 c	xix. 25, 25.	1 c d	v. 15.	7 a
iii. 4.	6 e	xx. 5.	1 m	v. 21.	4
iii. 5.	1 k	xx. 24. η	1 m	ix. 12.	1 d
iii. 13, 19.	1 m	xxi. 16.	6 b	ix. 24.	6 b
iv. 1, 5, 7.	1 k	xxi. 30.	1 m	li. 15.	1 m
v. 1.	1 m	xxiii. 23.	1 k	Ezek. iii. 6.	7 a
vi. 32.	4	xxiv. 3.	1 m	xxviii. 4.	1 h
vii. 4.	1 k	xxiv. 30.	4	Dan. i. 4.	1 h
viii. 1.	4	xxviii. 2, 11.	1 h	i. 17. λ	1 h
viii. 5, 5.	1 m	xxviii. 5, 5.	1 c	i. 20.	1 k
viii. 9.	1 g	xxviii. 16.	1 m	ii. 21.	1 k
viii. 9.	1 h	xxix. 19.	1 c	iv. 34.	3 c
viii. 14.	1 m	xxx. 2.	1 m	v. 11, 12, 14.	6 f
ix. 4, 16.	4	Eccles. ix. 11.	1 d	viii. 16, 17.	1 h
ix. 6, 10.	1 m	Isa. vi. 9, 10.	1 m	viii. 23, 27.	1 m
x. 13, 13.	1 d, 4	ii. 2.	1 k	ix. 2.	1 h
x. 23.	1 m	xi. 3.	5	ix. 13.	6 b
xi. 12.	1 m	xxvii. 11.	1 k	ix. 22.	1 k
xii. 11.	4	xxviii. 9.	1 c	ix. 25.	1 e
xiii. 15.	6 e	xxviii. 19.	1 f	x. 1, 1.	1 a k
xiv. 6.	1 m	xxix. 14.	1 k	x. 11.	1 g
xiv. 8.	1 f	xxix. 16.	1 e	xi. 12, 14.	1 f
xiv. 29.	1 m	xxix. 24.	3 a, 1 k	xi. 33, 35.	6 d
xiv. 33.	1 d	xxxii. 4.	1 c	xii. 8, 10, 10.	1 c
xv. 14.	1 d	xxxiii. 19. θ	1 k	Hos. iv. 14.	1 c
xv. 21.	1 m	xxxvi. 11.	7 b	xiii. 2.	1 l
xv. 32.	4	xl. 14, ι. 28.	1 m	xiv. 9.	1 l
xvi. 16.	1 k	xl. 21.	1 e	Obad. 7, 8.	1 m
xvi. 22.	1 k	xli. 20.	6 c	Micah iv. 12.	1 e
xvii. 18.	4	xliii. 10.	1 m		
xvii. 24.	1 m	xliv. 18, 18.	1 c, 6 b		

a marg. 'or, (when) thou hearest.' β lit. knew the knowledge. γ lit. that understood in hearing. δ marg. 'or, that they might instruct in.' ε lit. knowest understanding. ζ marg. 'or, (every one) that hath understanding.' η lit. and a man, how can he understand? θ lit. (of which there is) no understanding. ι marg. 'understandings.' κ lit. that know not to understand. λ marg. 'he made Daniel to understand.'

UNDERTAKE

עָרַב to become surety for any one. KAL *imp.* Isa. xxxviii. 14, marg. 'or, ease me.'

קָבַל to receive, to admit a law, precept, *i.e.* to observe it. PIEL *pret.* Esth. ix. 23.

UNDO, UNDONE

אָבַד to perish. KAL *pret.* Num. xxi. 29.

דָּמָה to cut off. NIPHAL *pret.* Isa. vi. 5.

נָתַר to be moved; to let loose; to shake off. HIPHIL *inf.* Isa. lviii. 6.

סוּר to turn aside; to remove; to leave undone. HIPHIL *pret.* Josh. xi. 15.

עָשָׂה to do. KAL *part.* Poel, *seq.* אֶת, Zeph. iii. 19, *i.e.* I will deal with.

UNDRESSED

נָזִיר *m.* consecrated, devoted; a Nazarite; transferred to the vine, which every seventh and also every fiftieth year was left unpruned: Lev. xxv. 5, 11.

UNEQUAL

תָּכַן see *Equal.* NIPHAL *fut.* Ezek. xviii. 25, 29.

UNFAITHFUL

בָּגַד to deal treacherously. KAL *fut.* Ps. lxxviii. 57. *part.* Poel, Prov. xxv. 19.

UNGIRD

פָּתַח to open; to loose. PIEL *fut.* Gen. xxiv. 32.

UNGODLY

בְּלִיַּעַל *m.* (see *Belial*), "ungodly," *lit.* of Belial: 2 Sam. xxii. 5: Ps. xviii. 4: Prov. xvi. 27; xix. 28.

חָסִיד *adj.* holy, godly: Ps. xliii. 1, *marg.* 'or, unmerciful.'

עֱוִיל *m.* evil, ungodly: Job xvi. 11.

רָשָׁע *adj.* wicked: 2 Chron. xix. 2: Job xxxiv. 18: Ps. i. 1, *marg.* 'or, wicked;' 4, 5, 6; iii. 7; lxxiii. 12.

UNHOLY

חֹל *adj.* profane: Lev. x. 10.

UNICORN

רְאֵם *m.* a wild and ferocious animal, frequent and well known in Palestine and the adjacent regions; thought by many to be the rhinoceros, or unicorn; by others the oryx, a large and fierce species of the antelope; but more generally, by learned men of the present day, to be the buffalo, bearing the like relation to the ox as the wild ass does to the domestic one, horned, and destroying men with his horns. The Lxx. has μονοκέρως, and the Vulg. *unicorn.* Num. xxiii. 22; xxiv. 8: Deut. xxxiii. 17, *lit.* an unicorn; Job xxxix. 9, 10: Ps. xxii. 21; xxix. 6, *lit.* son of unicorns; xcii. 10: Isa. xxxiv. 7, *marg.* 'or, rhinoceros.'

UNITE

יָחַד to become one, to be united, joined, *seq.* בְּ; to make one, to unite. KAL *fut.* Gen. xlix. 6. PIEL *imp.* Ps. lxxxvi. 11. יַחַד *m.* "together in unity," Ps. cxxxiii. 1.

UNJUST

אָוֶן *m.* iniquity: Prov. xi. 7.

עָוַל (see *Iniquity*), to deal unjustly. PIEL *fut.* Isa. xxvi. 10. עַוָּל *m.* Zeph. iii. 5. עָוֶל *m.* Ps. lxxxii. 2: Prov. xxix. 27. עַוְלָה *f.* Ps. xliii. 1.

UNLEAVENED

מַצָּה *f. pr.* sweetness, *concr.* sweet, *i.e.* not fermented, unleavened, ἄζυμον; unleavened bread: Gen. xix. 3, &c.

UNMINDFUL

שָׁיָה to forget. KAL *fut.* Deut. xxxii. 18.

UNOCCUPIED

חָדַל to cease; to cease to be what things were before. KAL *pret.* Judg. v. 6.

UNPROFITABLE

סָכַן to profit. KAL *fut.* Job xv. 3, *lit.* talk which profiteth not.

UNPUNISHED

נָקָה to be innocent; to pronounce innocent, to acquit. KAL *inf.* Jer. xlix. 12, *lit.* in being clear shall be clear. NIPHAL *inf.* Jer. xxv. 29, *lit.* being unpunished shall be unpunished. *fut.* Prov. xi. 21; xvi. 5; xvii. 5; xix. 5 and 9: Jer. xxv. 29, 29; xlix. 12, 12. PIEL *inf.* Jer. xxx. 11; xlvi. 28. *fut.* Jer. xxx. 11; xlvi. 28.

UNRIGHTEOUS

אָוֶן *m.* iniquity: Isa. x. 1; lv. 7, *marg.* 'man of iniquity.'

חָמָס *m.* violence: Exod. xxiii. 1, *lit.* witness of violence.

עָוַל to do evil, to act wickedly; see *Iniquity.* PIEL *part.* Ps. lxxi. 4. עַוָּל *m.* Job xxvii. 7. עָוֶל *m.* Lev. xix. 15, 35: Deut. xxv. 16. עַוְלָה *f.* Ps. xcii. 15. עוֹלָה *f.* Ps. xcii. 15 (כתיב).

צֶדֶק *m.* righteousness: Jer. xxii. 13, *lit.* not righteousness.

UNSATIABLE

שָׂבְעָה *f.* satiety, fulness: Ezek. xvi. 28, *lit.* without thy satisfaction.

UNSAVOURY

פָּתַל to twist; to show oneself crooked, crafty, perverse. HITHPAEL *fut.* 2 Sam. xxii. 27.

תָּפֵל *m.* anything unseasoned, unsavoury: Job vi. 6.

UNSEARCHABLE

חֵקֶר *m.* searching: Job v. 9: Ps. cxlv. 3: Prov. xxv. 3.

UNSHOD

יָחֵף *adj.* barefoot: Jer. ii. 25.

UNSTABLE

פַּחַז *m.* the original word פָּחַז implies precipitate motion, as of a stream breaking through impediments, or running down a declivity; its derivations have the import of rash, light, dissolute, licentious: Gen. xlix. 4. Gr. ἐξύβρισας ὡς ὕδωρ. Chald. but because thou hast followed thine own will, as water poured out. Sam. and Syr. thou hast been violent, and flowed down like water. Gesenius, a boiling up as of water, *sc.* art thou, *i.e.* thou didst boil up like water with lust and passion, referring to his incest. Symm. ὑπέρζεσας. Vulg. *effusus es.*

UNSTOP

פָּתַח to open. NIPHAL *fut.* Isa. xxxv. 5.

UNTEMPERED

תָּפֵל *m.* unsavoury; applied contemptuously to mortar: Ezek. xiii. 10, 11, 14, 15; xxii. 28; probably such as is not duly mixed, that has not power in it to hold, neither strength nor coherence, and therefore insufficient to keep up a wall, being soon washed away with the rain; such were the pretended visions and predictions of the false prophets: Ezek. xiii. 10, 11, 14, 15; xxii. 28. See *Foolish.*

UNWALLED

פְּרָזִי *m.* country, rustic (see *Village*): Deut. iii. 5. פְּרָזוֹת *f. pl.* unwalled (towns): Esth. ix. 19.

UNWISE

חָכָם *adj.* wise: Deut. xxxii. 6, *lit.* not wise: Hos. xiii. 13, *id.*

UNWITTINGLY

דַּעַת *f.* knowledge: Josh. xx. 3, *lit.* without knowledge; 5, *lit. id.*

שְׁגָגָה *f.* ignorance: Lev. xxii. 14.

UP

זָרַח to rise, as the sun; to be up. KAL *inf.* Judg. ix. 33.

קוּם to arise. KAL *imp.* Gen. xix. 14; xliv. 4: Exod. xxxii. 1: Josh. vii. 13: Judg. iv. 14; viii. 20; ix. 32; xix. 28: 1 Sam. ix. 26. *fut.* 2 Sam, xxiv. 11.

UPBRAID

חָרַף to upbraid, reproach, scorn. PIEL *pret.* Judg. viii. 15.

UPHARSIN

פְּרַם Ch. to divide. P'AL *part. active,* Dan. v. 25. See *Peres.*

UPHOLD

1 סָמַךְ to lean; to uphold, to sustain, to help, *pr.* to let lean upon; *seq. acc.* לְ and *dupl. acc.* Ps. li. 14. KAL ᵃ *pret.* ᵇ *imp.* ᶜ *fut.* ᵈ *part.* Poel.

2 סָעַד to prop, to uphold; to support. KAL *pret.*

3 קוּם to stand up; to make to stand. HIPHIL *fut.*

4 תָּמַךְ to take hold of; to attain, to acquire; to hold up, to support, *seq.* בְּ. KAL ᵃ *pret.* ᵇ *fut.*

Job iv. 4.	3	Ps. lxiii. 8.	4 a	Isa. xli. 10.	4 a
Ps. xxxvii. 17, 24.	1 d	cxix. 116.	1 b	xlii. 1.	4 b
xli. 12.	4 a	cxlv. 14.	1 d	lxiii. 5, 5.	1 d a
li. 12.	1 c	Prov. xx. 28.	2	Ezek. xxx. 6.	1 d
liv. 4.	1 d	xxix. 23.	4 b		

UPPER

עֵלִי *adj.* higher, upper: Josh. xv. 19: Judg. i. 15. עֶלְיוֹן *adj.* high, higher, upper: Gen. xl. 17: Josh. xvi. 5: 2 Kings xviii. 17: 1 Chron. vii. 24: 2 Chron. viii. 5; xxxii. 30: Isa. vii. 3; xxxvi. 2: Ezek. xlii. 5.

UPRIGHT

1 יָשַׁר to be straight, right; to be even, level. KAL ᵃ *pret.* PIEL ᵇ *fut.* ᶜ יָשָׁר *adj.* straight, right; upright, righteous, just: 1 Sam. xxix. 6, &c. ᵈ יֹשֶׁר *m.* straightness, rightness; right, duty, what is right and proper; of persons, uprightness, integrity; often with לֵב, לְבָב. ᵉ יִשְׁרָה *f.* integrity. ᶠ מִישׁוֹר *m.* straightness, of a way; evenness, of a level region; *trop.* Ps. cxliii. 10. ᵍ מֵישָׁרִים *m. pl.* straightness, rightness, of a way; uprightness, sincerity; justice; evenness, hence happiness: Isa. xxvi. 7.

2 נָכוֹחַ *adj.* what lies in a straight direct line; what is right, agreeable to truth and righteousness.

3 עֹמֶד *m.* standing, place where one stands.

4 קוֹמְמִיּוּת *adv.* upright, erect.

5 מִקְשָׁה *f.* beaten or turned work, as of a column, upright.

6 תָּמַם to be complete, whole; to be whole-minded, upright, blameless; to show oneself upright, to deal uprightly with any one; with עִם. KAL ᵃ *fut.* HITHPAEL ᵇ *fut.*

תָּם ᶜ *adj.* whole, perfect, upright; only in a moral sense. ᵈ תֹּם *m.* integrity of mind, uprightness, innocence. ᵉ תָּמִים *adj.* whole-minded, upright, innocent, blameless.

No. 1 c, *Upright*, not included.

Lev. xxvi. 13.	4	Ps. xix. 13.	6 a	Prov. xv. 21.	1 b
Deut. ix. 5.	1 d	xxv. 21.	1 d	xxviii. 6.	6 d
2 Sam. xxii. 24.	6 e	xxxvii. 18.	6 e	xxviii. 10, 18.	6 d
xxii. 26, 26.	6 b	lviii. 1.	1 g	xxix. 10.	6 c
1 Kings iii. 6.	1 e	lxxv. 2.	1 g	Eccles. xii. 10.	1 d
ix. 4.	1 d	lxxxiv. 11.	6 e	Cant. i. 4. a	1 g
1 Chron. xxix. 17,		cxi. 8.	1 c	Isa. xxvi. 7, 7.	1 g c
17.	1 g d	cxix. 7.	1 d	xxvi. 10.	2
Job iv. 6.	6 d	cxliii. 10.	1 f	xxxiii. 15. β	1 g
xii. 4.	6 e	Prov. ii. 7.	6 d	lvii. 2.	2
xxxiii. 3, 23.	1 d	ii. 13.	1 d	Jer. x. 5.	3
Ps. ix. 8.	1 g	x. 9, 29.	6 d	Dan. viii. 18.	3
xv. 2.	6 e	xi. 20.	6 e	x. 11.	3
xviii. 23.	6 e	xiii. 6.	6 d	Amos v. 10.	6 e
xviii. 25, 25.	6 e b	xiv. 2.	1 d	Hab. ii. 4.	1 a

a marg. 'or, they love thee uprightly.'   *β marg.* 'in uprightnesses.'

UPRISING

קוּם to stand up. KAL *inf.* Ps. cxxxix. 2.

UPROAR

הָמָה to make a noise, to rage, to be tumultuous. KAL *part.* Poel, 1 Kings i. 41.

UPSIDE DOWN

פָּנִים *m. pl.* face: 2 Kings xxi. 13, *lit.* upon its face; Isa. xxiv. 1, *marg.* 'perverteth the face thereof.'

UPWARD

גָּבַהּ to be lifted up. HIPHIL *fut.* Job v. 7, *marg.* 'lift up to fly.'

מָרוֹם *m.* height: Isa. xxxviii. 14.

URGE

אָלַץ to urge, to press. PIEL *fut.* Judg. xvi. 16.

חָזַק to be strong, to be strong upon any one, *seq.* עַל. KAL *fut.* Exod. xii. 33; the same word which is so frequently applied to the hardening of Pharaoh.

חֲצַף Ch. to be hard, rough; to be harsh, severe. APHEL *part.* Dan. iii. 22.

פָּצַר to blunt, to make dull; to urge, to press any one, *seq.* בְּ of person, with prayers, entreaties, *comp. obtundere precibus.* KAL *fut.* Gen. xxxiii. 11: Judg. xix. 7: 2 Kings ii. 17; v. 16.

פָּרַץ to break forth; to press upon, to urge with entreaties, *seq.* בְּ. KAL *fut.* 2 Kings v. 23.

URIM

אוּרִים *m. pl. lit.* lights. It has been matter of frequent discussion among the learned what we are to understand by the Urim and Thummim "put in the breast-plate of judgment," Exod. xxviii. 30; whether these two words refer to the stones inserted in the breast-plate, or to some further appendage of that ornament. The language of God to Moses seems to imply something distinct from

the precious stones ; and Bonar, on Leviticus, supposes that the words אוּרִים and תֻּמִּים were inserted in the centre of the breast-plate. The Jewish writers, and most learned critics, believe the Urim and Thummim to mean the twelve precious stones set in the breast-plate which the High Priest was to put on when he went in before the Lord : Exod. xxviii. 30 : Lev. viii. 8 : Num. xxvii. 21 : Deut. xxxiii. 8 : 1 Sam. xxviii. 6 : Ezra ii. 63 : Neh. vii. 65.

USE

1 אָמַר to say ; to use (speech). KAL *fut.*

2 דָּבַר to speak. PIEL *fut.*

3 מְלָאכָה *f.* ministry, work, service.

4 לִמּוּד *adj.* taught.

5 לָקַח to take. KAL *part.* Poel.

6 מָשַׁל to use a proverb ; to use (a proverb). KAL a *inf.* b *part.* Poel.

7 עָשָׂה to do. KAL a *pret.* NIPHAL b *fut.*

8 עֲבוֹדָה *f.* service.

9 עָשַׁק to oppress, to use (oppression). KAL *pret.*

10 קָסַם to divine, to use (divination). KAL a *inf.* b *fut.* c *part.* Poel.

11 מִשְׁפָּט judgment ; right ; manner, custom, use.

Lev. vii. 24, 24.	7 b, 3	Prov. xviii. 23. β	2	Ezek. xviii. 3.	6 a
Deut. xviii. 10.	10 c	Jer. ii. 24.	4	xxi. 21.	10 a
2 Kings xvii. 17.	10 b	xxiii. 31.	5	xxii. 29.	9
1 Chron. xxviii. 15.	8	xxxi. 23.	1	xxxv. 11.	7 a
Ps. cxix. 132. a	11	Ezek. xviii. 2.	6 b		

a *marg.* 'according to the custom toward those,' &c.   β *lit.* speaketh with intreaties.

USURY, USURER

1 נָשָׁא to lend on usury, *seq.* בְּ. KAL a *part.* b מַשָּׁא *m.* usury.

2 נָשָׁה to lend on usury, *seq. acc.* of thing, and בְּ of person. KAL a *pret.* b *part.* Poel.

3 נָשַׁךְ to bite ; to vex ; to lend on usury ; since not only the lending on usury but even the taking of interest was regarded as sordid and oppressive : in HIPHIL, to take usury of any one, with לְ of person. Lat. *usura vorax.* —Lucan. i. 171. KAL a *fut.* HIPHIL b *fut.* c נֶשֶׁךְ *m.* interest.

Exod. xxii. 25, 25.	2 b, 3 c	Neh. v. 7, 10.	1 b	Isa. xxiv. 2. β	1 a
Lev. xxv. 36, 37.	3 c	Ps. xv. 5.	3 c	xv. 10, 10.	2 a
Deut. xxiii. 19, }		Prov. xviii. 8.	3 e	Ezek. xviii. 8, 13, 17.	3 c
19,19,19,19. }	c a	Isa. xxiv. 2. a	2 b	xxii. 12.	3 c
xxiii. 20, 20.	3 b				

a "taker of usury."   β "giver of usury."

UTMOST, UTTERMOST

1 אַחֲרוֹן *adj.* hinder, hindermost, latter, in opposition to foremost, former. a אַחֲרִית *f.* the last or extreme part, uttermost part.

2 אֶפֶס *m.* end, extremity ; uttermost parts.

3 כָּנָף *com.* wing ; extremity.

4 קָצָץ to cut off, to cut asunder. KAL a *part.* Paül. b קֵץ end, utmost border : Jer. l. 26, *marg.* 'end.' c קָצֶה *f.* end,

extremity. d קָצֶה *m.* end, extremity, remotest parts. e קְצָוָה *f. td.* f קִיצוֹן *adj.* last.

Exod. xxvi. 4.	4 f	Deut. xxxiv. 2.	1	Ps. cxxxix. 9.	1 a
xxxvi. 11, 17.	4 f	Josh. xv. 1, 5, 21.	4 d	Isa. xlix. 18.	4 d
Num. xi. 1.	4 d	1 Sam. xiv. 2.	4 d	xxiv. 16.	3
xx. 16.	4 d	1 Kings vi. 24, 24.	4 c	Jer. ix. 26. a	4 a
xxii. 36, 41.	4 d	2 Kings vii. 5, 8.	4 d	xxv. 23. a	4 a
xxiii. 13.	4 d	Neh. i. 9.	4 d	xlix. 32. a	4 a
xxxiv. 3.	4 d	Ps. ii. 8.	2	l. 26.	4 b
Deut. xi. 24.	1	lxv. 8.	4 e	Joel ii. 20.	1
xxx. 4.	1				

a *marg.* 'cut off into corners.'

UTTER, UTTERLY

1 אָסַף to gather, to take away. KAL *inf.*

2 חִיצוֹן *adj.* outer, exterior.

3 חֹרֶב *m.* drought, waste.

4 כָּלִיל *adj.* complete, finished, perfect ; the whole.

5 מְאֹד *m.* as *adv.* mightily, vehemently, exceedingly.

6 מַשְׁחִית *f.* destruction.

Ps. cxix. 8, 43.	5	Ezek. xxix. 10. a	3	Ezek. xliv. 19, 19.	2
Isa. ii. 18.	4	xl. 31, 37.	2	xlvi. 20, 21.	2
Ezek. ix. 6.	6	xlii. 1, 3, 7, 8, 9, 14.	2	Zeph. i. 2. β	1

a *marg.* 'wastes of waste.'   β *marg.* 'by taking away.' See *Consume.*

UTTER

1 אָלַף to teach. PIEL *fut.*

2 אָמַר to say. KAL *fut.*

3 מִבְטָא *m.* something rashly uttered.

4 דָּבַר to speak. KAL a *part.* Poel. PIEL b *pret.* c *inf.* d *imp.* e *fut.*

5 הָגָה to mutter ; to speak ; to meditate. KAL a *fut.* POAL b *inf.*

6 יָצָא to go forth ; to cause to go forth. HIPHIL a *inf.* b *imp.* c *fut.* d *part.*

7 מָלַל to speak, to talk, tell, relate. PIEL a *pret.* b *fut.*

8 מָשַׁל to use parables ; to utter (a parable). KAL *imp.*

9 נָבַע to flow, as a brook ; used of speech ; to utter, to publish, to declare. HIPHIL *fut.*

10 נָגַד to show, to tell, to declare, to announce. HIPHIL a *pret.* b *fut.*

11 נָתַן to give. KAL a *pret.* b *inf.* c *fut.* NIPHAL d *pret.*

12 עָנָה to answer. KAL *fut.*

13 פּוּחַ to blow, to breathe ; to utter. HIPHIL *fut.*

14 פָּצָה to open. KAL *pret.*

Lev. v. 1.	10 b	Ps. xlvi. 6.	11 a	Isa. xxxii. 6.	4 c
Num. xxx. 6, 8.	3	lxvi. 14.	14	xlviii. 20.	6 b
Josh. ii. 14, 20.	10 b	lxxviii. 2.	9	lix. 13.	5 b
Judg. v. 12.	4 d	xciv. 4.	2	Jer. i. 16.	4 b
xi. 11.	4 e	cvi. 2.	7 b	x. 13.	11 b
2 Sam. xxii. 14.	11 c	cxix. 171.	9	xxv. 30.	11 c
Neh. vi. 19. a	6 d	cxlv. 7.	9	xlviii. 34.	11 a
Job viii. 10.	6 o	Prov. i. 20.	11 c	li. 16.	11 b
xv. 2.	12	i. 21.	4	li. 55.	11 d
xv. 5.	1	x. 18.	6 d	Ezek. xxiv. 3.	8
xxvi. 4.	10 a	xiv. 5.	13	Joel ii. 11.	11 a
xxvii. 4.	5 a	xxiii. 33.	4 e	iii. 16.	11 c
xxxiii. 3.	7 a	xxix. 11.	4 c	Amos i. 2.	11 c
xlii. 3.	10 a	Eccles. i. 8.	4 c	Micah vii. 3.	4 a
Ps. xix. 2.	9	v. 2.	6 a	Hab. iii. 10.	11 a

a *lit.* had been uttering.

VAGABOND

נוּד to be driven about, to wander, to be a fugitive. KAL *part.* Poel, Gen. iv. 12, 14.

נוּעַ to wander about. KAL *inf.* and *fut.* Ps. cix. 10, *lit.* and wandering let his children wander.

VAIL, VEIL

מִטְפַּחַת *f.* a wide upper garment of a woman, mantle, cloak; rather similar to the Arab hyke or Roman toga, which covered the head and great part of the person; which would hold six measures of barley: Ps. iii. 15, *marg.* 'or, sheet or apron.'

מַסְוֶה *m.* a covering, vail for the face: Exod. xxxiv. 33, 34, 35.

מַסְכָה *f.* a covering: Isa. xxv. 7.

פָּרֹכֶת *f.* vail, curtain, *sc.* of separation, which separated the Holy of Holies from the outer sanctuary in the tabernacle: Exod. xxvi. 31, &c.

צָעִיף *m.* a vail; or a woman's garment in which she could cover and disguise herself: Gen. xxiv. 65; xxxviii. 14, 19.

רָדִיד *m. pr.* something expanded; hence of a wide and thin female garment, a veil; which is the same with ἐξουσία, 1 Cor. xi. 10, since רָדַד is nearly of the same meaning with רָדָה, to have dominion over. The vail is a sign of modesty, humility, and subjection. In Armenia the unmarried cover only the chin, the married half of their faces, and this, in their idea, as a token of subjection. Calmet supposes this to be the veil of married women, the especial token of submission and dependence. To lift up the vail of a virgin is reckoned a gross insult; but to take away the veil of a married woman, one of the greatest indignities she can receive. Cant. v. 7: Isa. iii. 23.

VAIN, VANITY

1 דַּי *m.* sufficiency.

2 אָוֶן *m.* nothingness, vanity, a vain and empty thing; it implies mostly a false good; specially of the nothingness of idols, and of everything pertaining to idolatry; hence iniquity, &c.

3 הֶבֶל used of that which soon vanishes away, like vapour, or a bubble; to breathe, to become vain, insignificant and worthless. KAL [a] *fut.* HIPHIL [b] *part.* הֶבֶל [c] *com.* a breath, breathing, *e.g.* of air, a gentle breeze, Isa. lvii. 13. Vulg. well, *aura*; Lxx. less well, καταιγίς; oftener breath of the mouth, Aqu. ἀτμίς, Symm. ἀτμός; so very often of anything evanescent, transient, frail. Hence the signification vanity, something vain, empty, fruitless; specially of idols: Deut. xxxii. 21, &c. הֶבֶל [d] *m.* vanity.

4 חִנָּם *adv.* to no purpose, in vain.

5 כָּזַב to lie; of what deceives and disappoints. NIPHAL *pret.*

6 נָבַב to be hollow, empty, foolish. KAL *part.* Paül.

7 רוּחַ *com.* breath, wind.

8 רִיק *adj.* empty; *adv.* in vain, to no purpose. [a] רֵיק and רַק *adj. id.* [b] רֵיקָם *adv.* emptily.

9 שָׁוְא *m.* evil; specially falsehood, a lie; emptiness, vanity, nothingness; ἄκαρπον, Eph. v. 11; of idols, Jonah ii. 8, &c.; taking (up) the name of God in vain includes false as well as light swearing.

10 שָׂפָה *f.* lip; "vain words," *lit.* word of the lips, a phrase to express inconsiderate speech; *comp.* Prov. xiv. 23.

11 שֶׁקֶר *m.* a lie, falsehood; deception, a vain thing, anything which deceives and disappoints the hope.

12 תֹּהוּ *m.* wasteness, desolateness; emptiness, vanity; a vain thing, worthless.

No. 3 c, *Vanity*, not included.

Exod. v. 9.	11	Ps. xii. 2.	9	Isa. xli. 29.		2
xx. 7, 7.	9	xxiv. 4.	9	xliv. 9.		12
Lev. xxvi. 16, 20.	8	xxvi. 4.	9	xlv. 18, 19.		12
Deut. v. 11, 11.	8	xxxiii. 17.	11	xlix. 4, 4.		8, 3 c
xxxii. 47.	8 a	xxxix. 6.	3 c	lviii. 9.		2
Judg. ix. 4.	8 a	xli. 10.	9	lix. 4.		12
xi. 3.	8 a	lx. 11.	9	lxv. 23.		8
1 Sam. xii. 21, 21.	12	lxii. 10.	3 a	Jer. ii. 5, 5.		3 c a
xxv. 21.	11	lxxiii. 13.	9	ii. 30.		9
2 Sam. vi. 20.	8	lxxxix. 47.	9	iii. 23.		11
2 Kings xvii. 15, 15.	3 c a	cviii. 12.	9	iv. 14.		2
xviii. 20.	10	cxix. 37.	9	iv. 30.		9
2 Chron. xiii. 7.	8 a	cxxvii. 1, 1, 2.	9	vi. 29.		9
Job vii. 3.	9	cxxxix. 20.	9	viii. 8, 8.		11
ix. 29.	3 c	cxliv. 8, 11.	9	x. 3.		3 c
xi. 11.	9	Prov. i. 17.	9	xviii. 15.		9
xi. 12.	6	xi. 11.	8 a	xxiii. 16.		3 b
xv. 2.	7	xxii. 8.	2	xlvi. 11.		9
xv. 31, 31.	9	xxviii. 19.	8 a	l. 9.		8 b
xv. 35.	2	xxx. 8.	9	li. 58. β		1, 8
xvi. 3.	7	xxxi. 30.	3 c	lii. 8.		9
xxi. 34.	3 a c	Eccles. i. 2, 2, 2.		Lam. ii. 14.		3 c
xxvii. 12. a	3 a c	2, 2.	3 e d c d c	iv. 17.		3 c
xxxi. 5.	9	vi. 12.	3 c	Ezek. vi. 10.		4
xxxv. 13.	9	xii. 8.	3 d	xiii. 6, 7, 8, 9, 23.		9
xxxv. 16.	8	Isa. i. 13.	9	xxi. 29.		9
xxxix. 16.	8	v. 18.	9	xxii. 28.		9
xli. 9.	5	xxx. 7.	3 c	Hos. xii. 11.		9
Ps. ii. 1.	8	xxx. 28.	9	Hab. ii. 13.		9
iv. 2.	8	xxxvi. 5.	10	Zech. x. 2, 2.		2, 3 c
x. 7.	2	xl. 17, 23.	12	Mal. iii. 14.		9

α *lit.* are ye vain in vanity? β *lit.* in the sufficiency of vanity.

VALE, VALLEY

1 בִּקְעָה *f.* a valley, a cleft of the mountain; *opp.* to mountains and hills; often also a plain.

2 גַּיְא *com.* a valley, so called as the place where waters flow together.

3 נַחַל *m.* a stream, brook, torrent; a valley watered by a brook or torrent, similar to the term wady.

4 עֵמֶק *m.* a valley; properly, a long, low plain, adapted to the culture of grain, and also convenient for battles: Gen. xiv. 3, &c.

5 שְׁפֵלָה *f.* low country, as *opp.* to mountains; with *art.* the low country or plain along the Mediterranean from Joppa to Gaza.

No. 4 not included.

Gen. xxvi. 17, 19.	3	Josh. xi. 2.	5	2 Kings iii. 16, 17.	3
Num. xxi. 12.	2	xi. 8.	5	xiv. 7.	2
xxi. 20.	2	xi. 16, 16.	5	xxiii. 10.	2
xxiv. 6.	3	xi. 17.	1	1 Chron. iv. 14, 39.	2
xxxii. 9.	3	xii. 7.	1	xviii. 12.	2
Deut. i. 7.	3	xii. 8.	5	2 Chron. i. 15.	5
i. 24.	3	xv. 8, 8, 8.	2, 2, 4	xiv. 10.	2
iii. 16.	3	xv. 33.	5	xxv. 11.	2
iii. 29.	2	xviii. 16, 16, 16.	2, 4, 2	xxvi. 9.	2
iv. 46.	2	xix. 14, 27.	2	xxvii. 3.	2
viii. 7.	1	Judg. i. 9.	2	xxxiii. 6.	2
xi. 11.	1	xvi. 4.	3	xxxiii. 14.	3
xxi. 4, 4, 6.	3	1 Sam. xiii. 18.	2	Neh. ii. 13, 15.	2
xxxiv. 3.	1	xv. 5.	3	iii. 13.	2
xxxiv. 6.	2	xvii. 3, 52.	2	xi. 30, 35.	2
Josh. viii. 11.	2	2 Sam. viii. 13.	2	Job xxi. 33.	2
ix. 1.	5	1 Kings x. 27.	5	xxx. 6.	3
x. 40.	5	2 Kings ii. 16. a	2		

Ps. xxiii. 4.	2	Isa. lvii. 5.	3	Ezek. xxxi. 12.	2
lx. title.	2	lxiii. 14.	1	xxxii. 5.	2
civ. 8.	1	Jer. ii. 23.	2	xxxv. 8.	2
civ. 10.	3	vii. 31, 32, 32.	2	xxxvi. 4, 6.	2
Prov. xxx. 17.	3	xix. 2, 6, 6.	3	xxxvii. 1, 2.	1
Cant. vi. 11.	3	xxxii. 35.	2	xxxix. 11, 11, 15.	3
Isa. vii. 19.	3	xxxii. 44.	5	Joel iii. 18.	3
xxii. 1, 5.	2	xxxiii. 13.	5	Micah i. 6.	2
xxviii. 1, 4.	2	Ezek. vi. 3.	3	Zech. xii. 11.	1
xl. 4.	2	vii. 16.	2	xiv. 4, 5, 5.	2
xli. 18.	1				

a lit. one of the valleys.

VALIANT, VALOUR

1   אַבִּיר   *adj.* strong, mighty.

2   אִישׁ   *m.* man ; it connotes valour and dignity ; "a valiant man."

3   אֲרְאֵל   *m. prob.* the same as אֲרִיאֵל lion of God, hero.

4   בֵּן   *m.* son.

5   גָּבַר   to be or become strong, mighty, to prevail. KAL *a pret.* גִּבּוֹר *b adj.* strong, mighty, valiant, impetuous.

6   חָזֵק   to be strong ; to behave oneself valiantly. HITHPAEL *fut.*

7   חַיִל   *m.* strength, might, valour ; "valiant," *lit.* son of valour.

8   כַּבִּיר   *adj.* great, vast, mighty.

Num. xxiv. 18.	7	2 Sam. xvii. 10.	4, 7	1 Chron. xviii. 1.	7
Josh. i. 14.	7	xvii. 10.	7	2 Chron. xiii. 3.	7
vi. 2.	7	xxiii. 20.	7	xiv. 8.	7
viii. 3.	7	xxiv. 9.	7	xvii. 13, 14, 16, 17.	7
x. 7.	7	1 Kings i. 42.	7	xxv. 6.	7
Judg. iii. 29.	7	xi. 28.	7	xxvi. 12, 17.	7
vi. 12.	7	2 Kings v. 1.	7	xxviii. 6.	4, 7
xi. 1.	7	xxiv. 14.	7	xxxii. 21.	7
xviii. 2.	7	1 Chron. v. 18.	4, 7	Neh. xi. 6, 14.	7
xx. 44, 46.	7	v. 24.	7	Ps. lx. 12.	7
xxi. 10. *a*	4, 7	vii. 2, 5.	5 b	cviii. 13.	7
1 Sam. xiv. 52.	7	vii. 7, 9, 11, 40.	7	cxviii. 15, 16.	7
xvi. 18.	7	viii. 40.	7	Cant. iii. 7, 7.	5 b
xviii. 17.*β*	4, 7	x. 12.	7	Isa. x. 13.	1, 8
xxvi. 15.	2	xi. 22.	7	xxxiii. 7.*γ*	8
xxxi. 12.	5 b	xi. 26.	5 b	Jer. ix. 3.	5 a
2 Sam. ii. 7.	4, 7	xii. 21, 25, 28, 30.	7	xlvi. 15.	1
xi. 16.	7	xix. 23.	7	Nah. ii. 3.	7
xiii. 28.	4, 7	xxvi. 6, 30, 31, 32.	7		

a lit. out of the sons of valour.   *β or,* be a son of valour.   *γ marg.* 'messengers, according to Rabbinical usage of the word.'

VALUE

אֱלִיל   *m.* nought, empty, vain, of no value : Job xiii. 4.

סָלָה   to suspend a balance, to weigh. PUAL *fut.* Job xxviii. 16, 19.

עָרַךְ   to set in order, to compare, to estimate. HIPHIL *pret.* Lev. xxvii. 8, 12. *fut.* Lev. xxvii. 8. עֵרֶךְ *m.* estimation : Lev. xxvii. 12.

VANISH

יָלַךְ   to go, depart. KAL *fut.* Job vii. 9.

מָלַח   in Niphal, to pass away, to vanish. *pret.* Isa. li. 6.

סָרַח   to pour forth ; to be poured out, *metaph.* spilled, lost. NIPHAL *pret.* Jer. xlix. 7.

צָמַת   to cut off. NIPHAL *pret.* Job vi. 17.

VAPOUR

אֵד   *m.* vapour (see *Mist*) : Job xxxvi. 27.

נָשִׂיא   *m.* rising ; vapour rising from the earth : Ps. cxxxv. 7 : Jer. x. 13 ; li. 16.

עָלָה   to ascend. KAL *part.* Poel, Job xxxvi. 33, *or,* the rising (tempest), *i.e.* as prognostics of rain. This seems to be

what our version indicates ; but Schultens enumerates no less than twenty-eight interpretations of vv. 32, 33.

קִיטוֹר   *m.* smoke : Ps. cxlviii. 8.

VAUNT

פָּאַר   to be beautiful ; to glorify ; to vaunt oneself, to glory. HITHPAEL *fut.* Judg. vii. 2.

VEHEMENT

חֲרִישִׁי   *adj.* silent, still, hence sultry : Jonah iv. 8, *marg.* ' or, silent.'

VEIN

מוֹצָא   *m.* place of going forth ; vein, or mine : Job xxviii. 1.

VENGEANCE

נָקַם   to take vengeance. KAL *part.* Poel, Ps. xcix. 8, Nah. i. 2. NIPHAL *imp.* Jer. l. 15. HOPHAL *fut.* Gen. iv. 15. נָקָם *m.* vengeance : Deut. xxxii. 35, 41, 43 : Ps. lviii. 10 : Prov. vi. 34 : Isa. xxxiv. 8 ; xxxv. 4 ; xlvii. 3 ; lix. 17 ; lxi. 2 ; lxiii. 4 : Ezek. xxiv. 8 ; xxv. 12, 15 : Micah v. 15. נְקָמָה *f. id.* Judg. xi. 36 : Ps. xciv. 1 (*marg.* ' God of revenges '), 1 ; cxlix. 7 : Jer. xi. 20 ; xx. 12 ; xlvi. 10 ; l. 15, 28, 28 ; li. 6, 11, 11, 36 : Lam. iii. 60 : Ezek. xxv. 14, 14, 17, 17.

VENISON

צַיִד   *m.* food taken in hunting : Gen. xxv. 28 ; xxvii. 3, 5, 7, 19, 25, 31, 33. צֵידָה *f. id.* Gen. xxvii. 3 (כתיב).

VENOM

רֹאשׁ   *m.* (see *Gall*), poison of serpents : Deut. xxxii. 33.

VENT

פָּתַח   to open. NIPHAL *fut.* Job xxxii. 19.

VENTURE

תֹּם   *m.* simplicity : 1 Kings xxii. 34, 2 Chron. xviii. 33 : see also *Full.*

VERILY, VERITY, VERIFY

אָמַן   to support, bear ; to be supported ; to be firm, faithful, sure. NIPHAL *fut.* Gen. xlii. 20 : 1 Kings viii. 26 : 2 Chron. vi. 17. אֱמוּנָה *f.* firmness, stability ; faithfulness, fidelity : Ps. xxxvii. 3. אֱמֶת *f.* truth : Ps. cxi. 7.

אָמַר   to say. KAL *inf.* Judg. xv. 2.

קָנָה   to buy. KAL *inf.* 1 Chron. xxi. 24.

VERMILION

שָׁשַׁר   *m.* red colour ; vermilion : Jer. xxii. 14 : Ezek. xxiii. 14.

VERY

גָּדוֹל   *adj.* great : Gen. xxvii. 33.

דַּי   *m.* sufficiency : Hab. ii. 13, 13.

מְאֹד   mightily, vehemently, exceedingly : Gen. i. 31, &c.

מְעַט   *m.* little : Isa. xvi. 14, *lit.* little, small ; xxix. 17.

עֶצֶם   *f.* bone (see *Selfsame*) : Josh. x. 27 : Ezek. ii. 3.

שַׂגִּיא   Ch. *adj.* great : Dan. ii. 12.

VESSEL

כְּלִי *m.* apparatus, implement, furniture, of general import: Gen. xliii. 11 : Exod. xxv. 39 ; xxvii. 3, 19 ; xxx. 27, 27, 28 ; xxxv. 13, 16 ; xxxvii. 16, 24 ; xxxviii. 3, 3, 30 ; xxxix. 36, 37, 39, 40 ; xl. 9, 10 : Lev. vi. 28 : viii. 11 ; xi. 32, &c.

מָאן Ch. *m.* vase, vessel, utensil : Ezra v. 14, 15 ; vi. 5 ; vii. 19 ; Dan. v. 2, 3, 23.

נֵבֶל *m.* bottle : Isa. xxx. 14, *marg.* 'bottle of potters.'

VESTMENT, VESTURE, VESTRY

בֶּגֶד *m.* a covering, cloth, garment : Gen. xli. 42.

כְּסוּת *f.* covering : Deut. xxii. 12.

לְבוּשׁ *m.* garment, vestment : 2 Kings x. 22 : Ps. xxii. 18 ; cii. 26. מַלְבּוּשׁ *m.* 2 Kings x. 22.

מֶלְתָּחָה *f.* wardrobe, vestry, *sc.* of the king : 2 Kings x. 22.

VEX

1 בָּהַל to be suddenly seized with fear ; to be troubled and amazed. NIPHAL [a] *pret.* [b] *fut.* PIEL [c] *fut.*

2 דָּחַק to thrust, to push, as is done in a great crowd ; to oppress. KAL *part.* Poel.

3 מְהוּמָה *f.* confusion, consternation, tumult.

4 הָמַם to put in commotion, consternation, to disturb. KAL *pret.*

5 זוּעַ to shake, to agitate ; to disquiet. PILPEL [a] *part.* [b] זְוָעָה *f.* agitation, commotion.

6 יָגָה to grieve, to afflict ; to vex. HIPHIL *fut.*

7 יָנָה to be violent, raging, cruel ; to treat with violence, to maltreat, oppress : see *Oppress.* HIPHIL [a] *pret.* [b] *fut.*

8 יָצַר to be straitened ; to be in distress. KAL *fut.*

9 כָּעַס to be indignant, vexed, to take ill ; to vex, to grieve, to trouble any one ; to provoke. HIPHIL *pret.*

10 מָרַר to be bitter ; to make bitter, irritate, to grieve. KAL [a] *pret.* HIPHIL [b] *pret.*

11 עָצַב to grieve. PIEL *pret.*

12 עָשָׂה to do. KAL *pret.*

13 מוּצָק *m.* something narrow, scanty ; straitness, distress.

14 צָרַר to bind up, to press upon, persecute, distress. KAL [a] *pret.* [b] *inf.* [c] *fut.* [d] *part.* Poel. HIPHIL [e] *fut.*

15 קוּץ to loathe, to be weary ; to harass or give great uneasiness. HIPHIL *fut.*

16 קָצַר to be shortened, straitened. KAL *fut.*

17 רָעַע to be evil ; to do evil. HIPHIL [a] *fut.* [b] רַע *adj.* evil.

18 רְעוּת *f.* vexation. [a] רַעְיוֹן *m. id.*

19 רָעַע to break or dash in pieces ; to harass, to oppress a people. KAL *fut.*

20 רָשַׁע to do wickedly. HIPHIL *fut.*

21 שֶׁבֶר *m.* breaking.

Exod. xxii. 21.		7 b	Num. xxiii. 55.	14 a	2 Sam. xii. 18.	12, 17 b
Lev. xviii. 18.		14 b	Deut. xxviii. 20.	3	xiii. 2.	8
xix. 33.		7 b	Judg. ii. 18.	2	2 Kings iv. 27.	1
Num. xx. 15.		17 a	x. 8.	19	2 Chron. xv. 5.	3
xxv. 17.		14 b	xvi. 16.	16	xv. 6.	4
xxv. 18.		14 d	1 Sam. xiv. 47.	20	Neh. ix. 27.	14 e

Job xix. 2.		6	Eccles. ii. 22.		18 a	Isa. xxviii. 19.		5 b
xxvii. 2.		10 b	ii. 26.		18	lxiii. 10.		11
Ps. ii. 5.		1 c	iv. 4, 6.		18	lxv. 14.		21
vi. 2, 3.		1 a	iv. 16.		18 a	Ezek. xxii. 5.		3
vi. 10.		1 b	vi. 9.		18	xxii. 7, 29.		7 a
Eccles. i. 14.		18	Isa. vii. 6.		15	xxxii. 9.		9
i. 17.		18	ix. 1.		13	Hab. ii. 7.		5 a
ii. 11, 17.		18	xi. 13.		14 c			

VIAL

פַּךְ *m.* a flask or vial, from which the oil comes out by drops : 1 Sam. x. 1.

VICTORY

יָשַׁע to save ; to get the victory. HIPHIL *pret.* Ps. xcviii. 1. תְּשׁוּעָה *f.* 2 Sam. xix. 2, deliverance ; xxiii. 10, 12.

נֵצַח *m.* strength, power, glory ; victory : 1 Chron. xxix. 11 : Isa. xxv. 8.

VICTUALS

1 אֹכֶל *m.* eating, *i. e.* the act of eating ; food. [a] מַאֲכָל *m.* food, victual.

2 אֲרֻחָה *f.* an appointed portion of food or provision, a ration, delivered out daily or at a certain fixed time.

3 מָזוֹן *m.* food.

4 מִחְיָה *f.* means of life, sustenance.

5 כּוּל to sustain ; to provide victuals. PILPEL *pret.*

6 לֶחֶם *m.* whatever is eaten, any kind of food ; bread.

7 צַיִד *m.* food got in hunting ; food of any kind, specially provision for a journey. [a] צֵידָה *f. id.*

8 שֶׁבֶר *m.* corn.

Gen. xiv. 11.		1	Judg. vii. 8.	7 a	2 Chron. xi. 11.		1 a
Exod. xii. 39.		7 a	xvii. 10.	4	xi. 23.		3
Lev. xxv. 37.		1	xx. 10.	7 a	Neh. x. 31.		8
Deut. xxiii. 19.		1	1 Sam. xxii. 10.	7 a	xiii. 15.		7
Josh. i. 11.		7 a	1 Kings iv. 7, 27.	5	Jer. xl. 5.		2
ix. 11.		7 a	xi. 18.	6	xliv. 17.		6
ix. 14.		7					

VIEW

בִּין to understand, consider. KAL and HIPHIL *fut.* Ezra viii. 15.

נֶגֶד before, against, over against. מִנֶּגֶד : 2 Kings ii. 7.

רָאָה to see, to look on. KAL *imp.* Josh. ii. 1.

רָגַל to spy out, to search a country. PIEL *imp.* Josh. vii. 2. *fut.* Josh. vii. 2.

שָׁבַר to look, *seq.* בְּ to look upon attentively, to inspect, to view. KAL *part.* Poel, Neh. ii. 13, *lit.* was viewing ; 15, *lit. id.*

VILE

1 בָּזָה to despise. NIPHAL [a] *part.* [b] נִמְבְּזָה *adj. f.* the vile, the bad, spoken of flocks.

2 זָלַל to shake, to shake out, to squander ; and as one shakes out and casts away only worthless things ; hence, to be abject, vile, despised. KAL [a] *part.* Poel. [b] זַלּוּת *f.* contempt, a despising, vileness. Gesenius would render this verse, The wicked walk on every side like the risings of a tempest on the sons of men ; from זָלַל to shake.

3 טָמֵה to be unclean, defiled; to be reputed vile. NIPHAL ᵃ*pret.* Job xviii. 3, *i.e.* impious, wicked, comp. xiv. 4.

4 כָּאָה to be cast down, dejected; to be desponding, humble; in Niph. the smitten, the abject; *comp.* abjects. NIPHAL *pret.*

5 מָאַם to despise. NIPHAL *part.*

6 נָבֵל to act foolishly, to be vile and despised. PIEL, to make vile; ᵃ*pret.* ᵇ נָבָל *adj.* foolish. ᶜ נְבָלָה *f.*

7 קָלָה to be light; to be made light of, to be contemned. NIPHAL *pret.*

8 קָלַל to be light, not heavy; to be lightly esteemed, insignificant, vile; sometimes, *intens.* to be despised, contemned. KAL ᵃ*pret.* NIPHAL ᵇ*pret.* PIEL ᶜ*part.*

9 שֹׁעָר *adj.* horrible, *i.e.* bad, foul, loathsome, of figs.

Deut. xxv. 3.		7	Job xxx. 8.	4	Jer. xxix. 17.		9
Judg. xix. 24.		6 c	xl. 4.	8 a	Lam. i. 11.		2 a
1 Sam. iii. 13.		8 c	Ps. lxi. 8.	2 b	Dan. xi. 21.		1 a
xv. 9.		1 b	xv. 4.	5	Nah. i. 14.		8 a
2 Sam. vi. 22.		8 b	Isa. xxxii. 5, 6.	6 b	iii. 6.		6 a
Job xviii. 3.		3	Jer. xv. 19.	2 a			

VILLAGE

1 בַּת *f.* daughter.

2 חָצֵר *m.* court; a village, hamlet, Lat. *villa, pagus, i.e.* farm-buildings, farm-hamlet, usually erected round an open space or court, *e.g.* in the neighbourhood of cities. Spoken also of the moveable villages or encampments of nomadic tribes, who usually pitch their tents in a circle, or so as to form an enclosure. Exod. viii. 13, &c.

3 כְּפָר *m.* village. ᵃ כֹּפֶר *m. id.* ᵇ כְּפִיר *id.*

4 פְּרָז *m.* country regions, open country. ᵃ פְּרָזוֹן *m. id.* פְּרָזוֹת *f.* "unwalled villages." ᶜ פְּרָזִי *m.* one living in a village. פְּרוֹזִים (כתיב) *id.*

No. 2 not included.

Num. xxi. 25, 32.		1	2 Chron. xxviii. 18,		Neh. xi. 30, 30.	2, 1
xxxii. 42.		1	18, 18.	1	Esth. ix. 19.	4 c
Judg. v. 7, 11.		4 a	Neh. xi. 2.	3 b	Cant. vii. 11.	3
1 Sam. vi. 18.		3 a	xi. 25, 25, 25, 25.	1, 2, 2, 1	Ezek. xxxviii. 11.	4 b
1 Chron. xxvii. 25.		3	xi. 27, 28, 31.	2	Hab. iii. 14.	4

VILLANY

נְבָלָה *f.* folly, with the notion of wickedness; hence, shameful deed: Isa. xxxii. 6: Jer. xxix. 23.

VINE

גֶּפֶן *m.* a plant having young and pendulous shoots; especially a vine, a grape-vine, more fully vine of wine, Num. vi. 4. Rarely spoken of other similar plants, as the wild vine, or vine of the field, bearing wild cucumbers. A noble vine is put as an emblem of men of noble and generous disposition, Jer ii. 21, *comp.* Isa. v. 2; and, *vice versa*, a strange vine, vine of Sodom, stands for men of ignoble and degenerate character, Jer. ii. 21, Deut. xxxii. 32.—Gen. xl. 9, 10, &c.: 2 Kings xviii. 31, put for the fruit of the vine.

כֶּרֶם *com.* (see *Vineyard*): Cant. ii. 15, 15: Jer. xxxi. 5.

יַיִן *m.* wine: Num. vi. 4: Judg. xiii. 14, *lit.* vine of the wine.

שֹׂרֵק *m.* a vine of a fine and nobler kind, distinguished no less

by the luxuriance of its growth than by the richness and delicacy of its fruit, at this day called *serki* in Morocco; *metaph.* Israel, in their origin.—*Gesenius.* Probably so called from its blue or purple grapes: Isa. v. 2: Jer. ii. 21. שֹׂרֵקָה *f. id.* choice vine: Gen. xlix. 11.

VINEYARD, VINEDRESSERS

כַּנָּה *f.* a stock, root, or plant: Ps. lxxx. 15.

כֶּרֶם *m.* a field or park of the nobler plants or trees, cultivated in the manner of a garden or orchard; so כֶּרֶם זַיִת olive-yard: Judg. xv. 5. דֶּרֶךְ כְּרָמִים the way leading to gardens and orchards, *i.e.* to a cultivated and inhabited land, *opp.* to the desert, Job xxiv. 18; specially a vineyard, Exod. xxii. 5, Deut. xx. 6, xxviii. 30, &c.; fully כֶּרֶם חֶמֶר wine-garden, Isa. xxvii. 2. In the prophets a vineyard is a frequent emblem of the people of Israel, Isa. iii. 14, v. 1, &c., xxvii. 2, *sq.*, *comp.* Matt. xx. 1, *sq.*, xxi. 28, Luke xx. 9; figuratively the Church of God, Jer. xii. 10.—Gen. ix. 20, &c. כֹּרְמִים *m. pl.* vine-dressers: 2 Kings xxv. 12: 2 Chron. xxvi. 10: Isa. lxi. 5: Jer. lii. 16: Joel i. 11.

VINEGAR

חֹמֶץ *m.* vinegar; Syr. and Lxx. sour grapes: Num. vi. 3, 3: Ruth ii. 14: Ps. lxix. 21: Prov. x. 26; xxv. 20.

VINTAGE

בָּצַר to cut off; to gather grapes; to fence. KAL *part.* Paül, Zech. xi. 2 (כתיב). בָּצִיר *m.* a cutting off, vintage: Lev. xxvi. 5, 5: Judg. viii. 2: Isa. xxiv. 13; xxxii. 10: Jer. xlviii. 32: Micah vii. 1: Zech. xi. 2 (קרי).

כֶּרֶם *m.* (see *Vineyard*): Job xxiv. 6.

VIOL

נֵבֶל *m.* (see *Psaltery*): Isa. v. 12; xiv. 11: Amos v. 23; vi. 5.

VIOLATE, VIOLENCE, VIOLENT

1 גָּזַל to pluck off or away, to tear away, to take by force, by open violence, oftener by fraud or injustice of any kind, *e.g.* the property or possessions of others, to seize upon, to take by force, to claim as one's own; especially of the rich and powerful, who seize upon the possessions of the poor by fraud and violence. KAL ᵃ*pret.* ᵇ*part.* Paül. ᶜ גָּזֵל *m.* rapine. ᵈ גָּזֵל *m.* violence, violent perverting. ᵉ גְּזֵלָה *f. id.*

2 חָמַס to do violence to any one, to oppress, to wrong; properly, to be sharp, eager, vehement; to act violently, either in thought, word, or deed, in any respect against truth, right, justice, and goodness; whether it be in the case of other men or our own. KAL ᵃ*pret.* ᵇ*fut.* חָמָס *m.* violence, oppression, wrong; a genitive or suffix after this word may refer either to him who does the wrong or to him who suffers it.

3 עָרִיץ *adj.* terrible; powerful; violent, fierce, lawless, a tyrant.

4 עָשַׁק to oppress, to treat with violence and injustice. KAL *part.* Paül.

מְרוּצָה 5 *f.* running, oppression ; or for מְרֻצָה crushing.

Gen. vi. 11, 13.	2 c	Prov. x. 6, 11.	2 c	Ezek. xviii. 7, 12, 16.	1 e	
xxi. 25.	1 a	xiii. 2.	2 c	xviii. 18.	1 d	
Lev. vi. 2.	1 c	xvi. 29.	2 c	xxii. 26.	2 a	
vi. 4. α	1 e a	xxviii. 17.	4	xxviii. 16.	2 c	
Deut. xxviii. 31.	1 b	Eccles. v. 8.	1 d	xlv. 9.	2 c	
2 Sam. xxii. 3, 49. β	2 c	Isa. liii. 9.	2 c	Joel iii. 19.	2 c	
Job xx. 19.	1 a	lix. 6.	2 c	Amos iii. 10.	2 c	
xxiv. 2.	1 a	lx. 18.	2 c	vi. 3.	2 c	
Ps. vii. 16.	2 c	Jer. vi. 7.	2 c	Obad. 10.	2 c	
xi. 5.	2 c	xx. 8.	2 c	Jonah iii. 8.	2 c	
xviii. 48.	2 c	xxii. 3.	2 b	Micah ii. 2.	1 a	
lv. 9.	2 c	xxii. 17.	5	vi. 12.	2 c	
lviii. 2.	2 c	li. 35, 46.	2 c	Hab. i. 2, 3, 9.	2 c	
lxxii. 14.	2 c	Lam. iii. 6.	2 b	ii. 8, 17, 17.	2 c	
lxxiii. 6.	2 c	Ezek. vii. 11, 23.	2 c	Zeph. i. 9.	2 c	
lxxxvi. 14.	3	viii. 17.	2 c	iii. 4.	2 a	
cxl. 1, γ 4, 11.	2 c	xii. 19.	2 c	Mal. ii. 16.	2 c	
Prov. iv. 17.	2 c					

a lit. the spoil which he took violently away. *β lit.* the man of violences.
γ lit. man of violences.

VIPER

אֶפְעֶה *m.* viper, adder, any poisonous serpent : Job xx. 16 : Isa.
xxx. 6 ; lix. 5.

VIRGIN

בְּתוּלָה *f.* a virgin, pure and unspotted ; a virgin just married, a
young spouse ; cities or countries which have never
been conquered or brought into subjection are called
virgins : Gen. xxiv. 16, &c. בְּתוּלִים *m. pl.* virginity ;
signs, tokens of virginity : Lev. xxi. 13 : Deut. xxii. 15,
17, 20 : Judg. xi. 37, 38 : Ezek. xxiii. 3, 8.

עַלְמָה *f.* a young woman of marriageable age, yet under the care
of her parents ; as it were, hidden from the public :
Gen. xxiv. 43 : Cant. i. 3 ; vi. 8 : Isa. vii. 14 : with the
definite article הָ.

VIRTUOUS

חַיִל *m.* strength ; *trop.* moral strength, good quality, integrity,
virtue : Ruth iii. 11 : Prov. xii. 4 ; xxxi. 10, 29, *marg.*
' or, gotten riches.'

VISAGE, VISION

אַנְפִּין 1 Ch. face.

חִזָּיוֹן 2 *m.* vision, night-vision, or dream ; prophetic vision ; oracle
or prophecy. [a] חָזוּת *f.* [b] חֶזְיוֹן *f.* [c] חִזָּיוֹן *m.* a vision,
revelation. [d] חֵזוּ Ch. *m.* [e] מַחֲזֶה *m.*

רָאָה 3 to see, to see in vision, *i.e.* to be taught of God in vision
as the prophets. KAL [a] *inf.* [b] רֹאֶה *m.* vision. [c] מַרְאָה
f. id. [d] מַרְאֶה *m. id.*

תֹּאַר 4 *m.* appearance, form, visage.

Gen. xv. 1.	2 e	Isa. xxviii. 7.	3 b	Dan. iii. 19.	1
xlvi. 2.	3 c	xxix. 7.	2	iv. 5, 9, 10, 13.	2 d
Num. xii. 6.	3 c	xxix. 11.	2 b	vii. 1, 2, 7, 13, 15.	2 d
xxiv. 4.	2 e	lii. 14.	3 d	viii. 1, 2, 2, 13, 15,	
1 Sam. iii. 1.	2	Jer. xiv. 14.	2	17.	2
iii. 15.	3 c	xxiii. 16.	2	viii. 16, 27.	3 d
2 Sam. vii. 17.	2 c	Lam. ii. 9.	2	viii. 26, 26.	3 d, 2
1 Chron. xvii. 15.	2	iv. 8.	4	ix. 21, 24.	2
2 Chron. ix. 29.	2 a	Ezek. i. 1.	3 c	ix. 23.	3 d
xxvi. 5.	3 a	vii. 13, 26.	2	x. 1.	3 d
xxxii. 32.	2	viii. 3.	3 c	x. 7, 7, 8, 16.	3 c
Job iv. 18.	2 c	viii. 4.	3 d	x. 14.	2
vii. 14.	2 c	xi. 24, 24.	3 d	Hos. xii. 10.	2
ix. 8.	2 c	xii. 22, 23, 24, 27.	2	Joel ii. 28.	2 c
xxxiii. 15.	2 c	xiii. 7.	2 e	Obad. 1.	2
Ps. lxxxix. 19.	2	xiii. 16.	2	Micah iii. 6.	2
Prov. xxii. 18.	2	xl. 2.	3 c	Nah. i. 1.	2
Isa. i. 1.	2	xliii. 3, α 3, 3.	3 d d c d	Hab. ii. 2, 3.	2
xxi. 2.	2 b	Dan. i. 17.	2	Zech. xiii. 4.	2 c
xxii. 1, 5.	2 c	ii. 19, 28.	2 d		

a "appearance of the vision."

VISIT

פָּקַד to visit ; in a kind sense, to go to see, to visit for various
purposes ; in a hostile sense, to go to any, *i.e.* to come
or fall upon, to attack ; *seq.* עַל of person, to punish, to
visit with punishment ; also *seq.* אֶל and *acc.* The sin
to be punished is put in the accusative, and often with
עַל of person. This word includes both a judicial and a
merciful visitation, Exod. iii. 16, where the word 'seen'
may be left out in the second clause as unnecessary.
KAL [a] *pret.* [b] *inf.* [c] *imp.* [d] *fut.* [e] *part.* Poel. NIPHAL
[f] *fut.* HOPHAL [g] *pret.* [h] פְּקֻדָּה *f.* visitation, punishment ;
care, vigilance, providence, custody, watch.

Gen. xxi. 1.	a	Ps. xvii. 3.	a	Jer. xxiii. 2, 2.	a e	
l. 24.	b d	lix. 5.	b	xxiii. 12.	h	
l. 25.	b d	lxv. 9.	a	xxvii. 22.	h	
Exod. iii. 16.	b a	lxxx. 14.	c	xxix. 10.	h	
iv. 31.	a	lxxxix. 32.	c	xxxii. 5.	h	
xiii. 19.	b d	cvi. 4.	a	xlvi. 21.	a	
xx. 5.	a	Prov. xix. 23.	f	xlviii. 44.	h	
xxxii. 34.	a	Isa. x. 3.	h	xlix. 8.	a	
xxxiv. 7.	a	xxiii. 17.	a	l. 27.	h	
Lev. xviii. 25.	a	xxiv. 22.	f	l. 31.	h	
Num. xiv. 18.	a	xxvi. 14, 16.	a	li. 18.	h	
xvi. 29, 29.	f h	xxix. 6.	f	Lam. iv. 22.	h	
Deut. v. 9.	a	Jer. iii. 16.	b	Ezek. xxxviii. 8.	h	
Judg. xv. 1.	d	v. 9, 29.	g	Hos. ii. 13.	h	
Ruth i. 6.	a	vi. 6.	g	viii. 13.	h	
1 Sam. ii. 21.	a	vi. 15.	h	ix. 7.	h	
Job v. 24.	a	viii. 12.	h	ix. 9.	h	
vii. 18.	d	ix. 9.	d	Amos iii. 14, 14.	b a	
x. 12.	d	ix. 15.	d	Micah vii. 4.	h	
xxxi. 14.	d	xi. 23.	h	Zeph. ii. 7.	h	
xxxv. 15.	d	xiv. 10.	d	Zech. x. 3.	a	
Ps. viii. 4.	d	xv. 15.	c	xi. 16.	d	

VOICE

קוֹל *m.* any sound, noise, or voice, in a very extensive sense :
Gen. iii. 8, &c., sometimes equivalent to meaning, scope,
or purport : Exod. iv. 8 : Ps. xix. 3. קָל Ch. *m.* Dan.
iv. 31 ; vi. 20 ; vii. 11 : with the definite article הָ.

רְנָנָה *f.* singing aloud ; joyful voice : Job iii. 7.

VOID

אָבַד 1 to perish. KAL *part.* Poel.

בֹּהוּ 2 *m.* emptiness, voidness, *conc.* empty, void.

בָּקַק 3 to pour out, to empty, to make void. KAL *pret.*

מְבוּקָה 4 *f.* emptiness.

גֹּרֶן 5 *m.* a place made level, an area.

חָסֵר 6 *adj.* wanting, lacking.

נָאַר 7 to abhor, to reject. PIEL *pret.*

פָּרַר 8 to break, to break in pieces ; to break a covenant ; to
make vain, to bring to nought, to frustrate ; to annul,
to abolish. HIPHIL [a] *pret.* [b] *inf.* [c] *fut.*

רֵיקָם 9 *adv.* emptily ; vainly, void, to no purpose, without effect.

Gen. i. 2.	2	2 Chron. xviii. 9.	5	Prov. xvii. 18.	6
Num. xxx. 12.	8 b c	Ps. lxxxix. 39.	7	xxiv. 30.	6
xxx. 12.	8 a	cxix. 126.	8 a	Isa. lv. 11.	9
xxx. 15.	8 b c	Prov. vii. 7.	6	Jer. iv. 23.	2
Deut. xxxii. 28.	1	x. 13.	6	xix. 7.	3
1 Kings xxii. 10.	5	xii. 12.	6	Nah. ii. 10.	4
		xii. 11.	6		

VOLUME

מְגִלָּה *f.* roll : Ps. xl. 7.

VOLUNTARY

נְדָבָה *f.* willingness, voluntary gift, offering: Lev. vii. 16: Ezek. xlvi. 12, 12.

רָצוֹן *m.* good-will, voluntary will: Lev. i. 3.

VOMIT

קוֹא to spue out, to vomit forth. HIPHIL *pret.* Prov. xxv. 16. *fut.* Lev. xviii. 25: Job xx. 15: Prov. xxiii. 8: Jonah ii. 10. קִיא *m.* vomit: Isa. xix. 14; xxviii. 8: Jer. xlviii. 26. קָא *m. id.* Prov. xxvi. 11.

VOW

נָדַר to vow, *i.e.* to promise voluntarily to give or do something; the primary idea is that of setting apart, consecrating. KAL ᵃ*pret.* ᵇ*inf.* ᶜ*imp.* ᵈ*fut.* ᵉ*part.* Poel. ᶠ נֵדֶר and נֶדֶר *m.* a vow: Gen. xxviii. 20, &c.

f not included.

Gen. xxviii. 20, 20.	f d	Deut. xii. 17, 17.	f d	Ps. lxxvi. 11.		c
xxxi. 13, 13.	a f	xxiii. 21, 21.	d f	cxxxii. 2.		a
Lev. xxvii. 8.	e	xxiii. 22.	b	Eccles. v. 4, 4, 4.		d f d
Num. vi. 2, 2.	b f	xxiii. 23.	a	v. 5, 5.		d
xxi. 21, 21.	d f d	Judg. xi. 30, 30.	d f	Isa. xix. 21, 21.		a f
xxii. 2, 2.	d f	xi. 39, 39.	f a	Jer. xliv. 25, 25,		
xxx. 2, 2.	d f	1 Sam. i. 11, 11.	d f	25, 25.	}	f a f f
xxx. 3, 3.	d f	2 Sam. xv. 7, 7.	f a	Jonah ii. 9.		a
xxx. 10.	a	xv. 8, 8.	a f	Mal. i. 14.		e
Deut. xii. 11, 11.	f d					

VULTURE

אַיָּה *f.* the name of a clamorous bird of prey, unclean, and keen-sighted. Lxx. and Vulg. sometimes vulture, sometimes kite. The opinion of Bochart is not improbable, that it is a species of falcon, Eng. merlin. Job xxviii. 7.

דָּאָה *f.* a species of ravenous bird, having a rapid flight. Lxx. γύψ; Vulg. *milvus.* Lev. xi. 14.

דַּיָּה *f.* a bird of prey inhabiting ruins. Bochart understands the black vulture; better the kite or falcon, so called from its swift flight: Deut. xiv. 13: Isa. xxxiv. 15.

WAFER

צָפִיחִת *f.* a flat cake, so called from its spreading out: Exod. xvi. 31.

רָקִיק *m.* a thin cake, supposed to have been baked on the outside of a heated pitcher, as used by the Arabs at this day: Exod. xxix. 2, 23: Lev. ii. 4; vii. 12; viii. 26: Num. vi. 15, 19.

WAG

נוּד to shake, *e.g.* the head in pity, or as expressive of contempt, scorn, and insult. HIPHIL *fut.* Jer. xviii. 16.

נוֹעַ to nod, to move to and fro, to shake, *e.g.* the head, in scorn and insult. HIPHIL *fut.* Lam. ii. 15: Zeph. ii. 15.

WAGES

חִנָּם *adv.* freely, without wages: Jer. xxii. 13.

פְּעֻלָּה *f.* labour, wages of labour: Lev. xix. 13.

שָׂכַר to hire, to earn wages. HITHPAEL *part.* Hag. i. 6, 6.

שָׂכָר *m.* hire, wages, reward: Gen. xxx. 28; xxxi. 8: Exod. ii. 9: Ezek. xxix. 18, 19: Mal. iii. 5. מַשְׂכֹּרֶת *f. id.*: Gen. xxix. 15; xxxi. 7, 41.

WAGON

עֲגָלָה *f.* a wain, car, any wheel-carriage: Gen. xlv. 19, 21, 27; xlvi. 5: Num. vii. 3, 3, 6, 7, 8.

רֶכֶב *m.* chariot: Ezek. xxiii. 24.

WAIL

נָהָה to wail, lament; to wail for the dead in loud lamentations. KAL *imp.* Ezek. xxxii. 18. נְהִי *m.* Jer. ix. 10, 18, 19, 20. נֶהִ *m.* Ezek. vii. 11. נִי *m.* Ezek. xxvii. 32; but eleven MSS. and several printed editions, Lxx. and Arab., Theod. and Syr., exhibit the reading בְּנֵיהֶם their sons, which is perhaps better; *comp.* xxxii. 16, 2 Sam. i. 18.—*Gesenius.*

סָפַד to smite the breast, to mourn, to wail for the dead as hired mourners do. KAL *fut.* Micah i. 8. מִסְפֵּד *m.* lamentation: Esth. iv. 3: Ezek. xxvii. 31: Amos v. 16, 16, 17: Micah i. 8.

WAIT

1 אָרַב to lie in wait, in ambush, in order to make a sudden attack. KAL ᵃ*pret.* ᵇ*inf.* ᶜ*imp.* ᵈ*fut.* ᵉ*part.* Poel. PIEL ᶠ*part.* HIPHIL ᵍ*fut.* ʰ אֹרֶב *m.* a lying in wait. ⁱ אֹרֶב *m. id.* ᵏ מַאֲרָב *m.* lying in wait.

2 דּוּמִיָּה *f.* silence. ᵃ דּוּמָם *adv.* "quietly wait."

3 דָּמַם to be dumb, silent, still; to wait in silent expectation. KAL *imp.*

4 חוּל (see *Pain, Grieve, Abide, Rest*), the same with יָחַל. KAL ᵃ*pret.* HITHPOLEL ᵇ*imp.*

5 חָכָה to look, *seq.* לְ to look for, to wait, to desire. KAL ᵃ*part.* Poel. PIEL ᵇ*pret.* ᶜ*inf.* ᵈ*imp.* ᵉ*fut.* ᶠ*part.*

6 יָד *com.* hand.

7 יָחַל to wait, to hope; importing properly a long and patient waiting, a lingering hope, still expecting and earnestly desiring, though hitherto with delay and disappointment; mostly *seq.* לְ. NIPHAL ᵃ*pret.* PIEL ᵇ*pret.* ᶜ*fut.* ᵈ*part.* HIPHIL ᵉ*pret.* ᶠ*fut.*

8 עָמַד to stand, to stand still, to wait. KAL ᵃ*fut.* ᵇ*part.* Poel.

9 עָקֵב *m.* heel; lying in wait.

10 פָּנִים *m. pl.* face. לִפְנֵי before, used of waiters.

11 צָבָא to go forth to war, *trop.* of the temple service. KAL ᵃ*inf.* ᵇ צָבָא *m.* service.

12 צָדָה to fix the eyes upon; to lie in wait, to hunt after. KAL ᵃ*pret.* ᵇ צְדִיָּה *f.* lying in wait.

13 צָפָה to look about, to view from a distance, to watch; *seq.* אֶל to look out for, *i.e.* to select. KAL *part.* Paül.

14 קָוָה to hope strongly, to trust, implying firmness and constancy of mind, to hope for, to wait for, to expect anything; to hope that a thing will be effected, and to wait steadily and patiently till it is effected; *seq.* אֵת, אֶל, and

ל, also *acc.* and *dat.* KAL ᵃ *part.* Poel. PIEL ᵇ *pret.* ᶜ *inf.* ᵈ *imp.* ᵉ *fut.*

15 רִיב to strive. KAL *fut.*

16 שָׂבַר to look; to expect; to hope; *seq.* אֶל. PIEL *fut.*

17 שׁוּר to look around or about; to lay wait. KAL *fut.*

18 שָׁמַר to keep, to watch, to guard; to watch or wait for an advantage; to wait, to attend upon. KAL ᵃ *pret.* ᵇ *inf.* ᶜ *fut.* ᵈ *part.* Poel.

19 שָׁרַת to wait upon, to serve, to minister unto. PIEL *part.*

Gen. xlix. 18.	14 b	Job xxix. 21, 23.	7 b	Prov. xx. 22.	14 d	
Exod. xxi. 13.	12 a	xxx. 26.	7 c	xxiii. 28.	1 d	
Num. iii. 10.	18 a	xxxi. 9.	1 a	xxiv. 15.	1 d	
viii. 24.	11 a	xxxii. 4.	5 b	xxvii. 18.	18 d	
viii. 25.	11 b	xxxii. 11, 16.	7 e	Isa. viii. 17.	5 b	
xxxv. 20, 22.	12 b	xxxviii. 40.	1 h	xxv. 9, 9.	14 b	
Deut. xix. 11.	1 a	Ps. x. 9, 9.	1 d	xxvi. 8.	14 b	
Josh. viii. 4.	1 e	xxv. 3.	14 a	xxx. 18, 18.	5 e a	
viii. 13.	9	xxv. 5, 21.	14 b	xxxiii. 2.	14 b	
Judg. ix. 25.	1 f	xxvii. 14, 14.	14 d	xl. 31.	14 a	
ix. 32.	1 c	xxxiii. 20.	5 b	lii. 4.	7 c	
ix. 34, 43.	1 d	xxxvii. 7.	4 b	xlix. 23.	14 a	
ix. 35.	1 k	xxxvii. 14.	14 d	li. 5.	14 e	
xvi. 2.	1 d	xxxvii. 34.	14 a	lix. 9.	14 e	
xvi. 9, 12.	1 e	xxxix. 7.	14 b	lx. 9.	14 e	
xx. 29, 33, 36, 37,		xl. 1.	14 b c	lxiv. 4.	5 f	
-37, 38.	1 e	lii. 9.	14 e	Jer. v. 26.	17	
xxi. 20.	1 a	lvi. 6.	14 b	ix. 8.	1 i	
1 Sam. xv. 5.	1 g, or 15	lix. 3.	1 a	xiv. 22.	14 e	
xxii. 8, 13.	1 e	lix. 9.	18 c	Lam. iii. 10.	1 e	
1 Kings xx. 38.	8 a	lxii. 1.	2	iii. 25.	14 a	
2 Kings v. 2.	10	lxii. 5.	3	iii. 26.	2 a	
vi. 33.	7 f	lxv. 1.	2	iv. 19.	1 a	
1 Chron. vi. 32.	8 a	lxix. 3.	7 d	Ezek. xix. 5.	7 a	
vi. 33.	8 b	lxix. 6.	14 a	Dan. xii. 12.	5 f	
xxiii. 20.	8	lxxi. 10.	18 d	Hos. vi. 9.	5 c	
2 Chron. v. 11.	18 b	civ. 27.	16	vii. 6.	1 b	
vii. 6.	8 b	cvi. 13.	5 b	xii. 6.	14 d	
xvii. 19.	19	cxix. 95.	14 b	Micah i. 12.	4 a	
Ezra viii. 31.	1 e	cxxx. 5, 5.	14 b	v. 7.	7 c	
Neh. xii. 44.	8 b	cxlv. 15.	16	vii. 2.	1 d	
Job vi. 19.	14 b	Prov. i. 11, 18.	1 d	vii. 7.	7 f	
xiv. 14.	7 c	vii. 12.	1 d	Hab. ii. 3.	5 d	
xv. 22.	13	viii. 34.	18 b	Zeph. iii. 8.	5 d	
xvii. 13.	14 e	xii. 6.	1 b	Zech. xi. 11.	18 d	
xxiv. 15.	18 a					

WAKE, WAKEN

1 עוּר to wake, to be awake. KAL ᵃ *part.* Poel. NIPHAL ᵇ *fut.* HIPHIL ᶜ *imp.* ᵈ *fut.*

2 קוּץ to awake from sleep. HIPHIL *fut.*

3 שְׁמֻרוֹת *f. pl.* watchings.

4 שָׁקַד to wake, to be sleepless; to watch. KAL *pret.*

Ps. lxxvii. 4.ᵃ	3	Isa. l. 4, 4.	1 d	Joel iii. 12.	1 b
cxxvii. 1.	4	Jer. li. 39, 57.	2	Zech. iv. 1, 1.	1 d b
Cant. v. 2.	1 a	Joel iii. 9.	1 c		

ᵃ *lit.* the watches of mine eyes.

WALK

1 דָּרַךְ to tread, to go, to walk. KAL ᵃ *pret.* HIPHIL ᵇ *fut.*

2 הָלַךְ to go, to walk, to go forth. Piel, to walk assiduously, carefully, perseveringly. KAL ᵃ *pret.* ᵇ *inf.* ᶜ *fut.* ᵈ *part.* Poel. PIEL ᵉ *pret.* ᶠ *imp.* ᵍ *fut.* ʰ *part.* HIPHIL ⁱ *part.* HITHPAEL ᵏ *pret.* ˡ *inf.* ᵐ *imp.* ⁿ *fut.* ᵒ *part.* הֲלַךְ Ch. Pʼal ᵖ *part.* APHEL ᵠ *part.* ʳ מַהֲלַךְ *m.* journey. הֲלִיכָה *f.* goings, progress.

3 יָלַךְ of the same signification with הָלַךְ. KAL ᵃ *inf.* ᵇ *imp.* ᶜ *fut.* HIPHIL ᵈ *pret.* ᵉ *fut.*

4 סָבַב to go about, walk about. KAL *imp.*

Gen. iii. 8.	2 o	2 Chron. vi. 16,		
v. 22, 24.	2 n	16.	3 a, 2 a	
vi. 9.	2 k	vi. 27.	3 c	
xiii. 17.	2 m	vi. 31.	3 c	
xvii. 1.	2 m	vii. 17, 17.	3 c, 2 a	
xxiv. 40.	2 k	xi. 17.	2 a	
xxiv. 65.	2 d	xvii. 3, 4.	2 a	
xlviii. 15.	2 d	xx. 32.	3 c	
Exod. ii. 5.	2 d	xxi. 6, 13.	3 c	
xiv. 29.	2 a	xxi. 12.	2 a	
xvi. 4.	3 c	xxii. 3, 5.	2 a	
xviii. 20.	2 d	xxviii. 2.	3 c	
xxi. 19.	2 k	xxxiv. 2.	3 c	
Lev. xviii. 3.	3 c	xxxiv. 31.	3 c	
xviii. 4.	3 a	Neh. v. 9.	3 c	
xx. 23.	3 a	x. 29.	3 c	
xxvi. 3, 21.	3 c	Esth. ii. 11.	2 o	
xxvi. 12.	2 k	Job i. 7.	2 l	
xxvi. 23, 24, 27, 28,		ii. 2.	2 l	
40.	2 a	xviii. 8.	2 n	
xxvi. 41.	3 c	xxii. 14.	2 n	
Deut. iii. 7.	3 c	xxix. 3.	3 c	
v. 33.	3 c	xxxi. 5, 7.	2 a	
vi. 7.	2 n	xxxi. 26.	2 d	
viii. 6.	3 a	xxxiv. 8.	3 c	
viii. 19.	2 a	xxxviii. 16.	2 k	
x. 12.	3 a	Ps. i. 1.	2 a	
xi. 19, 22.	3 a	xii. 8.	2 n	
xiii. 4.	3 c	xv. 2.	2 d	
xiii. 5.	3 a	xxiii. 4.	2 d	
xix. 9.	3 c	xxvi. 1.	2 a	
xxiii. 14.	3 a	xxvi. 3.	2 k	
xxvi. 17.	3 a	xxvi. 11.	2 a	
xxviii. 9.	3 c	xxxix. 6.	2 n	
xxix. 19.	3 c	xlviii. 12.	4	
xxx. 16.	3 a	lv. 14.	2 g	
Josh. v. 6.	2 a	lvi. 13.	2 l	
xviii. 8.	2 m	lxxiii. 9.	2 n	
xxii. 5.	3 a	lxxviii. 10.	3 a	
Judg. ii. 17.	3 c	lxxxi. 12.	3 c	
ii. 22.	3 a	lxxxi. 13.	2 g	
v. 6.	3 c	lxxxii. 5.	2 n	
v. 10.	2 d	lxxxiv. 11.	2 g	
xi. 16.	3 c	lxxxvi. 11.	3 a	
1 Sam. ii. 30.	3 c	lxxxix. 15.	2 g	
ii. 35.	2 k	lxxxix. 30.	3 a	
viii. 3, 5.	2 a	xci. 6.	2 n	
xii. 2, 2.	2 o k	ci. 2.	2 n	
2 Sam. iii. 29.	2 o	ci. 6.	2 n	
vii. 6.ᵃ	2 o	civ. 3.	2 g	
vii. 7.	2 n	cxv. 7.	2 g	
x. 2.	2 n	cxvi. 9.	2 n	
1 Kings ii. 3, 4.	3 a	cxix. 1.	2 a	
ii. 42.	3 c	cxix. 3.	2 n	
iii. 3.	3 a	cxix. 45.	2 n	
iii. 6.	3 c	cxxviii. 1.	2 a	
iii. 14, 14.	3 c, 2 a	cxxxviii. 7.	3 c	
vi. 12, 12.	3 c a	cxlii. 3.	2 g	
viii. 23.	2 d	cxliii. 8.	3 c	
viii. 25, 25.	3 a, 2 a	Prov. i. 15.	3 c	
viii. 36.	3 a	ii. 7.	2 d	
viii. 58, 61.	3 a	ii. 13.	3 a	
ix. 4, 4.	3 c, 2 a	ii. 20.	3 c	
xi. 33, 38.	2 a	iii. 23.	3 c	
xv. 3, 26, 34.	2 a	vi. 12.	2 d	
xvi. 2, 26.	3 c	x. 9, 9.	2 d, 3 c	
xvii. 19, 31.	3 a	xiii. 20.	2 d	
xxii. 43, 52.	3 c	xiv. 2.	2 d	
2 Kings iv. 35.	3 c	xv. 21.	3 a	
viii. 18, 27.	3 c	xix. 1.	2 d	
x. 31.	3 a	xx. 7.	2 o	
xiii. 6, 11.	2 a	xxviii. 6, 18, 26.	2 d	
xvi. 3.	3 c	Eccles. ii. 14.	2 d	
xvii. 8.β	3 c	iv. 15.	2 h	
xvii. 19, 22.	3 c	vi. 8.	2 b	
xx. 3.	2 k	xi. 9.	2 d	
xxi. 21, 21.	3 c, 2 a	Isa. ii. 3, 5.	3 c	
xxi. 22.	2 a	iii. 16, 16.	3 c, 2 b	
xxii. 2.	2 a	viii. 11.	3 a	
xxiii. 3.	3 a	ix. 2.	2 d	
1 Chron. xvii. 6.	2 k	xx. 2.	2 d	
xvii. 8.	2 n	xx. 3.	2 a	
2 Chron. vi. 14.	2 d	xxx. 2.	2 d	

ᵃ *lit.* but was walking.   β *lit.* went after.

Isa. xxx. 21.	3 b
xxxiii. 15.	2 d
xxxv. 9.	2 a
xxxviii. 3.	2 k
xl. 31.	3 c
xlii. 5.	2 d
xlii. 24.	2 b
xliii. 2.	2 a
l. 10.	3 c
l. 11.	3 b
lvii. 2.	2 d
lix. 9.	2 g
lxv. 2.	2 d
Jer. ii. 5.	2 a
ii. 8.	2 a
iii. 17, 18.	3 b c
vi. 16, 16.	3 b c
vi. 25.	2 d
vi. 28.	2 d
vii. 6, 24.	2 b
vii. 9.	2 b
viii. 23.	2 a
viii. 2.	2 a
ix. 13.	2 c
ix. 14.	2 a
x. 23.	2 d
xi. 8.	3 c
xiii. 10, 10.	2 d, 3 c
xvi. 11.	3 c
xvi. 12.	2 d
xviii. 12.	3 c
xviii. 15.	2 d
xxiii. 14.	2 b
xxiii. 17.	2 d
xxvi. 4.	3 a
xxxi. 9.	3 e
xxxii. 23.	3 c
xlii. 3.	2 d
xliv. 10, 23.	3 a
Lam. v. 18.	2 e
Ezek. v. 6, 7.	2 e
xi. 12.	2 a
xi. 20.	3 c
xi. 21.	2 d
xvi. 47.	2 e
xviii. 9.	2 a
xviii. 17.	2 g
xx. 13, 16, 21.	3 c
xx. 19.	3 b
xxiii. 31.	2 k
xxxiii. 15.	2 d
xxxvi. 12.	3 d
xxxvi. 27.	3 c
xxxvii. 24.	3 c
xlii. 4.	2 r
Dan. iii. 25.	2 q
iv. 29.	2 p
iv. 37.	2 q
Hos. v. 11.	3 a
xi. 10.	3 c
xiv. 9.	3 c
Joel iii. 18.	3 c
Amos ii. 4.	3 c
iii. 3.	3 c
Micah ii. 7, 11.	3 a
iv. 2, 5, 5.	3 a
vi. 8.	3 a
vi. 16.	3 c
Nah. ii. 5.	2 a
ii. 11.	2 a
Hab. iii. 15.	1 b
Zeph. i. 17.	1 b
Zech. i. 10.	2 l
i. 11, 11.	2 k
iii. 7, 7.	2 i, 3 c
vi. 7, 7, 7.	2 l m n
x. 12.	2 n
Mal. ii. 6.	2 a
iii. 14.	2 a

WALL

1 אֻשַּׁרְנָא Ch. *m.* a wall, so called because it is upright.

2 בָּצַר to cut off, to make inaccessible. KAL *part.* Patil.

3 גָּדֵר *com.* a wall, specially a wall of a vineyard in addition to

a hedge, see Isa. v. 5 ; a walled place, enclosure. ᵃ גְּדֵר *m.* wall, fence. ᵇ גְּדֵרָה *f. id.*

4 חֵיל *m.* rampart ; *marg.* ' or, ditch.'

5 חַיִץ *m.* a wall, side of a house ; *marg.* ' or, a slight wall.'

6 חוֹמָה *f.* a wall which surrounds. Often for the wall of a city, rarely of other buildings, Lam. ii. 7 ; *metaph.* of a maiden, chaste and difficult of access, Cant. viii. 9, 10 ; *dual*, two walls, hence, between the two walls, 2 Kings xxv. 4, Jer. xxxix. 4 ;—these were near the king's gardens below Siloam, and may refer to the wall on the east of Zion and the eastern wall of the city ; see Robinson's Palestine, i. p. 460. In Isa. xxii. 11 the same expression seems to refer to the western part of Jerusalem, and may perhaps denote the first and second walls mentioned in Josephus.—B. J. v. iv. 2 ; Biblioth. Sacr. i. p. 199. Zech. ii. 5, "a wall of fire," may be an allusion to kindling fires as a protection against wild beasts in the night.—Exod. xiv. 22, &c.

7 חָרוּץ *m.* something cut in or dug out ; a trench of a fortified city.

8 כֹּתֶל *m.* a wall. ᵃ כְּתַל Ch. *m. id.*

9 קִיר *m.* a wall, of a city, of a house, of a garden, wall side, Josh. ii. 15 ; and so probably 2 Kings iv. 10, a little wall chamber built against the side of the house.

10 שׁוּר *m.* a wall. ᵃ שׁוּר Ch. *m. id.* ᵇ שָׁרוֹת *f. pl.* walls. ᶜ שׁוֹר *m.* an ox : Gen. xlix. 6, *marg.* ' or, houghed oxen ;' as it is rendered in the Gr. and Sam. in reference to the affair of the Shechemites. Bush considers the ox as symbolical of Joseph ; *comp.* Deut. xxxiii. 17. Jerus. Targum, " In their wilfulness they sold Joseph their brother, who is likened to an ox."

No. 6 not included.

Gen. xlix. 6.	10 c	2 Kings ix. 10.	9	Jer. v. 10.	10 b
xlix. 22.	10	ix. 8, 33.	9	Ezek. iv. 3.	9
Lev. xiv. 37, 37, 39.	9	xx. 2.	9	viii. 8, 8, 10.	9
Num. xiii. 28.	2	1 Chron. xxix. 4.	9	xii. 5, 7, 12.	9
xxii. 24, 24.	3	2 Chron. iii. 7, 7, 11,		xiii. 10.	5
xxii. 25, 25.	9	12.	9	xiii. 12, 14, 15, 15.	9
xxxv. 4.	9	Ezra ix. 12, 13, 16.	10 a	xxxiii. 14.	9
Deut. i. 28.	2	v. 3, 9.	1	xxxiii. 30.	9
xxxiii. 17.	10 c	v. 8.	8 a	xli. 5, 6, 6, 9, 12, 13,	
1 Sam. xviii. 11.		ix. 9.	3	17, 20, 22, 25.	9
xix. 10, 10.	9	Job xxiv. 11.	10	xlii. 7.	9
xx. 25.	9	Ps. xviii. 29.	10	xlii. 10.	3 a
xxv. 22, 34.	9	lxii. 3.	9	xlii. 12.	3 b
2 Sam. xxii. 30.	10	cxxii. 7.	4	xliii. 8.	9
1 Kings iv. 33.		Prov. xxiv. 31.	3 a	Dan. v. 5.	8 a
vi. 5, 5, 6, 15, 15,		Cant. ii. 9.	8	ix. 25.	7
16, 27, 27, 29.	9	Isa. v. 5.	9	Hos. ii. 6.	3
xiv. 10.	9	xxii. 5.	9	Amos v. 19.	9
xvi. 11.	9	xxv. 4.	9	Micah vii. 11.	3
xxi. 21.	9	xxviii. 2.	9	Hab. ii. 11.	9
xxi. 23.	4	lix. 10.	9		

WALLOW

גָּלַל to roll ; to roll oneself or be rolled, to wallow, *i.e.* be stained. HITHPOEL *part.* 2 Sam. xx. 12.

סָפַק to strike ; also, according to Syr. and Gesenius, to vomit, to vomit forth. KAL *pret.* Jer. xlviii. 26.

פָּלַשׁ to roll ; to roll oneself, to wallow, *e.g.* in ashes. HITHPAEL *imp.* Jer. vi. 26 ; xxv. 34. *fut.* Ezek. xxvii. 30.

WANDER

1 הָלַךְ to go, to walk, to go forth. KAL ᵃ *pret.* ᵇ *inf.*

2 נָדַד to move, to wander, to flee. KAL ᵃ *inf.* ᵇ *part.* Poel.

3 נוּד to be moved, to be driven about, to wander, to flit from place to place. KAL ᵃ *inf.* ᵇ נוֹד *m.* wandering.

4 נוּעַ to be agitated ; to wander about. KAL ᵃ *pret.* ᵇ *inf.* ᶜ *fut.* (כתיב). HIPHIL ᵈ *fut.*

5 צָעָה to bend, to incline ; applied to gait and manner ; see *Travel ;* to be inclined, bent, bowed down ; it is applied to harlots. KAL ᵃ *part.* Poel. PIEL ᵇ *pret.*

6 רָעָה to feed. KAL *part.* Poel, *lit.* be feeding.

7 שָׁנָה to wander, to go astray ; to err. KAL ᵃ *fut.* HIPHIL ᵇ *fut.* ᶜ *part.*

8 תָּעָה to go astray, to wander ; to err. KAL ᵃ *pret.* ᵇ *fut.* ᶜ *part.* Poel. HIPHIL ᵈ *pret.* ᵉ *fut.*

Gen. xx. 13.	8 d	Ps. lvi. 8.	3 b	Isa. xlvii. 15.	8 a
xxi. 14.	8 b	lix. 15.	4 d, or c	Jer. ii. 20.	5 a
xxxvii. 15.	8 c	cvii. 4.	8 a	xiv. 10.	4 b
Num. xiv. 33.	6	cvii. 40.	8 d	xlviii. 12, 12.	5 a b
xxxii. 13.	4 d	cxix. 10.	7 b	xlix. 5.	2 b
Deut. xxvii. 18.	7 c	Prov. xxi. 16.	8 c	Lam. iv. 14, 15.	4 a
Josh. xiv. 10.	1 a	xxvi. 2.	3 a	Ezek. xxxiv. 6.	7 a
Job xii. 24.	8 d	xxvii. 8, 8.	2 b	Hos. ix. 17.	3 a
xv. 23.	2 b	Eccles. vi. 9.	1 b	Amos iv. 8.	4 a
xxxviii. 41.	8 b	Isa. xvi. 2, 3.	2 b	viii. 12.	4 a
Ps. lv. 7.	2 a	xvi. 8.	8 a		

WANT

1 אֶפֶס *m.* cessation.

2 חָדַל to leave off, to cease, to desist. KAL *fut.*

3 חָסַר to diminish, to cut short ; to be diminished, to fail, to be wanting ; to want, to be in want, to suffer need. KAL ᵃ *pret.* ᵇ *fut.* ᶜ חָסֵר *adj.* wanting, destitute of. ᵈ חֶסֶר *m.* deficiency, want. ᵉ חֹסֶר *m. id.* ᶠ חֶסְרוֹן *m.* much want. ᵍ חַסִּיר Ch. *adj.* deficient, of weight. ʰ מַחְסוֹר *m.* want, deficiency ; want, need, poverty.

4 כָּרַת to cut off. NIPHAL *fut.* " shall not want," *lit.* there shall not be cut off from.

5 פָּקַד to review, to muster, to number ; also to miss in reviewing, numbering. KAL ᵃ *pret.* NIPHAL ᵇ *fut.*

Deut. xv. 8.	3 b	Prov. ix. 4, 16.	3 c	Eccles. vi. 2.	3 c
xxviii. 48, 57.	3 e	x. 19.	2	Cant. vii. 2.	3 b
Judg. xviii. 10.	3 h	x. 21.	3 c	Isa. xxxiv. 16.	5 a
xix. 19, 20.	3 h	xiii. 25.	3 b	Jer. xxxiii. 17, 18.	4
2 Kings x. 19, 19.	5 b	xiv. 28.	1	xxxv. 19.	4
Job xxx. 3.	3 d	xxi. 5.	3 h	xliv. 18.	3 a
Ps. xxiii. 1.	3 b	xxii. 16.	3 h	Ezek. iv. 17.	3 a
xxxiv. 9.	3 h	xxiv. 34.	3 h	Dan. v. 27.	3 g
xxxiv. 10.	3 b	xxvii. 16.	3 c	Amos iv. 6.	3 e
Prov. vi. 11.	3 h	Eccles. i. 15.	3 f		

WANTON

שָׁקַר to look, to look about, *i.e.* in the manner of wanton and immodest females. PIEL *part.* Isa. iii. 16.

WAR, WARRIOR

1 אִישׁ *m.* man ; " to have war," *lit.* to be a man of war.

2 אֱנוֹשׁ *m.* man ; " war against thee," *lit.* the men of thy war.

3 חַיִל *m.* strength, army ; valour ; " meet for war," *lit.* sons of power.

4 לָחַם to eat ; to consume ; to fight, to war ; more usual in Niphal. Soldiers in war or battle are hyperbolically said to devour their enemies, as Joshua the Canaanites, Num. xiv. 9 ; and the sword also is said to devour,

Ezek. xxi. 33, Isa. i. 20; see *Fight*. NIPHAL ᵃ*pret.* ᵇ*inf.* ᶜ*fut.* ᵈ*part.* ᵉ םָחָל war. ᶠ הָמָחְלִמ *f.* warring, fighting; fight, battle; war: Gen. xiv. 2, &c.

5   ןאָס This very difficult word has given occasion to numerous conjectures : our version takes it in the sense of conflict ; Gesenius, and most modern critics, understand it of one defended by the military shoe to keep him from the clay and mire ; Fürst entirely rejects this as a mere conjecture, and supposes the root to mean to sharpen, to pierce, and the noun to be the weapon used in battle for piercing or slaying ; others, tracing a reference to the oppression and conquest of the Midianites, have proposed renderings accordingly; see Gussetius and Rosenmüller, *in loc.* Seb. Schmidt renders the passage prophetically, in contrast with the history of Gideon's attack on the Midianites, "Every tumult shall be tumultuously thrown into perturbation by an earthquake." KAL *part.* Poel.

6   הָשָׂע to do, &c. KAL *part.* Poel, "warriors," *lit.* making war.

7   אָבָצ to go forth to war, as a soldier, to make war against any one, *seq.* לַע. KAL ᵃ*fut.* ᵇ*part.* Poel. ᶜ אָבָצ *m.* an army, host ; war, warfare, military service ; an appointed time of service.

8   לֵבֳק *m.* what is over against.

9   בָרְק *m.* encounter, battle, war. בָרְק Ch. *m. id.*

No. 4 f not included.

Num. i. 3, 20, 22, 24,		Judg. xi. 27.	4 b	2 Chron. xxv. 5.	7 c	
26, 28, 30, 32, 34,		1 Sam. xxviii. 1.	7 c	xxvi. 6.	4 c	
36, 38, 40, 45.	7 c	xxviii. 15.	4 d	xxvi. 11.	7 c	
xxvi. 2.	7 c	2 Sam. viii. 1.	1, 7 b	xxviii. 12.	7 c	
xxxi. 3, 4, 5, 6, 6,		1 Kings xii. 21.	6, 2 f	xxxiii. 14.	3	
21, 32, 36, 53.	7 c	xiv. 19.	4 a	Job x. 17.	7 c	
xxxi. 7.	7 a	xx. 1.	4 c	Ps. lv. 21.	9	
xxxi. 42.	7 b	xxi. 45.	4 a	lxviii. 30.	9	
xxxii. 27.	7 c	2 Kings vi. 8.	4 d	cxliv. 1.	9	
Deut. iii. 18.	3	xiv. 28.	4 a	Eccles. ix. 18.	9	
xx. 19.	4 b	xix. 8.	4 d	Isa. ix. 5.	5	
xxiv. 5.	7 c	1 Chron. v. 18.	4 f, 7 c	xxxvii. 8.	4 d	
Josh. iv. 13.	7 c	vii. 11, 40.	7 c	xxxvii. 9.	4 d	
x. 5.	4 c	xii. 8, 23, 24, 25,		xl. 2.	7 c	
xxii. 12.	7 c	27.	7 c	xl. 12.	2, 4 f	
xxiv. 9.	4 c	xviii. 10.	1, 4 f	Jer. xxi. 2.	4 d	
Judg. v. 8.	4 e	2 Chron. xi. 1.	6, 4 f	Ezek. xxvi. 9.	8	
xi. 4.	4 c	xvii. 10.	4 a	Dan. vii. 21.	9 a	
xi. 5.	4 a	xvii. 18.	7 c			

WARD

תיִבּ *m.* house : 2 Sam. xx. 3, *lit.* a house of ward.

רַגֹּס *m.* prison ; cage of a lion : Ezek. xix. 9.

תֶּרֻקְפּ *f.* custody : Jer. xxxvii. 13.

רָמְשִׁמ *m.* watch, guard ; ward, prison : Gen. xl. 3, 4, 7 ; xli. 10 ; xlii. 17 : Lev. xxiv. 12 : Num. xv. 34 : 1 Chron. xxvi. 16, 16 : Neh. xii. 24, 24, 25. תֶרֶמְשִׁמ *f.* watch, guard, custody : 2 Sam. xx. 3 : 1 Chron. ix. 23 ; xii. 29 ; xxv. 8 ; xxvi. 12 : Neh. xii. 45, 45 ; xiii. 30 : Isa. xxi. 8.

WARDROBE

דֶגֶבּ *m.* garment : 2 Kings xxii. 14 : 2 Chron. xxxiv. 22.

WARE, WARES

יִלְכּ *m.* a general name for tools, vessels, furniture, &c. : Jonah i. 5.

הָעֵנְכּ *f.* package, bundle, bale, from עַנָכּ to bind up : Jer. x. 17.

תוחָקִּמ *m.* wares, merchandise : Neh. x. 31.

רֶכֶמ *m.* ware, anything to be sold : Neh. xiii. 16. רָכְּמִמ *m. id.* Neh. xiii. 20.

ןוֹבָּעׅ *m.* commerce ; wares so obtained : Ezek. xxvii. 33.

הֶשֲׂעַמ *m.* work, deed, &c. : Ezek. xxvii. 16, 18, "wares of thy making."

WARM

1   בַרָז to be dissolved by the heat of the sun, to flow down, to be dissipated.

2   םַמָח to wax warm. KAL ᵃ*pret.* ᵇ*inf.* ᶜ*fut.* PIEL ᵈ*fut.* HITHPAEL ᵉ*fut.* ᶠ םָח *adj.* hot. ᵍ םֹח *m.* heat.

3   םַחָי to be or become warm. KAL *fut.*

2 Kings iv. 34.	2 c	Job xxxix. 14.	2 d	Isa. xliv. 16, 16.	2 c a
Job vi. 17.	1	Eccles. iv. 11.	3	xlvii. 14.	2 b
xxxi. 20.	2 e	Isa. xliv. 15.	2 c	Hag. i. 6.	2 g
xxxvii. 17.	2 f				

WARN

רַהָז to shine ; to enlighten ; to teach ; to admonish, to take warning, to beware of anything, to desist from anything, *seq.* ןִמ. NIPHAL *part.* Ps. xix. 11 : Ezek. iii. 21 ; xxxiii. 4, 5, 6, 6. HIPHIL *pret.* 2 Kings vi. 10 : 2 Chron. xix. 10 : Ezek. iii. 17, 18, 19, 20, 21 ; xxxiii. 3, 7, 9. *inf.* Ezek. iii. 18 ; xxxiii. 8.

דוּע to testify. HIPHIL *fut.* Jer. vi. 10.

WARP

יִתְשׁ *m.* the warp in a loom which drinketh as it were the woof or shoot in weaving : Lev. xiii. 48, 49, 51, 52, 53, 56, 57, 58, 59.

WASH

1   חַדָּה to thrust away, to cast off ; to cast out ; to wash away. HIPHIL *fut.*

2   סַבָכּ to tread ; hence to wash or cleanse garments by treading them in a trough : to wash spiritually, Ps. li. 2, of which ceremonial washing was typical. PIEL ᵃ*pret.* ᵇ*imp.* ᶜ*fut.* PUAL ᵈ*pret.* HOTHPAEL ᵉ*inf.*

3   םִיַמ *m. dual,* water.

4   ץַחָר to wash, to lave ; to bathe the body, &c. ; it is applied also to moral cleansing. KAL ᵃ*pret.* ᵇ*inf.* ᶜ*imp.* ᵈ*fut.* ᵉ*part.* PUAL ᶠ*pret.* HITHPAEL ᵍ*pret.* ʰ ץַחַר *m.* washing. ᶦ הָצְחַר *f.* washing-place for sheep.

5   ףַטָשׁ to overflow ; to wash or rinse copiously ; to wash away. KAL ᵃ*fut.*

Gen. xviii. 4.	4 c	Lev. viii. 6.	4 d	Lev. xvii. 15.	2 a
xix. 2.	4 c	viii. 21.	4 d	xvii. 16.	2 c
xxiv. 32.	4 b	ix. 14.	4 b	xxii. 6.	4 a
xliii. 24, 31.	4 d	xi. 25, 28, 40, 40.	2 c	Num. viii. 7.	2 a
xlix. 11.	2 a	xiii. 6, 34, 54.	2 a	viii. 21.	2 c
Exod. ii. 5.	4 b	xiii. 55, 56.	2 e	xix. 7, 10, 19.	2 a
xix. 10.	2 a	xiii. 58.	2 c	xix. 8, 21.	2 c
xix. 14.	2 c	xiv. 8, 8.	2 a, 4 a	xxxi. 24.	2 a
xxix. 4, 17.	4 a	xiv. 9, 9.	2 a, 4 a	Deut. xxi. 6.	4 d
xxx. 18.	4 b	xiv. 47, 47.	2 c	xxiii. 11.	4 d
xxx. 19, 21.	4 a	xv. 5, 6, 7, 10, 21,		Judg. xix. 21.	4 d
xxx. 20.	4 d	22.	2 c	Ruth iii. 3.	4 a
xl. 12, 31.	4 a	xv. 8, 11, 13, 27.	2 a	1 Sam. xxv. 41.	4 b
xl. 30.	4 b	xv. 16.	2 a	2 Sam. xi. 2.	4 e
Lev. i. 9, 13.	4 d	xv. 17.	2 d	xi. 8.	4 c
vi. 27.	2 c	xvi. 4, 24.	4 a	xii. 20.	4 d
		xvi. 26, 28.	2 c	xix. 24.	2 a

1 Kings xxii. 38,		Ps. xxvi. 6.	4 d	Cant. v. 12.	4 e
38.	5 a, 4 a	li. 2.	2 b	vi. 6.	4 i
2 Kings v. 10.	4 a	li. 7.	2 c	Isa. i. 16.	4 c
v. 12.	4 a	lviii. 10.	4 d	iv. 4.	4 a
v. 13.	4 c	lx. 8. a	4 h	Jer. ii. 22.	2 c
2 Chron. iv. 6, 6, }	4 b, 1,	lxxiii. 13.	4 d	iv. 14.	2 b
6. }	4 b	cviii. 9. a	4 h	Ezek. xvi. 4.	4 f
Neh. iv. 23.	3	Prov. xxx. 12.	4 f	xvi. 9, 9.	4 d, 5 a
Job ix. 30.	4 g	Cant. iv. 2.	4 i	xxiii. 40.	4 a
xiv. 19.	5 a	v. 3.	4 a	xl. 38.	1
xxix. 6.	4 b				

a lit. the pot of my washing.

WASTE

1 בָּלָה to wax old by use. PIEL trans. to consume: inf.

2 בָּלַק to empty out, to make empty; onomatopoetic, imitating the sound of emptying out a bottle. KAL a part. Poel. PUAL b part.

3 בָּעַר to feed upon, to eat up, to consume. PIEL inf.

4 בָּתָה f. desolation.

5 חָלַשׁ pr. to be prostrate; to be weak, frail, to waste away. KAL fut.

6 חָרַב to be dried up, to be dry; to be laid waste, to lie desert, e.g. lands, cities, since dry places quickly become waste and desert. Also to be wasted, destroyed, of a people, and trans. to waste, destroy. KAL a inf. b imp. c fut. NIPHAL d part. HIPHIL e pret. f fut. g part. HOPHAL h pret. i part. k חָרֵב adj. dry, waste. l חָרְבָּה f. desolation. m חֹרֶב m. dryness; desolation.

7 תּוֹלָל m. (r. יָלַל to howl), vexer, tormentor; abstr. vexation, the acts of one who extorts lamentation from others: Ps. cxxxvii. 3, lit. our tormentors, oppressors.

8 כָּלָה to be finished, ended, consumed, spent. KAL a pret. b fut.

9 כִּרְסֵם to cut down or off, to lay waste, to devour; as the wild boar a vineyard: fut.

10 נָצָה to lay waste, properly to tear in pieces, to pull down. KAL fut.

11 רָעָה to feed. KAL pret.

12 שָׁאָה to make a noise; to fall with a crash, e.g. a house, hence to be laid waste; see Desolation, Destruction. KAL a pret. HIPHIL b inf.

13 שׁוֹאָה f. a storm, tempest; desolation. a מְשׁוֹאָה f. id.

14 שָׁדַד to practise violence; to destroy, to lay waste, to desolate. PIEL a part. PUAL b pret. c שֹׁד m. destruction, ruin.

15 שׁוּד to treat with violence, to lay waste. KAL fut.

16 שָׁחַת to corrupt, destroy. HIPHIL a fut. b part.

17 שָׁמֵם to be astonished, properly struck dumb, to be laid waste, to be made desolate, since desolate places are silent and quiet. NIPHAL a pret. b part. HIPHIL c pret. d fut. e שַׁמָּה f. astonishment, desolation. f שְׁמָמָה f. id.

18 תֹּהוּ m. wasteness; emptiness.

19 תּוֹלָל m. some derive this word from תָּלַל to raise a mound, to lay on heaps.

20 תָּמַם to be finished; consumed. KAL inf.

Lev. xxvi. 31, 33.	6 l	Deut. xxxii. 10.	18	1 Chron. xx. 1.	16 a		
Num. xiv. 33.	20	1 Kings xvii. 14.	8 b	Neh. ii. 3, 17.	6 k		
xxi. 30.	17 d	xvii. 16.	8 a	Job xiv. 10.	5		
xxiv. 22.	3	2 Kings xix. 25.	12 b	xxx. 3.	13 a		
Deut. ii. 14.	20	1 Chron. xvii. 9.	1	xxxviii. 27.	13 a		

Ps. lxxix. 7.	17 c	Isa. lii. 9.	6 l	Ezek. xxix. 10. a	6 m l
lxxx. 13.	9	liv. 16.	16 b	xxix. 12.	6 i
xci. 6.	15	lviii. 12.	6 l	xxx. 7.	6 d
cxxxvii. 3.	7 or 19	lix. 7.	14 c	xxx. 12.	17 c
Prov. xviii. 9.	16 b	lx. 12.	6 a c	xxxiii. 24, 27.	6 l
xix. 26.	14 a	lx. 18.	14 c	xxxv. 4.	6 l
Isa. v. 6.	4	lxi. 4, 4.	6 m l	xxxvi. 4, 10, 33.	6 l
v. 17.	6 m	lxiv. 11.	6 l	xxxvi. 35, 38.	6 k
vi. 11.	12 a	Jer. iv. 15.	17 e	xxxviii. 8.	6 l
xv. 1, 1.	14 b	iv. 7.	10	Joel i. 7.	17 e
xix. 5.	6 c	xvii. 17.	6 l	i. 10, 10.	14 b
xxiii. 1, 14.	14 b	xliv. 6.	6 l	Amos vii. 9.	6 c
xxiv. 1.	2 a	xlix. 13, 13.	6 l m	ix. 14.	17 b
xxxiii. 8.	17 a	l. 21.	6 c	Micah vi. 6. β	11
xxxiv. 10.	6 c	Ezek. v. 14.	6 l	Nah. ii. 1.	2 b
xxxvii. 18.	6 e	vi. 6.	6 l	iii. 7.	14 b
xxxvii. 26.	12 a	xii. 20.	6 c	Zeph. i. 15.	13
xlii. 15.	6 f	xix. 7.	6 c	Hag. i. 4, 9.	6 k
xlix. 19.	6 l	xxvi. 2.	6 h	Mal. i. 3.	17 f
li. 3.	6 l	xxix. 9.	6 l		

a marg. 'wastes of waste.'   β marg. 'eat up.'

WATCH

1 נָצַר to watch, to guard, to keep. KAL part. Poel.

2 צָפָה to look about, to view from a distance. The primary idea is that of inclining or bending forward in order to behold; part. a watchman stationed on a tower; metaph. of prophets, who, like watchmen, announce future things as revealed to them in vision, comp. Hab. ii. 1; in a still wider sense, Isa. lvi. 10. Hence specially (a) to look out for anything, to await, Hos. ix. 8, Ephraim awaiteth, sc. response, help, comp. Lam. iv. 17, Ps. v. 3; (β) to watch, to observe closely, seq. acc., seq. בְּ, seq. בֵּין, to observe and judge between; (γ) to lie in wait, seq. לְ, Ps. xxxvii. 32; (δ) seq. אֶל to look out for, i.e. to select. Piel, to look about, to watch, seq. acc. Nah. ii. 1. Seq. אֶל of that for which one looks about, which he expects, e.g. help, Lam. iv. 17; בְּ, Micah vii. 7; absol. Ps. v. 3, I will await. KAL a inf. b fut. c part. Poel. PIEL d pret. e imp. f fut. g part. h צְפִיָּה f. a watch-tower. i צָפִית f. id. k מִצְפֶּה m. watch-tower.

3 עִיר Ch. m. watcher, a name for the angels in the later Hebrew as keeping watch over the affairs of men. Suiceri Thes. Eccl., art. ἐγρήγορος.

4 קִיץ to awake. HIPHIL pret.

5 שָׁמַר to keep, to watch, to guard; to keep in view, i.e. to observe, to mark; sometimes in a bad sense, to watch narrowly, to spy out. KAL a inf. b fut. c part. Poel. d שָׁמְרָה f. watch, guard. e מִשְׁמָר m. watch, guard. f מִשְׁמֶרֶת f. id. g אַשְׁמוּרָה and אַשְׁמֹרָה f. a watch, φυλακή, a part of the night so called from the military watches. Among the ancient Hebrews there were only three night-watches; the first, Lam. ii. 19, the middle, Judg. vii. 19, and the third, Exod. xiv. 24, 1 Sam. xi. 11.

6 שָׁקַד to wake, to be sleepless, to watch; trop. seq. עַל to watch over anything, to give attention to it, to watch at, e.g. doors, to lie in wait for, as the leopard, Jer. v. 6. KAL a pret. b inf. c imp. d fut. e part. Poel.

Gen. xxxi. 49.	2 b	2 Sam. xviii. 24, 25, 26,		Ezra viii. 29.	6 c
Exod. xiv. 24.	5 g	26, 27.	2 c	Neh. iv. 9.	5 e
Judg. vii. 19, 19.	5 g c	2 Kings ix. 17, 18, 20.	2 c	vii. 3, 3.	5 f e
1 Sam. iv. 13.	2 g	xi. 5, 6, 7.	5 f	xii. 9.	5 f
ii. 11.	5 g	xvii. 9.	1	Job vii. 12.	5 b
xiv. 16.	2 c	xviii. 8.	2 c	xiv. 16.	5 b
xix. 11.	2 c	2 Chron. xx. 24.	5 k	Ps. xxxvii. 32.	2 c
2 Sam. xiii. 34.	2 c	xxiii. 6.	5 f	lix. title.	5 b

Ps. lxiii. 6.	5 g	Isa. xxi. 11, 11, 12.	5 c	Jer. li. 12, 12.	5 c e
xc. 4.	5 g	xxix. 20.	6 e	Lam. ii. 19.	5 g
cii. 7.	6 a	lii. 8.	2 c	iv. 17, 17.	2 d h
cxix. 148.	5 g	lvi. 10.	2 c	Ezek. iii. 17.	2 c
cxxvii. 1.	5 c	lxii. 6.	5 c	vii. 6. a	4
cxxx. 6, 6.	5 c	Jer. iv. 16.	1	xxxiii. 2, 6, 6, 7.	2 c
cxli. 3.	5 d	v. 6.	6 e	Dan. iv. 13, 17, 23.	3
Prov. viii. 34.	6 b	vi. 17.	2 c	Hos. ix. 8.	2 c
Cant. iii. 3.	5 c	xx. 10.	5 c	Micah vii. 4.	2 g
v. 7.	5 c	xxxi. 6.	1	Nah. ii. 1.	2 e
Isa. xxi. 5, 5.	2 a i	xxxi. 28, 28.	6 a d	Hab. ii. 1, 1.	5 f, 2 f
xxi. 6.	2 g	xliv. 27.	6 e		
xxi. 8.	2 k				

a marg. 'awaketh against thee.'

WATER

1 זַרְזִיף *m.* a pouring rain, violent shower.

2 יָרָא to cast or pour out water. HIPHIL *fut.*, or, according to some, HOPHAL *fut.*

3 מַיִם *m. dual,* waters, water. Spoken of the waters of the ocean, Ps. xviii. 15, *comp.* 2 Sam. xxii. 16; of the ocean above the firmament, Gen. i. 7, Ps. xxix. 3, civ. 3, cxlviii. 4; of water held in the clouds, Job xxvi. 8, Ps. xviii. 11; of rain, Job v. 10, &c. Joined with the name of a place it denotes waters situated near that place, a fountain, stream, torrent, lake, marsh, &c. *Trop.* water, *i.e.* juice of poppies, Jer. viii. 14; water of the feet, urine, Isa. xxxvi. 12; water of a man, put for the *semen virile,* Isa. xlviii. 1; his offspring, *comp.* Num. xxiv. 7, Ps. lxviii. 26; (see *Fountain.*) In poetry water is the emblem (α) of abundance, multitude, Ps. lxxix. 3, lxxxviii. 17, Isa. xi. 9, Hab. ii. 14; (β) of great and overwhelming dangers, Ps. xviii. 16, xxxii. 6, lxix. 1, 2, 14; (γ) of terror, Josh. vii. 5, *opp.* is a heart like stone, Job xli. 24; (δ) of weakness, debility, Ps. xxii. 14; (ε) of lust, as likened to boiling water, Gen. xlix. 4.—Gen. i. 2, &c., Job xxvi. 10, *lit.* the face of the waters.

4 מָסָה to melt, to flow down; to make to flow down. HIPHIL *fut.*

5 תְּעָלָה *f.* a channel, trench, in which water goes up from a stream, to water or inundate the fields; a water-course; elegantly used of God dividing the supply of rain from the clouds.

6 צִנּוֹר *m.* a cataract, waterfall, so called from its rushing sound; a waterspout.

7 רָוָה to drink to the full, to be satisfied; to make to drink in, to water, *e.g.* the fields. PIEL *a imp. b fut.* HIPHIL *c pret. d part. e* רָוֶה *adj.* soaked, satiated. *f* רִיּ *m.* a watering, rain.

8 שׁוּק to run; to run over, to overflow; to cause to overflow with plenty, *e.g.* the earth. POLEL *fut.*

9 שָׁקָה to drink; to give to drink, to let drink; to water cattle, to water the ground. HIPHIL *a pret. b inf. c imp. d fut. e part. f* מַשְׁקֶה *m.* a watered country.

No. 3, *Water,* not included.

Gen. ii. 6.	9 a	Job xxxvii. 11.	7 f	Eccles. ii. 6, 6.	3, 9 b
ii. 10.	9 b	xxxviii. 25.	5	Isa. xvi. 9.	7 b
xiii. 10.	9 f	Ps. vi. 6.	4	xxvii. 3.	9 d
xxix. ii. 10.	9 d	xlii. 7.	6	lv. 10.	7 c
xxix. 3.	9 a	lxv. 9, 9.	8, 3	lviii. 11, 11, 11.	7 e, 3, 3
xxix. 7.	9 c	lxv. 10.	7 a	Jer. xxxi. 12.	7 e
Exod. ii. 16.	9 b	lxxii. 6.	1	Ezek. xvii. 7.	9 b
ii. 17, 19.	9 d	civ. 13.	9 e	xxxii. 6.	9 a
Deut. xi. 10.	9 a	Prov. xi. 25, 25.	7 d, 2	Joel iii. 18, 18.	3, 9 a

WAVE.

נוּף to lift up, to elevate; to lift up the hand repeatedly, to move or wave the hand up and down, to wave; see *Offer.* HIPHIL *a pret. b inf. c fut.* HOPHAL *d pret. e* תְּנוּפָה *f.* a waving, a wave-offering.

Exod. xxix. 24, 24.	a e	Lev. ix. 21, 21.	a e	Lev. xxiii. 12.	b
xxix. 26, 26.	a e	x. 14.	e	xxiii. 15, 17.	e
xxix. 27, 27.	a e	x. 15, 15, 15.	e b e	xxiii. 20, 20.	a e
Lev. vii. 30, 30.	b e	xiv. 12, 12.	a e	Num. v. 25.	a
vii. 34.	e	xiv. 21.	e	vi. 20, 20, 20.	a e e
viii. 27, 27.	c e	xiv. 24, 24.	a e	xviii. 11, 18.	e
viii. 29, 29.	c e	xxiii. 11, 11.	a c		

WAVE

1 בָּמָה *f.* high place, height; applied to waves.

2 גַּל *com.* rolling waves, billows.

3 דֳּכִי *m.* a crushing, dashing, beating together of waves; hence a raging, roaring noise.

4 מִשְׁבָּר *m.,* only in *pl.,* waves which break upon the shore, breakers.

2 Sam. xxii. 5.	4	Ps. lxxix. 9.	2	Jer. v. 22.	2
Job ix. 8.	1	xciii. 3.	3	xxxi. 35.	2
xxxviii. 11.	2	xciii. 4.	4	li. 42, 55.	2
Ps. xlii. 7.	4	cvii. 25, 29.	2	Ezek. xxvi. 3.	2
lxv. 7.	2	Isa. xlviii. 18.	2	Jonah ii. 3.	2
lxxxviii. 7.	4	li. 15.	2	Zech. x. 11.	2

WAX

דּוֹנַג *m.* wax: Ps. xxii. 14; lxviii. 2; xcvii. 5: Micah i. 4.

WAX

הָלַךְ to go. KAL *inf.* 1 Chron. xi. 9, *marg.* 'went in going and increasing.' *part.* Poel, 2 Sam. iii. 1, *lit.* going and strong; 1, *lit.* going and weak: 2 Chron. xvii. 12, *lit.* was going and great: Esth. ix. 4, *lit.* going and great.

יָלַךְ to go. KAL *fut.* 1 Chron. xi. 9, *lit.* went in going.

WAY

1 אָבַד to perish. KAL *pret.* Jer. xxv. 35.

2 אָרַח to be on the way; *part.* wayfaring man, traveller. KAL *a part.* Poel. *b* אֹרַח *com.* a way, path, road; *metaph.* way, manner of life and conduct, ways or paths of any one, *i.q.* his condition, lot. *c* אָרְחָא Ch. *f.* ways, *i.e. metaph.* counsels of God; affairs, destinies of any one.

3 אֶרֶץ *com.* the earth, ground; "a little way," *lit.* a little piece of ground.

4 בּוֹא to come. KAL *inf.* Gen. xxiv. 62, "from the way of."

5 דֶּרֶךְ *com. pr.* the act of treading, walking, going; a going, way, journey; a way, path, in which one treads, goes; with יָר wayside; a way, *i.e.* course, manner, in which one walks, lives, which one follows; specially a way of living, acting one's walk, conduct, life; to walk in the way of any one, to imitate his conduct. Also to walk in the way of the Lord, spoken of men, a way or conduct which Jehovah approves, and in which men ought to walk; spoken of God, his mode of acting, agency, Ps. xviii. 30; *pl.* ways of God, *i.e.* his works, Job xxvi. 14, xl. 19; way of worshipping God, worship, religion, *comp.* ὁδός, Acts xix. 9, 23; so Amos viii. 14, Ps. cxxxix.

24, comp. Jer. xviii. 15; way everlasting and similar phrases seem to refer to the will of God respecting us, Ps. cxxxix. 24. Sometimes passive, way, manner of one's experience, *i. q.* lot, how it goes with one, Ps. xxxvii. 5; so Job iii. 23, Amos ii. 7.—Gen. iii. 24, &c.

6 הָלַךְ to go. KAL ᵃ*part.* Poel. ᵇ הֲלִיכָה *f.* step, way. ᶜ הֵילְכָה *f.* (כתיב).

7 נָסַע to remove, to journey, to be on the way. KAL *pret.*

8 נָתִיב *m.* a trodden way, beaten way; hence footpath, byway.

9 מְסִלָּה *f.* highway.

10 עָבַר to pass. KAL *part.* Poel, "wayfaring man," *lit.* he that passeth along the road.

11 מַעְגָּל *m.* a track, rut; way, path; with יָד wayside. ᵃ מַעְגָּלָה *f. id.*

12 צִיּוּן *m.* a pillar, as a way-mark, guide.

13 קָרָא to meet. KAL *inf.* Exod. v. 20, "in the way."

14 רָחַק to be far off, a good way. HIPHIL ᵃ*pret.* ᵇ*inf.*

15 תָּעָה to go astray, to be out of the way. KAL *pret.*

No. 5 not included.

Gen. xxi. 16.	14 b	Ps. xliv. 18.	2 b	Prov. xxxi. 27.	6 b, or c
xxiv. 62.	4	lxxviii. 50.	8	Isa. xxvi. 7, 8.	2 b
xxxv. 16.	3	lxxxv. 5.	9	xxvii. 7, 7.	15
xxxviii. 21.	5	cxix. 9, 15, 101,		xxx. 11.	2 b
xlviii. 7.	3	104, 128.	2 b	xxxiii. 8.	10, 2 b
Exod. v. 20.	13	cxl. 5.	11	xxxv. 8, 8.	6 a, 5
Judg. v. 6.	2 b	cxli. 3.	2 b	xxxv. 8.	6, 5
xviii. 22.	14 a	Prov. i. 19.	2 b	xxxv. 8.	2 b
xix. 17.	2 a	ii. 15.	2 b	Jer. iv. 7.	7
1 Sam. iv. 13.	5	v. 6.	11 a	ix. 2.	2 a
2 Sam. xii. 4.	5 a	viii. 20.	2 b	xiv. 8.	2 a
2 Kings v. 19.	3	ix. 15.	2 b	xxv. 35.	5
Job xvi. 22.	2 b	x. 17.	2 b	xxxi. 21.	12
xviii. 10.	8	xii. 28.	2 b	Dan. iv. 37.	2 c
xix. 8.	2 b	xv. 10, 19, 24.	2 b	v. 23.	2 c
xxii. 15.	2 b	xvii. 23.	2 b	Hab. iii. 6.	6 b
xxx. 12.	2 b	xxii. 25.	2 b	Zech. x. 2.	7
xxxiv. 11.	2 b				

WEAK

1 אָמַל to wither, to languish; to be in extremity of weakness and decay. KAL ᵃ*part.* Paül. ᵇ אֻמְלָל *adj.* wasting with disease.

2 דַּל *adj.* weak, feeble, powerless; see *Wax.*

3 הָלַךְ to walk, to go. KAL *part.* Poel.

4 חָלָה to be worn down in strength, to be weak, to be sick. KAL ᵃ*pret.* PUAL ᵇ*pret.*

5 חָלַשׁ to prostrate, to weaken. KAL ᵃ*part.* Poel. ᵇ חַלָּשׁ *m.* weak person.

6 יָלַךְ to go. KAL *fut.* "weak as water," *lit.* go into water.

7 כָּשַׁל to stumble, to fall; applied to knees weak and tottering. KAL *pret.*

8 עָנָה to be afflicted; to afflict. PIEL *pret.*

9 רַךְ *adj.* tender.

10 רָפָה to be slackened, to become feeble. KAL ᵃ*fut.* PIEL ᵇ*pret.* ᶜ*part.* ᵈ רָפֶה *adj.* weak.

Num. xiii. 18.	10 d	Neh. vi. 9.	10 a	Isa. xiv. 12.	5 a
Judg. xvi. 7, 11, 17.	4 a	Job iv. 3.		xxxv. 3.	10 d
2 Sam. iii. 1, 1. a	2, 3	xii. 21.	10 b	Jer. xxxviii. 4.	10 c
iii. 39.		Ps. vi. 2.	1 b	Ezek. vii. 17.	
xvii. 2.	10 d	cii. 23.	8	xvi. 30.	1 a
2 Chron. xv. 7.	10 a	cix. 24.	7	xxi. 7.	
Ezra iv. 4.	10 c	Isa. xiv. 10.	4 b	Joel iii. 10.	5 b

a lit. going and weak, *i. e.* continually weaker.

WEALTH, WEALTHY

1 הוֹן *m.* riches, wealth, substance.

2 חַיִל *m.* strength, power; wealth, riches; comprehending all in which a man's power consists: Gen. xxxiv. 29. Gr. σώματα, slaves; comp. Rev. xviii. 13.

3 טוֹב *adj.* good.

4 יָטַב to be well, prosperous; to do good, to use well; to give wealth. HIPHIL *fut.*

5 כֹּחַ *m.* strength, might, power; *trop.* ability, *i. e.* wealth, riches.

6 נְכָסִים *m. pl.* riches, treasures.

7 רְוָיָה *f.* abundant moisture, abundance.

8 שָׁלֵו *adj.* secure, tranquil, at rest; especially of one enjoying quiet prosperity.

Gen. xxxiv. 29.	2	Job xxi. 13.	3	Prov. xiii. 22.	2
Deut. viii. 17, 18.	2	xxxi. 25.	2	xviii. 11.	1
Ruth ii. 1.	2	Ps. xlix. 6, 10.	2	xix. 4.	1
1 Sam. ii. 32.	4	lxvi. 12.	7	Eccles. v. 19.	6
2 Kings xv. 20.	2	cxii. 3.	1	vi. 2.	6
2 Chron. i. 11, 12.	6	Prov. v. 10.	5	Jer. xlix. 31.	8
Ezra ix. 12.	3	x. 15.	1	Zech. xiv. 14.	2
Esth. x. 3.	3	xiii. 11.	1		

WEAN

גָּמַל to ripen; *trans.* to wean a child; by a beautiful and appropriate figure this word is used both of vegetable and animal œconomy, but, as Michaelis observes, it is difficult to say which is the primary reference. KAL ᵃ*pret.* ᵇ*inf.* ᶜ*fut.* ᵈ*part.* Paül. NIPHAL ᵉ*inf.* ᶠ*fut.*

Gen. xxi. 8, 8.	f e	1 Sam. i. 24.	a	Isa. xi. 8.	d
1 Sam. i. 22.	d f	1 Kings xi. 20.	d	xxviii. 9.	d
i. 23, 23.	b	Ps. cxxxi. 2, 2.	d	Hos. i. 8.	c

WEAPON

1 אָזֵן *m.* furniture, utensil: Deut. xxiii. 13, *or,* thou shalt have a little spade among thy furniture.

2 כְּלִי *m.* a general name for all vessels, tools, instruments, &c.

3 נֶשֶׁק *m.* armour, weapon, collectively weapons.

4 שֶׁלַח *m.* a missile weapon, as sent against an enemy.

Gen. xxvii. 3.	2	2 Chron. xxiii. 7.	2	Jer. xxi. 4.	2
Num. xxxv. 18.	2	xxiii. 10.	4	xxii. 7.	2
Deut. i. 41.	2	Neh. iv. 17.	4	li. 25.	2
xxiii. 13.	1	Job xx. 24.	3	li. 20.	2
Judg. xviii. 11, 16, 17.	2	Eccles. ix. 18.	2	Ezek. ix. 1, 2.	2
1 Sam. xxi. 8.	2	Isa. xiii. 5.	2	xxxii. 27.	2
2 Sam. i. 27.	2	liv. 17.	2	xxxix. 9, 10.	3
2 Kings xi. 8.	2				

WEAR

1 בְּלָא Ch. to affliot, to vex; to wear out, *i. e.* to persecute with the purpose of entire annihilation. PAEL *fut.*

2 לָבַשׁ to put on. KAL ᵃ*pret.* ᵇ*fut.*

3 נָבֵל to fade, as the leaf of a tree for want of moisture. KAL ᵃ*inf.* ᵇ*fut.*

4 נָשָׂא to bear. KAL ᵃ*inf.* ᵇ*part.* Poel.

5 שָׁחַק to rub or wear away. KAL *pret.*

Exod. xviii. 18.	3 b a	1 Sam. xxii. 18.	4 b	Isa. iv. 1.	2 b
Deut. xxii. 11.	2 b	Esth. vi. 8.	2 a	Dan. vii. 25.	1
1 Sam. i. 28.	4 a	Job xiv. 19.	5	Zech. xiii. 4.	2 b
xiv. 3.	4 b				

WEARY

1 מָרַח to impose a burden, so as to weary. Hiphil *fut.* Job xxxvii. 11, by a striking figure representing the service imposed on the clouds. Others suppose the meaning of the verb to be to cast down, or to drive forward ; but it is probable that the true meaning is to weary or tire.

2 יָגַע to labour, to toil, especially with wearisome and painful effort ; it seems also to imply dislike or disgust ; *seq.* בְּ. Kal ᵃ *pret.* ᵇ *fut.* Piel ᶜ *fut.* Hiphil ᵈ *pret.* ᵉ יָגֵעַ *adj.* wearied. ᶠ יְגִיעָה *f.* weariness. ᵍ יָגִיעַ *adj.* wearied.

3 יָעַף to be wearied, faint, either with running, or, also, with severe labour, and also thirst ; hence to be wearied out, exhausted. Kal ᵃ *pret.* ᵇ *fut.* ᶜ יָעֵף *adj.* fatigued.

4 כֹּחַ *m.* strength ; *marg.* ' wearied (in) strength.'

5 לָאָה to be wearied, exhausted, *seq.* לְ *c. inf.* to labour in vain, not to be able, Gen. xix. 11 ; Hiph. to weary out, to tire one's patience. Kal ᵃ *fut.* Niphal ᵇ *pret.* Hiphil ᶜ *pret.* ᵈ *inf.* ᵉ *fut.* ᶠ מַתְלָאָה, contracted from מַה־תְלָאָה, what a weariness.

6 נָקַט to be weary of, to loathe ; *seq.* בְּ. Kal *pret.*

7 עוּף to cover, to cover over or be covered with darkness ; see *Faint.* Kal *fut.*

8 עָיֵף to languish, to faint, to fail. Kal ᵃ *pret.* ᵇ עָיֵף *adj.* languid, faint, weary, of one fatigued with travel or labour, and oppressed also with thirst.

9 עָמָל *m.* trouble, and pain of the severest kind.

10 קוּץ to loathe, to feel disgust, to abhor anything. Kal ᵃ *pret.* ᵇ *fut.*

11 שָׂבַע to be satisfied, satiate. Kal *fut.*

Gen. xix. 11.	5 a	Ps. lxix. 3.	2 a	Isa. l. 4.	3 c
xxvii. 46.	10 a	Prov. iii. 11.	10 b	lvii. 10.	2 a
Deut. xxv. 18.	2 e	xxv. 17.	11	Jer. ii. 24.	3 b
Judg. iv. 21.	7	Eccles. x. 15.	2 c	iv. 31.	8 a
viii. 15.	3 c	xii. 12.	2 f	vi. 11.	5 b
2 Sam. xvi. 14.	8 b	Isa. i. 14.	5 b	ix. 5.	5 b
xvii. 2.	2 e	v. 27.	8 b	xii. 5.	5 b
xvii. 29.	8 b	vii. 13, 13.	5 d e	xv. 6.	5 b
xxiii. 10.	2 a	xvi. 12.		xx. 9.	5 b
Job iii. 17.	2 g, 4	xxviii. 12.	8 b	xxxi. 25.	8 b
vii. 3. a	9	xxxii. 32.	8 b	li. 58, 64.	3 a
x. 1.	6	xl. 28, 30, 31.	2 b	Ezek. xxiv. 12.	5 c
xvi. 7.	5 c	xliii. 22.	2 a	Micah vi. 3.	5 c
xxii. 7.	8 b	xliii. 23, 24.	2 d	Hab. ii. 13.	3 b
xxxvii. 11.	1	xlvi. 1.	8 b	Mal. i. 13.	5 f
Ps. vi. 6.	2 a	xlvii. 13.	5 b	ii. 17, 17.	2 d
lxviii. 9.	5 b				

a lit. of trouble.

WEASEL

חֹלֶד *m.* a weasel, so called from its swift gliding motion, or from its gliding into holes. So Lxx., Vulg., Targ. Jon., and so Talmud ; Syr. and Arab. signify a mole, as Bochart understands the word. Lev. xi. 29.

WEATHER

זָהָב *m.* gold ; *metaph.* of the golden brightness of the sky so remarkable in Egypt and other dry sandy Eastern countries ; or specially for the sun itself. Job xxxvii. 22, " Fair weather."

יוֹם *m.* day : Prov. xxv. 20.

WEAVE

אָרַג to plait, to braid ; of the spider, whence Gr. ἀράχνη ; to weave with a shuttle. Kal *fut.* Judg. xvi. 13 : Isa. lix. 5. *part.* Poel, Exod. xxviii. 32, *lit.* work of the weaver ; xxxv. 35 ; xxxix. 22, *lit.* work of the weaver, 27 : 1 Sam. xvii. 7 : 2 Sam. xxi. 19 : 2 Kings xxiii. 7 : 1 Chron. xi. 23 ; xx. 5 : Isa. xix. 9 ; xxxviii. 12.

WEB

בַּיִת *m.* house : Job viii. 14, *marg.* ' spider's house.'

מַסֶּכֶת *f.* the thread, the warp, in weaving : Judg. xvi. 13, 14.

קוּרִים *m. pl.* fine threads, spiders' webs : Isa. lix. 5, 6.

WEDGE

לָשׁוֹן *com.* tongue ; wedge or bar of gold : perhaps a golden ornament of considerable size : Josh. vii. 21, 24.

WEDLOCK

נָאַף to commit adultery, to break wedlock. Kal *part.* Poel, Ezek. xvi. 38.

WEED

סוּף *m.* rush, reed, sedge, sea-weed : Jonah ii. 5.

WEEK

שָׁבוּעַ *m.* a seven, se'nnight, ἑβδομάς, *i.e.* a week ; (1) properly a week of days, seven days, Dan. x. 2, " three full weeks." Pentecost was called the festival of weeks from the seven weeks reckoned from the passover ; but in Ezek. xlv. 21 the festival of sevens of days is the passover, as being celebrated each time during seven whole days : (2) week of years, seven years, Dan. ix. 24, &c. ; *comp. hebdomas annorum*, Gell, N. A. iii. 10, Aristot. Polit. vii. 16. *Sing.* Gen. xxix. 27, 28 : Dan. ix. 27, 27. *Dual,* Lev. xii. 5. *Plur. m.* Dan. ix. 24, 25, 25, 26 ; x. 2, *lit.* weeks days ; 3, *lit. id. Plur. f.* Exod. xxxiv. 22 : Num. xxviii. 26 : Deut. xvi. 9, 9, 10, 16 ; 2 Chron. viii. 13 : Jer. v. 24.

WEEP

1 בָּכָה to drop, to distil, to flow in drops ; specially to weep, and in this sense common to all the kindred languages and dialects ; often of a people making lamentation under public calamities, also of the sorrow of a penitent. *Seq. acc.* to weep for any one, to mourn, to lament ; especially for one dead ; also *seq.* עַל of person or thing, אֶל and לְ. Further *seq.* עַל is to come weeping to any one, Num. xi. 13, Judg. xiv. 16 ; also to weep upon any one, *i. e.* in his embrace, Gen. xlv. 15 ; l. 1. Kal ᵃ *pret.* ᵇ *inf.* ᶜ *imp.* ᵈ *fut.* ᵉ *part.* Poel. Piel ᶠ *part.* ᵍ בָּכֶה *m.* weeping. ʰ בְּכִי *m.* weeping.

2 דָּמַע to weep, to shed tears. Kal ᵃ *inf.* ᵇ *fut.*

3 נָתַן to give. Kal *fut.*

Gen. xxi. 16.	1 d	Gen. xlv. 14, 14.	1 d a	Num. xxv. 6.	1 e
xxiii. 2.	1 b	xlv. 15.	1 d	Deut. i. 45.	1 d
xxvii. 38.	1 d	xlvi. 29.	1 d	xxxiv. 8, 8.	1 d h
xxix. 11.	1 d	l. 1, 17.	1 d	Judg. ii. 4.	1 d
xxxiii. 4.	1 d	Exod. ii. 6.	1 e	xiv. 16, 17.	1 d
xxxvii. 35.	1 d	Num. xi. 4, 13, 20.	1 d	xx. 23, 26. a	1 d
xlii. 24.	1 d	xi. 10.	1 e	xxi. 2. a	1 d h
xliii. 30, 30.	1 b d	xi. 18.	1 a	Ruth i. 9, 14.	1 d
xlv. 2.	3, 1 h	xiv. 1.	1 d	1 Sam. i. 7, 8.	1 d

1 Sam. i. 10.	1 b d	Neh. i. 4.	1 d	Jer. ix. 1.	1 d
xi. 4, 5.	1 d	viii. 9, 9.	1 d e	ix. 10.	1 h
xx. 41.	1 d	Esth. iv. 3.	1 d	xiii. 17.	1 d
xxiv. 16.	1 d	Job ii. 12.	1 h	xiii. 17.	2 a b
xxx. 4, 4.	1 d b	xvi. 16.	1 h	xxii. 10.	1 d
2 Sam. i. 12.	1 d	xxvii. 15.	1 d	xxii. 10.	1 b c
i. 24.	1 c	xxx. 25.	1 a	xxxi. 9, 16.	1 h
iii. 16, 34.β	1 b	xxx. 31.	1 e	xxxi. 15, 15.	1 h f
iii. 32, 32.	1 d	Ps. vi. 11.	1 h	xli. 6.	1 e
xii. 21, 22.	1 d	xxx. 5.	1 h	xlviii. 5.δ	1 h
xiii. 36, 36.γ	1 d a h	lxix. 10.	1 d	xlviii. 32, 32.	1 d h
xv. 23.	1 e	cii. 9.	1 h	l. 4.	1 e
xv. 30, 30.	1 e b	cxxvi. 6.	1 b	Lam. i. 2.ε	1 b d
xviii. 33.	1 d	cxxxvii. 1.	1 a	i. 16.	1 e
xix. 1.	1 e	Eccles. iii. 4.	1 b	Ezek. viii. 14.	1 f
2 Kings viii. 11.	1 d	Isa. xv. 2, 3.	1 h	xxiv. 16, ζ 23.	1 h
viii. 12.	1 e	xv. 5.	1 h	xxvii. 31.	1 h
xiii. 14.	1 d	xvi. 9.	1 h	Hos. xii. 4.	1 a
xx. 3.	1 d h	xxii. 4, 12.	1 h	Joel i. 5.	1 h
xxii. 19.	1 d	xxx. 19.	1 b d	ii. 12.	1 h
2 Chron. xxxiv. 27.	1 d	xxxiii. 7.	1 d	ii. 17.	1 d
Ezra iii. 12.	1 e	xxxviii. 3.	1 d h	Micah i. 10.	1 b d
iii. 13.	1 h	lxv. 19.	1 h	Zech. vii. 3.	1 d
x. 1, 1.	1 e a g	Jer. iii. 21.	1 h	Mal. ii. 13.	1 h

α *lit.* wept a great weeping. β *lit.* added to weep. γ *lit.* with a great weeping greatly. δ *lit.* in weeping shall go up weeping. ε *lit.* in weeping she weepeth. ζ *lit.* and thou shalt not weep.

WEIGH, WEIGHT

1 אֶבֶן *com.* a stone; a weight of a balance, even when not made of stone; since anciently, as at the present day, the Orientals often made use of stones for weights; *comp.* Eng. stone, for a weight of fourteen pounds.

2 נֵטֶל *m.* a burden, load.

3 פָּלַס to bring a thing to an exactness by a level; to weigh, which is done by making the balance even. PIEL ᵃ*fut.* ᵇ פֶּלֶס *m.* a balance, so called from being even, level.

4 שָׁקַל to poise, to weigh; the primary idea being to suspend the balance. KAL ᵃ*pret.* ᵇ*inf.* ᶜ*fut.* NIPHAL ᵈ*pret.* ᵉ*fut.* ᶠ מִשְׁקוֹל *m.* weight. ᵍ מִשְׁקָל *m.* weighing, act of weighing, weight.

5 תָּכַן to make even, to level; to poise, to weigh by the equilibrium of the balance. KAL ᵃ*part.* Poel. NIPHAL ᵇ*pret.* PIEL ᶜ*pret.*

6 תְּקַל Ch. to poise, to weigh. P'IL *pret.*

Gen. xxiii. 16.	4 c	1 Kings x. 14.	4 g	Prov. xi. 1.	1
xxiv. 22, 22.	4 g	2 Kings xxv. 16.	4 g	xvi. 2.	5 a
xliii. 21.α	4 g	1 Chron. xx. 2.	4 g	xvi. 11, 11.	3 b, 1
Lev. xix. 35.	4 g	xxi. 25.	4 g	xx. 10.	1
xix. 36.	1	xxii. 3, 14.	4 g	xx. 23.	1
xxvi. 26.	4 g	xxviii. 14, 14, 15, 15, 15, 16, 17, 17, 18.	4 g	xxvii. 2.	2
Num. vii. 13, 19, 25, 31, 37, 43, 49, 55, 61, 67, 73, 79.	4 g	2 Chron. iii. 9.	4 g	Isa. xxvi. 7.	3 a
Deut. xix. 13, 15.	1	iv. 18.	4 g	xl. 12.	4 a
Josh. vii. 21.	4 g	ix. 13.	4 g	xlvi. 6.	4 c
Judg. xvi. 5.	4 g	Ezra viii. 25, 26, 29.	4 g	Jer. xxxii. 9, 10.	4 c
1 Sam. ii. 3.	5 b	viii. 30, 34, 34.	4 g	lii. 20.	4 c
xvii. 5.	4 g	viii. 33.	4 d	Ezek. iv. 10, 16.	4 f
2 Sam. xii. 30.	4 g	Job vi. 2.	4 b e	v. 1.	4 g
xiv. 26, 26.	4 a, 1	xxviii. 15.	4 g	Dan. v. 27.	6
xxi. 16. 16.	4 g	xxviii. 25, 25.	4 g, 5 c	Micah vi. 11.	1
1 Kings vii. 47.	4 g	Ps. lviii. 2.	3 a	Zech. v. 8.	1
				ix. 12.	4 c

α *lit.* in its weight.

WELFARE

טוֹב *adj.* good: Neh. ii. 10.

יְשׁוּעָה *f.* salvation; welfare, prosperity: Job xxx. 15.

שָׁלוֹם *m.* peace: Gen. xliii. 27: Exod. xviii. 7: 1 Chron. xviii. 10: Ps. lxix. 22: Judg. xxxviii. 4.

WELL

1 בְּאֵר *f.* a well, a pit of clear spring water; a pit in which any-thing springeth up; a deep pit, in which a person may be swallowed up and drowned: Gen. xvi. 14, &c.

2 בּוֹר *m.* a pit; a cistern hewn out of stone.

3 עַיִן *com.* the eye; a well or fountain with water springing up in it, which is like an eye in the ground, clear and bright. ᵃ מַעְיָן *m.* a place of fountains, a fountain.

4 מָקוֹר *m.* a fountain, opened by digging; well-spring.

No. 1 not included.

Gen. xxiv. 13, 16, 29, 30, 42, 43, 45.	3	2 Sam. iii. 26.	2	Neh. ix. 25.	2
xlix. 22.	3	xxiii. 15, 16.	2	Ps. lxxiv. 6.	3 a
Exod. xv. 27.	3	2 Kings iii. 19, 25.	3 a	Prov. x. 11.	4
Deut. vi. 11.	2	1 Chron. xi. 17, 18.	2	xvi. 22.	4
Josh. xviii. 15.	3 a	2 Chron. xxvi. 10.	2	xviii. 4.	4
1 Sam. xix. 22.	2	Neh. ii. 13.	3	Isa. xii. 3.	3 a

WELL

1 טוֹב to be good, well. KAL ᵃ*pret.* HIPHIL ᵇ*pret.* ᶜ*part.* ᵈ טוֹב *adj.* good. ᵉ טוּב *m.* goodness.

2 יָטַב to be good, well; *impers.* Hiphil, to make or do well what one does, in the best manner, with an extraordinary degree of attention, earnestness, activity, diligence. Hence, joined with a verb, or standing before an infinitive mood or a gerund, it takes the place and nature of an adverb in our language, and is to be understood as it happens to be applied: to do good to any one, to benefit; *seq. dat.* of person, עִם of person, *seq.* אֶת and *accus.* of person. Once in a bad sense, Ps. xlix. 18, *i.e.* indulgest thine appetites. KAL ᵃ*fut.* HIPHIL ᵇ*pret.* ᶜ*inf., abs.* used as an adverb, well, rightly, greatly. ᵈ*fut.* ᵉ*part.*

3 יָפֶה *adj.* fair; well favoured; see *Favour.*

4 כֵּן *part. adj.* upright, erect; uprightly, right, well.

5 כֵּן *m.* a stand, base, pedestal; of the base or socket of a ship's mast: Isa. xxxiii. 23, *i.e.* they could not make fast the base of their mast.—*Barnes.*

6 לֵב *m.* heart; see *Mark, Look.*

7 מְאֹד *m.,* as an *adv.,* mightily, vehemently; exceedingly, right well.

8 מַעֲשֶׂה *m.* work; "well set hair," *lit.* the work of the curling tool.

9 מֶרְקָחָה *f.* a spicing, seasoning; see *Spice.*

10 שָׁלוֹם *m.* peace.

Gen. iv. 7, 7.	2 d	Ruth iii. 1.	2 a	Ps. cxxviii. 2.	1 d
xii. 13.	2 a	iii. 13.	1 d	cxxxix. 14.	7
xxix. 6, 6.	10	1 Sam. i. 10.	1 d	Prov. xi. 10.γ	1 e
xxix. 17.	3	xvi. 16,α 23.	1 a	xxvii. 23.	6
xxxii. 9.	2 d	xvi. 17.	2 e	xxx. 29.	1 c
xxxvii. 14, 14.	10	xx. 7.	1 d	Eccles. viii. 12, 13.	1 d
xxxix. 6.	3	xxiv. 18, 19.	1 d	Isa. i. 17.	2 c
xl. 14.	10	xxv. 31.	2 b	iii. 10.	1 d
xli. 2, 4, 18.	10	2 Sam. iii. 13.	1 d	iii. 24.	8
xliii. 27.	10	xviii. 28.	10	xxxiii. 23.	5
Exod. i. 20.	2 d	1 Kings ii. 18.	1 d	Jer. i. 12.	2 b
x. 29.	3	viii. 18.	1 b	vii. 23.	2 a
Num. xi. 18.	1 a	xviii. 24.	1 d	xv. 11.	1 d
Deut. iv. 40.	2 a	2 Kings iv. 23, 26, 26, 26, 26.	1 a	xxii. 15, 16.	1 d
v. 16, 29.	2 a	v. 21, 22.	10	xxxviii. 20.	2 a
v. 33.	1 a	ix. 11.	1 d	xl. 9.	2 a
vi. 3, 18.	2 a	x. 30.	1 b	xlii. 6.	2 a
xii. 25, 28.	2 a	xxv. 24.	10	xliv. 17.	1 d
xv. 16.	1 a	2 Chron. vi. 8.	1 d	Ezek. xxiv. 10.	9
xviii. 17.	2 b	xii. 12.β	1 d	xxxiii. 32.	1 c
xix. 13.	1 a	Ps. xlviii. 13.	1 a	xliv. 5, 5.	6
xxii. 7.	2 a	xlix. 18.	2 d	Dan. i. 4.	8
Judg. ix. 16.	1 d	lxxviii. 29.	1 d	Jonah iv. 4, 9, 9.	2 c
		cxix. 65.	1 d	Nah. iii. 4.	1 d
				Zech. viii. 15.	2 c

α *lit.* it shall be well with thee. β *lit.* there were good things. γ *lit.* in the good of.

WEN

יָבֵל *adj.* flowing, running, *sc.* with matter, as a sore, *i. e.* having running sores, ulcers ; spoken of a flock, Lev. xxii. 22. Vulg. *pupulas habens*, having pimples, pustules.

WENCH

שִׁפְחָה *f.* maidservant, handmaid, slave : 2 Sam. xvii. 17.

WEST

1   יָם *m.* sea ; it is also used for the west, westward, because the Mediterranean lies to the west of Palestine : Gen. xii. 8, &c.

2   מָבוֹא *com.* the going down, applied to the setting of the sun, and so to the west, westward.

3   מַעֲרָב *m.* the west, the place where the sun goes down. מַעֲרָבָה *f. id.*

4   שֶׁמֶשׁ *com.* sun ; with מָבוֹא, the going down, sunset.

No. 1 not included.

Josh. xxiii. 4.	2, 4	2 Chron. xxxiii. 14.	3	Isa. xlv. 6.	3 a
1 Chron. vii. 28.	3	Ps. lxxv. 6.	3	lix. 19.	3
xii. 15.	3	ciii. 12.	3	Dan. viii. 5.	3
xxvi. 16, 18, 30.	3	cvii. 3.	3	Zech. viii. 7.	2, 4
2 Chron. xxxii. 30.	3	Isa. xliii. 5.	3		

WET

צְבַע Ch. to dip in, to immerse ; to wet, to moisten. PAEL *part.* Dan. iv. 25. ITHPAEL *fut.* Dan. iv. 15, 23, 33 ; v. 21.

רָטַב to be wet, moistened with rain. KAL *fut.* Job xxiv. 8.

WHALE

תַּנִּין *m.* a great fish, sea monster ; *or*, rather, any reptile or animal of large dimensions, whether of the sea or land : Gen. i. 21 : Job vii. 12. תַּנִּים *m. pl.* Ezek. xxxii. 2.

WHEAT

בַּר and בָּר *m.* corn, grain, properly that which has been cleansed (*comp.* Jer. iv. 11) and is stored up in garners or sold : Jer. xxiii. 28 : Joel ii. 24 : Amos v. 11 ; viii. 5, 6.

דָּגָן *m.* corn, grain of any kind, properly increase : Num. xviii. 12 : Jer. xxxi. 12.

חִטָּה *f.* wheat ; in the singular mostly of the plant as growing in the fields ; *plur.* the grains, *collect.* grain : Gen. xxx. 14, &c.

חִנְטִין Ch. *m. pl.* wheat, probably from its sweetness above other grain : Ezra vi. 9 ; vii. 22.

רִיפוֹת *f. pl.* pounded corn or grain, grits : Prov. xxvii. 22.

WHEEL

אָבְנָיִם *f. dual*, a pair of stones, and spoken of a potter's wheel. It appears to have consisted of two stones, one above and the other below, and is so depicted on Egyptian monuments.—Wilkinson's Manners and Customs of the Ancient Egyptians, iii. p. 164. Jer. xviii. 3, *marg.* 'frames *or* seats.'

אוֹפָן *m.* a wheel of a sledge or carriage : Exod. xiv. 25, &c.

גַּלְגַּל *m.* a wheel of a chariot, also of a well ; a rolling thing :

Isa. xvii. 13.—Ps. lxxxiii. 13 : Eccles. xii. 6 : Isa. v. 28 : Jer. xlvii. 3 : Ezek. x. 2, 6, 13 ; xxiii. 24 ; xxvi. 10. גִּלְגָּל Ch. *m.* Dan. vii. 9. גַּלְגַּל *m.* Isa. xxviii. 28.

פַּעַם *com.* tread of the foot ; step ; paces of a chariot, or of the horses drawing it : Judg. v. 28.

WHELP

בֵּן *m.* son : Job iv. 11 ; xxviii. 8.

גּוּר *com.* a whelp, *sc.* of a lion : Jer. li. 38 : Nah. ii. 12. גּוּר *m.* a whelp, cub ; so called as still a suckling ; specially of a lion's whelp, different from כְּפִיר, *i. e.* a young lion already weaned, and beginning to seek prey for itself. Once of the whelp of the jackal. Gen. xlix. 9 : Deut. xxxiii. 22 : Ezek. xix. 2, 3, 5 : Nah. ii. 11.

WHET

לָטַשׁ to sharpen. KAL *pret.* Ps. vii. 12.

קָלַל to be light ; Pilpel, to shake ; to polish. PILPEL *pret.* Eccles. x. 10.

שָׁנַן to sharpen. KAL *pret.* Deut. xxxii. 41 : Ps. lxiv. 3.

WHIP

שׁוֹט *m.* (see *Scourge*) : 1 Kings xii. 11, 14 : 2 Chron. x. 11, 14 : Prov. xxvi. 3 : Nah. iii. 2.

WHIRL

הָלַךְ to go. KAL *part.* Poel, Eccles. i. 6, "it whirleth about continually."

סָבַב to go about. KAL *part.* Poel, Eccles. i. 6, *lit.* turning about, turning about, going.

WHIRLWIND

1   סוּפָה *f.* a whirlwind, which cometh suddenly, with great violence, sweeping all away before it ; it implies also great swiftness, Isa. v. 28 ; and waste, Hos. viii. 7 ; in Amos and Nahum, rendered by the Lxx. συντέλεια.

2   סָעַר to be violently agitated, to rush on as a tempest ; to scatter as with a whirlwind. KAL *ᵃ fut.* Hab. iii. 14, *marg.* 'were tempestuous.' PIEL *ᵇ fut.* PUAL *ᶜ fut.* *ᵈ* סַעַר *m.* a storm, tempest. *ᵉ* סְעָרָה *f. id.*

3   רוּחַ *com.* wind : Ezek. i. 4, *lit.* a wind of storm.

4   שָׂעַר to take away as with a whirlwind. KAL *ᵃ fut.* HITHPAEL *ᵇ fut.*

2 Kings ii. 1, 11.	2 e	Isa. xxi. 1.	1	Dan. xi. 40.	4 b
Job xxxvii. 9.	1	xl. 24.	2 e	Hos. viii. 7.	1
xxxviii. 1.	2 e	xli. 16.	2 e	xiii. 3.	2 c
xl. 6.	2 e	lxvi. 15.	1	Amos i. 14.	1
Ps. lviii. 9:	4 a	Jer. iv. 13.	1	Nah. i. 3.	1
Prov. i. 27.	1	xxiii. 19, 19.	2 e d	Hab. iii. 14.	2 a
x. 25.	1	xxv. 32.	2 d	Zech. vii. 14.	2 b
Isa. v. 28.	1	xxx. 23, 23.	2 e d	ix. 14.	2 e
xvii. 13.	1	Ezek. i. 4.	3, 2 e		

WHISPER

לָחַשׁ to whisper, to mutter, either so as not to be heard distinctly, or with a secret design. HITHPAEL *fut.* Ps. xli. 7. *part.* 2 Sam. xii. 19.

צָפַף to peep, to chirp, as a small bird. Gr. πιπίζω, τιτίζω. Like the Gr. τρίζω, it is transferred to the voice of the manes or shades, which the wizards professed to imitate. PILPEL *fut.* Isa. xxix. 4.

נִרְגָּן *m.* garrulous; a whisperer, tale-bearer, calumniator: Prov. xvi. 28.

WHIT

דָּבָר *m.* word: 1 Sam. iii. 18, *marg.* 'all the things, *or,* words.'

כָּלִיל *adj.* wholly: Deut. xiii. 16.

WHITE

1 דַּר *m.* a species of marble, resembling pearl.

2 חוּר *m.* fine white linen. ᵃ חִוָּר Ch. *adj.* ᵇ חֹרִי *m.* white bread made of white flour. See *Hole.*

3 לָבֵן to be white; to make white; *metaph.* to purify, to cleanse from the filth of sin. HIPHIL ᶜ *pret.* ᵇ *inf.* ᶜ *fut.* HITHPAEL ᵈ *fut.* ᵉ לָבָן *adj.* white, Gen. xxx. 35, &c. ᶠ לָבָן *adj. id.*

4 צָחַח to be bright, to be of a dazzling white. KAL ᵃ *pret.* ᵇ צַח *adj.* bright, white.

5 צַחַר *m.* whiteness, of wool. ᵃ צָחֹר *adj.* white, of she-asses; probably those of a very light colour. The asses used in Egypt by the wealthier Copts and others are almost perfectly white.

6 רִיר *m.* spittle, slaver; white (of an egg).

No. 3 e not included.

Gen. xl. 16.		2 b	Job vi. 6.		6	Ezek. xxvii. 18.		5
xlix. 12.		3 f	Ps. li. 7.		3 c	Dan. vii. 9.		2 a
Judg. v. 10.		5 a	Cant. v. 10.		4 b	xi. 35.		3 b
Esth. i. 6, 6.		1, 2	Isa. i. 18.		3 c	xii. 10.		3 d
viii. 15.		2	Lam. iv. 7.		4 a	Joel i. 7.		3 a

WHOLE, WHOLESOME, WHOLLY

1 חָיָה to live, to live again, to become well. KAL *inf.*

2 יוֹם *m.* day, used pleonastically after words denoting a certain space of time, and rendered "whole."

3 כָּלָה to be completed. PIEL *fut.*

4 כָּלִיל *adj.* complete; the whole, wholly.

5 מָלָא to fill, to make full: in Piel, joined with another verb, it has an adverbial force, also with אַחֲרֵי, to follow fully. PIEL ᵃ *pret.*

6 מִקְשָׁה *f.* wreathed, or turned work, "of a whole piece."

7 רָפָא to heal. KAL ᵃ *fut.* NIPHAL ᵇ *inf.* ᶜ מַרְפֵּא *m.* healing; sound, wholesome.

8 שָׁלֵם *adj.* whole, sound, perfect; whole, safe, unharmed. ᵃ שָׁלוֹם *m.* sound, whole.

9 תָּמַם to complete, to perfect; to be finished. KAL ᵃ *inf.* ᵇ תָּמִים *adj.*

Lev. iii. 9.		9 b	Num. xxxii. 11, 12.		5 a	Josh. xiv. 8, 9, 14.		5 a
vi. 22, 23.		4	Deut. i. 36.		5 a	Judg. xix. 2.		2
xix. 9.		3	xxvii. 6.		8	1 Sam. vii. 9.		4
xxv. 29.α		9 a	xxxiii. 10.β		4	Job v. 18.		7 a
Num. iv. 6.		4	Josh. v. 8.		1	Ps. li. 19.		4
x. 2.		6	viii. 31.		8	Prov. i. 12.		9 b
xi. 20, 21.		2	x. 13.		9 b	xv. 4.		7 c

Jer. xiii. 19.		8 a	Ezek. xv. 5.		9 b	Amos i. 6.		8
xix. 11.		7 b	Dan. x. 3.γ		2	i. 9.		8

α lit. until the year be finished. *β* "whole burnt sacrifice."
γ lit. three weeks days.

WHORE

1 אִשָּׁה *f.* a woman.

2 זָנָה to commit fornication, to play the whore or harlot; properly and chiefly spoken of a female, whether married or unmarried. *Constr.* with *acc.* of the male paramour, also *seq.* בְּ with אֶל, and very often *seq.* אַחֲרֵי. On the other hand, the husband from whom a woman departs in playing the whore, against whom she commits this crime, is put with מִן, Ps. lxxiii. 27; מֵאַחֲרֵי, Hos. i. 2; מִתַּחַת, iv. 12; and תַּחַת, Ezek. xxiii. 5 (*comp.* Num. v. 19, 29); מֵעַל, Hos. ix. 1; and עַל, Judg. xix. 2, Ezek. xvi. 15. Rarely this verb is applied to men. Num. xxv. 1, *seq.* אֶל. *Trop.* of idolatry; the relation existing between God and the Israelitish people being everywhere shadowed forth by the prophets under the emblem of the conjugal union, see Hos. i. and ii., Ezek. xvi. and xxiii., so that the people in worshipping other gods are compared to a harlot and adulteress. It is also said of superstitions connected with idolatry, Lev. xx. 6, as to consult wizards, &c. is to depart from the faith and trust which are due to God. KAL ᵃ *pret.* ᵇ *inf.* ᶜ *fut.* KAL ᵈ *part.* Poel. PUAL ᵉ *pret.* HIPHIL ᶠ *pret.* ᵍ *inf.* ʰ *fut.* זְנוּנִים *m. pl.* whoredom. ᵏ זְנוּת *f.* whoredom, fornication, only *trop.* of idolatry, or of any breach of fidelity towards God, *e.g.* of a murmuring and seditious people. ˡ תַּזְנוּת *f.* fornication, whoredom, *metaph.* for idol worship.

3 קְדֵשָׁה *f. pr.* sacred, consecrated; devoted to wickedness.

Gen. xxxviii. 24.		2 i	2 Chron. xxi. 13, 13.		2 h g	Ezek. xxiii. 14, 17,
Exod. xxxiv. 15.		2 d	Ps. lxxiii. 27.		2 c	18, 19.		2 l
xxxiv. 16, 16.		2 a f	cvi. 39.		2 c	xxiii. 27.		2 k
Lev. xvii. 7.		2 d	Prov. vi. 26.		2 c	xxiii. 29, 29.		2 l i
xix. 29, 29.		2 g c	xxiii. 27.		2 d	xxiii. 30.		2 b
xx. 5, 5.		2 d b	Isa. lvii. 3.α		2 a	xxiii. 35, 43.		2 l
xxi. 7.		2 d	Jer. iii. 2, 9.		2 k	xliii. 7, 9.		2 k
xxi. 9.		2 b	iii. 3.β		1, 2 d	Hos. i. 2, 2.		2 i
Num. xv. 33.		2 k	Ezek. vi. 9, 9.		2 d	i. 2.		2 b c
xv. 39.		2 d	xvi. 17, 28.		2 c	ii. 2, 4.		2 f
xxv. 1.		2 b	xvi. 20, 22, 25, 26.		2 l	iv. 10.		2 f
Deut. xxii. 21.		2 b	xvi. 30.		2 d	iv. 11.		2 k
xxiii. 17.		3	xvi. 33, 33.		2 d l	iv. 12, 12.		2 i c
xxiii. 18.		2 d	xvi. 34, 34.		2 l e	iv. 13.		2 c
xxxi. 16.		2 a	xvi. 36.		2 l	iv. 14, 14.		2 c d
Judg. ii. 17.		2 a	xx. 30.		2 d	iv. 18.		2 g f
viii. 27, 33.		2 c	xxiii. 3, 3.		2 c a	v. 3.		2 f
ix. 2.		2 c	xxiii. 7, 8, 8.		2 l	vi. 10.		2 k
2 Kings ix. 22.		2 i	xxiii. 11, 11.		2 l i	Nah. iii. 4, 4.		2 i
1 Chron. v. 25.		2 l					

α lit. and she will commit whoredom. *β lit.* a woman a whore.

WICKED

1 אָוֶן *m.* nothingness, vanity, especially in a moral sense; having evidently some affinity with אַיִן, nothing: yet some derive it from אָוָה, to desire; to lust; hence inward wickedness, that which has its foundation in corrupt affections, in which sense Ps. cxix. 133 is certainly to be understood; see *Iniquity.* Wicked men are those who pursue that which is vain and false with lawless desire, casting off the fear of God, and so come at length to trouble and sorrow.

2 אָנֵשׁ see *Desperate*. KAL *part.* Paül.

3 בְּלִיַּעַל *m.* (see *Belial*), worthlessness, badness, wickedness; "wicked," *lit.* of Belial.

4 דָּבָר *m.* word, matter, &c.

5 הַוָּה *f.* desire, cupidity; fall, ruin, calamities, a sinking of the mind into a corrupt, depraved state, into a gulf of lusts and insatiable desires. Also calamities, which one prepares for another, hence mischief, wickedness.

6 זִמָּה *f.* mischief meditated, plotted, and designed; such wickedness as shows itself to be fixed and settled in the heart, audacious, daring wickedness; specially of crimes arising from unchastity, as rape, incest. ª מְזִמָּה *f.* meditation, thought; oftener, in a bad sense, evil counsel, wicked purpose.

7 חֶסֶד *m.* This word, implying zeal, earnestness, is sometimes used in a bad sense, not only kindness towards, but zeal against, reproach; hence a wicked thing.

8 עָוָה to act perversely. HIPHIL *pret.*

9 עַוָּל *m.* (see *Iniquity*), evil, wicked, ungodly. ª עַוְלָה *f. id.* ᵇ עוֹלָה *f. id.*

10 עָמָל *m.* labour, toil; trouble, vexation, sorrow. ª עָמֵל *adj.* troublesome.

11 עֶצֶב *m.* labour, sorrow: Ps. cxxxix. 24, *marg.* 'way of pain, or grief,' *i. e.* that which causes grief.

12 רָעַע to break, to break in pieces; to be evil, bad; to do ill, to act wickedly. HIPHIL ª *pret.* ᵇ *inf.* ᶜ *fut.* ᵈ *part.* ᵉ רַע *adj.* bad, evil, worthless; morally bad, evil, wicked. ᶠ רֹעַ *m.* evil; evil, in a moral sense wickedness, depravity.

13 רָשַׁע There can be no doubt but that the general meaning of this word is, to be wicked, impious, ungodly, in *opp.* to צָדַק; but there is difficulty in ascertaining the primary sense. I fully acquiesce in that which has been mostly adopted, to be in a restless, unquiet state, answering to the description in Isa. lvii. 20, 21, tossed with various evil passions, distracted by many forms of wickedness, and having no peace of conscience. This agrees with the interpretation of the Rabbins, Aben-Ezra and Kimchi; and in Job xxxiv. 29 it has the meaning of giving trouble, in *opp.* to quietness. It is descriptive of the wicked, in respect to their internal state, their violent commotions within, the disquietude springing from sinful desires, which constantly impels them to fresh misdeeds.—*Hengstenberg.* Taylor adds this signification, to confound all right and wrong, just and unjust, truth and falsehood, good and evil; or to think and act as if there were no difference of persons, things, or actions. This is to throw the state of human affairs into the greatest confusion, this is to be wicked, or do wrong. KAL ª *pret.* ᵇ *fut.* HIPHIL ᶜ *pret.* ᵈ *inf.* ᵉ *fut.* ᶠ *part.* ᵍ רָשָׁע *adj.* unjust, guilty, wrong-doer; wicked, ungodly, impious; spoken of those who forsake the way of righteousness, and follow after many evil ways, Exod. ix. 27, Ps. i. 1, ·4, xxxvii. 10, Isa. xlviii. 22, lvii. 20, 21, Ezek. xxxiii. 8, 9, 11, 19; who

plot against and persecute the righteous, Ps. x. 2, xxxvii. 12, 32, Jer. v. 26; who borrow and pay not again, Ps. xxxvii. 21; is terrible in strength and violence, Ps. xxxvii. 35; who acquires wealth in order to sin, Prov. x. 16; who comes to an unhappy end, Prov. ii. 22, 1 Sam. ii. 9.—Gen. xviii. 23, &c. ʰ רֶשַׁע *m.* injustice, unrighteousness; specially fraud, falsehood; wickedness, ungodliness; *opp.* צֶדֶק, Ps. xlv. 7. ⁱ רִשְׁעָה *f.* ᵏ מִרְשַׁעַת *f.* wickedness, *concr.* wicked woman, as *scelus* for *scelesta*.

No. 13 g not included.

Gen. vi. 5.	12 e	Job xxiv. 20.	9 a	Eccles. vii. 17.	13 b
xiii. 13.	12 e	xxvii. 4.	9 a	vii. 25.	13 h
xix. 7.	12 c	xxix. 17.	9	viii. 8.	13 h
xxxviii. 7.	12 e	xxxi. 3.	9	Isa. ix. 18.	13 i
xxxix. 9.	12 e	xxxiv. 8,β 10.	13 h	xlvii. 10.	12 e
Lev. xviii. 17.	6	xxxiv. 12.	13 e	lviii. 4, 6.	13 h
xix. 29.	6	xxxiv. 18.	3	Jer. i. 16.	12 e
xx. 14, 14.	6	xxxiv. 36.	1	ii. 19, 33.	12 e
xx. 17.	7	xxxv. 8.	13 h	iii. 2.	12 e
Deut. ix. 4, 5.	13 i	Ps. v. 4.	13 i	iv. 14, 18.	12 e
ix. 18.	12 e	v. 9.	12 e	v. 28.	12 e
ix. 27.	6	ix. 9, 9.	12 e, 13 g	vi. 7, 29	12 e
xiii. 11. a	12 e, 4	x. 15, 15.	13 h g	vii. 12.	12 e
xv. 9.	3	xviii. 21.	13 a	viii. 6.	12 e
xvii. 2, 5.	12 e	xxii. 16.	12 d	xii. 4.	12 e
xxiii. 9.	12 e	xxvii. 12.	12 d	xiv. 16.	12 e
xxviii. 20.	12 f	xxviii. 4.	12 f	xiv. 20.	13 h
Judg. ix. 56.	12 e	xlv. 7.	13 h	xv. 21.	12 e
xx. 3, 12.	12 e	lii. 7.	5	xvii. 9.	2
1 Sam. xii. 17, 20.	12 e	lv. 11.	5	xxii. 22.	12 e
xii. 25.	12 b	lv. 15.	12 e	xxiii. 11, 14.	12 e
xxiv. 13, 13.	12 h g	lviii. 2.	9 b	xxxiii. 5.	12 e
xxv. 39.	12 e	lix. 5.	1	xliv. 3, 5, 9, 9, 9,	
xxx. 22.	12 e	lxiv. 2.	12 d	9.	12 e
2 Sam. iii. 34.	9 a	lxxiii. 8.	12 e	Lam. i. 22.	12 e
iii. 39.	12 e	lxxiv. 3.	12 a	Ezek. iii. 19, 19,	
vii. 10.	9 a	lxxxiv. 10.	13 h	19.	13 g h g
xxii. 22.	13 a	lxxxix. 22.	9 a	v. 6.	13 i
xxiv. 17.	8	xcii. 11.	12 d	vii. 11.	13 h
1 Kings i. 52.	12 e	xciv. 23.	12 e	viii. 9.	12 e
ii. 44, 44.	12 e	ci. 3.	3	xi. 2.	12 e
viii. 47.	13 a	ci. 4.	12 e	xiii. 22, 22.	13 g, 12 e
xxi. 25.	12 e	ci. 8, 8.	13 g, 1	xvi. 23, 57.	12 e
2 Kings xvii. 11.	12 e	cvi. 6.	13 c	xviii. 20.	13 i
xxi. 6.	12 e	cvii. 34.	12 e	xviii. 27, 27.	13 g
xxi. 11.	12 a	cxxv. 3.	13 h	xx. 44.	12 e
1 Chron. xvii. 9.	9 a	cxxxix. 20.	6 a	xxx. 12.	12 e
2 Chron. vi. 37.	13 a	cxli. 4. γ	13 h	xxxi. 11.	13 h
vii. 14.	12 e	Prov. ii. 14.	12 e	xxxiii. 12, 12,	
xx. 35.	13 c	iv. 17.	13 h	12.	13 i g h
xxii. 3.	13 d	vi. 12, 18.	1	xxxiii. 19, 19.	13 g i
xxiv. 7.	13 k	viii. 7.	13 h	Dan. ix. 5.	13 c
Neh. ix. 33.	13 c	x. 2.	13 h	ix. 15.	13 a
ix. 35.	12 e	xi. 5, 5.	13 g	xi. 32.	13 f
Esth. vii. 6.	12 e	xi. 21.	12 e	xii. 10, 10, 10.	13 g c g
ix. 25.	12 e	xii. 3.	13 h	Hos. vii. 1, 2, 3.	12 e
Job iv. 8.	10	xii. 13.	12 e	ix. 15, 15.	12 e f
ix. 29.	13 b	xiii. 6.	13 i	x. 13.	13 h
x. 7.	13 b	xiv. 32, 32.	13 g, 12 e	x. 15.δ	12 e
x. 15.	13 a	xv. 26.	12 e	Joel iii. 13.	12 e
xi. 11.	1	xvi. 12.	13 g	Jonah i. 2.	12 e
xi. 14.	9 a	xvii. 4.	12 d	Micah vi. 10, 10.	13 h g
xiii. 7.	9 a	xxi. 12, 12,		vi. 11.ε	13 h
xviii. 21.	9	12.	13 g g, 12 e	Nah. i. 1, 15.	3
xx. 12.	12 e	xxi. 27, 27.	13 g, 6	iii. 19.	12 e
xx. 22.	10 a	xxvi. 23, 26.	12 e	Zech. v. 8.	13 i
xxi. 30.	12 e	Eccles. iii. 16.	13 h	Mal. i. 4.	13 i
xxii. 5.	12 e			iii. 15.	13 i
xxii. 15.	12 e	viii. 15, 15.	13 g, 12 e	iv. 1.ζ	13 i

ª *lit.* according to this evil thing. β *lit.* men of wickedness. γ *lit.* works in wickedness. δ *marg.* 'the evil of your evil' (*comp.* Rom. vii. 13). ε *lit.* balances of wickedness. ζ *lit.* do wickedness.

WIDE

חֶבֶר *com.* society, company, community: Prov. xxi. 9; xxv. 24.

יָד *com.* hand: 1 Chron. iv. 40, *lit.* large of hands: Ps. civ. 25, *lit.* wide of spaces.

מִדָּה *f.* measure: Jer. xxii. 14, *lit.* a house of measures.

רָחַב to be or become wide, large, spacious. HIPHIL *imp.* Ps.

lxxxi. 10. *fut.* Ps. xxxv. 21 : Isa. lvii. 4. רָחָב *adj.* broad, large : 1 Chron. iv. 40 : Job xxx. 14 : Ps. civ. 25. רֹחַב *m.* breadth, width : Ezek. xli. 10.

WIDOW, WIDOWHOOD

אַלְמֹן *m.* widowhood, *trop.* of a state deprived of its king : Isa. xlvii. 9. אַלְמָנָה *f.* widow : Gen. xxxviii. 11, &c. אַלְמָנוּת *f. const.* widowhood : Gen. xxxviii. 14, 19 : 2 Sam. xx. 3 : Isa. liv. 4.

אִשָּׁה *f.* a woman : 1 Kings vii. 14.

WIFE

אִשָּׁה *f.* a woman ; a wife : Gen. ii. 24, &c.

בַּעַל to have dominion ; to marry. KAL *part.* Paül, Gen. xx. 3, *marg.* 'married to a husband :' Isa. liv. 1, "married wife."

נָשִׁים *f. pl.* of אִשָּׁה, wives : Gen. iv. 19, &c. נָשִׁין Ch. *f. pl.* Dan. vi. 24.

יְבֶמֶת *f.* a brother's wife : Deut. xxv. 7, 7, 9.

שֵׁגָל *f.* Ch. the king's wives : Dan. v. 2, 3, 23.

WILD

1 אִיִּים *m.* wild beasts called thoes, or jackal, about the size of a fox, so called from their howling ; numerous in the Eastern countries ; "wild beasts of the islands."

2 זִיז *m.* any wild beasts that stroll about for prey or food ; see *Abound.*

3 פֶּרֶא *com.* wild ass ; see *Ass.*

4 צִיִּים *m. pl.* inhabitants of the desert, men, or animals, such as jackals, ostriches, wild beasts ; *marg.* ' Ziim.'

5 שָׂדֶה *m.* field ; "wild," *lit.* of the field, *or,* in the field.

Gen. xvi. 12.	3	2 Chron. xxv. 18.	5	Isa. xiii. 21.	1
Lev. xxvi. 22.	5	Job xxxix. 15.	5	xiii. 22.	4
2 Sam. ii. 18.	5	Ps. l. 11.	5	xxxiv. 14, 14.	4, 1
2 Kings iv. 39, 39.	5	lxxx. 13.	5	Jer. l. 39, 39.	4, 1
xiv. 9.	5	Isa. xiii. 21.	4	Hos. xiii. 8.	5

WILDERNESS

1 אֶרֶץ *com.* the earth.

2 מִדְבָּר *m.* pasture land, open fields, *i.e.* an uninhabited tract or region, untilled, and adapted only to pasture, Joel ii. 22, Ps. lxv. 12, Jer. xxiii. 10, Joel i. 19, Isa. xlii. 11 ; often, also, a desert, a sterile and solitary region, Isa. xxxii. 15, xxxv. 1, l. 2, Jer. iv. 11, &c. ; also of a region desolated by violence, Isa. xiv. 17, lxiv. 10, Joel ii. 3, iii. 19. With the *art.* everywhere the great Arabian desert, Gen. xiv. 6, xvi. 7, Exod. iii. 1, xiii. 18, Deut. xi. 24 ; of which the different parts are distinguished by separate proper names. *Metaph.* Hos. ii. 3, I have made her as a desert, *i.e.* naked, destitute of everything ; Jer. ii. 31, " have I been a wilderness to Israel ? " *i.e.* have I commanded them to worship me for naught ? have I been barren towards them ? ix. 12 ; Isa. xxvii. 10.—Gen. xiv. 6, &c.

3 יְשִׁימוֹן *m.* desolate, waste, desert.

4 עֲרָבָה *f.* arid tract, sterile region, desert ; see *Plain.*

5 צִיָּה *f.* drought ; dry places. צִיִּים *m. pl.* dwelling in the wilderness.

6 תֹּהוּ *m.* wasteness ; waste, desolate, *marg.* ' or, void place.'

No. 2 not included.

Deut. xxxii. 10.	3	Ps. lxviii. 7.	3	Prov. xxi. 19.	1, 2
Job xii. 24.	6	lxxii. 9.	5 a	Isa. xxiii. 13.	5 a
xxiv. 5.	4	lxiv. 14.	5 a	xxxiii. 9.	4
xxx. 3.	5	lxxviii. 17.	5	Jer. li. 43.	4
xxxix. 6.	4	cvii. 40.	6	Amos vi. 14.	4

WILE, WILILY

נֵכֶל *m.* deceit : Num. xxv. 18. See *Beguile.*

עָרְמָה *f.* craftiness, guile : Josh. ix. 4.

WILL

1 אָבָה to be willing, to acquiesce, consent ; to be well-affected to, Ps. lxxxi. 11, to desire ; to be inclined to in will, desire, and affection ; always with a negative particle, except in Isa. i. 19, Job xxxix. 9 ; implying an opposition to the will, either of another person or one's own ; that will either actually put forth, or such as might have been anticipated.—*Gussetius.* KAL ᵃ *pret.* ᵇ *fut.* ᶜ *part.* Poel.

2 אֵהִי *adv.* where.

3 חָפֵץ to delight. KAL ᵃ *pret.* ᵇ *fut.* ᶜ חָפֵץ *adj.* willing, delighting. ᵈ חֵפֶץ *m.* delight, desire.

4 יָאַל to will, to desire ; of one who undertakes that which he wills, however difficult, implying active volition, *i. q.* to take upon oneself, to assay ; also of one willing to yield ; see *Consent.* HIPHIL ᵃ *pret.* ᵇ *fut.*

5 יָדַע to know. KAL *pret.* Eccles. iv. 13, *marg.* 'knoweth 1 ᵗ to be admonished.'

6 לֵב *m.* heart.

7 נָדַב to impel ; to impel oneself, to be of a willing mind ; to give willingly. KAL ᵃ *pret.* ᵇ *fut.* HITHPAEL ᶜ *part.* ᵈ נְדָבָה *f.* willingness ; a voluntary gift. נָדִיב *adj.* willing, voluntary, ready, prompt ; liberal ; noble, generous.

8 נֶפֶשׁ *com.* soul.

9 צְבָא Ch. to be inclined, prone ; to will, to please. PᵞAL ᵃ *pret.* ᵇ *inf.* ᶜ *fut.* ᵈ *part.*

10 רְעוּת *f.* Ch. wish, will.

11 רָצוֹן *m.* will, pleasure, choice ; selfwill.

Gen. xxiv. 5, 8.	1 b	Judg. xi. 17.	1 a	1 Chron. x. 4.	1 a
xlix. 6.	11	xix. 10, 25.	1 a	xi. 18, 19.	1 a
Exod. x. 27.	1 a	xix. 13.	11	xix. 19.	1 a
xxv. 2. a	7 b	Ruth iii. 13.	3 b	xxviii. 9.	3 c
xxxv. 5, 22.	7 e	1 Sam. ii. 25.	3 a	xxviii. 21.	7 e
xxxv. 21, 29.	7 a	xv. 9.	11	xxix. 5.	7 c
Lev. i. 3.	11	xxii. 17.	1 a	2 Chron. xxi. 7.	11
xix. 5.	11	xxvi. 23.	1 a	xxxv. 8.	7 d
xxii. 19, 29.	11	xxxi. 4.	11	Ezra vii. 18.	10
xxvi. 21.	1 b	2 Sam. ii. 21.	1 a	Neh. ix. 24.	11
Deut. i. 26.	1 a	vi. 10.	1 a	Esth. ix. 5.	11
ii. 30.	1 a	xii. 17.	1 a	Job ix. 3.	3 b
x. 10.	1 a	xiii. 14, 16, 25.	1 a	ix. 19.	1 b
xxi. 14. β	8	xiv. 29, 29.	1 a	Ps. xxvii. 12.	8
xxiii. 5.	1 a	xiii. 16, 17.	1 a	xxxv. 25.	8
xxv. 7.	1 a	1 Kings xiii. 33.	3 c	xl. 8.	11
xxix. 20.	11	xiii. 49.	11	xli. 2.	8
Josh. xvii. 12.	4 b	2 Kings viii. 19.	11	lxxxi. 11.	1 a
xxiv. 10.	1 a	xiii. 23.	1 a	cx. 3.	7 d
Judg. i. 27, 35.	4 b	xxiv. 4.	1 a	cxliii. 10.	11

Prov. i. 25, 30.	1 a	Isa. xlii. 24.	1 a	Dan. v. 19, 19, 19, 19.	9 d
xxi. 1.	3 b	Lam. iii. 33.	6	v. 21.	9 c
xxxi. 13.	3 d	Ezek. iii. 7, 7.	1 b c	vii. 19.	9 a
Eccles. iv. 13.	5	xvi. 27.	8	viii. 4.	11
Isa. i. 19.	1 b	xx. 8.	1 a	xi. 3, 16, 36.	11
xviii. 12.	1 a	Dan. iv. 17, 25, 32.	9 c	Hos. v. 11.γ	4 a
xxx. 9, 15.	1 a	iv. 35.	9 b	xiii. 10, 14, 14.δ	2

a lit. whom his heart maketh liberal. β "whither she will;" *lit.* to her **soul.** γ *lit.* he was willing to walk. δ *or,* where—where—?

WILLOW

עֲרָב *m.* willows, osiers: Lev. xxiii. 40: Job xl. 22: Ps. cxxxvii. 2: Isa. xv. 7; xliv. 4.

צַפְצָפָה *f.* according to the Rabbins, a willow, *salix:* Ezek. xvii. 5.

WIMPLE

מִטְפַּחַת *f.* a wide upper garment of a woman; mantle, cloak: Isa. iii. 22.

WIN

בָּקַע to rend asunder, of a city, to rend, *sc.* its walls, to break open, to take by storm, to subdue. KAL *inf.* 2 Chron. xxxii. 1.

לָקַח to take; to take or captivate any one by blandishments, wisdom, &c. KAL *part.* Poel, Prov. xi. 30, *marg.* 'taketh.'

WIND

רוּחַ *f.,* rarely *m.,* breath, air, wind: Gen. viii. 1, &c. רוּחַ Ch. *com.* Dan. ii. 35; vii. 2.

WINDING

סָבַב to turn oneself, to wind about. NIPHAL *pret.* Ezek. xli. 7. מוּסָב *m.* a winding about, or wall that surrounds: Ezek. xli. 7.

WINDOW

1 אֲרֻבָּה *f.* net-work, lace-work, and so a lattice; a window as closed by a lattice and not with glass, Eccles. xii. 3; a dove-house, dove-cote, as shut in with lattice-work, Isa. lx. 8; windows of heaven, *i.e.* sluices, flood-gates, which are opened to let fall the rain in torrents or waterspouts.

2 חַלּוֹן *com.* a window, hole for the light; a small latticed window or balcony, looking into the street; windows commonly looked into the court. The former is referred to in Judg. v. 28, Cant. ii. 9. A large window is meant in 2 Kings ix. 30, 32, out of which Jezebel was cast; Jer. xxii. 14, *marg.* 'or, my windows;' God's windows, so called because they were windows in an upper chamber, set apart for prayer and devotion, looking towards Jerusalem, and through which they looked when praying to God. Such a chamber and such windows Daniel had and used in Babylon.

3 כַּוִּין Ch. *m. pl.* windows.

4 צֹהַר *m.* light: Gen. vi. 16, light shalt thou make for the ark, *i.e.* windows; possibly one continued aperture for light, of one cubit breadth, surrounding the ark, along its upper part throughout; Gr. φῶτες, *comp.* viii. 6, from which this differs. The Rabbins conceived it to be some precious stone, dispensing light; see *Bush.*

5 שְׁמָשׁוֹת *f. pl.* windows admitting the rays of the sun; *or,* according to modern critics, battlements, pinnacles.

6 שָׁקַף *m.* a light; window to look out of. a שְׁקָפִים *m. pl. id.*

Gen. vi. 16.	4	1 Kings vii. 5.	6	Isa. lx. 8.	1
vii. 11.	1	2 Kings ii, 2, 19.	1	Jer. ix. 21.	2
viii. 2.	1	ix. 30, 32.	2	xxii. 14.	2
viii. 6.	2	iii. 17.	2	Ezek. xl. 16, 16, 22, 25,	
xxvi. 8.	2	1 Chron. xv. 29.	1	25, 29, 33, 36.	2
Josh. ii. 15, 18, 21.	2	Prov. vii. 6.	2	xli. 16, 16, 26.	2
Judg. v. 28.	2	Eccles. xii. 3.	1	Dan. vi. 10.	3
1 Sam. xix. 12.	2	Cant. ii. 9.	2	Joel ii. 9.	2
2 Sam. vi. 16.	2	Isa. xxiv. 18.	1	Zeph. ii. 14.	2.
1 Kings vi. 4.	2	liv. 12.	5	Mal. iii. 10.	1
vii. 4.	6 a				

WINE

1 חֶמֶר *m.* wine, from its fermentation or effervescence; "red wine;" see *Red.* a חֲמַר Ch. *m.*

2 יַיִן *m.* wine, from its fermenting and effervescing: Gen. ix. 21, &c. Figuratively, the wrath of God, or great calamities and sufferings, which disturb the mind with anguish and horror, as wine disturbs the head of the drunkard: Ps. lx. 3, Isa. li. 21; and because dreadful judgments are appointed by God's providence, the cup of this wine is said to be in his hand, and he causeth the nations to drink of it: Ps. lxxv. 8: Isa. li. 21: Jer. xxv. 15, &c.

3 יֶקֶב *m.* wine-press: the wine gathered in at the end of the vintage, Deut. xvi. 13, *comp.* Exod. xxiii. 16.

4 תִּירוֹשׁ *m.* must, new wine, so called because it gets possession of the brain, inebriates.

5 מִמְסָךְ *m.* mixed wine, spiced wine.

6 סָבָא to drink to excess. KAL a *part.* Poel, " (wine) bibbers." b סֹבֶא *m.* wine.

7 עֵנָב *m.* grapes.

8 עָסִיס *m.* new wine, the product of the same year, like new wheat; sweet wine.

9 שֵׁכָר *m.* strong drink; strong wine.

10 שְׁמָרִים *m. pl.* lees of wine; lees racked off or fined, *i.e.* generous old wine purified from the lees.

No. 2 not included.

Gen. xxvii. 28, 37.	4	Ezra vii. 22.	1 a	Jer. xxxi. 12.	4
Num. xviii. 12.	4	Neh. v. 11.	4	Dan. v. 1, 2, 4, 23.	1 a
xxviii. 12.	9	x. 37, 39.	4	Hos. ii. 8.	4
Deut. vii. 13.	4	xiii. 5, 12.	4	ii. 9, 22.	4
xi. 14.	4	Ps. iv. 7.	4	iii. 1.	7
xii. 17.	4	Prov. iii. 10.	4	iv. 11, 11.	2, 4
xiv. 23.	4	xxiii. 20.	2, 6 a	vii. 14.	4
xvi. 13.	3	xxx. 30, 30.	2, 5	ix. 2.	4
xviii. 4.	4	Isa. i. 22.	6 b	Joel i. 5, 5.	2, 8
xxxiii. 51.	4	xxiv. 7.	4	i. 10.	4
xxxiii. 28.	4	xxv. 6, 6.	10	ii. 19, 24.	4
Judg. ix. 13.	4	xxvii. 2.	1	iii. 18.	8
2 Kings xviii. 32.	4	xxxvi. 17.	4	Amos ix. 13.	4
2 Chron. xxxi. 5.	4	xlix. 26.	8	Micah vi. 15, a 15.	4, 2
xxxii. 28.	4	lxii. 8.	4	Hag. i. 11.	4
Ezra vi. 9.	1 a	lxv. 8.	4	Zech. ix. 17.	4

a "sweet wine."

WINE-FAT, WINE-PRESS

1 גַּת *f.* a press, wine-press, or rather trough, in which they put the new gathered grapes, and trod them with their feet, to force out the juice for wine, which runs into the vat, יֶקֶב, ὑπολήνιον, see below; the same seems to have been used by Gideon for threshing wheat secretly, Judg. vi. 11; *metaph.* the severe anger and vengeance of God, Lam. i. 15.

2 יֶקֶב *m.* a wine-fat, ὑπολήνιον, the vat or receptacle into which the must or new wine flowed from the press, נַת. It was often excavated in the earth, or even in a rock. Also the wine-press, the upper vat or receptacle in which the grapes were trodden out or pressed.

3 פּוּרָה *f.* press, in which the grape was broken and crushed.

Num. xviii. 27, 30.	2	Neh. xiii. 15.	1	Jer. xlviii. 33.	2
Deut. xv. 14.	2	Job xxiv. 11.	2	Lam. i. 15.	1
Judg. vi. 11.	1	Isa. v. 2.	2	Hos. ix. 2.	2
vii. 25.	2	lxiii. 2.	1	Zech. xiv. 10.	2
2 Kings vi. 27.	2	lxiii. 3.	3		

WING

1 אֵבֶר *m.* wing, pinion; either because of its strength, or because it covers and protects the body. ᵃ אֶבְרָה *f.* a wing, *collect.* wings, feathers.

2 גַּף Ch. *m.* a wing.

3 בַּעַל *m.* master, owner; "hath wings," *lit.* the master of wings.

4 כָּנָף *com.* a wing of a fowl; *metaph.* the dominions of a great empire; the wings of God, the defence and protection of his people, Ps. xci. 4; the wings, the light, the expanded rays of the sun, as often represented on the Theban and other temples in Egypt with wide outspreading wings, or the spreading beams of the morning, Ps. cxxxix. 9, Mal. iv. 2; the wings of the wind, and of the morning, the expansive swiftness with which they move, Gen. i. 21, *lit.* fowl of wing.—Exod. xix. 4, &c.

5 צִיץ *m.* brightness; a flower; a wing.

No. 4. not included.

Deut. xxxii. 11, 11.	4, 1 a	Eccles. x. 20.	3, 4	Ezek. xvii. 3, 3.	4, 1
Job xxxix. 13, 13.	4, 1 a	Isa. xl. 31.	1	Dan. vii. 4, 4, 6.	2
Ps. lv. 6.	1	Jer. xlviii. 9.	5		

WINK

קָרַץ to cut asunder; to pinch; to press the eyelids; to wink, as significative of insidious designs. KAL *fut.* Ps. xxxv. 19. *part.* Poel, Prov. vi. 13, x. 10.

רָזַם to wink with the eyes, as a gesture of pride and insolence. KAL *fut.* Job xv. 12.

WINNOW

זָרָה to scatter; to winnow. KAL *part.* Poel, Ruth iii. 2, Isa. xxx. 24.

WINTER

חֹרֶף *m.* autumn, the season when fruits are gathered. Not unfrequently it includes also the winter, so that summer and winter is put also for the whole year: Gen. viii. 22: Ps. lxxiv. 17: Jer. xxxvi. 22: Amos iii. 15: Zech. xiv. 8. חָרַף *v. denom.* KAL *fut.* Isa. xviii. 6.

סְתָו (כתיב), *or,* סְתָיו (קרי), *m.* winter; a word taken from the Chald.: Cant. ii. 11.

WIPE

מָחָה to stroke, to rub over, to wipe; to wipe off, to wipe away. KAL *pret.* 2 Kings xxi. 13, 13, *marg.* 'he wipeth;' Prov. xxx. 20: Isa. xxv. 8. *fut.* 2 Kings xxi. 13. NIPHAL *fut.* Prov. vi. 33. HIPHIL *fut.* Neh. xiii. 14.

WIRE

פָּתִיל *m.* a thread, line, cord: Exod. xxxix. 3.

WISE, WISDOM

1 בִּין to discern, to perceive; to discern mentally, to understand; to have understanding, to be intelligent, wise; *part.* as *particip. adj.* intelligent, discreet, wise, often joined with חָכָם, *opp.* to words signifying folly. KAL and HIPHIL ᵃ *fut.* HIPHIL ᵇ *part.* ᶜ בִּינָה *f.* understanding. ᵈ תְּבוּנָה *f. id.*

2 חָכַם to be or become wise. The word denotes the acquisition of the habit of wisdom: Prov. ix. 9. The latter import is more frequent, applied to the acquisition of wisdom by experience, to the discrimination of good and evil, the receiving of instruction, and the exercising of correct judgment; yet it occasionally carries with it the meaning of cunning, subtilty, wiliness, Ps. cv. 20. Hithpael to be wise in one's own eyes, *seq.* ל to outwit, to deceive. KAL ᵃ *pret.* ᵇ *imp.* ᶜ *fut.* PIEL ᵈ *fut.* PUAL ᵉ *part.* HIPHIL ᶠ *part.* HITHPAEL ᵍ *fut.* חָכָם ᵸ *adj. i. q.* Gr. σοφός, wise; specially (1) knowing, skilful, skilled in the arts (see *Cunning*), 2 Chron. ii. 12; more fully, wise-hearted, Exod. xxviii. 3; xxxi. 6; xxxv. 10; xxxvi. 1, 2, 8; (2) wise, *i. e.* intelligent, φρόνιμος, sensible, judicious, endued with reason, and using it, Deut. iv. 6; xxxii. 6: Prov. x. 1; xiii. 1: Hos. xiv. 9; often coupled with נָבוֹן, Deut. iv. 6, and *opp.* נָבָל, אֱוִיל, כְּסִיל, xxxii. 6; Prov. xvii. 28: Eccles. vi. 8. Also sagacious, shrewd, never at a loss (see *Subtil*), Jer. xviii. 18: Isa. xix. 11; xxix. 14: wise from the experience of life and human affairs, Prov. i. 6: Eccles. xii. 11; also skilled in divine things, Gen. xli. 8; and hence also spoken of magicians and enchanters, Exod. vii. 11; *comp.* Chald. Further, skilful to judge, wise in judging, 1 Kings ii. 9; and hence cunning, artful, Job v. 13; firm and constant in mind, consistent, Isa. xxxi. 2. The wide circle of virtues and mental endowments which the Hebrews comprised under this word, is best gathered from the history of those whose wisdom became proverbial among the Hebrews, *e. g.* Solomon, 1 Kings v. 7, &c.; Daniel, Ezek. xxviii. 3; the Egyptians, 1 Kings iv. 30. Thus the wisdom of Solomon is manifested in his acute judgment, 1 Kings iii. 16, &c.; x. 1, &c.; in his knowledge of very many objects, especially of nature, v. 13; in the multitude of verses and sentences which he either composed himself or retained in his memory, v. 12, Prov. i. 1; in a right judgment as to human affairs, &c. Elsewhere wisdom also includes skill in civil affairs, Isa. xix. 11; the faculty of prophesying, and of interpreting dreams, Dan. v. 11; and the art of enchantment and magic, Exod. vii. 11. A higher and more enlightened wisdom is ascribed to angels, 2 Sam. xiv. 20; to God, Job ix. 4; xxviii. 12, &c. The seat of wisdom is the heart, Prov. xvi. 23; xi. 29; xvi. 21. *Plur.* wise men, magi, magicians, Eccles. ix. 17: Gen. xli. 8: Jer. l. 35: Esth. i. 13.—Gen. xli. 33, &c. ⁱ חָכְמָה *f.* skill in an art, dexterity; wisdom; differs from בִּינָה ᵏ as that which is acquired, Prov. xxx. 2, 3:

Exod. xxviii. 3, &c. ^k חָכְמָה Ch. *f.* wisdom. ^l חָכְמוֹת *f.*
id. indicating wisdom, κατ' ἐξοχήν, *sapientia hypostatica*,
in which all the treasures of wisdom and knowledge are
concealed.—*Hengstenberg.* ^m חָכְמוֹת *f. id.* חַכִּים Ch.
adj. wise.

3 טְעֵם Ch. *m.* taste ; intellectual taste, judgment, discernment,
understanding.

4 תּוּשִׁיָּה *f.* (see *Is*), substance ; counsel, wisdom, understanding ;
sound wisdom.

5 לֵב *m.* heart ; to which is ascribed intelligence, wisdom. ^a לָבַב
v. denom. to take heart, to be bold, daring. NIPHAL
fut.

6 עָרְמָה *f.* craftiness, guile ; subtilty, prudence.

7 פָּקֵחַ *adj. pr.* open-eyed, seeing.

8 שָׂכַל to look at, to behold, to view ; *trop.* to be prudent, circumspect, to act prudently, wisely ; to prosper. KAL
^a *pret.* HIPHIL ^b *inf.* ^c *imp.* ^d *fut.* ^e *part.* ^f שֶׂכֶל *m.* in-
telligence, understanding, wisdom.

No. 2 h *Wise*, 2 i *Wisdom*, not included.

Gen. iii. 6.	8 b	Ps. ci. 2.	8 d	Prov. xix. 20.	2 c	
Exod. i. 10.	2 g	cv. 22.	2 d	xx. 1.	2 c	
xxiii. 8.	7	cxix. 98.	2 d	xxi. 11, 11.	2 c h	
Deut. xxxii. 29.	2 a	cxxxvi. 5.	1 d	xxiii. 4.	1 c	
1 Sam. xviii. 5.	8 d	Prov. i. 3.		xxiii. 9.	8 f	
xviii. 14, 15.	8 e	i. 20.ε	2 1	xxiii. 15.	2 a	
xviii. 30.	8 a	ii. 7.	4	xxiii. 19.	2 b	
1 Kings iv. 31.	2 c	iii. 21.	4	xxiv. 7.	2 1	
1 Chron. xxii. 12.	8 f	vi. 6.	4	xxvii. 11.	2 b	
xxvi. 14.α	8 f	viii. 5.	6	xxviii. 7.	1 b	
xxvii. 32.	1 b	viii. 14.	4	xxx. 24.η	2 h e	
2 Chron. xi. 23.	1 a	viii. 33.	2 b	Eccles. ii. 15.	2 a	
Ezra vii. 25.	2 k	ix. 1.	2	ii. 19, 19.	2 h a	
Job iv. 21.β	2 i	ix. 9, 9.	2 h c	vii. 10.	2 h	
vi. 13.	4	ix. 12, 12.	2 a	vii. 16.	2 g	
xi. 12.	5 a	x. 5, 19.	8 e	vii. 23, 23.	2 i c	
xii. 16.	4	x. 21.	5		5	
xxii. 2.γ	8 e	xi. 12.	5	Dan. ii. 12, 13, 14, 18,		
xxxii. 10.	2 c	xii. 8.	8 f	24, 24, 27, 48.	2 n	
xxxiv. 35.	8 b	xiii. 20, 20.	2 h c	ii. 14.	3	
xxxv. 11.	4	xiv. 1.ζ	2 m	ii. 20, 23, 30.	2 k	
xxxvi. 5.	5	xiv. 35.	8 e	ii. 21, 21.	2 k n	
xxxix. 26.	1 c	xv. 21.	5	iv. 6, 18.	2 n	
Ps. ii. 10.	8 c	xv. 24.	8 e	v. 7, 8, 15.	2 n	
xix. 7.	4	xvi. 20.	8 e	v. 11, 11, 14.	2 k	
xxxvi. 3.	8 b	xvii. 2.	8 e	xii. 3,θ 10.	8 e	
xlix. 3.	2 1	xvii. 10.	1 b	Micah vi. 9.	4	
lviii. 5.δ	2 e	xviii. 1.	4	Zech. ix. 2.	2 a	
xciv. 8.	8 d	xix. 8.	5			

α *lit.* in wisdom. β *lit.* not in wisdom. γ *marg.* 'or, if he may be
profitable, (doth his) good success (depend) thereon.' δ *marg.* 'or, be the
charmer never so cunning.' ε *marg.* 'wisdoms.' ζ *lit.* wisdom of women.
η *marg.* 'wise, made wise.' θ *marg.* 'or, teachers.'

WISH

חָפֵץ *adj.* willing, desiring, delighting in : Ps. xl. 14.

פֶּה *m.* mouth : Job xxxiii. 6, *marg.* 'mouth.'

שָׁאַל to ask. KAL *inf.* Job xxxi. 30. *fut.* Jonah iv. 8.

מַשְׂכִּית *f.* image, figure ; imagination, conceit : Ps. lxxiii. 7, *marg.*
'pass the thoughts of the heart.'

WIST, WIT, WOT

יָדַע to know. KAL *pret.* Gen. xxi. 26 ; xxxix. 8 ; xliv. 15 :
Exod. xvi. 15 ; xxxii. 1, 23 ; xxxiv. 29 : Lev. v. 17, 18 :
Num. xxii. 6 : Josh. ii. 4, 5 ; viii. 14 : Judg. xvi. 20.
inf. Gen. xxiv. 21, "to wit :" Exod. ii. 4, *id.*

חָכְמָה *f.* wisdom : Ps. cvii. 27, *marg.* 'all their wisdom is swallowed up.'

WITCH

כָּשַׁף to use magic formulas, incantations, to mutter, to practise
sorcery. PIEL *pret.* 2 Chron. xxxiii. 6. *part.* Exod.
xxii. 18 : Deut. xviii. 10. כְּשָׁפִים *m. pl.* 2 Kings ix. 22 :
Micah v. 12 : Nah. iii. 4, 4.

קֶסֶם *m.* divination : 1 Sam. xv. 23.

WITHDRAW

1 אָסַף to collect, to gather ; to gather up, *i.e.* to contract, to
draw up or back, to withdraw. KAL ^a *pret.* ^b *imp.*
NIPHAL ^c *fut.*

2 גָּרַע to take away, to detract, to withhold. KAL *fut.*

3 חָלַץ to draw off ; to withdraw oneself, to depart. KAL *pret.*

4 חָמַק to turn about, to go away, to depart. KAL *pret.*

5 יָנַח to put or place, to lay down, and leave at rest. HIPHIL
fut.

6 יָקַר to be precious, to make precious, or, as we say, to make
scarce ; to make rare, so as to be more valued. HI-
PHIL *imp.*

7 נָדַח to thrust, to impel ; to seduce, draw away. HIPHIL *fut.*

8 נָתַן to give. KAL *fut.*

9 סוּר to turn aside, to depart. HIPHIL *inf.*

10 סָרַר to slide back ; see *Rebel.* KAL *part.* Poel.

11 רָחַק to be far off ; to remove far away. HIPHIL *imp.*

12 שׁוּב to return ; to cause to return. HIPHIL ^a *pret.* ^b *fut.*

Deut. xiii. 13.	7	Job xxxvi. 7.	2	Lam. ii. 8.	12 a
1 Sam. xiv. 19.	1 b	Ps. lxxiv. 11.	12 b	Ezek. xviii. 8.	12 b
Neh. ix. 29.a	8, 10	Prov. xxv. 17.β	6	xx. 22.	12 a
Job ix. 13.	12 b	Eccles. vii. 18.	5	Hos. v. 6.	3
xiii. 21.	11	Cant. v. 6.	4	Joel ii. 10.	1 a
xxxiii. 17.	9	Isa. lx. 20.	1 c	iii. 15.	1 a

a *marg.* 'they gave a withdrawing shoulder.' β *marg.* 'or, let thy
foot be seldom in thy.'

WITHER

1 יָבֵשׁ to be or become dry, to dry up. KAL ^a *pret.* ^b *inf.* ^c *fut.*
HIPHIL ^d *pret.*

2 נָבֵל to wither, to fade and fall away. KAL *fut.*

3 צָנַם to be hard, dry, barren. KAL *part.* Paül.

4 קָמַל to pine away and die. KAL *pret.*

Gen. xli. 23.a	3	Isa. xix. 6.	4	Ezek. xvii. 10.	1 b c
Job viii. 12.	1 c	xix. 7.	1 c	xvii. 10.	1 c
Ps. i. 3.	2	xxvii. 11.	1 b	xix. 12.	1 a
xxxvii. 2.	2	xl. 7, 8.	1 a	Joel i. 12, 12.	1 a d
xc. 6.	1 a	xl. 24.	1 c	i. 17.	1 d
cii. 4, 11.	1 a	Jer. xii. 4.	1 c	Amos i. 2.	1 a
cxxix. 6.	1 a	Lam. iv. 8.	1 a	iv. 7.	1 a
Isa. xv. 6.	1 a	Ezek. xvii. 9, 9.	1 a c	Jonah iv. 7.	1 c

a *marg.* 'or, small.'

WITHHOLD

1 בָּצַר to cut off ; to cut off access, to restrain, to prevent.
NIPHAL *fut.*

2 חָבַל to pledge, or take to pledge ; to retain a pledge. KAL
pret.

3 חָשַׂךְ to hold back, to restrain ; to keep back, to withhold.
KAL ^a *pret.* ^b *fut.* ^c *part.* Poel.

4 יָנַח to rest ; to cause to rest, to withhold. HIPHIL *fut.*

5 כְּלָא to shut up, to restrain. KAL *fut.*

6 מָנַע to keep back, to withhold, to restrain; *seq. acc.* of thing, and מִן of person, rarely *seq.* לְ of person; *seq. acc.* and מִן of thing. KAL ᵃ*pret.* ᵇ*imp.* ᶜ*fut.* ᵈ*part.* Poel. NIPHAL ᵉ*pret.* ᶠ*fut.*

7 עָצַר to shut up, to close; to hold back, to hinder, to detain. KAL ᵃ*inf.* ᵇ*fut.*

Gen. xx. 6.	3 b	Job xxxi. 16.	6 c	Prov. xxiii. 13.	6 c
xxii. 12, 16.	3 a	xxxviii. 15.	6 f	Eccles. ii. 10.	6 a
xxiii. 6.	5	xlii. 2. α	1	xi. 6.	4
xxx. 2.	6 a	Ps. xxi. 2.	6 a	Jer. ii. 25.	6 b
1 Sam. xxv. 26.	6 a	xl. 11.	5	iii. 3.	6 f
2 Sam. xiii. 13.	6 c	lxxxiv. 11.	6 c	v. 25.	6 a
Neh. ix. 20.	6 a	Prov. iii. 27.	6 c	Ezek. xviii. 16.β	2
Job iv. 2.	7 a	xi. 24.	3	Joel i. 13.	6 e
xii. 15.	7 b	xi. 26.	6 d	Amos iv. 7.	6 a
xxii. 7.	6 c				

a marg. 'be hindered.'   *β marg.* 'pledged, *or,* taken to pledge.'

WITHIN

1 בֶּטֶן *f.* belly; the mind and affections.

2 בַּיִת *m.* house; inside, inner part, within.

3 חֶדֶר *m.* chamber.

4 חֵיק *m.* bosom.

5 פָּנִים *m. pl.* face. פָּנִים α *adv.* פְּנִימִי *adj.* inner.

6 קֶרֶב *m.* the midst, middle, inner part.

7 תָּוֶךְ *m.* middle. בְּתוֹךְ in the middle, among, within: Gen. ix. 21, &c.

No. 7 not included.

Gen. vi. 14.	2	2 Kings vi. 30.	2	Isa. xxvi. 9.	6
xviii. 12.	6	vii. 11.	6	lxiii. 11.	6
xxv. 22.	6	2 Chron. iii. 4.	5 a	Jer. iv. 14.	6
xxxix. 11.	2	Job xix. 27.β	4	xxiii. 9.	6
Exod. xxv. 11.	2	xx. 14.	6	Lam. i. 20.	6
xxvi. 33.	2	xxxii. 18.	1	Ezek. i. 27.	2
xxxvii. 2.	2	Ps. xxxvi. 1.	6	ii. 10.	5
Lev. x. 18.	5 a	xxxix. 3.	6	vii. 15.	6
xiv. 41.	2	xlv. 13.	5 a	xi. 19.	6
xvi. 2, 12, 15.	2	li. 10.	6	xxxvi. 26, 27.	6
Num. xviii. 7.	2	lv. 4.	6	xl. 7, 8, 43.	2
Deut. xxviii. 43.	6	xciv. 19.	6	xl. 16.	5 a
xxxii. 25.α	3	ci. 2, 7.	6	xli. 9.	2
2 Sam. xxv. 37.	6	ciii. 1.	6	xli. 17.	5 b
1 Kings vi. 15, 16.	2	cix. 22.	6	xliv. 17.	2
vi. 18, 19, 21, 29, 30.	5 a	cxlvii. 13.	6	Zeph. iii. 3.	6
vii. 8, 9, 31.	2	Prov. xxii. 18.γ	1	Zech. xii.	6
		xxvi. 24.	6		

α *marg.* 'from the chambers.'   β *marg.* 'in my bosom.'
γ *marg.* 'in thy belly.'

WITHOUT

1 אָחוֹר *m.* the hinder part, backside.

2 אֶפֶס *m.* end; *adv.* no more, no further.

3 בַּיִת *m.* house.

4 בִּלְעֲדֵי *part.* not unto, nothing to or for; without.

5 גַּבַּחַת *f.* baldness in front: Lev. xiii. 55, "(bare) without," *marg.* 'in the forehead.'

6 חוּץ *m.* whatever is out of doors or abroad: Gen. vi. 14, &c. חִיצוֹן ᵃ *adj.* outer, exterior.

7 סוּר to turn aside. KAL *part.* Poel, "is without," *marg.* 'departeth from.'

No. 6 not included.

Gen. xli. 44.	4	2 Kings xviii. 25.	4	Isa. lii. 4.	2
Lev. xiii. 55.	5	2 Chron. xxxiii. 14.	6 a	Jer. xliv. 19.	4
1 Kings vi. 29, 30.	6 a	Job viii. 6.	2	xlii. 17.	1
2 Kings xi. 15.	3	Prov. xi. 22.	7	xli. 17, 17.	6, 6 a
xvi. 18.	6 a	Isa. xxxvi. 10.	4	Dan. viii. 25.	2

WITHS

יֶתֶר *m.* a card, rope, made of the tough fibres of trees: Judg. xvi. 7 (*marg.* 'moist, *or,* new cords'), 8, 9.

WITHSTAND

1 חָזַק to be strong, to strengthen; to strengthen oneself. HITHPAEL ᵃ*pret.* ᵇ*inf.*

2 יָצַב to set, put, or place; to set oneself, to take a stand. HITHPAEL *inf.* with עִם in opposition.

3 עָמַד to stand; *seq.* עַל to withstand. KAL ᵃ*pret.* ᵇ*inf.* ᶜ*fut.* ᵈ*part.* Poel.

4 שָׂטָן *m.* an adversary.

Num. xxii. 32. α	4	2 Chron. xx. 6.	2	Eccles. iv. 12.	3 c
2 Chron. xiii. 7.β	1 a	xxvi. 18.δ	3 c	Dan. x. 13.δ	3 d
xiii. 8.γ	1 b	Esth. ix. 2.ε	3 a	xi. 15, 15.	3 c b

a marg. 'to be an adversary unto thee.' *β lit.* strengthen himself before them. *γ lit.* strengthen yourselves before the kingdom. *δ lit.* stood against. *ε lit.* stand before them.

WITNESS

1 עוּד to turn back; to say again and again, hence to affirm, and specially to testify, to exhort. Hiph. to testify, to bear witness; to cause to testify, to take witnesses, to take any one as witness, hence to call as witness, to invoke, *seq.* בְּ against any one. KAL ᵃ*fut.* (כתיב). HIPHIL ᵇ*pret.* ᶜ*fut.* ᵈעֵד *m.* witness, testimony, Messiah is God's witness: Isa. lv. 4: John xviii. 37: Gen. xxxi. 44, &c. ᵉעֵדָה *f.* testimony. ᶠעֵרוּת *f. id.*

2 עָנָה to answer, to answer as a witness, to bear witness. KAL ᵃ*pret.* ᵇ*imp.* ᶜ*fut.*

3 שָׁמַע to hear. KAL *part.* Poel.

No. 1 d not included.

Gen. xxi. 30.	1 e	Josh. xxiv. 27, 27.	1 e	Job xvi. 8, 8.	1 d, 2 c
xxxi. 52, 52.	1 d e	Judg. xi. 10. α	3	xxix. 11.	1 c
Num. xvii. 7, 8.	1 f	1 Sam. xii. 3.	2 b	Isa. iii. 9.	2 a
xviii. 2.	1 f	1 Kings xxi. 10, 13.	1 c	Lam. ii. 13, 13.	1 c, or a
Deut. iv. 26.	1 b	2 Chron. xxiv. 6.	1 f	Mal. ii. 14.	1 b

a marg. 'be the hearer.'

WITTINGLY

שָׂכַל to be wise; "to guide wittingly." PIEL *pret.* Gen. xlviii. 14.

WIZARD

יִדְּעֹנִי *m.* knowing, wise, and hence a wizard, sorcerer; a wizard spirit, spirit of divination, by which wizards were supposed to be attended: Lev. xx. 27. Lxx. ἐγγαστρίμυθους.—Lev. xix. 31; xx. 6, 27: Deut. xviii. 11: 1 Sam. xxviii. 3, 9: 2 Kings xxi. 6; xxiii. 24: 2 Chron. xxxiii. 6: Isa. viii. 19; xix. 3.

WOE

אוֹי *subst.* wailing, lamentation, Prov. xxiii. 29; *interj.* woe, of sorrow, grief, *c. dat.* woe to me; rarely *c. accus.*; of threatening, imprecation, Num. xxi. 29.—Num. xxi. 29: 1 Sam. iv. 7, 8: Isa. iii. 9, 11; vi. 5; xxiv. 16: Jer. iv. 13, 31; vi. 4; x. 19; xiii. 27; xv. 10; xlv. 3; xlviii. 46: Lam. v. 16: Ezek. xvi. 23, 23; xxiv. 6, 9: Hos. vii. 13; ix. 12. אוֹיָה *interj.* Ps. cxx. 5.

אִי a howling, wailing; *interj.* Eccles. iv. 10 ; x. 16.

אַלְלַי *interj.* expressive of grief : Job x. 15 : Micah vii. 1.

הָהּ *interj.* expressing grief ; "woe worth :" Ezek. xxx. 2.

הוֹי *part. interj.* of threatening, *seq.* nominal : Isa. v. 8, 11, 18, 20, 21 ; xxviii. 1 ; xxix. 1, 15 ; xxx. 1 ; xxxi. 1 : *seq.* אֶל, Jer. xlviii. 1 ; עַל, l. 27, Ezek. xiii. 3 ; לְ, xiii. 18 ; of grief, Isa. xvii. 12 ; of exhortation, ho, Isa. xviii. 1.—Also in Isa. v. 22 ; x. 1 ; xxxiii. 1 ; xlv. 9, 10 : Jer. xxii. 13 ; xxiii. 1 : Ezek. xxxiv. 2 : Amos v. 18 ; vi. 1 : Micah ii. 1 : Nah. iii. 1 : Hab. ii. 6, 9, 12, 15, 19 : Zeph. ii. 5 ; iii. 1 : Zech. xi. 17.

הִי *m.* wailing, lamentation, woe : Ezek. ii. 10.

WOEFUL

אָנַשׁ to be sick, desperate, incurable. KAL *part.* Paül, Jer. xvii. 16.

WOLF

זְאֵב *m.* a wolf, from its tawny colour ; ravenous and fierce, destroying and devouring in a most voracious manner, going out to seek his prey in the evening : Gen. xlix. 27 : Isa. xi. 6 ; lxv. 25 : Jer. v. 6 : Ezek. xxii. 27 : Hab. i. 8 : Zeph. iii. 3.

WOMAN

אִשָּׁה *f.* a woman, female, of any age or condition, married or unmarried ; as the name of the sex, female ; with the *art. collect.* women, the female sex ; a wife. As a term of reproach to a man who is weak, cowardly, effeminate : Isa. xix. 16 ; iii. 12 : Jer. li. 30 : Nah. iii. 13 : joined in apposition with various nouns, as in Josh. ii. 1, &c. *Plur.* נָשִׁים : Gen. xiv. 16, &c.

נְקֵבָה *f.* female : Lev. xv. 33 : Num. xxxi. 15 : Jer. xxxi. 22.

שִׁפְחָה *f.* a maidservant, or slave ; women servants ; bondwomen : Gen. xx. 14 ; xxxii. 5, 22 : Deut. xxviii. 68 : 2 Chron. xxviii. 10 : Esth. vii. 4.

WOMB

1 בֶּטֶן *f.* belly ; womb : Gen. xxv. 23, &c.

2 מֵעִים *m. pl.* bowels.

3 רֶחֶם *com.* womb. רַחַם *m.* the belly, the womb, the seat of affection and tender feeling.

No. 1 not included.

Gen. xx. 18.	3 a	1 Sam. i. 5, 6.	3 a	Ps. cx. 3.	3 a
xxix. 31.	3 a	Job iii. 11.	3 a	Prov. xxx. 16.	3
xxx. 22.	3 a	x. 18.	3 a	Isa. xlvi. 3.	3 a
xlix. 25.	3	xxiv. 20.	3 a	Jer. i. 5.	3 a
Exod. xiii. 2.	3 a	xxxi. 15, 15.	1, 3 a	xx. 17, 17, 18.	3 a
Num. viii. 16.	3 a	xxxviii. 3.	3 a	Ezek. xx. 26.	3
xii. 12.	3 a	Ps. xxii. 10.	3 a	Hos. ix. 14.	3 a
Ruth i. 11.	2	lviii. 3.	3 a		

WONDER

1 מוֹפֵת *m.* a miracle, prodigy, from יָפַת to persuade. Spoken chiefly of miracles, wonders, exhibited by God and his messengers to produce conviction ; often joined with signs. Since prodigies were accounted as tokens of divine authority, this word also signifies a sign, token, proof, *e.g.* of the divine protection, and of the divine

justice in punishing the wicked. Spoken also of a sign given by a prophet in confirmation of his prediction or promise. A sign of something future, a portent, omen : Isa. viii. 18 ; xx. 3 : Zech. iii. 8.

2 פָּלָא to separate, to distinguish ; to make distinguished, extraordinary, wonderful. NIPHAL [a] *pret.* [b] *part.* HIPHIL [c] *pret.* [d] *inf.* [e] *part.* [f] פָּלִיא *adj.* wonderful. [g] פֶּלֶא *m.* marvellousness, a miracle ; wonderful, a title of the Messiah, Isa. lx. 6. [h] פִּלְאִי *adj.* wonderful : Ps. cxxxix. 6 (כתיב). [i] מִפְלָאָה *f.* miracle.

3 פָּלָה to separate, distinguish ; make wonderful. NIPHAL *pret.*

4 שָׁעָה to look at, to behold with attention. HITHPAEL *part.*

5 שָׁמֵם to be astonished. HITHPOLEL [a] *fut.* [b] שַׁמָּה *f.* astonishment.

6 תָּמַהּ to be astonished, to wonder ; sometimes in a stronger sense, to be struck with fear and amazement ; to be in consternation. KAL [a] *imp.* [b] *fut.* HITHPAEL [c] *imp.* [d] תְּמַהּ Ch. wonder, miracle.

Gen. xxiv. 21.	4	Job xlii. 3.	2 b	Ps. cxxxix. 14.	3
Exod. iii. 20.	2 b	Ps. xxvi. 7.	2 b	cxlv. 5.	2 b
iv. 21.	1	xl. 5.	2 b	Prov. xxx. 18.	2 a
vii. 3.	1	lxxi. 7.	1	Isa. viii. 18.	a 1
xi. 9, 10.	2 g	lxxii. 18.	2 b	ix. 6.	2 g
xv. 11.	2 g	lxxiii. 18.	2 b	xx. 3.	1
Deut. iv. 34.	1	lxxv. 1.	2 b	xxv. 1.	2 b
vi. 22.	1	lxxvii. 11, 14.	2 g	xxviii. 29.	2 c
vii. 19.	1	lxxviii. 4, 11, 32.	2 b	xxix. 9.	6 a
xiii. 1, 2.	1	lxxviii. 43.	1	xxix. 14.	2 g
xxvi. 8.	1	lxxxvi. 10.	2 b	lix. 16.	5 a
xxviii. 46.	1	lxxxviii. 10, 12.	2 g	lxiii. 5.	5 a
xxviii. 59.	2 b	lxxxix. 5.	2 g	Jer. iv. 9.	5 b
xxxiv. 11.	1	xcvi. 3.	2 b	v. 30.	5 b
Josh. iii. 5.	2 b	cv. 2.	2 b	xxi. 2.	2 b
Judg. xiii. 19. a	2 e	cv. 5, 27.	1	xxxii. 20, 21.	1
2 Sam. i. 26.	2 a	cvi. 7, 22.	2 b	Lam. i. 9.	2 g
1 Chron. xvi. 9.	2 b	cvii. 8, 15, 21, 24,	2 b	Dan. iv. 2, 3.	6 d
xvi. 12.	1	31.	2 b	vi. 27.	6 d
2 Chron. ii. 9.	2 d	cxi. 4.	2 b	viii. 24.	6 b
xxxii. 31.	1	cxix. 18, 27.	2 b	xii. 6.	2 g
Neh. ix. 10.	1	cxix. 129.	2 g	Joel ii. 26.	2 d
ix. 17.	2 b	cxxxv. 9.	1	ii. 30.	1
Job ix. 10.	1	cxxxvi. 4.	2 b	Hab. i. 5.	6 c
xxxvii. 14.	2 b	cxxxix. 6.	2 f, or h	Zech. iii. 8.	1
xxxvii. 16.	2 i				

a *lit.* acted wonderfully in doing.

WONT

דָּבַר to speak. PIEL *inf.* 2 Sam. xx. 18, *lit.* speaking they will speak.

חֲזָה Ch. to see. P'AL *part. passive*, Dan. iii. 19, *i. e.* more than ever was seen.

סָכַן to be familiar, to cherish ; to become familiar, to be accustomed, to be wont, *seq.* gerund. HIPHIL *pret.* Num. xxii. 30. *inf.* Num. xxii. 30, *lit.* being wont was I ever wont.

WOOD

אָע Ch. *m.* wood : Dan. v. 4, 23.

חֹרֶשׁ *m.* a thick wood, thicket, forest, either as being to be cut, or from the Chald. to be entangled, interwoven : 1 Sam. xxiii. 15, 16, 18, 19.

יַעַר *m.* redundance, or overflowing ; a thicket of trees, so called from the exuberance and luxuriousness of trees and shrubs ; hence generally a wood, a forest ; in 2 Sam. xviii. 8, put for a morass in the wood, in which many were lost. Spoken of the sanctuary or tabernacle, Ps.

cxxxii. 6; in the fields of the wood, implying a region of Ephraim covered with forests, where Shiloh was situated; or in allusion to the name of the city, Kirjath-Jearim, where the ark was kept twenty years: Deut. xix. 5: Josh. xvii. 15, 18: 1 Sam. xiv. 25, 26: 2 Sam. xviii. 6, 8, 17: 2 Kings ii. 24: 1 Chron. xvi. 33: Ps. lxxx. 13; lxxxiii. 14; xcvi. 12; cxxxii. 6: Eccles. ii. 6: Cant. ii. 3: Isa. vii. 2: Ezek. xxxiv. 25: Micah vii. 14. יְעוֹרִים *m. pl. id.* Ezek. xxxiv. 25 (כתיב).

עֵץ *m.* tree, wood, anything made of wood: Ezek. xxi. 10, "every tree," *i.e.* all idols, *comp.* Jer. ii. 27; *pl.* sticks of wood, as prepared for fuel: Gen. xxii. 3, 9: Lev. i. 7; iv. 12.—Gen. vi. 14, &c.

WOOF

עֵרֶב *m.* the woof, weft, in weaving, which is thrown with the shuttle between, and intermixed with all the threads of the warp: Lev. xiii. 48, 49, 51, 52, 53, 56, 57, 58, 59.

WOOL

עֲמַר Ch. *m.* wool: Dan. vii. 9.

צֶמֶר *m.* wool, perhaps so called as being shorn: Lev. xiii. 47, *lit.* a garment of wool; 48, 52, 59: Deut. xxii. 11: Judg. vi. 37: 2 Kings iii. 4: Ps. cxlvii. 16: Prov. xxxi. 13: Isa. i. 18; li. 8: Ezek. xxvii. 18; xxxiv. 3; xliv. 17: Hos. ii. 5, 9.

שַׁעַטְנֵז *m.* linen and woollen: Lev. xix. 19.

WORD

1   אֹמֶר *m.* what is said, a word, discourse, *i. q.* דָּבָר, but with the exception of Josh. xxiv. 27, only in poetic style; especially of the words of God: Gen. xlix. 21, goodly words, words of grace, *i.e.* pleasant, persuasive. [a] אֹמֶר *m.* enunciation, expression, saying. [b] אִמְרָה *f.* word, declaration, discourse. [c] אִמְרָה *f. id.* [d] מַאֲמַר Ch. *m.* edict, commandment.

2   דָּבַר to speak. PIEL [a] *inf.* [b] דָּבָר *m.* a word, *verbum,* λόγος. This term we know is applied to the Son of God in the New Testament, and has been so understood by some of the ancient Jews. It is a remarkable circumstance that the expression "word's sake," in 2 Sam. vii. 21, is changed in 1 Chron. xvii. 19 to "servant's sake." *Collect.* for words, speech, discourse: Gen. xv. 1, &c. [c] דַּבְּרוֹת *f. pl.* sayings.

3   מִלָּה *f.* a word; speech, discourse; command, promise, doctrine, oracle, revelation, a message, thing, &c. [a] מִלָּה Ch. *f.* saying, decree.

4   פֶּה *m.* mouth, speech.

5   פִּתְגָם Ch. *m.* word; specially rescript, sentence.

No. 2 b not included.

Gen. xli. 40.	4	Deut. xxi. 5.	4	2 Sam. xxiii. 2.	3
xlix. 21.	1	xxxii. 1.	4	1 Kings xvi. 26, 26.	4, 2 b
Num. iii. 16, 51.	4	xxxiii. 3.	2 c	xvii. 1.*a*	4, 2 b
iv. 45.	4	xxxiii. 9.	1 c	1 Chron. xxi. 23.	4
xx. 24.	4	xxxiv. 5.	4	Ezra vi. 11.	5
xxii. 18.	4	Josh. xix. 50.	4	Job iv. 4.	3
xxiv. 4, 16.	1	xxii. 9.	4	vi. 10, 25.	3
xxvii. 21, 21.	4	xxiv. 27.	1	vi. 26.	3
xxxvi. 5.	4	2 Sam. xxii. 31.	1 c	viii. 8.	1

Job viii. 10.	3	Ps. xix. 14.	1	Prov. xvi. 24.	1
xii. 11.	3	liv. 2.	1	xvii. 27.	1
xv. 13.	3	lxviii. 11.	1 a	xix. 7, 27.	1
xvi. 4.	3	lxxviii. 1.	1	xxii. 21, 21.	1
xviii. 2.	3	cv. 19, 19.	2 b, 1 c	xxiii. 9.	3
xix. 2, 23.	3	cvii. 11.	3	xxiii. 12.	1
xxii. 22.	3	cxix. 11, 38, 41, 50,	3	xxv. 5.	1 c
xxiii. 5.	3	58, 67, 76, 82, 103,		Isa. v. 24.	1 c
xxiii. 12.	3	116, 133, 140,		xxxii. 7.	1
xxvi. 4.	3	148, 154, 158, 162,		xli. 26.	1
xxxii. 12.	3	170, 172.	1 c	Jer. v. 13.	2 a
xxxii. 14.	3	cxxxviii. 2.	1 c	Lam. ii. 17.	1 b
xxxiii. 3.	1	cxxxviii. 4.	1	Dan. ii. 9.	3 a
xxxiii. 8.	3	cxxxix. 4.	3	iii. 28.	3 a
xxxiv. 2, 3, 16.	3	cxli. 6.	1	iv. 17.	1 d
xxxiv. 37.	1	Prov. i. 2, 21.	1	iv. 31.	3 a
xxxv. 16.	3	ii. 1, 16.	1	v. 10.	3 a
xxxvi. 4.	3	iv. 5.	1	vi. 14.	3 a
xxxviii. 2.	3	v. 7.	1	vii. 11, 25.	3 a
Ps. v. 1.	1	vi. 2, 2.	1	Hos. i. 2.	2 a
xii. 6, 6.	1 c	vii. 1, 5, 24.	1	vi. 5.	1
xviii. 30.	1 c	viii. 8.	1	Hab. iii. 9.	1 a
xix. 4.	3	xv. 26.	1		

a lit. according to the mouth of my word.

WORK

1   אָמָן *m.* a skilful, trusty workman; or architect, artist.

2   דָּבָר word; thing, matter, affair, business.

3   הָלַךְ to go; applied to the motion of inanimate things. KAL *part.* Poel.

4   חָרַשׁ to cut; to grave; to work, fabricate, to devise, &c. KAL [a] *part.* Poel. [b] חָרָשׁ *m.* a graver in stone, a workman in iron, brass, stone, wood, an artisan, artificer.

5   חָשַׁב to think, to meditate, to purpose; to think out, to invent, to devise; hence an inventive worker. KAL [a] *part.* Poel, "cunning workman." [b] מַחֲשָׁבָת *f.* work of art or skill, "cunning work."

6   גָּזִית *f.* a cutting or hewing of stone.

7   יְגִיעַ *m.* labour.

8   יָד *com.* hand.

9   יֵצֶר *m.* formation; thing formed, work; an image, idol.

10   תּוּשִׁיָּה *f.* purpose, undertaking, enterprise; counsel, wisdom, understanding: Isa. xxviii. 29, *lit.* who maketh wonderful his counsel, and vast his understanding.—*Gesenius.*

11   מְלָאכָה *f.* ministry, service, properly on which any one is sent or employed in ordinary life; their work, labour, business. Lxx. ἔργον, ἐργασία. Specially work, labour, of an artisan, chiefly of an architect or others employed in building; business of the public, of the king, &c.; service, ministry, of the Levites; work of God in creation, so of divine judgments. Work as wrought, thing done or made.

12   עָבַד to labour, to work, to do work. KAL [a] *imp.* [b] *fut.* [c] *part.* Poel. PUAL [d] *pret.* HIPHIL [e] *inf.* עָבַד Ch. P'AL [f] *pret.* [g] *part. active.* [h] עָבָד *m.* work, deed. [i] עֲבוֹדָה *f.* work, labour, business; service, ministry. [k] עֲבִידָה Ch. *f.* work. [l] מַעֲבָד *m.* work, doing. [m] מַעֲבָד Ch. *m. id.*

13   עָלַל to perform a work, to accomplish, to execute; to do a deed. HITHPAEL [a] *pret.,* *seq.* בְּ of persons; see *Abuse.* [b] מַעֲלָל *m.* works, deeds, nearly of the same force as *facinora;* acts, exploits, designs, either good or bad. [c] עֲלִילָה *f.* an action. [d] עֲלִילִיָה *f. id.*

14 עָלָה to ascend. HIPHIL *fut.*

15 עָמֵל *adj.* labouring, toiling; labourer.

16 עָשָׂה to work, to labour, to do. KAL [a] *pret.* [b] *inf.* [c] *imp.* [d] *fut.* [e] *part.* Poel, workmen, *lit.* doers of work. NIPHAL [f] *pret.* [g] מַעֲשֶׂה *m.* work, *i.e.* labour, business, occupation; work, *i.e.* deed, act, *facinus*, something done; work, *i.e.* something made, created: Gen. v. 29, &c.

17 פָּעַל to work emphatically, with attention and diligence, as a workman at his trade. KAL [a] *pret.* [b] *fut.* [c] *part.* Poel. [d] פֹּעַל *m.* work, action, practice. [e] פְּעֻלָּה *f.* work, employment, wages; or, as it might have been rendered in Prov. xi. 18, reward. מִפְעָל *m.* work, doings. [g] מִפְעָלָה *f. id.*

18 קָשַׁר to conspire. KAL *pret.*

19 רָקַם to embroider. PUAL *pret.*

20 מִשְׁבְּצוֹת *f. pl.*; see *Ouches.*

21 שׂוּם to set, place. KAL *pret.*

No. 16 g not included.

Gen. ii. 2, 2, 3.	11	1 Sam. xi. 13.	16 a	Ezra vi. 22.	11
xxxiv. 7.	16 a	xiv. 14.	16 d	x. 13.	11
Exod. v. 9, 11.	12 i	xiv. 45, 45.	16 a	Neh. ii. 16.	11
v. 18.	12 a	xix. 5.	16 d	iii. 5.	12 i
x. 2.	13 a	2 Sam. xviii. 13.	16 a	iv. 6.	16 b
xii. 16.	11	xxiii. 10, 12.	16 d	iv. 11, 15.	11
xiv. 31.	8	1 Kings v. 16.		iv. 17, 17.	16 e, 11
xx. 9, 10.	11	16, 16.	11, 16 e, 11	iv. 19, 21.	16 e, 11
xxxi. 3, 14, 15, 15.	11	14, 14, 14. } 11, 16 d, 11		v. 5, 16.	11
xxxi. 4, 4.	5 b, 16 b	vii. 22, 22.	16 g, 11	vi. 3, 3, 9.	11
xxxi. 5, 5.	16 b, 11	vii. 40, 51.	16 d	vi. 16, 16.	11, 16 f
xxxiv. 21.	12 b	ix. 23, 23, 23.	11, 16 e, 11	vii. 70, 71.	11
xxxv. 2, 2, 21, 24, 29, 31, 33.	11	xvi. 20.	18	ix. 18, 26.	16 d
xxxv. 32, 32.	5 a, 16 b	xvi. 25.	16 d	ix. 35.	13 b
xxxv. 35, 35, } 16 b, 11,		xxi. 20, 25.	16 d	x. 33.	11
35, 35, 35. } 5 a, 11,		2 Kings iii. 2.	16 d	xi. 12.	11
5 b		xii. 11, 11.	11, 16 e, 11	xiii. 10.	11
xxxvi. 1, 1, 1.	16 a b, 11	xii. 14.	16 e, 11	Job vii. 2.	17 d
xxxvi. 2, 3.	11	xii. 15.	16 e, 11	x. 3.	7
xxxvi. 4, 4.	11	xvii. 11.	16 d	xii. 9.	16 a
4.	16 e, 11, 11	xxi. 6.	16 b	xxiii. 14.	16 b
xxxvi. 5, 6, 7.	11	xxii. 5, 5, 9.	11	xxiv. 5.	17 d
xxxvi. 8, 8, 8.	16 e, 11, 16 g	1 Chron. iv. 21. α	12 i	xxxi. 3.	17 b
xxxviii. 23.	5 a	iv. 23.	11	xxxiii. 29.	17 c
xxxviii. 24, 24.	11	vi. 49.	11	xxxiv. 8, 22.	17 c
xxxix. 3, 3.	16 b g	ix. 13, 19, 33. β	11	xxxiv. 11.	17 c
xxxix. 6.	16 d	xvi. 37.	2	xxxiv. 25.	12 l
xxxix. 32, 42.	12 i	xxii. 2.	6	xxxvi. 9, 24.	17 d
xxxix. 43.	11	xxii. 15.	16 e, 11	xxxvi. 23.	17 a
xl. 33.	11	xxii. 15, 15.	4 b, 11	Ps. v. 5.	17 c
Lev. xi. 32.	11	xxiii. 4, 24.	11	vi. 8.	17 c
xiii. 51.	11	xxv. 1. γ	11	ix. 16.	17 d
xvi. 29.	11	xxvii. 26.	11	xiv. 1.	13 c
xx. 12.	16 a	xxviii. 13, 19, 20, 21.	11	xiv. 4.	17 c
xxiii. 3, 3, 7, 8, 21, 25, 28, 30, 31, 35,		xxix. 1, 5, 6.	11	xv. 2.	17 c
36.	11	2 Chron. ii. 7, 14.	16 b	xviii. 4.	17 e
Num. iv. 3.	11	ii. 18.	12 e	xxviii. 3.	17 e
iv. 30, 35, 39, 43.	12 i	iii. 14.	14	xxviii. 5.	17 e
xxiii. 23.	17 a	iv. 11.	11	xxxi. 19.	17 a
xxviii. 18, 25, 26.	11	v. 1.	11	xxxvi. 12.	17 c
xxix. 1, 7, 12, 35.	11	viii. 9, 16.	11	xxxvii. 1.	16 e
Deut. v. 13, 14.	11	xv. 7.	17 e	xliv. 13.	17 d
xiii. 14.	16 f	xvi. 5.	11	xlv. 13.	20
xv. 19.	12 b	xvi. 6.	16 d	xlvi. 8.	17 g
xvi. 8.	11	xxiv. 12, 12.	11, 4 b	lii. 2.	16 e
xvii. 2.	16 d	xxiv. 13.	16 e, 11	liii. 4.	17 c
xvii. 4.	16 f	xxiv. 13, 13.	16 d, 11, 11	lviii. 2.	17 b
xxi. 3.	12 d	xxiv. 34.	11	lix. 2.	17 c
xxii. 21.	16 a	xxxi. 20.	16 d	lxiv. 9.	17 c
xxxi. 18.	16 a	xxxiii. 6. δ	16 b	lxiv. 9.	17 g
xxxii. 4.	17 d	xxxiv. 10.	16 e, 11	lxvi. 5.	17 a
xxxiii. 11.	17 d	xxxiv. 10.	16 e, 11	lxviii. 28.	11
Josh. vii. 11.	16 a	xxxiv. 12.	16 e	lxxiii. 28.	17 g
ix. 4.	16 d	xxxiv. 13, 13.	16 e, 11	lxxiv. 12.	11
Judg. v. 26.	15	xxxiv. 17.	16 e, 11	lxxvii. 11.	13 b
xx. 10.	16 a	Ezra iii. 69.	11	lxxvii. 12.	17 d
Ruth ii. 12.	17 d	iii. 8.	11	lxxviii. 7.	13 b
ii. 19, 19, 19.	16 a	iii. 9.	16 e, 11	lxxviii. 11.	13 c
1 Sam. vi. 6.	13 a	iv. 24.	12 k	lxxviii. 43.	21
viii. 16.	11	v. 8.	12 k	xc. 16.	17 d
		vi. 7.	12 k	xcii. 4, 4.	17 d, 16 g
				xcii. 7, 9.	17 c

Ps. xciv. 4, 16.	17 c	Eccles. ix. 1.	12 h	Jer. xxxi. 16.	17 e
xcv. 9.	17 d	Cant. vii. 1.	1	xxxii. 19.	13 d
ci. 3.	16 b	Isa. v. 12.	17 d	xlviii. 10.	11
ci. 7.	16 e	xix. 9.	11	l. 25.	11
civ. 23.	17 d	xxvi. 12, 12.	17 a, 16 g	l. 29.	17 d
cxi. 3.	17 d	xxvi. 18.	16 d	Ezek. xv. 3, 4, 5, 5.	11
cxix. 126. ε	16 b	xxviii. 29.	10	xx. 9, 14, 22.	16 b
cxxv. 5.	17 c	xxxii. 6.	11	xx. 44.	16 b
cxxxix. 15. ζ	19	xl. 10.	17 e	xxviii. 13.	11
cxli. 4, 4.	13 c, 17 c	xl. 19, 20.	4 b	xxix. 20.	16 a
cxli. 9.	17 c	xli. 4.	17 a	xxxiii. 26.	16 a
cxliii. 5, 5.	17 d, 16 g	xli. 24.	17 d	Dan. iv. 2.	12 f
cxlv. 5.	2	xliii. 13.	17 e	iv. 37.	12 m
Prov. viii. 22.	17 f	xliv. 11.	11	vi. 27.	12 g
x. 29.	17 c	xliv. 12, 12.	17 b	xi. 23.	16 d
xi. 18, 18.	16 e, 17 e	xlv. 9, 11.	17 a b	Hos. vi. 8.	17 c
xviii. 9.	11	xlix. 4.	11	viii. 6.	4 b
xx. 11.	17 d	lxi. 8.	17 e	Jonah i. 11, η 13.	3
xxi. 8.	17 d	lxii. 11.	17 e	Micah i. 1.	11
xxi. 25.	17 c	lxiv. 5.	16 e	Hab. i. 5, 5.	17 c d
xxiv. 12, 29.	17 d	lxv. 7.	17 e	ii. 18.	9
xxiv. 27.	11	Jer. x. 3, 3.	16 g, 4 b	iii. 2.	17 d
xxvi. 28.	16 d	x. 9, 9.	16 g, 4 b	Zeph. iii. 3.	17 a
xxxi. 13.	16 d	xi. 15.	16 b	Hag. i. 14.	11
Eccles. ii. 11, 11.	16 g a	xvii. 22, 24.	11	ii. 4.	11
ii. 17, 17.	16 g f	xviii. 3, 3.	16 e, 11	Mal. iii. 16.	16 c
iii. 9.	16 g	xxii. 13.	17 d		16 e

[a] *lit.* of the work of. [β] *lit.* for night and day on them in work. [γ] *lit.* men of work. [δ] *lit.* he multiplied to work. [ε] *or*, it is time to work for the Lord. [ζ] *lit.* embroidered. [η] *marg.* 'went, *or*, grew more and more tempestuous.'

WORLD

1 אֶרֶץ *com.* the earth, the ground; a land, a country.

2 חֶדֶל *m.* place of rest, region of the dead, *hades*; some take it by paronomasia for חֶלֶד; see below: Isa. xxxviii. 11. See an able disquisition of the meaning in Scheidii Dissert. in Cant. Hiskiæ, pp. 49–58. Barnes, "amongst the inhabitants of the land of stillness."

3 חֶלֶד *m.* the world, the age of man, as transitory and of short duration.

4 עוֹלָם *m.* perpetual, everlasting: also world. Compare also the old English expression in which both ideas seem to be connected: "ever shall be, world without end."

5 תֵּבֵל *f.* the earth, as fertile and inhabited, the habitable globe, world, οἰκουμένη; the whole earth, the world in general, especially where the founding of it is mentioned; *meton.* for the inhabitants of the earth.

No. 5 not included.

Ps. xvii. 14.	3	Eccles. iii. 11.	4	Isa. lxii. 11.	1
xxii. 27.	1	Isa. xxiii. 17.	1	lxiv. 4. β	4
xlix. 1.	3	xxxviii. 11.	2	Jer. xxv. 26.	1
lxxiii. 12.	4	xlv. 17. α	4		

[a] *lit.* to the ages of perpetuity. [β] "since the beginning of the world."

WORM

1 זָחַל to creep, to crawl. KAL *part.*

2 סָס *m.* a moth in clothes.

3 רִמָּה *f.* a worm, *collect.* worms, as bred in putrid substances.

4 תּוֹלֵע *m.* a worm, especially such as is generated in putrid substances. [a] תּוֹלֵעָה and תּוֹלַעַת, *f.* the *coccus* worm or insect, *coccus ilicis*, Linn., and hence *meton.* crimson or deep scarlet colour; also as above found in putrid substances. Used of the Messiah, foretelling his sufferings and treatment, Ps. xxii. 6.

Exod. xvi. 20.	4	Job xxi. 26.	3	Isa. xli. 14.	4 a
xvi. 24.	4	xxiv. 20.	3	li. 8.	2
Deut. xxviii. 39.	4 a	xxv. 6, 6.	3, 4 a	lxvi. 24.	4 a
Job vii. 5.	4 a	Ps. xxii. 6.	4 a	Jonah iv. 7.	4 a
xvii. 14.	3	Isa. xiv. 11, 11.	3, 4 a	Micah vii. 17.	1

WORMWOOD

לַעֲנָה *f.* wormwood ; perhaps so called as being noxious and poisonous (*comp.* Deut. xxix. 17, Rev. viii. 10, 11), as bitter herbs were commonly so regarded by the Hebrews : Deut. xxv. 18 : Prov. v. 4 : Jer. ix. 15 ; xxiii. 15 : Lam. iii. 15, 19 : Amos v. 7.

WORSE

זָעֵף to be angry ; to be morose, gloomy, sad. KAL *part.* Poel, Dan. i. 10, *marg.* ' sadder.'

נָגַף to smite ; applied to the overthrow and defeat of an army ; to be put to the worse. NIPHAL *pret.* 1 Chron. xix. 16, 19. *fut.* 2 Kings xiv. 12 ; 2 Chron. vi. 24, *marg.* ' or, smitten ;' xxv. 22, *marg.* 'smitten.'

רָעַע to be evil ; to do ill, to do evil to any one, to afflict. KAL *pret.* 2 Sam. xix. 7. HIPHIL *pret.* Jer. vii. 26, xvi. 12. *fut.* Gen. xix. 9 : 1 Kings xvi. 25. רַע *adj.* evil, 2 Chron. xxxiii. 9 : Ezek. vii. 24.

WORSHIP

1   סְגַד Ch. to fall down in worship of idols, *seq.* לְ; yet the meaning does not seem to be confined to the act of prostration, but to imply all profound adoration ; see Isa. xlvi. 6. P'AL *pret.* *fut.* *part.*

2   עָצַב to form, to fashion, hence עָצָב, an image. Hiphil may therefore be *denom.* to have to do with images, to worship. Hiphil *inf.*

3   עָבַד to work, to serve ; to serve God, to worship him. KAL *part.* Poel.

4   שָׁחָה to bow down, to bow down before God, to worship, to pay adoration, even without prostration. HITHPAEL ^a *pret.* ^b *inf.* ^c *imp.* ^d *fut.* ^e *part.*

Gen. xxii. 5.	4 d	2 Kings xvii. 16, 36.	4 d	Isa. ii. 8.	4 d
xxiv. 26, 48, 52.	4 d	xviii. 22.	4 d	ii. 20.	4 b
Exod. iv. 31.	4 d	xix. 37.	4 e	xxvii. 13.	4 a
xii. 27.	4 d	xxi. 3, 21.	4 d	xxxvi. 7.	4 d
xxiv. 1.	4 a	1 Chron. xvi. 29.	4 c	xxxvii. 38.	4 e
xxxii. 8.	4 d	xxx. 20.	4 d	xliv. 15, 17.	4 d
xxxiii. 10.	4 a	2 Chron. vii. 3, 22.	4 d	xlvi. 6.	4 d
xxxiv. 8, 14.	4 d	vii. 19.	4 a	xlix. 7.	4 d
Deut. iv. 19.^a	4 a	xx. 18.	4 b	lxvi. 23.	4 b
viii. 19.	4 a	xxix. 28.	4 e	Jer. i. 16.	4 d
xi. 16.	4 a	xxix. 29, 30.	4 d	vii. 2.	4 b
xvii. 3.	4 d	xxxii. 12.	4 d	viii. 2.	4 a
xxvi. 10.	4 a	xxxiii. 3.	4 d	xiii. 10.	4 d
xxix. 26.	4 d	Neh. viii. 6.	4 d	xvi. 11.	4 d
xxx. 17.	4 a	ix. 3, 6.	4 e	xxii. 9.	4 d
Josh. v. 14.	4 d	Job i. 20.	4 d	xxv. 6.	4 b
Judg. vii. 15.	4 d	Ps. v. 7.	4 d	xxvi. 2.	4 b
1 Sam. i. 3.	4 b	xxii. 27, 29.	4 d	xliv. 19.	2
i. 19, 28.	4 d	xxix. 2.	4 d	Ezek. viii. **16.**	4 e
xv. 25, 31.	4 d	xlv. 11.	4 c	xlvi. 2, 3.	4 a
xv. 30.	4 a	lxvi. 4.	4 d	xlvi. 9.	4 b
2 Sam. xii. 20.	4 d	lxxxi. 9.	4 d	Dan. ii. 46.	1 a
xv. 32.	4 d	lxxxvi. 9.	4 d	iii. 5, 6, 10, 11, 15,	
1 Kings ix. 6.	4 a	xcv. 6.	4 d	15, 18, 28.	1 b
ix. 9.	4 d	xcvi. 9.	4 c	iii. 7, 12, 14.	1 c
xi. 33.	4 d	xcvii. 7.	4 c	Micah v. 13.	4 d
xvi. 31.	4 d	xcix. 5, 9.	4 c	Zeph. i. 5, 5.	4 e
xxii. 53.	4 d	cvi. 19.	4 d	ii. 11.	4 d
2 Kings v. 18.	4 b	cxxxii. 7.	4 d	Zech. xiv. 16, 17.	4 b
x. 19, 21, 22, 23, 23.	3	cxxxviii. 2.	4 d		

a lit. shouldest be driven and shouldest worship.

WORTH, WORTHY

1   אַדִּיר *adj.* see *Glory.*

2   אִישׁ *m.* man.

---

3   אַף *m.* nose ; *dual,* face, countenance ; two persons.

4   בֵּן *m.* son : 1 Sam. xxvi. 16, *lit.* sons of death.

5   חַיִל *m.* strength, might, power ; wealth, riches.

6   מִכְסָה *f.* number ; computed value.

7   מְחִיר *m.* price.

8   מָלֵא *adj.* full.

9   קָטֹן to be little, small. KAL *pret.*

10   שָׂכָר *m.* hire.

11   מִשְׁפָּט *m.* judgment ; "worthy of death," *lit.* judgment of death.

Gen. xxiii. 9.	8	Deut. xxi. 22.	11	1 Kings i. 52.γ	4, 5
xxxii. 10.	9	xxv. 2.	4	ii. 26.	2
Lev. xxvii. 23.	6	Ruth iv. 11.	5	xxi. 2.	7
Deut. xv. 18.α	10	1 Sam. i. 5.β	3	Jer. xxvi. 11, 16.	11
xix. 6.	11	xxvi. 16.	4	Nah. ii. 5.	1

a lit. for the double of the hire of an hired servant.   β *marg.* 'double,'
lit. one portion of two faces.   γ *lit.* if he shall be for a son of valour.

WOULD   (See also WILL)

אַחֲלֵי a particle of wishing ; would God : 2 Kings v. 3.

נָתַן to give ; " would to God," Heb., who will give. KAL *fut.* Exod. xvi. 3 : Num. xi. 29 : Deut. xxviii. 67, 67 : Judg. ix. 29 : 2 Sam. xviii. 33.

WOUND

1   בָּצַע to cut, to wound. KAL *fut.*

2   דַּכָּה *f.* a crushing ; Deut. xxiii. 1, wounded or mutilated by crushing, *sc.* in the testicle, in order to produce emasculation.

3   דָּקַר to thrust through, to pierce, to stab, as with a sword, spear. PUAL *part.*

4   הָלַם to smite or strike as with a hammer. HITHPAEL *part.* Prov. xviii. 8, xxvi. 22, *marg.* ' like as when men are wounded.' These passages are supposed to be referable to this root by a transposition of the letters ה and ל ; see below.

5   מָזוֹר *m.* binding up of a wound ; *meton.* a wound, sore, *sc.* to be pressed and bound up. מָזוֹר, Obad. 7 ; but according to Lxx., Vulg., Chald., Syr., falsehood, treachery, plot ; others, a net, snare.

6   חַבּוּרָה *f.* a stripe, weal, bruise, *i.e.* the mark or print of blows in the skin, in which the blood and humours appear, spoken of the consequences of sin, and the sense of divine wrath.

7   חוּל to be in great pain, as one that has been wounded. KAL and HIPHIL *fut.*

8   חָלַל to pierce, to wound ; to stab ; it is applied to the wounding or penetrating the heart with sorrow. KAL ^a *pret.* POEL ^b *part.* POAL ^c *part.* ^d חָלָל *adj.* pierced, wounded.

9   חָלָה to be sick. HOPHAL, *lit.* to be made sick ; *pret.*

10   חֵץ *m.* arrow, arrow-wound, by the arrow of God.

11   לָהַם to swallow greedily ; according to the opinion of Schultens, spoken of pleasant meats or drinks greedily swallowed, dainty morsels. HITHPAEL *part.* Prov. xviii. 8, xxvi. 22, *marg.* ' like as when men are wounded ;' see above.

12   מָחַץ to smite through and through, to give a deep and deadly wound ; to draw much blood. KAL ^a *pret.*

13 נֶגַע *m.* a stroke, blow.

14 נָכֵא *adj.* smitten, afflicted.

15 נָכָה to smite, to strike, to wound. HIPHIL [a] *pret.* [b] *fut.* HOPHAL [c] *pret.* [d] מַכָּה *f.* a beating, smiting; a stroke, a blow.

16 עַצֶּבֶת *f.* grief, sorrow.

17 פָּצַע to cut, to cleave. KAL [a] *pret.* [b] *inf.* [c] *part.* Paül. [d] פֶּצַע *com.*, perhaps an open wound.

Gen. iv. 23.	17 d	Job xxxiv. 6.	10	Isa. li. 9.	8 b
Exod. xxi. 25, 25.	17 d	Ps. xviii. 38.	12 b	liii. 5.	8 c
Deut. xxiii. 1.	17 c, 2	xxxviii. 5.	6	Jer. vi. 7.	15 d
xxxii. 39.	12 a	lxiv. 7. a	15 d	x. 19.	15 d
Judg. ix. 40.	8 d	lxviii. 21.	12 b	xv. 18.	15 d
1 Sam. xvii. 52.	8 d	lxix. 26.	8 a	xxx. 12, 17.	15 d
xxxi. 3.	7	cix. 22.	8 a	xiv. 14, 14.	15 a d
2 Sam. xxii. 39.	12 b	cx. 6.	12 a	xxxvii. 10.	3
1 Kings xx. 37.	17 b	cxlvii. 3.	16	li. 52.	8 d
xxii. 34.	9	Prov. vi. 33.	13	Lam. ii. 12.	8 d
xxii. 35.	15 d	vii. 26.	8	Ezek. xxvi. 15.	8 d
2 Kings viii. 28.	15 b	xviii. 8.	4 or 11	xxviii. 23.	8 d
viii. 29.	15 d	xviii. 14.	14	xxx. 24. β	8 d
ix. 15.	15 d	xx. 30.	17 d	Hos. v. 13, 13.	5
1 Chron. x. 3.	7	xxiii. 14.	17 d	Joel ii. 8.	1
2 Chron. xviii. 33.	9	xxvi. 22.	4 or 11	Obad. 7.	5 a
xxii. 6.	15 d	xxvii. 6.	17 d	Micah i. 9.	15 d
xxxv. 23.	9	Cant. v. 7.	17 a	Nah. iii. 19.	15 d
Job v. 18.	8	Isa. i. 6.	17 d	Hab. iii. 13.	12 a
ix. 17.	17 d	xxx. 26.	15 d	Zech. xiii. 6, 6.	15 d c
xxiv. 12.	8 d				

a *lit.* shall their wounds be.   β "deadly wounded."

WRAP

1 גָּלַם to roll or wrap together, to fold. KAL *fut.*

2 חָבַשׁ to bind, to gird about. KAL *part.* Paül.

3 כָּנַס to gather together, to wrap around. HITHPAEL *inf.*

4 לוּט to wrap, to muffle, to cover. KAL [a] *part.* Paül. HIPHIL [b] *fut.*

5 מָעֹט *adj.* smooth, bare, hence polished, sharp.

6 סָבַךְ to interweave, to entwine. PUAL *fut.*

7 עָבַת to be interwoven, interlaced; spoken of trees with thick foliage. PIEL *fut.* Micah vii. 3, *i. e.* entangle, pervert. Taylor, so they wrap it up or wreathe it, namely, the avarice and corruption of the prince and judge, and the falsehood and cruel oppression of the great man; they twist it, this complicated evil, together into one strong body, and so proceed in their unjust practices without control; *comp.* Isa. v. 18.

8 עָלַף to cover, to wrap up. HITHPAEL *fut.*

9 שָׂרַג to interweave. PUAL *fut.*

Gen. xxxviii. 14.	8	Job viii. 17.	6	Ezek. xxi. 15.	5
1 Sam. xxi. 9.	4 a	xl. 17.	9	Jonah ii. 5.	2
1 Kings xix. 13.	4 b	Isa. xxviii. 20.	3	Micah vii. 3.	7
2 Kings ii. 8.	1				

WRATH

1 אַף *m.* the member with which we breathe, the nose; anger which shows itself in hard breathing. Schultens adds the notion of pride and arrogance. It is used, however, of the anger of God.

2 זָעַף to be angry; to be morose, gloomy, sad; implying displeasure and pain of mind; see *Indignation.* KAL [a] *inf.* [b] *fut.* [c] זַעַף *m.* anger.

3 חָרָה to burn, to be kindled, inflamed, spoken only of anger, with אַף expressed or understood, *seq.* בְּ, rarely אֶל or עַל. Sometimes these formulas express the feeling of grief, sadness, rather than anger; and hence are rendered in the Lxx. by the verb λυπέομαι, as Gen. iv. 5, Jonah iv. 4, 9, Neh. v. 6. KAL [a] *pret.* [b] *inf.* [c] *fut.* [d] חָרוֹן *m.* a burning, something burning; especially of anger, with אַף, glow of anger, burning anger, fierce wrath.

4 חֵמָה *f.* heat, heat of anger, *i. q.* anger, wrath; especially that which is sudden and immediate in execution: Prov. xvi. 14, as a messenger of immediate death.

5 כָּעַס to be indignant, vexed, take ill; to be angry. KAL [a] *fut.* [b] כַּעַס *m.* vexation, anger.

6 כַּעַשׂ *m.* the same in meaning as כַּעַס.

7 עָבַר to pass over; to overflow, of wrath. HITHPAEL, to be wroth with, *seq.* בְּ once *seq.* עִם of the Messiah. [a] *pret.* [b] *fut.* [c] עֶבְרָה *f.* outpouring, overflowing of wrath; hence for wrath itself, *i. e.* outburst of wrath; specially of God's wrath.

8 קָצַף to break out or forth in anger, or great displeasure. KAL [a] *pret.* [b] *inf.* [c] *fut.* HIPHIL [d] *pret.* [e] *inf.* [f] *part.* [g] קֶצֶף *m.* anger, wrath of God. [h] קְצַף Ch. *m.* anger.

9 רָגַז to be moved, disturbed, to be thrown into commotion; to be moved with anger, to be wroth. KAL [a] *fut.* Ch. APHEL [b] *pret.* [c] רֹגֶז *m.* fury, anger.

Gen. iv. 5.	3 c	2 Chron. xxiv. 18.	8 g	Ps. lxxviii. 62.	7 a
iv. 6. a	3 a	xxvi. 19, 19.	2 b a	lxxix. 7.	4
xxxi. 36.	3 c	xxviii. 9. γ	4	lxxxv. 3.	7 c
xxxiv. 7.	3 c	xxviii. 11, 13.	1	lxxxviii. 7.	3 d
xxxix. 19.	1	xxix. 8.	8 g	lxxxviii. 16. δ	3 d
xl. 2.	8 c	xxix. 10.	1	lxxxix. 38.	7 a
xli. 10.	8 a	xxx. 8.	1	lxxxix. 46.	4
xlix. 7.	7 c	xxxii. 25, 26.	8 g	xc. 7.	4
xx. 20.	4	xxxiv. 21, 25.	4	xc. 9, 11.	7 c
Exod. xv. 7.	3 d	xxxvi. 16.	1	xcv. 11.	7 c
xvi. 20.	8 c	Ezra v. 12.	9 b	cii. 10.	8 g
xxii. 24.	1	viii. 23.	8 h	cvi. 23.	4
xxxii. 10, 11, 12.	3 c	viii. 22.	1	cvi. 40.	4
Lev. x. 6.	8 c	x. 14.	8 g	cx. 5.	1
Num. i. 53.	8 g	Neh. iv. 1, 7.	3 c	cxxiv. 3.	1
xi. 33.	1	xiii. 18.	3 d	cxxxviii. 7.	1
xvi. 15.	8 c	Esth. i. 12.	8 c	Prov. iv. 4, 23.	7 c
xvi. 22.	8 c	i. 18.	8 g	xii. 16.	5 b
xvi. 46.	8 c	ii. 1.	4	xiv. 29.	1
xviii. 5.	8 g	ii. 21.	4	xiv. 35.	7 c
xxv. 11.	4	iii. 5.	8 a	xv. 1, 18. ε	4
xxxi. 14.	8 c	vii. 7, 10.	4	xvi. 14.	4
Deut. i. 34.	8 c	Job v. 2.	6	xix. 12.	2 c
iii. 26.	7 b	xiv. 13.	1	xix. 19. ζ	4
ix. 7, 8.	8 d	xiv. 13.	1	xxi. 14.	4
ix. 19.	8 a	xix. 11.	1	xxi. 24.	7 c
ix. 22. β	8 f	xix. 29.	1	xxiv. 18.	1
xi. 17.	1	xx. 23, 28.	1	xxvii. 3.	5 b
xxix. 23, 28.	4	xxi. 20.	4	xxvii. 4. a	4
xxxii. 27.	5 b	xxi. 30.	7 c	xxix. 8.	1
Josh. ix. 20.	8 g	xxxii. 2, 2, 3, 5.	3 c	xxx. 33.	1
xxii. 18.	8 c	xxxvi. 13.	1	Eccles. v. 17.	1
xxii. 20.	8 g	xxxvi. 18.	4	Isa. ix. 19.	7 c
1 Sam. xviii. 8.	3 b c	xl. 11.	1	x. 6.	7 c
xx. 7.	1	xli. 7.	1	xiii. 9, 13.	7 c
xxviii. 18.	8 c	Ps. ii. 5, 12.	1	xiv. 6.	7 c
xxix. 4.	8 c	xviii. 7.	3 a	xvi. 6.	7 c
2 Sam. iii. 8.	3 c	xxi. 9.	1	xxviii. 21.	9 a
xi. 20.	4	xxvii. 8.	4	xlvii. 6.	8 a
xiii. 21.	3 c	xxxviii. 1.	4	liv. 8.	8 g
xxii. 8.	3 a	lv. 3.	8 g	liv. 9.	8 b
2 Kings v. 11.	8 c	lviii. 9.	1	lvii. 16.	8 c
xiii. 19.	8 c	lix. 13.	3 d	lvii. 17, 17.	8 a c
xxiii. 13, 17.	4	lix. 13.	4	lx. 10.	8 g
xxiii. 26.	3 d	lxix. 24.	8 g	lxiv. 5.	8 c
1 Chron. xxvii. 24.	8 g	lxxvi. 10, 10.	4	lxiv. 9.	8 c
2 Chron. xii. 7.	4	lxxviii. 21, 59.	7 b	Jer. vii. 29.	7 c
xii. 12.	1	lxxviii. 31.	1	x. 10.	8 g
xvi. 10.	5 a	lxxviii. 38.	4	xviii. 20.	8 g
xix. 2, 10.	8 g	lxxviii. 49.	7 c		4

Jer. xxi. 5.	8 g	Ezek. vii. 12, 14.	3 d	Hos. xiii. 11.	7 c
xxxii. 37.	8 g	vii. 19.	7 c	Amos i. 11.	7 c
xxxvii. 15.	8 c	xiii. 15.	4	Hab. iii. 2.	9 c
xlviii. 30.	7 c	xxi. 31.	7 c	iii. 8.	7 c
l. 13.	8 g	xxii. 21, 31.	7 c	Zeph. i. 15, 18.	7 c
Lam. ii. 2.	7 c	xxxviii. 19.	7 c	Zech. vii. 12.	8 g
iii. 1.	7 c	Hos. v. 10.	7 c	viii. 14.	8 e
v. 22.	8 a				

a lit. does it kindle to thee?   *β lit.* were provoking to wrath.   *γ lit.* in the wrath of.   *δ* "fierce wrath."   *ε lit.* a man of wrath.   *ζ lit.* the great of wrath.

WREATH

גְּדִלִים   *m. pl.* properly, twisted threads ; fringes ; festoons on the capitals of columns : 1 Kings vii. 17.

עֲבֹת   *com.* anything interwoven ; a cord, braid, wreath, of small rods woven together : Exod. xxviii. 14, 14, 22, 24, 25 ; xxxix. 15, 17, 18.

שְׂבָכָה   *f.* a net ; lattice, lattice-work, balustrade, especially upon or around the capitals of columns : 2 Kings xxv. 17, 17 : 2 Chron. iv. 12, 13, 13.

שָׂרַג   to interweave. HITHPAEL *fut.* Lam. i. 14.

WREST

נָטָה   to stretch out ; to turn aside ; to wrest, pervert right. HIPHIL *inf.* Exod. xxiii. 2. *fut.* Exod. xxiii. 6 : Deut. xvi. 19.

עָצַב   to vex ; to wrest. PIEL *fut.* Ps. lvi. 5.

WRESTLE

אָבַק   to wrestle, from אָבָק, dust ; so Gr. from κόνις, κονίζεσθαι, συγκονιοῦσθαι ; from πάλη, very light dust, παλαίειν, συμπαλαίειν. Wrestlers having been first anointed to increase their strength, were afterwards sprinkled with fine sand or dust to give a firmer hold. The ground was also strewed with sand to break the fall. NIPHAL *inf.* Gen. xxxii. 25. *fut.* Gen. xxxii. 24.

פָּתַל   to twist ; to be twisted, to wrestle, which implies a mutual twisting and intertwining of the limbs. NIPHAL *pret.* Gen. xxx. 8. נַפְתּוּלִים *m. pl.* struggles : Gen. xxx. 8.

WRETCHEDNESS

רַע   *adj.* evil : Num. xi. 15.

WRING

1   מִיץ   *m.* pressure ; translated in the same verse by churning, forcing.

2   מָלַק   to break, to crack, but not so as to separate, *e.g.* the neck of a fowl. KAL *pret.*

3   מָצָה   to suck, to suck out ; to drink out greedily ; to press out moisture, *seq.* מִן from anything. KAL *a pret.* *b fut.* NIPHAL *c pret.* *d fut.*

Lev. i. 15, 15.	2, 3 c	Judg. vi. 38.	3 b	Prov. xxx. 33.	1
v. 8.	2	Ps. lxxiii. 10.	3 d	Isa. li. 17.	3 a
v. 9.	3 d	lxxv. 8.	3 b		

WRINKLE

קָמַט   to lay fast hold of, to compress ; to make wrinkled, to fill with wrinkles. KAL *fut.* Job xvi. 8.

WRITE

1   כָּתַב   properly, to cut in, to grave ; generally, to write, with an *acc.* of that which is written, also to write a book, &c. The material or book upon or in which one writes is often put after עַל ; also after אֶל and בְּ. So, too, with an *acc.* to inscribe, to write upon anything, to cover with writing ; here belongs Isa. xliv. 5 ; see *Subscribe.* The instrument *stylus* is put with בְּ ; he to or for whom one writes is put with לְ, אֶל, עַל. To write up, to inscribe in a register, *e.g.* men, inhabitants, soldiers. KAL *a pret.* *b inf.* *c imp.* *d fut.* *e part.* Poel. *f part.* Paül. NIPHAL *g fut.* *h part.* PIEL *i pret.* *k* כָּתָב *m.* writing, record. כָּתָב P'AL *l pret.* *m fut.* *n part. active.* *o part. passive.* כְּתָב P Ch. *m.* writing, edict. מִכְתָּב q *m.* writing, ordinance.

2   סָפַר   to write ; to number ; see *Scribe.* KAL *part.* Poel.

3   רְשַׁם   Ch. to write. P'AL *part. passive.*

Exod. xvii. 14.	1 c	2 Kings xxii. 13.	1 f	Esth. viii. 9, 9, 9.	1 g k k
xxiv. 4.	1 d	xxiii. 3, 21, 24, 28.	1 f	viii. 10.	1 d
xxiv. 12.	1 a	xxiv. 5.	1 f	viii. 13.	1 k
xxxi. 18.	1 f	1 Chron. iv. 41.	1 f	ix. 20, 29.	1 d
xxxii. 15, 15.	1 f	ix. 1.	1 f	ix. 23.	1 a
xxxii. 16, 16.	1 q	xvi. 40.	1 f	ix. 27.	1 k
xxxii. 32.	1 a	xxiv. 6.	1 d	ix. 32.	1 h
xxxiv. 1.	1 a	xxviii. 19.	1 k	x. 2.	1 f
xxxiv. 27.	1 c	xxix. 29.	1 f	Job xiii. 26.	1 d
xxxiv. 28.	1 d	2 Chron. ii. 11.	1 k	xix. 23.	1 g
xxxix. 30, 30.	1 d q	ix. 29.	1 f	xxxi. 35.	1 a
Num. v. 23.	1 a	xii. 15.	1 f	Ps. xl. 7.	1 f
xi. 26.	1 f	xiii. 22.	1 f	xlv. 1.	2
xvii. 2, 3.	1 d	xvi. 11.	1 f	lxix. 28.	1 g
xxxiii. 2.	1 d	xx. 34.	1 f	lxxxvii. 6.	1 b
Deut. iv. 13.	1 d	xxi. 12.	1 q	cii. 18.	1 g
v. 22.	1 d	xxiii. 18.	1 f	cxxxix. 16.	1 f
vi. 9.	1 a	xxiv. 27.	1 f	cxlix. 9.	1 f
ix. 10.	1 f	xxv. 4, 26.	1 f	Prov. iii. 3.	1 c
x. 2.	1 d	xxvi. 22.	1 a	vii. 3.	1 c
x. 4, 4.	1 d q	xxvii. 7.	1 f	xxii. 20.	1 a
xi. 20.	1 a	xxviii. 26.	1 f	Eccles. xii. 10.	1 f
xvii. 18.	1 a	xxx. 1.	1 a	Isa. iv. 3.	1 c
xxiv. 1, 3.	1 a	xxx. 5, 18.	1 f	viii. 1.	1 c
xxvii. 3, 8.	1 a	xxxi. 3.	1 f	x. 1.	1 i
xxviii. 58, 61.	1 f	xxxii. 17.	1 a	x. 19.	1 d
xxix. 20, 21, 27.	1 f	xxxii. 32.	1 f	xxx. 8.	1 c
xxx. 10.	1 f	xxxiii. 19.	1 f	xxxviii. 9.	1 q
xxxi. 19.	1 c	xxxiv. 21, 24, 31.	1 f	lxv. 6.	1 f
xxxi. 9, 22.	1 d	xxxiv. 4, 4.	1 k q	Jer. xvii. 1.	1 f
xxxi. 24.	1 b	27.	1 f	xvii. 13.	1 g
Josh. i. 8.	1 f	xxxvi. 8.	1 f	xxii. 30.	1 c
viii. 31, 34.	1 f	xxxvi. 22.	1 q	xxv. 13.	1 c
viii. 32, 32.	1 d a	Ezra i. 1.	1 q	xxx. 2.	1 c
x. 13.	1 f	iii. 2, 4.	1 f	xxxi. 33.	1 d
xiii. 6.	1 f	iv. 6.	1 a	xxxvi. 2, 6, 17, 27,	
xxiv. 26.	1 d	iv. 7, 7, 7.	1 a k f	29.	1 a
Judg. v. 14. *a*	2	iv. 8.	1 l	xxxvi. 4, 32.	1 d
1 Sam. x. 25.	1 d	v. 7.	1 o	xxxvi. 18.	1 e
2 Sam. i. 18.	1 f	v. 10.	1 m	xxxvi. 28.	1 c
xi. 14, 15.	1 d	vi. 2.	1 o	xlv. 1.	1 b
1 Kings ii. 3.	1 f	vi. 18.	1 p	li. 60, 60.	1 d f
xi. 41.	1 f	viii. 34.	1 g	Ezek. ii. 10, 10.	1 f
xiv. 19, 29.	1 f	Neh. vi. 6.	1 f	ix. 2, 3.	1 g
xv. 7, 23, 31.	1 f	vii. 5.	1 f	xiii. 9, 9.	1 g k
xvi. 5, 14, 20, 27.	1 f	viii. 14, 15.	1 f	xxiv. 2.	1 c
xxi. 8, 9.	1 d	ix. 38.	1 e	xxxvii. 16, 16.	1 c
xxi. 11.	1 f	x. 34, 36.	1 f	xxxvii. 20.	1 c
xxi. 39, 45.	1 f	xii. 23.	1 f	xliii. 11.	1 c
2 Kings i. 18.	1 f	xiii. 1.	1 f	Dan. v. 5, 5.	1 n
viii. 23.	1 f	Esth. i. 19.	1 g	v. 7, 8, 15, 16, 17.	1 p
x. 1, 6.	1 d	i. 22.	1 k	v. 24, 24.	1 p, 3
x. 34.	1 f	ii. 23.	1 g	v. 25, 25.	1 p, 3
xii. 19.	1 f	iii. 9.	1 g	vi. 8, 9, 10.	1 p
xiii. 8, 12.	1 f	iii. 12, 12, 12.	1 g k h	vi. 25.	1 l
xiv. 6, 15, 18, 28.	1 f	iii. 14.	1 k	vii. 1.	1 l
xv. 6, 11, 15, 21,		iv. 8.	1 k	ix. 11, 13.	1 f
26, 31, 36.	1 f	vi. 2.	1 f	xii. 1.	1 f
xvi. 19.	1 f	viii. 5, 5.	1 g a	Hos. viii. 12.	1 d
xvii. 37.	1 a	viii. 8, 8, 8.	1 c k h	Hab. ii. 2.	1 c
xx. 20.	1 f			Mal. iii. 16.	1 g
xxi. 17, 25.	1 f				

a or, numberer.

WRONG

1 חָמַס to do violence to any one, to oppress, to wrong. KAL [a] *fut.* [b] *part.* Poel. [c] חָמָס *m.* violence, that which is obtained by violence.

2 סָרָה *f.* turning away; transgression of law, fault, crime.

3 עָוָה to act perversely, to sin. KAL *pret.*

4 עַוָּתָה *f.* a bending or bowing down of any one, *i. e.* oppression.

5 עָקַל to twist, to wrest, to pervert. PUAL *part.*

6 עָשַׁק to oppress. KAL *inf.*

7 רַע *adj.* evil.

8 רָשָׁע *adj.* wicked: Exod. ii. 13, "him that did the wrong."

9 מִשְׁפָּט *m.* judgment.

10 שֶׁקֶר false.

Gen. xvi. 5.		1 c	Job xix. 7.	1 c	Ps. cxix. 86.		10
Exod. ii. 13. α		8	xxi. 27. β	1 a	Prov. viii. 36.		1 b
Deut. xix. 16.		2	Ps. xxxv. 19.	10	Jer. xxii. 13. γ		9
Judg. xi. 27.		7	xxxviii. 19.	10	Lam. iii. 59.		4
1 Chron. xii. 17.		1 c	lxix. 4.	10	Ezek. xxii. 29.		9
xvi. 21.		6	cv. 14.	6	Hab. i. 4.		5
Esth. i. 16.		3					

α "him that did the wrong," *comp.* Acts vii. 26. "imagine." β "wrongfully γ *lit.* without judgment.

YEAR

יוֹם *m.* day; in the *plur.* time, without reference to single days. Sometimes the signification is restricted to a definite space of time, viz. a year; as the Syriac and Chaldee denote both time and a year, and as in Eng. also several words signifying time, weight, measure, are likewise used to denote certain specific times, weights, measures: Exod. xiii. 10, 10, "full year;" Lev. xxv. 29; Num. ix. 22; Josh. xiii. 1, 1; Judg. xi. 40, "yearly," *lit.* from days to days, *marg.* 'from year to year;' xvii. 10, xxi. 19, *lit.* from days to days; 1 Sam. i. 3, *lit. id.;* 21, *lit.* of days; ii. 19, 19, 19, *lit. id.;* xx. 6, *lit. id.;* xxvii. 7, *marg.* '(a year of) days;' 2 Sam. xiv. 26, *lit.* the end of days to days; 1 Kings i. 1; Amos iv. 4, *marg.* '(years) of days.'

שָׁנָה *f.* a year; properly, repetition, *sc.* of the course of the sun, or of the seasons, as spring, harvest, winter, &c.; *comp.* Lat. *annus,* properly, *i.q. annulus,* a ring, circle; Gr. ἐνιαυτός.—Gen. i. 14, &c. שָׁנָה Ch. *f.* Ezra iv. 24; v. 11, 13; vi. 3, 15: Dan. v. 31; vii. 1.

YEARN

כָּמַר to be warm, to burn, *e.g.* one's love, to yearn; *seq.* עַל and אֶל. NIPHAL *pret.* Gen. xliii. 30, 1 Kings iii. 26.

YELL

נָעַר to shake; to roar, *e.g.* the young lion. KAL *pret.* Jer. li. 38, *marg.* 'or, shake themselves.' The Rabbinical meaning, to yell or bray, is doubtful.

נָתַן to give. KAL *pret.* Jer. ii. 15.

קוֹל *m.* voice: Jer. ii. 15.

YELLOW

יְרַקְרַק *adj.* greenish; paleness, yellowness of gold: Ps. lxviii. 13.

צָהֹב *adj.* gold-coloured, yellow, of hair: Lev. xiii. 30, 32, 36.

YESTERDAY, YESTERNIGHT

אֶמֶשׁ *adv.* properly the past night; also yesterday. It implies strictly the last part of the preceding natural day (not the civil), *i. e.* the evening and night of yesterday, and is thence transferred so as to denote evening and night in general: Gen. xix. 34; xxxi. 29, 42: 2 Kings ix. 26.

תְּמוֹל *adv.* yesterday; often coupled with שִׁלְשׁוֹם, "day before yesterday:" Exod. v. 14, *lit.* as yesterday the third day: 1 Sam. xx. 27: 2 Sam. xv. 20: Job viii. 9. אֶתְמוֹל aforetime, of old; yesterday: Ps. xc. 4, *lit.* the day of yesterday.

YIELD

1 גָּמַל to wean; applied to the producing of ripe or mature fruit; to make good; see *Reward.* KAL *fut.*

2 זָרַע to scatter seed, to sow; to scatter or yield its seed is said of a seed-bearing plant or tree. KAL [a] *part.* Poel. HIPHIL [b] *part.*

3 יָד *com.* hand; "yield yourselves," *marg.* 'give the hand.' See 1 Chron. xxix. 24, Ezra x. 19.

4 יְהַב Ch. to give. P'AL *pret.*

5 יָסַף to add, to increase, augment. HIPHIL [a] *inf.* [b] *fut.*

6 נָטָה to stretch out, to incline, to cause to incline. HIPHIL *pret.*

7 נָשָׂא to bear. KAL *fut.*

8 נָתַן to give. KAL [a] *pret.* [b] *inf.* [c] *imp.* [d] *fut.*

9 עָשָׂה to do, &c. KAL [a] *pret.* [b] *inf.* [c] *fut.* [d] *part.* Poel.

10 רָבָה to multiply; to yield much. HIPHIL *part.*

11 מַרְפֵּא healing, cure of diseases; tranquillity, placidness of mind.

Gen. i. 11, 11.	2 b, 9 d	Num. xvii. 8.	1	Eccles. x. 4.		11
i. 12, 12.	2 b, 9 d	Deut. xi. 17.	8 d	Isa. v. 10, 10.		9 c
i. 29.	2 a	2 Chron. xxx. 8.	8 c, 3	Jer. xvii. 8.		9 b
iv. 12. α	5 b, 8 b	Neh. ix. 37.	10	Ezek. xxxiv. 27, 27.	8 a d
xlix. 20.	8 d	Ps. lxvii. 6.	8 a	xxxvi. 8.		7
Lev. xix. 25.	5 a	lxxv. 12.	8 d	Dan. iii. 28.		4
xxv. 19.	8 a	cvii. 37.	9 c	Hos. viii. 7, 7.		9 c
xxvi. 4, 4.	8 a d	Prov. vii. 21.	6	Joel ii. 2.		8 a
xxvi. 20, 20.	8 d	xii. 12.	8 d	Hab. iii. 17.		9 a

α *lit.* it shall not add to give.

YOKE

מוֹט *m.* a bar, or pole; see *Staff:* a yoke: Nah. i. 13. מוֹטָה *f.* Isa. lviii. 6, 9: Jer. xxvii. 2; xxviii. 10, 12, 13, 13: Ezek. xxx. 18.

עֹל *m.* once עוֹל, Jer. v. 5; a yoke, the curved piece of wood upon the neck of draught animals, by which they are fastened to the pole or beam. Often *trop.* as the emblem of servitude.—Gen. xlvii. 40, &c.

צֶמֶד *m.* a pair, a yoke; as much land as a yoke of oxen can plough in a day: 1 Sam. xi. 7; xiv. 14: 1 Kings xix. 19, 21: Job i. 3; xlii. 12: Jer. li. 23.

YOUNG, YOUTH

1 אֶפְרֹחִים *m. pl.* the young of birds, a brood.

2 בָּחוּר *m.* a youth, young man, properly a chosen youth, implying strength, beauty, &c. ᵃ בְּחוּרוֹת *f. pl.* youth. ᵇ בְּחֻרִים *m. pl. id.*

3 בֵּן *m.* son; "young," *lit.* mostly, son of. ᵇ בֵּן Ch. son.

4 גּוֹזָל *m.* a young bird, *e.g.* a dove, or pigeon, Gen. xv. 9; an eaglet, Deut. xxxii. 11.

5 גּוּר *m.* a whelp, cub; so called as still a suckling.

6 חֹרֶף *m.* autumn; *metaph.* ripe, manly age.

7 יוֹם *m.* day.

8 יֶלֶד *m.* one born; a boy, a child; a youth, young man. ᵃ יַלְדוּת *f.* childhood, youth.

9 נַעַר *m.* a boy; spoken of an infant just born, of a boy, and of a youth near twenty years of age; often *emphat.* to express a tender age. ᵃ נַעֲרָה *m.* youth. ᵇ נַעֲרָה *f.* girl, young woman. ᶜ נְעוּרִים *m. pl.* youth. ᵈ נְעוּרוֹת *f. pl. id.*

10 עוּל to give milk, to suckle. KAL *part.* Poel, "ewes great with young." ᵃ עֲוִיל *m.* young children.

11 עֲלוּמִים *m. pl.* youth, youthful age; of the youth of a people, Isa. liv. 4. In Job xx. 11 our translators seem to have followed the Vulgate, inserting "of the sin" of his youth. Gesenius, with the Lxx., Chald., and Syr., would render the sentence, "his bones are full of youth," *i.e.* of youthful strength. The authorised version, however, is preferable, being more agreeable to the Hebrew and to the context. Compare also Ezek. xxxii. 27.

12 עֶלֶם *m.* a youth, a young man.

13 עֹפֶר *m.* fawn, *i.e.* young deer, roe, gazelle.

14 פַּר *m.* a young bullock, a steer.

15 פְּרֹחָה *f.* progeny of beasts; contemptuously for low and wicked men.

16 צָעִיר *adj.* small; in age, young; in number, few. ᵃ צְעִירָה *f. id.*

17 קָטָן *adj.* little, small; young. ᵃ קָטֹן *adj. id.*

18 שַׁחֲרוּת *f.* dawn of life; youth.

19 שִׁלְיָה *f.* after-birth, the membrane that envelopes the fœtus, and follows the birth.

Gen. iv. 23.	8	Gen. xlvi. 34.	9 c	Num. viii. 8, 8.	3
viii. 21.	9 c	xlviii. 14.	16	xi. 27.	9
ix. 24.	17	xlviii. 19.	17	xi. 28.	2 b
xiv. 24.	9	Exod. x. 9.	9	xv. 24.	9
xv. 9.	4	xxiv. 5.	9	xxviii. 11, 19, 27.	3
xviii. 7.	9	xxxiii. 11.	9	xxix. 2, 8, 13, 17.	3
xix. 4. α	9	Lev. i. 14.β	3	xxx. 3, 16.	9 c
xix. 31, 34, 38.	16	iv. 3.γ 14.γ	3	Deut. xxii. 6, 6.	1
xxii. 3, 5, 19.	9	v. 7.δ 14.δ	3	xxii. 6, 6.	9
xxv. 23.	16	ix. 2.ε	3	xxviii. 50.	9
xxvii. 15, 42.	17	xii. 6.ζ 8.ζ	3	xxviii. 57.	19
xxix. 16, 18.	17	xiv. 22, 30.	3	xxxii. 11.	4
xxix. 26.	16	xv. 14, 29.	3	xxxii. 25.	2
xxxiii. 13.	10	xvi. 3.	3	Josh. vi. 21, η 23.	9
xxxiv. 19.	9	xxii. 13.	9 c	vi. 26.	16
xli. 12.	9	xxii. 28.	3	Judg. i. 13.	17
xlii. 13, 15, 20, 32, 34.	17	xxiii. 18.ε	3	iii. 9.	17
		Num. vi. 10.δ	3	vi. 25.θ	14
xliii. 29.	17	vii. 15, ε 21, 27, 33, 39, 45, 51, 57, 63,	3	viii. 14, 20, 20.	9
xliii. 33, 33.	16, 16 a			ix. 5.	17
xliv. 2,12, 23, 26, 26.	17	69, 75, 81.	3	ix. 54, 54.	9
				xiv. 10.	2

Judg. xv. 2.	17	2 Chron. xxxvi. 17, 17.	2	Isa. xxiii. 4.	2
xvii. 7, 11, 12.	9	Ezra vi. 9.	3 a	xxxi. 8.	2
xviii. 3, 15.	9	Esth. ii. 2, 3.	9 b	xl. 11.	10
xix. 19.	9	iii. 13. α	9	xl. 30, 30.	9, 2
xxi. 12.	9 b	viii. 10.	3	xlvii. 12, 15.	9 c
Ruth ii. 9, 9, 15, 21.	9	Job i. 19.	9	liv. 4.	11
iii. 10.	9	xiii. 26.	9 c	liv. 6.	9
iv. 12.	9 b	xix. 18.	10 a	lxii. 5.	2
1 Sam. i. 24.ι	9	xx. 11.	11	Jer. ii. 2.	9 c
ii. 17.	9	xxix. 4.	6	iii. 4, 24, 25.	9 c
viii. 16.	2	xxix. 8.	9	vi. 11.	2
ix. 2.	2	xxx. 1.	16, 7	vi. 21.	2
ix. 11.	9 b	xxx. 12.	15	xi. 22.	2
xiv. 1, 6.	9	xxxi. 18.	9 c	xv. 8.	2
xiv. 49.	17	xxxii. 6.	16, 7	xviii. 21.	2
xvi. 11.	17	xxxiii. 25.	11	xxii. 21.	9 c
xvii. 14.	17	xxxvi. 14.	9 a	xxxi. 12.	3
xvii. 33, 33.	9, 9 c	xxxviii. 41.	8	xxxi. 13.	2
xvii. 42, 55, 58.	9	xxxix. 3.	8	xxxi. 19.	2
xx. 22.	12	xxxix. 4, 16.	3	xxxii. 30.	9 d
xxi. 4, 5.	9	xxxix. 30.	1	xlviii. 11.	9 c
xxv. 5, 5, 8, 8, 9, 12, 14, κ 25, 27.	9	Ps. xxv. 7.	9 c	xlviii. 15.	2
xxvi. 22.	9	xxix. 6.	3	xlix. 26.	2
xxx. 13, 17.	9	xxxvii. 25.	9	l. 30.	2
2 Sam. i. 5, 6, 13, 15.	9	lxxi. 5, 17.	9 c	li. 3.	2
ii. 14, 21.	9	lxxvii. 63.	2	li. 22, 22.	9, 2
vi. 22.	9	lxxviii. 71.	10	Lam. i. 15, 18.	2
ix. 12.	17	lxxxiv. 3.	2	ii. 21, 21.	9, 2
xiii. 32, 34.	9	lxxxviii. 15.	9 a	iii. 27.	9 c
xiv. 21.	9	lxxxix. 45.	11	iv. 3.	5
xvi. 2.	9	ciii. 5.	9 c	v. 13, 14.	2
xviii. 5, 12, 15, 29, 32, 32.	9	cx. 3.	8 a	Ezek. iv. 14.	9 c
xix. 7.	9 c	cxix. 9.	9	ix. 6.	2
1 Kings i. 2.	9 b	cxxvii. 4.	2	xvi. 22, 43.	9 c
xi. 28.	9	cxxix. 1, 2.	9 c	xvi. 46.	17
xii. 8, 10, 14.	8	cxliv. 12.	9 c	xvi. 60.	9 c
xvi. 34.	16	cxlvii. 9.	3	xvi. 61.	17
xviii. 12.	9 c	cxlviii. 12.	2	xxiii. 3, 8, 19, 21, 21.	9 c
Prov. i. 4.	9			xxiii. 6, 12, 23.	2
xx. 14, 15, 17, 19.	9	ii. 17.	9 c	xxx. 17.	2
2 Kings iv. 22.	9	v. 18.	9 c	xliii. 19.γ	3, 14
v. 22.	9	vii. 7, 7.	3, 9	xliii. 23.γ	3, 14
xx. 17.	9	xx. 29.	2	xliii. 25.γ	3, 14
viii. 12.	2	Eccles. xi. 9, 9,	2, 8 a, 2 a	xlv. 18.γ	3, 14
ix. 4, 4.	9	xi. 10.	18	xlvi. 6.γ	3, 14
1 Chron. xii. 28.	9	xii. 1.	2 a	Hos. ii. 15.	9 c
xxii. 5.	9	Cant. ii. 9, 17.	13	Joel i. 8.	2
xxiv. 31.	17	iv. 5.	13	ii. 28.	2
xxix. 1.	9	vii. 3.	13	Amos ii. 11.	2
2 Chron. xx. 8, 10, 14.	8	vii. 3.	13	iv. 10.	2
xiii. 7.	9	vii. 14.	13	viii. 13.	2
xiii. 9.λ	3, 14	Isa. ix. 17.	2	Zech. ii. 4.	9
xxi. 17.	9	xi. 7.	8	ix. 17.	2
xxii. 1.	17	xiii. 18.	2	xi. 16.μ	9
xxxiv. 3.	9	xx. 4.	9	xiii. 5.	9 c
				Mal. ii. 14, 15.	9 c

α *lit.* from the youth and to the old man.   β *lit.* sons of the dove.   γ *lit.* a steer the son of a bull.   δ *lit.* sons of.   ε *lit.* son of a bull.   ζ *lit.* son of a bull.   η *lit.* and from the youth and to the old man.   θ *lit.* a steer ox.   ι *lit.* and the child was a child.   κ *lit.* one young man of the young men.   λ *lit.* with a steer the son of a bull.   μ Perhaps *lit.* the wanderer.

ZEAL

קָנָא to be jealous; to envy; to burn with zeal; followed by לְ to be zealous for any one's cause; with בְּ of the object of zeal or envy. PIEL *pret.* Num. xxv. 13. *inf.* Num. xxv. 11, 2 Sam. xxi. 2. קִנְאָה *f.* jealousy, envy, zeal: Num. xxv. 11, "zealous for my sake," *lit.* with my zeal; 2 Kings x. 16; xix. 31: Ps. lxix. 9; cxix. 139: Isa. ix. 7; xxxvii. 32; lix. 17; lxiii. 15: Ezek. v. 13.

ZIF

זִו *m.* The name of the second Hebrew month, from the new moon of May to that of June, as though it were the month of flowers; from the root, זָוָה, implying splendour: 1 Kings vi. 1, 37.

ZOPHIM

צָפָה to look out; to watch. KAL *part.* Poel, *lit.* watchmen; Num. xxiii. 14: 1 Sam. i. 1.

ENGLISH AND HEBREW INDEX

** This Index is designed to furnish the reader with the various renderings of the several Hebrew words referred to in this work. The number of renderings is given in figures. The phrases which are not the direct rendering of the original, or which are to be referred to some other word in combination, are separated by a line. The expressions which give the peculiar force of the infinitive used intensively are placed separately. *Freq.* = frequent in such rendering.

אָב Abi-*ezrite* 3, chief 3, father *freq.*, forefather 1, principal 1——desire 1, family 2, patrimony 1.

אָב desire 1.

אָב Ch. father 9.

אֵב fruit 1, greenness 1.

אֵב Ch. fruit 3.

אָבַד *Kal*, broken 1, to be destroyed 4, destruction *inf.* 1, to fail 2, to lose 1, to be lost 8, to perish 79, to be perished 12, to be ready to perish 4, to be undone 1, to be void of 1——not to escape 1, to have no way to *flee* 1; *Inf. intens.* surely (perish) 2, utterly (perish) 1; *Piel*, to destroy 33, to be destroyed 1, to lose 1, to perish 1, to cause to perish 2, to make to perish 1, to spend 1; *Inf. intens.* utterly (destroy) 1; *Hiphil*, to destroy 24, to cause to perish 1, to take *from* 1.

אֲבַד Ch. *P'al*, to perish 1; *Aphel*, to destroy 4, to perish 1; *Hophal*, to be destroyed 1.

אֹבֵד perish 2.

(כ) אֲבֵדָה destruction 1.

אֲבֵדָה that which was lost 1, lost thing 1.

אַבְדוֹן destruction 6.

אַבְדָן destruction 1.

אָבְדָן destruction 1.

אָבָה *Kal*, to consent 3, to rest content 1, to will 46, to be willing 4.

אֲבֶה swift 1.

אֲבוֹי sorrow 1

אֵבוּס crib 3.

אַבְחָה point 1.

אֲבַטִּחִים melons 1.

אָבִיב Abib 7, ear 1, green ears of corn 1.

אֶבְיוֹן beggar 1, needy 35, poor 24, poor man 1.

אֲבִיוֹנָה desire 1.

אַבִּיר angel 1, bull 4, chiefest 1, mighty 3, mighty one 1, stout 2, strong 3, valiant 2.

אָבִיר mighty 6.

אָבַךְ *Hithpael*, to mount up 1.

אָבַל *Kal*, to lament 1, to mourn 17; *Hiphil*, to make to lament 1, to cause a mourning 1; *Hithpael*, to feign self to be a mourner 1, to lament 1, to mourn 17.

אָבֵל mourn 4, mourner 2, mourning 2.

אָבֵל plain 1.

אֵבֶל mourning 24.

אֶבֶן divers weights 3, stone *freq.*, stony 1, weight 4——carbuncle 1, mason 1, plummet 1.

אֶבֶן Ch. stone 8.

אַבְנֵט girdle 9.

אָבְנַיִם stools 1, wheels 1.

אָבַס *Kal*, fatted 1, stalled 1.

אֲבַעְבֻּעֹת blains 2.

אָבָק dust 4, small dust 1, powder 1.

אָבַק *Niphal*, to wrestle 2.

אֲבָקָה powder 1.

אָבַר *Hiphil*, to fly 1.

אֶבְרָה wing 3.

אֶבְרָה feather 2, wing 2.

אַבְרֵךְ bow the knee 1.

אֲגֻדָּה bunch 1, burden 1, troop 2.

אֱגוֹז nut 1.

אֲגוֹרָה piece of *silver* 1.

אֲגָלִים drops 1.

אֲגַם pond 3, pool 4, reed 1, standing *water* 2.

אַגְמוֹן bulrush 1, caldron 1, hook 1, rush 2.

אַגָּן bason 1, cup 1, goblet 1.

אֲגַפִּים bands 7.

אָגַר *Kal*, to gather 3.

אִגְּרָא Ch. letter 3.

אֶגְרוֹף fist 2.

אַגַּרְטְלִים chargers 2.

אִגֶּרֶת letter 10.

אֵד mist 1, vapour 1.

אָדַב *Hiphil*, to grieve 1.

אָדוֹן Adoni 3, Lord 26, lord *freq.*, master *freq.*, owner 1, O sir 1.

אַדִּיר excellent 4, famous 2, gallant 1, glorious 1, goodly 1, lordly 1, mighty 6, noble 7, principal 3, worthies 1.

אָדָם Adam *freq.*, another 1, low 1, man *very freq.*, man of low degree 1, mean man 3, person 8——common sort 1, hypocrite 1.

אָדַם *Kal*, to be ruddy 1; *Pual*, to be dyed red 5, to be red 1, to be made red 1; *Hiphil*, to be red 1; *Hithpael*, to be red 1.

אָדֹם red 7, ruddy 1.

אֹדֶם sardius 3.

אֲדַמְדָּם reddish 4, somewhat reddish 2.

אֲדָמָה country 1, earth 53, ground 43, husbandman 2, husbandry 1, land 125.

אַדְמֹנִי & אֲדַמְנִי red 1, ruddy 2.

אֶדֶן foundation 1, socket 53.

אֲדֹנָי Lord *freq.*, my Lord 1.

אָדַר *Niphal*, to be glorious 1, to become glorious 1; *Hiphil*, to make honourable 1.

אֲדָר Adar 7.

אֲדָר Ch. Adar 1.

אֶדֶר goodly 1, robe 1.

אֲדַרְגָּזְרַיָּא Ch. judges 2.

אַדְרַזְדָּא Ch. diligently 1.

אִדָּרִין Ch. threshing-floors 1.

אֲדַרְכֹּנִים drams 2.

אֶדְרָע Ch. force 1.

אַדֶּרֶת garment 4, glory 1, goodly 1, mantle 5, robe 1.

אָדַשׁ *Kal*, to thresh 1.

אָהַב & אָהֵב *Kal*, beloved 5, friend 11, to like 1, in love 1, to love *freq.*, lover 4; *Niphal*, lovely 1; *Piel*, friends 1, lover 14.

אַהֲבָה love 33, to love 7.

אֹהֲבִים lovers 1, loving 1.

אֹהָבִים loves 1.

אֱהִי (where) I will be 3.

אָהַל *Hiphil*, to shine 1.

אָהַל *Kal*, to pitch a tent 1, to remove a tent 1; *Piel*, to pitch a tent 1.

אֹהֶל covering 1, dwelling 1, dwelling place 2, (dwelling) place 1, home 1, tabernacle *freq.*, tent *freq.*

אֲהָלוֹת & אֲהָלִים aloes 3, trees of lign aloes 1.

אוֹב bottle 1, familiar spirit 8, to have familiar spirit 7.

אוּבָל or אָבֵל river 3.

אוּד brand 1, firebrand 2.

אוֹדֹת because of 5, cause 2.

אָוָה *Piel*, to desire 9, to long 1, to lust after 1; *Hithpael*, to covet 2, to desire 6, to desire greatly 1, to be desirous 1, to long 2, to lust 3, to point out 1.

אוֹי alas 1, woe 23.

אוֹיָה woe 1.

אֱוִיל fool 20, foolish 5, foolish man 1.

אוּל mighty 1, strength 1.

אֱוִלִי foolish 1.

אוּלָם or אֻלָם porch 34.

אוּלָם in very deed 2.

אִוֶּלֶת folly 13, foolishly 1, foolishness 10.

אָוֶן affliction 3, aven 6, Ben-oni 1, evil 1, false 1, idol 1, iniquity 47, mischief 31, mourners 1, mourning 1, nought 1, sorrow 1, unjust 1, unrighteous 2, vain 1, vanity 6, wicked 2, wickedness 5.

אוֹן force 1, goods 1, might 2, strength 7, substance 1.

אֳנִיּוֹת ships 1.

אוֹפַן fitly 1, wheel 33.

אוּץ *Kal*, to haste 3, to make haste 1, to hasten 1, hasty 2, to be narrow 1; *Hiphil*, to hasten 1, to labour 1.

אוֹצָר armoury 1, cellar 2, garner 1, store 2, storehouse 2, treasure 61, treasury 10.

אוֹר *Kal*, to be enlightened 2, to be light 1, to have light 1, to shine 2; *Niphal*, to be enlightened 1, glorious 1,—— break of day 1; *Hiphil*, to enlighten 2, to give light 11, to kindle 1, to light 1, to lighten 4, to set on fire 1, to shew light 2, to shine 2, to cause to shine 5, to make to shine 5.

אוֹר bright 2, clear 1, flood 1, herbs 1, light 114, lightning 1, morning 1, sun 1,—— day 2.

אוּר fire 5, light 1, Urim 7.

אוּרָה herb 2, light 2.

אֻרְוֹת cotes 1.

אַוָּה desire 3, lust after 1, pleasure 1.

אוֹת ensign 2, mark 1, miracle 2, sign 60, token 14.

אוֹת *Niphal*, to consent 4.

אָזָא & אֲזָה Ch. *P'al*, to heat 1, to be heated 1, hot 1.

אַד Ch. *P'al*, to be gone 2.

אֵזוֹב hyssop 10.

אֵזוֹר girdle 14.

אַזְכָּרָה memorial 7.

אָזַל *Kal*, to fail 1, to gad about 1, to be gone 2, to be spent 1; *Pual*, to go to and fro 1.

אֲזַל Ch. *P'al*, to go 6, to go up 1.

אָזַן *Piel*, to give good heed 1; *Hiphil*, to give ear 32, to hear 2, to hearken unto 6, to perceive by the ear 1.

אֹזֶן weapon 1.

אֹזֶן audience 7, ear *freq.*, hearing 5,—— to advertise 1, to displease 1, to hear 2, to reveal 1, to tell 1, shew 6.

אֲזִקִּים chains 2.

אָזַר *Kal*, to bind about 1, to gird up 3, to be girded 2; *Niphal*, to be girded 1; *Piel*, to compass about 1, to gird 2, to gird with 3; *Hithpael*, to gird self 3.

אֶזְרוֹעַ arm 2.

אֶזְרָח bay tree 1, born 5, born *in the land* 2, born of or in the country 2, one of...own country 3, homeborn 1, born in the land 1, of...own nation 1.

אָח another 24, brother *freq.*, brotherly 1, kindred 1, like 1, other 1.

אָח hearth 3.

אָח Ch. brother 1.

אָחַד *Hithpael*, to go one way or other 1.

אֶחָד a, an 67, alike 1, alone 1, altogether 1, another, any, apiece 1, a certain 9, few 3, first 36, only 4, other 30, a portion for 12, some, together 5.

אָחוּ flag 1, meadow 2.

אַחֲוָה declaration 1.

אַחֲוָה brotherhood 1.

אַחֲוָיָה Ch. shewing 1.

אָחוֹר till afterward 1, back 14, back part 1, backside 1, backward 11, behind 5, hereafter 1, hinder part 3, time to come 1, without 1.

אָחוֹת another 6, the other 1, sister *freq.*, together 1.

אָחַז *Kal*, to bar 1, to catch 1, to catch hold 1, to come upon 1, to fasten 2, to handle 1, to hold 11, to lay hold 3, portion 2, to rest 1, to surprise 1, to take 15, to take hold 15,—— to be affrighted 1; *Niphal*, to be caught 1, to be possessed 1, to have possession 2, to get possessions 1, to take possession 1, to be taken 1; *Piel*, to hold back 1; *Hophal*, to be fastened 1.

אֲחֻזָּה possession 66.

אֲחִידָן Ch. hard sentences 1.

אֹחִים doleful creatures 1.

אַחֲלַי & אַחֲלֵי O that 1; would God 1.

אַחְלָמָה amethyst 2.

אַחְמְתָא Ch. Achmetha 1.

אָחַר *Kal*, to stay there 1, to tarry longer 1; *Piel*, to continue 1, to defer 3, to delay 1, to hinder 1, to be late 1, to be slack 2, to tarry 6.

אַחַר back 1, back from 1, backside 1, to follow 10, follow after 1, following 21, hinder end 1, posterity 4, pursuing 2, remnant 1,—— to persecute 1.

אַחֵר another 34, another man 1, following 1, next 2, other 103, strange 1.

אַחֲרוֹן to come 9, following 1, hinder 1, hindermost 1, last 20, latter 8, rereward 1, utmost 2, uttermost 1.

אַחֲרֵי Ch. after 1.

אַחֲרִי Ch. another 5, other 1.

אַחֲרֵין Ch. at last 1.

אַחֲרִית end 21, hindermost 1, last 6, last end 4, latter 11, latter end 8, latter time 1, length 1, posterity 3, remnant 1, residue 1, reward 2, uttermost 1.

אַחֲרִית Ch. latter 1.

אָחֳרָן Ch. another 2, other 3.

אֲחֹרַנִּית back again 1, backward 6.

אֲחַשְׁדַּרְפְּנַיָּא Ch. princes 9.

אֲחַשְׁדַּרְפְּנִים lieutenants 4.

אֲחַשְׁתְּרָנִים camels 2.

אַט gently 1, secret 1, softly 2.

אָטָד Atad 2, bramble 3, thorn 1.

אֵטוּן fine linen 1.

אִטִּי softly 1.

אִטִּים charmers 1.

אָטַם *Kal*, narrow 4, to shut 1, to stop 2; *Hiphil*, to stop 1.

אָטַר *Kal*, to shut 1.

אִטֵּר left handed 2.

אִי country 1, island 6, isle 30.

אִי woe 2.

אֹיֵב *Kal*, enemy 280, to be an enemy 1, foe 2.

אֵיבָה enmity 3, hatred 2.

אֵיד calamity 17, destruction 7.

אַיָּה kite 2, vulture 1.

אִיִּים wild beast of the islands 3.

אַיָּל hart 7.

אַיִל lintel 1, post 21, ram *freq.*

אֵילִים mighty 4, mighty men 1, oaks 11, trees 2.

אֱיָל strength 1.

אַיָּלָה hind 8.

אֱיָלוּת strength 1.

אֵלַמִּים & אֵילַמִּים arches 13.

אִילָן Ch. tree 6.

אַיֶּלֶת Aijeleth 1, hind 2.

אָיֹם terrible 3.

אֵימָה dread 1, fear 5, horror 1, idol 1, terrible 2, terror 7.

אַיִן (not), to be gone 2.

אֵיפָה divers measures 2, ephah 34, measure 2.

אִישׁ another 5, a certain 4, fellow 1, *footman* 5, friend 1, good man 1, great man 1, high 1, high degree 1, husband 69, Ishi 1, male 2, man *very freq.*, mankind 1, mighty man 2, (valiant) man 1, people 1, person 12, some, worthy 1,—— adversary 2, bear 1, champion 2, consent 1, counsellor 1, destroyer 1, elder 1, eloquent 1, evil speaker 1, that giveth 1, have war 2, husbandman 1, lender 1, liar 1,

none 1, oppressor 1, prophet 1, reprover 1, slothful 1, steward 1, stranger 6, at great strife 1,——husbandman 2.

אִישׁ Hithpael, to shew selves men 1.

אִישׁן apple of the eye 3, black 1, obscure 1.

אִיתוֹן entrance 1.

אֵיתָן & אֵתָן Ethanim 1, hard 1, mighty 4, rough 1, strength 2, strong 5.

אַכְזָב liar 1, lie 1.

אַכְזָר cruel 3, fierce 1.

אַכְזָרִי cruel 7, cruel one 1.

אַכְזְרִיּוּת cruel 1.

אׇכְלָה meat 1.

אָכַל Kal, to burn up 1, to consume 26, to devour 95, to devour up 1, devourer 1, to dine 1, to eat 566, to eat up 19, eater 1, to feed 2, food 1, to be higher 1, meat 4; Inf. intens. at all (eat) 1, freely (eat) 2, in...wise (eat) 1, indeed (eat) 1, in plenty (eat) 1, quite (devour) 1; Niphal, to be consumed 2, to be devoured 5, to be eaten 36; Inf. intens. at all (eaten) 2; Piel, to consume 1; Pual, to be consumed 3, to be devoured 2; Hiphil, to consume 1, to cause to eat 3, to give to eat 1, to feed 12, to lay meat 1.

אֲכַל Ch. P'al, to devour 4, to eat 1,——to accuse 2.

אֹכֶל eating 4, food 16, mealtime 1, meat 18, prey 2, victuals 3.

אׇכְלָה to consume 1, to devour 3, to eat 2, food 1, fuel 3, meat 8.

אָכַף Kal, to crave 1.

אֶכֶף hand 1.

אִכָּר husbandman 5, plowman 2.

אֵל El 2, God 212, god 15, idols 1, might 1, mighty 4, mighty one 1, power 4, strong 1,——goodly 1, great 1.

אֶלְגָּבִישׁ great hailstones 3.

אַלְגּוּמִּים algum trees 3.

אָלָה Kal, to lament 1.

אָלָה Kal, to curse 1, to swear 2; Hiphil, to adjure 1, to cause to swear 1, to make to swear 1.

אָלָה curse 14, cursing 4, execration 2, oath 14, swearing 2.

אֵלָה oak 1.

אֵלָה Elah 3, elm 1, oak 11, teil tree 1.

אֱלָהּ Ch. El 1, God 78, god 15.

אֱלֹהִים angels 1, El-elohe-Israel 1, God very freq., goddess 2, godly 1, god 240, judge 5,—— exceeding 1, great 1, mighty 2, very great 1.

אֱלוֹהַּ God 52, god 5.

אֱלוּל Elul 1.

אַלּוֹן Allon-bachuth 1, oak 8.

אֵלוֹן plain 9.

אַלּוּף & אַלֻּף captain 1, chief 1, chief friend 2, duke 57, friends 1, governor 3, guide 4, ox 2.

אָלַח Niphal, to become filthy 3.

אַלְיָה rump 5.

אֱלִיל idol 17, image 1, of no value 1, thing of nought 1.

אַלְלַי woe 2.

אָלַם Niphal, to be dumb 7, to be put to silence 1; Piel, to bind 1.

אֵלֶם congregation 1.

אִלֵּם dumb 5, dumb man 1.

אַלְמֻגִּים almug tree 3.

אֲלֻמָּה sheaf 5.

אֵלַמּוֹת arches 2.

אַלְמָן forsaken 1.

אַלְמֹן widowhood 1.

אַלְמָנָה widow 53.

אַלְמָנוֹת desolate houses 1, desolate palaces 1.

אַלְמָנוּת widow 1, widowhood 3.

אַלְמֹנִי one 1, such 2.

אָלַף Kal, to learn 1; Piel, to teach 2, to utter 1.

אָלַף Hiphil, to bring forth thousands 1.

אֶלֶף family 1, kine 4, oxen 3, thousand freq.

אֶלֶף & אֲלַף Ch. thousand 3.

אָלַץ Piel, to urge 1.

אַלְקוּם no rising up 1.

אֵם dam 5, mother freq.,——parting 1.

אָמָה bondmaid 2, bondwoman 4, handmaid 23, maid 8, maidservant 19.

אַמָּה cubit very freq., measure 1, post 1.

אֻמָּה Ch. nation 8.

אָמוֹן one brought up 1.

אָמוֹן multitude 2, populous 1.

אֱמוּן faith 1, faithful 3, truth 1.

אֱמוּנָה also אֱמֻנָה faith 1, faithful 2, faithful man 3, faithfully 5, faithfulness 18, set office 5, stability 1, steady 1, truly 1, truth 13, verily 1.

אֵימִים & אֵמִים nations 1, people 2.

אַמִּין Ch. cubits 4.

אַמִּיץ & אָמִץ courageous 1, mighty 1, strong 3, strong one 4.

אָמִיר bough 1, branch 1.

אָמַל Kal, weak 1; Pulal, to languish 14, to be waxed feeble 1.

אֻמְלַל feeble 1.

אֻמְלַל weak 1.

אָמַן Kal, to bring up 3, bringer up 1, faithful 3, nurse 3, nursing father 1; Niphal, to be established 7, to be faithful 17, to be of long continuance 1, to be nursed 1, to stand fast 1, to be stedfast 2, to be sure 9, to be surely 1, to be trusty 1, to be verified 3,——to fail 1; Hiphil, to have assurance 1, to believe 45, to be sure 1, to trust 1, to put trust 2.

אָמַן Hiphil, to turn to the right 1.

אֲמַן Ch. Aphel, to believe 1, faithful 1, sure 1.

אׇמָּן cunning workman 1.

אָמֵן Amen 27, so be it 1, truth 2.

אֹמֶן truth 1.

אׇמְנָה certain portion 1, sure 1.

אׇמְנָה brought up 1.

אׇמְנוֹת pillars 1.

אׇמְנָם no doubt 1, indeed 2, surely 1, it is true 1, truly 1, of a truth 3.

אֻמְנָם indeed 3, of a surety 1, in very deed 1.

אָמַץ Kal, to be courageous 2, to be of good courage 9, to prevail 1, to be strong 4; Piel, to confirm 1, to establish 1, to fortify 1, to harden 2, to increase (strength) 1, to make obstinate 1, to strengthen 9, to

make strong 3; Hiphil, to strengthen 2; Hithpael, to make speed 2, to be stedfastly minded 1, to strengthen self 1.

אֹמֶץ stronger 1.

אׇמְצָה strength 1.

אֲמָצִים bay 2.

אָמַר Kal, to answer 99, to appoint 3, to bid 13, to call 2, to certify 1, to challenge 1, to charge 1, to command 29, to commune 1, to consider 1, to declare 1, to demand 1, to desire 2, to determine 1, to give commandment 1, to intend 3, to name 3, to promise 6, to publish 1, to purpose 2, to report 2, to require 1, to say very freq., to speak 180, to suppose 1, to talk 1, to tell 41, to think 14, to use speech 1, to utter 1,——at the commandment 1; Inf. intens. expressly (say) 1, indeed (say) 1, plainly (say) 1, still (say) 1, that is 1, verily (think) 1, yet (say) 1; Niphal, to be called 5, to be said 13, to be termed 2, to be told 2; Hiphil, to avouch 2; Hithpael, to boast self 1.

אֲמַר Ch. P'al, to command 12, to declare 1, to say 45, to speak 4, to tell 9.

אֹמֶר answer 1, saying 2, speech 2, word 42,——appointed unto him 1.

אֹמֶר promise 1, speech 2, thing 1, word 2.

אִמְרָה word 1.

אִמְרָה commandment 1, speech 7, word 28.

אִמְּרִין Ch. lambs 3.

אֶמֶשׁ in former time 1, yesterday 3, yesternight 1.

אֱמֶת assured 1, assuredly 1, establishment 1, faithful 1, faithfully 2, right 3, sure 1, true—truly—truth 115, verity 1.

אַמְתַּחַת sack 15.

אֲמִתְנִי Ch. terrible 1.

אָנָּא & אָנָּה I beseech thee 7, we beseech thee 1, O 2, Oh 1, I pray thee 2.

אָנָה Kal, to lament 1, to mourn 1.

אָנָה Piel, to deliver 1; Pual, to befall 1, to happen 1; Hithpael, to seek a quarrel 1.

אֱנוֹשׁ another 1, certain 11, divers 1, fellow 1, husband 3, man 518, certain man 1,

mortal man 1, people 1, person 2, servant 1, some, —— archer 1, *bloodthirsty* 1, brethren 1, chapman 1, counsellor 1, famous 1, familiar 1, to be in flower of their age 1, friend 1, some of them, stranger 1, their trade 2.

אָנַח *Niphal*, to groan 1, to mourn 1, to sigh 10.

אֲנָחָה groaning 4, mourning 1, sighing 6.

אֳנִי galley 1, navy 5, navy of ships 1.

אֲנִיָּה lamentation 1, sorrow 1.

אֳנִיָּה ship 30, ship*men* 1.

אֲנָךְ plumbline 4.

אָנַן *Hithpael*, to complain 2.

אָנַס *Kal*, to compel 1.

אֲנַס Ch. *P'al*, to trouble 1.

אָנַף *Kal*, to be angry 7, to be displeased 1; *Hithpael*, to be angry 6.

אֲנָפָה heron 2.

אַנְפִּין Ch. face 1, visage 1.

אָנַק *Kal*, to cry 1, to groan 1; *Niphal*, to cry 2.

אֲנָקָה crying out 1, ferret 1, groaning 1, sighing 2.

אָנַשׁ *Kal*, desperate 1, incurable 5, desperately wicked 1, woeful 1; *Niphal*, to be very sick 1.

אֱנָשׁ Ch. man 2, whosoever 2.

אֱנָשׁ Ch. man 1.

אָסוּךְ pot 1.

אָסוֹן mischief 5.

אָסוּר band 2,——prison 1.

אֱסוּר Ch. band 2, imprisonment 1.

אָסִיף & אָסָף ingathering 2.

אָסִיר bound in 1, those which are bound 1, prisoner 10.

אַסִּיר prisoner 3.

אֲסָמִים barns 1, storehouses 1.

אָסַף *Kal*, to assemble 9, to bring 2, to consume with 3, to destroy 1, to fetch 1, to gather 43, to gather in 8, to gather together 17, to gather up 3, to lose 1, to put all together 1, to recover (*another of leprosy*) 4, to be rereward 1, to take 2, to take away 5, to take up 1, to withdraw 3; *Inf. intens.* surely (assemble) 1, surely (consume) 1, utterly (consume) 1; *Niphal*, to

assemble 1, to assemble selves 4, to assemble selves together 4, to be assembled 3, to be brought 2, to be brought together 1, to be brought in 1, to be gathered 23, to be gathered together 13, to gather selves together 14, to gather selves 3, to gather together 3, to be gathered up again 1, to get him 1, to be gotten 1, to put up self 1, to be received 1, to be taken 1, to be taken away 4, to withdraw self 1; *Inf. intens.* generally (gathered) 1; *Piel*, to gather 2, to receive 1, rereward 4, to take into 1; *Pual*, to be gathered 4, to be gathered together 1; *Hithpael*, to be gathered together 1.

אֹסֶף gathering 2, have gathered 1.

אֲסֵפָה are gathered together 1.

אֲסֻפּוֹת assemblies 1.

אֲסֻפִּים Asuppim 2, thresholds 1.

אֲסַפְסֻף mixt multitude 1.

אָסְפַּרְנָא Ch. fast 1, forthwith 1, with speed 1, speedily 4.

אָסַר *Kal*, to bind 41, to bind selves 1, to gird 2, to harness 1, to hold 1, to make ready 4, to order 1, to prepare 1, prison 3, prisoner 2, to put in bands 1, to set in array 1, to tie 4; *Inf. intens.* fast (bind) 2; *Niphal*, to be bound 4, to be kept 1; *Pual*, to be bound 2.

אֵסָר & אִסָּר binding 1, bond 10.

אֱסָר Ch. decree 7.

עָא Ch. timber 3, wood 2.

אַף anger 176, to be angry 1, countenance 1, face 22, forehead 1, nose 12, nostril 13, snout 1, wrath 42, —— forbearing 1, *long*suffering 4, worthy 1.

אָפַד *Kal*, to bind 1, to gird 1.

אֲפֻדָּה ephod 2, ornament 1.

אַפֶּדֶן palace 1.

אָפָה *Kal*, to bake 10, bake*meats* 1, baker 11; *Niphal*, to be baken 3.

אֵפוֹד & אֵפֹד ephod 49.

אֲפִילֹת not grown up 1.

אָפִיק brook 1, channel 3, mighty 1, river 10, stream 2, strong pieces 1,——scales 1.

אָפֵל very dark 1.

אֹפֶל darkness 7, obscurity 1, privily 1.

אֲפֵלָה dark 1, darkness 6, gloominess 2, thick (darkness) 1.

אָפְנִים fitly 1.

אָפֵס *Kal*, to be clean gone 1, to be at an end 1, to fail 2, to be brought to nought 1.

אֶפֶס ankle 1, end 13, nothing 3, a thing of nought 1, uttermost parts 1, want 1.

אֶפַע of nought 1.

אֶפְעֶה viper 3.

אָפַף *Kal*, to compass 5.

אָפַק *Hithpael*, to force self 1, to refrain self 5, to be restrained 1.

אֵפֶר ashes 22.

אֲפֵר ashes 2.

אֶפְרֹחִים young 2, young ones 2.

אַפִּרְיוֹן chariot 1.

אַפִּתֹם Ch. revenue 1.

אֶצְבַּע finger 30, toe 2.

אֶצְבְּעָן Ch. fingers 1, toes 2.

אַצִּיל armhole 2, great 1.

אֲצִילִים chief men 1, nobles 1.

אָצַל *Kal*, to keep 1, to reserve 1, to take 1; *Niphal*, to be straitened 1; *Hiphil*, to take 1.

אֵצֶל hard by 1, near 2, near unto 1.

אֶצְעָדָה bracelet 1, chain 1.

אָצַר *Kal*, to lay up in store 2, to store up 1, to make treasurer 1; *Niphal*, to be treasured 1.

אֶקְדָּח carbuncle 1.

אַקּוֹ wild goat 1.

אֶרְאֵל valiant one 1.

אָרַב *Kal*, ambush 5, to lay wait 8, to lie in ambush 2, to lie in wait 23; *Piel*, ambushment 1, lier in wait 1; *Hiphil*, to lay wait 1.

אֶרֶב den 1, to lie in wait 1.

אֹרֶב wait 1.

אַרְבֶּה grasshopper 4, locust 20.

אֲרֻבָּה chimney 1, window 8.

אַרְבוֹת spoils 1.

אָרַג *Kal*, to weave 13.

אֶרֶג beam 1, weaver's shuttle 1.

אַרְגָּן purple 1.

אַרְגְּוָנָא Ch. scarlet 3.

אַרְגָּז coffer 3.

אַרְגָּמָן purple 36.

אָרָה *Kal*, to gather 1, to pluck 1.

אֲרֻכָה & אֲרוּכָה health 4, made up 1, perfected 1.

אָרוֹן & אָרֹן ark 195, chest 6, coffin 1.

אֲרָיוֹת & אֲרָוֹת stalls 3.

אֶרֶז cedar 66, cedar tree 6.

אַרְזָה cedar work 1.

אֲרָזִים made of cedar 1.

אָרַח *Kal*, company 1, to go 1, travelling company 1, wayfaring 1, wayfaring man 3.

אֹרַח byways 1, highway 1, manner 1, path 23, race 1, rank 1, traveller 1, troop 1, way 30.

אֹרְחָא Ch. way 2.

אֲרֻחָה allowance 2, diet 2, dinner 1, victuals 1.

אֲרִי & אַרְיֵה lion 78, young lion 1,——to pierce 1.

אֲרִיאֵל & אֲרִיאֵיל & אֲרִאֵל altar 2, Ariel 6, lionlike men 2.

אַרְיֵה Ch. lion 10.

אָרַךְ *Kal*, to be long 1, to become long 1, to be prolonged 1; *Hiphil*, to defer 1, to draw out 3, to lengthen 2, to be lengthened 1, to be long 1, to make long 1, to prolong 13, to be prolonged 4, to tarry 1, to tarry long 1,——to outlive 1, to overlive 1.

אֲרַךְ Ch. to be meet 1.

אֶרֶךְ *long*suffering 4, long*winged* 1, patient 1, slow to *anger* 8, slow to *wrath* 1.

אָרֹךְ high 1, length *freq.*, long 22,——for ever 2.

אַרְכָּא Ch. lengthening 1.

אֲרֻכָּה long 3.

אַרְכָה Ch. prolonged 1.

אַרְכֻּבָה Ch. knee 1.

אַרְמוֹן castle 1, palace 31.

אֹרֶן ash 1.

אַרְנֶבֶת hare 2.

אֲרַע Ch. earth 20, inferior 1.

אַרְעִית Ch. bottom 1.

אֶרֶץ country 140, earth *very freq.*, field 1, ground 96, land *very freq.*, way 3, world 4, ——common 1, nations 1, wilderness 1.

בּוּז contempt 7; contemptuously 1, despised 2, shamed 1.

בּוּזָה despised 1.

בּוּךְ Niphal, to be entangled 1, to be perplexed 2.

בּוּל Bul 1, food 1, stock 1.

בּוּס Kal, to loath 1, to tread down 4, to tread under 1, to tread under foot 1; Polel, to tread under foot 1, to tread down 1; Hophal, to be trodden under foot 1; Hithpael, to be polluted 2.

בּוּץ fine linen 7, white linen 1.

בּוּקָה empty 1.

בּוֹקֵר herdman 1.

בּוֹר cistern 4, dungeon 10, (כ) fountain 1, pit 42, well 9, ——dungeon 2.

בּוּר Kal, to declare 1.

בּוֹשׁ Kal, to be ashamed 71, to be confounded 21, to put to confusion 1, to become dry 1, with shame 1; Inf. intens. at all (ashamed) 2; Piel, to delay 1, to be long 1; Hiphil, to be ashamed 1, to make ashamed 2, to shame 1, to bring to shame 1, to cause shame 4, to put to shame 1; Hithpael, to be ashamed 1.

בּוּשָׁה shame 4.

בּוּת Ch. P'al, to pass the night 1.

בַּז & בַּז booty 1, Maher-shalal-hash-baz 1, prey 18, spoil 4, spoiled 2.

בָּזָא Kal, to spoil 2.

בָּזָה Kal, to despise 31, to disdain 1,——to think scorn 1; Niphal, to be contemned 1, contemptible 3, to be despised 4, vile person 1; Hiphil, to despise 1.

בְּזֹה to despise 1.

בִּזָּה prey 4, spoil 6.

בָּזַז Kal, to catch 1, to gather 1, to prey upon 1, for a prey 2, to take for a prey 5, to make a prey 1, to rob 5, robber 1, to spoil 9, to take spoil 4, to take 7, to take away 2; Niphal, to be spoiled 2; Inf. intens. utterly (spoiled) 1; Pual, to be robbed 1.

בִּזָּיוֹן contempt 1.

בָּזָק flash of lightning 1.

בָּזַר Kal, to scatter 1; Piel, to scatter 1.

בָּחַן tower 1.

בַּחַן tower 1.

בָּחוּר choice young man 1, chosen 1, young 1, young man 42,——hole 1.

בְּחוּרוֹת youth 2.

בָּחִיר choose 1, chosen 8, elect 4.

בָּחַל Kal, to abhor 1; Pual, (כ) gotten hastily 1.

בָּחַן Kal, to examine 1, to prove 5, to tempt 1, to be tried 1, to try 17; Niphal, to be proved 2, to be tried 1; Pual, trial 1.

בַּחַן tower 1.

בֹּחַן tried 1.

בָּחַר Kal, to appoint 1, choice 2, to choose 152, to choose out 5, excellent 1, to have rather be 1, to require 1; Niphal, acceptable 1, choice 3, to be chosen 3; Pual, (כ) to be joined 1.

בַּחֲרִים young men 1.

בָּטָא & בָּטָה Kal, to speak 1; Piel, to pronounce 2, to speak unadvisedly 1.

בָּטַח Kal, to be bold 1, careless 3, to put confidence 4, to be confident 2, to hope 1, to be secure 4, to be sure 1, to trust 87, to put trust 11, to trust safely 1; Hiphil, to make to hope 1, to cause to trust 1, to make to trust 3.

בֶּטַח assurance 1, boldly 1, without care 1, careless 5, confidence 1, hope 1, safe 2, safely 17, in safety 9, secure 3, surely 1.

בִּטְחָה confidence 1.

בִּטָּחוֹן confidence 2, hope 1.

בַּטֻּחוֹת to be secure 1.

בָּטֵל Kal, to cease 1.

בְּטֵל Ch. P'al, to cease 2, to cause to cease 2, to make to cease 1, to be hindered 1.

בֶּטֶן belly 30, body 8, as soon as they be born 1, within me 1, within thee 1, womb 30.

בָּטְנִים nuts 1.

בִּין Kal & Hiphil, to consider 3, diligently 1, (ק) to direct 1, to discern 1, to feel 1, to inform 1, to instruct 2, to have intelligence 1, to know 1, to look well 1, to mark 1, to perceive 5, prudent 1, to regard 5, to understand 35, to cause to understand 1, to make to understand 1, to give understanding 1, to view 1, to deal wisely 1; Niphal, discreet 2, eloquent 1, to be prudent 7, understanding 5, to have understanding 4, man of understanding 3; Polel, to instruct 1; Hiphil, to consider 4, to be cunning 1, to discern 1, to perceive 1, skilful 1, can skill 1, to teach 3, to understand 12, to cause to understand 1, to make to understand 3, understanding 7, to give understanding 5, to have understanding 6, wise 2, wise man 1; Hithpolel, to attend 1, to consider 14, to consider diligently 1, to perceive 1, to regard 1, to think 1, to understand 3, to get understanding 1.

בִּינָה knowledge 1, meaning 1, understanding 32, to understand 1, wisdom 1,——perfectly 1.

בִּינָה Ch. understanding 1.

בֵּיצִים eggs 6.

בַּיִר fountain 1.

בִּירָה palace 16.

בִּירָה Ch. palace 1.

בִּירָנִיּוֹת castles 2.

בַּיִת Beth-dagon, Beth-emek, Beth-ezel, Beth-shemesh, court 1, (כ) daughter 1, door 1, family 5, forth of 1, hangings 1, home 25, homeborn 1, house very freq., household freq., inside 1, inward 7, palace 1, place 16, temple 11, web 1,——dungeon 2, great as would contain 1, prison 19, steward 2, tablet 1, ward 1.

בַּיִת Ch. house freq.

בִּיתָן palace 3.

בָּכָא Baca 1, mulberry tree 4.

בָּכָה Kal, to bewail 5, Bochim 1, to complain 1, to make lamentation 1, to mourn 2, to weep 102,——with tears 1; Inf. intens. at all (weep) 1, more (weep) 1; sore (weep) 3; Piel, to weep 2.

בֶּכֶה (weeping) 1,——sore 1.

בְּכוֹר eldest 2, eldest (son) 1, eldest son 2, firstborn freq., firstling 9.

בִּכּוּר firstfruit 14, firstripe 2, firstripe fig 1, hasty fruit 1.

בְּכוֹרָה birthright 9, firstborn 1, firstling 5.

בִּכּוּרָה firstripe 1, firstripe fruit 1.

בַּכֻּרָה firstripe 1.

בְּכוּת Allon-bachuth 1.

בְּכִי overflowing 1, to weep 28, continual weeping 1,——sore 4.

בְּכִירָה firstborn 6.

בְּכִית mourning 1.

בָּכַר Piel, to make firstborn 1, to bring forth new fruit 1; Pual, to be firstling 1; Hiphil, to bring forth first child 1.

בֶּכֶר & בִּכְרָה dromedary 2.

בַּל Ch. heart 1.

בְּלָא Ch. Pael, to wear out 1.

בָּלַל Hiphil, to comfort 1, to take comfort 1, to recover strength 1, to strengthen 2.

בָּלַהּ Piel, (כ) to trouble 1.

בָּלָה Kal, to consume 1, to become old 1, to wax old 9; Piel, to consume 1, to enjoy long 1, to make old 1, to spend (כ) 1, to waste 1.

בָּלֶה old 5.

בַּלָּהָה terror 9, trouble 1.

בְּלוֹ Ch. tribute 3.

בְּלוֹא old 3.

בְּלִי corruption 1.

בְּלִיל corn 1, fodder 1, provender 1.

בְּלִימָה nothing 1.

בְּלִיַּעַל belial 16, evil 1, naughty 1, ungodly 2, ungodly men 2, wicked 5.

בָּלַל Kal, to be anointed 1, to confound 2, to mingle 37, to give provender 1, to temper 1; Hiphil,——to fade 1; Hithpoel, to mix self 1.

בָּלַם Kal, to be held in 1.

בָּלַם Kal, to gather 1.

בָּלַע Kal, to devour 2, to eat up 1, to swallow 1, to swallow down 3, to swallow up 13; Niphal, to be swallowed up 2; Piel, to cover 1, to destroy 8, to devour 2, to spend up 1, to swallow up 11; Pual, to be destroyed 1, to be swallowed up 2; Hithpael, to be at an end 1.

בֶּלַע devouring 1, that which he hath swallowed up 1.

בָּלַק Kal, to make waste 1; Pual, to be waste 1.

בָּמָה Bamah 1, Bamoth-baal 1, height 1, high place 101, wave 1.

בֵּן age 3, anointed one 1, appointed to 3, arrow 2, Benjamin 1, Ben-oni 1, one born 2, bough 2, branch 1, breed 1, calf 2,

children *very freq.*, colt 2, (בְּ) daughter 1, foal 1, man 21, meet 1, in a night 2, old 132, people 1, son *very freq.*, whelp 2, worthy 3, young — young one — youth 54, —— afflicted 1, arrow 2, bullock 1, young bullock 1, calf 2, young calf 1, came up in 1, common 1, corn 1, father 1, of first *year* 51, first-born 1, very fruitful 1, hostage 2, kid 1, lamb 2, man *freq.*, mighty 1, nephew 1, people 5, rebel 1, robber 1, servant born 1, soldier 1, spark 1, steward 1, stranger 12, them of (the East) 1, tumultuous one 1, valiant*est* 6.

בֵּן Ch. children 6, son 3, young 1, —— captive 1.

בָּנָה *Kal*, to build 328, to begin to build 1, to build up 11, to make 3, to repair 2, to set up 1; *Inf. intens.* surely (build) 1; *Niphal*, to be built 25, to be built up 2, to obtain children 1, to have children 1, to be set up 1.

בְּנָא & בְּנָה Ch. *P'al*, to build 14, to make 1; *Ithp'il*, to be builded 7.

בִּנְיָה building 1.

בָּנִים —— champion 2.

בִּנְיָן building 7.

בִּנְיָן Ch. building 1.

בְּנַס Ch. *P'al*, to be angry 1.

בֹּסֶר unripe grape 1.

בֹּסֶר sour grape 4.

בָּעָה *Kal*, to cause to boil 1, to enquire 2; *Niphal*, to be sought up 1, to swell out 1.

בְּעָא & בְּעָה *P'al*, to ask 3, to desire 3, to make petition 1, to pray 1, to request 1, to seek 3.

בָּעוּ Ch. petition 2.

בְּעוּתִים terrors 2.

בָּעַט *Kal*, to kick 2.

בְּעִי grave 1.

בְּעִיר beast 4, cattle 2.

בָּעַל *Kal*, Beulah 1, to have dominion 1, to have dominion over 1, to be husband 3, married wife 1, to be married 2, to marry 4, —— wife 1; *Niphal*, to be married 2.

בַּעַל Baal 1, captain 1, chief man 1, those to whom it is due 1, given to 2, great 1, husband 11, lord 2, man 26, master 5, owner 14, person 1, —— adversary 1, archer 1, babbler 1, bird

1, confederate 1, to have...to do 1, creditor 1, dreamer 1, furious 2, hairy 1, horseman 1, married 1, sworn 1.

בַּעַל Ch. —— chancellor 3.

בַּעֲלָה that hath 2, mistress 2.

בָּעַר *Kal*, to be brutish 3, to burn 26, to burn up 1, to be burned 2, to heat 1, to kindle 8; *Niphal*, to be brutish 2, to become brutish 2; *Piel*, to bring away 1, to burn 9, to eat up 3, to feed 1, to kindle 4, to put away 13, to set on fire 1, to take away 7, to waste 1; *Pual*, to burn 1; *Hiphil*, to burn up 1, to cause to be eaten 1, to kindle 1, to set *on fire* 1, to take away 1.

בַּעַר brutish 4, foolish 1.

בְּעֵרָה fire 1.

בָּעַת *Niphal*, to be afraid 3; *Piel*, to affright 1, to make afraid 7, to terrify 3, to trouble 2.

בְּעָתָה trouble 2.

בֹּץ mire 1.

בִּצָּה fen 1, mire 1, miry place 1.

בָּצִיר vintage 8.

בָּצָל onion 1.

בָּצַע *Kal*, to covet 2, to cut 1, to gain 1, to get *gain* 1, to be given to covetousness 2, greedy 2, to be wounded 1; *Piel*, to cut off 2, to finish 1, to fulfil 1, to gain greedily 1, to perform 1.

בֶּצַע covetousness 10, dishonest gain 2, gain 7, lucre 1, profit 3.

בָּצֵק *Kal*, to swell 2.

בָּצֵק dough 4, flour 1.

בָּצַר *Kal*, to cut off 1, defenced 5, to be fenced 16, to gather 4, grape gatherer 3, mighty things 1, strong 1, (בְּ) vintage 1, to be walled 1, to be walled up 1; *Niphal*, to be restrained 1, to be withholden 1; *Piel*, to fortify 2.

בֶּצֶר defence 1, gold 1.

בֶּצֶר gold 1.

בָּצְרָה Bozrah 1.

בִּצָּרוֹן strong hold 1.

בַּצֹּרֶת dearth 1, drought 1.

בַּקְבֻּק bottle 2, cruse 1.

בְּקִיעַ breach 1, cleft 1.

בָּקַע *Kal*, to break into 1, to break through 2, to cleave 5, to divide 4, to hatch 1, to

rend 1, to rip up 1, to win 1; *Niphal*, to break forth 1, to break out 2, to be broken in pieces 1, to be broken up 4, to be ready to burst 1, to cleave 1, to cleave asunder 1, to be divided 1, to be rent 2, to be rent asunder 1; *Piel*, to cleave 4, to cut out 1, to hatch 1, to rend 2, to rip up 2, to tear 1; *Pual*, to be made breach 1, to be rent 1, to be ripped up 1; *Hiphil*, to make a breach 1, to break through 1; *Hophal*, to be broken up 1; *Hithpael*, to be cleft 1, to be rent 1.

בֶּקַע bekah 1, half a shekel 1.

בִּקְעָא Ch. plain 1.

בִּקְעָה plain 7, valley 12, open valley 1.

בָּקַק *Kal*, empty 1, emptier 1, to make empty 1, to empty out 1, to make void 1; *Niphal*, to be emptied 1, to fail 1; *Inf. intens.* utterly (emptied) 1; *Polel*, to empty 1.

בָּקַר *Piel*, to enquire 2, to make enquiry 1, to search 1, to seek 1, to seek out 2.

בְּקַר Ch. *Pael*, to enquire 1, to be made search 3; *Ithpael*, to be made search 1.

בָּקָר beeve 7, bull 1, cattle 1, great cattle 1, herd 44, kine 2, ox 78, —— bullock 42, calf 4, cow 2, heifer 2.

בֹּקֶר day 3, early 3, morning *freq.*, morrow 7, —— day 1.

בַּקָּרָה seeketh out 1.

בִּקֹּרֶת be scourged 1.

בָּקַשׁ *Piel*, to ask 2, to beg 1, to beseech 2, to desire 1, to enquire 3, to get 1, to procure 1, to request 1, to make request 3, to require 14, to seek 193; *Pual*, to be made inquisition 1, to be sought for 2.

בַּקָּשָׁה request 9.

בַּר son 4.

בַּר choice 1, clean 3, clear 1, pure 2.

בָּר & בַּר corn 9, wheat 5.

בַּר Ch. old 1, son 7.

בַּר Ch. field 8.

בֹּר cleanness 4, purely 1, pureness 1.

בָּרָא *Kal*, to create 33, Creator 2, creator 1, to make 2; *Niphal*, to be created 9, to be done 1; *Piel*, to choose 2, to cut down 2, to dispatch 1; *Hiphil*, to make selves fat 1.

בַּרְבֻּרִים fowl 1.

בָּרַד *Kal*, to hail 1.

בָּרָד hail 27, hailstones 2.

בָּרֹד grisled 4.

בָּרָה *Kal*, to choose 1, to eat 3; *Piel*, meat 1; *Hiphil*, to cause to eat 1, to give *meat* 1.

בְּרוֹמִים rich apparel 1.

בְּרוֹשׁ fir 7, fir tree 13.

בְּרוֹתִים fir 1.

בָּרוּת meat 1.

בַּרְזֶל ax-head 1, head *of a hatchet* 1, iron 73, —— smith 1.

בָּרַח *Kal*, to be fled 4, to flee 49, to flee away 3, to make haste 1, to run away 1, to shoot 1; *Inf. intens.* fain (flee) 1; *Hiphil*, to chase 1, to chase away 1, to drive away 1, to make to flee 1, to put to flight 1, to reach 1.

בְּרִי fat 1.

בָּרִיא fat 7, fed 1, firm 1, plenteous 1, rank 2.

בְּרִיאָה new thing 1.

בִּרְיָה meat 3.

בָּרִיחַ crooked 1, nobles 1, piercing 1.

בְּרִיחַ bar 40, fugitive 1.

בְּרִית confederacy 2, covenant *very freq.*, league 15, to be in league 2, —— confederate 1.

בֹּרִית sope 2.

בָּרַךְ *Kal*, to bless 72, to kneel 1, to kneel down 1, to salute 1; *Inf. intens.* still (bless) 1; *Niphal*, to be blessed 3; *Piel*, to blaspheme 2, to bless 217, to congratulate 1, to curse 4, to praise 1, to be praised 1, to salute 4, to thank 1; *Inf. intens.* abundantly (bless) 1, altogether (bless) 2, at all (bless) 1, greatly (bless) 1, indeed (bless) 1; *Pual*, to be blessed 13; *Hiphil*, to make to kneel down 1; *Hithpael*, to bless self 4, to be blessed 3.

בְּרַךְ Ch. *P'al*, to bless 1, to kneel 1; *Pael*, to bless 3.

בֶּרֶךְ knee 25.

בְּרַךְ Ch. knee 1.

בְּרָכָה Berachah 2, blessed 3, blessing *freq.*, liberal 1, pool 1, present 3.

בְּרֵכָה fishpool 1, pool 16.

בָּרַק *Kal*, to cast forth 1.

גָּמַר Ch. *P'al*, perfect 1.

גַּן garden 42.

גָּנַב *Kal*, to carry away 1, to steal 25, to steal away 5; *Niphal*, to be stolen 1; *Piel*, to steal 2; *Pual*, to be secretly brought 1, to be stolen away 2; *Inf. intens.* indeed (stolen) 1; *Hithpael*, to steal away 2, to get by stealth 1.

גַּנָּב thief 17.

גְּנֵבָה theft 2.

גַּנָּה garden 12.

גִּנָּה garden 4.

גְּנָזִים chests 1, treasuries 2.

גִּנְזִין Ch. treasure 3.

גַּנְזַךְ treasury 1.

גָּנַן *Kal*, to defend 5; *Hiphil*, to defend 3.

גָּעָה *Kal*, to low 2.

גָּעַל *Kal*, to abhor 6, to lothe 3; *Niphal*, to be vilely cast away 1; *Hiphil*, to fail 1.

גֹּעַל lothing 1.

גָּעַר *Kal*, to corrupt 1, to rebuke 12, to reprove 1.

גְּעָרָה rebuke 1, rebuking 12, reproof 2.

גָּעַשׁ *Kal*, to shake 2; *Pual*, to be troubled 1; *Hithpael*, to be moved 1, to shake 2, to be shaken 3, to toss selves 1; *Hithpoel*, to be moved 2.

גַּף highest places 1, himself 2.

גַּף Ch. wing 3.

גֶּפֶן vine 54, vinetree 1.

גֹּפֶר gopher 1.

גָּפְרִית brimstone 7.

גֵּר alien 1, sojourner 1, stranger *freq.*

גָּרָב scab 1, scurvy 2.

גַּרְגַּר berry 1.

גַּרְגְּרוֹת neck 4.

גָּרַד *Hithpael*, to scrape self 1.

גָּרָה *Piel*, to stir up 3; *Hithpael*, to contend 3, to meddle 4, to be stirred up 3, to strive 1.

גֵּרָה cud 11.

גֵּרָה gerah 5.

גָּרוֹן aloud 1, mouth 1, neck 2, throat 4.

גֵּרוּת habitation 1.

גָּרַז *Niphal*, to be cut off 1.

גַּרְזֶן axe 4.

גָּדֹל (כ') man of great 1.

גָּרַם *Kal*, to gnaw the bone 1; *Piel*, to break (bones) 2.

גֶּרֶם bone 3, strong 1, top 1.

גְּרַם Ch. bone 1.

גֹּרֶן barn 1, barnfloor 1, corn 1, cornfloor 1, floor 11, threshingfloor 19, threshingplace 1, void place 2.

גָּרַס *Kal*, to break 1; *Hiphil*, to break 1.

גָּרַע *Kal*, to clip 1, to diminish 7, to minish 1, to restrain 2, thing taken 1, to withdraw 1; *Niphal*, to be abated 1, to be diminished 1, to be done away 1, to be kept back 1, to be taken 2, to be taken away 1; *Piel*, to make small 1.

גָּרַף *Kal*, to sweep away 1.

גָּרַר *Kal*, to catch 1, to destroy 1; *Niphal*, to chew 1; *Poal*, to saw 1; *Hithpoel*, continuing 1.

גֶּרֶשׂ beaten corn 1, corn beaten 1.

גָּרַשׁ *Kal*, to cast up 1, divorced 3, to drive out 1, put away 2; *Niphal*, to be cast out 2, troubled 1; *Piel*, to cast out 6, to drive away 2, to drive out 20, to expel 1, to thrust out 6; *Inf. intens.* surely (thrust out) 1; *Pual*, to be driven forth 1, to be thrust out 1.

גֶּרֶשׁ put forth 1.

גְּרֻשָׁה exaction 1.

גָּשַׁם *Hiphil*, to cause rain 1.

גֶּשֶׁם rain 26, great rain 1, much rain 1, shower 5.

גְּשֵׁם Ch. body 5.

גֻּשָׁם rained upon 2.

גָּשַׁשׁ *Piel*, to grope 2.

גַּת press 1, winefat 1, winepress 3.

גִּתִּית Gittith 3.

דָּאַב *Kal*, to mourn 1, to sorrow 1, sorrowful 1.

דַּאֲבָה sorrow 1.

דְּאָבוֹן sorrow 1.

דָּאג (כ') fish 1.

דָּאַג *Kal*, to be afraid 3, to be careful 1, to sorrow 1, to be sorry 1, to take thought 1.

דְּאָגָה care 1, carefulness 2, fear 1, heaviness 1, sorrow 1.

דָּאָה *Kal*, to fly 4.

דָּאָה vulture 1.

דֹּב & דּוֹב bear 12.

דֹּב Ch. bear 1.

דֹּבֶא strength 1.

דָּבַב *Kal*, to cause to speak 1.

דִּבָּה defaming 1, evil report 3, infamy 1, slander 3.

דְּבוֹרָה bee 4.

דְּבַח Ch. *P'al*, to offer sacrifices 1.

דֶּבַח Ch. sacrifice 1.

דִּבְיוֹנִים dove's dung 1.

דְּבִיר oracle 16.

דְּבֵלָה cake of figs 3, lump of figs 2.

דָּבֵק & דָּבַק *Kal*, to abide fast 1, to cleave 28, to follow close 1, to follow hard 1, to be joined together 1, to keep fast 2, to keep self 2, to stick 2, to take 1; *Pual*, to cleave fast together 1, to be joined 1; *Hiphil*, to cause to cleave 1, to make cleave 2, to follow hard after 4, to overtake 3, to pursue hard 1, to cause to stick 1; *Hophal*, to cleave 1.

דְּבַק Ch. *P'al*, to cleave 1.

דָּבֵק cleave 1, joining 1, stick closer 1.

דֶּבֶק joint 2, sodering 1.

דָּבַר *Kal*, to bid 1, to commune 1, to promise 1, to say 3, to speak 23, to talk 10, to tell 1, to utter 1; *Niphal*, to speak 3, to talk 1; *Piel*, to answer 1, to appoint 1, to bid 3, to command 4, to commune 19, to declare 2, to destroy 1, to give 3, to name 1, to promise 29, to pronounce 14, to publish 1, to rehearse 1, to say 119, to speak 377, to be spokesman 1, to talk 2, to teach 2, to tell 24, to think 1, to use intreaties 1, to utter 6, would (to speak) 2; *Inf. intens.* well (speak) 1, wont (to speak) 1; *Pual*, to be spoken 1, to be spoken for 1; *Hiphil*, to subdue 2; *Hithpael*, to speak 4.

דָּבָר act 52, advice 1, affair 2, answer 10, book 7, business 8, care 1, case 1, cause 8, commandment 20, communica-

---

tion 2, counsel 1, dealing 1, decree 1, deed 5, done 1, due 1, duty 2, effect 1, errand 3, evilfavouredness 1, hurt 1, language 1, manner 15, matter 63, message 3, oracle 1, ought 2, parts 1, portion 4, promise 6, provision 1, purpose 1, question 2, rate 5, reason 1, report 2, request 2, saying 34, sentence 3, soil 1, some *uncleanness* 1, somewhat to say 1, sort 1, speak-speech 10, talk 2, task 2, thing *freq.*, thought 1, tidings 4, whit 1, word *freq.*, work 2, —— to answer 8, chronicles 7, to commune 2, to confer 1, dearth 1, disease 1, eloquent 1, glory 1, harm 1, iniquity 1, judgment 1, lie 2, lying 1, power 1, to serve 1, sign 1, song 1, wickedness 1.

דֶּבֶר murrain 1, pestilence 47, plague 1.

דֹּבֶר fold 1, manner 1.

דִּבְרָה cause 1, end 1, estate 1, order 1, regard 1.

דִּבְרָה Ch. intent 1.

דַּבְּרוֹת words 1.

דֹּבְרוֹת floats 1.

דְּבַשׁ honey 52, honeycomb 2.

דַּבֶּשֶׁת bunches *of camels* 1.

דָּג fish 19.

דָּגָה fish 15.

דָּגָה *Kal*, to grow 1.

דָּגַל *Kal*, to set up banners 1, chiefest 1; *Niphal*, with banners 2.

דֶּגֶל banner 1, standard 13.

דָּגָן corn 37, cornfloor 1, wheat 2.

דָּגַר *Kal*, to gather 1, to sit 1.

דַּד breast 2, teat 2.

דָּדָה *Hithpael*, to go softly 1, to go with 1.

דְּהַב Ch. gold 14, golden 9.

דָּהַם *Niphal*, to be astonied 1.

דָּהַר *Kal*, to pranse 1.

דַּהֲרָה pransing 2.

דּוּג *Hiphil*, to cause sorrow 1.

דַּוָּג (כ') fisher 1, fisher 1.

דּוּגָה fishhook 1.

דּוֹד beloved 33, father's brother 2, love 8, uncle 16, wellbeloved 1.

דּוֹדָה aunt 1, father's sister 1, uncle's wife 1.

ı; *Hiphil*, to bend ı, to make go over ı, to guide ı, to lead 4, to lead forth ı, to make to go ı, to thresh ı, to tread ı, to tread down ı, to make to walk ı.

דֶּרֶךְ along 2, away ı, because of ı, conversation 2, custom ı, *eastward* ı, highway ı, journey 23, manner 8, pass by 3, *pathway* ı, through ı, toward 31, way *freq.*,——to journey ı, passengers ı.

דַּרְכְּמוֹנִים drams 4.

דְּרָע Ch. arm ı.

דָּרַשׁ *Kal*, to ask ı, to care for 2, to enquire 38, to make inquisition 2, *necromancer* ı, to question ı, to regard ı, to require 13, to search 7, to seek 88; *Inf. intens.* diligently (seek) ı, surely (require) ı; *Niphal*, to be enquired 5, to be required ı, to be sought ı, to be sought for ı; *Inf. intens.* at all (enquired of) ı.

דָּשָׁא *Kal*, to spring ı; *Hiphil*, to bring forth ı.

דֶּשֶׁא at grass ı.

דֶּשֶׁא grass 5, tender grass 2, green ı, herb 4, tender herb 2.

דָּשֵׁן *Kal*, to wax fat ı; *Piel*, to accept ı, to anoint ı, to take away the ashes from ı, to make fat ı, to receive ashes ı; *Pual*, to be made fat 4; *Hothpael*, to be made fat ı.

דָּשֵׁן fat 3.

דֶּשֶׁן fatness 7.

דֶּשֶׁן ashes 8.

דָּת commandment 2, commission ı, decree 9, law 9, manner ı.

דָּת Ch. decree 3, law 11.

דִּתְאָ Ch. tender grass 2.

דְּתָבַר Ch. counsellor ı.

הַבְהֲבִים offerings ı.

הֶבֶל *Kal*, to be vain 4; *Hiphil*, to make vain ı.

הֶבֶל vain—vanity 69,——altogether ı.

הֶבֶל vanity 3.

הָבְנִים ebony ı.

הָבַר *Kal*, astrologers ı.

הָגָה *Kal*, to imagine 2, to meditate 6, to mourn 4, to mutter ı, to roar ı, to speak 4, to study 2, to talk ı, to utter ı; *Inf. intens.* sore (mourn) ı; *Poal*, to utter ı; *Hiphil*, to mutter ı.

הָגָה *Kal*, to stay ı, to take away ı.

הָגָה mourning ı, sound ı, tale ı.

הָגוּת meditation ı.

הָגִיג meditation ı, to be musing ı.

הִגָּיוֹן device ı, Higgaion ı, meditation ı, solemn sou[nd] ı.

הֶגְיוֹן directly ı.

הָד sounding again ı.

הַדָּבְרִין Ch. counsellors 4.

הָדָה *Kal*, to put ı.

הֲדֹם footstool 6.

הָדַךְ *Kal*, to tread down ı.

הַדָּם Ch. pieces 2.

הֲדַס & הֲדַס myrtle 2, myrtle tree 4.

הָדַף *Kal*, to cast away ı, to cast out 2, to drive 3, to expel ı, to thrust 3, to thrust away ı.

הָדַר *Kal*, to countenance ı, crooked place ı, glorious ı, to honour 2; *Niphal*, to be honoured ı; *Hithpael*, to put forth self ı.

הֲדַר Ch. *Pael*, to glorify ı, to honour 2.

הָדָר beauty 4, comeliness 3, excellency 2 glorious ı, glory 6, goodly ı, honour 5, majesty 7.

הָדָר glory ı.

הֲדַר Ch. honour 2, majesty ı.

הֲדָרָה beauty 4, honour ı.

הָהּ woe worth! ı.

הֹוָה calamity 4, iniquity ı, mischief ı, mischievous ı, mischievous thing ı, naughtiness ı, naughty ı, noisome ı, perverse thing ı, substance ı, very wickedness 3.

הֹוָה mischief 3.

הֹוִי alas 2, ah 7, ho 3, O 3, woe 36.

הוּף Ch. *P'al*, to bring again ı, to come ı, to go ı, to go up ı.

הוֹלֵלָה madness 4.

הוֹלֵלוּת madness ı.

הוּם *Kal*, to destroy ı; *Niphal*, to be moved ı, to ring again 2; *Hiphil*, to make a noise 2.

הוּן *Hiphil*, to be ready ı.

הוֹן enough 2, to be rich ı, riches 10, substance 7, wealth 5,——for nought ı.

הָזָה *Kal*, to sleep ı.

הִי woe ı.

הִידוֹת thanksgiving ı.

הֵידָד shout ı, shouting 8.

הַיָּה (כ) calamity 2.

הֵיכָל palace 10, temple 70.

הֵיכָל Ch. palace 5, temple 8.

הֵילֵל Lucifer ı.

הֵילְכָה (כ) way ı.

הִין hin 22.

הָכַר *Hiphil*, to make selves strange ı.

הַכָּרָה shew ı.

הָלָא *Niphal*, to be cast far off ı.

הָלְאָה back ı, forward 5, henceforward ı.

הִלּוּלִים merry ı, praise ı.

הֲלִיךְ step ı.

הֲלִיכָה company ı, going 2, walk ı, way 2.

הָלַךְ *Kal*, to come 16, continually ı, to be conversant ı, to depart 3, to enter ı, to get thee ı, to go 217, to go about ı, to go along ı, to go away 3, to go forward ı, to go on 3, to go out 2, to be gone 14, to be gone up ı, to sound long ı, to march ı, to pass ı, to pass away 4, to prosper ı, to run 3, to run along ı, to take ı, to walk—to walk along ı10, to wander 2, to wax 5, *wayfaring* man ı, to whirl ı, to work 2,——to be at the point ı, to be eased ı, to follow 8, greater 2, more and more ı, to send ı, tale-bearer ı, traveller ı; *Inf. intens.* all along ı, along (went) 2, apace (came) ı, continually 3, forth (went) ı, forward (went) ı, needs (become) ı, on (went) 5, quite (gone) ı, speedily (go) ı, still (went on) ı, surely (depart) ı, surely (go) ı; *Niphal*, to be gone ı; *Piel*, to exercise self ı, to go 8, to cause to go ı, to lead ı, to run ı, to travel ı, to walk 12; *Hiphil*, places to walk ı; *Hithpael*, to behave self ı, to be conversant ı, to depart ı, to go 8, to go abroad ı, to go up and down 2, to go on still ı, to be wont to haunt ı, to move self ı, to run ı, travel ı, to walk—to walk abroad—to walk on—to walk to and fro—to walk up and down 44,——to follow ı.

הֲלַךְ Ch. *P'al*, to walk ı; *Aphel*, to walk 2.

הֵלֶךְ traveller ı,——dropped ı.

הֲלָךְ Ch. custom 3.

הָלַל *Kal*, fool ı, foolish 2, to deal foolishly ı, to shine ı; *Piel*, to boast 2, to celebrate ı, to commend ı, to praise 105, to sing praise 4; *Poel*, to make fools ı, mad ı, mad against ı, to make mad 2; *Pual*, to be commended ı, to be given to marriage ı, to be praised 5, worthy to be praised 2, renowned ı; *Hiphil*, to give *light* ı, to shine 2; *Hithpael*, to boast 2, to make boast ı, to boast selves 5, to glory 14, to be praised ı; *Hithpoel*, to be mad 3, to feign self mad ı, to rage 2.

הָלַם *Kal*, to beat ı, to beat down ı, to break down 2, to be broken 2, to be overcome with ı, to smite ı, to smite with the hammer ı.

הַלְמוּת hammer ı.

הֵם any of theirs ı.

הָמָה *Kal*, clamorous ı, concourse ı, to cry aloud ı, to be disquieted 4, loud ı, to mourn ı, to be moved ı, to make a noise 6, to rage 2, to roar 8, to sound 3, to be troubled 2, to make a tumult ı, tumultuous ı, being in an uproar ı.

הָמוֹן abundance 3, company ı, Hamon-gog 2, many 3, multitude 62, noise 4, riches ı, rumbling ı, sounding ı, store 2, tumult 4.

הֶמְיָה noise ı.

הֲמֻלָּה speech ı, tumult ı.

הָמַם *Kal*, to break ı, to consume ı, to crush ı, to destroy 4, to discomfit 5, to trouble ı, to vex ı.

הָמַן *Kal*, to multiply ı.

הַמְנִיךְ Ch. chain 3.

הֲמָסִים melting ı.

הֲנָחָה release ı.

הָסָה *Piel*, to hold peace 2, silence ı, to keep silence 2, to be silent ı, to hold tongue ı; *Hiphil*, to still ı.

זַן Ch. kind 4.

זָנָב tail 11.

זִנֵּב Piel, to smite the hindmost 2.

זָנָה Kal, to commit whoredom 1, to commit fornication 2, to be an harlot 23, to play the harlot 15, whore 7, to play the whore 3, to commit whoredom 10, to fall to whoredom 1, to go a whoring 17, whorish 2; Inf. intens. great (lit. in whoring) 1; Pual, to commit whoredom 1; Hiphil, to cause to commit fornication 1, to cause to be a whore 1, whoredom 1, to commit whoredom 3, to make to go a whoring 2; Inf. intens. continually (commit whoredom) 1.

זְנוּנִים whoredom 11.

זְנוֹת armour 1.

זְנוּת whoredom 9.

זָנַח Kal, to cast off 15, to remove far off 1; Hiphil, to cast away 1, to cast off 2, to turn far away 1.

זָנַק Piel, to leap 1.

זֵעָה sweat 1.

זָוָה to be removed 6, trouble 1.

זְעֵיר little 5.

זְעֵיר Ch. little 1.

זָעַךְ Niphal, to be extinct 1.

זָעַם Kal, to abhor 2, abominable 1, to be angry 1, to defy 3, indignation 1, to have indignation 3; Niphal, angry 1.

זַעַם anger 1, indignation 20, rage 1.

זָעַף Kal, to fret 1, to be sad 1, worse liking 1, to be worth 2.

זָעֵף displeased 2.

זַעַף indignation 2, rage 2, raging 1, wrath 1.

זָעַק Kal, to call 1, to cry 47, to cry out 11, to cry unto 1; Niphal, to assemble selves 1, to be called together 1, to come with such a company 1, to be gathered 2, to be gathered together 1; Hiphil, to assemble 2, to call 1, to cry 1, to make to cry 1, to gather together 1, to cause to be proclaimed 1.

זְעֵק Ch. P'al, to cry 2.

זְעָקָה cry 17, crying 1.

זֶפֶת pitch 3.

זִקִּים chains 3, fetters 1, firebrands 1.

זָקָן beard 19.

זָקֵן Kal, aged man 1, to be old 21, old man 1, to wax old 2; Hiphil, to be old 1, to wax old 1.

זָקֵן aged 3, ancient 14, ancient man 1, elder 115, eldest 1, old 24, old man 19, old men 1, old women 1, senator 1.

זֹקֶן age 1.

זָקְנָה to be old 3, old age 3.

זְקֻנִים old age 4.

זָקַף Kal, to raise 1, to raise up 1.

זְקַף Ch. P'al, to be set up 1.

זָקַק Kal, to fine 1, to pour down 1; Piel, to purge 1; Pual, purified 1, refined 3.

זֵר crown 11.

זָרָא loathsome 1.

זָרַב Pual, to wax warm 1.

זָרָה Kal, to cast away 1, to fan 3, to scatter 2, to strew 1, to winnow 2; Niphal, to be dispersed 1, to be scattered 1; Piel, to compass 1, to disperse 7, to fan 1, to scatter 15, to scatter away 1, to spread 1; Pual, to be scattered 1, to spread 1.

זְרוֹעַ arm 82, mighty 1, power 3, shoulder 2, strength 1, to help 1.

זֵרוּעַ sowing 1, things that are sown 1.

זַרְזִיף water 1.

זַרְזִיר ——greyhound 1.

זָרַח Kal, to arise 8, to rise 4, to rise up 2, to be risen 2, to shine 1, as soon as is up 1.

זֶרַח rising 1.

זֶרֶם Kal, to carry away as with a flood 1; Poal, to pour out 1.

זֶרֶם flood 1, overflowing 1, shower 1, storm 3, tempest 3.

זִרְמָה issue 2.

זָרַע Kal, to bear 1, to set with 1, to sow 43, to yield 1; Niphal, to conceive 1, to be sown 5; Pual, to be sown 1; Hiphil, to conceive seed 1, to yield 2.

זֶרַע child 2, fruitful 1, seed freq., seed time 1, sowing time 1, ——carnally 3.

זְרַע Ch. seed 1.

זֵרֹעִים pulse 1.

זֵרְעֹנִים pulse 1.

זָרַק Kal, to be here and there 1, to scatter 2, to sprinkle 29, strow 1; Pual, to be sprinkled 2.

זָרַר Poel, to sneeze 1.

זֶרֶת span 7.

חֹב bosom 1.

חָבָא Niphal, to be hid 2, to hide self 11, to do secretly 1,——held their peace 1; Pual, to hide selves 1; Hiphil, to hide 6; Hophal, to be hid 1; Hithpael, to be hid 4, to hide selves 6.

חָבַב Kal, to love 1.

חָבָה Kal, to hide self 1; Niphal, to hide selves 4.

חַבּוּלָה Ch. hurt 1.

חַבּוּרָה & חַבֻרָה blueness 1, bruise 1, hurt 1, stripe 2, wound 1.

חָבַט Kal, to beat 1, to beat off 1, to beat out 1, to thresh 1; Niphal, to be beaten out 1.

חֶבְיוֹן hiding 1.

חָבַל Kal, band 2, to deal corruptly 1, to offend 1, to lay to pledge 1, to take to pledge 4, to take a pledge of 2, to take a pledge 2, to take for a pledge 1, to withhold 1; Inf. intens. at all (take to pledge) 1, very (deal corruptly) 1; Niphal, to be destroyed 1; Piel, to bring forth 2, to destroy 5, to spoil 1, to travail with 1; Pual, to be corrupt 1, to be destroyed 1.

חֲבַל Ch. Pael, to destroy 2, to hurt 1; Ithpael, to be destroyed 3.

חֶבֶל & חֵבֶל band 1, coast 4, company 2, cord 16, country 1, destruction 1, line 7, lot 3, pain 1, pang 2, portion 4, region 3, rope 3, snare 1, sorrow 10, tackling 1.

חֲבֹל pledge 3.

חֲבַל Ch. hurt 1.

חֲבָל Ch. damage 1, hurt 1.

חֹבֵל mast 1.

חֹבֵל pilot 4, shipmaster 1.

חֲבֹלָה pledge 1.

חֲבַצֶּלֶת rose 2.

חָבַק Kal, to embrace 2, to fold 1; Piel, to embrace 10.

חִבֻּק folding 2.

חָבַר Kal, charmer 1, to couple together 1, to be coupled 1, to be coupled together 1, to be joined 4, to be joined together 1, ——charming 1; Piel, to couple 8, to join self 1; Pual, to be compact 1, to be coupled together 1, to have fellowship with 1, to be joined 1, to be joined together 1; Hiphil, to heap up 1; Hithpael, to join self 2, to join selves together 1, league 1.

חֶבֶר companion 1.

חָבֵר companion 7, fellow 4, knit together 1.

חֲבַר Ch. companion 1, fellow 2.

חֶבֶר company 1, enchantment 2, ——charmer 2, charming 1, wide 2.

חֲבַרְבֻּרוֹת spots 1.

חַבְרָה Ch. fellow 1.

חֶבְרָה company 1.

חֲבֶרֶת companion 1.

חֹבֶרֶת which coupleth 2, coupling 2.

חָבַשׁ Kal, to bind 4, to bind up 6, to gird about 1, to govern 1, healer 1, to put 2, to saddle 13, to be wrapped about 1; Piel, to bind 1, to bind up 1; Pual, to be bound up 2.

חֲבִתִּים pans 1.

חַג & חָג feast 52, feast day 2, sacrifice 3, solemn feast 3, solemnity 1.

חָגָּא terror 1.

חָגָב grasshopper 4, locust 1.

חָגַג Kal, to celebrate 1, to dance 1, to hold a feast 1, to keep a feast 1, to keep holy day 1, to keep (a feast) 8, to reel to and fro 1, to keep a solemn feast 1.

חֲגָוִים clefts 3.

חֲגוֹר girded with 1, girdle 3.

חֲגֹרָה apron 1, armour 1, to gird 1, girdle 3.

חָגַר Kal, to be able to put on 1, to be afraid 1, appointed 3, to gird 25, to gird self 3, to gird on 5, to gird up 2, to be girded 1, to restrain 1, ——on every side 1.

חַד Ch. a 4, first 4, one 5, together 1.

חַד sharp 4.

חָדַד Kal, to be fierce 1, to sharpen 1; Hiphil, to sharpen 1; Hophal, to be sharpened 3.

חָדָה *Kal*, to be joined 1, to rejoice 1; *Piel*, to make glad 1.

חַדּוּדִים sharp 1.

חֶדְוָה gladness 1, joy 1.

חֶדְוָה Ch. joy 1.

חֲדִין Ch. breast 1.

חָדַל *Kal*, to cease 19, to be ceased 1, to end 1, to fail 1, to forbear 20, to forsake 1, to leave 5, to leave off 5, to let alone 2, to rest 1, to be unoccupied 1, to want 1.

חָדֵל he that forbeareth 1, frail 1, rejected 1.

חֶדֶל world 1.

חֵדֶק brier 1, thorn 1.

חָדַר *Kal*, to enter a privy chamber 1.

חֶדֶר bedchamber 5, chamber 17, innermost part 2, inward part 2, parlour 1, within 1,—inner chamber 4, south 1.

חָדָשׁ *Piel*, to renew 6, to repair 3; *Hithpael*, to be renewed 1.

חָדָשׁ fresh 1, new *freq.*

חֹדֶשׁ month *freq.*, new moon *freq.*,—another 1.

חֲדַת Ch. new 1.

חוֹב debtor 1.

חוֹב *Piel*, to make endanger 1.

חוֹג *Kal*, to compass 1.

חוּג circle 1, circuit 1, compass 1.

חוּד *Kal*, to put forth 4.

חָוָה *Piel*, to shew 6.

חָוָא & חָוָה Ch. *Pael*, to shew 4; *Aphel*, to shew 10.

חַוּוֹת Bashan-havoth-jair 2, Havoth-jair 1, small town 1, town 3.

חוֹחַ bramble 1, thicket 1, thistle 5, thorn 5.

חוּט Ch. *Aphel*, to join 1.

חוּט cord 1, fillet 1, line 1, thread 4.

חוּל & חִיל *Kal*, to abide 1, to be afraid 1, to be in anguish 1, to bring forth 1, to travail with child 1, to dance 1, to fall grievously 1, to fall with pain 1, to fear 2, to grieve 1, to be grievous 1, to hope 1, to look 1, to be in pain 4, to have pain 1, to be pained 2, to be much pained 1, to be sore pained 1, to rest 1, to shake 2, to sorrow 1, to be sorrowful 1, to stay 2, to tarry 1, to travail 3, to tremble 1, to wait carefully 1, to be wounded 2; *Inf. intens.* great (have pain) 1; *Polel*, to bear 1, to calve 1, to make to calve 1, to dance 1, to drive away 1, to form 5, to be formed 1, to trust 1; *Pulal*, to be brought forth 2, to be made 1, to be shapen 1; *Hophal*, to be made to bring forth 1; *Hithpolel*, grievous 1, to travail with pain 1, to wait patiently 1; *Hithpalpel*, to be grieved 1.

חוֹל sand 23.

חוּם brown 4.

חוֹמָה wall *freq.*

חוּס *Kal*, to pity 6, to have pity 1, to regard 1, to spare 16.

חוֹף coast *of the sea* 2, haven 2, shore 2, *sea* side 1.

חוּץ abroad 21, field 2, forth 2, highway 1, out 7, out of 9, out from 2, outside 2, outward 1, street 44, without 71.

חֹק ('כ) bosom 1.

חָוַר *Kal*, to wax pale 1.

חוּר network 1.

חוֹר cave 1, hole 6.

חוּר white 2.

חוֹר hole 2.

חִוָּר Ch. white 1.

חוֹרִים nobles 13.

חוּשׁ *Kal*, to haste 4, to make haste 8, to hasten 1, Maher-shalal-hash-baz 1, ready 1; *Hiphil*, to haste 1, to make haste 1, to hasten 3.

חוֹתָם seal 5, signet 9.

חָזָה *Kal*, to behold 7, to look 3, to prophesy 2, to provide 1, to see 38.

חֲזָה & חֲזָא Ch. *P'al*, to behold 6, to have *a dream* 1, to see 23, to be wont 1.

חָזֶה breast 13.

חֹזֶה agreement 1, prophet 1, seer 19, stargazer 1.

חֵזוּ Ch. look 1, vision 11.

חָזוֹן vision 35.

חִזָּיוֹן visions 1.

חֶזְוָה Ch. sight 2.

חָזוּת agreement 1, notable 1, notable one 1, vision 2.

חִזָּיוֹן vision 9.

חֲזִיז bright cloud 1, lightning 2.

חֲזִיר boar 1, swine 6.

חָזַק *Kal*, to catch hold 1, to be confirmed 1, to be constant 1, to be of good courage 6, to be courageous 3, to be encouraged 1, to be established 1, to harden 1, to be hardened 3, to prevail 8, to be recovered 1, to be sore 3, to wax sore 1, to be stout 1, to strengthen 1, to be strengthened 2, to be strong 2, to wax strong 1. to be sure 1, to be urgent 1; *Piel*, to aid 1, to amend 1, to encourage 6, to fasten 1, to fortify 3, to make hard 1, to harden 9, to help 1, to maintain 1, to mend 1, to repair 13, to give strength 1, to strengthen 21, to make strong 2; *Hiphil*, to catch 4, to catch hold 2, to cleave 1, to confirm 2, to constrain 1, to continue 1, to force 1, to hold 11, to hold fast 5, to lay hold 8, to lean 1, to obtain 1, to prevail 2, to receive 1, to relieve 1, to repair 34, to retain 4, to seize 1, to strengthen 3, to be strong 1, to make strong 4, to take 9, to take hold 15, to take fast hold 1,—calker 2, help 1; *Hithpael*, to be of good courage 1, to take courage 1, to encourage self 2, to hold 1, to play the men 1, to become mighty 1, to wax mighty 1, to strengthen self 9, to be strengthened 3, to be strong 1, to make self strong 1, to shew self strong 1, to behave selves valiantly 1, to withstand 2.

חָזָק harder 1, hottest 1, loud 1, mighty 20, sore 3, stiffhearted 1, strong 28,—impudent 1.

חָזֵק stronger 1,—wax louder 1.

חֹזֶק strength 1.

חֹזֶק strength 5.

חָזְקָה force 2, mightily 2, to repair 1, sharply 1.

חֶזְקָה strength 1, strengthen self 1, strong 1, was strong 1.

חָח bracelet 1, chain 2, hook 4.

חַחִי ('כ) hook 1.

חָטָא *Kal*, to bear the blame 2, to commit *sin* 6, to do *sin* 2, to be in fault 1, to do harm 1, to offend 4, to sin 165, to trespass 1; *Piel*, to cleanse 8, to bear the loss 1, to offer for sin 2, to purge 1, to purify 2, to make reconciliation 1; *Hiphil*, to miss 1, to make an offender 1, to cause to sin 2, to make to sin 29; *Hithpael*, to be purified 2, to purify 9.

חֵטְא fault 1, grievously 1, offence 1, punishment of sin 1, sin 30.

חַטָּא offender 1, sinful 1, sinner 16.

חֲטָאָה sin 2, sinful 1.

חַטָּאָה Ch. sin-offering 1.

חַטָּאָה sin 7, sin-offering 1.

חַטָּאת punishment 3, purification for sin 2, sin 169, sin-offering *freq.*

חָטַב *Kal*, to cut down 1, to hew 7; *Pual*, to be polished 1.

חֲטֻבוֹת carved 1.

חִטָּה wheat 30.

חֲטִי Ch. sin 1.

חֲטָיָא Ch. sin-offering 1.

חָטַם *Kal*, to refrain 4.

חָטַף *Kal*, to catch 3.

חֹטֶר rod 2.

חַי alive 31, appetite 1, beast 76, wild beast 1, Beer-lahai-roi 1, company 1, congregation 2, living creature 15, life 152, lifetime 1, live 2, to live 105, lively 1, living 86, living thing 2, maintenance 1, multitude 1, to be old 1, quick 5, raw 6, running 7, springing 1, troop 1,—age 1, merry 1, old 1.

חַי Ch. life 2, that liveth 1, living 4.

חִידָה dark saying 3, dark sentence 1, dark speech 1, hard question 1, proverb 1, riddle 9.

חָיָה *Kal*, to live 148, to recover 10, to revive 1, to be whole 1,—God save 8; *Inf. intens.* certainly (recover) 1, surely (recover) 1, surely (live) 9; *Piel*, to keep alive 5, to leave alive 1, to make alive 2, to give life 2, to preserve life 1, to let live 1, to suffer to live 1, to nourish 1, to nourish up 1, to preserve 4, to preserve alive 2, to quicken 14, to repair 1, to revive 6, to save 11, to save alive 13, to save life 1; *Hiphil*, to keep alive 3, to make alive 1, to let live 1, to make to live 1, to promise life 1, to restore to life 4, to revive 2, to save 1, to save alive 6, to save lives 2.

חֲיָא & חַיָּה Ch. *P'al*, to live 5; *Aphel*, to keep alive 1.

חַיָּה lively 1.

חֵיוָא Ch. beast 20.

חַיּוּת ——living 1.

חָיָה *Kal*, to live 22, to save life 1.

חַיִל able 4, activity 1, army 56, band of men 1, band of soldiers 1, company 1, forces 13, great forces 1, goods 2, host 29, might 7, power 9, riches 11, strength — strong 17, substance 8, train 1, valiant — valiantly — valour 63, virtuous — virtuously 4, war 2, wealth 10, worthily 1, worthy 1.

חַיִל Ch. aloud 3, army 2, power 1, ——most *mighty* 1.

חֵיל army 1, bulwark 1, host 2, rampart 2, trench 1, wall 2, ——poor 1.

חִיל pain 3, pang 2, sorrow 1.

חִילָה sorrow 1.

חֵילָה bulwark 1.

חִין comely 1.

חַיִץ wall 1.

חִיצוֹן outer 1, outward 7, utter 12, without 5.

חֵיק bosom 32, bottom 3, lap 1, midst 1, within 1.

חִישׁ (ב׳) *Kal*, to make haste 1.

חִישׁ soon 1.

חֵךְ mouth 9, roof of the mouth 5, taste 4.

חָכָה *Kal*, to wait 1; *Piel*, to long 1, to tarry 2, to wait 10.

חַכָּה angle 2, hook 1.

חַכִּים Ch. wise 14.

חַכְלִילִי red 1.

חַכְלִילוּת redness 2.

חָכַם *Kal*, to be wise — to shew self wise 19; *Piel*, to teach wisdom 1, to make wiser 2; *Pual*, never so wisely 2, —— exceeding 1; *Hiphil* to make wise 1; *Hithpael*, to make self wise 1, to deal wisely 1.

חָכָם cunning 6, cunning man 4, subtil 1, *unwise* 2, wise *freq.*

חָכְמָה skilful 1, wisdom *freq.*, wisely 2, wit 1.

חָכְמָה Ch. wisdom 8.

חַכְמוֹת wisdom 4.

חַכְמוֹת every wise *woman* 1.

חֹל common 2, profane 2, profane place 2, unholy 1.

חָלָא *Kal*, to be diseased 1.

חֶלְאָה scum 5.

חָלָב milk 42, sucking 1, —— cheese 1.

חֵלֶב fat *freq.*, fatness 4, grease 1, marrow 1, —— best 5, finest 2.

חֶלְבְּנָה galbanum 1.

חֶלֶד age 2, short time 1, world 2.

חֹלֶד weasel 1.

חָלָה *Kal*, to be diseased 1, to be grieved 1, to be sick — to fall sick 27, sore 2, to be sorry 1, woman in travail 1, to be weak — to become weak 3; *Niphal*, diseased 2, grief 1, to be grieved 1, to be grievous 4, to put selves to pain 1, to be sick 1; *Piel*, to beseech 6, infirmity 1, to intreat 3, to lay 1, to pray 3, to make prayer 1, to make suit 1, to make supplication 1; *Pual*, to become weak 1; *Hiphil*, to put to grief 1, to make sick 3; *Hophal*, to be wounded 3; *Hithpuel*, to fall sick 1, to make self sick 2.

חַלָּה cake 14.

חֲלוֹם dream 63, dreamer 1, dream*er* 1.

חַלּוֹן window 31.

חֲלוֹף ——destruction 1.

חֲלוּשָׁה being overcome 1.

חַלְחָלָה pain 1, great pain 1, much pain 1.

חָלַט *Hiphil*, to catch 1.

חֲלִי jewel 1, ornament 1.

חֳלִי disease 7, grief 4, is sick 1, sickness 12.

חֶלְיָה jewel 1.

חָלִיל pipe 6.

חָלִילָה be far 9, forbid 4, —— God forbid 8.

חֲלִיפָה change 11, course 1.

חֲלִיצָה armour 1, spoil 1.

חֶלְכָה poor 2, (ב׳) poor 1.

חָלַל *Kal*, player on instruments 1, to be wounded 1; *Niphal*, to be defiled 1, to be polluted 4, to profane self 2, to be profaned 2, —— to take inheritance 1; *Piel*, to defile 8, to pipe 1, to pollute 18, to profane 30, to cast as profane 1, to prostitute 1, to slay 1, to stain 1, —— to break 3, to eat as common things 1, to eat 1, to gather the grape thereof 1; *Pual*, to be profaned

1, slain 1; *Poel*, to wound 1; *Poal*, to be wounded 1; *Hiphil*, to begin 52, to pollute 1, to sorrow 1, —— to break 1, first 1; *Hophal*,——men began 1.

חָלָל kill 2, profane 2, slain — slain man 79, wounded — deadly wounded 10.

חָלַם *Kal*, to dream 26; *Hiphil*, to cause to be dreamed 1.

חָלַם *Kal*, in good liking 1; *Hiphil*, to recover 1.

חֲלַם Ch. dream 22.

חֶלְמוּת egg 1.

חַלָּמִישׁ flint 3, flinty 1, rock 1.

חָלַף *Kal*, to abolish 1, to change 2, to be changed 1, to cut off 1, to go on forward 1, to grow up 2, to be over 1, to pass 2, to pass away 1, to pass on 1, to pass through 1, to strike through 2; *Piel*, to change 2; *Hiphil*, to alter 1, to change 5, to renew — to be renewed 3, to sprout 1.

חֲלַף Ch. *P'al*, to pass 4.

חָלַץ *Kal*, armed 8, armed man 2, ready armed 2, armed soldier 1, army 1, to draw out 1, to loose 2, prepared 1, ready prepared 1, to put off 1, to withdraw self 1; *Niphal*, to arm selves 1, to go armed 2, to be delivered 4; *Piel*, to deliver 12, to take away 2; *Hiphil*, to make fat 1.

חֲלָצַיִם loins 9, reins 1.

חָלַק *Kal*, to distribute 2, to divide 6, to be divided 3, to give 1, to impart 1, to part 1, to have part 1, partner 1, to take away a portion 1, to receive 1, to be smoother 1; *Niphal*, to distribute 1, to divide 1, to divide self 1, to be divided 4, to be parted 1; *Piel*, to deal 2, to distribute 1, to divide 21, to part 2; *Pual*, to be divided 3; *Hiphil*, to flatter 6, to separate self 1, to smooth 1; *Hithpael*, to divide 1.

חָלָק flattering 2, Halak 1, smooth 2.

חֲלַק Ch. portion 3.

חֵלֶק flattery 1, flattering 1, inheritance 1, part 22, portion 40, smooth 1, ——partaker 1.

חָלָק smooth 1.

חֶלְקָה field 3, flattering 2, flattery 1, ground 1, Helkath-hazzurim 1, parcel 5, part 1, piece 2, piece *of ground* 1, piece of land 2, plat 1, portion 6, slippery place 1, smooth 1, smooth thing 1.

חֲלֻקָּה division 1.

חֲלָקּוֹת flatteries 1.

חֲלַקְלַקּוֹת flatteries 2, slippery 2.

חָלַשׁ *Kal*, to discomfit 1, to waste away 1, to weaken 1.

חַלָּשׁ weak 1.

חָם father-in-law 4.

חָם hot 1, warm 1.

חֹם heat 9, to be hot 4, to be warm 1.

חֵמָא fury 1.

חֲמָא & חֵמָא Ch. fury 2.

חֶמְאָה butter 9.

חָמַד *Kal*, beauty 1, to covet 4, delectable thing 1, to delight 1, to desire 8, to lust 1; *Niphal*, to be desired 3, to be pleasant 1; *Piel*,——great delight 1.

חֶמֶד desirable 3, pleasant 2, ——red wine 1.

חֶמְדָּה desire 4, goodly 1, pleasant 11, precious 1.

חַמָּה heat 1, sun 5.

חֵמָה anger 1, bottles 1, hot displeasure 3, furious 5, furiously 1, fury 64, heat 1, indignation 1, poison 6, rage 2, wrath — wrathful — to be wroth 36.

חֶמְאָה butter 1.

חֲמוּדוֹת greatly beloved 3, goodly 1, pleasant 1, pleasant thing 1, precious 2, precious thing 1.

חָמוּץ oppressed 1.

חָמוּק joint 1.

חֲמוֹר ass 95, he-ass 1, heaps 1.

חֲמוֹרָתַיִם heaps 1.

חָמוֹת mother-in-law 11.

חֹמֶט snail 1.

חָמִיץ clean 1.

חֲמִישִׁי & חֲמִשִׁי fifth — fifth part —— fifth time *freq.*

חָמַל *Kal*, to have compassion 5, to pity 8, to have pity 10, to spare 18.

חֶמְלָה merciful 1, pity 1.

חָמַם *Kal*, to get heat 1, to have heat 1, to be hot 1, to wax hot 1, to be warm 1, to warm at 1, to warm self 2, to wax warm

חָצֵר (כ') Piel, to blow 1, to sound 3, trumpeter 1.

חֲצֹצְרָה trumpet 28, trumpeter 1.

חָצַר Piel, trumpeter 1; Hiphil, to blow 1, to sound 4.

חָצֵר court freq., town 1, village freq.

חַצְרֵר (כ') Piel, to sound 1.

חֹק appointed 1, bound 1, commandment 1, convenient 1, custom 2, decree 7, decreed 1, due 4, law 4, measure 1, ordinance 9, ordinary 1, portion 3, set time 1, statute freq., task 1, ——necessary 1.

חָקָה Pual, carved work 1, pourtrayed 2; Hithpael, to set a print 1.

חֻקָּה appointed 1, custom 2, manner 1, ordinance 22, rite 1, statute freq.

חָקַק Kal, to appoint 1, to decree 1, governor 1, to grave 2, to note 1, to pourtray 2, to set 1; Poel, to decree 1, governor 1, lawgiver 6; Pual, law 1; Hophal, to be printed 1.

חֵקֶק decree 1, thought 1.

חָקַר Kal, to search 11, to make search 1, to search out 7, to seek 1, to sound 1, to try 1; Niphal, to be found out 2, to be searched 1, to be searched out 1; Piel, to seek out 1.

חֵקֶר finding out 1, number 1, search 3, searched out 1, searching 3, unsearchable 3.

חֲרָאִים dung 1.

חָרֵב & חָרַב Kal, to decay 1, to be desolate 2, to be dried up 4, to be dry 2, to slay 1, to waste 1, to be laid waste 4, to lie waste 1, to be wasted 2; Inf. intens. utterly (wasted) 1; Niphal, desolate 1, to be slain 1, to be wasted 1; Pual, to be dried 2; Hiphil, to destroy 1, destroyer 1, to dry up 6, to lay waste 1, to make waste 3; Hophal, to be laid waste 2; Inf. intens. surely (slain) 1.

חֲרַב Ch. Hophal, to be destroyed 1.

חָרֵב desolate 2, dry 2, waste 6.

חֶרֶב axe 1, dagger 3, knife 5, mattock 1, sword freq., tool 1.

חֹרֶב desolation 1, drought 3, dry 3, heat 6, waste 3, ——utterly 1.

חָרְבָּה decayed place 1, desert 3, desolate 2, desolate place 5, desolation 8, destruction 1, waste 15, laid waste 2, waste place 6.

חָרְבָּה dry 1, dry ground 3, dry land 4.

חֶרָבוֹן drought 1.

חָרַג Kal, to be afraid 1.

חַרְגֹּל beetle 1.

חָרַד Kal, to be afraid 8, to be careful 1, to quake 1, to tremble 13; Hiphil, to make afraid 12, to discomfit 1, to fray 1, to fray away 2.

חָרֵד afraid 1, tremble 5.

חֲרָדָה care 1, fear 2, quaking 1, trembling 5, ——exceedingly 1.

חָרָה Kal, to be angry 9, to burn 1, to be displeased 4, to grieve 1, to be hot 5, to wax hot 5, to be kindled 43, to be wroth 14; Inf. intens. very (wroth) 1; Niphal, to be incensed 2; Hiphil, to kindle 1, ——earnestly 1; Tiphel, to close 1, to contend 1; Hithpael, to fret self 4.

חֲרוּזִים chains 1.

חָרוּל nettle 3.

חָרוֹן sore displeasure 1, fierce 23, fierceness 9, fury 1, wrath 5, fierce wrath 1, wrathful 1.

חָרוּץ decision 2, fine gold 1, gold 6, sharp pointed things 2, threshing instrument 2, wall 1.

חָרוּץ diligent 5.

חַרְחֻר extreme burning 1.

חֶרֶט graving tool 1, pen 1.

חַרְטֹם Ch. magician 5.

חַרְטֻמִּים magician 11.

חֳרִי fierce 3, heat 1,——great 2.

חֹרִי white 1.

חֲרִיטִים bags 1, crisping-pins 1.

חָרִים (כ') dung 2.

חָרִיץ harrow 2,——cheese 1.

חָרִישׁ earing 1, earing time 1, ground 1.

חֲרִישִׁי vehement 1.

חָרַךְ Kal, to roast 1.

חֲרַךְ Ch. Ithpael, to singe 1.

חֲרַכִּים lattice 1.

חָרַם Kal, to have a flat nose 1; Hiphil, to make accursed 1, to consecrate 1, to destroy 2, utterly to destroy 40, to devote 1, utterly to slay 1, utterly to make away 1; Inf. intens. utterly (destroy) 2; Hophal, utterly to be destroyed 1, to be devoted 1, to be forfeited 1.

חֵרֶם accursed 3, accursed thing 10, curse 4, cursed thing 3, dedicated thing 1, things which should have been utterly destroyed 1, appointed to utter destruction 1, devoted 3, devoted thing 2, net 9, utter destruction 1.

חֶרְמֵשׁ sickle 2.

חֶרֶם itch 1, sun 3.

חַרְסוּת or חַרְסִית (כ') east 1.

חָרַף Kal, to reproach 4, to winter 1; Niphal, betrothed 1; Piel, to blaspheme 1, to defy 8, to jeopard 1, to rail 1, to reproach 23, to upbraid 1.

חֹרֶף cold 1, winter 3, winterhouse 2, youth 1.

חֶרְפָּה rebuke 2, reproach 67, reproachfully 1, shame 3.

חָרַץ Kal, to bestir self 1, to decide 1, decreed 1, determined 1, maimed 1, to move 2; Niphal, to be determined 5.

חֲרַץ Ch. loin 1.

חַרְצֻבּוֹת bands 2.

חַרְצַנִּים kernel 1.

חָרַק Kal, to gnash 5.

חָרַר Kal, to burn 1, to be burned 2; Niphal, to be angry 1, to be burned 5, to be dried 1; Pilpel, to kindle 1.

חֲרֵרִים parched places 1.

חֶרֶשׂ earth 1, earthen 8, potsherd 5, sherd 2, ——stone 1.

חָרַשׁ Kal, to be deaf 1, to devise 5, to ear 1, graven 1, to hold peace 3, to imagine 1, to keep silence 3, to plow 11, plower 1, plowman 2, to be silent 1, worker 1; Niphal, to be plowed 2; Hiphil, to cease 1, to conceal 1, to leave off speaking 1, to hold peace 23, to rest 1, secretly to practise 1, to keep silence 3, to speak not a word 1, to be still 1, to hold tongue 4; Inf. intens. altogether (hold peace) 3; Hithpael, to be quiet 1.

חָרָשׁ artificer 2, carpenter 8, craftsman 4, engraver 3, maker 1, skilful 1, smith 3, worker 1, workman 6, such as wrought 1,——carpenter 4, mason 2, smith 1.

חֵרֵשׁ deaf 9.

חָרָשׁ artificer 1, Charashim 1, craftsmen 2, secretly 1.

חֹרֵשׁ artificer 1.

חֹרֶשׁ bough 1, forest 1, shroud 1, wood 4.

חֲרֹשֶׁת carving 2, cutting 2.

חָרַת Kal, graven 1.

חָשַׂךְ Kal, to assuage 1, to forbear 1, to hinder 1, to hold back 1, to keep 1, to keep back 3, to punish 1, to refrain 3, to reserve 1, to spare 8. to withhold 4,—— to be darkened 1; Niphal, to be assuaged 1, to be reserved 1.

חָשַׂף Kal, to make bare 4, to discover 2, to draw out 1, to take 1, uncover 2,——clean 1.

חָשִׂף little flock 1.

חָשַׁב Kal, to conceive 1, to count 4, cunning 8, cunning man 1, cunning workman 2, to devise 20, to esteem 2, to find out 1, to forecast 1, to hold 1, to imagine 7, to impute 2, to invent 1, to mean 1, to purpose 6, to regard 2, to think 16; Niphal, to be accounted 5, to be counted 17, to be esteemed 3, to be imputed 2, to be reckoned 2, reckoning to be made 1; Piel, to make account of 1, to consider 1, to count 2, to devise 2, to forecast 1, to imagine 2, to be like 1, to reckon 4, to think 1, to think on 1; Hithpael, to be reckoned 1.

חֲשַׁב Ch. P'al, to repute 1.

חֵשֶׁב curious girdle 8.

חִשָּׁבוֹן account 1, device 1, reason 1.

חִשְּׁבֹנוֹת engines 1, inventions 1.

חָשָׁה Kal, to hold peace 3, to keep silence 2, to be silent 1, to be still 1; Hiphil, to hold peace 6, to still 1, to be still 2.

חֲשׁוֹךְ Ch. darkness 1.

חֲשַׁח Ch. P'al, careful 1, to have need of 1.

חַשְׁחוּת be needful 1.

חֲשֵׁיכָה darkness 5.

חָשַׁךְ Kal, to be black 1, to be dark 3, to be darkened 7, to be dim 1; Hiphil, to make dark 2, to darken 2, to cause darkness 1, to hide 1.

חָשֵׁךְ mean 1.

חֹשֶׁךְ dark 7, darkness 69, night 1, obscurity 2.

חֶשְׁכָּה dark 1.

חֲשֵׁכָה dark 1.

חָשַׁל Niphal, feeble 1.

חֲשַׁל Ch. P'al, to subdue 1.

חַשְׁמַל amber 3.

חַשְׁמַנִּים princes 1.

חֹשֶׁן breastplate 25.

חָשַׁק Kal, to have a delight 1, to desire 2, to have a desire 1, to long 1, to set love 2, in love to 1; Piel, to fillet 3; Pual, to be filleted 2.

חֵשֶׁק desire 3, pleasure 1.

חֲשֻׁקִים fillets 8.

חִשֻּׁקִים felloes 1.

חֲשֵׁרָה dark 1.

חִשֻּׁרִים spokes 1.

חָשַׁשׁ chaff 2.

חַת broken 1, dismayed 1, dread 1, fear 1.

חָתָה Kal, to heap 1, to take 2, to take away 1.

חִתָּה terror 1.

חִתּוּל roller 1.

חִתְחַתִּים fears 1.

חִתִּית terror 8.

חָתַךְ Niphal, to be determined 1.

חִתֵּל Pual, to be swaddled 1; Hophal, Inf. intens. at all (swaddled) 1.

חֲתֻלָּה swaddling-band 1.

חָתַם Kal, (כ') to make an end 1, to seal 16, to seal up 6; Niphal, to be sealed 2; Piel, to mark 1; Hiphil, to be stopped 1.

חֲתַם Ch. P'al, to seal 1.

חֹתֶמֶת signet 1.

חָתַן Kal, father-in-law 21, mother-in-law 1; Hithpael, to make affinity 1, to join in affinity 2, to make marriages 3, to be son-in-law 5.

חָתָן bridegroom 8, husband 2, son-in-law 10.

חֲתֻנָּה espousal 1.

חָתַף Kal, to take away 1.

חֶתֶף prey 1.

חָתַר Kal, to dig 7, to dig through 1, to row 1.

חָתַת Kal, to be afraid 2, to be amazed 1, to be broken down 2, to be broken in pieces 5, to be chapt 1, to be dismayed 6; Niphal, to be abolished 1; to be affrighted 1, to be afraid 3, to be beaten down 1, to be broken 1, to be broken to pieces 1, to be discouraged 1, to be dismayed 20, to go down 1; Piel, to be broken 1, to scare 1; Hiphil, to make afraid 1, to break 1, to confound 1, to cause to be dismayed 1, to terrify 1.

חָתַת casting down 1.

טְאֵב Ch. P'al, to be glad 1.

טָב Ch. fine 1, good 1.

טְבוּלִים dyed attire 1.

טַבּוּר middle 1, midst 1.

טָבַח Kal, to kill 4, slaughter 3, to make slaughter 1, to slay 3.

טַבָּח cook 2, guard 1.

טַבָּח Ch. guard 1.

טֶבַח slaughter 9, —— beast 1, slay 1, sore 1.

טִבְחָה flesh 1, slaughter 2.

טַבָּחוֹת cooks 1.

טָבַל Kal, to dip 15, to plunge 1; Niphal, to be dipped 1.

טָבַע Kal, to sink 4, to be sunk 2; Pual, to be drowned 1; Hophal, to be fastened 1, to be settled 1, to be sunk 1.

טַבַּעַת ring freq.

טֵבֵת Tebeth 1.

טָהוֹר clean 50, fair 2, pure—pureness 42.

טָהֵר Kal, to be clean 25, to be made clean 1, to be cleansed 4, to be pure 2, to be purged 2; Piel, to make clean 1, to pronounce clean 10, to cleanse 21, to purge 3, purifier 1, to purify 3; Pual, to be cleansed 1; Hithpael, to be clean 1, to be made clean 1, to make selves clean 1, to cleanse selves 2, to be cleansed 12, to be purified 1, to purify selves 2.

טֹהַר to have clean 1, pureness 1.

טֹהַר clearness 1, purifying 2.

טֹהַר glory 1.

טָהֳרָה cleansing 7, purification 2, purifying 3, —— is cleansed 1.

טוּא Pilpel, to sweep 1.

טוֹב Kal, to be better 1, to be good 3, to seem good 2, to be goodly 1, to be well 5, to go well 1, —— to please 6; Hiphil, to do better 1, to cheer 1, to do good 4, to make goodly 1, to play well on 1, well 1, to do well 4.

טוֹב beautiful 2, best 8, better 71, bountiful 1, cheerful 1, at ease 1, fair 9, fair word 1, to favour 1, to be in favour 1, fine 3, glad 2, good freq., good deed 1, goodly 11, goodness 16, goods 2. graciously 1, joyful 1, kind 1, kindly 2, kindness 1, as it liketh 1, liketh best 1, loving 1, merry 7, pleasant 2, pleasure 2, pleasing 1, precious 3, prosperity 6, ready 1, sweet 1, wealth 3, welfare 1, well 21, —— pleaseth 6.

טוּב fair 1, gladness 1, good 9, good thing 2, goodness 14, goods 3, joy 1, to go well with 1.

טָוָה Kal, to spin 2.

טוּחַ Kal, to daub 7, to overlay 1, to plaister 1, to shut 1; Niphal, to be plaistered 1.

טוֹטָפוֹת frontlets 3.

טוּל Pilpel, to carry away 1; Hiphil, to cast 2, to cast forth 4, to cast out 2, to send out 1; Hophal, to be cast 1, to be cast down 1, to be utterly cast down 1, to be cast out 1.

טוּר row 26.

טוּר Ch. mountain 2.

טוּשׁ Kal, to haste 1.

טְוָת Ch. fasting 1.

טָחָה Piel, bowshot 1.

טָחַן to grind 1.

טְחֹרִים emerods 8.

טֻחוֹת inward parts 2.

טָחַן Kal, to grind 8.

טַחֲנָה grinding 1.

טִיחַ daubing 1.

טִיט clay 3, dirt 2, mire 8.

טִין Ch. miry 2.

טִירָה castle 3, goodly castle 1, habitation 1, palace 2, row 1.

טַל dew 31.

טַל Ch. dew 5.

טָלָא Kal, with divers colours 1, spotted 6; Pual, clouted 1.

טְלָאִים lambs 1.

טָלֶה lamb 2.

טַלְטֵלָה captivity 1.

טָלַל Piel, to cover 1.

טְלַל Ch. Aphel, to have shadow 1.

טָמֵא Kal, to defile self 6, to be defiled 8, to be polluted 2, to be unclean 60, to be made unclean 1, to take uncleanness 1; Niphal, to defile self 1, to be defiled 12, to pollute selves 1, to be polluted 3; Piel, to defile 31, to be defiled 1, to pollute 5, to pronounce unclean 12, as unclean 1; Inf. intens. utterly (unclean) 1; Pual, to be polluted 1; Hithpael, to defile selves 8, to be defiled 2, to be polluted 2, to be unclean 1, to make selves unclean 2; Hothpael, to be defiled 1.

טָמֵא defiled 5, polluted 1, pollution 1, unclean 80, —— infamous 1.

טֻמְאָה filthiness 7, unclean 3, uncleanness 26.

טָמָה Niphal, to be defiled 1, to be reputed vile 2.

טָמַן Kal, to hide 23, to lay privily 4, in secret 1; Niphal, to hide 1; Hiphil, to hide 2.

טֶנֶא basket 4.

טָנַף Piel, to defile 1.

טָעָה Hiphil, to seduce 1.

טָעַם Kal, to perceive 1, to taste 10; Inf. intens. but (taste) 1.

טְעַם Ch. P'al, to make to eat 1, to feed 1.

טַעַם advice 1, behaviour 2, decree 1, discretion 1, judgment 1, reason 1, taste 5, understanding 1.

טְעֵם Ch. account 1, commandment 2, matter 1, —— to be commanded 1.

טְעֵם Ch. commandment 2, decree 13, to taste 1, wisdom 1, —— chancellor 3, to command 3, to regard 2.

טָעַן Kal, to lade 1.

טָעַן Pual, thrust through 1.

טַף children 9, little children 3, families 1, little ones 28.

טָפַח Piel, to span 1, to swaddle 1.

טֶפַח coping 1, hand-breadth 3.

טֹפַח hand-breadth 4, hand-broad 1.

טְפָחִים span long 1.

טָפַל *Kal*, to forge 1, forger 1, to sew up 1.

טִפְסַר captain 2.

טָפַף *Kal*, to mince 1.

טְפַר Ch. nail 2.

טָפַשׁ *Kal*, to be fat 1.

טָרַד *Kal*, continual 2.

טְרַד Ch. *P'al*, to drive 4.

טָרַח *Hiphil*, to weary 1.

טֹרַח cumbrance 1, trouble 1.

טְרִי new 1, putrifying 1.

טָרַף *Kal*, to catch 2, prey 1, to ravin 4, to tear 8, to tear in pieces 3; *Inf. intens.* without doubt (rent) 1, surely (torn) 1; *Niphal*, to be torn in pieces 2; *Poal*, to be rent in pieces 1, torn in pieces 1; *Hiphil*, to feed 1.

טָרָף pluckt off 1.

טֶרֶף leaf 1, meat 3, prey 18, spoil 1.

טְרֵפָה ravin 1, torn 6, torn in pieces 1, torn of beasts 1.

יָאַב *Kal*, to long 1.

יָאָה *Kal*, to appertain 1.

יְאֹר brook 5, flood 6, river 53, stream 1.

יָאַל *Niphal*, to dote 1, to be foolish 1, to do foolishly 1, to become fools 1.

יָאַל *Hiphil*, to assay 1, to begin 1, to be content 7, to please 4, to take upon 2, would 3,—willingly 4.

יָאַשׁ *Niphal*, to despair 1, one that is desperate 1, to be no hope 3; *Piel*, to cause to despair 1.

יָבַב *Piel*, to cry 1.

יְבוּל fruit 3, increase 10.

יָבַל *Hiphil*, to bring 5, to carry 1, to lead 1; *Hophal*, to be brought forth 6, to be brought forth 1, to be carried 3, to be led forth 1.

יְבַל Ch. *Aphel*, to bring 2, to carry 1.

יוּבָל stream 1, *watercourse* 1.

יָבָל having a wen 1.

יָבָם husband's brother 2.

יָבַם *Piel*, to perform the duty of a husband's brother 2, to marry 1.

יְבֵמֶת brother's wife 3, sister-in-law 2.

יָבֵשׁ *Hiphil*, to be ashamed 7, to be confounded 9, to shame 1, to do shamefully 1.

יָבֵשׁ *Kal*, to be dried 2, to be dried up 10, to be dry 2, to dry up 4, to wither 16, to be withered 3, to be withered away 1; *Inf. intens.* clean (dried up) 1, utterly (wither) 1; *Piel*, to dry 1, to make dry 1, to dry up 1; *Hiphil*, to be dried up 2, to make dry 1, to dry up 11, to be withered 1, to be withered away 1.

יָבֵשׁ dried 1, dried away 1, dry 7.

יַבָּשָׁה dry ground 1, dry land 2, dry (ground) 2, dry (land) 8, land 1.

יַבֶּשֶׁת dry (land) 2.

יַבֶּשֶׁת Ch. earth 1.

יָגֵב (ק) *Kal*, husbandman 1.

יְגֵבִים fields 1.

יָגָה *Niphal*, to be afflicted 1, sorrowful 1; *Piel*, to grieve 1; *Hiphil*, to afflict 3, to cause grief 1, to vex 1.

יָגָה *Hiphil*, to be removed 1.

יָגוֹן grief 2, sorrow 12.

יָגֵעַ weary 1.

יְגִיעַ labour 15, work 1.

יָגַע *Kal*, to faint 1, to labour 11, to be weary 7, to be wearied 1; *Piel*, to make to labour 1, to weary 1; *Hiphil*, to weary 4.

יָגַע laboured for 1.

יָגֵעַ full of labour 1, weary 2.

יְגִעָה weariness 1.

יְגַר Ch. Jegar-*sahadutha* 1.

יָגֹר *Kal*, to be afraid 5, to fear 2.

יָד be able 12, axletree 1, border 2, charge 1, coast 6, custody 1, debt 1, dominion 3, force 2, hand *very freq.*, labour 1, ledge 2, means 4, ministry 2, near 2, ordinance 1, parts 4, paw 2, place 8, power 1, service 1, side 11, sore 1, state 2, stay 4, draw with strength 1, stroke 1, tenon 2, times 2, work 1,—be able 1, arm-holes 2, bounty 1, broad 1, consecrate 17, creditor 1, enough 1, fellowship 1, to help 1, instruments 1, large 3, order 2, presumptuously 1, snare 1, submitted 1, swear 4, throwing 1, thumb 2, to wait on 1, wax rich 1, wide 2, yield 1.

יַד Ch. hand 16, power 1.

יְדָא Ch. *Aphel*, to thank 1, to give thanks 1.

יָד *Kal*, to cast 3.

יְדִדוּת dearly beloved 1.

יָדָה *Kal*, to shoot 1; *Piel*, to cast 1, to cast out 1.

יָדָה *Hiphil*, to confess 7, to praise 53, to thank 5, to be thankful 1, to give thanks 32, thanksgiving 2; *Hithpael*, continuance 1, daily, confession 2.

יָדִיד amiable 1, beloved 7, loves 1, well-beloved 2.

יָדַע *Kal*, to acknowledge 5, acquaintance—acquainted with 3, to advise 1, to be aware 2, can discern 3, can have 1, can skill 6, can tell 5, cannot 1, to come to *understanding* 1, to comprehend 1, to consider 7, could 2, cunning 4, to be diligent 1, to discern 4, endued with 2, to feel 3, to have *knowledge* 2, to have *understanding* 2, to be *ignorant* 3, to know 664, knowledge 2, to have knowledge 10, to take knowledge 3, to be known 1, to mark 3, to perceive 18, to be privy to 1, to regard 1, to have respect 1, skilful—man of skill 6, to be sure 5, to understand 11, to wist 7, to wit 2, to wot 6,—could they 2, to be learned 3, to lie by man 1, at unawares 1, will be 1; *Inf. intens.* assuredly (know) 1, certainly (know) 6, for a certainty (know) 1, for certain (know) 2, for a certain (know) 1; *Niphal*, to be discovered 1, to be famous 1, to be instructed 1, to be known 34, to make self known 4; *Piel*, to cause to know 1; *Poal*, to appoint 1; *Pual*, acquaintance 4, familiar friend 1, kinsfolk 1, (כ) kinsman 1, (כ) to be known 1; *Hiphil*, to acknowledge 1, to answer 1, to declare 6, to cause to discern 1, to cause to know 5, to let know 2, to make know 8. to give knowledge 1, to make known 17, to make to be known 1, to shew 17, to teach 8, to tell 2,—prognosticator 1; *Hophal*, to come to knowledge 1, known 1; *Hithpael*, to make self known 2.

יְדַע Ch. *P'al* to know 22; *Aphel*, to certify 4, to make known 19, to teach 1.

יִדְּעֹנִי wizard 11.

יָהַב *Kal*, to ascribe 1, to bring 2, to come on 1, to give 24, go to 4, to set 1, to take 1, burden 1.

יְהַב Ch. *P'al*, to deliver 1, to give 17, to lay 1, to yield 1,—to prolong 1; *Ithp'al*, to be given 6, to be paid 1.

יְהַד *Hithpael*, to become Jews 1.

יָהִיר haughty 1, proud 1.

יַהֲלֹם diamond 3.

יוֹבֵל jubilee 21, ram's *horn* 1, rams' horn 4, trumpet 1.

יוּבָל river 1.

יוֹם age 6, ago 2, alway 8, *birth-day*, continuance 1, daily, daily, day *very freq.*, day by day, every day, each day, days agone, now-a-days, two days, even now, full year 1, life 4, long 1, as long as 10, so long as (I) live 2, now 4, presently 2, season 3, so long 1, space 3, time 65, process of time 3, to-day, weather 1, year 19, yesterday,——afternoon 1, always, chronicles 37, continually 10, elder 2, end, evening 1, ever 3, everlasting 1, evermore 1, for ever 18, full 9, old 2, outlived 1, overlived 1, perpetually 2, prolong, remaineth 1, to require 1, required, Sabbath, time, at any time, at this time, when at time, at all times, as at other times, in trouble 1, whole age 4, year, younger 2.

יוֹם Ch. day 13, time 2.

יוֹמָם daily 2, day 20, by day 18, in the day 1, by daytime 1, in the daytime 7.

יָוֵן mire 1, miry 1.

יוֹנָה dove 21, pigeon 10.

יוֹנֶק tender plant 1.

יוֹנֶקֶת branch 4, tender branch 1, young twigs 1.

יוֹרָה former *rain* 1, first rain 1.

יוֹתֵר better 1, further 1, more 3, moreover 1, over 2, profit 1.

יָזַן *Hophal*, fed 1.

יֶזַע anything that causeth sweat 1.

יָחַד *Kal*, to be joined 2, to be united 1; *Piel*, to unite 1.

יַחַד & יַחְדָּיו & יַחְדָּו alike 5, altogether 5, at all 1, at once 2, both 1, knit 1, likewise 1, only 1, together *freq.*, withal 2.

יָחִיד only child 1, darling 2, desolate 1, only 6, solitary 1, only son 1.

יָחִיל should hope 1.

יָחַל *Niphal*, to stay 1, (כ) to tarry 1, to wait 1; *Piel*, to hope 13, to cause to hope 1, to make to hope 1, to trust 2, to

wait 7; *Hiphil*, to hope 6, to have hope 7, to be pained 1, to tarry 3, to wait 4.

יָחַם *Kal*, to conceive 2, to get heat 1, to be hot 2, to be warm 1; *Piel*, to conceive 4.

יַחְמוּר fallow deer 2.

יָחֵף barefoot 4, being unshod 1.

יָחַר *Kal*, (בַ) to tarry longer 1.

יָחַשׂ *Kal*, to be reckoned by genealogies 2; *Hithpael*, genealogy 6, genealogy to be reckoned 2, number after genealogy 1, number throughout the genealogy 1, to be reckoned by genealogies 8.

יַחַשׂ genealogy 1.

יָטַב *Kal*, to be accepted 2, to seem best 1, to be made better 1, to find favour 1, to be glad 1, to be good 2, to be merry 4, to please 5, to be well 12, to go well 4,—— to be content 1, to please 8, to please well 1; *Hiphil*, to amend 4, to use aright 1, to benefit 1, to be better 1, to make better 1, to make cheerful 1, to be comely 1, diligent 1, diligently 1, to do *goodness* 1, to dress 1, earnestly 1, to do good 18, to make good 1, to make merry 1, to please 1, to shew more *kindness* 1, skilfull 1, very small 1, to make sweet 1, thoroughly 1, to tire 1, to trim 1, to give wealth 1, can well 1, to deal well 3, to do well 8, to entreat well 1, to have well *said* 1, to have well *seen* 1, to have well *spoken* 1; *Inf. intens.* surely (do good) 1, throughly (amend) 1, very (plainly) 1.

יְטַב *Ch.* *P'al*, to seem good 1.

יַיִן banqueting 1, vine 1, wine *freq.*, wine *bibber* 1,——vine 1.

יָכַח *Niphal*, to dispute 1, to reason together 1, to be reproved 1; *Hiphil*, to appoint 2, to argue 1, to chasten 1, to convince 1, to correct 3, correction 1, daysman 1, to judge 1, to maintain 1, to plead 2, to reason 2, to rebuke 13, to reprove 25; *Inf. intens.* surely (reprove) 1, in any wise (rebuke) 1; *Hophal*, to be chastened 1; *Hithpael*, to plead 1.

יָכֹל *Kal*, to be able 44, to attain 2, can 53, can away with 1, can——could 47, to endure 3, may——might 18, to overcome 1, to have power 1, to prevail 22, to suffer 1; *Inf. intens.* any at all (have power) 1, any ways (able) 1, still (prevail) 1.

יְכֵל *Ch.* *P'al*, to be able 4, can 5, could 2, to prevail 1.

יָלַד *Kal*, to bear 153, to beget 28, birth 1, born 4, to bring forth 19, to bring forth children 1, to bring forth young 1, to bring up 1, to calve 1, child 3, to be delivered of a child 1, to be delivered 5, time of delivery 1, to gender 1, to hatch 1, labour 2, to travail—woman in travail—woman that travaileth —travailing woman—travail with child 20; *Niphal*, to be begotten 1, one's birth 1, to be born 33, to be brought forth 1, to come 1, to be the son of 1; *Piel*, midwife 9, to do the office of a midwife 1; *Pual*, to be born 26, to be brought forth 1, to be brought up 1; *Hiphil*, to beget 181, to bring forth 1, to make to bring forth 1, to cause to bring forth 2; *Hophal*, birthday 1, to be born 1; *Hithpael*, to declare pedigrees 1.

יֶלֶד boy 2, child 12, fruit 1, son 3, young man—young one 10.

יַלְדָה damsel 1, girl 2.

יַלְדוּת childhood 1, youth 2.

יִלּוֹד born 7.

יָלִיד born 6, children 4, home-born 1, son 3.

יָלַךְ *Kal*, away 1, to come 80, to come away 2, to depart 66, to flow 3, to get 17, to get away 3, to get hence 1, to go 630, to go away 12, to go in 1, to go on 2, to go (one's) way 9, to go out 1, to be gone 10, to go up 1, to go up and down 1, to grow 1, to be let down 1, to march 1, to prosper 1, to run 1, to spread 2, to take *journey* 1, to vanish 1, to walk 123, to wax 1,——again 1, to follow 21, to pursue 1, to be weak 2; *Hiphil*, to bear 1, to bring 12, to carry 5, to carry away 1, to go 1, to cause to go 2, to make go 1, to lead 17, to lead forth 1, to cause to run 1, to take away 1, to cause to walk 2.

יָלַל *Hiphil*, to howl 28, to make to howl 1, to be howlings 1, ——Lucifer 1.

יֵלֵל howling 1.

יְלָלָה howling 5.

יָלַע *Kal*, to devour 1.

יַלֶּפֶת scabbed 2.

יֶלֶק cankerworm 6, caterpillar.

יַלְקוּט scrip 1.

יָם sea *freq.*, sea *shore*, south 1, west *freq.*, west side, western 1, westward 3,—— seafaring man 1.

יָם *Ch.* sea 3.

יָמִין right—right hand—right side 134, south 3,——left-handed 2.

יְמִינִי (בֵּ) right 1, on the right hand 1.

יֵמִם mules 1.

יָמַן *Hiphil*, to go to the right 1, to go on the right hand 1, to turn to the right hand 1, to use the right hand 1.

יְמָנִי right 33, on the right hand 1.

יָמַר *Hiphil*, to boast selves 1, to change 1.

יָמַשׁ *Hiphil*, (בַּ) to feel 1.

יָנָה *Kal*, to destroy 1, oppressing 3, oppressor 1, proud 1; *Hiphil*, to oppress 8, to thrust out by oppression 1, to vex 4, to do no wrong 1.

יָנַח *Hiphil*, to bestow 1, to cast down 1, to lay 8, to lay down 1, to lay up 10, to leave 21, to leave off 1, to let alone 4, to let remain 1, to pacify 1, to place 3, to put 5, to set 3, to set down 2, to suffer 5, to withdraw 1, to withhold 1; *Hophal*, to be left 3, to be set 1.

יְנִיקוֹת young twigs 1.

יָנַק *Kal*, to suck—sucking child —suckling 19; *Hiphil*, milch 1, nurse 5, to nurse 2, nursing mother 1, to give suck 4, to make to suck 1.

יַנְשׁוּף great owl 2, owl 1.

יָסַד *Kal*, to establish 2, to found 7, to lay the foundation 9, to lay (foundation) 1; *Niphal*, to take counsel 2, foundation 1, foundation to be laid 1; *Piel*, to appoint 1, to found 1, to lay for a foundation 1, to lay the foundation 5, to ordain 2; *Pual*, foundation 1, foundation to be laid 1, set 1; *Hophal*, foundation to be laid 1, to be instructed 1, ——sure (foundation) 1.

יְסָד ——began 1.

יְסוֹד bottom 9, foundation 10, repairing 1.

יְסוּדָה foundation 1.

יָסוּר (בַּ) they that depart from 1.

יִסּוֹר instruct 1.

יָסַךְ *Kal*, to be poured 1.

יָסַף *Kal*, to add 9, any more 1, to bring more 1, to cease 1, to come more 1, to exceed 1, to increase 3, to proceed 1, to put 1,——again 6, further 1, more 9; *Niphal*, to be added 1, to increase 1, to join 1, to be put 2, ——more 1; *Hiphil*, to add 19, any more 10, to come again 1, to continue 2, to do again 1, to be done 1, to exceed 3, to get more 1, to give 1, to give moreover 1, to increase 10, to increase more and more 1, to be increased 1, to make 1, to bring more 2, to do more 1, to make more 2, to put more 1, to be yet the more 1, to proceed 1, to proceed further 1, to prolong 2, to be put 2, to be *stronger* 1, to yield 2,——again 48, to conceive again 1, further 2, henceforth 2, longer 1, more—any more— more and more—the more—yet more—much more *freq.*

יְסַף *Ch.* *Hophal*, to be added 1.

יָסַר *Kal*, to chastise 2, to instruct 1, to reprove 1; *Niphal*, to be chastised 1, to be corrected 1, to be instructed 2, to be reformed 1; *Nithpael*, to be taught 1; *Piel*, to bind 1, to chasten 8, to chastise 9, to correct 6, to instruct 5, to punish 1, to teach 1; *Inf. intens.* sore (chasten) 1; *Hiphil*, to chastise 1.

יָעַד *Kal*, to appoint 3, to betroth 2; *Niphal*, to be agreed 1, to make an appointment 1, to assemble selves 1, to be assembled 3, to gather selves 1, to gather selves together 1, to be gathered together 2, to meet 9, to be met together 1; *Hiphil*, to appoint a time 2, to set a time 1; *Hophal*, set 2.

יָעָה *Kal*, to sweep away 1.

יְעוֹרִים (בֵּ) woods 1.

יָעַז *Niphal*, fierce 1.

יָעַט *Kal*, to cover 1.

יְעַט *Ch.* *P'al*, counsellors 2; *Ithpael*, to consult together 1.

יָעִים shovels 9.

יָעַל *Hiphil*, to set forward 1, can do good 1, to profit 17, to have profit 2, to be profitable 1; *Inf. intens.* at all (profit) 1.

יַעֲלָה roe 1.

יְעֵלִים wild goats 3.

יַעֲנָה ——owl 8.

יְעֵנִים ostriches 1.

יָעֵף **Kal**, to faint 4, to be weary 2, to weary self 2; *Hophal*, to be caused to fly 1.

יָעֵף faint 2, weary 2.

יָעֵף swiftly 1.

יָעַץ *Kal*, to advertise 1, to consult 3, to counsel 6, to give counsel 3, to take counsel 2, to give (counsel) 6, to take (counsel) 3, counsel 1, counsellor 22, to determine 2, to devise 2, to guide 1, to purpose 5; *Niphal*, to give advice 1, to take advice 1, to advise 1, well advised 1, to consult 5, to give counsel 2, to take counsel 9; *Hithpael*, to consult 1.

יַעַר forest 38, honeycomb 1, wood 19.

יַעְרָה forest 1, honeycomb 1.

יָפָה *Kal*, to be beautiful 1, to be fair 3; *Piel*, to deck 1; *Pual*, to be fairer 1; *Hithpael*, to make self fair 1.

יָפֶה beauty 1, beautiful 3, comely 1, fair 22, fair one 2, fairest 2, pleasant 1, well 5, ——beautiful 4, goodly 1.

יְפֵה־פִיָּה very fair 1.

יָפַח *Hithpael*, to bewail self 1.

יָפֵחַ as breathe out 1.

יָפַח beauty 1.

יֳפִי beauty 18.

יָפַע *Hiphil*, to be light 1, to shew self 1, to shine 2, to cause to shine 2, to shine forth 2.

יִפְעָה brightness 2.

יָצָא *Kal*, to appear 1, to break out 1, to bring forth 1, to come 10, to come abroad 1, to come out—to be come out *most freq.*, to come without 2, to come forth—to be come forth *very freq.*, to depart 12, to be departed 3, departure 1, in the end of 2, to escape 2, to fail 2, to fall 2, to fall out 2, to follow 1, to get away 1, to get forth 1, to get hence 1, to get out 4, get (out) 2, to go 3, to go away 1, able to go 1, to go abroad 1, to go forth 147, able to go forth 14, to go on 3, fit to go out for 1, to go out 298, to be gone out 17, to be gone forth 11, to grow 1, to issue 2, to issue out 5, to be laid out 1, to lie out 3, to proceed 16, to be risen 1, to shoot forth 1, to spread 1, to spring out 2, to stand out 1, ——after 1, begotten 1, to be condemned 1, to *and fro* (going forth) 1; *Inf. intens.* as do 1, assuredly (go forth) 1, scarce (gone) 1, surely (come out) 1, surely (go forth) 1, at any time (come) 1; *Hiphil*, to bear out 1, to bring forth 122, to bring in and out 1, to bring out 95, to bring up 5, to carry forth 11, to carry 1, to carry out 8, (צ to send with commandment 1, to draw forth 3, to exact 1, to fetch forth 1, to fetch out 1, to cause to go forth 1, to cause to go out 1, to let go out 1, to have forth 2, to have out 1, to lay out 1, to lead out 3, to pluck out 2, to pull out 1, to put away 2, to take forth 1, to take out 1, to utter 6; *Hophal*, to be brought forth 5.

יְצָא *Ch. Shaphel*, to be finished 1.

יָצַב *Hithpael*, to present selves 9, remaining 1, to resort 1, to set 1, to set selves 5, to stand 21, to be able to stand 3, can stand 1, to stand fast 1, to stand forth 1, to stand still 2, to stand up 30, to withstand 1.

יְצַב *Ch. Pael*, truth 1.

יָצַג *Hiphil*, to establish 1, to leave 1, to make 2, to present 1, to put 2, to set 8; *Hophal*, to be stayed 1.

יִצְהָר anointed 1, oil 22.

יָצוּעַ bed 4, (בְּ) chamber 3, couch 1.

יָצִיא to come forth 1.

יַצִּיב *Ch.* certain 1, certainty 1, true 2, truth 1.

יָצִיעַ chamber 3.

יָצַע *Hiphil*, to make bed 1, to spread 1; *Hophal*, to be spread 1,——to be laid 1.

יָצַק *Kal*, to cast 11, to cleave fast 1, to be firm 2, to grow 1, to be hard 1, molten 1, to pour 19, to pour out 4, to run out 1; *Hiphil*, to lay out 1, to set down 1; *Hophal*, molten 5, to be overflown 1, to be poured 2, to pour out 1, stedfast 1.

יְצֻקָה when it was cast 1.

יָצַר *Kal*, to fashion 4, to form 26, to frame 3, to make 3, Maker 2, maker 2, potter 17, to purpose 1,——earthen 1; *Niphal*, to be formed 1; *Pual*, to be fashioned 1; *Hophal*, to be formed 1.

יָצַר *Kal*, to be distressed 4, to be narrow 1, to be straitened 2, to be in straits 1, to be vexed 1.

יֵצֶר frame 1, thing framed 1, imagination 5, mind 1, work 1.

יְצֻרִים members 1.

יָצַת *Kal*, to be burned 3, to kindle 1; *Niphal*, to be burned 4, to be burned up 1, to be desolate 1, to be kindled 2; *Hiphil*, to burn 1, to set on fire 7, to kindle 9, to set *fire* 1.

יֶקֶב fats 2, presses 2, press-fat 1, wine 1, wine-press 10.

יָקַד *Kal*, to burn 2, to kindle 1, ——from the hearth 1; *Hophal*, to burn 2, to be burning 3.

יְקַד *Ch. P'al*, burning 8.

יְקֵדָה *Ch.* burning 1.

יְקָהָה gathering 1, to obey 1.

יְקוֹד burning 2.

יְקוּם living substance 1, substance 1.

יָקוֹשׁ fowler 1.

יָקוּשׁ fowler 2, snare 1.

יַקִּיר dear 1.

יַקִּיר *Ch.* noble 1, rare 1.

יָקַע *Kal*, to be alienated 2, to depart 1, to be out of joint 1; *Hiphil*, to hang 1, to hang up 2; *Hophal*, to be hanged 1.

יָקַץ *Kal*, to awake 10, to be awaked 1.

יָקַר *Kal*, to be precious 7, to be prised 1, to be set by 1; *Hiphil*, to make precious 1, to withdraw 1.

יָקָר brightness 1, clear 1, costly 4, excellent 2, fat 1, honourable woman 1, precious 25, reputation 1.

יְקָר honour 8, to honour 4, precious 1, precious things 3, price 1.

יְקָר *Ch.* glory 5, honour 2.

יָקֹשׁ *Kal*, fowler 1, to lay *snare* 1, to lay a snare 1; *Niphal*, to be snared 4; *Hophal*, snared 1.

יָרֵא *Kal*, to shoot 1; *Hiphil*, to shoot 1, shooter 1,——to be watered 1.

יָרֵא *Kal*, to be afraid 76, to dread 1, durst not 1, to fear 183, to reverence 2,——to see 1; *Niphal*, dreadful 5, to be feared 4, fearful 2, fearfully 1, to be had in reverence 1, reverend 1, terrible 24, terrible acts 1, terrible things 4, terribleness 1; *Piel*, to affright 1, to make afraid 2, to put in fear 2.

יָרֵא afraid 3, to fear 59, fearful 2.

יִרְאָה afraid 1, fear 42, fearfulness 1,——dreadful 1, exceedingly 1.

יָרַד *Kal*, to come down 103, to descend 19, to fall 103, to get down 9, to go down 148, to go downward 1, to be gone down 12, to light 1, to light down 1, to run down 7, to sink 1, to be subdued 1,—— abundantly 1; *Inf. intens.* indeed (come down) 1; *Hiphil*, to bring down 39, to carry down 2, to cast down 4, to cause to come down 2, to let fall down 1, to let go down 1, to hang down 1, to let down 5, to put down 1, to put off 1, to cause to run down 1, to let run down 1, to take down 7; *Hophal*, to be brought down 4, (בְּ) to go down 1, to be taken down 1.

יָרָה *Kal*, archers 2, to cast 4, to lay 1, shoot 7,——former rain 1; *Inf. intens.* through 1; *Niphal*, to be shot 1; *Hiphil*, to cast 1, to direct 1, to inform 1, to instruct 1, to rain 1, to shew 1, to shoot 9, to teach 46,——archers 2.

יָרֵא *Kal*, to be afraid 1.

יָרוֹק green thing 1.

יָרֵחַ moon 26.

יֶרַח month 11, moon 2.

יְרַח *Ch.* month 2.

יָרַט *Kal*, to be perverse 1, to turn over 1.

יָרִיב that contend 1, that contendeth 1, that strive 1.

יְרִיעָה curtain 53.

יָרֵךְ loins 2, shaft 3, side 7, thigh 21,——body 1.

יַרְכָה border 2, coast 2, parts 2, quarters 1, sides 21.

יַרְכָה *Ch.* thigh 1.

יָרַע *Kal*, to be evil 2, to be grieved 4, to be grievous 3, to do harm 1, to go ill 2, to be sad 1,——to displease 9.

יָרַק *Kal*, to spit 2; *Inf. intens.* but (spit) 1.

יָרָק green 2, herbs 3.

יֶרֶק grass 1, green 3, green thing 2.

יֵרָקוֹן mildew 5, paleness 1.

יְרַקְרַק greenish 2, yellow 1.

יָרַשׁ *Kal*, (בְּ) to drive out 1, to enjoy 2, to be heir 10, to inherit 21, inheritor 1, to pos-

כּוֹכָב star *freq.*, star*gazers* 1.

כּוּל *Kal*, to comprehend 1 ; *Pilpel*, to abide 1, to contain 3, to feed 6, forbearing 1, to guide 1, to nourish 4, to make provision 1, to sustain 3, to provide sustenance 1, to provide victuals 2 ; *Polpal*, to be present 1 ; *Hiphil*, to be able to abide—can abide 2, to bear 1, to contain 3, to hold 2, holding in 1, to receive 2.

כֻּמָּז tablets 2.

כּוּן *Niphal*, certain 2, certainty 1, to be directed 1, to be established 27, faithfulness 1, to be fashioned 1, to be fitted 1, to be fixed 4, to be meet 1, to be set in order 1, to prepare 1, (כ) to prepare (*selves*) 1, to be prepared 7, ready 8, right 4, to be set forth 1, to be stable 2, to stand 2, to tarry 1, in very deed 1 ; *Polel*, to confirm 2, to establish 14, to fashion 2, to ordain 1, to prepare 2, to prepare self 1, to be ready 1, to make ready 3, to stablish 3 ; *Pulal*, to be ordered 1, to be prepared 1 ; *Hiphil*, to set aright 1, to confirm 1, to direct 3, to establish 13, firm 2, to frame 1, to order 1, preparation 1, to make preparation 1, to prepare 68, to provide 4, to make provision 1, to make ready 5, to set 3, to set fast 2, to stablish 1 ; *Hophal*, to be established 2, fastened 1, to be prepared 3 ; *Hithpolel*, to be established 2, to prepare selves 1, to be prepared 1.

כַּוָּנִים cakes 2.

כּוֹס cup 31, little owl 2, owl 1.

כּוּר furnace 9.

כּוֹרִין Ch. measures 1.

כּוֹשָׁרוֹת ——chains 1.

כָּזַב *Kal*, liar 1 ; *Niphal*, to be found a liar 1, to be in vain 1 ; *Piel*, to fail 1, to lie 11 ; *Hiphil*, to make a liar 1.

כָּזָב deceitful 1, false 1, leasing 2, lie 23, lying 2,——liar 1.

כֹּחַ ability 2, able 3, chameleon 1, force 3, fruits 1, might 7, power 47, powerful 1, strength 50, substance 1, wealth 1,——weary 1.

כָּחַד *Niphal*, to be cut down 1, to be cut off 5, desolate 1, to be hid 4 ; *Piel*, to conceal 4, to hide 11 ; *Hiphil*, to cut off 5, to hide 1.

כָּחַל *Kal*, to paint 1.

כָּחַשׁ *Kal*, to fail 1 ; *Niphal*, to be found liars 1 ; *Piel*, to

belie 1, to deceive 1, to deny 5, to dissemble 1, to fail 2, to deal falsely 1, to lie 5, to submit selves 3 ; *Hithpael*, to submit selves 1.

כַּחַשׁ leanness 1, lies 4, lying 1.

כְּחָשִׁים lying 1.

כִּי burning 1.

כִּיד destruction 1.

כִּידוֹד sparks 1.

כִּידוֹן lance 1, shield 2, spear 5, target 1.

כִּידוֹר battle 1.

כִּיּוֹר hearth 1, laver 20, pan 1, scaffold 1.

כִּילַי churl 2.

כֵּילַפּוֹת hammers 1.

כִּימָה Pleiades 2, seven stars 1.

כִּים bag 4, (כ) cup 1, purse 1.

כִּירַיִם ranges for pots 1.

כִּישׁוֹר spindle 1.

כִּכָּר loaf 4, morsel 1, piece 2, plain 12, talent 48.

כַּכְּרִין Ch. talents 1.

כֹּל all, enough 1.

כָּלָא *Kal*, to forbid 1, to keep 1, to keep back 1, to refrain 2, to retain 1, to shut up 4, to be stayed 2, to withhold 2 ; *Niphal*, to be restrained 2, to be stayed 1 ; *Piel*, to finish 1.

כֶּלֶא prison 10.

כִּלְאַיִם divers seeds 1, diverse kind 1, mingled 1, mingled seed 1.

כֶּלֶב dog 32.

כָּלָה *Kal*, to be accomplished 3, to cease 2, to consume 1, to consume away 2, to be consumed 15, to be determined 4, to be done 1, end 1, to be an end of 1, to be ended 3, to fail 17, to faint 2, to finish 1, to be finished 5, to be fulfilled 1, to be spent 3, to waste 2 ; *Piel*, to accomplish 9, to consume 41, to destroy 1, to destroy utterly 2, to have done 7, to be done 1, to end 3, to make an end 46, to be expired 1, to cause to fail 1, to finish 7, to fulfil 2, fully 1, to leave 2, to leave off 1, to long 1, to bring to pass 1, to pluck 1, to wholly reap 1, to make clean riddance 1, to spend 5, to quite take away 1,—— to have (eaten) 1 ; *Pual*, to be ended 1, to be finished 1.

כָּלָה altogether 3, to consume 1, consume utterly 1, be consumed 1, consummation 1, consumption 2, was determined 1, end 1, full end 8, utter end 2, riddance 1.

כָּלֶה fail 1.

כַּלָּה bride 9, daughter-in-law 17, spouse 8.

כְּלוּא (ק) ——prison 2.

כְּלוּב basket 2, cage 1.

כְּלוּלוֹת espousals 2.

כֶּלַח full age 1, old age 1.

כְּלַי churl 2.

כְּלִי armour 28, armourbearer 17, artillery 1, bag 2, carriage 3, furniture 8, instrument 39, jewels 20, that is made of 1, that which pertaineth 1, pot 1, sacks 1, stuff 14, thing 12, tool 1, vessels *freq.*, wares 1, weapons 20,——furnish 1, one from another 1, psaltery 2.

כְּלִיא (כ) ——prison 2.

כִּלָּיוֹן consumption 1, failing 1.

כְּלָיוֹת kidneys 18, reins 13.

כָּלִיל all 2, every whit 1, flame 1, perfect 3, perfection 1, utterly 1, whole burnt offering 1, whole burnt sacrifice 1, wholly 4.

כָּלַל *Kal*, to perfect 1, to make perfect 1.

כְּלַל Ch. *Shaphel*, to finish 1, to make up 2, to set up 2 ; *Ishtaphel*, to set up 2.

כָּלַם *Niphal*, to be ashamed 11, to blush 2, to be confounded 10, to be put to confusion 1, to be put to shame 2 ; *Hiphil*, to make ashamed 1, to blush 1, to hurt 1, to reproach 2, to shame 1, to do shame 1, to put to shame 3 ; *Hophal*, to be confounded 1, to be hurt 1.

כְּלִמָּה confusion 6, dishonour 3, reproach 1, shame 20.

כְּלִמוּת shame 1.

כָּמַהּ *Kal*, to long 1.

כַּמֹּן cummin 3.

כָּמַס *Kal*, to be laid up in store 1.

כָּמַר *Niphal*, to be black 1, to be kindled 1, to yearn 2.

כְּמָרִים Chemarims 1, idolatrous priests 1, priests 1.

כְּמִרִירִים blackness 1.

כֵּן base 2, estate 4, foot 8, office 1, place 1, well 1.

כֵּן lice 4,——manner 1.

כֵּן aright 1, right 1, state 1, well 1.

כָּנָה *Piel*, to give flattering titles 2, to surname 1, to surname (himself) 1.

כַּנָּה ——vineyard 1.

כִּנּוֹר harp 42.

כֵּנִים true 5.

כִּנָּם lice 2.

כָּנַס *Kal*, to gather 3, to gather together 3, to heap up 1 ; *Piel*, to gather 2, to gather together 1 ; *Hithpael*, to wrap self 1.

כָּנַע *Niphal*, to be brought into subjection 6, to be brought under 1, to humble self 16, to be humbled 2, to be subdued 5 ; *Hiphil*, to bring down 3, to bring low 2, to subdue 6.

כִּנְעָה wares 1.

כְּנַעַן merchant 2, traffic 1, trafficer 1.

כְּנַעֲנִי Canaanite 1, merchant 2.

כָּנַף *Niphal*, to be removed 1.

כָּנָף border 2, corner 2, end 2, feathered 1, flying 1, overspreading 1, skirt 14, uttermost part 1, wing *freq.*, winged 1, —— bird 1, one another 1, quarters 1, sort 2.

כְּנַשׁ Ch. *P'al*, to gather together 1 ; *Ithpael*, to be gathered together 2.

כְּנָת companion 1.

כְּנָת Ch. companion 7.

כֵּס ——sworn 1.

כִּסֵּא appointed 1.

כִּסֵּא seat 7, stool 1, throne *freq.*

כָּסָה *Kal*, to conceal 1, to cover 2 ; *Niphal*, to be covered 2 ; *Piel*, to close 1, to conceal 3, to cover 119, to flee to hide 1, to hide 5, to overwhelm 2 ; *Pual*, to be clothed 1, to cover 1, to be covered 5 ; *Hithpael*, clad self 1, to cover self 1, to be covered 4.

כְּסֶה time appointed 1.

כִּסֶּה throne 3.

כָּסוּי covering 2.

כְּסוּת covering 5, raiment 1, vesture 1.

כָּסַח *Kal,* to be cut down 1, to be cut up 1.

כְּסִיל constellation 1, fool 61, foolish 8, Orion 3.

כְּסִילוּת foolish 1.

כָּסַל *Kal,* to be foolish 1.

כֶּסֶל confidence 1, flanks 6, folly 2, hope 3, loins 1.

כִּסְלָה confidence 1, folly 1.

כִּסְלֵו Chisleu 2.

כָּסַם *Kal,* to poll 1; *Inf. intens.* only 1.

כֻּסֶּמֶת fitches 1, rie 2.

כָּסַס *Kal,* to make count 1.

כָּסַף *Kal,* to have desire 1, to be greedy 1; *Niphal,* desired 1, to long 2; *Inf. intens.* sore (long) 1.

כֶּסֶף money 112, price 3, silver *freq.,* silverlings 1.

כְּסַף Ch. money 1, silver 12.

כְּסָתוֹת pillows 2.

כָּעַס *Kal,* to be angry 2, to be grieved 1, to take indignation 1, to have sorrow 1, to be wroth 1; *Piel,* to provoke 1, to provoke to anger 1; *Hiphil,* to provoke 2, to provoke to anger 43, to provoke unto wrath 1, to vex 1.

כַּעַס anger 2, angry 1, grief 6, provocation 4, provoking 1, sorrow 2, spite 1, wrath 3, ——sore 1.

כַּעַשׂ grief 1, indignation 1, sorrow 1, wrath 1.

כְּעֵת Ch. at such a time 1.

כַּף branch 1, cloud 1, hand 124, hand*ful* 3, handle 1, hand*led* 1, hollow 1, middle 1, palm 6, paw 1, power 1, sole 18, spoon 23, ——apiece 1, foot (breadth) 1.

כָּפָה *Kal,* to pacify 1.

כִּפָּה branch 3.

כְּפוֹר bason 6, hoarfrost 2, hoary frost 1.

כֵּפִים rocks 2.

כָּפִים beam 1.

כְּפִיר lion 6, village 1, young *lion* 1, young lions 24.

כָּפַל *Kal,* to double 4; *Niphal,* to be doubled 1.

כֶּפֶל double 2.

כָּפַן *Kal,* to bend 1.

כָּפָן famine 2.

כָּפַף *Kal,* to bow down 1, to be bowed down 2; *Niphal,* to bow self 1.

כָּפַר *Kal,* to pitch 1; *Piel,* to appease 1, to make atonement 5, to be made atonement 1, to make an atonement 65, to make the atonement 1, to forgive 2, to be merciful 2, to be pacified 1, to pacify 1, to pardon 1, to purge 2, to purge away 1, to put off 1, to reconcile 3, to make reconciliation 4; *Pual,* to be made atonement 1, to be cleansed 1, to be disannulled 1, to be purged 4; *Hithpael,* to be forgiven 1, to be purged 1.

כְּפָר village 2.

כֹּפֶר bribe 2, camphire 2, pitch 1, ransom 8, satisfaction 2, sum of money 1, village 1.

כִּפֻּרִים atonement 8.

כַּפֹּרֶת mercy-seat 27.

כָּפַשׁ *Hiphil,* to cover 1.

כְּפַת Ch. *P'il,* to be bound 1; *Pael,* to bind 3.

כַּפְתּוֹר knop 16, lintel 1, upper lintel 1.

כַּר captain 1, furniture 1, lamb 10, pasture 1, large pasture 1, ram 2.

כֹּר cor 1, measure 7.

כְּרָא Ch. *Ithp'el,* to be grieved 1.

כַּרְבֵּל clothed 1.

כַּרְבְּלָא Ch. hat 1.

כָּרָה *Kal,* to make a banquet 1, to buy 2, to dig 11, to open 1, to pierce 1, to prepare 1,——to make 2; *Niphal,* to be digged 1.

כָּרָה provision 1.

כְּרוּב cherub 28, cherubims *freq.*

כָּרוֹז Ch. herald 1.

כְּרַז Ch. *Aphel,* to make a proclamation 1.

כָּרִי captains 2.

כְּרִיתוּת divorce 1, divorcement 3.

כְּרֻב compass 2.

כַּרְכֹּם saffron 1.

כִּרְכָּרוֹת swift beasts 1.

כֶּרֶם vines 3, vineyard *freq.,* increase of the vineyards 1, vintage 1.

כַּרְמִיל crimson 3.

כֹּרְמִים vinedressers 5.

כַּרְמֶל Carmel 7, full ears of corn 1, full ears 1, green ears 1, fruitful field 6, fruitful place 1, plentiful 1, plentiful field 2.

כָּרְסֵא Ch. throne 3.

כִּרְסֵם to waste 1.

כָּרַע *Kal,* to bow 10, to bow down 8, to bow selves 4, to be brought down 1, to couch 1, to fall 1, feeble 1, kneeling 1, to sink down 1, to stoop down 1; *Hiphil,* to cast down 1, to bring low 1, to smite down 1, to subdue 2; *Inf. intens.* very (bring low) 1.

כְּרָעַיִם legs 9.

כַּרְפַּס green 1.

כָּרַר *Pilpel,* to dance 2.

כָּרֵשׂ belly 1.

כָּרַת *Kal,* to be confederate 1, to covenant 2, to make covenant 1, to cut 6, to cut down 18, to cut off 15, to destroy 1, feller 1, to hew 2, to hew down 2, to make a league 1, to make 83; *Niphal,* to be chewed 1, to be cut down 1, to be cut off 58, to be cut out 1, to fail 6, to be freed 1, to perish 1; *Inf. intens.* utterly (cut off) 1, ——to want 3; *Pual,* to be cut 1, to be cut down 1; *Hiphil,* to cut down 1, to cut off 73, to destroy 3,——to lose 1; *Hophal,* to be cut off 1.

כָּרֹת cottages 1.

כְּרֻתוֹת beams 3.

כְּרֵתִי Cherethims 1, Cherethites 8.

כֶּשֶׂב lamb 4, sheep 9.

כִּשְׂבָּה lamb 1.

כָּשָׂה *Kal,* to be covered 1.

כַּשִּׂיל axes 1.

כָּשַׁל *Kal,* to be decayed 1, to fail 1, to fall 12, (ב) to cause to fall 1, to fall down 1, to be fallen 1, feeble 1, to be ruined 1, to stumble 8, to be weak 1; *Inf. intens.* utterly (fall) 1; *Niphal,* to be cast down 2, to fall 10, feeble 1, to be overthrown 1, to stumble 10; *Piel,* to bereave 1; *Hiphil,* to cast down 1, to cause to fall 2, to make to fall 3, to be the ruin of 1, to cause to stumble 2; *Hophal,* overthrown 1.

כִּשָּׁלוֹן fall 1.

כָּשַׁף *Piel,* sorcerers 3, witch 2, to use witchcraft 1.

כַּשָּׁף sorcerer 1.

כְּשָׁפִים sorceries 2, witchcrafts 4.

כָּשֵׁר *Kal,* to prosper 1, to be right 1; *Hiphil,* to direct 1.

כִּשְׁרוֹן equity 1, good 1, right 1.

כָּתַב *Kal,* to describe 6, recorded 1, to subscribe 4. to write 193; *Niphal,* to be written 17; *Piel,* to prescribe 1, to write 1.

כְּתָב register 2, scripture 1, writing 14.

כְּתָב Ch. prescribing 1, writing 10, written 1.

כְּתַב Ch. *P'al,* to write 8.

כְּתֹבֶת ——any *marks* 1.

כָּתִית beaten 4, pure 1.

כֹּתֶל wall 1.

כְּתַל Ch. wall 2.

כָּתַם *Niphal,* to be marked 1.

כֶּתֶם gold 2, fine gold 4, pure gold 1. golden wedge 1, most *fine gold* 1.

כֻּתֹּנֶת & כְּתֹנֶת coat 23, garment 5, robe 1.

כָּתֵף arm 2, corner 2, shoulder 22, shoulderpiece 4, side 35, undersetter 4.

כָּתַר *Piel,* to beset round 1, to inclose round 1, to suffer 1; *Hiphil,* to compass about 2, to be crowned 1.

כֶּתֶר crown 3.

כֹּתֶרֶת chapiter 24.

כָּתַשׁ *Kal,* to bray (*in a mortar*) 1.

כָּתַת *Kal,* to beat 1, to beat down 1, to be broken in pieces 1, to crush 1, to stamp 1; *Piel,* to beat 3, to break in pieces 1, to smite 1; *Pual,* to be destroyed 1; *Hiphil,* to destroy 1, to discomfit 1; *Hophal,* to be beaten down 1, to be beaten to pieces 1, to be destroyed 1, to be smitten 1.

לָאָה *Kal,* to faint 1, to be grieved 1, to weary self 1; *Niphal,* to grieve 1, to lothe 1. to be wearied 1, to be weary 6, to weary selves 1; *Hiphil,* to weary 5, to make weary 1.

לְאֹם & לְאוֹם nation 10, people 25.

לָאַט *Kal,* to cover 1.

לָאט softly 1.

לֵב brokenhearted 1, comfortably 4 consent 1, courageous 1, friendly 2, hardhearted 1, heart very freq., wise hearted 6, kindly 2, merryhearted 1, midst 12, mind 11, minded 1, regard 4, stiffhearted 1, stouthearted 2, take heed 1, understanding 20, willingly 9, willing hearted 2, wisdom 6, —— bethink themselves 1, care for 2, considered 4, double heart 2, heed 1, look well 1, mark well 3, regarded 3, unawares 1, well 4.

לֵב Ch. heart 1.

לְבָאוֹת lionesses 1.

לְבָאִים lions 1.

לָבַב Niphal, to be wise 1; Piel, to make cakes 1, to make (cakes) 1, to ravish the heart 1.

לֵבָב breast 1, comfortably 1, courage 1, fainthearted 2, heart freq., midst 1, mind 4, tenderhearted 1, understanding 3, —— bethink selves 1, consider 5, unawares 1.

לְבַב Ch. heart 7.

לְבִבוֹת cakes 3.

לַבָּה flame 1.

לִבָּה heart 8.

לְבוֹנָה frankincense 15, incense 6.

לְבוּשׁ apparel 8, clothed with 1, clothing 9, garment 9, raiment that he had put on 1, vestment 1, vesture 2.

לְבוּשׁ Ch. garment 2.

לְבַט Niphal, to fall 3.

לָבִיא lion 4, great lion 3, old lion 2, stout lion 1, young (lion) 1.

לְבִיא lioness 1.

לָבֵן Kal, to make brick 1, to make brick 2; Hiphil, to be white 2, to be made white 1, to make white 1; Hithpael, to be made white 1.

לָבֵן white 28.

לָבֵן white 1.

לְבָנָה moon 3.

לְבֵנָה altars of brick 1, brick 9, tile 1.

לִבְנֶה poplar 2.

לִבְנָה paved 1.

לָבַשׁ & לָבֵשׁ Kal, to be apparelled 1, armed 1,

to array self 1, to clothe 3, to clothe self with 3, clothed in 3, to be clothed with 26, to come upon 3, that he had put on 32, to wear 4; Pual, in apparel 1, to be arrayed 1; Hiphil, to arm 2, to array 4, to clothe 3, to clothe with 13, to clothe in 1, to put—to put upon 9.

לְבֵשׁ Ch. P'al, to be clothed 2; Aphel, to clothe 1.

לֹג log of oil 5.

לָה Ch. as nothing 1.

לַהַב blade 2, bright 1, flame 8, glittering 1.

לֶהָבָה & לֶהָבֶת flame 13, flaming 5, head (of a spear) 1.

לַהַג study 1.

לָהָה Kal, to faint 1; Hithpael, mad 1.

לַהַט Kal, to be set on fire 1, flaming 1; Piel, to burn 3, to burn up 2, to set on fire 3, to kindle 1.

לַהַט flaming 1.

לְהָטִים enchantments 1.

לַהֵם Hithpael, as wounds 2.

לְהָקָה company 1.

לָוָה Kal, to abide with 1, to borrow 5; Niphal, to cleave 1, to join self 4, to be joined 6; Hiphil, to lend 8, lender 1.

לוּז Kal, to depart 1; Niphal, froward 2, perverse 1, perverseness 1; Hiphil, to depart 1.

לוּז hazel 1.

לוּחַ board 4, plate 1, table 38.

לוּט Kal, cast 1, wrapped 1; Hiphil, to wrap 1.

לוֹט covering 1.

לִוְיָה ornament 2.

לִוְיָתָן leviathan 5, —— mourning 1.

לוּלִים winding stairs 1.

לִין & לוּן Kal, to abide 4, to abide all night 6, to continue 1, to dwell 1, to endure 1, to grudge 1, to be left 1, to lie all night 3, to lodge 29, to lodge all night 1, to lodge in 2, to lodge this night 1, to lodging 1, to remain 7, to tarry 1, to tarry all night 1, to tarry the night 3; Niphal, to murmur 4, (ב) to murmur 3; Hiphil, to lodge

1, to cause to lodge 1, to murmur 8, to make to murmur 1; Hithpalpel, to abide 2.

לוּעַ Kal, to swallow down 1, to be swallowed up 1.

לִיץ Kal, mocker 1, to scorn 1, scorner 14, scornful 1; Hiphil, ambassador 1, to have in derision 1, interpreter 2, to make a mock 1, to scorn 3, teacher 1; Hithpalpel, mocker 1.

לוּשׁ Kal, to knead 5.

לְזוּת perverse 1.

לַח green 6, moist 1.

לֵחַ natural force 1.

לָחוּם while...is eating 1, flesh 1.

לְחִי cheek 9, two cheeks 1, cheek bone 1, jaw 7, jawbone 3, Lehi 1, Ramath-lehi 1.

לָחַךְ Kal, to lick up 1; Piel, to lick 3, to lick up 2.

לָחַם Kal, to devour 1, to eat 5, to fight 3, to fight against 1; Niphal, to fight 145, to overcome 2, to prevail 1, to war 10, to make war 8; Inf. intens. ever (fight) 1.

לֶחֶם war 1.

לֶחֶם bread 249, feast 21, food 1, fruit 1, loaf 5, meat 18, provision 1, shewbread 8, victuals 2, —— eat 1.

לְחֶם Ch. feast 1.

לְחֵנָה Ch. concubine 3.

לָחַץ Kal, to afflict 1, to crush 1, to force 1, to hold fast 1, to oppress 13, oppressors 1; Niphal, to thrust self 1.

לַחַץ affliction 5, oppression 7.

לָחַשׁ Piel, charmer 1; Hithpael, to whisper 1, to whisper together 1.

לַחַשׁ charmed 1, ear-ring 1, enchantment 1, orator (eloquent) 1, prayer 1.

לָט enchantment 3, privily 1, secretly 1, softly 1.

לֹט myrrh 2.

לְטָאָה lizard 1.

לָטַשׁ Kal, instructer 1, to sharpen 2, to whet 1; Pual, sharp 1.

לִיּוֹת additions 3.

לַיִל midnight 6, night freq., night season 2.

לֵילְיָא Ch. night 4.

לִילִית screech owl 1.

לַיִשׁ lion 1, old lion 2.

לָכַד Kal, to catch 4, to catch self 1, to take 77; Inf. intens. at all (take) 1; Niphal, to be holden 1, to be taken 35; Hithpael, to be frozen 1, to stick together 1.

לֶכֶד being taken 1.

לֻלָאֹת loops 13.

לָמַד Kal, to learn 22, skilful 1; Inf. intens. diligently learn) 1; Piel, to instruct 2, to teach 64; Pual, expert 1, to be instructed 1, to be taught 2, unaccustomed 1.

לִמּוּד accustomed 1, disciple 1, learned 2, taught 1, used 1.

לֹעַ throat 1.

לָעַב Hiphil, to mock 1.

לָעַג Kal, to have in derision 2, to laugh 2, to mock 5, to laugh to scorn 3; Niphal, stammering 1; Hiphil, to mock 2, to mock on 1, to laugh to scorn 2.

לַעַג derision 2, had in derision 1, scorn 2, scorning 2.

לָעֵג mocker 1, stammering 1.

לָעַז Kal, strange language 1.

לָעַט Hiphil, to feed 1.

לַעֲנָה hemlock 1, wormwood 7.

לַפִּיד brand 1, burning lamp 1, firebrand 2, lamp 8, lightning 1, torch 2.

לָפַת Kal, to take hold 1; Niphal, to turn aside 1, to turn self 1.

לָצוֹן scornful 2, scorning 1.

לֵץ Kal, to scorn 1.

לָקַח Kal, to accept 1, to bring 25, to buy 3, to carry away 5, drawn 1, to fetch 30, to get 6, to marry 4, to place 1, to put 1, to receive 62, to reserve 1, to seize 1, to seize upon 1, to send for 1, to take—to take away 793, to use 1, to win 1; Niphal, to be brought 1, to be taken 6, to be taken away 3; Pual, to be taken 7, to be taken away 1, to be taken up 1; Hophal, to be fetched 1, to be taken 4, to be taken away 1; Hithpael, infolding 1, mingled 1.

לֶקַח doctrine 4, learning 4, fair speech 1.

לָקַט Kal, to gather 13, to glean 1; Piel, to gather 8, to

gather up 2, to glean 11 ; *Pual*, to be gathered 1 ; *Hithpael*, to be gathered 1.

לֶקֶט gleaning 2.

לָקַק *Kal*, to lap 2, to lick 3; *Piel*, to lap 2.

לָקַשׁ *Piel*, to gather 1.

לֶקֶשׁ latter growth 2.

לְשַׁד fresh 1, moisture 1.

לָשׁוֹן bay 3, language 10, talkers 1, tongue *freq.*, wedge 2, —— babbler 1, fire 1, evil speaker 1.

לִשְׁכָּה chamber 46, parlour 1.

לֶשֶׁם ligure 2.

לָשַׁן *Piel*, to slander 1 ; *Poel*, ('ב) to slander 1 ; *Hiphil*, accuse 1.

לִשָּׁן Ch. language 7.

לֶתֶךְ half homer 1.

מֵאֲבוּס storehouse 1.

מְאֹד diligent 5, especially 1, exceeding 19, exceedingly 12, far 3, fast 1, good 3, great 12, greatly 49, might 1, mightily 2, mighty 2, much 6, quickly 1, right well 1, so much 2, never so much 1, so much 1, sore 23, utterly 2, very 137, very sore 2, well 2, ——louder and louder 1, very much 1.

מֵאָה hundred, hundred*fold*, hundredth, Meah 1, —— sixscore.

מְאָה Ch. hundred.

מַאֲוַיִּים desires 1.

מְאוּם blemish 1, blot 1.

מְאוּמָה fault 1, *nothing* 9, ought 5, somewhat 1, anything 14,——nought 1.

מָאוֹר bright 1, light 18.

מְאוּרָה den 1.

מֹאזְנַיִם balances 15.

מֹאזְנַיִן Ch. balances 1.

מַאֲכָל *bake*meats 1, food 5, fruit 1, meat 22, victual 1.

מַאֲכֶלֶת knife 4.

מַאֲכֹלֶת fuel 2.

מַאֲמַצִּים forces 1.

מַאֲמָר commandment 2, decree 1.

מֵאמַר Ch. appointment 1, word 1.

מָאן Ch. vessel 7.

מֵאֵן *Piel*, to refuse 40 ; *Inf. intens.* utterly (refuse) 1.

מָאֵן refuse 4.

מֵאֲנִים which refuse 1.

מָאַס *Kal*, to abhor 4, to cast away 7, to cast off 3, to contemn 2, to despise 24, to disdain 1, to loathe 1, to refuse 9, to reject 21 ; *Inf. intens.* (reject) 2 ; *Niphal*, to be refused 1, reprobate 1, vile person 1.

מָאַס *Niphal*, to become loathsome 1, to melt away 1.

מַאֲפֶה baken 1.

מַאֲפֵל darkness 1.

מַאְפֵּלְיָה darkness 1.

מָאַר *Hiphil*, fretting 3, pricking 1.

מַאֲרָב lie in ambush 1, ambushment 2, lurking-place 1, lying in wait 1.

מְאֵרָה curse 4, cursing 1.

מִבְדָּלוֹת separate cities 1.

מָבוֹא by which came 1, as cometh 1, coming in 2, as men enter into 1, entering 3, entrance into 2, entrance of 1, entry 6, where … goeth 1, going down 5,——westward 2.

מְבוּכָה perplexity 2.

מַבּוּל flood 13.

מְבוּנִים ('ב) taught 1.

מְבוּסָה treading down 1, trodden down 1, trodden under foot 1.

מַבּוּעַ fountain 1, spring 2.

מְבוּקָה void 1.

מִבְחוֹר choice 2.

מִבְחָר choice 7, choicest 1, chosen 4.

מַבָּט expectation 2.

מֶבָּט expectation 1.

מִבְטָא uttered out of 1, that which … uttered with 1.

מִבְטָח confidence 9, hope 1, sure 1, trust 4.

מַבְלִינִית comfort self 1.

מִבְנֶה frame 1.

מִבְצָר defenced 4, fenced 11, most fenced 1, fortress 6,

strong 2, stronghold 12, most strong 1.

מִבְרָח fugitive 1.

מִבְשִׁים secrets 1.

מְבַשְּׁלוֹת boiling-places 1.

מִגְבָּלֹת ends 1.

מִגְבָּעוֹת bonnets 4.

מֶגֶד pleasant 3, precious fruits 1, precious things 4.

מִגְדָּל castle 1, flower 1, pulpit 2, tower 47.

מִגְדֹּל tower 3.

מִגְדָּנוֹת precious things 4, presents 1.

מָגוֹר fear 6, Magor-*missabib* 1, terror 2.

מָגוּר dwelling 2, pilgrimage 4, where sojourn 1, be a stranger 4.

מְגוֹרָה fear 1.

מְגוּרָה barn 1, fear 2.

מַגְזֵרָה axe 1.

מַגָּל sickle 2.

מְגִלָּה roll 20, volume 1.

מְגִלָּה Ch. roll 1.

מְגַמָּה sup up 1.

מָגַן *Piel*, to deliver 3.

מָגֵן armed 2, buckler 8, defence 2, ruler 1, shield *freq.*,—— scale 1.

מִגְנָה sorrow 1.

מִגְעֶרֶת rebuke 1.

מַגֵּפָה plague 21, slaughter 3, stroke 1, —— to be plagued 1.

מָגַר *Kal*,——terrors 1 ; *Piel*, to cast down 1.

מְגַר Ch. *Pael*, to destroy 1.

מְגֵרָה axe 1, saw 3.

מִגְרָעוֹת narrowed rests 1.

מְגְרָפָה clods 1.

מִגְרָשׁ cast out 1, suburb *freq.*

מַד armour 2, clothes 1, garment 4, judgment 1, measure 2, raiment 2, ('ב) stature 1.

מִדְבַּח Ch. altar 1.

מִדְבָּר desert 13, south 1, speech 1, wilderness *freq.*

מָדַד *Kal*, to measure 42, to mete 1 ; *Niphal*, to be measured 3 ; *Piel*, to measure 2,

to mete out 2 ; *Polel*, to measure 1 ; *Hithpolel*, to stretch self 1.

מֻדַּד be gone 1.

מִדָּה garment 1, measure 27, measuring 10, meteyard 1, piece 7, size 3, stature 3, great stature 1, tribute 1, wide 1.

מִדָּה toll 1, tribute 2.

מַדְהֵבָה golden city 1.

מַדְוֶ garment 2.

מַדְוֶה disease 2.

מַדּוּחִים causes of banishment 1.

מָדוֹן contention 3, ('ב) contentions 2, ('ב) contentious 3, discord 1, strife 7.

מָדוֹן stature 1.

מָדוֹר Ch. dwelling 3.

מְדוּרָה pile 1, pile for fire 1.

מְדֻחָה ruin 1.

מַדְחֵפֹת to overthrow 1.

מַדַּי sufficiently 1.

מְדִינָה province 44, —— every province 9.

מְדִינָה Ch. province 11.

מִדְיָנִים brawling 2, contentions 4, contentious 3.

מַדְכֵבָה mortar 1.

מַדְמֵנָה dunghill 1.

מִדְיָנִים discord 2, strife 1.

מַדָּע & מַדַּע knowledge 4, science 1, thought 1.

מַדְקָרוֹת piercings 1.

מְדֹר Ch. dwelling 1.

מַדְרֵגָה stairs 1, steep places 1.

מִדְרָךְ *foot* breadth 1.

מִדְרָשׁ story 2.

מַדְרֵשָׁה threshing 1.

מָהַהּ *Hithpalpel*, to delay 1, to linger 2, to stay selves 1, to tarry 5.

מְהוּמָה destruction 3, discomfiture 1, trouble 3, tumult 2, vexation 2, vexed 1.

מָהִיר diligent 1, hasting 1, ready 2.

מָהַל *Kal*, mixed 1.

מַהֲלָךְ journey 3, walk 1.

מַהֲלָל praise 1.

מַהֲלֻמּוֹת stripes 1, strokes 1.

מְהֻמֹרוֹת deep pits 1.

מַהְפֵּכָה overthrew 3, overthrow 2, overthrown 1.

מַהְפֶּכֶת prison 2, stocks 2.

מָהַר Kal, to hasten 1; Niphal, to be carried headlong 1, fearful 1, hasty 1, rash 1; Piel, to haste 23, to cause to make haste 1, in haste 1, to make haste 13, to hasten 5, to be hasty 1, Maher-*shalal-hash-baz* 1, to fetch quickly 1, to make ready quickly 1, to be ready 2, to be so soon 1, to make speed 2, swift 2,——hastily 2, quickly 1, shortly 1, soon 1, speedily 1, straightway 1, suddenly 1.

מָהַר Kal, to endow 1; Inf. intens. surely 1.

מַהֵר hasteth 1.

מַהֵר hastily 2, at once 1, quickly 8, soon 1, speedily 4, suddenly 1.

מֹהַר dowry 3.

מְהֵרָה hastily 1, quickly 9, shortly 1, soon 1, make speed 1, with speed 1, speedily 4, swiftly 1.

מַהֲתַלּוֹת deceits 1.

מוֹאָל (ב) over against 1.

מוֹבָא coming in 2.

מוּג Kal, to consume 1, to faint 1, to melt 2; Niphal, to be dissolved 3, to faint 2, to be fainthearted 1, to melt away 2; Polel, to dissolve 1, to make soft 1; Hithpolel, to melt 2, to be melted 1.

מוֹדַע & מֹדַע kinsman 1, kinswoman 1.

מוֹדַעַת kindred 1.

מוֹט Kal, to be carried 1, to be fallen in decay 1, falling down 1, to be moved 2, to be ready 1, to be removed 1, to shake 1, to slide 1, to slip 2; Inf. intens. exceedingly (is moved) 1; Niphal, to be out of course 1, to fall 1, to be moved 17, to slip 1, to be removed 3; Hiphil, to cast 1, (ב) to fall 1; Hithpael, to be moved 1.

מוֹט bar 2, be moved 2, staff 1, yoke 1.

מוֹטָה bands 2, heavy 1, staves 1, yoke 8.

מוּךְ Kal, to be waxen poor 4, to be poorer 1.

מוּל Kal, to circumcise 13; Niphal, to circumcise selves 1, to be circumcised 16; Inf. intens. must needs (be circumcised) 1; Polel, to be cut down 1; Hiphil, to destroy 3; Hithpolel, to cut in pieces 1.

מוּל forefront 4, to *God*-ward 1, toward 3.

מוֹלֶדֶת begotten 1, born 2, issue 1, kindred 11, native 1, nativity 6.

מוּלָה circumcision 1.

מוּם blemish 16, blot 1, spot 3.

מוּסָב winding about 1.

מוּסָד foundation 2.

מוּסָדָה foundation 1, grounded 1.

מוֹסָדוֹת foundations 13.

מוּסָךְ covert 1.

מוֹסֵר bands 6, bonds 5.

מוּסָר bond 1, chasten*eth* 1, chastening 3, chastisement 3, check 1, correction 8, discipline 1, doctrine 1, instruction 30, rebuker 1.

מוֹעֵד appointed 3, appointed sign 1, appointed time 11, assembly 2, place of assembly 1, solemn assembly 1, congregation 149, solemn day 1, feast 6, appointed feast 1, set feast 5, solemn feast 9, season 8, appointed season 4, due season 1, solemn 1, solemnity 4, synagogue 1, time 4, set time 6.

מוֹעָד appointed time 1.

מוֹעָדוֹת solemn feast 1.

מוּעָדָה appointed 1.

מוּעֶדֶת out of joint 1.

מוּעָף dimness 1.

מוֹעֵצוֹת counsels 6, devices 1.

מוּעָקָה affliction 1.

מוֹפֵת miracle 2, sign 8, wonder 23, wondered at 1.

מוּץ Kal, extortioner 1.

מוֹצָא brought out 2, bud 1, that which came out 1, east 1, that go forth into 1, going forth 4, goings out 5, that which is gone out 1, outgoing 1, proceeded out 2, spring 5, vein 1, *water*-course 1, *water*-springs 2.

מוֹצָאוֹת draught-house 1, goings forth 1.

מוּצָק casting 1, hardness 1.

מוּצָק & מוּצַק is straitened 1, straitness 1, vexation 1.

מוּצֶקֶת when it was cast 1, pipe 1.

מוּק Hiphil, to be corrupt 1.

מוֹקֵד burning 1, hearth 1.

מוֹקְדָה burning 1.

מוֹקֵשׁ be ensnared 1, gin 3, snare 20, is snared 1, trap 2.

מוּר Niphal, to be changed 1; Hiphil, to change 11, to exchange 1, to be removed 1; Inf. intens. at all (change) 2.

מוֹרָא dread 1, fear 6, that ought to be feared 1, terribleness 1, terror 3.

מוֹרַג threshing instrument 3.

מוֹרָד going down 3, steep place 1, thin 1.

מוֹרָה razor 3.

מוֹרָה (ב) fear 1.

מוֹרֶה former rain 2, rain 1.

מוֹרָשׁ possession 2, thoughts 1.

מוֹרָשָׁה heritage 1, inheritance 2, possession 6.

מוּשׁ Kal, to depart 8, to remove 2, to be removed 1; Hiphil, to cease 1, to depart 3, (ב) depart 1, to go back 1, to remove 3, to take away 1.

מוּשׁ Kal, to feel 1; Hiphil, to feel 1, to handle 1.

מוֹשָׁב assembly 1, to dwell in 1, dwelling 12, dwelling-place 4, that dwelt in 1, wherein dwelt 1, habitation 12, inhabited place 1, seat 7, sitting 2, situation 2, sojourning 1.

מוֹשְׁכוֹת bands 1.

מוֹשָׁעוֹת salvation 1.

מוּת Kal, to be dead 122, dead body 4, dead man 2, one dead 3, death 7, (ב) to be put to death 1, worthy of death 1, to die 426, to be like to die 1, necromancer 1, to be slain 1, very suddenly 1,——for yours 1; Inf. intens. must needs (die) 1, surely (be put to death) 28, surely (die) 20; Polel, to slay 9; Hiphil, to put to death 19, to destroy 2, to cause to die 1, to kill 32, to slay 81,——crying 1; Inf. intens. at all (put to death) 1, in no wise (slay) 1, surely (kill) 1; Hophal, to be put to death 57, to die 1, to be slain 10.

מוּת be dead 8, dead*ly* 1, **death** freq., die 22, to slay 1.

מוּת Ch. death 1.

מוּת death 1.

מוֹתָר plenteousness 1, pre-eminence 1, profit 1.

מִזְבֵּחַ altar *freq.*

מֶזֶג liquor 1.

מְזֶה burnt with 1.

מָזֶה garner 1.

מְזוּזָה post 14, door-post 2, side-post 3.

מָזוֹן meat 1, victual 1.

מָזוֹן Ch. meat 2.

מָזוֹר be bound up 1, **wound 2.**

מָזוֹר wound 1.

מֵזַח & מֵזִיחַ girdle 1, **strength 2.**

מַזְלֵג flesh-hook 2.

מַזְלְגוֹת flesh-hooks 5.

מַזָּלוֹת planets 1.

מְזִמָּה devices 3, discretion 4, intents 1, witty inventions 1, lewdness 1, mischievous 1, mischievous device 1, thought 3, wicked device 3, wickedly 1.

מִזְמוֹר psalm *freq.*

מַזְמֵרוֹת pruning-hooks 4.

מְזַמְּרוֹת snuffers 5.

מִזְעָר few 1, small 1, very 2.

מְזָרֶה fan 2.

מַזָּרוֹת Mazzaroth 1.

מְזָרִים north 1.

מִזְרָח east 30, east end 1, **east side 5**, eastward 20, rising (of the sun) 7, rising of the sun 1, sunrising 9, sunrising 1.

מִזְרָע thing sown 1.

מִזְרָק bason 25, bowl 21.

מֹחַ marrow 1.

מֵחִים fat ones 1, fatlings 1.

מָחָא Kal, to clap 2; Piel, to clap 1.

מְחָא Ch. P'al, to smite 2; Pael, to stay 1; Ithp'al,——to be hanged 1.

מַחֲבֵא hiding-place 1.

מַחֲבֹאִים lurking-places 1.

מַחְבְּרוֹת couplings 1, joinings 1.

מַחְבֶּרֶת coupling 8.

מַחֲבַת pan 5.

מַחְגֹּרֶת girding 1.

מָחָה *Kal,* to blot 2, to blot out 9, to destroy 2, to put out 2, to wipe 4, to wipe away 1; *Inf. intens.* utterly (put out) 1; *Niphal,* to be abolished 1, to be blotted out 4, to be destroyed 3, to be put out 1, to be wiped away 1; *Hiphil,* to blot out 1, to destroy 1, to wipe out 1.

מָחָה *Pual,* full of marrow 1.

מָחָה *Kal,* to reach unto 1.

מְחוּגָה compass 1.

מָחוֹז haven 1.

מָחוֹל dance 5, dancing 1.

מְחוֹלָה company 1, dances 5, dancing 2.

מַחֲזֶה vision 3.

מֶחֱזָה light 4.

מְחִי engines 1.

מִחְיָה preserve life 1, quick 2, recover selves 1, reviving 2, sustenance 1, victuals 1.

מְחִיר gain 1, hire 1, price 11, sold 1, worth 1.

מַחֲלָה disease 1, infirmity 1.

מַחֲלָה disease 1, sickness 3.

מְחִלּוֹת caves 1.

מַחֲלָיִים diseases 1.

מַחֲלָפוֹת locks 2.

מַחֲלָפִים knives 1.

מַחֲלָצוֹת changeable suits of apparel 1, change of raiment 1.

מַחֲלֹקֶת Ch. course 1.

מַחֲלֹקֶת company 1, course 33, division 8, portion 1, *Sela*-hammahlekoth 1.

מַחֲלַת Mahalath 2.

מֶחֶמְאָת ——butter 1.

מַחְמָד beloved 1, desire 3, goodly 1, lovely 1, pleasant 3, pleasant thing 4.

(כ) מַחֲמַדִּים pleasant things 2.

מַחְמָל pitieth 1.

מַחֲנֶה army 4, bands 2, battle 1, camp 134, company 6, drove 1, host 61, Mahanaim 1, Mahaneh-*dan* 1, tents 5.

מַחֲנָק strangling 1.

מַחֲסֶה hope 2, refuge 13, place of refuge 2, shelter 2, trust 1.

מַחְסוֹם bridle 1.

מַחְסוֹר lack 1, need 1, penury 1, poor 1, poverty 1, want 8.

מָחַץ *Kal,* to be dipped 1, to pierce 1, to pierce through 1, to smite 1, to smite through 2, to strike through 1, to wound 7.

מַחַץ stroke 1.

מַחְצֵב hewed 1, hewn 2.

מַחֲצָה half 2.

מַחֲצִית half 14, half so much 1, mid*day* 1.

מָחַק *Kal,* to smite off 1.

מֶחְקָר deep place 1.

מָחָר *time* to come 1, time to come 6, to-morrow 44.

(כ) מַחֲרָאוֹת draught-house 1.

מַחֲרֵשָׁה mattock 2.

מַחֲרֶשֶׁת share 1.

מׇחֳרָת morrow 23, morrow after 6, next *day* 1, next day 2.

מַחְשֹׂף made appear 1.

מַחֲשָׁבָה device 1, purpose 1.

מַחֲשֶׁבֶת cunning 1, cunning works 2, curious works 1, device 11, devised by 1, imaginations 3, invented 1, means 1, purposes 5, thoughts 28.

מַחְשָׁךְ dark 1, dark place 2, darkness 4.

מַחְתָּה censer 15, fire-pan 4, snuff-dish 3.

מְחִתָּה destruction 7, dismaying 1, ruin 1, terror 2.

מַחְתֶּרֶת breaking up 1, secret search 1.

מְטָה & מְטָא Ch. *P'al,* to come 5, to reach 3.

מַטְאֲטֵא besom 1.

מַטְבֵּחַ slaughter 1.

מַטָּה beneath 7, down 1, downward 5, less 1, very low 1, under 1, underneath 2.

מַטֶּה rod 49, staff 16, tribe 182.

מִטָּה bed 28, bed*chamber* 2, bier 1.

מַטֶּה perverseness 1.

מִטְוֶה spun 1.

מִטּוֹת stretching out 1.

מְטִיל bar 1.

מַטְמֹן hidden riches 1, treasure 1, hid treasures 2.

מַטָּע plantation 1, planting 3, plants 2.

מַטְעַמּוֹת dainties 1, dainty meats 1.

מַטְעַמִּים savoury meat 6.

מִטְפַּחַת vail 1, wimple 1.

מָטַר *Niphal,* to be rained upon 1; *Hiphil,* to rain 10, to cause to rain 6.

מָטָר rain 38.

מַטָּרָא mark 1.

מַטָּרָה mark 2, prison 13.

מֵיטָב best 6.

מִיכַל brook 1.

מַיִם washing 1, water *very freq.,* water-*course* 2, water-*flood* 1, watering 1, water-*springs* 2, ——piss 2.

מִין kind 31.

(כ) מֵיסַךְ covert 1.

מִיץ churning 1, forcing 1, wringing 1.

מֵישׁוֹר equity 2, even place 1, plain 15, right 1, righteously 1, straight 1, made straight 1, uprightness 1.

מֵישָׁרִים agreement 1, aright 1, that are equal 1, equity 4, right things 3, righteously 1, sweetly 1, upright 1, uprightly 3, uprightness 3.

מֵיתָר cord 8, string 1.

מַכְאוֹב grief 2, pain 2, sorrow 12.

מִכְבָּר grate 6.

מַכְבֵּר thick cloth 1.

מַכָּה beaten 1, blow 1, plague 11, slaughter 14, smote 1, sore 1, stripe 2, stroke 2, wound 14, wounded 1.

מְכַוֶּה that burneth 1, burning 4.

מָכוֹן dwelling-place 2, foundations 1, habitation 2, place 11, settled place 1.

מְכוֹנָה base 22.

מְכוּרָה birth 2, habitation 1, nativity 1.

מָכַךְ *Kal,* to be brought low 1; *Niphal,* to decay 1; *Hophal,* to be brought low 1.

מִכְלָה fold 2, *sheepfold* 1.

מִכְלוֹל most gorgeously 1, all sorts 1.

מִכְלוֹת perfect 1.

מִכְלָל perfection 1.

מַכְלֻלִים all sorts 1.

מַכֹּלֶת food 1.

מִכְמַנִּים treasures 1.

מִכְמָר net 1.

מִכְמֹר net 1.

מִכְמֶרֶת drag 2.

מִכְמֹרֶת nets 1.

מְכֹנָה base 1.

מִכְנָסַיִם breeches 5.

מֶכֶס tribute 6.

מִכְסָה number 1, worth 1.

מִכְסֶה covering 16.

מְכַסֶּה clothing 1, to cover 1, that which covereth 1.

מָכַר *Kal,* to sell 56, to sell away 1; *Inf. intens.* at all (sell) 1; *Niphal,* to sell self 3, to be sold 16; *Hithpael,* to sell self 3, to be sold 1.

מֶכֶר to pay 1, price 1, ware 1.

מֻכָּר acquaintance 2.

מִכְרָה *salt*-pits 1.

מְכֵרָה habitation 1.

מִכְשׁוֹל caused to fall 1, offence 2, ruin 2, stumbling-block 1, ——*nothing* offend 1.

מַכְשֵׁלָה ruin 1, stumbling-block 1.

מִכְתָּב writing 9.

מַכְתֵּה bursting 1.

מִכְתָּם Michtam 6.

מַכְתֵּשׁ hollow place 1, mortar 1.

מָלָא & מָלֵא *Kal,* to be accomplished 5, to be at an end 1, to be expired 3, to fill 11, to fill with 4, to be filled 4, to be filled with 5, to fulfil 1, to be fulfilled 7, to be full of 39, to be full 5, to become full 1, to be fully set 1, fulness 1, to gather 1, to *overflow* 1, to presume 1, to replenish 2, to be replenished 1, to be satisfied 1, space 1, —— to consecrate 17; *Niphal,* to be accomplished 1, to be fenced 1, to be filled 2, to be filled with 19, to be fulfilled 1, to be full of 10, to be replenished 2; *Piel,*

to accomplish 1, to confirm 1, to fill—to fill with 56, to be filled with 1, to fulfil 14, to give in full tale 1, to have full of 1, to go fully 1, (בְ) fulness 1, to furnish 1, to gather together 1, to *overflow* 1, to replenish 2, to satisfy 1, to set 4, to take a *hand*ful 1,—to consecrate—to be consecrated 14, to draw full 1, to *follow* wholly 7; *Pual*, set 1; *Hithpael*, to gather selves 1.

מְלָא Ch. *P'al*, to fill 1; *Ithpael*, to be full 1.

מָלֵא fill 1, filled 1, filled with 1, full 10, full of 46, full with 1, fully 1, multitude 1, as is worth 1,—she that is with child 1.

מְלֹא fill 2, full 12, fulness 7, *hand*fuls 5, multitude 2,—all along 1, that whereof was full 1, all that is in 1, all that is therein 6, all that therein is 1.

מְלֵאָה fruit 1, first of ripe fruit 1, fulness 1.

מִלֻּאָה inclosings 2, settings 1.

מִלֻּאִים consecration 11, to be set 4.

מַלְאָךְ ambassador 4, angel 111, messenger 9.

מַלְאַךְ Ch. angel 2.

מְלָאכָה business 12, goods 2, labour 1, thing made 1, occupation 1, stuff 1, thing 2, use 1, work 126, manner of work 1, workmanship 3, manner of workmanship 2, workmen 9,—cattle 1, industrious 1, occupied 1, officer 1.

מַלְאֲכוּת message 1.

מְלֵאת ——fitly 1.

מַלְבּוּשׁ apparel 4, raiment 3, vestment 1.

מַלְבֵּן brickkiln 3.

מִלָּה byword 1, matter 1, anything to say 1, what to say 1, to speak 2, speaking 2, speech 5, talking 1, word 23,——answer 1.

מִלָּה Ch. commandment 1, matter 5, thing 11, word 7.

מַלּוּחַ mallows 1.

מְלוּכָה kingdom 18, king's 2, royal 4.

מָלוֹן inn 3, place where...lodge 1, lodging 2, lodging-place 2.

מְלוּנָה cottage 1, lodge 1.

מָלַח *Kal*, to season 1; *Pual*, to be tempered together 1; *Hophal*, to be salted 1; *Inf. intens.* at all (salted) 1.

מָלַח *Niphal*, to vanish away 1.

מֶלַח salt 28.

מְלַח Ch. *P'al*,——to have maintenance 1.

מְלַח Ch. salt 2,——maintenance 1.

מַלָּח mariner 4.

מְלֵחָה barren land 1, barrenness 1, salt *land* 1.

מְלָחִים rotten rags 2.

מִלְחָמָה battle 151, fight 4, fighting 1, war *freq.*

מָלַט *Niphal*, to deliver self 1, to be delivered 11, to escape 42, to be escaped 8, to let get away 1; *Inf. intens.* speedily (escape) 1; *Piel*, to deliver 20, to lay 1, to let alone 1, to save 5; *Inf. intens.* surely (deliver) 1; *Hiphil*, to be delivered 1, to preserve 1; *Hithpael*, to be escape 1, to leap out 1.

מֶלֶט clay 1.

מְלִילָה ears 1.

מְלִיצָה interpretation 1, taunting 1.

מָלַךְ *Kal*, to be king 5, ... be queen 1, to reign—to begin to reign 284, to rule 1; *Inf. intens.* surely (be king) 1; *Niphal*, to consult 1; *Hiphil*, to make king 39, to set a *king* 1, to set up *king* 1, to make *king* 6, to make queen 1, to make to reign 1; *Hophal*, to be made king 1.

מֶלֶךְ king *very freq.*, Moloch 1, royal 2.

מֶלֶךְ Ch. king *freq.*, royal 1.

מְלַךְ Ch. counsel 1.

מַלְכֹּדֶת trap 1.

מַלְכָּה queen 35.

מַלְכָּה Ch. queen 2.

מַלְכוּ Ch. kingdom *freq.*, kingly 1, realm 3, reign 4.

מַלְכוּת empire 1, kingdom *freq.*, realm 4, reign 21, royal 14.

מְלֶכֶת queen 5.

מָלַל *Kal*, to speak 1; *Piel*, to say 1, to speak 1, to utter 2.

מְלַל Ch. *Pael*, to say 1, to speak 4.

מַלְמָד goad 1.

מָלַץ *Niphal*, to be sweet 1.

מֶלְצַר ——Melzar 2.

מָלַק *Kal*, to wring off 2.

מַלְקוֹחַ booty 1, jaws 1, prey 6.

מַלְקוֹשׁ latter rain 8.

מֶלְקָחַיִם tongs 3.

מְלְקָחַיִם snuffers 1, tongs 2.

מֶלְתָּחָה vestry 1.

מַלְתָּעוֹת great teeth 1.

מַמְּגֻרוֹת barns 1.

מְמַדִּים measures 1.

מָמוֹת deaths 2.

מַמְזֵר bastard 2.

מִמְכָּר sale 2, that which cometh of sale 1, that which... sold 6, ware 1,——ought 1.

מִמְכֶּרֶת ——sold as 1.

מַמְלָכָה kingdom *freq.*, king's 1, reign 2, royal 4.

מַמְלָכוּת kingdom 8, reign 1.

מִמְסָךְ drink offering 1, mixed wine 1.

מֶמֶר bitterness 1.

מַמְרֹרִים bitterness 1.

מִמְשַׁח anointed 1.

מִמְשָׁל dominion 2, that ruled 1.

מֶמְשָׁלָה dominion 11, government 1, power 1, to rule 4.

מִמְשָׁק breeding 1.

מַמְתַּקִּים sweet 1, most sweet 1.

מָן manna 14.

מִן Ch. part 6, partly 2.

מְנַגִּינָה music 1.

מִנְדָּה Ch. toll 2.

מַנְדַּע Ch. knowledge 2, reason 1, understanding 1.

מָנָה *Kal*, to count 1, to number 8, to tell 3; *Niphal*, to be numbered 6; *Piel*, to appoint 2, to be appointed 1, to prepare 5, to set 1; *Pual*, to be appointed 1.

מְנָא & מְנָה Ch. *P'al*, Mene 2, to number 1; *Pael*, to ordain 1, to set 3.

מָנָה such things as belonged 1, part 3, portion 10.

מָנֶה maneh 1, pound 4.

מִנְהָג driving 2.

מִנְהָרוֹת dens 1.

מָנוֹד shaking 1.

מָנוֹחַ rest 6, place of rest 1.

מְנוּחָה comfortable 1, ease 1, quiet 1, rest 17, resting-place 2, still 1.

מָנוֹן son 1.

מָנוֹס apace 1, escape 1, way to flee 1, flight 1, refuge 4.

מְנוּסָה fleeing 1, flight 1.

מָנוֹר beam 4.

מְנוֹרָה candlestick 42.

מִנְּזָרִים crowned 1.

מִנְחָה gifts 7, meat offering *freq.*, meat (offering) 1, oblation 5, offering 33, present 28, sacrifice 5.

מִנְחָה Ch. meat offering 1, oblation 1.

מֶנִי number 1.

מִנִּים stringed instruments 1.

מֹנִים times 2.

מִנְיָן Ch. number 1.

מִנְלֶה perfection 1.

מָנַע *Kal*, to deny 2, to keep 1, to keep back 4, to refrain 2, to restrain 1, to withhold 14; *Niphal*, to hinder 1, to be withholden 3.

מַנְעוּל lock 6.

מִנְעָל shoes 1.

מַנְעַמִּים dainties 1.

מְנַעְנְעִים cornets 1.

מְנַקִּיּוֹת bowls 3, cups 1.

מְנָת portion 7.

מָס is afflicted 1.

מַס discomfited 1, levy 4, taskmasters 1, tributary 5, tribute 12.

מֵסַב that compass about 1, round about 2, places round about 1, at table 1.

מַסְגֵּר prison 3, smith 4.

מִסְגֶּרֶת border 14, close place 2, hole 1.

מַסָּד foundation 1.

מִסְדְּרוֹן porch 1.

מִפְתָּח opening 1.

מִפְתָּן threshold 8.

מֹץ chaff 8.

מָצָא Kal, to befall 3, to be befallen 2, to bring 1, to catch 1, to come on 1, to come to 1, to come unto 1, to come upon 5, to find 245, to find occasion 1, to find out 18, to be found 4, to get 5, to get hold upon 1, to hit 2, to light on 1, to light upon 1, to meet 4, to meet with 1, ready 1, to receive 1, to speed 1, to suffice 3, to take hold on 1,——to be able 3, serve occasion 1; Niphal, certainly (found) 1, to come to 1, to come to hand 1, to be enough 1, to be found 115, to be here 1, to be left 2, to be present 17,——to have 1, to be here 1, present 1; Hiphil, to cause to come 1, to deliver 2, to cause to find 1, to present 3.

מַצָּב garrison 7, station 1, place ... where stood 2.

מֻצָּב mount 1.

מַצָּבָה garrison 1.

מְצָבָה army 1.

מַצֵּבָה garrison 1, image 19, pillar 12, standing image 2.

מַצֶּבֶת pillar 4, substance 2.

מְצָד & מָצֹד castle 1, fort 1, hold 3, munition 1, stronghold 5.

מָצָה Kal, to suck 1, to wring 1, to wring out 2; Niphal, to be wrung out 3.

מַצָּה unleavened bread 35, unleavened cakes 5, without leaven 1, unleavened 12.

מַצָּה contention 1, debate 1, strife 1.

מִצְהֲלוֹת neighing 2.

מָצוֹד bulwark 1, net 1, snare 1.

מָצוּד net 1.

מְצוֹדָה hold 1, munition 1, net 1.

מְצוּדָה castle 1, defence 1, fort 1, fortress 6, hold 6, to be hunted 1, net 1, snare 2, stronghold 1, strong place 1.

מִצְוָה commanded 1, which was commanded 1, commandment very freq., law 1, ordinance 1, precept 4.

מְצוֹלָה bottom 1, deep 2.

מְצוּלָה deep 6, depth 2.

מָצוֹק anguish 1, distress 1, straitness 4.

מָצוּק pillar 1, situate 1.

מְצוּקָה anguish 1, distress 6.

מָצוֹר besieged 4, besieged place 2, bulwark 1, defence 2, fenced 1, fortified 1, fortress 2, siege 13, strong 2, stronghold 1, tower 1.

מְצוּרָה fenced 5, fort 1, munition 1, stronghold 1.

מַצּוּת contended 1.

מֵצַח brow 1, forehead 10,——impudent 1.

מִצְחָה greaves 1.

מְצֻלָּה bottom 1.

מְצִלּוֹת bells 1.

מְצִלְתַּיִם cymbals 13.

מִצְנֶפֶת diadem 1, mitre 11.

מַצָּע bed 1.

מִצְעָד going 1, step 2.

מִצְעִירָה little 1.

מִצְעָר little one 2, Mizar 1, small 1, little while 1, small company 1.

מִצְפֶּה watch-tower 2.

מַצְפֻּנִים hidden things 1.

מָצַץ Kal, to milk out 1.

מֵצַר distress 1, pain 1, strait 1.

מִצְרֵף fining-pot 2.

מַק rottenness 1, stink 1.

מַקָּבָה hammer 3.

מַקֶּבֶת hammer 1, hole 1.

מִקְדָּשׁ chapel 1, hallowed part 1, holy place 2, sanctuary 69.

מַקְהֵלוֹת congregations 1.

מַקְהֵלִים congregations 1.

מִקְוֵא linen yarn 4.

מִקְוֶה abiding 1, gathering together 1, hope 4, plenty of water 1, pools 1.

מִקְוֶה ditch 1.

מָקוֹם country 1, place very freq., room 3, space 1,——home 3, open 1, whithersoever 1.

מָקוֹר fountain 11, issue 1, spring 3, well 1, well-spring 2.

מֶקַח taking 1.

מַקָּחוֹת ware 1.

מֻקְטָר to burn upon 1.

מְקַטְּרוֹת altars for incense 1.

מִקְטֶרֶת censer 2.

מַקֵּל handstaff 1, rod 7, staff 10.

מִקְלָט refuge 20.

מִקְלַעַת carved 1, carving 1, figures 1, graving 1.

מִקְנֶה cattle 63, flock 4, herd 1, possession 5, purchase 1, substance 2.

מִקְנָה bought 7, possession 1, price 2, purchase 5.

מִקְסָם divination 2.

מִקְצוֹעַ corner 6, turning 5.

מַקְצֻעוֹת planes 1.

מִקְצָעֹת corners 2.

מָקַק Niphal, to consume away 3, to be corrupt 1, to be dissolved 1, to pine away 4; Hiphil, to consume away 1.

מִקְרָא assembly 1, calling 1, convocation 19, reading 1.

מִקְרֶה something befallen 1, befalleth 3, chance 1, event 3, hap to light on 1, happeneth 1.

מִקְרֶה building 1.

מִקְרֶה ——summer 2.

מִקְשָׁה beaten 1, beaten out of one piece 1, beaten work 6, upright 1, whole piece 1.

מִקְשָׁה garden of cucumbers 1.

מִקְשֶׁה ——well set hair 1.

מַר bitter 22, bitterly 3, bitterness 9, chafed 1, discontented 1, heavy 1, Mara 2,——angry 1, great (bitterness) 1.

מָר drop 1.

מֹר myrrh 12.

מָרָא Kal, to be filthy 1; Hiphil, to lift up self 1.

מָרֵא Ch. Lord 2, lord 2.

מַרְאָה looking-glass 1, vision 11.

מַרְאֶה apparently 1, appearance 37, appeareth 1, beautiful 1, beauty 1, countenance 11, fair 2, favoured 7, form 1, goodly 1, to look on 1, to look to 1, to look upon 4, looketh 1, pattern 1, to see 2, seem 1, sight 18, visage 1, vision 11,——as soon as 1.

מֻרְאָה crop 1.

מְרַאֲשֹׁת bolster 6, at his head 1, pillows 2.

מַרְאָשֹׁת principalities 1.

מַרְבַדִּים coverings of tapestry 2.

מַרְבֶּה great 1, increase 1.

מַרְבֶּה much 1.

מַרְבִּית greatest part 1, greatness 1, increase 2, multitude 1.

מַרְבֵּץ place to lie down 1.

מַרְבֵּץ couching-place 1.

מַרְבֵּק stall 2,——fat 1, fatted 1.

מַרְגּוֹעַ rest 1.

מַרְגְּלוֹת feet 3, at the feet 2.

מַרְגֵּמָה sling 1.

מַרְגֵּעָה refreshing 1.

מָרַד Kal, to rebel 24, rebellious 1.

מְרַד Ch. rebellion 1.

מֶרֶד rebellion 1.

מְרַד Ch. rebellious 2.

מַרְדּוּת ——rebellious 1.

מִרְדָּף persecuted 1.

מָרָה Kal, bitter 1, to be disobedient 1, to disobey 1, grievously 1, rebel 1, to rebel 12, rebellious 4, to be rebellious 2; Inf. intens. grievously (rebel) 1; Hiphil, to change 1, to be disobedient 1, provocation 1, to provoke 7, to rebel 9, rebellious 3.

מָרָה bitterness 1.

מֹרָה grief 1.

מָרוּד cast out 1, misery 2.

מָרוֹחַ broken 1.

מָרוֹם above 5, far above 1, dignity 1, haughty 1, height 10, high 7, most high 1, on high 20, high ones 1, high place 4, highest places 1, loftily 1, upward 1.

מֵרוֹץ race 1.

מְרוּצָה course 2, running 2, violence 1.

מְרוּקִים purifications 1.

מַרְזֵחַ mourning 1.

מִרְזֵחַ banquet 1.

מָרַח Kal, to lay for a plaister 1.

to go 4, to go away 2, to go forth 2, to go onward 1, to go out 1, to journey 29, to take journey 10, to be journeying 1, to march 1, to remove—to be removed 26, to set forth 2, to take (journey) 1, to be on his way 1, to go their way 1; *Inf. intens.* still (going on) 1; *Niphal*, to be departed 1, to go away 1; *Hiphil*, to cause to blow 1, to bring 3, to make go forth 1, to remove 2, to set aside 1.

נָסַק *Kal*, to ascend up 1.

נְסַק Ch. *Aphel*, to take up 2; *Hophal*, to be taken up 1.

נְעוּרוֹת youth 1.

נְעוּרִים childhood 1, youth 45.

נָעִים pleasant 9, pleasures 2, sweet 2.

נָעַל *Kal*, to bolt 2, inclosed 1, to lock 2, to shoe 1, shut up 1; *Hiphil*, to shoe 1.

נַעַל dryshod 1, shoe 18, shoe-latchet 1, pair of shoes 2.

נָעֵם *Kal*, to pass in beauty 1, to be delight 1, to be pleasant 5, to be sweet 1.

נֹעַם beauty 4, pleasant 2, pleasantness 1.

נַעֲמָנִים pleasant 1.

נַעֲצוּץ thorn 2.

נָעַר *Kal*, to shake 2, to shake off 1, shaken out 1, to yell 1; *Niphal*, to shake self 1, to be shaken 1, to be tossed up and down 1; *Piel*, to overthrow 2, to shake 1; *Hithpael*, to shake self 1.

נַעַר babe 1, boy 1, child 51, lad 32, servant 54, young 14, young man *freq.*, youth 4.

נֹעַר child 2, youth 2.

נַעֲרָה damsel 34, maid 7, maiden 15, young maiden 1, young 4, young woman 1.

נְעֹרֶת tow 2.

נָפָה border 1, coast 1, region 1, sieve 1.

נָפַח *Kal*, to blow 4, to breathe 2, to give up 1, seething 2; *Pual*, blown 1; *Hiphil*, to cause to lose life 1, to snuff 1.

נְפִילִים giants 3.

נֹפֶךְ emerald 4.

נָפַל *Kal*, to be accepted 2, to be cast down 1, to die 1, to fail 5, to fall 262, to fall away

5, to fall down 23, ready to fall 1, to be fallen 39, to be fallen down 1, fugitive 1, to have *inheritance* 1, inferior 2, to keep bed 1, to lie 2, to lay along 2, to lie down 1, to light 2, to light down 1, to be lost 2, lying 1, to be overthrown 3, to perish 1, to rot 2,——hast lost 1, to present 1; *Inf. intens.* surely (fall) 1; *Hiphil*, to cast 6, to be cast 1, to cast down 7, to cast in 1, to cast *lots* 10, to cast out 1, to cease 1, to divide 1, to divide by lot 5, to let fail 1, to cause to fall 4, to let fall 1, to make fall 1, to fell 3, to cause to lie down 1, to overthrow 1, to overwhelm 1, to present 4, to make to rot 1, to slay 1, to smite out 1, to throw down 1; *Hithpael*, to cast self down 1, to fall 1, to fall down 3; *Pilel*,——to be judged 1.

נְפַל Ch. *P'al*, to fall 3, to fall down 7, to have occasion 1.

נֵפֶל & נֶפֶל untimely birth 3.

נָפַץ *Kal*, to break 2, dispersed 1, to be overspread 1, to be scattered 2; *Piel*, to break 1, to dash 2, to dash in pieces 1, to cause to be discharged 1, to break in pieces 9, to scatter 1; *Pual*, to be beaten in sunder 1.

נֶפֶץ scattering 1.

נְפַק Ch. *P'al*, to come forth 4, to go forth 1, to be gone forth 1; *Aphel*, to take forth 1, to take out 4, to be taken out 1.

נִפְקָא Ch. expenses 2.

נָפַשׁ *Niphal*, to refresh selves 1, to be refreshed 2.

נֶפֶשׁ any 10, appetite 2, beast 3, body 7, breath 1, creature 9, dead—dead body 3, deadly 1, desire 5, discontented 1, ghost 2, heart 15, hearty 1, life 117, lust 2, man 2, me 3, mind 15, mortally 1, person 30, pleasure 4, self 19, soul *freq.*, thing 2, will 4, yourselves 6,——angry 1, fish 1, greedy 1, life in jeopardy 1, jeopardy of life 1, man 1, slay 1, tablet 1, she will 1, would have it 1.

נֶפֶת country 1.

נֹפֶת honeycomb 4,—— honeycomb 1.

נַפְתּוּלִים wrestlings 1.

נֵץ blossom 1, hawk 3.

נָצָא *Kal*, to flee 1.

נָצַב *Niphal*, appointed 1, best state 1, deputy 1, officer 6,

to present 1, to be set over 4, to be settled 1, to stand 12, to stand still 1, to stand up 1, to stand upright 2, best state 1; *Hiphil*, to erect 1, to establish 1, to lay 1, to rear up 1, to set 9, to set up 3, to sharpen 1, to stablish 1, to make to stand 1; *Hophal*, pillar 1, set up 1,—— Huzzab 1.

נֵצֶב haft 1.

נְצִבָה Ch. strength 1.

נָצָה *Niphal*, to strive 1, to strive together 4; *Hiphil*, to strive 3.

נָצָה *Kal*, to be laid waste 1; *Niphal*, ruinous 2.

נִצָּה flower 2.

נוֹצָה feather 1.

נָצַח *Niphal*, perpetual 1; *Piel*, to excel 1, chief musician 56, to oversee 1, overseer 2, to set forward 4, chief singer 1.

נְצַח Ch. *Ithpael*, preferred 1.

נֶצַח & נֵצַח alway 1, always 2, constantly 1, end 2, ever 24, evermore 1, perpetual 3, strength 2, victory 2,——never 5.

נֶצַח blood 1, strength 1.

נָצִיב garrison 9, officer 2, pillar 1.

נָצִיר preserved 1.

נָצַל *Niphal*, to deliver self 2, to be delivered 12, to be escaped 1, to be preserved 1, to be taken out 1; *Piel*, to deliver 1, to spoil 2, to strip off 1; *Hiphil*, to defend 1, to deliver 168, to part 1, to recover 6, to rescue 2, to rid 3, to save 1, to take 3, to take away 1,——to escape 1; *Inf. intens.* at all (deliver) 2, without fail (recover) 1, surely (deliver) 2; *Hophal*, plucked 2; *Hithpael*, to strip selves 1.

נְצַל Ch. *Aphel*, to deliver 2, to rescue 1.

נִצָּן flower 1.

נָצַץ *Kal*, to sparkle 1.

נָצַר *Kal*, besieged 2, hidden thing 1, to keep 38, monument 1, to observe 1, to preserve 13, preserver 1, subtil 1, watcher 1, watchman 3.

נֵצֶר branch 1.

נְקֵא Ch. pure 1.

נָקַב *Kal*, to appoint 1, to blaspheme 3, to bore 1, to curse

6, with holes 1, to name 2, to pierce 3, to strike through 1; *Niphal*, to be expressed 6.

נֶקֶב pipe 1.

נְקֵבָה female 18, maid-child 1, woman 3.

נָקֹד speckled 9.

נֹקֵד herdman 1, sheepmaster 1.

נְקֻדּוֹת studs 1.

נִקֻּדִים cracknels 1, mouldy 2.

נָקָה *Kal*, altogether (unpunished) 1; *Niphal*, to be blameless 1, to be clear 2, to be cut off 1, to be desolate 1, to be free 2, to be guiltless 2, to be innocent 4, to be quit 1, to be unpunished 10; *Inf. intens.* utterly (unpunished) 1; *Piel*, to acquit 3, to cleanse 3, to clear 2, to hold guiltless 3, to hold innocent 1, to leave unpunished 4; *Inf. intens.* at all (acquit) 1, by no means (clear) 2, altogether (unpunished) 1, wholly (unpunished) 1.

נָקַהּ *Kal*, to be weary 1.

נָקִי blameless 2, clean 1, clear 1, exempted 1, free 1, guiltless 4, innocent 30, quit 2.

נָקִיא innocent 2.

נִקָּיוֹן cleanness 1, innocency 4.

נָקִיק hole 3.

נָקַם *Kal*, to avenge 5, to avenge selves 1, to revenge 2, to take *vengeance* 2, to take vengeance 2; *Inf. intens.* surely (punished) 1; *Niphal*, to avenge self 3, to be avenged 4, to be punished 1, to revenge 1, to revenge self 1, to take *vengeance* 1, to take vengeance 1; *Piel*, to avenge 1, to take *vengeance* 1; *Hophal*, to be avenged 1, to be punished 1, vengeance to be taken 1; *Hithpael*, to be avenged 3, avenger 2.

נָקָם quarrel 1, vengeance 15,——avenged 1.

נְקָמָה revenge 2, revenging 1, vengeance 19,——avenge 5.

נָקַע *Kal*, to be alienated 3.

נָקַף *Kal*, to kill 1; *Piel*, to cut down 1, to destroy 1; *Hiphil*, to compass 6, to compass about 1, to go round 1, to go round about 1, to be gone round about 1, going about 1, to be gone about 1, to inclose 1, to round 1.

נָקַף shaking 2.

נִקְפָּה rent 1.

נָקַר *Kal*, to pick out 1, to thrust out 1; *Piel*, to be pierced 1, to put out 2; *Pual*, to be digged 1.

נְקָרָה cleft 1, clift 1.

נָקַשׁ *Kal*, to be snared 1; *Niphal*, to be snared 1; *Piel*, to catch 1, to lay snares 1; *Hithpael*, to lay a snare 1.

נְקַשׁ *Ch. P'al*, to smite 1.

נֵר candle 9, lamp 32, light 1.

נִר plowing 1.

נִרְגָּן tale-bearer 3, whisperer 1.

נֵרְדְּ spikenard 3.

נָשָׂא *Kal*, to accept 12, to arise 1, *armour*-bearer 18, to bear 156, to be able to bear 2, can bear 1, to bear up 2, to be borne 1, to bring 21, to bring forth 3, to burn 1, to be burned 1, to carry 25, to carry away 7, to cast 1, to contain 1, to ease 1, (בְּ) to exact 1, to exalt 1, to fetch 2, to forgive 16, to hold up 1, to lade 3, laden with 1, to be laid 3, to lay 1, to lift up 137, to marry 1, to obtain 4, to offer 1, to be partial 1, to pardon 4, to raise 1, to raise up 1, to receive 3, to regard 5, to respect 3, to set—to set up 10, to spare 3, to stir up 3, to suffer 5, to take—to take away—to take up 116, to wear 3, to yield 1,—continued 2, to go on 1, honourable 3, honourable man 1, to swear 4; *Inf. intens.* needs (be borne) 1, utterly (take away) 1; *Niphal*, to be borne 3, to be carried 3, to be exalted 3, to be extolled 1, high 2, to lift up self 3, to be lifted up 14, lofty 1, to be magnified 1, to take away 1; *Piel*, to advance 2, to carry 1, to exalt 1, to furnish 1, to further 1, to give 1, to help 2, to lift up 1, to take away 1,—to desire 1, to have a desire 1; *Hiphil*, to suffer to bear 1, to bring 1; *Hithpael*, to exalt self 3, to be exalted 2, to lift up self 4.

נְשָׂא *Ch. P'al*, to carry away 1, to take 1; *Ithpael*, to make insurrection 1.

נְשֵׂאת gift 1.

נָשַׂג *Hiphil*, ability 1, to be able 3, to attain 1, to attain unto 1, to get 1, to be able to get 3, can get 2, to take hold 1, to take hold of 2, to take hold on 1, to take hold upon 1, to lay at 1, to obtain 2, to overtake 23,

to put 1, to reach 2, to remove 1, to wax rich 1, to take 1; *Inf. intens.* surely (overtake) 1.

נְשׂוּאָה carriage 1.

נָשִׂיא captain 12, chief 9, cloud 1, governor 1, prince 95, ruler 6, vapour 3.

נָשַׂק *Niphal*, to be kindled 1; *Hiphil*, to burn 1, to kindle 1.

נָשָׁא *Kal, Inf. intens.* utterly (forget) 1; *Niphal*, to be deceived 1; *Hiphil*, to beguile 1, to deceive 10, to seize 1; *Inf. intens.* greatly (deceive) 1.

נָשָׁא *Kal*, to exact 1, giver of usury 1,—to be in debt 1; *Hiphil*, to exact 1.

נָשַׁב *Kal*, to blow 1; *Hiphil*, to cause to blow 1, to drive away 1.

נָשָׁה *Kal*, to forget 2; *Niphal*, to be forgotten 1; *Piel*, to make forget 1; *Hiphil*, to deprive 1, to exact 1.

נָשָׁה *Kal*, creditor 2, to exact 3, extortioner 1, to lend 1, usurer 1, to lend on usury 2, taker of usury 1; *Hiphil*, to lend 2.

נָשֶׁה which shrank 2.

נְשִׁי debt 1.

נְשִׁיָּה forgetfulness 1.

נָשִׁים wives—women *freq.*, married 3, marry 2, woman *freq.*

נְשִׁין *Ch.* wives 1.

נְשִׁיקָה kiss 2.

נָשַׁךְ *Kal*, to bite 10, to be lent upon usury 1; *Piel*, to bite 2; *Hiphil*, to lend upon usury 3.

נֶשֶׁךְ usury 12.

נִשְׁכָּה chamber 3.

נָשַׁל *Kal*, to cast 1, to cast out 1, to loose 1, to put off 1, to put out 1, to slip 1; *Piel*, to drive 1.

נָשַׁם *Kal*, to destroy 1.

נְשָׁמָה blast 3, breath 12, to breathe 2, that breathed 2, that breatheth 1, inspiration 1, soul 1, spirit 2.

נִשְׁמָא *Ch.* breath 1.

נָשַׁף *Kal*, to blow 2.

נֶשֶׁף dark 1, dawning of the day 1, dawning of the morning 1, night 3, twilight 6.

נָשַׁק *Kal*, armed 2, armed men 1, to kiss 25, to be ruled 1; *Piel*, to kiss 5; *Hiphil*, touched 1.

נֶשֶׁק & נֵשֶׁק armed men 1, armour 3, armoury 1, battle 1, harness 1, weapon 3.

נֶשֶׁר eagle 26.

נְשַׁר *Ch.* eagle 2.

נָשַׁת *Kal*, to fail 2; *Niphal*, to fail 1.

נִשְׁתְּוָן letter 2.

נִשְׁתְּוָן *Ch.* letter 3.

נְתוּנִים (כ׳) Nethinims 1.

נָתַח *Piel*, to cut 4, to cut in pieces 4, to divide 1, to hew in pieces 1.

נֵתַח parts 1, pieces 12.

נָתִיב path 3, way 2.

נְתִיבָה path 19, path*way* 1,—travel*lers* 1.

נְתִינִים Nethinims 17.

נְתִינִין *Ch.* Nethinims 1.

נָתַךְ *Kal*, to be poured 2, to be poured forth 2, to be poured out 3; *Niphal*, to drop 1, to be melted 1, to be molten 1, to be poured 1, to be poured forth 1, to be poured out 3; *Hiphil*, to gather 1, to gather together 1, to melt 2, to pour out 1; *Hophal*, to be melted 1.

נָתַן *Kal*, to add 2, to apply 2, to appoint 11, to ascribe 4, to assign 2, to bestow 3, to be bestowed 1, to bring 13, to bring forth 2, to bring hither 1, to cast 4, to cause 11, to charge 3, to come 1, to commit 5, to consider 1, to count 1, to deliver 156, to deliver up 3, to direct 1, to distribute 1, to fasten 5, to frame 1, to give 1040, to give forth 1, to give over 1, to give unto 1, to give up 6, wholly given 2, gift 1, to grant 15, to be granted 2, to hang 1, to hang up 2, to be healed 1, to lay 30, to lay unto charge 1, to lay up 3, to leave 2, to give leave 1, to lend 1, to let 5, to let out 1, to lift up 2, to be made 1, to make 106, to make of 2, to occupy 3, to offer 2, to ordain 2, having the oversight 1, to pay 4, to perform 1, to place 4, to plant 2, to pour 1, to present 1, to print 1, to pull away 1, to put 191, to put forth 1, to recompense 11, to render 1, to requite 1, to restore 1, to send—to send forth—to send out 13, to set—to set forth 101, to shew 7, to shoot forth—to shoot up 3, to strike 1, to *submit* 1, to suffer 18, to thrust 1, to tie 1, to trade 4, to turn 2, to utter 11, to yield 15,—aloud 1, to avenge 4, to cry 1, to cry out 1, to be given 1, to lie 4, make (set) 1, O that 16, to pull 1, to be put 1, to sing 1, to slander 1, take heed 2, to weep 1, to withdraw 1, would God—would to God 6, to yell 1; *Inf. intens.* doubtless (deliver) 1, without fail (deliver) 1, indeed (deliver) 1, surely (give) 2, willingly (give) 1; *Niphal*, to be cast 1, to be caused 1, to be committed 1, to be delivered 18, to be done 1, to be given 45, to be given up 1, to be granted 4, to be laid 1, to be made 1, to be put 1, to be set 1, to be uttered 1; *Inf. intens.* surely (be delivered) 1, surely (be given) 1; *Hophal*, to be delivered 1, to be given 4, to be gotten 1, to be put up 1, to be taken up 1.

נְתַן *Ch. P'al*, to bestow 2, to give 4, to pay 1.

נָתַם *Kal*, to mar 1.

נָתַע *Niphal*, to be broken 1.

נָתַץ *Kal*, to beat down 3, to break down 15, to break out 1, to cast down 2, to destroy 5, to pull down 2, to throw down 1, to be thrown down 2; *Niphal*, to be broken down 1, to be thrown down 1; *Piel*, to break down 5, to overthrow 1, to throw down 1; *Pual*, to be cast down 1; *Hophal*, to be broken down 1.

נָתַק *Kal*, broken 1, to draw 1, to pluck 1; *Niphal*, to be broken 5, to be broken off 1, to be drawn away 1, to be lifted up 1, to be plucked away 1, to be rooted out 1; *Piel*, to break 3, to break in sunder 1, break asunder 1, to burst 4, to pluck off 1, to pull 1; *Hiphil*, to draw 1, to pull out 1; *Hophal*, to be drawn away 1.

נֶתֶק dry scall 1, scall 13.

נָתַר *Kal*, to be moved 1; *Piel*, to leap 1; *Hiphil*, to drive asunder 1, to loose 2, to let loose 1, to undo 1,—to make 1.

נְתַר *Ch. Aphel*, to shake off 1.

נֶתֶר nitre 2.

נָתַשׁ *Kal*, to destroy 1, to pluck 1, to pluck out 2, to pluck up 7, to root out 2, to root up 1, to pluck up by the roots 1; *Inf. intens.* utterly (pluck up) 1; *Niphal*, to be forsaken 1, to be plucked up 2, to be pulled up 1; *Hophal*, to be plucked up 1.

סַלּוֹנִים thorns 1.

סָלַח *Kal,* to forgive 19, to pardon 13, to spare 1 ; *Niphal,* to be forgiven 13.

סַלָּח ready to forgive 1.

סְלִיחָה forgiveness 2, pardon 1.

סָלַל *Kal,* to cast up 6, to extol 1, made plain 1, to raise up 2 ; *Pilpel,* to exalt 1 ; *Hithpoel,* to exalt self 1.

סֹלְלָה bank 3, mount 8.

סֻלָּם ladder 1.

סַלְסִלּוֹת baskets 1.

סֶלַע rock 56, ragged rock 1, Sela 1, Sela-*hammahlekoth* 1, Selah 1, stone 1, stony 1, stronghold 1.

סָלְעָם bald locust 1.

סָלַף *Piel,* to overthrow 4, to pervert 3.

סֶלֶף perverseness 2.

סְלִק *Ch. P'al,* to come up 3 ; *P'il,* to come 1, to come up 1.

סֹלֶת fine flour 35, flour 15,——fine meal 1.

סְמָדַר tender grape 3.

סַמִּים sweet 14, sweet spices 2.

סָמַךְ *Kal,* established 1, to lay 18, to lean 1, to lie hard 1, to put 5, to set self 1, to stand fast 1, stayed 1, to sustain 3, to uphold 9 ; *Niphal,* to be borne up 1, to be holden up 1, to lean 2, to rest selves 1, to stay self 1 ; *Piel,* to stay 1.

סֶמֶל & סֵמֶל figure 1, idol 2, image 2.

סָמַן *Niphal,* appointed 1.

סָמַר *Kal,* to tremble 1 ; *Piel,* to stand up 1.

סָמָר rough 1.

סְנֶה bush 6.

סַנְוֵרִים blindness 3.

סַנְסִנִּים boughs 1.

סְנַפִּיר fins 5.

סָס worm 1.

סָעַד *Kal,* to comfort 3, to establish 1, to hold up 3, to refresh self 1, to strengthen 3, to be upholden 1.

סְעַד *Ch. Aphel,* helping 1.

סָעָה *Kal,*—— storm 1.

סָעִיף branch 1, outmost branch 1, clift 1, top 3.

סָעַף *Piel,* to lop 1.

סְעַפָּה bough 2.

סְעִפִּים thoughts 1.

סְעִפִּים opinions 1.

סָעַר *Kal,* tossed with tempest 1, to be tempestuous 2, to come out as a whirlwind 1 ; *Niphal,* to be sore troubled 1 ; *Piel,* to scatter with a whirlwind 1 ; *Pual,* to drive with the whirlwind 1.

סַעַר tempest 5, whirlwind 3.

סְעָרָה storm 1, stormy 4, tempest 1, whirlwind 1, whirlwind 9.

סַף bason 4, bowl 2, cup 1, door 13, door-post 1, gate 2, post 2, threshold 8.

סָפַד *Kal,* to lament 11, to mourn 15, mourner 1, to wail 1 ; *Niphal,* to be lamented 2.

סָפָה *Kal,* to consume 1, to be consumed 1, to destroy 3 ; *Niphal,* to be consumed 4, to be destroyed 2, to perish 2 ; *Hiphil,* to heap 1.

סָפָה *Kal,* to add 3, to augment 1, to put 1 ; *Niphal,* to be joined 1.

סָפַח *Kal,* to put 1 ; *Niphal,* to cleave 1 ; *Piel,* to put 1 ; *Pual,* to be gathered together 1 ; *Hithpael,* abiding 1.

סַפַּחַת scab 2.

סָפִיחַ such things as grow of themselves 1, things which grow 1, which groweth of its own accord 1, which groweth of itself 2.

סְפִינָה ship 1.

סַפִּיר sapphire 11.

סֵפֶל bowl 1, dish 1.

סָפַן *Kal,* cieled 2, to cover 3, seated 1.

סִפֻּן cieling 1.

סָפַף *Hithpolel,* to be doorkeeper 1.

סָפַק *Kal,* to clap 2, to smite 3, to strike 1, to wallow 1.

סֶפֶק sufficiency 1.

סָפַר *Kal,* to count 5, to number 16, to reckon 1, scribe 50, to tell 3, to tell out 1, writer 4, ——penknife 1 ; *Niphal,* to be

---

counted 1, to be numbered 5, to be told 2 ; *Piel,* to commune 1, to declare 22, to be declared 1, to number 1, to be numbered 1, to shew forth 6, to speak 2, to talk 1, to tell 31, to tell of 1 ; *Pual,* to be accounted 1, to be declared 1, to be told 3.

סְפַר *Ch.* scribe 6.

סֵפֶר bill 4, book 137, evidence 8, learning 2, letter 28, register 1, scroll 1,——learn*ed* 3.

סְפַר *Ch.* book 4, roll 1.

סְפָר numbering 1.

סְפֹרָה number 1.

סִפְרָה book 1.

סָקַל *Kal,* to stone 10 ; *Inf. intens.* surely (be stoned) 2 ; *Niphal,* to be stoned 4 ; *Piel,* to cast *stones* 1, to gather out *stones* 1, to gather out stones 1, to throw *stones* 1 ; *Pual,* to be stoned 1.

סַר heavy 1, sad 1.

סִרָבִים briers 1.

סַרְבָּלִין *Ch.* coats 2.

סָרָה rebellion 2, revolt 2, revolt*ed* 1, to turn away 1, wrong 1,——continual 1.

סָרַח *Kal,* exceeding in 1, to hang 2, spreading 1, to stretch selves 2 ; *Niphal,* to be vanished 1.

סֶרַח remnant 1.

סִרְיֹן brigandine 2.

סָרִים chamberlain 13, eunuch 17, officer 12.

סָרְכִין *Ch.* presidents 5.

סֶרֶן lord 21, plates 1.

סַרְעַפָּה bough 1.

סָרַף *Piel,* to burn 1.

סַרְפָּד brier 1.

סָרַר *Kal,* backsliding 1, rebellious 6, revolter 2, revolting 1, to slide back 1, stubborn 4, withdrew 1,——pull away 1.

סְתָו or סְתָיו winter 1.

סָתַם *Kal,* closed up 1, hidden 1, secret 1, to shut up 2, to stop 5 ; *Niphal,* to be stopped 1 ; *Piel,* to stop 2.

סָתַר *Kal,* (כ) to hide self 1 ; *Niphal,* to be absent 1, to be hid 10, to hide self 15, to be kept close 2, secret 2 ; *Piel,* to hide 1 ; *Pual,* secret 1 ; *Hiphil,*

---

to conceal 1, to hide 42, to keep secret 1 ; *Inf. intens.* surely (hide) 1 ; *Hithpael,* to be hid 1, to hide self 4.

סְתַר *Ch. P'al,* to destroy 1 ; *Pael,* secret things 1.

סֵתֶר backbiting 1, covering 1, covert 5, hiding-place 3, privily 1, secret 8, secret place 6, secretly 9,——disguis*eth* 1.

סִתְרָה protection 1.

עָב thick beam 1, thick 1.

עָב clay 1, cloud 22, thick cloud 7, thicket 1,——thick 1.

עָב thick plank 1.

עָבַד *Kal,* to be bondmen 1, bondservice 1, to bring to pass 1, to compel 1, to do 14, to dress 2, to ear 1, to execute 1, to keep 1, to labour 2, labouring man 1, servant 3, to be servants 1, to become servants 1, to serve 214, to make to serve 1, to serve self 1, to do service 3, to use service 1, to till 6, tiller 2, (ב) to transgress 1, to work 1, to do work 2, that work in 1, worshipper 5,——husbandman 1 ; *Niphal,* to be eared 1, to be served 1, to be tilled 2 ; *Pual,* to be made to serve 1, to be wrought 1 ; *Hiphil,* to keep in bondage 1, to cause to serve 3, to make to serve 3, to set a work 1 ; *Hophal,* to serve 4.

עֲבַד *Ch. P'al,* to do 10, keep 1, to make 5, to move 1, to work 2 ; *Ithpeal,* to be done 3, executed 1, to go on 1, to be made 2,——to be cut 2.

עֶבֶד bondman 20, *bondservant* 1, man-servant *freq.,* servant *very freq.,* (נ'א') sides 1, ——bondage 10.

עֲבֵד *Ch.* servant 7.

עָבֵד work 1.

עֲבֻדָּה household 1, store of servants 1.

עַבְדוּת bondage 3.

עָבָה *Kal,* to be grown thick 1, to be thicker 2.

עֲבוֹדָה act 2, bondage 8, effect 1, labour 1, ministering 1, ministry 1, office 1, to serve 1, service *freq.,* all manner of service 1, any manner of service 1, every kind of service 1, servile 11, servitude 2, tillage 2, use 1, work 10,——bondservant 1, wrought 1.

עֲבוֹט pledge 4.

עֲבוּר old corn 2.

עָבַט Kal, to borrow 1, to fetch (*a pledge*) 1; *Piel*, to break (*ranks*) 1; *Hiphil*, to lend 2; *Inf. intens.* surely (lend) 1.

עֲבָטִים thick clay 1.

עֲבִי thick 1.

עֳבִי thick 1, thickness 3.

עֲבִידָה Ch. affairs 2, service 1, work 3.

עָבַר Kal, to alienate 1, to be altered 1, to be charged 1, to come by 1, to come 7, to be come 1, to come over 5, to be come over 5, coming on 1, current 1, to be delivered 1, to enter 1, to escape 1, to fail 2, to get over 1, to go 24, to go away 1, to go beyond 2, to go by 3, to go forth 2, to go his way 1, to go in 1, to go on 6, to go over 51, to go through 9, to be gone 3, to be gone over 9, to have more 1, to overcome 1, to overpass 1, to be overpast 2, to overrun 2, to pass 83, to be passed 2, to pass along 8, to pass away 10, to pass away from 1, to pass beyond 1, to pass by 35, to pass on 19, to pass out 1, to pass over 81, to be passed over 6, to pass through 21, passage 1, passenger 5, passing 6, to be past 9, to perish 1, sweet smelling 1, to transgress 18, transgressor 1, *wayfaring man* 1; *Inf. intens.* speedily (pass over) 1; *Niphal*, to be passed over 1; *Piel*, to gender 1, to make partition 1; *Hiphil*, to alienate 1, beyond 1, to bring 3, to bring over 4, to bring through 1, to carry over 3, to conduct 1, to conduct over 1, to convey over 1, to do away 1, to make go 2, to have away 1, to lay 1, to pass 2, to make to pass by 1, to cause to pass 12, to make to pass 11, to pass through 1, to cause to pass through 4, to make to pass through 1, to put away 4, to remove 1, to send over 2, to set apart 1, to cause to sound 1, to make sound 1, to take 2, to take away 3, to make to transgress 1, to translate 1, to turn away 2,——to proclaim 1, to cause to be proclaimed 1, to make proclamation 4, raiser of taxes 1, to shave 1; *Inf. intens.* at all (bring over) 1; *Hithpael*, to meddle 1, to provoke to anger 1, to rage 1, to be wroth 5.

עֵבֶר passage 2, quarter 1, side—other side — this side 61, straight 3.

עֲבַר Ch. this side 7.

עֲבָרָה ferry-boat 1, ('כ) plains 2.

עֶבְרָה anger 1, rage 2, wrath 31.

עָבֵשׁ Kal, to be rotten 1.

עָבַת Piel, to wrap up 1.

עָבֹת thick 4.

עֲבֹת band 4, thick bough 3, thick branch 1, wreathen chains 2, cord 5, rope 3, wreathen 8.

עָגַב Kal, to dote 6, lover 1.

עֲגָבָה inordinate love 1.

עֲגָבִים much love 1, very lovely 1.

עֻגָּה & עֻגָּה cake 6, cake upon the hearth 1.

עָגוּר swallow 2.

עָגִיל ear-rings 2.

עָגֹל round 6.

עֵגֶל bullock 2, calf 33.

עֶגְלָה calf 1, (young) cow 1, heifer 10,——heifer 2.

עֲגָלָה cart 15, chariot 1, wagon 9.

עָגַם Kal, to grieve 1.

עָגַן Niphal, to stay 1.

עַד eternity 1, ever 42, everlasting 2, evermore 1, old 1, perpetually 1,——world without end 1.

עַד prey 3.

עֵד Galeed 2, witness 69.

עָדָה Kal, to adorn 1, to be adorned 1, to deck 2, to deck self 3, to be decked 1, to pass by 1; *Hiphil*, to take away 1.

עֲדָה & עֲדָא Ch. *P'al*, to alter 2, to be departed 1, to pass 1, to pass away 1; *Aphel*, to have...taken away 3, to remove 1, to take 1.

עֵדָה assembly 9, company 13, congregation 124, multitude 1, people 1, swarm 1.

עֵדָה testimony 22, witness 4.

עֵדוּת Shoshannim-eduth 1, Shushan-eduth 1, testimony 55, witness 4.

עֲדִי mouth 2, ornament 11,——excellent 1.

עֲדִים filthy 1.

עֲדִין given to pleasures 1.

עֵדֶן Hithpael, to delight selves 1.

עֶדֶן delicates 1, delight 1, pleasure 1.

עֶדְנָה pleasure 1.

עִדָּן Ch. time 13.

עָדַף Kal, to be more 1, odd number 1, that were over and above 2, overplus 1, to remain 4; *Hiphil*, to have over 1.

עָדַר Niphal, to fail 4, to lack 1, to be lacking 1; *Piel*, to lack 1.

עָדַר Kal, to keep rank 1; *Niphal*, to be digged 2.

עֵדֶר drove 4, flock 32, herd 2.

עֲדָשִׁים lentiles 4.

עוּב Hiphil, to cover with a cloud 1.

עוּג Kal, to bake 1.

עָב & עוּגָב organ 4.

עוּד Kal, to take to witness 1; *Piel*, to rob 1; *Hiphil*, to admonish 1, to charge 2, to protest 5, to call to record 2, to take to record 1, to take *witnesses* 3, to testify 14, to give warning 1, to witness 1, to witness against 1, to bear witness against 1, to give witness to 1, to be witness 1, to take to witness for 1; *Inf. intens.* earnestly (protest) 1, solemnly (protest) 2; *Hophal*, to be testified 1; *Pilel*, to lift up 1, to relieve 1; *Hithpalel*, to stand upright 1.

עָוָה Kal, to commit iniquity 1, to do wrong 1; *Niphal*, to be bowed down 1, perverse 1, to be of a perverse 1, to be troubled 1; *Piel*, to make crooked 1,——to turn 1; *Hiphil*, to do amiss 1, to commit iniquity 3, to do perversely 2, to pervert 2, to do wickedly 1.

עַוָּה ——overturn 3.

עוּז Hiphil, to gather 1, to gather selves 1, to gather selves to flee 1, to retire 1.

עֲוָיָא Ch. iniquity 1.

עֲוִיל ungodly 1.

עָוִיל young child 1, little one 1.

עוּל Kal, ewes great with young 1, milch 2, with young 2.

עוּל sucking child 1, infant 1.

עָוַל Piel, to deal unjustly 1, unrighteous 1.

עַוָּל unjust 1, unrighteous 1, wicked 3.

עֶוֶל & עָוֶל iniquity 16, unjust 1, unjustly 1, unrighteously 1, unrighteousness 2.

עַוְלָה iniquity 18, perverseness 1, unrighteousness 1, wickedly 1, wickedness 6,——unjust 1, wicked 1.

עֹלָה iniquity 2, ('כ) unrighteousness 1, wickedness 1.

עוֹלֵל & עֹלֵל babe 2, child 14, infant 3, little one 1, young child 1.

עוֹלָם alway 2, always 3, ancient 5, ancient time 1, any more 2, continuance 1, ('כ) Elam 1, eternal 1, ever 270, ever of old 1, everlasting 1, everlasting 63, evermore 14, lasting 1, long 2, long time 1, old 13, of old 9, of old time 2, perpetual 20, at any time 1, old time 1, world 2, beginning of the world 1,——never 15, world without end 1.

עָוֹן fault 2, iniquity freq., mischief 1, punishment 6, punishment of iniquity 4, sin 1.

עוֹנָה furrow 1, duty of marriage 1.

עִוְּעִים ——perverse 1.

עוּף Kal, to be faint 2, to wax faint 1, to flee away 1, to fly 14, to fly away 3, to shine forth 1, weary 1,——('כ) to set 1; *Polel*, to brandish 1, to fly 4; *Hiphil*, ('כ) to fly away 1,——to set 1; *Hithpolel*, to fly away 1.

עוֹף that flieth 1, bird 9, flying 2, fowl 59.

עוֹף Ch. fowl 2.

עוֹפֶרֶת lead 9.

עוּץ Kal, to take advice 1, to take *counsel* together 1.

עוּק Hiphil, to be pressed 2.

עָוַר Piel, to blind 2, to put out 3.

עוֹר hide 2, leather 1, skin freq.

עוּר Kal, to arise 1, to awake 16, to awake up 1, to stir up 1, to wake 1,——master 1; *Niphal*, to be raised 2, to be raised up 3, to be wakened 2; *Polel*, to awake 3, to lift up 3, to raise up 4, to stir up 4; *Hiphil*, to awake 3, to raise 3, to raise up 6, to stir up 15, to stir up self 1, to wake 2, to wake up 1, to waken 2; *Hithpolel*, to awake 2, to lift up self 1, to stir up self 2.

עוּר Niphal, to be made naked 1.

עוּר Ch. chaff 1.

עֹלָם Ch. ever 13, everlasting 4, never 1, old 2.

עֶלֶם young man 2, stripling 1.

עַלְמָה damsel 1, maid 2, virgin 4.

עֲלָמוֹת Alamoth 2.

עָלַס Kal, to rejoice 1; Niphal, ——goodly 1; Hithpael, to solace selves 1.

עָלַע Piel, to suck up 1.

עֲלַע Ch. rib 1.

עֻלַּף Pual, to faint 1, overlaid 1; Hithpael, to faint 2, to wrap self 1.

עֻלְפֶּה fainted 1.

עָלַץ Kal, to be joyful 1, to rejoice 6, to triumph 1.

עַם & עָם Ammi 2, Amminadib 1, folk 2, Lo-ammi 1, men 1, nation 17, people freq.,——people 5.

עַם Ch. people 15.

עָמַד Kal, to abide 4, to abide behind 1, to arise 2, to cease 1, to continue 6, to dwell 1, to be employed 1, to endure 8, to leave 2, to be over 1, to be present 1, to remain 8, to stand 367, to be able to stand — to stand by — to stand fast — to stand firm — to stand still — to stand up—to stay 367, to be at a stay 17, to tarry 2, to wait 5, to withstand — to withstand 6, —— to serve 2; Hiphil, to appoint 12, to confirm 2, to establish 5, to make 2, to ordain 1, to place 1, to present 4, to present self 1, to raise up 2, to repair 1, to set—to set forth—to set over—to set up 46, to settle 1, to cause to stand 1, to make to stand 1, to make to be at a stand 1, to stay 1; Hophal, to be presented 1, stayed up 1.

עֳמָד ——that I take 1.

עֳמָד place 6, I stood 1, where I stood 1, upright 2.

עֶמְדָּה standing 1.

עַמּוּד pillar freq.,——apiece 1.

עַמִּיק Ch. deep 1.

עָמִיר handful 1, sheaf 3.

עָמִית another 2, fellow 1, neighbour 9.

עָמַל Kal, to labour 8, to take labour 3.

עָמָל grievance 1, grievousness 1, iniquity 1, labour 25, mischief 9, miserable 1, misery 4, pain 2, painful 1, perverseness 1, sorrow 2, toil 1, travail 3, trouble 2, wearisome 1, wickedness 1.

עָמֵל that laboureth 4, that is in misery 1, to take labour 2, wicked 1, workmen 1.

עָמַם Kal, to hide 2; Hophal, to become dim 1.

עָמַס Kal, are borne 1, to burden selves with 1, to lade 2, to load 1, heavy loaden 1; Hiphil, to lade 1, to put 1.

עָמַק Kal, to be deep 1; Hiphil, deep 2, to make deep 1, to seek deep 1, to do deeply 2, in the depth 1, to be profound 1.

עָמֵק deeper 1, depth 1, strange 2.

עֹמֶק deep 14, deep things 1, ——exceeding deep 1.

עֵמֶק dale 2, vale 4, valley 63.

עֹמֶק depth 1.

עָמַר Piel, to bind sheaves 1; Hithpael, to make merchandise 2.

עֹמֶר omer 6, sheaf 8.

עֲמַר Ch. wool 1.

עָמַשׂ Kal, laded 1.

עֵנָב grapes 17, ripe grapes 1, wine 1.

עָנַג Pual, delicate 1; Hithpael, delicateness 1, to have delight 1, to delight self 5, to be delighted 1, to sport selves 1.

עָנֹג delicate 3.

עֹנֶג delight 1, pleasant 1.

עָנַד Kal, to bind 1, to tie 1.

עָנָה Kal, to give account 1, to afflict 1, to answer—to cause to answer—to give answer—to make answer 241, to bear witness 2, to be brought low 1, to cry 2, to hear 41, to lift up 1, to say unto 1, to shout 1, to give a (shout) 1, to sing 5, to sing together by course 1, to speak 8, to testify 12, to utter 1, to witness 52, to bear witness 1,——scholar 1; Niphal, to answer 2, to be answered 1, to be heard 2.

עָנָה Kal, to abase self 1, to be afflicted 2, to be exercised 2, gentleness 1, to be troubled 1; Niphal, to be afflicted 3, to humble self 1; Piel, to afflict 37, to deal hardly with 1, to defile 1, to force 5, to humble 10, to hurt 1, Leannoth 1, to ravish 1, to sing 2, to weaken 1; Inf. intens. in any wise (afflict) 1; Pual, to be afflicted 4, afflictions 1; Hiphil, to afflict 2, to answer 1; Hithpael, to afflict selves 1, to be afflicted 2, to chasten self 1, to submit self 1.

עֲנָה Ch. P'al, to answer 16, to speak 14.

עֲנֵה Ch. P'al, poor 1.

עָנָו humble 5, lowly 2, meek 12, (כ) poor 4, poor 1.

עֲנָוָה gentleness 1, humility 3, meekness 1.

עֲנָוָה gentleness 1, meekness 1.

עֱנוּת affliction 1.

עָנִי afflicted 15, (כ) humble 2, lowly 1, (כ) lowly 2, poor 59, (כ) poor 1.

עֹנִי afflicted 1, affliction 33, trouble 3.

עָנִיו meek 1.

עִנְיָן business 2, travail 6.

עָנַן Piel, to bring a cloud 1; Poel, enchanter 1, Meonenim 1, to observe times 5, soothsayer 2, sorceress 1.

עָנָן cloud 81, cloudy 6.

עֲנַן Ch. cloud 1.

עֲנָנָה cloud 1.

עָנָף bough 3, branch 4.

עֲנַף Ch. bough 1, branch 3.

עָנֵף full of branches 1.

עָנַק Kal, to compass about as a chain 1; Hiphil, to furnish 1; Inf. intens. liberally (furnish) 1.

עֲנָק chain 3.

עָנַשׁ Kal, to amerce 1, condemned 2, to punish 1, to be punished 1; Inf. intens. surely (punished) 1; Niphal, to be punished 3.

עֹנֶשׁ punishment 1, tribute 1.

עֲנַשׁ Ch. confiscation 1.

עָסִיס juice 1, new wine 2, sweet wine 2.

עָסַס Kal, to tread down 1.

עֳפָאִים branches 1.

עֳפִי Ch. leaves 3.

עָפַל Pual, to be lifted up 1; Hiphil, to presume 1.

עֹפֶל (כ) emerods 6, fort 1, Ophel 5, stronghold 1, tower 1.

עַפְעַפִּים dawning 1, eyelids 9.

עָפַר Piel, to cast dust 1.

עָפָר ashes 2, dust 91, earth 8, ground 1, morter 1, powder 3, rubbish 1.

עֹפֶר young roe 2, young hart 3.

עֵץ gallows 8, helve 1, plank 1, staff 4, stalk 1, stick 14, stock 4, timber 23, tree freq., wood freq.,——carpenter 4, pine 1.

עָצַב Kal, to displease 1, to grieve 2; Niphal, to be grieved 5, to be hurt 1, to be sorry 1; Piel, to make 1, to vex 1, to wrest 1; Hiphil, to grieve 1, to worship 1; Hithpael, to be grieved 1, it grieved 1.

עֲצַב Ch. P'al, lamentable 1.

עֶצֶב idol 16, image 1.

עֶצֶב labour 1.

עֹצֶב grievous 1, idol 1, labour 2, sorrow 3.

עֹצֶב idol 1, sorrow 2, wicked 1.

עִצָּבוֹן sorrow 2, toil 1.

עַצֶּבֶת sorrow 4, wound 1.

עָצָה Kal, to shut 1.

עָצֶה backbone 1.

עֵצָה tree 1.

עֵצָה advice 1, advisement 1, counsel 84, counsellor 2, purpose 2.

עָצוּם great 1, mighty 15, much 1, strong 12, strong one 1, ——feeble 1.

עָצֵל Niphal, to be slothful 1.

עָצֵל slothful 14, sluggard 6.

עַצְלָה slothfulness 2.

עַצְלוּת idleness 1.

עָצַם Kal, to be great 1, to be increased 4, to be mightier 1, to be mighty 2, to wax mighty 2, to be more 2, to shut 1, to be strong 3, to become strong 1; Piel, to break his bones 1, to close 1; Hiphil, to make stronger 1.

עֶצֶם body 2, bone freq., same—selfsame 16, strength 1,——life 1, very 2.

עֹצֶם might 1, strong 1, substance 1.

עָצְמָה abundance 1, strength 2.

עֲצָמוֹת strong 1.

עָצַר Kal, to be able 3, to close up 2, to detain 2, to keep

self close 1, to keep still 1, kept 1, to prevail 1, to recover 1, to refrain 1, to restrain 1, to retain 3, to shut 1, to shut up 13, to slack 1, to stop 1, to withhold 1, to withhold self 1,——to be *able* 2, to reign 1; *Inf. intens.* fast (closed) 1; *Niphal*, detained 1, to be shut up 2, to be stayed 7.

עֹצֶר barren 1, oppression 1, prison 1.

עֵצֶר ——magistrate 1.

עֲצָרָה solemn assembly 3, solemn meeting 1.

עֲצֶרֶת assembly 1, solemn assembly 6.

עָקַב *Kal*, to take by the heel 1, to supplant 2; *Inf. intens.* utterly (supplant) 1; *Piel*, to stay 1.

עָקֵב footstep 3, heel 7, *horsehoofs* 1, at the last 1, liers in wait 1, step 1.

עָקֹב crooked 1, deceitful 1, polluted 1.

עֵקֶב end 2, reward 3.

עָקָה subtilty 1.

עָקַד *Kal*, to bind 1.

עָקֹד ringstraked 7.

עָקָה oppression 1.

עָקַל *Pual*, wrong 1.

עֲקַלְקַל *byways* 1, crooked ways 1.

עֲקַלָּתוֹן crooked 1.

עָקַר *Kal*, to pluck up 1; *Niphal*, to be rooted up 1; *Piel*, to dig down 1, to hough 4.

עֲקַר Ch. *Ithp'al*, to be plucked up by the roots 1.

עֵקֶר stock 1.

עָקָר barren 9, barren woman 1, ——male or female barren 1.

עִקַּר Ch. stump 3.

עַקְרָב scorpion 6.

עָקַשׁ *Kal*, to prove perverse 1; *Niphal*, that is perverse 1; *Piel*, to make crooked 1, to pervert 2.

עִקֵּשׁ crooked 1, froward 6, perverse 4.

עִקְּשׁוּת ——froward 2.

עָר city 4, enemy 2.

עָר Ch. enemy 1.

עָרַב *Kal*, to become *surety* 1, to engage 1, to mortgage 1,

---

occupiers 1, to occupy 1, to be pleasant 1, to be pleasing 1, to take pleasure 1, to be surety 2, to be surety for 5, to become surety for 1, to put in surety 1, to be sweet 5, for to undertake 1; *Hithpael*, to intermeddle 1, to meddle with 2, to mingle selves 1, to be mingled 1, to give pledges 2.

עָרַב *Kal*, to be darkened 1, toward evening 1; *Hiphil*, evening 1.

עֲרַב Ch. *Pael*, mixed 2; *Ithpael*, to mingle selves 1, to be mixed 1.

עָרֵב sweet 2.

עָרֹב divers sorts of flies 2, swarm 7.

עֶרֶב mixed 1, mixed multitude 1, woof 9.

עֶרֶב Arabia 1, even 70, evening 49, evening*tide* 3, even*tide* 1, eventide 1, night 4, mingled people 4,——day 1.

עָרָב willows 5.

עֹרֵב raven 10.

עֲרָבָה Arabah 2, *Beth*-arabah 1, champaign 1, desert 9, evenings 1, heavens 1, plain 42, wilderness 5.

עֵרָבָה pledge 1, surety 1.

עֵרָבוֹן pledge 3.

עָרַג *Kal*, to cry 1, to pant 2.

עָרֹד Ch. wild ass 1.

עָרָה *Niphal*, to be poured 1; *Piel*, to leave destitute 1, to discover 2, to empty 2, to rase 2, to uncover 2; *Hiphil*, to discover 1, to pour out 1, to uncover 1; *Hithpael*, to make self naked 1, to spread self 1.

עֲרוּגָה bed 2, furrow 2.

עָרוֹד wild ass 1.

עֶרְוָה nakedness 51, shame 1, unclean 1, uncleanness 1.

עֶרְוָה Ch. dishonour 1.

עָרוֹם naked 16.

עָרוּם crafty 2, prudent 8, subtil 1.

עֲרוֹעֵר heath 1.

עָרוּץ cliffs 1.

עָרוֹת paper reeds 1.

עֶרְיָה bare 4, naked 1,—— quite (naked) 1.

עֲרִיסָה dough 4.

עֲרִיפִים heavens 1.

עָרִיץ mighty 1, oppressor 3, in great power 1, strong 1, terrible 13, violent 1.

עֲרִירִי childless 4.

עָרַךְ *Kal*, to put in array 7, to put selves in array 6, to put the battle in array 1, to set in array 8, to set in array against 1, to set selves in array 3, to compare 2, to direct 2, to equal 2, to esteem 1, expert in *war* 3, to furnish 2, to handle 1, to join *battle* 1, to ordain 2, to order 8, to lay in order 6, to put in order 1, to be reckoned up in order 1, to set in order 6, to prepare 5; *Hiphil*, to estimate 2, to tax 1, to value 3.

עֵרֶךְ equal 1, estimation 24, order 1, things that are to be set in order 1, price 1, proportion 1, suit 1, taxation 1,——set at 1, value*st* 1.

עָרֵל *Kal*, to count as uncircumcised 1; *Niphal*, foreskin to be uncovered 1.

עָרֵל uncircumcised 34, uncircumcised person 1.

עָרְלָה foreskins 13, —— uncircumcised 2.

עָרַם *Kal, Inf. intens.* very (subtilly) 1; *Hiphil*, to beware 1, to take crafty *counsel* 1, to be prudent 1, to deal subtilly 1.

עָרַם *Niphal*, to be gathered together 1.

עֹרֶם craftiness 1.

עָרְמָה guile 1, prudence 1, subtilty 1, wilily 1, wisdom 1.

עֲרֵמָה heap of corn 1, heap 8, sheaf 1.

עַרְמוֹן chesnut-tree 2.

עַרְעָר destitute 1, heath 1.

עָרַף *Kal*, to drop 1, to drop down 1.

עָרַף *Kal*, that is beheaded 1, to break down 1, to break neck 2, to cut off neck 1, to strike off neck 1.

עֹרֶף back 8, neck 17, *stiffnecked* 9.

עֲרָפֶל dark cloud 1, dark 1, darkness 3, gross darkness 2, thick darkness 8.

עָרַץ *Kal*, to be affrighted 1, to be afraid 2, to break 1, to dread 1, to fear 1, to oppress 1,

---

to prevail 1, to shake terribly 2, to be terrified 1; *Niphal*, to be feared 1; *Hiphil*, to be afraid 1, (be) dread 1, to fear 1.

עָרַק *Kal*, fleeing 1, sinews 1.

עָרַר *Kal*, to make bare 1; *Poel*, to raise up 1; *Pilpel, Inf. intens.* utterly 1; *Hithpalpel*, to be broken 1.

עֶרֶשׂ bed 5, bedstead 2, couch 3, ——bed 1.

עֵשֶׂב grass 16, herb 17.

עֲשַׂב Ch. grass 5.

עָשָׂה *Kal*, to accomplish 2, to advance 1, to appoint 2, apt for 1, to be at (agreement) 1, to bear 4, to bestow 5, to bring forth 10, to bring to pass 4, bruising 1, to be busy 1, to cause 1, that have the charge 1, to commit 45, to deal 50, to deal with 2, to deck 1, to do— to be done *freq.*, to dress 11, ready dressed 1, to effect 1, to execute 28, to exercise 1, to fashion 1, *fighting* men 1, to fit 1, ('ב) to fly 1, to fulfil 4, to furnish 1, to gather 1, to get 13, to give 1, to go about 1, to govern 1, to grant 1, to hold *a feast* 1, to keep 43, to labour 3, to maintain 1, to make 652, to make up 1, to make ready 2, to observe 4, to be occupied 1, to offer 47, to ordain 5, to pare 1, to perform 18, to practise 4, to prepare 36, to procure 4, to provide 2, to put 1, to requite 1, to sacrifice 3, to serve 1, to set 3, to shew 44, to spend 1, to take 2, to trim 1, to undo 1, to use 1, to vex self 1, to be *warriors* 1, to work 85, to yield 9, ——to consume 1, to displace 1, to feast 1, to finish 1, to hinder 1, to be industrious 1, to journey 1, officer 1, to sin 1, to vex 1; *Inf. intens.* certainly (do) 1, certainly (make) 2, indeed (do) 1, surely (deal) 1, surely (shew) 2, throughly (execute) 1; *Niphal*, to become 1, to be committed 3, to be done *freq.*, to be dressed 1, to be executed 1, to be put in execution 1, to be followed 1, to be given 1, to be holden 2, to be kept 3, to make 1, to be made 12, to be meet 2, to be occupied 1, to be offered 2, to come to pass 1, to be performed 2, to be prepared 2, to be used 1, to be wrought 4; *Piel*, to bruise 1; *Pual*, to be made 1.

עָשׂוֹר ten 1, instruments of ten strings 3, tenth 12.

פֶּחָה captain 9, deputy 2, governor 17.

פֶּחָה Ch. captain 4, governor 6.

פָּחַז Kal, light 2.

פַּחַז unstable 1.

פַּחֲזוּת lightness 1.

פָּחַח Hiphil, to be snared 1.

פֶּחָם coals 3.

פֶּחָר Ch. potter 1.

פַּחַת hole 1, pit 8, snare 1.

פְּחֶתֶת fret inward 1.

פִּטְדָה topaz 4.

פָּטִיר free 1.

פַּטִּישׁ hammer 3.

פַּטִּישׁ Ch. hosen 1.

פָּטַר Kal, to dismiss 1, free 1, to let out 1, open 4, to slip away 1; Hiphil, to shoot out 1.

פֶּטֶר firstling 4, that openeth 7.

פִּטְרָה such as open 1.

פְּטֵשׁ Ch. (ב) hosen 1.

פִּיד destruction 2, ruin 1.

פֵּיָה edge 1.

פִּיחַ ashes 2.

פִּילֶגֶשׁ concubine 36, paramour 1.

פִּימָה collops 1.

פִּיפִיּוֹת teeth 1,——two-edged 1.

פִּיק ——smite together 1.

פַּךְ box 2, vial 1.

פָּכָה Piel, to run out 1.

פָּלָא Niphal, hard 1, to arise... too hard 1, to be too hard 3, hidden 1, things too high 1, marvellous 1, to be marvellous 3, marvellous things 4, marvellous works 4, marvellously 1, marvels 1, miracles 1, to be wonderful 3, wonderful works 6, wonders 8, great wonders 1, wondrous things 3, wondrous works 11; Picl, to accomplish 1, performing 1; Hiphil, to shew marvellous 1, marvellous work 1, to do a marvellous work 1, to be marvellously... 1, to separate 1, to make singular 1, wonderful 1, to be wonderful 1, to make wonderful 1, wondrously 1; Hithpael, to shew self marvellous 1.

פֶּלֶא marvellous thing 1, wonder 8, wonderful 3, wonderfully 1.

פִּלְאִי (ב) secret 1, (ב) wonderful 1.

פָּלַג Niphal, to be divided 2; Piel, to divide 2.

פְּלַג Ch. P'al, divided 1.

פֶּלֶג river 9, stream 1.

פְּלַג Ch. dividing 1.

פְּלֻגָּה division 2, river 1.

פְּלַגָּה division 1.

פְּלֻגָּה Ch. division 1.

פְּלָדָה torch 1.

פָּלָה Niphal, to be separated 1, to be wonderfully made 1; Hiphil, to put a difference 1, to shew marvellous 1, to set apart 1, to sever 2.

פָּלַח Kal, to cut 1; Piel, to bring forth 1, to cleave 1, to shred 1, to strike through 1.

פְּלַח Ch. P'al, minister 1, to serve 9.

פֶּלַח piece 6.

פֻּלְחָן Ch. service 1.

פָּלַט Kal, to escape 1; Piel, to calve 1, to deliver 19, to be delivered 1, to cause to escape 1; Hiphil, to carry away safe 1, to deliver 1.

פֶּלֶט escape 1, that have escaped 2.

פַּלֵּט deliverance 1, escape 1.

פְּלִי secret 1.

פְּלִיא wonderful 1.

פָּלִיט escape 6, that escape 7, that had escaped 1, to be escaped 4, fugitive 1.

פָּלֵיט that escape 1, that escaped 1.

פְּלֵיטָה deliverance 5, escape 13, that is escaped 8, escaping 1, remnant 1.

פָּלִיל judge 3.

פְּלִילָה judgment 1.

פְּלִילִי judge 1, judgment 1.

פֶּלֶךְ distaff 1, part 8, staff 1.

פָּלַל Piel, to judge 2, to execute judgment 1, to think 1; Hithpael, to intreat 1, to make (prayer) 1, to pray 74, to make prayer 1, prayer be made 1, to make supplication 1.

פַּלְמוֹנִי certain 1.

פְּלֹנִי such 3.

פָּלַס Piel, to make 1, to ponder 3, to weigh 2.

פֶּלֶס scales 1, weight 1.

פָּלַץ Hithpael, to tremble 1.

פַּלָּצוּת fearfulness 1, horror 2, trembling 1.

פָּלַשׁ Hithpael, to roll self 1, to wallow self 3.

פְּלֵתִי Pelethites 7.

פֻּם Ch. mouth 6.

פֵּן corner 2.

פַּנַּג Pannag 1.

פָּנָה Kal, to appear 1, at eventide 1, to behold 1, to come on 1, dawning 1, to go away 1, to look 43, to mark 1, to be passed away 1, to regard 4, to respect 2, to have respect 4, to return 1, to turn — to turn aside—to turn away—to turn face — to turn self — to be turned 53, corner 1, right early 1; Piel, to cast out 1, to empty 1, to prepare 6; Hiphil, to look back 3, to turn 3, to turn self 1, to be turned back 1; Hophal, to lie 1, to turn back 1.

פִּנָּה bulwark 1, chief 2, corner 22, stay 1, tower 2.

פְּנִינִים (ב) rubies 1.

פָּנִים afore 2, aforetime 2, anger 3, countenance 30, edge 1, face very freq., favour 4, fear of 9, forefront 3, forefront 4, forefront 4, forepart 4, form 1, former time 1, forward 1, front 2, heaviness 1, as long as 1, look 1, looketh 1, looks 2, (ב) mouth 1, mouth 1, of old 1, old time 1, open 13, person 20, presence 75, prospect 6, was purposed 1, right forth 1, shewbread 7, sight 40, state 1, to make unto supplication 1, upside 2,—— to accept 4, battle 1, beseech 6, to deny 1, to disappoint 1, endure 1, enquire 1, to fear 3, honourable 1, impudent 1, meet 3, to meet 3, to be partial 1, to please 2, to regard 1, to say nay 3, street 1, toward 6, to wait on 1.

פְּנִים inner part 1, inward 2, within 10.

פְּנִימִי inner 30, inward 1, within 1.

פְּנִינִים rubies 6.

פָּנַק Piel, to delicately bring up 1.

פַּס Ch. part 2.

פָּסַג Piel, to consider 1.

פִּסָּה handful 1.

פָּסַח Kal, to halt 1, to pass over 3, passing over 1; Niphal, to become lame 1; Piel, to leap 1.

פֶּסַח passover 46, passover-offering 3.

פִּסֵּחַ lame 14.

פְּסִילִים carved images 3, graven images 18, quarries 2.

פַּסִּים (many) colours 3, divers colours 2.

פָּסַל Kal, to grave 1, to hew 5.

פֶּסֶל carved image 2, graven image 29.

פְּסַנְטֵרִין Ch. psaltery 1.

פְּסַנְתֵּרִין Ch. psaltery 3.

פָּסַס Kal, to fail 1.

פָּעָה Kal, to cry 1.

פָּעַל Kal, to commit 1, to do 10, doer 1, evildoer 1, to make 5, to ordain 1, to work 37.

פֹּעַל act 3, deed 2, to do 1, getting 1, maker 1, work 30.

פְּעֻלָּה labour 2, reward 1, wages 1, work 10.

פָּעַם Kal, to move 1; Niphal, to be troubled 3; Hithpael, to be troubled 1.

פַּעַם anvil 1, corner 3, foot 7, footstep 1, going 1, now 6, oftentimes 2, order 1, rank 1, step 4, time—second time—this time 59, twice 5, wheel 1,—— thrice 4, two times 1.

פַּעֲמוֹן bell 7.

פָּעַר Kal, to gape 1, to open 2, to open wide 1.

פָּצָה Kal, to deliver 1, to gape 1, to open 10, to rid 2, to utter 1.

פָּצַח Kal, to break forth 5, to break forth into joy 1, to make a loud noise 1; Piel, to break 1.

פְּצִירָה ——file 1.

פָּצַל Piel, to pill 2.

פְּצָלוֹת strakes 1.

פָּצַם Piel, to break 1.

צַיִד food 1, hunting 5, provision 2, that which he took in hunting 1, venison 8, victuals 2, ——catcheth 1, hunter 3.

צַיָּד hunter 1.

צֵידָה meat 1, provision 2, (כ) venison 1, victuals 6.

צִיָּה barren 1, drought 1, dry 8, dry land 1, dry place 1, solitary place 1, wilderness 2.

צִיּוֹן dry place 2.

צִיּוּן sign 1, title 1, waymark 1.

צִיִּים wild beasts of the desert 3, inhabiting the wilderness 1, that dwell in the wilderness 2.

צִינֹק stocks 2.

צִיץ blossom 1, flower 10, plate 3, wing 1.

צִיצָה flower 1.

צִיצִת fringe 3, lock 1.

צִיר Hithpael, to make as if had been ambassadors 1.

צִיר (כ) beauty 1, idol 1.

צִיר ambassador 4, hinge 1, messenger 2, pain 1, pang 3, sorrow 1.

צֵל defence 3, shade 1, shadow 45.

צְלָא Ch. Pael, to pray 2.

צָלָה Kal, to roast 3.

צָלוּל cake 1.

צָלַח Kal, to break out 1, to come 6, to come mightily 2, to go over 1, to be good 1, to be meet 1, to be profitable 1, to prosper 11, prosperously 1 ; Hiphil, prosperously to effect 1, to prosper 34, to cause to prosper 1, to make to prosper 1, to send prosperity 1, to be prosperous 1, to make prosperous 1.

צְלַח Ch. Aphel, to promote 1, to prosper 3.

צְלֹחָה pan 1.

צְלֹחִית cruse 1.

צַלַּחַת bosom 2, dish 1.

צְלִי roast 3.

צָלִיל cake 1.

צָלַל Kal, to quiver 1, to tingle 3.

צָלַל Kal, to sink 1

צָלַל Kal, to begin to be dark 1 ; Hiphil, shadowing 1.

צֵלֶל shadow 4.

צֶלֶם image 16, vain shew 1.

צֶלֶם & צְלֵם Ch. form 1, image 16.

צַלְמָוֶת shadow of death 18.

צָלַע Kal, to halt 4.

צֵלָע beam 1, board 2, chamber 11, corner 2, leaf 1, plank 1, rib 2, side 19, side chamber 9,——halting 1.

צֶלַע adversity 1, to halt 1, halting 1.

צֶלְצַל cymbal 3, locust 1, shadowing 1, spear 1.

צָמֵא Kal, to be athirst 2, to thirst 5, to suffer thirst 1, to be thirsty 2.

צָמָא thirst 15, thirsty 1.

צָמֵא thirst 1, that thirsteth 1, thirsty 7.

צִמְאָה thirst 1.

צִמָּאוֹן drought 1, dry ground 1, thirsty land 1.

צָמַד Niphal, to join self 2, to be joined 1 ; Pual, fastened 1 ; Hiphil, to frame 1.

צֶמֶד acre 1, couple 4, together 1, two asses 1, yoke 5, yoke of oxen 2.

צָמָה thirst 1.

צַמָּה locks 4.

צִמּוּקִים bunches of raisins 2, clusters of raisins 2.

צָמַח Kal, to bring forth 1, to grow 4, to grow up 1, to be grown up 1, to spring 2, to spring forth 3, to spring up 2 ; Piel, to grow again 1, to be grown 3 ; Hiphil, to bear 1, to bring forth 1, to cause to bud forth 1, to make to bud 2, to cause to grow 1, to make to grow 3, to cause to grow up 1, to cause to spring forth 3, to spring up 1.

צֶמַח branch 1, Branch 4, bud 3, that which grew upon 1, where grew 1, spring 1, springing 1.

צָמִיד bracelet 6, covering 1.

צַמִּים robber 2.

צְמִיתֻת ever 2.

צָמַק Kal, dry 1.

צֶמֶר wool 11, woollen 5.

צַמֶּרֶת highest branch 2, top 3.

צָמַת Kal, to cut off 1 ; Niphal, to be cut off 1, to vanish 1 ; Piel, to consume 1 ; Pilel, to cut off 1 ; Hiphil, to cut off 5, to destroy 5.

צֵן thorn 2.

צֹנֶה & צֹנֶא sheep 2.

צִנָּה hook 1.

צִנָּה buckler 5, shield 10, target 5.

צִנָּה cold 1.

צָנוֹף (כ) diadem 1.

צִנּוֹר gutter 1, waterspout 1.

צָנַח Kal, to fasten 1, to light from off 2.

צְנִינִים thorns 2.

צָנִיף diadem 2, hood 1, mitre 1.

צָנַם Kal, withered 1.

צָנַע Kal, lowly 1 ; Hiphil, humbly 1.

צָנַף Kal, to be attired 1, to violently turn 1 ; Inf. intens. surely (turn) 1.

צְנֵפָה ——toss 1.

צִנְצֶנֶת pot 1.

צִנְתָּרוֹת pipes 1.

צָעַד Kal, to go 3, to march 2, to march through 1, to run over 1 ; Hiphil, to bring 1.

צַעַד going 1, pace 1, step 11, ——go 1.

צְעָדָה going 2, ornament of the legs 2.

צָעָה Kal, captive exile 1, travelling 1, to wander 1, wanderer 1 ; Piel, to cause to wander 1.

צָעוֹר (כ) little one 2.

צָעִיף vail 3.

צָעִיר least 4, little 3, little one 2, small 1, small one 1, younger 7, youngest 3, —— young 1.

צְעִירָה youth 1.

צָעַן Kal, to be taken down 1.

צַעֲצֻעִים image work 1.

צָעַק Kal, to cry 43, to cry out 3 ; Inf. intens. at all (cry) 1 ; Niphal, to be called together 1, to gather 1, to gather selves together 3, to be gathered together 1 ; Piel, to cry 1 ; Hiphil, to call together 1.

צְעָקָה cry 19, crying 2.

צָעַר Kal, to be brought low 1, little one 1, to be small 1.

צָפַד Kal, to cleave 1.

צָפָה Kal, to behold 2, to look 1, to look well 1, Ramathaim-zophim 1, to be waited for 1, to watch 3, to keep the watch 1, watchman 17, Zophim 2 ; Piel, to cover 4, to espy 1, to garnish 1, to look 1, to look up 1, to overlay 39, to watch 3, watchman 2 ; Pual, covered 1, overlaid 1.

צָפָה ——swimmest 1.

צִפּוּי covering 3, overlaying 2.

צָפוֹן north freq., north side 12, north wind 1, northern 1, northward 24.

צְפוֹנִי northern 1.

צָפוּעַ (כ) dung 1.

צִפּוֹר bird 32, fowl 6, sparrow 2.

צַפַּחַת cruse 7.

צְפִיָּה watching 1.

צָפִיחִת wafers 1.

צָפִין (כ) hid 1.

צָפִיעַ dung 1.

צָפִיר goat 1, he-goat 3, he-goat 2.

צָפִיר Ch. he-goat 1.

צְפִירָה diadem 1, morning 2.

צָפִית watch-tower 1.

צָפַן Kal, to esteem 1, hidden one 1, to hide 11, to hide selves 1, to keep secretly 1, to lay up 8, to lurk privily 2, secret 1, secret place 1, to be privily set 1 ; Niphal, to be hid 1, to be hidden 2 ; Hiphil, to hide 2, (כ) to hide selves 1.

צֶפַע cockatrice 1.

צִפְעוֹנִי adder 1, cockatrice 3.

צִפְעוֹת issue 1.

צָפַף Pilpel, to chatter 1, to peep 2, to whisper 1.

צַפְצָפָה willow tree 1.

צָפַר Kal, to depart early 1.

צְפַר Ch. bird 1, fowl 3.

צְפַרְדֵּעַ frog 13.

צִפֹּרֶן nail 1, point 1.

צֶפֶת chapiter 1.

צִקְלֹן husk 1.

צָר & צַר adversary 27, adversity 1, afflicted 1, affliction 3, anguish 1, distress 5, enemy 38, flint 1, foe 2, small 1, sorrow 1, strait 3, tribulation 1, trouble 15, that trouble 2.

צַר close 1, narrow 2.

צֹר flint 1, sharp stone 1.

צָרַב Niphal, to be burned 1.

צָרֶבֶת burning 2, inflammation 1.

צָרָה adversary 1, adversity 5, affliction 7, anguish 5, distress 7, tribulation 3, trouble 44.

צְרוֹר bag 3, bundle 4, least grain 1, small stone 1, ——bindeth 1.

צָרַח Kal, to cry 1; Hiphil, to roar 1.

צֳרִי & צְרִי balm 6.

צָרִיחַ high place 1, hold 3.

צָרַךְ to need 1.

צָרַע Kal, leper 4, leprous 1; Pual, leper 10, leprous 5.

צִרְעָה hornet 3.

צָרַעַת leprosy 35.

צָרַף Kal, to cast 1, finer 1, founder 5, goldsmith 2, to melt 1, pure 2, to purge away 1, to refine 2, to be refined 1, to try 9, to be tried 1; Niphal, to be tried 1; Piel, refiner 2.

צֹרְפִי goldsmith 1.

צָרַר Kal, adversary 3, to afflict 3, to bind 4, to bind up 4, to be in distress 2, to be distressed 4, enemy 1, narrower 1, to oppress 1, to shut up 1, to be in a strait 3, to be in trouble 2, to vex 5; Pual, bound up 1; Hiphil, to be in affliction 1; to besiege 4, distress 1, to distress 1, to bring distress 1, pangs 2, to vex 1.

קֵא vomit 1.

קָאַת cormorant 2, pelican 3.

קַב cab 1.

קָבַב Kal, to curse 7; Inf. intens. at all (curse) 1.

קֵבָה maw 1.

קֻבָּה belly 1.

קֻבָּה tent 1.

קִבֻּץ company 1.

קְבוּרָה burial 4, burying-place 1, grave 4, sepulchre 5.

קָבַל Piel, to choose 1, to receive 6, to take 3, to undertake 1; Hiphil, to hold 1, to take hold 1.

קְבַל Ch. Pael, to receive 1, to take 2.

קֻבָל war 1.

קָבַע Kal, to rob 4, to spoil 2.

קֻבַּעַת dregs 2.

קָבַץ Kal, to assemble 2, to gather 15, to gather together 17, to gather up 1, to heap 1; Niphal, to assemble 1, to assemble selves 3, gather together 1, to gather selves together 10, to be gathered 5, to be gathered together 10, to resort 1; Piel, to bring together 1, to gather 42, to gather together 4, to gather up 1, to take up 1; Inf. intens. surely (gather) 1; Pual, to be gathered 1; Hithpael, to gather selves 1, to gather selves together 3, to gather together 1, to be gathered together 3.

קְבֻצָה ——gather 1.

קָבַר Kal, to bury 85, ——to be buried 2; Inf. intens. in any wise (bury) 1; Niphal, to be buried 39; Piel, to bury 6; Pual, to be buried 1.

קֶבֶר burying-place 6, grave 35, Kibroth-hattaavah 5, sepulchre 26.

קָדַד Kal, to bow 2, to bow down head 5, to bow the head 6, to stoop 2.

קִדָּה cassia 2.

קַדְמִים ancient 1.

קֹדֶשׁ holy 62, Holy One 41, saint 12.

קָדַח Kal, to burn 1, to kindle 2, to be kindled 2.

קַדַּחַת burning ague 1, fever 1.

קָדִים east 50, east wind 10, eastward 7, eastward 1.

קַדִּישׁ Ch. holy 4, holy one 3, saint 7.

קָדַם Piel, to come before 5, to flee before 1, to go before 2, to meet 2, to prevent 13,——to disappoint 1; Hiphil, to prevent 2.

קֶדֶם aforetime 1, ancient 6, ancient time 2, east 22, east side 4, eastward 1, eternal 2, everlasting 1, forward 1, old 17, past 1,——ever 1.

קֶדֶם east 12, east end 1, east part 2, east side 1, eastward 10.

קְדָם Ch. presence 1, —— it pleased 1, I thought 1.

קַדְמָה afore 1, antiquity 1, former estate 3, old estate 1.

קַדְמָה Ch. aforetime 1, ago 1.

קִדְמָה east 3, eastward 1.

קַדְמוֹן east 1.

קַדְמוֹנִי ancient 1, they that went before 1, east 4, former 2, old 1, things of old 1.

קַדְמַי Ch. first 3.

קָדְקֹד crown 1, crown of the head 6, pate 1, scalp 1, top of head 2.

קָדַר Kal, to be black 3, to be blackish 1, to be dark 2, to be darkened 1, heavily 1, to mourn 5; Hiphil, to make dark 2, to cause to mourn 1; Hithpael, to be black 1.

קַדְרוּת blackness 1.

קְדֹרַנִּית mournfully 1.

קָדֵשׁ & קָדַשׁ Kal, to be defiled 1, to be hallowed 3, to be holier 1, to be holy 5, to be sanctified 1; Niphal, to be hallowed 1, to be sanctified 10; Piel, to consecrate 2, to hallow 14, to keep holy 1, holy place 1, to prepare 6, proclaim 1, to sanctify 51; Pual, to be consecrated 1, to be sanctified 1, sanctified one 1; Hiphil, to appoint 1, to bid 1, to dedicate 9, to hallow 7, to prepare 1, to sanctify 24; Inf. intens. wholly (dedicate) 1; Hithpael, to be kept 1, to be purified 1, to be sanctified 2, to sanctify selves 20.

קָדֵשׁ sodomite 5, unclean 1.

קֹדֶשׁ consecrated 1, consecrated things 1, dedicated things 12, hallowed 2, hallowed things 7, holiness 29, holy very freq., holy portion 1, saint 1, sanctuary 68,——most holy 33, most holy things 6.

קְדֵשָׁה harlot 4, whore 1.

קָהָה Kal, to be set on edge 3; Piel, to be blunt 1.

קָהַל Niphal, to assemble selves 3, to assemble together 2, to be assembled 1, to gather selves together 8, to be gathered 2, to be gathered together 3; Hiphil, to assemble 5, to gather 4, to gather together 10, to be gathered together 1.

קָהָל assembly 17, company 17, congregation 86, multitude 3.

קְהִלָּה assembly 1, congregation 1.

קֹהֶלֶת preacher 7.

קָו & קַו line 20, rule 1,—— meted out 2.

קוֹא Kal, to spue 1; Hiphil, to spue out 2, to vomit 1, to vomit out 2, to vomit up 1, to vomit up again 1.

קוֹבַע helmet 2.

קָוָה Kal, to wait for 2, to wait on 2, to wait upon 1; Niphal, to be gathered 1, to be gathered together 1; Piel, to look 1, to tarry 1, to wait 22, to wait for 2, to wait on 2; Inf. intens. patiently (wait) 1.

קֶוֶה (כ') line 3.

קוֹחַ prison 1.

קוּט Kal, to be grieved 1,—— very (little) 1; Niphal, to lothe selves 3; Hithpolel, to be grieved 2.

קוּט Kal, to be cut off 1.

קוֹל bleating 1, crackling 1, cry 5, fame 1, lightness 1, lowing 1, noise 48, proclaim 2, proclamation 3, sound 39, thunder 12, thundering 2, voice freq.,——aloud 4, to cry 5, to hold peace 1, to sing 1, to speak 1, to yell 1.

קוּם Kal, to abide 1, to arise 211, to arise up 3, to be assured 1, continue 2, to endure 1, enemy 1, to be established 5, to get up 2, to hold 1, to be performed 1, to remain 1, to rise 62, to rise against 1, to rise up 83, to rise up again 1, to rise up against 7, to be risen 4, to be risen up 10, to be set 1, to stand 27, to stand up 19, to succeed 1, to be made sure 2, up 9, to be up 1, uprising 1,——to be clearer 1, to be dim 1; Inf. intens. surely (stand) 1; Piel, to confirm 5, to decree 1, to enjoin 1, to ordain 1, to perform 1, to stablish 1, to strengthen 1; Polel, to raise up 3, to be risen up 1; Hiphil, to accomplish 1, to make to arise up 1, to confirm 4, to continue 1, to establish 22, to make good 1, to help up 1, to lift up 3, to help to lift up again 1, to make 1, to perform 2, to pitch 1, to raise 6, to raise up 32, to rear 2, to rear up 8, to be reared up 1, to rouse up 1, to set 4, to set up 23, to stablish 2, to make to stand 1, to stir up 4, to uphold 1; Inf. intens. but newly (set) 1, surely (help) 1, surely (accomplish) 1; Hophal, to be per-

formed 1, to be raised up 1, to be reared up 1; *Hithpael*, to rise up 2, to rise up against 2.

קוּם Ch. *P'al*, to arise 5, to rise up 3, to stand 5; *Pael*, to establish 1; *Aphel*, to appoint 1, to establish 2, to make 1, to raise up self 1, to set 3, to set up 10; *Hophal*, to be made to stand 1.

קוֹמָה height 30, high 5, stature 7, tall 2,——along 1.

קוֹמְמִיּוּת upright 1.

קוֹן *Polel*, to lament 7, mourning woman 1.

קוֹף ape 2.

קוּץ *Hiphil*, to arise 1, to awake 17, to be awaked 1, to wake 1, to watch 1.

קוּץ *Kal*, to summer 1.

קוּץ *Kal*, to abhor 3, to be distressed 1, to be grieved 1, to loathe 1, to be weary 2; *Hiphil*, to vex 1.

קוֹץ thorn 12.

קוָצוֹת locks 2.

קוּר *Kal*, to dig 2; *Hiphil*, to cast out 2; *Pilpel*, breaking down 1, to destroy 1.

קוֹרָה beam 4, roof 1.

קוּרִים web 2.

קוֹשׁ *Kal*, to lay a snare 1.

קַט very 1.

קֶטֶב destroying 1, destruction 2.

קֹטֶב destruction 1.

קְטוֹרָה incense 1.

קָטַל *Kal*, to kill 1, to slay 2.

קְטַל Ch. *P'al*, to be slain 1, to slay 1; *Pael*, to slay 2; *Ithp'al*, to be slain 1; *Ithpael*, to be slain 1.

קֶטֶל slaughter 1.

קָטֹן *Kal*, to be a small thing 2, to be not worthy 1; *Hiphil*, to make small 1.

קָטָן least 6, less 2, little 11, little one 1, small 11, small quantity 1, small things 1, smallest 1, young 1, younger 10, youngest 2.

קָטֹן least 4, less 3, lesser 1, little 11, small 19, younger 4, youngest 12.

קָטַף *Kal*, to crop off 2, to cut up 1, to pluck 1; *Niphal*, to be cut down 1.

קָטַר *Piel*, to burn 1, to burn incense 37, to offer a sacrifice 1, to offer incense 3; *Inf. intens.* not fail (burn) 1; *Pual*, perfumed 1; *Hiphil*, to burn 50, to burn incense 15, to burn incense upon 2, to burn sacrifice 1, to kindle 1, to offer 2; *Hophal*, to be burnt 1, incense 1.

קָטַר *Kal*, joined 1.

קְטַר Ch. doubt 2, joint 1.

קִטֵּר incense 1.

קְטֹרֶת incense 54, perfume 3, sweet incense 2.

קִיא vomit 3.

קָיָה *Kal*, spue 1.

קַיִט Ch. summer 1.

קִיטוֹר smoke 3, vapour 1.

קִים substance 1.

קִים Ch. statute 2.

קָיָם Ch. stedfast 1, sure 1.

קִימָה rising up 1.

קַיִן spear 1.

קִינָה lamentation 18.

קַיִץ summer 10, summer fruit 9, summer house 1.

קִיצוֹן outmost 1, uttermost 3.

קִיקָיוֹן gourd 5.

קִיקָלוֹן shameful spewing 1.

קִיר side 4, town (wall) 1, wall 66,——mason 2, very 1.

קִיתָרֹס Ch. (כ) harp 4.

קַל light 1, swift 9, swiftly 2.

קָל Ch. sound 4, voice 3.

קָלָה *Niphal*, (כ) to be gathered together 1.

קָלָה *Kal*, dried 1, parched 1, to roast 1; *Niphal*, loathsome 1.

קָלָה *Niphal*, base 1, to be contemned 1, to be despised 1, to be lightly esteemed 1, to seem vile 1; *Hiphil*, to set light (by one) 1.

קָלוֹן confusion 1, dishonour 1, ignominy 1, reproach 1, shame 13.

קַלַּחַת caldron 2.

קָלַט *Kal*, lacking in his parts 1.

קָלִיא & קָלִי parched corn 6.

קָלַל *Kal*, to be abated 1, to be despised 2, to be lightly esteemed 2, to be swifter 4, to be vile 2; *Niphal*, to be easy 1, to be a light thing 5, to seem a light thing 1, to be swift 1, to be more vile 1,——slightly 2; *Piel*, to curse 39, to revile 1, to make vile 1; *Pilpel*, to make bright 1, to whet 1; *Pual*, to be accursed 1, to be cursed 2; *Hiphil*, to lightly afflict 1, to bring into contempt 1, to despise 1, to ease 2, to be easier 1, to lighten 2, to make lighter 3, to make somewhat lighter 1, to set light (by one) 1; *Hithpalpel*, to move lightly 1.

קָלָל burnished 1, polished 1.

קְלָלָה accursed 1, curse 27, cursing 5.

קָלַס *Piel*, to scorn 1; *Hithpael*, to mock 2, to scoff 1.

קֶלֶס derision 3.

קַלָּסָה mocking 1.

קָלַע *Kal*, to carve 3, to sling 1, to sling out 1; *Piel*, to sling 1, to sling out 1.

קֶלַע sling 4, slingstone 2.

קַלָּע slinger 1.

קְלָעִים hangings 15, leaves (of a door) 1.

קַלְקַל light 1.

קִלְּשׁוֹן forks 1.

קָמָה corn 2, grown up 2, stalk 1, standing corn 5.

קִמּוֹשׂ & קִימוֹשׂ nettles 2.

קֶמַח flour 4, meal 10.

קָמַט *Kal*, to fill with wrinkles 1; *Pual*, to be cut down 1.

קָמַל *Kal*, to be hewn down 1, to wither 1.

קָמַץ *Kal*, to take an handful 1, to take *an handful* 3.

קֹמֶץ hand*ful* 2, handful 2.

קִמָּשׂוֹן thorns 1.

קֵן nest 12, room 1.

קָנָא *Piel*, to be envious 4, to envy 9, to be jealous 10, to move to jealousy 1, to provoke to jealousy 1, zeal 1, to be zealous 2; *Inf. intens.* very (jealous) 2; *Hiphil*, to move to jealousy 2, to provoke to jealousy 1.

קְנָא Ch. *P'al*, to buy 1.

קַנָּא jealous 6.

קִנְאָה envied 1, envy 7, jealousy 25, zeal 9,——sake 1.

קָנָה *Kal*, to attain 1, to buy 51, to get 16, owner 1, to possess 2, possessor 3, to purchase 5, to recover 1, to redeem 1; *Inf. intens.* surely (buy) 1, verily (buy) 1; *Niphal*, to be bought 1, to be possessed 1; *Hiphil*, to teach to keep cattle 1.

קָנָה *Hiphil*, to provoke to jealousy 1.

קָנֶה balance 1, bone 1, branch 24, calamus 3, cane 2, reed 28, stalk 2,——spearman 1.

קַנּוֹא jealous 2.

קִנְיָן getting 2, goods 2, riches 1, substance 4,—— with money 1.

קִנָּמוֹן cinnamon 3.

קָנַן *Piel*, to make nest 4; *Pual*, to make nest 1.

קָסַם *Kal*, divination 1, to divine 7, diviner 7, prudent 1, soothsayer 1, to use *divination* 3.

קֶסֶם divination 8, reward of divination 1, divine sentence 1, witchcraft 1.

קָסַס *Poel*, to cut off 1.

קֶסֶת ink-horn 3.

קַעֲקַע ——marks 1.

קְעָרָה charger 14, dish 3.

קָפָא *Kal*, to be congealed 1, (כ) dark 1, that are settled 1; *Hiphil*, to curdle 1.

קִפָּאוֹן dark 1.

קָפַד *Piel*, to cut off 1.

קִפֹּד bittern 3.

קְפָדָה destruction 1.

קִפּוֹז great owl 1.

קָפַץ *Kal*, to shut 2, to shut up 1, to stop 2; *Niphal*, to be taken out of the way 1; *Piel*, skipping 1.

קֵץ after 10, border 3, end 51, infinite 1, utmost border 1,——process 1.

קָצַב *Kal*, to cut down 1, shorn 1.

קֶצֶב bottom 1, size 2.

קָצָה *Kal*, cutting off 1; *Piel*, to cut off 1, to cut short 1; *Hiphil*, to scrape 1, to scrape off 1.

קָצָה coast 1, corner 1, edge 2, end 22, lowest 3, part 1, quarters 1, selvedge 2, uttermost part 2.

קָצֶה after 1, border 3, brim 1, brink 1, edge 6, end 52, frontier 1, outmost coast 1, outside 3, quarter 2, shore 1, side 1, utmost 5, utmost part 2, uttermost 2, uttermost part 7, ——some 1.

קֵצָה end 4, infinite 1.

קֵצוּ end 3.

קָצוֹה ('כ) edge 1, ('כ) end 1, end 1, uttermost part 1.

קֶצַח fitches 3.

קָצִין captain 3, guide 1, prince 4, ruler 4.

קְצִיעוֹת cassia 1.

קָצִיר bough 3, branch 2, harvest 47, harvest man 1, harvest time 1.

קָצַע Hiphil, to cause to be scraped 1; Hophal, corner 1.

קָצַף Kal, to be angry 2, to be displeased 3, wrath come 1, to be wroth 22; Hiphil, to anger 1, to provoke to wrath 4; Hithpael, to fret selves 1.

קְצַף Ch. P'al, to be furious 1.

קֶצֶף foam 1, indignation 3, wrath 23,——sore 2.

קְצַף Ch. wrath 1.

קְצָפָה barked 1.

קָצַץ Kal, to cut off 1,——utmost 3; Piel, to cut 1, to cut asunder 1, to cut in pieces 2, to cut in sunder 1, to cut off 4; Pual, cut off 1.

קְצַץ Ch. Pael, to cut off 1.

קָצַר Kal, to cut down 1, to be much discouraged 1, to be grieved 1, harvest man 1, to lothe 1, mower 1, to reap 31, to be shortened 6, to be shorter 1, to be straitened 1, to be troubled 1, to be vexed 1, to be waxed short 1,——shorter 1; Inf. intens. at all (shortened) 1; Piel, to shorten 1; Hiphil, ('כ) to reap 1, to shorten 1.

קָצֵר few 1, hasty 1, small 2, soon 1.

קֹצֶר anguish 1.

קְצָת end 3, part 1,——some 1.

קְצָת Ch. end 2, partly 1.

קַר cold 2, ('כ) excellent 1.

קֹר cold 1.

קָרָא Kal, to bewray (self) 1, that are bidden 2, to call 460, to call for 1, to call upon 8, to cry 90, to cry unto 4, En-hakkore 1, ('כ) famous 1, to give names 3, guest 4, to invite 3, to be mentioned 1, to name 1, to give a name 1, to be named 1, to preach 2, to proclaim 36, to make proclamation 1, to pronounce 1, to publish 1, to read 36, renowned 2, to say 1,——to be famous 1; Niphal, to call selves 1, to be called 51, to be called forth 1, to be cried 1, to be famous 1, to be named 5, to read 1, to be read 1, to be renowned 1,——to be named 1; Pual, to be called 6, to be cried 1.

קָרָה Kal, to befall 5, to come 2, to be come 1, to come upon 1, to fall out 1, to happen 1, to help 1, to meet 73, to meet with 1, to seek 1,——against 41, against he come 1, in the way 1; Niphal, to chance 1, to happen to be 1, to meet 2,——by chance 1; Hiphil, to cause to come 1.

קְרָא Ch. P'al, to cry 3, to read 7; Ithp'al, to be called 1.

קֹרֵא partridge 2.

קָרֵב & קָרַב Kal, to approach 8, to come 9, to come near 32, to come nigh 10, to come together 1, to draw near 11, to draw nigh 7, to go 4, to go near 2, to be at hand 3, to be joined 1, to be near 1, to offer 1, to stand by 1; Niphal, to be brought 2; Piel, to cause to approach 1, to bring near 1, to go near 1, to be at hand 1, to join 1, to produce 1, to make ready 1; Hiphil, to bring 56, to bring forth 1, to bring near 4, to cause to be brought 1, to be come near 5, to cause to come near 4, to draw near 1, to cause to draw near 2, to draw nigh 1, to lay 1, to offer 104, to present 1, to be presented 1, to take 1.

קָרֵב approach 1, that came 1, which come near 4, that cometh nigh 2, drew near 2,——cometh any thing near 1.

קְרֵב Ch. P'al, to come 5, to come near 4; Pael, to offer 1; Aphel, to bring near 1, to offer 2.

קְרָב battle 5, war 4.

קְרָב Ch. war 1.

קֶרֶב bowels 1, unto charge 1, inward (thought) 1, inward part 3, inward thought 1, in-

wards 19, midst 72, purtenance 1,——to eat 1, to eat up 1, heart 1.

קָרֵבָה approaching 1, to draw near 1.

קָרְבָּן oblation 12, is offered 1, offering freq., sacrifice 1.

קֻרְבָּן offering 2.

קַרְדֹּם axe 5.

קָרָה cold 5.

קָרָה Kal, to befall 4, to come to pass unto 1, to happen 6, to meet 1, hap was 1; Niphal, to come 1, to happen 1, to meet 4; Piel, to lay beams 3, to make beams 1, to floor 1; Hiphil, to appoint 1, to bring 1, to send good speed 1.

קָרֶה uncleanness that chanceth 1.

קָרוֹב allied 1, approach 2, them that come nigh 1, at hand 6, kinsfolk 1, kinsman 1, near 35, near of kin 2, neighbour 5, next 1, nigh 12, nigh at hand 1, more ready 1, short 2, shortly 1,——any of kin 1, newly 1.

קָרַח Kal, to make (oneself) bald 1, to make baldness 1; Niphal, to make self bald 1; Hiphil, to make self bald 1; Hophal, made bald 1.

קֶרַח crystal 1, frost 3, ice 2.

קֹרַח ice 1.

קֵרֵחַ bald 1, bald head 2.

קָרְחָה bald 1, baldness 9, utterly 1.

קָרַחַת bald head 3, bare within 1.

קְרִי contrary 7.

קָרִיא famous 2, ('כ) renowned 1.

קְרִיאָה preaching 1.

קִרְיָה city 29.

קִרְיָא & קִרְיָה Ch. city 9.

קָרַם Kal, to cover 2.

קָרַן Kal, to shine 3; Hiphil, to have horns 1.

קֶרֶן horn 75,——hill 1.

קֶרֶן Ch. cornet 4, horn 10.

קָרַס Kal, to stoop 2.

קְרָסִים taches 10.

קַרְסֻלַּיִם feet 2.

קָרַע Kal, to cut 1, to cut out 1, to rend 52, to tear 4; Inf. intens. surely (rend) 1; Niphal, to be rent 5.

קְרָעִים pieces 3, rags 1.

קָרַץ Kal, to move 1, to wink 3; Pual, to be formed 1.

קֶרֶץ destruction 1.

קְרַץ Ch. ——to accuse 1.

קַרְקַע bottom 1, floor 6.

קֶרֶשׁ bench 1, board 50.

קֶרֶת city 5.

קַשְׂוָה & קַשָּׂה cover 3, cup 1.

קְשִׂיטָה piece of money 2, piece of silver 1.

קַשְׂקֶשֶׂת mail 1, scale 7.

קַשׁ stubble 16.

קִשֻּׁאִים cucumbers 1.

קָשַׁב Kal, to hearken 1; Hiphil, to attend 10, to cause to hear 1, to cause to be heard 1, to hearken 26, to give heed 3, to incline 1, to mark 2, to mark well 1, to regard 1.

קֶשֶׁב hearing 1, much heed 1, that regarded 1,——diligently 1.

קַשָּׁב attent 2, attentive 1.

קַשֻּׁב attentive 2.

קָשָׁה Kal, to be cruel 1, to be fiercer 1, to be hard 1, to seem hard 1, to be sore 1; Niphal, hardly bestead 1; Piel, to have hard labour 1; Hiphil, to make grievous 2, to be in hard labour 1, to ask a hard thing 1, to harden 12, would hardly 1, to make stiff 1, to stiffen 1, to be stiffnecked 2.

קָשֶׁה churlish 1, cruel 3, grievous 3, hard 4, too hard 1, hard things 1, hardhearted 1, heavy 1, obstinate 1, prevailed 1, rough 1, roughly 5, sore 2 sorrowful 1, stiff 2, stiffnecked 5 stubborn 1,——impudent 1, in trouble 1.

קְשׁוֹט Ch. truth 2.

קָשַׁח Hiphil, to harden 1, to be hardened 1.

קֹשֶׁט certainty 1.

קֹשְׁטְ truth 1.

קְשִׁי stubbornness 1.

קָשַׁר Kal, to bind 11, bound 1, bound up 1, conspirator 1, to conspire 15, to make conspiracy 5, stronger 1, to work treason 1; Niphal, to be joined together 1; to be knit 1; Piel, to bind 2; Pual, stronger 1; Hithpael, to conspire 3.

קֶשֶׁר confederacy 2, conspiracy 9, tréason 5.

קְשָׁרִים attire 1, head-bands 1.

קָשַׁשׁ *Kal*, to gather together 1; *Poel*, to gather 6; *Hithpoel*, to gather selves together 1.

קֶשֶׁת bow 67, bowman 1, bowshot 1,——archer 5, arrow 1.

קַשָּׁת archer 1.

קַתְרוֹם Ch. harp 4.

רָאָה *Kal*, to advise self 1, to approve 1, to behold 83, to consider 22, to discern 1, to enjoy 3, to espy 1, to have experience 1, to foresee 2, to gaze 1, to take heed 2, *Jehovah*-jireh 1, Lo 3, to look 93, to look on 10, to look out 2, to look up 1, to look upon 4, to mark 1, meet 1, to perceive 5, to provide 4, to regard 4, to respect 2, to have respect 3, to see 575, to shew 6, to spy 6, to stare 1, to view 1, visions 1,——to be in *presence* 1, joyfully 1, to be near 1, sight of others 1, to think 1; *Inf. intens.* certainly (see) 1, indeed (look) 1, surely (seen) 1; *Niphal*, to appear 66, to be looked upon 1, to present self 1, to seem 1, to be seen 27, to shew self 4, to be shewed 1, to be spied 1; *Pual*, to be seen 1; *Hiphil*, to make to enjoy 1, to cause to see 1, to let see 2, to shew 57, to be shewed 1; *Hophal*, to be shewed 4; *Hithpael*, to look one another 2, to look one upon another 1, to see one another 2.

רָאָה glede 1.

רָאָה see 1.

רֹאָה vision 1.

רְאוּת beholding 1.

רְאִי looking-glass 1.

רְאִי gazing stock 1, to look to 1, to see 1, to be seen 1, that seeth 2.

רִאשֹׁן (כ׳) first 2.

רְאִית (כ׳) beholding 1.

רָאַם *Kal*, to be lifted up 1.

רְאֵם unicorn 9.

רָאמוֹת coral 2.

רֵאשׁ poverty 2.

רֵאשׁ Ch. chief 1, head 12, sum 1.

רֹאשׁ band 2, beginning 14, to behead 1, captain 10, chapter 4, chief 90, chief man 4, chief things 1, chief place 1, chiefest place 1, company 2, end 2, end (of staves) 2, excellest 1, first 6, forefront 1, head *very freq.*, height 1, high among 2, on high 1, high *priest* 1, highest part 1, principal 5, ruler 2, sum 9, top 75,——every *man* 1, to lead 1, poor 1.

רֹאשׁ gall 8, hemlock 1, poison 1, venom 1.

רֵאשָׁה beginning 1.

רֹאשָׁה headstone 1.

רִאשׁוֹן aforetime 1, ancestor 1, beginning 4, eldest 1, first 128, fore*fathers* 1, foremost 3, former 26, former things 6, of old time 2, past 1.

רִאשֹׁנִי first 1.

רֵאשִׁית beginning 18, chief 8, chiefest 1, first 9, first part 1, first time 1, first*fruits* 1, firstfruits 11, principal thing 1.

רַאֲשֹׁת bolster 1.

רַב abound 2, in abundance——abundantly 7, *Bath*-rabbim 1, captain 24, common 1, elder 1, enough 8, exceedingly 2, full 1, great 128, increase 2, long 10, long enough 2, manifold 3, many 190, many a time 1, do many 2, have many 1, many things 1, master 1, mighty 5, more 12, much 30, too much 4, very much 1, multiply 1, multitude 7, officer 1, oftentimes 1, plenteous 3, populous 1, prince 2, process of *time* 1, *ship*master 1, suffice 3, sufficient 1.

רַב archer 2.

רַב Ch. captain 1, chief 1, great 9, lord 1, master 2, stout 1.

רֹב abundance 39, abundantly 6, all 1, excellent 1, great 9, great number 1, greatly 1, greatness 8, (כ׳) greatness 1, huge 1, to be increased 1, long 2, many 3, more in number 1, most 1, much 7, multitude 69, plentifully 1, plenty 3, very *age* 1,——common *sort* 1.

רָבַב *Kal*, to be increased 3, to be manifold 1, to be many 7, to be more 2, to be multiplied 3, to multiply 1; *Pual*, ten thousands 1.

רְבָב *Kal*, to shoot 2.

רְבָבָה many 1, millions 1, ten thousand 13,——multiply 1.

רָבַד *Kal*, to deck 1.

רָבָה *Kal*, to be in authority 1, to excel 1, to be greater 1, to grow up 1, to increase 12, to be increased 5, to be long 3, to be many 2, to be more in number 1, to be so much 1, to be much greater 1, to be multiplied 12, to multiply 16,——archer 1, greatness 1, process *of time* 1; *Piel*, to bring up 1, to increase 2, to nourish 1; *Hiphil*, to bring in abundance 4, to enlarge 1, exceeding 2, to be full of 1, great 4, to make great 3, to heap 1, to increase 21, to give many 2, to have many 3, to make many 5, to use many 1, any more 1, to give more 1, to give the more 2, to have more 1, to ask much 1, to gather much 1, much more 2, to take much 1, to yield much 1, to multiply 43, to make to multiply 1, to be multiplied 1, over much 2, plenteous 1, plenty 1, sore 2, store 1, throughly 1, very 1,——abundantly 1, to continue 1, great 1, many 13, to be many 1, many a time 1, more 4, more and more 1, much 23, very much 1; *Inf. intens.* exceedingly (multiply) 1, greatly (multiply) 1.

רְבָה Ch. *P'al*, to grow 2, to be grown 3; *Pael*, to make a great man 1.

רִבּוֹא & רְבוּ eighteen thousand, forty thousand, (כ׳) great things 1, ten thousand 2, twenty thousand,—— sixscore thousand, threescore thousand 1.

רִבּוּ Ch. ——ten thousand times ten thousand 2.

רִבּוּ Ch. greatness 2, majesty 3.

רִבּוֹת twenty thousand,—— twenty thousand.

רְבִיבִים showers 6.

רָבִיד chain 2.

רְבִיעִי foursquare —— fourth fourth part *freq.*

רְבִיעִי Ch. fourth 5.

רְבַךְ *Hophal*, baken 1, fried 1, that which is fried 1.

רָבַע *Kal*, to lie down to 2; *Hiphil*, to let gender 1.

רָבַע *Kal*, foursquare 1, square 1, squared 1; *Pual*, foursquare 2, square 1.

רֶבַע lying down 1.

רֶבַע fourth part 2, sides 3, squares 2.

רֹבַע fourth part 2.

רְבָעִים fourth 4.

רָבַץ *Kal*, to couch 2, to couch down 1, to fall down 1, to lie 8, to lie down 11, to sit 1; *Hiphil*, to make a fold 1, lay 1, to cause to lie down 2, to make to lie down 1, to make to rest 1.

רֶבֶץ where each lay 1, to lie down in 1, resting-place 2.

רַבְרַב Ch. great 7, great things 1, very great things 1.

רַבְרְבָן Ch. lords 6, princes 2.

רֶגֶב clods 2.

רָגַז *Kal*, to be afraid 1, to stand in awe 1, to be disquieted 1, to fall out 1, to fret 1, to move—to be moved 7, to quake 1, to rage 1, to tremble 10, to be troubled 3, to be wroth 1; *Hiphil*, to disquiet 2, to provoke 1, to shake 3, to make to tremble 1; *Hithpael*, rage 4.

רְגַז Ch. *Aphel*, to provoke unto wrath 1.

רֹגֶז Ch. rage 1.

רֹגֶז trembling 1.

רֹגֶז fear 1, noise 1, rage 1, trouble 3, troubling 1, wrath 1.

רְגָזָה trembling 1.

רָגַל *Kal*, to backbite 1; *Piel*, to espy out 1, to search 1, to slander 1, to spy 12, to spy out 8, to view 2; *Tiphal*, to teach to go 1.

רֶגֶל after 4, *broken*footed, foot *freq.*, footstool 5, legs 1, times 4,——be able to endure 1, coming 1, follow 5, great toe 2, haunt 1, journey 1, piss 2, possession 1.

רֶגֶל Ch. foot 7.

רַגְלִי on foot 1, footmen 5, footmen 6.

רָגַם *Kal*, to stone 16; *Inf. intens.* certainly (stone) 1.

רִגְמָה council 1.

רָגַן *Kal*, to murmur 1; *Niphal*, to murmur 2.

רָגַע *Kal*, to be broken 1, to divide 3; *Niphal*, to rest 1; *Hiphil*, to find ease 1, to be a moment 1, to rest 1, cause to rest 1, to give rest 1, to make to rest 1, to make suddenly 2.

רֶגַע that are quiet 1.

רֶגַע instant 2, moment 18, space 1, suddenly 1.

רָנַשׁ Kal, to rage 1.

רְנַשׁ Ch. Aphel, to assemble 2, to assemble together 1.

רְנַשׁ company 1.

רִנְשָׁה insurrection 1.

רָדַד Kal, to be spent 1, to subdue 2; Hiphil, to spread 1.

רָדָה Kal, to come to have dominion 1, to have dominion 6, to prevail against 1, to reign 1, to rule 9, to bear rule 3, to rule over 1; Piel, to make to have dominion 2; Hiphil, to make to rule 1.

רָדָה Kal, to take 2.

רָדִיד vail 1, veil 1.

רָדַם Niphal, to be fast asleep 2, cast into a dead sleep 1, in a deep sleep 1, to be in a deep sleep 1, sleeper 1, that sleepeth 1.

רָדַף Kal, to chase 10, to put to flight 1, to follow 9, to follow after 5, to follow on 1, to hunt 1, to persecute 19, persecutor 7, to pursue 76; Niphal, to be past 1, to be under persecution 1; Piel, to follow 1, follow after 3, to persecute 1, to pursue 4; Pual, to be chased 1; Hiphil, to chase 1.

רָהַב Kal, to behave self proudly 1, to make sure 1; Hiphil, to overcome 1, to strengthen 1.

רָהָב proud 1.

רַהַב proud 2, Rahab 3, strength 1.

רֹהַב strength 1.

רָהָה Kal, to be afraid 1.

רַהַט gallery 1, gutter 2, trough 1.

רָהִיט rafter 1.

רֵו Ch. form 2.

רוּד Kal, to be lord 1, to rule 1; Hiphil, to have the dominion 1.

רוּד Hiphil, mourn 1.

רָוָה Kal, to be made drunk 1, to take the fill 1, to be abundantly satisfied 1; Piel, to be bathed 1, to satiate 1, to satisfy 1, to be soaked 1, to water 1, to water abundantly 1; Hiphil, to make drunken 1, to fill 1, to satiate 1, to water 2.

רָוֶה drunkenness 1, watered 2.

רָוָה Kal, to be refreshed 2; Pual, large 1.

רֶוַח enlargement 1, space 1.

רוּחַ Hiphil, to accept 1, to smell 8, to make of quick understanding 1,——to touch 1.

רוּחַ air 1, anger 1, blast 4, breath 28, courage 1, mind 5, spirit freq., spiritual 1, tempest 1, whirlwind 1, wind freq., ——cool 1, quarters 1, side 6, vain 2.

רוּחַ Ch. mind 1, spirit 8, wind 2.

רְוָחָה breathing 1, respite 1.

רָוָה runneth over 1, wealthy 1.

רוּם Kal, to breed (worms) 1, to exalt self 2, to be exalted 20, to go up 1, haughty 1, high 17, to be high 4, high ones 1, too high 1, to be higher 2, to be lifted up 9, to be lift up 1, to be lofty 3, loud 1, to mount up 1, proud 1, tall 4,——presumptuously 1; Polel, to bring up 2, to exalt 11, to extol 2, to lift up on high 1, to set up on high 1, to lift up 4, to promote 1, to set up 3; Polal, to be exalted 2, to be extolled 1; Hiphil, to exalt 12, (ב) to be exalted 1, to give 5, to heave 3, to make on high 1, to hold up 2, to levy 1, to lift 1, to lift up 27, to offer 12, to offer up 4, promotion 1, to be promotion of 1, to set up 5, to take 3, to take away 1, to take off 3, to take up 7, (ב) to be taken away 1,——aloud 1; Hophal, to be heaved up 1, to be taken away 1, to be taken off 1; Hithpolel, to exalt self 1.

רוּם Ch. P'al, to extol 1, to be lifted up 1; Aphel, to set up 1; Hithpolel, to lift up self 1.

רוּם haughtiness 3, height 1, ——high 2.

רוּם Ch. height 5.

רוֹם on high 1.

רוֹמָה haughtily 1.

רוֹמֵם to be extolled 1, high 1.

רוּעַ Niphal, to be destroyed 1, to smart 1; Polal, to be shouting 1; Hiphil, to blow an alarm 1, to cry 3, to cry alarm 1, to cry aloud 1, to cry out 2, to make a joyful noise 7, to shout 18, to shout for joy 1, to sound an alarm 2, to triumph 1; Hithpolel, to shout for joy 1, triumph 2.

רוּף Polel, to tremble 1.

רוּץ Kal, to break down 1, footman 1, guard 14, posts 8, to run 10, (ב) to make run away 1, to run through 1; Hiphil, to divide speedily 1, to bring hastily 1, to run 1, to make run away 2, soon to stretch out 1.

רוּק Hiphil, to cast out 1, to draw 3, to draw out 5, to empty 5, to make empty 1, to pour out 1,——to arm 1; Hophal, to be emptied 1, to be poured forth 1.

רוּר Kal, to run 1.

רֹאשׁ gall 1.

רוּשׁ Kal, to lack 1, needy 1, poor 18, poor man 3; Hithpolel, to make self poor 1.

רָז Ch. secret 9.

רָזָה Kal, to famish 1; Niphal, to wax lean 1.

רָזֶה lean 2.

רָזוֹן leanness 2,——scant 1.

רָזוֹן prince 1.

רָזִי leanness 2.

רָזַם Kal, to wink at 1.

רָזֵן Kal, prince 5, ruler 2.

רָחַב Kal, to be enlarged 1, to be an enlarging 1; Niphal, large 1; Hiphil, to enlarge 14, to be enlarged 1, to make large 1, to make room 1, to make wide 1, to open wide 2.

רָחָב broad 6, large 5, at liberty 1, proud 3, wide 3,——large 3, wide 1.

רַחַב breadth 1, broad place 1.

רֹחַב breadth freq., broad 22, largeness 1, thick 1, thickness 2, wideness 1.

רְחוֹב broad place 1, broad way 2, street 40.

רַחוּם full of compassion 5, merciful 8.

רָחוֹק afar off 28, far 31, far abroad 1, far off 14, long 1, long ago 3, of old 2, space 1, great while to come 2.

רָחִיט (ב) rafter 1.

רֵחַיִם mill 2, millstones 2, nether millstone 1.

רָחִיק Ch. far 1.

רָחֵל ewe 2, sheep 2.

רָחַם Kal, to love 1; Piel, to have compassion 1, to have compassion on 4, to have compassion upon 3, merciful 1, to have mercy 13, to have mercy on 6, to shew mercy 3, to have mercy upon 6, to pity 2, to have pity 1; Inf. intens. surely (have mercy) 1; Pual, Lo-ruhamah 2, to find mercy 1, to have mercy 1, to obtain mercy 1, Ruhamah 3.

רָחָם gier-eagle 2.

רַחַם damsel 1, womb 4.

רֶחֶם matrix 5, womb 21.

רְחָמָה gier-eagle 1.

רֻחָמָה ——two damsels 2.

רַחֲמִים bowels 2, compassion 4, tender love 1, mercies 14, great mercies 1, tender mercies 11, mercy 4, to be pitied 1, pity 1.

רַחֲמִין Ch. mercies 1.

רַחֲמָנִי pitiful 1.

רָחַף Kal, to shake 1; Piel, to flutter 1, to move 1.

רָחַץ Kal, to bathe 6, to bathe self 12, to wash 46, to wash self 5; Pual, to be washed 2; Hithpael, to wash self 1.

רַחַץ washpot 2.

רְחַץ Ch. Hithp'il, to trust 1.

רַחְצָה washing 2.

רָחַק Kal, to be far 14, to be far away 1, to get far 1, to be far off 2, to go far off 1, to be far removed 1, to be too far 2, to flee far 1, to go far away 1, to be gone far 1, to be gone away far 1, to keep (oneself) far 1,——to refrain 1; Niphal, (ב) to be loosed 1; Piel, to put away far 1, to remove far 2, to remove far away 1; Hiphil, to be afar off 1, to put away far 1, to drive far 1, far 1, to put far away 3, to cast far off 1, to wander far off 1, to put far 3, to go far 1, to go far away 1, a good way off 1, to put away 1, to remove far 5, to remove far off 1, to be a good way 1, to withdraw far 1; Inf. intens. very (go far) 2.

רָחֵק that are far from 1.

רָחַשׁ Kal, to indite 1.

רַחַת shovel 1.

רָטַב Kal, to be wet 1.

רָטֹב green 1.

רֶמֶט fear 1.

רְמְפַּשׁ to be fresh 1.

רְטַשׁ Piel, to dash 1, to dash to pieces 1 ; Pual, to be dashed in pieces 3, to be dashed to pieces 1.

רִי watering 1.

רִיב Kal, to chide 6, to complain 1, to contend 12, to debate 1, to debate with 1, to plead 27, to rebuke 1, to strive 13,—— Jareb 2, to lay wait 1 ; Inf. in tens. ever (strive) 1, throughly (plead) 1 ; Hiphil, adversary 1, to strive 1.

רִיב cause 24, chiding 1, to contend 1, contention 2, controversy 13, (כ) multitude 1, pleading 1, strife 14, strive 2, striving 1, suit 1,—— adversary 1.

רֵיחַ savour 45, scent 2, smell 11.

רֵיחַ Ch. smell 1.

רֵיעַ friend 1.

רִיפוֹת ground corn 1, wheat 1.

רִיק empty 6, to no purpose 1, in vain 6, vain thing 1, vanity 2.

רֵק & רִיק emptied 1, empty 5, vain 5, vain fellows 1, vain men 1.

רֵיקָם without cause 2, empty 12, in vain 1, void 1.

רִיר spittle 1, white of an egg 1.

רִישׁ poverty 3.

רֵישׁ poverty 2.

רִישׁוֹן (כ) former 1.

רַךְ fainthearted 1, soft 3, tender 9, tender one 1, tender-hearted 1, weak 1.

רֹךְ tenderness 1.

רָכַב Kal, to get (oneself) up 1, on horseback 2, to ride—to ride in—to ride in a chariot—to ride on—to ride upon 55; Hiphil, to bring 1, to carry 3, to bring on horseback 1, to put 3, to cause to ride 7, to make to ride 3, to set 2.

רֶכֶב chariot 114, millstone 2, upper millstone 1, (כ) multitude 1, wagon 1.

רַכָּב chariot man 1, driver of a chariot 1, horseman 1.

רִכְבָּה chariots 1.

רָכוּב chariot 1.

רְכֻשׁ goods 12, riches 5, substance 11.

רָכִיל slanders 2, tale-bearer 3, carry tales 1,—— tale-bearer 1.

רָכַךְ Kal, to be softer 1, to be tender 2 ; Niphal, to faint 2, to be fainthearted 1 ; Pual, to be mollified 1 ; Hiphil, to make soft 1.

רֹכֵל Kal, merchant 17, spice merchant 1.

רְכֻלָּה merchandise 2, traffic 2.

רָכַס Kal, to bind 2.

רֶכֶס pride 1.

רְכָסִים rough places 1.

רָכַשׁ Kal, to gather 1, to get 4.

רֶכֶשׁ dromedary 1, mule 2, swift beast 1.

רָמָה Kal, to carry 1, to throw 2,——bowmen 4 ; Piel, to beguile 2, to betray 1, to deceive 5.

רָמָה high place 4.

רְמָה Ch. P'al, to cast 4, to be cast 1, to be cast down 1, to impose 1 ; Ithp'el, to be cast 5.

רִמָּה worm 7.

רִמּוֹן pomegranate 30, pomegranate tree 2.

רָמוּת height 1.

רֹמַח buckler 1, javelin 1, lancet 1, spear 12.

רְמִיָּה deceit 2, deceitful 4, deceitfully 3, false 1, guile 1, idle 1, slack 1, slothful 2.

רַמָּךְ dromedary 1.

רָמַם Kal, to be exalted 2 ; Niphal, to be exalted 1, to get (oneself) up 1, to lift up selves 1, to be lifted up 1, to mount up 1.

לְמֵמוּת lifting up of self 1.

רָמַס Kal, oppressor 1, to stamp upon 2, to trample 1, to trample under foot 1, to tread 4, to tread down 7, to tread upon 2 ; Niphal, to be trodden 1.

רָמַשׂ Kal, creep 11, move 6.

רֶמֶשׂ that creepeth 1, creeping thing 15, moving thing 1.

רֹן song 1.

רָנָה Kal, to rattle 1.

רִנָּה cry 12, gladness 1, joy 2, proclamation 1, rejoicing 1, shouting 1, sing — singing 11, triumph 1.

רָנַן Kal, to cry 2, to cry out 1, to rejoice 1, to shout 2, to shout for joy 1, to sing 12 ; Piel, to cry out 1, to greatly rejoice 1, to be joyful 1, to rejoice 7, to shout for joy 3, to sing aloud 3, to sing for joy 1, to sing 6, to sing out 1, to triumph 1 ; Inf. intens. aloud for joy (shout) 1 ; Pual, to be singing 1 ; Hiphil, to rejoice 1, to make to rejoice 1, to shout for joy 1, to sing aloud 1, to cause to sing for joy 1 ; Hithpolel, to shout 1.

רְנָנָה joyful 1, joyful voice 1, singing 1, triumphing 1.

רְנָנִים ——goodly 1.

רְסִיסִים drops 1.

רְסִיסִים breaches 1.

רֶסֶן bridle 4.

רָסַס Kal, to temper 1.

רַע adversity 4, affliction 6, bad 13, calamity 1, displeasure 4, distress 1, evil 445, evil-favouredness 1, grief 1, grievous 2, harm 5, heavy 1, hurt 20, hurtful 1, ill 6, ill-favoured 2, mischief 22, mischievous 1, misery 1, naught 3, naughty 1, noisome 2, sad—sadly 3, sore 9, sorrow 1, trouble 10, vex 1, wicked—wicked ones—wickedly 32, wickedness 55, worse 1, worst 1, wretchedness 1, wrong 1,—— to displease 3, exceedingly 1, great wickedness 1, harm 5, not to please 2, to smart 1.

רֵעַ noise 1, shouted 1,—— aloud 1.

רֵעַ brother 1, companion 5, fellow 10, friend 41, husband 1, lover 1, neighbour 104,——another 23, other 2.

רֵעַ thought 2.

רֹעַ badness 2, evil 11, naughtiness 1, sadness 1, sorrow 1, wickedness 3,——to be so bad 1, to be so evil 1.

רָעֵב Kal, to be famished 1, to hunger 1, to have hunger 1, to suffer hunger 2, to be hungry 4 ; Hiphil, to suffer to famish 1, to suffer to hunger 1.

רָעָב dearth 5, famine freq., hunger 8,——famished 1.

רָעֵב hunger bitten 1, hungry 21.

רְעָבוֹן famine 3.

רַעַד Kal, to tremble 1 ; Hiphil, to tremble 2.

רַעַד trembling 2.

רְעָדָה fear 1, fearfulness 1, trembling 2.

רָעָה Kal, companion 2, to keep company with 1, to devour 1, to eat up 3, to evil entreat 1, to be fed 1, to feed 73, herdman 7, to keep sheep 6, pastor 7, Shepherd 1, shepherd 59, shepherd 3, to wander 1, to waste 1,——to break 1, shearing house 1 ; Piel, to use as friend 1 ; Hiphil, to feed 1 ; Hithpael, to make friendship with 1.

רֵעָה friend 3.

רֵעָה companion 2, fellow 1.

רֹעָה broken 1.

רְעוּת mate 2, neighbour 2,——another 2.

רְעוּת vexation 7.

רְעוּת Ch. pleasure 1, will 1.

רְעִי pasture 1.

רֹעִי shepherd 2.

רֵעֶה (כ) fellows 1, love 9.

רַעְיוֹן vexation 3.

רַעְיוֹן Ch. cogitation 1, thought 5.

רָעַל Hophal, to be terribly shaken 1.

רַעַל mufflers 1, trembling 1.

רָעַם Kal, to roar 3, to be troubled 1 ; Hiphil, to make to fret 1, to thunder 8.

רַעַם thunder 6.

רַעְמָה thunder 1.

רַעֲנָן flourishing 1, fresh 1, green 18.

רַעֲנַן Ch. flourishing 1.

רָעַע Kal, to associate selves 1, to break 2, to break in pieces 1, to be broken 2, to be evil 2, ill 1, to be worse 1,——to displease 2, to be displeased 1 ; Inf. intens. utterly (broken) 1 ; Hiphil, to afflict 5, to bring evil 2, to do evil 14, evil doer 12, to evil entreat 2, evil man 1, to do harm 3, to hurt 7, to do hurt 1, to behave selves ill 1, to deal ill 1, to do mischief 1, to punish 1, to vex 1, wicked—wicked doer—to do wickedly 11, to deal worse—to do worse 4 ; Inf. intens. indeed (do evil) 1, still (do wickedly) 1 ; Hithpolel, to be broken down 1, to shew self friendly 1.

רָעַע Ch. *P'al*, to break 1, to bruise 1.

רָעַף *Kal*, to distil 1, to drop 2, to drop down 1; *Hiphil*, to drop down 1.

רָעַץ *Kal*, to dash in pieces 1, to vex 1.

רָעַשׁ *Kal*, to be moved 1, to quake 1, to remove 1, to shake 11, to tremble 8; *Niphal*, to be moved 1; *Hiphil*, to make afraid 1, to shake 4, to make to shake 1, to make to tremble 1.

רַעַשׁ commotion 1, confused noise 1, earthquake 6, fierceness 1, quaking 1, rattling 1, rushing 3, shaking 3.

רָפָא *Kal*, to cure 1, to heal 30, to be healed 1, physician 5, to make whole 1; *Niphal*, to be healed 16, to be made whole 1; *Piel*, to heal 6, to cause to be healed 1, to repair 1; *Inf. intens.* thoroughly (heal) 1; *Hithpael*, to be healed 3.

רָפָא giant 13, **Rephaim 4,** Rephaims 4.

רְפֻאוּת health 1.

רְפֻאוֹת healed 1, medicines 2.

רְפָאִים dead 7, deceased 1.

רָפַד *Kal*, to spread 1; *Piel*, to comfort 1, to make *a bed* 1.

רָפָה *Kal*, to be abated 1, to consume 1, to draw *toward evening* 1, to be faint 1, to be feeble 3, to wax feeble 3, to let go 1, to be slack 1, to be weak 1, to be weakened 1; *Niphal*, idle 3; *Piel*, to let down 2, to weaken 3; *Hiphil*, to cease 1, to fail 3, to forsake 2, to leave 1, to let alone 4, to let go 3, to give respite 1, to slack 1, to stay 3, to be still 1; *Hithpael*, to faint 1, to be slack 1, to be slothful 1.

רָפֶה giant 4.

רָפֶה weak 4.

רְפִידָה bottom 1.

רִפְיוֹן feebleness 1.

רָפַס *Hithpael*, to humble self 1, to submit self 1.

רְפַס Ch. *P'al*, to stamp 2.

רְפָסֹדוֹת flotes 1.

רָפַק *Hithpael*, to lean 1.

רָפַשׂ *Kal*, to foul 2; *Niphal*, troubled 1.

רֶפֶשׁ mire 1.

רְפָתִים stalls 1.

רַץ piece 1.

רָצָא *Kal*, to run 1.

רָצַד *Piel*, to leap 1.

רָצָה *Kal*, to accept 17, to be acceptable 1, to accomplish 1, to set affection 1, to approve 1, to consent with 1, to delight 4, to delight self 1, to enjoy 3, to have a favour 1, to be favourable 3, to like 1, (כ) to observe 1, to please 2, to be pleased with 4, to have pleasure 1, to take pleasure 5; *Niphal*, to be accepted 6, to be pardoned 1; *Piel*, to seek to please 1; *Hiphil*, to enjoy 1; *Hithpael*, to reconcile self 1.

רָצוֹן acceptable 8, acceptance 1, to be accepted 4, as.. would 1, delight 5, desire 3, favour 15, good pleasure 1, good will 2, own will 3, pleasure 4, self will 1, voluntary will 1, what would 1, will 5.

רָצַח *Kal*, to be put to death 1, to kill 6, man-slayer 2, to murder 13, to slay 18; *Niphal*, to be slain 2; *Piel*, to murder 4; *Pual*, to be slain 1.

רֶצַח slaughter 1, sword 1.

רָצַע *Kal*, to bore 1.

רָצַף *Kal*, being paved 1.

רֶצֶף baken on coals 1.

רִצְפָה live coal 1, pavement 7.

רָצַץ *Kal*, to be broken 3, bruised 2, to crush 2, to be discouraged 1, to oppress 3; *Niphal*, to break 1, to be broken 1; *Piel*, to break 1, to oppress 2; *Poel*, to oppress 1; *Hiphil*, to break 1; *Hithpolel*, to struggle together 1.

רַק lean 1, lean*fleshed* 1, thin 1.

רֹק to spit 1, spitting 1, spittle 1.

רָקַב *Kal*, to rot 2.

רָקָב rotten thing 1, rottenness 4.

רִקָּבוֹן rotten 1.

רָקַד *Kal*, to dance 1, to skip 2; *Piel*, to dance 3, to jump 1, to leap 1; *Hiphil*, to make to skip 1.

רַקָּה temples 5.

רָקַח *Kal*, apothecary 4, to compound 1, to make *ointment* 1; *Pual*, prepared 1; *Hiphil*, to spice 1.

רֶקַח spiced 1.

רֹקַח confection 1, ointment 1.

רַקָּח apothecary 1.

רַקֻּחָה confectionary 1.

רִקֻּחִים perfumes 1.

רָקִיעַ firmament 17.

רָקִיק cake 1, wafer 7.

רָקַם *Kal*, embroiderer 2, needlework 6; *Pual*, curiously wrought 1.

רִקְמָה broidered 2, broidered work 5, divers colours 2, needlework 1, needlework on both sides 1, raiment of needlework 1.

רָקַע *Kal*, to spread abroad 2, to spread forth 1, to stamp 2, to stretch out 1; *Piel*, to beat 1, to be made broad 1, to spread over 1; *Pual*, spread into plates 1; *Hiphil*, to spread out 1.

רְקֻעִים broad 1.

רָקַק *Kal*, to spit 1.

רִשְׁיוֹן grant 1.

רָשַׁם *Kal*, to be noted 1.

רְשַׁם Ch. *P'al*, to sign 4, to be signed 1, to be written 2.

רָשַׁע *Kal*, to be wicked 4, to deal wickedly 1, to wickedly depart 2, to do wickedly 1, to commit wickedness 1; *Hiphil*, to condemn 15, to make trouble 1, to vex 1, to do wickedly 7, to do wickedly against 1.

רָשָׁע guilty 1, ungodly 8, wicked *freq.*, that did wrong 1, ——condemned 1.

רֶשַׁע iniquity 1, wicked 4, wickedness 30.

רִשְׁעָה fault 1, wickedly 1, wickedness 13.

רֶשֶׁף arrow 1, burning coals 1, burning heat 1, coals 3, hot thunderbolts 1,——spark 1.

רָשַׁשׁ *Poel*, to impoverish 1; *Pual*, to be impoverished 1.

רֶשֶׁת net 20, net-work 2.

רַתּוֹק chain 1.

רַתּוּקָה chain 1.

רָתַח *Piel*, to make to boil 1; *Pual*, to boil 1; *Hiphil*, to make to boil 1.

——well (*to boil*) 1.

(כ) רַתִּיקָה chains 1.

רָתַם *Kal*, to bind 1.

רֹתֶם juniper 2, juniper tree 2.

רָתַק *Niphal*, to be loosed 1; *Pual*, to be bound 1.

רְתֻקוֹת chains 1.

רֶתֶת trembling 1.

שְׂאֹר leaven 4, leavened bread 1.

שְׂאֵת be accepted 1, dignity 1, excellency 2, highness 1, raise up self 1, raiseth up himself 1, rising 7.

שָׂבָךְ net 1.

שְׂבָכָה checker 1, lattice 1, network 7, snare 1, wreath 3, wreathen-work 2.

שַׂבְּכָא Ch. sackbut 3.

שָׂבַע & שָׂבֵעַ *Kal*, to have enough 3, to fill selves 1, to be filled 10, to be filled full 1, to be filled with 9, to be full 7, to be full of 6, to the full 1, to have plenty of 2, to be satiate 1, to be satisfied 30, to be satisfied with 7, to be sufficed 1, to be weary of 1; *Piel*, to satisfy 2; *Hiphil*, to fill 5, to satisfy 8, to satisfy with 2.

שֶׂבַע abundance 1, plenteous 2, plenteousness 1, plenty 4.

שָׂבֵעַ full 2, full of 6, satisfied 1, satisfied with 1.

שֹׂבַע fill 1, full 3, fulness 1, satisfying 1, to be sufficed 1.

שָׂבְעָה enough 1, to have enough 1, till...be full 1, to satisfy 1, sufficiently 1, unsatiable 1.

שִׂבְעָה fulness 1.

שָׂבַר *Kal*, to view 2; *Piel*, to hope 3, to tarry 1, to wait 2.

שֵׂבֶר hope 2.

שָׂנָא *Hiphil*, to increase 1, to magnify 1.

שְׂנָא Ch. *P'al*, to grow 1, to be multiplied 2.

שָׂנַב *Kal*, to be exalted 1, to be too strong 1; *Niphal*, to be exalted 4, to be excellent 1, to be high 3, lofty 1, to be safe 1; *Piel*, to defend 2, to set on high 2, to set up on high 1, to set up 1; *Pual*, to be safe 1; *Hiphil*, to exalt 1.

שָׂנָה *Kal*, to grow 2, to increase 1; *Hiphil*, to increase 1.

שַׂנִּיא excellent 1, great 1.

שַׂנִּיא Ch. exceeding 1, great 3, greatly 1, many 2, much 4, sore 1, very 1.

שָׂדַד *Piel*, to break the clods 2, to harrow 1.

שָׂדֶה country 17, field *freq.*, ground 4, land 10, soil 1, ——wild 8.

שָׂדַי field 13.

שְׂדֵרָה board 1, range 3.

שֶׂה cattle 8, lesser cattle 1, small cattle 1, ewe 1, goat 1, lamb 17, sheep 18.

שָׂהֵד record 1.

שָׂהֲדוּתָא Ch. *Jegar*-sahadutha 1.

שַׂהֲרֹנִים ornaments 2, round tires like the moon 1.

שׂוֹבֶךְ thick boughs 1.

שׂוּג *Niphal*, to turn back 1.

שׂוּג *Pilpel*, to make to grow 1.

שׂוּחַ *Kal*, to meditate 1.

שׂוּט *Kal*, to turn aside 1.

שׂוּךְ *Kal*, to make an hedge 1, to hedge up 1; *Polel*, to fence 1.

שׂוֹךְ bough 1.

שׂוֹכָה bough 1.

שׂוּם & שִׂים *Kal*, to appoint 19, to bring 5, to call (*a name*) 1, to cast in 1, to change 1, to charge 1, to commit 1, to consider 2, to convey 1, determined 1, to dispose 2, to do 2, to get 1, to give 11, to heap up 1, to hold 1, to impute 1, to be laid 1, to lay 64, to lay down 1, to lay up 3, to leave 1, to look 2, to be made 1, to make 122, to make out 1, to mark 2, to ordain 3, to order 2, to overturn 1, to place 1, to be placed 1, to preserve 1, to purpose 1, to put—to put in—to put on—to put to 183, to rehearse 1, to reward 1, to set—to cause to be set—to set on to set up 130, to shed 1, to shew 2, to take 3, to turn 5, to work 1,——care for 2, to consider 8, to disguise 1, to leave 1, to name 1, to paint 1, to regard 2, stedfastly 1, to tell 1, to tread down 1; *Inf. intens.* any wise (set) 1, wholly (set) 1; *Hiphil*, regarding 1,——on 1; *Hophal*, to be set 1.

שׂוּם Ch. *P'al*, to give 1, laid 1, to make 14, to set 1,——to command 3, to make 1, to regard 2; *Ithp'al*, to be given 1, to be laid 1, to be made 1.

שׂוּר *Kal*, to depart 1.

שׂוּר *Kal*, to have power 1, to reign 1; *Hiphil*, to make princes 1.

שׂוּר *Kal*, to cut 1.

שׂוֹרָה principal 1.

שׂוּשׂ & שִׂישׂ *Kal*, to be glad 4, greatly (rejoice) 1, to joy 1, to make mirth 1, to rejoice 21.

שֵׂחַ thought 1.

שָׂחָה *Kal*, to swim 2; *Hiphil*, to make to swim 1.

שָׂחוּ to swim in 1.

שְׂחוֹק derision 5, laughed to scorn 1, laughing 1, laughter 6, mocked 1, sport 1.

שָׂחַט *Kal*, to press 1.

שָׂחַק *Kal*, to deride 1, to have in derision 1, to laugh 10, to mock 2, to rejoice 1, to scorn 2, to make sport 1; *Piel*, that make merry 2, mocker 1, to rejoice 10, to be in sport 1, to make sport 1; *Hiphil*, to laugh to scorn 1.

שָׂט revolter 1.

שָׂטָה *Kal*, to decline 1, to go aside 4, to turn 1.

שָׂטַם *Kal*, to hate 5, to oppose self against 1.

שָׂטַן *Kal*, to be an adversary 5, to resist 1.

שָׂטָן adversary 7, Satan 19, to withstand 1.

שִׂטְנָה accusation 1.

שִׂיא excellency 1.

שִׂיב *Kal*, to be gray-headed 2.

שִׂיב Ch. *P'al*, elders 5.

שֵׂיב age 1.

שֵׂיבָה gray hairs 5, gray-headed 1, grey head 1, hoar hairs 1, hoar head 2, to be hoary 1, hoary head 2, old age 6.

שִׂיג pursu*ing* 1.

שִׂיד *Kal*, to plaister 2.

שִׂיד lime 2, plaister 2.

שִׂיחַ *Kal*, to commune 1, to complain 2, to meditate 5, to pray 1, to speak 4, to talk 4, to talk with 1; *Polel*, to declare 1, to muse 1.

שִׂיחַ bush 2, plant 1, shrubs 1.

שִׂיחַ babbling 1, communication 1, complaint 9, meditation 1, prayer 1, talk 1.

שִׂיחָה meditation 2, prayer 1.

שֵׂךְ pricks 1.

שַׂךְ tabernacle 1.

שֵׂכָּה barbed irons 1.

שֶׂכְוִי heart 1.

שְׂכִיָּה picture 1.

שַׂכִּין knife 1.

שָׂכִיר hired 2, hired men 1, hired servant 8, hireling 6.

שְׂכִירָה that is hired 1.

שָׂכַךְ *Kal*, cover 1.

שָׂכַל *Kal*, to behave self wisely 1; *Piel*, to guide wittingly 1; *Hiphil*, to consider 2, to consider wisely 2, expert 1, to have good success 1, to instruct 3, to be instructed 1, Maschil 13, to prosper 8, prudent 2, to deal prudently 1, skilful 1, skill 1, to give skill 1, to teach 2, to understand 14, to make to understand 1, to have understanding 2, wisdom—wise—to be wise—to make wise—wisely—to behave self wisely—to wisely consider 19.

שְׂכַל Ch. *Ithpael*, to consider 1.

שֵׂכֶל & שֶׂכֶל discretion 1, knowledge 1, policy 1, prudence 1, sense 1, understanding 7, wisdom 3, wise 1.

שִׂכְלוּת folly 1.

שָׂכְלְתָנוּ Ch. understanding 3.

שָׂכַר *Kal*, to hire 14, to reward 2; *Inf. intens.* surely (hire) 1; *Niphal*, to hire out selves 1; *Hithpael*, to earn wages 1.

שָׂכָר fare 1, hire 9, price 2, reward 1, reward*ed* 2, wages 6, worth 1.

שֶׂכֶר reward 1, sluice 1.

שָׂלָו or שְׂלָיו quails 4.

שַׂלְמָה clothes 3, garment 8, raiment 5.

שְׂמֹאול left 35, left hand 18, left side 1.

שְׂמֹאל *Hiphil*, left 1, to go to the left 1, to turn to the left 1,——on the left 1, to the left 1.

שְׂמֹאלִי left 9.

שָׂמַח & שָׂמֵחַ *Kal*, to be glad 34, to joy 2, to have joy 3, to be merry 1, to rejoice 84; *Piel*, to cheer 1, to cheer up 1, to make glad 11, to make joyful 2, to make merry 1, to rejoice 5, to cause to rejoice 1, to make to rejoice 4; *Inf. intens.* very (glad) 1; *Hiphil*, to make to rejoice 1.

שָׂמֵחַ glad 2, to be glad 2, joyful 3, merrily 1, merry 2, making merry 1, merry*hearted* 1, rejoice 5, rejoicing 1.

שִׂמְחָה glad 2, gladness 32, joy 44, joyfulness 1, mirth 8, pleasure 1, to r*e*joice 3, rejoicing 2,——exceeding 2, exceedingly 1.

שְׂמִיכָה mantle 1.

שִׂמְלָה apparel 2, cloth 2, clothes 6, clothing 2, garment 6, raiment 11.

שְׂמָמִית spider 1.

שָׂנֵא *Kal*, enemy 3, foe 1, to hate 119, to be hateful 1, odious 1; *Inf. intens.* utterly (hate) 2; *Niphal*, to be hated 2; *Piel*, to hate 15.

שְׂנֵא Ch. *P'al*, to hate 1.

שִׂנְאָה to hate 2, hatefully 1, hatred 13, —— exceedingly 1.

שָׂנִיא hated 1.

שָׂעִיר devil 2, goat *freq.*, hairy 2, kid 28, rough 1, satyr 2.

שְׂעִירָה kid 2.

שְׂעִירִם small rain 1.

שְׂעִפִּים thoughts 2.

שָׂעַר *Kal*, to be afraid 2, to be horribly afraid 1, to fear 1, to take away as with a whirlwind 1; *Niphal*, to be tempestuous 1; *Piel*, to hurl as a storm 1; *Hithpael*, to come like a whirlwind 1.

שַׂעַר storm 1,——affrighted 1, horribly 1, sore 1.

שֵׂעָר hair 1.

שֵׂעָר hair 24, hairy 2,——rough 1.

שְׂעַר Ch. hair 3.

שַׂעַר storm 1, tempest 1.

שְׂעָרָה hair 7.

שְׂעֹרָה barley 34.

שָׂפָה band 1, bank 10, binding 1, border 3, brim 8, brink 5, edge 8, language 7, lip *freq.*, prating 2, *seashore* 5, shore 1, side 3, speech 6, talk 1,——vain *words* 2.

שָׂפַח *Piel*, to smite with the scab 1.

שָׂפָם beard 1, upper lip 1, lips 3.

שָׂפַן Kal, treasures 1.

שָׂפַק Kal, to clap 1; Hiphil, to please selves 1.

שָׂפַק Kal, to suffice 1.

שֶׂפֶק stroke 1, sufficiency 1.

שַׂק sack 6, sackcloth 42.

שָׂקַד Niphal, to be bound 1.

שָׂקַר Piel, wanton 1.

שַׂר captain 125, chief captain 3, captain that had rule 1, chief 33, general 1, governor 6, keeper 3, lord 1, master 1, prince 208, principal 2, ruler 33, steward 1, taskmaster 1.

שָׂרַג Pual, to be wrapped together 1; Hithpael, to be wreathed 1.

שָׂרַד Kal, to remain 1.

שָׂרָד service 4.

שֶׂרֶד line 1.

שָׂרָה Kal, to have power as a prince 1, to have power 1.

שָׂרָה lady 2, princess 2, queen 1.

שְׂרוֹךְ latchet 1, shoelatchet 1.

שְׂרוּקִים principal plants 1.

שָׂרַט Kal, to make cuttings 1; Inf. intens.——pieces (cut in) 1; Niphal, to be cut in pieces 1.

שֶׂרֶט cuttings 1.

שָׂרֶטֶת cuttings 1.

שָׂרִיגִים branches 3.

שָׂרִיד to be left 3, remain 12, remaining 9, remnant 2, rest 1,——alive 1.

שָׂרִיק fine 1.

שָׂרַךְ Piel, traversing 1.

שָׂרַע Kal, to have any thing superfluous 1, thing superfluous 1; Hithpael, to stretch out self 1.

שַׂרְעַפִּים thoughts 2.

שָׂרַף Kal, to burn 98, to burn up 2, to cause to be burned 1, to kindle 1, to make a burning 1,——to be burnt 1; Inf. intens. utterly (burned) 1; Niphal, to be burnt 14; Pual, to be burnt 1.

שָׂרָף fiery 2, seraphims 2, fiery serpent 3.

שְׂרֵפָה burning 9, burnt 2,——to be burnt 1, throughly 1.

שָׂרַק speckled 1.

שֹׂרֵק choicest vine 1, noble vine 1.

שֹׂרֵקָה choice vine 1.

שָׂרַר Kal, to rule 2, to bear rule 1; Hithpael, to make self a prince 1; Inf. intens. altogether (make self a prince) 1.

שָׂשׂוֹן gladness 3, joy 15, mirth 3, rejoicing 1.

שָׂתַם Kal, to shut out 1.

שָׂתַר Niphal,—— to have in (one's) secret parts 1.

שָׁאַב Kal, to draw water 19.

שָׁאַג Kal, to roar 21; Inf. intens. mightily (roar) 1.

שְׁאָגָה roaring 7.

שָׁאָה Kal, to be wasted 1; Niphal, to be desolate 1, to rush 1, to make a rushing 1; Hiphil, to lay waste 2; Hithpael, wondering 1.

שָׁאֲוָה (כ') desolation 1.

שְׁאוֹל grave 31, hell 31, pit 3.

שָׁאוֹן noise 8, pomp 1, rushing 3, tumult 4,——horrible 1, tumultuous 2.

שְׁאָט despite 1, despiteful 2.

שְׁאִיָּה destruction 1.

שָׁאַל Kal, to ask 88, to ask counsel 5, to ask counsel 3, to ask on 1, to beg 1, to borrowed 1, to lay to charge 1, to consult 2, to demand 4, to desire 9, to enquire 22, to lent 2, to pray 1, to request 3, to require 1, to wish 1, wishing 1,——to borrow 1, to greet 1, to salute 5; Inf. intens. straitly (ask) 1, surely (ask) 1; Niphal, to ask leave 2, to obtain leave 1; Inf. intens. earnestly (ask) 1; Piel, ask counsel 1, to beg 1; Hiphil, to lend 2.

שָׁאֵל Ch. P'al, to ask 3, to demand 1, to require 2.

שְׁאֵלָא Ch. demand 1.

שְׁאֵלָה loan 1, petition 10, request 3.

שָׁאַן Pilel, to be at ease 2, to be quiet 2, to rest 1.

שַׁאֲנָן that is at ease 6, quiet 2, tumult 2.

שָׁאַף Kal, to desire 1, to earnestly desire 1, to devour 1, to haste 1, to pant 2, to snuff up 2, to swallow up 6.

שָׁאַר Kal, to remain 1; Niphal, to be left 43, to remain 45, remnant 4, the rest 2; Hiphil, to leave 32, to leave a remnant 1, to be left 1, to let 3, to reserve 1.

שְׁאָר other 1, remnant 11, residue 4, rest 10, Shear-jashub 1.

שְׁאָר Ch. whatsoever more 1, residue 2, rest 9.

שְׁאֵר body 1, flesh 7, food 1, kin 1, near kin 1, kinsman 1, near kinswoman 2, near of kin 1, nigh of kin 1.

שַׁאֲרָה near kinswoman 1.

שְׁאֵרִית that had escaped 1, be left 1, posterity 1, to remain 3, remainder 2, remnant 43, residue 13, rest 3.

שְׁאֵת desolation 1.

שְׁבָבִים broken in pieces 1.

שָׁבָה Kal, captive 3, to bring away captive 1, to carry away captive 5, to lead captive 3, to lead away captive 1, to take captive 5, to carry captive 3, to carry away 6, to carry away captive 6, to take away 1, to take captive 2, to take (prisoners) 1,——to carry captives 2; Niphal, to be carried away captive 1, to be taken captive 3, to be carried captives 3, to be driven away 1.

שְׁבוּ agate 2.

שָׁבוּעַ seven 1, week 19.

שְׁבוּעָה curse 1, oath 28,——sworn 1.

שְׁבוּת (כ') captivity 26.

שָׁבַח Piel, to commend 1, to keep in 1, to praise 5, to still 1; Hiphil, to still 1; Hithpael, to glory 1, to triumph 1.

שְׁבַח Ch. Pael, to praise 5.

שֵׁבֶט dart 1, pen 1, rod 34, sceptre 10, staff 2, tribe freq.,——correction 1.

שְׁבָט Sebat 1.

שְׁבַט Ch. tribe 1.

שְׁבִי captive 10, captivity 35, prisoners 2, that was taken 1,——to take away 1.

שָׁבִיב spark 1.

שְׁבִיב Ch. flame 2.

שִׁבְיָה captives 8, captivity 1.

שְׁבִיל path 2.

שְׂבִיסִים cauls 1.

שְׁבִיעִי seventh, seventh time.

שְׁבִית captives 1, captivity 6, (כ) captivity 7.

שֹׁבֶל leg 1.

שַׁבְּלוּל snail 1.

שִׁבֹּלֶת branch 1, channel 1, ears of corn 3, ears 11, flood 2, Shibboleth 1, waterflood 1.

שָׁבַע Kal, to swear 1; Niphal, to swear 154; Hiphil, to adjure 3, to charge 5, to charge by an oath 1, to charge with an oath 3, to take an oath (from another) 3, to swear (another) 2, to cause to swear 2, to make to swear 10,——to feed to the full 1; Inf. intens. straitly (swear) 2.

שֶׁבַע & שִׁבְעָה seven, seven times, sevenfold, seventeen, seventeenth, seventh, Shebah,—— by sevens.

שִׁבְעָה Ch. seven, seven times.

שִׁבְעִים seventy, threescore and fifteen, threescore and fourteen, threescore and seventeen, threescore and sixteen, threescore and ten, threescore and thirteen,——threescore and twelve.

שִׁבְעָנָה seven.

שִׁבְעָתַיִם (כ') seven, seven times, sevenfold.

שָׁבַץ Piel, to embroider 1; Pual, to be set 1.

שָׁבָץ anguish 1.

שְׁבַק Ch. P'al, to leave 3, to let alone 1; Ithpael, to be left 1.

שָׁבַר Kal, to break 46, to break up 1, to crush 1, to destroy 2, to quench 1, to tear 2; Niphal, to break 2, to be broken 45, to be broken down 1, to be broken off 1, brokenhearted 1, to be destroyed 7, to be hurt 2; Piel, to break 27, to break down 4, to break in pieces 5; Inf. intens. quite (break down) 1; Hiphil, bring to the birth 1; Hophal, to be hurt 1.

שָׁבַר Kal, to buy 14, to sell 1; Hiphil, to sell 5.

שֶׁבֶר & שֵׁבֶר affliction 2, breach 7, breaking 3, brokenfooted 1, brokenhanded 1, bruise 2, crashing 1, destruction 21, hurt 4, interpretation 1, vexation 1.

שֶׁבֶר corn 8, victuals 1.

שִׁבְּרוֹן breaking 1, destruction 1.

שְׁבַשׁ Ch. Ithpael, to be astonied 1.

שָׁבַת Kal, to cease 14, to celebrate 1, to keep 1, to rest 10, to keep sabbath 1; Niphal, to cease 4; Hiphil, to cause to cease 18, to let cease 1, to make to cease 10, to cause to fail 1, to make to fail 1, to suffer to be lacking 1, to leave 1, to put away 2, to put down 1, to make to rest 1, to rid 1, to still 1, to take away 1.

שֶׁבֶת to cease 1, to sit still 1, loss of time 1.

שַׁבָּת sabbath 107,——sabbath 1, every sabbath 3.

שַׁבָּתוֹן rest 8, sabbath 3.

שָׁגַג Kal, deceived 1, to err 1, to go astray 1, to sin ignorantly 1.

שְׁגָגָה error 2, ignorance 12, at unawares 4, unwittingly 1.

שָׁגָה Kal, to be deceived 1, to err 11, to go astray 1, to sin through ignorance 1, to wander 1,——to be ravished 2; Hiphil, deceiver 1, to cause to go astray 1, to let wander 1, to make to wander 1.

שָׁגַח Hiphil, to look 2, to narrowly look 1.

שְׁגִיאוֹת errors 1.

שִׁגָּיוֹן Shiggaion 1, Shigionoth 1.

שָׁגַל Kal, (כ) to lie with 1; Niphal, (כ) to be ravished 2; Pual, (כ) to be lien with 1.

שֵׁגָל queen 2.

שֵׁגָל Ch. wife 2.

שָׁגַע Pual, mad 4, mad man 1; Hithpael, to be mad 1, to play the mad man 1.

שִׁגָּעוֹן furiously 1, madness 2.

שֶׂגֶר that cometh of 1, increase 4.

שַׁד breast 18, pap 1, teat 1.

שֵׁד devil 2.

שֹׁד breast 3.

שֹׁד desolation 2, destruction 7, oppression 1, robbery 2, spoil—to spoil—spoiled—spoiler—spoiling 11, wasting 2.

שָׁדַד Kal, dead 1, destroy 1, to be destroyed 1, destroyer 1, to oppress 1, robber 2, to spoil 22; Inf. intens. utterly (spoiled) 1; Niphal, to be spoiled 1; Piel, to spoil 1, to waste 1; Pual, to be laid waste 5, to be spoiled 13, to be wasted 2; Poel, to spoil 1; Hophal, to be spoiled 2.

שִׁדָּה musical instrument 1,——all sorts (of musical instruments).

שַׁדַּי Almighty 48.

שְׁדֵמָה blasted 1.

שְׁדֵמָה field 5.

שָׁדַף Kal, blasted 3.

שְׁדֵפָה blasted 1.

שִׁדָּפוֹן blasting 5.

שְׁדַר Ch. Ithpael, to labour 1.

שֹׁהַם onyx 11.

שָׁו (כ) vanity 1.

שׁוֹא destruction 1.

שָׁוְא false 5, falsely 1, lie 1, lying 2, vain 22, vanity 22.

שׁוֹאָה desolate 2, desolation 7, to destroy 1, destruction 2, storm 1, wasteness 1.

שׁוּב Kal, to (do anything) again 2, averse 1, (כ) to bring 1, to bring again 12, to bring back 3, to cease 1, to come again—to become again 16, to come back 3, to convert 1, to be converted 1, converts 1, to get (oneself) again 1, to get (oneself) back again 1, to go again 13, to go back 8, to go home 1, to go out 2, to be gone back 2, Jashub 1, to see no more 1, to be past 1, (כ) to be rendered 1, to repent 3, to be restored—to be restored again 4, to retire 1, to return—to return again—(כ) to cause to return—to be returned 371, to reverse 3, (כ) to reward 1, Shear-jashub 1, to turn—to turn again—to turn away—to turn back—to turn back again—to turn backward—to turn from—to be turned—to be turned away—to be turned back—turning 181,——again 29, continually 1; Inf. intens. in any wise (go back) 1, at all (turn) 2, certainly (return) 2, still (in returning) 159, to and fro (went) 1; Polel, to bring again 3, to pervert 1, to restore 1, restorer 1, to slide back 1, to turn away 1, to turn back 2, to turn self again 1, turning away 1; Pulal, to be brought back 1; Hiphil, to answer 1, to cause to return 1, to bring 9, to bring again 68, to bring back 13, to bring back again 1, to bring home 3, to bring home again 2, to call to mind 1, to carry again 3, to carry back 3, to convert 1, to deliver 1, to deliver again 4, to draw back 2, to draw back 1, to fetch home again 1, to give 2, to give again 2, to hinder 2, to let 1, to pull in again 1, to put —to put again—to put up again 6, to recall 1, to recompense 7, to recover 6, to refresh 1, to relieve 3, to render—to render again—to be rendered 20, to report 1, to requite 5, to rescue 1, to restore—to restore again 39, to return—to cause to return—causing to return—to make to return 36, to reverse 3, to reward 3, to send back 1, to set again 1, to take 1, to take back 1, to take off 1, to turn—to turn away—to be turned—to turn back—to cause to turn—to make to turn 59, to withdraw 4,——again 1, to answer 5, to answer again 2, to bethink 2, to consider 9, to deny 1, to pay 1, to say nay 3; Inf. intens. in any case (bring again) 1, in any case (deliver) 1, in any wise (return) 1, certainly (requite) 1, needs (bring) 1, surely (bring) 1; Hophal, to be brought again 3, to be recompensed 1, to be restored 1.

שׁוֹבָב backsliding 2, frowardly 1, (כ) turn away 1.

שׁוֹבֵב backsliding 2.

שׁוּבָה returning 1.

שׁוּד Kal, to waste 1.

שָׁוָה Kal, to avail 1, to be compared 2, to countervail 1, to be equal 1, to be like 1, profit 1, to profit 1; Piel, to behave 1, to bring forth 1, to lay 3, to make like 2, to make plain 1, to reckon 1, to set 1; Hiphil, to equal 1, to make equal 1, Nithpael, to be alike 1.

שָׁוָה Piel,——(כ) substance 1.

שְׁוָה Ch. Pael, to be made like 1; Ithpael, to be made 1.

שׁוּחַ Kal, to be bowed down 1, to incline 1; Hiphil, to be humbled 1.

שׁוּחָה ditch 1, pit 4.

שׁוּט Kal, to despise 3.

שׁוּט Kal, to go 1, to go about 1, to go through 1, going to or fro 2, mariner 1, rower 1; Polel, to run to and fro 5; Hithpolel, to run to and fro 1.

שׁוֹט scourge 5, whip 6.

שׁוּל hem 6, skirt 4, train 1.

שׁוֹלָל spoiled 2, stripped 1.

שׁוּם garlick 1.

שָׁוַע Piel, to cry 17, to cry aloud 1, to cry out 2, to shout 1.

שׁוֹעַ bountiful 1, crying 1, rich 1.

שׁוּעַ crying 1, riches 1.

שֶׁוַע cry 1.

שַׁוְעָה cry 11.

שׁוּעָל fox 7.

שׁוֹעֵר doorkeeper 2, porter 35.

שׁוּף Kal, to break 1, to bruise 2, to cover 1.

שׁוֹפָר cornet 4, trumpet 68.

שׁוֹק hip 1, leg 4, shoulder 13, thigh 1.

שָׁקַק Polel, to water 1; Hiphil, to overflow 2.

שׁוּק street 4.

שׁוֹר bull 1, bullock 12, cow 2, ox 61,——wall 1.

שִׁיר Kal, to go 1, to sing 1.

שׁוּר Kal, to behold 5, to lay wait 1, to look 2, to observe 2, to perceive 1, to regard 1, to see 4.

שׁוּר enemies 1.

שׁוּר wall 4.

שׁוּר Ch. wall 3.

שׁוֹשָׁן lily 8, Shoshannim 2, Shoshannim-Eduth 1.

שׁוּשַׁן lily 1, Shushan-Eduth 1.

שׁוֹשַׁנָּה lily 4.

שֵׁיזַב Ch. Peel or Peil, to deliver 9.

שָׁזַף Kal, to look upon 1, to see 2.

שָׁזַר Hophal, twined 21.

שַׁח ——humble 1.

שָׁחַד Kal, to hire 1, to give reward 1.

שֹׁחַד bribe 3, bribery 1, gift 10, present 4, reward 7.

שָׁחָה Kal, to bow down 1; Hiphil, to make to stoop 1; Hithpael, to humbly beseech 1, to bow down 8, to bow down self 8, to bow self 35, to crouch 1, to fall down 3, to fall flat 1, to do obeisance 5, to make obeisance 4, to do reverence 5, to worship 99.

safely 4, salute 1, welfare 5, well
—be well 14,—— do 5, fare
1, friend 1, to greet 1, perfect
peace 1, to salute 6, all is well
1, wholly 1.

שִׁלּוּם recompence 2, reward 1.

שְׁלוֹשָׁה & שָׁלֹשׁ third, thirteen,
thirteenth,three,
——fork 1, oftentimes 1, thrice 4.

שְׁלוֹשִׁים thirtieth, thirty.

שָׁלַח Kal, to appoint 1, to give
1, to lay 13, to let go 1,
let loose 1, to put—to put forth
—to put in—putting forth—to
put out 37, to send—to send
again—to send away—to send
forth—to send out—sending—
sent 493, to shoot out 1, to
stretch forth—to stretch out 13 ;
Inf. intens. earnestly (send) 1 ;
Niphal, to be sent 1 ; Piel, to
bring 1, to bring on the way 1,
to cast 5, to cast away 1, to cast
out 6, to conduct 1, depart 4,
to give up 1, to grow long 1, to
lay 1, to let depart 2, to let
down 2, to let go 74, to let go
away 2, to let loose 2, to push
away 1, to put away—to put in
—to put out 1, to reach forth 1,
to send—to send away—to send
forth—to send out 137, to set 5,
to shoot—to shoot forth 4, to
sow 3, to spread out 1 ; Inf. intens. any wise (let go) 2 ; Pual,
to be cast 1, cast out 1, forsaken
1, left 1, to be put away 1, to
be sent 4, to be sent away 1 ;
Hiphil, to send 5.

שְׁלַח Ch. P'al, to put 1, to send
12, to be sent 1.

שֶׁלַח dart 1, plant 1, sword 3,
weapon 2,——put off 1.

שִׁלֻּחֹת branches 1.

שֻׁלְחָן table 70.

שָׁלַט Kal, to have power 1, to
rule 1, to bear rule 1, to
have rule 2 ; Hiphil, to have
dominion 2, to give power 2.

שְׁלֵט Ch. P'al, to have the
mastery 1, to have power
1, to bear rule 1, to be ruler 2 ;
Aphel, to make ruler 2.

שֶׁלֶט shield 7.

שִׁלְטוֹן power 2.

שִׁלְטוֹן Ch. ruler 2.

שָׁלְטָן Ch. dominion 14.

שַׁלֶּטֶת imperious 1.

שְׁלִי quietly 1.

שִׁלְיָה young one 1.

שַׁלִּיט governor 1, mighty 1, that
hath power 1, ruler 1.

שַׁלִּיט Ch. captain 1, to be lawful 1, to rule 6, ruler 2.

שָׁלִישׁ captain 11, excellent things
1, great lord 1, great measure 1, instrument of music 1,
lord 3, measure 2, prince 1.

שְׁלִישִׁי third, third part, third
rank, third time, ('כ)
three, three years old 4.

שָׁלַךְ Hiphil, to adventure 1, to
cast 72, to cast away 10,
to cast down 9, to cast forth 4,
to cast off 2, to cast out 9, to
cast (lots) 2, to hurl 1, to pluck
1, to throw 1 ; Hophal, cast 2,
to be cast 4, to be cast down 2,
to be cast out 4, to be thrown 1.

שָׁלָךְ cormorant 2.

שַׁלֶּכֶת when cast 1.

שָׁלַל Kal, to let fall 1, to spoil
6, to make a spoil 1, to
take spoil 5 ; Inf. intens. of purpose (let fall) 1 ; Hithpolel, to make
self a prey 1, to be spoiled 1.

שָׁלָל Maher-shalal-hash-baz 2,
prey 10, spoil 63.

שָׁלֵם Kal, to be ended 2, to be
finished 2, to be at peace
1, to be at peace with 1, peaceable 1, to prosper 1 ; Piel, to
make amends 1, to finish 1, full
2, to give again 1, to make good
6, to pay 20, to pay again 1, to
perform 3, to make prosperous 1,
to recompense 9, to render 9, to
repay 5, to be repayed 2, to requite 5, to make restitution 6,
to restore 8, to reward 9 ; Inf.
intens. full (make restitution) 1,
surely (make good) 1, surely (requite) 1, surely (pay) 1 ; Pual,
that is perfect 1, to be performed
1, to be recompensed 2, to be
rewarded 1 ; Hiphil, to make an
end 2, to make peace 7, to make
to be at peace 1, perform 3 ; Hophal, to be at peace 1.

שְׁלֵם Ch. P'al, to be finished 1 ;
Aphel, to deliver 1, to
finish 1.

שְׁלָם Ch. peace 4.

שָׁלֵם full 2, just 1, made ready
1, peaceable 1, perfect 16,
perfected 1, quiet 1, whole 4.

שֶׁלֶם peace-offering freq., peace
(offering) 2.

שִׁלֵּם recompense 1.

שִׁלְמָה reward 1.

שִׁלְמֹנִים rewards 1.

שָׁלַף Kal, to draw 21, to draw
off 1, to be drawn 1, to
grow up 1, to pluck off 1.

שִׁלֵּשׁ Piel, to do the third time
2, to stay three days 1, to
divide into three parts 1 ; Pual,
three 1, three years old 3, three-
fold 1.

שָׁלִישׁ ('כ) excellent things 1,
three days 1,——before-
time 4, time past 8.

שְׁלִישִׁים third 5.

שֵׁם fame 4, famous 4, infamous
1, name very freq., renown
7, report 1,——base 1.

שֻׁם Ch. name 11, (to) name 1.

שָׁמַד Niphal, to be destroyed 19,
to be overthrown 1, to
perish 1 ; Inf. intens. utterly (destroyed) 1 ; Hiphil, to destroy
66, to bring to nought 1, pluck
down 1 ; Inf. intens. utterly (destroy) 1.

שְׁמַד Ch. Aphel, to consume 1.

שַׁמָּה astonishment 13, desolate
10, desolation 12, waste 3,
wonderful thing 1.

שְׁמוּעָה bruit 1, doctrine 1, fame
2, mentioned 1, news 1,
report 4, rumour 9, tidings 8.

שָׁמַט Kal, to discontinue 1, to
release 1, to let rest 1, to
shake 1, to stumble 1, to throw
down 2 ; Niphal, to be overthrown 1 ; Hiphil, to release 1.

שְׁמִטָּה release 5.

שָׁמַיִם air 21, heaven very freq.,
——astrologers 1.

שְׁמַיִן Ch. heaven 38.

שְׁמִינִי eighth, Sheminith 3.

שָׁמִיר adamant 1, adamant stone
1, briers 8, diamond 1.

שָׁמֵם Kal, to be astonied 1, to
be astonished 11, to be an
astonishment 1, to be desolate
13, to be laid desolate 1, to make
desolate 2, desolate places 1, desolation 5,—— to destroy 1 ; Niphal, to be astonied 1, to be
astonished 11, to be desolate 17,
to be laid desolate 1, to be made
desolate 1, to be destitute 1,
waste 1, to lie waste 1 ; Polel,
astonied 2, to make desolate 2 ;
Hiphil, to make amazed 1, astonished 1, to make desolate 7, to
bring into desolation 1, to bring
unto desolation 1, to destroy 1,
to make desolate 1, to lay waste
2, to make waste 1 ; Hophal, to
be astonished 1, to lie desolate 4 ;

Hithpolel, to be astonished 1, to
be desolate 1, to destroy self 1,
to wonder 2.

שְׁמֵם Ch. Ithpolel, to be astonied 1.

שָׁמֵם desolate 2.

שְׁמָמָה desolate 40, ('כ) laid desolate 1, utterly desolate 1,
desolation 13, waste 1.

שִׁמָּמָה desolation 1, most desolate 1.

שִׁמָּמוֹן astonishment 2.

שָׁמַן Kal, to wax fat 1, to be
waxen fat 2 ; Hiphil, to become fat 1, to make fat 1.

שָׁמֵן fat 8, lusty 1, plenteous 1.

שֶׁמֶן anointing 1, fatness 1, oil
freq., oiled 2, ointment 13,
olive 4,——fat 2, fat thing 2,
fruitful 1, pine 1.

שְׁמֹנָה & שְׁמֹנֶה eight, eighteen,
eighteenth,eighth.

שְׁמֹנִים eightieth, eighty, four-
score.

שָׁמַע & שֵׁמַע Kal, to consent 1,
to consider 1, to
be content 1, to discern 2, to
give ear 1 to hear 731, to hear
tell 1, to hearken 196, to listen
1, to be obedient 6, to obey 81,
to perceive 1, to regard 1, to
understand 9, whosoever heareth
1, witness 1 ; Inf. intens attentively (hear) 1, carefully (hearken)
1, certainly (heard) 1, diligently
(hear) 2, diligently (hearken) 4,
diligently (obey) 1, indeed (hear)
1, indeed (obey) 2, surely (hear)
1 ; Niphal, to be heard 36, to be
obedient 1, to obey 1, to be per-
ceived 1, to be published 1, to
be reported 2 ; Piel, to call together 1, to gather together 1 ; Hiphil, to call together 2, to declare 3, to hear 2, to cause to
hear 5, to let hear 1, to make
to hear 4, to cause to be heard
6, to let be heard 1, to make to
be heard 3, to make noise 1, to
make a noise 1, to proclaim 1,
to make a proclamation 1, to
publish 16, to shew 6, to shew
forth 7, to sound 2, to make a
sound 2, to tell 4,——to sing
loud 1.

שְׁמַע Ch. P'al, to hear 8 ; Ith-
puel, to obey 1.

שֵׁמַע bruit 1, fame 5, hear 2,
hearing 1, loud 1, report
5, speech 1, tidings 2.

שֹׁמַע fame 4.

שֶׁמֶץ a little 2.

שִׁמְצָה shame 1.

שַׁקְעֲרוּרֹת hollow strakes 1.

שָׁקַף Niphal, to appear 1, to look 7, to look down 1, to look forth 1; Hiphil, to look 4, to look down 5, to look out 3.

שֶׁקֶף windows 1.

שְׁקֻפִים windows 1,—— narrow lights 1.

שָׁקַץ Piel, to abhor 1, to make abominable 2, to have in abomination 2, to detest 1; Inf. intens. utterly (detest) 1.

שֶׁקֶץ abominable 2, abomination 9.

שָׁקַק Kal, to have appetite 1, to long 1, to range 1, to run 1, to run to and fro 1; Hithpalpel, to justle one against another 1.

שָׁקַר Kal, to deal falsely 1; Piel, to fail 1, to deal falsely 1, to lie 3.

שֶׁקֶר without a cause 1, deceit 1, deceitful 2, false 21, falsehood 12, falsely 13, feignedly 1, liar 1, lie 28, lying 22, vain—vain thing 6, wrongful 4,—— lie 1, lying 1.

שֹׁקֶת trough 2.

שֹׁר navel 2.

שְׁרָא Ch. P'al, to dissolve 1, to dwell 1, loose 1; Pael, to begin 1, to dissolve 1; Ithpael, to be loosed 1.

שָׁרָב heat 1, parched ground 1.

שַׁרְבִיט sceptre 4.

שָׁרָה Kal, to direct 1; Piel,—— (ק) remnant 1.

שְׁרוּקֹת (כ') hissing 1.

שֵׁרוֹת walls 1.

שֵׁרוֹת bracelets 5.

שְׁרוּת (כ') remnant 1.

שִׁרְיָה habergeon 1.

שִׁרְיוֹן coat of mail 1, coat of mail 1, habergeons 2.

שִׁרְיָן breastplate 1, harness 2.

שְׁרִיקוֹת bleatings 1, (ק) hissing 1.

שָׁרִיר navel 1.

שְׁרִירוּת imagination 9, lust 1.

שְׁרֵמוֹת (כ') fields 1.

שָׁרַץ Kal, to breed abundantly 1, to bring forth abundantly 4, to bring forth in abundance 1, to creep 6, to increase abundantly 1, to move 1.

שֶׁרֶץ creep 1, creeping thing 11, move 1, moving creature 1.

שָׁרַק Kal, hiss 12.

שְׁרֵקָה hissing 7.

שָׁרַר Kal, enemies 4.

שֹׁרֶר navel 1.

שֵׁרֵשׁ Piel, to root out 2; Pual, to be rooted out 1; Poel, to take root 1; Poal, to take root 1; Hiphil, to cause to take root 2, to take root 1.

שֹׁרֶשׁ root 31,——bottom 1, deep 1, heel 1.

שֹׁרֶשׁ Ch. roots 3.

שַׁרְשְׁרָה chain 1.

שֵׁרֹשִׁי (ק) שְׁרֹשׁוּ (כ') Ch. banishment 1.

שַׁרְשְׁרָה chain 7.

שֵׁרֵת Piel, to minister 62, to minister to 1, to minister unto 17, servant 5, to serve 8, to do service 3, servitor 1, to wait on 1.

שָׁרֵת minister 1, ministry 1.

שֵׁשׁ fine linen 21, fine twined linen 16, marble 2, silk 1,——blue 1.

שֵׁשׁ & שִׁשָּׁה six freq., sixteen, sixteenth, sixth.

שִׁשָּׁא Piel, to leave but the sixth part 1.

שִׁשָּׁה Piel, to give the sixth part 1.

שִׁשִּׁי (כ') fine linen 1.

שִׁשִּׁי sixth, sixth part.

שִׁשִּׁים sixty, threescore.

שָׁשַׁר vermilion 2.

שָׁת foundation 1, purpose 1.

שֵׁת buttocks 2.

שֵׁת & שָׁת Ch. six, sixth.

שָׁתָה Kal, to banquet 1, to drink 210,—— drunkard 1; Inf. intens. assuredly (drunken) 1, certainly (drunk) 1, surely (drunk) 1; Niphal, to be drunk 1.

שְׁתָה Ch. P'al, to drink 5.

שְׁתִי drunkenness 1, warp 9.

שְׁתִיָּה drinking 1.

שְׁתִין Ch. threescore 5.

שָׁתַל Kal, to plant 10.

שְׁתַל plant 1.

שָׁתַם Kal,——to be open 2.

שָׁתַן Hiphil, to piss 6.

שָׁתַק Kal, to be calm 2, to cease 1, to be quiet 1.

שָׁתַת Kal, to be laid 1, to set 1.

תָּא chamber 2, little chamber 10.

תָּאַב Kal, to long 2.

תָּאַב Piel, to abhor 1.

תַּאֲבָה longing 1.

תָּאָה Piel, to point out 3.

תְּאוֹ wild ox 1.

תַּאֲוָה utmost bound 1, dainty 1, desire 14, Kibroth-hattaavah 5, lust 1, lusting 1, pleasant 1,——exceedingly 1, greedily 1.

תְּאוֹמִים twins 4.

תַּאֲלָה curse 1.

תָּאַם Kal, coupled 1, coupled together 1; Hiphil, to bear twins 2.

תְּאֵנָה occasion 1.

תְּאֵנָה fig 15, fig-tree 23.

תְּאֵנָה occasion 1.

תַּאֲנִיָּה heaviness 1, mourning 1.

תַּאֲנִים lies 1.

תָּאַר Kal, to be drawn 5; Piel, to mark out 2.

תֹּאַר countenance 1, form 3, goodly 1, visage 1,——beautiful 2, comely 1, fair 1, favoured 2, goodly 2, resemble 1.

תְּאַשּׁוּר box 1, box-tree 1.

תֵּבָה ark 28.

תְּבוּאָה fruit 13, gain 1, increase 23, revenue 5.

תָּבֻן understanding 1.

תְּבוּנָה discretion 1, reason 1, skilfulness 1, understanding 37, wisdom 1.

תְּבוּסָה destruction 1.

תֵּבֵל habitable part 1, world 35.

תֵּבֵל confusion 2.

תַּבְלִית destruction 1.

תְּבַלֻּל blemish 1.

תֶּבֶן chaff 1, straw 15, stubble 1.

תַּבְנִית figure 1, form 3, likeness 5, pattern 9, similitude 2.

תַּבְעֵרָה ——Taberah 2.

תְּבַר Ch. P'al, broken 1.

תַּנְמוּל benefit 1.

תִּגְרָה blow 1.

תִּדְהָר pine 1, pine-tree 1.

תְּדִירָא Ch. continually 2.

תֹּהוּ confusion 3, empty place 1, without form 2, nothing 1, nought 1, thing of nought 1, vain 4, vanity 4, waste 1, wilderness 2.

תְּהוֹם deep 20, deep place 1, depth 15.

תְּהִלָּה praise 56.

תִּהֲלָה folly 1.

תַּהֲלֻכָה ——go 1.

תַּהְפֻּכוֹת froward 3, froward things 2, very froward 1, frowardness 3, perverse things 1.

תָּו desire 1, mark 2.

תּוֹא wild bull 1.

תּוּב Ch. P'al, to return 3; Aphel, to answer 2, to be restored 1, to return 2, to return an answer 1.

תּוּבְנָה (כ') understanding 1.

תּוּגָה heaviness 3, sorrow 1.

תּוֹדָה confession 2, praise 4, sacrifice of praise 2, thank-offering 3, companies of them that give thanks 3, thanksgiving 18.

תְּוָה Ch. P'al, to be astonied 1.

תָּוָה Piel, to scrabble 1; Hiphil, to limit 1, to set a mark 1.

תּוֹחֶלֶת hope 6.

תָּוֶךְ between, half 1, middle 7, midnight 1, midst freq., midst among 1, within.

תּוֹכֵחָה punishment 1, rebuke 4.

תּוֹכַחַת argument 1, correction 1, reasoning 1, rebuke 3, reproof 16,——chastened 1, be reproved 1, often reproved 1.

תּוֹלֵדוֹת birth 1, generations 38.

תּוֹלֵל that wasted 1.

תּוֹלָע crimson 1, scarlet 1, worms 1.

תּוֹלַעַת & תּוֹלָע worm 6,——scarlet 33.

תַּעֲנִית heaviness 1.

תָּעַע Pilpel, deceiver 1 ; Hith-palpel, to misuse 1.

תַּעֲצֻמוֹת power 1.

תַּעַר penknife 1, rasor 4, scab-bard 1, shave 1, sheath 6.

תַּעֲרֻבוֹת ——hostages 2.

תַּעְתֻּעִים errors 2.

תֹּף tabret 8, timbrel 9.

תִּפְאֶרֶת & תִּפְאָרָה beautiful 6, beauty 10, bravery 1, comely 1, excellent (majesty) 1, fair 2, glorious 3, glory 22, honour 4.

תַּפּוּחַ apple 3, apple-tree 3.

תְּפוֹצָה dispersion 1.

תְּפִינִים baken (pieces) 1.

תָּפֵל foolish things 1, unsavoury 1, untempered 5.

תִּפְלָה folly 2, foolishly 1.

תְּפִלָּה prayer 76.

תִּפְלֶצֶת terribleness 1.

תָּפַף Kal, to play with timbrels 1 ; Poel, to taber 1.

תָּפַר Kal, to sew 2, to sew to-gether 1 ; Piel, women that sew 1.

תָּפַשׂ Kal, to catch 3, to handle 8, to be handled 1, to hold 1, laid over 1, to lay hold on 3, to take 29, to take hold 2 ; Inf. intens. surely (be taken) 1 ; Ni-phal, to be caught 1, to be stopped 1, to be surprised 2, to be taken 11, —— taking 1 ; Piel, to take hold 1.

תֹּפֶת tabret 1.

תִּפְתָּיֵא Ch. sheriffs 2.

תִּקְוָה expectation 7, expected 1, hope 23, line 2, thing that I long for 1.

תְּקוּמָה power to stand 1.

תְּקוֹמֵם rise up against 1.

תָּקוֹעַ trumpet 1.

תְּקוּפָה circuit 1, come about 1, end 2.

תַּקִּיף mightier 1.

תַּקִּיף Ch. mighty 2, strong 3.

תְּקַל Ch. P'al, Tekel 2 ; P'il, to be weighed 1.

תָּקַן Kal, to be made straight 1 ; Piel, to set in order 1, to make straight 1.

תְּקַן Ch. Hophal, to be esta-blished 1.

תָּקַע Kal, to blow a trumpet 46, to cast 1, to clap 2, to fasten 5, to pitch tent 3, to smite 1, to sound 2, to strike

3, to thrust 2, ——suretyship 1 ; Niphal, to be blown 2, to strike 1.

תֶּקַע sound 1.

תָּקַף Kal, to prevail against 3.

תְּקַף Ch. P'al, to be hardened 1, to be strong 2, to become strong 1 ; Pael, to make firm 1.

תְּקָף authority 1, power 1, strength 1.

תְּקָף Ch. might 1, strength 1.

תַּרְבּוּת increase 1.

תַּרְבִּית increase 5, unjust gain 1.

תֻּרְגַּם interpreted 1.

תַּרְדֵּמָה deep sleep 7.

תְּרוּמָה gift 1, heave-offering 24, heave shoulder 4, obla-tion 18, offered 1, offering 28.

תְּרוּמִיָּה oblation 1.

תְּרוּעָה alarm 6, blow 1, blowing of trumpets 1, blowing the trumpets 1, joy 2, jubile 1, loud noise 1, rejoicing 1, shout 10, to shout 1, shouting 8, joy-ful sound 1, sounding 1, high sounding 1.

תְּרוּפָה medicine 1.

תִּרְזָה cypress 1.

תְּרֵין Ch. second, two, ——twelve.

תָּרְמָה privily 1.

תַּרְמוּת (כ) deceit 1.

תַּרְמִית deceit 4, deceitful 1.

תֹּרֶן beacon 1, mast 2.

תְּרַע Ch. gate 1, mouth 1.

תָּרָע Ch. porter 1.

תַּרְעֵלָה astonishment 1, trem-bling 2.

תְּרָפִים idolatry 1, idols 1, images 7, teraphim 6.

תַּרְשִׁישׁ beryl 7.

תִּרְשָׁתָא Tirshatha 5.

תְּשׂוּמֶת fellowship 1.

תְּשֻׁאוֹת crying 1, noise 1, shout-ings 1, stirs 1.

תַּשְׁבֵּץ broidered 1.

תְּשׁוּבָה answer 2, be expired 3, return 3.

תְּשׁוּעָה deliverance 5, help 5, safety 4, salvation 17, victory 2.

תְּשׁוּקָה desire 3.

תְּשׁוּרָה present 1.

תְּשִׁיעִי ninth.

תֵּשַׁע & תִּשְׁעָה nine, nineteen, nineteenth, ninth.

תִּשְׁעִים ninety.

APPENDIX

EXAMPLES OF THE FIGURE PARONOMASIA

*** This figure occurs frequently in the poetical books of the Sacred Scriptures, as in all Oriental writings. It is found also in the New Testament, and in some of the best classical authors. Grammarians describe it as a play upon words; but this should not lead us to think lightly of its use, since it has evidently been adopted to give point to a sentence or to assist the memory. The best hermeneutical writers have been careful to call the reader's attention to the use of this figure, and to the emphasis frequently given by it to certain words and phrases. It has therefore been thought desirable to subjoin the following examples, taken chiefly from a learned dissertation by Jo. Christoph. Decker, who points out the importance, in an exegetical point of view, of attention to this figure, not only in the correct interpretation of words, but, in some cases, as to the correct reading. The figure consists in the use of words similar in sound, sometimes synonymous in signification, sometimes of contrary meaning. Not seldom unusual words are introduced and formed for the sake of a more striking contrast. The reader is requested to consult the body of this work to obtain a more distinct idea of the force and meaning of words used in this figure of speech.

Gen. ix. 6.—Whoso sheddeth man's הָאָדָם blood, by man בָּאָדָם shall his blood be shed; for in the image of God made he man אֶת־הָאָדָם.

27.—God shall enlarge יַפְתְּ Japhet לְיֶפֶת.

xviii. 27.—Behold now I have taken upon me to speak unto the Lord, which *am but* dust עָפָר and ashes וָאֵפֶר.

xxvii. 36.—Is not he rightly named Jacob יַעֲקֹב? for he hath supplanted me וַיַּעְקְבֵנִי these two times.

xxix. 34.—And she conceived again, and bare a son; and said, Now this time will my husband be joined יִלָּוֶה unto me, because I have born him three sons: therefore was his name called Levi לֵוִי.

35.—And she conceived again, and bare a son; and she said, Now will I praise אוֹדֶה the LORD: therefore she called his name Judah יְהוּדָה.

xxxi. 20.—And Jacob stole away unawares to Laban: *lit.* stole away, or deceived, the heart לֵב of Laban לָבָן.

52.—This heap *be* witness עֵד, and *this* pillar *be* witness עֵדָה.

xxxii. 24.—And Jacob was left alone; and there wrestled וַיֵּאָבֵק a man with him.

       "An unusual word appears to have been used by the sacred writer in order to allude to the name of the river יַבֹּק, ver. 23."—*Ges. Lex.*

Gen. xli. 51.—And Joseph called the name of the firstborn Manasseh מְנַשֶּׁה: For God, *said he*, hath made me forget נַשַּׁנִי all my toil, and all my father's house.

52.—And the name of the second called he Ephraim אֶפְרָיִם: for God hath caused me to be fruitful הִפְרַנִי in the land of my affliction.

xlii. 35.—When *both* they and their father saw וַיִּרְאוּ the bundles of money, they were afraid וַיִּירָאוּ.

xlviii. 22.—Moreover I have given to thee one portion שְׁכֶם above thy brethren: see *Portion*, No. 13.

xlix. 8.—Judah יְהוּדָה, thou *art he* whom thy brethren shall praise יוֹדוּךָ, *lit.* shall praise thee.

16.—Dan דָּן shall judge יָדִין his people, as one of the tribes of Israel, *comp.* Gen. xxx. 6: And Rachel said, God hath judged me דָּנַנִי, and hath also heard my voice, and hath given me a son: therefore called she his name Dan דָּן.

19.—Gad גָּד, a troop גְּדוּד shall overcome him יְגוּדֶנּוּ: but he shall overcome יָגֻד at the last.

Exod. xxiii. 2.—Thou shalt not follow a multitude to *do* evil; neither shalt thou speak in a cause to decline לִנְטֹת after many to wrest לְהַטֹּת *judgment*.

       The same verb is used in different conjugations, transitively and intransitively.

Exod. xxxii. 18.—*It is* not the voice of *them that* shout עֲנוֹת for mastery, or shout Victory, neither *is it* the voice of *them that* cry עֲנוֹת for being overcome, *lit.* for overthrow: *but* the noise (*lit.* voice) of *them that* sing עַנּוֹת do I hear.

Num. v. 18.—And the priest shall have in his hand the bitter water הַמְאָרֲרִים that causeth the curse מֵי הַמָּרִים.

xviii. 2.—And thy brethren also of the tribe of Levi לֵוִי, the tribe of thy father, bring thou with thee, that they may be joined וְיִלָּוּ unto thee, and minister unto thee.

xx. 1.—The people abode in Kadesh בְּקָדֵשׁ. **12.** And the LORD spake unto Moses and Aaron, Because ye believed me not, to sanctify me לְהַקְדִּישֵׁנִי in the eyes of the children of Israel, therefore ye shall not bring this congregation into the land which I have given them. **13.** This is the water of Meribah; because the children of Israel strove with the LORD, and he was sanctified וַיִּקָּדֵשׁ in them.

xxiv. 21.—And he looked on the Kenites אֶת־הַקֵּינִי, and took up his parable, and said, Strong is thy dwelling-place, and thou puttest thy nest קִנֶּךָ in a rock.

As if the name קֵינִי Kenite were deduced from קֵן, a nest.

xxvii. 14.—Ye rebelled against my commandment in the desert of Zin, in the strife of the congregation, to sanctify me לְהַקְדִּישֵׁנִי at the water before their eyes: that is the water of Meribah in Kadesh קָדֵשׁ in the wilderness of Zin.

In the above passages there is continued paronomasia in allusion to the name of the place in which the children of Israel were at the time, viz., Kadesh.

Judg. x. 4.—And he (Jair) had thirty sons, that rode on thirty ass colts, שְׁלֹשִׁים עֲיָרִים, and they had thirty cities, וּשְׁלֹשִׁים עֲיָרִים לָהֶם.

xv. 16.—And Samson said, With the jawbone of an ass הַחֲמוֹר, heaps upon heaps חֲמוֹר חֲמֹרָתָיִם (*marg.* 'an heap, two heaps'), with the jaw of an ass הַחֲמוֹר have I slain a thousand men.

Ruth i. 20.—And she said unto them, Call me not Naomi נָעֳמִי (*marg.* 'that is, Pleasant'), call me Mara מָרָא (*marg.* 'that is, Bitter'): for the Almighty hath dealt very bitterly with me הֵמַר לִי מְאֹד.

1 Sam. i. 27, 28.—For this child I prayed; and the LORD hath given me my petition שְׁאֵלָתִי which I asked of him שָׁאַלְתִּי: therefore also I have lent him הִשְׁאִלְתִּיהוּ to the LORD; as long as he liveth he shall be lent שָׁאוּל to the LORD.

There is an allusion to the twofold import of the verb שָׁאַל, to *obtain* by petition, and to *lend*.

vi. 14.—And the cart came into the field of Joshua, a Bethshemite, and stood there, where *there was* a great stone אֶבֶן גְּדוֹלָה.

15.—And the Levites took down the ark of the LORD, and the coffer that *was* with it, wherein the jewels of gold *were*, and put *them* on the great stone הָאֶבֶן הַגְּדוֹלָה.

1 Sam. vi. 18.—*According to* the number of all the cities of the Philistines *belonging* to the five lords, *both* of fenced cities, and of country villages, even unto the great *stone* of Abel אֶבֶן הַגְּדוֹלָה, whereon they set down the ark of the LORD.

19.—And the people lamented וַיִּתְאַבְּלוּ, because the LORD had smitten *many* of the people with a great slaughter.

There is a doubt in respect to ver. 18, whether the reading ought to be אֶבֶן or אָבֵל; in the latter case אֶבֶן is to be understood as in our version; and the place is called אָבֵל, in reference to the mourning in ver. 18; and some suppose it was called אָבֵל הַגְּדוֹלָה, to distinguish it from another place called אָבֵל; others suppose the stone itself might afterwards be called אָבֵל.

xxv. 25.—Let not my lord, I pray thee, regard this man of Belial, *even* Nabal: for as his name *is*, so *is* he; Nabal נָבָל, *i.e. foolish,* is his name, and folly וּנְבָלָה is with him.

2 Sam. xxii. 11; Ps. xviii. 10.—And he rode וַיִּרְכַּב upon a cherub כְּרוּב, and did fly.

In allusion to the similar roots כָּרַב and רָכַב, as if כְּרוּב might be derived from the latter by a transposition of letters, *i.e.* רְכוּב, a divine steed.

42.—They looked יִשְׁעוּ, but *there was* none to save מוֹשִׁיעַ.

From the similar roots שָׁעָה to look, and יָשַׁע to save.

1 Kings viii. 66; 2 Chron. vii. 10.—And they blessed the king, and went unto their tents joyful and glad וְטוֹבֵי of heart for all the goodness הַטּוֹבָה that the LORD had done for David his servant, and for Israel his people.

The root טוֹב means both to be good and to be glad.

xviii. 21.—How long halt ye פֹּסְחִים between two opinions? if the LORD be God, follow him.

26.—And called on the name of Baal from morning even unto noon, saying, O Baal, hear us. But *there was* no voice, nor any that answered. And they leaped וַיְפַסְּחוּ upon the altar which was made.

Used scornfully of the superstitious gestures of the priests of Baal, and including in this application an allusion to the primary meaning, to halt.

Neh. ix. 24.—So the children went in and possessed the land, and thou subduedst וַתַּכְנַע before them the inhabitants of the land, the Canaanites הַכְּנַעֲנִים.

The verb כָּנַע, to be low, to humble, to subdue, is evidently used because of its resemblance to כְּנַעֲנִי, a Canaanite, *quasi* one humbled.

Job xi. 12.—For vain נָבוּב man would be wise יִלָּבֵב, though man be born *like* a wild ass's colt.

But man (is) empty (and) void of understanding, and man is born (like) a wild ass's colt; signifying the imbecility and dulness of the human understanding when compared with the Divine wisdom. There is a play of words in the use of the verbs נָבוּב and יִלָּבֵב, of a like origin.—*Gesenius.*

Job xxiv. 18.—He *is* swift קַל as the waters; their portion is cursed תְּקֻלַּל in the earth.

There is an elegant paronomasia between the words *swift*, or *light*, and *cursed*. They being both represented by one radical word, and the reason of it is, because those things that are light and contemptible are cursed, or in a cursed condition.—*Caryl.*

xxix. 16.—I *was* a father אָב to the poor לָאֶבְיוֹנִים: and the cause which I knew not I searched out.

אָב and אֶבְיוֹן are from the same root.

xxx. 3.—For want and famine *they were* solitary; fleeing into the wilderness in former time desolate שׁוֹאָה and waste וּמְשֹׁאָה.

19.—He hath cast me into the mire, and I am become like dust בֶּעָפָר and ashes וָאֵפֶר.

xxxviii. 27.—To satisfy the desolate שֹׁאָה and waste וּמְשֹׁאָה; and to cause the bud of the tender herb to spring forth.

Ps. xviii. 7.—The earth shook וַתִּגְעַשׁ and trembled וַתִּרְעַשׁ; the foundations also of the hills moved and were shaken וַיִּתְגָּעֲשׁוּ, because he was wrath.

41.—They cried יְשַׁוְּעוּ, but *there was* none to save *them* מוֹשִׁיעַ: *even* unto the LORD, but he answered them not.

xxv. 16.—Turn thee unto me, and have mercy upon me; for I *am* desolate and afflicted כִּי־יָחִיד וְעָנִי אָנִי.

The paronomasia is in the two last words, "and afflicted (am) I."

xxxii. 7.—Thou *art* my hiding place; thou shalt preserve me תִּצְּרֵנִי from trouble מִצַּר.

xxxix. 11.—When thou with rebukes dost correct man אִישׁ for iniquity, thou makest his beauty to consume away like a moth עָשׁ: surely every man *is* vanity.

xl. 3.—And he put a new song in my mouth, *even* praise unto our God: many shall see *it* יִרְאוּ, and fear וְיִירָאוּ, and shall trust in the LORD.

lii. 6.—The righteous also shall see וְיִרְאוּ, and fear וְיִירָאוּ, and shall laugh at him.

lvi. 8.—Thou tellest my wanderings נֹדִי: put thou my tears into thy bottle בְנֹאדֶךָ: *are they* not in thy book?

The play on the words rendered *wanderings*, and *bottle*, was intended to fix the attention of those using this Psalm on the deep consolation of our tears being noticed of God.

lxiv. 4.—That they may shoot in secret at the perfect: suddenly do they shoot at him יֹרֻהוּ, and fear יִירָאוּ not.

lxviii. 28.—Thy God hath commanded thy strength עֻזֶּךָ: strengthen עוּזָּה, O God, that which thou hast wrought for us.

Ps. xcvi. 5.—For all the gods כָּל־אֱלֹהֵי of the nations *are* idols אֱלִילִים: but the LORD made the heavens.

Prov. vi. 23.—For the commandment *is* a lamp; and the law וְתוֹרָה *is* light אוֹר; and reproofs of instruction *are* the way of life.

xii. 21.—There shall no evil אָוֶן happen יְאֻנֶּה to the just: but the wicked shall be filled with mischief.

The verb אָנָה is here used, not only because of its similarity to אָוֶן, iniquity, and evil, penal or accidental, but to shew that what the wicked account accidental to themselves, comes by the just judgment of God, and by God's permission or ordination to the righteous, whose afflictions or trials spring not out of the earth, or by chance.

xiii. 12.—Hope תּוֹחֶלֶת deferred maketh the heart sick מַחֲלָה: but *when* the desire cometh, *it* is a tree of life.

Eccles. i. 2.—Vanity of vanities, saith the Preacher, vanity of vanities; all הַכֹּל *is* vanity הָבֶל.

13.—And I gave my heart to seek and search out by wisdom concerning all *things* that are done under heaven: this sore travail עִנְיָן hath God given to the sons of man to be exercised לַעֲנוֹת therewith (*marg.* 'or, to afflict them').

vii. 1.—A good name שֵׁם is better than precious ointment מִשָּׁמֶן.

The entire form of this sentence is evidently intended to assist the memory, as well as to impress the mind טוֹב שֵׁם מִשֶּׁמֶן טוֹב.

6.—For as the crackling of thorns הַסִּירִים under a pot הַסִּיר, so *is* the laughter of the fool.

Isa. i. 23.—Thy princes שָׂרַיִךְ *are* rebellious סוֹרְרִים, and companions of thieves.

ii. 19, 21.—When he ariseth to shake terribly לַעֲרֹץ the earth הָאָרֶץ.

v. 7.—For the vineyard of the LORD of hosts *is* the house of Israel, and the men of Judah his pleasant plant: and he looked for judgment לְמִשְׁפָּט, but behold oppression מִשְׂפָּח (*marg.* 'a scab'); for righteousness לִצְדָקָה, but behold a cry צְעָקָה.

vii. 9.—If ye will not believe תַאֲמִינוּ, surely ye shall not be established תֵּאָמֵנוּ.

x. 18.—And he shall consume the glory of his forest, and of his fruitful field, both soul and body: and they shall be as when a standardbearer נֹסֵס fainteth מְסֹס.

This difficult passage has had various renderings assigned to it; probably the best signification is that which refers the figure to a man wasting away with sickness, whose strength and vigour are gone, and who becomes weak and helpless.—*Barnes.*

30.—Cause it to be heard unto Laish, O poor עֲנִיָּה Anathoth עֲנָתוֹת.

xiii. 4.—The noise of a multitude in the mountains, like as of a great people; a tumultuous noise of the kingdoms of nations gathered together: the LORD of hosts צְבָאוֹת

mustereth the host צָבָא of the battle : or, a host of battle.

Isa. xiii. 6; Joel i. 15.—Howl ye; for the day of the LORD *is* at hand; it shall come as a destruction כְּשֹׁד from the Almighty מִשַּׁדַּי.

xiv. 4.—That thou shalt take up this proverb against the king of Babylon, and say, How hath the oppressor ceased! the golden מַדְהֵבָה city ceased!

מַדְהֵבָה is supposed to be a sarcastic allusion to the boastful epithet often applied to Babylon, מַזְהֵבָה, by the change of a letter to make it more conformable to the Chaldee.

xv. 8.—For the cry is gone round about the borders of Moab; the howling thereof unto Eglaim, and the howling thereof יְלָלָתָהּ unto Beer-elim, בְּאֵר אֵלִים, *i.e.* the well of heroes, which may now be called the well of those that howl.

9.—For the waters of Dimon דִּימוֹן shall be full of blood דָּם; for I will bring more upon Dimon.

Some suppose that Dimon is the same with Dibon, a letter changed for the sake of a paronomasia; others, that it is the river referred to in 2 Kings iii. 20-22, which shall now really flow with blood.

xvii. 1.—The burden of Damascus. Behold, Damascus is taken away from *being* a city מֵעִיר, and it shall be a ruinous heap, מְעִי (for מֵעֲוִי).

The prophet uses an unaccustomed form for the sake of an allusion to the preceding מֵעִיר.

2.—The cities עָרֵי of Aroer עֲרֹעֵר *are* forsaken: they shall be for flocks, which shall lie down, and none shall make *them* afraid.

xxi. 2.—Go up עֲלִי, O Elam עֵילָם; besiege, O Media; all the sighing thereof have I made to cease.

xxii. 18.—He will surely צָנוֹף violently turn יִצְנָפְךָ and toss thee צְנֵפָה *like* a ball into a large country.

xxiv. 3.—The land shall be utterly הִבּוֹק emptied תִּבּוֹק, and utterly וְהִבּוֹז spoiled תִּבּוֹז : for the LORD hath spoken this word.

4.—The earth mourneth אָבְלָה *and* fadeth away נָבְלָה, the world תֵּבֵל languisheth אֻמְלְלָה *and* fadeth away נָבְלָה, the haughty people of the earth do languish אֻמְלָלוּ.

17, 18.—Fear פַּחַד, and the pit וָפַחַת, and the snare וָפָח, *are* upon thee, O inhabitant of the earth. And it shall come to pass, *that* he who fleeth from the noise of the fear הַפַּחַד shall fall into the pit הַפַּחַת; and he that cometh up out of the midst of the pit הַפַּחַת shall be taken in the snare בַּפָּח. See also Jer. xlviii. 43, 44.

xxv. 6.—And in this mountain shall the LORD of hosts make unto all people a feast מִשְׁתֵּה of fat things שְׁמָנִים, a feast מִשְׁתֵּה of wines on the lees שְׁמָרִים, of fat things שְׁמָנִים full of marrow מְמֻחָיִם, of wines on the lees שְׁמָרִים well refined.

Isa. xxix. 9.—Stay yourselves הִתְמַהְמְהוּ, and wonder וּתְמָהוּ; cry ye out הִשְׁתַּעַשְׁעוּ, and cry וָשֹׁעוּ : they are drunken, but not with wine; they stagger, but not with strong drink.

xxx. 16.—But ye said, No; for we will flee נָנוּס upon horses סוּס; therefore shall ye flee תְּנוּסוּן; and, We will ride upon the swift קָל; therefore shall they that pursue you be swift יִקַּלּוּ.

xxxii. 6.—For the vile person נָבָל will speak villany נְבָלָה, and his heart will work iniquity, to practise hypocrisy, and to utter error against the LORD, to make empty the soul of the hungry, and he will cause the drink of the thirsty to fail.

7.—The instruments כֵּלָיו of the churl כֵּלַי *are* evil: he deviseth wicked devices to destroy the poor with lying words, even when the needy speaketh right.

8.—But the liberal נָדִיב deviseth liberal things נְדִיבוֹת; and by liberal things עַל־נְדִיבוֹת shall he stand.

19.—When it shall hail וּבָרַד, coming down on בְּרֶדֶת the forest; and the city shall be low in a low place.

xli. 5.—The isles saw it רָאוּ, and feared וַיִּרָאוּ; the ends of the earth were afraid.

liv. 8.—In a little בְּשֶׁצֶף wrath קֶצֶף I hid my face from thee for a moment; but with everlasting kindness will I have mercy on thee.—See *Little*.

lvi. 10.—His watchmen *are* blind: they are all ignorant, they *are* all dumb dogs, they cannot bark לִנְבֹּחַ (see *Bark*); sleeping, lying down, loving to slumber.

lvii. 6.—Among the smooth *stones* of the stream בְּחַלְּקֵי־נַחַל *is* thy portion חֶלְקֵךְ; they, they *are* thy lot.

lxi. 3.—To appoint unto them that mourn in Zion, to give unto them beauty פְּאֵר for ashes אֵפֶר.

lxv. 11, 12.—That prepare a table for that troop, and that furnish the drink offering unto that number לַמְנִי. Therefore will I number וּמָנִיתִי you to the sword, and ye shall all bow down to the slaughter.

Jer. i. 11, 12.—The word of the LORD came unto me, saying, Jeremiah, what seest thou? And I said, I see a rod of an almond tree שָׁקֵד. Then said the LORD unto me, Thou hast well seen: for I will hasten שֹׁקֵד my word to perform it.

17.—Thou therefore gird up thy loins, and arise, and speak unto them all that I command thee: be not dismayed תֵּחַת at their faces מִפְּנֵיהֶם, lest I confound thee אֲחִתְּךָ before them לִפְנֵיהֶם.

ii. 5.—And have walked after vanity הַהֶבֶל, and are become vain וַיֶּהְבָּלוּ.

v. 23.—This people hath a revolting סוֹרֵר and a rebellious heart; they are revolted סָרוּ and gone.

vi. 1.—Blow תִּקְעוּ the trumpet in Tekoa בִּתְקוֹעַ.

28.—They *are* all grievous סָרֵי revolters סוֹרְרִים.

viii. 13.—I will surely אָסֹף consume them אֲסִיפֵם (*marg.* 'or, in gathering I will consume them'), saith the LORD: *there* shall *be* no grapes on the vine, nor figs on the fig tree.

Jer. x. 11.—The gods that have not made עֲבַדוּ the heavens and the earth, *even* they shall perish יֵאבַדוּ from the earth, and from under these heavens.

xix. 1, 2.—Thus saith the LORD, Go and get a potter's earthen חֶרֶשׂ bottle בַּקְבֻּק, and *take* of the ancients of the people, and of the ancients of the priests; and go forth into the valley of the son of Hinnom, which is by the entry of the east הַחַרְסוּת gate (or, pottery-gate, where broken pots, say some, were thrown: *comp.* 10).

7.—And I will make void וּבַקֹּתִי (in allusion to the word for bottle, בַּקְבֻּק) the counsel of Judah and Jerusalem.

xxii. 22.—The wind shall eat up תִּרְעֶה all thy pastors רֹעַיִךְ.

xxiii. 33.—When this people, or the prophet, or a priest, shall ask thee, saying, What *is* the burden מַשָּׂא of the LORD?

This word is used in two senses, either as a burden, or as an oracle; the former is here intended, speaking contemptuously of the prophet's message. It is against this sense and this use that the prophet remonstrates in his rebuke, ver. 34, &c.

36.—And the burden מַשָּׂא of the LORD shall ye mention no more: for every man's word shall be his burden מַשָּׂא (*i. e.* that for which God will call him to account); for ye have perverted the words of the living God.

37.—Thus shalt thou say (or, oughtest to say) to the prophet, What hath the LORD answered thee? and, What hath the LORD spoken?

38.—But since ye say, The burden מַשָּׂא of the LORD; therefore thus saith the LORD; Because ye say this word, The burden מַשָּׂא of the LORD, and I have sent unto you, saying, Ye shall not say, The burden מַשָּׂא of the LORD.

39.—Therefore, behold, I, even I, will utterly נָשָׁא forget וְנָשִׁיתִי you, and I will forsake you וּנְטַשְׁתִּי, and the city that I gave you and your fathers, *and cast you* out of my sight.

In the above verse there seems to be an allusion to what might be the meaning of מַשָּׂא, if it were pronounced with שׁ instead of שׂ, as if from נָשָׁא, to forget; and it might imply that the prophet's message was one that might be suffered to be forgotten.

xxx. 3.—For, lo, the days come, saith the LORD, that I will bring again וְשַׁבְתִּי the captivity אֶת־שְׁבוּת of my people Israel and Judah, saith the LORD.

See also, v. 18; xxxi. 23; xxxii. 44; xxxiii. 7, 11, 26; xlviii. 47; xlix. 6, 39: Deut. xxx. 3: Ezek. xvi. 53; xxix. 14; xxxix. 25: Amos ix. 14: Zeph. ii. 7; iii. 20: Ps. xiv. 7; liii. 6; lxxxv. 1; cxxvi. 1, 4: Job xlii. 10: Lam. ii. 14: Neh. viii. 17: 2 Chron. xxviii. 11; in all which a similar paronomasia is used.

xlviii. 2.—In Heshbon בְּחֶשְׁבּוֹן they have devised חָשְׁבוּ evil against it; come, and let us cut it off from *being* a nation. Also thou shalt be cut down תִּדֹּמִּי, O Madmen מַדְמֵן; the sword shall pursue thee.

Heshbon was a well fortified city of the Moabites and may have been so called from the skill shewn in its construction as a fortress, from חָשַׁב, to invent.

Jer. xlviii. 9.—Give wings unto Moab, that it may flee נָצֹא and get away תֵּצֵא: for the cities thereof shall be desolate, without any to dwell therein.

li. 2.—And will send unto Babylon fanners זָרִים, that shall fan her וְזֵרוּהָ, and shall empty her land.

20.—Thou *art* my battle ax מַפֵּץ *and* weapons of war: for with thee will I break in pieces וְנִפַּצְתִּי the nations, &c.

The same verb is repeated in the following verses.

Lam. iii. 47.—Fear פַּחַד and a snare וָפַחַת is come upon us, desolation and destruction.

Ezek. vii. 6.—An end קֵץ is come, the end הֵקֵץ is come: it watcheth הֵקִיץ for thee; behold, it is come.

xii. 10.—Say thou unto them, Thus saith the LORD GOD; This burden הַמַּשָּׂא concerneth the prince הַנָּשִׂיא in Jerusalem.

xxiv. 21.—I will profane my sanctuary, the excellency of your strength, the desire מַחְמַד of your eyes, and that which your soul pitieth וּמַחְמַל (Heb., the pity of your soul).

xxv. 16.—Behold, I will stretch out mine hand upon the Philistines, and I will cut off וְהִכְרַתִּי the Cherethims כְּרֵתִים.

xxxix. 9.—And they that dwell in the cities of Israel shall go forth, and shall set on fire and burn וְהִשִּׂיקוּ the weapons בְּנֶשֶׁק.

Dan. v. 26–28.—This is the interpretation of the thing: MENE מְנֵא; God hath numbered מְנָה thy kingdom, and finished it. TEKEL תְּקֵל; thou art weighed תְּקִילְתָּא in the balances, and art found wanting. PERES פְּרֵס; thy kingdom is divided פְּרִיסַת, and given to the Medes and Persians וּפָרָס.

Hos. ii. 23.—And I will sow her וּזְרַעְתִּיהָ unto me in the earth.

There is here an evident allusion to the name Jezreel יִזְרְעֵאל, *lit.* the seed of God.

viii. 7.—The bud צֶמַח shall yield no meal קֶמַח.

ix. 15.—Their princes שָׂרֵיהֶם are revolters סוֹרְרִים.

16.—Ephraim אֶפְרַיִם is smitten (*comp.* Ps. cii. 4; cxxi. 6: Jonah iv. 7), their root is dried up, they shall bear no fruit פְּרִי.

x. 1.—Israel *is* an empty vine, he bringeth forth fruit unto himself: according to the multitude כְּרֹב of his fruit he hath increased הִרְבָּה the altars; according to the goodness כְּטוֹב of his land they have made goodly הֵיטִיבוּ images.

xii. 11.—*Is there* iniquity *in* Gilead גִּלְעָד (*lit.* heap of testimony, Gen. xxxi. 52)? surely they are vanity: they sacrifice bullocks in Gilgal בַּגִּלְגָּל (*lit.* heap of heap); yea, their altars *are* as heaps כְּגַלִּים in the furrows of the field.

xiii. 15.—Though he (*i. e.* Ephraim, אֶפְרַיִם) be fruitful יַפְרִיא, an east wind shall come.

Amos v. 5.—But seek not Beth-el, nor enter into Gilgal, and pass not to Beer-sheba : for Gilgal הַגִּלְגָּל shall surely גָּלֹה go into captivity יִגְלֶה, and Beth-el וּבֵית אֵל shall come to nought לְאָוֶן, and so called, Hos. iv. 15, Beth-aven בֵּית אָוֶן.

viii. 1, 2.—And he said, Amos, what seest thou ? And I said, A basket of summer fruit קָיִץ (i.e. harvest of fruits, from קוּץ, to cut off, or gather ripe fruits). Then said the LORD unto me, The end הַקֵּץ is come upon my people of Israel; I will not again pass by them any more; i.e. they are now like the ripe fig, ready to be gathered, ripe for judgment.

Jonah iv. 6.—And the LORD GOD prepared a gourd, and made it to come up over Jonah, that it might be a shadow צֵל over his head, to deliver לְהַצִּיל him from his grief. So Jonah was exceeding glad of the gourd.

Micah i. 10.—In the house of Aphrah לְעַפְרָה roll thyself in the dust עָפָר (comp. Jer. vi. 26).

13.—O thou inhabitant of Lachish לָכִישׁ, bind the chariot to the swift beast לָרֶכֶשׁ.

Micah i. 14.—The houses of Achzib אַכְזִיב shall be a lie לְאַכְזָב to the kings of Israel.

Nah. ii. 10.—She is empty בּוּקָה, and void וּמְבוּקָה, and waste וּמְבֻלָּקָה.

Hab. ii. 18.—What profiteth the graven image that the maker thereof hath graven it ; the molten image, and a teacher of lies, that the maker of his work trusteth therein, to make dumb אֱלִילִים idols אֱלִילִים ?

Zeph. i. 2.—I will utterly אָסֹף consume אָסֵף (lit. by taking away I will make an end of) all things from off the land, saith the LORD.

ii. 4.—For Gaza עַזָּה shall be forsaken עֲזוּבָה,............. and Ekron עֶקְרוֹן shall be rooted out תֵּעָקֵר.

iii. 1.—Woe to her that is filthy מֹרְאָה and polluted, to the oppressing city !—See Filthy.

Zech. ix. 3.—And Tyrus צוֹר did build herself a strong hold מָצוֹר.

5.—Ashkelon shall see it תֵּרֶא, and fear וְתִירָא.